THE OFFICIAL®
PRICE GUIDE TO

Records

THE OFFICIAL®
PRICE GUIDE TO

Records

TENTH EDITION

JERRY OSBORNE

HOUSE OF COLLECTIBLES • NEW YORK

© 1993 by Jerry Osborne

This is a registered trademark of Random House, Inc.

All rights reserved under International and Pan-American Copyright Conventions.

Published by: House of Collectibles
201 East 50th Street
New York, New York 10022

Distributed by Ballantine Books, a division of Random House, Inc., New York, and simultaneously in Canada by Random House of Canada Limited, Toronto.

Cover design by Kristine V. Mills
Cover photo by George Kerrigan

Manufactured in the United States of America

Library of Congress Catalog Card Number: 92-75369

ISBN: 0-876-37905-6

Tenth Edition: March 1993

10 9 8 7 6 5 4 3 2 1

CONTENTS

ACKNOWLEDGMENTS

The single most important element in the updating and revision of a price and reference guide is reader input.

From dealers and collectors, based in every state and in nearly every country around the globe, we receive suggestions, additions and corrections. Every single piece of data we acquire from readers is carefully reviewed, with all appropriate and usable information utilized in the next edition of this guide.

As enthusiastically as we encourage your contribution, let us equally encourage that when you write, you'll either type or print your name clearly on both the envelope and contents. It's as frustrating for us to receive a mailing of useful information, and not be able to credit the sender, as it probably is for the sender to not see his or her name in the Acknowledgments section.

In compiling this edition, information supplied by the people whose names appear below was of great importance. To these good folks, our deepest gratitude is extended. The amount of data and investment of time, of course, varied, but without each and every one of them this book would have been something less than it is.

Here then, alphabetically listed, is the board of advisors and contributors to this edition:

Peter Aarts
Jeff Aaron
Joe Abbati
Billie Abbott
James Able
Ken Abruzzi
Bob Adamonis
Stan Adams
Jim Ahrens
Marilee Albertsen
Davie Allan
Ed Allan
David Allen
Jeff Allen
Kevin O. Allen
Robert C. Allen
Russ Allie
John R. Allman
Tony Almeida
Joseph Alterio
Judy Dale Alvarez
Dan Alvino
Amber's Records
Ivan Amirault
Gary Amos
Gary L. Anderson
Nick Andrea
Michael H. Andrews
Art Appelbaum
Gene Armato
Jose C. Arocas
Jim Arslanian
Billy Arthur Jr.
Tim Ashibende
Donnie Atwell
Tracy Au

James Aull
Gary D. Bahr
Rob Balboni
Irwin S. Balch
Jay Ball
Richard M. Balsam
Lonnie Bambas
Howard F. Banney
Raymond A. Baradat
Renato Barahona
Ed Baran
Nic Barber
Saul Barbosa
Alan L. Barclay
Brent Barker Jr.
John Barley
Vartkes K. Baroghlian
Robert Barr
Kevin Barrett
Stanley Barron
Jerry Barthelemy
Joseph M. Barvinchak
Kenneth Baumgartner
Chris Beachley
Jeff Beauchamp
Rick Behrend
Gary Behymer
Richard J. Bell
Russ Bell
Randal Bender
Maxine Bennett
Kevin Bensink
Jerry Bentsch
Andy Benyo
Randy Berger
Daniel S. Berkman

Richard H. Bernard
Kevin Beran
Lou Berryman
Michael L. Berryman
Peter Berryman
Lynn Best
Big B.
Ricky Bishop
Frank Black
Malcolm Blackard
Gary Blackman
Edward R. Blair
John Blair
Harry Blaisure
Tony Blascheck
Russell E. Blatt
Peter Blecha
Dale Blount
Steve Bobbrow
Bruce Bodread
Dee Bolt, III
Marilyn A. Bonomi
Jim Borders
John Boumila
Robert Bowling
Jim Bowman
Boxcar Bill
Bill Boyd
Stephen Braitman
Ronald E. Brackney
R. Lee Bracy Jr.
Bill Bram
Glenn Bray
M.R. Brenz
Leonard Brewster
Mike Bricker

Bill Brit
Ed Broderick
John Brooks
Richard Brooks
Fred Broughton
George Brouthers
Dick Brouwer
Ben Brown
Davis B. Brown
Jean Brown
Kip Brown
Pat Brown
Michael Bruck
John Bruno
Kelly K. Bub
Donald Budde
Dave Budlong
Ralph Bukofzer
Leonard J. Bukowski
Carol Buller
Doug Bunger
Billy J. Burdette
Dave Burke
Ken Burroughs
Robert Burroughs
Bud Buschardt
Roger Bush
A.G. Bustos
Gary Butler
Thomas E. Butler
Frank T. Cadicamo
Duane L. Cain
Leo Callaham
Al Camp
Harvey Campbell
Henry Campbell

Acknowledgments

Terry Campbell
Joni L. Caneye
Stephen Canner
Gerri Carey
Jeff Carlson
Alan Carner
Michael Carr
Pat Carr
Joseph L. Caruso
Tim Carver
Frank Castillo
Patrick M. Castle
Carol A. Catalina
Michael Celio
Jerry Chamberlain
Fred Chambers
Jeff Chandler
Don Charles
Rich Cherry
Presley M. Cheshire
Johnny Chesko
Dennis Chiesa
Pete Chilkewitz
Erik Christensen
Daniel J. Christy
Cory Church
Alexander Clark
Jonathan Clark
Mike Clark
Stephen M. Clark
Thomas Clark
Bob Claymier
Ron Clemmens
Robert B. Clere
Keith Clodfelter
Bob Clofalo
Al Cocorochio Jr.
Daniel R. Coennen
Wallace W. Cogan
Howard R. Cohen
Dan Colagiovanni
Bob Colgan
Collect-A-Hit
Bill Collins
Jeff Collins
Kathleen Collins
C.J. Comfort
Bob Compeau
John Conaty
Loren Cone
Katherine Connella
Joseph A. Conway
Wendy Cook
Andrew Cooper
Mick Cooper
Sissy Cooper
Stan Cooper
Roger Copelin
Ronald L. Cornelius
Herbert Cornell

Richard D. Cornell
Michael Corns
Rick Cortez
Lee Cotten
Perry Cox
Erik Cram
Dan Crawford
Kevin Crey
Mark Crocker
Richard Croteau
Sally Crowley
Rory Cubel
Ross Crump
Bill Cullvane
John Cunningham
Rick J. Cunningham
Linda Curie-Cohen
Chris Curran
Lou Curtiss
Jeffrey J. Custer
David Cutler
Michael Daddario
Ron Dailey
F.J. D'Amico
Nicky D'Andrea
Sherman Daniel
Neil T. Daniels
Sherry Daniel
Frank Davella
James J. Davenport
James Davidson
G.P. Davis
Gary Davis
Hank Davis
Ken Davis
Larry Davis
Lloyd Davis
Michael Davis
Norman Davis
Ron Davis
William P. Davis
Bill Deandrea
Warren Debenham
Vern Debes
Robert M. Deckert
Don DeClark
Jim Dedman
Cathy Dee
Tim Deibert
William Deibert
Michael J. Delazzer
Walter Della-Pietra
David W. Dellinger
Robert Delph
Lee Dempsey
Jack C. Denny
Joseph De Paola
Les Derby
Ray De Santis
Ted Despres

Michael Dean
David W. Desper
Dennis R. Desrosiers
Tom Deuber
Michael Devich
Dennis DeWitt
Howard DeWitt
J. Ralph DeWitt
Jack Dey
Randall T. Dickey
Edward Dickhart
Emil A. Didonato
Vic Diehl
Jack DiGiorgi
Janet Di Domenico
John Di Rocco
Dirt Cheap Sounds
Bobby Diskin
Ron Ditscyun
Ronald R. Ditty Jr.
Frank Dix
John Dixon
Terry Dobrucki
George Dochterman
L.R. Docks
David A. Dodge
J. Taylor Doggett
Andrea Doll
Edward D. Donati
Larry Donn
K.D. Doolittle
Doug Dornbos
Larry Dorothy
Fred Dougherty
Steve Dougherty
Dennis Dow
Ralph Doyle
Alice L. Drake
Mitch Drumm
Richard Dukett
Jim Durst
Walter Dutko
C.R. Dutrow III
Jennifer W. Dynes
Frances Easton
Terry Easton
Dave Eaton
John C. Ebner
Judith M. Ebner
Chuck Edwards
David Edwards
Dan Eieja
Denise Eieja
David J. Eimer
Maria Elena
Don Ell
Case Ellerbroek
P.W. Elliott
Bruce Elrod
Brian W. Emero

Bill Emery
Tom Engle
Jerry Engler
Judy Ennicco
L. Curt Erler
Jim Evans
John Evans
Larry Evans
Rockin' Ricky Fah
Jerry Falk
Merrell Fankhauser
Harry A. Farnham
T. Don Faught
Frank Fazio
Ron Feldhaus
Stan Feldman
Mike Fenech
David N. Ferguson
Robert D. Ferlingere
Vic Figlar
Philip M. Finlay
Larry Finn
Bill Finneran
Stan Fintz
John Fischer
J. Fisher
Russ Fisher
John Fiumara
Lindsey C. Flaherty
Peggy Flaherty
Eric Flaum
James E. Fogerty
Keith Fontaine
Austin Fontenot
Joe Fontanilla
Jerry Ford
Gerry Ford
Sven Forsberg
Ted Foster
Hardy Fox
Bob Frandy
Jeffery A. Frankel
Loretta Fraser
Mike French
Randy Fried
Bob Friedman
Jonathan Frisch
Fred Frommholz
Tony Frydrych
Don Fuller
Michael Fulner
Maxim W. Furek
Raymond Gaillardetz
Alex Galbraith
Mitchell Galinkin
Fred Gallant
Jean-Marc Gargiulo
Arnie Ganem
Maureen Ganem
Jerry Gant

Acknowledgments

Tony Gargiulo
Brian Gari
Julie Garrett
Robert C. Garthe
Lee J. Garvin
Joseph Gavin
David Gayle
Guy H. Geest
Frank S. Gengar
Scott Georgi
Don Gergler
Roger Gernert
Bill Gerulis
Richie C. Gesner
Joel W. Getschman
Tom Giacoponello
Jim Gibbons
James D. Gibson
Jim Gier
John Giglio
Gerry Giles
Russell H. Ginns
Steve Goddard
Ed Godin
Bruce Gollubier
Tony Gongora
Fernando Gonzalez
Franklin E. Goodale
Mark Lee Goodale
Teresa Goodpaster
Paul Goodstein
Ed Gordon
Timothy Gorman
Larry Goshen
Fred Goss
Susan Goyette
Thomas Grantland
Brian Granville
F. Gravereau
Bruce Gray
Charles T. Gray
Les Gray
John Green
Robert Green
James P. Greene
Cathy Greenfield
Denise M. Gregoire
Hal Greimann
Tom Grenfell
Paul Grenyo
Fred J. Griego
Christopher Gries
Gary Griffin
Will Griffith
Gary Griga
Elliott Griggers
Rob Grill
April H. Grimes
John L. Grimes
Marc Grobman

Skip Groff
Thomas Grosh
Pete Gross
Paul Grothem
Paul Gruber
Steven Grunberg
Kevin J. Grundwaski
Jean-Philippe
Guichard
James O. Guthrie
Kim Gutzke
Sally Haas
Buck Hafeman
Ivan Haffenden
Richard Hagensen
Daniel Hagstrom
Indra Haim
Amy Beth Hale
Don Haley
Bill Hall Jr.
Marshall S. Hall
Carolyn Hamilton
Cliff Hamilton
Brent Hample
Gary L. Hampton
John Hanager
Bob Hanley
Audrey Hansen
Luke Hansen
Lyle Hansen
Terry Hansen
Wes Hanson
Bob Hapgood
Jon Hardgrove
Joe Hardy
Hare's Records
Jim Harkey
David Harper
Wes Harris
Glen D. Harris
Les Harris
Michael Harris
Steven Harris
Brian Lee Hart
Chris Hartlaub
Dennis Hartman
Lannie Hartman
Peter Harvey
Robert Harvey
Walter F. Harwood
Midge Hasenbank
Frank Haskell
Ken Haskins
Benno Häupl
Marvin Hauschild
Don Haverstock
John V. Heath
Barry L. Heck
Jean Heffner
Jeff Henderson

Randall Henderson
Ben W. Hendricks
Jim Henkel
Bruce Henningsgaard
Rick Hensley
Walter Hering
Brehon Herlihy
Dennis V. Hickey
D.W. Hicklin
James Hill
John Hillyard
Chris Hindman IV
Richard Hite
Chuck Hlava
Patricia Hodge
Dick Hogan
Bruce J. Holt
Chris Hood
John V. Hooley
Catherine Hopkins
Ron Hopkins
Ron Hopkinson
Brenda S. Hornberg
Phillip D. Horner
Dennis A. Horseman
Alexander Horvath
Larry N. Houlieff
Terry Hounsome
Bob Hover
Doyal Howell
Paul M. Hubbard
Bill Hughes
Bob Hughes
Elaine Hughes
David Huisman
Ray Hummell III
Bill Humphreys
Edward Hunt
Lester Hunt
Kay Hutchison
Tom Huxhold
Dave Hyatt
Rocco Imbriano
Gail Ireland
Donald L. Irwin
Don Jackson
Paul Jacobs Jr.
Dorothy Jacobson
Alexander James
Mark James
Steven R. James
Carl Janusek
Nancy Janusek
Arnold Jeffcoat
David Lee Jenkins
John Jester
Chris Jiles
Aloha Johnson
David Johnson
Ed Johnson

Jon E. Johnson
Rich Johnson
Ron R. Johnson
Colin Johnston
Hugh Jones
Jack Jones
Jay Jones
Joyce Jones
Larry Jones
Linda Jones
Paula Jones
Ron Jones
Wayne Jones
The Jordanaires
Robert Joyce
Steve Joyce
Sandra Judd
Jukebox Music Club
Ed Juska Jr.
Ron Kagel
Jim Kallgren
Thomas Kaltenbach
Rex Kamstra
George H. Kane
George Kapral
Dick Karle
Norm Katuna
Leon Katzinger
Artie Kauffman
Lewis Kaufman
Mike Keating
J. Keener
Vaughn Keith
Clifford C. Kekelik
Ella A. Keller
Jim Keller
Randy Keller
Karen Kellers
Michael B. Kelly
Chris Kempf
Jerry Kendall
Timothy Kessler
Larry Ketchie
Eric Kidder
Fran Killian
Colin Kilts
Dave Kims
Rob Kinyour
Dick Kissell
Dave Kemp
Dominique King
John P. King
T. Russell Kirkscey
Don R. Kirsch
Dick Kissell
Harry Klein
Jeff Klein
Earl Kliethermes
Johnny Kline
Pete Kline

ix

Acknowledgments

Peter Knoll
Cub Koda
Rick Kolack
Candy Korn
Ron Kowal
Chris Krahn
Frank Kramer
Milt Krantz
Matthew Krause
Jeff Kreiter
Walt G. Kubis
Kerry Kudlacek
Mike Kuehl
Mark Kulik
Ed Kunsch
Peter Kurtz
Doug Kyle
Glenn A. LaFave
Darwin Lamm
George Langabeer
Mary-Kaye Lanzetta
George J. Lapata
Rosalind Lardieri
Keith Lee Larsen
Edward Lary
Edward Lasko
Al LaSoya
Richard Lattanzi
Creig Lavine
Jack Lawrence Jr.
Paul Lawrence
Alan Leatherwood
Kean Leiker
Ray LeBov
Brian Lee
Rich Lefer
Mario Legault
Douglas C. Lembke
Jeffrey M. Lemlich
P.F. Lesley
Scooter Lesley
Paul Levy
Craig Lewis
Dan Lewis
Denny S. Lewis
Stan Lewis
T.E. Lewis
Terry Lewis
Marc Lindauer
Michael D. Linder
Jeff Lindin
John A. Lindquist
Joe Lindsey
Kurt Linhof
David Link
Jerry D. Linn
Andria Lisle
Richard Liukko
Robert G. Livingston
George B. Lockwood

Ron Lofman
Steve Loftness
Ron Lohman
Cyndee Long
Mark D. Long
Earl F. Loomis
Daniel Lorenzi
Dante E. Lorenzi
Dan Lorenzo
Oron Lott
Lou Christie Int'l
Fan Club
Frank Loux
Gary J. Lovell
Bob Lowenthal
Nancy Lucas
Peter Lucas
David Luhn
Curt Lundgren
Rick Lynch
Lisa J. Lynn
Frank Lyon
Edward W. Macauley
Leon Mach
Michael Reid Mackay
Barry MacDougall
Jerry Maciaszek
Lee Mackenzie
Malcolm MacQuillan
Al Madden
Joseph C. Madrano
John D. Magee
Kenny Mahouski
James M. Mains
Eric Maloney
Mike Marcolongo
Jim Marien
Teri Marinko
Jay Marker
Mike Markesich
Thomas A. Markris
Ron Marks
John Marlowe
Don Marshall
Patricia Marsolais
Dave Marsteller
Garry Martin
James Martin
Jim Martin
Steven L. Martin
Harry Maselow
Tony Mastrianni
Harold D. Mathews
Gary Mathieu
Greg Matson
Ernest Ray Maxwell
Gary McAfee
Sandy McClafferty
Ron McClure
Ruth McColley

Charles McConkey
Dick McCormick
Gary McCormick
Renee A. McCoy
Robbie McCurdy
Ron McCorkle
Peter McCullough
Tom McCullough
Scott McGredy
Bruce McKnight
James R. McNalis
Stephen J. McParland
Ken McPeck
Bruce Medici
Jeffrey M. Melchionoo
Nick Mele
Mark James Meli
Jeff Melius
William C. Menor
Robert Mercer
Joseph Merrell
Chris Messner
Gloria Metroka
Robert Michalski
Patrick Michiels
Dale D. Mikolaczyk
Aaron Milenski
Ian Miles
Arlen Miller
Charlie Miller
Gary Miller
J.E. Miller
Wesley Millet III
Aaron Mintz
Bill Mitchell
Paul Mitchell
Paul Mochinal
Craig Moerer
Steve Mogle
Eric Mohler
Bob Moke
Steven Molinari
Michael Monahan
Don Monfredi
George Moonoogian
Robert Moore
Jay A. Moriello
Les Moss
Mark Moukton
Gordon Mulholland
Steve Muller
John Mullins
George Mull
John Mullins
Bob Munn
Bill Munroe
Brian Murphy
Keith Murphy
Mike Murray
Charles Murrell

Kim Murrie
Allen E. Mushin
Ed Muske
Derek J. Myers
Gary Myers
Reuben Nance Jr.
Jeff Naskrent
Richard Necaise
Dale R. Neidigh
John Neilson
Greg M. Nelson
Harry Nelson
Nedra Nelson
Gary Nemetz
Charlie Neu
H.M. Neulieb
Brian R. Nevill
Steve Newman
Steve K. Nichols
Bob Nines
Geoffrey Niswander
Joe Nix
Laura Nolph
Bob Norberg
Carole Norris
Richard Norris
John M. Nowell III
Dave Nowlen
Jose Y. Nunez
Joseph Nunzio
Norvald Nygaard
Richard Oberholtzer
K.J. O'Brien
Paul B. Odell
Tom B. Ogilvy
Gerald R. Ognjan
Mike Ohr
Geof O'Keefe
Mark Oldies
Jim Oldsberg
Walt Oliver
Cathi Olsen
Brad Olson
Herb Olson
Tim O'Mara
O'Neile
Peter Oprisko
Kaitlín M. O'Reilly
Jean Ortiz
Steve Osborne
Bill Osment
Greg Oswald
Johnny Otis
Ilse M. Ouellette
Bill Owens Jr.
James L. Padrick
Frank B. Paino
Mark Palmer
Paul Palmer
Philip Palmer

Acknowledgments

Pam and Tony
Austin Pankey
Jerry Papile
Joseph Papo
David Paschen
Don Wayne Patterson
Richard E. Patterson
Dave Patton
Al Pavlow
Gareth Pawlowski
Chris Peake
Richard H. Pearce
Victor Pearlin
Daniel Pearsall
Wade Pearson
Pat Peasley
Alex Peavey
Lee Pecue
George F. Peek
Bob Pegg
Sylvia Pentel
Joe Peplozskiniski
Robert B. Perkins
John Perretta
Jack Peterson
Susan M. Peterson
Henri-Pierre Petit
Leslie J. Pfenninger
Bob Phillips
Calman P. Phillips
L. Gene Phillips
Mark Phillips
Paul Phillips
Tom Pickles
Alex Pierce
Wayne Pigna
Alex Pilepic
Steve Pimper
Pink
Donna Lynne Pinto
Walter Piotrowski
Pete Pittman
Michael R. Pitts
Steve C. Plucker
Edward F. Polic
Steve Polwort
Robert A. Pomeren
Christopher Popa
Ron Porchal
F. Darryl Porter
Mary Potts
David Pournaras
Alfred J. Powell
David Powell
Dee Powell
J.J. Powell
Tom Powell
Tony Powell
Melvin Prestenback
Steve Preston

Tom Preston
Tom Prestopnik
Ken Price
Danny Prisco
Ed Primeau
Steve Propes
Richard A. Proplesch
John Proudfoot
Chester Prudhomme
James Pucel
Lynn Pulsipher
Peggy H. Purcell
Frank J. Queen
Bill Quilty
Gilbert Quintero
Allen Radwill
Dennis Raffelock
Peter A. Rafter
Lou Rallo
Steven I. Ramm
Robert Ramsdell
Ray Randall
Richie Ranno
Jim Raposa
Helmut Rauch
Frank Ravella
Jerry A. Rayburn
Eddie Reardon
Thomas Redd
Walker Reddick
Tessa Ricar
Norman Rice
Charlie Richards
Tom Richards
Kurt Richter
Steven S. Rickman
Mary A. Riggins
Shelby Riggs
Mikel Rindflish
Don Riswick
John Ritchie
Phillip L. Ritz
Paul Roark
Tom Robbins
Phil Roberts Jr.
Ted Roberts
David Robertson
Velpo F. Robertson Jr.
Cliff Robnett
Brenda Rodela
Norman Rodger
Luiz G.C. Rodrigues
Alice Rogers
April Rogers
Jim Ronat
Arthur Root
Nicholas D. Rosati
Prewitt Rose
Paul Rosedalc
Gary B. Rosen

Vernon Roske
Ric Ross
Sigurd K. Rottingen
Terry Rowan
Gary Rowe
Ron Rowe
Fred Rozakis
Jenny Rozakis
Eric Rubin
James von
  Rummelhoff
Bruce B. Runnels
Gene Rupprecht
Wayne Russell
Andrew C. Russo Jr.
Daniel T. Ruth
Greg Ruzich
Brenda Ryan
Marc Ryan
Richard T. Ryan
Ron Rybacki
Robert Rymarzick
William Sabath
Ramona Saben
Ed Salaman
Ron Salyer
Sonia Sanchez
Ed Sanders
Greg Sanders
Rich Sandler
Sue Sanford
Rob Santos
Tony Saraiva
Ron Sataloff
G. Dee Sayles
Nina Schacherer
James Scharnott
David Schiller
George F. Scheufel
Eugene E. Schlepp
Dave Schlobach
Bob Schmidt
Daniel J. Schmidt
Joe Schmidt
Frederick Schmid
Gary Schneider
Mario Schöppen
Henry G. Schroeder
James Schroedle
Bill Schuh
Phil Schwartz
James F. Sciarra
James Scios
Billy Scott
Joseph Scott
Paul Scott
Rowland Scott
Bill Screws
Kevin Segura
Steve Seim

Rodney Selby
David Sellers Sr.
Laura Serra
Charles Shackleford
Jawad Shaikh
Thomas J. Shannon
Frank Sharpe
Michael Sharritt
Greg Shaw
Kristy Shaw
Steve Shaw
Dan Shellenbarger
Benny Shelton
Pat Shields
Joe Shillair
Bob Shine
Lee Shockley
Jimmy Short
Vitaly Shukin
Brenda S. Sievers
Bertram H. Silman
Louis Silvani
Michael J. Silver
Mike Simko
Joseph F. Simon
Bill Simoneau
Kara Sjoblom
Lorrie Sjoquist
Max Skok
Neal F. Skok
Bob Skurzewski
David Slone
Brian Slywka
Jim Small
Al Smith
Bill R. Smith
Bruce Smith
Don Smith
Ed Smith
Jamie Smith
Jeffrey B. Smith
John Smith
Kenneth H. Smith
Neal Smith
Pat Smith
Robert Smith
Shawna-Kay Smith
Vivian Smith
Walter Smith
Richard C. Sneathen
John P. Snow
Robert Snyder
Mark G. Speck
Stephen Spence
Philip Spencer
N. Springer
Bobby R. Sprinkle
Jo L. Sprouse
Danny Spurgeon
John M. Squires

xi

Acknowledgments

Dennis Srnel
John Stainze
Courtney B. Starbird
Terry L. Stark
J. Staszewski
Tom Stein
Jee Cee Ste-Marie
Carlo Stevan
Michael Stevens
Jack Stevenson
Mike Stewart
Larry Stidom
Wayne Stierle
Benn Stimmel
Francine Stinson
Doug Stitt
Mark Stitz
Matt Stitzel
Bill Stone
Mildred Stowers
Richard Strite
Gene Strupe
Howell Q. Strye
Paul Studstill
Anthony Sturiale
Stu Sturgis
Kerry Sugden
Damian Sullivan
Edward Suranyi
Greg Surek
Marisa Suttile
Scott Sutton
Lennart Svedberg
Robert L. Swan
Howard A. Sweet
Rod Sweetland
Bill Swisher
Symba
Joel B. Tamayo
Stanley Tarence
Ed Tataryn
Alan Taylor
Jack Taylor
James Taylor
Eric Teisberg
Steve Terrell
Jeff Thames
Dee Anne Thomas
Donald Thomas
James Thomas
James R. Thompson
Jo Ann Thompson
Steve Thompson
Carol Thuot
Jack Tietjen
Jeffrey Tischler
Terry Titus
Cliff Todd
Joe Tomkus
P. M. Tortorice

Ron Tosser
Tom Tourville
Mike Townsend
George G. Trabant
Jerry Traeder
Dan Trebik
Bill Trent
Greg Trudeau
Cam Trulli
Dennis R. Trumbo
Ted Tucker
Larry Tuczynski
G. Dean Ufford
Lou Ukelson
F. Steven Underwood
Timothy T. Uttley
Phil Valentine
Starr Van Deusen
Nicholas Vasil
Mike Vaughan
Jamee Vaughn
Larry Vaughan
Mike Vaughan
Ronald Vaughan
Bernard Vasek
Jimmy Velvet
Tom Ventris Jr.
Billy Vera
Tony Verdi
Bill Verkoilen
Kris Vermeer
Very English &
   Rolling Stone
Richard Vining
James von Rummelhoff
Allan Vorta
Michael Voss
Tony Waitekus
James K. Walker
Max Waller
Michael Walsh
Patrick M. Walters
Michael L. Ward
Jason L. Warren
Alex Warschaw
Morrie Warshawski
Mike Waston
William Watts
Chuck Wax
Stephen D. Way
Jim Weaver
Mark Weber
Carrollyn Webster
Tom Weingart
Richard Weize
Mike "Lightnin" Wells
Jerry Wendel
Tom Wenzel
Jack Wesolowski
Don Wessel

Don Weston
Danny A. White
Gwen Whitford
Gladys Whitney
Barry Wickham
Scott Wikle
Mike Wilcox
Dean S. Wilkey
Barbara Williams
Danny J. Williams
Gary C. Williams
George D. Williams
Robert B. Williams
Peter Wilson
Tom Wilson
Eric Wincentsen
Jack Wise
George Wisner
Don Wiur
David R. Wolfe
Don Wiur
Robert Wolk
Mike Wolstein
Ed Wood
Woody Woodall
Rick Woodby
Barbara Wright
Dave Wright
Gordon J. Wrubel
Marvin K. Wyant
Joseph R. Yarolimek
Paul Yates
Richard C. Yeandle
Pat Yochim
Bill Yoder
Harry Young
Kenn Zach
Zee's Records
Pinhas Zilbergeld
Robert L. Zimlich
David E. Ziola

Records

INTRODUCTION

In determining what should be included in *The Official Price Guide to Records,* we've considered many factors. Our goal is to make the guide helpful, convenient, and applicable; for avid record connoisseurs as well as for those who are simply curious about the value of their old records.

As an author-publisher team, we have put together nearly 50 record guides and reference books over the past 15 years. As a result of this considerable experience, we have developed some basic criteria that serve as the foundation for the guide.

First, we had to establish which records most people would own—the answer being those records made by *charted artists.* Thus, we began with the national pop and rock charts published by *Billboard, Cash Box,* and other trade publications. Then, because there has been so much chart crossover since the development of rock and roll, particularly between the black (rhythm and blues, soul, dance, etc.) music surveys and the top pop hits, we have included these charts as well.

Whether a song charted as a *single,* an *extended play (EP),* or a *long-playing (LP)* record, and regardless of whether it charted as "Race," "Rhythm and Blues," "Soul," "Disco," "Dance music," or "Sepia," you'll find that record priced here.

Performers who regularly appear on other charts — such as "Jazz," "Adult Contemporary," "Country," "Gospel," and "Classical"—do occasionally cross over to the pop/rock and black charts, and all who have are also included in this edition. However, these music forms are intrinsically diverse enough to require separate publications for truly comprehensive coverage.

Why Certain Records Are Not Listed

It is important to keep in mind the aforementioned guidelines. Much of the mail we receive is from folks who fail to read the introductory material, then cannot comprehend why certain, often obscure, records are not in this edition. A country music fan, for example, might not understand why Eddy Arnold is listed in this book while Ernest Tubb is not. Similarly, the jazz buff might be bewildered when finding Dave Brubeck here but not Art Farmer. While both Tubb and Farmer had numerous hits on their respective charts, they have never appeared on the pop charts. Eddy Arnold and Dave Brubeck, on the other hand, placed both singles and albums on the pop charts.

Just because we're listing all of the aforementioned charted artists, however, does not mean we are listing *only* charted records by those artists. Once an artist is included in the guide, we list and price *every known release* by that performer. Using country singer Hank Thompson as an example, let's show how comprehensive the coverage in this guide really is:

Despite his prominence in country and western music, Hank Thompson had only one song on the *Billboard* Hot 100; a single that remained on the chart for just one week and only managed to reach #99. Nevertheless, having qualified for this guide with one charted appearance, every known single (45 and 78 rpm), extended play, and long-playing album by Hank Thompson, from 1946 to present, is documented and priced in this edition. The reason behind the extensiveness of this coverage is if people like a performer well enough to put one of his/her records on the chart, they may own other records by that artist—without regard to chart success.

In summary, everyone who made the pop/rock (1950-1988) or black music charts (1942-1988) is included here, with not only their charted records, but their *entire* recorded output. This often includes 78rpm issues made twenty or thirty years before the '50s and should effectively cover most of the records to be found in the library of the average person.

Unlike earlier editions of this guide, which included very few 78rpm singles, one can now price tens of thousands of 78s with this book; records originally issued as far back as the 1920s and as recently as 1962. Plus, for the first time in any record guide, this edition provides separate sections and pricing for simultaneously released 45s and 78s, a common practice for most labels in the '50s.

If you are seeking information on recordings not covered in this book, please write to the author (address on next page). We'll even provide you with information on upcoming titles now in various stages of production, one of which is *The Official Price Guide to Compact Discs,* for those needing to price CDs of the '80s and '90s.

How the Prices Are Determined

Record values shown in this new *Official Price Guide to Records* are averaged using information derived from a number of traditional sources. Most influential in arriving at current values is our established "marked copy" review program. Dozens of the world's most active dealers and collectors receive a copy of the most recent edition in which, throughout the year, they mark changing prices. When it's time to prepare a revised edition, all marked copies are returned to us for analysis and processing.

Besides the annotated copies, we receive hundreds of letters each year, from folks like yourself, suggesting corrections and/or additions to the guide.

Another extremely important source of pricing information is *DISCoveries* magazine, a monthly publication where hobbyists buy, sell, and trade music collectibles. We painstakingly review each issue of *DISCoveries,* as well as other industry publications, carefully comparing prices being asked to those shown in the most recent edition of the *Official Price Guide to Records.* If marketplace trading indicates prices in the guide need to be increased or decreased, the changes are made. With our frequent publishing schedule, it is never long before the corrected prices appear in print.

What makes this step in the pricing process so vital is that nothing more verifiably illustrates the out-of-print record marketplace than everyday sales lists placed by dealers from around the country and around the globe.

Record prices, as with most collectibles, can vary drastically from one area of the country to another. Having reviewers and annotators in every state, as well as in Europe, Asia, and beyond, enables us to present a realistic average of the highest and lowest current asking prices for an identically graded copy of each record.

Other sources of consequential information include: set sales and auction lists in other magazines as well as private sales list mailings, record convention trading, personal visits with collectors and to retail locations around the country, and hundreds of hours on the telephone with key advisors.

Although the record marketplace information in this edition was believed accurate at press time, it is ever subject to market changes. At any time, major bulk discoveries, quantity dumps, sudden increases wrought by an artist's death, overnight stardom that creates a greater demand for earlier material, and other such events and trends can easily affect scarcity and demand. Through diurnal research, keeping track of the day-to-day changes and discoveries taking place in the fascinating world of record collecting is a relatively simple and ongoing procedure.

To ensure the greatest possible accuracy, *Official Price Guide to Records* prices are averaged from data culled from all of the aforementioned sources.

How You Can Help

Obviously, we can never get too much input or too many reviewers. We wholeheartedly encourage you to submit whatever information you feel would be useful in building a better record guide. The quantity of data is not a factor. No amount is too little or too much. The extensive list of names in the Acknowledgments chapter indicate the growth of our advisor team, especially when compared to previous editions.

When preparing additions for the *Official Price Guide to Records,* please try to list records in generally the same format as is used in the guide: artist's name, label, catalog number, title, year of release (if known), and price range. Since our data base is computer stored alphabetically by artist, there's no need to note the *Official Price Guide to Records* page number.

Wax Fax

One frequently used method of forwarding data to us is by FAX. For your convenience, we now have a full-time, dedicated FAX line (206 385-6572). Use this service to quickly and easily transmit additions, corrections, price updates, and suggestions. Be sure to include your name, address, and phone number so we can acknowledge your contribution and, if necessary, contact you.

Whether it's a marked copy of the guide, a letter, or a FAX, type or clearly print your name so we may accurately credit you in the next edition. Please submit all additions, corrections, and suggestions to:

Jerry Osborne
P.O. Box 255
Port Townsend, WA 98368

About the Format

Our arrangement of listings is the most logical way to present so much information in such a convenient, easy-to-carry package. It is clearly a format— the *only* format— with unlimited potential for expansion.

The structure of the *Official Price Guide to Records* allows us to include all of the following in one multi-purpose guidebook: 7-inch 45rpm singles, both 33rpm and 45rpm; 78rpm singles; 12-inch singles, both 33rpm and 45rpm; extended play 33rpm and 45rpm EPs; long play 10, and 12-inch LPs; picture sleeves; promotional issues, and more.

Once you locate an artist's section, his/her records are listed alphabetically by LABEL. Individual listings for each label appear in numerical order. In many instances, listings that are numerical by catalog number are also chronological in sequence of release, but there are also times where this is not the case. This format is especially helpful when using the guide along with an artist or label discography. Since the year of release is also provided for each listing, the reader knows immediately the pattern being followed by the label at the time.

Once familiar with the format, you'll find it easy and functional. However, do take time to familiarize yourself with the array. Reading all of the introductory pages should answer most reader questions. Having exhausted the supplied introductory material, please feel free to write or call if you have a question about the guide.

The documenting and pricing of so many recordings is made possible by selectively economizing on space; listing individual titles when necessary but not when it's possible to group a number of equally valuable releases together on one line. Again, *any time* it is necessary to have a separate listing on a record in order to clearly and accurately present the information, we will do it. Also, whenever a specific catalog number is noted, whether listed as an exception or not, the title will also be given for easy identification.

One facet of our approach of great concern is the artist who had one or more records of a value indicated for a particular label or series, but who also had one release (or more) that is a notable exception. Every effort has been made to separately document such exceptions, however, due to the sheer bulk of information herein, some may be missed. If you know of any, let us know about them.

You will find that the expansion of an artist's section, moving more toward individual rather than grouped listings, will be as commonplace in subsequent volumes of this series, as with this edition. There are hundreds of artists with revised sections in this volume, listing many more individual titles and catalog numbers than ever before. With some performers, it is, or perhaps soon will be, necessary to list every single record separately.

The decision to expand a section is partly based on reader input. Many examples of individual pricing in this edition can be directly attributed to a letter or call suggesting the need to do so. We're always listening and would love to hear from *you*.

Grading and the Price Range

The pricing shown in this edition represents the PRICE RANGE for NEAR-MINT condition copies. The value range allows for the countless variables that affect record pricing. Often, the range will widen as the dollar amount increases, making a $750-$1000 range as logical as a $3-$5 range.

The standardized system of record grading, used and endorsed by Osborne Enterprises, the House of Collectibles, and buyers and sellers worldwide, is as follows:

MINT: A *mint* item must be absolutely perfect. Nothing less can be honestly described as mint. Even brand new purchases can easily be flawed in some manner and not qualify as mint. To allow for tiny blemishes, the highest grade used in our record guide series is *near-mint*. An absolutely pristine mint, or still sealed, item may carry a slight premium above the near-mint range shown in this guide.

VERY GOOD: Records in *very good* condition should have a minimum of visual or audible imperfections, which should not detract much from your enjoyment of owning them. This grade is halfway between good and near-mint.

GOOD: Practically speaking, the grade of *good* means that the item is good enough to fill a gap in your collection until a better copy becomes available. Good condition merchandise will show definite signs of wear and tear, probably evidencing that no protective care was given the item. Even so, records in good condition should play all the way through without skipping.

Most older records are going to be in something less than near-mint, or "excellent" condition. It is very important to use the near-mint price range in this guide only as a starting point in record appraising. Be honest about actual condition. Apply the same standards to the records you trade or sell as you would want one from whom you were buying to observe. Visual grading may be unreliable. Accurate grading may require playing the record (play-grading).

Use the following formula to determine values on lesser condition copies:

For VERY GOOD condition, figure about 60% to 80% of the near-mint price range given in this guide.

Some dealers now report that a VG+ record priced at $4 or $40 will sell ahead of a mint item priced at $5 or $50. Also, with many of the older pieces that cannot be found in

6

near-mint, VG or VG+ may be the highest grade available. This significantly narrows the gap between VG and the near-mint range.

For GOOD condition, figure about 20% to 40% of the near-mint price range given in this guide.

ThE BoTTom LiNE

All the price guides and reporting of previous sales in the world won't change the fundamental fact that true value is nothing more than what one person is willing to accept and what another is prepared to pay. Actual value is based on scarcity and demand. It's always been that way and always will.

A recording—or anything for that matter—can be 50 or 100 years old, but if no one wants it, the actual value will certainly be minimal. Just because something is old does not necessarily make it valuable. Someone has to want it!

On the other hand, a recent release, perhaps just weeks old, can have exceptionally high value if it has already become scarce and is by an artist whose following has created a demand. A record does not have to be old to be valuable.

RecoRd TypEs DEfiNEd

With the inconsistent language used by the record companies in describing an EP or an LP, we've determined that a language guideline of some sort was needed in order to compile a useful record guide.

Some labels call a 10-inch LP an "EP" if it has something less than the prescribed number of tracks found on their LPs. Others call an EP a "Little LP." A few companies have even created special names, associated only with their own label, for the basic record formats.

Having carefully analyzed all of this, we have adopted the following classifications of record configurations, which consistently categorize all types, sizes, and speeds in one section or another:

Singles: 78rpm are those that play at 78rpm! Though 78s are almost always 10-inch discs, a few 7-inch 78rpm singles have been made.

Singles: 7-Inch can be either 45rpm or 33 1/3 (always referred to simply as "33") speed singles. If a 7-inch single has more than one track on either side, then it's an EP.

Singles are priced strictly as a disc, with a separate section devoted to picture sleeves (which are often traded separately). If we know that picture sleeves exist for a given artist, a separate grouping will appear for the label, price, and applicable year of release. Should you know of picture sleeves not documented in this edition, please advise us accordingly.

There have been a few 5-inch discs manufactured, but for the sake of keeping singles with singles (and since we don't want to establish a "Singles: 5-Inch" category), such curios will be included with the 7-inch singles.

EPs: 7-Inch 33/45rpm are 7-inch discs that have more than one track on one or both sides. Even if labeled an "EP" by the manufacturer, if it's pressed on a 10, or 12-inch disc it's an LP in our book. Unless so noted, all EPs are presumed to be accompanied by their original covers, in a condition about equal to the disc. An appropriate adjustment in value should be made to compensate for any differences in this area. Exceptions, such as EPs with paper sleeves or no sleeve at all, are designated as such when known.

LPs: 10/12-Inch 33rpm is self explanatory. The only possible confusion that might exist here is with 12-inch singles. If it's 10 or 12 inches in diameter, and labeled, priced, and marketed as a 12-inch single (Maxi-Single, etc.), then that's where you'll find it in this guide, regardless of its speed. Often, 12-inch singles will have a 12-inch die-cut cardboard sleeve or jacket; but many have covers that are exactly like LP jackets, with photos of the artist, etc. Unless so noted, all LPs are presumed to be accompanied by their original covers, in a condition about equal to the disc. An appropriate adjustment in value should be made to compensate for any differences in this area.

Other record type headings used in this edition, such as **Picture Sleeves, Promotional Singles,** etc., should be crystal-clear.

Cross-referencing and Multiple Artists' Recordings

The cross-referencing in this edition should provide the easiest possible method of discovering other sections of the book where a particular artist is featured or appears in any capacity.

We've tried to hold to a minimum unexplained cross-references, opting to concentrate more on those cross-references for which the reader can effortlessly understand the rationalization. Minimized is the unnecessary duplication of cross-references. For example, it is not necessary to list every group in which Eric Clapton played, under each and every one of those sections. What we've done is simply indicate "Also see Eric Clapton," where you *will* find a complete cross-referencing to all other sections where he appears.

Some artists have several sections, one right after the other, because they were involved in different duets and/or compilation releases. In such instances, the primary artist (whose section begins first) is not cross-referenced after each and every subsequent section, but only after the last section wherein that artist is involved. This, in effect, blocks the beginning and the end of releases pertaining to that performer. If you don't find the listing you're searching for right away, remember to check the sections that follow, as the artist may have been joined by someone else on that recording causing it to appear in a separate section.

Artist headings and resultant cross-referencing appear in two different formats in this guide. For example:

LEWIS, Jerry Lee, Carl Perkins & Johnny Cash

Listings under this type heading are those wherein the artists perform *together*. Often these releases will also include solo tracks by one or all of the performers in addition to those on which they collaborate.

LEWIS, Jerry Lee / Carl Perkins / Johnny Cash

This heading, with names separated by a slash, indicates there are selections on *separate* tracks by each of the named artists, but they do not perform together.

The parameter set for these compilation releases is four different performers or less. Compilations containing five or more individual performers are, for purposes of compiling this edition, classified as **Various Artists** issues, which are documented in a separate price guide.

Whenever more than one act is featured on a record, cross-references appear under all of the other artists on the disc, who have a section of their own in this edition, directing the reader to the location of the listing in question. If you're looking up a record with a different artist on each side, and you don't find it under one artist, be sure to try looking for the flip-side artist.

Not all releases containing more than one artist are given separate sections. In some cases it makes more sense to include such records in the primary section for the most important artist. We will rarely create separate sections for multiple artist discs when the other performers on the issue do not have a section of their own in this edition.

To illustrate this point, Hank Williams Jr. had several duet issues with Lois Johnson; Gene Ammons shared an LP with Sonny Stitt. Even though Johnson and Stitt do not have individual sections in this book (they didn't make the *Billboard* pop singles or LPs charts), such recordings may be important to collectors of Williams and Ammons. For that reason, they are included in their respective artist's section.

On the other hand, a duet by Brenda Lee and Willie Nelson requires a separate section, since either or both may be of interest to the researcher. Also, both are individually pop-charted artists. There are a few isolated exceptions to this policy, simply because every section in this edition was separately prepared and customized in whatever manner necessary to provide the user with the most usable information.

Promotional Issues

Separate documenting and pricing of promotional issues is, in most cases, unnecessary. Because most of the records issued during the primary four decades covered in this guide were simultaneously pressed for promotional purposes, a separate listing of them would theoretically double the size of an already large book.

Rather, we've chosen to list promotional copies separately when we have the knowledge that an alternate price (either higher or lower) consistently is asked for them. For the most part, promos of everyday releases will fall into the same range—usually toward the high end—given for store stock copies. Some may stretch the range slightly, but not enough to warrant separate pricing. Premiums may be paid for promos that have different (longer, shorter, differently mixed, etc.) versions of tunes, even though the artist may not be particularly hot in the collecting marketplace.

When identified as a "Promotional issue," we are usually describing a record with a special promotional ("Not For Sale," "Dee Jay Copy," etc.) label or sleeve, and not a *designate* promo. Designate promos are identical to commercial releases, except they have been rubber or mechanically stamped, stickered, written on by hand, or in some way altered to accommodate their use for promotional purposes. There are very few designate promos listed in this edition, and those that are (such as in the Elvis Presley section) are clearly identified as such.

Colored Vinyl Pressings

Records known to exist on both black vinyl and colored vinyl (vinyl is the term used regardless of whether it's polystyrene or vinyl) are listed separately since there is usually a value difference. However, some colored vinyl releases were never pressed on black vinyl, and since there is no way to have the record other than on colored vinyl, it may or may not be specifically noted as being on colored vinyl.

Because the true color of some colored vinyl pressings may be a judgment call (is it red or is it dark pink . . . is it dark blue or is it purple?), we're using "colored vinyl" to indicate any pressings that are not standard black vinyl. Likewise for multi-color and clear vinyl issues.

Foreign Releases

This edition by design lists only U.S. releases. There is, however, an occasional exception. A handful of records that were widely distributed in the United States or sold via widespread U.S. advertising, even though manufactured outside the country, are included. Such anomalies would appear only in the more sophisticated sections of the guide.

There are also a few significant Canadian releases in this edition. The collectors' market for out-of-print Canadian records is mostly a U.S. market. The trading of rare Canadian discs between Canadian collectors is not nearly as widespread as those instances that involve a U.S. buyer or seller.

The millions of overseas releases certainly have collector value to fans in those countries as well as to stateside collectors. Unfortunately, the tremendous volume of material and the variances in pricing make it impossible to comprehensively document and price imports.

Bootlegs and Counterfeits

Bootleg and counterfeit records are not priced in this guide, though a few are cited, along with information on how to distinguish them from an original.

For the record, a bootleg recording is one illegally manufactured, usually containing material not previously available in a legitimate form. Often, with the serious collector in mind, a boot will package previously issued tracks that have achieved some degree of value or scarcity. If the material is easily available, legally, then there would be no gain for the bootlegger.

The counterfeit record is one manufactured as close as possible in sound and appearance to the source disc from which it was inspired. Not all counterfeits were created to fool an unsuspecting buyer into thinking he or she was buying an authentic issue, but some were. Many were designated in some way, such as a slight marking or variance, so as not to allow them to be confused with originals. Such a fake record primarily exists to fill a gap in the collector's file until the real thing comes along.

With both bootleg and with counterfeit records, the appropriate and deserving recipients of royalties are, of course, denied remuneration for their works.

Since most of the world's valuable records have been counterfeited, it is always a good idea to consult with an expert when there is any doubt. The trained eye can usually spot a fake.

This is not to say *unauthorized* releases are excluded from the book. There are many legitimate releases that are unauthorized by one entity or another; records that are neither bootleg or counterfeit. Unauthorized does not necessarily mean illegal.

Group Names and Personnel

One problem that we'll never completely solve involves the many instances where groups using the exact same name are lumped together with other groups who are completely different. Whenever known to be different, these groups are given separate sections; however, there are times when we simply do not know. If you can shed any light in this area, we'd love to hear from you. Thanks to readers, many such groups have been sorted since our last edition.

The listing sequence for artists using the same name is chronological. Thus, the ABC group, Silk, who had a release in 1969, is listed ahead of the Philadelphia International group, Silk, that first recorded in 1979.

As often as not, there will have been group members that have come and gone over the years. Reflecting this turnover in our listing of members' names may cause some confusion, when the reader sees 12 different members shown for a group named the Five Satins. We've tried, whenever possible, to list the original line-up first, followed by later members. Also, the lead singer is usually listed first. We welcome additional information on group members from readers. One of the most reliable sources of this data is the LP covers, which often list members. If you can fill in the members' names on any groups where we don't list that information, we'll see that it gets into our next edition. Hundreds of group members have been added since the ninth edition of this guide.

When group members' names are given, there is a likelihood that not all of the members named appear on *all* of the releases documented. It is also possible that not all of the members named ever recorded with all of the other members shown at the same time.

When names are given for a solo performer, those named are likely noteworthy sidemen.

As more and more group members are named in future editions, there will be added cross-referencing to reflect the constant shuffle of performers from one group to another.

PARENThETICAL NOTES

S ome of the information that may be found in parentheses following the artist heading has already been covered. However, other uses of this space include:

- Complete artist and group or artist and band names. Some artists were shown as being with one group on a few releases and with another on other issues. We've tried to present the information the way, or many ways, that it was shown on the actual record label.

- Variations of spelling or names for the same artist. With some artists, it's convenient to have everything in one section; however, when it is illogical to combine listings, perhaps because the performer was popular under more than one name (such as Johnny Cymbal and Derek), you'll find individual sections for each name. Cross-references will be used to help you locate things easily. Having "Kenneth Rogers" in parentheses is not intended to mean that Kenneth is Kenny's real name. Rather, we're letting you know that some releases credit him as Kenneth Rogers instead of Kenny Rogers.

- Names of guest performers who may or may not be credited on the actual label, but who we feel you should know were involved in some of the records listed in that section.

- Real names of artists, but only when we feel they need to be given. We have no desire to give the real names of everyone who has recorded under a pseudonym, but there are times when you do need this information, particularly when they have also recorded under their real name or when more than one person has recorded under the same pseudonym. To help sort things out, we will, when known, give you the real name of someone who has recorded under a nom de guerre, such as Guitar Slim (a.k.a. Johnny Winter).

- A few of the more prolific labels with lengthy names are abbreviated in this guide. They are:

ABC-PAR . . . . ABC-Paramount
MFSL . . . . Mobile Fidelity Sound Lab
RCA . . . . RCA Victor
20TH FOX . . . . 20th Century-Fox
U.A. . . . . United Artists
W.B. . . . . Warner Brothers

Oldies Labels and Reissues

A n effort has been made to include many "oldies" or reissue records in the guide. Though many reissues of this type are of no value beyond their current retail cost, some are. Look at some of the early RCA Victor Gold Standard Series Elvis Presley releases, for example. Once in a blue moon a tune will turn up in true stereo on a reissue label that previously was hard to find in stereo (such as *I Ran All The Way Home,* on Collectables). Otherwise, it's just our desire to report comprehensively on all artists that prompted the listing of reissues.

The main reason we've included these reissues is to eliminate confusion, especially among younger collectors. Often, they'll discover a hit tune on a label, like Lana or Lost-Nite, and think it's an original release predating the label that had the hit single.

If there are reissues numbered as part of a label's standard release series, and not documented in this edition, please tell us about them.

UsiNq This Guide: Additional Points

- Whenever possible, records worth $25 or so are listed individually with label, catalog number, and title.

- The alphabetization used makes finding any artist or label easy, but a few guidelines may speed the process along for you:

- Names that are simply letters (and are not intended to be pronounced as a word) are found at the beginning of the listings under each letter of the alphabet (i.e., ABC, AC-DC, GQ, SSQ, etc.). The same rule applies to acronyms and to initials (i.e., G.T.O, MFSB, etc.). When known, we'll parenthetically tell you what the abbreviation represents.

- Names are listed in the alphabetical order of the first word. This means you'll find **Rock Squad** before **Rocket.** Hyphenated words are looked upon as whole words (i.e., Mello-Kings is treated the same as Mellokings). Divided names (i.e., De Vorzon, El Dorados, etc.) are alphabetically listed as though they were a one-word name.

- Possessive names precede similarly spelled names that are not possessive. For example, KNIGHT'S would be found before KNIGHTS, regardless of what follows the comma.

- The articles "A" or "The" have been dropped from group names in this guide even though they may appear on the records as part of the name.

- With record labels, the listings appear in alphabetical/numeric/chronological order. Prefixes are generally not used (they make it more difficult to scan the numbers) unless they are necessary for identification. With some artists (Beatles, Elvis, etc.) it is essential at times because of constant reissues.

- Some sections make use of the label prefixes to sort things out, but most use a number series. If the numbers are duplicated by the label, or if any of a variety of confusing similarities exist, we may resort to the prefixes for clarity.

- Anytime we find that the monaural or the stereo issue of a particular record is in need of a separate listing (because there is a price difference for one that is outside the boundaries of the price range of the other), we will gladly provide same. If there is but one listing, this indicates that we have no reason to believe there is much difference in the two forms. A little application of the known variables will help in this area. For example, if the range is $20-$30 for a 1960 LP and you know that the stereo issue is in true stereo, it's safe to place the mono at the low end of the range ($20-$25) and the stereo at the high end ($25-$30). The calculation may be reversed for late '60s and for most electronically reprocessed issues.

- We believe the year or years of release given in the far-right column to be accurate. If we don't know the correct year, the column is left blank. In some cases the record may have been released in one year and debuted on the nation's music charts the following year. This is common for year-end issues and explains why you may remember a hit as being from 1966, although we list it as a 1965 release.

• When multiple years are indicated, such as "64-66," it means the records described on that line spanned the years 1964 through 1966. They may have had one issue in 1964 and another in 1966, or may have had eight releases during those years. It does *not* mean that we believe the release came out sometime between 1964 and 1966.

• Unusual though it may be, a few records have been issued with no artist or label given. You will find this on both singles and albums. These items are filed here by title.

• There are hundreds of double albums (two discs in one package) priced in the guide, but they are not necessarily identified as double LPs. They are, nevertheless, included in the price range.

Guidelines for Pricing Records Not Found in This Edition

Since it is impossible for us to include *every* record ever produced, a few guidelines may assist you in evaluating records not found in this edition:

Pop Singles on 45rpm: Most pop (i.e. non-rock) vocal and instrumental 45s from the '50s are available for under $10. From many rock-oriented dealers, pop singles can often be bought for less than $5. The few exceptions are likely to be folks with charted hits, and those will be found in the guide.

Pop music singles from the '60s to present are seldom going to sell for over $5; usually around $3.

Pop Singles on 78rpm: Most pop 78s are available for under $5. Until the late '40s or early '50s, an *album* was a gatefold binder with a number of 78s, usually in individual paper sleeves. Prices on these pop albums will vary, but most will fall in the $20-50 range.

Pop Long Play Albums: From the '50s, 12-inch pop LPs generally are found for under $30 to $40. Ten-inch LPs may go for $25 to $50. Pop vocalists with jazz releases (such as Johnny Mathis' first LP) are an exception, but should be found in this book.

Most pop LPs from the '60s to present can be found for $5 to $15.

Pop Extended Play Albums: Pop EPs are scarce, as are all EPs, but many are still very reasonable. Most can be found for under $10-25.

Easy Listening Music: The average easy listening record will be worth about half of the price ranges shown for Pop Music.

Country Music on 45rpm: Most country music vocal and instrumental 45s from the '50s are available for under $15; many for less than $10. Obvious exceptions are any that border on rockabilly or country rock. Don't take any country record for granted! Play both sides of every disc, as it is always possible you'll discover a great country rocker.

Country music singles from the '60s to present are seldom going to sell for over $5.

Country Music on 78rpm: Most of the country 78s should fall into the $10 to $40 range. There are, however, many older 78s with prices well into three figures; some even higher.

Country Music Long Play Albums: From the '50s, 12-inch LPs generally are found for under $30 to $60. Ten-inch LPs may go for $50 to $100. As always, the range will vary widely depending on the following and collectibility of the artist.

Most country LPs from the '60s to present can be found for $10 to $25. Again, there are exceptions.

Country Music Extended Play Albums: Very, very few country music EPs were big sellers, which means nearly all are rare. You may find they are in the same price range as the '50s LPs above; some will bring even more than LPs from the same time period.

Jazz Singles on 45rpm: Most jazz 45s from the '50s are available for under $10; perhaps less than $5. The few exceptions are likely to be artists with charted hits, which will be found in the guide.

Jazz singles from the '60s to present are seldom going to sell for over $5.

Jazz Singles on 78rpm: Most jazz 78s are available for under $20. Until the late '40s or early '50s, an *album* was a gatefold binder with a number of 78s, usually in individual paper sleeves. Prices on these jazz albums will vary, but most will fall in the $25 to $75 range.

Jazz Long Play Albums: From the '50s, 12-inch jazz LPs generally are found for under $50 to $100. Ten-inch LPs may go for $75 to $200.

Most jazz LPs from the '60s to present can still be found for $15 to $30.

Jazz Extended Play Albums: As with country, very few jazz EPs were big sellers. All are rare. You may find they are in the same price range as the '50s jazz LPs above; some will bring even more than LPs from the same time period.

Comedy and Personality Long Play Albums: From the '50s and '60s, 12-inch comedy and personality (not soundtrack or original cast) LPs generally are found for under $15 to $40.

Most comedy and personality LPs from the '70s to present can be had for $5 to $15.

In summary, there is no way these few paragraphs can constitute a complete price guide for the millions of non-rock records that exist. If such generic generalizations were possible, while guaranteeing unerring accuracy, the entire price guide would be about ten pages. It is the exceptions that make record pricing so complicated and difficult to document.

Our goal here is simply to provide a rough idea of the value of recordings that are outside the parameters of the guide.

What to Expect When Selling Your Records to a Dealer

As nearly everyone in the hobby knows, there is a noteworthy difference between the prices reported in this guide and the prices that one can expect a dealer to pay when buying records for resale. Unless a dealer is buying for a personal collection and without thoughts of resale, he or she is simply not in a position to pay full price. Dealers work on a percentage basis, largely determined by the total dollar investment, quality, and quantity of material offered as well as the general financial condition and inventory of the dealer at the time.

Another very important consideration is the length of time it will take the dealer to recover at least the amount of the original investment. The greater the demand for the stock and the better the condition, the quicker the return and therefore the greater the percentage that can be paid. Our experience has shown that, day-in and day-out, most dealers will pay from 25% to 50% of *guide* prices. And that's assuming they are planning to resell at guide prices. If they traditionally sell below guide, that will be reflected in what they can pay for stock.

If you have records to sell, it would be wise to check with several shops. In doing so you'll begin to get a good idea of the value of your collection to a dealer.

Also, consult the Directory of Buyers and Sellers in this guide for the names of many dealers who not only might be interested in buying, but from whom many collectible records are available for purchase.

Whether you wish to sell the records you have, or add out-of-print discs to your collection, check out *DISCoveries* magazine. Each issue is packed with ads, features, discographies, collecting tips and more. If getting into the record marketplace is important to you, *DISCoveries* is recommended. (*DISCoveries,* P.O. Box 309, Fraser, MI 48026. Sample issue available upon request).

Concluding Thoughts

The purpose of this guide is to report as accurately as possible the most recent prices asked and paid for records within the area of its coverage. There are two key words here that deserve emphasis: **Guide** and **Report.**

We cannot stress enough that this book is only a guide. There always have and always will be instances of records selling well above and below the prices shown within these pages. These extremes are recognized in the final averaging process; but it's still important to understand that just because we've reported a 30-year-old record as having a $25 to $50 near-mint value, doesn't mean that a collector of that material should be hesitant to pay $75 for it. How badly he or she wants it and how often it's possible to purchase it *at any price* should be the prime factors considered, not the fact that we last reported it at a lower price. Of course, we'd like to know about sales of this sort so that the next edition can reflect the new pricing information.

Our objective is to report and reflect record marketplace activity; not to *establish* prices. For that reason, and if given the choice, we'd prefer to be a bit behind the times rather than ahead. With this guide being regularly revised, it will never be long before the necessary changes are reported within these pages.

We encourage record companies, artist management organizations, talent agencies, publicists, and performers to make certain that we are on the active mailing list for new release information, press releases, bios, publicity photos, and anything pertaining to recordings.

There is an avalanche of helpful information in this guide to aid the collector in determining what is valuable and what may not be worth fooling with, but the wise fan will also keep abreast of current trends and news through the pages of the fanzines and publications devoted to his/her favorite forms of music. ❑

SAMPLE LISTING

(Excerpted from the Supremes section)

Artist
heading

SUPREMES
Shown on some
releases as ...

(Diana Ross and the Supremes)

Singles: 7–inch
Category

GEORGE ALEXANDER INC. (1079 "The Only Time
I'm Happy") 30-40   65
(Special premium record. Has a Supremes interview on the flip.)

MOTOWN (1027 "Your Heart
Belongs to Me") 15-25   62

Label names,
selection
numbers and
titles

MOTOWN (1044 "A Breath Taking, First Sight Soul
Shaking, One Night Love Making, Next Day
Heart Breaking Guy") 25-30   63

Near-mint
price range

MOTOWN (1044 "A Breath Taking Guy") 5-8   63
(Reissue, with shorter title.)

TAMLA (54038 "I Want a Guy") 70-90   61

Year of
release

Picture Sleeves

MOTOWN (1027 "Your Heart
Belongs to Me") 30-40   62

Promotional Singles

AMERICAN INT'L PICTURES ("Dr. Goldfoot
and the Bikini Machine") 20-40   66
(Single-sided disc, used to promote the film of the same name.)

LPs: 10/12–inch 33rpm

Helpful
explanatory
notes

MOTOWN (606 "Meet the Supremes") .. 200-300   63
(Front cover pictures each member sitting on a chair.)

MOTOWN (606 "Meet the Supremes") 30-35   63

Group
members

(Front cover pictures the head of each group member.)

Members: Diana Ross; Mary Wilson; Florence Ballard; Cindy Birdsong.
Also see BALLARD, Florence
Also see PRIMETTES
Also see ROSS, Diana
Also see WILSON, Mary

References to
other related
sections

A

A FLOCK of SEAGULLS:
see FLOCK of SEAGULLS

A TASTE of HONEY: see TASTE of HONEY

A's
Singles: 7–inch
ARISTA 3-5   79
LPs: 10/12–inch 33rpm
ARISTA 5-10   79-81
Members: Richard Bush; Rick DiFonzo; Michael Snyder; Terry
Bortman; Rocco Nolte.

A.B. SKHY
Singles: 7–inch
MGM 3-5   69-70
LPs: 10/12–inch 33rpm
MGM 10-12   69-70

ABC
Singles: 12–inch 33/45rpm
MERCURY 4-6   83-87
Singles: 7–inch
MERCURY 2-4   82-87
Picture Sleeves
MERCURY 2-4   82-87
LPs: 10/12–inch 33rpm
MERCURY 5-10   82-87

AC-DC
Singles: 12–inch 33/45rpm
ATLANTIC 5-10   79
(Promotional issue only.)
Singles: 7–inch
ATCO 3-5   77
ATLANTIC 2-5   77-85
Picture Sleeves
ATLANTIC 2-5   81-83
LPs: 10/12–inch 33rpm
ATCO 5-15   76-90
ATLANTIC 5-10   77-86
Members: Bonn Scott; Angus Young; Malcomb Young; Phil
Rudd; Cliff Williams; Brian Johnson.

ADC BAND
Singles: 7–inch
COTILLION 2-5   78-82
LPs: 10/12–inch 33rpm
COTILLION 5-10   78-82
Members: Michael Judkins; Arwell Mathew Jr; Audrey Mathew;
Mark Patterson.

AM-FM
Singles: 7–inch
DAKAR 2-4   82
Also see MASON, Vaughn

APB
Singles: 12–inch 33/45rpm
IMPORT 4-6   83

SLEEPING BAG 4-6   84
Singles: 7–inch
IMPORT 2-4   83
LPs: 10/12–inch 33rpm
MCA 5-10   83

AWB: see AVERAGE WHITE BAND

AALON
Singles: 7–inch
ARISTA 3-5   77
LPs: 10/12–inch 33rpm
ARISTA 5-10   77
Members: Aalon Butler; Ronnie Hammond.
Also see WAR

ABACO DREAM
Singles: 7–inch
A&M 4-6   69-70
Members: Paul Douglas; Dave Williams; Dennis Williams; Frank
Maid; Mike Sassano.

ABBA
Singles: 12–inch 33/45rpm
ATLANTIC 4-8   77-79
Singles: 7–inch
ATLANTIC 3-6   75-82
Picture Sleeves
ATLANTIC 3-6   77-82
LPs: 10/12–inch 33rpm
ATLANTIC (Except 300) 10-20   74-84
ATLANTIC (300 "Abba") 15-25   78
(Promotional issue only.)
CBS INT'L 8-12   80
EPIC 5-8   79
K-TEL.......................... 8-10   80
NAUTILUS (20 "Arrival") 15-25   82
(Half-speed mastered.)
SILVER EAGLE 8-10   84
Members: Anni-frid Lyngstad; Bjorn Ulvaeus; Benny Andersson;
Agnetha Faltskog.
Also see FALTSKOG, Agnetha
Also see FRIDA

**ABBA / Spinners / Firefall / England Dan and
John Ford Coley**
EPs: 7–inch 33/45rpm
WARNER SPECIAL PRODUCTS 5-10   78
(Coca-Cola/Burger King promotional issue. Issued
with paper sleeve.)
Also see ABBA
Also see ENGLAND DAN and John Ford Coley
Also see FIREFALL
Also see SPINNERS

ABBEY TAVERN SINGERS
Singles: 7–inch
HBR 4-8   66

ABBOTT, Billy, and the Jewels
Singles: 7–inch
PARKWAY 5-10   63-64

ABBOTT, Gregory
Singles: 12–inch 33/45rpm
COLUMBIA 4-6   86-88
Singles: 7–inch
COLUMBIA 2-4   86-88
Picture Sleeves
COLUMBIA 2-4   86-88
LPs: 10/12–inch 33rpm
COLUMBIA 5-10   87

ABDUL, Paula
(Paula Abdul with the Wild Pair)
Singles: 7–inch
VIRGIN 2-4   88-89
Picture Sleeves
VIRGIN 2-4   88-89
LPs: 10/12–inch 33rpm
VIRGIN 5-8   88-91

ABRAMS, Colonel
Singles: 12–inch 33/45rpm
MCA 4-6   85-87
STREETWISE 4-6   84
Singles: 7–inch
MCA 2-4   85-87
STREETWISE 2-4   84
LPs: 10/12–inch 33rpm
MCA 5-8   86

**ABRAMS, Miss, and the Strawberry Point
School Third Grade Class**
Singles: 7–inch
A&M 3-5   71
REPRISE 3-5   70
Picture Sleeves
REPRISE .... 3-5 - 70
LPs: 10/12–inch 33rpm
REPRISE 8-12   72

ACCENTS
(Featuring Robert Draper Jr.)
Singles: 7–inch
BRUNSWICK (55100 "Wiggle Wiggle") 8-15   58
BRUNSWICK (55123 "Ching a Ling") 10-15 58-59
CORAL 10-15   59
JUBILEE 5-10   59
Members: Robert Draper Jr.; Robert Armstrong; James Jackson;
Billy Hood; Arvid Garrett; Israel Goudeau Jr.

ACCEPT
Singles: 7–inch
PORTRAIT 2-4   84-89
Picture Sleeves
PORTRAIT 2-4   84-86
LPs: 10/12–inch 33rpm
PVC 5-10   83
PASSPORT 6-10   81
PORTRAIT 5-10   84-89

ACCUSED
EPs: 7–inch 33/45rpm
MARTHA SPLATTERHEAD 8-12   82

LPs: 10/12–inch 33rpm
COMBAT 5-10   87
Members: Blaine Cook; Tom Niemeyer; Dana Collins; Alex
Sibbald.

ACE
Singles: 7–inch
ABC 3-5   76-78
ANCHOR 3-5   75-77
LPs: 10/12–inch 33rpm
ANCHOR 8-12   75-77
Members: Paul Carrack; Fran Byrne; Tex Comer; Phil Harris;
Alan Bam King; Jon Woodhead.
Also see CARRACK, Paul

ACE, Buddy
Singles: 7–inch
DUKE 4-8   60-69
FIDELITY 6-12   59
PAULA 3-5   70-72
SPECIALTY 5-10   59

ACE, Johnny
(Johnny Ace and the Beale Streeters)
Singles: 78rpm
DUKE 10-15   52-55
Singles: 7–inch
ABC 2-4   73
DUKE 15-25   52-55
MCA 2-4   84
EPs: 7–inch 33/45rpm
DUKE (71 "Memorial Album") 15-25   63
(Jukebox issue only.)
DUKE (80 "Memorial Album") 150-200   55
DUKE (81 "Tribute Album") 150-200   55
LPs: 10/12–inch 33rpm
DUKE (70 "Memorial Album") 500-600   55
(10–inch LP.)
DUKE (71 "Memorial Album") 150-250   57
(No playing card shown on cover.)
DUKE (71 "Memorial Album") 60-80   61
(Playing card shown on cover.)
DUKE (X-71 "Memorial Album") 8-10   74
MCA 4-6   83

ACE, Johnny / Earl Forrest
Singles: 78rpm
FLAIR 20-35   53
Singles: 7–inch
FLAIR (1015 "Midnight Hours
Journey") 50-75   53
Also see ACE, Johnny
Also see FORREST, Earl

ACE SPECTRUM
Singles: 7–inch
ATLANTIC 3-5   74-76
LPs: 10/12–inch 33rpm
ATLANTIC 8-10   74-76
Members: Henry Zant; Troy Johnson; Rudy Gay; Elliot Isaac.

ACKLES, David
Singles: 7–inch
ELEKTRA 3-6   68-72

LPs: 10/12–inch 33rpm

COLUMBIA	5-10	73
ELEKTRA	8-12	69-72

ACKLIN, Barbara
Singles: 7–inch

BRUNSWICK	4-8	67-73
CAPITOL	3-5	74-75
ERIC	2-4	83

Picture Sleeves

BRUNSWICK	5-10	68

LPs: 10/12–inch 33rpm

BRUNSWICK	10-15	68-71
CAPITOL	5-10	75

Also see CHANDLER, Gene, and Barbara Acklin

ACT I
Singles: 7–inch

SPRING	3-5	73-74

LPs: 10/12–inch 33rpm

SPRING	5-10	74

AD LIBS
Singles: 7–inch

A.G.P.	4-8	66
BLUE CAT	5-10	65
CAPITOL	3-6	70
KAREN	4-8	66
PHILIPS	4-8	67
SHARE	3-6	69

Members: Mary Ann Thomas; Danny Austin; Hugh Harris; J.T. Taylor; Norm Donegan; Dave Watts.

ADAM and the Ants
Singles: 12–inch 33/45rpm

EPIC	4-8	81

Singles: 7–inch

EPIC	3-5	81

LPs: 10/12–inch 33rpm

EDITIONS EG	5-10	82
EPIC	8-10	81-82

Members: Adam Ant; Johnny Bivouac; Andy Watson; Dave Barb.
Also see ANT, Adam
Also see BOW WOW WOW

ADAMS, Bobby
Singles: 7–inch

BATTLE	4-8	63
COLPIX	5-10	61
HOMETOWN	3-6	70
PET (803 "I Want My Lovin")	15-25	58
PURDY	4-8	64

ADAMS, Bobby, and Norma Jean Carpenter
Singles: 7–inch

KINGSTAR	3-5	71

Also see ADAMS, Bobby

ADAMS, Bryan
(B.G. Adams)
Singles: 12–inch 33/45rpm

A&M	4-6	82-87
(Black vinyl.)		

A&M	5-10	84
(Colored vinyl.)		

Singles: 7–inch

A&M (Except 474)	2-5	80-87
(Black vinyl.)		
A&M (474 "Let Me Take You Dancing")	8-12	79
A&M (Colored vinyl)	4-6	

Picture Sleeves

A&M (Except 474)	3-5	80-87
A&M (474 "Let Me Take You Dancing")	10-15	79

LPs: 10/12–inch 33rpm

A&M	5-10	80-87

Also see DION
Also see SWEENY TODD

ADAMS, Bryan, and Tina Turner
Singles: 7–inch

A&M	2-4	85

Picture Sleeves

A&M	2-4	85

Also see ADAMS, Bryan
Also see TURNER, Tina

ADAMS, Faye
Singles: 78rpm

ATLANTIC	10-15	52-53
HERALD	10-15	53-57
IMPERIAL	8-12	55-57

Singles: 7–inch

ABC	2-4	73
ATLANTIC	20-35	52-53
COLLECTABLES	2-4	82
HERALD (Black vinyl)	10-20	53-57
HERALD (Colored vinyl)	25-50	53
IMPERIAL	10-20	55-57
LIDO	5-10	59-60
SAVOY	5-10	61
WARWICK	5-10	61

LPs: 10/12–inch 33rpm

COLLECTABLES	6-8	88
SAVOY	5-10	76
WARWICK (2031 "Shake a Hand")	50-75	61

ADAMS, Faye / Little Esther / Shirley and Lee
LPs: 10/12–inch 33rpm

ALMOR (103 "Golden Souvenirs")	10-20	

Also see ADAMS, Faye
Also see LITTLE ESTHER
Also see MORRIS, Joe, and His Orchestra
Also see SHIRLEY & LEE

ADAMS, Gayle
Singles: 7–inch

PRELUDE	2-4	80-81

LPs: 10/12–inch 33rpm

PRELUDE	5-10	82

ADAMS, Johnny
Singles: 7–inch

ARIOLA AMERICAN	2-4	78
ATLANTIC	3-5	71-72
HELP ME	2-5	74-76
J.B.	3-5	76

MODERN	4-8	67
PAID	2-4	84
RIC	5-10	59-62
RON	4-8	64-65
SSS INT'L	2-5	68-74
WATCH	4-8	63

LPs: 10/12–inch 33rpm

ARIOLA AMERICAN	5-10	78
CHELSEA	10-20	77
HELP ME	8-10	74-76
SSS INT'L	10-15	70

ADAMS, Johnny, and the Gondoliers
Singles: 7–inch

RIC (957 "Knocked Out")	10-20	59

Also see ADAMS, Johnny

ADAMS, Marie
(Marie Adams with Three Tons of Joy)
Singles: 78rpm

PEACOCK	5-10	51-54

Singles: 7–inch

CAPITOL	5-10	58
PEACOCK	10-20	51-54
VANTAGE	3-5	73

Also see OTIS, Johnny

ADDEO, Leo, and His Orchestra
LPs: 10/12–inch 33rpm

CAMDEN	5-10	61

ADDERLEY, Julian "Cannonball"
Singles: 7–inch

BLUE NOTE	4-8	59
CAPITOL	3-8	61-73
RIVERSIDE	4-6	61-64

EPs: 7–inch 33/45rpm

EMARCY	10-20	55

LPs: 10/12–inch 33rpm

BLUE NOTE	20-30	58
(Label reads "Blue Note Records Inc. - New York, U.S.A.")		
BLUE NOTE	15-25	66
(Label reads "Blue Note Records - A Division Of Liberty Records Inc.")		
CAPITOL (Except 2200 and 2300 series)	8-15	66-80
CAPITOL (2200 and 2300 series)	12-25	64-65
DOBRE	5-8	77
EMARCY (400 series)	8-12	76
EMARCY (36000 series)	30-40	55-58
EVEREST	8-12	71
FANTASY	8-12	73-75
LIMELIGHT	10-20	66
MERCURY (1000 series)	5-10	81
MERCURY (20000 and 60000 series)	15-30	61-62
MILESTONE	6-12	73-82
PACIFIC JAZZ	15-25	62
RIVERSIDE (032 through 142)	5-8	82-85
RIVERSIDE (200 through 400 series)	15-30	58-63
RIVERSIDE (1100 series)	20-30	59-60
RIVERSIDE (3000 series)	10-15	68
RIVERSIDE (9000 series)	15-25	60-63
SAVOY (2200 series)	8-12	76
SAVOY (12018 "Presenting Cannonball")	50-75	55
TRIP	5-10	75
VSP	10-20	65
WING	8-12	68

Also see WILSON, Nancy, and Julian "Cannonball" Adderley

ADDERLEY, Julian "Cannonball," and John Coltrane
LPs: 10/12–inch 33rpm

LIMELIGHT	10-20	65
MERCURY	15-25	61

Also see COLTRANE, John

ADDERLEY, Julian "Cannonball," and Sergio Mendes
LPs: 10/12–inch 33rpm

CAPITOL	10-15	68-71
EVEREST	5-10	73

Also see ADDERLEY, Julian "Cannonball"
Also see MENDES, Sergio

ADDRISI, Dick
Singles: 7–inch

VALIANT	6-12	66

Also see ADDRISI BROTHERS

ADDRISI BROTHERS
Singles: 7–inch

BELL	3-5	74
BRAD	10-20	58
BUDDAH	3-5	77
COLUMBIA	3-5	72-73
DEL-FI	8-15	59
ELEKTRA	2-4	81
IMPERIAL	5-10	60
POM POM	5-10	62
PRIVATE STOCK	3-5	75
SCOTTI BROTHERS	2-4	79
VALIANT	4-8	64-65
WARNER	3-8	62-68

Picture Sleeves

SCOTTI BROTHERS	2-4	79

LPs: 10/12–inch 33rpm

BUDDAH	5-10	77
COLUMBIA	5-10	72

Members: Dick Addrisi; Don Addrisi.
Also see ADDRISI, Dick

ADE, King Sunny
(King Sunny Ade and His African Beats)
Singles: 12–inch 33/45rpm

MANGO	4-6	83

Singles: 7–inch

MANGO	2-4	83

LPs: 10/12–inch 33rpm

MANGO	5-10	83

ADVANCE
Singles: 12–inch 33/45rpm
POLYDOR 4-6   83
Singles: 7–inch
POLYDOR 2-4   83

ADVENTURES
Singles: 12–inch 33/45rpm
CHRYSALIS 4-6   86
Singles: 7–inch
CHRYSALIS 2-4   86
Picture Sleeves
CHRYSALIS 2-4   86
LPs: 10/12–inch 33rpm
CHRYSALIS 5-10   86

AEROSMITH
Singles: 7–inch
COLUMBIA 2-5   73-80
GEFFEN 2-4   85-90
Picture Sleeves
GEFFEN 2-4   85-89
LPs: 10/12–inch 33rpm
COLUMBIA (Except KC-32005) 5-15   73-86
COLUMBIA (KC-32005 "Aerosmith") . 20-25   73
(Orange cover. Incorrectly shows *Walking the Dog*
as *Walking the Dig.*)
COLUMBIA (KC-32005 "Aerosmith") . 10-12   73
(Correctly lists *Walking the Dog.*)
GEFFEN 5-10   85-87
Promotional LPs
COLUMBIA (187 "Pure Gold") 50-55   76
(Boxed set of the group's first three LPs.)
Members: Steve Tyler; Tom Hamilton; Joey Kramer; Joe Perry;
Brad Whitford.
Also see PERRY, Joe, Project
Also see RUN - D.M.C.

AFRIKA BAMBAATAA:
see BAMBAATAA, Afrika

AFRIQUE
Singles: 7–inch
MAINSTREAM 3-5   73
LPs: 10/12–inch 33rpm
MAINSTREAM 8-12   73
Member: David T. Walker.

AFRO CUBAN BAND
Singles: 7–inch
ARISTA 2-4   78
LPs: 10/12–inch 33rpm
ARISTA 5-10   78

AFTER the FIRE
Singles: 12–inch 33/45rpm
EPIC 4-8   83
Singles: 7–inch
EPIC 2-4   83-84
LPs: 10/12–inch 33rpm
EPIC 5-10   82
Members: Peter Banks; Iver Piercy; Tim Haywell; Nick Battle.
Also see BANKS, Peter

AFTERBACH
Singles: 7–inch
COLUMBIA/ARC 2-4   81
LPs: 10/12–inch 33rpm
COLUMBIA/ARC 5-10   81

AFTERNOON DELIGHTS
Singles: 12–inch 33/45rpm
MCA 4-8   81
Singles: 7–inch
MCA 2-4   81
LPs: 10/12–inch 33rpm
MCA 5-10   81

AGENT ORANGE
Singles: 7–inch
ENIGMA 2-4   86
POSH BOY 2-4   81
LPs: 10/12–inch 33rpm
ENIGMA 5-10   86-87

A-HA
Singles: 7–inch
REPRISE 2-4   85-86
WARNER 2-4   85-87
Picture Sleeves
WARNER 2-4   85-87
LPs: 10/12–inch 33rpm
REPRISE 5-10   85-86
WARNER 5-10   85-88
Member: Morten Harket.

AIDA
Singles: 12–inch 33/45rpm
VANGUARD 4-6   84
Singles: 7–inch
VANGUARD 2-4   84
LPs: 10/12–inch 33rpm
VANGUARD 5-8   84

AIR SUPPLY
Singles: 7–inch
ARISTA 2-4   80-86
FLASHBACK 2-4   82
Picture Sleeves
ARISTA 2-4   80-86
LPs: 10/12–inch 33rpm
ARISTA 5-10   80-86
COLUMBIA 10-15   77
MFSL (113 "The One That You Love") 20-25   84
NAUTULIS (31 "Lost in Love") 15-25   82
Members: Graham Russell; Russell Hitchcock; David Moyse;
Criston Barker; Ralph Cooper; David Green; Frank Esler-Smith;
Rex Goh.
Also see HITCHCOCK, Russell

AIRWAVES
Singles: 7–inch
A&M 2-4   78-79
LPs: 10/12–inch 33rpm
A&M 5-10   78-79
Members: John David; Dave Charles; Ray Martinez.

AKENS, Jewel
Singles: 7–inch
AMERICAN INT'L ARTISTS	2-4	75
CAPEHART	5-10	61
COLGEMS	4-8	67
ERA	4-8	65
MINASA	4-8	65
RTV	3-5	72
LPs: 10/12–inch 33rpm
ERA	20-30	65

AKKERMAN, Jan
(Jan Akkerman and Kaz Lux)
Singles: 7–inch
ATLANTIC	2-4	77-79
LPs: 10/12–inch 33rpm
ATCO	10-12	73
ATLANTIC	5-10	76-79
SIRE	10-15	73

AL B. SURE!
Singles: 7–inch
WARNER	2-4	88-90
Picture Sleeves
WARNER	2-4	88
LPs: 10/12–inch 33rpm
WARNER	5-8	88-90

ALABAMA
(Alabama Band)
Singles: 7–inch
GRT	4-8	77
MDJ	3-5	79-80
RCA	2-5	80-90
SUN (Colored vinyl)	4-8	81
Picture Sleeves
GRT	10-20	77
RCA	2-4	80-87
LPs: 10/12–inch 33rpm
ABC/WATERMARK ("American Country Countdown Presents Alabama")	8-12	88
(No number used. Promotional issue only.)		
ALABAMA RECORDS (78 9-01 "The Alabama Band")	200-400	78
PLANTATION	40-60	81
RCA	5-10	80-90
SONNY	30-50	79

Members: Randy Owen; Jeff Cook; Teddy Gentry; R. Scott; Mark Herndon.
Also see RICHIE, Lionel, and Alabama
Also see WILD COUNTRY

ALAIMO, Chuck
(Chuck Alaimo Quartet)
Singles: 78rpm
KEN	5-10	57
MGM	5-10	57
Singles: 7–inch
KEN	10-20	57
MGM	10-20	57

ALAIMO, Steve
(Steve Alaimo and the Redcoats)
Singles: 7–inch
ABC	3-6	66-67
ABC-PAR	4-8	64-66
ATCO	3-6	67-71
CHECKER	6-12	61-63
DADE	8-12	59
DICKSON	8-12	60
ENTRANCE	3-5	71-72
ERIC	2-4	83
IMPERIAL	5-10	60-63
LIFETIME	20-30	58
MARLIN (Except 6064)	10-20	59
MARLIN (6064 "I Want You to Love Me")	10-20	59
EPs: 7–inch 33/45rpm
ABC-PAR (531 "Where the Action Is")	8-15	65
(Jukebox issue only.)		
LPs: 10/12–inch 33rpm
ABC-PAR	15-25	65-66
CHECKER	20-30	61-63
CROWN	10-15	63

ALAIMO, Steve, and Betty Wright
Singles: 7–inch
ATCO	3-6	69

Also see ALAIMO, Steve
Also see WRIGHT, Betty

ALARM
Singles: 7–inch
I.R.S.	2-4	83-90
Picture Sleeves
I.R.S.	2-4	83-89
LPs: 10/12–inch 33rpm
I.R.S.	5-10	83-91

Members: Mike Peters; Nigel Twist; Dave Sharp; Eddie MacDonald.

ALBERT, Eddie
Singles: 78rpm
KAPP	4-8	54-56
Singles: 7–inch
COLUMBIA	3-5	68
HICKORY	3-6	64-65
KAPP	5-10	54-56
Picture Sleeves
KAPP (134 "Little Child")	10-15	56
LPs: 10/12–inch 33rpm
COLUMBIA	8-12	68
HAMILTON	10-15	59

ALBERT, Eddie, and Sondra Lee
Singles: 7–inch
KAPF	5-10	56

Also see ALBERT, Eddie

ALBERT, Morris
Singles: 7–inch
RCA	3-5	75-76

LPs: 10/12–inch 33rpm
RCA 5-10   75-76

ALBERTI, Willy
Singles: 7–inch
EPIC 3-6   59
LONDON 3-6   59
LPs: 10/12–inch 33rpm
LONDON 5-15   59

ALBRIGHT, Gerald
Singles: 7–inch
ATLANTIC 2-4   87-88
LPs: 10/12–inch 33rpm
ATLANTIC 5-8   88

ALCATRAZZ
Singles: 7–inch
ROCSHIRE 4-8   83
Picture Sleeves
ROCSHIRE 8-15   83
LPs: 10/12–inch 33rpm
CAPITOL 15-25   85
ROCSHIRE 15-25   83-84
Members: Graham Bonnet; Steve Val; Yngwie Malmsteen.
Also see RAINBOW
Also see SCHENKER, Michael, Group

ALDO NOVA: see NOVA, Aldo

ALDRICH, Renee
Singles: 7–inch
JAM PACKED 2-4   87

ALDRICH, Ronnie
LPs: 10/12–inch 33rpm
LONDON PHASE 4 5-15   61-71

ALEEM
(Aleems)
Singles: 12–inch 33/45rpm
ATLANTIC 4-6   87
NIA 5-8   85
Singles: 7–inch
ATLANTIC 2-4   86-87
NIA 3-5   84-85
LPs: 10/12–inch 33rpm
ATLANTIC 5-10   87
Members: Taharqa Aleem; Tunde-Ra Aleem; Leroy Burgess.
Also see BLACK IVORY

ALEEMS: see ALEEM

ALEXANDER, Arthur
Singles: 7–inch
BUDDAH 3-5   75-76
DOT 5-10   62-64
MONUMENT 4-6   68
MUSIC MILL 3-6   77
SOUND STAGE 7 3-6   65-71
WARNER 3-5   72-73
EPs: 7–inch 33/45rpm
DOT ("You Better Move On") 25-35   62
(Number not known.)

LPs: 10/12–inch 33rpm
DOT (3434 "You Better Move On") . . 35-45   62
(Monaural.)
DOT (25434 "You Better Move On") . 40-55   62
(Stereo.)
WARNER 8-15   72

ALEXANDER, David
Singles: 7–inch
SOUNDTOWN 2-4   87

ALEXANDER, Goldie
Singles: 7–inch
ARISTA 2-4   82

ALEXANDER, Margie
Singles: 12–inch 33/45rpm
CHI-SOUND 4-8   77
Singles: 7–inch
ATLANTIC 3-5   71
CHI-SOUND 2-4   76-77
FUTURE STARS 3-5   74

ALFIE: see SILAS, Alfie

ALFONZO
(Alfonzo Jones)
Singles: 12–inch 33/45rpm
JOE-WES 4-6   83
Singles: 7–inch
JOE-WES 2-4   82
LARC 2-4   82
LPs: 10/12–inch 33rpm
LARC 5-10   83

ALI, Muhammad, and Frank Sinatra
LPs: 10/12–inch 33rpm
ST. JOHN'S (1 "Ali and His Gang
Fight Tooth Decay") 20-40
(Promotional issue only.)
Also see CLAY, Cassius
Also see SINATRA, Frank

ALICE COOPER: see COOPER, Alice

ALICE WONDER LAND
Singles: 7–inch
BARDELL 10-20   63
UNITED INTERNATIONAL 10-15

ALISHA
Singles: 12–inch 33/45rpm
VANGUARD 4-6   84-86
Singles: 7–inch
MCA 2-4   90
RCA 2-4   87
VANGUARD 2-4   84-86
Picture Sleeves
RCA 2-4   87
LPs: 10/12–inch 33rpm
MCA 5-8   90

ALIVE 'N KICKING
Singles: 7–inch
ROULETTE 4-8   70-71

LPs: 10/12-inch 33rpm
ROULETTE (42052 "Alive 'N Kickin") 20-30   70
ROULETTE (42052 "Alive 'N Kickin") 40-60   70
(Promotional issue.)

ALL POINTS BULLETIN BAND
Singles: 7-inch
LITTLE CITY 3-5   75-79

ALL SPORTS BAND
Singles: 7-inch
RADIO 2-4   81-82
LPs: 10/12-inch 33rpm
RADIO 5-10   81

ALLAN, Davie
(Davie Allan and the Arrows)
Singles: 7-inch
A.O.A............................ 3-6   76
CUDE (101 "War Path") 30-40   63
MARC (3223 "War Path") 20-30   63
MGM 3-6   71-73
MRC 3-5   84
PRIVATE STOCK 3-5   74
SIDEWALK 10-15   64
TOWER 5-10   65-68
WHAT 3-5   82
LPs: 10/12-inch 33rpm
ALKOR 5-10   84
ARROW DYNAMICS 8-12   85
TOWER 15-25   65-68
WHAT 5-10   83
Members: Davie Allan; Steve Pugh; Larry Brown; Paul Johnson;
Don Manning; Tony Allwine.
Also see ANNETTE
Also see CURB, Mike
Also see DALE, Dick
Also see HONDELLS
Also see NAYLOR, Jerry
Also see PARIS SISTERS
Also see PRISCILLA
Also see RONSTADT, Linda
Also see STAFFORD, Terry

ALLAN, Davie / Eternity's Children / Main Attraction / Sunrays
EPs: 7-inch 33/45rpm
TOWER (4557 "Selections from
April Albums") 25-50   68
(Promotional issue only.)
Also see ALLAN, Davie
Also see ETERNITY'S CHILDREN
Also see SUNRAYS

ALLEN, Annisteen
(Annisteen Allen and Her Home Town Boys)

Singles: 78rpm
CAPITOL 10-15   55
DECCA 10-15   56-57
FEDERAL 10-15   51-52
KING 10-15   46-54
Singles: 7-inch
CAPITOL 10-20   55

DECCA 10-20   56-57
KING 15-25   53-54
TRUE SOUND 5-8
WIG 5-10   59
Also see ALLEN, Ernestine

ALLEN, Annisteen, and Melvin Moore
Singles: 7-inch
TODD.......................... 5-10   59
Also see ALLEN, Annisteen

ALLEN, Dayton
LPs: 10/12-inch 33rpm
GRAND AWARD 10-15   60

ALLEN, Donna
Singles: 7-inch
OCEANA 2-4   88
TWENTY-ONE 2-4   86-87
LPs: 10/12-inch 33rpm
OCEANA 5-8   88
TWENTY-ONE 5-10   86-87

ALLEN, Ernestine
(Annisteen Allen)
Singles: 7-inch
TRU-SOUND 5-10   62
LPs: 10/12-inch 33rpm
TRU-SOUND 20-35   62
Also see ALLEN, Annisteen

ALLEN, Jonelle
Singles: 7-inch
ALEXANDER STREET 2-4   78

ALLEN, Lee
Singles: 78rpm
ALADDIN 8-15   56
EMBER 10-15   58
Singles: 7-inch
ALADDIN 10-20   56
COLLECTABLES 2-4   82
EMBER 8-12   58-59
EPs: 7-inch 33/45rpm
EMBER (103 "Walkin' with Mr. Lee") . 40-60   58
LPs: 10/12-inch 33rpm
EMBER (200 "Walkin' with Mr. Lee") 75-125   58
(Red label.)
EMBER (200 "Walkin' with Mr. Lee") . 60-80   58
("Logs" label. Ember logo is formed with logs.)
EMBER (Black label) 25-35   60
Also see BLASTERS
Also see DOMINO, Fats
Also see STRAY CATS

ALLEN, Peter
Singles: 12-inch 33/45rpm
A&M 4-8   79
Singles: 7-inch
A&M 2-5   74-82
ARISTA 2-4   83-84
METROMEDIA 3-5   71-73
LPs: 10/12-inch 33rpm
A&M 5-10   74-82

ARISTA 5-10   83-84
METROMEDIA 10-15   71-72

ALLEN, R. Justice
Singles: 7–inch
CATAWBA 2-4   86

ALLEN, Rance, Group
Singles: 7–inch
CAPITOL 2-5   77-79
GOSPEL TRUTH 3-5   72-73
STAX 2-4   78-81
TRUTH 3-5   74-75
LPs: 10/12–inch 33rpm
CAPITOL 5-10   77-79
GOSPEL TRUTH 8-12   72-74
MYRRH 5-10   84.
STAX 5-10   78-81
TRUTH 8-10   75
Members: Rance Allen; Thomas Allen; Steven Allen; Esau Allen; Linda Mendez; Annie Mendez; Judy Mendez.

ALLEN, Rex
Singles: 78rpm
DECCA (Except 30651) 4-8   52-57
DECCA (30651 "Knock Knock,
  Rattle") 8-15   56
MERCURY 5-10   49-55
Singles: 7–inch
BUENA VISTA 4-8   59
DECCA (Except 28000 through
  30000 series) 3-8   56-72
DECCA (28000 and 29000 series) . 5-10   52-56
DECCA (30000 series, except 30651) . 5-10   56
DECCA (30651 "Knock Knock, Rattle") 15-20   56
JMI 3-5   73
MERCURY 5-10   53-62
WILDCAT 4-6
Picture Sleeves
MERCURY 5-10   63
EPs: 7–inch 33/45rpm
DECCA 10-20   56
MERCURY 10-20   53-56
LPs: 10/12–inch 33rpm
BUENA VISTA 20-25   61
COLLECTOR'S CLASSICS 5-10
CORAL 5-10   73
DECCA (5000 series) 10-15   68-70
  (Decca LP numbers in this series preceded by a
  "7" or a "DL-7" are stereo issues.)
DECCA (8000 series) 20-30   56-58
DESIGN 10-15   62
DISNEYLAND 6-10   70
HACIENDA 20-25
JMI 5-10
MCA 5-10
MERCURY 10-20   62
PICKWICK/HILLTOP 10-15   65
VOCALION 6-10   70
WING 10-15   64-66

ALLEN, Richie
(Richie Allen and the Pacific Surfers)
Singles: 7–inch
ERA 5-10   61
IMPERIAL 8-15   60-63
TOWER 4-8   66
LPs: 10/12–inch 33rpm
IMPERIAL 40-70   63
Member: Richie Podolor.

ALLEN, Steve
Singles: 78rpm
BRUNSWICK 4-8   53
CORAL 4-8   55-56
Singles: 7–inch
BRUNSWICK 5-10   53
CORAL 5-10   55-56
DOT 4-8   59-66
DUNHILL (Except 4097) 3-5   67-68
DUNHILL (4097 "Here Comes Sgt.
  Pepper") 4-8   67
SIGNATURE 3-6   59-60
Picture Sleeves
DOT 5-10   65
EPs: 7–inch 33/45rpm
BRUNSWICK 10-20   53
CORAL 10-20   55-56
DECCA 15-20   55
WOODBURY'S 10-20
LPs: 10/12–inch 33rpm
COLUMBIA (2554 "Steve Allen") 20-30   56
  (10–inch LP.)
CORAL (100 "Jazz Story") 25-35   59
  (Narration by Steve Allen, music by various artists.)
CORAL (57000 series, except 57099) 15-20   55-56
CORAL (57099 "The James Dean
  Story") 35-50   56
  (With Bill Randle.)
CORAL (57400 series) 10-20   63
  (Monaural.)
CORAL (7-57400 series) 10-20   63
  (Stereo.)
DECCA 20-25   55
DOT (Except 3472 and 3517) 10-20   59-66
DOT (3472 "Steve Allen's Funny
  Fone Calls") 15-20   63
DOT (3517 "More Funny Fone Calls) 15-20   63
DUNHILL 8-10   67
EMARCY 15-20   58
HAMILTON 10-15   59-64
MERCURY 10-15   61
PETE 5-10   69
ROULETTE 15-20   59
SIGNATURE (Except 1004) 15-20   59
SIGNATURE (1004 "Man on
  the Street") 30-40   59
  (With Louis Nye, Tom Poston and Don Knotts.)
  Also see PRESLEY, Elvis

ALLEN, Steve, and Jayne Meadows
Singles: 78rpm
CORAL 4-8   55
Singles: 7–inch
CORAL 5-10   55
Also see ALLEN, Steve

ALLEN, Vee
Singles: 7–inch
LION 3-5   73
MCA 2-4   83
LPs: 10/12–inch 33rpm
MCA 5-10   83

ALLEN, Woody
Singles: 7–inch
U.A. 3-5   72
Picture Sleeves
U.A. 4-6   72
LPs: 10/12–inch 33rpm
BELL 10-15   67
CAPITOL 8-12   68
CASABLANCA 8-12   79
COLPIX 20-30   64-65
U.A. (800 series) 6-10   77
U.A. (9900 series) 8-12   72

ALLENS, Arvee
(Ritchie Valens)
Singles: 7–inch
DEL-FI (4114 "Fast Freight") 20-30   59
Also see VALENS, Ritchie

ALLEY CATS
Singles: 7–inch
PHILLES (108 "Puddin n' Tain") 15-20   62
Members: Chester Pipkin; Gary Pipkin; Bobby Sheen; Sheridan
Spencer; Brice Coefield; James Barker.
Also see PIPKINS
Also see SHEEN, Bobby

ALLISON, Gene
Singles: 78rpm
CALVERT 10-15   56
DECCA 5-10   57
VEE JAY 5-10   57
Singles: 7–inch
CALVERT 15-25   56
CHAMPION 5-10   59
CHEROKEE 5-10   59
DECCA 10-15   57
MONUMENT 4-8   65
VALDOT 4-8   62
VEE JAY 8-15   57-60
LPs: 10/12–inch 33rpm
VEE JAY (1009 "Gene Allison") . . . 100-125   59
(Maroon label.)
VEE JAY (1009 "Gene Allison") 25-40   59
(Black label.)

ALLISONS
Singles: 7–inch
TIP (1011 "Surfer Street") 15-20   63

ALLMAN, Duane
LPs: 10/12–inch 33rpm
CAPRICORN 8-12   72-74
Also see DEREK and the Dominos

ALLMAN, Duane and Gregg
Singles: 7–inch
BOLD 5-8   73
LPs: 10/12–inch 33rpm
BOLD (301 "Duane and Gregg
Allman") 20-25   72
(Gatefold cover.)
BOLD (301 "Duane and Gregg Allman") 8-10   73
(Standard cover.)
SPRINGBOARD 8-10   75
Also see ALLMAN, Duane
Also see ALLMAN, Gregg
Also see ALLMAN BROTHERS BAND
Also see ALLMAN JOYS

ALLMAN, Gregg
(Gregg Allman Band)
Singles: 7–inch
CAPRICORN 3-5   73-77
EPIC 2-4   87-89
LPs: 10/12–inch 33rpm
CAPRICORN 8-12   73-77
EPIC 5-10   87-89
ROBERT KLEIN ("Interview") 40-60   81
(Promotional issue only.)
Also see ALLMAN, Duane and Gregg
Also see ALLMAN and Woman
Also see ALLMAN BROTHERS BAND
Also see ALLMAN JOYS

ALLMAN and Woman
Singles: 7–inch
WARNER 3-5   77
LPs: 10/12–inch 33rpm
WARNER 8-10   77
Members: Gregg Allman; Cher.
Also see ALLMAN, Gregg
Also see CHER

ALLMAN BROTHERS BAND
Singles: 7–inch
ARISTA 2-4   80-81
CAPRICORN (Except 036) 2-5   71-79
CAPRICORN (036 "Jessica") 25-35   73
Picture Sleeves
ARISTA 3-5   81
EPs: 7–inch 33/45rpm
ATLANTIC 10-20   73
(Jukebox issue only.)
CAPRICORN 10-20   73
(Jukebox issue only.)
LPs: 10/12–inch 33rpm
ARISTA 5-10   80-81
ATCO 15-20   69-73
CAPRICORN (Except 802) 8-15   72-79
CAPRICORN (802 "The Allman Brothers
Band at the Fillmore East") 15-20   71
EPIC 5-8   90

K-TEL 5-10
MFSL (157 "Eat a Peach") 20-25   85
POLYDOR (6339 "Best of the
  Allman Brothers Band") 5-10   89
POLYDOR (839-417 "The Allman
  Brothers Band") 25-35   89
  (Six-LP boxed set, with booklet.)
  Members: Duane Allman; Gregg Allman; Dicky Betts; Les
  Dudek; David Goldflies; Paul Hornsby; Berry Oakley; Dan Toler;
  Johnny Sandlin; Butch Trucks; Johnny Johanson.
  Also see ALLMAN, Duane and Gregg
  Also see BETTS, Richard
  Also see DUDEK, Les
  Also see HOUR GLASS
  Also see SEA LEVEL

ALLMAN JOYS
            Singles: 7-inch
DIAL (4046 "Spoonful") 25-35   66
            LPs: 10/12-inch 33rpm
DIAL 10-15   73
  Members: Duane Allman; Gregg Allman; Ralph Balinger; Ronnie
  Wilkin; Tommy Amato; Jack Jackson; Bobby Dennis.
  Also see ALLMAN, Duane and Gregg

ALMEIDA, Laurindo
  (Laurindo Almeida and the Modern Jazz Quartet)
            Singles: 7-inch
ATLANTIC 4-6   64
CAPITOL 3-8   55-65
PACIFIC JAZZ 5-8   55
            EPs: 7-inch 33/45rpm
CAPITOL 5-15   56-59
CORAL 5-10   54-56
PACIFIC JAZZ 10-15   54
            LPs: 10/12-inch 33rpm
ATLANTIC 10-20   64
CAPITOL (Except 8000 series) 15-25   59-65
CAPITOL (8000 series) 20-35   56-58
CORAL 25-45   54-56
CRYSTAL CLEAR 5-8   80
DAYBREAK 5-10   73
DOBRE 5-10   76-77
INNER CITY 5-8   79
PACIFIC JAZZ (7 "Laurindo Almeida
  Quartet") 50-75   54
  (10-inch LP.)
PACIFIC JAZZ (13 "Laurindo Almeida
  Quartet, Vol. 2") 50-75   54
  (10-inch LP.)
SURREY 10-20   65
WORLD PACIFIC 25-40   56-62
  Also see BYRD, Charlie
  Also see DAVIS, Sammy, Jr., and Laurindo Almeida
  Also see GETZ, Stan, and Laurindo Almeida
  Also see SOMMERS, Joanie, and Laurindo Almeida

ALMEIDA, Laurindo / Chico Hamilton
            LPs: 10/12-inch 33rpm
JAZZTONE 10-20   64
  Also see ALMEIDA, Laurindo
  Also see HAMILTON, Chico

ALMOND, Marc
            Singles: 7-inch
CAPITOL 2-4   89
            Picture Sleeves
CAPITOL 2-4   89
            LPs: 10/12-inch 33rpm
CAPITOL 5-8   89
  Also see MARK - ALMOND BAND

ALPACA PHASE III
            Singles: 7-inch
ATLANTIC 3-5   74

ALPERT, Herb
  (Herb Alpert and the Tijuana Brass; Herbie Alpert)
            Singles: 12-inch 33/45rpm
A&M 4-6   79-84
  (Black vinyl.)
A&M 5-8   84
  (Colored vinyl.)
            Singles: 7-inch
A&M (Except 700 series) 2-5   66-87
A&M (700 series) 3-8   62-66
ANDEX 4-6   59
CAROL 4-6   59
ROWE/AMI 4-8   66
  ("Play Me" Sales Stimulator promotional issue.)
            Picture Sleeves
A&M (Except 700 series) 2-5   66-87
A&M (700 series) 3-6   65-66
            EPs: 7-inch 33/45rpm
A&M 4-8   65-66
  (Jukebox issues only.)
            LPs: 10/12-inch 33rpm
A&M (Except 100 series) 5-10   66-87
A&M (100 series) 8-15   62-66
MFSL (053 "Rise") 25-50   81
  Also see HALL, Lani, and Herb Alpert
  Also see LOU, Herb B.

ALPERT, Herb, and Hugh Masekela
            Singles: 7-inch
A&M/HORIZON 2-4   78
            Picture Sleeves
A&M/HORIZON 3-5   78
            LPs: 10/12-inch 33rpm
A&M/HORIZON 5-10   78
  Also see ALPERT, Herb
  Also see MASEKELA, Hugh

ALPHAVILLE
            Singles: 12-inch 33/45rpm
ATLANTIC 4-6   84-86
            Singles: 7-inch
ATLANTIC 2-4   84-88
            Picture Sleeves
ATLANTIC 2-4   84-88
            LPs: 10/12-inch 33rpm
ATLANTIC 5-10   84-86

ALSTON, Gerald
Singles: 7–inch
MOTOWN 2-4   88
LPs: 10/12–inch 33rpm
MOTOWN 5-8   88

ALVIN, Dave
(Dave Alvin and the Red Devils)
Singles: 7–inch
ENIGMA 5-8   87
LPs: 10/12–inch 33rpm
EPIC 5-10   87
  Also see BLASTERS

ALVIN LEE: see LEE, Alvin

ALWAYS, Billy
Singles: 7–inch
EPIC 2-4   88
WAYLO 2-4   82

AMAZING RHYTHM ACES
Singles: 7–inch
ABC 2-5   75-79
COLUMBIA 2-4   79
WARNER 2-4   80
LPs: 10/12–inch 33rpm
ABC 8-12   75-78
COLUMBIA 5-10   79
WARNER 5-10   80
  Members: Russell Smith; James Brown Jr; Byrd Burton; Stick Davis; Billy Earhart III; James Hooker; Butch McDade.

AMAZULU
Singles: 7–inch
MANGO 2-4   87
  Members: Ann Marie Ruddock; Sharon Bailey; Lesley Beach.

AMBASSADORS
Singles: 7–inch
ARCTIC 3-6   68-69
ATLANTIC 4-8   67-68
SOUND STAGE 7 4-8   67-68
TIME 4-8
LPs: 10/12–inch 33rpm
ARCTIC 10-15   69
  Members: Bobby Todd; Herley Johnson; Orlando Oliphant.
  Also see CREME D' COCOA

AMBOY DUKES
Singles: 7–inch
MAINSTREAM 6-12   67-69
LPs: 10/12–inch 33rpm
AUDIOFIDELITY (1005 "Journey to
  the Center of the Mind") 8-12   83
  (Picture disc.)
MAINSTREAM (801 "Journeys and
  Migrations") 15-20   74
MAINSTREAM (6104 "Amboy Dukes") 25-35   68
MAINSTREAM (6112 "Journey to
  the Center of the Mind") 25-35   68
MAINSTREAM (6118 "Migration") ... 25-35   68
MAINSTREAM (6125 "Best of
  the Original Amboy Dukes") 25-35   69

POLYDOR 10-20   70
  Members: Ted Nugent; Greg Arama; Rusty Day; John Drake; Steve Farmer; Dave Palmer; Andy Solomon; Rod Grange; K.J. Knight; John Angelos.
  Also see NUGENT, Ted

AMBROSIA
Singles: 7–inch
20TH FOX 3-5   74-78
WARNER 2-4   78-82
LPs: 10/12–inch 33rpm
NAUTILUS 10-15   81
  (Half-speed mastered.)
20TH FOX 8-10   74-78
WARNER 5-10   78-82
  Members: David Pack; Burleigh Drummond; Joe Puerta; Christopher North.
  Also see PACK, David
  Also see PARSONS, Alan, Project

AMECHE, Don, and Frances Langford
EPs: 7–inch 33/45rpm
COLUMBIA 8-15   61
  (Promotional only.)
LPs: 10/12–inch 33rpm
COLUMBIA (1000 and 8000
  series) 15-20   61-62
COLUMBIA (30000 series) 8-12   71

AMERICA
Singles: 7–inch
AMERICAN INT'L 3-5   79
CAPITOL 2-4   79-85
WARNER 3-5   72-77
Picture Sleeves
AMERICAN INT'L 3-6   79
CAPITOL 2-4   82-83
WARNER 3-5   72-74
LPs: 10/12–inch 33rpm
CAPITOL 5-10   79-85
WARNER (Except 2576) 8-12   72-77
WARNER (2576 "America") 15-25   71
  (Does NOT include *A Horse with No Name*.)
WARNER (2576 "America") 8-12   72
  (Has *A Horse with No Name*.)
  Members: Gerry Beckley; Dan Peek; Dewey Bunnell.
  Also see PEEK, Dan

AMERICAN BREED
Singles: 7–inch
ABC 3-5   75
ACTA 4-8   67-69
MCA 2-4   84
PARAMOUNT 3-5   70
Picture Sleeves
ACTA 5-10   68
LPs: 10/12–inch 33rpm
ACTA 15-20   67-68
  Members: Gary Loizzo; Al Ciner; Chuck Colbert; Lee Graziano; Kevin Murphy.
  Also see RUFUS

AMERICAN COMEDY NETWORK
LPs: 10/12–inch 33rpm
CRITIQUE 5-10   84

AMERICAN DREAM
Singles: 7–inch
AMPEX 3-5   70
DEMIK 4-8   68
LPs: 10/12–inch 33rpm
AMPEX 15-20   70
Members: Nick Jameson; Dooley Van Winkle; Nicky Indelicato;
Don Ferris; Mickey Brook.

AMERICAN FLYER
Singles: 7–inch
U.A. 2-5   76-77
Picture Sleeves
U.A. 3-5   76-77
LPs: 10/12–inch 33rpm
U.A. 8-10   76-77
Members: Eric Kaz; Steve Katz; Craig Fuller; Doug Yule.
Also see PURE PRAIRIE LEAGUE
Also see VELVET UNDERGROUND

AMERICAN GIRLS
Singles: 7–inch
I.R.S. 2-4   86
Picture Sleeves
I.R.S. 2-4   86
LPs: 10/12–inch 33rpm
I.R.S. 5-10   86

AMES, Ed
Singles: 7–inch
RCA 3-8   63-73
Picture Sleeves
RCA 3-8   67
LPs: 10/12–inch 33rpm
CAMDEN 4-8   72-73
RCA 5-15   64-77
Also see AMES BROTHERS

AMES, Nancy
Singles: 7–inch
ABC 3-5   68
EPIC 3-5   66-68
LIBERTY 3-6   61-65
SC 3-5   68
Picture Sleeves
EPIC 4-6   66
LPs: 10/12–inch 33rpm
EPIC 5-12   66-68
LIBERTY 8-18   61-65
Also see LOPEZ, Trini, with the Ventures and Nancy Ames

AMES BROTHERS
Singles: 78rpm
CORAL 4-8   50-53
RCA 3-8   53-57
Singles: 7–inch
CORAL 8-15   50-53
EPIC 3-6   62-63
RCA 5-15   53-62

Picture Sleeves
EPIC 4-8   62
RCA 10-15   60
EPs: 7–inch 33/45rpm
CORAL 10-20   50-53
RCA 10-20   53-61
LPs: 10/12–inch 33rpm
CORAL 15-30   53-62
EPIC 10-15   63
RCA (1000 series) 5-10   75
RCA (1200 through 2200 series) .. 15-30   55-61
RCA (2800 series) 8-15   64
RCA (6000 series) 5-10   72
VOCALION 5-10   68
Members: Ed Ames; Joe Ames; Gene Ames; Vic Ames.
Also see AMES, Ed
Also see COMO, Perry / Ames Brothers / Harry Belafonte /
Radio City Music Hall Orch.

AMESBURY, Bill
Singles: 7–inch
CASABLANCA 3-5   74-75
LPs: 10/12–inch 33rpm
CAPITOL 5-10   76
CASABLANCA 8-10   74

AMMONS, Gene
Singles: 78rpm
CHESS 4-8   50
DECCA 3-6   54
MERCURY 5-10   47-53
PRESTIGE 3-8   51-57
Singles: 7–inch
ARGO 4-8   62
DECCA 5-10   54
MERCURY 5-10   50-53
PRESTIGE (100 through 400 series) .. 3-8   60-68
PRESTIGE (700 series) 2-5   69-73
(This "700" series can easily be distinguished from
the early fifties "700" series that follows. The
company address is shown as in New Jersey. In
the '50s the company was in New York.)
PRESTIGE (713 through 921) 5-10   51-57
(Black vinyl.)
PRESTIGE (713 through 921) 10-20   51-57
(Colored vinyl.)
SAVOY 4-8   60
UNITED 5-10   53-54
EPs: 7–inch 33/45rpm
EMARCY 20-30   54
PRESTIGE 25-50   51
LPs: 10/12–inch 33rpm
ARGO 15-20   62
CHESS 15-25   59
EMARCY (400 series) 8-12   76
EMARCY (26000 series) 40-60   54
(10–inch LPs.)
ENJA 5-10   81
MERCURY 15-20   60-63
OLYMPIC 5-10   74
PRESTIGE (014 through 192) 5-10   82-85

PRESTIGE (7010 through 7132) 20-30   55-58
(Each of the following LPs in this series was
reissued using the original catalog number but a
different title: Prestige 7050, *All Star Jam Session*,
was reissued as *Woofin' and Tweetin;* Prestige
7039, *Hi-Fi Jam Session*, was reissued as *Happy
Blues*, and Prestige 7060, *Jammin' with Gene*, was
reissued as *Not Really the Blues*. These three
1960 reissues are valued in the $15-$25 range.)
PRESTIGE (7146 through 7287) 15-25   58-64
PRESTIGE (7300 and 7400 series) .. 10-20   65-68
PRESTIGE (7500 through 7800 series) 8-15   68-70
PRESTIGE (10000 series) 5-10   71-74
PRESTIGE (24000 series) 8-12   73-81
ROOTS 5-10   76
SAVOY 15-25   61
TRIP 5-10   73-75
VEE JAY 15-25   60
WING 10-20   60-63
Also see McDUFF, Brother Jack, and Gene Ammons

**AMMONS, Gene, and Richard "Groove"
Holmes**
LPs: 10/12–inch 33rpm
PACIFIC JAZZ (32 "Groovin' with
Jug") 15-25   61
Also see HOLMES, Richard "Groove"

AMMONS, Gene, and Sonny Stitt
Singles: 78rpm
PRESTIGE 4-8   50-51
Singles: 7–inch
PRESTIGE (700 series) 5-10   50-51
(Black vinyl.)
PRESTIGE (700 series) 10-20   50-51
(Colored vinyl.)
EPs: 7–inch 33/45rpm
PRESTIGE 25-50   51
LPs: 10/12–inch 33rpm
ARGO 15-25   63
CADET 10-20   67
CHESS 15-25   60
PRESTIGE (107 "Gene Ammons") . 60-100   51
(10–inch LP.)
PRESTIGE (112 "Gene Ammons with
Sonny Stitt") 60-100   51
(10–inch LP.)
PRESTIGE (127 "The Gene
Ammons Band") 60-100   52
(10–inch LP.)
PRESTIGE (149 "The Gene
Ammons Quartet") 50-100   51
(10–inch LP.)
PRESTIGE (7600 series) 6-10   69
PRESTIGE (10000 series) 5-10   76
VERVE (8400 series) 15-20   61-62
(Reads "MGM Records - a Division of
Metro-Goldwyn-Mayer, Inc." at bottom of label.)

VERVE (8800 series) 8-12   72
(Reads "Manufactured By MGM Record Corp.," or
mentions either Polydor or Polygram at bottom of
label.)
Also see AMMONS, Gene
Also see STITT, Sonny

AMUZEMENT PARK
(Amusement Park Band)
Singles: 7–inch
ATLANTIC 2-4   84-85
OUR GANG 2-4   82-83
LPs: 10/12–inch 33rpm
ATLANTIC 5-10   84
Members: Paul Richmond; Darryl Ellis; Aaron Jamal; Norval
Hodges; Fred Entesari; Reuben Locke Jr.; Rico McFarland.

ANA
Singles: 7–inch
PARC 2-4   87-90
Picture Sleeves
PARC 2-4   87

ANACOSTIA
Singles: 7–inch
COLUMBIA 3-5   72-75
MCA 2-4   77
ROULETTE 2-4   84
TABU 2-4   78-79
LPs: 10/12–inch 33rpm
MCA 5-10   77
TABU 5-10   78

ANDERSEN, Eric
Singles: 7–inch
ARISTA 2-4   75-77
COLUMBIA 2-4   72
WARNER 2-4   68-71
LPs: 10/12–inch 33rpm
ARISTA 5-10   75-77
COLUMBIA 8-10   72
VANGUARD 15-20   65-70
WARNER 10-15   68-70

ANDERSON, Al
Singles: 7–inch
VANGUARD 3-5   73
LPs: 10/12–inch 33rpm
TWIN/TONE 5-10   88
VANGUARD 10-15   73
Also see NRBQ
Also see WILDWEEDS

ANDERSON, Bill
(Bill Anderson and the Jordanaires)
Singles: 12–inch 33/45rpm
MCA 4-8   78
Singles: 7–inch
DECCA (30000 series) 5-10   58-59
DECCA (31000 series) 4-8   60-66
DECCA (32000 and 33000 series) ... 3-6   67-72
MCA 2-4   73-81
SOUTHERN TRACKS 2-4   82-87

SWANEE 2-4   85
TNT 4-6   59
Picture Sleeves
DECCA 4-8 63-69
EPs: 7–inch 33/45rpm
DECCA 5-10 63-65
LPs: 10/12–inch 33rpm
CORAL 4-6   73
DECCA (4192 through 4686) 15-20 62-65
DECCA (4771 through 5344) 10-15 66-72
(Decca LP numbers in this series preceded by a
"7" or a "DL-7" are stereo issues.)
DECCA (7100 series) 15-20   69
DECCA (7200 series) 10-12   72
EPIC 5-10 82-85
MCA 5-10 73-80
SOUTHERN TRACKS 5-10   84
VOCALION 8-12 68-71
Also see COE, David Allan, and Bill Anderson
Also see KERR, Anita

ANDERSON, Carl
Singles: 12–inch 33/45rpm
EPIC 4-6 82-86
Singles: 7–inch
EPIC 2-4 82-86
LPs: 10/12–inch 33rpm
EPIC 5-10 82-86
Also see LORING, Gloria, and Carl Anderson

ANDERSON, Elton
Singles: 7–inch
CAPITOL 4-8   62
LANOR 4-8   63
MERCURY 8-12 59-61
VIN 10-20   58

ANDERSON, Ernestine
Singles: 7–inch
MERCURY 2-4 60-62
SUE 2-4 63-64
EPs: 7–inch 33/45rpm
MERCURY 5-10   59
LPs: 10/12–inch 33rpm
MERCURY 15-25 58-60
OMEGA DISK 10-15   59
SUE 10-15   63
WING 10-15   64

ANDERSON, Jesse
Singles: 7–inch
CADET 4-6 67-68
JEWEL 3-5   72
THOMAS 3-5   70

ANDERSON, John
Singles: 7–inch
ACE of HEARTS 3-6   74
WARNER 2-5 77-88
LPs: 10/12–inch 33rpm
WARNER 5-8 77-88
Also see HAGGARD, Merle

Also see HARRIS, Emmylou

ANDERSON, Jon
Singles: 12–inch 33/45rpm
ATLANTIC 4-6   82
Singles: 7–inch
ATLANTIC 2-5 76-82
COLUMBIA 2-4   88
ELEKTRA (Except 69580) 2-4 84-85
ELEKTRA (69580 "Save All Your Love") . 2-4   85
(Black vinyl.)
ELEKTRA (69580 "Save All Your Love") . 4-8   85
(Colored vinyl, special Christmas edition.)
LPs: 10/12–inch 33rpm
ATLANTIC 5-10 76-82
COLUMBIA 5-10   88
ELEKTRA 5-10   85
Promotional LPs
ATLANTIC ("An Evening with Jon
Anderson") 20-30   76
(Jon Anderson interviews, and music from his *Olias
of Sunhillow* LP, as well as selections by Yes.)
Also see JON and Vangelis
Also see TANGERINE DREAM / Jon Anderson / Bryan Ferry
Also see YES

ANDERSON, Lale
Singles: 7–inch
KING 3-6 61-62
LPs: 10/12–inch 33rpm
UNIVERSE 5-15   61

ANDERSON, Laurie
Singles: 12–inch 33/45rpm
WARNER 4-6   81
Singles: 7–inch
WARNER 2-4 81-89
EPs: 7–inch 33/45rpm
WARNER 3-5   81
LPs: 10/12–inch 33rpm
WARNER (Except 25192) 5-10 82-89
WARNER (25192 "United States Live")35-45   85
(Five-LP set.)
Also see GLASS, Philip

ANDERSON, Leroy
Singles: 78rpm
DECCA 2-5 51-57
Singles: 7–inch
DECCA 3-6 51-62
EPs: 7–inch 33/45rpm
DECCA 5-10 51-58
LPs: 10/12–inch 33rpm
DECCA 5-15 51-63

ANDERSON, Liz and Lynn
Singles: 7–inch
RCA 3-5   68

ANDERSON, Lynn
(Lynn Anderson and Jerry Lane)
Singles: 7–inch
CHART 3-5 66-71

COLUMBIA	2-4	70-80
MERCURY	2-4	86
PERMIAN	2-4	83
RCA	3-5	68

Picture Sleeves

COLUMBIA	3-6	70-72

EPs: 7–inch 33/45rpm

COLUMBIA	4-8	72
(Promotional only.)		

LPs: 10/12–inch 33rpm

ALBUM GLOBE	5-10	76
CHART (Except 1050)	8-15	67-71
CHART (1050 "Lynn Anderson")	10-20	72
COLUMBIA	6-10	70-80
HARMONY	5-10	71-73
MOUNTAIN DEW	5-10	
PERMIAN	5-10	83
PICKWICK	5-10	
TIME-LIFE	5-10	81
Also see ANDERSON, Liz, and Lynn		

ANDERSON, Lynn, and Gary Morris
Singles: 7–inch

PERMIAN	2-4	83
Also see ANDERSON, Lynn		
Also see MORRIS, Gary		

ANDERSON, Michael
Singles: 7–inch

A&M	2-4	88

LPs: 10/12–inch 33rpm

A&M	5-8	88

ANDERSON, Roshell
Singles: 7–inch

EXCELLO	3-5	71
SUNBURST	3-5	73-74

ANDERSON, Vicki
(Vikki Anderson; Vickie Anderson)
Singles: 7–inch

BROWNSTONE	3-5	71-72
DELUXE	4-8	66
FONTANA	4-8	64
KING	3-6	66-70
SMASH	4-8	65
TUFF	3-6	67
Also see BROWN, James, and Vickie Anderson		

ANDREA TRUE CONNECTION:
see TRUE, Andrea

ANDREWS, Chris
Singles: 7–inch

ATCO	4-8	66
RCA	3-6	69

ANDREWS, Inez
(Inez Andrews and the Andrewettes)
Singles: 7–inch

MCA	2-4	84
SONG BIRD	2-4	64-73

LPs: 10/12–inch 33rpm

MCA	5-10	84

SAVOY	5-10	80-81

ANDREWS, Julie
Singles: 7–inch

BUENA VISTA	3-6	65
COLUMBIA	3-5	67
DECCA	3-5	67
LONDON	3-6	60
RCA	2-4	70

Picture Sleeves

BUENA VISTA	4-8	65

EPs: 7–inch 33/45rpm

RCA	10-20	56

LPs: 10/12–inch 33rpm

ANGEL	15-25	58
COLUMBIA (1700 and 8500 series)	15-25	62
COLUMBIA (31000 series)	8-12	72
HARMONY	8-10	70-72
RCA (1000 series)	8-12	70
RCA (1400 through 1600 series)	20-30	56-58
RCA (3800 series)	8-15	67
20TH FOX	8-15	68

ANDREWS, Julie, and Carol Burnett
LPs: 10/12–inch 33rpm

COLUMBIA (2200 and 5800 series)	15-25	62
COLUMBIA (31000 series)	8-15	72
Also see BURNETT, Carol		

ANDREWS, Julie, and Andre Previn / Vic Damone / Jack Jones / Marian Anderson
EPs: 7–inch 33/45rpm

RCA (277 "We Wish You		
a Merry Christmas")	3-5	69
(Radio Shack Special Collector's Edition.)		
Also see ANDREWS, Julie		
Also see DAMONE, Vic		
Also see JONES, Jack		
Also see PREVIN, Andre		

ANDREWS, Lee
(Lee Andrews and the Hearts)
Singles: 78rpm

ARGO	10-20	57
GOTHAM	25-50	56
MAIN LINE	30-60	57
RAINBOW	100-200	54

Singles: 7–inch

ARGO	20-35	57
CASINO (110 "Baby, Come Back")	20-30	58
CASINO (452 "Try the Impossible")	50-75	58
CHESS	10-15	57-58
COLLECTABLES	2-4	82
CRIMSON	4-8	67-68
GOTHAM (318 "Bluebird of		
Happiness")	100-125	56
GOTHAM (320 "Lonely Room")	100-125	56
GOTHAM (321 "Just Suppose")	100-125	56
GOWEN	5-10	61
GRAND	5-8	62
JORDAN	15-25	60
LANA	3-5	

LOST-NITE 3-5   65
MAIN LINE (102 "Long Lonely
    Nights") 150-200   57
    (Green label.)
MAIN LINE (102 "Long Lonely
    Nights") 100-150   57
    (Black label, with Philadelphia address shown.)
MAIN LINE (102 "Long Lonely
    Nights") 15-25   62
    (Black label, no address shown.)
MAIN LINE (105 "Teardrops") 8-10   62
PARKWAY 5-8   62-63
RAINBOW (252 "Maybe You'll Be
    There") 250-300   54
    (Black vinyl.)
RAINBOW (252 "Maybe You'll Be
    There") 500-600   54
    (Colored vinyl. Small print.)
RAINBOW (252 "Maybe You'll Be
    There") 5-10   62
    (Colored vinyl. Very large print.)
RAINBOW (256 "White Cliffs of
    Dover") 350-400   54
    (Yellow label.)
RAINBOW (256 "White Cliffs of Dover") 5-10   62
    (Blue label.)
RAINBOW (259 "The Bells of St.
    Mary's") 250-300   54
    (Yellow label.)
RAINBOW (259 "The Bells of St.
    Mary's") 5-10   62
    (Blue label.)
RCA 5-8   66
SWAN 5-8   61
U.A. (100 series) 10-20   58-59
U.A. (500 series) 5-8   63
            LPs: 10/12–inch 33rpm
COLLECTABLES 6-8   82-85
LOST-NITE (1 "Lee Andrews and
    the Hearts") 8-10   81
    (Colored vinyl 10–inch LP.)
LOST-NITE (2 "Lee Andrews and
    the Hearts") 8-10   81
    (Colored vinyl 10–inch LP.)
LOST-NITE (100 series) 10-20   65
POST 10-15
    Members: Lee Andrews; Arthur Thompson; Roy Calhoun;
    Wendell Calhoun; Butch Curry; Ted Weems.

ANDREWS, Patty
            Singles: 78rpm
CAPITOL 3-5   55-56
DECCA 4-8   50-54
            Singles: 7–inch
CAPITOL 4-8   55-56
DECCA 5-10   50-54
    Also see ANDREWS SISTERS

ANDREWS, Ruby
            Singles: 7–inch
ABC 3-5   76-77
ZODIAC 4-6   67-71
            LPs: 10/12–inch 33rpm
ABC 8-10   77
ZODIAC 10-15   72
    Also see STACKHOUSE, Ruby

ANDREWS SISTERS
            Singles: 78rpm
CAPITOL 3-5   56
DECCA 4-10   38-57
            Singles: 7–inch
ABC 2-4   74
CAPITOL 4-8   56
DECCA 5-10   50-57
DOT 3-5   64
KAPP 3-6   59
PARAMOUNT 2-4   73-74
            Picture Sleeves
DECCA 5-10   57
            EPs: 7–inch 33/45rpm
DECCA 5-15   51-58
            LPs: 10/12–inch 33rpm
ABC 5-10   74
CAPITOL 5-10   64
DECCA (4000 series) 8-12   67
    (Decca LP numbers in this series preceded by a
    "7" or a "DL-7" are stereo issues.)
DECCA (5000 series) 20-40   49-54
    (10–inch LPs.)
DECCA (8000 series) 15-25   55-58
DOT 6-12   61-67
HAMILTON 5-10   64-65
MCA 8-12   73
PARAMOUNT 5-10   73-74
    Members: Patty Andrews; Maxene Andrews; Laverne Andrews.
    Also see ANDREWS, Patty
    Also see CROSBY, Bing

ANGEL
            Singles: 7–inch
CASABLANCA 2-4   75-80
            LPs: 10/12–inch 33rpm
CASABLANCA 5-10   75-80
    Members: Barry Brandt; Frank Dimino; Greg Giuffria; Mickey
    Jones; Punky Meadows; Felix Robinson.
    Also see GIUFFRIA
    Also see WILSON, Carl

ANGEL, Johnny T: see JOHNNY T. ANGEL

ANGEL CITY
            Singles: 7–inch
EPIC 2-4   80-82
            LPs: 10/12–inch 33rpm
EPIC 5-10   80-82
MCA 5-10   85
    Members: Doc Neeson; Rick Brewster; John Brewster.

ANGELS

Singles: 7-inch

ASCOT	5-8	63
CAPRICE	5-10	61-62
COLLECTABLES	2-4	82
ERIC	2-4	74
POLYDOR	3-5	74
RCA	5-8	67-68
SMASH	4-8	63-64

Picture Sleeves

SMASH	8-15	63

LPs: 10/12-inch 33rpm

ASCOT (13009 "The Angels Sing 12 of Their Greatest Hits") (Monaural.)	20-30	64
ASCOT (16009 "The Angels Sing 12 of Their Greatest Hits") (Stereo.)	30-40	64
CAPRICE (LP-1001 "And the Angels Sing") (Monaural.)	40-50	62
CAPRICE (SLP-1001 "And the Angels Sing") (Stereo.)	50-75	62
SMASH (27039 "My Boyfriend's Back") (Monaural.)	30-40	63
SMASH (67039 "My Boyfriend's Back") (Stereo.)	50-75	63
SMASH (27048 "A Halo to You") (Monaural.)	30-40	63
SMASH (67048 "A Halo to You") (Stereo.)	40-60	63

Members: Linda Jansen; Barbara Allbut; Phyllis "Jiggs" Allbut; Peggy Santaglia.
Also see DUSK
Also see SEDAKA, Neil, and the Tokens / Angels / Jimmy Gilmer and the Fireballs
Also see STARLETS

ANIMALS

(Eric Burdon and the Animals; Original Animals)

Singles: 7-inch

ABKCO	2-4	75
COLLECTABLES	2-4	82
I.R.S.	2-4	83
JET	2-4	77
MGM	5-10	64-71
MGM CELEBRITY SCENE ("The Animals")	35-45	66

(Boxed set, five 45s with bio insert and title strips.)

Picture Sleeves

MGM (13264 "House of the Rising Sun")	10-20	64
MGM (13274 "I'm Crying")	10-15	64
MGM (13298 "Boom Boom")	10-15	64
MGM (13339 "Bring It on Home to Me")	8-12	65
MGM (13769 "San Franciscan Nights")	5-10	67
MGM (13868 "Monterey")	5-10	67

THE ANIMALS Bring It On Home To Me b/w For Miss Caulker K-13339

LPs: 10/12-inch 33rpm

ABKCO	8-12	73-76
ACCORD	5-10	82
I.R.S.	5-10	83-85
MGM	15-30	64-69
PICKWICK	5-10	71
SCEPTER/CITATION	5-10	76
SPRINGBOARD	5-10	72
U.A.	5-10	77
WAND	8-12	70

Members: Eric Burdon; Alan Price; Hilton Valentine; Chas Chandler; John Steel; John Weider.
Also see BURDON, Eric
Also see PRICE, Alan
Also see WEIDER, John

ANIMOTION

Singles: 12-inch 33/45rpm

MERCURY	4-6	85

Singles: 7-inch

CASABLANCA	2-4	86
MERCURY	2-4	84-85
POLYDOR	2-4	89

Picture Sleeves

CASABLANCA	2-4	86
MERCURY	2-4	84-85
POLYDOR	2-4	89

LPs: 10/12-inch 33rpm

CASABLANCA	5-10	86
MERCURY	5-10	84-85
POLYDOR	5-8	89

ANITA and the So-and-Sos

(Anita Kerr Singers)

Singles: 7-inch

RCA	5-8	62

Also see KERR, Anita

ANKA, Paul

Singles: 78rpm

ABC-PAR	10-20	57
RPM	10-20	56

Singles: 12-inch 33/45rpm

COLUMBIA	4-6	83

Singles: 7-inch

ABC-PAR (104 "Share Your Love")	15-25	58

(Promotional, fan club issue.)

ABC-PAR (296-1 "My Heart Sings")	25-35	58

(Stereo Compact 33 Single.)

ABC-PAR (9831 through 9956) 10-15   57-58
ABC-PAR (9987 "My Heart Sings") ... 8-12   58
(Monaural.)
ABC-PAR (9987 "My Heart Sings") .. 20-30   58
(Stereo.)
ABC-PAR (10011 "I Miss You So") 8-12   59
(Monaural.)
ABC-PAR (S-10011 "I Miss You So") . 20-30   59
(Stereo.)
ABC-PAR (10022 "Lonely Boy") 8-12   59
(Monaural.)
ABC-PAR (S-10022 "Lonely Boy") ... 20-30   59
(Stereo.)
ABC-PAR (10040 "Put Your
Head on My Shoulder") 8-12   59
(Monaural.)
ABC-PAR (S-10040 "Put Your
Head on My Shoulder") 20-30   59
ABC-PAR (10064 "It's Time to Cry") ... 8-12   59
(Monaural.)
ABC-PAR (S-10064 "It's Time to Cry") 20-30   59
(Stereo.)
ABC-PAR (10082 "Puppy Love") 5-10   60
(Monaural.)
ABC-PAR (S-10082 "Puppy Love") .. 20-30   60
(Stereo.)
ABC-PAR (10106 "My Home Town") .. 5-10   60
(Monaural.)
ABC-PAR (S-10106 "My Home Town") 20-30   60
(Stereo.)
ABC-PAR (10132 "Hello Young Lovers")5-10   60
(Monaural.)
ABC-PAR (10132 "Hello
Young Lovers") 20-30   60
(Stereo.)
ABC-PAR (10147 "Summer's Gone") .. 5-10   60
(Monaural.)
ABC-PAR (S-10147 "Summer's
Gone") 20-30   60
(Stereo.)
ABC-PAR (10168 "The Story of
My Love")...................... 5-10   61
(Monaural.)
ABC-PAR (S-10168 "The Story of
My Love")..................... 20-30   61
(Stereo.)
ABC-PAR (10194 through 10338) 5-10   61-62
BARNABY 3-5   71
BUDDAH 3-5   72-78
COLUMBIA 2-4   83-85
ERIC.......................... 3-5   74
FAME 3-5   73
RCA (Except 2000, 8000, 9000 and
10000 series) 2-5   67-79
RCA (2575 "I'm Glad There Is You") . 10-20   62
(Stereo Compact 33.)
RCA (37-7977 "Love Me Warm
and Tender") 10-20   62
(Compact 33 Single.)

RCA (47-7977 "Love Me Warm
and Tender") 4-8   62
RCA (8000 and 9000 series) 4-8   62-69
RCA (10000 series) 2-4   78-81
RPM (472 "I Confess") 25-35   56
RPM (499 "I Confess") 20-35   56
U.A. 2-4   75-77

Picture Sleeves

ABC-PAR 10-20   58-61
COLUMBIA 2-4   83
ERIC 2-4   74
RCA (Except 11000 series) 5-10   62-65
RCA (11000 series) 2-4   78
U.A. 3-5   75

EPs: 7–inch 33/45rpm

ABC 12-15
(Jukebox issue only.)
ABC-PAR 25-35   59
RCA 10-15   63
(Jukebox issue only.)
SIRE 10-12   74
(Jukebox issue only.)

LPs: 10/12–inch 33rpm

ABC-PAR (ABC-240 "Paul Anka") ... 25-35   58
(Monaural.)
ABC-PAR (ABCS-240 "Paul Anka") .. 35-50   58
(Stereo.)
ABC-PAR (ABC-296 "My Heart Sings")25-35   59
(Monaural.)
ABC-PAR (ABCS-296 "My Heart
Sings") 35-45   59
(Stereo.)
ABC-PAR (ABC-323 "Big 15") 25-35   60
(Monaural.)
ABC-PAR (ABCS-323 "Big 15") 35-45   60
(Stereo.)
ABC-PAR (ABC-347 "For
Young Lovers") 25-30   60
(Monaural.)
ABC-PAR (ABCS-347 "For
Young Lovers") 30-35   60
(Stereo.)
ABC-PAR (ABC-353 "Anka at
the Copa") 25-30   60
(Monaural.)
ABC-PAR (ABCS-353 "Anka at
the Copa") 30-35   60
(Stereo.)
ABC-PAR (ABC-360 "It's
Christmas Everywhere") 25-30   60
(Monaural.)
ABC-PAR (ABCS-360 "It's
Christmas Everywhere") 30-35   60
(Stereo.)
ABC-PAR (ABC-371 "Strictly
Instrumental") 20-30   61
(Monaural.)

ABC-PAR (ABCS-371 "Strictly
   Instrumental") 25-35   61
   (Stereo.)
ABC-PAR (ABC-390 "His Big
   15 Vol. 2") 20-30   61
   (Monaural.)
ABC-PAR (ABCS-390 "His Big
   15, Vol. 2") 25-35   61
   (Stereo.)
ABC-PAR (ABC-409 "His Big
   15, Vol. 3") 20-30   62
   (Monaural.)
ABC-PAR (ABCS-409 "His Big
   15, Vol. 3") 25-35   62
   (Stereo.)
ABC-PAR (ABC-420 "Diana") 20-30   62
   (Monaural.)
ABC-PAR (ABCS-420 "Diana") 25-30   62
   (Stereo.)
ACCORD 5-10   81
BUDDAH 6-10   71-76
CAMDEN 6-10   74
COLUMBIA 5-10   83-85
LIBERTY 5-10   81-83
PICKWICK 5-10   75
RCA (Except "LPM" and "LSP" series) . 5-10 75-81
RCA (2000 through 4000" series) ... 10-25 62-70
   (With "LPM" prefix. Monaural.)
RCA (2000 through 4000" series) ... 15-30 62-70
   (With "LSP" prefix. Stereo.)
RANWOOD 5-10   81
RIVERA (0047 "Paul Anka and
   Others") 25-40   63
   (Has two tracks by Paul Anka.)
RHINO 5-10   86
SIRE 10-12   74-78
U.A. 5-10   74-78
   Also see ANN-MARGRET
   Also see MARLO, Micki

ANKA, Paul, and Odia Coates
Singles: 12-inch 33/45rpm
EPIC 4-6   77
Singles: 7-inch
EPIC 2-4   76
U.A. 2-4   74-75
   Also see COATES, Odia

ANKA, Paul / Sam Cooke / Neil Sedaka
LPs: 10/12-inch 33rpm
RCA 15-20   64
   Also see COOKE, Sam
   Also see SEDAKA, Neil

ANKA, Paul, and Karla DeVito
Singles: 12-inch 33/45rpm
COLUMBIA 4-6   83
Singles: 7-inch
COLUMBIA 2-4   83

ANKA, Paul, George Hamilton IV and Johnny Nash
Singles: 7-inch
ABC-PAR 5-10   58
   Also see ANKA, Paul
   Also see HAMILTON, George
   Also see NASH, Johnny

ANNETTE
(Annette Funicello; Annette and the Afterbeats;
Annette and the Upbeats)
Singles: 78rpm
DISNEYLAND (102 "How Will I Know")15-25   58
Singles: 7-inch
BUENA VISTA (336, "Jo-Jo the Dog Faced
   Boy"/"Lonely Guitar") 10-15   59
BUENA VISTA (336, "Jo-Jo the Dog Faced
   Boy"/"Love Me Forever") 8-15   59
   (Note different flip side.)
BUENA VISTA (339 through 354) 8-15   59-60
BUENA VISTA (359 through 407) ... 15-25 60-62
BUENA VISTA (414 "Teenage
   Wedding") 20-30   63
BUENA VISTA (427 through 436) ... 15-25 63-64
BUENA VISTA (337 "Wah Watusi") .. 10-15   64
BUENA VISTA (438 "Something
   Borrowed") 15-25   65
BUENA VISTA (440 "The Monkey's
   Uncle") 10-20   65
   (With the Beach Boys.)
BUENA VISTA (442 through 475) ... 10-15 65-66
DISNEYLAND 8-10   57-58
JUGGY 8-10
STARVIEW 5-10   83
TOWER (326 "What's a Girl to Do") . 20-25   67
   (Name misspelled, shown as "Annettte.")
Picture Sleeves
BUENA VISTA (339 through 354) ... 10-20 59-60
BUENA VISTA (359 through 407) ... 20-30 60-62
BUENA VISTA (414 "Teenage
   Wedding") 50-100   63
BUENA VISTA (427 through 436) ... 15-30 63-64
BUENA VISTA (337 "Wah Watusi") .. 10-15   64
BUENA VISTA (438 "Something
   Borrowed") 20-30   65
BUENA VISTA (440 "The Monkey's
   Uncle") 15-25   65
BUENA VISTA (442 through 475) ... 10-15 65-66
BUENA VISTA (802 "Parent Trap") .. 20-30   61
DISNEYLAND 25-35   58
EPs: 7-inch 33/45rpm
BUENA VISTA (3301 "Annette") 40-60   59
DISNEYLAND (04 "Tall Paul") 30-40   58
DISNEYLAND (69 "Mickey Mouse Club
   Featuring Annette") 35-45   58
LPs: 10/12-inch 33rpm
BUENA VISTA (3301 "Annette") 35-50   59
BUENA VISTA (3302 "Annette Sings
   Anka") 35-50   60
   (With bonus color photo.)

BUENA VISTA (3302 "Annette Sings
Anka") 30-35   60
(Without bonus photo.)
BUENA VISTA (3303 through 3508) . . 25-40   60-64
BUENA VISTA (4037 "Annette
Funicello") 15-25   72
DISNEYLAND (Except 3906) 15-30   62-75
(Various Mouseketeer cast albums that include or
feature Annette.)
DISNEYLAND (3906 "*Snow White* As Told
by Annette") 20-40
MICKEY MOUSE (12 through 24) . . . 35-50   57-58
(Various Mouseketeer cast albums that include or
feature Annette.)
RHINO (Except 702) 8-10   84
RHINO (702 "Best of Annette") 12-15   84
(Picture disc.)
SILHOUETTE 10-15   81
STARVIEW (4001 "Country Album") . . 8-12   84
(Standard issue.)
STARVIEW (4001 "Country Album") . 15-20   84
(Limited edition series.)
　　Also see ALLAN, Davie
　　Also see AVALON, Frankie, and Annette
　　Also see BEACH BOYS

ANNETTE / Jimmy Dodd
Singles: 78rpm
DISNEYLAND (758 "How Will I
Know"/"Annette") 15-25   58
(10–inch single.)
DISNEYLAND (758 "How Will I
Know"/"Annette") 20-30   58
(Five–inch single.)
Picture Sleeves
DISNEYLAND (758 "How Will I
Know"/"Annette") 20-40   58

ANNETTE and Hayley Mills
LPs: 10/12–inch 33rpm
BUENA VISTA (3508 "Annette and
Hayley Mills") 300-400   62
(Issued with paper cover. Special products
release.)

Also see MILLS, Hayley

ANNETTE and Tommy Sands
Singles: 7–inch
BUENA VISTA (802 "Parent Trap") . . 10-20   61
(45 single.)
BUENA VISTA (802 "Parent Trap") . . 25-35   61
(Compact 33 Single.)
Picture Sleeves
BUENA VISTA (802 "Parent Trap") . . 15-25   61
　　Also see ANNETTE
　　Also see SANDS, Tommy

ANNIE G.
Singles: 12–inch 33/45rpm
MCA 4-6   84
Singles: 7–inch
MCA 2-4   84

ANN-MARGRET
Singles: 12–inch 33/45rpm
AVCO EMBASSY (4547 "Today") . . . 10-15   70
FIRST AMERICAN (1207 "Everybody
Needs Somebody Sometime") 5-10   81
MCA (1867 "Midnight Message") 5-10   80
(Promotional issue only.)
MCA (1867 "What I Do to Men") 5-10   80
OCEAN/ARIOLA AMERICA 4-8   79-80
RAM (1001 "Everybody Needs
Somebody Sometime") 5-10   81
RAM 4-8   81
Singles: 7–inch
FIRST AMERICAN 3-5   81
MCA 3-5   79-80
OCEAN/ARIOLA AMERICA 3-5   79-80
RCA (VLP-2251 "The Vivacious One") 30-50   62
(Five-disc, jukebox set. With title strips.)
RCA (7857 "Lost Love") 15-25   61
(With "37" prefix. Compact 33 Single.)
RCA (7857 "Lost Love") 5-10   61
(With "47" prefix.)
RCA (7894 "I Just Don't Understand") 15-25   61
(With "37" prefix. Compact 33 Single.)
RCA (7894 "I Just Don't Understand") . 5-10   61
(With "47" prefix.)
RCA (7952 "It Do
Me So Good") 15-25   61
(With "37" prefix. Compact 33 Single.)
RCA (7952 "It Do Me So Good") 5-10   61
(With "47" prefix.)
RCA (7986 through 9109) 5-10   61-66
Picture Sleeves
RCA (7894 "I Just Don't Understand") 10-15   61
RCA (7952 "It Do Me So Good") 10-15   61
RCA (7986 "What Am I
Supposed to Do") 10-20   61
RCA (8061 "Jim Dandy") 15-20   62
RCA (8168 "Bye Bye Birdie") 15-25   63
EPs: 7–inch 33/45rpm
RCA (2251 "The Vivacious One") . . . 15-25   62
RCA (2659 "Mr. Wonderful") 15-25   63

RCA (4358 "On the Way Up") 15-25   62
RCA (9058 "On the Way Up") 15-25   62
        LPs: 10/12–inch 33rpm
LHI 12-15   68-69
LAGNIAPPE 1959 ("Be My Guest") 100-200   59
  (Cast LP produced by the Boys Tri-Ship Club of
  New Trier High School. Includes *Tropical Heat
  Wave* by Ann-Margret Olson.)
MCA 5-10   80
NORTHWESTERN UNIVERSITY/
RCA (5760 "Among Friends") 50-100   60
  (Cast LP for the *Waa-Mu Show of 1960* from
  Northwestern University. Lists Ann-Margret Olson
  as a dancer.)
RCA (LPM-2399 "And Here She Is") . 10-20   61
  (Monaural.)
RCA (LSP-2399 "And Here She Is") .. 15-25   61
  (Stereo.)
RCA (LPM-2453 "On the Way Up") .. 10-20   62
  (Monaural.)
RCA (LSP-2453 "On the Way Up") .. 15-25   62
  (Stereo.)
RCA (LPM-2251 "The Vivacious One") 10-20   62
  (Monaural.)
RCA (LSP-2251 "The Vivacious One") 15-25   62
  (Stereo.)
RCA (LPM-2659 "Bachelor's
  Paradise") 10-20   63
  (Monaural.)
RCA (LSP-2659 "Bachelor's
  Paradise") 15-25   63
  (Stereo.)
RCA/NARM ("Tenth Anniversary
  Convention") 40-60   68
  (Has *Bye Bye Birdie* by Ann-Margret, plus tracks
  by the Limeliters, Al Hirt, Paul Anka, Homer and
  Jethro, Peter Nero, Eddy Arnold, John Gary, Chet
  Atkins, Floyd Cramer, Anita Kerr Singers, Boots
  Randolph, Myron Cohen, Barry Sadler, Henry
  Mancini, Jack Jones, and Harry Belafonte.
  Promotional, souvenir issue only.)
   Also see ANKA, Paul
   Also see ARNOLD, Eddy
   Also see ATKINS, Chet
   Also see BELAFONTE, Harry
   Also see COHEN, Myron
   Also see CRAMER, Floyd
   Also see HOMER and Jethro
   Also see JONES, Jack
   Also see KERR, Anita
   Also see LIMELITERS
   Also see MANCINI, Henry
   Also see NERO, Peter
   Also see RANDOLPH, Boots
   Also see SADLER, Barry Also see REESE, Della

ANN-MARGRET and John Gary
        LPs: 10/12–inch 33rpm
RCA (LPM-2947 "Broadway Hits") ... 10-20   64
  (Monaural.)
RCA (LSP-2947 "Broadway Hits") ... 15-25   64
  (Stereo.)

Also see GARY, John

ANN-MARGRET and Lee Hazlewood
        Singles: 7–inch
LHI 4-6   68-69
        LPs: 10/12–inch 33rpm
LHI (12007 "Cowboy and the Lady") . 15-20   69
  Also see HAZLEWOOD, Lee

ANN-MARGRET and Al Hirt
        Singles: 7–inch
RCA (VLP-2690 "Beauty and
  the Beard") 25-50   64
  (Five-disc, jukebox set. With title strips.)
RCA (9524 "Slowly") 5-10   68
        EPs: 7–inch 33/45rpm
RCA (LSP-2690 "Beauty and
  the Beard") 15-25   64
        LPs: 10/12–inch 33rpm
RCA (LPM-2690 "Beauty and
  the Beard") 10-20   64
  (Monaural.)
RCA (LSP-2690 "Beauty and
  the Beard") 15-25   64
  (Stereo.)
  Also see HIRT, Al

ANN-MARGRET / Kitty Kalen / Della Reese
        LPs: 10/12–inch 33rpm
RCA (2724 "3 Great Girls") 15-20   63
  Also see ANN-MARGRET
  Also see KALEN, Kitty
  Also see REESE, Della

ANQUETTE
        LPs: 10/12–inch 33rpm
LUKE SKYWALKER 5-8   88

ANT, Adam
        Singles: 12–inch 33/45rpm
EPIC 4-6   82-85
        Singles: 7–inch
EPIC 2-4   82-85
        LPs: 10/12–inch 33rpm
EPIC 5-10   82-85
MCA 5-8   90
  Also see ADAM and the Ants

ANTELL, Peter
        Singles: 7–inch
BOUNTY (103 "The Times They
  Are a-Changin" 15-25   65
CAMEO 5-10   62-63
  Also see WILD ONES

ANTHONY, Alan
        Singles: 7–inch
CHALET 2-4   82

ANTHONY, Mark
        Singles: 7–inch
TABU 2-4   88

ANTHONY, Markus
Singles: 7–inch
ROCK 'N' ROLL 2-4   86

ANTHONY, Ray, and His Orchestra
Singles: 78rpm
CAPITOL 2-5   49-57
Singles: 7–inch
CAPITOL 3-6   50-62
EPs: 7–inch 33/45rpm
CAPITOL 5-10   52-59
LPs: 10/12–inch 33rpm
CAPITOL 5-15   52-62
Also see BEACH BOYS
Also see SINATRA, Frank

ANTHONY and the Camp
Singles: 12–inch 33/45rpm
WARNER 4-6   86
Singles: 7–inch
WARNER 2-4   86
Picture Sleeves
WARNER 2-4   86
LPs: 10/12–inch 33rpm
WARNER 5-10   86

ANTHONY and the Imperials:
see LITTLE ANTHONY and the Imperials

ANTHRAX
LPs: 10/12–inch 33rpm
ISLAND 5-10   85-90
MEGAFORCE 5-10   87-91

ANTON, Susan
Singles: 7–inch
COLUMBIA 2-4   78
Picture Sleeves
COLUMBIA 2-4   78
Also see KNOBLOCK, Fred, and Susan Anton

AORTA
Singles: 7–inch
ATLANTIC (2545 "Strange") 10-20   68
COLUMBIA (44870 "Strange") 5-10   69
HAPPY TIGER (567 "Sandcastles") .. 10-15   70
LPs: 10/12–inch 33rpm
COLUMBIA (9785 "Aorta") 15-20   69
COLUMBIA (38000 series) 5-10
HAPPY TIGER (1010 "Aorta 2") 15-25   70
Members: Bill Herman; Billy Jones; Jim Donlinger; Jim Nyeholt.

APOLLO 100
Singles: 7–inch
MEGA 2-4   71-72
LPs: 10/12–inch 33rpm
MEGA 5-10   72

APOLLONIA 6
Singles: 12–inch 33/45rpm
WARNER 4-6   84-85
Singles: 7–inch
WARNER 2-4   84-85

Picture Sleeves
WARNER 2-4   84-85
LPs: 10/12–inch 33rpm
WARNER 5-10   84-85
Also see VANITY 6

APOLLOS
LPs: 10/12–inch 33rpm
CICADELIC 5-10   86

APPALACHIANS
Singles: 7–inch
ABC-PAR 4-8   62-63
GOLDIE 8-10

APPALOOSA
(Robin Batteaux)
LPs: 10/12–inch 33rpm
COLUMBIA 10-15   69
WHITE GOLD 5-10   82

APPLEJACKS
Singles: 7–inch
CAMEO (100 series) 5-10   57-60
CAMEO (200 and 300 series) 4-8   61-64
DECCA 5-10   54
PRESIDENT 5-10   56
TONE-CRAFT 5-10   55
Member: Dave Appell.

APRIL
(April Stevens)
Singles: 7–inch
A&M 3-5   74
Also see STEVENS, April

APRIL and Nino:
see TEMPO, Nino, and April Stevens

APRIL WINE
Singles: 7–inch
BIG TREE 3-5   72-75
CAPITOL 2-4   78-85
LONDON 2-4   76-78
Picture Sleeves
CAPITOL (Except 4975) 2-4   81-84
CAPITOL (4975 "Just Between You
and Me") 2-4   81
(Sleeve opens to a 22 x 15 poster.)
CAPITOL (4975 "Just Between You
and Me") 2-4   81
(Standard sleeve—no poster.)
LPs: 10/12–inch 33rpm
AQUARIUS 5-10
ATLANTIC 5-10   81
BIG TREE 10-15   72-75
CAPITOL 5-10   78-85
LONDON 10-12   76-77
Members: Steve Lang; Jerry Mercer; Myles Goodwyn; Brian
Greenway; Gary Moffet.

AQUARIAN DREAM
Singles: 7–inch
BUDDAH 3-5   76-77

ELEKTRA 2-4   78
LPs: 10/12–inch 33rpm
BUDDAH 8-10   76
ELEKTRA 5-10   78-79
  Members: Claude Bartee; Pete Bartee; Jacques Burvick; Mike
  Fowler; Valerie Horn; Gloria Jones; Pat Shannon.
  Also see CONNORS, Norman

AQUARIANS
Singles: 7–inch
UNI 3-6   69
LPs: 10/12–inch 33rpm
UNI 12-15   69

AQUATONES
Singles: 7–inch
FARGO 10-20   58-61
LPs: 10/12–inch 33rpm
FARGO (3001 "The Aquatones
  Sing") 125-175   64
  Members: Barbara Lee; Larry Vannata; Vic Castro; Russ Nagy;
  Mike Roma; Tom Vivona.

ARBORS
Singles: 7–inch
COLUMBIA 3-5   73
  (Black vinyl.)
COLUMBIA 5-10   73
  (Colored vinyl. Promotional issue only.)
DATE 4-6   66-70
  (Black vinyl.)
DATE 5-10   66-70
  (Colored vinyl. Promotional issue only.)
MERCURY 3-5   65
LPs: 10/12–inch 33rpm
DATE 12-15   67-68
VANGUARD 15-20   62

ARCADIA
Singles: 12–inch 33/45rpm
CAPITOL 4-6   85-86
Singles: 7–inch
CAPITOL 2-4   85-86
Picture Sleeves
CAPITOL 2-4   85-86
LPs: 10/12–inch 33rpm
CAPITOL 5-10   85-86
  Members: Roger Taylor; Simon LeBon.
  Also see DURAN DURAN
  Also see TAYLOR, Roger

ARCHIBALD
  (Archibald with Dave Bartholomew's Band)
Singles: 78rpm
COLONY (105 "Little Miss
  Muffett") 25-50   51
IMPERIAL 15-35   50-57
Singles: 7–inch
IMPERIAL (Except 5212) 20-50   52-57
IMPERIAL (5212 "Early Morning
  Blues") 50-75   52

ARCHIES
Singles: 7–inch
CALENDAR 4-8   68-69
ERIC 2-4   81
KIRSHNER 3-8   69-72
  (Includes 5 1/2–inch flexi-discs.)
RCA 3-8   72
Picture Sleeves
CALENDAR 5-15   68
KIRSHNER 5-10   69-71
LPs: 10/12–inch 33rpm
ACCORD 5-10   81
BACK-TRAC 5-10   85
BRYLEN (4415 "The Archies") 10-20   82
CALENDAR 12-25   68-70
51 WEST 5-10   79
KIRSHNER 12-25   69-71
RCA (0221 "The Archies") 15-25   70
  (Promotional issue only.)
  Members: Ron Dante, Jeff Barry, Toni Wine, plus assorted
  guests.
  Also see BLOOM, Bobby
  Also see GREENWICH, Ellie
  Also see KIM, Andy
  Also see STEVENS, Ray
  Also see TEMPO, Nino

ARCHIES / Johnny Thunder
Singles: 7–inch
COLLECTABLES 2-4
  Also see THUNDER, Johnny

ARDEN, Toni
Singles: 78rpm
COLUMBIA 3-6   49-54
DECCA 3-6   57-57
RCA 3-6   55-56
Singles: 7–inch
COLUMBIA 5-10   50-54
DECCA 5-10   57-59
MISHAWAKA 3-5
RCA 5-10   55-56
EPs: 7–inch 33/45rpm
DECCA 8-15   58
COLUMBIA 10-15   56
LPs: 10/12–inch 33rpm
DECCA 12-25   57-59

AREA CODE 615
Singles: 7–inch
POLYDOR 3-5   69-70
LPs: 10/12–inch 33rpm
POLYDOR 8-12   69-70

ARENA BRASS
LPs: 10/12–inch 33rpm
EPIC 10-15   62

ARGENT
Singles: 7–inch
DATE 3-6   70
EPIC 4-8   69-74

LPs: 10/12–inch 33rpm

EPIC	10-20	69-75
U.A.	5-10	76

Members: Rod Argent; Russ Ballard; Robert Henrit; Jim Rodford; John Verity.
  Also see BALLARD, Russ
  Also see ZOMBIES

ARKADE
Singles: 7–inch

DUNHILL	4-6	70-71

Picture Sleeves

DUNHILL	4-6	71

ARLEN, Harold, with "Friend"
LPs: 10/12–inch 33rpm

COLUMBIA (OL-6520 "Harold Sings Arlen")	25-35	66
(Monaural.)		
COLUMBIA (OS-2920 "Harold Sings Arlen")	20-40	66
(Stereo.)		
COLUMBIA (CSP-2920 "Harold Sings Arlen")	5-10	

Members: Harold Arlen; Barbra Streisand.
  Also see STREISAND, Barbra

ARMADA ORCHESTRA
LPs: 10/12–inch 33rpm

SCEPTER	4-8	75

ARMAGEDDON
Singles: 7–inch

CAPITOL	3-6	71-72
CREATIVE SOUND	4-6	71

LPs: 10/12–inch 33rpm

A&M	8-12	75
AMOS	15-20	70

Members: Keith Relf; Louis Cennamo; Martin Pugh.
  Also see RENAISSANCE
  Also see YARDBIRDS

ARMATRADING, Joan
Singles: 12–inch 33/45rpm

A&M	4-6	83

Singles: 7–inch

A&M	2-5	74-86

Picture Sleeves

A&M	3-5	83

LPs: 10/12–inch 33rpm

A&M	8-12	73-90

Promotional LPs

A&M (12 "Talk Under Ladders")	15-25	81

ARMEN, Kay
Singles: 78rpm

DECCA	4-8	42-58

Singles: 7–inch

DECCA	5-12	55-59

EPs: 7–inch 33/45rpm

MGM	10-20	54-55

LPs: 10/12–inch 33rpm

DECCA (5000 series)	20-40	54
(10–inch LP)		

DECCA (8000 series)	10-20	59
MGM (200 series)	20-40	54
MGM (3000 series)	15-30	55

ARMORED SAINT
Singles: 12–inch 33/45rpm

CHRYSALIS	4-6	86

Singles: 7–inch

CHRYSALIS	2-4	84-86

LPs: 10/12–inch 33rpm

CHRYSALIS	5-10	84-87

ARMS, Russell
Singles: 78rpm

EPIC	3-6	54-56
ERA	3-6	56-57

Singles: 7–inch

EPIC	5-10	54-56
ERA	5-10	56-57

LPs: 10/12–inch 33rpm

ERA	10-20	57

ARMSTEAD, Joshie Jo
Singles: 7–inch

DE LEX	4-8	62
GIANT	4-6	67-69
TRUTH	3-5	74

Also see IKETTES

ARMSTRONG, Chuck
Singles: 7–inch

R&R	3-5	76

ARMSTRONG, Louis
(Louis Armstrong and the All Stars)
Singles: 78rpm

CAPITOL	4-8	56
COLUMBIA (2500 through 2700 series)	15-25	32
COLUMBIA (40000 series)	4-8	56-66
DECCA	5-15	35-58
OKEH	20-30	26-31
RCA	4-8	56
VICTOR	10-20	33
VOCALION	10-20	36

Singles: 7–inch

A&M	2-4	88
ABC	2-5	67-73
AMSTERDAM	3-5	71
AUDIO FIDELITY	3-5	71
AVCO EMBASSY	3-5	71
BRUNSWICK	4-6	67-68
BUENA VISTA	3-6	68
CAPITOL	5-10	56
COLUMBIA	5-10	56-66
CONTINENTAL	3-5	71
DECCA (25000 series)	4-6	61-64
DECCA (27000 through 29000 series)	8-10	50-56
DECCA (30000 through 31000 series)	5-10	56-59
DOT	4-8	59
EPIC	3-6	69
KAPP	4-6	64-69

JAZZ PANORAMA

FIREWORKS
WITH
LOUIS ARMSTRONG

featuring: Louis Armstrong, cornet; Kid Ory, trombone;
Johnny Dodds, clarinet; Lil Hardin, piano; Baby Dodds, drums;
Johnny St. Cyr, banjo; Peter Briggs, bass; Lonnie Johnson, gtr.

1204 A   Side 1
                          Volume 2

1. Don't Forget To Mess Around
2. Fireworks
3. Skip The Gutter
4. Two Deuces
5. Knee Drops
6. Alligator Crawl

(1204A)

33-1/3 RPM MICROGROOVE
MANUFACTURED FOR JAZZ COLLECTORS

MGM	4-8	59-60
MERCURY	4-6	64-66
RCA	5-10	56
U.A.	3-6	68-69
VERVE	4-8	59-60

Picture Sleeves

A&M	2-4	88
BUENA VISTA	5-8	68
CONTINENTAL	3-6	71
KAPP	5-10	64
MGM	8-12	59
MERCURY	5-10	64

Note: Multi-disc, 1950s boxed sets are in the $15
to $25 range. At this time we do not have specific
numbers and titles.

EPs: 7–inch 33/45rpm

COLUMBIA	5-15	55-59
DECCA	8-15	55-57
RCA	10-20	53-59

LPs: 10/12–inch 33rpm

ABC	5-10	68-76
AMSTERDAM	5-10	70
AUDIO FIDELITY	15-25	60-64
BIOGRAPH	5-10	73
BRUNSWICK (58004 "Jazz Classics")	50-100	50
(10–inch LP.)		
BRUNSWICK (75000 series)	8-15	68-71
BUENA VISTA	8-12	68
CHIAROSCURO	5-10	77
COLUMBIA (500 through 900 series)	25-50	54-57
COLUMBIA (2600 series)	8-15	67
COLUMBIA (9400 series)	8-15	67
COLUMBIA (30000 series)	5-12	71-80
CORAL	5-10	73
DECCA (100 series)	15-25	65-66
DECCA (4000 series)	10-20	61-63
DECCA (5000 series)	25-50	51-54
(10–inch LPs.)		
DECCA (8000 series)	15-25	55-59

DECCA (9000 series)	8-15	67
(Decca LP numbers in this series preceded by a "7" or a "DL-7" are stereo issues.)		
EVEREST	5-10	71-76
GNP/CRESCENDO	8-12	77
GUEST STAR	5-10	64
HARMONY	5-10	69
JAZZ HERITAGE	5-10	80
JAZZ PANORAMA (1204 "Fireworks")	20-40	
JEMI	5-10	
KAPP	10-15	64
MCA	6-10	73-82
MERCURY	10-15	66
METRO	10-15	65
MILESTONE	5-10	74-75
OLYMPIC	5-10	74
PAUSA	5-10	83
RCA (1300 and 1400 series)	25-50	53-56
RCA (2300 through 2900 series)	10-20	61-64
(With "LPM" or "LSP" prefix.)		
RCA (2600 series)	5-10	77
(With "CPL1" prefix.)		
RCA (5500 series)	8-12	77
RCA (6000 series)	8-12	71
SAGA	5-10	72
STORYVILLE	5-10	80
TRIP	5-10	72
U.A.	8-15	68-69
VANGUARD	8-12	76
VERVE	15-20	60-64
VOCALION	5-10	68-69

Also see BARRY, John
Also see BRUBECK, Dave
Also see CROSBY, Bing, and Louis Armstrong
Also see FITZGERALD, Ella, and Louis Armstrong
Also see KAYE, Danny, and Louis Armstrong
Also see JENKINS, Gordon
Also see MILLS BROTHERS, and Louis Armstrong

ARMSTRONG, Louis, and Duke Ellington
Singles: 7–inch

ROULETTE	4-6	63

LPs: 10/12–inch 33rpm

MFSL (155 "Recording for the First Time")	15-25	85
ROULETTE (100 series)	8-12	71
ROULETTE (52000 series)	15-25	63

Also see ELLINGTON, Duke

ARMSTRONG, Louis, and Guy Lombardo
Singles: 7–inch

CAPITOL	3-6	66

Also see LOMBARDO, Guy

ARMSTRONG, Louis, and Oscar Peterson
Singles: 7–inch

VERVE	4-6	59

LPs: 10/12–inch 33rpm

VERVE	15-25	59

Also see ARMSTRONG, Louis
Also see PETERSON, Oscar

ARNELL, Ginny
Singles: 7–inch
DECCA 5-10   60
MGM 4-8   63-65
WARWICK 5-10   61
LPs: 10/12–inch 33rpm
MGM 15-25   64
Also see JAMIE and Jane

ARNIE'S LOVE
Singles: 12–inch 33/45rpm

ARNO, Audrey
Singles: 7–inch
DECCA 4-8   61

ARNOLD, Calvin
Singles: 7–inch
IX CHAINS 3-5   75
VENTURE 4-8   67-69

ARNOLD, Eddy
Singles: 78rpm
BLUEBIRD 25-50   45
RCA (Except 1800 through
   3100 series) 10-20   46-49
RCA (1800 through 3100
   series) 15-30   46-49
Singles: 7–inch
DIAMOND P (1009 "If the Whole World
   Stopped Lovin") 5-10   73
   (Promotional issue only.)
MGM 3-5   73-76
RCA (0100 through 0400 series) 8-15   50-51
   (Black vinyl. Black or turquoise labels.)
RCA (0100 through 0400 series) 20-40   50-51
   (Colored vinyl.)
RCA (0500 through 0700 series) 3-5   71-72
   (Orange labels.)
RCA (2000 series) 5-10   62
   (Compact 33 stereo single.)
RCA (3000 through 6000 series) 10-20   50-57
RCA (7000 series) 5-12   57-62
RCA (8000 and 9000 series) 3-8   62-71
RCA (10000 through 13000 series) 2-5   76-83
Picture Sleeves
RCA 8-15   56-66
EPs: 7–inch 33/45rpm
RCA (100 series) 10-12   61
   (With "LPC" prefix. Compact 33 Double.)
RCA (280 "Best Wishes") 10-20
   (Promotional issue only.)
RCA (200 through 900 series) 10-15   52-56
   (With "EPA" prefix.)
RCA (1100 and 1200 series) 15-20   55-56
   (With "EPB" prefix.)
RCA (1400 and 1500 series) 8-12   57
   (With "EPA" prefix.)
RCA (3000 series) 20-25   52-54
   (With "EPB" prefix.)

RCA (4000 and 5000 series) 6-12   57-59
   (With "EPA" prefix.)
LPs: 10/12–inch 33rpm
CAMDEN 5-10   72-74
   (With "ACL1" prefix.)
CAMDEN (CAL and CAS series) 8-15   60-72
   (With "CAL," "CAS" or "CXS" prefix.)
GREEN VALLEY 8-10   76
K-TEL 8-10   74
MGM 8-12   74-76
RCA (AHL1, ANL1, APL1,
   and AYL1 series) 5-10   73-81
RCA (CPL1 series) 8-12   83
RCA (209 "Eddy Arnold") 15-20   66
   (Promotional issue only.)
RCA (1100 through 2200 series) 20-30   55-60
   (Monaural. with "LPM" prefix.)
RCA (2300 through 2900 series) 12-20   60-64
   (Monaural. with "LPM" prefix.)
RCA (3000 series) 45-55   52-54
   (10–inch LPs. with "LPM" prefix.)
RCA (3000 series) 8-12   64-68
   (12–inch LPs. with "LPM" prefix.)
RCA (1900 through 3400 series) 15-25   60-65
   (Stereo. with "LSP" prefix. "LSP" numbers below
   1900 were reprocessed stereo issues of '50s LPs.
   They were issued in the '60s and are in the
   $10-$15 range.)
RCA (3500 through 4800 series) 10-20   66-73
RCA (6000 series) 8-12   70
SUNRISE 5-10   79
TIME-LIFE 5-10   81
   Also see ANN-MARGRET
   Also see PRESLEY, Elvis / Hank Snow / Eddy Arnold / Jim
   Reeves

ARRINGTON, Steve
(Steve Arrington's Hall of Fame)
Singles: 12–inch 33/45rpm
ATLANTIC 4-6   83-86
Singles: 7–inch
ATLANTIC 2-4   83-86
KONGLATHER 2-4   82
MANHATTAN 2-4   87
LPs: 10/12–inch 33rpm
ATLANTIC 5-10   83-86
   Also see SLAVE

ARROWS (With Davie Allan):
see ALLAN, Davie

ART ATTACK
Singles: 12–inch 33/45rpm
B.M.O. 4-6   83
Singles: 7–inch
B.M.O. 2-4   83
LPs: 10/12–inch 33rpm
B.M.O. 5-10   83

ART in AMERICA
Singles: 7–inch
PAVILLION 2-4   83

LPs: 10/12–inch 33rpm

CAPITOL 8-12 70-72
  Members: Tony Ashton; Kim Gardner; Roy Dyke.
  Also see BADGER

ASIA
Singles: 12–inch 33/45rpm

GEFFEN 4-6 82-85
Singles: 7–inch

GEFFEN 2-4 82-90
Picture Sleeves

GEFFEN 2-4 81-85
LPs: 10/12–inch 33rpm

GEFFEN 5-10 82-90
  Members: Steve Howe; Carl Palmer; John Wetton; Geoff
  Downes; Mandy Mayer.
  Also see EMERSON, LAKE & PALMER
  Also see HOWE, Steve, Band

ASLEEP at the Wheel
Singles: 7–inch

CAPITOL 2-4 75-79
EPIC 3-5 74
LPs: 10/12–inch 33rpm

CAPITOL 10-15 75-79
EPIC (BG-33000 series) 15-25 75
EPIC (EG-33000 series) 10-15
EPIC (KE-33000 series) 10-15 74
EPIC (PE-33000 series) 5-10
MCA 5-10 80-84
U.A. 15-25 73
  Member: Ray Benson.

ASPHALT JUNGLE
Singles: 7–inch

TEC 2-4 80

ASSEMBLED MULTITUDE
Singles: 7–inch

ATLANTIC 3-5 70-72
ERIC 2-4 81
LPs: 10/12–inch 33rpm

ATLANTIC 8-10 70

ASSOCIATION
Singles: 7–inch

COLUMBIA 3-5 72
ELEKTRA 2-4 81
JUBILEE 4-8 65
MUMS 3-5 73
RCA 3-5 75
VALIANT 4-8 66
WARNER 3-6 67-71
Picture Sleeves

VALIANT 5-10 66
LPs: 10/12–inch 33rpm

COLUMBIA 8-10 72
VALIANT 12-20 66
WARNER 8-12 67-71
  Members: Gary Alexander; Ted Bluechel Jr; Brian Cole; Russ
  Giguere; Terry Kirkman; Cliff Nivison; Larry Ramos; Richard
  Thompson; Jim Yester.
  Also see MAMAS and the Papas / Association / Fifth Dimension
  Also see MIKE & DEAN

ASTLEY, Jon
Singles: 7–inch

ATLANTIC 2-4 87-88
Picture Sleeves

ATLANTIC 2-4 87-88
LPs: 10/12–inch 33rpm

ATLANTIC 5-10 87

ASTLEY, Rick
Singles: 7–inch

RCA 2-4 87-91
Picture Sleeves

RCA 2-4 87-89
LPs: 10/12–inch 33rpm

RCA 5-8 87-91

ASTORS
Singles: 7–inch

STAX 5-10 65-67
  Members: Curtis Johnson; Richard Harris; Eddie Stanbeck; Sam
  Byrnes.

ASTRONAUTS
Singles: 7–inch

PALLADIUM (610 "Come Along
  Baby") 75-125 61
RCA 5-10 63-65
Picture Sleeves

RCA 20-30 63
EPs: 7–inch 33/45rpm

RCA 25-40 63
RCA WURLITZER DISCOTHEQUE . 30-40 64
  (Promotional issue only.)
LPs: 10/12–inch 33rpm

RCA 20-30 63-67
  Members: Stormy Patterson; Robert Demmon; Dennis Lindsey;
  James Gallagher; Richard Fifield.

ASTRONAUTS / Liverpool Five
LPs: 10/12–inch 33rpm

RCA (251 "Stereo Festival") 25-45
  (Promotional issue only.)
  Also see ASTRONAUTS
  Also see LIVERPOOL FIVE

ASWAD
LPs: 10/12–inch 33rpm

ISLAND 5-10 84
MANGO 5-10 84-88
  Members: Candy McKenzie; Brinsley Forde; Donald Griffiths;
  Courtney Hemmings; George Oban; Angus Gaye; Bunny
  McKenzie; Trevor Bow.

ASYLUM CHOIR
Singles: 7–inch

SHELTER 3-5 71
SMASH 4-6 69
LPs: 10/12–inch 33rpm

SHELTER (2000 series) 8-10 74
SHELTER (8000 series) 10-15 71
SHELTER (52000 series) 5-10 75
SMASH (67107 "Look Inside") 25-30 68
  (With toilet tissue cover.)

Also see ATKINS, Chet

ATLANTA
Singles: 7-inch

MCA	2-4	84-85
MDJ	2-4	83

Picture Sleeves

MDJ	2-4	83

LPs: 10/12-inch 33rpm

MCA	5-10	84

ATLANTA DISCO BAND
Singles: 7-inch

ARIOLA AMERICA	2-4	76

LPs: 10/12-inch 33rpm

ARIOLA AMERICA	5-10	76

ATLANTA RHYTHM SECTION
Singles: 7-inch

COLUMBIA	2-4	81
DECCA	3-5	72
MCA	2-4	73
POLYDOR	2-4	74-80

LPs: 10/12-inch 33rpm

COLUMBIA	5-10	81
DECCA	12-20	72
MCA	5-10	77
MFSL (038 "Champagne Jam")	25-50	79
POLYDOR	5-10	74-80

Members: Ronnie Hammond; Rodney Justo; Robert Nix; Barry Bailey; J.R. Cobb; Dean Daughtry; Paul Goddard.
Also see CANDYMEN
Also see CLASSICS IV
Also see MANILOW, Barry / Atlanta Rhythm Section

ATLANTIC STARR
Singles: 12-inch 33/45rpm

A&M	4-6	79-85

Singles: 7-inch

A&M	2-4	78-86
MANHATTAN	2-4	86
WARNER	2-4	87-89

Picture Sleeves

A&M	2-4	78-86
WARNER	2-4	87

LPs: 10/12-inch 33rpm

A&M	5-10	78-85
WARNER	5-10	87-89

Members: Sharon Bryant; David Lewis; Wayne Lewis; Jonathan Lewis; William Sudderth; Damon Rentie; Clifford Archer; Joe Phillips; Porter Carroll; Koran Daniels; Barbara Weathers.

ATOMIC ROOSTER
Singles: 7-inch

ELEKTRA	3-5	71-72

LPs: 10/12-inch 33rpm

ELEKTRA	10-20	71-73
PVC	5-10	83

Members: Chris Farlowe; Pete French; Steve Bolton; John Cann; Vincent Crane; Paul Hammond; Carl Palmer; Johnny Mandala; Rick Parnell.
Also see BROWN, Arthur

ATTACK, Art: see ART ATTACK

ATTILA
LPs: 10/12-inch 33rpm

BACK-TRAC	5-10	85
EPIC (30030 "Attila")	40-50	70

Members: Billy Joel; Jon Small.
Also see JOEL, Billy

ATTITUDE
Singles: 12-inch 33/45rpm

ATLANTIC	4-6	83

Singles: 7-inch

ATLANTIC	2-4	83

LPs: 10/12-inch 33rpm

ATLANTIC	5-10	83

ATTITUDES
Singles: 7-inch

DARK HORSE	3-5	75-76

Picture Sleeves

DARK HORSE	3-5	75

LPs: 10/12-inch 33rpm

DARK HORSE	5-10	76-77

Members: Danny Kortchmar; David Foster; Jim Keltner; Paul Stallworth.

AUDIENCE
Singles: 7-inch

ELEKTRA	3-5	71-72

LPs: 10/12-inch 33rpm

AUDIENCE	10-15	71-72
ELEKTRA	8-12	72

Members: Trevor Williams; Howard Werth; Pat Neubergh; Nick Judd; Tony Connor; Keith Gemmell.

AUDIO TWO
LPs: 10/12-inch 33rpm

FIRST PRIORITY	5-8	88

AUDREY
Singles: 78rpm

PLUS (104 "Dear Elvis")	10-20	56

Singles: 7-inch

PLUS (104 "Dear Elvis")	20-25	56

(Break-in novelty. Contains excerpts of Elvis' Sun recordings.)
Also see PRESLEY, Elvis

AUGER, Brian
(Brian Auger and the Trinity; Brian Auger's Oblivion Express)
Singles: 7-inch

ATCO	4-6	68-69
RCA	3-5	70-74

LPs: 10/12-inch 33rpm

ATCO	12-15	69
CAPITOL	10-12	69
POLYDOR	5-10	74
RCA	6-10	70-77
WARNER	5-10	77

AUGIE: see MEYERS, Augie

AUGUST, Jan

Singles: 78rpm

MERCURY 3-5   50-62

Singles: 7–inch

MERCURY 3-8   50-62

EPs: 7–inch 33/45rpm

MERCURY 5-10   50-56

LPs: 10/12–inch 33rpm

MERCURY 5-15   50-62
WING 5-10   59
   Also see HAYMAN, Richard, Orchestra

AURRA

Singles: 12–inch 33/45rpm

SALSOUL 4-6   82

Singles: 7–inch

DREAM 2-4   80
SALSOUL 2-4   81-83

LPs: 10/12–inch 33rpm

DREAM 5-10   80
SALSOUL 5-10   81-83
   Members: Curt Jones; Starleana Young; Steve Washington; Tom
   Lockett Jr.; Phillip Fields.
   Also see DEJA
   Also see SLAVE

AUSTIN, Gene

Singles: 78rpm

COLUMBIA 3-5   54-56
DECCA 3-5   56
VICTOR 4-8   25-35

Singles: 7–inch

COLUMBIA 4-8   54-56
DECCA 4-6   56
RCA 4-8   57

Picture Sleeves

RCA 5-10   57

EPs: 7–inch 33/45rpm

RCA 5-10   53

LPs: 10/12–inch 33rpm

DOT 8-15
RCA 10-20   53-57
X 10-20   54

AUSTIN, Patti

Singles: 12–inch 33/45rpm

QWEST 4-6   84-86

Singles: 7–inch

ABC 3-6   68
CTI 2-4   76-80
COLUMBIA 3-5   71-73
CORAL 4-8   65-68
QWEST 2-4   81-86
U.A. 2-4   69-70

LPs: 10/12–inch 33rpm

CTI 5-10   77-80
GRP 5-8   90
QWEST 5-10   81-86
   Also see JONES, Quincy
   Also see WALDEN, Narada Michael, and Patti Austin
   Also see YUTAKA

AUSTIN, Patti, and Jerry Butler

Singles: 7–inch

CTI 2-4   83
   Also see BUTLER, Jerry

AUSTIN, Patti, and James Ingram

Singles: 7–inch

QWEST 2-4   82-84
   Also see AUSTIN, Patti
   Also see INGRAM, James

AUSTIN, Sil

Singles: 78rpm

JUBILEE 4-6   54-55
MERCURY 3-5   56-65

Singles: 7–inch

JUBILEE 5-10   54-55
MERCURY 3-8   56-65
SSS INT'L 2-4   70
SEW CITY 3-6   66

EPs: 7–inch 33/45rpm

MERCURY 10-15   56-57

LPs: 10/12–inch 33rpm

MERCURY 10-25   59-67
SSS INT'L 8-10   70-82
WING 10-12   63-68

AUSTIN, Sil, and Red Prysock

Singles: 7–inch

MERCURY 4-6   61

LPs: 10/12–inch 33rpm

MERCURY (20434 "Battle Royal") . . 15-25   61
  (Monaural.)
MERCURY (60106 "Battle Royal") . . 20-30   61
  (Stereo.)
SSS INT'L 8-10   69
WING 10-12   63-68
   Also see AUSTIN, Sil

AUTOGRAPH

Singles: 7–inch

RCA 2-4   84-85

Picture Sleeves

RCA 2-4   84-85

LPs: 10/12–inch 33rpm

RCA 5-10   84-87
   Member: Steve Plunkett.

AUTOMATIC MAN

Singles: 7–inch

ISLAND 2-4   76-77

LPs: 10/12–inch 33rpm

ISLAND 5-10   76-77
   Members: Michael Schrieve; Todd Cochran; Doni Harvey; Pat
   Thrall.

AUTRY, Gene

Singles: 78rpm

CHAMPION 50-75
CLARION 50-75
CONQUEROR 25-75
COLUMBIA 5-10   45-56
DECCA 50-75

DIVA 50-75
HARMONY 20-30
OKEH 10-20   40-45
PERFECT 30-60
QRS (1044 "Living in
  the Mountains") 3500-4500   29
VELVET TONE 50-75
VOCALION 25-50   35-40

Singles: 7–Inch

COLUMBIA (20700 through
  21500 series) 5-10   50-56
COLUMBIA (38700 through
  40500 series) 5-10   50-55
COLUMBIA (44000 series) 3-5   68
MISTLETOE 3-5   74
REPUBLIC 3-5   69-76

EPs: 7–Inch 33/45rpm

COLUMBIA 40-50   51-56

LPs: 10/12–Inch 33rpm

BIRCHMONT 8-12
CHALLENGE 25-30   58
COLUMBIA (55 through 154) 80-100   51-55
  (10–inch LPs.)
COLUMBIA (600 series) 80-100   55
COLUMBIA (1000 series) 8-10   70-82
COLUMBIA (1500 series) 20-25   61
COLUMBIA (2500 series) 80-100   56
  (10–inch LPs.)
COLUMBIA (6137 "Merry Christmas") 40-60   50
  (10–inch LP.)
COLUMBIA (8000 series) 80-100
COLUMBIA (9001 "Western Classics") 40-60   51
  (10–inch LPs.)
COLUMBIA (9002 "Western
  Classics, Vol. 2") 40-60   51
  (10–inch LPs.)
COLUMBIA (15000 series) 8-10   81
COLUMBIA (37000 series) 5-10   82
DESIGN 8-10
ENCORE 6-10   80
GRT 10-15   77
GRAND PRIX 8-10

HALLMARK 8-12
HARMONY (7100 through
  7300 series) 20-30   56-65
HARMONY (9500 series) 15-25   59-64
HARMONY (11000 series) 10-15   64-66
HURRAH 5-10
MELODY RANCH 20-25   65
MISTLETOE 8-12   74
MURRAY HILL (897296;"Melody
  Ranch Radio Show") 45-55
  (Four-LP set.)
RCA (2600 series) 25-30   62
RADIOLA 5-10   75
REPUBLIC (1900 series) 5-10
REPUBLIC (6000 series) 5-15   76-78
STARDAY 6-10   78

AVALON, Frankie

Singles: 78rpm

CHANCELLOR 10-20   57-58
X 10-15   54

Singles: 7–Inch

ABC 2-4   74
AMOS 2-4   69
BOBCAT 2-4   83
CHANCELLOR (1 "Shy Guy") 15-20
  (Acnecare promotional special products issue.)
CHANCELLOR (1004 "Cupid") 15-20   57
CHANCELLOR (1011 through 1026) .. 8-12   57-58
CHANCELLOR (1031 "Venus") 10-15   58
  (Monaural)
CHANCELLOR (1031 "Venus") 15-25   58
  (Stereo.)
CHANCELLOR (1036 "Bobby Sox
  to Stockings") 8-12   59
  (Monaural.)
CHANCELLOR (1036 "Bobby Sox
  to Stockings") 15-25   59
  (Stereo.)
CHANCELLOR (1040 "Just Ask
  Your Heart") 8-12   59
  (Monaural.)
CHANCELLOR (1040 "Just Ask
  Your Heart") 15-25   59
  (Stereo.)
CHANCELLOR (1045 "Why") 8-12   59
  (Monaural.)
CHANCELLOR (1045 "Why") 15-25   59
  (Stereo.)
CHANCELLOR (1048 through
  1131) 5-10   60-63
CHANCELLOR (1134 "Come Fly
  with Me") 15-25   63
CHANCELLOR (1135 "Cleopatra") .. 10-15   63
CHANCELLOR (1139 "Beach Party") 10-15   64
COLLECTABLES 2-4   81
DE LITE 2-4   76-78
ERIC 2-4   73
MCA 2-4   84

AVALON, Frankie, and Annette
Singles: 12–Inch 33/45rpm

AVANT-GARDE
Singles: 7–Inch

AVERAGE, Johnny, Band:
  see JOHNNY AVERAGE BAND

AVERAGE WHITE BAND
(AWB)
Singles: 7–inch
ARISTA	2-4	80
ATLANTIC	2-4	74-80
MCA	3-5	73-74

LPs: 10/12–inch 33rpm
ARISTA	5-8	80
ATLANTIC (Except 19000 series)	8-12	74-76
ATLANTIC (19000 series)	5-10	77-80
MCA (Except 345)	8-10	73-75
MCA (345 "Show Your Hand")	15-20	73
(With "Jack-in-the-box" cover.)		
MCA (345 "Show Your Hand")	8-10	73
(With standard cover.)		

Members: Roger Ball; Malcolm Duncan; Steve Ferrone; Alan Gorrie; Robbie McIntosh; Onnie McIntyre.
Also see FOREVER MORE
Also see KARP, Charlie
Also see KING, Ben E., and the Average White Band

AXE
Singles: 7–inch
ATCO	2-4	82-84
MCA	2-4	79-80

LPs: 10/12–inch 33rpm
ATCO	5-10	82-84
MCA	5-10	79-80

Member: Bobby Barth.
Also see BABYFACE

AXTON, Hoyt
(Hoyt Axton and the Sherwood Singers)
Singles: 7–inch
A&M	2-5	73-76
BRIAR	4-8	61
CAPITOL	2-5	71-72
COLGEMS	3-6	67
COLUMBIA	3-5	69
ELEKTRA	2-4	81
HORIZON	4-6	62-63
JEREMIAH	2-4	79-83
MCA	2-4	77-78
20TH FOX	4-6	66
VEE JAY	4-6	64-65

Picture Sleeves
A&M	3-5	73-74

LPs: 10/12–inch 33rpm
A&M	5-10	73-77
ACCORD	5-10	82
ALLEGIANCE	5-10	84
BRYLEN	5-10	82
CAPITOL	8-10	71
COLUMBIA	8-10	69
EXODUS	10-15	66
HORIZON	15-20	62-63
JEREMIAH	8-10	79-82
LAKE SHORE	5-10	81
MCA	5-10	77-78
SURREY	15-18	65
VEE JAY	10-15	64-65

VEE JAY INTERNATIONAL (Except 1000 series)	5-10	74-77
VEE JAY INTERNATIONAL (1000 series)	10-12	74

AXTON, Hoyt, and the Chambers Brothers
Singles: 7–inch
HORIZON	4-8	62

LPs: 10/12–inch 33rpm
HORIZON	15-20	63

Also see AXTON, Hoyt
Also see CHAMBERS BROTHERS

AYERS, Roy
(Roy Ayers' Ubiquity)
Singles: 12–inch 33/45rpm
COLUMBIA	4-6	84-85
POLYDOR	4-6	79

Singles: 7–inch
COLUMBIA	2-4	84-86
POLYDOR	2-4	77

LPs: 10/12–inch 33rpm
ATLANTIC	8-12	68-76
COLUMBIA	5-10	84-86
ELEKTRA	5-10	78
POLYDOR	6-10	70-82

Also see UBIQUITY

AYERS, Roy, and Wayne Henderson
Singles: 7–inch
POLYDOR	2-4	79-80

LPs: 10/12–inch 33rpm
POLYDOR	5-10	80

Also see AYERS, Roy
Also see HENDERSON, Wayne

AZTEC CAMERA
Singles: 12–inch 33/45rpm
SIRE	4-6	84

Singles: 7–inch
SIRE	2-4	83-85

LPs: 10/12–inch 33rpm
SIRE	5-10	83-87

AZTEC TWO STEP
Singles: 7–inch
ELEKTRA	3-5	72-73
RCA	2-4	76-78

LPs: 10/12–inch 33rpm
ELEKTRA	10-12	72
RCA	5-10	76-80
WATERHOUSE	5-10	80

Members: Rex Fowler; Alan Schwartzberg; Neal Schulman.

AZTECA
Singles: 7–inch
COLUMBIA	3-5	72-73

LPs: 10/12–inch 33rpm
COLUMBIA	10-12	72-73

Members: Coke Escovedo; Tony Smith.
Also see ESCOVEDO, Coke
Also see MALO
Also see SANTANA

B

B.B.C.S. & A.
Singles: 7–inch
SAM 2-4   82

B.B. & Q. BAND
(Brooklyn, Bronx and Queens Band)
Singles: 12–inch 33/45rpm
CAPITOL 4-6   81-83
Singles: 7–inch
CAPITOL 2-5   81-83
IN YOUR FACE 2-4   86
LPs: 10/12–inch 33rpm
CAPITOL 5-10   81-83

B. BEAT GIRLS
Singles: 12–inch 33/45rpm
25 WEST 4-6   83
Singles: 7–inch
25 WEST 2-4   83

B. BUMBLE and the Stingers
Singles: 7–inch
MERCURY 4-8   66
RENDEZVOUS 5-10   61-63
Members: Billy Brumble; Ron Brady; Fred Richard; Ernie
Freeman.
Also see FREEMAN, Ernie

B-52s
Singles: 12–inch 33/45rpm
WARNER 4-6   86
Singles: 7–inch
B-52s (52 "Rock Lobster") 15-20   78
REPRISE 2-4 89-91
WARNER (Except 927) 2-4 79-86
WARNER (927 "Give Me Back My Man") 3-5   81
(Promotional issue only.)
Picture Sleeves
B-52s (52 "Rock Lobster") 15-20   78
REPRISE 2-4   89

WARNER 3-5 80-83
LPs: 10/12–inch 33rpm
REPRISE 5-8 89-91
WARNER 5-10 79-86
Members: Cindy Wilson; Keith Strickland; Fred Schneider III;
Ricky Wilson; Kate Pierson.

B-H-Y
(Baker-Harris-Young)
Singles: 7–inch
SALSOUL 3-5   79
LPs: 10/12–inch 33rpm
SALSOUL 5-10   79
Members: Ron Baker; Norman Harris; Earl Young.
Also see MFSB
Also see TRAMMPS

B.T. EXPRESS
Singles: 12–inch 33/45rpm
COAST to COAST 4-6   81
COLUMBIA 4-6   81
Singles: 7–inch
COAST to COAST 2-4   82
COLUMBIA 2-5 76-80
EARTHTONE 2-4   84
ROADSHOW 3-5 74-75
SCEPTER 3-6   74
LPs: 10/12–inch 33rpm
COAST to COAST 5-10   82
COLUMBIA 5-10 76-80
ROADSHOW 10-12 74-76
SCEPTER 8-10   74
Members: Carlos Ward; Bill Risbrook; Richard Thompson;
Michael Jones; Dennis Rowe; Leslie Ming; Barbara Joyce
Lomas.

BTO:
see BACHMAN-TURNER OVERDRIVE

BABE RUTH
Singles: 7–inch
CAPITOL 2-4   76
HARVEST 3-5 73-76
LPs: 10/12–inch 33rpm
HARVEST 5-10 73-76
Members: Ellie Hope; Steve Gurl; Jenny Haan; Dave Hewitt;
Ray Knott; Bernie Marsden; Alan Shacklock; Ed Spevock.

BABY JANE and the Rock-a-byes
Singles: 7–inch
SPOKANE 8-10   63
U.A. 5-10   62

BABY RAY
(Ray Eddlemon)
Singles: 7–inch
IMPERIAL 8-15 66-67
LPs: 10/12–inch 33rpm
IMPERIAL 15-20   67

BABY RAY and the Ferns
Singles: 7–inch
DONNA 25-35   63
Member: Frank Zappa.
Also see ZAPPA, Frank

BABYFACE

Singles: 7-inch
SOLAR 2-4   87-89
LPs: 10/12-inch 33rpm
SOLAR 5-8   89

BABYS

Singles: 7-inch
CHRYSALIS 2-4   77-81
Picture Sleeves
CHRYSALIS 2-4   80
LPs: 10/12-inch 33rpm
CHRYSALIS 5-10   77-81
Members: Mike Corby; John Waite; Tony Brock; Wally Stocker.
Also see WAITE, John

BACHARACH, Burt

Singles: 7-inch
A&M 3-5   68-74
CABOT 3-5
KAPP 3-6   63-65
LIBERTY 3-5   66
U.A. 3-5   67
Picture Sleeves
A&M 3-5   71
EPs: 7-inch 33/45rpm
A&M 4-8   68-73
LPs: 10/12-inch 33rpm
A&M (Except 1) 5-10   67-74
A&M (1 "Radio Interview") 8-15   74
(Promotional issue only.)
KAPP 8-15   65
MCA 5-10   73

BACHARACH, Burt / Glen Campbell / Dionne Warwick

LPs: 10/12-inch 33rpm
CHEVROLET (6658 "On the Move")   10-20   70
(Chevrolet promotional issue.)
Also see CAMPBELL, Glen
Also see WARWICK, Dionne

BACHELORS

Singles: 7-inch
LONDON 3-8   63-72
Picture Sleeves
LONDON 8-15   64-65
LPs: 10/12-inch 33rpm
LONDON 10-20   64-72
Members: Con Cluskey; Declan Stokes; John Stokes.

BACHMAN, Randy

Singles: 7-inch
POLYDOR 2-4   78
LPs: 10/12-inch 33rpm
POLYDOR 5-10   78
RCA (1100 series) 5-10   75
RCA (4300 series) 10-15   70
Also see BACHMAN-TURNER-BACHMAN
Also see BACHMAN-TURNER OVERDRIVE
Also see GUESS WHO
Also see IRONHORSE

BACHMAN-TURNER-BACHMAN

LPs: 10/12-inch 33rpm
REPRISE 8-10   75
Members: Randy Bachman; C.F. Turner; Robin Bachman.
Also see BACHMAN-TURNER OVERDRIVE
Also see BRAVE BELT

BACHMAN-TURNER OVERDRIVE

Singles: 7-inch
COMPLEAT 2-4   84-85
MERCURY 3-5   73-79
Picture Sleeves
MERCURY 3-5   74-75
LPs: 10/12-inch 33rpm
COMPLEAT 5-10   84-85
CURB 5-8   86
MERCURY 6-12   73-79
Members: Randy Bachman; C.F. Turner; Robin Bachman; Tim
Bachman; Jim Clench; Norman Durkee; Blair Thornton.
Also see BACHMAN, Randy

BACK STREET CRAWLER
(Crawler)

Singles: 7-inch
EPIC 2-4   77-78
LPs: 10/12-inch 33rpm
ATCO 10-12   75-76
EPIC (Except PAL-349001) 5-10   77-78
EPIC (PAL-349001 "Crawler") ... 25-30   78
(Picture disc.)
Members: Tony Braunagel; John Bundrick; Paul Kossoff; Mike
Montgomery; Geoff Whitehorn; Terry Wilson Slesser.
Also see FREE
Also see KOSSOFF, Paul

BACKTRACK

Singles: 7-inch
GOLDMINE 2-4   85
Member: John Hunt.

BACKUS, Jim
(Jim Backus and Friend; Jim Bakus; Mr. MaGoo with the Dennis Farnon Orchestra)

Singles: 7-inch
JUBILEE 6-12   58-59
EPs: 7-inch 33/45rpm
RCA (1362 "McGoo in Hi-Fi") ... 25-30   56
LPs: 10/12-inch 33rpm
DORE 8-10   74
RCA (1362 "McGoo in Hi-Fi") ... 30-50   56

BAD BOYS FEATURING K LOVE

Singles: 12-inch 33/45rpm
STARLITE 4-6   85

BAD COMPANY

Singles: 12-inch 33/45rpm
ATLANTIC 4-8   88
(Promotional only.)
Singles: 7-inch
ATLANTIC 2-4   86-89
SWAN SONG 2-5   74-84
Picture Sleeves
ATLANTIC 2-4   86-89

KAISER 5-10	59	
OKEH 5-10	57	
RED TOP 15-20	59	
TALLY HO 5-10	61	
VIM 5-10	57	

EPs: 10/12–inch 33rpm

EPIC (7190 "Dumplins") 50-75	57	

LPs: 10/12–inch 33rpm

KING 25-35	59	
Also see SELLERS, Johnny		
Also see TERRY, Sonny		

BAGBY, Doc / Luis Rivera
LPs: 10/12–inch 33rpm

KING 25-35	59	
Also see BAGBY, Doc		

BAILEY, Arthur
Singles: 12–inch 33/45rpm

ATLANTIC 4-6	84	

Singles: 7–inch

ATLANTIC 2-4	84	

BAILEY, J.R.
Singles: 7–inch

CALLA 4-6	68	
MAM 3-5	74	
MIDLAND INT'L 3-5	75	
RCA 3-5	76	
SPRING 2-4	84	
TOY 3-5	72-73	
U.A. 2-4	78	

LPs: 10/12–inch 33rpm

MAM 8-10	74	
U.A. 5-10	78	
Also see CADILLACS		

BAILEY, Pearl
Singles: 78rpm

COLUMBIA 4-8	46-50	
CORAL 3-6	52-55	
MERCURY 3-6	56	
ROULETTE 3-6	57	
SUNSET 3-6	56	
VERVE 3-6	56	

Singles: 7–inch

COLUMBIA (38000 series) 5-10	50	
COLUMBIA (43000 series) 3-6	66	
CORAL 5-10	52-55	
DECCA 3-6	64	
MERCURY 5-10	56	
PROJECT 3 3-5	68-70	
RCA (500 series) 3-5	71	
RCA (9400 series) 3-6	67	
ROULETTE 4-8	59-68	
SUNSET 5-10	56	
VERVE 5-10	56	

EPs: 7–inch 33/45rpm

COLUMBIA 10-20	52-56	
CORAL 10-20	54	
ROULETTE 10-15	57	

LPs: 10/12–inch 33rpm

ACCORD 5-10	83	
COLUMBIA (900 series) 20-35	57	
COLUMBIA (2600 series) 25-40	56	
(10–inch LPs.)		
COLUMBIA (6000 series) 25-40	50	
(10–inch LPs.)		
CORAL (56000 series) 25-40	54	
(10–inch LPs.)		
CORAL (57000 series) 20-30	57	
CO-STAR 15-20	58	
MERCURY (Except 100 series) 20-30	56-58	
MERCURY (100 series) 8-12	69	
PROJECT 3 5-10	70	
RCA (4500 series) 5-10	71	
ROULETTE (100 series) 8-12	71	
ROULETTE (25000 and 25100 series) 15-25	57-63	
ROULETTE (25200 and 25300 series) 10-15	64-65	
VOCALION 15-25	58	
WING 15-25	59-63	

BAILEY, Pearl, and Mike Douglas
Singles: 7–inch

PROJECT 3 3-6	68	
Also see BAILEY, Pearl		
Also see DOUGLAS, Mike		

BAILEY, Philip
Singles: 12–inch 33/45rpm

COLUMBIA 4-6	83-86	

Singles: 7–inch

COLUMBIA 2-4	83-86	
COLUMBIA 2-4	85	

LPs: 10/12–inch 33rpm

COLUMBIA 5-10	83-86	
Also see EARTH, WIND & FIRE		

BAILEY, Philip, and Phil Collins
Singles: 12–inch 33/45rpm

COLUMBIA 4-6	84	

Singles: 7–inch

COLUMBIA 2-4	84	

Picture Sleeves

COLUMBIA 2-4	84	
Also see BAILEY, Philip		
Also see COLLINS, Phil		

BAILEY, Razzy
(Razzle Bailey)
Singles: 7–inch

ABC-PAR 4-6	67	
B&K 8-12	59	
CAPRICORN 3-5	75	
ERASTUS 3-5	76	
MCA 2-4	84-86	
1-2-4 3-5	69	
PEACH 5-10	66	
RCA 2-4	77-84	
SOUNDS of AMERICA 2-4	86-88	

Picture Sleeves

RCA 2-4	80-81	

LPs: 10/12–inch 33rpm

MCA	5-10	85-86
PLANTATION	5-8	81
RCA	5-10	79-84

BAIO, Scott

Singles: 7–inch

RCA	2-4	82-83

LPs: 10/12–inch 33rpm

RCA	5-10	82-83

BAJA MARIMBA BAND

Singles: 7–inch

A&M	3-5	66-67
ALMO	3-6	63-66
BELL	3-5	73
SHOUT	2-4	81

Picture Sleeves

A&M	3-8	66-68

EPs: 7–inch 33/45rpm

A&M	4-8	68

LPs: 10/12–inch 33rpm

A&M	5-10	64-70
BELL	5-10	73

Member: Julius Wechter.
Also see DENNY, Martin
Also see MONTEZ, Chris

BAKER, Anita

Singles: 7–inch

BEVERLY GLEN	2-4	83-84
ELEKTRA	2-4	86-90

Picture Sleeves

ELEKTRA	2-4	86-88

LPs: 10/12–inch 33rpm

BEVERLY GLEN	5-10	83
ELEKTRA	5-10	86-90

Also see CHAPTER 8

BAKER, Bill

(Bill Baker and the Chestnuts; Bill Baker's Five Satins)

Singles: 7–inch

AUDICON	5-10	62
CORAL	5-10	60
ETC	5-10	63
ELGIN (007 "Won't You Tell Me, My Heart")	30-45	59
ELGIN (013 "Wonderful Girl")	75-100	59
MUSIC TONE	5-10	61-62
MUSICNOTE (119 "Teenage Triangle")	15-25	63
VIM (515 "Thank Heaven")	30-45	60

LPs: 10/12–inch 33rpm

DEL CAM (1000 "I'll Be Seeing You")	8-10	87

Also see FIVE SATINS

BAKER, George

(George Baker Selection)

Singles: 7–inch

COLOSSUS	4-6	70
WARNER	3-5	75-76

Picture Sleeves

COLOSSUS	5-8	70

LPs: 10/12–inch 33rpm

COLOSSUS	15-20	70
WARNER	10-15	76

BAKER, Ginger

(Ginger Baker's Air Force)

Singles: 7–inch

ATCO	3-5	70

LPs: 10/12–inch 33rpm

ATCO	12-15	70-72
AXIOM	8-12	90
SIRE	5-10	77
POLYDOR	8-10	72-79

Also see BAKER - GURVITZ ARMY
Also see BLIND FAITH
Also see CREAM
Also see WINWOOD, Steve

BAKER, Lavern

(Lavern Baker and the Gliders)

Singles: 78rpm

ATLANTIC	5-10	59-65
KING	5-10	55

Singles: 7–inch

ATLANTIC (1000 series, except 1004)	8-15	55-58
ATLANTIC (1004 "Soul on Fire")	15-25	53-54
ATLANTIC (2000 series)	5-10	59-65
BRUNSWICK	4-8	66
KING	10-20	55

EPs: 7–inch 33/45rpm

ATLANTIC (566 "Lavern Baker - Tweedle Dee")	50-75	56
ATLANTIC (588 "Lavern Baker - Jim Dandy")	50-75	57
ATLANTIC (617 "Lavern Baker - I Cried a Tear")	40-60	58

LPs: 10/12–inch 33rpm

ATCO	8-10	71
ATLANTIC (Except 8002, 8007 and 8030)	15-20	59-63
ATLANTIC (8002 "Lavern") (Black label.)	50-75	57
ATLANTIC (8002 "Lavern") (Red label.)	20-30	59
ATLANTIC (8007 "Lavern Baker")	40-60	57
ATLANTIC (8030 "Blues Ballads") (Black label.)	35-45	59
ATLANTIC (8030 "Blues Ballads") (White label.)	35-45	59
ATLANTIC (8030 "Blues Ballads") (Red label.)	20-30	59
BRUNSWICK	10-15	70

Also see KING CURTIS
Also see RHODES, Todd
Also see WILSON, Jackie, and Lavern Baker

BAKER, Lavern, and Ben E. King

Singles: 7–inch

ATLANTIC	5-10	60

Also see KING, Ben E.

BAKER, Lavern, and Jimmy Ricks
Singles: 7-inch
ATLANTIC 5-10   61
  Also see BAKER, Lavern
  Also see RICKS, Jimmy

BAKER, Tammy Faye
Singles: 7-inch
SUTRA 2-4   88
Picture Sleeves
SUTRA 2-4   88

BAKER, Teddy
Singles: 7-inch
CASABLANCA 2-4   81

BAKER - GURVITZ ARMY
Singles: 7-inch
ATCO 3-5   74-76
JANUS 3-5   75
LPs: 10/12-inch 33rpm
ATCO 8-10   75-76
JANUS 10-12   75
  Members: Ginger Baker; Adrian Gurvitz; Paul Gurvitz; Peter
  Lemer; John Norman; Snips.
  Also see BAKER, Ginger
  Also see GURVITZ, Adrian

BALAAM and the Angel
LPs: 10/12-inch 33rpm
VIRGIN 5-10   87

BALANCE
Singles: 7-inch
PORTRAIT 2-4   81-82
LPs: 10/12-inch 33rpm
PORTRAIT 5-10   81-82
  Also see BLUES MAGOOS

BALDRY, Long John
(Long John Baldry and the Hootchie Cootchie Men)
Singles: 7-inch
A&M 4-6   68
ASCOT 4-8   66-67
EMI AMERICA 2-4   79
WARNER 3-6   68-72
LPs: 10/12-inch 33rpm
ASCOT 15-25   65
CASABLANCA 5-10   75-76
EMI AMERICA 5-10   79-80
MUSICLINE 5-8   86
U.A. 8-10   71
WARNER 8-10   71-72

BALDRY, Long John, and Kathi McDonald
Singles: 7-inch
EMI AMERICA 2-4   79
Picture Sleeves
EMI AMERICA 2-4   79
  Also see BALDRY, Long John
  Also see McDONALD, Kathi

BALIN, Marty
Singles: 7-inch
CHALLENGE 20-25   62

EMI AMERICA 2-4   81-84
Picture Sleeves
EMI AMERICA 2-4   81
LPs: 10/12-inch 33rpm
EMI AMERICA 8-10   81-83
  Also see JEFFERSON AIRPLANE
  Also see JEFFERSON STARSHIP

BALL, Kenny
(Kenny Ball and His Jazzmen)
Singles: 7-inch
DECCA 3-5   67
GUYDEN 3-5   61
KAPP 3-5   62-64
Picture Sleeves
KAPP 4-8   62
LPs: 10/12-inch 33rpm
JAZZOLOGY 5-10   79
KAPP 10-25   62-64
  Members: Kenny Ball; Johnny Bennett; Dave Jones; Colin
  Bates; Vic Pitts; Ron Bowden; Diz Disley.

BALLADS
Singles: 7-inch
VENTURE 4-8   68

BALLARD, Hank
(Hank Ballard and the Midnight Lighters; Hank Ballard and the Dapps)
Singles: 7-inch
KING 4-6   68
PEOPLE 3-5   72
POLYDOR 3-5   72
SILVER FOX 3-5   70
STANG 3-5   75
LPs: 10/12-inch 33rpm
KING (1000 series) 10-15   69

BALLARD, Hank, and the Midnighters
Singles: 7-inch
GUSTO 2-4   78
KING (5100 through 5500
  series, except 5215) 8-12   59-62
KING (5215 "Sugaree") 8-12   59
  (Monaural.)

KING (S-5215 "Sugaree") 20-25   59
  (Stereo.)
LE JOINT 3-5   79

Picture Sleeves

KING 8-12   61

EPs: 7-inch 33/45rpm

FEDERAL (333 "Their Greatest Hits") 75-125   54
KING (333 "Their Greatest Hits") 25-35   58
KING (435 "Singin'
  and Swingin, Vol. 1") 25-35   59
KING (435 "Singin'
  and Swingin, Vol. 2") 25-35   59
KING (793 "Jumpin' Hank Ballard") .. 25-35   62
KING (7815 "1963 Sound of Hank
  Ballard and the Midnighters") 15-25   59

LPs: 10/12-inch 33rpm

FEDERAL (90 "Their Greatest
  Hits") 1500-2000   54
  (10-inch LP.)
FEDERAL (541 "Their Greatest
  Hits") 500-600   57
  (White cover.)
FEDERAL (541 "Their Greatest
  Hits") 400-500   57
  (Tan or red cover.)
KING (541 "Their Greatest Hits") ... 50-100   58
KING (581 "Midnighters, Vol. 2") ... 50-100   58
KING (600 through 800 series,
  except KS-740) 25-40   59-64
KING (KS-740 "Spotlight on
  Hank Ballard") 75-100   61
  (Stereo.)
KING (900 series) 15-20   65-68
KING (5000 series) 8-10   77
  Also see BALLARD, Hank
  Also see MIDNIGHTERS
  Also see ROYALS

BALLARD, Russ

Singles: 7-inch

EMI AMERICA 2-4   84-85
EPIC 2-5   74-80

LPs: 10/12-inch 33rpm

EMI AMERICA 5-8   84-85
EPIC 8-10   74-80
  Also see ARGENT
  Also see UNIT 4+2

BALLIN' JACK

Singles: 7-inch

COLUMBIA 3-5   71
MERCURY 3-5   73

LPs: 10/12-inch 33rpm

COLUMBIA 10-12   70-72
MERCURY 8-10   73-74

BALLOON FARM

Singles: 7-inch

LAURIE 4-8   68

BALTIMORE and Ohio Marching Band

Singles: 7-inch

JUBILEE 3-6   67

LPs: 10/12-inch 33rpm

JUBILEE 10-15   67

BALUM and the Angels

LPs: 10/12-inch 33rpm

VIRGIN 5-8   87

BAMA

Singles: 7-inch

FREE FLIGHT (Black vinyl) 3-5   79
FREE FLIGHT (Colored vinyl) 4-6   79
  (Promotional issues only.)

LPs: 10/12-inch 33rpm

FREE FLIGHT 5-10   79

BAMBAATAA, Afrika

**(Afrika Bambaataa and James Brown; Afrika
Bambaataa and the Soul Sonic Force; Afrika
Bambaataa and Family)**

Singles: 12-inch 33/45rpm

TOMMY BOY 4-6   83-86

Singles: 7-inch

TOMMY BOY 2-4   82-86

LPs: 10/12-inch 33rpm

TOMMY BOY 5-10   83-86
  Also see BROWN, James
  Also see SHANGO

BANANA SPLITS

Singles: 7-inch

DECCA 4-8   68-69

Picture Sleeves

DECCA 8-10   69-70

EPs: 7-inch 33/45rpm

KELLOGG 8-12   69

LPs: 10/12-inch 33rpm

DECCA 10-15   69

BANANARAMA

Singles: 12-inch 33/45rpm

LONDON 4-6   83-88

Singles: 7-inch

LONDON 2-4   82-88

Picture Sleeves

LONDON 2-4   82-88

LPs: 10/12-inch 33rpm

LONDON 5-10   83-88
  Members: Satch Dallin; Kevin Woodward; S. Fahey.
  Also see BAND AID

BAND

Singles: 7-inch

CAPITOL (Except 2000 series) 3-5   71-77
CAPITOL (2000 series) 4-8   67-70
WARNER 2-4   78

Picture Sleeves

CAPITOL 4-8   70

LPs: 10/12-inch 33rpm

CAPITOL (Except 2955) 10-15   69-85

CAPITOL (2955 "Music from
Big Pink") 15-20   68
MFSL (039 "Music from Big Pink") ... 25-50   80
WARNER (737 "The Last Waltz") 20-30   78
(Promotional issue only.)
WARNER (3146 "The Last Waltz") ... 15-20   78
(Three-LP set.)
Members: Levon Helm; Rick Danko; Garth Hudson; Richard
Manuel; Robbie Robertson; Jimmy Wieder.
Also see DANKO, Rick
Also see DYLAN, Bob
Also see HAWKINS, Ronnie
Also see HELM, Levon
Also see LEVON and the Hawks
Also see MILLER, Steve / Band / Quicksilver Messinger Service
Also see ROBERTSON, Robbie

BAND AID
Singles: 7-Inch
COLUMBIA (04749 "Do They Know It's
Christmas") 2-4   84
Picture Sleeves
COLUMBIA 3-5   84
Members: Bananarama; Paul McCartney; Boomtown Rats; Boy
George; Phil Collins; Duran Duran; Bob Geldof; Heaven 17; Kool
and the Gang; George Michael; John Moss; Spandau Ballet;
Status Quo; Sting; U2; Ultravox; Paul Weller; Paul Young.
Also see BANANARAMA
Also see BOOMTOWN RATS
Also see COLLINS, Phil
Also see CULTURE CLUB
Also see DURAN DURAN
Also see GELDORF, Bob
Also see HEAVEN 17
Also see KOOL and the Gang
Also see SPANDAU BALLET
Also see STATUS QUO
Also see STING
Also see STYLE COUNCIL
Also see U2
Also see ULTRAVOX
Also see WHAM
Also see YOUNG, Paul

BAND of GOLD
Singles: 7-Inch
RCA 2-4   85

BAND of the BLACK WATCH
Singles: 7-Inch
PRIVATE STOCK 3-5   75-76
LPs: 10/12-Inch 33rpm
PRIVATE STOCK 5-10   76

BANDANA
(BANDANNA)
Singles: 7-Inch
HAVEN 3-5   76
PARAMOUNT 3-5   73
WARNER 2-4   81-86
LPs: 10/12-Inch 33rpm
WARNER 5-10   86
Also see PLAYER

BANDIT
Singles: 7-Inch
ABC 3-5   75

ARISTA 3-5   77
LPs: 12/12-inch 33rpm
ABC 8-10   75
ARISTA 6-10   77
Members: Jim Diamond; Danny McIntosh; James Litherland;
Cliff Williams; Graham Broad.

BANDOLERO
Singles: 12-Inch 33/45rpm
SIRE 4-6   84
Singles: 7-Inch
SIRE 2-4   84
LPs: 10/12-Inch 33rpm
ECLIPSE 8-10   75

BANDWAGON
Singles: 7-Inch
EPIC 4-6   68

BANG
Singles: 7-Inch
CAPITOL 3-5   72-74
LPs: 10/12-Inch 33rpm
CAPITOL 8-12   72-73

BANGLES
Singles: 12-Inch 33/45rpm
COLUMBIA 4-6   85-88
Singles: 7-Inch
COLUMBIA 2-4   84-88
DEF JAM 2-4   87
DOWNKIDDIE (001 "Getting Out
of Hand") 5-10   81
Picture Sleeves
COLUMBIA 2-4   84-88
DEF JAM 2-4   87
DOWNKIDDIE (001 "Getting Out
of Hand") 10-20   81
(Back of sleeve shows Downkiddie Records as
being in Los Angeles, California.)
DOWNKIDDIE (001 "Getting Out
of Hand") 8-15   81
(Back of sleeve shows Downkiddie Records as
being in Torrance, California.)
LPs: 10/12-Inch 33rpm
COLUMBIA 5-10   84-90
I.R.S. 6-10   83
Members: Vicki Peterson; Debbi Peterson; Susanna Hoffs;
Annette Zilinskas; Michael Steele.
Also see BANGS

BANGOR FLYING CIRCUS
Singles: 7-Inch
DUNHILL 3-5   70
LPs: 10/12-Inch 33rpm
DUNHILL 12-15   69
Members: Michael Tegza; David Wolinski; Alan DeCarlo.

BANGS
Singles: 7-Inch
DOWNKIDDIE (001 "Getting Out
of Hand") 20-30   81

Picture Sleeves

DOWNKIDDIE (001 "Getting Out
of Hand") 30-50   81
Members: Vicki Peterson; Debbi Peterson; Susanna Hoffs.
Also see BANGLES

BANKS, Darrell
Singles: 7–inch

ATCO 4-6   67
COTILLION 4-6   68
REVILOT 5-10   66
SOULTOWN 4-8   66
LPs: 10/12–inch 33rpm
ATCO 15-20   67
VOLT 10-15   69

BANKS, Peter
Singles: 7–inch

CAPITOL 3-5   73
LPs: 10/12–inch 33rpm
CAPITOL 10-12   73
Also see AFTER the FIRE
Also see BLODWYN PIG
Also see FLASH
Also see YES

BANKS, Ron
Singles: 12–inch 33/45rpm
CBS ASSOCIATED 4-6   83
Singles: 7–inch
ABC 3-5   75
CBS ASSOCIATED 2-4   83
LPs: 10/12–inch 33rpm
CBS ASSOCIATED 5-10   83
Also see DRAMATICS

BANKS, Rose
Singles: 7–inch

MOTOWN 3-5   76
SOURCE 2-4   80
LPs: 10/12–inch 33rpm
MOTOWN 8-10   76
Also see SLY and the Family Stone

BANKS, Tony
Singles: 7–inch

ATLANTIC 2-4   83
CHARISMA 2-4   79
LPs: 10/12–inch 33rpm
ATLANTIC 5-10   83
CHARISMA 5-10   79
Also see GENESIS

BANKS & HAMPTON
Singles: 7–inch

WARNER 3-5   76-77
LPs: 10/12–inch 33rpm
WARNER 5-10   77
Members: Homer Banks; Carl Hampton.

BANZAII
Singles: 7–inch

SCEPTER 3-5   75

BARBARA and the Browns
Singles: 7–inch

CADET 4-8   66
SOUND of MEMPHIS 3-5   72
STAX 5-10   64
Member: Barbara Brown.

BARBARA and the Uniques
Singles: 7–inch

ABBOTT 3-5   72
ARDEN 3-5   70
NEW CHICAGO SOUND 3-5   70
20TH FOX 3-5   74
Members: Barbara Livsey; Gwen Livsey; Doris Lindsey.

BARBARA LYNN: see LYNN, Barbara

BARBARIANS
Singles: 7–inch

JOY 20-30   64
LAURIE 10-20 65-66
LPs: 10/12–inch 33rpm
LAURIE (2033 "The Barbarians") ... 50-60 66
RHINO 5-10   79
Also see ELEGANTS

BARBER, Chris
(Chris Barber's Jazz Band)
Singles: 7–inch

ATLANTIC 4-8   59
LAURIE 4-8   58-63
LONDON 4-6   62
Picture Sleeves
LAURIE 5-10   59
LPs: 10/12–inch 33rpm
ARCHIVE of FOLK MUSIC 8-12   68
ATLANTIC 15-25   59
COLPIX 15-25   59
LAURIE 15-25 59-62
Also see DR. JOHN and Chris Barber's Jazz and Blues Band

BARBER, Frank
Singles: 7–inch

VICTORY 2-4   82
LPs: 10/12–inch 33rpm
VICTORY 5-10   82

BARBIERI, Gato
Singles: 7–inch

A&M 3-5   76-79
U.A. 3-5   73
LPs: 10/12–inch 33rpm
A&M 5-10   76-79
ARISTA 8-10   75
FLYING DUTCHMAN 5-10   70-80
IMPULSE 8-10   73-75
U.A. 5-10   73

BARBOUR, Dave
Singles: 78rpm

CAPITOL 5-10   50-51
Singles: 7–inch
ARWIN 4-8   59

CAPITOL 5-10   50-51
EPs: 7–inch 33/45rpm
CAPITOL 5-15   54
DECCA 5-15   53
LPs: 10/12–inch 33rpm
DECCA 15-25   53

BARBOUR, Keith
Singles: 7–inch
BARNABY 3-5   71
EPIC 3-6   69-70
LPs: 10/12–inch 33rpm
EPIC 15-20   69

BARBUSTERS
Singles: 7–inch
CBS ASSOCIATED 2-4   87
Also see JETT, Joan, and the Blackhearts

BARCLAY, Eddie
Singles: 78rpm
RAMA 5-10   55
TICO 5-10   55
Singles: 7–inch
RAMA 5-10   55
TICO 5-10   55

BARCLAY JAMES HARVEST
Singles: 7–inch
HARVEST 3-5   73
MCA 3-5   76-77
POLYDOR 3-5   75-79
LPs: 10/12–inch 33rpm
HARVEST 8-12   73
MCA 8-10   77
POLYDOR 8-10   74-80
SIRE 10-15   70-71
Members: Les Holroyd; John Lees; John Pritchard; Stewart "Wolly" Wolstenholme.

BARDENS, Peter
LPs: 10/12–inch 33rpm
CAPITOL 5-10   87
VERVE/FORECAST 10-12   71
Also see CAMEL

BARDEUX
Singles: 7–inch
ENIGMA 2-4   89
SYNTHICIDE 2-4   88
Picture Sleeves
SYNTHICIDE 2-4   88
LPs: 10/12–inch 33rpm
ENIGMA 5-8   89
SYNTHICIDE 5-8   88

BARE, Bobby
(Bobby Bare and the All American Boys; Bobby Bare and the Hillsiders; Bobby Bare and Bobby Bare Jr; Bobby Bare and the Family; Bobby and Jeannie Bare)
Singles: 78rpm
CAPITOL 5-10   57
Singles: 7–inch
CAPITOL 10-15   57

COLUMBIA 2-5   78-85
EMI AMERICA 2-4   85-86
FRATERNITY (835 through 878) 10-15   58-61
FRATERNITY (885 through 892) 5-10   61
MERCURY 3-5   70-72
RCA (Except 8000 and 9000 series) ... 3-5   69-77
RCA (8000 and 9000 series) 4-8   62-68
RICE 3-5   73-74
Picture Sleeves
RCA 5-10   62-65
LPs: 10/12–inch 33rpm
CAMDEN 8-12   68-73
COLUMBIA 5-10   78-85
MERCURY 10-15   70-72
PICKWICK 5-10   75-80
PICKWICK/HILLTOP 10-15   65
RCA (ANL1 and APL1 series) 8-12   73-77
RCA (AYL1 series) 5-10   81
RCA (2776 through 3994) 15-20   63-69
(With "LPM" or "LSP" prefix.)
RCA (4000 series) 10-15   69-71
(With "LSP" prefix.)
RCA (6000 series) 10-15   73
SUN (136 "Greatest Hits") 15-25   74
U.A. 8-12   75-76
Also see ORBISON, Roy / Bobby Bare / Joey Powers
Also see PARSONS, Bill

BARE, Bobby, Liz Anderson and Norma Jean
Singles: 7–inch
RCA 4-6   67
LPs: 10/12–inch 33rpm
BARE TRACKS 8-12
RCA 12-20   67

BARE, Bobby, and Rosanne Cash
Singles: 7–inch
COLUMBIA 2-4   79
Also see CASH, Rosanne

BARE, Bobby, and Skeeter Davis
Singles: 7–inch
RCA (8000 and 9000 series) 3-6   65-70
LPs: 10/12–inch 33rpm
RCA 10-15   65-70
Also see DAVIS, Skeeter

BARE, Bobby, / Donna Fargo / Jerry Wallace
LPs: 10/12–inch 33rpm
OUT of TOWN DIST 5-10   82
Also see BARE, Bobby
Also see FARGO, Donna
Also see WALLACE, Jerry

BAR-KAYS
Singles: 12–inch 33/45rpm
MERCURY 4-6   79-85
Singles: 7–inch
MERCURY 2-5   76-84
STAX 2-4   78-81
VOLT 3-6   67-74
LPs: 10/12–inch 33rpm
MERCURY 5-10   76-87

STAX 5-10   78-81
VOLT 10-15   67-74
  Members: Jimmy King; Phalon Jones; Carl Cunningham; Ron
  Caldwell; Larry Dodson; James Alexander; Charles Allen;
  Vernon Burch; Ben Cauley; Donnelle Hagan; Harvey Henderson;
  Winston Stewart.
  Also see REDDING, Otis

BARKLEY, Tyrone
Singles: 7–inch

MIDSONG INT'L 2-4   79

BARNES, Cheryl
Singles: 7–inch

MILLENNIUM 2-4   77
POLYDOR 2-4   80
RCA 2-4   79

BARNES, J.J.
Singles: 7–inch

BUDDAH 3-6   69
GROOVESVILLE 4-6   67
INVASION 3-5   70
KABLE 5-10   60
MAGIC TOUCH 3-5   70
MICKAYS 4-8   62-63
PERCEPTION 3-5   74
REVILOT 4-6   68
RICH 4-8
RIC-TIC 4-8   65-66
RING 4-8   64
VOLT 4-6   69

LPs: 10/12–inch 33rpm
PERCEPTION 8-12   74

BARNES, J.J., and Steve Mancha
LPs: 10/12–inch 33rpm

VOLT (6001 "Rare Stamps") 10-15 69
  Also see BARNES, J.J.
  Also see HOLIDAYS
  Also see MANCHA, Steve

BARNES, Jimmy
(Jimmy Barnes and the Gibralters)
Singles: 7–inch

GIBRALTAR 8-12   59
SAVOY 5-10   59-60
  Also see BROWN, Nappy

BARNES, Jimmy
Singles: 7–inch

GEFFEN 2-4   86-88

Picture Sleeves

GEFFEN 2-4   88

LPs: 10/12–inch 33rpm

GEFFEN 5-10   86
  Also see COLD CHISEL

BARNUM, H.B.
Singles: 7–inch

CAPITOL 4-6   65-68
DECCA 3-5   71
ELDO 5-10   60-61
IMPERIAL 5-10   64
MUN RAB 5-10   59

RCA 5-10   61-63
ULTRA SONIC 5-10   60
U.A. 3-5   73

Picture Sleeves

RCA 5-10   62

LPs: 10/12–inch 33rpm

CAPITOL 12-20 65
RCA 15-20 62
TROPIC ISLE 15-25 59
  Also see ROBINS

BARRABAS
Singles: 7–inch

ATCO 3-5   75-76

LPs: 10/12–inch 33rpm

ATCO 5-10   75-76
RCA 8-10   72-73
  Members: Jo Tejada; Ricky Morales; Miquel Morales; Juan
  Videl; Daniel Louis; Ernest Duarte.

BARRACUDA
Singles: 7–inch

RCA (9660 "Dance at St. Francis") .. 10-20 68
Picture Sleeves
RCA (9660 "Dance at St. Francis") .. 20-35 68

BARRACUDA
Singles: 7–inch

20TH FOX 3-5   73

BARRACUDA
Singles: 12–inch 33/45rpm

EPIC 4-6   83

Singles: 7–inch

EPIC 2-4   83

BARRETT, Richard
(Richie Barrett; Richard Barrett and the Chantels;
Richard Barrett and the Sevilles)
Singles: 7–inch

ATLANTIC 5-10   62
GONE 15-25 59
MGM 15-25 58
METRO 10-15 58
SEVILLE 10-15 60
20TH FOX 8-12   59
  Also see CHANTELS

BARRETT, Syd
Singles: 12–inch 33/45rpm

CAPITOL 8-12   88
(Promotional only. With special cover.)
LPs: 10/12–inch 33rpm

CAPITOL 5-10   74-88
HARVEST (Except 11314) 10-20 70-74
HARVEST (11314 "Madcap Laughs") 20-30   70
  Members: Syd Barrett; Dave Gilmour; Roger Waters; Vic
  Seywell; Mike Ratledge.
  Also see PINK FLOYD

BARRETTO, Ray
Singles: 7–inch

ASCOT 3-6   66
ATLANTIC 2-4   77-78

FANIA	3-5	68-72
RIVERSIDE	4-8	61
ROULETTE	2-4	
TICO	4-8	63
U.A.	3-5	65-67

LPs: 10/12–inch 33rpm

ATLANTIC	5-10	76-78
CTI	5-10	81
FANIA	5-10	68-73
FANTASY	8-10	73
RIVERSIDE	10-15	61-66
TICO	10-15	62-63
U.A.	8-15	65-67

Also see LYTLE, Johnny, and Ray Barretto

BARRON KNIGHTS
Singles: 7–inch

DECCA	5-10	67
EPIC (Except 9835)	2-4	79
EPIC (9835 "Pop Go the Workers")	5-10	65
MERCURY	3-5	72

Members: Barron Anthony; Peanut Langford; Butch Baker; Dave Ballinger; Duko D'mond.

BARROW, Keith
Singles: 12–inch 33/45rpm

| COLUMBIA | 4-6 | 79 |

Singles: 7–inch

CAPITOL	2-4	80
COLUMBIA	2-4	76-79
JEWEL	3-5	73

LPs: 10/12–inch 33rpm

CAPITOL	5-10	80
UMBIA	5-10	77
JEWEL	8-10	73

BARRY, Claudja
Singles: 12–inch 33/45rpm

CHRYSALIS	4-6	79
EPIC	4-6	86-87
PERSONAL	4-6	83
TSR	4-6	85

Singles: 7–inch

CHRYSALIS	2-4	79-84
EPIC	2-4	86-87
MIRAGE	2-4	82
PERSONAL	2-4	83
SALSOUL	2-4	77-78

LPs: 10/12–inch 33rpm

CHRYSALIS	5-10	79-84
HANDSHAKE	5-10	82
SALSOUL	5-10	77-78

BARRY, Claudja, and Ronnie Jones
LPs: 10/12–inch 33rpm

| HANDSHAKE | 5-10 | 82 |

Also see BARRY, Claudja

BARRY, Jan: see BERRY, Jan

BARRY, Joe
Singles: 7–inch

ABC/DOT	2-4	77
JIN	10-15	60-62
NUGGET	4-8	
SMASH	4-8	61-62

Picture Sleeves

| SMASH | 10-15 | 61 |

LPs: 10/12–inch 33rpm

| ABC/DOT | 5-10 | 77 |

BARRY, John, Orchestra
Singles: 12–inch 33/45rpm

| CASABLANCA (20146 "The Chase") | 10-12 | 78 |

Singles: 7–inch

A&M	2-4	83
CAPITOL (4200 series)	4-6	59
CAPITOL (5400 series)	2-4	86
COLUMBIA	3-5	65-70
EPIC	2-4	72
KING	3-6	61
MCA	2-4	85
MGM	3-5	66
MERCURY	3-6	64
20TH FOX	3-5	64
U.A.	3-6	63-65
WARNER	3-5	68

Picture Sleeves

| U.A. | 5-10 | 65 |

LPs: 10/12–inch 33rpm

CAPITOL (2500 series)	10-15	66
COLUMBIA (1003 "Ready When You Are Mr. J.B.")	8-12	70
COLUMBIA (2493 "Great Movie Themes")	10-15	66
COLUMBIA (2708 "You Only Live Twice") (Stereo.)	8-12	67
COLUMBIA (9293 "Great Movie Themes")	10-15	66
COLUMBIA (9508 "You Only Live Twice") (Monaural.)	8-12	67
U.A. (91 "James Bond Tenth Anniversary")	8-12	72
U.A. (3424 "Goldfinger and Other Favorites")	8-12	65
U.A. (6424 "Goldfinger and Other Favorites")	10-12	65

Since publication of *The Official Price Guide to Movie/TV Soundtracks and Original Cast Albums*, with over 8,000 listings, this guide has dropped many soundtracks, including some by this artist.

Also see ARMSTRONG, Louis
Also see BASIE, Count
Also see BASSEY, Shirley
Also see JONES, Tom
Also see MONRO, Matt
Also see SINATRA, Nancy

BARRY, Len

Singles: 7–inch

AMY	4-6	68-69
BUDDAH	3-5	72
CAMEO	4-8	64
DECCA	4-8	65-66
MCA	2-4	83
MERCURY	4-8	64
PARAMOUNT	3-5	73
PARKWAY	4-8	65
RCA	4-6	67-68
SCEPTER	3-6	69-70

EPs: 7–inch 33/45rpm

DECCA (74720 "1-2-3")	8-15	65
(Jukebox issue only.)		

LPs: 10/12–inch 33rpm

BUDDAH	10-15	72
CAMEO	20-25	64
DECCA	20-25	65
RCA	15-20	67

Also see DOVELLS

BARRY and the Tamerlanes

Singles: 7–inch

VALIANT	5-10	63-65

LPs: 10/12–inch 33rpm

VALIANT (406 "I Wonder What She's Doing Tonight")	50-75	63

Members: Barry DeVorzon; Terry Smith; Bodie Chandler.
Also see DE VORZON, Barry

BARTLEY, Chris

Singles: 7–inch

BUDDAH	3-5	71
MUSICOR	3-5	72
VANDO	4-8	67-68

LPs: 10/12–inch 33rpm

VANDO	15-20	67

BARTON, Eileen

Singles: 78rpm

CORAL	4-8	51-56
MERCURY	4-8	53
NATIONAL	5-10	50

Singles: 7–inch

CORAL	5-10	51-56
CREST	4-8	62
MGM	5-8	59
MERCURY	5-10	53
20TH FOX	3-6	63
U.A.	4-8	59

EPs: 7–inch 33/45rpm

CORAL	5-10	54

LPs: 10/12–inch 33rpm

CORAL	15-25	54

BARTON, Lou Ann

Singles: 7–inch

ASYLUM	2-4	82

LPs: 10/12–inch 33rpm

ANTONE'S	5-10	89

ASYLUM	8-12	82

BARTZ, Gary
(Gary Bartz Nu Troop)

Singles: 7–inch

ARISTA	2-4	80
CAPITOL	2-4	77-78

LPs: 10/12–inch 33rpm

ARISTA	5-10	80
CAPITOL	5-10	77-78
CATALYST	5-10	76
MILESTONE	10-15	68-69
PRESTIGE	6-10	73-75
VEE JAY	5-10	78

BASIA

Singles: 7–inch

EPIC	2-4	88-90

LPs: 10/12–inch 33rpm

EPIC	5-8	88-90

BASIE, Count

Singles: 78rpm

COLUMBIA	5-10	43-51
CLEF	4-8	52-56
DECCA (Except 1300 through 3000 series)	5-10	41-53
DECCA (1300 through 3000 series)	8-15	37-40
MERCURY	4-8	52-53
OKEH	4-8	52

Singles: 7–inch

ABC-PAR	3-5	66
BRUNSWICK	3-5	67
CLEF	5-10	52-56
COLUMBIA (33000 series)	2-4	76
COLUMBIA (38000 and 39000 series)	5-10	50-51
COMMAND	3-5	67
DECCA	5-10	53
HAPPY TIGER	2-5	70
MERCURY	5-10	52-53
OKEH	5-10	52
REPRISE	3-6	63
ROULETTE (Except "SSR" series)	4-8	58-63
ROULETTE ("SSR" series)	8-15	59
(Stereo.)		
U.A.	3-5	66
VERVE	3-5	60-67

EPs: 7–inch 33/45rpm

BRUNSWICK	10-15	54
CAMDEN	8-15	58
CLEF	10-20	52-55
COLUMBIA	10-20	50
CORAL	10-20	
DECCA	10-20	53
EPIC	10-20	55
RCA (Except 5000 series)	10-20	54
RCA (5000 series)	8-12	59
ROULETTE	8-12	58-60
VERVE	10-15	56

LPs: 10/12–inch 33rpm

ABC	5-10	76
ABC-PAR	10-15	66
ACCORD	5-10	82-83
AMERICAN	15-25	57
BRIGHT ORANGE	5-10	73
BRUNSWICK (54000 series)	10-20	63-67
BRUNSWICK (58000 series)	25-35	54
(10–inch LPs.)		
CAMDEN	10-20	58-60
CIRCLE	40-50	54
CLEF (120 "Count Basie and His Orchestra")	100-200	52
(10–inch LP.)		
CLEF (148 "The Count Basie Big Band")	100-200	52
(10–inch LP.)		
CLEF (164 "The Count Basie Sextet")	100-200	52
(10–inch LP.)		
CLEF (626 "Dance Session")	50-100	53
CLEF (647 "Dance Session, Volume 2")	50-100	53
CLEF (633 "Basieana")	50-100	53
CLEF (666 "Basie")	50-100	54
CLEF (678 "Basie Swings - Joe Williams Sings")	50-100	55
CLEF (685 "Count Basie")	50-80	56
CLEF (700 series)	20-30	56
COLISEUM	8-12	67
COLUMBIA (700 and 900 series)	20-30	56-57
COLUMBIA (6079 "Dance Parade")	25-35	49
(10–inch LPs)		
COLUMBIA (31000 series)	10-12	72
COMMAND	10-15	66-71
DAYBREAK	6-10	71
DECCA (100 series)	15-25	64
DECCA (5000 series)	25-35	50-53
(10–inch LPs.)		
DECCA (8000 series)	10-15	65
DOCTOR JAZZ	5-10	85-86
DOT	8-12	68
EMARCY (26000 series)	30-45	54
(10–inch LPs.)		
EMUS	8-15	
EPIC (1000 and 1100 series)	25-35	54
(10–inch LPs.)		
EPIC	25-35	55
FLYING DUTCHMAN	6-10	71
HAPPY TIGER	8-12	70
HARMONY (7000 series)	10-20	60
HARMONY (11000 series)	5-10	67-69
IMPULSE	10-20	62
JAZZ PANORAMA	50-75	52
MCA	8-12	77-82
MGM	6-10	70
MFSL (129 "Basie Plays Hefti")	15-25	85
MPS	10-12	72

MERCURY (25000 series)	25-35	50-51
(10–inch LPs.)		
METRO	6-10	65-66
OLYMPIC	5-10	74
PABLO	5-10	74-83
PAUSA	5-10	83
PRESTIGE	5-10	82
RCA (500 series)	10-15	65
RCA (1100 series)	25-35	54
REPRISE	10-15	63-65
ROULETTE (100 series)	12-18	71
ROULETTE (52003 through 52106)	15-20	58-64
ROULETTE (52111/12/13 "The World of Count Basie")	30-40	64
(3-LP set.)		
SCEPTER	5-10	74
SOLID STATE	8-12	68
TRIP	5-10	75
U.A.	10-15	66
VSP	10-15	66
VANGUARD	15-25	57
VERVE	5-10	73-84

(Reads "Manufactured By MGM Record Corp.," or mentions either Polydor or Polygram at bottom of label.)

VERVE (2000 series)	20-30	56

(Reads "Verve Records, Inc." at bottom of label.)

VERVE (2500 series)	8-12	77-82
VERVE (2600 series)	5-10	82
VERVE (6000 series)	20-30	56

(Reads "Verve Records, Inc." at bottom of label.)

VERVE (8000 and 8100 series)	15-25	56-57

(Reads "Verve Records, Inc." at bottom of label.)

VERVE (8200 through 8400)	15-20	58-61

(Reads "Verve Records, Inc." at bottom of label.)

VERVE (8500 through 8600 series)	10-15	62-67

(Reads "MGM Records - a Division of Metro-Goldwyn-Mayer, Inc." at bottom of label.)

VERVE (8700 series)	6-10	69

(Reads "MGM Records - a Division of Metro-Goldwyn-Mayer, Inc." at bottom of label.)

VERVE (68000 series)	10-20	63-65

(Reads "MGM Records - a Division of Metro-Goldwyn-Mayer, Inc." at bottom of label.)

Also see BARRY, John
Also see BENNETT, Tony, and Count Basie
Also see BREWER, Teresa, and Count Basie
Also see CROSBY, Bing, and Count Basie
Also see DAVIS, Sammy, Jr., and Count Basie
Also see FITZGERALD, Ella, and Count Basie
Also see JACQUET, Illinois, and Count Basie
Also see MILLS BROTHERS, and Count Basie
Also see PRYSOCK, Arthur, and Count Basie
Also see SINATRA, Frank, and Count Basie
Also see STARR, Kay, and Count Basie
Also see WILSON, Jackie, and Count Basie

BASIE, Count, and Tony Bennett
EPs: 7–inch 33/45rpm

ROULETTE	6-10	59

LPs: 10/12–inch 33rpm

ROULETTE	10-20	59-63

Also see BENNETT, Tony

BASIE, Count, and Billy Eckstine
Singles: 7–inch
ROULETTE (Except "SSR" series) 4-8   59
ROULETTE ("SSR" series) 8-15   59
LPs: 10/12–inch 33rpm
ROULETTE 15-20   59
Also see ECKSTINE, Billy

BASIE, Count, and Duke Ellington
Singles: 7–inch
COLUMBIA 2-4   62
LPs: 10/12–inch 33rpm
ACCORD 5-10   82
COLUMBIA 15-20   62
Also see ELINGTON, Duke

BASIE, Count, and Maynard Ferguson
LPs: 10/12–inch 33rpm
ROULETTE 10-20   65
Also see FERGUSON, Maynard

BASIE, Count, and Benny Goodman
LPs: 10/12–inch 33rpm
ABC 8-12   73
VANGUARD 15-25   59
Also see GOODMAN, Benny

BASIE, Count, and Oscar Peterson
LPs: 10/12–inch 33rpm
PABLO 5-10   75-83
VERVE 15-20   59
Also see PETERSON, Oscar

BASIE, Count, and Sarah Vaughan
LPs: 10/12–inch 33rpm
ROULETTE 15-20   61

BASIE, Count, Sarah Vaughan and Joe Williams
Singles: 7–inch
ROULETTE 2-4   60
LPs: 10/12–inch 33rpm
ROULETTE 15-20   60
Joe Williams is also a featured vocalist on many of the recordings included in the section of listings for Count Basie.
Also see BASIE, Count
Also see VAUGHAN, Sarah

BASIL, Toni
Singles: 12–inch 33/45rpm
CHRYSALIS 4-6   82-85
Singles: 7–inch
A&M 5-10   66
CHRYSALIS 2-4   82-85
Picture Sleeves
CHRYSALIS 2-4   82-84
LPs: 10/12–inch 33rpm
CHRYSALIS 5-10   82-84

BASKERVILLE HOUNDS
Singles: 7–inch
AVCO EMBASSY 4-6   69

BUDDAH 10-20   67
DOT 10-20   67
TEMA ("Hold Me") 25-35   67
(No Number used.)
LPs: 10/12–inch 33rpm
DOT 15-20   67
Also see TALULA BABIES

BASS, Fontella
Singles: 7–inch
ABC 2-4   74
BOBBIN 5-10   61
CHECKER 5-10   65-66
CHESS 2-5   75-85
ERIC 3-5   73
GUSTO 2-4
MCA 2-4   83
PAULA 3-5   74
LPs: 10/12–inch 33rpm
CHECKER 15-20   66
PAULA 5-10   71

BASS, Fontella, and Bobby McClure
Singles: 7–inch
CHECKER 3-5   65-66
Also see McCLURE, Bobby

BASS, Fontella, and Tina Turner
Singles: 7–inch
SONJA (2006 "Poor Little Fool") 5-10   62
(Shown only as by Fontella Bass.)
VESUVIUS (1002 "Poor Little
Fool") 10-15
Also see BASS, Fontella
Also see TURNER, Tina

BASSEY, Shirley
Singles: 12–inch 33/45rpm
U.A. 4-6   79
Singles: 7–inch
EPIC 4-8   59
MGM 3-6   60
U.A. 2-5   61-79
LPs: 10/12–inch 33rpm
EPIC 10-20   62
LIBERTY 4-6   81-82
MGM 12-20   60
PHILIPS 10-15   65
SPRINGBORAD 5-10   75
U.A. 4-6   80
(With "LM" prefix.)
U.A. 10-15   62-72
(With "UAL" or "UAS" prefix.)
U.A. 5-10   73-79
(With "UA-LA" prefix.)
Also see BARRY, John

BATAAN, Joe
(Joe Bataan and the Mestizo Band)
Singles: 7–inch
SALSOUL 2-4   80
UPTITE 3-5   69

LPs: 10/12–inch 33rpm

SALSOUL 5-10   80-81

BATDORF, John
LPs: 10/12–inch 33rpm

20TH FOX 5-10   81
Also see SILVER

BATDORF & RODNEY
Singles: 7–inch

ARISTA 3-5   75
ASYLUM 3-5   72
ATLANTIC 3-5   71-72
LPs: 10/12–inch 33rpm

ATLANTIC 8-12   71
ARISTA 6-10   75
ASYLUM 8-10   72
Members: John Batdorf: Mark Rodney.
Also see BATDORF, John

BAUMANN, Peter
Singles: 12–inch 33/45rpm

PORTRAIT 4-6   82-83
Singles: 7–inch

PORTRAIT 2-4   83
LPs: 10/12–inch 33rpm

PORTRAIT 5-10   82-83
VIRGIN 8-10   77
Also see TANGERINE DREAM

BAXTER, Duke
Singles: 7–inch

MERCURY 3-5   70
VMC 5-10   69
LPs: 10/12–inch 33rpm

VMC 15-20   69

BAXTER, Les
(Les Baxter and His Orchestra and Chorus; Les
Baxter Balladeers)
Singles: 78rpm

CAPITOL 3-6   50-57
Singles: 7–inch

A/S 2-4   70
CAPITOL 4-8   50-61
GNP/CRESCENDO 3-5   64-69
LINK 3-5   64
REPRISE 3-5   62-63
Picture Sleeves

REPRISE (20120; "Theme From *The
Manchurian Candidate*" 40-60   62
(A Frank Sinatra collectible, as his name is shown
on this cover.)
EPs: 7–inch 33/45rpm

CAPITOL 5-10   51-56
GNP/CRESCENDO 5-10   67-69
RCA 5-10   52
REPRISE 4-8   64
LPs: 10/12–inch 33rpm

ALSHIRE 5-10   70-85

AMERICAN INTERNATIONAL (1028 "Dunwich
Horror") 20-25   70
(Soundtrack.)
CAPITOL (200 through 900 series) .. 10-20   51-58
CAPITOL (1000 through 1800 series) . 5-15   58-63
CAPITOL (11000 series) 4-6   77-79
GNP/CRESCENDO 5-10   69
RCA 15-25   52
REPRISE 10-15   62-63
VARESE SARABANDE (81103 "Dunwich
Horror") 8-10   79
Also see CROSBY, Bing, and Bob Hope

BAY CITY ROLLERS
Singles: 7–inch

ARISTA 2-4   75-78
BELL 3-5   72-76
FLASHBACK 2-4   80
Picture Sleeves

ARISTA 2-4   75-78
LPs: 10/12–inch 33rpm

ARISTA 5-10   75-79
Members: Les McKeowen; Eric Faulkner; Stuart Wood; Alan
Longmuir; Derek Longmuir; Billy Lyall; Pat McGlynn; Ian Mitchell.
Also see ROLLERS

BAYER, Carole: see SAGER, Carole Bayer

BAZUKA
(Tony Camillo's Bazuka)
Singles: 7–inch

A&M 2-5   75
VENTURE 2-4   79
LPs: 10/12–inch 33rpm

A&M 5-10   75

BEACH BOYS
Singles: 12–inch 33/45rpm

CAPITOL (9711 "Rock and Roll
to the Rescue") 10-15   86
(Promotional issue only.)
CAPITOL (9796 "California Dreamin") 10-15   86
(Promotional issue only.)
CAPITOL (15234 "Rock and Roll
to the Rescue") 5-10   86
CARIBOU (2080 "Getcha Back") 10-15   86
(Promotional issue only.)
CARIBOU (9028 "Here Comes
the Night") 5-10   79
CARIBOU (9028 "Here Comes
the Night") 20-25   79
(Promotional issue only.)
Singles: 7–inch

BROTHER 5-10   67
CANDIX (301 "Surfin") 150-250   61
(Label reads "Distributed by Era Record Sales
Inc.")
CANDIX (301 "Surfin") 200-250   61
(Label does NOT say "Distributed by Era Record
Sales Inc.")
CANDIX (331 "Surfin") 125-175   62
CAPITOL (2000 series except 2765) .. 5-10   67-69

CAPITOL (2765 "Cottonfields") 15-20   70
CAPITOL (3000 series) 3-5   74
CAPITOL (4000 series except 4880) .. 8-12   62-63
CAPITOL (4880 "Ten Little Indians") . 15-20   62
CAPITOL (5000 series, except
   5096 and 5312) 5-10   63-66
   (Orange/yellow labels.)
CAPITOL (5096 "Little Saint Nick") .. 12-18   63
CAPITOL (5312 "The Man with
   All the Toys") 12-18   63
CAPITOL (5000 series) 2-4   81-86
   (Black labels.)
CAPITOL (6000 series) 5-10   67-68
CAPITOL (44000 series) 2-4   89
CARIBOU 3-5   79-86
ELEKTRA 2-4   88
ODE '70 12-15   71
REPRISE (0101 through 0107") 4-6   73
   ("Back to Back" reissue series.)
REPRISE (0894 "Add Some Music
   to Your Day") 5-10   70
REPRISE (0929 "Slip on Through") ... 5-10   70
REPRISE (0957 "Tears in
   the Morning") 12-15   70
REPRISE (0998 "Cool, Cool Water") . 60-75   71
REPRISE (1015 "Long Promised
   Road") 20-25   71
REPRISE (1047 "Long Promised
   Road") 20-25   71
REPRISE (1058 "Surf's Up") 45-50   71
REPRISE (1091 "Cuddle Up") 25-30   72
REPRISE (1101 "Marcella") 25-30   72
REPRISE (1138 "Sail on Sailor") 8-12   73
REPRISE (1156 "California Saga") .. 10-15   73
REPRISE (1310 "I Can Hear Music") ... 3-5   74
REPRISE (1321 "Child of Winter") ... 20-30   74
REPRISE (1325 "Sail on Sailor") ... 5-10   75
REPRISE (1336 "Wouldn't It Be Nice") 5-10   75
REPRISE (1354 through 1394) 3-5   76-78
X (301 "Surfin") 200-300   61

Promotional Singles

CAPITOL (2360 "Bluebirds over
   the Mountain") 15-20   69
CAPITOL (2936/7 "Salt Lake City") 175-200   65
CAPITOL CUSTOM ("Spirit of
   America") 125-150   63
CARIBOU (557 "Here Comes the
   Night") 10-12   79
   (Blue vinyl.)
CARIBOU (557 "Here Comes the
   Night") 50-60   79
   (Special Edition autographed copies. Blue vinyl.)
CARIBOU (9026 "Here Comes the
   Night") 10-15   79
EVA-TONE (0300 "Living Doll") 2-4   87
   (Barbie Doll promotional issue.)
ODE '70 (66016 "Wouldn't It Be
   Nice-Live Version") 35-40   71
REPRISE (557-2 "Sail on Sailor") .. 75-100   73

REPRISE (0998 "Cool, Cool Water") . 45-50   71
REPRISE (1310 "I Can Hear Music") 30-50   74
WHAT'S IT ALL ABOUT (449/450 and
   507/508) 20-22
   (Public service radio station issues. Program disc
   449/450 has the Beach Boys on one side and Dr.
   Hook on the flip. 507/508 features the Beach Boys
   on one side and the Rolling Stones on the other.)
   Note: Promo singles not listed separately are
   presumed to fall into the same price range as
   commercial issues.

Picture Sleeves

BROTHER (1001 "Heroes and
   Villains") 50-100   67
CAPITOL (2068 "Darlin") 10-20   67
CAPITOL (4777 "Surfin' Safari") 20-30   62
CAPITOL (4880 "Ten Little Indians") 75-100   62
CAPITOL (5118 "Fun, Fun, Fun") ... 10-20   63
CAPITOL (5174 "I Get Around") ... 10-20   64
CAPITOL (5245 "When I Grow Up") . 10-20   64
CAPITOL (5306 "Dance, Dance,
   Dance") 10-20   64
CAPITOL (5372 "Do You Wanna
   Dance") 10-20   65
CAPITOL (5395 "Help Me Rhonda") . 10-20   65
CAPITOL (5464 "California Girls") ... 10-20   65
CAPITOL (5540 "The Little Girl
   I Once Knew") 10-20   65
CAPITOL (5561 "Barbara Ann") 90-125   65
CAPITOL (5676 "Good Vibrations") .. 10-20   66
CAPITOL (5245 "When I Grow Up") . 10-20   64
CARIBOU 3-6   79-86

EPs: 7–inch 33/45rpm

BROTHER (1 "Radio Spot Backing
   Tracks") 225-250   73
   (Promotional issue only.)
CAPITOL (189 "Best of the Beach
   Boys") 15-20   66
   (With "LLP" prefix. Jukebox issue only.)
CAPITOL (1981 "Surfer Girl") 45-55   63
CAPITOL (2186 "10 Little Indians") 300-325   64
   (One side of this EP contains selections by Ray
   Anthony.)
CAPITOL (2027 "Shut Down, Vol. 2") 45-55   64
CAPITOL (2269 "The Beach Boys
   Today") 50-75   65
   (Jukebox issue only.)
CAPITOL (2293/94 "Beach Boys'
   Party") 125-150   65
   (Jukebox issue only.)
CAPITOL (2545 "Best of the Beach
   Boys") 50-75   66
   (With "DU" prefix. Jukebox issue only.)
CAPITOL (2545 "Best of the Beach
   Boys") 15-20   66
CAPITOL (2754/55 "Brian Wilson Introduces
   Selections") 350-375   64
   (Promotional issue only. Includes selections from
   Beach Boys Concert and *Beach Boys Songbook*.)

CAPITOL (5267 "4 By the Beach
   Boys") 35-45   66
REPRISE (2118 "Mount Vernon and
   Fairway") 8-10   73
   (Originally packaged with Reprise LP 2118,
   "Holland.")
ROCK SHOPPE ("The Beach Years")75-100   75
   (Demo disc for "A Six Hour Radio Special." Also
   contains excerpts by Jan and Dean, Dick Dale and
   the Surfaris, narrated by Roger Christian.
   Promotional issue, pressed in a quantity of 200
   copies.)
WARNER (422 "Sunflower Promo
   Spots") 100-125   70
WARNER (534 "Vote '72") 35-45   72
   (Promotional issue only.)
WHAT'S IT ALL ABOUT 20-25
   (Promotional issue only.)

LPs: 10/12–inch 33rpm

ACCORD 5-10   83
BROTHER (9001 "Smiley Smile") ... 15-20   67
BROTHER/SUNKIST (9431 "25 Years of
   Good Vibrations") 10-20   86
   (Includes tour booklet. Sold at Beach Boys
   concerts.)
CAPITOL (133 "20/20") 10-20   69
CAPITOL (133 "20/20") 30-35   69
   (With "SKAO-8" prefix. Capitol Record Club issue.)
CAPITOL (253 "Close Up") 35-40   69
CAPITOL (442 "Good Vibrations") ... 20-25   70
CAPITOL (500 "All Summer Long/
   California Girls") 8-12   70
CAPITOL (701 "Dance, Dance, Dance/
   Fun, Fun, Fun") 8-12   71
CAPITOL (1808 through 1998) 15-25 63-67
   (With "DT" prefix.)
CAPITOL (1808 through 1998) 5-10 75-78
   (With "SM" prefix.)
CAPITOL (1808 through 1998) 20-35 62-63
   (With "T" or "ST" prefix.)
CAPITOL (2027 "Shut Down, Vol. 2") .. 8-15   63
   (With "DT" prefix.)
CAPITOL (2027 "Shut Down, Vol. 2") .. 5-10   75
   (With "SM" prefix.)
CAPITOL (2027 "Shut Down, Vol. 2") . 15-20   63
   (With "T" or "ST" prefix.)
CAPITOL (2110 "All Summer Long") . 25-30   64
   (With *Don't Break Down.* On this pressing, *Don't
   Back Down* was incorrectly shown as *Don't Break
   Down.*)
CAPITOL (2110 "All Summer Long") . 15-20   64
   (With "Don't Back Down" shown correctly.)
CAPITOL (2164 "Beach Boys' Christmas
   Album") 5-10   75
   (With "SM" prefix.)
CAPITOL (2164 "Beach Boys' Christmas
   Album") 20-35   64
   (With "T" or "ST" prefix.)

CAPITOL (2198 "Beach Boys
   Concert") 10-15   64
   (With "T" or "ST" prefix.)
CAPITOL (2198 "Beach Boys Concert") 5-10
   (With "SM" prefix.)
CAPITOL (2269 "The Beach Boys
   Today") 15-20   65
   (With "T" or "DT" prefix.)
CAPITOL (2354 "Summer Days and
   Summer Nights") 20-35   65
   (With "T" or "DT" prefix.)
CAPITOL (2398 "Beach Boys Party") 30-35   65
   (With "SMAS" prefix. Price includes 15 bonus
   photos. Deduct $8-12 if these photos are missing.)
CAPITOL (2398 "Beach Boys Party") 20-30   65
   (With "MAS" prefix. Price includes 15 bonus
   photos. Deduct $8-12 if these photos are missing.)
CAPITOL (2458 "Pet Sounds") 15-20   66
   (With "T" or "DT" prefix.)
CAPITOL (2545 "Best of the Beach
   Boys") 10-15   66
   (With "T" or "DT" prefix.)
CAPITOL (2706 "Best of the Beach
   Boys, Volume 2") 10-15   67
   (With "T" or "DT" prefix.)
CAPITOL (2813 "Beach Boys Deluxe
   Set") 100-125   67
   (With "TCL" prefix.)
CAPITOL (2813 "Beach Boys Deluxe
   Set") 35-40   67
   (With "DTCL" prefix.)
CAPITOL (2859 "Wild Honey") 10-15   67
   (With "T" or "DT" prefix.)
CAPITOL (ST-8-2891 "Smiley Smile") 60-75   69
   (With "ST-8" prefix. Capitol Record Club issue.)
CAPITOL (2893 "Stack-o-Tracks") . 100-150   68
   (With music-lyrics booklet.)
CAPITOL (2893 "Stack-o-Tracks") ... 50-75   68
   (Without music-lyrics booklet.)
CAPITOL (2893 "Stack-o-Tracks") . 100-125   69
   (With "ST-8" prefix. Capitol Record Club issue.)
CAPITOL (2895 "Friends") 10-15   68
CAPITOL (2945 "Best of the Beach
   Boys, Volume, 3") 35-40   68
CAPITOL (3352 "Sunflower") 30-35   70
   (With "SKAO-9" prefix. Capitol Record Club issue.)
CAPITOL (6994 "Golden Years of
   the Beach Boys") 25-30   75
   (TV mail-order offer.)
CAPITOL (48421 "Pet Sounds") 5-8   90
CAPITOL (11000 through 16000
   except 11384) 5-15 74-86
CAPITOL (11384 Spirit of America") . 15-20   75
CAPITOL (92639 "Still Cruisin") 5-10   89
CAPITOL (123946 "Best of
   the Beach Boys, Vol. 1") 20-25   74
   (RCA Record Club issue.)
CAPITOL (153477 "Rarities") 20-25   75
   (RCA Record Club issue.)

CAPITOL (233559 "Endless Summer") 20-25   74
(RCA Record Club issue.)
CAPITOL (233593 "American
Summer") 20-25   75
(RCA Record Club issue.)
CARIBOU 5-10   78-85
ERA 12-18   69
EVEREST 5-10   81
MFSL (116 "Surfer Girl") 15-25   84
PAIR 10-12   84
PICKWICK 8-12   72-75
REPRISE (2118 "Holland") 15-20   73
(With *Mount Vernon and Fairway* EP.)
REPRISE (2118 "Holland") 8-12   73
(Without *Mount Vernon and Fairway* EP.)
REPRISE (2166 "Wild Honey/20-20") . 8-10   74
REPRISE (2166 "Friends/
Smiley Smile") 8-10   74
REPRISE (2223 "Good Vibrations/Best
of the Beach Boys") 8-10   75
REPRISE (2251 "15 Big Ones") 8-10   76
REPRISE (2258 "Love You") 8-10   77
REPRISE (2268 "M.I.U. Album") 8-10   78
REPRISE (6382 "Sunflower") 8-12   70
REPRISE (6453 "Surf's Up") 20-25   71
(Capitol Record Club issue.)
REPRISE (6484 "The Beach Boys
in Concert") 8-10   73
RONCO 8-10   78
SEARS (608 "Summertime Blues") 100-125   70
(Sold only at Sears retail stores.)
SESSIONS 15-20   80
SPRINGBOARD (4021 "Greatest
Hits: 1961-1963") 8-12   72
WAND (688 "Greatest Hits") 10-15   72

Promotional LPs

BROTHER (9431 "Good Vibrations From
the Beach Boys") 10-15   86
(Sunkist promotional issue.)
CAPITOL (1 "Open House") 175-200   78
CAPITOL (2754/5 "Beach Boys'
Concert") 300-350   64
CAPITOL (3123 "Silver Platter
Service") 75-100   64
(With selections by the Hollyridge Strings.)
CAPITOL (3133 "Silver Platter
Service") 125-150   64
("Beach Boys Christmas Special.")
CAPITOL (3266 "Silver Platter
Service") 75-100   67
CARIBOU (1024 "Keepin' the Summer
Alive") 45-50   80
CRAWDADDY ("Brian Wilson
Interview") 90-100   77
(Issued only to radio stations only.)
MORE MUSIC (03-179-72 "Good
Vibrations from London") 50-60

MUTUAL RADIO ("Dick Clark Presents
the Beach Boys") 150-175   81
(Three-LP boxed set.)
REPRISE ("Radio Spot Backing Tracks for
Beach Boys in Concert") 225-250   73
Members: Brian Wilson; Carl Wilson; Dennis Wilson; Mike Love;
Al Jardine; Bruce Johnston; Ricky Fataar; Blondie Chaplin.
Note: Promos NOT listed separately are priced in the same
range as commercial issues.
  Also see ANNETTE
  Also see ANTHONY, Ray
  Also see BEATLES / Beach Boys / Buddy Holly
  Also see CAMPBELL, Glen
  Also see CHICAGO
  Also see CLAYTON, Merry
  Also see DALE, Dick / Surfaris / Surf Kings (Beach Boys)
  Also see DR. HOOK
  Also see EVERLY BROTHERS with the Beach Boys
  Also see FAT BOYS and the Beach Boys
  Also see JAN & DEAN / Beach Boys
  Also see JETT, Joan, and the Blackhearts
  Also see KENNY and the Cadets
  Also see PETERSEN, Paul
  Also see ROLLING STONES
  Also see ROTH, David Lee
  Also see SURVIVORS
  Also see WILSON, Brian
  Also see WILSON, Brian, and Mike Love
  Also see WILSON, Carl
  Also see WILSON, Dennis

BEACH BOYS / Jan & Dean
LPs: 10/12-inch 33rpm
CAPITOL (8149 "The Beach Boys/
Jan & Dean") 10-20   81
(Sold only at Radio Shack stores. Realistic
#S1-7010.)
EXACT 5-8   81
  Also see JAN & DEAN

BEACH BOYS and Little Richard
Singles: 7-inch
CRITIQUE 3-5   87
Picture Sleeves
CRITIQUE 3-5   87
  Also see LITTLE RICHARD

BEACH BOYS / Tony & Joe
Singles: 7-inch
ERA 3-5   70
  Also see TONY & JOE

BEACH BOYS with Frankie Valle and the 4 Seasons
Singles: 7-inch
FBI 3-5   84
  Also see 4 SEASONS

BEACH BOYS / Carl Wilson
LPs: 10/12-inch 33rpm
BROTHER (2083 "Pet Sounds"/
"So Tough") 10-20   72
  Also see BEACH BOYS

BEACH BUMS
Singles: 7-inch
ARE YOU KIDDING ME? 20-30   66
Member: Bob Seger.

Also see SEGER, Bob

BEACON STREET UNION
Singles: 7–inch

MGM 5-10   67-69
RTP 4-6   69

LPs: 10/12–inch 33rpm

MGM 15-25   68
Members: John Lincoln Wright; Robert Rhodes; Paul Tartachny; Wayne Ulaky; Richard Weisberg.

BEAR, Edward: see EDWARD BEAR

BEAR ESSENCE STARRING MARIANNA
Singles: 12–inch 33/45rpm

MOBY DICK 4-6   84

BEARS
LPs: 10/12–inch 33rpm

I.R.S. 8-10   87-88

BEASLEY, Walter
Singles: 12–inch 33/45rpm

POLYDOR 4-6   88

Singles: 7–inch

POLYDOR 2-4   87-88

LPs: 10/12–inch 33rpm

POLYDOR 5-10   87-88

BEAST
LPs: 10/12–inch 33rpm

COTILLION 10-12   69
EVOLUTION 8-10   70

BEAT, B: see B. BEAT GIRLS

BEAT FARMERS
LPs: 10/12–inch 33rpm

MCA/CURB 5-10   86-87
RHINO 5-10   85

BEATLES
Singles: 12–inch 33/45rpm

ULTIMIX (120: "Twist and Shout") ... 40-60   88
(Promotional issue only.)

Singles: 7–inch

AMERICOM ("Yellow Submarine") . 400-600   69
(Plastic "Pocket Disc" soundsheet. Number not known.)
AMERICOM (221 "Hey Jude") 200-400   69
(Plastic "Pocket Disc" soundsheet.)
AMERICOM (335 "Get Back") 200-400   69
(Plastic "Pocket Disc" soundsheet.)
AMERICOM (382 "Ballad of
John and Yoko") 200-400   69
(Plastic "Pocket Disc" soundsheet.)
APPLE 4-6   71-75
ATCO (6302 "Sweet Georgia Brown") 25-35   64
(Shown as by "The Beatles with Tony Sheridan.")
ATCO (6308 "Ain't She Sweet") 8-12   64
(Shown as "The Beatles - Vocal By John Lennon.")
ATLANTIC 2-4   83-86

CAPITOL (Orange, black or purple label) 2-4   75-86
(Includes reissues of 1964-1975 material and original pressings of 1975-1986 releases.)
CAPITOL (2056 "Hello Goodbye") 4-6   67
(Orange/yellow "swirl" label.)
CAPITOL (2056 "Hello Goodbye") 8-10   68
(Red/orange "target" label.)
CAPITOL (2138 "Lady Madonna") 4-6   68
(Orange/yellow "swirl" label.)
CAPITOL (2138 "Lady Madonna") 8-10   68
(Red/orange "target" label.)
CAPITOL (5100 "Movie Medley"/"Fab
Four on Film") 60-70   81
(First issued with *Movie Medley* backed with *Fab Four on Film,* which was the Beatles talking about the film *A Hard Day's Night.* With "B" prefix.)
CAPITOL (5100 "Movie Medley"/"I'm
Happy Just to Dance with You") 2-4   81
(With "B" prefix.)
CAPITOL (5107 "Movie Medley") 2-4   82
(With "B" prefix.)
CAPITOL (5189 "Love Me Do") 2-4   82
(With "B" prefix. This recent Capitol 5000 series differs from the 5000 series of 1964 by its use of the "B" prefix.)
CAPITOL (5112 through 5964) 8-15   64-67
(Price here is for orange/yellow swirl label issues.)
CAPITOL (5112 "I Want to Hold
Your Hand") 2-4   84
(*I Want to Hold Your Hand* was reissued as a STEREO single in 1984. Even though the reissue is on the orange/yellow label, it has black print around the border of the label. 1964 issues have this print in white letters.)
CAPITOL (5112 through 5964) 12-15   68
(Red/orange target label issues.)
CAPITOL (5555 "We Can Work It
Out") 450-500   68
(Red and white "Starline" label. Issued in error.)
CAPITOL (6061 through 6066) 25-35   65
(Green label "Starline" series.)
CAPITOL (6278 through 6300) 2-4   81
(Blue label "Starline" series.)
CAPITOL (72144 "All My Loving") .. 80-100   71
(An error in production created a U.S. pressing of the Canadian release, *All My Loving/This Boy.*)
CICADELIC/BIODISC 3-5   90
COLLECTABLES 2-4   82
DECCA (31382 "My Bonnie") ... 3000-5000   62
(Shown as by Tony Sheridan and the Beat Brothers. Note: Price is for a *COMMERCIAL,* not promotional, issue. Commercial copies are on Decca's black label with silver print and a multi-color stripe across the center of the label. Black and silver Decca labels without the other colors are bootlegs.)
IBC (0082 "Murray the 'K' and the
Beatles As It Happened") 4-6   76

MGM (13213 "My Bonnie") 15-20   64
(Shown as by the Beatles with Tony Sheridan.)
MGM (13227 "Why") 15-20   64
(Shown as by the Beatles with Tony Sheridan.)
MURRAY the "K" and the BEATLES
(33 Single) 20-25   64
(Reissued in 1976 as IBC 0082.)
OLDIES 45 5-10   64
SWAN (4152 "She Loves You") . . . 200-250   63
(White label, with red print. Titles are in quotes.
Does NOT have "Don't Drop Out" on label.)
SWAN (4152 "She Loves You") . . . 175-225   63
(White label, with red print. No quotes on titles.
Does NOT have "Don't Drop Out" on label.)
SWAN (4152 "She Loves You") . . . 150-200   63
(White label, with red print. No quotes on titles.
Says "Don't Drop Out" on label.)
SWAN (4152 "She Loves You") . . . 150-200   63
(White label, with blue print. No quotes on titles.
Says "Don't Drop Out" on label.)
SWAN (4152 "She Loves You") 10-20   64
(Black label.)
SWAN (4182 "Sie Liebt Dich") 35-45   64
(With "She Loves You" following "Sie Liebt Dich"
on the same line. White label with red print.)
SWAN (4182 "Sie Liebt Dich") 30-60   64
(With "She Loves You" under "Sie Liebt Dich" on a
separate line. White label with orange print.)
SWAN (4182 "Sie Liebt Dich") 25-35   64
(With "She Loves You" under "Sie Liebt Dich" on a
separate line. White label with red print.)
TOLLIE 15-25   64
(Black label.)
TOLLIE 25-30   64
(Yellow label with blue print.)
TOLLIE 30-40   64
(Yellow label with black print. Label name in
brackets.)
TOLLIE 12-18   64
(Yellow label with black print. Label name is either
in a box or is by itself, with no lines, box or
brackets.)
TOLLIE 20-25   64
(Yellow label with green print. Label name is all in
uppercase letters.)
TOLLIE 15-20   64
(Yellow label with green print. Label name is all in
lowercase letters.)
TOPAZ (1353 "Seattle
Press Conference") 4-6   89
VEE JAY (498 "Please Please Me") 500-600   63
(Showing group as the "BEATLES." With thin
lettering and oval label logo.)
VEE JAY (498 "Please Please Me") 350-400   63
(Showing group as the "BEATLES." With bold
lettering and oval label logo.)
VEE JAY (498 "Please Please Me") 500-600   63
(Showing group as the "BEATLES." With
'brackets' label logo.)

VEE JAY (498 "Please Please Me") 350-400   63
(Showing group as the "BEATLES." With thin
lettering and oval label logo.)
VEE JAY (498 "Please Please Me") 400-500   63
(Showing group as the "BEATLES." With 'brackets'
label logo.)
VEE JAY (498 "Please Please Me") 600-700   63
(Showing group as the "BEATLES." With thin
lettering and oval label logo. Catalog number, at
bottom of label, is preceded by the number
symbol: "#498.")
VEE JAY (522 "From Me to You") . 125-150   63
(Black label with horizontal silver lines.)
VEE JAY (522 "From Me to You") . . 75-100   63
(Black label. With rainbow circle.)
VEE JAY (581 "Please Please Me") 100-125   64
(Purple label.)
VEE JAY (581 "Please Please Me") . 50-75   64
(White label.)
VEE JAY (581 "Please Please Me") . 30-40   64
(Yellow label.)
VEE JAY (581 "Please Please Me") . 15-25   64
(Black label with horizontal silver lines.)
VEE JAY (581 "Please Please Me") . 15-25   64
(Black label. No rainbow circle.)
VEE JAY (581 "Please Please Me") . 20-25   64
(Black label with rainbow circle.)
VEE JAY (587 "Do You Want to Know
a Secret") 30-40   64
(Yellow label.)
VEE JAY (587 "Do You Want to Know
a Secret") 15-25   64
(Black label with horizontal silver lines.)
VEE JAY (587 "Do You Want to Know
a Secret") 15-25   64
(Black label. No horizontal lines. With either "Vee
Jay" or "VJ" logo.)
VEE JAY (587 "Do You Want to Know
a Secret") 25-30   64
(Black label. No rainbow circle. Brackets Vee Jay
logo.)
VEE JAY (587 "Do You Want to Know
a Secret") 15-20   64
(Black label. No rainbow circle. Oval Vee Jay logo.)
VEE JAY (587 "Do You Want to Know
a Secret") 12-16   64
(Black label with rainbow circle.)

Picture Sleeves

APPLE (Except 2531) 12-18   68-70
APPLE (2531 "Ballad of John and
Yoko") 15-20   69
ATCO (6308 "Ain't She Sweet") . . . 100-125   64
CAPITOL/HOLIDAY INN 800-900   64
(Promotional sleeve, pictures the four Beatles on
front and their first three Capitol LPs on the back.
Not known to have been issued containing any
particular single.)
CAPITOL (2056 "Hello Goodbye") . . . 18-20   67
CAPITOL (2138 "Lady Madonna") . . . 12-18   68

CAPITOL (PB-5189 "Love Me Do") .. 10-12   82
(With "PB" prefix. Promo copies of this issue were on commercial stock labels, but are quickly identified by the printing of an "Intro" time of :13 on the right side of the label. Also, store stock copies were B-5189, not PB-5189.)
CAPITOL (5624 "Twist and Shout") ... 8-10   86
CAPITOL (5810 "Penny Lane") 90-100   67
CAPITOL (5964 "All You Need
Is Love") 70-85   67
(This promo, as well as many Capitol issues by other artists, was shipped in a "Rush" paper sleeve. It's possible a slight premium may be placed on these sleeves, although they were NOT identified in any way as a Beatles item.)
CAPITOL (9076 "I Want to Hold
Your Hand") 8-10   84
CAPITOL (9758 "Movie Medley") 30-35   81
(With "SPRO" prefix.)
CAPITOL CUSTOM (2637 "Music City
KFWBeatles") 200-250   64
(Radio KFWB and Wallichs Music City promo disc, "The Beatles Talking"/"You Can't Do That.")
CARROL JAMES (3301 "The Carroll James
Interview with the Beatles") 8- 12   84
CREATIVE RADIO (B-1 "The Beatle
Invasion") 10-20
(Radio show demo. Flip side is "Inside Paul McCartney.")
DECCA (31382 "My Bonnie") 500-600   62
(Shown as by Tony Sheridan and the Beat Brothers. Pink label with black lettering.)
MBRF (55551 "Decade") 100-150   72
(Contains radio spots for the "Beatles 1962-1966" and "Beatles 1967- 1970.")
MGM (13213 "My Bonnie") 90-100   64
(Shown as by the Beatles with Tony Sheridan.)
MGM (13227 "Why") 75-125   64
(Shown as by the Beatles with Tony Sheridan.)

STRAWBERRY FIELDS FOREVER (21 "How Do
You Do It") 76
(Beatles convention souvenir issue. Colored vinyl. With insert.)
SWAN (4152 "She Loves You") ... 150-200   63
SWAN (4152 "I'll Get You") 175-225   64
(Single-sided pressing. Flip side has blank grooves.)
SWAN (4182 "Sie Liebt Dich") 125-150   64
TOLLIE (9001 "Twist and Shout") . 100-125   64
TOLLIE (9008 "Love Me Do") 100-125   64
TOPAZ (1353 "Seattle
Press Conference") 4-8   89
U.A. (2357 "A Hard Day's Night") . 800-1100   64
U.A. (42370 "Let It Be") 400-700   70
(Has three radio advertisements for the film.)
VEE JAY (8 "Anna"/"Ask Me
Why") 9000-12000   64
VEE JAY (498 "Please Please
Me") 350-450   63
VEE JAY (522 "From Me to You") . 100-150   63
VEE JAY (581 "Please Please Me,"
Purple label) 100-150   64
VEE JAY (581 "Please Please Me,"
White label) 100-125   64
VEE JAY (587 "Do You Want to Know
a Secret") 100-125   64
WHAT'S IT ALL ABOUT 15-20

Plastic Soundsheets/Flexi-Discs

AMERICOM ....:............. 350-450   69
(Four–inch "Pocket Discs.")
EVA-TONE (8464 "All My Loving") ... 5-10   82
(Back side reads either "Compliments of Musicland" or "Compliments of Discount.")
EVA-TONE (8464 "All My Loving") .. 15-20   82
(Back side reads "Compliments of Sam Goody.")
EVA-TONE (830771 "Till There
Was You") 3-5   83
EVA-TONE (420826 "All My Loving") . 5-10   82
(Back side reads either "Compliments of Musicland" or "Compliments of Discount.")
EVA-TONE (420826 "All My Loving") 15-20   82
(Back side reads "Compliments of Sam Goody.")
EVA-TONE (420827 "Magical Mystery
Tour") 5-10   82
(Back side reads either "Compliments of Musicland" or "Compliments of Discount.")
EVA-TONE (420827 "Magical Mystery
Tour") 15-20   82
(Back side reads "Compliments of Sam Goody.")
EVA-TONE (420828 "Rocky Raccoon") 5-10   82
(Back side reads either "Compliments of Musicland" or "Compliments of Discount.")
EVA-TONE (420828 "Rocky
Raccoon") 15-20   82
(Back side reads "Compliments of Sam Goody.")
EVA-TONE (1214825 "The Beatles
German Medley) 30-40   83

CAPITOL (ST-2553 "Yesterday and
Today") 5000-10000   66
(Stereo. FIRST STATE "Butcher Cover" issues.)
CAPITOL (T-2553 "Yesterday and
Today") 300-400   66
(Monaural. PASTE OVER or PEELED "Butcher
cover" copies.)
CAPITOL (ST-2553 "Yesterday and
Today") 400-500   66
(Stereo. PASTE OVER or PEELED "Butcher
cover" copies.)
Note: the wide range of values exists here due to
varied opinions on the practice of peeling the
"Trunk cover" from the "Butcher cover." The
expertise used in the peeling is also a major factor
affecting the value of these LPs.
CAPITOL (T-2553 "Yesterday and
Today") 30-40   66
(Monaural. "Trunk cover.")
CAPITOL (ST-2553 "Yesterday and
Today") 20-25   66
(Stereo. Black label with white print around border.
"Trunk cover.")
CAPITOL (ST-2553 "Yesterday and
Today") 20-25   69
(Green label.)
CAPITOL (ST-2553 "Yesterday and
Today") 8-12   76
(Orange label.)
CAPITOL (ST-2553 "Yesterday and
Today") 6-10   78
(Purple label.)
CAPITOL (ST-2553 "Yesterday and
Today") 5-10   84
(Black label with black print around border.)
CAPITOL (ST-8-2553 "Yesterday and
Today") 25-35   66-69
(Capitol Record Club issue.)
CAPITOL (T-2576 "Revolver") 30-40   66
(Monaural.)
CAPITOL (ST-2576 "Revolver") 20-25   66
(Stereo. Black label with white print around border.)
CAPITOL (ST-2576 "Revolver") 20-25   69
(Green label.)
CAPITOL (ST-2576 "Revolver") 8-12   76
(Orange label.)
CAPITOL (ST-2576 "Revolver") 6-10   78
(Purple label.)
CAPITOL (ST-2576 "Revolver") 5-10   84
(Black label with black print around border.)
CAPITOL (ST-8-2576 "Revolver") ... 25-35   66-69
(Capitol Record Club issue.)
CAPITOL (MAS-2653 "Sgt. Pepper's Lonely
Hearts Club Band") 50-100   67
(Monaural.)
CAPITOL (SMAS-2653 "Sgt. Pepper's Lonely
Hearts Club Band") 30-40   67
(Stereo. Black label with white print around border.)

CAPITOL (SMAS-2653 "Sgt. Pepper's Lonely
Hearts Club Band") 18-22   69
(Green label.)
CAPITOL (SMAS-2653 "Sgt. Pepper's Lonely
Hearts Club Band") 8-12   76
(Orange label.)
CAPITOL (SMAS-2653 "Sgt. Pepper's Lonely
Hearts Club Band") 6-10   78
(Purple label.)
CAPITOL (SMAS-2653 "Sgt. Pepper's Lonely
Hearts Club Band") 5-10   84
(Black label with black print around border.)
CAPITOL (MAL-2835 "Magical Mystery
Tour") 75-150   67
(Monaural.)
CAPITOL (SMAL-2835 "Magical Mystery
Tour") 30-40   67
(Stereo. Black label with white print around border.)
CAPITOL (SMAL-2835 "Magical Mystery
Tour") 18-22   69
(Green label.)
CAPITOL (SMAL-2835 "Magical Mystery
Tour") 8-12   76
(Orange label.)
CAPITOL (SMAL-2835 "Magical Mystery
Tour") 6-10   78
(Purple label.)
CAPITOL (SMAL-2835 "Magical Mystery
Tour") 5-10   84
(Black label with black print around border.)
CAPITOL (3403 "The Beatles/
1962-1966") 8-12   78
CAPITOL (3404 "The Beatles/
1967-1970") 8-12   78
CAPITOL (11537 "Rock 'N' Roll
Music") 12-18   76
CAPITOL (11638 "Beatles at the
Hollywood Bowl") 8-10   77
CAPITOL (11711 "Love Songs") 6-10   77
CAPITOL (11840 "Sgt. Pepper's Lonely
Hearts Club Band") 15-20   78
(Picture disc.)
CAPITOL (11841 "The Beatles") 20-30   78
(Colored vinyl.)
CAPITOL (11842 "The Beatles/
1962-1966") 20-25   78
CAPITOL (11843 "The Beatles/
1967-1970") 20-25   78
CAPITOL (11900 "Abbey Road,"
Picture disc) 20-30   78
CAPITOL (11921 "A Hard Day's Night") 8-10   79
(Purple label.)
CAPITOL (11921 "A Hard Day's Night") 5-10   84
(Black label with black print around border.)
CAPITOL (11922 "Let It Be") 8-10   79
(Purple label.)
CAPITOL (11922 "Let It Be") 5-10   84
(Black label with black print around border.)
CAPITOL (12009 "Rarities") 40-60   78

CAPITOL (12060 "The Beatles
   Rarities") 6-10   80
CAPITOL (12199 "Reel Music") 6-10   82
CAPITOL (12245 "The Beatles 20
   Greatest Hits") 8-12   82
   (Purple label.)
CAPITOL (12245 "The Beatles 20
   Greatest Hits") 5-10   84
   (Black label.)
CAPITOL (16020 "Rock 'N' Roll
   Music, Volume I") 5-10   80
CAPITOL (16021 "Rock 'N' Roll
   Music, Volume II") 5-10   80
CAPITOL (90043 "Past Masters,
   Vol. 1") 6-10   88
CAPITOL (90044 "Past Masters,
   Vol. 2") 6-10   88
CAPITOL/APPLE 10-12   68-75
   (A "Capitol/Apple" label is simply the Apple label
   with the Capitol logo near the bottom of the label.)
CAPITOL RECORD CLUB ISSUES (Except
   ST-8-2553) 25-35
   (Includes Record Club issues on the Capitol label
   only. Releases on other labels, available through
   the club, are listed by their label name.)
CAPITOL RECORD CLUB (ST-8-2553
   "Yesterday and Today") 40-45   66
CICADELIC 5-10   85-87
CLARION (601 "The Amazing Beatles and
   Other Great English Sounds") 60-75   66
   (Stereo. Back cover lists song titles. Also contains
   selections by the Swallows.)
CLARION (601 "The Amazing Beatles and
   Other Great English Sounds") 75-100   66
   (Stereo. Back cover does NOT list song titles. Also
   contains selections by the Swallows.)
CLARION (601 "The Amazing Beatles
   and Other Great English Sounds") . 50-75   66
   (Monaural. Also contains selections by the
   Swallows.)
CREATIVE RADIO ("The Beatle
   Invasion") 35-45
   (Three-LP set, includes 12x19 poster.)
GREAT NORTHWEST MUSIC CO ... 5-10   78
H.S.R.D. 8-12   82
HALL of MUSIC 12-18   81
HERITAGE SOUND 8-10   82
I-N-S RADIO NEWS ("American Tour
   with Ed Rudy #2") 12-18   80
LINGASONG 10-12   77
LLOYDS ("The Great American Tour-1965
   Live Beatlemania Concert") 125-175   65
   (With selections by the Liverpool Lads.)
MFSL (1 "The Beatles, the
   Collection") 375-425   82
   (14-LP boxed set. Includes booklet and alignment
   tool.)
MFSL (023 "Abbey Road") 25-50   79

MFSL (047 "Magical Mystery
   Tour") 20-40   81
MFSL (072 "The Beatles") 20-30   82
MFSL/UHQR (100 "Sgt. Pepper's Lonely
   Hearts Club Band") 200-400   82
   (Boxed set. Silver label, with "UHQR" near top.)
MFSL (100 "Sgt. Pepper's Lonely
   Hearts Club Band") 15-25   84
   (White label. No "UHQR" on label.)
MFSL (101 "Please Please Me") 15-25   84
MFSL (102 "With the Beatles") 15-25   84
MFSL (103 "A Hard Day's Night") ... 15-25   84
MFSL (104 "Beatles for Sale") 15-25   84
MFSL (105 "Help") 15-25   84
MFSL (106 "Rubber Soul") 15-25   84
MFSL (107 "Revolver") 15-25   84
MFSL (108 "Yellow Submarine") 15-25   84
MFSL (109 "Let It Be") 15-25   84
MGM (E-4215 "The Beatles with
   Tony Sheridan and Guests") 45-55   64
   (Monaural. With selections by Tony Sheridan and
   by the Titans.)
MGM (SE-4215 "The Beatles with
   Tony Sheridan and Guests") 75-100   64
   (Stereo. With selections by Tony Sheridan and by
   the Titans.)
METRO (M-563 "This Is Where It
   Started") 40-50   66
   (Also contains selections by Tony Sheridan and by
   the Titans.)
METRO (MS-563 "This Is Where It
   Started") 50-75   66
   (Also contains selections by Tony Sheridan and by
   the Titans.)
MUSIC INTERNATIONAL 5-10   85
PAC 15-20   81
PBR INT'L 20-30   78
PHOENIX 10 5-10   82
PHOENIX 20 5-10   83
PICKWICK (Except 90071) 8-12   78-79
PICKWICK (90071 "Recorded Live In
   Hamburg, 1962, Volume 3") 15-20   78
POLYDOR (4504 "In the Beginning,
   Circa 1960") 12-15   70
   (With gatefold cover.)
POLYDOR (4504 "In the Beginning,
   Circa 1960") 5-10   81-84
   (With standard cover.)
POLYDOR (93199 "In the Beginning,
   Circa 1960") 15-18   70
   (Capitol Record Club issue.)
RPN (RADIO PULSEBEAT NEWS) "American
   Tour with Ed Rudy #2") 40-50   64
   (This LP was occasionally issued with a "Teen
   Talk" booklet. The value of the booklet is
   approximately the same as for the LP. This edition
   has NO pictures of the Beatles on the LP cover.)

RPN (RADIO PULSEBEAT NEWS) ("1965
Talk Album, Ed Rudy with New
U.S. Tour") 50-75   65
RAVEN 5-10   81
SAVAGE (69 "The Savage Young
Beatles") 75-100   68
(Label is yellow. Cover is orange.)
SAVAGE (69 "The Savage Young
Beatles") 40-50   68
(Label is orange. Cover is yellow.)
SILHOUETTE 8-12   81-84
STERLING PRODUCTIONS (6481;
"I Apologize") 70-80   66
(Price includes bonus 8x10 photo, which
represents $5-15 of the value.)
U.A. (UAL-3366 "A Hard Day's Night") 25-30   64
(Monaural.)
U.A. (UAS-6366 "A Hard Day's Night") 30-40   64
(Stereo. Black label.)
U.A. (UAS-6366 "A Hard Day's Night") 20-25   68-70
(Stereo. Pink and orange or black and orange
label.)
U.A. (UAS-6366 "A Hard Day's Night") 10-15   71
(Stereo. Tan label.)
U.A. (UAS-6366 "A Hard Day's Night") 8-12   77
(Stereo. Orange and yellow label.)
U.A. (90828 "A Hard Day's Night") . . 75-100   65
(Capitol Record Club issue.)
VEE JAY (202 "Hear the Beatles
Tell All") 50-60   64
(Monaural. Black label with rainbow color-band.)
VEE JAY (202 "Hear the Beatles
Tell All") 5-10   79
(Stereo.)
VEE JAY (202 "Hear the Beatles
Tell All") 5-10   87
(Picture disc.)
VEE JAY (1062 "Introducing the
Beatles") 325-375   63
(Monaural. With *Love Me Do* and *P.S. I Love You.*
Back cover pictures 25 other Vee Jay albums.)
VEE JAY (1062 "Introducing the
Beatles") 800-1200   63
(Stereo. With *Love Me Do* and *P.S. I Love You.*
Back cover pictures 25 other Vee Jay albums.)
VEE JAY (1062 "Introducing the
Beatles") 250-400   63-64
(Monaural. With *Love Me Do* and *P.S. I Love You.*
Back cover is blank. May be regarded as a
promotional issue, however nothing on the LP
supports that theory.)
VEE JAY (1062 "Introducing the
Beatles") 600-800   63-64
(Stereo. With *Love Me Do* and *P.S. I Love You.*
Back cover is blank. May be regarded as a
promotional issue, however nothing on the LP
supports that theory.)

VEE JAY (1062 "Introducing the
Beatles") 100-150   64
(Monaural. With *Love Me Do* and *P.S. I Love You.*
Back cover lists contents. Has brackets style label
logo.)
VEE JAY (1062 "Introducing the
Beatles") 150-250   64
(Stereo. With *Love Me Do* and *P.S. I Love You.*
Back cover lists contents. Has brackets style label
logo.)
VEE JAY (1062 "Introducing the
Beatles") 60-75   64
(Monaural. With *Love Me Do* and *P.S. I Love You.*
Back cover lists contents. Oval style label logo.)
VEE JAY (1062 "Introducing the
Beatles") 150-200   64
(Stereo. With *Ask Me Why* and *Please Please Me.*
Covers either label style or design.)
VEE JAY (1062 "Introducing the
Beatles") 40-60   64
(Monaural, rainbow color-band label. With *Ask Me
Why* and *Please Please Me.*)
VEE JAY (1062 "Introducing the
Beatles") 65-80   64
(Monaural, black label, no color-band. With *Ask Me
Why* and *Please Please Me.* Has brackets style
label logo.)
VEE JAY (1062 "Introducing the
Beatles") 35-45   64
(Monaural, black label, no color-band. With *Ask Me
Why* and *Please Please Me.* Label logo has
neither oval nor brackets.)
VEE JAY (1092 "Songs, Pictures
and Stories") 50-75   64
(Monaural.)
VEE JAY (1092 "Songs, Pictures
and Stories") 150-200   64
(Stereo.)
VEE JAY (1092 "Songs and Pictures) . . 5-8
(Reissue.)

Promotional LPs

ABC/WATERMARK ("Ringo's Yellow
Submarine") 700-800   84
(Set of 24 LPs in eight boxed sets, featuring Ringo
Starr telling the story of the Beatles. Issued to
radio stations only.)
APPLE (SBC-100 "The Beatles'
Christmas Album") 90-100   70
(Special issue for Beatles fan club members.)
APPLE FILMS (004 "The Yellow
Submarine") 400-450   69
(Contains the advertisements used on radio
stations to promote the film.)
ATCO (33-169 "Ain't She Sweet") . 300-350   64
(Also contains selections by the Swallows.)
BACKSTAGE (Colored vinyl) 20-30   82
CAPITOL ("Help, Open-End
Interview") 550-650   65
(Issued with programmer's script.)

CAPITOL ("The Platinum Beatles
Collection") 475-500   84
(18-LP boxed set.)
CAPITOL (SPRO-8969 "Rarities") ... 35-40   78
CAPITOL (SMAS-11638 "Beatles at the
Hollywood Bowl") 90-100   77
CAPITOL (12199 "Reel Music") 45-55   82
(Colored vinyl.)
CAPITOL/EMI (BC-13 "The Beatles
Collection") 250-300   78
(14-LP boxed set.)
I-N-S RADIO NEWS (1 "Beatlemania
Tour Coverage") 150-200   64
(An open-end interview. Includes a script.)
LINGASONG (7001 "Live! At the
Star-Club") 90-100   77
(Blue vinyl.)
LINGASONG (7001 "Live! At the
Star-Club") 75-90   77
(Red vinyl.)
LINGASONG (7001 "Live! At the
Star-Club") 30-40   77
(Black vinyl.)
ORANGE (12880 "The Silver Beatles")35-45   85
RAVEN 15-20   81
U.A. (UA-HELP "United
Artists Presents 'Help!'") 400-450   65
(Contains the advertisements used on radio
stations to promote the film.)
U.A. (UA-HELP INT "Special Open-End
Interview") 500-550   65
(Price includes script and programming
information, which represents about $50-75 of the
value.)
U.A. (2359/60 "Special Beatles
Half Hour Open End Interview") . 500-550   64
(Price includes 12-pages of script and
programming information, which represents about
$50-75 of the value.)
U.A. (2362/63 "United Artists
Presents *A Hard Day's Night*") ... 400-450   64
(Contains the advertisements used on radio
stations to promote the film.)
U.A. (UAL-6366 "A Hard
Day's Night") 300-350   64
(White label.)
Members: John Lennon; Paul McCartney; George Harrison;
Pete Best; Ringo Starr.
  Also see BEST, Pete
  Also see CLAY, Tom
  Also see HARRISON, George
  Also see LENNON, John
  Also see MARTIN, George
  Also see McCARTNEY, Paul
  Also see PRESLEY, Elvis / Beatles
  Also see PRESTON, Billy
  Also see SHANKAR, Ravi
  Also see SILKIE
  Also see STARR, Ringo

BEATLES / Beach Boys / Buddy Holly
LPs: 10/12–inch 33rpm
CREATIVE RADIO SHOWS (Demo of
"Specials") 75-100   79
(Promotional issue only.)
  Also see HOLLY, Buddy

BEATLES / Beach Boys / Kingston Trio
Plastic Soundsheets/Flexi-Discs
EVA-TONE (8464 "Surprise Gift from the Beatles
Beach Boys and Kingston Trio") . 300-350   64
(Plastic soundsheet.)
EVA-TONE (8464 "Surprise Gift from the Beatles
Beach Boys and Kingston Trio") . 200-250   64
(Five–inch edition of the above plastic soundsheet.)
  Also see BEACH BOYS
  Also see KINGSTON TRIO

BEATLES / Jerry Blabber
Singles: 7–inch
QUEST 5-10   65

BEATLES / 4 Seasons
LPs: 10/12–inch 33rpm
VEE JAY (DX-30 "Beatles Vs.
the Four Seasons") 300-400   64
(Monaural.)
VEE JAY (DXS-30 "Beatles Vs.
the Four Seasons") 500-750   64
(Stereo.)
Price includes a bonus Beatles poster, which
represents $80 to $100 of the value.
  Also see 4 SEASONS

BEATLES / Frank Ifield
LPs: 10/12–inch 33rpm
VEE JAY (1085 "The Beatles and
Frank Ifield") 750-1000   64
(Monaural. Pictures the Beatles on cover.)
VEE JAY (1085 "The Beatles and
Frank Ifield") 2000-3000   64
(Stereo. Pictures the Beatles on cover.)
VEE JAY (1085 "Jolly What!
the Beatles and Frank Ifield") 75-90   64
(Monaural. Pictures an Englishman on cover.)
VEE JAY (1085 "Jolly What!
the Beatles and Frank Ifield") ... 150-200   64
(Stereo. Pictures an Englishman on cover.)
  Also see IFIELD, Frank

BEATLES / Loretta Lynn
Singles: 7–inch
VEE JAY (581 "Please Please Me"/"Before
I'm over You") 50-100   64
(This pairing is the result of a production error.)
  Also see BEATLES
  Also see LYNN, Loretta

BEATLES BLAST at STADIUM
(DESCRIBED BY ERUPTING FANS)
LPs: 10/12–inch 33rpm

AUDIO JOURNAL 10-20   66
(*Beatles Blast*, etc." is the title of the LP. Featuring
only noise, made by fans at a Shea Stadium
concert. No artists are credited.

BEATMASTER
Singles: 7–inch

TOMMY BOY 2-4   84

BEAU, Toby: see TOBY BEAU

BEAU BRUMMELS
Singles: 7–inch

AUTUMN 5-10	64-65
PEP 2-4	
RHINO 2-4	82
VAULT 4-6	67
WARNER 4-8	66-75

Picture Sleeves

PEP 2-4	
RHINO 2-4	82

LPs: 10/12–inch 33rpm

ACCORD 5-10   82
AUTUMN (103 "Introducing the
Beau Brummels") 40-50   65
AUTUMN (104 "Beau
Brummels, Vol. 2") 40-50   65
JAS 8-10
POST 8-10
RHINO 5-10   81-82
VAULT (114 "Best of the Beau
Brummels") 25-30   67
VAULT (121 "Beau Brummels,
Vol. 44") 15-20   68
WARNER (Except 1644) 20-25   67-75
WARNER (1644 "Beau
Brummels '66") 30-35   66
Members: Sal Valentino; Ron Elliott; Ron Meagher; Declan
Mulligan; John Petersen.

BEAU COUP
Singles: 7–inch

AMHERST 2-4   87
ROCK 'N' ROLL 2-4   84-85

BEAU-MARKS
Singles: 7–inch

MAINSTREAM 4-6   68
PORT 5-10   62
RUST 5-10   61
SHAD 10-15   60
TIME (1032 "Rockin' Blues") 20-30   61

BEAUMONT, Jimmy
(Jimmy Beaumont and the Skyliners)
Singles: 7–inch

BANG 5-8   66
CAPITOL 3-5   74
COLPIX 5-10   61

DRIVE 3-5   76
GALLANT 5-10
MAY 5-10   61-63
Also see SKYLINERS

BEAUVOIR, Jean
Singles: 12–inch 33/45rpm

COLUMBIA 4-6   86

Singles: 7–inch

COLUMBIA 2-4   86

Picture Sleeves

COLUMBIA 2-4   86

LPs: 10/12–inch 33rpm

COLUMBIA 5-10   86
Also see LITTLE STEVEN and the Disciples of Soul
Also see PLASMATICS

BE-BOP DELUXE
Singles: 7–inch

HARVEST 3-5   75-78

LPs: 10/12–inch 33rpm

HARVEST (Black vinyl) 5-10   76-78
HARVEST (Colored vinyl) 15-20   77-78

Promotional LPs

HARVEST (8531 "Be Bop's Biggest") 25-35   75
Members: Richard Brown; Robert Bryan; Nicholas
Chatterton-Dew; Andrew Clarke; Simon Fox; Paul Jeffreys;
Milton R. James; Bill Nelson; Ian Parkin; Charles Tumahai.

BECK, Jeff
(Jeff Beck Group; Jeff Beck with Terry Bozzio and
Tony Hymas)
Singles: 7–inch

EPIC (10000 series) 4-8   67-69
EPIC (50000 series) 3-6   75-76

LPs: 10/12–inch 33rpm

ACCORD 5-10   81
EPIC (Except 43000 series) 8-12   68-89
EPIC (43000 series) 15-20   80-82
(Half-speed mastered.)
MFP 8-10
SPRINGBOARD 5-10   75

Promotional LPs

EPIC (151 "Everything You Always
Wanted to Hear") 15-25   76
EPIC (850 "Then and Now") 25-30   80
Also see BECK, BOGERT & APPICE
Also see CLAPTON, Eric, Jeff Beck and Jimmy Page
Also see DONOVAN
Also see HALL, Jimmy
Also see HAMMER, Jan
Also see HARRISON, George / Jeff Beck / Dave Edmunds
Also see HONEYDRIPPERS
Also see LORD SUTCH
Also see POWELL, Cozy
Also see YARDBIRDS

BECK, Jeff, and Rod Stewart
Singles: 7–inch

EPIC 2-4   85

Picture Sleeves

EPIC 2-4   85

BECK, Jeff, Ronnie Wood and Rod Stewart
LPs: 10/12–inch 33rpm
EPIC (33779 "Truth") 10-15   75
Also see BECK, Jeff
Also see STEWART, Rod
Also see WOOD, Ron

BECK, Jimmy
Singles: 7–inch
ASTRA 5-10
CHAMPION 10-20   59

BECK, Joe
Singles: 7–inch
POLYDOR 2-4   77
LPs: 10/12–inch 33rpm
KUDU 8-10   75
POLYDOR 5-10   77
VERVE/FORECAST 10-15   69
Also see PHILLIPS, Esther, and Joe Beck

BECK, BOGERT & APPICE
Singles: 7–inch
EPIC 3-5   73
LPs: 10/12–inch 33rpm
EPIC 10-12   73
Members: Jeff Beck; Tim Bogert; Carmine Appice.
Also see BECK, Jeff
Also see CACTUS
Also see VANILLA FUDGE

BECK FAMILY
Singles: 7–inch
LE JOINT 2-4   79

BECKHAM, Bob
Singles: 7–inch
DECCA 4-6   59-63
MONUMENT 3-5   67
SMASH 3-5   65
Picture Sleeves
DECCA 5-10   59
LPs: 10/12–inch 33rpm
DECCA 15-20   59

BECKMEIER BROTHERS
Singles: 7–inch
CASABLANCA 2-4   79
LPs: 10/12–inch 33rpm
CASABLANCA 5-10   79
Members: Fred Beckmeier; Steve Beckmeier.

BEE, Jimmy
(Jimmy Bee with Ernie Fields Jr.'s Orchestra)
Singles: 7–inch
ALA 3-5   73
CALLA 3-5   76
KENT 3-5   70
HAMILTON 5-10   59
20TH FOX 5-8   66-67
U.A. 3-5   71
LPs: 10/12–inch 33rpm
ALA (1975 "Live") 10-15   73

BEE GEES
Singles: 7–inch
ATCO 3-8   67-72
ATLANTIC 3-5
RSO 2-5   73-84
WARNER 2-4   87-89
Picture Sleeves
RSO 3-5   83
EPs: 7–inch 33/45rpm
ATCO (4523 Horizontal") 15-25   68
(Promotional issue only. Tracks are from
Horizontal, though shown only as "Atco
LP 33-233" on this label.)
ATCO (4535 Odessa") 10-20   69
(Promotional issue only.)
ATCO (37264 "Rare, Precious and
Beautiful") 8-15   69
(Promotional issue only.)
RSO (200 "Greatest Hits") 5-10   79
(Promotional issue only.)
LPs: 10/12–inch 33rpm
ATCO (Except TL-ST-142) 12-25   67-72
ATCO (TL-ST-142 "Odessa") 30-50   69
(Promotional issue only.)
RSO (Except 1) 5-10   73-84
RSO (1 "Words and Music") 40-60
(Promotional issue only.)
WARNER 5-10   87-89
Members: Barry Gibb; Maurice Gibb; Robin Gibb; Vince
Melouney; Colin Petersen.
Also see GIBB, Andy
Also see GIBB, Barry
Also see GIBB, Maurice
Also see GIBB, Robin
Also see SANG, Samantha

BEECHER, Johnny, and His Buckingham Road Quintet
Singles: 7–inch
CHARTER 4-8   63
OMEGA 5-8   58
WARNER 3-5   63
LPs: 10/12–inch 33rpm
CHARTER 15-20   63

BEEFEATERS
Singles: 7–inch
ELEKTRA (45013 "Please Let Me
Love You") 50-75   64
Members: David Crosby; Gene Clark; Jim McGuinn.
Also see BYRDS

BEEFHEART, Captain:
see CAPTAIN BEEFHEART

BEGINNING of the END
Singles: 7–inch
ALSTON 3-5   71-72
LPs: 10/12–inch 33rpm
ALSTON 10-12   71-76

BELAFONTE, Harry
Singles: 78rpm

JUBILEE 6-12	54
RCA 4-8	57
ROOST (501 "Lean on Me") 10-15	49

Singles: 7–inch

COLUMBIA 2-4	81
JUBILEE 10-20	54
RCA (0300 series) 5-8	57
RCA (0400 through 0600 series) 3-5	71-72
RCA (4000 and 5000 series) 5-10	52-55
RCA (6000 and 7000 series) 4-8	55-62
RCA (8000 and 9000 series) 3-6	62-67

Picture Sleeves

RCA (Except 9200 series) 6-12	55-59
RCA (9200 series) 3-6	69

EPs: 7–inch 33/45rpm

CAPITOL 15-20	55
JUBILEE 20-30	54
RCA (Except 24) 10-20	54-61
RCA (SPD-24 "Best of Belafonte") . . 30-60	56
(Ten-EP boxed set, with inserts.)	

LPs: 10/12–inch 33rpm

BOOK of the MONTH RECORDS . . . 15-20	83
CAMDEN 5-10	73-74
COLUMBIA 5-10	81
CORONET 8-15	
RCA (0000 through 0900 series) 5-10	73
RCA (1000 through 1900 series) . . . 15-25	54-59
(With "LOP," "LPM" or "LSP" prefix.)	
RCA (2400 series) 5-10	78-81
(With "AYL1 or "CPL1" prefix.)	
RCA (2000 and 3000 series,	
except 2449) 10-20	60-67
(With "LPM" or "LSP" prefix.)	
RCA (2449 "The Midnight Special") . . 20-40	62
(Bob Dylan plays harmonica on the title track—his	
first appearance on record.)	
RCA (4000 series) 10-15	68-71
RCA (6000 series) 15-25	59-72
Also see ANN-MARGRET	
Also see COMO, Perry / Ames Brothers / Harry Belafonte /	
Radio City Music Hall Orch.	
Also see DYLAN, Bob	

BELAFONTE, Harry, and Lena Horne
LPs: 10/12–inch 33rpm

RCA 15-25	59
Also see HORNE, Lena	

BELAFONTE, Harry, and Miriam Makeba
LPs: 10/12–inch 33rpm

RCA 10-15	65
Also see MAKEBA, Miriam	

BELAFONTE, Harry, and Nana Mouskouri
LPs: 10/12–inch 33rpm

RCA 10-15	66
Also see BELAFONTE, Harry	
Also see MOUSKOURI, Nana	

BELEW, Adrian
Singles: 7–inch

ATLANTIC 2-4	89-90

Picture Sleeves

ATLANTIC 2-4	89

LPs: 10/12–inch 33rpm

ATLANTIC 5-8	89-90
ISLAND 5-10	82-83

BELL, Archie
(Archie Bell and the Drells)
Singles: 12–inch 33/45rpm

PHILADELPHIA INT'L 4-6	79
PLAYHOUSE 4-6	84

Singles: 7–inch

ATLANTIC 3-6	68-72
BECKETT 2-4	81-84
EAST-WEST 2-4	
GLADES 3-5	73
OVIDE 4-8	67
PHILADELPHIA INT'L 2-5	76-79
TSOP 3-5	75-76

LPs: 10/12–inch 33rpm

ATLANTIC 10-15	68-69
BECKETT 5-10	81-84
PHILADELPHIA INT'L 8-10	75-79
TSOP 5-8	75
Members: Archie Bell; Huey Butler; James Wise; Joe Cross; Lee	
Bell; Willie Parnell.	
Also see PHILADELPHIA INTERNATIONAL ALL STARS	

BELL, Benny
(Featuring Paul Wynn)
Singles: 78rpm

COCKTAIL PARTY SONGS (202 "Shaving	
Cream") 15-25	46

Singles: 7–inch

ENTERPRISE 4-8	62
VANGUARD 3-5	75

LPs: 10/12–inch 33rpm

BELL ENTERPRISES 10-20	
VANGUARD 10-15	75
ZION 10-20	

BELL, Jerry
Singles: 7–inch

MCA 2-4	80-81

BELL, Madeline
Singles: 7–inch

ASCOT 5-8	64-65
BRUT 3-5	73
MOD 4-6	67
PHILIPS 4-6	67-68
PYE 3-5	76

LPs: 10/12–inch 33rpm

PHILIPS 15-20	68
PYE 8-10	76
Also see BLUE MINK	
Also see MANN, Manfred	
Also see WATERS, Roger	

BELL, Maggie
Singles: 7–inch
ATLANTIC 3-5   73-74
SWAN SONG 3-5   76
LPs: 10/12–inch 33rpm
ATLANTIC 10-12   74
SWAN SONG 8-10   75

BELL, Maggie, and Bobby Whitlock
Singles: 7–inch
SWAN SONG 2-4   83-84
   Also see BELL, Maggie
   Also see WHITLOCK, Bobby

BELL, Randy
Singles: 7–inch
EPIC 2-4   84

BELL, Rueben
Singles: 7–inch
ALARM 2-5   75-77
DELUXE 3-5   72-73
MURCO (1046 "You're Gonna
   Miss Me") 25-50   68
SILVER FOX 4-6   69

BELL, Trudy
Singles: 7–inch
PHILIPS 5-10   62-63

BELL, Vincent
(Vinnie Bell and the Bell Men)
Singles: 7–inch
DECCA 4-6   67-70
INDEPENDENT (102 "Quicksand") .. 20-30   60
MUSICOR 4-6   64
VERVE 4-8   63
LPs: 10/12–inch 33rpm
DECCA 8-15   67-70
INDEPENDENT 20-30   60
MUSICOR 10-15   64
VERVE 10-15   64

BELL, William
Singles: 7–inch
KAT FAMILY 2-4   83-84
MERCURY 2-5   76-77
STAX (Except 100 series) 3-6   67-74
STAX (100 series) 5-10   61-67
WILBE 2-4   86
LPs: 10/12–inch 33rpm
KAT FAMILY 5-10   83-84
MERCURY 8-10   77
STAX 10-12   67-74

BELL, William, and Janice Bullock
Singles: 7–inch
WILBE 2-4   86
   Also see BULLOCK, Janice

BELL, William, and Judy Clay
Singles: 7–inch
STAX 4-6   68
   Also see CLAY, Judy

BELL, William, and Mavis Staples
Singles: 7–inch
STAX 4-6   69
   Also see STAPLES, Mavis

BELL, William, and Carla Thomas
Singles: 7–inch
STAX 4-6   69-70
   Also see BELL, William
   Also see THOMAS, Carla

BELL & JAMES
Singles: 12–inch 33/45rpm
A&M 4-6   79
LORIMAR 4-6   80
Singles: 7–inch
A&M 2-4   78-84
LORIMAR 2-4   80
Picture Sleeves
A&M 3-5   78-81
LPs: 10/12–inch 33rpm
A&M 5-10   79-84
   Members: Leroy Bell; Casey James.

BELL NOTES
Singles: 7–inch
AUTOGRAPH 10-20   60
ERIC 3-5   73
MADISON 5-10   60
TIME (Blue label) 15-20   59
TIME (Red label) 5-10   59-60
EPs: 7–inch 33/45rpm
TIME (100 "I've Had It") 60-100   59
   Members: Carl Bonura; Ray Ceroni; Lenny Giambalvo; Pete
   Kane; John Casey.

BELL SISTERS
(Bell Sisters and Phil Harris)
Singles: 78rpm
BERMUDA 4-6
RCA 3-5   50-53
Singles: 7–inch
BERMUDA 5-10
RCA 5-10   50-53
   Members: Kay Bell; Cynthia Bell.
   Also see HARRIS, Phil
   Also see RENE, Henri, and His Orchestra

BELLAMY, David
Singles: 7–inch
WARNER 3-5   75
   Also see BELLAMY BROTHERS

BELLAMY BROTHERS
(Bellamy Brothers and the Forester Sisters)
Singles: 7–inch
CURB 2-4   84
ELEKTRA 2-4   83
MCA/CURB 2-4   85-90
WARNER 2-4   76-83
LPs: 10/12–inch 33rpm
ELEKTRA 5-10   83
MCA/CURB 5-10   84-90
WARNER 8-10   76-83

Members: David Bellamy; Howard Bellamy.
Also see BELLAMY, David

BELLE, Regina
Singles: 7–inch
COLUMBIA 2-4   87-88
ELEKTRA 2-4   87-88
Picture Sleeves
ELEKTRA 2-4   88
LPs: 10/12–inch 33rpm
COLUMBIA 5-10   87-88
Also see BRYSON, Peabo

BELLE EPOQUE
Singles: 7–inch
BIG TREE 2-4   78

BELLE STARS
Singles: 12–inch 33/45rpm
WARNER 4-6   83-84
Singles: 7–inch
WARNER 2-4   83-84
LPs: 10/12–inch 33rpm
WARNER 5-10   83-84

BELLS
Singles: 7–inch
MGM 3-5   73
POLYDOR 3-5   70-73
LPs: 10/12–inch 33rpm
POLYDOR 10-15   71-72
Members: Jacki Ralph; Cliff Edwards; Frank Mills.
Also see MILLS, Frank

BELLUS, Tony
Singles: 7–inch
ABC 2-4   73
COLLECTABLES 2-4   81
KING 4-8   65
NRC 8-15   59-60
Picture Sleeves
NRC (035 "Hey Little Darlin") 25-40   59
NRC (051 "The Echo of an Old Song") 20-30   60
LPs: 10/12–inch 33rpm
NRC (8 "Robbin' the Cradle with
Tony Bellus") 50-100   60
SHI-FI (11 "Gems of Tony Bellus") ... 20-40

BELLY, P.J.
(Rob Gamble)
Singles: 7–inch
NOR VA JAK 2-4   87

BELMONTS
(Belmonts with Dion)
Singles: 7–inch
COLLECTABLES 2-4   81
CRYSTAL BALL 4-6   79
DOT 10-15   68
LAURIE 3-5   75
MOHAWK (106 "Teenage
Clementine") 25-50   57
ROULETTE 2-4
SABINA (Except 521) 10-20   61-64

SABINA (521 "Nothing in Return") ... 20-30   64
SABRINA 15-25   61
(Sabrina changed its name to Sabina in 1961.)
STRAWBERRY 3-5   76
SURPRISE (1000 "Tell Me Why") ... 40-60   61
U.A. (800 and 900 series) 10-15   65
U.A. (50000 series) 15-20   66
LPs: 10/12–inch 33rpm
BUDDAH (5123 "Cigars,
Acappella, Candy") 25-50   72
DOT (25949 "Summer Love") 25-30   69
SABINA (5001 "Carnival of Hits") ... 75-125   62
STRAWBERRY 10-15   78
Members: Carlo Mastrangelo; Fred Milano; Angelo D'Aleo;
Frank Lyndon.
Also see DION and the Belmonts
Also see SOUL, Jimmy / Belmonts

BELMONTS, Freddy Cannon and Bo Diddley
Singles: 12–inch 33/45rpm
ROCK and ROLL TRAVELLING SHOW   4-6
Also see BELMONTS
Also see CANNON, Freddy
Also see DIDDLEY, Bo

BELOUIS SOME
Singles: 12–inch 33/45rpm
CAPITOL 4-6   85
Singles: 7–inch
CAPITOL 2-4   85
LPs: 10/12–inch 33rpm
CAPITOL 5-10   85

BELOYD
Singles: 7–inch
20TH FOX 2-4   77

BELTONES
Singles: 78rpm
HULL 20-30   57
Singles: 7–inch
COLLECTABLES 2-4   81
HULL (721 "I Talk to My Echo") 75-100   57
(Black label)
HULL (721 "I Talk to My Echo") 25-50   58
(Red label)
ROULETTE 3-5   73

BELUSHI, John
Singles: 7–inch
MCA 2-4   78
Also see BLUES BROTHERS
Also see NATIONAL LAMPOON

BELVIN, Jesse
(Jesse Belvin and the Sharptones)
Singles: 78rpm
CASH 15-25   56
HOLLYWOOD 20-40   53-56
MODERN 10-20   56-57
SPECIALTY (435 "Confusin' Blues") . 25-35   52
SPECIALTY (500 series) 15-25   55
Singles: 7–inch
ALADDIN (3431 "Let Me Dream") ... 25-30   58

CASH (1056 "Beware") 60-100   56
(Reissued in 1959 as by the Capris.)
CLASS 8-12   60
COLLECTABLES 2-4   81
CUSTOM 4-8
ERIC 2-4   73
HOLLYWOOD (412 "Love Comes
   Tumbling Down" 150-250   53
HOLLYWOOD (1059 "Betty
   My Darling" 100-200   56
IMPACT 4-8   62
JAMIE 8-15   59
KENT 8-15   59
KNIGHT 10-15   59
MODERN 12-25   56-57
RCA (7387 "Funny") 15-25   58
RCA (47-7469 "Guess Who") 15-25   59
   (Monaural.)
RCA (61-7469 "Guess Who") 25-45   59
   (Stereo.)
RCA (7543 "Here's a Heart") .. 15-25   59
RCA (7596 "Give Me Love") 15-25   59
RCA (7675 "Deep in My Heart") . 15-25   60
SPECIALTY (435 "Confusin' Blues") 75-100   52
SPECIALTY (550 "Gone") 25-35   55
TENDER (518 "Beware") 25-30   59
EPs: 7-inch 33/45rpm
RCA (2089 "Just Jesse Belvin") ... 25-40   59
RCA (2105 "Mr. Easy") 25-40   60
LPs: 10/12-inch 33rpm
CAMDEN 15-20   66
CORONET 8-12
CROWN 20-25   60-63
RCA (0900 series) 8-10   75
RCA (LPM-2089 "Just Jesse Belvin") . 30-40   59
   (Monaural.)
RCA (LSP-2089 "Just Jesse Belvin") . 30-40   59
   (Stereo.)
RCA (LPM-2105 "Mr. Easy") 30-40   60
   (Monaural.)

RCA (LSP-2105 "Mr. Easy") 30-40   60
   (Stereo.)
UNITED 10-15
   Also see BENTON, Brook / Jesse Belvin
   Also see CHARGERS
   Also see CLIQUES
   Also see JESSE & MARVIN

BELVIN, Jesse, and the Five Keys / Feathers
Singles: 7-inch
CANDLELITE (427 "Love Song") 10-15
   Also see FIVE KEYS

BELVIN, Jesse, with Three Dots and a Dash
Singles: 78rpm
IMPERIAL 25-50   51
Singles: 7-inch
IMPERIAL (5164 "I'll Never Love
   Again") 150-250   51
   Also see BELVIN, Jesse

BENATAR, Pat
Singles: 12-inch 33/45rpm
CHRYSALIS 4-8   79-86
Singles: 7-inch
CHRYSALIS 2-5   79-91
SUNSHINE 5-10   78
TRACE (5293 "Day Gig") 20-30   74
Picture Sleeves
CHRYSALIS 2-5   79-89
LPs: 10/12-inch 33rpm
CHRYSALIS 5-10   79-91
MFSL (057 "In the Heat of the Night") 20-40   81

BENNETT, Boyd
(Boyd Bennett and the Rockets; Boyd Bennett and
the Southlanders)
Singles: 78rpm
KING 5-10   54-57
Singles: 7-inch
KING (1400 series) 20-30   54-55
   (Maroon labels.)
KING (1400 series) 10-20   56
   (Blue labels.)
KING (4000 series) 10-15   56-58
KING (5000 series) 5-10   58-63
MERCURY 5-10   59-61
EPs: 7-inch 33/45rpm
KING (377 "Boyd Bennett") 100-200   56
KING (383 "Rock and Roll with Boyd
   Bennett and His Rockets") 100-200   56
LPs: 10/12-inch 33rpm
KING (594 "Boyd Bennett") 800-1200   58

BENNETT, Joe, and the Sparkletones
Singles: 78rpm
ABC-PAR 5-10   57-58
Singles: 7-inch
ABC 2-4   73
ABC-PAR 15-20   57-58
PARIS 10-15   59-60
LPs: 10/12-inch 33rpm
MCA 5-10   83

BENNETT, Tony
Singles: 78rpm

COLUMBIA 4-8	50-57	

Singles: 7–inch

COLUMBIA (1600 series) 4-8		
(Colored vinyl. Promotional issue only.)		
COLUMBIA (06000 series) 2-4	86	
COLUMBIA (38000 through		
41000 series) 5-10	50-61	
COLUMBIA (42000 through		
45000 series) 3-8	61-70	
IMPROV 3-4	75-77	
MGM 3-5	73	
VERVE 3-5	72-73	

Picture Sleeves

COLUMBIA (1600 series) 5-10		
(Promotional issue only.)		
COLUMBIA (40000 and 41000 series) . 5-10	53-61	
COLUMBIA (42000 through 44000		
series) 3-6	61-67	
IMPROV 3-4	75	

EPs: 7–inch 33/45rpm

COLUMBIA 5-15	55-59	

LPs: 10/12–inch 33rpm

COLUMBIA (Except 600 through		
1200 series) 6-12	59-86	
COLUMBIA (600 through 1200 series) 10-25	55-59	
FANTASY 8-12		
HARMONY 5-10	69-73	
IMPROV 5-10	75-78	
MGM 6-10	73	
MGM/VERVE 6-10	72	
MFSL 20-30	84	
Also see GETZ, Stan		

BENNETT, Tony, and Count Basie
EPs: 7–inch 33/45rpm

COLUMBIA 6-10	59	

LPs: 10/12–inch 33rpm

COLUMBIA 10-20	59	
Also see BASIE, Count		

BENNETT, Tony / Al Tornello
LPs: 10/12–inch 33rpm

GUEST STAR 5-10	64	
Also see BENNETT, Tony		

BENNO, Marc
Singles: 7–inch

A&M 2-5	71-79	

LPs: 10/12–inch 33rpm

A&M 8-12	70-79	
MCA 5-10		
Also see ASYLUM CHOIR		

BENSON, George
Singles: 78rpm

GROOVE 5-10	54	

Singles: 12–inch 33/45rpm

WARNER 4-6	80-83	

Singles: 7–inch

A&M 3-6	68-70	

ARISTA 3-5	77	
CTI 3-5	75-78	
COLUMBIA 4-8	66-67	
GROOVE (0024 "It Should Have		
Been Me #2") 20-40	54	
PRESTIGE 4-8	64	
WARNER 2-4	76-89	

Picture Sleeves

ARISTA 3-5	77	
WARNER 2-4	78-86	

LPs: 10/12–inch 33rpm

A&M 8-12	68-76	
CTI 8-10	71-78	
COLUMBIA 8-10	66-67	
(With "CL" or "CS" prefix.)		
COLUMBIA 5-10	76	
(With "CG" or "PC" prefix.)		
MFSL (011 "Breezin") 25-50	78	
POLYDOR 5-10	76	
VERVE 10-12	69	
WARNER 5-10	75-89	
Also see FRANKLIN, Aretha, and George Benson		
Also see McDUFF, Brother Jack		

BENT FABRIC: see FABRIC, Bent

BENTLEY, Erlene
Singles: 12–inch 33/45rpm

MEGATONE 4-6	83	
TVI 4-6	84	

Singles: 7–inch

MEGATONE 2-4	83	

BENTON, Brook
Singles: 78rpm

EPIC 5-10	56	
OKEH 5-10	55	

Singles: 7–inch

ALL PLATINUM 2-5	76	
BRUT 3-5	73	
COTILLION 3-6	68-72	
EPIC 10-20	56	
MGM 3-5	72	
MERCURY (10000 series) 5-10	59-65	
(Stereo.)		
MERCURY (70000 series) 10-20	60-61	
(Monaural.)		
MUSICOR 2-5	77	
OKEH 10-20	55	
OLDE WORLD 2-4	77-78	
RCA 4-8	65-67	
REPRISE 4-6	67-68	
STAX 3-5	74	
VIK 8-15	57-58	

Picture Sleeves

MERCURY 5-10	60-64	
RCA 4-8	65	

EPs: 7–inch 33/45rpm

MERCURY 10-20	59-61	

LPs: 10/12–inch 33rpm

ALL PLATINUM 8-10	76	

BENTON, Brook / Jesse Belvin
LPs: 10/12–inch 33rpm

BENTON, Brook, and Damita Jo
Singles: 7–inch

BENTON, Brook / Chuck Jackson / Jimmy Soul
LPs: 10/12–inch 33rpm

BENTON, Brook / Jackie Jocko
LPs: 10/12–inch 33rpm

BENTON, Brook, and Dinah Washington
Singles: 7–inch

Picture Sleeves

EPs: 7–inch 33/45rpm

LPs: 10/12–inch 33rpm

BERG, Gertrude
LPs: 10/12–inch 33rpm

BERGEN, Polly
Singles: 78rpm

Singles: 7–inch

EPs: 7–inch 33/45rpm

LPs: 10/12–inch 33rpm

BERGEN, Polly / Fran Warren / Lynn Roberts
LPs: 10/12–inch 33rpm

BERLIN
Singles: 12–inch 33/45rpm

Singles: 7–inch

Picture Sleeves

LPs: 10/12–inch 33rpm

BERLIN PHILHARMONIC
Singles: 7–inch

BERMAN, Shelley
LPs: 10/12–inch 33rpm

METRO	8-12	65
VERVE (15000 series)	10-20	59-64

BERMUDAS
Singles: 7–inch

ERA	5-10	64

Member: Rickie Page.

BERNARD, Chuck
Singles: 7–inch

LAWRENCE	4-6	67
SATELLITE	5-8	65-66
ZODIAC	3-5	70-71

BERNARD, Rod
(Rod Bernard and the Twisters)
Singles: 7–inch

ABC	2-4	74
ARBEE	4-8	65-66
ARGO	8-10	59
COLLECTABLES	2-4	81
COPYRIGHT	4-6	68
CRAZY CAJUN	2-4	78
HALL	5-10	61-64
HALLWAY	5-10	61-64
JIN (105 "This Should Go on Forever")	25-40	59
JIN (200 series)	3-5	74-76
MERCURY	5-10	59-61
TEARDROP	5-10	64-65

LPs: 10/12–inch 33rpm

JIN (4007 "Rod Bernard")	50-75	

Also see SHONDELLS / Rod Bernard / Warren Storm / Skip Stewart

BERNSTEIN, Elmer, and His Orchestra
Singles: 78rpm

DECCA	3-6	56

Singles: 7–inch

AVA	3-8	62-65
CAPITOL	4-8	59-60
CHOREO	3-5	62
COLUMBIA	3-5	65
DECCA	4-8	56
DOT	3-5	66
U.A.	3-5	65-68

EPs: 7–inch 33/45rpm

CAPITOL	3-8	59

LPs: 10/12–inch 33rpm

CAPITOL	4-8	59-60
COLUMBIA	5-15	60
DOT 10-15	59	
HAMILTON	4-8	59

Also see CARR, Vikki

Since publication of *The Official Price Guide to Movie/TV Soundtracks and Original Cast Albums*, with over 8,000 listings, this guide has dropped many soundtracks, including some by this artist.

BERNSTEIN, Leonard, and His Orchestra
LPs: 10/12–inch 33rpm

CAMDEN	8-15	55-56

COLUMBIA (919 "What Is Jazz")	20-40	56

Since publication of *The Official Price Guide to Movie/TV Soundtracks and Original Cast Albums*, with over 8,000 listings, this guide has dropped many soundtracks, including some by this artist.

COLUMBIA (31000 series)	5-10	71

BERNSTEIN, Leonard, and Dave Brubeck
LPs: 10/12–inch 33rpm

COLUMBIA	12-25	60

Also see BERNSTEIN, Leonard, and His Orchestra
Also see BRUBECK, Dave

BERRY, Chuck
Singles: 78rpm

CHESS (1600 series)	30-60	55-58
CHESS (1700 through 1729)	50-100	58-59
CHESS (1737 "My Childhood Sweetheart")	75-125	59
CHESS (1747 "Too Pooped to Pop")	100-200	60

Singles: 7–inch

ATCO	2-4	79
CHESS (1604 through 1615)	15-25	55-56
CHESS (1626 through 1645)	10-20	56
CHESS (1653 through 1729)	10-15	57-59
CHESS (1737 through 1963)	5-10	59-69
CHESS (2000 and 9000 series)	3-5	70-73
ERIC	2-4	73
MERCURY	4-8	66-72
PHILO	8-15	66

("Hip Pocket" Record.)

Picture Sleeves

CHESS	10-20	64

EPs: 7–inch 33/45rpm

CHESS (5118 "After School Session")	40-60	57
CHESS (5118 "Head Over Heels")	75-100	57
CHESS (5119 "Rock and Roll Music")	40-60	58
CHESS (5121 "Sweet Little 16")	40-60	58
CHESS (5124 "Pickin' Berries")	40-60	58
CHESS (5126 "Sweet Little Rock and Roller")	40-60	58

LPs: 10/12–inch 33rpm

ACCORD	5-10	82
ATCO	5-10	79
BROOKVILLE	12-15	73
CHESS (Except 1400 and 9000 series)	10-20	66-76
CHESS (1426 "After School Session")	50-75	57
CHESS (1432 "One Dozen Berrys")	50-75	58
CHESS (1435 "Chuck Berry's on Top")	50-75	59
CHESS (1448 "Rockin' at the Hops")	50-75	59
CHESS (1456 "Chuck Berry's New Jukebox Hits")	25-40	61
CHESS (1465 "More Chuck Berry")	25-40	63
CHESS (1466 "Chuck Berry Twist")	20-25	62
CHESS (1480 "Chuck Berry on Stage")	20-25	63
CHESS (1485 "Chuck Berry's Greatest Hits")	25-30	64
CHESS (1488 "St. Louis to Liverpool")	20-25	64

CHESS (1495 "Chuck Berry
  in London") 25-30   65
CHESS (1498 "Fresh Berrys") 20-25   65
CHESS (9000 series) 5-10   85
CHESS/MCA 5-8   89
EVEREST 8-10   76
GUSTO 5-10   78
MCA 8-12   86-87
MAGNUM 10-12   69
MERCURY 15-25   67-72
PICKWICK 8-10   72
TRIP 8-10   78
UPFRONT 5-10   79
  Also see DIDDLEY, Bo, and Chuck Berry
  Also see MILLER, Steve

BERRY, Chuck, and Howlin' Wolf
LPs: 10/12–inch 33rpm

CHESS 15-20   69
  Also see BERRY, Chuck
  Also see HOWLIN' WOLF

BERRY, Jan
(Jan; Jan Barry)
Singles: 7–inch

A&M 5-10   77-78
LIBERTY (55845 "The Universal
  Coward") 10-15   66
ODE '70 (Except 66023 and 66034) . 15-20   72-77
ODE '70 (66023 "Mother Earth") 25-40   72
  (With insert note from Jan. Promotional issue only.)
ODE '70 (66023 "Mother Earth") 20-30   72
  (Without insert note from Jan.)
ODE '70 (66034 "Don't You Just
  Know It") 30-40   73
  (With Brian Wilson.)
RIPPLE (6101 "Tomorrow's
  Teardrops") 30-45   61
Picture Sleeves
LIBERTY (55845 "The Universal
  Coward") 100-125   66
  Also see JAN & ARNIE
  Also see JAN & DEAN
  Also see WILSON, Brian

BERTEI, Adele
Singles: 12–inch 33/45rpm

GEFFEN 4-6   83
Singles: 7–inch
GEFFEN 2-4   83

BEST, Peter
Singles: 7–inch

CAMEO (391 "Boys") 20-35   66
  (Shown as by "Peter Best, formerly of the Beatles.")
CAPITOL (2092 "Carousel of Love") . 20-35   67
HAPPENING (405 "Don't Play with
  Me Little Girl") 35-50   66
MR. MAESTRO (711 "I Can't Do
  Without You Now") 40-50   65
  (Shown as by "Best of the Beatles, Peter Best.")

MR. MAESTRO (712 "Casting
  My Spell") 40-50   65
  (Shown as by "Best of the Beatles, Peter Best.")
ORIGINAL BEATLES DRUMMER
  (800 "I'll Try Anyway") 40-50   64
Picture Sleeves
CAMEO (391 "Boys") 50-75   66
LPs: 10/12–inch 33rpm
BEST FAN CLUB 25-30   66
PHOENIX 10 10-15   82
SAVAGE (71 "Best of the Beatles") 100-125   65
  Also see BEATLES

BETHEA, Harmon
(Bethea; Bethea with the Maskman and the Agents)
Singles: 7–inch

DYNAMO 4-6   69-71
MUSICOR 3-5   70-74

BETTERS, Harold
Singles: 7–inch

GATEWAY 4-6   63-65
REPRISE 4-6   66-67
LPs: 10/12–inch 33rpm
GATEWAY 12-15   64-66
REPRISE 12-15   65-67

BETTS, Dickey: see BETTS, Richard

BETTS, Richard
(Dickey Betts and Great Southern; Dickey Betts Band)
Singles: 7–inch

ARISTA 2-5   77-78
CAPRICORN 3-5   74-76
LPs: 10/12–inch 33rpm
ARISTA 5-10   77-78
CAPRICORN 8-10   74
EPIC 5-8   88
  Also see ALLMAN BROTHERS BAND

BEVEL, Charles "Mississippi"
Singles: 7–inch

A&M 3-5   73-74
LPs: 10/12–inch 33rpm
A&M 8-10   73-74

BEVERLY & DUANE
Singles: 7–inch

ARIOLA AMERICA 2-5   78-79
  Members: Beverly Wheeler; Duane Williams.

BEVERLY SISTERS
Singles: 7–inch

MERCURY 5-10   60
LPs: 10/12–inch 33rpm
CAPITOL 10-20   61

BEY, Salome, and Brotherhood
Singles: 7–inch

BUDDAH 3-5   76

BIBLE
LPs: 10/12–inch 33rpm
CHRYSALIS 5-8   88

BICKERSONS:
see AMECHE, Don, and Frances Langford

BIDDU
(Biddu and Orchestra)
Singles: 7–inch
COLOSSUS . . . . 3-5　　70
EPIC . . . . 2-5　　75-77
LPs: 10/12–inch 33rpm
EPIC . . . . 5-10　　76-77

BIG AUDIO DYNAMITE
Singles: 12–inch 33/45rpm
COLUMBIA (1739 "James Brown") . . . 6-10　　89
(Promotional issue only.)
COLUMBIA (1899 "Contact") . . . . 5-8　　89
(Promotional issue only.)
COLUMBIA (2302 "Medicine Show") . . . 5-8　　86
(Promotional issue only.)
COLUMBIA (2520 "C'mon Every
　Beatbox") . . . . 5-8　　86
(Promotional issue only.)
COLUMBIA (2697 "Hollywood
　Boulevard") . . . . 5-8　　86
(Promotional issue only.)
COLUMBIA (8133 "Other 99") . . . . 5-8　　88
(Promotional issue only.)
COLUMBIA (5000 through 8000 series) . 4-6　　85-90
Singles: 7–inch
COLUMBIA (5000 series, except 5841) . 3-5　　85
COLUMBIA (5841 "Medicine Show") . . . 4-6　　85
(White label. Promotional issue only.)
COLUMBIA (6000 series, except 6053) . 3-5　　86
COLUMBIA (6053 "E=MC^2 ") . . . . 4-6　　85
(White label. Promotional issue only.)
COLUMBIA (8000 series) . . . . 3-5　　88
Picture Sleeves
COLUMBIA (5841 "Medicine Show") . . . 5-8　　85
(Promotional issue only.)
COLUMBIA (6053 "E=MC^2 ") . . . . 5-8　　85
(Promotional issue only.)
COLUMBIA (8094 "Other 99") . . . . 4-6　　88
LPs: 10/12–inch 33rpm
COLUMBIA . . . . 5-10　　85-89
Members: Mick Jones; Don Letts; Leo Williams; Greg Roberts;
Dan Donovan; Flea.
Also see BIG AUDIO DYNAMITE II
Also see CLASH

BIG AUDIO DYNAMITE II
Singles: 12–inch 33/45rpm
COLUMBIA (4044 "Rush Dance") . . . . . 5-8　　91
COLUMBIA (657640 "Rush") . . . . 5-10　　91
(Promotional issue only.)
LPs: 10/12–inch 33rpm
COLUMBIA . . . . 8-10　　91
Members: Mick Jones; Gary Stonadge; Chris Kavanagh; Nick
Hawkins.
Also see BIG AUDIO DYNAMITE

BIG BOPPER
(Jape Richardson; Jiles Perry Richardson Jr.)
Singles: 7–inch
D (1008 "Chantilly Lace") . . . . 100-150　　58
MERCURY (30072 "Chantilly Lace") . 20-30　　61
(Compact 33 single.)
MERCURY (70000 series) . . . . 8-15　　58-59
LPs: 10/12–inch 33rpm
MERCURY (20402 "Chantilly
　Lace") . . . . 250-300　　59
(Black label.)
MERCURY (20402 "Chantilly
　Lace") . . . . 250-300　　59
(Pink label. Promotional issue only.)
MERCURY (20402 "Chantilly Lace") 75-100　　64
(Red label.)
MERCURY (20402 "Chantilly Lace") 　10-15　　81
(Chicago "skyline" label.)
PICKWICK . . . . 20-30　　73
Also see DEL-VIKINGS / Diamonds / Big Bopper / Gaylords
Also see RICHARDSON, Jape

BIG BROTHER and the Holding Company
(Big Brother)
Singles: 7–inch
COLUMBIA . . . . 5-10　　68-71
MAINSTREAM . . . . 5-10　　67-68
Picture Sleeves
COLUMBIA . . . . 5-10　　68
LPs: 10/12–inch 33rpm
COLUMBIA . . . . 15-25　　68-71
MADE to LAST . . . . 5-10　　84
MAINSTREAM (6099 "Big Brother
　and the Holding Company") . . . . . . 20-35　　67
Members: Janis Joplin; David Getz; Sam Andrew; Peter Albin;
Jim Gurley; David Schallock; Nick Gravenites; Kathi McDonald;
Sam Andres.
Also see JOPLIN, Janis
Also see McDONALD, Kathi

BIG COUNTRY
Singles: 12–inch 33/45rpm
MERCURY . . . . 4-6　　83-86
Singles: 7–inch
MERCURY . . . . 2-4　　83-86
REPRISE . . . . 2-4　　88
Picture Sleeves
MERCURY . . . . 2-4　　83-84
LPs: 10/12–inch 33rpm
MERCURY . . . . 5-10　　83-86
REPRISE . . . . 5-8　　88

BIG MAYBELLE
(Mable Smith)
Singles: 78rpm
KING . . . . 5-10　　48-49
OKEH . . . . 5-15　　53-56
SAVOY . . . . 5-10　　56-58
Singles: 7–inch
BRUNSWICK . . . . 4-8　　63
CHESS . . . . 4-8　　66
OKEH . . . . 15-30　　53-56

PARAMOUNT 3-5   73
PORT 4-8   65
ROJAC 4-8   64-69
SAVOY 5-15   56-61
EPs: 7–inch 33/45rpm
EPIC (7071 "Big Maybelle
  Sings the Blues") 25-50   57
LPs: 10/12–inch 33rpm
BRUNSWICK 15-25   62-68
ENCORE 10-15   67
EPIC 8-10   83
PARAMOUNT 8-10   73
ROJAC 10-12   67-69
SAVOY (14005 "Big Maybelle
  Sings") 35-45   57
SAVOY (14011 "Blues, Candy
  and Big Maybelle") 35-45   57
SCEPTER 12-20   64
UPFRONT 8-10   73

BIG PIG
Singles: 7–inch
A&M 2-4   88
Picture Sleeves
A&M 2-4   88

BIG RIC
Singles: 7–inch
ROCK 'N' ROLL 2-4   83
SCOTTI BROTHERS 2-4   83
LPs: 10/12–inch 33rpm
SCOTTI BROTHERS 5-10   83-84

BIG SAMBO
(Big Sambo and the House Wreckers; Big Sam and
the House Wreckers)
Singles: 7–inch
ERIC 4-8   62

BIG THREE
Singles: 7–inch
FM 5-10   63
ROULETTE 4-8   66
TOLLIE 4-8   64
LPs: 10/12–inch 33rpm
ACCORD 5-10   82
FM 15-25   63-64
ROULETTE 15-20   68
Members: Cass Elliott; Tim Rose; Denny Dougherty.
Also see ELLIOTT, Cass
Also see MAMAS and the Papas

BILK, Mr. Acker
(With the Leon Young String Chorale)
Singles: 7–inch
ATCO 4-6   61-66
REPRISE 3-5   62
LPs: 10/12–inch 33rpm
ASCOT 8-15   62
ATCO 10-20   62-66

BILK, Mr. Acker, and Bent Fabric
LPs: 10/12–inch 33rpm
ATCO 8-12   65
Also see BILK, Mr. Acker
Also see FABRIC, Bent

BILL & TAFFY
Singles: 7–inch
RCA 3-6   74
LPs: 10/12–inch 33rpm
RCA 10-12   73-74
Members: Bill Danoff; Taffy Danoff.
Also see FAT CITY
Also see STARLAND VOCAL BAND

BILL BLACK'S COMBO: see BLACK, Bill

BILLION DOLLAR BABIES
Singles: 7–inch
POLYDOR (Except 14406) 4-6   77
POLYDOR (14406 "Too Young") 8-12   77
  (Promotional issue only.)
LPs: 10/12–inch 33rpm
POLYDOR (Except 022) 12-15   77
POLYDOR (022 "Battle Axe") 20-25   77
  (Promotional issue only.)
Also see COOPER, Alice

BILLY ALWAYS: see ALWAYS, Billy

BILLY and Baby Gap
Singles: 7–inch
TOTAL EXPERIENCE 2-4   85
Members: Billy Young; Anthony Walker
Also see GAP BAND

BILLY & LILLIE
(Billy & Lillie and the Thunderbirds)
Singles: 78rpm
SWAN 5-10   57
Singles: 7–inch
ABC 3-5   73
ABC-PAR (10421 "Love
  Me Sincerely") 15-25   63
CAMEO 4-8   66
COLLECTABLES 2-4   81
SWAN 6-12   57-61
Members: Billy Ford; Lillie Bryant.
Also see BRYANT, Lillie

BILLY & SUE
Singles: 7–inch
CREW 3-5   70
Members: William Oliver Swofford; Lesley Gore.
Also see GORE, Lesley
Also see OLIVER

BILLY and the Beaters
Singles: 7–inch
ALFA 2-4   81
LPs: 10/12–inch 33rpm
ALFA 5-10   81
Member: Billy Vera.
Also see VERA, Bill

BILLY JOE and the Checkmates
(Billy Joe Hunter)
Singles: 7-inch
DORE 4-8   61-66

BILLY SATELLITE
Singles: 7-inch
CAPITOL 2-4   84
Picture Sleeves
CAPITOL 2-4   84
LPs: 10/12-inch 33rpm
CAPITOL 5-10   84

BIMBO JET
Singles: 7-inch
SCEPTER 3-5   75

BIONIC BOOGIE
Singles: 12-inch 33/45rpm
RP 4-8
Singles: 7-inch
POLYDOR 2-4   77-78
LPs: 10/12-inch 33rpm
POLYDOR 5-10   78
Member: Gregg Diamond.

BIRD, J.
Singles: 12-inch 33/45rpm
WARRIOR 4-6   84

BIRDLEGS & PAULINE and Their Versatility Birds
Singles: 7-inch
CUCA (1125 "Spring") 20-35 63
(Shown as by Birdlegs and His Versatility Birds.)
VEE JAY (510 "Spring") 5-10   63
LPs: 10/12-inch 33rpm
CUCA (4000 "Birdlegs & Pauline") .. 50-100 63
Members: Sidney Banks; Pauline Banks.

BIRDSONG, Edwin
Singles: 12-inch 33/45rpm
PHILADELPHIA INT'L 4-6   78-79
SALSOUL 4-6   81-84

Singles: 7-inch
PHILADELPHIA INT'L 2-4   78
POLYDOR 3-5   71-72
SALSOUL 2-4   81-84
LPs: 10/12-inch 33rpm
PHILADELPHIA INT'L 5-10   78
POLYDOR 8-10   71-73

BIRKIN, Jane, and Serge Gainsbourg
Singles: 7-inch
FONTANA 3-6   69
LPs: 10/12-inch 33rpm
FONTANA 6-12   70

BISHOP, Elvin
(Elvin Bishop Group; Elvin Bishop and Crabshaw Rising)
Singles: 7-inch
CAPRICORN 3-5   74-79
EPIC 3-5   72-75
FILLMORE 3-5   70-71
WARNER 3-5   72
LPs: 10/12-inch 33rpm
ALLIGATOR 5-8   91
CAPRICORN 8-12   74-78
EPIC 8-12   72-75
FILLMORE 10-15 69-72
Also see BUTTERFIELD, Paul
Also see GRATEFUL DEAD / Elvin Bishop Group

BISHOP, Stephen
Singles: 7-inch
ABC 3-5   76-78
WARNER 2-4   80-83
Picture Sleeves
ABC (12435 "Animal House") 4-8   78
LPs: 10/12-inch 33rpm
ABC 6-12   76-78
MCA 5-10   80
WARNER 5-10   80
Also see GRUSIN, Dave
Also see NEWMAN, Randy

BISHOP, Stephen, and Yvonne Elliman
Singles: 7-inch
WARNER 2-4   80
Also see BISHOP, Stephen
Also see ELLIMAN, Yvonne

BITS & PIECES
Singles: 7-inch
MANGO 2-4   81
NASCO 3-5   73-74
PARAMOUNT 3-5   74

BIZ MARKIE
Singles: 7-inch
COLD CHILL 2-4   88-90
PRISM 2-4   86
Picture Sleeves
COLD CHILL 2-4   90
LPs: 10/12-inch 33rpm
COLD CHILL 5-8   88-90

BLACK, Bill
(Bill Black's Combo)
Singles: 7–inch
COLUMBIA	3-5	70
ECHO	3-5	72
GUSTO	2-4	83
HI (Except 2000 series)	3-6	67-78
HI (2000 series)	5-10	59-66
LONDON	2-4	84
MEGA	3-5	71-74
MOTOWN	2-4	83

Picture Sleeves
HI	5-10	60-62

EPs: 7–inch 33/45rpm
MEGA (192 "Jukebox Favorites")	5-10	72
(Jukebox issue.)		

LPs: 10/12–inch 33rpm
COLUMBIA	8-10	69-70
51 WEST	5-10	84
HI (6000 and 8000 series)	5-10	77-78
HI (12001 through 12005)	15-30	60-62
HI (12006 through 12041)	10-20	62-68
HI (32000 through 32010)	15-30	61-63
HI (32011 through 32110)	10-20	63-77
MEGA	5-10	71-74
ZODIAC	5-10	77
Also see PRESLEY, Elvis		

BLACK, Cilla
Singles: 7–inch
BELL	3-4	68
CAPITOL	5-10	64-66
DJM	3-6	68-70
EMI AMERICA	3-5	74
PRIVATE STOCK	3-5	75-76

LPs: 10/12–inch 33rpm
CAPITOL (T-2308 "Is It Love")	20-30	65
(Monaural.)		
CAPITOL (ST-2308 "Is It Love")	25-35	65
(Stereo.)		

BLACK, Clint
Singles: 7–inch
RCA	2-4	89-90

LPs: 10/12–inch 33rpm
RCA	5-8	89-90

BLACK, Jay
Singles: 7–inch
ATLANTIC	3-5	75
MIDSONG	2-4	80
MIGRATION	3-5	75
MILLENNIUM	2-5	78
PRIVATE STOCK	3-5	76
ROULETTE	3-5	76
U.A.	4-8	67

Picture Sleeves
U.A.	5-10	67
Also see JAY and the Americans		

BLACK, Jeanne
Singles: 7–inch
CAPITOL	3-6	60-62

LPs: 10/12–inch 33rpm
CAPITOL	15-20	60

BLACK, Marlon
Singles: 7–inch
AVCO EMBASSY	3-5	71
SHAKAT	3-5	74

BLACK, Oscar
Singles: 78rpm
ATLANTIC	15-20	51
GROOVE	5-10	54-55

Singles: 7–inch
ATLANTIC (956 "Troubled		
Mind Blues")	50-100	51
GROOVE	25-50	54-55
SAVOY	5-10	61

BLACK, Oscar, and Sue Allen
Singles: 78rpm
GROOVE	5-10	54-55

Singles: 7–inch
GROOVE	25-50	54-55
Also see BLACK, Oscar		

BLACK, Shelly
Singles: 7–inch
VIGOR	3-5	76-77

BLACK, Stanley
LPs: 10/12–inch 33rpm
LONDON PHASE 4	5-15	62-65

BLACK, Terry
Singles: 7–inch
DUNHILL	4-8	65-66
TOLLIE	5-10	64-65

Picture Sleeves
TOLLIE	5-10	65

BLACK, Terry, and Laurel Ward
Singles: 7–inch
KAMA SUTRA	3-5	72
Also see BLACK, Terry		

BLACK & BLUE
(Black 'N Blue)
Singles: 7–inch
GEFFEN	2-4	84-88
MERCURY	3-5	70

LPs: 10/12–inch 33rpm
GEFFEN	5-10	84-88

BLACK BLOOD
Singles: 7–inch
CHRYSALIS	2-5	77
MAINSTREAM	3-5	75

LPs: 10/12–inch 33rpm
CHRYSALIS	5-10	77
MAINSTREAM	8-10	75

BLACK FLAMES
Singles: 7–inch
DEF JAM 2-4   87

BLACK HEAT
Singles: 7–inch
ATLANTIC 3-5   72-74
LPs: 10/12–inch 33rpm
ATLANTIC 8-10   72-75

BLACK ICE
Singles: 7–inch
AMHERST 3-5   76
HDM 2-5   77
MONTAGE 2-4   81-84
LPs: 10/12–inch 33rpm
AMHERST 8-10   76
MONTAGE 5-10   82

BLACK IVORY
Singles: 7–inch
BUDDAH 2-5   75-84
KWANZA 3-5   74
PANORAMIC 2-4   85
PERCEPTION 3-5   72
TODAY 3-5   71-73
LPs: 10/12–inch 33rpm
BUDDAH 5-10   75-84
TODAY 10-12   72-73
Member: Leroy Burgess.
Also see ALEEM

BLACK MAMBA
Singles: 12–inch 33/45rpm
GARAGE 4-6   84

BLACK OAK ARKANSAS
(Black Oak)
Singles: 7–inch
ATCO 3-5   71-75
CAPRICORN 2-5   77-78
ENTERPRISE 3-5   70
MCA 3-5   75-77
LPs: 10/12–inch 33rpm
ATCO 8-15   71-84
CAPRICORN 8-10   77-78
MCA 8-12   75-77
STAX 10-15   77-78
Members: Jim Mangrum; Ruby Starr; Rickie Reynolds; Stanley
Knight; Harvey Jett; Jimmy Henderson; Pat Daugherty; Tom
Aldridge.

BLACK OAK ARKANSAS / Cooper Brothers
LPs: 10/12–inch 33rpm
CAPRICORN (0005 "I'd Rather Be
  Sailing") 10-15   78
  (Promotional issue only.)
  Also see BLACK OAK ARKANSAS
  Also see COOPER BROTHERS

BLACK PEARL
Singles: 7–inch
ATLANTIC 3-6   69
PROPHESY 3-6   70

LPs: 10/12–inch 33rpm
ATLANTIC 12-15   69
PROPHESY 15-20   70

BLACK SABBATH
Singles: 7–inch
I.R.S. 2-4   89
WARNER 3-5   70-76
LPs: 10/12–inch 33rpm
I.R.S. 5-8   89
WARNER (Except 1000 and
  2000 series) 5-10   76-84
WARNER (1000 and 2000 series) .. 8-15   70-76
WARNER 5-10   87
Members: Ozzy Osbourne; Tony Iommi; Kip Treavor; Bill Ward;
Ronnie Dio; Terry "Geezer" Butler.
Also see OSBOURNE, Ozzy

BLACK SATIN
Singles: 7–inch
BUDDAH 3-5   75
LPs: 10/12–inch 33rpm
BUDDAH (5654 "Black Satin") 8-10   76
BUDDAH (5654 "Black Satin") 25-35   76
(Promotional issue.)
Member: Fred Parris.
Also see FIVE SATINS

BLACK UHURU
Singles: 7–inch
ISLAND 2-4   84
LPs: 10/12–inch 33rpm
ISLAND 5-10   84
MANGO 5-10   80-85
MESA 5-8   90

BLACKBYRDS
Singles: 7–inch
FANTASY 2-5   74-84
LPs: 10/12–inch 33rpm
FPM 10-12   75
FANTASY 10-15   74-84
Members: Gary Hart; Joe Hall III; Stephe Johnson; Keith Killgo;
Orville Saunders; Kevin Toney.
Also see BYRD, Donald

BLACKFOOT
Singles: 7–inch
ATCO 2-4   79-84
LPs: 10/12–inch 33rpm
ANTILLES 5-10   78
ATCO 5-10   79-84
EPIC 8-10   76
ISLAND 10-12   75
Members: Rick Medlocke; Jackson Spires; Charlie Hargrett;
Greg Walker.
Also see LYNYRD SKYNYRD

BLACKFOOT, J.D.
(J. Blackfoot)
Singles: 7–inch
EDGE 2-4   86-87
PHILIPS 8-12   69
SOUND TOWN 3-5   83-86

LPs: 10/12–inch 33rpm
FANTASY 10-15   74-75
MERCURY 15-25   70
SOUND TOWN 5-10   84-85

BLACKJACK
Singles: 7–inch
POLYDOR 2-4   79-84
20TH FOX 3-5   76
LPs: 10/12–inch 33rpm
POLYDOR 5-10   79-80
Members: Michael Bolotin; Tony Battaglia; Bruce Kulick; Chuck
Kirkpatrick; Jan Mullaney.
Also see BOLTON, Michael

BLACKMORE, Ritchie
Singles: 7–inch
POLYDOR 3-5   75
LPs: 10/12–inch 33rpm
POLYDOR 8-10   75
Also see BLACKMORE'S RAINBOW
Also see LORD SUTCH

BLACKMORE'S RAINBOW
Singles: 7–inch
OYSTER 3-5   76
POLYDOR 3-5   75-79
LPs: 10/12–inch 33rpm
OYSTER 8-12   75-76
Members: Ritchie Blackmore; Roger Glover; Ronnie Dio.
Also see BLACKMORE, Ritchie
Also see DEEP PURPLE
Also see RAINBOW

BLACKSMOKE
Singles: 7–inch
CHOCOLATE CITY 3-5   76

BLACKWELL
Singles: 7–inch
ASTRO 3-6   69-70
BUTTERFLY 2-4   78
LPs: 10/12–inch 33rpm
ASTRO 8-10   69
BUTTERFLY 5-10   78

BLACKWELL, Charlie
Singles: 7–inch
WARNER 4-8   59

BLADES of GRASS
Singles: 7–inch
FINE (57027 "It Isn't Easy") 20-30   67
JUBILEE 4-8   67-68
LPs: 10/12–inch 33rpm
JUBILEE 12-20   67
Members: Bruce Ames; Marc Black; Frank DiChiara; Dave
Gordon.

BLAKE & HINES
Singles: 7–inch
MOTOWN 2-4   87

BLANC, Mel
(With the Sportsmen and Billy May)
Singles: 78rpm
CAPITOL (5221 "Seasons Greetings
from Capitol") 10-20   49
(Promotional issue only. Also has greetings from
other Capitol artists.)
CAPITOL 10-20   48-54
Singles: 7–inch
CAPITOL (Except PRO-15) 15-30   50-54
CAPITOL (PRO-15 "I Taut I Taw a
Record Dealer") 30-50   51
(Mel Blanc provides the voice of assorted cartoon
characters, though he is not credited on label.
Promotional issue only.)
WARNER 5-10   60
EPs: 7–inch 33/45rpm
CAPITOL (436 "Party Panic") 35-50   53
LPs: 10/12–inch 33rpm
CAPITOL (436 "Party Panic") 50-75   53
(10–inch LP.)
CAPITOL (3200 series) 15-30   61-63
GOLDEN 10-20   61
Also see HUNT, Pee Wee

BLANCHARD, Jack, and Misty Morgan
Singles: 7–inch
EPIC 2-4   73-75
MEGA 3-5   71-73
WAYSIDE 3-5   69-70
LPs: 10/12–inch 33rpm
MEGA 8-12   72
WAYSIDE 10-15   70

BLANCMANGE
Singles: 12–inch 33/45rpm
ISLAND 4-6   83-84
SIRE 4-6   84-85
Singles: 7–inch
ISLAND 2-4   83-84
SIRE 2-4   84-85
LPs: 10/12–inch 33rpm
ISLAND 5-10   82-84
SIRE 5-10   84-85

BLAND, Billy
Singles: 78rpm
OLD TOWN 5-10   55-57
Singles: 7–inch
ATLANTIC 2-4   84
COLLECTABLES 2-4   81
TIP TOP 10-15   58
OLD TOWN (1016 through 1035) ... 10-20   55-57
OLD TOWN (1076 through 1143) 6-12   60-63

BLAND, Bobby
(Bobby "Blue" Bland)
Singles: 78rpm
CHESS 10-20   54
MODERN 15-25   52

Singles: 7–inch

ABC	2-4	73-78
DUKE (105 "I.O.U. Blues")	75-100	54
DUKE (115 "No Blow No Show")	50-100	54
DUKE (141 "It's My Life, Baby")	30-60	56
DUKE (146 through 196)	15-30	57-58
DUKE (300 series)	5-10	60-66
DUKE (400 series)	4-8	66-72
DUNHILL	2-4	74
MCA	2-4	79-84
ST. LAWRENCE	4-8	

LPs: 10/12–inch 33rpm

ABC	5-10	75-78
ABC/DUKE	5-10	73
BLUESWAY	5-10	73
DUKE (74 through 78)	20-30	62-64
DUKE (79 through 89)	15-20	66-69
DUKE (90 through 92)	10-15	70-74
DUNHILL	8-10	73-74
MCA	5-10	79-84

BLAND, Bobby, and B.B. King
Singles: 7–inch

ABC	2-4	78
IMPULSE	3-5	76

LPs: 10/12–inch 33rpm

DUNHILL	10-12	74
IMPULSE	8-10	76
MCA	5-10	82

Also see KING, B.B.

BLAND, Bobby / Little Junior Parker
LPs: 10/12–inch 33rpm

DUKE (DLP-72 "The Barefoot Rock")	100-150	58
DUKE (X-72 "The Barefoot Rock")	10-12	74

Also see PARKER, Little Junior

BLAND, Bobby, and Ike Turner
Singles: 7–inch

KENT	5-10	62

Also see TURNER, Ike

BLAND, Bobby / Johnny Guitar Watson
LPs: 10/12–inch 33rpm

CROWN	15-20	63

Also see BLAND, Bobby
Also see WATSON, Johnny

BLANE, Marcie
Singles: 7–inch

LONDON	2-4	84
SEVILLE	5-10	62-65

BLAST, C.L.
Singles: 7–inch

ATLANTIC	3-6	69
COTILLION	2-4	80
PARK PLACE	2-4	85
STAX	4-8	67
UNITED	3-5	70-71

LPs: 10/12–inch 33rpm

COTILLION	5-10	80

BLASTERS
Singles: 7–inch

MCA	2-4	84
SLASH	3-5	81-85

Picture Sleeves

SLASH	2-4	81-85

LPs: 10/12–inch 33rpm

ROLLIN' ROCK (021 "American Music")	50-75	80
SLASH	8-12	81-85

Members: David Alvin; Phil Alvin; John Bazz; Gene Taylor; Bill Bateman; Steve Berlin; Lee Allen.
Also see ALLEN, Lee
Also see ALVIN, David
Also see HARTMAN, Dan / Blasters

BLAZE
Singles: 7–inch

EPIC	3-5	76-77
FRATERNITY	3-5	76

BLEND
Singles: 7–inch

MCA	2-4	78-79

LPs: 10/12–inch 33rpm

MCA	5-10	78-79

BLENDELLS
Singles: 7–inch

COLLECTABLES	2-4	81
COTILLION	4-8	68
ERA	3-5	73
RAMPART	8-10	64
REPRISE	4-8	64-65

BLENDERS
Singles: 7–inch

CORTLAND	5-10	62
MAR-V-LOUS	4-8	66
VISION (1000 "I Asked for Your Hand")	40-50	62
WITCH	10-15	63

BLESSING, Michael
(Michael Nesmith)
Singles: 7–inch

COLPIX (792 "Until It's Time for You to Go")	15-25	65

Also see NESMITH, Michael

BLEYER, Archie
(Archie Blyer and Marla Alba)
Singles: 78rpm

ARC	8-15	35
CADENCE	5-10	54-57
VOCALION	8-15	34

Singles: 7–inch

CADENCE	8-15	54-57

LPs: 10/12–inch 33rpm

CADENCE (3044 "Moonlight Serenade")	15-25	62
(Monaural.)		

CADENCE (25044 "Moonlight
  Serenade") 20-30   62
  (Stereo.)
    Also see CHORDETTES
    Also see GODFREY, Arthur, with Archie Bleyer
    Also see HAYES, Bill

BLIND FAITH
Singles: 7–inch
RSO 3-6   77
LPs: 10/12–inch 33rpm
ATCO (304A "Blind Faith") 20-30   69
  (Front cover pictures a nude girl.)
ATCO (304B "Blind Faith") 10-12   69
  (Front cover pictures the group.)
RSO 5-10   76
  (Reissue. Pictures nude girl.)
  Members: Eric Clapton; Ginger Baker; Steve Winwood; Rick
  Gretch.
    Also see BAKER, Ginger
    Also see CLAPTON, Eric
    Also see FAMILY
    Also see WINWOOD, Steve

BLODWYN PIG
Singles: 7–inch
A&M 3-6   69-70
LPs: 10/12–inch 33rpm
A&M (3000 series) 5-10   82
A&M (4000 series) 10-15   69-70
  Members: Blodwyn; Mick Abrahams; Peter Banks; Ron Berg;
  Clive Bunker; Jack Lancaster; Andy Pyle.
    Also see BANKS, Peter

BLONDIE
Singles: 12–inch 33/45rpm
CHRYSALIS 5-10   78-84
Singles: 7–inch
CHRYSALIS 2-5   77-84
PRIVATE STOCK 6-10   76-77
Picture Sleeves
CHRYSALIS 3-8   79-82
LPs: 10/12–inch 33rpm
CHRYSALIS (Except 5001) 5-10   76-84
CHRYSALIS (5001 "Parallel Lines") . 15-25   78
  (Picture disc.)
MFSL (050 "Parallel Lines") 20-40   81
PRIVATE STOCK 15-20   75
  Members: Deborah Harry; Clem Burke; Jimmy Destri; Chris
  Stein; Gary Valentine; Fred Smith; Nigel Harrison.
    Also see HARRY, Debbie

BLOOD, SWEAT & TEARS
Singles: 7–inch
ABC 2-4   78
COLUMBIA 3-5   69-77
Picture Sleeves
COLUMBIA 3-5   70-72
LPs: 10/12–inch 33rpm
ABC 5-10   77
COLUMBIA (Except 9619 and
  49000 series) 10-12   69-76
COLUMBIA (9619 "Child Is Father
  to the Man") 15-20   68

COLUMBIA (49000 series) 12-15   81
  (Half-speed mastered.)
LAX (1865 "Nuclear Blues") 5-10   80
  (Black vinyl.)
LAX (1865 "Nuclear Blues") 10-12   80
  (Colored vinyl. Promotional issue only.)
  Members: David Clayton-Thomas; Jerry Hyman; Fred Lipsius;
  Dick Halligan; Bobby Colomby; Lew Soloff; Chuck Winfield;
  Steve Katz; James Thomas Fielder.
    Also see CLAYTON-THOMAS, David
    Also see KOOPER, Al

BLOODROCK
Singles: 7–inch
CAPITOL 3-6   69-75
Promotional Singles
CAPITOL (3451 "Bloodrock
  Interview By Sol Smaizys") 4-8   72
LPs: 10/12–inch 33rpm
CAPITOL 10-20   69-75
  Members: Rick Cobb; Eddie Grundy; Steve Hill; Lee Pickens;
  Nick Taylor; Warren Ham; Jim Rutledge.

BLOODSTONE
Singles: 12–inch 33/45rpm
MOTOWN 4-6   79
T-NECK 4-6   82-85
Singles: 7–inch
EPIC 2-4   82
LONDON 3-5   73-76
MOTOWN 2-4   79
T-NECK 2-4   82-85
Picture Sleeves
LONDON 3-5   74-76
LPs: 10/12–inch 33rpm
LONDON 8-10   73-74
MOTOWN 5-10   78
T-NECK 5-10   82
  Members: Harry Williams; Charles McCormick; Charles Love;
  Steve Ferrone; Roger Lee Durham; Willis Draffen.

BLOOM, Bobby
Singles: 7–inch
EARTH 3-6   69
KAMA SUTRA 4-8   67
L&R 3-5   70
MGM 5-10   70-73
ROULETTE 3-5   70
WHITE WHALE 4-6   69
LPs: 10/12–inch 33rpm
BUDDAH 8-12   71
L&R 10-15   70
    Also see ARCHIES
    Also see MANN, Bobby
    Also see MUSIC EXPLOSION

BLOOMFIELD, Mike
LPs: 10/12–inch 33rpm
CLOUDS 5-10   78
COLUMBIA (9000 series) 12-15   69
COLUMBIA (37000 series) 6-10   81-83
GUITAR PLAYER 8-10   77
HARMONY 8-10   71

TAKOMA 5-10   77-81
WATERHOUSE 5-10   81
   Also see KGB

BLOOMFIELD, Mike, Dr. John and John Paul Hammond
LPs: 10/12–inch 33rpm

COLUMBIA 8-10   73
   Also see DR. JOHN

BLOOMFIELD, Mike, and Nick Graventes
LPs: 10/12–inch 33rpm

COLUMBIA 10-12   69
   Also see ELECTRIC FLAG

BLOOMFIELD, Mike, and Al Kooper
LPs: 10/12–inch 33rpm

COLUMBIA 12-20   68
MFSL (178 "Super Session") 15-25   85
   Also see KOOPER, Al
   Also see MOBY GRAPE

BLOOMFIELD, Mike, Al Kooper and Steve Stills
Singles: 7–inch

COLUMBIA 3-6   68
LPs: 10/12–inch 33rpm

COLUMBIA 10-15   68
MFSL 15-20   85
   Also see BLOOMFIELD, Mike
   Also see STILLS, Stephen

BLOSSOMS
Singles: 7–inch

BELL 4-8   69-70
CAPITOL 8-12   57-58
CHALLENGE 10-15   61-62
CLASSIC ARTISTS 3-5   89
EEOC (8472 "Things Are Changing") 75-100   65
  (Equal Employment Opportunity Center promo
  issue. Has Brian Wilson on piano.)
EPIC 3-5   77
LION 3-5   72
MGM 8-12   68
ODE 5-10   67-69
OKEH 5-10   62-63
REPRISE 4-8   65-67
Picture Sleeves

EEOC (8472 "Things Are Changing") 75-100   65
  (Promotional issue only.)
LPs: 10/12–inch 33rpm

LION 8-12   72
   Members: Darlene "Love" Wright; Gloria Jones; Fanita
   James-Barrett; Annette Williams; Nanette Williams-Jackson;
   Grazia Nitzsche; Jean King.
   Also see BOB B. SOXX and the Blue Jeans
   Also see EDDY, Duane
   Also see FABARES, Shelley
   Also see LOVE, Darlene
   Also see PRESLEY, Elvis
   Also see WILSON, Brian

BLOW, Kurtis
Singles: 12–inch 33/45rpm

MERCURY 4-6   80-86

Singles: 7–inch

MERCURY 2-4   80-86
POLYDOR 2-4   85
LPs: 10/12–inch 33rpm

MERCURY 5-10   80-86
   Also see KING DREAM CHORUS and Holiday Crew
   Also see KRUSH GROVE ALL STARS

BLOWFLY
Singles: 7–inch

WEIRD WORLD 2-4   80
LPs: 10/12–inch 33rpm

WEIRD WORLD 8-10   80

BLUE
Singles: 7–inch

IRIS 2-4
MCA/PIG (Colored vinyl) 4-6   77
  (Promotional issue only.)
RSO 3-5   73-75
ROCKET 3-5   77
LPs: 10/12–inch 33rpm

RSO 8-10   73
ROCKET 5-10   77
   Members: Tim Donald; Ian MacMillan; Jimmy McCullough; Hugh
   Nicholson.
   Also see MARMALADE

BLUE, David
(David Cohen)
Singles: 7–inch

ASYLUM 3-5   73
REPRISE 3-6   69
LPs: 10/12–inch 33rpm

ASYLUM 8-10   73-76
ELEKTRA 12-15   66
REPRISE 12-15   68

BLUE BARRON and His Orchestra
Singles: 7–inch

MGM 4-6   50-55
EPs: 7–inch 33/45rpm

MGM 4-8   54-55
LPs: 10/12–inch 33rpm

MGM 10-20   54

BLUE BELLES
(Starlets)
Singles: 7–inch

NEWTOWN 8-10   62
PEAK 5-10   62
Picture Sleeves

PEAK 15-25   62
   Members: Patti Labelle; Cindy Birdsong; Nona Hendryx; Sarah
   Dash.
   Also see LABELLE, Patti
   Also see PATTON, Robert G.
   Also see STARLETS

BLUE CHEER
Singles: 7–inch

MERCURY 3-5   76
PHILIPS 4-6   68-70

Picture Sleeves
PHILIPS 8-15   68

LPs: 10/12–inch 33rpm
PHILIPS (9000 series) 5-10   80
PHILIPS (600000 series) 20-40   68-71
Members: Leigh Stephens; Paul Whaley; Dick Peterson; Randy Holden; Tony Rainer; Bruce Stephens; Ralph Kellogg; Gary Yoder.

BLUE DIAMONDS
Singles: 7–inch
LONDON 4-8   62-63

BLUE HAZE
Singles: 7–inch
A&M 3-5   72-74

BLUE JAYS
(Leon Peels and the Bluejays)
Singles: 7–inch
CLASSIC ARTISTS 3-5   89
COLLECTABLES 2-4   81
ERA 2-4   72
MILESTONE 10-15   61-62
Member: Leon Peels.

BLUE JAYS / Little Caesar and the Romans
LPs: 10/12–inch 33rpm
MILESTONE (1001 "Blue Jays Meet Little
  Caesar and the Romans") 45-65   62
  (Black vinyl.)
MILESTONE (1001 "Blue Jays Meet Little
  Caesar and the Romans") 100-200   62
  (Colored vinyl.)
  Also see BLUE JAYS
  Also see LITTLE CAESAR and the Romans

BLUE MAGIC
Singles: 12–inch 33/45rpm
MIRAGE 4-6   83
Singles: 7–inch
ATCO 3-5   73-76
CAPITOL 2-4   81
LIBERTY 3-6   69
MIRAGE 2-4   83
WMOT 3-5
LPs: 10/12–inch 33rpm
ATCO 8-10   74-77
ATLANTIC 5-10   83
CAPITOL 5-10   81
COLLECTABLES 6-8   86
MIRAGE 5-10   83
Members: Ted Mills; Margie Joseph; Vernon Sawyer; Wendell Sawyer; Richard Pratt; Keath Beaton.
Also see JOSEPH, Margie

BLUE MINK
Singles: 7–inch
BELL 3-5   71-72
MCA 3-5   73-74
PHILIPS 3-6   69-70
Picture Sleeves
PHILIPS 4-8   70

LPs: 10/12–inch 33rpm
MCA 8-10   73
PHILIPS 12-15   69-70
Members: Madeline Bell; Roger Cook; Barry Morgan; Herbie Flowers; Alan Parker; Ann Odell; Roger Coulan; Ray Cooper.
Also see BELL, Madeline

BLUE NOTES
Singles: 78rpm
JOSIE 20-30   56-57
Singles: 7–inch
COLLECTABLES 2-4   81
JALYNNE 15-25   60
JOSIE (800 "If You Love Me") 75-100   56
JOSIE (814 "Letters") 50-75   57
JOSIE (823 "Retribution Blues") 40-60   57
RED TOP 5-8   63
3 SONS 10-20   62
UNI 4-8   69
VAL-UE 15-20   60
LPs: 10/12–inch 33rpm
COLLECTABLES 5-10   82
Members: Harold Melvin; Jesse Gillis Jr.; Roosevelt Brodie; Frank Peaker; Bernard Williams; John Atkins; Lawrence Brown.
Also see BLUENOTES
Also see MELVIN, Harold, and the Blue Notes

BLUE OYSTER CULT
Singles: 12–inch 33/45rpm
COLUMBIA 4-6   80
Singles: 7–inch
COLUMBIA 2-4   72-84
WHAT'S IT ALL ABOUT 8-12
  (Promotional issue only.)
Picture Sleeves
COLUMBIA (02000 and
  04000 series) 2-4   81-84
COLUMBIA (45000 series) 4-8   72
EPs: 7–inch 33/45rpm
COLUMBIA (40 "Bootleg EP") 20-25   72
LPs: 10/12–inch 33rpm
ABC RADIO ("A Night on the Road") . 35-50   81
  (Promotional issue only.)
COLUMBIA (Except 31000 through
  33000 series) 5-10   76-84
COLUMBIA (31000 through 33000
  series) 6-12   72-75
Members: Al Bouchard; Joe Bouchard; Eric Bloom; Alan Lanier; Donald "Buck Dharma" Roeser.

BLUE PRINT
Singles: 7–inch
FANTASY 2-4   83

BLUE RIDGE RANGERS
(John Fogerty)
Singles: 7–inch
FANTASY 3-5   72-73
LPs: 10/12–inch 33rpm
FANTASY 10-12   73
Also see FOGERTY, John

BLUE STARS
Singles: 78rpm
MERCURY 3-6   55-56
Singles: 7–inch
MERCURY 5-10   55-56

BLUE SWEDE
Singles: 7–inch
EMI AMERICA 3-5   73-75
Picture Sleeves
EMI AMERICA 3-5   73-74
LPs: 10/12–inch 33rpm
EMI AMERICA 8-10   74-75
Members: Bjorn Skifs; Jan Guldback; Bosse Liljedahl; Michael Areklew; Ladislau Balaz; Tommy Berglund; Hinke Ekestubble.

BLUENOTES
Singles: 7–inch
BROOKE 8-12   59-60
Picture Sleeves
BROOKE 15-25   60
Also see BLUE NOTES

BLUES BROTHERS
Singles: 7–inch
ATLANTIC 3-5   78-81
(Black vinyl.)
ATLANTIC 5-10
(Colored vinyl. Promotional issue only.)
Picture Sleeves
ATLANTIC 3-6   78-80
LPs: 10/12–inch 33rpm
ATLANTIC 10-15   78-81
Members: Dan Aykroyd; John Belushi.
Also see BELUSHI, John

BLUES IMAGE
Singles: 7–inch
ATCO 4-8   69-71
LPs: 10/12–inch 33rpm
ATCO 10-20   69-70
Members: Mike Pinera; Joe Lala; Frank Konte; Malcolm Jones; Manuel Bertematti.
Also see PINERA, Mike

BLUES MAGOOS
Singles: 7–inch
ABC 4-8   68-70
GANIM (1000 "Who Do You Love") .. 20-40   69
MERCURY (30000 series) 2-4   76
MERCURY (70000 series) 8-12   66-68
VERVE/FOLKWAYS (5006 "So I'm
   Wrong") 20-30   66
VERVE/FOLKWAYS (5044 "So I'm
   Wrong") 15-25   67
Picture Sleeves
MERCURY 10-20   67
LPs: 10/12–inch 33rpm
ABC 8-10   69-70
MERCURY (21096 "Psychedelic
   Lollipop") 30-40   66
   (Monaural.)

MERCURY (21104 "Electric
   Comic Book") 25-30   67
   (Monaural. With comic book insert.
   Deduct $5 if comic is missing.)
MERCURY (61096 "Psychedelic
   Lollipop") 25-40   66
   (Red label. Stereo.)
MERCURY (61096 "Psychedelic
   Lollipop") 5-10   66
   (Chicago "skyline" label.)
MERCURY (61104 "Electric
   Comic Book") 20-30   67
   (Stereo. With comic book insert.
   Deduct $5 if comic is missing.)
MERCURY (61167 "Basic
   Blues Magoos") 20-30   68
Members: Geoff Daking; Mike Esposito; Ron Gilbert; Ralph Scala; Emil Thielhelm.
Also see BALANCE
Also see FELIX and the Escorts

BLUES PROJECT
Singles: 7–inch
CAPITOL 5-8   72
MCA 3-5   73
VERVE/FOLKWAYS 10-15   66-67
LPs: 10/12–inch 33rpm
CAPITOL 10-15   72
ELEKTRA 5-10   80
MCA 8-10   73
MGM 8-12   70-74
VERVE/FOLKWAYS 15-25   66
VERVE/FORECAST 12-20   66-70
Members: Al Kooper; Roy Blumenfeld; David Cohen; Tommy Flanders; Richard Green; John Gregory; Don Gretmar; Danny Kalb; Steve Katz; Andy Kulbert; Bill Lussenden; Chicken Hirsch.
Also see KOOPER, Al
Also see SEATRAIN

BO, Eddie
Singles: 78rpm
ACE 5-10   56-57
APOLLO 8-12   55-56
Singles: 7–inch
ACE 10-15   56-59
APOLLO 15-25   55-56
AT LAST 4-8   63
BLUE JAY 4-8   64
BO-SOUND 3-5   71
CAPITOL 5-10   61
CHECKER 10-15   58
CHESS (Except 1600 series) 4-8   62
CHESS (1600 series) 10-15   58
CINDERELLA 4-8   63
RIC 5-10   59-62
SEVEN B 4-8   66-68
SCRAM 4-6   69
SWAN 5-10   62
Also see PARKER, Robert

BO, Eddie, and Inez Cheatham
Singles: 7-inch

SEVEN B 4-8		68

Also see BO, Eddie

BO DIDDLEY: see DIDDLEY, Bo

BOB & EARL
Singles: 7-inch

CLASS 5-10		59

Members: Earl Nelson; Bobby Byrd.
Also see BYRD, Bobby
Also see LEE, Jackie

BOB & EARL
Singles: 7-inch

ABC 2-4		73
CHENE 4-8		64
COLLECTABLES 2-4		81
CRESTVIEW 3-6		69
ISLAND 3-5		
LOMA 4-8		64
MARC 6-12		63-64
MIRWOOD 5-8		66
TEMPE 5-10		62
UNI 4-6		70
WHITE WHALE 5-10		69

LPs: 10/12-inch 33rpm

CRESTVIEW 15-20		69
TIP 20-25		64
UPFRONT 10-15		

Members: Earl Nelson; Bobby Relf.
Also see RELF, Bobby
Also see NELSON, Earl
Also see WHITE, Barry

BOB B. SOXX and the Blue Jeans
Singles: 7-inch

PHILLES 10-15		62-63

LPs: 10/12-inch 33rpm

PHILLES (4002 "Zip-a-Dee

Doo-Dah") 75-125		63

Members: Bobby Sheen; Darlene Love; Carolyn Willis; Fanita
James- Barrett.
Also see BLOSSOMS
Also see HONEY CONE
Also see LOVE, Darlene
Also see RONETTES / Crystals / Darlene Love / Bob B. Soxx
and the Blue Jeans
Also see SHEEN, Bobby

BOBBETTES
Singles: 78rpm

ATLANTIC 5-10		57

Singles: 7-inch

ATLANTIC 10-15		57-60
DIAMOND 5-8		62-65
END 5-10		61
GALLIANT 10-15		60
GONE 10-15		61
JUBILEE 5-8		62
KING 5-10		61-62
MAYHEW 3-5		72-74
RCA 4-8		66

TRIPLE-X 10-20		60

Members: Emma Pought; Jannie Pought; Heather Dixon; Laura
Webb; Helen Gathers.
Also see KING CURTIS

BOBBY and the Midnites
Singles: 7-inch

ARISTA 2-4		81
COLUMBIA 2-4		84

LPs: 10/12-inch 33rpm

ARISTA 5-10		81
COLUMBIA 5-10		84

Member: Bob Weir.
Also see WEIR, Bob

BOBBY LEE: see LEE, Bobby

BOBO, Willie
(Willie Bobo and the Bo-Gents)
Singles: 7-inch

BLUE NOTE 3-5		77
CAPITOL 3-5		76
JUPITER JAZZ 3-5		75
TICO 8-12		59
VERVE 4-8		65-69

LPs: 10/12-inch 33rpm

BLUE NOTE 5-10		77
COLUMBIA 8-10		78-79
MGM 5-10		
ROULETTE 15-25		63-64
SUSSEX 8-10		
TICO 10-20		
TRIP 5-10		
VERVE 10-20		65-69

Also see HANCOCK, Herbie, and Willie Bobo

BOCEPHUS
(Hank Williams Jr.)
Singles: 7-inch

VERVE (10540 "Meter Reader Maid") 20-30		67

Also see WILLIAMS, Hank, Jr.

BOFILL, Angela
Singles: 12-inch 33/45rpm

ARISTA 4-6		81-85

Singles: 7-inch

ARISTA 2-4		81-85
GRP 3-5		79

LPs: 10/12-inch 33rpm

ARISTA 5-10		81-85
GRP 8-10		78-79

BOHANNON
(Hamilton Bohannon)
Singles: 12-inch 33/45rpm

COMPLEAT 4-6		84-85
MERCURY 5-8		77-80
MCA 4-6		84
PHASE II 4-6		80-83

Singles: 7-inch

DAKAR 3-5		73-75
MERCURY 2-4		77-80
PHASE 2 2-4		80-83

LPs: 10/12–inch 33rpm
DAKAR 10-12   73-75
MERCURY 8-10   77-80
PHASE 2 5-10   80-83

BOHANNON, Hamilton, and Dr. Perri Johnson
Singles: 12–inch 33/45rpm
PHASE 2 4-6   81
Singles: 7–inch
PHASE 2 2-4   81
Also see BOHANNON

BOHN, Rudi
LPs: 10/12–inch 33rpm
LONDON PHASE 4 5-12   61

BOILING POINT
Singles: 7–inch
BULLET 3-5   78

BOLAN, Marc
LPs: 10/12–inch 33rpm
REPRISE (511 "Interview with Marc
  Bolan of T-Rex") 50-75   71
  (Promotional issue only.)
RHINO (Picture disc) 8-10
WHAT 5-10   82
Also see T. REX

BOLGER, Ray
Singles: 78rpm
DECCA 4-8   49-51
Singles: 7–inch
ARMOUR 3-6   63
DECCA 5-10   50-51
LPs: 10/12–inch 33rpm
DISNEYLAND 6-10   65

BOLIN, Tommy
Singles: 7–inch
NEMPEROR 3-5   76
LPs: 10/12–inch 33rpm
COLUMBIA 8-10   76
NEMPEROR (400 series) 10-12   75
NEMPEROR (37000 series) 5-10   81
Also see JAMES GANG
Also see ZEPHYR

BOLOTON, Michael: see BOLTON, Michael

BOLTON, Michael
(Michael Boloton)
Singles: 12–inch 33/45rpm
COLUMBIA 4-8   85
  (Promotional issue only.)
Singles: 7–inch
COLUMBIA 2-4   83-91
RCA 3-5   75-76
Picture Sleeves
COLUMBIA 2-4   88
LPs: 10/12–inch 33rpm
COLUMBIA 5-10   83-91
RCA 8-10   75-76

Also see BLACKJACK

BOMBERS
Singles: 7–inch
WEST END 3-5   79
LPs: 10/12–inch 33rpm
WEST END 8-12   79

BON JOVI
Singles: 7–inch
MERCURY 2-4   84-90
Picture Sleeves
MERCURY 2-4   84-89
LPs: 10/12–inch 33rpm
MERCURY 5-10   84-90
Members: Jon Bon Jovi; Richie Sambora; David Bryan; Alec
John Such; Tico Torres.

BON ROCK
Singles: 12–inch 33/45rpm
EARTHTONE 4-6   84
LPs: 10/12–inch 33rpm
EARTHTONE 5-10   84
Member: Keith Rogers.

BOND, Angelo
Singles: 7–inch
ABC 3-5   75-76
LPs: 10/12–inch 33rpm
ABC 8-10   75-77

BOND, Johnny
Singles: 78rpm
COLUMBIA (Except 21521) 4-6   50-56
COLUMBIA (21521 "The Little Rock
  Roll") 8-12   56
Singles: 7–inch
COLUMBIA (Except 21521) 8-12   50-56
COLUMBIA (21521 "The Little Rock
  Roll") 20-30   56
DITTO 5-10   59
LAMB and LION 3-5   74
MGM 3-5   73
REPUBLIC 4-8   60
SMASH 4-6   62
STARDAY (600 through 900 series) . . . 3-6   63-72
STARDAY (8000 series) 3-5   72
EPs: 7–inch 33/45rpm
COLUMBIA 10-15   58
REPUBLIC 10-15   60
LPs: 10/12–inch 33rpm
CMH 5-10   77
HARMONY 10-20   64-65
LAMB and LION 5-10   74
NASHVILLE 5-10   71
SHASTA 10-15
STARDAY (100 and 200 series) 20-25   61-64
STARDAY (300 series, except 354) . . 15-20   65-66
STARDAY (354 "Famous Hot
  Rodders I Have Known") 25-30   65
STARDAY (400 series) 10-15   67-71
STARDAY (900 series) 6-10   74

BONDS, Gary "U.S."
(U.S. Bonds)
Singles: 7–inch
ABC	2-4	73
ATCO	3-6	69
BLUFF CITY	3-5	74
BOTANIC	4-6	68
COLLECTABLES	2-4	81
EMi AMERICA	2-4	81-82
LEGRAND (1003 through 1020)	5-10	60-62
LEGRAND (1022 through 1041)	10-20	62-66
LEGRAND (1043 through 1046)	8-15	66-67
MCA	2-4	84
PRODIGAL	3-5	75
SUE	3-6	70

Picture Sleeves
EMI AMERICA	2-4	81-82
LEGRAND	8-15	61

LPs: 10/12–inch 33rpm
EMI AMERICA	5-10	81-82
LEGRAND (1000 series)	5-10	86
LEGRAND (3001 "Dance 'Till Quarter to Three")	40-60	61
LEGRAND (3002 "Twist Up Calypso")	40-60	62
LEGRAND (3003 "Greatest Hits")	40-60	62
MCA	5-10	84
PHOENIX	5-10	84
RHINO	5-10	84

Also see CHECKER, Chubby / Gary U.S. Bonds
Also see GREENWICH, Ellie
Also see JACKSON, Chuck
Also see KING, Ben E.
Also see SPRINGSTEEN, Bruce

BONDS, U.S: see BONDS, Gary "U.S."

BONE SYMPHONY
Singles: 12–inch 33/45rpm
CAPITOL	4-6	83

Singles: 7–inch
CAPITOL	2-4	83

LPs: 10/12–inch 33rpm
CAPITOL	5-10	83

BONES
Singles: 7–inch
MCA	3-5	73
SIGNPOST	4-6	72

LPs: 10/12–inch 33rpm
MCA	8-10	73
SIGNPOST	10-12	72

BONES, Elbow: see ELBOW BONES

BONEY M
Singles: 12–inch 33/45rpm
CARRERE	4-6	85
SIRE	4-6	79

Singles: 7–inch
ATCO	3-5	76-77
ATLANTIC	3-5	77
SIRE	2-4	78-79

Picture Sleeves
SIRE	2-4	79

LPs: 10/12–inch 33rpm
ATCO	10-12	76
ATLANTIC	8-10	77
SIRE	5-10	77-79

Members: Marcia Barrett; Bobby Farrell; Liz Mitchell; Maizie Williams.

BONNIE and the Treasures
(Featuring Charlott O'Hara)
Singles: 7–inch
PHI DAN (5505 "Home of the Brave")	30-40	65

BONNIE SISTERS
(With Mickey "Guitar" Baker and Randy Carlos)
Singles: 78rpm
RAINBOW	5-10	56

Singles: 7–inch
RAINBOW	10-20	56

BONO, Sonny: see SONNY

BONOFF, Karla
Singles: 7–inch
COLUMBIA	2-4	77-84

Picture Sleeves
COLUMBIA	2-4	77-84

LPs: 10/12–inch 33rpm
COLUMBIA	5-10	77-82

BONZO DOG BAND
(Bonzo Dog Doo-Dah Band)
Singles: 7–inch
IMPERIAL	3-6	69
LIBERTY	4-8	68
U.A.	3-5	71-72

LPs: 10/12–inch 33rpm
IMPERIAL	15-20	68-70
LIBERTY	5-10	83
U.A.	10-15	71-74

Members: Vivian Stanshall; Neil Innes; Roger Ruskin Spear; Hughie Flint; Tony Kaye; Dave Richards; Andy Roberts.
Also see RUTLES

BONZO GOES to WASHINGTON
Singles: 12–inch 33/45rpm
SLEEPING BAG	4-6	84

BOOGIE BOYS
Singles: 12–inch 33/45rpm
CAPITOL	4-6	84-88

Singles: 7–inch
CAPITOL	2-4	84-88

LPs: 10/12–inch 33rpm
CAPITOL	5-10	85-88

Member: William Stroman.

BOOGIE MAN ORCHESTRA
Singles: 7–inch
BOOGIE MAN	3-5	75

BOOK of LOVE
Singles: 12–inch 33/45rpm
SIRE	4-6	84-85

Singles: 7–inch

SIRE 2-4   84-90

Picture Sleeves

SIRE 2-4   88

LPs: 10/12–inch 33rpm

SIRE 5-10   86-91

BOOKER, James

Singles: 7–inch

PEACOCK 3-5   60-64

LPs: 10/12–inch 33rpm

ROUNDER 5-10   84
Also see LITTLE BOOKER

BOOKER, John Lee

(John L. Booker; John Lee Hooker)

Singles: 78rpm

CHANCE 25-75   51
CHESS 20-40   51
DELUXE 15-25   53
GONE (60 "Mad Man Blues") 30-50   51
MODERN 10-20   51
ROCKIN' 15-25   53

Singles: 7–inch

CHANCE (1108 "Miss Lorraine") .. 300-500   51
CHANCE (1110 "Graveyard Blues") 300-500   51
CHANCE (1122 "609 Boogie") 300-500   51
DELUXE (6004 "Blue Monday") 75-100   53
DELUXE (6032 "Pouring Rain") 50-100   53
DELUXE (6004 "Blue Monday") 50-100   53
DELUXE (6046 "My Baby Don't
Love Me") 50-100   53
MODERN (852 "Ground Hog Blues") . 50-75   51
ROCKIN' (525 "Pouring Down Rain") 75-100   53
Also see HOOKER, John Lee

BOOKER T. and Priscilla

Singles: 7–inch

A&M 3-5   71-73

LPs: 10/12–inch 33rpm

A&M 8-10   71-73
Members: Booker T. Jones; Priscilla Coolidge-Jones.

BOOKER T. and the MGs

Singles: 12–inch 33/45rpm

A&M 4-8   82-84

Singles: 7–inch

A&M 2-4   81-82
ASYLUM 3-5   77
EPIC 3-5   75
STAX (Except 100 series) 3-6   67-71
STAX (100 series) 4-8   62-66

LPs: 10/12–inch 33rpm

A&M 8-10   72-81
ASYLUM 5-10   77
ATLANTIC 10-12   68
ATLANTIC/ATCO (133 "Excerpts from
In the Christmas Spirit) 15-20   66
(Promotional issue only. One side has excerpts
from Soul Christmas, a various artists LP.)
EPIC 8-10   74
PICKWICK 5-10

STAX (700 series, except 70
and 713) 20-30   65-68
STAX (701 "Green Onions") 25-40   62
STAX (713 "In the Spirit
of Chirstmas") 25-35   66
(Hands and keyboard drawing on front cover. Back
has 1966 copyright date.)
STAX (713 "In the Spirit
of Chirstmas") 15-25   67
(Christmas ornament cover. Back has "© 1967.")
STAX (2000 series) 10-20   68-71
STAX (8000 series) 5-10   81-84
Members: Booker T. Jones; Steve Cropper; Al Jackson; Louis
Steinberg; Willie Hall.
Also see BOOKER T. and Priscilla
Also see MGs
Also see MAR-KEYS / Booker T. and the MGs
Also see RANDLE, Del
Also see SANTANA
Also see SIMON, PAUL

BOOM, Taka

Singles: 7–inch

ARIOLA 2-4   79
MIRAGE 2-4   85

LPs: 10/12–inch 33rpm

ARIOLA 5-10   79
Also see UNDISPUTED TRUTH

BOOMTOWN RATS

Singles: 7–inch

COLUMBIA 2-4   79-80

LPs: 10/12–inch 33rpm

COLUMBIA 5-10   79-85
MERCURY 8-12   77
Members: Bob Geldof; Pete Briquette; Gerry Cott; Simon Crowe;
Johnny Fingers; Garry Roberts.
Also see BAND AID
Also see GELDOF, Bob

BOONE, Daniel

Singles: 7–inch

EPIC 3-5   72
MERCURY 3-5   72-74
PYE 2-4   75

LPs: 10/12–inch 33rpm

MERCURY 10-12   72

BOONE, Debbie

Singles: 7–inch

LAMB and LION 2-4   80-84
WARNER 2-4   77-80

Picture Sleeves

WARNER 2-4   78

LPs: 10/12–inch 33rpm

LAMB and LION 5-10   80-84
WARNER 5-10   77-80
Also see BOONE, Pat, and the Boone Girls
Also see BOONE GIRLS

BOONE, Pat

Singles: 78rpm

DOT 4-8   55-58
REPUBLIC 5-10   54

Singles: 7-inch

ABC 2-4	74-75
BUENA VISTA 3-5	73
CAPITOL 3-5	70
CHEVROLET/RCA Victor (4988 "June	
Is Bustin' Out All Over") 10-15	58
(Promotional issue for Chevrolet dealers. Narration	
by Bob Lund.)	
DOT (200 series) 8-12	59-60
(Stereo.)	
DOT (15000 series) 5-10	55-57
(Maroon label.)	
DOT (15000 and 16000 series,	
except 16658) 4-8	57-66
(Black label.)	
DOT (16658 "Beach Girl") 5-10	64
(With Bruce Johnston and Terry Melcher.)	
DOT (17000 series) 3-6	66-75
HITSVILLE 3-5	76-77
LION 2-4	72
MC 2-4	77
MCA 2-4	84
MGM 3-5	71-73
MELODYLAND 3-5	74-76
ORCHID 2-4	89
REPUBLIC 10-15	54
SRG 2-4	88
TETRAGRAMMATON 3-5	69
WARNER 2-4	80-81

Picture Sleeves

DOT 8-12	57-62

EPs: 7-inch 33/45rpm

DOT 8-12	57-60

LPs: 10/12-inch 33rpm

ABC 5-10	74
BIBLE VOICE 5-10	70
CANDLELITE 6-10	
(Mail-order offer.)	
DOT (3000 series) 20-35	55-56
(Maroon label.)	
DOT (3000 series, except 3501) 10-20	57-67
(Black label. Monaural series.)	
DOT (3501 "Pat Boone Sings	
Guess Who") 25-35	63
DOT (9000 "April Love") 30-40	57
(Soundtrack.)	
DOT (25000 series, except	
25270 and 25501) 10-20	58-68
(Stereo series.)	
DOT (25270 "Moonglow") 10-20	60
(Black vinyl.)	
DOT (25270 "Moonglow") 30-50	60
(Colored vinyl.)	
DOT (25501 "Pat Boone Sings	
Guess Who") 25-40	63
FAMOUS TWINSET 5-8	74
HAMILTON 10-12	65
HITSVILLE 8-10	76
LAMB and LION 5-10	73-81

MC 5-10	77
MCA 5-10	82
MGM 5-10	73
PARAMOUNT 5-10	74
PICKWICK 5-10	
SUPREME 6-10	70
TETRAGRAMMATON 10-12	69
WORD 5-10	75-84
Also see BRUCE & TERRY	
Also see HUSKY, Ferlin / Pat Boone	
Also see JENKINS, Gordon, and His Orchestra	

BOONE, Pat and Shirley
(Pat Boone Family)

Singles: 7-inch

DOT 4-6	62-64
MGM 3-5	72
MELODYLAND 3-5	75
MOTOWN 3-5	74
WARNER 2-4	79

EPs: 7-inch 33/45rpm

DOT 5-10	59

LPs: 10/12-inch 33rpm

DOT 10-20	62
LION 5-10	72
WORD 5-10	71

BOONE, Pat, and the Boone Girls
Singles: 7-inch

LION 2-4	72
Also see BOONE, Pat and Shirley	
Also see BOONE GIRLS	

BOONE FAMILY: see BOONE, Pat and Shirley

BOONE GIRLS
(Boones)

Singles: 7-inch

LAMB and LION 2-4	77
LION 2-4	72
MGM 3-5	71-73
MOTOWN 3-5	75
WARNER 2-4	77

LPs: 10/12-inch 33rpm

LAMB and LION 5-10	77-83
Also see BOONE, Debbie	
Also see BOONE, Pat, and the Boone Girls	

BOOTEE, Duke
Singles: 7-inch

MERCURY 2-4	84

BOOTSY'S RUBBER BAND
(William "Bootsy" Collins; Bootsy)

Singles: 12-inch 33/45rpm

WARNER 4-6	79-82

Singles: 7-inch

WARNER 2-4	75-82

Picture Sleeves

WARNER 2-4	75-82

LPs: 10/12-inch 33rpm

WARNER 5-10	76-82

Members: William "Bootsy" Collins; Phelp Collins; Frankie
Waddy; Gary Cooper; Fred Wesley; Rick Gardner; Robert
Johnson; Maceo Parker; Gary Shider; Mike Hampton; Bennie
Worrell.
   Also see PARLIAMENT
   Also see SWEAT BAND
   Also see ZAPP

BOOTY PEOPLE
Singles: 7–inch
CALLA 3-5   76
LPs: 10/12–inch 33rpm
ABC 5-10   77

BORDERSONG
Singles: 7–inch
GREAT NORTHWEST (704 "She's a
  Good Woman") 10-20   76
LPs: 10/12–inch 33rpm
REAL GOOD (1001 "Morning") 75-100   75
Members: Ann Wilson; Nancy Wilson.
Also see HEART

BOSTIC, Earl
Singles: 78rpm
GOTHAM 5-10   46-48
KING 5-10   47-58
MAJESTIC 5-10   46
Singles: 7–inch
KING (500 series) 3-5   77
KING (4000 series, except 4491) 5-10   50-57
  (Black vinyl.)
KING (4491 "I Got Loaded") 25-35   52
KING (4000 series) 10-20   52-56
  (Colored vinyl.)
KING (5000 series) 4-8   57-65
KING (6000 series) 3-6   65-69
KING (15000 series) 2-5   72
EPs: 7–inch 33/45rpm
KING 8-15   52-62
LPs: 10/12–inch 33rpm
KING (72 "Earl Bostic and
  His Alto Sax") 50-100   52
KING (76 "Earl Bostic and
  His Alto Sax") 50-100   52
KING (77 "Earl Bostic and
  His Alto Sax") 50-100   52
KING (78 "Earl Bostic and
  His Alto Sax") 50-100   52
KING (79 "Earl Bostic and
  His Alto Sax") 50-100   52
KING (95 "Earl Bostic Plays Old
  Standards") 50-100   54
KING (103 "Earl Bostic and
  His Alto Sax") 50-100   54
KING (119 "Earl Bostic and
  His Alto Sax") 50-100   54
  (King 72 through 119 are 10–inch LPs.)
KING (500 series) 20-40   55-58
KING (600 through 1000 series) 8-15   59-70
PHILLIPS 8-12   68

BOSTIC, Earl, and Bill Doggett
Singles: 78rpm
KING 5-10   56
Singles: 7–inch
KING 10-15   56
  Also see BOSTIC, Earl
  Also see DOGGETT, Bill

BOSTIC, Sam
Singles: 7–inch
ATLANTIC 2-4   85

BOSTON
Singles: 7–inch
EPIC 3-5   76-79
MCA 2-4   85-87
Picture Sleeves
MCA 2-4   85-87
LPs: 10/12–inch 33rpm
EPIC (E99-34188 "Boston") 15-25   78
  (Picture disc.)
EPIC (HE-34188 "Boston") 12-15   80
  (Half-speed mastered.)
EPIC (PE-34188 "Boston") 15-25   76
EPIC (35000 series) 10-12   78
EPIC (HE-45000 series) 12-15   81
  (Half-speed mastered.)
MCA 5-10   85-87
Members: Brad Delp; Tom Scholz; Barry Goudreau; Sib
Hashian; Fran Sheehan.
  Also see GOUDREAU, Barry
  Also see ORION the HUNTER

BOSTON POPS ORCHESTRA
(Conducted by Arthur Fiedler)
Singles: 78rpm
RCA 2-5   50-57
Singles: 7–inch
RCA 3-8   50-65
Picture Sleeves
RCA (8378 "I Want to Hold Your Hand") 8-12   64
EPs: 7–inch 33/45rpm
RCA 4-8   50-61
LPs: 10/12–inch 33rpm
DEUTSCHE GRAMMOPHON 4-8   78
MIDSONG INT'L 4-8   79
POLYDOR 5-10   71-72
RCA 5-20   50-69
  Also see HIRT, Al, and the Boston Pops

BOSTON POPS ORCHESTRA
(Conducted by John Williams)
LPs: 10/12–inch 33rpm
PHILIPS 5-10   80-86
  Also see WILLIAMS, John

BOSWELL, Connee
Singles: 78rpm
BRUNSWICK 5-10   32-44
DECCA 5-10   35-56
Singles: 7–inch
CHARLES 4-8   62
DECCA 5-10   50-56

EPs: 7–inch 33/45rpm		
DECCA 5-15	56
RCA 5-10	57
LPs: 10/12–inch 33rpm		
DECCA 15-25	56
RCA 10-20	57

Also see BOSWELL SISTERS
Also see CROSBY, Bing, and Connee Boswell

BOTTOM & COMPANY
Singles: 7–inch

MOTOWN 3-5	74-75
LPs: 10/12–inch 33rpm		
GORDY 8-10	76

BOTTOM LINE
Singles: 7–inch

GREEDY 3-5	76
LPs: 10/12–inch 33rpm		
GREEDY 8-10	76

BOUNTY, Rick, and the Rockits
Singles: 7–inch

BOW (6144 "It'll Be Me") 75-100	58
MASSABESIC 3-5	86
Picture Sleeves		
MASSABESIC 3-5	86

BOURGEOIS-TAGG
Singles: 7–inch

ISLAND 2-4	86-87
LPs: 10/12–inch 33rpm		
ISLAND 5-10	86-87

Members: Brent Bourgeois; Larry Tagg.

BOW WOW WOW
Singles: 12–inch 33/45rpm

RCA 4-6	83
Singles: 7–inch		
RCA 2-4	81-84
Picture Sleeves		
RCA 2-4	82
LPs: 10/12–inch 33rpm		
HARVEST 5-10	82
RCA 5-10	81-84
Promotional LPs		
RCA "Special Radio Series") 10-15	81

Members: Annabella Lu Win; Matt Ashman; Dave Barbarossa;
Leroy Gorman.
Also see ADAM and the Ants

BOWEN, Jimmy
Singles: 78rpm

ROULETTE 5-10	57
Singles: 7–inch		
CAPEHART 5-10	61-62
CREST 5-10	61
REPRISE 5-10	64-66
ROULETTE (Except 4002) 10-20	57-60
ROULETTE (4002 "Party Doll") 20-30	57

(Credited to "Jimmy Bowen with the Rhythm
Orchids" though actually by Buddy Knox.)

Picture Sleeves		
CAPEHART (5005 "Teenage		
Dreamworld") 30-40	61
EPs: 7–inch 33/45rpm		
ROULETTE (302 "Jimmy Bowen") . . 40-50	57
LPs: 10/12–inch 33rpm		
REPRISE (6210 "Sunday Morning		
with the Comics") 20-25	66
ROULETTE (25004 "Jimmy Bowen") 75-100	57

Also see KNOX, Buddy / Jimmy Bowen

BOWIE, David
Singles: 12–inch 33/45rpm

EMI AMERICA 5-10	82-87
RCA 10-15	79-80
Promotional 12–inch Singles		
EMI AMERICA 8-15	82-87
RCA 15-25	79-80
Singles: 7–inch		
BACKSTREET 3-5	82
DERAM (85009 "Rubber Band") . . . 20-40	67
EMI AMERICA 3-5	83-87
LONDON (20079 "Laughing Gnome") 15-25	73
MERCURY (72949 "Space Oddity") 30-40	69
MERCURY (73075 "Memory of a		
Free Festival") 35-50	70
RCA 3-6	71-84
WARNER (5815 "Can't Help		
Thinking About Me") 50-75	66
Picture Sleeves		
BACKSTREET (1767 "Cat People") . . . 4-8	82
EMI AMERICA 3-5	83-87
RCA (0001 "Time") 200-400	73
RCA (0719 "Starman") 15-20	72
RCA (0876 "Space Oddity") 10-15	73
RCA (12078 "Ashes to Ashes") 10-15	80
RCA (12134 "Fashion") 5-10	80
RCA (13660 "White Light White Heat") . 3-5	83
RCA (13769 "1984") 3-5	80
Promotional Singles		
BACKSTREET 5-10	82
DERAM (85009 "Rubber Band") 30-40	67
EMI AMERICA (8158 through 8190) . . . 4-8	83-84
EMI AMERICA (8231 "Blue Jean") 4-8	84
EMI AMERICA (8246 through 8308) . . . 4-8	83-86
EMI AMERICA (8380 "Day in Day Out") 4-8	87
EMI AMERICA (8380 "Day in		
Day Out") 15-20	87
(Colored vinyl. Boxed edition.)		
EMI AMERICA (43000 series) 4-8	87
LONDON (20079 "Laughing Gnome") 15-25	73
MERCURY (311 "All the Madmen") . . 40-60	70
MERCURY (72949 "Space Oddity") . 30-50	69
MERCURY (73075 "Memory of a		
Free Festival") 40-60	70
RCA 5-12	71-84
WARNER (5815 "Can't Help Thinking		
About Me") 50-75	66
WHAT'S IT ALL ABOUT 10-20	

EPs: 7–inch 33/45rpm

RCA 20-25
(Promotional issues only.)

LPs: 10/12–inch 33rpm

DERAM (16003 "David Bowie") ... 100-125   67
(Monaural.)
DERAM (18003 "David Bowie") ... 100-150   67
(Stereo.)
EMI AMERICA 5-10   83-87
LONDON 10-20   73-85
MFSL (064 "Rise and Fall of
  Ziggy Stardust" 20-40   82
MFSL (083 "Let's Dance") 15-25   82
MERCURY (61246 "Man of Words/
  Man of Music") 75-100   69
MERCURY (61246 "Space Oddity") .. 10-15   72
MERCURY (61325 "The Man Who Sold
  the World") 25-40   71
PRECISION (1 "Don't Be Fooled
  By the Name") 20-25   81
  (10–inch LP.)
RCA (0291 "Bowie Pin Ups") 10-15   73
RCA (0576 "Diamond Dogs") 500-750   74
  (With "Dog Genitals" cover.)
RCA (0576 "Diamond Dogs") 10-15   74
  (With dog's genitals covered.)
RCA (0700 through 1300 series) 10-15   74-76
RCA (1732 "Changesone Bowie") . 100-125   76
  (With alternate take of *John, I'm Only Dancing*.)
RCA (1732 "Changesone Bowie") ... 10-20   76
  (With the commonly issued take of *John, I'm Only
  Dancing*.)
RCA (2000 through 2500) 10-15   77
RCA (2743 "Peter and the Wolf") 10-15   78
  (Black vinyl.)
RCA (2743 "Peter and the Wolf") 35-55   78
  (Colored vinyl.)
RCA (2900 through 4200 series) 5-10   79-82
RCA (4600 through 4800 series) 10-15   71-73
  (With "LSP" prefix.)
RCA (4700 through 4900
  series, except 4862) 5-10   83-84
  (With "AFL" or "CPL" prefix.)
RCA 4862 "Ziggy Stardust") 5-10   83
  (Black vinyl.)
RCA 4862 "Ziggy Stardust") 40-80   83
  (Clear vinyl.)
RYKODISC 8-12   87-90

Promotional LPs

DERAM (18003 "David Bowie") 200-300   67
EMI AMERICA (9960 "Let's Talk") ... 40-70   83
MERCURY (61246 "Man of Words/
  Man of Music") 75-125   69
RCA (0200 through 4800 series) 20-40   71-73
  (With programmer's strip on front cover.)
RCA (2697 "Bowie Now") 30-50   78
RCA (3016 "An Evening with
  David Bowie") 100-200   78
RCA (3545 "Bowie 1980") 50-75   80

RCA (3829 "RCA Special
  Radio Series") 30-50   80
RCA (3840 "David Bowie
  Interview") 35-50   80
RCA (11306 "Peter and the Wolf") ... 30-40   78
  Also see HOUSTON, Cissy
  Also see KHAN, Chaka
  Also see QUEEN and David Bowie
  Also see SPIDERS from Mars
  Also see TURNER, Tina
  Also see VANDROSS, Luther

BOWIE, David / Joe Cocker / Youngbloods
LPs: 10/12–inch 33rpm

MERCURY (SRD-2-29 "Zig Zag
  Festival") 40-60   70
  (Promotional issue only.)
  Also see COCKER, Joe
  Also see YOUNGBLOODS

BOWIE, David, and Bing Crosby
Singles: 7–inch

RCA 3-6   83

Picture Sleeves

RCA 4-8   . 83
  Also see CROSBY, Bing

BOWIE, David, and Mick Jagger
Singles: 12–inch 33/45rpm

EMI AMERICA (19200 "Dancing in the
  Streets") 8-12   85

Singles: 7–inch

EMI AMERICA (8288 "Dancing in the
  Streets") 2-4   85

Picture Sleeves

EMI AMERICA (8288 "Dancing in the
  Streets") 3-5   85
  Also see JAGGER, Mick

BOWIE, David, and the Pat Metheny Group
Singles: 12–inch 33/45rpm

EMI AMERICA 4-8   85

Singles: 7–inch

EMI AMERICA 2-4   85

LPs: 10/12–inch 33rpm

EMI AMERICA 5-10   85
  Also see METHENY, Pat

BOWIE, David / Iggy Pop
Singles: 12–inch 33/45rpm

RCA (10956 "Sound and Vision") ... 30-50   77
  (Promotional issue only.)
  Also see BOWIE, David
  Also see POP, Iggy

BOWLES, Rick
Singles: 7–inch

POLYDOR 2-4   82

LPs: 10/12–inch 33rpm

POLYDOR 5-10   82

BOX of FROGS
Singles: 7–inch

EPIC 2-4   84-86

LPs: 10/12–inch 33rpm

EPIC 5-10   84-86
Members: Chris Dreja; Jim McCarty; Jeff Beck.
Also see YARDBIRDS

BOX TOPS

Singles: 7–inch

BELL 3-5   70-71
GUSTO 2-4   84
HI 3-5   72-73
MALA 4-8   67-69
SPEHRE SOUND 4-8   67
STAX 3-5   74

LPs: 10/12–inch 33rpm

BELL 10-20   67-69
COTILLION 10-15   71
KORY 5-10   77
RHINO 5-10   82
Members: Alex Chilton; Rick Allen; Tom Boggs; Harold Cloud;
Bill Cunningham; John Evans; Swain Scharfar; Gary Talley;
Danny Smythe; Rick Stevens.

BOY GEORGE

Singles: 7–inch

VIRGIN 2-4   87-89

LPs: 10/12–inch 33rpm

VIRGIN 5-10   87-89
Also see CULTURE CLUB

BOY MEETS GIRL

Singles: 7–inch

A&M 2-4   85-89
RCA 2-4   88

Picture Sleeves

A&M 2-4   85-89

LPs: 10/12–inch 33rpm

A&M 5-10   85
RCA 5-8   88
Members: George Merrill; Shannon Rubicam.

BOYCE, Tommy

Singles: 7–inch

A&M (Except 826) 4-8   66
A&M (826 "In Case the Wind
  Should Blow") 10-12   66
CAPITOL 3-5   71
COLPIX 8-10   66
DOT 10-15   60
MGM 8-10   65
RCA (7000 series) 10-15   61
RCA (8000 series) 8-12   62-63
R-DELL 15-20   58
WOW 8-12   61

LPs: 10/12–inch 33rpm

CAMDEN 15-20   68
Also see CLOUD, Christopher

BOYCE, Tommy, and Bobby Hart
(Boyce and Hart)

Singles: 7–inch

A&M 4-8   67-69
AQUARIAN 3-6   68

Picture Sleeves

A&M 5-10   67-69
AQUARIAN 5-8   68

LPs: 10/12–inch 33rpm

A&M 10-20   67-69
Also see BOYCE, Tommy
Also see DOLENZ, JONES, BOYCE & HART

BOYD, Eddie
(Eddie Boyd and His Chess Men; Eddie Boyd Blues
Combo; Little Eddie Boyd and His Boogie Band)

Singles: 78rpm

CHESS 10-20   50-56
HERALD 40-60   52
J.O.B. 20-25   52-58
RCA 10-20   47-50

Singles: 7–inch

ART TONE 5-10   62
BEA and BABY 5-10   59
CHESS (1523 "Cool Kind Treatment") 25-50   52
CHESS (1533 "24 Hours") 25-50   53
CHESS (1541 "Third Degree") 25-50   53
CHESS (1552 "That's When I
  Miss You") 25-50   53
CHESS (1561 "Picture in the Frame") 20-40 54
CHESS (1573 "Hush Baby,
  Don't You Cry") 20-40   54
CHESS (1576 "Driftin") 20-40   54
CHESS (1582 "The Story of Bill") ... 15-30 55
CHESS (1595 "Real Good Feeling") . 15-30 55
CHESS (1606 "I'm a Prisoner") 15-30 55
CHESS (1634 "Just a Fool") 15-25 56
CHESS (1660 "I Got a Woman") ... 15-25 56
CHESS (Colored vinyl) 75-125   54
  (We are unable at this time to specify exactly which
  Chess numbers were pressed on colored vinyl.)
HERALD (406 "I'm Goin' Downtown") 75-125   52
J.O.B. (1007 "Five Long Years") 40-60   52
  (Black vinyl.)
J.O.B. (1007 "Five Long Years") ... 75-125   52
  (Colored vinyl.)
J.O.B. (1009 "It's Miserable to
  Be Alone") 40-60   53
J.O.B. (1114 "I Love You") 30-50   57
LA SALLE 5-10   61
MOJO 5-10
ORIOLE (1316 "Five Long Years") .. 20-30   58
PALOS 4-8   63-64
PUSH 5-10   62
RCA (50-0006 "What Makes These
  Things Happen to Me") 35-50   50
  (Colored vinyl.)

EPs: 7–inch 33/45rpm

ESQUIRE 15-20   60

LPs: 10/12–inch 33rpm

EPIC 20-25   69
LONDON 15-20   69
Also see GREEN, Peter

BOYD, Jimmy
(Little Jimmy Boyd)
Singles: 78rpm
COLUMBIA (Except 21571) 4-8	52-56
COLUMBIA (21571 "Rockin' Down the Mississippi") 10-15	56

Singles: 7–inch
CAPITOL 4-8	63
COLUMBIA (152 "I Saw Mommy Kissing Santa Claus") 10-20	52
COLUMBIA (21571 "Rockin' Down the Mississippi") 30-40	56
COLUMBIA (39000 and 40000 series) 10-20	52-56
IMPERIAL 3-6	66-67
MGM (12788 "Cream Puff") 40-50	59
TAKE TEN 4-8	63
VEE JAY 4-8	65

Picture Sleeves
COLUMBIA (152 "I Saw Mommy Kissing Santa Claus") 15-25	52

(With die-cut center hole.)
Also see LAINE, Frankie, and Jimmy Boyd

BOYD, Jimmy, and Rosemary Clooney
Singles: 78rpm
COLUMBIA 4-8	53

Singles: 7–inch
COLUMBIA (39000 series) 8-12	53
COLUMBIA (41000 series) 4-8	60

Also see BOYD, Jimmy
Also see CLOONEY, Rosemary

BOYD, Little Eddie: see BOYD, Eddie

BOYER, Bonnie
Singles: 12–inch 33/45rpm
COLUMBIA 4-6	79

Singles: 7–inch
COLUMBIA 2-4	79

LPs: 10/12–inch 33rpm
COLUMBIA 5-10	79

BOYER, Charles
Singles: 7–inch
VALIANT 3-6	65

LPs: 10/12–inch 33rpm
VALIANT 10-20	65

BOYLAN, Terence
Singles: 7–inch
ASYLUM 2-4	77-80

LPs: 10/12–inch 33rpm
ASYLUM 5-10	77-80
VERVE/FORECAST 12-15	69

BOYS BAND
Singles: 7–inch
ELEKTRA 2-4	82

Picture Sleeves
ELEKTRA 2-4	82

LPs: 10/12–inch 33rpm
ASYLUM 5-10	82

BOYS DON'T CRY
Singles: 12–inch 33/45rpm
PROFILE 4-6	86

Singles: 7–inch
PROFILE 2-4	86

LPs: 10/12–inch 33rpm
PROFILE 5-10	86

Member: Nick Richards.

BOYS In the BAND
Singles: 7–inch
SPRING 3-5	70

BOYS on the BLOCK
Singles: 7–inch
FANTASY 2-4	87

BOZE, Calvin
Singles: 78rpm
ALADDIN 10-20	50-52
G&G (1029 "Safronia B.") 30-50	46
SCORE 10-15	48

Singles: 7–inch
ALADDIN (3045 "Waitin' and Drinkin") 50-100	50
ALADDIN (3055 "Safronia B.") 50-100	50
ALADDIN (3065 "Lizzie Lou") 50-75	50
ALADDIN (3072 "Stinkin' from Drinkin") 40-60	50
ALADDIN (3079 "Beale Street on Saturday Night") 40-50	51
ALADDIN (3086 "Slippin' and Slidin") 40-50	51
ALADDIN (3100 "I've Got News for You") 40-50	51
ALADDIN (3110 "I'm Gonna Steam off the Stamp") 40-50	52
ALADDIN (3160 "Shamrock") 40-50	52
ALADDIN (3122 "My Friend Told Me") 40-50	52
ALADDIN (3132 "Good Time Sue") . . 40-50	52
ALADDIN (3147 "Looped") 40-50	52
ASTRA 5-10	
IMPERIAL 5-10	62

BRADLEY, James
(James Bradley and the Bill Smith Combo)
Singles: 7–inch
CHESS 5-10	60
MALACO 2-4	79-84
MANCO 5-10	61

LPs: 10/12–inch 33rpm
MALACO 5-10	84

BRADLEY, Jan
Singles: 7–inch
ADANTI 4-8	65
CHESS 4-8	62-68
DOYLEN 4-8	70
ERIC 2-4	73
FORMAL (Except 1044) 5-10	62-63
FORMAL (1044 "Mama Didn't Lie") . . 15-25	62
HOOTENANNY 5-8	62

NIGHT OWL	5-8	63
SOUND SPECTRUM	4-8	65

BRADLEY, Owen
(Owen Bradley Quintet)
Singles: 78rpm

CORAL	4-8	49-50
DECCA	3-8	54-57

Singles: 7–inch

CORAL	5-10	50
DECCA	5-10	54-61

EPs: 7–inch 33/45rpm

CORAL	10-20	54
DECCA	10-20	58

LPs: 10/12–inch 33rpm

CORAL	15-25	53-55
DECCA	15-25	58-60

BRADSHAW, Terry
Singles: 7–inch

BENSON	2-4	80
MERCURY	3-5	76

Picture Sleeves

BENSON	2-4	80

LPs: 10/12–inch 33rpm

BENSON	5-10	80
HEARTWARMING	5-10	82
MERCURY	6-12	76

BRADSHAW, Tiny
Singles: 78rpm

KING	5-10	50-55

Singles: 7–inch

GUSTO	2-4	80-83
KING (4300 through 4500 series) (Black vinyl.)	15-25	50-53
KING (4300 through 4500 series) (Colored vinyl.)	40-60	50-53
KING (4600 through 4800 series)	10-20	54-55

EPs: 7–inch 33/45rpm

KING	20-35	52-56

LPs: 10/12–inch 33rpm

KING (74 "Off and On")	100-150	52
KING (501 "Tiny Bradshaw")	50-100	55
KING (653 "Great Composer")	30-50	59
KING (953 "24 Great Songs")	20-30	66

BRAINSTORM
Singles: 12–inch 33/45rpm

TABU	4-6	77-79

Singles: 7–inch

RCA	2-4	82
TABU	2-4	76-79

LPs: 10/12–inch 33rpm

RCA	5-10	82
TABU	5-10	77-79

Members: Belita Woods; Charles Overton; Jeryl Bright; Larry Sims; Jerry Kent; Renell Gousalves; Willie Wooten; Lamont Johnson; Trenita Womack.

BRAM TCHAIKOVSKY:
see TCHAIKOVSKY, Bram

BRAMLETT, Bonnie
Singles: 7–inch

CAPRICORN	3-5	75-78
COLUMBIA	3-5	72-73
REFUGE	2-4	81

LPs: 10/12–inch 33rpm

CAPRICORN	8-10	75-78
COLUMBIA	10-12	72-73

Also see DELANEY & BONNIE
Also see LITTLE FEAT

BRAMLETT, Delaney
(Delaney and Bekka Bramlett; Delaney Bramlett and Blue Diamond)
Singles: 7–inch

COLUMBIA (45950 "Are You a Beatle Or a Rolling Stone")	5-10	73
CREAM	2-4	81
GNP/CRESCENDO	4-8	64-66
INDEPENDENCE	4-8	67

LPs: 10/12–inch 33rpm

COLUMBIA	8-10	72-73
MGM	8-10	75
PRODIGAL	8-10	77

Also see DELANEY & BONNIE
Also see RIO, Chuck, and Delaney

BRAND X
Singles: 7–inch

PASSPORT	2-4	78

LPs: 10/12–inch 33rpm

PASSPORT	5-10	76-84

Members: Phil Collins; John Goodsall; Percy Jones; Robin Lumley; Morris Pert.
Also see COLLINS, Phil

BRANDON, Bill
Singles: 7–inch

MOONSONG	3-5	72-73
PIEDMONT	3-5	76
PRELUDE	3-5	77-78
SOUTH CAMP	4-8	67
TOWER	4-8	68

BRANIGAN, Laura
Singles: 12–inch 33/45rpm

ATLANTIC	4-8	82-87

Singles: 7–inch

ATLANTIC	2-4	80-90
EMI AMERICA	2-4	84

Picture Sleeves

ATLANTIC	2-4	80-87

LPs: 10/12–inch 33rpm

ATLANTIC	5-10	82-90
EMI AMERICA	5-10	84

BRASS CONSTRUCTION
Singles: 12–inch 33/45rpm

CAPITOL	4-6	83
LIBERTY	4-6	82

Singles: 7–inch

CAPITOL	2-4	83
LIBERTY	2-4	82
U.A.	3-5	75-80

LPs: 10/12–inch 33rpm

CAPITOL	5-10	83
U.A.	5-10	75-80
LIBERTY	5-10	82

Members: Randy Muller; Wade Williamston; Joe Wong; Wayne Parris; Mickey Grudge; Morris Price; Jesse Ward; Sandy Billups; Larry Payton.

BRASS FEVER

Singles: 7–inch

IMPULSE	3-5	76-77

LPs: 10/12–inch 33rpm

IMPULSE	8-10	76

BRASS RING

Singles: 7–inch

ABC	3-5	70
DUNHILL (Except 4090)	4-6	66-69
DUNHILL (4090 "Love in the Open Air")	10-20	67
ITCO	3-5	69

Picture Sleeves

DUNHILL (4090 "Love in the Open Air")	15-25	67

(Billed on sleeve as "Paul McCartney's First NON Beatle Song.")

LPs: 10/12–inch 33rpm

DUNHILL	8-12	66-73
ITCO	6-10	70
PROJECT 3	6-10	72

Members: Phil Bodner.
Also see McCARTNEY, Paul

BRAUN, Bob

Singles: 7–inch

AUDIO FIDELITY	3-6	65
DECCA	4-8	62
FRATERNITY	3-6	64-66
KING	4-8	59
U.A.	3-5	67

Picture Sleeves

DECCA	4-8	62

EPs: 7–inch 33/45rpm

DECCA	5-10	63

LPs: 10/12–inch 33rpm

AUDIO FIDELITY	8-12	65
DECCA	10-20	62
U.A.	8-12	67
WRAYCO	5-10	71

BRAVE BELT

Singles: 7–inch

REPRISE	3-5	71-72

LPs: 10/12–inch 33rpm

REPRISE	15-20	71-75

Members: Chad Allan; Randy Bachman; Robert Bachman; C.F. Turner.
Also see BACHMAN-TURNER-BACHMAN

BRAVOS, Los: see LOS BRAVOS

BREAD

(David Gates and Bread)

Singles: 7–inch

ASYLUM	3-5	
ELEKTRA (Except 45666 and 45668)	3-5	70-77
ELEKTRA (45666 "Dismal Day")	5-8	69
ELEKTRA (45668 "Could I")	4-6	69

Picture Sleeves

ELEKTRA	4-8	70-72

LPs: 10/12–inch 33rpm

ELEKTRA (100 and 1000 series)	8-12	73-77
ELEKTRA (5000 series)	15-25	72-73
(Quadrophonic series.)		
ELEKTRA (74000 and 75000 series, except 75015)	10-15	69-73
ELEKTRA (75015 "Baby I'm a Want You")	15-25	72
(With die-cut cover.)		
ELEKTRA (75015 "Baby I'm a Want You")	10-15	72
(Standard cover.)		
K-TEL	5-10	82

Members: David Gates; James Griffin; Mike Botts; Larry Knechtel; Robb Royer.
Also see GATES, David

BREAK MACHINE

Singles: 12–inch 33/45rpm

SIRE	4-6	84

Singles: 7–inch

SIRE	2-4	84

BREAKFAST CLUB

Singles: 7–inch

MCA	2-4	87

Picture Sleeves

MCA	2-4	87

LPs: 10/12–inch 33rpm

MCA	5-10	87

BREAKWATER

Singles: 7–inch

ARISTA	3-5	79-80

LPs: 10/12–inch 33rpm

ARISTA	5-10	79-80

Members: Kae Williams; Lincoln Gilmore; James Jones; Gene Robinson Jr.; Vince Garnell; Greg Scott; John Braddock; Steve Green.

BREATHLESS

Singles: 7–inch

EMI AMERICA	2-4	79

LPs: 10/12–inch 33rpm

EMI AMERICA	5-10	79-80

BRECKER BROTHERS

Singles: 7–inch

ARISTA	3-5	75-80

LPs: 10/12–inch 33rpm

ARISTA	5-10	75-81

Members: Mike Brecker; Randy Brecker; Dave Sanborn.
Also see DREAMS

BREMERS, Beverly
Singles: 7-inch
BRUT 3-5
COLUMBIA 3-5   75-77
ERIC 2-4   83
SCEPTER 3-5   71-75
Picture Sleeves
SCEPTER 4-6   72
LPs: 10/12-inch 33rpm
SCEPTER 8-10   72

BRENDA & HERB
Singles: 7-inch
H&L 3-5   78
Members: Brenda Reid; Herb Rooney.
Also see EXCITERS

BRENDA & PETE:
see LEE, Brenda, and Pete Fountain

BRENDA and the Tabulations
Singles: 12-inch 33/45rpm
CHOCOLATE CITY 4-6   77
Singles: 7-inch
CHOCOLATE CITY 3-5   76-77
DIONN 5-10   67-69
EPIC 3-5   72-75
TOP and BOTTOM 4-6   69-71
LPs: 10/12-inch 33rpm
CHOCOLATE CITY 5-10   77
DIONN (2000 "Dry Your Eyes") 20-30   67
TOP and BOTTOM 15-20   70
Members: Brenda Payton; Jerry Joures; Eddie Jackson; Maurice
Coates; Dennis Dozier; Donald Ford; Deborah Martin; Lee
Smith; Kenneth Wright; Pat Mercer.

BRENDA LEE: see LEE, Brenda

BRENNAN, Walter
Singles: 7-inch
DOT 5-10   60
KAPP 3-5   71
LIBERTY 4-8   62-64
RPC 8-10   61
Picture Sleeves
DOT 10-15   60
LIBERTY 8-12   62-63
LPs: 10/12-inch 33rpm
DOT 15-25   60
EVEREST 15-20   60
HAMILTON 8-10   65
LIBERTY 15-25   62
LONDON 6-10   70
RPC 15-25   62
SUNSET 8-10   66
U.A. 5-10   75

BRENSTON, Jackie
(Jackie Brenston and His Delta Cats)
Singles: 78rpm
CHESS (Except 1458) 10-20   51-53

CHESS (1458 "Rocket 88") 30-40   51
(With Ike Turner. Fakes abound but original 45s do
not exist of this single.)
FEDERAL 5-10   56-57
Singles: 7-inch51
CHESS (1469 "In My Real
Gone Rocket") 150-250   51
CHESS (1496 "Leo the Louse") ... 100-150   52
CHESS (1532 "The Blues Got
Me Again") 50-100   53
FEDERAL 20-35   56-57
SUE 5-10   61
Also see TURNER, Ike

BRENSTON, Jackie / Muddy Waters
Singles: 7-inch
CHESS (113 "Rocket 88") 3-5
Also see BRENSTON, Jackie
Also see WATERS, Muddy

BREWER, Teresa
(Teresa Brewer and the Lancers; Teresa Brewer and
Mickey Mantle; Teresa Brewer and Bobby Wayne)
Singles: 78rpm
CORAL 5-10   52-57
LONDON 5-10   50-52
Singles: 7-inch
ABC 3-5   67
AMSTERDAM 3-5   72-73
CORAL (60000 and 61000 series) ... 10-20   52-58
CORAL (62000 and 65000 series) 5-10   58-64
DOCTOR JAZZ 2-4   83
FLYING DUTCHMAN 3-5   72
LONDON 8-12   50-52
PHILIPS 4-8   63-67
PROJECT 3 2-4   82
RCA (11882 "Merry Christmas") 3-6   79
(With picture label. Special products issue.)
SSS INT'L 3-5   68
SIGNATURE 2-4   74-83
Picture Sleeves
CORAL 5-10   58-60
SIGNATURE 2-4   80
EPs: 7-inch 33/45rpm
CORAL 8-15   55-60
LONDON 10-20   51
LPs: 10/12-inch 33rpm
AMSTERDAM 6-10   73-74
COLUMBIA 5-10   81
CORAL (7 "Best of Teresa Brewer") . 10-20   65
CORAL (56072 "A Bouquet of Hits
from Teresa Brewer") 25-40   52
(10-inch LP.)
CORAL (56093 "Till I Waltz
Again with You") 25-40   53
(10-inch LP.)
CORAL (57027 through 57297) 15-25   55-59
CORAL (57315 through 57351) 10-20   60-65
DOCTOR JAZZ 5-10   79-83
FLYING DUTCHMAN 6-10   73-74
IMAGE 5-10   78

LONDON (1006 "Teresa Brewer") ... 40-60   51
(10–inch LP.)
MCA 5-10   83
PHILIPS 10-15   63-67
PROJECT 3 5-10   82
RCA 5-10   75
SIGNATURE 5-10   74-75
VOCALION 8-12   69
WING 8-10   66

BREWER, Teresa, and Count Basie
LPs: 10/12–inch 33rpm

DOCTOR JAZZ 5-10   84
Also see BASIE, Count

BREWER, Teresa, and Duke Ellington
LPs: 10/12–inch 33rpm

COLUMBIA 5-10   81
FLYING DUTCHMAN 6-10   74
Also see BREWER, Teresa
Also see ELLINGTON, Duke

BREWER & SHIPLEY
Singles: 7–inch

A&M 4-8   68-69
BUDDAH 3-5   70
CAPITOL 3-5   74-75
KAMA SUTRA 3-5   70-73

Picture Sleeves

KAMA SUTRA 3-6   72

LPs: 10/12–inch 33rpm

A&M 12-15   68
ACCORD 5-10   83
CAPITOL 8-10   74-75
KAMA SUTRA 10-12   70-76
Members: Mike Brewer; Tom Shipley.

BRIAN & BRENDA
Singles: 7–inch

ROCKET 3-5   76-78
Members: Brian Russell; Brenda Russell.

BRICK
Singles: 12–inch 33/45rpm

BANG 4-6   79-82

Singles: 7–inch

BANG 2-4   76-82
MAINSTREET 3-5   76
STREET 3-5   76

LPs: 10/12–inch 33rpm

BANG 5-10   76-82
Members: Jimmy Brown; Regi Hargis; Eddie Irons; Ray
Ransom; Don Nevins.

BRIDES of FUNKENSTEIN
Singles: 7–inch

ATLANTIC 2-4   78-80

LPs: 10/12–inch 33rpm

ATLANTIC 5-10   78-80
Members: Lynn Mabry; Dawn Silva.
Also see PARLIAMENT

BRIDGES, Alicia
Singles: 12–inch 33/45rpm

SECOND WAVE 4-6   84
POLYDOR 4-6   78-79

Singles: 7–inch

A.V.I. 2-4   82
MEGA 3-5   72
POLYDOR 2-4   78-79
SECOND WAVE 2-4   84
ZODIAC 3-5   73

LPs: 10/12–inch 33rpm

POLYDOR 5-10   78-79

BRIDGEWATER, Dee Dee
Singles: 12–inch 33/45rpm

ELEKTRA 4-6   79-80

Singles: 7–inch

ELEKTRA 3-5   78-79

LPs: 10/12–inch 33rpm

ATLANTIC 8-10   76
ELEKTRA 5-10   78-80

BRIEF ENCOUNTER
Singles: 7–inch

CAPITOL 3-5   76-77
SEVENTY SEVEN 3-5   72-73
Members: Maurice Whittington; Gary Bailey; Larry Bailey;
Belmont Bailey; Monte Bailey.

BRIGGS, Lillian
Singles: 78rpm

EPIC 4-8   56

Singles: 7–inch

ABC-PAR 4-8   61
CORAL 5-10   59-60
EPIC 10-20   56

BRIGHT, Larry
Singles: 7–inch

BRIGHT 4-8   65
DEL-FI (Except 4204) 5-10   63-64
DEL-FI (4204 "Surfin' Queen") 10-20   63
DONNA 4-8   64
DOT 4-8   66
EDIT 5-10   62
HIGHLAND 5-10   61
JOJO 3-5   76
ORIGINAL SOUND 3-5   71
RENDEZVOUS 5-10   60
SOUND 3-5   71
TIDE (006 through 1083) 5-10   60-62
TIDE (2012 "Money") 4-8   66

BRIGHT, Larry / Humdingers
Singles: 7–inch

JAYE JOSEPH 4-8   64
Also see BRIGHT, Larry

BRIGHTER SIDE of DARKNESS
Singles: 7–inch

20TH FOX 3-5   72-75

LPs: 10/12–inch 33rpm

20TH FOX 8-10   73
Members: Darryl Lamont; Ralph Eskridge; Larry Washington; Randolph Murph.

BRILEY, Martin
Singles: 7–inch

EMI AMERICA 2-4   84
MERCURY 2-4   81-84
LPs: 10/12–inch 33rpm
MERCURY 5-10   81-85

BRILL, Marty, and Larry Foster
LPs: 10/12–inch 33rpm

COLPIX 10-20   65
LAURIE 15-20   62

BRIMMER, Charles
Singles: 7–inch

CHELSEA 3-5   75-76
LPs: 10/12–inch 33rpm
CHELSEA 8-10   76-77

BRINKLEY, Charles
Singles: 7–inch

MUSIC MACHINE 3-5   75

BRINKLEY & PARKER
Singles: 7–inch

DARNEL 3-5   74

BRISCOE, Jimmy, and the Little Beavers
Singles: 7–inch

ATLANTIC 3-5   71
J-CITY 3-5   72
PHI-KAPPA 3-5   73-75
SALSOUL 2-4   79
WANDERICK 3-5   77
LPs: 10/12–inch 33rpm
PHI-KAPPA 10-12   74
WANDERICK 8-10   77
Members: Jimmy Briscoe; Stanford Stansbury; Robert Makins; Kevin Brown; Maurice Pully.

BRISTOL, Johnny
Singles: 7–inch

ATLANTIC 3-5   76-78
HANDSHAKE 2-4   80-81
MGM 3-5   74-75
LPs: 10/12–inch 33rpm
ATLANTIC 5-10   76-78
HANDSHAKE 5-10   81
MGM 8-12   74-75
Also see STEWART, Amii, and Johnny Bristol

BRISTOL, Johnny, and Alton McClain
Singles: 7–inch

POLYDOR 2-4   80
Also see McCLAIN, Alton, and Destiny

BRISTOL, Johnny, and Spyder Turner
Singles: 7–inch

POLYDOR 2-4   83
Also see BRISTOL, Johnny
Also see TURNER, Spyder

BRISTOL, Marc
LPs: 10/12–inch 33rpm

KING NOODLE 5-10   87

BRITISH LIONS
Singles: 7–inch

RSO 3-5   78
LPs: 10/12–inch 33rpm
RSO 5-10   78
Members: John Fiddler; Dale Griffin; Overend Watts; Ray Major; Morgan Fisher.
Also see MOTT the HOOPLE

BRITT, Tina
Singles: 7–inch

EASTERN 5-8   65
MINIT 3-6   69
VEEP 4-8   68-69
LPs: 10/12–inch 33rpm
MINIT 12-20   69

BROADWAY
Singles: 7–inch

GRANITE 3-5   76
HILLTAK 2-4   78
LPs: 10/12–inch 33rpm
HILLTAK 8-10   79

BROMBERG, David
Singles: 7–inch

COLUMBIA 3-5   72-73
FANTASY 2-4   77-79
LPs: 10/12–inch 33rpm
ATLANTIC 5-10   80
COLUMBIA 8-12   72-77
FANTASY 8-12   76-80
Also see GRATEFUL DEAD
Also see HARRISON, George
Also see LOGGINS & MESSINA / David Bromberg
Also see SAHM, Doug

BRONNER BROTHERS
Singles: 7–inch

NEIGHBOR 2-4   84

BRONSKI BEAT
Singles: 12–inch 33/45rpm

MCA 4-6   84-86
Singles: 7–inch
MCA 2-4   84-86
Picture Sleeves
MCA 2-4   84
LPs: 10/12–inch 33rpm
MCA 5-10   85-86
Member: Steve Bronski.
Also see COMMUNARDS

BROOD, Herman
(Herman Brood and Wild Romance)
Singles: 7–inch

ARIOLA AMERICA 2-4   79
LPs: 10/12–inch 33rpm
ARIOLA AMERICA 8-10   79-80
TOWNHOUSE 5-10   82

BROOKINS, Robert
Singles: 12–inch 33/45rpm
MCA 4-6   86
Singles: 7–inch
MCA 2-4   86

BROOKLYN BRIDGE
(Johnny Maestro and the Brooklyn Bridge)
Singles: 7–inch
BUDDAH 4-8   68-72
ERIC 2-4   78
LPs: 10/12–inch 33rpm
BUDDAH 20-25   69-72
COLLECTABLES 5-10
  Members: Johnny Maestro; Fred Ferrara; Les Cauchi; Mike
  Gregorio; Tom Sullivan; Carolyn Wood; Jimmy Rosica; Richie
  Macioce; Artie Cantanzarita; Shelly Davis; Joe Ruvio.
  Also see MAESTRO, Johnny

BROOKLYN DREAMS
Singles: 12–inch 33/45rpm
CASABLANCA 4-6   79
MILLENNIUM 4-6   78
Singles: 7–inch
CASABLANCA 2-4   79-80
MILLENNIUM 3-5   77-78
LPs: 10/12–inch 33rpm
CASABLANCA 5-10   79-80
MILLENNIUM 8-10   77
  Members: Joe Esposito; Eddie Hokenson; Bruce Sudano.
  Also see ESPOSITO, Joe "Bean"
  Also see SUMMER, Donna

BROOKS, Donnie
Singles: 7–inch
CHALLENGE 4-8   66
COLLECTABLES 2-4   81
DJ 4-8   65
ERA 5-10   59-68
HAPPY TIGER 3-5   70-71
MIDSONG 3-5
OAK 3-5
REPRISE 3-5   64-65
YARDBIRD 3-6   68-69
Picture Sleeves
ERA 8-12   60-61
Promotional Singles
ERA ("Mission Bell"/"Doll House") ... 50-75   60
  (Distributed during a personal appearance.)
LPs: 10/12–inch 33rpm
ERA (105 "The Happiest") 30-40   61
OAK 8-10   71
WISHBONE 5-10   75
  Also see CARLTON, Larry

BROOKS, Garth
Singles: 7–inch
CAPITOL 2-4   90-91
LPs: 10/12–inch 33rpm
CAPITOL 5-8   90-91

BROOKS, Louis
(Louis Brooks and His Hi-Toppers)
Singles: 78rpm
EXCELLO 8-15   52-57
Singles: 7–inch
EXCELLO (2000 series) 25-50   52-53
EXCELLO (2100 series) 15-25   57-59

BROOKS, Nancy
Singles: 7–inch
ARISTA 2-4   79

BROOKS, Nancy / Bud Roman
Singles: 7–inch
TOPS 20-35

BROOKS, Ramona
Singles: 7–inch
MANHATTAN 3-5   77
U.A. 3-5   77
LPs: 10/12–inch 33rpm
MANHATTAN 8-10   78

BROOM, Bobby
Singles: 7–inch
ARISTA 2-4   81-84
GRP 2-4   81
LPs: 10/12–inch 33rpm
GRP 5-10   81

BROTHER to BROTHER
Singles: 7–inch
SUGAR HILL 2-4   81
TURBO 3-5   74-77
LPs: 10/12–inch 33rpm
SUGAR HILL 5-10   81
TURBO 10-12   74-77
  Members: Michael Burton; Bill Jones; Frankie Prescott; Yogi
  Horton.

BROTHERHOOD
Singles: 7–inch
COLUMBIA 3-5   70
DIAL 3-6   69
MCA 2-4   78
RCA 3-6   69
Picture Sleeves
RCA 4-8   69
LPs: 10/12–inch 33rpm
MCA 5-10   78
RCA 12-15   69
  Members: Drake Levin; Michael Smith; Phil Volk; Ron Collins.
  Also see REVERE, Paul, and the Raiders
  Also see WOMACK, Bobby

BROTHERHOOD of MAN
Singles: 7–inch
BELL 3-5   74
DERAM 3-5   70-72
PRIVATE STOCK 3-5   77
PYE 3-5   75-76
LPs: 10/12–inch 33rpm
DERAM 10-12   70

PYE 8-10   76

BROTHERLY LOVE
Singles: 7–inch
MUSIC MERCHANT 2-4   72

BROTHERS by CHOICE
Singles: 7–inch
ALA 2-4   78-80
FRETONE 3-5   75

BROTHERS FOUR
Singles: 7–inch
COLUMBIA (Except 43547) 4-8   59-69
COLUMBIA (43547 "Ratman and Bobbin
  in the Clipper Caper") 5-10   69
FANTASY 3-5   70
Picture Sleeves
COLUMBIA 5-10   60-63
LPs: 10/12–inch 33rpm
COLUMBIA 10-20   59-69
FANTASY 8-12   70
FIRST AMERICAN 5-10   81
HARMONY 6-10   69-72
  Members: Bob Flick; Dick Foley; John Paine; Mike Kirkland.

BROTHERS GUIDING LIGHT
(Brothers Guiding Light Featuring David)
Singles: 7–inch
MERCURY 3-5   73

BROTHERS JOHNSON
Singles: 12–inch 33/45rpm
A&M (Black vinyl) 4-6   78-85
A&M (Colored vinyl) 5-10   78-85
Singles: 7–inch
A&M 2-4   76-88
Picture Sleeves
A&M 2-5   76-85
LPs: 10/12–inch 33rpm
A&M (Except PR-4714) 5-10   76-85
A&M (PR-4714 "Blam") 15-25   79
  (Picture disc.)
  Members: Louis Johnson; George Johnson.
  Also see JONES, Quincy, and Brothers Johnson

BROTHERS of SOUL
Singles: 7–inch
BOO 4-6   68-70
  Members: Richard Knight; Robert Eaton; Fred Bridges.

BROWN, Al, and His Tunetoppers
(Al Brown's Tunetoppers)
Singles: 7–inch
AMY 5-10   60-61
EPs: 7–inch 33/45rpm
AMY (1 "Madison Dance Party") 35-45   60
LPs: 10/12–inch 33rpm
AMY (1 "Madison Dance Party") 45-50   60

BROWN, Alex
Singles: 12–inch 33/45rpm
MERCURY 4-6   85

Singles: 7–inch
MERCURY 2-4   85
ROXBURY 3-5   76

BROWN, Arthur
(Crazy World of Arthur Brown; Arthur Brown's
Kingdom Come)
Singles: 7–inch
ATLANTIC 4-8   68
TRACK 4-6   68-69
LPs: 10/12–inch 33rpm
ATLANTIC 15-20   68
GULL 8-10   75
PASSPORT 10-12   74
RECKLESS 5-10   88
TRACK 10-15   68
  Also see ATOMIC ROOSTER
  Also see PARSONS, Alan, Project

BROWN, Boots
(Boots Brown and His Blockbusters; Boots Brown
and the Pelugelpipers; Boots Brown and Dan Drew)
Singles: 78rpm
RCA 3-5   53-57
Singles: 7–inch
DOT 3-6   68
RCA 5-10   53-60
EPs: 7–inch 33/45rpm
GROOVE (1000 "Rock
  That Beat") 20-35   55
LPs: 10/12–inch 33rpm
GROOVE (1000 "Rock That Beat") . 50-100   55

BROWN, Buster
Singles: 78rpm
FIRE (1008 "Fannie Mae") 150-200   59
Singles: 7–inch
ABC 2-4   73
CHECKER 5-10   63
FIRE 5-10   59-62
GWENN 5-10   62
OLDIES 45 3-5
RCA 3-5   74
ROULETTE 2-4   72
SEROCK 4-8   63
LPs: 10/12–inch 33rpm
COLLECTABLES 6-8   88
FIRE (102 "The New King of
  the Blues") 100-200   60
  (Blue cover. Track listing includes *Blueberry Hill*
  and *When Things Go Wrong*.)
FIRE (102 "The New King of
  the Blues") 75-125   60
  (White cover. With *Blueberry Hill* and *When Things
  Go Wrong* replaced by *Going on a Picnic* and
  Corena.)
SOUFFLE 10-15   73

BROWN, Charles
(Charles Brown with Johnny Moore's Three Blazers)
Singles: 78rpm
ALADDIN 10-20   49-57

CASH 5-10   57
HOLLYWOOD 8-12   54
SWING TIME 15-25   52

Singles: 7–inch

ACE 5-10   59
ALADDIN (3076 "Black Night") 50-100   51
ALADDIN (3091 "I'll Always Be in
  Love with You") 25-50   51
ALADDIN (3092 "Seven Long
  Days") 25-50   52
ALADDIN (3116 "Hard Times") 25-50   52
ALADDIN (3120 "My Last Affair") 25-50   52
ALADDIN (3138 "Without Your
  Love") 25-50   52
ALADDIN (3157 "Rollin' Like a Pebble
  in the Sand") 50-75   52
ALADDIN (3163 "Evening Shadows") 25-50   53
ALADDIN (3176 "Take Me") 25-50   53
ALADDIN (3191 "Lonesome Feeling") 25-50   53
ALADDIN (3200 and 3300 series) . . . 15-30   53-58
CASH 15-25   57
EAST-WEST 10-20   58
GALAXY 5-8   66
HOLLYWOOD (1006 "Pleading For
  Your Love") 20-30   54
IMPERIAL 5-10   62-63
JEWEL 3-5   71-74
KING 5-10   60-64
LIBERTY 2-4   84
LILLY 5-10   62
MAINSTREAM 4-8   65
NOLA 5-10   63
STARDAY 3-6   69
SWING TIME (253 "I'll Miss You") . 50-100   52
SWING TIME (259 "Be Fair with Me") 50-100   52

LPs: 10/12–inch 33rpm

ALADDIN (702 "Mood Music") 200-300   52
  (10–inch LP. Black vinyl.)
ALADDIN (702 "Mood Music") 450-550   52
  (10–inch LP. Colored vinyl.)
ALADDIN (809 "Mood Music") 100-200   57
BIG TOWN 8-10   77-78
BLUESWAY 8-10   70
IMPERIAL (9178 "Million Sellers") . . 50-75   62
JEWEL 8-15   72
KING (775 "Christmas Songs") 30-50   61
KING (878 "The Great
  Charles Brown") 30-50   63
KING (5000 series) 5-10
MAINSTREAM (300 series) 8-12   72
MAINSTREAM (6000/56000 series) . 10-20   65
SCORE (4011 "Driftin' Blues") 100-150   57
    Also see CHARLES, Ray / Charles Brown
    Also see McCRACKLIN, Jimmy / T-Bone Walker / Charles
    Brown
    Also see MOORE, Johnny

BROWN, Charles / Basin Street Boys
Singles: 78rpm

CASH 5-10   57

Singles: 7–inch

CASH (1052 "Lost in the Night") 10-20   57

BROWN, Charles / Lloyd Glenn
Singles: 78rpm

HOLLYWOOD 5-10   54

Singles: 7–inch

HOLLYWOOD (1021 "Merry Christmas
  Baby") 20-30   54
    Also see GLENN, Lloyd

BROWN, Charles, and Jimmy McCracklin
LPs: 10/12–inch 33rpm

IMPERIAL (9257 "Best of the Blues") 25-50   64
    Also see McCRACKLIN, Jimmy

BROWN, Charles, and Amos Milburn
(BROWN, Charles / Amos Milburn)
Singles: 7–inch

ACE 5-10   59
KING (5000 series) 5-10   61
KING (6000 series) 3-5   75

LPs: 10/12–inch 33rpm

GRAND PRIX (421 "Original
  Blues Sound") 10-15   64
  (With Jackie Shane and Bob Marshall & the
  Crystals.)
    Also see BROWN, Charles
    Also see MILBURN, Amos

BROWN, Chuck
Singles: 7–inch

EXCELLO 4-8   62

BROWN, Chuck, and the Soul Searchers
Singles: 12–inch 33/45rpm

SOURCE 4-8   78-79

Singles: 7–inch

SOUL SEARCHERS 2-4   84
SOURCE 2-5   78-80
T.T.E.D. 2-4   84

LPs: 10/12–inch 33rpm

SOURCE 5-10   79

BROWN, Clyde
Singles: 7–inch

ATLANTIC 3-5   73-74

BROWN, Danny Joe, and the Danny Joe Brown Band
Singles: 7–inch

EPIC 2-4   81

LPs: 10/12–inch 33rpm

EPIC 5-10   81
    Also see MOLLY HATCHET

BROWN, Dee, and Lola Grant
Singles: 7–inch

SHURFINE 4-8   66

BROWN, Dennis
Singles: 12–inch 33/45rpm

A&M 4-6   82

Singles: 7–inch

A&M 2-4   81-82

LPs: 10/12–inch 33rpm

A&M 5-10   81-82

BROWN, Don
Singles: 7–inch

FIRST AMERICAN 3-5   77-78

BROWN, James
(James Brown and His Famous Flames; James Brown and the J.B.s)
Singles: 12–inch 33/45rpm

CHURCHILL 4-6   83
POLYDOR 4-6   78

Singles: 78rpm

FEDERAL (Except 12348) 10-15   56-58
FEDERAL (12348 "I Want
  You So Bad") 20-40   59

Singles: 7–inch

AUGUSTA 2-4   83
BACKSTREET 2-4   83
BETHLEHEM 8-15   69
CHURCHILL 2-4   83
FEDERAL (12000 series) 8-15   56-60
FEDERAL (S-12352 "I've Got
  to Change") 20-30   59
  (Stereo.)
FEDERAL (S-12361 "Good, Good
  Lovin") 20-30   59
  (Stereo.)
KING (5000 series) 5-10   60-65
KING (6000 series) 4-8   65-71
PEOPLE 3-6   71-76
POLYDOR 2-5   71-84
SCOTTI BROTHERS 2-4   86-88
SMASH 5-10   64-66
T.K. 2-4   80-81

Picture Sleeves

KING (5000 series) 5-10   64
POLYDOR 2-5   72-84
SCOTTI BROTHERS 2-4   85-86
SMASH 5-10   64

EPs: 7–inch 33/45rpm

KING 15-30 59-63
SMASH 10-20 65-66
  (Jukebox issues only.)

LPs: 10/12–inch 33rpm

AGUSTA SOUND 5-8
AUDIO FIDELITY (326 "James Brown") 8-12 83
CHURCHILL 5-10   83
HRB 8-10   73
KING (610 "Please, Please, Please") 75-125 59
  (Cover pictures a woman's legs.)
KING (635 "Try Me") 75-125   59
  (Cover pictures a woman with a smoking gun.)
KING (683 "James Brown and His
  Famous Flames *Think*") 75-125 60
  (Cover pictures a baby.)
KING (683 "James Brown and His
  Famous Flames *Think*") 20-30
  (Cover has pictures of James Brown.)

KING (743 "The Always Amazing James Brown
  and the Famous Flames") 50-75   61
  (Cover is pink and blue.)
KING (771 "Jump Around") 50-75   62
KING (780 "The Exciting
  James Brown") 50-75   62
KING (804 "James Brown and the Famous
  Flames Tour the U.S.A." 50-75   62
KING (826 "Apollo Theatre Presents
  the James Brown Show") 40-60   63
KING (851 "Prisoner of Love") 30-50   63
KING (883 "Pure Dynamite") 25-50   64
KING (900 series) 15-25 65-66
KING (1000 and 1100 series,
  except 1038) 10-15 67-71
KING (1038 "Thinking About Little
  Willie John") 30-35   68
POLYDOR 5-10   71-84
SCOTTI BROTHERS 5-8   86-88
SMASH 10-20 64-68
SOLID SMOKE 5-10   80-81
T.K. 5-10   80
  Also see BAMBAATAA, Afrika
  Also see BYRD, Bobby, and James Brown
  Also see J.B.s

BROWN, James, and Vicki Anderson
Singles: 7–inch

KING 4-6   67-70
  Also see ANDERSON, Vicki

BROWN, James, Band
Singles: 7–inch

KING 4-8   61
  Also see WESLEY, Fred, and the Horny Horns

BROWN, James, and Lyn Collins
Singles: 7–inch

POLYDOR 3-5   72
  Also see COLLINS, Lyn

BROWN, James, and Marva Whitney
Singles: 7–inch

KING 3-6   69
  Also see BROWN, James
  Also see WHITNEY, Marva

BROWN, Jim Edward
(Jim Edward Brown and Helen Cornelius)
Singles: 7–inch

RCA (Except 8000 and 9000 series) ... 2-5   69-81
RCA (8000 and 9000 series) 3-8   65-68

LPs: 10/12–inch 33rpm

RCA (Except 3000 and 4000 series) .. 5-10 73-81
RCA (3000 and 4000 series) 8-12 66-72
  (With "LPM" or "LSP" prefix.)
  Also see BROWNS

BROWN, Jocelyn
Singles: 12–inch 33/45rpm

JELLYBEAN 4-6   86
VINYL DREAMS 4-6   84
Singles: 7–inch

JELLYBEAN 2-4   86

WARNER 2-4   86-87
LPs: 10/12–inch 33rpm
JELLYBEAN 5-10   86
VINYL DREAMS 5-10   84

BROWN, Julie
Singles: 7–inch
RHINO 2-4   84
LPs: 10/12–inch 33rpm
RHINO 5-10   85

BROWN, Les, and His Orchestra
(Les Brown and His Band of Renown; Les Brown and
His Duke University Blue Devils)
Singles: 78rpm
BLUEBIRD 5-10   38-40
CAPITOL 3-5   56-57
COLUMBIA 5-10   42-57
CONQUEROR 5-10   41
CORAL 3-6   5
DECCA 5-10   36-40
OKEH 5-10   41-42
Singles: 7–inch
CAPITOL 3-8   56-59
COLUMBIA 5-10   50-60
CORAL 3-6   59
SIGNATURE..................... 3-6   60
EPs: 7-inch 33/45rpm
CAPITOL 5-10   56-58
COLUMBIA 5-10   54-56
CORAL 5-10   53-56
LPs: 10/12-inch 33rpm
CAPITOL 10-20 56-59
COLUMBIA 10-25 50-61
CORAL 15-30 55-60
HARMONY 8-15   59
KAPP 8-15   59
MEDALLION 8-15   61
Also see DAY, Doris

BROWN, Louise
Singles: 7–inch
WITCH 5-10   61

BROWN, Maxine
Singles: 7–inch
ABC 2-4   75
ABC-PAR 5-10   61-62
AVCO EMBASSY 3-5   71
COLLECTABLES 2-4   81
COMMONWEALTH UNITED 4-6   69-70
ERIC 2-4   83
NOMAR 5-10   61
WAND 5-10   63-67
WHAM 4-8
Picture Sleeves
WAND (135 "Ask Me") 10-15 63
WHAM (7036 "All in My Mind") 10-15
LPs: 10/12–inch 33rpm
COLLECTABLES 6-8   88
COMMONWEALTH UNITED 10-12 69

GUEST STAR 10-12 64
WAND 15-25 63-67
Also see JACKSON, Chuck, and Maxine Brown

BROWN, Maxine / Irma Thomas
LPs: 10/12–inch 33rpm
GRAND PRIX 12-15 64
Also see BROWN, Maxine
Also see THOMAS, Irma

BROWN, Miquel
Singles: 12–inch 33/45rpm
TSR 4-6   83
Singles: 7–inch
POLYDOR 2-4   79
TSR 2-4   83
LPs: 10/12–inch 33rpm
POLYDOR 5-10   78
TSR 5-10   85

BROWN, Nappy
(Nappy Brown and the Gibralters; Nappy Brown and
the Southern Sisters)
Singles: 78rpm
SAVOY 5-10   55-57
Singles: 7–inch
SAVOY (1100 series) 10-20 55
SAVOY (1500 series) 10-15 57-60
SAVOY (1600 series) 5-10   61-63
LPs: 10/12–inch 33rpm
SAVOY (14002 "Nappy Brown
Sings") 50-100 57
SAVOY (14025 "The Right Time") ... 40-60 60
SAVOY (14427 "Nappy Brown") 8-15 77
Also see BARNES, Jimmy

BROWN, Odell
(Odell Brown and the Organ-izers)
Singles: 7–inch
CADET 3-6   67-68
LPs: 10/12–inch 33rpm
CADET 10-15 67-69
PAULA 8-10   74

BROWN, Oscar, Jr.
Singles: 7–inch
ATLANTIC 3-5   74
COLUMBIA 5-10   60-62
FONTANA 4-8   65-66
MAD 8-12   59
LPs: 10/12–inch 33rpm
ATLANTIC 5-10
COLUMBIA 15-25 61-63
FONTANA 10-15 66

BROWN, Peter
Singles: 12–inch 33/45rpm
COLUMBIA 4-6   84
RCA 4-6   83
Singles: 7–inch
COLUMBIA 2-4   84
DRIVE 3-5   77-80
RCA 2-4   83

LPs: 10/12–inch 33rpm

COLUMBIA	5-10	84
DRIVE	5-10	78
RCA	5-10	82-83

BROWN, Peter, and Betty Wright
Singles: 7–inch

DRIVE	3-5	78

Also see BROWN, Peter
Also see WRIGHT, Betty

BROWN, Polly
Singles: 7–inch

ARIOLA AMERICA	3-5	75-76
BEL	3-5	73
GTO	3-5	74

Also see PICKETTYWITCH

BROWN, Randy
(Randy Brown and Company)
Singles: 12–inch 33/45rpm

MILLENNIUM	4-6	78

Singles: 7–inch

CHOCOLATE CITY	2-4	80-81
IX CHAINS	3-5	75
PARACHUTE	2-5	78-79
STAX	2-4	80
TRUTH	3-5	74-75

LPs: 10/12–inch 33rpm

CHOCOLATE CITY	5-10	80-81
PARACHUTE	5-10	78-79
STAX	5-10	80-81

BROWN, Ray, and the Whispers
Singles: 7–inch

GNP/CRESCENDO	8-12	65
PARKWAY	8-12	66

BROWN, Roy
(Roy Brown and His Mighty, Mighty Men)
Singles: 78rpm

DELUXE (1000 series)	15-25	47-48
DELUXE (3300 through 3318)	10-20	49-51
GOLD STAR	15-20	48
IMPERIAL	10-15	57
KING	10-20	52-57

Singles: 7–inch

BLUESWAY	4-8	67
DELUXE (3319 "Bar Room Blues")	150-200	51
(Black vinyl.)		
DELUXE (3319 "Bar Room Blues")	200-400	51
(Colored vinyl.)		
DELUXE (3323 "I've Got the Last		
Laugh Now")	75-100	51
(Black vinyl.)		
DELUXE (3323 "I've Got the Last		
Laugh Now")	150-250	51
(Colored vinyl.)		
FRIENDSHIP	5-10	
GUSTO	2-4	83
HOME of the BLUES	15-25	60-61
IMPERIAL	10-20	57

KING (4000 series)	25-50	52-56
KING (5000 series)	8-12	59-60
MERCURY	3-5	71
TRU-LOVE	4-6	

EPs: 7–inch 33/45rpm

KING (254 "Roy Brown")	50-100	53

LPs: 10/12–inch 33rpm

BLUESWAY	10-20	68-73
EPIC	10-15	71
INTERMEDIA	5-10	84
KING (956 "24 Hits")	35-45	66
KING (1100 series)	10-15	71
KING (5000 series)	8-10	79

Also see HARRIS, Wynonie / Roy Brown

BROWN, Ruth
(Ruth Brown and the Rhythmakers)
Singles: 78rpm

ATLANTIC (Except 800 series)	8-12	51-57
ATLANTIC (800 series)	10-20	49-50

Singles: 7–inch

ATLANTIC (919 "Teardrops from		
My Eyes")	200-250	50
ATLANTIC (948 "Shine On")	25-50	51
ATLANTIC (962 through 993)	20-30	52-53
ATLANTIC (1005 through 1091)	10-20	53-56
ATLANTIC (1100 series)	10-15	57-58
ATLANTIC (2000 series)	5-10	59-60
DECCA	4-8	64
NOSLEN	4-8	64
PHILIPS	5-10	62
SYKE	4-8	69

EPs: 7–inch 33/45rpm

ATLANTIC (505 "Ruth Brown Sings")	50-75	53
ATLANTIC (535 "Ruth Brown Sings")	50-75	53
ATLANTIC (585 "Ruth Brown Sings")	35-60	57
PHILIPS	10-15	62

LPs: 10/12–inch 33rpm

Atlantic apparently never issued *Ruth Brown Sings* (ALR-115, which would have been from 1951). We have yet verify the existence of even one copy of this LP)

ATLANTIC (1308 "Last Date with		
Ruth Brown")	50-70	59
ATLANTIC (SD-1308 "Last Date with		
Ruth Brown")	75-100	59
(Stereo.)		
ATLANTIC (8004 "Ruth Brown")	50-75	57
(Black label.)		
ATLANTIC (8004 "Ruth Brown")	30-40	60
(Red label.)		
ATLANTIC (8026 "Miss Rhythm")	35-50	59
(Black label.)		
ATLANTIC (8026 "Miss Rhythm")	35-50	59
(White label.)		
ATLANTIC (8026 "Miss Rhythm")	15-25	60
(Red label.)		
ATLANTIC (8080 "Best of Ruth		
Brown")	15-25	63

COBBLESTONE	8-10	72
DOBRE	5-10	78
MAINSTREAM (300 series)	8-10	72
MAINSTREAM (6000 series)	12-15	65
PHILIPS	12-15	62
SKYE	10-12	70

Also see JOHNSON, Buddy

BROWN, Savoy: see SAVOY BROWN

BROWN, Sawyer: see SAWYER BROWN

BROWN, Sharon
Singles: 12–inch 33/45rpm

PROFILE	4-6	83

Singles: 7–inch

PROFILE	2-4	82-83

BROWN, Shawn
Singles: 12–inch 33/45rpm

JWP	4-6	85

BROWN, Sheree
Singles: 12–inch 33/45rpm

CAPITOL	4-6	81

Singles: 7–inch

CAPITOL	2-4	81-82

LPs: 10/12–inch 33rpm

CAPITOL	5-10	81-82

BROWN, Shirley
Singles: 12–inch 33/45rpm

MERCURY	4-6	83

Singles: 7–inch

ABET	3-5	71
ARISTA	2-5	77-78
SOUND TOWN	2-4	84-85
STAX	2-4	79
TRUTH	3-5	74-76
20TH FOX	2-4	80

LPs: 10/12–inch 33rpm

ARISTA	5-10	77
COLUMBIA	10-15	68-72
SOUND TRACK	5-10	85
STAX	5-10	77-79
TRUTH	8-10	75

BROWN, Veda
Singles: 7–inch

RAKEN	3-5	75
STAX	3-5	73-74

BROWN, Wini
(Wini Brown and the Boyfriends)
Singles: 78rpm

COLUMBIA	4-8	51
MERCURY	15-25	52

Singles: 7–inch

COLUMBIA (872 "A Good Man Is Hard to Find")	10-20	51
JARO	10-15	60
MERCURY (5870 "Here in My Heart")	75-125	52

MERCURY (8270 "Be Anything")	75-125	52

Members: Wini Brown; Joe Van Loan; Percy Green; Fred Francis; Warren Suttles.
Also see VAN LOAN, Joe

BROWN, Wini, and Cootie Williams
LPs: 10/12–inch 33rpm

JARO (5001 "Around Midnight")	25-40	60

Also see BROWN, Wini

BROWN SUGAR
Singles: 7–inch

ABKCO	3-5	72
CAPITOL	3-5	76
CHELSEA	3-5	73-74

Member: Clydie King.

BROWNE, Duncan
Singles: 7–inch

IMMEDIATE	3-6	69
RAK	3-5	72
SIRE	2-4	79

LPs: 10/12–inch 33rpm

IMMEDIATE	10-15	68
SIRE	5-10	79

BROWNE, Jackson
Singles: 12–inch 33/45rpm

ASYLUM	4-6	81-82
ELEKTRA	4-8	89
(Promotional only.)		

Singles: 7–inch

ASYLUM	2-4	72-86
COLUMBIA	2-4	86
ELEKTRA	2-4	80-89

Picture Sleeves

ASYLUM	2-4	82-84
ELEKTRA	2-4	80

LPs: 10/12–inch 33rpm

ASYLUM (Except 5051)	8-10	72-86
ASYLUM (5051 "Jackson Browne")	10-15	72
(With burlap cover.)		
ASYLUM (5051 "Jackson Browne")	8-10	72
(Without burlap.)		
ELEKTRA ("Jackson Browne's First Album")	25-35	67
(Promotional issue only.)		
ELEKTRA (60830 "World in Motion")	5-8	89
MFSL (055 "Pretender")	20-40	81

Also see CLEMONS, Clarence
Also see LINDLEY, David

BROWNE, Tom
Singles: 12–inch 33/45rpm

ARISTA	4-6	83

Singles: 7–inch

ARISTA	2-4	83-84
GRP	2-4	79-82

LPs: 10/12–inch 33rpm

ARISTA	5-10	83-84
GRP	5-10	79-82

BROWNS

(Jim Edward Brown and Maxine Brown with the Louisiana Hayride Band)

Singles: 78rpm

FABOR	5-10	54-55
RCA	4-8	56-57

Singles: 7–inch

COLUMBIA	4-8	62
FABOR	10-15	54-55
RCA	6-12	56-61

Picture Sleeves

RCA	8-12	60

EPs: 7–inch 33/45rpm

RCA	10-20	57-60

LPs: 10/12–inch 33rpm

CAMDEN	8-12	65-68
RCA (1000 through 3000 series)	5-10	75-81
(With "ANL1" or "AYL1" prefix.)		
RCA (1438 Jim Edward, Maxine and Bonnie Brown")	35-55	57
(With "LPM" prefix.)		
RCA (2000 series)	15-30	59-65
(With "LPM" or "LSP" prefix.)		
RCA (3000 series)	12-20	65-67
(With "LPM" or "LSP" prefix.)		

Members: Jim Edward Brown; Maxine Brown; Bonnie Brown.
Also see BROWN, Jim Edward
Also see COOKE, Sam / Rod Lauren / Neil Sedaka / Browns

BROWNSVILLE STATION

Singles: 7–inch

BIG TREE	3-5	72-74
EPIC	3-5	79
HIDEOUT (1957 "Rock and Roll Holiday")	8-12	69
PALLADIUM	4-8	70
POLYDOR	3-5	70
PRIVATE STOCK	3-5	77
WARNER (7501 "That's Fine")	4-8	71

LPs: 10/12–inch 33rpm

BIG TREE	10-12	72-75
EPIC (Black vinyl)	8-10	78
EPIC (Colored vinyl)	10-20	78
(Promotional issue only.)		
PALLADIUM (1004 "Brownsville Station")	20-25	70
PRIVATE STOCK	8-10	77
WARNER	12-15	70

Members: Tony Driggins; Cub Koda; Michael Lutz; Henry Weck; Bruce Nazarian.
Also see SEGER, Bob

BRUBECK, Dave, Quartet

(Dave Brubeck Trio; Dave Brubeck Octet; Dave Brubeck Featuring Paul Desmond)

Singles: 78rpm

COLUMBIA	4-8	55-57
FANTASY	4-8	52-55

Singles: 7–inch

COLUMBIA (Except 40000 and 41000 series)	3-6	62-65
COLUMBIA (40000 and 41000 series)	5-10	55-61
FANTASY (500 series)	5-10	52-55

Picture Sleeves

COLUMBIA	5-10	61-63

EPs: 7–inch 33/45rpm

COLUMBIA	10-25	55-59
FANTASY	15-30	51-57

LPs: 10/12–inch 33rpm

ATLANTIC (79 "Fantasy Years")	8-12	74
COLUMBIA (566 "Jazz Goes to College")	50-75	54
COLUMBIA (590 "Dave Brubeck at Storyville")	50-75	54
COLUMBIA (622 "Brubeck Time")	40-60	55
COLUMBIA (699 "Jazz: Red Hot and Cool")	40-60	55
COLUMBIA (826 "Dave Brubeck Quintet at Carnegie Hall")	20-30	63
COLUMBIA (878 "Brubeck Plays Brubeck")	30-50	56
COLUMBIA (932 "Brubeck, Jay and Kai at Newport")	30-50	57
COLUMBIA (984 "Jazz Impressions of the U.S.A.")	30-50	57
COLUMBIA (1000 through 1200 series)	20-35	57-59
COLUMBIA (1300 through 2300 series)	12-25	59-65
COLUMBIA (6321 "Jazz Goes to College")	50-100	54
(10-inch LP.)		
COLUMBIA (6322 "Jazz Goes to College")	50-75	54
(10-inch LP.)		
COLUMBIA (6330 "Dave Brubeck at Storyville")	50-75	54
COLUMBIA (6331 "Dave Brubeck at Storyville")	50-75	54
(10-inch LP.)		
COLUMBIA (8000 series)	20-45	57-59
(Stereo series.)		
COLUMBIA (8100 through 9300 series)	15-30	59-66
(Stereo series.)		
CROWN	10-15	62-64
FANTASY (1 "Dave Brubeck Trio")	75-100	51
(10-inch LP.)		
FANTASY (2 "Dave Brubeck Trio")	75-100	51
(10-inch LP.)		
FANTASY (3 "Dave Brubeck Octet")	75-100	52
(10-inch LP.)		
FANTASY (5 "Dave Brubeck Quartet with Paul Desmond")	75-100	52
(10-inch LP.)		
FANTASY (7 "Dave Brubeck Quartet with Paul Desmond")	75-100	53
(10-inch LP.)		

FANTASY (8 "At Storyville") 75-100   53
(10-inch LP.)
FANTASY (10 "Jazz at
the Black Hawk") 75-100   53
(10-inch LP.)
FANTASY (11 "Jazz at Oberlin") 75-100   53
(10-inch LP.)
FANTASY (13 "Jazz at the
College of the Pacific") 75-100   54
(10-inch LP.)
FANTASY (16 "Old Sounds from
San Francisco") 75-100   55
(10-inch LP.)
FANTASY (204 "Dave Brubeck Trio") . 50-75   56
FANTASY (205 "Dave Brubeck Trio") . 50-75   56
FANTASY (210 "Jazz at
the Black Hawk") 50-75   56
FANTASY (223 "Jazz at the
College of the Pacific") 50-75   56
FANTASY (229 "Dave Brubeck
Quartet with Paul Desmond") 5-75   56
FANTASY (230 "Dave Brubeck
Quartet with Paul Desmond") 50-75   56
FANTASY (239 "Dave Brubeck
Octet") 50-75   56
FANTASY (240 "At Storyville") 50-75   57
FANTASY (245 "Jazz at Oberlin") . . 50-75   57
FANTASY (3300 series) 15-25   62
HORIZON 5-10   76
JAZZTONE (1272 "Dave Brubeck") . . 25-50   57
Members: Dave Brubeck; Paul Desmond; Cal Tjader; Dick
Collins; David Van Kriedt; Joe Morello; Eugene Wright.
Also see ARMSTRONG, Louis
Also see BERNSTEIN, Leonard, and Dave Brubeck
Also see TJADER, Cal

BRUBECK, Dave, and Paul Desmond
Singles: 7-inch
A&M 3-5   76
HORIZON 3-5   75
LPs: 10/12-inch 33rpm
HORIZON 6-10   74-75
As a member of Dave Brubeck's group, Paul
Desmond was often credited prominently on
releases which, for consistency, appear in the
Brubeck section.
Also see DESMOND, Paul

BRUBECK, Dave, and Gerry Mulligan
Singles: 7-inch
COLUMBIA 2-4   68
LPs: 10/12-inch 33rpm
COLUMBIA 8-15   68-73
VERVE 8-12   73
Also see BRUBECK, Dave
Also see MULLIGAN, Gerry

BRUCE, Jack
(Jack Bruce Band; Jack Bruce and Friends)
Singles: 7-inch
RSO 3-5   74-75

LPs: 10/12-inch 33rpm
ATCO 10-15   69-71
EPIC 5-10   80
POLYDOR 8-12   72
RSO 5-10   74-77
Also see CREAM
Also see MAYALL, John
Also see WEST, BRUCE & LAING

BRUCE, Jack, and Robin Trower
LPs: 10/12-inch 33rpm
CHRYSALIS 5-10   82
Also see BRUCE, Jack
Also see TROWER, Robin

BRUCE, Lenny
Singles: 7-inch
FANTASY (Black vinyl) 5-10
FANTASY (Colored vinyl) 10-15
Picture Sleeves
WARNER (598 "The Law, Language
and Lenny Bruce") 20-30   74
EPs: 7-inch 33/45rpm
FANTASY (2 "Curran
Theater Concert") 10-20
(Promotional issue only.)
LPs: 10/12-inch 33rpm
CAPITOL (2630 "Why Did Lenny
Bruce Die") 15-20   66
DOUGLAS 15-25   68-71
FANTASY (1 "Lenny Bruce") 50-75
(Promotional issue only.)
FANTASY (7001 "Lenny Bruce's
Interviews of Our Times") 30-40   58
(THICK red vinyl.)
FANTASY (7001 "Lenny Bruce's
Interviews of Our Times") 15-20
(Black vinyl.)
FANTASY (7001 "Lenny Bruce's
Interviews of Our Times") 8-12
(THIN red vinyl.)
FANTASY (7003 "The Sick Humor
of Lenny Bruce") 30-40   58
(THICK red vinyl.)
FANTASY (7003 "The Sick Humor
of Lenny Bruce") 15-20
(Black vinyl.)
FANTASY (7003 "The Sick Humor
of Lenny Bruce") 8-12
(THIN red vinyl.)
FANTASY (7007 "I Am Not a Nut,
Elect Me") 30-40   59
(THICK red vinyl.)
FANTASY (7007 "I Am Not a Nut,
Elect Me") 15-20
(Black vinyl.)
FANTASY (7007 "I Am Not a Nut,
Elect Me") 8-12
(THIN red vinyl.)

FANTASY (7011 "Lenny Bruce,
American") 30-40   62
(THICK red vinyl.)
FANTASY (7011 "Lenny Bruce,
American") 15-20
(Black vinyl.)
FANTASY (7011 "Lenny Bruce,
American") 8-12
(THIN red vinyl.)
FANTASY (7012 "The Best of
Lenny Bruce") 25-30   63
(THICK red vinyl.)
FANTASY (7012 "The Best of
Lenny Bruce") 15-20
(Black vinyl.)
FANTASY (7012 "The Best of
Lenny Bruce") 8-12
(THIN red vinyl.)
FANTASY (7017 "Thank You
Masked Man") 10-15   72
FANTASY (34201 "Lenny Bruce Live
at the Curran Theatre") 10-15   72
FANTASY (79003 "The Real Lenny
Bruce") 8-12   75
LENNY BRUCE RECORDS ("Recordings
Submitted As Evidence in the San Francisco
Obscenity Trial in March, 1962") .. 75-100   62
PHILLES (4010 "Lenny Bruce Is Out
Again") 50-75   66
REPRISE (6329 "The Berkeley
Concert") 15-20   69
U.A. (3580 "Midnight Concert") 15-20   67
U.A. (9800 "At Carnegie Hall") 15-20   71
WARNER (9101 "The Law, Language
and Lenny Bruce") 10-20   74
(Promotional issue only.)

BRUCE & TERRY
Singles: 7–inch
COLUMBIA 5-10   64-66
Members: Bruce Johnston; Terry Melcher.
Also see BOONE, Pat
Also see CALIFORNIA MUSIC
Also see HONDELLS
Also see NEWTON, Wayne
Also see RIP CHORDS
Also see SAGITTARIUS

BRUNSON, Tyrone "Tystick"
Singles: 12–inch 33/45rpm
BELIEVE in a DREAM 4-6   82-84
Singles: 7–inch
BELIEVE in a DREAM 2-4   82-84
LPs: 10/12–inch 33rpm
BELIEVE in a DREAM 5-10   82-84

BRYAN, Billy
(Gene Pitney)
Singles: 7–inch
BLAZE (351 "Going Back to My Love") 15-25   59
Also see PITNEY, Gene

BRYANT, Anita
Singles: 7–inch
CARLTON 4-8   58-61
COLUMBIA 4-8   61-67
DISNEYLAND 2-4
TRIP 3-5
Picture Sleeves
COLUMBIA 4-8   61-67
DISNEYLAND 3-5
EPs: 7–inch 33/45rpm
ACSP (1779 "See America with AC") .. 5-10
(Promotional issue for AC Spark Plugs.)
LPs: 10/12–inch 33rpm
CARLTON 10-20   59-61
COLUMBIA 8-15   62-67

BRYANT, Anita / Jo Stafford and Gordon MacRae
Singles: 7–inch
COLUMBIA 5-10   60
Also see MacRAE, Gordon, and Jo Stafford

BRYANT, Lillie
Singles: 7–inch
CAMEO 8-10   58
SWAN 5-10   59
Also see BILLY & LILLIE

BRYANT, Ray, Combo
Singles: 7–inch
CADET 3-6   66-67
COLUMBIA 4-8   60-64
SIGNATURE 4-8   60
Picture Sleeves
CADET 4-6   67
COLUMBIA 5-10   60
LPs: 10/12–inch 33rpm
CADET 10-20   66-67
COLUMBIA 15-30   60-62
EPIC (3279 "Ray Bryant Trio") 40-60   56
PRESTIGE/NEW JAZZ 15-25   62
SIGNATURE 15-25   60
SUE 15-30   60-64

BRYSON, Peabo
Singles: 7–inch
BULLET 3-5   76-77
CAPITOL 2-4   77-82
ELEKTRA 2-4   84-87
MCA 2-4   84
SHOUT 3-5   75
Picture Sleeves
CAPITOL 2-4   81
ELEKTRA 2-4   85
LPs: 10/12–inch 33rpm
BULLET 8-10   76
CAPITOL 5-10   78-84
COLUMBIA 5-8   91
ELEKTRA 5-10   84-86
Also see BELLE, Regina
Also see MANCHESTER, Melissa, and Peabo Bryson
Also see ZAGER, Michael, Moon Band, and Peabo Bryson

BRYSON, Peabo, and Natalie Cole
Singles: 7–inch
CAPITOL 2-4   79
LPs: 10/12–inch 33rpm
CAPITOL 5-10   79
  Also see COLE, Natalie

BRYSON, Peabo, and Roberta Flack
Singles: 7–inch
ATLANTIC 2-4   80
CAPITOL 2-4   83
Picture Sleeves
CAPITOL 2-4   83
LPs: 10/12–inch 33rpm
ATLANTIC 5-10   80
CAPITOL 5-10   83
  Also see BRYSON, Peabo
  Also see FLACK, Roberta

BUBBLE PUPPY
Singles: 7–inch
INTERNATIONAL ARTISTS (128
  "Hot Smoke and Sasafrass") 15-20   69
INTERNATIONAL ARTISTS (133
  "Beginning") 15-25   69
INTERNATIONAL ARTISTS (136
  "Days of Our Time") 15-25   70
INTERNATIONAL ARTISTS (138
  "Hurry Sundown") 15-25   69
Promotional Singles
INTERNATIONAL ARTISTS
  (Black vinyl) 25-40   69-70
INTERNATIONAL ARTISTS
  (Colored vinyl) 25-50   70
LPs: 10/12–inch 33rpm
INTERNATIONAL ARTISTS (10 "A
  Gathering of Promises")
  (Green label) 100-125   69
INTERNATIONAL ARTISTS (10 "A
  Gathering of Promises")
  (White label) 150-200   69
  (Promotional issue only.)
  Members: Red Prince; Todd Potter; Rory Cox; M. Taylor; Dave
  Fore.

BUCHANAN, Bill
Singles: 7–inch
GONE (5032 "The Thing") 15-25   58
U.A. 8-12   62
  Also see BUCHANAN & ANCELL
  Also see BUCHANAN & CELLA
  Also see BUCHANAN & GOODMAN
  Also see BUCHANAN & GREENFIELD

BUCHANAN, Roy
Singles: 7–inch
ALLIGATOR 2-4   85-86
ATLANTIC 2-4   76-78
BOMARC 10-15   61
POLYDOR 3-5   72-75
SWAN 4-8   61
LPs: 10/12–inch 33rpm
ALLIGATOR 5-10   85
ATLANTIC 5-10   76-77
BIOYA 30-40   71
POLYDOR 8-15   72-75
WATERHOUSE 5-10   81
  Also see CANNON, Freddy
  Also see GREGG, Bobby
  Also see HAWKINS, Dale

BUCHANAN & ANCELL
Singles: 78rpm
FLYING SAUCER 10-20   57
Singles: 7–inch
FLYING SAUCER 20-25   57
  Members: Bill Buchanan; Bob Ancell.
  Also see BUCHANAN, Bill

BUCHANAN & CELLA
Singles: 7–inch
ABC-PAR 10-20   59
  Member: Bill Buchanan.
  Also see BUCHANAN, Bill

BUCHANAN & GOODMAN
Singles: 78rpm
LUNIVERSE (Except 101X) 15-25   56-58
LUNIVERSE (101X "Back to Earth") . 25-50   56
RADIO-ACTIVE 8-15
Singles: 7–inch
COMIC 10-15   59
LUNIVERSE (Except 101X) 15-30   56-58
LUNIVERSE (101X "Back to Earth") 100-125   56
NOVELTY 10-15   59
RADIO-ACTIVE (101 "The Flying
  Saucer") 50-75   56
  Members: Bill Buchanan; Dickie Goodman.
  Also see BUCHANAN, Bill
  Also see GOODMAN, Dickie

BUCHANAN & GREENFIELD
Singles: 7–inch
NOVEL (711 "The Invasion") 15-20   64
  (Red label.)
NOVEL (711 "The Invasion") 3-5   72
  (Red and white label.)
  Members: Bill Buchanan; Howard Greenfield.
  Also see BUCHANAN, Bill

BUCHANAN BROTHERS
Singles: 7–inch
EVENT 3-6   69-71
LPs: 10/12–inch 33rpm
EVENT (101 "Medicine Man") 20-25   69
Members: Terry Cashman; Gene Pistilli; Tommy West.
Also see CASHMAN, PISTILLI & WEST

BUCK
Singles: 7–inch
PLAYBOY 3-5   75

BUCKEYE
Singles: 7–inch
POLYDOR 2-4   79
LPs: 10/12–inch 33rpm
POLYDOR 5-10   79

BUCKINGHAM, Lindsey
Singles: 7–inch
ASYLUM 2-4   81
ELEKTRA 2-4   84
WARNER 2-4   83
Picture Sleeves
ASYLUM 2-4   81
LPs: 10/12–inch 33rpm
ASYLUM 5-10   81
ELEKTRA 5-10   84
Also see BUCKINGHAM NICKS
Also see EGAN, Walter
Also see FLEETWOOD MAC
Also see STEWART, John

BUCKINGHAM NICKS
Singles: 7–inch
POLYDOR 3-5   73-79
Picture Sleeves
POLYDOR 3-5   73
LPs: 10/12–inch 33rpm
POLYDOR (5058 "Buckingham
  Nicks") 30-40   73
Members: Lindsey Buckingham; Stevie Nicks.
Also see BUCKINGHAM, Lindsey
Also see NICKS, Stevie

BUCKINGHAMS
Singles: 7–inch
COLUMBIA 4-8   67-70
RED LABEL 2-4   85
ROWE/AMI 10-20   66
("Play Me" Sales Stimulator promotional issue.)
SPECTRA-SOUND 10-20   67
U.S.A. 10-15   66-67
Picture Sleeves
COLUMBIA 8-15   67-68
LPs: 10/12–inch 33rpm
COLUMBIA 15-25   67-75
RED LABEL 5-10   85
U.S.A. (107 "Kind of a Drag") 50-75   67
  (With 13 tracks.)
U.S.A. (107 "Kind of a Drag") 30-40   67
  (With 12 tracks.)

Members: Dennis Tufano; Carl Giammerse; Nick Fortune; Marty
Grebb; Dennis Miccoli; Jon-Jon Poulos.
Also see TUFANO & GIAMMERSE

BUCKLEY, Tim
Singles: 7–inch
DISC REET 3-5   73-74
ELEKTRA 4-8   66-67
LPs: 10/12–inch 33rpm
DISC REET 8-10   73-74
ELEKTRA 15-20   66-70
RHINO 5-10   83
STRAIGHT 15-25   66-70
WARNER 10-15   70-72

BUCKNER & GARCIA
Singles: 12–inch 33/45rpm
COLUMBIA 4-6   82
Singles: 7–inch
BGO 4-6   81
COLUMBIA 2-4   81
Picture Sleeves
COLUMBIA 2-4   81
LPs: 10/12–inch 33rpm
COLUMBIA 5-10   82
Members: Jerry Buckner; Gary Garcia.
Also see WILLIS "The Guard" and Vigorish

BUCKWHEAT
Singles: 7–inch
LONDON 3-5   71-73
LPs: 10/12–inch 33rpm
LONDON 10-12   71-73

BUCKWHEAT ZYDECO:
see ZYDECO, Buckwheat

BUD & TRAVIS
Singles: 7–inch
LIBERTY 4-8   59-65
WORLD PACIFIC 5-8   59
LPs: 10/12–inch 33rpm
LIBERTY 10-20   59-65
SUNSET 8-15   67
Members: Bud Dashiel; Travis Edmonson.

BUENA VISTAS
Singles: 7–inch
MARQUEE 5-10   68
SWAN 10-15   66

BUFFALO REBELS
Singles: 7–inch
MAR-LEE 15-20   60-61
Also see REBELS
Also see ROCKIN' REBELS

BUFFALO SPRINGFIELD
Singles: 7–inch
ATCO 5-10   67-68
LPs: 10/12–inch 33rpm
ATCO (105 "Retrospective") 8-10   75
ATCO (200 "Buffalo Springfield") 30-50   66
  (Contains Baby Don't Scold Me.)

ATCO (200 "Buffalo Springfield") 15-25   67
(*Baby Don't Scold Me* replaced with *For What It's Worth.*)
ATCO (226 through 283) 20-30   67-69
ATCO (806 "Buffalo Springfield") 15-20   73
   Members: Stephen Stills; Neil Young; Jim Messina; Richie
   Furay; Jim Fielder; Doug Hastings; Dewey Martin; Bruce Palmer.
   Also see FURAY, Richie
   Also see MESSINA, Jim
   Also see POCO
   Also see STILLS, Stephen
   Also see YOUNG, Neil

BUFFETT, Jimmy
Singles: 7–inch
ABC 2-5   75-78
ASYLUM 2-4   80
BARNABY 3-5   70-72
DUNHILL 3-5   73-75
FULL MOON 2-4   80
MCA (Black vinyl) 2-4   79-86
MCA (Colored vinyl) 3-6   85
LPs: 10/12–inch 33rpm
ABC 8-10   76-78
BARNABY 10-15   70-77
DUNHILL 10-15   73-74
MCA 5-10   79-90
U.A. 8-10   75

BUFFETT, Mary
Singles: 12–inch 33/45rpm
MOBY DICK 4-6   84
Singles: 7–inch
MOBY DICK 2-4   84

BUGGLES
Singles: 7–inch
CARRERE 2-4   82
ISLAND 2-4   79-83
Promotional Singles
CARRERE ("Fade Away") 2-4   82
(Soundsheet. Originally included in a magazine.)
LPs: 10/12–inch 33rpm
CARRERE 5-10   82
ISLAND 5-10   80
   Members: Trevor Horn; Geoff Downes.
   Also see YES

BULAWAYO SWEET RHYTHM BOYS
Singles: 78rpm
LONDON 3-6   54
Singles: 7–inch
LONDON 5-10   54

BULL and the Matadors
Singles: 7–inch
TODDLIN' TOWN 5-10   68-69

BULLDOG
Singles: 7–inch
BUDDAH 3-5   72-74
DECCA 3-5   72
GUYDEN 3-5   71
MCA 3-5   73

LPs: 10/12–inch 33rpm
BUDDAH 8-12   74
DECCA 12-20   72
   Members: Gene Cornish; Dino Danelli; Billy Hocher; Eric
   Thorngren; John Turi.
   Also see RASCALS

BULLENS, Cindy
Singles: 7–inch
CASABLANCA 2-4   79-80
U.A. 2-4   78-79
LPs: 10/12–inch 33rpm
CASABLANCA 5-10   79
U.A. 5-10   78

BULLOCK, Janice
Singles: 7–inch
WRC 2-4   87
   Also see BELL, William, and Janice Bullock

BUMBLE, B:
see B. BUMBLE and the Stingers

BUMBLE BEE UNLIMITED
Singles: 7–inch
MERCURY 3-5   76-77
RCA 2-4   79
LPs: 10/12–inch 33rpm
RCA 5-10   79

BUNN, Allen
(Alden Bunn)
Singles: 78rpm
APOLLO 25-50   52
RED ROBIN 40-60   54
Singles: 7–inch
APOLLO (436 "She'll Be Sorry") ... 75-100   52
APOLLO (439 "Discouraged") 75-100   52
RED ROBIN (124 "My Kinda
   Woman") 175-225   54
   Also see LARKS
   Also see TARHEEL SLIM

BUONO, Victor
Singles: 7–inch
DORE 3-5   71
FAMILY 3-5   71
LPs: 10/12–inch 33rpm
DORE 5-10   71

BUOYS
Singles: 7–inch
POLYDOR 3-5   73
SCEPTER 3-6   69-71
Picture Sleeves
SCEPTER 4-6   71
LPs: 10/12–inch 33rpm
SCEPTER 8-10   71

BURCH, Ray
LPs: 10/12–inch 33rpm
YELLOWSTONE 8-10   72

BURCH, Vernon
Singles: 12–inch 33/45rpm
CHOCOLATE CITY	4-6	79-80
SPECTOR	4-6	81

Singles: 7–inch
CHOCOLATE CITY	2-4	78-80
COLUMBIA	2-4	77-78
SPECTOR	2-4	81-84
U.A.	3-5	75

LPs: 10/12–inch 33rpm
CHOCOLATE CITY	5-10	79-80
COLUMBIA	8-10	77-78
SPECTOR	5-10	81-84
U.A.	8-10	74-76

BURDON, Eric
(Eric Burdon Band)
Singles: 7–inch
CAPITOL	3-5	74

LPs: 10/12–inch 33rpm
CAPITOL	8-10	74-75
LAX	5-10	81-84
VERVE	10-12	72

Also see ANIMALS

BURDON, Eric, and War
Singles: 7–inch
ABC	3-5	76
CAPITOL	3-5	74-75
MGM	3-5	70

Picture Sleeves
MGM	4-6	70

LPs: 10/12–inch 33rpm
ABC	8-10	77
MGM (Except 4710)	10-15	70
MGM (4710 "Black Man's Burdon")	20-30	70

(Promotional issue only.)
Also see WAR

BURDON, Eric, and Jimmy Witherspoon
Singles: 7–inch
MGM	3-5	71

LPs: 10/12–inch 33rpm
MGM	10-15	71

Also see BURDON, Eric
Also see WITHERSPOON, Jimmy

BURGESS, Richard James
Singles: 12–inch 33/45rpm
CAPITOL	4-6	84

Singles: 7–inch
CAPITOL	2-4	84

LPs: 10/12–inch 33rpm
CAPITOL	5-10	84

BURKE, Keni
Singles: 7–inch
DARK HORSE	3-5	77-78
RCA	2-4	81-82

LPs: 10/12–inch 33rpm
DARK HORSE	8-10	77
RCA	5-10	81-82

Also see FIVE STAIRSTEPS

BURKE, Solomon
Singles: 12–inch 33/45rpm
SAVOY	4-6	84

Singles: 78rpm
APOLLO	5-10	56-57

Singles: 7–inch
ABC/DUNHILL	3-5	74
AMHERST	3-5	78
APOLLO	15-25	56-58
ATLANTIC	4-8	61-68
BELL	3-6	69-70
CHESS	3-5	75-77
DUNHILL	3-5	74
INFINITY	3-5	79
MGM	3-5	70-73
PRIDE	3-5	72-73
SINGULAR	5-10	60

LPs: 10/12–inch 33rpm
ABC/DUNHILL	10-12	74
APOLLO (498 "Solomon Burke")	60-100	62
ATLANTIC (8000 series)	25-45	62-64
ATLANTIC (8100 series)	15-30	65-68
BELL	12-20	69
CHESS	8-10	75-76
CLARION	12-20	64
INFINITY	5-10	79
KENWOOD	12-20	64
MGM	10-15	71-72
PRIDE	8-12	73
ROUNDER	5-10	84
SAVOY	5-10	81-83

Also see CHARLES, Ray / Somomon Burke
Also see SOUL CLAN

BURKE, Solomon, and Lady Lee
Singles: 7–inch
PRIDE	3-5	73

Also see BURKE, Solomon

BURNETT, Carol
LPs: 10/12–inch 33rpm
DECCA	15-25	61-64
COLUMBIA	8-12	71
RCA	10-15	67
TETRAGRAMMATON	8-12	69
VOCALION	8-12	68

Also see ANDREWS, Julie, and Carol Burnett

BURNETT, T-Bone
(J. Henry Burnett)
Singles: 7–inch
WARNER	2-4	83

LPs: 10/12–inch 33rpm
TAKOMA	5-10	80
WARNER	5-10	82-83

BURNETTE, Billy
(Billy Burnette and Jawbone)
Singles: 7–inch
A&M	3-5	76
COLUMBIA	2-4	80-81

MCA/CURB	2-4	86
POLYDOR	2-4	79
WARNER	3-6	69

LPs: 10/12-inch 33rpm

COLUMBIA	5-10	80-81
ENTRANCE	10-12	72
MCA/CURB	5-10	86
POLYDOR	5-10	79

Also see FLEETWOOD MAC

BURNETTE, Dorsey

Singles: 78rpm

ABBOTT	5-10	55

Singles: 7-inch

ABBOTT	15-30	55
CALLIOPE	3-5	77
CAPITOL	3-5	71-74
CEE-JAM (16 "Bertha-Lou")	25-50	58
COLLECTABLES	2-4	81
CONDOR	4-6	70
DOT	5-10	61
ELEKTRA	2-4	79-80
ERA	4-8	60-69
HAPPY TIGER	3-6	70
HICKORY	4-8	67
IMPERIAL	10-20	59-63
LIBERTY	3-6	69
MC	3-5	77
MEL-O-DY	4-8	64
MELODYLAND	3-5	75-76
MERRI	5-10	60
MOVIE STAR	4-8	
MUSIC FACTORY	3-6	68
REPRISE	5-8	62-63
SMASH	4-8	66
SURF (5019 "Bertha Lou")	50-75	57
U.S. NAVY ("Be a Navy Man")	10-20	

(U.S. Navy recruiting promotional issue.)

Picture Sleeves

ERA (3033 "The River and the Mountain")	15-25	61
REPRISE (246 "Four for Texas")	20-30	63
U.S. NAVY ("Be a Navy Man")	15-25	

(U.S. Navy recruiting promotional issue.)

LPs: 10/12-inch 33rpm

CALLIOPE	8-10	77
CAPITOL	10-12	72-73
DOT (3456 "Dorsey Burnette Sings")	20-40	63
(Monaural.)		
DOT (25456 "Dorsey Burnette Sings")	25-50	63
(Stereo.)		
ERA (EL-102 "Tall Oak Tree")	40-80	60
(Monaural.)		
ERA (ES-102 "Tall Oak Tree")	100-150	60
(Stereo.)		
ERA (800 series)	15-20	69
GUSTO	5-10	
TRIP	8-12	74

Also see BURNETTE, Johnny and Dorsey

BURNETTE, Johnny

Johnny Burnette and the Rock'n Roll Trio)

Singles: 78rpm

CORAL	15-25	56-57
VON (106 "Go Mule Go")	50-75	54

Singles: 7-inch

CAPITOL	8-12	63-64
CHANCELLOR	10-15	62
CORAL (61651 "Tear It Up")	50-75	56
CORAL (61675 "Midnight Train")	50-75	56
CORAL (61719 "Honey Hush")	50-75	56
CORAL (61758 "Lonesome Train")	50-75	56
CORAL (61829 "Eager Beaver Baby")	40-50	57
CORAL (61869 "Drinkin' Wine Spo-Dee-O-Dee")	40-50	57
CORAL (61918 "Rock Billy Boogie")	40-50	57

(All Coral 61000 series promotional issues are valued at the high end of the price range.)

FREEDOM (44001 "I'm Restless")	20-40	58
FREEDOM (44011 "Gumbo")	20-40	59
FREEDOM (44017 "Sweet Baby Doll")	20-40	59
LIBERTY	8-12	60
(Green and silver labels.)		
LIBERTY	5-10	60-62
(Multi-color labels.)		
LIBERTY ALL-TIME HITS	3-5	
MAGIC LAMP (515 "Bigger Man")	20-30	64
SAHARA	5-10	64
U.A.	2-4	84
VON (106 "Go Mule Go")	200-400	54

Picture Sleeves

LIBERTY (55285 "You're Sixteen")	15-20	60
LIBERTY (55298 "Little Boy Sad")	15-20	61
LIBERTY (55318 "Big, Big World")	15-20	61
MAGIC LAMP (515 "Bigger Man")	75-100	64

EPs: 7-inch 33/45rpm

LIBERTY (1004 "Dreamin'")	40-60	60
LIBERTY (1011 "Johnny Burnette's Hits")	50-75	61

LPs: 10/12-inch 33rpm

CORAL (57080 "Johnny Burnette and the Rock'n Roll Trio")	1000-1200	56

(Counterfeits can be identified by their lack of printing on the spine and hand-etched identification numbers in the trail-off. Originals have the numbers mechanically stamped. Canadian issues are worth at least as much as U.S. issues.)

LIBERTY (3179 "Dreamin'")	30-40	60
(Monaural.)		
LIBERTY (7179 "Dreamin'")	40-60	60
(Stereo.)		
LIBERTY (3183 "Johnny Burnette")	30-40	61
(Monaural.)		
LIBERTY (7183 "Johnny Burnette")	40-50	61
(Stereo.)		
LIBERTY (3190 "Johnny Burnette Sings")	30-40	61
(Monaural.)		

LIBERTY (7190 "Johnny Burnette
  Sings") 40-50   61
  (Stereo.)
LIBERTY (3206 "Johnny Burnette's Hits
  and Other Favorites") 30-40   62
  (Monaural.)
LIBERTY (7206 "Johnny Burnette's Hits
  and Other Favorites") 40-50   62
  (Stereo.)
LIBERTY (3255 "Roses Are Red") ... 30-40   62
  (Monaural.)
LIBERTY (7255 "Roses Are Red") ... 40-50   62
  (Stereo.)
LIBERTY (3389 "The Johnny
  Burnette Story") 30-40   64
  (Monaural.)
LIBERTY (7389 "The Johnny
  Burnette Story") 40-50   64
  (Stereo.)
LIBERTY (7300 series) 25-30   63
LIBERTY (10000 series) 5-10   81
MCA 5-10   82
SOLID SMOKE (Black vinyl) 5-10   78-80
SOLID SMOKE (Colored vinyl) 10-15   78
SUNSET 15-25   67
U.A. 10-15   75
  Members (Trio): Johnny Burnette; Dorsey Burnette; Paul
  Burlison.
  Also see BURNETTE, Dorsey
  Also see BURNETTE, Johnny
  Also see VEE, Bobby / Johnny Burnette / Ventures / Fleetwoods

BURNETTE, Johnny and Dorsey
(Burnette Brothers)
Singles: 7–inch
CORAL (62190 "Blues Stay
  Away from Me") 25-35   60
IMPERIAL 15-20   58
REPRISE 4-6   63
  Also see BURNETTE, Dorsey
  Also see BURNETTE, Johnny
  Also see TEXANS

BURNETTE, Rocky
(Rocky Burnette and the Rock 'N Roll Trio)
Singles: 7–inch
EMI AMERICA 2-4   80
LPs: 10/12–inch 33rpm
EMI AMERICA 5-10   80-82
GOODS 5-10   82
KYD 5-10   83

BURNING SENSATIONS
Singles: 7–inch
CAPITOL 2-4   83
LPs: 10/12–inch 33rpm
CAPITOL 5-10   83

BURNS, George
Singles: 7–inch
MERCURY 2-4   80-81
Picture Sleeves
MERCURY 2-4   80

LPs: 10/12–inch 33rpm
BUDDAH 6-10   72
MERCURY 5-10   80
PRIDE 5-10
  Also see MARTIN, Dean

BURNS, George, and Gracie Allen
LPs: 10/12–inch 33rpm
MARK '56 8-15
  Also see BURNS, George

BURRAGE, Harold
(Harold Barrage)
Singles: 78rpm
ALADDIN 10-15   52
COBRA 10-15   56-57
DECCA 10-15   50
STATES 10-20   54
Singles: 7–inch
ALADDIN (3194 "Sweet
  Brown Gal") 25-40   52
COBRA 15-25   56-58
DECCA (48175 "Hi-Yo") 25-50   50
FOXY 4-8   62
M-PAC 4-8   62-65
PASO 5-10   61
STATES (144 "Feel So Fine") 50-100   54
  (Black vinyl.)
STATES (144 "Feel So Fine") 100-200   50
  (Colored vinyl.)
VEE JAY 5-10   60
VIVID 4-8   64

BURRELL, Kenny
LPs: 10/12–inch 33rpm
CADET 10-20   66
VERVE 10-15   68

BURRELL, Kenny, and Jimmy Smith
LPs: 10/12–inch 33rpm
VERVE 10-15   68
  Also see BURRELL, Kenny
  Also see SMITH, Jimmy

BURRITO BROTHERS
Singles: 7–inch
CURB 2-4   81-84
EPIC 2-4   81
LPs: 10/12–inch 33rpm
A&M 8-10   80
CURB 5-10   81-82
  Also see FLYING BURRITO BROTHERS

BURROWS, Tony
Singles: 7–inch
BELL 3-5   70-72

BURTON, Jenny
Singles: 12–inch 33/45rpm
ATLANTIC 4-6   83-85
Singles: 7–inch
ATLANTIC 2-4   83-86
LPs: 10/12–inch 33rpm
ATLANTIC 5-10   83-85

BURTON, Jenny, and Patrick Jude
Singles: 7-inch
ATLANTIC 2-4   84
Also see BURTON, Jenny

BURTON, Richard
Singles: 7-inch
MGM 3-6   65

BUS BOYS
Singles: 7-inch
ARISTA 2-4   80-84
LPs: 10/12-inch 33rpm
ARISTA 5-10   80-82
Members: Gus Loundermon; Brian O'Neal; Kevin O'Neal; Michael Jones; Victor Johnson; Steve Felix.

BUSCH, Lou, Orchestra
Singles: 78rpm
CAPITOL 2-5   55-56
Singles: 7-inch
CAPITOL 4-8   55-56
Also see CARR, Joe "Fingers"

BUSH, Kate
Singles: 12-inch 33/45rpm
EMI AMERICA 4-6   85-86
Singles: 7-inch
COLUMBIA 2-4   89
EMI AMERICA 3-6   78-86
GEFFEN 2-4   87
HARVEST 4-8   78-79
Picture Sleeves
EMI AMERICA 4-6   85
HARVEST 8-12   78
LPs: 10/12-inch 33rpm
COLUMBIA 5-10   89
EMI AMERICA 6-12   78-86
HARVEST 10-15   78
Also see GABRIEL, Peter, and Kate Bush

BUSHKIN, Joe
LPs: 10/12-inch 33rpm
CAPITOL 15-25   56

BUSTERS
Singles: 7-inch
ARLEN 10-20   63-64
Members: Jack Baker; Fran Parda; Rick LaFrenier; Richard Eriksen; Tink Hermanson.

BUTANES
Singles: 7-inch
ENRICA 10-20   61

BUTCHER, Jon
(John Butcher Axis)
Singles: 7-inch
CAPITOL 2-4   85-89
POLYDOR 2-4   83-84
Picture Sleeves
CAPITOL 2-4   87
LPs: 10/12-inch 33rpm
CAPITOL 5-10   85-89

POLYDOR 5-10   83-84

BUTLER, Billy
(Billy Butler and Infinity; Billy Butler and the Chanters; Billy Butler and the Enchanters)
Singles: 7-inch
BRUNSWICK 4-8   66-68
CURTOM 3-5   76
OKEH 4-8   63-66
MEMPHIS 3-5   71
PRIDE 3-5   72-73
LPs: 10/12-inch 33rpm
EDSEL 5-10   86
OKEH 15-20   66
PRESTIGE 10-15   69-70
PRIDE 10-12   73
Members: Billy Butler; Earl Batts; Jess Tillman; Larry Wade; Phyllis Know.

BUTLER, Carl
Singles: 7-inch
COLUMBIA 4-6   61-63
LPs: 10/12-inch 33rpm
COLUMBIA 10-20   63
HARMONY 8-15   66-71

BUTLER, Carl and Pearl
Singles: 7-inch
COLUMBIA 4-6   63-69
LPs: 10/12-inch 33rpm
CMH 5-10   80
COLUMBIA 10-20   64-70
HARMONY 8-12   72
PEDACA 5-10
Also see BUTLER, Carl

BUTLER, Champ
Singles: 78rpm
COLUMBIA 3-8   50-54
CORAL 3-8   55-56
Singles: 7-inch
COLUMBIA 5-10   50-54
CORAL 5-10   55-56
GILLETTE 4-6   62
EPs: 7-inch 33/45rpm
COLUMBIA 8-15   53
LPs: 10/12-inch 33rpm
GILLETTE 10-20   62

BUTLER, Jerry
(Jerry Butler and the Impressions)
Singles: 78rpm
ABNER (1013 "For Your Precious
Love") 10-20   58
(Issued on 45 as FALCON 1013. The Abner 78 uses the Falcon 1013 number.)
Singles: 7-inch
ABNER 10-15   58-60
COLLECTABLES 2-4   81
ERIC 2-4   73
FALCON (1013 "For Your Precious
Love") 15-25   58

FOUNTAIN 2-4   82
MCA 2-4   83
MERCURY 3-8 67-74
MISTLETOE 3-5   75
MOTOWN 3-5 76-77
PHILADELPHIA INT'L 2-4 78-81
TRIP 3-5
VEE JAY (280 "For Your Precious
  Love") 500-600   58
VEE JAY (354 through 715) 5-10 60-66
VEE JAY (1971 "Aware of Love"} 15-25   63
  (Stereo compact 33 single.)
Picture Sleeves
VEE JAY 8-12 61-64
LPs: 10/12–inch 33rpm
ABNER (2001 "Jerry Butler
  Esquire") 75-125   59
BUDDAH 12-20   69
EXODUS 5-10
FOUNTAIN 5-10   82
DYNASTY 12-18
KENT 10-15   68
LOST-NITE 8-10   81
MERCURY 8-15 67-84
MOTOWN 5-10 76-77
PHILADELPHIA INT'L 5-10 78-81
POST 5-10
PRIDE 8-10   72
UPFRONT 8-10
SCEPTER 8-10
SIRE 8-12   77
SUNSET 10-12   68
TRIP 10-12 71-78
U.A. 8-10   75
VEE JAY (1000 series) 25-45 60-64
VEE JAY (1100 series) 20-30 64-65
  Members (Impressions): Jerry Butler; Sam Gooden; Richard
  Brooks; Arthur Brooks; Curtis Mayfield.
  Also see AUSTIN, Patti, and Jerry Butler
  Also see CHANDLER, Gene, and Jerry Butler
  Also see IMPRESSIONS
  Also see McPHATTER, Clyde / Little Richard / Jerry Butler
  Also see RIVERS, Johnny / 4 Seasons / Jerry Butler / Jimmy
  Soul

BUTLER, Jerry, and Brenda Lee Eager
Singles: 7–inch
MERCURY 2-4 71-73
LPs: 10/12–inch 33rpm
MERCURY 8-10   73
  Also see EAGER, Brenda Lee

BUTLER, Jerry, and Betty Everett
Singles: 7–inch
ABC 2-4   73
VEE JAY 3-5   64
LPs: 10/12–inch 33rpm
BUDDAH 10-15   69
TRADITION 5-10   82
VEE JAY 20-30   64
  Also see DELLS
  Also see EVERETT, Betty

BUTLER, Jerry, and Debra Henry
Singles: 7–inch
PHILADELPHIA INT'L 2-4   80
  Also see SILK

BUTLER, Jerry, and Stix Hooper
Singles: 7–inch
MCA 2-4   83
  Also see HOOPER, Stix

BUTLER, Jerry, and Thelma Houston
Singles: 7–inch
MOTOWN 3-5   77
LPs: 10/12–inch 33rpm
MOTOWN 5-10   77
  Also see BUTLER, Jerry
  Also see HOUSTON, Thelma

BUTLER, Jonathan
Singles: 7–inch
JIVE 2-4 86-88
Picture Sleeves
JIVE 2-4   87
LPs: 10/12–inch 33rpm
JIVE 5-10 86-88

BUTTERFIELD, Paul
(Butterfield Blues Band)
Singles: 7–inch
BEARSVILLE 3-5 73-81
ELEKTRA 4-8 67-69
Picture Sleeves
ELEKTRA 4-8   67
LPs: 10/12–inch 33rpm
AMHERST 5-8   86
BEARSVILLE 8-10 73-81
ELEKTRA 10-20 65-76
RED LIGHTNIN' ("An Offer You
  Can't Refuse") 30-40   72
  (One sided promotional LP.)
  Also see BISHOP, Elvin

BUTTERFLYS
Singles: 7–inch
RED BIRD 10-20   64

BUTTONS, Red
Singles: 78rpm
COLUMBIA 3-6   53
Singles: 7–inch
COLUMBIA 5-10   53

BUZZARD, Dr: see DR. BUZZARD

BUZZCOCKS
Singles: 7–inch

I.R.S. 2-4 79-80
LPs: 10/12–inch 33rpm
I.R.S. 5-10 79
Members: Pete Shelley; Steve Diggle; Howard Devoto; Steve
Garvey; John Maher.
Also see SHELLEY, Pete

BYRD, Bobby
(Robert Byrd and His Birdies; Bobby Byrd and the
Impalas; Bobby Day)
Singles: 78rpm

CASH 15-20 56
JAMIE 5-10 57
SAGE and SAND 5-10 55
SPARK 8-15
Singles: 7–inch
CASH (1031 "The Truth Hurts") 50-80 56
CORVET (1017 "Why") 35-45 58
JAMIE (1039 "Bippin' and Boppin'
Over You") 10-15 57
SAGE and SAND (203 "Please
Don't Hurt Me") 20-30 55
SPARK (501 "Bippin' and Boppin'
over You") 20-35 57
Also see BOB & EARL
Also see DAY, Bobby
Also see HOLLYWOOD FLAMES
Also see NUNN, Bobby

BYRD, Bobby
(Bobby Byrd and the Byrds)
Singles: 7–inch
BROWNSTONE 3-5 71-72
FEDERAL 4-8 63
INTERNATIONAL BROTHERS 3-5 75
KING 3-6 67-71
KWANZA 3-5 73
SMASH 4-8 64-65
ZEPHYR 8-12
LPs: 10/12–inch 33rpm
KING 10-15 70
Also see KING, Anna, and Bobby Byrd

BYRD, Bobby, and James Brown
Singles: 7–inch
KING 3-6 68
Also see BROWN, James
Also see BYRD, Bobby

BYRD, Charlie
Singles: 7–inch
RIVERSIDE 3-6 62-63
LPs: 10/12–inch 33rpm
COLUMBIA 15-25 65-69
OFFBEAT 25-35 59-60
RIVERSIDE 15-25 62-82
SAVOY 30-45 58
Also see ALMEIDA, Laurindo
Also see GETZ, Stan, and Charlie Byrd

BYRD, Charlie, and Woody Herman
LPs: 10/12–inch 33rpm
EVEREST 10-20 63
PICKWICK 6-12 66
Also see BYRD, Charlie
Also see HERMAN, Woody

BYRD, Donald
(Donald Byrd and 125th Street, N.Y.C.)
Singles: 7–inch
BLUE NOTE 3-5 75-77
ELEKTRA 2-4 78-82
LPs: 10/12–inch 33rpm
BETHLEHEM 15-25 60
BLUE NOTE 15-25 59-65
(Label reads "Blue Note Records Inc. - New York,
U.S.A.")
BLUE NOTE 10-20 66-77
(Label reads "Blue Note Records - a Division of
Liberty Records Inc.")
COLUMBIA (998 "Jazz Lab") 40-60 57
(With Gigi Gryce.)
COLUMBIA (1058 "Jazz Lab, Vol. 2,
Modern Jazz Perspective") 40-60 57
(With Gigi Gryce.)
ELEKTRA 5-10 78-82
JUBILEE (1059 "Jazz Lab") 40-60 57
(With Gigi Gryce.)
PRESTIGE (7062 "Two Trumpets") . 75-100 56
(Yellow label. With Art Farmer.)
PRESTIGE (7080 "Youngbloods") ... 60-80 57
(Yellow label. With Phil Woods.)
PRESTIGE (7092 "Three Trumpets") 60-80 57
(Yellow label. With Art Farmer and Idrees
Sulieman.)
REGENT (6056 "Jazz Eyes") 40-60 57
SAVOY (12032 "Byrd's Word") 40-60 56
(With Frank Foster.)
TRANSITION (4 "Byrd's Eye View") . 50-80 55
(With Hank Mobley.)
TRANSITION (5 "Byrd Jazz") 50-80 55
(With Yusef Lateef.)
TRANSITION (17 "Byrd Blows
on Beacon Hill") 50-80 56
VERVE 20-30 58
Also see BLACKBYRDS

BYRD, Gary
(Gary Byrd and the G.B. Experience)
Singles: 12–inch 33/45rpm
WONDIRECTION 4-6 83
Singles: 7–inch
RCA 3-5 73

BYRD, Jerry
Singles: 7–inch
MONUMENT 4-6 60-62
EPs: 7–inch 33/45rpm
DECCA 8-12 58
MERCURY 10-20 53-55

LPs: 10/12–inch 33rpm

DECCA	15-30	58
LEHUA	8-10	
MERCURY (Except 25000 series)	10-20	58-64
MERCURY (25000 series) (10–inch LPs.)	20-40	53-54
MONUMENT	12-25	61-63
WING	10-15	60-66

BYRDS

Singles: 7–inch

ASYLUM	3-5	73
COLUMBIA (1600 series)	4-6	73
COLUMBIA (43271 "Mr. Tambourine Man") (Black vinyl.)	5-10	65
COLUMBIA (43271 "Mr. Tambourine Man") (Colored vinyl. Promotional issue only.)	50-75	65
COLUMBIA (43332 "I'll Feel a Whole Lot Better") (Black vinyl.)	5-10	65
COLUMBIA (43332 "I'll Feel a Whole Lot Better") (Colored vinyl. Promotional issue only.)	50-75	65
COLUMBIA (43332 "All I Really Want to Do") (Black vinyl.)	5-10	65
COLUMBIA (43332 "All I Really Want to Do") (Colored vinyl. Promotional issue only.)	50-75	65
COLUMBIA (43434 "Turn Turn Turn") (Black vinyl.)	5-10	65
COLUMBIA (43434 "Turn Turn Turn") (Colored vinyl. Promotional issue only.)	50-75	65
COLUMBIA (43501 through 45761)	4-8	66-72
SCHOLASTIC	5-10	66

Picture Sleeves

COLUMBIA (Except 43271)	12-25	65-71
COLUMBIA (43271 "Mr. Tambourine Man") (Promotional issue only.)	100-150	65
COLUMBIA (43578 "Eight Miles High")	15-25	65
COLUMBIA (44157 "Have You Seen Her Face")	15-25	65

EPs: 7–inch 33/45rpm

COLUMBIA (10287 "The Byrds") (Columbia Special Products issue for the Scholastic Book Services.)	40-60	66
COLUMBIA (116003/4 "Fifth Dimension Open-End Interview") (Promotional issue only.)	50-75	66

LPs: 10/12–inch 33rpm

ASYLUM	8-10	73
COLUMBIA (2000 series)	20-25	65-67
COLUMBIA (9000 series)	15-25	65-69
COLUMBIA (30000 through 33000 series)	8-12	70-75
COLUMBIA (34000 through 37000 series)	5-10	75-84
COLUMBIA (46773 "The Byrds") (Four-LP set. Includes booklet.)	30-40	90
TOGETHER	15-20	69

Promotional LPs

BROADCAST ("Byrds Live")	35-45	81
COLUMBIA (2000 series) (White label.)	40-50	65-67
COLUMBIA (9000 series) (White label.)	35-45	65-69
COLUMBIA (116003/4 "Fifth Dimension" Interview Album)	100-125	66

Members: David Crosby; Gene Clark; Chris Hillman; Roger McGuinn; Mike Clark; Skip Battin; John Guerin; Kevin Kelley.
Also see BEEFEATERS
Also see CLARK, Gene
Also see CROSBY, David
Also see HILLMAN, Chris
Also see McGUINN, Roger
Also see PARSONS, Gram

BYRNE, David

Singles: 12–inch 33/45rpm

SIRE	4-6	82

LPs: 10/12–inch 33rpm

ECM	5-8	85
LUAKA BOP	5-8	89
SIRE	5-10	81

Also see ENO, Brian
Also see TALKING HEADS

BYRNES, Edd "Kookie," with Joanie Sommers and the Mary Kaye Trio

Singles: 7–inch

WARNER	5-10	59

Picture Sleeves

WARNER	8-12	59

Also see KAYE, Mary
Also see SOMMERS, Joanie

BYRNES, Edward

(Edd "Kookie" Byrnes; Edd Byrnes with Connie Stevens and Don Ralke's Orchestra; Edd Byrnes with Friend; Edd Byrnes and the Mary Kaye Trio.)

Singles: 7–inch

WARNER (5047 "Kookie Kookie")	5-10	59
WARNER (S-5047 "Kookie Kookie") (Stereo.)	10-20	59
WARNER (5087 through 5121)	5-10	59

Picture Sleeves

WARNER	15-20	59

LPs: 10/12–inch 33rpm

WARNER	20-30	59

Also see BYRNES, Edd "Kookie," with Joanie Sommers and the Mary Kaye Trio
Also see RALKE, Don
Also see STEVENS, Connie

BYRON, D.L.

Singles: 7–inch

ARISTA	2-4	80

LPs: 10/12–inch 33rpm

ARISTA	5-10	80

C

C., Fantastic Johnny:
see FANTASTIC JOHNNY C.

C and the Shells
Singles: 7–inch
COTILLION 2-4   3-6
ZANZEE 3-5   72
Members: Calvin White; Andrea Bolden; Lonzine Wright.
Also see SANDPEBBLES

C.C. and Company
Singles: 7–inch
SUSSEX 3-5   75
20TH CENTURY/WESTBOUND 3-5   75

C.C.S.
Singles: 7–inch
BELL 3-5   73
RAK 4-8   71
LPs: 10/12–inch 33rpm
RAK 15-20   71-72

C.J. and Co.
Singles: 7–inch
WESTBOUND 3-5   77-78
LPs: 10/12–inch 33rpm
WESTBOUND 5-10   77-78

C.L. BLAST: see BLAST, C.L.

C.O.D.s
Singles: 7–inch
ERIC 2-4   74
KELLMAC 5-10   65-66
Members: Larry Brownlee; Robert Lewis; Carl Washington.
Also see MYSTIQUE

C.Q.D.
Singles: 12–inch 33/45rpm
EMERGENCY 4-6   83

CACTUS
Singles: 7–inch
ATCO 5-8   70-72
LPs: 10/12–inch 33rpm
ATCO 20-25   70-72
Members: Carmine Appice; Tim Bogert; Pete French; Werner
Fritzschings; Duane Hitchings; Jerry Norris; Mike Pinera; Roland
Robinson; Rusty Day; Jim McCarty.
Also see BECK, BOGERT & APPICE
Also see NEW CACTUS BAND
Also see PINERA, Mike
Also see YARDBIRDS

CACTUS WORLD NEWS
Singles: 7–inch
MCA 2-4   86
LPs: 10/12–inch 33rpm
MCA 5-10   86

CADETS
MODERN (Except 971) 15-25   55-57
MODERN (971 "If It Is Wrong") 20-40   55
Singles: 7–inch
COLLECTABLES 2-4   81
MODERN (Except 971) 20-40   55-57
MODERN (971 "If It Is Wrong") 75-100   55
LPs: 10/12–inch 33rpm
CROWN (370 "The Cadets") 25-40   63
CROWN (5015 "Rockin' 'n Reelin') . 75-100   57
RELIC 10-15
Members: Ted Taylor; Aaron Collins; Will "Dub" Jones; Willie
Davis; Lloyd McGraw; Prentice Moreland; Tom Fox; Randolph
Jones.
Also see FLARES
Also see JACKS
Also see TAYLOR, Ted

CADILLAC, Flash:
see FLASH CADILLAC and the Continental Kids

CADILLACS
Singles: 78rpm
JOSIE (765 "Gloria") 25-50   54
JOSIE (769 "Wishing Well") 25-50   54
JOSIE (773 through 820) 15-30   55-57
Singles: 7–inch
ABC 2-4   73
ARCTIC (101 "Fool") 15-25   64
CAPITOL 8-12   62
JOSIE (765 "Gloria") 300-400   54
JOSIE (769 "Wishing Well") 350-450   54
JOSIE (773 "No Chance") 40-60   55
JOSIE (778 "Down the Road") 40-60   55
JOSIE (785 "Speedo") 25-50   55
JOSIE (792 "Zoom") 25-50   56
JOSIE (798 "Betty My Love") 25-50   56
JOSIE (800 series except 820) 10-20   56-60
JOSIE (820 "My Girl Friend") 25-50   57
JOSIE (900 series) 5-10   63
JUBILEE (9010 "Romeo") 30-50   62
(Stereo.)
LANA 3-5
MERCURY 15-25   61
SMASH 5-10   61
VIRGO 2-4   72-73
LPs: 10/12–inch 33rpm
CADAVER 5-10
HARLEM HITPARADE 10-12
JUBILEE (1045 "The Fabulous
Cadillacs") 300-400   57
(Blue label.)
JUBILEE (1045 "The Fabulous
Cadillacs") 200-250   59
(Flat black label.)
JUBILEE (1045 "The Fabulous
Cadillacs") 50-100   60
(Glossy black label.)
JUBILEE (1089 "The Crazy
Cadillacs") 150-250   58
(Flat black label.)

JUBILEE (1089 "The Crazy
Cadillacs") 75-125   60
(Glossy black label.)
JUBILEE (5009 "Twistin' with
the Cadillacs") 50-75   62
(Monaural.)
JUBILEE (5009 "Twistin' with
the Cadillacs") 75-125   62
(Stereo.)
MURRAY HILL (1195 "The Very Best
of the Cadillacs") 5-10   88
MURRAY HILL (1285 "The Cadillacs") 30-35
(Five-LP boxed set.)
Members: Earl "Speedo" Carroll; Jim "Papa" Clark; Gus
Willingham; Bobby Phillips; Laverne Drake; Charles Brooks;
James Bailey; Earl Wade.
Also see BAILEY, J.R.
Also see NEW YORK CITY
Also see ORIGINAL CADILLACS
Also see SCHOOLBOYS

CADILLACS / Orioles
LPs: 10/12–inch 33rpm
JUBILEE (1117 "The Cadillacs Meet
the Orioles") 75-100   61
Also see CADILLACS
Also see ORIOLES

CAESAR, Shirley
(Shirley Caesar and the Caesar Singers)
Singles: 7–inch
HOB/SCEPTER 3-5   73-75
ROADSHOW 2-5   77-78
LPs: 10/12–inch 33rpm
HOB 8-12   70-75
ROADSHOW 5-10   77
TRIP 5-10   77

CAESAR & CLEO
Singles: 7–inch
REPRISE 10-15   64-65
VAULT 15-25   63
Picture Sleeves
REPRISE (0419 "Let the Good
Times Roll") 25-50   65
Members: Salvatore "Sonny" Bono; Cher LaPiere.
Also see SONNY & CHER

CAESAR and the Romans:
see LITTLE CAESAR and the Romans

CAESARS
Singles: 7–inch
LANIE 4-8   67

CAFE
(With the Hearns Sisters)
Singles: 12–inch 33/45rpm
MONTAGE 4-6   84

CAFFERTY, John
(John Cafferty and the Beaver Brown Band)
Singles: 7–inch
SCOTTI BROTHERS 2-4   83-86

Picture Sleeves
SCOTTI BROTHERS 2-4   84-86
LPs: 10/12–inch 33rpm
SCOTTI BROTHERS 5-10   83-89

CAIN, Jonathan
(Jonathan Cain Band)
Singles: 7–inch
BEARSVILLE 3-5   76
OCTOBER 3-5   75-76
LPs: 10/12–inch 33rpm
BEARSVILLE 5-10   77
Also see CAIN, Tane
Also see JOURNEY

CAIN, Tane
Singles: 7–inch
RCA 2-4   82-83
LPs: 10/12–inch 33rpm
RCA 5-10   82
Also see CAIN, Jonathan

CAINE, General
Singles: 12–inch 33/45rpm
CAPITOL 4-6   84
TABU 4-6   82-84
Singles: 7–inch
CAPITOL 2-4   84
TABU 2-4   82-84
LPs: 10/12–inch 33rpm
TABU 5-10   82-84

CAIOLA, Al
Singles: 78rpm
RCA 4-8   53-55
REGENCY 4-8   56
Singles: 7–inch
AVLANCHE 2-4   73
PREFERRED 3-6   59-60
RCA 4-8   53-55
REGENCY 4-8   56
U.A. 3-6   60-68
EPs: 7–inch 33/45rpm
RCA 5-10   53
LPs: 10/12–inch 33rpm
ATCO 10-15   60
BAINBRIDGE 5-8   80
CAMDEN 8-12   62
CHANCELLOR 10-15   60
RCA 10-15   59
ROULETTE 10-15   60
SAVOY 15-25   56
TIME 10-20   60-61
TWO WORLDS 8-10   72
UNART 8-12   67
U.A. 10-15   60-69

CALDERA
Singles: 7–inch
CAPITOL 3-5   76
LPs: 10/12–inch 33rpm
CAPITOL 8-10   76-79

CALDWELL, Bobby

Singles: 12–inch 33/45rpm

MCA	4-6	84-85

Singles: 7–inch

CLOUDS	2-4	78-80
PBR INT'L	2-4	76
POLYDOR	2-4	82-83
MCA	2-4	84-85

LPs: 10/12–inch 33rpm

CLOUDS	5-10	78-80
MCA	5-10	84
POLYDOR	5-10	82

Also see CAPTAIN BEYOND

CALDWELL, Rue

Singles: 12–inch 33/45rpm

CRITIQUE	4-6	83

Singles: 7–inch

CRITIQUE	2-4	83

CALE, J.J.

Singles: 7–inch

LIBERTY (55840 "Dick Tracy")	5-10	66
MERCURY	2-4	83-84
SHELTER	2-5	71-81

LPs: 10/12–inch 33rpm

MCA	5-10	81
MERCURY	5-10	82-85
SHELTER	10-15	71-79
SILVERTONE	5-8	80

CALE, John

Singles: 7–inch

A&M	2-4	81
COLUMBIA	3-5	70
I.R.S.	2-4	79-80
REPRISE	3-5	72

Picture Sleeves

I.R.S.	2-4	79-80

LPs: 10/12–inch 33rpm

A&M	5-10	81
COLUMBIA	12-15	70-71
I.R.S.	5-10	79
ISLAND	8-10	75-77
PASSPORT	5-10	84
REPRISE	10-12	72-73
ZE	5-10	83

Also see EARTH OPERA
Also see VELVET UNDERGROUND

CALEN, Frankie

Singles: 7–inch

BEAR	4-8	62
EPIC	4-8	63-64
NRC (029 "Angel Face")	5-10	59
NRC (5008 "Angel Face")	5-10	59
SPARK	15-20	61
U.A.	4-8	62

CALHOON

Singles: 12–inch 33/45rpm

WARNER/SPECTOR	4-8	75

Singles: 7–inch

WARNER/SPECTOR	3-5	75-76

CALIFORNIA MUSIC

Singles: 7–inch

RCA/EQUINOX	10-15	74-76

Members: Dean Torrence; Bruce Johnston; Terry Melcher;
Kenny Hinkle.
Also see BRUCE & TERRY
Also see JAN & DEAN

CALIFORNIA RAISINS

Singles: 7–inch

ATLANTIC	2-4	88
PRIORITY (Black vinyl)	2-4	87-88
PRIORITY (7915 "What Does It Take to Win Your Love") (Colored vinyl.)	4-6	88

Picture Sleeves

PRIORITY	3-5	87-88

LPs: 10/12–inch 33rpm

PRIORITY	5-10	87-88

Member: Buddy Miles.
Also see MILES, Buddy

CALL

Singles: 12–inch 33/45rpm

ELEKTRA	4-6	86

Singles: 7–inch

ELEKTRA	2-4	86
MCA	2-4	89
MERCURY	2-4	83

Picture Sleeves

MCA	2-4	89

LPs: 10/12–inch 33rpm

ELEKTRA	5-10	86-87
MCA	5-8	89
MERCURY	5-10	82-83

CALLENDER, Bobby

Singles: 7–inch

CORAL	4-8	67
ROULETTE	4-8	63

LPs: 10/12–inch 33rpm

MGM	10-15	68

CALLIER, Terry

Singles: 12–inch 33/45rpm

ERECT	4-6	82

Singles: 7–inch

CADET	3-6	68-73
ELEKTRA	2-5	78-79

LPs: 10/12–inch 33rpm

CADET	10-12	72-73
CHESS	10-15	71
ELEKTRA	8-10	78-79

CALLOWAY, Cab

(Cab Calloway and His Cab Jivers; Cab Calloway and
His Caballiers)

Singles: 78rpm

ABC-PAR	4-8	56
BANNER	8-12	31-32

BELL 4-8 53-55
BLUEBIRD 5-10 49
BRUNSWICK 5-15 30-36
COLUMBIA 5-10 42-49
CONQUEROR 8-12 38-41
DOMINO 10-15 30
HI-TONE 5-8 49
JEWEL 8-12 31
MEL-O-DEE 10-20 31
MELOTONE 8-12 32-33
OKEH 5-10 40-42
ORIOLE 8-12 32-33
PERFECT 8-12 32
RCA 4-8 49
REGAL 5-12 31-51
ROMEO 8-12 32-33
SIGNATURE 5-8 49
VARIETY 8-12 33-37
VICTOR 5-15 33-34
VOCALION 5-10 38-40

Singles: 7-inch

ABC-PAR 10-15 56
BELL 10-15 53-55
CORAL 4-8 61-62
GONE 5-10 58
OKEH (6896 "Willow Weep for Me") . 20-30 52
RCA (007 "Rooming
    House Boogie") 50-75 49
RCA (8000 series) 4-6 62
RCA (11000 series) 3-5 78

EPs: 7-inch 33/45rpm

EPIC (7000 series) 10-20 53

LPs: 10/12-inch 33rpm

BRUNSWICK (58010 "Cab Calloway") 40-60 52
CORAL (57408 "Blues Make
    Me Happy") 15-20 62
    (Monaural.)
CORAL (757408 "Blues Make
    Me Happy") 20-30 62
    (Stereo.)
EPIC (3265 "Cab Calloway") 30-50 57
GONE (101 "Cotton Club Revue") ... 30-50 58
GUEST STAR 10-15
RCA (LPM-2021 "Hi De Hi De Ho") .. 15-25 60
    (Monaural.)
RCA (LSP-2021 "Hi De Hi De Ho") .. 25-35 60
    (Stereo.)

CALVERT, Eddie

Singles: 78rpm

CAPITOL 3-5 56
ESSEX 3-5 53-54

Singles: 7-inch

ABC-PAR 4-6 60-61
CAPITOL 5-10 56
ESSEX 4-8 53-54

LPs: 10/12-inch 33rpm

ABC-PAR 10-15 60-62

CAMBRIDGE, Godfrey

LPs: 10/12-inch 33rpm

EPIC 10-20 64-68

CAMBRIDGE STRINGS and Singers

Singles: 7-inch

LONDON 3-5 61

CAMEL

Singles: 7-inch

JANUS 3-5 74-77

LPs: 10/12-inch 33rpm

ARISTA 5-10 79
JANUS 8-10 74-77
PASSPORT 5-10 81
    Members: Peter Bardens; Doug Ferguson; Andy Latimer; Andy
    Ward.
    Also see BARDENS, Peter

CAMEO

Singles: 12-inch 33/45rpm

ATLANTA ARTISTS 4-6 83-86
CHOCOLATE CITY 4-6 78-80

Singles: 7-inch

ATLANTA ARTISTS 2-4 83-88
CHOCOLATE CITY 2-5 75-82

Picture Sleeves

ATLANTA ARTISTS 2-4 86-88

LPs: 10/12-inch 33rpm

ATLANTA ARTISTS 5-10 83-90
CHOCOLATE CITY 5-10 77-82
    Members: Tomi Jenkins; Larry Blackmon; Nathan Leftenant.
    Also see EAST COAST
    Also see SINGLETON, Charlie

CAMERON
(Rafael Cameron)

Singles: 7-inch

SALSOUL 2-4 80-82

LPs: 10/12-inch 33rpm

SALSOUL 5-10 80-82

CAMERON, G.C.

Singles: 7-inch

MALACO 2-4 83
MOTOWN 3-5 73-77
MOWEST 3-5 71-73

LPs: 10/12-inch 33rpm

MOTOWN 5-10 74-77
    Also see SPINNERS

CAMERON, Rafael: see CAMERON

CAMP, Hamilton
(Hamid Hamilton Camp and the Skymonters; Bob
Camp)

Singles: 7-inch

AMERICAN INT'L 3-5 71
WARNER 4-8 68

LPs: 10/12-inch 33rpm

ELEKTRA (200 series) 12-15 64
ELEKTRA (75000 series) 8-10 73
MOUNTAIN RAILROAD 5-10
WARNER 10-15 67-69

CAMPBELL, Debbie
Singles: 7–inch
PLAYBOY 3-5   75

CAMPBELL, Glen
(Glen Campbell with the Glen-Aires; Glen Campbell
and the Green River Boys)
Singles: 7–inch
ATLANTIC AMERICA 2-4   82-86
CAPEHART 10-20   61
CAPITOL (2000 and 3000 series) 3-6   68-74
CAPITOL (4000 series) 2-5   75-81
  (Orange or purple labels.)
CAPITOL (4783 through 5360) 5-10   61-65
  (Orange/yellow swirl labels.)
CAPITOL (5441 "Guess I'm Dumb") . 25-40   65
  (With Brian Wilson.)
CAPITOL (5504 through 5939) 3-8   65-67
CENECO 10-15
CREST 10-15   61-62
  (May be shown as Glen Cambpbell on some Crest
  labels.)
EVEREST 3-6   69
STARDAY 3-6   68
MCA 2-4   84-88
MIRAGE 2-4   81
WARNER 2-4   80
Picture Sleeves
CAPITOL (Except 4856 and 5279) 3-6   68-74
CAPITOL (4856 "Long Black
  Limousine") 10-15   62
CAPITOL (5279 "Summer, Winter,
  Spring and Fall") 8-12   64
EPs: 7–inch 33/45rpm
CAPITOL 5-10   68-69
  (Jukebox issues.)
CAPITOL/CHEVROLET (55 "The Glen
  Campbell Good Time Hour") 5-10
LPs: 10/12–inch 33rpm
ATLANTIC AMERICA 5-10   82-86
BUCKBOARD 8-10
CAPITOL (103 through 752) 8-15   68-71

CAPITOL (1810 "Big Bluegrass
  Special") 75-100   62
  (Shown as by the Green River Boys Featuring
  Glen Campbell.)
CAPITOL (1881 through 2392) 20-40   63-65
  (With "T" or "ST" prefix.)
CAPITOL (2809 through 2928) 8-15   67-68
  (With "T" or "ST" prefix.)
CAPITOL (2000 series) 5-10   78
  (With "SM" prefix.)
CAPITOL (11000 through 16000
  series) 5-10   72-82
CAPITOL (94000 series) 8-15   72
  (Capitol Record Club issues.)
CAPITOL (120000 series) 5-10
  (Capitol Record Club issues.)
CAPITOL CREATIVE PRODUCTS . . . 5-10
CUSTOM TONE 15-20
LONGINES ("Glen Campbell's
  Golden Favorites") 20-30   72
  (Six-LP, boxed set.)
PICKWICK 8-10   64-73
STARDAY 15-20   68-69
  Also see BACHARACH, Burt / Glen Campbell / Dionne Warwick
  Also see BEACH BOYS
  Also see CHAMPS
  Also see FABARES, Shelley
  Also see FOLKSWINGERS
  Also see FORD, Tennessee Ernie, and Glen Campbell
  Also see HONDELLS
  Also see MARTIN, Dean / Glen Campbell
  Also see RIP CHORDS
  Also see SAGITTARIUS
  Also see WILSON, Brian

CAMPBELL, Glen, and Rita Coolidge
Singles: 7–inch
CAPITOL 2-4   80
  Also see COOLIDGE, Rita

CAMPBELL, Glen, and Bobbie Gentry
Singles: 7–inch
CAPITOL 3-5   68-70
EPs: 7–inch 33/45rpm
CAPITOL 8-10   68
  (Jukebox issue only.)
LPs: 10/12–inch 33rpm
CAPITOL 8-10   68
  Also see GENTRY, Bobbie

**CAMPBELL, Glen / Lettermen / Ella
Fitzgerald / Sandler and Young**
LPs: 10/12–inch 33rpm
CAPITOL (56 "B.F. Goodrich Presents
  Christmas 1969") 10-15   69
  (Promotional, special products issue.)
    Also see FITZGERALD, Ella
    Also see LETTERMEN
    Also see SANDLER & YOUNG

CAMPBELL, Glen, and Anne Murray
Singles: 7–inch
CAPITOL 3-5   71-72

LPs: 10/12–inch 33rpm

CAPITOL 5-10   71-80

CAMPBELL, Glen / Anne Murray / Kenny Rogers / Crystal Gayle

CAPITOL/U.A. (11743-F-19 "Glen/Anne/
  Kenny/Crystal") 300-500   78
  (Four framed picture disc set. Promotional issue
  only.)
  Also see GAYLE, Crystal
  Also see MURRAY, Anne
  Also see ROGERS, Kenny

CAMPBELL, Glen, and Billy Strange
LPs: 10/12–inch 33rpm

SURREY 12-20   65
  Also see STRANGE, Billy

CAMPBELL, Glen, and Tanya Tucker
Singles: 7–inch

CAPITOL 2-4   81
  Also see CAMPBELL, Glen
  Also see TUCKER, Tanya

CAMPBELL, Jim
Singles: 7–inch

LAURIE 3-6   69-70

CAMPBELL, Jo Ann
Singles: 78rpm

ELDORADO 10-20   57
POINT 10-20   56

Singles: 7–inch

ABC-PAR 10-20   60-62
  (Monaural.)
ABC-PAR (10134 "Kookie
  Little Paradise") 20-40   60
  (Stereo.)
CAMEO 5-10   62-63
ELDORADO 15-20   57
GONE 10-20   59
POINT 15-25   56
RORI 4-8

LPs: 10/12–inch 33rpm

ABC-PAR (393 "Twistin' and
  Listenin") 40-50   62
  (Monaural.)
ABC-PAR (393 "Twistin' and
  Listenin") 50-60   62
  (Stereo.)
CAMEO (1026 "All the Hits
  of Jo Ann Campbell") 25-30   62
CORONET (199 "Starring Jo Ann
  Campbell") 25-30   62
END (306 "I'm Nobody's Baby") 40-60   59
  Also see JO ANN & TROY

CANDELA
Singles: 12–inch 33/45rpm

ARISTA 4-6   83

Singles: 7–inch

ARISTA 2-4   82-83

CANDY and the Kisses
Singles: 7–inch

CAMEO 10-15   64
COLLECTABLES 2-4   81
DECCA 4-8   68
R&L 10-15   63
SCEPTER 8-12   65-66
  Members: Candy Nelson; Suzanne Nelson; Jeanette Johnson.

CANDYMEN
Singles: 7–inch

ABC 4-8   67-69
LIBERTY 3-6   70

LPs: 10/12–inch 33rpm

ABC 15-25   67-68
  Members: Rodney Justo; Barry Bailey; Dean Daughtry; Billy
  Gilmore; Paul Goddard; John Adkins; Bob Nix.
  Also see ATLANTA RHYTHM SECTION
  Also see CLASSICS IV
  Also see ORBISON, Roy

CANE, Gary
(Gary Cane and His Friends)
Singles: 7–inch

SHELL 8-12   60-61

CANNED HEAT
(Heat Brothers)
Singles: 7–inch

ALA 2-4   84
ATLANTIC 3-5   74
LIBERTY 4-6   68-71
U.A. 3-5   71-73

Picture Sleeves

LIBERTY 4-8   67-69

LPs: 10/12–inch 33rpm

ACCORD 5-10   81
ALA 8-10   84
ATLANTIC 10-12   73-74
JANUS 12-15   69
LIBERTY (1000 series) 5-10   80
LIBERTY (7000 series) 15-20   67-69
LIBERTY (10000 series) 5-10   81
LIBERTY (11000 series) 10-15   69-70
PICKWICK 5-10
SCEPTER 10-15
SUNSET 10-15   71
U.A. 10-15   71-75
WAND 15-20   70
  Members: Bob Hite; Joel Scott Hill; Harvey Mandel; Mark Andex;
  Ed Bayer; Frank Cook; Richard Hite; Chris Morgan; James
  Shane; Gene Taylor; Larry Taylor; Henry Vestine; Alan Wilson;
  Nolfo De LaParra.
  Also see HOOKER, John Lee, and Canned Heat
  Also see LITTLE RICHARD
  Also see MANDEL, Harvey

CANNED HEAT and the Chipmunks
Singles: 7–inch

LIBERTY 15-25   68-70
  Also see CANNED HEAT
  Also see CHIPMUNKS

CANNIBAL and the Headhunters
Singles: 7–inch

AIRES	4-8	68
CAPITOL	3-6	69
COLLECTABLES	2-4	81
DATE	4-8	66
ERA	3-5	73
RAMPART	5-10	65-66

LPs: 10/12–inch 33rpm

DATE (3001 "Land of 1000 Dances")	20-25	66
RAMPART (3302 "Land of 1000 Dances")	40-50	65

Members: Frankie "Cannibal" Garcia; Robert Jaramillo; Joe Jaramillo; Richard Lopez.

CANNON, Ace
(Johnny "Ace" Cannon)
Singles: 7–inch

FERNWOOD	4-8	63-64
HI (2000 series)	5-8	61-66
HI (2100 through 2300 series)	3-6	66-76
MOTOWN	2-4	82
SANTO	4-8	62

Picture Sleeves

HI	5-10	62-63

EPs: 7–inch 33/45rpm

HI (1133 "In the Spotlight")	5-10	68

(Jukebox issue.)

LPs: 10/12–inch 33rpm

ALLEGIANCE	5-10	84
GUSTO	5-10	80
HI (007 through 040)	10-20	62-67

(Numbers in this series are preceeded by a "12" for mono or a "32" for stereo issues.)

HI (043 through 090)	6-10	68-75

(Numbers in this series are preceded by a "32," indicating stereo.)

HI (6000 and 8000 series)	8-10	77-79
MOTOWN	5-10	83

CANNON, Dean
Singles: 7–inch

VALIANT	4-8	63

CANNON, Freddy
(Freddie Cannon)
Singles: 7–inch

BUDDAH	3-5	71
CLARIDGE	3-5	74-76
ERIC	2-4	78
HQ ("Kennywood Park")	4-6	87

(KDKA promotional issue only. No number used.)

MCA	3-5	74
METROMEDIA	3-5	72
ROYAL AMERICAN	3-6	69-70
SIRE	4-6	69
SWAN	5-10	59-64
WARNER	4-8	64-67
WE MAKE ROCK and ROLL RECORDS	4-6	68

Picture Sleeves

HQ ("Kennywood Park")	5-8	87

(KDKA promotional issue only. No number used.)

SWAN	15-25	59-62
WARNER	10-20	64-65

LPs: 10/12–inch 33rpm

RHINO	5-10	82
SWAN (502 "The Explosive Freddy Cannon")	50-75	60

(Monaural.)

SWAN (502 "The Explosive Freddy Cannon")	65-90	60

(Stereo.)

SWAN (504 "Happy Shades of Blue")	50-75	62
SWAN (505 "Solid Gold Hits")	50-75	61
SWAN (507 "Palisades Park")	50-75	62
SWAN (511 "Freddy Cannon Steps Out")	50-75	62
WARNER (1544 "Freddie Cannon")	30-40	64
WARNER (1612 "Action")	30-40	64
WARNER (1628 "Greatest Hits")	30-40	64

Also see BUCHANAN, Roy
Also see DANNY and the Juniors
Also see G-CLEFS
Also see SLAY, Frank

CANNON, Freddy, and the Belmonts
Singles: 7–inch

MIA SOUND	4-6	81

Also see BELMONTS, Freddy Cannon and Bo Diddley
Also see CANNON, Freddy

CANO, Eddie
Singles: 7–inch

DUNHILL	3-6	66-67
GNP/CRESCENDO	4-6	62
REPRISE	4-8	62-65

LPs: 10/12–inch 33rpm

DUNHILL	10-15	67
GNP/CRESCENDO	8-15	61-62
RCA	8-15	62
REPRISE	8-15	62-65

CANTINA BAND
Singles: 7–inch

MILLENNIUM	5-8	81

Member: Lou Christie.
Also see CHRISTIE, Lou

CANTRELL, Lana
Singles: 7–inch

EAST COAST	2-4	74
POLYDOR	2-4	74-75
RCA	3-6	66-69

LPs: 10/12–inch 33rpm

RCA	8-15	67-69

CANYON
Singles: 7–inch

MAGNA-GLIDE	3-5	75

CAPALDI, Jim
Singles: 12–inch 33/45rpm
ISLAND 4-8   88
(Promotional only.)
RSO 4-6   79
Singles: 7–inch
ATLANTIC 2-4   83
ISLAND 3-5   72-88
RSO 2-4   78
Picture Sleeves
ATLANTIC 2-4   83
LPs: 10/12–inch 33rpm
ATLANTIC 5-10   83
CAPITOL 8-10   72
ISLAND 6-12 73-88
RSO 5-10 78-79
Also see TRAFFIC

CAPITOL'S MYSTERY ARTIST
(Nancy Wilson)
Singles: 7–inch
CAPITOL (1667 "Something
Wonderful Happens") 5-10   60
(Promotional issue only. Nancy's name is not
shown on label.)
Also see WILSON, Nancy

CAPITOLS
Singles: 7–inch
COLLECTABLES 2-4   81
KAREN 4-8   66-68
LPs: 10/12–inch 33rpm
ATCO 15-20   66
COLLECTABLES 6-8   88
SOLID SMOKE 5-10   85

CAPRELLS
Singles: 7–inch
ARIOLA AMERICA 3-5   76

CAPRIS
Singles: 7–inch
AMBIENT SOUND 3-6   82
COLLECTABLES 2-4   81
LOST NITE (101 "There's a Moon
Out Tonight") 20-30   60
(Pink label.)
LOST NITE (101 "There's a Moon
Out Tonight") 5-10   60
(Yellow label.)
MR. PEEKE (118 "Limbo") 8-12   63
OLD TOWN (1094 "There's a Moon
Out Tonight") 10-15   60
OLD TOWN (1099 "Where I
Fell in Love") 15-20   60
OLD TOWN (1103 "Why Do I Cry") .. 15-25   60
OLD TOWN (1107 "Girl in
My Dreams") 25-50   61
PLANET (1010 "There's a Moon
Out Tonight") 100-200 60

TROMMERS (101 "There's a Moon
Out Tonight") 25-30   60
LPs: 10/12–inch 33rpm
AMBIENT SOUND 5-10   82
COLLECTABLES 6-8   84
Members: Nick "Santos" Santamaria; Mike Mitchell; Vince
Narcardo; John Apostol; Frank Reina.

CAPTAIN & TENNILLE
Singles: 7–inch
A&M 3-5   75-78
BUTTERSCOTCH CASTLE (001 "The Way
I Want to Touch You") 50-75   73
JOYCE (101 "The Way I
Want to Touch You") 20-40   74
CASABLANCA 2-5   79-80
Picture Sleeves
A&M 4-6   75-78
LPs: 10/12–inch 33rpm
A&M 8-10 75-79
CAASABLANCA 5-10   79
Members: Daryl Dragon; Toni Tennille.
Also see TENNILLE, Toni
Also see YELLOW BALLOON

CAPTAIN BEEFHEART
(Captain Beefheart and His Magic Band)
Singles: 7–inch
A&M (794 "Diddy wah Diddy") 50-75   66
A&M (818 "Moonchild") 40-60   66
BUDDAH 4-8   67-69
MERCURY 3-5   74
REPRISE 3-6   72
VIRGIN 3-5   82
Promotional Singles
REPRISE (434 "Lick My Decals
Off, Baby") 40-50   70
REPRISE (447 "Talking About") ... 40-50   71
REPRISE (514 "Click Clack") 25-40   71
REPRISE (547 "Low Yo Yo Stuff") ... 40-50   72
(Issued with gatefold, EP-like, cover.)
LPs: 10/12–inch 33rpm
A&M 5-10   84
ACCORD 5-10   83
BIZARRE 10-12   72
BLUE THUMB (1 "Strictly Personal") . 15-20   68
(Black label.)
BLUE THUMB (1 "Strictly Personal") .. 8-12   69
(Tan label.)
BLUE THUMB (Tan label) 8-12   69
BUDDAH (1001 "Safe As Milk") 25-35   67
(Monaural. With 4" x 15" "Safe As Milk" bumper
sticker. Without sticker, deduct $10 to $15.)
BUDDAH (5001 "Safe As Milk") 25-30   67
(Stereo. With bumper sticker. Without sticker,
deduct $10-15.)
BUDDAH (5077 "Mirror Man") 10-15   71
BUDDAH (5063 "Safe As Milk") 8-10   70

D.I.R. (57 "Direct News, Week of 12-18-78") 25-40   78
(Contains five 5-minute radio programs, one of which has an interview with Don Van Vliet. Promotional issue only.)

EPIC 5-10   82

MERCURY (709 "Unconditionally Guaranteed") 8-12   74

MERCURY (1018 "Bluejeans and Moonbeams") 8-12   74

REPRISE (2027 "Trout Mask Replica") 8-12   77

REPRISE (2050 "Spotlight Kid") 10-15   72

REPRISE (2115 "Clear Spot") 10-20   72
(With embossed "Clear Spot" plastic bag.)

REPRISE (2115 "Clear Spot") 15-20   72
(White label. With printed inserts instead of standard cover. Promotional issue only.)

STRAIGHT (1053 "Trout Mask Replica") 30-40   68
(With lyrics sleeve.)

STRAIGHT (1053 "Trout Mask Replica") 20-25   68
(Without lyrics sleeve.)

STRAIGHT (6420 "Lick My Decals Off, Baby") 10-15   70

VIRGIN 5-10   80-82

WARNER 5-10   78

Members: Don "Captain Beefheart" Van Vliet; Doug Moon; Paul Blakely; Alex St. Claire; Jerry Handley; Ry Cooder; Jeff Cotton; John French; Bill "Zoot Horn Rollo" Harkleroad; Rockette Morton; Jimmy Semens; Jerry Handsley.
Also see COODER, Ry
Also see MOTHERS of INVENTION

CAPTAIN BEYOND
Singles: 7-inch
CAPRICORN 3-5   73
LPs: 10/12-inch 33rpm
CAPRICORN (Except 0105) 8-12   72-73
CAPRICORN (0105 "Captain Beyond") 35-50   72
(With 3-D cover.)

CAPRICORN (0105 "Captain Beyond") 15-25   72
(With standard cover.)

WARNER 8-10   77

Members: Bobby Caldwell; Rod Evans; Willie Daffern; Lee Dorman; Larry Reinhardt.
Also see CALDWELL, Bobby
Also see DEEP PURPLE
Also see IRON BUTTERFLY

CAPTAIN RAPP
Singles: 12-inch 33/45rpm
BECKET 4-6   83
Singles: 7-inch
BECKET 2-4   83

CAPTAIN SKY
(Daryl Cameron)
Singles: 12-inch 33/45rpm
WMOT 4-6   81
Singles: 7-inch
A.V.I. 2-5   79-82
TEC 2-4   80
TRIPLE 2-4   86
WMOT 2-4   81
LPs: 10/12-inch 33rpm
A.V.I. 5-10   78-82
TEC 5-10   80

CARA, Irene
Singles: 12-inch 33/45rpm
CASABLANCA 4-6   83
GEFFEN 4-6   83
Singles: 7-inch
CASABLANCA 2-4   83
GEFFEN 2-4   83-85
RSO 2-4   80
NETWORK 2-4   81
Picture Sleeves
GEFFEN 2-4   83
LPs: 10/12-inch 33rpm
GEFFEN 5-10   83-85
NETWORK 5-10   82
RSO 5-10   80

CARAVAN
Singles: 7-inch
BTM 3-5   75
DK 2-4   83
LONDON 3-5   71
LPs: 10/12-inch 33rpm
ARISTA 5-10   76
BTM 5-10   75
LONDON 12-15   71-75
VERVE/FORECAST 15-20   69

Members: Steve Miller; Richard Coughlan; Pye Hastings; John Perry; Geoff Richards; Jan Schelhaas; Dave Sinclair; Richard Sinclair; Mike Wedgewood.

CARAVELLES
Singles: 7-inch
SMASH 4-8   63-65

LPs: 10/12–inch 33rpm

SMASH (27044 "You Don't Have to
  Be a Baby to Cry") 20-30   63
  (Monaural.)
SMASH (67044 "You Don't Have to
  Be a Baby to Cry") 20-30   63
  (Stereo.)
  Members: Lois Wilkinson; Andrea Simpson.

CARDINALS

Singles: 78rpm

ATLANTIC 15-25   51-57

Singles: 7–inch

ATLANTIC (952 "I'll Always
  Love You") 75-100   51
ATLANTIC (958 "Wheel of
  Fortune") 75-100   52
ATLANTIC (972 "The Bump") 50-100   52
ATLANTIC (995 "You Are My
  Only Love") 75-100   53
ATLANTIC (1025 "Under a Blanket
  of Blue") 50-75   54
ATLANTIC (1054 "The Door Is
  Still Open") 25-50   55
ATLANTIC (1067 "Two Things
  I Love") 20-40   55
ATLANTIC (1079 "There Goes My
  Heart to You") 20-40   55
ATLANTIC (1090 "Off Shore") 20-40   56
ATLANTIC (1100 series) 15-25   56-57
  Members: Ernie Warren; Morodith Brothere; Leon Hardy; Donald
  Johnson; Jack "Sam" Aydelotte; Luther MacArthur; James
  Brown; Lee Tarver.

CAREFREES

Singles: 7–inch

LONDON INT'L (10614 "We Love
  You Beatles") 8-12   64
LONDON INT'L (10615 "Paddy Wack") . 4-8   64

Picture Sleeves

LONDON INT'L (10614 "We Love
  You Beatles") 10-20   64

LPs: 10/12–inch 33rpm

LONDON (379 "We Love You All") . . . 35-40   64
  Members: Lyn Cornell; Betty Prescott; Barbara Kay.

CAREY, Mariah

Singles: 7–inch

COLUMBIA 2-4   90

LPs: 10/12–inch 33rpm

COLUMBIA 5-8   90

CAREY, Tony

Singles: 7–inch

MCA 2-4   84
ROCSHIRE 2-4   83

LPs: 10/12–inch 33rpm

MCA 5-10   84
ROCSHIRE 5-10   83
  Also see PLANET P PROJECT
  Also see RAINBOW

CARGILL, Henson

Singles: 7–inch

ARCO 4-6   67
ATLANTIC 3-5   73-74
COPPER MOUNTAIN 2-4   79-80
ELEKTRA 3-5   75
MEGA 3-5   71-73
MONUMENT 4-6   67-70
RUFF 4-6
TOWER 3-6   68

LPs: 10/12–inch 33rpm

ATLANTIC 6-10   73
HARMONY 6-10   72
MEGA 6-10   72
MONUMENT 8-12   68-70

CARLA & RUFUS: see RUFUS & CARLA

CARLIN, George

Singles: 7–inch

LITTLE DAVID 3-5   72-75
RCA 4-8   67

Picture Sleeves

LITTLE DAVID 5-10   72

LPs: 10/12–inch 33rpm

ATLANTIC 5-10   81
CAMDEN 8-10   72
EARDRUM 5-10   84
ERA 8-12   72
LITTLE DAVID 5-10   72-85
RCA 10-15   67

CARLISLE, Belinda

Singles: 12–inch 33/45rpm

I.R.S. 4-6   86

Singles: 7–inch

I.R.S. 2-4   86-87
MCA 2-4   87-90

Picture Sleeves

MCA 2-4   87-88

LPs: 10/12–inch 33rpm

I.R.S. 5-10   86-87
MCA 5-10   87-90
  Also see GO-GOs

CARLISLE, Steve

Singles: 7–inch

MCA 2-4   81-82

LPs: 10/12–inch 33rpm

MCA 5-10   82

CARLOS, Walter

LPs: 10/12–inch 33rpm

COLUMBIA 8-12   69-72

CARLTON, Carl
(Little Carl Carlton)

Singles: 12–inch 33/45rpm

20TH FOX 4-6   80

Singles: 7–inch

ABC 3-5   73-76
BACK BEAT 3-6   68-75

CASABLANCA 2-4   86
GOLDEN WORLD 4-8   65
LANDO 4-8   65
MCA 2-4   84
MERCURY 3-5   77
RCA 2-4   82
20TH FOX 2-4   81-82

LPs: 10/12-inch 33rpm

ABC 10-12   74
BACK BEAT 10-15   73
CASABLANCA 5-10   86
RCA 5-10   82
20TH FOX 5-10   81

CARLTON, Larry

Singles: 7-inch

GRP 2-4   90
MCA 2-4   85-86
UNI 4-6   68-69
WARNER 2-5   78-83

LPs: 10/12-inch 33rpm

ATLANTIC 5-10   84
BLUE THUMB 10-12   73
GRP 5-8   90
MCA 5-10   85-87
UNI 12-18   68
WARNER 5-10   78-83
   Also see BROOKS, Donnie

CARMAN, Paull

Singles: 12-inch 33/45rpm

COLUMBIA 4-6   86

Singles: 7-inch

COLUMBIA 2-4   86-87

LPs: 10/12-inch 33rpm

COLUMBIA 5-10   86

CARMEN, Eric

Singles: 12-inch 33/45rpm

GEFFEN 4-6   85

Singles: 7-inch

ARISTA (Except 9000 series) 3-5   75-80
ARISTA (9000 series) 2-4   88
COOL 2-4   86
EPIC 3-6   70
GEFFEN 2-4   85
RCA 2-4   87

Picture Sleeves

ARISTA (0200 series) 3-5   77
ARISTA (9000 series) 2-4   88

LPs: 10/12-inch 33rpm

ARISTA (Except 4057) 5-10   77-88
ARISTA (AL-4057 "Eric Carmen") 8-10   75
ARISTA (AQ-4057 "Eric Carmen") ... 15-20   75
   (Quardophonic.)
GEFFEN 5-10   85
   Also see CHOIR
   Also see RASPBERRIES

CARN, Jean: see CARNE, Jean

CARNE, Jean
(Jean Carn)

Singles: 7-inch

ATLANTIC 2-4   88
MOTOWN 2-4   82
OMNI 2-4   86
PHILADELPHIA INT'L 2-4   77-80
TSOP 2-4   81

LPs: 10/12-inch 33rpm

OMNI 5-10   86
PHILADELPHIA INT'L 5-10   76-80
MOTOWN 5-10   82
TSOP 5-10   81
   Also see JOHNSON, Al, and Jean Carn
   Also see MILITELLO, Bobby

CARNES, Kim

Singles: 12-inch 33/45rpm

EMI AMERICA 4-6   80-85

Singles: 7-inch

A&M 3-5   75-82
AMOS 3-6   71-72
EMI AMERICA 2-4   79-86
ELEKTRA 2-4   84

Picture Sleeves

EMI AMERICA 2-4   80-86

LPs: 10/12-inch 33rpm

A&M (3000 series) 5-10   82
A&M (4000 series) 8-10   75-77
AMOS 12-18   71
EMI AMERICA 5-10   79-86
MCA 5-10   84
MFSL (073 "Mistaken Identity") 20-30   82
   Also see COTTON, Gene, and Kim Carnes
   Also see ROGERS, Kenny, and Kim Carnes
   Also see STRIESAND, Barbra, and Kim Carnes
   Also see U.S.A. for AFRICA

CARNES, Kim, and Dave Ellington

Singles: 7-inch

AMOS 3-5   72
   Also see CARNES, Kim

CARNIVAL

Singles: 7-inch

U.A. 3-5   71
WORLD PACIFIC 3-6   69

LPs: 10/12-inch 33rpm

WORLD PACIFIC 10-15   69
   Member: Terry Fisher.

CAROSONE, Renato

Singles: 7-inch

CAPITOL 4-8   58

CARPENTER, Carleton, and Debbie Reynolds

Singles: 78rpm

MGM 4-8   51

Singles: 7-inch

MGM 5-10   51

EPs: 7-inch 33/45rpm

MGM 5-15   51

Also see REYNOLDS, Debbie

CARPENTER, Thelma
Singles: 78rpm
COLUMBIA	4-8	50
MAJESTIC	5-10	45-46

Singles: 7–inch
COLUMBIA	10-15	50
CORAL (Except 62272)	5-10	60-62
CORAL (62272 "Heartaches")	20-30	61

LPs: 10/12–inch 33rpm
CORAL (57433 "Thinking of You Tonight") (Monaural.)	15-25	63
CORAL (7-57433 "Thinking of You Tonight") (Stereo.)	25-35	63

CARPENTERS
Singles: 7–inch
A&M (Except 2735)	3-6	69-82
A&M (2735) (Promotional issue only. Title not known.)	10-15	

Picture Sleeves
A&M (Except 2735)	3-6	70-81
A&M (2735 "Yesterday Once More") (Promotional issue only. With paper sleeve.)	10-15	

EPs: 7–inch 33/45rpm
A&M	10-15	72-85

LPs: 10/12–inch 33rpm
A&M (3000 series)	8-15	71-85
A&M (4000 series, except 4205)	8-15	70-83
A&M (4205 "Offering")	20-35	69
A&M (4205 "Ticket to Ride")	10-15	71
A&M (5100 series)	5-8	90
A&M (50000 series) (Quadraphonic series.)	15-25	74-75
A&M (6000 series)	8-12	85
MFP (50431 "Ticket to Ride")	10-15	70

Members: Karen Carpenter; Richard Carpenter; Tony Peluso.

CARR, Cathy
Singles: 78rpm
CORAL	4-8	53-56
FRATERNITY	4-8	55-56

Singles: 7–inch
ABC	2-4	73
COLLECTABLES	2-4	81
CORAL	5-10	53-56
FRATERNITY	5-10	55-56
LAURIE	5-10	62-63
ROULETTE (Except SSR-4152)	5-10	59-61
ROULETTE (SSR-4152 "I'm Gonna Change Him") (Stereo.)	10-15	59
SMASH	4-8	61

EPs: 7–inch 33/45rpm
BRUNSWICK	10-20	57

LPs: 10/12–inch 33rpm
DOT	15-25	66
FRATERNITY (1005 "Ivory Tower")	40-50	57

ROULETTE (R-25077 "Shy") (Monaural.)	25-40	59
ROULETTE (SR-25077 "Shy") (Stereo.)	30-50	59

CARR, James
Singles: 7–inch
ATLANTIC	3-5	71
GOLDWAX	4-8	65-69

LPs: 10/12–inch 33rpm
GOLDWAX	12-20	67-68

CARR, Jerry
Singles: 7–inch
CHERIE	2-4	81

CARR, Joe "Fingers"
(Lou Busch)
Singles: 78rpm
CAPITOL	3-6	50-57

Singles: 7–inch
CAPITOL	5-10	50-59
CORAL	3-6	63
DOT	3-6	66
WARNER	4-8	60-62

EPs: 7–inch 33/45rpm
CAPITOL	5-15	51-57

LPs: 10/12–inch 33rpm
CAPITOL (Except 2000 series)	12-25	51-61
CAPITOL (2000 series)	8-15	64
CORAL	8-15	63
DOT	8-15	66
WARNER	10-20	60-62

Also see BUSCH, Lou
Also see FRAZIER, Dallas, and Joe "Fingers" Carr
Also see PROVINE, Dorothy, and Joe "Fingers" Carr

CARR, Valerie
Singles: 7–inch
ATLAS	4-8	64
ROULETTE	5-10	58-61

LPs: 10/12–inch 33rpm
ROULETTE (25094 "Ev'ry Hour, Ev'ry Day")	25-35	59

CARR, Vikki
Singles: 7–inch
COLUMBIA	3-5	71-75
LIBERTY	4-8	62-69

Picture Sleeves
COLUMBIA	3-5	74
LIBERTY	4-8	67

LPs: 10/12–inch 33rpm
COLUMBIA	8-10	71-75
LIBERTY (Except 10000 series)	10-20	63-70
LIBERTY (10000 series)	5-10	81
SUNSET	8-12	
U.A.	5-10	71-80

Also see BERNSTEIN, Elmer

CARR, Wynona
Singles: 7–inch
REPRISE	5-10	61-63

SPECIALTY 5-10   59-60
LPs: 10/12–inch 33rpm
REPRISE 10-20   62
SPECIALTY 8-10   88

CARRACK, Paul
Singles: 12–inch 33/45rpm
CHRYSALIS 4-8   87
(Promotional only.)
Singles: 7–inch
CHRYSALIS 2-4   87
EPIC 2-4   82
Picture Sleeves
CHRYSALIS 2-4   87-88
LPs: 10/12–inch 33rpm
CHRYSALIS 5-10   87-89
EPIC 5-10   82
   Also see ACE
   Also see MIKE + the MECHANICS
   Also see SQUEEZE

CARRADINE, Keith
Singles: 7–inch
ABC 3-5   75
ASYLUM 3-5   78
VALA 2-4   83
LPs: 10/12–inch 33rpm
ASYLUM 8-10   76

CARROLL, Andrea
Singles: 7–inch
BIG TOP (515 "The Doolang") 30-40   64
BIG TOP (3156 "It Hurts to
   Be Sixteen") 8-12   63
EPIC (9438 "Young and Lonely") ... 50-100   61
   (Yellow label.)
EPIC (9438 "Young and Lonely") 50-75   61
   (White label. Promotional issue.)
EPIC (9450 "Please Don't
   Talk to the Lifeguard") 10-15   61
EPIC (9471 "Gee Dad") 15-20   61
EPIC (9523 "Fifteen Shades of Pink") 15-20   62
Picture Sleeves
EPIC (9471 "Gee Dad") 25-35   61
RCA (8618 "Sally Fool") 8-12   65
U.A. (982 "The World
   Isn't Big Enough") 8-15   66
U.A. (50039 "Hey Beach Boy") 8-15   66
LPs: 10/12–inch 33rpm
B.T. PUPPY (1017 "Side by Side") ... 20-30
   (With Beverly Warren.)

CARROLL, Andrea / Beverly Warren
LPs: 10/12–inch 33rpm
B.T. PUPPY (1017 "Andrea Carroll
   and Beverly Warren") 50-75   69
   Also see CARROLL, Andrea

CARROLL, Bernadette
Singles: 7–inch
COLLECTABLES 2-4   81
JULIA 4-8   62

LAURIE 5-10   63-64

CARROLL, Bob
Singles: 78rpm
BALLY 4-8   56-57
DERBY 4-8   53
MGM 4-8   55
Singles: 7–inch
BALLY 5-10   56-57
DERBY 5-10   53
DOT 3-6   66
MGM 5-10   55
MURBO 3-6   67
UNART 4-8   59
U.A. 4-8   59-59
Picture Sleeves
U.A. 5-10   58

CARROLL, Cathy
Singles: 7–inch
CHEER 10-15   63-64
DOT 4-8   66
MUSICOR 4-8   65
PHILIPS 4-8   63
TRIODEX 10-15   61
WARNER 5-10   62-63

CARROLL, David, Orchestra
Singles: 78rpm
MERCURY 3-5   53-57
Singles: 7–inch
MERCURY 4-8   53-62
EPs: 7–inch 33/45rpm
MERCURY 5-10   54-59
LPs: 10/12–inch 33rpm
MERCURY 8-18   53-62
WING 5-10   59
   Also see CONTINO, Dick

CARROLL, Jim
(Jim Carroll Band)
Singles: 12–inch 33/45rpm
ATLANTIC 4-8   83
   (Promotional only.)
Singles: 7–inch
A&M 3-5   72
ATCO 2-4   80-81
ATLANTIC 2-4   83
LPs: 10/12–inch 33rpm
A&M 10-15   71
ATCO 5-10   80-82
ATLANTIC 5-10   83

CARROLL, Ronnie
Singles: 7–inch
PHILIPS 4-8   63-66

CARROLL BROTHERS
Singles: 7–inch
CAMEO (140 "Red Hot") 50-75   58
CAMEO (200 series) 5-10   62
FELSTED 5-10   59

LPs: 10/12–inch 33rpm
CAMEO (1015 "College Twist Party") 25-35   62
Member: Pete Carroll.

CARS
Singles: 12–inch 33/45rpm
ELEKTRA 5-10   86
(Promotional issues only.)
Singles: 7–inch
ELEKTRA 3-5   78-88
Picture Sleeves
ELEKTRA 3-5   78-88
LPs: 10/12–inch 33rpm
ELEKTRA (Except 5E-567) 5-10   78-87
ELEKTRA (5E-567 "Shake It Up") .. 50-100   81
(Picture disc. Promotional issue only.)
NAUTILUS 15-20   82
(Half-speed mastered.)
Members: Ric Ocasek; Elliot Easton; Benjamin Orr; Greg
Hawkes; Dave Robinson.
Also see EASTON, Elliot
Also see OCASEK, Ric

CARSON, Kit
Singles: 78rpm
CAPITOL 4-8   55
Singles: 7–inch
CAPITOL 8-10   55

CARSON, Mindy
Singles: 78rpm
COLUMBIA 4-8   52-56
Singles: 7–inch
COLUMBIA 8-12   52-56
JOY 4-8   60
RCA 8-12   50-52
Also see MITCHELL, Guy, and Mindy Carson

CARTEE, Wayne
Singles: 7–inch
GROOVY 2-4   77

CARTER, Carlene
(Carlene Carter and Rockpile)
Singles: 7–inch
EPIC 2-4   83
WARNER 2-4   78-82
LPs: 10/12–inch 33rpm
EPIC 5-10   83
WARNER 5-10   78-82
Also see EDMUNDS, Dave, and Carlene Carter
Also see ORRALL, Robert Ellis
Also see ROCKPILE

CARTER, Clarence
Singles: 7–inch
ABC 3-5   75-76
ATLANTIC 4-8   68-72
FAME (Except 1000 series) 3-5   72-73
FAME (1000 series) 4-8   67
ICHIBAN 2-4   88
RONN 3-5   77
VENTURE 2-4   80-81

LPs: 10/12–inch 33rpm
ABC 8-10   74-76
ATLANTIC 10-20   68-71
BIG C 5-10   83
BRYLEN 5-10   84
FAME 10-12   73
ICHIBAN 5-10   88
VENTURE 5-10   80-81

CARTER, Clarence and Candi
Singles: 7–inch
ATLANTIC 3-5   72
Also see CARTER, Clarence

CARTER, Mel
Singles: 7–inch
ABKCO 2-4   84
AMOS 3-5   69-70
ARWIN 5-10   60
BELL 3-6   68-69
CREAM 2-4   81
DERBY 5-10   63
IMPERIAL 4-8   64-66
LIBERTY 4-6   67-68
MERCURY 4-8   62
PHILLIPS 4-8   62
ROMAR 3-5   73-74
LPs: 10/12–inch 33rpm
AMOS 10-12   70
DERBY (702 "When a Boy
Falls in Love") 50-100   63
IMPERIAL 15-20   65-66
LIBERTY 12-20   67
SUNSET 10-12   68-70

CARTER, Mel / Vic Dana
EPs: 7–inch 33/45rpm
ROWE/AMI 5-10
(Colored vinyl. Jukebox issue.)
Also see DANA, Vic

CARTER, Mel, and Clydie King
Singles: 7–inch
PHILIPS 4-8   62
Also see CARTER, Mel

CARTER, Ralph
Singles: 7–inch
MERCURY 3-5   75-76

CARTER, Ron
LPs: 10/12–inch 33rpm
MILESTONE 5-10   77-78
MOTOWN 5-8   84

CARTER, Valerie
Singles: 7–inch
COLUMBIA 2-4   77-79
LPs: 10/12–inch 33rpm
COLUMBIA 8-10   77-78
Also see LITTLE FEAT
Also see MONEY, Eddie, and Valerie Carter

CARTER, Valerie, and Henry Paul
Singles: 7-inch
ATLANTIC 2-4   82
Also see CARTER, Valerie

CARTER BROTHERS
Singles: 7-inch
COLEMAN 8-10   64
JEWEL 4-8   65-67
Members: Jerry Carter; Al Carter; Roman Carter.

CARTRELL, Della
Singles: 7-inch
RIGHT ON 3-5   71-72

CARTRIDGE, Flip
Singles: 7-inch
PARROT 4-8   66-67

CARUSO, Marian
Singles: 78rpm
DECCA 3-6   54-55
DEVON 3-6   52
Singles: 7-inch
DECCA 5-10   54-55
DEVON 5-10   52

CASCADES
Singles: 7-inch
ABC 2-4   73
ARWIN 4-8   66
CANBASE 3-5   72
CHARTER 10-15   64
COLLECTABLES 2-4   81
LIBERTY 4-8   65
PROBE 3-6   68
RCA 5-10   63-64
SMASH 4-8   67
UNI 3-6   69-70
VALIANT 5-10   62-63
WARNER 2-4
Picture Sleeves
PROBE 4-8   68
RCA 8-12   63
LPs: 10/12-inch 33rpm
BLOSSOM 10-15
CASCADES (6820 "What Goes On
    Inside the Cascades") 20-35
UNI 15-20   69
VALIANT (W-405 "Rhythm of
    the Rain") 40-60   63
    (Monaural.)
VALIANT (WS-405 "Rhythm of
    the Rain") 50-100   63
    (Stereo.)
    Also see LIND, Bob
    Also see YOUNG, Neil

CASCADES / Sir Douglas Quintet
Singles: 7-inch
TRIP 2-4
    Also see CASCADES
    Also see SIR DOUGLAS QUINTET

CASEY, Al
(Al Casey Combo; Al Casey and the K-C Ettes)
Singles: 78rpm
DOT 5-10   56-57
MCI 8-12   55
Singles: 7-inch
CHALLENGE 5-10   60
DOT (15524 "A Fool's Blues") 10-20   56
DOT (15563 "Guitar Man") 15-25   57
GREGMARK (5 "Caravan") 5-10   61
    (Shown as by Duane Eddy, but actually by Al
    Casey.)
HIGHLAND (1002 "Got the Teenage
    Blues") 25-40   60
HIGHLAND (1004 "Night Beat") 15-25   60
LIBERTY 10-20   58
MCI 10-20   55
RAMCO 8-10   61
STACY 10-15   62-64
U.A. 5-10   59
LPs: 10/12-inch 33rpm
STACY (100 "Surfin' Hootenany") ... 30-50   63
    (Black vinyl.)
STACY (100 "Surfin' Hootenany") . 100-125   63
    (Colored vinyl.)
    Also see CLARK, Sanford
    Also see EDDY, Duane
    Also see EXOTIC GUITARS
    Also see REYNOLDS, Jody

CASH, Alvin
(Alvin Cash and the Crawlers; Alvin Cash and the
Registers)
Singles: 7-inch
CHESS 3-5   70
COLLECTABLES 2-4   81
DAKAR 3-5   76
ERIC 2-4   73
MAR-V-LUS 4-8   65-67
SEVENTY SEVEN 3-5   72
TODDLIN' TOWN 3-5   68-69
XL ("Twine Time") 15-25   65
LPs: 10/12-inch 33rpm
MAR-V-LUS 15-20   65
SOUND STAGE "7" 10-15   73

CASH, Johnny
(Johnny Cash and the Tennessee Two; Johnny Cash
and the Tennessee Three)
Singles: 78rpm
SUN 5-10   55-57
Singles: 7-inch
CACHET 2-4   80
COLUMBIA (Except 41000 through
    43000 series) 2-5   67-85
COLUMBIA (41000 and 42000 series) 10-15   60-62
    (With "3" prefix. Compact 33 singles)
COLUMBIA (41000 and 42000 series) 5-10   58-64
    (With "4" prefix.)
COLUMBIA (43000 series) 4-8   64-66
SSS/SUN (Black vinyl) 2-4   69-70

SSS/SUN (Colored vinyl) 3-6   69-70
(Promotional issues only.)
SCOTTI BROS 2-4   82
SUN (200 series) 10-20   55-58
SUN (300 series) 5-10   58-62
EPs: 7–inch 33/45rpm
COLUMBIA (Except jukebox EPs) ... 10-20   58-60
COLUMBIA (Stereo jukebox EPs) ... 25-30   69
SUN 10-20   58
Picture Sleeves
COLUMBIA (Except 41000 and 42000
series) 3-5   67-85
COLUMBIA (41000 series) 10-15   58-61
COLUMBIA (42000 series) 5-10   61-64
COLUMBIA (44000 series) .... -36   68
SUN (295 "Guess Things
Happen That Way") 10-15   58
LPs: 10/12–inch 33rpm
COLUMBIA (29 "The World of
Johnny Cash") 8-12   70
COLUMBIA (363 "Legends and
Love Songs") 10-15   68
(Columbia Record Club issue.)
COLUMBIA (1200 through 1799) 15-30   58-61
(With "CL" prefix. Monaural.)
COLUMBIA (8100 through 8599) 20-40   58-61
(With "CS" prefix. Stereo.)
COLUMBIA (1800 through 2650) 10-20   62-68
(With "CL" prefix. Monaural.)
COLUMBIA (2004 "The Heart of
Johnny Cash") 15-25
((Columbia Star Series.)
COLUMBIA (8600 through 9450) 10-20   62-68
(With "CS" prefix. Stereo.)
COLUMBIA (9700 through 9943) 8-12   69-70
(With "CS" prefix.)
COLUMBIA (10000 series) 5-10   73
COLUMBIA (30000 through 38000
series) 5-15   70-82
COLUMBIA/SUFFOLK 8-10   79
DESIGN 5-8
DORAL 20-40
(Promotional mail-order LP from Doral cigarettes.)
HARMONY 8-12   69
LONGINES SYMPHONETTE 5-8
OUT of TOWN DIST 5-10   82
PICKWICK 5-10
PRIORITY 5-10   81-82
SSS/SUN 5-10   69-84
SHARE 5-10
STACK-O-HITS 5-8
SUN (1220 "Johnny Cash and His
Hot and Blue Guitar") 40-50   56
SUN (1235 "Songs That Made
Him Famous") 35-45   58
SUN (1240 "Greatest") 25-40   59
SUN (1245 "Johnny Cash Sings Hank
Williams and Other Favorties") 20-35   60

SUN (1255 "Now Here's
Johnny Cash") 20-30   61
SUN (1270 "All Aboard the
Blue Train") 20-30   63
SUN (1275 "Original Sun Sound
of Johnny Cash") 20-30   64
TRIP 8-10   74
U.A. 10-12   68
Also see RICH, Charlie
Also see ROBBINS, Marty / Johnny Cash / Ray Price
Also see STATLER BROTHERS

CASH, Johnny, and June Carter
(Johnny Cash and June Carter Cash)
Singles: 7–inch
COLUMBIA 2-5   67-83
LPs: 10/12–inch 33rpm
COLUMBIA (9500 series) 10-20   64-67
COLUMBIA (32000 series) 5-10   73
HARMONY 6-10   72
Also see JENNINGS, Waylon, Willie Nelson, Johnny Cash, and
Kris Kristofferson

CASH, Johnny, Rosanne Cash and the Everly Brothers
Singles: 7–inch
MERCURY (872 420-7 "Ballad of a
Teenage Queen") 2-4   89
Also see CASH, Rosanne
Also see EVERLY BROTHERS

CASH, Johnny / Roy Clark / Linda Ronstadt
LPs: 10/12–inch 33rpm
POINTED STAR (10178 "Concert
Behind Prison Walls") 10-15   78
(NAPA special products TV soundtrack.)
Also see CLARK, Roy
Also see RONSTADT, Linda

CASH, Johnny / Billy Grammer / Wilburn Brothers
LPs: 10/12–inch 33rpm
PICKWICK/HILLTOP 10-15   65
Also see GRAMMER, Billy

CASH, Johnny, and Levon Helm
Singles: 7–inch
A&M 2-4   80
Also see HELM, Levon

CASH, Johnny, and Waylon Jennings
Singles: 7–inch
COLUMBIA 2-4   78-86
EPIC 2-4   80
Also see JENNINGS, Waylon

CASH, Johnny, Carl Perkins and Jerry Lee Lewis
LPs: 10/12–inch 33rpm
COLUMBIA 5-10   82
Also see PERKINS, Carl, Jerry Lee Lewis, Roy Orbison and
Johnny Cash

CASH, Johnny / Tammy Wynette
LPs: 10/12–inch 33rpm
COLUMBIA (5418 "The King and
Queen") 10-15
(Columbia Musical Treasury issue.)
Also see CASH, Johnny
Also see WYNETTE, Tammy

CASH, Rosanne
Singles: 7–inch
COLUMBIA 2-4   80-90
EPs: 7–inch 33/45rpm
COLUMBIA 4-8   85
LPs: 10/12–inch 33rpm
COLUMBIA 6-10   79-90
Also see BARE, Bobby, and Rosanne Cash
Also see CASH, Johnny, Rosanne Cash and the Everly Brothers
Also see CROWELL, Rodney, and Rosanne Cash

CASH, Tommy
Singles: 7–inch
AUDIOGRAPH 2-4   83
ELEKTRA 3-5   75
EPIC 3-5   68-73
MONUMENT 2-4   77-79
MUSICOR 3-6   65
20TH FOX 2-4   76
U.A. 3-6   66-68
LPs: 10/12–inch 33rpm
ELEKTRA 5-10   75
EPIC 8-12   69-72
MONUMENT 5-10   78
U.A. 10-12   68

CA$HFLOW
Singles: 12–inch 33/45rpm
ATLANTA ARTISTS 4-6   86
Singles: 7–inch
ATLANTA ARTISTS 2-4   86
MERCURY 2-4   86
LPs: 10/12–inch 33rpm
ATLANTA ARTISTS 5-10   86

CASHMAN, Terry
(Terry Cashman and the Men)
Singles: 7–inch
BOOM (005 "Try Me") 8-10   66
LIFESONG 3-5   76-82
LPs: 10/12–inch 33rpm
LIFESONG 5-10   76-77

CASHMAN & WEST
Singles: 7–inch
ABC 2-4   74
DUNHILL 3-5   72-74
LIFESONG 3-5   75
LPs: 10/12–inch 33rpm
ABC 8-10   74
DUNHILL 8-12   72-74
Members: Terry Cashman; Tommy West.
Also see CROCE, Jim
Also see GENE & TOMMY
Also see MORNING MIST

CASHMAN, PISTILLI & WEST
Singles: 7–inch
ABC 4-6   68
CAPITOL 3-5   69-71
LPs: 10/12–inch 33rpm
ABC 12-15   68
CAPITOL 10-15   69-71
Members: Terry Cashman; Gene Pistilli; Tommy West.
Also see BUCHANAN BROTHERS
Also see CASHMAN, Terry

CASHMERE
Singles: 12–inch 33/45rpm
PHILLY WORLD 4-6   83
TNT 4-6   84
Singles: 7–inch
PHILLY WORLD 2-4   83-85
LPs: 10/12–inch 33rpm
PHILLY WORLD 5-10   83-85

CASINOS
(Gene Hughes and the Casinos; The Casinos and the
Saturns)
Singles: 7–inch
ABC 3-5   73
AIRTOWN (002 "That's the Way") ... 10-15   67
CERTRON 5-8   70
COLLECTABLES 2-4   81
FRATERNITY 5-10   65-71
ITZY (2 "Do You Recall") 20-30   63
MILLION 5-8   72
NAME (001 "Do You Recall") 200-300   62
OLYMPIC (251 "Do You Recall") ... 75-125   63
TERRY (115 "Gee Whiz") 25-50   64
TERRY (116 "That's the Way") ... 12-25   64
TRIP 3-5
U.A. 4-6   68
LPs: 10/12–inch 33rpm
FRATERNITY (1019 "Then You Can
Tell Me Goodbye") 20-30   67
Member: Gene Hughes.

CASLONS
Singles: 7–inch
AMY 10-20   61-62
SEECO 10-20   61

CASON, Rich, and the Galactic Orchestra
Singles: 12–inch 33/45rpm
PRIVATE I 4-6   84
Singles: 7–inch
LARC 2-4   83
PRIVATE I 2-4   84

CASPER
Singles: 7–inch
SUNFLOWER 3-5   71

CASPER
Singles: 7–inch
A.V.I. 2-4   84
ATLANTIC 2-4   83
LPs: 10/12–inch 33rpm
A.V.I. 5-10   84
ATLANTIC 5-10   83

CASS, Mama: see ELLIOTT, Cass

CASSIDY, David
Singles: 7–inch
BELL 3-5   71-73
ENIGMA 2-4   90
FLASHBACK 2-4   73
MCA 2-4   79
RCA 3-5   75-77
Picture Sleeves
BELL 3-5   71-73
ENIGMA 2-4   90
LPs: 10/12–inch 33rpm
BELL 10-15   72-74
ENIGMA 5-10   90
RCA 8-12   74-76
Also see PARTRIDGE FAMILY
Also see WILSON, Carl

CASSIDY, Shaun
Singles: 7–inch
WARNER 2-4   77-80
Picture Sleeves
WARNER 2-4   77-80
LPs: 10/12–inch 33rpm
WARNER 8-10   77-80

CASSIDY, Shaun, and Todd Rundgren's Utopia
Singles: 7–inch
WARNER 2-4   80
Also see CASSIDY, Shaun
Also see UTOPIA

CASTAWAYS
Singles: 7–inch
COLLECTABLES 2-4   81
ERA 2-4   72
ERIC 2-4   78
FONTANA 4-8   68

LANA 2-4
SOMA 5-12   65
Members: Richard Robey; Robert Folschon; Ron Hensley;
James Donna; Dennis Caswell.

CASTELLS
Singles: 7–inch
COLLECTABLES 2-4   80
DECCA 4-8   65-66
ERA 5-10   61-63
LAURIE 15-20   68
U.A. 4-8   68
WARNER (Except 5421) 4-8   64
WARNER (5421 "I Do") 50-60   64
(With Brian Wilson.)
LPs: 10/12–inch 33rpm
ERA (EL-109 "So This Is Love") 40-60   62
(Monaural.)
ERA (ES-109 "So This Is Love") 60-80   62
(Stereo.)
Members: Chuck Girard; Bob Ussery; Tom Hicks; Joe Kelly.
Also see WILSON, Brian

CASTER, Jimmy: see CASTOR, Jimmy

CASTLE, David
Singles: 7–inch
PARACHUTE 3-5   77-79
LPs: 10/12–inch 33rpm
PARACHUTE 8-10   77-79

CASTLE SISTERS
Singles: 7–inch
ROULETTE 5-10   59-60
TERRACE 5-10   62-63
TRIODEX 5-10   61
Picture Sleeves
TERRACE 10-15   62

CASTLEMAN, Boomer
(Boomer Clarke)
Singles: 7–inch
CREME 2-4   86
MUMS 3-5   75
SRO (218 "Summertime Blues") 4-6   86
(Promotional issue only.)
Also see LEWIS & CLARKE

CASTOR, Jimmy
(Jimmy Castor Bunch; Jimmy Castor Quintet)
Singles: 12–inch 33/45rpm
SALSOUL 4-6   83
Singles: 7–inch
ATLANTIC 3-5   74-77
CAPITOL 4-6   68-69
CLOWN 5-10   62
COMPASS 4-6   68
COTILLION 2-4   79
DECCA 4-8   66
DREAM 2-4   84-85
DRIVE 2-4   78
JET SET 4-8   65
KINETIC 3-6   70

LONG DISTANCE	2-4	81
RCA	3-5	71-73
SALSOUL	2-4	82
SLEEPING BAG	2-4	88
SMASH	4-8	66-67

LPs: 10/12–inch 33rpm

ATLANTIC	8-10	74-77
COTILLION	5-10	79
DREAM	5-10	83
DRIVE	5-10	78
LONG DISTANCE	5-10	80
PAUL WINLEY	5-15	
RCA	10-15	72-75
SMASH	15-20	67

Members: Jimmy Castor; Gerry Thomas; Doug Gibson; Lenny Fridie Jr.; Harry Jensen; Bobby Manigault.

CASTOR, Jimmy, and the Juniors
Singles: 78rpm

ATOMIC (100 "This Girl of Mine")	40-60	57
WING (90078 "I Promise")	25-35	56

Singles: 7–inch

ATOMIC (100 "This Girl of Mine")	100-200	57
WING (90078 "I Promise")	75-125	56

Also see CASTOR, Jimmy

CASWELL, Johnny
Singles: 7–inch

DECCA	4-8	66
LUV	4-8	67
SMASH	4-8	63-64

Also see CRYSTAL MANSION

CAT MOTHER
(Cat Mother and the All Night News Boys)
Singles: 7–inch

POLYDOR	3-6	69-72

LPs: 10/12–inch 33rpm

POLYDOR	20-30	69-73

CATE BROTHERS
(Cates Gang)
Singles: 7–inch

ASYLUM	3-5	76-78
ELEKTRA	2-4	77
METROMEDIA	3-5	70

LPs: 10/12–inch 33rpm

ASYLUM	5-10	75-77
ATLANTIC	5-10	79
METROMEDIA	10-12	70-73

Members: Earl Cate; Ernie Cate.

CATES, George
Singles: 78rpm

CORAL	3-6	51-57

Singles: 7–inch

CORAL	5-10	51-57
DOT	3-6	62
SIGNATURE	3-6	59-60

EPs: 7–inch 33/45rpm

CORAL	5-10	54-57

LPs: 10/12–inch 33rpm

CORAL	10-20	54-57

CATHY & JOE
Singles: 7–inch

SMASH	4-8	64-65

CATHY JEAN
(Cathy Jean and the Roomates)
Singles: 7–inch

ERIC	2-4	73
PHILIPS (Except 40014)	8-12	63
PHILIPS (40014 "Believe Me")	10-20	62
VALMOR	10-15	61-62

LPs: 10/12–inch 33rpm

VALMOR (78 "At the Hop")	400-500	62

(Reissue. Has titles printed on cover. Does not picture the group.)

VALMOR (789 "At the Hop")	350-450	61

(Pictures Cathy Jean and the Roomates. Note different number.)

Also see ROOMATES

CAVALIERE, Felix
Singles: 7–inch

BEARSVILLE	3-5	74-75
EPIC	2-4	80

LPs: 10/12–inch 33rpm

BEARSVILLE	10-12	74-75
EPIC (705 "Castles in the Air")	15-20	79

(Interview and music. Promotional issue only.)

EPIC (35990 "Castles in the Air")	5-10	79

Also see KARP, Charlie
Also see RASCALS

CAVALLARO, Carmen
Singles: 78rpm

DECCA	3-6	50-57

Singles: 7–inch

DECCA	3-8	50-61

EPs: 7–inch 33/45rpm

DECCA (Except 844)	5-10	50-59
DECCA (844 "The Eddy Duchin Story")	20-30	56

(Boxed three-EP set.)

LPs: 10/12–inch 33rpm

DECCA (Except "The Eddy Duchin Story")	10-20	50-61
DECCA (DL-8289 "The Eddy Duchin Story")	25-35	56

(Soundtrack. Monaural.)

DECCA (DL7-8289 "The Eddy Duchin Story")	25-30	59

(Soundtrack. Stereo.)

DECCA (8396 "The Eddy Duchin Story")	60-75	56

(Soundtrack. Also has music from three other shows.)

DECCA (DL-9121 "The Eddy Duchin Story")	10-15	65

(Soundtrack. Monaural.)

DECCA (DL7-9121 "The Eddy Duchin Story")	10-15	65

(Soundtrack. Stereo.)

VOCALION 10-15   59

CAZZ
(Robert Lewis)
Singles: 7–inch
NUMBER 2-4   78

CELEBRATION
(Celebration Featuring Mike Love)
Singles: 7–inch
MCA 2-4   78
PACIFIC ARTS 5-10   79
Promotional Singles
MCA (1982 "Almost Summer,
   KRTH 101 Version") 10-12   78
LPs: 10/12–inch 33rpm
MCA (3037 "Almost Summer") 8-10   78
   (Soundtrack.)
PACIFIC ARTS 8-12   79
   Members: Mike Love; Charles Lloyd; Steve Leach; Ron Altbach;
   Linda Mallah; Suzanne Wallach; Irene Cathaway; Al Perkins;
   Tim Weston.

CELI BEE and the Buzzy Bunch
Singles: 7–inch
APA 3-5   77-78
LPs: 10/12–inch 33rpm
APA 5-10   77-79

CELLOS
Singles: 78rpm
APOLLO 10-20   57
Singles: 7–inch
APOLLO (510 "Rang Tang Ding
   Dong") 30-40   57
   (No subtitle used.)
APOLLO (510 "Rang Tang Ding
   Dong") 15-25   57
   (With "I Am the Japanese Sandman" subtitle.)
APOLLO (515 "Under Your Spell") . . . 25-50   57
APOLLO (516 "The Be-Bop Mouse") . 25-50   57
APOLLO (524 "I Beg for Your Love") . 40-60   58
   Members: Cliff Williams; Ken Levinson; Alvin Campbell; Bill
   Montgomery; Alton Thomas.

CENTRAL LINE
Singles: 12–inch 33/45rpm
MERCURY 4-6   84-85
Singles: 7–inch
MERCURY 2-4   81-85
LPs: 10/12–inch 33rpm
MERCURY 5-10   82-85

CERRONE
Singles: 12–inch 33/45rpm
PAVILLION 4-6   82
Singles: 7–inch
ATLANTIC 2-4   79
COTILLION 2-5   77-78
PAVILLION 2-4   82
LPs: 10/12–inch 33rpm
ATLANTIC 5-10   79
COTILLION 5-10   77-79

PAVILLION 5-10   82

CERRONE and La Toya Jackson
Singles: 12–inch 33/45rpm
PALASS 4-6   86
   Also see CERRONE
   Also see JACKSON, La Toya

CETERA, Peter
Singles: 7–inch
FULL MOON 2-4   82-88
Picture Sleeves
FULL MOON 2-4   82-86
LPs: 10/12–inch 33rpm
FULL MOON 5-10   81-88
WARNER 5-8   86
   Also see CHER and Peter Cetera
   Also see CHICAGO
   Also see FALTSKOG, Agnetha, and Peter Cetera

CETERA, Peter, and Amy Grant
Singles: 7–inch
FULL MOON 2-4   86
   Also see CETERA, Peter
   Also see GRANT, Amy

CHABUKOS
Singles: 7–inch
MAINSTREAM 3-5   73

CHACKSFIELD, Frank, Orchestra
LONDON 3-6   53-57
Singles: 7-inch
LONDON 3-8   53-61
EPs: 7-Inch 33/45rpm
LONDON 4-8   53-61
LPs: 10/12-inch 33rpm
LONDON 5-15   53-61
RICHMOND 5-12   59-62

CHAD & JEREMY
Singles: 7–inch
COLLECTABLES 2-4   81
COLUMBIA (Except 43277) 4-8   65-68
COLUMBIA (43277 "Before and After") . 4-8   65
   (Black vinyl.)
COLUMBIA (43277 "Before and After") 10-15   65
   (Colored vinyl. Promotional issues only.)
ERIC 2-4   73
LANA 3-5
ROCSHIRE 2-4   84
TRIP 3-5
WORLD ARTISTS 5-10   64-65
Picture Sleeves
COLUMBIA 5-10   65-66
WORLD ARTISTS 8-12   64-65
LPs: 10/12–inch 33rpm
CAPITOL (2000 series) 15-20   66
CAPITOL (12000 and 16000 series) . . 5-10   80
COLUMBIA 20-25   65-68
FIDU 10-12
HARMONY 12-15   69
ROCSHIRE 5-10   84

SIDEWALK . . . . 12-20　69
TRADITION REST 10-12
WORLD ARTISTS (2002 "Yesterday's
　Gone") . . . . 20-40　64
　(Monaural.)
WORLD ARTISTS (2005 "Chad & Jeremy
　Sing for You") . . . . 20-40　65
　(Monaural.)
WORLD ARTISTS (3002 "Yesterday's
　Gone") . . . . 30-50　64
　(Stereo.)
WORLD ARTISTS (3005 "Chad & Jeremy
　Sing for You") . . . . 30-50　65
　(Stereo.)
　Members: Chad Stuart; Jeremy Clyde.

CHAIN REACTION
Singles: 7-inch
ARIOLA AMERICA . . . . 3-5　76
DATE . . . . 5-10　66
DELICKS . . . . 5-10　69
DIAL . . . . 5-10　68
GRT . . . . 4-6　70
VERVE . . . . 10-20　68

CHAIRMEN of the Board
(Chairmen)
Singles: 7-inch
INVICTUS . . . . 3-6　70-76
SURFSIDE . . . . 3-5　82
Picture Sleeves
INVICTUS . . . . 3-5　70-72
LPs: 10/12-inch 33rpm
INVICTUS . . . . 12-20　70-74
　Members: General Norman Johnson; Eddie Curtis; Harrison
　Kennedy; Danny Woods.
　Also see JOHNSON, General

CHAKA KHAN: see KHAN, Chaka

CHAKACHAS
Singles: 7-inch
AVCO EMBASSY . . . . 3-5　72
JANUS . . . . 3-5　74
POLYDOR . . . . 3-5　71-75
LPs: 10/12-inch 33rpm
AVCO EMBASSY . . . . 8-10　72
POLYDOR . . . . 8-12　72

CHAKIRIS, George
Singles: 7-inch
CAPITOL . . . . 3-6　62-65
HORIZON . . . . 4-6　62
Picture Sleeves
CAPITOL . . . . 5-10　63
LPs: 10/12-inch 33rpm
CAPITOL . . . . 10-20　62-65
HORIZON . . . . 15-20　62

CHAMBERLAIN, Richard
Singles: 7-inch
MCA . . . . 2-4　77
MGM . . . . 4-6　62-65

Picture Sleeves
MGM . . . . 5-10　62-65
LPs: 10/12-inch 33rpm
MGM . . . . 15-20　63-65
METRO . . . . 8-12　66

CHAMBERS BROTHERS
Singles: 7-inch
AVCO . . . . 3-5　74-75
COLUMBIA . . . . 4-8　67-73
TEAR DROP . . . . 3-5　74
VAULT . . . . 8-12　65-69
Picture Sleeves
COLUMBIA . . . . 4-8　68-69
LPs: 10/12-inch 33rpm
AVCO . . . . 8-12　74-75
COLUMBIA (20 "Love, Peace
　and Happiness") . . . . 20-25　69
COLUMBIA (2000 and 9000 series)　. 15-20　67-68
COLUMBIA (30000 series,
　except 31158) . . . . 10-20　71-75
COLUMBIA (31158 "Oh My God") . . . 40-50　72
FOLKWAYS 8-10
ROXBURY . . . . 8-10　76
VAULT (100 series) . . . . 15-20　67-70
VAULT (9000 series) . . . . 20-25　66
　Members: Joe Chambers; Willie Chambers; Lester Chambers;
　George Chambers.
　Also see AXTON, Hoyt, and the Chambers Brothers
　Also see PEANUT BUTTER CONSPIRACY / Ashes /
　Chambers Brothers

CHAMPAGNE
Singles: 7-inch
ARIOLA AMERICA . . . . 2-5　77-78

CHAMPAIGN
Singles: 12-inch 33/45rpm
COLUMBIA . . . . 4-6　83
Singles: 7-inch
COLUMBIA . . . . 2-4　81-85
LPs: 10/12-inch 33rpm
COLUMBIA . . . . 5-10　81-85
　Members: Rena Jones; Pauli Carman; Michael Day; Dana
　Walden; Michael Reed; Howard Reeder; Rocky Maffit.

CHAMPLIN, Bill
Singles: 7-inch
ELEKTRA . . . . 2-4　81-82
EPIC . . . . 2-5　78
LPs: 10/12-inch 33rpm
ELEKTRA . . . . 5-10　82
EPIC . . . . 5-10　78
　Also see SONS of CHAMPLIN

CHAMPS
Singles: 78rpm
CHALLENGE . . . . 10-20　58
Singles: 7-inch
CHALLENGE . . . . 5-10　58-65
ERIC . . . . 2-4　78
LANA 2-4
REPUBLIC . . . . 3-5　76

TEQUILA
(Chuck Rio) Jat Music Co.
I'LL BE THERE
(Dave Burgess) Golden West Melodies, Inc.
THE CHAMPS

EPs: 7–inch 33/45rpm
CHALLENGE (7100 "Tequila") 25-50   58
CHALLENGE (7101 "Caramba") 25-50   58
LPs: 10/12–inch 33rpm
CHALLENGE (601 "Go Champs
  Go!") 50-100   58
  (Black vinyl.)
CHALLENGE (601 "Go Champs
  Go!") 250-350   58
  (Colored vinyl.)
CHALLENGE (605 "Everybody's
  Rockin' with the Champs") 50-75   58
CHALLENGE (613 "Go Champs
  Go!") 40-60   62
CHALLENGE (614 "The Champs Play
  All American") 40-60   62
  (Monaural.)
CHALLENGE (2514 "The Champs Play
  All American") 50-75   62
  (Stereo.)
DESIGN SPOTLIGHT SERIES 10-15
INTERNATIONAL AWARD 10-20
POINT 10-20
SPECTRUM 10-20
  Members: Dave Burgess; Danny "Chuck Rio" Flores; Gene
  Alden; Dale Norris; Joe Burness; Van Norman; Jim Seals; Dash
  Crofts; Dean Beard; Bobby Morris; Glen Campbell; Jerry Cole;
  Keith MacKendrick; Chuch Downs; Rich Grissom; Keith
  MacKendrick; Mo Marshall; Dean McDaniel; Johnny Meeks;
  Gary Nieland; Curtis Paul; Jerry Puckett; Leon Sanders; Dave
  Smith; John Trombatore.
  Also see CAMPBELL, Glen
  Also see SEALS & CROFTS
  Also see VINCENT, Gene

CHAMPS / Cyclones
LPs: 10/12–inch 33rpm
DESIGN SPOTLIGHT SERIES 10-20
  Also see CHAMPS

CHAMPS' BOYS ORCHESTRA
Singles: 7–inch
JANUS 3-5   76

CHANDLER, Gene
(Eugene Dixon)
Singles: 12–inch 33/45rpm
20TH FOX 4-8   79
Singles: 7–inch
BRUNSWICK 4-8   67-68
CHECKER 4-8   66-69
CHI-SOUND 2-5   79-82
COLLECTABLES 2-4   81
CONSTELLATION 4-8   63-66
CURTOM 3-5   72-73
ERIC 2-4   73
FASTFIRE 2-4   86
MCA 2-4   84
MARSEL 3-5   76
MERCURY 3-5   70
SOLID SMOKE 2-4   84
20TH FOX 2-4   78-79
VEE JAY 5-10   61-63
LPs: 10/12–inch 33rpm
BRUNSWICK 12-15   67-69
CHECKER 15-20   67
CHI-SOUND/20TH FOX 5-10   78-79
CONSTELLATION 15-25   64-66
KENT 5-10   86
MERCURY 10-15   70
SOLID SMOKE 5-10   84
20TH FOX 5-10   78-81
UPFRONT 8-10
VEE JAY (1040 "The Duke of Earl") 50-100   62
  (Monaural.)
VEE JAY (1040 "The Duke of Earl") 100-150   62
  (Stereo.)
  At least six early Vee Jay tracks, including *Duke of
  Earl*, were actually by the Dukays, not just Gene
  Chandler.
  Also see DUKAYS
  Also see DUKE of EARL

CHANDLER, Gene, and Barbara Acklin
Singles: 7–inch
BRUNSWICK 4-8   68-69
  Also see ACKLIN, Barbara

CHANDLER, Gene, and Jerry Butler
(Gene and Jerry)
Singles: 7–inch
MERCURY 3-6   70
  Also see BUTLER, Jerry

CHANDLER, Gene, and Jamie Lynn
Singles: 7–inch
SALSOUL 2-4   83
  Also see CHANDLER, Gene

CHANDLER, Karen
Singles: 78rpm
CORAL 4-8   52-55
DECCA 4-6   56
Singles: 7–inch
CARLTON 4-8   60
CORAL 5-10   52-55

DECCA 5-10   56
DOT 3-5   67-68
MOHAWK 4-8   62
STRAND 4-8   61
SUNBEAM 4-8   59
TIVOLI 3-6   65
EPs: 7–inch 33/45rpm
CORAL 8-15   52
LPs: 10/12–inch 33rpm
STRAND 10-20   61
Also see FONTAINE, Eddie, and Karen Chandler

CHANDLER, Karen, and Jimmy Wakely
Singles: 78rpm
DECCA 4-8   56
Singles: 7–inch
DECCA 5-10   56
Also see CHANDLER, Karen
Also see WAKELY, Jimmy

CHANDLER, Kenny
Singles: 7–inch
AMY 4-8   63
COLLECTABLES 2-4   81
CORAL 4-8   62
EPIC 4-8   65-66
LAURIE 5-10   62-63
TOWER 4-8   67-68
U.A. 8-10   61

CHANGE
Singles: 12–inch 33/45rpm
ATLANTIC 4-6   84
RFC 4-6   83
Singles: 7–inch
ATLANTIC 2-4   81-85
RFC 2-4   80
WARNER 2-4   80
LPs: 10/12–inch 33rpm
ATLANTIC 5-10   81-85
RFC 5-10   80
WARNER 5-10   80
Members: Paolo Granolio; David Romani; James Robinson;
Deborah Cooper.
Also see VANDROSS, Luther

CHANGIN' TIMES
Singles: 7–inch
BELL 10-20   67

CHANNEL, Bruce
Singles: 7–inch
CHARAY 4-6   68
COLLECTABLES 2-4   81
ELEKTRA 2-4   80
KING 5-10   59-60
LE CAM (100 series) 5-10   64
LE CAM (953 "Hey Baby") 10-20   62
LE CAM (1100 and 7200 series) 3-5   77
MALA 4-8   67-68
MANCO (1035 "Run Romance Run") . 8-10   62
MEL-O-DY 4-8   64
NAP 3-5

SHAH 4-8   64
SMASH 4-8   62-63
SOFT 4-8
TEEN AGER (601 "Run
  Romance Run") 20-30   59
ZUMA 3-5   77
Picture Sleeves
SMASH 8-12   62-63
LPs: 10/12–inch 33rpm
SMASH (27008 "Hey! Baby") 30-50   62
(Monaural.)
SMASH (67008 "Hey! Baby") 25-40   62
(Stereo.)

CHANNEL, Bruce / Paul & Paula
Singles: 7–inch
ERA 2-4
Also see CHANNEL, Bruce
Also see PAUL & PAULA

CHANSON
Singles: 7–inch
ARIOLA AMERICA 2-4   78-79
LPs: 10/12–inch 33rpm
ARIOLA AMERICA 5-10   78

CHANTAYS
Singles: 7–inch
ABC 2-4   74
COLLECTABLES 2-4   81
DOT 4-8   63
DOWNEY (104 "Pipeline") 15-25   63
DOWNEY (108 "Monsoon") 15-20   63
DOWNEY (116 through 130) 10-20   63-65
MCA 2-4   84
LPs: 10/12–inch 33rpm
DOT (3516 "Pipeline") 25-30   63
(Monaural.)
DOT (25516 "Pipeline") 30-40   63
(Stereo.)
DOT (3771 "Two Sides of
  the Chantays") 25-30   63
(Monaural.)
DOT (25771 "Two Sides of
  the Chantays") 30-40   63
(Stereo.)
DOWNEY (1002 "Pipeline") 100-175   63
Members: Bob Marshall; Bob Welch; Bob Spickard; Brian
Carman; Steve Cahn; Warren Waters

CHANTELS
Singles: 78rpm
END 15-25   57
Singles: 7–inch
ABC 2-4   73
CARLTON 5-10   61
END (1001 "He's Gone") 35-60   57
(Black label.)
END (1005 "Maybe") 30-50   57
(Black label.)
END (White or gray label) 10-20   58-59
END (Multi-color label) 8-15   58-61

ERIC 2-4	73	
LANA 3-5		
LUDIX 5-10	63	
RCA 3-6	70	
ROULETTE 3-6	69-71	
TCF 4-8	65	
VERVE 4-8	66	

EPs: 7–inch 33/45rpm

END (201 "I Love You So") 100-125   58
END (202 "I Love You So") 75-100   58

LPs: 10/12–inch 33rpm

CARLTON (LP-144 "The Chantels on Tour/
  Look in My Eyes") 50-100   62
  (Monaural.)
CARLTON (STLP-144 "The Chantels on Tour/
  Look in My Eyes") 75-150   62
  (Stereo.)
END (301 "We're the Chantels") . . 500-600   58
  (Pictures the group on front cover.)
END (301 "The Chantels") 100-150   59
  (Pictures a juke box on front cover.)
END (312 "There's Our Song
  Again") 50-75   62
FORUM (9104 "The Chantels Sing
  Their Favorites") 25-40   64
ROULETTE 5-10
  Members: Arlene Smith; Lois Harris; Renee Minus; Sonia
  Gorring; Jackie Landry.
  Also see BARRETT, Richard

CHANTERS

Singles: 7–inch

DE LUXE (6162 "My My Darling") . . . 30-40   58
DE LUXE (6166 "Row Your Boat") . . . 25-35   58
  (Black label.)
DE LUXE (6166 "Row Your Boat") . . . 10-15
  (Yellow label.)
DE LUXE (6172 "Five Little Kisses") . 30-40   58
DE LUXE (6191 "No, No, No") 20-30   61
DE LUXE (6194 "My My Darling") . . . 20-30   61
DE LUXE (6200 "Row Your Boat") . . . 10-15   63
GUSTO 2-4   77
  Members: Bud Johnson Jr; Larry Pendegrass; Fred Paige;
  Bobby Thompson; Elliot Green.

CHAPIN, Harry

Singles: 7–inch

BOARDWALK 2-4   80-81
DUNHILL 2-4   88
ELEKTRA 3-5   72-79

LPs: 10/12–inch 33rpm

BOARDWALK 5-10   80
DUNHILL 5-10   88
ELEKTRA 8-12   72-79

CHAPLAIN, Paul

(Paul Chaplain and His Emeralds; Paul Chaplin)

Singles: 7–inch

ELGIN 5-10
HARPER 10-20   60-61

CHAPMAN, Tracy

Singles: 7–inch

ELEKTRA 2-4   88-89

Picture Sleeves

ELEKTRA 2-4   88-89

LPs: 10/12–inch 33rpm

ELEKTRA 5-8   88-89

CHAPTER 8

Singles: 12–inch 33/45rpm

ARIOLA AMERICA 4-8   79
BEVERLY GLEN 4-6   85

Singles: 7–inch

ARIOLA AMERICA 3-5   79-80
BEVERLY GLEN 2-4   85
  Members: Anita Baker; Michael Powell; David Washington;
  Carolyn Crawford; Valerie Pinkston.

LPs: 10/12–inch 33rpm

ARIOLA AMERICA 5-10   79
  Also see BAKER, Anita
  Also see CRAWFORD, Carolyn
  Also see DETROIT EMERALDS

CHARADE

(Featuring Jessica)

Singles: 12–inch 33/45rpm

PROFILE 4-6   83

CHARGERS

Singles: 7–inch

RCA (7301 "Old MacDonald") 15-25   58
RCA (7417 "Here in My Heart") 15-25   58
  Members: Jesse Belvin; James Scott; Ben Easley; Dunbar
  White; Johnny White; Mitchell Alexander; Jimmy Norman.
  Also see BELVIN, Jesse
  Also see NORMAN, Jimmy

CHARLENE

(Charlene Duncan)

Singles: 7–inch

MOTOWN 2-4   80-85
PRODIGAL 3-5   76-77

Picture Sleeves

PRODIGAL 3-5   77

LPs: 10/12–inch 33rpm

MOTOWN 5-10   82-85
PRODIGAL 8-10   76

CHARLENE and Stevie Wonder

Singles: 7–inch

MOTOWN 2-4   82
  Also see CHARLENE
  Also see WONDER, Stevie

CHARLES, Jimmy

(Jimmy Charles and the Revelletts)

Singles: 7–inch

ABC 2-4   73
COLLECTABLES 2-4   81
ERIC 2-4   79
MCA 2-4   84
PROMO 10-15   60
ROULETTE 2-4   71

Picture Sleeves
PROMO 15-25   60-61

CHARLES, Lee
Singles: 7–inch
BAMBOO 3-5   70-71
BRUNSWICK 3-6   69
HOT WAX 3-5   73
INVICTUS 3-5   74
REVUE 4-8   68

CHARLES, Ray
(Ray Charles and the Raelettes)
Singles: 78rpm
ATLANTIC 5-10   52-58
JAX 10-20   52
ROCKIN' 5-10   53
SWING BEAT 15-25   49
SWING TIME 10-20   50-53
ATLANTIC 10-15   52-58

Singles: 7–inch
ABC 3-8   66-73
ABC-PAR (Monaural) 4-8   60-66
ABC-PAR (Stereo) 10-15   61-62
ATLANTIC (976 "Roll with Me Baby") . 50-75   52
ATLANTIC (984 "The Sun's Gonna
Shine Again") 30-60   53
ATLANTIC (999 "Mess Around") 30-60   53
ATLANTIC (1000 series) 12-25   53-57
ATLANTIC (2000 series) 5-10   58-68
ATLANTIC (3000 series) 3-5   77-79
BARONET 4-8   62
COLUMBIA 2-4   82-87
CROSSOVER 3-5   73-78
HURRAH 8-12
IMPULSE 5-10   61
MAYFAIR (121 "Pony Boy") 4-8
(With "Uncle Stu.")
RCA 3-5   76
ROCKIN' (504 "Walkin' and Talkin") 100-200   53
SITTIN in WITH (641 "Baby Let me Hear
You Call My Name") 75-150   52
SWING TIME (250 "Baby Let Me
Hold Your Hand") 75-100   51
SWING TIME (274 "Kiss Me Baby") . 75-100   52
SWING TIME (300 "Baby Let Me
Hear You Call My Name") 75-100   52
SWING TIME (326 "The Snow
Is Falling") 50-100   53
TANGERINE 2-4   71
TIME 3-5   62

Picture Sleeves
ABC 3-6   68-70

EPs: 7–inch 33/45rpm
ABC-PAR 10-20   60-62
ATLANTIC 20-30   56-59

LPs: 10/12–inch 33rpm
ABC (Except 590) 10-12   66-73
ABC (590 "A Man and His Soul") 20-25   67
ABC-PAR (300 and 400 series) 15-25   60-64

ABC-PAR (400 and 500 series) 12-20   65-66
AHED 8-12
(TV mail-order offer.)
ATLANTIC (500 series) 10-15   73
ATLANTIC (900 "The Ray
Charles Story, Vols. 1 and 2") 30-40   62
(Combines Atlantic 8063 and 8064.)
ATLANTIC (1259 "The Great
Ray Charles") 45-60   57
ATLANTIC (1279 "Soul Brothers") ... 40-50   58
(With Milt Jackson.)
ATLANTIC (1289 "Ray Charles
at Newport") 40-50   58
ATLANTIC (1312 "Genius of
Ray Charles") 30-45   59
ATLANTIC (1360 "Soul Meeting") ... 20-35   62
(With Milt Jackson. Number would indicate a 1961
release, but not actually issued until 1962.)
ATLANTIC (1369 "Genius
After Hours") 20-35   61
ATLANTIC (1500 series) 8-10   70
ATLANTIC (3700 series) 20-22   82
ATLANTIC (7000 series) 12-15   64
ATLANTIC (8006 "Ray Charles") 45-60   57
(Black label.)
ATLANTIC (8006 "Ray Charles") 25-35   59
(Red label.)
ATLANTIC (8025 "Yes Indeed") 30-40   59
(Black label.)
ATLANTIC (8025 "Yes Indeed") 25-35   60
(Red label.)
ATLANTIC (8029 "What'd I Say") ... 30-40   59
(Black label.)
ATLANTIC (8029 "What'd I Say") ... 25-35   60
(Red label.)59
ATLANTIC (8039 "Ray Charles
in Person") 30-40   60
(Black label.)
ATLANTIC (8039 "Ray Charles
in Person") 25-35   60
(Red label.)
ATLANTIC (8052 "The Genius
Sings the Blues") 20-30   61
ATLANTIC (8054 "Dot the Twist") ... 20-30   61
ATLANTIC (8063 "The Ray
Charles Story, Vol. 1") 20-25   62
ATLANTIC (8064 "The Ray
Charles Story, Vol. 2") 20-25   62
ATLANTIC (8083 "The Ray
Charles Story, Vol. 3") 20-25   63
ATLANTIC (8094 "The Ray
Charles Story, Vol. 4") 20-25   64
ATLANTIC (19000 series) 5-10   77-80
BARONET 15-20   62
BLUESWAY 8-10   73
BULLDOG 5-10   84
COLUMBIA 5-10   83-86
CORONET 8-10
CROSSOVER 8-15   73-76

MGM (3000 series)	10-20	55-60
MGM (4000 series)	8-15	63-66
METRO	6-10	65
VOCALION	8-10	66

CHARLES, Ronnie
LPs: 10/12-inch 33rpm

20TH FOX	8-12	75

CHARLES, Rosevelt
LPs: 10/12-inch 33rpm

VANGUARD	10-20	64

CHARLES, Sonny
(Sonny Charles and Checkmates Ltd.)
Singles: 7-inch

A&M	4-8	68-73
CAPITOL	4-8	66-67
FRATERNITY	4-8	64
HIGHRISE	2-4	82
RCA	3-5	72

LPs: 10/12-inch 33rpm

HIGHRISE	5-10	82
A&M	15-25	69

Also see CHECKMATES LTD.

CHARLES, Tommy
Singles: 78rpm

DECCA	5-10	56
WILLETT	10-20	57

Singles: 7-inch

DECCA	8-15	56
WILLETT (111 "Hey There Baby")	40-60	57

CHARLESTON CITY ALL-STARS
LPs: 10/12-inch 33rpm

GRAND AWARD	5-15	57-59

CHARME
Singles: 7-inch

ATLANTIC	2-4	84
RCA	2-4	79-85

LPs: 10/12-inch 33rpm

RCA	5-10	79-85

CHARMETTES
(Charmetts)
Singles: 7-inch

FEDERAL	5-10	59
HI	5-10	59
KAPP	10-15	63-64
MALA	5-10	64
MARLIN	5-10	62
MELOMEGA	5-10	62
MONA	5-10	60
TRI DISC	5-10	62
WORLD ARTISTS	5-10	65

CHARMS
(Otis Williams and the Charms)
Singles: 78rpm

CHART	5-15	55-56
DELUXE	10-15	54-57
ROCKIN'	20-40	53

Singles: 7-inch

CHART (608 "Love's Our Inspiration")	15-25	55
CHART (613 "Heart of a Rose")	15-25	56
CHART (623 "I'll Be True")	15-25	56
DELUXE (6000 "Heaven Only Knows")	75-125	53
DELUXE (6014 "Happy Are We")	75-100	53
DELUXE (6034 "Bye-Bye Baby")	75-100	54
DELUXE (6050 "Quiet Please")	50-100	54
DELUXE (6056 "My Baby Dearest Darling")	50-100	54
DELUXE (6062 through 6098)	15-30	54-56
DELUXE (6100 series) (Monaural)	12-25	57-59
DELUXE (6100 series) (Stereo.)	25-45	59
GUSTO	2-4	77
KING	5-10	60-63
OKEH	4-8	65-66
ROCKIN' (516 "Heaven Only Knows")	200-350	53

EPs: 7-inch 33/45rpm

DELUXE (357 "Hits By the Charms")	150-200	55
DELUXE (364 "Hits By the Charms")	150-200	55
DELUXE (385 "Otis Williams and the Charms")	100-200	56
KING (357 "Hits By the Charms")	50-75	58
KING (364 "Hits By the Charms, Vol. 2")	50-75	58
KING (385 "Otis Williams and His Charms")	50-75	58

LPs: 10/12-inch 33rpm

DELUXE (570 "All Their Hits") (With color photo of the group on cover.)	300-400	58
KING (614 "This Is Otis Williams and the Charms")	100-125	59

Members: Otis Williams and the Charms; Otis Williams; Ron Bradley; Don Peark; Joe Renn; Richard Parker.
Also see WILLIAMS, Otis

CHARO
(Charo with the Salsoul Orchestra)
Singles: 7-inch

CAPITOL	3-5	76
SALSOUL	3-5	77-78

LPs: 10/12-inch 33rpm

SALSOUL	5-10	77-78

Also see SALSOUL ORCHESTRA

CHARTBUSTERS
Singles: 7-inch

BELL	4-8	67
CRUSADER	8-12	65
MUTUAL	5-10	64-65

CHARTS
Singles: 7-inch

ABC	2-4	73

COLLECTABLES 2-4
EVERLAST (5001 "Desiree") 25-50   57
EVERLAST (5002 "Dance Girl") 20-40   57
EVERLAST (5006 "You're
  the Reason") 20-40   58
EVERLAST (5008 "All Because
  of Love") 20-40   58
EVERLAST (5010 "My Diane") 20-40   58
EVERLAST (5026 "Desiree") 10-20   63
GUYDEN 5-10   59
VELVTONE 10-20
WAND (1112 "Desiree") 5-10   66
WAND (1124 "Livin' the Nightlife") 4-8   66

LPs: 10/12-inch 33rpm

COLLECTABLES 8-10   86
LOST-NITE...................... 8-12   81
Members: Joe Grier; Steve Brown; Ross Buford; Glen Jackson;
Leroy Binns.

CHASE

Singles: 7-inch

EPIC 3-5   71-76

LPs: 10/12-inch 33rpm

EPIC 10-12   71-76
Members: Bill Chase; Jerry Van Blair; Jay Burrid; Dennis
Johnson; Ted Piercefield: Phil Porter; Terry Richards; Angel
South; Alan Ware.

CHASE, Ellison

Singles: 7-inch

BIG TREE 3-5   76-77
COLUMBIA 2-4   82
MAGNA-GLIDE 3-5   75

LPs: 10/12-inch 33rpm

COLUMBIA/ARC 5-10   82

CHATER, Kerry

Singles: 7-inch

WARNER 3-5   76-78

LPs: 10/12-inch 33rpm

WARNER 5-10   77
Also see PUCKETT, Gary

CHAZ

Singles: 7-inch

PROMISE 2-4   82

CHEAP TRICK

Singles: 12-inch 33/45rpm

EPIC 4-6   83

Singles: 7-inch

ASYLUM 2-4   81
EPIC 2-5   77-90
PASHA 2-4   84

Picture Sleeves

EPIC (Except 50814) 2-5   79-88
EPIC (50814 "Voices") 4-8   79
  (Promotional issue only.)

EPs: 7-inch 33/45rpm

CSP 4-8   81
  (Nestles candy promotional issue.)

LPs: 10/12-inch 33rpm

EPIC 5-10   76-90

EPIC/NU-DISC 10-15   80
  (Includes bonus single.)
PASHA 5-10   84
Members: Robert Zander; Tom Petersson; Rick Nielson; Bun E.
Carlos.

CHEATHAM, Oliver

Singles: 7-inch

CRITIQUE 2-4   86-87
MCA 2-4   83

LPs: 10/12-inch 33rpm

MCA 5-10   83

CHECKER, Chubby

Singles: 7-inch

ABKCO 2-4   72
AMHERST 3-5   76
BUDDAH 4-6   69
MCA 2-4   82
PARKWAY (006 "The Jet") 5-10   62
PARKWAY (804 through 810) 8-12   59-60
PARKWAY (811 "The Twist"/"Toot") .. 10-20   60
  (White label.)
PARKWAY (811 "The Twist"/"Toot") ... 8-12   60
  (Orange label.)
PARKWAY (811 "The Twist"/
  "Twistin' U.S.A.") 5-10   61
  (Yellow/orange or orange label.)
PARKWAY (811 "The Twist") 15-20   61
  (Colored vinyl.)
PARKWAY (813 through 989) 5-10   60-66
20TH FOX 3-5   73-74

Picture Sleeves

PARKWAY 8-12   61-65

EPs: 7-inch 33/45rpm

PARKWAY 15-20   61
  (Includes Compact 33 Doubles.)

LPs: 10/12-inch 33rpm

ABKCO 8-10   72
D.C.M. 4-6
EVEREST 5-10   81
51 WEST 5-10   84
MCA 8-10   82
PARKWAY 15-30   60-66
Also see DREAMLOVERS
Also see FAT BOYS

CHECKER, Chubby / Gary U.S. Bonds

LPs: 10/12-inch 33rpm

EXACT 5-10   80
Also see BONDS, Gary "U.S."

CHECKER, Chubby, and Bobby Rydell

Singles: 7-inch

CAMEO (12 "Your Hits and Mine") .. 10-20   61
  (Promotional issue only.)
CAMEO (200 series) 5-10   61-62

Picture Sleeves

CAMEO 5-10   61

LPs: 10/12-inch 33rpm

CAMEO 20-30   61-63
Also see RYDELL, Bobby

CHECKER, Chubby, and Dee Dee Sharp
LPs: 10/12–inch 33rpm

CAMEO 20-30		62

Also see CHECKER, Chubby
Also see SHARP, Dee Dee

CHECKMATES LTD.
Singles: 7–inch

A&M 4-6		69
CAPITOL 4-8		66-67
FANTASY 2-5		77-78
GREEDY 3-5		77
RUSTIC 3-5		74

LPs: 10/12–inch 33rpm

A&M 15-20		69
CAPITOL 15-20		67
FANTASY 8-10		77
IKON 5-10		
POLYDOR 8-10		76
RUSTIC 8-10		74

Members: Sonny Charles; Bill Van Buskirk; Marvin Smith; Bobby
Stevens; Harvey Trees.
Also see CHARLES, Sonny

CHEECH & CHONG
Singles: 7–inch

A&M 2-4		
EPIC/ODE 3-5		77
MCA 2-4		85
ODE 3-5		71-77
WARNER 2-4		78

Picture Sleeves

A&M 2-4		
MCA 2-4		85
ODE 8-12		73-77
WARNER 2-4		78

EPs: 7–inch 33/45rpm

ODE (8 "Cheech & Chong") 5-8		71

LPs: 10/12–inch 33rpm

EPIC/ODE 8-10		77
MCA 5-8		85
ODE 8-12		71-76
WARNER 8-10		78-80

Members: Richard Marin; Thomas Chong.
Also see TAYLOR, Bobby

CHEE-CHEE & PEPPY
Singles: 7–inch

BUDDAH 3-5		71

LPs: 10/12–inch 33rpm

BUDDAH 10-15		72

Members: Dorothy Moore; Keith Bolling.
Also see MOORE, Dorothy

CHEEKS, Judy
Singles: 7–inch

DREAM 2-4		80
SALSOUL 2-4		78
U.A. 3-5		73

LPs: 10/12–inch 33rpm

SALSOUL 5-10		78
U.A. 8-10		73

CHEERS
Singles: 78rpm

CAPITOL 5-10		54-56
MERCURY 5-10		57

Singles: 7–inch

CAPITOL 10-20		54-56
MERCURY 8-15		57

EPs: 7–inch 33/45rpm

CAPITOL (584 "Bazoom") 50-75		55

Members: Bert Convy; Gil Garfield; Susan Allen.

CHEMAY, Joe
(Joe Chemay Band)
Singles: 7–inch

UNICORN 2-4		81

LPs: 10/12–inch 33rpm

UNICORN 5-10		81

CHEQUERED PAST
Singles: 7–inch

EMI AMERICA 2-4		84

LPs: 10/12–inch 33rpm

EMI AMERICA 5-10		84

Members: Clem Burke; Nigel Harrison.

CHER
(Cher Bono; Cher Allman)
Singles: 12–inch 33/45rpm

CASABLANCA 8-10		79-82

Singles: 7–inch

ATCO 3-6		69-72
ATLANTIC 4-6		69
CASABLANCA 3-5		79
COLUMBIA 3-5		82
GEFFEN 2-4		87-90
IMPERIAL 5-10		64-68
KAPP 3-5		71-72
LIBERTY 2-4		82
MCA 3-5		73-75
U.A. 3-5		71-72
WARNER 3-5		75-77
WARNER/SPECTOR 3-5		74

Picture Sleeves

COLUMBIA 3-5		82
GEFFEN 2-4		87-89

LPs: 10/12–inch 33rpm

ATCO 15-20		69
CASABLANCA (Except NBPIX-7133) . 8-12		79
CASABLANCA (NBPIX-7133 "Take Me Home") 25-30		79
(Picture disc.)		
COLUMBIA 5-10		82
GEFFEN 5-10		87-91
IMPERIAL 15-25		65-68
KAPP 12-15		71-72
LIBERTY 5-10		81
MCA 10-15		73-74
SPRINGBOARD 8-10		72
SUNSET 8-10		70
U.A. 8-10		71-75
WARNER 8-15		75-77

Also see ALLMAN & WOMAN
Also see CHERILYN / Cherilyn's Group
Also see MASON, Bonnie Jo
Also see SONNY & CHER

CHER and Peter Cetera
Singles: 7–inch

GEFFEN 2-4   89
Picture Sleeves
GEFFEN 2-4   89
Also see CETERA, Peter

CHER & NILSSON
Singles: 7–inch

SPECTOR 3-5   75
Members: Cher; Harry Nilsson.
Also see CHER
Also see NILSSON

CHERI
Singles: 12–inch 33/45rpm
21 4-6   83
Singles: 7–inch
21 2-4   83
VENTURE 2-4   82

CHERILYN / Cherilyn's Group
(Cher Bono)
Singles: 7–inch
IMPERIAL (66081 "Dream Baby") . . . 20-30   64
Also see CHER
ULTRA D'OR (8 "99½ Won't Do") . 100-150   56

CHERRELLE
(Cherrelle and Alexander O'Neal)
Singles: 12–inch 33/45rpm
TABU 4-6   84-86
Singles: 7–inch
TABU 2-4   84-88
LPs: 10/12–inch 33rpm
TABU 5-10   84-88
Also see O'NEAL, Alexander

CHERRY, Ava
Singles: 12–inch 33/45rpm
CAPITOL 4-6   82
Singles: 7–inch
CAPITOL 2-4   82
CURTOM 2-4   80
RSO 2-4   80
LPs: 10/12–inch 33rpm
RSO 5-10   80

CHERRY, Don
Singles: 78rpm
COLUMBIA 4-8   55-59
DECCA 5-10   50-56
Singles: 7–inch
COLUMBIA 5-10   55-59
DECCA 8-12   50-56
MONUMENT 2-5   65-78
STRAND 4-8   59
VERVE 4-8   62
WARWICK 4-8   60

EPs: 7–inch 33/45rpm
COLUMBIA 8-15   56
LPs: 10/12–inch 33rpm
COLUMBIA 15-25   56
HARMONY 10-15   59
MONUMENT 8-12   66-73
Also see DAY, Doris, and Don Cherry

CHERRY PEOPLE
Singles: 7–inch
HERITAGE 4-8   68-69
Picture Sleeves
HERITAGE 6-10   68
LPs: 10/12–inch 33rpm
HERITAGE 15-20   68

CHERYL LYNN: see LYNN, Cheryl

CHET, FLOYD & DANNY
ATKINS, Chet, Floyd Cramer and Danny Davis

CHEYNE
Singles: 12–inch 33/45rpm
MCA 4-6   85

CHIC
Singles: 12–inch 33/45
ATLANTIC 4-8   78-83
Singles: 7–inch
ATLANTIC 2-5   77-83
MIRAGE 2-4   82
Picture Sleeves
ATLANTIC 2-5   78-80
LPs: 10/12–inch 33rpm
ATLANTIC 5-10   77-82
Also see HONEYDRIPPERS
Also see NORMA JEAN
Also see RODGERS, Nile

CHIC / Leif Garrett / Roberta Flack / Genesis
EPs: 7–inch 33/45rpm
WARNER SPECIAL PRODUCTS 8-12   78
(Coca-Cola/Burger King promotional issue. Issued
with paper sleeve.)
Also see CHIC
Also see FLACK, Roberta
Also see GARRETT, Leif
Also see GENESIS

CHICAGO
Singles: 12–inch 33/45rpm
COLUMBIA 4-8   80
Singles: 7–inch
COLUMBIA 3-6   69-80
DGC 2-4   90
FULL MOON 2-4   82-86
REPRISE 2-4   88-89
WARNER 2-4   87
Picture Sleeves
COLUMBIA 3-6   70-77
FULL MOON 2-4   84-86
REPRISE 2-4   88-91
WARNER 2-4   87

EPs: 7–inch 33/45rpm

COLUMBIA 10-15 70-73
(Jukebox issues only.)

LPs: 10/12–inch 33rpm

ACCORD 5-10   81
COLUMBIA ("Chicago) 200-250 76
(No number used. Boxed set of first 10 LPs [17
discs]. Promotional issue only.)
COLUMBIA (8 "Chicago Transit
Authority") 25-35   69
COLUMBIA (24 "Chicago II") 20-30   70
COLUMBIA (C2-30110 "Chicago III") . 10-20   70
COLUMBIA (C2Q-30110 "Chicago III") 20-25   74
(Quadrophonic.)
COLUMBIA (30863 "Chicago IV") ... 15-20   71
COLUMBIA (CAX-30865
"Chicago IV") 20-30   71
(Four-LP boxed edition. Includes three posters,
booklet and card.)
COLUMBIA (CQ-30865 "Chicago IV") 20-30   74
(Quadrophonic.)
COLUMBIA (31102 through 38590) .. 8-15 72-82
(With "C2," "FC," "HC," "KC," "JC," or "PC" prefix.)
COLUMBIA (31102 through 34200) .. 15-25 74-76
(Quadrophonic. With "CQ," "C2Q," "GQ," or "PCQ"
prefix.)
COLUMBIA (43000 and 44000 series) 15-25   82
(Half-speed mastered.)
FULL MOON 5-10 82-86
MFSL (128 "Chicago Transit
Authority") 15-25   85
REPRISE 5-8 88-91
MAGNUM 10-12   78
WARNER 5-8   86
Members: Peter Cetera; Terry Kath; Robert Lamm; James
Pankow; Lee Loughnane; Daniel Seraphine; Walter Parazaider.
Also see BEACH BOYS
Also see CETERA, Peter

CHICAGO GANGSTERS
Singles: 7–inch

GOLD PLATE 3-5 75-76
RCA 3-5   78
RED COACH 3-5 74-75

LPs: 10/12–inch 33rpm

GOLD PLATE 10-12 75-76
Members: Sam McCant; James McCant; Larry McCant; Chris
McCant.

CHICAGO LOOP
Singles: 7–inch

DYNO VOICE 4-8 66-67
MERCURY 4-8 67-68

CHICAGO TRANSIT AUTHORITY:
see CHICAGO

CHICANO, El: see EL CHICANO

CHICORY
(Chicory Tip)
Singles: 7–inch

EPIC 3-5 72-73

LPs: 10/12–inch 33rpm

EPIC 10-12   72

CHIEFTAINS
Singles: 7–inch

ISLAND 3-5   76

LPs: 10/12–inch 33rpm

COLUMBIA 5-10 78-80
ISLAND 5-10 75-78

CHIFFONS
Singles: 7–inch

B.T. PUPPY 3-5   70
BIG DEAL (6003 "Tonight's the Night") 35-50   60
BUDDAH 4-8   71
LAURIE 5-10 63-76
REPRISE 10-15   62
WILDCAT (601 "Never Never") 10-20   61

LPs: 10/12–inch 33rpm

B.T. PUPPY (1011 "My Secret Love") 35-45   70
COLLECTABLES 5-10   87
LAURIE (2018 "He's So Fine") 35-50   63
LAURIE (2020 "One Fine Day") 35-50   63
LAURIE (LLP-2036 "Sweet
Talkin' Guy") 35-45   66
(Monaural.)
LAURIE (SLP-2036 "Sweet
Talkin' Guy") 40-50   66
(Stereo.)
LAURIE (4001 "Everything You Always
Wanted to Hear") 10-20   75
Members: Judy Craig; Barbara Lee; Patricia Bennett; Sylvia
Peterson.
Also see CHRISTIE, Lou, and the Classics / Isley Brothers /
Chiffons
Also see COASTERS / Crew-Cuts / Chiffons
Also see FOUR PENNIES

CHILD, Desmond, and Rouge
Singles: 12–inch 33/45rpm

CAPITOL 4-8   79

Singles: 7–inch

CAPITOL (Black vinyl) 2-4 79-82
CAPITOL (Colored vinyl) 4-6   79

LPs: 10/12–inch 33rpm

CAPITOL (Black vinyl) 5-10   79
CAPITOL (Colored vinyl) 15-20   79
Also see VIDAL, Maria

CHI-LITES
Singles: 12–inch 33/45rpm

LARC 4-8   83
PRIVATE 1 4-6   84

Singles: 7–inch

BLUE ROCK 4-8   65
BRUNSWICK 3-6 69-78
CHI-SOUND 2-4 80-82
EPIC 2-4   83
INPHASION 2-4   79
LARC 2-4   83
MERCURY 3-5 76-77
O'RETTA 3-5   70

PRIVATE I 2-4   84
REVUE 4-8   67-68
20TH FOX 2-4   81

LPs: 10/12–inch 33rpm
BRUNSWICK 10-15   69-74
CHI-SOUND 5-8   80-82
EPIC 5-10   83-84
LARC 5-10   83
MERCURY 5-10   77
PICKWICK 5-10
20TH FOX 5-10   80-81
    Members: Eugene Record; Creadel Jones; Robert Lester;
    Marshall Thompson; Danny Johnson.
     Also see JOHNSON, Danny
     Also see RECORD, Eugene
     Also see WILSON, Jackie, and the Chi-Lites

CHILLIWACK
Singles: 7–inch
A&M 3-5   72
MILLENNIUM 2-4   81-83
MUSHROOM 2-5   76-80
PARROT 3-5   71
SIRE 3-5   74-76

LPs: 10/12–inch 33rpm
A&M 10-15   71-73
MILLENNIUM 5-10   81-82
MUSHROOM 8-12   77-80
PARROT 15-20   70
SIRE 10-15   75
    Members: Bill Henderson; Howard Froese; Claire Lawrence;
    Glen Miller; Ross Turney.

CHILLTOWN
Singles: 12–inch 33/45rpm
A&M 4-6   83

CHIMES
Singles: 7–inch
ABC 2-4   75
COLLECTABLES 2-4   81
LAURIE 10-15   60
LIMELIGHT 10-20   63
METRO INT'L 5-10   63
MUSIC NOTE (1101 "Once in Awhile") 10-20   61
RESERVE (120 "When School
   Starts Again") 30-40   57
TAG (444 "Once in Awhile"/"Summer
   Night") 10-20   60
   (Maroon label.)
TAG (444 "Once in Awhile"/"Summer
   Night") 5-10   60
   (Green label.)
TAG (444 "Once in Awhile"/"Oh How
   I Love You So") 10-20   60
   (Though shown as by the Chimes, *Oh How I Love
   You So* is by the BiTones.)
TAG (445 "I'm in the Mood
   for Love") 5-10   61
TAG (447 "Let's Fall in Love") 8-10   61
TAG (450 "My Love") 10-20   62

CHINA CRISIS
Singles: 12–inch 33/45rpm
VIRGIN 4-6   82
WARNER 4-6   83
Singles: 7–inch
VIRGIN 2-4   82
WARNER 2-4   84
LPs: 10/12–inch 33rpm
A&M 5-10   87
WARNER 5-10   84-85

CHIP E. INC. FEATURING K. JOY
Singles: 12–inch 33/45rpm
D.J. INT'L 4-6   85

CHIPMUNKS
(Starring Alvin, Theodore, and Simon; Featuring David Seville)
Singles: 7–inch
AMERICAN TELECARD 10-15   64
   (Cardboard flexi-disc.)
LIBERTY (Except 77000 series) 5-10   58-74
LIBERTY (77000 series) 10-20   59
   (Stereo.)
MISTLETOE 3-5   75
SUNSET 3-6   68
U.A. 3-5   74
Picture Sleeves
LIBERTY 5-10   59-65
EPs: 7–inch 33/45rpm
LIBERTY 10-20   59-64
LPs: 10/12–inch 33rpm
LIBERTY (3132 "Let's All Sing
   with the Chipmunks") 20-30   59
   (Monaural. Black vinyl. Cover shows Chipmunks
   as animals. If Chipmunks are drawn as cartoon
   characters, deduct 50%.)
LIBERTY (3132 "Let's All Sing
   with the Chipmunks") 25-40   59
   (Monaural. Colored vinyl. Cover shows Chipmunks
   as animals. If Chipmunks are drawn as cartoon
   characters, deduct 50%.)
LIBERTY (3159 "Sing Again
   with the Chipmunks") 20-30   60
   (Monaural. Cover shows Chipmunks as animals. If
   Chipmunks are drawn as cartoon characters,
   deduct 50%.)
LIBERTY (3170 "Around the World
   with the Chipmunks") 20-30   60
   (Monaural. Cover shows Chipmunks as animals. If
   Chipmunks are drawn as cartoon characters,
   deduct 50%.)
LIBERTY (3200 through 3400 series) 10-20   61-65
   (Monaural.)
LIBERTY (7132 "Let's All Sing
   with the Chipmunks") 20-35   59
   (Stereo. Black vinyl. Cover shows Chipmunks as
   animals. If Chipmunks are drawn as cartoon
   characters, deduct 50%.)

LIBERTY (7132 "Let's All Sing
with the Chipmunks") 25-45   59
(Stereo. Colored vinyl. Cover shows Chipmunks as
animals. If Chipmunks are drawn as cartoon
characters, deduct 50%.)
LIBERTY (7159 "Sing Again
with the Chipmunks") 20-35   60
(Stereo. Cover shows Chipmunks as animals. If
Chipmunks are drawn as cartoon characters,
deduct 50%.)
LIBERTY (7170 "Around the World
with the Chipmunks") 20-35   60
(Stereo. Cover shows Chipmunks as animals. If
Chipmunks are drawn as cartoon characters,
deduct 50%.)
LIBERTY (7200 through 7400 series)   10-20   61-65
(Stereo.)
LIBERTY (10000 series) 5-10   82
PICKWICK 5-10   80
SUNSET 8-15   68-69
U.A. 5-10   74-76
    Also see CANNED HEAT and the Chipmunks
    Also see SEVILLE, David

CHIPMUNKS
**(Starring Alvin, Theodore, and Simon; Featuring
David Seville Jr.)**
          Singles: 7–inch
EXCELSIOR 2-4   80
RCA 2-4   81-82
          Picture Sleeves
EXCELSIOR 2-4   80
RCA 2-4   81
          LPs: 10/12–inch 33rpm
EXCELSIOR 5-10   80
PICKWICK INT'L 5-10   80
RCA 5-10   81-82

CHIYO and the Crescents:
see CRESCENTS

CHOCOLATE MILK
        Singles: 12–inch 33/45rpm
RCA 4-6   83
          Singles: 7–inch
RCA 2-5   75-83
          LPs: 10/12–inch 33rpm
RCA 5-10   77-82
    Members: Frank Richard; Amadee Castanell; Robert Doban; Joe
    Foxx; Mario Tio; Dwight Richards.

CHOCOLETE
        Singles: 12–inch 33/45rpm
SUPERTRONICS 4-6   85

CHOICE FOUR
          Singles: 7–inch
RCA 3-5   74-76
          LPs: 10/12–inch 33rpm
RCA 8-10   74-75
    Members: Pete Marshall; Ted Maduro; Bobby Hamilton; Charles
    Blagmore.

CHOICE MCs Featuring Fresh Gordon
        Singles: 12–inch 33/45rpm
TOMMY BOY 4-6   85

CHOIR
          Singles: 7–inch
CANADIAN AMERICAN (203 "It's
Cold Outside") 25-35   67
INTREPID 4-6   70
ROULETTE 10-15   67-68
          EPs: 7–inch 33/45rpm
BOMP 8-10   76
    Member: Eric Carmen.
    Also see CARMEN, Eric

CHOPS
        Singles: 12–inch 33/45rpm
ATLANTIC 4-6   84
          Singles: 7–inch
ATLANTIC 2-4   84
          LPs: 10/12–inch 33rpm
ATLANTIC 5-10   84

CHORDCATS
          Singles: 78rpm
CAT 10-15   54
          Singles: 7–inch
CAT (112 "Hold Me, Baby") 20-40   54
    Members: Carl Feaster; Claude Feaster; Jimmy Keys; Floyd
    McRae; William Edwards.
    Also see CHORDS

CHORDETTES
(Chordettes with Archie Bleyer)
          Singles: 78rpm
CADENCE 5-10   54-57
COLUMBIA 5-10   50-54
          Singles: 7–inch
BARNABY 3-5   70-76
CADENCE 8-15   54-63
COLUMBIA 10-15   50-54
ERIC 2-4   78
          Picture Sleeves
CADENCE 8-15   58-61
          EPs: 7–inch 33/45rpm
CADENCE 10-20   57-61
COLUMBIA (Except 201 through 401)   10-25   54-57
COLUMBIA (201 "Harmony Time") . . 30-40   50
(Four-disc boxed set.)
COLUMBIA (241 "Harmony Time,
Vol. 2") 30-40   51
(Four-disc boxed set.)
COLUMBIA (309 "Harmony Encores")   30-40   52
(Four-disc boxed set.)
COLUMBIA (401 "Your Requests") . . . 30-40   53
(Four-disc boxed set.)
          LPs: 10/12–inch 33rpm
BACK-TRAC 5-10
BARNABY 8-10   76
CADENCE (1002 "Close Harmony") . 20-30   55
CADENCE (3001 "The Chordettes") . 20-35   57

CADENCE (3020 "Barbershop
Harmonies") 20-30   58
CADENCE (3062 "Never on Sunday") 20-30   62
CADENCE (25062 "Never on
Sunday") 25-35   62
COLUMBIA (956 "Listen") 20-35   57
COLUMBIA (2519 "The Chordettes") . 25-35   56
(10-inch LP.)
COLUMBIA (6111 "Harmony Time") . . 30-40   50
(10-inch LP.)
COLUMBIA (6170 "Harmony Time,
Vol. 2") 30-40   51
(10-inch LP.)
COLUMBIA (6218 "Harmony
Encores") 30-40   52
(10-inch LP.)
COLUMBIA (6285 "Your Requests") . . 30-40   53
(10-inch LP.)
EVEREST 5-10   82
HARMONY 12-15   59
Members: Margie Needham; Janet Ertel; Carol Bushman; Lynn
Evans.
Also see BLEYER, Archie

CHORDS
Singles: 78rpm
CAT (104 "Sh-Boom"/"Cross over
the Bridge") 15-25   54
CAT (104 "Sh-Boom"/"Little Maiden") . 10-20   54
CAT (109 "Zippety Zum") 5-10   54
Singles: 7-inch
CAT (104 "Sh-Boom"/"Cross over
the Bridge") 50-75   54
CAT (104 "Sh-Boom"/"Little Maiden") . 20-40   54
CAT (109 "Zippety Zum") 15-25   54
Members: Carl Feaster; Claude Feaster; Jimmy Keys; Floyd
McRae; William Edwards.
Also see CHORDCATS
Also see SH-BOOMS

CHRIS & KATHY
Singles: 7-inch
MONOGRAM 10-15   64
Members: Chris Montez; Kathy Young.
Also see MONTEZ, Chris
Also see YOUNG, Kathy

CHRISTIAN, Chris
Singles: 7-inch
TESTA 5-10   59

CHRISTIE
Singles: 7-inch
EPIC 3-5   70-71
LPs: 10/12-inch 33rpm
EPIC 10-15   70
Members: Jeff Christie; Mike Blakely; Vic Elmes.

CHRISTIE, Dean
(Dean Christy)
Singles: 7-inch
MERCURY 4-8   63-64
SWL 5-10   62
SELECT (715 "Heart Breaker") 10-15   62

SELECT (718 "Teenage Jezebel") . . . 15-25   62
TOP FLIGHT (113 "So Much") 20-30

CHRISTIE, Janice
Singles: 12-inch
SUPERTRONICS 4-6   85-86

CHRISTIE, Lou
(Lou Christie and the Classics)
Singles: 12-inch 33/45rpm
PLATEAU (4551 "Guardian Angels") . 40-50   81
Singles: 7-inch
ABC 2-4   73
ALCAR (207 "Close Your Eyes") 15-20   63
ALCAR (208 "You're with It") 20-25   63
AMERICAN MUSIC MAKERS (006
"The Jury") 25-30
BUDDAH 5-15 68-72
C&C (102 "The Gypsy Cried") 75-100   62
CO & CE (235 "Outside the
Gates of Heaven") 5-10   66
COLPIX 6-12   64-66
COLUMBIA 10-15   67
EPIC 10-15   76
MGM (Except 13473) 5-10   65-66
MGM (13473 "Rhapsody in the Rain") 10-15   65
(With "making out in the rain" lyrics.)
MGM (13473 "Rhapsody in the Rain") . 5-10   65
(With "fell in love in the rain" lyrics.)
MIDLAND INT'L 10-15   76-77
MIDSONG 10-12   77
PLATEAU (4551 "Guardian Angels") . 40-50   81
ROULETTE (4457 "The Gypsy Cried") 15-20   62
(White label with color spokes.)
ROULETTE (4457 "The Gypsy Cried") 5-10   63
(Pink label.)
ROULETTE (4481 "Two Faces
Have I") 15-25   63
(White label with color spokes.)
ROULETTE (4481 "Two Faces
Have I") 5-10   63
(Pink label.)
ROULETTE (4457 through 4527) 5-10   62-63

ROULETTE (4545 "Stay") 10-15   64
ROULETTE (4554 "When You
  Dance") 20-25   64
SLIPPED DISC 10-15   76
THREE BROTHERS 5-15   73-75
WORLD (1002 "The Jury") 25-30

Picture Sleeves

COLPIX (799 "Big Time") 10-20   64
MGM (13473 "Rhapsody in the Rain") . 8-12   65
MGM (13533 "Painter") 8-12   66
MGM (13576 "If My Car
  Could Only Talk") 10-20   66

LPs: 10/12–inch 33rpm

BUDDAH (5052 "I'm Gonna
  Make You Mine") 10-15   69
BUDDAH (5073 "Paint America Love") 15-20   69
CO & CE (1231 "Lou Christie
  Strikes Back") 30-50   66
COLPIX (4001 "Lou Christie
  Strikes Again") 20-25   66
CSP (18260 "Lou Christie Does Detroit") 5-8
51 WEST ("Lou Christie Does Detroit") 10-15   83
MGM (4360 "Lightnin' Strikes") 12-18   66
MGM (4394 "Painter of Hits") 15-20   66
ROULETTE (25208 "Lou Christie") . . 50-60   63
  (Cover has a blue background.)
ROULETTE (25208 "Lou Christie") . . 30-40   63
  (Cover has white wall background.)
ROULETTE (25332 "Lou Christie
  Strikes Again") 20-30   63
  (Repackage of Co & Ce 1231, *Lou Christie Strikes*
  Back.)
THREE BROTHERS (2000 "Lou
  Christie") 15-20   74
  Also see CANTINA BAND
  Also see CLASSICS
  Also see CRITTERS / Young Rascals / Lou Christie
  Also see GORE, Leslie, and Lou Christie
  Also see LA RUE, D.C.
  Also see LUGEE and the Lions
  Also see MARCY JOE
  Also see SACCO

CHRISTIE, Lou / Dovells / Bobby Rydell / Tokens

LPs: 10/12–inch 33rpm

WYNCOTE 10-20
  Also see DOVELLS
  Also see RYDELL, Bobby
  Also see TOKENS

CHRISTIE, Lou, and the Classics / Isley Brothers / Chiffons

LPs: 10/12–inch 33rpm

SPIN-O-RAMA (173 "Lou Christie and
  the Classics") 20-30   66
  Also see CHIFFONS
  Also see ISLEY BROTHERS

CHRISTIE, Lou, and Pia Zadora

Singles: 7–inch

MIDSONG (72013 "Don't Knock
  My Love") 15-20

Also see CHRISTIE, Lou
Also see ZADORA, Pia

CHRISTIE, Susan

Singles: 7–inch

COLUMBIA 4-8   66-67

CHRISTMAS SPIRIT

Singles: 7–inch

WHITE WHALE (290 "Christmas Is My
  Time of Year") 50-75   69
  Members: Mark Volman; Howard Kaylan; Linda Ronstadt.
  Also see RONSTADT, Linda
  Also see TURTLES

CHRISTOPHER, Gavin

Singles: 7–inch

E.M.I. 2-4   88
ISLAND 3-5   76
MANHATTAN 2-4   86
RSO 2-4   79

LPs: 10/12–inch 33rpm

ISLAND 8-10   76
MANHATTAN 5-10   86
RSO 5-10   79

CHRISTOPHER, Paul and Shawn

Singles: 7–inch

CASABLANCA 3-5   75

CHRISTY, Chic

Singles: 7–inch

HAC 15-25   62
  Members: Lou Christie; Kay Chick; Susan Christie.
  Also see CHRISTIE, Lou

CHRISTY, Don
(Sonny Bono)

Singles: 7–inch

FIDELITY 10-15   60
GO 10-15   60
NAME 10-15   60
SPECIALTY 10-15   59
  Also see SONNY

CHRISTY, June

Singles: 78rpm

CAPITOL 3-8   51-57

Singles: 7–inch

CAPITOL (1800 through 3900
  series) 5-10   51-58
CAPITOL (4000 through 4800
  series) 3-8   59-62

EPs: 7–inch 33/4rpm

CAPITOL 5-15   53-55

LPs: 10/12–inch 33rpm

CAPITOL (516 "Something Cool") ... 25-40   54
  (With "H" prefix. 10–inch LP.)
CAPITOL (516 "Something Cool") ... 15-25   55
  (Green label. With "T" prefix.)
CAPITOL (516 "Something Cool") ... 10-20   60
  (Black label. With "T" or "ST" prefix.)
CAPITOL (516 "Something Cool") 5-10   75
  (With "SM" prefix.)

CAPITOL (600 through 900 series) .. 15-25   55-57
(Green label.)
CAPITOL (600 through 900 series) .. 10-15   60
(Black label.)
CAPITOL (1000 through 2400 series) 10-20   60-65
CAPITOL (11000 series) 5-10   79
DISCOVERY 5-10   82
SEABREEZE 5-10   80

CHRISTY, June, with Stan Kenton
EPs: 7-inch 33/45rpm
CAPITOL 5-10   56
LPs: 10/12-inch 33rpm
CAPITOL (656 "Duet") 20-35   56
(10-inch LP.)
Also see CHRISTY, June
Also see JONES, Jonah
Also see KENTON, Stan, and His Orchestra

CHUCKLES
(Featuring Teddy Randazzo)
Singles: 7-inch
ABC-PAR 5-10   61
Also see RANDAZZO, Teddy
Also see THREE CHUCKLES

CHUNG, Wang: see WANG CHUNG

CHURCH, Eugene
(Eugene Church and the Fellows)
Singles: 7-inch
CLASS 5-10   58-60
COLLECTABLES 2-4   81
KING 4-8   61-63
RENDEZVOUS 5-10   60
SPECIALTY 10-15   57
WORLD PACIFIC 4-8   67
Also see CLIQUES

CHURCHILL, Savannah
(Savannah Churchill and the Five Kings; Savannah
Churchill and the Striders; Savannah Churchill and
the Four Tunes)
Singles: 78rpm
ARGO 4-8   56
DECCA 4-8   53-55
KAY-RON 5-10   56
MANOR 5-10   45-48
RCA 5-10   51-52
REGAL (3309 "Once There Lived
a Fool") 25-50   50
REGAL (3313 "Wedding Bells") 5-10   50
Singles: 7-inch
ARGO 5-10   56
DECCA 5-10   53-55
JAMIE 4-8   60
KAY-RON 5-10   56
RCA 5-10   51-52
REGAL (3309 "Once There Lived
a Fool") 75-125   50
EPs: 7-inch 33/45rpm
CAMDEN (270 "Love and Sin") 35-50   55

CAMDEN (282 "Savannah
Churchill Sings") 35-50   55
Also see FOUR TUNES

CINDERELLA
Singles: 12-inch 33/45rpm
MERCURY 4-8   88
(Promotional only.)
Singles: 7-inch
MERCURY 2-4   86-90
Picture Sleeves
MERCURY 2-4   86-89
LPs: 10/12-inch 33rpm
MERCURY 5-10   86-90

CINDY & ROY
Singles: 12-inch 33/45rpm
CASABLANCA 4-8   79
Singles: 7-inch
CASABLANCA 2-4   79
LPs: 10/12-inch 33rpm
CASABLANCA 5-10   79

CIRCUS
Singles: 7-inch
METROMEDIA 3-5   72-73
LPs: 10/12-inch 33rpm
HEMISPHERE 10-15   74
METROMEDIA 15-25   73

CIRCUT
Singles: 12-inch 33/45rpm
4TH and BROADWAY 4-6   84-85

CISSEL, Chuck
Singles: 7-inch
ARISTA 2-4   79-80
LPs: 10/12-inch 33rpm
ARISTA 5-10   80

CISSEL, Chuck, and Marva King
Singles: 7-inch
ARISTA 2-4   82
Also see CISSEL, Chuck

CITY
LPs: 10/12-inch 33rpm
CHRYSALIS 5-10   86

CITY BOY
Singles: 7-inch
AIRBOY 2-5   77
ATLANTIC 2-4   79-81
MERCURY 3-5   76-78
LPs: 10/12-inch 33rpm
ATLANTIC 5-10   80
MERCURY 8-10   76-78
Members: Steve Broughton; Lol Mason; Mike Slamer; Max
Thomas; Roy Ward; Chris Dunn; Roger Kent.

CLANCY BROTHERS
(Clancy Brothers and Lou Killen; Clancy Brothers and
Robbie O'Connell)
LPs: 10/12-inch 33rpm
AUDIO FIDELITY 8-12   71-73

COLUMBIA 8-15	70	
VANGUARD 5-12	74-83	

CLANCY BROTHERS and Tommy Makem
Singles: 7–inch

COLUMBIA 3-6	62-69	

LPs: 10/12–inch 33rpm

COLUMBIA 10-20	62-69	
HARMONY 6-10	71-72	
SHANACHIE 5-10		
TRADITION 10-15	67-69	
Also see CLANCY BROTHERS		

CLANNAD
LPs: 10/12–inch 33rpm

RCA 5-10	84-88	

CLANTON, Ike
Singles: 7–inch

ACE 5-10	59-60	
MERCURY 4-8	62-63	
Also see DEL-VIKINGS / Ike Clanton		

CLANTON, Jimmy
(Jimmie Clanton)
Singles: 78rpm

ACE 10-15	57	

Singles: 7–inch

ABC 2-4	73	
ACE 5-10	57-63	
(Monaural.)		
ACE (567 "My Own True Love") 15-25	59	
(Stereo.)		
COLLECTABLES 2-4	81	
ERIC 2-4	73	
IMPERIAL 4-8	67-68	
LAURIE 4-6	69	
MALA 4-8	65	
OLDIES 45 3-5		
PHILIPS 4-8	63-64	
SPIRAL 3-5	71	
STARCREST 3-5	76	
STARFIRE 3-5	78	
VIN 4-8	62	

Promotional Singles

ACE (644 "Venus in Blue Jeans") 10-20	62	
ACE (51860 "The Slave") 8-15	60	
(Promotional, bonus disc with the *Jimmy's*		
Happy/Jimmy's Blue LP.)		
U.A. ("Teenage Millionaire") 5-10	62	
(Cardboard 5–inch flexi-disc.)		

Picture Sleeves

ACE (Except 51860) 8-15	59-63	
ACE (51860 "The Slave") 15-25	60	
(Promotional only, mail-order bonus offer to buyers		
of the *Jimmy's Happy/Jimmy's Blue* LP. All copies		
of this sleeve were autographed by Clanton.)		
PHILIPS 5-10	64	
STARCREST 4-6	76	

EPs: 7–inch 33/45rpm

ACE (Black vinyl) 20-35	59-61	

ACE (Colored vinyl) 35-50	60	

LPs: 10/12–inch 33rpm

ACE (100 "Jimmy's Happy/		
Jimmy's Blue") 60-80	60	
(Black vinyl.)		
ACE (100 "Jimmy's Happy/		
Jimmy's Blue") 75-125	60	
(Colored vinyl.)		
ACE (1001 "Just a Dream") 50-75	59	
ACE (1007 "Jimmy's Happy") 40-50	60	
ACE (1008 "Jimmy's Blue") 40-50	60	
ACE (1011 "My Best to You") 50-75	61	
ACE (1014 "Teenage Millionaire") ... 50-75	61	
ACE (1026 "Venus in Blue Jeans") .. 40-60	61	
PHILIPS 15-25	64	
Also see DALE, Jimmy		

CLANTON, Jimmy / Frankie Ford / Jerry Lee Lewis / Patsy Cline
EPs: 7–inch 33/45rpm

MEMORY LANE 3-5	92	
(Promotional issue only.)		
Also see CLINE, Patsy		
Also see FORD, Frankie		
Also see LEWIS, Jerry Lee		

CLANTON, Jimmy / Bristow Hopper
LPs: 10/12–inch 33rpm

DESIGN 10-20	

CLANTON, Jimmy, and Mary Ann Mobley
Singles: 7–inch

ACE 5-10	61	

Picture Sleeves

ACE 10-15	61	
Also see CLANTON, Jimmy		

CLAPTON, Eric
Singles: 12–inch 33/45rpm

WARNER (2248 "Forever Man") 5-10	
(Promotional issue only.)	

Singles: 7–inch

ATCO 4-6	70-71	
DUCK 2-4	83-86	
POLYDOR 3-5	72-73	
RSO 3-5	74-82	

Picture Sleeves

DUCK 2-4	85-89	
RSO 3-5	80-81	

LPs: 10/12–inch 33rpm

ATCO (329 "Eric Clapton") 20-30	70	
ATCO (803 "History of Eric Clapton")	20-30	72
DUCK 5-10	83-89	
MFSL (030 "Slowhand") 25-50	79	
MFSL (183 "Bluesbreakers") 15-20	87	
POLYDOR 8-12	72-73	
RSO 8-15	73-82	
Also see BLIND FAITH		
Also see COOLIDGE, Rita		
Also see CREAM		
Also see CURTIS, Sonny		
Also see DELANEY and Bonnie and Friends		
Also see DEREK and the Dominoes		

Also see GUY, Buddy, with Dr. John and Eric Clapton / Buddy
Guy with the J. Geils Band
Also see HARRISON, George
Also see LEVY, Marcy
Also see LOMAX, Jackie
Also see MAYALL, John
Also see RUSSELL, Leon
Also see STARR, Ringo
Also see TOWNSHEND, Pete, and Ronnie Lane
Also see WATERS, Roger
Also see YARDBIRDS

CLAPTON, Eric, Jeff Beck and Jimmy Page
LPs: 10/12–inch 33rpm

RCA (4624 "Guitar Boogie") 10-15   71
Also see BECK, Jeff
Also see PAGE, Jimmy

CLAPTON, Eric, and Tina Turner
Singles: 7–inch

DUCK 2-4   87

Picture Sleeves

DUCK 2-4   87
Also see CLAPTON, Eric
Also see TURNER, Tina

CLARK, Chris
Singles: 7–inch

MOTOWN 4-8   67-68
V.I.P. 5-10   65-67

LPs: 10/12–inch 33rpm

MOTOWN 12-15   67
WEED 10-15

CLARK, Claudine
(Claudine Clark and the Spinners)
Singles: 7–inch

CHANCELLOR 5-10   62-63
COLLECTABLES 2-4   81
ERIC 2-4   73
HERALD (521 "Teenage Blues") 20-30   58
JAMIE 4-8   64

LPs: 10/12–inch 33rpm

CHANCELLOR (5029 "Party Lights") . 40-60   62

CLARK, Dave, Five
(Dave Clark and Friends)
Singles: 7–inch

CONGRESS (212 "I Knew It All
the Time") 10-15   64
EPIC 5-10   64-72
JUBILEE (5476 "Chaquita") 10-20   64
LAURIE (3188 "I Walk the Line") 25-35   63
RUST (5078 "I Walk the Line") 20-30   64

Promotional Singles

EPIC (Black vinyl) 10-15   65-72
EPIC (Colored vinyl) 15-25   65

Picture Sleeves

CONGRESS (212 "I Knew It All
the Time") 15-25   64
EPIC 8-15   64-70

EPs: 7–inch 33/45rpm

COLUMBIA 20-40   64-65
EPIC 15-25   66
(Jukebox issues only.)

LPs: 10/12–inch 33rpm

CUSTOM (1098 "It's Happening") . . . 15-20
EPIC (24093 "Glad All Over") 75-125   64
(Instruments are not pictured on cover.)
EPIC (24093 "Glad All Over") 20-30   64
(Instruments are pictured on cover.)
EPIC (24104 "The Dave Clark
Five Return") 20-30   64
EPIC (24117 "American Tour") 20-30   64
EPIC (24128 "Coast to Coast") 20-30   64
EPIC (24139 "A Weekend in London") 20-30   65
EPIC (24162 "Having a
Wild Weekend") 20-30   65
EPIC (24178 "I Like It Like That") . . . 20-30   65
EPIC (24185 "Greatest Hits") 20-30   66
EPIC (24198 "Try too Hard") 20-30   66
EPIC (24212 "Satisfied with You") . . . 20-30   66
EPIC (24221 "More Greatest Hits") . . 20-30   66
EPIC (24236 "5 By 5") 20-30   67
EPIC (24312 "You Got What It Takes") 20-30   67
EPIC (24354 "Everybody Knows") . . . 20-30   68
EPIC (26000 series) 15-25   64-68
(Reprocessed stereo series.)
EPIC (30434 "Dave Clark Five") 35-50   71
EPIC (33459 "Glad All Over Again") . 20-25   75

Promotional LPs

EPIC (77238 "The Dave Clark
Interviews") 40-45   65
I-N-S RADIO NEWS (1006 "It's
Here Luv") 75-100   64
Members: Dave Clark; Mike Smith; Lenny Davidson; Denny
Payton; Rick Huxley.

CLARK, Dave, Five / Rick Astor and the Switchers
LPs: 10/12–inch 33rpm

CORTLEIGH (1073 "Dave Clark
Five") 15-25   66
(Has only two Dave Clark Five tracks.)

CLARK, Dave, Five / Lulu
Singles: 7–inch

EPIC (10260/65 "Everybody Knows"/
"Best of Both Worlds") 10-20   67
(Promotional issue only.)
Also see LULU

CLARK, Dave, Five / Playbacks
LPs: 10/12–inch 33rpm

CROWN (400 "Playbacks") 20-25   64
(Stereo.)
CROWN (5400 "Playbacks") 20-25   64
(Monaural.)
CROWN (473 "Chaquita - In
Your Heart") 20-25   65
(Stereo.)
CROWN (5473 "Chaquita - In
Your Heart") 20-25   65
(Monaural.)
(Crown LPs have only two DC5 tracks on each.)
Also see CLARK, Dave, Five

CLARK, Dee
Singles: 7–inch
ABC	2-4	73
ABNER (Monaural)	8-15	58-60
ABNER (Stereo)	20-25	59-60
CHELSEA	3-5	75
COLLECTABLES	2-4	83
ERIC	2-4	73
COLUMBIA	4-8	67
CONSTELLATION	4-8	63-65
FALCON	15-25	58
LIBERTY	3-5	70
MCA	2-4	84
ROCKY	3-5	73
VEE JAY (Monaural)	5-10	60-63
VEE JAY (Stereo)	15-25	60-63
U.A.	3-5	71
WAND	4-8	68
WARNER	3-5	73

Picture Sleeves
ABNER	15-25	59

EPs: 7–inch 33/45rpm
ABNER (900 "Dee Clark")	40-60	61
VEE JAY (900 "Dee Clark")	25-50	61

LPs: 10/12–inch 33rpm
ABNER (LP-2000 "Dee Clark") (Monaural.)	40-60	59
ABNER (SR-2000 "Dee Clark") (Stereo.)	50-75	59
ABNER (LP-2002 "How About That") (Monaural.)	40-60	59
ABNER (SR-2002 "How About That") (Stereo.)	50-75	59
SOLID SMOKE	5-10	84
SUNSET (5217 "Wondering")	10-15	68
VEE JAY (1019 "You're Looking Good")	20-30	60
VEE JAY (1028 "Dee Clark")	20-30	61
VEE JAY (1037 "Hold On, It's Dee Clark")	20-30	61
VEE JAY (1047 "The Best of Dee Clark")	20-30	64

Also see SAUNDERS, Red

CLARK, Gene
(Gene Clark and the Gosdin Brothers)
Singles: 7–inch
ASYLUM	3-5	74
COLUMBIA (43000 series)	5-8	66
RSO	2-4	77

LPs: 10/12–inch 33rpm
A&M	10-15	71
ASYLUM	8-10	74
COLUMBIA (2618 "Gene Clark") (Monaural.)	20-30	67
COLUMBIA (9418 "Gene Clark") (Stereo.)	25-35	67
COLUMBIA (31123 "Early L.A. Sessions")	10-15	72

RSO	5-10	77
RUMOR	3-5	80
TAKOMA	5-10	84

Also see BYRDS

CLARK, Petula
(Pet Clark)
Singles: 78rpm
CORAL	5-10	53-54
KING	5-10	54
MGM	5-10	55

Singles: 7–inch
CORAL	10-20	53-54
DUNHILL	3-5	74
ERIC	2-4	83
IMPERIAL	5-10	59-60
JANUS	3-5	76
KING	10-20	54
LAURIE	4-8	62-63
LONDON	4-8	62
MGM (12000 series)	10-20	55
MGM (14000 series)	3-6	72-74
ROWE/AMI	5-10	66

("Play Me" Sales Stimulator promotional issue.)
SCOTTI BROTHERS	2-4	82
WARNER	3-8	64-69
WARWICK	5-10	61

EPs: 7–inch 33/45rpm
WARNER	5-10	65-66

(Jukebox issues only.)

LPs: 10/12–inch 33rpm
GNP/CRESCENDO	8-10	73
IMPERIAL (9079 "Pet Clark") (Monaural.)	15-25	65
IMPERIAL (12027 "Pet Clark") (Stereo.)	20-30	65
LAURIE (2032 "In Love") (Monaural.)	20-25	65
LAURIE (S-2032 "In Love") (Stereo.)	25-35	65
LAURIE (2043 "Petula Clark Sings for Everybody") (Monaural.)	15-20	65
LAURIE (2043 "Petula Clark Sings for Everybody") (Stereo.)	20-25	65
MGM	8-12	72
PREMIER	15-25	64
SUNSET	10-20	66
WARNER	10-20	65-71

Also see FELICIANO, Jose / Petula Clark

CLARK, Roy
Singles: 7–inch
ABC	2-4	74-79
ABC/DOT	2-4	75-77
CAPITOL	4-8	61-66
CHURCHILL	2-4	82-84
DOT	2-5	68-74
MCA	2-4	79-84

EPIC (3008 "London Calling") 5-8   80
(Hall of Fame series.)
EPIC (3245 "Should I Stay") 15-20   82
(Single sided disc. Promotional issue only.)
EPIC (5749 "Train in Vain") 15-20   79
(10–inch single. Promotional issue only.)
EPIC (5799 "Clampdown") 15-20   79
(10–inch single. Promotional issue only.)
EPIC (8470 "Should I Stay") 5-8   82
(Hall of Fame series.)
EPIC (20000 series) 3-5   82
EPIC (30000 series) 3-5   82
EPIC (50000 series, except
50738, 50851 and 51013) 3-5   79-81
EPIC (50738 "White Man in
Hammersmith Palais") 5-10   79
EPIC (50851 "Train in Vain") 10-15   79
(Promotional issue only.)
EPIC (51013 "Hitsville UK") 10-15   80
(Promotional issue only.)

Picture Sleeves
EPIC (2479 "Rock the Casbah") 5-10   82
(With set of four stickers, add $3 to $5.)
EPIC (3061 "Should I Stay") 10-15   82
(Shown as "Special Limited Edition.")
EPIC (3547 "Should I Stay") 5-10   82
(Lists B-side, *Cool Confusion*.)
EPIC (3547 "Should I Stay") 10-15   82
(No B-side shown. Promotional issue only.)

LPs: 10/12–inch 33rpm
EPIC (913 "Sandinista Now") 15-20   80
(Promotional issue only.)
EPIC (952 "If Music Could Talk") 15-20   81
(Promotional issue only.)
EPIC (1574 "World According
to Clash") 30-35   82
Black cover, with printing.)
EPIC (1574 "World According
to Clash") 25-30   82
Black cover, with no printing.)
EPIC (35543 "Give 'Em Enough Rope") 5-10   78
(Blue label.)
EPIC (35543 "Give 'Em
Enough Rope") 10-15   78
(White label. Promotional issue only. With insert.)
EPIC (36060 "The Clash") 5-10   79
EPIC (36060 "The Clash") 15-20   79
(White label. Promotional issue only. With lyric
insert and bonus single, #1178 *Gates of the West*.)
EPIC (36328 "London Calling") 10-15   79
EPIC (36328 "London Calling") 15-20   79
(White label. Promotional issue only. With lyric
sleeve.)
EPIC (37037 "Sandinista") 15-20   80
(White label. Promotional issue only. With
Armagideon Times #3.)
EPIC (37037 "Sandinista") 10-15   80
(With *Armagideon Times #3*.)

EPIC (37689 "Combat Rock") 8-10   82
(Black label. Has "2000 flushes" segment in
Inoculated City.)
EPIC (37689 "Combat Rock") 5-8   82
(Blue label. "2000 flushes" segment is edited out of
Inoculated City.)
EPIC (37689 "Combat Rock") 10-15   82
(White label. Promotional issue only. With lyric
sleeve.)
EPIC (37689 "Combat Rock") 25-30   82
(Limited edition, camouflage vinyl. Promotional
issue only. With "Face the Future" sticker.)
EPIC (38540 "Black Market Clash") ... 5-10   80
EPIC (40017 "Cut the Crap") 5-10   85
EPIC (40017 "Cut the Crap") 10-15   85
(White label. Promotional issue only.)
EPIC (44035 "Story of the Clash") ... 10-15   88
EPIC/NU-DISC (36846 "Black
Market Clash") 10-15   80
(10–inch LP.)
Members: Joe Strummer; Mick Jones; Nick Sheppard; Pete
Howard; Paul Simonon; Topper Headon; Terry Chimes; Vince
White.
Also see BIG AUDIO DYNAMITE

CLASSIC SULLIVANS
Singles: 7–Inch
KWANZA 3-5   73

CLASSICS
Singles: 7–inch
STARR (508 "Close Your Eyes") .. 100-125   60
(Reissued on Alcar 207, as by Lou Christie and the
Classics.)
Members: Lou Christie; Kay Chick; Shirley Herbert; Ken Krease.
Also see CHRISTIE, Lou
Also see LUGEE and the Lions

CLASSICS
Singles: 7–Inch
COLLECTABLES 2-4   83
DART (1015 "Cinderella") 20-25   60
DART (1024 "Life Is But a Dream") .. 60-80   61
DART (1032 "Angel Angela") 20-25   61
ERIC 2-4   82
MERCURY 15-20   61
MUSIC NOTE 5-10   63
MUSICTONE 5-10
PICCOLO 5-10   65
STORK 5-10   64
STREAM LINE 5-10   61
Members: Emil Stuccio; Tony Victor; John Gamble; Jamie Troy.

CLASSICS IV
(Dennis Yost and the Classics IV; Classics)
Singles: 7–inch
ARLEN 10-20   64
CAPITOL 10-15   66-67
IMPERIAL 4-8   67-70
LIBERTY 3-5   70
MGM 3-5   75
MGM/SOUTH 3-5   72-73
U.A. 3-5   71

LPs: 10/12–inch 33rpm

ACCORD	5-10	81
IMPERIAL	12-20	68-69
LIBERTY (10000 series)	5-10	82-83
LIBERTY (11000 series)	10-12	70
MGM/SOUNDS of the SOUTH	8-10	73
SUNSET	10-12	70
U.A.	8-10	75

Members: Dennis Yost; James Cobb; Dean Daughtry; Wally Eaton; Auburn Burrell; Kim Venable; Joe Wilson.
Also see ATLANTA RHYTHM SECTION
Also see CANDYMEN
Also see YOST, Dennis

THE CHAMP SINGS!

STAND BY ME and I AM THE GREATEST

CASSIUS CLAY
ON COLUMBIA RECORDS

CLAY, Cassius
(Cassius Marcellus Clay Jr; Muhammed Ali)
Singles: 7–inch

COLUMBIA (43007 "Stand By Me")	10-20	64
COLUMBIA (75717 "Will the Real Sonny Liston Please Fall Down")	25-40	64
(Promotional issue only.)		

Picture Sleeves

COLUMBIA (43007 "Stand By Me")	25-35	64

LPs: 10/12–inch 33rpm

COLUMBIA (2093 "I Am the Greatest")	30-40	63
(Monaural.)		
COLUMBIA (8893 "I Am the Greatest")	35-45	63
(Stereo.)		

CLAY, Judy
Singles: 7–inch

ATLANTIC	3-5	69-70
EMBER	5-10	61-62
SCEPTER	4-8	64-66
STAX	4-6	68-69

Also see BELL, William, and Judy Clay
Also see VERA, Billy, and Judy Clay

CLAY, Otis
Singles: 12–inch 33/45rpm

PAULA	4-8	85

Singles: 7–inch

COTILLION	3-6	68-71
DAKAR	3-6	69
ELKA	3-5	75

HI	3-5	72-73
KAYVETTE	3-5	77
ONE-DERFUL	4-8	65-67

LPs: 10/12–inch 33rpm

HI	8-12	73-77

CLAY, Tom
(Tom Clay and the Blackberries; Tom Clay and the Raybor Voices)
Singles: 7–inch

BIG TOP	10-15	60
CHANT (103 "Never Before")	20-25	59
MOTOWN	2-4	81
MOWEST	3-5	71
OFFICIAL IBBB INTERVIEW ("Remember, We Don't Like Them, We Love Them")	15-25	64
(Tom Clay interviews the Beatles. Promotional issue only.)		

LPs: 10/12–inch 33rpm

MOWEST	10-15	71

Also see BEATLES

CLAYDERMAN, Richard
LPs: 10/12–inch 33rpm

COLUMBIA	5-8	84

CLAYTON, Merry
Singles: 7–inch

CAPITOL	4-8	63-65
MCA	2-4	80-88
ODE '70	3-5	70-76

LPs: 10/12–inch 33rpm

MCA	5-10	80
ODE (34000 series)	5-10	77
ODE (77000 series)	10-12	71-75

Also see BEACH BOYS
Also see SCOTT, Tom
Also see SMITH, Leslie, and Merry Clayton
Also see WYCOFF, Michael

CLAYTON, Willie
Singles: 7–inch

COMPLEAT	2-4	85

CLAYTON-THOMAS, David
Singles: 7–inch

COLUMBIA	3-5	72
DECCA	4-6	69
RCA	3-5	73

LPs: 10/12–inch 33rpm

ABC	5-10	78
COLUMBIA	10-15	72
DECCA	15-20	69
RCA	8-12	73-74

Also see BLOOD, SWEAT & TEARS

CLEAN LIVING
Singles: 7–inch

VANGUARD	3-5	72

LPs: 10/12–inch 33rpm

VANGUARD	8-10	72-73

CLEAR LIGHT
Singles: 7-inch
ELEKTRA 4-8   67
LPs: 10/12-inch 33rpm
ELEKTRA (4011 "Clear Light") 15-20   67
Members: Cliff DeYoung; Douglas Lubahn; Michael Ney; Ralph
Schuckett; Bob Seal; Dallas Taylor.

CLEFS of LAVENDER HILL
Singles: 7-inch
DATE 10-20   66-67
THAMES ("Stop! Get a Ticket") 25-35   66
(Number not known.)

CLEFTONES
(Herb Cox and the Cleftones)
Singles: 78rpm
GEE 15-25   56-57
Singles: 7-inch
ABC 2-4   73
CLASSIC ARTISTS 3-5   90
GEE (Red label) 15-25   56-58
GEE (Gray label) 5-10   61-63
ROULETTE (4000 series) 8-12   58-60
ROULETTE GOLDEN GOODIES 3-5
WARE 5-10   64
LPs: 10/12-inch 33rpm
GEE (GLP-705 "Heart and Soul") . 100-150   61
(Monaural.)
GEE (SGLP-705 "Heart and
Soul") 150-200   61
(Stereo.)
GEE (GLP-707 "For Sentimental
Reasons") 150-200   62
(Monaural.)
GEE (SGLP-707 "For Sentimental
Reasons") 200-250   62
(Stereo.)
Members: Herbie Cox; Berman Patterson; Bill McClain; Charles
James; Warren Corbin; Pat Span; Eugene Pearson.
Also see DRIFTERS
Also see HARPTONES / Cleftones

CLEMMONS, Angela
Singles: 12-inch 33/45rpm
PORTRAIT 4-6   82
Singles: 7-inch
EPIC 2-4   80
PORTRAIT 2-4   82-87
LPs: 10/12-inch 33rpm
PORTRAIT 5-10   82

CLEMONS, Clarence
(Clarence Clemons and the Red Bank Rockers)
Singles: 7-inch
COLUMBIA 2-4   83-85
LPs: 10/12-inch 33rpm
COLUMBIA 5-10   83-85
Also see BROWNE, Jackson
Also see FRANKLIN, Aretha
Also see SPRINGSTEEN, Bruce

CLIFF, Jimmy
Singles: 12-inch 33/45rpm
COLUMBIA 4-6   83-84
Singles: 7-inch
A&M 3-6   69-70
COLUMBIA 2-4   82-84
MANGO 3-5   73-75
MCA 3-5   81
REPRISE 3-5   74-77
VEEP 4-8   67-68
LPs: 10/12-inch 33rpm
A&M 10-20   70
COLUMBIA 5-10   82
ISLAND 8-10   74
MCA 5-10   80-81
MANGO 8-10   75
REPRISE 8-10   73-76
VEEP 15-20   69
WARNER 5-10   78

CLIFF, Jimmy, with Elvis Costello and the Attractions
Singles: 12-inch 33/45rpm
COLUMBIA 5-10   86
(Promotional issue only.)
Also see CLIFF, Jimmy
Also see COSTELLO, Elvis

CLIFFORD, Buzz
Singles: 7-inch
BOW 5-10
CAPITOL 4-8   67
COLUMBIA (41876 "Baby Sittin'
Boogie") 30-50   60
(With "3" prefix. Compact 33 Single.)
COLUMBIA (41979 "Simply Because") 30-50   61
(With "3" prefix. Compact 33 Single.)
COLUMBIA (42019 "I'll Never Forget") 30-50   61
(With "3" prefix. Compact 33 Single.)
COLUMBIA (42290 "Forever") 30-50   62
(With "3" prefix. Compact 33 Single.)
COLUMBIA (41774 "Hello Mr.
Moonlight") 10-15   60
(With "4" prefix.)
COLUMBIA (41876 "Baby Sitter
Boogie") 20-30   60
(Note slightly different title. With "4" prefix.)
COLUMBIA (41876 "Baby Sittin'
Boogie") 5-10   61
(With "4" prefix.)
COLUMBIA (41979 "Simply Because") 15-25   61
(With "4" prefix.)
COLUMBIA (42019 "I'll Never Forget") 15-25   61
(With "4" prefix.)
COLUMBIA (42177 "Moving Day") ... 5-10   61
(With "4" prefix.)
COLUMBIA (42290 "Forever") 15-25   62
(With "4" prefix.)
DOT 4-6   69-70
ERIC 2-4   83

RCA 4-8   66
ROULETTE 4-8   62-63
Picture Sleeves
COLUMBIA 15-20   61-62
LPs: 10/12–inch 33rpm
COLUMBIA (1616 "Baby Sittin'
Boogie") 40-60   61
(Monaural.)
COLUMBIA (8416 "Baby Sittin'
Boogie") 50-75   61
(Monaural.)
DOT 15-20   69

CLIFFORD, Linda
Singles: 12–inch 33/45rpm
CAPITOL 4-6   82
RSO 4-8   79
RED LABEL 4-6   85
Singles: 7–inch
CAPITOL 2-4   80-82
CURTOM 2-4   77-78
GEMIGO 3-5   75
PARAMOUNT 3-5   74
POLYDOR 3-5   73
RSO 2-4   79-80
RED LABEL 2-4   84-85
LPs: 10/12–inch 33rpm
CAPITOL 5-10   80-82
CURTOM 8-10   77-80
RSO 5-10   79-80
Also see MAYFIELD, Curtis, and Linda Clifford

CLIFFORD, Mike
Singles: 7–inch
AIR 3-5   71
AMERICAN INT'L 3-5   70
CAMEO 4-8   65-66
COLUMBIA 4-8   61-62
LIBERTY 5-10   59
SIDEWALK 4-8   67-68
U.A. 4-8   62-65
Picture Sleeves
COLUMBIA 5-10   61
LPs: 10/12–inch 33rpm
U.A. 15-25   65

CLIFFORD, Mike, and Patience and Prudence
Singles: 7–inch
LIBERTY 5-10   59
Also see CLIFFORD, Mike
Also see PATIENCE & PRUDENCE

CLIMAX
Singles: 7–inch
ARISTA 2-4   81
BELL 3-5   71
CAROUSEL 3-5   70-71
FLASHBACK 2-4   73
PARAMOUNT 3-5   70
PATTI PLATTERS 4-8   67
ROCKY ROAD 3-5   72

LPs: 10/12–inch 33rpm
ROCKY ROAD 12-15   72
Members: Sonny Geraci; John Bahler; Tom Bahler; Jon Jon
Gultman; Walt Nims.
Also see LOVE GENERATION
Also see OUTSIDERS

CLIMAX BLUES BAND
Singles: 7–inch
SIRE 3-5   71-79
WARNER 2-4   79-82
LPs: 10/12–inch 33rpm
SIRE (Except 6000 series) 10-15   69-76
SIRE (6000 series) 8-10   77-79
VIRGIN 5-10   83
WARNER 5-10   79-81
Members: Climax Chicago Blues Band; Colin Cooper; John
Cuffley; Peter Haycock; Derek Holt; Richard Jones; Arthur Wood.

CLINE, Patsy
Singles: 78rpm
CORAL 5-10   55-56
DECCA 5-10   57
Singles: 7–inch
CORAL 10-20   55-56
DECCA (25000 series) 3-8   65-69
DECCA (29963 through 30846) 8-12   57-59
DECCA (30929 "Gotta Lot of
Rhythm in My Soul") 10-15   59
DECCA (31000 series) 4-8   59-64
EVEREST (2000 series) 4-8   62-64
EVEREST (20005 "I Don't Wanta") .. 10-15   62
4 STAR (11 "Hidin' Out") 5-10   56
4 STAR (1033 "Life's Railway
to Heaven") 3-5   78
KAPP 4-8   65
MCA 3-5   73-80
STARDAY (7000 series) 4-8   65
STARDAY (8000 series) 3-5   71
Picture Sleeves
DECCA (Except 30221) 5-10   62-63
DECCA (30221 "Walkin After
Midnight") 15-20   62-63
EPs: 7–inch 33/45rpm
CORAL 20-30   58
DECCA 10-25   57-65
4 STAR 25-35   57
PATSY CLINE 25-35   57
LPs: 10/12–inch 33rpm
ACCORD 5-10   81
ALBUM GLOBE 5-10
ALLEGIANCE 5-10   84
COLUMBIA 12-15   69
(Columbia Musical Treasury issue.)
COUNTRY FIDELITY 5-10   82
DECCA (176 "The Patsy Cline Story") 25-40   63
(Includes booklet.)
DECCA (4200 series) 20-30   61-62
DECCA (4500 series) 15-25   64
DECCA (4800 series) 10-15   67
DECCA (8611 "Patsy Cline") 30-45   57

When I Get Through With You

c/w

Imagine That

PATSY CLINE

DECCA ◆
31377

EVEREST (300 series)	5-10	75
EVEREST (1200 series)	15-20	62-64
51 WEST	5-10	82
H.S.R.D.	8-10	84
LONGINES	8-12	
MCA	5-10	80-89
METRO	10-20	65
PICKWICK/HILLTOP	10-12	65-68
SEARS	10-15	
VOCALION	10-15	65-69

   Also see CLANTON, Jimmy / Frankie Ford / Jerry Lee Lewis /
     Patsy Cline
   Also see HAGGARD, Merle / Patsy Cline
   Also see KERR, Anita
   Also see REEVES, Jim, and Patsy Cline

CLINE, Patsy / Cowboy Copas / Hawkshaw Hawkins
LPs: 10/12–inch 33rpm

STARDAY	15-20	65

   Also see COPAS, Cowboy
   Also see HAWKINS, Hawkshaw

CLINE, Patsy / Hank Locklin / Miller
Brothers / Eddie Marvin
EPs: 7–inch 33/45rpm

4 STAR (136 Hidin' Out")	25-50	56

(Promotional 10–inch, 45 rpm. Not issued with
cover.)
   Also see LOCKLIN, Hank

CLINE, Patsy / Pete Pike / Jack
Bradshaw / Miller Brothers
EPs: 7–inch 33/45rpm

4 STAR (137 "Come on In")	25-50	56

(Promotional 10–inch, 45 rpm. Not issued with
cover.)
   Also see CLINE, Patsy
   Also see CLINE, Patsy / Hank Locklin / Miller Brothers / Eddie
    Marvin

CLINTON, George
(George Clinton Band)
Singles: 12–inch 33/45rpm

CAPITOL	4-6	82-86

Singles: 7–inch

ABC	2-4	74

CAPITOL	2-4	83-86
PAISLEY PARK	2-4	89

LPs: 10/12–inch 33rpm

ABC	8-10	74
CAPITOL	5-10	82-86
INVICTUS	10-12	73
PAISLEY PARK	5-8	89

   Also see PARLIAMENTS

CLIQUE
Singles: 7–inch

ABC	2-4	73
CINEMA (001 "Splash")	25-35	67
SCEPTER	10-20	67
WHITE WHALE	8-15	69-71

LPs: 10/12–inch 33rpm

WHITE WHALE (7126 "The Clique") .	20-25	69

CLIQUES
Singles: 78rpm

MODERN	10-15	56

Singles: 7–inch

MODERN (987 "The Girl
in My Dreams"	20-30	56

   Members: Jesse Belvin; Eugene Church.
   Also see BELVIN, Jesse
   Also see CHURCH, Eugene

CLOCKS
Singles: 7–inch

BOULEVARD	2-4	82

LPs: 10/12–inch 33rpm

BOULEVARD	5-10	82

CLOCKWORK
Singles: 12–inch 33/45rpm

PRIVATE I	4-6	84

Singles: 7–inch

PRIVATE I	2-4	84

CLOONEY, Rosemary
Singles: 78rpm

COLUMBIA	3-6	50-57

Singles: 7–inch

APCO	3-5	75
COLUMBIA	5-10	50-57
CORAL	4-8	59
DOT	3-6	68
GIBSON/COLUMBIA	10-15	55

("Musicards," with fold-out covers.)

MGM	3-8	59-65
RCA	3-6	60-61
REPRISE	3-6	63-64
SATURDAY EVENING POST (1055 "Hollywood's
Favorite Songbird")	15-20	54

(Promotional issue only. Includes interview script.)

Picture Sleeves

RCA	4-8	60

EPs: 7–inch 33/45rpm

COLUMBIA	10-20	51-56
MGM	5-10	58-60

LPs: 10/12–inch 33rpm

COLUMBIA (500 through 1200
series, except 6297) 15-25   54-58
COLUMBIA (6297 "While
We're Young") 25-35   51
(10–inch LP.)
CONCORD JAZZ 5-10   78-83
CORAL 10-15   59
HARMONY 8-15   59-68
MGM (Except 1000 series) 10-15   59-62
MGM (1000 series) 8-12   67
RCA 10-15   60-63
REPRISE 8-15   63-64
Also see BOYD, Jimmy, and Rosemary Clooney
Also see CROSBY, Bing, Louis Armstrong, Rosemary Clooney
and the Hi-Los
Also see GOODMAN, Benny, Trio, with Rosemary Clooney
Also see HERMAN, Woody

CLOONEY, Rosemary, and Bing Crosby
Singles: 7–inch
RCA 4-8   59
LPs: 10/12–inch 33rpm
CAMDEN 6-10   69
CAPITOL (2300 series) 8-12   65
CAPITOL (11000 series) 5-10   77
Also see CROSBY, Bing

CLOONEY, Rosemary, and Jose Ferrer
EPs: 7–inch 33/45rpm
MGM 10-20   58
Also see FERRER, Jose

CLOONEY, Rosemary, and the Hi-Los
EPs: 7–inch 33/45rpm
COLUMBIA 5-10   57
LPs: 10/12–inch 33rpm
COLUMBIA (1006 "Ring
Around Rosie") 20-25   57

CLOONEY, Rosemary, and Dick Haymes
LPs: 10/12–inch 33rpm
EXACT 5-10   80
Also see HAYMES, Dick

CLOONEY, Rosemary, and Guy Mitchell
(With Joanne Gilbert)
EPs: 7–inch 33/45rpm
COLUMBIA (377 "Red Garters") 15-20   54
(Soundtrack.)
LPs: 10/12–inch 33rpm
COLUMBIA (6282 "Red Garters") ... 40-50   54
(10–inch LP. Soundtrack.)
Also see MITCHELL, Guy

CLOONEY, Rosemary, and Perez Prado
Singles: 7–inch
RCA 4-8   60
LPs: 10/12–inch 33rpm
RCA 10-12   60
Also see CLOONEY, Rosemary
Also see PRADO, Perez

CLOUD, Christopher
(Tommy Boyce)
Singles: 7–inch
CHELSEA 3-5   72-73
LPs: 10/12–inch 33rpm
CHELSEA 10-15   73
Also see BOYCE, Tommy

CLOUT
Singles: 7–inch
EPIC 2-4   78-79
LPs: 10/12–inch 33rpm
EPIC 5-10   79-80

CLOVERS
Singles: 78rpm
ATLANTIC (900 series) 20-40   51-53
ATLANTIC (1000 series) 5-15   53-56
RAINBOW 100-150   51
Singles: 7–inch
ATLANTIC (934 "Don't You
Know I Love You") 100-150   51
ATLANTIC (944 "Fool, Fool, Fool") . 75-100   51
ATLANTIC (963 "One Mint Julep") .. 50-75   52
ATLANTIC (969 "Ting-A-Ling") 50-75   52
ATLANTIC (977 "I Played the Fool") . 50-75   52
ATLANTIC (989 "Yes It's You") 50-75   53
ATLANTIC (1000 "Good Lovin") 40-60   53
ATLANTIC (1010 "Comin' on") 30-50   53
ATLANTIC (1022 "Lovey Dovey") .. 30-50   54
ATLANTIC (1035 "Your Cash Ain't
Nothin' But Trash") 30-50   54
ATLANTIC (1046 "I Confess") 30-50   54
ATLANTIC (1052 "Blue Velvet") 25-50   54
ATLANTIC (1060 "Love Bug") 25-50   55
ATLANTIC (1073 "Nip Sip") 25-50   55
ATLANTIC (1083 "Devil Or Angel") .. 25-50   56
ATLANTIC (1094 "Your Tender Lips") 25-50   56
ATLANTIC (1100 series) 15-25   56-58
ATLANTIC (2000 series) 5-10   61
BRUNSWICK 5-10   63
JOSIE 4-8   68
POPLAR 15-25   58
PORT 5-10   65
PORWIN 5-10   63
RIPETE 2-4   88
U.A. 10-15   59-61
WINLEY (255 "Wrapped Up in
a Dream") 20-30   61
WINLEY (655 "I Need You Now") ... 20-30   62
EPs: 7–inch 33/45rpm
ATLANTIC (504 "The Clovers Sing") 75-100   56
ATLANTIC (537 "The Clovers Sing") 75-100   56
ATLANTIC (590 "The Clovers Sing") . 60-85   57
LPs: 10/12–inch 33rpm
ATCO 10-12   71
ATLANTIC (1248 "The Clovers") .. 150-250   56
ATLANTIC (8009 "The Clovers") .. 100-175   57
(Black label.)

ATLANTIC (8009 "The Clovers") 40-60   59
(Red label.)
ATLANTIC (8034 "The Clovers'
Dance Party") 50-80   59
GRAND PRIX 10-15   64
POPLAR (1001 "The Clovers in
Clover") 75-100   58
TRIP 8-10   72
U.A. (3033 "The Clovers in Clover") .. 50-75   59
(Monaural.)
U.A. (6033 "The Clovers in Clover") .. 50-75   59
(Stereo.)
U.A. (3099 "Love Potion
Number Nine") 50-75   60
(Monaural.)
U.A. (6099 "Love Potion
Number Nine") 75-100   60
(Stereo.)
Members: John "Buddy" Bailey; Harold Winley; Hal Lucas; Bill
Harris; Matthew McQuater; Charlie White; Billy Mitchell.
Also see JACKSON, Willis
Also see KING CURTIS
Also see MITCHELL, Billy

CLUB HOUSE
Singles: 12–inch 33/45rpm
ATLANTIC 4-6   83
Singles: 7–inch
ATLANTIC 2-4   83

CLUB NOUVEAU
Singles: 12–inch 33/45rpm
WARNER 4-6   86
Singles: 7–inch
TOMMY BOY 2-4   88
WARNER 2-4   86-88
LPs: 10/12-inch 33rpm
WARNER 5-10   86-88

COASTERS
Singles: 78rpm
ATCO 10-20   56-57
Singles: 7–inch
ATCO (6064 "Down in Mexico") 25-40   56
(Maroon label.)
ATCO (6073 "One Kiss Led
to Another") 20-30   56
(Maroon label.)
ATCO (6087 "Searchin") 15-25   57
(Maroon label.)
ATCO (6087 "Searchin") 10-15   57
(Yellow and white label.)
ATCO (6098 through 6192) 10-15   57-61
ATCO (6204 through 6407) 5-10   61-66
DATE 4-8   67-68
KING 3-5   71-73
TURNTABLE 3-6   69
EPs: 7–inch 33/45rpm
ATCO (4501 "Rock and Roll
with the Coasters") 45-70   58
ATCO (4503 "Keep Rockin") 45-70   58

ATCO (4506 "The Coasters") 30-50   59
ATCO (4507 "Top Hits") 30-50   59
LPs: 10/12-inch 33rpm
ATCO (101 "The Coasters") 75-100   58
(Yellow label.)
ATCO (101 "The Coasters") 25-50   59
(Yellow and white label.)
ATCO (111 "Greatest Hits") 50-75   59
ATCO (123 "One By One") 40-50   60
(Monaural.)
ATCO (SD-123 "One By One") 50-60   60
(Stereo.)
ATCO (135 "Coast Along") 30-40   59
(Monaural.)
ATCO (SD-135 "Coast Along") 40-50   59
(Stereo.)
ATCO (371 "Greatest Recordings") .. 10-20   71
ATLANTIC 10-12   82
CLARION 12-15   64
KING 10-12   71
POWER PAK 5-10   83
TRIP 8-10   72-76
Members: Bobby Nunn; Leon Hughes; Carl Gardner; Billy Guy;
Adolph Jacobs; Cornel Gunter; Will Jones; Earl Carroll; Ronnie
Bright; Jimmy Norman.
Also see HENDRICKS, Bobby
Also see KING CURTIS
Also see NORMAN, Jimmy
Also see NUNN, Bobby
Also see ROBINS

COASTERS / Crew-Cuts / Chiffons
LPs: 10/12-inch 33rpm
EXACT 5-10   80
Also see CHIFFONS
Also see CREW-CUTS

COASTERS / Drifters
LPs: 10/12-inch 33rpm
TVP 10-15
(TV mail-order offer.)
Also see DRIFTERS

COATES, Odia
Singles: 12–inch 33/45rpm
EPIC 4-6   77
Singles: 7–inch
BUDDAH 3-5   73
EPIC 2-4   78
U.A. 2-4   74-75
LPs: 10/12-inch 33rpm
U.A. 8-10   75
Also see ANKA, Paul, and Odia Coates

COBB, Joyce
Singles: 7–inch
CREAM 2-4   79-80
TRUTH 3-5   75

COBHAM, Billy
(Billy Cobham's Glass Menagerie; Billy Cobham with
the George Duke Band)
Singles: 12–inch 33/45rpm
COLUMBIA 4-6   80

Singles: 7–inch

| ATLANTIC | 3-5 | 75-77 |
| COLUMBIA | 2-4 | 78-80 |

LPs: 10/12–inch 33rpm

ATLANTIC	5-10	73-79
COLUMBIA	5-10	77-80
ELEKTRA	5-10	82-83

Also see DUKE, George
Also see SINGLETON, Charlie

COCA-NUTS
Singles: 7–inch

| "BRING IT BACK!" | 3-5 | 86 |

(No label name used.)

COCCIANTE, Richard
Singles: 7–inch

| 20TH FOX | 3-5 | 76 |

LPs: 10/12–inch 33rpm

| 20TH FOX | 5-10 | 76 |

COCHISE
Singles: 7–inch

| U.A. | 3-5 | 71 |

EPs: 7–inch 33/45rpm

| U.A. | 10-12 | 71 |

LPs: 10/12–inch 33rpm

| U.A. | 10-12 | 71 |

Member: Mick Grabham.

COCHRAN, Eddie
Singles: 78rpm

| CREST (1026 "Skinny Jim") | 50-100 | 56 |
| LIBERTY | 10-15 | 57 |

Singles: 7–inch

CAPEHART (5003 "Rough Stuff")	10-20	60
CREST (1026 "Skinny Jim")	150-200	56
LIBERTY (54000 series)	5-10	62
LIBERTY (55056 "Sittin' in the Balcony")	15-25	57
LIBERTY (55070 "Mean When I'm Mad")	15-25	58
LIBERTY (55087 "Drive in Show")	15-25	57
LIBERTY (55112 "Twenty Flight Rock")	20-30	58
LIBERTY (55123 "Jeannie Jeannie Jeannie")	20-30	58
LIBERTY (55138 "Pretty Girl")	15-25	58
LIBERTY (55144 "Summertime Blues")	15-25	58
LIBERTY (55166 "C'mon Everybody") (Green label.)	15-25	58
LIBERTY (55166 "C'mon Everybody") (Black label.)	10-20	58
LIBERTY (55177 "Teenage Heaven")	15-25	59
LIBERTY (55203 "Somethin' Else") (With horizontal silver lines.)	15-25	59
LIBERTY (55203 "Somethin' Else") (Without horizontal silver lines.)	10-20	59
LIBERTY (55217 "Hallelujah, I Love Her So")	10-20	59

LIBERTY (55242 "Cut Across Shorty") (Green label.)	15-25	60
LIBERTY (55242 "Cut Across Shorty") (Black label.)	10-20	61
LIBERTY (55278 "Sweetie Pie")	10-20	60
LIBERTY (55389 "Weekend")	20-30	61
CAPEHART (5003 "Rough Stuff")	25-50	60
LIBERTY (55070 "Mean When I'm Mad")	750-1000	58

EPs: 7–inch 33/45rpm

| LIBERTY (3061-1/2/3 "Singin' to My Baby") | 100-150 | 58 |

(Price is for any of three volumes.)

LPs: 10/12–inch 33rpm

LIBERTY (3061 "Singin' to My Baby") (Green label.)	200-300	58
LIBERTY (3061 "Singin' to My Baby") (Black label.)	40-60	60
LIBERTY (3172 "Memorial Album")	50-100	60
LIBERTY (3220 "Never to Be Forgotten") (Black label.)	50-100	62
LIBERTY (3220 "Never to Be Forgotten") (Yellow label. Promotional issue only.)	75-90	62
LIBERTY (10000 series)	5-10	81-83
SUNSET (1123 "Summertime Blues")	15-25	66
U.A. (428 "Very Best of Eddie Cochran")	10-15	75
U.A. (9959 "Legendary Masters")	15-20	71

Also see KEY, Troyce

COCHRAN, Hank
Singles: 7–inch

CAPITOL	2-4	78
DOT	3-5	70
ELEKTRA	2-4	80
GAYLORD	4-8	62-63
LIBERTY	4-8	62-63
MONUMENT	3-6	67-68
RCA	4-8	64-66

LPs: 10/12–inch 33rpm

CAPITOL	5-10	78
ELEKTRA	5-10	80
MONUMENT	10-15	68
RCA	10-20	65

COCHRAN, Hank, and Willie Nelson
Singles: 7–inch

| CAPITOL | 2-4 | 78 |

Also see COCHRAN, Hank
Also see NELSON, Willie

COCHRAN, Wayne
(Wayne Cochran and the C.C. Riders)
Singles: 7–inch

BETHLEHEM	3-5	70
CHESS	4-8	67-68
DECK	3-5	

EPIC	3-5	72
KING (5000 series)	5-10	63-65
KING (6000 series)	4-8	65-71
MERCURY	4-8	65-67
SCOTTIE	10-15	59
SOFT	4-8	65

Picture Sleeves

CHESS	4-8	67
MERCURY	5-10	65

LPs: 10/12–inch 33rpm

BETHLEHEM	12-15	70
CHESS	20-30	68
EPIC	8-10	72
KING	15-25	70

COCHRANE, Tom
(Tom Cochrane and Red Rider)
Singles: 7–inch

CAPITOL	2-4	86
RCA	2-4	88

LPs: 10/12–inch 33rpm

CAPITOL	5-10	86
RCA	5-8	88

Also see RED RIDER

COCK ROBIN
Singles: 12–inch 33/45rpm

COLUMBIA	4-6	85

Singles: 7–inch

COLUMBIA	2-4	85

LPs: 10/12–inch 33rpm

COLUMBIA	5-10	85-87

COCKBURN, Bruce
Singles: 7–inch

GOLD MOUNTAIN	2-4	84
MCA	2-4	86
MILLENNIUM	2-4	80

LPs: 10/12–inch 33rpm

EPIC	10-15	71-72
GOLD CASTLE	5-8	89
GOLD MOUNTAIN	5-10	84
ISLAND	8-10	77-78
MCA	5-10	86
MILLENNIUM	5-10	80-81
TRUE NORTH	8-10	77-78

COCKER, Joe
Singles: 7–inch

A&M	3-6	68-78
ASYLUM	2-4	78-79
CAPITOL	2-4	84-90
ISLAND	2-4	82-83
PHILIPS	10-15	65

Picture Sleeves

A&M	3-5	69-74
CAPITOL	2-4	84

LPs: 10/12–inch 33rpm

A&M (Except 3100 series)	8-15	69-77
A&M (3100 series)	5-10	82
ASYLUM (Except 145)	5-10	78-79

ASYLUM (145 "Luxury You Can Afford")	5-10	79
ASYLUM (145 "Luxury You Can Afford")	10-20	79
(Picture disc. Promotional issue only.)		
CAPITOL	5-10	84-90
ISLAND	5-8	82

Also see BOWIE, David / Joe Cocker / Youngbloods
Also see CRUSADERS
Also see GREASE BAND
Also see RUSSELL, Leon

COCKER, Joe, and Jennifer Warnes
Singles: 7–inch

ISLAND	2-4	82

Picture Sleeves

ISLAND	2-4	82

Also see COCKER, Joe
Also see WARNES, Jennifer

COCO, El: see EL COCO

CODAY, Bill
Singles: 7–inch

CRAYON	3-5	71
EPIC	3-5	73-75
GALAXY	3-5	71

CODY, Commander:
see COMMANDER CODY

COE, David Allan
Singles: 7–inch

COLUMBIA	2-5	74-86
SSS INT'L (Black vinyl)	3-5	71-72
SSS INT'L (Colored vinyl)	5-10	71-72
(Promotional issues only.)		

LPs: 10/12–inch 33rpm

COLUMBIA	5-10	72-86
SSS INT'L (9 "Penitentiary Blues")	25-40	70

Also see JONES, George, and David Allan Coe

COE, David Allan, and Bill Anderson
Singles: 7–inch

COLUMBIA	2-4	80

Also see ANDERSON, Bill

COE, David Allan, and Willie Nelson
Singles: 7–inch

COLUMBIA	2-4	86

Also see COE, David Allan
Also see NELSON, Willie
Also see NELSON, Willie / Jerry Lee Lewis / Carl Perkins / David Allan Coe

COFFEE
Singles: 7–inch

DELITE	2-4	80-82

COFFEY, Dennis
(Dennis Coffey and the Detroit Guitar Band; Dennis Coffey and Lyman Woodward Trio)
Singles: 7–inch

MAVERICK	3-6	69
SUSSEX	3-5	70-74
WARNER	3-5	74
20TH CENTURY/WESTBOUND	3-5	75-76

WESTBOUND 2-4   77-78
LPs: 10/12-inch 33rpm
SUSSEX 10-12   70-75
20TH CENTURY/WESTBOUND 8-10   75-76
WESTBOUND 5-10   77

COHEN, Leonard
Singles: 7-inch
COLUMBIA 3-6   68-73
LPs: 10/12-inch 33rpm
COLUMBIA 10-12   68-85
WARNER 8-12   77

COHEN, Myron
LPs: 10/12-inch 33rpm
RCA 10-15   66
Also see ANN-MARGRET

COLD BLOOD
Singles: 7-inch
ABC 3-5   75
REPRISE 3-5   72-73
SAN FRANCISCO 3-6   70
EPs: 7-inch 33/45rpm
SAN FRANCISCO 5-8   70
LPs: 10/12-inch 33rpm
ABC 8-10   76
REPRISE 10-12   72-73
SAN FRANCISCO 12-15   69-70
WARNER 8-10   74
Members: Lydia Pense; Michael Andreas; Rod Ellicott; Frank
Davis; Jerry Jonutz; Danny Hull; Larry Field.

COLD CHISEL
Singles: 7-inch
ELEKTRA 2-4   81
LPs: 10/12-inch 33rpm
ELEKTRA 5-10   80-82
Members: Jimmy Barnes; Don Walker; Steve Prestwich; Phil
Small; Ian Moss.

COLDER, Ben
(Sheb Wooley)
Singles: 7-inch
MGM 4-8   62-73
SUNBIRD 2-4   80
LPs: 10/12-inch 33rpm
MGM (Except 4100 series) 10-20   66-73
MGM (4100 series) 15-25   61-63
Also see WOOLEY, Sheb

COLE, Ann
(Ann Cole and the Suburbans)
Singles: 78rpm
BATON 4-8   56-57
TIMELY 4-8   54
Singles: 7-inch
BATON 10-20   56-57
MGM 5-10   60
ROULETTE 10-20   62
SIR 5-10   59-60
TIMELY 10-20   54
Also see SUBURBANS

COLE, Bobby
Singles: 7-inch
DATE 3-6   68-69

COLE, Cozy
(Cozy Cole and His All Stars; Cozy Cole and Gary
Chester; Cozy Cole and Pete Johnson; Cozy Cole and
Red Norvo)
Singles: 78rpm
MGM 3-6   54
Singles: 7-inch
ARTISTIQUE 4-8   61
BETHLEHEM 4-8   63
CHARLIE PARKER 4-8   62
CORAL 4-8   62-67
GRAND AWARD 5-8   58
KING 4-8   59-60
LOVE 5-10   58-59
MGM 5-10   54
MERCURY 5-8   58
RANDOM 4-8   60
Picture Sleeves
RANDOM 5-10   60
EPs: 7-inch 33/45rpm
AFTER HOURS 15-20   55
MGM 15-20   54
WALDORF 5-8
LPs: 10/12-inch 33rpm
AFTER HOURS 25-30   55
CHARLIE PARKER 15-20   62
COLUMBIA 10-15   66
CORAL 15-20   62-64
EVEREST 8-10   74
FELSTED 15-20   59
KING 20-25   59-60
LOVE 20-25   59
PARIS 20-25   58
SAVOY 8-12   72-77
TRIP 8-10   74
Also see SHEARING, George

COLE, Cozy, and Illinois Jacquet
LPs: 10/12-inch 33rpm
AUDITION 25-35   55
Also see COLE, Cozy
Also see JACQUET, Illinois

COLE, Nat "King"
(King Cole Trio; King Cole Quintet; Nat Cole Quartet)
Singles: 78rpm
AMMOR 15-25   42
ATLAS 10-20   43-45
CAPITOL (100 through 700 series) ... 5-10   43-49
CAPITOL (800 through 4600 series) .. 4-8   50-58
CAPITOL (15000 series) 3-8   47-49
DAVIS and SCHWEGLER 20-40   39-40
DECCA 10-20   42-47
DISC 15-25   42
EXCELSIOR 10-20   42-45
SAVOY 10-15   46
VARSITY 15-25   40

Singles: 7-inch

CAPITOL (Except 800 through
4200 series) 4-8   59-69
CAPITOL (800 through 4200 series) .. 5-15   50-59
(Purple labels.)
TAMPA (6 "Vom-Vim-Veedle") 8-12   57

Picture Sleeves

CAPITOL 5-10   59-66
TAMPA (6 "Vom-Vim-Veedle") 10-20   57

EPs: 7-inch 33/45rpm

CAPITOL 10-20   50-60
DECCA 10-20   56

LPs: 10/12-inch 33rpm

CAMAY 8-12
CAPITOL (Except 100 through
2900 series) 5-15   61-82
CAPITOL (H-156 "Nat 'King' Cole
at the Piano") 50-100   49
(10-inch LP.)
CAPITOL (H-177 "Nat 'King'
Cole Trio") 50-75   49
(10-inch LP.)
CAPITOL (H-220 "Nat 'King'
Cole Trio") 50-75   50
(10-inch LP.)
CAPITOL (H-332 "Penthouse
Serenade") 50-75   52
(10-inch LP.)
CAPITOL (H-357 "Unforgetable") 50-75   52
(10-inch LP.)
CAPITOL (100 through 900 series) .. 20-35   55-58
(With "T" prefix.)
CAPITOL (1000 through 2900 series) 10-20   58-68
CROWN 8-12   64
DECCA (8260 "In the Beginning") ... 35-50   56
DYNAMIC HOUSE 5-10   72
MCA 5-10   73
MARK '56 5-10   76
MONARCH ("Nat 'King' Cole") 75-100   53
(Colored vinyl.)
PICKWICK 4-8
SCORE (4019 "King Cole Trio") 20-40   58
SPINORAMA 10-15
VSP 10-15   66
WYNCOTE 10-15   63
Also see FOUR KNIGHTS
Also see KENTON, Stan
Also see MARTIN, Dean, and Nat "King" Cole
Also see PRESLEY, Elvis
Also see PRESLEY, Elvis / Frank Sinatra / Nat "King" Cole
Also see SINATRA, Frank / Nat King Cole

COLE, Nat "King" / Phil Flowers
LPs: 10/12-inch 33rpm

EXCELSIOR 5-10

COLE, Nat "King," and Stubby Kaye
Singles: 7-inch

CAPITOL 3-6   65

Picture Sleeves

CAPITOL 4-8   65

**COLE, Nat "King," and His Trio / George
Kingston**
LPs: 10/12-inch 33rpm

WYNCOTE 10-15
Also see COLE, Nat "King"

COLE, Nat "King," and George Shearing
LPs: 10/12-inch 33rpm

CAPITOL 20-30   61
Also see SHEARING, George, Quintet

COLE, Natalie
(Natalie Cole and George Shearing)
Singles: 12-inch 33/45rpm

EPIC 4-6   83
MODERN 4-6   85

Singles: 7-inch

CAPITOL 2-4   75-80
E.M.I. 2-4   88-90
EPIC 2-4   83
MANHATTAN 2-4   87
MODERN 2-4   85

Picture Sleeves

E.M.I. 2-4   88-89
MANHATTAN 2-4   87
MODERN 2-4   85

LPs: 10/12-inch 33rpm

CAPITOL 8-12   75-82
E.M.I. 5-8   89
ELEKTRA 5-8   91
EPIC 5-10   83
MANHATTAN 5-10   87
MFSL (032 "Thankful") 25-50   79
MFSL (081 "Natalie Cole Sings
George Shearing Plays") 20-30   82
MODERN 5-10   85
Also see BRYSON, Peabo, and Natalie Cole
Also see SHEARING, George, Quintet

COLE, Sami Jo
Singles: 7-inch

ELEKTRA 2-4   81

COLE, Tony
Singles: 7-inch

20TH FOX 2-4   73-74
LPs: 10/12-inch 33rpm
20TH FOX 8-10   73

COLEMAN, Albert
(Albert Coleman's Atlanta Pops)
Singles: 7-inch

EPIC 2-4   82

COLEMAN, Durell
Singles: 7-inch

ISLAND 2-4   85
LPs: 10/12-inch 33rpm
ISLAND 5-10   85

COLLAGE
Singles: 12-inch 33/45rpm

CONSTELLATION 4-6   86

MCA 4-6   85
SOLAR 4-6   83
Singles: 7–inch
CONSTELLATION 2-4   86
MCA 2-4   85
SOLAR 2-4   82-83
LPs: 10/12–inch 33rpm
CONSTELLATION 5-10   86
SOLAR 5-10   81-83

COLLAY and the Satellites
Singles: 7–inch
SHO-BIZ (1002 "Last Chance") 15-25   60

COLLEY, Keith
Singles: 7–inch
CHALLENGE 4-6   66-70
COLUMBIA 4-6   68
ERA 5-10   61-62
JAF 4-8
UNICAL 5-10   63-64
VEE JAY 4-8   65

COLLIER, Mitty
Singles: 7–inch
CHESS 5-10   61-68
ENTRANCE 3-5   72
ERIC 2-4   78
PEACHTREE 3-6   69-70
LPs: 10/12–inch 33rpm
CHESS 15-25   65-66
GOSPEL ROOTS 5-10   79

COLLINS, Albert
(Albert Collins and the Ice Breakers)
Singles: 12–inch 33/45rpm
ALLIGATOR (5 "Cold Snap") 5-10   86
(Promotional issue only.)
Singles: 7–inch
GREAT SCOTT (007 "Albert's Alley") . 15-25
HALL 5-10   64
HALL WAY 8-12   63
IMPERIAL 4-6   69
KANGAROO (104 "Collins Shuffle") .. 25-50   58
LIBERTY 3-5   70
TCF HALL 4-8   65-66
TUMBLEWEED 3-5   72-73
20TH FOX 4-6   68
LPs: 10/12–inch 33rpm
ALLIGATOR 5-10   79-87
BLUE THUMB 10-15   69
BRYLEN 5-10   84
IMPERIAL 10-15   69-70
TCF HALL (8002 "Cool Sound
   of Albert Collins") 30-35   65
TUMBLEWEED 10-15   71

COLLINS, Albert, Robert Cray and Johnny
Copeland / Albert Collins
Singles: 12–inch 33/45rpm
ALLIGATOR (5 "T-Bone Shuffle") 5-10   86
(Promotional issue only.)
LPs: 10/12–inch 33rpm
ALLIGATOR 5-10   86
Also see COLLINS, Albert
Also see CRAY, Robert

COLLINS, Dorothy
Singles: 78rpm
AUDIOVOX 4-8   54-55
CORAL 4-8   55-56
DECCA 4-8   52
MGM 4-8   50-51
Singles: 7–inch
AUDIOVOX 5-10   54-55
CORAL 5-10   55-56
DECCA 5-10   52
GOLD EAGLE 4-8   61
MGM 5-10   50-51
ROULETTE 4-6   63
TOP RANK 5-10   59-60
EPs: 7–inch 33/45rpm
CORAL 5-10   55-56
MGM 5-10   55
LPs: 10/12–inch 33rpm
CORAL 15-25   55-57
MOTIVATION 10-15   62
TOP RANK 10-15   60
VOCALION 5-10   65

COLLINS, Judy
Singles: 7–inch
ELEKTRA (Except 45008 through 45680)2-5   70-84
ELEKTRA (45008 through 45680) 4-8   64-69
Picture Sleeves
ELEKTRA (Except "The Hostage") 2-5   69-84
ELEKTRA ("The Hostage") 4-8   73
(Promotional issue only. Number not known.)
LPs: 10/12–inch 33rpm
ELEKTRA (Except 200 and
   300 series) 10-15 67-84
ELEKTRA (209 "Maid of
   Constant Sorrow") 30-40   61
ELEKTRA (222 "Golden Apples
   of the Sun") 25-35   62
ELEKTRA (243 "Judy Collins No. 3") . 20-30   63
(Monaural.)
ELEKTRA (7-243 "Judy Collins No. 3") 25-35   63
(Stereo.)
ELEKTRA (253 "Running for My Life") .. 5-8   80
ELEKTRA (300 series) 15-20   65-68
(Monaural.)
ELEKTRA (7-300 series) 15-20   65-72
(Stereo.)
ELEKTRA (60001 "Times of Our Lives") 5-8   82

COLLINS, Judy, and T.G. Sheppard
Singles: 7–inch
ELEKTRA 2-4   84
   Also see COLLINS, Judy
   Also see SHEPPARD, T.G.

COLLINS, Keanya
Singles: 7–inch
BLUE ROCK 3-6   69
ITCO 3-6   69

COLLINS, Lyn
(Lyn Collins and the Famous Flames)
Singles: 7–inch
PEOPLE 3-5   72-76
LPs: 10/12–inch 33rpm
PEOPLE 10-12   72-75
   Also see BROWN, James and Lyn Collins

COLLINS, Phil
Singles: 12–inch 33/45rpm
ATLANTIC 4-6   84-86
Singles: 7–inch
ATLANTIC 2-4   81-90
Picture Sleeves
ATLANTIC 2-4   81-90
LPs: 10/12–inch 33rpm
ATLANTIC 5-10   81-90
   Also see BAILEY, Philip, and Phil Collins
   Also see BAND AID
   Also see BRAND X
   Also see GENESIS

COLLINS, Phil, and Marilyn Martin
Singles: 7–inch
ATLANTIC 2-4   85
Picture Sleeves
ATLANTIC 2-4   85
   Also see COLLINS, Phil
   Also see MARTIN, Marilyn

COLLINS, Rodger
(Roger Collins)
Singles: 7–inch
FANTASY 3-5   73
GALAXY 3-8   66-73
POMPEII 3-6   69

COLLINS, William:
  see BOOTSY'S RUBBER BAND

COLLINS, Willie
Singles: 7–inch
CAPITOL 2-4   86

COLLINS & COLLINS
Singles: 7–inch
A&M 2-4   80
LPs: 10/12–inch 33rpm
A&M 5-10   80

COLLINS KIDS
Singles: 78rpm
COLUMBIA 5-15   55-57
Singles: 7–inch
COLUMBIA (21470 "Hush Money") .. 15-25   55

COLUMBIA (21514 "Rockaway Rock") 15-25   56
COLUMBIA (21543 "I'm in My Teens") 15-25   56
COLUMBIA (21560 "Rock and Roll
Polka") 15-25   56
COLUMBIA (40824 "Move
a Little Closer") 20-30   57
COLUMBIA (40921 "Hop, Skip
and Jump") 20-30   57
COLUMBIA (41012 "Party") 35-55   57
COLUMBIA (41087 "Hoy Hoy") 30-45   58
COLUMBIA (41149 "Mercy") 30-45   58
COLUMBIA (41225 "Whistle Bait") .. 35-55   58
COLUMBIA (41329 "Sugar Plum") ... 10-20   59
LPs: 10/12–inch 33rpm
COLUMBIA 5-10   83
   Members: Larry Collins; Lawrencine "Lorrie" Collins.

COLOMBO, Chris: see COLUMBO, Chris

COLONEL ABRAMS: see ABRAMS, Colonel

COLORS
Singles: 12–inch 33/45rpm
FIRST TAKE 4-6   83
Singles: 7–inch
BECKET 2-4   82

COLTER, Jessi
(Mirriam Johnson; Mirriam Eddy)
Singles: 7–inch
CAPITOL 2-5   75-82
RCA 3-6   69-72
LPs: 10/12–inch 33rpm
CAPITOL 5-10   75-81
RCA 8-12   70
   Also see EDDY, Duane and Mirriam
   Also see JENNINGS, Waylon, and Jessi Colter

COLTRANE, Alice
LPs: 10/12–inch 33rpm
IMPULSE 8-10   71-74
WARNER 5-10   77-78

COLTRANE, Alice, and Carlos Santana
LPs: 10/12–inch 33rpm
COLUMBIA 6-10   74
   Also see COLTRANE, Alice
   Also see SANTANA

COLTRANE, Chi
Singles: 7–inch
CLOUDS 3-5   78
COLUMBIA 3-5   72-73
LPs: 10/12–inch 33rpm
CLOUDS 5-10   77
COLUMBIA 8-12   72-73

COLTRANE, John
Singles: 78rpm
PRESTIGE 5-10   57
Singles: 7–inch
ATLANTIC 4-8   60-61
PRESTIGE 5-10   57-64

LPs: 10/12–inch 33rpm
ATLANTIC (1300 and 1400 series) . . 20-40	59-66	
BLUE NOTE (1577 "Blue Train") . . 100-150	51	

(Label gives New York street address for Blue Note Records.)

BLUE NOTE (1577 "Blue Train") 35-55	59

(Label reads "Blue Note Records Inc. - New York, U.S.A.")

COLTRANE (4950 "Cosmic Music") 150-200	66
COLTRANE (5000 "Cosmic Music") 150-200	66
IMPULSE (Except 6 through 77) 10-25	66-71
IMPULSE (6 through 77) 25-45	61-65
JAZZLAND 20-40	61
PRESTIGE (7043 "Two Tenors") . . . 50-100	56

(Yellow label.)

PRESTIGE (7043 "Two Tenors") 25-35	64

(Blue label.)

PRESTIGE (7105 "Coltrane") 50-100	57

(Yellow label.)

PRESTIGE (7105 "Coltrane") 25-35	57

(Blue label.)

PRESTIGE (7123 "John Coltrane with the Red Garland Trio") 50-75	57

(Yellow label.)

PRESTIGE (7123 "Traneing in") 25-35	64

(Blue label, logo on right. Reissue of *John Coltrane with the Red Garland Trio*.)

PRESTIGE (7123 "Traneing In") 15-25	69

(Blue label, logo at top.)

PRESTIGE (7142 "Soultrane") 40-70	58

(Yellow label.)

PRESTIGE (7158 "Cattin") 40-70	59

(Yellow label.)

PRESTIGE (7158 "Cattin") 25-35	64

(Blue label.)

PRESTIGE (7131 "Wheelin' and Dealin") 40-70	59

(Yellow label.)

PRESTIGE (7188 "Lush Life") 40-70	60

(Yellow label.)

PRESTIGE (7188 "Lush Life") 25-35	64

(Blue label.)

PRESTIGE (7200 series) 20-40	61-64

(Yellow label.)

PRESTIGE (7200 series) 15-25	64

(Blue label.)

PRESTIGE (7300 series) 15-25	65
U.A. 25-35	62

Also see ADDERLEY, Julian "Cannonball," and John Coltrane
Also see ELLINGTON, Duke, and John Coltrane

COLTRANE, John, and Miles Davis
LPs: 10/12–inch 33rpm
PRESTIGE 10-20	64

Also see DAVIS, Miles

COLTRANE, John, and Thelonious Monk
LPs: 10/12–inch 33rpm
JAZZLAND 20-30	61
MILESTONE 8-12	73

RIVERSIDE (Except 039) 10-20	65-68	
RIVERSIDE (039 "Thelonious Monk and John Coltrane") 5-10	82	

Also see COLTRANE, John
Also see MONK, Thelonious

COLTS
Singles: 78rpm
MAMBO 35-50	55
VITA 10-20	55-56

Singles: 7–inch
ANTLER (4003 "Never No More") . . . 20-40	57
ANTLER (4007 "Guiding Angel") 20-40	57
MAMBO (112 "Adorable") 100-200	55
PLAZA (505 "Sweet Sixteen") 10-15	62
VITA (112 "Adorable") 50-100	55
VITA (121 "Sweet Sixteen") 25-50	56
VITA (130 "Never No More") 25-50	56

Members: Joe Crunby; Rubin Crunby; Leroy Smith; Carl Moland.

COLTS / Red Coats
Singles: 7–inch
DEL-CO 15-25	59

Also see COLTS

COLUMBO, Chris
(Chris Colombo Quintet)
Singles: 7–inch
BATTLE 4-8	62
MAXX 3-6	64
STRAND 4-8	63

LPs: 10/12–inch 33rpm
MERCURY 5-10	75
STRAND 10-15	63

COMATEENS
Singles: 12–inch 33/45rpm
MERCURY 4-6	83-84

Singles: 7–inch
MERCURY 2-4	83-84

LPs: 10/12–inch 33rpm
CACHALOT 5-10	81
MERCURY 5-10	83

COMER, Tony and Crosswinds
Singles: 7–inch
VIDCOM 2-4	84

COMMANDER CODY
(Commander Cody and His Lost Planet Airmen)
Singles: 7–inch
ABC 3-5	75
ARISTA 3-5	77
DOT 3-5	73-74
MCA 2-4	83
PARAMOUNT 3-5	71-74
WARNER 3-5	75

LPs: 10/12–inch 33rpm
ARISTA 5-10	77
PARAMOUNT 10-12	71-74
WARNER 8-10	75-76

COMMODORES
Singles: 12–inch 33/45rpm
MOTOWN 4-8 79-85
POLYDOR 4-6 86
Singles: 7–inch
ATLANTIC 5-10 69
MOTOWN 2-5 74-85
(Black vinyl.)
MOTOWN (1307 "Machine Gun") 4-6 74
(Colored vinyl. Promotional issue only.)
MOWEST 3-5 72
POLYDOR 2-4 86
Picture Sleeves
MOTOWN 3-5 85
LPs: 10/12–inch 33rpm
MOTOWN (Except 39) 8-10 74-87
MOTOWN (39 "1978 Platinum Tour") . 15-20 78
(Promotional issue only.)
POLYDOR 5-10 86
Members: Lionel Ritchie; William King; Ronald LaPread; Tommy McClary; Walter Orange; Milan Williams.
Also see McCLARY, Thomas
Also see RICHIE, Lionel

COMMON BOND
LPs: 10/12–inch 33rpm
FRONTLINE 5-10 86-87

COMMUNARDS
Singles: 12–inch 33/45rpm
MCA 4-6 86
Singles: 7–inch
MCA 2-4 86-88
LPs: 10/12–inch 33rpm
MCA 5-10 86-88
Members: Jimmy Sommerville; Sara Jane Morris; Richard Coles.
Also see BRONSKI BEAT

COMO, Perry
Singles: 78rpm
RCA 5-10 43-58
Singles: 7–inch
RCA (237 "Supper Club Favorites") .. 15-25 49
(Three disc set.)
RCA (0100 through 0900 series) 3-6 69-73
RCA (VP-2000 series) 5-10 59
(Stereo.)
RCA (2800 through 7400 series) 8-18 48-59
RCA (7500 through 9700 series) 4-8 59-69
RCA (10000 through 13000 series) 2-5 74-83
Picture Sleeves
RCA (3800 through 7100 series) 10-20 53-58
RCA (7200 through 9700 series) 5-15 58-69
EPs: 7–inch 33/45rpm
RCA (Except SPD series) 10-25 52-70
RCA (SPD-27 "Perry Como") 40-60 56
(Boxed 10-EP set. Includes inserts and biography booklet.)

RCA (SPD-28 "Perry Como
Highlighter") 20-30 56
(Sampler from Kleenex Tissue. Includes picture cover.)
LPs: 10/12–inch 33rpm
CAMDEN 5-15 57-74
RCA (0100 through 4000 series) 5-10 73-83
(With "AFL1," "ANL1," "APL1," "AQL1," "AYL1" or "CPL1" prefix.)
RCA (1004 "Saturday Night
with Mr. C") 20-30 58
RCA (1007 "Golden Records") 20-30 58
RCA (LPM-1085 "So Smooth") 20-40 55
RCA (LPM-1172 "I Believe") 20-40 56
RCA (LPM-1176 "Relaxing with
Perry Como") 20-40 56
RCA (LPM-1177 "Sentimental Date
with Perry Como") 20-40 56
RCA (LPM-1191 "Perry Como Sings Hits from
Broadway Shows") 20-40 56
RCA (LPM-1243 Perry Sings
Christmas Music") 20-40 56
RCA (LPM-1463 We Get Letters") ... 20-30 57
RCA (LPM-1800 through
LPM-2900 series) 15-25 58-63
RCA (LSP-1085 through LSP-1463) . 10-20 62-68
(Electronic stereo reissues.)
RCA (LSP-1800 through
LSP-2900 series) 15-30 58-63
(Stereo.)
RCA (3013 "TV Favorites") 25-50 52
(10–inch LP.)
RCA (3044 "Supper Club Favorites") . 25-50 52
(10–inch LP.)
RCA (3124 "Broadway") 25-50 53
(10–inch LP.)
RCA (3133 "Christmas") 25-50 53
(10–inch LP.)
RCA (3188 "I Believe") 25-50 53
(10–inch LP.)
RCA (3224 "Golden Records") 25-50 54
(10–inch LP.)
RCA (3300 through 4500 series) 8-15 64-71
(With "LPM" or "LSP" prefix.)
READER'S DIGEST 8-15 75

COMO, Perry / Ames Brothers / Harry Belafonte / Radio City Music Hall Orch.
EPs: 7–inch 33/45rpm
RCA (SP-35 "Merry Christmas") 10-20 56
(Dealer giveaway. Issued with paper sleeve.)
Also see AMES BROTHERS
Also see BELAFONTE, Harry

COMO, Perry, and Eddie Fisher
Singles: 78rpm
RCA 4-8 52
Singles: 7–inch
RCA 5-10 52
Also see FISHER, Eddie

COMO, Perry, and the Fontane Sisters
Singles: 78rpm
RCA 4-8   50-51
Singles: 7–inch
RCA 8-15   50-51
Also see FONTANE SISTERS

COMO, Perry, and Jaye P. Morgan
Singles: 78rpm
RCA 4-8   55
Singles: 7–inch
RCA 5-10   55
Also see COMO, Perry
Also see MORGAN, Jaye P.

COMO, Sue
Singles: 7–inch
SMART 5-10   60

COMPAGNONS DE LA CHANSON, Les:
see LES COMPAGNONS DE LA CHANSON

COMSTOCK, Bobby
(Bobby Comstock and the Counts)
Singles: 7–inch
ASCOT 8-15   64-66
ATLANTIC 10-15   60
BLAZE (349 "Tennessee Waltz") 10-20   59
ERIC 2-4   73
FESTIVAL 10-15   61
JUBILEE 5-10   60-63
LAWN 8-12   62-64
MOHAWK 10-15   61
TRIUMPH 10-15   59
LPs: 10/12–inch 33rpm
ASCOT (16026 "Out of Sight") 30-45   66
BLAZE ("Tennessee Waltz") 100-150
Also see KING CURTIS

CON FUNK SHUN
Singles: 12–inch 33/45rpm
MERCURY 4-6   83-86
Singles: 7–inch
FRETONE 3-5   74
MERCURY 2-4   77-86
LPs: 10/12–inch 33rpm
51 WEST 5-10   83
MERCURY 5-10   76-86
Members: Mike Cooper; Louis McCall; Karl Fuller; Paul Harrell; Danny Thomas; Felton Pilate II.

CONCEPT
Singles: 7–inch
TUCKWOOD 2-4   85

CONDUCTOR
Singles: 7–inch
JAMIE 5-10   61
MONTAGE 2-4   82
LPs: 10/12–inch 33rpm
MONTAGE 5-10   82

CONEY HATCH
LPs: 10/12–inch 33rpm
MERCURY 5-10   83-85

CONLEE, John
Singles: 7–inch
ABC 2-4   78
ABC/DOT 2-4   76-77
COLUMBIA 2-4   86
MCA 2-4   79-86
LPs: 10/12–inch 33rpm
ABC 8-10   78
COLUMBIA 5-10   86
MCA 5-10   79-86

CONLEY, Arthur
Singles: 7–inch
ATCO 3-5   67-70
CAPRICORN 2-4   71-74
FAME 3-5   66
JOTIS 3-5   66
LPs: 10/12–inch 33rpm
ATCO 15-25   67-69
Also see SOUL CLAN

CONNICK, Harry, Jr.
(Harry Connick Jr. Trio)
LPs: 10/12–inch 33rpm
COLUMBIA 5-8   90-91

CONNIE
Singles: 12–inch 33/45rpm
SUNNYVIEW 4-6   85-86
Singles: 7–inch
SUNNYVIEW 2-4   85-86

CONNIFF, Ray, Orchestra and Chorus
Singles: 78rpm
COLUMBIA 3-5   56-57
Singles: 7–inch
COLUMBIA 3-8   56-82
Picture Sleeves
COLUMBIA 3-8   60-64
EPs: 7–inch 33/45rpm
COLUMBIA 5-10   56-59
LPs: 10/12–inch 33rpm
COLUMBIA 6-18   57-82
HARMONY 4-8   69

CONNOR, Chris
Singles: 78rpm
ATLANTIC 3-5   56-57
BETHLEHEM 4-6   54-55
Singles: 7–inch
ATLANTIC 4-8   56-62
BETHLEHEM (1200 and 1300
series) 5-10   54-55
BETHLEHEM (3000 series) 2-4   64
FM 3-6   63
EPs: 7–inch 33/45rpm
ATLANTIC 15-25   56-57
BETHLEHEM 20-40   54-56

LPs: 10/12–inch 33rpm

ABC-PAR 10-20	65-66
ATLANTIC (601 "George	
Gershwin Almanac") 40-60	57
ATLANTIC (1240 "He Loves Me	
He Loves Me Not") 40-50	57
ATLANTIC (1228 "Chris Connor") . . . 40-50	57
ATLANTIC (1286 "Jazz Date") 40-50	58
ATLANTIC (1290 "Chris Craft") 40-50	58
ATLANTIC (1307 "Sad Cafe") 30-40	59
(Monaural.)	
ATLANTIC (SD-1307 "Sad Cafe") . . . 35-45	59
(Stereo.)	
ATLANTIC (8014 "I Miss You So") . . . 40-50	58
ATLANTIC (8032 "Witchcraft") 30-40	59
(Monaural.)	
ATLANTIC (SD-8032 "Witchcraft") . . . 35-45	59
(Stereo.)	
ATLANTIC (8040 "In Person") 30-40	59
(Monaural.)	
ATLANTIC (SD-8040 "In Person") . . . 35-45	59
(Stereo.)	
ATLANTIC (8046 "A Portrait") 25-35	60
(Monaural.)	
ATLANTIC (SD-8046 "A Portrait") . . . 35-45	60
(Stereo.)	
ATLANTIC (8061 "Free Spirits") 20-30	62
(Monaural.)	
ATLANTIC (SD-8061 "Free Spirits") . . 25-35	62
(Stereo.)	
BETHLEHEM (20 "This Is Chris") . . . 40-50	55
(Maroon label.)	
BETHLEHEM (56 "Chris") 40-50	56
(Maroon label.)	
BETHLEHEM (1001 Lullabys	
of Birdland") 75-100	54
(10–inch LP.)	
BETHLEHEM (1002 Lullabys	
for Lovers, Vol. 2") 75-100	54
(10–inch LP.)	
BETHLEHEM (6000 series) 10-12	78
(Gray label.)	
BETHLEHEM (6004 "Lullabys	
of Birdland") 40-50	56
(Maroon label.)	
BETHLEHEM (6005 "Lullabys	
for Lovers") 40-50	56
(Maroon label.)	
BETHLEHEM (6006 "Bethlehem	
Girls") 40-50	56
(Maroon label.)	
FM 10-15	63

Also see FERGUSON, Maynard, and Chris Connor
Also see SIMONE, Nina, Chris Connor and Carmen McRae

CONNORS, Norman

Singles: 7–inch

ARISTA 2-4	78-81
BUDDAH 3-5	74-77
CAPITOL 2-4	88

LPs: 10/12–inch 33rpm

ARISTA 5-10	78-81
BUDDAH 10-12	75-78
NOVUS 5-10	81

Members: Michael Henderson; Pharoah Sanders; Jean Cain;
Phyllis Hyman.
Also see AQUARIAN DREAM
Also see HENDERSON, Michael
Also see HYMAN, Phyllis

CONTI, Bill

Singles: 7–inch

ARISTA 2-4	82
U.A. 3-5	77-78

LPs: 10/12–inch 33rpm

MCA 5-10	79
U.A. 8-12	78-79

CONTINENTAL 4
(Continental Four)

Singles: 7–inch

JAY WALKING 3-5	71-72

LPs: 10/12–inch 33rpm

JAY WALKING 10-15	71

Members: Fred Kelly; Anthony Burke; Ronnie McGregor; Larry
McGregor.

CONTINO, Dick

Singles: 78rpm

MERCURY 3-5	54-57

Singles: 7–inch

DOT 3-6	66-67
MERCURY 4-8	54-64

EPs: 7–inch 33/45rpm

MERCURY 5-10	55-59

LPs: 10/12–inch 33rpm

DOT 5-15	64-66
HAMILTON 5-10	64-66
MERCURY 8-15	56-63
WING 5-10	63

Also see CARROLL, David

CONTOURS

Singles: 12–inch 33/45rpm

MOTOWN 4-8	88

Singles: 7–inch

GORDY 5-10	62-67
MOTOWN (400 series) 2-4	82-88
MOTOWN (1008 "Whole Lotta	
Woman") 125-150	61
MOTOWN (1012 "Funny") 200-300	61
ROCKET 2-4	80

Picture Sleeves

MOTOWN 2-4 88	

LPs: 10/12–inch 33rpm

GORDY (901 "Do You Love Me") . . . 50-75	62
MOTOWN 5-10	82

Members: Bill Gordon; Sylvester Potts; Billy Hoggs; Joe
Billingslea; Hubert Johnson.
Also see EDWARDS, Dennis

CONTROLLERS
(Controllers with Valerie DeMece)
Singles: 12–inch 33/45rpm
MCA 4-6   85-86
Singles: 7–inch
JUANA 2-4   76-82
MCA 2-4   85-88
LPs: 10/12–inch 33rpm
JUANA 8-10   77-79
MCA 5-10   86
WINDHAM HILL 5-10   85
Members: Larry McArthur; Regie McArthur; Ricky Lewis; Leonard Brown.

CONVERTION
Singles: 7–inch
SAM 2-4   81
VANGUARD 2-4   83
LPs: 10/12–inch 33rpm
VANGUARD 5-10   83

CONWAY BROTHERS
Singles: 7–inch
ICHIBAN 2-4   87
PBT 2-4   86
PAULA 2-4   85

COODER, Ry
Singles: 7–inch
MUSICOR 4-8   66
REPRISE 3-6   69-72
WARNER 2-5   77-82
LPs: 10/12–inch 33rpm
MFSL (085 "Jazz") 25-50   82
REPRISE 8-12   72-76
WARNER 5-10   77-87
Also see CAPTAIN BEEFHEART
Also see LITTLE FEAT

COOK, Tony
Singles: 12–inch 33/45rpm
HALFMOON 4-6   84

COOKE, Dale
(Sam Cooke)
Singles: 78rpm
SPECIALTY 5-10   57
Singles: 7–inch
SPECIALTY 15-25   57
Also see COOKE, Sam

COOKE, SAM
(Sam Cooke and the Soul Stirrers)
Singles: 78rpm
KEEN 5-10   57
SPECIALTY 5-10   57
Singles: 7–inch
CHERIE 3-5   71
COLLECTABLES 2-4   81
KEEN (3-2000 and 4000 series) 8-12 57-61
(Monaural.)
KEEN (5-2000 series) 20-30 58-60
(Stereo.)

RCA (7000 and 8000 series) 5-10 60-66
(With "47" prefix.)
RCA (7000 series) 15-25 60-61
(Stereo. With "61" prefix.)
SPECIALTY (SPBX series) 12-15   87
(Boxed sets of six colored vinyl singles.)
SPECIALTY (500 and 600 series) 8-12 57-59
SPECIALTY (900 series) 3-5   70-72
Picture Sleeves
RCA 10-20   60-65
EPs: 7–inch 33/45rpm
KEEN (2001/2002/2003 "Songs By
Sam Cooke") 30-40   57
(Price is for any of three volumes.)
KEEN (2012/2013/2014 "Tribute to
the Lady") 20-30   59
(Price is for any of three volumes.)
KEEN (2006 "Encore") 20-40   58
KEEN (2008 "Encore, Vol. 2") 20-40 58
RCA (126 "Sam Cooke Sings") 10-20   61
(Compact 33.)
RCA (3373 "Sam Cooke") 15-20   64
(Jukebox issue.)
RCA (4375 "Another
Saturday Night") 15-25   63
LPs: 10/12–inch 33rpm
CAMDEN 8-10   68-74
CANDLELITE 15-20   74
(Mail-order offer.)
CHERIE 8-10   71
FAMOUS 10-20   69
KEEN (2001 "Sam Cooke") 35-45   58
KEEN (2003 "Encore") 35-45   58
KEEN (2004 "Tribute to the Lady") .. 30-40 59
KEEN (86101 "Hit Kit") 35-45   59
KEEN (86103 "I Thank God") 30-40   60
KEEN (86106 "Wonderful World") ... 30-40 60
PHOENIX 10 5-10   81
PICKWICK 5-10   76
RCA (2000 and 3000 series) 15-35 60-68
(With "LPM" or "LSP" prefix.)
RCA (2000 through 5000 series) 5-10 78-85
(With "AFL1," "ANL1" or "AYL1" prefix.)
RCA (7000 series) 8-12   86
SAR 3-5   61
SPECIALTY 8-12   69-89
TRIP 8-10   72-76
UPFRONT 8-10   73
Also see ANKA, Paul / Sam Cooke / Neil Sedaka
Also see CHARLES, Ray / Little Richard / Sam Cooke
Also see COOKE, Dale
Also see RAWLS, Lou

COOKE, Sam / Rod Lauren / Neil Sedaka / Browns
EPs: 7–inch 33/45rpm
RCA (33-99 "Compact 33 Double") .. 15-20 60
(With the same four songs on each side — mono
on one side, stereo on the reverse.)
Also see BROWNS

Also see LAUREN, Rod
Also see SEDAKA, Neil

COOKE, Sam / Lloyd Price / Larry Williams / Little Richard
LPs: 10/12–inch 33rpm
SPECIALTY (2112 "Our
  Significant Hits") 25-35   60
  (Black and gold label.)
  Also see COOKE, Sam
  Also see LITTLE RICHARD
  Also see PRICE, Lloyd
  Also see WILLIAMS, Larry

COOKE, Samona
Singles: 7–inch
EPIC 3-5   76-77
MERCURY 2-4   78

COOKER
(Norman Des Rosiers)
Singles: 7–inch
SCEPTER 3-5   73-74
LPs: 10/12–inch 33rpm
SCEPTER 8-10   74

COOKER, John Lee
(John Lee Hooker)
Singles: 7–inch
KING (4504 "Stomp Boogie") 50-75   52
  Also see HOOKER, John Lee

COOKIE and His Cupcakes
(Terry "Cookie" Clinton; Cookie and His Berry Cups)
Singles: 7–inch
CHESS 5-10   63
JUDD 10-20   59
KHOURY'S (703 "Matilda") 20-30   59
LYRIC 10-15   63-64
MERCURY 5-10   61
PAULA 4-8   65-68

COOKIE and His Cupcakes / Little Alfred
Singles: 7–inch
LYRIC 8-12   64
  Also see COOKIE and His Cupcakes

COOKIES
Singles: 7–inch
ABC 2-4   74
DIMENSION 10-20   62-64
ERIC 2-4   73
MCA 2-4   83
  Member: Earl-Jean McCree.
  Also see EARL-JEAN

COOKIES / Little Eva / Carole King
LPs: 10/12–inch 33rpm
DIMENSION (6001 "The Dimension
  Dolls, Vol. 1") 50-75   63
  Also see COOKIES
  Also see KING, Carole
  Also see LITTLE EVA

COOL HEAT
Singles: 7–inch
FORWARD 3-6   70
  Also see WIND

COOLEY, Eddie
(Eddie Cooley and the Dimples)
Singles: 78rpm
ROYAL ROOST 8-12   56-57
Singles: 7–inch
ABC 2-4   73
ROULETTE 5-10   60
ROYAL ROOST 10-20   56-57
TRIUMPH 8-12   59

COOLIDGE, Rita
Singles: 7–inch
A&M 3-5   71-83
PEPPER 4-8   68-69
Picture Sleeves
A&M 3-6   72-83
LPs: 10/12–inch 33rpm
A&M 5-10   71-83
Promotional LPs
A&M ("In-Store Sampler - Rita
  Coolidge") 10-15
  Also see CAMPBELL, Glen, and Rita Coolidge
  Also see CLAPTON, Eric

COOLIDGE, Rita, and Kris Kristofferson
Singles: 7–inch
A&M 3-5   73-74
MONUMENT 3-5   74-75
Picture Sleeves
A&M 3-5   73
LPs: 10/12–inch 33rpm
A&M 8-12   73-79
MONUMENT 8-10   74
  Also see COOLIDGE, Rita
  Also see KRISTOFFERSON, Kris

COOPER, Alice
(Alice Cooper Group)
Promotional Singles: 12–inch 33/45rpm
EPIC (1347 "I Got a Line on You") 5-8
EPIC (1663 "Poison") 5-8   89
EPIC (1686 "Trash") 5-8   89
EPIC (1890 "I'm Your Gun") 5-8   89
MCA (17177 "He's Back") 5-8   86
MCA (17205 "Give It Up") 5-8   86
WARNER (864 "Clones") 10-15   80
WARNER (1059 "I Like Girls") 5-8
Singles: 7–inch
ATLANTIC 3-5   75
EPIC 2-4   89-90
MCA 2-4   86-87
STRAIGHT (101 "Reflected") 15-25   69
STRAIGHT (7398 "Shoe Salesman")   15-20   70
WARNER 3-5   70-82
Promotional Singles
ATLANTIC 5-10   75
MCA 3-6   86-87

WARNER 8-12   70-80
Picture Sleeves
MCA 2-4   87
WARNER 4-8   72-80
EPs: 7-Inch 33/45rpm
WARNER 15-25   73
(Jukebox issues only.)
LPs: 10/12-inch 33rpm
ATLANTIC 5-10   75-78
EPIC 5-8   89
MFSL (063 "Welcome to
My Nightmare") 25-50   82
MCA 5-10   86-87
STRAIGHT (1051 "Pretties for You") . 30-40   69
(Cover has a drawing of a woman raising her
dress, with a yellow sticker covering her crotch
area. Price is for cover with sticker still intact.)
STRAIGHT (1051 "Pretties for You") . 20-30   69
(Cover shows the woman with the sticker removed
and panties showing.)
WARNER (Except 1883, 2567
and 2623) 8-12   73-84
WARNER (1883 "Love It to Death") .. 25-30   71
(Black cover has Cooper's right thumb showing
through his wrap. Does NOT have white block
reading "Including Their Hit *I'm Eighteen*.")
WARNER (1883 "Love It to Death") .. 15-20   71
(Black cover has Cooper's right thumb showing
through his wrap. Has white block reading
"Including Their Hit *I'm Eighteen*." Also includes
issue with huge white stripes at top and bottom of
cover.)
WARNER (1883 "Love It to Death") ... 5-10   71
(Black cover does NOT have Cooper's right thumb
showing through his wrap. Has the white block
reading "Including Their Hit *I'm Eighteen*.")
WARNER (2567 "Killer") 15-18   71
(With poster and 1972 calendar.)
WARNER (2567 "Killer") 5-10   72
(Without poster and calendar.)
WARNER (2623 "School's Out") 30-40   72
(With panties attached. Panties came in four
different colors: pink, white, yellow, and blue. Back
cover does not list titles.)
WARNER (2623 "School's Out") 15-20   72
(With panties attached. Back cover lists titles.)
WARNER (2623 "School's Out") 5-10   72
(With no paper panties. Back cover lists titles.)
WARNER (2685 "Billion Dollar Babies") 5-10   73
WARNER (BS4-2685 "Billion
Dollar Babies") 20-25   73
(Quad issue.)
WARNER (2748 "Muscle of Love") ... 5-10   73
WARNER (BBS4-2748 "Muscle
of Love") 20-25   73
(Quad issue.)
WARNER (2803 through 3581) 5-10   74-81
WARNER/STRAIGHT (1051 "Pretties
for You") 15-18   69

WARNER/STRAIGHT (1845 "Easy
Action") 30-35   70
(With the name "Alice Cooper" in black letters on
front cover.)
WARNER/STRAIGHT (1845 "Easy
Action") 5-10   70
(With the name "Alice Cooper" in white letters on
front cover.)
Promotional LPs
CHELSEA PROD ("Allison's Tea
House") 25-30   74
STRAIGHT (1051 "Pretties for You") . 45-55   69
(Cover has drawing of a woman raising her dress,
with a yellow sticker covering her crotch area.
Price is for cover with sticker still intact.)
STRAIGHT (1051 "Pretties for You") . 30-40   69
(Cover shows the woman with the sticker removed
and panties showing.)
STRAIGHT (1845 "Easy Action") 25-30   70
STRAIGHT (1883 "Love It to Death") 20-25   71
WARNER 20-40   71-78
(Includes all white label promo labels.)
WARNER/STRAIGHT ("Pretties
for You") 25-30   69
Members: Kane Roberts; Ken K. Mary.
Also see BILLION DOLLAR BABIES
Also see FROST
Also see NAZZ
Also see SPIDERS

COOPER, Les, and the Soul Rockers
Singles: 7-inch
ABC 2-4   73
ARRAWAK 4-8   65
ATCO 3-6   69
DIMENSION (1023 "Motor City") 10-15   64
ENJOY 4-8   65
EVERLAST 5-10   62
SAMAR 4-8   66
LPs: 10/12-inch 33rpm
EVERLAST (202 "Wiggle Wobble") .. 40-60   63

COOPER, Pat
LPs: 10/12-inch 33rpm
U.A. 10-15   66-69

COOPER BROTHERS
Singles: 7-inch
CAPRICORN 2-4   78-79
LPs: 10/12-inch 33rpm
CAPRICORN 5-10   78-79
Also see BLACK OAK ARKANSAS / Cooper Brothers

COPAS, Cowboy
(Lloyd Copas)
Singles: 78rpm
KING 5-10   46-57
Singles: 7-inch
KING (900 through 1500 series) 10-15   50-55
KING (4800 through 5200 series) ... 5-10   55-59
KING (5300 through 5700 series) 4-8   60-63
STARDAY (400 through 700 series) ... 4-8   60-66

| STARDAY (7000 series) | 3-6 | 64 |
| STARDAY (8000 series) | 2-4 | 71 |

EPs: 7-inch 33/45rpm

| KING | 15-25 | 52-53 |
| STARDAY | 10-20 | 60 |

LPs: 10/12-inch 33rpm

GUEST STAR	10-15	
KING (553 "All-Time Hits")	45-55	57
KING (556 "Favorite Sacred Songs")	40-50	57
KING (600 through 800 series)	25-35	59-64
KING (1000 series)	8-12	69
NASHVILLE	8-12	68-70
PICKWICK/HILLTOP	10-12	66
STARDAY (100 and 200 series)	20-30	60-64
STARDAY (300 series)	12-20	65-67
STARDAY (400 series)	8-12	68-70
Also see COPAS, Lloyd

COPAS, Cowboy / Hawkshaw Hawkins
LPs: 10/12-inch 33rpm

| KING | 10-20 | 63-66 |
Also see CLINE, Patsy / Cowboy Copas / Hawkshaw Hawkins
Also see COPAS, Cowboy
Also see HAWKINS, Hawkshaw

COPAS, Lloyd
Singles: 7-inch

| DOT (15735 "Circle Rock") | 60-80 | 58 |
Also see COPAS, Cowboy

COPELAND, Ken
Singles: 78rpm

| IMPERIAL | 4-8 | 57 |
| LIN (5007 "Fanny Brown") | 10-15 | 58 |

Singles: 7-inch

DOT	8-12	58
IMPERIAL	10-15	57
LIN (5007 "Fanny Brown")	20-30	58

COPELAND, Ken / Mints
Singles: 78rpm

| IMPERIAL | 8-12 | 57 |
| LIN | 10-15 | 56-57 |

Singles: 7-inch

IMPERIAL	10-15	57
LIN (5007 "Pledge of Love")	15-25	56
LIN (5017 "Fanny Brown")	20-30	57
Also see COPELAND, Ken

COPELAND, Stewart
LPs: 10/12-inch 33rpm

| A&M | 5-10 | 83-85 |
Also see POLICE

COPELAND, Stewart, and Stan Ridgway
Singles: 7-inch

| A&M | 2-4 | 83 |
Also see COPELAND, Stewart
Also see WALL of VOODOO

COPELAND, Vivian
Singles: 7-inch

| D'ORO | 3-6 | 69 |
| MALA | 4-8 | 67 |

COREA, Chick
Singles: 7-inch

| POLYDOR | 2-4 | 79 |

LPs: 10/12-inch 33rpm

BLUE NOTE	8-12	75-78
ECM	5-10	75-80
ELEKTRA	5-8	83
PACIFIC JAZZ	5-8	81
POLYDOR	6-12	76-78
VERVE	8-10	76
WARNER	5-8	80-81
Also see HANCOCK, Herbie, and Chick Corea
Also see RETURN to FOREVER

COREY, Jill
Singles: 78rpm

| COLUMBIA | 3-6 | 54-57 |

Singles: 7-inch

| COLUMBIA | 5-10 | 54-60 |
| MERCURY | 4-8 | 62 |

EPs: 7-inch 33/45rpm

| COLUMBIA | 8-12 | 55-57 |

LPs: 10/12-inch 33rpm

| COLUMBIA | 15-25 | 56-57 |

CORLEY, Al
Singles: 7-inch

| MERCURY | 2-4 | 85 |

CORLEY, Bob
Singles: 78rpm

| RCA | 3-5 | 56 |
| STARS | 10-15 | 55 |

Singles: 7-inch

| RCA | 5-10 | 56 |
| STARS | 20-25 | 55 |

CORNBREAD & BISCUITS
Singles: 7-inch

| MASKE | 5-10 | 60 |

CORNELIUS BROTHERS and Sister Rose
Singles: 7-inch

| PLATINUM | 8-12 | 70 |
| U.A. | 3-5 | 70-74 |

LPs: 10/12-inch 33rpm

| PICKWICK | 5-10 | 76 |
| U.A. | 10-15 | 72-76 |
Members: Ed Cornelius; Carter Cornelius; Rose Cornelius.

CORNELL, Don
Singles: 78rpm

| CORAL | 3-6 | 52-57 |

Singles: 7-inch

ABC-PAR	3-6	65
CORAL	5-10	52-57
DOT	4-8	59-60
JAYBEE	3-5	69
JUBILEE	3-6	62
SIGNATURE	4-8	59-60
20TH FOX	3-6	64

EPs: 7–Inch 33/45rpm
CORAL 5-10   54-56
LPs: 10/12–inch 33rpm
ABC-PAR 8-12   66
CORAL 15-25   54-57
DOT 10-15   59
MOVIETONE 5-10   66
SIGNATURE 10-15   59
VOCALION 8-15   59

CORNELL, Don, Johnny Desmond and Alan Dale
Singles: 78rpm
CORAL 3-6   53
Singles: 7–inch
CORAL 5-10   53
EPs: 7–inch 33/45rpm
CORAL 5-10   54
Also see CORNELL, Don
Also see DALE, Alan
Also see DESMOND, Johnny

CORNER BOYS
Singles: 7–inch
NEPTUNE 4-6   69
Members: Victor Drayton; Jerry Akines; Reginald Turner; Ernie
Brooks; Johnny Bellman.

CORPORATION
Singles: 7–inch
CAPITOL 10-15   69
MUSICOR 4-8   70
LPs: 10/12–inch 33rpm
AGE of AQUARIUS 20-25   69
CAPITOL 20-25   69

CORSAIRS
(Featuring Jay "Bird" Uzzell)
Singles: 7–inch
CHESS 5-10   62
ERIC........................... 2-4   78
SMASH 5-10   61
TUFF 5-10   61-64

CORTEZ, Dave "Baby"
(Baby Cortez)
Singles: 7–inch
ABC 2-4   74
ALL PLATINUM 3-5   72
ARGO 4-8   64
CHESS 4-8   63
CLOCK 5-10   59-62
COLLECTABLES 2-4   81
EMIT 4-8   62
ERIC........................... 2-4   73
FIRE 5-10   60
JULIA 15-25   62
OKEH (7100 series) 10-20   58
OKEH (7200 series) 4-8   64
ROULETTE 4-8   65-68
SOUND 3-5   71
T-NECK 3-6   69

WINLEY 4-8   62
EPs: 7–inch 33/45rpm
CLOCK 20-30   59-61
RCA (EPA-4342 "Dave 'Baby'
Cortez and His Happy Organ") 15-25   59
(Monaural.)
RCA (ESP-4342 "Dave 'Baby'
Cortez and His Happy Organ") 35-50   59
(Stereo.)
LPs: 10/12–inch 33rpm
CHESS 25-30   62
CLOCK 25-35   60-63
CORONET 10-15
CROWN 15-20   63
DESIGN 10-15
METRO 10-20   65
RCA (LPM-2099 "Dave 'Baby'
Cortez and His Happy Organ") 25-35   59
(Monaural.)
RCA (LSP-2099 "Dave 'Baby'
Cortez and His Happy Organ") 35-50   59
(Stereo.)
ROULETTE 15-20   65-66
Also see ISLEY BROTHERS and Dave "Baby" Cortez

CORTEZ, Dave "Baby" / Jerry's House Rockers
LPs: 10/12–inch 33rpm
CROWN 10-20   63
Also see CORTEZ, Dave "Baby"

CORY
Singles: 7–inch
PHANTOM 3-5   77

CORYELL, Larry
LPs: 10/12–inch 33rpm
ARISTA 5-10   76
VANGUARD 10-15   69
Also see ELEVENTH HOUR/ELVENTH HOUSE
Also see MOUZON, Alphonse, and Larry Croyell

COSBY, Bill
Singles: 12–inch 33/45rpm
MOTOWN (110 "Super Special
for Radio") 5-10   82
(Promotional issue only.)
Singles: 7–inch
CAPITOL 2-5   76-78
UNI 3-6   69-70
WARNER 3-5   65-67
EPs: 7–inch 33/45rpm
WARNER (274 "A Taste of Cosby") ... 5-10
(Promotional issue only.)
LPs: 10/12–inch 33rpm
CAPITOL 5-10   76-78
COLUMBIA (40270 "Music from
the Bill Cosby Show") 5-10   86
(Featuring Grover Washington Jr.)
GEFFEN 5-10   86
MCA 5-10   73
MOTOWN 5-10   82

PARTEE 5-10
TETRAGRAMMATON 6-10   69
UNI 5-10   69-72
WARNER (Except 249) 10-15   64-70
WARNER (249 "Best of Bill Cosby") . 15-20   69
(Promotional issue only.)
Also see ROSS, Diana, and Bill Cosby / Diana Ross with the Jackson Five
Also see WASHINGTON, Grover, Jr.

COSBY, Bill, and Ozzie Davis
LPs: 10/12–inch 33rpm
BLACK FORUM 8-12   72
Also see COSBY, Bill

COSTA, Don, Orchestra
Singles: 78rpm
ABC-PAR 2-5   56-57
ESSEX 2-5   55
Singles: 7–inch
ABC-PAR 3-6   56-57
COLUMBIA 3-5   62-63
DCP 3-5   64-65
ESSEX 4-8   55
JAMIE 3-6   59
MGM 2-5   66-72
MERCURY 3-5   68
U.A. 3-6   59-62
VERVE 3-5   67
Picture Sleeves
U.A. 5-10   60
VERVE 4-8   67
LPs: 10/12–inch 33rpm
ABC-PAR 10-20   56-61
COLUMBIA 8-12   62-63
DCP 5-10   64-65
HARMONY 5-10   65
MERCURY 5-10   68-69
U.A. 8-12   59-62
VERVE 5-10   67

COSTANDINOS, Alec R.
(With the Syncophonic Orchestra)
Singles: 7–inch
CASABLANCA 2-4   79
LPs: 10/12–inch 33rpm
CASABLANCA 5-10   78-79

COSTELLO, Elvis
(Elvis Costello and the Attractions; Costello Show)
Singles: 12–inch 33/45rpm
COLUMBIA 5-10   83-85
Singles: 7–inch
CBS (Black vinyl) 2-5   79
CBS (Colored vinyl) 10-20   79
COLUMBIA 3-5   77-86
WARNER 2-4   89
Promotional Singles
COLUMBIA 5-10   77-86
Picture Sleeves
COLUMBIA (Except 10919) 3-6   81-85

COLUMBIA (10919 "Accidents Will
  Happen") 15-20   78
(Promotional issue only.)
WARNER 2-4   89
EPs: 7–inch 33/45rpm
COLUMBIA (1171 "Live at
  Hollywood High") 10-20   78
(Bonus EP. Included with the LP Armed Forces.)
COLUMBIA (11251 "I Can't Stand
  Up for Falling Down") 10-20   80
COLUMBIA (11251 "I Can't Stand
  Up for Falling Down") 20-30   80
(White label. Promotional issue only.)
LPs: 10/12–inch 33rpm
COLUMBIA (30000 series,
  except 35709) 8-12   77-86
COLUMBIA (35709 "Armed Forces") . 15-25   79
(Includes the bonus EP Live At Hollywood High.)
COLUMBIA (35709 "Armed Forces") .. 8-12   79
(Without Live At Hollywood High EP.)
COLUMBIA (35709 "Armed Forces") . 30-40   79
(Colored vinyl.)
COLUMBIA/COSTELLO (35331 "This
  Year's Model") 20-30   78
COLUMBIA (40000 series,
  except 48157) 5-8   85-86
COLUMBIA (48157 "Imperial
  Bedroom") 30-40   82
(Half-speed mastered.)
WARNER 5-10   89-91
Promotional LPs
COLUMBIA ("My Aim Is True"/
  "This Year's Model") 75-125   79
(Picture disc. No number given.)
COLUMBIA (529 "Live at Hollywood
  High") 30-45   79
COLUMBIA (958 "Tom Snyder
  Interview") 25-35   81
COLUMBIA (1318 "Almost Blue") ... 25-35   81
COLUMBIA/COSTELLO (847 "Taking
  Liberties") 30-35   80
Also see CLIFF, Jimmy, with Elvis Costello and the Attractions
Also see HIATT, John
Also see NICK & ELVIS

COTTON, Gene
Singles: 7–inch
ABC 3-5   75-77
ARIOLA AMERICA 2-4   77-79
KNOLL 2-4   81-82
MYRRH 3-5   74
LPs: 10/12–inch 33rpm
ABC 8-10   76-77
ACCORD 5-10   83
ARIOLA AMERICA 5-10   78-79
BUDDAH 8-10   74-75
CAPITOL 8-10   71
IMPACT 15-20
KNOLL 5-10   81-82
MYRRH 8-10   73

COTTON, Gene, and Kim Carnes
Singles: 7-inch
ARIOLA AMERICA 2-4   78
Also see CARNES, Kim
Also see COTTON, Gene

COTTON, James
(James Cotton Blues Band; James Cotton with Matt "Guitar" Murphy and Luther Tucker)
Singles: 12-inch 33/45rpm
ERECT 4-6   82
Singles: 78rpm
SUN (199 "My Baby") 75-100   54
SUN (206 "Cotton Crop Blues") 50-75   54
Singles: 7-inch
BUDDAH 3-5   75
LOMA 10-15   66
SUN (199 "My Baby") 300-400   54
SUN (206 "Cotton Crop Blues") ... 250-350 54
VERVE/FOLKWAYS 4-8   67
VERVE/FORECAST 4-8   67-69
LPs: 10/12-inch 33rpm
ACCORD 5-10   83
ALLIGATOR 5-10   84
ANTONE'S 5-10   88
BUDDAH 10-12   74-76
CAPITOL 10-12   71
ERECT 5-10   82
INTERMEDIA 5-10   84
VANGUARD 10-15   68
VERVE/FOLKWAYS 10-20   67
VERVE/FORECAST 10-15   66-69
Also see WATERS, Muddy

COTTON, James, Carey Bell, Junior Wells, and Billy Branch
LPs: 10/12-inch 33rpm
ALLIGATOR (4790 "Harp Attack") 5-10   90
Also see WELLS, Junior

COTTON, Josie
Singles: 12-inch 33/45rpm
BOMP 5-10   80
ELEKTRA (11538 "Johnny Are
   You Queer") 5-10   82
Singles: 7-inch
ELEKTRA (Black vinyl) 2-4   82-84
ELEKTRA (Colored vinyl) 5-10   82
WEA (79292 "Johnny Are You Queer") . 3-5   82
Picture Sleeves
ELEKTRA 2-4   82-84
WEA (79292 "Johnny Are You Queer") . 3-5   82
LPs: 10/12-inch 33rpm
ELEKTRA 5-10   82

COTTON, LLOYD & CHRISTIAN
Singles: 7-inch
20TH FOX 3-5   75-76
LPs: 10/12-inch 33rpm
20TH FOX 8-12   75-76
Members: Darryl Cotton; Michael Lloyd; Chris Christian.

COUCHOIS
Singles: 7-inch
WARNER 2-4   79-80
LPs: 10/12-inch 33rpm
WARNER 5-10   79-80

COUGAR, John:
see MELLENCAMP, John Cougar

COULTER, Clifford
Singles: 7-inch
COLUMBIA 2-4   80
LPs: 10/12-inch 33rpm
COLUMBIA 5-10   80

COUNT BASIE: see BASIE, Count

COUNT FIVE
Singles: 7-inch
DOUBLE-SHOT 5-10   66-69
LPs: 10/12-inch 33rpm
DOUBLE-SHOT (1001 "Psychotic
   Reaction") 25-35   66
(Monaural.)
DOUBLE-SHOT (5001 "Psychotic
   Reaction") 30-40   66
(Stereo.)

COUNT 5
Singles: 7-inch
LES COUNTS (3447 "Count 5") 20-30

COUNTRY BOYS and City Girls
Singles: 7-inch
HAPPY FOX 3-5   76
Member: Lee Maye.

COUNTRY COALITION
Singles: 7-inch
ABC 3-5   70-73
ABC/BLUESWAY 3-5   70
LPs: 10/12-inch 33rpm
ABC/BLUESWAY 10-12   70

COUNTRY HAMS
Singles: 7-inch
EMI (3977 "Walking in the
   Park with Eloise") 10-20   74
Picture Sleeves
EMI (3977 "Walking in the
   Park with Eloise") 50-60   74
Promotional Singles
EMI (3977 "Walking in the
   Park with Eloise") 25-35   74
Members: Paul McCartney and Wings; Chet Atkins; Floyd Cramer.
Also see ATKINS, Chet
Also see CRAMER, Floyd
Also see McCARTNEY, Paul

COUNTRY JOE and the Fish
Singles: 7-inch
VANGUARD 5-10   67-69
Picture Sleeves
VANGUARD 8-15   68

EPs: 7-inch 33/45rpm

RAG BABY (1001 "Rag Baby") 30-40	66
RAG BABY (1002 "Rag Baby") 30-40	66
RAG BABY (1003 "Rag Baby") 30-40	66

LPs: 10/12-inch 33rpm

FANTASY 8-10	75-77
VANGUARD (Except 9266) 10-20	67-71
VANGUARD (9266 "I Feel Like	
I'm Fixin' to Die") 20-30	67
(With cut-out pictures and poster game.)	
VANGUARD (9266 "I Feel Like	
I'm Fixin' to Die") 10-20	67
(Without pictures and poster.)	
Also see McDONALD, Country Joe	

COUNTS

Singles: 78rpm

DOT 10-20	53-56
NOTE 20-40	56

Singles: 7-inch

DOT (1199 "Hot Tamales") 20-40	54
DOT (1188 "Darling Dear") 30-40	53
DOT (1210 "My Dear, My Darling") . . 30-40	54
DOT (1226 "Baby, I Want You") 30-40	54
DOT (1235 "Let Me Go Lover") 20-30	54
DOT (1243 "From This Day On") . . . 20-30	55
DOT (1265 "Sally Walker") 15-25	55
DOT (1275 "Heartbreaker") 15-25	56
DOT (16000 series) 5-10	60
NOTE (20000 "Sweet Names") 75-125	56

COUNTS

Singles: 7-inch

AWARE 3-5	74
WESTBOUND 3-5	72

LPs: 10/12-inch 33rpm

AWARE 8-10	75
AWARE/GRC 8-10	73
GRC 8-10	73
TCB 4-8	
WESTBOUND 8-10	72

COURTNEY, David

LPs: 10/12-inch 33rpm

U.A. 8-10	75

COURTNEY, Lou
(Lew Courtney)

Singles: 7-inch

BUDDAH 3-6	69
EPIC 3-5	73-75
IMPERIAL 4-8	63-64
PHILIPS 4-8	65
POP SIDE 4-8	67
RAGS 4-6	73
RIVERSIDE 4-8	66-67
VERVE 4-6	68

LPs: 10/12-inch 33rpm

EPIC 8-10	74
RCA 8-10	76
RIVERSIDE 15-20	67

COURTSHIP

Singles: 7-inch

CAPITOL 3-5	70
GLADES 3-5	72
TAMLA 3-5	72

COUSIN ICE

Singles: 7-inch

URBAN ROCK 4-6	85

COVAY, Don
(Don Covay and the Goodtimers; Don Covay and the Jefferson Lemon Blues Band; Don "Pretty Boy" Covay)

Singles: 7-inch

ARNOLD (1002 "Pony Time") 10-15	61
ATLANTIC 4-8	65-70
BIG TOP 5-10	60
BLAZE (350 "Standing in	
the Doorway") 15-20	58
CAMEO 5-10	62-63
COLUMBIA 5-10	61
LANDA 4-8	64
MERCURY 2-4	72-75
NEWMAN 2-4	80
PARKWAY 4-8	63-64
PHILADELPHIA INT'L 3-5	76
ROSEMART 4-8	64
SUE (709 "Believe It Or Not") 15-25	
U-VON 3-5	77

LPs: 10/12-inch 33rpm

ATLANTIC 15-25	65-69
JANUS 8-12	72
MERCURY 8-10	74
PHILADELPHIA INT'L 8-10	76
VERSATILE 8-10	78
Also see GOODTIMERS	
Also see PRETTY BOY	
Also see SOUL CLAN	

COVEN

Singles: 7-inch

BUDDAH 3-5	74
LION 3-5	71
MGM 3-5	71-73
MERCURY 3-6	69
SGC 5-8	68
WARNER 3-5	71-73

LPs: 10/12-inch 33rpm

BUDDAH 8-10	74
MGM 10-12	71-72
MERCURY 12-15	69
Member: Teresa Kelly.	

COVER GIRLS

Singles: 7-inch

CAPITOL 2-4	89-90
FEVER 2-4	87-88

Picture Sleeves

FEVER 2-4	87-88

LPs: 10/12-inch 33rpm

CAPITOL 5-8	89-90

FEVER 5-10   87

COWBOY COPAS: see COPAS, Cowboy

COWBOY CHURCH SUNDAY SCHOOL
Singles: 78rpm
DECCA 3-5   54-55
VOSS 3-5   54
Singles: 7–inch
DECCA 5-10   54-55
VOSS 5-10   54
Picture Sleeves
DECCA 10-20   55
EPs: 7–inch 33/45rpm
DECCA 8-12   55

COWSILLS
Singles: 7–inch
JODA (103 "All I Really
  Want to Be Is Me") 10-20   65
LONDON 2-4   71-72
MGM 3-5   67-71
PHILIPS 4-8   66-67
Picture Sleeves
MGM 4-8   67-69
PHILIPS 5-10   66
EPs: 7–inch 33/45rpm
MGM (1 "The Cowsills") 15-25   68
  (Promotional issue from the American Dairy
  Assocaition.)
LPs: 10/12–inch 33rpm
LONDON 8-10   71
MGM 10-12   67-71
WING 10-12   68
  Members: Bill Cowsill; Barry Cowsill; John Cowsill; Susan
  Cowsill; Bob Cowsill; Paul Cowsill; Barbara Cowsill.

COX, Wally
Singles: 78rpm
RCA 3-5   53
Singles: 7–inch
ARVEE 4-8   60
GEORGE 4-8   61
RCA (5278 "What a Crazy Guy") 5-10   53
WAND 3-5   70
Picture Sleeves
RCA (5278 "What a Crazy Guy") 10-20   53

COYOTE SISTERS
Singles: 7–inch
MOROCCO 2-4   84
Picture Sleeves
MOROCCO 2-4   84
LPs: 10/12–inch 33rpm
MOROCCO 5-10   84
  Members: Leah Kunkel; Marty Gwinn; Renee Armand.

CRABBY APPLETON
Singles: 7–inch
ELEKTRA 3-5   70-72
LPs: 10/12–inch 33rpm
ELEKTRA 8-10   70-71

CRACK the SKY
Singles: 12–inch 33/45rpm
GRUDGE 4-8   88
  (Promotional only.)
Singles: 7–inch
GRUDGE 2-4   88-90
LIFESONG 3-5   76-79
LPs: 10/12–inch 33rpm
GRUDGE 5-8   88-90
LIFESONG (Except 8000 series) 10-15   75-78
LIFESONG (8000 series) 5-10   81

CRADDOCK, Billy "Crash"
(Billy Craddock "Crash" Craddock; Billy Graddock)
Singles: 7–inch
ABC 2-5   72-78
ABC/DOT 3-5   75-77
CAPITOL 2-4   78-82
CARTWHEEL 3-5   71-72
CEE CEE 2-4   83
CHART 3-6   67-73
COLONIAL 8-12   58
COLUMBIA 5-10   59-60
DATE 8-12   58
KING (Except 5912) 4-8   64-65
KING (5912 "Betty Betty") 10-15   64
MERCURY 4-8   61-62
SKY CASTLE ("Smacky Mouth") 20-30
  (No number used. Shows Columbia identification
  numbers, 26671/26672.)
Picture Sleeves
COLUMBIA (41470 "Don't
  Destroy Me") 15-25   59
COLUMBIA (41619 "All I Want Is You") 15-25   60
EPs: 7–inch 33/45rpm
ABC 4-8   74
  (Jukebox issue only.)
LPs: 10/12–inch 33rpm
ABC 6-10   72-78
ABC/AT EASE 10-12   78
  (Special issue for the Armed Forces.)
ABC/DOT 8-10   76-77
CAPITOL 5-10   78-83
CARTWHEEL 10-12   71-72
CHART 8-12   73
HARMONY 10-12   73
KING (912 "I'm Tore Up") 45-55   64
STARDAY 8-10
MCA 5-10   82

CRAMER, Floyd
Singles: 78rpm
ABBOTT 3-5   53-54
MGM 2-5   55-57
Singles: 7–inch
ABBOTT 5-10   53-54
MGM 5-8   55-57
RCA (Except 7000 and 8000 series) .. 2-5   67-81
RCA (7000 and 8000 series) 4-8   61-66

Picture Sleeves
RCA 6-12   61-63
EPs: 7–inch 33/45rpm
MGM 8-12   57
RCA 5-10   61-63
LPs: 10/12–inch 33rpm
ALSHIRE 8-12   68
CAMDEN 6-12   65-74
MGM (3500 series) 15-20   57
MGM (4200 series) 10-15   64
MGM (4600 series) 8-12   70
RCA (0100 through 4000 series) 5-10   73-81
   (With "AHL1," ANL1," "APD1," "APL1," or "AYL1"
   prefix.)
RCA (2000 through 4000 series) 10-20   60-73
   (With "LPM" or "LSP" prefix.)
   Also see ANN-MARGRET
   Also see ATKINS, Chet, Floyd Cramer and Danny Davis
   Also see ATKINS, Chet, Floyd Cramer and Boots Randolph
   Also see COUNTRY HAMS
   Also see FRANCIS, Connie
   Also see PRESLEY, Elvis
   Also see REEVES, Jim

CRAMER, Floyd / Peter Nero / Frankie Carle
LPs: 10/12–inch 33rpm
RCA 10-15   63
   Also see CRAMER, Floyd
   Also see NERO, Peter

CRAMPS
Singles: 12–inch 33/45rpm
I.R.S. (1008 "The Crusher") 10-15   82
   (Issued with paper sleeve.)
Singles: 7–inch
I.R.S. (9021 "Goo Goo Muck") 4-8   81
I.R.S. (9021 "Goo Goo Muck") 35-50   81
   (Colored vinyl.)
ILLEGAL/I.R.S. (9014 "Garbageman") . 5-10   80
VENGEANCE (666 "Surfin' Bird") ... 50-75   78
VENGEANCE (668 "Human Fly") ... 50-75   78
Picture Sleeves
I.R.S. (9014 "Garbage Man") 10-20   80
I.R.S. (9021 "Goo Goo Muck") 10-20   81
ILLEGAL/I.R.S. (9014 "Garbageman") 10-15   80
EPs: 7–inch 33/45rpm
BIG BEAT (6 "Smell of Female") 10-15   83
LPs: 10/12–inch 33rpm
ENIGMA 5-10
ILLEGAL/I.R.S. (007 "Songs the
   Lord Taught Us") 10-15   79
   (Tracks on disc are different than those shown on
   the cover, and in a different sequence than shown
   on label.)
ILLEGAL/I.R.S. (012 "Off the Bone") . 15-20   83
   (With 3-D cover and glasses.)
ILLEGAL/I.R.S. (012 "Off the Bone") .. 5-10   83
   (With standard cover.)
ILLEGAL (501 "Gravest Hits") 10-20   79
ILLEGAL/I.R.S. (70016 "Psychedelic
   Jungle") 8-10   81

LAST RECORD 15-20   78
NST 5-10   85
MIDNIGHT 15-20   78
   Members: Lux Interior; Poison Ivy; Congo Powers; Bryan
   Gregory; Nick Knox; Ivy Rorschach.

CRAMPTON SISTERS
Singles: 7–inch
ABC 4-8   66
DCP 5-10   64

CRANE, Les
Singles: 7–inch
WARNER 3-5   71
Picture Sleeves
WARNER 4-8   71
LPs: 10/12–inch 33rpm
WARNER 5-10   71

CRAWFORD, Caroline
Singles: 7–inch
MERCURY 2-4   78-79
LPs: 10/12–inch 33rpm
MERCURY 5-10   78-79

CRAWFORD, Carolyn
Singles: 7–inch
MERCURY 2-4   79
MOTOWN 15-30   63-64
PHILADELPHIA INT'L 3-5   74-75
   Also see CHAPTER 8

CRAWFORD, Hank
Singles: 7–inch
ATLANTIC 3-8   61-70
KUDU 3-5   72
LPs: 10/12–inch 33rpms
ATLANTIC 10-20   61-73
KUDU 10-12   72-76

CRAWFORD, Johnny
Singles: 7–inch
ABC 2-4   73
CINDY 4-6
COLLECTABLES 2-4   81
DEL-FI 5-10   61-64
SIDEWALK 4-8   67-68
WYNNE (124 "Ask") 10-15   60
Picture Sleeves
DEL-FI 10-15   61-63
SIDEWALK 5-8   68
EPs: 7–inch 33/45rpm
GRASON (6515 "The Restless Ones") 10-15
LPs: 10/12–inch 33rpm
DEL-FI (1220 "The Captivating
   Johnny Crawford") 20-30   62
DEL-FI (1223 "A Young
   Man's Fancy") 20-30   62
DEL-FI (1224 "Rumors") 20-30   63
DEL-FI (1229 "His Greatest Hits") ... 20-30   63
DEL-FI (1248 "Greatest Hits Vol. 2") . 20-30   63
GUEST STAR 15-20   63
RHINO 5-10   82

SUPREME (110 "Songs from
The Restless Ones) 15-20   66
(Soundtrack. Monaural.)
SUPREME (210 "Songs from
The Restless Ones) 20-30   66
(Soundtrack. Stereo.)

CRAWFORD, Randy
Singles: 12-inch 33/45rpm
WARNER 4-6   83
Singles: 7-inch
COLUMBIA 3-5   72-73
MCA 2-4   81
WARNER 2-5   77-86
Picture Sleeves
COLUMBIA 3-5   72
LPs: 10/12-inch 33rpm
RCA 5-10   84
WARNER 8-10   76-89
Also see CRUSADERS
Also see JARREAU, Al, and Randy Crawford
Also see SPRINGFIELD, Rick, and Randy Crawford

CRAWLER: see BACK STREET CRAWLER

CRAY, Robert
(Robert Cray Band)
Singles: 12-inch 33/45rpm
MERCURY 4-8   88
(Promotional only.)
Singles: 7-inch
MERCURY 2-4   87-88
Picture Sleeves
MERCURY 2-4   87-88
LPs: 10/12-inch 33rpm
HIGHTONE 5-10   83-87
MERCURY 5-10   86
TOMATO 10-20   80
Also see COLLINS, Albert, Robert Cray and Johnny Copeland

CRAY, Robert, Band, with the Memphis Horns
LPs: 10/12-inch 33rpm
MERCURY 5-8   90
Also see CRAY, Robert
Also see MEMPHIS HORNS

CRAYTON, Pee Wee
Singles: 78rpm
ALADDIN 10-20   51
FLAIR 10-15   55
4 STAR 10-20   47
IMPERIAL 10-15   54-55
MODERN 8-12   49-51
POST 8-12   55
RECORDED in HOLLYWOOD 10-20   54
VEE JAY 8-12   56-57
Singles: 7-inch
ALADDIN (3112 "When It
Rains It Pours") 50-100   51
EDCO (1009 "Ev'ry Night 'Bout
This Time") 20-30
EDCO (1010 "Money Tree") 20-30

FLAIR (1061 "Central Avenue Blues") 10-20   55
(By Pee Wee Crayton even though shown as by
the Carroll County Boys. The flip, Dizzy, was by the
Carroll County Boys.)
FOX (10069 "Give Me
One More Chance") 15-25
GUYDEN 5-10   61
IMPERIAL (5288 "Do Unto Others") . 25-40   54
IMPERIAL (5297 "Win-o") 25-40   54
IMPERIAL (5321 "I Need Your Love") 25-40   54
IMPERIAL (5338 "My Idea About You") 25-40   55
IMPERIAL (5345 "Eyes Full of Tears") 25-40   55
IMPERIAL (5353 "Yours Truly") 25-40   55
JAMIE 3-5   61
MODERN 20-30   51
POST (2007 "I Must Go On") 20-30   55
RECORDED in HOLLYWOOD (408 "Pappy's
Blues") 50-75   54
RECORDED in HOLLYWOOD (426 "Baby
Pat the Floor") 50-75   54
SMASH 4-8   62
VEE JAY (214 "Frosty Night") 25-35   56
VEE JAY (252 "I Found Peace
of Mind") 25-35   57
VEE JAY (266 "Fiddle De Dee") 25-35   57
LPs: 10/12-inch 33rpm
CROWN (5175 "Pee Wee Crayton") . 40-50   59
MURRAY BROTHERS 5-10   83
VANGUARD 8-12   71

CRAZY ELEPHANT
Singles: 7-inch
BELL 4-8   69-70
SPHERE SOUND 4-6   69
LPs: 10/12-inch 33rpm
BELL 15-20   69

CRAZY HORSE
Singles: 7-inch
EPIC 3-5   72
M.O.C. 4-8
REPRISE 3-5   71-72
LPs: 10/12-inch 33rpm
EPIC 8-12   72-76
RCA 5-10   78
REPRISE 10-15   71-72
Members: Ralph Molina; Billy Talbot; Leon Whitsell; George
Whitsell; Ry Cooder; Mike Curtis; Greg Leroy; Bob Notkoff; Neil
Young.
Also see YOUNG, Neil

CRAZY OTTO
Singles: 78rpm
DECCA 3-5   55-57
Singles: 7-inch
DECCA 4-8   55-61
MGM 3-5   62
EPs: 7-inch 33/45rpm
DECCA 5-10   55-58
LPs: 10/12-inch 33rpm
DECCA 8-18   55-61

MGM 6-12		63
VOCALION 8-10		59
see BROWN, Arthur		

CREACH, Papa John
Singles: 7-inch

BUDDAH 3-5		76
DJM 2-4		79
GRUNT 3-5		71-72

LPs: 10/12-inch 33rpm

BUDDAH 8-12		75-77
DJM 6-10		77-78
GRUNT 10-15		71-74
Also see JEFFERSON STARSHIP		
Also see SUNRISE		

CREAM
Singles: 7-inch

ATCO 4-8		67-70

EPs: 7-inch 33/45rpm

ATCO ("Goodbye Cream") 10-15		69
(Promotional issue only.)		

LPs: 10/12-inch 33rpm

ATCO (206 "Fresh Cream") 25-35		67
(With I Feel Free. On RSO reissues, this track is		
replaced with Spoonful.)		
ATCO (206 "Fresh Cream") 10-20		67
(Without I Feel Free.)		
ATCO (232 "Disraeli Gears") 20-30		67
ATCO (291 "The Best of Cream") ... 20-30		69
ATCO (328 "Live Cream") 20-30		70
ATCO (700 "Wheels of Fire") 20-30		68
ATCO (7001 "Goodbye") 20-30		69
ATCO (7005 "Live Cream, Vol. 2") ... 20-30		72
MFSL (066 "Wheels of Fire") 30-40		82
POLYDOR 10-12		72-73
RSO (Except 015) 5-10		72-83
RSO (015 "Classic Cuts") 35-45		75
(Promotional issue only.)		
SPRINGBOARD 10-12		
Members: Eric Clapton; Jack Bruce; Ginger Baker.		
Also see BAKER, Ginger		
Also see BRUCE, Jack		
Also see CLAPTON, Eric		

CREATIVE SOURCE
Singles: 7-inch

POLYDOR 3-5		75
SUSSEX 3-5		73-74

LPs: 10/12-inch 33rpm

POLYDOR 8-10		75-76
SUSSEX 10-12		74
Members: Don Wyatt; Celeste Rhodes; Steve Flanagan;		
Barbara Berryman; Barbara Lewis.		

CREEDENCE CLEARWATER REVIVAL
Singles: 12-inch 33/45rpm

FANTASY (238 "Creedence Medley") 10-15		85
FANTASY (759 "I Heard It Through		
the Grapevine") 15-20		76
(Promotional issue only.)		

Singles: 7-inch

FANTASY (Except 2832) 3-6		69-85

FANTASY (2832 "45 Revolutions		
Per Minute") 40-60		70
SCORPIO (412 "Porterville") 15-25		68

Picture Sleeves

FANTASY (Except 2832) 5-10		69-76
FANTASY (2832 "45 Revolutions		
Per Minute") 20-25		70

LPs: 10/12-inch 33rpm

BEVERLY ("Willie and the		
Poor Boys") 75-100		
(Half-speed mastered. Number not known.)		
FANTASY (1 through 70) 8-15		73-78
FANTASY (4500 series) 5-10		80-85
(Includes reissues of 8382 through 9404.)		
FANTASY (8382 through 9404) 8-15		68-72
FANTASY (9418 through 9621) 5-10		72-82
K-TEL 8-12		78
MFSL (037 "Cosmo's Factory") 30-50		79
SWEET THUNDER (13 "Green		
River") 75-100		75
(Half-speed mastered.)		
WARNER SPECIAL PRODUCTS		
(3514 "Greatest Hits") 10-15		85
(TV mail-order offer.)		
Members: John Fogerty; Tom Fogerty; Doug Clifford; Stuart		
Cook.		
Also see FOGERTY, John		
Also see FOGERTY, Tom		
Also see GOLLIWOGS		
Also see HARRISON, Don		

CREME, Lol, and Kevin Godley:
see GODLEY, Kevin, and Lol Creme

CREME D'COCOA
Singles: 7-inch

VENTURE 2-4		78-80

LPs: 10/12-inch 33rpm

VENTURE 8-10		79
Also see EBONYS		

CRENSHAW, Marshall
Singles: 12-inch 33/45rpm

SHAKE (104 "Marshall Crenshaw") .. 20-25		81
WARNER 5-10		82

Singles: 7-inch

WARNER 2-4		82-85

LPs: 10/12-inch 33rpm

WARNER 5-10		82-85

CREOLE, Kid: see KID CREOLE

CRESCENDOS
Singles: 78rpm

NASCO 5-10		57

Singles: 7-inch

ABC 2-4		73
MCA 2-4		84
NASCO (6005 "Oh Julie") 10-20		57
NASCO (6009 "School Girl") 10-20		58
NASCO (6021 "Young and in Love") . 10-20		58
SCARLET 10-15		60-61
TAP (7027 "Oh Julie") 10-15		57

Picture Sleeves

NASCO (6009 "School Girl") 20-30   58
NASCO (6021 "Young and in Love") . 20-30   58
TAP (7027 "Oh Julie") 15-25   57
LPs: 10/12-inch 33rpm
GUEST STAR (1453 "Oh Julie") 20-30   20-30
Members: George Lanuis; Ken Brigham; James Hall; Tommy Fortner.

CRESCENTS
(Chiyo and the Crescents)
Singles: 7-inch
BREAK OUT (4 "Pink Dominos") 15-25   63
(With straight horizontal lines.)
BREAK OUT (4 "Pink Dominos") 15-20   63
(With jagged horizontal lines.)
ERA (3116 "Pink Dominos") 5-10   63

CRESTS
Singles: 78rpm
JOYCE 103 ("Sweetest One") 50-100   57
JOYCE 105 ("No One to Love") 75-125   57
Singles: 7-inch
ABC 2-4   73
APT 5-10   65
CAMEO 5-10   63-64
COED (Except 501) 10-20   58-62
COED (501 "Pretty Little Angel") 50-75   58
COLLECTABLES 2-4   81-83
CORAL (62403 "You Blew Out
  the Candles") 15-25   64
ERIC 2-4   73
JOYCE 103 ("Sweetest One") 100-150   57
(With the oversize letter "Y" in the Joyce logo.)
JOYCE 103" (Sweetest One") 15-25
(With all of the letters the same size in the Joyce logo.)
JOYCE 105"(No One to Love") ... 100-125   57
KING TUT 4-8
LANA 2-4
LOST-NITE 3-5
MUSICTONE 5-10   62
SELMA (311 "Guilty") 10-20   62
SELMA (4000 "Did I Remember") ... 20-30   63
TIMES SQUARE 5-10   62-64
TRANS ATLAS 10-20   62
TRIP 2-4
EPs: 7-inch 33/45rpm
COED (101 "The Angels
  Listened In") 300-350   59
LPs: 10/12-inch 33rpm
COED (901 "The Crests Sing
  All Biggies") 150-200   60
COED (904 "Best of the Crests") . 125-175   60
COLLECTABLES 8-12   82
POST 8-12
Members: Johnny Maestro; Tom Gough; Harold Torres; Jay Carter.
Also see MAESTRO, Johnny

CRETONES
Singles: 7-inch
PLANET 2-4   80-81
Picture Sleeves
PLANET 2-4   80
LPs: 10/12-inch 33rpm
PLANET 5-10   80-81

CREW-CUTS
Singles: 78rpm
MERCURY 4-6   54-57
Singles: 7-inch
ABC-PAR 4-6   63
CHESS 4-6   64
FIREBIRD 3-5   70
MERCURY 5-10   54-57
RCA 4-8   58-60
VEE JAY 4-6   63
WARWICK 4-8   60-61
WHALE 4-6   62
EPs: 7-inch 33/45rpm
MERCURY 10-20   54-57
LPs: 10/12-inch 33rpm
MERCURY 25-50   55-56
RCA 20-30   59-60
WING 15-25   59-60
Members: Ray Perkins; John Perkins; Rudi Maugeri; Pat Barrett.
Also see COASTERS / Crew-Cuts / Chiffons

CREW-CUTS / Junior Powell and Charlotte Grubic
LPs: 10/12-inch 33rpm
RCA CUSTOM ("The Crew-Cuts
  Have a Ball") 20-30   59
(Special products issue for Ebonite Co. One side has "Bowling Tips By Top Stars")
Also see CREW-CUTS

CREWE, Bob
(Bob Crewe Generation; Bob Crew and the Rays)
Singles: 78rpm
CORAL 3-6   56
Singles: 7-inch
ABC-PAR 5-10   61
DYNO VOICE 3-6   66-68
CORAL 8-10   56
CREWE 3-5   71
ELEKTRA 3-5   76-77
ERIC 2-4   73
JUBILEE 8-12   54
MELBA 8-12   57
METROMEDIA 3-5   72
SPOTLIGHT 15-25   56
20TH FOX 3-5   76
U.T. 8-12   59
VIK 5-10   57
WARWICK 5-10   59-61
Picture Sleeves
DYNO VOICE 3-6   67
LPs: 10/12-inch 33rpm
CGC 10-12   70

DYNO VOICE 10-12   67-68
ELEKTRA 8-10   76-77
GAMBLE 2-4   69
PHILIPS 10-15   67
WARWICK 15-25   60-61
  Also see LA ROSA, Julius, and the Bob Crew Generation

CRICKETS
Singles: 7–inch
BARNABY 15-25   72
BRUNSWICK (55124 "Love's Made
  a Fool of You") 15-25   59
BRUNSWICK (55153 "When You
  Ask About Love") 15-25   59
CORAL (62198 "More Than
  I Can Say") 15-25   60
EPIC (08028 "T-Shirt") 2-4   88
LIBERTY 10-20   61-65
MGM 10-15   73
MUSIC FACTORY 15-20   68
Promotional Singles
BRUNSWICK (55124 "Love's Made
  a Fool of You") 20-30   59
BRUNSWICK (55153 "When You
  Ask About Love") 20-30   59
CORAL (62198 "More Than
  I Can Say") 20-30   60
EPIC (08028 "T-Shirt") 2-4   88
EPs: 7–inch 33/45rpm
B.H.M.S. 3-6   78
CORAL (81192 "The Crickets") 75-100   63
  (With Buddy Holly on one track, *It's Too Late*.)
LPs: 10/12–inch 33rpm
BARNABY (30268 "Rockin' '50s
  Rock and Roll") 15-25   70
CORAL (57320 "In Style") 40-60   60
KOALA 8-10
LIBERTY (3272 "Something Old, Something New,
  Something Blue, Somethin' Else") .. 30-40   64
  (Monaural.)
LIBERTY (3351 "California Sun") 30-40   64
  (Monaural.)
LIBERTY (7272 "Something Old, Something New,
  Something Blue, Somethin' Else") .. 40-50   64
  (Stereo.)
LIBERTY (7351 "California Sun") 40-50   64
  (Stereo.)
VERTIGO 10-20   73
  Note: Records by Buddy Holly and the Crickets,
  even if shown only as by the Crickets, are listed in
  the BUDDY HOLLY section.
  Members: Sonny Curtis; Jerry Naylor; Glen D. Hardin; Jerry
  Allison; Joe Mauldin; Earl Sinks; David Box.
    Also see CURTIS, Sonny
    Also see HOLLY, Buddy
    Also see IVAN
    Also see JENNINGS, Waylon
    Also see NAYLOR, Jerry
    Also see PRESLEY, Elvis
    Also see VEE, Bobby, and the Crickets

CRISS, Peter
Singles: 7–inch
CASABLANCA 3-5   79-80
LPs: 10/12–inch 33rpm
CASABLANCA (Except PIX 7122) ... 20-30   78-80
CASABLANCA (PIX 7122 "Peter
  Criss") 40-50   79
  (Picture disc.)
    Also see KISS

CRISS, Sonny
Singles: 7–inch
IMPERIAL 5-10   60
PEACOCK 4-8   61
LPs: 10/12–inch 33rpm
IMPERIAL 20-25   63

CRITTERS
Singles: 7–inch
KAPP 5-10   65-69
MCA 2-4   84
MUSICOR (1044 "Georgianna") 10-20   65
PRANCER 4-8   68
PROJECT 3 4-8   67-69
Picture Sleeves
KAPP (769 "Mr. Dieingly Sad") 8-12   66
PROJECT 3 4-8   67-69
LPs: 10/12–inch 33rpm
BACK-TRAC 5-10   85
KAPP (1485 "Younger Girl") 20-30   66
  (Monaural.)
KAPP (3485 "Younger Girl") 25-35   66
  (Stereo.)
PROJECT 3 15-20   68

CRITTERS / Young Rascals / Lou Christie
LPs: 10/12–inch 33rpm
BOTIQUE 10-20   66
  (Tracks shown as by the Young Rascals are
  actually by Felix and the Escorts.)
    Also see CHRISTIE, Lou
    Also see CRITTERS

CROCE, Jim
Singles: 7–inch
ABC 3-5   72-74
LIFESONG 3-5   75-76
Picture Sleeves
ABC 4-6   73
EPs: 7–inch 33/45rpm
ABC 10-12   73
  (Jukebox issue only.)
LPs: 10/12–inch 33rpm
ABC 10-12   72-74
BURNS MEDIA (1-2 "The Faces
  I've Been") 40-60   75
  (Two-LP set. Promotional issue only.)
CASHWEST 8-10   77
COMMAND 12-15   74-75
LIFESONG 10-15   75-78

MFSL (079 "You Don't Mess
  Around with Jim") 25-50   82
  Also see CASHMAN & WEST
  Also see GREENWICH, Ellie

CROCE, Jim and Ingrid
(Jim and Ingrid)
Singles: 7–inch
CAPITOL 10-15   69
LPs: 10/12–inch 33rpm
CAPITOL (315 "Croce") 30-35   69
PICKWICK 5-10
  Also see CROCE, Jim

CROCHET, Cleveland
(Cleveland Crochet and the Sugar Bees; Cleveland
Crochet and His Hillbilly Ramblers)
Singles: 7–inch
GOLDBAND 5-10   60-61
LYRIC 5-10
LPs: 10/12–inch 33rpm
GOLDBAND (7749 "Cleveland Crochet and
  All the Sugar Bees") 35-50   61

CROCKETT, G.L.
(G. Davy Crockett)
Singles: 78rpm
CHIEF 10-20   57
Singles: 7–inch
CHECKER (1121 "Look Out Mabel") . 20-30   65
CHIEF (7010 "Look Out Mabel") 50-75   57
4 BROTHERS 5-10   65

CROCKETT, Howard
Singles: 78rpm
DOT 10-20   57
Singles: 7–inch
DOT (15593 "If You'll Let Me") 35-50   57
DOT (17000 series) 3-5   73
MANCO 5-10   60
MEL-O-DY 10-15   64

CROOK, General
Singles: 7–inch
CAPITOL 3-6   69
DOWN to EARTH 3-6   70-71
WAND 3-5   74
LPs: 10/12–inch 33rpm
CAPITOL 10-15   70
WAND 10-12   74

CROSBY, Beverly
Singles: 7–inch
BAREBACK 3-5   77

CROSBY, Bing
(Bing Crosby and the Andrews Sisters; Bing and Gary
Crosby)
Singles: 78rpm
BRUNSWICK 10-20   32-34
DECCA 5-15   34-57
KAPP 3-5   57
VICTOR 10-20   31

Singles: 7–inch
AMOS 3-5   69
CAPITOL 4-6   63
COLUMBIA 4-6   59
DAYBREAK 3-5   71
DECCA (23281 through 30828) 5-10   51-59
DECCA (31000 series) 4-8   61-65
KAPP 4-6   57
LONDON 2-4   77
MGM 4-6   60
POLYDOR 2-4   78
RCA 4-6   60
REPRISE 4-6   64-67
U.A. 3-5   75
VERVE 3-5
Picture Sleeves
DECCA 5-10   53-63
DAYBREAK 3-5   71
KAPP 4-8   57
EPs: 7–inch 33/45rpm
BRUNSWICK 5-15   50-55
COLUMBIA 8-12   50-57
DECCA ("Old Masters") 20-30
  (Boxed EP set. No number shown.)
DECCA (Except 1700) 6-15   50-59
DECCA (1700 "Deluxe Box Set") ... 75-100   54
  (17-EP set.)
RCA 5-10   57
THREE on ONE (407 "Bing Crosby Sings
  2 New Christmas Songs")
  (Though labeled "45 Extended Play," actually has
  only one song on each side. May not have been
  issued with cover.)
VERVE (5022 "Bing Sings While
  Bregman Swings") 8-15   59
  (With envelope/sleeve.)
LPs: 10/12–inch 33rpm
AMOS 8-10   69
ARGO 10-15   76
BIOGRAPH 5-10   73
BRUNSWICK (54000 series) 15-25   55
BRUNSWICK (58000 series) 25-40   52
  (10–inch LPs.)
CAPITOL (2300 series) 8-12   65
CAPITOL (11000 series) 5-10   77-78
CITADEL 5-10   78
COLUMBIA (43 "Bing in Hollywood") . 10-15   67
COLUMBIA (2502 "Der Bingle") 20-30   56
  (10–inch LP.)
COLUMBIA (6027 "Classics") 20-40   49
  (10–inch LP.)
COLUMBIA (6105 "Classics Vol. 2") . 20-40   50
  (10–inch LP.)
COLUMBIA (35000 series) 5-10   78-79
COLUMBIA SPECIAL PRODUCTS 5-8   77
DECCA (100 series) 15-30   54-65
DECCA (4000 series) 20-50   61-64
DECCA (5000 series) 15-25   49-55
  (10–inch LPs.)

DECCA (6000 series) 25-50 55-56
(10–inch LPs.)
DECCA (8000 series) 15-25 54-59
(Black label with silver print.)
DECCA (8000 series) 8-15 60-72
(Black label with horizontal rainbow stripe.)
DECCA (8700 series) 8-12 64
DECCA (9000 series) 10-20 61-62
(Decca LP numbers in this series preceded by a
"7" or a "DL-7" are stereo issues.)
ENCORE 8-10 68
GOLDEN 10-15 57-59
HARMONY (7000 series) 10-15 57
HARMONY (11000 series) 5-10 69
LONDON 5-10 77
MCA 5-10 77-82
MGM 10-15 61-64
METRO 5-10 65
P.I.P. 5-10 71
POLYDOR 5-10 77
RCA (500 series) 6-10 72
RCA (1400 through 2000 series) 10-20 57-59
(With "LPM" or "LSP" prefix.)
RCA (2000 series) 5-10 77
(With "CPL1" prefix.)
REPRISE 8-12 64
20TH FOX 5-10 79
U.A. 5-10 76
VOCALION (3600 series) 10-15 57
VOCALION (3700 series) 5-10 66
WARNER 10-15 60-62
X 15-25 54
Also see ANDREWS SISTERS
Also see BOWIE, David, and Bing Crosby
Also see CROSBY, Gary, Phillip, Dennis, Lindsay and Bing
Also see DORSEY, Jimmy
Also see SINATRA, Frank, Bing Crosby and Dean Martin
Also see YOUNG, Victor

CROSBY, Bing and Gary
Singles: 78rpm
DECCA 3-5 50-51
Singles: 7–inch
DECCA 4-8 50-51

CROSBY, Bing, and Louis Armstrong
Singles: 78rpm
CAPITOL 3-5 56
DECCA 3-5 51
Singles: 7–inch
CAPITOL 4-8 56
DECCA 4-8 51
MGM 3-5 60
LPs: 10/12–inch 33rpm
MGM (100 series) 5-10 70
MGM (3800 series) 10-20 60
SOUNDS RARE 5-10 83

CROSBY, Bing, Louis Armstrong, Rosemary Clooney and the Hi-Los
Singles: 7–inch
COLUMBIA (6277 "Music to Shave By") 5-10
(Special products flexi-disc from Remington.)
Also see ARMSTRONG, Louis
Also see CROSBY, Bing, and Louis Armstrong
Also see CLOONEY, Rosemary

CROSBY, Bing, and Fred Astaire
LPs: 10/12–inch 33rpm
U.A. 5-8 77

CROSBY, Bing, and Count Basie
LPs: 10/12–inch 33rpm
DAYBREAK 8-12 72
Also see BASIE, Count

CROSBY, Bing, and Connee Boswell
Singles: 78rpm
DECCA 4-8 38-40
LPs: 10/12–inch 33rpm
DECCA 15-25 52
Also see BOSWELL, Connee

CROSBY, Bing, and Judy Garland
Singles: 78rpm
DECCA 5-10 45
Also see GARLAND, Judy

CROSBY, Bing, and Bob Hope
Singles: 78rpm
DECCA 5-10 45
EPs: 7–inch 33/45rpm
CAPITOL CUSTOM (2263 "Vacation Road
to Minnesota") 5-10
(Issued to promote Minnesota tourism.)
Also see BAXTER, Les

CROSBY, Bing, and Louis Jordan
Singles: 78rpm
DECCA 5-10 45
Also see JORDAN, Louis

CROSBY, Bing, and Grace Kelly
Singles: 78rpm
CAPITOL 3-5 56
Singles: 7–inch
CAPITOL 5-10 56

CROSBY, Bing, and Peggy Lee
Singles: 78rpm
DECCA 3-5 52
Singles: 7–inch
DECCA 5-10 52
Also see LEE, Peggy

CROSBY, Bing, and the Mills Brothers
Singles: 78rpm
BRUNSWICK 5-10 32
Also see MILLS BROTHERS

CROSBY, Bing, and Frank Sinatra
Singles: 78rpm
CAPITOL 3-5 56

CROUCH, Andrae
(Andrae Crouch and the Disciples)
Singles: 7-inch
LIGHT	2-4	76-80
WARNER	2-4	81
LPs: 10/12-inch 33rpm
ACCORD	.82	5-8
LIGHT	5-8	68-82
WARNER	5-8	81

CROW
(David Wagner)
Singles: 7-inch
AMARET	3-6	69-72
LPs: 10/12-inch 33rpm
AMARET	10-15	69-73

CROWD PLEASERS
Singles: 7-inch
WESTBOUND	2-4	79
LPs: 10/12-inch 33rpm
WESTBOUND	5-10	79

CROWDED HOUSE
Singles: 12-inch 33/45rpm
CAPITOL	4-6	86
Singles: 7-inch
CAPITOL	2-4	86-88
Picture Sleeves
CAPITOL	2-4	87-88
LPs: 10/12-inch 33rpm
CAPITOL	5-10	86-88
Member: Neil Finn.
Also see SPLIT ENZ

CROWELL, Rodney
Singles: 7-inch
COLUMBIA	2-4	86-90
WARNER	2-4	78-82
LPs: 10/12-inch 33rpm
COLUMBIA	5-8	86-90
WARNER	5-10	78-81

CROWELL, Rodney, and Rosanne Cash
Singles: 7-inch
COLUMBIA	2-4	88
Also see CASH, Rosanne
Also see CROWELL, Rodney

CROWN HEIGHTS AFFAIR
Singles: 12-inch 33/45rpm
SBK	4-6	89
Singles: 7-inch
DELITE	3-5	75-82
RCA	3-5	73-74
LPs: 10/12-inch 33rpm
DELITE	5-10	75-82
RCA	10-12	74-78
Members: Phil Thomas; Ray Rock; Bert Reid; James Baynard;
Ray Reid; William Anderson; Howard Young; Muki Wilson.

CROWS
Singles: 78rpm
RAMA (3 "Seven Lonely Days")	20-40	53
RAMA (5 "Gee")	20-40	53
RAMA (10 "Heartbreaker")	50-100	53
RAMA (29 "Baby")	40-60	54
RAMA (30 "Miss You")	50-100	54
RAMA (50 "Baby Doll")	40-60	54
TICO (1082 "Mambo Shevitz")	40-60	51
Singles: 7-inch
RAMA (3 "Seven Lonely Days")	200-300	53
RAMA (5 "Gee")	40-60	53
(Black vinyl. Blue label. No clouds or lines around "Rama" logo.)		
RAMA (5 "Gee")	25-40	53
(Black vinyl. Blue label. With clouds and lines around "Rama" logo.)		
RAMA (5 "Gee")	150-200	53
(Colored vinyl.)		
RAMA (5 "Gee")	10-20	56
(Red label.)		
RAMA (10 "Heartbreaker")	200-250	53
(Black vinyl.)		
RAMA (10 "Heartbreaker")	400-450	53
(Colored vinyl.)		
RAMA (29 "Baby")	100-125	54
RAMA (30 "Miss You")	200-250	54
(Black vinyl.)		
RAMA (30 "Miss You")	400-450	54
(Colored vinyl.)		
RAMA (50 "Baby Doll")	125-175	54
TICO (1082 "Mambo Shevitz")	75-100	51
(Black vinyl.)		
TICO (1082 "Mambo Shevitz")	150-200	51
(Colored vinyl.)		
Members: Daniel "Sonny" Norton; Harold Major; Jerry Hamilton;
Mark Jackson; Bill Davis.
Also see HARPTONES / Crows
Also see JEWELS

CRUDUP, Big Boy
(Arthur "Big Boy" Crudup)
Singles: 78rpm
ACE (503 "I Wonder")	175-225	53
BLUEBIRD	8-12	41-46
CHAMPION (108 "I Wonder")	200-250	52
GROOVE	10-15	53-54
RCA	5-10	47-53
Singles: 7-inch
FIRE	5-10	62
GROOVE (0011 "I Love My Baby")	30-40	53
GROOVE (0026 "She's Got No Hair")	30-40	54
GROOVE (5005 "Mean Ol' Frisco")	30-40	54
RCA (0000 "That's All Right")	200-225	49
(Colored vinyl.)		
RCA (0001 "Boy Friend Blues")	50-100	49
(Colored vinyl.)		
RCA (0013 "Shout Sister, Shout")	50-100	49
(Colored vinyl.)		
RCA (0032 "Hoodoo Lady Blues")	50-100	50
(Colored vinyl.)		
RCA (0046 "Come Back Baby")	50-100	49
(Colored vinyl.)		

RCA (0074 "Dust My Broom") ..... 50-100 | 50
(Colored vinyl.)
RCA (0092 "Mean Old Santa Fe") .. 50-100 | 50
(Colored vinyl.)
RCA (0100 "Lonesome World to Me") 50-100 | 50
(Colored vinyl.)
RCA (0105 "She's Just
Like Caldonia") .... 50-100 | 50
(Colored vinyl.)
RCA (0117 "Nobody Wants Me") ... 50-100 | 50
(Colored vinyl.)
RCA (0126 "Roberta Blues") ...... 50-100 | 50
(Colored vinyl.)
RCA (0141 "Too Much Competition") 50-100 | 50
(Colored vinyl.)
RCA (4367 "Love Me Mama") ..... 50-100 | 51
RCA (4572 "Goin' Back to Georgia") . 50-75 | 52
RCA (4753 "Worried About You Baby") 50-75 | 52
RCA (4933 "Second Man Blues") .... 50-75 | 52
RCA (5070 "Pearly Lee") .... 50-75 | 52
RCA (5167 "Keep on Drinkin") ...... 50-75 | 53
RCA (5563 "My Wife and Women") .. 50-75 | 53

EPs: 7–inch 33/45rpm

CAMDEN (415 "Arthur 'Big Boy'
Crudup") .... 100-125 | 57

LPs: 10/12–inch 33rpm

COLLECTABLES .... 6-8 | 88
DELMARK .... 15-25 | 69
FIRE (103 "Mean Ol' Frisco") ..... 125-175 | 62
RCA .... 10-20 | 71
TRIP (7501 "Mean Ol' Frisco") .... 8-12 | 75
Also see CRUDUP, Percy Lee
Also see JAMES, Elmore

CRUDUP, Percy Lee
(Arthur Crudup)

Singles: 78rpm

CHECKER (754 "Open Your Book") .. 20-30 | 52
Also see CRUDUP, Big Boy

CRUISE, Pablo: see PABLO CRUISE

CRUM, Simon
(Ferlin Husky)

Singles: 78rpm

CAPITOL .... 4-8 | 55-57

Singles: 7–inch

ABC .... 3-5 | 74
CAPITOL .... 5-10 | 55-63

LPs: 10/12–inch 33rpm

CAPITOL (1880 "The Unpredictable
Simon Crum") .... 75-100 | 63
Also see HUSKY, Ferlin

CRUSADERS

Singles: 7–inch

ABC .... 2-4 | 78
BLUE THUMB .... 3-5 | 72-77
CHISA .... 3-5 | 71
MCA .... 2-4 | 79-86

LPs: 10/12–inch 33rpm

BLUE THUMB .... 10-12 | 73-77
GRP .... 5-8 | 91
MCA .... 8-10 | 79-86
MFSL (010 "Chain Reaction") ...... 25-50 | 78
(Half-speed mastered.)
MOTOWN .... 10-12 | 73
MOWEST .... 10-12 | 72
Also see COCKER, Joe
Also see CRAWFORD, Randy
Also see HOOPER, Stix
Also see JAZZ CRUSADERS
Also see SAMPLE, Joe

CRUSADERS and B.B. King

Singles: 7–inch

MCA .... 2-4 | 82

LPs: 10/12–inch 33rpm

MCA .... 8-10 | 82
Also see CRUSADERS
Also see KING, B.B.

CRYAN' SHAMES

Singles: 7–inch

COLUMBIA .... 4-8 | 66-70
DESTINATION .... 5-10 | 66

Picture Sleeves

COLUMBIA .... 8-12 | 67

LPs: 10/12–inch 33rpm

BACK-TRAC .... 5-10 | 85
COLUMBIA (2589 "Sugar and Spice") 20-25 | 66
(Monaural.)
COLUMBIA (2786 "A Scratch
in the Sky") .... 20-25 | 67
(Monaural.)
COLUMBIA (9389 "Sugar and Spice") 15-20 | 66
(Stereo.)
COLUMBIA (9586 "A Scratch
in the Sky") .... 15-20 | 67
(Stereo.)
COLUMBIA (9719 "Synthesis") ..... 15-20 | 69

CRYSTAL, Billy

Singles: 12–inch 33/45rpm

A&M .... 4-6 | 85

Singles: 7–inch

A&M .... 2-4 | 85

Picture Sleeves

A&M .... 3-5 | 85

LPs: 10/12–inch 33rpm

A&M .... 5-10 | 85

CRYSTAL GAYLE: see GAYLE, Crystal

CRYSTAL GRASS
Singles: 7-inch
POLYDOR 3-5	75
PRIVATE STOCK 3-5	76

LPs: 10/12-inch 33rpm
MERCURY 5-10	78
POLYDOR 8-10	75

CRYSTAL MANSION
Singles: 7-inch
CAPITOL 3-6	68-70
COLOSSUS 3-5	70-71
RARE EARTH 3-5	72
20TH FOX 2-4	79

LPs: 10/12-inch 33rpm
CAPITOL 12-15	69
RARE EARTH 10-12	72
20TH FOX 5-10	79
Also see CASWELL, Johnny

CRYSTALS
Singles: 7-inch
MICHELLE 4-8	67
PAVILLION 2-4	82
PHILLES (100 "There's No Other") ... 8-12	61
PHILLES (102 "Uptown") 8-12	62
PHILLES (105 "He Hit Me") 15-20	62
PHILLES (106 "He's a Rebel") 8-12	62
PHILLES (109 "He's Sure the Boy I Love") 8-12	62
PHILLES (111 "Let's Dance the Screw") 350-400	63
(White label promotional issue only. Copies with blue labels are counterfeits.)	
PHILLES (112 "Da Do Ron Ron") 8-12	63
PHILLES (115 "Then He Kissed Me") . 8-12	63
PHILLES (119 "Little Boy") 10-12	63
PHILLES (122 "All Grown Up") 10-12	64
U.A. 4-8	65-66

LPs: 10/12-inch 33rpm
PHILLES (4000 "The Crystals Twist Uptown") 150-250	62
(Monaural. Blue label.)	
PHILLES (4000 "The Crystals Twist Uptown") 250-300	62
(Monaural. White label. Promotional issue only.)	
PHILLES (4000 "The Crystals Twist Uptown") 400-500	62
(Stereo.)	
PHILLES (4001 "He's a Rebel") ... 150-250	63
PHILLES (4003 "The Crystals") ... 150-250	63
PHILLES (90722 "The Crystals Twist Uptown") 200-300	62
(Capitol Record Club issue.)	
Also see LOVE, Darlene
Also see RONETTES / Crystals / Darlene Love / Bob B. Soxx and the Blue Jeans

THE CRYSTALS

D. J. COPY
NOT FOR SALE

Mother Bertha
Music - BMI
P TCY 11
Time: 3:45

PHILLES RECORDS

LET'S DANCE
THE SCREW - PART I
(Phil Spector)
111
PHILLES RECORDS, A DIVISION OF PHIL SPECTOR PRODUCTIONS

CUBA, Joe
(Joe Cuba Sextet)
Singles: 7-inch
ROULETTE 3-5	71
TICO 4-6	66

LPs: 10/12-inch 33rpm
TICO 10-15	66-67

CUES
Singles: 78rpm
CAPITOL 5-10	55-56
JUBILEE 5-10	55
LAMP 5-10	54
PREP 8-10	57

Singles: 7-inch
CAPITOL 10-20	55-56
JUBILEE 15-20	55
LAMP 10-20	54
PREP 10-15	57
Members: Ollie Jones; Jimmy Breedlove; Abe DeCosta; Robey Kirk; Eddie Barnes.
Also see RAVENS

CUFF LINKS
Singles: 7-inch
ATCO 3-5	72
DECCA 3-6	69-71
MCA 2-4	84

Picture Sleeves
DECCA (32533 "Tracy") 5-10	69
(Gatefold sleeve. Promotional issue only.)	

LPs: 10/12-inch 33rpm
DECCA 15-25	69-70
Members: Ron Dante; Rupert Holmes.
Also see HOLMES, Rupert

CUGINI
Singles: 7-inch
SCOTTI BROTHERS 2-4	79

CULT
(Southern Death Cult; Death Cult)
Singles: 12-inch 33/45rpm
SIRE 4-6	85-86

Singles: 7-inch
SIRE 2-4	85-89

Picture Sleeves

SIRE 2-4   85-89
LPs: 10/12–inch 33rpm
SIRE 5-10   85-89
Members: Ian Astbury; Billy Duffy; Jamie Stewart; Les Warner.

CULTURE CLUB
(Featuring Boy George)
Singles: 12–inch 33/45rpm
EPIC/VIRGIN 4-6   82-86
Singles: 7–inch
EPIC/VIRGIN 2-4   82-86
Picture Sleeves
EPIC/VIRGIN 2-4   83-86
LPs: 10/12–inch 33rpm
EPIC/VIRGIN 5-10   82-86
Members: Boy George; Jon Moss; Roy Hay; Michael Craig.
Also see BAND AID
Also see BOY GEORGE

CUMMINGS, Burton
Singles: 7–inch
ALFA 2-4   81
PORTRAIT 3-5   76-78
Picture Sleeves
ALFA 2-4   81
EPs: 7–inch 33/45rpm
PORTRAIT 4-8   77
(Issued with a paper sleeve.)
LPs: 10/12–inch 33rpm
ALFA 5-10   81
PORTRAIT 8-10   76-78
Also see GUESS WHO

CUNHA, Rick
Singles: 7–inch
COLUMBIA 3-5   75
GRC 3-5   74
LPs: 10/12–inch 33rpm
COLUMBIA 8-10   75
GRC 10-12   74
Also see JENNINGS, Waylon

CUPIDS
Singles: 7–inch
AANKO (1002 "Brenda") 75-100   63
KC (115 "Brenda") 10-15   63

CURB, Mike
(Mike Curb and the Sidewalk Sounds; Mike Curb and
the Curbstones; Mike Curb and the Rebalairs; Mike
Curb Congregation; Mike Curb and the Waterfall)
Singles: 7–inch
BUENA VISTA 3-5   75
FORWARD 3-6   69
MGM 2-4   70
REPRISE (0287 "Hot Dawg") 10-20   64
SMASH (1938 "The Rebel") 10-15   64
TOWER 10-15   66
WARNER 3-5   77
Picture Sleeves
BUENA VISTA 5-10   75
FORWARD 4-8   69

LPs: 10/12–inch 33rpm
BUENA VISTA 8-12
COBURT 8-12   70
FORWARD 5-10
MGM 5-10   71
Also see ALLAN, Davie
Also see DAVIS, Sammy, Jr.
Also see OSMONDS

CURE
Singles: 12–inch 33/45rpm
ELEKTRA 4-6   85-86
SIRE 4-6   83-85
Singles: 7–inch
ELEKTRA 2-4   85-89
SIRE 2-4   83-85
Picture Sleeves
ELEKTRA 2-4   86-89
LPs: 10/12–inch 33rpm
A&M 8-10   81
ELEKTRA 5-10   85-89
PVC 8-10   80
SIRE 5-10   83-85
Members: Robert Smith; Laurence Tolhurst.

CURIOSITY KILLED the CAT
Singles: 7–inch
MERCURY 2-4   87
Picture Sleeves
MERCURY 2-4   87
LPs: 10/12–inch 33rpm
MERCURY 5-8   87

CURTIS, King: see KING CURTIS

CURTIS, Sonny
Singles: 78rpm
CORAL 5-10   53
Singles: 7–inch
A&M (1359 "The Lights of L.A.") 20-30   72
CAPITOL 8-12   75-76
CORAL (61023 "The Best Way to
Hold a Girl") 15-20   53
CORAL (62207 "Red Headed
Stranger") 20-25   60
DIMENSION 8-12   63-64
DOT 10-20   58
ELEKTRA 2-4   79-81
LIBERTY 10-15   64
MERCURY 8-12   73
OVATION 10-15   70
STEEM 2-4   85
VIVA 8-10   66-69
LPs: 10/12–inch 33rpm
ELEKTRA 8-15   79-81
IMPERIAL (9276 "Beatle Hits") 25-35   64
(Monaural.)
IMPERIAL (12276 "Beatle Hits") 30-40   64
(Stereo.)
VIVA (36012 "1st of Sonny Curtis") .. 20-30   68
VIVA (36021 "The Sonny Curtis Style") 20-30   69
Also see CLAPTON, Eric

Also see CRICKETS

CURTIS, T.C.
Singles: 12–inch 33/45rpm
SIRE 4-6   85

CURTOLA, Bobby
(Bobby Curtola and the Martells)
Singles: 7–inch
DEL-FI 5-10   61-63
KING 4-8   67
TARTAN 4-8   63-66
Picture Sleeves
DEL-FI 10-15   61-62

CUT
Singles: 7–inch
SUPERTRONICS 2-4   86

CUTTING CREW
Singles: 7–inch
VIRGIN 2-4   87-89
Picture Sleeves
VIRGIN 2-4   87-89
LPs: 10/12–inch 33rpm
VIRGIN 5-10   87-89

CYCLONES
Singles: 7–inch
TROPHY (500 "Bullwhip Rock") 15-25   58
Member: Bill Taylor.

CYMANDE
Singles: 7–inch
JANUS 3-5   72-73
LPs: 10/12–inch 33rpm
JANUS 10-12   72-74

CYMARRON
Singles: 7–inch
ENTRANCE 3-5   71-72
LPs: 10/12–inch 33rpm
ENTRANCE 10-12   71

CYMBAL, Johnny
Singles: 7–inch
AMARET 3-6   69
COLUMBIA 4-8   66
DCP (1135 "Go VW, Go") 10-15   65
KAPP 5-15   63-64
KEDLEN 10-15   63
MCA 2-4   84
MGM 8-15   60-61
MUSICOR 4-8   67
VEE JAY 4-8   63
Picture Sleeves
DCP (1135 "Go VW, Go") 15-25   65
LPs: 10/12–inch 33rpm
KAPP (1324 "Mr. Bass Man") 25-35   63
(Monaural.)
KAPP (3324 "Mr. Bass Man") 30-40   63
(Stereo.)
Also see DEREK

CYMBAL & CLINGER
Singles: 7–inch
CHELSEA 3-5   73
MGM 3-5   71
MARINA 3-5   71
LPs: 10/12–inch 33rpm
CHELSEA 10-12   72
Members: Johnny Cymbal; Peggy Clinger.
Also see CYMBAL, Johnny

CYMONE, Andre
Singles: 12–inch 33/45rpm
COLUMBIA 4-6   82-86
Singles: 7–inch
COLUMBIA 2-4   82-86
LPs: 10/12–inch 33rpm
COLUMBIA 5-10   82-86

CYRÉ
Singles: 7–inch
FRESH 2-4   87

CYRKLE
Singles: 7–inch
COLUMBIA (Except 43589) 5-10   65-68
COLUMBIA (43589 "Red Rubber Ball") 5-10   65
(Black vinyl.)
COLUMBIA (43589 "Red Rubber Ball")10-15   65
(Colored vinyl. Promotional issue only.)
Picture Sleeves
COLUMBIA 20-30   66-68
LPs: 10/12–inch 33rpm
COLUMBIA (2544 "Red Rubber Ball") 20-25   66
COLUMBIA (9344 "Red Rubber Ball") 25-30   66
COLUMBIA (2632 "Neon") 20-25   67
(Monaural.)
COLUMBIA (9432 "Neon") 20-30   67
(Stereo.)
FLYING DUTCHMAN/AMSTERDAM
(12007 "The Minx") 20-25   70
(Soundtrack.)

CYRKLE / Paul Revere and the Raiders
Singles: 7–inch
COLUMBIA (466 "Camaro"/"SS 396") 10-15   66
(Special Products Chevrolet promotional issue
only.)
Picture Sleeves
COLUMBIA (466 "Camaro"/"SS 396") 15-25   66
(Special Products Chevrolet promotional issue
only.)
COLUMBIA (43000 series) 5-10   66-67
Members: Don Danneman; Michael Losekamp; Marty Fried;
Tom Dawes; John Simon.
Also see CYRKLE
Also see REVERE, Paul, and the Raiders
Also see SIMON, Paul

D

"D" TRAIN
Singles: 12-inch 33/45rpm
PRELUDE 4-6   81-85
Singles: 7-inch
PRELUDE 2-4   81-85
LPs: 10/12-inch 33rpm
PRELUDE 5-10   82-85
Members: James "D Train" Williams; Hubert Eaves III.
Also see WILLIAMS, James "D Train"

D., Eddie: see EDDIE D.

D.A.
Singles: 7-inch
RASCAL (102 "Ready 'N Steady") ... 20-30   79
LPs: 10/12-inch 33rpm
FRONTLINE 5-10   85-86

DB's
LPs: 10/12-inch 33rpm
I.R.S. 5-10   87

DFX2
Singles: 7-inch
MCA 2-4   83
LPs: 10/12-inch 33rpm
MCA 5-10   83

D.J. DOC and Spyder D.
Singles: 7-inch
PROFILE 4-6   86

D.J. JAZZY JEFF and the Fresh Prince
Singles: 7-inch
JIVE 2-4   87-89
WORD-UP 2-4   86
Picture Sleeves
JIVE 2-4   88-89
LPs: 10/12-inch 33rpm
JIVE 5-10   87-89
Also see SIMPSONS

DMX, Davy: see DAVY DMX

D.O.X.
(Defenders of the Cross)
LPs: 10/12-inch 33rpm
FRONTLINE 5-10   86

DADDY DEWDROP
Singles: 7-inch
CAPITOL 3-5   75
INPHASION 2-4   78-79
SUNFLOWER 3-6   70-72
SUNFLOWER/MGM 3-5   73
LPs: 10/12-inch 33rpm
SUNFLOWER 12-15   71

DADDY O's
Singles: 7-inch
CABOT 5-10   58

DAHL, Steve, and the Teenage Radiation
Singles: 7-inch
COHO 2-4   79
OVATION 2-4   79
Picture Sleeves
OVATION 2-4   79

DAILY, E.G.
(Elizabeth G. Daily)
Singles: 12-inch 33/45rpm
A&M 4-6   86
Singles: 7-inch
A&M 2-4   86
LPs: 10/12-inch 33rpm
A&M 5-10   86

DAISY DILLMAN BAND: see DILLMAN BAND

DA'KRASH
Singles: 7-inch
CAPITOL 2-4   88
LPs: 10/12-inch 33rpm
CAPITOL 5-8   88

DALBELLO
Singles: 12-inch 33/45rpm
CAPITOL 4-6   84
Singles: 7-inch
CAPITOL 2-4   84

DALE, Alan
Singles: 78rpm
COLUMBIA 4-6   50-51
CORAL 3-6   52-56
DECCA 3-5   52
Singles: 7-inch
ABC-PAR 3-6   64
ADVANCE 3-6
COLUMBIA 5-10   50-51
CORAL (60000 and 61000 series) 5-10   52-56
CORAL (62000 series) 3-6   63
DECCA 4-8   52
EMKAY 3-6   62
FTP 3-6   61
MGM 4-8   59
SINCLAIR (1003 "A Teenage Girl") .. 15-25   61
EPs: 7-inch 33/45rpm
CORAL 5-15   52-56
LPs: 10/12-inch 33rpm
CORAL 15-25   55-56
FORD 10-15   63
U.A. 10-15   60
Also see CORNELL, Don, Johnny Desmond and Alan Dale

DALE, Dick
(Dick Dale and His Del-tones)
Singles: 7–inch

CAPITOL 8-12	63-64	
COLUMBIA 3-5	87	
CONCERT ROOM 4-8	63	
COUGAR 4-8	67	
CUPID 10-20	60	
DEL-TONE (5012 "Oh Wee Marie") .. 35-50	59	
DEL-TONE (5013 "Stop Teasing") ... 25-35	59	
DEL-TONE (5014 "Jessie Pearl") 35-50	60	
DEL-TONE (5017 through 5028) 10-15	61-63	
GNP/CRESCENDO 3-5	75	
RENDEZVOUS (204 "Reincarnation Parts 1 and 2") 8-12	62	
SATURN 10-15	63	
YES 10-20		

Promotional Singles

CAPITOL ("Thunder Wave"/ "Spanish Kiss") 8-10 64
(Bonus single, packaged with the *Surf Age* LP by Jerry Cole and His Spacemen.)
CAPITOL (2320 "Peppermint Man") .. 25-35 63
(Compact 33 Single.)

Picture Sleeves

CAPITOL (Except 2320) 12-25 63
CAPITOL (2320 "Peppermint Man") .. 35-45 63
(Promotional Compact 33 Single sleeve.)
COLUMBIA 4-6 87
YES 4-8

LPs: 10/12–inch 33rpm

BALBOA 5-10 83
CAPITOL (T-1930 "King of the Surf Guitar") 30-40 63
(Monaural.)
CAPITOL (ST-1930 "King of the Surf Guitar") 40-50 63
(Stereo.)
CAPITOL (T-2002 "Checkered Flag") . 25-35 63
(Monaural.)
CAPITOL (ST-2002 "Checkered Flag") 30-40 63
(Stereo.)
CAPITOL (T-2053 "Mr. Eliminator") .. 30-35 64
(Monaural.)
CAPITOL (ST-2053 "Mr. Eliminator") . 35-40 64
(Stereo.)
CAPITOL (T-2111 "Summer Surf") ... 40-50 64
(Monaural. With *Movin' Surf*, a bonus single by Jerry Cole and His Spacemen.)
CAPITOL (T-2111 "Summer Surf") ... 35-45 64
(Monaural. Without bonus single.)
CAPITOL (ST-2111 "Summer Surf") .. 45-55 64
(Stereo. With *Movin' Surf*, a bonus single by Jerry Cole and His Spacemen.)
CAPITOL (ST-2111 "Summer Surf") .. 40-50 64
(Stereo. Without bonus single.)
CAPITOL (T-2293 "Rock Out with Dick Dale Live At Ciro's") 30-35 65
(Monaural.)
CAPITOL (2293 "Rock Out with Dick Dale Live At Ciro's") 35-40 65
(Stereo.)
DEL-TONE (1001 "Surfer's Choice") . 30-40 61
DEL-TONE (1886 "Surfer's Choice") . 40-60 63
DUBTONE 15-20 63
GNP/CRESCENDO 8-12 75
Also see ALLAN, Davie
Also see BEACH BOYS / Dick Dale / Surfaris / Surf Kings

DALE, Dick / Jerry Cole / Super Stocks / Mr. Gasser and the Weirdos
EPs: 7–inch 33/45rpm

CAPITOL (2663 "The Big Surfing Sounds") 35-50 64
(Promotional issue only.)

DALE, Dick / Surfaris / Fireballs
LPs: 10/12–inch 33rpm

ALMOR (108 "World of Surfin") 10-20
ALMOR (109 "Hot Rod Drag City") .. 10-20
Also see FIREBALLS

DALE, Dick / Surfaris / Surf Kings (Beach Boys)
LPs: 10/12–inch 33rpm

GUEST STAR (1433 "Surf Kings") ... 20-30 63
(Credits the Beach Boys, though there are no tracks by the Beach Boys. Also, tracks credited to the Surfaris are by the Original Surfaris.)
GUEST STAR (1433 "Surf Kings") ... 15-20 63
(Does not credit the Beach Boys.)

DALE, Dick / Francine York
Singles: 7–inch

UNITED STATES ARMY (1301 "Enlistment Twist") 10-15 62
(Promotional issue only.)
Also see DALE, Dick

DALE, Jimmy
(Jimmy Clanton)
Singles: 7–inch

DREW-BLAN (1003 "My Pride and Joy") 15-25 61
Also see CLANTON, Jimmy

DALE & GRACE
Singles: 7–inch

COLLECTABLES 2-4		
ERIC 2-4		
GUYDEN 3-5	72	
HBR 4-8	66	
MICHELLE 5-10	63-64	
MONTEL 4-8	63-67	
MONTEL MICHELLE (942 "What Am I Living For") 4-8	64	
(Shows both label names.)		
TRIP 2-4		

LPs: 10/12–inch 33rpm

MONTEL (100 "I'm Leaving It Up to You") 35-50 64
Members: Dale Houston; Grace Broussard.

DALLARA, Tony
Singles: 7–Inch
MERCURY	5-10	58-60
VESUVIUS	4-8	61-62

LPs: 10/12–Inch 33rpm
VESUVIUS	8-10	62

DALTON, Kathy
Singles: 7–Inch
DISC REET	3-5	74

LPs: 10/12–Inch 33rpm
DISC REET	8-12	73-74

DALTON & DUBARRI
Singles: 7–Inch
ABC	3-5	76
COLUMBIA	3-5	73-74
HILLTAK	2-4	79

LPs: 10/12–Inch 33rpm
ABC	8-10	76
COLUMBIA	10-12	73-74
HILLTAK	5-10	79

DALTREY, Roger
Singles: 7–Inch
A&M	3-5	75-76
ATLANTIC	2-4	84-87
MCA	2-5	73-82
MCA/GOLDHAWKE	3-5	75-77
ODE	3-5	72-73
POLYDOR	2-4	80-81
TRACK	3-5	73

Picture Sleeves
ATLANTIC	2-4	84
POLYDOR	3-5	80

LPs: 10/12–Inch 33rpm
ATLANTIC	5-10	84-87
MCA	10-15	71-82
POLYDOR	5-8	80
TRACK	10-12	73
Also see WHO		

DALTREY, Roger, and Steve Gibbons
Singles: 12–Inch 33/45rpm
MCA	5-10	
(Promotional issue only.)		
Also see GIBBONS, Steve, Band		

DALTREY, Roger, and Rick Wakeman
Singles: 7–Inch
A&M	3-5	75

LPs: 10/12–Inch 33rpm
A&M	8-10	75
Also see DALTREY, Roger		
Also see WAKEMAN, Rick		

DAMIAN, Michael
Singles: 7–Inch
CYPRESS	2-4	89
LEG	2-4	81

Picture Sleeves
CYPRESS	2-4	89
LEG	2-4	81

LPs: 10/12–Inch 33rpm
CYPRESS	5-8	89

DAMARIS
Singles: 7–Inch
COLUMBIA	2-4	84

DAMIANO, Joe
(Josef Damiano)
Singles: 7–Inch
CHANCELLOR	5-10	59-60

DAMION & DENITA
LPs: 10/12–Inch 33rpm
ROCKET	5-10	80

DAMITA JO
(Damita Joe)
Singles: 7–Inch
EPIC (Black vinyl)	3-5	65-67
EPIC (Colored vinyl)	4-8	66
MELIC	3-6	64
MERCURY	4-8	60-64
RANWOOD	3-5	68-71
VEE JAY	3-6	65

Picture Sleeves
EPIC	4-8	65
MERCURY	5-10	61-63

EPs: 7–Inch 33/45rpm
MERCURY	5-10	60-61

LPs: 10/12–Inch 33rpm
CAMDEN	6-10	65
EPIC	8-15	65-67
MERCURY	12-25	61-63
RANWOOD	5-10	68
VEE JAY	10-15	65
Also see BENTON, Brook, and Damita Jo		

DAMITA JO and Billy Eckstine
Singles: 7–Inch
MERCURY	3-6	63
Also see ECKSTINE, Billy		

DAMITA JO with Steve Gibson and the Red Caps
Singles: 78rpm
RCA (6281 "Always")	5-10	55

Singles: 7–Inch
ABC-PAR	5-10	61
RCA (6281 "Always")	10-15	55

LPs: 10/12–Inch 33rpm
ABC-PAR (378 "Big 15")	40-50	61
Also see DAMITA JO		
Also see GIBSON, Steve		

DAMNATION
(Featuring Adam Blessing)
Singles: 7–Inch
U.A.	3-5	71-72

LPs: 10/12–Inch 33rpm
U.A.	10-15	69-71

DAMON, Liz
(Liz Damon's Orient Express)
Singles: 7–inch
ABC	3-5	73
ANTHEM	3-5	71-72
MAKAHA	3-6	70
WHITE WHALE	3-5	70

LPs: 10/12–inch 33rpm
MAKAHA	5-10	70
WHITE WHALE	8-12	71

DAMONE, Vic
Singles: 78rpm
COLUMBIA	3-6	56-57
MERCURY	3-6	50-55

Singles: 7–inch
CAPITOL	4-6	61-64
COLUMBIA	5-10	56-61
DOLTON	4-6	62
MGM	3-5	72-73
MERCURY	5-10	50-55
RCA	3-6	66-69
REBECCA	2-5	77
UNITED TALENT	3-5	70
WARNER	4-6	65-66

EPs: 7–inch 33/45rpm
COLUMBIA	5-10	56-58
MERCURY	8-12	50-56

LPs: 10/12–inch 33rpm
CAPITOL	10-15	62-64
COLUMBIA (900 through 1500 series)	15-25	56-61
COLUMBIA (1900 series)	10-15	62
COLUMBIA (8000 through 8300 series)	15-25	58-61
COLUMBIA (8700 series)	10-15	62
DOLTON	10-15	64
HARMONY	5-10	66-67
HOLLYWOOD	5-10	
MERCURY (Except 25000 series)	8-12	69
MERCURY (25000 series)	15-30	50-56
RCA	8-12	66-68
UNITED TALENT	5-10	
WARNER	10-15	65
WING	10-15	59-63

Also see ANDREWS, Julie and Andre Previn / Vic Damone /
Jack Jones / Marian Anderson
Also see FISHER, Eddie / Vic Damone / Dick Haymes

DANA, Bill
(Jose Jimenez)
Singles: 7–inch
A&M	4-8	65-66
KAPP	5-15	61-63
SIGNATURE	5-10	60

Picture Sleeves
KAPP	10-20	61-62

LPs: 10/12–inch 33rpm
A&M	8-12	68
CAPITOL	6-10	70

HBR	8-10	66
KAPP	12-25	60-64
ROULETTE	12-25	61
SIGNATURE	20-25	60

DANA, Vic
Singles: 7–inch
CASINO	3-5	76
COLUMBIA	3-5	71
DOLTON	4-8	61-65
LIBERTY	3-6	68-70
MGM	3-5	75

Picture Sleeves
DOLTON	5-10	62-66

LPs: 10/12–inch 33rpm
DOLTON	12-25	61-65
LIBERTY	8-15	67-70
SUNSET	8-10	67

Also see CARTER, Mel / Vic Dana

DANCER, PRANCER & NERVOUS
Singles: 7–inch
CAPITOL	5-10	59

Picture Sleeves
CAPITOL	8-10	59

Member: Russ Regan.

DANDLEERS: see DANLEERS

DANGERFIELD, Rodney
Singles: 12–inch 33/45rpm
RCA	4-6	83

Singles: 7–inch
RCA	2-4	83

Picture Sleeves
RCA	2-4	83

LPs: 10/12–inch 33rpm
DECCA	15-20	66
CASABLANCA	5-10	80
RCA	5-10	83
RHINO	5-10	80

DANIELS, Charlie, Band
(Charley Daniels and the Jaguars)
Singles: 7–inch
EPIC	2-5	76-86
HANOVER	10-15	59
KAMA SUTRA	3-5	73-76
PAULA (200 series)	4-8	66
PAULA (400 series)	3-5	76

EPs: 7–inch 33/45rpm
KAMA SUTRA (10 "Volunteer Jam")	5-8	74

(Bonus EP packaged with *Fire on the Mountain* LP.)

LPs: 10/12–inch 33rpm
CAPITOL (11000 series)	8-10	75
CAPITOL (16000 series)	5-10	80
EPIC (Except 273)	5-10	76-91
EPIC (273 "Everything You Always Wanted to Hear")	10-15	77

(Promotional issue only.)
KAMA SUTRA	10-15	73-76
MFSL (176 "Million Mile Reflections")	15-20	85

DANKO, Rick
Singles: 7–inch
ARISTA 2-4   78
LPs: 10/12–inch 33rpm
ARISTA 8-10   77
Also see BAND

DANKWORTH, Johnny
(Johnnie Dankworth)
Singles: 78rpm
CAPITOL 3-5   55-56
Singles: 7–inch
CAPITOL 4-8   55-56
FONTANA 3-5   63-66
20TH FOX 3-5   66
LPs: 10/12–inch 33rpm
FONTANA (Except 7559) 6-10   64-69
FONTANA (27559 "The Idol") 15-20   66
  (Soundtrack. Monaural.)
FONTANA (67559 "The Idol") 20-25   66
  (Soundtrack. Stereo.)
ROULETTE 10-15   60-61
TOP RANK 10-15   60

DANLEERS
(Dandleers)
Singles: 7–inch
ABC 2-4   75
AMP 3 (1005 " One Summer Night") ... 5-8
AMP 3 (2115 " One Summer Night") . 25-35   58
EPIC (9367 "Half a Block
  from an Angel") 15-25   60
EPIC (9421 "Little Lover") 15-25   60
EVEREST (19412 "Foolish") 20-30   61
LE MANS 4-8   64
MERCURY 10-20   58-59
SMASH 4-8   64
  Members: Jimmy Weston; Johnny Lee; Nat McCune; Willie
  Ephriam; Roosevelt Mays; Doug Ebron; Louis Williams; Terry
  Wilson; Frank Clemens; Bill Carey.

DANNY and the Juniors
(Danny and the Juniors Featuring Joe Terry)
Singles: 78rpm
ABC-PAR 10-20   57-58
Singles: 7–inch
ABC 2-4   73
ABC-PAR 8-12   57-59
CRUNCH 3-5   73
GOLDIES 45 3-5
GUYDEN 5-10   62
LUB 4-6   68
MCA 2-4
MERCURY 4-8   64
RONN 4-6   68
ROULETTE 2-4
SINGULAR (711 "At the Hop") 75-100   57
  (Blue label.)
SINGULAR (711 "At the Hop") 4-8
  (Black label.)
SWAN 8-12   60-62

TOPAZ 2-4   87
EPs: 7–inch 33/45rpm
ABC-PAR (11 "At the Hop") 250-350   58
Picture Sleeves
SWAN (4064 "Candy Cane
  Sugar Plum") 50-75   60
LPs: 10/12–inch 33rpm
MCA 5-10
  Members: Danny Rapp; Frank Maffei; Joe Terry; Dave White.
  Also see CANNON, Freddy

DANNY WILSON
Singles: 7–inch
VIRGIN 2-4   87
Picture Sleeves
VIRGIN 2-4   87
LPs: 10/12–inch 33rpm
VIRGIN 5-10   87

DANSE SOCIETY
Singles: 12–inch 33/45rpm
ARISTA 4-6   84
Singles: 7–inch
ARISTA 2-4   84

DANTE
(Dante and the Evergreens; Dante and His Friends)
Singles: 7–inch
A&M 5-10   66
IMPERIAL 15-25   61-62
MADISON 8-12   60-61
LPs: 10/12–inch 33rpm
MADISON (1002 "Dante and the
  Evergreens") 150-200   61

DANTE and His Friends:
see DANTE

DANTE and the Evergreens:
see DANTE

D'ARBY, Terence Trent
Singles: 7–inch
COLUMBIA 2-4   87-89
Picture Sleeves
COLUMBIA 2-4   87-89
LPs: 10/12–inch 33rpm
COLUMBIA 5-10   87-89

DARENSBOURG, Joe, and His Dixie Flyers
Singles: 7–inch
LARK 4-8   58-59
LPs: 10/12–inch 33rpm
DIXIELAND JUBILEE 5-10   75
GHB 5-10   77

DARIAN, Fred
(Freddy Darian)
Singles: 7–inch
DEL-FI 5-10   60
GARDENA 5-10   61
JAF 4-8   61-63
MAHALO 4-8   63
OKEH 5-10   59

RCA	5-10	59
U.A.	4-8	63

DARIN, Bobby
(Bobby Darin and the Jaybirds; Bobby Darin and the
Rinky Dinks; Bob Darin)
Singles: 78rpm

ATCO	10-15	57-58
DECCA	8-15	56-57

Singles: 7–inch

ATCO ("She's Tanfastic")	15-20	
(Promotional issue only. No number shown.)		
ATCO (6103 through 6127)	10-20	57-58
ATCO (6133 "Plain Jane")	10-20	59
(Monaural.)		
ATCO (SD-45-6133 "Plain Jane")	20-30	59
(Stereo.)		
ATCO (6149 through 6334)	5-10	59-65
ATLANTIC	4-8	65-67
CAPITOL	5-8	62-65
DECCA (29883 "Rock Island Line")	20-30	56
DECCA (29922 "Blue Eyed Mermaid")	30-50	56
DECCA (30031 "The Greatest		
Builder")	20-30	56
DECCA (30225 "Dealer in Dreams")	25-40	57
DECCA (30737 "Dealer in Dreams")	10-15	59
DIMENSION	3-6	70
DIRECTION	3-6	68-70
MOTOWN	3-5	71-72

Picture Sleeves

ATCO (Except 6211)	8-15	59-62
ATCO (6211 "Ave Maria")	75-100	61
CAPITOL	5-10	62-65

EPs: 7–inch 33/45rpm

ATCO (1001 "For Teenagers Only")	40-60	60
(Promotional issue only. Issued with paper sleeve.)		
ATCO (4502 "Bobby Darin")	35-45	58
ATCO (4504 "That's All")	25-35	59
ATCO (4505 "Bobby Darin")	30-45	59
ATCO (4508 "This Is Darin")	20-30	59
ATCO (4512 "At the Copa")	20-30	60
ATCO (4513 "For Teenagers Only")	30-50	60
CAPITOL CUSTOM/ARTISTIC (45 "Scripto		
Presents Bobby Darin")	20-30	63
(Promotional issue only. Issued with paper sleeve.)		
DECCA (2676 "Bobby Darin")	50-75	60

LPs: 10/12–inch 33rpm

ATCO (Except 102 and 131)	20-35	59-67
ATCO (102 "Bobby Darin")	40-60	58
ATCO (131 "The Bobby Darin Story")	35-40	61
(White cover.)		
ATCO (131 "The Bobby Darin Story")	10-15	72
(Black cover.)		
ATLANTIC	15-25	66-67
BAINBRIDGE	5-10	81
CANDLELITE	15-20	76
CAPITOL	20-25	62-66
CLARION	15-20	64
DIRECTION	12-20	68-70

IMPERIAL HOUSE	12-15	76
MOTOWN (100 series)	5-10	82
MOTOWN (700 and 800 series)	10-12	72-74
WARNER (3501 "The Original		
Bobby Darin")	20-30	76
(Three-LP mail-order offer.)		
Also see DING DONGS		
Also see RINKY DINKS		

DARLIN, Florraine
Singles: 7–inch

EPIC	8-10	62-63
RIC	4-8	64

DARNEL, Bill
(Bill Darnel and the Heathertones)
Singles: 78rpm

CORAL	3-5	50-51
DECCA	3-5	52-53

Singles: 7–inch

CORAL	5-10	50-51
DECCA	5-10	52-53
JUBILEE	4-8	59
LONDON (Except 1665)	5-10	56
LONDON (1665 "Rock-a-Boogie		
Baby")	10-15	56
PARIS	10-15	59
X	5-10	54-55

EPs: 7–inch 33/45rpm

X	10-20	55

LPs: 10/12–inch 33rpm

X	20-30	55

DARNELL, Larry
Singles: 78rpm

DELUXE	5-10	57
OKEH	5-10	51-53
REGAL	10-15	49-51
SAVOY	5-10	55

Singles: 7–inch

ANNA	15-20	60
ARGO	5-10	60
DELUXE	10-20	57
MISTY	4-6	
OKEH	10-20	51-53
REGAL	10-20	51
SAVOY (1151 "That's All		
I Want from You")	15-25	55
WARWICK	8-12	59

EPs: 7–inch 33/45rpm

EPIC (7072 "For You My Love")	30-40	61
Member: Mickey Baker.		

DARRELL, Johnny
Singles: 7–inch

CAPRICORN	3-5	74-75
CARTWHEEL	3-5	71-72
GUSTO	2-4	78
MONUMENT	3-5	73
U.A.	3-5	65-70

Picture Sleeves

U.A.	3-6	67

LPs: 10/12-inch 33rpm

CAPRICORN	6-10	75
GUSTO	5-10	
SUNSET	6-10	68-70
U.A.	8-12	66-70

DARRELL, Johnny / George Jones / Willie Nelson

LPs: 10/12-inch 33rpm

SUNSET	8-10	69

Also see DARRELL, Johnny
Also see JONES, George
Also see NELSON, Willie

DARREN, James
(Jimmy Darren)

Singles: 7-inch

ABC	2-4	74
BUDDAH	3-5	70
COLPIX (102 "There's No Such Thing")	5-10	58
COLPIX (113 "Gidget")	5-10	59
COLPIX (119 "Angel Face")	5-10	59
(Monaural.)		
COLPIX (SCP-119 "Angel Face")	10-20	59
(Stereo.)		
COLPIX (128 through 708)	5-10	59-63
COLPIX (758 "Punch and Judy")	10-20	64
COLPIX (765 "Married Man")	5-10	64
ERIC	2-4	
KIRSHNER	3-5	71-72
MCA	2-4	
MGM	3-5	73
PRIVATE STOCK	3-5	75-77
RCA	3-5	78
WARNER	4-8	65-68

Picture Sleeves

COLPIX	8-15	58-61

LPs: 10/12-inch 33rpm

COLPIX (406 "Album No. 1")	20-30	60
COLPIX (418 "Gidget Goes Hawaiian")	20-30	61
COLPIX (424 "For All Sizes")	20-30	62
COLPIX (428 "Love Among the Young")	20-30	62
KIRSHNER	10-20	71-72
WARNER	15-20	67

DARREN, James / Shelley Fabares / Paul Petersen

LPs: 10/12-inch 33rpm

COLPIX (444 "Teenage Triangle")	25-35	63
COLPIX (468 "More Teenage Triangle")	25-35	63

Also see DARREN, James
Also see FABARES, Shelley
Also see PETERSEN, Paul

DARTELLS

Singles: 7-inch

ARLEN (509 "Hot Pastrami")	8-12	63
(Black vinyl.)		

ARLEN (509 "Hot Pastrami")	20-30	63
(Colored vinyl.)		
ARLEN (513 "Dance Everybody, Dance")	10-15	63
DOT	4-8	63-64
HBR	4-8	66

LPs: 10/12-inch 33rpm

DOT (3522 "Hot Pastrami")	25-30	63
(Monaural.)		
DOT (25522 "Hot Pastrami")	25-30	63
(Stereo.)		

Member: Doug Phillips.

DASH, Sarah

Singles: 7-inch

KIRSHNER	2-4	79

LPs: 10/12-inch 33rpm

KIRSHNER	5-10	78

Also see LABELLE, Patti

DAVE & SUGAR
(Dave Rowland and Sugar)

Singles: 7-inch

ELEKTRA	2-4	81
RCA	2-5	75-82

LPs: 10/12-inch 33rpm

ELEKTRA	5-10	81
RCA	5-10	76-82

Members: Dave Rowland; Vicki Hackeman-Baker; Jackie Frantz; Sue Powell; Melissa Dean; Jamie Kaye.
Also see PRIDE, Charley

DAVID, F.R

Singles: 7-inch

CARRERE AMERICA	2-4	83

LPs: 10/12-inch 33rpm

CARRERE AMERICA	5-10	83

DAVID & JONATHAN

Singles: 7-inch

AMY	4-8	68
CAPITOL	4-8	66-67
20TH FOX	4-6	66

Picture Sleeves

CAPITOL	5-10	66

LPs: 10/12-inch 33rpm

CAPITOL (2473 "Michelle")	20-30	66

Members: Roger Greenaway; Roger Cook.
Also see WHITE PLAINS

DAVID & LEE

Singles: 7-inch

G.S.P. (1 "Sad September")	20-30	62

Members: David Gates; Leon Russell.
Also see GATES, David
Also see RUSSELL, Leon

DAVIDSON, John

Singles: 7-inch

COLUMBIA	3-6	66-71
MERCURY	3-5	73
20TH FOX	3-5	73-77

Picture Sleeves

COLUMBIA	4-6	66-69

LPs: 10/12–inch 33rpm

COLPIX	10-15	65
COLUMBIA	5-10	66-80
HARMONY	4-6	72
MERCURY	5-10	73
20TH FOX	5-10	74-76

DAVIE, Hutch
(Hutch Davie and His Honky-Tonkers)
Singles: 7–inch

ATCO	5-10	58-59
CANADIAN AMERICAN	4-8	61
CLARIDGE	4-8	66
CONGRESS	4-8	62
DYNO VOICE	3-6	68

LPs: 10/12–inch 33rpm

ATCO (105 "Much Hutch")	20-30	59

DAVIES, Dave
Singles: 7–inch

RCA	3-5	80
REPRISE	15-20	67-68
WARNER	2-4	83

Picture Sleeves

RCA (12089 "Wild Man")	10-15	80

LPs: 10/12–inch 33rpm

RCA	8-12	80-81
WARNER	5-10	83

Also see KINKS

DA VINCI, Paul
Singles: 7–inch

MERCURY	3-5	72-74

DAVIS, Betty
Singles: 7–inch

ISLAND	3-5	75-76
JUST SUNSHINE	3-5	73-74

LPs: 10/12–inch 33rpm

ISLAND	5-10	75
JUST SUNSHINE	6-10	73-74

DAVIS, Billy, Jr.
(Billy Davis)
Singles: 7–inch

ABC	3-5	75
COBBLESTONE	4-6	69
HI	4-8	68

LPs: 10/12–inch 33rpm

SAVOY	5-10	82

Also see FIFTH DIMENSION

DAVIS, Carl, and the Chi-Sound Orchestra
Singles: 7–inch

CHI-SOUND	3-5	77

DAVIS, Danny
(Danny Davis and the Nashville Brass; Danny Davis Orchestra; Danny Davis and the Titans; Danny Davis and the Nashville Strings)
Singles: 78rpm

BLUE JAY	3-5	54
HICKORY	3-5	54

MGM	3-6	51-53

Singles: 7–inch

BLUE JAY	4-8	54
CABOT	3-6	59
HICKORY	4-8	54
LIBERTY	3-6	59
MGM (11000 series)	5-10	51-53
MGM (13000 series)	3-5	62-65
RCA	2-4	69-84
THUNDER	3-6	59
VERVE	3-5	61

LPs: 10/12–inch 33rpm

MGM	8-18	61-65
RCA SPECIAL PRODUCTS (0176 "America 200 Years Young")	10-15	76

(Special Products issue for the Amana Corp.)

RCA	5-10	69-84

Also see ATKINS, Chet, Floyd Cramer and Danny Davis

DAVIS, Danny, and Byron Lee
Singles: 7–inch

MGM	4-6	64

DAVIS, Danny, the Nashville Brass, and Willie Nelson
Singles: 7–inch

RCA	2-4	80

LPs: 10/12–inch 33rpm

RCA	5-10	80

Also see DAVIS, Danny
Also see LOCKLIN, Hank
Also see NELSON, Willie, Danny Davis and the Nashville Brass
Also see NEWMAN, Jimmy C., Danny Davis and the Nashville Brass

DAVIS, Geater
Singles: 7–inch

HOUSE of ORANGE	3-5	70
SEVENTY	3-5	73

DAVIS, John, and the Monster Orchestra
Singles: 12–inch 33/45rpm

COLUMBIA	4-6	79

Singles: 7–inch

COLUMBIA	3-5	78-79
SAM	3-5	76-78

LPs: 10/12–inch 33rpm

COLUMBIA	5-10	79

DAVIS, Krystal
Singles: 12–inch 33/45rpm

URBAN ROCK	4-6	85

DAVIS, Mac
Singles: 7–inch

CAPITOL	4-8	65
COLUMBIA	3-5	70-78
CASABLANCA	2-4	80-85
JAMIE	5-10	62
MCA	2-4	86
VEE JAY	5-10	63

Picture Sleeves

COLUMBIA	3-5	70-75

LPs: 10/12–inch 33rpm

ACCORD	5-10	82
CASABLANCA	5-10	81-85
COLUMBIA	8-10	70-83
MCA	5-10	86
SPRINGBOARD	6-10	
TRIP	8-10	73

DAVIS, Miles
(Miles Davis Sextet)

Singles: 78rpm

BLUE NOTE	3-6	54-56
PRESTIGE	3-6	52-57

Singles: 7-inch

BLUE NOTE (1600 series)	5-10	54-56
COLUMBIA (02000 through 03000 series)	2-4	81-83
COLUMBIA (10000 series)	3-6	75
COLUMBIA (41000 through 46000 series)	3-8	61-74
PRESTIGE (100 through 400 series)	4-8	57-66
PRESTIGE (700 through 900 series)	5-10	52-55

EPs: 7-Inch 33/45rpm

BLUE NOTE	15-25	52
CAPITOL (459 "Jeru")	50-100	53
COLUMBIA	6-10	59
PRESTIGE	12-20	52-53

LPs: 10/12-Inch 33rpm

BLUE NOTE (100 series)	8-12	73
BLUE NOTE (1500 series)	25-50	56-58
(Label gives New York street address for Blue Note Records.)		
BLUE NOTE (1500 series)	15-25	58
(Label reads "Blue Note Records Inc. - New York, U.S.A.")		
BLUE NOTE (1500 series)	10-20	66
(Label shows Blue Note Records as a division of either Liberty or United Artists.)		
BLUE NOTE (5013 "Miles Davis")	100-150	52
(10-Inch LP.)		
BLUE NOTE (5022 "Tempus Fugit")	100-150	53
(10-Inch LP.)		
BLUE NOTE (5044 "Miles Davis")	100-150	54
(10-Inch LP.)		
CAPITOL (H-459 "Jeru")	100-150	53
(10-Inch LP.)		
CAPITOL (T-459 "Jeru")	35-50	53
CAPITOL (762 "Birth of Cool")	50-75	56
CAPITOL (1900 series)	10-20	63
CAPITOL (11000 series)	8-12	72
CAPITOL (16000 series)	5-10	81
COLUMBIA (20 "Friday and Saturday Nights in Person")	25-30	61
(Monaural.)		
COLUMBIA (26 "Bitches Brew")	8-12	70
COLUMBIA (820 "Friday and Saturday Nights in Person")	30-40	61
(Stereo.)		

COLUMBIA (900 through 1600 series)	20-35	57-61
(With six black Columbia "eye" logos on red label.)		
COLUMBIA (1800 through 2300 series)	15-25	61-65
COLUMBIA (8000 through 8400 series)	20-35	58-62
(With six black Columbia "eye" logos on red label.)		
COLUMBIA (8600 through 9800 series)	10-20	61-69
COLUMBIA (10000 series)	6-10	73
COLUMBIA (30000 series, except 36976)	6-12	70-85
COLUMBIA (36976 "The Miles Davis Collection")	30-40	80
(Six-LP set.)		
COLUMBIA (40000 series)	8-12	81-85
DEBUT (043 "Blue Moods")	5-8	83
DEBUT (120 "Blue Moods")	50-100	55
FANTASY	15-20	62
FONTANA	10-15	65
MFSL (177 "Someday My Prince Will Come")	15-25	85
MOODSVILLE	15-20	63
NEW JAZZ	10-15	64
PRESTIGE (004 through 093)	5-8	80-85
PRESTIGE (100 series)	50-100	52-54
(10-Inch LPs.)		
PRESTIGE (7007 through 7166)	40-60	55-59
(Yellow label.)		
PRESTIGE (7168 through 7281)	20-30	60-64
(Yellow label.)		
PRESTIGE (7000 through 7600 series)	6-12	64-69
(Blue label.)		
PRESTIGE (7700 through 7800 series)	6-12	70-71
PRESTIGE (24000 series)	8-12	72-78
SAVOY	12-20	61
TRIP	5-10	73
U.A.	8-10	71
WARNER	5-10	86-89

Also see COLTRANE, John, and Miles Davis
Also see FORREST, Jimmy

DAVIS, Miles, and Thelonious Monk
LPs: 10/12-Inch 33rpm

COLUMBIA	10-20	64

Also see DAVIS, Miles
Also see JACQUET, Illinois, and Miles Davis
Also see MONK, Thelonious

DAVIS, Miz

Singles: 7–inch

NEW	3-5	76

DAVIS, Paul

Singles: 7–inch

ARISTA	2-4	81-82
BANG (Except 500 series)	3-5	73-80
BANG (500 series)	3-6	68-72
FLASHBACK	2-4	82

SOLID GOLD 2-4   73
LPs: 10/12–inch 33rpm
ARISTA 5-10   81
BANG 10-12   72-82
  Also see OSMOND, Marie, and Paul Davis

DAVIS, Ruth
Singles: 7–inch
CLARIDGE 2-4   78
  Also see KIRKLAND, Bo, and Ruth Davis

DAVIS, Sammy, Jr.
(Sammy Davis)
Singles: 7–inch
A.L.B.B. (38032 "The House I
  Live In") 3-5
  (Promotional issue only.)
DECCA (25500 series) 3-6   62
DECCA (29000 through 31000 series) . 5-10   54-60
DECCA (32000 series) 3-5   69
ECOLOGY 2-4   71
MGM 2-5   71-79
VERVE 4-6   60
REPRISE 3-6   61-71
20TH FOX 3-5   75-76
WARNER 2-4   77
Picture Sleeves
A.L.B.B. (38032 "The House I
  Live In") 5-10
  (Promotional issue only.)
EPs: 7–inch 33/45rpm
CAPITOL 5-15   54
DECCA 8-12   54-55
LPs: 10/12–inch 33rpm
DECCA (100 series) 10-20   66
DECCA (4000 series) 10-20   61-65
DECCA (8100 through 8700 series) . . 20-30   54-58
DECCA (8900 series) 10-20   59
DECCA (9032 "Mr. Wonderful") 60-70   56
  (Soundtrack.)
HARMONY 5-10   69-71
MCA 5-10   77
MGM 5-10   72-73
MOTOWN 6-10   70
RCA (1086 "Three Penny Opera") . . . 15-25   64
REPRISE 10-20   61-69
20TH FOX (Except 5014) 5-10   76
20TH FOX (FXG-5014 "Of Love
  and Desire") 25-30   64
  (Soundtrack. Monaural.)
20TH FOX (SXG-5014 "Of Love
  and Desire") 35-40   64
  (Soundtrack. Stereo.)
WARNER 5-10   77
U.A. (5187 "Salt and Pepper") 15-20   68
  (Soundtrack.)
VOCALION 5-10   68
  Also see CURB, Mike
  Also see SINATRA, Frank, Sammy Davis Jr. and Dean Martin

DAVIS, Sammy, Jr., and Laurindo, Almeida
LPs: 10/12–inch 33rpm
REPRISE 10-15   67
  Also see ALMEIDA, Laurindo

DAVIS, Sammy, Jr., and Count Basie
Singles: 7–inch
VERVE 3-5   65
LPs: 10/12–inch 33rpm
MGM 6-10   73
VERVE 10-15   65
  Also see BASIE, Count

DAVIS, Sammy, Jr., and Carmen McRae
Singles: 7–inch
DECCA 5-10   55
EPs: 7–inch 33/45rpm
DECCA 5-10   59
LPs: 10/12–inch 33rpm
DECCA 10-20   59
  Also see McRAE, Carmen

DAVIS, Sammy, Jr., and Buddy Rich
LPs: 10/12–inch 33rpm
REPRISE 10-20   66
  Also see RICH, Buddy

DAVIS, Sammy, Jr. / Joya Sherril
LPs: 10/12–inch 33rpm
DESIGN 5-10
  Also see DAVIS, Sammy, Jr.

DAVIS, Skeeter
Singles: 7–inch
MERCURY 2-5   76-77
PART TWO 2-4   80
RCA (Except 7400 through 9600 series) 3-5   69-74
RCA (7400 through 8300 series) 4-8   59-64
RCA (8400 through 9600 series) 3-6   64-68
Picture Sleeves
RCA 4-8   63
EPs: 7–inch 33/45rpm
RCA 5-10   63
LPs: 10/12–inch 33rpm
CAMDEN 5-10   65-74
GUSTO 5-10   78
RCA (2000 and 3000 series,
  except 3790) 10-15   60-68
RCA (3790 "Skeeter Davis
  Sings Buddy Holly") 20-30   67
TUDOR 5-10   84
  Also see BARE, Bobby, and Skeeter Davis
  Also see HAMILTON, George, IV, and Skeeter Davis
  Also see JENNINGS, Waylon
  Also see POSEY, Sandy / Skeeter Davis
  Also see WAGONER, Porter, and Skeeter Davis

DAVIS, Skeeter, and NRBQ
Singles: 7–inch
ROUNDER 3-5   85
  Also see DAVIS, Skeeter
  Also see NRBQ

DAVIS, Spencer
(Spencer Davis Group; Spencer Davis and Peter Jameson)
Singles: 7-inch
ALLEGIANCE 2-4   84
ATCO 5-10   66
FONTANA 8-12   64
U.A. 4-8   66-72
VERTIGO 2-4   73-74
Picture Sleeves
U.A. 8-12   66-67
LPs: 10/12-inch 33rpm
ALLEGIANCE 5-10   84
DATE 10-12   70
FONTANA 20-30   66
ISLAND 5-10   83
MEDIARTS 10-12   71
RHINO 5-10   84
U.A. 15-30   67-75
VERTIGO 10-12   73-74
WING 10-15
    Members: Spencer Davis; Steve Winwood; Pete York; Brian Dexter; Ray Fenwick; Ken Salmon.
    Also see WINWOOD, Steve

DAVIS, Tim
Singles: 7-inch
METROMEDIA 3-5   72-73
LPs: 10/12-inch 33rpm
METROMEDIA 8-10   72-74
    Also see MILLER, Steve

DAVIS, Tyrone
Singles: 7-inch
ABC 4-6   68
COLUMBIA 2-5   76-81
DAKAR 3-6   68-77
EPIC 2-4   83
FUTURE 2-4   87-88
HIGHRISE 2-4   82-83
OCEAN FRONT 2-4   83-84
LPs: 10/12-inch 33rpm
COLUMBIA 8-10   76-81
DAKAR 10-15   69-76
EPIC 5-10   83
HIGHRISE 5-10   82

DAVY D: see DAVY DMX

DAWN
Singles: 7-inch
ARISTA 3-5   75
ELEKTRA 3-5   76-77
    Members: Joyce Wilson; Telma Hopkins.
    Also see DAWN (With Tony Orlando)

DAWN
(With Tony Orlando)
Singles: 7-inch
BELL 3-5   70-72
LPs: 10/12-inch 33rpm
BELL 10-12   70-71
    Members: Tony Orlando; Joyce Wilson; Telma Hopkins.

Also see DAWN
Also see ORLANDO, Tony, and Dawn

DAWSON, Cliff
Singles: 7-inch
BOARDWALK 2-4   82

DAWSON, Cliff, and Renee Diggs
Singles: 7-inch
BOARDWALK 2-4   83
    Also see DAWSON, Cliff
    Also see STARPOINT

DAY, Arlan
Singles: 7-inch
PASHA 2-4   81

DAY, Bobby
(Bobby Day and the Satellites; Bobby Day and the Blossoms; Bobby Byrd)
Singles: 78rpm
CLASS 5-10   57
Singles: 7-inch
CLASS 8-12   57-59
RCA 5-8   63-64
RENDEZVOUS 5-10   60-62
SURE SHOT 4-8   67
LPs: 10/12-inch 33rpm
CLASS (5002 "Rockin' with Robin") . 75-100   59
RHINO 5-10   84
    Also see BYRD, Bobby

DAY, Dennis
(Dennis Day with Jack Benny)
Singles: 78rpm
CAPITOL 3-5   56
RCA 3-5   50-54
Singles: 7-inch
CAPITOL 4-8   56
RCA 4-8   50-54
REPRISE 3-6   62
SHAMROCK 3-6   59
EPs: 7-inch 33/45rpm
CAPITOL 5-10   56
RCA 5-10   50-59
LPs: 10/12-inch 33rpm
BLUEBIRD 5-10   60
CAMDEN 5-10   64-66
CAPITOL 10-20   56
DESIGN 5-10
MASTERSEAL 10-20
RCA (3036 "My Wild Irish Rose") 15-25   52
REPRISE 5-10   63
ROULETTE 10-15   63

DAY, Doris
(Doris Day and the Mellomen; Doris Day and the Norman Luboff Choir)
Singles: 78rpm
COLUMBIA 4-8   47-57
Singles: 7-inch
ARWIN (68899 "David's Psalm") 5-10
COLUMBIA (38000 and 39000 series) 5-10   50-53

COLUMBIA (40000 through 44000
series) 4-8 54-67
Picture Sleeves
COLUMBIA 10-20 57-61
EPs: 7–inch 33/45rpm
COLUMBIA 10-30 50-59
LPs: 10/12–inch 33rpm
COLUMBIA (1 "Listen to Day") 20-30 60
COLUMBIA (600 through 1300 series) 15-30 55-59
COLUMBIA (1400 through 2100
series) 10-20 60-64
COLUMBIA (2500 series) 20-35 56
(10–inch LPs.)
COLUMBIA (6000 series) 25-50 49-55
(10–inch LPs.)
COLUMBIA (8000 through 8900
series) 15-30 58-64
COLUMBIA (2200 through 2300
series) 10-25 64-65
(Monaural.)
COLUMBIA (9000 through 9100
series) 15-35 64-65
(Stereo.)
HARMONY 8-12 66-72
Also see BROWN, Les, and His Orchestra

DAY, Doris, and Don Cherry
EPs: 7–inch 33/45rpm
COLUMBIA 10-20 56
Also see CHERRY, Don

DAY, Doris, and Frankie Laine
Singles: 78rpm
COLUMBIA 3-6 52
Singles: 7–inch
COLUMBIA 5-10 52
Also see LAINE, Frankie

DAY, Doris, and Andre Previn
LPs: 10/12–inch 33rpm
COLUMBIA 10-20 62
Also see PREVIN, Andre

DAY, Doris, and Johnnie Ray
Singles: 78rpm
COLUMBIA 3-6 52-53
Singles: 7–inch
COLUMBIA 5-10 52-53
Also see RAY, Johnnie

DAY, Doris / Frank Sinatra
EPs: 7–inch 33/45rpm
COLUMBIA (571 "Young
at Heart") 10-15 55
LPs: 10/12–inch 33rpm
COLUMBIA (6339 "Young at Heart") . 40-50 55
(Soundtrack. 10–inch LP.)
Also see DAY, Doris
Also see SINATRA, Frank

DAY, Morris
Singles: 12–inch 33/45rpm
WARNER 4-6 85-86

Singles: 7–inch
WARNER 2-4 85-88
Picture Sleeves
WARNER 2-4 85-88
LPs: 10/12–inch 33rpm
WARNER 5-10 85-88
Also see TIME

DAYBREAK
Singles: 7–inch
PRELUDE 2-4 80
UNI........................... 2-4 70

DAYE, Cory
Singles: 7–inch
N.Y.I. 2-4 79
LPs: 10/12–inch 33rpm
N.Y.I. 5-10 79

DAYE, Johnny
Singles: 7–inch
JOMADA 4-8 65-66
PARKWAY 4-8 66
STAX 4-6 68

DAYNE, Taylor
Singles: 7–inch
ARISTA 2-4 87-90
Picture Sleeves
ARISTA 2-4 87-90
LPs: 10/12–inch 33rpm
ARISTA 5-8 87-90

DAYTON
Singles: 7–inch
CAPITOL 2-4 82-85
LIBERTY 2-4 81-82
U.A. 2-4 80
LPs: 10/12–inch 33rpm
CAPITOL 5-10 83
LIBERTY 5-10 81-82
U.A. 5-10 80

DAZZ BAND
Singles: 12–inch 33/45rpm
GEFFEN 4-6 86
MOTOWN 4-8 80-85
Singles: 7–inch
GEFFEN 2-4 86
MOTOWN 2-4 80-85
RCA 2-4 88
LPs: 10/12–inch 33rpm
GEFFEN 5-10 86
MOTOWN 5-10 80-85
Also see KINSMAN DAZZ

D'COCOA, Creme: see CREME D'COCOA

DEACONS
Singles: 7–inch
CAMELOT 8-10
SHAMA 10-20 68

DEAD BOYS
Singles: 7-inch
SIRE 3-5   77-78
SIRE 5-10   77-78
(Promotional issues only.)
LPs: 10/12-inch 33rpm
BOMP 8-10   80
SIRE 15-25   77-78
Members: Stiv Bators; Jimmy Zero, John Blitz; Cheetah Chrome; Jeff Jizz.

DEAD KENNEDYS
Singles: 7-inch
ALTERNATIVE TENTACLES 4-8   83-86
LPs: 10/12-inch 33rpm
ALTERNATIVE TENTACLES 10-20   83-86
I.R.S. 10-12   81
Members: Jello Biafra; East Bay Ray; Deron Peligro; Klaus Fluoride.

DEAD MILKMEN
LPs: 10/12-inch 33rpm
ENIGMA 5-10   87-90

DEAD OR ALIVE
Singles: 12-inch 33/45rpm
EPIC 4-6   84-86
Singles: 7-inch
EPIC 2-4   84-89
Picture Sleeves
EPIC 2-4   84-89
LPs: 10/12-inch 33rpm
EPIC 5-10   84-89
Member: Pete Burns.

DEADLY NIGHTSHADE
Singles: 7-inch
PHANTOM 3-5   76
LPs: 10/12-inch 33rpm
PHANTOM 8-10   76

DEAL, Bill
(Bill Deal and the Rhondels)
Singles: 7-inch
BUDDAH 3-5   71-72
CHESLICK 4-6
COLLECTABLES 2-4
ERIC 2-4
HERITAGE 4-8   68-70
POLYDOR 3-5   70-73
RED LION 2-4   79
Picture Sleeves
HERITAGE 8-10   69
LPs: 10/12-inch 33rpm
HERITAGE 15-20   69
RHINO 5-10   86

DEAN, Alan
Singles: 78rpm
LONDON 3-5   51
MGM 3-5   51-56
RAMA 4-6   56-57

Singles: 7-inch
LONDON 5-10   51
MGM 4-8   51-56
RAMA 5-10   56-57

DEAN, Debbie
(Debbie Deane and the Petites; Debbie Dean and the Paulette Singers)
Singles: 7-inch
MOTOWN 25-35   61-62
TREVA 4-8   66
V.I.P. 4-8   66-68
Picture Sleeves
MOTOWN (1025 "Everybody's Talking
About My Baby") 30-60   62

DEAN, Hazell
(Hazel Dean)
Singles: 12-inch 33/45rpm
QUALITY 4-6   84
Singles: 7-inch
LONDON 3-5   76

DEAN, Jimmy
(Jimmie Dean)
Singles: 78rpm
COLUMBIA 4-8   57
4 STAR 4-8   54
MERCURY 4-8   56
Singles: 7-inch
CASINO 3-5   76
COLUMBIA (40000 through 43000 series,
except 42175) 5-10   57-66
COLUMBIA (42175 "Big Bad John") . 8-12   61
(Dean says: "At the bottom of this mine
lies one hell of a man.")
COLUMBIA (42175 "Big Bad John") ... 4-6   61
(Dean says: "At the bottom of this mine
lies a big, big man.")
COLUMBIA (45000 and 46000 series) . 3-5   74
4 STAR (1600 series) 5-10   54
4 STAR (1700 series) 4-8   59
KING 4-6   64
MERCURY 5-10   56
RCA 3-6   66-71
Picture Sleeves
COLUMBIA (Except 41025) 5-10   59-66
COLUMBIA (41025 "Little Sandy
Sleighfoot") 10-20   57
EPs: 7-inch 33/45rpm
COLUMBIA 8-12   57
LPs: 10/12-inch 33rpm
ACCORD 5-10   82
BRYLEN 5-10
CASINO 5-10   76
COLUMBIA (1025; Jimmy Dean's
Hour of Prayer") 20-30   57
COLUMBIA (1500 through 2500
series) 10-25   61-66
(Monaural.)

COLUMBIA (8000 and 9000 series) .. 10-25   61-68
(Stereo. With "CS" prefix.)
COLUMBIA (9200 series) 5-10
(With "PC" prefix.)
COLUMBIA (10000 series) 6-10   73
CROWN 10-15
GRT 5-10   77
GUEST STAR 8-10
HARMONY 8-12   60-69
KING 12-18   61
LA BREA (8014 "Bummin' Around
with Jimmy Dean") 20-30
MERCURY (20319 "Jimmy Dean Sings
His Television Favorites") 20-30   57
PICKWICK/HILLTOP 10-12   65
RCA 8-12   67-71
SPIN-O-RAMA 8-10
WING 8-12   64
WYNCOTE 8-10

DEAN, Jimmy / Johnny Horton
LPs: 10/12-inch 33rpm
STARDAY 15-20   65
Also see HORTON, Johnny

DEAN, Jimmy / Marvin Rainwater
LPs: 10/12-inch 33rpm
PREMIER (9054 "Showtime") 10-15

DEAN, Jimmy / Marvin Rainwater / Rusty Evans
LPs: 10/12-inch 33rpm
ALMOR 10-15
Also see RAINWATER, Marvin

DEAN, Jimmy, and Dottie West
Singles: 7-inch
RCA 3-5   71
LPs: 10/12-inch 33rpm
RCA 8-10   70
Also see DEAN, Jimmy
Also see WEST, Dottie

DEAN & JEAN
Singles: 7-inch
EMBER 5-10   59-62
RUST 4-8   63-65
Members: Welton Young; Brenda Lee Jones.
Also see JONES, Brenda

DEAN & MARC
Singles: 7-inch
BULLSEYE 8-10   59
HICKORY 4-8   63-65
MAY 4-8   63
Members: Dean Mathis; Marc Mathis.
Also see NEWBEATS

DEANE, Shelbra
Singles: 7-inch
CASINO 3-5   76-77

DE BARGE
(DeBarges)
Singles: 12-inch 33/45rpm
GORDY 4-6   85-86
Singles: 7-inch
GORDY 2-4   81-86
STRIPED H. 2-4   87
Picture Sleeves
GORDY 2-4   85-86
LPs: 10/12-inch 33rpm
GORDY 5-10   81-86
MOTOWN 4-6
Members: Eldra BeBarge; Marty DeBarge; James DeBarge;
Bunny De Barge.
Also see DE BARGE, Bunny
Also see DE BARGE, EL
Also see KING DREAM CHORUS and Holiday Crew

DE BARGE, Bunny
Singles: 12-inch 33/45rpm
GORDY 4-6   87
Singles: 7-inch
GORDY 2-4   87
LPs: 10/12-inch 33rpm
MOTOWN 5-8   87
Also see DE BARGE

DE BARGE, Chico
Singles: 12-inch 33/45rpm
MOTOWN 4-6   86-87
Singles: 7-inch
MOTOWN 2-4   86-88
Picture Sleeves
MOTOWN 2-4   86
LPs: 10/12-inch 33rpm
MOTOWN 5-10   86-87

DE BARGE, El
(El DeBarge with DeBarge)
Singles: 12-inch 33/45rpm
GORDY 4-6   86-87
Singles: 7-inch
GORDY 2-4   81-87
LPs: 10/12-inch 33rpm
GORDY 5-10   81-87
Also see DE BARGE

DEBBIE DEB
Singles: 12-inch 33/45rpm
JAMPACKED 4-6   85
SUNNYVIEW 4-6   84
Singles: 7-inch
JAMPACKED 2-4   87
Also see TRINERE / Freestyle / Debbie Deb

DE BLANC
Singles: 7-inch
ARISTA 3-5   75-76
Also see DYNASTY

DE BURGH, Chris
Singles: 7-inch
A&M 2-5   75-87

COLONIAL (430 "Sittin in
the Balcony") 15-20   57
(Has "45 RPM" on left side of label.)
COLONIAL (430 "Sittin in
the Balcony") 10-15   57
(Has "45 RPM" on right side of label.)
COLONIAL (430 "Sittin in the Balcony") 8-12   57
(No "45 RPM" on label. Reads "Dist. by AM-PAR
Record Corp.")
COLONIAL (435 "1000 Concrete
Blocks") 15-20   57
DOT 5-10   58

Picture Sleeves
COLONIAL (430 "Sittin in
the Balcony") 30-40   57
Also see LOUDERMILK, John D.

DEE, Kiki
Singles: 7-inch
LIBERTY 4-6   68
MCA 3-5   73-77
POSSE 2-4   81
RCA 2-4   81
RARE EARTH 3-5   71
ROCKET 3-5   73-79
TAMLA 3-6   70
WORLD PACIFIC 4-8   66
LPs: 10/12-inch 33rpm
LIBERTY (7600 series) 15-20   69
LIBERTY (10000 series) 5-10   81
MCA/ROCKET 8-12   73-74
RCA 5-10   81
ROCKET 8-10   77-78
TAMLA 15-20   70
Also see JOHN, Elton, and Kiki Dee

DEE, Lenny
Singles: 78rpm
DECCA 2-4   56-61
Singles: 7-inch
DECCA 3-5   56-61
EPs: 7-inch 33/45rpm
DECCA 4-8   59
LPs: 10/12-inch 33rpm
DECCA 5-15   55-70

DEE, Lola
Singles: 78rpm
BALLY 3-6   57
MERCURY 3-5   54-56
WING 5-10   55-56
Singles: 7-inch
BALLY 5-10   57
MERCURY 5-10   54-56
WING 10-20   55-56

DEE, Lola, and Rusty Draper
Singles: 78rpm
MERCURY 3-6   56
Singles: 7-inch
MERCURY 5-10   56

Also see DRAPER, Rusty

DEE, Neecy
Singles: 12-inch 33/45rpm
TNT 4-6   85

DEE, Tommy
(Tommy Dee with Carol Kay and the Teen-Aires)
Singles: 7-inch
CHALLENGE 8-10   60
CREST (Monaural) 5-10   59
CREST (Stereo) 15-25   59
PIKE 4-8   61
SIMS 10-15   66

DEE JAY and the Runaways
Singles: 7-inch
COULEE (109 "Love Bug Crawl") ... 20-35
IGL (100 "Jenny Jenny") 100-150   65
IGL (103 "Peter Rabbit") 20-40   66
SMASH 3-5   66
SONIC 4-6   68
STONE (45 "Don't You Ever") 20-30   66
Members: Denny Storey; John Senn; Gary Lind; Terry Klein;
Bob; Tom.

DEELE
Singles: 7-inch
SOLAR 2-4   83-88
LPs: 10/12-inch 33rpm
SOLAR 5-10   84-88
Members: Kenny Edmonds; Antonio Reid; Darnell Bristol; Kevin
Roberson; Carlos Green.

DEEP PURPLE
Singles: 12-inch 33/45rpm
MERCURY 4-8   87
Singles: 7-inch
GRP 3-5   73
MERCURY 2-4   84-87
TETRAGRAMMATON 5-10   68-69
WARNER 3-6   70-73
WARNER/PURPLE 2-4   74-75
Picture Sleeves
MERCURY 3-5   85
TETRAGRAMMATON 8-15   68
WARNER/PURPLE 3-5   74-75
LPs: 10/12-inch 33rpm
MERCURY 6-12   84-88
PASSPORT 5-10   88
PORTRAIT 5-10   82
RCA 5-8   90
SCEPTER/CITATION 8-10   72
TETRAGRAMMATON (102 "Shades
of Deep Purple") 20-30   68
TETRAGRAMMATON (107 "Book
of Taliesyn") 20-30   69
TETRAGRAMMATON (119 "Deep
Purple") 20-30   69
WARNER (Except 3000 series) 15-25   70-74
WARNER (3000 series) 5-10   77
WARNER/PURPLE 10-15   74-80

Members: Ritchie Blackmore; Jon Lord; Ian Paice; Rod Evans;
Nick Simper; Roger Glover; Ian Gillan; David Coverdale.
Also see BLACKMORE'S RAINBOW
Also see CAPTAIN BEYOND
Also see GILLAN, Ian
Also see GLOVER, Roger
Also see WHITESNAKE

DEEP VELVET
Singles: 7–inch
AWARE	3-5	73

DEES, Rick
(Rick Dees and His Cast of Idiots)
Singles: 12–inch 33/45rpm
RSO	4-8	78
STAX	4-8	78

Singles: 7–inch
ATLANTIC	2-4	86
FRETONE (040 "Disco Duck")	5-10	76
RSO (Except 860)	3-5	76-77
RSO (860 "He Ate Too Many Jelly Donuts")	8-10	77
RSO/POLYDOR	3-5	76-77
STAX	3-5	78

Picture Sleeves
ATLANTIC	2-4	86
STAX	3-5	78

LPs: 10/12–inch 33rpm
ATLANTIC	5-10	85
RSO	8-10	77

DEES, Sam
Singles: 7–inch
ATLANTIC	3-5	73-75
CHESS	3-5	71
LOLO	4-6	69
POLYDOR	2-4	78

LPs: 10/12–inch 33rpm
ATLANTIC	5-10	75

DEES, Sam, and Bettye Swann
Singles: 7–inch
BIG TREE	3-5	76

Also see DEES, Sam
Also see SWANN, Bettye

DEF LEPPARD
Singles: 12–inch 33/45rpm
MERCURY	4-8	80-87
(Promotional only.)		

Singles: 7–inch
MERCURY	2-4	80-88

EPs: 7–inch 33/45rpm
BLUDGEON RIFFOLA	10-15	78

Picture Sleeves
MERCURY (Except 811 215 7)	2-4	80-88
MERCURY (811 215 7 "Photograph")	3-6	83

LPs: 10/12–inch 33rpm
MERCURY	5-10	80-88

Members: Joe Elliott; Rick Allen; Steve Clark; Phil Collen; Rick
Savage.

DE FRANCO FAMILY
Singles: 7–inch
20TH FOX (Except 2214)	3-5	73-74
20TH FOX (2214 "We Belong Together")	4-8	75

Picture Sleeves
20TH FOX	3-5	73-74

LPs: 10/12–inch 33rpm
20TH FOX	8-12	73-74

Member: Tony DeFranco.

DEJA
Singles: 7–inch
VIRGIN	2-4	87-88

LPs: 10/12–inch 33rpm
VIRGIN	5-10	87-88

Members: Curt Jones; Starleana Young.
Also see AURRA
Also see SLAVE

DE JOHN SISTERS
Singles: 78rpm
COLUMBIA	3-6	57
EPIC	4-6	54-56
OKEH	4-8	53

Singles: 7–inch
COLUMBIA	10-15	57
EPIC	8-12	54-56
OKEH	10-15	53
SUNBEAM	8-12	59
U.A.	4-8	60

LPs: 10/12–inch 33rpm
U.A.	15-25	60

Members: Julie DeGiovanni; Dux DeGiovanni.

DEJONAY, Zena
Singles: 12–inch 33/45rpm
TVI	4-6	84

DEKKER, Desmond, and the Aces
Singles: 7–inch
UNI	3-6	69-70

LPs: 10/12–inch 33rpm
UNI	20-25	69

DELACARDOS
Singles: 7–inch
ELGEY (1001 "Letter to a School Girl")	30-40	59
IMPERIAL	5-10	63
SHELL	5-10	61-62
U.A.	10-15	61

DELANEY & BONNIE
(Delaney and Bonnie and Friends)
Singles: 7–inch
ATCO	3-6	70-72
COLUMBIA	3-5	72-73
ELEKTRA	3-5	69
INDEPENDENCE	4-8	67
STAX	4-8	68-69

LPs: 10/12–inch 33rpm
ATCO	15-25	70-72
COLUMBIA	15-25	72
ELEKTRA	15-25	69

GNP/CRESCENDO 15-25 70
STAX 15-25 69
Members: Delaney Bramlett; Bonnie Bramlett.
Also see BAD HABITS
Also see BRAMLETT, Bonnie
Also see CLAPTON, Eric
Also see LANI & BONI
Also see SHINDOGS
Also see WHITLOCK, Bobby

DELBERT & GLEN
Singles: 7–inch
CLEAN 3-5 72-73
LPs: 10/12–inch 33rpm
CLEAN 12-20 72-73
Members: Delbert McClinton; Glen Clark.
Also see McCLINTON, Delbert
Also see PRINE, John / Daryl Hall and John Oates / Barnaby
Bye / Delbert & Glen

DELEGATES
Singles: 7–inch
MAINSTREAM 5-10 72
LPs: 10/12–inch 33rpm
MAINSTREAM 10-15 73

DELEGATION
Singles: 12–inch 33/45rpm
SHADYBROOK 4-8 77
Singles: 7–inch
MCA 3-5 76
MERCURY 2-4 80-81
SHADYBROOK 2-4 77-79
LPs: 10/12–inch 33rpm
MERCURY 5-10 80-81
SHADYBROOK 5-10 79
Members: Ray patterson; Ricky Bailey; Bruce Dunbar.

DELFONICS
Singles: 7–inch
CAMEO 4-8 67
COLLECTABLES 2-4
FLASHBACK 3-5
MOON SHOT 4-8 68
PHILLY GROOVE 3-6 68-73
ROULETTE 3-5 73
LPs: 10/12–inch 33rpm
KORY 8-10 77
PHILLY GROOVE 10-20 68-74
POOGIE 5-10 81
COLLECTABLES 6-8 88
Members: Major Harris; William Hart; Wilbert Hart; Randy Cain;
Richie Daniels.
Also see HARRIS, Major

DEL FUEGOS
Singles: 7–inch
SLASH 2-4 85-87
Picture Sleeves
SLASH 2-4 86
LPs: 10/12–inch 33rpm
RCA 5-8 89
SLASH 5-10 85-87

DELIVERANCE
Singles: 7–inch
COLUMBIA 2-4 80

DELLS
Singles: 78rpm
VEE JAY (166 "Dreams of
Contentment") 50-75 55
VEE JAY (200 series) 10-20 56-57
Singles: 12–inch 33/45rpm
ABC 4-6 79
Singles: 7–inch
ABC 3-5 73-78
ARGO 5-10 62
CADET 3-6 67-75
CHESS 2-4 73
COLLECTABLES 2-4
MCA 2-4 79
MERCURY 3-5 75-77
PRIVATE I 2-4 84
20TH FOX 2-4 80-82
VEE JAY (166 "Dreams of
Contentment") 100-150 55
Note: Vee Jay 134, *Tell the World,* is listed in the
following section for DELLS / Count Morris.
VEE JAY (204 "Oh, What a Night") .. 25-35 56
VEE JAY (230 "Movin' On") 20-30 56
VEE JAY (236 "Why Do You
Have to Go?") 20-30 57
VEE JAY (251 "Distant Love") 20-30 57
VEE JAY (258 "Pain in My Heart") ... 20-30 57
VEE JAY (274 "The Springer") 15-20 58
VEE JAY (292 "I'm Calling") 15-25 58
VEE JAY (300 "Wedding Day") 40-60 58
VEE JAY (324 "Dry Your Eyes") 20-30 58
VEE JAY (338 through 712) 5-10 59-65
LPs: 10/12–inch 33rpm
ABC 8-10 78
BUDDAH 10-15 69
CADET 10-20 68-75
LOST-NITE 8-10 81
MERCURY 10-15 75-77
PRIVATE I 5-10 84
TRIP 10-12 73
20TH FOX 5-10 80-81
UPFRONT 10-15 68
VEE JAY (1010 "Oh What a Night") 400-500 59
(Maroon label, with thin circular ring.)
VEE JAY (1010 "Oh What a Night") 300-400 59
(Maroon label, with thick circular ring.)
VEE JAY (1010 "Oh What a Night") 100-200 61
(Black label. Monaural.)
VEE JAY (1010 "Oh What a Night") 100-200 61
(Black label. Stereo.)
VEE JAY (1141 "It's Not Unusual") 100-200 65
Members: Johnny Funches; Mike McGill; Marvin Junior; Vern
Allison; Johnny Carter.
Also see BUTLER, Jerry, and Betty Everett
Also see GREENE, Barbara
Also see SOUTH, Joe / Dells

DELLS / Count Morris
Singles: 78rpm
VEE JAY (134 "Tell the World") 75-150   55
Singles: 7-inch
VEE JAY (134 "Tell the World") ... 400-500   55
(Black vinyl.)
VEE JAY (134 "Tell the World") ... 700-900   55
(Colored vinyl.)
Also see DELLS

DELLS and the Dramatics
Singles: 7-inch
CADET 3-5   75
Also see DELLS
Also see DRAMATICS

DE LORY, Al
Singles: 7-inch
CAPITOL 2-5   68-71
EUREKA 3-5   61
PHI DAN 2-5   65
LPs: 10/12-inch 33rpm
CAPITOL 5-15   69-70

DELPHS, Jimmy
Singles: 7-inch
CARLA 4-8   67
KAREN 4-8   68

DEL-VIKINGS
(Dell-Vikings Featuring Krips Johnson)
Singles: 78rpm
DOT 10-15   57
FEE BEE 20-40   56-57
MERCURY 5-10   57
Singles: 7-inch
ABC 3-5   75
ABC-PAR (10208 "I'll Never
  Stop Crying") 10-15   61
ABC-PAR (10248 "I Hear Bells") 20-30   61
ABC-PAR (10278 "Kiss Me") 8-12   62
ABC-PAR (10304 "One More
  River to Cross") 10-15   62
ABC-PAR (10341 "Confession of Love")8-12   62
ABC-PAR (10385 "An Angel
  Up in Heaven") 25-35   63
ABC-PAR (10425 "Too Many Miles") .. 8-12   63
ALPINE (66 "The Sun") 25-35   60
BIM BAM BOOM 3-5   72
BLUE SKY 2-4
BROADCAST 2-4
COLLECTABLES 2-4   80
CRUISIN' 2-4
DRC (101 "Can't You See") 20-30
DOT (15000 series) 10-15   57
DOT (16000 series) 8-12   60-61
FEE BEE (173 "Welfare Blues") 3-5   77
FEE BEE (205 "Come Go with Me") . 50-80   56
(Has "45 RPM" on each side at top of label. With
two sets of thin, horizontal, double parallel lines.)

FEE BEE (205 "Come Go with Me") . 10-20   61
(Does not have "45 RPM." With one set of lines,
one thick, one thin.)
FEE BEE (206 "Down in Bermuda") . 40-60   57
FEE BEE (210 "What Made Maggie
  Run/Down By the Stream") 40-60   57
FEE BEE (210 "What Made Maggie
  Run/Uh Uh Baby") 40-60   57
FEE BEE (210 "What Made Maggie
  Run/When I Come Home") 50-75   57
FEE BEE (214 "Whispering Bells") .. 50-75   57
FEE BEE (218 "I'm Spinning") 50-75   57
FEE BEE (221 "Willette") 40-60   57
FEE BEE (227 "Tell Me") 15-25   59
FEE BEE (902 "True Love") 20-30   61
GATEWAY (743 "We Three") 15-25   64
GOLDIES 2-4
JOJO 3-6   76
LIGHTNING 2-4
LUNIVERSE (106 "Somewhere over
  the Rainbow") 35-50   57
LUNIVERSE (110 "Heaven
  in Paradise") 35-50   58
LUNIVERSE (113 "White Cliffs
  of Dover") 35-50   58
LUNIVERSE (114 "There I Go") 35-50   58
MCA 2-4
MERCURY (30000 series) 4-6   61
MERCURY (70000 series) 8-15   57-63
SCEPTER 4-6   72
SHIP 2-4
Picture Sleeves
ALPINE (66 "The Sun") 40-60   60
EPs: 7-inch 33/45rpm
DOT (1058 "Come Go with Us") .. 200-300   57
MERCURY (3359 "They Sing,
  They Swing") 50-100   57
MERCURY (3362 "They Sing,
  They Swing") 75-100   57
MERCURY (3363 "They Sing,
  They Swing") 75-100   57
LPs: 10/12-inch 33rpm
COLLECTABLES 6-8   80-83
DOT (3695 "Come Go with Me") ... 200-400   66
LUNIVERSE (1000 "Come Go
  with the Del Vikings") 300-400   57
MERCURY (20314 "They Sing,
  They Swing") 75-125   57
MERCURY (20353 "Del Vikings'
  Record Session") 75-125   58
Members: Kripp Johnson; Norman Wright; Clarence Quick; Don
Jackson; Gus Backus; Bill Blakely; David Lerchey.

DEL-VIKINGS / Ike Clanton
Singles: 7-inch
ERA 3-5
Also see CLANTON, Ike

DEL-VIKINGS / Diamonds / Big Bopper / Gaylords
Singles: 7–inch
MERCURY (53 "60 Second Spots") .. 20-40   58
(Promotional issue only.)
  Also see BIG BOPPER
  Also see DIAMONDS
  Also see GAYLORDS

DEL-VIKINGS / Sonnets
LPs: 10/12–inch 33rpm
CROWN (5368 "The Del-Vikings and
  the Sonnets") 20-30   63
(Tracks shown by the Sonnets are actually by
either the Meadowlarks or the Sounds.)
  Also see DEL-VIKINGS
  Also see JULIAN, Don, and the Meadowlarks

DE MARCO, Ralph
Singles: 7–inch
GUARANTEED 5-10   59
SHELLEY (1011 "Donna") 20-30   60
20TH FOX 4-8   62
Picture Sleeves
GUARANTEED 10-15   59

DE MATTEO, Nicky
(Nicky DeMatteo and the Sorrows)
Singles: 7–inch
ABC-PAR 5-10   61
CAMEO 5-10   65-66
DIAMOND 5-15   63
END (1021 "School House Rock") ... 15-25   58
GUYDEN 5-10   60
PARIS 8-12   59
TORE 8-12   59

DEMENSIONS
(Dimensions)
Singles: 7–inch
COLLECTABLES 2-4
CORAL (Except 65611) 10-20   61-63
CORAL (65611 "As Time Goes By") 4-8   67
MOHAWK (116 "Over the Rainbow") . 20-30   60
  (Maroon label.)
MOHAWK (116 "Over the Rainbow") . 10-20   60
  (Brown label.)
MOHAWK (116 "Over the Rainbow") .. 8-12   61
  (Red label.)
MOHAWK (121 "God's Christmas") .. 20-30   60
MOHAWK (123 "A Tear Fell") 25-35   60
OLD HIT 3-5
Picture Sleeves
CORAL (62344 "My Foolish Heart") .. 15-25   63
LPs: 10/12–inch 33rpm
CORAL (57430 "My Foolish Heart") . 75-100   63
  (Monaural.)
CORAL (7-57430 "My Foolish Heart")85-125   63
  (Stereo.)
MCA 5-10
  Member: Lenny Dell.

DENNY, Martin
Singles: 7–inch
LIBERTY (55000 series) 3-6   59-67
LIBERTY (56000 series) 2-4   69
LIBERTY (77000 series) 5-10   59-60
  (Stereo.)
Picture Sleeves
LIBERTY 5-10   59-63
EPs: 7–inch 33/45rpm
LIBERTY 5-10   59
LPs: 10/12–inch 33rpm
FIRST AMERICAN 5-10   81
LIBERTY 10-20   59-69
SUNSET 5-10   66-68
U.A. 5-10   74-80
  Also see BAJA MARIMBA BAND
  Also see ZENTER, Si

DENNY, Sandy
Singles: 7–inch
A&M 3-5   72-73
LPs: 10/12–inch 33rpm
A&M 8-12   71-72
ISLAND 8-10   74-76
  Also see FAIRPORT CONVENTION
  Also see LED ZEPPELIN

DENNY, Sandy, and the Strawbs
LPs: 10/12–inch 33rpm
PICKWICK 10-15   73
  Also see DENNY, Sandy
  Also see STRAWBS

DENVER, John
Singles: 12–inch 33/45rpm
RCA (11189 "Bet on the Blues") 5-10   77
(Promotional issue only.)
Singles: 7–inch
ALLEGIANCE 2-4
CHERRY MOUNTAIN (02 "Flying
  Or Me") 3-5   86
RCA (Except 0067 through 0955) 2-5   74-86
RCA (0067 through 0955) 4-8   70-74
Promotional Singles
EVA-TONE (106026 "Trees for America")3-5   86
RCA (2008 "Rocky Mountain High") .. 5-10   72
Picture Sleeves
ALLEGIANCE 2-4
CHERRY MOUNTAIN (02 "Flying
  Or Me") 3-5   86
RCA (Except 2008) 2-5   74-86
RCA (2008 "Rocky Mountain High") .. 5-10   72
(Promotional issue only.)
LPs: 10/12–inch 33rpm
HJD (66 "John Denver Sings") 200-300   66
  (Promotional issue only. Less than 300 copies
  made as Christmas gifts for friends.)
MOS ("Something to sing About") .. 50-100   66
  (Promotional issue only. No actual label name is
  used. Various artists LP with three Denver tracks
  not available elsewhere.)

MERCURY (704 "Beginnings") 10-15   72
(With illustration on cover.)
MERCURY (704 "Beginnings") 8-10   74
(With mountain scene photo on cover.)
RCA (0101 through 3449) 5-10   73-80
RCA (0075 "The John
Denver Radio Show") 20-30   74
(Single-sided LP. Promotional issue only.)
RCA (0683 "The Second John
Denver Radio Show") 20-30   74
RCA (4000 series) 10-15   69-72
(Orange labels.)
RCA (4000 and 5000 series) 5-10   81-85
(Black labels.)
RCA (5398 "The John Denver
Holiday Radio Show") 10-20   84
(Promotional issue only.)
WINDSTAR 5-8   90
  Also see DENVER, BOISE & JOHNSON
  Also see MITCHELL, Chad, Trio
  Also see MURPHEY, Michael
  Also see TRAVERS, Mary
  Also see WONDER, Stevie / John Denver

DENVER, John, and Placido Domingo
Singles: 7-inch
COLUMBIA 2-4   82
  Also see DOMINGO, Placido

DENVER, John, and Emmylou Harris
Singles: 7-inch
RCA 2-4   83
  Also see HARRIS, Emmylou

DENVER, John, and the Muppets
Singles: 7-inch
RCA 2-4   79
LPs: 10/12-inch 33rpm
RCA 5-10   79-83
  Also see MUPPETS

DENVER, John, and Olivia Newton-John
Singles: 7-inch
RCA 3-5   75
  Also see NEWTON-JOHN, Olivia

DENVER, John / Diana Ross
Singles: 7-inch
WHAT'S IT ALL ABOUT 4-8   81
(Public service, radio station issue.)
  Also see ROSS, Diana

DENVER, BOISE & JOHNSON
Singles: 7-inch
REPRISE (0695 "Take Me
to Tomorrow") 5-10   68
  Member: John Denver; Michael Johnson.
  Also see DENVER, John
  Also see JOHNSON, Michael

DEODATO
(Eumir Deodato)
Singles: 12-inch 33/45rpm
WARNER 4-6   84

Singles: 7-inch
CTI 2-4   73-77
MCA 2-4   74-76
WARNER 2-4   78-84
Picture Sleeves
CTI 2-4   73
LPs: 10/12-inch 33rpm
CTI 8-10   73-74
MCA 6-10   76
MUSE 8-10   73-76
WARNER 5-10   78-82

DEPECHE MODE
Singles: 12-inch 33/45rpm
SIRE 4-6   81-87
Singles: 7-inch
SIRE 2-4   81-90
Picture Sleeves
SIRE 2-4   85-88
LPs: 10/12-inch 33rpm
SIRE 5-10   81-90

DEREK
(Johnny Cymbal)
Singles: 7-inch
BANG 4-8   68-69
SOLID GOLD 2-4   73
  Also see CYMBAL, Johnny

DEREK & CYNDI
Singles: 7-inch
THUNDER 3-5   74
Picture Sleeves
THUNDER 3-5   74

DEREK and the Dominos
Singles: 7-inch
ATCO 3-5   70-72
RSO 2-4   73
LPs: 10/12-inch 33rpm
ATCO (704 "Layla") 20-30   70
POLYDOR 8-10   74
RSO 5-10   77
  Members: Eric Clapton; Jim Gordon; Carl Radle; Bobby
  Whitlock; Duane Allman.
  Also see ALLMAN, Duane
  Also see CLAPTON, Eric
  Also see WHITLOCK, Bobby

DERRINGER, Rick
(Derringer; Rick Derringer and the McCoys)
Singles: 7-inch
BLUE SKY 2-5   74-80
EPIC 2-4   83
LPs: 10/12-inch 33rpm
BLUE SKY 8-18   73-81
MERCURY 10-20   74
PASSPORT 5-10   83
  Also see McCOYS

DERRINGER, Rick, and the Edgar Winter Group
LPs: 10/12–inch 33rpm
BLUE SKY 8-10   75
  Also see DERRINGER, Rick
  Also see WINTER, Edgar

DE SANTO, Sugar Pie
Singles: 7–inch
BRUNSWICK 4-8   67-68
CADET 4-8   66
CHECK 8-12   60
CHECKER 4-8   63-66
GEDINSON 4-8   62
SOUL CLOCK 3-6   69
VELTONE 10-20   60
WAX 4-8   64
EPs: 7–inch 33/45rpm
CHECKER (2979 "Sugar Pie") 30-40   61
LPs: 10/12–inch 33rpm
CHECKER (2979 "Sugar Pie") 40-50   61
  Also see JAMES, Etta, and Sugar Pie DeSanto

DE SARIO, Teri
Singles: 7–inch
CASABLANCA 2-4   78
LPs: 10/12–inch 33rpm
CASABLANCA 5-10   80

DE SARIO, Teri, and K.C.
Singles: 7–inch
CASABLANCA 2-4   79-80
  Also see DE SARIO, Teri
  Also see K.C. and the Sunshine Band

DE SHANNON, Jackie
Singles: 7–inch
AMHERST 6-12   78
ATLANTIC 5-10   72-74
CAPITOL 5-10   71
COLUMBIA (Except 10221) 5-10   75
COLUMBIA (10221 "Boat to Sail") ... 10-15   76
  (With Brian Wilson.)
EDISON INT'L (416 "I Wanna
  Go Home") 50-100   60
EDISON INT'L (418 "Put My
  Baby Down") 50-100   60
IMPERIAL 4-8   65-70
LIBERTY (55000 series,
  except 55602) 15-25   60-64
LIBERTY (55602 "Little Yellow Roses") 8-10   63
  (Black vinyl.)
LIBERTY (55602 "Little Yellow Roses")15-25   63
  (Colored vinyl. Promotional issue only.)
LIBERTY (56000 series) 5-10   70
MGM 4-8   65
RCA 2-4   80
Picture Sleeves
LIBERTY (55526 "Faded Love") ... 75-100   63
LPs: 10/12–inch 33rpm
AMHERST (1010 "You're the
  Only Dancer") 15-25   77

ATLANTIC 10-15   72-74
CAPITOL 15-20   71
COLUMBIA 10-15   75
IMPERIAL (9286 "This Is
  Jackie De Shannon") 25-50   65
  (Monaural.)
IMPERIAL (9294 "You Won't
  Forget Me") 25-50   65
  (Monaural.)
IMPERIAL (9296 "In the Wind") 25-50   65
  (Monaural.)
IMPERIAL (9328 "Are You
  Ready for This") 25-50   66
  (Monaural.)
IMPERIAL (9344 "New Image") 25-50   67
  (Monaural.)
IMPERIAL (9352 "For You") 25-50   67
  (Monaural.)
IMPERIAL (12286 "This Is
  Jackie De Shannon") 25-50   65
  (Stereo.)
IMPERIAL (12294 "You Won't
  Forget Me") 25-50   65
  (Stereo.)
IMPERIAL (12296 "In the Wind") 25-50   65
  (Stereo.)
IMPERIAL (12328 "Are You
  Ready for This") 25-50   66
  (Stereo.)
IMPERIAL (12344 "New Image") 25-50   67
  (Stereo.)
IMPERIAL (12352 "For You") 25-50   67
  (Stereo.)
IMPERIAL (12386 "Me About You") .. 25-50   68
IMPERIAL (12404 "What the World
  Needs Now Is Love") 25-50   68
IMPERIAL (12415 "Laurel Canyon") . 25-50   68
IMPERIAL (12442 "Put a Little
  Love in Your Heart") 25-50   69
IMPERIAL (12453 "To Be Free") 25-50   70
LIBERTY (3320 "Jackie
  De Shannon") 50-100   63
  (Monaural.)
LIBERTY (3390 "Breakin' It Up On
  the Beatles Tour") 50-100   64
  (Monaural.)
LIBERTY (7320 "Jackie
  De Shannon") 75-100   63
  (Stereo.)
LIBERTY (7390 "Breakin' It Up on
  the Beatles Tour") 75-100   64
  (Stereo.)
LIBERTY (10000 series) 5-10   82
SUNSET 10-15   68-71
U.A. 8-10   75
  Also see DEE, Jackie
  Also see SHANNON, Jackie
  Also see WILSON, Brian

DESMOND, Johnny
Singles: 78rpm
CORAL	3-5	52-56
MGM	3-6	50-51

Singles: 7-inch
COLUMBIA	4-8	59-60
CORAL	5-10	52-56
DIAMOND	3-6	62
EDGEWOOD	3-6	62
MGM	5-10	50-51
MUSICANZA	2-4	
RCA	3-6	63
20TH FOX	3-6	64
VIGOR	2-4	73

Picture Sleeves
CORAL	5-10	55

EPs: 7-inch 33/45rpm
CORAL	8-15	54-56
MGM	10-20	52
P.R.I. (11 "So Nice")	5-10	

LPs: 10/12-inch 33rpm
CAMDEN	10-20	53-54
COLUMBIA	5-10	59-60
CORAL	15-25	55-56
LION	10-15	56
MGM	10-20	55
MAYFAIR	10-15	58
MOVIETONE	5-10	66
VOCALION	5-10	66

Also see CORNELL, Don, Johnny Desmond and Alan Dale

DESMOND, Paul
(Paul Desmond Quartet)
Singles: 7-inch
A&M	3-5	69-70
RCA VICTOR	3-8	62-63

LPs: 10/12-inch 33rpm
A&M	5-15	69-76
CTI	8-12	75
CAMDEN	8-12	73
DISCOVERY	5-8	81
FANTASY (21 "Paul Desmond")	40-60	54
(10-inch LP.)		
FANTASY (220 "Paul Desmond")	20-40	56
RCA (2400 and 2500 series)	15-25	62-63
RCA (2800 series)	5-10	78
RCA (3300 and 3400 series)	10-20	65-66
WARNER	20-30	60

Also see BRUBECK, Dave, and Paul Desmond
Also see MULLIGAN, Gerry, and Paul Desmond

DESTINATION
Singles: 7-inch
A.V.I.	3-5	77

LPs: 10/12-inch 33rpm
A.V.I.	8-10	77

DESTINATION
Singles: 12-inch 33/45rpm
BUTTERFLY	4-6	79

BUTTERFLY	2-4	79

LPs: 10/12-inch 33rpm
BUTTERFLY	5-10	79

DET REIRRUC and the Club Rappers
Singles: 12-inch 33/45rpm
CLUB	4-6	85

DETECTIVE
Singles: 7-inch
SWAN SONG	3-5	77-78

LPs: 10/12-inch 33rpm
SWAN SONG	10-12	77-78

Member: Michael Des Barres.

DETERGENTS
Singles: 7-inch
KAPP	5-10	66
ROULETTE	5-10	64-65

Picture Sleeves
ROULETTE (4590 "Leader of the Laundromat")	15-25	64

LPs: 10/12-inch 33rpm
ROULETTE (25308 "The Many Faces of the Detergents")	25-35	65

Members: Ron Dante; Tommy Wynn; Danny Jordan.

DETROIT
Singles: 7-inch
PARAMOUNT	3-5	70-71

LPs: 10/12-inch 33rpm
PARAMOUNT	10-15	71-72

Also see DETROIT WHEELS
Also see ROCKETS
Also see RYDER, Mitch, and the Detroit Wheels

DETROIT EMERALDS
Singles: 7-inch
RIC-TIC	4-8	68
WESTBOUND	3-5	70-78

LPs: 10/12-inch 33rpm
WESTBOUND	10-15	71-78

Members: Abrim Tilmon; Ivory Tilmon; Cleophus Tilmon;
Raymond Tilmon; James Mitchell; Paul Riser; Maurice King;
Johnny Allen.
Also see CHAPTER 8

DETROIT WHEELS
Singles: 7-inch
INFERNO	4-8	68

Also see DETROIT
Also see RYDER, Mitch, and the Detroit Wheels
Also see ROCKETS

DETROYT
Singles: 7-inch
TABU	2-4	84

DE VAUGHN, William
Singles: 7-inch
ROXBURY	3-5	74
TEC	2-4	80

LPs: 10/12-inch 33rpm
ROXBURY	8-10	74

TEC 5-10   80

DEVICE
Singles: 12–inch 33/45rpm
CHRYSALIS 4-8   86
(Promotional issue only.)
Singles: 7–inch
CHRYSALIS 2-4   86
Picture Sleeves
CHRYSALIS 2-4   86
LPs: 10/12–inch 33rpm
CHRYSALIS 5-8   86

DEVO
Singles: 12–inch 33/45rpm
ENIGMA 4-6   88
WARNER 4-8 80-85
Singles: 7–inch
ASYLUM 2-4   81
BOOJI BOY 3-5   78
ENIGMA 2-4   88
FULL MOON 2-4   81
WARNER 2-5 78-85
Promotional Singles
WARNER (49826 "Beautiful World") .. 8-12   81
(Space helmet shaped disc. With helmet photo.)
WARNER (49826 "Beautiful World") . 50-75   81
(Colored vinyl, space helmet shaped disc. No
photo. Experimental pressing only.)
Picture Sleeves
WARNER 2-5 79-85
LPs: 10/12–inch 33rpm
ENIGMA 5-10   88
WARNER 5-10 78-88
Members: Mark Mothersbaugh; Bob Mothersbaugh; David
Kendrick; Bob Casale; Gerald Casale.

DE VOL, Frank, Orchestra
(Frank De Vol and the Rainbow Strings)
Singles: 78rpm
CAPITOL 3-5 50-56
KEM 3-5   55
Singles: 7–inch
ABC-PAR 3-5 64-65
CAPITOL 3-6 50-56
COLGEMS 3-5   68
COLUMBIA 3-5 59-62
KEM 3-6   55
Picture Sleeves
COLGEMS 3-5   68
LPs: 10/12–inch 33rpm
ABC-PAR 5-10 65-66
COLGEMS (COM-108 "Guess Who's
Coming to Dinner") 20-25   68
(Soundtrack. Monaural.)
COLGEMS (COS-108 "Guess Who's
Coming to Dinner") 25-30   68
(Soundtrack. Stereo.)
COLGEMS (COMO-5006 "The
Happening") 15-20   67
(Soundtrack. Monaural.)

COLGEMS (COSO-5006 "The
Happening") 20-25   67
(Soundtrack. Stereo.)
COLUMBIA 8-10 59-63
HARMONY 5-10   65

DEVONS
Singles: 7–inch
KING 3-6   69

DE VORZON, Barry
Singles: 7–inch
COLUMBIA 8-12 59-61
RCA 10-20 57-59
WARNER 2-4   81
LPs: 10/12–inch 33rpm
A&M 5-10   76
ARISTA 5-10   76
Also see BARRY and the Tamerlanes

DE VORZON, Barry, and Perry Botkin Jr.
Singles: 7–inch
A&M 2-5 76-77
Picture Sleeves
A&M 3-5   76
LPs: 10/12–inch 33rpm
A&M 5-10   76
Also see DE VORZON, Barry
Also see McCOY BOYS

DEVOTIONS
Singles: 7–inch
DELTA (1001 "Rip Van Winkle") 50-75   61
KAPE 5-10
ROULETTE (4406 "Rip Van Winkle") 25-30   61
(White label.)
ROULETTE (4541 "Rip Van Winkle") . 6-10   64
(Orange label.)
ROULETTE (4556 "Sunday Kind
of Love") 15-20   64
ROULETTE (4580 "Snow White") ... 10-20   64
Members: Joe Pardo; Frank Pardo; Bob Weisbrod; Ray
Sanchez; Bob Havorka; Louis DeCarlo; Larry Frank

DEVOTO, Howard
Singles: 12–inch 33/45rpm
I.R.S. 4-6   86
Singles: 7–inch
I.R.S. 2-4   86
LPs: 10/12–inch 33rpm
I.R.S. 5-10   86

DEXY'S MIDNIGHT RUNNERS
Singles: 7–inch
EMI AMERICA 2-4   81
MERCURY 2-4 82-83
Picture Sleeves
MERCURY 5-10 82-83
LPs: 10/12–inch 33rpm
EMI AMERICA 5-10   81
MERCURY 5-10 82-83

DEY, Tracey
Singles: 7–inch
AMY	8-12	63-65
COLUMBIA	5-10	66
LIBERTY	10-20	63
VEE JAY	10-20	62

DE YOUNG, Cliff
Singles: 7–inch
MCA	3-5	73-75

Picture Sleeves
MCA	3-5	74

LPs: 10/12–inch 33rpm
MCA	10-12	73-75

DE YOUNG, Dennis
Singles: 12–inch 33/45rpm
MCA	4-8	88
(Promotional only.)		

Singles: 7–inch
A&M	2-4	83-86

Picture Sleeves
A&M	2-4	84-86

LPs: 10/12–inch 33rpm
A&M	5-10	84-86
MCA	5-8	88

Also see STYX

DIAMOND, Gregg
(Gregg Diamond's Starcruiser; Gregg Diamond's Bionic Boogie)
Singles: 12–inch 33/45rpm
POLYDOR	4-6	79

Singles: 7–inch
MARLIN	2-5	78
POLYDOR	2-4	79-80

LPs: 10/12–inch 33rpm
MARLIN	5-10	78
MERCURY	5-10	79
POLYDOR	5-10	77-78

DIAMOND, Joel
(Joel Diamond Experience)
Singles: 12–inch 33/45rpm
CASABLANCA	4-6	79

Singles: 7–inch
ATLANTIC	2-4	82
CASABLANCA	2-4	79-84
MOTOWN	2-4	81

LPs: 10/12–inch 33rpm
CASABLANCA	8-10	79

DIAMOND, Leo
Singles: 78rpm
AMBASSADOR	3-5	51
RCA	2-5	55

Singles: 7–inch
RCA	3-6	55

DIAMOND, Neil
Singles: 12–inch 33/45rpm
COLUMBIA (1586 "Heartlight")	6-10	82

Singles: 7–inch
BANG (100 series)	2-4	
("Best Hits" reissue series.)		
BANG (500 and 700 series)	3-8	66-73
CAPITOL	2-4	80-81
COLUMBIA (02600 through 06100 series)	2-4	81-86
COLUMBIA (10000 and 11000 series)	3-5	74-80
COLUMBIA (33000 series)	2-4	
("Hall of Fame" series.)		
COLUMBIA (42809 "Clown Town")	150-200	63
COLUMBIA (45000 series)	3-5	73-74
MCA (40000 series)	3-5	73
MCA (60000 series)	2-4	73
PHILCO	10-20	66-67
("Hip-Pocket" records.)		
SOLID ROCK	2-4	
UNI	3-6	68-72

Promotional Singles
BANG (Except 55075)	5-10	66-73
UNI (55075 "Two-Bit Manchild")	15-20	68
(Colored vinyl.)		
CAPITOL	3-5	80-81
COLUMBIA (1115 "Song Sung Blue")	3-6	77
COLUMBIA (1193 "September Morn")	3-6	79
(An alternate version.)		
COLUMBIA (02600 through 11000)	3-5	74-86
COLUMBIA (42809 "Clown Town")	100-200	63
COLUMBIA (45000 series)	4-8	73-74
MCA	3-5	73
UNI	5-10	68-72
WHAT'S IT ALL ABOUT	8-15	

Picture Sleeves
CAPITOL	3-5	80-81
COLUMBIA	3-6	73-86
UNI	4-8	68-70

EPs: 7–inch 33/45rpm
COLUMBIA (32919 "Serenade")	10-20	74
MCA (34989 "12 Greatest Hits")	10-20	74
UNI (34818 "Neil Diamond Gold")	10-20	71
UNI (34871 "Stones")	10-20	71

Note: all EPs listed were made for jukebox use.

LPs: 10/12–inch 33rpm
BANG (214 "The Feel of Neil Diamond")	50-100	66
BANG (217 "Just For You")	20-40	67
BANG (219 "Greatest Hits")	20-40	68
BANG (221 "Shilo")	40-50	70
BANG (224 "Do It")	30-40	71
BANG (227 "Double Gold")	20-35	73
CAPITOL	5-10	80
COLUMBIA (30000 series)	8-12	73-86
COLUMBIA (40000 series)	5-10	86-89
COLUMBIA (42550 "Jonathan Livingston Seagull")	15-25	81
(Half-speed mastered.)		
COLUMBIA (45025 "Best Years of Our Lives")	5-8	89

COLUMBIA (46525 "You Don't
Bring Me Flowers") 15-25   80
(Half-speed mastered.)
COLUMBIA (47628 "On the Way
to the Sky") 15-25   82
(Half-speed mastered.)
DIRECT-to-DISK 10-20
FROG KING (1 "Early Classics") 25-50   78
(Includes music and lyrics songbook. Columbia
Record Club issue.)
HARMONY (30023 "Chartbusters") .. 15-25   70
(A various artists LP, containing the 1963 Columbia
tracks, *Clown Town* and the otherwise unavailable
I've Never Been the Same.)
MCA 6-15   72-81
MFSL (024 "Hot August Night") 25-50   79
MFSL (071 "Jazz Singer") 20-30   82
UNI (11 Neil Diamond D.J. Sampler") 25-50   71
(Promotional souvenir issue only.)
UNI (1913 "Open-End Interview
with Neil Diamond") 25-50   72
(Promotional issue only.)
UNI (73030 "Velvet Gloves and Spit") 20-35   68
(Does not contain *Shilo*.)
UNI (73030 "Velvet Gloves and Spit") 15-25   70
(With *Shilo*.)
UNI (73047 "Brother Love's Traveling
Salvation Show") 20-35   69
UNI (73047 "Sweet Caroline/Brother Love's
Traveling Salvation Show") 15-25   69
UNI (73071 "Touching You,
Touching Me") 15-25   69
UNI (73084 "Gold") 15-25   70
UNI (73092 "Tap Root Manuscript") .. 15-25   70
(Some 70000 series LPs were reissued in the
90000 series, with the only change being the first
digit.)
UNI (93106 "Stones") 15-25   71
UNI (93136 "Moods") 15-25   72
    Also see NEIL & JACK
    Also see STREISAND, Barbra, and Neil Diamond

DIAMOND, Neil / Diana Ross and the Supremes
LPs: 10/12-inch 33rpm
MCA (734727 "It's Happening") 30-40   72
(One side of LP devoted to each artist.)
    Also see DIAMOND, Neil
    Also see SUPREMES

DIAMOND REO
Singles: 7-inch
BIG TREE 3-5   75
BUDDAH 3-5   77
LPs: 10/12-inch 33rpm
BIG TREE 8-10   75
KAMA SUTRA 8-10   76
PICCADILLY 5-10   79

DIAMONDS
Singles: 78rpm
CORAL 4-8   55-56
MERCURY 4-8   56-57
Singles: 7-inch
CORAL 5-10   55-56
MERCURY 5-10   56-62
Picture Sleeves
MERCURY (71291 "High Sign") 10-20   58
EPs: 7-inch 33/45rpm
BRUNSWICK 15-20   57
MERCURY 10-20   56-61
LPs: 10/12-inch 33rpm
MERCURY 20-40   57-60
WING 15-25   59
    Members: David Somerville; Phil Leavitt; Bill Reed; Ted Kowalski
    Also see DEL-VIKINGS / Diamonds / Big Bopper / Gaylords

DIAMONDS and Pete Rugolo
LPs: 10/12-inch 33rpm
MERCURY (60076 "The Diamonds
Meet Pete Rugolo") 45-55   59
    Also see DIAMONDS

DIANE RAY: see RAY, Diane

DIBANGO, Manu
Singles: 7-inch
ATLANTIC 3-5   73
LPs: 10/12-inch 33rpm
ATLANTIC 8-10   73

DICK & DEE DEE
Singles: 7-inch
DOT 4-8   68-69
LAMA 15-20   61
LIBERTY 5-10   61-62
U.A. 2-4
WARNER 4-8   62-69
Picture Sleeves
WARNER 10-20   63-64
LPs: 10/12-inch 33rpm
LIBERTY (3236 "Tell Me/The
Mountain's High") 40-50   62
(Monaural.)
LIBERTY (7236 "Tell Me/The
Mountain's High") 40-50   62
WARNER (1500 "Young and
in Love") 20-30   63
WARNER (1538 "Turn Around") 20-30   64
WARNER (1586 "Thou Shalt
Not Steal") 20-30   65
WARNER (1623 "Songs We've
Sung on Shindig") 20-30   65
    Members: Dick St. John; Dee Dee Sperling.

DICK & DON: see ADDRISI BROTHERS

DICK LEE: see LEE, Dick

DICKENS, Jimmy
(Little Jimmy Dickens)
Singles: 78rpm
COLUMBIA 4-8   50-57
Singles: 7-inch
COLUMBIA (10000 series) 2-4   76
COLUMBIA (20000 and 21000
series) 8-15   50-56
COLUMBIA (40000 series) 5-10   56
COLUMBIA (41000 series,
except 41173) 5-10   57-60
COLUMBIA (41173 "I Got a Hole
in My Pocket") 30-45   57
COLUMBIA (42000 through 44000
series) 4-8   60-67
DECCA 3-6   67-69
LITTLE GEM 3-5   75
PARTRIDGE 2-4   80
STARDAY 3-5   73
U.A. 3-5   70-72
EPs: 7-inch 33/45rpm
COLUMBIA (Except 2800 series) 15-20   52-57
COLUMBIA (2800 series) 10-15   57-58
LPs: 10/12-inch 33rpm
COLUMBIA (1047 "Raisin' the
Dickens") 40-50   57
COLUMBIA (1500 through 2500
series) 10-20   60-66
(Monaural.)
COLUMBIA (8300 through 9600
series) 15-25   60-68
(Stereo.)
COLUMBIA (10000 and 11000 series) . 6-10   70-73
COLUMBIA (38000 series) 5-10   84
DECCA 10-12   68-69
GUSTO 5-10
HARMONY (7000 series) 10-15   64-65
HARMONY (9000 series) 20-30   54
HARMONY (11000 series) 8-12   67
QCA 6-10   75

DICKEY DOO and the Don'ts
Singles: 7-inch
ASCOT 4-8   65
CASINO 3-5
DANNA 4-8   67
SWAN 8-12   58-59
U.A. 8-10   60-61
LPs: 10/12-inch 33rpm
U.A. (3094 "Madison and
Other Dances") 25-30   60
(Monaural.)
U.A. (3097 "Teen Scene") 25-30   60
U.A. (6094 "Madison and
Other Dances") 30-40   60
(Stereo.)
U.A. (6097 "Teen Scene") 30-40   60
(Stereo.)
Members: Gerry Granahan; Harvey Davis; Jerry Grant; Ray
Gangi; Joey Paige.

Also see GRANAHAN, Gerry

DICKIE LEE: see LEE, Dickie

DICTATORS
Singles: 7-inch
ASYLUM 2-4   77
LPs: 10/12-inch 33rpm
ASYLUM 8-12   77-78
EPIC 10-12   75

DIDDLEY, Bo
Singles: 78rpm
CHECKER 15-30   55-57
Singles: 7-inch
ABC 2-4   74
CHECKER (814 through 850) 15-25   55-56
CHECKER (860 through 896) 10-20   57-58
CHECKER (907 "Bo Meets
the Monster") 20-30   58
CHECKER (914 through 997) 5-10   59-62
CHECKER (1019 through 1200) 5-10   62-69
CHESS 3-5   71-72
RCA 3-5   76
EPs: 7-inch 33/45rpm
CHESS (5125 "Bo Diddley") 40-60   58
(With cardboard cover.)
CHESS (5125 "Bo Diddley") 30-40   58
(With paper cover.)
LPs: 10/12-inch 33rpm
ACCORD 5-10   82
CHECKER (1436 "Go Bo Diddley") . 75-100   57
CHECKER (2974 "Have Guitar
Will Travel") 50-75   59
CHECKER (2976 "Bo Diddley
in the Spotlight") 50-75   60
CHECKER (2977 "Bo Diddley
Is a Gunslinger") 65-75   61
CHECKER (2980 "Bo Diddley
in a Lover") 40-60   61
CHECKER (2982 "Bo Diddley's
a Twister") 40-50   62
CHECKER (2984 "Bo Diddley") 35-45   62
CHECKER (2985 "Bo Diddley
and Company") 40-60   63
CHECKER (2987 "Surfin' with
Bo Diddley") 35-45   63
(Most of the tracks on this LP are by the
Megatons.)
CHECKER (2988 "Bo Diddley's
Beach Party") 35-45   63
CHECKER (2989 "Bo Diddley's 16 All-Time
Greatest Hits") 25-35   63
CHECKER (2992 "Hey Good Lookin") 25-35   64
CHECKER (2996 "500% More Man") 25-35   64
CHECKER (3001 "The Originator") .. 25-35   66
CHECKER (3006 "Go Bo Diddley") .. 25-35   67
CHECKER (3007 "Boss Man") 40-60   67
CHECKER (3013 "The Black
Gladiator") 25-35   69

CHESS (1431 "Bo Diddley") 75-100   58
CHESS (50000 series) 10-20   71-74
CHESS (60000 series) 15-25   74
MCA/CHESS 5-8   88
RCA (1229 "20th Anniversary of
  Rock 'N Roll") 10-20   76
(With numerous guest stars.)
  Also see BELMONTS, Freddy Cannon and Bo Diddley
  Also see MOONGLOWS

DIDDLEY, Bo, and Chuck Berry
Singles: 7–inch
CHECKER (13370 "Bo's Beat") 4-8   64
LPs: 10/12–inch 33rpm
CHECKER (2991 "Two Great Guitars") 20-25   64
  Also see BERRY, Chuck

DIDDLEY, Bo, Howlin' Wolf and Muddy Waters
LPs: 10/12–inch 33rpm
CHECKER (3010 "Super Super
  Blues Band") 15-20   68
  Also see DIDDLEY, Bo
  Also see HOWLIN' WOLF
  Also see WATERS, Muddy

DIESEL
Singles: 7–inch
REGENCY 2-4   81
LPs: 10/12–inch 33rpm
REGENCY 8-10   81

DIFFORD & TILBROOK
Singles: 7–inch
A&M 2-4   84
LPs: 10/12–inch 33rpm
A&M 5-10   84
  Members: Chris Difford; Glenn Tilbrook.
  Also see SQUEEZE

DIFOSCO
(Difosco Erwin)
Singles: 7–inch
EARTHQUAKE 3-5   71
ROXBURY 3-5   76
20TH FOX 3-5   78
  Also see IRWIN, Big D.

DILLARD, Varetta
(Varetta Dillard and the Roamers; Varetta Dillard and
the Four Students)
Singles: 78rpm
GROOVE 5-10   55-56
SAVOY 5-10   53-55
Singles: 7–inch
CUB 4-8   60-61
GROOVE (0139 "Darling, Listen to
  the Words of This Song") 20-30   56
GROOVE (0152 through 0177) 12-25   56-57
RCA 10-15   57
SAVOY 10-20   53-55
TRIUMPH 8-12   59

DILLARDS
Singles: 7–inch
ANTHEM 3-5   71-72
CAPITOL 4-6   65
ELEKTRA 4-8   63-69
POPPY 3-5   74
U.A. 3-5   75
WHITE WHALE 3-5   70
LPs: 10/12–inch 33rpm
ANTHEM 6-10   72
ELEKTRA (200 series) 20-30   63-65
(Gold label.)
ELEKTRA (7-200 series) 20-30   63-65
(Gold label.)
ELEKTRA (7-200 series) 10-15
(Brown label.)
ELEKTRA (74000 series) 8-12   68
FLYING FISH 5-10   77-81
POPPY 8-12   73
20TH FOX 8-12   73
  Members: Doug Dillard; Rodney Dillard; Dean Webb; Mitch
  Jayne.

DILLARDS and John Hartford
LPs: 10/12–inch 33rpm
FLYING FISH 5-10
  Also see DILLARDS
  Also see HARTFORD, John

DILLMAN BAND
(Daisy Dillman Band)
Singles: 7–inch
RCA 2-4   81
U.A. 2-4   77-78
LPs: 10/12–inch 33rpm
RCA 5-10   81
U.A. 5-10   78

DI MEOLA, Al
(Al Di Meola Project)
Singles: 7–inch
COLUMBIA 2-4   76-84
LPs: 10/12–inch 33rpm
COLUMBIA 5-10   76-83
EMI 5-10   88
  Also see RETURN to FOREVER

DING DONGS
(Bobby Darin)
Singles: 7–inch
BRUNSWICK (55073 "Early in
  the Morning") 75-100   58
  Also see DARIN, Bobby

DINNING, Mark
Singles: 78rpm
MGM 4-8   57
Singles: 7–inch
CAMEO 4-8   64
HICKORY 4-8   65-66
MGM (Except 12775 and 12980) 5-10   57-63
MGM (12775 "Cutie Cutie") 10-15   59

MGM (12980 "Top 40, News,
   Weather and Sports") 15-20   61
   (With mention of Patrice Lumumba in lyrics.)
MGM (12980 "Top 40, News,
   Weather and Sports") 5-10   61
   (With no mention of Patrice Lumumba in lyrics.)
MGM GOLDEN CIRCLE 3-5
U.A. 3-5   67-68
                Picture Sleeves
MGM 10-15   60
             LPs: 10/12–inch 33rpm
MGM (E-3828 "Teen Angel") 40-60   60
   (Monaural.)
MGM (SE-3828 "Teen Angel") 50-75   60
   (Stereo.)
MGM (E-3855 "Wanderin") 40-60   60
   (Monaural.)
MGM (SE-3855 "Wanderin") 50-75   60
   (Stereo.)

DINO, DESI & BILLY
                Singles: 7–inch
COLUMBIA 3-6   69
UNI 3-6   69
REPRISE (Except 0965) 4-8   64-69
REPRISE (0965 "Lady Love") 10-15   70
                Picture Sleeves
REPRISE 5-10   65-68
             LPs: 10/12–inch 33rpm
REPRISE 15-25   65-66
UNI 12-20   69
   Members: Dino Martin; Desi Arnaz Jr; Billy Hinsche.

DINO, Kenny
             Singles: 12–inch 33/45rpm
KDK PRODUCTIONS ("Love Songs
   for Seka") 15-25   80
   (Picture disc with photo of adult-film star, Seka.)
                Singles: 7–inch
COLUMBIA 4-8   64
DOT 4-8   61
MUSICOR 5-10   61-62
RADNOR 4-6
SMASH 4-8   63-64

DINO, Paul
                Singles: 7–inch
ENTRE 4-8   63
PROMO 5-10   60-61

DIO
                Singles: 7–inch
WARNER 2-4   85-86
             LPs: 10/12–inch 33rpm
REPRISE 5-8   90
WARNER 5-10   85-87

DION
   (Dion DiMucci)
                Singles: 7–inch
ARISTA 2-4   89
BIG TREE/SPECTOR 3-5   76

COLUMBIA (3-42662 "Ruby Baby") . . 25-35   62
   (Compact 33 single.)
COLUMBIA (4-42662 "Ruby Baby") . . . 5-10   62
COLUMBIA (42776 "This Little
   Girl") 5-10   63
COLUMBIA (42810 "Be Careful of
   Stones You Throw") 5-10   63
   (Black vinyl.)
COLUMBIA (42810 "Be Careful of
   Stones You Throw") 20-30   63
   (Colored vinyl. Promotional issue only.)
COLUMBIA (42852 "Donna the
   Prima Donna") 5-10   63
   (Black vinyl.)
COLUMBIA (42852 "Donna the
   Prima Donna") 20-30   63
   (Colored vinyl. Promotional issue only.)
COLUMBIA (42917 through 44719) . . . 5-10   63-68
LAURIE (100 series) 2-4
LAURIE (3000 and 3100 series) 5-10   60-63
LAURIE (3400 series) 4-6   68-69
LIFESONG 3-5   78-79
MYRRH 3-5   85
SPECTOR 3-5   75
WARNER (Except 814) 3-6   69-79
WARNER (814 "The Wanderer") 5-10   79
   (Promotional issue only.)
WARNER/SPECTOR 3-5   75
                Picture Sleeves
ARISTA 2-4   89
COLUMBIA (Except 42662) 10-20   64-66
COLUMBIA (42662 "Ruby Baby") . . . 30-40   62
   (Promotional sleeve for *Ruby Baby*, but does not
   show title or number. Simply reads, "Dion Is Now
   on Columbia Records.")
COLUMBIA (42662 "Ruby Baby") . . . 10-15   62
   (Commercially issued sleeve.)
LAURIE 10-15   60-62
             LPs: 10/12–inch 33rpm
ABEL 8-10
ARISTA 6-12   77-89
COLLECTABLES 6-8   85-87
COLUMBIA 15-25   63-73
DAYSPRING 5-10   80
LAURIE (2004 "Alone with Dion") . . . 20-30   61
LAURIE (2009 "Runaround Sue") . . . 20-30   61
   (Black vinyl.)
LAURIE (2009 "Runaround Sue") . . 75-100   61
   (Colored vinyl.)
LAURIE (2012 "Lovers Who Wander") 20-30   62
LAURIE (2015 "Love Came to Me") . . 20-30   63
LAURIE (2017 "Sand and All
   Other Girls") 20-30   63
LAURIE (2019 "15 Million Sellers") . . 20-30   63
LAURIE (2022 "More of Dion's
   Greatest Hits") 20-30   63
LAURIE (2047 "Dion") 15-20   68
LAURIE (4000 series) 8-15
LIFESONG 5-10   78

WARNER 10-15   69-76
  Also see ADAMS, Bryan
  Also see DEE, Joey, and the Starliters / Dion
  Also see EDMUNDS, Dave
  Also see LANG, K.D.
  Also see REED, Lou
  Also see SIMON, Paul

DION / Glen Stuart Chorus
LPs: 10/12–inch 33rpm
ABEL 8-10

DION and the Belmonts
(Featuring Dion DiMucci)
Singles: 7–inch
ABC 4-8   66-67
COLLECTABLES 2-4
LAURIE (3013 "I Wonder Why") 25-30   58
  (Gary label.)
LAURIE (3013 "I Wonder Why") 15-20   58
  (Blue label.)
LAURIE (3013 "I Wonder Why") 5-8   59
  (Red and white label.)
LAURIE (3015 "No One Knows") 15-20   58
  (Blue label.)
LAURIE (3015 "No One Knows") 5-8   58
  (Red and white label.)
LAURIE (3021 "Don't Pity Me") 10-15   58
LAURIE (3027 "A Teenager in Love") .. 8-12   59
  (Monaural.)
LAURIE (S-3027 "A Teenager
  in Love") 20-30   59
  (Stereo.)
LAURIE (3035 through 3059) 8-15   59-60
MOHAWK (107 "Tag Along") 30-40   57
ROCK"N MANIA 3-5
Picture Sleeves
LAURIE 10-20   59-60
EPs: 7–inch 33/45rpm
LAURIE (301 "Their Hits") 50-75   59
LAURIE (302 "Where Or When") 40-60   59
LPs: 10/12–inch 33rpm
ABC (599 "Together Again") 15-25   67
ARISTA 8-12   84
COLLECTABLES 6-8   85
GRT 8-10   75
LAURIE (1002 "Presenting Dion
  and the Belmonts") 75-100   59
LAURIE (2002 "Presenting Dion
  and the Belmonts") 50-80   60
LAURIE (2006 "Wish Upon a Star") .. 30-40   60
LAURIE (2013 "Dion Sings His Greatest
  Hits - with the Belmonts") 20-30   62
LAURIE (2016 "By Special Request") 30-40   62
LAURIE (4001 "Everything You
  Always Wanted to Hear") 8-12   76
LAURIE (6000 "60 Greatest") 15-20
PICKWICK 8-10   75
WARNER 10-15   73
  Also see BELMONTS

DION and the Timberlanes
(Featuring Dion DiMuci)
Singles: 7–inch
JUBILEE (5294 "The Chosen Few") . 15-25   57
MOHAWK (105 "The Chosen Few") . 30-35   57
VIRGO 2-4   73
  Also see DION

DIONNE and Friends
Singles: 7–inch
ARISTA 2-4   85
  Members: Dionne Warwick; Elton John; Stevie Wonder; Gladys
  Knight.
  Also see JOHN, Elton
  Also see KNIGHT, Gladys
  Also see WARWICK, Dionne
  Also see WONDER, Stevie

DIPLOMATS
Singles: 7–inch
AROCK 4-8   64
DYNAMO 4-6   68-69
MAY 5-10   61
MINIT 4-8   66
WAND 4-8   65

DIRECT CURRENT
Singles: 7–inch
TEC 3-5   79

DIRE STRAITS
Singles: 12–inch 33/45rpm
WARNER 4-6   83
Singles: 7–inch
WARNER 2-4   79-88
Picture Sleeves
WARNER 2-4   80-86
LPs: 10/12–inch 33rpm
WARNER 5-10   78-88
  Member: Mark Knopfler.

DIRKSEN, Senator Everett McKinley
Singles: 7–inch
CAPITOL 3-6   66
Picture Sleeves
CAPITOL 4-8   66
LPs: 10/12–inch 33rpm
BELL 5-10   70
CAPITOL 10-15   66-67

DIRT BAND: see NITTY GRITTY DIRT BAND

DISCO FOUR
Singles: 12–inch 33/45rpm
PROFILE 4-6   83
Singles: 7–inch
PROFILE 2-4   82-83

DISCO-TEX and His Sex-o-lettes
Singles: 7–inch
CHELSEA 3-5   74-76
LPs: 10/12–inch 33rpm
CHELSEA 8-10   75-76
MUSICOR 5-10   79

DISCO 3
Singles: 12–inch 33/45rpm
SUTRA 4-6   83
Singles: 7–inch
SUTRA 2-4   84

DIVINYLS
Singles: 12–inch 33/45rpm
CHRYSALIS 4-6   85
Singles: 7–inch
CHRYSALIS 2-4   83-86
Picture Sleeves
CHRYSALIS 2-4   85
LPs: 10/12–inch 33rpm
CHRYSALIS 5-10   83-86
VIRGIN 5-8   91
Member: Christina Amphlett.

DIXIE CUPS
Singles: 7–inch
ABC-PAR 4-8   65-66
ANTILLES 2-4   87
LANA 3-5
RED BIRD 5-10   64-65
TRIP 2-4
Picture Sleeves
ANTILLES 2-4   87
EPs: 7–inch 33/45rpm
ABC-PAR 15-25 65
LPs: 10/12–inch 33rpm
ABC-PAR (ABC-525 "Riding High") .. 25-30 65
(Monaural.)
ABC-PAR (ABCS-525 "Riding High") . 30-40 65
(Stereo.)
RED BIRD (RB-100 "Chapel of Love") 35-45 64
(Monaural.)
RED BIRD (RBS-100 "Chapel
of Love") 50-75 64
(Stereo.)
RED BIRD (RB-103 "Iko Iko") 35-45 64
(Monaural.)
RED BIRD (RBS-103 "Iko Iko") 40-60 64
(Stereo.)
Members: Barbara Hawkins; Rosa Hawkins; Joan Johnson.

DIXIE DREGS
(Dregs)
Singles: 7–inch
ARISTA 2-4   80-82
CAPRICORN 2-4   77-79
LPs: 10/12–inch 33rpm
ARISTA 5-10   80-82
CAPRICORN 5-10   78-79
Member: Steve Morse.
Also see MORSE, Steve, Band

DIXIE DRIFTER
Singles: 7–inch
AMY 4-6   68
IX CHAINS 3-5   74
ROULETTE 4-8   65

DIXIE HUMMINGBIRDS
Singles: 78rpm
OKEH 3-5   53
Singles: 7–inch
ABC 2-5   73-74
OKEH 5-10   53
PEACOCK 3-6   59-74
LPs: 10/12–inch 33rpm
CONSTELLATION 5-10   64
GOSPEL ROOTS 5-10   80
PEACOCK 5-10   59-78

DIXIEBELLES
Singles: 7–inch
MONUMENT 3-5   72
SOUND STAGE 7 4-8   63-64
EPs: 7–inch 33/45rpm
SOUND STAGE 7 .... 15-20 63
LPs: 10/12–inch 33rpm
SOUND STAGE 7 .... 20-30 63
MONUMENT 15-20 65
Also see SMITH, Jerry

DIXON, Billy, and the Topics
(4 Seasons)
Singles: 7–inch
TOPIX (6002 "Trance") 20-30 60
TOPIX (6008 "Lost Lullabye") 30-40 60
Also see 4 SEASONS

DIXON, Floyd
(Floyd Dixon and His Band)
Singles: 78rpm
ALADDIN 10-20 50-52
CASH 10-15 54
CAT 10-15 54
MODERN 8-12   49-50
PEACOCK 8-12   50
SUPREME 10-15 47
SWING TIME 10-15 47
Singles: 7–inch
ALADDIN (3135 "Wine Wine Wine") 75-150 52
ALADDIN (3144 "Red Cherries") ... 75-100 52
(Black vinyl.)
ALADDIN (3144 "Red Cherries") .. 150-250 52
(Colored vinyl.)
ALADDIN (3151 "Tired, Broke
and Busted") 75-100 52
CASH (1057 "Oh Baby") 25-50 54
CAT (106 "Moonshine") 25-50 54
CAT (114 "Hey Bartender") 20-40 54
CHATTAHOOCHEE 4-8   64
CHECKER 10-20 58
DODGE 8-12   61
EBB 15-20 57
JELLO 10-15 60
KENT 8-12   58
SPECIALTY (468 "Hard Living Alone") 25-50 53
(Black vinyl.)

STREETWISE 2-4   84
WARNER 2-4   81
EPs: 7-inch 33/45rpm
ATCO (4521 "Dr. John") 5-10   72
(Promotional issue only.)
LPs: 10/12-inch 33rpm
A&M 8-10   79
ACCORD 5-10   81
ACE 10-12
ATCO (Except 200 and 300 series) ... 8-12   72-74
ATCO (200 and 300 series) 12-15   68-71
BAROMETER 10-12   74
CLEANCUTS 5-10   82-84
HORIZON 5-10   79
KARATE 8-10   78
SPRINGBOARD 10-12   72
TRIP 8-10   75-76
U.A. 8-10   75
WARNER 5-10   89
Also see BLOOMFIELD, Mike, Dr. John and John Paul Hammond
Also see GUY, Buddy, with Dr. John and Eric Clapton / Buddy Guy with the J. Geils Band
Also see REBENNACK, Mac
Also see SAHM, Doug
Also see SIMPSONS

DR. JOHN and Chris Barber's Jazz and Blues Band
LPs: 10/12-inch 33rpm
GREAT SOUTHERN 8-10   90
Also see BARBER, Chris

DR. JOHN and Libby Titus
Singles: 7-inch
WARNER 2-4   81
Also see DR. JOHN

DR. WEST'S MEDICINE SHOW and Junk Band
Singles: 7-inch
GO GO 4-8   66-67
GREGAR 4-8   68
ROWE/AMI 4-8   66
("Play Me" Sales Stimulator promotional issue.)
LPs: 10/12-inch 33rpm
GO GO (002 "The Eggplant That Ate Chicago") 20-30   67
GREGAR 12-20
Also see GREENBAUM, Norman

DODDS, Nella
Singles: 7-inch
WAND 4-8   64-66

DOGGETT, Bill
Singles: 78rpm
KING 3-6   53-57
Singles: 7-inch
ABC-PAR 3-6   64
CHUMLEY 2-4   74
COLUMBIA 4-8   62-63
GUSTO 2-4

KING (4000 series) 6-12   53-56
KING (5000 series) 5-10   56-65
KING (6000 series) 3-8   66-71
ROULETTE 3-6   67
SUE 4-6   64
WARNER 4-6   61
Picture Sleeves
COLUMBIA 5-10   62
EPs: 7-inch 33/45
KING 8-15   53-59
LPs: 10/12-inch 33rpm
ABC-PAR 10-15   65
COLUMBIA 10-20   62-63
HARMONY 10-15   67
KING (82 through 118) 20-40   52-55
(10-inch LPs.)
KING (500 through 900 series) 12-25   56-66
ROULETTE 10-15   66
STARDAY 5-10
WARNER 12-20   61-62
Members: Bill Butler; Clifford Scott.
Also see BOSTIC, Earl, and Bill Doggett
Also see FITZGERALD, Ella, and Bill Doggett
Also see JACQUET, Illinois

DOKKEN
(Don Dokken)
Singles: 7-inch
ELEKTRA 2-4   83-88
Picture Sleeves
ELEKTRA 2-4   87
LPs: 10/12-inch 33rpm
ELEKTRA 5-10   83-88
GEFFEN 5-8   90

DOLBY, Thomas
Singles: 12-inch 33/45rpm
CAPITOL 4-6   83-84
Singles: 7-inch
CAPITOL 2-4   83-84
HARVEST 2-4   82
Picture Sleeves
CAPITOL 2-4   83-84
LPs: 10/12-inch 33rpm
CAPITOL 5-10   83-84
EMI 5-8   88
HARVEST 5-10   83
Also see DOLBY'S CUBE

DOLBY'S CUBE
(Thomas Dolby)
Singles: 12-inch 33/45rpm
CAPITOL 4-6   84
Singles: 7-inch
CAPITOL 2-4   84
Also see DOLBY, Thomas

DOLCE, Joe
Singles: 7-inch
MCA 3-5   81
METROMEDIA 2-4   81

LPs: 10/12–inch 33rpm

MCA 5-8   81

DOLENZ, Micky
(Mickey Dolenz)

Singles: 7–inch

CHALLENGE (59353 "Don't Do It") .. 10-20   66
CHALLENGE (59372 "Huff Puff") 10-20   67
MGM 8-12   71-72
ROMAR 8-10   73-74

Picture Sleeves

CHALLENGE (59353 "Don't Do It") .. 10-20   66
CHALLENGE (59372 "Huff Puff") 20-30   67

LPs: 10/12–inch 33rpm

CHRYSALIS 8-10   79
    Also see MONKEES
    Also see NILSSON

DOLENZ, Micky, Davy Jones and Peter Tork
Singles: 7–inch

CHRISTMAS RECORDS 8-12   76
    (Fan club, mail-order issue. Issued with special poster.)
    Members: Micky Dolenz; David Jones; Peter Tork.
    Also see MONKEES

DOLENZ, JONES, BOYCE & HART
Singles: 7–inch

CAPITOL (4180 "I Remember
    the Feeling") 10-15   75
CAPITOL (4271 "I Love You") 10-15   75

LPs: 10/12–inch 33rpm

CAPITOL 10-15   76
    Members: Micky Dolenz; David Jones; Tommy Boyce; Bobby Hart.
    Also see BOYCE, Tommy, and Bobby Hart
    Also see DOLENZ, Micky
    Also see JONES, Davy, and Micky Dolenz

DOLLAR
Singles: 7–inch

CARRERE 2-4   79

DOLPHINS
Singles: 7–inch

EMPRESS 5-10   61
FRATERNITY 4-8   64-65
GEMINI 4-8   62
LAURIE 5-10   63
SHAD (5020 "Tell-Tale Kisses") 20-30   60
YORKSHIRE (125 "Surfing East
    Coast") 15-20   66

DOMINGO, Placido
Singles: 7–inch

CBS 2-4   81-84

LPs: 10/12–inch 33rpm

CBS 5-10   81-84
EMI 5-8   91
RCA 5-10   82
    Also see DENVER, John, and Placido Domingo

DOMINO, Fats
Singles: 78rpm

IMPERIAL 10-20   50-57

Singles: 7–inch

ABC 2-4   73
ABC-PAR 4-8   63-64
BROADMOOR 4-8   67
IMPERIAL (5099 "Korea Blues") .. 200-225   52
IMPERIAL (5167 "You Know I
    Miss You") 150-200   52
IMPERIAL (5180 "Goin' Home") .. 100-150   52
IMPERIAL (5197 "Poor Poor Me") .. 50-100   52
IMPERIAL (5209 "How Long") 50-100   52
    (Black vinyl.)
IMPERIAL (5209 "How Long") 150-250   52
    (Colored vinyl.)
IMPERIAL (5220 "Nobody
    Loves Me") 50-100   53
    (Black vinyl.)
IMPERIAL (5220 "Nobody
    Loves Me") 150-250   53
    (Colored vinyl.)
IMPERIAL (5231 "Going to
    the River") 50-100   53
    (Black vinyl.)
IMPERIAL (5231 "Going to
    the River") 150-250   53
    (Colored vinyl.)
IMPERIAL (5240 "Please Don't
    Leave Me") 40-80   53
IMPERIAL (5251 "You Said
    You Love Me") 40-80   53
IMPERIAL (5262 "Something's
    Wrong") 25-50   53
    (Black vinyl.)
IMPERIAL (5262 "Something's
    Wrong") 100-200   53
    (Colored vinyl.)
IMPERIAL (5272 "Little School Girl") . 20-40   54
IMPERIAL (5283 "Baby, Please") ... 20-40   54
IMPERIAL (5301 "You Can Pack
    Your Suitcase") 20-40   54
IMPERIAL (5313 "Love Me") 20-40   54
IMPERIAL (5323 "I Know") 20-40   54
IMPERIAL (5340 "Don't You Know") . 20-30   55
IMPERIAL (5348 through 5396) 10-20   55-56
IMPERIAL (5407 "Blueberry Hill") .. 10-15   56
    (Black vinyl.)
IMPERIAL (5407 "Blueberry Hill") .. 75-125   56
    (Colored vinyl.)
IMPERIAL (5417 through 5477) 10-15   56-57
IMPERIAL (5492 "Yes My Darling") ... 8-12   58
    (Black vinyl.)
IMPERIAL (5492 "Yes My Darling") . 75-125   58
    (Colored vinyl.)
IMPERIAL (5515 through 5980) 5-10   58-63
IMPERIAL (66000 series) 4-6   64
IMPERIAL GOLDEN SERIES 3-5
MERCURY 4-8   65
REPRISE 4-6   68-70
TOOT TOOT (001 "My Toot Toot") 3-5   85
    (With Doug Kershaw.)

U.A.	3-5	74
WARNER	3-5	80

Picture Sleeves

IMPERIAL (5428 "I'm Walkin")	15-25	57
IMPERIAL (5477 "The Big Beat")	15-20	57
IMPERIAL (5606 "I Want to Walk You Home")	10-20	59
IMPERIAL (5629 "Be My Guest")	10-20	59
MERCURY (72485 "It's Never too Late")	20-30	65

EPs: 7-inch 33/45rpm

ABC-PAR	15-25	64-65
IMPERIAL (Except 127)	25-50	56-57
IMPERIAL (127 "Fats Domino-America's Outstanding Piano Stylist") (Red, script logo label.)	50-100	53
IMPERIAL (127 "Fats Domino-America's Outstanding Piano Stylist") (Maroon label.)	25-50	56
MERCURY (Jukebox issues only.)	15-25	65

LPs: 10/12-inch 33rpm

ABC-PAR	15-20	63-65
CANDLELITE	12-15	76
EVEREST	8-10	74-77
GRAND AWARD	10-15	
HARLEM HITPARADE	8-10	75
HARMONY	10-15	69
IMPERIAL (Except 9004 through 9040)	20-40	58-63
IMPERIAL (9004 "Rock and Rollin")	60-100	56
IMPERIAL (9009 "Fats Domino Rock and Rollin")	60-100	56
IMPERIAL (9028 "This Is Fats Domino")	60-100	57
IMPERIAL (9038 "Here Stands Fats Domino")	60-100	57
IMPERIAL (9040 "This Is Fats")	60-100	57
LIBERTY	5-10	80-81
MERCURY (21039 "Fats Domino '65") (Monaural.)	15-20	65
MERCURY (61039 "Fats Domino '65") (Stereo.)	15-20	65
REPRISE (6304 "Fats Is Back")	20-30	68
REPRISE (6439 "Fats")	300-400	71
SUNSET	12-15	66-71
TOMATO	10-20	89
U.A.	8-10	71-80

Also see ALLEN, Lee
Also see PRICE, Lloyd

DOMINOES

Singles: 78rpm

FEDERAL (12001 "Do Something for Me")	20-40	50
FEDERAL (12010 "Harbor Lights")	100-200	50
FEDERAL (12022 "Sixty Minute Man")	20-30	51
FEDERAL (12039 "I Am with You")	20-30	51
FEDERAL (12059 "That's What You're Doing to Me")	20-30	52
FEDERAL (12068 "Have Mercy Baby")	20-30	52
FEDERAL (12072 "Love, Love, Love")	20-30	52

Singles: 7-inch

FEDERAL (12001 "Do Something for Me")	350-400	50
FEDERAL (12022 "Sixty Minute Man")	150-200	51
FEDERAL (12039 "I Am with You")	200-300	51
FEDERAL (12059 "That's What You're Doing to Me")	250-300	52
FEDERAL (12068 "Have Mercy Baby")	100-175	52
FEDERAL (12072 "Love, Love, Love")	100-125	52

For later Federal numbers, EPs, and LPs, see the Billy Ward and the Dominoes section.

GUSTO	2-4	

Members: Billy Ward; Clyde McPhatter; Charlie White; William Lamont; Bill Brown.
  Also see LITTLE ESTHER and the Dominoes
  Also see McPHATTER, Clyde
  Also see WARD, Billy, and the Dominoes

DON & DEWEY
(Don and Dewey with the Titans)

Singles: 78rpm

SHADE	5-10	56
SPECIALTY	5-10	57
SPOT	5-10	56

Singles: 7-inch

FIDELITY	5-10	60
HIGHLAND	5-10	62
RUSH	4-8	63
SHADE (1000 "Miss Sue")	20-30	56
SPECIALTY (SPBX series) (Boxed set of six colored vinyl 45s.)	12-15	86
SPECIALTY (599 "Jungle Hop")	10-15	57
SPECIALTY (600 series, except 617)	5-10	57-61
SPECIALTY (617 "Just a Little Lovin'")	10-15	57
SPOT	10-20	56

LPs: 10/12-inch 33rpm

SPECIALTY (2131 "They're Rockin' Till Midnight") (Black and gold label.)	10-15	70
SPECIALTY (2131 "They're Rockin' Till Midnight") (Black and white label.)	5-10	88

Members: Don Harris (aka Don Bowman); Dewey Terry.

DON & JUAN

Singles: 7-inch

BIG TOP	5-10	61-63
ERIC	2-4	
MALA	4-8	63-65
TERRIFIC	3-5	
TWIRL	4-8	66

Members: Roland Trone: Claude Johnson.
Also see GENIES

DON and the Goodtimes
(Don Gallucci)
Singles: 7–inch
BURDETTE (3 "Colors of Life") 10-20   66
DUNHILL 5-10   65
EPIC 5-10   67-68
JERDEN 8-12   66
PICCADILLY 5-10
WAND 5-10   64
Picture Sleeves
EPIC 10-15   67
LPs: 10/12–inch 33rpm
BURDETTE (300 "Greatest Hits") ... 40-50   66
EPIC (24311 "So Good") 15-20   67
   (Monaural.)
EPIC (26311 "So Good") 15-20   67
   (Stereo.)
PANORAMA (104 "Harpo") 30-40
PICCADILLY (3394 "Goodtime Music") 5-10   82
WAND (679 "Where the Action Is") .. 25-35   67
   Also see KINGSMEN
   Also see TOUCH

DON, DICK & JIMMY
Singles: 78rpm
CROWN 4-8   54-55
DOT 4-8   54
Singles: 7–inch
CROWN 8-12   54-55
DOT 8-12   54
LPs: 10/12–inch 33rpm
CROWN (5005 "Spring Fever") 25-35   57
DOT 15-25   59
MODERN (1205 "Spring Fever") 35-50   56
VERVE 15-25   59
   Members: Don Sutton; Dick Rock; Jimmy Cook.

DONALDSON, Bo, and the Heywoods
Singles: 7–inch
ABC 3-5   73-75
CAPITOL 3-5   76
FAMILY 3-5   72-74
PLAYBOY 3-5   77
Picture Sleeves
ABC 3-5   74
LPs: 10/12–inch 33rpm
ABC 5-10   74
FAMILY 8-12   73

DONALDSON, Lou
(Lou Donaldson Quintet)
Singles: 78rpm
BLUE NOTE 3-5   52-57
Singles: 7–inch
ARGO 4-6   63-65
BLUE NOTE (100 through 300 series) .. 3-5   73-74
BLUE NOTE (1500 and 1600 series) .. 5-10   52-58
BLUE NOTE (1700 through 1900 series) 4-8   58-72

LPs: 10/12–inch 33rpm
ARGO 10-20   63-65
BLUE NOTE 8-15   64-80
   (Label shows Blue Note Records as a division of
   either Liberty or United Artists.)
BLUE NOTE (1500 series) 25-50   57-58
   (Label gives New York street address for Blue Note
   Records.)
BLUE NOTE (1500 series) 15-25   58
   (Label reads "Blue Note Records Inc. - New York,
   USA.")
BLUE NOTE (1500 series) 10-20   66
   (Label shows Blue Note Records as a division of
   either Liberty or United Artists.)
BLUE NOTE (4000 and 84000 series) 15-25   58-63
   (Label reads "Blue Note Records Inc. - New York,
   U.S.A.")
BLUE NOTE (5000 series) 50-75   52-54
   (10–inch LPs.)
BLUE NOTE (5000 series) 50-75   52-54
   (10–inch LPs.)
CADET 8-12   65-71
COTILLION 5-10   76-77
SUNSET 5-10   69-71
TRIP 5-10   79

DONEGAN, Lonnie
(Lonnie Donegan and His Skiffle Group)
Singles: 78rpm
LONDON 3-6   56
MERCURY 3-6   56
Singles: 7–inch
ABC 2-4   76
APT 4-8   62
ATLANTIC 4-8   60-61
DOT 4-8   61
FELSTED 4-8   61
HICKORY 4-6   64-65
LONDON 8-12   56
MCA 2-4
MERCURY 5-10   56
LPs: 10/12–inch 33rpm
ABC-PAR 15-20   63
ATLANTIC 20-30   60
DOT (3159 "Lonnie Donegan") 25-35   59
DOT (3394 "Lonnie Donegan") 20-30   61
U.A. 10-12   77

DONNA LYNN: see LYNN, Donna

DONNER, Ral
(Ral Donner and the Starfires; Ral Donner with Scotty
Moore, D.J. Fontana and the Jordanaires)
Singles: 7–inch
ABC 2-4   73
CHICAGO FIRE 8-10   74
END 10-20   63
FONTANA 10-20   64-65
GONE (5102 "Girl of My Best Friend") 20-30   60
   (Black label.)

GONE (5100 series, except
5108 and 5119) 5-10   61-62
(Multi-color labels.)
GONE (5108 "To Love"/"And Then") . 15-25   61
(Shortly after this release, *You Don't Know What
You've Got* was issued using the same catalog
number.)
GONE (5108 "You Don't Know What
You've Got") 5-10   61
GONE (5114 "Please Don't Go") 8-12   61
GONE (5119 "School of
Heartbreakers") 20-25   61
GONE (5121 "She's Everything"/
"Because We're Young") 8-12   61
GONE (5121 "She's Everything"/
"Will You Love Me in Heaven") 10-15   61
(*Will You Love Me in Heaven* is by an unknown girl
group, though credited on the label to Ral Donner.)
GONE (5125 "To Love Someone/Will You Love Me
in Heaven") 8-12   61
(*Will You Love Me in Heaven* is sung by Ral
Donner.)
GONE (5129 "Loveless Life") 5-10   62
GONE (5133 "To Love") 8-10   61
MJ 4-6   70
MID-EAGLE 4-6   68-76
RED BIRD (057 "Love Isn't
Like That") 75-125   66
REPRISE (20135 "Christmas Day") .. 15-25   62
REPRISE (20141 "I Got Burned") ... 15-25   63
RISING SONS 4-6   68
ROULETTE 2-4   71
SCOTTIE (1310 "Tell Me Why") 50-75   59
SMASH (34774 "Good Lovin") 15-25   65
(Promotional issue only.)
STARFIRE (Colored vinyl) 4-6   78-79
STARFIRE (Black vinyl, except 114) ... 2-4   78-79
STARFIRE (114 "Rip It Up") 2-4   79
(Black vinyl.)
STARFIRE (114 "Rip It Up") 8-12   79
(Picture disc.)
SUNLIGHT 8-10   72
TAU (105 "Lonliness of a Star") 20-30   63
THUNDER (7801 "The Day the
Beat Stopped") 3-5   78
(Clear vinyl.)

Picture Sleeves

MJ 5-10   70
REPRISE (20141 "I Got Burned") ... 40-50   63
STARFIRE 2-4   78-79

LPs: 10/12–inch 33rpm

AUDIO RESEARCH 12-15   80
GONE (5012 "Takin' Care of
Business") 60-80   61
GONE (5033 "Elvis Scrapbook") 10-15
GYPSY 8-12   79
MURRAY HILL 5-10   88

STARFIRE (1004 "An Evening
with Ral Donner") 10-15   82
(Multi-color vinyl.)
Also see PRESLEY, Elvis

DONNER, Ral / Ray Smith / Bobby Dale
LPs: 10/12–inch 33rpm
CROWN 15-20   63
Also see SMITH, Ray

DONNER, Ral / Zantees
Singles: 7–inch
EVA-TONE/GOLDMINE 2-4   79
(Soundsheet.)
Also see DONNER, Ral

DONNIE and the Dreamers
Singles: 7–inch
DECCA (31312 "Carole") 30-40   61
WHALE (500 "Count Every Star") ... 15-25   61
WHALE (505 "My Memories of You") . 25-35   61

DONOVAN
(Donovan P. Leitch; Donovan with the Jeff Beck
Group)
Singles: 12–inch 33/45rpm
ALLEGIANCE (1437 "Donovan") 5-10   83
Singles: 7–inch
ALLEGIANCE 2-4   83
ARISTA 3-5   77
EPIC 4-8   66-76
(Black vinyl.)
EPIC (10045 "Sunshine Superman") . 10-15   66
(Colored vinyl. Promotional issue only.)
EPIC MEMORY LANE 3-5
HICKORY 8-15   65-68
Picture Sleeves
EPIC 5-10   66-71
LPs: 10/12–inch 33rpm
ALLEGIANCE 5-10   83
ARISTA 8-10   77
BELL 10-12   73
COLUMBIA 5-10   73
EPIC (Except 26439) 10-20   66-76
EPIC (BXN-26439 "Donovan's Greatest
Hits") 15-20   69
(Gatefold cover. Includes booklet.)
EPIC (PE-26439 "Donovan's Greatest
Hits") 5-10   77
HICKORY (123 "Catch the Wind") ... 20-40   65
HICKORY (127 "Fairy Tale") 20-40   65
HICKORY (135 "The Real Donovan") 20-40   66
HICKORY (143 "Like It Is") 20-40   68
HICKORY (149 "Best of Donovan") .. 20-40   69
JANUS 10-12   70-71
KORY 5-10   77
PYE 8-10   76
Also see BECK, Jeff

DOO, Dickey:
see DICKEY DOO and the Dont's

DOOBIE BROTHERS
Singles: 12-inch 33/45rpm
WARNER 4-8   79
Singles: 7-inch
ASYLUM 2-4   80
CAPITOL 2-4   89-90
SESAME STREET 2-4   81
WARNER 2-5   71-83
Picture Sleeves
CAPITOL 2-4   89
SESAME STREET 2-4   81
WARNER 2-5   72-80
LPs: 10/12-inch 33rpm
CAPITOL 5-8   89-91
MFSL (122 "Takin' It to the Streets") . 10-15   84
NAUTILUS (5 "Captain and Me") 25-35   80
(Half-speed mastered.)
NAUTILUS (18 "Minute By Minute") .. 15-20   81
(Half-speed mastered.)
PICKWICK 6-10   80
WARNER 6-12   71-83
Members: Michael McDonald; Tom Johnston; Patrick Simmons;
Bobby LaKind.
Also see JOHNSTON, Tom
Also see McDONALD, Michael
Also see SIMMONS, Patrick

DOOBIE BROTHERS, James Hall and James Taylor
Singles: 7-inch
ASYLUM 2-4   80
Also see TAYLOR, James

DOOBIE BROTHERS and Nicolette Larson
Singles: 7-inch
WARNER 2-4   79
Also see LARSON, Nicolette

DOOBIE BROTHERS / Kate Taylor and the Simon-Taylor Family
Singles: 7-inch
WARNER 2-4   80
Picture Sleeves
WARNER 2-4   80
Also see DOOBIE BROTHERS
Also see SIMON SISTERS
Also see TAYLOR, James
Also see TAYLOR, Kate
Also see TAYLOR, Livingston

DOOLITTLE BAND
(Dandy and the Doolittle Band)
Singles: 7-inch
COLUMBIA 2-4   80

DOORS
Singles: 7-inch
ELEKTRA (Except 45000 series) 2-4   79-83
ELEKTRA (45000 series) 4-8   67-72
Promotional Singles
ELEKTRA (45000 series) 8-15   67-72
Picture Sleeves
ELEKTRA 8-15   67-78

LPs: 10/12-inch 33rpm
ELEKTRA (500 series) 5-10   78-80
ELEKTRA (4007 "The Doors") 20-35   67
(Monaural.)
ELEKTRA (4014 "Strange Days") ... 15-25   67
(Monaural.)
ELEKTRA (5035 "Best of the Doors") 15-20   73
ELEKTRA (EKS-6001 "Weird Scenes
Inside the Gold Mine") 12-15   72
ELEKTRA (8E-6001 "Weird Scenes
Inside the Gold Mine") 8-12   73
ELEKTRA (9002 "Absolutely Live") .. 15-20   70
ELEKTRA (60000 series) 5-10   83-91
ELEKTRA (74007 "The Doors") 20-25   67
ELEKTRA (74014 "Strange Days") .. 15-25   67
ELEKTRA (74024 "Waiting for
the Sun") 15-20   68
ELEKTRA (75005 "The Soft
Parade") 10-20   69
ELEKTRA (75007 "Morrison Hotel/
Hard Rock Cafe") 12-15   70
ELEKTRA (74079 "Doors 13") 12-15   70
ELEKTRA (75011 "L.A. Woman") ... 25-35   71
(With die-cut cover.)
ELEKTRA (75011 "L.A. Woman") 5-10
(With standard cover.)
ELEKTRA (75017 "Other Voices") 8-12   71
ELEKTRA (75038 "Full Circle") 8-12   72
MFSL (051 "The Doors") 15-20   76
Members: Jim Morrison; Robbie Krieger; Ray Manzarek; John
Densmore.
Also see MANZAREK, Ray

DORADOS, El: see EL DORADOS

DORE, Charlie
Singles: 7-inch
CHRYSALIS 2-4   81
ISLAND 2-4   80-81
LPs: 10/12-inch 33rpm
ISLAND ....:................. 5-10   80-81

DORMAN, Harold
Singles: 7-inch
ABC 2-4   73
COLLECTABLES 2-4
RITA 8-10   60
SANTO 4-8   62
SUN 5-10   61-62
TINCE 5-10   60

DORSEY, Jimmy, Orchestra and Chorus
Singles: 78rpm
BELL 2-5   54
COLUMBIA 3-5   50-52
DECCA 2-6   35-57
FRATERNITY 2-5   57
MGM 2-5   54
OKEH 10-15   29
Singles: 7-inch
ABC 2-4   73

BELL 3-5	54	
COLUMBIA 3-6	50-52	
DECCA 3-6	51-67	
DOT 2-4	63	
EPIC 2-4	59	
FRATERNITY 2-5	57-60	
MGM 2-4	54	

EPs: 7-inch 33/45rpm

COLUMBIA 4-8	52-56	

LPs: 10/12-inch 33rpm

COLUMBIA 10-20	55-56	
CORAL 10-20	54	
DECCA 10-20	57-66	
EPIC 8-12	59	
FRATERNITY 10-20	57	
HINDSIGHT 5-10	81	
LION 10-20	56	
MCA 5-10	75	

Also see CROSBY, Bing, and Jimmy Dorsey

DORSEY, Lee

Singles: 7-inch

ABC 2-4	78	
ABC-PAR (10192 "Lotti Mo") 5-10	61	
ACE 8-10	61	
AMY 4-8	65-69	
CONSTELLATION 4-8	64	
FLASHBACK 3-5	65	
FURY 5-10	61-63	
GUSTO 2-4		
POLYDOR 3-5	70-72	
REX (1005 "Rock") 15-20	58	
ROULETTE 2-4		
SANSU 4-8	67	
SMASH 4-8	63	
SPRING 3-5	71	
VALIANT (1001 "Lotti Mo") 20-30	58	

LPs: 10/12-inch 33rpm

AMY (8010 "Ride Your Pony") 20-25	66	
AMY (8011 "The New Lee Dorsey") .. 20-25	66	
ARISTA 5-10	85	
FURY (1002 "Ya Ya") 35-45	62	
POLYDOR 10-12	70	
SPHERE SOUND (7003 "Ya Ya") ... 15-25	67	

DORSEY, Tommy, Orchestra
(Tommy Dorsey Orchestra Starring Warren Covington)

Singles: 78rpm

BELL 4-8	54	
(7-inch disc.)		
BLUEBIRD 3-6	40	
DECCA 2-5	52-64	
OKEH 10-15	29	
RCA 2-5	49-57	
VICTOR 3-6	35-48	

Singles: 7-inch

DECCA 2-4	52-64	
MCA 2-4	73	
RCA 2-4	50-57	

EPs: 7-inch 33/45rpm

COLUMBIA 4-8	52-56	
DECCA 4-8	52-63	
RCA 4-6	51-61	
WALDORF 4-8		

LPs: 10/12-inch 33rpm

ACCORD 5-10	82	
BRIGHT ORANGE 5-10	73	
CAMDEN (Except 200 series) 5-10	61-73	
CAMDEN (200 series) 10-20	53-55	
COLPIX 10-20	58-63	
COLUMBIA 10-20	58	
CORAL 5-10	73	
CORONET 5-10		
DECCA 10-20	52-60	
GOLDEN MUSIC SOCIETY 15-20	56	
HARMONY 5-10	65-72	
MCA 5-10	75-81	
MOVIETOWN 8-10	67	
RCA 10-20	51-82	
SPRINGBORAD 6-10	77	
20TH FOX 10-15	59-73	

Also see GARLAND, Judy / Tommy Dorsey
Also see SINATRA, Frank

DOSS, Kenny

Singles: 7-inch

BEARSVILLE 2-4	80	

LPs: 10/12-inch 33rpm

BEARSVILLE 5-10	80	

DOTTIE & RAY

Singles: 7-inch

LE SAGE 4-8	65	

DOUBLE

Singles: 12-inch 33/45rpm

A&M 4-8	86	

Singles: 7-inch

A&M 2-4	86	

Picture Sleeves

A&M 2-4	86	

LPs: 10/12-inch 33rpm

A&M 5-10	86	

Members: Kurt Maloo; Felix Haug.

DOUBLE ENTENTE

Singles: 12-inch 33/45rpm

COLUMBIA 4-6	84	

Singles: 7-inch

COLUMBIA 2-4	84	

DOUBLE EXPOSURE

Singles: 12-inch 33/45rpm

GOLD COAST 4-6	81	

Singles: 7-inch

SALSOUL 2-4	76-79	

LPs: 10/12-inch 33rpm

SALSOUL 8-10	76-79	

Members: James Williams; Joseph Harris; Leonard Davis;
Charles Whittington.

DOUBLE IMAGE
Singles: 7-inch
CBS ASSOCIATED 2-4   83
CURB 2-4   83
LPs: 10/12-inch 33rpm
ECM 5-10   79

DOUBLE VISION
Singles: 12-inch 33/45rpm
PROFILE 4-6   84

DOUCETTE
(Jerry Doucette)
Singles: 7-inch
MUSHROOM 2-4   77-79
LPs: 10/12-inch 33rpm
MUSHROOM 5-10   78-79

DOUGLAS, Carl
(Carl Douglas and the Big Stampede)
Singles: 7-inch
ERIC 2-4
OKEH 4-8   66-67
20TH FOX 3-5   74-75
LPs: 10/12-inch 33rpm
20TH FOX 10-15   74

DOUGLAS, Carol
Singles: 12-inch 33/45rpm
MIDSONG INT'L 4-6   78
Singles: 7-inch
MIDLAND INT'L 2-5   74-79
RCA 3-5   76
20TH FOX 2-4   81
Picture Sleeves
MIDLAND INT'L 2-5   77-88
LPs: 10/12-inch 33rpm
MIDLAND INT'L 8-10   75-80

DOUGLAS, Mike
Singles: 7-inch
BANANA 5-10
BLUE RIVER 4-6   66
DECCA 3-6   69
EPIC 4-6   65-67
IMAGE 3-5   77
MGM 2-4   71-73
PROJECT 3 3-5   68
STAX 3-5   74
Picture Sleeves
EPIC 4-8   65-66
LPs: 10/12-inch 33rpm
ATLANTIC 5-10   76
EPIC 10-15   65-67
HARMONY 8-12   68
Also see BAILEY, Pearl, and Mike Douglas

DOUGLAS, Ronny, and Bobby Lonero
Singles: 7-inch
COLUMBIA 3-5   71-72

DOVALE, Debbie
Singles: 7-inch
ROULETTE 8-15   63-64

DOVE, Ronnie
(Ronnie Dove and the Beltones)
Singles: 7-inch
ABC 2-4   74
DECCA (31288 "Party Doll") 8-10   61
DECCA (32000 and 33000 series) 3-5   71-73
DIAMOND 3-6   64-70
ERIC 2-4
HITSVILLE 3-5   76
JALO (1406 "Saddest Song") 15-20   62
MC 2-4   78
MCA 2-4   73
MELODYLAND 3-5   75-76
MOTION 2-4   81
MOON SHINE 2-4   83
SWAN 4-6   63
WRAYCO 3-5   71
Picture Sleeves
DIAMOND 4-8   65-66
LPs: 10/12-inch 33rpm
CERTRON 10-12   70
DIAMOND 15-25   65-70
MCA 8-10   73

DOVELLS
Singles: 7-inch
ABKCO 2-4   83
COLLECTABLES 2-4
DECCA 3-6   70
EVENT 3-6   70-74
MGM 4-6   66-73
PARKWAY (Except 819 and 827) 5-10   62-63
PARKWAY (819 "No No No") 10-15   61
PARKWAY (827 "Bristol Stomp"/
"Out in the Cold") 10-15   61
PARKWAY (827 "Bristol Stomp"/
"Letters of Love") 5-8   61
(Note different flip.)
SWAN 4-8   65
VERVE 3-5   73
Picture Sleeves
PARKWAY 5-10   62-63
LPs: 10/12-inch 33rpm
DOVCO 5-10   76
PARKWAY (7006 "The Bristol Stomp") 30-50   61
PARKWAY (7010 "All the Hits
of the Teen Groups") 25-40   62
PARKWAY (7021 "For Your
Hully Gully Party") 25-40   63
PARKWAY (7025 "You Can't
Sit Down") 25-40   63
WYNCOTE 10-20   65
Members: Len Barry; Arnie Satin; Jerry Summers; Danny
Brooks; Mike Dennis.
Also see BARRY, Len
Also see CHRISTIE, Lou / Len Barry and the Dovells / Bobby
Rydell / Tokens

Also see MAGISTRATES
Also see ORLONS / Dovells

DOWELL, Joe
Singles: 7–inch
JOURNEY 3-5   73
MONUMENT 4-6   66
SMASH 4-8   61-63
Picture Sleeves
JOURNEY 3-5   73
SMASH 5-10   61-62
LPs: 10/12–inch 33rpm
SMASH 15-25   61-62
WING 10-15   66

DOWNING, Al
(Big Al Downing)
Singles: 7–inch
CARLTON (489 "Miss Lucy") 20-30   58
CHALLENGE (59006 "Down on
  the Farm") 20-30   58
CHESS (1000 series) 5-10   62
CHESS (2000 series) 3-5   75
COLUMBIA 4-8   64
HOUSE of the FOX 3-5   71
JANUS 3-5   74
KANSOMA 4-8   62
LENOX 4-8   63
POLYDOR 3-5   76
SILVER FOX 2-4
TEAM 2-4   82-84
V-TONE 5-10   61
WARNER 2-4   78-80
WHITE ROCK (1111 "Down on
  the Farm") 50-100   58
WHITE ROCK (1113 "Miss Lucy") .. 50-100   58
LPs: 10/12–inch 33rpm
TEAM 5-10   83-85
Also see LITTLE ESTHER and Big Al Downing

DOWNING, Don
Singles: 7–inch
ABNER 4-8   62
CHAN 4-8
ROADSHOW 3-5   73
SCEPTER 3-5   74
LPs: 10/12–inch 33rpm
ROADSHOW 5-10   79

DOZIER, Gene, and the Brotherhood
Singles: 7–inch
MINIT 4-8   67-68
LPs: 10/12–inch 33rpm
MINIT 10-15   67

DOZIER, Lamont
Singles: 12–inch 33/45rpm
WARNER 4-8   79
Singles: 7–inch
ABC 3-5   73-76
COLUMBIA 2-4   81
INVICTUS 3-5   72-73

M&M 2-4   82
MEL-O-DY (102 "Dearest One") 25-40   62
LPs: 10/12–inch 33rpm
ABC 8-10   73-74
COLUMBIA 5-10   81
INVICTUS 8-12   74
M&M 5-10   82
WARNER 8-10   76-79
Also see HOLLAND, Eddie, and Lamont Dozier
Also see VOICE MASTERS

DRAFI
Singles: 7–inch
LONDON 4-8   66-67

DRAGON
Singles: 12–inch 33/45rpm
POLYDOR 4-6   84
Singles: 7–inch
POLYDOR 2-4   83-84
PORTRAIT 2-5   78-79
LPs: 10/12–inch 33rpm
POLYDOR 5-10   83
PORTRAIT 5-10   78

DRAKE, Charlie
Singles: 7–inch
U.A. (Except 398) 4-8   61-62
U.A. (398 "My Boomerang
  Won't Come Back") 15-20   61
  (With "Practiced till I was BLACK in the face" lyrics.)
U.A. (398 "My Boomerang
  Won't Come Back") 4-8   61
  (With "Practiced till I was BLUE in the face" lyrics.)

DRAKE, Guy
Singles: 7–inch
MALLARD 3-5   71
ROYAL AMERICAN 3-5   70
LPs: 10/12–inch 33rpm
OVATION 5-10   74
ROYAL AMERICAN 15-20   70

DRAKE, Pete
Singles: 7–inch
SMASH 3-6   64-65
STARDAY 3-5   66
STOP 3-5   68-70
LPs: 10/12–inch 33rpm
CANAAN 8-12   68
CUMBERLAND 12-20   63
PICKWICK/HILLTOP 8-12   67
MOUNTAIN DEW 8-10
SMASH 10-15   64-65
STARDAY 15-25   62-65
STOP 6-10   70

DRAMATICS
Singles: 7–inch
ABC 3-5   75-77
CADET 3-5   74
CAPITOL 2-4   82

CRACKERJACK 20-30	61	
FANTASY 2-4	86	
MAINSTREAM 3-5	75	
MCA 2-4	79-80	
VOLT 3-5	71-73	
WINGATE 5-8	67	

LPs: 10/12–inch 33rpm

ABC 8-10	75-78	
CADET 8-10	74	
CAPITOL 5-10	82	
FANTASY 5-10	86	
MCA 5-10	80	
STAX 8-10	77-78	
VOLT 10-12	72-74	

Members: Ron Banks; Elbert Wilkins; L.J. Reynolds; William Howard; Larry Demps; Lenny Mayes; Carl Smalls; Willie Ford.
Also see BANKS, Ron
Also see DELLS with the DRAMATICS
Also see REYNOLDS, L.J.
Also see UNDISPUTED TRUTH

DRAPER, Rusty
Singles: 78rpm

MERCURY 3-5	52-57	

Singles: 7–inch

MERCURY 4-8	52-62	
MONUMENT 3-5	63-70	

EPs: 7–inch 33/45rpm

MERCURY 10-15	54-56	

LPs: 10/12–inch 33rpm

GOLDEN CREST 5-10	73	
HARMONY 5-10	72	
MERCURY 10-20	54-62	
MONUMENT 8-12	65-75	
WING 8-12	63-64	

Also see DEE, Lola, and Rusty Draper

DREAM ACADEMY
Singles: 7–inch

MCA 2-4	79	
WARNER 2-4	85-86	

Picture Sleeves

WARNER 2-4	85-86	

LPs: 10/12–inch 33rpm

REPRISE 5-10	87	
WARNER 5-10	85-86	

DREAM SYNDICATE
LPs: 10/12–inch 33rpm

A&M 5-10	84	
SLASH 5-10		

Also see TEXTONES

DREAM WEAVERS
Singles: 78rpm

DECCA 3-5	55-56	

Singles: 7–inch

DECCA 5-10	55-56	

EPs: 7–inch 33/45rpm

DECCA 10-20	56	

Member: Wade Buff.

DREAMBOY
Singles: 7–inch

QWEST 2-4	83-84	

LPs: 10/12–inch 33rpm

QWEST 5-10	83-84	

DREAMLOVERS
Singles: 7–inch

CAMEO 8-12	64	
CASINO (1308 "Amazons and Coyotes") 10-15	64	
COLLECTABLES 2-4	82	
COLUMBIA (42698 "Sad Sad Boy") . 10-15	63	
COLUMBIA (42752 "Sad Sad Boy") ... 5-8	63	
COLUMBIA (42842 "Pretty Little Girl") 20-40	63	
DOWN ("If I Should Lose You") 40-60		
(Number not known.)		
END (1114 "If I Should Lose You") 8-12	62	
HERITAGE 10-15	61-62	
MERCURY 5-10	66-67	
SWAN (4167 "Amazons and Coyotes") 15-20	63	
(White label.)		
SWAN (4167 "Amazons and Coyotes") 8-12	63	
(Black label.)		
V-TONE 10-15	60-61	
WARNER 3-5	65	

LPs: 10/12–inch 33rpm

COLLECTABLES 6-8	82	
COLUMBIA (2020 "The Bird") 30-40	63	
(Monaural.)		
COLUMBIA (8820 "The Bird") 35-45	63	
(Stereo.)		
HERITAGE 8-12	79	

Members: Tommy Ricks; Cleveland Hammock; Cliff Dunn; Morris Gardner; Ray Dunn.
Also see CHECKER, Chubby

DREAMS
Singles: 7–inch

COLUMBIA 3-5	71-72	
D.C. 4-6	69	

LPs: 10/12–inch 33rpm

COLUMBIA 10-15	70-71	

Also see BRECKER BROTHERS

DREAMS SO REAL
LPs: 10/12–inch 33rpm

ARISTA 5-8	88	
FATHER'S HOUSE 8-10	86	
I.R.S. 5-10	87	

Members: Barry Marler; Drew Worsham; Trent Allen.

DREGS: see DIXIE DREGS

DRENNON, Eddie, and B.B.S. Unlimited
Singles: 7–inch

FRIENDS and CO 3-5	75	

DRESSLER, Len
Singles: 78rpm

MERCURY 4-8	56	

Singles: 7–inch

CAPITOL 3-6	63	

DRIFTERS / Lesley Gore / Roy Orbison / Los Bravos

EPs: 7–inch 33/45rpm

SWINGERS for COKE 15-20   66
(Promotional issue only. Each artist sings a song
about Coca Cola.)
Also see DRIFTERS
Also see GORE, Lesley
Also see LOS BRAVOS
Also see ORBISON, Roy

DRUPI

Singles: 7–inch

A&M 3-5   73

DRUSKY, Roy

Singles: 7–inch

CAPITOL 2-4   76
DECCA 3-6   60-62
MERCURY 3-5   63-72
PLANTATION 2-4   79-80

EPs: 7–inch 33/45rpm

DECCA 4-8   61-63

LPs: 10/12–inch 33rpm

CAPITOL 5-10   76
DECCA 12-20   61-62
HARMONY 10-12   65
MCA 4-8
MERCURY 10-20   64-72
PICKWICK/HILLTOP 8-12
PLANTATION 5-10   79-80
SCORPION 5-10   76
VOCALION 8-12   70
WING 10-15   64-66
Also see WELLS, Kitty, and Roy Drusky

DUALS

Singles: 7–inch

COLLECTABLES 2-4
INFINITY (032 "Big Race") 20-30   64
STAR REVUE (1031 "Stick Shift") ... 50-75   61
SUE (745 "Stick Shift") 10-15   61

LPs: 10/12–inch 33rpm

SUE (2002 "Stick Shift") 50-80   61
Members: John Lagemann; Henry Bellinger.

DUBS

Singles: 78rpm

GONE 10-15   57
JOHNSON (102 "Don't Ask Me
to Be Lonely") 100-200   57

Singles: 7–inch

ABC-PAR 8-15   59-61
CLASSIC ARTISTS 3-5   90
CLIFTON 3-5   73
END (1108 "This to Me Is Love") 20-30   62
GONE (5002 "Don't Ask Me to
Be Lonely") 35-50   57
(With double image, shadow-like lettering.)
GONE (5002 "Don't Ask Me
to Be Lonely") 15-25   57
(With normal lettering.)

GONE (5011 "Could This Be Magic") 15-25   57
GONE (5020 "Beside My Love") 15-25   58
GONE (5034 "Be Sure My Love") ... 15-25   58
GONE (5046 "Chapel of Dreams") .. 15-25   58
(Black label.)
GONE (5046 "Chapel of Dreams") .. 10-15   60
(Multi-color label.)
GONE (5138 "Is There a Love for Me") 15-25   62
(Black label.)
JOHNSON (97 "Connie") 4-6   73
JOHNSON (98 "Somebody Goofed") .. 4-6   73
JOHNSON (102 "Don't Ask Me
to Be Lonely") 500-750   57
JOSIE 8-12   63
LANA 3-5
MARK-X 8-12   60
OLDIES 45 3-5
ROULETTE 2-4
WILSHIRE 10-20   63

LPs: 10/12–inch 33rpm

CANDLELITE 10-15   73
MURRAY HILL 5-10   88
Members: Richard Blandon; Billy Carlisle; Cleveland Still; James
Millor; Tom Gardner; Tom Grate; Cordell Brown; Dave Shelley.

DUBS / Actuals

Singles: 78rpm

CANDLELITE (438 "We Three") 5-10   72

DUBS / Shells

LPs: 10/12–inch 33rpm

CANDLELITE 8-10
JOSIE (4001 "The Dubs Meet
the Shells") 75-150   62
Also see DUBS
Also see SHELLS

DUBSET

Singles: 12–inch 33/45rpm

ELEKTRA 4-6   84

DUCES of Rhythm and Tempo Toppers
(Featuring Little Richard)

Singles: 78rpm

PEACOCK 15-25   53-54

Singles: 7–inch

PEACOCK (1616 "Fool at the Wheel") 50-75   53
PEACOCK (1628 "Always") 50-75   54
Also see LITTLE RICHARD

DUCHIEN, Armand

Singles: 12–inch 33/45rpm

A&M 4-6   84

DUDEK, Les

Singles: 7–inch

COLUMBIA 3-5   77-78

LPs: 10/12–inch 33rpm

COLUMBIA 8-12   75-81
Also see ALLMAN BROTHERS BAND

DUDLEY, Dave

Singles: 78rpm

KING 4-8   55-56

Singles: 7-inch

COLUMBIA	2-4	78
CURIO	4-8	
GOLDEN RING	4-8	63
GOLDEN WING (3020 "Six Days on the Road") (Black vinyl.)	4-8	63
GOLDEN WING (3020 "Six Days on the Road") (Colored vinyl.)	10-20	63
JUBILEE	4-8	62
KING (4000 series)	8-12	55-56
KING (5000 series)	4-6	63
MERCURY	3-6	63-73
NRC	5-10	59
NEW STAR	4-8	62
RICE	2-4	73-78
STARDAY	5-10	60
SUN (Black vinyl)	2-4	79-80
SUN (Colored vinyl)	3-6	79-80
U.A.	3-5	75-76
VEE	5-10	61

LPs: 10/12-inch 33rpm

GOLDEN RING (110 "Six Days on the Road")	25-30	63
MERCURY	10-15	64-73
MOUNTAIN DEW	8-12	69
NASHVILLE	8-12	68
PLANTATION	5-10	81
RICE	2-4	78
SUN	5-10	80
U.A.	8-12	75-76
WING	8-12	68

Also see JAMES, Sonny / Dave Dudley / Sunny Williams

DUDLEY, Dave, and Tom T. Hall
Singles: 7-inch
MERCURY	2-4	70

Also see HALL, Tom T.

DUDLEY, Dave / Link Wray
LPs: 10/12-inch 33rpm
GUEST STAR	10-20	63

Also see DUDLEY, Dave
Also see WRAY, Link

DUDLEY, Kay
Singles: 7-inch
TEEN ED	4-8	61

DU DROPPERS
Singles: 78rpm
GROOVE	15-25	53-55
RCA	10-20	53
RED ROBIN	20-40	52-53

Singles: 7-inch
GROOVE (0001 "Dead Broke")	40-60	54
GROOVE (0013 "Just Whisper")	50-75	54
GROOVE (0036 "Let Nature Take It's Course")	30-40	54
GROOVE (0104 "Talk That Talk")	20-40	55
GROOVE (0120 "You're Mine Already")	20-40	55
RCA (5229 "I Wanna Know")	25-35	53
RCA (5321 "I Found Out")	25-30	53
RCA (5425 "Whatever You're Doin'")	25-30	53
RCA (5504 "Don't Pass Me By")	25-30	53
RED ROBIN (108 "Can't Do Sixty No More") (Black vinyl.)	100-125	52
RED ROBIN (108 "Can't Do Sixty No More") (Colored vinyl.)	200-300	52
RED ROBIN (116 "Come on and Love Me Baby")	100-125	53

EPs: 7-inch 33/45rpm
GROOVE (2 "Talk That Talk")	100-200	55
GROOVE (5 "Tops in Rhythm and Blues")	100-200	55

Members: Julius Ginyard; Willie Ray; Eddie Hashaw; Harvey Ray; Bob Kornegay; Prentice Moreland; Joe Van Loan; Charlie Hughes.
Also see GALE, Sunny, and the Du Droppers

DUKAYS
Singles: 7-inch
JERRY-O	5-10	64
NAT	8-12	61-62
OLDIES 45	3-5	
VEE JAY	5-8	62

Members: Eugene "Gene Chandler" Dixon; James Lowe; Earl Edwards; Ben Broyles; Shirley Jones; Charles Davis Claude McRae.
Also see ARTISTICS
Also see CHANCE, Nolan
Also see CHANDLER, Gene

DUKE, Doris
Singles: 7-inch
CANYON	3-5	70

DUKE, George
Singles: 12-inch 33/45rpm
ELEKTRA	4-6	85-86
EPIC	4-6	83

Singles: 7-inch
ELEKTRA	2-4	85-86
EPIC	2-4	77-83

LPs: 10/12-inch 33rpm
ELEKTRA	5-10	85-86
EPIC	5-10	77-83
MPS/BASF	8-10	74-76

Also see CLARKE, Stanley, and George Duke
Also see COBHAM, Billy
Also see MOTHERS of INVENTION

DUKE, Patty
Singles: 7-inch
U.A.	4-8	65-68

Picture Sleeves
U.A.	8-10	65

LPs: 10/12-inch 33rpm
U.A.	15-20	65-68

DUKE and the DRIVERS
Singles: 7-inch

ABC 3-5   75

LPs: 10/12-inch 33rpm

ABC 8-10   76

DUKE JUPITER
Singles: 7-inch

COAST to COAST 2-4   82
MOROCCO 2-4   84-85

LPs: 10/12-inch 33rpm

COAST TO COAST 5-10   82-83
MERCURY 5-10   80
MOROCCO 5-10   84

DUKE of EARL
(Gene Chandler)
Singles: 7-inch

VEE JAY 5-8   62
Also see CHANDLER, Gene

DUKES OF DIXIELAND
LPs: 10/12-inch 33rpm

AUDIO FIDELITY 5-15   55-61
COLUMBIA 5-10   62
EPIC 5-15   56
RCA VICTOR 5-10   59

DUKES of STRATOSPHERE
Singles: 12-inch 33/45rpm

GEFFEN (2840 "Vanishing Girl") 5-10   87
(Promotional issue only.)

LPs: 10/12-inch 33rpm

GEFFEN 5-10   87
Also see XTC

DUNCAN, Jamie
Singles: 7-inch

SOUTHERN GOLD 2-4   86

DUNCAN SISTERS
Singles: 12-inch 33/45rpm

EAR MARC 4-6   79

Singles: 7-inch

EAR MARC 2-4   79-80
HI 3-5   75

DUNDAS, David
Singles: 7-inch

CHRYSALIS 3-5   76-77

LPs: 10/12-inch 33rpm

CHRYSALIS 8-10   77

DUNLAP, Gene
Singles: 7-inch

HITT (182 "Made in the Shade") 30-50   58

DUNN and Bruce Street
Singles: 7-inch

DEVAKI 2-4   81-82
Members: Dunn Pearson; Bruce Gray

DUNN & McCASHEN
Singles: 7-inch

CAPITOL 3-6   69-70

LPs: 10/12-inch 33rpm

CAPITOL 10-12   69-70
COLUMBIA 12-15   71

DUPREE, Champion Jack
(Jack Dupree and His Band)
Singles: 78rpm

ALERT 10-15   46
APOLLO 10-15   49-50
CELEBRITY 10-15   46
CONTINENTAL 10-20   45
JOE DAVIS 10-15   46
KING 8-12   53-55
RED ROBIN 25-40   53-54
VIK 5-10   57

Singles: 7-inch

ATLANTIC 5-10   61
EVERLAST 4-8   64
FEDERAL 5-10   61
GUSTO 2-4
KING (4695 "Walkin' Upside
  Your Head") 10-20   53
KING (4706 "Rub a Little Boogie") ... 10-20   53
RED ROBIN (109 "Stumblin'
  Block Blues") 150-200   53
RED ROBIN (112 "Highway Blues") 150-200   53
RED ROBIN (130 "Drunk Again") . 150-200   54
VIK (260 "Dirty Woman") 20-30   57
VIK (279 "Old Time Rock and Roll") . 20-30   57

LPs: 10/12-inch 33rpm

ARCHIVE of FOLK MUSIC 10-15   68
ATLANTIC (8019 "Blues from
  the Gutter") 75-100   59
  (Green label.)
ATLANTIC (8019 "Blues from
  the Gutter") 40-60   59
  (Black label.)
ATLANTIC (8019 "Blues from
  the Gutter") 40-60   59
  (White label.)
ATLANTIC (8019 "Blues from
  the Gutter") 20-30   59
  (Red label.)
ATLANTIC (8045 "Natural and
  Soulful Blues") 30-40   61
  (Monaural.)
ATLANTIC (SD-8045 "Natural and
  Soulful Blues") 40-50   61
  (Stereo.)
ATLANTIC (8056 "Champion of
  the Blues") 30-40   61
  (Monaural.)
ATLANTIC (SD-8056 "Champion of
  the Blues") 40-50   61
  (Stereo.)
ATLANTIC (8255 "Blues from
  the Gutter") 8-10   70
BLUE HORIZON 10-15   69
EVEREST 8-12

FOLKWAYS (3825 "Women Blues
of Champion Jack Dupree") 20-30   61
GNP/CRESCENDO 8-12   74
JAZZMAN 5-10   82
KING (735 "Champion Jack Dupree
Sings the Blues") 50-60   61
KING (1084 "Walking the Blues") 10-15   70
LONDON 10-15   69
OKEH (12103 "Cabbage Greens") . . . 25-35   63
STORYVILLE 5-10   82
Members: Jack Dupree; Larry Dale; Al Lucas; Gene Moore;
Stick McGhee; Willie Jones; Pete Brown.
Also see McGHEE, Brownie
Also see McGHEE, Stick

DUPREE, Champion Jack, and Mickey Baker
LPs: 10/12–inch 33rpm
SIRE 10-15   69

DUPREE, Robbie
Singles: 7–inch
ELEKTRA 2-4   80-81
Picture Sleeves
ELEKTRA 2-4   80
LPs: 10/12–inch 33rpm
ELEKTRA 5-10   80-81

DUPREES
Singles: 7–inch
COED 5-10   62-65
COLLECTABLES 2-4   80
COLUMBIA 8-12   65-67
ERIC 2-4
HERITAGE 4-8   68-70
LOST-NITE 3-5
(Black vinyl.)
LOST-NITE 10-15
(Colored vinyl.)
RCA 3-6   75
Picture Sleeves
COLUMBIA 10-20   66
HERITAGE 4-8   68
LPs: 10/12–inch 33rpm
COED (905 "You Belong to Me") . . . 50-100   62
COED (906 "Have You Heard") 50-100   63
COLLECTABLES 6-8   80
HERITAGE (35002 "Total Recall") . . . 20-30   68
POST (1000 "The Duprees Sing") . . . 15-25
Members: Joey "Vann" Canzano; Mike Arnone; Tom Bialaglow;
John Salvato; Joe Santollo.
Also see ITALIAN ASPHALT and Pavement Company

DURAN DURAN
Singles: 12–inch 33/45rpm
CAPITOL 4-8   82-87
Singles: 7–inch
CAPITOL (Black vinyl) 2-4   82-90
CAPITOL (Colored vinyl) 5-10   86-87
(Promotional issues only.)
HARVEST 2-4   81-82
Picture Sleeves
CAPITOL 2-4   83-89

EPs: 7–inch 33/45rpm
HARVEST 15-20   82
LPs: 10/12–inch 33rpm
CAPITOL 5-10   82-90
HARVEST (12158 "Duran Duran") . . . 8-12   82
MFSL (182 "Seven and
the Ragged Tiger") 15-25   87
Members: John Taylor, Andy Taylor; Simon LeBon.
Also see ARCADIA
Also see BAND AID
Also see POWER STATION
Also see TAYLOR, Andy
Also see TAYLOR, John

DURANTE, Jimmy
Singles: 78rpm
BRUNSWICK 5-10   34
DECCA 4-8   44-57
Singles: 7–inch
DECCA 4-8   51-59
WARNER 2-4   63-70
EPs: 7–inch 33/45rpm
DECCA 5-10   54-56
MGM 5-10   53-55
VARSITY 5-10   55
LPs: 10/12–inch 33rpm
DECCA (9000 series) 15-25   54-56
DECCA (78000 series) 8-12   70
HARMONY 8-12   68
LIGHT 5-10   71
LION 15-20   56
MGM (3200 series) 15-25   55
MGM (4200 series) 10-15   64
ROULETTE 15-20   61
WARNER 10-15   63-67
Also see GOLDSBORO, Bobby / Jimmy Durante
Also see MARTIN, Dean
Also see PRESLEY, Elvis

DURY, Ian, and the Blockheads
Singles: 7–inch
STIFF (Except 1179) 2-4   79-81
STIFF (1179 "Hit Me with Your
Rhythm Stick") 3-5   79
(Promotional issue only. Bonus issued with the *Do
It Yourself* LP.)
(Promotional issue only.)
Picture Sleeves
STIFF/EPIC (Except 1179) 2-4   79-81
STIFF/EPIC (1179 "Hit Me with Your
Rhythm Stick") 3-5   78
(Promotional issue only. Bonus issue with the *Do It
Yourself* LP.)
STIFF/COLUMBIA (23 "Sweet
Gene Vincent") 4-6
(Yellow vinyl.)
LPs: 10/12–inch 33rpm
POLYDOR 5-10   81
STIFF/EPIC (Except 36104) 5-10   78-82

STIFF/EPIC (36104 "Do It Yourself") . 10-15   79
(Includes bonus single *Hit Me with Your Rhythm Stick*.)
Also see JANKEL, Chas

DUSK
Singles: 7–inch
BELL 4-6   71-72
Member: Peggy Santiglia.
Also see ANGELS

DUVALL, Huelyn
Singles: 78rpm
CHALLENGE 10-15   58
Singles: 7–inch
CHALLENGE (1012 "Comin' Or
Goin") 25-35   58
(Blue label.)
CHALLENGE (1012 "Comin' Or
Goin") 10-20   58
(Maroon label.)
CHALLENGE (59002 "Humdinger") . . 10-20   58
CHALLENGE (59014 "Little Boy Blue")15-25   58
CHALLENGE (59025 "Juliette") 10-20   58
CHALLENGE (59069 "Pucker Paint") 15-25   59
STARFIRE (600 "It's No Wonder") . . . 30-35   59
TWINKLE (506 "Beautiful Dreamer") . 40-60

DYER, Ada
Singles: 7–inch
MOTOWN 2-4   88

DYKE and the Blazers
Singles: 7–inch
ARTCO 8-10   67
ORIGINAL SOUND 4-8   67-70
LPs: 10/12–inch 33rpm
ORIGINAL SOUND (8876 "Funky Broadway") 30-3567
ORIGINAL SOUND (8877 "Dyke's
Greatest Hits") 20-30   67
Member: Arlester "Dyke" Christian.

DYLAN, Bob
(Bob Dylan with the Band)
Singles: 7–inch
ASYLUM 3-6   74
COLUMBIA (10106 "Tangled Up in
Blue") 8-12   75
COLUMBIA (10217 "Million Dollar
Bash") 8-12   75
COLUMBIA (10245 "Hurricane") 3-5   75
COLUMBIA (10298 "Mozambique") 3-5   75
COLUMBIA (10454 "Rita Mae") 8-12   77
COLUMBIA (10805 "Baby Stop Crying") 4-8   78
COLUMBIA (10851 "Changing of
the Guards") 8-12   78
COLUMBIA (11000 series) 2-5   79-80
COLUMBIA (13-0000 series) 2-4
COLUMBIA (18-0000 series) 2-4   81
COLUMBIA (38-0000 through 0400) ... 2-4   84-86
COLUMBIA (42656 "Mixed Up
Confusion") 275-325   63

COLUMBIA (42856 "Blowin' in
the Wind") 150-200   63
COLUMBIA (43242 "Subterranean
Homesick Blues") 10-20   65
(Gray label.)
COLUMBIA (43242 "Subterranean
Homesick Blues") 4-8   65
(Red label.)
COLUMBIA (43346 "Like a Rolling
Stone") 4-8   65
COLUMBIA (43389 "Positively
4th Street") 10-20   65
(Gray label.)
COLUMBIA (43389 "Positively
4th Street") 4-8   65
(Red label.)
COLUMBIA (43477 "Can You Please
Crawl Out Your Window") 10-12   65
COLUMBIA (43683 "I Want You") 4-8   66
COLUMBIA (43541 "One of Us
Must Know") 8-12   66
COLUMBIA (43592 "Rainy Day
Women #12 and 35) 4-8   66
COLUMBIA (43792 "Just Like
a Woman") 4-8   66
COLUMBIA (44069 "Leopard-Skin
Pill-Box Hat") 8-12   67
COLUMBIA (44826 "I Threw It
All Away") 8-10   69
COLUMBIA (44926 "Lay Lady, Lay") ... 4-8   69
COLUMBIA (45004 "Tonight I'll Be
Staying Here with You) 8-10   69
COLUMBIA (45199 "Wigwam") 5-10   69
COLUMBIA (45409 "Watching the
River Flow") 5-10   71
COLUMBIA (45516 "George Jackson") 8-10   71
COLUMBIA (45913 "Knockin' on
Heaven's Door") 3-5   73
COLUMBIA (45982 "A Fool Such As I") . 3-5   73
Picture Sleeves
COLUMBIA (02510 "Heart of Mine") ... 4-8   81
COLUMBIA (10245 "Hurricane") 25-50   75
COLUMBIA (11235 "Slow Train") 5-10   80
COLUMBIA (43242 "Subterranean
Homesick Blues") 300-500   65
(Promotional issue only.)
COLUMBIA (43242 "Subterranean
Homesick Blues") 40-60   65
(Columbia "Hit Pack" picture sleeve.)
COLUMBIA (43389 "Positively
4th Street") 25-35   65
COLUMBIA (43683 "I Want You") ... 20-25   66
Promotional Singles
ASYLUM 8-12   74
COLUMBIA (25 "All the Tired Horses") 30-40   70
COLUMBIA (1039 "If Not for You") .. 30-40   71
COLUMBIA (10106 "Tangled Up
in Blue") 10-20   75
COLUMBIA (10245 "Hurricane") 15-20   75

COLUMBIA (10245 "Hurricane") 20-30   75
(Compact 33 Single.)
COLUMBIA (10298 "Mozambique") ... 8-10   75
COLUMBIA (10454 "Rita Mae") 10-20   77
COLUMBIA (10805 "Baby Stop
Crying") 10-20   78
COLUMBIA (11000 series) 4-8   79-80
COLUMBIA (18-0000 series) 3-6   81
COLUMBIA (38-0000 through 0400) ... 3-5   84-86
COLUMBIA (42856 "Blowin' in
the Wind") 250-400   63
(Price includes "Rebel with a Cause," a letter-insert
introducing Dylan, which represents $100 to $200
of the value.)
COLUMBIA (43242 "Subterranean
Homesick Blues") 40-60   65
(Black vinyl.)
COLUMBIA (43242 "Subterranean
Homesick Blues") 50-75   65
(Colored vinyl.)
COLUMBIA (43346 "Like a Rolling
Stone") 40-60   65
(Black vinyl.)
COLUMBIA (43346 "Like a Rolling
Stone") 50-75   65
(Colored vinyl.)
COLUMBIA (43389 "Positively
4th Street") 30-40   65
(Black vinyl.)
COLUMBIA (43389 "Positively
4th Street") 50-75   65
(Colored vinyl.)
COLUMBIA (43389 "Positively
4th Street") 75-100   65
(Outtake promo. Has an alternate take of *Can You
Please Crawl Out Your Window*.)
COLUMBIA (43477 "Can You Please
Crawl Out Your Window") 40-60   65
COLUMBIA (43683 "I Want You") ... 30-45   66
(Black vinyl.)
COLUMBIA (43683 "I Want You") ... 50-75   66
(Colored vinyl.)
COLUMBIA (43541 "One of Us
Must Know") 40-55   66
COLUMBIA (43592 "Rainy Day
Women #12 and 35") 30-40   66
COLUMBIA (43792 "Just Like a
Woman") 30-40   66
(Black vinyl.)
COLUMBIA (43792 "Just Like A
Woman") 50-75   66
(Colored vinyl.)
COLUMBIA (44069 "Leopard-Skin
Pill-Box Hat") 30-40   67
COLUMBIA (44826 "I Threw It
All Away") 15-25   69
COLUMBIA (44926 "Lay Lady,
Lay") 15-25   69

COLUMBIA (45004 "Tonight I'll Be
Staying Here with You") 15-25   69
COLUMBIA (45199 "Wigwam") 15-25   69
COLUMBIA (45409 "Watching the
River Flow") 15-25   71
COLUMBIA (45516 "George Jackson")15-25   71
COLUMBIA (45913 "Knockin' on
Heaven's Door") 10-20   73
COLUMBIA (45982 "A Fool Such As I")10-20   73
COLUMBIA (75606 "Blowin' in
the Wind") 250-400   63
("Special Album Excerpt.")

EPs: 7–inch 33/45rpm

COLUMBIA (319 "Step Lively") ... 100-150   65
COLUMBIA (9128 "Bringing It All
Back Home") 125-175   65
(Jukebox issue only.)
COLUMBIA/PLAYBACK 75-100   73
(Promotional issue only. Contains four tracks by
four different artists.)

LPs: 10/12–inch 33rpm

ASYLUM (201 "Before the Flood") ... 10-15   74
ASYLUM (1003 "Planet Waves") 15-20   74
(Without cut corner.)
ASYLUM (1003 "Planet Waves") 8-10   74
(With cut corner.)
ASYLUM (EQ-1003 "Planet Waves") . 15-20   74
(Quadrophonic.)
COLUMBIA (C2L-41 "Blonde
on Blonde") 40-60   66
(Monaural. With "female photos" on inside of
jacket.)
COLUMBIA (C2L-41 "Blonde
on Blonde") 15-25   66
(Monaural. With Dylan photo replacing female
photos.)
COLUMBIA (C2S-841 "Blonde
on Blonde") 40-60   66
(Stereo. With "female photos" on inside of jacket.)
COLUMBIA (C2S-841 "Blonde
on Blonde") 15-25   66
(Stereo. With Dylan photo replacing female
photos.)
COLUMBIA (CL-1779 "Bob Dylan") 125-175   62
(Monaural. Red and black label with six Columbia
"eye" boxes.)

COLUMBIA (CL-1779 "Bob Dylan") . . 20-30   62
(Monaural. Red label, without six Columbia "eye"
boxes.)

COLUMBIA (CL-1986 "The
Freewheelin' Bob Dylan") 2000-3000   63
(Monaural. With *Let Me Die in My Footsteps,
Talkin' John Birch Society Blues, Gamblin' Willie's
Dead Man's Hand,* and *Rocks and Gravel,* which
may also be shown as *Solid Gravel.* We suggest
verification of the above tracks by listening to the
LP, rather than accepting the information printed
on the label. In fact, some copies of the rare
pressing have reissue labels. Identification
numbers of this press are XLP-58717-1A and
XLP-58718-1A.)

COLUMBIA (CL-1986 "The
Freewheelin' Bob Dylan") 20-30   63
(Monaural. With the above tracks replaced by four
others.)

COLUMBIA (CL-2105 "The Times They
Are A-Changin") 20-30   64
(Monaural.)

COLUMBIA (CL-2193 "Another
Side of Bob Dylan") 15-20   64
(Monaural.)

COLUMBIA (CL-2328 "Bringin'
It All Back Home") 15-25   65
(Monaural.)

COLUMBIA (CL-2389 "Highway
61 Revisited") 100-125   65
(Monaural. With alternate take of *From a Buick 6.*
The alternate take begins with a harmonica riff.
This pressing has a "-1" at the end of the
identification number, stamped in the vinyl trailoff.)

COLUMBIA (CL-2389 "Highway
61 Revisited") 10-15   65
(Monaural.)

COLUMBIA (KCL-2663 "Bob
Dylan's Greatest Hits") 15-25   67
(Monaural.)

COLUMBIA (CL-2804 "John Wesley
Harding") 60-100   68
(Monaural.)

COLUMBIA (CS-8579 "Bob Dylan") 150-200   62
(Stereo. Red and black label with six Columbia
"eye" boxes.)

COLUMBIA (CS-8579 "Bob Dylan") . . 25-40   62
(Stereo. Red label, without six Columbia "eye"
boxes.)

COLUMBIA (PC-8579 "Bob Dylan") . . . 5-10

COLUMBIA (CS-8786 "The
Freewheelin' Bob Dylan") 20-30   63
(Stereo.)

COLUMBIA (PC-8786 "The
Freewheelin' Bob Dylan") 5-10

COLUMBIA (CS-8905 "The Times They
Are A-Changin") 20-30   64
(Stereo.)

COLUMBIA (CS-8993 "Another
Side of Bob Dylan") 15-25   64
(Stereo.)

COLUMBIA (CS-9128 "Bringin'
It All Back Home") 15-25   65
(Stereo.)

COLUMBIA (CS-9189 "Highway
61 Revisited") 100-150   65
(Stereo. With alternate take of *From a Buick 6.* The
alternate take begins with a harmonica riff. This
pressing has a "-1" at the end of the identification
number, stamped in the vinyl trailoff.)

COLUMBIA (CS-9189 "Highway
61 Revisited") 10-20   65
(Stereo.)

COLUMBIA (KCS-9463 "Bob
Dylan's Greatest Hits") 15-25   67
(Stereo.)

COLUMBIA (CS-9604 "John Wesley
Harding") 20-30   68
(Stereo.)

COLUMBIA (KCS-9825 "Nashville
Skyline") 8-12   69

COLUMBIA (C2X-30050 "Self
Portrait") 50-60   70
(With "360-Degree Stereo" at bottom of label.)

COLUMBIA (C2X-30050 "Self
Portrait") 10-15   70
(Without "360-Degree Stereo" at bottom of label.)

COLUMBIA (KC-30290 "New Morning") 8-10   70

COLUMBIA (KC-31120 "Greatest Hits
Vol. 2") 10-12   71

COLUMBIA (KC-32460 "Pat Garrett
and Billy the Kid") 8-10   73
(Soundtrack.)

COLUMBIA (KC-32747 "Dylan") 8-10   73

COLUMBIA (CQ-32872 "Nashville
Skyline") 25-35   74
(Quadrophonic.)

COLUMBIA (PC-33235 "Blood on
the Tracks") 25-35   75
(With mural pictured on the back cover.)

COLUMBIA (PC-33235 "Blood on
the Tracks") 8-12   75
(With liner notes on the back cover.)

COLUMBIA (PC2-33682 "The
Basement Tapes") 10-12   75

COLUMBIA (PC-33893 "Desire") 8-10   76

COLUMBIA (PCQ-33893 "Desire") . . 25-35   76
(Quadrophonic.)

COLUMBIA (PC-34349 "Hard Rain") . . 8-10   76

COLUMBIA (JC-35453 "Street Legal") 8-10   78

COLUMBIA (PC2-36067 "Bob Dylan
at Budokan") 8-10   79

COLUMBIA (FC-36120 "Slow
Train Comin") 8-10   79

COLUMBIA (FC-36553 "Saved") 8-10   80

COLUMBIA (FC-37496 "Shot of Love") 8-10   81

COLUMBIA (PC-38819 "Infidels") 8-10   83

COLUMBIA (C5X-38830"Biograph") . 20-30   85
(Boxed set of five LPs, includes 36-page booklet.)
COLUMBIA (FC-39944 "Real Live") . . . 5-10   84
COLUMBIA (FC-40110 "Empire
Burlesque") 5-10   85
COLUMBIA (OC-40439 "Knocked Out
Loaded") 5-10   86
COLUMBIA (OC-40957 "Down in
the Groove") 5-10   88
COLUMBIA (HC-43235 "Blood on
the Tracks") 20-30   83
(Half-speed mastered.)
COLUMBIA (45281 "Oh Mercy") 5-10   89
COLUMBIA (46794 "Under the
Red Sky") 5-10   90
COLUMBIA (47382 "The Bootleg Series
Volumes 1 - 3") 15-20   89
COLUMBIA (HC-49825 "Nashville
Skyline") 20-30   81
(Half-speed mastered.)
FOLKWAYS (5322 "Bob Dylan
Vs. A.J. Weberman") 100-175
ISLAND (1 "Before the Flood") 25-30   74
MFSL (114 "The Times They
Are a-Changing") 10-15
Promotional LPs
ASYLUM (201 "Before the Flood") . . . 25-40   74
ASYLUM (1003 "Planet Waves") 25-40   74
COLUMBIA (422 "Renaldo and
Clara") 25-35   76
(Soundtrack.)
COLUMBIA (798 "Saved") 25-35   80
COLUMBIA (1259 "Dylan London
Interview") 25-35   80
COLUMBIA (1263 "Shot of Love") . . . 25-35   81
COLUMBIA (1471 "Electric Lunch") . . 15-25   83
COLUMBIA (1770 "Infidels") 10-20   83
COLUMBIA (C2L-41 "Blonde
on Blonde") 60-75   66
(Monaural. With "female photos" on inside of
jacket.)
COLUMBIA (C2S-841 "Blonde
on Blonde") 60-75   66
(Stereo. With "female photos" on inside of jacket.)
COLUMBIA (CL-1779 "Bob Dylan") 200-300   62
(Monaural.)
COLUMBIA (CL-1986 "The
Freewheelin' Bob Dylan") 2000-3000   63
(Monaural. With *Let Me Die in My Footsteps,
Talkin' John Birch Society Blues, Gamblin' Willie's
Dead Man's Hand,* and *Rocks and Gravel,* which
may also be shown as *Solid Gravel.* We suggest
verification of the above tracks by listening to the
LP, rather than accepting the information printed
on the label. In fact, some copies of the rare
pressing have reissue labels. Identification
numbers of this press are XLP-58717-1A and
XLP-58718-1A.)

COLUMBIA (CL-1986 "The
Freewheelin' Bob Dylan") 75-100   63
(Monaural. With the above tracks replaced by four
others.)
COLUMBIA (CL-2105 "The Times
They Are A-Changin") 75-100   64
COLUMBIA (CL-2193 "Another
Side of Bob Dylan") 60-75   64
(Monaural.)
COLUMBIA (CL-2328 "Bringin'
It All Back Home") 60-75   65
(Monaural.)
COLUMBIA (CL-2389 "Highway
61 Revisited") 60-75   65
(Monaural.)
COLUMBIA (KCL-2663 "Bob
Dylan's Greatest Hits") 60-75   67
(Monaural.)
COLUMBIA (CL-2804 "John Wesley
Harding") 50-60   68
(Monaural.)
COLUMBIA (CS-8579 "Bob Dylan") 200-300   62
(Stereo.)
COLUMBIA (CS-8786 "The
Freewheelin' Bob Dylan") 75-100   63
(Stereo.)
COLUMBIA (CS-8905 "The Times
They Are A-Changin") 75-100   64
(Stereo.)
COLUMBIA (CS-8993 "Another
Side of Bob Dylan") 60-75   64
(Stereo.)
COLUMBIA (CS-9128 "Bringin'
It All Back Home") 60-75   65
(Stereo.)
COLUMBIA (CS-9189 "Highway
61 Revisited") 60-75   65
(Stereo.)
COLUMBIA (KCS-9463 "Bob
Dylan's Greatest Hits") 60-75   67
(Stereo.)
COLUMBIA (KCS-9825 "Nashville
Skyline") 50-60   69
COLUMBIA (30050 "Self Portrait") . . 50-60   70
COLUMBIA (31120 "Greatest Hits
Vol. 2") 10-20   71
COLUMBIA (32460 "Pat Garrett
and Billy the Kid") 15-25   73
(Soundtrack.)
COLUMBIA (32747 "Dylan") 10-15   73
COLUMBIA (33235 "Blood on
the Tracks") 20-25   75
COLUMBIA (33682 "The
Basement Tapes") 10-15   75
COLUMBIA (33893 "Desire") 10-15   76
COLUMBIA (34349 "Hard Rain") 10-15   76
COLUMBIA (35453 "Street Legal") . . 10-15   78
COLUMBIA (36067 "Bob Dylan
at Budokan") 10-20   79

COLUMBIA (36120 "Slow
Train Comin") 10-15   79
COLUMBIA (36553 "Saved") 10-15   80
COLUMBIA (37496 "Shot of Love") .. 10-15   81
COLUMBIA (38819 "Infidels") 10-15   83
COLUMBIA (39944 "Real Live") 10-15   84
COLUMBIA (40110 "Empire
Burlesque") 10-15   85
COLUMBIA (40439 "Knocked Out
Loaded") 10-15   86
COLUMBIA (43235 "Blood on
the Tracks") 25-35   83
(Half-speed mastered.)
COLUMBIA (49825 "Nashville
Skyline") 25-35   81
(Half-speed mastered.)
FOLKWAYS (5322 "Bob Dylan Vs.
A.J. Weberman") 75-100
ISLAND (1 "Before the Flood") 25-35   74
WESTWOOD ONE ("Dylan on
Dylan") 150-175   84
(Five-LP set. Issued for radio broadcast only.)
WESTWOOD ONE ("Dylan on
Dylan") 100-125   84
(Three-LP set. Shorter version of the above show.)
Also see BAND
Also see BELAFONTE, Harry
Also see HARRISON, George
Also see SAHM, Doug
Also see TRAVELING WILBURYS
Also see U.S.A. for AFRICA

DYLAN, Bob, and the Grateful Dead
LPs: 10/12-inch 33rpm
COLUMBIA (45056 "Dylan and
the Dead") 5-10   89
Also see GRATEFUL DEAD

**DYLAN, Bob, and the Heartbreakers /
Michael Rubini**
Singles: 7-inch
MCA 2-4   86
Also see DYLAN, Bob
Also see PETTY, Tom, and the Heartbreakers

DYNAMIC BREAKERS
Singles: 12-inch 33/45rpm
SUNNYVIEW 4-6   85
Singles: 7-inch
SUNNYVIEW 2-4   85

DYNAMIC CORVETTES
Singles: 7-inch
ABET 3-5   75

DYNAMICS
Singles: 7-inch
ARC (4450 "Enchanted Love") 15-25   59
CAPRI (104 "No One But You") 50-75   59
DELTA 10-15   59
DYNAMIC 12-25   59-62
GUARANTEED 5-10   59
IMPALA (501 "Moonlight") 25-35   58

LAVERE 8-12   61
LIBAN 10-20   62
LIBERTY 8-12   63
REPRISE 8-12   63
SEECO (6001 "Moonlight") 15-25   59
U.S.A. (769 "Summertime") 15-20   64
WARNER RECORDS (1016 "A Hundred
Million Lies") 50-75   59

DYNA-SORES
Singles: 7-inch
RENDEZVOUS 8-12   60
Member: Jimmy Norman.
Also see NORMAN, Jimmy

DYNASTY
Singles: 7-inch
SOLAR 2-4   79-88
LPs: 10/12-inch 33rpm
SOLAR 5-10   79-82
Members: Kevin Spencer; Nidra Beard; Linda Carriere; Leon
Sylvers.
Also see DE BLANK

DYNATONES
Singles: 7-inch
HBR 4-8   66
ST. CLAIR 8-10   66
LPs: 10/12-inch 33rpm
HBR 20-25   66

DYNELL, Johnny, and the New York 88
Singles: 12-inch 33/45rpm
ACME 4-6   83-84

DYSON, Clifton
Singles: 12-inch 33/45rpm
MOTOWN 4-8   79
Singles: 7-inch
MOTOWN 2-4   79
NETWORK 2-4   82
LPs: 10/12-inch 33rpm
AFTER HOURS 5-10   82
NETWORK 5-10   82

DYSON, Ronnie
Singles: 12-inch 33/45rpm
COTILLION 4-6   83
Singles: 7-inch
COLUMBIA 2-5   69-78
COTILLION 2-4   82-83
Picture Sleeves
COLUMBIA 3-5   73-75
LPs: 10/12-inch 33rpm
COLUMBIA 8-10   70-79
COTILLION 5-10   82-83

E

E., Sheila
(Sheila Escovedo)
Singles: 12-inch 33/45rpm
WARNER 4-6   84-85
Singles: 7-inch
PAISLEY PARK 2-4   85-87
WARNER 2-4   84-85
LPs: 10/12-inch 33rpm
PAISLEY PARK 5-10   85-87
WARNER 5-10   84-91
  Also see KRUSH GROOVE ALL-STARS
  Also see PRINCE

EBN/OZN
Singles: 12-inch 33/45rpm
ELEKTRA 4-6   84
Singles: 7-inch
ELEKTRA 2-4   84
LPs: 10/12-inch 33rpm
ELEKTRA 5-10   84
  Members: Ebn; Ozn.

ELO:
  see ELECTRIC LIGHT ORCHESTRA

EQ
Singles: 12-inch 33/45rpm
ATLANTIC 4-6   86

E.U.
(Experience Unlimited)
Singles: 7-inch
ISLAND 2-4   86
MANHATTAN 2-4   88
Picture Sleeves
MANHATTAN 2-4   88
LPs: 10/12-inch 33rpm
ISLAND 5-10   86
VIRGIN 5-8   89

EAGER, Brenda Lee
(Brenda Lee Eager and Peaches)
Singles: 12-inch 33/45rpm
PRIVATE I 4-6   84
Singles: 7-inch
MERCURY 3-5   72-74
PLAYBOY 3-5   75
PRIVATE I 2-4   84
  Also see BUTLER, Jerry, and Brenda Lee Eager

EAGLES
Singles: 7-inch
ASYLUM 3-5   72-80
FULL MOON 2-4   81
Picture Sleeves
ASYLUM 3-5   72-80

LPs: 10/12-inch 33rpm
ASYLUM 8-12   72-82
MFSL (126 "Hotel California") 20-30   84
  Members: Don Felder; Glenn Frey; Don Henley; Randy Meisner;
  Timothy B. Schmit; Joe Walsh; Bernie Leadon.
  Also see FELDER, Don
  Also see FREY, Glenn
  Also see HENLEY, Don
  Also see LEADON, Bernie
  Also see LEE, Johnny / Eagles
  Also see MEISNER, Randy
  Also see NEWMAN, Randy
  Also see POCO
  Also see RONSTADT, Linda
  Also see SCHMIT, Timothy B.
  Also see SIMMONS, Patrick
  Also see VITALE, Joe
  Also see WALSH, Joe

EARLAND, Charles
(Charles Earland's Odyssey; Charlie Earland Jr.)
Singles: 7-inch
COLUMBIA 2-4   81-82
MERCURY 3-5   76
PRESTIGE 3-5   70-74
QUAKER TOWN 4-8   64
LPs: 10/12-inch 33rpm
COLUMBIA 5-10   80
MERCURY 5-10   76-78
MUSE 5-10   80
PRESTIGE 5-10   70-75
RARE BIRD 5-10   71
TRIP 5-10   73

EARLE, Steve
(Steve Earle and the Dukes)
Singles: 12-inch 33/45rpm
MCA 4-6   86
Singles: 7-inch
EPIC 2-4   84-85
MCA 2-4   86-90
UNI 2-4   88
Picture Sleeves
EPIC 2-4   84
EPs: 7-inch 33/45rpm
LSI 5-10   82
LPs: 10/12-inch 33rpm
MCA 5-10   86-90
UNI 5-8   88

EARL-JEAN
(Earl Jean McCree)
Singles: 7-inch
COLPIX 4-8   64
  Also see COOKIES
  Also see KING, Ben E.

EARLS
Singles: 12-inch 33/45rpm
WOODBURY 6-10   76-77
Singles: 7-inch
ABC 5-10   68
ATLANTIC 2-4
BARRY 4-8   63
CLIFTON 3-5   74

EARLS / Pretenders

EARONS

EARTH OPERA

EARTH QUAKE:
see EARTHQUAKE

EARTH, WIND & FIRE

EARTH, WIND & FIRE and the Emotions

EARTH, WIND & FIRE and Ramsey Lewis

EARTHQUAKE
(Earth Quake)

Also see KIHN, Greg, Band / Earthquake / Modern Lovers /
   Rubinoos
Also see KIHN, Greg, Band / Earthquake / Rubinoos /
   Jonathan Richman

EAST, Thomas
(Thomas East and the Fabulous Playboys)
Singles: 7–inch
LION 3-5   73
MGM 3-5   73
TODDLIN' TOWN 4-8   68-69

EAST COAST
Singles: 7–inch
RSO 3-5   79
   Members: Gregory Johnson; Larry Blackmon; Gary Dow; Eric
   Rurham; Anthony Lockett; Arnett Leftenant; Nathan Leftenant.
   Also see CAMEO

EAST L.A. CAR POOL
Singles: 7–inch
GRC 3-5   75

EASTBOUND EXPRESSWAY
Singles: 7–inch
AVI 2-4   78-79

EASTON, Elliot
Singles: 7–inch
ELEKTRA 2-4   85
LPs: 10/12–inch 33rpm
ELEKTRA 5-10   85
   Also see CARS

EASTON, Sheena
Singles: 12–inch 33/45rpm
EMI AMERICA 4-6   81-86
Singles: 7–inch
EMI AMERICA 2-4   81-86
LIBERTY 2-4   81
MCA 2-4   88-91
RCA 2-4   89
Picture Sleeves
EMI AMERICA 3-6   81-86
RCA 2-4   89
LPs: 10/12–inch 33rpm
EMI AMERICA 5-10   81-86
MCA 5-8   88-91

EASTON, Sheena, and Kenny Rogers
Singles: 7–inch
LIBERTY 2-4   83
LPs: 10/12–inch 33rpm
LIBERTY 5-10   84
   Also see EASTON, Sheena
   Also see ROGERS, Kenny

EASTWOOD, Clint
Singles: 7–inch
CAMEO (240 "Rowdy") 10-20   63
CERTRON 4-6   70
GOTHIC (005 "Unknown Girl") 10-20   61
PARAMOUNT 4-8   69
WARNER 2-4   81

Picture Sleeves
CAMEO (240 "Rowdy") 30-50   63
CERTRON 5-8   70
GOTHIC (005 "Unknown Girl") 10-20   61
LPs: 10/12–inch 33rpm
CAMEO (1056 "Cowboy Favorites") 75-125   63
   Also see CHARLES, Ray, and Clint Eastwood
   Also see HAGGARD, Merle, and Clint Eastwood
   MARVIN, Lee / Lee Marvin and Clint Eastwood

EASTWOOD, Clint, and T.G. Sheppard
Singles: 7–inch
WARNER 2-4   84
   Also see EASTWOOD, Clint
   Also see SHEPPARD, T.G.

EASY STREET
Singles: 7–inch
CAPRICORN 3-5   76
LPs: 10/12–inch 33rpm
CAPRICORN 8-10   76-77

EASYBEATS
Singles: 7–inch
ASCOT 8-12   66
RARE EARTH 4-8   69
U.A. 5-8   67-69
Picture Sleeves
ASCOT 10-20   66
LPs: 10/12–inch 33rpm
RARE EARTH (517 "Easy Ridin") . . . 10-20   70
RHINO 5-10   85
U.A. (3588 "Friday on My Mind") 30-40   67
   (Monaural.)
U.A. (6588 "Friday on My Mind") 30-40   67
   (Stereo.)
U.A. (6667 "Falling off
   the Edge of the World") 30-40   68
   Also see FLASH and the Pan

EBB TIDE
(Ebb K. Harrison, Sr.)
Singles: 7–inch
SOUND GEMS 3-5   75-76

EBONEE WEBB
(Ebony Web)
Singles: 7–inch
CAPITOL 2-4   81-84
HI 3-5   70-73
LPs: 10/12–inch 33rpm
CAPITOL 5-10   81-84

EBONY
Singles: 12–inch 33/45rpm
QUALITY/RFC 4-6   84

EBONY, IVORY & JADE
Singles: 7–inch
COLUMBIA 3-5   75

EBONY RHYTHM FUNK CAMPAIGN
Singles: 7–inch
INNOVATION 3-5   75

MCA 3-5   72
LPs: 10/12–inch 33rpm
UNI 5-10   72

EBONY WEB: see EBONEE WEBB

EBONYS
Singles: 7–inch
BUDDAH 3-5   76
PHILADELPHIA INT'L 3-5 71-74
LPs: 10/12–inch 33rpm
PHILADELPHIA INT'L 8-10   73
Members: Jenny Holmes; David Beasley; James Tuten; Clarence Vaughn.
Also see CREME D'COCOA

ECHO and the Bunnymen
Singles: 12–inch 33/45rpm
SIRE 5-10 81-86
Singles: 7–inch
SIRE 2-4 81-86
LPs: 10/12–inch 33rpm
SIRE 5-10 81-87

ECHOES
Singles: 7–inch
ASCOT 15-20   65
COLUMBIA 5-10   60
FELSTED (8614 "Angel of Love") ... 30-40   61
SRG (101 "Baby Blue") 25-40   60
SEG-WAY (103 "Baby Blue") 8-12   61
SEG-WAY (106 "Sad Eyes") 8-12   61
SEG-WAY (1002 "Angel of My Heart") 15-20   62
EPs: 7–inch 33/45rpm
CRYSTAL BALL 4-6
Members: Harry Doyle; Tom Morrissey; Tom Duffy.

ECHOES / Four Esquires
Singles: 7–inch
ROULETTE 3-5
Also see ECHOES
Also see FOUR ESQUIRES

ECKSTINE, Billy
Singles: 78rpm
DELUXE 10-15   45
MGM 4-8 47-56
NATIONAL 5-10 45-48
RCA 4-8   56
Singles: 7–inch
A&M 3-5   76
ENTERPRISE 3-5 70-74
MGM 6-12 50-56
MERCURY 4-8 59-64
MOTOWN 3-6 65-68
RCA 4-8   56
ROULETTE 4-6 59-60
Picture Sleeves
MERCURY 5-10   62
EPs: 7–inch 33/45rpm
EMARCY 10-20 54-55
KING 10-20   53
MGM 10-20 50-56

MOTOWN 5-10   65
RENDITION 15-25   50
LPs: 10/12–inch 33rpm
AUDIO LAB (1549 "Mr. B") 30-40   60
EMARCY (26025 "Blues for Sale") 50-100   54
(10–inch LP.)
EMARCY (26027 "Love Songs of Mr. B") 50-100   54
EMARCY (36010 "I Surrender Dear") 30-60   55
EMARCY (36029 "Blues for Sale") .. 25-50   55
EMARCY (36030 "Love Songs of Mr. B") 50-100   55
EMARCY (36129 "Imagination") 25-50   55
ENTERPRISE 5-10 71-74
KING (12 "The Great Mr. B") 75-125   52
(10–inch LP.)
MGM (219 "Tenderly") 30-50   53
(10 Inch LP.)
MGM (257 "I Let a Song Go Out of My Heart") 40-60   55
(10 Inch LP.)
MGM (3176 "Mr. B with a Beat") 15-25   55
MGM (3209 "Rendezvous") 15-25   55
MGM (3275 "That Old Feeling") 15-25   55
MERCURY 15-25 57-64
METRO 10-15   65
MOTOWN 10-15 65-69
NATIONAL (2001 "Billy Eckstine Sings") 75-125   50
(10–inch LP.)
REGENT 20-40 56-57
ROULETTE 15-25   60
SAVOY 8-10 76-79
TRIP 5-10   75
WING 8-12   67
Also see BASIE, Count, and Billy Eckstine
Also see DAMITA JO and Billy Eckstine

ECKSTINE, Billy, and Quincy Jones
Singles: 7–inch
MERCURY 3-6   62
LPs: 10/12–inch 33rpm
MERCURY 15-25   62
Also see JONES, Quincy

ECKSTINE, Billy /Arthur Prysock
LPs: 10/12–inch 33rpm
GUEST STAR 5-10   64
Also see PRYSOCK, Arthur

ECKSTINE, Billy, and Sarah Vaughan
Singles: 7–inch
MERCURY 4-8 57-59
LPs: 10/12–inch 33rpm
GUEST STAR 5-10   64
LION 15-25   59
MERCURY (20316 "Best of Irving Berlin") 20-30   57
Also see ECKSTINE, Billy
Also see VAUGHAN, Sarah

ECSTASY, PASSION & PAIN
Singles: 12–inch
ROULETTE 4-6   84
Singles: 7–inch
ROULETTE 2-4   74-76
LPs: 10/12–inch 33rpm
ROULETTE 8-10   74
Members: Barbara Roy; Bill Gardner; Joseph Williams Jr.; Althea Smith; Alan Tizer.
Also see ROY, Barbara

EDDIE, John
Singles: 7–inch
COLUMBIA 2-4   86
Picture Sleeves
COLUMBIA 2-4   86
LPs: 10/12–inch 33rpm
COLUMBIA 5-10   86

EDDIE & BETTY
Singles: 7–inch
LARK 5-10   59
SIX THOUSAND 10-15   57
WARNER 5-10   59
LPs: 10/12–inch 33rpm
WARNER 15-20   59
Members: Eddie Cole; Betty Cole.

EDDIE & DUTCH
Singles: 7–inch
IVANHOE 3-5   70

EDDIE & ERNIE
Singles: 7–inch
CHESS 4-8   66
EASTERN 4-8   65-66
REVUE 3-5   69
Members: Eddie Campbell; Ernie Johnson.

EDDIE & FREDDIE
Singles: 7–inch
OCTOBER 3-5   77

EDDIE and the Tide
(Eddie Rice)
Singles: 12–inch 33/45rpm
SPIN 4-8   88
(Promotional only.)
Singles: 7–inch
ATCO 2-4   85

EDDIE D.
Singles: 12–inch 33/45rpm
PHILLY WORLD 4-6   85
Singles: 7–inch
PHILLY WORLD 2-4   85

EDDY, Duane
(Duane Eddy and the Rebels; Duane Eddy and the Rebelettes; Duane Eddy and His Rock-a-billies; Duane Eddy and His Twangy Guitar)
Singles: 78rpm
FORD (500 "Ramrod") 15-25   57
JAMIE 10-20   58

Singles: 7–inch
BIG TREE 3-5   72
CAPITOL 2-4   87
COLPIX 5-10   65-66
CONGRESS 3-5   70
ELEKTRA 3-5   77
FORD (500 "Ramrod") 25-30   57
GREGMARK (5 "Caravan") 5-10   61
(Credited to Duane Eddy, but actually by Al Casey.)
JAMIE (73 "Peter Gunn") 25-50   61
(Compact 33 single.)
JAMIE (1100 series) 8-15   58-61
(Monaural.)
JAMIE (1100 series) 15-25   59-60
(Stereo.)
JAMIE (1200 series) 5-10   61-62
RCA 5-10   61-65
REPRISE 5-15   66-68
UNI 4-6   70
Picture Sleeves
CAPITOL 2-4   87
COLPIX 15-25   66
JAMIE 15-25   59-61
RCA 10-15   62-64
EPs: 7–inch 33/45rpm
JAMIE 20-40   59-60
RCA/WURLITZER
DISCOTHEQUE MUSIC 15-25   64
LPs: 10/12–inch 33rpm
CAMDEN 8-15
CAPITOL 8-10   87
COLPIX (490 "Duane A-Go-Go") 25-30   65
COLPIX (494 "Duane Eddy
Does Bob Dylan") 25-30   65
JAMIE (Except 3000, 3011 and
3026) 15-30   59-63
JAMIE (3000 "Have Twangy Guitar
Will Travel") 20-40   58
(White cover.)
JAMIE (3000 "Have Twangy Guitar
Will Travel") 15-30   58
(Red cover.)

JAMIE (3011 "Songs of Our Heritage") 50-75   60
(Colored vinyl.)
JAMIE (3011 "Songs of Our Heritage") 20-30   60
(Gatefold cover. Black vinyl.)
JAMIE (3011 "Songs of Our Heritage") 15-20   61
(Standard cover. Black vinyl.)
JAMIE (3026 "16 Greatest Hits") 15-20   64
RCA ("LPM"/"LSP" series) 20-30   62-66
RCA ("ANL1" series) 5-10   78
REPRISE 15-20   66-67
SIRE 10-15   75
   Members: Duane Eddy; Steve Douglas.
   Also see ART of NOISE
   Also see BLOSSOMS
   Also see CLARK, Sanford, and Duane Eddy
   Also see FOGERTY, John
   Also see JIMMY & DUANE
   Also see THOMAS, B.J.

EDDY, Duane and Mirriam
Singles: 7–inch
REPRISE (0622 "Guitar on My Mind") 10-15   67
   Also see COLTER, Jessi
   Also see EDDY, Duane

EDELMAN, Randy
Singles: 7–inch
ARISTA 2-5   77-79
LION 3-5   73
MGM 3-5   73
SUNFLOWER 3-5   71-72
20TH FOX 3-5   74-76
LPs: 10/12–inch 33rpm
ARISTA 5-10   77-79
LION 8-10   73
MGM 8-10   72
SUNFLOWER 8-12   71
20TH FOX 8-10   74-78

EDEN'S CHILDREN
Singles: 7–inch
ABC 4-6   68
LPs: 10/12–inch 33rpm
ABC 10-15   68

EDGE, Graeme
(Graeme Edge Band)
Singles: 7–inch
LONDON 3-5   77
THRESHOLD 3-5   74
LPs: 10/12–inch 33rpm
LONDON 8-10   77
THRESHOLD 8-10   75
   Also see GURVITZ, Adrian
   Also see MOODY BLUES

EDISON LIGHTHOUSE
Singles: 7–inch
BELL 3-5   70-71

EDMUNDS, Dave
(Dave Edmunds Band)
Singles: 12–inch 33/45rpm
COLUMBIA (Except 1725) 4-8   85-87
(Promotional tissue only.)
COLUMBIA (1725 "Information") 8-12   84
(Picture disc. Promotional issue only.)
Singles: 7–inch
COLUMBIA 2-4   80-85
MAM 3-6   70-71
RCA 3-6   73-74
SWAN SONG 3-5   77-81
Promotional Singles
COLUMBIA (1576 "Run Rudolph Run") . 4-6   82
(Compact 33 single.)
COLUMBIA (03428 "Run Rudolph Run") 3-5   82
Picture Sleeves
COLUMBIA 2-4   85
SWAN SONG 3-5   81
LPs: 10/12–inch 33rpm
ATLANTIC (320 "College Network") . 35-45
(Promotional issue only.)
CAPITOL 5-8   90
COLUMBIA (Except 1725) 5-10   80-87
COLUMBIA (1725 "Information") 15-25   83
(Picture disc. Promotional issue only.)
MAM (3 "Rockpile") 30-40   72
RCA (4000 series) 5-10   82
RCA (5000 series) 10-12
SWAN SONG 8-10   77-81
   Also see DION
   Also see EDMUNDS, Dave
   Also see HARRISON, George / Jeff Beck / Dave Edmunds
   Also see LEWIS, Huey, and the News
   Also see LOWE, Nick, and Dave Edmunds

EDMUNDS, Dave, and Carlene Carter
Singles: 7–inch
WARNER 2-4   80
   Also see CARTER, Carlene

EDSELS
Singles: 7–inch
ABC 2-4   75
CAPITOL 10-20   61-62
DOT (16311 "My Whispering Heart") . 15-20   62
DUB (2843 "Lama Rama Ding Dong") 30-50   58
DUB (2843 "Rama Lama Ding Dong") 10-20   58
(Note variation of title.)
EMBER 10-15   61
LOST-NITE 4-6
MUSICTONE 5-10   64
ROULETTE (4151 "Do You Love Me") 15-20   59
TAMMY (1010 "What Brought
Us Together") 20-30   60
TAMMY (1014 "Three
Precious Words") 20-30   61
TAMMY (1023 "The Girl I Love") 15-25   61
TWIN 10-12   61
   Members: George Jones Jr; Larry Green; James Reynolds;
   Marshall Sewell; Harry Green.

EDWARD BEAR
Singles: 7–inch
CAPITOL 3-5   70-74
Picture Sleeves
CAPITOL 3-5   72-73
LPs: 10/12–inch 33rpm
CAPITOL 8-10   70-73

EDWARDS, Alton
Singles: 12–inch 33/45rpm
COLUMBIA 4-6   82
Singles: 7–inch
COLUMBIA 2-4   82

EDWARDS, Bobby
Singles: 7–inch
BLUEBONNET 5-10   59
CAPITOL 4-8   61-63
CHART 4-6   68
CREST 5-10   61
MANCO 4-8   62
MUSICOR 4-8   65
POLARIS 3-5

EDWARDS, Dee
Singles: 12–inch 33/45rpm
COTILLION 4-6   79
Singles: 7–inch
COTILLION 2-4   78-80
D TOWN 4-8   65
RCA 3-5   72
LPs: 10/12–inch 33rpm
COTILLION 5-10   80

EDWARDS, Dennis
Singles: 12–inch 33/45rpm
GORDY 4-6   84
Singles: 7–inch
GORDY 2-4   84-85
MOTOWN 2-4
LPs: 10/12–inch 33rpm
GORDY 5-10   84-85
Also see CONTOURS
Also see TEMPTATIONS

EDWARDS, Jayne
Singles: 12–inch 33/45rpm
PROFILE 4-6   83-84
Singles: 7–inch
PROFILE 2-4   83-84
LPs: 10/12–inch 33rpm
PROFILE 5-10   84

EDWARDS, Jimmy
(Jimmie Edwards)
Singles: 78rpm
MERCURY 5-10   57
Singles: 7–inch
MERCURY 8-12   57-58
RCA 5-10   59-60

EDWARDS, John
Singles: 7–inch
AWARE 3-5   73-74
BELL 3-5   72
COTILLION 3-5   76-77
LPs: 10/12–inch 33rpm
AWARE 5-10   74
CREED 5-10   75
GENERAL/GRC 5-10   74

EDWARDS, Jonathan
Singles: 7–inch
ATCO 3-5   72-73
CAPRICORN 3-5   71
WARNER 2-4   77
LPs: 10/12–inch 33rpm
AMERICAN MELODY 5-8
ATCO 8-10   72-74
CAPRICORN 10-12   71
REPRISE 8-10   74
WARNER 8-10   77

EDWARDS, Tom
Singles: 7–inch
CORAL 5-8   57

EDWARDS, Tommy
Singles: 78rpm
MGM 4-8   51-58
TOP 10-20   49-50
Singles: 7–inch
MGM (10000 and 11000 series) 5-10   51-55
MGM (12000 and 13000 series) 4-8   55-65
MGM (50000 series) 10-15   59
(Stereo.)
Picture Sleeves
MGM 8-12   60
EPs: 7–inch 33/45rpm
MGM (Except 1001) 10-15   59
MGM (1001 "It's All In the Game") ... 15-25   52
LPs: 10/12–inch 33rpm
LION 10-15   59
MGM 15-25   58-63
METRO 8-12   65
REGENT 20-30   58

EDWARDS, Vincent
Singles: 7–inch
CAPITOL 4-8   62
COLPIX 4-8   65
DECCA (Monaural) 4-8   62-63
DECCA (Stereo 33 series) 5-10   62
KAMA SUTRA 4-6   67
RUSS-FI (1 "Oh Babe") 5-10   59
RUSS-FI (7001 "Why Did You
Leave Me") 4-8   62
Picture Sleeves
COLPIX 4-8   65
DECCA 5-10   62
KAMA SUTRA 4-8   67

EPs: 7–inch 33/45rpm
DECCA 8-10   62
LPs: 10/12–inch 33rpm
DECCA 10-20   62-63

EGAN, Walter
Singles: 7–inch
BACKSTREET 2-4   83
COLUMBIA 2-4   77-79
Picture Sleeves
BACKSTREET 2-4   83
LPs: 10/12–inch 33rpm
BACKSTREET 5-8   83
COLUMBIA 5-10   77-80
Also see BUCKINGHAM, Lindsey
Also see NICKS, Stevie

EGG CREAM
Singles: 7–inch
PYRAMID 3-5   77
LPs: 10/12–inch 33rpm
PYRAMID 5-10   77
Member: Andy Adams.

EGYPTIAN COMBO
Singles: 7–inch
MGM 4-8   66
NORMAN 4-8   64-65

801
LPs: 10/12–inch 33rpm
EDITIONS E.G 5-10   86
Members: Phil Manzanera; Brian Eno.
Also see ENO, Brian
Also see MANZANERA, Phil

8TH DAY
(Eighth Day)
Singles: 7–inch
A&M 2-4   83
INVICTUS 3-5   71-72
KAPP 4-8   67-69
Picture Sleeves
KAPP 5-8   68
LPs: 10/12–inch 33rpm
A&M 5-10   83
INVICTUS 8-10   71-73
KAPP 10-15   68
Members: Melvin Davis; Tony Newton; Bruce Nazarion; Michael
Anthony; Anita Sherman; Carole Stallings; Lynn Harter.

EL CHICANO
Singles: 7–inch
GORDO 3-6   70
KAPP/GORDO 3-5   70-72
MCA 3-5   73-75
RFR 2-4   82
SHADYBROOK 2-4   77-78
LPs: 10/12–inch 33rpm
KAPP 10-12   70-72
MCA 8-10   73-74
Also see TIERRA

EL COCO
(Coco)
Singles: 12–inch 33/45rpm
A.V.I. 4-8   76-85
Singles: 7–inch
A.V.I. 2-5   75-85
LPs: 10/12–inch 33rpm
A.V.I. 5-10   75-85

EL DEBARGE: see DE BARGE, El

EL DORADOS
Singles: 78rpm
VEE JAY (115 "Baby I Need You") . . . 10-20   54
VEE JAY (118 "Annie's Answer") 20-40   54
(With Hazel McCollum.)
VEE JAY (127: "One More Chance") . 35-60   54
VEE JAY (147 "At My Front Door") . . 10-20   55
VEE JAY (165 "I'll Be Forever
Lovin' You") 10-20   55
VEE JAY (180 through 302) 10-20   56-57
Singles: 7–inch
COLLECTABLES 2-4
VEE JAY (115 "Baby I Need You") . . . 50-75   54
(Black vinyl.)
VEE JAY (115 "Baby I Need You") . 250-400   54
(Colored vinyl.)
VEE JAY (118 "Annie's Answer") 50-75   54
(Black vinyl. With Hazel McCollum.)
VEE JAY (118 "Annie's Answer") . . 150-225   54
(Colored vinyl.)
VEE JAY (127: "One More Chance")125-175   54
VEE JAY (147 "At My Front Door") . . 20-30   55
VEE JAY (165 "I'll Be Forever
Lovin' You") 20-30   55
VEE JAY (180 "Now That You've
Gone") 20-30   56
VEE JAY (197 "A Fallen Tear") 30-40   56
VEE JAY (211 "Bim Bam Boom") 30-40   56
VEE JAY (250 "Tears on My Pillow") . 20-30   57
VEE JAY (263 "Three Reasons
Why") 75-100   58
VEE JAY (302 "Lights Are Low") . . . 50-100   58
LPs: 10/12–inch 33rpm
LOST-NITE 5-10   81
VEE JAY (1001 "Crazy Little
Mama") 300-400   58
(Maroon label.)
VEE JAY (1001 "Crazy Little
Mama") 150-250   58
(Black label.)
(Vee Jay 1001 also has two tracks by the
Magnificants.)
Members: Pirkle Lee Moses Jr; Arthur Bassett; Louis Bradley;
James Maddox; Jewel Jones; Richard Nickens; Johnny Carter;
Ted Long; John McCall; Douglas Brown.
Also see MAGNIFICENTS

ELAINE & ELLEN
Singles: 7–inch
OVATION 2-4   80

ELBERT, Donnie
Singles: 78rpm
DELUXE	5-10	57

Singles: 7–inch
ALL PLATINUM	3-5	72
AVCO	3-5	72
COMMAND PERFORMANCE	3-5	
CUB	4-8	63
DELUXE	10-20	57-58
GATEWAY	4-8	64-65
GUSTO	2-4	
JALYNNE (107 "Mommie's Gone")	15-25	60
JALYNNE (110 "Lucille")	5-10	62
RARE BULLET	3-5	70
RED TOP	15-20	
TRIP	3-5	
VEE JAY	5-15	60

LPs: 10/12–inch 33rpm
ALL PLATINUM	10-15	71
DELUXE	10-15	71
KING (629 "The Sensational Donnie Elbert Sings")	50-100	59
SUGARHILL	5-10	81
TRIP	8-10	72

ELBOW BONES and the Racketeers
Singles: 12–inch 33/45rpm
EMI AMERICA	4-6	83

Singles: 7–inch
EMI AMERICA	2-4	84

Members: Ginchy Dan; Stephanie Fuller.

ELECTRIC EXPRESS
Singles: 7–inch
KEY-VAC	4-8	
LINCO	4-8	71

ELECTRIC FLAG
(Electric Flag Music Band)
Singles: 7–inch
ATLANTIC	3-5	74-75
COLUMBIA	4-8	67
SIDEWALK	8-12	67

Picture Sleeves
COLUMBIA	5-10	67

LPs: 10/12–inch 33rpm
ATLANTIC	8-10	74
COLUMBIA	10-15	68-71

Also see BLOOMFIELD, Mike, and Nick Gravenites
Also see MILES, Buddy, Express

ELECTRIC INDIAN
Singles: 7–inch
MARMADUKE	5-10	69
U.A.	3-6	69

LPs: 10/12–inch 33rpm
U.A.	10-15	69

Also see MFSB

ELECTRIC LIGHT ORCHESTRA
(ELO)
Singles: 12–inch 33/45rpm
JET	10-15	78

Singles: 7–inch
JET/CBS	2-5	77-86
JET/U.A. (Except 1000)	3-5	77
JET/U.A. (1000 "Telephone Line")	4-8	77
(Colored vinyl. Promotional issue only.)		
MCA	2-4	80
U.A.	2-4	72-77

Picture Sleeves
JET	3-5	78-79
JET/CBS	2-4	86
JET/U.A.	3-5	77
MCA	2-4	80
U.A.	3-6	74-77

LPs: 10/12–inch 33rpm
JET/CBS (Except 40000 series)	5-10	78-86
JET/CBS (40000 series)	20-25	80-83
(Half-speed mastered.)		
U.A.	10-15	72-76
U.A./JET (Except 123 and 823)	8-12	76-77
U.A./JET (123 "Olé ELO")	25-35	76
(Colored vinyl. Promotional issue only.)		
U.A./JET (823 "Out of the Blue")	10-15	76
(Black vinyl.)		
U.A./JET (823 "Out of the Blue")	30-40	76
(Colored vinyl. Promotional issue only.)		

Also see LYNNE, Jeff
Also see NEWTON-JOHN, Olivia, and the Electric Light Orchestra
Also see WOOD, Roy

ELECTRIC MIND
Singles: 12–inch 33/45rpm
EMERGENCY	4-6	83

ELECTRIC PRUNES
Singles: 7–inch
REPRISE (PRO-277 "Sanctus")	35-45	67
(Promotional issue only.)		
REPRISE (PRO-0305 "Help Us")	25-35	68
(Promotional issue only.)		
REPRISE (0473 "Little Olive")	25-35	66
REPRISE (0532 "I Had too Much to Dream")	10-15	66
REPRISE (0564 "Get Me to the World on Time")	10-20	67
REPRISE (0594 "Dr. Do Good")	10-20	67
REPRISE (0607 "The Great Banana Hoax")	10-20	67
REPRISE (0652 "You Never Had It Better")	20-30	68
REPRISE (0805 "Hey Mr. President")	10-20	69
REPRISE (0833 "Violet Rose")	25-35	69
REPRISE (0858 "Love Grows")	15-20	69

LPs: 10/12–inch 33rpm
REPRISE (6248 "I Had Too Much to Dream")	20-30	67
REPRISE (6262 ("Undreground")	20-30	67

REPRISE (6257 "Mass in F Minor") .. 20-30   67
REPRISE (6262 "Release of an Oath")15-25   68
REPRISE (6342 "Just Good
  Rock 'N' Roll") 15-25   69

ELECTRONIC CONCEPT ORCHESTRA
LPs: 10/12–inch 33rpm

LIMELIGHT 5-10   69
MERCURY 5-10   70
Member: Eddie Higgins.

ELEGANTS
(Vito and the Elegants)
Singles: 7–inch

ABC 2-4   73
ABC-PAR (10219 "Tiny Cloud") 15-20   61
APT (25005 "Little Star") 20-30   58
  (Silver print on black label.)
APT (25005 "Little Star") 10-20   58
  (White or multi-color label.)
APT (25017 "Goodnight") 20-30   58
APT (25029 "Payday") 15-25   59
BIM BAM BOOM 5-10   74
  (Black vinyl.)
BIM BAM BOOM 2-4   74
  (Colored vinyl.)
CRYSTAL BALL 3-5
HULL (732 "Little Boy Blue") 35-40   60
LAURIE (3283 "Barbara Beware") ... 8-12   65
LAURIE (3298 "Wake Up") 15-25   65
MCA 2-4
PHOTO (2662 "A Dream Can
  Come True") 15-20   63
ROULETTE 2-4   71
U.A. 10-15   60-61
Picture Sleeves

CRYSTAL BALL 3-5
PHOTO (2662 "A Dream Can
  Come True") 30-40   63
  (Includes printed insert, which represents $10-$15
  of the value.)
LPs: 10/12–inch 33rpm

CRYSTAL BALL 8-12   90
MURRAY HILL 8-10
  Members: Vito Picone; Frank Tardagno; Carman Romano;
  Jimmy Moschella; Artie Venosa.
  Also see BARBARIANS

ELEKTRIK DRED
Singles: 7–inch

SOUNDS of FLORIDA 2-4   83

ELEKTRO, Eve
Singles: 12–inch 33/45rpm

BLACK SUIT 4-6   84

ELEPHANTS MEMORY
Singles: 7–inch

APPLE (1854 "Liberation
  Special") 4-8   72
BUDDAH 4-8   69
METROMEDIA 3-6   70-71

RCA 3-5   74
Promotional Singles

APPLE (1854 "Liberation Special") .. 15-25   72
Picture Sleeves

APPLE (1854 "Liberation Special") ... 5-10   72
METROMEDIA 4-8   70
LPs: 10/12–inch 33rpm

APPLE 10-15   72
BUDDAH 10-15   69-74
METROMEDIA 10-12   70
MUSE 8-10
RCA 8-10   74
  Also see LENNON, John

ELEVENTH HOUSE
LPs: 10/12–inch 33rpm

ARISTA 5-10   75
VANGUARD (40036 "Introducing the Eleventh
  House with Larry Coryell") 10-20
  (Quadrophonic.)
VANGUARD (79342 "Introducing the Eleventh
  House with Larry Coryell") 8-12
  Members: Larry Coryell; Kenny Nolan.
  Also see CORYELL, Larry

ELGART, Larry
(Larry Elgart and His Manhattan Swing Orchestra)
Singles: 78rpm

DECCA 2-4   54-55
Singles: 7–inch

DECCA 3-6   54-55
MGM 2-5   61-62
RCA 2-5   59-83
EPs: 7–inch 33/45rpm

BRUNSWICK 5-10   54
DECCA 5-10   54-55
LPs: 10/12–inch 33rpm

BRUNSWICK 15-25   54
  (10–inch LPs.)
CAMDEN 5-10   60-73
DECCA 10-20   54-55
MGM 8-12   60-62
RCA 5-10   59-83

ELGART, Les
(Les Elgart and His Orchestra)
Singles: 78rpm

COLUMBIA 2-5   53-57
Singles: 7–inch

COLUMBIA (40000 series,
  except 40180) 3-6   53-62
COLUMBIA (40180 "Bandstand
  Boogie") 15-20   54
COLUMBIA (56767 "Bandstand Twist") 5-10   62
  (Promotional issue only.)
GOLD-MOR 2-4   73
EPs: 7–inch 33/45rpm

COLUMBIA 5-10   53-59
LPs: 10/12–inch 33rpm

COLUMBIA 10-20   53-62
HARMONY 5-10   66

ELGART, Les and Larry
Singles: 7–inch
COLUMBIA 2-4   64-68
SWAMPFIRE 2-4   69
Picture Sleeves
COLUMBIA 3-5   65
LPs: 10/12–inch 33rpm
COLUMBIA (Except 38000 series) 8-15   57-68
COLUMBIA (38000 series) 5-10   82
HARMONY 5-10   68-73
SWAMPFIRE 5-10   70
Also see ELGART, Larry
Also see ELGART, Les

ELGINS
Singles: 7–inch
V.I.P. 4-8   66-71
LPs: 10/12–inch 33rpm
V.I.P. (400 "Darling Baby") 20-30   66
Members: Saundra Mallet; Cleo Miller; Robert Flemming; John Dawson; Norbert McClean.

ELI'S SECOND COMING
Singles: 7–inch
SILVER BLUE 3-5   76-78
Members: Bobby Eli.
Also see MFSB

ELLEDGE, Jimmy
Singles: 7–inch
4 STAR 3-5   75
HICKORY 3-5   65-67
LITTLE DARLIN' 3-5   68
RCA (Except 8012) 4-8   61-64
RCA (8012 "Can't You
See It in My Eyes") 10-20   62
SIMS 3-6   64
Picture Sleeves
RCA 5-10   62-63

ELLIMAN, Yvonne
Singles: 7–inch
DECCA 3-5   71-72
MCA 2-4
RSO 3-5   74-79
LPs: 10/12–inch 33rpm
DECCA 10-15   72
MCA 8-12   73
RSO 6-10   77-79
Also see BISHOP, Stephen, and Yvonne Elliman

ELLINGTON, Duke
Singles: 78rpm
CAPITOL 2-5   53-56
COLUMBIA 2-5   50-53
RCA 2-5   51-55
Singles: 7–inch
BELL 2-4   73
BETHLEHEM 3-6   58-60
CAPITOL (2000 series) 4-8   53-56
COLUMBIA (33000 series) 2-4   76
COLUMBIA (39000 series) 5-10   50-53

COLUMBIA (40000 through
42000 series) 3-6   58-61
RCA (0300 series) 2-4   74
RCA (4000 through 6000 series) 4-8   51-55
REPRISE 3-5   67
EPs: 7–inch 33/45rpm
BRUNSWICK 10-20   54
CAPITOL 10-20   53-56
COLUMBIA 10-20   50-56
RCA.......................... 10-20   52-60
ROYALE 10-20
LPs: 10/12–inch 33rpm
ALLEGIANCE 5-8   84
ALLEGRO 25-50   54
(10–inch LPs.)
ATLANTIC 5-10   71-82
BASF 5-10   73
BETHLEHEM 15-30   56-57
BRIGHT ORANGE 5-10   73
BRUNSWICK (54000 series) 15-30   56
BRUNSWICK (58000 series) 30-50   54
(10–inch LPs.)
CAMDEN (400 series) 15-25   58
CAPITOL (400 series) 25-50   53
(With "H" prefix. 10–inch LPs.)
CAPITOL (400 through 600 series) .. 25-40   55-57
CAPITOL (1600 series) 10-20   61
(With "T" prefix.) .
CAPITOL (11000 series) 5-10   72-77
CAPITOL (16000 series) 4-6   81
COLUMBIA (27 "The Ellington
Era, Volume 1) 25-40   63
COLUMBIA (39 "The Ellington
Era, Volume 2, 1927-1940) 25-40   66
COLUMBIA (500 through 900 series) 20-30   54-57
COLUMBIA (1085 through 2029
except 1360) 15-30   57-63
(Monaural.)
COLUMBIA (1360 "Anatomy of a
Murder") 35-50   59
(Soundtrack. Monaural.)
COLUMBIA (4000 series) 25-50   55

COLUMBIA (6000 series) 30-60   50
(10–inch LPs.)
COLUMBIA (8053 through 9600,
except 8166) 10-20   57-68
(Stereo.)
COLUMBIA (8166 "Anatomy of a
Murder") 45-60   59
(Soundtrack. Stereo.)
COLUMBIA (14000 series) 5-10   79
(Columbia Special Products series.)
COLUMBIA (32000 through
38000 series) 5-10   73-82
COLUMBIA SPECIAL PRODUCTS ... 8-10   82
DECCA 8-15   67-70
DOCTOR JAZZ 5-8   84
EVEREST 5-10   70-73
FANTASY 6-12   71-75
FLYING DUTCHMAN 5-10   69
HARMONY 5-10   67-71
IMPULSE (Except 9200 series) ... 15-20   62
IMPULSE (9200 series) 8-12   73
ODYSSEY 8-12   68
PABLO 5-10   76-80
PRESTIGE 6-12   73-77
RCA (500 series) 10-20   64-69
RCA (0700 through 2000 series) 5-8   75-78
(With "ANL1" or "APL1" prefix.)
RCA (1000 series) 25-40   54
(With "LJM" or "LPT" prefix.)
RCA (1300 through 2800 series) 10-30   57-66
(With "LPM" or "LSP" prefix.)
RCA (3000 series) 25-50   52-53
(10–inch LPs.)
RCA (3500 through 3900 series) 8-15   66-68
RCA (4000 series) 8-10   81
RCA (6009 "The Indispensible
Duke Ellington") 20-30   61
RCA (6042 "This Is Duke Ellington") . 10-15   71
REPRISE 10-20   63-68
RIVERSIDE (Except 100 series) 10-20   62-64
RIVERSIDE (100 series) 15-30   56-59
RON-LETTE 15-30   58
SOLID STATE 5-10   70
SUNSET 5-10   69
TRIP 5-10   75-76
U.A. (Except 14000 and 15000 series) 5-10   72
U.A. (14000 and 15000 series) 15-25   62
VERVE 10-15   67
X (3037 "Duke Ellington") 25-50   55
(10–inch LP.)
   Also see ARMSTRONG, Louis, and Duke Ellington
   Also see BASIE, Count, and Duke Ellington
   Also see BREWER, Teresa, and Duke Ellington
   Also see FITZGERALD, Ella, and Duke Ellington
   Also see HIBBLER, Al, and Duke Ellington
   Also see JACKSON, Mahalia, and Duke Ellington
   Also see SINATRA, Frank, and Duke Ellington

ELLINGTON, Duke, and John Coltrane
LPs: 10/12–inch 33rpm
IMPULSE 15-25   63

Also see COLTRANE, John

ELLINGTON, Duke, and Johnny Hodges
LPs: 10/12–inch 33rpm
PRESTIGE 8-10   81
VERVE (Except 8800 series) 15-30   59-60
VERVE (8800 series) 8-12   73
   Also see ELLINGTON, Duke
   Also see HODGES, Johnny

ELLIOT, Cass
(Mama Cass)
Singles: 7–inch
DUNHILL 3-6   68-70
RCA 3-5   71-73
LPs: 10/12–inch 33rpm
DUNHILL 10-20   68-72
PICKWICK 8-12
RCA 10-15   72-73
   Also see BIG THREE
   Also see MAMAS and the Papas
   Also see MASON, Dave, and Mama Cass
   Also see MUGWUMPS

ELLIOT, Mike, and Bud Latour
Singles: 7–inch
MCA 2-4   86
(Promotional issues only.)
TRI-FIVE 2-4   86

ELLIS, Jimmy
Singles: 7–inch
BOBLO 5-10   77-78
CHALLENGER 4-6   73
DRADCO 8-10   64
KRISTAL 2-4   85
MCA 3-5   73
SOUTHERN TRACKS 2-4   86-87
SUN 3-6   72-77
TONY LAWRENCE 2-4   83-84
Picture Sleeves
BOBLO (536 "I'm Not Trying
to Be Like Elvis") 10-20   78
EPs: 7–inch 33/45rpm
JIMMY ELLIS FAN CLUB
("Merry Christmas") 4-6   81
LPs: 10/12–inch 33rpm
BOBLO (829 "By Request, Ellis
Sings Elvis") 75-125   77
ROLLER SKATE 8-10   82
   Also see LEWIS, Jerry Lee, Carl Perkins and Charlie Rich

ELLIS, Ray, Orchestra
Singles: 78rpm
COLUMBIA 3-8   57
Singles: 7–inch
COLUMBIA 3-8   57
MGM 3-5   59-60
RCA 3-5   61
LPs: 10/12–inch 33rpm
HARMONY 5-10   59
MGM 5-10   59-60
RCA 5-10   61

ELLIS, Shirley
Singles: 7–inch
COLUMBIA 4-8   67
CONGRESS 4-8   63-65
Picture Sleeves
CONGRESS 5-10   64-65
LPs: 10/12–inch 33rpm
COLUMBIA 15-20   67
CONGRESS 20-25   64-65

ELLISON, Lorraine
Singles: 7–inch
LOMA 3-5   67-68
MERCURY 4-8   65-66
SHARP 4-8   63
WARNER 3-6   66-69
LPs: 10/12–inch 33rpm
WARNER (1000 series) 15-20   67-69
WARNER (2000 series) 8-10   74

ELMO & ALMO
Singles: 7–inch
DADDY BEST 3-6   67

ELUSION
Singles: 7–inch
COTILLION 2-4   81
LPs: 10/12–inch 33rpm
COTILLION 5-10   81

ELY, Joe
Singles: 7–inch
MCA 2-4   77-81
SOUTHCOAST 2-4   81
LPs: 10/12–inch 33rpm
MCA 5-10   77-81
SOUTHCOAST 5-10   81

EMERSON, Keith
LPs: 10/12–inch 33rpm
BACKSTREET 5-10   81

EMERSON, Keith, and the Nice
Singles: 7–inch
MERCURY 3-5   72
LPs: 10/12–inch 33rpm
MERCURY 12-15   72
Also see EMERSON, Keith
Also see EMERSON, LAKE & PALMER
Also see NICE

EMERSON, LAKE & PALMER
Singles: 7–inch
ATLANTIC 3-5   77-80
COTILLION 3-5   71-72
MANTICORE 3-5   74
POLYDOR 2-4   86
Promotional Singles
ATLANTIC ("Brain Salad Surgery") 2-4   78
Picture Sleeves
POLYDOR 2-4   86
LPs: 10/12–inch 33rpm
ATLANTIC (Except 281) 8-10   77-80

ATLANTIC (281 "Emerson, Lake
and Palmer") 12-15   77
(With the London Philharmonic Orchestra. Also
contains interviews with the three members.
Promotional issue only.)
COTILLION 12-15   71-72
MFSL (031 "Pictures at an Exhibition") 15-25   80
MANTICORE 10-12   73-74
Members: Keith Emerson; Greg Lake; Carl Palmer.
Also see ASIA
Also see EMERSON, LAKE & POWELL

EMERSON, LAKE & POWELL
Singles: 7–inch
POLYDOR 2-4   86
LPs: 10/12–inch 33rpm
POLYDOR 5-10   86
Members: Keith Emerson; Greg Lake; Cozy Powell.
Also see EMERSON, Keith
Also see EMERSON, LAKE & PALMER
Also see LAKE, Greg
Also see POWELL, Cozy

EMMERSON, Les
Singles: 7–inch
LION 3-5   73

EMOTIONS
Singles: 7–inch
BRAINSTORM 4-6   68
CALLA 4-8   65
JASON SCOTT 4-8
KAPP 5-10   62-63
KARATE 4-8   64
LAURIE (3167 "Starlit Night") 10-15   63
20TH FOX 10-15   63-64
VARDAN 4-8   65
LPs: 10/12–inch 33rpm
MAGIC CARPET 8-10
Members: Joe Favale; Tony Maltese; Don Colluri; Larry
Cusamanno; Joe Nigro; Sal Covais.

EMOTIONS
Singles: 12–inch 33/45rpm
RED LABEL 4-6   84
Singles: 7–inch
ARC 2-4   80-81
COLUMBIA 2-5   76-81
STAX 2-4   77-79
MOTOWN 2-4   85
RED LABEL 2-4   84
TWIN STACKS 4-8   68
VOLT 3-6   69-74
LPs: 10/12–inch 33rpm
ARC 5-8   79-81
COLUMBIA 5-10   76-81
MOTOWN 5-10   85
RED LABEL 5-10   84
STAX 5-10   77-79
VOLT 10-20   69-74
Members: Sheila Hutchinson; Wanda Hutchinson; Jeanette
Hutchinson.
Also see EARTH, WIND & FIRE and the Emotions

EMPERORS
Singles: 7–inch
BRUNSWICK 4-8   67
MALA 5-10   66-67
SABRA ("I Want My Woman") 25-35
(Number not known.)
TWO PLUS TWO 5-10   66

ENCHANTERS
Singles: 7–inch
BALD EAGLE (3001 "Come on Baby,
Let's Do the Stroll") 15-25   58
BAMBOO 10-15   61
EP-SOM (103 "I Need Your Love") . 100-150   62
J.J.&M. (1562 "Oh Rose Marie") .. 100-150   62
MUSITRON (1072 "I Lied to
My Heart") 30-40   61
ORBIT (532 "Touch of Love") 15-20   59
SHARP (105 "We Make Mistakes") . 10-20   60
STARDUST (102 "Raindrops") 300-500
TOM TOM (301 "Surf Blast") 25-35   63
WARNER 5-10   64

ENCHANTMENT
Singles: 7–inch
COLUMBIA 2-4   82-84
DESERT MOON 3-5   76
RCA 2-4   80
ROADSHOW 3-5   77-78
U.A. 3-5   76-77
LPs: 10/12–inch 33rpm
COLUMBIA 5-10   82
RCA 5-10   80
ROADSHOW 8-10   77-79
U.A. 8-10   77
    Members: Bobby Green; Mickey Clanton; Joe Thomas; Davis
    Banks; Emanuel Johnson.

ENDGAMES
Singles: 12–inch 33/45rpm
FLIP 4-6   83
MCA 4-6   83
Singles: 7–inch
MCA 2-4   84
LPs: 10/12–inch 33rpm
MCA 5-10   84

ENERGETICS
Singles: 7–inch
ATLANTIC 2-4   79
LPs: 10/12–inch 33rpm
ATLANTIC 5-10   79

ENERGY
Singles: 7–inch
SHOUT 3-5   74

ENGLAND DAN & JOHN FORD COLEY
Singles: 7–inch
A&M 3-5   71-77
BIG TREE 2-5   76-80
MCA 2-4   80

LPs: 10/12–inch 33rpm
A&M 10-12   71-73
BIG TREE 8-10   76-79
MCA 5-10   80
    Members: Dan Seals; John Ford Coley.
    Also see ABBA / Spinners / Firefall / England Dan and John
      Ford Coley
    Also see SEALS, Dan
    Also see SOUTHWEST F.O.B.

ENGLE, Priscilla
LPs: 10/12–inch 33rpm
FRONTLINE 5-10   86

ENGLISH, Barbara Jean
Singles: 7–inch
ALITHIA 3-5   73-74
LPs: 10/12–inch 33rpm
ALITHIA 8-10   73

ENGLISH, Jackie
Singles: 7–inch
VENTURE 2-4   80

ENGLISH, Scott
(Scott English and the Accents; Scott English and the
Dedications)
Singles: 7–inch
DOT (16099 "White Cliffs of Dover") . 10-15   60
JANUS (171 "Brandy") 8-10   71
JANUS (192 "Woman in My Life") 3-5   72
JOKER (777 "Ugly Pills") 15-25   62
SPOKANE (4003 "High on a Hill") 8-15   64
SPOKANE (4007 "Here Comes
the Pain") 10-20   64
SULTAN (4003 "High on a Hill") 15-25   63
SULTAN (5500 "Rags to Riches") ... 20-30   61

ENGLISH BEAT
Singles: 12–inch 33/45rpm
I.R.S. 4-6   83-85
Singles: 7–inch
I.R.S. 2-4   83-85
LPs: 10/12–inch 33rpm
I.R.S. 5-10   82-85
SIRE 5-10   80-81
    Members: Andy Cox; David Steele.
    Also see FINE YOUNG CANNIBALS

ENGLISH CONGREGATION
Singles: 7–inch
ATCO 3-5   72
SIGNPOST 3-5   73
LPs: 10/12–inch 33rpm
SIGNPOST 8-10   73

ENNIS, Ethel
Singles: 78rpm
JUBILEE 4-8   56
Singles: 7–inch
JUBILEE 5-10   56
LPs: 10/12–inch 33rpm
CAPITOL 15-25   58
JUBILEE 15-30   56-63

RCA 10-20   64

ENO, Brian
(Eno)
Singles: 7-inch
ISLAND 3-5   72
LPs: 10/12-inch 33rpm
ANTILLES 8-10   73-78
EDITIONS E.G. 5-10   81-82
ISLAND 8-10   73-78
PVC 5-10   79
SIRE 5-10   81
   Also see BYRNE, David
   Also see 801
   Also see FRIPP & ENO
   Also see ROXY MUSIC

ENTERTAINERS IV
Singles: 7-inch
DORE 4-8   66

ENTWISTLE, John
(John Entwistle's Rigor Mortis; John Entwistle's Ox)
Singles: 7-inch
DECCA 3-5   72
TRACK 3-5   73
LPs: 10/12-inch 33rpm
ATCO 5-10   81
DECCA 10-15   71-72
MCA/TRACK 8-10   72-75
   Also see TOWNSHEND, Pete, and Ronnie Lane
   Also see WHO

EON
Singles: 7-inch
ARIOLA AMERICA 2-4   78
LPs: 10/12-inch 33rpm
ARIOLA AMERICA 5-10   78
SCEPTER 8-10   73

EPIC SPLENDOR
Singles: 7-inch
HOT BISCUIT 4-8   67-68
Picture Sleeves
HOT BISCUIT 5-10   67

EPOQUE, Belle: see BELLE EPOQUE

EPPS, Preston
Singles: 7-inch
ADMIRAL 4-8   65
EMBASSY 4-8   62
JO JO 3-6   69
MAJESTY 4-8
ORIGINAL SOUND (Except 4) 5-10   60-61
ORIGINAL SOUND (4 "Bongo Rock") . 8-10 60
   (Monaural.)
ORIGINAL SOUND (4 "Bongo Rock") 10-20 60
   (Stereo.)
TOP RANK 5-10   59
EPs: 7-inch 33/45rpm
ORIGINAL SOUND (1001 "Bongo
   Rock") 15-25   60

LPs: 10/12-inch 33rpm
ORIGINAL SOUND (5002 "Bongo
   Bongo Bongo") 30-40   60
   (Monaural.)
ORIGINAL SOUND (8851 "Bongo
   Bongo Bongo") 30-50   60
   (Stereo.)
ORIGINAL SOUND (5009 "Surfin'
   Bongos") 25-40   63
   (Monaural.)
ORIGINAL SOUND (8872 "Surfin'
   Bongos") 25-50   63
   (Stereo.)
TOP RANK (349 "Bongola") 30-50   61

EQUALS
Singles: 7-inch
PRESIDENT 5-10   67-68
RCA 4-6   68
LPs: 10/12-inch 33rpm
LAURIE (2045 "Unequalled") 20-25   67
PRESIDENT 15-25   68-69
RCA 10-15   68
   Member: Eddy Grant.
   Also see GRANT, Eddy

ERAMUS HALL
Singles: 12-inch 33/45rpm
CAPITOL 4-6   84
Singles: 7-inch
CAPITOL 2-4   84
LPs: 10/12-inch 33rpm
CAPITOL 5-10   84

ERIC
Singles: 12-inch 33/45rpm
MEMO 4-6   84

ERIC B. and Rakim
Singles: 7-inch
4TH and B'WAY 2-4   87-88
ZAKIA 2-4   86
LPs: 10/12-inch 33rpm
4TH and B'WAY 5-10   87
MCA 5-8   90
UNI 5-8   88

ERNIE / Sesame Street Kids
(With Jim Henson as "Ernie")
Singles: 7-inch
COLUMBIA 3-5   70
   Also see HENSON, Jim

ERUPTION
Singles: 12-inch 33/45rpm
ARIOLA AMERICA 4-8   78
HANSA 4-8
Singles: 7-inch
ARIOLA AMERICA 2-4   78
LPs: 10/12-inch 33rpm
ARIOLA AMERICA 5-10   78

ERWIN, Dee
(Difosco Erwin; Big Dee Erwin)
Singles: 7–inch
CUB 4-8   68
ROULETTE 4-8   65
  Also see DIFOSCO
  Also see IRWIN, Big Dee

ESCORTS
Singles: 7–inch
ALITHIA 3-5   73-74
LPs: 10/12–inch 33rpm
ALITHIA 8-10   73-74
  Members: Reginald Hayes; Robert Arrington; Laurence Franklin; Stephen Carter; William Dugger; Frank Heard; Marion Murphy.

ESCOVEDO, Coke
Singles: 7–inch
MERCURY 3-5   76-77
LPs: 10/12–inch 33rpm
MERCURY 5-10   76-77
  Also see AZTECA
  Also see SANTANA

ESMERALDA, Santa
Singles: 12–inch 33/45rpm
CASABLANCA 4-8   77-78
Singles: 7–inch
CASABLANCA 2-5   77-78
LPs: 10/12–inch 33rpm
CASABLANCA 5-10   77-80
  Member: Leroy Gomez.

ESPOSITO, Joe "Bean"
Singles: 7–inch
CASABLANCA 2-4   83
  Also see BROOKLYN DREAMS

ESQUIRES
Singles: 7–inch
B&G 4-8
BUNKY 4-8   67-68
CAPITOL 3-6   69
JU-PAR 3-5   76
LAMARR 3-5   71
SALEM 5-10   65
TOWER 5-10   65
WAND 4-8   68-69
LPs: 10/12–inch 33rpm
BUNKY (300 "Get on Up
  and Get Away") 20-25   68
  Members: Millard Edwards; Gilbert Alvis; Betty Moorer; Sam Pace; Harvey Scales; Shawn Taylor.

ESSENCE
Singles: 7–inch
EPIC 3-5   75-77
LPs: 10/12–inch 33rpm
SAVOY 5-10   78

ESSEX
Singles: 7–inch
BANG 4-8   66
ROULETTE 5-8   63-64

LPs: 10/12–inch 33rpm
ROULETTE (25234 "Easier Said
  Than Done") 25-35   63
ROULETTE (25235 "A Walkin'
  Miracle") 20-35   63
ROULETTE (25246 "Young and
  Lively") 20-30   64
  Members: Anita Humes; Walter Vickers; Rodney Taylor; Billie Hill; Rudolph Johnson.

ESSEX, David
Singles: 7–inch
COLUMBIA 3-5   73-76
RSO 2-4   79
UNI 4-8   67
Picture Sleeves
COLUMBIA 3-5   73-74
UNI 5-10   67
LPs: 10/12–inch 33rpm
COLUMBIA (CQ-32560 "Rock On") .. 15-25   74
  (Quadrophonic)
COLUMBIA (KC-32560 "Rock On") .. 15-20   73
COLUMBIA (33289 "David Essex") ... 8-15   74
COLUMBIA (33813 "All the
  Fun of the Fair") 8-15   75
MERCURY 5-10   83

ESTEFAN, Gloria:
  see MIAMI SOUND MACHINE

ETERNALS
Singles: 7–inch
COLLECTABLES 2-4
HOLLYWOOD (68 "Rockin' in
  the Jungle") 10-20   59
  (White or blue label.)
HOLLYWOOD (68 "Rockin' in
  the Jungle") 8-10   59
  (Yellow label.)
HOLLYWOOD (70 "Babalu's
  Wedding Day") 15-20   59
  (Red label.)
HOLLYWOOD (70 "Babalu's
  Wedding Day") 8-12   59
  (Blue label.)
WARWICK (611 "Blind Date") 10-15   60
  Members: Charles Girona; Alex Miranda; Fred Hodge; Ernie Sierra; Arnold Torres; George Villanueva.

ETERNITY'S CHILDREN
Singles: 7–inch
A&M 5-8   67
TOWER 4-6   68-69
Picture Sleeves
TOWER 5-10   68
LPs: 10/12–inch 33rpm
TOWER (5123 "Eternity's Children") . 20-25   68
TOWER (5144 "Timeless") 20-25   68
  Also see ALLAN, Davie / Eternity's Children / Main Attraction / Sunrays

ETTA & HARVEY
Singles: 7-inch
CHESS 5-10   60
Members: Etta James; Harvey Fuqua.
Also see HARVEY and the Moonglows
Also see JAMES, Etta

ETZEL, Roy
(Roy Etzel and the Jupiter Serenaders)
Singles: 7-inch
HICKORY 4-8   63
MGM 4-6   65-67
PRESIDENT 4-8   61
TIME 4-8   61
LPs: 10/12-inch 33rpm
MGM 8-12   65

EUBANKS, Jack
Singles: 7-inch
MONUMENT 4-8   61-64
LPs: 10/12-inch 33rpm
MONUMENT 10-20   66

EUCLID BEACH BAND
Singles: 7-inch
EPIC/CLEVELAND INT'L 2-4   78-79
SCENE 3-5   78
LPs: 10/12-inch 33rpm
EPIC 5-10   79

EUNICE
(With the Earl Palmer Combo; Eunice Russ Frost)
Singles: 7-inch
CLASSIC ARTISTS 3-5   89
Also see GENE & EUNICE

EUROGLIDERS
Singles: 7-inch
COLUMBIA 2-4   84
LPs: 10/12-inch 33rpm
COLUMBIA 5-10   84
Member: Grace Knight.

EUROPE
Singles: 12-inch 33/45rpm
EPIC 4-8   86
(Promotional only.)
Singles: 7-inch
EPIC 2-4   86-88
LPs: 10/12-inch 33rpm
EPIC 5-10 86-88
Members: Joey Tempest; John Leven; Mic Michaeli; Kee
Marcello; Ian Haughland.

EURYTHMICS
Singles: 12-inch 33/45rpm
RCA 4-6   83-86
Singles: 7-inch
ARISTA 2-4   89-91
RCA 2-4   83-88
Picture Sleeves
ARISTA 2-4   89
RCA 2-4   83-88

LPs: 10/12-inch 33rpm
ARISTA 5-8   89-91
RCA 5-10   83-88
Members: Annie Lennox; Dave Stewart.
Also see LENNOX, Annie, and Al Green
Also see TOURISTS

EURYTHMICS and Aretha Franklin
Singles: 12-inch 33/45rpm
RCA 4-6   85
Singles: 7-inch
RCA 2-4   85
Also see EURYTHMICS
Also see FRANKLIN, Aretha

EVANS, Linda
Singles: 7-inch
ARIOLA 3-5   79

EVANS, Margie
Singles: 7-inch
ICA 3-5   77
U.A. 3-5   73

EVANS, Paul
(Paul Evans and the Curls)
Singles: 7-inch
ATCO 5-10   59-60
CARLTON 5-10   61-62
CINNAMON INT'L 2-4   80
COLLECTABLES 2-4
COLUMBIA 3-6   68
DECCA 5-10   58
DOT 3-5   73
EPIC 4-8   64-65
GUARANTEED 5-10 59-60
KAPP 4-8   62-63
LAURIE 3-5   71
MERCURY 3-5   74-75
MUSICOR 3-5   77
RCA 8-10   57
RANWOOD 3-5   72
SPRING 2-4   78-79
LPs: 10/12-inch 33rpm
CARLTON (129 "Hear Paul Evans
   in Your Home Tonight") 25-35   61
   (Monaural.)
CARLTON (129 "Hear Paul Evans
   in Your Home Tonight") 35-50   61
   (Stereo.)
CARLTON (130 "Folk Songs
   of Many Lands") 20-25   61
   (Monaural.)
CARLTON (130 "Folk Songs
   of Many Lands") 20-30   61
   (Stereo.)
GUARANTEED (1000 "Fabulous
   Teens") 30-45   60
   (Monaural.)
GUARANTEED (1000 "Fabulous
   Teens") 40-50   60
   (Stereo.)

KAPP (1346 "21 Years in
a Tennessee Jail") 20-25   64
(Monaural.)
KAPP (1475 "Another Town,
Another Jail") 20-30   66
(Monaural.)
KAPP (3346 "21 Years in
a Tennessee Jail") 20-45   64
(Stereo.)
KAPP (3475 "Another Town,
Another Jail") 20-30   66

EVANS, Paul and Mimi
Singles: 7–inch
EPIC 4-8   64
Also see EVANS, Paul

EVASIONS
Singles: 7–inch
SAM 2-4   81

EVE
LPs: 10/12–inch 33rpm
LHI 10-12   70

EVE ELEKTRO: see ELEKTRO, Eve

EVERETT, Betty
(Betty Everett and the Daylighters)
Singles: 7–inch
ABC 4-6   66-67
C.J. 5-10   61-64
COBRA 10-20   57-58
COLLECTABLES 2-4
DOTTIE (1126 "Tell
Me Darling") 15-20
ERIC 2-4
FANTASY 3-5   70-74
OLDIES 45 3-5
ONE-DERFUL 4-8   62
UNI 3-6   68-69
VEE JAY 4-8   63-65
LPs: 10/12–inch 33rpm
FANTASY 8-10   75
SUNSET 10-15   68
UNI 10-15   69
VEE JAY (1077 "It's in His Kiss") 25-50   64
VEE JAY (1122 "The Very Best
of Betty Everett") 25-35   65
Also see BUTLER, Jerry, and Betty Everett

EVERETT, Betty / Ketty Lester
LPs: 10/12–inch 33rpm
GRAND PRIX 10-15   64
Also see LESTER, Ketty

EVERETT, Betty / Impressions
LPs: 10/12–inch 33rpm
CUSTOM 10-15   64
Also see EVERETT, Betty
Also see IMPRESSIONS

EVERETT, Leon
Singles: 7–inch
ORLANDO 2-4   80-86
RCA 2-4   81-84
TRUE 5-10   77
LPs: 10/12–inch 33rpm
ORLANDO 5-10   86
RCA 5-10   81-84
TRUE (1002 "Goodbye King of
Rock and Roll") 15-20   77
(Price includes 18 x 23 bonus poster of Elvis
Presley. Deduct $4-$8 if poster is missing.)

EVERLY, Don
Singles: 7–inch
ABC/HICKORY 3-5   75-77
HICKORY/MGM 3-5   76
ODE 3-5   70-74
LPs: 10/12–inch 33rpm
ABC/HICKORY 8-10   76-77
ODE 8-12   70-74
Also see HARRIS, Emmylou
Also see KIMBERLY, Adrian

EVERLY, Phil
Singles: 7–inch
CAPITOL 2-4   83
CURB 2-4   80-81
ELEKTRA 2-4   79
PYE 3-5   73-76
RCA 3-5   73
LPs: 10/12–inch 33rpm
ELECTRA 5-10   79
PYE 8-10   75-76
RCA 8-10   73

EVERLY BROTHERS
Singles: 78rpm
CADENCE 20-30   57-58
COLUMBIA 20-30   56
Singles: 7–inch
BARNABY 2-4   70-76
CADENCE 10-15   57-61
(Silver and maroon, or blue labels)
CADENCE 5-10   61-62
(Red label.)
COLUMBIA (21496 "The Sun Keeps
Shining") 75-100   56
ERIC 2-4
MERCURY 2-4   84-86
RCA 3-6   72-73
WARNER (5151 "Cathy's Clown") 8-10   60
(Monaural.)
WARNER (S-5151 "Cathy's Clown") . 20-30   60
(Stereo.)
WARNER (5163 through 5833) 5-10   60-69
WARNER (5857 "Fifi the Flea") 15-25   67
(Shown by "Don Everly Brother" on one side, and
as "Phil Everly Brother" on the flip.)
WARNER (5901 through 7425) 4-8   67-70

Promotional Singles

BARNABY	3-6	70-76
CADENCE	15-25	57-62
(Black vinyl.)		
CADENCE (1348 "All I Have		
to Do Is Dream")	25-50	
(Colored vinyl.)		
COLUMBIA (21496 "The Sun Keeps		
Shining")	35-50	56
MERCURY	3-5	84-86
RCA	4-8	72-73
WARNER (5151 "Cathy's Clown")	35-45	60
(Colored vinyl.)		
WARNER (5163 "So Sad")	35-45	60
(Colored vinyl.)		
WARNER (5199 "Ebony Eyes")	35-45	61
(Colored vinyl.)		

Picture Sleeves

CADENCE (1337 "Wake Up		
Little Susie")	50-100	57
CADENCE (1355 "Problems")	20-40	58
CADENCE (1369 "Till I Kissed You")	20-40	59
CADENCE (1376 "Let It Be Me")	20-40	60
WARNER (5151 "Cathy's Clown")	15-25	60
WARNER (5163 "So Sad")	15-20	60
WARNER (5199 "Ebony Eyes")	15-20	61
WARNER (5220 "Temptation")	15-20	61
WARNER (5250 "Crying in the Rain")	10-20	62
WARNER (5273 "That's Old		
Fashioned")	10-20	62
WARNER (5297 "Don't Ask Me		
to Be Friends")	10-20	62
MERCURY	3-5	84

EPs: 7–inch 33/45rpm

CADENCE (4 "Dream with the		
Everly Brothers")	25-35	61
CADENCE (104 "The Everly		
Brothers")	30-50	57
CADENCE (105 "The Everly		
Brothers")	30-50	57
CADENCE (107 "The Everly		
Brothers")	30-50	58
CADENCE (108/109/110 "Songs Our		
Daddy Taught Us")	25-45	58
(Price is for any of three volumes.)		
CADENCE (111 "The Everly		
Brothers")	25-45	59
CADENCE (118 "The Everly		
Brothers")	25-35	59
CADENCE (121 "Very Best of		
The Everly Brothers")	25-35	60
CADENCE (333 "Rockin' with		
the Everly Brothers")	25-35	61
WARNER (1381-1 "Foreverly		
Yours")	15-25	60
(Black vinyl.)		
WARNER (1381-1 "Foreverly Yours")	15-25	60
(Colored vinyl. Promotional issue only.)		

WARNER BROS. RECORDS

33⅓ RPM STANDARD GROOVE
33⅓ RPM STANDARD GROOVE
(Note: Live Copy To Be Supplied By Local Announcer)

THE EVERLY BROTHERS
SPECIALLY PREPARED SHORT TRACKS
from the ALL-NEW EVERLY BROTHERS
ALBUM # W/WS 1418

PRO 134

Cut 1. 1:09 MY MAMMY (Donaldson-Young) Bourne Inc. ASCAP From The Warner Bros. Film "The Jazz Singer"
Cut 2. 1:19 HI-LILI, HI-LO (Kaper-Deutch) Robbins Mus. Corp. ASCAP From The MGM Film "Lili"
Cut 3. 1:02 MUS'RAT (Travis-Ann-Hensley) American Mus. Inc. BMI
Cut 4. 1:20 NOW IS THE HOUR (Maori Farewell Song) (Kaihan-Scott-Stewart) Leeds Music Corp. ASCAP
Cut 5. 1:16 LOVE IS WHERE YOU FIND IT (Brown-Brent) Leo Feist Inc. ASCAP From The MGM film "The Kissing Bandit"

WARNER (1381-2 "Especially		
for You")	15-25	60
WARNER (5501 "The Everly Brothers		
Plus Two Oldies")	15-25	61

LPs: 10/12–inch 33rpm

ARISTA	8-12	84
BARNABY (350 "Original		
Greatest Hits")	10-15	70
BARNABY (30260 "End of an Era")	10-15	71
BARNABY (4000 series)	6-10	77
CADENCE (3003 "The Everly		
Brothers")	75-125	58
CADENCE (3016 "Songs Our Daddy		
Taught Us")	50-75	58
CADENCE (3025 "The Everly		
Brothers' Best")	75-100	59
(Blue cover.)		
CADENCE (3040 "The Fabulous Style		
of the Everly Brothers")	50-75	60
CADENCE (3059 "Folk Songs")	35-40	63
CADENCE (3062 "15 Everly Hits")	45-65	63
CADENCE (25040 "The Fabulous Style		
of the Everly Brothers")	75-100	60
(Stereo.)		
CADENCE (25059 "Folk Songs")	35-40	63
(Stereo.)		
CADENCE (25062 "15 Everly Hits")	45-65	63
(Stereo.)		
CANDLELITE	10-15	76
HARMONY	10-12	68-70
MERCURY	5-10	84-86
PAIR	8-12	84
PASSPORT	5-10	84-86
RCA	8-12	72
RHINO (214 "All They Had to		
Do Was Dream")	5-10	85
RHINO (258 "Heartache		
and Memories")	8-10	85
(Picture disc.)		
RONCO	8-10	
WARNER (1381 "It's Everly		
Time")	25-40	60

WARNER (1395 "A Date with
the Everly Brothers") 30-40   60
(With gatefold cover and eight "wallet pix" cut-out
photos.)
WARNER (1395 "A Date with
the Everly Brothers") 15-20   61
(With standard cover.)
WARNER (1418 "Songs for Both Sides
of an Evening") 25-30   61
WARNER (1430 "Instant Party") 20-30   62
WARNER (1471 "Golden Hits") 20-30   62
WARNER (1483 "Christmas with
the Everly Brothers") 20-25   61
WARNER (1513 "Great Country
Hits") 20-25   63
WARNER (1554 "Very Best of
the Everly Brothers") 15-20   64
(Yellow cover. Green label.)
WARNER (1554 "Very Best of
the Everly Brothers") 10-15   70
(Blue cover. Green label.)
WARNER (1554 "Very Best of
the Everly Brothers") 8-12   72
(Blue cover. "Skyline" label.)
WARNER (1578 "Rock 'N Soul") 20-25   65
WARNER (1585 "Gone Gone Gone") 20-25   65
WARNER (1605 "Beat and Soul") ... 15-25   65
WARNER (1620 "In Our Image") 15-25   66
WARNER (1646 "Two Yanks
in London") 15-25   66
(With the Hollies.)
WARNER (1676 "The Hit Sound
of the Everly Brothers") 15-20   67
WARNER (1708 "The Everly
Brothers Sing") 15-25   67
WARNER (1752 "Roots") 15-25   68
WARNER (1858 "The Everly
Brothers Show") 12-15   70

Promotional LPs

WARNER (134 "The Everly
Brothers") 75-100   61
(One sided, 10–inch LP with five tracks from *The
Everly Brothers - Both Sides of an Evening* [WB
1418]. Promotional issue only.)
WARNER (135 "Souvenir
Sampler, 10 Songs") 50-80   61
(Has Don and Phil discussing *The Everly Brothers
- Both Sides of an Evening*. Has an LP discount
coupon on sleeve. Promotional pressing.)
WARNER (1381 "It's Everly Time") . 50-100   60
WARNER (1395 "A Date with
the Everly Brothers") 75-100   60
(With gatefold cover and eight "wallet pix" cut-out
photos.)
WARNER (1418 "Both Sides of
an Evening") 50-75   61
WARNER (1430 "Instant Party") 50-75   62
WARNER (1471 "Golden Hits") 50-75   62

WARNER (1483 "Christmas with
the Everly Brothers") 50-75   61
WARNER (1513 "Great Country
Hits") 30-60   63
WARNER (1554 "Very Best of
the Everly Brothers") 30-60   64
(Yellow cover.)
WARNER (1578 "Rock'N Soul") 30-60   65
WARNER (1585 "Gone Gone Gone") 30-60   65
WARNER (1605 "Beat 'N Soul") 25-50   65
WARNER (1620 "In Our Image") 25-50   66
WARNER (1646 "Two Yanks
in London") 25-50   66
WARNER (1676 "The Hit Sound
of the Everly Brothers") 25-50   67
WARNER (1708 "The Everly
Brothers Sing") 25-50   67
WARNER (1752 "Roots") 20-40   68
WARNER (1858 "The Everly
Brothers Show") 20-30   70
Members: Don Everly; Phil Everly.
Also see CASH, Johnny, Rosanne Cash and the Everly Brothers
Also see EVERLY, Don
Also see EVERLY, Phil
Also see HOLLIES

EVERLY BROTHERS with the Beach Boys
Singles: 7–inch
CAPITOL (44297 "Don't Worry Baby") .. 2-5   88
Picture Sleeves
CAPITOL (44297 "Don't Worry Baby") .. 3-5   88
Also see BEACH BOYS

EVERY FATHER'S TEENAGE SON
Singles: 7–inch
BUDDAH 4-8   67

EVERY MOTHER'S SON
Singles: 7–inch
MGM 4-8   67-68
POLYDOR 2-4
Picture Sleeves
MGM 4-8   67
LPs: 10/12–inch 33rpm
MGM 10-20   67

EVERYTHING IS EVERYTHING
Singles: 7–inch
VANGUARD APOSTOLIC 4-6 69
LPs: 10/12–inch 33rpm
VANGUARD 15-20 69

EXCELLENTS
Singles: 7–inch
BLAST (205 "Coney Island Baby") ... 15-25 62
(Red label.)
BLAST (205 "Coney Island Baby") ... 10-15 62
(Red and white label.)
BLAST (205 "Coney Island Baby") ... 40-60 62
(White label.)
(Promotional issue only.)
BLAST (205 "Coney Island Baby") ... 10-15 65
(Purple label.)
COLLECTABLES 2-4
MERMAID (106 "Love No One
But You") 75-100 64
(Label pictures a mermaid.)
MERMAID (106 "Love No One
But You") 25-50
(Mermaid not pictured.)
OLD TIMER 4-8 64

EXCELS
Singles: 7–inch
GONE 15-20 60
RSVP (111 "Can't Help
Lovin' That Girl of Mine") 20-30 61

EXCITERS
Singles: 7–inch
BANG 4-8 66
LIBERTY 2-4
ROULETTE 4-8 64
RCA 4-8 68-69
SHOUT 4-8 66-67
TODAY 3-5 70
U.A. 5-10 62-63
Picture Sleeves
ROULETTE 8-15 64
LPs: 10/12–inch 33rpm
RCA 10-12 69
ROULETTE 15-20 66
SUNSET 10-12 70
TODAY 8-10 71
U.A. (3264 "Tell Him") 25-40 63
(Monaural.)
U.A. (6264 "Tell Him") 35-50 63
(Stereo.)
Members: Brenda Reid; Herb Rooney.
Also see BRENDA & HERB

EXECUTIVE
Singles: 7–inch
20TH FOX 2-4 81

EXECUTIVE SUITE
Singles: 7–inch
BABYLON 3-5 73-74

JUBILEE 4-6 69
U.A. 3-5 75

EXILE
Singles: 7–inch
ATCO 3-5 77
COLUMBIA 3-6 69-70
EPIC 2-4 83-86
MCA/CURB 2-4 85-86
WARNER/CURB 2-4 78-81
WOODEN NICKEL 3-5 72-73
LPs: 10/12–inch 33rpm
EPIC 5-10 83-86
MCA/CURB 5-8 85-86
RCA 5-10 78
WARNER 5-10 78-81
WOODEN NICKEL 8-10 73
Members: J.P. Pennington; Les Taylor; Sonny LeMaire; Marlon
Hargis; Steve Goetzman.

EXITS
Singles: 7–inch
GEMINI 4-8 67

EXODUS
LPs: 10/12–inch 33rpm
ARISTA 5-10 87
CAPITOL 5-8 90
COMBAT 5-8 87-89

EXOTIC GUITARS
Singles: 7–inch
RANWOOD 3-5 68-70
LPs: 10/12–inch 33rpm
RANWOOD 5-10 68-70
Member: Al Casey.
Also see CASEY, Al
Also see PLATTERS / Exotic Guitars

EXPOSE
Singles: 12–inch 33/45rpm
ARISTA 4-6 85-89
Singles: 7–inch
ARISTA 2-4 85-90
Picture Sleeves
ARISTA 2-4 87-89
LPs: 10/12–inch 33rpm
ARISTA 5-10 86-89
Members: Jeanette Jurado; Gioia Bruno; Ann Curless.

EXPRESS, B.T: see B.T. EXPRESS

EYE to EYE
Singles: 7–inch
WARNER 2-4 82-83
LPs: 10/12–inch 33rpm
WARNER 5-10 82-83
Also see MARSHALL - HAIN

EZO
LPs: 10/12–inch 33rpm
GEFFEN 5-10 87

F

F., Simon
(Simon Fellowes)
Singles: 7–inch
REPRISE 2-4   87

FCC
(Funky Communication Committee)
Singles: 7–inch
FREE FLIGHT (Black vinyl) 2-4   79
FREE FLIGHT (Colored vinyl) 3-5   79
(Promotional issue only.)
LPs: 10/12–inch 33rpm
FREE FLIGHT 5-8   79
RCA 5-10   80

FLB: see FAT LARRY'S BAND

F.R. DAVID: see DAVID, F.R.

FABARES, Shelley
Singles: 7–inch
COLPIX (Except 721) 5-10   62-64
COLPIX (721 "Football Season's
Over") 50-100   64
DUNHILL (4001 "My Prayer") 15-25   65
DUNHILL (4041 "See Ya 'Round
on the Rebound") 15-25   65
ERIC 2-4
VEE JAY (632 "Lost Summer Love") . 15-25   64
Picture Sleeves
COLPIX (621 "Johnny Angel") 50-100   62
COLPIX (636 "Johnny Loves Me") ... 40-60   62
LPs: 10/12–inch 33rpm
COLPIX (426 "Shelley") 35-45   62
(Monaural.)
COLPIX (426 "Shelley") 45-55   62
(Stereo.)
COLPIX (431 "The Things We
Did Last Summer") 35-45   62
(Monaural.)
COLPIX (431 "The Things We
Did Last Summer") 45-55   62
(Stereo.)
Also see BLOSSOMS
Also see CAMPBELL, Glen
Also see DARREN, James / Shelley Fabares / Paul Petersen
Also see PETERSEN, Paul, and Shelley Fabares

FABIAN
(Fabian and the Fabulous Four)
Singles: 7–inch
ABC 2-4   74
CHANCELLOR (1020 "I'm in Love") . 15-20   58
CHANCELLOR (1024 "Be My
Steady Date") 15-20   58
CHANCELLOR (1029 "I'm a Man") .. 10-15   58
(Monaural.)

CHANCELLOR (1029 "I'm a Man") .. 15-25   58
(Stereo.)
CHANCELLOR (1033 "Turn Me
Loose") 10-15   59
(Monaural.)
CHANCELLOR (1033 "Turn Me
Loose") 15-25   59
(Stereo.)
CHANCELLOR (1037 "Tiger") 10-15   59
(Monaural.)
CHANCELLOR (1037 "Tiger") 15-25   59
(Stereo.)
CHANCELLOR (1041 "Come on
and Get Me") 8-12   59
(Monaural.)
CHANCELLOR (1041 "Come on
and Get Me") 15-25   59
(Stereo.)
CHANCELLOR (1044 "Hound
Dog Man") 8-12   59
(Monaural.)
CHANCELLOR (1044 "Hound
Dog Man") 15-25   59
(Stereo.)
CHANCELLOR (1047 "String Along") . 8-12   60
(Monaural.)
CHANCELLOR (1047 "String Along") 15-25   60
(Stereo.)
CHANCELLOR (1061 through 1092) .. 8-15   60-61
COLLECTABLES 2-4
CREAM 3-5   77
DOT 5-10   62
ERIC 2-4
Picture Sleeves
CHANCELLOR (1029 "I'm a Man") .. 10-20   58
CHANCELLOR (1033 "Turn Me
Loose") 10-20   59
CHANCELLOR (1037 "Tiger") 10-20   59
CHANCELLOR (1041 "Come on
and Get Me") 10-20   59
CHANCELLOR (1044 "Hound
Dog Man") 10-20   59
CHANCELLOR (1047 "String Along") 10-20   60
CHANCELLOR (1051 "Strollin' in
the Springtime") 10-20   60
CHANCELLOR (1055 "King of Love") 10-20   60
CHANCELLOR (1061 "Kissin' and
Twistin") 10-20   60
CHANCELLOR (1067 "Hold On") ... 10-20   61
CHANCELLOR (1079 "You're Only
Young Once") 10-20   61
CHANCELLOR (1084 "A Girl
Like You") 15-25   61
CHANCELLOR (1092 "Wild Party") .. 15-25   61
CREAM 3-5   77
EPs: 7–inch 33/45rpm
CHANCELLOR (301 "Hound Dog
Man") 15-25   60

CHANCELLOR (5003 "Hold That
Tiger!") 15-25   59
(Black label. Price for any of three volumes.)
CHANCELLOR (5003 "Excerpts from *Hold
That Tiger!*") 25-40   59
(With paper sleeve. White label. Promotional issue
only.)
CHANCELLOR (5005 "The Fabulous
Fabian") 20-30   60
CHANCELLOR (9802 "Young and
Wonderful") 20-30   60

LPs: 10/12–inch 33rpm

ABC 10-12   73
CHANCELLOR (5003 "Hold That
Tiger") 25-35   59
(Monaural.)
CHANCELLOR (5003 "Hold That
Tiger") 35-45   59
(Stereo.)
CHANCELLOR (5005 "The
Fabulous Fabian") 25-35   59
(Monaural.)
CHANCELLOR (5005 "The
Fabulous Fabian") 35-45   59
(Stereo.)
CHANCELLOR (5012 "The Good
Old Summertime") 25-35   60
(Monaural.)
CHANCELLOR (5012 "The Good
Old Summertime") 35-45   60
(Stereo.)
CHANCELLOR (5019 "Rockin' Hot") . 40-50   61
CHANCELLOR (5024 "16 Fabulous
Hits") 40-50   62
CHANCELLOR (69802 "Young and
Wonderful") 25-35   60
EVEREST 5-10   83
MCA 5-10   85
TRIP 8-10   77
U.A. 10-12   75
Also see 4 DATES

FABIAN / Frankie Avalon
Singles: 7–inch

CHANCELLOR/WIBG 99 ("When the Saints
Go Marchin' In") 25-50   61
(Colored vinyl. Radio station special products
issue. No number used. Flip is by the Live Five,
who were the WIBG dee jays.)
LPs: 10/12–inch 33rpm

CHANCELLOR (5009 "Hit Makers") . . 40-50   60
MCA 5-10   85
Also see AVALON, Frankie
Also see FABIAN

FABRIC, Bent
Singles: 7–inch

ATCO 4-6   62-65
Picture Sleeves

ATCO 5-8   62

LPs: 10/12–inch 33rpm

ATCO 8-15   62-63
Also see BILK, Mr. Acker, and Bent Fabric

FABRIQUE, Tina
Singles: 12–inch 33/45rpm

PRISM 4-6   84

FABULOUS COUNTS
Singles: 7–inch

MOIRA 3-6   68-70
LPs: 10/12–inch 33rpm

COTILLION 10-12   69

FABULOUS FARQUAHR
(Farquahr)
Singles: 7–inch

ELEKTRA 3-5   71
VERVE/FORECAST 4-8   68-69
WARNER 3-6   70
LPs: 10/12–inch 33rpm

ELEKTRA 8-10   70
VERVE/FORECAST 10-15   69

FABULOUS POODLES
Singles: 7–inch

EPIC 3-5   79
LPs: 10/12–inch 33rpm

EPIC 5-10   76-79

FABULOUS RHINESTONES
Singles: 7–inch

JUST SUNSHINE 3-5   72
LPs: 10/12–inch 33rpm

JUST SUNSHINE 8-10   72-73

FABULOUS THUNDERBIRDS
Singles: 7–inch

CBS ASSOCIATED 2-4   86-89
CHRYSALIS 2-4   79-81
ELEKTRA 2-4   88
Picture Sleeves

CBS ASSOCIATED 2-4   86-87
LPs: 10/12–inch 33rpm

CBS ASSOCIATED 5-10   86-89
CHRYSALIS 5-10   79-81
TAKOMA 10-15   79
Members:Kim Wilson; Jimmie Vaughan; Preston Hubbard; Fran
Christina.
Also see SANTANA
Also see VAUGHAN BROTHERS

FACE to FACE
Singles: 12–inch 33/45rpm

EPIC 4-6   84
PORTRAIT 4-6   84
Singles: 7–inch

EPIC 2-4   84
MERCURY 2-4   88
PORTRAIT 2-4   84
LPs: 10/12–inch 33rpm

EPIC 5-10   84
MERCURY 5-8   88

FACENDA, Tommy
Singles: 7-inch
ATLANTIC 15-20   59
LEGRANDE 5-10   59
NASCO 5-10   58
Also see KING CURTIS

FACES
Singles: 7-inch
WARNER 3-6   71-75
LPs: 10/12-inch 33rpm
MERCURY 8-12   73
WARNER 10-20   70-76
Members: Rod Stewart; Ron Wood; Ronnie Lane.
Also see McLAGAN, Ian
Also see SMALL FACES
Also see STEWART, Rod
Also see WOOD, Ron

FACHIN, Erla
Singles: 7-inch
CRITIQUE 2-4   88
Picture Sleeves
CRITIQUE 2-4   88

FACTS of LIFE
Singles: 7-inch
KAYVETTE 3-5   76-77
LPs: 10/12-inch 33rpm
KAYVETTE 8-10   77
Members: Jean Davis; Keith William; Chuck Carter.

FAGEN, Donald
Singles: 7-inch
WARNER 2-4   82-88
Picture Sleeves
WARNER 2-4   82-88
LPs: 10/12-inch 33rpm
MFSL (120 "Nightfly") 15-25   84
WARNER 5-10   82-88
Also see STEELY DAN

FAGEN, Donald, and Walter Becker
LPs: 10/12-inch 33rpm
PVC 5-10   85
Also see FAGEN, Donald

FAGIN, Joe
Singles: 7-inch
MILLENNIUM 2-4   82

FAIR, Yvonne
Singles: 7-inch
DADE 4-8   63
KING 4-8   62
MOTOWN 3-5   74-76
SMASH 4-8   66
SOUL 3-6   70
LPs: 10/12-inch 33rpm
MOTOWN 5-10   76

FAIRCHILD, Barbara
Singles: 7-inch
CAPITOL 2-4   86
COLUMBIA 2-4   69-78

DOWN HOME 2-4   80
KAPP 3-5   68
LPs: 10/12-inch 33rpm
AUDIOGRAPH 5-10   82
COLUMBIA 8-12   70-78
PAID 5-10   81
Also see WALKER, Billy, and Barbara Fairchild

FAIRGROUND ATTRACTION
Singles: 7-inch
RCA 2-4   88
Picture Sleeves
RCA 2-4   88
LPs: 10/12-inch 33rpm
RCA 5-8   88

FAIRPORT CONVENTION
Singles: 7-inch
A&M 3-5   71-72
LPs: 10/12-inch 33rpm
A&M 10-12   69-74
COTILLION 10-15   70
VARRICK/ROUNDER 5-10   86
ISLAND 8-10   74-75
Also see DENNY, Sandy
Also see MATTHEWS, Ian
Also see THOMPSON, Richard

FAIRWEATHER
(Andy Fairweather-Low)
LPs: 10/12-inch 33rpm
NEON 8-10   71
Also see FAIRWEATHER-LOW, Andy

FAIRWEATHER-LOW, Andy
Singles: 7-inch
A&M 3-5   75-77
LPs: 10/12-inch 33rpm
A&M 8-10   74-76
WARNER 5-10   80
Also see FAIRWEATHER
Also see WILLIE and the Poor Boys

FAITH, Adam
Singles: 7-inch
AMY 4-8   64-65
CAPITOL 4-8   65-66
CUB 5-10   59
DOT 4-8   62
LPs: 10/12-inch 33rpm
AMY (8005 "Adam Faith") 20-30   65
MGM (3951 "England's Top Singer") . 25-30   61
WARNER 8-12   74

FAITH, Gene
Singles: 7-inch
VIRTUE 3-6   69-70

FAITH, Percy, Orchestra
Singles: 78rpm
COLUMBIA 2-4   50-57
Singles: 7-inch
COLUMBIA 3-8   50-76

Picture Sleeves
COLUMBIA 5-8   60
EPs: 7-Inch 33/45rpm
COLUMBIA 5-10   50-59
ROYALE 5-10
LPs: 10/12-Inch 33rpm
COLUMBIA 5-15   51-82
HARMONY 5-10   68-72
Also see SANDERS, Felicia

FAITH BAND
Singles: 7-Inch
MERCURY/VILLAGE 2-5   78-79
VILLAGE 3-5   78
LPs: 10/12-Inch 33rpm
BROWN BAG 10-12   73
MERCURY 5-10   78-79
VILLAGE 8-10   77

FAITH NO MORE
Singles: 7-Inch
SLASH 2-4   90
LPs: 10/12-Inch 33rpm
SLASH 5-8   90

FAITHFULL, Marianne
Singles: 12-Inch 33/45rpm
ISLAND 4-6   83
Singles: 7-Inch
ISLAND 2-4   79
LONDON (Except 1022) 4-8   64-72
LONDON (1022 "Sister Morphine") . 75-100   69
(With the Rolling Stones.)
Picture Sleeves
LONDON 5-10   65
LPs: 10/12-Inch 33rpm
ISLAND 5-10   79-90
LONDON 15-25   65-69
Also see ROLLING STONES

FALANA, Lola
Singles: 7-Inch
RCA 2-4   75
REPRISE 5-10   67

FALCO
Singles: 12-Inch 33/45rpm
A&M 4-6   83-86
Singles: 7-Inch
A&M 2-4   83-86
Picture Sleeves
A&M 2-4   86
LPs: 10/12-Inch 33rpm
A&M 5-10   83-86

FALCONS
Singles: 7-Inch
ANNA (1110 "Just for Your Love") ... 20-40   60
ATLANTIC 5-10   62-63
BIG WHEEL 4-8   66
CHESS (1743 "Just for Your Love") .. 10-15   59

FALCON (1006 "Now That
  It's Over") 75-100   57
FLICK (001 "You're So Fine") 75-125   59
FLICK (008 "You Must Know
  I Love You") 20-30   60
KUDO (661 "This Heart of Mine") ... 30-40   58
LIBERTY 2-4
LU PINE 8-12   62-64
MERCURY (70940 "Baby That's It") . 15-20   56
SILHOUETTE (522 "Can This
  Be Christmas") 40-50   57
(Flip side, *Sent Up*, is Silhouette 521, a number
  also used for a Charmers release.)
UNART (2013 "You're So Fine") 8-12   59
UNART (2013-S "You're So Fine") ... 15-25   59
(Stereo.)
UNART (2022 "Country Shack") 8-12   59
U.A. 5-10   59-60
EPs: 7-Inch 33/45rpm
U.A. (10010 "The Falcons") 40-60   59
  Members: Wilson Pickett; Eddie Floyd; Arnet Robinson; Joe
  Stubbs; Ben Rice; Lance Finnie.
  Also see FLOYD, Eddie
  Also see PICKETT, Wilson

FALTERMEYER, Harold
Singles: 7-Inch
MCA 2-4   85
Picture Sleeves
MCA 2-4   85
  Also see LABELLE, Patti, and Harold Faltermeyer

FALTERMEYER, Harold, and Steve Stevens
Singles: 12-Inch 33/45rpm
COLUMBIA 4-8   86
(Promotional issue only.)
Singles: 7-Inch
COLUMBIA 2-4   86
  Also see FALTERMEYER, Harold

FALTSKOG, Agnetha
Singles: 7-Inch
POLYDOR 2-4   83
Picture Sleeves
POLYDOR 3-5   83
LPs: 10/12-Inch 33rpm
POLYDOR 5-10   83
  Also see ABBA

FALTSKOG, Agnetha, and Peter Cetera
Singles: 7-Inch
ATLANTIC 2-4   88
Picture Sleeves
ATLANTIC 2-4   88
  Also see CETERA, Peter
  Also see FALTSKOG, Agnetha

FAME: see KIDS from "FAME"

FAME, Georgie
(Georgie Fame and the Blue Flames)
Singles: 7-Inch
EPIC 3-6   68-70
IMPERIAL 4-8   65-67

ISLAND 3-5   75
EPs: 7–inch 33/45rpm
EPIC 5-10   68
(Jukebox issues only.)
LPs: 10/12–inch 33rpm
EPIC 10-20   68-70
IMPERIAL 15-20   65-66
ISLAND 8-10   75

FAMILY
Singles: 7–inch
LITTLE CITY 3-5   77
U.A. 3-5   71-73
LPs: 10/12–inch 33rpm
REPRISE 15-20   68-70
U.A. 10-12   71-73
Members; Rick Gretch; John Weider.
Also see BLIND FAITH
Also see WEIDER, John

FAMILY
Singles: 12–inch 33/45rpm
PAISLEY PARK 4-6   85
Singles: 7–inch
PAISLEY PARK 2-4   85
LPs: 10/12–inch 33rpm
PAISLEY PARK 5-10   85

FAMILY PLANN
Singles: 7–inch
DRIVE 3-5   75

FANCY
Singles: 7–inch
BIG TREE 3-5   74
POISON RING 3-6   71
LPs: 10/12–inch 33rpm
BIG TREE 8-10   74
POISON RING 12-20   71
RCA 5-10   79
Members:Al Ranaudo; Billy Durso.

FANNY
Singles: 7–inch
CASABLANCA 3-5   74-75
REPRISE 3-5   70-73
LPs: 10/12–inch 33rpm
CASABLANCA 8-10   74
REPRISE 10-12   70-73
Members: Jean Millington; June Millington; Alice de Buhr; Nickey
Barclay; Patti Quatro; Wendy Haas; Brie Howard.

FANTASTIC FIVE KEYS
Singles: 7–inch
CAPITOL 5-10   62
Also see FIVE KEYS

FANTASTIC FOUR
Singles: 7–inch
EASTBOUND 3-5   73-74
RIC-TIC 4-8   66-68
SOUL 4-6   68-70
EASTBOUND 3-5   74
WESTBOUND 3-5   75-79

LPs: 10/12–inch 33rpm
SOUL 10-12   69
20TH FOX/WESTBOUND 8-10   76
WESTBOUND 8-10   75-78
Members: Joe Pruitt; James Epps; Robert Pruitt; Toby Childs;
Ernest Newsome; Cleveland Horn.

FANTASTIC FOUR / Wingate's Love-in Strings
Singles: 7–inch
RIC-TIC 4-8   67
Also see FANTASTIC FOUR

FANTASTIC JOHNNY C.
(Johnny Corley)
Singles: 7–inch
KAMA SUTRA 3-5   70
PHIL L.A. of SOUL 4-8   67-73
LPs: 10/12–inch 33rpm
PHIL L.A. of SOUL 15-20   68

FANTASTICS
Singles: 7–inch
BELL 3-5   71-72
DERAM 3-6   69

FANTASY
Singles: 7–inch
IMPERIAL 3-6   69
LIBERTY 3-5   70
LPs: 10/12–inch 33rpm
LIBERTY 10-15   70

FANTASY
Singles: 12–inch 33/45rpm
QUALITY 4-6   83
Singles: 7–inch
PAVILLION 2-4   81
LPs: 10/12–inch 33rpm
PAVILLION 5-10   81-82

FANTAYZEE, Haysl:
see HAYSI FANTAYZEE

FARAGHER BROTHERS
Singles: 7–inch
ABC 3-5   76-77
POLYDOR 2-4   79
LPs: 10/12–inch 33rpm
ABC 5-10   79
POLYDOR 5-10   78-79

FARDON, Don
Singles: 7–inch
CHELSEA 3-5   73
GNP/CRESCENDO 4-8   68
LPs: 10/12–inch 33rpm
DECCA 10-12   70
GNP/CRESCENDO 15-20   68

FARGO, Donna
Singles: 7–inch
ABC 2-4   78
ABC/DOT 3-5   74-77

FATBACK
(Fatback Band)
Singles: 12–inch 33/45rpm
SPRING 4-6 84
Singles: 7–inch
COTILLION 2-4 83-85
EVENT 3-5 74-76
PERCEPTION 3-5 72-74
POLYDOR 2-4 79
SPRING 2-5 76-85
LPs: 10/12–inch 33rpm
COTILLION 5-10 83-85
EVENT 8-10 74-76
PERCEPTION 8-10 72
POLYDOR 5-10 79
SPRING 5-10 76-84
 Members: Bill Curtis; Johnny King; George Williams; Johnny Flippin; Earl Shelton; George Adam; Fred Demerey; George Victory; Gerry Thomas.

FATES WARNING
LPs: 10/12–inch 33rpm
ENIGMA 5-10 87
METAL BLADE 5-8 88-89

FAX, Tony
Singles: 7–inch
CALLA 3-6 68

FAYE, Alma
Singles: 12–inch 33/45rpm
CASABLANCA 4-6 79
Singles: 7–inch
CASABLANCA 2-4 79

FAZE-O
Singles: 7–inch
SHE 2-4 77-79
LPs: 10/12–inch 33rpm
SHE 5-10 77-79

FEARON, Phil
Singles: 7–inch
COOLTEMPO 2-4 86
ISLAND 2-4 86

FEATHER
Singles: 7–inch
WHITE WHALE 3-5 70
LPs: 10/12–inch 33rpm
COLUMBIA 10-12 70

FEATHERBED
(Barry Manilow)
Singles: 7–inch
BELL (133 "Could It Be Magic") 15-25 71
BELL (971 "Amy") 15-25 71
 Also see MANILOW, Barry

FEE WAYBILL: see WAYBILL, Fee

FEEL
Singles: 12–inch 33/45rpm
SUTRA 4-6 83

Singles: 7–inch
SUTRA 2-4 82-83

FEELGOOD, DR: see DR. FEELGOOD

FEELIES
A&M 5-8 88

FELDER, Don
Singles: 7–inch
ASYLUM 2-4 83
FULL MOON/ASYLUM 2-4 81
MCA 2-4
Picture Sleeves
FULL MOON/ASYLUM 2-4 81
LPs: 10/12–inch 33rpm
ASYLUM 5-10 83
ELEKTRA 5-8 83
 Also see EAGLES

FELDER, Wilton
Singles: 7–inch
ABC 2-4 78
MCA 2-4 79-85
LPs: 10/12–inch 33rpm
ABC 5-10 78
MCA 5-10 80-85
PACIFIC JAZZ 8-12 69
 Also see JAZZ CRUSADERS
 Also see TASTE of HONEY

FELDER, Wilton, and Bobby Womack
Singles: 7–inch
MCA 2-4 80-85
Picture Sleeves
MCA 2-4 80-85
 Also see FELDER, Wilton
 Also see WOMACK, Bobby

FELDMAN, Victor
(Victor Feldman All Stars; Victor Feldman Quartet; Victor Feldman Trio; Vic Feldman)
Singles: 7–inch
AVA 3-5 63
INFINITY 3-5 62
PACIFIC JAZZ 3-5 66
VEE JAY 3-5 64
LPs: 10/12–inch 33rpm
AVA 10-20 63
CONTEMPORARY 15-25 58-60
INTERLUDE 15-20 59
MODE 20-30 58
NAUTILUS 10-20 82
 (Half-speed mastered.)
PACIFIC JAZZ 10-15 67-68
PALTO ALTO 5-10 83-84
RIVERSIDE 15-20 61
VEE JAY 15-25 59-65
WORLD PACIFIC 15-25 62

FELICIANO, Jose
Singles: 7–inch
ALA 2-4 80
MOTOWN 2-4 81-83

PRIVATE STOCK	3-5	76-77
RCA	3-6	64-75

LPs: 10/12–inch 33rpm

CAMDEN	8-10	72
MOTOWN	5-10	81
PRIVATE STOCK	6-10	76-77
RCA	8-15	65-76

FELICIANO, Jose / Petula Clark
EPs: 7–inch 33/45rpm

TK (334 "Mackenna's Gold")	10-20	69
Also see CLARK, Petula		

FELICIANO, Jose, and Quincy Jones
LPs: 10/12–inch 33rpm

RCA (4096 "Mackenna's Gold")	15-25	69
(Soundtrack.)		
Also see FELICIANO, Jose		
Also see JONES, Quincy		

FELIX & JARVIS
Singles: 7–inch

RFC/QUALITY	2-4	82-83

FELLER, Dick
Singles: 7–inch

ASYLUM	3-5	74-75
U.A.	2-4	72-80

LPs: 10/12–inch 33rpm

ASYLUM	6-10	75
AUDIOGRAPH ALIVE	5-10	84
U.A.	8-12	73

FELLINI, Suzanne
Singles: 7–inch

CASABLANCA	2-4	80

LPs: 10/12–inch 33rpm

CASABLANCA	5-10	80

FELONY
Singles: 7–inch

ROCK 'N' ROLL	2-4	83-84

LPs: 10/12–inch 33rpm

ROCK 'N' ROLL	5-10	83

FELTS, Narvel
Singles: 78rpm

MERCURY	5-10	57

Singles: 7–inch

ABC	2-4	76
ABC/DOT	3-5	75-77
CINNAMON	3-5	73-74
COLLAGE	2-4	79
COMPLEAT	2-4	82-83
EVERGREEN	2-4	82-86
GMC	2-4	81
GROOVE	4-8	63
HI (2100 series)	4-8	67
HI (2300 series)	3-5	76
KARI	2-4	80
LOBO	2-4	82
MCA	2-4	79
MERCURY	8-12	57

PINK	10-15	59-60

LPs: 10/12–inch 33rpm

ABC	5-10	78
ABC/DOT	8-10	75-77
CINNAMON	8-10	73-74
HI	8-10	76

FELTS, Narvel / Red Sovine / Mel Tillis
LPs: 10/12–inch 33rpm

POWER PAK	5-10	
Also see FELTS, Narvel		
Also see SOVINE, Red		

FEMALE BODY INSPECTORS
Singles: 12–inch 33/45rpm

WARNER	4-6	86

Singles: 7–inch

WARNER	2-4	86

FENDER, Freddy
(Baldemar Huerta)
Singles: 7–inch

ABC	2-4	76-79
ABC/DOT	4-6	75-77
ARV INT'L	3-5	75
ARGO	10-15	60
DISCOS DOMINANTE	5-10	
DUNCAN	10-20	59
GRT	4-8	75-76
GOLDBAND	4-8	
IMPERIAL	8-12	60
MCA	2-4	82
NORCO	4-8	63-65
STARFLITE	2-4	79-80
WARNER	2-4	83

LPs: 10/12–inch 33rpm

ABC	5-10	78-79
ABC/DOT	8-10	75-77
ACCORD	5-10	81
GRT	8-10	75
STARFLITE	5-10	80

FENDER, Freddy, and Noel VIII
Singles: 7–inch

NORCO (107 "Magic of Love")	4-8	65
SOCK-O (101 "Magic of Love")	10-15	65
Also see FENDER, Freddy		

FENDERMEN
Singles: 7–inch

COLLECTABLES	2-4	
CUCA (1003 "Mule Skinner Blues")	50-75	60
DAB	4-8	
ERA	3-5	72
ERIC	2-4	
KOALA	2-4	
SOMA	6-10	60-61

LPs: 10/12–inch 33rpm

SOMA (1240 "Mule Skinner Blues")	800-1200	60
Members: Phil Humphrey; Jim Sundquist.		

FERGUSON, Helena
Singles: 7–inch
COMPASS 4-8   67-68

FERGUSON, Jay
Singles: 7–inch
ASYLUM 3-5   77-79
CAPITOL 2-4   82
LPs: 10/12–inch 33rpm
ASYLUM 8-10   76-79
CAPITOL 5-10   80-82
Also see JO JO GUNNE
Also see SPIRIT

FERGUSON, Johnny
Singles: 7–inch
MGM 5-10   59-60

FERGUSON, Maynard
(Maynard Ferguson Sextet)
Singles: 78rpm
CAPITOL 3-5   50-51
EMARCY 3-5   54
MERCURY 2-4   55
Singles: 12–inch 33/45rpm
COLUMBIA 4-6   79
Singles: 7–inch
CAMEO 3-5   63
CAPITOL 5-10   50-51
COLUMBIA 2-4   71-82
EMARCY 5-10   54
MAINSTREAM 3-5   71-72
MERCURY 5-10   55
ROULETTE 4-8   59-62
EPs: 7–inch 33/45rpm
EMARCY 5-15   54-57
LPs: 10/12–inch 33rpm
BETHLEHEM 5-10   78
CAMEO 15-20   63
COLUMBIA 5-10   71-82
EMARCY (400 series) 5-10   76
EMARCY (1000 series) 5-10   81
EMARCY (26017 "Hollywood
  Party") 50-100   54
  (10–inch LP.)
EMARCY (26024 "Dimensions") ... 50-100   54
  (10–inch LP.)
EMARCY (36000 series) 20-40   55-57
ENTERPRISE 8-12   68
MAINSTREAM (300 series) 6-10   71-72
MAINSTREAM (6000 series) 15-20   64
  (Stereo.)
MAINSTREAM (56000 series) 10-20   64
  (Monaural.)
MERCURY 12-20   60
PALTO ALTO 5-10   83
PRESTIGE 8-12   69
ROULETTE 12-25   58-72
SKYLARK (17 "Great Jazz Solos") .. 25-50   53
TRIP 5-10   74
Also see BASIE, Count, and Maynard Ferguson

Also see KENTON, Stan
Also see MANN, Herbie / Maynard Ferguson

FERGUSON, Maynard, and Chris Connor
Singles: 7–inch
ATLANTIC 4-6   61
LPs: 10/12–inch 33rpm
ATLANTIC (8049 "Double Exposure") 25-35   61
  (Monaural.)
ATLANTIC (SD-8049 "Double
  Exposure") 35-45   61
  (Stereo.)
ROULETTE (52068 "Two's Company") 40-60   58
Also see CONNOR, Chris
Also see FERGUSON, Maynard

FERKO STRING BAND
Singles: 78rpm
MEDIA 3-5   55
SAVOY 3-5   55
Singles: 7–inch
ARGO 3-5   63
MEDIA 4-8   55
SAVOY 4-8   55
LPs: 10/12–inch 33rpm
ABC-PAR 10-15   63
ALSHIRE 4-6   76
REGENT 12-20   56-59
SURE 6-12   65-73

FERRANTE & TEICHER
Singles: 78rpm
COLUMBIA 2-5   53
ENTRE 3-6   53
Singles: 7–inch
ABC-PAR 3-6   58-62
COLUMBIA 4-8   53
ENTRE 5-10   53
U.A. 2-5   59-79
Picture Sleeves
U.A. (Except 231 to 300) 4-8   63-69
U.A. (231 to 300) 5-10   60-61
EPs: 7–inch 33/45rpm
ABC-PAR 4-8   58-60
MGM 10-20   54
U.A. 4-8   69
LPs: 10/12–inch 33rpm
ABC 5-10   73-76
ABC-PAR 8-15   58-66
COLUMBIA 8-15   55-73
DORAL 10-20
  (Promotional mail-order issue, from Doral
  cigarettes.)
GUEST STAR 4-8   64
HARMONY 5-10   64-70
LIBERTY 5-10   81-84
MGM 20-40   54
METRO 5-10   66
MISTLETOE 4-6   75
SUNSET 5-10   70-71
WESTMINSTER 12-20   55-58

UNART 5-10   67
U.A. 5-15   60-80
URANIA 4-8
Members: Arthur Ferrante; Louis Teicher.

FERRARI
Singles: 12–inch 33/45rpm
SUGAR HILL 4-6   82

FERRER, Jose
(Jose Ferrer and the Ferrers)
Singles: 78rpm
COLUMBIA 3-5   54-55
Singles: 7–inch
COLUMBIA 4-8   54-55
EPIC 3-5   68
RCA 4-6   60
Picture Sleeves
RCA 4-6   60
LPs: 10/12–inch 33rpm
MGM 8-12   62-65
Also see CLOONEY, Rosemary, and Jose Ferrer

FERRY, Bryan
Singles: 12–inch 33/45rpm
WARNER 4-6   85
Singles: 7–inch
ATLANTIC 2-4   74-79
REPRISE 2-4   88
WARNER 2-4   85
Picture Sleeves
REPRISE 2-4   88
LPs: 10/12–inch 33rpm
ATLANTIC 10-12   72-78
REPRISE 5-10   87
WARNER 5-10   85
Also see ROXY MUSIC
Also see TANGERINE DREAM / Jon Anderson / Bryan Ferry

FEVA, Sandra
Singles: 7–inch
CATAWBA 2-4   87
KRISMA 2-4   86
VENTURE 2-4   79-81
LPs: 10/12–inch 33rpm
VENTURE 5-10   81

FEVER
Singles: 12–inch 33/45rpm
FANTASY 4-6   79-82
JDC 4-6   85
Singles: 7–inch
FANTASY 2-4   79-82
LPs: 10/12–inch 33rpm
FANTASY 5-10   79-80

FEVER TREE
Singles: 7–inch
AMPEX 10-20   70
MAINSTREAM 5-10   67
UNI (Except 55060) 10-20   68-69
UNI (55060 "San Francisco Girls") 8-12   68
(Black vinyl.)

UNI (55060 "San Francisco Girls") .. 20-40   68
(Colored vinyl. Promotional issue only.)
LPs: 10/12–inch 33rpm
AMPEX 12-20   70
MCA 8-10   76
UNI (73024 "Fever Tree") 20-30 68
UNI (73040 "Another Time,
   Another Place") 15-25   68
UNI (73067 "Creation") 15-25   70
Members: Dennis Keller; Rob Landes; E.E. Wolfe; John Tuttle.

FIDELITYS
Singles: 7–inch
BATON 10-15   58
SIR 10-20   59-60

FIEDLER, Arthur:
   see BOSTON POPS ORCHESTRA

FIELD, Sally
Singles: 7–inch
COLGEMS 4-6   67-68
Picture Sleeves
COLGEMS 4-8   67
LPs: 10/12–inch 33rpm
COLGEMS 10-20   67

FIELDS, Ernie
Singles: 7–inch
CAPITOL 4-6   64
RENDEZVOUS 4-8   59-62
LPs: 10/12–inch 33rpm
RENDEZVOUS (1309 "In the Mood") 30-40   60

FIELDS, Kim
Singles: 7–inch
CRITIQUE 2-4   84

FIELDS, Richard "Dimples"
Singles: 12–inch 33/45rpm
RCA 4-6   84-85
Singles: 7–inch
BOARDWALK 2-4   81-83
COLUMBIA 2-4   87
RCA 2-4   84-85
LPs: 10/12–inch 33rpm
BOARDWALK 5-10   81-82
RCA 5-10   84

FIELDS, W.C.
LPs: 10/12–inch 33rpm
AMERICAN 5-10   75
COLUMBIA 6-10   69-77
DECCA 8-12   68
HARMONY 6-10   70
HUDSON 15-25   60
MARK '56 (571 "Original Radio
   Broadcasts") 30-50   78
(Picture disc.)

FIELDS, W.C., and Mae West
LPs: 10/12–inch 33rpm
HARMONY 6-10   70

PROSCENIUM 15-20   60
  Also see FIELDS, W.C.
  Also see WEST, Mae

FIELDS, W.C., Memorial Electric String Band
Singles: 7-inch

HBR 4-8   66
MERCURY 5-10   66

FIESTA
Singles: 7-inch

ARISTA 2-4   78

FIESTAS
Singles: 7-inch

COLLECTABLES 2-4
OLD TOWN (1062 through 1122) 10-20   59-60
OLD TOWN (1127 through 1189) 5-10   62-65
RESPECT 3-5   75
STRAND (25046 "Julie") 20-30   61
VIGOR 2-4   74
  Members: Tom Bullock; Eddie Morris; Sam Ingalls; Preston Love.
  Also see ROBERT & JOHNNY / Fiestas

FIFTH ANGEL
LPs: 10/12-inch 33rpm

EPIC 5-8   88

FIFTH DIMENSION
Singles: 7-inch

ABC 3-5   75-76
ARISTA 3-5   75
BELL 3-5   70-74
MOTOWN 2-4   78-79
SOUL CITY 4-8   66-70
SUTRA 2-4   83
Picture Sleeves
SOUL CITY 4-8   67-69
LPs: 10/12-inch 33rpm
ABC 8-10   75
ARISTA 8-10   75
BELL 8-12   70-74
KORY 8-10   77
MOTOWN 5-10   78-79
RHINO 5-10   86
SOUL CITY 10-15   67-70
  Members: Marilyn McCoo; Billy Davis Jr; Lamonte McLemore;
  Florence LaRue; Ron Townson.
  Also see DAVIS, Billy, Jr.
  Also see MAMAS and the Papas / Association / Fifth Dimension
  Also see McCOO, Marilyn, and Billy Davis Jr.

FIFTH ESTATE
Singles: 7-inch

JUBILEE 4-8   67-69
RED BIRD 5-10   66
LPs: 10/12-inch 33rpm
JUBILEE (8005 "Ding Dong
  the Witch Is Dead") 20-30   67

50 GUITARS of TOMMY GARRETT
Singles: 7-inch

LIBERTY 3-5   66-68

LPs: 10/12-inch 33rpm
LIBERTY 5-15   61-71
MUSICOR 5-10   76-78
U.A. 5-8   73
  Also see GARRETT, Tommy

52ND STREET
Singles: 12-inch 33/45rpm

A&M 4-6   83
MCA 4-6   85-87
PROFILE 4-6   84
Singles: 7-inch
MCA 2-4   85-86
LPs: 10/12-inch 33rpm
MCA 5-10   86

FIGURES on the BEACH
Singles: 12-inch 33/45rpm
METRO AMERICAN 4-6   84
Singles: 7-inch
SIRE 2-4   89
Picture Sleeves
SIRE 2-4   89

FILE 13
Singles: 12-inch 33/45rpm
PROFILE 4-6   84

FINE YOUNG CANNIBALS
Singles: 12-inch 33/45rpm
I.R.S. 4-6   86-89
Singles: 7-inch
I.R.S. 2-4   86-90
Picture Sleeves
I.R.S. 2-4   86-89
LPs: 10/12-inch 33rpm
I.R.S. 5-10   86-90
  Members: Roland Gift; Danny Cox; David Steele.
  Also see ENGLISH BEAT

FINESSE & SYNQUIS
LPs: 10/12-inch 33rpm
MCA 5-8   88

FINISHED TOUCH
Singles: 7-inch
MOTOWN 2-4   78
LPs: 10/12-inch 33rpm
MOTOWN 5-10   78

FINN, Tim
Singles: 7-inch
A&M 2-4   83
LPs: 10/12-inch 33rpm
A&M 5-10   83
  Also see SPLIT ENZ

FINNEGAN, Larry
Singles: 7-inch
CORAL 4-8   62
OLD TOWN 5-10   62-63
RIC 8-10   64

FINNEY, Albert
Singles: 7–inch
MOTOWN 2-4   77
LPs: 10/12–inch 33rpm
MOTOWN 5-10   77

FIONA
(Fiona Flanagan; Fiona with Kip Winger)
Singles: 7–inch
ATLANTIC 2-4   84-89
Picture Sleeves
ATLANTIC 2-4   89
LPs: 10/12–inch 33rpm
ATLANTIC 5-10   84-89

FIORILLO, Elisa
Singles: 7–inch
CHRYSALIS 2-4   88-90
Picture Sleeves
CHRYSALIS 2-4   88
LPs: 10/12–inch 33rpm
CHRYSALIS 5-8   88

FIRE & RAIN
Singles: 7–inch
MERCURY 3-5   73
LPs: 10/12–inch 33rpm
MERCURY 8-10   73

FIRE INC.
Singles: 7–inch
MCA 2-4   84
Picture Sleeves
MCA 2-4   84

FIREBALLET
Singles: 7–inch
PASSPORT 3-5   75-76
LPs: 10/12–inch 33rpm
PASSPORT 8-10   75-76

FIREBALLS
Singles: 7–inch
ATCO 4-8   67-70
DOT 4-8   63-67
KAPP (248 "Fireball") 75-100 59
TOP RANK (2008 "Torquay") 8-12   59
TOP RANK (2026 "Bulldog") 8-12   59
 (Monaural.)
TOP RANK (2026-ST "Bulldog") . 15-25 59
 (Stereo.)
TOP RANK (2038 "Foot Patter") . 8-12 60
 (Monaural.)
TOP RANK (2038-ST "Foot Patter") . 15-25 60
 (Stereo.)
TOP RANK (2054 "Vaquero") 8-12   61
TOP RANK (2081 "Sweet Talk") . 8-12   61
TOP RANK (3003 "Rik-A-Tik") .. 8-12   61
WARWICK 5-10   61
EPs: 7–inch 33/45rpm
TOP RANK (1000 "The Fireballs") ... 50-75 60

LPs: 10/12–inch 33rpm
ATCO 10-14 68
TOP RANK (324 "The Fireballs") 45-55 60
TOP RANK (343 "Vaquero") 45-60 60
 (Monaural.)
TOP RANK (643 "Vaquero") 50-75 60
 (Stereo.)
WARWICK (2042 "Here Are the
 Fireballs") 45-60 61
Members: Chuck Tharp; George Tomsco; Dan Trammell; Eric
Budd; Stan Lark; Doug Roberts; Jimmy Gilmer; Keith
McCormick.
 Also see DALE, Dick / Surfaris / Fireballs
 Also see GILMER, Jimmy
 Also see STRING-A-LONGS

FIREFALL
Singles: 7–inch
ATLANTIC 3-5   76-82
Picture Sleeves
ATLANTIC 3-5   78-79
LPs: 10/12–inch 33rpm
ATLANTIC 5-10   76-83
Members: Rick Roberts; Jock Bartley; Larry Burnette; Mike
Clark; Scott Kirkpatrick; Dave Muse; Mark Andes; Peter Graves.
 Also see ABBA / Spinners / Firefall / England Dan and John
 Ford Coley
 Also see MANILOW, Barry / Firefall

FIREFLIES
Singles: 7–inch
CANADIAN AMERICAN 8-12   60
ERIC 2-4
HAMILTON 4-8   63
RIBBON 8-12   59-60
TAURUS (355 "You Were Mine") 8-12 62
TAURUS (366 "My Prayer For You") . 10-15 62
LPs: 10/12–inch 33rpm
TAURUS (1002 "You Were Mine") .. 75-125 61
 (Monaural.)
TAURUS (1002 "You Were Mine") . 250-350 61
 (Stereo.)
Members: Ritchie Adams; Lee Reynolds; John Viscelli; Paul
Giacolone.

FIREFLY
Singles: 7–inch
A&M 3-5   75
EMERGENCY 2-4   81

FIRESIGN THEATRE
Singles: 7–inch
COLUMBIA (Except 34) 3-6   69
COLUMBIA (34 "This Side") 4-8   70
 (Single-sided, promotional disc.)
Picture Sleeves
COLUMBIA (34 "This Side") 5-10   70
LPs: 10/12–inch 33rpm
BUTTERFLY 5-10   77
COLUMBIA 8-15   69-74
EPIC 5-10   74
MORWAY 5-8   85
RHINO 5-10   79-82

Members: Phil Proctor; John Fresno; Philip Austin; David Ossman; Cy Faryar.

FIRM

Singles: 7–inch
ATLANTIC 2-4   85-86
Picture Sleeves
ATLANTIC 2-4   85-86
LPs: 10/12–inch 33rpm
ATLANTIC 5-10   85-86
Members: Jimmy Page; Paul Rodgers; Tony Franklin; Chris Slade.
   Also see BAD COMPANY
   Also see MANN, Manfred
   Also see PAGE, Jimmy
   Also see RODGERS, Paul

FIRST CHOICE

Singles: 12–inch 33/45rpm
FIRST CHOICE 4-6   83
SALSOUL 4-6   84
Singles: 7–inch
GOLD MINE 2-5   77-79
PHILLY GROOVE 3-5   73-74
WAND 3-5   72
WARNER 3-5   76
LPs: 10/12–inch 33rpm
GOLD MINE 5-10   77-80
KORY 8-10   77
PHILLY GROOVE 8-10   73-74
Members: Rochelle Fleming; Annette Guest; Joyce Jones.

FIRST CIRCLE

Singles: 7–inch
EMI AMERICA 2-4   87

FIRST CLASS

Singles: 7–inch
ALL PLATINUM 3-5   76-77
EBONY SOUNDS 3-5   75
TODAY 3-5   74
UK 3-5   74-75
LPs: 10/12–inch 33rpm
ALL PLATINUM 5-10   76
PARK-WAY 5-10   80
SUGARHILL 5-10   81
Members: Harold Bell; Fred Marshall; Sylvester Redditt; Tony Yarbrough.

FIRST EDITION

Singles: 7–inch
REPRISE 4-8   67-68
LPs: 10/12–inch 33rpm
REPRISE 12-20   67-68
Members: Kenny Rogers; Mike Settle; Thelma Lou Camacho; Terry Williams; Mickey Jones.
   Also see NEW CHRISTY MINSTRELS
   Also see ROGERS, Kenny, and the First Edition

FIRST FAMILY

Singles: 7–inch
POLYDOR 3-5   74

FIRST FIRE

LPs: 10/12–inch 33rpm
TORTOISE INT'L 5-10   78

FIRST FOUR

Singles: 7–inch
STRATA 4-8   65

FIRST GEAR

LPs: 10/12–inch 33rpm
MYRRH 8-10   72

FIRST LOVE

Singles: 12–inch 33/45rpm
CHYCAGO INT'L 4-6   82
Singles: 7–inch
CHYCAGO INT'L 2-4   82
CIM 2-4   83
DAKAR 2-4   80
LPs: 10/12–inch 33rpm
CHYCAGO INT'L 5-10   82

FISCHOFF, George
(George Fischoff Keyboard Komplex; George Fischoff and the Peppers; George Fischoff and the Luv Ens)
Singles: 7–inch
COLUMBIA 3-5   77
DRIVE 2-4   79
HERITAGE 2-4   81
P.I.P. 3-5   75
RANWOOD 3-5   76
REWARD 2-4   84
U.A. 3-5   72-74

FISHBONE

LPs: 10/12–inch 33rpm
COLUMBIA 5-8   91

FISHER, Eddie

Singles: 78rpm
RCA 2-5   50-57
Singles: 7–inch
ABC-PAR 2-4   61
DOT 2-5   65-66
MUSICOR 2-4   69
RCA (3000 through 6000 series) 5-10   50-57
RCA (7000 through 9000 series) 3-8   57-68
RAMROD 4-6   60-63
7 ARTS 4-6   61
TRANS ATLAS 4-6   62
Picture Sleeves
RCA (5000 series) 15-25   53-55
RCA (6000 series) 10-15   55-57
RAMROD 4-8   60
EPs: 7–inch 33/45rpm
RCA 10-20   51-58
LPs: 10/12–inch 33rpm
CAMDEN 6-10   63
DOT 10-15   65-67
HAMILTON 6-10   66
RCA (1024 through 2504) 15-30   55-62

RCA (3025 through 3231) 20-35 52-54
  (10–inch LPs.)
RCA (3375 "Best of Eddie Fisher") ... 10-15 65
RCA (3700 and 3800 series) 10-20 66-67
RAMROD (1 "At the Winter Garden") . 10-20 63
RAMROD (6001 "Scent of Mystery") . 50-60 60
  (Soundtrack. Monaural.)
RAMROD (6001 "Scent of Mystery") . 75-85 60
  (Soundtrack Stereo.)
  Also see COMO, Perry, and Eddie Fisher

FISHER, Eddie / Vic Damone / Dick Haymes
LPs: 10/12–inch 33rpm
ALMOR 10-15
  Also see DAMONE, Vic
  Also see HAYMES, Dick

FISHER, Eddie, and Debbie Reynolds
EPs: 7–inch 33/45rpm
RCA (4018 "Bundle of Joy") 15-25 56
  (Soundtrack.)
LPs: 10/12–inch 33rpm
RCA (1399 "Bundle of Joy") 40-50 56
  (Soundtrack.)
  Also see FISHER, Eddie
  Also see REYNOLDS, Debbie

FISHER, Mary Ann
Singles: 7–inch
FIRE 5-10 59-60
IMPERIAL 4-8 62
SEG-WAY 4-8 61

FISHER, Miss Toni: see FISHER, Toni

FISHER, Toni
(Miss Toni Fisher)
Singles: 7–inch
BIG TOP 5-10 62
CAPITOL 4-8 67
COLLECTABLES 2-4
COLUMBIA 5-10 61
ERA 3-5 72
SIGNET 5-10 59-64
SMASH 4-8 63
LPs: 10/12–inch 33rpm
SIGNET (509 "The Big Hurt") 30-40 60

FISHER, Willie
Singles: 7–inch
TIGRESS 3-5 77

FIT
Singles: 7–inch
A&M 2-4 88

FITZGERALD, Ella
Singles: 78rpm
DECCA (800 through 3000 series) ... 10-15 36-41
DECCA (18000 through 26000 series) . 5-10 42-49
VERVE 3-5 54-57
Singles: 7–inch
CAPITOL 3-5 67-68
DECCA (27000 and 28000 series) ... 10-20 50-53

DECCA (29000 series) 8-15 54-56
DECCA (30000 series except 30405) . 5-10 56-67
DECCA (30405 "Goody Goody") 15-25 57
PABLO 2-4 75
PRESTIGE 3-5 69
REPRISE 3-5 69-71
VERVE (10000 series) 5-10 56-59
VERVE (10100 through 10300 series,
  except 10340) 4-6 60-65
VERVE (10340 "Ringo Beat") 8-12 64
Picture Sleeves
VERVE 5-10 59-60
EPs: 7–inch 33/45rpm
DECCA 15-30 50-58
VERVE 10-25 56-61
LPs: 10/12–inch 33rpm
ATLANTIC 5-10 72
BAINBRIDGE 5-10 81
CAPITOL (2000 series) 8-15 67-68
CAPITOL (11000 series) 5-10 78
CAPITOL (16000 series) 4-6 82
COLUMBIA 5-10 73
CORAL 4-8 73
DECCA (156 "The Best of Ella
  Fitzgerald") 25-35 58
  (Black label with silver print.)
DECCA (156 "The Best of Ella
  Fitzgerald") 15-20 65
  (Black label with horizontal rainbow band.)
DECCA (4000 series) 10-20 61-67
DECCA (5084 "Souvenir Album") .. 75-125 49
  (10–inch LP.)
DECCA (5300 "Gershwin Songs") .. 75-125 51
  (10–inch LP.)
DECCA (8000 series) 20-40 55-59
EVEREST 5-10 73
MCA 5-10 76-82
MGM 5-10 70
MPS 5-10 72
METRO 10-15 65-66
OLYMPIC 5-10 74
PABLO 5-10 75-83
REPRISE 8-12 69-71
VERVE (29 "Ella Fitzgerald Sings the George and
  Ira Gershwin Songbook") 30-40 64
  (Five-LP reissue of Verve 4029.)
VERVE (2500 and 2600 series) 5-10 76-82
  (Reads "Manufactured By MGM Record Corp.," or
  mentions either Polydor or Polygram at bottom of
  label.)
VERVE (4001 through 4009) 25-50 56
  (Reads "Verve Records, Inc." at bottom of label.)
VERVE (4010 "Ella Fitzgerald Sings the Duke
  Ellington Song Book") 75-125 56
  (Four-LP set.)
VERVE (4013 through 4015) 20-40 57
  (Reads "Verve Records, Inc." at bottom of label.)
VERVE (4019 "Ella Fitzgerald Sings the Irving Berlin
  Songbook") 20-40 58

VERVE (4020 through 4028) 20-40   58-59
(Reads "Verve Records, Inc." at bottom of label.)
VERVE (4029 "Ella Fitzgerald Sings the George and
Ira Gershwin Songbook") 40-60   59
(Five-LP set, containing individual LPs 4024
through 4028.)
VERVE (4036 through 4071) 10-20   59-66
VERVE (6000 series) 20-35   57-59
(Reads "Verve Records, Inc." at bottom of label.)
VERVE (6100 series) 15-20   60
(Reads "Verve Records, Inc." at bottom of label.)
VERVE (8200 series) 20-30   58
(Reads "Verve Records, Inc." at bottom of label.)
VERVE (64036 through 64071) 10-20   59-66
VERVE (67000 and 68000 series) 8-15   67-73
VERVE (2610000 series) 20-30   83
VOCALION 6-10   67
   Also see CAMPBELL, Glen / Lettermen / Ella Fitzgerald /
   Sandler and Young
   Also see RIDDLE, Nelson

FITZGERALD, Ella, and Louis Armstrong
EPs: 7–inch 33/45rpm
VERVE 15-30   56
LPs: 10/12–inch 33rpm
METRO 5-10   67
VERVE (4003 "Ella and Louis") 40-60   56
VERVE (4006 "Ella and Louis Again")50-100   56
VERVE (4011 "Porgy and Bess") 25-50   57
(Monaural.)
VERVE (6040 "Porgy and Bess") 40-65   57
(Stereo.)
VERVE (8811 "Ella and Louis") 5-10   72
   Also see ARMSTRONG, Louis

FITZGERALD, Ella, and Count Basie
LPs: 10/12–inch 33rpm
PABLO 5-10   79
VERVE 15-20   63
   Also see BASIE, Count

FITZGERALD, Ella / Bill Doggett
Singles: 7–inch
DECCA 2-5   53
LPs: 10/12–inch 33rpm
VERVE 10-20   62
   Also see DOGGETT, Bill

FITZGERALD, Ella, and Duke Ellington
Singles: 7–inch
VERVE 2-4   66
LPs: 10/12–inch 33rpm
VERVE 10-20   65-67
   Also see ELLINGTON, Duke

FITZGERALD, Ella / Billie Holiday
LPs: 10/12–inch 33rpm
MCA 5-10   76
VERVE (6022 "At Newport") 40-50   58
(Stereo.)
VERVE (8234 "At Newport") 30-40   58
(Monaural.)

FITZGERALD, Ella / Billie Holiday / Lena Horne
LPs: 10/12–inch 33rpm
COLUMBIA (2531 "Ella, Lena
and Billie") 75-100   56
(10–inch LP.)
   Also see HOLIDAY, Billie
   Also see HORNE, Lena

FITZGERALD, Ella, and the Ink Spots
Singles: 78rpm
DECCA (18000 series) 4-8   44-45
EPs: 7–inch 33/45rpm
DECCA 5-10   53
   Also see INK SPOTS

FITZGERALD, Ella, and Antonio Carlos Jobim
LPs: 10/12–inch 33rpm
PABLO 5-10   81
   Also see JOBIM, Antonio Carlos

FITZGERALD, Ella, and Louis Jordan
Singles: 78rpm
DECCA (23000 series) 4-8   46
   Also see JORDAN, Louis

FITZGERALD, Ella, and Peggy Lee
LPs: 10/12–inch 33rpm
DECCA (8166 "Pete Kelly's Blues") .. 40-60   56
   Also see LEE, Peggy

FITZGERALD, Ella, and Oscar Peterson
LPs: 10/12–inch 33rpm
PABLO 5-10   76
   Also see FITZGERALD, Ella
   Also see PETERSON, Oscar

FIVE AMERICANS
Singles: 7–inch
ABC-PAR 5-10   65
ABNAK (Except 109) 8-15   67-69
(Black vinyl.)
ABNAK (Except 109) 15-25   67-69
(Colored vinyl.)
ABNAK (109 "I See the Light") 15-25   65
(Black vinyl.)
ABNAK (109 "I See the Light") 30-40   65
(Colored vinyl.)
HBR 5-10   65-66
JETSTAR 10-15   65
Picture Sleeves
ABNAK (126 "Guided Tour") 10-15   68
HBR (468 "Evol–Not Love") 10-20   66
LPs: 10/12–inch 33rpm
ABNAK 20-30   67-68
HBR (8503 "I See the Light") 30-35   66
(Monaural.)
HBR (9503 "I See the Light") 35-40   66
(Stereo.)

FIVE BLOBS
Singles: 7–inch
COLUMBIA 5-10   58
JOY 10-15   59

Member: Bernie Nee.

FIVE BY FIVE
Singles: 7–inch
PAULA 5-15   67-70
LPs: 10/12–inch 33rpm
PAULA 15-20   69

5 CHANELS
(Chanels)
Singles: 7–inch
DEB 8-10   58

FIVE DU-TONES
Singles: 7–inch
ONE-DERFUL 5-10   63-65

FIVE EMPREES
(Five Empressions)
Singles: 7–inch
FREEPORT 5-10   65-66
GOLD STANDARD 4-8
(Colored vinyl.)
SMASH 4-8   66
LPs: 10/12–inch 33rpm
FREEPORT (3001 "The Five Emprees
[Little Miss Sad]") 35-45   65
(Monaural.)
FREEPORT (3001 "Little Miss Sad") . 20-30   66
(Reissue.)
FREEPORT (4001 "The Five Emprees [Little
Miss Sad]") 30-40   65
(Stereo.)
FREEPORT (4001 "Little Miss Sad") . 25-35   66
(Reissue.)
Also see FIVE EMPRESSIONS

FIVE EMPRESSIONS
(Five Emprees)
Singles: 7–inch
FREEPORT 8-12   65
Also see FIVE EMPREES

FIVE FLIGHTS UP
Singles: 7–inch
T.A. 3-5   70-71

FIVE KEYS
(Rudy West and the Five Keys)
Singles: 78rpm
ALADDIN (3085 "With a Broken
Heart") 100-200   51
ALADDIN (3099 "The Glory of
Love") 100-200   51
ALADDIN (3113 "It's Christmas
Time") 150-250   51
ALADDIN (3118 "Yes Sir, That's
My Baby") 50-100   52
ALADDIN (3127 "Red Sails in
the Sunset") 75-125   52
ALADDIN (3131 "Mistakes") 200-350   52
ALADDIN (3136 "I Hadn't Anyone
Til You") 75-125   52

ALADDIN (3158 "I Cried for You") . 200-300   52
ALADDIN (3167 "Can't Keep
from Crying") 150-250   53
ALADDIN (3175 "There Ought
to Be a Law") 75-125   53
ALADDIN (3190 "These Foolish
Things") 50-100   53
ALADDIN (3204 "Teardrops in
Your Eyes") 50-100   53
ALADDIN (3214 "My Saddest
Hour") 50-100   53
ALADDIN (3228 "Someday
Sweetheart") 50-100   54
ALADDIN (3245 "Deep in My
Heart") 50-100   54
ALADDIN (3263 "My Love") 100-150   55
ALADDIN (3312 "Story of Love") 40-60   56
CAPITOL 5-15   54-57
GROOVE (0031 "I'll Follow You") . 400-600   51
Singles: 7–inch
ALADDIN (3099 "The Glory of
Love") 350-500   51
ALADDIN (3113 "It's Christmas
Time") 500-750   51
ALADDIN (3118 "Yes Sir, That's
My Baby") 400-600   52
ALADDIN (3127 "Red Sails in
the Sunset") 750-850   52
ALADDIN (3131 "Mistakes") 500-750   52
ALADDIN (3136 "I Hadn't Anyone
Til You") 500-750   52
ALADDIN (3158 "I Cried for You") . 300-600   52
ALADDIN (3167 "Can't Keep
from Crying") 300-500   53
ALADDIN (3175 "There Ought
to Be a Law") 250-500   53
ALADDIN (3190 "These Foolish
Things") 750-1000   53
ALADDIN (3204 "Teardrops in
Your Eyes") 250-500   53
ALADDIN (3214 "My Saddest
Hour") 300-500   53
(Flat blue label.)
ALADDIN (3214 "My Saddest
Hour") 250-350   53
(Glossy blue label.)
ALADDIN (3228 "Someday
Sweetheart") 300-500   54
ALADDIN (3245 "Deep in My
Heart") 300-500   54
ALADDIN (3263 "My Love") 150-250   55
ALADDIN (3312 "Story of Love") 150-250   56
CAPITOL (2945 "Ling Ting Tong") ... 15-25   54
CAPITOL (3032 "Close Your Eyes") . 15-25   55
CAPITOL (3127 "The Verdict") 10-20   55
CAPITOL (3185 "I Wish I'd Never
Learned to Read") 10-20   55
CAPITOL (3267 "Gee Whittakers") .. 10-20   55
CAPITOL (3318 "What Goes On") ... 10-20   56

CAPITOL (3392 "I Dreamt I
Dwelt in Heaven") 10-20   56
(Standard 45rpm hole.)
CAPITOL (3392 "I Dreamt I
Dwelt in Heaven") 20-25   56
(LP-size, ¼-inch hole. Purple label.)
CAPITOL (3392 "I Dreamt I
Dwelt in Heaven") 25-30   56
(LP-size, ¼-inch hole. White label. Promotional
issue only.)
CAPITOL (3455 "Peace and Love") .. 10-20   56
CAPITOL (3502 "Out of Sight,
Out of Mind") 10-20   56
CAPITOL (3597 "Wisdom of a Fool") . 10-20   56
CAPITOL (3660 "Let There Be You") . 10-20   57
CAPITOL (3710 "Four Walls") 8-12   57
CAPITOL (3738 "This I Promise You") . 8-12   57
CAPITOL (3786 "Face of an Angel") .. 8-12   57
CAPITOL (3830 "Do Anything") 8-12   57
CAPITOL (3861 "From Me to You") .. 5-10   58
CAPITOL (3948 "With All My Heart") . 5-10   58
CAPITOL (4009 "Handy Andy") 5-10   58
CAPITOL (4092 "Our Great Love") ... 5-10   58
CLASSIC ARTISTS 3-5   89
GROOVE (0031 "I'll Follow You") 2500-3000   51
GUSTO 2-4
IMPERIAL 3-5   62
KING (5221 "I Took Your
Love for a Toy") 15-25   59
KING (5273 through 5877) 8-15   59-64
LANDMARK 3-5   73
OWL 3-5   73
SEG-WAY (1008 "Out of Sight
Out of Mind") 8-12   62

EPs: 7-inch 33/45rpm

CAPITOL (572 "The Five Keys") ... 75-125   55
CAPITOL (828 "The Five Keys
on Stage") 100-150   57
(Pictures one group member's thumb in a
phallic-like position.)
CAPITOL (828 "The Five Keys
on Stage") 50-100   57
(Reworked cover, with thumb removed from
picture.)

LPs: 10/12-inch 33rpm

ALADDIN (806 "The Best of the
Five Keys") 500-750   56
(Maroon label.)
CAPITOL (828 "The Five Keys
on Stage") 150-200   57
(In cover photo, group member on left is holding
his right hand in in a phallic-like position.)
CAPITOL (828 "The Five Keys
on Stage") 75-125   57
(Reworked cover, with offending hand removed
from the picture.)
CAPITOL (1769 "The Fantastic
Five Keys") 75-125   62
(With "T" prefix.)

CAPITOL (1769 "The Fantastic
Five Keys") 8-10   77
(With "M" prefix.)
GREAT GROUP CLASSICS 8-12
HARLEM HITPARADE 10-15   72
KING (688 "The Five Keys") 200-300   60
KING (692 "Rhythm and Blues Hits:
Past and Present") 200-300   60
SCORE (4003 "On the Town") 350-450   57
Members: Rudy West; Ripley Ingram; Maryland Pierce; Dickie
Smith; Ray Loper; Bernie West; Ulysses Hicks; Thomas Threat.
Also see BELVIN, Jesse, and the Five Keys / Feathers
Also see FANTASTIC FIVE KEYS

FIVE MAN ELECTRICAL BAND
Singles: 7-inch

CAPITOL 4-8   68-69
LION 3-5   72-73
LIONEL 3-5   71
MGM 4-8   70
POLYDOR 3-5   74

LPs: 10/12-inch 33rpm

CAPITOL 15-20   69
LION 10-12   73
LIONEL 10-15   70-71
MGM 10-15   70
PICKWICK 5-10

FIVE ROYALES
(5 Royales)

Singles: 78rpm

APOLLO 10-25   51-55
KING 8-15   54-56

Singles: 7-inch

ABC-PAR 5-10   62
APOLLO (441 "Courage to Love")" .. 50-75   52
(Black vinyl.)
APOLLO (441 "Courage to Love")" 100-150   52
(Colored vinyl.)
APOLLO (443 "Baby, Don't Do It") .. 50-75   52
APOLLO (446 "Help Me, Somebody") 50-75   53
APOLLO (448 "Laundromat Blues") . 50-75   53
APOLLO (449 "I Want to Thank You") 40-60   53
APOLLO (452 "I Do") 35-45   54
APOLLO (454 "Cry Some More") ... 35-45   54
APOLLO (458 "What's That") 30-40   54
APOLLO (467 "With All Your Heart") . 30-40   55
GUSTO 2-4
HOME of the BLUES 5-10   60-62
KING (4740 through 4785) 30-40   54-55
KING (4806 through 4973) 20-30   55-56
KING (5000 series) 8-15   57-64
SMASH 5-8   64-65
TODD 5-10   63
VEE JAY 5-10   61-62

LPs: 10/12-inch 33rpm

APOLLO (488 "The Rockin'
5 Royales") 800-1100   59
(Green cover.)

APOLLO (488 "The Rockin'
5 Royales") 500-1000 59
(Yellow cover.)
KING (580 "Dedicated to You") ... 250-400 58
KING (616 "The 5 Royales Sing
for You") 150-250 59
KING (678 "The 5 Royales") 150-250 60
KING (955 "24 All Time Hits") 30-60 66
    Members: Johnny Tanner; Eugene Tanner; Lowman Pauling; Jim
    Moore; Otto Jeffries; Obadiah "Scoop" Carter.
    Also see JOHN, Little Willie / 5 Royales / Earl (Connelly) King /
    Midnighters

FIVE SATINS
(5 Satins)

Singles: 78rpm

EMBER 8-15 56-57
STANDORD (100 "All Mine") 50-100 56
STANDORD (200 "In the Still of
the Nite") 75-125 56

Singles: 7-inch

ABC 2-4 73
CANDLELITE 3-5
CHANCELLOR 10-15 62
COLLECTABLES 2-4
CUB 10-15 60-61
EMBER (1005 "In the Still
of the Nite") 100-200 56
(Has Ember label pasted over Standord label. Can
be identified by the identification number 6106 in
the vinyl trail-off.)
EMBER (1005 "In the Still
of the Nite") 15-25 56
EMBER (1005 "[I'll Remember] in the Still
of the Nite") 50-100 56
(White label. Promotional issue.)
EMBER (1005 "[I'll Remember] in the Still
of the Nite") 20-30 59
(Red label. Reads "Special Demand Release.")
EMBER (1005 "[I'll Remember] in the Still
of the Nite") 15-25 60
(Multi-color "logs" label.)
EMBER (1005 "[I'll Remember] in the Still
of the Nite") 5-10 61
(Black label.)
EMBER (1008 "Wonderful Girl") 10-20 56
EMBER (1014 "Oh, Happy Day") ... 10-20 57
EMBER (1019 "To the Aisle") 10-20 57
EMBER (1025 "Our Anniversary") ... 10-20 57
(Red label.)
EMBER (1025 "Our Anniversary") 5-10 57
(Black label.)
EMBER (1028 "Million to One") 15-20 58
EMBER (1038 "A Night
to Remember") 10-15 58
EMBER (1056 through 1070) 5-10 59-61
ELEKTRA 3-6 82
FIRST (104 "When Your Lover
Comes Along") 15-25 59
(Orange label.)

FIRST (104 "When Your Lover
Comes Along") 10-20 59
(Green label.)
FLASHBACK 3-5 65
KIRSHNER 3-5 73-74
KLIK 5-10 73
LANA 3-5
NIGHTTRAIN 4-6 70
RCA 3-6 71
ROULETTE 5-8 64
SAMMY (103 "No One Knows") 20-30
STANDORD (100 "All Mine") 300-450 56
(Red label. Copies on a maroon-brown label are
unauthorized reissues.)
STANDORD (200 "In the Still of
the Nite") 800-1200 56
(Red label. Reads "Produced By Martin Kuegull.")
STANDORD (200 "In the Still of
the Nite") 400-500 56
(Red label.)
STANDORD (5051 "All Mine") 25-40
TIME MACHINE 4-8 62
TIMES SQUARE 10-15 63
(Colored vinyl.)
U.A. 10-20 61
WARNER 5-10 63

EPs: 7-inch 33/45rpm

EMBER (100 "The Five Satins Sing") 50-75 60
(Red label.)
EMBER (100 "The Five Satins Sing") 25-35 61
(Black or multi-color label.)
EMBER (101 "The Five
Satins Sing, Vol. 2") 50-75 60
(Red label.)
EMBER (101 "The Five
Satins Sing, Vol. 2") 25-35 61
(Black or multi-color label.)
EMBER (102 "The Five
Satins Sing, Vol. 3") 50-75 60
(Red label.)
EMBER (102 "The Five
Satins Sing, Vol. 3") 25-35 61
(Black or multi-color label.)
EMBER (104 "In the Still
of the Night") 150-250 61

LPs: 10/12-inch 33rpm

CELEBRITY SHOWCASE 10-12 70
COLLECTABLES 5-10 84
EMBER (100 "The Five Satins
Sing") 200-300 57
(Red label. Group is pictured on front cover.)
EMBER (100 "The Five Satins
Sing") 50-100 58
(Multi-color label. Black vinyl.)
EMBER (100 "The Five Satins
Sing") 500-750 58
(Multi-color label. Colored vinyl.)

EMBER (100 "The Five Satins
Sing") .... 35-50 ... 60
(Black label.)
EMBER (401 "The Five Satins
Encore") .... 50-75 ... 60
(Black label.)
EMBER (401 "The Five Satins
Encore") .... 35-50 ... 61
(Multi-color label.)
LOST-NITE .... 6-10 ... 81
MT. VERNON (108 "The Five
Satins Sing") 20-30
RELIC 8-10
  Members: Fred Parris; Louis Peebles; Stan Dortch; Jim
  Freeman; Nate Moseley; Bill Baker; Jimmy Curtis; Nate
  Marshall; Ed Martin; John Brown; Tom Killebrew; Al Denby; Jess
  Murphy; Wes Forbes; Richard Freeman.
   Also see BAKER, Bill
   Also see BLACK SATIN
   Also see GRANAHAN, Gerry
   Also see NEW YORK CITY
   Also see NEW YORKERS
   Also see PARRIS, Fred
   Also see SOUTHSIDE JOHNNY and the ASBURY DUKES

FIVE SATINS / Pharotones
Singles: 7–inch
TIMES SQUARE .... 5-10 ... 63
  Also see FIVE SATINS

FIVE SPECIAL
Singles: 7–inch
ELEKTRA .... 2-4 ... 79-80
LPs: 10/12–inch 33rpm
ELEKTRA .... 5-10 ... 79

FIVE STAIRSTEPS
(Stairsteps; Five Stairsteps and Cubie)
Singles: 7–inch
BUDDAH .... 4-6 ... 67-68
COLLECTABLES 2-4
CURTOM .... 4-6 ... 68-69
GOLD 4-6
WINDY C .... 4-8 ... 66-67
Picture Sleeves
BUDDAH .... 4-8 ... 67-68
LPs: 10/12–inch 33rpm
BUDDAH .... 10-12 ... 68-70
COLLECTABLES .... 6-8 ... 85
CURTOM .... 8-10 ... 69
WINDY C .... 10-15 ... 67
  Members: Clarence Burke Jr.; James Burke; Keni Burke; Dennis
  Burke; Cubie Burke; Aloha Burke.
   Also see BURKE, Keni
   Also see INVISIBLE MAN'S BAND
   Also see STAIRSTEPS

FIVE STAR
Singles: 12–inch 33/45rpm
RCA .... 4-6 ... 85-86
Singles: 7–inch
RCA .... 2-4 ... 85-87
Picture Sleeves
RCA .... 2-4 ... 86

LPs: 10/12–inch 33rpm
RCA .... 5-10 ... 85-86

5000 VOLTS
Singles: 7–inch
PHILIPS .... 3-5 ... 75
PRIVATE STOCK .... 3-5 ... 76

FIXX
Singles: 12–inch 33/45rpm
MCA .... 4-6 ... 82-86
Singles: 7–inch
MCA .... 2-5 ... 82-90
Picture Sleeves
MCA .... 2-5 ... 83-89
LPs: 10/12–inch 33rpm
MCA (Except 8642) .... 5-10 ... 82-91
MCA (8642 "Talkabout") 8-12
(Interviews with Fixx. Promotional issue only.)
RCA .... 5-8 ... 89
  Members: Cy Curnin; Adam Woods; Danny Brown; Alfi Agies;
  Jamie West; Rupert Greenall.

FLACK, Roberta
Singles: 7–inch
ATLANTIC .... 2-5 ... 69-88
MCA .... 2-4 ... 81
VIVA .... 2-4 ... 83
Picture Sleeves
ATLANTIC .... 2-4 ... 78-82
LPs: 10/12–inch 33rpm
ATLANTIC .... 5-10 ... 69-88
VIVA .... 5-10 ... 83
   Also see BRYSON, Peabo, and Roberta Flack
   Also see CHIC / Leif Garrett / Roberta Flack / Genesis
   Also see McCANN, Les

FLACK, Roberta, and Donny Hathaway
Singles: 7–inch
ATLANTIC .... 2-4 ... 71-80
LPs: 10/12–inch 33rpm
ATLANTIC .... 5-10 ... 72-80
   Also see HATHAWAY, Donny

FLACK, Roberta, and Eric Mercury
Singles: 7–inch
ATLANTIC .... 2-4 ... 83
   Also see FLACK, Roberta
   Also see MERCURY, Eric

FLAGG, Fannie
LPs: 10/12–inch 33rpm
RCA .... 10-15 ... 66

FLAMIN' GROOVIES
Singles: 7–inch
BOMP .... 3-5 ... 74
EPIC .... 4-6 ... 69-70
KAMA SUTRA .... 3-5 ... 71
Picture Sleeves
BOMP .... 4-8 ... 74
EPs: 7–inch 33/45rpm
SKYDOG 5-10

LPs: 10/12–inch 33rpm

BUDDAH	10-12	77
EPIC (26487 "Supernazz")	35-45	69
KAMA SUTRA (2021 "Flamingo")	15-25	70
(Pink label.)		
KAMA SUTRA (2021 "Flamingo")	10-15	
(Blue label.)		
KAMA SUTRA (2031 "Teenage Head")	15-25	71
(Pink label.)		
KAMA SUTRA (2031 "Teenage Head")	10-15	
(Blue label.)		
SIRE	10-12	76-79
SNAZZ (2371 "Sneakers")	60-80	68
(10–inch LP.)		
VOXX	5-10	

Members: Roy Loney; Cyril Jordan; George Alexander; Tim Lynch; Danny Mihm; Chris Wilson; James Farrell; David Wright.

FLAMING EMBER
Singles: 7–inch

HOT WAX	3-6	69-70

LPs: 10/12–inch 33rpm

HOT WAX	10-15	70-71

Members: Joe Sladich; Jerry Plunk; Bill Ellis; Jim Bugnel.

FLAMINGOS
Singles: 78rpm

CHANCE (1133 "Someday, Someway")	50-100	53
CHANCE (1140 "That's My Desire")	50-100	53
CHANCE (1145 "Golden Teardrops")	50-100	53
CHANCE (1149 "Plan for Love")	50-100	53
CHANCE (1154 "Cross over the Bridge")	50-100	54
CHANCE (1162 "Blues in the Letter")	50-100	54
CHECKER (815 "When")	15-25	55
CHECKER (821 "Please Come Back Home")	15-30	55
CHECKER (830 "I'll Be Home")	15-30	56
CHECKER (837 through 915)	8-15	56-57
DECCA	5-10	57
PARROT (808 "Dream of a Lifetime")	50-100	54
PARROT (812 "I'm Yours")	75-150	55

Singles: 7–inch

ABC	3-5	73
CHANCE (1133 "If I Can't Have You")	300-400	53
(Black vinyl.)		
CHANCE (1133 "If I Can't Have You")	500-750	53
(Colored vinyl.)		
CHANCE (1140 "That's My Desire")	300-400	53
(Black vinyl.)		
CHANCE (1140 "That's My Desire")	500-750	53
(Colored vinyl.)		

CHANCE (1145 "Golden Teardrops")	400-500	53
(Black vinyl.)		
CHANCE (1145 "Golden Teardrops")	1000-1500	53
(Colored vinyl.)		
CHANCE (1149 "Plan for Love")	400-500	53
(Yellow and black label.)		
CHANCE (1149 "Plan for Love")	300-400	53
(Blue and silver label.)		
CHANCE (1154 "Cross over the Bridge")	300-400	54
CHANCE (1162 "Blues in the Letter")	250-350	54
CHECKER (815 "When")	25-50	55
CHECKER (821 "Please Come Back Home")	25-50	55
CHECKER (830 "I'll Be Home")	25-50	56
CHECKER (837 "Kiss from Your Lips")	20-30	56
CHECKER (846 "The Vow")	20-30	56
CHECKER (853 "Would I Be Crying")	20-30	56
CHECKER (915 "Dream of a Lifetime")	10-20	59
CHECKER (1084 "Lover Come Back to Me")	5-10	64
CHECKER (1091 "Goodnight Sweetheart")	5-10	64
CHESS	2-4	73
COLLECTABLES	2-4	
DECCA	8-15	57-59
END (1035 "Please Wait for Me")	20-40	58
(Title later changed to *Lovers Never Say Goodbye*.)		
END (1035 "Lovers Never Say Goodbye")	10-20	58
END (1040 "But Not for Me")	10-15	58
END (1044 "At the Prom")	10-15	58
END (1046 "I Only Have Eyes For You"/"At the Prom")	10-15	59
END (1046 "I Only Have Eyes for You"/ "Goodnight Sweetheart")	15-25	59
(Note different flip.)		

END (1046 "I Only Have
Eyes for You") 20-30   59
(Stereo.)
END (1055 "Love Walked In") 8-12   59
(Monaural.)
END (1055 "Love Walked In") 20-30   59
(Stereo.)
END (1062 through 1124) 6-12   59-62
JULMAR 4-6   69
PARROT (808 "Dream of a
Lifetime") 250-300   54
(Black vinyl.)
PARROT (808 "Dream of a
Lifetime") 750-1000   54
(Colored vinyl.)
PARROT (811 "I Really Don't
Want to Know") 500-750   55
(Black vinyl.)
PARROT (811 "I Really Don't
Want to Know") 3000-4000   55
(Colored vinyl.)
PARROT (812 "I'm Yours") 250-300   55
(Black vinyl.)
PARROT (812 "I'm Yours") 750-1000   55
(Colored vinyl.)
PHILIPS 4-8   66
POLYDOR 3-5   70
RONZE 3-5   71-76
ROULETTE 5-8   63
TIMES SQUARE 8-12   64
VEE JAY 5-10   61
WORLDS 3-5   75

EPs: 7–inch 33/45rpm

END (205 "Goodnight Sweetheart") .. 40-60   59
(Monaural.)
END (205 "Goodnight Sweetheart") .. 50-85   59
(Stereo.)

LPs: 10/12–inch 33rpm

CHECKER (1433 "Flamingos") 75-125   59
(Monaural.)
CHECKER (3005 "Flamingos") 25-50   66
(Stereo.)
CHESS 8-10   76
CONSTELLATION 15-20   64
EMUS 8-10
END (304 "Flamingo Serenade") 30-50   59
(Monaural.)
END (304 "Flamingo Serenade") 50-75   59
(Stereo.)
END (307 "Flamingo Favorites") 20-35   60
(Monaural.)
END (307 "Flamingo Favorites") 25-40   60
(Stereo.)
END (308 "Requestfully Yours") 20-35   60
(Monaural.)
END (308 "Requestfully Yours") 25-40   60
(Stereo.)

END (316 "The Sound
of the Flamingos") 20-35   62
(Monaural.)
END (316 "The Sound
of the Flamingos") 25-40   62
(Stereo.)
LOST-NITE 5-10   81
MEKA 10-15
PHILLIPS 15-25   66
RONZE 10-15   72-73
SOLID SMOKE 5-10   82
Members: Sollie McElroy; John Carter; Zeke Carey; Jake Carey;
Paul Wilson; Nate Nelson; Tommy Hunt; Terry Johnson.
Also see HUNT, Tommy

FLAMINGOS / Moonglows
LPs: 10/12–inch 33rpm

VEE JAY (1052 "The Flamingos
Meet the Moonglows") 30-40   62
Also see FLAMINGOS
Also see MOONGLOWS

FLANAGAN, Ralph
Singles: 78rpm

RCA 2-5   50-57

Singles: 7–inch

CORAL 3-6   61
IMPERIAL 3-8   59
RCA 4-8   50-57

EPs: 7–inch 33/45rpm

CAMDEN 4-8   54
RCA 5-10   51-57

LPs: 10/12–inch 33rpm

CAMDEN 10-20   54
GOLDEN ERA 4-8   76
IMPERIAL 8-15   58-59
RCA 10-20   51-57

FLARES
(Flairs)
Singles: 7–inch

COLLECTABLES 2-4
FELSTED (8604 "Loving You") 8-12   60
FELSTED (8607 "Jump and Bump") .. 8-12   60
PRESS 4-8   62-63

Picture Sleeves

FELSTED (8607 "Jump and Bump") . 20-30   60

LPs: 10/12–inch 33rpm

PRESS (73001 "Encore of
Foot Stompin' Hits") 25-35   61
(Monaural.)
PRESS (83001 "Encore of
Foot Stompin' Hits") 30-40   61
(Stereo.)
Members: Aaron Collins; Willie Davis; Tom Miller; Randy Jones.
Also see CADETS

FLARES / Ramrocks
Singles: 7–inch

FELSTED (8624 "Foot Stompin") 6-10   61
Also see FLARES
Also see RAMROCKS

FLASH
Singles: 7–inch
CAPITOL 3-5   72
LPs: 10/12–inch 33rpm
CAPITOL (11000 series) 5-10   77
(With "SM" prefix.)
CAPITOL (11000 series) 8-10   72-73
(With "SMAS" or "ST" prefix.)
Also see BANKS, Peter

FLASH and the Pan
Singles: 12–inch 33/45rpm
EPIC 4-6   81-83
Singles: 7–inch
EPIC 2-4   79-83
LPs: 10/12–inch 33rpm
EPIC 5-10   79-82
Members: Harry Vanda; George Young.
Also see EASYBEATS

FLASH CADILLAC and the Continental Kids
Singles: 7–inch
EPIC 4-8   72-74
PRIVATE STOCK 4-6   74-77
LPs: 10/12–inch 33rpm
EPIC 10-12   72-74
PRIVATE STOCK 8-10   75
Also see WOLFMAN JACK

FLASHCATS
Singles: 7–inch
BOGUS 2-4   86
Also see JACKSON, Bull Moose

FLATT, Lester, and Earl Scruggs
Singles: 78rpm
COLUMBIA 3-6   51-57
MERCURY 4-8   49-53
Singles: 7–inch
COLUMBIA (20000 and 21000
series) 5-10   51-56
COLUMBIA (40000 through 42000
series) 4-8   56-63
COLUMBIA (43000 through 45000
series) 3-6   64-67
MERCURY 10-15   50-53
Picture Sleeves
COLUMBIA 4-8   62-68
MERCURY 4-6   68
EPs: 7–inch 33/45rpm
COLUMBIA 8-15   57-60
LPs: 10/12–inch 33rpm
COLUMBIA (30 "Flatt and
Scruggs") 8-12   75
COLUMBIA (400 series) 12-15   69
COLUMBIA (1000 and 2000 series,
except 1019) 10-20   60-68
COLUMBIA (1019 "Foggy Mountain
Jamboree") 25-40   57
COLUMBIA (8000 and 9000 series) .. 10-20   60-70
(With "CS" prefix.)

COLUMBIA (8000 and 9000 series) .. 5-10
(With "PC" prefix.)
COLUMBIA (10000 series) 6-12   73
COLUMBIA (30000 through 37000
series) 5-12   70-82
COPPER CREEK 5-10
COUNTY 5-10
EVEREST 5-10   71-82
51 WEST 5-10
HARMONY 8-15   60-71
MERCURY (20000 series) 20-35   58-63
(Monaural.)
MERCURY (60000 series) 20-30   63
(Stereo.)
MERCURY (61000 series) 10-15   68
NASHVILLE 8-10   70
PICKWICK/HILLTOP 8-12   68
POWER PAK 5-10
ROUNDER
WING 8-12   68
Also see SCRUGGS, Earl

FLATT, Lester, Earl Scruggs, and Doc Watson
LPs: 10/12–inch 33rpm
COLUMBIA 10-15   67
Also see FLATT, Lester, and Earl Scruggs
Also see WATSON, Doc

FLAVOR
Singles: 7–inch
COLUMBIA 4-6   68
Picture Sleeves
COLUMBIA 4-6   68
LPs: 10/12–inch 33rpm
JU-PAR 8-10   77

FLAVOUR, La: see LA FLAVOUR

FLEETWOOD, Mick
LPs: 10/12–inch 33rpm
RCA 5-10   81
Also see FLEETWOOD MAC

FLEETWOOD MAC
Singles: 12–inch 33/45rpm
WARNER (652 "Go Your Own Way") . 15-25   76
(Promotional issue only.)
Singles: 7–inch
BLUE HORIZON 4-8   70
DJM 4-8   73
EPIC (10351 "Black Magic
Woman") 5-10   68
EPIC (10368 "Stop Messin'
Around") 5-10   68
EPIC (10436 "Albatross") 3-5   69
EPIC (11029 "Albatross") 3-5   73
EPIC (139609 "Albatross") 4-8
(Promotional issue only.)
REPRISE 3-6   69-76
WARNER (Except 8304) 2-4   77-90
WARNER (8304 "Go Your Own Way") . 8-12   76

Picture Sleeves

EPIC (139609 "Albatross") 5-10
(Promotional issue only.)
WARNER 3-6   77-88

LPs: 10/12–Inch 33rpm

BLUE HORIZON (3801 "Fleetwood Mac
in Chicago") 20-25   70
BLUE HORIZON (4803 "Blues Jam
in Chicago, Vol. 1") 20-25   70
BLUE HORIZON (4805 "Blues Jam
in Chicago, Vol. 2") 20-25   70
BLUE HORIZON (66227 "Blues Jam
at Chess") 20-25   69
BLUE HORIZON (83110 "Mr.
Wonderful") 20-25
EPIC (Except 33740) 15-25   68-71
EPIC (33740 "English Rose") 8-12   73
EPIC (33740 "Fleetwood Mac/
English Rose") 8-12   74
MFSL (012 "Fleetwood Mac") 30-60   78
MFSL (119 "Mirage") 20-30   84
NAUTILUS (8 "Rumours") 20-30   80
(Half-speed mastered.)
REPRISE (Except 6368) 8-15   70-77
REPRISE (6368 "Then Play On") 15-25   69
(Without Oh Well.)
REPRISE (6368 "Then Play On") 10-15   69
(With Oh Well.)
SIRE 8-10   75-77
VARRICK 5-10   85
WARNER 8-12   77-90
Members: Mick Fleetwood; John McVie; Peter Green; Jeremy
Spencer; Danny Kirwin; Christine McVie; Bob Welch; Bob
Weston; Dave Walker; Lindsay Buckingham; Stevie Nicks; Rick
Vito; Billy Burnette.
  Also see BUCKINGHAM, Lindsay
  Also see BURNETTE, Billy
  Also see FLEETWOOD, Mick
  Also see GREEN, Peter
  Also see MAYALL, John
  Also see McVIE, Christine
  Also see NICKS, Stevie
  Also see WELCH, Bob

FLEETWOOD MAC / Danny Kirwan
Singles: 7–Inch
DJM 4-8   73
  Also see FLEETWOOD MAC

FLEETWOODS
Singles: 7–Inch
DOLPHIN (1 "Come Softly to Me") ... 10-20   59
DOLTON (1 "Come Softly to Me") 8-10   59
DOLTON (3 "Graduation's Here") 3-6   59
(Monaural.)
DOLTON (3 "Graduation's Here") 10-15   59
(Stereo. With "S" prefix.)
DOLTON (5 through 315) 5-10   59-66
LIBERTY (55188 "Come Softly to Me") 5-10   59
(Monaural.)
LIBERTY (77188 "Come Softly to Me") 10-15   59
(Stereo.)

U.A. 2-4   74
Picture Sleeves
DOLTON (22 "Runaround") 8-12   60
EPs: 7–Inch 33/45rpm
DOLTON (502 "The Fleetwoods") ... 20-30   60
LPs: 10/12–Inch 33rpm
DOLTON (2001 "Mr. Blue") 25-35   59
(Monaural.)
DOLTON (8001 "Mr. Blue") 30-40   59
(Stereo.)
DOLTON (2002 through 2039) 20-30   60-65
(Monaural.)
DOLTON (8002 through 8039) ... 20-35   60-65
(Stereo.)
LIBERTY 5-10   82-83
SUNSET 10-15   66
U.A. 8-10   75
Members: Gary Troxel; Barbara Ellis; Gretchen Christopher.
  Also see VEE, Bobby / Johnny Burnette / Ventures / Fleetwoods

FLEMONS, Wade
(Wade Flemons and the Newcomers)
Singles: 7–Inch
VEE JAY (Maroon label) 8-12   58-59
VEE JAY (Black label) 4-8   61-63
LPs: 10/12–Inch 33rpm
VEE JAY (1011 "Wade Flemons") ... 40-50   59
(Maroon label.)
VEE JAY (1011 "Wade Flemons") ... 15-25   61
(Black label.)
  Also see EARTH, WIND & FIRE

FLENOY, Julian
Singles: 7–Inch
KMA 2-4   86

FLESH for LULU
Singles: 12–Inch 33/45rpm
MCA 4-6   85
Singles: 7–Inch
MCA 2-4   85
LPs: 10/12–Inch 33rpm
CAPITOL 5-10   87
MCA 5-10   85
Members: Nick Marsh; James Mitchell; Rocco Barker; Kevin
Mills; Derek Grenning.

FLESHTONES
Singles: 7–Inch
I.R.S. 2-4   81-82
LPs: 10/12–Inch 33rpm
I.R.S. 5-10   81-82
Members: Jonithan Weiss; Marek Pakulski; Keith Streng; Bill
Milhiser; Peter Zaremba.
  Also see VIPERS

FLETCHER, Darrow
Singles: 7–Inch
CONGRESS 3-5   70
CROSSOVER 2-4   75-79
GROOVY 4-8   66
REVUE 4-6   68
UNI 3-5   70-71

FLETCHER, Dusty
Singles: 78rpm
NATIONAL 8-12   47

FLETCHER, Lois
Singles: 7–inch
PLAYBOY 3-5   74

FLINT, Shelby
Singles: 7–inch
CADENCE 5-10   58
VALIANT 4-8   60-66
LPs: 10/12–inch 33rpm
VALIANT (401 "Shelby Flint") 25-40   61
VALIANT (403 "Shelby Flint
  Sings Folk") 25-35   61
  (Monaural.)
VALIANT (WS-403 "Shelby Flint
  Sings Folk") 35-50   61
  (Stereo.)
VALIANT (5003 "Cast Your
  Fate to the Wind") 15-25   66
  (Monaural.)
VALIANT (25003 "Cast Your
  Fate to the Wind") 20-30   66
  (Stereo.)

FLIP CARTRIDGE: see CARTRIDGE, Flip

FLIRTATIONS
Singles: 7–inch
DERAM 4-6   69
PARROT 4-8   68
LPs: 10/12–inch 33rpm
DERAM 15-20   69

FLIRTS
Singles: 12–inch 33/45rpm
CBS ASSOCIATES 4-6   86
Singles: 7–inch
CBS ASSOCIATES 2-4   86
O RECORDS 2-4   82
LPs: 10/12–inch 33rpm
CBS ASSOCIATES 5-10   86
O RECORDS 5-10   82

FLOATERS
Singles: 7–inch
ABC 2-4   77-79
Picture Sleeves
ABC 2-4   77
LPs: 10/12–inch 33rpm
ABC 5-10   77-79
Members: Charles Clark; Paul Mitchell; Ralph Mitchell; Larry
Cunningham; Jonathan Murray.

FLOATING BRIDGE
Singles: 7–inch
VAULT 5-10   69
LPs: 10/12–inch 33rpm
VAULT (124 "The Floating
  Bridge") 20-30   69

FLOCK
Singles: 7–inch
COLUMBIA 4-6   69-70
DESTINATION 5-10   66-67
U.S.A 4-8   68
LPs: 10/12–inch 33rpm
COLUMBIA 10-15   69-71
MERCURY 8-10   75

FLOCK of SEAGULLS
Singles: 12–inch 33/45rpm
JIVE 4-6   82-83
Singles: 7–inch
JIVE 2-4   82-86
Picture Sleeves
JIVE 2-4   82-84
LPs: 10/12–inch 33rpm
JIVE 5-10   82-86

FLOOD, Dick
(Dick Flood and the Pathfinders)
Singles: 7–inch
EPIC 4-6   61-62
KAPP 3-6   65
MONUMENT 4-8   59-60
NASCO 3-5   71-72
NUGGET 3-6   68
TOTEM 3-6   67

FLOS
Singles: 7–inch
SUPERSTAR I. 2-4   87

FLOTSAM & JETSAM
Singles: 12–inch 33/45rpm
ELEKTRA 4-8   88
  (Promotional only.)
Singles: 7–inch
ELEKTRA 2-4   88
LPs: 10/12–inch 33rpm
ELEKTRA 5-8   88
MCA 5-8   90

FLOYD, Eddie
Singles: 7–inch
ATLANTIC 4-8   65
LUPINE 5-10   63
MALACO 3-5   77
MERCURY 3-5   78
SAFICE 4-8   64
STAX 3-8   66-75
LPs: 10/12–inch 33rpm
ATCO 8-10   74
MALACO 5-10   77
STAX 10-20   67-79
  Also see FALCONS
  Also see MOORE, Dorothy, and Eddie Floyd
  Also see REDDING, Otis / Carla Thomas / Sam & Dave / Eddie
  Floyd

FLOYD, Eddie, and Mavis Staples
Singles: 7–inch
STAX 3-6   69

Also see FLOYD, Eddie
Also see STAPLES, Mavis

FLOYD, King: see KING FLOYD

FLYING BURRITO BROTHERS
Singles: 7–inch
A&M 3-6   69-70
COLUMBIA 3-5   76
LPs: 10/12–inch 33rpm
A&M 10-15   69-76
COLUMBIA 8-10   75-76
REGENCY 5-10   80
Also see BURRITO BROTHERS
Also see HILLMAN, Chris
Also see PARSONS, Gram

FLYING LIZARDS
Singles: 7–inch
VIRGIN 2-4   79
Picture Sleeves
VIRGIN 2-4   79
LPs: 10/12–inch 33rpm
VIRGIN 5-10   80

FLYING MACHINE
Singles: 7–inch
CONGRESS 4-8   69-70
RAINY DAY 4-8   67
LPs: 10/12–inch 33rpm
JANUS 10-15   69
Also see TAYLOR, James

FOCUS
Singles: 7–inch
ATCO 3-5   75
SIRE 3-5   73
LPs: 10/12–inch 33rpm
ATCO 8-10   74-75
SIRE 8-10   72-77
Also see AKKERMAN, Jan

FOCUS
Singles: 7–inch
EMI AMERICA 2-4   87

FOCUS and P.J. Proby
LPs: 10/12–inch 33rpm
HARVEST 5-10   78
Also see FOCUS
Also see PROBY, P.J.

FOGELBERG, Dan
Singles: 7–inch
COLUMBIA 4-6   73
EPIC 3-5   74-75
FULL MOON/EPIC 2-5   75-82
FULL MOON 2-4   82-87
Picture Sleeves
FULL MOON/EPIC 2-4   80-87
LPs: 10/12–inch 33rpm
COLUMBIA 10-15   72
EPIC 8-10   74-78
EPIC/FULL MOON 8-10   75-82
FULL MOON 5-10   82-90

FOGELBERG, Dan, and Tim Weisberg
Singles: 7–inch
FULL MOON/EPIC 2-4   78-80
LPs: 10/12–inch 33rpm
FULL MOON/EPIC 5-10   78
Also see FOGELBERG, Dan
Also see WEISBERG, Tim

FOGERTY, John
Promotional Singles: 12–inch 33/45rpm
WARNER (2234 "Old Man
Down the Road") 5-10   84
WARNER (2267 "Rock and Roll
Girls") 5-10   85
WARNER (2337 "I Can't Help
Myself") 5-10   85
WARNER (2362 "Vanz Kant Danz) ... 5-10   85
WARNER (2363 "Vanz Kant
Danz-Edit") 5-10   85
WARNER (2514 "Eye of the Zombie") . 5-10   86
Singles: 7–inch
ASYLUM 3-5   75-76
FANTASY 3-6   73
WARNER 2-4   84-86
Picture Sleeves
WARNER 2-4   84-87
LPs: 10/12–inch 33rpm
ASYLUM (1046 "John Fogerty") 5-10   75
WARNER (25203 "Centerfield") 10-15   84
(Last track is titled *Zanz Kant Danz.*)
WARNER (25203 "Centerfield") 5-8   85
(Last track is *Vanz Kant Danz.*)
WARNER (25449 "Eye of the Zombie") . 5-8   85
Also see BLUE RIDGE RANGERS
Also see CREEDENCE CLEARWATER REVIVAL
Also see EDDY, Duane

FOGERTY, Tom
(Tommy Fogerty and the Blue Velvets)
Singles: 7–inch
FANTASY 3-5   71-82
ORCHESTRA ("Now You're
Not Mine") 35-50   62
(Catalog number unknown.)
ORCHESTRA (1010 "Have You
Ever Been Lonely") 35-50   61
ORCHESTRA (6177 "Come On
Baby") 35-50   61
(Despite the higher number, this was the first
Orchestra single.)
Picture Sleeves
FANTASY 3-5   71
LPs: 10/12–inch 33rpm
FANTASY 8-10   72-81
Members: Tom Fogerty; John Fogerty; Doug Clifford; Stuart
Cook.
Also see CREEDENCE CLEARWATER REVIVAL
Also see SAUNDERS, Merl

FOGHAT
Singles: 7–inch
BEARSVILLE 2-5   72-80

FONTAINE, Eddie, and Gerry Granahan
Singles: 7–inch
SUNBEAM 10-15   58
  Also see FONTAINE, Eddie
  Also see GRANAHAN, Gerry

FONTAINE, Frankie
(Frank Fontaine)
Singles: 7–inch
ABC-PAR 3-6   62-65
CAPITOL 3-6   63
Picture Sleeves
ABC-PAR 5-8   62
CAPITOL 5-8   63
LPs: 10/12–inch 33rpm
ABC-PAR 10-20   62-66
MGM 6-10   67

FONTANA, Wayne
Singles: 7–inch
BRUT 3-5   73
MGM 4-8   66-67
METROMEDIA 4-6   69
LPs: 10/12–inch 33rpm
MGM (4459 "Wayne Fontana") 15-25   67

FONTANA, Wayne, and the Mindbenders
Singles: 7–inch
FONTANA 5-10   65
LPs: 10/12–inch 33rpm
FONTANA (27542 "The Game
  of Love") 30-35   65
  (Monaural.)
FONTANA (67542 "The Game
  of Love") 35-40   65
  (Stereo.)
  Members: Wayne Fontana; Graham Gouldman; Bob Land; Paul
  Hancox; Eric Stewart; Rick Rothwell; James O'Neil.
  Also see FONTANA, Wayne
  Also see MINDBENDERS

FONTANE SISTERS
Singles: 78rpm
DOT 3-6   54-60
RCA 4-8   51-54
Singles: 7–inch
DOT 5-10   54-60
RCA 8-12   51-54
Picture Sleeves
RCA (5524 "Kissing Bridge") 10-15   54
EPs: 7–inch 33/45rpm
DOT 10-15   56-57
LPs: 10/12–inch 33rpm
DOT (Except 108) 15-25   56-63
DOT (108 "The Fontane Sisters") ... 25-40   55
  (10–inch LP.)
  Members: Bea Fontane; Marge Fontane; Geri Fontane.
  Also see COMO, Perry, and the Fontane Sisters

FOOLS
Singles: 12–inch 33/45rpm
PVC 4-6

Singles: 7–inch
EMI AMERICA 2-4   80-81
Picture Sleeves
EMI AMERICA 3-5   80
LPs: 10/12–inch 33rpm
EMI AMERICA (Except 9393) 5-10   80-81
EMI AMERICA (9393 "April Fools
  Day") 10-15   80
  (Promotional issue only.)

FOOLS GOLD
Singles: 7–inch
COLUMBIA 3-5   77
MORNING SKY 3-5   76
LPs: 10/12–inch 33rpm
COLUMBIA 8-10   77
MORNING SKY 8-10   76

FORBERT, Steve
Singles: 7–inch
NEMPEROR 2-4   79-82
LPs: 10/12–inch 33rpm
NEMPEROR 5-10   79-82

FORCE MDs
Singles: 12–inch 33/45rpm
TOMMY BOY 4-6   84-86
Singles: 7–inch
TOMMY BOY 2-4   84-88
LPs: 10/12–inch 33rpm
TOMMY BOY 5-10   84-87

FORD, Dee Dee
Singles: 7–inch
ABC-PAR 4-8   63
TODD 5-10   59
  Also see GARDNER, Don, and Dee Dee Ford

FORD, Ernie: see FORD, Tennessee Ernie

FORD, Frankie
Singles: 7–inch
ABC 2-4   73-74
ACE 8-15   58-60
BRIARMEADE 3-5
CINNAMON 3-5
COLLECTABLES 2-4   81
CONSTELLATION 4-8   63
DOUBLOON 4-8   67
IMPERIAL 5-10   60-62
PAULA 3-5   71
SYC 2-4   82
20TH FOX 4-8
Picture Sleeves
ACE (592 "Chinatown") 15-25   60
EPs: 7–inch 33/45rpm
ACE (105 "Best of Frankie Ford") ... 50-75   59
LPs: 10/12–inch 33rpm
ACE (1005 "Let's Take a
  Sea Crusie") 75-125   59
BRIARMEADE 8-10   76
  Also see CLANTON, Jimmy / Frankie Ford / Jerry Lee Lewis /
  Patsy Cline

Also see SMITH, Huey

FORD, Lita

Singles: 7–inch

MERCURY 2-4   84
RCA 2-4   88-90

Picture Sleeves

RCA 2-4   88-90

LPs: 10/12–inch 33rpm

MERCURY 5-10   84
RCA 5-8   88-90
Also see RUNAWAYS

FORD, Lita, and Ozzy Osbourne

Singles: 7–inch

RCA 2-4   89

Picture Sleeves

RCA 2-4   89
Also see FORD, Lita
Also see OSBOURNE, Ozzy

FORD, Mary: see PAUL, Les, and Mary Ford

FORD, Pennye

Singles: 12–inch 33/45rpm

TOTAL EXPERIENCE 4-6   84-85

Singles: 7–inch

TOTAL EXPERIENCE 2-4   84-85

LPs: 10/12–inch 33rpm

TOTAL EXPERIENCE 5-10   85

FORD, Robben

LPs: 10/12–inch 33rpm

WARNER 5-8   88

FORD, Tennessee Ernie

Singles: 78rpm

CAPITOL (1 "Sixteen Tons") 4-6   69
(Promotional "Special Commemorative Pressing"
for Ford's 20th year on Capitol.)
CAPITOL (1200 through 2900 series) .. 3-6   50-57
CAPITOL (40000 series) 3-8   49-50

Singles: 7–inch

CAPITOL (1275 through 2900 series) . 5-10   50-54
(Purple labels. Ford's many "Boogie" titles
represent the higher end of this price range.)
CAPITOL (2000 through 4100 series) .. 2-4   70-75
(Orange labels.)
CAPITOL (3000 through 4400 series) .. 4-8   54-60
CAPITOL (4500 through 5700 series) .. 3-5   61-67

Picture Sleeves

CAPITOL 5-10   55-60

EPs: 7–inch 33/45rpm

CAPITOL (Except 413) 5-10   55-61
CAPITOL (413 "Backwoods Boogie
and Blues") 20-30   53

LPs: 10/12–inch 33rpm

CAPITOL (Except 888) 5-15   56-80
CAPITOL (888 "Ol' Rockin' Ern") 35-50   57
EVEREST 5-10
Also see LAWRENCE, Steve / Tennessee Ernie Ford
Also see LEE, Brenda / Tennessee Ernie Ford
Also see STARR, Kay, and Tennessee Ernie Ford

FORD, Tennessee Ernie, and Glen Campbell

LPs: 10/12–inch 33rpm

CAPITOL 10-12   75
Also see CAMPBELL, Glen

FORDHAM, Julia

LPs: 10/12–inch 33rpm

VIRGIN 5-8   88-90

FORECAST

Singles: 12–inch 33/45rpm

RCA 4-6   83

Singles: 7–inch

ARIOLA 2-4   80
RCA 2-4   83

LPs: 10/12–inch 33rpm

RCA 5-10   83

FOREIGNER

Singles: 7–inch

ATLANTIC 2-4   77-90
ATLANTIC/WARNER 2-4   79

Picture Sleeves

ATLANTIC 2-4   78-88

LPs: 10/12–inch 33rpm

ATLANTIC 5-10   77-91
GEFFEN 5-10   85
MFSL (052 "Double Vision") 25-50   81
Members: Lou Gramm; Rick Wills; Mick Jones; Dennis Elliott;
Ian McDonald; Al Greenwood.
Also see BAD COMPANY
Also see NEW JERSEY MASS CHOIR
Also see SPYS

FOREST, Earl: see FORREST, Earl

FOREST, Jimmy

(Jimmy Forrest)

Singles: 78rpm

UNITED 5-10   52-55

Singles: 7–inch

PRESTIGE 4-6   61-62
TRIUMPH 4-8   59
UNITED (Except 113) 5-10   52-55
UNITED (110 "Night Train") 10-15   52
(Black vinyl.)
UNITED (110 "Night Train") 20-30   52
(Colored vinyl.)

LPs: 10/12–inch 33rpm

NEW JAZZ (8250 "Forrest Fire") 25-50   60
NEW JAZZ (8293 "Soul Street") 25-50   62
PRESTIGE 20-30   61-62
(Yellow label.)
PRESTIGE 10-20   64
(Blue label.)
UNITED 002 "Night Train") 75-100   57
(10–inch LP.)
Also see DAVIS, Miles

FORESTER SISTERS

Singles: 7–inch

WARNER 2-4   84-91

LPs: 10/12–inch 33rpm

WARNER 5-8 85-91
Members: Kathy Forester; Kim Forester; June Forester; Christy Forester.

FOREVER MORE
Singles: 7–inch

RCA 3-5 69-70

LPs: 10/12–inch 33rpm

RCA 10-15 69-70
Also see AVERAGE WHITE BAND

FORMATIONS
Singles: 7–inch

BANK 5-10 68
MGM 3-5 68-69
Members: Victor Drayton; Jerry Akines; Reginald Turner; Ernie Brooks; Johnny Bellman.

FORREST
Singles: 12–inch 33/45rpm

PROFILE 4-6 83

FORREST, Earl
(Earl Forest)
Singles: 78rpm

DUKE (Except 103) 5-10 52
DUKE (103 "Rock the Bottle") 10-20 52
METEOR 25-45 53

Singles: 7–inch

DUKE (108 "Whoopin' and Hollerin") . 25-35 52
DUKE (113 "Last Night's Dream") . . . 20-30 53
DUKE (121 "Out on a Party") 120-30 54
DUKE (130 "Your Kind of Love") 20-30 54
DUKE (300 series) 4-8 62-63
METEOR (5005 "I Wronged
a Woman") 50-100 53
Also see ACE, Johnny / Earl Forrest

FORREST, Jimmy: see FOREST, Jimmy

FORTUNES
Singles: 7–inch

CAPITOL 3-5 71-74
LONDON 2-4
PRESS 5-10 65-66
U.A. 4-8 67-68
WORLD PACIFIC 3-5 70

LPs: 10/12–inch 33rpm

CAPITOL 8-10 71-73
COCA-COLA ("It's the Real Thing") . . 30-40
(Special products issue.)
PRESS (73002 "The Fortunes") 20-25 65
(Monaural.)
PRESS (83002 "The Fortunes") 25-30 65
(Stereo.)
WORLD PACIFIC 8-10 70

FORUM
Singles: 7–inch

MIRA 10-15 67
PENTHOUSE 10-20 66

LPs: 10/12–inch 33rpm

MIRA 15-20 67

Members: Phil Campos; Rene Nole; Riselle Vaine.

FOSTER, Bruce
Singles: 7–inch

MILLENIUM 3-5 77

Picture Sleeves

MILLENIUM 5-10 77

LPs: 10/12–inch 33rpm

MILLENIUM 8-15 77

FOSTER, David
Singles: 7–inch

ATLANTIC 2-4 85-88

Picture Sleeves

ATLANTIC 2-4 85-88

LPs: 10/12–inch 33rpm

ATLANTIC 5-10 86-88
MFSL (123 "The Best of Me") 15-25 84

FOSTER, David, and Olivia Newton-John
Singles: 7–inch

ATLANTIC 2-4 86
Also see FOSTER, David
Also see NEWTON-JOHN, Olivia

FOSTER, Ian
Singles: 7–inch

MCA 2-4 87

FOSTER & LLOYD
LPs: 10/12–inch 33rpm

RCA 5-10 86-89

FOTOMAKER
Singles: 7–inch

ATLANTIC 3-5 78-79

LPs: 10/12–inch 33rpm

ATLANTIC 5-10 78-79
Members: Gene Cornish; Dino Dannelli; Wally Bryson.
Also see RASCALS
Also see RASPBERRIES

FOUNDATIONS
Singles: 7–inch

UNI 3-6 67-71

LPs: 10/12–inch 33rpm

UNI 15-20 68-69

FOUNTAIN, Pete
Singles: 7–inch

CORAL 3-5 58-62

LPs: 10/12–inch 33rpm

CORAL 5-15 59-69
FIRST AMERICAN 4-8 78
GUEST STAR 4-8 64
Also see HIRT, Al, and Pete Fountain
Also see LEE, Brenda, and Pete Fountain

FOUNTAIN, Roosevelt, and the Pens of Rhythm
Singles: 7–inch

PRINCE-ADAMS 4-8 62-63

FOUR ACES
DECCA 4-8 51-57
FLASH 10-20 50

MERION 10-20	52	
VICTORIA 8-12	51	

Singles: 7-Inch

ABC-PAR 3-6	60	
DECCA (25000 series) 3-5	61-64	
DECCA (27000 and 28000 series) 5-10	51-53	
DECCA (29000 through 31000 series) 4-8	54-60	
FLASH (103 "Who's to Blame") 10-20	50	
MERION (104 "Wanted") 10-15	52	
RADNOR 2-4	69	
VICTORIA (101 "Sin") 10-20	51	
(Black vinyl.)		
VICTORIA (101 "Sin") 25-50	51	
(Colored vinyl.)		
VICTORIA (102 "There's a Christmas Tree in Heaven") 10-20	51	

Picture Sleeves

ABC-PAR 4-8	60	

EPs: 7-Inch 33/45rpm

DECCA 10-20	52-59	

LPs: 10/12-Inch 33rpm

ACCORD 5-10	81-82	
DECCA (4013 "The Golden Hits") ... 15-25	60	
DECCA (5429 "The Four Aces") 20-40	52	
(10-inch LP.)		
DECCA (8122 through 8693) 15-30	55-58	
DECCA (8766 "The Swingin' Aces") .. 15-25	58	
(Monaural.)		
DECCA (8766 "The Swingin' Aces") .. 20-30	58	
(Stereo. With "DL-7" prefix.)		
DECCA (8855 "Hits from Broadway") . 15-25	59	
(Monaural.)		
DECCA (8855 "Hits from Broadway") . 20-30	59	
(Stereo. With "DL-7" prefix.)		
DECCA (8944 "Beyond the Blue Horizon") 10-20	59	
(Monaural.)		
DECCA (8944 "Beyond the Blue Horizon") 15-25	59	
(Stereo.)		
MCA 5-10	74	
RADNOR 5-8		
U.A. 10-15	61	
VOCALION 5-10	69	
WESTOWN 5-8		

Members: Al Alberts; Louis Silvestri; Dave Mahoney; Sol Vocarro. Also see LEE, Brenda / Bill Haley and the Comets / Kalin Twins / Four Aces

FOUR ACES / Four Lads / Four Preps
LPs: 10/12-Inch 33rpm

EXACT 5-10	80	

Also see FOUR ACES
Also see FOUR LADS
Also see FOUR PREPS

FOUR BLAZES
Singles: 7-Inch

UNITED (114 "Mary Jo") 30-50	52	
(Black vinyl.)		

UNITED (114 "Mary Jo") 75-100	52	
(Colored vinyl.)		
UNITED (125 "Night Train") 15-25	52	
UNITED (127 "Stop Boogie Woogie") 15-25	52	
UNITED (146 "Not Any More Tears") . 15-25	53	
UNITED (158 "Ella Louise") 15-25	53	
UNITED (168 "My Great Love Affair") 15-25	54	
UNITED (177 "Do the Do") 15-25	54	
UNITED (191 "She Needs to Be Loved") 15-25	55	
(Reissued as by the Blasers.)		

Member: Tommy Braden.

FOUR BUDDIES
Singles: 78rpm

SAVOY 15-30	50-53	

Singles: 7-Inch

SAVOY (769 "I Will Wait") 200-300	50	
SAVOY (779 "Don't Leave Me Now") 100-150	51	
SAVOY (789 "My Summer's Gone") 100-150	51	
SAVOY (817 "Heart And Soul") ... 100-150	51	
SAVOY (845 "You're Part of Me") .. 75-125	52	
SAVOY (866 "What's the Matter with Me") 75-125	52	
SAVOY (888 "My Mother's Eyes") .. 50-100	53	
SAVOY (891 "I'd Climb the Highest Mountain") 50-75	53	

Members: Leon Harrison; Greg Carroll; Bert Palmer; Tommy Smith.

FOUR COINS
Singles: 78rpm

EPIC 3-6	54-59	

Singles: 7-Inch

COLUMBIA 3-6	67	
EPIC 5-10	54-59	
JOY 3-6	64	
JUBILEE 3-6	61-62	
MGM 4-8	60-61	
VEE JAY 4-8	62-63	

Picture Sleeves

EPIC 5-10	57	

EPs: 7-Inch 33/45rpm

EPIC 5-10	55-58	

LPs: 10/12-Inch 33rpm

EPIC 10-20	55-58	
MGM 10-15	61	
ROULETTE 10-15	65	

FOUR DATES
Singles: 7-Inch

CHANCELLOR 8-12	58	

Also see FABIAN

FOUR ESQUIRES
Singles: 78rpm

CADENCE 4-8	55	
PARIS 4-8	57	
PILGRIM 4-8	56	

Singles: 7–inch

CADENCE 5-10	55
PARIS 8-15	57
PILGRIM 5-10	56
TERRACE 4-8	63

Also see ECHOES / Four Esquires

FOUR FELLOWS
Singles: 78rpm

DERBY 20-40	54
GLORY 10-20	55-57

Singles: 7–inch

DERBY (862 "I Tried") 200-300	54
GLORY (231 "I Wish I Didn't Know You") 30-40	55
GLORY (234 "Soldier Boy") 20-30	55
GLORY (236 "Angels Say") 20-30	55
GLORY (238 "Fallen Angel") 20-30	56
GLORY (241 "Petticoat Baby") 30-40	56
GLORY (242 "Darling You") 50-75	56
GLORY (244 "I Sit in My Window") .. 20-30	56
GLORY (248 "You Don't Know Me") . 20-30	56
GLORY (250 "Give Me Back My Broken Heart") 25-35	57
GLORY (263 "You're Still in My Heart") 20-30	57
NESTOR (27 "Remember") 100-200	58

Members: David Jones; Ted Williams; Larry Banks; Jim McGowan.

450 SL
Singles: 7–inch

GOLDEN BOY 2-4	85

FOUR FRESHMEN
Singles: 78rpm

CAPITOL 2-5	50-57

Singles: 7–inch

CAPITOL 3-8	50-65
DECCA 3-5	67
LIBERTY 3-5	68

Picture Sleeves

CAPITOL 3-8	63

EPs: 7–inch 33/45rpm

CAPITOL 5-10	54-59

LPs: 10/12–inch 33rpm

CAPITOL (With "SM" prefix) 5-10	75-79
CAPITOL (522 through 992) 15-30	54-58
(With "T" prefix.)	
CAPITOL (1000 and 2000 series) ... 10-20	58-64
(With "T" or "ST" prefix.)	
LIBERTY 5-10	68-82
SUNSET 5-10	70

Members: Don Barbour; Ross Barbour; Ken Errair; Bob Flanagan.

FOUR JACKS and a JIll
Singles: 7–inch

RCA 4-8	68

LPs: 10/12–inch 33rpm

RCA 10-15	68

FOUR KNIGHTS
Singles: 78rpm

CAPITOL 5-10	51-57
CORAL 8-12	49
DECCA 10-15	46-47

Singles: 7–inch

CAPITOL (346 "Spotlight Songs") ... 30-50	52
(Boxed set of three 45 rpm singles.)	
CAPITOL (1587 through 1914) 15-30	51-52
CAPITOL (1930 through 2517) 10-20	52-53
CAPITOL (2654 "Oh Baby Mine") ... 20-30	53
CAPITOL (2654 "I Get So Lonely") ... 8-12	53
(Note title change.)	
CAPITOL (2782 through 3730) 8-12	54-57
CORAL (61936 through 62110) 5-10	58-59
DECCA (48018 "He'll Understand and Say Well Done") 50-75	52
SOUVENIR 4-8	62

EPs: 7–inch 33/45rpm

CAPITOL (346 "Spotlight Songs") ... 50-75	52
(Two-EP set.)	
CAPITOL (414 "The Four Knights Sing") 40-60	53
CAPITOL (506 "I Get So Lonely") ... 40-60	54

LPs: 10/12–inch 33rpm

CAPITOL (H-346 "Spotlight Songs") 100-200	52
(10–inch LP.)	
CAPITOL (T-346 "Spotlight Songs") . 50-75	55
CORAL (57221 "The Four Knights") 50-100	58
CORAL (57309 "Million Dollar Baby") 30-60	60
(Monaural.)	
CORAL (757309 "Million Dollar Baby") 50-75	60
(Stereo.)	

Members: Gene Alford; John Wallace; Clarence Dixon; Oscar Broadway.
Also see COLE, Nat "King"
Also see HUNT, Pee Wee

FOUR LADS
Singles: 78rpm

COLUMBIA 3-5	52-58
OKEH 4-6	52

Singles: 7–inch

COLUMBIA 4-8	52-60
DOT 3-5	62
FONA 2-4	77-78
KAPP 3-6	60-61
OKEH 5-10	52
U.A. 3-5	63-69

Picture Sleeves

COLUMBIA 10-15	56-59
KAPP 4-8	60

EPs: 7–inch 33/45rpm

COLUMBIA 5-15	55-59

LPs: 10/12–inch 33rpm

COLUMBIA (912 "On the Sunny Side") 20-30	56
COLUMBIA (1045 "The Four Lads Sing Frank Loesser") 20-30	57

COLUMBIA (1111 "Four on the Aisle") 15-25   58
(Monaural.)
COLUMBIA (1223 "Breezin' Along") . . 15-25   58
(Monaural.)
COLUMBIA (1235 "Greatest Hits") . . . 15-25   58
COLUMBIA (1299 through 1550) 10-20   59-60
(Monaural.)
COLUMBIA (2576 "Stage Show") . . . 20-30   56
(10–inch LP.)
COLUMBIA (6329 "Stage Show") . . . 25-40   54
(10–inch LP.)
COLUMBIA (8035 "Breezin' Along") . . 20-30   58
(Stereo.)
COLUMBIA (8047 "Four on the Aisle") 20-30   58
(Stereo.)
COLUMBIA (8106 through 8350) 15-25   59-60
(Stereo.)
DOT 10-15   62-63
KAPP 10-15   61
HARMONY 5-10   69
U.A. 8-12   64
VIKING 5-10
Members: Frankie Busseri; Jimmy Arnold; Connie Coderini;
Bernie Toorish.
Also see FOUR ACES / Four Lads / Four Preps
Also see LAINE, Frankie, and the Four Lads
Also see RAY, Johnnie

FOUR LOVERS
Singles: 78rpm
EPIC (9255 "My Life for Your Love") 50-100   57
RCA 10-15   56-57
Singles: 7–inch
EPIC (9255 "My Life for Your Love") 150-200   57
MAGIC CARPET 3-5
RCA (6518 "You're the
Apple of My Eye") 20-25   56
RCA (6519 "Honey Love") 20-25   56
RCA (6646 "Jambalaya") 15-25   56
RCA (6768 "Happy Am I") 15-25   57
RCA (6812 "Shake a Hand") 20-25   57
RCA (6819 "Night Train") 15-20   57
EPs: 7–inch 33/45rpm
RCA (869 "The Four Lovers") 150-200   56
RCA (871 "Joyride") 350-450   56
LPs: 10/12–inch 33rpm
RCA (1317 "Joyride") 400-600   56
Members: Frankie Valli; Tom Devito; Nick Devito; Hank Majewski.
Also see 4 SEASONS
Also see VALLI, Frankie

FOUR LOVERS / Homer & Jethro
EPs: 7–inch 33/45rpm
RCA (47 "The Four Lovers/
Homer & Jethro") 30-50   56
(Promotional only. Not issued with cover.)
Also see HOMER & JETHRO

FOUR LOVERS / Teddi King
EPs: 7–inch 33/45rpm
RCA (64 "The Four Lovers/
Teddi King") 30-50   56
(Promotional only. Not issued with cover.)

FOUR PENNIES
Singles: 7–inch
LAURIE 3-5
RUST (5070 "When the Boy's Happy") 15-25   63
RUST (5071 "My Block") 15-25   63
Members: Judy Craig; Barbara Lee; Patricia Bennett; Sylvia
Peterson.
Also see CHIFFONS

FOUR PREPS
Singles: 78rpm
CAPITOL 3-6   56-57
Singles: 7–inch
CAPITOL (3576 through 5074,
except 4568) 5-10   56-63
CAPITOL (4568 "Dream Boy, Dream") 20-30   61
CAPITOL (5143 "A Letter to
the Beatles") 15-25   64
CAPITOL (5178 through 5921) 4-8   64-67
Picture Sleeves
CAPITOL 8-12   61-62
EPs: 7–inch 33/45rpm
CAPITOL 8-15   56-58
LPs: 10/12–inch 33rpm
CAPITOL 15-25   58-67
Members: Bruce Belland; Glen Larson; Marv Ingraham; Ed
Cobb; Don Clarke.
Also see FOUR ACES / Four Lads / Four Preps
Also see KINGSTON TRIO / Four Preps

4 SEASONS
(Four Seasons; Frankie Valli and the 4 Seasons)
Singles: 7–inch
BOB CREWE PRESENTS 10-15   70
(Promotional issue only.)
COLLECTABLES 2-4   81
COLUMBIA (6675 "Big Man's World") 25-35   64
(Promotional soundsheet.)
CREWE (333 "And That Reminds Me") . 4-8   69
GONE (5122 "Bermuda") 20-40   61
MCA/CURB 3-5   85-86
MOTOWN 5-10   73
MOWEST 5-10   72
OLDIES 45 4-8   62-63
PHILIPS (40166 through 40662) 4-8   64-69
PHILIPS (40688 "Lay Me Down") . . . 15-25   70
PHILIPS (40694 "Where Are
My Dreams") 20-25   70
RAINBOW 4-8   62
SEASONS 4-EVER (Black vinyl) 4-6   71
SEASONS 4-EVER (Colored vinyl) . . 10-12   71
VEE JAY (456 through 562) 5-10   62-63
VEE JAY (576 "Stay"/"Peanuts") 40-50   63
VEE JAY (582 "Stay"/
"Goodnight My Love") 5-10   64

VEE JAY (597 "Alone") 10-15   64
(Yellow label.)
VEE JAY (597 "Alone") 8-10   64
(Black label.)
VEE JAY (597 "Alone") 5-8   64
(Multi-color label.)
VEE JAY (608 through 719) 10-15 64-66
WABC RADIO (77 "Cousin Brucie
Go Go") 75-100   64
(Special products custom pressing. Colored vinyl.)
WXYZ-DETROIT (121003 "Jody
Reynolds' Theme") 50-75   65
(Special products custom pressing.)
WARNER 3-5 75-80
WIBBAGE (WIBG "Jody
Reynolds' Theme") 50-75   65
(Special products custom pressing.)

Picture Sleeves

CREWE (333 "And That Reminds Me 10-15   69
PHILIPS (Except 40542) 10-20 64-70
PHILIPS (40542 "Saturday's Father") 20-30   68
(Fold-out sleeve.)
PHILIPS (40542 "Saturday's Father") . 5-10   68
(Standard sleeve.)
VEE JAY (539 "Candy Girl") 15-25   64

EPs: 7–inch 33/45rpm

MAGIC CARPET 4-8
PHILIPS (2705 "Edizone D'Oro") 20-30   68
(Jukebox issue.)
VEE JAY (901 "Peanuts + 3") 20-35   64
VEE JAY (902 "Alone + 3") 20-35   64

LPs: 10/12–inch 33rpm

ARISTA 8-12   84
GUEST STAR 10-20   64
K-TEL 15-20   77
LONGINES (95833 "Greatest Hits of Frankie
Valli and the 4 Seasons") 20-30
(TV mail-order offer.)
MCA 5-10   85
MOTOWN 5-10   80
MOWEST 10-12
PHILLIPS (200124 "Dawn and 11 Other
Great Hits") 15-20   64
(Monaural.)
PHILLIPS (200129 "Born to Wander") 15-20   64
(Monaural.)
PHILLIPS (200146 "Rag Doll") 15-20   64
(Monaural.)
PHILLIPS (200150 "All the Song Hits") 15-20   64
(Monaural.)
PHILLIPS (200164 "The 4 Seasons
Entertain You") 15-20   65
(Monaural.)
PHILLIPS (200193 "Big Hits By Burt Bacharach, Hal
David and Bob Dylan") 50-65   65
(Photos of group on front and back cover.
Monaural.)

PHILLIPS (200193 "Big Hits By Burt Bacharach,
Hal David and Bob Dylan") 15-20   65
(No group photos on cover. Monaural.)
PHILLIPS (200196 "Gold Vault
of Hits") 15-20   65
(Monaural.)
PHILLIPS (200201 "Working My Way
Back to You") 15-20   66
(Monaural.)
PHILLIPS (200221 "2nd Gold Vault
of Hits") 15-20   66
(Monaural.)
PHILLIPS (200222 "Lookin' Back") . . 15-20   66
(Monaural.)
PHILLIPS (200223 "Christmas Album")15-25   66
(Stereo.)
PHILLIPS (200243 "New Gold Hits") . 15-20   67
(Monaural.)
PHILLIPS (600124 "Dawn and 11 Other
Great Hits") 15-20   64
(Stereo.)
PHILLIPS (600129 "Born to Wander") 15-20   64
(Stereo.)
PHILLIPS (600146 "Rag Doll") 15-20   64
(Stereo.)
PHILLIPS (600150 "All the Song Hits")15-20   64
(Stereo.)
PHILLIPS (600164 "The 4 Seasons
Entertain You") 15-20   65
(Stereo.)
PHILLIPS (600193 "Big Hits By Burt Bacharach,
Hal David and Bob Dylan") 50-65   65
(Photos of group on front and back cover. Stereo.)
PHILLIPS (600193 "Big Hits By Burt Bacharach,
Hal David and Bob Dylan") 15-20   65
(No group photos on cover. Stereo.)
PHILLIPS (600196 "Gold Vault
of Hits") 15-20   65
(Stereo.)
PHILLIPS (600201 "Working My Way
Back to You") 15-20   66
(Stereo.)
PHILLIPS (600221 "2nd Gold Vault
of Hits") 15-20   66
(Stereo.)
PHILLIPS (600222 "Lookin' Back") . . 15-20   66
(Stereo.)
PHILLIPS (600223 "Christmas Album")15-25   66
(Stereo.)
PHILLIPS (600243 "New Gold Hits") . 15-20   67
(Stereo.)
PHILLIPS (600290 "Genuine Imitation
Life Gazette") 35-45   69
(Yellow cover.)
PHILLIPS (600290 "Genuine Imitation
Life Gazette") 10-15   69
(White cover.)
PHILLIPS (341 "Half and Half") 110-15   70
PHILLIPS (2-6501 "Edizone D'Oro") . 20-25   68

  Members: Frankie Valli; Tom Devito; Nick Devito; Hank
  Majewski; Bob Gaudio; Charlie Calello; Nick Massi; Joe Long;
  Don Ciccione; Bill Deloach; Paul Wilson.
  Also see BEACH BOYS with Frankie Valli and the Four Seasons
  Also see BEATLES / 4 Seasons
  Also see DIXON, Billy, and the Topics
  Also see FOUR LOVERS
  Also see RASCALS / Buggs / Four Seasons / Johnny Rivers
  Also see RIVERS, Johnny / 4 Seasons / Jerry Butler / Jimmy
   Soul
  Also see ROYAL TEENS
  Also see SANTOS, Larry
  Also see SIMON, Paul
  Also see VALLI, Frankie
  Also see WONDER WHO

4 SEASONS / Connie Francis / Barbara Brown and the Buggs
LPs: 10/12-inch 33rpm

  Also see FRANCIS, Connie

4 SEASONS / Little Royal
Singles: 7-inch

4 SEASONS / Scarlets
Singles: 7-inch

4 SEASONS / Shirelles
Singles: 7-inch

  (Coca-Cola radio spots, for radio station use.)
  Also see JAN & DEAN / Roy Orbison / 4 Seasons / Shirelles
  Also see SHIRELLES

4 SEASONS / Ray Stevens
Singles: 7-inch

  Also see 4 SEASONS

  Also see STEVENS, Ray

FOUR SONICS
Singles: 7-inch

FOUR SPORTSMEN
Singles: 7-inch

FOUR TOPS
Singles: 12-inch 33/45rpm

Singles: 7-inch

  (Topps Chewing Gum promotional item.
  Single-sided, cardboard flexi, picture disc. Issued
  with generic paper sleeve.)

Picture Sleeves

LPs: 10/12-inch 33rpm

  Members: Levi Stubbs; Lawrence Payton; Abdul "Duke" Fakir;
  Obie Benson.
  Also see HOLLAND - DOZIER
  Also see PAYTON, Lawrence
  Also see SUPREMES and Four Tops

FOUR TOPS / Temptations

LPs: 10/12-inch 33rpm

SILVER EAGLE 6-10   87
   Also see FOUR TOPS
   Also see TEMPTATIONS

FOUR TUNES

Singles: 78rpm

ARCO 5-10	50
COLUMBIA 5-10	48
JUBILEE 5-10	53-57
MANOR 5-10	46-49
RCA 5-15	49-53

Singles: 7-inch

JUBILEE (5128 "Marie") 10-20   53
JUBILEE (5132 through 5276) 8-15   53-57
JUBILEE (6000 "Marie") 5-8   59
KAY-RON (1000 "I Want to Be Loved") 15-20   54
KAY-RON (1005 "I Understand") 15-20   54
RCA (0008 "You're Heartless") 100-150   49
   (Colored vinyl.)
RCA (0016 "My Last Affair") 100-150   49
   (Colored vinyl.)
RCA (0042 "I'm Just a
   Fool in Love") 100-150   49
   (Colored vinyl.)
RCA (0072 "Am I Blue") 75-125   50
   (Colored vinyl.)
RCA (0085 "Old Fashioned Love") .. 75-125   50
   (Colored vinyl.)
RCA (0131 "May That Day
   Never Come") 75-125   51
RCA (3881 "Do I Worry") 30-40   50
RCA (3967 "Cool Water") 25-35   50
RCA (4102 "Wishing You
   Were Here Tonight") 25-35   51
RCA (4241 "I Married an Angel") 15-25   51
RCA (4280 "It's No Sin") 20-30   51
RCA (4305 "Early in the Morning") ... 15-25   51
RCA (4427 "I'll See You
   in My Dreams") 20-30   51
RCA (4489 "Come What May") 10-20   52
RCA (4663 "I Wonder") 10-20   52
RCA (4828 "They Don't Understand") 10-20   52
RCA (4968 "I Don't Want to Set
   the World on Fire") 20-30   52
RCA (5532 "Don't Get Around
   Much Anymore") 15-25   53
VIRGO 2-4   72

EPs: 7-inch 33/45rpm

RCA (586 "Four Tunes") 50-75   54

LPs: 10/12-inch 33rpm

JUBILEE (1039 "12 x 4") 50-75   57
   Members: Jim Nabbie; Danny Owens; William "Pat" Best; Jimmy
   Gordon; Deek Watson.
   Also see CHURCHILL, Savannah

FOUR TUNES / Shadows

LPs: 10/12-inch 33rpm

CHICAGO 8-10   88
   Also see FOUR TUNES

FOUR VOICES

Singles: 78rpm

COLUMBIA 3-5   55-57

Singles: 7-inch

ABC-PAR 4-8   61
COLUMBIA 4-8   55-60
PEACOCK 3-6   62

FOUR-EVERS

Singles: 7-inch

CHATTAHOOCHEE 4-8   64
COLUMBIA (42303 "You Belong
   to Me") 30-50   62
COLUMBIA (42303 "You Belong
   to Me") 75-100   62
   (With "3" prefix. Compact 33 Single.)
COLUMBIA (43886 "A Lovely Way
   to Spend an Evening") 5-10   66
CONSTELLATION 10-15   65
CRYSTAL BALL 3-6
JAMIE 5-10   63
JASON SCOTT 3-5
RED BIRD 10-15   66
SMASH (1853 "It's Love") 10-15   63
SMASH (1887 "Please Be Mine") ... 10-20   63
SMASH (1887 "Be My Girl") 10-20   64
   (Same catalog number used on both issues above.)
SMASH (1921 "Doo Be Dum") 10-15   63

FOWLEY, Kim

Singles: 7-inch

CAPITOL 3-5   72-73
CREATIVE FAMILY 15-25
IMPERIAL 4-8   68-69
LIVING LEGEND 10-15   65-66
LOMA 5-10   66
REPRISE 4-8   67
TOWER 4-8   67

LPs: 10/12-inch 33rpm

CAPITOL 10-15   72-74
IMPERIAL 15-20   68-69
PVC 5-10   79
TOWER 15-20   67
   Also see KING LIZARD

FOX

Singles: 7-inch

ARIOLA/GTO 3-5   75
GTO 3-5   74

LPs: 10/12-inch 33rpm

ARIOLA AMERICA 8-10   75

FOX, Charles

Singles: 7-inch

HANDSHAKE 2-4   81

FOX, Samantha

Singles: 12-inch 33/45rpm

JIVE 4-6   86

Singles: 7-inch

JIVE 2-4   86-89

Picture Sleeves
JIVE 2-4 86-89
LPs: 10/12–inch 33rpm
JIVE 5-10 86-88

FOX, Virgil
LPs: 10/12–inch 33rpm
DECCA 10-12 71

FOXX, Inez
(Inez and Charlie Foxx)
Singles: 7–inch
DYNAMO 4-6 67-70
LANA 3-5
MUSICOR 4-8 66-68
SUE 4-8 65
SYMBOL 5-10 63-64
VOLT 3-5 72-73
U.A. 3-5 74
LPs: 10/12–inch 33rpm
DYNAMO 10-15 67
SUE (1037 "Inez and Charlie Fox") .. 20-25 65
(Monaural.)
SUE (1037 "Inez and Charlie Fox") .. 25-30 65
(Stereo.)
SYMBOL (4400 "Mockingbird") 35-45 63
VOLT 8-10 73
Also see PLATTERS / Inez and Charlie Foxx / Jive Five / Tommy Hunt

FOXX, Redd
(Redd Foxx and Hattie Noel)
Singles: 78rpm
DOOTO (Except 416) 3-5 57-61
DOOTO (416 "Real Pretty Mama") .. 10-15 57
DOOTONE 3-5 56-57
SAVOY 5-10 46
Singles: 7–inch
DOOTO (Except 416) 5-10 57-61
DOOTO (416 "Real Pretty Mama") .. 15-25 57
DOOTONE 8-12 56-57
EPs: 7–inch 33/45rpm
DOOTO 5-10 57-61
DOOTONE 5-10 56-57
LPs: 10/12–inch 33rpm
ATLANTIC 5-10 75
AUTHENTIC 15-25 55-56
DOOTO 5-15 60-74
DOOTONE 10-20 57
KING 5-10 69-71
LAFF 5-10 79
LOMA 8-12 66-68
MF 5-8
RCA 5-10 72
WARNER 8-10 69

FOZZIE BEAR: see KERMIT / Fozzie Bear

FRAMPTON, Peter
Singles: 7–inch
A&M (Except 1988) 2-5 74-81

A&M (1988 "Tried to Love") 3-6 77
(With Mick Jagger.)
A&M (1988 "Tried to Love") 10-15 77
(White label, promotional issue.)
ATLANTIC 2-4 86
Picture Sleeves
A&M (Except 1988) 2-5 74-81
A&M (1988 "Tried to Love") 4-6 77
ATLANTIC 2-4 86
LPs: 10/12–inch 33rpm
A&M (3000 and 4000 series) 6-12 72-82
ATLANTIC 5-10 86-89
Promotional LPs
A&M (3703 "Frampton Comes Alive") 10-15 79
(Picture disc.)
A&M (4704 "I'm in You") 15-25 77
(Picture disc.)
ATLANTIC (848 "Frampton Is Alive") .. 8-15 86
Also see FRAMPTON'S CAMEL
Also see JAGGER, Mick
Also see STARR, Ringo

FRAMPTON'S CAMEL
(Peter Frampton)
Singles: 7–inch
A&M 5-10 72-73
LPs: 10/12–inch 33rpm
A&M 10-20 73
Also see FRAMPTON, Peter
Also see HUMBLE PIE

FRANCE JOLI: see JOLI, France

FRANCHI, Sergio
Singles: 7–inch
LAX 2-4 79
METROMEDIA 2-4 71-72
RCA 3-6 62-67
U.A. 3-5 69-70
LPs: 10/12–inch 33rpm
FOUR CORNERS 6-10 66
RCA 5-15 62-77
U.A. 5-10 70

FRANCIS, Connie
Singles: 78rpm
MGM 4-8 55-58
Singles: 7–inch
GSF 3-5 73
IVANHOE 3-5
MGM CELEBRITY SCENE (CS6-5 "Connie
Francis") 30-40 66
(Boxed set of five singles with bio insert and title
strips.)
MGM (3000 series) 3-5 71
MGM (12015 "Freddy") 25-50 55
MGM (12056 "Oh, Please
Make Him Jealous") 25-50 55
MGM (12122 through 12555) 12-25 55-57
MGM (12588 through 13116) 5-10 58-63
MGM (13127 through 14034
except 13550) 4-8 64-69

MGM (13550 "A Nurse in the
U.S. Army Corp") 20-25   66
(Promotional issue only.)
MGM (14500 series) 3-5   81
MGM (50000 series) 12-25   59-60
(Stereo singles.)
POLYDOR 2-4   83

Picture Sleeves

MGM (12000 series, except 12738) . . . 5-15   58-61
MGM (12738 "My Happiness") 10-15   58
(Pink sleeve.)
MGM (12738 "My Happiness") 15-25   58
(Black and white sleeve.)
MGM (13000 series,
except 13505 and 13773) 5-10   61-68
MGM (13505 "Empty Chapel") 10-20   66
MGM (13773 "My Heart Cries for You")10-20   67
MGM (14000 series,
except 14058 and 14091) 3-6   68-69
MGM (14058 "Gone Like the Wind") . 10-20   69
MGM (14091 "Mr. Love") 10-20   69

EPs: 7–inch 33/45

MGM 10-20   58-62

LPs: 10/12–inch 33rpm

LEO 12-15
LION 12-15
MGM (100 series) 10-15   70
MGM (3700 series) 25-35   58-60
MGM (3800 and 3900 series) 20-35   60-61
MGM (4000 series) 15-25   62-69
MGM (5400 series) 5-10
MGM (10000 series) 8-12   71
MGM (91000 series) 10-15
(Capitol Record Club series.)
MATI-MOR (8002 "Brylcreem Presents Sing
Along with Connie Francis") 15-25   61
(Promotional issue. With the Jordanaires.)
METRO 10-15   65-66
MGM/SESSIONS 10-12   75
POLYDOR 5-10   83
Also see CRAMER, Floyd
Also see 4 SEASONS / Connie Francis / Barbara Brown and
   the Buggs
Also see RANDOLPH, Boots

FRANCIS, Connie, and Marvin Rainwater
Singles: 78rpm

MGM 5-10   57

Singles: 7–inch

MGM 10-15   57
Also see FRANCIS, Connie
Also see RAINWATER, Marvin

FRANCIS, Connie, and Hank Williams Jr.
LPs: 10/12–inch 33rpm

MGM 15-25   64
Also see FRANCIS, Connie
Also see WILLIAMS, Hank, Jr.

FRANKE and the Knockouts
Singles: 7–inch

MCA 2-4   84

MILLENNIUM 2-4   81-82

LPs: 10/12–inch 33rpm

MCA 5-10   84
MILLENNIUM 5-10   81-82

FRANKIE and the Spindles
Singles: 7–inch

ROC-KER 4-8   68

FRANKIE GOES to HOLLYWOOD
Singles: 12–inch 33/45rpm

ISLAND 4-6   84-86

Singles: 7–inch

ISLAND 2-4   84-86

Picture Sleeves

ISLAND 2-4   84-85

LPs: 10/12–inch 33rpm

ISLAND 5-10   84-86
Members: Holly Johnson; Paul Rutherford.

FRANKLIN, Aretha
Singles: 12–inch 33/45rpm

ARISTA 4-6   84-86

Singles: 7–inch

ARISTA 2-4   80-89
ATLANTIC (2000 series) 3-6   67-74
ATLANTIC (3000 series) 2-4   74-79
ATLANTIC (13000 series) 2-4
CHECKER 5-10   60
COLUMBIA (Except 44000 series) 4-8   60-67
COLUMBIA (44000 series) 3-5   67-68
CHESS 2-4   73

Picture Sleeves

ARISTA 2-4   85-87
COLUMBIA 5-10   62-63

EPs: 7–inch 33/45rpm

COLUMBIA 5-10   64
(Jukebox issues.)

LPs: 10/12–inch 33rpm

ARISTA 5-10   80-89
ATLANTIC (Except "QD" series) 8-15   67-79
ATLANTIC ("QD" series) 12-18   73
(Quadrophonic.)
BATTLE 5-15
CANDLELITE 8-10   77
CHECKER 15-20   65
COLUMBIA (12 "Aretha Franklin") . . . 10-15   68
COLUMBIA (1612 through 2281) 12-25   61-64
(Monaural.)
COLUMBIA (2300 through 2700
series) 10-20   65-67
(Monaural.)
COLUMBIA (8402 through 9081) 15-30   61-64
(With "CS" prefix. Stereo.)
COLUMBIA (9100 through 9700
series) 10-15   65-69
(With "CS" prefix. Stereo.)
COLUMBIA (10000 series) 5-10   73
COLUMBIA (30000 series) 5-10   72-82
HARMONY 10-12   68-71

UPFRONT 5-10   79
  Also see CLEMONS, Clarence
  Also see EURYTHMICS and Aretha Franklin
  Also see GRAHAM, Larry
  Also see SANTANA
  Also see SIMON, Paul
  Also see SWEET INSPIRATIONS
  Also see WOLF, Peter

FRANKLIN, Aretha, and George Benson
Singles: 7-inch
ARISTA 2-4   81
Picture Sleeves
ARISTA 2-4   81
  Also see BENSON, George

FRANKLIN, Aretha, with James Cleveland and the Southern California Community Choir
EPs: 7-inch 33/45rpm
ATLANTIC (1025 "Amazing Grace") ... 4-8   72
(Promotional issue only.)
LPs: 10/12-inch 33rpm
ATLANTIC 6-10   72

FRANKLIN, Aretha, and Whitney Houston
Singles: 7-inch
ARISTA 2-4   89
Picture Sleeves
ARISTA 2-4   89
  Also see HOUSTON, Whitney

FRANKLIN, Aretha, and Elton John
Singles: 7-inch
ARISTA 2-4   89
Picture Sleeves
ARISTA 2-4   89
  Also see JOHN, Elton

FRANKLIN, Aretha, and George Michael
Singles: 7-inch
ARISTA 2-4   87
Picture Sleeves
ARISTA 2-4   87
  Also see FRANKLIN, Aretha
  Also see MICHAEL, George

FRANKLIN, Bobby
(Bobby Franklin and Insanity; Boby Franklin)
Singles: 7-inch
BABY 3-5   75
COLUMBIA 3-5   76
THOMAS 3-6   69

FRANKLIN, Carolyn
Singles: 7-inch
RCA 3-5   69-73
LPs: 10/12-inch 33rpm
RCA 10-12   69-73

FRANKLIN, Doug
(Doug Franklin and the Bluenotes)
Singles: 7-inch
COLONIAL 5-10   58-59

FRANKLIN, Erma
Singles: 7-inch
BRUNSWICK 3-5   69
EPIC 4-8   61-63
SHOUT 4-6   67-68
LPs: 10/12-inch 33rpm
BRUNSWICK 10-15   69
EPIC 15-20   62

FRANKLIN, Rodney
Singles: 7-inch
COLUMBIA 2-4   80-86
LPs: 10/12-inch 33rpm
COLUMBIA 5-10   80-86

FRANKS, Michael
Singles: 7-inch
REPRISE 3-5   76
WARNER 2-4   77-83
LPs: 10/12-inch 33rpm
JOHN HAMMOND 5-10
REPRISE 5-10   76-90
WARNER 5-10   77-87

FRANTICS
Singles: 7-inch
BOLO 4-8   62
DOLTON 5-10   59-61
SEAFAIR 4-8   64
  Also see MOBY GRAPE

FRASER, Andy
Singles: 7-inch
ISLAND 2-4   84
Picture Sleeves
ISLAND 2-4   84
  Also see FREE

FRAZIER, Dallas
Singles: 78rpm
CAPITOL 3-5   54
Singles: 7-inch
CAPITOL (2000 through 2400 series) .. 3-5   67-69
CAPITOL (2800 and 2900 series) 6-10   54
CAPITOL (5500 series) 4-6   65
JAMIE 4-8   59
MERCURY 4-6   64
MUSIKRON 4-8   61
RCA 3-5   71-73
20TH FOX 3-5   75
LPs: 10/12-inch 33rpm
CAPITOL 10-20   66-67
RCA 8-12   70-71

FRAZIER, Dallas, and Joe "Fingers" Carr
Singles: 78rpm
CAPITOL 3-5   54
Singles: 7-inch
CAPITOL 5-10   54
EPs: 7-inch 33/45rpm
CAPITOL 8-12   54
  Also see CARR, Joe "Fingers"
  Also see FRAZIER, Dallas

FREBERG, Stan
(Stan Freberg Show)
Singles: 78rpm
CAPITOL 5-15   50-57
Singles: 7-inch
BELFAST SPARKLING WATER (1515
"Invisible Bubbles") 50-75
(Product commercials for radio use.)
BIG SOUND (2 "Jockey's Little
Helper") 35-50
(Product commercials for radio use.)
BUBBLE UP (2227 "Music to
Bubble Up By") 20-30
(Product commercials for radio use.
BUTTERNUT COFFEE (2000 "Instant Sales for
Instant Butternut by Instant Freberg")40-50
(Product commercials for radio use.
BUTTERNUT COFFEE (2237 "Amazing
Butternut Coffee") 25-35
(Product commercials for radio use.)
CAPITOL (415 "Wun'erful Wun'erful")   10-15   57
(Single-sided, promotional issue.)
CAPITOL (1200 through 3100
series, except 2125) 10-20   50-54
CAPITOL (2125 "Abe Snake for
President") 30-40   52
CAPITOL (3200 through 5700 series) . 5-15   54-66
COCA COLA BOTTLING CO. (2227 "Music
to Bubble-Up By") 30-50
(Product commercials for radio use.)
CONTADINA (4476 "The Whole
Peeled Bounce") 35-50
(Product commercials for radio use. With the Hi
Lo's.)
MILKY WAY (23300 "Tom Sweet and
His Milky Way Machine") 35-50
PITTSBURGH PAINT (1/2 "Four
Pittsburgh Paint commercials") 20-30
(Product commercials for radio use.)
RADIO (2225 "Who Listens to Radio") 25-40
(Promotional spots for advertising with radio.)
SOUTHERN BAPTIST CHURCH (101578 "Southern
Baptist Radio and TV Commission") 15-20
(Product commercials for radio use.)
STAINLESS STEEL (1369 "Stainless
Steel") 35-50
(Product commercials for radio use.)
STAN FREBERG on COMMERCIALS
("Rubblemeyer Farms") 40-60
(Promotional issue only. Commercial parodies,
comparing right and wrong production of radio
spots.)
TERMINIX (3540 "Floor Show, Now
Going on at Your House") 30-40
(Product commercials for radio use.)
UNITED PRESBYTERIAN CHURCH (101578 "The
Presbyterian Church") 15-20
(Product commercials for radio use.)

ZEE (2020 "Zee with Freberg - Hey
You Up There") 35-50
(Product commercials for radio use.)
ZEE (24005 "Zee Spot Commercials") 35-50
(Product commercials for radio use.)
Picture Sleeves
BUBBLE UP (2227 "Music to
Bubble Up By") 85-100
(Gatefold sleeve.)
CAPITOL (415 "Wun'erful Wun'erful")   15-20   57
(Promotional issue only.)
CAPITOL (4097 "Green Christmas") .. 6-12   58
CAPITOL (4329 "The Old Payola
Roll Blues") 15-20   60
CAPITOL (5726 "Flackman and
Reagan") 10-15   66
H.I.S. (122667 "Funny Record by
Stan Freberg for H.I.S.") 35-50
(Product commercials for radio use.)
PITTSBURGH PAINT (1/2 "Four
Pittsburgh Paint commercials") 20-30
(Reads: "The Stations Representatives Assn.
presents: Some Exciting new commercials for
Radio!")
RADIO (2225 "Who Listens to Radio") 25-40
(Promotional spots for using radio advertising.)
SOUTHERN BAPTIST CHURCH (101578 "Southern
Baptist Radio and TV Commission") 15-20
(Product commercials for radio use.)
TERMINIX (3540 "Floor Show") 10-20
(Product commercials for radio use.)
ZEE (2020 "Zee Here, Mr. Freberg") . 35-50
(Product commercials for radio use.)
EPs: 7-inch 33/45rpm
CAPITOL (496 "Any Requests") 20-30   54
CAPITOL (628 "Real St. George") ... 15-25   55
CAPITOL (731 "Elderly Man River") . 35-50   58
CAPITOL (732 "The Best of the
Stan Freberg Show") 40-50   58
(Promotional issue only.)
CAPITOL (1101 "Omaha") 15-25   59
CAPITOL (1589 "Stan Freberg") 25-40   61
(Compact 33.)
CAPITOL (3192 "Ugly Duckling") 15-25
SWIMSUITSMANSHIP (2080
"Swimsuitsmanship") 100-125
(Promotional issue only. Cover reads: "Fit Facts
and Figures You and Rose Marie Reid.")
UNITED PRESBYTERIAN CHURCH
(1400 "Is God Dead?") 30-45
(Product commercials for radio use.)
LPs: 10/12-inch 33rpm
BEKINS (27713 "Bekins Presents
the Sound of Moving") 35-50
(Product commercials for radio use.)
BUTTERNUT COFFEE (2000 "Instant
Butternut Coffee") 40-60
(Product commercials for radio use.)

CAPITOL (777 "A Child's Garden
   of Freberg") 20-40   57
CAPITOL (1035 "The Best of the
   Stan Freberg Shows") 40-60   58
CAPITOL (1242 "Stan Freberg
   with the Original Cast") 20-35   59
   (With "T" prefix.)
CAPITOL (1242 "Stan Freberg
   with the Original Cast") 12-20   69
   (With "DT" prefix.)
CAPITOL (1242 "Stan Freberg
   with the Original Cast") 5-10   75
   (With "SM" prefix.)
CAPITOL (1573 "Stan Freberg Presents the
   United States of America, Volume
   1 - the Early Years") 25-25   61
   (With "W" or "SW" prefix.)
CAPITOL (1694 "Face the
   Funnies") 25-35   62
CAPITOL (1816 "Madison Avenue
   Werewolf") 25-35   62
CAPITOL (2020 "Best of Stan
   Freberg") 15-25   64
CAPITOL (2551 "Freberg
   Underground") 15-25   66
   (With "T" or "ST" prefix.)
CAPITOL (2551 "Freberg
   Underground") 5-10   75
   (With "SM" prefix.)
CAPITOL (3264 "Mickey Mouse's
   Birthday Party") 15-25   63
CAPITOL (11000 series) 5-10   78
CAPITOL (80700 "Uncle Stan
   Wants You") 60-80   61
   (Promotional issue for the LP series, *Stan Freberg
   Presents the United States of America*.)
COCA COLA (2468 "The Freedle Family
   Singers") 175-200
COLUMBIA (105948 "Hey, Look
   Us Over") 60-75
   (Promotional issue only. With booklet.)
FREBERG LTD. (2343 "Woburn-Salada
   Tea") 35-50
   (Product commercials for radio use.)
KAISER FOIL (22077 "A Kaiser Foil
   Salesman Faces Life") 125-175
   (10-inch LP. Product commercials for radio use.)
MEADOWGOLD (2152 "Meadowgold
   Dairies") 85-100
   (Product commercials for radio use.)
OREGON (2039 "Oregon
   Soundtrack") 125-150
   (Product commercials for radio. Includes press kit.)
RADIO (3 "Radio Briefings") 35-50
   (Promotional spots for using radio advertising.)
RADIO (1499 "More Here Than
   Meets the Ear") 30-45
   (Promotional spots for using radio advertising.)

RADIO (2226 "Who Listens to Radio") 35-50
   (Promotional spots for using radio advertising.)
TV GUIDE (2889 "TV Guide Spots") . 60-75
   (Product commercials for radio use.)
   Note: Advertising agency discs containing
   commercials for radio station use are listed by
   product name, since there are no other label
   names used.
   Members: Stan Freberg; Daws Butler; June Foray; George
   Burns; Jesse White; Peter Leeds; Paul Frees; Billy May.

FRED, John
(John Fred and His Playboy Band)
Singles: 7-inch
JEWEL 5-10   64-65
MONTEL 10-15   59-62
N-JOY 8-12
PAULA 4-8   65-69
UNI 3-6   69-70
LPs: 10/12-inch 33rpm
PAULA 15-25   66-68
UNI 10-15   70

FRED and the New J.B.s
Singles: 7-inch
PEOPLE 3-5   75

FREDDIE and the Dreamers
Singles: 7-inch
CAPITOL (5053 "I'm Telling You Now") 15-20   63
CAPITOL (5137 "You Were
   Made for Me") 15-20   63
ERIC 2-4
MERCURY 4-8   64-65
SUPER K 3-6   70
TOWER 4-8   65
Picture Sleeves
MERCURY 5-10   65
EPs: 7-inch 33/45rpm
MERCURY (74 "Interview with
   the Dreamers") 20-30   65
   (Promotional issue only.)
MERCURY (60161 "Fun Loving Freddie and
   the Dreamers") 20-30   65
   (Jukebox issue only.)
LPs: 10/12-inch 33rpm
CAPITOL 8-10   76-79
MERCURY 20-30   65-66
TOWER (5003 "I'm Telling
   You Now") 15-25   65
   (Also has tracks by Linda Laine and the Sinners,
   Four Just Men, Heinz, and Mike Rabin & the
   Toggery Five.)
   Also see JONES, Tom / Freddie and the Dreamers / Johnny
   Rivers

FREDDIE and the Dreamers / Beat Merchants
Singles: 7-inch
TOWER 4-8   65
   Also see FREDDIE and the Dreamers

FREDERICK
Singles: 12–inch 33/45rpm
HEAT 4-6   85

FREDERICK II
Singles: 7–inch
VULTURE 3-5   71

FREE
Singles: 7–inch
A&M 3-6   70-71
ISLAND 3-5   72
Picture Sleeves
A&M 4-6   70
LPs: 10/12–inch 33rpm
A&M 8-15   69-75
ISLAND (Except 7) 8-10   73
ISLAND (7 "The Free Story") 25-30   73
(Includes booklet. Promotional issue only.)
Members: Andy Fraser; Paul Rodgers; Simon Kirke; Paul Kossoff.
  Also see BACK STREET CRAWLER
  Also see BAD COMPANY
  Also see FRASER, Andy
  Also see KOSSOFF, Paul
  Also see RODGERS, Paul
  Also see WILLIE and the Poor Boys

FREE EXPRESSION
Singles: 7–inch
VANGUARD 2-4   81

FREE MOVEMENT
Singles: 7–inch
COLUMBIA 3-5   71
DECCA 3-5   71
LPs: 10/12–inch 33rpm
COLUMBIA 8-10   72

FREEMAN, Bobby
Singles: 7–inch
ABC 2-4   73
AUTUMN 4-8   63-64
DOUBLE SHOT 3-6   69-70
GUSTO 2-4
JOSIE 10-15   58-62
KING 5-10   60-65
LOMA 4-8   67
RNOR 2-4
VIRGO 2-4   72
Picture Sleeves
RNOR 5-10
LPs: 10/12–inch 33rpm
AUTUMN (102 "C'mon and Swim") .. 20-30   64
JOSIE (4007 "Get in the Swim") 15-25   65
JUBILEE (1086 "Do You
  Wanna Dance") 35-50   59
  (Monaural.)
JUBILEE (1086 "Do You
  Wanna Dance") 50-75   59
  (Stereo.)
JUBILEE (5010 "Twist with
  Bobby Freeman") 20-30   62

KING (930 "The Lovable Style
  of Bobby Freeman") 30-35   65

FREEMAN, Bobby, and Chuck Jackson
LPs: 10/12–inch 33rpm
GRAND PRIX 15-20   64
  Also see FREEMAN, Bobby
  Also see JACKSON, Chuck

FREEMAN, Ernie
(Ernie Freeman Combo)
Singles: 78rpm
CASH 3-6   56
Singles: 7–inch
AVA 4-8   64
CASH 8-12   56
IMPERIAL (Except 5752) 5-10   57-62
IMPERIAL (5752 "Theme from Igor") .. 8-12   61
KING 5-10   60
LIBERTY 4-8   62
LPs: 10/12–inch 33rpm
DUNHILL 10-15   67
IMPERIAL 15-25   57-62
LIBERTY 10-20   62-63
  Members: Ernie Freeman; Irvin Ashby; Joe Comfort; R. Martinez.
  Also see B. BUMBLE and the Stingers
  Also see OTIS, Johnny
  Also see SIR CHAUNCEY
  Also see WITHERSPOON, Jimmy

FREEMAN, John
Singles: 7–inch
DAKAR 3-5   77

FREESTYLE
(Freestyle Express)
Singles: 7–inch
MUSIC SPECIALISTS 2-4   84-86
  Also see TRINERE / Freestyle / Debbie Deb

FREEZ
Singles: 12–inch 33/45rpm
STREETWISE 4-6   83
Singles: 7–inch
STREETWISE 2-4   83
LPs: 10/12–inch 33rpm
STREETWISE 5-10   83
  Also see ROCCA, John

FREHLEY, Ace
Singles: 7–inch
CASABLANCA 3-5   78
LPs: 10/12–inch 33rpm
CASABLANCA (Except PIX-7121) .. 20-30   78-80
CASABLANCA (PIX-7121 "Ace
  Frehley") 40-50   79
  (Picture disc.)
MEGAFORCE 5-10   87-89
  Also see KISS

FREHLEY'S COMET
LPs: 10/12–inch 33rpm
MEGAFORCE 5-8   88

FRENCH, Don
Singles: 7–inch
LANCER 5-10   59

FRESH, Doug E., and the Get Fresh Band
Singles: 12–inch 33/45rpm
REALITY 4-6   85
Singles: 7–inch
REALITY 2-4   85-88
LPs: 10/12–inch 33rpm
REALITY 5-8   88

FRESH BAND
Singles: 12–inch 33/45rpm
ARE 'N BE 4-6   84

FRESH 3 MCs
Singles: 12–inch 33/45rpm
PROFILE 4-6   84
Singles: 7–inch
PROFILE 2-4   84
LPs: 10/12–inch 33rpm
PROFILE 5-10   84

FREY, Glenn
Singles: 12–inch 33/45rpm
MCA 4-6   84-85
Singles: 7–inch
ASYLUM 2-4   82
MCA 2-4   84-89
Picture Sleeves
ASYLUM 2-4   82
MCA 2-4   85-88
LPs: 10/12–inch 33rpm
ASYLUM 5-10   82
MCA 5-10   84-89
Also see EAGLES

FRIDA
Singles: 7–inch
ATLANTIC 3-5   82
LPs: 10/12–inch 33rpm
ATLANTIC 5-10   82
Also see ABBA

FRIEDMAN, Dean
Singles: 7–inch
LIFESONG 2-4   77-78
LPs: 10/12–inch 33rpm
LIFESONG 5-10   77-78
RECORD CO-OP 5-10   82

FRIEDMAN, Kinky
Singles: 7–inch
ABC 3-5   75
EPIC 2-4   76
SUNRISE 2-4   83
LPs: 10/12–inch 33rpm
ABC 5-10   74
EPIC 5-10   76
VANGUARD 5-10   73

FRIEND & LOVER
Singles: 7–inch
ABC 4-8   67
CADET CONCEPT 3-5
VERVE/FORECAST 4-8   68
LPs: 10/12–inch 33rpm
VERVE/FORECAST 12-15   68
Members: James Post; Cathy Post.

FRIENDS of DISTINCTION
Singles: 7–inch
RCA 3-5   69-73
LPs: 10/12–inch 33rpm
COLLECTABLES 5-10   88
RCA 10-15   69-73
Members: Floyd Butler; Jessica Cleaves; Harry Elston; Charlene
Gibson; Barbara Jean Love.

FRIJID PINK
Singles: 7–inch
LION 3-6   72
LONDON 3-5
PARROT 4-8   69-71
LPs: 10/12–inch 33rpm
FANTASY 8-10   74
LION 8-10   72
PARROT 15-25   70

FRIPP, Robert
LPs: 10/12–inch 33rpm
EDITIONS E.G. 5-10   79-81
POLYDOR 5-10   79-81
Also see KING CRIMSON

FRIPP, Robert, and Andy Summers
LPs: 10/12–inch 33rpm
A&M 5-10   82-84
Also see FRIPP, Robert
Also see POLICE

FRIPP & ENO
LPs: 10/12–inch 33rpm
ANTILLES 8-10   73
Members: Robert Fripp; Brian Eno.
Also see ENO, Brian
Also see FRIPP, Robert

FRIZZELL, Lefty
Singles: 78rpm
COLUMBIA 4-8   50-57
Singles: 7–inch
ABC 2-4   73-75
COLUMBIA (20000 and 21000 series)   5-10   50-56
COLUMBIA (40000 and 41000 series) .   4-8   56-61
COLUMBIA (42000 through 45000
  series) 3-6   61-72
EPs: 7–inch 33/45rpm
COLUMBIA 10-20   51-59
LPs: 10/12–inch 33rpm
ABC 8-12   73-77
COLUMBIA (1342 "The One and
  Only Lefty Frizzell") 30-40   59
COLUMBIA (2169 "Saginaw,
  Michigan") 20-30   64

COLUMBIA (2386 "The Sad Side
of Life") 15-25   65
COLUMBIA (2488 "Lefty Frizzell's
Greatest Hits") 15-25   66
(Monaural.)
COLUMBIA (2772 "Puttin' On") 15-25   67
COLUMBIA (8969 "Saginaw,
Michigan") 25-35   64
COLUMBIA (9019 "Songs of
Jimmie Rodgers") 50-100   51
(10-inch LP.)
HARMONY (9021 "Listen to Lefty") . 50-100   52
(10-inch LP.)
COLUMBIA (9186 "The Sad Side
of Life") 20-25   65
COLUMBIA (9288 "Lefty Frizzell's
Greatest Hits") 20-25   66
(Stereo. With "CS" prefix.)
COLUMBIA (9288 "Lefty Frizzell's
Greatest Hits") 5-10
(With "PC" prefix.)
COLUMBIA (9572 "Puttin' On") 20-25   67
COLUMBIA (10000 series) 5-12   73-83
COLUMBIA (30000 series) 5-12   75-82
HARMONY (7241 "Songs of
Jimmie Rodgers") 25-40   60
HARMONY (11000 series) 8-15   66-68
MCA 8-12   82
ROUNDER 5-10   80-83
   Also see PRICE, Ray / Lefty Frizzell / Carl Smith
   Also see SMITH, Carl / Lefty Frizzell / Marty Robbins

FROGMEN
Singles: 7-inch
ASTRA (1009 "Underwater") 25-35   61
ASTRA (1010 "Beware Below") 25-35   61
CANDIX (314 "Underwater") 15-25   61
CANDIX (326 "Beware Below") 15-25   61
SCOTT (101 "Tioga") 10-20   64
SCOTT (102 "Underwater") 10-20   64
TEE JAY (131 "Sea Hunt") 15-25   64
(Black vinyl.)
TEE JAY (131 "Sea Hunt") 25-50   64
(Colored vinyl.)

FROMAN, Jane
Singles: 78rpm
CAPITOL 2-5   52-56
Singles: 7-inch
CAPITOL 3-6   52-56
EPs: 7-inch 33/45rpm
CAPITOL 5-15   52-56
LPs: 10/12-inch 33rpm
CAPITOL 15-25   52-56
   Also see MARTIN, Dean / Jane Froman

FROST
(Dick Wagner and Frost)
Singles: 7-inch
DATE 5-10   68
VANGUARD 4-8   69-70

LPs: 10/12-inch 33rpm
VANGUARD 10-20   69-70
   Also see COOPER, Alice

FROST, Frank, with the Night Hawks
Singles: 7-inch
JEWEL 4-8   66-67
PHILLIPS INT'L 8-12   61
LPs: 10/12-inch 33rpm
JEWEL 8-10   74
PHILLIPS INT'L. (1975 "Hey
Boss Man!") 800-1200   61

FROST, Thomas and Richard
Singles: 7-inch
IMPERIAL 3-6   69
UNI 3-6   72
LPs: 10/12-inch 33rpm
UNI 8-10   72

FROZEN GHOST
Singles: 7-inch
ATLANTIC 2-4   87
LPs: 10/12-inch 33rpm
ATLANTIC 5-10   87

FUGS
(Village Fugs)
Singles: 7-inch
ESP 4-8   66
LPs: 10/12-inch 33rpm
BROADSIDE (304 "Ballads of Contemporary
Protest, Point of Views, and General
Dissatisfaction") 35-50   66
ESP (1018 "The Fugs First Album") .. 20-25   66
(Reissue of Broadside 304.)
ESP (1028 "The Fugs) 20-25   66
ESP (1038 "Virgin Fugs") 20-25   67
ESP (2018 "Fugs Four") 20-25   67
PVC 5-10   82
REPRISE 10-20   67-70
   Members: Ed Saunders; John Anderson; Lee Crabtree; Pete
   Kearney; Tuli Kupferberg; Vinny Leary; Ken Weaver; Pete
   Stampfel; Steve Weber.

FULL FORCE
Singles: 12-inch 33/45rpm
COLUMBIA 4-6   85-86
Singles: 7-inch
COLUMBIA 2-4   85-87
LPs: 10/12-inch 33rpm
COLUMBIA 5-10   85-87
   Also see LISA LISA

FULLER, Bobby
(Bobby Fuller Four; Bobby Fuller with Jim Reese and
the Embers; Bobby Fuller and the Fanatics)
Singles: 7-inch
ABC 2-4   73
HI-TONE 4-8
DONNA (1403 "Those Memories
of You") 25-35   65

EASTWOOD (0345 "Not Fade
Away") 15-25   62
ERIC 2-4
EXETER (122 "Wine, Wine, Wine") . 50-100   64
EXETER (124 "I Fought the Law") .. 75-125   64
EXETER (126 "Fool of Love") 50-100   64
LIBERTY 10-15   65
MUSTANG 5-10   65-66
TODD (1090 "Saturday Night") 15-25
YUCCA (141 "You're in Love") 25-35   62
YUCCA (144 "My Heart Jumped") ... 25-35   62

LPs: 10/12–inch 33rpm
MUSTANG (900 "KRLA King of
the Wheels") 60-75   66
(Monaural.)
MUSTANG (900 "KRLA King of
the Wheels") 75-100   66
(Stereo.)
MUSTANG (901 "I Fought the Law") . 35-45   66
(Monaural.)
MUSTANG (901 "I Fought the Law") . 45-55   66
(Stereo.)
RHINO 5-10   81
VOXX 5-10   84
Members: Bobby Fuller; Randy Fuller; Duane Quirico; Jim
Reese; Dalton Powell; Johnny Barbata.

FULLER, Bobby / Seeds
Singles: 7–inch
TRIP 3-6
Also see FULLER, Bobby
Also see SEEDS

FULLER, Jerry
Singles: 7–inch
BELL 3-5   72
CHALLENGE (Except 59052) 5-10   60-66
CHALLENGE (59052 "Betty My
Angel") 15-25   59
COLUMBIA 3-5   70
LIN 10-15   58-59

LPs: 10/12–inch 33rpm
LIN (100 "Teenage Love") 25-35   60
MCA 5-10   79

FULLER, Jerry, and Diane Maxwell
Singles: 7–inch
CHALLENGE 5-10   60
Also see FULLER, Jerry
Also see MAXWELL, Diane

FULSON, Lowell
(Lowell Folsom; Lowel Fulsom)
Singles: 78rpm
ALADDIN 25-35   51
BIG TOWN 8-12   46-47
CASH 5-10   57
CHECKER 5-10   54-57
DOWN TOWN 5-10   49
GILT EDGE 5-10   51
HOLLYWOOD 5-10   55
PARROT 20-30   53

RPM 5-10   50
SCOTTY'S RADIO 8-12   46
SWING TIME 5-10   46-53
TRILON 8-12   47-48

Singles: 7–inch
ALADDIN (3088 "Double Trouble
Blues") 50-75   53
ALADDIN (3104 "Night and Day") 50-7551
ALADDIN (3104 "Stormin' & Rainin") . 40-60   53
(Black vinyl.)
ALADDIN (3104 "Stormin' and
Rainin") 75-125   53
(Colored vinyl.)
ALADDIN (3217 "Don't Leave Me") .. 25-50   53
ALADDIN (3233 "Blues Never Fail") . 25-50   53
CASH 15-25   57
CHECKER (804; Reconsider Baby") . 15-25   54
CHECKER (812 "Check Yourself") .. 15-25   55
CHECKER (820 through 937) 10-20   55-59
CHECKER (952 through 1046) 8-12   60-62
GRANITE 2-4   76
HOLLYWOOD (1029 "Rocking After
Midnight") 20-30   55
JEWEL 3-6   69-73
KENT 3-8   64-70
MOVIN' 4-8   64
PARROT (787 "I've Been Mistreated") 50-75   53
(Black vinyl.)
PARROT (787 "I've Been
Mistreated") 75-125   53
(Colored vinyl.)
SWING TIME (289 "Let's Live Right") 20-30   51
SWING TIME (295 "Guitar Shuffle") . 20-30   51
SWING TIME (301 "The Highway
Is My Home") 20-30   51
SWING TIME (308 "Black
Widow Spider") 20-30   51
SWING TIME (315 "Raggedy
Daddy Blues") 20-30   52
SWING TIME (320 "Ride Until the
Sun Goes Down") 20-30   52
SWING TIME (325 "Upstairs") 20-30   52
SWING TIME (330 "I Love My Baby") 20-30   52
SWING TIME (335 "Cash Box
Boogie") 20-30   53
SWING TIME (338 "I've Been
Mistreated") 20-30   52

Picture Sleeves
KENT 5-8   67

LPs: 10/12–inch 33rpm
ARHOOLIE 10-12   62
BIG TOWN 5-10   78
CHESS (408 "Hung Down Head") ... 15-20
JEWEL 8-10   70-73
KENT 10-15   65-71
UNITED 8-12
Members: Lowell Fulson; Lloyd Glenn; Earl Brown; Bob Harvey;
Bill Hadnott.
Also see GLENN, Lloyd

FUN & GAMES
Singles: 7–inch
UNI 4-8   68
LPs: 10/12–inch 33rpm
UNI 12-15   68

FUN BOY THREE
Singles: 7–inch
CHRYSALIS 2-4   82-83
LPs: 10/12–inch 33rpm
CHRYSALIS 5-10   82-83
Also see SPECIALS

FUN FUN
Singles: 12–inch 33/45rpm
TSR 4-6   84-85

FUNICELLO, Annette: see ANNETTE

FUNK, Professor: see PROFESSOR FUNK

FUNK DELUXE
Singles: 7–inch
SALSOUL 2-4   83-84
LPs: 10/12–inch 33rpm
SALSOUL 5-10   83

FUNKADELIC
(Featuring George Clinton)
Singles: 7–inch
WARNER 2-4   78-79
WESTBOUND 3-6   69-76
Picture Sleeves
WARNER 2-4   78-81
LPs: 10/12–inch 33rpm
20TH CENTURY/WESTBOUND 8-15   75
WARNER 5-10   76-81
WESTBOUND (215 "Let's Take It
to the Stage") 30-50   75
WESTBOUND (227 "Tales of
Kidd Funkadelic") 30-50   76
WESTBOUND (1001 "On the Verge") 30-50   74
WESTBOUND (2000 "Funkadelic") . . 40-50   70
WESTBOUND (2001 "Free
Your Mind") 30-50   70
WESTBOUND (2007 "Maggot Brain") 40-60   71
WESTBOUND (2020 "America Eats
Its Young") 30-50   72
WESTBOUND (2022 "Cosmic Slop") . 30-50   73
Also see PARLIAMENTS

FUNKADELIC
Singles: 7–inch
LAX 2-4   81
LPs: 10/12–inch 33rpm
LAX 5-10   81
Note: This group was formed by three former
members of the preceding Westbound/Warner
Bros. band.
Also see FUNKADELIC (Featuring George Clinton)
Also see JUNIE

FUNKY COMMUNICATION COMMITTEE:
see FCC

FUNKY KINGS
Singles: 7–inch
ARISTA 3-5   76
LPs: 10/12–inch 33rpm
ARISTA 5-10   76

FUNN
Singles: 7–inch
MAGIC 2-4   81

FURAY, Richie
Singles: 7–inch
ASYLUM 2-4   77-79
LPs: 10/12–inch 33rpm
ASYLUM 5-10   76-82
Also see BUFFALO SPRINGFIELD
Also see POCO
Also see SOUTHER - HILLMAN - FURAY

FURIOUS FIVE
Singles: 12–inch 33/45rpm
SUGAR HILL 4-6   84-85

FURIOUS FIVE and the Sugarhill Gang
Singles: 12–inch 33/45rpm
SUGAR HILL 4-6   81
Also see FURIOUS FIVE
Also see SUGARHILL GANG

FURYS
Singles: 7–inch
MACK IV 8-10   63

FUSE ONE
LPs: 10/12–inch 33rpm
CTI 5-10   82

FUTURE
Singles: 7–inch
HOUSTON INT'L 2-4   87

FUTURES
Singles: 7–inch
AVALANCHE 2-4
GAMBLE 3-5   73
PHILADELPHIA INT'L 2-4   81
LPs: 10/12–inch 33rpm
PHILADELPHIA INT'L 5-10   81
Members: James King; Kenny Crwe; Harry McGilkerry; Frank
Washington; John King.
Also see MASON, Barbara

FUZZ
Singles: 7–inch
CALLA 3-5   71
ROULETTE 3-5
LPs: 10/12–inch 33rpm
CALLA 10-12   71
Members: Sheila Young; Barbara Gilliam; Val Williams.

G

G., Kenny
(Kenny Gorelick)
Singles: 7-Inch
ARISTA 2-4   83-90
Picture Sleeves
ARISTA 2-4   87-90
LPs: 10/12-inch 33rpm
ARISTA 5-10   83-89
Also see LORBER, Jeff

G., Kenny, and Kashif
Singles: 7-Inch
ARISTA 2-4   85
Also see G., Kenny
Also see KASHIF

G., Kenny, and Lenny Williams
Singles: 7-Inch
ARISTA 2-4   83-86
Also see G., Kenny
Also see WILLIAMS, Lenny

G.L.O.B.E. and Whiz Kid
Singles: 12-Inch 33/45rpm
TOMMY BOY 4-6   83
Singles: 7-Inch
TOMMY BOY 2-4   83

GQ
Singles: 7-Inch
ARISTA 2-4   79-82
LPs: 10/12-inch 33rpm
ARISTA 5-10   79-81

G.T.
Singles: 12-Inch 33/45rpm
A&M 4-6   83
Singles: 7-Inch
A&M 2-4   83
LPs: 10/12-inch 33rpm
A&M 5-8   83

GTR
Singles: 12-Inch 33/45rpm
ARISTA 4-6   86
Singles: 7-Inch
ARISTA 2-4   86
Picture Sleeves
ARISTA 2-4   86
LPs: 10/12-inch 33rpm
ARISTA 5-10   86
Members: Max Bacon; Steve Howe; Steve Hackett; Phil
Spalding; Jonathan Mover.
Also see HACKETT, Steve
Also see HOWE, Steve
Also see MARILLION

GABOR SZABO: see SZABO, Gabor

GABRIEL
Singles: 7-Inch
ABC 3-5   76-77
EPIC 2-4   78-79
LPs: 10/12-inch 33rpm
ABC 8-10   75-76
EPIC 5-10   78

GABRIEL, Peter
Singles: 12-Inch 33/45rpm
GEFFEN 4-6   82-86
Singles: 7-Inch
ATCO 3-5   77
ATLANTIC 3-5   78
GEFFEN 2-4   82-90
MERCURY 2-4   80
WTG 2-4   89
WARNER 2-4   86
Picture Sleeves
GEFFEN 2-4   82-86
LPs: 10/12-inch 33rpm
ATCO 10-12   77
ATLANTIC 8-10   78
GEFFEN 5-10   82-90
MERCURY 5-10   80
Also see GENESIS

GABRIEL, Peter, and Kate Bush
Singles: 7-Inch
GEFFEN 2-4   87
Picture Sleeves
GEFFEN 2-4   87
Also see BUSH, Kate

GABRIEL and the Angles
Singles: 7-Inch
AMY (823 "Zing Went the Strings
of My Heart") 25-35   61
NORMAN 8-12   61-62
SWAN 5-10   62-63

GADABOUTS
Singles: 78rpm
MERCURY 4-8   54-56
WING 4-8   55
Singles: 7-Inch
JARO 5-10   60
MERCURY 8-12   54-56
WING 5-10   55

GADSON, James
Singles: 7-Inch
CREAM 3-5   72
Also see SOUL RUNNERS

GADSON, Mel
Singles: 7-Inch
BIG TOP 10-20   60

GAGE, Yvonne
Singles: 7-Inch
CIM 2-4   84

GAGNON, Andre
Singles: 7–inch
LONDON 3-5   76

GAIL, Sunny: see GALE, Sunny

GAINES, Earl
(Earl Gains)
Singles: 7–inch
CHAMPION 5-10	58-60
DELUXE 4-6	68-69
HBR 4-8	66
HOLLYWOOD 4-8	67
SEVENTY SEVEN 3-5	73

LPs: 10/12–inch 33rpm
DELUXE 10-15	69
EXCELLO 3-5	62
HBR 10-15	66

GAINES, Rosie
Singles: 7–inch
EPIC 2-4   85

GALE, Eric
Singles: 7–inch
COLUMBIA 2-4   78-80
LPs: 10/12–inch 33rpm
COLUMBIA 5-10	77-80
ELEKTRA 5-10	83
KUDU 8-10	73

Also see GRUSIN, Dave

GALE, Sunny
(Sunny Gale and the Saints and Sinners Dixieland
Band; Sunny Gail)
Singles: 78rpm
DECCA 3-6	56-57
DERBY 3-6	52
RCA 3-5	52-56

Singles: 7–inch
BLAINE 3-5	65
CANADIAN AMERICAN 3-6	63-64
DECCA 5-10	56-59
DERBY 8-12	52
RCA (4000 through 6000 series) 6-12	52-56
RCA (9000 series) 3-5	68
RIVERSIDE 3-5	63
STAGE 4-8	62
TERRACE 3-6	62
THIMBLE 2-4	74
WARWICK 4-8	60-61

EPs: 7–inch 33/45rpm
KING 5-10	
RCA 5-10	56

LPs: 10/12–inch 33rpm
CANADIAN AMERICAN 10-20	64
RCA (1277 "Sunny and Blue") 20-30	56
WARWICK (2018 "Sunny") 15-25	60

Also see WILCOX, Eddie

GALE, Sunny, and the Du Droppers
Singles: 78rpm
RCA 5-10   53

Singles: 7–inch
RCA (5543 "The Note in the Bottle") . 10-20   53
Also see DU DROPPERS
Also see GALE, Sunny

GALLAGHER, Rory
LPs: 10/12–inch 33rpm
ATCO 10-12	71-72
CHRYSALIS 5-10	75-80
MERCURY 5-10	82
POLYDOR 8-10	72-75
SPRINGBOARD 8-12	76

Also see TASTE

GALLAGHER & LYLE
Singles: 7–inch
A&M 2-4   73-78
LPs: 10/12–inch 33rpm
A&M 8-10	73-78
CAPITOL (SM-10000 series) 5-10	77
CAPITOL (ST-11000 series) 8-12	72

Members: Ben Gallagher; Graham Lyle.
Also see McGUINNESS - FLINT

GALLAHADS
Singles: 78rpm
CAPITOL 3-5	55
JUBILEE 3-5	56
VIK 3-5	57

Singles: 7–inch
CAPITOL 5-10	55
JUBILEE 5-10	56
VIK 5-10	57

GALLERY
Singles: 7–inch
SUSSEX 3-5   72
Picture Sleeves
SUSSEX (239 "I Believe in Music") 4-6   72
LPs: 10/12–inch 33rpm
SUSSEX 10-12   72-73
Member: Jim Gold.

GALLOP, Frank
Singles: 7–inch
ABC-PAR 5-10   58

Bob Booker & George Foster Present
THE SON OF IRVING
Starring
FRANK GALLOP
MUSICOR
MU 1191

| KAPP | 4-6 | 66 |
| MUSICOR | 4-6 | 66 |

Picture Sleeves

| MUSICOR | 4-8 | 66 |

LPs: 10/12–inch 33rpm

| MUSICOR | 10-15 | 66 |

GALLOWAY, Leata
Singles: 7–Inch

| COLUMBIA | 2-4 | 88 |

GAMBLE, Dee Dee Sharp:
see SHARP, Dee Dee

GAME THEORY
EPs: 7–Inch 33/45rpm

| ENIGMA | 4-6 | 82-86 |

LPs: 10/12–inch 33rpm

| ENIGMA | 5-10 | 82-86 |

Members: Scott Miller; Gil Ray; Shelley LaFreniere; Guillaume Gassuan; Donteet Thayer.

GAMMA
Singles: 7–inch

| ELEKTRA | 2-4 | 79-82 |

LPs: 10/12–inch 33rpm

| ELEKTRA | 5-10 | 79-82 |

Also see MONTROSE

GANG of FOUR
Singles: 12–inch 33/45rpm

| WARNER | 4-6 | 80-84 |

Singles: 7–inch

| WARNER | 2-4 | 80-84 |

LPs: 10/12–inch 33rpm

| WARNER | 5-10 | 80-83 |

Also see SHRIEKBACK

GANG'S BACK
Singles: 7–inch

| HANDSHAKE | 2-4 | 82 |

GANGSTERS
Singles: 7–inch

| HEAT | 2-4 | 79-81 |
| MONTAGE | 2-4 | 82 |

LPs: 10/12–inch 33rpm

| MONTAGE | 5-10 | 82 |

GANTS
Singles: 7–inch

| LIBERTY | 10-15 | 65-67 |

LPs: 10/12–inch 33rpm

| LIBERTY | 15-25 | 65-66 |

GAP, Billy and Baby:
see BILLY and Baby Gap

GAP BAND
Singles: 12–inch 33/45rpm

| PASSPORT | 4-6 | 83 |
| TOTAL EXPERIENCE | 4-6 | 82-86 |

Singles: 7–inch

| A&M | 3-5 | 75 |
| CAPITOL | 2-4 | 89 |

MEGA	2-4	84
MERCURY	2-4	79-84
PASSPORT	2-4	83
RCA	2-4	87
SHELTER	3-5	74
TATTOO	3-5	77
TOTAL EXPERIENCE	2-4	82-87

Picture Sleeves

| TOTAL EXPERIENCE | 2-4 | 82 |

LPs: 10/12–inch 33rpm

CAPITOL	5-8	89
MERCURY	5-10	79-80
PASSPORT	5-10	83
SHELTER	8-10	74
TATTOO	8-10	77
TOTAL EXPERIENCE	5-10	82-86

Members: Charles Wilson; Ronnie Wilson; Robert Wilson.
Also see BILLY and Baby Gap

GARCIA, Jerry
(Jerry Garcia Band)
Singles: 7–inch

DOUGLAS	3-6	73
ROUND	4-6	72-74
WARNER	4-6	72

LPs: 10/12–inch 33rpm

ARISTA	5-10	78-82
ROUND	8-10	74-75
U.A.	8-10	76
WARNER (2582 "Garcia")	35-45	72

Also see DYLAN, Bob, and the Grateful Dean
Also see GRATEFUL DEAD
Also see IT'S a BEAUTIFUL DAY
Also see JEFFERSON AIRPLANE
Also see OLD and in the Way
Also see ROWANS
Also see SAUNDERS, Merl, Jerry Garcia, John Kahn and Bill Vitt

GARCIA, Jerry, and Robert Hunter
Singles: 7–inch

| ROUND (102 "Sampler for Dead Heads") | 20-30 | 74 |

(Includes letter about the Grateful Dead LP, *The Mars Hotel,* and some miniature LP covers. Promotional fan club issue.)

| ROUND (102 "Sampler for Dead Heads") | 15-20 | 74 |

(Price for disc without inserts.)
Also see GARCIA, Jerry
Also see GRATEFUL DEAD

GARDNER, Dave
(Brother Dave Gardner)
Singles: 7–inch

DECCA (30627 "Slick Slacks")	15-30	58
OJ	5-10	57
RCA	3-8	59-61

LPs: 10/12–inch 33rpm

CAMDEN	5-10	73
CAPITOL	15-25	63
RCA	15-25	60-64
TOWER	10-20	67

GARDNER, Don, and Dee Dee Ford
Singles: 7–inch

FIRE	5-10	62
FLASHBACK	3-5	65
KC	5-10	62
LUDIX	4-8	63
RED TOP	4-8	63
TRU-GLO-TOWN	4-8	66

LPs: 10/12–inch 33rpm

FIRE (105 "Need Your Lovin")	50-100	62
SUE (1044 "Don Gardner and Dee Dee Ford in Sweden")	20-30	66

Also see FORD, Dee Dee
Also see WASHINGTON, Baby, and Don Gardner

GARDNER, Joanna
Singles: 7–inch

PHILLY WORLD	2-4	85

GARDNER, Reggie
Singles: 7–inch

CAPITOL	3-5	71

GARDNER, Taana
Singles: 7–inch

WEST END	2-4	81

GARFUNKEL, Art
Singles: 7–inch

COLUMBIA	2-4	73-81

Picture Sleeves

COLUMBIA	2-4	81

LPs: 10/12–inch 33rpm

COLUMBIA (30000 series)	8-12	73-81
(With "FC," "JC," "KC" or "PC" prefix.		
COLUMBIA (30000 series)	10-20	73-75
(With "CQ" or "PCQ" prefix. Quad issues.)		
COLUMBIA (40000 series)	5-8	88
COLUMBIA (47000 series)	10-20	78
(Half-speed mastered.)		

Also see GARR, Artie
Also see SIMON & GARFUNKEL
Also see TAYLOR, James

GARI, Frank
Singles: 7–inch

ATLANTIC	4-8	62
CAPITOL	4-6	68
CRUSADE	5-10	60-62
RIBBON	5-10	59

Picture Sleeves

CRUSADE	10-15	61-62

GARLAND, Judy
Singles: 78rpm

CAPITOL	3-5	56-57
COLUMBIA	3-5	53-54
DECCA (Except 2000 through 4000 series)	5-10	42-55
DECCA (2000 through 4000 series)	10-15	39-42

Singles: 7–inch

ABC	3-5	67
CAPITOL	5-10	56-63

COLUMBIA (40000 series)	8-15	53-54
DECCA (25000 series)	4-8	65
DECCA (29000 series)	8-10	55
WARNER	3-5	63

Promotional Singles

CAPITOL ("After You've Gone"/ "When You're Smiling")	10-20	59

Picture Sleeves

CAPITOL ("After You've Gone"/ "When You're Smiling")	15-25	59

(Sleeve reads "Two of the Top Tunes from *Garland at the Grove*.")

EPs: 7–inch 33/45rpm

CAPITOL (676 "Miss Show Business")	10-20	55
CAPITOL (734 "Judy")	10-20	56
CAPITOL (835 "Alone")	10-20	57
CAPITOL (1569 "Judy at Carnegie Hall")	10-15	62
COLUMBIA (1201 "A Star Is Born")	15-20	54
(Soundtrack.)		
COLUMBIA (2598 "Judy Garland")	20-30	57
COLUMBIA (7621 "Born in a Trunk")	25-50	56
DECCA (620 "Judy Garland at the Palace/ Greatest Performances")	10-20	55
DECCA (661 "The Wizard of Oz")	15-25	51
DECCA (2050 "Judy Garland, Vol. 2")	12-20	53
MGM (268 "If You Feel Like Singing, Sing")	10-20	54
MGM (1038 "Get Happy")	10-20	55
MGM (1116 "Look for the Silver Lining")	10-20	55
MGM (1122 "Judy Garland")	10-20	55

LPs: 10/12–inch 33rpm

ABC (620 Judy Garland at Home at the Palace")	10-15	67
ABC (30007 "Judy Garland the ABC Collection")	5-10	76
AEI (3101 "Meet Me in St. Louis"/ the Harvey Girls")	10-15	
(Soundtrack. Reissue.)		
ACCESSOR	8-15	
AUDIOFIDELITY (311 "Judy Garland")	8-10	83
(Picture disc.)		
C.I.T.	8-12	
CAPITOL (676 "Miss Show Business")	30-40	55
(With "W" prefix.)		
CAPITOL (676 "Miss Show Business")	10-20	63
(With "SW" prefix.)		
CAPITOL (734 "Judy")	25-35	56
(With "T" prefix.)		
CAPITOL (734 "Judy")	10-20	63
(With "DT" prefix.)		
CAPITOL (835 "Alone")	25-35	57
(With "T" prefix.)		
CAPITOL (835 "Alone")	10-20	63
(With "DT" prefix.)		
CAPITOL (1036 "Judy in Love")	20-35	58
CAPITOL (1118 "Garland at the Grove")	40-60	59

CAPITOL (1188 "The Letter") 25-35   59
(With John Ireland.)
CAPITOL (1467 "Judy - That's
Entertainment") 20-35   60
CAPITOL (1569 "Judy at Carnegie
Hall") 20-35   61
CAPITOL (1710 "The Garland Touch") 20-30   62
CAPITOL (1861 "I Could Go On
Singing") 25-30   63
(Soundtrack. With "W" prefix.)
CAPITOL (1861 "I Could Go On
Singing") 35-40   63
(Soundtrack. With "SW" prefix.)
CAPITOL (1941 "Our Love Letter") .. 15-20   63
(With John Ireland.)
CAPITOL (1999 "The Hits of
Judy Garland") 20-30   64
(With "T" or "ST" prefix.)
CAPITOL (1999 "The Hits of
Judy Garland") 5-10   75
(With "SM" prefix.)
CAPITOL (2062 "Just for Openers") .. 15-25   64
CAPITOL (2988 "Judy Garland
Deluxe Set") 20-35   68
CAPITOL (11763 "Alone") 5-10   78
CAPITOL (11876 "Judy - That's
Entertainment") 5-10   79
CAPITOL (12034 "Just for Openers") .. 5-10   80
CAPITOL (16175 "The Hits of
Judy Garland") 4-6   81
COLUMBIA (762 "Born in a Trunk") . 50-100   56
(10-inch LP.)
COLUMBIA (1101 "A Star Is Born") .. 20-25   58
(Soundtrack.)
COLUMBIA (1201 "A Star Is Born") .. 35-45   54
(Soundtrack. Deluxe boxed edition.)
COLUMBIA (8740 "A Star Is Born") .. 20-30   63
(Soundtrack.)
COLUMBIA (10011 "A Star Is Born") .. 5-12   73
(Soundtrack.)
COLUMBIA/CSP (8740 "A Star Is
Born") 5-10
(Soundtrack.)
COMPUNSONIC 8-12
DRG 10-20
DECCA (5 "Collector's Items:
1936-1945") 15-25   70
DECCA (172 "The Best of Judy
Garland") 15-20   63
(Monaural.)
DECCA (7-172 "The Best of Judy
Garland") 15-20   63
(Stereo.)
DECCA (4199 "The Magic of Judy
Garland") 15-20   61
DECCA (5152 "The Wizard of Oz") .. 25-50   52
(Soundtrack. 10-inch LP.)
DECCA (6020 "Judy Garland at
the Palace") 35-45   55

DECCA (8190 "Judy Garland - Greatest
Performances") 35-45   55
DECCA (8387 "The Wizard of Oz") .. 20-35   56
(Soundtrack. One side, *The Song Hits from
Pinocchio*, does not feature Judy.)
DECCA (8498 "Meet Me in St. Louis"/
"The Harvey Girls") 60-70   57
(Soundtrack. Different show on each side.)
DECCA (75150 "Judy Garland's
Greatest Hits") 8-12   69
DECCA (78387 "The Wizard of Oz") . 10-15   67
(Soundtrack.)
51 WEST 5-10
HARMONY (11366 "A Star Is Born") . 10-15   69
(Soundtrack.)
JUNO (1000 "Judy - London 1969") .. 6-12   69
MCA (4003 "The Best of
Judy Garland") 10-15   73
MGM (1 "Golden Years at MGM") ... 15-25   69
MGM (21 "The Pirate") 50-75   51
(Soundtrack. With Gene Kelly. 10-inch LP.)
MGM (82 "Judy Garland Sings") ... 50-100   51
MGM (113 "Judy Garland") 8-12   70
MGM (3149 "Judy Garland") 35-45   54
MGM (3234 "The Pirate") 25-30   55
(Soundtrack. With Gene Kelly.)
MGM (3464 "The Wizard of Oz") 35-45   61
(Soundtrack.)
MGM (3771 "Words and Music") 15-25   60
MGM (3989 "The Judy Garland
Story, Volume 1") 15-20   61
MGM (3996 "The Wizard of Oz") 15-20   61
(Soundtrack.)
MGM (4005 "The Judy Garland
Story, Volume 2") 15-20   61
MGM (4204 "The Very Best of
Judy Garland") 12-20   64
MARK '56 (632 "Live in
San Francisco") 50-75   79
(Picture disc.)
METRO (505 "Judy Garland") 10-15   65
METRO (581 "Judy Garland
in Song") 10-15   66
PARAGON 5-10
PHOENIX 10 8-12
PICKWICK 5-10
RADIANT 6-12
RADIOLA 5-10
SPRINGBOARD 5-10
STANYAN 5-10   74
STAR TONE 5-10
TRIP (9 "16 Greatest Hits - Judy
Garland") 5-10   76
TROPHY 5-10
Also see CROSBY, Bing, and Judy Garland
Also see MARTIN, Dean
Also see YOUNG, Victor

GARLAND, Judy / Tommy Dorsey
Singles: 78rpm
VOGUE ("The Trolley Song") 500-750   46
(Picture disc.)
<small>Also see DORSEY, Tommy</small>

GARLAND, Judy, and Liza Minnelli
Singles: 7–inch
CAPITOL 4-6   65
LPs: 10/12–inch 33rpm
CAPITOL (2295 "Live at the London
  Palladium") 15-20   65
CAPITOL (11191 "Live at the London
  Palladium") 5-10   73
MFSL (048 "Live at the London
  Palladium") 20-35   81
TROLLEY CAR 5-10
<small>Also see GARLAND, Judy
Also see MINNELLI, Liza</small>

GARLOW, Clarence
Singles: 78rpm
ALADDIN 8-15   52
FEATURE 10-15   51-54
FOLK STAR 5-10   54
FLAIR 10-20   54
GOLDBAND 5-10   56-57
LYRIC 10-15   51
MACY'S 5-10   49
Singles: 7–inch
ALADDIN (3179 "New Bon
  Ton Roula") 50-75   52
ALADDIN (3225 "You Got Me Crying") 50-75   52
FEATURE (3005 "If I Keep
  on Worrying") 40-60   54
FLAIR (1021 "Crawfishin") 50-75   54
FOLK STAR (1130 "Za Belle") 25-40   54
FOLK STAR (1199 "No, No Baby") ... 25-40   54
GOLDBAND 10-20   56-57

GARNER, Erroll
(Erroll Garner Trio)
Singles: 78rpm
COLUMBIA 3-8   50-57
MERCURY 4-8   54
Singles: 7-Inch
ABC-PAR 3-6   61-62
COLUMBIA 3-8   50-70
MGM 3-5   66-69
MERCURY (70000 series) 4-8   54
MERCURY (72000 and
  73000 series) 3-6   63-71
REPRISE 3-6   63
EPs: 7-Inch 33/45rpm
ATLANTIC 5-15   52-56
BRUNSWICK 5-15   53
COLUMBIA 5-15   50-59
EMARCY 5-15   56
KING 5-15   54
MERCURY 5-15   54-56
SAVOY 5-15   51-55

LPs: 10/12-Inch 33rpm
ABC-PAR 15-25   61
ATLANTIC (109 "Rhapsody") 50-100   49
  (10–inch LP.)
ATLANTIC (112 "Piano Solos") 50-100   50
  (10–inch LP.)
ATLANTIC (128 "Passport to Fame") 50-100   51
  (10–inch LP.)
ATLANTIC (138 "Piano Solos") 50-100   52
  (10–inch LP.)
ATLANTIC (1227 "Greatest Garner") . 30-40   56
BARONET 15-25   61
BLUE NOTE (5000 series) 20-40   52-53
  (10–inch LP.)
COLUMBIA (535 "At the Piano") 45-65   53
  (Red and gold label.)
COLUMBIA (535 "At the Piano") 30-50   56
  (Red and black label.)
COLUMBIA (583 "Gems") 40-60   54
  (Red and gold label.)
COLUMBIA (583 "Gems") 30-50   56
  (Red and black label.)
COLUMBIA (617 "Gonest") 40-60   55
  (Red and gold label.)
COLUMBIA (617 "Gonest") 30-50   56
  (Red and black label.)
COLUMBIA (651 "Music for
  Tired Lovers") 25-50   55
  (Red and gold label.)
COLUMBIA (883 "Concert By
  the Sea") 25-50   56
COLUMBIA (939 through 1587) 15-35   57-61
COLUMBIA (2540 "Garnerland") ... 30-50   56
  (10–inch LP.)
COLUMBIA (6139 "Piano Moods") .. 50-75   50
COLUMBIA (6173 "Gems") 50-75   51
COLUMBIA (8000 series) 15-25   60
COLUMBIA (9000 series) 6-12   70
COLUMBIA SPECIAL PRODUCTS 5-8   79
DIAL (205 "Garner Trio") 75-100   50
  (10–inch LP.)
DIAL (902 "Gaslight Session") 60-80   50
  (10–inch LP.)
EMARCY (26000 series) 20-40   54
  (10–inch LP.)
EMARCY (36000 series) 20-30   55-56
ENRICA 15-25   59
EVEREST 5-10   70
GRAND AWARD 20-35   56
HARMONY 8-12   68
JAZZTONE 20-35   57
KING (265-17 "Erroll Garner") 50-75   54
  (10–inch LP.)
KING (540 "Erroll Garner") 25-35   58
LONDON 8-12   72-73
MGM 10-20   65-68
MERCURY (20009 "At the Piano") .. 50-75   50
MERCURY (20055 "Mambo") 40-60   54
MERCURY (20063 "Solitaire") 40-60   54

MERCURY (20090 "Afternoon of
an Elf") 40-60   55
MERCURY (20662 through 20859) . . 15-25   62-63
(Monaural.)
MERCURY (25117 "At the Piano") ... 50-75   51
(10-inch LP.)
MERCURY (25157 "Gone with
Garner") 50-75   51
(10-inch LP.)
MERCURY (60662 through 60859) . . 20-30   62-63
(Stereo.)
MERCURY (61000 series) 8-12   70
REPRISE 12-25   63
RONDO-LETTE 15-25   58
ROOST (10 "Piano Magic") 30-60   52
(10-inch LP.)
ROOST (2213 "Giants") 25-40   56
SAVOY (1100 series) 5-10   78
SAVOY (2000 series) 5-10   76
SAVOY (12002 "Erroll Garner") 30-50   55
SAVOY (12003 "Erroll Garner,
Vol. 2") 30-50   55
SAVOY (12008 "Erroll Garner") 30-50   55
SAVOY (15000 "At the Piano") 75-125   49
(10-inch LP.)
SAVOY (15001 "At the Piano, Vol. 2")75-125   50
(10-inch LP.)
SAVOY (15002 "At the Piano, Vol. 3")75-125   50
(10-inch LP.)
SAVOY (15004 "At the Piano, Vol. 4")75-125   50
(10-inch LP.)
SAVOY (15026 "At the Piano, Vol. 5")75-125   50
(10-inch LP.)
TRIP 5-10   74
WING 10-20   62
Also see STARR, Kay / Erroll Garner

GARNETT, Gale
(Gale Garnett and the Gentle Reign)
Singles: 7-inch
COLUMBIA 3-6   68
RCA 4-8   64-67
Picture Sleeves
RCA 4-8   64
LPs: 10/12-inch 33rpm
COLUMBIA 8-12   68-69
RCA 10-15   64-66

GARR, Artie
(Art Garfunkel)
Singles: 7-inch
OCTAVIA (8002 "Private Love") 20-30   61
WARWICK (515 "Beat Love") 20-30   59
Also see GARFUNKEL, Art

GARRAFFA, Donna
Singles: 12-inch 33/45rpm
ARTIST INT'L 4-6   85

GARRETT, Lee
Singles: 7-inch
CHRYSALIS 3-5   76

GARRETT, Leif
Singles: 7-inch
ATLANTIC 3-5   77-78
SCOTTI BROS 2-4   78-81
Picture Sleeves
ATLANTIC....................... 3-5   77-78
SCOTTI BROS 2-4   78-81
LPs: 10/12-inch 33rpm
ATLANTIC 5-10   77
SCOTTI BROS 5-10   78-81
Also see CHIC / Roberta Flack / Leif Garrett / Genesis

GARRETT, Scott
(Scott Garret)
Singles: 7-inch
LAURIE (Except 3029) 5-10   59
LAURIE (3029 "Love Story") 20-30   59
(With the Mystics.)
OKEH 5-10   60
Also see MYSTICS

GARRETT, Siedah
Singles: 12-inch 33/45rpm
QWEST 4-6   85
Singles: 7-inch
QWEST 2-4   85-88
Picture Sleeves
QWEST 2-4   85-88

GARRETT, Tommy
(Tommy Garrett and 25 Pianos)
LPs: 10/12-inch 33rpm
LIBERTY 8-15   62
Also see 50 GUITARS of TOMMY GARRETT

GARRETT, Vernon
Singles: 78rpm
MODERN 4-8   57
Singles: 7-inch
ICA............................ 3-5   77
KAPP 3-5   70
MODERN 8-12   57
VENTURE 4-6   69

GARRETT, Vernon, and Marie Franklin
Singles: 7-inch
VENTURE 3-5   76

GARRETT'S CREW
Singles: 7-inch
CLOCKWORK 2-4   83

GARY, John
Singles: 7-inch
ACE 3-5   62
BIG B 3-5   64
FRATERNITY 3-6   59-66
RCA 3-5   63-71
ST. JAMES 3-5   63

EPs: 7–inch 33/45rpm

RCA (2804 "John Gary") 4-8   63
(Stereo Compact 33.)

LPs: 10/12–inch 33rpm

CAMDEN 5-10	68	
CHURCHILL 4-8	77	
METRO 5-10	65	
RCA 5-15	63-78	

Also see ANN-MARGRET and John Gary

GARY & DAVE
Singles: 7–inch

LONDON 3-5   73

GARY and the Hornets
Singles: 7–inch

SMASH 4-8   66-68

Picture Sleeves

SMASH 5-10   66-67

GARY O'
LPs: 10/12–inch 33rpm

CAPITOL 5-10   81

GARY'S GANG
Singles: 12–inch 33/45rpm

COLUMBIA 4-8	79	
RADAR 4-6	83	

Singles: 7–inch

COLUMBIA 2-4	79	
RADAR 2-4	83	

LPs: 10/12–inch 33rpm

COLUMBIA 5-10   79

Members: Gary Turnier; Eric Matthew.

GASCA, Luis
LPs: 10/12–inch 33rpm

BLUE THUMB 8-10   72

GATES, David
(David Gates and the Accents)
Singles: 7–inch

ARISTA 2-4	81	
DEL-FI (4206 "No One Really Loves a Clown") 10-20	63	
EAST WEST (123 "Walkin' and Talkin'") 75-100	59	
ELEKTRA 3-5	73-80	
MALA (413 "You'll Be My Baby") 40-50	60	
MALA (418 "Happiest Man Alive") ... 40-50	61	
MALA (427 "Jo-Baby") 40-50	61	
PERSEPCTIVE (7500 "Jo-Baby") . 50-100	58	
(No catalog number — identification number used here.)		
PLANETARY (108 "Once Upon a Time") 10-15	65	
ROBBINS (1008 "Jo-Baby") 35-45	61	

Picture Sleeves

ELEKTRA 3-5   77

LPs: 10/12–inch 33rpm

ARISTA 5-10	81	
ELEKTRA 8-15	73-80	

Also see ASHLEY, Del

Also see BREAD
Also see DAVID & LEE

GATLIN, Larry
(Larry Gatlin and the Gatlin Brothers Band; Larry Gatlin with Family and Friends; Gatlin Quartet)
Singles: 7–inch

COLUMBIA 2-4	79-86	
MONUMENT 3-5	73-78	

LPs: 10/12–inch 33rpm

COLUMBIA 5-10	79-86	
MONUMENT 5-10	74-78	
SWORD and SHIELD (9009 "The Old Country Church") 25-50	61	

(By the Gatlin Quartet, which included sister Donna.)
Members: Larry Gatlin; Steve Gatlin; Rudy Gatlin.

GAYE, Marvin
Singles: 12–inch 33/45rpm

COLUMBIA 4-6   83-85

Singles: 7–inch

COLUMBIA 2-4	82-85	
DETROIT FREE PRESS ("The Teen Beat Song") 25-35	66	
(Promotional issue only.)		
MOTOWN 2-4		
MOTOWN/TOPPS (6 "How Sweet It Is to Be Loved By You") 50-75	67	
(Topps Chewing Gum promotional item. Single-sided, cardboard flexi, picture disc. Issued with generic paper sleeve.)		
TAMLA (1800 series) 2-4	86	
TAMLA (54041 "Let Your Conscience Be Your Guide") 20-30	61	
TAMLA (54055 "Sandman") 45-55	62	
TAMLA (54063 "Soldier's Plea") 10-20	62	
TAMLA (54068 through 54170) 4-8	62-68	
TAMLA (54176 through 54280) 3-6	68-77	

Picture Sleeves

TAMLA (1800 series) 2-4	86	
TAMLA (54095 "Try It Baby") 4-8	64	
TAMLA (54101 "Baby, Don't You Do It") 4-8	64	
TAMLA (54280 "Got to Give It Up") 3-6	77	

LPs: 10/12–inch 33rpm

COLUMBIA	5-10	82-85
KORY	8-10	76-77
MOTOWN	8-12	64-83
NATURAL RESOURCES	5-10	78
TAMI A (221 "Soulful Moods")	50-75	61
TAMLA (239 "That Stubborn Kind of Fella")	40-60	63
TAMLA (242 "On Stage")	20-35	63
TAMLA (251 "When I'm Alone I Cry")	20-35	64
TAMLA (252 through 299)	15-30	64-69
TAMLA (300 series)	8-12	70-81
TAMLA (6100 series)	5-10	86

Also see MARTHA and the Vandellas
Also see MOONGLOWS

GAYE, Marvin / Gladys Knight and the Pips
Singles: 7–inch

MOTOWN	4-8	68

Also see KNIGHT, Gladys

GAYE, Marvin, and Diana Ross
Singles: 7–inch

MOTOWN	3-5	73-74

LPs: 10/12–inch 33rpm

MOTOWN	8-12	73

Also see ROSS, Diana

GAYE, Marvin, and Tammi Terrell
Singles: 7–inch

TAMLA	4-8	67-70

LPs: 10/12–inch 33rpm

MOTOWN	5-10	80-82
TAMLA	10-15	67-70

Also see TERRELL, Tammi

GAYE, Marvin, and Mary Wells
Singles: 7–inch

MOTOWN	4-8	64

Picture Sleeves

MOTOWN	4-8	64

LPs: 10/12–inch 33rpm

MOTOWN (613 "Marvin and Mary - Together")	20-25	64

Also see WELLS, Mary

GAYE, Marvin, and Kim Weston
Singles: 7–inch

TAMLA	4-8	64-67

LPs: 10/12–inch 33rpm

TAMLA (270 "Marvin Gaye and Kim Weston")	20-25	66

Also see GAYE, Marvin
Also see WESTON, Kim

GAYLE, Crystal
Singles: 7–inch

COLUMBIA	2-4	79-82
DECCA	3-6	70-72
ELEKTRA	2-4	82
MCA	2-4	77
U.A.	2-5	74-80
WARNER	2-4	83-90

Picture Sleeves

COLUMBIA	3-4	79-82
U.A.	3-4	77-79

LPs: 10/12–inch 33rpm

COLUMBIA	5-10	79-83
ELEKTRA	5-10	82
LIBERTY	5-10	80-82
MCA	5-10	78
MFSL (043 "We Must Believe in Magic")	20-40	80
U.A. (Except "Somebody Loves You picture disc")	5-10	75-80
U.A. ("Somebody Loves You")	75-100	78
(Picture disc. Promotional issue only. One of a four-artist, four-LP set.)		
WARNER	5-10	83-90

Also see CAMPBELL, Glen / Anne Murray / Kenny Rogers / Crystal Gayle
Also see RABBITT, Eddie, and Crystal Gayle

GAYLE, Crystal, and Gary Morris
Singles: 7–inch

WARNER	2-4	85

Also see MORRIS, Gary

GAYLE, Crystal, and Tom Waits
LPs: 10/12–inch 33rpm

COLUMBIA	5-10	82

Also see GAYLE, Crystal
Also see WAITS, Tom

GAYLORD, Ronnie
Singles: 78rpm

MERCURY	3-5	54-55
WING	3-5	55-56

Singles: 7–inch

MERCURY	4-8	54-55
WING	4-8	55-56

EPs: 7–inch 33/45rpm

MERCURY	5-10	55

Also see GAYLORD & HOLIDAY

GAYLORD & HOLIDAY
Singles: 7–inch

NATURAL RESOURCES	2-4	77
PALMER	3-6	67
PRODIGAL	2-4	76
VERVE	4-8	66

LPs: 10/12–inch 33rpm

NATURAL RESOURCES	5-10	76
PRODIGAL	5-10	75
VMI	5-10	72

Members: Ronnie Gaylord; Burt Holiday.
Also see GAYLORD, Ronnie
Also see GAYLORDS

GAYLORDS
Singles: 78rpm

MERCURY	4-6	52-62

Singles: 7–inch

MERCURY	5-10	52-62
TIME	4-8	64

EPs: 7–inch 33/45rpm
MERCURY 5-15   54-56
LPs: 10/12-inch 33rpm
MERCURY (Except 25198) 12-25   55-63
MERCURY (25198 "By Request") . . . 20-30   55
(10-inch LP.)
TIME 10-15   64
WING 10-20   59-64
Members: Don Rea; Burt (Holiday) Bonaldi; Billy Christ.
Also see GAYLORD & HOLIDAY
Also see DEL-VIKINGS / Diamonds / Big Bopper / Gaylords

GAYNOR, Gloria
Singles: 12–inch 33/45rpm
POLYDOR 4-6   78
SILVER BLUE 4-6   83
Singles: 7–inch
COLUMBIA 3-5   73
JOCIDA 4-8   65
MGM 3-5   74-75
POLYDOR 2-5   76-81
SILVER BLUE 2-4   83
LPs: 10/12-inch 33rpm
ATLANTIC 5-10   82
MGM 8-10   75
POLYDOR 5-10   76-80

GAYTEN, Paul
Singles: 78rpm
ARGO 5-10   57
CHECKER 5-10   55-56
DELUXE 5-10   47-49
OKEH 5-10   52-55
REGAL 5-10   49-51
Singles: 7–inch
ANNA 5-10   59-60
ARGO 10-15   57-58
CHECKER (801 through 836) 10-20   55-56
CHECKER (872 through 880) 5-10   57-58
OKEH 10-15   52-55

G-CLEFS
Singles: 78rpm
PARIS 4-8   57
PILGRIM 4-8   56
Singles: 7–inch
LOMA 4-8   66
PARIS (502 "Symbol of Love") 15-25   57
PARIS (502 "Symbol of Love") 10-20   57
PILGRIM (715 "Ka Ding Dong") 15-25   56
(Purple label, no pilgrims.)
PILGRIM (715 "Ka Ding Dong") 8-12   56
(Red label with pilgrims.)
PILGRIM (720 "Cause You're Mine") . 10-20   56
REGINA 10-15   64
ROULETTE 2-4
TERRACE 5-10   61-63
VEEP 4-8   65-66
Also see CANNON, Freddy

GEDDES, David
Singles: 7–inch
ATCO 3-5   75
BIG TREE 3-5   75
H&L 3-5   77
ZODIAC 3-5   77
LPs: 10/12–inch 33rpm
BIG TREE 8-10   75

GEE, Spoonie: see SPOONIE GEE

GEILS, J., Band
(Geils)
Singles: 12–inch 33/45rpm
EMI AMERICA 4-8   82-84
Singles: 7–inch
ATLANTIC 3-5   71-78
EMI AMERICA 2-4   78-84
PRIVATE I 2-4   85
Picture Sleeves
ATLANTIC 3-5   73-78
EMI AMERICA 2-4   78-84
PRIVATE I 2-4   85
LPs: 10/12–inch 33rpm
ATLANTIC (Black vinyl) 8-12   70-80
ATLANTIC (Colored vinyl) 15-20   73
EMI AMERICA 5-10   78-84
NAUTILUS (25 "Love Stinks") 15-20   82
(Half-speed mastered.)
Also see GUY, Buddy, with Dr. John and Eric Clapton / Buddy
Guy with the J. Geils Band
Also see WOLF, Peter

GELDOF, Bob
Singles: 7–inch
ATLANTIC 2-4   86
Picture Sleeves
ATLANTIC 2-4   86
LPs: 10/12–inch 33rpm
ATLANTIC 5-10   86
Also see BAND AID
Also see BOOMTOWN RATS

GEM
Singles: 7–inch
STREETKING 2-4   84

GENE & DEBBE
Singles: 7–inch
HICKORY 3-5   70
TRX 4-6   67-69
LPs: 10/12–inch 33rpm
TRX (1001 "Here and Now") 15-25   68
Members: Gene Thomas; Debbe Nevills.
Also see THOMAS, Gene

GENE & EUNICE
Singles: 78rpm
ALADDIN 4-8   55
COMBO 4-8   55
Singles: 7–inch
ALADDIN 10-20   55
CASE 5-10   59

COLLECTABLES 2-4
COMBO 10-20   55
ERA 3-5   72
LILLY 4-8   62
U.A. 2-4

EPs: 7-inch 33/45rpm

CASE (100 "Gene & Eunice") 25-35   59
(Issued with paper sleeve.)
Members: Gene Forrest; Eunice Levy.
Also see EUNICE

GENE & JERRY
Singles: 7-inch
DIAL 4-8   63
ROULETTE 4-8   63
LPs: 10/12-inch 33rpm
ROULETTE 10-15   64

GENE (Chandler) & JERRY (Butler):
see CHANDLER, Gene, and Jerry Butler

GENE & TOMMY
Singles: 7-inch
ABC 4-8   67
Members: Terry Cashman; Tommy West.
Also see CASHMAN & WEST

GENE & WENDELL
Singles: 7-inch
PHILIPS 4-8   62-63
RAY STARR 5-10   61-62

GENE LOVES JEZEBEL
Singles: 12-inch 33/45rpm
GEFFEN 4-6   86
Singles: 7-inch
GEFFEN 2-4   86-90
Picture Sleeves
GEFFEN 2-4   88
LPs: 10/12-inch 33rpm
GEFFEN 5-10   86-90
Members: Michael Aston; Jay Aston; James Stevenson; Chris
Bell; Peter Rizzo.
Also see THOMPSON TWINS

GENE the HAT
Singles: 7-inch
CHECKER 5-10   61
DEAUVILLE 4-8   62
GEE 4-8   62

GENELLS
Singles: 7-inch
DEWEY (101 "Linda, Please Wait") . . 15-25   63

GENERAL CAINE: see CAINE, General

GENERAL KANE
Singles: 12-inch 33/45rpm
MOTOWN 5-10   86
Singles: 7-inch
MOTOWN 2-4   86-87
LPs: 10/12-inch 33rpm
MOTOWN 5-10   86

GENERAL PUBLIC
Singles: 12-inch 33/45rpm
I.R.S. 4-6   84-86
Singles: 7-inch
I.R.S. 2-4   84-86
Picture Sleeves
I.R.S. 2-4   84
LPs: 10/12-inch 33rpm
I.R.S. 5-10   84-86

GENESIS
Singles: 12-inch 33/45rpm
ATLANTIC 4-6   86
Singles: 7-inch
ATCO 3-5   76-77
ATLANTIC 2-4   78-87
CHARISMA 4-6   73
PARROT (3018 "Silent Sun") 10-15   68
(Promotional issue only.)
Picture Sleeves
ATLANTIC 2-5   78-87
Promotional Singles
ATCO 3-5   76-77
ATLANTIC 2-4   78-86
CHARISMA 4-8   73
PARROT 10-15   68
EPs: 7-inch 33/45rpm
ATLANTIC (1800 "Spot the Pigeon") . . 5-10   77
(Promotional issue only.)
LPs: 10/12-inch 33rpm
ABC 8-10   74
ATCO 8-15   74-77
ATLANTIC 5-10   78-86
BUDDAH (5659 "Best of Genesis") . . 10-15   76
CHARISMA 8-12   72-79
IMPULSE 15-25   70
LONDON (600 series) 10-15   74
LONDON (50000 series) 5-10   77
MCA 5-10   78
MFSL (062 "Trick of the Tail") 25-50   82
Members: Phil Collins; Peter Gabriel; Tony Banks; Steve
Hackett; Anthony Phillips; Mike Rutherford.
Also see BANKS, Tony
Also see CHIC / Roberta Flack / Leif Garrett / Genesis
Also see COLLINS, Phil
Also see GABRIEL, Peter
Also see HACKETT, Steve
Also see PHILLIPS, Anthony
Also see RUTHERFORD, Mike

GENIES
Singles: 7-inch
ERIC 2-4
HOLLYWOOD 10-15   59
SHAD (5002 "Who's That Knocking")   10-15   59
(Pink label.)
SHAD (5002 "Who's That Knocking") . 5-10   59
(Blue label.)
WARWICK 8-12   60-61
Members: Eugene Pitt; Roy Charles Hammond; Claude
Johnson; Roland Trone; Jay Washington.
Also see DON & JUAN

Also see JIVE FIVE
Also see ROY C.

GENTLE GIANT
Singles: 7–inch
CAPITOL 3-5   74-78
COLUMBIA 3-5   72-73
LPs: 10/12–inch 33rpm
CAPITOL 5-10   74-80
COLUMBIA 8-10   72-73
VERTIGO 10-15   71
Members: Derek Shulman; Ray Shulman; Phil Shulman; Gary Green; Kerry Minnear; Tony Visconti; John Weathers; Martin Smith.

GENTLE PERSUASION
Singles: 7–inch
CAPITOL 2-4   83
WARNER 5-10   78

GENTRY, Bobbie
Singles: 7–inch
BRUNSWICK 3-5   75
CAPITOL 3-6   67-76
WARNER 2-5   76-78
Picture Sleeves
CAPITOL 3-6   67-72
LPs: 10/12–inch 33rpm
CAPITOL (Except "SM" series) 8-15   67-71
CAPITOL ("SM" series) 5-10   81
WARNER ("Ode to Billie Joe: Radio Salute to Bobbie Gentry") 15-20   76
(Promotional issue only.)
Also see CAMPBELL, Glen, and Bobbie Gentry
Also see REYNOLDS, Jody, and Bobbie Gentry

GENTRYS
Singles: 7–inch
BELL 4-8   68
CAPITOL 3-5   72
MGM (Except 13690) 4-8   65-67
MGM (13690 "There's a Love") 8-10   67
STAX 3-5   74
SUN (1108 through 1122) 3-6   70-71
(Black vinyl.)
SUN (1108 through 1122) 10-15   70-71
(Colored vinyl. Promotional issues only.)
SUN (1126 "God Save Our Country")   10-20   71
YOUNGSTOWN (600 "Little Drops of Water") 15-25   65
YOUNGSTOWN (601 "Keep On Dancing") 15-25   65
Picture Sleeves
MGM 5-10   65
LPs: 10/12–inch 33rpm
MGM 20-30   65-70
SUN 20-30   70
Members: Larry Raspberry; Jimmy Johnson; Bruce Bowles; Pat Neal.

GENTY
Singles: 7–inch
VENTURE 2-4   80

GEORGE, Barbara
Singles: 7–inch
AFO 5-10   61-62
SUE 4-8   62-63
U.A. 3-5   74
LPs: 10/12–inch 33rpm
AFO (5001 "I Know" 50-75   62

GEORGE, Lowell
Singles: 7–inch
WARNER 2-5   78-79
LPs: 10/12–inch 33rpm
WARNER 5-10   78-79
Also see LITTLE FEAT

GEORGE (Jones) & GENE (Pitney):
see JONES, George, and Gene Pitney

GEORGIA SATELLITES
Singles: 12–inch 33/45rpm
ELEKTRA 4-8   89
(Promotional only.)
Singles: 7–inch
ELEKTRA 2-4   86-89
LPs: 10/12–inch 33rpm
ELEKTRA 5-10   86-89
Member: Dan Baird.

GEORGIO
Singles: 7–inch
MACOLO 2-4   87
MOTOWN 2-4   87
Picture Sleeves
MOTOWN 2-4   87
LPs: 10/12–inch 33rpm
MOTOWN 5-10   87

GERARD, Danyel
Singles: 7–inch
COLUMBIA 4-6   72
MGM/VERVE 3-5   72
LPs: 10/12–inch 33rpm
VERVE 8-12   71

GERRARD, Donny
Singles: 7–inch
GREEDY 3-5   76-77
ROCKET 3-5   76
LPs: 10/12–inch 33rpm
GREEDY 8-10
Also see SKYLARK

GERRY and the Pacemakers
Singles: 7–inch
ERIC 2-4
LAURIE (3196 "I Like It") 10-15   63
LAURIE (3233 "How Do You Do It") ... 8-12   64
LAURIE (3251 through 3370) 5-10   64-67
LPs: 10/12–inch 33rpm
ACCORD 5-10   81
CAPITOL 5-10   79
LAURIE 15-25   64-66
U.A. 20-25   65

Member: Gerry Marsden.
Also see MARTIN, George, and His Orchestra

GESTURES
Singles: 7–inch
SOMA 5-10   64-65

GET WET
Singles: 7–inch
BOARDWALK 2-4   81
Picture Sleeves
BOARDWALK 2-4   81
LPs: 10/12–inch 33rpm
BOARDWALK 5-10   81

GETZ, Stan
(Stan Getz Quintet)
CLEF 3-5   53-54
DAWN 3-5   54
MERCURY 3-5   53
NORGRAN 3-5   54-55
PRESTIGE 3-5   50-53
ROOST 3-5   50-53
Singles: 7–inch
CLEF 4-8   53-54
COLUMBIA 2-4   75-80
DAWN 4-8   54
MGM 3-5   65
MERCURY 4-8   53
NORGRAN 4-8   54-55
PRESTIGE 4-8   50-53
ROOST 4-8   50-53
VERVE 3-6   60-72
EPs: 7–inch 33/45rpm
CLEF 10-20   53
DALE 15-25   51
NORGRAN (11 through 155) 20-30   53-55
NORGRAN (2000-6 "At the Shrine") 50-100   55
(Six-EP boxed set.)
PRESTIGE (1309 "Stan Getz") 20-40   52
ROOST 15-25   50-53
LPs: 10/12–inch 33rpm
A&M 5-8   90
AMERICAN RECORDING
 SOCIETY 20-30   57
BARONET 10-20   62
BLUE RIBBON 10-20   61
CLEF (137 "Stan Getz Plays") 75-100   53
(10–inch LP.)
CLEF (143 "Artistry of Stan Getz") . . 75-100   53
(10–inch LP.)
COLUMBIA 5-10   74-82
CONCORD JAZZ 5-10   81
CROWN (5002 ""Groovin' High") 20-35   57
DALE (21 "Retrospect") 100-150   51
(10–inch LP.)
INNER CITY 5-10   78
JAZZ MAN 5-10   82
JAZZTONE 20-30   57
MGM (Except 4312) 5-10   70

MGM (4312 "Mickey One") 12-20   65
(Soundtrack.)
METRO 10-15   65
MODERN (1202 "Groovin' High") . . . 35-50   56
NEW JAZZ 15-25   59
NORGRAN (4 "Stan Getz") 100-150   53
(10–inch LP.)
NORGRAN (1000
 "Interpretations") 50-100   54
NORGRAN (1008 "Interpretations,
 Vol. 2") 50-100   54
NORGRAN (1029 "Interpretations,
 Vol. 3") 50-100   55
NORGRAN (1032 "West Coast
 Jazz") 40-60   55
NORGRAN (1087 "Stan Getz '57") . . 40-60   57
NORGRAN (2000-2 "At the Shrine") 100-200   55
(With booklet.)
PRESTIGE (102 "Stan Getz") 100-200   52
(10-inch LPs)
PRESTIGE (7002 through 7022) 25-50   56
(Yellow label.)
PRESTIGE (7252 through 7256) 25-50   56
(Yellow label.)
PRESTIGE (7000 series) 8-18   64-68
(Blue label.)
PRESTIGE (24000 series) 8-12   72-79
ROOST (103 "The Stan Getz Years") 30-40   64
ROOST (402 "Stan Getz") 100-150   50
(10-inch LPs)
ROOST (404 "Stan Getz and
 the Swedish All Stars") 100-125   51
(10–inch LPs)
ROOST (407 "Jazz at Storyville") . . 75-100   53
(10–inch LPs)
ROOST (411 "Jazz at
 Storyville, Vol. 2") 75-100   54
(10–inch LP.)
ROOST (420 "Jazz at
 Storyville, Vol. 3") 75-100   54
(10–inch LP.)
ROOST (417 "Chamber Music") . . . 75-100   54
(10–inch LP.)
ROOST (2207 "Sounds of Stan Getz") 25-40   56
ROOST (2249 through 2258) 20-30   63
ROULETTE 8-12   71-72
SAVOY (1100 series) 5-10   77
SAVOY (9004 "All Star Series) . . . 100-150   51
(10–inch LPs)
SEECO (7 "Highlights in
 Modern Jazz") 75-125   54
(10–inch LP.)
VSP 8-12   66-67
VERVE 25-50   57-60
(Reads "Verve Records, Inc." at bottom of label.)
VERVE 15-30   61-72
(Reads "MGM Records - a Division of
Metro-Goldwyn-Mayer, Inc." at bottom of label.)

VERVE 5-10   73-84
(Reads "Manufactured By MGM Record Corp.," or
mentions either Polydor or Polygram at bottom of
label.)
Also see BENNETT, Tony
Also see HAMPTON, Lionel, and Stan Getz
Also see HOLIDAY, Billie, and Stan Getz
Also see TJADER, Cal, and Stan Getz

GETZ, Stan, and Laurindo Almeida
Singles: 7–inch
VERVE 4-6   66
LPs: 10/12–inch 33rpm
VERVE 10-15   66
Also see ALMEIDA, Laurindo

GETZ, Stan, and Charlie Byrd
Singles: 7–inch
MGM 2-4   78
VERVE 3-5   62
LPs: 10/12–inch 33rpm
VERVE 15-25   62
Also see BYRD, Charlie

GETZ, Stan, and Astrud Gilberto
Singles: 7–inch
MGM 2-4   78
VERVE 3-6   64-65
LPs: 10/12–inch 33rpm
VERVE 15-25   64
Also see GILBERTO, Astrud

GETZ, Stan, and Oscar Peterson
LPs: 10/12–inch 33rpm
VERVE 20-40   57-60
(Reads "Verve Records, Inc." at bottom of label.)
VERVE 10-20   61-72
(Reads "MGM Records - a Division of
Metro-Goldwyn-Mayer, Inc." at bottom of label.)
Also see GETZ, Stan
Also see PETERSON, Oscar

GIANT STEPS
Singles: 7–inch
A&M 2-4   88-89
LPs: 10/12–inch 33rpm
A&M 5-8   88

GIBB, Andy
Singles: 7–inch
RSO 2-4   77-81
Picture Sleeves
RSO 2-4   77-78
LPs: 10/12–inch 33rpm
RSO 5-10   77-80
Also see BEE GEES
Also see NEWTON-JOHN, Olivia, and Andy Gibb

GIBB, Andy, and Victoria Principal
Singles: 7–inch
RSO 3-5   81
Picture Sleeves
RSO 5-10   81
Also see GIBB, Andy

GIBB, Barry
Singles: 7–inch
ATCO 3-5   77
MCA 2-4   84
Picture Sleeves
MCA 2-4   84
LPs: 10/12–inch 33rpm
MCA 5-10   84
Also see BEE GEES
Also see STREISAND, Barbra, and Barry Gibb
Also see WARWICK, Dionne

GIBB, Maurice
Singles: 7–inch
ATCO 3-5   70
Also see BEE GEES

GIBB, Robin
Singles: 7–inch
ATCO 3-5   69-71
EMI AMERICA 2-4   85
MIRAGE 2-4   84
POLYDOR 2-4   83
RSO 3-5   78
SESAME STREET 3-5   78
Picture Sleeves
EMI AMERICA 2-4   85
MIRAGE 2-4   84
POLYDOR 2-4   83
SESAME STREET 3-5   78
LPs: 10/12–inch 33rpm
ATCO 8-10   70
MIRAGE 5-10   84
POLYDOR 5-10   83
Also see BEE GEES
Also see LEVY, Marcy, and Robin Gibb

GIBBONS, Steve, Band
Singles: 7–inch
MCA/GOLD HAWKE 3-5   76-78
POLYDOR 3-5   78
LPs: 10/12–inch 33rpm
MCA 8-10   76-77
POLYDOR 5-10   78-80
Also see DALTREY, Roger, and Steve Gibbons

GIBBS, Doug
Singles: 7–inch
OAK 3-5   72

GIBBS, Georgia
Singles: 78rpm
CORAL 3-5   50-51
Singles: 7–inch
BELL 4-6   64-66
CORAL 8-12   50-51
EPIC (Except 9606) 4-8   63-64
EPIC (9606 "Tater Poon") 8-15   63
IMPERIAL 4-8   60
KAPP 4-8   59
MERCURY 5-10   51-57
RCA 4-8   57-67
ROULETTE 4-8   58-59

DERBY 5-10   52
MGM 5-10   51-55
EPs: 7–inch 33/45rpm
JD 8-12

GIBSON, Jon
LPs: 10/12–inch 33rpm
FRONTLINE 5-10   86

GIBSON, Johnny
(Johnny Gibson Trio)
Singles: 7–inch
BIG TOP 4-8   61-63
TWIRL 4-8
Also see JOHNNY and the Hurricanes

GIBSON, Steve
(Steve Gibson and the Red Caps; Steve Gibson and
the Original Red Caps)
Singles: 78rpm
ABC-PAR 8-12   56-57
BEACON 10-20   44
MERCURY 6-12   47-54
RCA 5-10   51-55
Singles: 7–inch
ABC-PAR 8-15   56-60
BAND BOX 4-8   62
HI LO 15-20   58
HUNT 10-15   59
JAY DEE (796 "It Hurts Me
  But I Like It") 20-30   54
MERCURY (5380 "I'll Never Love
  Anyone Else") 75-125   50
MERCURY (8038 "San Antonio
  Rose") 40-60   51
MERCURY (8069 "Wedding Bells") . . 40-60   51
MERCURY (8146 "Blueberry
  Hill") 40-60   51
MERCURY (70389 "Wedding Bells") 30-40   54
RCA (0127 "I'm to Blame") 30-45   51
RCA (0138 "Would I Mind") 30-45   51
RCA (3986 "The Thing") 40-50   50
RCA (4076 "Three Dollars
  and Ninety-Eight Cents") 30-40   51
RCA (4294 "Shame") 30-40   51
RCA (4670 "Two Little Kisses") 20-30   52
RCA (5103 "Truthfully") 20-30   52
RCA (5130 "Big Game Hunter") 20-30   53
RCA (5987 through 6345) 10-15   55
ROSE 8-12   59-60
STAGE (3001 "Blueberry Hill") 15-25
EPs: 7–inch 33/45rpm
MERCURY (3215 "Blueberry Hill") . 100-200   52
LPs: 10/12–inch 33rpm
MERCURY (25115 "You're Driving
  Me Crazy") 100-200   52
  (10–inch LP. Title on label is *Harmony Time*.)
MERCURY (25116 "Blueberry
  Hill") 100-200   52
  (10–inch LP. Title on label is *Singing and Swinging*.)
  Also see DAMITA JO with Steve Gibson and the Red Caps

Also see GIBSON, Steve

GIBSON BROTHERS
Singles: 12–inch 33/45rpm
ISLAND 4-6   79
Singles: 7–inch
ISLAND 2-4   79
LPs: 10/12–inch 33rpm
HOMESTEAD 5-8   90
ISLAND 5-8   79

GIDEA PARK
Singles: 7–inch
PROFILE 2-4   82
  Member: Adrian Baker.

GILBERT, Regina, and Jan Midkiff
Singles: 7–inch
FOUNTAIN 3-5   86
  Members: Regina Gilbert; Jan Midkiff; Don Capps; Randy
  Foushee; Daniel Shumate.

GILBERTO, Astrud
Singles: 7–inch
CTI 3-5   71
VERVE 3-5   67-70
LPs: 10/12–inch 33rpm
IMAGE 5-10   78
PERCEPTION 5-10   72
VERVE 8-15   65-70
  Also see GETZ, Stan, and Astrud Gilberto
  Also see JOBIM, Antonio Carlos
  Also see JONES, Quincy
  Also see WANDERLEY, Walter

GILBERTO, Astrud, and Stanley Turrentine
LPs: 10/12–inch 33rpm
CTI 5-10   71
  Also see GILBERTO, Astrud
  Also see TURRENTINE, Stanley

GILDER, Nick
Singles: 7–inch
CHRYSALIS 3-5   76-79
Picture Sleeves
CHRYSALIS. 3-5   78
LPs: 10/12–inch 33rpm
CASABLANCA 5-10   80
CHRYSALIS 5-10   77-79
  Also see SWEENY TODD

GILKYSON, Terry
(Terry Gilkyson and the Easy Riders; Terry Gilkyson
and the South Coasters)
Singles: 78rpm
COLUMBIA 3-5   54-57
DECCA 4-6   51-52
Singles: 7–inch
COLUMBIA 5-10   54-57
DECCA 5-10   51-52
Picture Sleeves
COLUMBIA (40817 "Marianne") 10-15   57
EPs: 7–inch 33/45rpm
COLUMBIA 5-15   57
DECCA 5-15   53

LPs: 10/12-inch 33rpm

DECCA (5263 "Folk Songs by a
Solitary Singer") 20-40   50
DECCA (5305 "Solitary Singer") 20-40   51
  (10–inch LP.)
DECCA (5457 "Golden Minutes
of Folk Music") 20-30   53
  (10–inch LP.)
KAPP 10-20   60-63
  Members: Terry Gilkyson; Rich Dehr.
  Also see MARTIN, Dean

GILL, Johnny
Singles: 7-inch
COTILLION 2-4   83-85
MOTOWN 2-4   90
Picture Sleeves
MOTOWN 2-4   90
LPs: 10/12-inch 33rpm
COTILLION 5-10   83-85
MOTOWN 5-8   90
  Also see LATTISAW, Stacy, and Johnny Gill
  Also see NEW EDITION

GILL, Vince
Singles: 7-inch
MCA 2-4   90-91
RCA 2-4   84-89
LPs: 10/12-inch 33rpm
MCA 5-8   90-91
RCA 5-8   84-89

GILLAN, Ian
(Gillan)
Singles: 7-inch
OYSTER 3-5   76
LPs: 10/12-inch 33rpm
ISLAND 5-10   77-78
OYSTER 8-10   76
VIRGIN 5-10   80
  Also see DEEP PURPLE

GILLEY, Mickey
(Mickey Gilley and the Urban Cowboy Band)
Singles: 7-inch
ACT 1 4-8   66
ASYLUM 2-4   80
ASTRO (Except 100 series) 3-5   71-73
ASTRO (100 series) 10-20   63-65
DARYL 4-8   63
DOT (15706 "Call Me Shorty") 50-75   58
EPIC 2-4   78-86
ERIC 4-6   64
GOLDBAND 4-8   64
GRT 3-5   70
KHOURY'S (712 "Drive-In Movie") ... 15-20   59
LYNN 10-20   60-61
MINOR (106 "Ooh Wee") 60-80   57
PAULA (Except 400 series) 4-6   66-68
PAULA (400 series) 2-4   74-84
PLAYBOY 3-5   74-77
POTOMAC 10-15   60

PRINCESS 8-12   62
RESCO 3-5   74
REX (1007 "Grapevine") 20-25   58
SABRA 10-15   61
SAN 10-15   63
SUPREME 8-12   62
TCF HALL 4-8   65
LPs: 10/12-inch 33rpm
ASTRO (Except 101) 8-10   73-78
ASTRO (101 "Lonely Wine") 75-150   64
EPIC 5-10   79-86
PAULA (Except 2000 series) 5-10   81
PAULA (2195 "Down the Line") 20-25   67
PAULA (2224 "Mickey Gilley at
His Best") 10-12   74
PAULA (2234 "Mickey Gilley") 8-10   78
PLAYBOY 8-12   74-78
  Also see CHARLES, Ray, and Mickey Gilley
  Also see HAGGARD, Merle / Mickey Gilley / Willie Knight

GILLEY, Mickey, and Barbi Benton
Singles: 7-inch
PLAYBOY 3-5   75
Picture Sleeves
PLAYBOY 3-5   75

GILLEY, Mickey, and Johnny Lee
Singles: 7-inch
EPIC 2-4   81
  Also see LEE, Johnny
  Also see NELSON, Willie / Johnny Lee / Mickey Gilley

GILLEY, Mickey, and Charly McClain
Singles: 7-inch
EPIC 2-4   83-84
  Also see GILLEY, Mickey

GILMER, Jimmy
(Jimmy Gilmer and the Fireballs)
Singles: 7-inch
ABC 2-4   74
ATCO 4-8   68
DECCA 10-15   59
DOT 4-8   63-66
HAMILTON 4-8   63
WARWICK (547 "True Love Ways") . 10-20   60
LPs: 10/12-inch 33rpm
ATCO 10-12   68-69
CROWN 15-20   63
DOT (3512 "Torquay") 15-25   63
  (Monaural.)
DOT (3545 "Sugar Shack") 15-25   63
  (Monaural.)
DOT (3577 "Buddy's Buddy") 40-50   64
  (Monaural.)
DOT (3643 "Lucky 'Leven") 15-25   63
  (Monaural.)
DOT (3668 "Folkbeat") 15-25   63
  (Monaural.)
DOT (3709 "Campusology") 15-25   63
  (Monaural.)

DOT (25512 "Torquay") 20-30   63
(Stereo.)
DOT (25545 "Sugar Shack") 20-30   63
(Stereo.)
DOT (25577 "Buddy's Buddy") 75-100   64
(Stereo.)
DOT (25643 "Lucky 'Leven") 20-30   63
(Stereo.)
DOT (25668 "Folkbeat") 20-30   63
(Stereo.)
DOT (25709 "Campusology") 20-30   63
(Stereo.)
DOT (25856 "Firewater") 20-30   63
Also see FIREBALLS
Also see JIM & MONICA
Also see SEDAKA, Neil, and the Tokens / Angels / Jimmy
  Gilmer and the Fireballs

GILMOUR, David
Singles: 12–inch 33/45rpm
COLUMBIA 4-6   84-86
Singles: 7–inch
COLUMBIA 2-4   84-86
Picture Sleeves
COLUMBIA 2-4   84
LPs: 10/12–inch 33rpm
COLUMBIA 5-10   78-85
Also see PINK FLOYD

GILREATH, James
Singles: 7–inch
JOY 4-8   63-64

GILSTRAP, Jim
Singles: 7–inch
BELL 3-5   74
ROXBURY 3-5   75-76
LPs: 10/12–inch 33rpm
ROXBURY 5-10   75-76

GINIE LYNN: see LYNN, Ginie

GINO & GINA
Singles: 7–inch
BRUNSWICK 4-8   61
MERCURY 10-15 58

GIOVANNI, Nikki, and the New York Community Choir
LPs: 10/12–inch 33rpm
RIGHT-ON 4-8   71

GIPSY KINGS
LPs: 10/12–inch 33rpm
MUSICIAN 5-8   88-89

GIRLFRIENDS
Singles: 7–inch
COLPIX 10-15 63-64
MELIC 5-10   63
PIONEER 10-15 60
Members: Carolyn Willis; Gloria Goodson; Nannette Jackson.
Also see HONEY CONE

GIRLS CAN'T HELP IT
LPs: 10/12–inch 33rpm
SIRE 5-10   84

GIRLSCHOOL
Singles: 7–inch
MERCURY 2-4   82
LPs: 10/12–inch 33rpm
MERCURY 5-10   82
STIFF AMERICA 5-10   82

GIRLTALK
Singles: 7–inch
GEFFEN 2-4   84

GIUFFRIA
(Gregg Giuffria)
Singles: 12–inch 33/45rpm
MCA 4-8   84
(Promotional only.)
Singles: 7–inch
MCA 2-4   84-85
MCA/CAMEL 2-4   85-86
Picture Sleeves
MCA 2-4   84-85
LPs: 10/12–inch 33rpm
MCA 5-10   84-85
MCA/CAMEL 5-10   85-86
Also see ANGEL

GIVENS FAMILY
Singles: 7–inch
PJ 2-4   86
SUGAR HILL 2-4   85

GLADIOLAS
Singles: 78rpm
EXCELLO 15-25 57
Singles: 7–inch
EXCELLO (2101 "Little Darlin") 25-50   57
EXCELLO (2110 "Run, Run Little Joe")25-50   57
EXCELLO (2120 "I Wanta Know") ... 25-50   57
EXCELLO (2136 "Say You'll Be Mine") 20-40   58
Members: Maurice Williams; Norman Wade; Bill Massey; Willie
Jones; Earl Gainey; Bobby Robinson.
Also see WILLIAMS, Maurice, and the Zodiacs

GLADSTONE
Singles: 7–inch
ABC 2-4   72
LPs: 10/12–inch 33rpm
ABC 8-10   72-73

GLAHE, Will, and His Orchestra
Singles: 78rpm
LONDON 2-4   55-57
Singles: 7–inch
LONDON 2-4   55-60
LPs: 10/12–inch 33rpm
LONDON 5-15   55-60

GLASS, Philip
LPs: 10/12–inch 33rpm
CBS 5-10   82-86

Also see ANDERSON, Laurie
Also see RONSTADT, Linda

GLASS BOTTLE
Singles: 7-Inch
AVCO 3-5   71
AVCO EMBASSY 3-5   70
LPs: 10/12-Inch 33rpm
AVCO 8-12   71
Member: Gary Criss.

GLASS FAMILY
Singles: 7-Inch
JDC 2-4   78

GLASS HARP
LPs: 10/12-Inch 33rpm
DECCA 8-10   71-72
MCA 5-10
Member: Phil Keaggy.

GLASS HOUSE
Singles: 7-Inch
INVICTUS 2-4   69-72
LPs: 10/12-Inch 33rpm
INVICTUS 8-10   71-72
KIRSHNER 8-10   71
Members: Scherrie Payne; Ty Hunter; Larry Mitchell; Pearl
Jones; Eric Dunham.
Also see HUNTER, Ty
Also see PAYNE, Scherrie

GLASS MOON
Singles: 7-Inch
RADIO 2-4   82
LPs: 10/12-Inch 33rpm
RADIO 5-10   80-82

GLASS TIGER
Singles: 12-Inch 33/45rpm
MANHATTAN 4-6   86
Singles: 7-Inch
EMI/MANHATTAN 2-4   88
MANHATTAN 2-4   86-87
Picture Sleeves
EMI/MANHATTAN 2-4   88
MANHATTAN 2-4   86-87
LPs: 10/12-Inch 33rpm
EMI/MANHATTAN 5-8   88
MANHATTAN 5-10   86

GLAZER, Tom
(Tom Glazer and the Children's Do-Re-Mi Chorus;
Tom Glazer with Dotty Evans and Robin Morgan)
COLUMBIA 5-10   53-55
CORAL 5-10   56
Singles: 7-Inch
COLUMBIA 5-10   53-55
CORAL 5-10   56
KAPP 4-8   63-64
U.A. 4-8   66-67
Picture Sleeves
KAPP 5-10   63

LPs: 10/12-Inch 33rpm
CAMDEN 5-10   64-65
KAPP 10-15 63-64
COLUMBIA 20-30   55
HARMONY 10-15   59
MERCURY 15-25   55
MOTIVATION 5-10   62
RIVERSIDE 10-15   61
U.A. 10-15   66
WASHINGTON 10-15   59
WONDERLAND 10-15   63

GLEASON, Jackie
(Jackie Gleason's Orchestra)
Singles: 78rpm
CAPITOL 3-5   52-57
DECCA (27000 series) 3-5   51
Singles: 7-Inch
CAPITOL 5-10 52-62
DECCA (27000 series) 4-8   51
EPs: 7-Inch 33/45rpm
CAPITOL (Except 511) 5-15 53-60
CAPITOL (511 "And Awa-a-ay
We Go") 50-75   54
(Double EP set.)
CAPITOL (511 "And Awa-a-ay
We Go") 75-100 54
(With and "EBF" prefix. Boxed two-EP set.)
LPs: 10/12-Inch 33rpm
CAPITOL (Except 511) 5-15 53-69
CAPITOL (511 "And Awa-a-y
We Go") 75-100 54
(10-inch LP. Songs by Jackie, sung in character
by: Joe the Bartender; The Loud Mouth; Ralph
Kramden; Fenwick Babbitt; Reggie Van Gleason
III, and the Poor Soul.)
Also see MARTIN, Dean / Jackie Gleason

GLENCOVES
Singles: 7-Inch
SELECT 5-8   63-64

GLENN, Darrell
Singles: 78rpm
DOT 3-6   56
RCA 3-6   54
Singles: 7-Inch
COLUMBIA 3-6   66-67
DOT 10-15   56
FASHION 5-10   60
LONGHORN 4-8   65
NRC 8-12   58
POMPEII 3-6   68-69
RCA 5-10   54
ROBBIE 3-6   64
TWINKLE (505 "That's Right") 30-50
VALLEY 5-10   53
LPs: 10/12-Inch 33rpm
NRC 12-20   59

GLENN, Garry
Singles: 7–inch
MOTOWN 2-4   87

GLENN, Lloyd
Singles: 78rpm
ALADDIN 3-6   56-57
HOLLYWOOD 4-8   54
SWING TIME 5-10   52-54
Singles: 7–inch
ALADDIN 8-12   56-59
HOLLYWOOD 10-15   54
IMPERIAL 4-8   62
SWING TIME 20-30   52-54
LPs: 10/12–inch 33rpm
ALADDIN (808 "Chica-Boo") 50-75   56
  (Black vinyl.)
ALADDIN (808 "Chica-Boo") 150-200   56
  (Colored vinyl.)
BLACK and BLUE 8-10   77
IMPERIAL (9174 "Chica-Boo") 30-40   62
  (Monaural.)
IMPERIAL (12174 "Chica-Boo") 30-40   62
  (Stereo.)
SCORE (4006 "Piano Stylings") 50-100   56
SCORE (4020 "After Hours") 50-100   57
SWING TIME (1901 "Lloyd
  Glenn") 125-150   54
  (10–inch LP.)
  Also see BROWN, Charles / Lloyd Glenn
  Also see FULSON, Lowell

GLITTER, Gary
(Gary Glitter and the Glitter Band)
Singles: 7–inch
ARISTA 3-5   75
BELL 3-5   72-74
LPs: 10/12–inch 33rpm
BELL 8-10   72
EPIC 6-10   81
  Also see GLITTER BAND

GLITTER BAND
Singles: 7–inch
ARISTA 3-5   75-76
LPs: 10/12–inch 33rpm
ARISTA 8-10   76
  Member: Pete Gill.
  Also see GLITTER, Gary
  Also see MOTORHEAD

GLORIES
Singles: 7–inch
DATE 10-15   67-68
  Members: Yvonne Gearing; Betty Stokes; Mildred Vaney.

GLOVER, Roger
Singles: 7–inch
21 2-4   84
UK 8-10   75
LPs: 10/12–inch 33rpm
POLYDOR 5-10   78
21 5-10   84

U.K. 8-10   75
  Also see DEEP PURPLE
  Also see RAINBOW

GO WEST
Singles: 7–inch
CHRYSALIS 2-4   85-87
EMI 2-4   90
Picture Sleeves
CHRYSALIS 2-4   85-87
EMI 2-4   90
LPs: 10/12–inch 33rpm
CHRYSALIS 5-10   85-87

GOANNA
Singles: 7–inch
ATCO 2-4   83
LPs; 10/12–inch 33rpm
ATCO 5-10   83

GODFATHERS
LPs: 10/12–inch 33rpm
EPIC 5-8   88-89

GODFREY, Arthur
Singles: 78rpm
COLUMBIA 2-5   50-56
DECCA (29000 series) 2-4   55
Singles: 7–inch
COLUMBIA 5-10   50-56
CONTEMPO 3-6   63-64
DECCA (29000 series) 5-8   55
MGM 3-6   66
MTA 3-5   69
SIGNATURE 4-8   60
VEE JAY 3-6   65
Picture Sleeves
MGM 5-10   66
EPs: 7–inch 33/45rpm
COLUMBIA 8-15   52-56
LPs: 10/12–inch 33rpm
ADMIRAL 8-12   67
CAMDEN 8-12   66-67
CAPITOL 8-15   62
COLUMBIA 10-20   53-61
CONTEMPO 8-15
HARMONY 10-15   59
RCA 5-10   73
SIGNATURE 8-15   60
  Also see MARINERS

GODFREY, Arthur, with Archie Bleyer
EPs: 7–inch 33/45rpm
CADENCE 10-20   54
LPs: 10/12–inch 33rpm
CADENCE (540 "Christmas with Godfrey
  and the Little Godfreys") 30-40   54
  (10–inch LP.)
  Also see BLEYER, Archie
  Also see GODFREY, Arthur

GODFREY, Ray
Singles: 7-inch
ABC	4-8	67
COLUMBIA	4-8	67
J&J	5-10	60
PEACH	10-15	62
SIMS	4-8	63
SPRING	4-6	70
TOLLIE	5-10	65
YONAH	5-10	61

GODLEY, Kevin, and Lol Creme
(Godley and Creme)
Singles: 12-inch 33/45rpm
POLYDOR	4-8	85

Singles: 7-inch
MERCURY	3-5	77
MIRAGE	2-4	82
POLYDOR	2-4	85

LPs: 10/12-inch 33rpm
MERCURY	10-15	77
MIRAGE	5-10	82
POLYDOR	5-10	85
Also see SCAFFOLD
Also see 10CC

GODSPELL
(Robin Lamont and Original "Godspell" Cast)
Singles: 7-inch
BELL	3-5	72

GODWIN, Peter
Singles: 12-inch 33/45rpm
POLYDOR	4-6	83

GODZ
Singles: 7-inch
MILLENIUM	3-5	78

LPs: 10/12-inch 33rpm
CASABLANCA	5-10	78
MILLENIUM/CASABLANCA	5-10	78

GOFFIN, Louise
Singles: 7-inch
ASYLUM	3-5	79
ELEKTRA	3-5	79

LPs: 10/12-inch 33rpm
ASYLUM	5-10	79-81

GO-GOs
Singles: 12-inch 33/45
I.R.S	4-8	82

Singles: 7-inch
I.R.S. (Except 8001)	2-5	81-85
I.R.S. (8001 "We Got the Beat")	4-8	82
(Picture disc.)		

Picture Sleeves
I.R.S.	2-5	81-85

LPs: 10/12-inch 33rpm
I.R.S.	5-10	81-90
Members: Belinda Carlisle; Charlotte Caffey; Jane Wiedlin; Margot Olaverria; Elissa Bello; Gina Schock; Kathy Valentine.
Also see CARLISLE, Belinda

Also see TEXTONES
Also see VENTURES
Also see WIEDLIN, Jane

GOLD, Andrew
Singles: 7-inch
ASYLUM	3-5	76-78

Picture Sleeves
ASYLUM	3-5	77-78

LPs: 10/12-inch 33rpm
ASYLUM	5-10	75-80
Also see SIMPSONS
Also see WAX

GOLD, Marty, and His Orchestra
Singles: 7-inch
KAPP	3-5	58-59
RCA	3-5	60-61

EPs: 7-inch 33/45rpm
KAPP	4-8	59
VIK	5-10	56-57

LPs: 10/12-inch 33rpm
KAPP	8-12	59
RCA	8-12	59-63
VIK	10-20	56-57

GOLDDIGGERS
Singles: 7-inch
METROMEDIA	3-5	69
RCA	3-5	72

LPs: 10/12-inch 33rpm
METROMEDIA	8-12	69
RCA	5-10	71
Also see MARTIN, Dean

GOLDE, Frannie
Singles: 7-inch
ATLANTIC	3-5	77
BIG TREE	3-5	76
PORTRAIT	3-5	79

GOLDEN EARRING
Singles: 7-inch
ATLANTIC	3-5	70
MCA	3-5	76-78
POLYDOR (2000 series)	2-4	79
POLYDOR (14000 series)	3-6	69
TRACK	3-5	74-75
21	2-4	82-86

Picture Sleeves
21	3-5	84

LPs: 10/12-inch 33rpm
ATLANTIC	15-20	69
CAPITOL (164 "Miracle Mirror")	30-35	69
CAPITOL (2823 "Winter Harvest")	30-35	67
CAPITOL (11315 "Golden Earring")	10-12	74
DWARF	10-20	
MCA	6-10	75-81
POLYDOR	5-10	79-80
TRACK (396 "Moontan")	20-25	73
(With nude showgirl on cover.)		
TRACK (396 "Moontan")	10-12	73
(Showgirl not nude on cover.)		

TRACK (2139 "Switch") 8-12   75
21 5-10   82-86

GOLDEN GATE STRINGS
(With Stu Phillips)
LPs: 10/12–inch 33rpm
EPIC 5-10   67
    Also see HOLLYRIDGE STRINGS

GOLDSBORO, Bobby
Singles: 7–inch
CURB 2-4   80-82
EPIC 3-5   77
LAURIE 5-8   62-63
U.A. (Except 672 through 980) 4-6   66-73
U.A. (672 through 980) 5-8   63-66
VISTA 3-5   74
Picture Sleeves
U.A. (Except 710) 4-8   66-74
U.A. (710 "Whenever He Holds You") . 8-12   64
LPs: 10/12–inch 33rpm
CURB 5-10   80-82
DORAL 15-25
    (Promotional mail-order issue, from Doral
    cigarettes.)
EPIC 8-10   77
K-TEL 5-10
LIBERTY 5-10   81
SUNSET 5-10
U.A. 10-20   64-76
    Also see ORBISON, Roy
    Also see REEVES, Del, and Bobby Goldsboro

GOLDSBORO, Bobby / Jimmy Durante
Singles: 7–inch
LIGHT (608 "We Gotta Start Lovin") ... 4-8   71
    Also see DURANTE, Jimmy

GOLLIWOGS
Singles: 7–inch
FANTASY 15-25   65
SCORPIO 15-25   64-68
LPs: 10/12–inch 33rpm
FANTASY 10-15   75
    Also see CREEDENCE CLEARWATER REVIVAL

Scorpio

Time 2:26
Creece-BMI

404
(P-2505)

BROWN-EYED GIRL
Wild Group
THE GOLLIWOGS

GOMM, Ian
Singles: 7–inch
STIFF 2-4   79
LPs: 10/12–inch 33rpm
STIFF 5-10   79-80

GONE ALL STARS
Singles: 7–inch
GONE 10-15   58
ROULETTE 3-5   71
EPs: 7–inch 33/45rpm
GONE (101 "Dancin' Bandstand") ... 35-55   58

GONZALES, Terri
Singles: 7–inch
BECKET 2-4   82

GONZALEZ
Singles: 12–inch 33/45rpm
CAPITOL 4-6   79
Singles: 7–inch
CAPITOL 2-4   78-79
LPs: 10/12–inch 33rpm
CAPITOL 5-10   78-80

GOOD QUESTION
Singles: 7–inch
PAISLEY PARK 2-4   88

GOODEES
Singles: 7–inch
HIP 4-8   68-69
LPs: 10/12–inch 33rpm
HIP 10-15   69

GOODIE
Singles: 12–inch 33/45rpm
TOTAL EXPERIENCE 4-6   82-84
Singles: 7–inch
TOTAL EXPERIENCE 2-4   82-84
LPs: 10/12–inch 33rpm
TOTAL EXPERIENCE 5-10   83

GOODIES
Singles: 7–inch
20TH FOX 3-5   75

GOODING, Cuba
Singles: 12–inch 33/45rpm
STREETWISE 4-6   83
Singles: 7–inch
MOTOWN 3-5   78-79
STREETWISE 2-4   83
LPs: 10/12–inch 33rpm
MOTOWN 5-10   78-79
    Also see MAIN INGREDIENT

GOODMAN, Benny, Orchestra
Singles: 78rpm
COLUMBIA (Except 2856) 5-15   33-56
COLUMBIA (2856 "Your Mother's
    Son-In-Law") 30-50   34
    (Colored plastic. Vocal by Billie Holiday.)
MELOTONE 10-20   31

VICTOR (Except 25808) 5-15   36-58
VICTOR (25808 "Popcorn Man") . 750-1000   39
Singles: 7-inch
CHESS 4-6   59
COLUMBIA (Except 250) 4-8   50-56
COLUMBIA (250 "1938 Carnegie
  Hall Concert") 25-35
  (Boxed set.)
COMMAND 3-5   67
DECCA 3-5   62
RCA 4-8   50-59
EPs: 7-inch 33/45rpm
BRUNSWICK 5-10   54
CAPITOL 5-10   55-56
COLUMBIA 5-10   50-58
DECCA (798 "The Benny Goodman
  Story") 10-15   56
MGM 4-8   59
RCA 5-10   50-59
LPs: 10/12-inch 33rpm
ABC 5-10   76
BRIGHT ORANGE 5-10   73
BRUNSWICK 10-20   54
CAMDEN 5-10   63-65
CAPITOL 5-15   55-78
CENTURY 5-10   79
CHESS 5-15   59
COLPIX 8-12   62
COLUMBIA (Except 160) 5-15   50-82
COLUMBIA (160 "The Famous 1938
  Carnegie Hall Concert") 25-40
  (Two-LP boxed set. Includes cardboard inner
  sleeves.)
COMMAND 5-10   67
DECCA (188 "The Benny Goodman
  Story, Volumes 1 and 2") 25-35
DECCA (8252 "The Benny Goodman
  Story, Volume 1") 20-30   56
DECCA (8253 "The Benny Goodman
  Story, Volume 2") 20-30   56
DECCA (7-8252 "The Benny Goodman
  Story, Volume 1") 15-20   59
  (Reprocessed stereo reissue.)
DECCA (7-8253 "The Benny Goodman
  Story, Volume 2") 15-20   59
  (Reprocessed stereo reissue.)
EVEREST 5-10   73
HARMONY 5-10   59-60
LONDON 5-10   72-78
LONDON/PHASE 4 5-10   71-72
MCA 5-10   80
MGM 5-15   59
MARK '56 5-10   77
MEGA 5-10   72-74
MUSICMASTERS 5-10
PAUSA 5-10   83
PRESTIGE 5-10   69
QUINTESSENCE 4-8   79
RCA (Except 6703) 5-15   50-78

RCA (6703 "The Golden Age
  of Swing") 15-20   55
SUNBEAM 5-10   73
TIME-LIFE (354 "Into the '70s" 10-20   72
  (Three-LP boxed set. Includes booklet.)
WESTINGHOUSE ("World Favorites") 20-30   58
  ((No number used.)
X 10-15   54
   Also see BASIE, Count, and Benny Goodman
   Also see HOLIDAY, Billie
   Also see LEE, Peggy

GOODMAN, Benny, Trio, with Rosemary Clooney
Singles: 78rpm
COLUMBIA 3-5   50-56
Singles: 7-inch
COLUMBIA 5-10   56
LPs: 10/12-inch 33rpm
COLUMBIA 15-25   56
   Also see CLOONEY, Rosemary
   Also see GOODMAN, Benny, Orchestra

GOODMAN, Dickie
Singles: 7-inch
AUDIO SPECTRUM 10-20   64
CASH 4-6   75
COTIQUE 4-8   69
DIAMOND 10-15   62
EXTRAN 5-8   82
GOODNAME 3-5   88
HOTLINE 4-6   79
J.M.D 15-20   62
JANUS 3-6   77
M.D 10-20   61
MARK-X 10-20   61
MONTAGE 3-5   82
PRELUDE 3-5   80
RAINY WEDNESDAY 4-8   73-75
RAMGO 8-12   70
RED BIRD 10-15   66
RHINO 3-5   84
RORI 10-15   61
SHARK 4-6   79
SHELL 3-5   84
SHOCK 4-6   77
20TH FOX 10-15   63
TWIRL 10-15   66
WACKO 3-5   81
Z-100 3-5   84
LPs: 10/12-inch 33rpm
CASH (6000 "Mr. Jaws") 25-30   75
COMET (69 "My Son the Joke") 20-30   64
IX CHAINS 12-15   73
RHINO 5-10   83
RORI (3301 "Many Heads of
  Dickie Goodman") 50-65   62
   Also see BUCHANAN & GOODMAN

GOODMAN, Jerry, and Jan Hammer
LPs: 10/12–inch 33rpm
NEMPEROR 8-10   74
  Also see HAMMER, Jan

GOODMAN, Steve
Singles: 7–inch
ASYLUM 3-5   75-81
BUDDAH 3-5   72-73
LPs: 10/12–inch 33rpm
ASYLUM 5-10   75-80
BUDDAH 8-12   71-76
RED PAJAMAS 5-10   83-87

GOODMAN, Steve, and Phoebe Snow
Singles: 7–inch
ASYLUM 2-4   80
  Also see GOODMAN, Steve
  Also see SNOW, Phoebe

GOODTIMERS
Singles: 7–inch
ARNOLD 5-10   61
EPIC 4-8   61
  Member: Don Covay.
  Also see COVAY, Don

GOODWIN, Don
Singles: 7–inch
SILVER BLUE 3-5   73

GOODWIN, Ron
Singles: 78rpm
CAPITOL 3-5   56-57
Singles: 7–inch
CAPITOL 4-8   56-59
KING 3-6   61
LPs: 10/12–inch 33rpm
CAPITOL 8-15   57-60
  Also see VINCENT, Gene / Frank Sinatra / Sonny James / Ron
  Goodwin

GOODY GOODY
Singles: 7–inch
ATLANTIC 3-5   78
LPs: 10/12–inch 33rpm
ATLANTIC 5-10   78

GOON SQUAD
Singles: 12–inch 33/45rpm
EPIC 4-6   85
Singles: 7–inch
EPIC 2-4   85

GOOSE CREEK SYMPHONY
(Goose Creek)
Singles: 7–inch
CAPITOL 3-6   70-72
LPs: 10/12–inch 33rpm
CAPITOL 10-15   70-72
COLUMBIA 8-12   74
RLO 8-12

GORDON, Robert
(Robert Gordon and Link Wray)
Singles: 12–inch 33/45rpm
PRIVATE STOCK 10-15   78
RCA 8-12   81
  (Promotional issue only.)
Singles: 7–inch
PRIVATE STOCK 4-6   77-78
RCA (Black vinyl) 3-5   79-81
RCA (Colored vinyl) 8-12   79-81
  (Promotional issue only.)
Picture Sleeves
PRIVATE STOCK (45203 "Fire") 5-10   79
RCA (11471 "It's Only Make Believe") . 5-10   79
LPs: 10/12–inch 33rpm
PRIVATE STOCK 8-10   77-78
RCA (Black vinyl) 5-10   79-82
RCA (Colored vinyl) 20-30   79
Promotional LPs
RCA (3411 "Robert Gordon"/"Live
  from paradise in Boston") 35-45   79
  Also see WRAY, Link

GORDON, Roscoe
Singles: 78rpm
CHESS (1487 "Booted") 20-40   52
DUKE (101 "Tell Daddy") 30-50   52
DUKE (106 through 129) 10-20   53-54
FLIP (227 "Just Love Me Baby") ... 50-100   55
RPM (322 "Roscoe's Boogie") 20-30   50
RPM (336 "A Dime a Dozen") 20-30   50
RPM (344 through 384) 15-25   51-53
SUN (Except 227 and 237) 10-20   56-58
SUN (227 "Just Love Me Baby") ... 50-100   55
SUN (237 "The Chicken") 30-60   56
Singles: 7–inch
ABC-PAR 5-10   62-63
CHESS (1487 "Booted") 100-125   52
COLLECTABLES 2-4   81
DUKE (106 "T-Model Boogie") 40-60   53
DUKE (109 "Too Many Women") 25-50   53
DUKE (114 "Ain't No Use") 25-50   53
DUKE (129 "Three Cent Love') 25-50   54
DUKE (300 series) 5-10   60
FLIP (227 "Just Love Me Baby") .. 200-300   55
FLIP (237 "The Chicken") 20-30   56
OLD TOWN 4-6   64
RPM (322 "Roscoe's Boogie") 50-100   50
RPM (324 "Saddle the Cow") 75-100   50
RPM (336 "Dime a Dozen") 50-100   50
RPM (344 "Booted") 40-60   51
RPM (350 "No More Doggin'") 40-60   51
RPM (358 "New Orleans Wimmen") . 40-60   51
RPM (365 "What You Got on
  Your Mind") 40-60   51
RPM (369 "Trying") 40-60   52
RPM (373 "Lucille") 40-60   52
RPM (379 "Just in from Texas") 40-60   52
RPM (384 "We're All Loaded") 40-60   52

SUN (Except 227 and 237) 15-25 56-58
SUN (227 "Just Love Me Baby") .. 400-500 55
SUN (237 "The Chicken") 100-150 56
VEE JAY 5-10 59-61

GORE, Lesley
Singles: 7–inch
A&M 3-6 75-76
CREWE 3-6 70-71
MERCURY (72119 through 72206) ... 5-10 63
MERCURY (72245 "Je Ne Sais Plus") 10-20 64
MERCURY (72259 through 72726) 5-10 64-67
MERCURY (72842 through 72969) .. 10-15 68-69
MOWEST 3-6 72
Picture Sleeves
A&M 5-10 75-76
MERCURY 10-15 63-67
LPs: 10/12–inch 33rpm
A&M 8-10 75
MERCURY (8000 series) 5-10 80
MERCURY (20000 and 60000 series) 20-30 63-68
MOWEST 8-10 72
POLYDOR 5-10 85
WING 10-20 67-69
Also see BILLY & SUE
Also see DRIFTERS / Leslie Gore / Roy Orbison / Los Bravos

GORE, Leslie, and Lou Christie
Singles: 7–inch
MANHATTAN (50039 "Since I
Don't Have You") 5-8 86
Also see CHRISTIE, Lou
Also see GORE, Leslie

GORE, Michael
Singles: 7–inch
CAPITOL 2-4 84

GORL, Robert
Singles: 7–inch
ELEKTRA 2-4 84

GORME, Eydie
Singles: 78rpm
ABC-PAR 3-5 55-62
Singles: 7–inch
ABC-PAR 4-8 55-62
CALENDAR 3-6 67

COLUMBIA 3-8 62-68
(Black vinyl.)
COLUMBIA (43082 "I Want You
to Be My Baby") 5-10 64
(Colored vinyl.)
CORAL 5-10 53-55
GALA 3-5 76
MGM 3-5 71-73
RCA 3-5 69-70
U.A. 3-6 60-76
Picture Sleeves
COLUMBIA 4-8 62-63
LPs: 10/12–inch 33rpm
ABC-PAR 15-25 57-65
APPLAUSE 4-6 81
COLUMBIA 10-20 63-73
GALA 5-8 76
HARMONY 5-10 68-71
MGM 5-10 71
RCA 5-10 68-70
U.A. 10-20 61-62
VOCALION 8-15 63
Also see LAWRENCE, Steve, and Eydie Gorme

GOUDREAU, Barry
Singles: 7–inch
PORTRAIT 2-4 79
LPs: 10/12–inch 33rpm
PORTRAIT 5-10 79
Also see BOSTON

GOULET, Robert
Singles: 7–inch
ABC 2-5 74
ARTISTS of AMERICA 2-5 75
COLUMBIA (Black vinyl) 3-6 61-70
COLUMBIA (Colored vinyl) 5-10 63
MGM 3-5 73
MERLIN 3-5 71
PARAMOUNT 3-5 74
Picture Sleeves
ABC 3-6 74
COLUMBIA (Except 59227) 3-6 62-65
COLUMBIA (59227 "The Moon
Was Yellow") 5-10 63
(Promotional issue only.)
EPs: 7–inch 33/45rpm
COLUMBIA (9096 "Robert Goulet") 4-8 65
(Jukebox issue.)
LPs: 10/12–inch 33rpm
ARTISTS of AMERICA 5-10 76
COLUMBIA 5-15 61-73
HARMONY 5-10 71-72
MERLIN 5-10 71
ORINDA 5-10 78

GRACE, Fredi, and Rhinestone
Singles: 7–inch
RCA 2-4 82

COLUMBIA
NOT FOR SALE
RADIO STATION COPY
45 RPM
4-42661
JZSP 58839
Publisher:
Aldon Music, Inc.
(BMI) 1962
TIME: 2:29
BLAME IT ON THE BOSSA NOVA
- B. Mann - C. Weil -
EYDIE GORME
Arr. & Cond. by Marion Evans
Prod. by Al Kasha
©"COLUMBIA" MARCAS REG. PRINTED IN U.S.A.

GRACE, Leda
Singles: 7–inch
POLYDOR 2-4   81

GRACIE, Charlie
Singles: 78rpm
CADILLAC 15-25   53-54
CAMEO 10-15   57
SOCK & SOUL 4-6   70
20TH CENTURY 10-20   55
Singles: 7–inch
ABKCO 3-5   75
CADILLAC (141 "Boogie Woogie
   Blues") 60-100   53
CADILLAC (144 "Rockin'
   and Rollin") 60-100   54
CAMEO 10-15   57-59
CORAL 5-10   59
DIAMOND 4-8   65
FELSTED 4-8   61
PRESIDENT 4-8   62
SOCK and SOUL 3-5
ROULETTE 4-8   59-61
20TH CENTURY (5035 "Honey
   Honey") 35-50   55

GRADDOCK, Billy: see CRADDOCK, Billy

GRADUATES
Singles: 7–inch
CORSICAN 10-20   59
SHAN-TODD 10-20   59
Picture Sleeves
CORSICAN 20-30   59

GRAHAM, Jaki
Singles: 12–inch 33/45rpm
CAPITOL 4-6   86
Singles: 7–inch
CAPITOL 2-4   86
LPs: 10/12–inch 33rpm
CAPITOL 5-10   86

GRAHAM, Jaki, and David Grant
Singles: 12–inch 33/45rpm
CAPITOL 4-6   86
Singles: 7–inch
CAPITOL 2-4   86
   Also see GRAHAM, Jaki
   Also see GRANT, David

GRAHAM, Larry
(Larry Graham and Graham Central Station; Graham
Central Station)
Singles: 7–inch
ARISTA 2-4   87
WARNER 2-5   74-83
Picture Sleeves
WARNER 3-5   80
LPs: 10/12–inch 33rpm
WARNER 5-10   73-83
   Also see FRANKLIN, Aretha
   Also see SLY and the Family Stone

GRAINGERS
Singles: 7–inch
BC 2-4   81

GRAMM, Lou
Singles: 7–inch
ATLANTIC 2-4   87-90
Picture Sleeves
ATLANTIC 2-4   87
LPs: 10/12–inch 33rpm
ATLANTIC 5-10   87-89

GRAMMER, Billy
Singles: 7–inch
DECCA 4-8   61-66
EPIC 4-6   66-67
EVEREST 5-8   60
MERCURY 3-6   68-69
MONUMENT (Except 400 series) 3-5   75-76
MONUMENT (400 series) 5-10   59-63
RICE 4-6   67
STOP 3-5   69
EPs: 7–inch 33/45rpm
DECCA 5-10   64
LPs: 10/12–inch 33rpm
CLASSIC CHRISTMAS 5-10   77
DECCA 10-15   62-64
EPIC 8-12   67
MONUMENT (4000 "Travelin' On") .. 15-20   59
   (With *Lost in a Small Cafe.*)
MONUMENT (8039 "Travelin' On") ... 8-12   66
   (*Lost in a Small Cafe* replaced by *Gotta Travel On.*)
STONEWAY 5-10   75
VOCALION 6-12   68
   Also see CASH, Johnny / Billy Grammer / Wilburn Brothers

GRANAHAN, Gerry
Singles: 7–inch
CANADIAN AMERICAN 5-10   60
CAPRICE (Except 108) 5-10   61
CAPRICE (108 "Dance Girl, Dance") . 50-75   61
   (With the Wildwoods [a.k.a. Five Satins].)
GONE 8-12   59-60
SUNBEAM 15-20   58-59
VEEP 4-8   65
Picture Sleeves
GONE (5081 "Look For Me") 15-25   60
   Also see DICKY DOO and the Don'ts
   Also see FIVE SATINS
   Also see FONTAINE, Eddie, and Gerry Granahan

GRANATA, Rocca, and the International Quintet
Singles: 7–inch
LAURIE 3-6   59
Picture Sleeves
LAURIE 5-8   59

GRAND CANYON
Singles: 7–inch
BANG 4-6   74
FAITHFUL VIRTUE 3-5   70

GRAND FUNK RAILROAD
(Grand Funk)

Singles: 7–inch

CAPITOL (Black vinyl)	3-6	69-76
CAPITOL (Colored vinyl)	5-8	73
(Promotional issue only.)		
FULL MOON	2-4	81
MCA	3-5	76-77

Picture Sleeves

CAPITOL	3-6	71-76
FULL MOON	2-4	81
MCA	3-5	76

LPs: 10/12–inch 33rpm

CAPITOL (307 through 853)	8-15	69-71
CAPITOL (11000 series, except 11207)	6-12	72-76
CAPITOL (11207 "We're an		
American Band")	6-10	73
(Black vinyl.)		
CAPITOL (11207 "We're an		
American Band")	20-30	73
(Colored vinyl. Promotional issue only.)		
CAPITOL (12000 and 16000 series) . .	5-10	80-81
FULL MOON	5-10	81-83
MCA	8-10	76

Members: Mark Farner; Don Brewer; Mel Schacher; Craig Frost.
Also see KNIGHT, Terry, and the Pack

GRANDMASTER FLASH and the Furious Five
(Grandmaster Melle Mel and the Furious Five;
Grandmaster and Melle Mel; Grandmaster Flash)

Singles: 12–inch 33/45

ATLANTIC	4-6	84
ELEKTRA	4-6	85-86
SUGAR HILL	4-6	80-85

Singles: 7–inch

ATLANTIC	2-4	84
ELEKTRA	2-4	85-87
MCA	2-4	85
SUGAR HILL	3-5	80-85

Picture Sleeves

ATLANTIC	2-4	84

LPs: 10/12–inch 33rpm

ELEKTRA	5-10	86-88
SUGAR HILL	5-10	82-85

Also see KING DREAM CHORUS and Holiday Crew
Also see MELLE MEL and Duke Bootee

GRANDMIXER D. ST.

Singles: 12–inch 33/45rpm

ISLAND	4-6	83

Singles: 7–inch

ISLAND	2-4	83

GRANT, Amy

Singles: 7–inch

A&M	2-4	85-90
MYRRH	2-5	80-85

Picture Sleeves

A&M	2-4	85-88

LPs: 10/12–inch 33rpm

A&M	5-10	85-91

MYRRH	5-10	80-85

Also see CETERA, Peter, and Amy Grant

GRANT, David

Singles: 12–inch 33/45rpm

CHRYSALIS	4-6	83

Singles: 7–inch

CAPITOL	2-4	86
CHRYSALIS	2-4	83

Also see GRAHAM, Jaki, and David Grant

GRANT, Earl

Singles: 78rpm

PRINCE	4-8	56

Singles: 7–inch

DECCA	3-8	58-70
PRINCE (1201 "One-Way Street")	5-10	56
(Black vinyl.)		
PRINCE (1201 "One-Way Street") ...	10-20	56
(Colored vinyl.)		

EPs: 7–inch 33/45rpm

DECCA	5-10	59-62

LPs: 10/12–inch 33rpm

DECCA	8-18	59-70
MCA	5-10	76
VOCALION	5-10	69-70

GRANT, Eddy

Singles: 12–inch 33/45rpm

EPIC	4-6	80-82
PORTRAIT	4-6	83-85

Singles: 7–inch

EPIC	2-4	79-80
PORTRAIT	2-4	83-85

Picture Sleeves

PORTRAIT	2-4	84

LPs: 10/12–inch 33rpm

EPIC	5-10	79-80
PORTRAIT	5-10	83-85

Also see EQUALS

GRANT, Eleanor

Singles: 7–inch

CBS ASSOCIATED	2-4	84-85
CATAWBA	2-4	83
COLUMBIA	2-4	76

GRANT, Gogi

Singles: 78rpm

ERA	3-5	55-56
RCA	3-5	52-57

Singles: 7–inch

CHARTER	4-6	63
ERA	5-10	55-56
LIBERTY	4-8	60-61
MONUMENT	3-6	66-67
PETE	3-6	68-69
RCA	5-10	52-58
20TH FOX	4-6	61-62

Picture Sleeves

20TH FOX	5-10	61

GRANT, Janie

GRANT, Tom

GRAPEFRUIT

GRAPES of WRATH

GRAPPELLI, Stephane, and David Grisman

GRAPPELLI, Stephane, and Barney Kessel

GRASS ROOTS

(Rob Grill and the Grass Roots)

GRATEFUL DEAD

Members: Jerry Garcia; Ron McKernan; Bob Weir; Bill
Kreutzman; Phil Lesh; Mickey Hart; Tom Constanten; Ned Lagin;
Robert Hunter; Keith Godchaux; Donna Godchaux; Brent
Mydland.
Also see BROMBERG, David
Also see CROSBY, David
Also see GARCIA, Jerry
Also see GARCIA, Jerry, and Robert Hunter
Also see HART, Mickey
Also see KANTER, Paul, and Grace Slick
Also see NEW RIDERS of the Purple Sage
Also see SILVER
Also see WEIR, Bob

GRATEFUL DEAD / Elvin Bishop Group
Singles: 7-inch
Also see BISHOP, Elvin
Also see GRATEFUL DEAD

GRAVES, Billy
Singles: 7-inch

GRAVES, Carl
Singles: 7-inch
Also see SKYLARK

GRAY, Claude
Singles: 7-inch

GRAY, Diva, and Oyster
Singles: 7-inch

LPs: 10/12–Inch 33rpm
COLUMBIA 5-10   79

GRAY, Doble
Singles: 12–inch 33/45rpm
INFINITY 5-8   79
Singles: 7–Inch
ARISTA 2-4   83
CAPITOL (Except 5853) 2-4   86
CAPITOL (5853 "River Deep,
   Mountain High") 5-8   67
CAPRICORN 3-5   76-77
CHARGER 4-8   64-66
COLLECTABLES 2-4   81
CORDAK 5-8   62-64
DECCA 3-5   73
ERIC 2-4
GUSTO 2-4   85
INFINITY 3-5   78-79
JAF 4-8   63
MCA 2-4   73-75
REAL FINE 5-10   62
ROBOX 2-4   81
STRIPE 8-12   60-61
WHITE WHALE 4-6   69
LPs: 10/12–inch 33rpm
CAPITOL 5-10   86
CAPRICORN 8-10   76
CHARGER 15-20   65
DECCA 8-10   73
INFINITY 6-10   79
MCA 8-10   73-74
ROBOX 5-10   81
STRIPE 10-12

GRAY, Dolores
Singles: 78rpm
DECCA 3-5   51-55
Singles: 7–inch
DECCA 5-10   51-55
LPs: 10/12–inch 33rpm
CAPITOL (897 "Warm Brandy") 15-25   57

GRAY, Glen, and the Casa Loma Orchestra
Singles: 78rpm
CAPITOL 3-5   56-57
DECCA 3-5   55
Singles: 7–inch
CAPITOL 4-8   56-58
DECCA 4-8   55
EPs: 7–inch 33/45rpm
CAPITOL 5-10   56-58
LPs: 10/12–inch 33rpm
CAPITOL 5-15   56-63

GRAY, Maureen
Singles: 7–inch
CHANCELLOR 15-25   61-62
LANDA 8-12   62
MERCURY 4-8   63-64

GRAYSON, Kim
Singles: 7–inch
SOUNDWAVES 2-4   87
Picture Sleeves
SOUNDWAVES 2-4   87

GREAN, Charles
(Charles Randolph Grean Sounde)
Singles: 7–inch
DOT 3-6   67
RANWOOD 2-5   69-79
LPs: 10/12–inch 33rpm
RANWOOD 6-12   69-70

GREASE BAND
Singles: 7–inch
SHELTER 3-5   71
LPs: 10/12–inch 33rpm
SHELTER 8-10   71
   Member: Henry McCullough.
   Also see COCKER, Joe
   Also see McCARTNEY, Paul

GREAT BELIEVERS
Singles: 7–inch
CASCADE (365 "Comin' Up Fast") .. 40-60   64
   Member: Johnny Winter.
   Also see WINTER, Johnny

GREAT!! SOCIETY!!
Singles: 7–inch
COLUMBIA (44583 "Sally Go 'Round
   the Roses") 10-15   68
NORTHBEACH (1001 "Someone to
   Love") 75-150   66
   Member: Grace Slick.
   Also see JEFFERSON AIRPLANE
   Also see SLICK, Grace

GREAT WHITE
Singles: 7–inch
CAPITOL 2-4   86-90
EMI AMERICA 2-4   84
Picture Sleeves
CAPITOL 2-4   86-89
LPs: 10/12–inch 33rpm
CAPITOL 5-10   86-91
EMI AMERICA 5-10   84
ENIGMA 5-8   88
GREENWORLD 5-10   85

GREAVES, R.B.
Singles: 7–inch
ATCO 3-5   69-70
BAREBACK 3-5   77
MGM 3-5   73
MIDSONG 2-4   80
SUNFLOWER 3-5   72
20TH FOX 3-5   74
LPs: 10/12–inch 33rpm
ATCO 15-20   69

GRECCO, Cyndi
Singles: 7–inch
PRIVATE STOCK 3-5   76-77

GRECH, Rick
Singles: 7–inch
RSO 3-5   73
LPs: 10/12–inch 33rpm
RSO 5-10   73

GRECO, Buddy
(Buddy Greco Trio)
Singles: 78rpm
CORAL 3-6   51-55
KAPP 3-5   56
Singles: 7–inch
CORAL 5-10   51-55
EPIC 4-8   58-67
HERALD 5-8   59
KAPP 5-8   56
MGM 3-5   71-72
REPRISE 3-6   66-68
SCEPTER 3-5   69
Picture Sleeves
EPIC 4-8   64-65
EPs: 7–inch 33/45rpm
CORAL 5-10   55
LPs: 10/12–inch 33rpm
CORAL 15-25   55
EPIC 10-15   60-66
HARMONY 8-12   68
KAPP 10-15   61
REPRISE 8-12   67
SCEPTER 5-10   69-73
VOCALION 8-12   64

GREELEY, George
Singles: 7–inch
WARNER 3-5   59-62
Picture Sleeves
WARNER 3-5   62
EPs: 7–inch 33/45rpm
CAPITOL 5-10   56
LPs: 10/12–inch 33rpm
CAPITOL 5-15   56
RAVE 10-20   56
WARNER 5-10   59-61

GREEN, Al
(Al Greene and the Soul Mates)
Singles: 7–inch
A&M 2-4   87
BELL 3-5   72-73
FLASHBACK 3-5
HI 3-5   70-78
HOT LINE 8-12   67
MOTOWN 2-4   82-85
Picture Sleeves
HI 3-5   78
LPs: 10/12–inch 33rpm
A&M 5-10   87

BELL 8-10   72
HI 10-12   69-78
HOT LINE (1500 "Back Up Train") ... 20-30   67
KORY 8-10   77
MELODY 5-10
MOTOWN 5-10   82-85
MYRRH 5-10   80 83
Also see LENNOX, Annie, and Al Green

GREEN, Darren
Singles: 7–inch
RCA 3-5   73-74

GREEN, Garland
Singles: 7–inch
CASINO 3-5   76
COTILLION 3-6   71
GAMMA 4-8   67
OCEAN FRONT 2-4   83
RCA 3-5   77
REVUE 4-6   68
SPRING 3-5   74-75
UNI 4-6   69
LPs: 10/12–inch 33rpm
OCEAN FRONT 5-10   83
RCA 8-10   74-78
UNI 10-12   70

GREEN, Grant
LPs: 10/12–inch 33rpm
BLUE NOTE 15-25   61-65
(Label reads "Blue Note Records Inc. - New York,
U.S.A.")
BLUE NOTE 10-15   66-71
(Label reads "Blue Note Records - a Division of
Liberty Records Inc.")
VERVE 10-18   65
VERSATILE 5-10   78

GREEN, Jack
Singles: 7–inch
RCA 2-4   80
LPs: 10/12–inch 33rpm
RCA 5-10   80
Also see PRETTY THINGS
Also see T. REX

GREEN, Peter
LPs: 10/12–inch 33rpm
REPRISE 8-10   71
SAIL 5-10   79-80
Also see BOYD, Eddie
Also see FLEETWOOD MAC

GREEN, Sonny
Singles: 7–inch
HILL 3-5   73

GREEN BERETS
Singles: 7–inch
UNI 3-5   70

GREEN RIVER BOYS: see CAMPBELL, Glen

GREENBAUM, Norman
Singles: 7-inch
GREGAR 4-6	69-70
REPRISE 3-5	70-71

Picture Sleeves
REPRISE 5-8	69

LPs: 10/12-inch 33rpm
GREGAR 15-20	70
REPRISE 12-15	69-72

Also see DR. WEST'S MEDICINE SHOW and Junk Band

GREENBERG, Steve
Singles: 7-inch
TRIP 4-6	69

GREENE, Al: see GREEN, Al

GREENE, Barbara
Singles: 7-inch
ATCO (5260 "Long Tall Sally") 25-30	62
RENEE 8-10	68
VIVID 4-8	64

Also see DELLS

GREENE, Jack
(Jack Greene and the Jolly Green Giants)
Singles: 7-inch
DECCA 3-6	65-72
EMH 2-4	83-84
FRONTLINE 2-4	80
MCA 3-5	73-74

LPs: 10/12-inch 33rpm
CORAL 4-8	73
DECCA 8-15	66-71
51 WEST 5-10	84
FRONTLINE 5-10	80
MCA 5-10	73

GREENE, Jack, and Jeannie Seely
Singles: 7-inch
DECCA 3-5	69-72

LPs: 10/12-inch 33rpm
DECCA 8-12	70-72
MCA 4-6	73
PINNACLE 5-10	78
RDS 5-10	79

Also see GREENE, Jack
Also see SEELY, Jeannie

GREENE, Laura
Singles: 7-inch
SOUND TREK 2-4	80

GREENE, Lorne
Singles: 7-inch
COLUMBIA 3-6	69
GRT 3-5	70-71
RCA 4-8	62-66

Picture Sleeves
RCA 5-10	63-65

LPs: 10/12-inch 33rpm
CAMDEN 5-10	70
MGM 5-10	71

RCA 10-20	63-66

GREENWICH, Ellie
(Ellie Gaye)
Singles: 7-inch
BELL 4-8	69
RED BIRD (034 "You Don't Know") .. 10-20	65
RCA 10-20	
U.A. 8-12	67
VERVE 4-6	70-73

LPs: 10/12-inch 33rpm
U.A. (6648 "Ellie Greenwich Composes, Producers and Sings") 30-40	68
VERVE 10-15	73

Also see ARCHIES
Also see BONDS, Gary "U.S."
Also see CROCE, Jim
Also see RAINDROPS

GREENWOOD, Lee
(Lee Greenwood Affair)
Singles: 7-inch
DOT 3-6	69
MCA 2-4	81-88
PARAMOUNT 3-5	71

Picture Sleeves
MCA 2-4	83

LPs: 10/12-inch 33rpm
MCA 5-10	82-88

Also see MANDRELL, Barbara, and Lee Greenwood

GREENWOOD COUNTY SINGERS
(Greenwoods)
Singles: 7-inch
DECCA 4-6	64-66
KAPP 4-6	64-66

Picture Sleeves
KAPP 4-6	64

LPs: 10/12-inch 33rpm
DECCA 10-15	64
KAPP 10-15	64-66
RCA 8-12	70

GREER, Big John, and the Four Students
Singles: 78rpm
GROOVE 5-10	55

Singles: 7-inch
GROOVE (0131 "A Man and a Woman") 10-20	55

Also see GREER, John

GREER, John
(Big John Greer)
Singles: 78rpm
RCA 10-20	49-53

Singles: 7-inch
RCA (0007 "Drinkin' Wine Spoo-Dee-O-Dee") 35-50	49
(Colored vinyl.)	
RCA (0029 "If I Told You Once") 35-50	49
(Colored vinyl)	
RCA (0051 "Rocking Jenny Jones") . 35-50	50
(Colored vinyl)	

RCA (0076 "I'll Never Do That Again") 35-50   50
(Colored vinyl.)
RCA (0096 "Cheatin'") 35-50   50
(Colored vinyl.)
RCA (0104 "Red Juice") 35-50 50
(Colored vinyl.)
RCA (0108 "Once There Lived a Fool")15-25   51
RCA (0113 "Why Did You Go") 15-25   51
RCA (0125 "Clambake Boogie") 15-25   51
RCA (0137 "Rockin' with Big John") .. 15-25   51
RCA (4293 "Have Another Drink") ... 15-25   51
RCA (4348 "Got You on My Mind") ... 15-25   51
RCA (4484 "Strong Red Whiskey") .. 15-25   52
RCA (5037 "I'm the Fat Man") 15-25   52
RCA (5170 "You Played on My Piano") 15-25   53
RCA (5259 "Ride Pretty Baby") 15-25   53
RCA (5531 "Drinkin' Fool") 15-25   53
<small>Also see GREER, Big John, and the Four Students</small>

GREGG, Bobby
(Bobby Gregg and His Friends; Bobby Grego)
Singles: 7-inch
COTTON 8-12   62
EPIC 4-8   62-66
LPs: 10/12-inch 33rpm
EPIC (24051 "Let's Stomp and
Wild Weekend") 20-25   63
(Monaural.)
EPIC (26051 "Let's Stomp and
Wild Weekend") 25-30   63
(Stereo.)
<small>Also see BUCHANAN, Roy</small>

GREGORY, Dick
Singles: 7-inch
VEE JAY 4-8   62
LPs: 10/12-inch 33rpm
COLPIX 10-20   61-64
POPPY 8-15   69-73
VEE JAY 10-20   62-64

GREY & HANKS
Singles: 7-inch
RCA 3-5   78-80
LPs: 10/12-inch 33rpm
RCA 5-10   79-80
<small>Members: Zane Grey; Len Hanks</small>

GRIFFIN
Singles: 7-inch
QWEST 2-4   84

GRIFFIN, Billy
Singles: 7-inch
ATLANTIC 2-4   86
COLUMBIA 2-4   83-86
LPs: 10/12-inch 33rpm
COLUMBIA 5-10   84-86
<small>Also see MIRACLES</small>

GRIFFIN, Merv
(Merv Griffin and the Griffin Family Singers)
Singles: 78rpm
COLUMBIA 3-5   53
RCA 3-5   51-52
Singles: 7-inch
CAMEO 3-5   63-64
CARLTON 4-8   61
COLUMBIA 5-10   53
CORAL 3-6   66
DOT 3-5   68
GRIFFIN 3-5   73
MGM 4-6   65-67
MERCURY 4-6   62
METROMEDIA 3-5   70
RCA 5-10   51-52
EPs: 7-inch 33/45rpm
RCA (3000 series) 5-10   52
LPs: 10/12-inch 33rpm
CAMEO 8-15   64
CARLTON 10-20   61
MGM 8-15   65-66
METROMEDIA 5-10   69
RCA (3000 series) 15-25   52
(10-inch LPs.)
<small>Also see MARTIN, Freddy, and His Orchestra</small>

GRIFFIN, Reggie, and Technofunk
Singles: 7-inch
SWEET MOUNTAIN 2-4   82

GRIFFIN BROTHERS
(Griffin Brothers Featuring Tommy Brown; Griffin
Brothers Featuring Margie Day)
Singles: 78rpm
DOT 5-10   50-52
Singles: 7-inch
DOT (1071 "Weeping and Crying") .. 25-40   51
DOT (1094 "It'd Surprise You") 20-30   51
DOT (1095 "The Teaser") 20-30   51
DOT (1104 "I'm Gonna Jump in
the River") 20-30   52
DOT (1105 "Coming Home") 20-30   52
DOT (1108 "Ace in the Hole") 35-45   52
DOT (1114 "My Story") 15-25   53
DOT (1117 "I Wanna Go Back") 15-25   53
DOT (1144 "My Story") 15-25   53
DOT (1145 "Black Bread") 15-25   53
DOT (16000 series) 5-10   60
<small>Members: Jimmy Griffin; Edward "Buddy" Griffin.</small>

GRIFFITH, Andy
(Deacon Andy Griffith)
Singles: 78rpm
CAPITOL 5-10   53-57
Singles: 7-inch
CAPITOL (2500 series) 4-6   69
CAPITOL (2600 through 3600 series) 10-20   53-57
CAPITOL (4000 and 5000 series) 4-8   59-63
(Purple or orange/yellow swirl labels.)

CAPITOL (4000 series) 3-5   76
(Orange labels.)
COLONIAL ("What It Was—Was
Football") 15-25   53
(Number not known.)
COLUMBIA 5-10   72

EPs: 7-Inch 33/45rpm
CAPITOL 20-30   54-61

LPs: 10/12-Inch 33rpm
CAPITOL (872 "Face in the Crowd") . 35-50   57
(Soundtrack.)
CAPITOL (962 "Just for Laughs") ... 35-45   58
CAPITOL (1100 through 1600 series) 30-40   59-61
CAPITOL (2000 series) 15-25   64-67
COLUMBIA 5-10   72

GRIFFITH, Johnny, Inc.
Singles: 7-Inch
RCA 3-5   73

GRIM REAPER
Singles: 7-Inch
RCA/EBONY 2-4
RCA/EBONY/EVA-TONE 5-10   85
(Soundsheet. Promotional issue only.)
RCA 2-4   85
Picture Sleeves
RCA/EBONY 2-4
LPs: 10/12-Inch 33rpm
RCA 5-10   84-87

GRIN
Singles: 7-Inch
A&M 3-5   74
SPINDIZZY 3-5   71-72
THUNDER 3-5
LPs: 10/12-Inch 33rpm
A&M 8-10   73
COLUMBIA 5-10
SPINDIZZY 8-10   71-73
Member: Nils Lofgren.
Also see LOFGREN, Nils

GRINDERSWITCH
Singles: 7-Inch
ATCO 3-5   77-78
LPs: 10/12-Inch 33rpm
ATCO 8-10   77
CAPRICORN 8-10   74-76

GRISMAN, David
LPs: 10/12-Inch 33rpm
ROUNDER 5-8   83
WARNER 5-10   80-81
Also see GRAPPELLI, Stephane, and David Grisman

GROCE, Larry
Singles: 7-Inch
PEACEABLE 3-5   75
WARNER 3-5   75
LPs: 10/12-Inch 33rpm
DAYBREAK 8-10   71-72
WARNER 8-10   76

GROSS, Henry
Singles: 7-Inch
A&M 3-5   74-75
LIFESONG 3-5   76-78
LPs: 10/12-Inch 33rpm
ABC-PAR 8-10   71
A&M 8-10   73-75
CAPITOL 5-10   81
LIFESONG 8-10   76-78
Also see SHA NA NA

GROUND HOG
(Joe Richardson)
Singles: 7-Inch
GEMIGO 3-5   74

GROVE, Harry, Trio
Singles: 78rpm
LONDON 3-5   52
Singles: 7-Inch
LONDON 4-6   52
LPs: 10/12-Inch 33rpm
LONDON 10-20   52

GRUSIN, Dave
(Dave Grusin Quintet; Dave Grusin and the NY/LA Dream Band)
Singles: 7-Inch
DECCA 3-6   68-69
EPIC 4-8   63
WARNER 2-4   83
LPs: 10/12-Inch 33rpm
COLUMBIA 10-20   65
EPIC 15-25   62
GRP 5-10   80-89
POLYDOR 5-10   77
SHEFFIELD LAB 8-15   77-82
VERSATILE 5-10   78
Also see BISHOP, Stephen
Also see GALE, Eric
Also see RITENOUR, Lee

GUADALCANAL DIARY
LPs: 10/12-Inch 33rpm
ELEKTRA 5-10   86-89
Members: Rhett Crowe; Murray Attaway; John Poe; Jeff Walls.

GUARALDI, Vince
(Vince Guaraldi Trio)
Singles: 7-Inch
FANTASY 4-6   62-66
LPs: 10/12-Inch 33rpm
FANTASY (3200 series) 20-30   56-58
FANTASY (3300 series) 15-25   62-66
FANTASY (8000 series) 15-25   62
FANTASY (8300 series) 10-20   63-66
MFSL (112 "Jazz Impressions
of Black Orpheus") 20-40   84
WARNER 8-12   68-69

GUARD, Dave, and the Whiskeyhill Singers
Singles: 7-Inch
CAPITOL 4-8   62

LPs: 10/12–inch 33rpm

CAPITOL 15-20   62
   Members: Dave Guard; Cyrus Faryar; Judy Hensky; David
   "Buck" Wheat.
   Also see KINGSTON TRIO

GUCCI CREW II

LPs: 10/12–inch 33rpm

GUCCI 5-8   89

GUESS WHO

Singles: 7–inch

AMY 10-20   67
FONTANA 10-15   69
HILLTAK 3-5   78-79
RCA 3-6   69-76
SCEPTER (1295 "Shakin' All Over") .. 8-12   65
SCEPTER (12000 series) 10-20   65-66

Picture Sleeves

RCA 4-8   70

LPs: 10/12–inch 33rpm

HILLTAK 5-10   79
MGM 12-15   69
PICKWICK 8-10   72
PIP 8-10   71
PRIDE 8-10   73
RCA (Except "AYL1" and
  LSP-4000 series) 8-12   73-80
RCA ("AYL1" series) 5-10   80
RCA (4141 through 4830) 12-25   69-72
  (With "LSP" prefix.)
SCEPTER 8-10   73
SPRINGBOARD 8-10   72
WAND 12-15   69
   Members: Chad Allen; Burton Cummings; Randy Bachman;
   Domenic Troiano.
   Also see BACHMAN, Randy
   Also see CUMMINGS, Burton
   Also see WOLFMAN JACK

GUESS WHO / Discotays

Singles: 7–inch

SCEPTER (1295 "Shakin' All Over") . 15-20   65
   Also see GUESS WHO

GUIDRY, Greg

Singles: 7–inch

COLUMBIA 2-4   82

LPs: 10/12–inch 33rpm

COLUMBIA/BADLAND 5-10   82

GUITAR, Bonnie

Singles: 78rpm

DOT 3-6   57
4 STAR 3-6   56

Singles: 7–inch

ABC 3-5   74
COLUMBIA 3-5   72
DOLTON 5-10   59
DOT (15000 series) 8-12   57-59
DOT (16000 series) 4-6   66-67
FABOR 4-6   64
4 STAR 8-12   56

JERDEN 5-10   63
MCA 2-4   74
PARAMOUNT 3-5   70
RCA 10-20   61-62
RADIO 5-10   58

LPs: 10/12–inch 33rpm

CAMDEN 6-12   69
DOT (Except 3069) 10-15   59-68
DOT (3069 "Moonlight and Shadows") 15-20   57
HAMILTON 8-12   65
PARAMOUNT 8-12   70
PICKWICK 6-12   70

CRYING IN MY HEART
(Elton Anderson)
GUITAR SLIM

GUITAR SLIM
(Johnny Winter)

Singles: 7–inch

DIAMOND JIM (204 "Crying in
  My Heart") 75-100   62
  (Reissued as by Texas "Guitar" Slim.)
   Also see TEXAS "GUITAR" SLIM
   Also see WINTER, Johnny

GUNHILL ROAD

Singles: 7–inch

KAMA SUTRA 3-5   73
MERCURY 3-5   72

LPs: 10/12–inch 33rpm

KAMA SUTRA 8-10   72
MERCURY 8-10   71

GUNS 'N' ROSES

Singles: 7–inch

GEFFEN 2-4   88-89

Picture Sleeves

GEFFEN 2-4   88-89

EPs: 7–inch 33/45rpm

UZI SUICIDE ("Live Like a Suicide") . 50-75   86

LPs: 10/12–inch 33rpm

GEFFEN (Except 24148) 5-10   88-89
GEFFEN (24148 "Appetite
  for Destruction") 30-40   87
  (With robot/rape painting on cover.)

GEFFEN (24148 "Appetite
for Destruction") 5-8   87
(With skulls and cross cover.)

GUNTER, Shirley
(Shirley Gunter and the Flairs; Shirley Gunter and the
Queens)
Singles: 78rpm
FLAIR (Except 1076) 8-15   54-55
FLAIR (1076 "How Can I Tell You") .. 10-20   55
MODERN 5-10   56
Singles: 7–inch
FLAIR (Except 1076) 10-20
FLAIR (1076 "How Can I Tell You") .. 30-60   55
MODERN 10-20   56
TANGERINE 4-8   65
Member (Queens): Zola Taylor.

GURVITZ, Adrian
Singles: 7–inch
JET 3-5   79
Also see BAKER - GURVITZ ARMY
Also see EDGE, Graeme
Also see PARRISH & GURVITZ

GUTHRIE, Arlo
Singles: 7–inch
REPRISE 3-6   67-77
LPs: 10/12–inch 33rpm
REPRISE 8-10   67-76
U.A. 10-15   69
WARNER 5-10   77-81
Also see SEEGER, Pete, and Arlo Guthrie

GUTHRIE, Gwen
Singles: 12–inch 33/45rpm
GARAGE 4-6   85
ISLAND 4-6   83-85
Singles: 7–inch
GARAGE 2-4   85
ISLAND 2-4   82-85
POLYDOR 2-4   86-87
WARNER 2-4   88
Picture Sleeves
POLYDOR 2-4   86
LPs: 10/12–inch 33rpm
GARAGE 5-10   85
ISLAND 5-10   85
POLYDOR 5-8   86
Also see HOWARD, George
Also see LIMIT

GUY
Singles: 7–inch
UPTOWN 2-4   88-89

GUY, Bob
(Frank Zappa)
Singles: 7–inch
DONNA (1380 "Letter from Jeepers") 50-75   61
Also see ZAPPA, Frank

GUY, Buddy
(Buddy Guy and His Band)
Singles: 7–inch
ARTISTIC 10-15   58-59
CHESS 5-10   60-65
LPs: 10/12–inch 33rpm
BLUE THUMB 8-10   70
CHESS 10-12   69
VANGUARD 12-15   68
Also see WELLS, Junior, and Buddy Guy

GUY, Buddy, with Dr. John and Eric Clapton / Buddy Guy with the J. Geils Band
Singles: 7–inch
ATCO (6890 "A Man of Many Words") .. 4-8   72
Also see CLAPTON, Eric
Also see DR. JOHN
Also see GEILS, J., Band

GYPSIES
Singles: 7–inch
CAPRICE 4-8   66
OLD TOWN 4-8   64-66
Members: Betty Pearce; Ernestine Pearce; Shirley Pearce;
Lestine Johnson.

GYPSY
Singles: 7–inch
METROMEDIA 3-5   70
RCA 3-5   72
LPs: 10/12–inch 33rpm
METROMEDIA 8-10   70-71
RCA 8-10   72-73
Also see WALSH, James, Gypsy Band

H

HACKETT, Buddy
Singles: 78rpm
CORAL 3-5   53-56
Singles: 7–Inch
CORAL 5-10   53-56
LAUREL 4-8   60
LPs: 10/12–Inch 33rpm
CORAL 8-15   65
DOT 10-15   59

HACKETT, Steve
Singles: 7–inch
CHARISMA 2-4   80
CHRYSALIS 3-5   76-79
EPIC 2-4   81
LPs: 10/12–inch 33rpm
CHARISMA 5-10   80
CHRYSALIS 5-10   76-79
EPIC 5-10   81
  Also see GTR
  Also see GENESIS

HAGAR, Sammy
Singles: 7–inch
CAPITOL 3-5   76-79
COLUMBIA 2-4   87
GEFFEN (Except 29246) 2-4   82-87
GEFFEN (29246 "Two Sides of Love") . 2-4   84
  (Black vinyl.)
GEFFEN (29246 "Two Sides of Love") . 4-8   84
  (Colored vinyl.)
Picture Sleeves
CAPITOL 3-5   79
COLUMBIA 2-4   87
GEFFEN 2-4   82-87
LPs: 10/12–Inch 33rpm
CAPITOL 5-10   77-82
GEFFEN 5-10   82-87
  Also see MONTROSE
  Also see VAN HALEN

HAGAR, SCHON, AARONSON, SHRIEVE
Singles: 7–inch
GEFFEN 2-4   85
Picture Sleeves
GEFFEN 2-4   85
LPs: 10/12–Inch 33rpm
GEFFEN 5-10   84
  Members: Sammy Hagar; Neal Schon; Ken Aaronson; Michael
  Shrieve.
  Also see HAGAR, Sammy
  Also see SCHON, Neal, and Jan Hammer
  Also see SANTANA

HAGEN, Nina
(Nina Hagen Band)
Singles: 12–inch 33/45rpm
COLUMBIA 4-6   84-85
Singles: 7–inch
COLUMBIA 2-4   80-85
LPs: 10/12–inch 33rpm
COLUMBIA 5-10   80-83

HAGGARD, Merle
(Merle Haggard and the Strangers; Merle Haggard and
Bonnie Owens)
Singles: 7–inch
CAPITOL 3-8   65-77
COLUMBIA 2-4   83
EPIC 2-4   81-89
MCA 2-5   77-85
MERCURY 2-4   83
TALLY 10-20   63-65
Picture Sleeves
CAPITOL 4-8   67-71
MCA 2-5   77-80
EPs: 7–inch 33/45rpm
CAPITOL 8-15   71
  (Jukebox issues only.)
LPs: 10/12–Inch 33rpm
ALBUM GLOBE 5-10
CAPITOL (168 through 735) 8-15   69-71
  (With a "T," "ST," "STBB" or "SWBB" prefix.)
CAPITOL (168 through 735) 4-8   69-71
  (With "SKAO" or SM" prefix.)
CAPITOL (796 "Merle Haggard's Strangers
  and Friends Honky Tonkin'") 20-30   71
CAPITOL (803 "Land of Many
  Churches") 50-75   71
CAPITOL (823 "Truly the Best of
  Merle Haggard") 40-60   71
CAPITOL (835 "Someday We'll
  Look Back") 8-12   71
CAPITOL (882 "Let Me Tell You
  About a Song") 8-12   72

CAPITOL (2300 through 2900 series)	15-25	65-68
(With "T," "ST" or "SKAO" prefix.)		
CAPITOL (2700 through 2900 series)	.5-10	
(With "SM" prefix.)		
CAPITOL (11000 through 16000 series)	5-10	72-82
EPIC	5-10	81-86
MCA	4-8	77-84
MERCURY	5-10	83
PICKWICK/HILLTOP	8-12	
SONGBIRD	5-10	81

Also see ANDERSON, John

HAGGARD, Merle / Patsy Cline
LPs: 10/12–inch 33rpm

OUT of TOWN DIST	5-10	82

Also see CLINE, Patsy

HAGGARD, Merle, and Clint Eastwood
Singles: 7–inch

ELEKTRA	2-4	80

Picture Sleeves

ELEKTRA	2-4	80

Also see EASTWOOD, Clint

HAGGARD, Merle / Mickey Gilley / Willie Knight
LPs: 10/12–inch 33rpm

OUT of TOWN DIST	5-10	82

Also see GILLEY, Mickey

HAGGARD, Merle / Sonny James
LPs: 10/12–inch 33rpm

CAPITOL	12-15	

Also see JAMES, Sonny

HAGGARD, Merle, and George Jones
Singles: 7–inch

EPIC (03405 "C.C. Waterback")	2-4	82
EPIC (03405 "C.C. Waterback")	4-8	82
(Picture disc.)		

LPs: 10/12–inch 33rpm

EPIC	5-10	82

Also see JONES, George

HAGGARD, Merle, and Willie Nelson
Singles: 7–inch

EPIC	2-4	83

LPs: 10/12–inch 33rpm

EPIC	5-10	83

Also see NELSON, Willie

HAGGARD, Merle, and Johnny Paycheck
Singles: 7–inch

EPIC	2-4	81

Also see HAGGARD, Merle
Also see PAYCHECK, Johnny

HAHN, Carol
Singles: 12–inch 33/45rpm

NICKLE	4-6	83

HAHN, Joyce
Singles: 78rpm

CADENCE	3-5	57

Singles: 7–inch

CADENCE	4-8	57

HAIRCUT ONE HUNDRED
Singles: 7–inch

ARISTA	2-4	82

LPs: 10/12–inch 33rpm

ARISTA	5-10	82

Member: Nick Heyward.
Also see HEYWARD, Nick

HAIRSTON, Curtis
Singles: 12–inch 33/45rpm

PRETTY PEARL	4-6	83

Singles: 7–inch

ATLANTIC	2-4	87
PRETTY PEARL	2-4	84-85

HALEY, Bill
(Bill Haley and the Comets; Bill Haley and the Saddlemen; Bill Haley and His Saddle Men; Bill Haley and the Four Aces of Western Swing; Bill Haley with Reno Browne and Her Buckaroos)
Singles: 78rpm

ATLANTIC (727 "I'm Gonna Dry Ev'ry Tear with a Kiss")	250-350	50
COWBOY (1201 "Too Many Parties Too Many Pals")	300-400	48
COWBOY (1202 "Candy Kisses")	300-400	49
COWBOY (1203 "The Covered Wagon Rolled Right Along")	250-300	49
COWBOY (1204 "Behind the Eight Ball")	250-300	50
COWBOY (1205 "Candy Kisses")	200-300	50
COWBOY (1701 "Candy Kisses")	250-350	49
COWBOY (1701 "My Sweet Little Girl from Nevada")	250-350	49
(By Reno Browne and Her Buckaroos featuring Bill Haley. The Cowboy 1701 number is used twice.)		
DECCA (29124 "Rock Around the Clock")	50-100	54
(Black label with gold print.)		

DECCA (29124 "Rock Around
the Clock") 25-50   54
(Black label with silver print.)
DECCA (29204 "Shake, Rattle
and Roll") 50-80   54
(Black label with gold print.)
DECCA (29204 "Shake, Rattle
and Roll") 25-50   54
(Black label with silver print.)
DECCA (29317 through 30530) 15-30   54-57
DECCA (30592 through 30781) 20-40   58
DECCA (30844 "I Got a Woman") . . . 25-50   59
DECCA (30873 "A Fool Such As I") . . 40-60   59
DECCA (30926 "Caledonia") 50-75   59
DECCA (30956 "Ooh, Look-a-There
Ain't She Pretty") 50-100   59
ESSEX 15-25   52-55
HOLIDAY (105 "Rocket 88") 50-100   51
HOLIDAY (108 "Green Tree Boogie") 50-100   51
HOLIDAY (111 "A Year Ago This
Christmas") 50-100   51
HOLIDAY (113 "Jukebox
Cannonball") 50-100   51
KEYSTONE (5101 "Deal Me
a Hand") 250-350   50
KEYSTONE (5102 "Susan Van
Dusan") 250-350   50

Singles: 7–inch

APT (25081 "Burn That Candle") 15-20   65
APT (25087 "Haley A-Go-Go") 15-20   65
ARZEE 8-12   77
DECCA (29000 series) 20-35   54-56
(With silver lines on both sides of the name Decca.)
DECCA (29000 series) 10-20   54-56
(With a star and silver lines under the name
Decca.)
DECCA (30000 series) 10-20   56-59
DECCA (31000 series) 5-10   60-64
DECCA (72000 series) 4-6   69
Note: Essex 102, *Rock Around the Clock,* is a
bootleg.
ESSEX (303 "Rock the Joint") 500-750   52
(Colored vinyl.)
ESSEX (303 "Rock the Joint") 50-75   52
(Black vinyl.)
ESSEX (305 "Rocking Chair on
the Moon") 50-100   52
ESSEX (310 "Real Rock Drive") 50-100   52
ESSEX (321 "Crazy Man Crazy") 30-50   52
ESSEX (327 "Fractured") 30-40   53
ESSEX (332 "Live It Up") 25-35   53
ESSEX (340 "Ten Little Indians") 25-35   53
ESSEX (348 "Chattanooga
Choo-Choo") 20-30   54
ESSEX (374 "Jukebox Cannonball") . 40-60   54
ESSEX (381 "Rocket 88") 100-125   55
ESSEX (399 "Rock the Joint") 35-50   55
GONE (5111 "Spanish Twist") 15-25   61
GONE (5116 "Riviera") 15-25   61

HOLIDAY (105 "Rocket 88") 250-350   51
HOLIDAY (108 "Green Tree
Boogie") 250-350   51
HOLIDAY (111 "A Year Ago This
Christmas") 250-350   51
HOLIDAY (113 "Jukebox
Cannonball") 250-350   51
JANUS 8-12   71
JUKEBOX 2-4   90
KAMA SUTRA 5-10   70
KASEY 10-15   61
MCA 3-5   74-80
NEWTOWN (5013 "Tenor Man") 10-15   63
NEWTOWN (5014 "Midnight in
Washington") 10-15   63
NEWTOWN (5024 "Dance Around
the Clock") 10-15   63
NEWTOWN (5025 "Tandy") 10-15   63
OLD GOLD 3-5   82
RADIO ACTIVE 4-8   70
TRANSWORLD (200 and 300 series) 60-75   54
TRANSWORLD (718 "Real Rock
Drive") 50-75   53
U.A. 5-10   69
WARNER (5145 "Candy Kisses") . . . 10-20   60
WARNER (5154 "Chick Safari") 10-20   60
WARNER (5171 "So Right Tonight") . 10-20   60
WARNER (5228 "Flip, Flop and Fly") . 10-20   60
WARNER (7124 "Rock Around
the Clock") 8-12   68

Picture Sleeves

ARZEE 8-12   77
DECCA (30314 "Billy Goat") 40-60   57
DECCA (30530 "Mary, Mary Lou") . . . 25-35   58

EPs: 7–inch 33/45rpm

ARZEE (137 "Bill Haley Sings") 20-30   77
CLAIRE (4779 "Bill Haley and
the Comets") 15-20   78
DECCA (2168 "Shake, Rattle
and Roll") 40-60   54
DECCA (2209 "Dim, Dim the Lights") 40-60   55
DECCA (2322 "Rock and Roll") 40-60   56
DECCA (2398/2399/2400 "He Digs Rock
and Roll") 40-60   56
(Price is for any of three volumes.)
DECCA (2416/2417/2418 "Rock'n Roll
Stage Show") 40-50   56
(Price is for any of three volumes.)
DECCA (2532 "Rockin' the Oldies") . . 30-40   57
DECCA (2533 "Rock 'N' Roll Party") . 30-40   57
DECCA (2534 "Rockin' and Rollin") . . 30-40   57
DECCA (2564 "Rockin' Around the
World") 30-40   57
DECCA (2576 "Rockin' Around
Europe") 30-40   57
DECCA (2577 "Rockin' Around
the Americas") 30-40   57

DECCA (2615/2616 "Rockin' the
Joint") 30-40   58
(Price is for either of two volumes.)
DECCA (2638 "Bill Haley's Chicks") .. 30-40   58
DECCA (2670 "Bill Haley and
His Comets") 30-40   59
DECCA (2671 "Strictly Instrumental") 30-40   59
DECCA (72638 "Bill Haley's Chicks") . 50-75   59
(Stereo.)
DECCA (72670 "Bill Haley and
His Comets") 50-75   59
(Stereo.)
DECCA (72671 "Strictly Instrumental") 50-75   59
(Stereo.)
ESSEX (102 "Dance Party") 50-100   54
ESSEX (117/118/119 "Rock with Bill Haley
and the Comets") 50-100   54
(Price is for any of three volumes.)
SOMERSET (460 "Rock with Bill Haley
and the Comets") 40-60   55
TRANSWORLD (117/118/119 "Rock with Bill Haley
and the Comets") 50-100   54
(Price is for any of three volumes. May be titled *For
Your Dance Party*.)

LPs: 10/12–Inch 33rpm

ACCORD 5-10   81-82
ALSHIRE 8-10   79
AMBASSADOR 8-15   70-87
BUDDAH 5-10   84
CORAL 8-10   73
DECCA (5560 "Shake, Rattle
and Roll") 250-350   54
(10–inch LP.)
DECCA (7211 "Golden Hits") 12-18   72
DECCA (8225 "Rock Around
the Clock") 75-125   55
(All black label with silver print.)
DECCA (8225 "Rock Around
the Clock") 20-40   60
(Black label with rainbow color stripe. Reads
"M'F'D by Decca Records Inc. New York, U.S.A.")
DECCA (8225 "Rock Around
the Clock") 15-20   68
(Black label with rainbow color stripe. Reads "Mfr'd
by Decca Records, a Div. of MCA Inc. New York,
U.S.A.")
DECCA (8315 "He Digs Rock
and Roll") 50-100   56
DECCA (8345 "Rock'n Roll
Stage Show") 50-100   56
DECCA (8569 "Rockin' the Oldies") . 50-100   57
DECCA (8692 "Rockin' Around
the World") 50-75   58
DECCA (8775 "Rockin' the Joint") .. 50-75   58
DECCA (8821 "Bill Haley's
Chicks") 40-60   58
DECCA (8964 "Strictly Instrumental") 35-50   60
DECCA (75027 "Greatest Hits") 12-20   68

DECCA (78225 "Rock Around
the Clock") 50-75   59
(All black label with silver print.)
DECCA (78225 "Rock Around
the Clock") 50-75   59
(Black label with rainbow color stripe.)
DECCA (78692 "Rockin' Around
the World") 20-30   62
DECCA (78821 "Bill Haley's Chicks") 50-80   58
DECCA (78964 "Strictly Instrumental") 40-65   60
ESSEX (202 "Rock with Bill Haley and
the Comets") 200-300   54
EXACT 5-10   80
51 WEST 5-10   83
GNP/CRESCENDO 8-12   74-76
GREAT NORTHWEST 8-12   81
GUEST STAR 12-20   65
JANUS 8-12   72
JOKER 5-10   81
KAMA SUTRA (2014 "Bill Haley's
Scrapbook") 20-30   70
KAMA SUTRA (2014 "Bill Haley's
Scrapbook") 20-30   70
KOALA 8-10   79
MCA 6-10   73-88
PAIR 5-8   86
PHOENIX 5-10   81
PICKWICK 8-10   71-74
ROULETTE 15-20   62
SILHOUETTE 5-10   81
SOMERSET (1300 "Rock and Roll
Dance Party") 75-100   55
(Besides Bill Haley, has tracks by Bunny Paul and
the Harptones, Ken Carson, Dinning Sisters,
Swingers, Don Costa, Aristocrats, Escorts, and the
House Rockers.)
SOMERSET (4600 "Rock with Bill
Haley and the Comets") 75-125   55
SPRINGBOARD 8-10   77
SUN 10-15   80
TRANSWORLD (202 "Rock with Bill Haley
and the Comets") 200-300   56
VOCALION 15-25   63
WARNER (W-1378 "Bill Haley
and His Comets") 25-35   60
(Monaural.)
WARNER (WS-1378 "Bill Haley
and His Comets") 35-45   60
(Stereo.)
WARNER (W-1391 "Haley's
Jukebox") 25-35   60
(Monaural.)
WARNER (WS-1391 "Haley's
Jukebox") 35-45   60
(Stereo.)
Also see KINGSMEN
Also see LEE, Brenda / Bill Haley and the Comets / Kalin Twins
/ Four Aces
Also see LOPEZ, Trini / Scott Gregory

HALEY, Bill / Boots Randolph
Singles: 7–inch
LOGO (7005 "Yakety Sax") 8-12   61
  Also see HALEY, Bill
  Also see RANDOLPH, Boots

HALL, Daryl
(Daryl Hall with Gulliver)
Singles: 7–inch
AMY 4-8   69
CHELSEA 3-6   76
RCA 2-4   80-87
Picture Sleeves
RCA 2-4   80-86
LPs: 10/12–inch 33rpm
RCA 5-10   80-86
  Also see U.S.A. for AFRICA

HALL, Daryl, and Ruth Copeland
Singles: 7–inch
RCA 2-4   76
  Also see HALL, Daryl

HALL, Daryl, and John Oates
(Hall and Oates)
Singles: 12–inch 33/45rpm
RCA 4-8   78-85
Singles: 7–inch
ARISTA 2-4   88-90
ATLANTIC 3-5   72-77
CHELSEA 3-5   76
RCA 2-5   76-84
Picture Sleeves
ARISTA 2-4   88
RCA 2-5   77-85
Promotional Singles
RCA (Colored vinyl) 5-8   85
  (One side by Daryl Hall and one side by John
  Oates.)
LPs: 10/12–inch 33rpm
ARISTA 5-8   88-90
ATLANTIC 8-12   72-77
CHELSEA 10-12   76
MFSL (069 "Abandoned
  Luncheonette") 20-30   82
RCA (Black vinyl) 5-10   75-84
RCA (Colored vinyl) 10-12   78
Promotional LPs
RCA ("Special Radio Series") 15-25   81
  Also see PRINE, John / Daryl Hall and John Oates / Barnaby
  Bye / Delbert and Glen
  Also see WHOLE OATS

HALL, Daryl, John Oates, David Ruffin and Eddie Kendrick
Singles: 7–inch
RCA 2-4   85
Picture Sleeves
RCA 2-4   85
LPs: 10/12–inch 33rpm
RCA 5-8   85
  Also see KENDRICK, David
  Also see RUFFIN, David

HALL, Ellis, Jr.
Singles: 7–inch
H.C.R.C. 2-4   83

HALL, Jimmy
Singles: 7–inch
EPIC 3-5   80-82
LPs: 10/12–inch 33rpm
EPIC 5-10   80
  Also see BECK, Jeff
  Also see WET WILLIE

HALL, John
(John Hall Band)
Singles: 7–inch
ASYLUM 3-5   78
COLUMBIA 3-5   79
EMI AMERICA 2-4   81-83
LPs: 10/12–inch 33rpm
ASYLUM 5-10   78
COLUMBIA 8-10   70
EMI AMERICA 5-10   81-82
  Also see ORLEANS

HALL, Lani
Singles: 7–inch
A&M 2-5   71-85
Picture Sleeves
A&M 2-5   72-85
LPs: 10/12–inch 33rpm
A&M 5-10   72-85
  Also see MENDES, Sergio

HALL, Lani, and Herb Alpert
Singles: 7–inch
A&M 2-4   81
  Also see ALPERT, Herb
  Also see HALL, Lani

HALL, Larry
Singles: 7–inch
GOLD LEAF 4-8   62
HOT (1 "Sandy") 15-25   59
STRAND 5-10   59-62
LPs: 10/12–inch 33rpm
STRAND (1005 "Sandy") 40-50   60

HALL, Randy
Singles: 7–inch
MCA 2-4   84-88
LPs: 10/12–inch 33rpm
MCA 5-10   84

HALL, Tom T.
(Tom T. Hall and the Storytellers)
Singles: 7–inch
MERCURY (Except 70000 series) 2-4   77-86
MERCURY (70000 series) 3-6   67-77
RCA 2-5   77-81
LPs: 10/12–inch 33rpm
MERCURY (500 through 1100 series) . 5-10   73-77
MERCURY (5000 through 8000 series) 5-10   78-84
MERCURY (61000 series) 8-15   69-71
MERCURY (80000 series) 5-10   83-86

OUT of TOWN DIST 5-10   82
RCA 5-10   78-81
   Also see DUDLEY, Dave, and Tom T. Hall
   Also see PAGE, Patti, and Tom T. Hall

HALL, Tom T., and Earl Scruggs
Singles: 7–inch

COLUMBIA 2-4   82
LPs: 10/12–inch 33rpm
COLUMBIA 5-10   82
   Also see HALL, Tom T.
   Also see SCRUGGS, Earl

HALL & OATES:
see HALL, Daryl, and John Oates

HALLORAN, Jack, Singers
Singles: 7–inch
DOT 3-5   63

HALOS
Singles: 7–inch
7 ARTS 10-15   61
TRANS ATLAS 5-8   62
LPs: 10/12–inch 33rpm
WARWICK (2046 "The Halos") 50-100   62
   Member: Arthur Crier.
   Also see KING, Ben E.
   Also see LEE, Curtis
   Also see MANN, Barry

HAMILTON, Bobby
Singles: 7–inch
APT 8-12   58-59
DECCA 5-10   59
DIANA 5-10   59

HAMILTON, Chico
(Chico Hamilton Trio; Chico Hamilton Quartet; Chico Hamilton Quintet; Chico Hamilton and the Players)
Singles: 7–Inch
COLUMBIA 4-6   61
CORAL 4-6   62
ENTERPRISE 3-5   74
IMPULSE 4-6   64-67
PACIFIC JAZZ (600 series) 5-10   54-55
PACIFIC JAZZ (88000 series) 4-6   66
EPs: 7-Inch 33/45rpm
DECCA 15-25   57
PACIFIC JAZZ 20-40   55-56
LPs: 10/12-Inch 33rpm
BLUE NOTE 5-10   75
COLUMBIA 15-25   60-62
CROWN 10-20   63
DECCA (8614 "Jazz from Sweet
   Smell of Success") 25-40   57
DISCOVERY 5-8   81
ELEKTRA 5-8   80
EVEREST 5-8   79
FLYING DUTCHMAN 8-10   71
IMPULSE 10-20   63-71
INSTANT 10-20   64
MERCURY 5-10   77
ODYSSEY 10-20   68

PACIFIC JAZZ (17 "The Chico
   Hamilton Trio") 75-100   55
   (10–inch LP.)
PACIFIC JAZZ (39 "Spectacular!") . . 15-25   62
PACIFIC JAZZ (1209 "Chico
   Hamilton Quintet") 50-75   55
PACIFIC JAZZ (1216 "In Hi Fi") 50-75   56
PACIFIC JAZZ (1220 "Chico
   Hamilton Trio") 50-75   57
PACIFIC JAZZ (1225 "Chico
   Hamilton Quintet") 50-75   57
PACIFIC JAZZ (20000 series) 10-20   68
REPRISE 15-25   63
SESAC 35-55   59
   (Promotional issue only.)
SOLID STATE 10-15   68-69
SUNSET 8-15   68
WARNER (1245 "With Strings
   Attached") 50-75   58
WARNER (1271 "Goings East") 50-75   58
WARNER (1344 "Three Faces
   of Chico") 40-60   59
WORLD PACIFIC (1000 and
   1200 series) 25-40   58-60
   Also see ALMEIDA, Laurindo / Chico Hamilton

HAMILTON, Chico, and Charles Lloyd
LPs: 10/12-Inch 33rpm
COLUMBIA 10-15   68
   Also see HAMILTON, Chico
   Also see LLOYD, Charles, Quartet

HAMILTON, George, IV
(George Hamilton IV and the Country Gentlemen)
Singles: 78rpm
ABC-PAR 3-6   56-65
COLONIAL 8-12   56
Singles: 7–inch
ABC 2-4   78
ABC/DOT 2-4   77
ABC-PAR (9000 series) 10-20   56-59
ABC-PAR (10000 series) 5-10   59-65
COLONIAL (420 "A Rose and
   a Baby Ruth") 40-60   56
GRT 3-5   76
MCA 2-4   79-80
RCA 3-8   61-74
Picture Sleeves
ABC-PAR 10-15   65
EPs: 7–inch 33/45rpm
ABC-PAR 8-12   58
LPs: 10/12–inch 33rpm
ABC 8-10   72-77
ABC-PAR 25-40   58-63
CAMDEN 8-10   68-73
HARMONY 8-10   70
LAMB and LION 8-10   74
MCA 5-10   80
RCA ("APL1" series) 8-10   74-76
RCA ("LPM" and "LSP" series) 10-15   61-73
   Also see ANKA, Paul, George Hamilton IV and Johnny Nash

HAMILTON, George, IV, and Skeeter Davis
LPs: 10/12-inch 33rpm
RCA 10-12   70
  Also see DAVIS, Skeeter
  Also see HAMILTON, George, IV

HAMILTON, Roy
Singles: 78rpm
EPIC 3-5   54-57
Singles: 7-inch
AGP 4-8   69
CAPITOL 4-8   67
EPIC 8-15   54-62
MGM 5-10   63-65
RCA 5-10   65-67
Picture Sleeves
EPIC 5-10   60-62
EPs: 7-inch 33/45rpm
EPIC 10-20   55-59
LPs: 10/12-inch 33rpm
EPIC (Except 1103) 10-25   57-67
EPIC (1103 "The Voice of
  Roy Hamilton") 30-40   55
  (10-inch LP.)
MGM 10-20   63-64
RCA 10-20   66

HAMILTON, Russ
Singles: 78rpm
KAPP 4-8   57
Singles: 7-inch
KAPP 5-10   57-64
MGM 4-8   60
LPs: 10/12-inch 33rpm
KAPP (1076 "Rainbow") 45-55   57

HAMILTON, JOE FRANK & DENNISON
Singles: 7-inch
PLAYBOY 3-5   76-77
Picture Sleeves
PLAYBOY 3-5   76
LPs: 10/12-inch 33rpm
PLAYBOY 8-10   76-77
Members: Dan Hamilton; Joe Frank Carollo; Alan Dennison.

HAMILTON, JOE FRANK & REYNOLDS
Singles: 7-inch
ABC 3-5   72
DUNHILL 3-5   71
PLAYBOY 3-5   75-76
Picture Sleeves
PLAYBOY 3-5   76
LPs: 10/12-inch 33rpm
DUNHILL 8-10   71-72
PLAYBOY 8-10   75-77
Members: Dan Hamilton; Joe Frank Carollo; Tom Reynolds.
  Also see HAMILTON, JOE FRANK & DENNISON
  Also see T-BONES

HAMLISCH, Marvin
Singles: 12-inch 33/45rpm
U.A. 4-6   77

Singles: 7-inch
A&M 3-5   74-76
ARISTA 2-4   79
MCA 2-5   74-83
PLANET 2-4   80
U.A. 2-4   71-77
LPs: 10/12-inch 33rpm
MCA 5-10   74
SOUTHERN CROSS 5-10   83

HAMMEL, Karl, Jr.
Singles: 7-inch
ARLISS (1007 "Summer Souvenirs") . 10-20   61
ARLISS (1011 "Sittin' Alphabetically") 30-40   61
LAURIE 5-10   63
20TH FOX 4-8   66

HAMMER, Jan
(Jan Hammer Group)
Singles: 12-inch 33/45rpm
MCA 4-6   85
Singles: 7-inch
ASYLUM 2-4   79
MCA 2-4   85
NEMPEROR 3-5   76-78
LPs: 10/12-inch 33rpm
ECM 5-10
MPS 5-10   76
NEMPEROR 5-10   74-86
VANGAURD 5-10   77
  Also see BECK, Jeff
  Also see GOODMAN, Jerry, and Jan Hammer
  Also see SCHON, Neal, and Jan Hammer

HAMMER, M.C.
(Hammer)
Singles: 7-inch
CAPITOL 2-4   88-90
LPs: 10/12-inch 33rpm
CAPITOL 5-8   88-90

HAMMOND, Albert
Singles: 7-inch
EPIC 3-5   76
MUMS 3-5   72-75
LPs: 10/12-inch 33rpm
COLUMBIA 5-10   81-82
EPIC 8-10   77
MUMS 8-10   72-74
  Also see MAGIC LANTERNS
  Also see SPRINGSTEEN, Bruce / Albert Hammond / Loudon
  Wainwright, III / Taj Mahal

HAMPSHIRE, Keith
(Keith Hampshire and the Ladys)
Singles: 7-inch
A&M 3-5   72-74
RCA 3-5   71

HAMPTON, Lionel
Singles: 7-inch
CLEF 4-8   55
BRUNSWICK 3-5   74

COLUMBIA 3-4   76
DECCA (Except 140 and 154) 50-53
DECCA (140 "Moonglow") 15-25   51
(Four disc boxed set)
DECCA (154 "Just Jazz") 15-25   53
(Four disc boxed set)
GLAD HAMP 4-6   60-67
IMPULSE 3-6   65
MGM 4-8   51-61
NORGREN 4-6   56

EPs: 7–inch 33/45rpm

CLEF 10-30   53-56
COLUMBIA 8-15   56
DECCA 8-15   51-53
EMARCY 8-12   56
EPIC 8-12   56
GLAD HAMP 5-10   62
MGM 10-20   56
MERCURY 8-15   55
NORGREN 10-30   55
RCA 8-15   54-57

LPs: 10/12–inch 33rpm

AMERICAN RECORDING SOCIETY (403
"Swinging Jazz") 75-100   56
(Includes booklet.)
AUDIO FIDELITY 15-25   57-59
BLUENOTE (5046 "Rockin' and
Groovin") 75-100   53
(10–inch LP.)
BRUNSWICK 74
CAMDEN (400 and 500 series) 15-25   58-59
CLEF (142 "Lionel Hampton Quartet") 50-75   53
(10–inch LP.)
CLEF (611 "Lionel Hampton Quartet") 40-60   53
CLEF (628 "Lionel Hampton Quintet") 40-60   54
CLEF (642 "Lionel Hampton Quintet") 40-60   54
CLEF (667 "Quartet/Quintet") 40-60   55
CLEF (670 "Big Band") 40-60   55
CLEF (673 "Big Band") 40-60   55
CLEF (735 "Flying Home") 40-60   56
CLEF (736 "Swingin' with Hamp") ... 40-60   56
CLEF (744 "Hamp's Big Four") 40-60   56
CLEF (709 "Lionel Hampton Trio") ... 40-60   56
COLUMBIA (711 "Wailin at
the Trianon") 35-45   56
COLUMBIA (1304 through 1661) 15-25   59-61
(Monaural.)
COLUMBIA (8110 through 8461) 20-30   59-61
(Stereo.)
CONTEMPORARY (3502 "Lionel Hampton
Swings in Paris") 40-60   55
CORAL 15-25   63
DECCA (4000 series) 20-30   61-63
(Monaural.)
DECCA (7-4000 series) 20-30   61-63
(Stereo.)
DECCA (5320 "Boogie Woogie") 40-60   51
(10–inch LP.)

DECCA (7013 "Just Jazz") 30-50   53
(10–inch LP.)
DECCA (8200 series) 25-35   56
DECCA (9000 series) 20-30   58
DECCA (79000 series) 10-15   69
EMARCY (26037 "In Paris") 40-60   53
(10–inch LP.)
EMARCY (26038 "Crazy Hamp") 40-60   53
(10–inch LP.)
EMARCY (36032 "In Paris") 30-40   53
EMARCY (36034 "Crazy Hamp") 30-40   56
EPIC (3190 "Lionel Hampton Apollo
Hall Concert 1954") 40-50   56
EPIC (16027 "Many Splendored
Vibes") 20-30   62
(Monaural.)
EPIC (17027 "Many Splendored
Vibes") 25-35   62
(Stereo.)
GENE NORMAN PRESENTS (15 "Lionel
Hampton with the Jazz All Stars") .. 40-60   57
GLAD HAMP (1001 through 1009) .. 10-20   61-65
GLAD HAMP (1020 and 1021) 5-10   80
GLAD HAMP (3000 series) 10-20   62
HARMONY (7000 series) 15-25   58-61
HARMONY (32000 series) 5-10   73
IMPULSE 15-25   65
LAURIE 5-10   78
MCA 5-8   75-82
MGM (285 "Oh Rock") 50-75   51
(10–inch LP.)
MGM (3386 "Oh Rock") 25-35   56
MUSE 5-8   79
NORGREN (1080 "Lionel Hampton
and His Giants") 50-75   55
PERFECT (12002 "Hampton Swings") 30-50   59
RCA (1000 "Hot Mallets") 40-60   54
RCA (1422 "Jazz Flamenco")30-40 57
RCA (LPM-2318 "Swing Classics") .. 25-30   61
(Monaural.)
RCA (LSP-2318 "Swing Classics") .. 30-35   61
(Stereo.)
RCA (3900 series) 10-15   68
RCA (5536 "The Complete
Lionel Hampton") 50-60   76
(Six LP boxed set.)
SUTRA 5-10   81
VERVE (2018 "Lionel Hampton
Plays Love Songs") 40-50   56
VERVE (2500 series) 5-10   82
VERVE (8019 through 8228) 20-35   57-58
WHO'S WHO in JAZZ 78-81

HAMPTON, Lionel and Stan Getz
LPs: 10/12–inch 33rpm
NORGREN (1037 "Hamp and Getz") 75-100   55
VERVE (8128 "Hamp and Getz") 40-60   57
Also see GETZ, Stan

HAMPTON, Lionel and Dinah Washington
LPs: 10/12-inch 33rpm
DECCA (8088 "All American
Award Concert") 40-60   54
   Also see HAMPTON, Lionel
   Also see WASHINGTON, Dinah

HANCOCK, Herbie
Singles: 12-inch 33/45rpm
COLUMBIA 4-6   79-85
Singles: 7-inch
BLUE NOTE 3-6   62-65
COLUMBIA 2-5   74-88
WARNER 3-5   69-72
LPs: 10/12-inch 33rpm
BLUE NOTE 15-25   62-65
   (Label reads "Blue Note Records Inc. - New York,
   U.S.A.")
BLUE NOTE 8-15   66-71
   (Label shows Blue Note Records as a division of
   either Liberty or United Artists.)
COLUMBIA 6-12   67-85
WARNER 8-15   70-74
   Also see SANTANA
   Also see SUMMERS, Bill

HANCOCK, Herbie, and Willie Bobo
LPs: 10/12-inch 33rpm
BLUE NOTE 5-10   73
   Also see BOBO, Willie
   Also see HANCOCK, Herbie

HANCOCK, Herbie, and Chick Corea
LPs: 10/12-inch 33rpm
COLUMBIA 5-10   79
POLYDOR 8-10   79
   Also see COREA, Chick
   Also see HANCOCK, Herbie

HANDY, John
(John Handy Quartet; John Handy Quintet)
Singles: 7-inch
IMPULSE 3-5   76-77
COLUMBIA 4-6   66-69
LPs: 10/12-inch 33rpm
IMPULSE 5-10   76-77
COLUMBIA 10-15   66-68
RCA 10-15   67
ROULETTE (52000 series) 15-25   60
ROULETTE (52100 series) 10-15   66-67
WARNER 5-10   78

HANDY, John, III
LPs: 10/12-inch 33rpm
ROULETTE (100 series) 5-10   76
ROULETTE (52000 series) 15-25   60
ROULETTE (52100 series) 10-20   66-67

HANSON & DAVIS
Singles: 12-inch 33/45rpm
FRESH 4-6   85-86
Singles: 7-inch
FRESH 2-4   86

HANSSON, Bo
Singles: 7-inch
CHARISMA 3-5   73
SIRE 3-5   76-77
LPs: 10/12-inch 33rpm
FAMOUS CHARISMA 8-10   72-73
PVC 5-10   79
SIRE 8-10   76-77

HAPPENINGS
Singles: 7-inch
ABC 2-4   73
B.T. PUPPY 4-8   66-69
BIG TREE 3-5   72
JUBILEE 3-6   69-71
MIDLAND INT'L 3-5   77
MUSICORE 3-5   72
VIRGO 2-4   72
Picture Sleeves
B.T. PUPPY (532 "Why Do Fools
Fall in Love") 5-10   67
LPs: 10/12-inch 33rpm
B.T. PUPPY (1001 "Happenings") ... 15-25   66
B.T. PUPPY (1003 "Psycle") 15-25   67
B.T. PUPPY (1004 "Golden Hits") ... 25-35   68
JUBILEE (8028 "Piece of Mind") 15-20   69
JUBILEE (8030 "Greatest Hits") 15-20   69
   Member: Bob Miranda; Tom Guliano; Ralph DeVito; Dave Libert;
   Bernie Laporte; Mike LaNeue.
   Also see TOKENS / Happenings

HARBOR, Pearl: see PEARL HARBOR

HARD TIMES
Singles: 7-inch
WORLD PACIFIC 5-10   66-68
LPs: 10/12-inch 33rpm
WORLD PACIFIC 15-25   66-68
   Also see STEPPENWOLF

HARDCASTLE, Paul
Singles: 12-inch 33/45rpm
CHRYSALIS 4-6   85-86
PROFILE 4-6   84
Singles: 7-inch
CHRYSALIS 2-4   85-86
PROFILE. 2-4   84-85
Picture Sleeves
CHRYSALIS 2-4   85
LPs: 10/12-inch 33rpm
CHRYSALIS 5-10   86
PROFILE. 5-10   85

HARDEN TRIO
Singles: 7-inch
COLUMBIA 2-4   65-68
PAPA JOE 2-4   72
LPs: 10/12-inch 33rpm
COLUMBIA 10-15   66-68
HARMONY 8-12   70
   Members: Arlene Harden; Bobby Harden; Robbie Harden.

HARDIN, Tim
Singles: 7–inch

COLUMBIA 3-5	69-72
VERVE/FOLKWAYS 3-5	66-70
VERVE/FORECAST 3-5	67-71

LPs: 10/12–inch 33rpm

ATCO 8-15	67
COLUMBIA 6-12	69-81
MGM 6-10	70-74
POLYDOR 5-10	81
VERVE/FORECAST 10-15	66-69

HARDLY WORTHIT PLAYERS
(Featuring Senator Bobby and Senator McKinley)
Singles: 7–inch

PARKWAY 4-8	67

LPs: 10/12–inch 33rpm

PARKWAY 10-20	66-67
Also see SENATOR BOBBY	

HARDY, Hagood
Singles: 7–inch

CAPITOL 3-5	75-78
HERITAGE 3-5	71

LPs: 10/12–inch 33rpm

CAPITOL 4-8	75-76

HARDY BOYS
Singles: 7–inch

RCA 3-5	69-70

LPs: 10/12–inch 33rpm

RCA 8-10	69-70

HAREWOOD, Dorian
Singles: 7–inch

EMERIC 2-4	88

LPs: 10/12–inch 33rpm

EMERIC 5-8	88

HARLEM RIVER DRIVE
(Harlem River Drive Featuring Eddie Palmieri)
Singles: 7–inch

ARISTA 3-5	75
ROULETTE 3-5	70-72

LPs: 10/12–inch 33rpm

ROULETTE 8-10	71
TICO 5-10	72
Members: Eddie Palmieri; Jimmy Norman.	
Also see NORMAN, Jimmy	

HARLEY, Steve
(Steve Harley and Cockney Rebel)
Singles: 7–inch

CAPITOL 3-5	78
EMI 3-5	75-77

LPs: 10/12–inch 33rpm

CAPITOL 5-10	78
EMI 5-10	75-77

HARMONICATS
(Jerry Murad's Harmonicats)
Singles: 78rpm

MERCURY 3-5	50-57

Singles: 7–inch

COLUMBIA 3-5	61-67
MERCURY 4-8	50-60

Picture Sleeves

COLUMBIA 5-10	60

EPs: 7–inch 33/45rpm

MERCURY 5-10	50-61

LPs: 10/12–inch 33rpm

COLUMBIA 8-15	61-67
HARMONY 5-10	66
MERCURY 5-15	50-69
WING 5-10	59-64
Members: Jerry Murad; Al Fiore; Don Les.	

HARNELL, Joe
(Joe Harnell and His Orchestra; Joe Harnell and His Trio)
Singles: 7–inch

COLUMBIA 3-5	66-68
EPIC 3-6	59-60
KAPP 3-5	61-65
MCA 2-4	78
MEDALLION 3-5	61-62
MOTOWN 3-5	69-70

Picture Sleeves

KAPP 4-8	63

LPs: 10/12–inch 33rpm

CAPITOL 5-8	77
COLUMBIA 5-10	66
EPIC 5-15	59-63
KAPP 5-15	63-66
MEDALLION 5-15	61
MOTOWN 5-10	70

HARNEY, Ben, and Sheryl Lee Ralph
Singles: 7–inch

GEFFEN 2-4	83

HAROLD, Prince: see PRINCE HAROLD

HARPER, Janice
Singles: 7–inch

CAPITOL 5-10	58-60
PREP 5-10	57
RCA 4-6	66

LPs: 10/12–inch 33rpm

CAPITOL 15-20	58-60

HARPERS BIZARRE
Singles: 7–inch

FOREST BAY CO 3-5	76
WARNER 3-6	67-72

EPs: 7–inch 33/45rpm

WARNER 4-8	68
(Jukebox issues only.)	

LPs: 10/12–inch 33rpm

FOREST BAY CO 8-10	76
WARNER 10-20	67-68
Members: Ted Templeman; John Petersen; Dick Yount; Dick	
Scoppettone; John Peterson.	

HARPO, Slim
Singles: 78rpm
EXCELLO 4-8   57
Singles: 7–inch
ABC 2-4   73
EXCELLO (2100 series, except 2113) . 5-10   59-61
EXCELLO (2113 "I'm a King Bee") 8-12   57
EXCELLO (2200 series) 4-6   62-68
EXCELLO (2300 series) 3-5   69-71
LPs: 10/12–inch 33rpm
EXCELLO (Except 8003 and 8005) . . 10-20   68-70
EXCELLO (8003 "Raining in My
Heart") 30-50   61
EXCELLO (8005 "Baby, Scratch
My Back") 20-30   66

HARPTONES
(Harp-Tones)
Singles: 78rpm
ANDREA 10-20   56
BRUCE 15-25   53-55
GEE 10-20   57
PARADISE 20-30   56
RAMA 10-20   56-57
TIP TOP 10-20   56
Singles: 7–inch
AMBIENT SOUND 4-6   82
ANDREA (100 "What Is Your
Decision") 20-30   56
(With chain-like horizontal lines.)
ANDREA (100 "What Is Your
Decision") 15-25   56
(With straight horizontal lines.)
BRUCE (101 "A Sunday Kind
of Love") 300-500   53
("Bruce" in script lettering.)
BRUCE (101 "A Sunday Kind
of Love") . . . . :. . . 25-50   53
("Bruce" in block lettering.)
BRUCE (102 "My Memories of You") . 25-50   54
(With straight horizontal lines.)
BRUCE (102 "My Memories of You") . 10-15   54
(With jagged horizontal lines.)
BRUCE (104 "I Depended on You") . . 40-60   54
BRUCE (109 "Forever Mine") 30-60   54
(With the Shytans.)
BRUCE (113 "Since I Fell for You") . . 30-50   54
BRUCE (128 "I Almost Lost My Mind") 30-50   55
COED (540 "Answer Me My Love") . . 10-15   60
COMPANION (102 "All in Your Mind") 20-25   61
COMPANION (103 "Foolish Me") 20-30   61
CUB (9097 "Devil in Velvet") 10-15   61
GEE (1045 "Cry Like I Cried") 15-25   57
KT (201 "Sunset") 20-30   63
PARADISE (101 "Life Is But
a Dream") 50-75   56
(Maroon label.)

PARADISE (101 "Life Is But
a Dream") 20-30   56
(Purple label.)
PARADISE (103 "My Success") 50-75   56
PARADISE (103 "It All Depends
on You") 50-75   56
(Maroon label.)
PARADISE (103 "It All Depends
on You") 20-30   56
(Purple label.)
RAMA (203 "Three Wishes") 20-30   56
RAMA (214 "The Masquerade
Is Over") 20-30   56
RAMA (221 "The Shrine of
Saint Cecilia") 20-30   57
RAVEN (8001 "Sunday Kind of Love") 10-15   62
ROULETTE 3-5   71
TIP TOP (401 "My Memories of You") 25-35   56
WARWICK (512 "Love Me
Completely") 15-25   59
WARWICK (551 "No Greater
Miracle") 15-25   59
EPs: 7–inch 33/45rpm
BRUCE (201 "The Sensational
Harptones") 5000-10000   54
LPs: 10/12–inch 33rpm
AMBIENT SOUND (37718 "Love
Needs") 8-12   82
HARLEM HITPARADE (5006 "The
Harptones") 10-15
RARE BIRD 8-10
RELIC 8-10
Members: Willie Winfield; Nicky Clark; Bill Brown; Bill Dempsey;
Bill Galloway; Raoul Cita; Jimmy Beckum; Lynn Daniels; Vicki
Burgess; Margaret Moore; Fred Taylor.

HARPTONES / Cleftones
Singles: 7–inch
ROULETTE 2-4
Also see CLEFTONES

HARPTONES / Crows
LPs: 10/12–inch 33rpm
ROULETTE 15-20   72
Also see CROWS

HARPTONES / Paragons
LPs: 10/12–inch 33rpm
MUSICNOTE 20-30   64
Also see HARPTONES
Also see PARAGONS

HARRELL, Grady
Singles: 7–inch
MCA 3-5   85

HARRIS, Betty
Singles: 7–inch
JUBILEE 8-10   63-69
PROM 2-4
SSS INT'L 3-6   69
SANSU 4-8   66-68

HARRIS, Bobby
Singles: 7-inch
ATLANTIC 4-8   65
Also see LUNDY, Pat, and Bobby Harris

HARRIS, Brenda Jo
Singles: 7-inch
ROULETTE 4-6   68

HARRIS, Damon
Singles: 12-inch 33/45rpm
WMOT 4-6   78-79
Singles: 7-inch
WMOT 3-5   78-79
LPs: 10/12-inch 33rpm
WMOT 5-10   78
Also see IMPACT
Also see TEMPTATIONS

HARRIS, David
Singles: 7-inch
PLEASURE 3-5   74

HARRIS, Eddie
Singles: 7-inch
ABC 3-5   73
ATLANTIC 3-6   65-77
COLUMBIA 4-6   64
VEE JAY 5-8   61-63
WARNER 2-4   81
LPs: 10/12-inch 33rpm
ANGELACO 5-10   81
ATLANTIC 6-12   65-81
BUDDAH 8-12   69
COLUMBIA 10-20   64-68
CRUSADERS 5-10   82
GNP/CRESCENDO 5-10   73
HARMONY 5-10   72
RCA 5-10   78
SUNSET 5-10   69
TRIP 5-10   73
VEE JAY (3016 through 3028) 20-35   61-62
VEE JAY (3031 through 3034) 15-25   63
Also see McCANN, Les, and Eddie Harris

HARRIS, Eddie, and John Klemmer
LPs: 10/12-inch 33rpm
CRUSADERS 5-8   82
Also see HARRIS, Eddie
Also see KLEMMER, John

HARRIS, Emmylou
(Emmylou Harris and the Hot Band)
Singles: 7-inch
JUBILEE 5-10   69-70
REPRISE (Except 1341) 3-5   75-77
REPRISE (1341 "Light of the Stable") .. 4-6   75
WARNER 2-5   77-86
Picture Sleeves
REPRISE 3-5   75-77
WARNER 2-4   80-86
LPs: 10/12-inch 33rpm
EMUS 10-15   79

JUBILEE (8031 "Gliding Bird") 60-80   69
MFSL (015 "Quarter Moon
   in a Ten-Cent Town") 30-40   78
REPRISE 8-10   75
WARNER 5-10   77-87
Members: James Burton; Glen D. Hardin; Emory Gordy; Ronnie
Tutt.
Also see ANDERSON, John
Also see CRICKETS
Also see DENVER, John
Also see EVERLY, Don
Also see LITTLE FEAT
Also see ORBISON, Roy, and Emmylou Harris / Craig Hundley
Also see OWENS, Buck, and Emmylou Harris
Also see PARSONS, Gram
Also see PARTON, Dolly
Also see PARTON, Dolly, Linda Ronstadt, and Emmylou Harris
Also see PRESLEY, Elvis
Also see RONSTADT, Linda, and Emmylou Harris
Also see TUCKER, Tanya
Also see WINCHESTER, Jesse
Also see YOUNG, Neil

HARRIS, Gene
(Gene Harris and the Three Sounds)
Singles: 7-inch
BLUE NOTE 3-5   71-77
LPs: 10/12-inch 33rpm
BLUE NOTE 5-10   71-77

HARRIS, Huey "Baby"
Singles: 7-inch
PROFILE 2-4   85

HARRIS, Major
Singles: 7-inch
ATLANTIC 3-5   75-76
OKEH 3-6   69
POP ART 2-4   83
WMOT 3-5   76-81
LPs: 10/12-inch 33rpm
ATLANTIC 8-10   75
RCA 5-10   78
WMOT 8-10   76
Also see DELFONICS

HARRIS, Peppermint:
see PEPPERMINT HARRIS

HARRIS, Phil
Singles: 78rpm
ARA 4-8   46
RCA 3-6   50-54
Singles: 7-inch
COLISEUM 3-5   68
MEGA 2-4   73
MONTCLARE 2-4   76
RCA 5-10   50-54
REPRISE 3-5   62
VISTA 3-5   67-70
Picture Sleeves
MONTCLARE 3-5   76
EPs: 7-inch 33/45rpm
RCA 5-10   53-60

LPs: 10/12–inch 33rpm

CAMDEN 8-12	63
MEGA 5-10	72-74
RCA (1900 series) 10-20	59
RCA (3000 series) 20-30	53-54
ZODIAC 5-10	77
Also see BELL SISTERS	

HARRIS, Richard

Singles: 7–inch

ATLANTIC 3-5	74-75
DUNHILL 3-6	68-75

Picture Sleeves

DUNHILL (Except 4134) 4-6	72
DUNHILL (4134 "MacArthur Park") 3-6	68
DUNHILL (4134 "MacArthur Park") . . . 8-12	68
(Specially printed promotional sleeve.)	

EPs: 7–inch 33/45rpm

DUNHILL 4-6	68
(Jukebox issues only.)	

LPs: 10/12–inch 33rpm

ATLANTIC 6-10	74-75
DUNHILL 8-15	68-73

HARRIS, Rolf

Singles: 7–inch

EPIC (Except 9721) 4-8	63-66
EPIC (9721 "Ringo for President") . . . 10-15	64
MGM 3-5	70
20TH FOX 8-12	60-61

Picture Sleeves

EPIC 8-12	63-64

LPs: 10/12–inch 33rpm

EPIC 20-30	63-64

HARRIS, Sam

Singles: 12–inch 33/45rpm

MOTOWN 4-6	84-86

Singles: 7–inch

MOTOWN 2-4	84-86

Picture Sleeves

MOTOWN 2-4	84-86

LPs: 10/12–inch 33rpm

MOTOWN 5-10	84-86

HARRIS, Thurston

(Thurston Harris and the Sharps)

Singles: 78rpm

ALADDIN 4-6	57

Singles: 7–inch

ALADDIN 10-15	57-61
CUB 4-8	62
DOT 4-8	62-63
IMPERIAL 4-8	63
REPRISE 4-8	64

HARRIS, Tony

Singles: 78rpm

EBB 5-10	56-57

Singles: 7–inch

EBB 10-15	56-57

HARRIS, Wynonie

(Wynonie Harris and Lucky Millinder)

Singles: 78rpm

ALADDIN 10-20	47
APOLLO 10-20	45-46
BULLET 10-20	46
HAMP-TONE 10-20	45
KING 10-20	47-57
PHILO 10-20	45

Singles: 7–inch

KING (4210 "Good Rockin' Tonight") . 50-75	52
KING (4461 "Bloodshot Eyes") 50-75	51
KING (4468 "I'll Never Give Up") 50-75	51
KING (4485 "Lovin' Machine") 50-75	51
(Black vinyl.)	
KING (4485 "Lovin' Machine") 200-250	51
(Colored vinyl.)	
KING (4507 "My Playful Baby's Gone")50-75	51
KING (4526 "Keep on Churnin'") 50-75	52
KING (4555 "Night Train") 50-75	52
KING (4565 "Adam Come and	
Get Your Rib") 50-75	52
KING (4592 "Rot Gut") 50-75	52
KING (4593 "Bad News, Baby") 50-75	52
KING (4620 "Wasn't That Good") 40-60	53
KING (4635 "The Deacon Don't	
Like It") 40-60	53
KING (4668 "Please, Louise") 40-60	53
KING (4685 "Quiet Whiskey") 40-60	53
KING (4716 "Shake That Thing") 40-60	54
KING (4724 "Don't Take My Whiskey	
Away from Me") 40-60	54
KING (4763 "Christina") 25-40	54
KING (4774 "Good Mambo Tonight") . 25-40	54
KING (4789 "Mr. Dollar") 25-40	54
KING (4814 "Drinkin' Sherry Wine") . . 25-40	54
KING (4826 "Wine, Wine,	
Sweet Wine") 25-40	54
KING (4839 "Shotgun Wedding") 25-40	54
KING (4900 and 5000 series) 15-25	56-57
KING (5050 "Big Old Country Fool") . 10-20	57
KING (5073 "There's No Substitute	
for Love") 10-20	57
KING (5100 through 5400 series) 5-10	58-60
ROULETTE 4-8	60

EPs: 7–inch 33/45rpm

KING (260 "Wynonie Harris") 300-400	54

LPs: 10/12–inch 33rpm

KING (1086 "Good Rockin' Blues") . . 10-15	72
Also see MILBURN, Amos / Wynonie Harris / Crown Prince Waterford	
Also see MILLINDER, Lucky, and His Orchestra	

HARRIS, Wynonie / Roy Brown

LPs: 10/12–inch 33rpm

KING (607 "Battle of the Blues") . . 100-200	58
KING (627 "Battle of	
the Blues, Vol. 2") 100-200	58

HARRIS, Wynonie / Roy Brown / Eddie Vinson
LPs: 10/12–inch 33rpm
KING (668 "Battle of
the Blues, Vol. 4") 200-300   60
Also see BROWN, Roy
Also see HARRIS, Wynonie

HARRISON, Don, Band
Singles: 7–inch
ATLANTIC 4-8   76
MERCURY 4-8   77
LPs: 10/12–inch 33rpm
ATLANTIC 8-10   76
MERCURY 8-10   77
Members: Don Harrison; Doug Clifford; Stu Cook.
Also see CREEDENCE CLEARWATER REVIVAL.

HARRISON, George
Singles: 12–inch 33/45rpm
DARK HORSE (949 "All Those
Years Ago") 25-30   81
(Promotional issue only. Includes title sleeve.)
DARK HORSE (1075 "Wake Up My
Love") 20-25   82
(Promotional issue only. Includes title sleeve.)
DARK HORSE (2845 "Got My Mind
Set on You") 15-20   87
(Promotional issue only. Includes picture cover.)
DARK HORSE (2885 "When We
Was Fab") 15-20   88
(Promotional issue only.)
DARK HORSE (2889 "Devil's Radio") 15-20   87
(Promotional issue only. Includes picture cover.)
Singles: 7–inch
APPLE (1828 "What Is Life") 4-6   71
APPLE (1836 "Bangla Desh") 4-6   71
APPLE (1862 "Give Me Love") 4-6   73
APPLE (1877 "Dark Horse") 4-6   74
APPLE (1879 "Ding Dong Ding Dong") . 4-6   74
APPLE (1884 "You") 3-5   75
APPLE (1885 "This Guitar") 4-6   75
APPLE (2995 "My Sweet Lord") 4-6   70
CAPITOL (Orange label) 5-15   76
CAPITOL (Purple label) 3-5   78
CAPITOL (Black label) 3-6   83-87
CAPITOL STARLINE 3-5   77-87
DARK HORSE (0410 "All Those
Years Ago") 3-5   81
DARK HORSE (8294 "This Song") 4-6   76
DARK HORSE (8313 "Crackerbox
Palace") 2-4   77
DARK HORSE (8763 "Blow Away") 2-4   79
DARK HORSE (8844 "Love Comes to
Everyone") 3-5   79
DARK HORSE (27913 "This Is Love") . 3-5   88
DARK HORSE (28131 "When We
Was Fab") 2-4   88
DARK HORSE (28178 "Got My Mind
Set on You") 2-4   87

DARK HORSE (29744 "I Really
Love You") 15-20   83
DARK HORSE (29864 "Wake Up
My Love") 3-5   82
DARK HORSE (49725 "All Those
Years Ago") 2-4   81
DARK HORSE (49785 "Teardrops") ... 3-5   81
WARNER (22807 "Cheer Down") 2-4   89
Picture Sleeves
APPLE (1828 "What Is Life") 20-30   71
APPLE (1836 "Bangla Desh") 10-15   71
APPLE (1877 "Dark Horse") 40-60   74
APPLE (1879 "Ding Dong Ding Dong") 10-15   74
APPLE (1884 "You") 10-15   75
APPLE (2995 "My Sweet Lord") 15-25   70
DARK HORSE (8294 "This Song") .. 15-20   76
DARK HORSE (8294 "This Song") .. 40-50   76
(Special promotional sleeve issued with promo
single. Price in cludes insert flyer with "The Story
Behind *This Song,* which represents about
$15-$20 of the value.)
DARK HORSE (8763 "Blow Away") 4-6   79
DARK HORSE (8844 "Love Comes
to Everyone") 250-350   79
DARK HORSE (27913; "This Is Love") . 3-5   88
DARK HORSE (28131 "When We
Was Fab") 2-4   88
DARK HORSE (28178 "Got My Mind
Set on You") 2-4   87
DARK HORSE (49725 "All Those
Years Ago") 2-4   81
WARNER (22807 "Cheer Down") 2-4   89
Promotional Singles
APPLE (1862 "Give Me Love") 25-35   73
APPLE (1879 "Ding Dong Ding Dong") 25-30   74
APPLE (1877 "Dark Horse") 30-40   74
APPLE (1879 "Ding Dong Ding Dong") 20-30   74
APPLE (1884 "You") 25-35   75
APPLE (1885 "This Guitar") 25-35   75
APPLE/20TH FOX (791 "Concert
for Bangla Desh") 400-500   71
(Four radio spots. Issued only to radio stations.)
DARK HORSE (8294 "This Song") .. 10-15   76
DARK HORSE (8313 "Crackerbox
Palace") 10-15   77
DARK HORSE (8763 "Blow Away") .. 10-12   79
DARK HORSE (8844 "Love Comes
to Everyone") 10-15   79
DARK HORSE (27913 "This Is Love") 10-12   88
DARK HORSE (28131 "When We
Was Fab") 10-12   88
DARK HORSE (28178 "Got My Mind
Set on You") 10-15   87
DARK HORSE (29744 "I Really Love
You") 10-12   83
DARK HORSE (29864 "Wake Up
My Love") 10-12   82
DARK HORSE (49725 "All Those
Years Ago") 8-10   81

DARK HORSE (49725 "All Those
Years Ago") 10-12   81
DARK HORSE (49785"Teardrops") . . 10-12   81
WARNER (22807 "Cheer Down") 8-12   89
LPs: 10/12–inch 33rpm
APPLE (639 "All Things Must
Pass") 30-40   70
(Three-LP boxed set. Includes bonus poster.)
APPLE (3350 "Wonderwall Music") . . 15-25   68
APPLE (3385 "Concert for
Bangla Desh") 30-40   71
(Three-LP boxed set. Includes 64-page booklet.
Also has music by Eric Clapton, Bob Dylan, Leon
Russell, Ringo Starr; Ravi Shankar, and others.)
APPLE (3410 "Living in the Material
World") 10-12   73
APPLE (3418 "Dark Horse") 10-15   73
APPLE (3420 "Extra Texture") 10-12   75
CAPITOL (639 "All Things Must Pass")15-25   76-78
(Orange or purple labels. Three-LP boxed set.
Includes bonus poster.)
CAPITOL (639 "All Things Must Pass")25-35   83
(Black label. 3-LP boxed set. Includes bonus
poster.)
CAPITOL (11578 "The Best of George
Harrison") 8-12   76
(Custom label with six photos of Harrison. Also
contains tracks by the Beatles that feature George.)
CAPITOL (11578 "The Best of George
Harrison") 30-40   77
(Orange label.)
CAPITOL (11578 "The Best of George
Harrison") 8-10   78-83
(Purple or black labels.)
CAPITOL (12248 "Concert For Bangla
Desh") 250-300   82
(2-LP set.)
CAPITOL (16000 series) 10-20   81
DARK HORSE (3005 "Thirty-Three
and 1/3") 8-10   76
DARK HORSE (3255 "George
Harrison") 8-10   79
DARK HORSE (3492 "Somewhere in
England") 5-10   81
DARK HORSE (23734 "Gone Troppo") 8-12   82
DARK HORSE (25643 "Cloud Nine") . . 8-10   87
DARK HORSE (25726 "Best of
Dark Horse") 8-10   89
ZAPPLE (3358 "Electronic Music") . . 15-25   69
Promotional LPs
DARK HORSE ("Dark Horse Radio
Special") 175-225   74
DARK HORSE (649 "A Personal Music
Dialogue with George Harrison
At 33 1/3") 30-40   76
DARK HORSE (23734 "Gone Troppo")20-25   82
(An audiophile Quiex II vinyl pressing.)
  Also see BEATLES
  Also see BROMBERG, David

  Also see CLAPTON, Eric
  Also see DYLAN, Bob
  Also see HODGE, Chris
  Also see RUSSELL, Leon
  Also see SCOTT, Tom
  Also see SHANKAR, Ravi
  Also see TRAVELING WILBURYS

**HARRISON, George / Jeff Beck / Dave
Edmunds**
Singles: 12–inch 33/45rpm
COLUMBIA (2034 "I Don't Want to
Do It") 10-20   85
(Has one song by each artist.)
COLUMBIA (2085 "I Don't Want to
Do It") 10-20   85
(Promotional issue only. Has the Harrison song on
both sides.)

Singles: 7–inch
COLUMBIA (04887 "I Don't Want to
Do It") 2-4   85
Promotional Singles
COLUMBIA (04887 "I Don't Want to
Do It") 8-12   85
(Has the Harrison song on both sides.)

**HARRISON, George / Dave Edmunds / Jeff
Beck**
Singles: 12–inch 33/45rpm
COLUMBIA (2034 "I Don't Want to
Do It") 10-20   85
(Promotional issue only.)
  Also see BECK, Jeff
  Also see EDMUNDS, Dave
  Also see HARRISON, George

HARRISON, Jerry
(Jerry Harrison and the Casual Gods)
LPs: 10/12–inch 33rpm
FLY/SIRE 5-8   90
SIRE 5-8   88

HARRISON, Noel
Singles: 7–inch
LONDON 4-8   65-67
REPRISE 3-6   67-70
LPs: 10/12–inch 33rpm
LONDON 15-20   66-67
REPRISE 10-15   67-69
RIVERSIDE 10-12

HARRISON, Reggie:
see HIPPIES / Reggie Harrison

HARRISON, Wes
Singles: 7–inch
PHILIPS 8-12   63
LPs: 10/12–inch 33rpm
PHILIPS 15-25   63

HARRISON, Wilbert
(Wilbert Harrison and the Roamers; Wilbert Harrison
and His Kansas City Playboys; Wilburt Harrison)
Singles: 78rpm
DELUXE 10-20   52-53

Singles: 7–inch

ABC 2-4	73
BRUNSWICK 3-5	74
CONSTELLATION 4-8	64
DELUXE (6002 "This Woman	
of Mine") 40-50	52
DELUXE (6031 "Gin & Coconut Milk") 40-50	53
DOC 5-10	62
FURY 5-10	59-62
GLADES 8-12	59
HOUSE of SOUND 4-6	
NEPTUNE 4-8	61
PORT 4-8	65
ROCKIN' (526 "This Woman	
of Mine") 75-100	52
ROULETTE 3-5	67
SSS INT'L 3-5	71
SAVOY (1100 series) 10-20	54
SAVOY (1500 series) 5-10	59
SEA HORN 4-8	63
SUE (11 "Let's Work Together") 5-8	69
(Company address at bottom of label.)	
SUE (11 "Let's Work Together") 4-6	69
(Company address at top.)	
SUE (11 "Let's Work Together") 3-5	69
(Company address on left side.)	

LPs: 10/12–inch 33rpm

BUDDAH 8-12	71
CHELSEA 8-10	77
JUGGERNAUT 8-12	71
RELIC 5-10	90
SPHERE SOUND 25-40	65
SUE 15-25	70
WET SOUL 10-15	70

HARRY, Debbie
(Deborah Harry)
Singles: 12–inch 33/45rpm

CHRYSALIS 4-6	81-83
GEFFEN 4-6	85-86

Singles: 7–inch

CHRYSALIS 3-5	81-83
GEFFEN 2-4	85-87

Picture Sleeves

CHRYSALIS 3-5	81
GEFFEN 2-4	86-87

LPs: 10/12–inch 33rpm

CHRYSALIS 5-10	81
GEFFEN 5-10	86
SIRE 5-8	89
Also see BLONDIE	
Also see WIND in the WILLOWS	

HART, Bonnie
Singles: 7–inch

BADGER 3-5	88

HART, Corey
Singles: 7–inch

EMI 2-4	90
EMI AMERICA 2-4	84-87

EMI MANHATTAN 2-4	88

Picture Sleeves

EMI AMERICA 2-4	84-86

LPs: 10/12–inch 33rpm

EMI 5-8	90
EMI AMERICA 5-10	84-86
EMI MANHATTAN 5-8	89

HART, Freddie
(Freddie Hart and the Heartbeats)
Singles: 78rpm

CAPITOL 3-6	53-55
COLUMBIA (Except 21512) 2-5	56-63
COLUMBIA (21512 "Dig Boy, Dig") ... 5-10	56

Singles: 7–inch

CAPITOL (2500 through 3000 series) .. 4-8	53-55
(Purple labels.)	
CAPITOL (2600 through 4600 series) .. 2-4	70-79
(Orange labels.)	
COLUMBIA (Except 21512) 3-6	56-63
COLUMBIA (21512 "Dig Boy, Dig") .. 25-35	56
KAPP 3-5	65-72
MCA 2-4	73
MONUMENT 3-6	63-64
SUNBIRD 2-4	80-81

Picture Sleeves

KAPP 3-5	68
SUNBIRD 2-4	80

LPs: 10/12–inch 33rpm

BRYLEN 5-10	84
CAPITOL 5-10	70-79
COLUMBIA (1700 series) 20-25	62
COLUMBIA (13000 series) 10-12	72
CORAL 5-8	73
HARMONY 8-12	67-73
KAPP 8-15	65-69
MCA 8-12	75
PICKWICK/HILLTOP 8-12	
SUNBIRD 5-10	80
VOCALION 8-10	72

HART, Freddie / Sammi Smith / Jerry Reed
LPs: 10/12–inch 33rpm

HARMONY 6-10	72
Also see HART, Freddie	
Also see REED, Jerry	
Also see SMITH, Sammi	

HART, Mickey
Singles: 7–inch

WARNER 4-8	71-72

LPs: 10/12–inch 33rpm

RELIX 5-10	85
WARNER 10-20	72
Also see GRATEFUL DEAD	
Also see WOLFF, Henry, Nancy Hennings and Mickey Hart	

HART, Mickey, Airto and Flora Purim
LPs: 10/12–inch 33rpm

REFERENCE 8-10	83
Also see HART, Mickey	
Also see PURIM, Flora	

HART, Rita
Singles: 12-inch 33/45rpm
ENVELOPE. 4-6   84

HART, Rod
Singles: 7-inch
IBC 2-4   80
PHOENIX SUN 3-6   68
PLANTATION 3-5   76-77
LPs: 10/12-inch 33rpm
PLANTATION 5-10   76

HARTFORD, John
Singles: 7-inch
AMPEX 3-5   71
RCA 4-6   66-70
LPs: 10/12-inch 33rpm
FLYING FISH 5-10   76-84
RCA 8-12   67-70
WARNER 8-10   71-72
    Also see DILLARDS and John Hartford

HARTLEY, Keef, Band
Singles: 7-inch
DERAM 3-5   70-73
LPs: 10/12-inch 33rpm
DERAM 10-12   69-73
    Also see MAYALL, John

HARTMAN, Dan
Singles: 12-inch 33/45rpm
BLUE SKY 4-6   78-81
MCA 4-6   84-85
Singles: 7-inch
BLUE SKY 2-5   76-81
MCA 2-4   84-85
PORTRAIT 2-4   81
Picture Sleeves
MCA 2-4   84-85
LPs: 10/12-inch 33rpm
BLUE SKY (Except 246) 5-10   76-81
BLUE SKY (246 "Who Is
    Dan Hartman") 8-15   75
    (Promotional issue only.)
MCA 5-10   84-85
    Also see WINTER, Edgar

HARTMAN, Dan / Blasters
Singles: 7-inch
MCA 2-4   84
Picture Sleeves
MCA 2-4   84
    Also see BLASTERS
    Also see HARTMAN, Dan

HARVEST, Barclay James:
    see BARCLAY JAMES HARVEST

HARVEST, King: see KING HARVEST

HARVEY
(Harvey Fuqua)
Singles: 7-inch
CHESS 8-12   59-61

TRI-PHI 10-15   62-63
    Also see HARVEY and the Moonglows
    Also see NEW BIRTH

HARVEY, Alex
(Sensational Alex Harvey Band)
Singles: 7-inch
ATLANTIC 3-5   75
CAPITOL 3-5   72
VERTIGO 3-5   73-75
LPs: 10/12-inch 33rpm
CAPITOL 8-12   72
ATLANTIC 8-10   75
VERTIGO 8-10   73-75

HARVEY, Steve
Singles: 12-inch 33/45rpm
LONDON 4-6   84
Singles: 7-inch
LONDON 2-4   84

HARVEY and the Moonglows
(Featuring Harvey Fuqua)
Singles: 7-inch
CHESS 8-12   58-59
    Also see ETTA & HARVEY
    Also see HARVEY
    Also see MOONGLOWS

HARVEY BOYS
Singles: 78rpm
CADENCE 3-5   57
Singles: 7-inch
CADENCE 5-10   57

HASHIM
Singles: 12-inch 33/45rpm
CUTTING EDGE 4-6   84

HASLAM, Annie
Singles: 7-inch
SIRE 3-5   78
LPs: 10/12-inch 33rpm
SIRE 8-12   77
    Also see RENAISSANCE

HASSAN and 7-11
Singles: 7-inch
EASY STREET 2-4   84

HASSLES
Singles: 7-inch
U.A. 8-12   67-69
Picture Sleeves
U.A. 10-12   67-69
LPs: 10/12-inch 33rpm
LIBERTY 8-10   81
U.A. (6631 "The Hassles") 20-30   68
U.A. (6699 "Hour of the Wolf") 20-30   68
    Members: William (Billy) Joel; Howard Blauvelt; Jonathan Small;
    Richard McKenner; John Dizek.
    Also see JOEL, Billy

HATCHER, Roger
Singles: 7-inch
BROWN DOG 3-5   76

HATFIELD, Bobby
Singles: 7-inch
MOONGLOW 5-10   63
VERVE 4-8   68-69
WARNER 3-5   72
LPs: 10/12-inch 33rpm
MGM 10-12   71
Also see RIGHTEOUS BROTHERS

HATHAWAY, Donny
Singles: 7-inch
ATCO 3-6   69-78
LPs: 10/12-inch 33rpm
ATCO 8-10   70-78
ATLANTIC 5-10   80
Also see FLACK, Roberta, and Donny Hathaway

HATHAWAY, Donny, and June Conquest
Singles: 7-inch
CURTOM (1971 "I Thank You") 3-5   72
(Previously issued as by June and Donnie.)
Members: Donny Hathaway; June Conquest.
Also see JUNE & DONNIE

HATHAWAY, Donny, and Margie Joseph
Singles: 7-inch
ATCO 3-5   72
Also see HATHAWAY, Donny
Also see JOSEPH, Margie

HAVENS, Richie
Singles: 7-inch
A&M 3-5   77
DOUGLAS 4-8   68
ELEKTRA 2-4   80
MGM 3-5   70
ODE '70 3-5   72
STORMY FOREST 3-5   70-74
VERVE/FOLKWAYS 4-8   66-68
VERVE/FORECAST 4-8   68-69
LPs: 10/12-inch 33rpm
A&M 8-10   76
DOUGLAS 12-15   68
ELEKTRA 5-10   80
MGM 8-10   70
ODE '70 8-10   73
RBI 5-10   87
STORMY FOREST 10-12   69-74
VERVE/FOLKWAYS 12-15   67-68
VERVE/FORECAST 12-15   67-69

HAWK
(Jerry Lee Lewis)
Singles: 7-inch
PHILLIPS INT'L 15-20   60
Also see LEWIS, Jerry Lee

HAWKINS, Dale
(Dale Hawkins with the Escapades)
Singles: 78rpm
CHECKER 10-20   56-57
Singles: 7-inch
ABC-PAR 4-8   65

ATLANTIC 5-10   61-62
BELL 4-8   69
CHECKER (800 series) 20-25   56-57
(Maroon label with checkerboard design at top.)
CHECKER (800 series) 8-12   57-58
(Maroon label with Checker name on side.)
CHECKER (900 series) 5-10   58-61
LINCOLN 4-8
TILT 5-10   61
ZONK 8-12   62
Picture Sleeves
CHECKER (944 "Poor Little
Rhode Island") 40-60   60
LPs: 10/12-inch 33rpm
BELL (6036 "L.A., Memphis
and Tyler, Texas") 20-30   69
CHESS (1429 "Suzy-Q") 200-300   58
ROULETTE (R-25175 "Let's All Twist at the Miami
Beach Peppermint Lounge") 40-60   62
(Monaural.)
ROULETTE (SR-25175 "Let's All Twist at the Miami
Beach Peppermint Lounge") 50-80   62
(Stereo.)
Also see BUCHANAN, Roy

HAWKINS, Edwin, Singers
Singles: 7-inch
BUDDAH 3-5   71-72
PAVILION 3-6   69
LPs: 10/12-inch 33rpm
BUDDAH 8-12   71-72
PAVILION 10-12   69
Members: Edwin Hawkins; Walter Hawkins; Tramaine Hawkins;
Daniel Hawkins; Elaine Kelley; Norma King; Dorothy Morrison;
Barbara Gill; Shirley Miller; Edwin Miller; Donald Henderson.
Also see MELANIE
Also see MORRISON, Dorothy

HAWKINS, Erskine
Singles: 78rpm
BLUEBIRD 5-10   39-44
BRUNSWICK 4-8   53
DECCA 4-6   56
CORAL 4-8   50-54
KING 5-10   51-52
VICTOR/RCA 5-10   45-52
VOCALION 5-10   36-37
Singles: 7-inch
BRUNSWICK 5-10   53
DECCA 5-10   56
CORAL 5-10   52-54
KING (4514 "Steel Guitar Rag") 15-20   52
(Black vinyl.)
KING (4514 "Steel Guitar Rag") 30-40   52
(Colored vinyl.)
KING (4522 "Down Home Jump") ... 15-20   52
(Black vinyl.)
KING (4522 "Down Home Jump") ... 30-40   52
(Colored vinyl.)
KING (4574 "New Gin Mill Special") . 15-20   52

KING (4597 "The Way You
Look Tonight") 15-20   52
KING (4686 "Double Shot") 15-20   53
EPs: 7–inch 33/45rpm
RCA 10-20   59
LPs: 10/12–inch 33rpm
CORAL 30-50   54
DECCA 20-30   61
IMPERIAL 20-30   62
RCA 25-40   60

HAWKINS, Erskine, and the Four Hawks
Singles: 78rpm
KING 10-20   53
Singles: 7–inch
KING (4671 "My Baby, Please") 50-75   53
KING (4686 "Double Shot") 25-50   53
Also see HAWKINS, Erskine

HAWKINS, Hawkshaw
Singles: 78rpm
KING 3-6   46-53
RCA 2-5   55-57
Singles: 7–inch
COLUMBIA 4-6   59-62
KING (900 through 1100 series) 5-10   50-53
KING (5000 series) 4-6   60-64
RCA 5-10   55-59
STARDAY 3-5   71
EPs: 7–inch 33/45rpm
KING 8-12   53
LPs: 10/12–inch 33rpm
CAMDEN 10-15   64-66
GLADWYNNE (2006 "Country and Western
Cavalcade") 60-80
HARMONY 10-15   63
KING (500 series) 20-35   58-59
KING (800 series) 15-25   63-64
KING (1000 series) 8-12   69
LA BREA (8020 "Hawkshaw Hawkins") 60-80
NASHVILLE 8-12   69
STARDAY 5-10
Also see CLINE, Patsy / Cowboy Copas / Hawkshaw Hawkins
Also see COPAS, Cowboy / Hawkshaw Hawkins

HAWKINS, Jennell
Singles: 7–inch
AMAZON 4-8   61-63
DYNAMIC 4-8   61
DYNAMITE 4-8   61
OLDIES 45 3-5
LPs: 10/12–inch 33rpm
AMAZON (AM-1001 "Many Moods
of Jenny") 20-30   61
(Monaural.)
AMAZON (AS-1001 "Many Moods
of Jenny") 25-40   61
(Stereo.)
AMAZON (AM-1002 "Moments to
Remember") 20-30   62
(Monaural.)

AMAZON (AS-1002 "Moments to
Remember") 25-40   62

HAWKINS, Ronnie
(Ronnie Hawkins and the Hawks)
Singles: 7–inch
COTILLION 3-5   70-71
HAWK 5-10
MONUMENT 3-5   72-73
ROULETTE (4154 "Forty Days") 10-15   59
ROULETTE (SSR-4154 "Forty Days") 20-30   59
(Stereo.)
ROULETTE (4177 "Mary Lou") 10-15   59
ROULETTE (SSR-4177 "Mary Lou") . 20-30   59
(Stereo.)
ROULETTE (4209 through 4502) 5-10   59-63
LPs: 10/12–inch 33rpm
ACCORD 5-10   83
COTILLION 10-15   70-71
MONUMENT 8-12   72-75
ROULETTE (25078 "Ronnie Hawkins")50-75   59
(Black vinyl. Monaural.)
ROULETTE (SR-25078 "Ronnie
Hawkins") 75-100   59
(Black vinyl. Stereo.)
ROULETTE (25078 "Ronnie
Hawkins") 175-225   59
(Colored vinyl.)
ROULETTE (25102 "Mr. Dynamo") .. 50-75   60
(Black vinyl. Monaural.)
ROULETTE (SR-25102 "Mr.
Dynamo") 75-100   60
(Black vinyl. Stereo.)
ROULETTE (25102 "Mr.
Dynamo") 175-225   60
(Colored vinyl.)
ROULETTE (25120 "Folk Ballads") .. 50-75   60
(Monaural.)
ROULETTE (SR-25120 "Folk
Ballads") 75-100   60
(Stereo.)
ROULETTE (25137 "Songs of Hank
Williams") 50-75   60
(Monaural.)
ROULETTE (SR-25137 "Songs of Hank
Williams") 75-100   60
(Stereo.)
ROULETTE (42045 "Best of Ronnie
Hawkins") 25-35   70
U.A. 5-10   79
Also see BAND
Also see LENNON, John
Also see LEVON and the Hawks

HAWKINS, Roy
Singles: 78rpm
DOWN TOWN (2018 "Christmas
Blues") 10-20   48
DOWN TOWN (2020 "It's too Late to
Change") 10-20   48

DOWN TOWN (2024 "Forty Jim") ... 10-20	48
DOWN TOWN (2025 "Quarter to	
One") 10-20	48
MODERN 8-15	48-54
RPM 5-10	54

Singles: 7–inch

KENT 4-8	62
MODERN (826 "The Thrill Is Gone") . 35-55	51
MODERN (852 "Gloom and Misery	
All Around") 35-55	51
MODERN (853 "I Don't Know Just	
What to Do") 35-55	51
MODERN (859 "Highway 59") 20-30	52
MODERN (869 "Doin' All Right") 20-30	52
MODERN (898 "Bad Luck Is Falling") 20-30	54
RPM (440 "Is It Too Late") 15-25	54
RHYTHM (120 "I Hate to Be Alone") . 30-40	58

HAWKINS, Sam
(Sam Hawkins and the Crystals)
Singles: 7–inch

ARNOLD 3-5	63
BLUE CAT 5-8	65
DECCA 5-10	59-61
GONE 10-15	59
SHELL 4-8	

HAWKS
Singles: 7–inch

COLUMBIA 2-4	81

LPs: 10/12–inch 33rpm

COLUMBIA 5-10	81

HAWKWIND
Singles: 7–inch

ATCO 3-5	75
U.A. 3-5	71-73

LPs: 10/12–inch 33rpm

ATCO 8-10	75
SIRE 5-10	78
U.A. 10-15	71-74

Also see MOTORHEAD

HAWLEY, Deane
(Deane Hawley and the Crystals)
Singles: 7–inch

DORE 5-10	59-61
LIBERTY 5-10	61-62
SUNDOWN 4-8	
VALOR 5-10	
WARNER 4-8	64

HAYES, Bill
(Bill Hayes with Archie Bleyer's Orchestra)
Singles: 78rpm

ABC-PAR 5-10	57
ABC-PAR (9895 "Bop Boy") 10-20	58
CADENCE 4-6	55-56
MGM 3-5	55

Singles: 7–inch

ABC-PAR (Except 9895) 8-12	57
ABC-PAR (9895 "Bop Boy") 35-50	58

ABLE 4-8	
BARNABY 3-5	76
CADENCE 5-10	55-56
DAYBREAK 3-5	74
KAPP 5-8	59
MGM 5-10	55
SHAW 4-6	65

Picture Sleeves

CADENCE 10-15	55

EPs: 7–inch 33/45rpm

MGM 10-20	55

LPs: 10/12–inch 33rpm

ABC-PAR 20-30	57
DAYBREAK 5-10	74
KAPP 10-15	60

Also see BLEYER, Archie

HAYES, Isaac
Singles: 12–inch 33/45rpm

COLUMBIA 4-6	85-86

Singles: 7–inch

ABC 3-5	77
BRUNSWICK 4-8	64
COLUMBIA 2-4	85-87
ENTERPRISE 3-6	69-74
HBS 3-5	75-76
POLYDOR 2-4	78-80
SAN AMERICAN 3-5	70
STAX 3-5	78

LPs: 10/12–inch 33rpm

ABC-PAR 8-10	75-77
ATLANTIC 8-10	72
COLUMBIA 5-10	86
ENTERPRISE 10-12	68-75
HBS 8-12	75-77
POLYDOR 5-10	77-81
STAX 5-10	77-82

HAYES, Isaac, and Millie Jackson
Singles: 7–inch

POLYDOR 2-4	79-80

LPs: 10/12–inch 33rpm

POLYDOR 5-10	79

Also see JACKSON, Millie

HAYES, Isaac, and David Porter
Singles: 7–inch

ENTERPRISE 3-5	72

Also see PORTER, David

HAYES, Isaac, and Dionne Warwick
Singles: 7–inch

ABC 3-5	77

LPs: 10/12–inch 33rpm

HBS 8-12	77

Also see HAYES, Isaac
Also see WARWICK, Dionne

HAYES, Linda
(Linda Hayes with Tony Williams; Linda Hayes and the Platters; Linda Hayes with the Flairs)
Singles: 78rpm

ANTLER 5-10	56

DECCA	5-10	55
HOLLYWOOD (Except 1032)	5-10	53-55
HOLLYWOOD (1032 "Our Love Is		
Forever Blessed")	10-15	55
KING	5-10	55
RECORDED in HOLLYWOOD	5-10	53

Singles: 7-inch

ANTLER	10-20	56
DECCA	10-20	55
HOLLYWOOD (Except 1032)	15-25	53-55
HOLLYWOOD (1032 "Our Love Is		
Forever Blessed")	30-40	55
KING (4752 "My Name Ain't Annie")	30-40	54
KING (4773 "Please Have Mercy")	20-30	55

Also see MOORE, Johnny, and Linda Hayes
Also see PLATTERS

HAYES, Peter Lind, and Mary Healy
Singles: 7-inch

COLUMBIA	4-8	55
ESSEX	4-8	53
KAPP	4-8	56

HAYES, Richard
Singles: 7-inch

ABC-PAR	8-15	56
COLUMBIA	4-8	60-61
CONTEMPO	4-6	64
DECCA	4-6	61
MERCURY	5-10	50-55

EPs: 7-inch 33/45rpm

MERCURY	8-15	54

LPs: 10/12-inch 33rpm

MERCURY	10-20	55

HAYES, Richard, and Kitty Kallen
Singles: 7-inch

MERCURY	5-10	50-51

Also see HAYES, Richard
Also see KALLEN, Kitty

HAYMAN, Richard, Orchestra
(Richard Hayman and Jan August)
Singles: 7-inch

COMMAND	3-5	69
MGM	3-6	65
MERCURY	3-6	50-62
MUSICOR	3-5	73

EPs: 7-inch 33/45rpm

MERCURY	4-8	51-59

LPs: 10/12-inch 33rpm

ASCOT	5-10	64
COMMAND	5-10	69
MAINSTREAM	5-10	67
MERCURY	10-20	51-64
TIME	5-10	63-64
WING	5-10	62-64

Also see AUGUST, Jan

HAYMES, Dick
Singles: 78rpm

CAPITOL	3-5	56

DECCA	4-8	43-54

Singles: 7-inch

CAPITOL	5-10	56
GNP/CRESCENDO	3-5	75
DECCA	5-10	50-54
WARWICK	3-6	60

EPs: 7-inch 33/45rpm

CAPITOL	5-10	56
DECCA	5-10	50-54

LPs: 10/12-inch 33rpm

AUDIOPHILE	5-10	78
CAPITOL	10-20	56
CORAL	4-6	73
DAYBREAK	5-10	74
DECCA	10-20	50-54
GLENDALE	5-10	84
MCA	5-10	76-83
WARWICK	8-15	60

Also see CLOONEY, Rosemary, and Dick Haymes
Also see FISHER, Eddie / Vic Damone / Dick Haymes
Also see JAMES, Harry, and Dick Haymes

HAYSI FANTAYZEE
Singles: 7-inch

RCA	2-4	83

Picture Sleeves

RCA	2-4	83

LPs: 10/12-inch 33rpm

RCA	5-10	83

Members: Kato Garner; Jeremiah Healy.

HAYWARD, Justin
Singles: 7-inch

COLUMBIA	3-5	78
DERAM	3-5	77
RED BIRD	10-15	66

LPs: 10/12-inch 33rpm

DERAM	10-20	77-80

Also see MOUSKOURI, Nana

HAYWARD, Justin, and John Lodge
Singles: 7-inch

THRESHOLD	3-5	75

LPs: 10/12-inch 33rpm

THRESHOLD	12-15	75

Also see HAYWARD, Justin
Also see LODGE, John
Also see MOODY BLUES

HAYWARD, Leon: see HAYWOOD, Leon

HAYWOOD, Leon
(Leon Hayward)
Singles: 12-inch 33/45rpm

CASABLANCA	4-6	83
MCA	4-8	79
20TH FOX	4-6	80

Singles: 7-inch

ATLANTIC	3-5	71-72
CAPITOL	3-5	69-70
CASABLANCA	2-4	83
COLUMBIA	3-5	76-77
DECCA	4-6	67-68

EPIC 2-4 80-81
FAT FISH 4-6   66
GALAXY 4-6   67
IMPERIAL 4-8 65-66
MCA 2-5 77-79
MODERN 2-4   84
20TH FOX 2-5 74-80

LPs: 10/12–Inch 33rpm

CASABLANCA 5-10   83
DECCA 8-12   67
GALAXY 8-12   67
MCA 5-10 78-79
20TH FOX 5-10 73-80

HAZARD, Robert
Singles: 7–Inch

RCA 2-4   83

LPs: 10/12–Inch 33rpm

RCA 5-10   83

HAZE
Singles: 7–Inch

ASI 3-5   75

LPs: 10/12–Inch 33rpm

ASI 8-10   74

HAZLEWOOD, Lee
Singles: 7–Inch

CAPITOL 3-5   72
JAMIE 5-10   60
LHI 4-6   68
MCA 2-4 79-80
MGM 4-6 66-67
REPRISE 4-6 65-68
SMASH 5-8   61

LPs: 10/12–Inch 33rpm

CAPITOL 8-10   72
HARMONY 8-12   67
MGM 10-15 66-67
MERCURY 10-15   63
REPRISE 10-15 64-65

Also see ANN-MARGRET and Lee Hazlewood
Also see SHACKLEFORDS
Also see SINATRA, Nancy, and Lee Hazlewood

HEAD, Murray
(Murray Head with the Trinidad Singers; Murry Head)
Singles: 12–Inch 33/45rpm

CHESS 4-6   85

Singles: 7–Inch

A&M 3-5   76
CAPITOL 4-6   67
CHESS 2-4   85
DECCA 3-6 69-71

Picture Sleeves

DECCA 3-5 70-71

LPs: 10/12–Inch 33rpm

A&M 8-10   76
COLUMBIA 5-10   72

HEAD, Roy
(Roy Head and the Traits)
Singles: 7–Inch

ABC 3-5 73-79
ABC/DOT 3-5 76-77
AVION 2-4   83
BACK BEAT 4-8 65-67
CHURCHILL 2-4   81
DUNHILL 3-5   70
ELEKTRA 2-4 79-80
MEGA 3-5   74
MERCURY 4-6   68
NSD 2-4   82
SCEPTER 4-8 65-66
SHANNON 3-5   75
TMI 3-5 71-73
TNT 8-10   65

LPs: 10/12–Inch 33rpm

ABC 8-10 73-78
DUNHILL 10-12   70
ELEKTRA 5-10 79-80
SCEPTER (532 "Treat Me Right") ... 15-25   65
  (Monaural.)
SCEPTER (532 "Treat Me Right") ... 20-30   65
  (Stereo. With an "SS" prefix.)
TMI 8-10   72
TNT (101 "Roy Head and the
  Traits") 100-150   65
(Counterfeits can be identified by their content.
They include *Treat Her Right,* as well as other later
Head tracks on side two. Originals do not have
these.)
  Also see TRAITS

HEAD EAST
Singles: 7–Inch

A&M 3-5 75-79

LPs: 10/12–Inch 33rpm

A&M 5-10 75-80
ALLEGIANCE 5-10   83

HEADBOYS
Singles: 7–Inch

RSO 3-5   79

LPs: 10/12–Inch 33rpm

RSO 5-10   79

HEADPINS
Singles: 7–Inch

ATCO 3-5   82
SOLID GOLD 3-5   83

LPs: 10/12–Inch 33rpm

ATCO 5-10   82
SOLID GOLD 5-8   83

HEALEY, Jeff
(Jeff Healey Band)
Singles: 7–Inch

ARISTA 2-4   89

Picture Sleeves

ARISTA 2-4   89

LPs: 10/12–inch 33rpm

ARISTA 5-8   89-90

HEAP, Jimmy
(Jimmy Heap and the Melody Masters; Jimmy Heap and Perk Williams)

Singles: 78rpm

CAPITOL 4-6   53-55

Singles: 7–inch

CAPITOL 10-15   53-55
D.............................. 8-10   59
DART 5-10   60
FAME (502 "Little Jewell") 200-250   58
FAME (509 "Night Cap") 8-15   61
FAME (510 "Go Get Em") 8-15   61
FAME (511 "Flint Rock") 8-15   61
IMPERIAL 4-8   60

HEART

Singles: 12–inch 33/45rpm

CAPITOL 4-6   85
MUSHROOM 4-8   76
PORTRAIT 4-8   77-79

Promotional 12–inch Singles

MUSHROOM (7023 "Dreamboat Annie) 8-10   76
PORTRAIT (16445 "Straight On") 8-10   78

Singles: 7–inch

CAPITOL 2-4   85-90
EPIC 2-5   81-83
MUSHROOM 3-6   76-79
PORTRAIT 3-5   77-79

Picture Sleeves

CAPITOL 2-4   85-90

LPs: 10/12–inch 33rpm

CAPITOL 5-10   85-90
CAPITOL RADIO STAR ("Audio
   Cue Card") 10-15   87
   (Radio interview. Promotional issue only.)
EPIC 5-10   80-83
MUSHROOM (MRS-5005 "Dreamboat
   Annie") 8-12   76
MUSHROOM (MRS-5008 "Magazine") 50-75   77
   (First issue. Last track on Side One is *Magazine*.)
MUSHROOM (MRS-5008 "Magazine") 5-10   77
   (Second issue. First track on Side Two is
   Magazine. There are also other differences in song
   order.)
MUSHROOM (MRS-1-SP "Magazine") 8-12   78
   (Picture Disc.)
MUSHROOM (MRS-2-SP "Dreamboat
   Annie") 10-15   79
   (Picture Disc.)
NAUTILUS 20-25   80
   (Half-speed mastered.)
PORTRAIT (30000 series) 5-10   77-81
PORTRAIT (40000 series) 12-15   81
   (Half-speed mastered.)
   Members: Nancy Wilson; Ann Wilson; Howard Leese; Steve
   Fossen; Roger Fisher; Mike Derosier; Mark Andes; Denny
   Carmassi.
   Also see BORDERSONG

Also see SPIRIT
Also see WILSON, Ann and the Daybreaks

HEART BEATS QUINTET
(With Russell Jacquet and His Orchestra)

Singles: 10–inch

CANDLELITE (437 "Tormented") 10-20   72
   (Colored vinyl 45 rpm.)
CANDLELITE (437 "Tormented") 8-15   72
   (Black vinyl 45 rpm.)

Singles: 7–inch

CANDLELITE (1135 "Tormented") 3-5   76
NETWORK (71200 "Tormented") ... 50-100   55
   (Black vinyl. Pastel yellow label.)
NETWORK (71200 "Tormented") 25-50
   (Black vinyl. Bright yellow label.)
NETWORK (71200 "Tormented") 10-15
   (Colored vinyl.)
   Members: James Sheppard; Albert Crump; Vernon Walker;
   Wally Roker; Rob Adams.
   Also see HEARTBEATS
   Also see JACQUET, Russell

HEART of GOLD BAND

LPs: 10/12–inch 33rpm

RELIX 5-10   86
   Members: Keith Godchaux; Donna Godchaux.

HEARTBEATS

GEE 5-10   57
HULL 10-20   55-56
RAMA 5-10   56-57

Singles: 7–inch

COLLECTABLES 2-4
GEE (1043 "When I Found You") 15-20   57
GEE (1047 "After New Year's Eve") . 15-20   57
   (Red label.)
GEE (1047 "After New Year's Eve") .. 5-10   57
   (Gray label.)
GEE (1061 "People Are Talking") 5-10   60
GEE (1062 "Darling, How Long") 5-10   60
GUYDEN (2011 "One Million Years") . 15-20   59
   (Yellow label.)
GUYDEN (2011 "One Million Years") . 10-15   59
   (Purple label.)
HULL (711 "Crazy for You") 100-150   55
   (White label. Promotional issue only.)
HULL (711 "Crazy for You") 50-100   55
   (Pink label.)
HULL (711 "Crazy for You") 20-40   55
   (Black label.)
HULL (713 "Darling How Long") ... 50-100   56
HULL (716 "People Are Talking") ... 50-100   56
HULL (720 "A Thousand Miles
   Away") 100-150   56
   (Black label.)
HULL (720 "A Thousand Miles Away") 20-30   56
   (Red label.)
RAMA (216 "A Thousand Miles Away") 15-20   56
RAMA (222 "I Won't Be the
   Fool Anymore") 25-35   57

RAMA (231 "Everybody's Somebody's
Foo") 15-25   57
ROULETTE (4000 series) 5-10   58-59
LPs: 10/12–inch 33rpm
EMUS 8-10
ROULETTE (25107 "A Thousand
Miles Away") 75-125   60
ROULETTE (25107 "A Thousand
Miles Away") 5-8   81
(Has a "1981" copyright date at the bottom of back
cover.)
Members: James Sheppard; Albert Crump; Vernon Walker;
Wally Roker; Rob Adams.
Also see HEART BEATS QUINTET

HEARTBEATS / Shep and the Limelights
LPs: 10/12–inch 33rpm
ROULETTE (115 "Echoes of a
Rock Era") 35-45   72
Also see HEARTBEATS
Also see SHEP and the Limelights

HEARTS
Singles: 78rpm
BATON 5-10   55-56
Singles: 7–inch
BATON 10-20   55-56
J&S 15-25   57-58
LAVENDER 5-10   62
TUFF 5-10   63
ZELLS 5-10   63
LPs: 10/12–inch 33rpm
ZELLS (337 "I Feel Good") 100-200   63
Members: Justine "Baby" Washington; Rex Garvin; Pat Ford;
Cinda Filder; Mry Jefferson; Levrgn Ray.
Also see WASHINGTON, Baby

HEARTSFIELD
Singles: 7–inch
MERCURY 3-5   74
LPs: 10/12–inch 33rpm
COLUMBIA 5-10   77
MERCURY 8-10   73-75

HEARTSMAN, Johnny
Singles: 7–inch
MUSIC CITY 5-10   57

HEAT
Singles: 7–inch
MCA 3-5   79-81
LPs: 10/12–inch 33rpm
MCA 5-10   79-81

HEATH, Ted
Singles: 78rpm
LONDON 2-4   50-61
Singles: 7–inch
LONDON 3-6   50-61
EPs: 7–inch 33/45rpm
LONDON 4-8   51-56
LPs: 10/12–inch 33rpm
LONDON 5-15   50-62
RICHMOND 4-8   62

HEATH, Walter
Singles: 7–inch
BUDDAH 3-5   74

HEATH BROTHERS
Singles: 7–inch
COLUMBIA 3-5   79-81
LPs: 10/12–inch 33rpm
COLUMBIA 5-10   79-81

HEATHERTON, Joey
Singles: 7–inch
CORAL 10-20   64-65
DECCA 10-20   66
MGM 4-8   72-73
Picture Sleeves
CORAL (62422 "That's How
It Goes") 15-25   64
MGM 4-8   72
LPs: 10/12–inch 33rpm
MGM 8-12   72

HEATWAVE
Singles: 12–inch 33/45rpm
EPIC 4-8   77-82
Singles: 7–inch
EPIC 3-5   77-82
LPs: 10/12–inch 33rpm
EPIC 5-10   77-82
Member: Keith Wilder; Rod Temperton; Ernie Berger; John
Wilder; Eric Johns.

HEAVEN & EARTH
Singles: 7–inch
GEC 3-5   76
MERCURY 2-5   78-80
TEC 2-4   80
WMOT 2-4   81
LPs: 10/12–inch 33rpm
MERCURY 5-10   78-79
WMOT 5-10   81
Members: Dwight Dukes; Dean Williams; James Dukes; Keith
Steward.

HEAVEN BOUND
Singles: 7–inch
MGM 3-5   71
LPs: 10/12–inch 33rpm
MGM 8-12   72
Members: Tony Scotti.

HEAVEN 17
Singles: 12–inch 33/45rpm
ARISTA 4-6   83-84
Singles: 7–inch
ARISTA 2-4   83-84
LPs: 10/12–inch 33rpm
ARISTA 8-10   83
VIRGIN 5-10   87
Also see BAND AID

HEAVY D. and the Boyz
Singles: 12–inch 33/45rpm
MCA 4-6   86

Singles: 7–inch

MCA	2-4	86-88

LPs: 10/12–inch 33rpm

MCA	5-10	86-87
UPTOWN	5-8	89

HEBB, Bobby

Singles: 7–inch

BOOM	4-6	66
CADET	3-5	72
FM	4-8	61
LAURIE	3-5	75
PHILIPS	4-6	66
RICH	5-10	60
SCEPTER	4-6	66

Picture Sleeves

PHILIPS	4-8	66

LPs: 10/12–inch 33rpm

EPIC	10-12	70
PHILLIPS	15-20	66

HEBB, Bobby / Billy Sha-Rae

Singles: 7–inch

LAURIE	2-4	

Also see HEBB, Bobby
Also see SHA-RAE, Billy

HEDGEHOPPERS ANONYMOUS

Singles: 7–inch

PARROT	4-8	65-66

Also see KING, Jonathan

HEFTI, Neal

(Neal Hefti and His Orchestra; Neal Hefti Quintet; Neal Hefti and the Mello-Larks)

Singles: 78rpm

CORAL	3-5	51-57
EPIC	3-5	55-56

Singles: 7–inch

COLUMBIA	3-5	65
CORAL	4-6	51-59
DOT	3-5	67-68
EPIC	4-6	55-56
RCA	3-5	66
REPRISE	3-5	62
U.A.	3-5	65-66

Picture Sleeves

RCA	4-8	66-67
RCA GOLD STANDARD SERIES	2-4	89

EPs: 7–inch 33/45rpm

CORAL	4-8	52-56
X	4-8	55

LPs: 10/12–inch 33rpm

COLUMBIA	8-15	60
CORAL	10-20	52-60
EPIC	10-15	56
RCA (3621 "Hefti in Gotham City")	10-20	66
REPRISE	8-15	62
20TH FOX	8-12	64
U.A. (573 "Definitely Hefti")	8-15	67
X	10-15	55

Since publication of *The Official Price Guide to Movie/TV Soundtracks and Original Cast Albums*, with over 8,000 listings, this guide has dropped many soundtracks, including some by this artist.

HEIGHT, Donald

Singles: 7–inch

DAKAR	3-5	76
JUBILEE	4-6	63-69
KING	4-8	60
OLD TOWN	4-8	64
RCA	4-6	65
ROULETTE	4-6	65
SHOUT	4-6	66-68
SOOZEE	4-8	62

HEIGHT, Ronnie

Singles: 7–inch

BAMBOO	5-10	61
DORE	5-10	59
ERA	5-10	59-61

HEINTJE

Singles: 7–inch

MGM	3-6	70

LPs: 10/12–inch 33rpm

MGM	8-10	70

HELIX

LPs: 10/12–inch 33rpm

CAPITOL	5-10	83-87
GRUDGE	5-8	90

HELLO PEOPLE

Singles: 7–inch

ABC/DUNHILL	3-5	75-76
PHILIPS	4-6	68

Picture Sleeves

PHILIPS	5-8	68

LPs: 10/12–inch 33rpm

ABC/DUNHILL	8-10	74
ABC-PAR	8-10	75
MEDIARTS	12-15	70
PHILLIPS	15-20	68

HELLOWEEN

LPs: 10/12–inch 33rpm

MX	10-15	86
RCA	5-10	87-89

HELM, Levon

(Levon Helm and the RCO All-Stars)

Singles: 7–inch

A&M	2-4	80
ABC	3-5	78
CAPITOL	2-4	82
MCA	2-4	80

LPs: 10/12–inch 33rpm

ABC-PAR	5-10	77-78
A&M	5-10	80
CAPITOL	5-10	82
MCA	5-10	80

Also see BAND

Also see CASH, Johnny, and Levon Helm
Also see LEVON and the Hawks

HELMS, Bobby
Singles: 78rpm
DECCA 5-10   56-57
Singles: 7–inch
BLACK ROSE 2-4   83-84
CAPITOL 3-5   70
CERTRON 3-5   70
COLUMBIA 3-6   64
DECCA (Except 29947) 5-10   57-62
DECCA (29947 "Tennessee Rock and
Roll") 20-30   56
GUSTO 3-5   74
KAPP 4-6   65-67
LARRICK 3-5   75
LITTLE DARLIN' 3-6   67-79
MCA 2-4
MILLION 3-5   72
MISTLETOE 3-5   74
PLAYBACK 2-4
Picture Sleeves
CERTRON 4-6   70
DECCA (30194 "Fraulein") 15-20   57
DECCA (30513 "Jingle Bell Rock") ... 8-15   57
EPs: 7–inch 33/45rpm
DECCA 10-20   57-59
LPs: 10/12–inch 33rpm
CERTRON 8-10   70
COLUMBIA 12-15   63
DECCA (8638 "Bobby Helms Sings to
My Special Angel") 30-40   57
HARMONY 10-12   67
KAPP 10-15   66
LITTLE DARLIN' 10-12   68
MCA 5-10   83
MISTLETOE 5-10   74
VOCALION 10-12   65
Also see KERR, Anita

HELMS, Jimmie
Singles: 7–inch
EAST WEST (114 "It Was Ours") 20-30   58
FOREST 4-8   63
SCOTTIE 10-15   59
SYMBOL 4-8   63

HENDERSON, Finis
Singles: 7–inch
MOTOWN 2-4   83
LPs: 10/12–inch 33rpm
MOTOWN 5-10   83
Also see WEAPONS of PEACE

HENDERSON, Joe
Singles: 7–inch
ABC 3-5   73
KAPP 4-6   64
RIC 4-6   64
TODD 4-8   62-63
VIRGO 3-5   72

LPs: 10/12–inch 33rpm
TODD 20-25   62

HENDERSON, Michael
Singles: 12–inch 33/45rpm
EMI AMERICA 4-6   86
Singles: 7–inch
BUDDAH 2-5   76-83
EMI AMERICA 2-4   86
LPs: 10/12–inch 33rpm
ACCORD 5-10
BUDDAH 8-12   76-83
EMI AMERICA 5-10   86
Also see CONNORS, Norman
Also see HYMAN, Phyllis, and Michael Henderson

HENDERSON, Ron, and Choice of Colour
Singles: 7–inch
CHELSEA 3-5   77

HENDERSON, Skitch
EPs: 7–inch 33/45rpm
CAPITOL 10-20   50-54
COLUMBIA 5-15   65
DECCA 5-15   56
LPs: 10/12–inch 33rpm
CAPITOL (H-110 "Keyboard Sketches) 25-45   50
(10–inch LP.)
CAPITOL (502 "A Man and His Music") 15-25   54
COLUMBIA 5-15   65
DECCA (8000 series) 10-25   56
SEECO (62 "Skitch Henderson") 25-45
SEECO (401 "Latin Favorites") 20-35   56

HENDERSON, Wayne
(Wayne Henderson and the Freedom Sounds)
Singles: 7–inch
POLYDOR 3-5   78-79
LPs: 10/12–inch 33rpm
ABC 5-10   77
ATLANTIC 8-12   67-68
POLYDOR 5-10   78-79
Also see AYERS, Roy, and Wayne Henderson

HENDERSON, Willie
(Willie Henderson and the Soul Explosions)
Singles: 7–inch
BRUNSWICK 3-6   70
PLAYBOY 3-5   74
LPs: 10/12–inch 33rpm
BRUNSWICK 10-12   69-74

HENDRICKS, Bobby
Singles: 7–inch
MGM 4-8   63
MERCURY 4-8   61
SUE 5-10   58-60
Also see COASTERS
Also see DRIFTERS

HENDRIX, Jimi
Singles: 7–inch
AUDIO FIDELITY (167 "No
Such Animal") 10-15

REPRISE (Except 0572 and 0665) . . . 5-10   67-72
REPRISE (0572 "Hey Joe") 20-30   67
REPRISE (0665 "Up from the Skies") 10-15   68
TRIP 2-4   72

Promotional Singles

REPRISE (Except 0572 and 0665) . . . 6-10   67-72
REPRISE (0572 "Hey Joe") 25-30   67
REPRISE (0665 "Up from the Skies") 10-20   68

Picture Sleeves

AUDIO FIDELITY (167 "No
Such Animal") 15-25
REPRISE (0572 "Hey Joe") 60-80   67

EPs: 7–inch 33/45rpm

REPRISE (595 "And a Happy
New Year") 75-100   74
(Promotional issue only. Issued with paper sleeve.)

LPs: 10/12–inch 33rpm

ABC (82-41 "Jimi Hendrix:
A Tribute") 150-200   82
(Five LPs plus cue sheets. Promotional issue only.)
ACCORD 5-10   81
BBC ROCK HOUR/LONDON WAVELENGTH
("Jimi Hendrix Special") 50-75   81
CAPITOL (12000 series) 5-8   86
CAPITOL (15000 series) 4-6   86
(Mini LP.)
CRAWDADDY 200-250   75
PICKWICK 5-10   75
WESTWOOD ONE ("Psychedelic Psnack
[Psalute to Jimi Hendrix]") 20-25   89
(Promotional issue only.)
NUTMEG (1001 "High, Live 'N Dirty") 15-20   78
(Colored vinyl.)
REPRISE (840 "Jimi Hendrix - Christmas
Medley") 40-50   79
(Promotional issue only.)
REPRISE (2025 "Smash Hits") 25-35   69
(Orange and brown label. Price includes bonus
poster, which represents about
$15-$20 of the value.)
REPRISE (2025 "Smash Hits") 8-10   71
(Brown label.)
REPRISE (2029 "Historic
Performances") 8-10   70
REPRISE (2034 "The Cry of Love") . . . 8-10   71
REPRISE (2040 "Rainbow Bridge") . . 10-15   71
REPRISE (2049 "In the West") 10-15   72
REPRISE (2103 "War Heroes") 10-15   72
REPRISE (2204 "Crash Landing") . . . 10-15   75
REPRISE (2229 "Midnight Lightning") 10-15   75
REPRISE (2245 "Essential Jimi
Hendrix") 8-12   78
REPRISE (2276 "Smash Hits") 5-10   77
REPRISE (2293 "Essential Jimi
Hendrix, Vol. 2") 50-100   79
(Includes the bonus single, *Gloria*,
extended version.)

REPRISE (2293 "Essential Jimi
Hendrix, Vol. 2") 10-15   79
(Without the bonus single.)
REPRISE (2299 "Nine to the Universe") 5-10   80
REPRISE (R-6261 "Are You
Experienced") 35-65   67
(Monaural. Green, pink and yellow label.)
REPRISE (6261 "Are You
Experienced") 12-20   68
(Orange and brown label.)
REPRISE (6261 "Are You
Experienced") 5-10   71
(Brown label.)
REPRISE (R-6281 "Axis: Bold
As Love") 175-225   68
(Monaural. Orange and brown label.)
REPRISE (RS-6281 "Axis: Bold
As Love") 15-20   68
(Stereo. Green, pink and yellow label.)
REPRISE (RS-6281 "Axis: Bold
As Love") 5-10   71
(Brown label.)
REPRISE (6307 "Electric Ladyland") . 12-15   68
(Orange and brown label.)
REPRISE (6307 "Electric Ladyland") . . 8-10   71
(Brown label.)
REPRISE (6481 "From the film
Jimi Hendrix") 15-20   73
(Soundtrack.)
REPRISE (22306 "Jimi Hendrix
Concerts") 8-10   82
REPRISE (25119 "Kiss the Sky") 5-10   84
REPRISE (25358 "Jimi Plays
Monterey") 5-10   86
RHINO 5-10   82
ROLLING STONE PRODUCTIONS (82-24 "The
Jimi Hendrix Profile") 50-100   82
(Two LPs plus cue sheets. Promotional issue only.)
RYKO 10-15   87-88
SHOUT 10-15   72
(White label with red and blue printing.)
SHOUT 8-10
(Yellow label.)

NO SUCH ANIMAL
(J. Hendrix)
Part I
PROMOTION
COPY
NOT FOR SALE
AF-167-A
Bates Music
Publ. Corp.
BMI 2:27
AUDIO FIDELITY
JIMI HENDRIX
A PRODUCT OF AUDIO FIDELITY RECORDS, INC.

SPRINGBOARD 8-10   72
TRIP 8-10   72-74
U.A. 8-10   75
WESTWOOD ONE ("Rock and Roll Never Forgets
    Jimi Hendrix") 150-200   83
    (Five LPs plus cue sheets. Promotional issue only.)
WESTWOOD ONE ("Jimi Hendrix, Live
    and Unreleased") 400-500   88
    (Eight LPs plus cue sheets. Promotional issue
    only.)
    Also see REDDING, Otis / Jimi Hendrix

HENDRIX, Jimi, and the Isley Bros.
LPs: 10/12–inch 33rpm
T-NECK 10-15   71
    Also see ISLEY BROTHERS

HENDRIX, Jimi, and Curtis Knight
LPs: 10/12–inch 33rpm
CAPITOL (659 "Flashing") 8-10   70
CAPITOL (2856 "Get That Feeling") . 10-15   67
CAPITOL (2894 "Flashing") 10-15   68
51 WEST 5-10   82

HENDRIX, Jimi, and Little Richard
Singles: 7–inch
ALANNA 3-6   72
LPs: 10/12–inch 33rpm
ALANNA 10-12   72
EVEREST 6-10   74
PICKWICK 6-10   73
    Also see LITTLE RICHARD

HENDRIX, Jimi, and Buddy Miles
LPs: 10/12–inch 33rpm
CAPITOL (472 "Band of Gypsies") ... 10-12   70
    Also see MILES, Buddy

HENDRIX, Jimi, and Lonnie Youngblood
LPs: 10/12–inch 33rpm
MAPLE (6004 "Two Great Experiences
    Together") 20-25   71
    Also see HENDRIX, Jimi
    Also see YOUNGBLOOD, Lonnie

HENDRIX, Patti
Singles: 7–inch
HILLTAK 3-5   78
20TH FOX 3-5   74

HENDRYX, Nona
Singles: 12–inch 33/45rpm
RCA 4-6   83-86
Singles: 7–inch
EMI AMERICA 2-4   87
EPIC 3-5   77
RCA 2-4   83-87
Picture Sleeves
EMI AMERICA 2-4   87
LPs: 10/12–inch 33rpm
EMI AMERICA 5-8   87
EPIC 5-10   77
RCA 5-10   83-87
    Also see LABELLE, Patti

HENHOUSE FIVE PLUS TOO
Singles: 7–inch
WARNER/AHAB 3-5   76-77
    Member: Ray Stevens.
    Also see STEVENS, Ray

HENLEY, Don
Singles: 12–inch 33/45rpm
GEFFEN 4-6   85
Singles: 7–inch
ASYLUM 2-4   82-83
GEFFEN 2-4   84-89
Picture Sleeves
ASYLUM 2-4   82
GEFFEN 2-4   84-90
LPs: 10/12–inch 33rpm
ASYLUM 5-10   82-83
GEFFEN 5-10   84-89
    Also see EAGLES
    Also see NICKS, Stevie, and Don Henley

HENRY, Clarence
(Clarence "Frogman" Henry)
Singles: 78rpm
ARGO 10-15   56-57
Singles: 7–inch
ARGO (5200 series) 10-15   56-58
ARGO (5300 and 5400 series) 5-10   59-63
DIAL 4-6   67
PARROT 4-8   64-66
CHESS 3-5   73
ERIC 3-5   73
MAISON DE SOUL 3-5   77
LPs: 10/12–inch 33rpm
ARGO (4009 "You Always Hurt
    the One You Love") 50-75   61
CADET 20-30
    (Some Cadet LPs were packaged in Argo covers,
    using the same numbers.)
ROULETTE 15-20   69

HENSLEY, Ken
Singles: 7–inch
MERCURY 3-5   73
LPs: 10/12–inch 33rpm
MERCURY 8-10   73
WARNER 8-10   75
    Also see URIAH HEEP

HENSON, Jim
(Jim Henson's Muppets)
Singles: 7–inch
COLUMBIA 3-5   72
SIGNATURE 5-8   60
Singles: 12–inch 33/45rpm
COLUMBIA 5-10   71
    Also see ERNIE
    Also see KERMIT / Fozzie Bear
    Also see MUPPETS

HERB the "K"
Singles: 7–inch
PRIVATE I 2-4   85

HERMAN, Keith
Singles: 7-inch
RADIO 2-4   79

HERMAN, Woody, and His Orchestra
Singles: 78rpm
CAPITOL 2-4   54-56
MARS 2-4   52-53
Singles: 7-inch
CADET 2-5   69
CAPITOL 3-6   54-56
CENTURY 2-4   79
CHURCHILL 2-4   79
COLUMBIA 2-4   65-76
FANTASY 2-4   73-74
MCA 2-4   73
MARS 4-8   52-53
PHILIPS 3-5   62
EPs: 7-inch 33/45rpm
CAPITOL 5-10   55-56
COLUMBIA 8-12   52-54
DECCA 5-10   56
MGM 5-10   55
LPs: 10/12-inch 33rpm
ACCORD 5-10   82
ATLANTIC (1300 series) 10-20   60
ATLANTIC (90000 series) 5-10   82
BRIGHT ORANGE 5-10   73
CADET 8-12   69-71
CAPITOL 5-10   72-75
  (With "M" or "SM" prefix.)
CAPITOL 10-25   55-62
  (With a "T" or "ST" prefix.)
CENTURY 5-10   78
CHESS 5-10   76
COLUMBIA (500 series) 15-25   55
COLUMBIA (2300 and 2400 series) ... 5-15   65-66
COLUMBIA (2500 series) 15-25   52-54
  (10-inch LPs.)
COLUMBIA (6000 series) 15-25   49-55
COLUMBIA (9000 series) 5-15   65-67
COLUMBIA (32000 series) 5-10   74
CONCORD JAZZ 5-10   81-83
CROWN 10-15   59
DECCA (4000 series) 8-15   64
DECCA (8000 series) 10-25   56
EVEREST (Except 200 and 300
  series) 10-20   59-63
EVEREST (200 and 300 series) 5-10   74-78
FPM 5-10   75
FANTASY 5-10   71-81
HARMONY 5-10   72
JAZZLAND 10-20   60
MGM 10-25   55
METRO 5-12   65
PHILIPS 10-15   62-65
ROULETTE 10-20   59
SURREY 8-12   66
TREND 5-10   81

TRIP 5-10   75
VSP 8-12   66-67
VERVE 8-15   63-68
WHO'S WHO in JAZZ 5-10   78
WING 5-10
  Also see BYRD, Charlie, and Woody Herman
  Also see CLOONEY, Rosemary

HERMAN'S HERMITS
Singles: 7-inch
ABKCO 2-4
BUDDAH 3-5   74-76
MGM 4-6   64-69
PRIVATE STOCK 3-5   75
Picture Sleeves
MGM 5-12   65-67
LPs: 10/12-inch 33rpm
ABKCO 5-10   73-76
MGM (Except 4478) 10-20   65-68
MGM (E-4478 "Blaze") 35-45   67
  (Monaural.)
MGM (SE-4478 "Blaze") 10-20   67
  (Stereo.)
  Members: Peter Noone; Derek Leckenby; Karl Green; Keith
  Hopwood; Barry Whitwham.
  Also see PAGE, Jimmy

HERNANDEZ, Patrick
Singles: 12-inch 33/45rpm
COLUMBIA 4-6   79
Singles: 7-inch
COLUMBIA 2-4   79
LPs: 10/12-inch 33rpm
COLUMBIA 5-10   79

HEROES
Singles: 12-inch 33/45rpm
RCA 4-8   87
Singles: 7-inch
RCA 2-4   87
LPs: 10/12-inch 33rpm
POLYDOR 5-10   80
RCA 5-10   87

HESITATIONS
Singles: 7-inch
B.T. PUPPY 4-8   68
GWP 4-8   69
KAPP 5-10   66-68
LPs: 10/12-inch 33rpm
KAPP 10-15   67-68
  Member: Leonard Veal.

HEWETT, Howard
Singles: 7-inch
ARISTA 2-4   88
ELEKTRA 2-4   85-90
Picture Sleeves
ELEKTRA 2-4   86
LPs: 10/12-inch 33rpm
ELEKTRA 5-8   85-90
  Also see SHALAMAR
  Also see WARWICK, Dionne, and Howard Hewett

HEYETTES
Singles: 7–inch
LONDON 3-5   76
Picture Sleeves
LONDON 5-10   76
LPs: 10/12–inch 33rpm
LONDON 5-10   76

HEYWARD, Nick
Singles: 7–inch
ARISTA 2-4   83-84
LPs: 10/12–inch 33rpm
ARISTA 5-10   83
Also see HAIRCUT ONE HUNDRED

HEYWOOD, Eddie
Singles: 78rpm
DECCA 3-5   53
MERCURY 3-5   55-57
Singles: 7–inch
DECCA 4-6   53
LIBERTY 3-5   61-63
MERCURY 3-6   55-61
20TH FOX 3-5   63
EPs: 7–inch 33/45rpm
COLUMBIA 4-8   52
DECCA 4-8   56
MERCURY 4-8   55-56
LPs: 10/12–inch 33rpm
BRUNSWICK 10-15   55
CAPITOL 5-10   67-69
COLUMBIA 10-20   52
CORAL 10-15   55
DECCA 10-15   56
EPIC 10-15   56
LIBERTY 8-12   62-63
MERCURY 10-15   55-60
RCA 10-12   59
SUNSET 5-10   66
VOCALION 5-10   66
WING 8-12   59-64
Also see HOLIDAY, Billie, and Eddie Heywood
Also see WINTERHALTER, Hugo, and His Orchestra

HIATT, John
Singles: 12–inch 33/45rpm
A&M 4-8   87
(Promotional only.)
GEFFEN 4-8   85
(Promotional only.)
Singles: 7–inch
A&M 2-4   87-90
GEFFEN 2-4   85
MCA 2-4   79-90
LPs: 10/12–inch 33rpm
A&M 5-10   87-90
GEFFEN ("Riot with Hiatt") 25-35
(Promotional issue only.)
Also see COSTELLO, Elvis

HIBBLER, Al
Singles: 78rpm
ALADDIN 4-6   56
ATLANTIC 5-10   51
CLEF 3-5   54
COLUMBIA 3-5   50
DECCA 3-5   55-57
MERCURY 3-5   52-56
MIRACLE 5-10   48
NORGRAN 3-5   54-55
ORIGINAL 4-8   55
Singles: 7–inch
ALADDIN 5-10   56
ATLANTIC (925 "The Blues Came
Tumbling Down") 30-40   51
ATLANTIC (932 "Travelin' Light") 30-40   51
ATLANTIC (945 "This Is Always") ... 30-40   51
ATLANTIC (1071 "Danny Boy") 15-25   55
CLEF 4-8   54
COLUMBIA 5-10   50
DECCA 4-8   55-59
MCA 2-4   74
MERCURY 4-8   52-56
NORGRAN 4-8   54-55
ORIGINAL 5-10   55
REPRISE 4-6   61-62
SATIN 3-6   66
TOP RANK 4-6   60
VEGAS 3-6   67
EPs: 7–inch 33/45rpm
CLEF 10-15   51
DECCA 5-10   55-57
NORGRAN 10-15   53
RCA 5-10   55
LPs: 10/12–inch 33rpm
ATLANTIC 10-20   56
CLEF 15-25   54
DECCA (8000 series) 10-20   56-59
DECCA (75000 series) 5-10   69
LMI 8-12   65
MCA 5-10   76
NORGRAN (4 "Favorites") 30-40   53
REPRISE 8-15   61
TRIP 4-8   77
VERVE 10-20   55
Also see HOLIDAY, Billie, and Al Hibbler
Also see McSHANN, Jay

HIBBLER, Al, and Duke Ellington
Singles: 7–inch
COLUMBIA (33000 series) 2-4   76
LPs: 10/12–inch 33rpm
COLUMBIA 15-25   56
Also see ELLINGTON, Duke
Also see HIBBLER, Al

HICKEY, Ersel
Singles: 7–inch
APOLLO (761 "Upside Down Love") . 15-25   62
BLACK CIRCLE 3-5   72

EPIC 10-15   58-60
JANUS 3-5   71
KAPP 8-12   61
LAURIE 8-12   63
MAGNUM 2-4   84
RAMESES 3-5   76
TOOT 8-12
UNIFAX 3-5   74
EPs: 7-inch 33/45rpm
EPIC (7206 "Ersel Hickey in
   Lover's Land") 75-100   58

HICKS, Clair
Singles: 12-inch 33/45rpm
KN 4-6   84

HICKS, Dan, and His Hot Licks
Singles: 7-inch
BLUE THUMB 3-5   73-74
LPs: 10/12-inch 33rpm
BLUE THUMB 8-10   71-73
EPIC 10-12   69
WARNER 5-10   78

HIDDEN STRENGTH
Singles: 7-inch
U.A. 3-5   76

HI-FI FOUR
Singles: 78rpm
KING 4-6   56
Singles: 7-inch
KING 10-15   56

HIGGINS, Bertie
Singles: 7-inch
CBS ASSOCIATED 2-4   85
KAT FAMILY 2-4   81-82
SOUTHERN TRACKS 2-4   87
LPs: 10/12-inch 33rpm
KAT FAMILY 5-10   82

HIGGINS, Monk
(Monk Higgins and the Specialties)
Singles: 7-inch
BUDDAH 3-5   74
CHESS 3-6   67
SOLID STATE 3-6   68
ST. LAWRENCE 4-6   66
U.A. 3-5   72-73
LPs: 10/12-inch 33rpm
BUDDAH 5-10   74
SOLID STATE 8-12   69
U.A. 8-10   72
Also see MASON, Barbara

HIGH INERGY
Singles: 12-inch 33/45rpm
GORDY 4-6   83
Singles: 7-inch
GORDY (Black vinyl) 2-5   77-83
GORDY (Colored vinyl) 3-6
(Promotional only.)

LPs: 10/12-inch 33rpm
GORDY 5-10   77-83
Also see ROBINSON, Smokey, and Barbara Mitchell

HIGH KEYS
Singles: 7-inch
ATCO 8-10   63-64
VERVE 4-8   66

HIGHLIGHTS
(Featuring Frank Pizani)
Singles: 78rpm
BALLY 4-8   56-57
Singles: 7-inch
BALLY 8-12   56-58
Also see PIZANI, Frank

HIGHTOWER, Willie
Singles: 7-inch
CAPITOL 4-6   69
FAME 3-5   70

HIGHWAYMEN
Singles: 7-inch
ABC-PAR 4-6   65-66
LIBERTY 2-4   81
U.A. 4-8   61-64
LPs: 10/12-inch 33rpm
ABC-PAR 8-15   66
LIBERTY 5-8   82
U.A. 15-20   61-65
Members: Steve Butts; Chan Daniels; Gil Robbins; Dave Fisher.

HILL, Bunker
Singles: 7-inch
MALA (Except 464) 5-8   62
MALA (464 "The Girl Can't Dance") ... 8-12   63

HILL, Dan
Singles: 7-inch
COLUMBIA 2-4   87
EPIC 2-4   80-81
20TH FOX 3-5   75-79
Picture Sleeves
20TH FOX 3-5   78
LPs: 10/12-inch 33rpm
EPIC 5-10   80-81
20TH FOX 5-10   75-80

HILL, Dan, and Vonda Sheppard
Singles: 7-inch
COLUMBIA 2-4   87
LPs: 10/12-inch 33rpm
COLUMBIA 5-10   87
Also see HILL, Dan

HILL, David
Singles: 78rpm
ALADDIN 3-6   57
RCA 3-6   57
Singles: 7-inch
ALADDIN 5-10   57
KAPP 5-10   59
RCA 5-10   57-58

HILL, Jessie
Singles: 7–inch
DOWNEY 5-10   64
MINIT 8-12   60-62
YOGI-MAN (607 "Hey Now Mama") .. 10-15
LPs: 10/12–inch 33rpm
BLUE THUMB 8-10   72

HILL, Lonnie
Singles: 7–inch
URBAN SOUND 2-4   84-85
LPs: 10/12–inch 33rpm
URBAN SOUND 5-10   85

HILL, Z.Z.
Singles: 7–inch
ATLANTIC 4-6   69-70
AUDREY 3-5   71-72
COLUMBIA 3-5   77-78
HILL 3-5   71-73
KENT 4-8   64-71
M.H. 4-8   63
M.H.R 3-5   75
MALACO 2-4   82-84
MAILBU 2-4
MESA 4-8   64
MANKIND 3-5   71-72
QUINCY 3-5   70
RARE BULLET 2-4   84
U.A. 3-5   73-75
LPs: 10/12–inch 33rpm
COLUMBIA 5-10   78-79
KENT 10-15   69-71
MALACO 5-10   82-84
MANKIND 8-12   71
U.A. 8-10   72-75

HILLAGE, Steve
Singles: 7–inch
ATLANTIC 3-5   76-77
LPs: 10/12–inch 33rpm
ATLANTIC 8-10   76-77
VIRGIN 8-10   75

HILLMAN, Chris
Singles: 7–inch
ASYLUM 3-5   76-77
LPs: 10/12–inch 33rpm
ASYLUM 5-10   76-77
SUGAR HILL 5-10   82-84
  Also see BYRDS
  Also see FLYING BURRITO BROTHERS
  Also see McGUINN & HILLMAN
  Also see SOUTHER - HILLMAN - FURAY BAND

HILLSIDE SINGERS
Singles: 7–inch
METROMEDIA 3-5   71-72
LPs: 10/12–inch 33rpm
METROMEDIA 8-12   71

HILLTOPPERS
(Hill Toppers)
Singles: 78rpm
DOT 3-5   52-57
Singles: 7–inch
ABC 2-4   74
DOT (15000 series) 5-10   52-60
DOT (16000 series) 4-6   63
3-J 3-6   66
EPs: 7–inch 33/45rpm
DOT 5-12   54-56
LPs: 10/12–inch 33rpm
DOT (105 "The Hilltoppers") 30-40   54
  (10–inch LP.)
DOT (106 "The Hilltoppers") 30-40   54
  (10–inch LP.)
DOT (3003 "Tops in Pops") 20-30   55
DOT (3029 "Towering Hilltoppers") .. 20-30 56
DOT (3073 "The Hilltoppers") 20-30   57
SOUVENIR 8-15   73
  Members: Jimmy Sacca; Billy Vaughn; Don McGuire; Seymour
  Spiegelman.
  Also see VAUGHN, Billy

HINDSIGHT
Singles: 7–inch
VIRGIN 2-4   88

HINE, Eric
Singles: 7–inch
MONTAGE 2-4   81

HINES, Gregory
Singles: 7–inch
EPIC 2-4   87-88
  Also see VANDROSS, Luther, and Gregory Hines

HINES, J., and the Fellows
Singles: 7–inch
DELUXE 3-5   73

HINTON, Joe
(Little Joe Hinton)
Singles: 7–inch
ARVEE 4-8   61
BACKBEAT 5-10   59-65
HOTLANTA 8-10   74
Picture Sleeves
BACKBEAT 8-15   59-65
LPs: 10/12–inch 33rpm
BACKBEAT (60 "Funny") 20-25   65
DUKE 8-10   73

HIPPIES / Reggie Harrison
Singles: 7–inch
PARKWAY (863 "Memory Lane") 8-10   63
  Also see STEREOS
  Also see TAMS

HIROSHIMA
Singles: 12–inch 33/45rpm
EPIC 4-6   85
Singles: 7–inch
ARISTA 2-4   80-84

EPIC 2-4   85
LPs: 10/12-inch 33rpm
ARISTA 5-10   79-84
EPIC 5-10   83-89

HIRT, Al
Singles: 7-inch
CORAL 3-5   65
GWP 2-5   69-70
MONUMENT 2-4   74
RCA 3-6   61-68
Picture Sleeves
RCA 4-8   61-66
EPs: 7-inch 33/45rpm
RCA 4-8   62
LPs: 10/12-inch 33rpm
ACCORD 4-8   82
AUDIO FIDELITY 10-15   59-61
CAMDEN 5-10   67-71
CORAL 8-15   65
GWP 5-10   70-71
METRO 5-10   65
MONUMENT 5-8   74
RCA (Except 3309) 5-15   61-78
RCA (LPM-3309 "Best of Al Hirt") 10-15   65
(Monaural. Has Ann-Margret on one track.)
RCA (LSP-3309 "Best of Al Hirt") 15-20   65
(Stereo. Has Ann-Margret on one track.)
VOCALION 5-10   70
Also see ANN-MARGRET and Al Hirt

HIRT, Al, and the Boston Pops Orchestra
LPs: 10/12-inch 33rpm
RCA 10-15   64
Also see BOSTON POPS ORCHESTRA

HIRT, Al, and Pete Fountain
Singles: 7-inch
CORAL 3-6   61
EPs: 7-inch 33/45rpm
CORAL 4-8   62
LPs: 10/12-inch 33rpm
CORAL 8-15   61-62
MGM 8-15   64
MONUMENT 5-10   75
VERVE 10-20   61
Also see FOUNTAIN, Pete

HIRT, Al / Henry Mancini / Perez Prado
LPs: 10/12-inch 33rpm
RCA 8-15   63
Also see MANCINI, Henry
Also see PRADO, Perez

HIRT, Al, and Hugo Montenegro
LPs: 10/12-inch 33rpm
RCA (4275 "Viva Max") 15-20   70
(Soundtrack.)
Also see MONTENEGRO, Hugo

HIRT, Al, and Boots Randolph
Singles: 7-inch
MONUMENT 3-5   75

Also see HIRT, Al
Also see RANDOLPH, Boots

HITCHCOCK, Robyn
(Robyn Hitchcock and the Egyptians)
Singles: 7-inch
A&M 2-4   88-90
LPs: 10/12-inch 33rpm
A&M 5-8   88-90

HITCHCOCK, Russell
Singles: 7-inch
ARISTA 2-4   88
LPs: 10/12-inch 33rpm
ARISTA 5-10   88
Also see AIR SUPPLY

HO, Don
(Don Ho and the Aliis)
Singles: 7-inch
HEL 3-5   77
MEGA 2-5   74-75
REPRISE 3-6   65-71
LPs: 10/12-inch 33rpm
MEGA 4-8   74
REPRISE 5-15   65-70

HODGE, Chris
(Chris Hodge with George Harrison)
Singles: 7-inch
APPLE 4-6   72-73
RCA 3-5   73-75
Picture Sleeves
APPLE 5-8   72
Also see HARRISON, George

HODGES, Charles
Singles: 7-inch
ALTO 10-15   65
CALLA 3-5   70
Also see HUNT, Geraldine, and Charlie Hodges

HODGES, Eddie
Singles: 7-inch
AURORA 4-6   65-66
BARNABY 3-5   76
CADENCE 8-15   61-62
COLUMBIA 4-8   62-63
DECCA 5-10   59
MGM 4-8   64
Picture Sleeves
CADENCE 10-15   61
COLUMBIA 5-10   63
Also see MILLS, Hayley, and Eddie Hodges

HODGES, Johnny
Singles: 7-inch
CLEF 5-10   53-56
COLUMBIA 5-10   51
GROOVE 5-10   56
MERCURY 5-10   51-53
NORGRAN 5-10   54-56
VMC 3-6   68
VERVE 4-8   57-67

EPs: 7-Inch 33/45rpm

ATLANTIC 20-30	54
EPIC 15-25	55
NORGRAN 25-50	54
RCA (3000 "Alto Sax") 50-75	52

LPs: 10/12-Inch 33rpm

AMERICAN RECORDING (421 "Johnny	
Hodges and the Ellington All Stars") 40-60	57
CLEF (111 "Johnny Hodges	
Collates") 100-200	52
(10–inch LP.)	
CLEF (128 "Johnny Hodges	
Collates, Vol. 2") 100-200	52
(10–inch LP.)	
ENCORE 10-15	68
EPIC (3105 "Hodge Podge") 50-75	55
EPIC (22000 series) 8-12	74
IMPULSE 10-20	65
INSTANT 15-20	64
MCA 5-10	82
NORGRAN (1 "Swing with	
Johnny Hodges") 150-250	53
(10–inch LP.)	
NORGRAN (1004 "Memories of	
Ellington") 100-200	54
NORGRAN (1009 "More Johnny	
Hodges") 100-200	54
NORGRAN (1024 "Dance Bash") . 100-200	55
NORGRAN (1045 "Creamy") 100-200	56
NORGRAN (1048 "Castle Rock") .. 100-200	56
NORGRAN (1055 "Ellingtonia") 75-150	56
NORGRAN (1059 "In a	
Tender Mood") 75-150	56
NORGRAN (1060 "Used to	
Be Duke") 75-150	56
NORGRAN (1061 "The Blues") 75-150	56
PABLO 5-10	78
RCA (500 series) 10-20	66
RCA (3000 "Alto Sax") 200-300	52
(10–inch LP.)	
RCA (3800 series) 10-20	67
VSP 10-20	66-67
VERVE (8179 "Perdido") 50-100	57
VERVE (8180 "In a Mellow Tone") .. 50-100	57
VERVE (8203 "Duke's in Bed") 50-100	57
VERVE (8271 "Big Sound") 50-100	58
(Reads "Verve Records, Inc." at bottom of label.)	
VERVE (8271 "Big Sound") 15-25	
(Reads "MGM Records - A Division Of	
Metro-Goldwyn-Mayer, Inc." at bottom of label.)	
VERVE (8314 through 8358) 25-45	59-60
(Reads "Verve Records, Inc." at bottom of label.)	
VERVE (8314 through 8358) 15-25	61-69
(Reads "MGM Records - A Division Of	
Metro-Goldwyn-Mayer, Inc." at bottom of label.)	
VERVE 8-15	74-79
(Reads "Manufactured By MGM Record Corp.," or	
mentions either Polydor or Polygram at bottom of	
label.)	

Also see ELLINGTON, Duke, and Johnny Hodges
Also see MULLIGAN, Gerry, and Johnny Hodges

HODGES, Johnny, and Lawrence Welk
LPs: 10/12-Inch 33rpm

DOT 10-20	66

Also see WELK, Lawrence

HODGES, Johnny, and Wild Bill Davis
LPs: 10/12-Inch 33rpm

RCA 10-20	65-67
VERVE 15-30	61-66

Also see HODGES, Johnny

HODGES, JAMES & SMITH
Singles: 12–Inch 33/45rpm

LONDON 4-8	79

Singles: 7–inch

LONDON 3-5	76-79
20TH FOX 3-5	75

LPs: 10/12–inch 33rpm

LONDON 5-10	78

Members: Pat Hodges; Denita James; Jessica Smith.

HODGSON, Roger
Singles: 7–inch

A&M 2-4	84

LPs: 10/12–inch 33rpm

A&M 5-10	84-87

Also see SUPERTRAMP

HOG HEAVEN
Singles: 7–inch

ROULETTE 3-5	71

LPs: 10/12–inch 33rpm

ROULETTE 10-12	71

Members: Ron Rosman; Mike Vale; Peter Lucia; Eddie Gray.
Also see JAMES, Tommy, and the Shondells

HOGG, Andrew
Singles: 78rpm

EXCLUSIVE (89 "He Knows How Much	
We Can Bear") 20-30	47

Also see HOGG, Smokey

HOGG, Smokey
(Andrew Hogg)
Singles: 78rpm

BULLET 15-25	48
COLONY 10-20	50
COMBO 10-15	52
CROWN 8-12	54
EXCLUSIVE 15-25	47
FEDERAL 15-25	53
FIDELITY 10-20	52
IMPERIAL 5-10	50-53
INDEPENDENT 10-20	49
MACY'S 8-12	49
MERCURY 10-20	51
METEOR 20-30	54
MODERN 10-20	48-52
RAY'S RECORD 15-25	52
RECORDED in HOLLYWOOD 5-10	52
SHOW TIME 10-20	54

COLUMBIA (6163 "Billie Holiday
  Favorites") 100-200   51
  (10–inch LP.)
COLUMBIA (1157 "Lady in Satin") . . . 30-40   58
COLUMBIA (30000 series) 8-15   72-73
DECCA (100 series) 10-20   65-72
DECCA (5345 "Lover Man") 100-150   52
  (10–inch LP.)
DECCA (8215 "The Lady Sings") 50-75   56
DECCA (8701 "Blues Are Brewin") . . . 50-75   58
DECCA (75000 series) 8-15   68
ESP 8-12   71-73
EVEREST 5-10   73-75
HARMONY 5-10   73
JAZZTONE (1209 "Billie Holiday
  Sings") 30-40   56
JOLLY ROGER (5020 "Billie
  Holiday") 75-100   54
KENT 5-10   73
MCA 5-10   73
MFSL (201 "In Rehearsal") 15-25   87
MGM (100 series) 6-10   70
MGM (3700 series) 20-40   59
MGM (4900 series) 5-10   74
MAINSTREAM 10-20   65
METRO 10-20   65
MONMOUTH-EVERGREEN 5-10   72
PARAMOUNT 5-10   73
PICKWICK 5-10
RIC 10-20   64
SCORE 25-50   57
SOLID STATE 8-12   69
TRIP 5-10   73
U.A. (5600 series) 5-10   72
U.A. (14000 and 15000 series) 20-30   62
VSP 8-15   66
VERVE 20-40   57-60
  (Reads "Verve Records, Inc." at bottom of label.)
VERVE 10-25   61-72
  (Reads "MGM Records - a Division of
  Metro-Goldwyn-Mayer, Inc." at bottom of label.)
VERVE 5-10   73-84
  (Reads "Manufactured By MGM Record Corp.," or
  mentions either Polydor or Polygram at bottom of
  label.)
  Also see FITZGERALD, Ella / Billie Holiday / Lena Horne

HOLIDAY, Billie, and Stan Getz
LPs: 10/12–inch 33rpm

DALE (25 "Billie and Stan") 150-200   51
  (10–inch LP.)
  Also see GETZ, Stan
  Also see GOODMAN, Benny, Orchestra
  Also see LYNNE, Gloria / Nina Simone / Billie Holiday

HOLIDAY, Billie, and Eddie Heywood
LPs: 10/12–inch 33rpm

COMMODORE (20005 "Billie
  Holiday, Volume 1") 100-150   50
  (10–inch LP.)

COMMODORE (20006 "Billie
  Holiday, Volume 2") 100-150   50
  (10–inch LP.)
COMMODORE (30008 "Billie
  Holiday, Volume 1") 40-60   59
COMMODORE (30011 "Billie
  Holiday, Volume 2") 40-60   59
  Also see HEYWOOD, Eddie

HOLIDAY, Billie, and Al Hibbler
LPs: 10/12–inch 33rpm

IMPERIAL 20-30   62
SUNSET 8-15   67
  Also see HIBBLER, Al
  Also see HOLIDAY, Billie

HOLIDAY, Chico
Singles: 7–inch

CORAL 3-6   61-63
KARATE 3-6   65
NEW PHOENIX 8-10
RCA 4-8   59
SHAMLEY 3-5   69

HOLIDAY, Jimmy
Singles: 7–inch

DIPLOMACY 4-8   65
EVEREST 4-8   63-65
KENT 4-6   68
MINIT 4-8   66-68
LPs: 10/12–inch 33rpm
MINIT 15-25   66

HOLIDAY, Jimmy, and Clydie King
Singles: 7–inch

MINIT 4-8   67
  Also see HOLIDAY, Jimmy

HOLIDAYS
Singles: 7–inch

GOLDEN WORLD 5-8   66
  Members: Edwin Starr; Steve Mancha; J.J. Barnes.
  Also see BARNES, J.J., and Steve Mancha
  Also see STARR, Edwin

HOLIEN, Danny
Singles: 7–inch

TUMBLEWEED 3-5   72

HOLLAND, Amy
Singles: 7–inch

CAPITOL 2-4   80-83
Picture Sleeves
CAPITOL 2-4   80
LPs: 10/12–inch 33rpm
CAPITOL 5-10   80-83
  Also see McDONALD, Michael

HOLLAND, Brian
(Bryant Holland)
Singles: 7–inch

INVICTUS 3-5   72-73
KUDO 10-15   58
  Also see HOLLAND - DOZIER

HOLLAND, Eddie
Singles: 7–inch

MERCURY	15-25	58
MOTOWN	10-25	61-64
TAMLA (102 "Merry-Go-Round")	100-150	59
U.A.	8-12	59-61

Picture Sleeves

MOTOWN	10-20	62

LPs: 10/12–inch 33rpm

MOTOWN (604 "Eddie Holland")	35-50	63

HOLLAND, Eddie, and Lamont Dozier
Singles: 7–inch

MOTOWN	8-12	63

Also see DOZIER, Lamont
Also see HOLLAND, Eddie
Also see HOLLAND - DOZIER

HOLLAND – DOZIER
(Holland-Dozier with the Four Tops)
Singles: 7–inch

INVICTUS	3-5	72-73
MOTOWN	15-20	63

Members: Brian Holland; Lamont Dozier
Also see FOUR TOPS
Also see HOLLAND, Brian
Also see HOLLAND, Eddie, and Lamont Dozier

HOLLIDAY, Jennifer
Singles: 12–inch 33/45rpm

GEFFEN	4-6	83-86

Singles: 7–inch

GEFFEN	2-4	82-87

Picture Sleeves

GEFFEN	2-4	85-86

LPs: 10/12–inch 33rpm

GEFFEN	5-10	82-86

HOLLIES
Singles: 12–inch 33/45rpm

EPIC	4-8	77

Singles: 7–inch

ATLANTIC	2-4	83
EPIC (10000 series, except 10716)	3-8	67-74
EPIC (10716 "Survival of the Fittest")	8-10	71
EPIC (50000 series)	3-5	75-78
IMPERIAL (66026 through 66070)	10-15	64-65
IMPERIAL (66099 "Yes I Will")	20-40	65
IMPERIAL (66119 through 66258)	5-10	66-68
IMPERIAL (66271 "If I Needed Someone")	20-40	65
LIBERTY (55674 "Stay")	25-40	64

Picture Sleeves

ATLANTIC	3-5	83
EPIC	4-8	67-68
IMPERIAL	5-10	67

LPs: 10/12–inch 33rpm

ATLANTIC	5-10	83
CAPITOL	5-10	80
EPIC (24315 "Evolution") (Monaural.)	15-25	67

EPIC (26315 "Evolution") (Stereo.)	15-20	67
EPIC (26538 "He Ain't Heavy He's My Brother")	10-15	70
EPIC (30255 "Moving Finger")	10-15	71
EPIC (KE-30958 "Distant Light")	10-20	72
EPIC (AL-30958 "Distant Light")	5-10	77
EPIC (31000 through 35000 series)	6-12	73-78
IMPERIAL	25-50	64-67
LIBERTY	5-10	84

Also see CLARKE, Allan
Also see EVERLY BROTHERS
Also see NASH, Graham
Also see PARSONS, Alan, Project
Also see SPRINGSTEEN, Bruce / Johnny Winter / Hollies

HOLLIES / Peter Sellers
Singles: 7–inch

U.A. (50079 "After the Fox")	10-20	66

LPs: 10/12–inch 33rpm

U.A. (286 "After the Fox") (Soundtrack.)	8-10	74
U.A. (4148 "After the Fox") (Soundtrack. Monaural.)	15-25	66
U.A. (5148 "After the Fox") (Soundtrack. Stereo.)	25-35	66

Also see HOLLIES

HOLLOWAY, Brenda
(Brenda Holloway and the Carrolls)
Singles: 7–inch

BREVIT	5-10	63
CATCH	5-10	64
DONNA	5-10	62
TAMLA	4-8	64-67

Picture Sleeves

TAMLA	5-10	65

LPs: 10/12–inch 33rpm

TAMLA (257 "Every Little Bit Hurts")	25-35	65

HOLLOWAY, Brenda, and Jess Harris
Singles: 7–inch

BREVIT	4-8	63

Also see HOLLOWAY, Brenda

HOLLOWAY, Loleatta
(Loleatta Holloway and the Salsoul Orchestra)
Singles: 12–inch 33/45rpm

SALSOUL	4-8	83
STREETWISE	4-8	84

Singles: 7–inch

AWARE	3-5	73-75
GRC	3-5	73
GALAXY	3-5	71
GOLD MINE	3-5	76-77
SALSOUL	2-4	77-83

LPs: 10/12–inch 33rpm

GOLD MINE	5-10	77

Also see SALSOUL ORCHESTRA

HOLLOWAY, Loleatta, and Bunny Sigler
Singles: 7–inch

GOLD MINE	3-5	78

Also see HOLLOWAY, Loleatta
Also see SIGLER, Bunny

HOLLY, Buddy
(Buddy Holly and the Crickets; Buddy Holly and the Three Tunes)

Singles: 12-Inch 33/45rpm
SOLID SMOKE 5-10   79

Singles: 78rpm
BRUNSWICK (55009 "That'll Be
the Day") 75-125   57
BRUNSWICK (55035 "Oh Boy") ... 75-125   58
BRUNSWICK (55053 "Maybe Baby") 75-125   58
BRUNSWICK (55072 "Think It Over") 75-125   58
BRUNSWICK (55094 "It's So
Easy") 75-125   58
CORAL (61852 "Words of Love") .. 100-150   57
CORAL (61885 "Peggy Sue") 75-125   57
CORAL (61947 "Listen to Me") 75-125   58
CORAL (61985 "Rave On") 75-125   58
CORAL (62006 "Early in
the Morning") 75-125   58
CORAL (62051 "Heartbeat") 75-125   58
DECCA (29854 "Blue Days - Black
Nights") 75-125   56
DECCA (30166 "Modern Don Juan") 75-125   56
DECCA (30434 "That'll Be the Day") 75-125   57
DECCA (30543 "Love Me") 75-125   58
DECCA (30650 "Ting-A-Ling") 75-125   58

Singles: 7-inch
BRUNSWICK (55009 "That'll Be
the Day") 25-35   57
BRUNSWICK (55035 "Oh Boy") 25-35   58
BRUNSWICK (55053 "Maybe Baby") 20-30   58
BRUNSWICK (55072 "Think It Over") 20-30   58
BRUNSWICK (55094 "It's So Easy") . 20-30   58
CORAL (61852 "Words of Love") .. 150-200   57
CORAL (61885 "Peggy Sue") 20-30   57
CORAL (61947 "Listen to Me") 20-30   58
CORAL (61985 "Rave On") 20-30   58
CORAL (62006 "Early in the
Morning") 20-30   58
CORAL (62051 "Heartbeat") 20-30   58
CORAL (62074 "It Doesn't Matter
Anymore") 20-30   59
CORAL (62134 "Peggy Sue Got
Married") 30-40   59
(Orange label.)
CORAL (62134 "Peggy Sue Got
Married") 10-20   62
(Yellow label.)
CORAL (62210 "True Love Ways") .. 30-40   60
CORAL (62329 "Reminiscing") 20-30   62
CORAL (62352 "Bo Diddley") 25-35   63
CORAL (62369 "Brown Eyed
Handsome Man") 25-35   63
CORAL (62390 "Rock Around
with Ollie Vee") 30-40   64
CORAL (62407 "Maybe Baby") 30-40   64
CORAL (62448 "Slippin' and Slidin'") . 50-75   65

CORAL (62554 "Rave On") 25-35   68
CORAL (62558 "Love Is Strange") .. 15-25   69
CORAL (65618 "That'll Be the Day") . 15-25   69
DECCA (29854 "Blue Days - Black
Nights") 100-150   56
(With silver lines on both sides of the name Decca.)
DECCA (29854 "Blue Days - Black
Nights") 75-100   56
(With a star and silver lines under the name
Decca.)
DECCA (30166 "Modern Don Juan") 100-150   56
(With silver lines on both sides of the name Decca.)
DECCA (30166 "Modern Don Juan") 75-100   56
(With a star and silver lines under the name
Decca.)
DECCA (30434 "That'll Be
the Day") 100-150   57
(With silver lines on both sides of the name Decca.)
DECCA (30434 "That'll Be
the Day") 75-100   57
(With a star and silver lines under the name
Decca.)
DECCA (30543 "Love Me") 100-150   58
(With silver lines on both sides of the name Decca.)
DECCA (30543 "Love Me") 75-100   58
(With a star and silver lines under the name
Decca.)
DECCA (30650 "Ting-A-Ling") 100-150   58
(With silver lines on both sides of the name Decca.)
DECCA (30650 "Ting-A-Ling") 75-100   58
(With a star and silver lines under the name
Decca.)
MCA 3-5   73-78

Promotional Singles
BRUNSWICK (55009 "That'll Be
the Day") 40-60   57
BRUNSWICK (55035 "Oh Boy") 40-60   58
BRUNSWICK (55053 "Maybe Baby") 40-60   58
BRUNSWICK (55072 "Think It Over") 40-60   58
BRUNSWICK (55094 "It's So Easy") . 40-60   58
CORAL (61852 "Words of Love") . 100-150   57
CORAL (61885 "Peggy Sue") 50-75   57
CORAL (61947 "Listen to Me") 50-75   58
CORAL (61985 "Rave On") 50-75   58
CORAL (62006 "Early in
the Morning") 50-75   58

CORAL (62051 "Heartbeat") 50-75   58
CORAL (62074 "It Doesn't Matter
   Anymore") 50-75   59
CORAL (62134 "Peggy Sue Got
   Married") 50-75   59
CORAL (62210 "True Love Ways") .. 50-75   60
CORAL (62329 "Reminiscing") 40-60   62
CORAL (62352 "Bo Diddley") 40-60   63
CORAL (62369 "Brown Eyed
   Handsome Man") 40-60   63
CORAL (62390 "Rock Around
   with Ollie Vee") 40-60   64
CORAL (62407 "Maybe Baby") 40-60   64
CORAL (62448 "Slippin' and Slidin'") . 40-60   65
CORAL (62554 "Rave On") 25-50   68
CORAL (62558 "Love Is Strange") ... 20-30   69
   (Price doubles if accompanied by dee jay insert
   sheet.)
CORAL (65618 "That'll Be the Day") . 20-30   69
DECCA (29854 "Blue Days - Black
   Nights") 100-150   56
DECCA (30166 "Modern Don Juan")100-150   56
DECCA (30434 "That'll Be the Day")100-150   57
DECCA (30543 "Love Me") 100-150   58
DECCA (30650 "Ting-A-Ling") 100-150   58

Picture Sleeves

CORAL (62558 "Love Is Strange") ... 10-15   69
MCA 3-5   78

EPs: 7-Inch 33/45rpm

BRUNSWICK (71036 "The Chirping
   Crickets") 300-350   57
   (With printed back cover.)
BRUNSWICK (71036 "The Chirping
   Crickets") 350-450   57
   (With blank back cover.)
BRUNSWICK (71038 "The Sound
   of the Crickets") 100-200   58
CORAL (81169 "Listen to Me") 200-300   58
CORAL (81182 "The Buddy
   Holly Story") 150-250   59
CORAL (81191 "Buddy Holly") 150-250   62
CORAL (81193 "Brown Eyed
   Handsome Man") 100-200   63
DECCA (2575 "That'll Be the Day") 500-750   58
   (With liner notes on the back cover.)
DECCA (2575 "That'll Be the Day") 400-600   58
   (With EP ads on the back cover.)

LPs: 10/12-Inch 33rpm

BRUNSWICK (54038 "The Chirping
   Crickets") 200-300   57
CORAL (8 "Best of Buddy Holly") ... 75-125   66
CORAL (57210 "Buddy Holly") 100-150   58
   (Maroon label.)
CORAL (57210 "Buddy Holly") 25-50   63
   (Black label.)
CORAL (57279 "The Buddy
   Holly Story") 75-100   59
   (Maroon label. With red and black print on the back
   cover.)

CORAL (57279 "The Buddy
   Holly Story") 50-75   59
   (Maroon label. With black print on the back cover.)
CORAL (57279 "The Buddy
   Holly Story") 30-40   63
   (Black label. With pictures of other LPs on the back
   cover.)
CORAL (57326 "The Buddy
   Holly Story Vol. II") 100-125   60
   (Maroon label.)
CORAL (57326 "The Buddy
   Holly Story Vol. II") 25-50   63
   (Black label.)
CORAL (57405 "Buddy Holly
   and the Crickets") 50-75   62
   (Maroon label.)
CORAL (57405 "Buddy Holly
   and the Crickets") 25-45   63
   (Black label.)
CORAL (57426 "Reminiscing") 50-75   63
   (Maroon label.)
CORAL (57426 "Reminiscing") 20-40   63
   (Black label.)
CORAL (57450 "Showcase") 40-50   64
CORAL (57463 "Holly In the Hills") . 75-100   65
CORAL (57492 "Buddy Holly's
   Greatest Hits") 75-100   67
CORAL (757279 "The Buddy
   Holly Story") 25-35   63
   (Stereo.)
CORAL (757405 "Buddy Holly
   and the Crickets") 50-75   62
   (Maroon label. Stereo.)
CORAL (757405 "Buddy Holly
   and the Crickets") 25-45   63
   (Black label. Stereo.)
CORAL (757463 "Holly In the Hills") . 40-60   65
   (Stereo.)
CORAL (757504 "Giant") 40-80   69
   (Stereo.)
CREATIVE RADIO ("The Day the
   Music Died") 25-30
   (Two-LP set, includes poster.)
DECCA (207 "A Rock and Roll
   Collection") 15-20   72
DECCA (8707 "That'll Be the Day") 250-350   58
   (Black label.)
DECCA (8707 "That'll Be the Day") 150-250   61
   (Multi-color label.)
MCA (Except 6-80000) 8-12   75-85
MCA (6-80000 "The Complete
   Buddy Holly") 30-40   81
   (Six-LP boxed set.)
VOCALION (3811 "The Great
   Buddy Holly") 90-110   67
   (Monaural.)
VOCALION (73811 "The Great
   Buddy Holly") 20-30   67
   (Reprocessed stereo.)

VOCALION (73923 "Good Rockin'
Buddy Holly") 100-125   71
(Reprocessed stereo.)
Promotional LPs
BRUNSWICK (54038 "The Chirping
Crickets") 300-350   57
CORAL (Except 757504) 50-75   58-65
CORAL (757504 "Giant") 35-45   69
DECCA (8707 "That'll Be the Day") 350-450   58
(Pink label.)
PICK (1111 "Buddy Holly and the
Picks") 10-12   86
Also see BEATLES / Beach Boys / Buddy Holly
Also see CRICKETS
Also see JENNINGS, Waylon
Also see PETTY, Norman, Trio
Also see PRESLEY, Elvis / Buddy Holly

HOLLY, Pete, and the Looks
Singles: 7–inch
BOMP 2-4   87
Picture Sleeves
BOMP 2-4   87

HOLLY and the Italians
(Featuring Holly Beth Vincent)
Singles: 7–inch
OVAL 3-5
VIRGIN 2-4   82
Picture Sleeves
OVAL 3-5
LPs: 10/12–inch 33rpm
VIRGIN 5-10   81-82

HOLLYRIDGE STRINGS
(Stu Phillips and the Hollyridge Strings)
Singles: 7–inch
CAPITOL 3-6   61-68
LPs: 10/12–inch 33rpm
CAPITOL 5-15   64-78
Also see GOLDEN GATE STRINGS
Also see PHILLIPS, Stu

HOLLYWOOD ARGYLES
Singles: 7–inch
ABC 2-4   74
CHATTAHOOCHEE 4-8   65
ERA 3-5   72
FELSTED 4-8   63
FINER ARTS 4-8   61
LUTE 5-10   60
PAXLEY 4-8   61
LPs: 10/12–inch 33rpm
LUTE (9001 "Alley Oop") 250-350   60
Member: Gary Paxton.
Also see NEW HOLLYWOOD ARGYLES

HOLLYWOOD ARGYLES / Phil Flowers
Singles: 7–inch
WHAT 3-5
Also see HOLLYWOOD ARGYLES

HOLLYWOOD FLAMES
Singles: 78rpm
DECCA 15-30   54-55
EBB 5-10   57-59
LUCKY (001 "One Night with a Fool") 50-100   54
LUCKY (006 "Peggy") 50-100   54
LUCKY (009 "Let's Talk It Over") 40-60   54
MONA-LEE 10-20   59
MONEY (202 "I'm Leaving") 25-50   54
SWING TIME (345 "Let's Talk It Over") 50-75   53
SWING TIME (346 "Go and Get
Some More") 50-75   54
Singles: 7–inch
ATCO 5-10   59-60
CHESS 10-15   61
DECCA (29285 "Peggy") 50-60   54
DECCA (48331 "Let's Talk It Over") . . 50-60   55
EBB 10-15   57-59
GOLDIE 5-8   62
LUCKY (001 "One Night with
a Fool") 200-300   54
LUCKY (006 "Peggy") 200-300   54
LUCKY (009 "Let's Talk It Over") . . 150-225   54
MONEY (202 "I'm Leaving") 200-300   54
SWING TIME (345 "Let's Talk
It Over") 300-400   53
SWING TIME (346 "Go and Get
Some More") 300-400   54
SYMBOL 5-10   65-66
VEE JAY 8-12   63
LPs: 10/12–inch 33rpm
SPECIALTY 6-10   88
Members: David Ford; Bobby Byrd; Gaynel Hodge; Clyde Tillis;
Earl Nelson; Curtis Williams; Don Height; Ray Brewster; John
Berry; George Home.
Also see BYRD, Bobby

HOLLYWOOD STARS
Singles: 7–inch
ARISTA 3-5   77
LPs: 10/12–inch 33rpm
ARISTA 8-10   77
Also see KINKS / Hollywood Stars

HOLLYWOOD STUDIO ORCHESTRA
Singles: 7–inch
U.A. 4-8   59
LPs: 10/12–inch 33rpm
U.A. 10-15   61

HOLM, Michael
Singles: 7–inch
MERCURY 3-5   74

HOLMAN, Eddie
Singles: 7–inch
ABC 3-5   69-71
AGAPE 2-4   82
ASCOT 4-8   63
BELL 4-6   68
GSF 3-5   73
PARKWAY 10-20   65-67

SALSOUL 3-5	77	
SILVER BLUE 3-5	74	

LPs: 10/12–inch 33rpm

ABC-PAR 10-12	70	
SALSOUL 5-10	77	

HOLMES, Cecil
(Cecil Holmes' Soulful Sounds)
Singles: 7–inch

BUDDAH 3-5	73	

LPs: 10/12–inch 33rpm

BUDDAH 6-12	73	

HOLMES, Clint
Singles: 7–inch

EPIC 3-5	73	

LPs: 10/12–inch 33rpm

EPIC 10-12	73	

HOLMES, Jake
Singles: 7–inch

COLUMBIA 3-5	71-72	
POLYDOR 3-5	70	
TOWER 4-6	67	

Picture Sleeves

TOWER 4-6	67	

LPs: 10/12–inch 33rpm

POLYDOR 8-12	70	
TOWER 10-15	67	

HOLMES, Jan
Singles: 7–inch

JAY JAY 2-4	85	

HOLMES, Leroy, Orchestra
Singles: 78rpm

MGM 3-5	51-57	

Singles: 7–inch

MGM 4-8	51-61	
METRO 3-6	59	
U.A. 3-5	67-68	

Picture Sleeves

U.A. 4-8	67	

EPs: 7–inch 33/45rpm

MGM 4-8	52-56	
U.A. (10041 "Leroy Holmes and His Orchestra") . . . . 4-8 (Promotional issue only.)	67	

LPs: 10/12–inch 33rpm

LION 5-10	59-60	
MGM 5-15	52-62	
U.A. 4-8	67-68	

HOLMES, Richard "Groove"
Singles: 7–inch

BLUE NOTE 3-5	71	
FLYING DUTCHMAN 3-5	76	
PACIFIC JAZZ 4-8	61-69	
PRESTIGE 3-6	66-69	

LPs: 10/12–inch 33rpm

BLUE NOTE 5-10	71	
FLYING DUTCHMAN 5-10	75-76	

GROOVE MERCHANT 5-10	72-75	
LOMA 10-15	66	
MUSE 5-10	78-80	
PACIFIC JAZZ (Except 20000 series) 15-25	61-62	
PACIFIC JAZZ (20000 series) 8-15	68-69	
PRESTIGE 8-15	66-70	
VERSATILE 5-10	78	
WARNER 10-20	64	
WORLD PACIFIC JAZZ 8-12	70	

Also see AMMONS, Gene, and Richard "Groove" Holmes
Also see JONES, Brenda, and "Groove" Holmes
Also see McGRIFF, Jimmy
Also see WITHERSPOON, Jimmy

HOLMES, Richard "Groove," and Les
McCann
LPs: 10/12–inch 33rpm

PACIFIC JAZZ 15-25	62	

Also see HOLMES, Richard "Groove"
Also see McCANN, Les

HOLMES, Rupert
Singles: 7–inch

EPIC 3-6	74-76	
INFINITY 3-5	79	
MCA 2-4	80-81	
PRIVATE STOCK 2-4	78	

Picture Sleeves

EPIC 2-4	75	

LPs: 10/12–inch 33rpm

ELEKTRA 5-10	81	
EPIC 8-12	74-75	
INFINITY 5-10	79	
MCA 5-10	80	
PRIVATE STOCK 5-10	78	

Also see CUFF LINKS
Also see STREET PEOPLE

HOMBRES
Singles: 7–inch

VERVE/FORECAST 4-6	67-68	

LPs: 10/12–inch 33rpm

VERVE/FORECAST 15-20	67	

HOMER & JETHRO
Singles: 78rpm

KING 5-15	46-53	
FEDERAL 8-15	51	
RCA 5-10	50-58	

Singles: 7–inch

BLUEBIRD 4-8	59	
KING 3-6	63	
RCA (0100 series) . . . . 20-30 (Colored vinyl.)	50	
RCA (0100 through 0400 series) . . . . 10-20 (Black vinyl.)	50	
RCA (0500 series) 3-5	71	
RCA (4200 through 7500 series) 8-18	51-59	
RCA (47-7600 through 47-9900 series) . 4-8	59-70	
RCA (61-7744 "Sink the Bismarck") . . 10-20	60	

EPs: 7–inch 33/45rpm

AUDIO LAB 10-20	59	

KING	10-20	53-54
RCA	10-20	53-57

Picture Sleeves

RCA (5000 series)	8-12	53
RCA (8000 series)	3-6	64

LPs: 10/12-Inch 33rpm

AUDIO LAB (1513 "Musical Madness")	25-35	58
CAMDEN	10-20	62-71
DIPLOMAT	8-12	
GUEST STAR	10-15	63
KING (639 "They Sure Are Corny")	20-30	59
KING (800 series)	10-20	63
KING (1000 series)	8-12	67
NASHVILLE	8-12	69
RCA (1412 "Barefoot Ballads")	30-40	57
RCA (1516 "Worst of Homer & Jethro")	40-50	57
(Monaural. With "LPM" prefix.)		
RCA (1880 "Life Can Be Miserable")	25-35	58
(Monaural. With "LPM" prefix.)		
RCA (1880 "Life Can Be Miserable")	35-50	58
(Stereo. With "LSP" prefix.)		
RCA (2100 through 2900 series)	10-20	60-64
(Monaural. With "LPM" prefix.)		
RCA (2100 through 2900 series)	15-25	60-64
(Stereo. With "LSP" prefix.)		
RCA (3112 "Homer & Jethro		
Fracture Frank Loesser")	40-50	53
(10-inch LP.)		
RCA (3300 through 4600 series)	8-15	65-72

Members: Henry "Homer" Haynes; Kenneth "Jethro" Burns.
Also see ANN-MARGRET
Also see FOUR LOVERS / Homer & Jethro

HONDELLS

Singles: 7-Inch

AMOS	4-8	69-70
COLUMBIA	5-10	67-68
MERCURY (72324 "Little Honda")	10-15	64
MERCURY (72366 "My Buddy Seat")	10-15	64
MERCURY (72405 "Little Sidewalk		
Surfer Girl")	8-12	65
MERCURY (72443 "Sea of Love")	8-12	65
MERCURY (72479 "Sea Cruise")	5-10	65
MERCURY (72523 "Follow Your		
Heart")	5-10	66
MERCURY (72563 "Younger Girl")	5-10	67
MERCURY (72605 "Kissin' My		
Life Away")	5-10	67

Promotional Singles

MERCURY (72324 "Hot Rod High")	20-25	64
(Shows Hot Rod High as the "A" side.)		
MERCURY (72324 "Little Honda")	15-20	64
(Shows Little Honda as the "A" side.)		
MERCURY (72366 "My Buddy Seat")	15-20	64
MERCURY (72405 through 72605)	8-12	65-67

Picture Sleeves

MERCURY (72366 "My Buddy Seat")	10-20	64
MERCURY (72479 "Sea Cruise")	10-20	65

LPs: 10/12-Inch 33rpm

MERCURY (20940 "Go, Little Honda")	20-25	64
(Monaural.)		
MERCURY (60940 "Go, Little Honda")	25-30	64
(Stereo.)		
MERCURY (20982 "The Hondells")	20-25	64
(Monaural.)		
MERCURY (20982 "The Hondells")	25-30	65
(Stereo.)		

Members: Chuck Girard; Richard Burns; Brian Wilson; Wayne
Edwards; Glen Campbell; Joe Kelly; Bruce Johnston; Terry
Melcher; Jerry Naylor; Gary Usher.
Also see ALLEN, Davie
Also see BRUCE & TERRY
Also see CAMPBELL, Glen
Also see NAYLOR, Jerry
Also see WILSON, Brian

HONDELLS / Del Shannon / Martha and the Vandellas

EPs: 7-Inch 33/45rpm

PEPSI-COLA (8256 "Pepsi-Cola Ad		
Radio Youth Market, 1966")	15-20	66
(Promotional issue only.)		

Also see MARTHA and the Vandellas
Also see SHANNON, Del

HONDELLS / Dusty Springfield

Singles: 7-Inch

COLLECTABLES	2-4	86

Also see HONDELLS
Also see SPRINGFIELD, Dusty

HONEY CONE

Singles: 7-Inch

HOT WAX	3-6	69-76

LPs: 10/12-Inch 33rpm

HOT WAX	8-10	70-72

Members: Edna Wright; Carolyn Willis; Shellie Clark; Sharon
Cash.
Also see BOB B SOXX and the Blue Jeans
Also see GIRLFRIENDS

HONEYCOMBS

Singles: 7-Inch

INTERPHON	5-10	64-65
WARNER	5-10	65-66

Picture Sleeves

INTERPHON (7713 "I Can't		
Stop")	10-20	64

LPs: 10/12-Inch 33rpm

INTERPHON (88001 "Here Are		
the Honeycombs")	20-30	64
VEE JAY (88001 "Here Are		
the Honeycombs")	35-45	64

Members: Honey Lantree; John Lantree; Martin Murray; Denis
D'Ell; Alan Ward.

HONEYCONES

Singles: 7-Inch

EMBER	8-12	58-59

HONEYCUTT, Miki

Singles: 7-Inch

PAULA	3-5	77

HONEYDRIPPERS
Singles: 7–inch
ESPARANZA 2-4   84-85
Picture Sleeves
ESPARANZA 2-4   84-85
LPs: 10/12–inch 33rpm
ESPARANZA 5-10   84

Members: Jeff Beck; Jimmy Page; Robert Plant; Nile Rodgers.
Also see BECK, Jeff
Also see CHIC
Also see PAGE, Jimmy
Also see PLANT, Robert
Also see RODGERS, Nile

HONEYMOON SUITE
Singles: 7–inch
WARNER 2-4   84-88
Picture Sleeves
WARNER 2-4   84-88
LPs: 10/12–inch 33rpm
WARNER 5-10   84-88

HOOK, Dr: see DR. HOOK

HOOKER, Frank, and the Positive People
Singles: 7–inch
PANORAMA 2-4   79-80

HOOKER, John Lee
Singles: 78rpm
CHART 5-10   53
CHESS 20-40   52-54
JVB 15-30   53
MODERN 5-15   48-56
REGAL 8-12   50-51
SENSATION 8-12   49-50
SPECIALTY 5-10   54
VEE JAY 8-15   55-60
Singles: 7–inch
ABC 3-5   71-73
BATTLE 4-8   62
BLUESWAY 4-6   67-69
CHART 10-15   53
CHESS (1505 "High Priced
  Woman") 150-250 52
CHESS (1513 "Walkin' the Boogie") . 40-80 52

CHESS (1562 "It's My Own Fault") .. 30-50   54
CHESS (1900 series) 4-8   66
ELMOR 5-8
FEDERAL 5-10   60
FORTUNE 5-10   60
GALAXY 4-8   63
HI-Q 4-8   61
JVB (30 "Boogie Rambler") 50-75   53
JEWEL 3-5   70-77
KING 3-5   70
LAUREN 4-8   61
MODERN (835 "How Can You Do It") 30-60   51
MODERN (862 "Cold Chills
  All over Me") 30-60   52
MODERN (886 "Bluebird Blues") 30-60   52
MODERN (893 "New Boogie Chillen") 30-60   52
MODERN (897 "Rock House Boogie") 30-60   53
MODERN (901 "It's a Stormin'
  and Rainin") 25-50   53
MODERN (908 "Love Money
  Can't Buy") 25-50   53
MODERN (916 "Too Much Boogie") . 25-50   53
MODERN (923 "Down Child") 25-50   54
MODERN (931 "I Wonder Little
  Darling") 25-50   54
MODERN (935 "I Tried Hard") 20-40   54
MODERN (942 "Cool Little Car") 20-40 54
MODERN (948 "Half a Stranger") ... 20-40   55
MODERN (958 "You Receive Me") .. 20-40   55
MODERN (966 "Hug and Squeeze") . 20-40   55
MODERN (978 "Lookin' for a Woman")20-40   56
SPECIALTY (528 "Everybody's Blues")20-40   54
STARDAY 3-5   70
STAX 4-6   69
VEE JAY (Maroon label) 15-25   55-60
VEE JAY (Black label) 5-10   60-65
EPs: 7–inch 33/45rpm
IMPULSE 8-10   66
(Jukebox issues only.)
LPs: 10/12–inch 33rpm
ABC 8-12   71-74
ARCHIVE of FOLK MUSIC 10-12   68
ATCO (151 "Don't Turn Me
  from Your Door") 20-25   63
(Monaural.)
ATCO (SD-151 "Don't Turn Me
  from Your Door") 25-30   63
(Stereo.)
ATLANTIC 8-10   72
BATTLE 10-12
BLUESWAY 10-15   66-73
BRYLEN 5-10   84
BUDDAH 12-15   69
CHAMELEON 5-8   89
CHESS (1438 "House of the Blues") . 25-35 61
CHESS (1454 "John Lee Hooker Plays
  and Sings the Blues") 25-35   61
CHESS (1500 series) 15-20   66
CROWN 10-20   62-63

CUSTOM 10-15
EVEREST 5-10   79-83
EXODUS 8-10
FANTASY 8-10   72-77
FORTUNE 8-12   69
GNP/CRESCENDO 8-10   74
GALAXY (201 "John Lee Hooker") ... 20-30   63
GREEN BOTTLE 10-12   72
IMPULSE 12-15   66
JEWEL 10-12   71
KENT 10-12   71
KING (727 "John Lee Hooker
    Sings Blues") 30-50   61
KING (1000 series) 10-12   70
MCA 5-10   83
MUSE 5-10   80
SPECIALTY 10-15   70
    (Black and gold label.)
SPECIALTY 5-10   88
    (Black and white label.)
STAX (2000 series) 10-12   69
STAX (4000 series) 8-10   77
TOMATO 5-10   78
TRADITION 10-12   69
TRIP 8-10   73-78
UNITED 10-12
U.A. 12-15   71-73
VEE JAY (1007 "I'm John Lee
    Hooker") 40-60   59
    (Maroon label.)
VEE JAY (1007 "I'm John Lee
    Hooker") 20-30   61
    (Black label.)
VEE JAY (1023 through 1043) 25-40   60-62
VEE JAY (1049 through 1078) 15-25   62-64
VERVE/FOLKWAYS 10-15   66
WAND 10-12   70
    Also see BOOKER, John Lee
    Also see COOKER, John Lee
    Also see JOHN LEE
    Also see JOHNNY LEE
    Also see McGHEE, Sticks / John Lee Hooker
    Also see TEXAS SLIM
    Also see WILLIAMS, Johnny

HOOKER, John Lee, and Canned Heat
Singles: 7-Inch
U.A. 3-5   71
LPs: 10/12-inch 33rpm
LIBERTY 10-15   71
RHINO 5-10   82
    Also see CANNED HEAT

HOOKER, John Lee / Lightnin' Hopkins / J. Carroll
LPs: 10/12-inch 33rpm
GUEST STAR 15-20   64
    Also see HOPKINS, Lightnin'

HOOKER, John Lee, and Little Eddie Kirkland
Singles: 78rpm
MODERN 5-10   52

Singles: 7-inch
MODERN (876 "It's Hurts Me So ") .. 30-60   52

HOOKER, John Lee / Eddie Kirkland / Eddie Burns / Sylvester Cotton
LPs: 10/12-inch 33rpm
UNITED (7783 "Detroit Blues") 10-20
    Also see HOOKER, John Lee

HOOPER, Stix
Singles: 7-inch
MCA 2-4   79-82
LPs: 10/12-inch 33rpm
MCA 5-10   79-82
    Also see BUTLER, Jerry, and Stix Hooper
    Also see CRUSADERS

HOOTERS
Singles: 7-inch
COLUMBIA 2-4   85-89
MONTAGE 2-4   83
Picture Sleeves
COLUMBIA 2-4   85-87
LPs: 10/12-inch 33rpm
COLUMBIA 5-10   85-89
    Also see LAUPER, Cyndi

HOPE, Ellie
Singles: 12-inch 33/45rpm
QUALITY 4-6   83

HOPE, Lynn
(Lynn Hope Quintet)
Singles: 78rpm
ALADDIN 4-6   54-56
PREMIUM 3-6   50
Singles: 7-inch
ALADDIN 10-20   54-56
KING 5-10   60
LPs: 10/12-inch 33rpm
ALADDIN (707 "Lynn Hope and His
    Tenor Sax") 100-150   55
    (10-inch LP.)
ALADDIN (850 "Lynn Hope") 75-100   56
IMPERIAL 15-20   62
KING 15-25   61
SCORE (4015 "Tenderly") 25-50   57

HOPKIN, Mary
(Mark Hopkins)
Singles: 7-inch
APPLE/AMERICOM (238 "Those
    Were the Days") 150-250   69
    (Four-inch flexi, "pocket disc.")
APPLE 4-8   68-72
ESKEE 4-8   66
RCA 3-5   76
Promotional Singles
APPLE 8-12   68-72
ESKEE 4-8   66
RCA 3-5   76
Picture Sleeves
APPLE 5-10   68-70

LPs: 10/12–inch 33rpm

AIR	8-10	72
APPLE	10-15	69-72

HOPKINS, Lightnin'
(Lightning Hopkins)

Singles: 78rpm

ACE	5-10	56
ALADDIN (3063 through 3262)	25-50	50
CHART	4-8	55
DECCA	5-10	53
GOLD STAR (Except 671)	5-10	47-50
GOLD STAR (671 "Henny Penny Blues")	20-25	50
HARLEM	10-20	54-55
HERALD	5-10	54-55
LIGHTNING	20-30	55
MERCURY	5-10	52
MODERN	8-12	47-49
RPM	5-10	52-54
SITTIN' in WITH	5-10	51-53
TNT	20-30	53-54

Singles: 7–inch

ACE (516 "My Little Kewpie Doll")	20-30	56
ALADDIN (3063 "Shotgun")	75-100	50
ALADDIN (3077 "Moonrise Blues")	75-100	50
ALADDIN (3096 "Abilene")	75-100	51
ALADDIN (3117 "You Are Not Going to Worry My Life Anymore")	75-100	52
ALADDIN (3262 "My California")	50-75	54
ARHOOLIE	4-8	65
BLUESVILLE	4-8	60-63
CANDID	4-8	60-62
CHART	10-20	55
DART	5-10	60
DECCA (28841 "The War Is Over")	15-25	53
DECCA (48306 "Merry Christmas")	15-25	53
DECCA (48312 "Highway Blues")	15-25	53
DECCA (48321 "I'm Wild About You, Baby")	15-25	53
FIRE	4-8	61
FLASHBACK	3-6	65
HARLEM (2321 "Contrary Mary")	100-150	54
HARLEM (2324 "Lightnin's Boogie")	100-150	54
HARLEM (2331 "Fast Life")	100-150	55
HARLEM (2336 "Old Woman Blues")	100-150	55
HERALD (425 "Lightnin's Boogie")	20-30	54
HERALD (428 "Lightnin's Special")	20-30	54
HERALD (436 "Sick Feeling Blues")	20-30	54
HERALD (443 "Nothin' But the Blues")	20-30	54
HERALD (449 "They Wonder Who I Am")	20-30	55
HERALD (500 series)	10-20	59-60
IMPERIAL	10-15	62
IVORY	8-12	61
JAX (315 "No Good Woman") (Colored vinyl.)	150-250	53

JAX (318 "Automobile") (Colored vinyl.)	150-250	53
JAX (321 "Contrary Mary") (Colored vinyl.)	150-250	54
JAX (635 "Coffee Blues") (Colored vinyl.)	100-200	54
JAX (642 "You Caused My Heart to Weep") (Colored vinyl.)	100-200	54
JEWEL	3-6	68-72
KENT	3-5	
KIMBERLEY	5-10	60
LIGHTNING (104 "Unsuccessful Blues")	250-350	55
MERCURY (70081 "Ain't It a Shame")	50-75	52
MERCURY (70191 "My Mama Told Me")	50-75	52
MERCURY (8274 "Sad News from Korea")	50-75	52
MERCURY (8293 "Gone with the Wind")	50-75	52
PRESTIGE	4-8	60-67
RPM (337 "Beggin' You to Stay")	25-40	51
RPM (346 "Jake Head")	50-75	52
RPM (351 "Don't Keep My Baby Long")	50-75	52
RPM (359 "Needed Time")	50-75	52
RPM (378 "Another Fool in Town")	50-75	53
RPM (388 "Black Cat")	50-75	53
RPM (398 "Sante Fe")	50-75	54
SHAD	5-10	59
SITTIN' in WITH (621 "New York Boogie") (Colored vinyl.)	150-250	51
SITTIN' in WITH (635 "Coffee Blues") (Colored vinyl.)	150-250	52
SITTIN' in WITH (642 "You Caused My Heart to Weep") (Colored vinyl.)	150-250	52
SITTIN' in WITH (644 "Jailhouse Blues") (Colored vinyl.)	150-250	52
SITTIN' in WITH (647 "Dirty House") (Colored vinyl.)	150-250	52
SITTIN' in WITH (652 "Papa Bones Boogie") (Colored vinyl.)	150-250	52
SITTIN' in WITH (658 "Broken Hearted Blues") (Colored vinyl.)	150-250	53
SITTIN' in WITH (660 "I've Been A Bad Man") (Colored vinyl.)	150-250	53
SITTIN' in WITH (661 "Down to the River") (Colored vinyl.)	150-250	53
TNT (8002 "Late in the Evening")	200-300	54
TNT (8003 "Leavin' Blues")	200-300	54

TNT (8010 "Moanin' Blues") 200-300	55	
VAULT 3-5	70	

Even among blues experts there is confusion over which of the Jax and Sittin' in With singles were pressed on colored plastic, which were on black, and which came both ways. Any additional information will appear in future editions.

LPs: 10/12–inch 33rpm

ARHOOLIE 10-15	68	
BARNABY 8-10	71	
BULLDOG 12-15	65	
CANDID 20-30	61	
COLLECTABLES 6-8	88	
CROWN 20-25	61	
DART 10-15		
EVEREST (241 "Lightnin' Hopkins") . 10-15	69	
EVEREST (342 "Autobiography In Blues") 5-10	79	
FANTASY 8-10	72-81	
FIRE (104 "Mojo Hand") 75-100	62	
GUEST STAR 15-20	64	
HARLEM HITPARADE 5-10		
HERALD (1012 "Lightnin' and the Blues") 100-200	60	
IMPERIAL 20-30	62	
INTERNATIONAL ARTISTS (6 "Free Form Patterns") 50-100	68	
JAZZ MAN 5-10	82	
JEWEL 10-12	67-70	
MAINSTREAM 8-10	71-74	
MOUNT VERNON 15-20		
OLYMPIC 8-10	73	
PICKWICK 8-10		
POPPY 12-15	69	
PRESTIGE 10-15	65-70	
PRESTIGE/BLUESVILLE 20-25	61-64	
RHINO 5-10	82	
SCORE (4022 "Lightnin Hopkins Strums the Blues") 50-75	59	
SOUL PARADE 8-10		
TIME 25-30	60-62	
TOMATO 5-10	77	
TRADITION (1035 through 1040) . . . 20-30	60	
TRADITION (1056 through 2000) . . . 10-15	67-72	
TRIP 5-10	71-78	
UNITED 8-10		
UPFRONT 8-12		
VAULT 10-12	69	
VEE JAY 20-30	62	
VERVE 15-20	62	
VERVE/FOLKWAYS 12-15	65-67	

Also see HOOKER, John Lee / Lightnin' Hopkins / Johnny Carroll

HOPKINS, Lightnin,' and Sonny Terry
Singles: 7–inch

PRESTIGE BLUESVILLE 4-8	61	

LPs: 10/12–inch 33rpm

PRESTIGE BLUESVILLE 15-20	61-63	

Also see TERRY, Sonny

HOPKINS, Lightnin' / Brownie McGhee & Sonny Terry
LPs: 10/12–inch 33rpm

HORIZON (WP-1617 "Blues Hoot") . . 20-25	63	
(Monaural.)		
HORIZON (ST-1617 "Blues Hoot") . . 25-30	63	
(Stereo.)		

Also see McGHEE, Brownie, and Sonny Terry

HOPKINS, Lightnin,' and Thunder Smith
Singles: 78rpm

ALADDIN (165 "West Coast Blues") 50-100	47	
ALADDIN (167 "Katie Mae Blues") . 50-100	47	
ALADDIN (168 "Feel So Bad") 50-100	47	

Also see HOPKINS, Lightnin'

HOPKINS, Nicky
Singles: 7–inch

COLUMBIA 3-5	72	

LPs: 10/12–inch 33rpm

COLUMBIA 8-10	73	
ROLLING STONE 10-12	72	

Also see JEFFERSON AIRPLANE
Also see LORD SUTCH
Also see QUICKSILVER
Also see ROLLING STONES

HORAN, Eddie
Singles: 7–inch

HDM 3-5	78	
MGM 3-5	74	

HORN, Trevor, Paul Morley and the Art of Noise
Singles: 7–inch

ISLAND 2-4	86	

Also see ART of NOISE

HORNE, Jimmy "Bo"
Singles: 12–inch 33/45rpm

SUNSHINE SOUND 4-8	79	

Singles: 7–inch

ALSTON 3-5	75-77	
SUNSHINE SOUND 3-5	77-80	

LPs: 10/12–inch 33rpm

SUNSHINE SOUND 5-10	78-80	

HORNE, Lena
Singles: 78rpm

RCA 3-5	52-57	

Singles: 7–inch

BUDDAH 3-5	71	
CHARTER 4-6	63	
DRG 2-4	86	
GRYPHON 3-5	76	
MCA 2-4	78	
RCA (4000 through 7000 series) . . 5-10	52-61	
20TH FOX 4-6	63-64	
U.A. 3-6	65-66	

Picture Sleeves

RCA 4-8	62	

EPs: 7–inch 33/45rpm

MGM 5-10	54-55	

RCA 5-10	56-59	

LPs: 10/12–inch 33rpm

BUDDAH 5-10	71
CAMDEN 10-20	56
CHARTER 10-15	63
CORONET 5-10	
DRG 5-10	86
GRYPHON 5-10	75-76
LIBERTY 5-8	81
MFSL (094 "Lady and Her Music") ... 20-40	82
MGM 15-30	54-55
POLYDOR 4-8	
QWEST 5-10	81
RCA (Except 4300 series) 10-30	52-63
RCA (4300 series) 4-8	81
SPRINGBOARD 4-8	77
TOPS 15-30	56
20TH FOX 8-15	64
U.A. 8-15	65-66

Also see BELAFONTE, Harry, and Lena Horne
Also see FITZGERALD, Ella / Billie Holiday / Lena Horne

HORNE, Lena, and Michel Legrand
LPs: 10/12–inch 33rpm

GRYPHON 5-10	75

Also see LEGRAND, Michel

HORNE, Lena, and Gabor Szabo
LPs: 10/12–inch 33rpm

SKYE 8-12	70

Also see HORNE, Lena
Also see SZABO, Gabor

HORNSBY, Bruce, and the Range
Singles: 7–inch

RCA 2-4	86-90

Picture Sleeves

RCA 2-4	87-88

LPs: 10/12–inch 33rpm

RCA 5-10	86-90

HORSLIPS
Singles: 7–inch

DJM (Except 1036) 3-5	77-79
DJM (1036 "Sure the Boy Was Green") . 4-8	77
(Colored vinyl.)	
MERCURY 3-5	79
RCA 3-5	75

LPs: 10/12–inch 33rpm

ATCO 10-12	73-74
DJM 5-10	77-79
MERCURY 5-10	79-80
RCA 8-10	74

HORTON, Jamie
Singles: 7–inch

ERIC 3-5	68
JOY 8-12	59-61

HORTON, Johnny
Singles: 78rpm

ABBOTT 5-10	51-52
COLUMBIA 5-10	56-57

CORMAC	
MERCURY 5-10	54-55

Singles: 7–inch

ABBOTT (100 "Candy Jones") 20-30	51
ABBOTT (101 "Happy Millionaire") .. 20-30	51
ABBOTT (102 "Plaid and Calico") ... 20-30	51
ABBOTT (103 "Birds and Butterflies") 20-30	51
ABBOTT (104 "Go and Wash") 20-30	51
ABBOTT (105 "Shadows on	
the Old Bayou") 20-30	51
ABBOTT (106 "Words") 20-30	51
ABBOTT (107 "Long Rocky Road") .. 20-30	52
ABBOTT (108 "Somebody's Rockin'	
My Broken Heart") 20-30	52
ABBOTT (109 "Rhythm in	
My Baby's Walk") 20-30	52
ABBOTT (135 "Plaid and Calico") ... 15-20	53
CORMAC (1193 "Plaid and Calico") 50-100	51
CORMAC (1197 "Birds and	
Butterflies") 50-100	51
COLUMBIA (21504 "Honky Tonk	
Man") 10-20	56
COLUMBIA (21538 "I'm a One	
Woman Man") 10-15	56
COLUMBIA (40813 "I'm Coming	
Home") 15-25	57
COLUMBIA (40919 "She Knows Why") 8-12	57
COLUMBIA (40986 "I'll Do It	
Every Time") 8-12	57
COLUMBIA (41043 "Lover's Rock") . 15-25	57
COLUMBIA (41110 "Honky Tonk	
Hardwood Floor") 30-50	58
COLUMBIA (41210 "All Grown Up") . 10-15	58
COLUMBIA (41308 through 44156) ... 5-10	58-67
DOT (15996 "Plaid and Calico") 8-12	59
MERCURY (6412 "The Devil Sent	
Me You") 15-25	52
MERCURY (6418 "The Rest	
of Your Life") 15-25	52
MERCURY (70014 "I Won't Forget") . 15-25	52
MERCURY (70100 "Tennessee	
Jive") 15-25	53
MERCURY (70156 "S.S. Lureline") .. 15-25	53
MERCURY (70198 "You You You") .. 15-25	53
MERCURY (70227 "All for the	
Love of a Girl") 15-25	53
MERCURY (70325 "Move Down	
the Line") 15-25	54
MERCURY (70399 "The Door of	
Your Mansion") 15-25	54
MERCURY (70462 "No True Love") . 15-25	54
MERCURY (70636 "Ridin' the	
Sunshine Special") 15-25	55
MERCURY (70707 "Big Wheels	
Rollin'") 15-25	55

Picture Sleeves

COLUMBIA (Except 41308) 8-12	59-64

COLUMBIA (41308 "When It's
Springtime in Alaska") 10-20   59
(Blue and white sleeve. Promotional only.)
DOT 5-10   59

EPs: 7–inch 33/45rpm
COLUMBIA 15-25   57-60
MERCURY 15-25   55
SESAC (1201 "Free and Easy
Songs") 30-40   59
(Promotional issues only.)

LPs: 10/12–inch 33rpm
BRIAR INT'L (104 "Done Rovin") . . 100-150
COLUMBIA (CL-1300 through CL-1700
series) 20-30   60-62
(Monaural.)
COLUMBIA (CL-2200 series) 10-20   65
(Monaural.)
COLUMBIA (CS-8000 series) 25-30   60-63
(Stereo.)
COLUMBIA (PC-8000 series) 5-10
COLUMBIA (9000 series) 15-20   65-69
(Stereo. With "CS" prefix.)
COLUMBIA (30000 series) 10-15   71
CROWN 12-15   63
CUSTOM 8-12
DOT (3221 "Johnny Horton") 25-40   59
(Monaural.)
DOT (25221 "Johnny Horton") 15-25   66
(Stereo.)
HARMONY 10-12   70-71
MERCURY (20478 "The Fantastic
Johnny Horton") 25-40   59
PICKWICK/HILLTOP 10-15   65-68
SEARS 10-15
(Promotional issue only.)
SESAC (1201 "Free and Easy
Songs") 100-150   59
(Promotional issue only.)
Also see DEAN, Jimmy / Johnny Horton
Also see PRICE, Ray / Johnny Horton / Carl Smith / George
Morgan

HORTON, Johnny / Sonny James
LPs: 10/12–inch 33rpm
CUSTOM 8-12
Also see JAMES, Sonny
Also see HORTON, Johnny

HOSANNA
Singles: 7–inch
CALLA 3-5   76

HOT
Singles: 7–inch
BIG TREE 3-5   77-79
LPs: 10/12–inch 33rpm
BIG TREE 5-10   77-79
Members: Gwen Owens; Cathy Carson; Juanita Curiel.

HOT BUTTER
Singles: 7–inch
MUSICOR 3-5   72

LPs: 10/12–inch 33rpm
MUSICOR 8-10   72-74
Members: Steve Jerome; Bill Jerome; Johnny Abbott; Stan Free;
Dave Mullaney.

HOT CHOCOLATE
(Hot Chocolate Band)
Singles: 7–inch
APPLE 5-10   69
BELL 3-5   74
BIG TREE 3-5   75-77
EMI AMERICA 2-4   82
INFINITY 3-5   78-79
RAK 3-5   72-73
LPs: 10/12–inch 33rpm
BIG TREE 8-10   74-77
EMI AMERICA 5-10   82
INFINITY 5-10   78-79
Members: Errol Brown; Tony Wilson; Harvey Hinsley; Larry
Ferguson; Tony Conner; Patrick Olive.

HOT CUISINE
Singles: 7–inch
PRELUDE 2-4   81

HOT LINE
Singles: 12–inch 33/45rpm
MEMO 4-6   84
Singles: 7–inch
RED COACH 3-5   74

HOT SAUCE
Singles: 7–inch
VOLT 3-5   72-74

HOT STREAK
Singles: 12–inch 33/45rpm
EASY STREET 4-6   83

HOT TUNA
Singles: 7–inch
GRUNT 3-6   71-76
Picture Sleeves
GRUNT 4-8   72
LPs: 10/12–inch 33rpm
GRUNT 10-20   72-78
RCA (3000 series) 5-10   81
RCA (4000 series) 10-15   70-71
RELIX ("Acoustic Hot
Tuna Splashdown") 10-15   84
(No number used.)
Members: Paul Cassady; Jorma Kaukonen.
Also see JOPLIN, Janis / Hot Tuna
Also see KAUKONEN, Jorma

HOTBOX
Singles: 12–inch 33/45rpm
POLYDOR 4-6   84
Singles: 7–inch
POLYDOR 2-4   84

HOTEL
Singles: 7–inch
MCA 2-4   79-80
MERCURY 3-5   78

LPs: 10/12–inch 33rpm

MCA 5-10   79-80

HOTHOUSE FLOWERS
Singles: 7–inch

LONDON 2-4   88-90

LPs: 10/12–inch 33rpm

LONDON 5-10   88-90
Members: Liam O'Maonlai; Fiachna O'Braonain; Peter O'Toole; Leo Barnes.

HOTLEGS
Singles: 7–inch

CAPITOL (Except 3043) 3-5   70-71
CAPITOL (3043 "Run Baby, Run") ... 10-15   71

LPs: 10/12–inch 33rpm

CAPITOL 15-20   71
Members: Eric Stewart; Kevin Godley; Lol Cream.
Also see 10CC

HOT-TODDYS
Singles: 7–inch

CORSICAN 10-20   59
SHAN-TODD 15-25   59
STRAND 8-12   60
Also see ROCKIN' REBELS

HOUR GLASS
Singles: 7–inch

LIBERTY 8-10   68

Picture Sleeves

LIBERTY 10-15   68

LPs: 10/12–inch 33rpm

LIBERTY 15-20   67-68
U.A. 10-15   73
Members: Duane Allman; Gregg Allman.
Also see ALLMAN BROTHERS BAND

HOUSE of LORDS
Singles: 7–inch

RCA/SIMMONS 2-4   89

Picture Sleeves

RCA/SIMMONS 2-4   89

LPs: 10/12–inch 33rpm

RCA/SIMMONS 5-8   88
SIMMONS 5-8   90

HOUSE of LOVE
LPs: 10/12–inch 33rpm

FONTANA 5-8   90
RELATIVITY 5-8   88

HOUSEMARTINS
LPs: 10/12–inch 33rpm

ELEKTRA 5-10   87-88

HOUSTON, Cissy
(Sissie Houston)
Singles: 7–inch

COLUMBIA 2-4   79-80
COMMONWEALTH UNITED 3-5   70
JANUS 3-5   71
KAPP 4-8   67
PRIVATE STOCK 3-5   77-78

LPs: 10/12–inch 33rpm

COLUMBIA 5-10   79-80
JANUS 8-10   70
PRIVATE STOCK 5-10   77-78
Also see BOWIE, David
Also see MANN, Herbie, and Cissy Houston
Also see SWEET INSPIRATIONS

HOUSTON, David
Singles: 78rpm

RCA 5-10   56-57

Singles: 7–inch

BLACK ROSE 2-4   82
COLONIAL 3-5   78
COUNTRY INT'L 2-4   80
DERRICK 2-4   79
ELEKTRA 3-5   78-79
EXCELSIOR 2-4   81
EPIC 3-8   63-76
NRC 5-10   59
PHILLIPS INTERNATIONAL 4-8   61
RCA (6611 "Sugar Sweet") 10-20   56
RCA (6696 "Blue Prelude") 10-15   56
RCA (6927 "One and Only") 25-40   57
RCA (7001 "Teenage
   Frankie and Johnny") 10-20   57
SOUNDWAVES 2-4   83
STARDAY 2-4   77
SUN (400 series) 5-10   66
SUN (1100 series) 3-5   72

Picture Sleeves

EPIC 4-8   66-69

LPs: 10/12–inch 33rpm

CAMDEN 8-12   66
COLUMBIA 6-10   73
DELTA 5-10   82
EPIC 5-15   64-76
EXACT 5-10   80
EXCELSIOR 5-10   81
51 WEST 5-10   84
GUEST STAR 6-12   64
GUSTO 5-10   78
HARMONY 8-12   70-72
STARDAY 6-10   77
Also see JAMES, Sonny / David Houston
Also see JONES, George / Buck Owens / David Houston /
Tommy Hill.

HOUSTON, David, and Barbara Mandrell
Singles: 7–inch

EPIC 3-5   70-74

LPs: 10/12–inch 33rpm

EPIC 8-15   72-75
Also see MANDRELL, Barbara

HOUSTON, David, and Tammy Wynette
Singles: 7–inch

EPIC 4-6   67

LPs: 10/12–inch 33rpm

EPIC 8-12   67
51 WEST 5-10   82
Also see HOUSTON, David

Also see WYNETTE, Tammy

HOUSTON, Don
Singles: 7–inch
THUNDER .... 5-10　　　59

HOUSTON, Thelma
(Thelma Houston and Pressure Cooker)
Singles: 12–inch 33/45rpm
MCA .... 4-6　　　83
Singles: 7–inch
CAPITOL .... 4-8　　　66
DUNHILL (Except 11) .... 3-5　　　70
DUNHILL (11 "Everybody Gets to
　Go to the Moon") .... 4-6　　　69
　(Special Apollo 11 Mission promotional issue.)
MCA .... 2-4　　　83
MOTOWN .... 2-4　　74-78
MOWEST .... 2-4　　71-73
RCA .... 2-4　　80-81
TAMLA .... 2-4　　76-79
Picture Sleeves
DUNHILL (11 "Everybody Gets to
　Go to the Moon") .... 4-6　　　69
　(Special Apollo 11 Mission promotional issue.)
LPs: 10/12–inch 33rpm
DUNHILL .... 10-12　　69
MCA .... 5-10　　　83
MOTOWN .... 5-10　　81-82
MOWEST .... 8-10　　　72
RCA .... 5-10　　80-81
SHEFFIELD (2 "I've Got the
　Music in Me") .... 25-30　　74
SHEFFIELD (200 "I've Got the
　Music in Me") .... 5-10　　　82
TAMLA .... 5-10　　76-79
MYRRH .... 8-10　　　74
Also see BUTLER, Jerry, and Thelma Houston

HOUSTON, Whitney
Singles: 12–inch 33/45rpm
ARISTA .... 4-6　　85-88
Singles: 7–inch
ARISTA .... 2-4　　85-90
Picture Sleeves
ARISTA .... 2-4　　85-88
LPs: 10/12–inch 33rpm
ARISTA .... 5-10　　85-90
Also see FRANKLIN, Aretha, and Whitney Houston
Also see KING DREAM CHORUS and Holiday Crew
Also see PENDERGRASS, Teddy

HOWARD, Camille, Trio
(Camille Howard)
Singles: 78rpm
FEDERAL .... 4-8　　　53
IMPERIAL .... 4-8　　　53
SPECIALTY .... 5-10　　51-53
VEE JAY .... 4-8　　　56
Singles: 7–inch
FEDERAL (12125 "Excite Me,
　Daddy") .... 20-30　　53

FEDERAL (12134 "Hurry Back, Baby") 20-30　　53
FEDERAL (12147 "You're Lower
　Than a Mole") .... 20-30　　53
IMPERIAL .... 15-25　　53
SPECIALTY (443 "Old Baldy Boogie") 20-30　　53
SPECIALTY (449 "Bacarolle Boogie") 20-30　　53
VEE JAY .... 10-20　　56
Members: Camille Howard; Roy Milton; Dallas Bartley.
Also see MILTON, Roy

HOWARD, Don
Singles: 78rpm
ESSEX .... 3-5　　　52
MERCURY .... 3-5　　　56
Singles: 7–inch
ESSEX .... 5-10　　　52
MERCURY .... 4-8　　　56

HOWARD, Eddy
Singles: 78rpm
MERCURY .... 3-5　　50-57
Singles: 7–inch
MERCURY .... 5-10　　50-61
MISHAWAKA .... 3-5　　　72
EPs: 7–inch 33/45rpm
MERCURY .... 5-10　　50-59
LPs: 10/12–inch 33rpm
IMPERIAL .... 8-15　　　61
MERCURY .... 10-20　　50-65
WING .... 5-10　　60-63

HOWARD, George
(George Howard with Gwen Guthrie)
Singles: 12–inch 33/45rpm
MCA .... 4-6　　　86
Singles: 7–inch
MCA .... 2-4　　86-90
PALO ALTO .... 2-4　　　83
TBA .... 2-4　　84-86
LPs: 10/12–inch 33rpm
GRP .... 5-8　　　91
MCA .... 5-10　　86-90
PALO ALTO .... 5-10　　　83
TBA .... 5-10　　84-86
Also see GUTHRIE, Gwen

HOWARD, Miki
Singles: 7–inch
ATLANTIC .... 2-4　　86-90
LPs: 10/12–inch 33rpm
ATLANTIC .... 5-10　　86-90
Also see SIDE EFFECT

HOWARD, Miki, and Gerald Levert
Singles: 7–inch
ATLANTIC .... 2-4　　　88
Also see HOWARD, Miki

HOWE, Steve, Band
Singles: 7–inch
ATLANTIC .... 3-5　　75-79
LPs: 10/12–inch 33rpm
ATLANTIC .... 5-10　　75-79

Also see ASIA
Also see GTR
Also see YES

HOWLIN' WOLF
(Chester Burnett)
Singles: 78rpm
CHESS 15-25   51-57
RPM 20-30   51
Singles: 7–Inch
CHESS (1528 "My Last Affair") 75-100   53
CHESS (1557 "All Night Boogie") ... 40-60   53
CHESS (1566 "No Place to Go") 40-60   54
CHESS (1575 "Baby, How Long") ... 40-60   54
CHESS (1584 "I'll Be Around") 25-50   55
CHESS (1593 "Who Will Be Next") . 25-50   55
CHESS (1600 series) 15-25   55-57
CHESS (1700 through 1900 series) ... 5-10   58-66
CHESS (2000 series) 3-6   67-71
LPs: 10/12–Inch 33rpm
CADET 10-12   69
CHESS (Except 1400 and 1500 series) 8-10   71-77
CHESS (1434 "Moaning in
the Moonlight") 60-90   58
(Black label.)
CHESS (1469 "Howlin' Wolf") 50-70   62
(Black label.)
CHESS (1500 series, except 1502) .. 15-20   67-69
CHESS (1502 "Real Folk Blues") 25-35   66
CHESS/MCA (Except 9332) 5-8   89
CHESS/MCA (9332 "Howlin' Wolf") .. 35-45   91
(Five LP boxed set, with 32-page booklet.)
CROWN 15-20   62
CUSTOM 10-12
KENT 10-15   67
RPM (347 "My Baby Stole Off") ... 100-200   51
UNITED 8-10
Also see BERRY, Chuck, and Howlin' Wolf
Also see DIDDLEY, Bo, Howlin' Wolf and Muddy Waters
Also see ROBINSON, Freddy
Also see WATERS, Muddy, and Howlin' Wolf

HUANG CHUNG:
see WANG CHUNG

HUBBARD, Freddie
Singles: 12-Inch 33/45rpm
FANTASY 4-8   81
Singles: 7-Inch
ATLANTIC 3-5   69
BLUE NOTE 4-8   61-64
COLUMBIA 3-7   74-76
LPs: 10/12-Inch 33rpm
ATLANTIC 8-15   67-76
BLUE NOTE 15-25   60-65
(Label reads "Blue Note Records Inc. - New York, U.S.A.")
BLUE NOTE 8-15   66-76
(Label shows Blue Note Records as a division of either Liberty or United Artists.)
CTI 6-12   70-75
COLUMBIA 5-10   74-83

ELEKTRA 5-8   82
ENJA 5-8   81
FANTASY 5-8   81-83
IMPULSE 10-20   63-73
LIBERTY 5-8   81
PABLO 5-8   82-83
PAUSA 5-8   82

HUBBARD, Freddie, and Oscar Peterson
LPs: 10/12-Inch 33rpm
PABLO 5-10   80
Also see PETERSON, Oscar

HUBBARD, Freddie, and Stanley Turrentine
LPs: 10/12-Inch 33rpm
CTI 6-12   74
Also see HUBBARD, Freddie
Also see TURRENTINE, Stanley

HUDMON, R.B., Jr.
Singles: 7-Inch
ATLANTIC 3-5   76-77
CAPITOL 3-5   71
COTILLION 3-5   78
1-2-3 3-6   68-70
LPs: 10/12-Inch 33rpm
COTILLION 5-10   78

HUDSON, Al
(Al Hudson and the Soul Partners)
Singles: 12-Inch 33/45rpm
ABC 4-8   77
Singles: 7-Inch
ABC 3-5   76-79
ATCO 3-5   75-76
LPs: 10/12-Inch 33rpm
ABC 8-10   77
Also see ONE WAY

HUDSON, David
Singles: 7-Inch
ALSTON 2-4   80
LPs: 10/12-Inch 33rpm
ALSTON 5-10   80

HUDSON, "Emperor" Bob, and Lawrence Welk
Singles: 7-Inch
RANWOOD 3-5   72
Also see HUDSON & LANDRY
Also see WELK, Lawrence

HUDSON, Lavine
Singles: 7-Inch
VIRGIN 2-4   88

HUDSON, Pookie
(Pookie Hudson and the Spaniels)
Singles: 7-Inch
CHESS 4-8   66
DOUBLE-L 8-12   63
JAMIE (1319 "This Gets to Me") .. 25-50   66
NEPTUNE 5-10   61
PARKWAY 8-12   62
Also see SPANIELS

HUDSON & LANDRY
Singles: 7–inch
DORE 3-5   71-74
LPs: 10/12–inch 33rpm
DORE 10-20   71-75
Members: Bob Hudson; Ron Landry.
Also see HUDSON, "Emperor" Bob, and Lawrence Welk

HUDSON BROTHERS
Singles: 7–inch
ARISTA 3-5   76-78
CASABLANCA 3-5   74
MCA/ROCKET 3-5   74-76
Picture Sleeves
MCA/ROCKET 3-5   75
LPs: 10/12–inch 33rpm
CASABLANCA 8-10   74
PLAYBOY 8-10   72
MCA/ROCKET 8-10   74-75
Members: Bill Hudson; Brett Hudson; Mark Hudson.

HUES CORPORATION
Singles: 7–inch
RCA 3-5   73-75
WARNER 3-5   77
LPs: 10/12–inch 33rpm
RCA 8-10   73-77
WARNER 5-10   77-78
Members: St. Clair Lee; H. Ann Kelly; Tommy Brown; Karl
Russell; Fleming Williams.

HUFF, Terry
(Terry Huff and Special Delivery)
Singles: 7–inch
MAINSTREAM 3-5   76
PHILADELPHIA INT'L 2-4   80
LPs: 10/12–inch 33rpm
MAINSTREAM 5-10   76

HUGH, Grayson
Singles: 7–inch
RCA 2-4   89-90
LPs: 10/12–inch 33rpm
RCA 5-8   88

HUGHES, Freddie
(Fred Hughes)
Singles: 7–inch
BRUNSWICK 3-6   69-71
COLLECTABLES 2-4   81
EXODUS 4-8   66
MINASA (709 "One Step Too Far") .. 15-25   65
VEE JAY 5-10   65
WAND 4-8   68-69
WEE 4-8
LPs: 10/12–inch 33rpm
BRUNSWICK 8-12   70
WAND 10-15   68

HUGHES, Jimmy
Singles: 7–inch
ATLANTIC 4-6   68
COLLECTABLES 2-4   81

FAME 4-8   64-67
GUYDEN 4-8   62
VOLT 3-6   69-71
LPs: 10/12–inch 33rpm
ATCO 10-15   67
STAX 5-10   85
VEE JAY 15-20   64
VOLT 10-12   69

HUGHES, Rhetta
Singles: 12–inch 33/45rpm
ARIA 4-6   83
Singles: 7–inch
ARIA 2-4   83
COLUMBIA 4-6   67-68
SUTRA 2-4   80
TETRAGRAMMATON 4-6   68-69
LPs: 10/12–inch 33rpm
SUTRA 5-10   80
TETRAGRAMMATON 10-12   69

HUGHES, Rhetta, and Tennyson Stephens
LPs: 10/12–inch 33rpm
COLUMBIA 12-18   65
Also see HUGHES, Rhetta
Also see STEPHENS, Tennyson

HUGHES - THRALL
Singles: 7–inch
BOULEVARD 2-4   82
Members: Glenn Hughes; Pat Thrall.

HUGO & LUIGI
(Hugo & Luigi Chorus)
Singles: 78rpm
MERCURY 3-5   55-56
Singles: 7–inch
MERCURY 5-10   55-56
RCA 4-8   59-60
ROULETTE 4-8   58
Picture Sleeves
ROULETTE 5-10   58
LPs: 10/12–inch 33rpm
FORUM 5-10   60
MERCURY 5-15   56
RCA 5-10   60-63
ROULETTE 5-12   59
WING 5-10   60
Members: Hugo Peretti; Luigi Creatore.

HULIN, T.K.
Singles: 7–inch
SMASH 4-8   63
L.K. (1001 "Little Bitty Boy") 100-200
L.K. (1119 "Baby, Be My Steady") ... 15-25   63
LPs: 10/12–inch 33rpm
STARLITE 10-12

HULLABALOOS
Singles: 7–inch
ROULETTE 4-8   64-65
Picture Sleeves
ROULETTE 10-20   64-65

LPs: 10/12–inch 33rpm
ROULETTE (25297 "England's Newest
  Singing Sensations") 25-30   65
ROULETTE (25310 "The Hullabaloos
  on Hullabaloo") 25-30   65

HUMAN BEINZ
(Human Beinz with the Mammals)
Singles: 7–inch
CAPITOL 4-8   67-69
GATEWAY 5-10   66-67
Picture Sleeves
CAPITOL 8-15   68
LPs: 10/12–inch 33rpm
CAPITOL (2906 "Nobody But Me") .. 15-25   68
CAPITOL (2926 "Evolutions") 20-25   68
GATEWAY (3012 "Nobody But Me") . 25-35   68

HUMAN BODY
Singles: 7–inch
BEARSVILLE 2-4   84

HUMAN LEAGUE
Singles: 12–inch 33/45rpm
A&M 4-6   82-86
Singles: 7–inch
A&M 2-4   82-86
VIRGIN/A&M 2-4   90
Picture Sleeves
A&M 2-4   82-85
LPs: 10/12–inch 33rpm
A&M 5-10   82-86
  Members: Phil Oakey; Ian Marsh; Martin Ware; Colin Thurston.
  Also see LEAGUE UNLIMITED ORCHESTRA
  Also see MORODER, Giorgio, and Phil Oakey

HUMBLE PIE
Singles: 7–inch
A&M 3-5   71-75
ATCO 2-4   80
IMMEDIATE 4-8   69
Picture Sleeves
A&M 4-8   71-72
LPs: 10/12–inch 33rpm
A&M 8-12   70-82
ACCORD 5-10   82
ATCO 5-10   80-81
IMMEDIATE 10-15   68-72
  Members: Steve Marriott; Peter Frampton; Greg Ridley; B.J.
  Cole; Jerry Shirley; Lyn Dobson.
  Also see FRAMPTON, Peter
  Also see SMALL FACES

HUMPERDINCK, Engelbert
(Gerry Dorsey)
Singles: 7–inch
EH (1 "For My Friends") 10-15
  (Promotional issue only. Contents unknown.)
EPIC 2-5   76-83
PARROT 3-6   67-73
Picture Sleeves
PARROT 3-6   67-71

LPs: 10/12–inch 33rpm
EPIC 5-10   76-83
PARROT 8-15   67-74

HUMPHREY, Bobbi
Singles: 12–inch 33/45rpm
EPIC 4-8   78-79
Singles: 7–inch
BLUE NOTE 3-5   72-76
EPIC 3-5   77-79
LPs: 10/12–inch 33rpm
BLUE NOTE 5-10   71-76
EPIC 5-10   78-79

HUMPHREY, Della
Singles: 7–inch
ARCTIC 4-6   68

HUMPHREY, Paul, and His Cool Aid Chemists
Singles: 7–inch
LIZARD 3-6   70-71
LPs: 10/12–inch 33rpm
LIZARD 8-12   71

HUMPHRIES, Teddy
Singles: 7–inch
KING (5000 series) 5-10   59
  (Monaural.)
KING (S-5000 series) 10-15   59
  (Stereo.)

HUNT, Geraldine
Singles: 7–inch
ABC 4-6   67
BOMBAY 4-8   64
CHECKER 4-8   62
PRISM 2-4   80
ROULETTE 3-5   70-73

HUNT, Geraldine, and Charlie Hodges
Singles: 7–inch
CALLA 3-5   70
  Also see HODGES, Charles
  Also see HUNT, Geraldine

HUNT, Pee Wee
Singles: 78rpm
CAPITOL 3-5   50-57
Singles: 7–inch
CAPITOL 5-10   50-62
SAVOY 5-10   51
EPs: 7–inch 33/45rpm
CAPITOL 5-10   50-56
SAVOY 5-10   51
LPs: 10/12–inch 33rpm
CAPITOL 4-8   78
  (With an "SM" prefix.)
CAPITOL 15-30   50-63
  (With a "T" or "ST" prefix.)
GLENDALE 4-8   78
SAVOY (15042 "Dixieland") 25-35   54
  (10–inch LP.)
TOPS 15-25   57

Also see BLANC, Mel
Also see FOUR KNIGHTS

HUNT, Tommy
Singles: 7-inch
ATLANTIC 4-8   65
CAPITOL 4-8   66
DYNAMO 4-8   67
SCEPTER 4-8   61-63
LPs: 10/12-inch 33rpm
DYNAMO (8001 "Greatest Hits") 15-25   67
SCEPTER (506 "I Just Don't Know
  What to Do with Myself") 25-35   62
  Also see FLAMINGOS
  Also see PLATTERS / Inez and Charlie Foxx / Jive Five /
  Tommy Hunt

HUNTER, Ian
Singles: 7-inch
CHRYSALIS 2-4   79
COLUMBIA 3-5   75
LPs: 10/12-inch 33rpm
CHRYSALIS 5-10   79-81
COLUMBIA 8-10   75-79
  Also see MOTT the HOOPLE

HUNTER, Ian, and Mick Ronson
LPs: 10/12-inch 33rpm
MERCURY 5-8   89
  Also see HUNTER, Ian
  Also see RONSON, Mick

HUNTER, Ivory Joe
(Ivory Joe Hunter and the Ivorytones)
Singles: 78rpm
ATLANTIC 5-10   55-58
EXCLUSIVE 8-12   45
4 STAR 8-12   48
KING 5-12   47-57
MGM 5-10   49-54
PACIFIC 10-15   45-47
Singles: 7-inch
ATLANTIC 8-12   55-58
CAPITOL 4-8   61-62
DOT 5-10   58-59
GOLDISC 5-10   60
KING (4424 "False Friend Blues") ... 25-35   51
KING (4443 "She's Gone Blues") 25-35   51
KING (4455 "Old Gal and New
  Gal Blues") 25-35   51
KING (5200 series) 5-10   59
MGM (500 series) 2-4   78
MGM (8011 "I Almost Lost My Mind") . 25-35   49
MGM (10000 and 11000 series) 15-25   49-54
MGM (10578 "I Almost Lost My Mind") 20-30   49
PARAMOUNT 3-5   73
SMASH 4-8   63
SOUND STAGE 7 4-6   68
STAX 5-8   64
VEE JAY 4-8   62
VEEP 4-8   67
EPs: 7-inch 33/45rpm
ATLANTIC (589 "Ivory Joe Hunter") .. 30-40   58

ATLANTIC (608 "Rock with
  Ivory Joe Hunter") 30-50   58
KING (265 "Ivory Joe Hunter") 30-50   54
MGM (1376/7/8 "I Get That
  Lonesome Feeling") 20-40   57
  (Price is for any of three volumes.)
LPs: 10/12-inch 33rpm
ATLANTIC (8008 "Ivory Joe Hunter") 50-80   58
  (Black Label.)
ATLANTIC (8008 "Ivory Joe Hunter") 40-60   59
  (Red Label.)
ATLANTIC (8015 "Ivory Joe Hunter Sings
  the Old and the New") 50-80   58
  (Black Label.)
ATLANTIC (8015 "Ivory Joe Hunter Sings
  the Old and the New") 40-60   59
  (Red Label.)
DOT 15-25   64
EPIC 8-10   71
EVEREST 8-10   74
GOLDISC (403 "Fabulous Ivory
  Joe Hunter") 25-35   61
GRAND PRIX 10-15
HOME COOKING 5-10   89
KING (605 "16 Greatest Hits") 50-80   58
LION 15-20
MGM (3488 "I Get That
  Lonesome Feeling") 50-80   57
PARAMOUNT 8-10   74
SAGE (603 "Ivory Joe Hunter") 25-35   59
SMASH 15-20   63
SOUND (603 "Ivory Joe Hunter") 50-80   57
  Also see CHARLES, Ray / Ivory Joe Hunter / Jimmy Rushing

HUNTER, Ivory Joe / Memphis Slim
LPs: 10/12-inch 33rpm
STRAND (1123 "The Artistry of
  Ivory Joe Hunter") 15-25

HUNTER, John
Singles: 7-inch
PRIVATE I 2-4   84-85
LPs: 10/12-inch 33rpm
PRIVATE I 5-10   85

HUNTER, Tab
Singles: 78rpm
DOT 4-8   56-57
Singles: 7-inch
DOT 5-10   56-62
WARNER (Monaural) 5-10   58-59
WARNER (Stereo) 10-15   59
  (With "S" prefix.)
Picture Sleeves
WARNER 8-12   58-60
EPs: 7-inch 33/45rpm
WARNER (EA-1221 "Tab Hunter") .. 15-25   58
  (Monaural. Has one track not heard on stereo
  version.)

WARNER (ESB-1221 "Tab Hunter") . . 20-35   58
(Stereo. Has one track not heard on mono
version.)
LPs: 10/12-inch 33rpm
DOT (3370 "Young Love") 25-30   61
(Monaural.)
DOT (25370 "Young Love") 20-30   61
(Stereo. Has some rerecorded tracks for stereo,
that are the original recordings on the mono
version.)
WARNER 25-35   58-60

HUNTER, Ty
(Ty Hunter and the Voice Masters)
Singles: 7-inch
ANNA (1114 "Everything About You") . 10-15   60
ANNA (1123 "Everytime") 10-15   60
CHECK MATE 5-10   61
CHESS 4-8   62-64
Also see GLASS HOUSE
Also see ORIGINALS
Also see VOICE MASTERS

HUNTER MUSKETT
LPs: 10/12-inch 33rpm
BRADLEY (1003 "Hunter Muskett") . . 35-45   73
Members: Danny Thompson; Jim McCarty; Chris George; Doug
Morter; Roger Trevit; Terry Hiscock; Mike Giles; Ken Freeman.

HUNTLEY, Chet, and David Brinkley
LPs: 10/12-inch 33rpm
RCA 8-15   64-66

HUNTSBERRY, Howard
Singles: 7-inch
MCA 2-4   88
LPs: 10/12-inch 33rpm
MCA 5-8   88

HURBY'S MACHINE
LPs: 10/12-inch 33rpm
SOUND CHECK 5-8   88

HURD, Debra
Singles: 7-inch
GEFFEN 2-4   83

HURRICANE
LPs: 10/12-inch 33rpm
ENIGMA 5-8   88-90

HURT, Jim
Singles: 7-inch
SCOTTI BROTHERS 2-4   80

HURT 'EM BAD and the S.C. Band
Singles: 7-inch
PROFILE 2-4   82

HUSKEY, Ferlin: see HUSKY, Ferlin

HUSKY, Ferlin
(Ferlin Husky and the Hush Puppies; Ferlin Husky
and the Coon Creek Girls; Ferlin and Bettie Husky;
Ferlin Huskey)
Singles: 78rpm
CAPITOL 4-8   52-57
Singles: 7-inch
ABC 3-5   73-75
CAPITOL (2000 through 3400) 3-6   67-72
(Orange labels.)
CAPITOL (2300 through 4300) 5-10   52-60
(Purple labels.)
CAPITOL (4400 through 5900) 4-8   60-67
CACHET 2-4   80
FIRST GENERATION 2-4   78
KING 4-8   60-61
EPs: 7-inch 33/45rpm
CAPITOL 10-20   57-60
Picture Sleeves
CAPITOL 4-8   62-68
LPs: 10/12-inch 33rpm
ABC 5-10   73-75
AUDIOGRAPH ALIVE 5-10   82
CAPITOL (718 "Songs of the
Home and Heart") 35-45   56
CAPITOL (880 "Boulevard of
Broken Dreams") 30-40   57
CAPITOL (1200 through 2800 series) 10-20   60-68
(With "T" or "ST" prefix.)
CAPITOL (1200 through 2800 series) . 5-10   68-75
(With "DT" or "SM" prefix.)
FIRST GENERATION 5-8   78
KING (647 "Country Tunes Sung
from the Heart") 25-35   59
KING (728 "Easy Livin") 25-35   60
PICKWICK 6-12
PICKWICK/HILLTOP 8-12   65
Also see CRUM, Simon
Also see OWENS, Buck / Faron Young / Ferlin Husky
Also see PRESTON, Terry
Also see SHEPARD, Jean, and Ferlin Husky

HUSKY, Ferlin / Pat Boone
Singles: 7-inch
U.S.A.F. 5-10   60
(Promotional issue only.)
Also see BOONE, Pat
Also see HUSKY, Ferlin

HUTCH, Willie
Singles: 7-inch
DUNHILL 4-8   65
MAVERICK 4-8   68
MOTOWN 3-5   73-82
RCA 4-6   69
WHITFIELD 3-5   78-79
Picture Sleeves
MOTOWN 3-5   75
LPs: 10/12-inch 33rpm
MOTOWN 5-10   73-82
RCA 10-12   69

WHITFIELD 5-10   78-79

HUTSON, Leroy
(Leroy Hutson and the Free Spirit Symphony)
Singles: 7–inch

CURTOM 3-5   73-78
RSO 3-5   79

LPs: 10/12–inch 33rpm

CURTOM 8-10   73-78
Also see IMPRESSIONS

HUTTON, Danny
Singles: 7–inch

HBR 4-8   65
MGM 4-8   66
Picture Sleeves

HBR 10-15   65
MGM 8-12   66
LPs: 10/12–inch 33rpm

MGM 8-10   70
Also see THREE DOG NIGHT

HYDE, Paul, and the Payolas
Singles: 7–inch

A&M 2-4   85
I.R.S. 2-4
Picture Sleeves

A&M 2-4   85
I.R.S. 2-4
LPs: 10/12–inch 33rpm

A&M 5-10   85

HYLAND, Brian
Singles: 7–inch

ABC 3-5   73
ABC-PAR 4-8   61-64
DOT 4-6   67-69
KAPP 4-8   60-61
LEADER 10-15   60
MCA 2-4   73
PHILIPS 4-8   64-67
ROWE/AMI 5-10   66
("Play Me" Sales Stimulator promotional issue.)
ROULETTE 2-4
UNI 3-5   70-72
Picture Sleeves

ABC-PAR 8-15   61-63

KAPP (Except 352) 10-20   60-61
KAPP (352 "Four Little Heels") 20-30   60
(Black and white sleeve. Promotional issue only.)
KAPP (352 "Four Little Heels") 10-20   60
(Color sleeve.)
PHILIPS 4-8   64-67
LPs: 10/12–inch 33rpm

ABC-PAR 20-25   61-64
DOT 10-12   69
KAPP (1202 "The Bashful Blonde") . . 25-30   60
(Monaural.)
KAPP (3202 "The Bashful Blonde") . . 30-40   60
PHILIPS 15-20   64-66
PICKWICK 5-10
PRIVATE STOCK 5-10   77
UNI 8-10   71
WING 10-12   67

HYMAN, Dick
(Dick Hyman Trio; Dick Hyman and His Electric Eclectics)
Singles: 78rpm

MGM 2-4   54-57
Singles: 7–inch

COLUMBIA 3-5   74-75
COMMAND 3-6   61-70
EVEREST 4-6   60
MGM 4-8   54-62
RCA 2-4   62
LPs: 10/12–inch 33rpm

ATLANTIC 5-10   75
COLUMBIA 5-10   74
COMMAND 5-15   60-73
EVEREST 5-10   60
FAMOUS DOOR 5-10   73
MCA 5-10   77
MGM 10-20   54-63
PROJECT 3 5-10   71
RCA 4-8   80-83
SUNSET 5-10   66

HYMAN, Phyllis
Singles: 12–inch 33/45rpm

ARISTA 4-6   83
Singles: 7–inch

ARISTA 2-5   78-83
BUDDAH 3-5   77
DESERT MOON 3-5   76
PHILADELPHIA INT'L 2-4   86
LPs: 10/12–inch 33rpm

ARISTA 5-10   79-83
BUDDAH 5-10   77
PHILADELPHIA INT'L 5-10   86

HYMAN, Phyllis, and Michael Henderson
Singles: 7–inch

ARISTA 2-4   81
Also see CONNORS, Norman
Also see HENDERSON, Michael
Also see HYMAN, Phyllis

I

I LEVEL
Singles: 12–inch 33/45rpm
VIRGIN 4-6   82-84
Singles: 7–inch
VIRGIN 2-4   82-84
LPs: 10/12–inch 33rpm
VIRGIN 5-10   83

I.R.T.
(Interboro Rhythm Team)
Singles: 12–inch 33/45rpm
RCA 4-6   84
Singles: 7–inch
RCA 2-4   84

IAN, Janis
Singles: 7–inch
CAPITOL 3-5   71
CASABLANCA 2-4   80
COLUMBIA 3-5   74-81
POLYDOR 3-5   78
VERVE 3-5
VERVE/FOLKWAYS 4-8   66-67
VERVE/FORECAST 4-6   68-69
Picture Sleeves
COLUMBIA 3-6   75
LPs: 10/12–inch 33rpm
CAPITOL 8-12   71-75
COLUMBIA 8-10   74-81
MGM 8-10   70
POLYDOR 8-10   75
VERVE/FOLKWAYS 10-15   67
VERVE/FORECAST 10-15   68-69

ICE - T
Singles: 7–inch
SIRE 2-4   88-90
Picture Sleeves
SIRE 2-4   88
LPs: 10/12–inch 33rpm
SIRE 5-10   87-91

ICEHOUSE
Singles: 12–inch 33/45rpm
CHRYSALIS 4-6   81-86
Singles: 7–inch
CHRYSALIS 2-4   81-88
Picture Sleeves
CHRYSALIS 2-4   81-88
LPs: 10/12–inch 33rpm
CHRYSALIS 5-10   81-88

ICICLE WORKS
Singles: 7–inch
ARISTA 2-4   84

LPs: 10/12–inch 33rpm
ARISTA 5-10   84

ICON
LPs: 10/12–inch 33rpm
CAPITOL 5-10   84
Members: Steve Clifford; Dan Wexler; Pat Dixon; John Aquilino; Tracy Wallach; Jerry Harrison.

IDEALS
Singles: 7–inch
SATELLITE 5-8   66
Members: Sam Stewart; Reggie Jackson; Leonard Mitchell.

IDES of MARCH
Singles: 7–inch
KAPP 4-6   69
PARROT 5-10   66-67
RCA 3-5   72-73
WARNER 3-6   69-71
LPs: 10/12–inch 33rpm
RCA 8-12   72-73
WARNER 10-15   70-71
Members: Jim Peterik; Mike Borch; Ray Herr; Bob Bergland; Chuck Soumar; John Larson; Larry Millas.

IDLE RACE
Singles: 7–inch
LIBERTY (55997 "Here We Go
Round the Lemon Tree") 10-15   67
LPs: 10/12–inch 33rpm
LIBERTY (7603 "Birthday Party") . . . 25-30   69
SUNSET 8-12   72
Members: Jeff Lynne; Greg Masters; Roger Spencer; Dave Pritchard.
Also see LYNNE, Jeff

IDOL, Billy
Singles: 12–inch 33/45rpm
CHRYSALIS 4-6   81-86
Singles: 7–inch
CHRYSALIS 2-4   81-90
Picture Sleeves
CHRYSALIS 2-4   83-90
LPs: 10/12–inch 33rpm
CHRYSALIS (1377 "Billy Idol") 10-20   82
(Promotional issue only.)
CHRYSALIS (4000 "Don't Stop") 8-10   81
CHRYSALIS (20000 series) 5-8   90
CHRYSALIS (40000 series) 5-10   82-87

IF
Singles: 7–inch
CAPITOL 3-5   70-74
METROMEDIA 3-5   72
LPs: 10/12–inch 33rpm
CAPITOL 10-12   69-74
METROMEDIA 8-10   72-73

IFIELD, Frank
Singles: 7–inch
CAPITOL 4-6   63-65
HICKORY 3-6   66-71
MAM 3-5   71

VEE JAY	4-8	62-63
WARNER	3-5	79

LPs: 10/12–inch 33rpm

CAPITOL	10-20	63
HICKORY	8-10	66-68
VEE JAY	10-20	62

Also see BEATLES / Frank Ifield

Alhambra

Lado A

MO-771
45 R. P. M.

℗ 1972.

A VECES LLEGAN CARTAS
(M. Alejandro)
JULIO IGLESIAS

IGLESIAS, Julio
Singles: 7–inch

ALAHAMBRA	3-6	72-75
COLUMBIA	2-4	83-89

LPs: 10/12–inch 33rpm

COLUMBIA	5-10	83-90

IGLESIAS, Julio, and Willie Nelson
(Willie Nelson and Julio Iglesias)
Singles: 7–inch

COLUMBIA (Except 04495)	2-4	84
COLUMBIA (04495 "As Time Goes By")	8-12	84
(Promotional issue only.)		

Picture Sleeves

COLUMBIA (Except 04495)	2-4	84
COLUMBIA (04495 "As Time Goes By")	10-15	84
(Promotional issue only.)		

Also see NELSON, Willie

IGLESIAS, Julio, and Diana Ross
Singles: 7–inch

COLUMBIA	2-4	84

Picture Sleeves

COLUMBIA	2-4	84

Also see ROSS, Diana

IGLESIAS, Julio, and Stevie Wonder
Singles: 7–inch

COLUMBIA	2-4	88

Picture Sleeves

COLUMBIA	2-4	88

Also see IGLESIAS, Julio
Also see WONDER, Stevie

IGGY and the Stooges: see POP, Iggy

IKETTES

ATCO	4-8	61-62

INNIS	4-8	64
MODERN	4-8	64-66
PHI-DAN	4-8	
POMPEII	4-8	68
TEENA	4-8	63
U.A.	3-6	71-72

LPs: 10/12–inch 33rpm

MODERN	15-20	65
U.A.	8-10	73-75

Members: Delores Johnson; Eloise Hester; Joshie Jo Armstead; Vanetta Fields; Jessie Smith; Robbie Montgomery.
Also see ARMSTEAD, Joshie Jo
Also see MIRETTES
Also see TURNER, Ike and Tina

ILLINOIS SPEED PRESS
Singles: 7–inch

COLUMBIA	4-8	68-70

LPs: 10/12–inch 33rpm

COLUMBIA	10-15	69-70

Members: Paul Cotton; Rob Lewine; Fred Page; Kal David; Mike Anthony.
Also see POCO

ILLUSION
Singles: 7–inch

DYNO VOICE	4-8	68
STEED	4-6	69-71

LPs: 10/12–inch 33rpm

STEED	10-20	69-70

ILLUSION
Singles: 7–inch

ISLAND	3-5	77-78

LPs: 10/12–inch 33rpm

ISLAND	5-10	77-78

ILLUSION
Singles: 7–inch

SUGAR HILL	2-4	82

ILLUSTRATED MAN
Singles: 7–inch

CAPITOL	2-4	84

IMAGINATION
Singles: 12–inch 33/45rpm

ELEKTRA	4-6	84

Singles: 7–inch

ELEKTRA	2-4	83
MCA	2-4	82-83
RCA	2-4	87

LPs: 10/12–inch 33rpm

MCA	5-10	82

IMPACT
Singles: 7–inch

ATCO	3-5	76
FANTASY	3-5	77-78

LPs: 10/12–inch 33rpm

ATCO	8-10	75
FANTASY	5-10	77

Members: Damon Harris; John Simms; Donald Tilghman; Charles Timmons.
Also see HARRIS, Damon

IMPALAS
(Featuring Joe "Speedo" Frazier)
Singles: 7–inch
CUB (Except 9022) 8-10   59-60
CUB (9022 "I Ran All the Way Home") 20-25   59
CUB (9022 "Sorry I Ran All
  the Way Home") 8-10   59
  (The difference between the two previous listings is
  the use of "Sorry" in the title.)
HAMILTON 10-15   59
MGM 3-5   64-78
EPs: 7–inch 33/45rpm
CUB (5000 "Sorry, I Ran All
  the Way Home") 100-150   59
LPs: 10/12–inch 33rpm
CUB (CUB-8003 "Sorry, I Ran All
  the Way Home") 100-150   59
  (Monaural.)
CUB (CUBS-8003 "Sorry, I Ran All
  the Way Home") 150-250   59
  (Stereo.)

IMPALAS / Horst Jankowski and His Orchestra
Singles: 7–inch
COLLECTABLES 2-4   85
  Also see IMPALAS
  Also see JANKOWSKI, Horst, and His Orchestra

IMPELLITTERI
LPs: 10/12–inch 33rpm
RELATIVITY 5-8   88

IMPERIALS
Singles: 7–inch
CAPITOL 8-12   63
CARLTON 10-15   61
END (1027 "Tears on My Pillow") 15-20   58
  (First pressing. Reissues were credited to "Little
  Anthony and the Imperials.")
LIBERTY 8-12   58
  Also see LITTLE ANTHONY and the Imperials

IMPERIALS
Singles: 7–inch
OMNI 3-5   78

IMPRESSIONS
Singles: 12–inch 33/45rpm
20TH FOX 4-8   79
Singles: 7–inch
ABC 4-8   66-68
ABC-PAR 5-10   61-66
ABNER 10-20   59-60
ADORE (901 "Popcorn Willie") 25-45   64
BANDERA (2504 "Listen") 20-25   59
CHI-SOUND 3-5   81
COTILLION 3-5   76-77
CURTOM 3-6   68-76
MCA 2-4   87
PORT 5-10   62
SWIRL 10-15   62

20TH FOX 3-5   81
VEE JAY (424 through 621) 6-12   61-64
  (Vee Jay 280, *For Your Precious Love*, appears in
  the Jerry Butler section.)
Picture Sleeves
CURTOM 4-8   68
EPs: 7–inch 33/45rpm
CURTOM (20 "Do You Want to Win") . 5-10   70
  (Promotional issue only.)
LPs: 10/12–inch 33rpm
ABC 10-15   66-76
ABC-PAR 15-20   63-66
COTILLION 8-10   76
CURTOM 8-10   68-76
MCA 5-10   82
PICKWICK 8-10   75
SCEPTER/CITATION 8-10
SIRE 8-12   76
20TH FOX 5-10   79-81
UPFRONT 8-10
  Members: Curtis Mayfield; Sam Gooden; Richard Brooks; Fred
  Cash; Leroy Hutson; Reggie Torlan; Ralph Johnson; Nate Evans.
  Also see EVERETT, Betty / Impressions
  Also see HUTSON, Leroy
  Also see MAYFIELD, Curtis
  Also see MYSTIQUE

IMPRESSIONS / Jerry Butler
LPs: 10/12–inch 33rpm
SIRE 5-10   77
  Also see BUTLER, Jerry
  Also see IMPRESSIONS

IMPRESSORS
Singles: 7–inch
CUB (9010 "Do You Love Her") 10-20   58
ONYX (514 "Is It Too Late") 30-40   57

IN CROWD
Singles: 7–inch
BRENT 5-10   65
HICKORY 10-15   65
MUSICOR (1111 "Do the Surfer Jerk") 10-20   65
RONN 10-20
SWAN 4-8   65
TOWER 5-8   65-66
VIVA 4-8   66-67

INCREDIBLE BONGO BAND
Singles: 7–inch
MGM 3-5   73
PRIDE 3-5   72-74
LPs: 10/12–inch 33rpm
PRIDE 8-10   73-74

INCREDIBLE STRING BAND
LPs: 10/12–inch 33rpm
ELEKTRA 8-12   67-72
REPRISE 8-12   72-74

INCREDIBLES
Singles: 7–inch
AUDIO ARTS 4-8   66-68
CLASS 4-8   66

TETRAGRAMMATON 3-6   69
LPs: 10/12–inch 33rpm
AUDIO ARTS 10-12   70

INDEEP
Singles: 12–inch 33/45rpm
SOUND of NEW YORK 4-6   83-85
Singles: 7–inch
SOUND of NEW YORK 2-4   83-85
LPs: 10/12–inch 33rpm
SOUND of NEW YORK 5-10   83

INDEPENDENTS
Singles: 7–inch
WAND 3-6   72-74
LPs: 10/12–inch 33rpm
WAND 8-12   72-74
Members: Chuck Jackson; Maurice Jackson; Eric Thomas; Helen Curry.

INDIA
Singles: 12–inch 33/45rpm
WEST END 4-6   83

INDIOS TABAJARAS, Los:
see LOS INDIOS TABAJARAS

INDIVIDUALS
Singles: 7–inch
P.I.P. 3-5   75
21 3-5

INDUSTRY
Singles: 7–inch
CAPITOL 2-4   83

INFINITY
(Infinity Featuring Billy Butler)
Singles: 7–inch
FOUNTAIN 4-6   69
MERCURY 3-5   70
UNI 3-5   72
Members: Billy Butler; Earl Batts; Jess Tillman; Larry Wade; Phyllis Know.

INFORMATION SOCIETY
Singles: 78rpm
TOMMY BOY 2-4   88-90
Picture Sleeves
TOMMY BOY 2-4   88
LPs: 10/12–inch 33rpm
TOMMY BOY 5-8   88-90

INGMANN, Jorgen
Singles: 78rpm
MERCURY 4-8   56
Singles: 7–inch
ATCO 4-8   60-66
MERCURY 5-10   56
PARROT 4-8   64
U.A. INT'L 4-6   68
LPs: 10/12–inch 33rpm
ATCO 20-30   62
MERCURY 20-30   56
U.A. INT'L 8-12   68

INGRAM
Singles: 7–inch
H&L 3-5   77
LPs: 10/12–inch 33rpm
H&L 8-10   77

INGRAM, James
Singles: 12–inch 33/45rpm
QWEST 4-6   83
Singles: 7–inch
MCA 2-4   87
QWEST 2-4   83-86
WARNER 2-4   90
Picture Sleeves
QWEST 2-4   83-86
LPs: 10/12–inch 33rpm
QWEST 5-10   83-86
WARNER 5-8   90
Also see AUSTIN, Patti, and James Ingram
Also see JONES, Quincy, and James Ingram
Also see ROGERS, Kenny, Kim Carnes and James Ingram
Also see RONSTADT, Linda, and James Ingram
Also see U.S.A. for AFRICA

INGRAM, James, and Michael McDonald
Singles: 7–inch
QWEST 2-4   83
Also see INGRAM, James
Also see McDONALD, Michael

INGRAM, Luther
(Luther Ingram and the G-Men)
Singles: 7–inch
DECCA 4-8   65
ERIC 2-4
HIB 4-8   67
KO KO 3-6   67-78
PROFILE 2-4   86-87
SMASH 4-8   66
LPs: 10/12–inch 33rpm
KO KO 8-10   71-76
Note: the Ko Ko label name may be shown as one word (Koko) on some issues.

INK SPOTS
(Charlie Fuqua's Ink Spots)
Singles: 78rpm
BLUEBIRD 10-20   36
DECCA (800 series) 10-15   36
DECCA (1000 through 4000 series) .. 5-10   36-42
DECCA (18000 through 30000 series) . 3-8   42-57
Singles: 7–inch
DECCA 5-10   50-61
GRAND AWARD 5-10   56
VERVE 4-8   60
X-TRA 4-8   60
EPs: 7–inch 33/45rpm
DECCA 5-15   54-56
GRAND AWARD 5-15   56
TOPS (606 "Ink Spots") 10-15   59
(Two-EP set.)
WALDORF MUSIC HALL 5-15   55

Members: Bill Kenny; Orville Jones; Herb Kenny; Charlie Fuqua; Ivory "Deek" Watson; Bernie Mackey; Cliff Givens; Billy Bowen. Also see FITZGERALD, Ella, and the Ink Spots Also see KENNY, Bill

INK SPOTS

Members: James Holmes; Charlie Fuqua; Harry Jackson; Isaac Royal; Leon Antoine.

INMAN, Autry

INMATES

INNER CITY

INNER CITY JAM BAND

INNER LIFE

Singles: 7–inch

PERSONAL	2-4	84
PRELUDE	2-5	79-80
SALSOUL	2-4	83

INNERVISION
Singles: 7–inch

ARIOLA AMERICA	3-5	77
PRIVATE STOCK	3-5	75

INNOCENCE
Singles: 7–inch

KAMA SUTRA	4-8	66-67

LPs: 10/12–inch 33rpm

KAMA SUTRA	15-20	67

Members: Pete Anders; Vinnie Poncia.

INNOCENCE in DANGER
Singles: 12–inch 33/45rpm

EPIC	4-6	84

Singles: 7–inch

EPIC	2-4	84

INNOCENTS
Singles: 7–inch

DECCA	10-15	63
ERA	3-5	72
INDIGO	8-12	60-62
PORT	4-8	
REPRISE (20112 "Oh How I Miss My Baby/Be Mine")	15-20	62
REPRISE (20125 "Oh How I Miss My Baby/You're Never Satisfied")	8-12	62
TRANS WORLD	10-15	60
WARNER (5450 "My Heart Stood Still")	15-25	64

LPs: 10/12–inch 33rpm

INDIGO (503 "Innocently Yours")	50-75	61

Members: Darron Stankey; Al Candaleria; Jim West.
Also see YOUNG, Kathy

INSIDERS
Singles: 12–inch 33/45rpm

EPIC	4-8	87

(Promotional only.)

Singles: 7–inch

EPIC	2-4	87

Picture Sleeves

EPIC	2-4	87

LPs: 10/12–inch 33rpm

EPIC	5-10	87

INSTANT FUNK
Singles: 12–inch 33/45rpm

SALSOUL	4-8	79-83

Singles: 7–inch

SALSOUL	2-5	78-83
TSOP	3-5	75-77

LPs: 10/12–inch 33rpm

SALSOUL	5-10	79-83
TSOP	5-10	76

INTERLUDE
Singles: 7–inch

STAR VISION INT'L	2-4	80

INTERNATIONAL ALL STARS
LPs: 10/12–inch 33rpm

LONDON	5-10	61

INTRIGUES
Singles: 7–inch

TOOT	4-8	68
YEW	3-6	69-71

LPs: 10/12–inch 33rpm

YEW	10-15	70

INTRIGUES
Singles: 7–inch

WORLD TRADE	2-4	85

INTRIQUE
Singles: 7–inch

COOLTEMPO	2-4	87

INTRUDERS
(Intruders Trio)
Singles: 7–inch

FAME	5-10	59

INTRUDERS
Singles: 7–inch

EXCEL	4-8	
GAMBLE	4-6	66-73
GOWEN	5-10	62
PHILADELPHIA INT'L	3-5	72
RIPETE	3-5	85
TSOP	3-5	74-75

Picture Sleeves

GAMBLE	4-8	66

LPs: 10/12–inch 33rpm

GAMBLE	10-15	67-73
TSOP	8-10	75

Members: Sam Brown; Eugene Doughtry; Phil Terry; Robert Edwards; Bobby Starr.

INVINCIBLES
Singles: 7–inch

DOUBLE SHOT	4-8	66
INVINCIBLE	4-8	66
LOMA	4-8	66
RAMPART	4-6	69
WARNER	4-8	64-67

INVISIBLE MAN'S BAND
Singles: 7–inch

BOARDWALK	2-4	81-82
MANGO	2-4	80
MOVE'N GROOVE	2-4	83

LPs: 10/12–inch 33rpm

BOARDWALK	10-20	81
MANGO	5-8	80

Members: Clarence Burke; Ken Burke; James Burke; Dennis Burke.
Also see FIVE STAIRSTEPS

INVITATIONS
Singles: 7–inch
DIAMOND 5-10   68
DYNO VOICE 5-10   65-66
MGM 5-10   66

INVITATIONS
Singles: 7–inch
SILVER BLUE 3-5   74

INXS
Singles: 12–inch 33/45rpm
ATCO 4-6   84
ATLANTIC 4-6   85-86
Singles: 7–inch
ATCO 2-4   83-85
ATLANTIC 2-4   85-90
Picture Sleeves
ATCO 2-4   83-84
ATLANTIC 2-4   85-90
LPs: 10/12–inch 33rpm
ATCO 5-10   83-85
ATLANTIC 5-10   85-90
Members: Micheal Hutchence; Tim Farriss; Andrew Farriss; Jon Farriss; Gary Beers; Kirk Pengilly.

IRIS, Donnie
Singles: 7–inch
HME 2-4   85
MCA 2-4   80-83
Picture Sleeves
HME 2-4   85
MCA 2-4   82-83
LPs: 10/12–inch 33rpm
HME 5-10   85
MCA 5-10   80-83
MIDWEST 5-10   80
Also see JAGGERZ

IRISH ROVERS
Singles: 7–inch
DECCA 3-6   68-70
LPs: 10/12–inch 33rpm
CLEVELAND INT'L 5-8   81
DECCA 8-15   68-72
MCA 5-10   73-77
SANDCASTLE 5-10   76
Also see ROVERS

IRON BUTTERFLY
Singles: 7–inch
ATCO 3-6   68-71
MCA 2-4   75
EPs: 7–inch 33/45rpm
ATCO (4524 "Iron Butterfly") 20-30   68
(Promotional issue only. Issued with paper sleeve.)
LPs: 10/12–inch 33rpm
ATCO (Except 227) 10-15   68-71
ATCO (227 "Heavy") 15-20   68
MCA 8-10   75
Members: Doug Ingle; Mike Pinera; Larry Reinhardt; Ron Bushy; Lee Dorman; Erik Brann.
Also see CAPTAIN BEYOND

45 RPM
ATCO RECORDS
EP-C-4524-A
D. J. COPY
SP
VOCAL
Produced by
Charles Greene &
Brian Stone
A York/Pala
Records, Inc.
Production
1 - GET OUT OF MY LIFE, WOMAN (Time: 3:24)
(Allen Toussaint) Marsaint, BMI
2 - UNCONSCIOUS POWER (Time: 2:29)
(Ingle-Weis-Bushy) Ten East-Cotillion, BMI
IRON BUTTERFLY
From ATCO LP 33-227
Division of ATLANTIC RECORDS, 1841 B'way., N. Y., N. Y.

Also see PINERA, Mike

IRON MAIDEN
Singles: 7–inch
CAPITOL (Except V-15375) 2-4   88
CAPITOL (V-15375 "Can I
Play with Madness") 5-8   88
(Picture/shaped disc.)
LPs: 10/12–inch 33rpm
CAPITOL (Except "SEAX" series) 5-10   82-88
CAPITOL (SEAX-12215 "Number of
the Beast") 15-25   82
(Picture disc.)
CAPITOL (SEAX-12306 "Piece of
Mind") 20-30   83
(Picture disc.)
EPIC 5-8   90
HARVEST 5-10   80-82

IRONHORSE
Singles: 7–inch
SCOTTI BROS 2-4   79-80
LPs: 10/12–inch 33rpm
SCOTTI BROS 5-10   79-80
Member: Randy Bachman.
Also see BACHMAN, Randy

IRWIN, Big Dee
(Difosco Erwin; Dee Irwin; Big Dee Irwin with Little Eva)
Singles: 7–inch
BLISS 5-10
DIMENSION 5-10   63-64
FAIRMOUNT 4-8   66
IMPERIAL 4-8   68
ROTATE 4-8   65
Also see DIFOSCO
Also see ERWIN, Dee
Also see LITTLE EVA
Also see PASTELLS

IRWIN, Dee, and Mamie Galore
Singles: 7–inch
IMPERIAL 4-8   68-69
Also see IRWIN, Big Dee

ISAAK, Chris
LPs: 10/12–inch 33rpm
REPRISE 5-8   89
WARNER 5-10   87

ISLANDERS
(Featuring Randy Starr)
Singles: 7–inch
MAYFLOWER 5-10   59-60
LPs: 10/12–inch 33rpm
MAYFLOWER 20-30   60
Also see STARR, Randy

ISLEY BROTHERS
(Isley Brothers Featuring Ronald Isley)
Singles: 78rpm
TEENAGE (1004 "Angels Cried") 20-30   57
Singles: 12–inch 33/45rpm
T-NECK 4-8   79-83
Singles: 12–inch 33/45rpm
WARNER 4-6   87
Singles: 7–inch
ATLANTIC 5-10   61-65
CINDY (3009 "Don't Be Jealous") ... 40-50   58
GONE (5022 "Everybody's Gonna
  Rock and Roll") 20-30   58
GONE (5048 "My Love") 20-30   59
MARK-X (7003 "Rockin' MacDonald) . 20-35   57
MARK-X (8000 "Rockin' MacDonald) . 10-20   58
RCA (447-0500 series) 4-6   61
  (Black label with dog on top.)
RCA (447-0500 series) 3-5   65
  (Black label with dog on side.)
RCA (47-7000 series) 5-10   59-60
RCA (61-7588 "Shout") 10-20   59
  (Stereo.)
T-NECK (Except 501) 2-5   69-84
T-NECK (501 "Testify") 4-8   64
TAMLA 4-8   66-69
TEENAGE (1004 "Angels Cried") .. 100-150   57
U.A. 4-8   63-64
VEEP 4-8   66
WAND 5-10   62-63
WARNER 2-4   85-88
LPs: 10/12–inch 33rpm
BUDDAH 10-12   76
CAMDEN 8-10   73-75
COLLECTABLES 6-8   88
MOTOWN 5-10   80-82
PHILADELPHIA INT'L 5-10   78
PICKWICK 5-10   77
RCA (LPM-2156 "Shout!") 35-45   59
  (Monaural.)
RCA (LSP-2156 "Shout!") 45-55   59
  (Stereo.)
SCEPTER 10-20   66
SUNSET 8-10   69
T-NECK (Except 137) 8-10   69-84

T-NECK (137 "Everything You Always
  Wanted to Hear") 10-15   76
  (Promotional issue only.)
TAMLA 12-15   66-69
TRIP 8-10   76
U.A. (500 series) 8-10   75
U.A. (6000 series) 20-25   63
WAND (WD-653 "Twist and Shout") . 20-30   62
  (Monaural.)
WAND (WDS-653 "Twist and Shout) 30-40   62
  (Stereo.)
WARNER 5-10   85-87
  Members: Ron Isley; Rudy Isley; O'Kelly Isley; Ernie Isley;
  Marvin Isley.
  Also see CHRISTIE, Lou, and the Classics / Isley Brothers /
  Chiffons
  Also see HENDRIX, Jimi, and the Isley Brothers
  Also see ISLEY - JASPER - ISLEY
  Also see RASCALS / Isley Brothers

ISLEY BROTHERS and Dave "Baby" Cortez
LPs: 10/12–inch 33rpm
T-NECK 8-10   69
  Also see CORTEZ, Dave "Baby"

ISLEY BROTHERS / Go-Go's
EPs: 7–inch 33/45rpm
RCA/WURLITZER 10-15   64
  (Promotional issue only.)
  Also see GO-GOs

ISLEY BROTHERS / Marvin & Johnny
LPs: 10/12–inch 33rpm
CROWN 10-20   63
  Also see MARVIN & JOHNNY

ISLEY - JASPER - ISLEY
Singles: 12–inch 33/45rpm
CBS ASSOCIATED 4-6   85-86
Singles: 7–inch
CBS ASSOCIATED 2-4   85-87
LPs: 10/12–inch 33rpm
CBS ASSOCIATED 5-10   85-86
  Members: Marvin Isley; Chris Isley; Ernie Isley.
  Also see ISLEY BROTHERS

IT's a BEAUTIFUL DAY
(Featuring David LaFlamme)
Singles: 7–inch
COLUMBIA 4-8   69-73
SAN FRANCISCO SOUND 8-12   70
LPs: 10/12–inch 33rpm
COLUMBIA (1058 "Marrying Maiden") 15-20   70
COLUMBIA (9768 "It's a
  Beautiful Day") 20-30   69
COLUMBIA (30734 "Choice Quality
  Stuff/Anytime") 10-15   71
COLUMBIA (31338 "Live at
  Carnegie Hall") 10-15   72
COLUMBIA (32181 "It's a Beautiful
  Day ... Today") 10-15   73
COLUMBIA (32660 "A 1001 Nights") . 30-40   73
  (Promotional issue only.)

SAN FRANCISCO SOUNDS (11790 "It's
 a Beautiful Day") 25-35   70
 Also see GARCIA, Jerry
 Also see LA FLAMME, David
 Also see PABLO CRUISE

ITALIAN ASPHALT and Pavement Company
(Duprees)
Singles: 7–inch
COLOSSUS 3-5   70
Picture Sleeves
COLOSSUS 4-6   70
LPs: 10/12–inch 33rpm
COLOSSUS 8-10   70
 Also see DUPREES

IVAN
(Jerry Ivan Allison)
Singles: 7–inch
CORAL (62017 "Real Wild Child") ... 35-45   59
CORAL (62081 "Frankie
 Frankenstein") 50-75   59
CORAL (65607 "Real Wild Child") ... 20-25   67
 Also see CRICKETS

IVAN / Johnny Tillotson
Singles: 7–inch
OLDIES 45 4-8   64
 Also see IVAN
 Also see TILLOTSON, Johnny

IVES, Burl
(Burl Ives and the Trinidaddies)
Singles: 78rpm
COLUMBIA 3-8   50-51
DECCA 3-8   48-57
Singles: 7–inch
BELL 3-5   70
BIG TREE 3-5   71
BUENA VISTA 4-6   63
COLUMBIA (39000 series) 5-10   50-51
COLUMBIA (44000 series) 3-6   68-69
COLUMBIA (70000 series) 3-6   69
CYCLONE 3-5   70
DECCA (25000 series) 4-6   66-69
DECCA (27000 through 30000 series) . 5-10   50-59
DECCA (31000 through 33000 series) . 3-8   60-73
DISNEYLAND 4-6   64
MCA 3-5   73-74
MONKEY JOE 3-5   78
Picture Sleeves
BUENA VISTA 4-8   63
DECCA 4-8   62
U.A. 4-8   62
EPs: 7–inch 33/45rpm
COLUMBIA 5-15   51-55
DECCA 5-15   49-65
LPs: 10/12–inch 33rpm
BELL 5-10   71
CAEDMON 4-6   72
COLUMBIA (628 "Wayfaring
 Stranger") 20-35   55

COLUMBIA (1459 "Return of the Wayfaring
 Stranger") 15-25   60
COLUMBIA (2570 "Children's
 Favorites") 20-35   55
 (10–inch LP.)
COLUMBIA (6058 "Wayfaring
 Stranger") 25-40   50
 (10–inch LP.)
COLUMBIA (6109 "Wayfaring
 Stranger, Vol. 2") 25-40   51
 (10–inch LP.)
COLUMBIA (6144 "Wayfaring
 Stranger, Vol. 3") 25-40   51
 (10–inch LP.)
COLUMBIA (9000 series) 8-12   68-69
CORAL 4-8   73
DECCA (100 series) 15-25   61
DECCA (4000 series) 10-20   62-68
 (Decca LP numbers in this series preceded by a
 "7" or a "DL-7" are stereo issues.)
DECCA (5013 "Ballads and
 Folk Songs") 20-40   49
 (10–inch LP.)
DECCA (5080 "Ballads and
 Folk Songs, Vol. 2") 20-40   49
 (10–inch LP.)
DECCA (5490 "Women – Songs of
 the Fair Sex") 20-30   53
 (10–inch LPs)
DECCA (8000 series) 10-20   55-59
DISNEYLAND 8-12   63-64
EVEREST 5-10   78
HARMONY 8-15   59-70
MCA 5-10   73-75
SUNSET 5-10   70
UNART 6-12   67
U.A. 10-20   59-62
WORD 5-10   63-66
 Also see MILLS, Hayley, and Burl Ives

IVEYS
(Badfinger)
Singles: 7–inch
APPLE (1803 "Maybe Tomorrow") ... 10-15   69
APPLE/AMERICOM (301 "Maybe
 Tomorrow") 150-250   69
 (Four–inch flexi, "pocket disc.")
 Also see BADFINGER

IVY LEAGUE
Singles: 7–inch
CAMEO 5-10   65-66
LPs: 10/12–inch 33rpm
CAMEO (2000 "Tossing and
 Turning") 20-30   65
 Member: John Carter.
 Also see OHIO EXPRESS

IVY THREE
Singles: 7–inch
SHELL 10-20   60-61

J

J. BIRD: see BIRD, J.

J.B.s
(J.B.'s Internationals)
Singles: 7–inch
PEOPLE 3-5   72-76
POLYDOR 3-5   77-78
LPs: 10/12–inch 33rpm
PEOPLE 5-8   72-75
Also see BROWN, James

J.D. DREWS: see DREWS, J.D.

J.J. FAD
Singles: 7–inch
RUTHLESS 2-4   88
Picture Sleeves
RUTHLESS 2-4   88
LPs: 10/12–inch 33rpm
RUTHLESS 5-8   88

JACK, Ballin': see BALLIN' JACK

JACKIE and the STARLITES
Singles: 78rpm
FIRE/FURY (1000 "They Laughed
   at Me") 20-40   57
Singles: 7–inch
FIRE/FURY (1000 "They Laughed
   at Me") 75-125   57
FURY 10-15   62
HULL 15-20   63
MASCOT (128 "For All We Know") ... 15-20   62
MASCOT (130 "You Keep Telling Me") 20-25   63
MASCOT (131 "Walking from School") 15-20   63
LPs: 10/12–inch 33rpm
LOST-NITE 5-8   81
Member: Jackie Rue.
   Also see STARLITES

JACKIE LEE: see LEE, Jackie

JACKS
Singles: 78rpm
RPM (Except 428 and 433) 5-10   55-56
RPM (428 "Why Don't You Write Me"/
   "Smack Dab in the Middle") 15-25   55
RPM (428 "Why Don't You Write Me"/
   "My Darling") 10-20   55
   (Note different flip side.)
RPM (433 "I'm Confessin") 10-20   55
Singles: 7–inch
KENT 5-10   60
RPM (428 "Why Don't You Write Me"/
   "Smack Dab in the Middle") 75-100   55

RPM (428 "Why Don't You Write Me"/
   "My Darling") 25-40   55
   (Note different flip side.)
RPM (433 "I'm Confessin") 35-45   55
RPM (444 "This Empty Heart") 25-35   55
RPM (454 "How Soon") 20-30   56
RPM (458 "Why Did I Fall in Love") .. 25-35 56
RPM (467 "Lets Make Up") 25-35   56
LPs: 10/12–inch 33rpm
BEST 15-25
CROWN (372 "The Jacks") 30-50   62
   (Stereo.)
CROWN (5021 "Jumpin' with
   the Jacks") 50-75   56
CROWN (5372 "The Jacks") 30-50   62
   (Monaural.)
RPM (3006 "Jumpin' with
   the Jacks") 200-250   56
RELIC 10-15
   Members: Willie Davis; Ted Taylor; Aaron Collins; Will Jones;
   Lloyd McCraw; Prentice Moreland.
   Also see CADETS

JACKS, Susan
Singles: 7–inch
EPIC 2-4   80
MERCURY 3-5   75-76
LPs: 10/12–inch 33rpm
EPIC 5-8   80
Also see POPPY FAMILY

JACKS, Terry
Singles: 7–inch
BELL 3-5   74
FLASHBACK 3-5   75
LONDON 3-5   73
PRIVATE STOCK 3-5   75-76
LPs: 10/12–inch 33rpm
BELL 8-10   74
Also see POPPY FAMILY

JACKSON, Bull Moose
(Bull Moose Jackson and His Buffalo Bearcats; Bull
Moose Jackson and the Flashcats; Moose Jackson)
Singles: 78rpm
ENCINO 5-10   57
KING 8-15   45-55
MGM 5-10   47
QUEEN 8-12   45-46
Singles: 7–inch
BOGUS 4-6   85
ENCINO (1004 "Understanding") 25-35   57
KING (4181 "I Love You,
   Yes I Do") 20-30   51
KING (4189 "I Want a Bowlegged
   Woman") 20-30   51
KING (4451 "Trust in Me") 20-30   51
KING (4462 "Unless") 20-30   51
KING (4472 "Cherokee Boogie") 20-30   51
KING (4493 "I'll Be Home for Xmas") 20-30   51
KING (4524 "Nosey Joe") 35-50   52

1. Terry Stafford's hit singles *Suspicion* and *I'll Touch a Star* highlight his 1964 Crusader album — particularly uncommon in stereo. **2.** One of the most valuable rock and roll albums ever is the Johnny Burnette Trio's *Rock'n Roll.* This 1956 release is also one of the first rock albums ever issued. **3.** As with Terry Stafford, Ral Donner gained fame by singing in an Elvis style. No one was more successful at it than Ral. **4.** Easily one of the most influential duos in rock history, Don and Dewey's recordings are a must for any '50s and '60s collection. All of their significant tracks are on this attractively packaged 1970 album. **5.** Billy Storm hit the charts in 1959 with *I've Come of Age.* On his first LP, Billy does a 16-minute version of *Lover Come Back to Me* that consumes one entire side of the disc. **6.** When originally released in 1966, Booker T. and the MGs' Christmas album had this dreadfully unadorned cover. When reissued the following year (1967), a slightly more artistic cover was utilized.

1.

2.

3.

4.

5.

6.

1. Aretha Franklin's first album came out on Columbia, six years before she changed her hairstyle, signed with Atlantic, and won R-E-S-P-E-C-T as the Queen of Soul. **2.** Johnny Maestro, former voice of the Crests, fronted the Brooklyn Bridge on this 1969 release.
3. This 1974 LP spotlighted many of Loretta Lynn's biggest hits. Issued only to radio stations, it is considered a prize by her followers. **4.** *Waylon Jennings at JD's* came out in 1964. Contrary to the title's implication, this is a collection of studio tracks and not live recordings. **5.** If this cover strikes you as different than the one you're used to seeing on *Elvis — For LP Fans Only,* you are very observant. When reissued in 1965, RCA applied roughly the same cover slick to the back as to the front, sans the label logo and some other printing. Pictured here is the back cover. **6.** Historic performances by Otis Redding and the Jimi Hendrix Experience were issued twice — with completely different front covers but identical back covers. This, the more psychedelic of the two, is the rarer edition.

1.

2.

3.

4.

5.

6.

1. Otis Redding's first album, *Pain in My Heart*, came out in 1964, three years before *Dock of the Bay*. By the time the world recognized his talent, he was gone. **2.** Everything by Frank Zappa and the Mothers of Invention is collectible — perhaps as much for their zany covers as for the music. **3.** This 1973 promotional issue, unsuspecting as it may be, is one of the most valuable albums in this guide. Why? Because only a handful were made by RCA for in-house use, and it has a segment of songs by Elvis Presley. Collectors will pay handsomely for this peculiar item. **4.** *Before and After*, a 1965 release, was the eighth Fleetwoods' album and came out a couple of years after the group's last chart hit. **5.** Wilson Pickett teamed with Bobby Womack and composed *I'm a Midnight Mover* and *I Found True Love*, both of which are among the ten soulful tracks on this 1968 issue. **6.** Strangely, most of the artists with hit rock and roll singles in the mid-'50s had no albums, yet many who had no big hits, like Buddy Johnson, were well represented on the long play format.

1.

2.

3.

4.

5.

6.

1. As with many of the Decca albums of the '50s, *The Kalin Twins* has a linen-like, textured front cover. **2.** Though three of Carl Perkins' chart hits involve clothing — *Blue Suede Shoes*, *Pink Pedal Pushers*, and *Pointed Toe Shoes* — his debut album for Columbia has none of them. It does, however, offer some classic '50s rock and roll tunes. **3.** Since it's not likely a U.S. issue of *River Deep – Mountain High* will be discovered, some have asked to see a color picture of the British release of this mysterious 1966 album. **4.** Another controversial '60s album is *The Summit*. Once thought not to exist at all, it has since been learned that copies were indeed made — but only in Great Britain. This remarkable collection teams the talents of Frank Sinatra, Dean Martin, Bing Crosby, and Sammy Davis, Jr. **5.** Robert Crumb's distinctive cartoon art made *Cheap Thrills* one of the most recognizable albums ever. In contrast, the entire back cover is a photo of Big Brother's legendary lead vocalist, Janis Joplin. **6.** *One Dozen Berrys*, rock and roll pioneer Chuck Berry's second album, sports an imaginative and very berry cover.

1. The Jacks had but one album. Unfortunately, it was on Crown, who's frugal approach to LP packaging was seldom eclipsed. **2.** Les and Mary are, of course, Les Paul and Mary Ford — they were so popular in the mid-'50s that no last names were necessary. Les Paul's contributions to guitar artistry cannot be overstated. **3.** When producer Sam Montel first overheard Dale Houston and Grace Broussard singing Don and Dewey's *I'm Leaving It Up to You*, he knew they were on to something. He recorded them and within weeks they had the No. 1 song in the country. **4.** Bo Diddley album covers often had little or nothing to do with the music. Perhaps the unidentified "company" on *Bo Diddley & Company* is merely there to support one of Bo's guitars. **5.** The same selections and fundamental cover art can be found on three different Lloyd Glenn albums; on Aladdin, Score (pictured), and Imperial. **6.** On this surprising release, the versatile Don Gibson is musically surrounded by Spanish guitars, featuring guest pickers of no less renown than Chet Atkins.

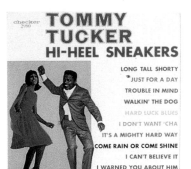

1.

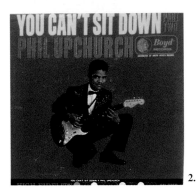

2.

3.

4.

5.

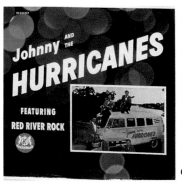

6.

1. Tommy Tucker's *Hi-Heel Sneakers* is a seldom-seen album. Not coincidentally, this 1964 release offers an equally seldom-seen glimpse of real high-heel sneakers. **2.** On *You Can't Sit Down, Part Two*, Phil Upchurch is pictured with a guitar — odd, since the star on *You Can't Sit Down* is clearly an unidentified saxophonist. **3.** Lloyd Price had a half-dozen R&B hits on Specialty before hitting pay dirt with ABC-Paramount in 1957. This 1959 LP showcases fourteen of his early tracks. **4.** Six of the twelve tunes on *Rock 'N Soul* were chart hits for Solomon Burke, whose gospel/soul vocals were always stellar. **5.** Though several name British acts became far more popular the following year, the winner of England's 1963 Melody Maker Newcomer of the Year Award was Billy J. Kramer. *Trains and Boats and Planes* is the third LP for Billy J. Kramer and the Dakotas. **6.** When *Red River Rock* came out in 1959, every Johnny and the Hurricanes member was still a teenager. At that time they were considered the hottest instrumental group in the country, a title they soon relinquished to the Ventures.

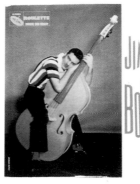

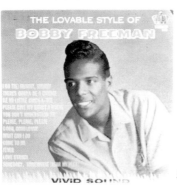

1. Based just on the cover, one would think Dee Clark to be the man pictured. Of course, the couple are merely models. Clark is not even shown on the back cover. **2.** James Ray registered two chart hits and one LP on Caprice, issued in early 1962. As with many albums, the music far outstrips the creativity of the cover. Thankfully, times have changed — posing while holding a cigarette is now considered unsightly. **3.** Benny Goodman's famous 1938 Carnegie Hall jazz concert is captured on a two-disc, Columbia Masterworks issue. **4.** Roulette deemed 20-year-old Jimmy Bowen worthy of an album release in 1957. Years later, Bowen would become one of the most distinguished country music moguls in Nashville. **5.** Bobby Freeman placed four hits in the Top 40, for three different record labels. His King hit *(I Do the) Shimmy, Shimmy* is the lead track on *The Lovable Style of Bobby Freeman.* **6.** *The Everly Brothers*, subtitled "14 Songs for Both Sides of an Evening," relies on an often-used concept — one side for dancing (uptempo), one for dreaming (ballads).

1.

2.

3.

4.

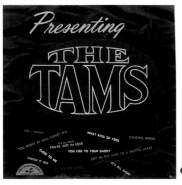

5.

6.

Here are six albums that for a variety of reasons have no front cover picture of the record-ing artists — not an infrequent practice in the '50s and '60s. **1.** *Baby Scratch My Back* by Slim Harpo (1966). Slim is pictured on the back cover. **2.** *Freddie Cannon* (1964). Warner Bros. lists the singer as Freddie instead of Freddy. **3.** *Jimmy Reed Now Appearing* (1960). The above two covers list song titles, whereas this one shows merely a marquee. Reed is not pictured anywhere. **4.** *Hear the Beatles Tell All* (1964). Not that anyone in 1964 didn't know what the Beatles looked like, but it still seems that Vee Jay would have plastered them on the front cover. **5.** *Songs of the West* by the Norman Luboff Choir (1955). Dis-tinctive in that there is no printing whatsoever on the front cover — only a picturesque cat-tle drive scene. We're fairly certain it's not the cows doing the singing here. **6.** *Presenting the Tams* (1964). At first glance, one might be unsure what that red thing is. Closer inspec-tion reveals it to be, of all things, a tam. The Tams — not one is wearing a tam — are shown on the back.

KING (4535 "Let Me Love You
All Night") 20-30   52
KING (4551 "Bearcat Blues") 20-30   52
KING (4580 "Big Ten-Inch Record") .. 40-60   52
KING (4600 through 4800 series) ... 10-20   53-55
SEVEN ARTS 5-10   61
WARWICK 5-10   60

Picture Sleeves
BOGUS 2-4   85

EPs: 7-Inch 33/45rpm
KING (211 "Bull Moose Jackson Sings
His All-Time Hits") 40-60   52
KING (261 "Bull Moose Jackson Sings His
All-Time Hits, Vol. 2") 40-60   54

LPs: 10/12-Inch 33rpm
AUDIO LAB (1524 "Bullmoose
Jackson") 75-100   59
BOGUS 5-8   85
Also see FLASHCATS

JACKSON, Chuck
(Chuck Jackson and the Vikings)
Singles: 7-Inch
ABC 3-5   73-74
ALL PLATINUM 3-5   75-77
AMY 8-12   62
ATCO 5-8   61
BELTONE 5-10   61
DAKAR 3-5   72
EMI AMERICA 2-4   80
FEE BEE 10-15   60
MOTOWN 4-6   68
SCEPTER 3-5   73
SUGAR HILL 2-4   81
VIBRATION 3-5   77
V.I.P. 3-6   69-71
WAND 4-8   61-67

Picture Sleeves
WAND 5-10   63

LPs: 10/12-Inch 33rpm
ABC 8-10   73
ALL PLATINUM 8-10   76
EMI-AMERICA 5-8   80
MOTOWN 10-15   68-69
SCEPTER 8-10   72
SPINORAMA 10-12
U.A. 8-10   75
V.I.P. 8-10   70
WAND (Except 680) 15-25   61-67
WAND (680 "Dedicated to the King") . 20-30 66
Also see BENTON, Brook / Chuck Jackson / Jimmy Soul
Also see BONDS, Gary "U.S."
Also see FREEMAN, Bobby, and Chuck Jackson

JACKSON, Chuck, and Maxine Brown
Singles: 7-Inch
WAND 4-8   65-67
LPs: 10/12-Inch 33rpm
COLLECTABLES 6-8   88
WAND 15-25   65-66
Also see BROWN, Maxine

JACKSON, Chuck / Percy Sledge
Singles: 7-Inch
TRIP 3-5
Also see SLEDGE, Percy

JACKSON, Chuck, and Tammi Terrell
LPs: 10/12-Inch 33rpm
WAND 15-25   67
Also see TERRELL, Tammi

JACKSON, Chuck / Young Jesse
LPs: 10/12-Inch 33rpm
GUEST STAR 8-12   64
Also see JACKSON, Chuck

JACKSON, Clarence
Singles: 7-Inch
R&R 2-4   85

JACKSON, Deon
Singles: 7-Inch
ABC 3-5   75
ATLANTIC 4-8   63-64
CARLA 4-8   66-69
LPs: 10/12-Inch 33rpm
ATCO 15-20   66
COLLECTABLES 6-8   88

JACKSON, Ernest
Singles: 7-Inch
STONE 3-5   73

JACKSON, Freddie
Singles: 12-Inch 33/45rpm
CAPITOL 4-6   85-86
Singles: 7-Inch
CAPITOL 2-4   85-90
Picture Sleeves
CAPITOL 2-4   85-87
LPs: 10/12-Inch 33rpm
CAPITOL 5-8   85-90
Also see MOORE, Melba, and Freddie Jackson

JACKSON, George
Singles: 78rpm
ATLANTIC (1024 "Uh-Huh") 10-15   53
RPM 3-6   55
Singles: 7-Inch
ATLANTIC (1024 "Uh-Huh") 25-35   53
CAMEO 4-8   66
DOT 4-8   65
DOUBLE R 4-8
HI (2100 series) 4-8   67
HI (2200 series) 3-5   72-73
MERCURY 4-8   67-68
RPM 10-20   55

JACKSON, J.J.
(J.J. Jackson and the Jackels; J.J. Jackson and the
Jackals)
Singles: 7-Inch
ABC 3-5   73
CALLA 4-8   66-67
EVEREST 4-8   62

LOMA 4-8   67-68
MAGNA 3-5   75
PRELUDE 5-10   59
STORM 5-10   59
WARNER 4-6   69
LPs: 10/12–inch 33rpm
CALLA 15-25   67
CONGRESS 15-20   68
PERCEPTION 10-15   69-70
WARNER 10-20   69

JACKSON, Janet
Singles: 12–inch 33/45rpm
A&M 4-6   82-90
Singles: 7–inch
A&M 2-4   82-90
Picture Sleeves
A&M 2-4   82-87
LPs: 10/12–inch 33rpm
A&M 5-8   82-90

JACKSON, Jenny
Singles: 7–inch
FARR 3-5   76

JACKSON, Jermaine
Singles: 12–inch 33/45rpm
ARISTA 4-6   84-89
MOTOWN 4-8   80-83
Singles: 7–inch
ARISTA 2-4   84-89
MOTOWN 3-5   72-83
Picture Sleeves
ARISTA 4-6   84-89
MOTOWN 3-5   81
LPs: 10/12–inch 33rpm
ARISTA 5-8   84-89
MOTOWN 5-8   72-82
Also see JACKSONS
Also see ORIGINALS and Jermaine Jackson

JACKSON, Jermaine, and Michael Jackson
Singles: 12–inch 33/45rpm
ARISTA 4-6   84
Also see JACKSON, Michael

JACKSON, Jermaine, and Pia Zadora
Singles: 7–inch
CURB 2-4   85
Also see JACKSON, Jermaine
Also see ZADORA, Pia

JACKSON, Joe
Singles: 12–inch 33/45rpm
A&M 4-6   82-86
Singles: 7–inch
A&M (Except 18000) 2-5   79-86
A&M (18000 "I'm the Man") 10-15   79
(Boxed set of five 45s with sleeves and poster.
Labeled "The 7–inch Album.")
Picture Sleeves
A&M 2-5   80-86

LPs: 10/12–inch 33rpm
A&M (3666 "Look Sharp") 12-25   79
(Double 10–inch LP set. Includes "Look Sharp"
button. Deduct $4 to $6 if button is missing.)
A&M (3900 series) 5-8   87
A&M (4000 and 5000 series) 5-10   79-89
A&M (6000 series) 8-12   86-88
MFSL (080 "Night and Day") 20-30   82
VIRGIN 5-8   91

JACKSON, LaToya
Singles: 12–inch 33/45rpm
LARC 4-6   83
PRIVATE I 4-6   84
Singles: 7–inch
LARC 2-4   83
POLYDOR 2-4   80-81
PRIVATE I 2-4   84-86
LPs: 10/12–inch 33rpm
POLYDOR 5-8   80-81
PRIVATE I 5-8   84
Also see CERRONE and LaToya Jackson

JACKSON, Mahalia
Singles: 78rpm
APOLLO 3-5   50-57
COLUMBIA 3-5   55-57
Singles: 7–inch
APOLLO (200 through 500 series) ... 5-10   50-59
APOLLO (600 through 700 series) 4-6   59-62
COLUMBIA 4-8   55-70
GRAND AWARD 4-8   58-59
KENWOOD 3-6   64-69
Picture Sleeves
APOLLO 4-8   62
EPs: 7–inch 33/45rpm
APOLLO 5-10   54-59
COLUMBIA 5-10   55-60
LPs: 10/12–inch 33rpm
APOLLO (201/2 "Spirituals") 15-20   54
APOLLO (482 "No Matter
How You Pray") 10-15   59
APOLLO (499 "Mahalia Jackson") ... 10-15   62
APOLLO (1001 "Command
Performance") 10-15   61
AUDIOFIDELITY 4-8
(Reissue of Apollo 499.)
CAEDMON 4-8   73
COLORTONE 5-8
(Reissue of Grand Award 265.)
COLUMBIA (CL-600 through CL-2100
series) 10-20   55-64
COLUMBIA (CL-2400 through CL-2600
series) 5-15   66-67
COLUMBIA (CS-8000 through CS-8900
series) 10-20   59-64
(Stereo.)

COLUMBIA (CS-9200 through CS-9900
  series) 5-15   66-69
  (Stereo. Reissues, with a "CSP," "JCS" or "PC"
  prefix, are in the $5 to $10 range.)
COLUMBIA (10000 series) 4-8   73
COLUMBIA (30000 series) 5-10   71-72
GRAND AWARD (265 "Spirtuals") 5-10   66
  (Reissue of Grand Award 326.)
GRAND AWARD (326 "Spirtuals") ... 15-25   55
HARMONY 5-10   68-72
KENWOOD 5-10   64-73
PRIORITY 4-6   82

JACKSON, Mahalia, and Duke Ellington
LPs: 10/12-inch 33rpm
COLUMBIA (CL-1162 "Black, Brown
  and Beige") 15-25   58
  (Monaural.)
COLUMBIA (CS-8015 "Black, Brown
  and Beige") 25-40   58
  (Stereo.)
COLUMBIA (JCS-1162 "Black, Brown
  and Beige") 5-10
  Also see ELLINGTON, Duke
  Also see JACKSON, Mahalia

JACKSON, Marlon
LPs: 10/12-inch 33rpm
CAPITOL 5-8   87

JACKSON, Michael
Singles: 12-inch 33/45rpm
EPIC 4-8   79-87
Singles: 7-inch
EPIC 2-5   79-88
MCA (1786 "Someone in the Dark") .. 25-50   83
  (Promotional issue only.)
MOTOWN 2-5   71-88
Picture Sleeves
EPIC 2-5   82-88
MCA (1786 "Someone in the Dark") .. 25-50   83
  (Promotional issue only.)
MOTOWN 3-5   72
LPs: 10/12-inch 33rpm
EPIC (35000 through 40000) 5-8   79-87
EPIC (45000 series) 10-15   80
  (Half-speed mastered.)
MOTOWN 5-10   72-85
  Also see JACKSON, Jermaine, and Michael Jackson
  Also see JACKSONS
  Also see JONES, Quincy
  Also see McCARTNEY, Paul, and Michael Jackson
  Also see ROCKWELL
  Also see ROSS, Diana, and Michael Jackson
  Also see U.S.A. for AFRICA
  Also see WONDER, Stevie, and Michael Jackson

JACKSON, Michael, and Mick Jagger / Jacksons
Singles: 12-inch 33/45rpm
EPIC (5022 "State of Shock") 8-12   84
  (With special cover.)

EPIC (5022 "State of Shock") 15-20   84
  (Promotional issue with cover.)
Singles: 7-inch
EPIC (4503 "State of Shock") 3-5   84
Picture Sleeves
EPIC (4503 "State of Shock") 3-5   84
  Also see JACKSON, Michael
  Also see JACKSONS
  Also see JAGGER, Mick

JACKSON, Mick
Singles: 7-inch
ATCO 3-5   78

JACKSON, Millie
Singles: 7-inch
GEFFEN 2-4   87
JIVE 2-4   86-88
MGM 3-6   69
SPRING 3-5   71-83
LPs: 10/12-inch 33rpm
JIVE 5-8   86
SPRING 5-8   73-83
POLYDOR 5-8   79
  Also see HAYES, Isaac, and Millie Jackson
  Also see WHODINI

JACKSON, Moose:
  see JACKSON, Bull Moose

JACKSON, Paul, Jr.
Singles: 7-inch
ATLANTIC 2-4   88

JACKSON, Python Lee:
  see PYTHON LEE JACKSON

JACKSON, Randy
Singles: 7-inch
EPIC 3-5   78

JACKSON, Rebbie
Singles: 12-inch 33/45rpm
COLUMBIA 4-6   84-86
Singles: 7-inch
COLUMBIA 2-4   84-86
Picture Sleeves
COLUMBIA 2-4   84
LPs: 10/12-inch 33rpm
COLUMBIA 5-8   84-86

JACKSON, Rebbie, and Robin Zander
Singles: 7-inch
COLUMBIA 2-4   86
  Also see JACKSON, Rebbie

JACKSON, Roddy
Singles: 7-inch
SPECIALTY 8-12   58-59

JACKSON, Shawn
Singles: 7-inch
PLAYBOY 3-5   74

JACKSON, Stonewall
Singles: 7-inch
COLUMBIA (Except 41000 series) 3-8	61-73
COLUMBIA (41000 series) 4-8	58-61
FIRST GENERATION 2-4	81
GRT 3-5	74
LITTLE DARLIN' 3-5	78-79
MGM 3-5	73
PHONORAMA 2-4	83

Picture Sleeves
COLUMBIA (41393 "Waterloo") 8-10   59

EPs: 7-inch 33/45rpm
COLUMBIA 5-10   59

LPs: 10/12-inch 33rpm
AUDIOGRAPH ALIVE 5-8	82
COLUMBIA (1391 "The Dynamic Stonewall Jackson") .... 20-30 (Monaural.)	59
COLUMBIA (1700 through 2700 series) 8-15 (Monaural.)	62-67
COLUMBIA (8186 "The Dynamic Stonewall Jackson") .... 25-40 (Stereo.)	59
COLUMBIA (8500 through 9900 series) 8-15 (Stereo.)	62-70
COLUMBIA (10000 series) 5-8	73
COLUMBIA (30000 series) 5-10	70-72
FIRST GENERATION 5-8	78
GRT 5-10	75-76
HARMONY 8-12	66-74
LITTLE DARLIN' 5-8	79
MYRRH 5-8	76
PHONORAMA 5-8	
RURAL RHYTHM 5-10	
SUNBIRD 5-8	80

JACKSON, Walter
Singles: 7-inch
BRUNSWICK 3-5	73
CHI-SOUND 3-5	76-78
COLUMBIA (02000 series) 2-4	81
COLUMBIA (42000 series) 4-8	62-63
COTILLION 3-6	69
EPIC 4-8	66-68
KELLI-ARTS 2-4	83
OKEH 4-8	64-67
20TH FOX 3-5	79

Picture Sleeves
OKEH 4-8   66-67

LPs: 10/12-inch 33rpm
CHI-SOUND 8-10	76-78
COLUMBIA 5-8	81
EPIC 8-10	77
OKEH 10-20	65-69
20TH FOX 5-8	79

JACKSON, Wanda
(Wanda Jackson and the Party Timers)
Singles: 78rpm
CAPITOL 15-25   56-57

Singles: 7-inch
DECCA 10-20	54-55
ABC 3-5	75
CAPITOL (2000 through 3000 series) .. 3-8 (Orange or orange/yellow labels.)	67-72
CAPITOL (3400 through 4500 series) 10-20 (Purple labels.)	56-61
CAPITOL (4600 through 5900 series) .. 4-8	61-67
DECCA 20-40	54-55
JIN 3-6	
MYRRH 2-4	73-75

Picture Sleeves
CAPITOL 5-10   62-66

EPs: 7-inch 33/45rpm
CAPITOL (1041 "Wanda Jackson") .. 25-50   58

LPs: 10/12-inch 33rpm
CAPITOL (100 through 600 series) ... 8-15	69-71
CAPITOL (1041 "Wanda Jackson") . 50-100	58
CAPITOL (1384 "Rockin' with Wanda") 50-100	60
CAPITOL (1511 "There's a Party Goin' On") .... 75-100 (With "T" prefix. Monaural.)	61
CAPITOL (1511 "There's a Party Goin' On") .... 100-125 (With "ST" prefix. Stereo.)	61
CAPITOL (1596 "Right Or Wrong") .. 25-35 (With "T" prefix. Monaural.)	61
CAPITOL (1596 "Right Or Wrong") .. 35-45 (With "ST" prefix. Stereo.)	61
CAPITOL (1776 "Wonderful Wanda") 15-25 (With "T" prefix. Monaural.)	62
CAPITOL (1776 "Wonderful Wanda") 20-30 (With "ST" prefix. Stereo.)	62
CAPITOL (1911 "Love Me Forever") . 15-25 (With "T" prefix. Monaural.)	63
CAPITOL (1911 "Love Me Forever") . 20-30 (With "ST" prefix. Stereo.)	63
CAPITOL (2030 "Two Sides of Wanda Jackson") .... 35-40 (With "T" prefix. Monaural.)	64
CAPITOL (2030 "Two Sides of Wanda Jackson") .... 40-45 (With "ST" prefix. Stereo.)	64
CAPITOL (2300 through 2900 series) 10-20	65-68
CAPITOL (11000 series) 5-8	72-73
DECCA (4224 "Lovin' Country Style") 40-50	62
GUSTO 5-8	80
MYRRH 5-8	73-76
PICKWICK/HILLTOP 8-12	65-68
VARRICK/ROUNDER 5-8	87
VOCALION 8-12	69
WORD 4-8	77

JACKSON, Willis
(Willis "Gator Tail" Jackson and His Orchestra; Vocal By the 4'Gaters)
Singles: 78rpm
APOLLO 5-10   50

ATLANTIC 15-25	51-53	

JACOBS, Hank
Singles: 7-inch
IMPERIAL	5-10	62
SUE	4-8	63-64

LPs: 10/12-inch 33rpm
SUE (1023 "So Far Away")	20-30	64

JACQUET, Illinois
(Illinois Jacquet and His All-Stars; Jacque Rabbit; Illinois Jacquet with Russell Jacquet)
Singles: 78rpm
ARA	5-10	46
ALADDIN	5-10	45-54
APOLLO	5-10	46-47
MERCURY	4-8	52
PHILO	5-10	45
RCA	5-10	48-51
SAVOY	5-10	46

Singles: 7-inch
ALADDIN	10-20	53-54
ARGO	4-8	63-65
MERCURY	10-15	52
PRESTIGE	3-6	68-69
RCA (0011 "Black Velvet") (Colored vinyl.)	20-30	49
RCA (0021 "Big Foot") (Colored vinyl.)	20-30	49
RCA (0047 "Blue Satin") (Colored vinyl.)	20-30	49
RCA (0087 "My Old Gal") (Colored vinyl.)	20-30	49
RCA (0097 "Slow Down, Baby") (Colored vinyl.)	15-20	49
VERVE	4-8	62

EPs: 7-inch 33/45rpm
APOLLO (602 "Jam Session")	50-75	50
CLEF (126 "Illinois Jacquet Collates")	25-40	51
CLEF (143 "Illinois Jacquet Collates")	25-40	51
CLEF (166 "Illinois Jacquet Collates, No. 2")	20-40	52
CLEF (167 "Illinois Jacquet Collates, No. 2")	20-40	52
CLEF (207 "Jazz Moods")	20-40	54
CLEF (374 "Illinois Jacquet and His Orchestra")	20-40	55
RCA (3236 "Black Velvet")	40-60	53
SAVOY	20-30	50-53

LPs: 10/12-inch 33rpm
ACCORD	5-8	82
ALADDIN (800 series)	50-60	56
APOLLO (104 "Jam Session")	150-250	50
ARGO	15-25	63-65
CLEF (112 "Illinois Jacquet Collates")	100-125	51
(10-inch LP. Has Mercury label with Clef logo and number.)		

CLEF (129 "Illinois Jacquet Collates, No. 2")	100-125	52
(10-inch LP. Has Mercury label with Clef logo and number.)		
CLEF (622 "Jazz Moods")	50-100	54
CLEF (676 "Illinois Jacquet and His Orchestra")	50-75	55
CLEF (680 "The Kid and the Brute")	50-75	55
CLEF (700 "Jazz Moods")	40-60	56
CLEF (702 "Groovin")	40-60	56
CLEF (750 "Swing's the Thing")	40-60	56
EPIC	15-25	63
GRAND AWARD (315 "Uptown Jazz")	20-35	56
IMPERIAL	15-25	62
JRC	5-8	79
PRESTIGE	8-12	69-75
RCA (3236 "Black Velvet") (10-inch LP.)	50-75	53
ROULETTE	20-30	60
SAVOY (15024 "Tenor Sax") (10-inch LP.)	50-100	53
TRIP	5-8	79
VERVE (2500 series)	5-10	82-87
VERVE (8000 series)	25-50	57-58
(Reads "Verve Records, Inc." at bottom of label.)		
VERVE (8000 series)	10-20	61-65
(Reads "MGM Records - a Division of Metro-Goldwyn-Mayer, Inc." at bottom of label.)		

Members: Illinois Jacquet; Johnny Otis; Russell Jacquet; Arthur Dennis; Henry Coker; Sir Charles; Ulysses Livingston; William Hadnott.
Also see COLE, Cozy, and Illinois Jacquet
Also see DOGGETT, Bill
Also see HEART BEATS QUINTET
Also see OTIS, Johnny
Also see X-RAYS

JACQUET, Illinois, and Count Basie
LPs: 10/12-inch 33rpm
CLEF (701 "Port of Rico")	40-60	56

Also see BASIE, Count

JACQUET, Illinois, and Miles Davis
EPs: 7-inch 33/45rpm
ALADDIN (504 "Illinois Jacquet and His Tenor Sax")	50-65	54
ALADDIN (511 "Illinois Jacquet and His Tenor Sax")	50-65	54

LPs: 10/12-inch 33rpm
ALADDIN (708 "Illinois Jacquet and His Tenor Sax") (10-inch LP.)	100-150	54

Also see DAVIS, Miles

JACQUET, Illinois / Lester Young
EPs: 7-inch 33/45rpm
ALADDIN (501 "Battle of the Saxes")	50-65	54

LPs: 10/12-inch 33rpm
ALADDIN (701 "Battle of the Saxes")	100-150	54
(10-inch LP. Black vinyl.)		

ALADDIN (701 "Battle of
the Saxes") 200-250   54
(10–inch LP. Colored vinyl.)
ALADDIN (803 "Illinois Jacquet and
His Tenor Sax") 60-80   56
(Has the eight tracks from *Battle of the Saxes,* plus
four others.)

JACQUET, Russell
(Russell Jacquet and His All Stars; Russell Jacquet
and His Yellow Jackets; Russell Jacquet and His
Bopper Band)
Singles: 78rpm
GLOBE 5-10   45
JEWEL 4-8   47
KING 4-8   49-50
MODERN MUSIC 4-8   46
SENSATION 4-8   48
EPs: 7–inch 33/45rpm
KING (308 "Russell Jacquet and
His All Stars") 50-75   53
KING (309 "Russell Jacquet and
His All Stars") 50-75   53
LPs: 10/12–inch 33rpm
KING (8 "Russell Jacquet and
His All Stars") 75-125   53
(10–inch LP.)
Also see HEART BEATS QUINTET
Also see JACQUET, Illinois

JADE WARRIOR
Singles: 7–inch
VERTIGO 2-4   71-72
LPs: 10/12–inch 33rpm
ANTILLES 5-8   78
ISLAND 8-10   74-76
VERTIGO 10-12   71-72

JAGGER, Chris
LPs: 10/12–inch 33rpm
ASYLUM 8-10   73-74

JAGGER, Mick
Singles: 12–inch 33/45rpm
COLUMBIA (2060 "Lucky in Love") 4-8   85
(With special cover.)
COLUMBIA (2060 "Lucky in Love") .. 15-20   85
(Promotional issue with special cover.)
COLUMBIA (5181 "Just Another Night") 4-8   85
(With special cover.)
COLUMBIA (5181 "Just Another
Night") 15-20   85
(Promotional issue with special cover.)
COLUMBIA (6926 "Let's Work") 5-10   87
COLUMBIA (7492 "Throwaway") 5-10   87
EPIC (5931 "Ruthless People") 10-15   86
(With special cover.)
Singles: 7–inch
COLUMBIA (04743 "Just Another
Night") 3-5   85
COLUMBIA (04893 "Lucky in Love") ... 3-5   85
COLUMBIA (07306 "Let's Work") 3-5   87

COLUMBIA (07653 "Throwaway") 3-5   87
EPIC (06211 "Ruthless People") 3-5   86
Picture Sleeves
COLUMBIA (04743 "Just Another
Night") 3-5   85
COLUMBIA (04893 "Lucky in Love") ... 3-5   85
COLUMBIA (07306 "Let's Work") 3-5   87
COLUMBIA (07653 "Throwaway") 3-5   87
EPIC (06211 "Ruthless People") 3-5   86
Promotional Singles
COLUMBIA (04743 "Just Another
Night") 8-10   85
COLUMBIA (04893 "Lucky in Love") .. 8-10   85
COLUMBIA (07306 "Let's Work") 8-10   87
COLUMBIA (07653 "Throwaway") ... 8-10   87
EPIC (06211 "Ruthless People") 5-10   86
LPs: 10/12–inch 33rpm
COLUMBIA (39940 "She's the Boss") . 8-10   85
COLUMBIA (40919 "Primitive Cool") .. 8-10   87
EPIC 8-12   86
LONDON WAVELENGTH (006
"The Mick Jagger Special") 75-100   81
(Promotional issue only.)
ROLLING STONES (164 "Interview
with Mick Jagger") 75-100   71
(Promotional issue only.)
U.A. (300 "Ned Kelly") 10-15   74
(Soundtrack.)
U.A. (5213 "Ned Kelly") 15-20   70
(Soundtrack.)
Also see BOWIE, David, and Mick Jagger
Also see FRAMPTON, Peter
Also see JACKSON, Michael, and Mick Jagger
Also see ROLLING STONES
Also see SIMON, Carly
Also see TOSH, Peter, and Mick Jagger
Also see WEST, Leslie
Also see WOLF, Peter, and Mick Jagger

JAGGERZ
Singles: 7–inch
GAMBLE 4-8   68
KAMA SUTRA 3-6   70
WOODEN NICKEL 3-5   75
LPs: 10/12–inch 33rpm
KAMA SUTRA 10-15   70
WOODEN NICKEL 8-10   75
Members: Dominic Ierace (a.k.a. Donnie Iris); Jim Puglinro; Jim
Ross; Bill Maybray; Ben Faiella.
Also see IRIS, Donnie
Also see Q

JAGS
Singles: 7–inch
ISLAND 3-5   79-80
Picture Sleeves
ISLAND 3-5   79-80
LPs: 10/12–inch 33rpm
ISLAND 5-8   80-81

JAISUN
Singles: 7–inch
JETT SETT 3-5   78

JAK
Singles: 7–Inch
EPIC 2-4   84-86
LPs: 10/12–inch 33rpm
EPIC 5-8   85

JAKKI
Singles: 7–Inch
PYRAMID 3-5   76
WEST END 3-5

JAM
Singles: 7–Inch
POLYDOR 2-5   78-83
Picture Sleeves
POLYDOR 3-5   80-83
LPs: 10/12–Inch 33rpm
POLYDOR 5-8   77-83
Also see STYLE COUNCIL

JAMAICA BOYS
Singles: 7–Inch
WARNER 2-4   87-88

JAMAL, Ahmad
(Ahmad Jamal Trio; Ahmad Jamal Quintet)
Singles: 7–Inch
ARGO 4-8   57-65
CADET 3-6   66-68
CHESS 3-5   73
PARROTT 5-10   55
20TH FOX 3-5   73-80
EPs: 7–Inch 33/45rpm
ARGO 8-15   59-61
LPs: 10/12–Inch 33rpm
ABC 8-12   68
ARGO (610 through 662) 20-40   56-60
ARGO (667 through 758) 15-25   61-65
CADET 10-25   65-73
CATALYST 5-10   76
EPIC (600 series) 15-30   63-65
EPIC (3212 "Ahmad Jamal Trio") 30-50   56
EPIC (3600 series) 20-30   59
IMPULSE 10-20   69-73
MOTOWN 5-10   80
PERSONAL CHOICE 5-8   82
SHUBRA 5-8   83
20TH FOX 5-10   73-80
WHO'S WHO in JAZZ 5-10   81

JAMES, Bob
(Bob James Trio)
Singles: 7–Inch
CTI 3-5   74-77
COLUMBIA 2-5   79-83
TAPPAN ZEE/COLUMBIA 2-5   77-85
Picture Sleeves
COLUMBIA 3-5   79-80
LPs: 10/12–Inch 33rpm
CTI 5-10   74-77
COLUMBIA 5-8   83
ESP 10-15   65

MERCURY 15-25   63
TAPPAN ZEE/COLUMBIA 5-10   77-85

JAMES, Bob, and Earl Klugh
Singles: 7–Inch
CAPITOL 2-4   82
TAPPAN ZEE/COLUMBIA 3-5   79
LPs: 10/12–Inch 33rpm
CAPITOL 5-8   82
MFSL (124 "2 of a Kind") 20-30   84
TAPPAN ZEE/COLUMBIA 5-10   79
Also see KLUGH, Earl

JAMES, Bob, and David Sanborn
LPs: 10/12–Inch 33rpm
WARNER 5-8   86-88
Also see JAMES, Bob
Also see SANBORN, David

JAMES, Elmore
(Elmore James and His Broomdusters; Elmo James)
Singles: 78rpm
ACE 10-20   53
CHECKER 20-30   53
CHIEF 5-10   57
FLAIR 10-20   54-56
METEOR (5000 "I Believe") 20-30   53
METEOR (5003 "Sinful Woman") 20-30   53
MODERN (983 "Wild About You") ... 10-20   56
TRUMPET (146 ("I Believe My Time
  Ain't Long") 15-25   52
VEE JAY 5-8   57
Singles: 7–Inch
ACE (508 "My Time Ain't Long") .. 100-200   53
CHECKER (777 "Country Boogie") 200-400   53
CHESS 4-6   60
CHIEF (7001 "The Twelve
  Year Old Boy") 25-50   57
CHIEF (7004 "It Hurts Me Too") 25-50   57
CHIEF (7006 "Cry for Me Baby") 25-50   57
ENJOY 10-15   65
FIRE 10-20   60-62
FLAIR (1011 "Early in the
  Morning") 150-200   54
FLAIR (1014 "Can't Stop Lovin") .. 150-200   54
FLAIR (1022 "Strange Kinda
  Feeling") 100-150   55
FLAIR (1031 "Make My Dreams
  Come True") 100-200   55
FLAIR (1039 "Sho'nuff, I Do") 100-200   55
FLAIR (1048 "Dark and Dreary") .. 100-200   56
FLAIR (1057 "Standing at
  the Crossroads") 100-200   55
FLAIR (1062 "Late Hours
  at Midnight") 75-100   56
FLAIR (1069 "Happy Home") 75-100   56
FLAIR (1074 "Dust My Blues") 75-100   56
FLAIR (1079 "Blues Before Sunrise") 75-100   56
FLASHBACK 3-6   65
JEWEL (764 "Dust My Broom") 4-8   66

JEWEL (783 "Catfish Blues") 4-8   66
(Though credited to Elmo James, the flip sides of
Jewel 764 and 783 are actually by Big Boy
Crudup.)
KENT 4-8   60-67
METEOR (5000 "I Believe") 100-200   53
METEOR (5003 "Sinful Woman") .. 100-200   53
MODERN (983 "Wild About You") . 100-200   56
M-PAC 4-8
S&M 4-8
SOUND 4-8
PHERE SOUND 4-8   65
VEE JAY 8-12   57

LPs: 10/12-inch 33rpm

BELL 10-12   68-69
BLUE HORIZON 10-12
CHESS 10-12   69
COLLECTABLES 6-8   88
CROWN (5168 "Blues After Hours") . 40-50   61
CUSTOM 8-12
INTERMEDIA 5-8   84
KENT (5022 "Original Folk Blues") .. 20-30   64
KENT (9000 series) 10-20   67-69
KENT TREASURE SERIES 5-8   86
RELIC 5-10   88
SPHERE SOUND (7002 "The Sky
  Is Crying") 25-35
SPHERE SOUND (7008 "I Need
  You") 25-35
TRIP 8-10   71-78
UNITED 10-12
UPFRONT 8-10
  Also see CRUDUP, Big Boy

JAMES, Elmore, and John Brim
LPs: 10/12-inch 33rpm

CHESS 10-15   69
  Also see JAMES, Elmore

JAMES, Etta
(Etta "Miss Peaches" James)
Singles: 78rpm

MODERN 8-15   55-56

Singles: 7-inch

ABC 3-5   74
ARGO 4-8   60-64
CADET 3-5   67-72
CHESS 3-5   73-76
KENT 8-15   58-60
MODERN (900 series) 10-20   55-56
MODERN (1000 series) 5-10   57-58
T-ELECTRIC 3-5   80
WARNER 3-5   78

LPs: 10/12-inch 33rpm

ARGO 20-30   61-65
CADET 10-15   67-71
CHESS 10-12   71-76
CROWN 20-30   61-63
INTERMEDIA 5-8   84

KENT (3002 "Miss Etta James") 15-25   61
  (Black vinyl.)
KENT (3002 "Miss Etta James") 30-40   61
  (Colored vinyl.)
T-ELECTRIC 5-8   80
UNITED 10-12
WARNER 5-8   78
WESTBOUND 8-10
  Also see ETTA & HARVEY

JAMES, Etta, and Sugar Pie DeSanto
Singles: 7-inch

CADET 4-8   65-66
  Also see DE SANTO, Sugar Pie
  Also see JAMES, Etta

JAMES, Harry, and His Orchestra
Singles: 78rpm

BRUNSWICK 3-6   38
COLUMBIA 3-6   40-57
VARIETY 4-8   40

Singles: 7-inch

COLUMBIA (33000 series) 3-5   76
COLUMBIA (38000 through
  40000 series) 5-8   50-56
DOT 3-6   65-66
GOLD-MOR 3-5   73
MGM 4-6   59-63

EPs: 7-inch 33/45rpm

COLUMBIA 5-15   50-56

LPs: 10/12-inch 33rpm

BAINBRIDGE 5-8   83
BRIGHT ORANGE 5-8   73
CAPITOL (600 through 1500 series) . 15-30   55-61
  (With "T" or "ST" prefix.)
CAPITOL (1500 series) 10-20   62
  (With "DT" prefix.)
CAPITOL (1500 series) 5-8   77
  (With "M" prefix.)
COLUMBIA 10-30   50-67
COLUMBIA SPECIAL PRODUCTS 5-8   79
DOT 8-15   66-67
HARMONY 10-20   59-72
LONDON 5-10   68
MGM 10-20   59-65
METRO 8-15   65-67
SHEFFIELD LAB 5-8   77-79
  Also see KALLEN, Kitty
  Also see SINATRA, Frank

JAMES, Harry, and Dick Haymes
LPs: 10/12-inch 33rpm

CIRCLE 5-8   81
  Also see HAYMES, Dick
  Also see JAMES, Harry, and His Orchestra

JAMES, Jesse
Singles: 7-inch

T.T.E.D. 2-4   87
20TH FOX 3-8   67-75
UNI 4-6   69
ZEA (ZAY) 3-5   70-71

LPs: 10/12–inch 33rpm
20TH FOX 8-10   67

JAMES, Jimmy, and the Vagabonds
Singles: 7–inch
ATCO 4-8   67-68
PYE 3-5   75-76
LPs: 10/12–inch 33rpm
ATCO 10-15   67
PYE . . . . : 5-8   75

JAMES, Joni
Singles: 78rpm
MGM (222 "Let There Be Love") . . 100-200   53
(Four disc boxed set.)
MGM (234 "Award Winning Album") 100-200   54
(Four disc boxed set.)
MGM (272 "Little Girl Blue") 100-200   54
(Four disc boxed set.)
MGM (11000 and 12000 series) 10-20   52-58
SHARP (46 "Let There Be Love") . . . 25-50   52
SHARP (50 "You Belong to Me") 25-50   52
Singles: 7–inch
MGM (16 through 19) 20-40   59-60
(Stereo compact 33 singles.)
MGM (11223 through 12660) 15-25   52-58
MGM (12706 "There Goes My Heart") 10-15   58
(Monaural.)
MGM (12706 "There Goes My Heart") 20-30   58
(Stereo. Unusual numbering—most MGM stereo
45s are in the 50000 series. Billed as the industry's
"First Single Stereo Disc.".)
MGM (12746 through 13304) 10-20   59-64
MGM (13288 "Sentimental Me") 50-75   64
(Promotional issue only.)
MGM (50111 "There Must Be a Way") 15-25   59
(Stereo.)
MGM/GOLDEN CIRCLE (101
through 104) 5-10   61
SHARP (46 "Let There Be Love") . 150-250   52
SHARP (50 "You Belong to Me") . . 100-200   52
Picture Sleeves
MGM (12565 "Never Till Now") 10-20   57

MGM (12706 "There Goes My Heart") 25-50   58
MGM (12779 "I Still Get a Thrill") 10-20   59
MGM (12895 "We Know") 10-20   60
MGM (12933 "My Last Date") 10-20   60
MGM (12948 "Be My Love") 10-20   61
MGM (13037 "You Were Wrong") . . . 10-20   62
EPs: 7–inch 33/45rpm
MGM (222 "Let There Be Love") 50-75   53
MGM (234 "Award Winning Album") . 50-75   54
MGM (272 "Little Girl Blue") 50-75   54
MGM (326 "When I Fall in Love") . . . 20-40   55
(EPs 222 through 326 are two-disc sets.)
MGM (1160 "When I Fall in Love") . . . 10-20   55
MGM (1172 "Have Yourself
a Merry Little Christmas") 25-50   55
MGM (1211 through 1617) 10-20   56-58
MGM (1652/3/4 "Songs of
Hank Williams") 10-15   59
(Monaural. Price is for any of three volumes.)
MGM (1652/3/4 "Songs of
Hank Williams") 30-40   59
(Stereo. Price is for any of three volumes.)
MGM (1656/7/8 "100 Strings
and Joni") 10-15   59
(Monaural. Price is for any of three volumes.)
MGM (1656/7/8 "100 Strings
and Joni") 30-40   59
(Stereo. Price is for any of three volumes.)
MGM (1672/3/4 "Joni Swings Sweet") 10-15   59
(Monaural. Price is for any of three volumes.)
MGM (1672/3/4 "Joni Swings Sweet") 30-40   59
(Stereo. Price is for any of three volumes.)
MGM (3328 "In the Still of the Night") 20-35   56
MGM (3533 "Songs by Jerome Kern
and Harry Warren") 20-35   57
LPs: 10/12–inch 33rpm
MGM (222 "Let There Be Love") . . . 75-125   53
(10–inch LP.)
MGM (234 "Award Winning Album") 75-125   54
(10–inch LP.)
MGM (272 "Little Girl Blue") 75-125   54
(10–inch LP.)
MGM (3240 "When I Fall in Love") . . 30-50   55
MGM (3328 "In the
Still of the Night") 30-50   56
MGM (3346 "Award Winning
Album, Vol. 1") 30-50   56
MGM (3347 "Little Girl Blue") 30-50   56
MGM (3348 "Let There Be Love") . . . 30-50   56
MGM (3449 "Songs by Victor
Young and Frank Losser") 30-50   56
MGM (3468 "Merry Christmas") 30-50   56
MGM (3528 "Give Us This Day") 25-45   57
MGM (3533 "Songs by Jerome Kern
and Harry Warren") 25-45   57
MGM (3602 "Among My Souvenirs") . 25-45   58
MGM (3623 "Ti Voglio Bene") 25-45   58
MGM (3706 "Award Winning
Album, Vol. 1") 25-45   58

MGM (E-3718 "Je T'Aime") 25-45   58
(Monaural.)
MGM (SE-3718 "Je T'Aime") 35-55   58
(Stereo.)
MGM (E-3729 "Songs by
Hank Williams") 25-45   59
(Monaural.)
MGM (SE-3729 "Songs by
Hank Williams") 35-55   59
(Stereo.)
MGM (E-3749 through E-4286) 20-30   59-65
(Monaural.)
MGM (SE-3749 through SE-4286) ... 20-35   59-65

JAMES, Rick
(Rick James and the Stone City Band)
Singles: 12–inch 33/45rpm
GORDY 4-6   79-85
MOTOWN 4-6   78-85

Singles: 7–inch
GORDY 2-5   78-85
MOTOWN 2-4   86
REPRISE 2-4   88

Picture Sleeves
GORDY 3-5   79-85

LPs: 10/12–inch 33rpm
GORDY 5-8   78-86
REPRISE 5-8   88
  Also see STONE CITY BAND
  Also see TEMPTATIONS and Rick James

JAMES, Rick, and Friend
(Rick James and Smokey Robinson)
Singles: 7–inch
GORDY 3-5   83

JAMES, Rick, and Smokey Robinson
Singles: 7–inch
GORDY 3-5   83
  Also see JAMES, Rick
  Also see JAMES, Rick, and Friend
  Also see ROBINSON, Smokey

JAMES, Rick, and Roxanne Shante
Singles: 7–inch
REPRISE 2-4   88
  Also see SHANTE, Roxanne

JAMES, Sonny
(Sonny James and the Southern Gentlemen; Sonny
James, the Southern Gentlemen)
Singles: 78rpm
CAPITOL 4-8   52-57
Singles: 7–inch
CAPITOL (2000 through 3900) 3-5   67-74
(Orange labels.)
CAPITOL (2200 through 3800) 5-10   52-57
(Purple labels.)
CAPITOL (3900 through 5900) 4-8   58-67
(Purple or orange/yellow swirl labels.)
CAPITOL (6000 series) 2-4
COLUMBIA 3-5   72-78
DIMENSION 2-4   82

DOT 4-6   62
GROOVE 4-8   61
MONUMENT 3-5   79
NRC 5-8   60
RCA 4-8   61-62
Picture Sleeves
CAPITOL (Except 4268) 4-8   65-71
CAPITOL (4268 "Who's Next in Line) . 6-10   59
COLUMBIA 3-5   72-75
DIMENSION 3-5   76
NRC (050 "Jenny Lou") 10-15   60
EPs: 7–inch 33/45rpm
CAPITOL 8-15   57-58
CAPITOL CREATIVE PRODUCTS ... 5-10   68
LPs: 10/12–inch 33rpm
ABC 5-8   77
BROOKVILLE 8-12   75
CAMDEN 8-12
CAPITOL (100 through 800) 8-12   68-71
CAPITOL (779 "The Southern
Gentleman") 25-35   57
CAPITOL (867 "Sonny") 20-30   57
CAPITOL (988 "Honey") 20-30   58
CAPITOL (1100 series) 15-25   59
CAPITOL (2000 through 2800) 8-15   64-68
CAPITOL (11000 series) 5-8   72-73
COLUMBIA 5-10   72-78
CROWN 8-12
DIMENSION 5-8   82
DOT 15-20   62
GUEST STAR 10-15   64
HAMILTON 8-12   65
MONUMENT 5-8   79
PICKWICK 5-8   76
PICKWICK/HILLTOP 8-12   69
TVP 8-12   75
  Also see HAGGARD, Merle / Sonny James
  Also see HORTON, Johnny / Sonny James
  Also see VINCENT, Gene / Frank Sinatra / Sonny James / Ron
  Goodwin

JAMES, Sonny / Dave Dudley / Sunny Williams
LPs: 10/12–inch 33rpm
DIPLOMAT 5-10
  Also see DUDLEY, Dave

JAMES, Sonny / David Houston
LPs: 10/12–inch 33rpm
PICKWICK/HILLTOP 8-12   67
  Also see HOUSTON, David

JAMES, Sonny / Seekers
Singles: 7–inch
CAPITOL (5375 "I'll Keep Holding On"/
"I'll Never Find Another You") 4-8   65
(These two tracks were unintentionally pressed
back-to-back.)
  Also see JAMES, Sonny
  Also see SEEKERS

JAMES, Tommy
(Tommy James and the Shondells)
Singles: 7-inch
ABC	3-5	73
FANTASY	2-4	75-80
MCA	3-5	74
MILLENNIUM	3-5	79-81
ROULETTE	4-8	66-73
TWENTY-ONE	2-4	83

Picture Sleeves
FANTASY	3-5	76
MILLENNIUM	3-5	71
ROULETTE	5-10	66-67
TWENTY-ONE	2-4	83

LPs: 10/12-inch 33rpm
FANTASY	8-10	76-80
MILLENNIUM	5-8	80
ROULETTE	10-20	66-72
SCEPTER	8-10	73
SCEPTER/CITATION	5-8	82
TWENTY-ONE	5-8	83

Members: Tommy James; Mike Vale; Ed Gray; Ron Rosman; Pete Lucia.
Also see HOG HEAVEN
Also see SHONDELLS

JAMES BOYS
Singles: 7-inch
PHIL L.A. of SOUL	4-6	68

Also see MFSB

JAMES GANG
Singles: 7-inch
ABC	3-5	70-72
ATCO	3-5	74-75
BLUESWAY	4-6	69

LPs: 10/12-inch 33rpm
ABC	10-12	70-73
ATCO	8-10	74-76
BLUESWAY	10-15	69
COMMAND	8-10	74
MCA	5-8	

Members: Joe Walsh; Tommy Bolin; Dominic Troiano.
Also see BOLIN, Tommy
Also see WALSH, Joe

JAMESON, Cody
Singles: 7-inch
ATCO	3-5	77

JAMESON, Nick
Singles: 7-inch
MOTOWN	2-4	86

LPs: 10/12-inch 33rpm
MOTOWN	5-8	86

JAMESTOWN MASSACRE
Singles: 7-inch
WARNER	3-5	72

JAMIE & JANE
Singles: 7-inch
DECCA (30862 "Strolling")	15-20	59
DECCA (30934 "Faithful Our Love")	15-20	59

Members: Gene Pitney; Ginny Arnell.
Also see ARNELL, Ginny
Also see PITNEY, Gene

JAMIES
Singles: 7-inch
EPIC	5-10	58-63
EPIC (11000 series)	2-4	74
U.A.	4-6	59

Picture Sleeves
EPIC (9281 "Summertime Summertime")	15-20	58-63

JAMME
Singles: 7-inch
DUNHILL	3-5	70

LPs: 10/12-inch 33rpm
DUNHILL	10-12	70

Members: Keith Adey; Don Adey.

JAMMERS
Singles: 7-inch
SALSOUL	2-4	82-83

JAMUL
Singles: 7-inch
LIZARD	3-5	70

LPs: 10/12-inch 33rpm
LIZARD	10-12	70

JAN & ARNIE
(With Don Ralke's Orchestra)
Singles: 78rpm
ARWIN (108 "Jennie Lee")	150-250	58

Singles: 7-inch
ARWIN (108 "Jennie Lee")	15-25	58
ARWIN (111 "Gas Money")	15-25	58
ARWIN (113 "I Love Linda")	15-25	58
DOT (16116 "Gas Money")	10-20	58
DORE (522 "Baby Talk")	150-200	59

(By Jan & Dean though shown on first pressings as by Jan & Arnie.)

EPs: 7-inch 33/45rpm
DOT (1097 "Jan & Arnie")	350-450	60

Members: Jan Berry; Arnie Ginsburg.
Also see BERRY, Jan
Also see JAN & DEAN
Also see RALKE, Don

JAN & DEAN
Singles: 7-inch
CAPITOL (89 "Jennie Lee")		

(By Jan & Dean instead of Jan & Arnie.)
CHALLENGE (9120 "Wanted: One Girl")	10-20	61
CHALLENGE (9111 "Heart and Soul"/ "Those Words")	25-35	61
CHALLENGE (9111 "Heart and Soul"/ "Midsummer Night's Dream")	10-20	61

(Note different flip side.)
CHALLENGE (59111 "Heart and Soul")	10-20	61
COLUMBIA (44036 "Yellow Balloon")	15-25	67
DORE	15-25	59-61

J&D (1 "Oh What a Beautiful
Morning") 150-200   87
(Private, limited, promotional, red vinyl pressing by
Dean Torrence which he used as Christmas gifts.
With Chris Farmer and Phil Bardowell.)
J&D (401 "California Lullabye") 20-30   66
J&D (402 "Like a Summer Rain") 20-30   66
JAN & DEAN (10 "Hawaii") 45-60   66
JAN & DEAN (11 "Fan Tan") 50-75   66
LIBERTY (55397 "A Sunday Kind
of Love") 10-20   61
LIBERTY (55454 "Tennessee") 10-20   62
LIBERTY (55496 "Who Put the Bomp")20-30   62
LIBERTY (55522 "She's Still Talkin'
Baby Talk") 50-75   62
LIBERTY (55531 "Linda") 8-12   63
LIBERTY (55580 through 55727) 5-10   63-64
LIBERTY (55766 through 55923) 8-12   63-66
MAGIC LAMP (401 "California
Lullabye") 15-25   66
ODE (66111 "Fun City") 15-25   75
U.A. 10-20   72-76
WARNER (7151 "Only a Boy") 25-35   67
WARNER (7219 "I Know My Mind") . . 25-35   68

Picture Sleeves

DORE (555 "We Go Together") 35-50   60
DORE (576 "Gee") 75-100   60
LIBERTY (Except 55766 and 55849) . 15-25   63-65
LIBERTY (55766 "From All Over
the World") 80-125   65
LIBERTY (55849 "Folk City") 20-30   65
U.A. (50859 "Jenny Lee") 15-25   71

EPs: 7–inch 33/45rpm

ARTISTIC (227 "Original
Golden Hits") 40-50   65
(Also has tracks by Jerry Wallace, Champs, Ray
Sharpe, Fireflies, Rosie and the Originals, and
Gene & Eunice. A Mail-order offer.)

LPs: 10/12–inch 33rpm

AUDIO ENCORE 5-8   89
COLUMBIA (9461 "Save for a
Rainy Day") 1500-2000   67
(At least one sale of this LP has been confirmed. It
DOES exist but is probably not a U.S. issue.
Tracks are remixed from what is heard on the J&D
LP of the same title. Does have one track, *Lullaby
in the Rain,* which is not on the J&D LP.)
DEADMAN'S CURVE ("Live at
Keystone Berkeley") 15-25   78
(With Papa Doo Ron Ron.)
DESIGN/STEREO SPECTRUM 10-20   64
DORE (101 "Jan & Dean") 150-250   60
(Price includes a 12"x12" Jan & Dean color photo,
which represents $50 to $75 of the value.)
EMI 10-15   86
EMI/LIBERTY 10-20   90
EXACT 5-8   80
EXCELSIOR 10-15   80
IMPERIAL HOUSE 5-8   80

DEADMAN'S CURVE RECORDS
C1978
SIDE ONE
JAN AND DEAN
LIVE AT KEYSTONE
BERKELEY

INTERNATIONAL AWARD
SERIES 8-10
J&D (101 "Save for a Rainy Day") . 200-250   67
K-TEL 5-10   70-89
LIBERTY (3248 through 3403) 20-25   62-65
(Monaural.)
LIBERTY (3414 "Pop Symphony
Number 1") 40-45   65
(Monaural.)
LIBERTY (3417 through 3460) 20-25   65-66
(Monaural.)
LIBERTY (7248 through 7403) 20-30   62-65
(Stereo.)
LIBERTY (7414 "Pop Symphony
Number 1") 40-50   65
(Stereo.)
LIBERTY (7417 through 7460) 20-30   65-66
(Stereo.)
LIBERTY (10000 series) 8-12   81-82
MAGIC CARPET 10-12
PAIR (1071 "California Gold") 10-15
RHINO 5-8   82
SILVER EAGLE (1039 "Silver
Summer") 25-35   86
(Mail-order offer.)
SUNSET 10-15   67
U.A. 10-12   71-79
Members: Jan Berry; Dean Torrence.
Also see BEACH BOYS
Also see BEACH BOYS / Jan & Dean
Also see BERRY, Jan
Also see CALIFORNIA MUSIC
Also see JAN & ARNIE

JAN & DEAN / Roy Orbison / 4 Seasons / Shirelles

EPs: 7–inch 33/45rpm

COKE ("Let's Swing the Jingle
for Coca-Cola") 25-45   65
(Coca-Cola radio spots. Issued to radio
stations only.)
Also see 4 SEASONS
Also see ORBISON, Roy
Also see SHIRELLES

JAN & DEAN / Soul Surfers
LPs: 10/12–inch 33rpm
L-J (101 "Jan & Dean with the
Soul Surfers") 35-45   63
  Also see JAN & DEAN

JAN & KJELD
Singles: 7–inch
ALONCA 4-6	66
IMPERIAL 5-10	59
JARO INT'L 5-10	60
KAPP 5-10	60-61

Picture Sleeves
JARO INT'L 5-10	60
KAPP 5-10	60

LPs: 10/12–inch 33rpm
KAPP (1190 "Banjo Boy") 20-30   60

JANE, Baby: see BABY JANE

JANE'S ADDICTION
LPs: 10/12–inch 33rpm
TRIPLE X 10-20
(Clear vinyl.)
WARNER 5-8   88-90

JANIS, Johnny
Singles: 78rpm
ABC-PAR 4-8   57
Singles: 7–inch
ABC-PAR 5-10	57
BOMARC 5-10	59-60
COLUMBIA 5-10	60
CORAL 5-10	55
MONUMENT 4-6	66-68

LPs: 10/12–inch 33rpm
ABC-PAR (140 "For the First Time") . 35-50	57
COLUMBIA 15-20	61
MONUMENT 10-15	65

JANKEL, Chas
Singles: 12–inch 33/45rpm
A&M 4-6   83
Singles: 7–inch
A&M 2-4   82
LPs: 10/12–inch 33rpm
A&M 5-8   82
  Also see DURY, Ian, and the Blockheads

JANKOWSKI, Horst, and His Orchestra
Singles: 7–inch
MERCURY 3-6   65-68
Picture Sleeves
MERCURY 3-6   65
LPs: 10/12–inch 33rpm
MERCURY 5-15   65-69
  Also see IMPALAS / Horst Jankowski and His Orchestra

JARMELS
Singles: 7–inch
LAURIE 6-12   61-63
LPs: 10/12–inch 33rpm
COLLECTABLES 6-8   87

JARRE, Jean-Michael
Singles: 12–inch 33/45rpm
POLYDOR 4-6   86
Singles: 7–inch
POLYDOR 2-5   78-86
LPs: 10/12–inch 33rpm
DREYFUS 5-8	85-86
POLYDOR 5-8	77-86
  Also see U.S.A. for AFRICA

JARREAU, Al
Singles: 7–inch
MCA 2-4	87
RAYNARD (10024 "Shake Up") 50-100	
REPRISE 3-5	76
WARNER 2-5	77-86

Picture Sleeves
MCA 2-4	87
WARNER 3-5	83-84

LPs: 10/12–inch 33rpm
MFSL (019 "All Fly Home") 25-50	78
REPRISE 5-10	76-88
WARNER 5-10	77-86
  Also see U.S.A. for AFRICA

JARREAU, Al, and Randy Crawford
Singles: 7–inch
WARNER 2-4   82
  Also see CRAWFORD, Randy
  Also see JARREAU, Al

JARRETT, Keith
LPs: 10/12–inch 33rpm
ATLANTIC 8-10	75
ECM 8-12	76-80
IMPULSE 8-10	75-77

JARVIS, Carol
Singles: 78rpm
BALLY 4-6	57
DOT 4-6	57

Singles: 7–inch
BALLY 5-10	57
DOT 5-10	57-59
ERA 5-10	60-61

JARVIS, Marion
Singles: 7-inch
ROXBURY 3-5   74

JASMIN
Singles: 12-inch 33/45rpm
TVI 4-6   84

JASON and the Scorchers
(Jason and the Nashville Scorchers)
Singles: 7-inch
EMI AMERICA 2-4   84-86
PRAXIS 10-15   83-84
LPs: 10/12-inch 33rpm
EMI AMERICA 5-8   84-86
Member: Jason Ringenberg.

JASPER, Chris
Singles: 7-inch
CBS ASSOCIATED 2-4   87-88
LPs: 10/12-inch 33rpm
CBS ASSOCIATED 2-4   87

JAY, Dee: see DEE JAY

JAY, Jazzy: see JAZZY JAY

JAY, Morty
(Morty Jay and the Surfin' Cats)
Singles: 7-inch
LEGEND 8-12   63
20TH FOX 4-8   63
Picture Sleeves
LEGEND 10-15   63

JAY and the Americans
(Featuring Jay Black)
Singles: 7-inch
FUTURA 3-5   72
U.A. (353 through 992) 4-8   61-66
U.A. (50000 series) 3-5   66-71
Picture Sleeves
U.A. 5-10   65-66
LPs: 10/12-inch 33rpm
RHINO 5-8   86
SUNSET 10-12   69-70
UNART 8-12   68
U.A. (300 series) 5-8   75
U.A. (1000 series) 5-8   80
U.A. (3222 "She Cried") 20-25   62
(Monaural.)
U.A. (3300 "At the Cafe Wha") 20-25   63
(Monaural.)
U.A. (3407 "Come a Little Bit Closer") 15-25   64
(Monaural.)
U.A. (3417 through 3562) 15-20   64-67
(Monaural.)
U.A. (6222 "She Cried") 20-30   62
(Stereo.)
U.A. (6300 "At the Cafe Wha") 20-30   63
(Stereo.)
U.A. (6407 "Come a Little Bit Closer") 20-25   64
(Stereo.)

U.A. (6417 through 6719) 10-20   64-69
Also see BLACK, Jay

JAY and the Techniques
(Featuring Jay Proctor)
Singles: 7-inch
EVENT 3-5   76
GORDY 3-5   72
SMASH 4-8   67-69
Picture Sleeves
SMASH 4-8   67-68
LPs: 10/12-inch 33rpm
EVENT 8-10   75
SMASH 15-20   67-68

JAYE, Jerry
Singles: 7-inch
CARLTON 15-25   64
COLUMBIA 3-5   75
HI (2100 series) 4-8   67-68
HI (2300 series) 3-5   76-77
LABEL 5-10   59
MEGA 3-5   71-74
RAINTREE 3-5   72
STEPHANY (1320 "Sugar Dumplin') . 20-30   58
LPs: 10/12-inch 33rpm
HI (32000 series) 15-20   67
HI (32100 series) 5-8   76

JAYE, Miles
Singles: 7-inch
ISLAND 2-4   87-89
LPs: 10/12-inch 33rpm
ISLAND 5-8   87-89
MCA 5-8   87

JAYHAWKS
Singles: 78rpm
ALADDIN 5-10   57
FLASH (Except 105) 5-10   56
FLASH (105 "Counting My Teardrops")20-40   56
Singles: 7-inch
ALADDIN (3393 "Everyone Should
 Know") 50-75   57
EASTMAN (792 "Start the Fire") 40-60   59
EASTMAN (798 "New Love") 40-60   59
FLASH (105 "Counting My
 Teardrops") 100-150   56
FLASH (109 "Stranded in the Jungle") 15-20   56
FLASH (111 "Love Train") 15-20   56
OLDIES 45 3-5
Members: James Johnson; Carl Fisher; Dave Govan; Carver
Bunkern; Richard Owens.
Also see MARATHONS
Also see PALMER, Earl
Also see VIBRATIONS

JAYNETTS
Singles: 7-inch
J&S 4-8   65
TUFF 4-8   63-64

LPs: 10/12–inch 33rpm

TUFF (13 "Sally, Go 'Round
the Roses") 50-75   63
(Includes *Dear Abby* by the Hearts.)
Members: Ethel Davis; Johnnie Louise; Mary Sue Wells; Ada
Ray; Yvonne Bushnell.
Also see JOHNNIE & JOE

JAZZ CRUSADERS
Singles: 7–inch

CHISA 3-5   70-71
PACIFIC JAZZ 4-8   62-68
WORLD PACIFIC 4-8   64-65

LPs: 10/12–inch 33rpm

BLUE NOTE 5-10   75-80
CHISA 8-12   70
LIBERTY 8-12   70
PACIFIC JAZZ (27 through 87) 20-35   61-64
PACIFIC JAZZ (10000 and 20000
series) 10-20   65-69
PAUSA 5-8   82
WORLD PACIFIC 8-15   65
Members: Wilton Felder; Nesbert Hooper; Wayne Henderson;
Joe Sample.
Also see CRUSADERS
Also see FELDER, Wilton

JAZZY JAY
Singles: 7–inch

ATLANTIC 2-4   84

JEAN, Cathy: see CATHY JEAN

JEAN, Earl: see EARL-JEAN

JEAN and the Darlings
Singles: 7–inch

VOLT 4-8   67-69

JECKYLL, Dr: see DR. JECKYLL

JEFF & ALETA
Singles: 7–inch

SRI 3-5   80

JEFFERSON
Singles: 7–inch

DECCA 4-6   69
JANUS 4-6   69

LPs: 10/12–inch 33rpm

JANUS 10-15   69

JEFFERSON, Morris
Singles: 7–inch

PARACHUTE 3-5   78

LPs: 10/12–inch 33rpm

PARACHUTE 5-8   78

JEFFERSON AIRPLANE
Singles: 7–inch

ELEKTRA 2-4   88
GRUNT (0500 through 0511) 3-5   71-72
GRUNT (10988 "White Rabbit") 10-20   77
(Colored vinyl. Promotional issue only.)
RCA (0150 through 0343) 4-6   69-70

RCA (5156 "White Rabbit") 4-8   87
(Colored vinyl. Promotional issue only.)
RCA (8769 through 9644) 5-10   66-68
(Dog on side of label.)
RCA (9000 series) 2-4   89
(Dog near top of label.)

Picture Sleeves

GRUNT (0500 "Pretty As You Feel") .. 5-10   71
GRUNT (0506 "Long John Silver") .. 10-15   72
GRUNT (11196 through 13872) 3-8   78-84
RCA (Except 5156) 8-12   68-70
RCA (5156 "White Rabbit") 4-8   87
(Promotional issue only.)

LPs: 10/12–inch 33rpm

EPIC 5-8   89
GRUNT (0147 "Thirty Seconds over
Winterland") 10-15   73
GRUNT (1001 "Bark") 30-60   71
GRUNT (1007 "Long John Silver") .. 30-60   72
GRUNT (1255 "Flight Log") 10-15   77
GRUNT (0437 "Early Flight") 10-15   74
GRUNT (4386 "Bark") 10-15   82
PAIR 8-10   84
RCA (0320 ("Volunteers") 12-15   73
(Quadrophonic.)
RCA (1511 "After Bathing at Baxters") 20-30   67
(Black label.)
RCA (1511 "After Bathing at Baxters") 10-12   71
(Orange label.)
RCA (3584 "Jefferson
Airplane Takes off") 75-125   66
(Has 12 tracks.)
RCA (3584 "Jefferson
Airplane Takes off") 15-20   66
(Has 11 tracks.)
RCA (3584 "Jefferson
Airplane Takes off") 10-12   69
(Orange label.)
RCA (3661 "Worst of Jefferson Airplane") 5-8   80
RCA (3739 "Jefferson
Airplane Takes off") 5-8   80
RCA (3766 "Surrealistic Pillow") 20-30   67
(Black label.)

RCA (3766 "Surrealistic Pillow") 10-12   69
(Orange label.)
RCA (3797 "Crown of Creation") 5-8   80
RCA (3798 "Bless Its
Pointed Little Head") 5-8   80
RCA (3867 "Volunteers") 5-8   81
RCA (4058 "Crown of Creation") 10-15   68
RCA (4133 "Bless Its
Pointed Little Head") 10-20   69
(Includes artwork insert.)
RCA (4238 "Volunteers") 10-15   69
RCA (4448 "Blows Against
the Empire") 10-20   70
(Black vinyl. Price includes booklet insert, which
represents about $4 to $6 of the value.)
RCA (4448 "Blows Against
the Empire") 75-100   70
(Clear vinyl. Promotional issue only.)
RCA (LSP-4459 "Worst of
Jefferson Airplane") 10-15   70
RCA (AFL1-4459 "Worst of
Jefferson Airplane") 5-8
Members: Signe Anderson; Marty Balin; Paul Kantner; Jack
Casady; Jorma Kaukonen; Skip Spence; Grace Slick; Craig
Chaquico; Joey Covington; Papa John Creach; Spencer Dryden;
Dave Freiberg.
    Also see BALIN, Marty
    Also see CREACH, Papa John
    Also see CROSBY, David
    Also see GARCIA, Jerry
    Also see GREATII SOCIETYII
    Also see HOPKINS, Nicky
    Also see JEFFERSON STARSHIP
    Also see KBC BAND
    Also see KANTNER, Paul, and Grace Slick
    Also see KAUKONEN, Jorma
    Also see QUICKSILVER
    Also see SLICK, Grace
    Also see STILLS, Stephen

JEFFERSON STARSHIP
Singles: 7-inch
GRUNT 2-5   74-84
Picture Sleeves
GRUNT 3-5   77-83
LPs: 10/12-inch 33rpm
GRUNT (0717 through 1557) 10-15   74-76
GRUNT (1255 "Flight Log,
1966-1976") 15-20   77
(With simulated leather cover. Also contains
Jefferson Airplane, Hot Tuna, Grace Slick and Paul
Kanter tracks.)
GRUNT (1255 "Flight Log,
1966-1976") 10-20   81
(With standard cover.)
GRUNT (2515 through 3247) 10-15   78-79
GRUNT (3363 "Gold") 15-20   79
(Picture disc.)
GRUNT (3452 through 6413) 6-12   79-87
RCA 5-8   81-89

Members: Grace Slick; Marty Balin; Paul Kantner; Aynsley
Dunbar; Pete Sears; Mickey Thomas; John Barbata.
Note: Cross references that already appear under Jefferson
Airplane are not duplicated below.
    Also see HOT TUNA
    Also see JEFFERSON AIRPLANE
    Also see KANTNER, Paul, and Jefferson Starship
    Also see STARSHIP

JEFFREE
Singles: 7-inch
MCA 3-5   78-79
LPs: 10/12-inch 33rpm
MCA 5-8   79

JEFFREY, Joe
(Joe Jeffrey Group)
Singles: 7-inch
WAND 4-6   69
LPs: 10/12-inch 33rpm
WAND 10-15   69

JEFFREYS, Garland
Singles: 7-inch
A&M 3-5   77-79
ARISTA 3-5   75
ATLANTIC 3-5   73
EPIC 2-4   81-83
LPs: 10/12-inch 33rpm
A&M 5-8   77-79
ATLANTIC 8-10   73
EPIC 5-8   81-83

JEFFREYS, Garland, and Phoebe Snow
Singles: 7-inch
A&M 3-5   78
Picture Sleeves
A&M 3-5   78
    Also see JEFFREYS, Garland
    Also see SNOW, Phoebe

JELLY BEANS
Singles: 7-inch
ESKEE 4-8   65
RED BIRD 5-10   64

JELLYBEAN
("Jellybean" Benitez)
Singles: 12-inch 33/45rpm
EMI AMERICA 4-6   84-86
Singles: 7-inch
CHRYSALIS 2-4   87
EMI AMERICA 2-4   84-86
LPs: 10/12-inch 33rpm
CHRYSALIS 5-8   87
EMI AMERICA 5-8   84-86

JENKINS, Donald
(Donald Jenkins and the Delighters)
Singles: 7-inch
CORTLAND 5-10   63
DUCHESS 4-8   65

JENKINS, Gordon, and His Orchestra
Singles: 78rpm
DECCA 3-6   50-56

Singles: 7-inch
COLUMBIA 4-6   64
DECCA 5-10   50-56
KAPP 4-8   60-64
TIME 4-6   62
X 4-8   55

EPs: 7-inch 33/45rpm
DECCA 5-15   51-56

LPs: 10/12-inch 33rpm
CAPITOL (700 series) 15-25   56
(With "T" prefix.)
CAPITOL (700 series) 10-15   61
(With "DT" prefix.)
CAPITOL (700 series) 4-8   75
(With "SM" prefix.)
COLUMBIA 10-20   62-63
CORAL 5-8   73
DECCA 15-30   51-63
(Decca LP numbers in this series preceded by a
"7" or a "DL-7" are stereo issues.)
DOT 5-10   66
GWP 5-10   71
MCA 5-8   73-75
SUNSET 5-10   67
TIME 10-15   62-64
   Also see ARMSTRONG, Louis
   Also see BOONE, Pat
   Also see LEE, Peggy
   Also see WEAVERS

JENKINS, Gus
(Gus Jinkins)
Singles: 78rpm
COMBO 8-12   54
FLASH 4-8   56-57

Singles: 7-inch
CATALINA 4-8   63
COMBO (87 "I Been Working") 30-50   54
FLASH 8-12   56-57
GENERAL ARTIST 4-8   64-69
PIONEER INT'L 5-10   59-62
SAR 4-8   64
TOWER 4-8   64-65

JENKINS, Kechia
Singles: 7-inch
PROFILE 2-4   88

JENKINS, Norma
Singles: 7-inch
DESERT MOON 2-4   76

JENNIFER
(Jennifer Warnes)
Singles: 7-inch
PARROT 4-6   67-70
LPs: 10/12-inch 33rpm
PARROT 10-20   68-70
   Also see WARNES, Jennifer

JENNINGS, Waylon
(Waylon Jennings and the Waylors; Waylon Jennings
and the Kimberlys; Waylon Jennings and the Crickets)
Singles: 7-inch
A&M (739 "Four Strong Winds") 8-10   64
A&M (722 "Rave On") 10-15   63
BAT (121636 "White Lightning") 30-50   62
BAT (121639 "Dream Baby") 25-35   62
BRUNSWICK (55130 "Jole Blon") . 100-150   59
   (Maroon label. With Buddy Holly and
   King Curtis.)
BRUNSWICK (55130 "Jole Blon") .. 75-100   59
   (Yellow label. Promotional issue only.)
RCA (Except 8572 through 9642) 3-5   69-80
RCA (8572 through 9642) 4-8   65-68
RAMCO 5-10   67
TREND '61 (102 "Another Blue Day") 20-25   61
TREND '63 (106 "The Stage") 50-75   63

Picture Sleeves
RCA 3-5   79-80

LPs: 10/12-inch 33rpm
A&M (4238 "Don't Think Twice") 25-30   69
BAT (1001 "Waylon Jennings
   at JD's") 200-300   64
   (500 copies were pressed on Bat, then another
   500 were done on Sounds Ltd.)
CAMDEN 8-15   67-76
EPIC 5-8   90
MCA 4-6
PICKWICK 5-10   75
RCA (0240 through 3378) 5-10   73-79
RCA (3406 "Greatest Hits") 15-20   79
   (Picture disc.)
RCA (3493 "What Goes Around
   Comes Around") 5-10   79
RCA (3523 "Folk Country") 15-25   66
RCA (3602 "Music Man") 5-10   80
RCA (3620 "Leavin' Town") 20-30   66
RCA (3660 "Waylon Sings
   Ol' Harlan") 15-20   67
RCA (3663 "Are You Ready
   for the Country") 5-8   80
RCA (3736 "Nashville Rebel") 15-25   66
   (Soundtrack.)
RCA (3737 "Good Hearted Woman") ... 5-8   80
RCA (3825 "Love of the
   Common People") 15-25   67
RCA (3897 "Honky Tonk Heroes") ... 5-8   81
RCA (3918 "Hangin' On") 15-20   68
RCA (3942 "This Time") 5-8   81
RCA (4023 "Only the Greatest") 15-20   68
RCA (4072 "Dreaming My Dreams") ... 5-8   81
RCA (4073 "The Ramblin' Man") 5-8   81
RCA (4085 "Jewels") 15-20   68
RCA (4137 "Just to Satisfy You") 15-20   69
RCA (4163 "Waylon Live") 5-8   81
RCA (4164 "I've Always
   Been Crazy") 5-8   81
RCA (4180 "Country Folk") 15-25   69

RCA (4247 "Black on Black") 5-8   82
RCA (4250 "Music Man") 5-8   82
RCA (4260 "Waylon") 10-15   70
RCA (4341 "Best of Waylon Jennings") 8-10   77
RCA (4418 "Singer of Sad Songs") .. 10-15   70
RCA (4487 "The Taker/Tulsa") 10-15   71
RCA (4567 "Cedartown Georgia") ... 10-15   71
RCA (4647 "Good Hearted Woman") . 10-15   72
RCA (4673 "It's Only Rock and Roll") ... 5-8   83
RCA (4751 "Ladies Love Outlaws") .. 10-15   72
RCA (4826 "Waylon and Co.") 5-8   83
RCA (4828 "Best of Waylon Jennings") . 5-8   83
RCA (4854 "Lonesome, On'ry
  and Mean") 10-15   73
SOUNDS (1001 "Waylon Jennings
  at JD's") 200-250   64
  (First issued on Bat.)
TIME-LIFE 5-8   81
VOCALION 15-20   69
  Also see CASH, Johnny, and Waylon Jennings
  Also see CRICKETS
  Also see CUNHA, Rick
  Also see DAVIS, Skeeter
  Also see HOLLY, Buddy
  Also see KIMBERLYS
  Also see KING CURTIS
  Also see MANDRELL, Barbara
  Also see U.S.A. for AFRICA

JENNINGS, Waylon, and Jesse Colter
Singles: 7-inch
RCA 3-5   69-71
LPs: 10/12-inch 33rpm
RCA (3931 "Leather and Lace") 5-8   81
  Also see COLTER, Jesse

JENNINGS, Waylon, and Willie Nelson
(Waylon and Willie)
Singles: 7-inch
COLUMBIA 2-4   83
MCA 2-4   86
RCA 2-5   76-86
LPs: 10/12-inch 33rpm
AURA 5-8   83
COLUMBIA 5-8   83
RCA (2686 "Waylon and Willie") 5-10   78
RCA (2686 "Waylon and Willie") 20-25   78
  (Colored vinyl. Promotional issue only.)
RCA (4455 "Waylon and Willie II") 5-8   82

JENNINGS, Waylon, Willie Nelson, Jessi Colter, and Tompall Glaser
LPs: 10/12-inch 33rpm
RCA (1321 "The Outlaws") 5-10   76

JENNINGS, Waylon, Willie Nelson, Johnny Cash, and Kris Kristofferson
Singles: 7-inch
COLUMBIA 2-4   85-90
LPs: 10/12-inch 33rpm
COLUMBIA 5-8   85-90
  Also see CASH, Johnny
  Also see KRISTOFFERSON, Kris

Also see NELSON, Willie

JENNINGS, Waylon / Johnny Paycheck
LPs: 10/12-inch 33rpm
OUT of TOWN DIST 5-8   82
  Also see PAYCHECK, Johnny

JENNINGS, Waylon, and Jerry Reed
Singles: 7-inch
RCA 2-4   83
  Also see REED, Jerry

JENNINGS, Waylon, and Hank Williams Jr.
Singles: 7-inch
RCA 2-4   83
  Also see JENNINGS, Waylon
  Also see WILLIAMS, Hank, Jr.

JENSEN, Kris
Singles: 7-inch
A&M 3-5   70
COLPIX 5-10   59
HICKORY 4-8   62-65
KAPP 4-8   61
LEADER 5-10   60-61
Picture Sleeves
HICKORY 10-15   62-64
LPs: 10/12-inch 33rpm
HICKORY (110 "Torture") 40-50   62

JEROME, Henry, and His Orchestra
Singles: 7-inch
DECCA 3-5   60-64
EPs: 7-inch 33/45rpm
DECCA 4-6   61
LPs: 10/12-inch 33rpm
DECCA 5-12   60-64
ROULETTE 5-15   59

JERRY, Mungo: see MUNGO JERRY

JESSE & MARVIN
Singles: 78rpm
SPECIALTY 15-25   52
Singles: 7-inch
SPECIALTY (447 "Dream Girl") 50-75   52
  (Black vinyl.)
SPECIALTY (447 "Dream Girl") ... 100-200   52
  (Colored vinyl.)
  Members: Jesse Belvin; Marvin Phillips.
  Also see BELVIN, Jesse
  Also see MARVIN & JOHNNY

JESSE'S GANG
Singles: 7-inch
GEFFEN 2-4   87
JES SAY 4-6   85

JESTERS
Singles: 78rpm
WINLEY 10-15   57
Singles: 7-inch
ABC 2-4   73
AMY 3-5   62
COLLECTABLES 2-4

CYCLONE (5011 "I Laughed") 25-45   58
LOST-NITE 4-6   63
WINLEY (218 "So Strange") 25-35   57
   (With "Winley" in ³⁄₁₆-inch letters.)
WINLEY (218 "So Strange") 8-12   61
   (With "Winley" in ¼-inch letters.)
WINLEY (221 "I'm Falling in Love") . 35-45   57
   (With "Winley" in ³⁄₁₆-inch letters.)
WINLEY (221 "I'm Falling in Love") .. 10-15   61
   (With "Winley" in ¼-inch letters.)
WINLEY (225 "The Plea") 35-40   58
   (With "Winley" in ³⁄₁₆-inch letters.)
WINLEY (225 "The Plea") 10-15   61
   (With "Winley" in ¼-inch letters.)
WINLEY (242 "The Wind") 30-40   60
WINLEY (248 "That's How It Goes") . 40-50   61
   (Colored vinyl.)
WINLEY (248 "That's How It Goes") . 20-30   61
   (Black vinyl.)
WINLEY (252 "Come Let
   Me Show You") 20-30   61
     LPs: 10/12-inch 33rpm
COLLECTABLES 6-8   86
LOST-NITE 5-8   81
   Members: Len McKay; Adam Jackson; Jimmy Smith; Noel
   Grant; Leo Vincent; Melvin Lewis; Don Lewis.

JESTERS / Paragons
     LPs: 10/12-inch 33rpm
JOSIE 50-100
JUBILEE (1098 "Jesters
   Meet the Paragons") 100-150   59
PAUL WINLEY PRODUCTIONS (102 "Jesters
   Meet the Paragons") 20-25   65
WINLEY (6003 "War: Jesters
   Meet the Paragons") 50-100   60
   Also see JESTERS
   Also see PARAGONS

JESUS and Mary Chain
     Singles: 7-inch
WARNER 2-4   87-89
     LPs: 10/12-inch 33rpm
REPRISE 5-8   86
WARNER 5-8   87-89

JETBOY
     LPs: 10/12-inch 33rpm
MCA 5-8   88

JETE, Le: see LE JETE

JETER, Genobia
     Singles: 12-inch 33/45rpm
RCA 4-6   86
     Singles: 7-inch
RCA 2-4   86-87
     LPs: 10/12-inch 33rpm
RCA 5-8   86

JETER, Genobia, and Glenn Jones
     Singles: 7-inch
RCA 2-4   87

Also see JONES, Glenn

JETHRO TULL
     Singles: 12-inch 33/45rpm
CHRYSALIS 4-8   88-89
   (Promotional only.)
     Singles: 7-inch
CHRYSALIS 3-5   72-88
CHRYSALIS/REPRISE 4-8   69-72
     Picture Sleeves
CHRYSALIS 3-5   74
     EPs: 7-inch 33/45rpm
CHRYSALIS 8-12   71
     LPs: 10/12-inch 33rpm
CHRYSALIS (Except CH4 and V5X
   series) 6-12   73-89
CHRYSALIS (CH4 series) 10-12   73-74
   (Quadrophonic issues.)
CHRYSALIS (V5X-41653 "Twenty
   Years of Jethro Tull") 25-35   88
   (Five-LP set.)
MFSL (061 "Aqualung") 25-50   82
MFSL (092 "Broadsword and
   the Beast") 20-30   82
REPRISE 10-15   69-72
REPRISE/CHRYSALIS (2106 "Living
   in the Past") 15-20   72
   (Price includes bonus, color booklet.)
     Promotional LPs
CHRYSALIS (623 "Radio Show") ... 10-20   76
   (Music/interview with Ian Anderson about *Mu*.)
   Members: Ian Anderson; Clive Bunker; Glen Cormick; John
   Evan; Barry Barlow; David Palmer; John Glascock; Jeff
   Hammond; Mick Abrahams.
   Also see WILD TURKEY

JETS
     Singles: 12-inch 33/45rpm
MCA 4-6   85-88
     Singles: 7-inch
MCA 2-4   85-89
     Picture Sleeves
MCA 2-4   86-88
     LPs: 10/12-inch 33rpm
MCA 5-8   85-89
   Members: Elizabeth Wolfgram and the Wolfgram family.

JETT, Joan, and the Blackhearts
     Singles: 12-inch 33/45rpm
BLACKHEART/CBS 4-8   88
   (Promotional only.)
MCA 4-8   83
     Singles: 7-inch
BLACKHEART/CBS 2-4   83-90
BOARDWALK 3-5   81-82
MCA 3-5   83
     Picture Sleeves
BLACKHEART/CBS 2-4   83-88
BOARDWALK 3-5   81-82
MCA 3-5   83

U.A. 5-10   64-66
LPs: 10/12–inch 33rpm
AMBIENT SOUND 5-8   82
COLLECTABLES 6-8   85
RELIC 8-10
U.A. (3455 "The Jive Five") 25-30   65
(Monaural.)
U.A. (6455 "The Jive Five") 30-35   65
(Stereo.)
   Members: Eugene Pitt; Norm Johnson; Richard Harris; Jerry
   Hannah; Billy Prophet; Johnny Watson; Casey Spencer;
   Webster Harris.
   Also see GENIES
   Also see PLATTERS / Inez and Charlie Foxx / Jive Five /
    Tommy Hunt

JIVIN' GENE
(Jivin' Gene and the Jokers)
Singles: 7–inch
ABC 3-5   73
CHESS 4-8   64
HALL WAY 3-5   64
JIN (109 "Going Out with the Tide") .. 15-25   59
JIN (116 "Breakin' Up
Is Hard to Do") 15-25   59
MERCURY 6-10   59-62
TFC/HALL 4-8   65
   Member: Gene Bourgeois.

JO, Damita: see DAMITA JO

JO, Marcy: see MARCY JOE

JO, Sami: see SAMI JO

JO ANN & TROY
Singles: 7–inch
ATLANTIC 8-12   64
   Members: Jo Ann Campbell; Troy Seals.
   Also see CAMPBELL, Jo Ann

JO JO GUNNE
Singles: 7–inch
ASYLUM 3-5   72
LPs: 10/12–inch 33rpm
ASYLUM (Except 5071) 8-10   72-74
ASYLUM (5071 "Jumpin' the Gunne") 10-15   73
(With gatefold cover.)
ASYLUM (5071 "Jumpin' the Gunne") . 8-10   73
(With standard cover.)
   Member: Jay Ferguson.
   Also see FERGUSON, Jay

JOBIM, Antonio Carlos
Singles: 7–inch
A&M 4-6   67
CTI 3-5   70
MCA 3-5   74
VERVE 4-6   63-64
LPs: 10/12–inch 33rpm
A&M 8-12   67-70
CTI 8-12   70-71
CAPITOL 10-20   64
DISCOVERY 5-8   82
MCA 5-8   73

VERSATILE 5-8   78
VERVE (Except 3000 series) 10-20   63
VERVE (3000 series) 5-8   82
WARNER 8-15   65-80
   Also see FITZGERALD, Ella, and Antonio Carlos Jobim
   Also see GILBERTO, Astrud
   Also see SINATRA, Frank, and Antonio Carlos Jobim

JOBOXERS
Singles: 7–inch
RCA 2-4   83
LPs: 10/12–inch 33rpm
RCA 5-8   83

JOE, Billy: see BILLY JOE

JOE, Marcy: see MARCY JOE

JOE & ANN
Singles: 7–inch
ACE 5-10   60-62

JOE & EDDIE
Singles: 7–inch
CAPITOL 4-8   59
GNP/CRESCENDO 4-8   62-65
LPs: 10/12–inch 33rpm
GNP/CRESCENDO 8-15   63-66
   Members: Joe Gilbert; Eddie Brown.

JOEL, Billy
Singles: 12–inch 33/45rpm
COLUMBIA 4-8   83
Singles: 7–inch
COLUMBIA (2628 "She's Got a Way") .. 4-6   81
(Promotional issue only.)
COLUMBIA (02518 through 06526) 2-4   81-86
COLUMBIA (10000
and 11000 series) 3-5   74-80
COLUMBIA (40000 series) 3-5   73-74
COLUMBIA (70000 series) 2-4   89
EPIC 2-4   86
FAMILY (0900 "She's Got a Way") ... 10-20   73
FAMILY (0906 "Tomorrow Is Today") . 10-20   73
Picture Sleeves
COLUMBIA (Except 02628) 2-5   79-90
COLUMBIA (02628 "She's Got a Way") . 4-6   81
(Promotional issue only.)
LPs: 10/12–inch 33rpm
COLUMBIA (30000 and 40000 series) 5-10   73-89
(With "FC," "KC," "PC," "QC," or "TC" prefix.)
COLUMBIA (30000 series) 10-15   74-76
(With "CQ" or "PCQ" prefix. Quad issues.)
COLUMBIA (HC-40000 series) 10-15   80-87
(Half-speed mastered.)
FAMILY PRODUCTIONS (2700 "Cold
Spring Harbor") 35-45   71
Promotional LPs
COLUMBIA (326 "Souvenir") 25-35   75
COLUMBIA (402 "Interchords") 25-35   77
SKYCLAD (102 "A Tribute to Billy Joel") 6-8   91
(Clear vinyl. Intentionally has no music—by Billy
Joel or anyone. Limited edition of 666 copies.)

BILLY JOEL

...kfully, ...O music by: Phil Collins, Cope...
...nley, ...va Delegation, Marshmallow C...

Also see ATTILA
Also see HASSLES
Also see KHAN, Steve
Also see U.S.A. for AFRICA

JOEL, Billy, and Ray Charles
Singles: 7–inch
COLUMBIA 2-4 87
 Also see CHARLES, Ray
 Also see JOEL, Billy

JOESKI LOVE
Singles: 7–inch
VINTERTAINMENT 2-4 86

JOHANSEN, David
Singles: 7–inch
BLUE SKY 3-5 78-82
LPs: 10/12–inch 33rpm
BLUE SKY 5-8 78-82
 Also see NEW YORK DOLLS

JOHN, Dr: see DR. JOHN

JOHN, Elton
Singles: 12–inch 33/45rpm
GEFFEN 4-8 83-85
 (Promotional only.)
MCA 4-8 78-88
 (Promotional only.)
Singles: 7–inch
CONGRESS (6017 "Lady Samatha") . 20-30 69
CONGRESS (6022 "Border Song") .. 20-30 70
DJM (70008 "Lady Samatha") 40-60 69
EPIC 2-4 87
GEFFEN 3-5 81-86
MCA (40000 through 40505) 3-6 72-76
MCA (40892 through 40973) 3-5 78
MCA (40993 "Song for Guy") 4-6 78
 (Promotional issue only.)
MCA (41042 through 41293) 3-5 79-80
MCA (53196 through 53000 series) 2-4 87-90
MCA/ROCKET 3-5 76-77
ROCKET 3-5 76-77
UNI 3-6 70-72
VIKING (1010 "From Denver to L.A.") 35-50 69
 (Flip is by the Barbara Moore Singers.)

Picture Sleeves
GEFFEN 3-5 81-86
MCA (40000 through 40505) 3-6 74-75
MCA (40892 through 40973) 3-5 78
MCA (40993 "Song for Guy") 4-6 78
 (Promotional issue only.)
MCA (41042 through 41293) 3-5 79-80
MCA (53196 through 53000 series) 2-4 87-88
MCA/ROCKET 3-5 76-77
ROCKET 3-5 76-77
EPs: 7–inch 33/45rpm
MCA (Except 40105) 8-10 73
 (Jukebox issues.)
MCA (40105 "Saturday Night's
 Alright for Fighting") 3-5 73
 (Single with two tracks on side two. Not issued with
 EP cover.)
UNI 10-12 70
 (Jukebox issue only.)
LPs: 10/12–inch 33rpm
COLUMBIA SPECIAL PRODUCTS 5-8 81
DJLP (403 "Empty Sky") 20-25 69
 (U.K. issue, distributed in the U.S.A.)
GEFFEN 5-8 81-87
MCA (1995 "A Single Man") 35-45 79
 (Promotional issue picture disc. "B" side pictures
 Elton from the rear.)
MCA (2100 through 2130) 6-10 73-75
MCA (2142 "Captain Fantastic and
 the Brown Dirt Cowboy") 10-12 75
 (Includes poster, lyrics booklet, bio scrapbook and
 comic insert. Deduct $3 to $5 if these items are
 missing.)
MCA (2142 "Captain Fantastic") ... 50-100 79
 (Colored vinyl. Promotional issue only.)
MCA (2163 through 5121) 5-10 75-80
MCA (6000 series) 5-8 88-89
MCA (8000 series) 10-12 87
MCA (10003 "Goodbye Yellow
 Brick Road") 10-12 73
MCA (13921 "Thom Bell Sessions") .. 5-10 79
MCA (14591 "A Single Man") 8-12 79
 (Picture disc.)
MCA (37000 series) 4-8 79
MCA/ROCKET (Except 1953) 10-12 76-77
MCA/ROCKET (1953 "Get Up
 and Dance") 20-25 77
 (Promotional issue only.)
NAUTILUS (10003 "Goodbye Yellow
 Brick Road") 30-40 82
 (Half-speed mastered.)
PARAMOUNT 8-12 71
SASSON/GEFFEN (2176 "Sasson
 Presents Elton John") 20-30 81
 (Single-sided, four-track LP. Promotional issue
 only.)
UNI (73090 "Elton John") 15-20 70
 (Includes booklet.)

UNI (73096 "Tumbleweed
   Connection") 15-20   71
   (Includes booklet.)
UNI (93105 "11-17-70") 15-20   71
UNI (93120 "Madman Across
   the Water") 15-20   71
   (Includes booklet.)
UNI (93135 "Honky Chateau") 15-20   72
VIKING (105 "The Games") 150-175   70
   (Soundtrack. With Francis Lai and the Barbara
   Moore Singers.)
   Also see DIONNE and Friends
   Also see FRANKLIN, Aretha, and Elton John
   Also see MICHAEL, George
   Also see OLSSON, Nigel
   Also see RUSH, Jennifer, and Elton John
   Also see SEDAKA, Neil
   Also see STARR, Ringo

JOHN, Elton, and Kiki Dee
Singles: 7–inch
ROCKET 3-5   76
Picture Sleeves
ROCKET 3-5   76
   Also see DEE, Kiki

JOHN, Elton, and Lesley Duncan
Singles: 7–inch
MCA (1938 "Love Song") 15-20   76
   (Promotional issue only.)

JOHN, Elton / John Lennon
Singles: 7–inch
MCA (40364 "Philadelphia Freedom") .. 3-5   75
Picture Sleeves
MCA (40364 "Philadelphia Freedom") .. 3-5   75
MCA (40364 WFIL radio "Philadelphia
   Freedom") 30-40   75
   (Promotional issue only.)
   Also see LENNON, John

JOHN, Elton / Tina Turner
Singles: 7–inch
POLYDOR (002 "Pinball Wizard") ... 25-35   75
   (Promotional issue only.)
   Also see JOHN, Elton
   Also see TURNER, Tina

JOHN, Little Willie
Singles: 78rpm
KING 4-8   56-57
Singles: 7–inch
GUSTO 2-4   87
KING (4818 through 5394) 8-15   56-60
KING (5428 through 5949) 4-8   61-64
EPs: 7–inch 33/45rpm
KING (423 "Talk to Me") 25-35   58
Picture Sleeves
GUSTO ("Fever") 2-4   87
LPs: 10/12–inch 33rpm
BLUESWAY 10-15   73
KING (564 "Fever") 70-90   56
   (With brown cover.)

KING (564 "Fever") 20-40   59
   (With blue cover.)
KING (596 "Talk to Me") 40-60   58
KING (603 "Mr. Little Willie John") ... 40-60   58
KING (691 "In Action") 100-125   60
KING (739 "Sure Things") 20-40   61
KING (767 "The Sweet, the Hot,
   the Teenage Beat") 20-40   61
KING (802 "Come On and Join
   Little Willie John") 20-30   62
KING (895 "These Are My
   Favorite Songs") 20-30   64
KING (949 "All Originals") 20-30   66
KING (1081 "Free At Last") 20-30   70
   Also see WILLIAMS, Paul

JOHN, Little Willie / Drifters
Singles: 7–inch
ATLANTIC (89189 "Fever") 2-4   89
Picture Sleeves
ATLANTIC (89189 "Fever") 2-4   89
   Also see DRIFTERS

JOHN, Little Willie / 5 Royales / Earl King / Midnighters
EPs: 7–inch 33/45rpm
KING (387 "Rock and Roll
   Hit Parade") 75-100   56
   Also see 5 ROYALES
   Also see JOHN, Little Willie
   Also see KING, Earl (Connelly)
   Also see MIDNIGHTERS

JOHN, Mable
Singles: 7–inch
STAX 4-8   66-68
TAMLA (54031 "Who Wouldn't Love
   a Man Like That") 30-40   60
TAMLA (54040 "No Love") 20-30   61
TAMLA (54050 "Take Me") 20-30   61
TAMLA (54081 "Who Wouldn't Love
   a Man Like That") 10-15   63

JOHN, Pope: see POPE JOHN
Singles: 7–inch

JOHN, Robert
(Bobby Pedrick Jr.)
Singles: 12–inch 33/45
CBS ASSOCIATED 4-6   84
Singles: 7–inch
A&M 3-5   70-72
ARIOLA 3-5   78
ATLANTIC 3-5   72-73
COLUMBIA 4-8   68-69
EMI AMERICA 2-4   79-80
MOTOWN 2-4   83
LPs: 10/12–inch 33rpm
COLUMBIA 10-20   68
EMI AMERICA 5-8   79-82
HARMONY 8-10   72
   Also see PEDRICK, Bobby

JOHN & ERNEST
Singles: 7–inch
RAINY WEDNESDAY 4-8   73
Members: John Free; Ernest Smith.

JOHN LEE
(John Lee Hooker; John Lee's Groundhogs)
Singles: 78rpm
GOTHAM 10-15   53
Singles: 7–inch
PLANET 4-8   67
Also see HOOKER, John Lee

JOHNNIE & JOE
Singles: 7–inch
ABC-PAR 8-15   60
AMBIENT SOUND 3-5   82
CHESS (1654 "Over the Mountain") . 10-20   57
(Silver and blue label.)
CHESS (1654 "Over the Mountain") . . 8-10   60
(Blue or multi-color label.)
CHESS (1769 "Across the Sea") 8-12   60
GONE (5024 "Who Do You Love") . . . 15-25   61
J&S (Except 1664) 10-15   57-59
J&S (1664 "Over the Mountain") . . 30-40   57
(With horizontal lines across label.)
J&S (1664 "Over the Mountain") 10-15   62
(Without horizontal lines across label.)
LPs: 10/12–inch 33rpm
AMBIENT SOUND 5-8   82
Members: Johnnie Louise Richardson; Joe Rivers.
Also see JAYNETTS

JOHNNY and the Distractions
Singles: 7–inch
A&M 2-4   82
LPs: 10/12–inch 33rpm
A&M 5-8   82

JOHNNY and the Expressions
Singles: 7–inch
JOSIE 4-8   65-66

JOHNNY and the Hurricanes
Singles: 7–inch
ABC 3-5   73
ATILA 5-10   64
BIG TOP 5-10   60-63
JA-DA 4-8
JEFF 5-10   64
MALA 4-8   63
TWIRL (1001 "Crossfire") 20-40   59
WARWICK (502 "Crossfire") 15-20   59
("Warwick" in sans-serif, or block style print.)
WARWICK (502 "Crossfire") 10-15   59
("Warwick" in serif style print, but does not extend
across entire label. "Crossfire" in quotes.)
WARWICK (502 "Crossfire") 8-10   59
("Warwick" in serif style print, extending across
entire label. No quotes on Crossfire.)
WARWICK (509 "Red River Rock") 8-10   59
(Monaural.)

THE BEATNIK FLY
(T. King - I. Mack)
JOHNNY and THE HURRICANES
M-520

WARWICK (509-ST "Red River Rock") 20-30   59
(Stereo.)
WARWICK (513 "Reville Rock") 5-10   59
(Monaural.)
WARWICK (513-ST "Reville Rock") . . 20-30   59
(Stereo.)
WARWICK (520 "Beatnik Fly") 8-10   60
("Warwick" in serif style print.)
WARWICK (520 "Beatnik Fly") 5-8   60
(With Warwick horse and scroll logo.)
Picture Sleeves
BIG TOP (3036 "Down Yonder") 10-15   60
BIG TOP (3051 "Rocking Goose") . . . 10-15   60
BIG TOP (3056 "You Are
My Sunshine") 10-15   60
BIG TOP (3063 "Ja-Da") 10-15   61
BIG TOP (3076 "Old Smokie") 10-15   61
WARWICK (520 "Beatnik Fly") 10-20   60
EPs: 7–inch 33/45rpm
WARWICK (700 "Johnny and
the Hurricanes") 50-75   59
LPs: 10/12–inch 33rpm
ATILA (1030 "Live at the Star Club") 75-125   64
(Price includes fan club insert.)
BIG TOP (1302 "The Big Sound of Johnny
and the Hurricanes") 45-55   60
(Monaural.)
BIG TOP (ST-1302 "The Big Sound of Johnny
and the Hurricanes") 75-100   60
(Stereo.)
TWIRL (5002 "Beatnik Fly") 70-90   59
WARWICK (W-2007 "Johnny and
the Hurricanes") 50-75   59
(Monaural.)
WARWICK (WST-2007 "Johnny and
the Hurricanes") 75-100   59
(Stereo.)
WARWICK (W-2010 "Stormsville") . . 45-60   60
(Monaural.)
WARWICK (WST-2010 "Stormsville") 55-80   60
(Stereo.)
Members: Johnny Paris; Paul Tesluk; Dave Yorko; Lionel "Butch"
Mattice; Bill Savitch.
Also see GIBSON, Johnny

JOHNNY and the Jammers
Singles: 7–inch
DART (131 "School Day Blues") . . 150-200   59
Member: Johnny Winter.
Also see WINTER, Johnny

JOHNNY AVERAGE BAND
Singles: 7–inch
BEARSVILLE 3-5   81
LPs: 10/12–inch 33rpm
BEARSVILLE 5-8   81
Member: Nikki Wills.

JOHNNY HATES JAZZ
Singles: 7–inch
VIRGIN 2-4   88
Picture Sleeves
VIRGIN 2-4   88
LPs: 10/12–inch 33rpm
VIRGIN 5-8   88

JOHNNY LEE
(John Lee Hooker)
Singles: 78rpm
DELUXE 10-15   52
Singles: 7–inch
DELUXE (6009 "(I Came to
See You Baby") 75-100   52
Also see HOOKER, John Lee

JOHNNY - O
Singles: 7–inch
DORE 5-10   59

JOHNNY T. ANGEL
Singles: 7–inch
BELL 3-5   74

JOHNS, Sammy
Singles: 7–inch
GRC 3-5   73-75
REAL WORLD 3-5   80
WARNER/CURB 3-5   76
LPs: 10/12–inch 33rpm
GRC 8-10   75

JOHNSON, Al
Singles: 7–inch
COLUMBIA 3-5   80
LPs: 10/12–inch 33rpm
COLUMBIA 5-8   80

JOHNSON, Al, and Jean Carn
Singles: 7–inch
COLUMBIA 3-5   80
Also see CARNE, Jean
Also see JOHNSON, Al

JOHNSON, Benny
Singles: 7–inch
TODAY 3-5   73

JOHNSON, Betty
Singles: 78rpm
BALLY 4-6   56-57

BELL (1054 "This Is the Thanks I Get") 5-10   54
(Seven-inch 78.)
RCA 4-6   55
Singles: 7–inch
ATLANTIC 5-10   58-60
BALLY 5-10   56-57
BELL 3-5   71
COED 5-10   60
DOT 5-10   60
NEW-DISC 10-20
RCA (6000 series) 5-10   55
RCA (8000 series) 4-8   63
REPUBLIC 5-10   60-61
WORLD ARTISTS 4-8   63
EPs: 7–inch 33/45rpm
RCA 8-12   57
LPs: 10/12–inch 33rpm
ATLANTIC (8017 "Betty Johnson") . . 15-25   58
ATLANTIC (8027 "Songs You Heard
When You Fell in Love") 15-25   59
BALLY (12011 "The Touch") 30-45   57

JOHNSON, Bubber
(Bubber Johnson and the Dreamers)
Singles: 78rpm
KING 4-8   55-57
MERCURY 10-15   52
Singles: 7–inch
KING (4000 series) 8-15   55-56
KING (5000 series) 5-10   57-60
MERCURY (8285 "Forget if You Can") 35-45   52
LPs: 10/12–inch 33rpm
KING (569 "Come Home") 40-55   57
KING (624 "Sweet Love Songs") 30-40   59

JOHNSON, Buddy
(Buddy Johnson and His Orchestra)
Singles: 78rpm
ATLANTIC 4-6   53
DECCA 4-8   42-54
MERCURY 4-6   53-56
RCA 4-6   56
Singles: 7–inch
ATLANTIC 5-10   53
DECCA (24996 "You Got to Walk
That Chalk Line") 15-25   50
DECCA (28907 "Talkin' About Another
Man's Wife") 10-20   53
DECCA (29058 "Handful of Stars") . . 10-20   54
MERCURY 5-10   53-56
RCA 5-10   56
ROULETTE 4-8   59
WING 5-10   56
LPs: 10/12–inch 33rpm
FORUM 10-15
MERCURY (20072 "Buddy Johnson
Wails") 25-35   58
(Monaural.)

MERCURY (60072 "Buddy Johnson
   Wails") 35-55   58
   (Stereo.)
MERCURY (20209 "Rock 'N' Roll") . . 30-40   58
MERCURY (20322 "Walkin") 20-30   58
WING (1211 "Rock 'N Roll
   Stage Show") 10-20   63
WING (12005 "Rock 'N Roll") 35-50   56
   Also see BROWN, Ruth
   Also see PRYSOCK, Arthur

JOHNSON, Buddy and Ella
Singles: 78rpm
MERCURY 4-6   56-57
Singles: 7-inch
MERCURY 5-10   56-61
ROULETTE 4-8   59
LPs: 10/12-inch 33rpm
MERCURY (20347 "Swing Me") 25-35   58
ROULETTE (R-25085 "Go Ahead and
   Rock and Roll") 20-30   59
   (Monaural.)
ROULETTE (SR-25085 "Go Ahead and
   Rock and Roll") 30-40   59
   Also see JOHNSON, Buddy

JOHNSON, Danny
Singles: 7-inch
FIRST AMERICAN 3-5   79
LPs: 10/12-inch 33rpm
FIRST AMERICAN 5-8   79
   Also see CHI-LITES

JOHNSON, General
(General Johnson and the Chairmen; Norman
Johnson)
Singles: 12-inch 33/45rpm
ARISTA 4-8   78
Singles: 7-inch
ARISTA 3-5   76-78
INVICTUS 3-5   71
SURFSIDE 3-5   80
LPs: 10/12-inch 33rpm
SURFSIDE (1001 "Success") 5-10   80
   Also see CHAIRMEN of the Board
   Also see SHOWMEN

JOHNSON, Howard
Singles: 12-inch 33/45rpm
A&M 4-6   82-85
Singles: 7-inch
A&M 2-4   82-85
LPs: 10/12-inch 33rpm
A&M 5-8   82-85
   Also see NITEFLYTE

JOHNSON, James Arthur
Singles: 7-inch
TUXEDO MUSIC 2-4   86

JOHNSON, Janice Marie
Singles: 7-inch
CAPITOL 2-4   84
   Also see TASTE of HONEY

JOHNSON, Jesse
(Jesse Johnson's Revue)
Singles: 12-inch 33/45rpm
A&M 4-6   85-88
   (Black vinyl.)
A&M 5-8   85-88
   (Colored vinyl.)
Singles: 7-inch
A&M 2-4   85-88
OLD TOWN 3-5   66
Picture Sleeves
A&M 2-4   85-88
LPs: 10/12-inch 33rpm
A&M 5-8   85-88
   Also see STONE, Sly
   Also see TIME

JOHNSON, Jimmy
(Jimmy Johnson and His Band featuring Hank
Alexander)
Singles: 7-inch
MAGNUM 4-8   65

JOHNSON, Kevin
Singles: 7-inch
MAINSTREAM 3-5   73

JOHNSON, L.V.
Singles: 7-inch
ICA 2-4   80-81

JOHNSON, Lonnie
(Lonnie Johnson and Victoria Spivey)
Singles: 78rpm
ALADDIN 4-8   47
ARCO 4-8
BLUEBIRD 4-8   44
DISC 4-8   46-47
GROOVE 4-8   55
HOLIDAY 4-8   48
KING 4-8   47-57
PARADISE 4-8   52
RCA 4-8   46-50
RAMA 4-8   56
SCORE 4-8   49
Singles: 7-inch
FEDERAL 5-10   60
GROOVE (5003 "He's a
   Jelly-Roll Baker") 15-25   55
KING (4201 "Tomorrow Night") 20-30   51
KING (4500 through 4600 series) . . . 15-25   51-53
KING (4700 through 4900 series) 5-10   54-56
KING (5000 series) 4-8   57-65
KING (6000 series) 3-5   70
PRESTIGE 4-8   60-64
RAMA (9 "My Woman Is Gone") 15-25   53
   (Black vinyl.)
RAMA (9 "My Woman Is Gone") 30-60   53
   (Colored vinyl.)
RAMA (14 "Stick with Me Baby") 15-25   53
RAMA (19 "It's Been So Long") 15-25   53
RAMA (20 "This Love of Mine") 15-25   53

EPs: 7–inch 33/45rpm
KING (267 "Lonnie Johnson") 25-40   54

LPs: 10/12–inch 33rpm
COLLECTOR'S CLASSICS 10-15
KING (520 "Lonesome Road") 75-100   56
KING (958 "12 Bar Blues") 15-20   66
KING (1083 "Tomorrow Night") 10-15   70
PRESTIGE 10-15   69
PRESTIGE BLUESVILLE 20-30   60-63
ROOTS N' BLUES 5-8   90

JOHNSON, Lonnie, and Elmer Snowden
LPs: 10/12–inch 33rpm
PRESTIGE BLUESVILLE 20-30   61

JOHNSON, Lonnie / George Dawson's Chocolateers
Singles: 78rpm
PARADE 4-8   52
Also see JOHNSON, Lonnie

JOHNSON, Lou
Singles: 7–inch
BIG HILL 4-8   64-66
BIG TOP 4-8   62-67
COTILLION 4-6   68-69
HILLTOP 4-8   64
VOLT 3-5   71
LPs: 10/12–inch 33rpm
COTILLION 10-12   69
VOLT 8-10   71

JOHNSON, Marv
Singles: 7–inch
GORDY 4-8   65-68
TAMLA (101 "Come To Me") ... 150-200   59
U.A. 5-10   59-64
EPs: 7–inch 33/45rpm
U.A. (10,007 "Marv Johnson") 30-40   60
U.A. (10,009 "Marv Johnson") 30-40   60
LPs: 10/12–inch 33rpm
U.A. (3081 "Marvelous
    Marv Johnson") 25-30   60
    (Monaural.)
U.A. (3081 "More Marv Johnson") ... 25-30   60
    (Monaural.)
U.A. (3187 "I Believe") 25-30   62
    (Monaural.)
U.A. (6081 "Marvelous
    Marv Johnson") 30-35   60
    (Stereo.)
U.A. (6081 "More Marv Johnson") ... 30-35   60
    (Stereo.)
U.A. (6187 "I Believe") 30-35   62
    (Stereo.)

JOHNSON, Michael
Singles: 7–inch
ATCO 3-5   73
EMI AMERICA 3-5   78-80

Picture Sleeves
EMI AMERICA 3-5   78
LPs: 10/12–inch 33rpm
ATCO 8-10   73
EMI AMERICA 5-8   78-82
Also see DENVER, BOISE & JOHNSON
Also see SYLVIA and Michael Johnson

JOHNSON, Orlando, and Trance
Singles: 12–inch 33/45rpm
EASYSTREET 4-6   83

JOHNSON, Paul
Singles: 7–inch
EPIC 2-4   · 88

JOHNSON, Robert
Singles: 7–inch
INFINITY 3-5   78
LPs: 10/12–inch 33rpm
INFINITY 5-8   78

JOHNSON, Rozetta
Singles: 7–inch
CLINTONE 3-5   70

JOHNSON, Ruby
Singles: 7–inch
NEBS 4-8   65
VOLT 4-8   66
V-TONE 8-10   60

JOHNSON, Syl
Singles: 12–inch 33/45rpm
BOARDWALK 4-6   82
Singles: 7–inch
FEDERAL 5-10   59-62
HI 3-5   73-76
SHAMA 3-5   77
TMP-TING 4-8   65
TWILIGHT 4-8   67-68
TWINIGHT 3-6   69
LPs: 10/12–inch 33rpm
HI 8-10   73-75
TWINIGHT 10-15   68

JOHNSON, Troy
Singles: 7–inch
KALLISTA 2-4   86

JOHNSTON, Tom
Singles: 7–inch
WARNER 3-5   79-81
LPs: 10/12–inch 33rpm
WARNER 5-8   81
Also see DOOBIE BROTHERS

JOINER, ARKANSAS JUNIOR HIGH SCHOOL BAND
Singles: 7–inch
LIBERTY 5-10   60-61

JOLI, France
Singles: 12–inch 33/45rpm
EPIC 4-6   83-85

Singles: 7-inch
EPIC	2-4	83-85
PRELUDE	3-5	79-82

LPs: 10/12-inch 33rpm
EPIC	5-8	83-85
PRELUDE	5-8	79-80

JOLLY, Pete
(Pete Jolly Trio)
Singles: 7-inch
A&M	3-5	68-69
AVA	4-6	63-64
COLUMBIA	3-6	66
MAINSTREAM	3-6	69

LPs: 10/12-inch 33rpm
A&M	8-12	68-71
AVA	10-20	63-64
CHARLIE PARKER	15-20	62
COLUMBIA	10-20	65
MGM	8-15	63
METROJAZZ	15-25	60
RCA (1100 through 1300 series)	20-30	55-57
TRIP	5-8	75

Also see MONTEZ, Chris

JOLO
Singles: 12-inch 33/45rpm
MEGATONE	4-6	84

JON & ROBIN
(Jon & Robin and the In Crowd)
Singles: 7-inch
ABNAK	4-8	67-68

LPs: 10/12-inch 33rpm
ABNAK	15-20	67-68

Members: Jon Abnor; Robin Abnor.

JON & VANGELIS
Singles: 7-inch
POLYDOR	3-5	77-83

LPs: 10/12-inch 33rpm
POLYDOR	5-8	80-83

Members: Jon Anderson; Vangelis.
Also see ANDERSON, Jon
Also see VANGELIS

JONAE, Gwen
Singles: 12-inch 33/45rpm
ARIAL	4-6	83
C&M	4-6	83

JONES, Brenda
(Brenda Lee Jones)
Singles: 7-inch
FLYING DUTCHMAN	3-5	76
MERCURY	3-5	74
RUST	4-8	66
WAVE	2-4	82

Also see DEAN & JEAN
Also see LEE, Brenda

JONES, Brenda, and "Groove" Holmes
Singles: 7-inch
FLYING DUTCHMAN	3-5	76

Also see HOLMES, Richard "Groove"
Also see JONES, Brenda

JONES, Brian
LPs: 10/12-inch 33rpm
ROLLING STONES (49100 "Pipes of Pan")	10-15	71

Promotional LPs
ROLLING STONES (49100 "Pipes of Pan")	30-35	71

(Includes poster and cue sheets.)
Also see ROLLING STONES

JONES, Corky
(Buck Owens)
Singles: 78rpm
DIXIE	15-25	56
PEP	20-40	56

Singles: 7-inch
DIXIE (505 "Rhythm and Booze")	75-100	56
PEP (107 "Hot Dog")	100-150	56

Also see OWENS, Buck

JONES, Davy
(David Jones)
Singles: 7-inch
BELL	8-10	71-72
COLPIX	10-20	65
MGM	10-15	72-73
MY FAVORITE MONKEE-DAVY JONES SINGS ("A Little Bit Me, a Little Bit You")	50-100	67

(Promotional issue only. No number used.)

Picture Sleeves
COLPIX (784 "What Are We Going to Do")	20-30	65

LPs: 10/12-inch 33rpm
BELL (6067 "Davy Jones")	15-25	71
COLPIX (CP-493 "David Jones")	20-25	65

(Monaural.)
COLPIX (SCP-493 "David Jones")	25-30	65

(Stereo.)
Also see MONKEES

JONES, Davy, and Mickey Dolenz
Singles: 7-inch
BELL	8-10	71
MCA	3-5	78

Picture Sleeves
MCA	3-5	78

Also see JONES, Davy
Also see DOLENZ, Micky
Also see NILSSON, Harry

JONES, Etta
Singles: 7-inch
KING	4-8	61-62
PRESTIGE	4-8	60-65
20TH FOX/WESTBOUND	3-5	75

LPs: 10/12-inch 33rpm
GRAND PRIX	8-12	
KING (544 "Etta Jones Sings")	40-60	58
KING (707 "Etta Jones Sings")	35-50	61
MUSE	5-8	77-81

PRESTIGE (7100 and 7200 series) .. 25-50 | 60-63
(Yellow labels.)
PRESTIGE (7100 and 7200 series) .. 15-25 | 65
(Blue labels.)
PRESTIGE (7400 through 7700
series) .... 10-20 | 67-70
ROULETTE .... 10-20 | 66
20TH FOX/WESTBOUND .... 5-10 | 75

JONES, George
(George Jones and the Jones Boys; George Jones
and Sonny Burns; George Jones and Jeanette Hicks)
Singles: 78rpm
DIXIE .... 15-25 | 56
MERCURY .... 4-8 | 57
STARDAY .... 5-10 | 54-57
Singles: 7–inch
D.............................. 4-8 | 65-66
EPIC .... 2-5 | 72-82
MERCURY (71000 and 72000 series) . 5-10 | 57-64
MUSICOR .... 3-6 | 65-71
PROMOTIONAL COPIES ("The
Race Is On") .... 15-25 | 64
(No label name other than "Promotional Copies," is
shown on disc.)
RCA .... 3-5 | 72-74
STARDAY (Except 100 and 200 series) . 3-8 | 64-71
STARDAY (100 and 200 series) ..... 10-20 | 54-57
(Black vinyl.)
STARDAY (264 "Just One More") ... 25-35 | 56
(Colored vinyl.)
U.A. .... 4-6 | 62-67
Picture Sleeves
MERCURY .... 8-12 | 62-64
MUSICOR .... 4-8 | 65
U.A. .... 4-8 | 62-63
EPs: 7–inch 33/45rpm
DIXIE (501 "Why Baby Why") ...... 25-50 | 56
(Not issued with cover.)
DIXIE (505 "Heartbreak Hotel") ..... 25-50 | 56
(Not issued with cover.)
DIXIE (525 "Don't Do This to Me") ... 15-25 | 59
(Has one George Jones track. Not issued with
cover.)
MERCURY .... 10-20 | 61
RECORD of the MONTH (280 "Heartbreak
Hotel") 30-40
(Colored vinyl.)
STARDAY .... 8-15 | 65
(Jukebox issues.)
LPs: 10/12–inch 33rpm
ACCORD .... 4-6 | 82
ALBUM GLOBE .... 5-8 | 81
ALLEGIANCE .... 4-8 | 84
AMBASSADOR 5-8
BUCKBOARD .... 5-8 | 76
BULLDOG 8-10
CAMDEN .... 5-8 | 72-74
COLUMBIA .... 5-8 | 80-83

EPIC .... 5-10 | 72-82
EVEREST .... 5-8 | 79
51 WEST .... 5-8 | 79-82
GRASS COUNTRY 8-10
GUEST STAR .... 20-30 | 63
GUSTO .... 5-8 | 78-81
I&M .... 5-8 | 82
KOALA 5-8
K-TEL 5-8
LIBERTY .... 5-8 | 82
MERCURY (8000 series) .... 5-10 | 72
MERCURY (20306 "14 Country
Favorites") .... 35-45 | 58
MERCURY (20462 "Country Church
Time") .... 35-45 | 59
MERCURY (20477 "White Lightning") 35-45 | 59
MERCURY (20621 through 20836) .. 20-30 | 60-63
(Monaural.)
MERCURY (20906 through 21048) .. 10-20 | 64-65
(Monaural.)
MERCURY (60257 through 60836) .. 20-35 | 60-63
(Stereo.)
MERCURY (60906 through 61048) .. 15-25 | 64-65
(Stereo.)
MOUNTAIN DEW 5-8
MUSIC DISC .... 6-10 | 69
MUSICOR .... 8-15 | 65-77
MUSICOR/RCA .... 8-10 | 74-75
NASHVILLE .... 6-10 | 70-71
PHOENIX 10 .... 5-8 | 81
PHOENIX 20 .... 5-8 | 81
PICADILLY .... 5-8 | 81
PICKWICK .... 4-8 | 80
PICKWICK/HILLTOP .... 8-12 | 69
POWER PAK .... 5-8 | 75
RCA .... 5-10 | 72-75
ROUNDER .... 5-8 | 82
RUBY 5-8
SEARS 8-12
STARDAY (100 series, except 101) .. 25-35 | 60-62
STARDAY (101 "The Grand Ole
Opry's New Star") .... 50-100 | 58
STARDAY (300 series) .... 15-30 | 65-66
STARDAY (400 series, except 401) ... 8-12 | 69
STARDAY (401 "George Jones Song
Book and Picture Album") .... 30-35 | 67
(With 32-page song booklet.)
STARDAY (401 "George Jones Song
Book and Picture Album") .... 15-20 | 68
(Without song booklet.)
STARDAY (3000 series) .... 5-8 | 77
STARDAY (90000 series) 8-12
SUNRISE 5-8
TIME-LIFE .... 5-8 | 81-82
TRIP .... 5-8 | 76
TROLLY CAR 5-8
UNART .... 8-12 | 67-68
U.A. (85 "Superpak") .... 10-15 | 71
U.A. (100 series) .... 5-8 | 73

U.A. (3000 series) 10-20 62-67
(Monaural.)
U.A. (6000 series) 12-25 62-69
(Stereo.)
WHITE LIGHTNING 12-18
WING 8-12 64-68
WING/PICKWICK 4-6
  Also see CHARLES, Ray, George Jones and Chet Atkins
  Also see DARRELL, Johnny / George Jones / Willie Nelson
  Also see HAGGARD, Merle, and George Jones
  Also see JONES, Thumper
  Also see PARTON, Dolly / George Jones
  Also see SMITH, Hank, and the Nashville Playboys

JONES, George, and David Allan Coe
Singles: 7-inch
COLUMBIA 2-4 81
  Also see COE, David Allan

JONES, George, and Melba Montgomery
Singles: 7-inch
MUSICOR 4-6 66-67
U.A. 4-6 63-66
LPs: 10/12-inch 33rpm
BUCKBOARD 5-8 76
GUEST STAR 20-30
LIBERTY 4-6 82
MUSIC DISC 6-10 69
MUSICOR 8-12 66-74
MUSICOR/RCA 8-10 74
U.A. (200 series) 5-8 73
U.A. (3000 series) 10-20 63-66
(Monaural.)
U.A. (6000 series) 12-25 63-66
(Stereo.)
  Also see MONTGOMERY, Melba

JONES, George / Buck Owens / David Houston / Tommy Hill.
LPs: 10/12-inch 33rpm
NASHVILLE 10-15
  Also see HOUSTON, David
  Also see OWENS, Buck

JONES, George, and Johnny Paycheck
Singles: 7-inch
EPIC 2-5 78-80
LPs: 10/12-inch 33rpm
EPIC 5-8 80
  Also see PAYCHECK, Johnny

JONES, George, and Gene Pitney
(George and Gene, with the Jordanaires)
Singles: 7-inch
MUSICOR 4-6 65-66
Picture Sleeves
MUSICOR 4-6 65
LPs: 10/12-inch 33rpm
DESIGN 6-10
INTERNATIONAL AWARD 8-10
MUSIC DISC 10-12 69

MUSICOR (3044 "George Jones and
Gene Pitney") 15-25 65
(Front cover shows title as "For the First Time! Two
Great Stars, George Jones and Gene Pitney.")
MUSICOR (3044 "George Jones and
Gene Pitney") 15-20 65
(Front cover shows title as "Recorded in Nashville,
Tennessee, George Jones and Gene Pitney.")
MUSICOR (3065 "It's Country
Time Again") 10-20 65
  Also see PITNEY, Gene

JONES, George, Gene Pitney, and Melba Montgomery
LPs: 10/12-inch 33rpm
MUSICOR 10-20 66
(Contains duets by these artists, but there are no
tracks where all three perform together.)
  Also see MONTGOMERY, Melba

JONES, George, and Ernest Tubb
Singles: 7-inch
FIRST GENERATION 2-4 81

JONES, George, and Tammy Wynette
(George, Tammy and Tina)
Singles: 7-inch
EPIC 2-5 71-80
LPs: 10/12-inch 33rpm
COLUMBIA 5-8 81
EPIC 8-12 71-81
TVP 5-8
  Also see JONES, George
  Also see WYNETTE, Tammy

JONES, Glenn
Singles: 12-inch 33/45rpm
RCA 4-6 83-85
Singles: 7-inch
JIVE 2-4 87-88
RCA 2-4 83-87
Picture Sleeves
JIVE 2-4 87
LPs: 10/12-inch 33rpm
JIVE 5-8 87
RCA 5-8 83-84
  Also see JETER, Genobia, and Glenn Jones
  Also see WARWICK, Dionne, and Glenn Jones

JONES, Grace
Singles: 12-inch 33/45rpm
ISLAND 4-6 83
MANHATTAN 4-6 85
Singles: 7-inch
BEAM JUNCTION 3-5 76-77
ISLAND 2-5 78-83
MANHATTAN 2-4 85-86
Picture Sleeves
MANHATTAN 2-4 86
LPs: 10/12-inch 33rpm
ISLAND 5-8 77-82
MANHATTAN 5-8 85-86

JONES, Howard
Singles: 12–inch 33/45rpm
ELEKTRA 4-6   83-85
Singles: 7–inch
ELEKTRA 2-4   83-89
Picture Sleeves
ELEKTRA 2-4   84-89
LPs: 10/12–inch 33rpm
ELEKTRA 5-8   83-89

JONES, Ignatius
Singles: 12–inch 33/45rpm
WARNER 4-6   83
Singles: 7–inch
WARNER 2-4   83

JONES, Jack
Singles: 7–inch
CAPITOL 4-8   59-60
KAPP 4-6   60-67
POLYDOR 2-4   83
RCA 3-6   67-77
Picture Sleeves
CAPITOL 4-8   59
KAPP 4-6   63-69
LPs: 10/12–inch 33rpm
CAMDEN 5-8   73
CAPITOL 10-20   59-64
KAPP 10-20   61-69
MCA 5-8   77
MGM 5-8   79
RCA 5-10   67-77
Also see ANDREWS, Julie and Andre Previn / Vic Damone /
Jack Jones / Marian Anderson
Also see ANN-MARGRET

JONES, Jimmy
(Jimmy Jones and the Jones Boys; Jimmie Jones and
the Savoys)
Singles: 7–inch
ARROW (717 "Heaven in
Your Eyes") 50-100   57
BELL 4-8   67
CUB 5-10   59-62

EPIC (9339 "Whenever
You Need Me") 50-75   59
MGM 3-5   78
PARKWAY 4-8   66
ROULETTE (4232 "Lover") 15-25   60
SAVOY (1586 "With All My Heart") . . 10-15   60
VEE JAY 4-8   63
Picture Sleeves
CUB (9072 "That's When I Cried") . . . 15-20   60
LPs: 10/12–inch 33rpm
JEN JILLUS 5-10   77
MGM (E-3847 "Good Timin") 35-45   60
(Monaural.)
MGM (SE-3847 "Good Timin") 45-60   60
(Stereo.)

JONES, Joe
Singles: 7–inch
ABC 3-5   73
RIC 5-10   60
ROULETTE 5-10   60-61
LPs: 10/12–inch 33rpm
PRESTIGE 10-15   69
ROULETTE (R-25143 "You Talk too
Much") 25-30   61
(Monaural.)
ROULETTE (SR-25143 "You Talk too
Much") 30-40   61
(Stereo.)

JONES, Johnny
Singles: 7–inch
FURY 4-8   68

JONES, Jonah
(Jonah Jones Quartet)
Singles: 78rpm
GROOVE 3-8   56
Singles: 7–inch
BETHLEHEM 4-6   59
CAPITOL 4-6   58-63
DECCA 3-6   65
GROOVE 5-10   56
EPs: 7–inch 33/45rpm
BETHLEHEM 5-15   55
CAMDEN 5-8   69
CAPITOL 5-10   58-59
GROOVE 5-15   56
RCA 5-10   59
LPs: 10/12–inch 33rpm
ANGEL 20-30   56
BETHLEHEM 20-40   55-60
CAPITOL (1000 through 2800 series) 10-25   58-67
(With "T" or "ST" prefix.)
CAPITOL (1600 series) 5-8   77
(With "SM" prefix.)
CAPITOL (11000 series) 5-8   75
DECCA 10-20   65-67
GROOVE 30-40   56
INNER CITY 5-8   81

MOTOWN 8-12   69
RCA 15-25   59-63
  Also see CHRISTY, June

JONES, Kay Cee
Singles: 78rpm
AMERICAN 4-8   56
DECCA 4-8   57
Singles: 7-inch
AMERICAN 8-12   56
CHANCELLOR 5-10   59
DECCA 5-10   57

JONES, Klinte
Singles: 7-inch
OH MY 4-6   84

JONES, Linda
(Linda Jones and the Whatnauts)
Singles: 7-inch
ATCO 4-8   65
BLUE CAT 4-8   65
COTIQUE 4-6   69
LOMA 5-10 67-68
NEPTUNE 4-6   69
STANG 3-5   72
TURBO 3-5   72
WARNER 4-6   69
LPs: 10/12-inch 33rpm
LOMA (5907 "Hyptomized") 15-25 67
TURBO 10-15 72

JONES, Michael
LPs: 10/12-inch 33rpm
NARADA LOTUS 5-8   88

JONES, Oran "Juice"
(Juice)
Singles: 7-inch
DEF JAM 2-4   86-87
LPs: 10/12-inch 33rpm
DEF JAM 5-8   86

JONES, Quincy
Singles: 7-inch
A&M 3-5   69-81
ABC 3-6   68
BELL 3-6   69
COLGEMS 3-6   68
IMPULSE 4-8   62
MERCURY 4-8   59-66
RCA 3-6   69
REPRISE 3-5   72
UNI 3-6   69
U.A. 3-5   70
Picture Sleeves
A&M 3-5   77-81
COLGEMS 4-8   68
LPs: 10/12-inch 33rpm
A&M 5-10 69-82
ABC (700 series) 8-12 73

ABC-PAR (149 "How I
  Feel About Jazz") 75-100 56
ABC-PAR (186 "Go West, Man") ... 75-100 57
ALLEGIANCE 5-8   84
COLGEMS 20-30 68
EMARCY (36083 "Jazz Abroad") ... 75-100 56
IMPULSE (11 "The Quintessence") .. 15-25 62
IMPULSE (9300 series) 8-12 78
LIBERTY 10-20 67
MFSL (078 "You've Got It Bad") 20-30 82
MERCURY (623 "Ndeda") 15-20 72
MERCURY (2014 "Around the World") 20-30 61
  (Monaural.)
MERCURY (20444 "Birth of a Band") 40-50 59
  (Monaural.)
MERCURY (20561 "Great,
  Wide World") 40-50 60
  (Monaural.)
MERCURY (20612 "I Dig Dancers") . 40-50 60
  (Monaural.)
MERCURY (20653 "Quincy Jones
  at Newport '61") 20-30 61
  (Monaural.)
MERCURY (20751 "Big Band
  Bossa Nova") 20-30 62
  (Monaural.)
MERCURY (20799 "Hip Hits") 20-30 63
  (Monaural.)
MERCURY (20863 through 21070) .. 10-20 64-66
  (Monaural.)
MERCURY (6014 "Around the World") 25-35 61
  (Stereo.)
MERCURY (60444 "Birth of a Band") 45-60 59
  (Stereo.)
MERCURY (60561 "Great,
  Wide World") 45-55 60
  (Stereo.)
MERCURY (60612 "I Dig Dancers") . 45-55 60
  (Stereo.)
MERCURY (60653 "Quincy Jones
  at Newport '61") 25-35 61
  (Stereo.)
MERCURY (60751 "Big Band
  Bossa Nova") 25-35 62
  (Stereo.)
MERCURY (60799 "Hip Hits") 25-35 63
  (Stereo.)
MERCURY (60863 through 61070) .. 15-25 64-66
PRESTIGE (172 "Sweden-American
  All Stars") 200-250 53
  (10-inch LP.)
QWEST 5-8   89
TRIP 5-8   74-76
U.A. 10-15 70
VERVE 15-20 67
WING 6-12 69
  Also see ASHFORD and SIMPSON
  Also see AUSTIN, Patti
  Also see ECKSTINE, Billy, and Quincy Jones

Also see FELICIANO, Jose, and Quincy Jones
Also see GILBERTO, Astrud
Also see JACKSON, Michael
Also see RIPERTON, Minnie
Also see U.S.A. for AFRICA
Also see VAUGHAN, Sarah, and Quincy Jones
Also see WASHINGTON, Dinah

JONES, Quincy, and Brothers Johnson
Singles: 7-inch
A&M 3-5   75
Also see BROTHERS JOHNSON

JONES, Quincy, and Trevin Campbell
Singles: 7-inch
QWEST 2-4   90

JONES, Quincy, with Ray Charles and Chaka Khan
Singles: 7-inch
QWEST 2-4   89
Picture Sleeves
QWEST 2-4   89
Also see CHARLES, Ray
Also see KHAN, Chaka

JONES, Quincy, and James Ingram
Singles: 7-inch
A&M 3-5   81
Also see INGRAM, James
Also see JONES, Quincy

JONES, Rickie Lee
Singles: 7-inch
WARNER 2-5   79-84
Picture Sleeves
WARNER 2-5   84
EPs: 10-inch 33/45rpm
WARNER (23805 "Girl at
  Her Volcano") 10-15   83
LPs: 10/12-inch 33rpm
GEFFEN 5-8   89
MFSL (089 "Rickie Lee Jones") 25-50   82
WARNER 5-8   79-84

JONES, Shirley
Singles: 7-inch
PHILADELPHIA INT'L 2-4   86-87
LPs: 10/12-inch 33rpm
PHILADELPHIA INT'L 5-8   86
Also see JONES GIRLS

JONES, Spencer
Singles: 12-inch 33/45rpm
NEXT PLATINUM 4-6   83
Singles: 7-inch
PROFILE 2-4   86

JONES, Spike
(Spike Jones and the City Slickers)
Singles: 78rpm
BLUEBIRD 10-20   42-43
RCA 5-15   46-55
VICTOR 8-12   44-45
Singles: 7-inch
LIBERTY 4-8   59-65

RCA (0500 series) 3-5   71
RCA (3287-89 "Spike
  Jones Favorites") 35-50   49
  (Three-disc boxed set.)
RCA (3600 through 6000 series) 10-20 49-55
  (Black vinyl.)
RCA (Colored vinyl) 20-40
WARNER 5-10   59
Picture Sleeves
RCA 20-30   53-54
EPs: 7-inch 33/45rpm
RCA 20-30   51-59
VERVE 15-25   56-57
LPs: 10/12-inch 33rpm
GLENDALE 5-8   78
LIBERTY 15-25   60-65
MGM 8-12   70
RCA (18 "Spike Jones
  Plays the Charleston") 50-100   51
RCA (1000 series) 5-8   75
RCA (2200 series) 15-25   60
RCA (2300 series) 5-8   77
RCA (3054 "Bottoms Up") 40-60   52
RCA (3128 "Spike Jones
  Kids the Classics") 40-60   53
RCA (3200 series) 8-12   71
RCA (3700 series) 4-8   80
RCA (3800 series) 10-15   67
  (With "LPM" or "LSP" prefix.)
RCA (3800 series) 5-8   81
  (With "AYL1" prefix.)
U.A. 5-8   75
VERVE (Except 8500 series) 20-40   56-59
VERVE (8500 series) 12-20   63
WARNER 15-25   59-60
Also see KATZ, Mickey, and His Orchestra

JONES, Tamiko
Singles: 7-inch
A&M 3-6   68-69
ARISTA 3-5   75
ATLANTIC 4-6   66
ATLANTIS 3-5   77
CONTEMPO 3-5   76
DECEMBER 4-6   67
GOLDEN WORLD 4-6   66
POLYDOR 3-5   79
SUTRA 2-4   86
20TH FOX 3-5   74
LPs: 10/12-inch 33rpm
A&M 10-12   68
DECEMBER 10-12   68

JONES, Tamiko, and Herbie Mann
Singles: 7-inch
ATLANTIC 4-6   66
LPs: 10/12-inch 33rpm
ATLANTIC 8-15   67
Also see JONES, Tamiko
Also see MANN, Herbie

JONES, Thelma
Singles: 7–inch
BARRY 4-8   66-68
COLUMBIA 3-5   78

JONES, Thumper
(George Jones)
Singles: 78rpm
STARDAY (240 "Rock-It") 20-30   56
Singles: 7–inch
STARDAY (240 "Rock-It") 75-100   56
EPs: 7–inch 33/45rpm
DIXIE (502 "Thumper Jones") 20-30   58
  (Contains three Jones tracks. Not issued with
  cover.)
LPs: 10/12–inch 33rpm
TEENAGE HEAVEN 8-12
  Also see JONES, George

JONES, Tom
Singles: 7–inch
EPIC 3-5   76-80
LONDON 3-5   77
MCA 3-5   79
MERCURY 2-4   81-85
PARROT 3-8   65-75
SYMBOL 4-8   65
TOWER 4-8   65
Picture Sleeves
PARROT (9737 through 9801) 4-8   65
PARROT (40000 series) 3-6   69-71
LPs: 10/12–inch 33rpm
EPIC 8-12   70-76
LONDON 5-8   77
MERCURY 5-8   81-85
PARROT 10-20   65-74
  Also see ART of Noise and Tom Jones
  Also see BARRY, John

JONES, Tom / Freddie and the Dreamers / Johnny Rivers
LPs: 10/12–inch 33rpm
TOWER (5007 "Three at the Top") . . . 15-20   65
  Also see FREDDIE and the Dreamers
  Also see JONES, Tom
  Also see RIVERS, Johnny

JONES GIRLS
Singles: 7–inch
CURTOM 3-5   75
EPIC 2-4   81
PARAMOUNT 3-5   74
PHILADELPHIA INT'L 3-5   79-82
RCA 2-4   83
LPs: 10/12–inch 33rpm
PHILADELPHIA INT'L 5-8   79-81
RCA 5-8   83
  Members: Shirley Jones; Brenda Jones; Valorie Jones.
  Also see JONES, Shirley

JONESES
Singles: 7–inch
MERCURY 3-5   74-83

VMP 3-5   72
Picture Sleeves
MERCURY 3-5   75
LPs: 10/12–inch 33rpm
EPIC 5-8   77
MERCURY 5-8   74-83
  Members: Glenn Dorsey; Harold Taylor; Cy Brooks; Ernest Holt;
  Wendell Noble; Reginald Noble; Larry Noble; Sam White.

JONZUN, Michael
Singles: 12–inch 33/45rpm
A&M 4-6   85
  (Black vinyl.)
A&M 5-8   85
  (Colored vinyl.)
Singles: 7–inch
A&M 2-4   85
  Also see JONZUN CREW

JONZUN CREW
Singles: 12–inch 33/45rpm
A&M 4-6   84-85
TOMMY BOY 4-6   82-85
Singles: 7–inch
A&M 2-4   84-85
TOMMY BOY 2-4   82-85
LPs: 10/12–inch 33rpm
A&M 5-8   84-85
TOMMY BOY 5-8   83-85
  Members: Michael Jonzun; Soni Jonzun; Steve Thorpe; Gordy
  Worthy.
  Also see JONZUN, Michael

JOPLIN, Janis
(Janis Joplin with Big Brother and Full Tilt)
Singles: 7–inch
COLUMBIA 4-8   69-72
SIMON and SHUSTER ("Janis") 3-5
  (Soundsheet. Included with the book *Janis*.)
LPs: 10/12–inch 33rpm
COLUMBIA (KCS-9913 "I Got Dem 'Ol Kozmic
  Blues Again, Mama") 20-25   69
COLUMBIA (PC-9913 "I Got Dem 'Ol Kozmic
  Blues Again, Mama") 5-8
COLUMBIA (30000 series) 10-15   71-75
  (With "KC" or "PG" prefix.)
COLUMBIA (30000 series) 12-20   74
  (With "CQ" prefix. Quad.)
COLUMBIA (30000 series) 5-8   82-84
  (With "PC" prefix.)
MEMORY 5-10
  Also see BIG BROTHER and the Holding Company

JOPLIN, Janis / Hot Tuna
LPs: 10/12–inch 33rpm
GRUNT ("The Last Interview") 25-35   72
  (Promotional issue only. Includes bonus Joplin
  home recording.)
  Also see HOT TUNA
  Also see JOPLIN, Janis

JORDAN, Frank
Singles: 7–inch
A-STREET 3-5   86

JORDAN, Jerry
(Jordans)
Singles: 7–inch
MCA 3-5   75-76
LPs: 10/12–inch 33rpm
MCA 5-8   75-76

JORDAN, Lonnie
Singles: 7–inch
BOARDWALK 2-4   82
MCA 3-5   78
U.A. 3-5   76-77
LPs: 10/12–inch 33rpm
MCA 5-8   78
Also see WAR

JORDAN, Louis
(Louis Jordan's Elk Rendezvous Band; Louis Jordan
and His Tympani 5)
Singles: 78rpm
DECCA (7500 through 8600 series) ... 5-10   38-43
DECCA (18000 through 30000 series) .. 4-8   44-50
VIK 4-8   56
Singles: 7–inch
ALADDIN (3223 "Whiskey Do
  Your Stuff") 20-30   54
ALADDIN (3227 "Ooo-Wee") 20-30   54
ALADDIN (3242 "A DollarDown") 25-35   54
ALADDIN (3246 "Messy Bessie") ... 20-30   54
ALADDIN (3249 "Louis' Blues") 20-30   54
ALADDIN (3264 "Put Some Money
  in the Pot") 20-30   54
ALADDIN (3270 "Fat Back and
  Corn Liquor") 20-30   54
ALADDIN (3279 "Gal, You Need
  a Whippin") 20-30   54
DECCA (20000 through 30000 series) 15-25 50-54
LOU-WA 5-10   60
MERCURY 10-20   56-58
PZAZZ 4-6   68
TANGERINE 4-8   62-66
VIK 8-12   56
WARWICK 5-10   60-61
X 8-12   55
EPs: 7–inch 33/45rpm
DECCA 15-25   56
MERCURY 15-25   57
LPs: 10/12–inch 33rpm
CLASSICAL JAZZ 5-8   82
DECCA (5035 "Greatest Hits") 10-20   68
DECCA (8551 "Let the Good
  Times Roll") 30-40   56
MCA 5-8   75-80
MERCURY (20242 "Somebody Up
  There Digs Me") 25-30   57
MERCURY (20331 "Man, We're
  Wailin") 25-30   58

SCORE (4007 "Go Blow Your Horn") . 65-85   57
TANGERINE 12-15   64
TRIP 8-10   75
WING 15-20   63
Also see CROSBY, Bing, and Louis Jordan
Also see FITZGERALD, Ella, and Louis Jordan

JORDAN, Stanley
LPs: 10/12–inch 33rpm
BLUE NOTE 5-8   85-87
EMI 5-8   88

JORDAN, Tenita
Singles: 7–inch
CBS ASSOCIATED 2-4   85

JORDANS: see JORDAN, Jerry

JOSEPH, David
Singles: 12–inch 33/45rpm
MANGO 4-6   83
Singles: 7–inch
MANGO 2-4   83

JOSEPH, Margie
(Margie Joseph and Blue Magic)
Singles: 12–inch 33/45rpm
H.C.R.C. 4-6   83
Singles: 7–inch
ATCO 3-5   75
ATLANTIC 3-5   72-78
COTILLION 2-5   76-84
H.C.R.C. 2-4   82-83
OKEH 4-8   68
VOLT 3-5   68-71
LPs: 10/12–inch 33rpm
ATLANTIC 8-10   73-74
H.C.R.C. 5-8   83
VOLT 10-12   71
Also see BLUE MAGIC
Also see HATHAWAY, Donny, and Margie Joseph

JOSIAS, Cory
Singles: 12–inch 33/45rpm
SIRE 4-6   83

JOURNEY
Singles: 7–inch
COLUMBIA 2-5   74-87
GEFFEN 2-4   85
Picture Sleeves
COLUMBIA 3-5   80-87
GEFFEN 2-4   85
EPs: 7–inch 33/45rpm
CSP 4-6   81
  (Nestle's candy promotional issue.)
LPs: 10/12–inch 33rpm
COLUMBIA (662 "LiveSampler") 12-15   75
  (Promotional issue only.)
COLUMBIA (914 "Journey") 12-15   75
  (Promotional issue only.)
COLUMBIA (30000 series) 5-10   75-82

COLUMBIA (46000 and 47000
series) 12-15 81-82
(Half-speed mastered.)
MFSL (144 "Escape") 40-60 85
Members: Steve Perry; Neal Schon; Aynsley Dunbar; Gregg
Rolie; Ross Valory; Robert Fleishman.
Also see CAIN, Jonathan
Also see PERRY, Steve
Also see SCHON, Neal, and Jan Hammer

JOVI, Bon: see BON JOVI

JOY, Roddie
Singles: 7-inch
PARKWAY 4-8 66-67
RED BIRD 5-10 65

JOY DIVISION
LPs: 10/12-inch 33rpm
FACTORY 5-8 81
QWEST 5-8 88

JOY of COOKING
(The Joy)
Singles: 7-inch
BROWNSVILLE 3-5 71
CAPITOL 3-5 71-73
FANTASY 3-5 77-78
LPs: 10/12-inch 33rpm
CAPITOL 8-10 71-72
FANTASY 5-10 77-78
Members: Terry Garthwaite; Toni Brown.

JUDAS PRIEST
Singles: 7-inch
COLUMBIA 3-5 79-84
Picture Sleeves
COLUMBIA 3-5 81
LPs: 10/12-inch 33rpm
COLUMBIA (Except picture discs) 5-8 77-90
COLUMBIA (99-1543 "Screaming
for Vengeance") 10-20 84
(Picture disc.)
COLUMBIA (99-1851 "Love Bites") .. 15-20 84
(Picture disc.)
COLUMBIA (39926 "Great Vinyl
and Concert Hits") 10-20 84
(Picture disc.)
JANUS 6-10 76
OVATION 5-8 80
RCA 5-8 83-84
VISA 5-8 78-81
Members: Rob Halford; K.K. Downing; Glenn Tipton; Ian Hill;
Dave Holland.

JUDDS
Singles: 7-inch
RCA 2-5 83-88
RCA/CURB 2-4 89-90
Promotional Singles
RCA 5-10 83-88
(Black vinyl.)
RCA (13673 "Had a Dream") 15-20 83
(Colored vinyl.)

RCA (13923 "Why Not Me") 10-20 84
(Colored vinyl.)
RCA (13673 "Had a Dream") 15-20 83
(Colored vinyl.)
LPs: 10/12-inch 33rpm
RCA 5-8 83-88
RCA/CURB 5-8 89-90
Members: Naomi Judd; Wynonna Judd.

JUICY
Singles: 12-inch 33/45rpm
ATLANTIC 4-8 83-84
PRIVATE I 4-6 85
Singles: 7-inch
ARISTA 2-4 83
ATLANTIC 2-4 83-84
CBS ASSOC 2-4 86
PRIVATE I 2-4 85-86
LPs: 10/12-inch 33rpm
ARISTA 5-8 83
ATLANTIC 5-8 84
Members: Jerry Barnes; Katreese Barnes

JUKES:
see SOUTHSIDE JOHNNY and the Asbury Jukes

JULIA LEE: see LEE, Julia

JULIAN, Don and the Meadowlarks
Singles: 78rpm
DOOTO 10-20 57
DOOTONE 20-30 55-56
RPM (399 "Love Only You") 25-50 54
RPM (406 "LSMFT Blues") 50-100 54
Singles: 7-inch
CLASSIC ARTISTS 3-5 89
DOOTO (424 "Blue Moon") 30-40 57
DOOTONE (359 "Heaven and
Paradise") 50-75 55
DOOTONE (367 "Always and
Always") 40-60 55
(Red label.)
DOOTONE (367 "Always and
Always") 30-40 55
(Maroon label.)
DOOTONE (372 "This Must
Be Paradise") 40-60 55
DOOTONE (394 "Please Love
a Fool") 30-50 56
DOOTONE (405 "I Am a Believer") .. 50-75 56
DYNAMITE (1112 "Heaven Only
Knows") 15-25 62
ORIGINAL SOUND (3 "Please Say
You Want Me") 20-30 58
ORIGINAL SOUND (12 "There's
a Girl") 15-25 58
RPM (399 "Love Only You") 125-200 54
RPM (406 "LSMFT Blues") 125-200 54
EPs: 7-inch 33/45rpm
DOOTO (203 "Don Julian and the
Meadowlarks") 25-50 58

DOOTONE (203 "Don Julian and the
Meadowlarks") 100-150   56
Members: Don Julian; Ronald Barrett; Earl Jones; Randy Jones;
Glen Reagan; Freeman Bralton; Benny Patricks.
Also see DEL-VIKINGS / Sonnets
Also see LARKS
Also see PENGUINS / Meadowlarks / Medallions / Dootones

JULIE
(Julie Budd)
Singles: 7–inch
A&M 2-4   84-85
TOM CAT 3-5   76

JULUKA
Singles: 7–inch
WARNER 2-4   83-84
LPs: 10/12–inch 33rpm
WARNER 5-8   83-84

JUMBO
Singles: 7–inch
PRELUDE 3-5   77
LPs: 10/12–inch 33rpm
PYE 5-8   77

JUMP 'N the SADDLE BAND
Singles: 7–inch
ATLANTIC 2-4   83
Picture Sleeves
ATLANTIC 2-4   83

JUNE & DONNIE
Singles: 7–inch
CURTOM (1935 "I Thank You Baby") . . . 4-6   68
Members: June Conquest; Donny Hathaway.
Also see HATHAWAY, Donny, and June Conquest

JUNGKLAS, Rob
Singles: 7–inch
MANHATTAN 2-4   87
Picture Sleeves
MANHATTAN 2-4   87
LPs: 10/12–inch 33rpm
MANHATTAN 5-8   86

JUNGLE BROTHERS
LPs: 10/12–inch 33rpm
IDLERS 5-8   88

JUNIE
(Walter Morrison; Junie Morrison)
Singles: 7–inch
COLUMBIA 2-4   81
EASTBOUND 3-5   74
20TH FOX/WESTBOUND 3-5   75-76
LPs: 10/12–inch 33rpm
20TH FOX/WESTBOUND 5-8   76
Also see FUNKADELIC
Also see MORRISON, Junie
Also see OHIO PLAYERS

JUNIOR
(Junior Giscombe)
Singles: 12–inch 33/45rpm
LONDON 4-6   84

MERCURY 4-6   83
Singles: 7–inch
CASABLANCA 2-4   83
LONDON 2-4   84-88
MERCURY 2-4   82-86
LPs: 10/12–inch 33rpm
MERCURY 5-8   82-83

JU-PAR UNIVERSAL ORCHESTRA
Singles: 7–inch
JU-PAR 3-5   77

JUPITER, Duke: see DUKE JUPITER

JUST US
Singles: 7–inch
ATLANTIC 3-5   71
COLPIX 4-8   66
KAPP 4-8   66-67
MINUTEMAN 4-8   66
Picture Sleeves
KAPP 4-8   66
LPs: 10/12–inch 33rpm
KAPP 10-15   66

JUST - ICE
LPs: 10/12–inch 33rpm
FRESH FIVE 5-8   88

JUSTIS, Bill
(Bill Justis and the Jury; Bill Justis Orchestra)
Singles: 78rpm
PHILLIPS INT'L 5-10   57
Singles: 7–inch
BELL 3-5   70
MONUMENT 3-5   76
PHILLIPS INT'L 5-10   57-59
PLAY ME 5-10   59
MCA 3-5   77
MONUMENT 4-8   66
NRC 4-8   60
SMASH 4-8   63-65
Picture Sleeves
SMASH 4-8   63
LPs: 10/12–inch 33rpm
HARMONY 8-10   72
PHILLIPS INT'L (1950 "Cloud 9") . . . 25-30   57
SMASH 15-20   62-66
SUN 8-10   69

JUVET, Patrick
Singles: 12–inch 33/45rpm
CASABLANCA 4-6   78-79
Singles: 7–inch
CASABLANCA 3-5   78-79
LPs: 10/12–inch 33rpm
CASABLANCA 5-8   78-79

K

KBC BAND
Singles: 7–inch
ARISTA 2-4   86
Picture Sleeves
ARISTA 2-4   86
LPs: 10/12–inch 33rpm
ARISTA 5-8   86
Members: Paul Kantner; Marty Balin; Jack Casady.
Also see JEFFERSON AIRPLANE

KC and the Sunshine Band
(KC; Sunshine Band)
Singles: 12–inch 33/45rpm
EPIC 4-6   82
MECA 4-6   83-85
SUNSHINE SOUND 4-6   81
Singles: 7–inch
CASABLANCA 2-4   80-83
EPIC 2-4   81-83
MECA 2-4   83-85
SUNSHINE SOUND 2-4   81
TK 3-5   73-81
Picture Sleeves
TK 3-5   76-78
LPs: 10/12–inch 33rpm
CASABLANCA 5-8   81
EPIC 5-8   81-82
MECA 5-8   84
SUNSHINE SOUND 5-8   81
TK 8-10   74-80
Also see DE SARIO, Teri, and K.C.
Also see WRIGHT, Betty

KGB
Singles: 7–inch
MCA 3-5   76
LPs: 10/12–inch 33rpm
MCA 8-10   76
Members: Mike Bloomfield; Barry Goldberg; Rick Gretch;
Carmine Appice; Ray Kennedy.
Also see BLOOMFIELD, Mike
Also see KENNEDY, Ray

K.I.D.
Singles: 12–inch 33/45rpm
SAM 4-6   81
Singles: 7–inch
SAM 3-5   81

KTP
Singles: 7–inch
MERCURY 2-4   87

KADO, Ernie: see K-DOE, Ernie

KADOR, Ernest: see K-DOE, Ernie

KAEMPFERT, Bert, and His Orchestra
Singles: 7–inch
DECCA 3-8   60-71
Picture Sleeves
DECCA 3-6   66
EPs: 7–inch 33/45rpm
DECCA 4-8   61
LPs: 10/12–inch 33rpm
CADENCE 10-15   61
DECCA 10-15   59-72
MCA 5-10   73-76

KAJAGOOGOO
(Kaja)
Singles: 12–inch 33/45rpm
EMI AMERICA 4-6   83-85
Singles: 7–inch
EMI AMERICA 2-4   83-85
Picture Sleeves
EMI AMERICA 2-4   83
LPs: 10/12–inch 33rpm
EMI AMERICA 5-8   83-85
Also see LIMAHL

KALEIDOSCOPE
Singles: 7–inch
A&M 3-5   73
EPIC (10117 "Elevator Man") 15-25   67
EPIC (10219 "Little Orphan Nannie") . 15-25   67
EPIC (10239 "I Found Out") 15-25   67
EPIC (10332 "Just a Taste") 15-25   68
EPIC (10481 "Lie to Me") 15-25   69
EPIC (10500 "Tempe, Arizona") 15-25   69
LPs: 10/12–inch 33rpm
BACK-TRAC 5-8   85
EPIC (24304 "Side Trips") 50-100   67
(Monaural.)
EPIC (24333 "Beacon from Mars") .. 40-60   67
(Monaural.)
EPIC (26304 "Side Trips") 50-75   67
(Stereo.)
EPIC (26333 "Beacon from Mars") .. 50-75   67
(Stereo.)
EPIC (26467 "Incredible
Kaleidoscope") 20-40   69
EPIC (26508 "Bernice") 15-20   70
PACIFIC ARTS 5-10   78
Members: David Lindley; Solomon Feldthouse; John Vidican;
John Welsh; Rick O'Neil; Brian Monsour; Chris Darrow.
Also see WILLIAMS, Larry, and Johnny Guitar Watson

KALIN TWINS
Singles: 7–inch
DECCA 5-10   58-62
Picture Sleeves
DECCA (30977 "Why Don't You
Believe Me") 8-12   59

EPs: 7–inch 33/45rpm

DECCA (2623 "Kalin Twins") 25-50   58
DECCA (2641 "Forget Me Not") 25-50   59

LPs: 10/12–inch 33rpm

DECCA (8812 "Kalin Twins") 50-75   58
VOCALION 10-20   66
   Members: Hal Kalin; Herb Kalin.
   Also see LEE, Brenda / Bill Haley and the Comets / Kalin Twins
   / Four Aces

KALLEN, Kitty

Singles: 78rpm

DECCA 4-8   54-57
COLUMBIA 4-8   54
MERCURY 4-8   51-54

Singles: 7–inch

BELL 4-6   67
DECCA 5-10   54-59
COLUMBIA (40000 series) ... 5-10   54
COLUMBIA (41000 series) 4-8   59-61
MGM 4-6   65
MERCURY 5-10   51-54
PHILIPS 4-6   66
RCA 4-8   63
20TH-CENTURY-FOX 4-8   64
U.A. 4-8   65

Promotional Singles

DECCA (78094 "Personal Introduction By
   Kitty Kallen to '54 Christmas
   Seal Song") 8-12   54
   (Single-sided promotional pressing.)

EPs: 7–inch 33/45rpm

DECCA 10-15   54-56
COLUMBIA 10-15   54
MERCURY 10-15   55

LPs: 10/12–inch 33rpm

COLUMBIA 10-20   60-61
DECCA (8397 "It's a Lonesome
   Old Town") 20-30   56
MCA 4-8   83
MERCURY (25206 "Pretty Kitty
   Kallen Sings") 30-50   55
   (10–inch LP.)
MOVIETONE 8-12   67
RCA 10-20   63
20TH-CENTURY-FOX 10-15   64
VOCALION 10-20   59
WING 10-15   63
   Also see ANN-MARGRET / Kitty Kallen / Della Reese
   Also see HAYES, Richard, and Kitty Kallen
   Also see JAMES, Harry, and His Orchestra

KALLEN, Kitty, and Georgie Shaw

Singles: 78rpm

DECCA 4-8   55

Singles: 7–inch

DECCA 5-10   55
   Also see KALLEN, Kitty
   Also see SHAW, Georgie

KALLMANN, Gunter, Chorus

Singles: 7–inch

4 CORNERS 4-6   65-68

LPs: 10/12–inch 33rpm

4 CORNERS 8-12   65-68
POLYDOR 5-10   70

KALYAN

Singles: 7–inch

MCA 3-5   77

LPs: 10/12–inch 33rpm

MCA 8-10   77

KAMIKAZE

Singles: 12–inch 33/45rpm

A&M 4-6   84

Singles: 7–inch

A&M 2-4   84

KAMON, Karen

Singles: 7–inch

COLUMBIA 2-4   84

Picture Sleeves

COLUMBIA 2-4   84

KANE, Big Daddy

LPs: 10/12–inch 33rpm

COLD CHILL 5-8   88-90

KANE, Madleen

Singles: 12–inch 33/45rpm

CHALET 4-6   82
TSR 4-6   85

Singles: 7–inch

CHALET 2-4   82
WARNER 3-5   78-79

Picture Sleeves

WARNER 3-5   78-79

LPs: 10/12–inch 33rpm

CHALET 5-8   82
WARNER 5-8   78-79

KANE, Paul
(Paul Simon)

Singles: 7–inch

TRIBUTE (128 "Carlos Dominguez") . 50-75   63
   (Copies crediting "Paul Simon" as the singer are
   bootlegs.)
   Also see SIMON, Paul

KANE GANG

Singles: 12–inch 33/45rpm

LONDON 4-6   86

Singles: 7–inch

CAPITOL 2-4   87
LONDON 2-4   86

Picture Sleeves

CAPITOL 2-4   87

LPs: 10/12–inch 33rpm

CAPITOL 5-8   87
LONDON 5-8   86
POLYGRAM 5-8   85

KANO
Singles: 7-inch

EMERGENCY 3-5   80
MIRAGE 2-4   81
LPs: 10/12-inch 33rpm
EMERGENCY 5-8   81
MIRAGE 5-8   81

KANSAS
Singles: 12-inch 33/45rpm

CBS ASSOCIATED 5-10   83
(Promotional only.)
MCA 4-8   88
(Promotional only.)
Singles: 7-inch
CBS ASSOCIATED 2-4   83
KIRSHNER 3-5   74-82
MCA (17290 "Power") 3-6   87
(CD mix on vinyl. Promotional issue only.)
MCA (50000 series) 2-4   86-87
Picture Sleeves
CBS ASSOCIATED 2-4   83
KIRSHNER 3-5   82
MCA 2-4   86-87
LPs: 10/12-inch 33rpm
CBS ASSOCIATED 5-8   83-84
KIRSHNER (30000 series) 8-12   74-82
KIRSHNER (40000 series) 15-25 81-82
(Half-speed mastered.)
MCA 5-8   86-88
Promotional LPs
BURNS MEDIA ("Two for the Show") . 15-25 78
KIRSHNER (34929 "Point of
Know Return") 50-75 79
(Picture disc.)
KIRSHNER (555 "Two for the Show") 10-15   78
Members: Dave Hope; Rich Williams; Phil Ehart; Kerry Livgren;
Robbie Shakespeare; Steve Walsh; Terry Brock.
Also see MORSE, Steve, Band
Also see STREETS
Also see WALSH, Steve

KANTNER, Paul
Singles: 7-inch

MALACO 3-5   79

KANTNER, Paul, and Grace Slick
Singles: 7-inch

GRUNT 3-5   72
Picture Sleeves
GRUNT 3-6   72
LPs: 10/12-inch 33rpm
GRUNT (0100 series) 8-10   71
GRUNT (2002 "Sunfighter") ... 10-15 71
(Includes booklet.)
GRUNT (4000 series) 5-8   82
Also see GRATEFUL DEAD
Also see JEFFERSON AIRPLANE
Also see SLICK, Grace

KANTNER, Paul, and the Jefferson Starship
Singles: 7-inch

RCA 3-6   71
Also see KANTNER, Paul
Also see JEFFERSON STARSHIP

KAPLAN, Gabriel
Singles: 7-inch

ABC 3-5   74
ELEKTRA 3-5   76-77
Picture Sleeves
ELEKTRA 3-5   77
LPs: 10/12-inch 33rpm
ABC 8-10   74

KAREN, Kenny
(Ken Karen)
Singles: 7-inch

BIG TREE 3-5   73
COLUMBIA (3-42264 "Oh Susie,
Forgive Me") 15-25 62
(Compact 33 Single.)
COLUMBIA (3-42452 "To Sandy,
with Love") 15-25 62
(Compact 33 Single.)
COLUMBIA (3-42638 "16 Years
Ago Tonight") 15-25 62
(Compact 33 Single.)
COLUMBIA (4-42264 "Oh Susie,
Forgive Me") 5-10   62
COLUMBIA (4-42452 "To Sandy,
with Love") 5-10   62
COLUMBIA (4-42638 "16 Years
Ago Tonight") 5-10   62
STRAND 5-10   59-60
Picture Sleeves
COLUMBIA (42264 "Oh Susie,
Forgive Me") 10-15 62
COLUMBIA (42452 "To Sandy,
with Love") 10-15 62

KARI, Sax
Singles: 78rpm

APOLLO 5-8   47
CHECKER 4-6   54
GREAT LAKES 5-10   54
STATES 4-8   53
Singles: 7-inch
CONTOUR 8-12   59
GREAT LAKES (1205 "Train
Ride") 25-50 54
JOB (1118 "Chocolate Fizz") . 25-50 57
STATES 10-20 53

KARI, Sax / Lena Gordon
Singles: 78rpm

CHECKER 4-8   54
Singles: 7-inch
CHECKER (803 "Disc Jockey
Jamboree") 15-25 54
Also see KARI, Sax

KARI, Sax, and the Quailtones
Singles: 78rpm
JOSIE 20-30   55
Singles: 7-inch
JOSIE (779 "Tears of Love") 100-150   55

KARL, Frankie, and the Dreams
Singles: 7-inch
D.C. 5-10   68

KARMA
LPs: 10/12-inch 33rpm
A&M 8-10   77

KARP, Charlie
(Charlie Karp and the Name Droppers)
LPs: 10/12-inch 33rpm
GRUDGE 5-8   87
Members: Charlie Karp; Mark Epstein; Reggy Marks; Tyger MacNeal; John Goldschmid; Dan Aldrich; Roger Ball; Corky Laing; Felix Cavaliere; Frank Sims; Jeff Bova.
Also see AVERAGE WHITE BAND
Also see CAVALIERE, Felix
Also see MILES, Buddy

KASANDRA
(Kasandrea and the Midnight Riders)
Singles: 7-inch
CAPITOL 4-8   68
IMPERIAL 5-10   60
LPs: 10/12-inch 33rpm
CAPITOL 10-15   68

KASENETZ - KATZ SINGING ORCHESTRAL CIRCUS
(Kasenetz-Katz Super Cirkus; Kasenetz-Katz Fighter Squadron)
Singles: 7-inch
BELL (966 "When He Comes") 5-10   71
(With 10CC.)
BUDDAH 4-8   68
EPIC 3-5   77
MAGNA-GLIDE 3-5   75
SUPER K 3-5   69-71
LPs: 10/12-inch 33rpm
BUDDAH 10-15   68
Also see MUSIC EXPLOSION
Also see NELSON, Teri
Also see 1910 FRUITGUM COMPANY
Also see OHIO EXPRESS
Also see 10CC

KASHIF
Singles: 12-inch 33/45rpm
ARISTA 4-6   83-86
Singles: 7-inch
ARISTA 2-4   83-88
LPs: 10/12-inch 33rpm
ARISTA 5-8   83-87
Also see G., Kenny, and Kashif
Also see MOORE, Melba, and Kashif
Also see WARWICK, Dionne, and Kashif

KASHIF and Mell'sa Morgan
Singles: 7-inch
ARISTA 2-4   87
Also see MORGAN, Meli'sa

KATFISH
Singles: 7-inch
BIG TREE 3-5   75

KATRINA and the Waves
Singles: 7-inch
CAPITOL 2-4   85-86
SBK 2-4   89
Picture Sleeves
CAPITOL 2-4   85-86
SBK 2-4   89
LPs: 10/12-inch 33rpm
CAPITOL 5-8   85-86
SBK 5-8   89

KATZ, Mickey, and His Orchestra
Singles: 78rpm
CAPITOL 4-6   51-57
Singles: 7-inch
CAPITOL 5-10   51-62
EPs: 7-inch 33/45rpm
CAPITOL 10-15   53-56
LPs: 10/12-inch 33rpm
CAPITOL (Except SM-298) 15-30   53-65
CAPITOL (SM-298 "Mickey Katz") 5-8   78
Also see JONES, Spike

KAUKONEN, Jorma
(Jorma Kaukonen and Vital Parts)
Singles: 7-inch
GRUNT 3-5   73
LPs: 10/12-inch 33rpm
GRUNT 8-12   73
RCA 5-10   79-81
Also see HOT TUNA
Also see JEFFERSON AIRPLANE

KAY, John
(John Kay and Steppenwolf; John Kay and the Sparrows)
Singles: 7-inch
DUNHILL 3-5   72-73
MERCURY 3-5   78
LPs: 10/12-inch 33rpm
COLUMBIA 10-20   69
DUNHILL 8-10   72-73
MERCURY 5-8   78
QWIL 5-8   87
Also see STEPPENWOLF

KAY GEES: see KAY-GEES

KAYAK
Singles: 7-inch
JANUS 3-5   78
MERCURY 2-4   80
LPs: 10/12-inch 33rpm
HARVEST 8-10   74
JANUS 5-10   75-79

MERCURY 5-8   80
   Also see WERNER, Max

KAYE, Danny
Singles: 78rpm
COLUMBIA 3-6   50-54
DECCA 3-6   50-56
Singles: 7–inch
COLUMBIA 5-10   50-54
DECCA 5-10   50-56
REPRISE 4-8   62
Picture Sleeves
REPRISE 5-10   62
EPs: 7–inch 33/45rpm
CAPITOL 5-10   58
COLUMBIA 10-20   49-54
DECCA 8-15   54-57
LPs: 10/12–inch 33rpm
CAMDEN 15-25   57
CAPITOL 15-25   58
COLUMBIA (6000 series) 20-40   49-54
  (10–inch LPs.)
DECCA (100 series) 10-20   63
DECCA (5000 series) 20-30   54
  (10–inch LPs.)
DECCA (8000 series) 20-30   54-59
DECCA (78000 series) 10-15   67
GOLDEN 5-10   62
HARMONY (7000 series) 15-25   57
HARMONY (7300 series) 8-15   64

KAYE, Danny, and Louis Armstrong
Singles: 7–inch
DOT 4-8   59-64
Picture Sleeves
DOT 5-10   59
   Also see ARMSTRONG, Louis
   Also see KAYE, Danny

KAYE, Mary
(Mary Kaye Trio)
Singles: 78rpm
CAPITOL 3-6   52
DECCA 3-6   55-56
RCA 3-6   54
Singles: 7–inch
BLUE-J 4-8
CAMELOT 4-6   67
CAPITOL 5-10   52
DECCA 5-10   55-56
LECTRON 4-6   65
RCA 5-10   54
VERVE 4-8   60
WARNER 4-8   59
EPs: 7–inch 33/45rpm
DECCA 5-10   56
LPs: 10/12–inch 33rpm
COLUMBIA 8-15   62
DECCA 10-25   56
MOVIETONE 8-12   67
20TH FOX 8-15   64

VERVE 10-15   60-62
WARNER 10-20   59
   Also see BYRNES, Edd "Kookie," with Joanie Sommers and the
   Mary Kaye Trio

KAYE, Sammy, and His Orchestra
Singles: 78rpm
COLUMBIA 3-6   50-57
Singles: 7–inch
COLUMBIA 5-10   50-60
DECCA 4-6   60-70
PROJECT 3 3-5   72
EPs: 7–inch 33/45rpm
COLUMBIA 5-15   50-60
DECCA 4-6   64
RCA 5-15   52-53
LPs: 10/12–inch 33rpm
CAMDEN 10-25   53-56
COLUMBIA 10-25   50-62
DECCA 8-15   60-70
HARMONY 5-10   59-68
MCA 5-10   74
PROJECT 3 5-8   72
RCA 5-10   68-72
VOCALION 5-10   71

KAY-GEES
Singles: 7–inch
DE-LITE 3-5   78-79
GANG 3-5   74-76
LPs: 10/12–inch 33rpm
DELITE 5-8   78-79
GANG 5-10   75

KAYLI, Bob
(Robert Gordy)
Singles: 7–inch
ANNA (1104 "Never More") 15-25   59
CARLTON (482 "Everyone Was
  There") 10-15   58
GORDY (7008 "Hold On Pearl") 20-30   62
TAMLA (54051 "Small Sad Sam") . . . 15-25   61

K-DOE, Ernie
(Ernest Kador; Ernie Kado)
Singles: 78rpm
SPECIALTY 5-10   55
Singles: 7–inch
DUKE 4-8   64-69
EMBER 5-10   59-61
INSTANT 4-8   63-64
MINIT 5-10   59-63
SPECIALTY 10-20   55
LPs: 10/12–inch 33rpm
JANUS 8-10   71
MINIT (0002 "Mother in Law") 50-80   61
   Also see SPELLMAN, Benny
   Also see THOMAS, Irma / Ernie K-Doe / Showmen / Benny
   Spellman.

KEANE BROTHERS
Singles: 12–inch 33/45rpm
ABC 4-8   79

KELLY, Paul
Singles: 7–inch
DIAL	4-8	65-68
HAPPY TIGER	3-5	70
PHILIPS	4-8	66-68
WARNER	3-5	73-76

Picture Sleeves
PHILIPS	4-8	66

LPs: 10/12–inch 33rpm
HAPPY TIGER	8-10	70
WARNER	8-10	72-76

Also see TEX, Joe

KELLY BROTHERS
Singles: 7–inch
EXCELLO	4-8	67-69
SIMS	4-8	65-67

LPs: 10/12–inch 33rpm
EXCELLO	10-20	68

Also see KING PINS

KELTON, Gene
Singles: 7–inch
AVATAR	2-4	87

KEMP, Johnny
Singles: 7–inch
COLUMBIA	2-4	86-89

Picture Sleeves
COLUMBIA	2-4	86-89

LPs: 10/12–inch 33rpm
COLUMBIA	5-8	86-89

KENDALL, Jeannie
(Jeanie Kendall)
Singles: 7–inch
DOT	3-5	72-73

Also see KENDALLS

KENDALL SISTERS
Singles: 7–inch
ARGO	4-6	57-58

KENDALLS
Singles: 7–inch
DOT	3-5	72-73
MCA/CURB	2-4	86
MERCURY	2-4	81-85
OVATION	3-5	77-80
STOP	3-5	70
U.A.	3-5	75-76
VARSITY	10-15	69

LPs: 10/12–inch 33rpm
DOT	8-12	72
GUSTO	5-8	78
MCA/CURB	5-8	86
MERCURY	5-8	81-85
OVATION	5-10	77-80
STOP	10-15	70
POWER PAK	5-8	74

Members: Jeannie Kendall; Royce Kendall.
Also see KENDALL, Jeannie

KENDRICK, Nat, and the Swans
Singles: 7–inch
DADE (1000 series)	5-10	59-60
DADE (5000 series)	4-8	63

Members: Nat Kendrick; J.C. Adams; Bobby Roach; Fats
Gonder: Bernard Odum.

KENDRICKS, Eddie
(Eddie Kendrick)
Singles: 7–inch
ARISTA	3-5	78-80
ATLANTIC	2-4	80-81
CORNER STREET	2-4	84
RCA	2-4	85-88
TAMLA	3-5	71-77

LPs: 10/12–inch 33rpm
ARISTA	5-8	78
ATLANTIC	5-8	81
MOTOWN	5-8	75-82
MS. DIXIE	5-8	83
TAMLA	8-10	71-78

Also see HALL, Daryl, John Oates, David Ruffin and Eddie
Kendrick
Also see RUFFIN, David, and Eddie Kendricks
Also see TEMPTATIONS

KENDRICKS, Linda
Singles: 12–inch 33/45rpm
AIRWAVE	4-6	84

Singles: 7–inch
AIRWAVE	2-4	84

KENNEDY, Edward M.
LPs: 10/12–inch 33rpm
RCA	8-15	65

KENNEDY, Jacqueline
LPs: 10/12–inch 33rpm
AUDIO FIDELITY (703 "Jacqueline Kennedy")	8-15	66

(Jackie's story as well as excerpts of some of her
speeches given as First Lady.)

KENNEDY, John Fitzgerald
LPs: 10/12–inch 33rpm
CAEDMON	5-10	64
CHALLENGE	8-15	64
COLPIX	10-20	64
COLUMBIA	10-20	65
DECCA	10-20	63
DIPLOMAT	5-15	63
DOCUMENTARIES UNLIMITED	10-20	63
GATEWAY	8-15	64
HARMONIA	8-15	64
LEGACY	10-20	65
PALACE	8-15	64
PHILIPS	8-15	64
PICKWICK	8-12	63
PREMIER	10-20	63
RCA	8-15	64
REGINA	5-15	64
SOMERSET	5-15	63

20TH FOX 10-20   63

Most of the albums listed above were released as a tribute of some type to President Kennedy after his assassination on November 22, 1963. Most contain excerpts of his speeches.

KENNEDY, John Fitzgerald / Richard M. Nixon
LPs: 10/12-Inch 33rpm
COLUMBIA 10-15   68
Also see KENNEDY, John Fitzgerald

KENNEDY, Joyce
Singles: 7-inch
A&M 2-4   84-85
LPs: 10/12-inch 33rpm
A&M 5-8   84
Also see MOTHER'S FINEST

KENNEDY, Joyce, and Jeffrey Osborne
Singles: 7-inch
A&M 2-4   84
Also see KENNEDY, Joyce
Also see OSBORNE, Jeffrey

KENNEDY, Mike
Singles: 7-inch
ABC 3-5   72
LPs: 10/12-inch 33rpm
ABC 8-10   72
Also see LOS BRAVOS

KENNEDY, Ray
Singles: 7-inch
ARC 3-5   80
LPs: 10/12-inch 33rpm
CREAM 10-12   72
Also see KGB

KENNEDY, Robert Francis
LPs: 10/12-Inch 33rpm
COLUMBIA 8-15   68

KENNER, Chris
Singles: 78rpm
BATON 5-10   55
IMPERIAL 5-10   57
Singles: 7-inch
BATON (220 "Don't Let Her
Pin That Charge") 15-25   55
IMPERIAL 10-20   57-58
INSTANT 5-10   61-64
PRIGAN 10-15   61
RON 5-10   61
UPTOWN 4-8   65
VALIANT (3229 "I Like It Like
That") 25-35   61
LPs: 10/12-inch 33rpm
ATLANTIC (8117 "Land of
1,000 Dances") 15-25   66

KENNY, Bill
(Bill Kenny and the Song Spinners)
Singles: 78rpm
DECCA 3-5   50-53
VIK 3-5   56
X 3-5   55
Singles: 7-inch
DECCA 5-10   50-53
MERCURY 4-8   62
TEL 4-8   59
VIK 5-8   56
WARWICK 4-8   60
X 5-8   55
LPs: 10/12-inch 33rpm
DECCA (5333 "Precious Memories") . 15-25   51
(10-inch LP.)
MERCURY 10-15   62
Also see INK SPOTS

KENNY & JOHNNY
Singles: 7-inch
PHILADELPHIA INT'L 2-4   86
Members: Kenny Whitehead; Johnny Whitehead.
Also see WHITEHEAD, Kenny and Johnny

KENNY and the Cadets
Singles: 7-inch
RANDY (422 "Barbie") 350-500   62
(Black vinyl.)
RANDY (422 "Barbie") 500-750   62
(Colored vinyl.)
Members: Brian Wilson; Carl Wilson; Al Jardine; Audree Wilson.
Also see BEACH BOYS

KENNY G: see G., Kenny

KENT, Al
Singles: 7-inch
BARITONE 4-8   60
WINGATE 4-8   65
WIZARD 5-10   59

KENTON, Stan, and His Orchestra
Singles: 78rpm
CAPITOL 3-6   45-57
Singles: 7-inch
CAPITOL (Purple labels) 4-10   50-61
CAPITOL (Orange and Yellow labels) . . 3-6   61-68
EPs: 7-inch 33/45rpm
CAPITOL 5-15   50-59
LPs: 10/12-inch 33rpm
BRIGHT ORANGE 5-8   73
CAPITOL (H-155 "Encores") 50-75   49
(10-inch LP.)
CAPITOL (T-155 "Encores") 25-50   55
CAPITOL (H-167 "Artistry in Rhythm") 50-75   49
(10-inch LP.)
CAPITOL (T-167 "Artistry in Rhythm") 25-50   55
(With "T" prefix.)
CAPITOL (DT-167 "Artistry
in Rhythm") 5-10   69
(Stereo.)

CAPITOL (SM-167 "Artistry in Rhythm") 5-8	75	
CAPITOL (H-172 "Progressive Jazz") 50-75	50	
(10–inch LP.)		
CAPITOL (T-172 "Progressive Jazz") . 25-50	55	
CAPITOL (H-190 "Milestones") 50-75	50	
(10–inch LP.)		
CAPITOL (T-190 "Milestones") 25-50	55	
CAPITOL (H-248 "Stan Kenton		
Presents") 50-75	50	
(10–inch LP.)		
CAPITOL (T-248 "Stan Kenton		
Presents") 25-50	55	
CAPITOL (H-353 "City of Glass") 50-75	52	
(10–inch LP.)		
CAPITOL (T-353 "City of Glass") 25-50	55	
CAPITOL (H-358 "Classics") 50-75	52	
(10–inch LP.)		
CAPITOL (T-358 "Classics") 25-50	55	
CAPITOL (H-386 "This Is an		
Orchestra") 50-75	53	
(10–inch LP.)		
CAPITOL (H-462 "Standards") 50-75	53	
(10–inch LP.)		
CAPITOL (T-462 "Standards") 25-50	55	
CAPITOL (H-525 "Showcase") 50-75	54	
(10–inch LP.)		
CAPITOL (W-525 "Showcase") 25-75	55	
CAPITOL (H-526 "Showcase") 50-75	54	
(10–inch LP.)		
CAPITOL (W-526 "Showcase") 25-50	55	
CAPITOL (305 "Hair") 5-10	69	
CAPITOL (600 through 1200 series) . 15-25	56-59	
CAPITOL (1300 through 2900 series) 10-20	60-68	
CAPITOL (11000 and 12000 series) ... 5-8	72-80	
CAPITOL (16000 series) 4-6	81	
CREATIVE WORLD 5-8	71-80	
HINDSIGHT 4-8	84	
LONDON 5-8	72-77	
MARK '56 5-8	77	
MFSL (091 "Stan Kenton		
Plays Wagner") 15-25	82	

Also see CHRISTY, June, and Stan Kenton
Also see COLE, Nat "King"
Also see FERGUSON, Maynard

KENTON, Stan, and Tex Ritter
LPs: 10/12–inch 33rpm

CAPITOL (T-1757 "Stan Kenton		
and Tex Ritter") 40-60	62	
(Monaural.)		
CAPITOL (ST-1757 "Stan Kenton		
and Tex Ritter") 50-75	62	
(Stereo.)		

Also see KENTON, Stan
Also see RITTER, Tex

KERMIT
(Jim Henson)
Singles: 7–inch
ATLANTIC 3-5   79

KERMIT / Fozzie Bear
(Jim Henson)
Singles: 7–inch
ATLANTIC 3-5   80

Also see KERMIT
Also see HENSON, Jim
Also see MUPPETS

KERR, Anita
(Anita Kerr Singers; Anita Kerr Quartette)
Singles: 78rpm
DECCA 3-6   51-57
Singles: 7–inch

AMPEX 3-5	71
DECCA (27000 through 30000 series) 5-10	51-60
DECCA (31000 through 33000 series) . 3-6	60-72
DOT 3-5	69-70
RCA 3-8	63-75
WARNER 3-6	66-68

LPs: 10/12–inch 33rpm

AMPEX 5-8	71
BAINBRIDGE 4-6	81
CAMDEN 5-10	68
CENTURY 4-8	79
DECCA 8-15	60-69
DOT 5-10	69-70
RCA 8-15	62-77
VOCALION 5-10	70
WARNER 8-12	66
WORD 4-8	75-77

There are hundreds of artists whose recordings
contain the background vocals of the Anita Kerr
Singers, some of whom are cross referenced
below.

Also see ANDERSON, Bill
Also see ANITA and the So-and-Sos
Also see ANN-MARGRET
Also see ATKINS, Chet
Also see CLINE, Patsy
Also see FOLEY, Red
Also see HELMS, Bobby
Also see LEE, Brenda
Also see LITTLE DIPPERS
Also see PRESLEY, Elvis
Also see REEVES, Jim

KERR, George
Singles: 7–inch
ALL PLATINUM 3-5   70

KERSHAW, Nik
LPs: 10/12–inch 33rpm
MCA 5-8   84-85

KEY, Troyce
Singles: 7–inch
WARNER 10-20   58-59

Also see COCHRAN, Eddie
Also see VELOURS

KHAN, Chaka
Singles: 12–inch 33/45rpm
WARNER 4-6   79-87
Singles: 7–inch
ATLANTIC 2-4   78-87

KILZER, John
LPs: 10/12–inch 33rpm

GEFFEN	5-8	88

KIM, Andy
Singles: 7–inch

ABC	3-5	74
CAPITOL	3-5	74-76
RED BIRD	4-8	65
STEED	3-6	68-71
TCF	4-8	64
20TH FOX	4-8	68
UNI	3-5	72-73
U.A.	4-8	63

Picture Sleeves

CAPITOL	3-5	74
STEED	4-6	69-71

LPs: 10/12–inch 33rpm

CAPITOL	8-12	74-75
DUNHILL	8-12	74
STEED	10-15	68-71
UNI	8-12	72-73

Also see ARCHIES

KIMBERLY, Adrian
(Don Everly)
Singles: 7–inch

CALLIOPE (6501 "Pomp and Circumstance")	10-20	61
CALLIOPE (6503 "Greensleeves")	25-35	61
CALLIOPE (6504 "Draggin' Dragon")	25-35	61

Also see EVERLY, Don

KIMBERLYS
Singles: 7–inch

CANADIAN AMERICAN	4-8	62-63
COLUMBIA	4-8	65-66
HAPPY TIGER	3-5	70-71
RCA	3-5	69

LPs: 10/12–inch 33rpm

HAPPY TIGER	8-12	70

Also see JENNINGS, Waylon

KIMBLE, Neal
Singles: 7–inch

VENTURE	4-8	68

KIME, Warren, and His Brass Impact Orchestra
LPs: 10/12–inch 33rpm

COMMAND	5-10	67

KIMMEL, Tom
Singles: 7–inch

MERCURY	2-4	87

Picture Sleeves

MERCURY	2-4	87

LPs: 10/12–inch 33rpm

MERCURY	5-8	87

KINDLER, Steven
LPs: 10/12–inch 33rpm

GLOBAL PACIFIC	5-8	88

KINETICS
LPs: 10/12–inch 33rpm

ETIQUETTE	5-8	86

Members: Roger Rogers; Daniel Davison; Roger Baldwin; Denney Goodhew.

KING
(Paul King)
Singles: 12–inch 33/45rpm

EPIC	4-6	85

Singles: 7–inch

EPIC	2-4	85

Picture Sleeves

EPIC	2-4	85

LPs: 10/12–inch 33rpm

ELEKTRA	5-8	80-81
EPIC	5-8	85

KING, Albert
Singles: 78rpm

PARROT	10-20	50

Singles: 7–inch

BOBBIN	5-10	59-62
COUN-TREE	4-8	65
KING	4-8	61-63
PARROT (798 "Bad Luck Blues")	100-125	53
STAX	3-8	66-74
TOMATO	3-5	78-79
UTOPIA	3-5	76-77

LPs: 10/12–inch 33rpm

ATLANTIC	8-12	69-82
FANTASY	5-8	
KING (852 "Big Blues")	40-60	63
KING (1000 series)	10-12	69
STAX (Except 723 and 2000 series)	8-12	72-81
STAX (723 "Born Under a Bad Sign")	15-25	67
STAX (2000 series)	10-15	68-71
STAX (8000 series)	5-10	90
TOMATO	5-8	77-79
UTOPIA	8-10	76-77

Also see LITTLE MILTON and Albert King

KING, Albert, and Otis Rush
LPs: 10/12–inch 33rpm
CHESS 10-15   69
　Also see KING, Albert
　Also see RUSH, Otis

KING, Anna
Singles: 7–inch
LUDIX 4-8   63
MALIBU 4-8   61
RUST 4-8   64
SMASH 4-8   64-65
LPs: 10/12–inch 33rpm
SMASH (27059 "Back to Soul") 15-20   64
　(Monaural.)
SMASH (67059 "Back to Soul") 20-25   64
　(Stereo.)

KING, Anna, and Bobby Byrd
Singles: 7–inch
SMASH 4-8   64
　Also see BYRD, Bobby
　Also see KING, Anna

KING, B.B.
Singles: 78rpm
BULLET (309 "Miss Martha King") ... 25-50   49
BULLET (315 "Got the Blues") 25-50   49
RPM 5-10   50-57
Singles: 7–inch
ABC 3-8   66-78
ABC-PAR 4-8   62-66
BLUESWAY 4-6   67-70
KENT (300 series) 5-10   58-64
KENT (400 series) 4-8   64-68
KENT (4000 and 5000 series) 3-5
MCA 2-4   80-85
PAULA 2-4   81
RPM (339 "3 O'clock Blues") 25-50   52
RPM (348 "Fine Looking Woman") .. 25-50   52
RPM (355 "Shake It Up and Go") 25-50   52
RPM (363 "You Didn't Want Me") 25-50   52
RPM (360 "Someday, Somewhere") . 20-40   52
RPM (380 "Woke Up This Morning") . 20-40   53
RPM (374 "Story from My
　Heart and Soul") 20-40   53
RPM (386 "Please Love Me") 20-40   53
RPM (391 "Neighbourhood Affair") ... 20-40   53
RPM (395 "Why Did You Love Me") .. 20-40   53
RPM (403 through 501) 10-20   54-57
Picture Sleeves
BLUESWAY 4-6   69
MCA 2-4   85
EPs: 7–inch 33/45rpm
ABC-PAR 8-10   63
　(Jukebox issue only.)
LPs: 10/12–inch 33rpm
ABC 8-10   70-78
ABC-PAR 15-25   63-65
ACCORD 5-8   82
BLUESWAY 10-15   67-73

COMMAND 10-12   74
CROWN (Except 147) 15-25   59-63
CROWN (147 "B.B. King Wails") 15-25   60
　(Black vinyl.)
CROWN (147 "B.B. King Wails") ... 75-125   60
　(Colored vinyl.)
CRUSADERS 5-8   82
CUSTOM 8-10
FANTASY 5-8   81
GALAXY 15-20   63
KENT 10-15   64-73
MCA 5-8   79-85
PICKWICK 5-10
UNITED 10-12
　Also see BLAND, Bobby, and B.B. King
　Also see CRUSADERS, and B.B. King
　Also see SIMPSONS

KING, B.B., Jr., and the Blues Messengers
Singles: 7–inch
L. BROWN 4-8   64

KING, Ben E.
Singles: 7–inch
ATLANTIC 3-5   75-81
ATCO (Except 6100 and 6200 series) .. 4-6   64-69
ATCO (6100 and 6200 series) 4-8   60-64
ELEKTRA 3-5   76
MANDALA 3-5   72-73
MAXWELL 3-6   69
Picture Sleeves
ATLANTIC 3-5   86
LPs: 10/12–inch 33rpm
ATCO (133 "Spanish Harlem") 20-30   61
　(Monaural.)
ATCO (SD-133 "Spanish Harlem") .. 30-40   61
　(Monaural.)
ATCO (137 "For Soulful Lovers") 20-30   62
　(Monaural.)
ATCO (SD-137 "For Soulful Lovers") . 25-35   62
　(Stereo.)
ATCO (142 "Don't Play That Song") . 20-30   62
　(Monaural.)
ATCO (SD-142 "Don't Play
　That Song") 25-35   62
　(Stereo.)
ATCO (165 "Greatest Hits") 20-30   64
　(Monaural.)
ATCO (SD-165 "Greatest Hits") 25-35   64
　(Stereo.)
ATCO (174 "Seven Letters") 20-30   65
　(Monaural.)
ATCO (SD-174 "Seven Letters") 25-35   65
　(Stereo.)
ATLANTIC 8-12   75-81
KING 10-15
MANDALA 8-12   72
MAXWELL 10-15   70
　Also see BAKER, Lavern, and Ben E. King
　Also see BONDS, Gary "U.S."
　Also see DRIFTERS

Also see EARL-JEAN
Also see HALOS
Also see LITTLE EVA
Also see SOUL CLAN

KING, Ben E., and the Average White Band
Singles: 7–inch
ATLANTIC 3-5   77
LPs: 10/12–inch 33rpm
ATLANTIC 8-10   77
Also see AVERAGE WHITE BAND

KING, Ben E., and Dee Dee Sharp
Singles: 7–inch
ATCO 4-8   68
Also see KING, Ben E.
Also see SHARP, Dee Dee

KING, Bobby
(Featuring Alfie Silas)
Singles: 7–inch
MOTOWN 2-4   84
RODEO 10-15
Also see SILAS, Alfie

KING, Carole
Singles: 7–inch
ABC 3-5   74
ABC-PAR (9921 "Goin' Wild") 30-40   58
ABC-PAR (9986 "Baby Sittin") 30-40   59
ALPINE (57 "Oh, Neil") 50-75   60
ATLANTIC 3-5   82-83
AVATAR 3-5   77-78
CAPITOL 3-5   77-80
COMPANION (2000 "It Might As Well
   Rain Until September") 40-60   62
DIMENSION (1009 "He's a Bad
   Boy") 10-20   63
DIMENSION (1004 "School Bells
   Are Ringing") 10-20   63
DIMENSION (2000 "It Might As Well
   Rain Until September") 5-10   62
ODE 3-5   71-76
RCA (7560 "Short Mort") 35-45   59
TOMORROW (7502 "A Road to
   Nowhere") 10-15   66
Picture Sleeves
AVATAR 3-5   77
CAPITOL 3-5   77-80
ODE 3-5   71-75
LPs: 10/12–inch 33rpm
ATLANTIC 5-8   82-83
AVATAR 8-12   78
CAPITOL (Except 11000 series) 5-8   80
CAPITOL (11000 series) 8-10   77-79
EMUS 5-8   79
EPIC/ODE (30000 series) 5-8   78-80
EPIC/ODE (40000 series) 12-15   80
   (Half-speed mastered.)
ODE 10-12 70-78
Also see COOKIES / Little Eva / Carole King
Also see SHIRELLES

KING, Claude
Singles: 7–inch
CINNAMON 3-5   74
COLUMBIA 3-8   61-71
DEE JAY (1248 "Run Baby, Run") ... 30-50   57
TRUE 3-5   77-80
Picture Sleeves
COLUMBIA 4-8   61-69
LPs: 10/12–inch 33rpm
COLUMBIA 10-20 62-70
GUSTO 5-8   80
HARMONY 8-12   68
TRUE 8-10   77
Also see YOUNG, Faron / Carl Perkins / Claude King

KING, Earl
(Earl Connelly King)
Singles: 78rpm
KING 4-8   55
Singles: 7–inch
KING 8-12   55
Also see JOHN, Little Willie / 5 Royales / Earl King / Midnighters

KING, Evelyn "Champagne"
Singles: 12–inch 33/45rpm
PRIVATE I 4-6   85
RCA 4-8   78-86
Singles: 7–inch
EMI 2-4   90
EMI-MANHATTAN 2-4   88-86
RCA 2-4   78-86
Picture Sleeves
RCA 2-4   78-86
LPs: 10/12–inch 33rpm
EMI 5-8   90
EMI-MANHATTAN 5-8   88
RCA 5-8   77-86

KING, Freddie
(Freddy King)
Singles: 78rpm
EL-BEE 10-20   56
Singles: 7–inch
COTILLION 3-6   68-70
EL-BEE (157 "Country Boy") 50-75   56
FEDERAL 4-8   60-65
GUSTO 3-5   78
KING 3-5   69
LPs: 10/12–inch 33rpm
COTILLION 10-15 69-70
KING (762 "Freddy King Sings
   the Blues") 30-40   61
KING (773 "Let's Hide Away
   and Dance Away") 35-50   61
KING (821 "Bossa Nova and Blues") . 20-30   62
KING (856 "Freddy King Goes Surfin") 20-30   63
KING (900 series) 15-20 65-66
KING (1000 series) 10-15   69
MCA 5-8
RSO 8-10 74-77
SHELTER 8-10 71-75

Also see ROGERS, Jimmy, and Freddie King

KING, Freddie, and Lulu Reed
Singles: 7–inch
FEDERAL 4-8   62

KING, Freddie / Lulu Reed / Sonny Thompson
LPs: 10/12–inch 33rpm
KING (777 "Boy-Girl-Boy") 20-30   62
Also see KING, Freddie
Also see RUSSELL, Leon
Also see THOMPSON, Sonny

KING, Johnny
Singles: 7–inch
DOT 5-10   58
GUY 4-8   61
MONTICELLO 5-10   59
TIARA 5-10   59

KING, Jonathan
Singles: 7–inch
PARROT 4-8   65-72
UK 3-5   73-74
UK/BIG TREE 3-5   75
LPs: 10/12–inch 33rpm
PARROT (71013 "Jonathan King
Or Then Again") 25-30   67
UK 10-20   72-73
Also see HEDGEHOPPERS ANONYMOUS

KING, Marcel
Singles: 12–inch 33/45rpm
A&M 4-6   84
Singles: 7–inch
A&M 2-4   84

KING, Marva
Singles: 7–inch
TRI-WORLD 2-4   88

KING, Morgana
Singles: 78rpm
MERCURY 4-6   56
Singles: 7–inch
MAINSTREAM 4-8   64
MERCURY 5-10   56
PARAMOUNT 3-5   73-74
REPRISE 4-6   66-67
20TH FOX 4-8   59
VERVE 4-6   68
WING 5-10   56
Picture Sleeves
PARAMOUNT 3-5   73
LPs: 10/12–inch 33rpm
ASCOT 15-25   65-66
CAMDEN 15-25   60
EMARCY (36079 "For You, for Me,
Forever More") 30-50   56
MAINSTREAM (300 series) 5-10   72
MAINSTREAM (6000 series) 15-25   64-65
MERCURY (20231 "Morganna King
Sings the Blues") 30-40   57

MUSE 5-8   79-82
PARAMOUNT 5-10   73
REPRISE 15-25   65-67
TRIP 5-8   74
U.A. (3028 "Folk Songs ala King") ... 30-40   59
(Monaural.)
U.A. (3028 "Folk Songs ala King") ... 40-50   59
(Stereo.)
U.A. (30020 "Let Me Love You") 30-40   60
VERVE 10-15   68
WING 10-20   65

KING, Pee Wee
(Pee Wee King with Redd Stewart; Pee Wee King and New Golden West Cowboys)
Singles: 78rpm
BLUEBIRD 4-6   49
RCA 3-6   50-55
Singles: 7–inch
BRIAR 4-8   61
JARO 4-8   60
CUCA 4-8   64-66
LANDA 4-8   61
RCA 5-10   50-55
STARDAY 4-6   64-71
TODD 4-6   59
LPs: 10/12–inch 33rpm
BRIAR (102 "Golden Olde-Tyme
Dances") 50-60   62
CAMDEN 8-15   65-71
CAPITOL 10-20   66
NASHVILLE 8-12
RCA 5-8   77
STARDAY (200 series) 10-20   64
STARDAY (900 series) 8-10   75

KING, Peggy
Singles: 78rpm
COLUMBIA 3-5   54-56
MGM 3-5   52
Singles: 7–inch
BUENA VISTA 4-8   62
BULLET 3-5   71
COLUMBIA 5-10   54-56
MGM 5-10   52
ROULETTE 4-8   61
Picture Sleeves
BUENA VISTA 4-8   62
EPs: 7–inch 33/45rpm
COLUMBIA 8-12   55
LPs: 10/12–inch 33rpm
COLUMBIA 15-25   55
IMPERIAL 10-20   59
Also see VALE, Jerry, Peggy King and Felicia Sanders

KING, Rev. Martin Luther, Jr.
Singles: 7–inch
DOOTO 4-6   68
GORDY 4-6   68
MERCURY 4-6   68

LPs: 10/12–inch 33rpm

BLACK FORUM	5-10	70
BUDDAH	8-15	69
CREED	8-12	68-71
DOTTO	8-15	62-68
EXCELLO	8-15	68
GORDY	8-15	63-68
MERCURY	8-15	68
MR. MAESTRO	10-15	63
NASHBORO	5-8	72
20TH FOX	8-15	63-68
UNART	8-12	68

These recordings contain speeches or excerpts of speeches by King.
Also see LANDS, Liz / Martin Luther King

KING, Sleepy: see SLEEPY KING

KING, Willard
(Will King)

Singles: 7–inch

CAPITOL	3-5	73
TOTAL EXPERIENCE	2-4	85

KING BISCUIT BOY
(King Biscuit Boy with Crowbar)

Singles: 7–inch

EPIC	3-5	75
PARAMOUNT	3-5	70-73

LPs: 10/12–inch 33rpm

EPIC	8-10	74
PARAMOUNT	10-15	70-73

KING COLE TRIO: see COLE, Nat "King"

KING CRIMSON

Singles: 12–inch 33/45rpm

WARNER	4-6	84

Singles: 7–inch

ATLANTIC	3-5	70-74
WARNER	2-4	81-84

LPs: 10/12–inch 33rpm

ATLANTIC (Except 18000 and 19000 series)	10-20	69-74
ATLANTIC (18000 and 19000 series)	8-10	74-75
EDITIONS	5-10	
MFSL (075 "In the Court of the King Crimson King")	25-50	82
WARNER	5-8	81-84
WIZARDO	10-12	
WORLD RECORD CLUB	12-15	

Members: Greg Lake; Robert Fripp; Boz Burrell; Bill Bruford.
Also see BAD COMPANY
Also see FRIPP, Robert
Also see LAKE, Greg
Also see YES

KING CURTIS
(King Curtis and the Kingpins; King Curtis and the Nobel Knights; King Curtis Combo)

Singles: 78rpm

GEM	10-15	54
MONARCH	15-20	53
RPM	10-15	53

Singles: 7–inch

ABC-PAR	4-8	60
ALCOR	4-8	62
ATCO	4-8	59-71
CAPITOL	4-8	62-65
ENJOY	4-8	62
EVEREST	4-8	61
GEM (208 "Tenor in the Sky")	35-50	54
KING	4-8	62
MONARCH (702 "Wine Head")	40-65	53
NEW JAZZ	3-5	61
RPM (383 "Boogie in the Moonlight")	25-50	53
SEG-WAY	10-15	61
TRU-SOUND	4-8	61-63

Picture Sleeves

CAPITOL (5377 "Bill Bailey")	5-8	65

EPs: 7–inch 33/45rpm

ATCO	4-8	68
(Jukebox issues only.)		
CAPITOL	8-15	63

LPs: 10/12–inch 33rpm

ATCO (113 "Have Tenor Sax Will Blow")	75-100	59
(Monaural.)		
ATCO (SD-113 "Have Tenor Sax Will Blow")	100-125	59
(Stereo.)		
ATCO (189 through 385)	10-20	66-72
CAMDEN	10-15	68
CAPITOL (2000 series)	10-20	64-68
CAPITOL (11000 series)	5-8	78-79
CLARION	8-10	
COLLECTABLES	6-8	88
ENJOY (2001 "Soul Twist")	30-50	62
EVEREST (1121 "Azure")	20-30	61
HARLEM HIT PARADE	8-10	
MOUNT VERNON	10-12	
NEW JAZZ (8237 "New Scene")	20-30	60
PRESTIGE (7200 series)	15-20	62
PRESTIGE (7700 series)	8-12	69-70
RCA	15-20	
TRU-SOUND	15-20	62

The studio tenor saxophone work of King Curtis is featured on the recordings of many artists, a few of whom are referenced below.
Also see BAKER, Lavern
Also see BENTON, Brook
Also see BOBBETTES
Also see CLOVERS
Also see COASTERS
Also see COMSTOCK, Bobby
Also see DARIN, Bobby
Also see FACENDA, Tommy
Also see JENNINGS, Waylon
Also see KING PINS
Also see LED ZEPPELIN / King Curtis
Also see McPHATTER, Clyde
Also see MITCHELL, Freddie
Also see PAT and the Satellites
Also see PRETTY BOY
Also see RESTIVO, Johnny
Also see SEDAKA, Neil

Also see SHARPE, Ray
Also see SHIRELLES, and King Curtis
Also see TURNER, Joe
Also see TURNER, Sammy

KING DIAMOND
LPs: 10/12–inch 33rpm
ROADRACER 5-8   87-90

KING DREAM CHORUS and Holiday Crew
Singles: 12–inch 33/45rpm
MERCURY 4-6   86
Singles: 7–inch
MERCURY 2-4   86
Members: Kurtis Blow; El De Barge; Fat Boys; Grandmaster Melle Mel; Whitney Houston; Stacy Lattisaw; Lisa Lisa and Full Force; Teena Marie; Menudo; Stephanie Mills; New Edition; Run-DMC; James Taylor; Whodini.
Also see BLOW, Kurtis
Also see DE BARGE
Also see FAT BOYS
Also see GRANDMASTER FLASH and the Furious Five
Also see HOUSTON, Whitney
Also see LATTISAW, Stacy
Also see LISA LISA
Also see MARIE, Teena
Also see MENUDO
Also see MILLS, Stephanie
Also see NEW EDITION
Also see RUN-D.M.C.
Also see TAYLOR, James
Also see WHODINI

KING FAMILY
Singles: 7–inch
WARNER 3-5   65
LPs: 10/12–inch 33rpm
CAPITOL 5-15   65
WARNER 5-15   65

KING FLOYD
(King Floyd and the Three Queens)
Singles: 7–inch
CHIMNEYVILLE 3-5   70-76
ORIGINAL SOUND 4-8   64
PULSAR 4-8
UPTOWN 4-8   66
LPs: 10/12–inch 33rpm
ATCO 8-10   73
CHIMNEYVILLE 8-10   72
COTILLION 8-12   71
PULSAR 10-12   69

KING HANNIBAL
(James T. Shaw)
Singles: 7–inch
AWARE 3-5   73
LPs: 10/12–inch 33rpm
AWARE 8-10   73

KING HARVEST
Singles: 7–inch
A&M 3-5   75-76
PERCEPTION 3-5   72-73
LPs: 10/12–inch 33rpm
A&M 10-15   75
PERCEPTION 8-12   73

Also see WILSON, Carl

KING KOBRA
Singles: 7–inch
REQUEST 4-8   63

KING LIZARD
(Kim Fowley)
Singles: 7–inch
ORIGINAL SOUND 8-12   75
Also see FOWLEY, Kim

KING PINS
Singles: 7–inch
ATCO 4-8   67
FEDERAL 4-8   63-64
VEE JAY 4-8   63
LPs: 10/12–inch 33rpm
KING (865 "It Won't Be This
Way Always") 25-35   63
Also see KELLY BROTHERS
Also see KING CURTIS

KING PLEASURE: see PLEASURE, King

KING RICHARD'S FLUEGEL KNIGHTS
Singles: 7–inch
MTA 3-6   66-68
LPs: 10/12–inch 33rpm
MTA 5-10   67-70

KING TEE
LPs: 10/12–inch 33rpm
CAPITOL 5-8   89-90

KINGBEES
(Nino Tempo and the Kingbees)
Singles: 7–inch
RSO 3-5   80-81
Picture Sleeves
RSO 3-5   80-81
LPs: 10/12–inch 33rpm
RSO 5-8   80-81
Members: Jamie; Michael; Rex.
Also see TEMPO, Nino

KINGDOM COME
Singles: 7–inch
POLYDOR 2-4   88
LPs: 10/12–inch 33rpm
POLYDOR 5-8   88-89

KINGFISH
Singles: 7–inch
JET 3-5   78
ROUND 3-5   76
LPs: 10/12–inch 33rpm
ACCORD 5-8   81
JET 8-10   77
ROUND 10-20   76
Members: Bob Weir; David Torbert; Matt Kelly.
Also see KELLY, Matt
Also see NEW RIDERS of the PURPLE SAGE
Also see WEIR, Bob

KINGS
Singles: 7–inch
ELEKTRA 3-5   80-81
LPs: 10/12–inch 33rpm
ELEKTRA 5-8   80-81

KINGS of the SUN
Singles: 12–inch 33/45rpm
RCA 4-8   88-89
Singles: 7–inch
RCA 2-4   88-90
LPs: 10/12–inch 33rpm
RCA 5-8   88-90

KING'S X
Singles: 12–inch 33/45rpm
MEGAFORCE 4-8   88
(Promotional only.)
LPs: 10/12–inch 33rpm
MEGAFORCE 5-8   88-90

KINGSMEN
Singles: 7–inch
EAST WEST 10-20   58
Also see HALEY, Bill

KINGSMEN
Singles: 7–inch
CAPITOL 3-5   72
EARTH 4-6   69
ERIC 3-5
JERDEN (712 "Louie Louie") 40-60   63
WAND (Except 1107 and 1115) 5-10   63-68
WAND (1107 "It's Only the Dog") 10-15   65
WAND (1115 "Killer Joe") 8-12   65
Picture Sleeves
WAND (1118 "The Krunch") 10-20   66
LPs: 10/12–inch 33rpm
ARISTA 8-10   81
HEAVY WEIGHT 20-25   67
PICADILLY 5-8   80
RHINO 5-8
SCEPTER/CITATION 8-12   72
WAND (657 "The Kingsmen
  in Person") 30-35   64
WAND (659 "The Kingsmen,
  Vol. 2") 50-100   64
  (Without *Death of an Angel*.)
WAND (659 "The Kingsmen, Vol. 2") . 25-35   64
  (With *Death of an Angel*.)
WAND (662 "The Kingsmen, Vol. 3") . 25-30   65
WAND (670 through 681) 20-25   65-67
  Members: Lynn Easton; Mike Mitchell; Don Gallucci; Norm
  Sundholm; Gary Abbot; Jack Ely; Barry Curtis; Dick Peterson.
  Also see DON and the Goodtimes

KINGSTON TRIO
Singles: 7–inch
CAPITOL (856 "The Merry Minuet") .. 10-20   59
  (Promotional issue only.)
CAPITOL (1400 and 1800 series) 5-15   60-63
  (Compact 33 Singles.)

CAPITOL (2006 "Farewell Adelita") .. 10-15   60
  (Special products giveaway for Welgrume
  Sportswear.)
CAPITOL (2782 "Molly Dee") 10-15   59
  (Promotional issue only.)
CAPITOL (3970 through 4114) 5-10   58-59
CAPITOL (4167 "The Tijuana Jail") ... 5-10   59
CAPITOL (S-4167 "The Tijuana Jail") 10-20   59
  (Stereo.)
CAPITOL (4221 "M.T.A.") 5-10   59
CAPITOL (4221 "M.T.A.") 20-30   59
  (Promotional "Special Preview Record." Label
  pictures the Trio.)
CAPITOL (4271 "A Worried Man") 5-10   59
CAPITOL (4303 "Coo Coo-U") 5-10   59
CAPITOL (S-4303 "Coo Coo-U") 10-20   59
  (Stereo.)
CAPITOL (4338 through 5166) 4-8   59-64
CAPITOL (6000 series) 3-6   62-65
CAPITOL/LION OF TROY (2006 "Farewell
  Adelita") 8-12   60
  (Capitol Special Products issue for Lion of Troy
  shirt buyers.)
DECCA 4-8   64-66
TETRAGRAMMATON 4-6   69
NAUTILUS 4-6   79
XERES 3-5   82
Picture Sleeves
CAPITOL (2006 "Farewell Adelita") .. 10-15   60
  (Special products issue for Welgrume Sportswear.)
CAPITOL (2782 "Molly Dee") 10-20   59
  (Promotional issue only.)
CAPITOL (4338 "El Matador") 10-15   60
CAPITOL (4740 "Scotch and Soda") . 10-15   62
CAPITOL (4842 "One More Town") .. 10-15   62
CAPITOL/LION OF TROY (2006 "Farewell
  Adelita") 10-15   60
  (Capitol Special Products issue for Lion of Troy
  shirt
DECCA (31702 "Hope You
  Understand") 15-25   65
DECCA (31790 "Yes, I Can Feel It") . 15-25   65
DECCA (31860 "Runaway Song") ... 15-25   65
XERES 3-5   82
EPs: 7–inch 33/45rpm
CAPITOL 10-25   58-61
CAPITOL CUSTOM (2670 "Cool
  Cargo") 15-25   60
  (Special products issue for 7-Up.)
LPs: 10/12–inch 33rpm
CANDLELITE (6971 "Historic
  Recordings") 15-25
CAPITOL (500 series) 8-15   70
CAPITOL (T-996 "The Kingston Trio") 25-40   58
  (Monaural.)
CAPITOL (DT-996 "The Kingston
  Trio") 10-15   69
  (Reprocessed stereo.)
CAPITOL (1107 "From the Hungry i") 25-35   59

CAPITOL (ST-1183 "Stereo Concert") 25-35 — 59
CAPITOL (T-1199 "At Large") . . . . 20-25 — 59
(Monaural.)
CAPITOL (ST-1199 "At Large") . . . . . 20-30 — 59
CAPITOL (T-1258 "Here We
Go Again") . . . . 20-25 — 59
(Monaural.)
CAPITOL (ST-1258 "Here We
Go Again") . . . . 20-30 — 59
(Stereo.)
CAPITOL (T-1352 "Sold Out") . . . . . . 20-25 — 60
(Monaural.)
CAPITOL (ST-1352 "Sold Out") . . . . . 20-30 — 60
(Stereo.)
CAPITOL (T-1407 "String Along . . . . . 20-25 — 60
(Monaural.)
CAPITOL (ST-1407 "String Along . . . . 20-30 — 60
(Stereo.)
CAPITOL (T-1446 through T-2081) . . 15-20 — 60-64
(Monaural.)
CAPITOL (ST-1446 through ST-2081) 15-25 — 60-64
(Stereo.)
CAPITOL (T-2180 "The Folk Era") . . . 25-35 — 64
(Mono. Three-LP set with bound-in booklet.)
CAPITOL (ST-2180 "The Folk Era") . . 30-40 — 64
(Stereo. Three-LP set with bound-in booklet.)
CAPITOL (T-2280 through T-2614) . . 10-20 — 65-66
(Monaural.)
CAPITOL (ST-2280 through ST-2614) 15-25 — 65-66
(Stereo.)
CAPITOL (11000 series) . . . . 5-8 — 79
CAPITOL (16000 series) . . . . 4-6 — 81
DECCA (4000 series) . . . . 15-20 — 64-65
(Monaural.)
DECCA (7-4000 series) . . . . 15-25 — 64-65
(Stereo.)
INTERMEDIA . . . . 5-8 — 85
NAUTILUS . . . . 15-25 — 79
PICKWICK 5-10
TETRAGRAMMATON . . . . 10-15 — 69
XERES . . . . 5-10 — 82
Members: John Stewart; Dave Guard; Nick Reynolds; Bob
Shane.
Also see BEATLES / Beach Boys / Kingston Trio
Also see GUARD, Dave, and the Whiskeyhill Singers
Also see NEW KINGSTON TRIO
Also see STEWART, John
Also see STEWART, John, and Nick Reynolds

KINGSTON TRIO / Four Preps
Singles: 7-inch
U.S.A.F. (103 "El Matador") . . . . 10-20 — 60
(Promotional, radio station issue only.)
Also see FOUR PREPS

KINGSTON TRIO / Dinah Shore
Singles: 7-inch
U.S.A.F. (129 "Everglades") . . . . 10-20 — 60
(Promotional, radio station issue only.)
Also see SHORE, Dinah

KINGSTON TRIO / Frank Sinatra
EPs: 7-inch 33/45rpm
CAPITOL (2229 "Excerpts from
Great New Releases") . . . . 25-50 — 62
(Promotional issue only.)
Also see KINGSTON TRIO
Also see SINATRA, Frank

KINISON, Sam
LPs: 10/12-inch 33rpm
WARNER . . . . 5-8 — 86-90

KINKS
Singles: 12-inch 33/45rpm
ARISTA . . . . 4-8 — 79-83
Singles: 7-inch
ARISTA . . . . 3-6 — 77-85
CAMEO (308 "Long Tall Sally") . . . . 75-100 — 64
CAMEO (345 "Long Tall Sally") . . . . . 40-60 — 65
CAMEO (348 "You Still Want Me") . 100-200 — 65
ERIC 3-5
MCA . . . . 3-5 — 86
RCA . . . . 4-6 — 72-76
REPRISE (0306 through 0647) . . . . . . 5-8 — 65-67
REPRISE (0691 through 0847) . . . . . 8-12 — 68-69
REPRISE (0930 through 1094) . . . . . . 4-8 — 70-72
Promotional Singles
ARISTA (Except 5) . . . . 3-6 — 77-85
ARISTA (5 "Sleepwalker") . . . . 10-15 — 77
(Colored vinyl.)
CAMEO (308 "Long Tall Sally") . . . . . 50-75 — 64
CAMEO (345 "Long Tall Sally") . . . . . 35-45 — 65
CAMEO (348 "You Still Want Me") . 100-150 — 65
REPRISE (0306 through 0647) . . . . . 10-20 — 65-67
REPRISE (0691 through 0847) . . . . . 10-15 — 68-69
REPRISE (0930 through 1094) . . . . . . 6-12 — 70-72
Picture Sleeves
ARISTA 3-5 80-84
EPs: 7-inch 33/45rpm
ARISTA (22 "The Kinks Misfit Record") 20-25 — 78
(Promotional issue only.)
CAMEO . . . . 4-6 — 78
REPRISE (352 "Arthur") . . . . 10-20 — 69
(Promotional issue only.)
LPs: 10/12-inch 33rpm
ARISTA . . . . 6-12 — 77-86
COMPLEAT 5-8
MCA . . . . 5-8 — 86-89
MFSL (070 "Misfits") . . . . 20-30 — 82
PICKWICK . . . . 5-10 — 72-79
PYE . . . . 8-10 — 75-76
RCA (Except "AYL1" series) . . . . 10-15 — 71-76
RCA VICTOR ("AYL1" series) . . . . 5-8 — 80-82
REPRISE (2127 "The Great Lost
Kinks Album") . . . . 20-30 — 73
REPRISE (R-6143 "You Really
Got Me") . . . . 50-100 — 64
(Monaural.)

REPRISE (RS-6143 "You Really
Got Me") 20-30   64
(Stereo.)
REPRISE (R-6158 "Kinks Size") 50-75   65
(Monaural.)
REPRISE (RS-6158 "Kinks Size") ... 20-30   65
(Stereo.)
REPRISE (R-6173 "Kinda Kinks") ... 50-75   65
(Monaural.)
REPRISE (RS-6173 "Kinda Kinks") .. 20-30   65
(Stereo.)
REPRISE (R-6184 "Kinks Kinkdom") . 50-75   65
(Monaural.)
REPRISE (RS-6184 "Kinks Kinkdom") 20-30   65
(Stereo.)
REPRISE (R-6197 "The Kink
Kontroversy") 50-75   66
(Monaural.)
REPRISE (RS-6197 "The Kink
Kontroversy") 20-30   66
(Stereo.)
REPRISE (R-6217 "The Kinks'
Greatest Hits") 50-75   66
(Monaural.)
REPRISE (RS-6217 "The Kinks'
Greatest Hits") 20-30   66
(Stereo.)
REPRISE (R-6228 "Face to Face") .. 50-75   66
(Monaural.)
REPRISE (RS-6228 "Face to Face") . 20-30   66
(Stereo.)
REPRISE (R-6260 "The Live Kinks") . 50-75   67
(Monaural.)
REPRISE (RS-6260 "The Live Kinks") 20-30   67
(Stereo.)
REPRISE (R-6279 "Something Else") 50-75   67
(Monaural.)
REPRISE (RS-6279 "Something
Else") 20-30   67
(Stereo.)
REPRISE (6327 "Village Green
Preservation Society") 25-35   69
REPRISE (6366 "Arthur") 15-20   69
(Price includes lyrics insert.)
REPRISE (6423 "Lola Vs.
the Powerman") 12-15   69
(Blue and white cover.)
REPRISE (6423 "Lola Vs.
the Powerman") 6-10   69
(Black, blue and white cover.)
REPRISE (6454 "The Kink Kronikles") . 8-12   69
(Original Reprise Kinks LPs from the sixties were
on a multi-colored label. All 11 of these LPs have
been repressed on the brown Reprise label and
are valued at $10 to $15.)
Promotional LPs
ARISTA (Except 69) 10-15   77-84
ARISTA (69 "Low Budget Radio
Interview") 40-50   79

REPRISE (2127 "The Great Lost
Kinks Album") 50-75   73
REPRISE (R-6143 "You Really
Got Me") 50-100   64
(White label, monaural.)
REPRISE (R-6158 "Kinks Size") .. 100-200   65
(White label, monaural.)
REPRISE (R-6173 "Kinda Kinks") . 100-200   65
(White label, monaural.)
REPRISE (R-6184 "Kinks
Kingdom") 100-200   65
(White label, monaural.)
REPRISE (R-6197 "The Kink
Kontroversy") 100-200   66
(White label, monaural.)
REPRISE (R-6217 "The Kink's
Greatest Hits") 100-200   66
(White label, monaural.)
REPRISE (R-6228 "Face to Face") . 75-150   66
(White label, monaural.)
REPRISE (R-6260 "The Live
Kinks") 75-150   67
(White label, monaural.)
REPRISE (R-6279 "Something
Else") 75-150   67
REPRISE (RS-6000 series) 30-60   64-72
(White label, stereo.)
WARNER (328 Complete "Kinks Kit"/"Then
Now And In-Between") 325-375   69
(Boxed set, includes *Then Now and In-Between*
LP, button, pin, postcard, letter, decal, and other
promotional materials.)
WARNER (328 "Then Now
and In-Between") 75-100   69
(Price for LP only.)
Members: Ray Davies; Dave Davies; Mick Avory; Peter Quaife;
John Dalton; John Gosling; John Beecham; Mike Cotton.
Also see DAVIES, Dave

KINKS / Hollywood Stars
Singles: 7-inch
ARISTA (5 "Sleepwalker") 8-10   77
Picture Sleeves
ARISTA (5 "Sleepwalker") 10-15   77
Also see HOLLYWOOD STARS
Also see KINKS

KINNEY, Fern
Singles: 7-inch
ATLANTIC 4-6   68
MALACO 3-5   79-80

KINSMAN DAZZ
Singles: 7-inch
20TH FOX 3-5   78-79
LPs: 10/12-inch 33rpm
20TH FOX 5-8   79
Also see DAZZ BAND

KIRBY, Kathy
Singles: 7-inch
ASCOT 4-6   67

LONDON 4-8	62-65	
PARROT 4-8	65-66	

KIRBY STONE FOUR:
see STONE, Kirby, Four

KIRK, Jim, and the TM Singers
Singles: 7–Inch

CAPITOL 3-5	80	

Picture Sleeves

CAPITOL 3-5	80	

KIRKLAND, Bo
Singles: 7–Inch

CLARIDGE 3-5	75	

KIRKLAND, Bo, and Ruth Davis
(Bo and Ruth)
Singles: 7–Inch

CLARIDGE 3-5	75-78	

LPs: 10/12–Inch 33rpm

CLARIDGE 5-10	76	

Also see DAVIS, Ruth
Also see KIRKLAND, Bo

KIRTON, Lew
Singles: 7–Inch

BELIEVE 2-4	83	
MARLIN 3-5	77	

KISS
Singles: 12–Inch 33/45rpm

CASABLANCA 10-20	78-82	
MERCURY 10-20	83-88	

Singles: 7–Inch

CASABLANCA 4-8	74-82	
MERCURY (Except 0002) 3-6	85-88	
MERCURY (0002 "World Without Heroes") 10-20	81	
(Picture disc.)		
POLYGRAM (832-903 "Crazy Nights") 8-12	87	
(Picture disc.)		

Picture Sleeves

CASABLANCA (858 "Flaming Youth") . 8-10	75	
CASABLANCA (2365 "I Love It Loud") . 8-10	81	
MERCURY 4-8	85-87	

LPs: 10/12–Inch 33rpm

CASABLANCA (7006 "Hotter Than Hell") 15-25	74	
CASABLANCA (7016 "Dressed to Kill") 10-20	75	
CASABLANCA (7020 "Alive") ... 10-20	75	
CASABLANCA (7025 "Destroyer") ... 10-20	75	
CASABLANCA (7032 "The Originals") 40-55	76	
CASABLANCA (7037 "Rock and Roll Over") 15-20	76	
(With bonus sticker.)		
CASABLANCA (7037 "Rock and Roll Over") 10-15	76	
(Without sticker.)		
CASABLANCA (7057 "Love Gun") ... 30-60	77	
(Price includes stand-up, cardboard gun.)		

CASABLANCA (7057 "Love Gun") .. 10-20	77	
(Without cardboard gun.)		
CASABLANCA (7076 "Alive II") 30-40	77	
(With booklet/tatoos.)		
CASABLANCA (7076 "Alive II") 15-20	77	
(Without booklet/tatoos.)		
CASABLANCA (7100 "Double Platinum") 30-40	78	
(With platinum award.)		
CASABLANCA (7100 "Double Platinum") 15-20	78	
(Without platinum award.)		
CASABLANCA (7152 "Dynasty") 15-20	79	
(With poster.)		
CASABLANCA (7152 "Dynasty") 10-15	79	
(Without poster.)		
CASABLANCA (7225 "Kiss Unmasked") 15-20	80	
(With poster.)		
CASABLANCA (7225 "Kiss Unmasked") 10-15	80	
(Without poster.)		
CASABLANCA (7261 "Music from the Elder") 25-50	81	
CASABLANCA (7270 "Creatures of the Night") 15-20	82	
(With make up.)		
MERCURY (Except 836887) 5-10	83-88	
MERCURY (836887 "Smashes, Thrashes and Hits") 15-20	88	
(Picture disc.)		
MERCURY (838913 "Hot in the Shade")5-10	89	
CASABLANCA (9001 "Kiss") 15-25	74	

Promotional LPs

CASABLANCA (76 "Kiss Tour Album") 20-30	76	
CASABLANCA (7001 "Kiss") 40-60	74	
(Without *Kissin' Time*)		
CASABLANCA (7032 "The Originals") 60-80	76	
(With inserts.)		
CASABLANCA (20137 "Criss, Frehley, Simmons, Stanley") 20-30	78	

Members: Gene Simmons; Ace Frehley; Paul Stanley; Peter Criss; Bruce Kulick; Eric Carr; Vinnie Vincent.
Also see CRISS, Peter
Also see FREHLEY, Ace
Also see SIMMONS, Gene
Also see STANLEY, Paul
Also see VINCENT, Vinnie, Invasion

KISSING the PINK
Singles: 7–Inch

ATLANTIC 3-5	83	
MERCURY 2-4	87	

Picture Sleeves

MERCURY 2-4	87	

LPs: 10/12–Inch 33rpm

ATLANTIC 5-8	83	
MERCURY 5-8	87	

KISSOON, Mac and Katie
Singles: 7-inch
ABC 3-5   71
BELL 3-5   72
MCA/STATE 3-5   75-76
LPs: 10/12-inch 33rpm
MCA/STATE 8-12   76
   Also see WATERS, Roger

KITARO
(Mansanori Takahashi)
Singles: 12-inch 33/45rpm
GEFFEN 4-8   86
   (Promotional only.)
Singles: 7-inch
GEFFEN 2-4   86
LPs: 10/12-inch 33rpm
GEFFEN 5-8   85-90
GRAMAVISION 5-8   85-86

KITT, Eartha
Singles: 12-inch 33/45rpm
STREETWISE 4-6   83
Singles: 78rpm
RCA 3-6   53-57
Singles: 7-inch
DECCA 4-6   65
KAPP 4-8   59-66
RCA 5-10   53-57
STREETWISE 2-4   83
Picture Sleeves
RCA 10-15   54-55
EPs: 7-inch 33/45rpm
RCA 10-20   53-57
LPs: 10/12-inch 33rpm
CAEDMON 5-10   69
DECCA 10-15   65
GNP/CRESCENDO 10-15   65
KAPP 10-20   59-60
MGM 10-20   62
PHILIPS 8-15   68
RCA 15-30   53-57
STANYAN 5-10   72

KITTY and the Haywoods
Singles: 7-inch
MERCURY 3-5   77
LPs: 10/12-inch 33rpm
MERCURY 8-10   77

KIX
Singles: 7-inch
ATLANTIC 2-4   81-89
Picture Sleeves
ATLANTIC 2-4   89
LPs: 10/12-inch 33rpm
ATLANTIC 5-8   81-89

KLAATU
Singles: 12-inch 33/45rpm
CAPITOL 2-4   80
   (Promotional only.)

Singles: 7-inch
CAPITOL 3-5   77-80
ISLAND 4-6   75
Picture Sleeves
CAPITOL 3-5   77
LPs: 10/12-inch 33rpm
CAPITOL 8-12   76-80
   Members: John Woloschuk; Cary Draper; David Long;; Dino
   Tome.

KLEEER
Singles: 7-inch
ATLANTIC 2-5   79-85
LPs: 10/12-inch 33rpm
ATLANTIC 5-8   79-85
   Members: Paul Crutchfield; Richard Lee; Norm Durham.
   Also see UNIVERSAL ROBOT BAND

KLEIN, Robert
Singles: 7-inch
BRUT 4-8   73
CASABLANCA 3-5   79
LPs: 10/12-inch 33rpm
BRUT 8-12   73

KLEIN & MBO
Singles: 12-inch 33/45rpm
ATLANTIC 4-6   83
Singles: 7-inch
ATLANTIC 2-4   83

KLEMMER, John
Singles: 7-inch
ABC 3-5   76
LPs: 10/12-inch 33rpm
ABC 5-10   75-79
CADET CONCEPT 8-12   69
CHESS 8-12   76
ELEKTRA 5-8   80-83
MCA 5-10   79-82
NAUTILUS 5-8   80-81
NOVUS 5-8   79
   Also see HARRIS, Eddie, and John Klemmer

KLINT, Pete, Quintet
Singles: 7-inch
MERCURY 4-6   67

KLIQUE
Singles: 12-inch 33/45rpm
MCA 4-6   81-85
Singles: 7-inch
MCA 2-4   81-85
LPs: 10/12-inch 33rpm
MCA 5-8   81-85
   Members: Howard Huntsberry; Deborah Hunter; Isaac Suthers.

KLOCKWISE
Singles: 7-inch
SINBAN 2-4   84-85

KLOWNS
Singles: 7-inch
RCA 3-5   70

Picture Sleeves
RCA .... 3-5　70

LPs: 10/12–inch 33rpm
RCA .... 8-10　70

KLUGH, Earl
Singles: 7–inch
BLUE NOTE .... 3-5　77
LIBERTY .... 2-4　81

LPs: 10/12–inch 33rpm
BLUE NOTE .... 5-8　76-77
CAPITOL .... 5-8　83-84
LIBERTY .... 5-8　80-81
MFSL (025 "Finger Paintings") ...... 20-40　79
MFSL (076 "Late Night") .... 20-30　82
MFSL/UHQR (025 "Finger Paintings") 30-50　79
　(Boxed set.)
U.A. .... 5-10　78-80
WARNER .... 5-8　84-91
　Also see JAMES, Bob, and Earl Klugh
　Also see LAWS, Hubert, and Earl Klugh

KLYMAXX
Singles: 12–inch 33/45rpm
CONSTELLATION .... 4-6　84-87
MCA .... 4-6　84-86
Singles: 7–inch
CONSTELLATION .... 2-4　84-87
MCA .... 2-4　84-86
SOLAR .... 3-5　81-83
Picture Sleeves
CONSTELLATION .... 2-4　85-87
MCA .... 4-6　84-86
LPs: 10/12–inch 33rpm
CONSTELLATION .... 5-8　85-87
MCA .... 5-8　90
SOLAR .... 5-8　81-83
　Members: Lorena Hardiman; Ann Williams; Cheryl Coolen;
　Robbin Grider; Lynn Malsby; Joyce Irby; Bernadette Cooper;
　Judy Takeuchi.

KNACK
Singles: 7–inch
CAPITOL (4000 series) .... 3-5　79-81
Picture Sleeves
CAPITOL (4731 "My Sharona") .... 4-8　79
CAPITOL (4771 "Good Girls Don't") .... 3-5　79
CAPITOL (4822 "Baby Talks Dirty") ... 8-10　80
CAPITOL (5054 "Pay the Devil") ..... 8-10　80
LPs: 10/12–inch 33rpm
CAPITOL .... 8-10　79-81
　Members: Doug Fieger; Bruce Gary; Berton Averre; Prescott
　Niles.
　Also see SKY

KNICKERBOCKERS
Singles: 7–inch
CHALLENGE (59268 "All I Need
　Is You") .... 10-20　65
CHALLENGE (59293 through 59384) . 5-10　65-67
ERIC 3-5

LPs: 10/12–inch 33rpm
CHALLENGE (621 "Jerk and
　Twine Time") .... 45-55　66
CHALLENGE (622 "Lies") .... 45-55　66
CHALLENGE (12664 "Lloyd Thaxton Presents
　the Knickerbockers") .... 45-55　65
LANA 3-5
SUNDAZED .... 5-10　89
　Members: Buddy Randell; Beau Charles; Jimmy Walker; John
　Charles.

KNIGHT, Frederick
Singles: 7–inch
JUANA .... 2-4　81
MAXINE .... 4-6　69
STAX .... 3-5　72
TRUTH .... 3-5　75
LPs: 10/12–inch 33rpm
STAX .... 8-10　73

KNIGHT, Gladys
(Gladys Knight and the Pips)
Singles: 12–inch 33/45rpm
COLUMBIA .... 4-8　79-85
MCA .... 4-6　86
Singles: 7–inch
ABC .... 3-5　73
BUDDAH .... 3-5　73-79
COLUMBIA .... 3-5　79-85
ENJOY .... 4-8　64
ERIC .... 3-5　78
FLASHBACK .... 3-5　67
FURY .... 10-15　61-63
MCA .... 2-4　86-88
MAXX .... 4-8　64-65
SOUL .... 4-8　67-74
VEE JAY .... 5-10　61-63
Picture Sleeves
BUDDAH .... 3-5　73-75
COLUMBIA .... 3-5　81
MCA .... 2-4　87
LPs: 10/12–inch 33rpm
ACCORD .... 5-8　81-82
ALLEGIANCE .... 5-8　84
BELL .... 10-15　68-75
BUDDAH .... 8-12　73-78
COLUMBIA .... 5-8　79-85
51 WEST 5-8
FURY (1003 "Letter Full of Tears") .. 75-100　62
LOST-NITE .... 5-8　81
MCA .... 5-8　87
MCP .... 8-10　76
MAXX (3000 "Gladys Knight
　and the Pips") .... 20-30　64
MOTOWN (Except 792) .... 5-8　80-82
MOTOWN (792 "Anthology") .... 8-12　74
NATURAL RESOURCES .... 5-8　78
PICKWICK .... 8-10　73
RELIC .... 5-10　90
SOUL .... 10-15　67-75

SPHERE SOUND (7006 "Gladys Knight
  and the Pips") 20-30   65
SPRINGBOARD 8-10   75
TRIP 8-10   73
U.A. 10-15   75
UPFRONT 10-12
VEE JAY 10-15   76
  Also see DIONNE and Friends
  Also see GAYE, Marvin / Gladys Knight and the Pips
  Also see PIPS

KNIGHT, Gladys, and Johnny Mathis
Singles: 7–inch
COLUMBIA 3-5   80
  Also see KNIGHT, Gladys
  Also see MATHIS, Johnny

KNIGHT, Holly
Singles: 7–inch
COLUMBIA 2-4   88

KNIGHT, Jean
(Jean Knight and Premium)
Singles: 7–inch
CHELSEA 3-5   75
COTILLION 2-4   81-82
DIAL 3-5   74
JETSTREAM 4-8   65
MIRAGE 2-4   85
OLA 3-5   77
OPEN 3-5   76
SOULIN 2-4   81-85
STAFF 3-5   72
STAX 3-5   71-73
TRIBE 4-8   65
Picture Sleeves
MIRAGE 2-4   85
LPs: 10/12–inch 33rpm
COTILLION 5-8   81
MIRAGE 5-8   85
STAX 10-15   71

KNIGHT, Jerry
Singles: 7–inch
A&M 2-4   80-83
Picture Sleeves
A&M 2-4   80
LPs: 10/12–inch 33rpm
A&M 5-8   80-81
  Also see OLLIE & JERRY
  Also see RAYDIO

KNIGHT, Marie
Singles: 78rpm
DECCA 4-8   54
MERCURY 4-8   56
WING 4-8   56
Singles: 7–inch
DECCA (48315 "You Got a Way
  of Making Love") 10-20   54
DIAMOND 4-8   63
MERCURY 10-15   56
MUSICOR 4-8   65-66

OKEH 4-8   61-65
WING 8-12   56
Picture Sleeves
OKEH 5-10   61
LPs: 10/12–inch 33rpm
CARLTON (119 "Lift Every
  Voice and Sing") 20-30   60
  Also see MARIE & REX

KNIGHT, Robert
Singles: 7–inch
DOT 4-8   61
ELF 4-8   68-69
MONUMENT 3-5   74
RISING SONS 4-8   67-68
LPs: 10/12–inch 33rpm
RISING SONS (17000 "Everlasting
  Love") 15-25   67

KNIGHT, Sonny
Singles: 78rpm
ALADDIN 8-12   53
DOT 4-8   56
SPECIALTY 4-8   57
Singles: 7–inch
A&M 4-8   63-64
ALADDIN (3195 "Dear Wonderful") .. 20-30   53
ALADDIN (3207 "What Officer") 20-30   53
AURA 4-8   64-65
DOT (15507 "Confidential") 10-15   56
  (Maroon label.)
DOT (15507 "Confidential") 5-10   57
  (Black label.)
EASTMAN 15-25   59
FIFO 4-8   61
MERCURY 4-8   62
ORIGINAL SOUND (2 "Once in
  Awhile") 10-15   58
SPECIALTY 8-12   57
STARLA (Except 1) 8-12   58-59
STARLA (1 "Dedicated to You") ... 15-20   57
VITA (137 "Confidential") 15-25   56
WORLD PACIFIC (Except 403) 4-8   66
WORLD PACIFIC (403 "If You Want
  This Love") 5-10   64
  (Reissued several months later on Aura 403.)
Picture Sleeves
AURA (4505 "Love Me") 10-15   64
LPs: 10/12–inch 33rpm
AURA 15-20   64

KNIGHT, Terry
(Terry Knight and the Pack)
Singles: 7–inch
A&M 4-8   65
ABKCO 3-5   75
CAMEO 4-8   67
CAPITOL 5-10   69
FRATERNITY 4-8   67
LUCKY ELEVEN 5-10   66-67

LPs: 10/12–inch 33rpm

ABKCO 10-15   72
CAMEO (2007 "Reflections") 25-30   67
LUCKY ELEVEN (8000 "Terry Knight
  and the Pack") 20-25   66
  Also see GRAND FUNK RAILROAD

KNIGHT BROTHERS
Singles: 7–inch

CHECKER 5-8   63-66
MERCURY 4-6   67-68
  Member: Peter Knight.

KNIGHTSBRIDGE STRINGS
Singles: 7–inch

MONUMENT 3-6   66
TOP RANK 4-8   59-60
LPs: 10/12–inch 33rpm
MONUMENT 5-10   66-69
PURIST 5-10   64
RIVERSIDE 5-12   62-64
SESAC 8-15
TOP RANK 5-15   59-60
  Also see RANDOLPH, Boots

KNOBLOCK, Fred
Singles: 7–inch

SCOTTI BROS 2-4   80-82
LPs: 10/12–inch 33rpm
SCOTTI BROS 5-8   80-82

KNOBLOCK, Fred, and Susan Anton
Singles: 7–inch

SCOTTI BROS 3-5   80
  Also see ANTON, Susan
  Also see KNOBLOCK, Fred

KNOCKOUTS
Singles: 7–inch

COS-DE (1003 "Sweet Talk") 15-25   60
MGM 4-8   61

KNOX, Buddy
(Buddy Knox and the Rhythm Orchids)
Singles: 78rpm

ROULETTE 10-15   57
Singles: 7–inch
ABC 3-5   73
LIBERTY 4-8   60-64
REPRISE 4-8   65-66
ROULETTE (4002 "Party Doll") . . . 20-30   57
  (With roulette wheel on label.)
ROULETTE (4002 "Party Doll") 8-12   57
  (Without roulette wheel.)
ROULETTE (4009 "Rock Your Little
  Baby to Sleep") 20-30   57
  (With roulette wheel on label.)
ROULETTE (4009 "Rock Your Little
  Baby to Sleep") 8-12   57
  (Without roulette wheel.)
ROULETTE (4018 through 4262) 5-10   57-60
RUFF 4-8   65
U.A. 4-6   68-71

Picture Sleeves
LIBERTY (55305 "Ling Ting Tong") . . 10-20   61
EPs: 7–inch 33/45rpm
ROULETTE (301 "Buddy Knox") 50-75   57
LPs: 10/12–inch 33rpm
ACCORD 5-8   82-83
LIBERTY (3251 "Golden Hits") 20-30   62
  (Monaural.)
LIBERTY (7251 "Golden Hits") 25-35   62
  (Stereo.)
ROULETTE (25003 "Buddy Knox") . 75-100   57
U.A. 10-15   69

KNOX, Buddy / Jimmy Bowen
(With the Rhythm Orchids)
Singles: 78rpm

ROULETTE 15-25   57
TRIPLE-D (797 "Party Doll"/"I'm
  Stickin' with You") 50-100   57
Singles: 7–inch
ROULETTE (4001 "My Baby's Gone"/"I'm
  Stickin' with You") 30-50   57
TRIPLE-D (797 "Party Doll"/"I'm
  Stickin' with You") 300-400   57
LPs: 10/12–inch 33rpm
MURRAY HILL 5-8
ROULETTE (25048 "Buddy Knox and
  Jimmy Bowen") 75-125   58
  Also see BOWEN, Jimmy
  Also see KNOX, Buddy

KOENEMANN, Randy, with Midwests Best
Singles: 7–inch

L. PARKS 2-4   87

KOFFIE
Singles: 12–inch 33/45rpm

PAN DISC 4-6   83
Singles: 7–inch
PHILIPS 4-8   68

KOFFMAN, Moe,
(Moe Koffman Quartette; Moe Koffman Quintet; Moe Koffman Septette)
Singles: 7–inch

ABC 3-5   73
ASCOT 4-6   62
ATCO 4-6   65
GOLD EAGLE 4-8   61
JUBILEE 3-8   58-68
PALETTE 4-6   60-63
VIRGO 3-5   72
LPs: 10/12–inch 33rpm
ASCOT 10-15   62
JANUS 5-8   78
JUBILEE (1000 series) 15-25   57-58
JUBILEE (8000 series) 8-12   68
U.A. 15-25   62-63

LPs: 10/12–inch 33rpm

U.A. 5-8   80
  Members: Bruce Blackman; Bob Gauthler.
  Also see STARBUCK

KOSSOFF, Paul
LPs: 10/12–inch 33rpm

DJM 10-12   77
ISLAND 8-10   73-75
  Also see BACK STREET CRAWLER
  Also see FREE

KOSSOFF / Kirke / Tetsu / Rabbit
LPs: 10/12–inch 33rpm

ISLAND 8-10   72
  Members: Paul Kossoff; Simon Kirke.
  Also see FREE
  Also see KOSSOFF, Paul

KOSTELANETZ, Andre, and His Orchestra
Singles: 78rpm

COLUMBIA 3-5   50-57
Singles: 7–inch
COLUMBIA 4-8   50-61
EPs: 7–inch 33/45rpm
COLUMBIA 5-10   50-59
LPs: 10/12–inch 33rpm
COLUMBIA 5-15   50-71

KOTTKE, Leo
Singles: 7–inch

CAPITOL 3-5   75
LPs: 10/12–inch 33rpm
CAPITOL (Except 16000 series) 8-12   71-76
CAPITOL (16000 series) 5-8   81
CHRYSALIS 5-10   76-81
OBLIVION 15-20
SYMPOSIUM 10-12   70
TAKOMA 8-12   71-74

KOTTKE, Leo, John Fahey and Peter Lang
LPs: 10/12–inch 33rpm

TAKOMA 8-10   74
  Also see KOTTKE, Leo

KRAFTWERK
Singles: 12–inch 33/45rpm

WARNER 4-6   83
Singles: 7–inch
CAPITOL 3-5   76-78
VERTIGO 3-5   75
WARNER 2-4   81-83
Picture Sleeves
WARNER 2-4   81-83
LPs: 10/12–inch 33rpm
CAPITOL 8-10   75-78
MERCURY 5-8   77
VERTIGO 8-10   73-75
WARNER 5-8   80-86

KRAMER, Billy J., and the Dakotas
Singles: 7–inch

EPIC 4-8   68
ERIC 3-5

IMPERIAL 4-8   64-66
LIBERTY (55586 "Do You Want to Know a
  Secret"/"I'll Be on My Way") 8-12   63
LIBERTY (55626 "Bad to Me") 8-10   64
LIBERTY (55643 "I'll Keep You
  Satisfied") 8-10   64
LIBERTY (55667 "Do You Want to
  Know a Secret"/"Bad to Me") 5-8   64
Picture Sleeves
IMPERIAL (66051 "From a
  Window") 10-15   64
LPs: 10/12–inch 33rpm
CAPITOL 8-10   78-79
IMPERIAL (9267 "Little Children") ... 25-35   64
  (Monaural.)
IMPERIAL (9273 "I'll Keep
  You Satisfied") 25-35   64
  (Monaural.)
IMPERIAL (9291 "Trains and Boats
  and Planes") 25-35   65
  (Monaural.)
IMPERIAL (12267 "Little Children") .. 25-40   64
  (Stereo.)
IMPERIAL (12273 "I'll Keep
  You Satisfied") 25-40   64
  (Stereo.)
IMPERIAL (12291 "Trains and Boats
  and Planes") 25-40   65
  (Stereo.)

KRANZ, George
Singles: 12–inch 33/45rpm

PERSONAL 4-6   83
Singles: 7–inch
PERSONAL 2-4   83

KRISTOFFERSON, Kris
Singles: 7–inch

A&M 2-4   73
COLUMBIA 3-5   77-81
EPIC 4-8   67
MONUMENT 3-5   70-81
Picture Sleeves
A&M 2-4   73
EPs: 7–inch 33/45rpm
MONUMENT (532 "Kristofferson") 5-10   71
  (Promotional issue only.)

LPs: 10/12–inch 33rpm

COLUMBIA 5-8   77-81
MONUMENT 8-12   70-76
   Also see COOLIDGE, Rita, and Kris Kristofferson
   Also see JENNINGS, Waylon, Willie Nelson, Johnny Cash, and
      Kris Kristofferson
   Also see NELSON, Willie, and Kris Kristofferson

KROKUS

Singles: 7–inch

ARIOLA AMERICA 2-4   81
ARISTA 2-4   82-86

Picture Sleeves

ARISTA 2-4   84-86

LPs: 10/12–inch 33rpm

ARIOLA AMERICA 5-8   81
ARISTA 5-8   82-86
   Dani Crivelli; Chris Von Rohr; Marc Storace;
   Fernando Von Arb; Mark Kohler.
MCA 5-8   88

KRUSH GROOVE ALL STARS

Singles: 12–inch 33/45rpm

WARNER 4-6   85
   Also see BLOW, Kurtis
   Also see E., Sheila
   Also see FAT BOYS
   Also see RUN D.M.C.

KRYSTAL

Singles: 7–inch

EPIC 2-4   84
MAGIC TOUCH 2-4
SPRING 3-5   79

KRYSTAL GENERATION

Singles: 7–inch

BUDDAH 4-6   69
MR. CHAND 3-5   71
   Members: Joyce Smith; Darlene Arnold; Mary Shelley; Mary
   Lead; Wylie Dixon; Walter "Simtec" Simmons.
   Also see SIMTEC & WYLIE

KRYSTOL

Singles: 12–inch 33/45rpm

EPIC 4-6   84-86

Singles: 7–inch

EPIC 2-4   84-86

LPs: 10/12–inch 33rpm

EPIC 5-8   86

KUBAN, Bob

(Bob Kuban and the In-Men; Bob Kuban Band)
Singles: 7–inch

ERIC 3-5
MUSICLAND U.S.A. (Except 20,001) .. 4-8   66-67
MUSICLAND U.S.A. (20,001 "The
   Cheater") 8-10   66
   ("Vocal by Walter Scott" shown on both sides.)
MUSICLAND U.S.A. (20,001 "The
   Cheater") 3-6   66
   ("Vocal by Walter Scott" shown only on flip, *Try Me
   Baby.*)

MUSICLAND U.S.A. (20,001 "The
   Cheater") 3-6   66
   ("Vocal by Walter Scott" not on either side.)
NORMAN 4-8   65-66
   (Walter Scott may be shown as "Little Walter.")
REPRISE 4-6   70

LPs: 10/12–inch 33rpm

MUSICLAND U.S.A. (3500 "Look Out for
   the Cheater") 25-35   66
   Members: Walter Scott; Bob Kuban; John Krenski; Greg Hoeltzel.

KUF-LINX

(Kuff-Linx)
Singles: 78rpm

CHALLENGE 8-10   58
Singles: 7–inch
CHALLENGE (1013 "So Tough") 10-15   57
   (Blue or white label.)
CHALLENGE (1013 "So Tough") 5-10   58
CHALLENGE (59004 "Service
   with a Smile") 8-12   58
CHALLENGE (59015 "Climb
   Love's Mountain") 15-25   58
   Member: Johnny Jennings.

KULIS, Charlie

Singles: 7–inch

PLAYBOY 3-5   75

KWICK

Singles: 12–inch 33/45rpm

CAPITOL 4-6   83
Singles: 7–inch
CAPITOL 2-4   83
EMI AMERICA 2-4   80-82
LPs: 10/12–inch 33rpm
CAPITOL 5-8   83
EMI AMERICA 5-8   80-81
   Members: Terry Bartlett; Bert Brown; William Sumlin; Vince
   Williams.
   Also see NEWCOMERS

KYM

Singles: 12–inch 33/45rpm

AWARD 4-6   84
Singles: 7–inch
AWARD 2-4   84

L

L.A. BOPPERS
Singles: 7–inch
MCA	2-4	82
MERCURY	3-5	80-81

LPs: 10/12–inch 33rpm
MCA	5-8	82
MERCURY	5-10	80-81

L.A. DREAM TEAM
Singles: 12–inch 33/45rpm
MCA	4-6	86

Singles: 7–inch
MCA	2-4	86

LPs: 10/12–inch 33rpm
MCA	5-8	86-87

Members: Rudy Pardee; Chris Wilson.

L.A. GUNS
LPs: 10/12–inch 33rpm
VERTIGO	5-8	88-89

L.A. JETS
Singles: 7–inch
RCA	3-5	76

LPs: 10/12–inch 33rpm
RCA	8-10	76

L.L. COOL J
(Ladies Love Cool James; James Todd Smith)
Singles: 12–inch 33/45rpm
COLUMBIA	4-6	85-86

Singles: 7–inch
COLUMBIA	2-4	85-86
DEF JAM	2-4	87-90

LPs: 10/12–inch 33rpm
COLUMBIA	5-8	85
DEF JAM	5-8	87-90

L.T.D.
(Love, Togetherness and Devotion)
Singles: 7–inch
A&M	3-5	76-80
MONTAGE	2-4	83

Picture Sleeves
A&M	3-5	76-78

LPs: 10/12–inch 33rpm
A&M	8-10	74-81
MONTAGE	5-8	83
SPRINGBOARD	8-10	77

Member: Jeffrey Osborne.
Also see OSBORNE, Jeffrey

LTG EXCHANGE
Singles: 7–inch
FANIA	3-5	74
WAND	3-5	74

LABAN
Singles: 7–inch
CRITIQUE	2-4	86

LABELLE, Patti
(Patti Labelle and the Blue Belles; Labelle)
Singles: 12–inch 33/45rpm
EPIC	4-8	78-79
MCA	4-6	85
PHILADELPHIA INT'L	4-6	83-85

Singles: 7–inch
ATLANTIC	4-8	65-70
EPIC	3-5	74-80
KING	4-8	63
MISTLETOE	3-5	73
PHILADELPHIA INT'L	2-4	81-85
MCA	2-4	85-87
NEWTOWN	4-8	62-63
NICETOWN	4-8	64
PARKWAY	4-8	64
RCA	3-5	73
TRIP	3-5	71
WARNER	3-5	71-72

LPs: 10/12–inch 33rpm
ATLANTIC	15-25	65-67
EPIC	8-10	74-82
MCA	5-8	85-89
MISTLETOE	10-20	
NEWTOWN (631 "Sweethearts of the Apollo")	50-75	63
NEWTOWN (632 "Sleigh Bells, Jingle Bells and Blue Bells")	50-75	63
PARKWAY (7043 "On Stage")	30-40	64
PHILADELPHIA INT'L	5-8	81-85
RCA (0200 series)	8-10	73
RCA (4100 series)	5-8	82
TRIP	8-10	71-75
U.A.	8-10	74-75
UPFRONT	10-15	
WARNER	8-10	71-72

Also see BLUE BELLES
Also see DASH, Sarah
Also see HENDRIX, Nona
Also see NYRO, Laura
Also see WOMACK, Bobby, and Patti Labelle

LABELLE, Patti / Harold Faltermeyer
Singles: 7–inch
MCA	2-4	85

Also see FALTERMEYER, Harold

LABELLE, Patti, and Michael McDonald
Singles: 7–inch
MCA	2-4	86

Also see McDONALD, Michael

LABELLE, Patti, and Grover Washington Jr.
Singles: 7–inch
ELEKTRA	2-4	82

Also see LABELLE, Patti
Also see WASHINGTON, Grover, Jr.

LA BOUNTY, Bill
Singles: 7–inch

20TH FOX	3-5	75-76
WARNER	3-5	78

LABYRINTH
Singles: 7–inch

21	2-4	85

Member: Julie Loco.

LACE
Singles: 7–inch

WING	2-4	87

LPs: 10/12–inch 33rpm

WING	5-8	87

LADD, Cheryl
Singles: 12–inch 33/45rpm

CAPITOL (8894 "Skinnydippin")	10-15	78

(Promotional issue only.)

Singles: 7–inch

CAPITOL	3-5	76-79

Picture Sleeves

CAPITOL	3-5	78-79
WARNER	4-6	74

LPs: 10/12–inch 33rpm

CAPITOL	8-10	78-79

Also see VALLI, Frankie, and Cheryl Ladd

LADIES CHOICE
Singles: 7–inch

STREETWISE	2-4	83

LADY
Singles: 7–inch

MEGA	2-4	82

LADY FLASH
Singles: 7–inch

RSO	3-5	76

LPs: 10/12–inch 33rpm

RSO	8-12	76

Members: Monica Burruss; Debra Byrd; Reparata.
Also see MANILOW, Barry

LAFAYETTES
Singles: 7–inch

RCA	5-10	62

LA FLAMME, David
Singles: 7–inch

AMHERST	3-5	76-77

Picture Sleeves

AMHERST	3-5	76

LPs: 10/12–inch 33rpm

AMHERST	8-10	76-78

Also see IT'S a BEAUTIFUL DAY

LA FLAVOUR
Singles: 12–inch 33/45rpm

SWEET CITY	8-10	80

Singles: 7–inch

MERCURY	3-5	79
SWEET CITY	3-5	80

LPs: 10/12–inch 33rpm

SWEET CITY	5-8	80

LA FORGE, Jack
(Jack LaForge and His Orchestra)
Singles: 7–inch

LYRIC	3-5	65-66
REGINA	3-5	63-66
RIO	4-6	62

LPs: 10/12–inch 33rpm

AUDIO FIDELITY	6-12	66
PURPLETONE	8-15	62
REGINA	8-15	63-65

LAID BACK
Singles: 12–inch 33/45rpm

SIRE	4-6	84-85
WARNER	4-6	83

Singles: 7–inch

SIRE	2-4	84-85
WARNER	2-4	83-84

LPs: 10/12–inch 33rpm

SIRE	5-8	84

Members: Timothy Stahl; John Guldberg.

LAINE, Cleo
Singles: 7–inch

RCA	3-5	74-80

LPs: 10/12–inch 33rpm

BUDDAH	8-10	74
FONTANA	10-15	66
GNP/CRESCENDO	5-10	74
QUINTESSENCE	5-8	80
RCA	5-10	73-80

Also see CHARLES, Ray, and Cleo Laine

LAINE, Frankie
Singles: 78rpm

MERCURY	4-8	47-51
COLUMBIA	4-8	51-57

Singles: 7–inch

ABC	3-5	67-69
AMOS	3-5	70-71
CAPITOL	4-8	64-66
COLUMBIA (39367 through 41486)	5-15	51-59
COLUMBIA (41613 through 42966)	4-8	60-64
MAINSTREAM	3-5	75
MERCURY (5000 series)	8-15	50-51
SUNFLOWER	3-5	72
WARNER	3-5	74

Picture Sleeves

COLUMBIA	10-20	56-57

EPs: 7–inch 33/45rpm

COLUMBIA	5-15	52-59
MERCURY	8-15	51-54

LPs: 10/12–inch 33rpm

ABC (600 series)	8-15	67-69
ABC (30000 series)	5-8	76
AMOS	8-12	70-71
CAPITOL	10-15	65
COLUMBIA (600 through 1200 series)	15-30	54-58

COLUMBIA (1300 through 1900
series) 10-20 59-63
(Monaural.)
COLUMBIA (2500 series) 20-30 56
(10–inch LPs.)
COLUMBIA (6000 series) 20-40 53-54
(10–inch LPs.)
COLUMBIA (8100 through 8700
series) 10-20 59-63
(Stereo.)
HARMONY 8-15 65-71
HINDSIGHT 4-8 84
MERCURY (20000 series) 15-30 54-61
MERCURY (25000 series) 20-40 51-52
(10–inch LPs.)
MERCURY (60000 series) 10-20 61
TOWER 8-15 67
TRIP 5-8 75
WING 8-15 60-67
Also see DAY, Doris, and Frankie Laine

LAINE, Frankie, and Jimmy Boyd
Singles: 78rpm
COLUMBIA 4-8 53
Singles: 7–inch
COLUMBIA 5-10 53
Also see BOYD, Jimmy

LAINE, Frankie, and the Four Lads
Singles: 78rpm
COLUMBIA 4-8 54
Singles: 7–inch
COLUMBIA 5-10 54
EPs: 7–inch 33/45rpm
COLUMBIA 5-15 56
LPs: 10/12–inch 33rpm
COLUMBIA 20-30 56
Also see FOUR LADS

LAINE, Frankie, and Jo Stafford
Singles: 78rpm
COLUMBIA 4-8 51-53
Singles: 7–inch
COLUMBIA 5-10 51-53
EPs: 7–inch 33/45rpm
COLUMBIA 5-15 54
LPs: 10/12–inch 33rpm
COLUMBIA 20-30 54
Also see LAINE, Frankie
Also see STAFFORD, Jo

LAKE
Singles: 7–inch
CARIBOU 3-5 81
COLUMBIA 3-5 77-79
LPs: 10/12–inch 33rpm
CARIBOU 5-8 81
COLUMBIA 5-10 77-79

LAKE, Greg
Singles: 7–inch
ATLANTIC 3-5 75-77

CHRYSALIS 3-5 81
LPs: 10/12–inch 33rpm
CHRYSALIS 5-10 81
Also see EMERSON, LAKE & PALMER
Also see KING CRIMSON

LAKESIDE
Singles: 7–inch
SOLAR 3-5 78-87
LPs: 10/12–inch 33rpm
ABC-PAR 8-10 77
SOLAR 5-8 77-84

LA LA
Singles: 7–inch
ARISTA 2-4 87

LA LA, Prince: see PRINCE LA LA

LAMAS, Lorenzo
Singles: 7–inch
SCOTTI BROTHERS 2-4 84-85

LAMB, Kevin
Singles: 7–inch
ARISTA 3-5 78

LAMBERT, Guy: see PRESLEY, Elvis

LAMONT, Lee
Singles: 7–inch
BACK BEAT 4-8 64-66

L'AMOUR
Singles: 12–inch 33/45rpm
BROCCOLLI 4-6 84

LAMP SISTERS
Singles: 7–inch
DUKE 4-8 68-69

LANCE, Herb
(Herb Lance and the Classics)
Singles: 78rpm
DELUXE 8-12 57
SITTIN' in WITH 10-20 49
Singles: 7–inch
DELUXE 10-20 57
MALA 5-10 59-60
PROMO 8-12 61
LPs: 10/12–inch 33rpm
CHESS 15-25 66

LANCE, Major
Singles: 12–inch 33/45rpm
KAT FAMILY 4-6 82
Singles: 7–inch
COLUMBIA 3-5 77
CURTOM 3-5 70
DAKAR 4-6 69
EPIC 4-8 66
KAT FAMILY 2-4 82
MERCURY (71582 "Phyllis") 15-30 60
OKEH (Except 7200) 5-10 63-67
OKEH (7200 "Think Nothing About It") 25-50 64

OSIRIS 3-5   75
PLAYBOY 3-5   74-75
SOUL 3-5   78
VOLT 3-5   72
Picture Sleeves
OKEH 4-8   63-64
EPs: 7–inch 33/45rpm
OKEH 10-15   64
(Jukebox issue only.)
LPs: 10/12–inch 33rpm
BACK-TRAC 5-8   85
CONTEMPO 10-12
KAT FAMILY 5-8   83
OKEH 15-20   63-64
SOUL 5-8   78

LANDIS, Jerry
(Paul Simon)
Singles: 7–inch
AMY (875 "The Lone Teen Ranger") . 25-35   62
CANADIAN AMERICAN (130 "I'm
Lonely") 20-30   61
MGM (12822 "Anna Belle") 25-35   59
WARWICK (552 "Just a Boy") 25-35   60
WARWICK (558 "Just a Boy") 25-35   60
WARWICK (619 "Play Me
a Sad Song") 25-35   61
Also see SIMON, Paul

LANDS, Liz / Martin Luther King
Singles: 7–inch
GORDY (7023 "We Shall Overcome") . 8-12   63
Also see KING, Rev. Martin Luther, Jr.

LANDS, Liz, and the Temptations
Singles: 7–inch
GORDY (7030 "Keep Me") 8-12   64
Also see LANDS, Liz
Also see TEMPTATIONS

LANE, Mickey Lee
Singles: 7–inch
MALA 5-8   68
SWAN 5-10   64-66

LANE, Robin, and the Chartbusters
Singles: 7–inch
WARNER 3-5   80-81
Picture Sleeves
WARNER 3-5   80
LPs: 10/12–inch 33rpm
WARNER 5-8   80-81
Members: Robin Lane; Leroy Radcliffe; Asa Brebner; Scott
Baeren wald; Tim Jackson.

LANE BROTHERS
Singles: 78rpm
RCA 5-10   57
Singles: 7–inch
LEADER 5-8   60
RCA 5-10   57-58

LANE BROTHERS / Julius La Rosa
EPs: 7–inch 33/45rpm
RCA 5-10   57
(Promotional issue only.)
Also see LANE BROTHERS
Also see LA ROSA, Julius

LANG, K.D.
Singles: 7–inch
SIRE 2-4   88-90
LPs: 10/12–inch 33rpm
SIRE 5-8   88-90
Also see ORBISON, Roy, and K.D. Lang

LANI & BONI
Singles: 7–inch
GARPAX (4084 "Cherry Pie") 10-15   64
Members: Delaney Bramlett; Bonnie Bramlett.
Also see DELANEY & BONNIE

LANIER & CO.
Singles: 7–inch
LARC 2-4   82-83
LPs: 10/12–inch 33rpm
LARC 5-8   83

LANIN, Lester, and His Orchestra
Singles: 78rpm
EPIC 3-5   56-57
Singles: 7–inch
EPIC 4-8   56-62
EPs: 7–inch 33/45rpm
EPIC 4-8   56-58
LPs: 10/12–inch 33rpm
EPIC 5-15   56-62

LANSON, Snooky
Singles: 78rpm
DECCA 3-5   52
DOT 3-5   55-56
LONDON 3-5   50-51
REPUBLIC 3-5   53
Singles: 7–inch
DECCA 5-10   52
DOT 5-10   55-56
LONDON 5-10   50-51
REPUBLIC 5-10   53
STARDAY 3-6   68
LPs: 10/12–inch 33rpm
CAMDEN (200 series) 10-20   55
DOT 10-15   60
STARDAY 5-10   68

LANZ, David
(David Lanz and Paul Speer)
LPs: 10/12–inch 33rpm
NARADA 5-8   88

LANZA, Mario
Singles: 78rpm
RCA 3-5   50-57
Singles: 7–inch
RCA (0400 series) 3-5   71

RCA (3200 through 8500 series) 5-10	51-59
RCA (1300 series) 4-6	50

Picture Sleeves

RCA (3300 "The Loveliest		
Night of the Year") 15-25	51
RCA (4209 "Song of India") 15-25	51

EPs: 7–inch 33/45rpm

RCA (Except 1837) 8-15	53-61
RCA (1837 "Student Prince") 15-25	54
(Soundtrack.)		

LPs: 10/12–inch 33rpm

CAMDEN (Except 400 series) 5-15	63
CAMDEN (400 series) 10-20	57
(With "CAL" prefix. Monaural.)		
CAMDEN (400 series) 8-15	63
(With "CAS" prefix. Stereo.)		
RCA (75 "The Toast of New Orleans") 45-60	51
(Soundtrack. (10–inch LP.)		
RCA (86 through 1181) 20-30	51-53
RCA (1750 "A Legendary		
Performer") 5-8	76
RCA (1837 "Student Prince") 35-45	54
(Soundtrack.)		
RCA (1860 through 2090) 15-25	54-57
(Black label.)		
RCA (1860 through 2090) 6-12	68
(Orange label.)		
RCA (2211 "Seven Hills of Rome") ... 20-30	58
(Soundtrack songs on side one, other Mario Lanza songs on side two.)		
RCA (2331 through 2333) 15-25	59-61
(Black label.)		
RCA (2331 through 2333) 6-12	68
(Orange label.)		
RCA (2338 "For the First Time") 20-30	59
(Soundtrack.)		
RCA (2339 through 2790) 10-20	60-64
(Black label.)		
RCA (2339 through 2790) 6-12	68
(Orange label.)		
RCA (2800 series) 4-8	78
RCA (2900 through 3200) 8-15	68-71
RCA (4158 "The Mario		
Lanza Collection") 35-45	81
(Five-LP boxed set.)		

LARKIN, Billy
(Billy Larkin and the Delegates)
Singles: 78rpm

MELODY 20-30	56

Singles: 7–inch

BRYAN 3-5	75
CASINO 3-5	76
MELODY (103 "Rock-it,		
Davy Crockett") 50-75	56
MERCURY 3-5	78-79
SUNBIRD 3-5	81
WORLD PACIFIC 4-8	66

LPs: 10/12–inch 33rpm

AURA 15-25	65-66
BRYAN 5-10	75
WORLD PACIFIC 10-20	65-69

LARKS
Singles: 78rpm

APOLLO (427 "Eyesight to		
the Blind") 50-100	51
APOLLO (429 "Little Side Car") 50-75	51
APOLLO (430 "Ooh . . . It Feels		
So Good") 50-75	51
APOLLO (435 "My Lost Love") 50-75	51
APOLLO (437 "Darlin'") 50-75	52
APOLLO (475 "Honey from		
the Bee") 20-40	55
APOLLO (1177 "My Heart Cries		
for You") 50-75	51
APOLLO (1180 "Hopefully		
Yours") 50-75	51
APOLLO (1184 "My Reverie") 50-75	51
APOLLO (1189 "Shadrack") 50-75	52
APOLLO (1190 "Stolen Love") 50-75	52
APOLLO (1194 "Hold Me") 50-75	52
LLOYDS (108 "Margie") 40-60	54
LLOYDS (110 "If It's a Crime") 40-60	54
LLOYDS (111 "When You're Near") .. 20-40	54
LLOYDS (112 "No Other Girl") 50-75	54
LLOYDS (114 "Forget It") 20-40	54
LLOYDS (115 "Johnny Darlin'") 20-40	54

Singles: 7–inch

APOLLO (429 "Little Side Car") ... 400-600	51
APOLLO (430 "Ooh . . . It Feels		
So Good") 400-600	51
APOLLO (435 "My Lost Love") ... 400-600	51
APOLLO (437 "Darlin'") 500-750	52
APOLLO (475 "Honey from		
the Bee") 150-250	55
APOLLO (1180 "Hopefully Yours") . 400-600	51
APOLLO (1184 "My Reverie") ... 750-1000	51
(Black vinyl)		
APOLLO (1184 "My Reverie") .. 1000-1500	51
(Colored vinyl.)		
APOLLO (1189 "Shadrack") 400-600	52
APOLLO (1190 "Stolen Love") 400-600	52
(Black vinyl)		
APOLLO (1190 "Stolen Love") ... 750-1000	52
(Colored vinyl)		
APOLLO (1194 "Hold Me") 400-600	52
LLOYDS (108 "Margie") 300-500	54
LLOYDS (110 "If It's a Crime") 250-350	54
LLOYDS (111 "When You're Near") 150-250	54
LLOYDS (112 "No Other Girl") 400-500	54
LLOYDS (114 "Forget It") 150-250	54
LLOYDS (115 "Johnny Darlin'") ... 150-200	54

Members: Gene Mumford; Allen Bunn; Ray Barnes; Thermon Ruth; Dave McNeil; Hadie Rowe; Orville Brooks.
Also see BUNN, Allen

LARKS
(Don Julian and the Larks)
Singles: 7–inch

JERK 4-8	65	
MONEY 4-8	64-71	

LPs: 10/12–inch 33rpm

AMAZON (1009 "Greatest Hits") 45-55	63	
MONEY 15-20	65-67	

Also see JULIAN, Don, and the Meadowlarks

LARKS
Singles: 7–inch

CROSS FIRE 10-15		
GUYDEN 5-10	63	
SHERYL 10-15	61	
STACY 4-8	63	
VIOLET 10-15	63	

LA ROSA, Julius
Singles: 78rpm

CADENCE 3-6	53-55	

Singles: 7–inch

ABC 4-6	67	
BARNABY 3-5	70	
CADENCE (1200 series) 5-10	53-55	
CADENCE (1400 series) 4-8	63-64	
KAPP 4-8	60-62	
MGM 4-6	66	
MGM CELEBRITY SCENE (CS5-5		
"Julius LaRosa") 10-20	66	
(Boxed set of five singles with bio insert and title		
strips.)		
METROMEDIA 3-5	70	
RCA (0900 series) 3-5	73	
RCA (6000 and 7000 series) 5-10	56-58	
ROULETTE 4-8	59	

EPs: 7–inch 33/45rpm

CADENCE 5-15	54-58	
RCA (EPA-841 "Julius LaRosa") 5-10	56	
RCA (EPB-1299 "Julius LaRosa") ... 15-25	56	

LPs: 10/12–inch 33rpm

CADENCE (1007 "Julie's Best") 20-30	55	
FORUM 10-15	60	
KAPP 10-15	61	
MGM 10-15	66-67	
METROMEDIA 5-10	71	
RCA (1299 "Julius LaRosa") 20-30	56	
ROULETTE 10-20	59	

Also see LANE BROTHERS / Julius La Rosa

LA ROSA, Julius, and the Bob Crewe Generation
Singles: 7–inch

CREWE 3-6	69	

Also see CREWE, Bob
Also see LA ROSA, Julius

LARRICE
Singles: 12–inch 33/45rpm

STREETWISE 4-6	84	

LARRY & JOHNNY
Singles: 7–inch

JOLA (1000 "Beatle Time") 10-15	64	

Members: Larry Williams; Johnny "Guitar" Watson.
Also see WILLIAMS, Larry, and Johnny Watson

LARRY LEE: see LEE, Larry

LARSEN, Neil
Singles: 7–inch

A&M 3-5	79	
WARNER 2-4	83	

LPs: 10/12–inch 33rpm

A&M 5-8	79	
HORIZON 8-10	78-79	
WARNER 5-8	83	

Also see LARSEN - FEITEN BAND

LARSEN - FEITEN BAND
Singles: 7–inch

WARNER 3-5	80	

LPs: 10/12–inch 33rpm

WARNER 5-8	80	

Members: Neil Larsen; Buzz Feiten.
Also see LARSEN, Neil

LARSON, Nicolette
Singles: 7–inch

MCA 2-4	86	
WARNER 3-5	78-82	

LPs: 10/12–inch 33rpm

MCA 5-8	86	
WARNER 5-8	78-82	

Also see DOOBIE BROTHERS and Nicolette Larson
Also see WINCHESTER, Jesse
Also see YOUNG, Neil

LA RUE, D.C.
Singles: 12–inch 33/45rpm

CASABLANCA 4-6	79-80	
PYRAMID 4-8	78-79	

Singles: 7–inch

CASABLANCA 3-5	79-80	
PYRAMID 4-6	76-79	

LPs: 10/12–inch 33rpm

CASABLANCA 5-8	79-80	
PYRAMID 5-10	76-79	

Also see CHRISTIE, Lou

LA SALLE, Denise
Singles: 7–inch

ABC 3-5	77-79	
CHESS 4-8	68	
MCA 3-5	79-80	
MALACO 2-4	81-85	
WESTBOUND 3-5	71-75	

LPs: 10/12–inch 33rpm

ABC 8-10	77-78	
MCA 5-8	80	
MALACO 5-8	81-85	
WESTBOUND 8-10	72-75	

LASLEY, David
Singles: 7–inch
EMI AMERICA . . . . 2-4　82-84

LASSER, Max
(Max Lasser's Ark)
LPs: 10/12–inch 33rpm
CBS . . . . 5-8　88

LASSIES
Singles: 78rpm
DECCA . . . . 4-8　56
Singles: 7–inch
DECCA . . . . 8-12　56

LAST, James
Singles: 7–inch
POLYDOR . . . . 3-5　71-82
LPs: 10/12–inch 33rpm
POLYDOR . . . . 5-10　72-81

LAST POETS
Singles: 7–inch
DOUGLAS . . . . 3-5　71
LPs: 10/12–inch 33rpm
BLUE THUMB . . . . 8-12　72-73
DOUGLAS . . . . 10-15　70-71
JUGGERNAUT . . . . 10-15　71

LAST WORD
Singles: 7–inch
ATCO . . . . 4-8　67-68
BOOM . . . . 4-8　66
LPs: 10/12–inch 33rpm
ATCO . . . . 10-20　68

LATEEF, Yusef
(Yusef Lateef Quintet)
Singles: 7–inch
ATLANTIC . . . . 3-5　68-70
IMPULSE . . . . 3-6　64
NEW JAZZ . . . . 4-8　60
PRESTIGE . . . . 3-6　63-69
LPs: 10/12–inch 33rpm
ATLANTIC . . . . 8-15　68-76
CTI . . . . 5-8　77-79
CADET . . . . 10-15　69
CHARLIE PARKER . . . . 20-30　62
EVEREST . . . . 5-10　74
IMPULSE (56 through 9125) . . . . 10-20　63-66
IMPULSE (9200 and 9300 series) . . . 73-78
MILESTONE . . . . 8-12　73
MOODSVILLE . . . . 25-35　61
NEW JAZZ . . . . 25-40　59-61
PRESTIGE (7122 "The Sounds
 of Yusef Lateef") . . . . 50-100　57
 (Yellow label.)
PRESTIGE (7400 through
 7800 series) . . . . 10-20　66-71
PRESTIGE (24000 series) . . . . 8-15　72-74
RIVERSIDE (300 series) . . . . 20-30　60
 (Monaural.)

RIVERSIDE (3000 series) . . . . 10-20　68
RIVERSIDE (9300 series) . . . . 25-35　60
 (Stereo.)
SAVOY (2200 series) . . . . 8-12　76-79
SAVOY (12000 series) . . . . 25-50　56-58
SAVOY (13000 series) . . . . 25-50　58
TRIP . . . . 5-10　73
VERVE (8217 "Before Dawn") . . . . . 50-100　57
 (Reads "Verve Records, Inc." at bottom of label.)
VERVE (8217 "Before Dawn") 25-35
 (Reads "MGM Records - a Division of
 Metro-Goldwyn-Mayer, Inc." at bottom of label.)

LATIMORE, Benny
(Latimore)
Singles: 7–inch
ATLANTIC . . . . 4-6　69
DADE . . . . 4-8　67-68
GLADES . . . . 3-5　73-79
MALACO . . . . 2-4　83-86
LPs: 10/12–inch 33rpm
GLADES . . . . 6-10　73-78
MALACO . . . . 5-8　83-86

LATTISAW, Stacy
Singles: 7–inch
COTILLION . . . . 3-5　79-84
MOTOWN . . . . 2-4　86-88
LPs: 10/12–inch 33rpm
COTILLION . . . . 5-8　79-84
MOTOWN . . . . 5-8　86-88
 Also see KING DREAM CHORUS and Holiday Crew

LATTISAW, Stacy, and Johnny Gill
Singles: 7–inch
COTILLION . . . . 3-5　84-85
LPs: 10/12–inch 33rpm
COTILLION . . . . 5-8　84
 Also see GILL, Johnny
 Also see LATTISAW, Stacy

LAUGHING SOUP DISH
Singles: 7–inch
VOXX . . . . 2-4　87
LPs: 10/12–inch 33rpm
VOXX . . . . 5-8　87

LAUPER, Cyndi
Singles: 12–inch 33/45rpm
PORTRAIT . . . . 4-6　83-87
Singles: 7–inch
PORTRAIT . . . . 2-4　83-87
Picture Sleeves
EPIC . . . . 5-8　89
PORTRAIT . . . . 2-4　83-87
LPs: 10/12–inch 33rpm
PORTRAIT . . . . 5-8　83-86
 Also see HOOTERS
 Also see U.S.A. for AFRICA

LAURA & JOHNNY
Singles: 7–inch
SILVER FOX . . . . 4-6　69

LAURA LEE: see LEE, Laura

LAURAN, Niki
Singles: 12–inch 33/45rpm
WAVE 4-6   83

LAUREN, Rod
Singles: 7–inch
CHANCELLOR 4-8   62
RCA 5-10   59-62
Picture Sleeves
RCA 5-10   59-60
LPs: 10/12–inch 33rpm
RCA (LPM-2176 "I'm Rod Lauren") .. 20-30   61
(Monaural.)
RCA (LSP-2176 "I'm Rod Lauren") .. 30-40   61
(Stereo.)
Also see COOKE, Sam / Rod Lauren / Neil Sedaka / Browns

LAURENCE, Paul
Singles: 12–inch 33/45rpm
CAPITOL 4-6   86
Singles: 7–inch
CAPITOL 2-4   85-86
LPs: 10/12–inch 33rpm
CAPITOL 5-8   86

LAURIE, Annie
Singles: 78rpm
DELUXE 5-10   47-49
REGAL 5-10   49
OKEH 5-10   55
SAVOY 5-10   56
Singles: 7–inch
DELUXE 8-15   57-60
DOVE 4-6   68
GUSTO 3-5   78
OKEH 10-15   55
RITZ 4-8   62
SAVOY 10-15   56
LPs: 10/12–inch 33rpm
AUDIO LAB (1510 "It Hurts to Be
in Love") 40-50   58

LAURIE, Linda
Singles: 7–inch
ANDIE 5-10   60
GLORY 5-10   59
KEETCH 4-8   64
RECONA 4-8   63
RUST 4-8   60-63

LAURIE SISTERS
Singles: 78rpm
MERCURY 4-6   54-55
VIK 4-6   56
Singles: 7–inch
MGM 5-10   59-60
MERCURY 5-10   54-55
PORT 4-8   63
VIK 5-10   56

LPs: 10/12–inch 33rpm
CAMDEN (CAL-545 "Hits of the
Great Girl Groups") 15-25   60
(Monaural.)
CAMDEN (CAS-545 "Hits of the
Great Girl Groups") 25-35   60
(Stereo.)

LAVERNE & SHIRLEY
Singles: 7–inch
ATLANTIC 3-6   76-77
LPs: 10/12–inch 33rpm
ATLANTIC 8-10   76
Members: Penny Marshall; Cindy Williams.

LAVETTE, Betty
(Betty Lavett; Bettye LaVette)
Singles: 7–inch
ATCO 3-5   72
ATLANTIC 4-8   62-63
BIG WHEEL 4-8   66
CALLA 4-8   65
EPIC 3-5   75
KAREN 4-6   68-69
LUPINE 4-8   64
MOTOWN 3-5   81-82
SSS INT'L 3-5   71
SILVER FOX 4-6   69
TCA 3-5   71
WEST END 4-8
LPs: 10/12–inch 33rpm
MOTOWN 5-8   81

LAWRENCE, Eddie
Singles: 78rpm
CORAL 3-5   56-57
Singles: 7–inch
CORAL 4-8   56-63
EPIC 4-6   65
SHASTA 4-8   60
SIGNATURE 4-8   60
Picture Sleeves
CORAL 5-10   56
EPIC 4-8   65
LPs: 10/12–inch 33rpm
CORAL 12-25   55-62
EPIC 8-15   65
SIGNATURE 10-20   59

LAWRENCE, Steve
Singles: 78rpm
CORAL 4-8   55-57
KING 4-8   52-53
Singles: 7–inch
ABC 3-5   73
ABC-PAR 5-10   58-60
CALENDAR 4-8   67-68
COLUMBIA 4-8   62-68
CORAL 5-15   55-59
KING (1200 series) 5-10   53
KING (5000 series) 4-8   60-64

KING (15000 series) 5-10   52-53
MGM 3-5   71-73
RCA 3-6   69-70
ROULETTE 3-5   73
STAGE 2 2-4   84
20TH FOX 3-5   75-77
U.A. (200 and 300 series) 4-8   60-61
U.A. (900 through 1100 series) 3-5   76-78
WARNER 3-5   78

Picture Sleeves

COLUMBIA 4-8   62-63
STAGE 2 2-4   84
U.A. 5-10   60-61

EPs: 7–inch 33/45rpm

COLUMBIA 5-10   64-69
(Jukebox issues only.)
CORAL 5-10   60
(Jukebox issues only.)
KING 10-20   53
RCA 4-8   70

LPs: 10/12–inch 33rpm

ABC-PAR 20-30   57-60
APPLAUSE 5-10   81
COLUMBIA 10-25   63-68
COLUMBIA RECORD CLUB 8-15   75
CORAL (57050 "About That Girl") ... 20-40   56
CORAL (57182 "Songs By
  Steve Lawrence") 20-30   57
CORAL (57204 "Here's Steve
  Lawrence") 20-30   57
CORAL (57268 "All About Love") 20-30   58
  (Monaural.)
CORAL (57434 "Songs
  Everybody Knows") 12-20   62
  (Monaural.)
CORAL (757268 "All About Love") ... 20-40   58
  (Stereo.)
CORAL (757434 "Songs
  Everybody Knows") 15-25   62
  (Stereo.)
GALA 5-10   77
GUEST STAR 5-10   64
HARMONY 6-12   68-71
KING (593 "Steve Lawrence") 25-35   58
MGM 5-10   71
RCA 6-12   69-70
SESAC 10-20   59
  (Promotional issues only.)
SPINORAMA 8-15
U.A. 10-20   61-64
VERSATILE 5-8   77
VOCALION 5-12   66-69

LAWRENCE, Steve / Tennessee Ernie Ford
LPs: 10/12–inch 33rpm

CAMAY 15-25   60
  Also see FORD, Tennessee Ernie

LAWRENCE, Steve, and Eydie Gorme
(Steve & Eydie)
Singles: 78rpm

CORAL 4-8   55

Singles: 7–inch

CALENDAR 4-6   68
COLUMBIA 4-8   62-67
CORAL 5-10   55
MGM 3-5   72-73
RCA 3-5   68-69

EPs: 7–inch 33/45rpm

ABC 5-10   60
  (Jukebox issues only.)
ADVERTISING COUNCIL (5071
  "Celebrity Spots") 15-30
  (Promotional issue only. Includes other artists.)
COLUMBIA 5-10   64-69
  (Jukebox issues only.)
CORAL 10-15   58

LPs: 10/12–inch 33rpm

ABC 5-10   73-76
ABC/LONGINES ("Romantic
  Treasury") 30-45   67
  (Six-LP boxed set.)
ABC-PAR 15-25   59-64
CBS 10-15   63
CALENDAR 8-15   68
COLUMBIA 10-20   63-67
CORAL (57336 "Steve & Eydie") 15-25   60
ENCORE 5-8   84
HARMONY 5-10   64-71
MCA 5-10
MGM 5-10   72-73
PICKWICK 5-10
RCA 6-12   69-72
STAGE 2 5-10   78-84
U.A. 10-20   61-62
VOCALION 5-12   67
  Also see GORME, Eydie
  Also see OSMONDS, Steve Lawrence and Eydie Gorme

LAWRENCE, Steve / Trini Lopez
LPs: 10/12–inch 33rpm

DIPLOMAT 10-15   65
  Also see LAWRENCE, Steve
  Also see LOPEZ, Trini

LAWRENCE, Vicki
Singles: 7–inch

BELL 3-5   73-74
FLASHBACK 3-5   74
PRIVATE STOCK 3-5   75-76
U.A. 3-5   71

LPs: 10/12–inch 33rpm

BELL 8-12   73
WINDMILL 5-10   79

LAWS, Debra
Singles: 7–inch

ELEKTRA 3-5   80-81

LPs: 10/12–inch 33rpm

ELEKTRA 5-8   81

LAWS, Eloise
Singles: 7–inch

ABC 3-5   77-78
CAPITOL 2-4   82
COLUMBIA 4-6   68-70
INVICTUS 3-5   75-77
LIBERTY 3-5   80-81
MUSIC MERCHANT 3-5   72-73
Picture Sleeves
LIBERTY 3-5   80
LPs: 10/12–inch 33rpm
ABC 8-10   77-78
CAPITOL 5-8   82
INVICTUS 5-10   76
LIBERTY 5-8   80

LAWS, Hubert
Singles: 7-Inch

ATLANTIC 4-6   65
CTI 3-5   70-75
COLUMBIA 2-4   78
LPs: 10/12-Inch 33rpm
ATLANTIC 8-18   66-81
CTI 8-15   70-77
COLUMBIA 5-10   76-80

LAWS, Hubert, and Earl Klugh

COLUMBIA 5-10   80
   Also see KLUGH, Earl
   Also see LAWS, Hubert

LAWS, Ronnie
(Ronnie Laws and Pressure)
Singles: 7–inch

BLUE NOTE 3-5   75-77
CAPITOL 2-4   83-84
LIBERTY 3-5   80-81
U.A. 3-5   75-80
LPs: 10/12–inch 33rpm
BLUE NOTE 6-12   75-77
CAPITOL 5-8   83
LIBERTY 5-10   81
U.A. 5-10   75-80
   Also see EARTH, WIND & FIRE

LAYNA, Magda
Singles: 12–inch 33/45rpm

MEGATONE 4-6   83

LAYNE, Joy
Singles: 78rpm

MERCURY 4-6   57
Singles: 7–inch
LUCKY FOUR 4-8   61
MERCURY 5-10   57

LAZY COWGIRLS
Singles: 7–inch

BOMP 2-4   87

Picture Sleeves
BOMP 2-4   87
LPs: 10/12–inch 33rpm
BOMP 5-8   87

LAZY RACER
Singles: 7–inch
A&M 3-5   79-80
LPs: 10/12–inch 33rpm
A&M 5-10   79-80

LEACH, Billy
Singles: 7–inch
BALLY 5-10   57

LEADON, Bernie
(Bernie Leadon and the Michael Georgiades Band)
Singles: 7–inch
ASYLUM 3-5   77
LPs: 10/12–inch 33rpm
ASYLUM 8-10   77
   Also see EAGLES

LEAGUE UNLIMITED ORCHESTRA
Singles: 7–inch
A&M 2-4   82
LPs: 10/12–inch 33rpm
A&M 5-8   82
   Also see HUMAN LEAGUE

LEAPY LEE
Singles: 7–inch
CADET 4-6   69
DECCA 4-8   68-71
MAM 3-5   72
MCA 3-5   75
Picture Sleeves
MCA 3-5   75
LPs: 10/12–inch 33rpm
DECCA 12-20 68

LEATHERWOLF
LPs: 10/12–inch 33rpm
ISLAND 5-8   88-89

LEAVES
Singles: 7–inch
CAPITOL 4-8   66
MIRA (202 "Too Many People"/
   "Love Minus Zero") 8-10   65
(Reissued on Mira 227 as *Too Many People/Girl
from the East*.)
MIRA (207 "Hey Joe, Where You
   Gonna Go") 10-12 65
(Reissued on Mira 222 with the shorter title, *Hey
Joe*.)
MIRA (213 through 234) 4-8   66
PANDA (1003 "Hey Joe") 8-12   82
(Colored vinyl, leaf-shaped disc.)
LPs: 10/12–inch 33rpm
CAPITOL (T-2638 "All the
   Good That's Happening") 15-25 67
(Monaural.)

CAPITOL (ST-2638 "All the
Good That's Happening") 25-35   67
(Stereo.)
MIRA (LP-3005 "Hey Joe") 25-35   66
(Monaural.)
MIRA (LPS-3005 "Hey Joe") 30-40   66
(Stereo.)
  Members: John Beck; Bob Arlin; Jim Pons; Tom Ray; Bill
  Rheinhart; Robert Reiner.
  Also see MOTHERS of INVENTION
  Also see TURTLES

LEAVILLE, Otis
(Otis Leavill)
Singles: 7–inch
BLUE ROCK 4-8   65
BRUNSWICK 4-8   67
COLUMBIA 4-8   66
DAKAR 4-6   69-70
LIMELIGHT 4-8   64
LUCKY 4-8   64
SMASH 4-8   68

LEAVY, Calvin
Singles: 7–inch
BLUE FOX 3-5   70

LE BLANC, Lenny
Singles: 7–inch
BIG TREE 3-6   76-77
CAPITOL 3-5   81
LPs: 10/12–inch 33rpm
BIG TREE 8-12   76-77
CAPITOL 5-10   81

LE BLANC & CARR
Singles: 7–inch
BIG TREE 3-5   77-78
LPs: 10/12–inch 33rpm
ATLANTIC (003 "Live from the
Atlantic Studios") 8-12   78
(Promotional issue only.)
BIG TREE 8-10   77
  Members: Lenny LeBlanc; Pete Carr.
  Also see LE BLANC, Lenny

LED ZEPPELIN
Singles: 7–inch
ATLANTIC (2613 "Good Times
Bad Times") 10-15   69
ATLANTIC (2690 "Whole Lotta
Love") 5-8   69
(Edited version [3:12].)
ATLANTIC (2777 "The Immigrant Song"/
"Hey Hey, What Can I Do") 15-25   70
(Has "Do What Thou Wilt Shall Be the Whole of
the Law" etched in the vinyl trail-off.)
ATLANTIC (2777 "The Immigrant Song"/
"Hey Hey, What Can I Do") 10-15   70
(Does not have "Do What Thou Wilt Shall Be the
Whole of the Law" etched in the vinyl trail-off.)
ATLANTIC (2849 "Black Dog") 5-10   71
ATLANTIC (2865 "Rock and Roll") ... 5-10   72
ATLANTIC (2970 "Over the Hills
and Far Away") 5-10   73
ATLANTIC (2986 "D'yer Mak'er") 5-10   73
ATLANTIC (13116 "Whole Lotta Love") . 4-6
ATLANTIC (13131 "The Immigrant
Song") 4-6
ATLANTIC (13129 "Black Dog") 4-6
ATLANTIC (13130 "Rock and Roll") ... 4-6
Note: Atlantic 13000 numbers are "Oldies Series"
reissues.
SWAN SONG (70102 "Trampled
Under Foot") 4-6   75
SWAN SONG (70110 "Candy
Store Rock") 4-6   76
SWAN SONG (71003 "Fool in the Rain") 4-6   76
Picture Sleeves
ATLANTIC (175 "Stairway to
Heaven") 50-75   72
(Promotional issue only.)
Promotional Singles
ATLANTIC (157 "Gallows Pole") 50-75   71
ATLANTIC (175 "Stairway to
Heaven") 50-75   72
ATLANTIC (269 "Stairway to
Heaven") 20-30   77
ATLANTIC (1019 "Dazed and
Confused") 75-100   69
(With picture sleeve.)
ATLANTIC (2613 "Good Times
Bad Times") 25-35   69
(Black and white label.)
ATLANTIC (2613 "Good Times
Bad Times") 20-30   69
(Red and white label.)
ATLANTIC (2690 "Whole Lotta Love"/
"Living Loving Maid") 15-25   69
ATLANTIC (2690 "Whole Lotta Love" [5:33] /
Whole Lotta Love" (3:12]) 25-35   69
ATLANTIC (2777 "The Immigrant Song"/
"The Immigrant Song") 15-25   70

ATLANTIC (2777 "The Immigrant Song"/
Blank) 15-25   70
(Side two is a blank pressing.)
ATLANTIC (2849 "Black Dog") 15-20   71
ATLANTIC (2865 "Rock and Roll") ... 15-20   72
ATLANTIC (2970 "Over the Hills
and Far Away") 10-20   73
ATLANTIC (2986 "D'yor Mak'er") 10-20   73
SWAN SONG (70102 "Trampled
Under Foot") 10-15   75
SWAN SONG (70110 "Candy
Store Rock") 10-15   76
SWAN SONG (71003 "Fool in
the Rain") 10-15   76
(Blue label. Side one runs 6:08; side two is edited
[3:20].) SWAN SONG (71003 "Fool in
the Rain") 8-12   76
(White label. Both sides run 6:08.)

EPs: 7–inch 33/45rpm
ATLANTIC (7-7208 "Led Zeppelin") .. 50-75   71
(Jukebox issue only.)
ATLANTIC (7-7255 "Houses of
the Holy") 50-75   73
(Jukebox issue only.)

LPs: 10/12–inch 33rpm
ATLANTIC (7201 "Led Zeppelin III") . 10-15   70
ATLANTIC (7208 "Led Zeppelin IV") . 10-15   71
(Their fourth LP, though no title is actually shown
on cover.)
ATLANTIC (7225 "Houses of
the Holy") 15-20   73
(With "Led Zeppelin paper band around cover.)
ATLANTIC (7225 "Houses of
the Holy") 10-15   73
(Without "Led Zeppelin paper band around cover.)
ATLANTIC (8216 "Led Zeppelin") .. 50-100   69
(Pink and brown label.)
ATLANTIC (8216 "Led Zeppelin") ... 10-20   69
(Red and green label.)
ATLANTIC (8236 "Led Zeppelin II") .. 10-15   69
ATLANTIC (19126 "Led Zeppelin") .. 5-10   72
ATLANTIC (19127 "Led Zeppelin II") .. 5-10   72
ATLANTIC (19128 "Led Zeppelin III") . 5-10   72
ATLANTIC (19129 "Led Zeppelin IV") . 5-10   72
ATLANTIC (19130 "Houses of
the Holy") 5-10   73
MFSL (065 "Led Zeppelin II") 25-50   82
SWAN SONG (2-200 "Physical
Graffiti") 10-15   75
SWAN SONG (2-201 "The Song
Remains the Same") 10-15   76
(Embossed print on cover. With bound-in
eight-page booklet. Soundtrack.)
SWAN SONG (2-201 "The Song
Remains the Same") 8-12   76
(Standard, not-embossed, cover.)
SWAN SONG (8416 "Presence") 8-12   76
SWAN SONG (16002 "In Through
the Out Door") 8-12   79

SWAN SONG (90051 "Coda") 8-10   82

Promotional LPs
ATLANTIC (7201 "Led Zeppelin III") . 25-40   70
(White label. Monaural.)
ATLANTIC (7201 "Led Zeppelin III") . 15-25   70
(White label. Stereo.)
ATLANTIC (7208 "Led Zeppelin IV") . 15-25   71
(White label. No title actually shown on cover;
however, it was their fourth LP.)
ATLANTIC (7225 "Houses of
the Holy") 25-40   73
(White label. Monaural.)
ATLANTIC (7225 "Houses of
the Holy") 15-25   73
(White label. Stereo.)
ATLANTIC (8216 "Led Zeppelin") ... 20-40   69
(White label.)
ATLANTIC (8236 "Led Zeppelin II") .. 20-40   69
(White label.)
SWAN SONG (200 "Physical
Graffiti") 15-20   75
(With "FT" suffix.)
SWAN SONG (2-201 "The Song
Remains the Same") 15-20   76
(With "MO" suffix.)
SWAN SONG (8416 "Presence") ... 10-20   76
(With "MO" suffix.)
SWAN SONG (16002 "In Through
the Out Door") 10-15   79
(With "MO" suffix.)
SWAN SONG (90051 "Coda") 10-12   82
(With designate promo stamping on back cover.)
Members: Robert Plant; Jimmy Page; John Paul Jones; John
Bonham.
  Also see DENNY, Sandy
  Also see PAGE, Jimmy
  Also see PLANT, Robert

LED ZEPPELIN / King Curtis
Singles: 7–inch
ATLANTIC/ATCO (2690/6779 "Whole
Lotta Love") 40-50   71
(Promotional issue only. Atlantic label on Zep side;
Atco label on flip—King Curtis' version of same
song.)
  Also see KING CURTIS
  Also see LED ZEPPELIN

LEDERNACKEN
Singles: 12–inch 33/45rpm
4TH and BROADWAY 4-6   84

LEE, Alvin
(Alvin Lee and Company; Alvin Lee and Ten Years
Later)
Singles: 7–inch
COLUMBIA 3-5   74
RSO 3-5   79
LPs: 10/12–inch 33rpm
ATLANTIC 5-8   80-81
COLUMBIA 10-12   73-75
LONDON 8-10   78

RSO 10-12   77-79
21 RECORDS 5-8   86
  Also see TEN YEARS AFTER

LEE, Alvin, and Mylon LeFevre
Singles: 7–inch
COLUMBIA 3-5   74
LPs: 10/12–inch 33rpm
COLUMBIA 10-12   73
  Also see LEE, Alvin

LEE, Bobby
Singles: 7–inch
A-B-S (106 "Miss Mary") 150-200
CUCA 4-8   62
DECCA 5-10   60-61
FALEW 4-8   64
PORT 4-8   67
RAMCO 4-8   67
SUE 4-8   66

LEE, Brenda
(Brenda Lee Jones)
Singles: 78rpm
APOLLO 10-15   56
Singles: 7–inch
APOLLO (490 "I Ain't Gonna
  Give Nobody None") 10-20   56
  Also see JONES, Brenda

LEE, Brenda
(Brenda Lee and the Jordanaires)
Singles: 78rpm
DECCA 10-20   56-58
Singles: 7–inch
DECCA (30050 "Jambalaya") 20-30   56
DECCA (30107 "Christy Christmas") . 15-25   56
DECCA (30198 "One Step at a Time") 15-20   57
DECCA (30333 "Dynamite") 15-20   57
DECCA (30411 "One Teenager
  to Another") 10-20   57
DECCA (30535 "Rock-A-Bye
  Baby Blues") 10-20   57
DECCA (30673 "Ring-A My Phone") . 20-30   58
DECCA (30776 "Rockin' Around
  the Christmas Tree") 10-15   58
DECCA (30806 "Bill Bailey") 10-15   59
DECCA (30967 "Sweet Nothin's") 8-12   59
(Price range of 30050 through 30967 is for black,
pink or green label originals. Pink and green were
promotional only. Decca multi-color labels in that
series are $4 to $8 reissues.)
DECCA (31093 through 32330) 5-10   60-68
DECCA (32428 through 32975) 4-6   69-72
DECCA (34330 "Interview") 10-20   72
(Promotional issue only.)
DECCA (88215 "I'm Gonna Lasso
  Santa Claus") 20-30   56
(Decca "Children's Series.")
ELEKTRA 3-5   78
MCA 3-5   73-86

Picture Sleeves
WARNER 2-4   91
DECCA (30776 "Rockin' Around
  the Christmas Tree") 15-25   59
DECCA (30967 "Sweet Nothin's") ... 25-35   59
DECCA (31093 through 32428) 5-15   60-69
DECCA (34000 series) 5-10   62
(Compact 33 stereo.)
DECCA (88215 "I'm Gonna Lasso
  Santa Claus") 30-40   56
(For either 45 or 78 rpm single sleeve.)
EPs: 7–inch 33/45rpm
DECCA 10-20   60-65
LPs: 10/12–inch 33rpm
CORAL 5-10   73
DECCA (4039 through 4104) 20-30   60-61
(Monaural.)
DECCA (4176 through 4755) 15-25   61-66
(Monaural.)
DECCA (4757 "10 Golden Years") ... 15-20   66
(Gatefold cover. Monaural.)
DECCA (4757 "10 Golden Years") ... 10-15
(Standard cover. Monaural.)
DECCA (4825 through 4955) 10-15   66-68
(Monaural.)
DECCA (8873 "Grandma, What
  Great Songs You Sang") 25-35   59
(Monaural.)
DECCA (74039 through 74104) 25-35   60-61
(Stereo.)
DECCA (74176 through 74755) 20-30   61-66
(Stereo.)
DECCA (74757 "10 Golden Years") .. 20-25   66
(Gatefold cover. Stereo.)
DECCA (74757 "10 Golden Years") .. 10-15
(Standard cover. Stereo.)
DECCA (74825 through 75232) 10-15   66-70
(Stereo.)
DECCA (78873 "Grandma, What
  Great Songs You Sang") 30-40   59
(Stereo.)
MCA (Except 700 series) 8-10   73-86
MCA (700 series) 5-8
VOCALION 10-12   67-70
  Also see KERR, Anita
  Also see MOORE, Bob
  Also see RANDOLPH, Boots

LEE, Brenda / Carl Dobkins, Jr.
EPs: 7–inch 33/45rpm
DECCA (38169 "Datesetters, U.S.A.") 15-25   60
(Celanese Special Products issue.)
  Also see DOBKINS, Carl, Jr.

LEE, Brenda / Bill Haley and the Comets / Kalin Twins / Four Aces
EPs: 7–inch 33/45rpm
DECCA (7-2661 "Top Teen Hits") 15-25   59
(Stereo.)
  Also see FOUR ACES
  Also see HALEY, Bill

Also see KALIN TWINS

LEE, Brenda / Tennessee Ernie Ford
LPs: 10/12-inch 33rpm
DECCA (9226 "The Brenda Lee/Tennessee Ernie
  Ford Show for Christmas Seals")   .. 20-30
  (Promotional issue only.)
  Also see FORD, Tennessee Ernie

LEE, Brenda, and Pete Fountain
Singles: 7-inch
DECCA 4-6   68
EPs: 7-inch 33/45rpm
DECCA (734528 "Brenda and Pete") .. 5-10   68
  (Jukebox issue.)
LPs: 10/12-inch 33rpm
DECCA 10-15   68
  Also see FOUNTAIN, Pete

LEE, Brenda, and the Oak Ridge Boys
Singles: 7-inch
MCA 3-5   82
  Also see OAK RIDGE BOYS

LEE, Brenda, and Willie Nelson
Singles: 7-inch
MONUMENT 3-5   83
  Also see LEE, Brenda
  Also see NELSON, Willie

LEE, Curtis
Singles: 7-inch
ABC 3-5   74
DUNES 8-15   60-63
HOT (7 "Gotta Have You") 25-35   60
MCA 2-4
MIRA 4-8   67
ROJAC 4-8   67
SABRA (517 "Let's Take a Ride") 10-20   61
WARRIOR (1555 "With All My Heart") 10-20   59
Picture Sleeves
DUNES (2003 "Pledge of Love") 20-25   61
  Also see HALOS

LEE, Dick
Singles: 78rpm
ESSEX 4-8   54
VIK 4-8   56
X 4-8   55
Singles: 7-inch
ABC 4-6   67
BLUE BELL 4-8   61
CAPITOL 4-6   68
CENTAUR 5-8   59
DOT 4-8   66
ESSEX 5-10   54
FELSTED 5-8   60
KAPP 4-6   69
MGM 5-10   59
METRO 4-8   65
ROULETTE 4-8   62-63
20TH FOX 4-8   65
VIK 5-10   56

X 5-10   55
Picture Sleeves
FELSTED 8-12   60

LEE, Dickey
(Dickey Lee With the Collegiates; Dickie Lee)
Singles: 78rpm
SUN (280 "Good Lovin") 10-20   57
SUN (297 "Dreamy Nights") 10-20   57
TAMPA 10-15   57
Singles: 7-inch
ABC 3-5   73
ATCO 4-8   68
DIAMOND 4-8   69
DICKIE LEE STORY 15-20   77
  (No label name or number. Promotional issue only.)
DOT 10-15   60
ERIC 3-5
MERCURY 3-5   79-82
RCA 3-5   70-78
RENDEZVOUS (188 "Stay
  True Baby") 15-25   62
SMASH 4-8   62-64
SUN (280 "Good Lovin") 15-25   57
SUN (297 "Dreamy Nights") 20-30   57
TCF 4-8   65
TCF HALL 4-8   64-65
TAMPA (131 "Dream Boy") 15-25   57
TRACIE 4-8   67
LPs: 10/12-inch 33rpm
RCA 6-12   71-76
MERCURY 5-8   79-80
SMASH 20-25   62
TCF HALL 15-20   65

LEE, Jackie
(Jackie Lee and His Orchestra)
Singles: 78rpm
CORAL 3-5   53
Singles: 7-inch
CORAL 4-8   53

LEE, Jackie
(Earl Nelson)
Singles: 7-inch
FAYETTE 4-8   64
KEYMAN 4-8   67-68
MIRWOOD 4-8   65-66
SWAN 5-10   59
UNI 3-5   70
LPs: 10/12-inch 33rpm
MIRWOOD 15-25   66
  Also see BOB & EARL

LEE, Jimmy, and Artis
Singles: 78rpm
MODERN 10-20   52
Singles: 7-inch
MODERN (885 "Let's Talk
  It Over") 25-35   52

LEE, Johnny
Singles: 7–inch
ABC/DOT	3-5	75
ASTRO	3-5	80
ASYLUM	3-5	80-82
EPIC	3-5	81
FULL MOON/WARNER	2-4	80-86
GRT	3-5	76-78

Picture Sleeves
ASYLUM	3-5	80

LPs: 10/12–inch 33rpm
ACCORD	5-8	83
ASYLUM	5-10	80-81
FULL MOON/WARNER	5-8	80-86
GRT	8-10	77
JMS	8-12	
PLANTATION	5-10	81

Also see GILLEY, Mickey, and Johnny Lee
Also see NELSON, Willie / Johnny Lee / Mickey Gilley

LEE, Johnny / Eagles
Singles: 7–inch
ASYLUM	3-5	80-81

Picture Sleeves
ASYLUM	3-5	80

Also see EAGLES
Also see LEE, Johnny

LEE, Julia
(Julia Lee and Her Boyfriends)
Singles: 78rpm
CAPITOL	5-15	46-52

Singles: 7–inch
CAPITOL (Except 2203)	10-15	50-52
CAPITOL (2203 "Last Call for Alcohol")	15-20	52

EPs: 7–inch 33/45rpm
CAPITOL (EBF-228 "Party Time")	30-50	50

LPs: 10/12–inch 33rpm
CAPITOL (H-228 "Party Time") (10–inch LP.)	50-75	50
CAPITOL (T-228 "Party Time")	35-55	55

LEE, Laura
Singles: 7–inch
ARIOLA AMERICA	3-5	76
CHESS	4-8	67-69
COTILLION	4-6	69
HOT WAX	3-5	71-72
INVICTUS	3-5	74
RIC TIC	4-8	66

LPs: 10/12–inch 33rpm
CHESS	8-12	72
HOT WAX	8-12	72-73
INVICTUS	8-12	74

LEE, Leapy: see LEAPY LEE

LEE, Leon
Singles: 7–inch
CROSSOVER	3-5	74

LEE, Michele
Singles: 7–inch
ABC-PAR	4-8	62-63
COLUMBIA	4-8	65-69

LPs: 10/12–inch 33rpm
COLUMBIA	10-20	66-68

LEE, Nickie
Singles: 7–inch
DADE	4-8	67
MALA	4-8	68-69

LEE, Peggy
(Peggy Lee with Benny Goodman's Orchestra)
Singles: 78rpm
CAPITOL	5-15	41-58
OKEH	5-10	41-42

Singles: 7–inch
A&M	3-5	75
ATLANTIC	3-5	74
CAPITOL (801 through 2000 series)	8-12	49-51
CAPITOL (2100 through 3400 series)	3-6	68-72
CAPITOL (3800 through 5900 series)	4-8	58-67
CAPITOL (90000 series)	4-8	
COLUMBIA	3-5	76
DECCA (25000 series)	4-6	64
DECCA (28000 and 29000 series)	4-8	52-58
DECCA (30000 series)	4-8	58-59

EPs: 7–inch 33/45rpm
CAPITOL (Except 100 series)	10-20	57-59
CAPITOL (100 series)	20-40	52
COLUMBIA	20-40	50-51
DECCA	15-30	52-55

LPs: 10/12–inch 33rpm
A&M	5-8	75
ATLANTIC	5-8	74
CAPITOL (183 "A Natural Woman")	8-12	69
CAPITOL (H-155 "Rendezvous with Peggy") (10–inch LP.)	50-75	52
CAPITOL (T-155 "Rendezvous with Peggy")	25-50	55
CAPITOL (H-204 "My Best to You")	50-75	52
CAPITOL (377 through 810)	5-10	69-71
CAPITOL (864 "The Man I Love")	20-40	56
CAPITOL (979 "Jump for Joy")	20-40	57
CAPITOL (T-1049 through T-1969) (Monaural.)	15-25	58-63
CAPITOL (ST-1049 through ST-1969) (Stereo.)	20-30	58-63
CAPITOL (T-2096 through T-2887) (Monaural.)	10-20	64-68
CAPITOL (ST-2096 through ST-2887)	10-20	64-68
CAPITOL (11000 series)	5-10	72-79
CAPITOL (16000 series)	4-8	80
COLUMBIA (6033 "Benny Goodman and Peggy Lee") (10–inch LP.)	40-60	50
DRG	5-8	79

DECCA (DXB-164 "Best of
Peggy Lee") 15-25   60
(Monaural.)
DECCA (DXSB7-164 "Best of
Peggy Lee") 10-20   66
(Stereo.)
DECCA (DL-4000 series) 10-15   64
(Monaural.)
DECCA (DL7-4000 series) 15-20   64
(Stereo.)
DECCA (5482 "Black Coffee") 50-75   53
(10-inch LP.)
DECCA (5539 "Songs in
an Intimate Style") 50-75   53
(10-inch LPs.)
DECCA (8411 "Dream Street") 30-50   56
DECCA (8358 "Black Coffee") 30-50   57
DECCA (8591 "Sea Shells") 30-50   58
DECCA (8816 "Miss Wonderful") 20-40   59
EVEREST 5-8   74
GLENDALE 4-8   82
HARMONY (7000 series) 15-25   58
HARMONY (30000 series) 5-10   70
MERCURY 5-8   77
VOCALION 6-12   66-70
Also see CROSBY, Bing, and Peggy Lee
Also see FITZGERALD, Ella, and Peggy Lee
Also see GOODMAN, Benny, Orchestra
Also see JENKINS, Gordon, and His Orchestra

LEE, Peggy, and Dean Martin
Singles: 78rpm
CAPITOL 8-12   49
Also see MARTIN, Dean

LEE, Peggy, and George Shearing
Singles: 7-inch
CAPITOL 4-8   59
LPs: 10/12-inch 33rpm
CAPITOL (1219 "Beauty and the
Beat") 20-30   59
(Capitol logo on left side of label.)
CAPITOL (1219 "Beauty and the
Beat") 10-20   62
(Capitol logo at the top of label.)
Also see SHEARING, George, Quintet

LEE, Peggy, and Mel Torme
Singles: 78rpm
CAPITOL 5-10   49
Singles: 7-inch
CAPITOL 8-12   49
Also see LEE, Peggy
Also see TORME, Mel

LEE, Roberta
Singles: 78rpm
DECCA 4-6   51-54
TEMPO 4-8   50-51
X 4-6   54
Singles: 7-inch
DECCA 5-10   51-54

TEMPO 5-10   50-51
TOWER 4-6   68
X 5-10   54

LEE, Toney
Singles: 12-inch 33/45rpm
RADAR 4-6   83
Singles: 7-inch
CRITIQUE 2-4   85

LEE & PAUL
Singles: 7-inch
COLUMBIA 5-10   59-65
Members: Lee Pockriss; Paul Vance.
Also see VANCE, Paul

LEFEVRE, Raymond, and His Orchestra
Singles: 7-inch
ATLANTIC 4-6   61
4 CORNERS 4-6   67-68
JAMIE 4-6   60
KAPP 3-8   58-66
MERCURY 4-8   60
VERVE 4-6   62
LPs: 10/12-inch 33rpm
ATLANTIC 8-15   61
BUDDAH 5-10   71-72
4 CORNERS 5-10   67-68
KAPP 8-15   59-66
MONUMENT 6-12   67

LEFT BANKE
Singles: 7-inch
CON AMERICA 5-8   78
SMASH (Except 2243) 5-8   66-69
SMASH (2243 "Myrah") 30-40   69
Picture Sleeves
SMASH (Except 2243) 10-20   67
SMASH (2243 "Myrah") 30-40   69
LPs: 10/12-inch 33rpm
RHINO 5-8   85
SMASH (27088 "Walk Away Renee") 20-30   67
(Monaural.)
SMASH (67088 "Walk Away Renee") 25-35   67
(Stereo.)
SMASH (67113 "Left Banke Too") ... 25-35   69
MERCURY 5-8   81
Members: Michael Brown; George Cameron; Tom Finn; Steve
Martin; Rick Brand.
Also see STORIES

LEGACY
Singles: 7-inch
BRUNSWICK 3-5   82
PRIVATE I 2-4   85

LEGRAND, Michel, and His Orchestra
Singles: 7-inch
A&M 2-4   83
BELL 3-5   71-72
COLUMBIA 4-8   55-59
DECCA 3-6   68
FLASHBACK 3-5   73

MCA	3-5	73-76
MGM	3-6	67-68
PHILIPS	4-6	63-66
20TH FOX	3-5	77
U.A.	3-5	70
WARNER	3-6	68-76

Picture Sleeves

MGM	8-15	67

EPs: 7–inch 33/45rpm

COLUMBIA	5-10	56-59

LPs: 10/12–inch 33rpm

BELL	5-10	72-74
COLUMBIA	10-20	55-71
GRYPHON	5-8	75-79
HARMONY	5-10	66-74
KORY	4-8	77
MCA	8-15	73-76
MERCURY	8-15	65
PABLO	4-8	83
PHILIPS	8-15	62-64
SPRINGBOARD	4-8	77
20TH FOX	5-10	77
U.A.	6-12	69
VERVE	8-15	68-72
WARNER	6-12	71-76

Also see HORNE, Lena, and Michel Legrand
Also see VAUGHAN, Sarah
Since publication of *The Official Price Guide to Movie/TV Soundtracks and Original Cast Albums,* with over 8,000 listings, this guide has dropped many soundtracks, including some by this artist.

LEHRER, Tom
Singles: 7–inch

REPRISE	3-6	69

LPs: 10/12–inch 33rpm

LEHRER (101 "Songs By Tom Lehrer")	40-60	52
(10–inch LP.)		
LEHRER (102 "More Songs By Tom Lehrer")	20-30	59
LEHRER (202 "An Evening Wasted with Tom Lehrer")	20-30	59
REPRISE	10-20	65-66

LE JETE
Singles: 12–inch 33/45rpm

MEGATONE	4-6	83

LEKAKIS, Paul
Singles: 7–inch

ZYX	2-4	87

LEMMONS, Billy
Singles: 7–inch

ARIOLA AMERICA	3-5	77

LEMON PIPERS
Singles: 7–inch

BUDDAH	4-8	67-69
CAROL	8-12	
ERIC	3-5	78

Picture Sleeves

BUDDAH	5-10	68

LPs: 10/12–inch 33rpm

BUDDAH	12-20	68

Members: Ivan Browne; Bill Bartlett; Paul Lenka; Bill Albaugh; Steve Walmsley; Reg Nave.
Also see 1910 FRUITGUM COMPANY / Lemon Pipers
Also see RAM JAM

LENNON, John
(John and Yoko; Plastic Ono Band)
Singles: 12–inch 33/45rpm

CAPITOL (9585/6 "Imagine"/ "Come Together")	25-35	86
(Promotional issue only.)		
CAPITOL (9894 "Happy Xmas")	150-200	86
(Promotional issue only.)		
CAPITOL (9917 "Rock and Roll People")	20-30	86
(Promotional issue only.)		
CAPITOL (9929 "Happy Xmas")	35-45	86
(Promotional issue only.)		
CAPITOL (79453 "Stand By Me")	20-25	88
(Promotional issue only.)		
GEFFEN (919 "Starting Over")	35-45	80
(Promotional issue only.)		
GEFFEN (1079 "Happy Xmas")	25-30	82
(Price range includes special sleeve. Promotional issue only.)		
POLYDOR (250 "Nobody Told Me")	25-30	83

Singles: 7–inch

AMERICOM (435 "Give Peace a Chance")	200-400	69
(Plastic "Pocket Disc" soundsheet.)		
APPLE (1809 "Give Peace a Chance")	4-6	69
APPLE (1813 "Cold Turkey")	4-8	69
APPLE (1818 "Instant Karma")	4-6	70
APPLE (1827 "Mother")	5-10	70
APPLE (1830 "Power to the People")	4-6	71
APPLE (1840 "Imagine")	4-6	71
APPLE (1842 "Happy Xmas")	8-12	71
(Label pictures John and Yoko.)		
APPLE (1842 "Happy Xmas")	5-8	71
(Standard Apple label.)		
APPLE (1848 "Woman Is the Nigger of the World")	4-6	72
(With Elephant's Memory.)		
APPLE (1868 "Mind Games")	4-6	73
APPLE (1874 "Whatever Gets You Through the Night")	4-6	74
APPLE (1878 "#9 Dream")	4-6	74
APPLE (1881 "Stand By Me")	4-6	75
CAPITOL	10-15	78
(Orange labels.)		
CAPITOL	3-5	78-84
(Purple or black labels.)		
CAPITOL STAR LINE	2-4	77-78
GEFFEN (0408 "Starting Over")	3-5	83
GEFFEN (0415 "Watching the Wheels")	3-5	83

GEFFEN (29855 "Happy Xmas") 3-5   82
GEFFEN (49604 "Starting Over") 3-5   80
GEFFEN (49644 "Woman") 3-5   80
GEFFEN (49695 "Watching the
  Wheels") 3-5   81
ORANGE PEEL (70078 "Interview") . 12-15   81
  (John is interviewed by David Peel. Picture disc.)
POLYDOR 3-5   84-86

Promotional Singles

APPLE (1809 "Give Peace a Chance") 8-12   69
APPLE (1813 "Cold Turkey") 20-25   69
APPLE (1818 "Instant Karma") 20-25   70
  (With *Instant Karma* on both sides of disc.)
APPLE (1818 "Instant Karma") ... 150-200   70
  (With *Instant Karma* only on one side of disc. Flip
  is a blank pressing.)
APPLE (1827 "Mother") 25-35   70
APPLE (1830 "Power to the People") 15-25   71
APPLE (1840 "Imagine") 10-15   71
APPLE (1848 "Woman Is the
  Nigger of the World") 12-15   72
APPLE (1868 "Mind Games") 30-40   73
APPLE (1874 "Whatever Gets You
  Through the Night") 25-35   74
APPLE (1878 "#9 Dream") 25-35   74
APPLE (1878 "What You Got") 50-75   74
  (Two separate promo singles have the same
  catalog number [1878]. On commercial issues
  these tracks were back to back.)
APPLE (1881 "Stand By Me") 25-35   75
APPLE (1883 "Ain't That a Shame") 100-200   75
APPLE (1883 "Slippin' and Sliddin'") 100-200   75
  (There were two separate promo singles using the
  same 1883 catalog number.)
APPLE (47663/4 "Happy Xmas") .. 200-400   71
  (White label with black print.)
CAPITOL (57849 "Imagine") 30-50   92
COTILLION (104/5 "John Lennon on
  Ronnie Hawkins") 30-35   70
  (John Lennon promotes a 1970 Ronnie Hawkins
  Cotillion release.)
EVA-TONE ("John Lennon
  Radio Play") 200-400   69
  (Soundsheet only. Originally included with a boxed
  set issue of *Aspen* Magazine. Price for complete
  set would be double that of just the Lennon disc.)
EVA-TONE (101075 "The
  Rock Generation") 20-30   76
  (Issued with the book *The Rock Generation*. Has a
  brief Lennon interview.)
GEFFEN (29855 "Happy Xmas") 8-12   82
GEFFEN (49604 "Starting Over") 10-15   80
GEFFEN (49644 "Woman") 8-12   80
GEFFEN (49695 "Watching the
  Wheels") 10-12   81
KYA ("KYA 1969 Peace Talk") 50-60   69
  (Radio KYA's Tom Campbell and Bill Holley's
  telephone interview with John Lennon.)
POLYDOR 8-15   84-86

QUAKER 10-15   86
  (Soundsheet, issued with Quaker Granola Dipps.)
QUAYE/TRIDENT (3419 "Rock 'N'
  Roll") 300-350   75
  (Contains a one minute radio spot for the "Rock 'N'
  Roll" LP. Issued to radio stations only.)
WHAT'S IT ALL ABOUT 15-20

Picture Sleeves

APPLE (1809 "Give Peace a Chance") 10-15   69
APPLE (1813 "Cold Turkey") 50-75   69
APPLE (1818 "Instant Karma") 10-15   70
APPLE (1827 "Mother") 75-125   70
APPLE (1830 "Power to the People") 15-20   71
APPLE (1842 "Happy Xmas") 10-15   71
APPLE (1848 "Woman Is the Nigger
  of the World") 10-15   72
APPLE (1868 "Mind Games") 6-10   73
GEFFEN (29855 "Happy Xmas") 3-5   82
GEFFEN (49604 "Starting Over") 2-4   80
GEFFEN (49644 "Woman") 2-4   80
GEFFEN (49695 "Watching the Wheels") 2-4   81
POLYDOR 2-4   84

LPs: 10/12-inch 33rpm

ADAM VIII LTD. (8018 "John Lennon Sings
  Great Rock and Roll Hits, Roots") 200-300   75
APPLE (3361 "Wedding Album") ... 75-125   69
  (Price range is for complete boxed set with all
  inserts.)
APPLE (3362 "Live Peace in
  Toronto") 30-40   70
  (With 16-page photo/calendar.)
APPLE (3362 "Live Peace in
  Toronto") 10-15   70
  (Without calendar.)
APPLE (3372 "John Lennon, Plastic
  Ono Band") 15-20   70
APPLE (3379 "Imagine") 15-20   71
  (Includes bonus poster and photo card.)
APPLE (3392 "Sometime in New
  York City") 20-25   72
APPLE (3414 "Mind Games") 10-15   73
APPLE (3416 "Walls and Bridges") .. 10-15   74
APPLE (3419 "Rock 'N' Roll") 10-15   75
APPLE (3421 "Shaved Fish") 10-15   75
APPLE/TETRAGRAMMATON (5001 "Two
  Virgins") 100-125   68
  (With brown paper outer sleeve.)
APPLE/TETRAGRAMMATON (5001 "Two
  Virgins") 60-100   68
  (Without paper outer sleeve.)
APPLE/TETRAGRAMMATON (5001 "Two
  Virgins") 10-15
  (Reissue, with brown paper outer sleeve that does
  NOT cover entire jacket.)
CAPITOL 5-15   75-88
GEFFEN 10-15   80-82
MFSL 15-25   85
  (Half-speed mastered.)

NAUTILUS (47 "Double Fantasy") ... 25-35   82
(Half-speed mastered.)
POLYDOR 5-8   84
SILHOUETTE (10014 "Reflections
and Poetry") 10-15   84
ZAPPLE (3357 "Life with the Lions") . 20-25   69
Promotional LPs
APPLE (3392 "Sometime In New
York City") 200-400   72
GEFFEN (2023 "John Lennon
Collection") 30-40   82
(Quiex II "Limited Edition Pressing.")
POLYDOR (817 238-1 "Heart Play") . 15-25   83
(Includes program notes and copy of a letter from
Yoko on her stationary.)
SILHOUETTE (10014 "Reflections
and Poetry") 40-50   84
    Also see BEATLES
    Also see ELEPHANT'S MEMORY
    Also see HAWKINS, Ronnie
    Also see JOHN, Elton / John Lennon
    Also see ONO, Yoko
    Also see PEEL, David, and the Lower East Side / John Lennon
    and Yoko Ono

LENNON, Julian
Singles: 12–inch 33/45rpm
ATLANTIC 5-8   85
Singles: 7–inch
ATLANTIC 3-5   84-89
Picture Sleeves
ATLANTIC 3-5   84-85
LPs: 10/12–inch 33rpm
ATLANTIC 5-10   84-89

LENNON SISTERS
Singles: 78rpm
BRUNSWICK 4-6   57
CORAL 4-6   56
Singles: 7–inch
BRUNSWICK 5-10   57-59
CORAL 5-10   56
DOT 4-8   58-67
MERCURY 3-6   68
LPs: 10/12–inch 33rpm
BRUNSWICK 10-20   57
DOT 5-15   59-67
HAMILTON 5-12   64
MERCURY 8-12   68-69
RANWOOD 4-8   68-81
VOCALION 5-10   69-70
WING 5-10   69
    Members: Kathy Lennon; Peggy Lennon; Janet Lennon; Dianne
    Lennon.
    Also see WELK, Lawrence

LENNOX, Annie, and Al Green
Singles: 7–inch
A&M 2-4   88
Picture Sleeves
A&M 2-4   88
    Also see EURYTHMICS
    Also see GREEN, Al

LEON LEE: see LEE, Leon

LEONETTI, Tommy
Singles: 78rpm
CAPITOL 4-6   54-56
VIK 4-8   57
Singles: 7–inch
ATLANTIC 5-8   60
CAPITOL 5-10   54-56
COLUMBIA 4-6   67-73
DECCA 4-6   68-69
EPIC 3-5   74
RCA 3-8   59-77
20TH FOX 3-5   77
VIK 5-10   57
Picture Sleeves
COLUMBIA 4-8   68
LPs: 10/12–inch 33rpm
CAMDEN 10-20   59
RCA 10-20   64-67

LE PAMPLEMOUSSE
Singles: 12–inch 33/45rpm
A.V.I. 4-8   78-85
Singles: 7–inch
A.V.I. 3-5   77-85
LPs: 10/12–inch 33rpm
A.V.I. 5-8   78-85

LEPPARD, Def: see DEF LEPPARD

LE ROUX
(Louisiana's LeRoux)
Singles: 7–inch
CAPITOL 3-6   78
RCA 3-5   82-83
LPs: 10/12–inch 33rpm
CAPITOL 5-8   78-81
RCA 5-8   82

LES COMPAGNONS DE LA CHANSON
Singles: 7–inch
CAPITOL 4-6   59-60

LESEAR, Anne
Singles: 7–inch
H.C.R.C. 3-5   84

LESTER, Bobby
Singles: 7–inch
CHECKER 5-10   59
COLUMBIA 3-5   70
LPs: 10/12–inch 33rpm
COLUMBIA 10-15   70

LESTER, Bobby, and the Moonglows
Singles: 7–inch
CHESS 5-8   62
LPs: 10/12–inch 33rpm
CHESS (1471 "Best of Bobby Lester
and the Moonglows") 30-40   62
    Also see MOONGLOWS

LESTER, Bobby, and the Moonlighters
Singles: 78rpm
CHECKER 10-15   54
Singles: 7-inch
CHECKER (806 "So All Alone") 50-75   54
(Checkerboard top label.)
CHECKER (806 "So All Alone") 10-20   58
(Vertical logo.)
Also see LESTER, Bobby

LESTER, Jerry
Singles: 78rpm
CORAL 4-6   50
Singles: 7-inch
CORAL 5-10   50

LESTER, Ketty
Singles: 7-inch
COLLECTABLES 2-4
ERA 5-8   62-63
EVEREST 4-8   62
PETE 4-6   68-69
RCA 4-6   64
TOWER 4-6   65-66
LPs: 10/12-inch 33rpm
AVI 5-8   80
ERA (EL-108 "Love Letters") 25-35   62
(Monaural.)
ERA (ES-108 "Love Letters") 30-40   62
(Stereo.)
MEGA 5-8   85
PETE 10-15   69
RCA 10-20   64-65
SHEFFIELD 8-10   77
TOWER 10-15   66
Also see EVERETT, Betty, and Ketty Lester

LET'S ACTIVE
LPs: 10/12-inch 33rpm
I.R.S. 5-8   84-86

LETTERMEN
Singles: 7-inch
ALPHA-OMEGA 2-5   78-88
APPLAUSE 2-4   83
CAPITOL 3-8   61-76
WARNER 5-8   60
Picture Sleeves
CAPITOL 5-10   61-68
LPs: 10/12-inch 33rpm
ALPHA-OMEGA 5-15   77-88
APPLAUSE 5-8   82
CANDELITE 5-10
CAPITOL (138 through 836) 5-15   68-71
CAPITOL (1669 through 2934) 10-20   62-68
(With "T" or "ST" prefix.)
CAPITOL (2500 and 2700 series) 4-8
(With "SM" prefix.)
CAPITOL (11000 series) 5-10   71-75
CAPITOL (16000 series) 4-8   80-83

LONGINES (220 "Time for Us") 15-30
(Five-LP boxed set.)
LONGINES (220 "From the Lettermen,
with Love") 5-8   72
(Bonus LP, issued with the above box set.)
PICKWICK 5-8   77
Members: Tony Butala; James Pike; Bob Engemann; Gary Pike;
Donny Pike; Chad Nichols; Don Campo.
Also see CAMPBELL, Glen / Lettermen / Ella Fitzgerald /
Sandler and Young
Also see PETER & GORDON / Lettermen
Also see TONY, BOB & JIMMY

LEVEL 42
Singles: 7-inch
A&M 2-4   84
POLYDOR 2-4   82-88
LPs: 10/12-inch 33rpm
A&M 5-8   84
POLYDOR 5-8   82-88
Members: Mark King; Mike Lindup; Phil Gould; Boon Gould;
Krys Mach.

LEVERT
Singles: 7-inch
ATLANTIC 2-4   86-88
TEMPRE 3-5   85
LPs: 10/12-inch 33rpm
ATLANTIC 5-8   86-90
Members: Sean Levert; Gerald Levert; Marc Gordon.

LEVINE, Hank
(Hank Levine and the Minature Men)
Singles: 7-inch
ABC-PAR 4-8   61
DOLTON 4-8   62-63
TOPS 4-8   60
Also see MINIATURE MEN

LEVON and the Hawks
(Featuring Levon Helm)
Singles: 7-inch
ATCO 10-20   65-68
Also see BAND
Also see HELM, Levon
Also see HAWKINS, Ronnie

LEVY, Marcy
Singles: 7-inch
EPIC 3-5   82
LPs: 10/12-inch 33rpm
EPIC 8-15   82
Also see CLAPTON, Eric

LEVY, Marcy, and Robin Gibb
Singles: 7-inch
RSO 2-4   80
Picture Sleeves
RSO 3-5   80
Also see GIBB, Robin
Also see LEVY, Marcy

LEWIS, Barbara
Singles: 7-inch
ATLANTIC 4-8   62-67
ENTERPRISE 3-5   70-71

REPRISE 3-5   73
LPs: 10/12–inch 33rpm
ATLANTIC (8086 through 8173) 20-35   63-68
ATLANTIC (8286 "Best of Barbara
    Lewis") 10-15   71
COLLECTABLES 6-8   88
ENTERPRISE 10-12   70
SOLID SMOKE 8-10

LEWIS, Bobby
Singles: 78rpm
SPOTLIGHT 10-15   56
Singles: 7–inch
ABC-PAR 4-8   64
BELTONE 5-10   61-62
ERIC 2-4
LANA 3-5
ROULETTE 5-10   59
SPOTLIGHT (394 "Mumbles Blues") . 10-20   56
LPs: 10/12–inch 33rpm
BELTONE (4000 "Tossin'
    and Turnin") 50-100   61

LEWIS, Gary, and the Playboys
Singles: 7–inch
LIBERTY (Except 56144) 4-8   64-69
LIBERTY (56144 "I Saw Elvis
    Presley Last Night") 10-15   69
Picture Sleeves
LIBERTY 4-8   65-67
EPs: 7–inch 33/45rpm
LIBERTY (227 "Doin' the Flake") 10-20   65
    (Liberty/Kellogg's Premium Record. Issued with
    paper sleeve.)
LPs: 10/12–inch 33rpm
GUSTO 5-8   72
LIBERTY (Except 10000 series) 15-30   65-69
LIBERTY (10000 series) 5-8   81
SUNSET 12-15   69
U.A. (Except 1000 series) 8-10   75
U.A. (1000 series) 5-8   81

LEWIS, Huey, and the News
Singles: 12–inch 33/45rpm
CHRYSALIS 4-8   84-89
Singles: 7–inch
CHRYSALIS 2-5   80-89
Promotional Singles
CHRYSALIS (43065 "Hip to
    Be Square") 10-15   85
    (Four disc set, each of a different color vinyl.)
LPs: 10/12–inch 33rpm
CHRYSALIS 5-8   80-89
MFSL 15-20   85
   Members: Huey Lewis; Bill Gibson; Mario Cipollina; Sean
   Hopper; Chris Hayes; Johnny Colla.
   Also see EDMUNDS, Dave
   Also see SAN FRANCISCO ALL STARS
   Also see U.S.A. for AFRICA

LEWIS, J.G.
Singles: 7–inch
IX CHAINS 4-6   76

LEWIS, Jerry
Singles: 78rpm
CAPITOL 4-6   50-53
DECCA 4-6   56-57
Singles: 7–inch
CAPITOL 5-10   50-53
DECCA 4-8   56-62
DOT 4-8   60
LIBERTY 4-8   63
EPs: 7–inch 33/45rpm
CAPITOL 6-12   56
DECCA 6-10   56
LPs: 10/12–inch 33rpm
CAPITOL 10-15   64
DECCA 15-25   56
DOT 10-15   60
VOCALION 8-12   66
   Also see MARTIN, Dean, and Jerry Lewis

LEWIS, Jerry Lee
(Jerry Lee Lewis and His Pumping Piano)
Singles: 78rpm
SUN 10-20   56-58
Singles: 7–inch
AMERICA SMASH 3-5   86
BUDDAH 3-6   71
ELEKTRA 3-5   79-82
MCA 3-5   82-83
MERCURY 3-6   70-82
SCR 3-5   85
SSS/SUN 3-5   69-84
   (Includes numbers below 100 and over 1000.)
SMASH (1857 through 2122) 5-10   63-67
SMASH (2146 through 2257) 4-8   68-70
SUN (259 "Crazy Arms") 15-25   56
SUN (267 through 296) 8-15   56-58
SUN (300 series) 5-10   58-65
Picture Sleeves
SUN (281 "Great Balls of Fire") 15-25   57
SUN (296 "High School Confidential") 15-25   57
EPs: 7–inch 33/45rpm
MERCURY (6 "Special Radio Cuts from *Would You
    Take Another Chance on Me*") 15-25   71
    (Promotional issues only.)
MERCURY (14 "Special Radio Cuts from *The Killer
    Rocks On*") 15-25   72
    (Promotional issues only.)
SCR 10-15   86
SSS/SUN (108 "Golden Cream
    of the Country") 15-25   69
    (Jukebox issue only.)
SSS/SUN (114 "A Taste of Country") . 15-25   69
    (Jukebox issue only.)
SMASH (2 "Jerry Lee Lewis") 20-25   64
SMASH (28 "Open-End Inverview") . . 30-40   64
    (Promotional issue only.)

LEWIS, Jerry Lee / Curly Bridges / Frank Motley

LEWIS, Jerry Lee / Johnny Cash

LEWIS, Jerry Lee, and Friends

Members: Jerry Lee Lewis; Jimmy Ellis; Charlie Rich.
Also see RICH, Charlie

LEWIS, Jerry Lee and Linda Gail
Singles: 7–inch
SMASH 3-6   69-70
SUN 5-10   63
LPs: 10/12–inch 33rpm
SMASH 15-25   69

LEWIS, Jerry Lee / Roger Miller / Roy Orbison
LPs: 10/12–inch 33rpm
PICKWICK 8-10
Also see MILLER, Roger
Also see ORBISON, Roy

LEWIS, Jerry Lee, Carl Perkins and Charlie Rich
LPs: 10/12–inch 33rpm
SSS/SUN (1018 "Trio +") 8-10   78
(With Jimmy Ellis.)
Also see LEWIS, Jerry Lee, and Friends
Also see PERKINS, Carl

LEWIS, Jerry Lee / Charlie Rich / Johnny Cash
LPs: 10/12–inch 33rpm
POWER PAK 8-10
Also see CASH, Johnny, Carl Perkins and Jerry Lee Lewis
Also see LEWIS, Jerry Lee

LEWIS, Jimmy
(Jimmy Lewis and the L.A. Street Band)
Singles: 7–inch
HOTLANTA 3-5   75
MCA 2-4   84
LPs: 10/12–inch 33rpm
HOTLANTA 5-10   74

LEWIS, Marcus
Singles: 7–inch
AEGIS 2-4   88

LEWIS, Ramsey
(Ramsey Lewis Trio; Ramsey Lewis and Co.)
Singles: 12–inch 33/45rpm
COLUMBIA 4-6   79-85
Singles: 7–inch
ABC 3-5   74
ARGO 4-8   58-65
CADET 3-6   65-72
CHESS 3-5   73
COLUMBIA 2-5   72-87
EMARCY 4-8   59
EPs: 7–inch 33/45rpm
ARGO (687 "The Sound
  of Christmas") 15-25   61
LPs: 10/12–inch 33rpm
ARGO (611 "Gentleman of Swing") .. 40-60   58
ARGO (627 "Gentleman of Jazz") ... 40-60   58
ARGO (642 "Ramsey Lewis Trio
  with Len Winchester") 30-50   59
ARGO (645 "An Hour with the
  Ramsey Lewis Trio") 25-50   59

ARGO (665 "Stretching
  Out") 25-50   60
ARGO (680 "From the Soil") 25-50   61
ARGO (687 "The Sound
  of Christmas") 25-50   61
ARGO (693 "The Sound of Spring") . 25-35   62
ARGO (700 series) 20-40   62-65
CADET 10-20   65-72
COLUMBIA 6-12   72-85
EMARCY (36150 "Down to Earth") .. 25-45   59
  (Monaural.)
EMARCY (80029 "Down to Earth") .. 35-60   59
  (Stereo.)
TRIP 5-8   75
Members: Ramsey Lewis; Eldee Young; Red Holt.
Also see EARTH, WIND & FIRE and Ramsey Lewis
Also see WILSON, Nancy
Also see YOUNG HOLT UNLIMITED

LEWIS, Smiley
Singles: 78rpm
COLONY (106 "Sad Life") 20-40   52
COLONY (110 "Where Were You") .. 20-40   52
DELUXE (3099 "Turn Your Volume
  on, Baby") 20-40   47
IMPERIAL 12-25   50-57
Singles: 7–inch
DOT 5-8   64
IMPERIAL (5194 "The Bells Are
  Ringing") 50-100   52
IMPERIAL (5208 "Gumbo Blues") .. 50-100   52
IMPERIAL (5224 "Gypsy Blues") ... 50-100   54
IMPERIAL (5234 "Play Girl") 50-75   53
  (Black vinyl.)
IMPERIAL (5234 "Play Girl") 100-200   53
  (Colored vinyl.)
IMPERIAL (5241 "Caldonia's Party") . 50-75   53
IMPERIAL (5252 "Little Fernandez") . 50-75   53
IMPERIAL (5268 "Down the Road") . 50-75   54
IMPERIAL (5279 "I Love You for
  Sentimental Reasons") 50-75   54
IMPERIAL (5296 "Can't Stop
  Loving You") 50-75   54
IMPERIAL (5316 "Too Many Drivers") 50-75   54
IMPERIAL (5325 "Jailbird") 50-75   54
IMPERIAL (5349 "Real Gone Lover") . 30-60   55
IMPERIAL (5356 "I Hear You
  Knocking") 20-40   55
IMPERIAL (5372 "Queen of Hearts") . 20-40   55
IMPERIAL (5380 "One Night") 20-40   56
IMPERIAL (5389 "She's Got Me Hook,
  Line and Sinker") 20-40   56
IMPERIAL (5404 "Down Yonder
  We Go Ballin") 20-40   56
IMPERIAL (5418 "Shame,
  Shame, Shame") 20-40   56
IMPERIAL (5431 through 5820) 10-20   57-62
KNIGHT 10-15   59
LOMA 5-10   65
OKEH 5-10   62

LPs: 10/12–inch 33rpm
IMPERIAL (9141 "I Hear You
Knocking") 150-200   61

LEWIS & CLARKE
(Lewis and Clarke Expedition)
Singles: 7–inch
CHARTMAKER 4-8   66
COLGEMS 4-8   67-68
Picture Sleeves
COLGEMS 5-10   67
LPs: 10/12–inch 33rpm
COLGEMS 12-18   67
Members: Travis Lewis; Boomer Clarke (Castleman); John London.
Also see CASTLEMAN, Boomer
Also see MURPHEY, Michael

LIA
Singles: 7–inch
VIRGIN 2-4   88

LIA, Orsa
Singles: 7–inch
INFINITY 3-5   79
RCA 4-6   68

LIBERACE
Singles: 78rpm
COLUMBIA 3-6   52-57
DECCA 3-6   52
Singles: 7–inch
A.V.I. 3-5   76-77
COLUMBIA (39000 through 41000
series) 5-10   52-58
CORAL 4-6   59-61
DECCA (28000 series) 5-10   52
DOT 4-6   64-67
MGM 3-5   73
WARNER 3-5   71
Picture Sleeves
COLUMBIA 10-15   54
EPs: 7–inch 33/45rpm
COLUMBIA 5-15   52-56
DECCA (28000 series) 8-15   52
LPs: 10/12–inch 33rpm
ABC 5-8   74
A.V.I. 5-8   73-79
COLUMBIA (500 through 1200 series) 15-30   53-58
COLUMBIA (6000 series) 20-30   52
(10–inch LP.)
COLUMBIA (9800 series) 5-10   69
CORAL 8-15   59-64
DECCA 5-10   72
DOT 8-15   63-68
FORWARD 5-10   69
HARMONY 8-15   59-70
HAMILTON 5-10   65
MISTLETOE 5-8   74
PARAMOUNT 5-10   73-74
TRIP 4-8   76
VOCALION 5-10   68

WARNER 5-10   71
Also see PRESLEY, Elvis

LIEBERMAN, Lori
Singles: 7–inch
CAPITOL 3-5   72-75
MILLENIUM 3-5   78
LPs: 10/12–inch 33rpm
CAPITOL 8-12   72-74

LIFESTYLE
Singles: 7–inch
MCA 3-5   77
LPs: 10/12–inch 33rpm
MCA 8-10   77

LIGGETT, Otis
Singles: 12–inch 33/45rpm
EMERGENCY 4-6   83
Singles: 7–inch
EMERGENCY 3-5   83

LIGGINS, Jimmy
(Jimmy Liggins and His 3-D Music)
Singles: 78rpm
ALADDIN 10-15   54
SPECIALTY 10-20   47-54
Singles: 7–inch
ALADDIN (3250 "I Ain't Drunk") 25-50   54
ALADDIN (3251 "No More Alcohol") . 25-50   54
DUPLEX 4-6
SPECIALTY (434 "Brown Skin Baby") 25-50   49
SPECIALTY (470 "Drunk") 20-40   53
(Black vinyl.)
SPECIALTY (470 "Drunk") 50-75   53
(Colored vinyl.)
SPECIALTY (484 "Going Away") 20-40   54

LIGGINS, Joe
(Joe Liggins and His Honeydrippers)
Singles: 78rpm
DOT 5-10
EXCLUSIVE 10-20   45-48
SMASH 8-12   54
SPECIALTY 10-15   49-54
Singles: 7–inch
ALADDIN (3368 "Justina") 15-25   56
MERCURY (70440 "Yeah, Yeah,
Yeah") 15-25   54
SPECIALTY (338 "The Honey
Dripper") 20-30   49
SPECIALTY (379 "Little Joe's Boogie") 20-30   51
SPECIALTY (392 "Frankie Lee") ... 20-30   51
SPECIALTY (402 "Whiskey, Gin
and Wine") 20-30   52
SPECIALTY (409 "Louisiana Woman") 20-30   52
SPECIALTY (413 "So Alone") 20-30   52
SPECIALTY (426 "Boogie Woogie
Lou") 20-30   52
SPECIALTY (430 "Tanya") 20-30   52
SPECIALTY (441 "Goin' Back
to New Orleans") 20-30   52

SPECIALTY (453 "Freight Train
  Blues") 20-30   53
SPECIALTY (465 "Farewell Blues") . . 20-30   53
SPECIALTY (474 "Everyone's Down
  on Me") 20-30   53
SPECIALTY (529 "Whiskey, Women
  and Loaded Dice") 20-40   54
   Also see MILTON, Roy / Joe Liggins

LIGHT, Enoch, and His Orchestra
**(Terry Snyder and the All-Stars; Command All-Stars;
Enoch Light and the Light Brigade)**
Singles: 7-inch
COMMAND 3-6   61
LPs: 10/12-inch 33rpm
COMMAND 5-15 59-66
GRAND AWARD 5-15   59
PROJECT 5-10 67-71

LIGHTFOOT, Gordon
(Gord Lightfoot)
Singles: 7-inch
ABC-PAR 8-18   62
REPRISE 3-5 70-77
U.A. 3-8 65-69
WARNER (Except 5621) 2-5 78-86
WARNER (5621 "For Lovin' Me") ... 5-8   65
Picture Sleeves
U.A. (50152 "The Way I Feel") 5-10   67
LPs: 10/12-inch 33rpm
LIBERTY 5-8   80
MFSL (018 "Sundown") 25-50   78
PICKWICK 5-8   79
REPRISE (Except 2237) 8-12 70-76
REPRISE (2237 "Gord's Gold") 10-15   75
U.A. (Except 3400/6400 series) 5-10 69-74
U.A. (3400 series) 10-15 66-69
  (Monaural.)
U.A. (6400 series) 10-20 66-69
  (Stereo.)
WARNER 5-8 78-86

LIGHTHOUSE
Singles: 7-inch
EVOLUTION 3-5 71-72
POLYDOR 4-6 73-74
RCA 2-4 69-70
LPs: 10/12-inch 33rpm
EVOLUTION 10-15 71-72
JANUS 8-10   76
POLYDOR 8-12 73-74
RCA 10-15 69-70

LIMAHL
(Chris Hamill)
Singles: 12-inch 33/45rpm
EMI AMERICA 4-6 85-86
Singles: 7-inch
EMI AMERICA 2-4 85-86
LPs: 10/12-inch 33rpm
EMI AMERICA 5-8 85-86
   Also see KAJAGOOGOO

LIME
Singles: 12-inch 33/45rpm
PRISM 4-6   83
TSR 4-6   85
Singles: 7-inch
PRISM 3-5   83
LPs: 10/12-inch 33rpm
PRISM 5-8   83

RCA VICTOR
SIDE II
INTRODUCING .....
Band 1: THE LIMELITERS
Band 2: BARRY MARTIN
Band 3: PENNY AND JEAN
Band 4: GORDON TERRY
Band 5: THE UNIVERSALS

LIMELITERS
Singles: 7-inch
ELEKTRA 5-10 60-61
RCA 4-8 61-64
WARNER 3-6   68
Picture Sleeves
RCA 5-10 61-63
EPs: 7-inch 33/45rpm
RCA ("Introducing . . .") 10-15   61
  (Introduces 11 new RCA acts with about 30
  seconds of music by: Limeliters, Cables; Toni
  Harper; Gary Judis; Cleo Jons; Baker Knight;
  Langan Sisters; Barry Martin; Penny and Jean;
  Gordon Terry; Universals. Promotional issue only.)
LPs: 10/12-inch 33rpm
CAMDEN 5-10   74
ELEKTRA 15-25 60-61
LEGACY 8-10   70
PICKWICK 5-8   72
RCA (Except 2336) 10-20 61-68
RCA (2336 "Pure Gold") 5-8   77
STAX 6-10   74
WARNER 8-15   68
   Members: Glen Yarbrough; Lou Gottlieb; Alex Hassilev; Ernie
   Sheldon.
   Also see ANN-MARGRET
   Also see YARBROUGH, Glen

LIMIT
Singles: 12-inch 33/45rpm
PORTRAIT 4-6   84
Singles: 7-inch
ARISTA 3-5   82
PORTRAIT 2-4   84
   Also see GUTHRIE, Gwen

LIMITED WARRANTY
Singles: 7–inch
ATCO 2-4   86

LIMMIE and Family Cookin'
Singles: 7–inch
AVCO 3-6   72

LIND, Bob
Singles: 7–inch
CAPITOL 3-5   71
VERVE/FOLKWAYS 4-6   66
WORLD PACIFIC 4-8   65-66
LPs: 10/12–inch 33rpm
CAPITOL 10-15   71
VERVE/FOLKWAYS 10-20   66
WORLD PACIFIC 10-20   66
    Also see CASCADES

LINDEN, Kathy
Singles: 7–inch
CAPITOL 4-8   62-63
FELSTED 5-10   58-59
MONUMENT 5-10   60-61
NATIONAL 4-8
RECORD PROD. CORP 4-8   61
Picture Sleeves
FELSTED 8-15   58-59
MONUMENT 4-8   60-61
EPs: 7–inch 33/45rpm
FELSTED (35001 "Hits") 35-45   58
LPs: 10/12–inch 33rpm
FELSTED (7501 "That Certain Boy") . 40-60   59

LINDISFARNE
Singles: 7–inch
ATCO 3-5   78
ELEKTRA 3-5   72-73
LPs: 10/12–inch 33rpm
ATCO 8-12   78
ELEKTRA 10-15   71-74

LINDLEY, David
(David Lindley and El Rayo)
Singles: 7–inch
ASYLUM 3-5   81
LPs: 10/12–inch 33rpm
ASYLUM 5-10   81
ELEKTRA 5-8   88
    Also see BROWNE, Jackson

LINDSAY, Mark
Singles: 7–inch
COLUMBIA 3-6   69-75
GREEDY 3-6   76
WARNER 3-6   77
LPs: 10/12–inch 33rpm
COLUMBIA 10-15   70-71
    Also see REVERE, Paul, and the Raiders

LINER
Singles: 7–inch
ATCO 3-5   79

LPs: 10/12–inch 33rpm
ATCO 5-10   79

LINK - EDDY COMBO
Singles: 7–inch
REPRISE 5-10   61
    Member: Al Garcia.

LINKLETTER, Art
Singles: 7–inch
CAPITOL 3-5   69
EPs: 7–inch 33/45rpm
COLUMBIA 5-10   56
WORD 3-5   69
LPs: 10/12–inch 33rpm
CAPITOL 8-15   61
COLUMBIA 15-25   56
HARMONY 8-15   59
20TH FOX 8-15   63-66
WORD 5-10   68

LIONS & GHOSTS
LPs: 10/12–inch 33rpm
EMI AMERICA 5-8   87

LIPPS, INC.
Singles: 7–inch
CASABLANCA 3-5   79-83
LPs: 10/12–inch 33rpm
CASABLANCA 5-8   79-81

LIQUID GOLD
Singles: 12–inch 33/45rpm
CRITIQUE 4-6   83
PARACHUTE 4-8   79
Singles: 7–inch
CRITIQUE 2-4   83
PARACHUTE 3-5   79
LPs: 10/12–inch 33rpm
PARACHUTE 5-10   79

LIQUID LIQUID
Singles: 12–inch 33/45rpm
99 RECORDS 4-6   83

LIQUID SMOKE
Singles: 7–inch
AVCO EMBASSY 3-5   70
LPs: 10/12–inch 33rpm
AVCO EMBASSY 10-12   70

LISA
Singles: 12–inch 33/45rpm
MOBY DICK 4-6   83-84

LISA LISA
(Lisa Lisa and Cult Jam with Full Force)
Singles: 12–inch 33/45rpm
COLUMBIA 4-6   85-86
Singles: 7–inch
COLUMBIA 2-4   85-88
LPs: 10/12–inch 33rpm
COLUMBIA 5-8   84-89
    Member: Lisa Velez.

Also see FULL FORCE
Also see KING DREAM CHORUS and Holiday Crew

LITES, Shirley
Singles: 12–inch 33/45rpm
WEST END 4-6   83

LITTLE, Rich
Singles: 7–inch
BOARDWALK 2-4   82
MERCURY 3-5   71
LPs: 10/12–inch 33rpm
BOARDWALK 5-8   82
CAEDMON 5-10   72
KARR 8-15   68
MERCURY 8-10   71
PIZZA HUT ("Pizza Hut '73") 15-20
(Souvenir of an annual company meeting.
Promotional issue only. No Number used.)

LITTLE ANTHONY and the Imperials
(Anthony and the Imperials; Imperials)
Singles: 7–inch
APOLLO 8-12   61
AVCO 3-5   74-75
DCP 4-8   64-66
END (1027 "Tears on My Pillow") 10-20   58
(Shown only as by "The Imperials.")
END (1027 "Tears on My Pillow") 5-10   58
(Shown by "Little Anthony and the Imperials.")
END (1036 "So Much") 10-15   58
END (1038 "The Diary") 15-20   59
END (1039 through 1104") 8-15   58-61
JANUS 3-5   71-72
MCA 2-4   80
OLD HIT 2-4
PCM 2-4   83
PURE GOLD 3-5   76
ROULETTE 4-8   61-63
U.A. 3-6   69-70
VEEP 4-8   66-68
Picture Sleeves
DCP 8-12   65
VEEP 8-12   66
EPs: 7–inch 33/45rpm
END (203 "Little Anthony and
the Imperials") 50-75   58
END (204 "We Are the Imperials
Featuring Little Anthony") 50-75   59
LPs: 10/12–inch 33rpm
ACCORD 5-10   83
AVCO 8-10   74
DCP 15-25   64-66
END (303 "We Are the Imperials
Featuring Little Anthony") 50-100   59
END (311 "Shades of the '40s") 40-60   60
FORUM CIRCLE 10-15
LIBERTY 5-8   81
ROULETTE 20-25   65
SUNSET 10-12   70
U.A. (Except 1000 series) 10-15 69-74

U.A. (1000 series) 5-8   80
VEEP 15-20   66-68
Members: Anthony Gourdine; Clarence Collins; Sam Strain;
Tracy Lord; Ernie Wright; Gloucester Rogers.
Also see IMPERIALS
Also see O'JAYS

LITTLE ANTHONY and the Imperials / Platters
LPs: 10/12–inch 33rpm
EXACT 5-10   80
Also see LITTLE ANTHONY and the Imperials
Also see PLATTERS

LITTLE BEAVER
Singles: 7–inch
CAT 3-5   72-76

LITTLE BILL and the Bluenots
Singles: 7–inch
DOLTON 10-20   59
TOPAZ 10-20
LPs: 10/12–inch 33rpm
CAMELOT (102 "The Fiesta Club Presents Little
Bill and the Blue Notes") 50-75   60
Members: Bill Engelhart; Buck England; Tom Morgan.

LITTLE BOOKER
(James Booker)
Singles: 78rpm
IMPERIAL 15-25   54
Singles: 7–inch
ACE 10-20   58
IMPERIAL (5293 "Thinkin'
'Bout My Baby") 50-75   54
Also see BOOKER, James

LITTLE CAESAR
Singles: 78rpm
BIG TOWN 10-20   53
RPM 10-20   53
RECORDED in HOLLYWOOD 10-20   53
Singles: 7–inch
BIG TOWN (106 "Big Eyes") 20-40   53
BIG TOWN (110 "What Kind of
Fool Is He") 20-40   53
RPM (393 "Chains of Love
Have Disappeared") 20-40   53
RECORDED in HOLLYWOOD (234 "The
River") 25-50   53
RECORDED in HOLLYWOOD (235 "Goodbye
Baby") 25-50   53
RECORDED in HOLLYWOOD (236 "Talking
to Myself") 25-50   53
RECORDED in HOLLYWOOD (237 "Atomic
Love") 25-50   53

LITTLE CAESAR and the Consuls
Singles: 7–inch
MALA 8-12   65

LITTLE CAESAR and the Romans
Singles: 7–inch
DEL-FI 10-15   61

LPs: 10/12–inch 33rpm
DEL-FI (1218 "Memories of Those
  Oldies But Goodies") 50-75   61
  Members: Carl Burnett; David Johnson; Leroy Sanders; Johnny
  Simmons.
  Also see BLUE JAYS / Little Caesar and the Romans

LITTLE DIPPERS
(Anita Kerr Singers)
Singles: 7–inch
DOT 4-6   64
UNIVERSITY 5-8 59-60
  Also see KERR, Anita

LITTLE ESTHER
(Esther Phillips; Little Esther Phillips; Little Esther
with the Earle Warren Orchestra; Little Esther with the
Johnny Otis Orchestra)
Singles: 78rpm
DECCA 8-12   54
FEDERAL 10-20   51
SAVOY 5-10   56
Singles: 7–inch
ATLANTIC 4-8 64-67
DECCA (28804 "Talkin' All
  Out of My Head") 20-30   54
DECCA (48305 "Stop Cryin'") 20-30   54
DECCA (48314 "He's a No
  Good Man") 40-60   54
FEDERAL (12023 "I'm a Bad Girl") .. 25-50   51
FEDERAL (12042 "Crying and
  Sighing") 25-50   51
FEDERAL (12055 "Crying Blues") ... 25-50   52
FEDERAL (12063 "Summertime") ... 25-50   52
FEDERAL (12065 "Better Beware") .. 25-50   52
FEDERAL (12078 "Aged and Mellow") 25-50   52
FEDERAL (12090 "Ramblin' Blues") .. 25-50   52
FEDERAL (12122 "You Took My Love
  too Fast") 25-50   53
FEDERAL (12126 "Hound Dog") 25-50   53
FEDERAL (12142 "Cherry Wine") ... 25-50   53
KUDU 3-5 72-76
LENOX 5-10 62-63
MERCURY 3-5 77-79
ROULETTE 3-6   69
SAVOY (1100 series) 10-15   56
SAVOY (1500 series) 5-10 58-59
WARWICK 5-8 60-61
WINNING 3-5   83
LPs: 10/12–inch 33rpm
ATLANTIC (1500 and 1600 series) ... 8-12 70-76
ATLANTIC (8100 series) 15-30 65-66
KING (622 "Memory Lane") 800-1200   59
KUDU 8-12 72-76
LENOX (227 "Release Me") 30-50   62
MERCURY 5-10 78-81
YORKSHIRE 8-12
  Also see ADAMS, Faye / Little Esther / Shirley and Lee
  Also see PHILLIPS, Esther, and Joe Beck

LITTLE ESTHER, who was voted the top recording star in the rhythm and blues field in the 1950 Cash Box poll, has now reached the ripe old age of sixteen.

LITTLE ESTHER and the Dominoes
(With the Earle Warren Orchestra)
Singles: 78rpm
FEDERAL (12036 "Heart to Heart") .. 40-60   51
Singles: 7–inch
FEDERAL (12036 "Heart to Heart") 250-350   51
  Also see LITTLE ESTHER with the Earle Warren Orchestra
  (With the Dominoes)
  Also see LITTLE ESTHER and Clyde McPhatter

LITTLE ESTHER and Big Al Downing
Singles: 7–inch
LENOX 5-10   63
  Also see DOWNING, Al

LITTLE ESTHER & Junior with the Johnny Otis Orchestra / Johnny Otis Orchestra with the Vocaleers
Singles: 78rpm
SAVOY (824 "Get Together Blues") .. 10-20   51
  Also see VOCALEERS

LITTLE ESTHER and Little Willie Littlefield
Singles: 78rpm
FEDERAL 10-15   52
Singles: 7–inch
FEDERAL (12108 "Last Laugh
  Blues") 25-50   52
FEDERAL (12115 "Turn the Lamps
  Down Low") 25-50   52
  Also see LITTLEFIELD, Little Willie

LITTLE ESTHER and Clyde McPhatter
Singles: 7–inch
FEDERAL (12344 "Heart to Heart") .. 15-25   58
  Also see LITTLE ESTHER and the Dominoes
  Also see McPHATTER, Clyde

LITTLE ESTHER and Bobby Nunn
Singles: 78rpm
FEDERAL (12100 "Saturday
  Night Daddy") 20-30   52
FEDERAL (12122 "You Took My
  Love Too Fast") 10-20   53
Singles: 7–inch
FEDERAL (12100 "Saturday
  Night Daddy") 35-50   52

FEDERAL (12122 "You Took My
Love too Fast") 150-200   53
Also see NUNN, Bobby

LITTLE ESTHER and Mel Walker
(With the Johnny Otis Orchestra)
Singles: 78rpm
FEDERAL 10-15   52
SAVOY 10-15   50
Singles: 7–inch
FEDERAL (12055 "Ring-A-Ding Doo") 25-50   52
SAVOY (735 "Mistrustin' Blues") 25-50   50
SAVOY (759 "Deceivin' Blues") 25-50   50
Also see OTIS, Johnny
Also see WALKER, Mel

LITTLE ESTHER with the Earle Warren Orchestra
(With the Dominoes)
Singles: 78rpm
FEDERAL (12016 "The Deacon
Moves In") 50-75   51
FEDERAL (12036 "Heart") 40-60   51
Singles: 7–inch
FEDERAL (12016 "The Deacon
Moves In") 300-400   51
FEDERAL (12036 "Heart") 250-350   51
Also see DOMINOES
Also see LITTLE ESTHER and the Dominoes

LITTLE EVA
Singles: 7–inch
ABC 3-5   74
AMY 4-8   65-66
BELL 3-5   72
DIMENSION 5-10   62-65
MCA 2-4   80
SPRING 3-5   70
VERVE 4-8   66
Picture Sleeves
DIMENSION (1035 "Makin' with
the Magilla") 20-30   64
LPs: 10/12–inch 33rpm
DIMENSION (DLP-6000
"L-L-L-L-Locomotion") 35-55   62
(Monaural.)
DIMENSION (DLPS-6000
"L-L-L-L-Locomotion") 50-75   62
(Stereo.)
Also see COOKIES / Little Eva / Carole King
Also see IRWIN, Big Dee
Also see KING, Ben E.

LITTLE FEAT
Singles: 7–inch
WARNER 3-6   70-78
LPs: 10/12–inch 33rpm
MFSL (013 "Waiting for Columbus") . 75-125   78
WARNER (984 "Hoy Hoy") 15-20   81
(Promotional issue only.)
WARNER (1890 through 2884) 8-15   70-76
WARNER (3015 through 3538) 6-12   77-81
WARNER (25000 and 26000 series) ... 5-8   88-90

Members: Lowell George; Ken Gradney; Richard Hayward;
Kenny Gradney; Sam Clayton; Roy Estrada; Fred Tackett; Paul
Barrere; Bill Payne.
Also see BRAMLETT, Bonnie
Also see CARTER, Valerie
Also see GEORGE, Lowell
Also see HARRIS, Emmylou
Also see MOTHERS of INVENTION
Also see TOWER of POWER
Also see ZEVON

LITTLE JO ANN
Singles: 7–inch
KAPP 8-12   62

LITTLE JOE and the Thrillers
(Little Joe; Little Joe the Thriller)
Singles: 7–inch
ENJOY 4-8   64
EPIC (9292 "It's too Bad We
Had to Say Goodbye") 10-15   58
MGM 3-5   70-73
OKEH 8-12   56-61
PEANUT 5-10
REPRISE 5-8   63
ROSE 5-8   63
TWENTIETH CENTURY (1214 "For Sentimental
Reasons") 15-25   61
EPs: 7–inch 33/45rpm
EPIC (7198 "Little Joe and
the Thrillers") 75-100   58
Members: Joe Cook; Richard Frazier; Farris Hill; Don Burnett;
Harry Pascle.

LITTLE JOE BLUE
Singles: 7–inch
CHECKER 4-8   66
MOVIN' 4-8   66

LITTLE JOEY and the Flips
(Joey Hall)
Singles: 7–inch
JOY 8-10   62

LITTLE JUNIOR'S BLUE FLAMES
(Junior Parker)
Singles: 78rpm
SUN ...., 25-50   53
Singles: 7–inch
SUN (187 "Feelin' Good") 75-100   53
SUN (192 "Love My Baby") 75-100   53
Also see PARKER, Little Junior

LITTLE MAC and the Boss Sounds
Singles: 7–inch
ATLANTIC 4-8   65
Member: Ann Mason.

LITTLE MILTON
(Milton Campbell)
Singles: 78rpm
METEOR 25-50   57
SUN 40-60   53-54
Singles: 7–inch
BOBBIN 10-20   59-61

CHECKER	4-8	62-71
CHESS	3-6	73-76
GLADES	3-5	76-78
MCA	2-4	83
MALACO	2-4	84-86
METEOR (5040 "Let's Boogie Baby")	50-75	57
METEOR (5045 "Let My Baby Be")	50-75	57
STAX	3-5	72-82
SUN (194 "Beggin' My Baby")	50-100	53
SUN (200 "If You Love Me")	100-200	54
SUN (220 "Homesick for My Baby")	150-300	55

LPs: 10/12-inch 33rpm

CHECKER (2995 "We're Gonna Make It")	20-30	65
CHECKER (3002 "Big Blues")	20-30	66
CHECKER (3011 "Grits Ain't Groceries")	15-20	69
CHECKER (3012 "If Walls Could Talk")	15-20	70
CHESS	10-15	72-76
GLADES	8-10	76-77
MCA	5-8	83
MALACO	5-8	84-86
STAX	8-12	73-81

LITTLE MILTON and Albert King
LPs: 10/12-inch 33rpm

STAX	5-10	79

Also see KING, Albert
Also see LITTLE MILTON

LITTLE RICHARD
(Little Richard and His Band)
Singles: 78rpm

PEACOCK	15-25	53
RCA	20-40	52
SPECIALTY	10-20	56-57

Singles: 7-inch

ABC	3-5	73
ATLANTIC	4-8	63
BELL	3-5	73
BRUNSWICK	4-6	68
CORAL	4-8	63
END	10-15	59
GREEN MOUNTAIN	3-5	73
KENT	3-5	73
MCA	2-4	86
MANTICORE	3-5	75
MERCURY	4-8	61
MODERN	10-15	57-58
(Black label.)		
MODERN	4-8	66-67
(Red or white label.)		
OKEH	4-6	66-69
PEACOCK (1658 "Little Richard's Boogie")	20-40	53
PEACOCK (1673 "Maybe I'm Right")	20-40	54
RCA (4392 "Taxi Blues")	100-150	51
RCA (4582 "Get Rich Quick")	100-150	52
RCA (4772 "Why Did You Leave Me")	100-150	52

RCA (5025 "Please Have Mercy on Me")	100-150	52
REPRISE	3-6	70-72
SPECIALTY (561 through 664)	10-20	56-59
SPECIALTY (670 through 699)	5-10	59-64
SPECIALTY (SPBX series)	15-20	85
(Boxed sets of six colored vinyl 45s.)		
TRIP	3-5	71
VEE JAY	4-8	64
WARNER	3-5	87

Picture Sleeves

MODERN (1018 "Holy Mackeral")	10-20	57
OKEH (7251 "Poor Dog")	8-10	66
SPECIALTY (606 "Jenny Jenny")	15-25	57
SPECIALTY (611 "Keep a Knockin")	15-25	57
SPECIALTY (624 "Good Golly Miss Molly")	15-25	58
SPECIALTY (633 "Ooh! My Soul")	15-25	58

EPs: 7-inch 33/45rpm

CAMDEN (416 "Little Richard")	100-150	56
CAMDEN (446 "Little Richard Rocks")	75-125	56
KAMA SUTRA (17 "Little Richard")	10-20	70
SPECIALTY (400 "Here's Little Richard")	30-40	56
SPECIALTY (401 "Here's Little Richard")	30-40	56
SPECIALTY (402 "Here's Little Richard")	30-40	56
SPECIALTY (403 "Little Richard")	30-40	57
SPECIALTY (404 "Little Richard")	30-40	57
SPECIALTY (405 "Little Richard")	30-40	57

LPs: 10/12-inch 33rpm

ACCORD	5-10	81
AUDIO ENCORES	20-25	80
BUDDAH	10-12	69
CAMDEN (420 "Little Richard")	100-150	56
CAMDEN (2430 "Every Hour")	10-15	70
CORAL	20-30	63
CROWN	15-25	63
CUSTOM	10-12	
EPIC	10-12	71
EVEREST	5-8	82
EXACT	5-10	80-81
51 WEST	5-8	
GRT	5-8	77
GOLD DISC	10-12	
GUEST STAR	10-15	64
KAMA SUTRA	10-12	70
MERCURY	20-25	61
MODERN	10-20	66
OKEH	10-20	67
PICKWICK	10-12	72
REPRISE	10-12	70-72
ROULETTE	10-15	68
SCEPTER	10-12	
SPECIALTY (100 "Here's Little Richard")	250-300	57
(Reissued as Specialty 2100.)		

SPECIALTY (2100 "Here's Little
Richard") 30-50   57
SPECIALTY (2103 "Little Richard") .. 30-50   57
SPECIALTY (2104 "The Fabulous
Little Richard") 30-50   58
SPECIALTY (2111 "Biggest Hits") ... 15-25   63
SPECIALTY (2113 "Grooviest 17
Original Hits") 10-15   68
SPECIALTY (2154 "The Essential Little
Richard") 8-12   84
SPIN-O-RAMA 10-15
SUMMIT 10-12
TRIP 10-12   71-78
20TH FOX 15-25   63
UNITED 8-10
U.A. 8-10   75
UPFRONT 8-10   77
VEE JAY 10-20   64-65
VEE JAY/DYNASTY 10-12
WARNER 5-8   87
WING 10-20   64
Also see BEACH BOYS and Little Richard
Also see CANNED HEAT
Also see CHARLES, Ray / Little Richard / Sam Cooke
Also see COOKE, Sam / Lloyd Price / Larry Williams / Little
Richard
Also see HENDRIX, Jimi, and Little Richard
Also see DUCES of RHYTHM and Tempo Toppers
Also see McPHATTER, Clyde / Little Richard / Jerry Butler

LITTLE RICHARD / Sister Rosetta
LPs: 10/12–inch 33rpm
GUEST STAR 10-15
Also see LITTLE RICHARD

LITTLE RICHIE
Singles: 7–inch
SOUND STAGE 7 4-8   66

LITTLE RIVER BAND
(LRB)
Singles: 12–inch 33/45rpm
CAPITOL 4-6   83
Singles: 7–inch
CAPITOL 2-4   79-85
HARVEST 3-5   76-78
Picture Sleeves
CAPITOL 3-5   81-83
LPs: 10/12–inch 33rpm
CAPITOL 5-8   79-85
HARVEST 5-8   75-80
MFSL 20-30   79
Also see SHORROCK, Glen

LITTLE ROYAL and the Swingmasters
Singles: 7–inch
TRI-US 3-5   72-73

LITTLE SISTER
Singles: 7–inch
STONE FLOWER 3-5   70-72
LPs: 10/12–inch 33rpm
STONE FLOWER 10-12   70

LITTLE STEVEN and the Disciples of Soul
Singles: 7–inch
EMI AMERICA 3-5   82-84
LPs: 10/12–inch 33rpm
EMI AMERICA 5-8   82-84
MANHATTAN 5-8   87
Also see BEAUVOIR, Jean
Also see SPRINGSTEEN, Bruce

LITTLE SYLVIA
(Sylvia Vanderpool)
Singles: 78rpm
CAT (102 "Fine Love") 10-15   53
JUBILEE 10-15   52
Singles: 7–inch
CAT (102 "Fine Love") 15-25   53
JUBILEE (5093 "Drive, Daddy,
Drive") 25-35   52
Also see MICKEY & SYLVIA
Also see SYLVIA

LITTLE WALTER
(Little Walter and His Jukes; Little Walter and His
Night Caps; Little Walter and His Night Cats; Little
Walter Trio; Marion Walter Jacobs)
Singles: 78rpm
CHANCE 25-50   52
CHECKER 10-20   52-57
ORA NELLE (711 "Ora Nelle Blues") . 50-75   47
Singles: 7–inch
CHANCE (1116 "Ora Nelle Blues") 250-350   52
CHECKER (758 "Juke") 20-30   52
CHECKER (764 "Mean Old World") . 20-30   52
CHECKER (770 "Off the Wall") 20-30   53
(Black vinyl.)
CHECKER (770 "Off the Wall") 75-100   53
(Colored vinyl.)
CHECKER (780 "Quarter to Twelve") 15-25   53
CHECKER (786 "Lights Out") 15-25   53
CHECKER (793 "Rocker") 15-25   54
CHECKER (799 "You Better
Watch Yourself") 15-25   54
(Black vinyl.)
CHECKER (799 "You Better
Watch Yourself") 50-75   54
(Colored vinyl.)
CHECKER (800 series) 10-20   54-58
CHECKER (900 through 1100 series) . 8-15   58-65
LPs: 10/12–inch 33rpm
CHESS (Except 1428) 10-20   69-74
CHESS (1428 "Best of Little Walter") 50-100   57

LITTLE WILLIE JOHN: see JOHN, Little Willie

LITTLEFIELD, Little Willie
Singles: 78rpm
EDDIE'S (1202 "Little Willie's Boogie") 10-20   48
EDDIE'S (1205 "Chicago Bound") ... 20-30   48
EDDIE'S (1212 "Swanee River") 20-30   49
FEDERAL 15-25   52-57
MODERN 15-25   49-50
RHYTHM 15-25   56

Singles: 7–inch

BULLS-EYE 10-15   58
FEDERAL (12101 "Sticking on
    You, Baby") 50-75   52
FEDERAL (12110 "K.C. Loving") 50-75   52
FEDERAL (12137 "The Midnight Hour
    Was Shining") 50-75   53
FEDERAL (12148 "Miss K.C.'s Fine") 50-75   53
FEDERAL (12163 "Please Don't
    Go-o-o-o-oh") 50-75   53
FEDERAL (12174 "Falling Tears") ... 50-75   54
FEDERAL (12221 "Jim Wilson's
    Boogie") 25-50   55
FEDERAL (12300 series) 10-20   57-59
RHYTHM (108 "Ruby-Ruby") 25-50   56
    Also see LITTLE ESTHER and Little Willie Littlefield

LITTLEFIELD, Little Willie / Goree Carter
Singles: 78rpm
FREEDOM (1502 "Littlefield Boogie") 15-25   49
    Also see LITTLEFIELD, Little Willie

LIVE
Singles: 7–inch
T.S.O.B. 3-5   81

LIVERPOOL FIVE
Singles: 7–inch
RCA 5-10   65-67
LPs: 10/12–inch 33rpm
RCA (LPM-3583 "The Liverpool
    Five Arrive") 20-25   66
    (Monaural.)
RCA (LSP-3583 "The Liverpool
    Five Arrive") 20-30   66
    (Stereo.)
RCA (LPM-3682 "Out of Sight") 20-25   67
    (Monaural.)
RCA (LSP-3682 "Out of Sight") 20-30   67
    (Stereo.)
    Also see ASTRONAUTS / Liverpool Five

LIVIGNI, John
Singles: 7–inch
RAINTREE 3-5   75

LIVIN' PROOF
Singles: 7–inch
JU-PAR 3-5   77

LIVING COLOR
LPs: 10/12–inch 33rpm
EPIC 5-8   88-90

LIVING STRINGS
Singles: 7–inch
COMMAND 3-5   59
GRAND AWARD 3-5   59
LPs: 10/12–inch 33rpm
CAMDEN 5-10   60-62
COMMAND 5-10   59
GRAND AWARD 5-10   59

LIZARD, King: see KING LIZARD

LIZZY BORDEN
LPs: 10/12–inch 33rpm
ENIGMA/METAL BLADE 5-8   86-89

LLOYD, Charles, Quartet
LPs: 10/12–inch 33rpm
ATLANTIC 10-15   67
    Also see HAMILTON, Chico

LLOYD, Ian
Singles: 7–inch
POLYDOR 3-5   76
SCOTTI BROTHERS 2-4   79
LPs: 10/12–inch 33rpm
POLYDOR 5-10   76
SCOTTI BROTHERS 5-8   79
    Also see STORIES

LOAF, Meat: see MEAT LOAF

LOBO
(Kent Lavole)
Singles: 7–inch
BIG TREE 3-5   71-75
ELEKTRA 3-5   80
EVERGREEN 3-5
FLASHBACK 3-5   73
MCA 2-4   79
MARIANNE 3-5   77
WARNER 3-5   76-78
LPs: 10/12–inch 33rpm
BIG TREE 10-15   71-75
CALUMET 10-15   73
MCA 5-10   79

LOCKLIN, Hank
Singles: 78rpm
DECCA 4-8   52
4 STAR 4-8   52-54
RCA 4-8   55-57
Singles: 7–inch
COUNTRY ARTISTS 2-4   83
DECCA (29000 series) 5-10   52
4 STAR (1500 and 1600 series) 5-10   52-54
KING (5000 series) 4-8   59
MGM 3-5   74
PLANTATION 3-5   76-77
RCA (0030 through 0900 series) 3-5   72-74
RCA (6100 through 7600 series) 5-10   55-59
RCA (7700 through 9900 series) 4-8   60-71
EPs: 7–inch 33/45rpm
RCA 8-15   58-61
LPs: 10/12–inch 33rpm
CAMDEN 8-15   62-74
DESIGN 10-15   62
INTERNATIONAL AWARD 8-12
KING (600 and 700 series) 15-25   61
MGM 5-10   75
METRO 10-15   65
PICKWICK/HILLTOP 8-15   65-68

PLANTATION 5-8   77-81
RCA (Except 1600 series) 10-20   62-71
RCA (1673 "Foreign Love") 25-35   58
SEARS 10-15
WRANGLER 15-25   62
   Also see CLINE, Patsy / Hank Locklin / Miller Brothers / Eddie
   Marvin
   Also see SNOW, Hank / Hank Locklin / Porter Wagoner

LOCKLIN, Hank, with Danny Davis and the Nashville Brass
Singles: 7–inch

RCA 3-6   69-70
LPs: 10/12–inch 33rpm
RCA 8-10   70
   Also see DAVIS, Danny
   Also see LOCKLIN, Hank

LOCKSMITH
Singles: 7–inch

ARISTA 3-5   80
LPs: 10/12–inch 33rpm
ARISTA 5-10   80

LODGE, John
Singles: 7–inch

LONDON 3-5   77
LPs: 10/12–inch 33rpm
LONDON 8-10   76-77
   Also see HAYWARD, Justin, and John Lodge
   Also see MOODY BLUES

LOFGREN, Nils
Singles: 7–inch

A&M 3-5   75-77
LPs: 10/12–inch 33rpm
A&M (Except 8362) 8-10   75-82
A&M (8362 "Authorized Bootleg") ... 25-30   76
   (Promotional issue only.)
BACKSTREET 5-8   81
COLUMBIA 5-8   85
EPIC 8-10   76
RYKODISC 5-8   91
   Also see GRIN

LOGG
Singles: 7–inch

SALSOUL 3-5   81
LPs: 10/12–inch 33rpm
SALSOUL 5-8   81

LOGGINS, Dave
Singles: 7–inch

EPIC 3-5   74-81
VANGUARD 4-6   72-74
LPs: 10/12–inch 33rpm
CAPITOL 5-8   84
EPIC 8-10   74-81
VANGUARD 8-12   72
   Also see MURRAY, Anne, and Dave Loggins

LOGGINS, Kenny
Singles: 12–inch 33/45rpm

COLUMBIA 4-8   81-86

Singles: 7–inch
COLUMBIA 2-5   77-87
LPs: 10/12–inch 33rpm
COLUMBIA (Except 45387) 6-12   72-88
COLUMBIA (45387 "Nightwatch") ... 10-15   81
   (Half-speed mastered.)
   Also see U.S.A. for AFRICA

LOGGINS, Kenny, and Stevie Nicks
Singles: 7–inch

COLUMBIA 3-5   78
   Also see NICKS, Stevie

LOGGINS, Kenny, and Steve Perry
Singles: 7–inch

COLUMBIA 3-5   82
   Also see LOGGINS, Kenny
   Also see PERRY, Steve

LOGGINS & MESSINA
Singles: 7–inch

COLUMBIA 3-5   72-76
LOS ANGELES KINGS/
  COLUMBIA (10444 "Angry Eyes") ... 3-5   76
   (Promotional issue for "Columbia/Kings Record
   Night" at the L.A. Forum.)
Picture Sleeves
LOS ANGELES KINGS/
  COLUMBIA (10444 "Angry Eyes") ... 3-5   76
   (Promotional issue for "Columbia/Kings Record
   Night" at the L.A. Forum.)
LPs: 10/12–inch 33rpm
COLUMBIA (30000 series) 8-10   72-82
COLUMBIA (44000 series) 10-15   82
   (Half-speed mastered.)
   Members: Kenny Loggins; Jim Messina.
   Also see LOGGINS, Kenny
   Also see MESSINA, Jim

LOGGINS & MESSINA / David Bromberg
LPs: 10/12–inch 33rpm

COLUMBIA 8-15   72
   (Promotional only.)
   Also see BROMBERG, David
   Also see LOGGINS & MESSINA

LOLITA
Singles: 7–inch

4 CORNERS 4-6   65
KAPP 5-8   60-61
Picture Sleeves
KAPP 10-15   61
LPs: 10/12–inch 33rpm
KAPP 15-25   61

LOMAX, Jackie
Singles: 7–inch

APPLE (1802 "Sour Milk Sea") 10-20   68
APPLE (1807 "New Day") 10-15   69
APPLE (1819 "How the
  Web Was Woven") 4-8   70
CAPITOL 3-5   77
EPIC 4-8   68
WARNER 3-5   71-73

Promotional Singles
APPLE (1802 "Sour Milk Sea") 20-30   68
Picture Sleeves
APPLE (1819 "How the
Web Was Woven") 5-10   70
LPs: 10/12–inch 33rpm
APPLE (3354 "Is This
What You Want") 12-20   69
CAPITOL 5-10   76-77
WARNER 8-12   71-72
  Also see BADGER
  Also see CLAPTON, Eric
  Also see McCARTNEY, Paul
  Also see STARR, Ringo

LOMBARDO, Guy
(Guy Lombardo and His Royal Canadians)
Singles: 78rpm
BRUNSWICK 4-8   32-34
COLUMBIA 4-8   27-31
DECCA 3-8   34-57
VICTOR 3-6   36-38
Singles: 7-Inch
CAPITOL 3-6   59-67
DECCA 3-8   50-73
EPs: 7-inch 33/45rpm
CAPITOL 5-10   56-59
DECCA 5-10   50-59
RCA 5-10   60
LPs: 10/12-Inch 33rpm
CAMDEN 10-30   54-65
CAPITOL (Except 739 through 1598) . 5-15   61-81
CAPITOL (739 through 1598) 10-25   56-61
DECCA 10-30   50-67
LONDON 5-8   73
MCA 5-8   75
RCA 5-8   72-77
VOCALION 5-10   66-68
  Also see ARMSTRONG, Louis, and Guy Lombardo

LONDON, Julie
Singles: 78rpm
LIBERTY 4-6   55-57
Singles: 7–inch
BETHLEHEM 4-8   59
LIBERTY 4-8   55-68
Picture Sleeves
LIBERTY 8-12   61
EPs: 7-inch 33/45rpm
BETHLEHEM 10-20   59
LIBERTY 10-20   56-57
LPs: 10/12–inch 33rpm
GUEST STAR 5-10   64
LIBERTY (3006 "Julie Is Her Name") . 20-25   56
LIBERTY (3012 "Lonely Girl") 20-25   56
LIBERTY (9002 "Calendar Girl") 25-35   56
LIBERTY (3027 "Julie Is Her Name") . 20-25   57
  (Monaural. Black vinyl.)
LIBERTY (7027 "Julie Is Her Name") . 40-60   59
  (Stereo. Colored vinyl.)

LIBERTY (3043 through 3514) 12-25   57-67
  (Monaural.)
LIBERTY (7100 through 7546) 15-30   57-68
  (Stereo.)
SUNSET 8-15   66-68
U.A. 5-10   75

LONDON, Julie, and the Bud Shank Quintet
LPs: 10/12–inch 33rpm
LIBERTY 10-15   66
  Also see LONDON, Julie
  Also see SHANK, Bud

LONDON, Laurie
Singles: 7–inch
CAPITOL 8-10   58-59
ROULETTE 5-10   59
EPs: 7–inch 33/45rpm
CAPITOL (10182 "Laurie London") .. 20-30   58
CAPITOL (10191 "Laurie London") .. 20-30   58
LPs: 10/12–inch 33rpm
CAPITOL (1016 "Laurie London") ... 30-50   58

LONDON SYMPHONY ORCHESTRA
(London Symphony Orchestra with Ian Anderson)
Singles: 7–inch
RCA (14262 "Elegy") 2-4   86
LPs: 10/12–inch 33rpm
RCA (4000 series) 5-8   83
RCA (7067 "A Classic Case") 8-10   86
RSO 5-8   79

LONE JUSTICE
Singles: 7–inch
GEFFEN 2-4   85-87
LPs: 10/12–inch 33rpm
GEFFEN 5-8   85-86
  Member: Tony Gilkyson.

LONG, Shorty
Singles: 78rpm
RCA 4-8   56
Singles: 7–inch
RCA 5-10   56
VALLEY (108 "I Got Nine
Little Kisses") 50-75

LONGET, Claudine
Singles: 7–inch
A&M 3-6   66-70
BARNABY 3-5   70-73
LPs: 10/12–inch 33rpm
A&M 5-12   67-69
BARNABY 5-10   70-72

LONGMIRE, Wilbert
Singles: 7–inch
TAPPAN ZEE 3-5   79-80
LPs: 10/12–inch 33rpm
TAPPAN ZEE 5-8   79-80

LOOKING GLASS
Singles: 7–inch
EPIC 3-5   72-74

LPs: 10/12–inch 33rpm
EPIC 10-12   72-73

LOOSE CHANGE
Singles: 7–inch
CASABLANCA 3-5   79-80
LPs: 10/12–inch 33rpm
CASABLANCA 5-10   79

LOOSE ENDS
Singles: 12–inch 33/45rpm
MCA 4-6   85-86
Singles: 7–inch
MCA 2-4   85-90
LPs: 10/12–inch 33rpm
MCA 5-8   85-90

LOOSE JOINTS
Singles: 12–inch 33/45rpm
4TH and BROADWAY 4-6   84
Singles: 7–inch
4TH and BROADWAY 2-4   84

LOPEZ, Denise
LPs: 10/12–inch 33rpm
A&M 5-8   88

LOPEZ, Trini
Singles: 12–inch 33/45rpm
ROULETTE 5-8   77
Singles: 7–inch
CAPITOL 3-5   71-72
D.R.A. 5-10   61
GRIFFIN 3-5   73-75
KING (5173 "Nola") 10-15   59
KING (5187 "Rock On") 15-25   59
KING (5198 "Here Comes Sally") 10-15   59
KING (5234 through 5487) 8-15   59-61
KING (5800 series) 5-10   63-64
KING (6000 series) 4-8   65-66
MARIANNE 3-5   77
PRIVATE STOCK 3-5   75
REPRISE 4-8   63-71
ROULETTE 3-5   77
UNITED MODERN 4-8   64
VOLK (101 "The Right to Rock") 15-25   58
Picture Sleeves
REPRISE 5-10   62-66
EPs: 7–inch 33/45rpm
COLUMBIA/WARNER (124178 "Trini
Lopez Sings His Greatest Hits") 4-8   67
(Coca-Cola/Fresca special products issue.)
FRESCA 8-12   67
(Promotional issue only.)
KING (483 "Teenage Idol") 10-20   63
REPRISE 8-12   63-68
LPs: 10/12–inch 33rpm
CAPITOL 5-10   72
EXACT 5-8   81
GRIFFIN 8-10   72
HARMONY 8-10   70

KING 10-20   63
REPRISE 10-20   63-69
ROULETTE 5-8   78
SILVER EAGLE 5-10   82
WEA LATINA 5-8   91
Also see LAWRENCE, Steve / Trini Lopez

LOPEZ, Trini / Scott Gregory
LPs: 10/12–inch 33rpm
GUEST STAR (1499 "Trini Lopez / Scott
Gregory [Bill Haley]") 30-50   64
Also see HALEY, Bill

LOPEZ, Trini, with the Ventures and Nancy Ames
LPs: 10/12–inch 33rpm
REPIRSE (6361 "The Trini
Lopez Show") 10-15   70
Also see LOPEZ, Trini
Also see VENTURES

LOR, Denise
Singles: 78rpm
LIBERTY 3-5   56
MAJAR 4-6   54
MERCURY 3-5   55
Singles: 7–inch
LIBERTY 4-8   56
MAJAR 5-10   54
MERCURY 4-8   55
EPs: 7–inch 33/45rpm
MERCURY 5-10   55

LORBER, Jeff
(Jeff Lorber Fusion)
Singles: 12–inch 33/45rpm
ARISTA 4-6   85
Singles: 7–inch
ARISTA 3-5   79-85
INNER CITY 3-5   78
WARNER 2-4   86
LPs: 10/12–inch 33rpm
ARISTA 5-8   79-85
INNER CITY 5-10   78
WARNER 5-8   86
Members: Kenny Gorelick; Karyn White; Michael Jeffries.
Also see G., Kenny
Also see UNLIMITED TOUCH

LORD, C.M.
Singles: 12–inch
MONTAGE 4-6   82-84
WAVE 4-6   83
Singles: 7–inch
CAPITOL 3-5   76
MONTAGE 2-4   82-84
LPs: 10/12–inch 33rpm
CAPITOL 8-10   76
MONTAGE 5-8   84

LORD ROCKINGHAM'S XI
Singles: 7–inch
LONDON 5-10   58

LORD SUTCH
(Lord Sutch and His Heavy Friends)
LPs: 10/12–inch 33rpm
COTILLION (9015 "Lord Sutch
and His Heavy Friends") 20-30   70
COTILLION (9049 "Hands of
Jack the Ripper") 15-25   72
Also see BECK, Jeff
Also see BLACKMORE, Ritchie
Also see HOPKINS, Nicky
Also see MOON, Keith
Also see PAGE, Jimmy

LORELEIS
Singles: 78rpm
SPOTLIGHT 5-8   55
Singles: 7–inch
BRUNSWICK 3-5   64
SPOTLIGHT 5-10   55

LOREN, Bryan
Singles: 12–inch 33/45rpm
PHILLY WORLD 4-6   83-84
Singles: 7–inch
PHILLY WORLD 2-4   83

LORETTA LYNN: see LYNN, Loretta

LORING, Gloria
Singles: 7–inch
MGM 3-5   72
LPs: 10/12–inch 33rpm
ATLANTIC 5-8   86

LORING, Gloria, and Carl Anderson
Singles: 7–inch
CARRERE 2-4   86
LPs: 10/12–inch 33rpm
EPIC 5-8   85
Also see ANDERSON, Carl

LOS ADMIRADORES
LPs: 10/12–inch 33rpm
COMMAND 8-15   60

LOS BRAVOS
Singles: 7–inch
LONDON 2-4
PARROT 4-8   68
PRESS 4-8   66-68
LPs: 10/12–inch 33rpm
PARROT (71021 "Bring a Little Lovin") 15-25   68
PRESS (83003 "Black Is Black") 20-25   66
Member: Mike Kennedy.
Also see DRIFTERS / Lesley Gore / Roy Orbison / Los Bravos
Also see KENNEDY, Mike

LOS INDIOS TABAJARAS
Singles: 7–inch
RCA 4-6   63-64
LPs: 10/12–inch 33rpm
RCA (LPM-1788 "Sweet and Savage") 20-30   58
(Monaural.)
RCA (LSP-1788 "Sweet and Savage") 25-40   58
(Stereo.)

RCA (2800 and 2900 series) 8-15   63-64
Members: Natalicio; Antenor Moreyra Lima (aka Musaperi and
Herundy).

LOS LOBOS
Singles: 12–inch 33/45rpm
SLASH 5-8   86
(Promotional issue only.)
Singles: 7–inch
SLASH 2-4   83-90
LPs: 10/12–inch 33rpm
SLASH 5-8   83-90
Member: David Hidalgo.

LOS POP-TOPS: see POP-TOPS

LOST GENERATION
Singles: 7–inch
BRUNSWICK 3-5   70-71
INNOVATION 3-5   74
LPs: 10/12–inch 33rpm
BRUNSWICK 10-12   70

LOU, Bonnie
Singles: 78rpm
KING 4-6   55
Singles: 7–inch
FRATERNITY 5-10   58
KING 5-10   55

LOUDERMILK, John D.
Singles: 7–inch
COLUMBIA 5-10   58-60
MUSIC IS MEDICINE 3-5   78-79
RCA 4-8   61-69
WARNER 3-5   71
Picture Sleeves
COLUMBIA (41165 "Yearbook") 10-20   58
RCA (8101 "Road Hog") 5-10   62
LPs: 10/12–inch 33rpm
MUSIC IS MEDICINE 5-8   78
RCA 15-25   61-69
WARNER 8-12   71
Also see DEE, Johnny

LOUDNESS
LPs: 10/12–inch 33rpm
ATCO 5-8   85-87

LOUISIANA'S LE ROUX: see LE ROUX

LOVE
Singles: 7–inch
BLUE THUMB 4-6   69-70
ELEKTRA (45603 through 45608) 5-8   66-67
ELEKTRA (45613 "Que Vida") 15-25   67
ELEKTRA (45629 through 45700) 5-8   68-70
RSO 4-6   74-75
LPs: 10/12–inch 33rpm
BLUE THUMB 12-15   69-70
ELEKTRA (4001 "Love") 25-40   66
(Monaural.)
ELEKTRA (4005 "Da Capo") 25-40   66
(Monaural.)

ELEKTRA (4013 "Forever Changes")   25-40   67
(Monaural.)
ELEKTRA (74001 "Love") 25-35   66
(Stereo.)
ELEKTRA (74005 "Da Capo") 25-35   67
(Stereo.)
ELEKTRA (74013 "Forever Changes") 20-30   67
(Stereo.)
ELEKTRA (74049 "Four Sail") 20-30   69
(Stereo.)
ELEKTRA (74058 "Revisited") . . . . . . : 20-30   70
(Gatefold cover.)
ELEKTRA (74058 "Revisited") 5-8   81
(Standard cover.)
MCA 5-8   82
RSO 8-10   74
RHINO (251 "Love Live") 8-10   82
RHINO (800 "Best of Love") 5-8   80
  Members: Arthur Lee; Tjay Contrelli; John Echols; Bryan
  Maclean; Don Conka; Ken Forssi.

LOVE, Candace
Singles: 7-inch
AQUARIUS 4-8   68

LOVE, Darlene
Singles: 7-inch
COLUMBIA 3-5   88
PHILLES (111 "The Boy I'm Gonna Marry"/
  "My Heart Beat a Little Bit Faster") . 12-18   63
PHILLES (111 "The Boy I'm Gonna Marry"/
  "Playing for Keeps") 8-12   63
PHILLES (114 "Wait Till My
  Bobby Gets Home") 10-15   63
PHILLES (117 "A Fine, Fine Boy") 8-15   63
PHILLES (119 "Christmas, Baby
  Please Come Home") 15-25   63
PHILLES (123 "He's a Quiet Guy") . . 30-50   64
PHILLES (125 "Christmas, Baby
  Please Come Home") 15-25   64
REPRISE 4-8   66
RHINO 5-8   86
WARNER/SPECTOR 3-6   74-77
Picture Sleeves
COLUMBIA 3-5   88
LPs: 10/12-inch 33rpm
COLUMBIA (40605 "Paint
  Another Picture") 8-12   88
  Also see BLOSSOMS
  Also see BOB B. SOXX and the Blue Jeans
  Also see CRYSTALS
  Also see RONETTES / Crystals / Darlene Love / Bob B. Soxx
  and the Blue Jeans

LOVE, Darlene / Annie Golden
Singles: 7-inch
ELEKTRA 3-5   85
Picture Sleeves
ELEKTRA 3-5   85
  Also see LOVE, Darlene

LOVE, Le Juan
Singles: 7-inch
LUKE SKY. 2-4   88

LOVE, Ronnie
Singles: 7-inch
D TOWN 5-10
DOT 5-10   60-61
STARTIME (5003 "Shakin' and
  a Breakin") 20-30   61

LOVE, Rudy, and the Love Family
Singles: 7-inch
CALLA 3-5   76
LPs: 10/12-inch 33rpm
CALLA 5-10   76

LOVE, Vikki, with Nuance
Singles: 12-inch 33/45rpm
4TH and BROADWAY 4-6   85
Singles: 7-inch
4TH and BROADWAY 2-4   85
  Also see NUANCE

LOVE and KISSES
Singles: 7-inch
CASABLANCA 3-5   77-79
LPs: 10/12-inch 33rpm
CASABLANCA 8-10   77-79

LOVE & ROCKETS
Singles: 7-inch
BIG TIME 2-4   86
LPs: 10/12-inch 33rpm
BEGGARS BANQUET 5-8   89
BIG TIME 5-8   86-87
  Members: David Jor; Kevin Haskins; Daniel Ash.

LOVE BUG STARSKI
Singles: 12-inch 33/45rpm
ATLANTIC 2-4   85
FEVER 4-6   83

LOVE CHILD'S AFRO CUBAN BLUES BAND
(Love Child's Latin Soul Afro Blues Band)
Singles: 7-inch
A&M 3-6   69
ROULETTE 3-5   75
LPs: 10/12-inch 33rpm
ROULETTE 5-10   75

LOVE CLUB
Singles: 12-inch 33/45rpm
WEST END 4-6   83

LOVE COMMITTEE
Singles: 7-inch
ARIOLA AMERICA 3-5   75-76
GOLD MIND 3-5   77-78

LOVE GENERATION
Singles: 7-inch
IMPERIAL 4-8   67-68
LPs: 10/12-inch 33rpm
IMPERIAL 10-15   68

U.A. 8-10   77
   Also see CLIMAX

LOVE, PEACE & HAPPINESS
Singles: 7–inch
RCA 3-5   71-72
LPs: 10/12–inch 33rpm
RCA 8-10   71

LOVE UNLIMITED
(Love Unlimited Orchestra)
Singles: 7–inch
CASABLANCA 3-5
MCA 2-4
20TH FOX 3-5   73-77
UNI 3-5   72
UNLIMITED GOLD 2-5   77-84
LPs: 10/12–inch 33rpm
20TH FOX 8-10   74-76
UNI 5-10   72
UNLIMITED GOLD 5-8   77-84
   Also see WHITE, Barry

LOVELITES
Singles: 7–inch
BANDERA 8-10   67
LOCK 4-8   69
LOVELITE 3-6   70-71
PHI-DAN 10-15   66
20TH FOX 3-6   73
UNI 3-6   69-70
LPs: 10/12–inch 33rpm
UNI 10-15   70

LOVELY, Ike
Singles: 7–inch
WAND 3-5   73

LOVERBOY
Singles: 7–inch
COLUMBIA 2-4   81-87
Picture Sleeves
COLUMBIA 3-5   81-87
LPs: 10/12–inch 33rpm
COLUMBIA (Except 169961) 5-10   80-89
COLUMBIA (169961 "Loverboy") 10-15   82
   Members: Mike Reno; Matthew Frenette; Paul Dean; Doug
   Johnson; Scott Smith.
   Also see RENO, Mike, and Ann Wilson

LOVERDE
Singles: 12–inch 33/45rpm
MOBY DICK 4-6   83

LOVERS
Singles: 78rpm
DECCA 5-10   56
Singles: 7–inch
ALADDIN (3419 "Tell Me") 15-25   58
DECCA (29862 "Don't Touch Me") . . . 15-25   56
IMPERIAL 5-10   62-63
KELLER (101 "Party Line") 20-40   61
LAMP (2005 "Darling, It's Wonderful") 10-15   58
LAMP (2013 "I Wanna Be Loved") . . . 15-20   58

LAMP (2018 "Tell Me") 15-20   58
POST (10007 "Darling, It's Wonderful") 5-10   63
   Member: Tarheel Slim.
   Also see TARHEEL SLIM

LOVERS
Singles: 7–inch
MARLIN 3-5   77

LOVESMITH
(Michael Lovesmith)
Singles: 7–inch
MOTOWN 2-4   81-85
LPs: 10/12–inch 33rpm
MOTOWN 5-8   81

LOVETT, Lyle
Singles: 7–inch
MCA 2-4   86-90
LPs: 10/12–inch 33rpm
MCA 5-10   86-90

LOVETTE, Eddie
Singles: 7–inch
STEADY 4-8   69
LPs: 10/12–inch 33rpm
STEADY 8-10   70

LOVICH, Lene
Singles: 7–inch
STIFF 3-5   79-83
LPs: 10/12–inch 33rpm
STIFF 5-8   79-83

LOVIN' SPOONFUL
Singles: 7–inch
ERIC 2-4   78
KAMA SUTRA 3-8   65-72
Picture Sleeves
KAMA SUTRA 5-10   65-67
LPs: 10/12–inch 33rpm
BACK-TRAC 5-8   85
BUDDAH 8-10   73
51 WEST 5-8
GRT 8-15   76
GUSTO 5-8
KAMA SUTRA (750 "24 Karat Hits") . 10-15   68
KAMA SUTRA (2000 series) 8-15   70-76
KAMA SUTRA (8000 series) 15-25   65-69
KAMA SUTRA (91102 "Best of
  the Lovin' Spoonful") 8-10

NASHVILLE CATS
b/w Full Measure
THE LOVIN' SPOONFUL

KA-219

Kama Sutra
MGM RECORDS
A Product of Koppelman-Rubin Associates, Inc.   Produced by Erik Jacobsen

Members: John Sebastian; Zalman Yanovsky; Joe Butler; Steve Boone; Jerry Yester.
Also see SEBASTIAN, John

LOW, Gary
Singles: 12–inch 33/45rpm
QUALITY 4-6   83

LOWE, Bernie
(Bernie Lowe Orchestra)
Singles: 7–inch
CAMEO 4-8   58-63
LPs: 10/12–inch 33rpm
CAMEO 15-25   62-63

LOWE, Jim
Singles: 78rpm
DOT 4-8   55-57
MERCURY 4-8   53-54
Singles: 7–inch
BUDDAH 4-6   68
DECCA 4-8   60-61
DOT (15300 through 16200 series) ... 5-10   55-60
DOT (16600 series) 4-8   64
MERCURY 5-10   53-54
20TH FOX 4-8   63
U.A. 4-6   67
EPs: 7–inch 33/45rpm
DOT 10-20   57
MERCURY 10-20   57
LPs: 10/12–inch 33rpm
DOT (3051 "The Green Door") 25-35   57
DOT (3114 "Wicked Women") 25-35   58
DOT (3681 "The Green Door") 10-20   66
  (Monaural.)
DOT (25681 "The Green Door") 10-20   66
  (Stereo.)
MERCURY (20246 "Door of Fame") . 25-35   57

LOWE, Nick
(Nick Lowe and Rockpile; Nick Lowe and His Cowboy Outfit)
Singles: 7–inch
COLUMBIA 2-5   78-86
LPs: 10/12–inch 33rpm
COLUMBIA 5-10   78-86
REPRISE 5-8   90
  Also see NICK & ELVIS

LOWE, Nick, and Dave Edmunds
Singles: 7–inch
COLUMBIA 3-5   81
EPs: 7–inch 33/45rpm
COLUMBIA (1219 "Nick Lowe and Dave Edmunds
  Sing the Everly Brothers") 5-10   80
  (Promotional issue only.)
  Also see EDMUNDS, Dave
  Also see LOWE, Nick
  Also see ROCKPILE

LOWRELL
Singles: 7–inch
AVI 3-5   78-80
  Also see SIMON, Lowrell

LOZ NETTO: see NETTO, Loz

L'TRIMM
LPs: 10/12–inch 33rpm
ATLANTIC 5-8   88

LUBOFF, Norman, Choir
Singles: 78rpm
COLUMBIA 3-5   54-59
Singles: 7-Inch
COLUMBIA 3-6   54-59
EPs: 7-Inch 33/45rpm
COLUMBIA 4-8   54-59
LPs: 10/12-Inch 33rpm
COLUMBIA 5-15   54-60
HARMONY 5-10   61
RCA 5-10   61-62

LUCAS, Carrie
Singles: 12–inch 33/45rpm
CONSTELLATION 4-6   84-85
Singles: 7–inch
CONSTELLATION 2-4   84-85
SOLAR 3-5   79-82
SOUL TRAIN 3-5   77
LPs: 10/12–inch 33rpm
CONSTELLATION 5-8   85
SOLAR 5-10   79-82
SOUL TRAIN 8-10   77

LUCAS, Carrie, and the Whispers
Singles: 7–inch
CONSTELLATION 2-4   85
  Also see LUCAS, Carrie
  Also see WHISPERS

LUCAS, Frank
Singles: 7–inch
ICA 3-5   77-78

LUCAS, Matt
Singles: 7–inch
DOT 4-8   63-64
RENE 10-15   63
SMASH 4-8   63

LUGEE and the Lions
Singles: 7–inch
ROBBEE (112 "The Jury") 50-75   61
  Members: Lou Christie; Kay Chick; Amy Sacco; Bill Faveck.
  Also see CHRISTIE, Lou
  Also see CLASSICS

LUGO, Danny, and the Destinations
Singles: 12–inch 33/45rpm
C&M 4-6   84

LUKE, Robin
Singles: 7–inch
BERTRAM INTERNATIONAL (206 "Susie
  Darlin") 20-40   58
BERTRAM INTERNATIONAL (208
  through 212) 15-25   58-59
DOT 5-10   58-61

Picture Sleeves

BERTRAM INTERNATIONAL (206 "Susie
Darlin'") 40-60   58
DOT (16096 "Everlovin") 10-20   60

EPs: 7–inch 33/45rpm

DOT (1092 "Susie Darlin") 50-75   60

LUKE, Robin, and Roberta Shore
Singles: 7–inch

DOT 4-8   62
Also see LUKE, Robin

LULU
(Lulu and the Luvers)
Singles: 7–inch

ALFA 3-5   81-82
ATCO 3-6   69-72
CHELSEA 3-5   73-75
EPIC 4-8   67-68
PARROT (9000 series) 5-10   64-65
PARROT (40000 series) 4-8   67
ROCKET 3-5   78

Picture Sleeves

ALFA (7006 "I Could Never
Miss You More") 3-6   81
(Pictures Lulu without a headband.)
ALFA (7006 "I Could Never
Miss You More") 3-5   81
(Pictures Lulu wearing a headband.)
EPIC 4-8   67-68

LPs: 10/12–inch 33rpm

ALFA 5-8   81
ATCO 10-12 70-72
CAPRICORN 8-10   74
CHELSEA 10-12 73-77
EPIC 10-15 67-70
HARMONY 10-12 70
PARROT (61016 "From Lulu
with Love") 50-100 67
(Monaural.)
PARROT (71016 "From Lulu
with Love") 50-100 67
(Stereo.)
PICKWICK 8-10   73
ROCKET 5-8   78
Also see CLARK, Dave, Five / Lulu

LUMAN, Bob
Singles: 78rpm

IMPERIAL 15-25 57

Singles: 7–inch

CAPITOL 10-20 58
EPIC 2-5   68-77
HICKORY (1200 series) 4-8   63-64
HICKORY (1300 through 1500 series) .. 3-5 65-70
IMPERIAL (5705 "Red Cadillac and
a Black Mustache") 10-20 60
(Black label. Reissue of 8311.)
IMPERIAL (8311 "Red Cadillac and
a Black Mustache") 35-55 57
(Maroon label.)

IMPERIAL (8313 "Red Hot") 40-60   57
(Maroon label.)
IMPERIAL (8313 "Red Hot") 30-40   59
(Black label.)
IMPERIAL (8315 "Make Up
Your Mind Baby") 20-30   57
(Maroon label.)
IMPERIAL (8315 "Make Up
Your Mind Baby") 10-15   59
(Black label.)
POLYDOR 3-5   77-78
WARNER 5-15   59-62

Picture Sleeves

WARNER 15-25 60-62

EPs: 7–inch 33/45rpm

HICKORY (124-006 "Selections from
Livin' Lovin' Sounds") 10-20   65
(Promotional "Six-Pac" issue only.)
ROLLIN' ROCK (34 "Bob Luman") 5-8
WARNER (1396 "Let's Think
About Livin") 50-75   60
WARNER (5506 "Bob Luman") 50-75   60
(Promotional issue only.)

LPs: 10/12–inch 33rpm

EPIC 8-15   68-77
HARMONY 10-15 72
HICKORY (124 "Livin' Lovin' Sounds") 15-25 65
HICKORY (4000 series) 8-12   74
POLYDOR 8-12   78
WARNER (W-1396 "Let's Think
About Livin") 30-40   60
(Monaural.)
WARNER (WS-1396 "Let's Think
About Livin") 40-60   60
(Stereo.)

LUMAN, Bob, and Sue Thompson
Singles: 7–inch

HICKORY 4-8   63
Also see LUMAN, Bob
Also see THOMPSON, Sue

LUNAR FUNK
Singles: 7–inch

BELL 3-5   72

LUND, Art, and His Orchestra
Singles: 78rpm

CORAL 3-5   52-57
MGM 3-6   47-55

Singles: 7–inch

CORAL 4-8   52-58
MGM 5-10   50-55
U.A. 3-6   65

EPs: 7–inch 33/45rpm

MGM 5-10   54-55

LPs: 10/12–inch 33rpm

MGM 10-20 55

LUNDBERG, Victor
Singles: 7–inch
LIBERTY 4-6   67
LPs: 10/12–inch 33rpm
LIBERTY 10-15   68

LUNDY, Pat
(Pat Lundi)
Singles: 7–inch
COLUMBIA 4-6   67-68
DELUXE 4-6   69
HEIDI 4-8   65
LEOPARD 3-5
PYRAMID 3-5   76
RCA 3-5   73
TOTO 4-8   62
VIGOR 3-5   75
LPs: 10/12–inch 33rpm
COLUMBIA 10-15   68
PYRAMID 5-8   76

LUNDY, Pat, and Bobby Harris
Singles: 7–inch
HEIDI 4-8   65
Also see HARRIS, Bobby
Also see LUNDY, Pat

LUSHUS DAIM and the Pretty Vain
Singles: 7–inch
MOTOWN 2-4   85
LPs: 10/12–inch 33rpm
MOTOWN 5-8   85

LUTHER
Singles: 7–inch
COTILLION 3-5   76-77
LPs: 10/12–inch 33rpm
COTILLION 8-10   77

LY-DELLS
Singles: 7–inch
MASTER (111 "Genie of the Lamp")   75-125   61
MASTER (251 "Wizard of Love") 30-40   61
ROULETTE 10-15   63
SCA (18001 "Book of Songs") 20-30   62
SOUTHERN SOUND (122 "Hide
   and Seek") 25-35   65
LPs: 10/12–inch 33rpm
CLIFTON 8-10

LYLE, Bobby
Singles: 7–inch
CAPITOL 3-5   78

LYMAN, Arthur
(Arthur Lyman Group)
Singles: 7–inch
GNP/CRESCENDO 3-5   64-75
HI FI 4-6   59-69
LPs: 10/12–inch 33rpm
GNP/CRESCENDO 8-15   63-75
HI FI 10-20   58-69
OLYMPIC 5-8   79

LYME & CYBELLE
Singles: 7–inch
WHITE WHALE 5-10   66-67
Also see ZEVON, Warren

LYMON, Frankie
(Frankie Lymon and the Teenagers)
Singles: 78rpm
GEE 10-15   55-57
Singles: 7–inch
ABC 2-4   73
BIG KAT 4-8   68
COLUMBIA 4-8   64
GEE (1002 "Why Do Fools
   Fall in Love") 30-40   55
   (Red label with gold print.)
GEE (1002 "Why Do Fools
   Fall in Love") 10-20   55
   (Red label with black print.)
GEE (1012 through 1039) 10-20   56-59
MURRAY HILL 3-5
ROULETTE 8-12   58-61
TCF 5-8   64
Picture Sleeves
BIG KAT (7008 "I Want You
   to Be My Girl") 5-10   68
EPs: 7–inch 33/45rpm
GEE (601 "The Teenagers
   Go Rockin'") 75-125   56
GEE (601 "The Teenagers
   Go Romantic") 75-125   56
ROULETTE (304 "Frankie Lymon
   at the London Palladium") 50-75   58
LPs: 10/12–inch 33rpm
GEE (701 "The Teenagers Featuring
   Frankie Lymon") 200-300   57
   (Red label.)
GEE (701 "The Teenagers Featuring
   Frankie Lymon") 50-100   61
   (Gray label.)
MURRAY HILL (148 "Frankie Lymon
   and the Teenagers") 35-55
   (Boxed, five-LP set, with booklet and bonus single.)
ROULETTE (25013 "Frankie Lymon
   at the London Palladium") 50-65   58
ROULETTE (25036 "Rock and
   Roll") 50-75   58
ROULETTE (25250 "Frankie Lymon's
   Greatest") 25-35   64
   Members: Frankie Lymon; Herman Santiago; Sherman Garnes;
   Jim Merchant; Joe Negroni.
   Also see TEENAGERS

LYMON, Lewis, and the Teenchords
(Louis Lymon and the Teenchords)
Singles: 78rpm
END 10-20   57
FURY 10-20   57
Singles: 7–inch
END (1003 "Too Young") 25-35   57
END (1007 "I Found Out Why") 25-30   57

END (1113 "Too Young") 8-12   62
FURY (1000 "I'm So Happy") 35-45   57
  (Maroon label.)
FURY (1000 "I'm So Happy") 15-20
  (Yellow label.)
FURY (1003 "Please Tell the Angels") 40-60   57
JUANITA (101 "Dance Girl") 25-35   58
LPs: 10/12–inch 33rpm
COLLECTABLES 6-8   88
LOST-NITE 5-10   81
  Members: Lewis Lymon; Ralph Vaughan; David Lyttle; Ross
  Rocco; Lyndon Harold; Jimmy Castor; John Pruitt; Ed Pellegrino.

LYNCH, Ray
LPs: 10/12–inch 33rpm
MUSIC WEST 5-10   89

LYNDELL, Linda
Singles: 7–inch
VOLT 4-8   68

LYNN, Barbara
Singles: 7–inch
ATLANTIC 3-5   67-72
COLLECTABLES 2-4
JAMIE 4-8   62-65
TRIBE 4-8   66-67
LPs: 10/12–inch 33rpm
ATLANTIC 10-20   68
JAMIE 20-30   62-64

LYNN, Barbara, and Lee Maye
Singles: 7–inch
JAMIE 4-8   65
  Also see LYNN, Barbara

LYNN, Cheryl
Singles: 12–inch 33/45rpm
COLUMBIA 4-6   78-85
Singles: 7–inch
COLUMBIA 3-5   78-85
MANHATTAN 2-4   87
PRIVATE I 2-4   85
LPs: 10/12–inch 33rpm
COLUMBIA 5-10   78-84

LYNN, Cheryl, and Luther Vandross
Singles: 7–inch
COLUMBIA 3-5   82
  Also see LYNN, Cheryl
  Also see VANDROSS, Luther

LYNN, Donna
Singles: 7–inch
CAPITOL (Except 5127) 4-8   63-65
CAPITOL (5127 "My Boyfriend Got
  a Beatle Haircut") 15-20   64
EPIC 4-8   63
PALMER 4-8   67
LPs: 10/12–inch 33rpm
CAPITOL 15-25   64

LYNN, Ginie
Singles: 7–inch
ABC 3-5   78

LYNN, Loretta
(Loretta Lynn and the Coal Miners)
Singles: 7–inch
DECCA (31000 series) 4-8   62-66
DECCA (32000 series) 3-6   66-71
MCA 2-5   73-86
ZERO (107 "I'm a Honky Tonk Girl") . 35-60   60
ZERO (110 "New Rainbow") 50-100   61
ZERO (112 "The Darkest Day") 50-100   61
Picture Sleeves
DECCA (31000 series) 8-12   66
DECCA (32000 series) 4-6   70
MCA 3-5   78
EPs: 7–inch 33/45rpm
DECCA 10-20   64-65
LPs: 10/12–inch 33rpm
CORAL 5-8   73
COUNTRY MUSIC MAGAZINE 15-20   76
  (Mail-order LP sold by *Country Music* magazine.)
DECCA (DL-4457 "Loretta Lynn
  Sings") 50-75   63
  (Monaural.)
DECCA (DL7-4457 "Loretta Lynn
  Sings") 65-80   63
  (Stereo.)
DECCA (DL-4541 through DL-5000) . 15-25   64-68
  (Monaural.)
DECCA (DL7-4541 through DL7-5000) 15-30   64-68
  (Stereo.)
DECCA (75084 "Your Squaw Is
  on the Warpath") 25-35   69
  (Has *Barney.*)
DECCA (75084 "Your Squaw Is
  on the Warpath") 15-20   69
  (Without *Barney.*)
DECCA (75115 through 75381) 10-20   69-72
L.L. 20-25   76
MCA 5-10   73-86
TEE VEE 8-12   78
TROLLEY CAR 8-10   81
VOCALION 8-15   68-72
Promotional LPs
MCA (1934 "Loretta Lynn's
  Greatest Hits") 25-35   74
  (Cover shows title as simply *Loretta Lynn.*)
MCA (35013 "Allis-Chalmers Presents
  Loretta Lynn") 25-35   78
MCA (35018 "Crisco Presents Loretta
  Lynn's Country Classics") 25-35   79
  Also see BEATLES / Loretta Lynn
  Also see PIERCE, Webb / Loretta Lynn
  Also see STARR, Kenny
  Also see TWITTY, Conway

LYNN, Loretta / Tammy Wynette
LPs: 10/12–inch 33rpm
RADIANT 5-8   81

Also see LYNN, Loretta
Also see WYNETTE, Tammy

LYNN, Vera
Singles: 78rpm
LONDON 3-5   51-57
Singles: 7-inch
ARCO 4-6   67
DJM 4-6   69
LONDON 5-10   51-64
U.A. 4-6   67
EPs: 7-inch 33/45rpm
LONDON 5-10   52-56
LPs: 10/12-inch 33rpm
LONDON 10-20   52-64
MGM 8-12   61
U.A. 5-10   67

LYNNE, Gloria
Singles: 7-inch
CANYON 3-5   70
EVEREST 4-8   59-66
FONTANA 4-6   64-69
HI FI 4-6   66
IMPULSE 3-5   76
MERCURY 3-5   72
SEECO 4-8   61
LPs: 10/12-inch 33rpm
CANYON 5-10   70
DESIGN 10-15   62
EVEREST (300 series) 5-10   75
EVEREST (1000 series) 20-30   58-65
  (Stereo.)
EVEREST (5000 series) 15-25   58-65
  (Monaural.)
FONTANA 10-20   64-69
HI FI 10-15   66
IMPULSE 5-10   76
MERCURY 8-12   69-72
SUNSET 8-15   66-67
UPFRONT 5-10   72

LYNNE, Gloria / Nina Simone / Billie Holiday
LPs: 10/12-inch 33rpm
ALMOR 10-15
  Also see HOLIDAY, Billie
  Also see SIMONE, Nina

LYNNE, Jeff
(Jeff Lynn)
Singles: 12-inch 33/45rpm
JET 5-8   77
Singles: 7-inch
JET 3-5   77
REPRISE 5-8   90
TWIN-SPIN 10-15   65
VIRGIN 2-4   84
  Also see ELECTRIC LIGHT ORCHESTRA
  Also see IDLE RACE
  Also see MOVE
  Also see TRAVELING WILBURYS

LYNYRD SKYNYRD
Singles: 7-inch
ATNIA 3-6   78
MCA (Except 1966) 3-6   74-78
MCA (1966 "Gimmie Back My Bullets") 8-12   77
  (Promotional concert souvenir issue.)
EPs: 7-inch 33/45rpm
MCA 10-15   76
  (Promotional issue only.)
LPs: 10/12-inch 33rpm
MCA (2000 and 3000 series,
  except 3029) 8-10   75-78
MCA (3029 "Street Survivors") 30-40   77
  (Front cover pictures the group in flames.)
MCA (3029 "Street Survivors") 8-10   77
  (Pictures the group without flames.)
MCA (5000 series) 5-8   79-82
MCA (6000 series) 10-15   76-81
MCA (8000 series) 8-12   88
MCA (10000 series) 10-15   79-81
MCA (37000 series) 5-8   79-82
MCA (42000 series) 5-8   87
MCA/SOUNDS of the SOUTH
  (300 and 400 series) 8-15   73-74
Promotional LPs
MCA (2170 "Gimmie Back My Bullets") 25-35   76
  (White label. Concert souvenir copy.)
  Members: Ronnie Van Zant; Gary Rossington; Allen Collins;
  Steve Gaines; Cassie Gaines; Ed King; Rick Medlocke; Greg
  Walker; Leon Wildeson; Billy Powell; Artimus Pyle; Bob Burns.
  Also see BLACKFOOT
  Also see ROSSINGTON - COLLINS BAND
  Also see STRAWBERRY ALARM CLOCK

LYTLE, Johnny
(Johnny Lytle Quintet; Johnny Lytle Trio)
Singles: 7-inch
PACIFIC JAZZ 4-6   68
RIVERSIDE 4-8   63
SOLID STATE 4-6   68
TUBA 4-8   65-66
LPs: 10/12-inch 33rpm
JAZZLAND 15-25   60-62
MILESTONE 5-10   72
MUSE 5-8   78-81
PACIFIC JAZZ 8-15   67
RIVERSIDE 10-20   63-68
SOLID STATE 8-15   67-69
TUBA 10-15   66

LYTLE, Johnny, and Ray Barretto
LPs: 10/12-inch 33rpm
JAZZLAND 15-25   62
  Also see BARRETTO, Ray
  Also see LYTLE, Johnny

M

M
(Robin Scott)
Singles: 12–Inch 33/45rpm
SIRE 8-10   79
Singles: 7–Inch
SIRE 3-5   79-81
Picture Sleeves
SIRE 3-5   79
LPs: 10/12–Inch 33rpm
SIRE 8-10   79-82

M., Boney: see BONEY M

M/A/R/R/S
Singles: 7–Inch
4TH and B'WAY 2-4   87-88

M.C. CHILL
Singles: 12–Inch 33/45rpm
FEVER 4-6   86

M.C. HAMMER: see HAMMER, M.C.

M.C. SHAN
(Featuring T.J. Swan)
Singles: 7–Inch
COLD CHILL 2-4   87

MC-5
(Motor City 5)
Singles: 7–Inch
A² (333 "Looking at You") 15-25   67
AMG (1000 "I Can Only
  Give You Everything") 20-30   66
  (Promotional issue only.)
AMG (1001 "I Can Only
  Give You Everything") 20-30   66
ATLANTIC (2678 "Tonight") 4-8   69
ATLANTIC (2724 "American Rose") 4-8   69
ELEKTRA (45648 "Kick Out the Jams") 5-10   69
Picture Sleeves
A² (333 "Looking at You") 40-60   67
LPs: 10/12–Inch 33rpm
ATLANTIC 10-15   70-71
ELEKTRA (74042 "Kick Out
  the Jams") 30-35   69
  (Title track has X-rated intro. Back cover has liner
  notes.)
ELEKTRA (74042 "Kick Out
  the Jams") 12-15   69
  (Title track has censored intro. Back cover has no
  liner notes.)

MC SHY-D
LPs: 10/12–Inch 33rpm
LUKE SKYWALKER 5-8   87

MFSB
(Mothers, Fathers, Sisters, Brothers)
Singles: 7–Inch
PHILADELPHIA INT'L 3-5   74-78
TSOP 3-5   81
LPs: 10/12–Inch 33rpm
PHILADELPHIA INT'L 8-10   73-78
TSOP 5-8   80
  Members: Norman Harris; Ronnie Baker; Bobby Eli; Bobby
  Martin; Earl Young; Don Renaldo; Albert Barone; Charles
  Apollonia; Angelo Petrella; Diana Barnett; Davis Barnett; Romeo
  Distefano; Rudy Maliazia; Christine Reeves; Joe Donofrio; Leno
  Zachery; Joe DeAngelis; Danny Ellions; Scott Temple; Milton
  Phibbs; Frederich Jainer; Fred Linge; Ricci Genovese; Edward
  Cascerelle; Rocco Bene; Robert Hartzell; Karl Chambers;
  Roland Chambers; Dexter Wansel; Ron Harding; Terri Wells;
  James Smith; Evon Solot; Larry McKenna; Clifford Rudd; Miguel
  Fuentes; Evette Benton; John Usry; Dennis Harris; Don
  Renaldo; Marc Rubin; Derek Graves; Lenny Pakula; John Faith;
  Alphonso Carey; Billy Johnson; Steve Green; Leon Huff;
  Carleton Kent; Quinton Joseph; Carla Benson; Bob Malach;
  David Cruse; Steve Gold; Barbara Ingram; Joel Bryant.
  Also see ELECTRIC INDIAN
  Also see ELI'S SECOND COMING
  Also see JAMES BOYS
  Also see NOBLES, Cliff
  Also see PEOPLE'S CHOICE
  Also see PHILADELPHIA INTERNATIONAL ALL STARS
  Also see THREE DEGREES
  Also see TRAMMPS

MGs
(Memphis Group)
Singles: 7–Inch
STAX 3-5   73
LPs: 10/12–Inch 33rpm
STAX 8-12   73
  Also see BOOKER T. and the MGs

M+M: see MARTHA and the Muffins

M.O.D.
LPs: 10/12–Inch 33rpm
CAROLINE 5-8   88
MEGAFORCE 5-8   87-89

MABLEY, Moms
Singles: 7–Inch
MERCURY 3-5   69-71
EPs: 7–Inch 33/45rpm
CHESS 5-10   63
LPs: 10/12–Inch 33rpm
CHESS 15-25   61-64
MERCURY 10-20   64-70

MABLEY, Moms, and Pigmeat Markham
LPs: 10/12–Inch 33rpm
CHESS 10-20   64-71
  Also see MABLEY, Moms
  Also see MARKHAM, Pigmeat

MABON, Willie
(Willie Mabon and His Combo)
Singles: 78rpm
CHESS 10-20   52-56
FEDERAL 10-20   57

Singles: 7–inch

CHESS (1531 "I Don't Know") 100-200		53
(Colored vinyl.)		
CHESS (1531 "I Don't Know") 20-40		53
(Black vinyl.)		
CHESS (1538 "I'm Mad") 20-40		53
CHESS (1548 "You're a Fool") 20-40		53
CHESS (1554 "I Got to Go") 20-40		53
CHESS (1564 "Would You, Baby") ... 20-40		54
CHESS (1580 "Poison Ivy") 20-40		54
DELTA (3004 "Light Up Your Lamp") ... 5-8		
FEDERAL (12306 "Light Up		
Your Lamp") 15-25		57
FORMAL 4-6		62
MAD (1298 "I Gotta Go Now") 10-20		60
MAD (1300 "I Don't Know") 10-20		60
PARROT (1050 "I Don't Know") ... 150-250		53
U.S.A. 5-8		63-65

LPs: 10/12–inch 33rpm

CHESS (1439 "Willie Mabon") 50-100   59

MAC, Fleetwood: see FLEETWOOD MAC

MAC BAND
(Featuring the Campbell Brothers)
Singles: 7–inch

MCA 2-4   88

LPs: 10/12–inch 33rpm

MCA 5-8   88

MacARTHUR, James
Singles: 7–inch

SCEPTER 4-8	62-63
TRIODEX 5-10	61

MacDONALD, Jeanette, and Nelson Eddy
EPs: 7–inch 33/45rpm

RCA (Except 220) 4-8	61
RCA (220 "Rose Marie") 10-20	52

LPs: 10/12–inch 33rpm

RCA (16 "Rose Marie") 40-50	52
RCA (526 "Rose Marie") 10-20	66
RCA (1000 series) 5-10	75
RCA (1700 series) 10-20	59
RCA (2400 series) 5-8	77
RCA (3900 series) 5-8	81

MacDONALD, Ralph
Singles: 12–inch 33-45rpm

POLYDOR 4-6   84-85

Singles: 7–inch

MARLIN 3-5	76-79
POLYDOR 2-4	84-85

LPs: 10/12–inch 33rpm

MARLIN 6-10	76-79
POLYDOR 5-8	84-85

MACEO and All the Kings Men
Singles: 7–inch

EXCELLO 3-5	72
HOUSE of FOX 3-5	70

LPs: 10/12–inch 33rpm

EXCELLO 8-12   72

MACEO and the Macks
Singles: 7–inch

PEOPLE 3-5   73-74

LPs: 10/12–inch 33rpm

PEOPLE 8-12   74

MACHINATIONS
Singles: 12–inch 33/45rpm

A&M 4-6   83

Singles: 7–inch

A&M 3-5   83

LPs: 10/12–inch 33rpm

A&M 5-8   83

MACHINE
Singles: 7–inch

RCA 3-5   79-80

LPs: 10/12–inch 33rpm

RCA 5-10   80

MacGREGOR, Byron
Singles: 7–inch

CAPITOL 3-5	75
WESTBOUND 3-5	74

LPs: 10/12–inch 33rpm

WESTBOUND 5-10   74

MacGREGOR, Mary
Singles: 7–inch

ARIOLA 3-5	78
ARIOLA AMERICA 3-5	76-77
RSO 3-5	79-80

LPs: 10/12–inch 33rpm

ARIOLA AMERICA 8-10   77

MACHO
Singles: 7–inch

PRELUDE 3-5   78

LPs: 10/12–inch 33rpm

PRELUDE 5-10   78

MACK, Lonnie
(Lonnie Mack and Pismo)
Singles: 7–inch

ABC 3-5	73
A.M.G. 3-6	
BARRY 3-5	
CAPITOL 3-5	77
COLLECTABLES 2-4	
ELEKTRA 3-5	71
FRATERNITY 5-10	63-68
ROULETTE 3-5	75

LPs: 10/12–inch 33rpm

ALLIGATOR 5-8	85-86
CAPITOL 8-10	77
ELEKTRA 10-20	69-71
FRATERNITY (SF-1014 "Wham of		
That Memphis Man") 25-35	63
(Monaural.)		

FRATERNITY (SSF-1014 "Wham of
That Memphis Man") 35-55   63
(Stereo.)
TRIP 8-10   75
Members: Lonnie Mack; Jim Keltner; Tim Drummond.

MACK, Lonnie, and Rusty York
LPs: 10/12-inch 33rpm
QCA 10-15   73
Also see MACK, Lonnie
Also see YORK, Rusty

MACK, Warner
Singles: 78rpm
DECCA 5-10   57
Singles: 7-inch
DECCA (30301 through 31684) 4-8   57-64
DECCA (31774 through 33045) 3-6   57-64
KAPP 4-6   61-62
MCA 3-5   73-76
PAGEBOY 3-5   77-81
SCARLET 4-8   60
TOP RANK 4-8   60
EPs: 7-inch 33/45rpm
DECCA 5-8   65
LPs: 10/12-inch 33rpm
CORAL 5-8   73
DECCA 8-18   65-70
KAPP 10-20   61-66

MacKENZIE, Giselle
Singles: 78rpm
CAPITOL 3-5   51-54
VIK 3-5   56
X 3-5   55
Singles: 7-inch
CAPITOL 5-10   51-54
EVEREST 4-8   60
MERCURY 4-8   63
VIK 5-10   56
X 5-10   55
Picture Sleeves
VIK 5-10   56
X 5-10   55
EPs: 7-inch 33/45rpm
CAPITOL 5-10   53-69
VIK 5-10   56
LPs: 10/12-inch 33rpm
CAMDEN 10-20   59
EVEREST 10-20   60
GLENDALE 5-8   78
MERCURY 10-20   63
RCA 10-20   59
SUNSET 8-12   67
VIK 15-25   56

MacRAE, Gordon
Singles: 78rpm
CAPITOL 3-5   53-57
Singles: 7-inch
CAPITOL 4-8   53-68

EPs: 7-inch 33/45rpm
CAPITOL 5-10   54-57
ROYALE 5-10
LPs: 10/12-inch 33rpm
CAPITOL 10-20   54-69

MacRAE, Gordon, and Jo Stafford
Singles: 7-inch
CAPITOL 4-8   62
LPs: 10/12-inch 33rpm
CAPITOL (1600 and 1900 series) ... 10-20   62-63
CAPITOL (11000 series) 4-8   79
Also see BRYANT, Anita / Jo Stafford and Gordon MacRae
Also see MacRAE, Gordon
Also see STAFFORD, Jo

MAD LADS
Singles: 7-inch
MARK-FI (1934 "Why") 20-30   62
CAPITOL 5-8   64
STAX 5-10   64
VOLT (100 series) 5-10   65-68
VOLT (4000 series) 3-6   69-73
LPs: 10/12-inch 33rpm
COLLECTABLES 6-8   86
VOLT (400 series) 15-25   66
VOLT (6000 series) 10-15   69-73

MAD RIVER
Singles: 7-inch
CAPITOL 5-10   68-69
EPs: 7-inch 33/45rpm
WEE (10021 "Mad River") 25-50   68
LPs: 10/12-inch 33rpm
CAPITOL (185 "Paradise Bar
and Grill") 25-35   69
CAPITOL (2985 "Mad River") 25-35   68
Members: David Robinson; Tom Manning; Lawrence Hammond;
Rick Bochner; Greg Dewey; Ron Wilson.

MADAGASCAR
Singles: 7-inch
ARISTA 2-4   81-82

MADAME X
Singles: 7-inch
ATLANTIC 2-4   87
LORIMAR 2-4   88
LPs: 10/12-inch 33rpm
ATLANTIC 5-8   87

MADDOX, Johnny
(Johnny Maddox and the Rhythmasters)
Singles: 78rpm
DOT 3-6   50-57
Singles: 7-inch
ABC 3-5   74
DOT 4-8   50-63
EPs: 7-inch 33/45rpm
DOT 5-10   52-56
LPs: 10/12-inch 33rpm
DOT 10-25   55-67
HAMILTON 10-15   64

PARAMOUNT 5-10   74

MADE in U.S.A.
Singles: 7–inch
DE-LITE 3-5   77

MADIGAN, Betty
Singles: 78rpm
CORAL 3-6   57
JAY DEE 3-6   54
MGM (11000 series) 3-6   53-56
Singles: 7–inch
CORAL 4-8   57-59
JAY DEE 5-10   54
MGM (11000 series) 5-10   53-56
MGM (13000 series) 4-6   66-67
20TH FOX 4-6   64
U.A. 4-8   60-61
EPs: 7–inch 33/45rpm
JAY DEE 5-10   54
MGM 5-10   57
LPs: 10/12–inch 33rpm
CORAL 10-20   62
MGM 10-20   57-69

MADNESS
Singles: 12–inch 33/45rpm
GEFFEN 4-6   83
STIFF 8-12
(Promotional issues only.)
Singles: 7–inch
GEFFEN 2-4   83-84
SIRE 3-5   80-81
LPs: 10/12–inch 33rpm
GEFFEN 5-8   83-84
SIRE 5-8   80-81

MADONNA
Singles: 12–inch 33/45rpm
SIRE 4-8   83-88
Singles: 7–inch
GEFFEN 2-5   85
SIRE 2-5   83-90
Picture Sleeves
SIRE 2-5   83-89
LPs: 10/12–inch 33rpm
SIRE (Except 25157) 5-8   83-90
SIRE (25157 "Like a Virgin") 5-8   83
(Black vinyl.)
SIRE (1-25157 "Like a Virgin") 75-125   83
(Colored vinyl. Promotional issue only.)

MADURA
LPs: 10/12–inch 33rpm
COLUMBIA 10-15   71-73

MAESTRO, Johnny
Singles: 7–inch
APT (25075 "She's All Mine Alone") . . 10-20   65
BUDDAH 5-10   71-72
CAMEO 10-15   63-64
COED (549 "What a Surprise") 10-20   61

COED (552 "Mr Happiness") 10-15   61
COED (557 "I.O.U.") 20-30   61
COED (562 "Besame Baby") 75-100   61
COLLECTABLES 2-4
PARKWAY 8-12   66-67
U.A. (474 "Before I Loved Her") 20-30   62
LPs: 10/12–inch 33rpm
BUDDAH (5091 "The Johnny
   Maestro Story") 25-35   71
(Price includes inserts.)
HARVEY 10-15   81
   Also see BROOKLYN BRIDGE
   Also see CRESTS
   Also see MASTERS, Johnny

MAGAZINE 60
Singles: 7–inch
BAJA 2-4   86

MAGGARD, Cledus
(Cledus Maggard and the Citizen's Band)
Singles: 7–inch
MERCURY 3-5   75-79
LPs: 10/12–inch 33rpm
MERCURY 5-10   76

MAGIC LADY
Singles: 12–inch 33/45rpm
A&M 4-6   82
Singles: 7–inch
A&M 2-4   82
MOTOWN 2-4   88
LPs: 10/12–inch 33rpm
A&M 5-8   82
ARISTA 5-8   80

MAGIC LANTERN
LPs: 10/12–inch 33rpm
CHAPARRAL (201 "Haymarket
   Square") 200-300   68
   Members: Gloria Lambert;Marc Swenson; Robert Homa; John
   Kowslowski.

MAGIC LANTERNS
Singles: 7–inch
ATLANTIC 4-6   68-70
BIG TREE 3-5   71
CHARISMA 3-5   72
EPIC 4-8   66
LPs: 10/12–inch 33rpm
ATLANTIC 12-15   69
   Members: Jim Bilsbury; Bev Beveridge; Mike "Ozzy" Osborne;
   Peter Garner; Harry Paul Ward; Albert Hammond.

MAGIC MUSHROOM
Singles: 7–inch
A&M 5-10   66
EAST COAST 5-10
PHILIPS 5-10   67
WARNER 10-15   66

MAGIC ORGAN
(Jerry Smith)
Singles: 7-Inch
RANWOOD 3-5   72-77
LPs: 10/12-Inch 33rpm
RANWOOD 4-8   72-83
SUNNYVALE 4-6   79
Also see SMITH, Jerry

MAGIC TOUCH
Singles: 7-Inch
BLACK FALCON 3-5   71

MAGISTRATES
Singles: 7-Inch
MGM 4-8   68-69
Member: Jean Hillary.
Also see DOVELLS

MAGNIFICENT MEN
Singles: 7-Inch
CAPITOL 4-8   66-68
MERCURY 3-6   69
LPs: 10/12-Inch 33rpm
CAPITOL 10-20   67-68
MERCURY 8-12   70
Members: Bob Angelucci; Dave Buff; Buddy King; Tom Pane.

MAGNIFICENTS
Singles: 78rpm
VEE JAY 10-20   56-58
Singles: 7-Inch
CHECKER (1016 "Do You Mind") 5-10   62
COLLECTABLES 2-4
KANSOMA (03 "Do You Mind") 5-10   62
VEE JAY (183 "Up on the Mountain")   30-60   56
VEE JAY (208 "Caddy Bo") 40-75   56
VEE JAY (235 "Off the Mountain") .. 30-60   57
VEE JAY (281 "Don't Leave Me") 50-75   58
VEE JAY (367 "Up on the Mountain")   10-15   60
Also see EL DORADOS

MAGNUM FORCE
Singles: 7-Inch
PAULA 2-4   85
LPs: 10/12-Inch 33rpm
WIZARD 5-8   78

MAHAL, TAJ: see TAJ MAHAL

MAHARIS, George
Singles: 7-Inch
EPIC 4-6   62-66
Picture Sleeves
EPIC 4-6   62-64
LPs: 10/12-Inch 33rpm
EPIC 10-15   62-66

MAHOGANY
Singles: 12-Inch 33/45rpm
WEST END 4-6   83
Singles: 7-Inch
WEST END 2-4   83

MAHOGANY RUSH
Singles: 7-Inch
COLUMBIA 3-5   76-82
20TH FOX 3-5   74-75
LPs: 10/12-Inch 33rpm
COLUMBIA 8-12   76-82
20TH FOX 10-12   73-75
Member: Frank Marino.
Also see MARINO, Frank

MAHONEY, Skip, and the Casuals
Singles: 7-Inch
ABET 3-5   76-77
D.C. INT'L 3-5   74

MAI TAI
Singles: 12-Inch 33/45rpm
MERCURY 4-6   87
Singles: 7-Inch
CRITIQUE 2-4   86
MERCURY 2-4   87
LPs: 10/12-Inch 33rpm
MERCURY 5-8   87
Members: Carol DeWindt; Jettie Well; Mildred Douglas.

MAIN ATTRACTION
Singles: 7-Inch
RCA 2-4   86
LPs: 10/12-Inch 33rpm
RCA 5-8   86

MAIN INGREDIENT
Singles: 7-Inch
RCA 3-5   69-81
ZAKIA 2-4   86
Picture Sleeves
RCA 3-6   70-81
LPs: 10/12-Inch 33rpm
COLLECTABLES 5-8   88
RCA 8-12   70-81
Members: Don McPherson; Luther Simmons; Tony Sylvester;
Cuba Gooding.
Also see GOODING, Cuba
Also see POETS

MAINSTREETERS
Singles: 7-Inch
EVENT 3-5   73

MAJESTY
Singles: 7-Inch
GOLDEN BOY 2-4   85

MAJOR LANCE: see LANCE, Major

MAJORS
Singles: 7-Inch
IMPERIAL 8-15   62-64
LPs: 10/12-Inch 33rpm
IMPERIAL (9222 "Meet the Majors") . 25-35   63
(Monaural.)
IMPERIAL (12222 "Meet the Majors") 25-35   63
(Stereo.)
Members: Ricky Cordo; Eugene Glass; Idella Morris; Frank
Troutt; Ronald Gathers.

MAKEBA, Miriam
Singles: 7-inch
KAPP 4-8   62
MERCURY 4-6   66
RCA 4-8   64
REPRISE 4-6   67-68
LPs: 10/12-inch 33rpm
KAPP 10-20   62
MERCURY 10-15   66
PETERS INT'L 5-8   81
RCA 10-20   60-68
REPRISE 10-15   67
 Also see BELAFONTE, Harry, and Miriam Makeba
 Also see MANHATTAN BROTHERS and Miriam Makeba

MAKEM, Tommy:
 see CLANCY BROTHERS and Tommy Makem

MALCOLM X
Singles: 7-inch
TOMMY BOY 2-4   83-84
LPs: 10/12-inch 33rpm
DOUGLAS 8-15   68-71

MALICE
LPs: 10/12-inch 33rpm
ATLANTIC 5-8   87
ENIGMA 5-8

MALMKVIST, Siw
 (Siw Malmkvist and Umberto Marcato)
Singles: 7-inch
JUBILEE 4-6   64
KAPP 4-8   61

MALO
Singles: 7-inch
TRAQ 3-5   81
WARNER 3-5   72-73
LPs: 10/12-inch 33rpm
WARNER 8-12   72-74
 Also see AZTECA
 Also see SANTANA, Jorge

KMALMSTEEN, Yngwie J.
LPs: 10/12-inch 33rpm
POLYDOR 5-8   88

MALTBY, Richard, and His Orchestra
Singles: 78rpm
VIK 3-5   56
X 3-5   54-55
Singles: 7-inch
COLUMBIA 4-8   59
ROULETTE 4-8   60-61
VIK 5-10   56
X 5-10   54-55
Picture Sleeves
VIK 10-15   56
EPs: 7-inch 33/45rpm
COLUMBIA 5-10   59
VIK 5-10   56
X 5-10   54-55

LPs: 10/12-inch 33rpm
CAMDEN 10-20   60-62
COLUMBIA 10-20   59
HARMONY 10-20   61
ROULETTE 10-20   60-62
VIK (1051 "Hue-Fi Moods") 20-30   56
VIK (1068 "Manhattan Bandstand") .. 20-30   56
X (1038 "Make Mine Maltby") 20-30   56

MAMA CASS: see ELLIOT, Cass

MAMA'S BOYS
LPs: 10/12-inch 33rpm
JIVE 5-8   84-87

MAMAS and the Papas
Singles: 7-inch
ABC 3-5   70
DUNHILL 4-8   65-72
MCA 3-5   80-82
Picture Sleeves
DUNHILL (4020 "California
 Dreamin") 50-100   65
 (Promotional issue only.)
DUNHILL (4083 "Creeque Alley") ... 25-35   67
 (Promotional issue only.)
DUNHILL (4113 "Dancing Bear") 4-8   67
EPs: 7-inch 33/45rpm
ABC 8-15   71
 (Promotional issues only.)
DUNHILL 15-20   65
LPs: 10/12-inch 33rpm
ABC 6-10   76
DUNHILL 8-18   66-73
MCA 5-8   80-82
PICKWICK 6-10   72
 Members: John Phillips "Mama" Cass Elliot; Denny Doherty;
 Michelle Gilliam.
 Also see BIG THREE
 Also see ELLIOT, Cass
 Also see McGUIRE, Barry
 Also see PHILLIPS, John

**MAMAS and the Papas / Association / Fifth
Dimension**
LPs: 10/12-inch 33rpm
TEE VEE/WARNER SPECIAL
 PRODUCTIONS 10-20   79
 Also see ASSOCIATION
 Also see FIFTH DIMENSION
 Also see MAMAS and the Papas

MAN PARRISH: see PARRISH, Man

MANCHA, Steve
Singles: 7-inch
GROOVE CITY 4-8
GROOVESVILLE 4-8   65-67
WHEELSVILLE 4-8   65
 Also see BARNES, J.J., and Steve Mancha

MANCHESTER, Melissa
Singles: 12-inch 33/45rpm
ARISTA 4-6   82

Since publication of *The Official Price Guide to Movie/TV Soundtracks and Original Cast Albums*, with over 8,000 listings, this guide has dropped many soundtracks, including some by this artist.
Also see ANN-MARGRET
Also see HIRT, Al / Henry Mancini / Perez Prado
Also see MATHIS, Johnny, and Henry Mancini

Picture Sleeves

MCA 2-5		79-85

LPs: 10/12-inch 33rpm

ABC 8-10		78-79
ABC/DOT 8-12		76-77
COLUMBIA 8-15		71-81
COLUMBIA SPECIAL PRODUCTS 5-8		82
EMI 5-8		88
MCA 5-10		79-86
SONGBIRD 5-8		82
TIME-LIFE 5-8		81

Also see HOUSTON, David, and Barbara Mandrell
Also see JENNINGS, Waylon

MANDRELL, Barbara, and Lee Greenwood
Singles: 7-inch

MCA 2-4		84

LPs: 10/12-inch 33rpm

MCA 5-8		84

Also see GREENWOOD, Lee

MANDRELL, Barbara, and the Oak Ridge Boys
Singles: 7-inch

MCA 2-4		86

Also see MANDRELL, Barbara
Also see OAK RIDGE BOYS

MANDRILL
Singles: 7-inch

ARISTA 3-5		77-80
LIBERTY 2-4		83
MONTAGE 2-4		82
POLYDOR 3-5		71-74
U.A. 3-5		75-76

LPs: 10/12-inch 33rpm

ARISTA 8-10		77-80
LIBERTY 5-8		83
POLYDOR 10-12		71-75
U.A. 8-10		75

Also see MASSER, Michael, and Mandrill

MANFRED MANN: see MANN, Manfred

MANGANO, Silvana
Singles: 78rpm

MGM 3-6		53

Singles: 7-inch

MGM 5-10		53

MANGIONE, Chuck
(Chuck Mangione Quintet; Gap and Chuck Mangione)
Singles: 7-inch

A&M 3-5		75-80
COLUMBIA 2-4		82-84
MERCURY 3-5		71-77

Picture Sleeves

A&M 3-5		78-80

LPs: 10/12-inch 33rpm

A&M 5-10		75-81
COLUMBIA 5-8		82-84
JAZZLAND (84 "Recuerdo") 40-50		62

JAZZLAND (984 "Recuerdo") 45-60		62
(Stereo.)		
MFSL 25-50		82
MERCURY 6-12		71-78
MILESTONE 5-8		77
RIVERSIDE (371 "Jazz Brothers") ... 40-50		61

MANHATTAN BROTHERS and Miriam Makeba
Singles: 78rpm

LONDON 3-6		56

Singles: 7-inch

LONDON 5-10		56

Also see MAKEBA, Miriam

MANHATTAN TRANSFER
Singles: 7-inch

ATLANTIC 3-5		75-85

LPs: 10/12-inch 33rpm

ATLANTIC 8-10		75-87
COLLECTABLES 6-8		88
MFSL 25-50		78

Members: Tim Hauser; Alan Paul; Gary Chester; Garnett Brown; Ken Buttrey; Cheryl Bentyne; Janis Siegel; Don Roberts.

MANHATTANS
Singles: 12-inch 33/45rpm

COLUMBIA 4-6		84-85

Singles: 7-inch

AVANTI 8-12		63
CAPITOL 8-12		61-62
CARNIVAL 5-15		64-69
COLUMBIA 2-5		73-87
DELUXE 3-5		69-73

LPs: 10/12-inch 33rpm

CARNIVAL (201 "Dedicated to You") 100-150		66
CARNIVAL (202 "For You and Yours") 100-150		66
COLUMBIA 8-12		73-85
DELUXE 10-15		70-72
SOLID SMOKE 5-8		81

Members: George Smith; Ken Kelly; Sonny Bivens; Winfred Scott; Richard Taylor; Regina Bell.

MANILOW, Barry
Singles: 12-inch 33/45rpm

ARISTA 5-10		78-87

Singles: 7-inch

ARISTA 2-5		74-90
BELL 3-5		73-74
FLASHBACK 2-4		76
RCA 2-4		86

Promotional Singles

ARISTA (11 "It's Just Another New Year's Eve") 4-8		77
ARISTA (9318 "Paradise Cafe") 3-5		84
(Clear vinyl.)		

Picture Sleeves

ARISTA (Except 11) 2-5		78-85

COLUMBIA	8-18	65-81
EMBRYO	8-12	70-71
EPIC (3395 "Salute to the Flute")	60-80	57
EPIC (3499 "Herbie Mann")	50-70	58
FINNADAR	5-10	76
INTERLUDE	20-35	59
JAZZLAND (5 "Californians")	35-55	60
MILESTONE	8-12	73
MODE (114 "Flute Fraternity")	40-60	57
NEW JAZZ (8211 "Just Wailin")	50-60	58
PREMIER	20-30	63
PRESTIGE (7101 "Flute Souffle")	75-100	57
PRESTIGE (7124 "Flute Flight")	75-100	57
PRESTIGE (7136 "Mann in the Morning")	75-100	58
PRESTIGE (7432 "Best of Herbie Mann")	20-30	65
RIVERSIDE (03 "Blues for Tomorrow")	5-8	82
RIVERSIDE (234 "Sultry Serenade")	50-75	57
RIVERSIDE (245 "Great Ideas")	50-75	57
RIVERSIDE (3000 series)	8-12	69
ROULETTE	10-15	67
SAVOY (1100 series)	5-8	76
SAVOY (12107 "Mann Alone")	30-40	57
SAVOY (12108 "Yardbird Suite")	35-50	57
SOLID STATE	8-12	68
SURREY	10-15	65
U.A. (4000 and 5000 series)	20-40	59
U.A. (5300 series)	8-10	72
U.A. (14000 and 15000 series)	20-40	62-63
VSP	8-15	66
VERVE	20-40	57-61

(Reads "Verve Records, Inc." at bottom of label.)

VERVE	15-25	63

(Reads "MGM Records - A Division of Metro-Goldwyn-Mayer, Inc." at bottom of label.)

VERVE	5-10	69-73

(Reads "Manufactured By MGM Record Corp.," or mentions either Polydor or Polygram at bottom of label.)

Also see JONES, Tamiko, and Herbie Mann

MANN, Herbie, and Cissy Houston
Singles: 7–inch

ATLANTIC	3-5	76

Also see HOUSTON, Cissy

MANN, Herbie / Maynard Ferguson
LPs: 10/12–inch 33rpm

ROULETTE	8-12	71

Also see FERGUSON, Herbie
Also see MANN, Herbie

MANN, Johnny, Singers
Singles: 7–inch

DECCA	3-5	66
EPIC	3-5	72
EUREKA	4-8	60
LIBERTY	4-6	62-68

LPs: 10/12–inch 33rpm

EPIC	5-10	72

LIBERTY	10-20	59-69
LIGHT	5-10	76
SUNSET	5-10	66-70
U.A.	5-10	71

Also see ZENTNER, Si

MANN, Manfred
(Manfred Mann's Earth Band)
Singles: 7–inch

ARISTA	2-4	84-85
ASCOT (Except 2157 and 2165)	6-12	64-68
ASCOT (2157 "Do Wah Diddy Diddy")	3-5	64
ASCOT (2165 "Sha La La")	4-8	64
MERCURY	3-6	66-69
POLYDOR	3-5	71-74
PRESTIGE	8-10	64
U.A.	4-8	66
WARNER	3-5	76-81

EPs: 7–inch 33/45rpm

U.A. (10030 "Manfred Mann")	10-20	64

(Promotional issue only. Not issued with cover.)

Picture Sleeves

ASCOT	10-20	64
MERCURY	8-15	68

LPs: 10/12–inch 33rpm

ARISTA	5-8	83
ASCOT (13015 "Manfred Mann")	25-35	64

(Monaural.)

ASCOT (13018 "Five Faces of Manfred Mann")	25-35	65

(Monaural.)

ASCOT (13024 "Mann Made")	25-35	66

(Monaural.)

ASCOT (16015 "Manfred Mann")	35-45	64

(Stereo.)

ASCOT (16018 "Five Faces of Manfred Mann")	35-45	65

(Stereo.)

ASCOT (16024 "Mann Made")	35-45	66

(Stereo.)

CAPITOL	5-8	80
EMI AMERICA	10-12	77
JANUS	12-15	74
MERCURY	15-20	68
POLYDOR	10-15	70-74
U.A.	20-35	66-68
WARNER	5-8	74-81

Members: Manfred Mann; Mike D'Abo; Paul Jones; Tom McGuinness; Mick Rogers; Mick Vickers; Chris Slade; Colin Pattenden; Mike Hugg; Steve York; Mick Rogers.
Also see BELL, Madeline
Also see FIRM
Also see McGUINNESS - FLINT
Also see THOMPSON, Chris, and Night

MANNA, Charlie
Singles: 7–inch

DECCA	4-6	61
JUBILEE	4-6	65

Picture Sleeves

DECCA	4-8	61

LPs: 10/12–inch 33rpm

DECCA	10-20	61-62
VERVE	10-15	66

MANNHEIM STEAMROLLER
LPs: 10/12–inch 33rpm

AMERICAN GRAMAPHONE	5-8	83-90

MANONE, Wingy, and His Orchestra
Singles: 78rpm

COLUMBIA	3-5	54
DECCA	4-8	57

Singles: 7–inch

COLUMBIA	5-10	54
DECCA	8-12	57
IMPERIAL	4-6	62
KEM	4-6	61

EPs: 7–inch 33/45rpm

COLUMBIA	5-10	54
VIK	5-10	56

LPs: 10/12–inch 33rpm

IMPERIAL	8-15	62
MCA	5-10	83
PRESTIGE	5-10	70
RCA	5-10	69
SAVOY	5-10	73
STORYVILLE	5-10	83
VIK	10-20	56

MANTOVANI
(Mantovani and His Orchestra)
Singles: 78rpm

LONDON (Except 1761)	3-5	51-65
LONDON (1761 "Let Me Be Loved")	4-6	57

Singles: 7–inch

LONDON (Except 1761)	3-8	51-65
LONDON (1761 "Let Me Be Loved")	4-8	57

Picture Sleeves

LONDON (Except 1761)	4-8	57-65
LONDON (1761 "Let Me Be Loved")	30-45	57

(*Let Me Be Loved* is the main theme from the film, *The James Dean Story.* Sleeve pictures Dean.)
EPs: 7–inch 33/45rpm

LONDON	4-8	51-59

LPs: 10/12–inch 33rpm

BAINBRIDGE	5-10	82
LONDON	8-18	51-72

Also see PRESLEY, Elvis

MANTRA
Singles: 7–inch

CASABLANCA	2-4	81

LPs: 10/12–inch 33rpm

CASABLANCA	5-10	81

MANTRONIX
Singles: 12–inch 33/45rpm

SLEEPING BAG	4-6	85

LPs: 10/12–inch 33rpm

CAPITOL	5-8	88-90
SLEEPING BAG	5-8	86

MANU DIBANGO: see DIBANGO, Manu

MANZANERA, Phil
(Phil Manzanera Quiet Sun; Phil Manzanera and 801; Manzanera)
Singles: 12–inch 33/45rpm

EDITIONS E.G.	5-8	82

LPs: 10/12–inch 33rpm

ANTILLES	8-10	
ATCO	8-10	
EDITIONS E.G.	5-8	82
POLYDOR	8-10	78

Also see ROXY MUSIC

MANZAREK, Ray
Singles: 7–inch

MERCURY	4-6	73-74

LPs: 10/12–inch 33rpm

A&M	5-10	84
MERCURY	8-12	74-75

Also see DOORS

MARA, Tommy
Singles: 7–inch

B&F	5-10	60
FELSTED	5-10	58-59

MARATHONS
Singles: 7–inch

ARGO (5389 "Peanut Butter")	5-10	61
ARVEE (5027 "Peanut Butter")	10-12	61

(Other Arvee releases by the Marathons are actually by a different group. See the following section.)

CHESS (1790 "Peanut Butter")	5-10	61
PLAZA	5-10	62

EPs: 7–inch 33/45rpm

MARK '56 ("Laura Scudder's Magic Record")	4-8	69

(Laura Scudder's potato chip mail-order, coupon giveaway item. Has three tracks, including *Peanut Butter,* imbedded in a single band on each side. When needle begins tracking, it's unknown which song will play. Price includes paper picture sleeve.)
LPs: 10/12–inch 33rpm

ARVEE (428 "Peanut Butter")	50-75	61

Members: James Johnson; Carl Fisher; Dick Owens; Dave Govan; Don Bradley.
Also see JAYHAWKS
Also see VIBRATIONS

MARATHONS
Singles: 7–inch

ARVEE (Except 5027)	5-10	61-62

(Arvee 5027 is by a different group and is listed in the preceeding section.)

MARCELS
Singles: 7–inch

COLPIX (186 through 687)	10-20	61-63
COLPIX (694 "One Last Kiss")	50-75	63
ERIC	2-4	
QUEEN BEE	10-15	73

ST. CLAIR 5-10
Picture Sleeves
COLPIX (186 "Blue Moon") 30-50   61
COLPIX (612 "Heartaches") 30-50   61
COLPIX (624 "Merry Twistmas") 40-60   61
LPs: 10/12–inch 33rpm
COLPIX (416 "Blue Moon") 75-125   61
(Gold label.)
COLPIX (416 "Blue Moon") 30-50   63
(Blue label.)
MURRAY HILL 8-10
Members: Cornelius Harp; Fred Johnson; Ron Mundy; Gene Bricker; Richard Knauss; Walt Maddox; Al Johnson.

MARCH, Little Peggy
(Peggy March)
Singles: 7–inch
RCA 4-8   62-71
Picture Sleeves
RCA 10-20   63
EPs: 7–inch 33/45rpm
RCA 15-25   63
LPs: 10/12–inch 33rpm
RCA (Except 2732) 15-20   65-68
RCA (LPM-2732 "I Will Follow Him") . 50-60   63
(Monaural.)
RCA (LSP-2732 "I Will Follow Him") . 55-70   63
(Stereo.)

MARCH, Little Peggy, and Bennie Thomas
LPs: 10/12–inch 33rpm
RCA 15-20   65

MARCH, Peggy, and Gary Marshal
Singles: 7–inch
RCA 4-8   66
Also see MARCH, Little Peggy

MARCHAN, Bobby
(Bobby Marchon; Bobby Marchan and the Tick Tocks; Bobby Marchan and the Clowns)
Singles: 78rpm
ACE 5-10   56
ALADDIN 5-10   53
DOT 5-10   54
GALE 5-10   57
Singles: 7–inch
ABC 3-5   73
ACE 10-20   56
ALADDIN (3189 "Just a Little Walk") . 25-35   53
CAMEO 4-8   66-67
DIAL 4-8   64-74
DOT (1203 "Just a Little Ol' Wine") . 20-25   54
FIRE 5-10   59-62
FLASHBACK 3-5   65
GALE 8-12   57
GAMBLE 4-6   68
MERCURY 3-5   77
SPHERE SOUND 4-8   65
VOLT 4-8   63
LPs: 10/12–inch 33rpm
COLLECTABLES 5-8   88

SPHERE SOUND (7004 "There's Something
on Your Mind") 30-50   64

MARCHAN, Bobby, and the Clowns
Singles: 7–inch
ACE 5-10   59
Also see MARCHAN, Bobby
Also see SMITH, Huey

MARCY JO and Eddie Rambeau
Singles: 7–inch
ROBBEE 5-10   62
SWAN 10-20   63
Also see MARCY JOE
Also see RAMBEAU, Eddie

MARCY JOE
(Marcy Jo)
Singles: 7–inch
ROBBEE 5-10   61
SWAN 8-12   62
Also see CHRISTIE, Lou

MARDONES, Benny
Singles: 7–inch
POLYDOR 3-5   80
PRIVATE STOCK 3-5   78
LPs: 10/12–inch 33rpm
POLYDOR 5-8   80

MARESCA, Ernie
Singles: 7–inch
LAURIE 5-10   66
RUST 8-12   64
SEVILLE 8-12   60-65
LPs: 10/12–inch 33rpm
SEVILLE (87001 "Shout! Shout!
[Knock Yourself Out])" 40-80   62

MARGRET, Ann: see ANN-MARGRET

MARIACHI BRASS
LPs: 10/12–inch 33rpm
WORLD PACIFIC 6-12   66
Member: Chet Baker.

MARIE, Diane
Singles: 12–inch 33/45rpm
PRELUDE 4-6   83

MARIE, Teena
Singles: 12–inch 33/45rpm
EPIC 4-6   83-85
Singles: 7–inch
EPIC 2-4   83-88
GORDY 3-5   79-81
MOTOWN 2-4
LPs: 10/12–inch 33rpm
EPIC 5-8   83-90
GORDY 5-10   79-81
Also see KING DREAM CHORUS and Holiday Crew

MARIE & REX
Singles: 7–inch
CARLTON 5-10   59
Members: Marie Knight; Rex Garvin.

Also see KNIGHT, Marie

MARIGOLDS

Singles: 78rpm

EXCELLO 10-20   55

Singles: 7–inch

EXCELLO (2057 "Rollin' Stone") 20-40   55
EXCELLO (2061 "Two Strangers) ... 20-40   55
EXCELLO (2078 "Foolish Me") 20-40   56
EXCELLO (2091 "It's You, Darling,
   It's You") 20-40   56
Members: Johnny Bragg; Henry Jones; Hal Hebb; Willie Wilson.

MARILLION

Singles: 7–inch

CAPITOL 2-4   83-87

LPs: 10/12–inch 33rpm

CAPITOL 5-8   83-87
Members: Fish; Steve Hogarth; Steve Rothany; Mark Kelly; Pete
Trewavas; Ian Mosely.
Also see GTR

MARIMBA CHIAPAS

Singles: 78rpm

CAPITOL 3-6   56

Singles: 7–inch

CAPITOL 5-8   56

MARINERS

Singles: 78rpm

CADENCE 3-5   55-56
COLUMBIA 3-5   50-55

Singles: 7–inch

CADENCE 5-10   55-56
COLUMBIA 5-10   50-55
TIARA 4-8   58

EPs: 7–inch 33/45rpm

COLUMBIA 5-10   51-55

LPs: 10/12–inch 33rpm

CADENCE 15-25   56
COLUMBIA 15-25   51-55
EPIC 10-20   59
HARMONY 10-20   59
Also see GODFREY, Arthur

MARINO, Frank

(Frank Marino and Mahogany Rush)
Singles: 7–inch

COLUMBIA 3-5   77-81

LPs: 10/12–inch 33rpm

COLUMBIA 5-10   77-81
Also see MAHAGONY RUSH

MARK - ALMOND BAND

Singles: 7–inch

ABC 3-5   75
BLUE THUMB 3-5   72
COLUMBIA 3-5   72-73

LPs: 10/12–inch 33rpm

A&M 8-10   78
ABC 8-10   76
BLUE THUMB 8-12   70-73
COLUMBIA 8-10   72-73

MCA 5-8
PACIFIC ARTS 8-10   81
Members: Jon Mark; Johnny Almond.

MARK II

Singles: 7–inch

WYE 5-10   60-61
Member: Winston Cogswell.

MARK IV

Singles: 7–inch

COSMIC 10-15   58
MERCURY (71000 series) 5-10   59
MERCURY (73000 series) 3-5   72-73

LPs: 10/12–inch 33rpm

MERCURY 10-12   73

MARKETTS

(Mar-Kets)
Singles: 7–inch

LIBERTY 8-12   62
MERCURY 3-5   73
UNI 4-6   69
UNION 15-20   61-62
WARNER (Except 5391) 4-8   63-66
WARNER (5391 "Outer Limits") 5-10   63
WARNER (5391 "Out of Limits") 4-8   63
  (Note title change.)
WORLD PACIFIC 4-8   67

LPs: 10/12–inch 33rpm

DORE 5-8   82
LIBERTY (3226 "Surfer's Stomp") ... 25-30   62
  (Monaural.)
LIBERTY (3226 "Surfing Scene") ... 20-25   62
  (Monaural. Reissue.)
LIBERTY (7226 "Surfer's Stomp") ... 30-35   62
  (Stereo.)
LIBERTY (7226 "Surfing Scene") ... 25-30   62
  (Stereo.) Reissue.
MERCURY 10-15   73
PHONORAMA 5-8   84
WARNER (W-1509 "Take to Wheels") 20-25   63
  (Monaural.)
WARNER (WS-1509 "Take to
  Wheels") 25-30   63
  (Stereo.)
WARNER (W-1537 "Out of Limits") .. 20-25   64
  (Monaural.)
WARNER (WS-1537 "Out of Limits") . 25-30   64
  (Stereo.)
WARNER (W-1642 "Batman Theme") 20-30   66
  (Monaural.)
WARNER (WS-1642 "Batman
  Theme") 25-30   66
  (Stereo.)
WORLD PACIFIC 15-20   67
Members: Ben Benay; Mike Henderson; Ray Pohlman; Tommy
Tedesco; Bill Pittman; Gene Pello; Tom Hensley; Richard
Hobaica.
Also see NEW MARKETTS

MAR-KEYS
Singles: 7-inch
SATELITE (107 "Last Night") 10-15   61
STAX 4-8   61-66
LPs: 10/12-inch 33rpm
ATLANTIC 20-25   61-62
STAX 10-20   66-71
Members: Donald Dunn; Steve Cropper; Don Nix.

MAR-KEYS / Booker T. and the MGs
LPs: 10/12-inch 33rpm
STAX (720 "Back to Back") 12-18   67
Also see BOOKER T. and the MGs
Also see MAR-KEYS

MARKHAM, Pigmeat
Singles: 7-inch
ABC 3-5   74
CHESS 4-8   64-70
WIG 6-12
LPs: 10/12-inch 33rpm
CHESS 10-20   61-69
JEWEL 5-10   72-73
Also see MABLEY, Moms, and Pigmeat Markham

MARKS, Guy
Singles: 7-inch
ABC 4-6   68
ARIOLA AMERICA 3-5   76
RADNOR 3-5   70
LPs: 10/12-inch 33rpm
ABC 10-20   66-68

MARLEY, Bob, and the Wailers
(Wailers)
Singles: 7-inch
COTILLION 3-5   81
ISLAND 2-5   76-84
SHELTER 3-5   71
Picture Sleeves
ISLAND 2-4   83
LPs: 10/12-inch 33rpm
CALLA (1200 series) 10-15   76
CALLA (34000 series) 8-10   77
COTILLION 5-8   81
ISLAND (11 "Babylon By Bus") 10-12   78
ISLAND (9000 series except 9329) .. 8-12   75-80
ISLAND (9329 "Catch a Fire") 15-25   75
(Shaped cover.)
ISLAND (9329 "Catch a Fire") 8-10   75
(Standard cover.)
ISLAND (90000 series) 5-8   83-86
Also see TOSH, Peter

MARLEY, Ziggy, and the Melody Makers:
see MELODY MAKERS

MARLEY MARL
LPs: 10/12-inch 33rpm
COLD CHILL 5-8   88

MARLO, Micki
Singles: 78rpm
ABC-PAR 5-10   57

CAPITOL 4-8   54-56
Singles: 7-inch
ABC-PAR (Except 9841) 5-10   57
ABC-PAR (9841 "What
You've Done to Me") 10-20   57
(With "Vocal assist by Paul Anka.")
ABC-PAR (9841 "What
You've Done to Me") 5-10   57
(Has singer humming the lines done by Paul Anka
on first pressing.)
CAPITOL 5-10   54-56
LPs: 10/12-inch 33rpm
ABC-PAR 15-25   60
Also see ANKA, Paul

MARLOWE, Marion
(Marion Marloe with Frank Parker)
Singles: 78rpm
CADENCE 4-6   55-56
COLUMBIA 4-6   53-54
Singles: 7-inch
CADENCE 5-10   55-56
COLUMBIA 5-10   53-54
EPs: 7-inch 33/45rpm
COLUMBIA 6-12   53-55
LPs: 10/12-inch 33rpm
BARNABY 5-8   76
COLUMBIA 20-35   53-55
HARMONY 10-15   60

MARMALADE
Singles: 7-inch
ARIOLA AMERICA 3-5   76
EMI 3-5   74
EPIC 4-8   67-69
LONDON 3-6   70-71
LPs: 10/12-inch 33rpm
EPIC 10-15   70
G&P 8-10   81
LONDON 10-15   70
Member: Junior Campbell.
Also see BLUE

MARSALIS, Branford
(Branford Marsalis Quartet Featuring Terence Blanchard)
LPs: 10/12-inch 33rpm
COLUMBIA 5-8   84-90

MARSALIS, Wynton
LPs: 10/12-inch 33rpm
COLUMBIA 5-8   82-91
WHO'S WHO IN JAZZ 5-8   83

MARSH, Little Toni
Singles: 12-inch 33/45rpm
PRISM 4-6   83

MARSHALL - HAIN
Singles: 7-inch
HARVEST 3-5   78
LPs: 10/12-inch 33rpm
HARVEST 5-8   78

Members: Julian Marshall; Kit Hain.
Also see EYE to EYE

MARSHALL TUCKER BAND
Singles: 7–inch
CAPRICORN 3-5 73-78
WARNER 3-5 79-80
Picture Sleeves
WARNER 3-5 79
LPs: 10/12–inch 33rpm
CAPRICORN 10-12 73-78
WARNER 8-10 79-83

MARTERIE, Ralph, and His Orchestra
Singles: 78rpm
MERCURY 3-5 50-57
Singles: 7–inch
MERCURY 4-8 50-60
U.A. 3-6 61-62
EPs: 7–inch 33/45rpm
MERCURY 5-10 50-59
LPs: 10/12–inch 33rpm
MERCURY 8-18 50-60
U.A. 5-10 61-62
WING 5-10 56-60

MARTHA and the Muffins
(M+M)
Singles: 12–inch 33/45rpm
RCA 4-6 83-84
Singles: 7–inch
DINDISC/VIRGIN 3-5 80
RCA 2-4 83-84
LPs: 10/12–inch 33rpm
CURRENT 5-8 84
RCA 5-8 83
VIRGIN 5-8 80

MARTHA and the Vandellas
(Martha Reeves and the Vandellas)
Singles: 7–inch
GORDY (7011 "I'll Have to
Let Him Go") 10-15 62
GORDY (7014 through 7025) 5-10 62-63
GORDY (7027 through 7110) 4-8 64-72
MOTOWN 2-4
MOTOWN/TOPPS (7 "Dancing in
the Street") 50-75 67
MOTOWN/TOPPS (14 "Heat Wave") . 50-75 67
(Topps Chewing Gum promotional item.
Single-sided, cardboard flexi, picture disc. Issued
with generic paper sleeve.)
Picture Sleeves
GORDY (7033 "Dancing in the Street") 8-12 64
LPs: 10/12–inch 33rpm
ERA 5-10 79
GORDY (902 "Come and Get
These Memories") 40-60 63
(Monaural.)

GORDY (GS-902 "Come and Get
These Memories") 50-75 63
(Stereo.)
GORDY (907 "Heat Wave") 30-50 63
(Monaural.)
GORDY (GS-907 "Heat Wave") 35-55 63
(Stereo.)
GORDY (915 through 925) 20-40 65-67
GORDY (926 through 958) 15-20 68-72
MOTOWN (Except 100 and 200
series) 12-15 74
MOTOWN (100 and 200 series) 5-8 81-82
Members: Martha Reeves; Rosalind Ashford; Annette Beard.
Also see GAYE, Marvin
Also see HONDELLS / Del Shannon / Martha and the Vandellas
Also see REEVES, Martha
Also see VELVELETTES

MARTIKA
LPs: 10/12–inch 33rpm
COLUMBIA 5-8 89

MARTIN, Bobbi
Singles: 7–inch
BUDDAH 3-5 71-72
CORAL 4-6 61-67
GREEN MENU 3-5 75
MGM 3-5 73
MAYPOLE 5-8 60
U.A. 4-6 68-70
Picture Sleeves
CORAL 4-8 65
EPs: 7–inch 33/45rpm
CORAL 5-10 65
LPs: 10/12–inch 33rpm
BUDDAH 5-10 71
CORAL 10-20 65
SUNSET 5-10 71
U.A. 8-12 68-70
VOCALION 5-10 70

MARTIN, Dean
Singles: 78rpm
APOLLO (1088 "Oh Marie") 25-50 47
APOLLO (1116 "Santa Lucia") 25-50 48
CAPITOL (545 through 2001) 5-15 49-52
CAPITOL (2037 "Hey, Brother,
Pour the Wine") 15-20 54
(Seven–inch 78 rpm. Promotional issue only.)
CAPITOL (2071 through 3841) 5-15 52-57
CAPITOL (15000 series) 10-20 48-49
DIAMOND (2035 "Which Way
Did My Heart Go") 40-60 46
DIAMOND (2036 "I Got the Sun
in the Morning") 40-60 46
EMBASSY (124 "One Foot
in Heaven") 100-150 49
Singles: 7–inch
CAPITOL (401 "Dean Martin Sings") 50-100 53
(Four-disc boxed set.)

CAPITOL (247 "Silver Bells") 10-15   66
(Promotional issue only.)
CAPITOL (691 through 981) 10-15   49-50
CAPITOL (987 "Sleep Warm") 50-100   59
(Promotional issue only.)
CAPITOL (1002 through 1458) 10-15   50-51
CAPITOL (1609 "I Met a Girl") 50-100   60
(Promotional issue only.)
CAPITOL (1703 through 3238) 8-15   51-55
CAPITOL (3295 through 4570) 5-10   55-61
CAPITOL (6000 series) 4-6   64
CAPITOL (44153 "That's Amore") 2-4   88
MCA 3-5   85
REPRISE (190 through 193) 4-8   64
(Compact 33 singles. Promotional issues only.)
REPRISE (200 "Sophia") 150-200   65
(Promotional issue only.)
REPRISE (0252 through 1178) 3-6   64-73
REPRISE (20,000 series) 4-8   62-63
REPRISE (40,000 series) 10-15   62
(Stereo 33 singles.)
TEXAS DESERT CIRCUS WEEK (2160 ("It's 1200
Miles from Texas to Palm Springs") 50-100   58
(Single-sided promotional disc. No actual label
name. Made especially for play in Palm Springs,
promoting a circus. Incorrect title is shown on
label. Should read *It's 1200 Miles from Palm
Springs to Texas.*)
WARNER 2-4   83

Picture Sleeves

CAPITOL (987 "Sleep Warm") 100-200   59
CAPITOL (1609 "I Met a Girl") 50-100   60
(Promotional issue only. Sleeve reads: "From the
Soundtrack of the Motion Picture *Bells are
Ringing*.")
CAPITOL (4028 "Volare") 15-25   58
CAPITOL (4222 "On an Evening
in Roma") 15-25   59
REPRISE (20,116 "Who's Got
the Action") 15-20   62

EPs: 7–inch 33/45rpm

CAPITOL (EAP-401 "Dean Martin
Sings") 25-50   53
(Price is for either of two volumes.)
CAPITOL (EBF-401 "Dean Martin
Sings") 75-125   53
(Double EP boxed set.)
CAPITOL (481 "Sunny Italy") 25-50   53
CAPITOL (576 "Swingin'
Down Yonder") 20-40   59
(Price is for any of three volumes.)
CAPITOL (701 "Memories Are Made
of This") 25-50   55
CAPITOL (702 "Artists and Models") . 25-50   55
CAPITOL (806 "Hollywood Or Bust") . 25-50   57
CAPITOL (840 "Ten Thousand
Bedrooms") 25-50   57
CAPITOL (849 "Pretty Baby") 20-40   58
(Price is for any of three volumes.)

CAPITOL (702 "Artists and Models") . 25-50   55
CAPITOL (939 "Return to Me") 20-40   58
CAPITOL (1027 "Volare") 20-40   58
CAPITOL (1285 "A Winter Romance") 20-40   59
(Price is for any of three volumes.)
CAPITOL (1580 "Dean Martin") 20-30   61
(Compact Double 33.)
CAPITOL (EAP-1659 "Dino - Italian
Love Songs") 15-25   61
CAPITOL (SU-1659 "Dino - Italian
Love Songs") 15-25   61
(Jukebox issue.)
CAPITOL (9123 "Dean Martin") 25-50   54
18 TOP HITS (27 "Dean Martin") 20-40   54-55
(Price for either 45 and 78 rpm EPs.)
LLOYDS (705 "Dean Martin") 25-50   54
(Mail-order bonus issue.)
REPRISE 10-20   62-73
(Jukebox 33 compact issues.)

LPs: 10/12–inch 33rpm

CAPITOL (100 series) 8-15   69
CAPITOL (300 series) 8-15   69
CAPITOL (H-401 "Dean Martin
Sings") 50-100   53
(10–inch LP.)
CAPITOL (T-401 "Dean Martin Sings") 25-50   55
(Red cover.)
CAPITOL (TT-401 "Dean Martin
Sings") 10-20   59
(Pink cover.)
CAPITOL (523 "Return to Me"/"You're
Nobody Til Somebody Loves You") .. 8-12   70
CAPITOL (576 "Swingin' Down
Yonder") 30-40   55
CAPITOL (849 through 2601) 15-30   57-66
(With "T" or "ST" prefix.)
CAPITOL (849 through 2601) 8-15   63-65
(With "DT" prefix.)
CAPITOL (2815 "Dean Martin
Deluxe Set") 15-25   67
(Three-LP boxed set.)
CAPITOL (2941 "Favorites") 8-12   68
COSMIC (450 "Dean Martin") 15-20
LONGINES (5234 "Memories Are
Made of This") 25-50   73
(Five-LP boxed set. Includes booklet.)
LONGINES (5235 "That's Amore") ... 8-15   73
PAIR 6-10   83
PICKWICK 6-12
REPRISE 8-18   63-78
S.M.I. 10-20
SEARS 15-25
TALKING BOOK (58007 "Look:
December 26, 1967") 50-75   67
(Produced by the American Foundation for the
Blind. Plays at 16⅔ rpm. Has interview with Dean
on one side and an interview with Tom Stoppard
on the reverse.)
TEE VEE 10-20   78

TOWER 15-30   65-66
WALDORF (27 "Dean Martin Sings") . 20-40   53
(10–inch LP.)
WARNER 5-8   83
Promotional LPs
DEAN MARTIN TESTIMONIAL
DINNER 200-250   59
(Presented by the Friars Club, and sold as a
"Collectors Item" for $25 at the dinner. Three LPs
in triple pocket jacket. No actual label name used.
With guest appearances by Jimmy Durante, Joey
Bishop, Tony Martin, George Burns, Dinah Shore,
Mort Sahl, Judy Garland; Sammy Cahn, Danny
Thomas, Sammy Davis Jr., Bob Hope, Frank
Sinatra and others.)
REPRISE (246 Dean Martin
Radio Sampler") 35-50   66

MARTIN, Dean / Glen Campbell
LPs: 10/12–inch 33rpm
ZENITH/CAPITOL SPECIAL
PRODUCTS 10-20   72
(Issued with paper cover.)

MARTIN, Dean / Jeff Clark / Arlene James
EPs: 45/78rpm
POPULAR (1035 "Oh Marie") 8-15   54
(78 rpm. Not issued with special cover.)
VICTORY (1031 "Walking My Baby
Back Home") 8-15   54
(78 rpm. Not issued with special cover.)
POPULAR (1035 "Oh Marie") 10-20   54
(45 rpm. Not issued with special cover.)
VICTORY (1031 "Walking My Baby
Back Home") 20-40   54
(45 rpm. Colored vinyl. Not issued with special
cover.)

MARTIN, Dean, and Nat "King" Cole
Singles: 78rpm
CAPITOL 4-6   54
Singles: 7–inch
CAPITOL 5-10   54

MARTIN, Dean / Jane Froman
Singles: 78rpm
CAPITOL 4-6   53

Singles: 7–inch
CAPITOL (20030 "Who's Your Little
Who Zis") 8-15   53
(Promotional issue only.)

MARTIN, Dean / Jackie Gleason
LPs: 10/12–inch 33rpm
CAPITOL SPECIAL MARKETS 8-10

MARTIN, Dean / Rock Hudson
Singles: 7–inch
NATIONAL FEATURES (2785
"Showdown") 20-30   73
(Interviews with Showdown film stars. Promotional
issue only. Includes script.)

MARTIN, Dean / Red Ingle and the Natural Seven
Singles: 78rpm
CAPITOL (726 "Vieni Su") 8-15   49
(Promotional issue only.)

MARTIN, Dean, and Jerry Lewis
Singles: 78rpm
CAPITOL (15000 series) 5-10   48
NATIONAL MASK and PUPPET CORP.
("Puppet Show") 10-20
(Promotional issue only.)
EPs: 7–inch 33/45rpm
CAPITOL (533 "Living It Up") 100-150   54
CAPITOL (752 "Pardners") 75-125   56

MARTIN, Dean / Nicolini Lucchesi
LPs: 10/12–inch 33rpm
AUDITION (5936 "Dean Martin Sings,
Niccolini Lucchesi Plays") 25-50   56

MARTIN, Dean, and Ricky Nelson
Singles: 7–inch
WARNER (2262 "My Rifle,
My Pony and Me") 200-300   59
(Promotional issue only.)
Also see NELSON, Rick

MARTIN, Dean, and the Nuggets
Singles: 78rpm
CAPITOL 4-6   55
Singles: 7–inch
CAPITOL 5-10   55

MARTIN, Dean, and Helen O'Connell
Singles: 78rpm
CAPITOL 4-6   51
Singles: 7–inch
CAPITOL 5-10   51
Also see O'CONNELL, Helen

MARTIN, Dean / Patti Page
LPs: 10/12–inch 33rpm
DECCA (79224 "Christmas Seals
for 1962") 30-40   62
(Public service program for TB. Dean's show on
one side, Patti's on flip.)
DECCA (79235 "Christmas Seals
for 1962") 20-30   62
(Public service program for TB. Dean's and Patti's
shows on one side, flip has Si Zenter and Vaughn
Monroe.)
Also see MONROE, Vaughn
Also see PAGE, Patti
Also see ZENTER, Si

MARTIN, Dean, and Line Renaud
Singles: 78rpm
CAPITOL 4-6   55
Singles: 7–inch
CAPITOL 5-10   55

MARTIN, Dean / Nelson Riddle
EPs: 7–inch 33/45rpm
CAPITOL (1063 "Rio Bravo") 50-75   59
(Promotional only. Issued with special paper
sleeve.)
Also see RIDDLE, Nelson

MARTIN, Dean, and Margaret Whiting
Singles: 78rpm
CAPITOL 4-6   50
Singles: 7–inch
CAPITOL 5-10   50
Also see MARTIN, Dean
Also see WHITING, Margaret

MARTIN, Derek
Singles: 7–inch
BUTTERCUP 4-8
CRACKERJACK 5-10   63
ROULETTE 4-8   65
SUE 4-8   66
VOLT 4-8   68

MARTIN, Eric
(Eric Martin Band)
Singles: 7–inch
CAPTIOL 2-4   85
ELEKTRA 2-4   83
LPs: 10/12–inch 33rpm
ELEKTRA 5-8   83

MARTIN, Freddy, and His Orchestra
Singles: 78rpm
RCA 3-5   50-56
Singles: 7–inch
CAPITOL 4-6   63
DECCA 4-6   67-68
KAPP 4-6   61
RCA 5-8   50-56
EPs: 7–inch 33/45rpm
CAMDEN 5-10   54-56
RCA 5-10   50-54
LPs: 10/12–inch 33rpm
CAMDEN 10-20   54-56
CAPITOL 5-15   59-79
DECCA 5-10   67
KAPP 5-15   61-66
MCA 4-8   73-75
RCA 8-20   51-72
Also see GRIFFIN, Merv

MARTIN, George, and His Orchestra
Singles: 7–inch
U.A. (745 "Ringo's Theme") 10-15   64
U.A. (750 "A Hard Day's Night") 15-25   64
U.A. (800 series) 4-6   65
U.A. (50148 "Love in the Open Air") . 20-25   67
Picture Sleeves
U.A. (745 "Ringo's Theme") 40-60   64
U.A. (750 "A Hard Day's Night") ... 250-350   64
Promotional Singles
U.A. (745 "Ringo's Theme") 10-15   64
(White label.)
LPs: 10/12–inch 33rpm
U.A. (377 "Off the Beatle Track") 30-40   64
U.A. (383 "A Hard Day's Night") 20-30   64
U.A. (420 "George Martin") 15-25   65
U.A. (448 "Help") 20-30   65
U.A. (539 "The Beatle Girls") 25-35   66
U.A. (647 "London By George") 10-15   68
Also see BEATLES
Also see GERRY and the Pacemakers

MARTIN, Janis
Singles: 78rpm
RCA (Except 6652) 8-15   56-57
RCA (6652 "My Boy Elvis") 10-20   56
Singles: 7–inch
BIG DUTCH 3-5   77
PALETTE 5-10   61
RCA (6400 and 6500 series) 15-25   56
RCA (6652 "My Boy Elvis") 25-30   56
RCA (6700 through 7300 series) 10-20   56-58

EPs: 7–inch 33/45rpm
RCA (4093 "Just Squeeze Me") 75-100   58

MARTIN, Janis / Hank Snow
EPs: 7–inch 33/45rpm
RCA (76 "Love Me to Pieces") 15-25   56
(Promotional issue only.)
Also see MARTIN, Janis
Also see SNOW, Hank

MARTIN, Kenny
Singles: 7–inch
BIG TOP 5-10   60
FEDERAL 8-12   59-60
PJ 4-8   66

MARTIN, Marilyn
Singles: 7–inch
ATLANTIC 2-4   86-87
LPs: 10/12–inch 33rpm
ATLANTIC 5-8   86-87
Also see COLLINS, Phil, and Marilyn Martin

MARTIN, Moon
(John Martin)
Singles: 7–inch
CAPITOL 3-5   78-79
LPs: 10/12–inch 33rpm
CAPITOL 5-10   78-82

MARTIN, Nancy
Singles: 7–inch
ATLANTIC 2-4   82

MARTIN, Paul
Singles: 7–inch
ASCOT 5-10   65
IMPEX 4-8   66

MARTIN, Ray, Orchestra
Singles: 7–inch
RCA 3-6   61-62
U.A. 4-8   58
Picture Sleeves
RCA 4-8   61
U.A. 5-10   58
LPs: 10/12–inch 33rpm
CAMDEN 5-10   67-70
LONDON 8-12   63
MONUMENT 5-10   67
RCA 10-15   61

MARTIN, Steve
Singles: 7–inch
WARNER 3-5   77-79
Picture Sleeves
WARNER 3-5   78
LPs: 10/12–inch 33rpm
WARNER 5-10   77-81

MARTIN, Tony
Singles: 78rpm
RCA 3-6   50-57

Singles: 7–inch
CHART 3-5   70
DOT 4-6   61-66
DUNHILL 3-6   67
MOTOWN 4-6   64-66
NAN 4-6   64
PARK AVENUE 4-6   63
RCA 5-10   50-60
EPs: 7–inch 33/45rpm
DECCA 5-10   51-56
MERCURY 5-10   54-56
RCA 5-10   51-57
LPs: 10/12–inch 33rpm
CAMDEN 10-20   59-60
CHART 5-10   70
CHARTER 10-15   63
CORAL 5-8   73
DECCA 15-25   51-56
DOT 10-15   61-62
MERCURY 10-20   54-61
RCA 15-25   51-60
20TH FOX 10-15   64
WING 10-15   59-60
Also see MARTIN, Dean

MARTIN, Trade
Singles: 7–inch
COED 6-12   62-64
GEE 5-10   59
RCA 4-8   66-67
ROULETTE 5-10   60
STALLION 4-6
TOOT 4-6   68
LPs: 10/12–inch 33rpm
BUDDAH 10-15   72

MARTIN, Vince
(Vince Martin and the Tarriers; Vince Martin and Fred Neil)
Singles: 78rpm
GLORY 3-6   56
Singles: 7–inch
ABC-PAR 5-10   59
GLORY 8-12   56
ELEKTRA 4-8   64
LPs: 10/12–inch 33rpm
CAPITOL 5-10   73
ELEKTRA 10-20   64
Also see TARRIERS

MARTINDALE, Wink
Singles: 7–inch
ABC/DOT 3-5   76
DOT 4-8   59-66
RANWOOD 3-5   73
Picture Sleeves
DOT 5-10   59-60
LPs: 10/12–inch 33rpm
DOT 15-25   59-66
HAMILTON 10-20   64

MARTINDALE, Wink, and Robin Ward
Singles: 7-inch
DOT 4-8   63-64
LPs: 10/12-inch 33rpm
DOT 15-25   64
Also see MARTINDALE, Wink
Also see WARD, Robin

MARTINE, Layng, Jr.
Singles: 7-inch
BARNABY 3-5   71
DATE 5-10   66
GENERAL INT'L 4-8   66
PLAYBOY 3-5   76

MARTINO, Al
Singles: 78rpm
BBS 4-6   52
CAPITOL 3-5   52-57
Singles: 7-inch
BBS (101 "Here in My Heart") 5-10   52
  (Black vinyl.)
BBS (101 "Here in My Heart") 10-20   52
  (Colored vinyl.)
CAPITOL (Except 2122 through 4593) . 3-6   62-81
CAPITOL (Except F-2122 through
  F-4593) 5-10   52-61
20TH FOX 4-8   59-64
Picture Sleeves
CAPITOL 5-10   63-66
LPs: 10/12-inch 33rpm
CAPITOL 5-20   62-80
GUEST STAR 5-10   64
MOVIETONE 5-10   67
SPRINGBOARD 5-8   78
20TH FOX 10-20   59-65

MARVELETTES
Singles: 7-inch
MOTOWN 3-5
MOTOWN/TOPPS (12 "Please
  Mr. Postman") 50-75   67
  (Topps Chewing Gum promotional item.
  Single-sided, cardboard flexi, picture disc. Issued
  with generic paper sleeve.)
TAMLA 4-8   61-71
Picture Sleeves
TAMLA 10-15   61-64
LPs: 10/12-inch 33rpm
MOTOWN (Except 100 series) 12-18   75
MOTOWN (100 series) 5-8   82
TAMLA (228 "Please Mr. Postman") . 50-100   61
TAMLA (229 The Marvelettes Sing") 50-100   62
TAMLA (231 "Playboy") 50-100   62
TAMLA (237 "Marvelous Marvelettes")50-100   63
TAMLA (243 "On Stage") 50-75   63
TAMLA (253 through 288) 20-30   66-68
TAMLA (300 series) 12-18   70
Members: Gladys Horton; Kathy Anderson; Georgeanna Tillman;
Wanda Young; Juanita Cowart.

MARVELOWS
(Mighty Marvelows)
Singles: 7-inch
ABC 4-8   66-69
ABC-PAR 8-10   64-66
LPs: 10/12-inch 33rpm
ABC 15-20   68
Members: Melvin Mason; Frank Paden; Johnny Paden; Jesse
Smith; Sonny Stevenson; Andrew Thomas.

MARVIN & JOHNNY
Singles: 78rpm
ALADDIN 10-15   56
MODERN 10-20   54-56
RAYS 10-15   54
SPECIALTY 10-15   53-55
Singles: 7-inch
ALADDIN 15-25   56
ERIC 2-4
FELSTED 4-8   63
FIREFLY 10-15   60
JAMIE 5-10   61
MODERN 20-40   54-56
RAYS 15-25   54
SPECIALTY (Except 479) 25-40   53-55
SPECIALTY (479 "Baby Doll") 30-40   53
  (Black vinyl.)
SPECIALTY (479 "Baby Doll") 50-80   53
  (Colored vinyl.)
SWINGIN 8-12   61
LPs: 10/12-inch 33rpm
CROWN (5381 "Marvin and
  Johnny") 35-55   63
Members: Marvin Phillips; Johnny Dean.
Also see ISLEY BROTHERS / Marvin & Johnny
Also see JESSE & MARVIN

MARX, Groucho
Singles: 78rpm
DECCA 4-8   51
YOUNG PEOPLE'S RECORDS 3-6   54
Singles: 7-inch
A&M 3-5   73
DECCA 10-20   51
YOUNG PEOPLE'S RECORDS 5-10   54
LPs: 10/12-inch 33rpm
A&M 5-10   72
DECCA (5405 "Horray for
  Captain Spaulding") 100-150
  (10-inch LP.)

MARX, Richard
Singles: 7-inch
MANHATTAN 2-4   87
LPs: 10/12-inch 33rpm
EMI 5-8   89
MANHATTAN 5-8   87

MARY JANE GIRLS
Singles: 12-inch 33/45rpm
GORDY 4-6   83-85
MOTOWN 4-6   85-87

Singles: 7–inch
GORDY 2-4   83-87
Picture Sleeves
GORDY 2-4   85
LPs: 10/12–inch 33rpm
GORDY 5-8   83-87
Members: Joane "Jo Jo" McDuffie; Candice "Candy" Ghant; Kim "Maxi" Wuletich, Yvette "Corvette" Marine.

MAS, Carolyn
Singles: 7–inch
MERCURY 3-5   79
LPs: 10/12–inch 33rpm
MERCURY 5-10   79

MASCARA
Singles: 12–inch 33/45rpm
OH MY 4-6   84

MASEKELA, Hugh
(Hugh Masekela and the Union of South Africa)
Singles: 12–inch 33/45rpm
JIVE AFRIKA 4-6   84
Singles: 7–inch
BLUE THUMB 3-5   74
CASABLANCA 3-5   75-77
CHISA 3-6   67-71
JIVE AFRIKA 2-4   84
MGM 3-6   66-68
MERCURY 3-8   63-68
UNI 3-6   67-69
LPs: 10/12–inch 33rpm
BLUE THUMB 5-10   72-74
CASABLANCA 5-10   75-77
CHISA 8-15   67-71
IMPULSE 5-10   78
MGM 8-15   66-68
MERCURY 8-18   63-67
UNI 8-12   67-69
UPFRONT 5-8   77
VERVE 8-15   68
WING 6-12   68
Also see ALPERT, Herb, and Hugh Masekela

MASHMAKHAN
Singles: 7–inch
EPIC 3-6   70
JAMIE 4-8   69
LPs: 10/12–inch 33rpm
EPIC 10-12   70-71

MASKED MARAUDERS
Singles: 7–inch
DEITY 4-8   69
LPs: 10/12–inch 33rpm
DEITY 15-20   69

MASKMAN and the Agents
Singles: 7–inch
DYNAMO 4-8   68-69
GAMA 4-8   68
LPs: 10/12–inch 33rpm
DYNAMO 10-15   69

MASON, Barbara
(Barbara Mason and the Futures)
Singles: 12–inch 33/45rpm
WEST END 4-8   83-84
Singles: 7–inch
ARCTIC 4-8   64-68
BUDDAH 3-5   71-75
CHARGER 4-8   65
CRUSADER 4-8   64
NATIONAL GENERAL 3-5   70
PHONORAMA 3-5   84
PRELUDE 3-5   78
WMOT 3-5   80-81
WEST END 3-5   83-84
LPs: 10/12–inch 33rpm
ARCTIC 15-25   65-68
BUDDAH 8-12   72-75
GNC 10-15   70
NATIONAL GENERAL 10-15   70
PHONORAMA 5-8   84
PRELUDE 8-10   78
WMOT 8-10   81
WARNER 8-12   77
WIND 8-10   81
Also see FUTURES
Also see HIGGINS, Monk

MASON, Barbara, and Bunny Sigler
Singles: 7–inch
WARNER 3-5   77
Also see MASON, Barbara
Also see SIGLER, Bunny

MASON, Bonnie Jo
(Cher)
Singles: 7–inch
ANNETTE (1000 "Ringo, I Love You") 50-75   64
Also see CHER

MASON, Dave
Singles: 7–inch
ABC 3-5   74
BLUE THUMB 3-5   70-78
COLUMBIA 3-5   73-81
MARBLE 2-4   83
LPs: 10/12–inch 33rpm
ABC 8-10   75
BLUE THUMB (19 "Alone Together") . 10-12   70
(Black vinyl.)
BLUE THUMB (19 "Alone Together") . 20-25   70
(Colored vinyl.)
BLUE THUMB (34 through 54) 10-15   72-73
BLUE THUMB (800 series) 8-10   75
BLUE THUMB (6000 series) 8-10   74-78
COLUMBIA (Black vinyl) 8-10   73-81
COLUMBIA (Colored vinyl) 10-15   73-81
(Promotional issue only.)
ISLAND 5-8   83
Also see MERRYWEATHER, Neil
Also see TRAFFIC

MASON, Dave, and Cass Elliot
Singles: 7–inch
DUNHILL 2-4   70-71
LPs: 10/12–inch 33rpm
BLUE THUMB 12-15   71
Also see ELLIOT, Cass
Also see MASON, Dave

MASON, Harvey
Singles: 7–inch
ARISTA 3-5   76-81
LPs: 10/12–inch 33rpm
ARISTA 5-10   78-81

MASON, Jackie
Singles: 7–inch
VERVE 3-6   62
EPs: 7–inch 33/45rpm
VERVE (5076 "The Greatest Comedian in
the World Only Nobody Knows It") .. 8-10   62
(Promotional issue only.)
LPs: 10/12–inch 33rpm
VERVE 8-18   62-64
WARNER 5-8   87

MASON, Nick
(Nick Mason's Fictitious Sports)
Singles: 12–inch 33/45rpm
COLUMBIA 4-6   85
Singles: 7–inch
COLUMBIA 3-5   81-85
LPs: 10/12–inch 33rpm
COLUMBIA 5-8   81-85
Also see PINK FLOYD

MASON, Nick, and Rick Fenn
Singles: 7–inch
COLUMBIA 2-4   85
LPs: 10/12–inch 33rpm
COLUMBIA 5-8   85
Also see MASON, Nick

MASON, Vaughan
(Vaughan Mason and Crew)
Singles: 12–inch 33/45rpm
BRUNSWICK 4-6   80
Singles: 7–inch
BRUNSWICK 2-4   80-81
LPs: 10/12–inch 33rpm
BRUNSWICK 5-8   80
Also see AM-FM

MASON, Vaughan, and Butch Dayo
Singles: 12–inch 33/45rpm
SALSOUL 4-6   83
Singles: 7–inch
SALSOUL 2-4   82-83
LPs: 10/12–inch 33rpm
SALSOUL 5-8   83
Also see MASON, Vaughan

MASON DIXON DANCE BAND
Singles: 7–inch
ALEXANDER STREET 3-5   79

MASON PROFFIT
Singles: 7–inch
AMPEX 3-5   71
HAPPY TIGER 4-6   70
LPs: 10/12–inch 33rpm
AMPEX 8-10   71
HAPPY TIGER 8-12   70-71
WARNER 8-10   72-73
Members: John Talbot; Terry Talbot.

MASQUERADERS
Singles: 7–inch
ABC 3-5   75
AMERICAN GROUP 3-5   69
BANG 2-4   80
BELL 4-8   68
HI 3-5
HOT BUTTERED SOUL 3-5   75-76
TOWER 4-8   66
WAND 4-8   67
Members: Lee Hatim; Robert Wrightsil; David Sanders; Harold
Thomas; Sam Hutchins.

MASS PRODUCTION
Singles: 7–inch
COTILLION 3-5   76-83
LPs: 10/12–inch 33rpm
COTILLION 5-8   76-83

MASSER, Michael, and Mandrill
Singles: 7–inch
ARISTA 3-5   77
Also see MANDRILL

MASSEY, Wayne
Singles: 7–inch
POLYDOR 3-5   80

MASSEY, Wayne, and Charly McClain
Singles: 7–inch
EPIC 2-4   85-86
Also see MASSEY, Wayne

MASSIAH, Maurice
Singles: 12–inch 33/45rpm
RFC/QUALITY 4-6   83

MASTER PLAN
Singles: 7–inch
CRUSH 2-4   88

MASTERDON COMMITTEE
Singles: 12–inch 33/45rpm
PROFILE 4-6   86-87
Singles: 7–inch
PROFILE 2-4   86-87
LPs: 10/12–inch 33rpm
PROFILE 5-8   86

MASTERPIECE
Singles: 7–inch
WHITFIELD 3-5   80
LPs: 10/12–inch 33rpm
WHITFIELD 5-10   80

MASTERS, Johnny
(Johnny Maestro)
Singles: 7–inch
COED (527 "Say It Isn't So") 15-20   60
Also see MAESTRO, Johnny

MASTERS, Sammy
Singles: 78rpm
DECCA 3-5   57
4 STAR 5-10   57
Singles: 7–inch
DECCA 8-12   57
DOT 5-10   60-66
4 STAR (1695 "Pink Cadillac") 30-50   57
4 STAR (1697 "Whop-T-Bop") 30-50   57
GALAHAD 4-8   62-72
KAPP 4-8   64
LODE 5-10   60-61
WARNER 5-10   60
EPs: 7–inch 33/45rpm
4 STAR (26 "Sammy Masters") 50-75   57
(Promotional issue only. Not issued with cover.)

MASTERS of CEREMONY
LPs: 10/12–inch 33rpm
4TH and BROADWAY 2-4   88

MATHEWS, Tobin
(Tobin Mathews and Co.; Tobin Matthews)
Singles: 7–inch
CHIEF 5-10   60-61
COLUMBIA 4-8   63
U.S.A. 4-8   61

MATHIS, Johnny
Singles: 78rpm
COLUMBIA 3-5   57-58
Singles: 7–inch
AURAVISION 5-10
(Cardboard flexi-discs. Columbia Record Club
promotional issues.)
COLUMBIA (Except 40000 series) 3-5   74-85
COLUMBIA (41000 and 42000 series) . . 4-8   58-63
COLUMBIA (44000 through 46000
series) 3-6   67-74
MERCURY 4-6   63-66
Picture Sleeves
COLUMBIA (40993 "Chances Are") . . . 8-12   57
COLUMBIA (41060 through 42799) 3-8   58-63
MERCURY 3-6   63-66
EPs: 7–inch 33/45rpm
COLUMBIA (Except 8800 series) 5-15   57-59
COLUMBIA (8871 through 8873) 10-20   56
LPs: 10/12–inch 33rpm
COLUMBIA (Except 887) 5-15   57-87
COLUMBIA (887 "Johnny Mathis") . . . 35-50   56
CONCERT 8-12
(TV mail-order offer.)
MFSL 15-20   85
MERCURY 8-18   64-67
Also see KNIGHT, Gladys, and Johnny Mathis

MATHIS, Johnny, and Henry Mancini
LPs: 10/12–inch 33rpm
COLUMBIA 5-8   87
Also see MANCINI, Henry

MATHIS, Johnny, and Dionne Warwick
Singles: 7–inch
ARISTA 3-5   82
Also see WARWICK, Dionne

MATHIS, Johnny, and Deniece Williams
Singles: 7–inch
COLUMBIA 2-5   78-84
LPs: 10/12–inch 33rpm
COLUMBIA (35435 "That's What
Friends Are For") 15-25   78
(Picture disc. Promotional issue only.)
COLUMBIA (35435 "That's What
Friends Are For") 5-10   78
(Standard vinyl disc.)
Also see MATHIS, Johnny
Also see WILLIAMS, Deniece

MATHIS, Kathy
Singles: 7–inch
TABU 2-4   87

MATLOCK, Ronn
Singles: 7–inch
COTILLION 3-5   79

MATTHEWS, Dave
LPs: 10/12–inch 33rpm
PEOPLE 10-15   71

MATTHEWS, Ian
Singles: 7–inch
DECCA 3-5   70-71
COLUMBIA 3-5   76-77
ELEKTRA 3-5   73
MUSHROOM 3-5   78-79
VERTIGO 3-5   71-72
LPs: 10/12–inch 33rpm
CAPITOL 8-10   71
COLUMBIA 8-10   77
DECCA 8-12   71
ELEKTRA 8-10   73-74
MUSHROOM (Except 5012) 8-10   78
MUSHROOM (5012 "Stealin' Home") 20-25   78
(Picture disc. Promotional issue only.)
MUSHROOM (5012 "Stealin' Home") . 8-10   78
(Standard vinyl disc.)
VERTIGO 10-12   71-72
Also see FAIRPORT CONVENTION
Also see MATTHEWS' SOUTHERN COMFORT

MATTHEWS, Milt
Singles: 7–inch
H&L 3-5   78

MATTHEWS' SOUTHERN COMFORT
(Featuring Ian Matthews)
Singles: 7–inch
DECCA 3-5   71

LPs: 10/12-inch 33rpm		
DECCA 10-15	70-71
MCA 5-10	78
Also see MATTHEWS, Ian		
Also see SOUTHERN COMFORT		

MATYS BROS.
Singles: 78rpm

ESSEX 3-6	54

Singles: 7-inch

ESSEX 5-10	54
SELECT 4-6	62
SOUND 4-6	

MAUDS
Singles: 7-inch

DUNWICH 5-10	67
MERCURY 4-8	67-69
RCA 3-6	70

LPs: 10/12-inch 33rpm

MERCURY 15-25	67

MAURIAT, Paul
Singles: 7-inch

PHILIPS 3-5	67-71

Picture Sleeves

PHILIPS 3-5	68

LPs: 10/12-inch 33rpm

PHILIPS 8-18	67-71

MAXAYN
Singles: 7-inch

CAPRICORN 3-5	72-74

LPs: 10/12-inch 33rpm

CAPRICORN 8-10	72-74

MAXWELL, Diane
Singles: 7-inch

CAPITOL 4-8	61
CHALLENGE 5-10	59

LPs: 10/12-inch 33rpm

CHALLENGE (607 "Almost Seventeen") 30-35	59
(Monaural.)		
CHALLENGE (2501 "Almost Seventeen") 35-45	59
(Stereo.)		
Also see FULLER, Jerry, and Diane Maxwell		

MAXWELL, Robert
(Bobby Maxwell)
Singles: 78rpm

MGM 3-5	57
MERCURY 3-5	52
TEMPO 3-5	51-52

Singles: 7-inch

DECCA 3-6	64
MGM 4-8	57
MERCURY 5-10	52
TEMPO 5-10	51-52

EPs: 7-inch 33/45rpm

MGM 5-10	57
MERCURY 5-10	52

TEMPO 5-10	51-52

LPs: 10/12-inch 33rpm

DECCA 8-15	64
MGM 10-15	57
TEMPO 10-20	52

MAY, Billy, and His Orchestra
Singles: 78rpm

CAPITOL 3-5	50-56

Singles: 7-inch

CAPITOL 5-10	50-56

EPs: 7-inch 33/45rpm

CAPITOL 5-10	50-56

LPs: 10/12-inch 33rpm

CAPITOL 8-18	50-56

MAY, Brian
(Brian May and Friends)
Singles: 7-inch

CAPITOL 2-4	83

LPs: 10/12-inch 33rpm

CAPITOL 5-8	83
Also see QUEEN		
Also see REO SPEEDWAGON		
Also see VAN HALEN		

MAYALL, John
(John Mayall and the Blues Breakers Featuring Eric Clapton)
Singles: 7-inch

IMMEDIATE 4-8	67
LONDON 5-10	66-68
POLYDOR 3-6	69-74

LPs: 10/12-inch 33rpm

ABC 8-12	76-78
BLUE THUMB 8-12	74
DJM 8-12	79
ISLAND 5-8	90
LONDON 10-15	67-78
MCA 5-8	
POLYDOR 10-12	69-74
Also see BRUCE, Jack		
Also see CLAPTON, Eric		
Also see FLEETWOOD MAC		
Also see HARTLEY, Keef, Band		
Also see TAYLOR, Mick		

MAYANA
Singles: 12-inch 33/45rpm

ATLANTIC 4-6	83

Singles: 7-inch

ATLANTIC 2-4	83

MAYBE MENTAL
LPs: 10/12-inch 33rpm

PLACEBO 6-10	84-86

MAYER, Nathaniel
(Nathaniel Mayer and the Fabulous Twilights; Nathaniel Mayer and the Fortune Braves)
Singles: 7-inch

FORTUNE (487 "Hurting Love") 15-20	62
FORTUNE (500 series) 10-20	62-69
U.A. 5-10	62

McCALLUM, David
Singles: 7–inch
CAPITOL 4-8   66
Picture Sleeves
CAPITOL 5-10   66
LPs: 10/12–inch 33rpm
CAPITOL 10-15   66

McCANN, Les
Singles: 7–inch
ATLANTIC 3-5   69-75
LIMELIGHT 4-6   65
PACIFIC JAZZ 4-8   60-65
WORLD PACIFIC 3-6
LPs: 10/12–inch 33rpm
ATLANTIC 5-10   69-75
LIMELIGHT 10-20   65
PACIFIC JAZZ 15-25   60-65
Also see FLACK, Roberta
Also see HOLMES, Richard "Groove," and Les McCann
Also see RAWLS, Lou, and Les McCann Ltd.

McCANN, Les, and Eddie Harris
Singles: 7–inch
ATLANTIC 3-5   69-70
LPs: 10/12–inch 33rpm
ATLANTIC 5-10   69-71
Also see HARRIS, Eddie
Also see McCANN, Les

McCANN, Peter
Singles: 7–inch
COLUMBIA 3-5   79
20TH FOX 3-5   77
LPs: 10/12–inch 33rpm
20TH FOX 8-10   77

McCARTNEY, Paul
(Wings; Paul McCartney and Wings; Paul and Linda McCartney)
Singles: 12–inch 33/45rpm
CAPITOL (15212 "Spies Like Us") 5-8   85
CAPITOL (15235 "Press") 4-8   86
COLUMBIA (03019 "Take It Away") ... 5-10   82
COLUMBIA (05077 "No More
Lonely Nights") 5-8   84
("Playout version.")
COLUMBIA (05077 "No More
Lonely Nights") 10-15   84
("Special Dance Mix.")
COLUMBIA (10940 "Goodnight
Tonight") 10-20   79
COLUMBIA (39927 "No More
Lonely Nights") 8-12   84
(Picture disc.)
PROFILE (7147 "Let It Be") 5-8   87
Promotional 12–inch Singles
CAPITOL (8574 "Maybe I'm Amazed") 40-50   77
CAPITOL (9556 "Spies Like Us") 20-25   85
CAPITOL (9763 "Press") 10-15   86
CAPITOL (9797 "Angry") 10-15   86

COLUMBIA (775 "Coming Up") 50-60   80
(Red label.)
COLUMBIA (775 "Coming Up") 45-55   80
(White label.)
COLUMBIA (1940 "No More
Lonely Nights") 10-15   84
("Ballad" version.)
COLUMBIA (1990 "No More
Lonely Nights") 10-15   84
("Special Dance Mix.")
COLUMBIA (05077 "No More
Lonely Nights") 10-15   84
("Ballad version.")
COLUMBIA (10940 "Goodnight
Tonight") 10-20   79
PROFILE (7147 "Let It Be") 10-15   87
Singles: 7–inch
APPLE (1829 "Another Day") 4-6   71
APPLE (1837 "Uncle Albert
Admiral Halsey") 4-6   71
APPLE (1847 "Give Ireland Back
to the Irish") 4-6   72
APPLE (1851 "Mary Had a Little Lamb") 4-6   72
APPLE (1857 "Hi Hi Hi") 4-6   72
APPLE (1861 "My Love") 4-6   73
APPLE (1863 "Live and Let Die") 4-6   73
APPLE (1869 "Helen Wheels") 4-6   73
APPLE (1871 "Jet"/"Mamunia") 5-10   74
APPLE (1871 "Jet"/"Let Me Roll It") 4-6   74
APPLE (1873 "Band on the Run") 4-6   74
APPLE (1875 "Junior's Farm") 4-6   74
CAPITOL (1829 "Another Day") 2-4
CAPITOL (1837 "Uncle Albert
Admiral Halsey") 2-4
CAPITOL (1847 "Give Ireland Back
to the Irish") 2-4
CAPITOL (1851 "Mary Had a
Little Lamb") 2-4
CAPITOL (1857 "Hi Hi Hi") 2-4
CAPITOL (1861 "My Love") 2-4
CAPITOL (1863 "Live and Let Die") 2-4
CAPITOL (1869 "Helen Wheels") 2-4
CAPITOL (1871 "Jet") 2-4
CAPITOL (1873 "Band on the Run") ... 2-4
CAPITOL (1875 "Junior's Farm") 2-4
CAPITOL (4091 "Listen to What
the Man Said") 3-5   75
CAPITOL (4145 "Letting Go") 3-5   75
CAPITOL (4175 "Venus and Mars
Rock Show") 3-5   75
CAPITOL (4256 "Silly Love Songs") ... 3-5   76
(Capitol custom label.)
CAPITOL (4256 "Silly Love Songs") ... 2-4
(Black label.)
CAPITOL (4293 "Let 'Em In") 3-5   76
(Capitol custom label.)
CAPITOL (4293 "Let 'Em In") 2-4
(Black label.)
CAPITOL (4385 Maybe I'm Amazed") .. 3-5   77

LPs: 10/12–inch 33rpm

APPLE (3363 "McCartney") 15-20   70
  (Label shows Paul's full name beneath LP title.)
APPLE (3363 "McCartney") 10-15   70
  (Label doesn't show Paul's name beneath LP title.)
APPLE (3375 "Ram") 10-15   71
APPLE (3386 "Wild Life") 10-15   71
APPLE (3409 "Red Rose
  Speedway") 10-15   73
APPLE (3415 "Band on the Run") ... 10-15   73
  (Price includes bonus poster.)
CAPITOL (3363 "McCartney") 8-10
CAPITOL (3375 "Ram") 8-10
CAPITOL (3386 "Wildlife") 8-10
CAPITOL (3409 "Red Rose Speedway") 8-10
CAPITOL (3415 "Band on the Run") .. 8-10
  (Price includes bonus poster.)
CAPITOL (11525 "Wings at the
  Speed of Sound") 8-10   76
CAPITOL (11593 "Wings over
  America") 12-15   76
CAPITOL (11905 "Greatest Hits") 5-10   78
  (Price includes bonus poster.)
CAPITOL (11419 "Venus and Mars") . 10-15   75
  (Price includes bonus posters and stickers.)
CAPITOL (11777 "London Town") ... 10-15   78
  (Price includes bonus poster.)
CAPITOL (11901 "Band on the
  Run") 20-30   78
  (Picture disc.)
CAPITOL (12475 "Press to Play") 8-10   87
CAPITOL (48287 "All the Best!") 10-15   87
CAPITOL (91653 "Flowers in the Dirt") . 5-8   89
CAPITOL (94778 "Tripping the
  Live Fantastic") 10-12   90
CAPITOL (95379 "Tripping the
  Live Fantastic - Highlights") 5-10   90
COLUMBIA (36057 "Back to the Egg") 5-10   79
COLUMBIA (36478 "McCartney") 5-10   80
COLUMBIA (36479 "Ram") 5-10   80
COLUMBIA (36480 "Wild Life") 5-10   80
COLUMBIA (36481 "Red Rose
  Speedway") 5-10   80
COLUMBIA (36482 "Band on the Run") 5-10   80
COLUMBIA (36511 "McCartney II") .. 15-20   80
  (Issued with bonus single [1204] *Coming Up*,
  which represents $4-$8 of the above price range.)
COLUMBIA (36801 "Venus and
  Mars") 5-8   80
  (Price includes bonus posters.)
COLUMBIA (36987 "The McCartney
  Interview") 8-10   80
COLUMBIA (37409 "Wings at the
  Speed of Sound") 5-8   81
COLUMBIA (37462 "Tug of War") 5-8   82
  (With Stevie Wonder on *Ebony and Ivory*.)
COLUMBIA (39149 "Pipes of Peace") .. 5-8   83
  (With Michael Jackson on *Say Say Say*.)

COLUMBIA (39613 "Give My
  Regards to Broad Street") 5-8   84
COLUMBIA (46482 "Band on
  the Run") 10-15   80
  (Half-speed mastered.)
LIBERTY (50100 Live and Let Die) ... 5-8   84
  (With McCartney on title track only.)
LONDON (76007 "The Family Way") . 50-60   67
  (Soundtrack. Monaural.)
LONDON (82007 "The Family Way") . 60-70   67
  (Soundtrack. Stereo.)
U.A. (100 "Live and Let Die") 15-20   73
  (Copies with cut corners are valued at about
  one-half of the above price range. McCartney is
  heard on title track only.)

Promotional LPs

APPLE (3375 "Ram") 80-100   71
  (Monaural.)
APPLE (6210 "Brung to Ewe By") . 175-200   71
COLUMBIA (821 "The McCartney
  Interview") 40-50   80
COLUMBIA (36057 "Back to the Egg") 15-20   79
COLUMBIA (36511 "McCartney II") .. 15-20   80
WARNER ("The Family Way") 150-200   67
  (10–inch LP. Ad spots for radio stations.)
  Also see BEATLES
  Also see BRASS RING
  Also see COUNTRY HAMS
  Also see GREASE BAND
  Also see LOMAX, Jackie
  Also see NEWMAN, Thunderclap
  Also see PERKINS, Carl
  Also see SUZY and the Red Stripes

McCARTNEY, Paul, and Michael Jackson

Singles: 12–inch 33/45rpm

COLUMBIA (1758 "Say Say Say") ... 10-15   83
COLUMBIA (04169 "Say Say Say") 5-8   83

Promotional 12–inch Singles

COLUMBIA (04169 "Say Say Say") .. 12-18   83

Singles: 7–inch

COLUMBIA (04168 "Say Say Say") 2-4   83
EPIC (03288 "The Girl Is Mine") 2-4   82
EPIC (03372 "The Girl Is Mine") 5-8   82
  (Single-sided pressing with small, LP size, hole.)

Picture Sleeves

COLUMBIA (04168 "Say Say Say") 2-4   83

Promotional Picture Sleeves

COLUMBIA (04168 "Say Say Say") 5-8   83
EPIC (03288 "The Girl Is Mine") 5-8   82

Promotional Singles

COLUMBIA (04168 "Say Say Say") 5-8   83
EPIC (03288 "The Girl Is Mine") 5-8   82
  (Label shows identification number as 169138.)
EPIC (03288 "The Girl Is Mine") 10-15   82
  (Label shows identification number as 169202.
  Also reads "New Edited Version.")
  Also see JACKSON, Michael

McCARTNEY, Paul / Rochestra / Who / Rockpile
Singles: 12–inch 33/45rpm
ATLANTIC (388 "Every Night") 60-80   81
(Promotional issue only.)
Also see ROCKPILE
Also see WHO

McCARTNEY, Paul, and Stevie Wonder
Singles: 12–inch 33/45rpm
COLUMBIA (02878 "Ebony and Ivory") . 5-8   82
Promotional 12–inch Singles
COLUMBIA (1444 "McCartney") 25-30   82
Singles: 7–inch
COLUMBIA (02860 "Ebony and Ivory") . 2-4   82
Promotional Singles
COLUMBIA (02860 "Ebony and Ivory") 8-12   82
Picture Sleeves
COLUMBIA (02860 "Ebony and Ivory") . 2-4   82
Promotional Picture Sleeves
COLUMBIA (02860 "Ebony and Ivory") . 5-8   82
Note: Stevie Wonder appears only on *Ebony and Ivory.*
Also see McCARTNEY, Paul
Also see WONDER, Stevie

McCLAIN, Alton, and Destiny
Singles: 7–inch
POLYDOR 3-5   79-81
LPs: 10/12–inch 33rpm
POLYDOR 5-10   79-81
Also see BRISTOL, Johnny, and Alton McClain

McCLAIN, Janice
Singles: 12–inch 33/45rpm
MCA 4-6   86
Singles: 7–inch
MCA 2-4   86
RFC 2-4   80
LPs: 10/12–inch 33rpm
MCA 5-8   86

McCLARY, Thomas
Singles: 7–inch
MOTOWN 2-4   84-85
LPs: 10/12–inch 33rpm
MOTOWN 5-8   85
Also see COMMODORES

McCLINTON, Delbert
Singles: 7–inch
BOBILL 4-8   67
BROWNFIELD 4-8   65
CAPITOL 3-5   80-81
CAPRICORN 3-5   78
LPs: 10/12–inch 33rpm
ACCORD 5-8   81
CAPITOL 5-8   81
CAPRICORN 5-8   79
INTERMEDIA 5-8   84
MCA 5-8   81
POLYDOR 5-8   79
Also see DELBERT & GLEN

McCLINTON, O.B.
Singles: 7–inch
MERCURY 3-5   76
LPs: 10/12–inch 33rpm
ENTERPRISE 8-10   72-74

McCLURE, Bobby
Singles: 7–inch
CHECKER 4-8   66-67
Also see BASS, Fontella, and Bobby McClure

McCONNELL, C. Lynda
Singles: 12–inch 33/45rpm
ATLANTIC 4-6   84
Singles: 7–inch
ATLANTIC 2-4   84

McCOO, Marilyn
Singles: 7–inch
RCA 2-4   83
LPs: 10/12–inch 33rpm
RCA 5-8   83

McCOO, Marilyn, and Billy Davis, Jr.
Singles: 12–inch 33/45rpm
COLUMBIA 4-6   79
Singles: 7–inch
ABC 3-5   76-78
COLUMBIA 3-5   78
LPs: 10/12–inch 33rpm
ABC 8-10   76-77
COLUMBIA 5-10   78
Also see FIFTH DIMENSION
Also see McCOO, Marilyn

McCORMICK, Gayle
Singles: 7–inch
DECCA 3-5   72
DUNHILL 3-5   71-72
MCA 3-5   73
LPs: 10/12–inch 33rpm
DECCA 10-12   72
DUNHILL 10-12   71
FANTASY 8-10   74
Also see SMITH

McCOY, Charlie
Singles: 7–inch
CADENCE 4-8   61-62
MONUMENT 3-6   68-78
LPs: 10/12–inch 33rpm
EPIC 5-8   82
MONUMENT 5-10   69-78

McCOY, Freddie
Singles: 7–inch
PRESTIGE 4-6   67

McCOY, Van
(Van McCoy and the Soul City Symphony)
Singles: 12–inch 33/45rpm
MCA 4-8   79
Singles: 7–inch
AMHERST 3-5

AVCO	3-5	74-75
CGC	3-5	70
COLUMBIA	4-8	65-66
EPIC	3-6	69
H&L	3-5	76
LIBERTY	4-8	62
MCA	3-5	78-79
ROCK 'N	8-12	61
SILVER BLUE	3-5	73

LPs: 10/12-inch 33rpm

AVCO	8-10	74-75
BUDDAH	8-10	72-75
COLUMBIA	12-18	66
H&L	8-10	76
MCA	8-10	77-79

McCOY BOYS

Singles: 7-inch

VERVE	8-12	60

Members: Gil Garfield; Perry Botkin, Jr; Ray Campi.
Also see DE VORZON, Barry, and Perry Botkin, Jr.

McCOYS

Singles: 7-inch

BANG	5-10	65-67
MERCURY	8-15	68
SOLID GOLD	2-4	73

LPs: 10/12-inch 33rpm

BANG	25-35	65-66
MERCURY	15-25	68-69

Also see DERRINGER, Rick
Also see STRANGELOVES

McCRACKLIN, Jimmy

(Jimmy McCracklin and His Blues Blasters; Jimmie McCracklin)

Singles: 78rpm

ALADDIN	10-15	51
CAVATONE	10-20	47
COURTNEY	10-20	45
DOWN TOWN	10-20	48
EXCELSIOR	10-20	45
GLOBE	10-20	45
HOLLYWOOD	10-15	55
MODERN	10-15	49
PEACOCK	10-15	52-54
RPM	10-15	50
SWING TIME	10-15	51-52
TRILON	10-15	49

Singles: 7-inch

ART-TONE	5-10	61-62
CHECKER	10-15	58
CHESS	4-8	62
GEDINSON'S	4-8	61
HI	5-10	60
HOLLYWOOD	15-25	55
IMPERIAL	4-8	62-67
IRMA	10-15	
KENT	4-8	62
LIBERTY	3-5	70
MERCURY	8-12	59-61

MINIT	4-8	67-70
MODERN (926 "Blues Blasters Boogie")	20-30	54
MODERN (934 "Darlin' Share Your Love")	20-30	54
MODERN (951 "Forgive Me Baby")	20-30	54
MODERN (967 "Gonna Tell Your Mother")	20-30	55
PEACOCK (1605 "My Days Are Limited")	20-30	52
PEACOCK (1615 "Share and Share Alike")	20-30	53
PEACOCK (1634 "The End")	20-30	53
PEACOCK (1639 "The Cheater")	20-30	53

LPs: 10/12-inch 33rpm

CHESS (1464 "Jimmy McCracklin Sings")	40-60	62
CROWN	15-20	61
IMPERIAL	20-35	63-66
MINIT	12-18	67-69
STAX	8-12	72-81

Also see BROWN, Charles, and Jimmy McCracklin

McCRACKLIN, Jimmy / T-Bone Walker / Charles Brown

LPs: 10/12-inch 33rpm

IMPERIAL (9257 "Best of the Blues, Vol. 1")	15-25	64

Also see BROWN, Charles

McCRAE, George

Singles: 7-inch

GOLD MOUNTAIN	2-4	84
T.K.	3-5	74-79

LPs: 10/12-inch 33rpm

CAT	8-10	76
GOLD MOUNTAIN	5-8	84
TK	8-10	74-77

McCRAE, George and Gwen

Singles: 7-inch

CAT	3-5	76

Also see McCRAE, George
Also see McCRAE, Gwen

McCRAE, Gwen

Singles: 7-inch

ATLANTIC	2-4	81-83
BLACK JACK	2-4	84
CAT	3-5	74-75

LPs: 10/12-inch 33rpm

ATLANTIC	5-8	81-83
CAT	8-10	74-76

Also see McCRAE, George and Gwen

McCRARYS

Singles: 7-inch

CAPITOL	2-4	80-82
PORTRAIT	3-5	78-79

LPs: 10/12-inch 33rpm

CAPITOL	5-8	80
PORTRAIT	5-10	78

Members: Sam McCrary; Linda McCrary; Al McCrary; Charity McCrary.

McCULLOUGH, Ullanda
Singles: 7–inch
ATLANTIC 3-5   81

McCURN, George
Singles: 7–inch
A&M 4-8   63-64
LIBERTY 4-8   62
REPRISE 4-6   66
LPs: 10/12–inch 33rpm
A&M 15-25   63

McDANIEL, Donna
Singles: 7–inch
MIDLAND INT'L 3-5   77

McDANIELS, Gene
(Eugene McDaniels)
Singles: 7–inch
COLUMBIA 4-6   66-67
LIBERTY 4-8   60-65
MGM 3-5   73
ODE '70 3-5   75
LPs: 10/12–inch 33rpm
ATLANTIC 10-15   70-71
LIBERTY 15-25   60-67
ODE '70 8-12   75
SUNSET 10-15   66
U.A. 8-12   75

McDEVITT, Charles, Skiffle Group
(Featuring Nancy Wiskey)
Singles: 7–inch
CHIC 5-10   57
ORIOLE 5-10   57

McDONALD, Country Joe
Singles: 7–inch
FANTASY 3-5   75-79
VANGUARD 3-6   71-74
LPs: 10/12–inch 33rpm
FANTASY 5-10   75-79
MFSL 25-50   81
PICCADILLY 10-15   78
VANGUARD 8-12   69-76
Also see COUNTRY JOE and the Fish

McDONALD, Kathi
Singles: 7–inch
CAPITOL 3-6   74
LPs: 10/12–inch 33rpm
CAPITOL 10-20   74
Also see BALDRY, Long John, and Kathi McDonald
Also see BIG BROTHER and the Holding Company

McDONALD, Michael
Singles: 7–inch
MCA 2-4   86
WARNER 2-4   82-85
Picture Sleeves
WARNER 2-4   82-85

LPs: 10/12–inch 33rpm
MCA 5-8   86
MFSL 15-25   85
REPRISE 5-8   90
WARNER 5-8   82-85
Also see DOOBIE BROTHERS
Also see HOLLAND, Amy
Also see LABELLE, Patti, and Michael McDonald
Also see MEMPHIS HORNS
Also see PACK, David
Also see STEELY DAN
Also see WOOD, Lauren

McDONALD, Michael, and James Ingram
Singles: 7–inch
QWEST 2-4   83
Also see INGRAM, James
Also see McDONALD, Michael

McDOWELL, Carrie
Singles: 7–inch
MOTOWN 2-4   87

McDOWELL, Ronnie
Singles: 7–inch
EPIC 2-5   79-85
GRT 3-5   77
MCA/CURB 2-4   86
SCORPION (Except 0533) 3-5   77-79
SCORPION (0533 "Only the
  Lonely") 4-8   77
LPs: 10/12–inch 33rpm
DICK CLARK 8-10   79
EPIC 5-10   79-85
MCA/CURB 5-8   86
SCORPION 10-12   77-79
STRAWBERRY 8-10

McDUFF, Brother Jack
Singles: 7–inch
CADET 3-6   68
BLUE NOTE 3-6   69
LPs: 10/12–inch 33rpm
BLUE NOTE 8-12   69
PRESTIGE (7000 series) 25-50   60-64
(Yellow label.)
PRESTIGE (7000 series) 15-25   64-65
(Blue label.)
Also see BENSON, George

McDUFF, Brother Jack, and Gene Ammons
LPs: 10/12–inch 33rpm
PRESTIGE 30-50   61
(Yellow label.)
Also see AMMONS, Gene

McDUFF, Brother Jack, and Willis Jackson
LPs: 10/12–inch 33rpm
PRESTIGE 15-25   66
Also see JACKSON, Willis
Also see McDUFF, Brother Jack

McENTIRE, Reba
Singles: 7–inch
MCA 2-4   84-90

MERCURY	2-5	76-83

LPs: 10/12–inch 33rpm

MCA	5-8	84-90
MERCURY (Except 1177)	8-18	79-83
MERCURY (1177 "Reba McEntire")	30-40	77

McFADDEN, Bob
(Bob McFadden and Dor)
Singles: 7–inch

BRUNSWICK	8-10	59
CORAL	8-10	60

Picture Sleeves

BRUNSWICK	15-25	59

LPs: 10/12–inch 33rpm

BRUNSWICK (54056 "Songs Our Mummy Taught Us")	75-125	59
(Monaural.)		
BRUNSWICK (7-54056 "Songs Our Mummy Taught Us")	100-150	59
(Stereo.)		

Also see McKUEN, Rod

McFADDEN & WHITEHEAD
Singles: 12–inch 33/45rpm

PHILADELPHIA INT'L	4-8	79
SUTRA	4-6	

Singles: 7–inch

CAPITOL	2-4	82-83
PHILADELPHIA INT'L	3-5	79
SUTRA	2-4	
TSOP	2-4	80

LPs: 10/12–inch 33rpm

CAPITOL	5-8	83
PHILADELPHIA INT'L	5-8	79
TSOP	5-8	80

Members: Gene McFadden; John Whitehead.

McFARLAND, Gary
LPs: 10/12–inch 33rpm

SKYE	8-12	69

McFERRIN, Bobby
Singles: 7–inch

EMI	2-4	88-90

LPs: 10/12–inch 33rpm

BLUE NOTE	5-10	87
EMI	5-8	88-90

McGEE, Parker
Singles: 7–inch

BIG TREE	3-5	77

LPs: 10/12–inch 33rpm

BIG TREE	5-10	76

McGHEE, Brownie
(Brownie McGhee and His Jook Block Busters; Brownie McGhee and His Sugar Men)
Singles: 78rpm

ALERT	10-15	46-47
DERBY	8-12	52
DISC	8-12	47
DOT	8-12	53
ENCORE	8-12	53

HARLEM	10-20	52
LONDON	8-12	51
PAR	8-12	52
RED ROBIN	8-12	52-53
SAVOY	8-12	50-57
SAVOY (5000 series)	10-15	44-48
SITTIN' in WITH	5-10	48

Singles: 7–inch

DOT (1184 "Cheatin' and Lying")	20-30	53
HARLEM (2323 "Christina")	30-40	52
HARLEM (2329 "Bluebird")	30-40	52
JACKSON (2304 "Mean Old Frisco")	100-125	52
(Colored vinyl.)		
JAX (304 "I Feel So Good")	75-100	52
(Colored vinyl.)		
JAX (307 "Meet You in the Morning")	75-100	52
(Colored vinyl.)		
JAX (310 "Stranger's Blues")	75-100	52
(Colored vinyl.)		
JAX (312 "I'm 10,000 Years Old")	75-100	52
(Colored vinyl.)		
JAX (322 "New Bad Blood")	75-100	52
(Colored vinyl.)		
RED ROBIN (111 "Don't Dog Your Woman")	100-200	53
SAVOY (800 series)	15-25	51-52
SAVOY (1100 through 1500 series)	8-18	55-59

LPs: 10/12–inch 33rpm

FOLKWAYS (Except 20, 30 and 2000 series)	8-10	
FOLKWAYS (20, 30 and 2000 series)	20-40	54-55
STORYVILLE	5-8	
VANGUARD	8-10	

Though sometimes not credited, many of the above feature Sonny Terry on harmonica.
Also see DUPREE, Champion Jack

McGHEE, Brownie, and Sonny Terry
Singles: 78rpm

SAVOY (5000 series)	10-15	44-48

Singles: 7–inch

PRESTIGE BLUESVILLE	4-8	60-62

LPs: 10/12–inch 33rpm

A&M	8-10	73
BLUESWAY	10-12	69-73
EVEREST	10-12	69
FANTASY (3000 series)	15-25	61-62
(Black vinyl.)		
FANTASY (3000 series)	25-50	61-62
(Colored vinyl.)		
FANTASY (8000 series)	15-20	62
(Black vinyl.)		
FANTASY (8000 series)	25-40	62
(Colored vinyl.)		
FANTASY (24000 series)	8-10	72-81
FOLKWAYS (2000 and 3000 series)	20-30	55-61
FOLKWAYS (31000 series)	8-10	
FONTANA	10-15	69

MAINSTREAM (6000 series) 15-20   65
MAINSTREAM (300 series) 8-10   71
MUSE 5-8   81
OLYMPIC 8-10   73
PRESTIGE (1000 series) 25-30   60
PRESTIGE (7000 series) 8-10   69-70
PRESTIGE BLUESVILLE 20-25   60-62
PRESTIGE FOLKLORE 12-15
ROULETTE 25-35   59
SAVOY (1100 series) 5-8   84
SAVOY (12000 series) 8-10   73
SAVOY (14000 series) 25-30   58
SHARP (2003 "Down Home Blues") . 25-50   59
SMASH 15-20   65
VERVE 20-25   61
VERVE/FOLKWAYS 15-20   65
WORLD PACIFIC 25-30   60
    Also see HOPKINS, Lightnin' / Brownie McGhee & Sonny Terry
    Also see McGHEE, Brownie
    Also see TERRY, Sonny

McGHEE, Stick
(Stick McGhee and His Buddies; Stick McGhee and
the Ramblers; Sticks McGhee)
Singles: 78rpm
ATLANTIC 10-20   49-52
DECCA (48104 "Drinkin' Wine
    Spo-Dee-O-Dee") 15-25   47
ESSEX 8-12   52
HARLEM (1018 "Blues Mixture") 15-25   47
KING 8-12   53-55
LONDON 25-50   51
SAVOY 8-12   55
Singles: 7-inch
ATLANTIC (955 "Wee Wee Hours") .. 50-75   52
ATLANTIC (991 "New Found Love") . 40-60   52
GUSTO 2-4
HERALD 5-10   60
KING (4610 "Little Things We
    Used To Do") 25-40   53
KING (4628 "Blues in My Heart") ... 25-40   53
KING (4672 "Dealin' from the Bottom) 24-40   53
KING (4700 "I'm Doin' All the Time") . 25-40   53
KING (4783 "Double Crossin' Liquor") 25-40   55
KING (4800 "Get Your Mind
    Out of the Gutter") 25-40   55
LONDON (978 "You Gotta Have Something
    on the Ball") 100-150   51
SAVOY 15-25   55

McGHEE, Sticks / John Lee Hooker
LPs: 10/12-inch 33rpm
AUDIO LAB (1520 "Highway of
    Blues") 100-125   59
    Also see DUPREE, Champion Jack
    Also see HOOKER, John Lee
    Also see McGHEE, Stick

McGILPIN, Bob
Singles: 7-inch
BUTTERFLY 3-5   77-78

LPs: 10/12-inch 33rpm
BUTTERFLY (Black vinyl) 5-10   78-79
BUTTERFLY (Colored vinyl) 12-18   78
CASABLANCA 5-8   80

McGOVERN, Maureen
Singles: 7-inch
CASABLANCA 3-5
EPIC 3-5   78
MAIDEN VOYAGE 3-5
20TH FOX 3-5   73-75
WARNER 3-5   79-80
WOODEN NICKEL 3-5   73
LPs: 10/12-inch 33rpm
20TH FOX 8-12   73-75
WARNER 5-10   79

McGRIFF, Edna
Singles: 78rpm
JUBILEE 10-15   51-53
Singles: 7-inch
CAPITOL 4-8   64-65
JUBILEE (5062 "Note Droppin' Papa") 20-30   51
JUBILEE (5073 "Heavenly Father") .. 20-30   52
JUBILEE (5087 "It's Raining") 20-30   52
JUBILEE (5089 "In a Chapel by the
    Side of the Road") 20-30   52
JUBILEE (5099 "Good") 20-30   52
JUBILEE (5109 "Edna's Blues") 20-30   53
    (Black vinyl.)
JUBILEE (5109 "Edna's Blues") 50-75   53
    (Colored vinyl.)
WILLOW 5-10   61

McGRIFF, Edna, and Sonny Til
Singles: 78rpm
JUBILEE (5090 "Once in a While") .. 10-15   52
Singles: 7-inch
JUBILEE (5090 "Once in a While") .. 20-30   52
    Also see McGRIFF, Edna
    Also see TIL, Sonny

McGRIFF, Jimmy
(Jimmy McGriff Trio)
Singles: 7-inch
BLUE NOTE 3-5   71
CAPITOL 3-5   70-71
COLLECTABLES 2-4
GROOVE MERCHANT 3-5   75
JELL (100 series) 5-10   62
JELL (500 series) 4-8   65
MILESTONE 2-4   83
SOLID STATE 4-6   66-70
SUE 4-8   62-64
U.A. 3-5   71-78

LPs: 10/12-inch 33rpm
BLUE NOTE 8-12   70-71
COLLECTABLES 6-8   88
51 WEST 5-8
GROOVE MERCHANT 8-12   71-76
LRC 8-10   77-78

MILESTONE	5-8	81-83
SOLID STATE	10-15	66-70
SOUL SUGAR	10-12	70
SUE	20-30	62-65
U.A.	8-12	71
VEEP	10-15	68

Also see HOLMES, Richard "Groove"
Also see PARKER, Little Junior, and Jimmy McGriff

McGUFFEY LANE
Singles: 7-inch
ATCO	2-4	81-82

LPs: 10/12-inch 33rpm
ATCO	5-10	82

McGUINN, Roger
Singles: 7-inch
COLUMBIA	3-5	73-77

LPs: 10/12-inch 33rpm
ARISTA	5-8	90
COLUMBIA	8-10	77

Also see MITCHELL, Chad, Trio

McGUINN and HILLMAN
LPs: 10/12-inch 33rpm
CAPITOL	5-8	80

Members: Roger McGuinn; Chris Hillman.
Also see HILLMAN, Chris
Also see McGUINN, Roger

McGUINN, CLARK & HILLMAN
Singles: 7-inch
CAPITOL	3-5	79

LPs: 10/12-inch 33rpm
CAPITOL	5-8	79-82

Members: Roger McGuinn; Gene Clark; Chris Hillman.
Also see BYRDS
Also see McGUINN & HILLMAN

McGUINNESS - FLINT
Singles: 7-inch
CAPITOL	3-5	70-71

LPs: 10/12-inch 33rpm
CAPITOL	10-12	70-71

Members: Tom McGuinness; Hughie Flint.
Also see MANN, Manfred

McGUIRE, Barry
(Barry McGuire and the Horizon Singers)
Singles: 7-inch
ABC	3-5	70
DUNHILL	4-8	65-66
HORIZON	4-8	63
ODE '70	3-5	70
MCA	3-5	
MOSAIC	4-8	61-62
MYRRH	3-5	73
ROULETTE	3-5	

Picture Sleeves
DUNHILL	5-10	65

LPs: 10/12-inch 33rpm
BIRDWING	5-8	80
DUNHILL	20-30	65
HORIZON	15-25	63

MYRRH	5-8	73-75
ODE '70	8-10	70
SPARROW	5-8	79
SURREY	12-15	65

Also see MAMAS and the Papas
Also see NEW CHRISTY MINSTRELS

McGUIRE, Barry, and Barry Kane
Singles: 7-inch
HORIZON	4-8	62

LPs: 10/12-inch 33rpm
HORIZON	15-25	62
SURREY	12-18	66

McGUIRE, Phyllis
Singles: 7-inch
REPRISE	4-6	64-65
ORPHEUM	4-6	68

LPs: 10/12-inch 33rpm
ABC-PAR	10-20	66

Also see McGUIRE SISTERS

McGUIRE SISTERS
Singles: 78rpm
CORAL	4-8	54-58

Singles: 7-inch
ABC-PAR	4-6	66
CORAL (Except 61000 series)	4-8	58-65
CORAL (61000 series)	5-10	54-58
MCA	2-4	
REPRISE	4-6	63-65

Picture Sleeves
CORAL	5-15	56-61

EPs: 7-inch 33/45rpm
CORAL	5-15	55-60

LPs: 10/12-inch 33rpm
ABC-PAR	10-20	66
CORAL (6 "Best of the McGuire Sisters")	15-25	65
CORAL (56123 "By Request")	25-50	55
CORAL (57000 series)	15-25	56-65
MCA	5-8	78
VOCALION	10-20	60-67

Members: Phyllis McGuire; Dorothy McGuire; Christine McGuire.
Also see McGUIRE, Phyllis

McIAN, Peter
Singles: 7-inch
COLUMBIA/ARC	3-5	80

LPs: 10/12-inch 33rpm
COLUMBIA/ARC	5-8	80

McKEE, Lonett
Singles: 7-inch
SUSSEX	3-5	74

McKENDREE SPRING
Singles: 7-inch
DECCA	3-6	69-72
MCA	3-5	73
PYE	3-5	76

LPs: 10/12-inch 33rpm
DECCA	10-15	69-72

MCA 8-10   73
PYE 8-10   75-76

McKENZIE, Bob and Doug
Singles: 7–inch
MERCURY 3-5   82
LPs: 10/12–inch 33rpm
MERCURY 5-10   81

McKENZIE, Scott
(McKenzie's Musicians)
Singles: 7–inch
CAPITOL 4-8   65-67
EPIC 3-6   67-72
ODE 4-8   67-71
LPs: 10/12–inch 33rpm
ODE (44000 series) 15-25   67
ODE (34000 series) 8-10   77
ODE (77000 series) 10-15   70

McKUEN, Rod
(Rod McKuen and the Keytones; Rod McKuen and the Horizon Singers)
Singles: 7–inch
A&M 4-8   63
BUDDAH 3-5   73-74
DECCA 5-10   59
HORIZON 4-8   63
JUBILEE 4-8   62
KAPP 4-8   61
LIBERTY 8-12   56
RCA 4-8   66-67
SPIRAL 4-8   61-62
VISTA 3-5   71
WARNER 3-6   68-72
Picture Sleeves
VISTA 3-5   71
WARNER 3-5   71
LPs: 10/12–inch 33rpm
DECCA (4900 series) 10-15   68
DECCA (8800 series) 20-30   59
DECCA (75000 series) 10-12   69
CAPITOL 15-20   64
HARMONY 8-10   71
HI FI 20-30   58-59
EPIC (600 and 3800 series) 15-20   62
EPIC (26000 series) 10-12   68
EVEREST 10-12   68
HORIZON 15-25   63
IN 15-20   64
JUBILEE 20-25   62
KAPP (1200 and 3200 series) 15-25   61
KAPP (1500 and 3500 series) 10-20   67
LIBERTY (Except 3011) 10-15   67
LIBERTY (3011 "Songs for a
  Lazy Afternoon") 25-40   56
RCA 10-20   65-69
STANYAN 10-15   66-72
SUNSET 8-10   70
TRADITION 10-12   68
VISTA 8-10   71

WARNER 8-15   67-76
Also see McFADDEN, Bob
Also see SAN SEBASTIAN STRINGS

McLAGAN, Ian
Singles: 7–inch
MERCURY 3-5   79
LPs: 10/12–inch 33rpm
MERCURY 5-10   79
Also see FACES
Also see SMALL FACES

McLAIN, Tommy
Singles: 7–inch
COLLECTABLES 2-4
JIN (Except 197) 4-8   66-69
JIN (197 "Sweet Dreams") 5-10   66
MSL 4-8   66

McLANE, Jimmy
Singles: 7–inch
SWAY 4-8   61

McLAREN, Malcom
(Malcom McLaren and the World's Famous Supreme Band)
Singles: 12–inch 33/45rpm
ISLAND 4-6   83-85
Singles: 7–inch
ISLAND 2-4   83-85
LPs: 10/12–inch 33rpm
ISLAND 5-8   83-85

McLAUGHLIN, John
LPs: 10/12–inch 33rpm
COLUMBIA 5-10   72-83
DOUGLAS 8-12   72
POLYDOR 8-15   69-72
WARNER 5-8   81

McLAUGHLIN, Pat
LPs: 10/12–inch 33rpm
CAPITOL 5-8   88

McLAURIN, Bette
(Bette McLaurin and the Four Fellows; Bette McLaurin and the Striders; Betty McLaurin)
Singles: 78rpm
CENTRAL 5-10   54
CORAL 5-10   53
DERBY (700 series) 5-10   50-52
DERBY (804 "My Heart Belongs
  to Only You") 10-20   52
GLORY 10-15   55
JUBILEE 5-10   55
Singles: 7–inch
CAPITOL 5-10   59
CENTRAL 10-15   54
CORAL 10-15   53
DERBY (700 series) 10-20   50-52
DERBY (804 "My Heart Belongs
  to Only You") 50-75   52
GLORY (233 "Grow Old Along
  with Me") 15-25   55

GLORY (237 "Just Come a
Little Bit Closer") .... 15-25　　55
GLORY (241 "I'm Past Sixteen") .... 15-25　　55
JUBILEE .... 10-20　　55
O GEE .... 5-10　　59
PULSE .... 4-8　　65

McLEAN, Don
Singles: 7-inch
ARISTA .... 3-5　　78
LIBERTY 3-5
MILLENNIUM .... 3-5　　81-83
RCA .... 2-4　　83
U.A. .... 3-5　　71-75
Picture Sleeves
U.A. .... 3-5　　71-73
LPs: 10/12-inch 33rpm
CASABLANCA .... 8-10　　79
LIBERTY .... 5-8　　82-83
MILLENNIUM .... 5-8　　81
U.A. .... 10-12　　71-74
Promotional LPs
RCA ("Special Radio Series") .... 10-15　　81

McLEAN, Penny
Singles: 7-inch
ATCO .... 3-5　　75-76
Also see SILVER CONVENTION

McLEAN, Phil
Singles: 7-inch
VERSATILE .... 4-8　　61-62

McLOLLIE, Oscar
(Oscar McLollie and the Honey Jumpers; Oscar Lollie)
Singles: 78rpm
CLASS .... 5-10　　57
MERCURY .... 5-10　　51-56
MODERN .... 10-20　　52-55
WING .... 10-15　　56
Singles: 7-inch
CLASS .... 5-10　　57-59
MERCURY (70000 series) .... 10-15　　56
MODERN (902 "Honey Jump") ..... 30-40　　52
MODERN (915 "Be Cool, My Heart") . 25-35　　52
MODERN (920 "Falling in
Love with You") .... 25-35　　54
MODERN (928 "Mama Don't Like") .. 20-30　　54
MODERN (932 "Hot Banana") ...... 20-30　　54
MODERN (940 "Love Me Tonight") .. 20-30　　54
MODERN (943 "Dig That Crazy
Santa Claus") .... 20-30　　54
MODERN (950 "Hey Lolly Lolly") .... 20-30　　55
MODERN (955 "Eternal Love") ..... 20-30　　55
MODERN (970 "Convicted") .... 20-30　　55
WING .... 10-15　　56
LPs: 10/12-inch 33rpm
CROWN (5016 "Oscar McLollie and His
Honey Jumpers") .... 150-200　　56

McLOLLIE, Oscar, and Jeanette Baker
Singles: 7-inch
CLASS .... 5-10　　58

McLOLLIE, Oscar, and Nancy Lamarr
Singles: 7-inch
SAHARA .... 4-8　　63
Also see McLOLLIE, Oscar

McLYTE
LPs: 10/12-inch 33rpm
FIRST PRIORITY .... 5-8　　89

McMAHON, Gerard
Singles: 7-inch
FULL MOON .... 2-4　　83
LPs: 10/12-inch 33rpm
FULL MOON .... 5-8　　83

McNALLY, Larry John
Singles: 7-inch
ARC .... 2-4　　81

McNAMARA, Robin
Singles: 7-inch
STEED .... 3-5　　69-71
LPs: 10/12-inch 33rpm
STEED .... 10-15　　70

McNEELY, Big Jay
**(Big Jay McNeely and His Blue Jays; Big Jay McNeely
with Little Sonny Warner)**
Singles: 78rpm
ALADDIN .... 10-20　　49
BAYOU .... 15-25　　53
FEDERAL .... 10-15　　52-54
EXCLUSIVE .... 10-20　　46
IMPERIAL .... 10-20　　51-52
SAVOY .... 10-15　　48-49
VEE JAY .... 10-15　　55
Singles: 7-inch
BAYOU (014 "Hometown Jamboree") 40-60　　53
BAYOU (018 "Catastrophe") ...... 40-60　　53
FEDERAL (12102 "The Goof") ..... 20-30　　52
FEDERAL (12111 "Earthquake") .... 20-30　　52
FEDERAL (12141 "Nervous, Man
Nervous") .... 20-30　　53
FEDERAL (12151 "3-D") .... 20-30　　53
FEDERAL (12168 "Mule Walk") ..... 20-30　　54
FEDERAL (12179 "Hot Cinders") ... 20-30　　54
FEDERAL (12186 "Let's Work") ..... 20-30　　54
FEDERAL (12191 "Beachcomber") .. 20-30　　54
IMPERIAL (5219 "Deacon's Express") 25-35　　53
SWINGIN' .... 5-10　　59-61
VEE JAY (142 "Big Jay's Hop") .... 25-35　　55
WARNER .... 4-8　　63
EPs: 7-inch 33/45rpm
FEDERAL (246 "Go! Go! Go!
with Big Jay McNeely") .... 100-200　　53
FEDERAL (301 Big Jay
McNeely, Vol. 2") .... 100-150　　54

FEDERAL (332 Wild Man of
the Saxophone") 100-150   54
FEDERAL (373 Just Crazy") 75-100   55
LPs: 10/12-inch 33rpm
COLLECTABLES 5-8   88
FEDERAL (96 "Big Jay McNeely") . 600-800   54
(10-inch LP.)
FEDERAL (530 "Big Jay In 3-D") .. 250-350   57
KING (650 "Big Jay in 3-D") 50-75   59
SAVOY (15045 "Rhythm and Blues
Concert") 250-350   55
(10-inch LP.)
WARNER (W-1523 "Big Jay McNeely")25-35   63
(Monaural.)
WARNER (WS-1523 "Big Jay
McNeely") 30-40   63
(Stereo.)
Also see OTIS, Johnny

McNEELY, Big Jay / Paul Williams
Singles: 78rpm
SAVOY 10-15   49-55
Singles: 7-inch
SAVOY (1100 series) 10-20   55
Also see McNEELY, Big Jay
Also see WILLIAMS, Paul

McNEIR, Ronnie
Singles: 7-inch
CAPITOL 2-4   84
PRODIGAL 3-5   75
LPs: 10/12-inch 33rpm
CAPITOL 5-8   84

McNICHOL, Kristy and Jimmy
Singles: 7-inch
RCA 3-5   78
Picture Sleeves
RCA 3-5   78
LPs: 10/12-inch 33rpm
RCA 5-10   78

M'COOL, Shamus
Singles: 7-inch
PERSPECTIVE 2-4   81

McPHATTER, Clyde
Singles: 78rpm
ATLANTIC 10-15   56-57
Singles: 7-inch
AMY 4-8   65-67
ATLANTIC (1000 series) 10-20   56-58
ATLANTIC (2000 series) 8-12   58-60
DECCA 4-6   70
DERAM 4-8   68-69
MGM 5-10   59-60
MERCURY 5-10   60-65
Picture Sleeves
MGM 10-15   60
MERCURY 5-10   60-65
EPs: 7-inch 33/45rpm
ATLANTIC (584 "Clyde McPhatter") .. 50-75   58

ATLANTIC (605 "Rock with
Clyde McPhatter") 50-75   58
ATLANTIC (618 "Clyde McPhatter") . 50-75   59
LPs: 10/12-inch 33rpm
ALLEGIANCE 5-8
ATLANTIC (8024 "Love Ballads") . 100-150   59
(Black label.)
ATLANTIC (8024 "Love Ballads") ... 25-50   59
(Red label.)
ATLANTIC (8031 "Clyde") 50-100   59
ATLANTIC (8077 "Best of
Clyde McPhatter") 25-35   63
DECCA 15-25   70
MGM (E-3775 "Let's Start
Over Again") 30-40   59
(Monaural.)
MGM (SE-3775 "Let's Start
Over Again") 40-50   59
(Stereo.)
MGM (E-3866 "Greatest Hits") 30-40   60
(Monaural.)
MGM (SE-3866 "Greatest Hits") 40-50   60
(Stereo.)
MERCURY 20-35   60-64
WING 20-30   62
Also see DOMINOES
Also see DRIFTERS
Also see KING CURTIS
Also see LITTLE ESTHER and Clyde McPhatter

McPHATTER, Clyde / Little Richard / Jerry Butler
LPs: 10/12-inch 33rpm
PICKWICK (3233 "Rhythm and Blues
and Greens") 15-20
Also see BUTLER, Jerry
Also see LITTLE RICHARD
Also see McPHATTER, Clyde

McPHERSON, Wyatt "Earp"
Singles: 7-inch
SAVOY 4-8   61

McPHERSON, Wyatt "Earp," and Paul Williams
Singles: 7-inch
BATTLE 4-8   63
Also see McPHERSON, Wyatt "Earp"
Also see WILLIAMS, Paul

McRAE, Carmen
Singles: 78rpm
DECCA 3-6   55-57
VENUS 4-8   54
Singles: 7-inch
COLUMBIA 4-6   62
DECCA 5-10   55-57
VENUS 5-10   54
Picture Sleeves
COLUMBIA 4-8   62

LPs: 10/12–inch 33rpm

BETHLEHEM (1023 "Carmen
McRae") 75-125   54
(10–inch LP.)
COLUMBIA 15-25   61-65
DECCA (8100 through 8800 series) .. 40-60   55-58
(Black and silver label.)
DECCA (8100 through 8800 series) .. 15-25   64
(Black label with horizonal rainbow stripe.)
FOCUS 15-25   65
KAPP 20-40   58-59
MAINSTREAM 10-20   65-67
TIME 15-25   63
　Also see DAVIS, Sammy, Jr., and Carmen McRae
　Also see SIMONE, Nina, Chris Connor and Carmen McRae

McSHANN, Jay
(Jay McShann and His Orchestra; Jay McShann and
His Combo; Jay McShann and his Trio; Jay McShann
Quartet; Jay McShann's Kansas City Stompers; Jay
McShann and His Jazz Men; Jay McShann's Sextet)
Singles: 78rpm

ALADDIN 5-10   50
CAPITOL 10-15   44-45
DECCA 10-15   41-43
DOWN BEAT 5-10   48-49
MERCURY 5-10   45-46
MODERN 5-10   50
PHILO/ALADDIN 10-15   45
PREMIER 8-12   45
SWING TIME 5-10   48-50
VEE JAY 4-8   55-56

Singles: 7–inch

VEE JAY 5-15   55-56

EPs: 7–inch 33/45rpm

DECCA (742 "Kansas City
Memories") 30-45   54

LPs: 10/12–inch 33rpm

CAPITOL 12-18   67
DECCA (5503 "Kansas City
Memories") 125-175   54
(10–inch LP. With Charlie Parker, Al Hibbler, Walter
Brown, and Paul Paul Quinichette.)
DECCA (9000 series) 10-15   68
　Also see HIBBLER, Al
　Also see WITHERSPOON, Jimmy

McSHANN, Jay, With Johnny Moore's Three
Blazers
Singles: 78rpm

MODERN 8-12   50
　Also see MOORE, Johnny

McSHANN, Jay, and Priscilla Bowman
Singles: 78rpm

VEE JAY 5-10   55

Singles: 7–inch

VEE JAY 10-15   55
　Also see McSHANN, Jay

McSHY D
LPs: 10/12–inch 33rpm
LUKE SKYWALKER 5-8   87

McVIE, Christine
Singles: 7–inch
WARNER 2-4   84
LPs: 10/12–inch 33rpm
SIRE 8-10   76
WARNER 5-8   84
　Also see FLEETWOOD MAC
　Also see PERFECT, Christine
　Also see NEWMAN, Randy

McWILLIAMS, Paulette
Singles: 7–inch
FANTASY 3-5   77

MEAD, Sister Janet
Singles: 7–inch
A&M 3-5   74

MEADER, Vaughn
LPs: 10/12–inch 33rpm
CADENCE 10-20   62-63
KAMA-SUTRA 8-15

MEADOWS BROTHERS
Singles: 7–inch
KAYVETTE 2-4   87

MEAGAN
Singles: 7–inch
NEXT PLATINUM 4-6   84

MEAN MACHINE
Singles: 7–inch
SUGAR HILL 2-4   81

MEAT LOAF
(Marvin Lee Aday)
Singles: 7–inch
EPIC 2-5   77-83
RSO 3-5   74
LPs: 10/12–inch 33rpm
CLEVELAND INT'L 5-8   81-83
EPIC (30000 series, except 34974) .. 5-10   77-80
EPIC (34974 "Bat Out of Hell") 5-10   77
EPIC (34974 "Bat Out of Hell") 15-20   77
(Picture disc. With bats on front cover.)
EPIC (34974 "Bat Out of Hell") 25-30   77
(Picture disc. Without bats on front cover.
Promotional issue only.)
EPIC (40000 series) 12-15   80
(Half-speed mastered.)
　Also see FOLEY, Ellen
　Also see STONEY and Meat Loaf

MEAT PUPPETS
LPs: 10/12–inch 33rpm
SST 5-8   81-87
　Members: Curt Kirkwood; Cris Kirkwood; Derrick Bostrom.

MECO
(Meco Monardo)
Singles: 12–inch 33/45rpm
ARISTA 4-6   83
Singles: 7–inch
ARISTA 2-4   82-83
MILLENNIUM 3-5   77-78
RSO 3-5   80
LPs: 10/12–inch 33rpm
ARISTA 5-8   82-84
MILLENNIUM 5-10   77-78
RSO 5-8   80

MEDEIROS, Glenn
Singles: 7–inch
AMHERST 2-4   87
LPs: 10/12–inch 33rpm
AMHERST 5-8   87
MCA 5-8   90

MEDLEY, Bill
Singles: 7–inch
A&M 3-5   71-73
LIBERTY 3-5   81
MGM 4-8   68
PARAMOUNT 3-5   71
PLANET 2-4   82-83
RCA 2-4   83-85
REPRISE 4-8   65
U.A. 3-5   78-80
VERVE 4-8   67
LPs: 10/12–inch 33rpm
A&M 8-12   71-73
LIBERTY 5-10   81
MGM 10-20 68-70
PLANET 8-10   82
RCA 5-8   83-85
U.A. 8-10   78-80
Also see RIGHTEOUS BROTHERS

MEDLEY, Bill, and Jennifer Warnes
Singles: 7–inch
RCA 2-4   87
Also see MEDLEY, Bill
Also see WARNES, Jennifer

MEDLIN, Joe
Singles: 7–inch
BRUNSWICK 4-8   61
MERCURY 4-8   59-60

MEGADETH
LPs: 10/12–inch 33rpm
CAPITOL 5-8   86-90
Members: Dave Mustaine; Dave Ellefson; Gar Samuelson.

MEGATONS
Singles: 7–inch
CHECKER 5-10   62
DODGE 10-15   62
FOREST 4-8   63
JELL 4-8   62

MEGATRONS
Singles: 7–inch
ACOUSTICON 5-10   59
AUDICON 5-10   59-61

MEISNER, Randy
Singles: 7–inch
ASYLUM 3-5   78
EPIC 3-5   80-82
LPs: 10/12–inch 33rpm
ASYLUM 8-10   78
EPIC 5-10   80-82
Also see EAGLES
Also see NELSON, Rick
Also see POCO

MEL & KIM
Singles: 7–inch
ATLANTIC 2-4   87

MEL & TIM
Singles: 7–inch
BAMBOO 4-6   69-70
COLLECTABLES 2-4
ERIC 2-4
STAX 3-5   72-74
LPs: 10/12–inch 33rpm
BAMBOO 10-15   70
STAX 8-12   72-74
Members: Mel Harden; Tim McPherson.

MELACHRINO, George, and His Orchestra
Singles: 78rpm
RCA 3-5   50-57
Singles: 7–inch
RCA 4-8   50-59
EPs: 7–inch 33/45rpm
RCA 5-10   50-59
LPs: 10/12–inch 33rpm
RCA 10-20 50-61

MELANIE
(Melanie and the Edwin Hawkins Singers)
Singles: 7–inch
ABC 3-5   75
ATLANTIC 3-5   77
BUDDAH 3-6   69-73
CASABLANCA 3-5   74
COLUMBIA 4-8   67-68
ERIC 2-4   78
MCA 2-4
MIDSONG INT'L 3-5   78
NEIGHBORHOOD 3-5   71-75
PORTRAIT 2-4   81
STORK 5-10   70
(Promotional issue only.)
TOMATO 3-5   78-79
Picture Sleeves
BUDDAH 2-4   70-74
NEIGHBORHOOD 2-4   72-73

EPs: 7–inch 33/45rpm

BUDDAH 5-8   70
(Jukebox issue.)

LPs: 10/12–inch 33rpm

ABC 8-10	75	
ACCORD 5-8	81-82	
ATLANTIC 8-10	76	
BLANCHE 5-8	82	
BUDDAH 10-15	69-77	
51 WEST 5-8	79	
MCA/MIDSONG 5-10	77-78	
NEIGHBORHOOD 8-10	71-75	
PICKWICK 8-10	71	
TOMATO 5-10	79	

Also see HAWKINS, Edwin, Singers

MELLAA

Singles: 7–inch

LARC 2-4   83

MELLE MEL and Duke Bootee
Singles: 12–inch 33/45rpm

SUGAR HILL 4-6   82
Also see GRANDMASTER FLASH and the Furious Five

MELLENCAMP, John Cougar
(John Cougar; John Mellencamp)
Singles: 7–inch

MERCURY 2-4	87-90	
RIVA (Except 211) 2-5	79-85	
RIVA (211 "Hand to Hold on To") 2-4	82	
RIVA (211 "Hand to Hold on To") 10-15	82	
(Picture disc.)		

Picture Sleeves

RIVA 2-4   82-85

LPs: 10/12–inch 33rpm

MAIN MAN (601 "Kid Inside") 5-8   83
MAIN MAN (4001 "Kid Inside") 40-60   83
(Picture disc.)
MERCURY (Except 349) 5-8   87-90
MERCURY (349 "Let It All Hang") ... 25-35   87
(Interview LP. Promotional issue only.)
RIVA 5-10   79-85

MELLO-KINGS
(Mellokings; Mellotones)
Singles: 78rpm

HERALD (502 "Tonite Tonite") 15-25   57
(Shows the group as "The Mellotones".)
HERALD (502 "Tonite Tonite") 5-10   57
(Shows the group as "The Mello-Kings.")

Singles: 7–inch

COLLECTABLES 2-4
FLASHBACK 2-4   65
HERALD (502 "Tonite Tonite") 150-200   57
((Shows the group as "The Mellotones.")
HERALD (502 "Tonite Tonite") 15-25   57
((Shows the group as "The Mello-Kings." Has logo
in script print inside the flag.)

HERALD (502 "Tonite Tonite") 8-12
((Shows the group as "The Mello-Kings." Has logo
in block print inside the flag.)
HERALD (507 through 567) 10-20   57-61
LESCAY 10-15   62

EPs: 7–inch 33/45rpm

HERALD (451 "The Fabulous
Mello-Kings") 200-250   60

LPs: 10/12–inch 33rpm

COLLECTABLES 6-8   84
HERALD (1013 "Tonight Tonight") . 200-300   60
Members: Larry Esposita; Bob Scholl; Jerry Scholl; Eddie Quinn;
Neil Areana.

MELLO-MOODS
(Mellow Moods; Mellomoods; With the Schubert
Swanson Trio)
Singles: 78rpm

PRESTIGE (799 "Call on Me") 75-150   53
PRESTIGE (856 "I'm Lost") 75-150   53
ROBIN (104 "I Couldn't Sleep
a Wink Last Night") 200-300   52
ROBIN (105 "Where Are You") ... 150-200   52

Singles: 7–inch

HAMILTON (143 "I'm Lost") 8-10
PRESTIGE (799 "Call on Me") 500-600   53
PRESTIGE (856 "I'm Lost") 500-600   53
ROBIN (104 "I Couldn't Sleep a
Wink Last Night") 600-800   52
ROBIN (105 "Where Are You") ... 600-800   52
Members: Ray "Buddy" Wooten; Bobby Williams; Monte Owens;
Bobby Baylor; Jimmy Bethea.

MELLO-TONES
Singles: 78rpm

FASCINATION ("Rosie Lee") 25-40   57
GEE 8-12   57

Singles: 7–inch

FASCINATION ("Rosie Lee") 100-125   57
GEE 10-20   57

MELODIANS
Singles: 12–inch 33/45rpm

REAL AUTHENTIC SOUND 4-6   84

LPs: 10/12–inch 33rpm

REAL AUTHENTIC SOUND 5-8   84

MEL-O-DOTS
Singles: 78rpm

APOLLO (1192 "One More Time") .. 50-100   52

Singles: 7–inch

APOLLO (1192 "One More Time") 750-1000   52

MELVIN, Harold
(Harold Melvin and the Bluenotes)
Singles: 12–inch 33/45rpm

PHILADELPHIA INT'L 4-8   80
SOURCE 4-8   79-80

Singles: 7–inch

ABC 3-5   77-78
ARCTIC 5-8   67
LANDA 5-10   64-65

MCA 3-5   81
PHILADELPHIA INT'L 3-5   72-79
PHILLY WORLD 2-4   84-85
SOURCE 3-5   79-80
Picture Sleeves
PHILADELPHIA INT'L 3-5   72-75
LPs: 10/12–inch 33rpm
ABC 8-10   77
MCA 5-8   81
PHILADELPHIA INT'L 8-12   72-76
PHILLY WORLD 5-8   84-85
SOURCE 5-10   80
   Also see BLUE NOTES
   Also see PAIGE, Sharon
   Also see PENDERGRASS, Teddy

MEMPHIS HORNS
Singles: 7–inch
RCA 3-5   76-78
LPs: 10/12–inch 33rpm
RCA 5-10   77-78
   Members: Wayne Jackson; Andrew Love.
   Also see CRAY, Robert, Band, with the Memphis Horns
   Also see McDONALD, Michael
   Also see POINTER SISTERS

MEN at WORK
Singles: 12–inch 33/45rpm
COLUMBIA 4-6   82-83
Singles: 7–inch
COLUMBIA 3-5   82-83
LPs: 10/12–inch 33rpm
COLUMBIA (1650 "Cargo World
  Premier Weekend") 10-15   83
  (Promotional issue only.)
COLUMBIA (ARC-37978 "Business
  As Usual") 5-10   82
COLUMBIA (PAL-37978 "Business
  As Usual") 30-40   83
  (Picture disc.)
COLUMBIA (38167 "Business As Usual") 5-8   82
COLUMBIA (38660 "Cargo") 5-8   83
COLUMBIA (47978 "Business
  As Usual") 10-15   85
  (Half-speed mastered.)
COLUMBIA (48660 "Cargo") 10-15   85
   Members: Colin Hay; Ron Strykert; Jerry Speiser; John Rees;
   Greg Ham.

MEN WITHOUT HATS
Singles: 12–inch 33/45rpm
BACKSTREET 4-6   83
MCA 4-6   83-84
Singles: 7–inch
BACKSTREET 2-4   83
MCA 2-4   83-84
MERCURY 2-4   87
LPs: 10/12–inch 33rpm
BACKSTREET 5-8   83
MCA 5-8   84
MERCURY 5-8   87

MENAGE
Singles: 12–inch 33/45rpm
PROFILE 4-6   83-85
Singles: 7–inch
PROFILE 2-4   83-85
LPs: 10/12–inch 33rpm
PROFILE 5-8   83

MENDES, Sergio
(Sergio Mendes and Brasil '66; Sergio Mendes and
Brasil '77; Sergio Mendes Trio)
Singles: 12–inch 33/45rpm
A&M 4-6   82
Singles: 7–inch
A&M (807 through 1257) 3-6   66-71
A&M (1279 through 2700 series) 2-5   71-85
ATLANTIC 4-6   67-68
BELL 3-5   73
ELEKTRA 3-5   75-80
Picture Sleeves
A&M (807 through 1257) 3-6   66-71
LPs: 10/12–inch 33rpm
A&M (Except 4100 series) 5-12   69-84
A&M (4100 series) 10-15   66-69
ATLANTIC 15-25   65-68
BELL 8-10   73-74
CAPITOL (T-2294 "In a Brazilian Bag") 40-50   65
  (Monaural.)
CAPITOL (ST-2294 "In a Brazilian Bag)50-60   65
  (Stereo.)
ELEKTRA 8-10   75-79
EVEREST 8-10   74
MFSL 15-25   84
PHILIPS 10-12   68
TOWER (T-5052 "In a Brazilian Bag") 30-40   65
  (Monaural.)
TOWER (ST-5052 "In a Brazilian Bag")40-50   65
  (Stereo.)
   Also see ADDERLEY, Julian "Cannonball," and Sergio Mendes
   Also see HALL, Lani

MENUDO
Singles: 7–inch
RCA 2-4   84-85
LPs: 10/12–inch 33rpm
RCA 5-8   84-85
   Also see KING DREAM CHORUS and Holiday Crew

MERC & MONK
Singles: 7–inch
MANHATTAN 3-5   85
   Members: Eric Mercury; Thelonious Monk.
   Also see MERCURY, Eric
   Also see MONK, Thelonious

MERCURY, Eric
LPs: 10/12–inch 33rpm
AVCO EMBASSY 10-15   69
CAPITOL 5-10   81
ENTERPRISE 8-12   72-73
   Also see FLACK, Roberta, and Eric Mercury
   Also see MERC & MONK

MERCURY, Freddie
Singles: 12–inch 33/45rpm
COLUMBIA 4-6   84
Singles: 7–inch
COLUMBIA 2-5   84-85
Picture Sleeves
COLUMBIA (04869 "I Was Born
to Love You") 3-5   85
(Promotional issue only.)
LPs: 10/12–inch 33rpm
COLUMBIA 5-8   85
Also see QUEEN

MERCURY, Freddie / Giorgio Moroder
Singles: 12–inch 33/45rpm
COLUMBIA 4-6   84
Also see MERCURY, Freddie
Also see MORODER, Giorgio

MERCY
Singles: 7–inch
SUNDI 4-8   69
WARNER 4-8   69
LPs: 10/12–inch 33rpm
SUNDI 15-20   69
WARNER 10-15   69

MERMAIDS: see MURMAIDS

MERMAN, Ethel, Dick Haymes
Singles: 78rpm
DECCA 3-5   51
Singles: 7–inch
DECCA 5-10   51

MERRY-GO-ROUND
Singles: 7–inch
A&M 4-8   67-69
LPs: 10/12–inch 33rpm
A&M 15-30   67
RHINO 5-8   85
Members: Emitt Rhodes; Joel Larson; Gary Kato; Bill Reinhart.
Also see RHODES, Emitt

MERRYWEATHER:
see MERRYWEATHER, Neil

MERRYWEATHER, Neil
(Merryweather)
Singles: 7–inch
CAPITOL 3-6   69
LPs: 10/12–inch 33rpm
CAPITOL 10-20   69
MERCURY 10-15   74-75
Also see MASON, Dave
Also see MILLER, Steve

**MERRYWEATHER, Neil, and John
Richardson**
LPs: 10/12–inch 33rpm
KENT 10-15   72

MERRYWEATHER & CAREY
LPs: 10/12–inch 33rpm
RCA 8-12   71

Members: Neil Merryweather; Lynn Carey.
Also see MERRYWEATHER, Neil

MESA
Singles: 7–inch
ARIOLA AMERICA 3-5   77

MESSENGERS
Singles: 7–inch
BEAM 5-10   64
ERA 4-8   65
HOME MADE (01 "Right On") 15-25
MGM 4-8   64-65
RARE EARTH 3-6   71
SOUL 4-8   67
LPs: 10/12–inch 33rpm
RARE EARTH (509 "The Messengers") 8-12   69
(With standard cover.)
RARE EARTH (509 "The
Messengers") 20-25   69
(With rounded-top cover. Promotional issue.)

MESSINA, Jim
(Jim Messina and the Jesters)
Singles: 7–inch
AUDIO FIDELITY 15-25   64
COLUMBIA 3-5   79-80
VIV 10-15
WARNER 3-5   81-83
LPs: 10/12–inch 33rpm
AUDIO FIDELITY (7037 The
Dragsters") 45-55   64
COLUMBIA 5-8   79
THIMBLE 10-12   73
WARNER 5-8   81-83
Also see BUFFALO SPRINGFIELD
Also see LOGGINS & MESSINA
Also see POCO
Also see YOUNG, Neil, and Jim Messina

MESSINA, Jim, and Pauline Wilson
Singles: 7–inch
WARNER 3-5   81
Also see MESSINA, Jim

METAL CHURCH
LPs: 10/12–inch 33rpm
ELEKTRA 5-8   86-89

METALLICA
LPs: 10/12–inch 33rpm
ELEKTRA 5-8   84-88
ENIGMA 5-8   84
MEGAFORCE 8-10   84-86
Members: James Hetfield; Jason Newsted; Kirk Hammett; Lars
Ulrich.

METERS
Singles: 7–inch
JOSIE 3-6   69-71
REPRISE 3-5   74-76
WARNER 3-5   77
LPs: 10/12–inch 33rpm
ISLAND 8-10   75

JOSIE 10-12   69-70
REPRISE 8-10   72-75
VIRGO 8-10   75
WARNER 8-10   77
  Also see NEVILLE BROTHERS

METHENY, Pat
Singles: 7–inch
ECM 2-4   79-84
LPs: 10/12–inch 33rpm
ECM 5-10   76-84
EMI AMERICA 5-8   85
GEFFEN 5-8   87-90
WARNER 5-8   83
  Also see BOWIE, David, and the Pat Metheny Group

METROS
Singles: 7–inch
1-2-3 4-6   69
RCA 4-8   66-67
LPs: 10/12–inch 33rpm
RCA 10-20   67

MEYERS, Augie
(Augie)
Singles: 7–inch
ATLANTIC AMERICA 2-4   88
AXBAR 2-4   83
PARAMOUNT 3-6   73
TEXAS RE-CORD CO 3-5   75-79
SUPER BEET (Except 102) 2-4   87
SUPER BEET (102 "Velma from
  Selma") 5-10   87
SUPER BEET (102 "Mathilda") 2-4   87
  (Both of above are numbered 102.)
Selma.)
VOL 4-8   68
LPs: 10/12–inch 33rpm
ATLANTIC AMERICA 5-8   88
PARAMOUNT 15-20   73
POLYDOR 10-20   71
SUPER BEET 5-8   87
TEXAS RE-CORD CO 10-15   75
  Also see LEWIS, Jerry Lee
  Also see NELSON, Willie
  Also see VINCENT, Gene

MIAMI
Singles: 7–inch
DRIVE 3-5   74-76
LPs: 10/12–inch 33rpm
DRIVE 5-10   76
  Member: Robert Moore.

MIAMI DISCO BAND
Singles: 7–inch
SALSOUL 3-5   79
  Member: Beverly Barkley.

MIAMI SOUND MACHINE
(Gloria Estefan and the Miami Sound Machine)
Singles: 12–inch 33/45rpm
EPIC 4-6   84-90

Singles: 7–inch
EPIC 2-4   84-91
Picture Sleeves
EPIC 2-4   85-88
LPs: 10/12–inch 33rpm
EPIC 5-8   84-91
  Members: Marcos Avila; Kiki Garcia; Gloria Estefan; Emilio
  Estefan Jr.

MICHAEL, George
Singles: 12–inch 33/45rpm
COLUMBIA 4-6   84-87
Singles: 7–inch
ARISTA 2-4   87
COLUMBIA 2-4   84-90
LPs: 10/12–inch 33rpm
COLUMBIA 5-8   84-90
  Also see FRANKLIN, Aretha, and George Michael
  Also see JOHN, Elton
  Also see WHAM!

MICHAELS, Lee
Singles: 7–inch
A&M 4-6   67-71
COLUMBIA 3-5   73
Picture Sleeves
A&M 4-6   70-71
LPs: 10/12–inch 33rpm
A&M (Except 3158 and 4140) 10-15   67-73
A&M (3158 "Lee Michaels") 5-8   82
A&M (4140 "Carnival of Life") 15-25   67
COLUMBIA 10-12   73-75
Promotional LPs
COLUMBIA ("Lee Michaels in Hawaii") 35-45   75

MICHELE LEE: see LEE, Michele

MICKEY & SYLVIA
Singles: 78rpm
GROOVE (175 "Love Is Strange") ... 10-15   56
RAINBOW 10-15   55
VIK 5-10   57
Singles: 7–inch
ALL PLATINUM 3-6   69
GROOVE (175 "Love Is Strange") ... 10-20   56
RCA (47-7774 "Sweeter As the
  Day Goes By") 8-12   60
RCA (61-7774 "Sweeter As the
  Day Goes By") 15-25   60
  (Stereo.)
RCA (47-7811 "What Would I Do") ... 8-12   60
RCA (61-7811 "What Would I Do") .. 15-25   60
  (Stereo.)
RCA (37-7877 "Love Lesson") 20-30   61
  (Compact 33 Single.)
RCA (47-7877 "Love Lesson") 8-12   61
RCA (8500 series) 8-12   65
RAINBOW (316 "I'm So Glad") 15-25   55
RAINBOW (318 "Rise Sally Rise") ... 15-25   55
VIK 10-15   57-58
WILLOW 8-12   61-62

EPs: 7-inch 33/45rpm

GROOVE (18 "Love Is Strange") . . . 50-100   57
VIK (262 "Mickey & Sylvia") 40-60   57
LPs: 10/12-inch 33rpm
CAMDEN (863 "Love Is Strange") . . . 35-50   65
RCA 10-15   73
VIK (1102 "New Sounds") 100-200   57
   Members: Mickey Baker; Sylvia Vanderpool.
   Also see LITTLE SYLVIA
   Also see SYLVIA

MICO WAVE
Singles: 7-inch
COLUMBIA 2-4   87-88

MIDLER, Bette
Singles: 7-inch
ATLANTIC 2-5   72-90
Picture Sleeves
ATLANTIC 2-5   72-85
LPs: 10/12-inch 33rpm
ATLANTIC 5-10   72-90
   Also see REDD, Sharon, Ula Hedwig and Charlotte Crossley
   Also see U.S.A. for AFRICA

MIDNIGHT OIL
Singles: 12-inch 33/45rpm
COLUMBIA 4-6   84
Singles: 7-inch
COLUMBIA 2-4   84-89
LPs: 10/12-inch 33rpm
COLUMBIA 5-8   84-90

MIDNIGHT STAR
Singles: 12-inch 33/45rpm
SOLAR 4-6   82-86
Singles: 7-inch
SOLAR 2-4   80-88
LPs: 10/12-inch 33rpm
SOLAR 5-8   82-88

MIDNIGHT STRING QUARTET
LPs: 10/12-inch 33rpm
VIVA 5-10   66-68

MIDNIGHTERS
Singles: 78rpm
FEDERAL 10-20   54-57
Singles: 7-inch
FEDERAL (12169 "Work with
  Me Annie") 25-35   54
  (Silver top label.)
FEDERAL (12169 "Work with
  Me Annie") 10-15   55
  (Green label.)
FEDERAL (12177 "Give It Up") 20-30   54
FEDERAL (12185 "Sexy Ways") 25-30   54
FEDERAL (12195 "Annie Had
  a Baby") 25-35   54
FEDERAL (12200 "Annie's Aunt
  Fannie") 20-30   54
FEDERAL (12202 "Tell Them") 20-30   54
FEDERAL (12205 "Moonrise") 25-35   54

FEDERAL (12210 "Ashamed of
  Myself") 20-30   55
FEDERAL (12220 "Switchie, Witchie,
  Titchie") 20-30   55
FEDERAL (12224 "Henry's Got
  Flat Feet") 20-30   55
FEDERAL (12227 "It's Love, Baby") . 20-25   55
FEDERAL (12230 "Give It Up") 15-20   55
FEDERAL (12240 "That House on
  the Hill") 15-25   55
FEDERAL (12243 "Don't Change Your
  Pretty Ways") 15-25   55
FEDERAL (12251 through 12339) . . . 10-20   56-58
   Members: Henry Booth; Hank Ballard; Sonny Woods; Charles
   Sutton; Lawson Smith; Alonzo Tucker. May be shown on some
   early releases as "The Midnighters, Formerly the Royals."
   Also see BALLARD, Hank, and the Midnighters
   Also see JOHN, Little Willie / 5 Royales / Earl King / Midnighters
   Also see ROYALS

MIDNIGHTERS, Thee:
see THEE MIDNIGHTERS

MIDWAY
Singles: 12-inch 33/45rpm
PERSONAL 4-6   84
Singles: 7-inch
PERSONAL 2-4   84

MIGHTY CLOUDS of JOY
Singles: 12-inch 33/45rpm
EPIC 4-6   79
Singles: 7-inch
ABC 3-5   76-77
DUNHILL 3-5   74-75
EPIC 3-5   79-80
MYRRH 2-4   82
PEACOCK 3-6   61-73
LPs: 10/12-inch 33rpm
ABC 5-8   75-76
DUNHILL 5-8   74
EPIC 5-8   79
MYRRH 5-8   81-83
PEACOCK 5-10   65-73
PRIORITY 5-8   82

MIGHTY FIRE
Singles: 7-inch
ELEKTRA 2-4   81-82
ZEPHYR 3-5   80
LPs: 10/12-inch 33rpm
ELEKTRA 5-8   81-82

MIGHTY FLEA
Singles: 7-inch
ELDO 4-8   67

MIGHTY HANNIBAL
(James T. Shaw)
Singles: 7-inch
DECCA 4-8   65
JOSIE 4-8   66-67
LOMA 4-8   68

SHURFINE 4-8   66

MIGHTY MARVELOWS: see MARVELOWS

MIGHTY POPE
Singles: 7–inch
PRIVATE STOCK 3-5   77

MIKE & BILL
Singles: 7–inch
ARISTA 3-5   75

MIKE + the MECHANICS
Singles: 7–inch
ATLANTIC 2-4   86-90
LPs: 10/12–inch 33rpm
ATLANTIC 5-8   86-90
Members: Mike Rutherford; Paul Carrack; Paul Young; Peter
Van Hooke; Adrian Lee.
Also see CARRACK, Paul
Also see RUTHERFORD, Mike
Also see SAD CAFE
Also see YOUNG, Paul

MIKKI
Singles: 7–inch
EMERALD INT'L 2-4   82-83
POP ART 2-4   84

MILBURN, Amos
(Amos Milburn and the Aladdin Chickenshackers)
Singles: 78rpm
ALADDIN (100 and 200 series) 15-25   45-47
ALADDIN (3000 series) 10-20   48-56
Singles: 7–inch
ALADDIN (3014 "Chicken Shack
Boogie") 75-125   50
ALADDIN (3018 "Bewildered") 50-100   50
ALADDIN (3068 "Bad Bad Whiskey") 50-75   50
ALADDIN (3080 "Let's Rock Awhile") . 50-75   51
ALADDIN (3090 "Everybody Clap
Hands") 50-75   51
ALADDIN (3093 "Ain't Nothing
Shaking") 50-75   51
ALADDIN (3105 "Boogie Woogie") . . 50-75   51
ALADDIN (3124 "Drinkin'
and Thinkin") 40-60   52
ALADDIN (3125 "Flying Home") 40-60   52
ALADDIN (3133 "Roll Mr. Jelly") 40-60   52
ALADDIN (3150 "Greyhound") 40-60   52
ALADDIN (3159 "Rock, Rock, Rock") 40-60   52
ALADDIN (3164 "Let Me Go Home,
Whiskey") 30-50   53
ALADDIN (3168 "Please, Mr.
Johnson") 30-50   53
ALADDIN (3197 "One Scotch, One
Bourbon, One Beer") 30-50   53
ALADDIN (3218 "Good Good
Whiskey") 25-45   53
ALADDIN (3226 "Rocky Mountain") . . 25-45   54
ALADDIN (3240 "Milk and Water") . . . 25-45   54
ALADDIN (3248 "Glory of Love") 25-45   54

ALADDIN (3253 "Vicious Vicious
Vodka") 25-45   54
ALADDIN (3269 "One Two Three
Everybody") 25-45   54
ALADDIN (3293 "My Happiness
Depends on You") 25-45   55
ALADDIN (3306 "House Party") 25-45   55
ALADDIN (3332 "Chicken Shack") . . 20-40   56
IMPERIAL 5-10   62
KING (5000 series) 5-10   60-61
KING (6000 series) 4-8   67
LE CAM 4-8   62
MOTOWN (1038 "My Baby Gave
Me Another Chance") 15-25   63
LPs: 10/12–inch 33rpm
ALADDIN (704 "Rockin' the
Boogie") 300-500   55
(Black vinyl. 10–inch LP.)
ALADDIN (704 "Rockin' the
Boogie") 500-1000   55
(Colored vinyl. 10–inch LP.)
ALADDIN (810 "Rockin' the
Boogie") 200-300   56
IMPERIAL (9176 "Million Sellers") . . . 50-75   62
MOTOWN (608 "The Blues Boss") 250-500   63
SCORE (4012 "Let's Have a Party") 100-200   57
Also see BROWN, Charles, and Amos Milburn

**MILBURN, Amos / Wynonie Harris / Velma
Nelson / Crown Prince Waterford**
LPs: 10/12–inch 33rpm
ALADDIN (703 "Party After Hours"). 300-500   56
(Black vinyl. 10–inch LP.)
ALADDIN (703 "Party After Hours")500-1000   56
(Colored vinyl. 10–inch LP.)
Also see HARRIS, Wynonie
Also see MILBURN, Amos

MILES, Buddy
(Buddy Miles Express; Buddy Miles Band)
Singles: 7–inch
CASABLANCA 3-5   75-76
COLUMBIA 3-5   73-74
MERCURY 3-6   68-71
LPs: 10/12–inch 33rpm
CASABLANCA 8-10   75
COLUMBIA 8-12   73-74
MERCURY 10-15   68-72
Also see CALIFORNIA RAISINS
Also see ELECTRIC FLAG
Also see HENDRIX, Jimi
Also see KARP, Charlie
Also see SANTANA, Carlos, and Buddy Miles

MILES, Garry
(Garry Miles and the Statues; Gary Miles)
Singles: 7–inch
LIBERTY (54000 series) 5-8   68
LIBERTY (55000 series) 10-15   60-64
Picture Sleeves
LIBERTY (55261 "Look for a Star") . . 10-20   60

EPs: 7–inch 33/45rpm

LIBERTY (1005 "Look for a Star") ... 50-75   60
Also see STATUES

MILES, John
Singles: 12–inch 33/45rpm
LONDON 5-8   77-80
Singles: 7–inch
ARISTA 3-5   78
LONDON 3-5   76-77
WEA 2-4   85
LPs: 10/12–inch 33rpm
ARISTA 5-10   78
LONDON 5-10   76-80
WEA 5-8   85
Also see PARSONS, Alan, Project

MILES, Lenny
Singles: 7–inch
GROOVE 5-10   62
SCEPTER 5-10   61

MILITELLO, Bobby
Singles: 7–inch
GORDY 2-4   82-83
LPs: 10/12–inch 33rpm
GORDY 5-8   82-83
Member: Jean Carn.
Also see CARNE, Jean

MILLER, Chuck
Singles: 78rpm
MERCURY 5-10   55-58
Singles: 7–inch
MERCURY 8-15   55-58
LPs: 10/12–inch 33rpm
MERCURY (20195 "After Hours") ... 40-60   56
(10–inch LP.)

MILLER, Clint
Singles: 7–inch
ABC-PAR 10-20   58
BIG TOP 5-10   59
HEADLINE 5-10   60-61
LENOX 4-8   62

MILLER, Frankie
Singles: 78rpm
COLUMBIA 3-6   54-56
Singles: 7–inch
COLUMBIA 5-10   54-56
STARDAY 4-8   59-67
U.A. 4-6   62
EPs: 7–inch 33/45rpm
STARDAY 8-12   60
LPs: 10/12–inch 33rpm
AUDIO LAB (1562 "Fine Country
    Singing") 20-30   63
STARDAY (134 "Country Music's
    New Star") 25-40   61
STARDAY (199 "Country Style") ... 25-35   62
STARDAY (338 "Blackland Farmer") . 15-25   65
U.A. 15-25   62

MILLER, Frankie
(Frankie Miller Band)
Singles: 7–inch
CAPITOL 2-4   82
CHRYSALIS 3-5   75-79
LPs: 10/12–inch 33rpm
CAPITOL 5-10   82
CHRYSALIS 8-12   73-80

MILLER, Glenn, and His Orchestra
(New Glenn Miller Orchestra with Ray McKinley;
Buddy DeFranco and the Glenn Miller Orchestra)
Singles: 78rpm
BLUEBIRD 5-10   38-44
BRUNSWICK 5-10   37-38
COLUMBIA 5-10   35
DECCA 15-25   37
RCA 4-8   47-58
VICTOR 5-10   42-46
Singles: 7–inch
EPIC 3-6   65-69
RCA 3-10   50-67
EPs: 7–inch 33/45rpm
EPIC 5-15   54-56
RCA (Except 6700 series) 5-15   50-61
RCA (6700 "Anthology
    Limited Edition, Vol. 1") 25-50   56
RCA (6701 "Anthology
    Limited Edition, Vol. 2") 25-50   56
RCA (6702 "Army Air Force Band") .. 20-30   56
LPs: 10/12–inch 33rpm
BRIGHT ORANGE 5-8   73
CAMDEN 5-10   63-74
COLUMBIA 5-8   82
EPIC (1000 and 3000 series) 20-40   54-56
EPIC (16000 series) 12-25   60
EPIC (24000 and 26000 series) ... 10-20   65-66
EVEREST (Except 4004) 5-8   82
EVEREST (4004 "Glenn Miller") 20-30   82
(Five-LP boxed set.)
GREAT AMERICAN GRAMOPHONE . 5-10   77
HARMONY 5-10   70
KORY 5-8   77
MOVIETONE 8-15   67
RCA (16 through 30) 25-50
(10–inch LPs.)
RCA (0600 through 3800 series) 5-10   74-81
(With "ANL," "AYL" or "CPL" prefix.)
RCA (LPT-3000 series) 25-50   52-54
(10–inch LP.)
RCA (1000 through 1500 series) 20-40   54-57
(Black label.)
RCA (1100 through 1500 series) 5-10   68-69
(Orange label.)
RCA (1600 through 3900 series) 10-25   58-68
(Black label. With "LPM" or "LSP" prefix.)
RCA (1900 through 4100 series) 5-10   68-69
(Orange label.)
RCA (5000 series) 5-10   75-80

RCA (6000 series) 5-15   69-73
RCA (6100 series) 15-30   59-63
RCA (6700 "Anthology
  Limited Edition, Vol. 1") 75-100   56
  (Five-LP set with booklet and special gold or silver
  case.)
RCA (6700 "Anthology
  Limited Edition, Vol. 1") 50-75   62
  (Reissue.)
RCA (6701 "Anthology
  Limited Edition, Vol. 2") 75-100   56
  (Five-LP set with booklet and special gold or silver
  case.)
RCA (6701 "Anthology
  Limited Edition, Vol. 2") 50-75   62
  (Reissue.)
RCA (6702 "Army Air Force Band") .. 50-75   56
SPRINGBOARD 4-8   77
20TH FOX (100 series) 20-30   59
20TH FOX (900 series) 5-10   73
20TH FOX (3000 series) 15-25   59
20TH FOX (3100 series) 10-15   65
20TH FOX (4100 series) 10-15   65
20TH FOX (72000 series) 6-12   73

MILLER, Jody
Singles: 7-inch
CAPITOL 4-8   63-70
EPIC 3-5   70-79
Picture Sleeves
CAPITOL 5-10   65
LPs: 10/12-inch 33rpm
CAPITOL (1913 "Wednesday's Child
  Is Full of Woe") 15-25   63
CAPITOL (2349 through 2996) 10-20   65-69
CAPITOL (11000 series) 5-10   73
EPIC 5-10   70-77
PICKWICK/HILLTOP 10-15   66
  Also see PAYCHECK, Johnny, and Jody Miller

MILLER, Marcus
Singles: 12-inch 33/45rpm
WARNER 4-6   83-84
Singles: 7-inch
WARNER 2-4   83-84

MILLER, Mrs. Elva
(Mrs. Miller)
Singles: 7-inch
AMARET 4-8   69-70
CAPITOL 5-10   66
LPs: 10/12-inch 33rpm
AMARET 10-20   69
CAPITOL 20-35   66-67

MILLER, Mitch
(Mitch Miller's Orchestra and Chorus; Mitch Miller and
the Sing-Along Gang)
Singles: 78rpm
COLUMBIA 3-6   50-57

Singles: 7-inch
COLUMBIA 4-10   50-65
DECCA 3-6   65-66
DIAMOND 3-6   68
GOLD-MOR 3-5   73
U.A. 3-6   68
Picture Sleeves
COLUMBIA 5-8   59-63
EPs: 7-inch 33/45rpm
COLUMBIA 5-10   55-61
LPs: 10/12-inch 33rpm
ATLANTIC 5-8   70
COLUMBIA (Except 2780/6380) 5-20   56-82
COLUMBIA (2780 "Major Dundee") .. 35-45   65
  (Soundtrack. Monaural.)
COLUMBIA (6380 "Major Dundee") .. 45-55   65
  (Soundtrack. Stereo.)
DECCA 5-12   66
HARMONY 5-12   65-71

MILLER, Ned
Singles: 78rpm
DOT 5-10   57
Singles: 7-inch
CAPITOL (2000 series) 3-6   68
CAPITOL (4600 series) 4-8   61
CAPITOL (5400 and 5800 series) ... 3-8   65-67
DOT (15000 series,
  except 15601) 5-10   57
DOT (15601 "From a Jack to a King") 10-15   57
FABOR 4-6   62-65
JACKPOT 5-10   59
REPUBLIC 3-5   69-70
LPs: 10/12-inch 33rpm
CAPITOL 10-15   65-67
FABOR (1001 "From a Jack
  to a King") 15-25   63
  (Black vinyl.)
FABOR (1001 "From a Jack
  to a King") 50-75   63
  (Colored vinyl.)
PLANTATION 5-8   81
REPUBLIC 8-10   70

MILLER, Roger
Singles: 7-inch
BUENA VISTA 3-5   70
COLUMBIA 3-5   73-74
DECCA 5-10   59
ELEKTRA 2-4   81
MCA 2-4   86
MERCURY 3-5   70-72
MUSICOR 4-8   65
RCA (7000 series) 5-10   60-63
RCA (8000 series) 4-6   65
SMASH 3-8   64-76
STARDAY 4-6   65
WINDSONG 3-5   77
Picture Sleeves
BUENA VISTA 4-6   70

MILLS, Hayley, and Jimmie Bean
EPs: 7-inch 33/45rpm
DISNEYLAND 15-25   60

MILLS, Hayley, and Maurice Chevalier
Singles: 7-inch
BUENA VISTA 5-8   62
Also see MILLS, Hayley

MILLS, Hayley, and Eddie Hodges
Singles: 7-inch
BUENA VISTA 5-8   63
Picture Sleeves
BUENA VISTA 10-15   64
Also see HODGES, Eddie

MILLS, Hayley, and Burl Ives
(With Eddie Hodges and Deborah Walley)
Singles: 7-inch
BUENA VISTA (4023 "Summer Magic") . 5-8   63
(Alcoa Wrap promotional issue.)
Picture Sleeves
BUENA VISTA (4023 "Summer
Magic") 10-15   63
(Alcoa Wrap promotional issue.)
Also see IVES, Burl
Also see MILLS, Hayley

MILLS, Stephanie
Singles: 12-inch 33/45rpm
CASABLANCA 4-6   82-85
MCA 4-6   85-86
20TH FOX 4-8   79-81
Singles: 7-inch
ABC 3-5   74
CASABLANCA 2-4   82-86
MCA 2-4   85-89
MOTOWN 3-5   75
PARAMOUNT 3-5   74
20TH FOX 3-5   79-81
LPs: 10/12-inch 33rpm
ABC 8-10   75
CASABLANCA 5-8   82-85
MCA 5-8   86-89
MOTOWN (800 series) 8-10   75
MOTOWN (6000 series) 5-8   82
20TH FOX 5-10   79-81
Also see KING DREAM CHORUS and Holiday Crew

MILLS, Stephanie, and Teddy Pendergrass
Singles: 7-inch
20TH FOX 3-5   81
Also see MILLS, Stephanie
Also see PENDERGRASS, Teddy

MILLS, Yvonne, and the Sensations
Singles: 78rpm
ATCO 8-15   56-57
Singles: 7-inch
ATCO 15-25   56-58
Also see SENSATIONS

MILLS BROTHERS
Singles: 78rpm
BANNER 5-10   34
BRUNSWICK 5-10   31-47
CONQUEROR 5-10
DECCA (100 through 4300 series) ... 5-10   34-42
DECCA (11000 through 24000 series) . 5-10   42-57
Singles: 7-inch
ABC 3-5   74
DECCA 5-15   50-61
DOT (15000 series) 4-8   58-59
DOT (17000 series) 3-6   68-69
MCA 3-5   73-74
PARAMOUNT 3-5   71-72
RANWOOD 3-5   73-76
EPs: 7-inch 33/45rpm
DECCA 5-15   50-63
DOT 5-10   58-59
LPs: 10/12-inch 33rpm
ABC 5-8   74
DECCA (100 series) 10-15   66
DECCA (4000 series) 10-20   61-67
DECCA (5000 series) 20-40   49-55
(10-inch LPs.)
DECCA (7000 series) 20-30   55
DECCA (8000 series) 15-30   55-59
DECCA (75000 series) 5-10   70
DOT 5-15   58-70
EVEREST 5-10   75-77
GNP/CRESCENDO 5-8   73
PARAMOUNT 5-10   72-74
RANWOOD 5-10   74-81
SONGBIRD 6-12   74
VOCALION 5-10   66-69
Members: Herb Mills; Harry Mills; Donald Mills; John Mills.
Also see CROSBY, Bing, and the Mills Brothers

MILLS BROTHERS, and Louis Armstrong
Singles: 7-inch
DECCA 4-6   61
Also see ARMSTRONG, Louis

MILLS BROTHERS, and Count Basie
LPs: 10/12-inch 33rpm
ABC 5-8   74
DOT 8-12   68
Also see BASIE, Count
Also see MILLS BROTHERS

MILSAP, Ronnie
Singles: 7-inch
BOBLO 3-5   77
CHIPS 4-6   70
FESTIVAL 3-5   77
RCA 2-5   74-91
SCEPTER 4-8   65-69
WARNER (5405 "It Went to Your Head")5-10   63
WARNER (8000 series) 3-5   75-76
Picture Sleeves
RCA 2-5   79-85

LPs: 10/12–inch 33rpm

BUCKBOARD 8-10	76
CRAZY CAJUN 8-10	75
51 WEST 5-8	
HSRD 8-10	82
RCA 5-10	74-91
TRIP 8-10	76
WARNER 8-10	71-75

Also see PRESLEY, Elvis

MILTON, Roy
(Roy Milton and His Band; Roy Milton and His Solid
Senders; Roy Milton Sextet)
Singles: 78rpm

DOOTONE 10-15	55-56
DELUXE 8-12	
HAMP-TONE 10-20	45
JUKE BOX 20-25	46
KING 5-10	56-57
ROY MILTON (111 "Groovin' with Joe")15-25	46
ROY MILTON (207 "Them There Eyes") 15-25	46
SPECIALTY 5-10	47-55

Singles: 7–inch

CENCO 5-10	61
DOOTONE 20-40	55-56
KING (4900 and 5000 series) 10-15	56-58
KING (5600 series) 5-10	62
SPECIALTY (414 "Short, Sweet and Snappy") 20-40	50
SPECIALTY (429 "So Tired") 20-40	51
SPECIALTY (436 "Flying Saucer") ... 20-40	52
SPECIALTY (438 "Night and Day") .. 20-40	52
SPECIALTY (446 "Believe Me Baby") 50-75	52
SPECIALTY (458 "Some Day") ..... 20-30 (Black vinyl.)	53
SPECIALTY (458 "Some Day") ..... 50-75 (Colored vinyl.)	53
SPECIALTY (464 "Let Me Give You All My Love") .... 20-30 (Black vinyl.)	54
SPECIALTY (464 "Let Me Give You All My Love") .... 50-75 (Colored vinyl.)	54
SPECIALTY (480 through 545) 15-25	54-55
SPECIALTY (700 series) 4-6	69
WARWICK 5-10	60

LPs: 10/12–inch 33rpm

KENT (554 "The Great Roy Milton") 35-45	63

Also see HOWARD, Camille, Trio

MILTON, Roy / Joe Liggins
Singles: 78rpm

SPECIALTY 5-10	53

Singles: 7–inch

SPECIALTY 15-25	53

Also see LIGGINS, Joe
Also see MILTON, Roy

MIMMS, Garnet
(Garnet Mimms and the Enchanters; Garnet Mimms
and the Trucking Co.)
Singles: 7–inch

ARISTA 3-5	77
GSF 3-5	72
LIBERTY 2-4	81
U.A. 4-8	63-66
VEEP 4-8	66
VERVE 3-5	68-70

Picture Sleeves

U.A. 5-10	63

LPs: 10/12–inch 33rpm

ARISTA 5-10	78
GRAND PRIX 15-20	63
GUEST STAR (1907 "Garnet Mimms") 20-25	64
U.A. 20-30	63-66

Members: Garnet Mimms; Samuel Bell; Charles Boyer; Zola
Pearnell.

MIMMS, Garnet / Maurice Monk
LPs: 10/12–inch 33rpm

GRAND PRIX 15-20	63

Also see MIMMS, Garnet

MINA
Singles: 7–inch

TIME 4-8	61

MINDBENDERS
Singles: 7–inch

FONTANA 5-10	65-67

LPs: 10/12–inch 33rpm

FONTANA 20-25	66

Members: Eric Stewart.
Also see FONTANA, Wayne, and the Mindbenders

MINEO, Sal
Singles: 78rpm

EPIC 8-12	57

Singles: 7–inch

DECCA 4-8	64
EPIC 8-15	57-59
FONTANA 4-8	65

Picture Sleeves

EPIC 10-15	57-59

EPs: 7–inch 33/45rpm

EPIC 20-30	57-58

LPs: 10/12–inch 33rpm

EPIC (3405 "Sal") 30-50	58

MINIATURE MEN
Singles: 7–inch

DOLTON 5-10	62

Also see LEVINE, Hank

MINISTRY
Singles: 12–inch 33/45rpm

ARISTA 4-6	83
SIRE 4-6	86
WAX TRAX 4-6	85

Singles: 7–inch

ARISTA 2-4	83

SIRE 2-4	86-89
WAX TRAX 2-4	85

LPs: 10/12–inch 33rpm

ARISTA 5-8	83
SIRE 5-8	86-89

MINK DE VILLE
Singles: 7–inch

ATLANTIC 2-4	81-84
CAPITOL 3-5	77-78

LPs: 10/12–inch 33rpm

ATLANTIC 5-8	81-83
CAPITOL 5-8	77-82

MINNEAPOLIS GENIUS 94 EAST
Singles: 7–inch

HOT PINK 2-4	86

MINNELLI, Liza
Singles: 7–inch

A&M 3-6	68-71
ABC 3-5	73
CADENCE 5-10	63
CAPITOL (4900 through 5700 series) . 5-10	63-65
COLUMBIA 3-5	72-75
U.A. 3-5	77

LPs: 10/12–inch 33rpm

A&M 10-15	68-73
ABC (752 "Cabaret") 10-15	72
(Soundtrack. With Joel Grey.)	
ARISTA (4069 "Lucky Lady") 8-10	76
(Soundtrack.)	
CADENCE (4012 "Best Foot Forward")30-40	63
(Monaural. Original cast.)	
CADENCE (24012 "Best Foot	
Forward") 40-60	63
(Stereo. Original cast.)	
CAPITOL (T-2100 and T-2400 series) 10-20	64-66
(Monaural.)	
CAPITOL (ST-2100 and	
ST-2400 series) 15-25	64-66
(Stereo.)	
CAPITOL (2200 series) 5-8	78
CAPITOL (11000 series) 5-10	72-78
COLUMBIA 8-15	72-77
DRG (6101 "The Act") 8-10	78
EPIC 5-8	89
MCA (752 "Cabaret") 5-8	
(Soundtrack. With Joel Grey.)	
STET 8-10	
TELARC 10-12	87

Also see GARLAND, Judy, and Liza Minnelli

MINOGUE, Kylie
LPs: 10/12–inch 33rpm

GEFFEN 5-8	88

MINOR DETAIL
Singles: 7–inch

POLYDOR 2-4	83-84

LPs: 10/12–inch 33rpm

POLYDOR 5-8	83

Members: John Hughes; Willie Hughes.

MINTS:
see COPELAND, Ken / Mints

MIRABAI
LPs: 10/12–inch 33rpm

ATLANTIC 5-10	75

MIRACLES
(Smokey Robinson and the Miracles; Miracles Featuring Bill Smokey Robinson)
Singles: 12–inch 33/45rpm

COLUMBIA 4-6	77

Singles: 7–inch

CHESS (119 "Bad Girl") 3-5	84
CHESS (1734 "Bad Girl") 10-20	59
CHESS (1768 "All I Want") 10-20	60
COLUMBIA 3-5	77-78
END (1016 "Got a Job") 30-40	58
END (1029 "Money") 20-40	58
END (1084 "Money") 10-15	61
MOTOWN (G1 "Bad Girl") 350-400	59
MOTOWN (400 and 500 series) 3-5	
MOTOWN (2207 "Bad Girl") 400-450	59
MOTOWN/TOPPS (11 "Shop Around") 50-75	67
(Topps Chewing Gum promotional item	
Single-sided, cardboard flexi, picture disc. Issued	
with generic paper sleeve.)	
ROULETTE 3-5	
STANDARD GROOVE (13090 "I Care	
About Detroit") 75-100	68
(Promotional issue only.)	
TAMLA (009 "The Christmas Song") 175-200	63
(Promotional issue only.)	
TAMLA (54028 "Way Over There"/	
"Depend on Me") 75-100	60
(With alternate take of *Way Over There,* not	
available elsewhere.)	
TAMLA (54028 "Way Over There"/	
"Depend on Me") 25-35	60
(With the hit version of *Way Over There,* the same	
as is heard on their Tamla LPs.)	

TAMLA (54028 "The Feeling Is So Fine"/
"You Can Depend on Me") 325-350   60
(Issued twice, first with the standard version of *You
Can Depend on Me*, then with an alternate take.
The alternate can be identified by the letter "A"
following the identification number in the trail-off.
There is no reportable difference in value.)

TAMLA (54034 "Shop Around") 75-125   60
(With horizontal lines across top half of label. Has
an alternate take of *Shop Around*. Identification
number is 45-H55518 A-2.)

TAMLA (54034 "Shop Around") 25-35   60
(With globe logo. Has the alternate take of *Shop
Around*. Identification number is 45-H55518 A-2.)

TAMLA (54034 "Shop Around") 15-25   60
(Has the hit version of *Shop Around*. Identification
number is 45-L1 3.)

TAMLA (54034 "Shop Around") 5-10   60
(Has the hit version of *Shop Around*. Identification
number is 45-L1 3. With or without horizontal lines.)

TAMLA (54036 "Ain't It Baby") 10-15   61
TAMLA (54044 "Mighty Good Lovin") . 10-15   61
TAMLA (54048 "Everybody's Gotta
Pay Some Dues") 5-10   61
TAMLA (54053 through 54069) 5-10   62
TAMLA (54073 through 54194) 4-8   62-70
TAMLA (54199 through 54268) 3-5   70-76
Picture Sleeves
TAMLA (54044 "Mighty Good Lovin") . 15-25   61
TAMLA (54059 "I'll Try Something
New") 15-25   62
TAMLA (54073 through 54194) 5-10   62-70
LPs: 10/12–inch 33rpm
COLUMBIA 8-10   77-78
IMPERIAL HOUSE 8-12   79
MOTOWN (Except 793) 5-8   82-84
MOTOWN (793 "Anthology") 12-18   74
NATURAL RESOURCES 5-10   78
TAMLA (220 "Hi! We're the
Miracles") 200-250   61
(White label.)
TAMLA (220 "Hi! We're the
Miracles") 150-200   61
(Yellow label with globes.)
TAMLA (223 "Cookin' with
the Miracles") 125-150   62
(White label.)
TAMLA (223 "Cookin' with
the Miracles") 100-125   62
(Yellow label with globes.)
TAMLA (224 "Shop Around") 100-150   62
TAMLA (230 "I'll Try Something
New") 75-125   62
TAMLA (236 "Christmas with
the Miracles") 100-200   63
TAMLA (238 "The Fabulous
Miracles") 75-125   63
TAMLA (241 "On Stage") 50-100   63

TAMLA (245 "Mickey's Monkey") ... 50-100   63
(Monaural.)
TAMLA (245 "Mickey's Monkey") .. 100-150   63
(Stereo.)
TAMLA (254 "Greatest Hits
from the Beginning") 25-35   63
(Monaural.)
TAMLA (254 "Greatest Hits
from the Beginning") 35-45   63
(Stereo.)
TAMLA (267 through 297) 12-20   65-70
TAMLA (301 through 344) 10-15   71-76
Members: William "Smokey" Robinson; Pete Moore; Bobby
Rogers; Ron White; Claudette Rogers
Also see GRIFFIN, Billy
Also see ROBINSON, Smokey
Also see RON & BILL

MIRAN, Wayne, and Rush Release
Singles: 7–inch
ROULETTE 3-5   75

MIRETTES
Singles: 7–inch
REVUE 4-8   67-69
UNI............................. 3-6   69
LPs: 10/12–inch 33rpm
REVUE 12-18   68
UNI........................... 10-15   69
Members: Vanetta Fields; Jessie Smith; Robbie Montgomery.
Also see IKETTES

MISS ABRAMS: see ABRAMS, Miss

MISS THANG
Singles: 12–inch 33/45rpm
TOMMY BOY 4-6   86

MISS TONI FISHER: see FISHER, Miss Toni

MISSING PERSONS
Singles: 12–inch 33/45rpm
CAPITOL 4-6   82-86
Singles: 7–inch
CAPITOL 2-4   82-86
Picture Sleeves
CAPITOL 2-5   82-84
EPs: 7–inch 33/45rpm
KOMOS 5-8   80
LPs: 10/12–inch 33rpm
CAPITOL 5-8   82-86
Members: Dale Bozzio; Terry Bozzio; Warren Cuccurullo.
Also see MOTHERS of INVENTION

MISSION
Singles: 7–inch
PARAMOUNT 3-5   74

MISSION U.K.
LPs: 10/12–inch 33rpm
MERCURY....................... 5-8   87-90

MISSOURI
Singles: 7–inch
PANAMA 3-5   78

POLYDOR 3-5   79
LPs: 10/12-inch 33rpm
PANAMA 8-12   77
POLYDOR 5-10   79

MR. BIG
Singles: 7-inch
ARISTA 2-4   77-91
LPs: 10/12-inch 33rpm
ARISTA 5-10   76-91

MR. MISTER
Singles: 7-inch
RCA 2-4   84-87
LPs: 10/12-inch 33rpm
RCA 5-8   84-87
Members: Richard Page; Pat Mastelotto; Steve Farris; Steve George.
Also see PAGES

MR. T.
(Lawrence Tero)
Singles: 12-inch 33/45rpm
COLUMBIA (9C9-39911 "Mr. T's
Commandments") 8-12   84
Singles: 7-inch
COLUMBIA 2-4   84
MCA 2-4   84
LPs: 10/12-inch 33rpm
COLUMBIA 5-8   84
MCA 5-8   84

MISTRESS
Singles: 7-inch
RSO 3-5   79
LPs: 10/12-inch 33rpm
RSO 5-10   79

MITCHELL, Billy
(Billy Mitchell Group)
Singles: 78rpm
ATLANTIC 20-40   51-52
Singles: 7-inch
ATLANTIC (933 "My Love,
My Desire") 100-200   51
CALLA 4-6   69
JUBILEE 5-10   61
RON 5-10   61-62
U.A. 5-10   60
WARWICK 5-10   59
Also see CLOVERS
Also see MORRIS, Joe, and His Orchestra

MITCHELL, Bobby
(Bobby Mitchell and the Toppers)
Singles: 78rpm
IMPERIAL (5200 series) 20-40   53
IMPERIAL (5250 through 5309) 15-25   53-54
IMPERIAL (5300 and 5400 series) ... 10-15   55-57
Singles: 7-inch
IMPERIAL (5236 "I'm Cryin") 100-150   53
IMPERIAL (5250 "One Friday
Morning") 100-150   53

IMPERIAL (5270 "Baby's Gone") 50-75   54
IMPERIAL (5282 "Angel Child") 50-75   54
IMPERIAL (5295 "The Wedding
Bells Are Ringing") 50-75   54
IMPERIAL (5309 "I'm a Young Man")   50-75   54
IMPERIAL (5326 "I Wish I Knew") ... 30-40   55
IMPERIAL (5346 "I Cried") 20-30   55
IMPERIAL (5378 through 5558) 10-20   56-58
IMPERIAL (5900 series) 5-10   63
RON 5-10   61
SHOW-BIZ 5-10   59

MITCHELL, Chad
Singles: 7-inch
AMY 3-6   68-69
WARNER 4-8   66-67
LPs: 10/12-inch 33rpm
BELL 10-15   69
WARNER 10-20   66-67

MITCHELL, Chad, Trio
Singles: 7-inch
COLPIX 5-10   59-61
KAPP 5-8   61-63
MAY 4-8   62
MERCURY 4-8   63-64
Picture Sleeves
KAPP 10-15   61
MERCURY 8-12   63-65
LPs: 10/12-inch 33rpm
COLPIX 20-30   60
KAPP 15-25   61-64
MERCURY 15-20   63-64
Members: Chad Mitchell; Joe Frazier; Mike Kobluk; Jim [Roger] McGuinn.
Also see McGUINN, Roger
Also see MITCHELL, Chad
Also see MITCHELL TRIO

MITCHELL, Chad, Trio, and the Gatemen
LPs: 10/12-inch 33rpm
COLPIX 20-25   64
Also see MITCHELL, Chad, Trio

MITCHELL, Freddie, and Orchestra
Singles: 78rpm
ABC-PAR 3-5   57
BRUNSWICK 4-6   53
CORAL 4-6   53
DERBY 4-8   49-52
MERCURY 4-6   52
Singles: 7-inch
ABC-PAR 4-8   57-61
BRUNSWICK 5-10   53
CORAL 5-10   53
DERBY 5-10   49-52
MERCURY 5-10   52
ROCK 'N ROLL 5-8
LPs: 10/12-inch 33rpm
TRIP 10-15
X (1030 "Boogie Bash") 40-60   56
Also see KING CURTIS

MITCHELL, Guy
Singles: 78rpm
COLUMBIA 3-8   50-57
Singles: 7–inch
COLUMBIA 5-10   50-62
ERIC 2-4   83
JOY 4-8   62-63
REPRISE 4-6   66
STARDAY 3-6   67-69
Picture Sleeves
COLUMBIA 5-15   56-62
EPs: 7–inch 33/45rpm
COLUMBIA 5-15   54-57
LPs: 10/12–inch 33rpm
COLUMBIA (1211 "Guy in Love") 20-30   58
(Monaural.)
COLUMBIA (1226 "Greatest Hits") ... 25-35   59
COLUMBIA (1552 "Sunshine
Guitar") 15-25   60
(Monaural.)
COLUMBIA (6231 "Open Spaces") .. 25-50   53
(10–inch LP.)
COLUMBIA (8011 "Guy in Love") 30-40   58
(Stereo.)
COLUMBIA (8352 "Sunshine Guitar") 20-30   60
(Stereo.)
KING (644 "Sincerely Yours") 150-250   59
NASHVILLE 5-10   70
STARDAY 8-12   68-69
Also see CLOONEY, Rosemary, and Guy Mitchell

MITCHELL, Guy, and Mindy Carson
Singles: 78rpm
COLUMBIA 3-6   52-53
Singles: 7–inch
COLUMBIA 5-10   52-53
Also see CARSON, Mindy

MITCHELL, Guy / Eileen Rodgers
EPs: 7–inch 33/45rpm
COLUMBIA 10-15   56
Also see RODGERS, Eileen
Also see MITCHELL, Guy

MITCHELL, Joni
Singles: 7–inch
ASYLUM 3-5   72-80
ELEKTRA 3-5   75
GEFFEN 2-4   82-91
REPRISE 3-6   68-72
LPs: 10/12–inch 33rpm
ASYLUM 8-10   72-80
GEFFEN 5-8   82-91
REPRISE 10-20   68-71

MITCHELL, Joni, and the L.A. Express
LPs: 10/12–inch 33rpm
ASYLUM 8-10   74
Also see MITCHELL, Joni

MITCHELL, Kim
Singles: 7–inch
BRONZE 2-4   85
LPs: 10/12–inch 33rpm
BRONZE 5-8   85

MITCHELL, McKinley
Singles: 7–inch
BOXER 10-15   59
CHIMNEYVILLE 3-5   77-78
ONE-DERFUL 5-10   62-65

MITCHELL, Philip
(Prince Philip Mitchell)
Singles: 7–inch
ATLANTIC 3-5   78-79
EVENT 3-5   75
ICHIBAN 2-4   86

MITCHELL, Rubin
Singles: 7–inch
CAPITOL 3-6   67-68
Picture Sleeves
CAPITOL 4-8   67
LPs: 10/12–inch 33rpm
CAPITOL 10-15   67

MITCHELL, Willie
(Willie Mitchell and the Four Kings)
Singles: 7–inch
HI 4-8   62-69
HOME of the BLUES 5-10   60-61
MOTOWN 3-5
STOMPER TIME (1160 "Tell It
to Me, Baby") 40-60
Picture Sleeves
HI 5-8   68
LPs: 10/12–inch 33rpm
BEARSVILLE 5-8   81
HI (12010 through 12042) 10-20   63-68
(Monaural.)
HI (32010 through 32058) 10-25   63-71
(Stereo.)
HI (8000 series) 5-8   77
MOTOWN 8-10   82

MITCHELL TRIO
Singles: 7–inch
MERCURY 4-8   65-66
REPRISE 4-8   67
Picture Sleeves
MERCURY 5-10   63-66
LPs: 10/12–inch 33rpm
MERCURY (21049 "That's the
Way It's Gonna Be") 15-20   65
(Monaural.)
MERCURY (21067 "Violets of Dawn") 15-20   65
(Monaural.)
MERCURY (61049 "That's the
Way It's Gonna Be") 20-25   65
(Stereo.)

MERCURY (21067 "Violets of Dawn") 20-25   65
(Stereo.)
REPRISE (6354 "Alive") 15-20   67
  Members: Chad Mitchell; Joe Frazier; Mike Kobluk; John
  Denver; David Boise.
   Also see DENVER, John
   Also see MITCHELL, Chad, Trio

MITCHUM, Robert
(Robert Mitchum and the Calypso Band)
Singles: 78rpm
CAPITOL 5-10   57-58
Singles: 7–inch
CAPITOL (Except 3986) 5-10   57
CAPITOL (3986 "The Ballad of
  Thunder Road") 8-12   58
  (Purple label.)
CAPITOL (3986 "The Ballad of
  Thunder Road") 4-8   62
  (Orange/yellow label.)
MONUMENT 4-6   67
EPs: 7–inch 33/45rpm
CAPITOL (853 "Calypso Is Like So") . 15-25   57
  (Price is for any of three volumes.)
LPs: 10/12–inch 33rpm
CAPITOL (853 "Calypso Is Like So") . 35-55   57
MONUMENT 10-15   67

MIXTURES
Singles: 7–inch
SIRE 3-5   71

MOB
Singles: 7–inch
COLOSSUS 3-5   71-72
MERCURY 4-8   68
PRIVATE STOCK 3-5   76-77
Picture Sleeves
COLOSSUS 3-6   71-72
LPs: 10/12–inch 33rpm
COLOSSUS 10-15   71
PRIVATE STOCK 8-12   75

MOBY GRAPE
Singles: 7–inch
COLUMBIA 5-10   67-69
Picture Sleeves
COLUMBIA 20-25   67
LPs: 10/12–inch 33rpm
COLUMBIA (Except 2698/9498) 10-15   68-72
COLUMBIA (2698 "Moby Grape") . . . 35-45   67
  (Monaural. Cover pictures Don Stevenson's middle
  finger over washboard. Price includes bonus
  poster, which represents about $5 to $10 of the
  value.)
COLUMBIA (2698 "Moby Grape") . . . 10-20   67
  (Monaural. Cover pictures Don Stevenson's hand
  closed. Price includes bonus poster.)

COLUMBIA (9498 "Moby Grape") . . . 40-50   67
  (Stereo. Cover pictures Don Stevenson's middle
  finger over washboard. Price includes bonus
  poster, which represents about $5 to $10 of the
  value.)
COLUMBIA (9498 "Moby Grape") . . . 10-20   67
  (Stereo. Cover pictures Don Stevenson's hand
  closed. Price includes bonus poster.)
ESCAPE 8-10   78
HARMONY 10-12   70-71
REPRISE 10-12   71
SAN FRANCISCO SOUND 10-15   83
Promotional LPs
COLUMBIA (MGS-1 "Grape Jam") . . 10-20   68
  (With Mike Bloomfield and Al Kooper.)
ESCAPE (95018 "Live Grape") 15-25   78
  (Colored vinyl.)
  Members: Don Stevenson; Jerry Miller; Peter Lewis; Skip
  Spence; Jeff Blackburn.
   Also see BLOOMFIELD, Mike, and Al Kooper
   Also see FRANTICS

MOCEDADES
Singles: 7–inch
TARA 3-5   74
LPs: 10/12–inch 33rpm
TARA 5-10   74

MODEL 500
Singles: 12–inch 33/45rpm
METROPLEX 4-6   85

MODELS
Singles: 12–inch 33/45rpm
GEFFEN 4-6   86
Singles: 7–inch
GEFFEN 2-4   86
LPs: 10/12–inch 33rpm
GEFFEN 5-8   86
WINDSONG 5-8   80

MODERN ENGLISH
Singles: 12–inch 33/45rpm
SIRE 4-6   82-86
Singles: 7–inch
SIRE 2-4   82-86
LPs: 10/12–inch 33rpm
SIRE 5-8   83-86
TVT 5-8   90

MODERN ROCKETRY
Singles: 12–inch 33/45rpm
MEGATONE 4-6   83

MODERNAIRES
(Modernaires with Paula Kelly)
Singles: 78rpm
COLUMBIA 3-5   50
CORAL 3-5   51-56
Singles: 7–inch
CAPITOL 3-6   69
COLUMBIA (38000 series) 5-10   50
CORAL 5-10   51-56

MERCURY 4-8   59
U.A. 4-6   62
EPs: 7–inch 33/45rpm
CORAL 5-10   51-55
LPs: 10/12–inch 33rpm
COLUMBIA 10-25   50-66
CORAL 15-25   51-55
LIBERTY 5-10   84
MERCURY 8-12   60
ROSS 5-10   79
U.A. 10-20   61-62
WING 10-15   62
   Members: Paula Kelly; John Drake; Allan Copeland; Francis
   Scott; Hal Dickenson.

MODUGNO, Domenico
Singles: 7–inch
DECCA 4-8   58-64
MCA 3-5   78
MGM 4-6   66
RCA 4-6   68-72
U.A. INT'L 4-6   67
EPs: 7–inch 33/45rpm
DECCA 5-10   58
LPs: 10/12–inch 33rpm
DECCA 15-25   58-61
RCA 10-15   66
U.A. INT'L 8-12   67

MODULATIONS
Singles: 7–inch
BUDDAH 3-5   74-75

MOJO MEN
(Mojo)
Singles: 7–inch
AUTUMN 8-12   65-66
GRT 4-8   69
REPRISE 5-10   66-68
LPs: 10/12–inch 33rpm
GRT (10003 "Mojo Magic") 15-20   69

MOLLY HATCHET
Singles: 7–inch
EPIC 2-5   79-86
EPs: 7–inch 33/45rpm
CSP 4-8   81
   (Nestles candy promotional issue.)
LPs: 10/12–inch 33rpm
EPIC (Except picture discs) 5-10   78-87
EPIC (694 "Flirtin' with Disaster") 20-30   79
   (Picture disc. Promotional issue only.)
EPIC (884 "Beatin the Odds") 20-25   80
   (Picture disc. Promotional issue only.)
EPIC (1320 "Take No Prisoners") 15-20   81
   (Picture disc. Promotional issue only.)
EPIC (35347 "Molly Hatchet") 25-30   78
   (Picture disc. Promotional issue only.)
EPIC (36110 "Flirtin' with Disaster") .. 20-30   79
   (Picture disc. Promotional issue only.)
   Members: Danny Joe Brown; Jimmy Farrar.
   Also see BROWN, Danny Joe

MOM & DADS
Singles: 7–inch
GNP/CRESCENDO 3-5   71-80
LPs: 10/12–inch 33rpm
GNP/CRESCENDO 5-10   71-87

MOMENT of TRUTH
Singles: 7–inch
ROULETTE 3-5   75

MOMENTS
Singles: 7–inch
ERA 5-10   63-64
HIT 4-8   63
WORLD ARTISTS 4-8   64
   Also see SHACKLEFORDS

MOMENTS
(Moments and Whatnauts)
Singles: 7–inch
STANG 3-6   68-78
SUGAR HILL 2-4   80-81
LPs: 10/12–inch 33rpm
STANG 8-12   70-78
VICTORY 5-8   82
   Also see O'JAYS / Moments
   Also see RAY, GOODMAN & BROWN

MONAE, Tia
Singles: 12–inch 33/45rpm
FIRST TAKE 4-6   84

MONARCHS
Singles: 7–inch
ERWIN (1069 "Surge") 15-25   64

MONDAY, Julie
Singles: 7–inch
RAINBOW 4-8   66
SSS INT'L 3-6   68

MONDAY AFTER
Singles: 7–inch
BUDDAH 3-5   76

MONEY, Eddie
Singles: 12–inch 33/45rpm
COLUMBIA 4-6   84
Singles: 7–inch
CBS (165196 "Maybe I'm a Fool") ... 20-40   79
   (Picture disc. Promotional issue only.)
COLUMBIA 3-5   78-89
POLYDOR 2-4   85
Picture Sleeves
COLUMBIA 3-5   82-84
LPs: 10/12–inch 33rpm
COLUMBIA 6-9   77-89
POLYDOR 5-8   85

MONEY, Eddie, and Zane Buzby
Singles: 7–inch
COLUMBIA 3-5   79

MONEY, Eddie, and Valerie Carter
Singles: 7–inch
COLUMBIA 3-5   80
  Also see CARTER, Valerie

MONEY, Eddie, and Valerie Carter
Singles: 7–inch
COLUMBIA 3-5   80
  Also see CARTER, Valerie

MONEY, Eddie, and Ronnie Spector
Singles: 7–inch
COLUMBIA 3-5   86
  Also see MONEY, Eddie
  Also see SPECTOR, Ronnie

MONGO SANTAMARIA:
see SANTAMARIA, Mongo

MONITORS
Singles: 7–inch
BUDDAH 3-5   72
MOTOWN 3-5
SOUL 4-6   68
V.I.P. 4-8   65-68
LPs: 10/12–inch 33rpm
SOUL 10-20   69

MONK, T.S.
(Thelonious Monk Jr.)
Singles: 7–inch
MIRAGE 2-4   80-82
LPs: 10/12–inch 33rpm
MIRAGE 5-8   81-82

MONK, Thelonious
Singles: 7–inch
COLUMBIA 3-6   63-69
PRESTIGE 3-8   60-69
EPs: 7–inch 33/45rpm
PRESTIGE 20-40   52
LPs: 10/12–inch 33rpm
BLACK LION 5-10   74
BLUE NOTE (100 through 500 series) . 6-12 73-76
BLUE NOTE (1510 "Genius of
  Modern Music, Vol. 1") 40-60   56
  (Label has Lexington Ave. street address for Blue
  Note Records.)
BLUE NOTE (1510 "Genius of
  Modern Music, Vol. 1") 30-40   58
  (Label reads, "Blue Note Records Inc. New York,
  U.S.A.")
BLUE NOTE (1510 "Genius of
  Modern Music, Vol. 1") 10-20
  (Label reads "Blue Note Records - a Division of
  Liberty Records Inc.")
BLUE NOTE (1511 "Genius of
  Modern Music, Vol. 2") 40-60   56
  (Label has Lexington Ave. street address for Blue
  Note Records.)

BLUE NOTE (1511 "Genius of
  Modern Music, Vol. 2") 30-40   58
  (Label reads, "Blue Note Records Inc. New York,
  U.S.A.")
BLUE NOTE (1511 "Genius of
  Modern Music, Vol. 2") 10-20
  (Label reads "Blue Note Records - a Division of
  Liberty Records Inc.")
BLUE NOTE (5002 "Theolonious
  Monk") 175-275   52
  (10–inch LP.)
BLUE NOTE (5009 "Theolonious
  Monk") 175-275   52
  (10–inch LP.)
COLUMBIA (1900 through
  2600 series) 12-25   63-67
  (Monaural.)
COLUMBIA (8700 through
  9800 series) 15-30   63-69
  (Stereo.)
COLUMBIA (32000 through
  38000 series) 5-15   74-83
EVEREST 5-10   78
MILESTONE 5-15   75-84
PAUSA 5-10   83
PRESTIGE (142 "Thelonious
  Monk Trio") 75-125   52
  (10–inch LP.)
PRESTIGE (180 "Thelonious Monk
  with Frank Foster") 75-125   54
  (10–inch LP.)
PRESTIGE (189 "Thelonious Monk
  with Art Blakey") 50-100   54
  (10–inch LP.)
PRESTIGE (7053 through 7245) 30-60   56-62
  (Yellow labels.)
PRESTIGE (7000 through
  7600 series) 15-25   65-69
  (Blue labels.)
PRESTIGE (24000 series) 8-12   72
RIVERSIDE (12-201 through
  12-323) 30-60   55-60
RIVERSIDE (400 series) 15-30   62-67
RIVERSIDE (1100 series) 25-50   58-60
RIVERSIDE (3000 series) 10-20   68-69
RIVERSIDE (9400 series) 15-30   62-63
TOMATO 5-10   78
TRIP 5-10   73
  Also see COLTRANE, John, and Thelonious Monk
  Also see DAVIS, Miles, and Thelonious Monk
  Also see MERC & MONK
  Also see MULLIGAN, Gerry, and Thelonious Monk

MONK, Thelonious, and Sonny Rollins
EPs: 7–inch 33/45rpm
PRESTIGE 20-40   52
LPs: 10/12–inch 33rpm
PRESTIGE (166 "Thelonious Monk
  and Sonny Rollins") 100-200   52
  (10–inch LP.)

PRESTIGE (200 series) 30-60	57-58
PRESTIGE (7000 series) 30-60	57-59
PRESTIGE (1100 series) 30-60	58

MONKEES
Singles: 12–Inch 33/45rpm
ARISTA 8-12	86
(Promotional issue only.)	

Singles: 7–inch
ARISTA (0201 "Daydream Believer") . . . 4-8	76
ARISTA (9000 series) 3-5	76-86
COLGEMS 5-10	66-70
FLASHBACK 3-5	73
RHINO 2-4	87

Picture Sleeves
COLGEMS (1000 series) 10-20	66-68
COLGEMS (5000 series) 15-25	69-70

EPs: 7–Inch 33/45rpm
COLGEMS (Cardboard discs) 5-10	67
(Single-sided, four track discs, originally attached	
to cereal boxes. Not issued with covers, although	
discs were illustrated.)	
COLGEMS (101 "The Monkees") 50-75	66
COLGEMS (102 "More of	
the Monkees") 50-75	67

LPs: 10/12–inch 33rpm
ARISTA (4000 series) 8-10	76
ARISTA (8000 series) 5-8	86
BELL (6081 "Refocus") 20-30	73
COLGEMS (COM-101 "Monkees") . . 20-30	66
(Monaural. With *Papa Jean's Blues*.)	
COLGEMS (COS-101 "Monkees") . . . 30-40	66
(Stereo. With *Papa Jean's Blues*.)	
COLGEMS (COM-101 "Monkees") . . 15-25	66
(Monaural. With *Papa Gene's Blues*.)	
COLGEMS (COS-101 "The Monkees") 20-30	66
(Stereo. With *Papa Gene's Blues*.)	
COLGEMS (COM-102 "More of	
the Monkees") 15-25	67
(Monaural.)	
COLGEMS (COS-102 "More of	
the Monkees") 20-30	67
(Stereo.)	
COLGEMS (COM-103	
"Headquarters") 15-25	67
(Monaural.)	
COLGEMS (COS-103	
"Headquarters") 20-30	67
(Stereo.)	
COLGEMS (COM-104 "Pisces, Aquarius,	
Capricorn and Jones") 15-25	67
(Monaural.)	
COLGEMS (COS-104 "Pisces, Aquarius,	
Capricorn and Jones") 20-30	67
(Stereo.)	
COLGEMS (COM-109 "The Birds, The Bees,	
and the Monkees") 50-75	68
(Monaural.)	

COLGEMS (COS-109 "The Birds, The Bees,		
and the Monkees") 20-30	68
(Stereo.)	
COLGEMS (113 "Instant Replay") . . . 25-35	69
COLGEMS (115 "The Monkees	
Greatest Hits") 40-50	69
COLGEMS (117 "The Monkees	
Present") 60-75	69
COLGEMS (119 "Changes") 75-100	70
COLGEMS (329 "Golden Hits") . . . 100-125	71
(RCA Special Products issue.)	
COLGEMS (1001 "A Barrel Full	
of Monkees") 50-75	71
COLGEMS (5008 "Head") 35-45	68
LAURIE HOUSE 20-30	73
(Mail-order offer.)	
PAIR (0188 "The Monkees") 15-25	82
RCA (329 "Golden Hits") 50-75	72
RCA (7000 series) 8-10	
RHINO 5-10	82-87

Members: Michael Nesmith; Davy Jones; Micky Dolenz; Peter Tork.
Also see DOLENZ, Micky
Also see DOLENZ, JONES & TORK
Also see JONES, Davy
Also see NESMITH, Michael

MONOTONES
Singles: 7–inch
ARGO (Except 5339) 10-15	58-59
ARGO (5339 "Tell It to the Judge") . . 15-20	59
CHESS 3-5	73
COLLECTABLES 2-4	
ERIC 3-5	
HICKORY 5-10	64-65
HULL (735 "Reading the Book	
of Love") 50-60	60
HULL (743 "Daddy's Home But	
Momma's Gone") 15-20	61
MASCOT (124 "Book of Love") . . . 125-200	57
ROULETTE 3-5	73

Members: Warren Davis; Frank Smith; John Raynes; George Malone; Charles Patrick; James Patrick.

MONRO, Matt
Singles: 7–inch
CAPITOL 3-6	66-72
LIBERTY 3-8	62-66
U.A. 3-5	74
WARWICK 4-8	61

LPs: 10/12–inch 33rpm
CAPITOL 8-15	67-70
LIBERTY 10-20	62-66
LONDON (1611 "Blue and	
Sentimental") 20-30	57
WARWICK (2045 "My Kind of Girl") . . 15-25	61

Also see BARRY, John

MONROE, Marilyn
Singles: 78rpm
RCA (Except 5745) 10-15	54-55

WHO IS SHE

SHE'S GORGEOUS! HER NAME IS A HOUSEHOLD WORD! YOU GUESS! ASK YOUR LISTENERS TO GUESS!

ANSWER IN NEXT WEEK'S D.J. KIT

Simon House Indi - BMI

NOT FOR SALE

RCA VICTOR
PROMOTION DISC

Simon House   (20-5745)
-ASCAP   54-VB-3143

THE RIVER OF NO RETURN
(Ken Darby-Lionel Newman)
(from the 20th Century-Fox CinemaScope Prod.
"River Of No Return")

MARILYN MONROE
with Orchestral Accompaniment
Time: 2:14

RCA (5745 "River of No Return") 15-25   54
  (With picture of Marilyn on label. Promotional only.)
RCA/SIMON HOUSE (5745 "River of
  No Return") 25-50   54
  (With "Who Is She?" label. Promotional issue only.)
U.A. 5-10   59

Singles: 7–inch
RCA (Except 5745) 10-20   54-55
RCA (5745 "River of No Return") 15-25   54
  (With picture of Marilyn on label. Promotional only.)
20TH FOX (311 "River of No Return") . 5-10   62
U.A. 5-10   59

Picture Sleeves
RCA (5745 "River of No Return") 25-50   54
RCA (6033 "Heat Wave") 25-50   55
20TH FOX (311 "River of No Return") 25-50   62

EPs: 7–inch 33/45rpm
MGM (208 "Gentlemen Prefer
  Blondes") 15-25   53
  (Soundtrack. With Jane Russell.)
RCA (593 "There's No Business
  Like Show Business") 10-20   55
U.A. (1005 "Some Like It Hot") 10-15   59

LPs: 10/12–inch 33rpm
ASCOT (13500 "Some Like It Hot") .. 15-20   64
  (Monaural. Soundtrack.)

ASCOT (16500 "Some Like It Hot") .. 25-30   64
  (Stereo. Soundtrack. Also has selections from
  other films.)
COLUMBIA (1527 "Let's Make Love") 20-30   60
  (Monaural. Soundtrack.)
COLUMBIA (8327 "Let's Make Love") 30-40   60
  (Stereo. Soundtrack.)
COLUMBIA/CSP (8327 "Let's Make
  Love") 8-10
  (Soundtrack. With Yves Montand and Frankie
  Vaughan.)
MGM (208 "Gentlemen Prefer
  Blondes") 40-60   53
  (10–inch LP.)
MGM (3231 "Gentlemen Prefer
  Blondes") 25-35   55
  (Soundtrack. With Jane Russell. One side has
  music from *Till the Clouds Roll By*.)
MOVIETONE (72016 "Unforgettable") 10-20   67
STET 8-10
20TH FOX (5000 "Marilyn") 40-60   62
  (Add $25 to $50 if accompanied by bonus poster.)
U.A. (272 "Some Like It Hot") 8-10   74
  (Soundtrack.)
U.A. (4030 "Some Like It Hot") 25-35   59
  (Monaural. Soundtrack.)
U.A. (5030 "Some Like It Hot") 40-50   59
  (Stereo. Soundtrack.)

MONROE, Vaughn
Singles: 78rpm
BLUEBIRD 5-10   40-42
RCA 3-8   47-58
VICTOR 4-8   42-47
Singles: 7–inch
DOT 3-6   62-63
JUBILEE 4-6   61
MGM 4-6   60
RCA 5-8   50-59
ROD 3-5   68
U.A. 4-6   60
Picture Sleeves
RCA 10-15   57
EPs: 7–inch 33/45rpm
CAMDEN 5-10   56
RCA 5-10   50-56
LPs: 10/12–inch 33rpm
CAMDEN 15-25   56
DOT 10-20   62-64
HAMILTON 10-20   65
KAPP 10-20   65
RCA (11 through 3066) 20-40   50-53
  (10–inch LPs.)
RCA (1400 through 1700 series) 15-25   56-58
  (12–inch LPs.)
RCA (1100 series) 5-10   75
RCA (3800 series) 10-15   67
RCA (6000 series) 5-10   72
Also see MARTIN, Dean / Patti Page

MONROES
Singles: 7-inch
ALFA 2-4   82
LPs: 10/12-inch 33rpm
ALFA 5-8   82

MONTANA ORCHESTRA
LPs: 10/12-inch 33rpm
MJS 5-8   81

MONTANA SEXTET
Singles: 12-inch 33/45rpm
PHILLY SOUND 4-6   83

MONTANAS
Singles: 7-inch
INDEPENDENCE 5-10   67-69
WARNER 4-8   66-68

MONTCLAIRS
Singles: 7-inch
PAULA 3-5   71-74
LPs: 10/12-inch 33rpm
PAULA 8-12   72

MONTE, Lou
Singles: 78rpm
RCA (Except 6704) 3-5   53-56
RCA (6704 "Elvis Presley
   for President") 10-15   56
Singles: 7-inch
GWP 3-5   71-72
RCA (5382 through 6600 series) 8-12   53-56
RCA (6700 through 7600
   series, except 6704) 5-10   56-60
RCA (6704 "Elvis Presley
   for President") 15-25   56
RCA (8700 through 9000 series) 4-8   65-67
RAGALIA 3-6   69
REPRISE 4-8   62-65
ROULETTE 4-8   60-61
Picture Sleeves
REPRISE 5-8   62-63
EPs: 7-inch 33/45rpm
RCA (Except 18) 8-12   57-59
RCA (18 "Elvis Presley for President") 20-30   56
   (Promotional issue only. Not issued with cover.)
LPs: 10/12-inch 33rpm
CAMDEN 15-20   58
HARMONY 10-15   68
RCA (1600 through 1900 series) 20-35   57-59
RCA (3000 series) 10-20   66-67
ROULETTE 15-25   60
REPRISE 15-25   61-65

MONTENEGRO, Hugo
(Hugo Montenegro's Orchestra and Chorus)
Singles: 7-inch
RCA 3-5   64-75
TIME 4-6   61-63
20TH FOX 5-8   59

LPs: 10/12-inch 33rpm
CAMDEN 10-20   62
GWP 5-10   70
MAINSTREAM 10-15   67-68
MOVIETONE 8-12   67
PICKWICK 5-10
RCA (0025 through 2300 series) 5-10   72-77
RCA (LOC-1113 "Hurry Sundown") .. 35-40   67
   (Monaural. Soundtrack.)
RCA (LSO-1113 "Hurry Sundown") .. 40-50   67
   (Stereo. Soundtrack.)
RCA (2900 series) 10-15   64
RCA (LPM-3475 "The Man
   from Uncle") 25-35   65
   (Monaural. Soundtrack.)
RCA (LSP-3475 "The Man
   from Uncle") 30-40   65
   (Stereo. Soundtrack.)
RCA (LPM-3574 "The Man
   from Uncle, Volume 2") 30-40   66
   (Monaural. Soundtrack.)
RCA (LSP-3574 "The Man
   from Uncle, Volume 2") 35-45   66
   (Stereo. Soundtrack.)
RCA (3500 through 4600 series) 5-15   66-71
RCA (6000 series) 5-10   71
TIME 8-15   60-64
20TH FOX 5-15   59-68
   Also see HIRT, Al, and Hugo Montenegro

MONTEZ, Chris
Singles: 7-inch
A&M 4-6   65-68
COLLECTABLES 2-4
ERA 3-5   72
ERIC 2-4
JAMIE 3-5   73
MONOGRAM 5-10   62-64
PARAMOUNT 3-5   71-73
LPs: 10/12-inch 33rpm
A&M 10-20   66-67
MONOGRAM (100 "Let's Dance") ... 45-65   63
   Members: Joel Hill; Carol Kaye; Julius Wechter; Pete Jolly; Tom Tedesco; Hal Blaine.
   Also see BAJA MARIMBA BAND
   Also see CHRIS & KATHY
   Also see JOLLY, Pete

MONTGOMERY, Melba
Singles: 7-inch
CAPITOL 3-5   69-76
COMPASS 2-4   86
ELEKTRA 3-5   73-75
MUSICOR 3-6   66-69
U.A. (500 through
   900 series) 4-8   63-66
U.A. (1000 and 1100 series) 3-5   77
Picture Sleeves
MUSICOR 4-8   66
LPs: 10/12-inch 33rpm
CAPITOL 8-12   69-75

ELEKTRA 5-10	73-75
MUSICOR 10-20	66-68
UNART 8-12	67
U.A. (Except 600 series) 10-20	64
U.A. (600 series) 5-10	78

Also see JONES, George, and Gene Pitney and Melba Montgomery
Also see JONES, George, and Melba Montgomery
Also see PITNEY, Gene, and Melba Montgomery
Also see WEST, Dottie / Melba Montgomery

MONTGOMERY, Tammy
(Tammi Terrell)
Singles: 7-inch

CHECKER 5-10	64
SCEPTER 5-10	61
TRY ME 5-10	63
WAND 5-10	62

Also see TERRELL, Tammi

MONTGOMERY, Wes
(Wes Montgomery Quartet)
Singles: 7-inch

A&M 3-5	67-70
PACIFIC JAZZ 4-8	60
RIVERSIDE 4-8	61-64
VERVE 4-6	65-68

LPs: 10/12-inch 33rpm

A&M 10-15	67-70
ACCORD 5-8	82
BLUE NOTE 6-12	75
MGM 10-15	70
MILESTONE 8-15	73-83
PACIFIC JAZZ (5 "Montgomeryland") 35-45	60
PACIFIC JAZZ (10000 and 20000	
series) 10-20	66-68
RIVERSIDE (034 through 089) 5-8	82-83
RIVERSIDE (300 and 400 series) . . . 15-30	59-67
RIVERSIDE (3000 series) 10-15	68-69
VERVE 10-20	65-72

(Reads "MGM Records - A Division of
Metro-Goldwyn-Mayer, Inc." at bottom of label.)

VERVE 5-10	73-84

(Reads "Manufactured By MGM Record Corp.," or
mentions either Polydor or Polygram at bottom of
label.)
Also see MONTGOMERY BROTHERS
Also see SMITH, Jimmy, and Wes Montgomery

MONTGOMERY BROTHERS
Singles: 7-inch

RIVERSIDE 4-8	61

LPs: 10/12-inch 33rpm

FANTASY 20-35	60-62
PACIFIC JAZZ 20-30	61
RIVERSIDE 20-30	61
WORLD PACIFIC (1240 "Montgomery	
Brothers") 35-55	58

Members: Wes Montgomery; Buddy Montgomery; Monk
Montgomery.
Also see MONTGOMERY, Wes
Also see SHEARING, George, and the Montgomery Brothers

MONTRE-EL, Jackie
Singles: 7-inch

ABC 4-8	68

MONTROSE
Singles: 7-inch

WARNER 3-5	74-77

LPs: 10/12-inch 33rpm

ENIGMA 5-8	87
WARNER 8-12	73-78

Members: Ronnie Montrose; Sammy Hagar.
Also see HAGAR, Sammy

MONTROSE, Ronnie
Singles: 7-inch

WARNER 3-5	78

LPs: 10/12-inch 33rpm

WARNER 5-10	78

Also see GAMMA
Also see MONTROSE
Also see WINTER, Edgar

MONTY PYTHON
Singles: 7-inch

ARISTA 3-5	80

LPs: 10/12-inch 33rpm

ARISTA 5-10	75-82
MCA 5-8	83
WARNER 5-10	79
PYE 5-10	75

Members: John Cleese; Graham Chapman; Eric Idle; Michael
Palin; Terry Jones; Terry Gilliam.
Also see RUTLES

MONYAKA
Singles: 12-inch 33/45rpm

EASY STREET 4-6	83

MOODY BLUES
Singles: 7-inch

DERAM 3-6	68-72
LONDON (200 series) 3-5	78
LONDON (1000 series) 5-10	67
LONDON (9000 series, except 9726) 10-15	65-66
LONDON (9726 "Go Now") 5-10	65
LONDON (20000 series) 8-12	66
POLYDOR 2-4	86-88
THRESHOLD (600 series) 2-4	81-85
THRESHOLD (67000 series) 3-5	70-72

Picture Sleeves

POLYDOR 2-4	86
THRESHOLD (600 series) 2-4	81-85
THRESHOLD (67000 series) 3-5	70-72

LPs: 10/12-inch 33rpm

DERAM (18012 "Days of Future	
Passed") 10-20	68
DERAM (18017 "In Search of the	
Lost Chord") 10-20	68
(Gatefold cover.)	
DERAM (18017 "In Search of the	
Lost Chord") 5-10	
(Standard cover.)	

DERAM (18025 "On the Threshold
of a Dream") 10-20   69
(Gatefold cover.)
DERAM (18025 "On the Threshold
of a Dream") 5-10   69
(Standard cover.)
DERAM (18051 "In the Beginning") .. 10-20   69
DERAM (820006 "Days of Future
Passed") 5-10
LONDON (428 "Go Now") 20-25   65
(Stereo.)
LONDON (690 "Caught Love") 10-20   77
LONDON (708 "Octave") 8-10   78
(Black vinyl.)
LONDON (708 "Octave") 20-25   78
(Colored vinyl. Promotional issue only.)
LONDON (3428 "Go Now") 25-45   65
(Monaural.)
MFSL (042 "Days of Future Past") .. 25-50   80
MFSL (151 "Seventh Sojourn") 15-25   85
POLYDOR 5-8   88-91
THRESHOLD 6-12   69-86
Members: Michael Pinder; Ray Thomas; Graeme Edge; Denny
Laine; Brian Hines; Clint Warwick; John Lodge; Justin Hayward;
Patrick Moraz.
Also see EDGE, Graeme
Also see HAYWARD, Justin, and John Lodge
Also see LODGE, John
Also see MORAZ, Patrick
Also see PINDER, Michael
Also see THOMAS, Ray

MOON, Keith
Singles: 7–inch
TRACK 3-5   75
LPs: 10/12–inch 33rpm
MCA 8-10   75
Also see LORD SUTCH
Also see NELSON, Rick
Also see WHO

MOONEY, Art, and His Orchestra
Singles: 78rpm
MGM 3-5   50-57
VOGUE (Except 711 and 713) 25-40   46-48
(Picture discs.)
VOGUE (711 "I've Been Working
on the Railroad") 50-100   46
(Picture discs.)
VOGUE (713 "I've Been Working
on the Railroad") 50-100   46
(Picture discs.)
Singles: 7–inch
DECCA 3-6   61-62
KAPP 3-6   64-65
MGM (Except 12312) 4-8   50-64
MGM (12312 "Rebel Without a Cause") 5-10   56
RIVERSIDE 3-5   62
Picture Sleeves
MGM (12312 "Rebel Without a Cause"/
"East of Eden") 20-30   56
(Billed as a "Tribute to James Dean.")

EPs: 7–inch 33/45rpm
MGM 5-10   55-56
LPs: 10/12–inch 33rpm
DECCA 10-15   62
KAPP 10-15   64
MGM 10-25   55-61
RCA 8-12   67

MOONGLOWS
Singles: 78rpm
CHAMPAGNE (7500 "I Just Can't
Tell No Lie") 75-125   52
CHANCE 1147 "Whistle My Love") 750-100   53
CHANCE (1150 "Just a Lonely
Christmas") 75-100   53
CHANCE (1152 "Secret Love") 75-100   54
CHANCE (1152 "I Was Wrong") ... 75-100   54
CHANCE (1161 "219 Train") 75-100   54
CHESS (1500 series) 10-20   54-55
CHESS (1600 series) 8-15   55-57
Singles: 7–inch
BIG P 3-5   71
CHAMPAGNE (7500 "I Just Can't
Tell No Lie") 350-450   52
CHANCE (1147 "Whistle My
Love") 1000-1500   53
(Colored vinyl.)
CHANCE (1150 "Just a Lonely
Christmas") 800-1200   53
(Colored vinyl.)
CHANCE (1152 "Secret Love") .. 750-1000   54
(Blue and silver label.)
CHANCE (1152 "Secret Love") ... 500-700   54
(Yellow and black label.)
CHANCE (1156 "I Was Wrong") . 750-1000   54
(Yellow and black label.)
CHANCE (1156 "I Was Wrong") .. 300-400   55
(White and black label.)
CHANCE (1161 "219 Train") 500-700   54
(White and black label.)
CHESS (1581 "Sincerely") 40-60   54
CHESS (1589 "Most of All") 40-60   54
CHESS (1598 "Foolish Me") 30-40   55
CHESS (1605 "Starlite") 30-40   55
CHESS (1611 In My Diary") 30-40   55
CHESS (1619 "We Go Together") ... 30-40   56
CHESS (1629 "See Saw") 25-35   56
CHESS (1646 "Over and Over Again") 20-35   56
CHESS (1651 "I'm Afraid the
Masquerade Is Over") 20-30   56
CHESS (1661 "Please Send Me
Someone to Love") 20-30   57
CHESS (1669 "The Beating of
My Heart") 20-30   57
CHESS (1681 "Too Late") 10-20   58
CHESS (1689 "Soda Pop") 10-15   58
CHESS (1701 "This Love") 10-15   58
CHESS (1717 "I'll Never Stop
Wanting You") 10-15   58

BLAZE (101 "Miss Mosey") 20-30
HOLLYWOOD (1031 "Why Johnny
Why") 20-30   55
HOLLYWOOD (1045 "Christmas Eve
Baby") 20-30   55
HOLLYWOOD (1056 "I Send My
Love") 20-30   56
MODERN (800 and 900 series) 15-25   53
RCA (0009 "This Is One Time Baby") . 25-50   50
(Colored vinyl.)
RCA (0018 "Bop-A-Bye Baby") 25-50   50
(Colored vinyl.)
RCA (0026 "Walkin' Blues") 25-50   50
(Colored vinyl.)
RCA (0031 "Shuffle Shuck") 25-50   50
(Colored vinyl.) ....
RCA (0043 "So Long") 25-50   50
(Colored vinyl.) ....
RCA (0073 "Misery Blues") 25-50   50
(Colored vinyl.) ....
RCA (0086 "Rain-Check") 25-50   50
(Colored vinyl.) ....
RCA (0095 "Jumping Jack") 25-50   50
(Colored vinyl.)
RENDEZVOUS 5-10   60
Members: Johnny Moore; Charles Brown; Eddie Williams.
Also see BROWN, Charles
Also see DIXON, Floyd, and Johnny Moore's Three Blazers
Also see McSHANN, Jay, and Johnny Moore's Three Blazers

MOORE, Johnny, and Linda Hayes
Singles: 7-inch
HOLLYWOOD (1031 "Why, Johnny [Ace]
Why 30-40   55
Also see HAYES, Linda
Also see MOORE, Johnny

MOORE, Lee
Singles: 7-inch
SOURCE 3-5   79

MOORE, Melba
Singles: 12-inch 33/45rpm
CAPITOL 4-6   83-86
EPIC 4-8   79-80
Singles: 7-inch
BUDDAH 3-5   75-78
CAPITOL 2-4   82-87
EMI AMERICA 2-4   81-82
EPIC 3-5   78-80
MERCURY 3-6   69-72
MUSICOR 4-8   66
LPs: 10/12-inch 33rpm
ACCORD 5-10   81
BUDDAH 8-10   75-79
CAPITOL 5-8   83-86
EMI AMERICA 5-10   81
EPIC 5-10   78-80
MERCURY 10-15   70-72
Also see THOMAS, Lillo, and Melba Moore

MOORE, Melba, and Freddie Jackson
Singles: 7-inch
CAPITOL 2-4   86-88
Also see JACKSON, Freddie

MOORE, Melba, and Kashif
Singles: 7-inch
CAPITOL 2-4   86
Also see KASHIF
Also see MOORE, Melba

MOORE, Rene
Singles: 7-inch
POLYDOR 2-4   88
LPs: 10/12-inch 33rpm
POLYDOR 5-8   88

MOORE, Tim
Singles: 7-inch
ASYLUM 3-5   74-79
DUNHILL 3-5   73
LPs: 10/12-inch 33rpm
ASYLUM 5-10   74-75

MOORE, Vinnie
LPs: 10/12-inch 33rpm
SQUAWK 5-8   88

MORAZ, Patrick
LPs: 10/12-inch 33rpm
ATLANTIC 8-12   76
CHRISIMA 5-8   78
IMPORT 8-10   77
PASSPORT 5-8
Also see MOODY BLUES
Also see YES

MORGAN, Denroy
Singles: 12-inch 33/45rpm
BECKET 4-6   81-82
Singles: 7-inch
BECKET 3-5   81

MORGAN, Jane
Singles: 78rpm
KAPP 3-6   54-57
Singles: 7-inch
ABC 4-6   67-68
EPIC 4-6   65-68
COLPIX 4-8   63-65
KAPP 5-10   54-62
RCA 3-5   69-70
EPs: 7-inch 33/45rpm
KAPP 5-10   55-59
Picture Sleeves
COLPIX 5-10   63
ELEKTRA 2-4   82
EPIC 4-8   65
KAPP 5-12   57-59
LPs: 10/12-inch 33rpm
ABC 5-10   68
COLPIX 10-20   63-66
EPIC 10-15   65-67

KAPP 10-20   56-63
MCA 5-10   73
RCA (Except 1160) 8-12   69-70
RCA (1160 "Marry Me, Marry Me") ... 10-15   69
   (Soundtrack.)
HARMONY 5-8   70
   Also see WILLIAMS, Roger, and Jane Morgan

MORGAN, Jaye P.
Singles: 78rpm
DECCA 3-6   54-55
DERBY 3-6   53
RCA 3-6   54-56
Singles: 7–inch
ABC-PAR 4-6   65
BEVERLY HILLS 3-5   69-72
DECCA 5-10   54-55
DERBY 5-10   53
GIGOLO 3-5
MGM 4-8   59-63
RCA 5-10   54-56
EPs: 7–Inch 33/45rpm
DECCA 10-20   55
DERBY 10-20   53
LPs: 10/12–inch 33rpm
BAINBRIDGE 5-10   82
BEVERLY HILLS 5-8   70
MGM 15-25   59-61
RCA (1155 "Jaye P. Morgan") 20-30   55
   Also see COMO, Perry, and Jaye P. Morgan
   Also see PRESLEY, Elvis / Jaye P. Morgan

MORGAN, Lee
Singles: 7–Inch
BLUE NOTE 4-6   64-69
BUZZ 3-5   79-80
VEE JAY 4-8   60
LPs: 10/12–Inch 33rpm
BLUE NOTE (200 series) 8-12   74
BLUE NOTE (900 and 1000 series) ... 5-10   79-81
BLUE NOTE (1500 series) 25-50   56-58
   (Label gives New York street address for Blue Note Records.)
BLUE NOTE (1500 series) 15-25   58
   (Label reads: "Blue Note Records Inc. - New York, USA.")
BLUE NOTE (1500 series) 10-20   66
   (Label shows Blue Note Records as a division of either Liberty or United Artists.)
BLUE NOTE (4000 series) 20-40   61
   (Label gives New York street address for Blue Note Records.)
BLUE NOTE (4000 series) 15-25   62
   (Label reads: "Blue Note Records Inc. - New York, USA.")
BLUE NOTE (4000 series) 10-20   66
   (Label shows Blue Note Records as a division of either Liberty or United Artists.)

BLUE NOTE (4100 through 4200 series) 15-25   63
   (Label reads: "Blue Note Records Inc. - New York, USA.")
BLUE NOTE (4100 through 4200 series) 10-20   66-67
   (Label shows Blue Note Records as a division of either Liberty or United Artists.)
BLUE NOTE (84000 series) 20-40   61
   (Label gives New York street address for Blue Note Records.)
BLUE NOTE (84000 series) 15-25   62
   (Label reads: "Blue Note Records Inc. - New York, USA.")
BLUE NOTE (84000 series) 10-20   66
   (Label shows Blue Note Records as a division of either Liberty or United Artists.)
BLUE NOTE (84100 through 84200 series) 15-25   63-69
   (Label reads: "Blue Note Records Inc. - New York, USA.")
BLUE NOTE (84100 through 84300 series) 10-20   66-70
   (Label shows Blue Note Records as a division of either Liberty or United Artists.)
BLUE NOTE (89000 series) 10-15   71
GNP/CRESCENDO 6-12   73
JAZZLAND 15-25   62
MCA 5-8   74
PACIFIC JAZZ 5-8   81
PRESTIGE 5-8   81
SAVOY (12091 "Introducing Lee Morgan") 50-75   56
SUNSET 5-10   69
TRADITION 8-15   68
TRIP 6-10   73
VEE JAY 25-50   60-65

MORGAN, Mell'sa
Singles: 12–inch 33/45rpm
CAPITOL 4-6   86
Singles: 7–inch
CAPITOL 2-4   86-88
LPs: 10/12–inch 33rpm
CAPITOL 5-8   86-87
   Also see KASHIF and Meli'sa Morgan

MORGAN, Russ, and His Orchestra
Singles: 78rpm
DECCA 3-5   50-56
Singles: 7–inch
DECCA 5-10   50-56
EVEREST 4-6   61
VEE JAY 4-6   64-65
EPs: 7–inch 33/45rpm
DECCA 5-10   51-56
LPs: 10/12–inch 33rpm
CAPITOL 10-15   62
CIRCLE 5-10   81
DECCA 10-30   51-67

EVEREST 10-15	60-63	
GNP/CRESCENDO 5-10	73	
MCA 5-10	73	
PICKWICK ....,..... 5-10	65	
SUNSET 8-12	66	
VEE JAY 10-15	65	

MORGAN BROTHERS
Singles: 7-inch
MGM 4-8	58-60	
RCA 5-10	55	

MORISETTE, Johnnie
Singles: 7-inch
SAR 5-10	60-63

MORLEY, Cozy
Singles: 78rpm
ABC-PAR 10-15	57

Singles: 7-inch
ABC-PAR 10-20	57

MORMON TABERNACLE CHOIR
Singles: 7-inch
COLUMBIA 3-5	59

Picture Sleeves
COLUMBIA 4-8	59

LPs: 10/12-inch 33rpm
COLUMBIA 5-10	59-76
RCA 5-10	60

MORNING MIST
Singles: 7-inch
EVENT 3-5	71

Members: Terry Cashman; Tommy West.
Also see CASHMAN & WEST

MORNING, NOON & NIGHT
Singles: 7-inch
ROADSHOW 3-5	77

LPs: 10/12-inch 33rpm
ROADSHOW 8-10	77

MORODER, Giorgio
(Giorgio)
Singles: 12-inch 33/45rpm
COLUMBIA 4-6	84
MCA 4-6	84

Singles: 7-inch
BACKSTREET 2-4	
CASABLANCA 3-5	79-80
COLUMBIA 2-4	84
DUNHILL 3-5	72
EMI AMERICA 2-4	84
MCA 2-4	84
POLYDOR 3-5	80
VIRGIN 2-4	

LPs: 10/12-inch 33rpm
CASABLANCA 5-10	77-79
DUNHILL 10-12	72
POLYDOR 5-10	80

Also see MERCURY, Freddie / Giorgio Moroder
Also see SUMMER, Donna

MORODER, Giorgio, and Phil Oakey
Singles: 12-inch 33/45rpm
VIRGIN 4-6	84

Also see HUMAN LEAGUE
Also see MORODER, Giorgio

MORRILL, Kent
Singles: 7-inch
BRC 4-8	71
CONGRESS 5-10	69
ETIQUETTE.................... 10-15	63

LPs: 10/12-inch 33rpm
CREAM 10-12	
SUSPICIOUS 5-8	88

Also see WAILERS

MORRIS, David, Jr.
Singles: 7-inch
BUDDAH 3-5	76
PHILIPS 4-8	68

MORRIS, Gary
Singles: 7-inch
WARNER 2-4	80-88

LPs: 10/12-inch 33rpm
WARNER 5-8	82-88

Also see ANDERSON, Lynn, and Gary Morris
Also see GAYLE, Crystal, and Gary Morris

MORRIS, Joe, and His Orchestra
(Joe Morris Orch. Featuring Mr. Stringbean)
Singles: 78rpm
ATLANTIC (Except 950, 954 and 974) 5-10	47-57	
ATLANTIC (950 "If I Had Known") ... 20-30	51	
ATLANTIC (954 "Someday You'll Be Sorry") 10-20	52	
ATLANTIC (974 "Bald Headed Woman") 10-20	52	
DECCA 4-8	49-50	
MANOR 5-10	46-47	

Singles: 7-inch
ATLANTIC (950 "If I Had Known") .. 75-125	51	
(Vocals by Billy Mitchell and Teddy Smith.)		
ATLANTIC (954 "Someday You'll Be Sorry") 50-100	52	
(Vocal by Billy Mitchell.)		
ATLANTIC (974 "Bald Headed Woman") 50-100	52	
(Vocal by Billy Mitchell.)		
ATLANTIC (1100 series) 10-15	57	
HERALD (Except 420) 10-20	53-54	
HERALD (420 "Travelin' Man") 20-30		
(Black vinyl.)		
HERALD (420 "Travelin' Man") 40-60		
(Colored vinyl.)		

Also see ADAMS, Faye
Also see MITCHELL, Billy

MORRIS, Joe, and His Orchestra
(Featuring Billy Mitchell)
Singles: 78rpm
ATLANTIC 10-15	51-52

Singles: 7-inch

ATLANTIC 20-40   51-52
  Also see MITCHELL, Billy

MORRIS, Joe, and His Orchestra
(Featuring Laurie Tate)
Singles: 78rpm

ATLANTIC 10-15   51-52
Singles: 7-inch
ATLANTIC (965 "Rock Me Daddy") .. 20-40   52

MORRIS, Marlowe, Quintet
Singles: 7-inch

COLUMBIA 4-8   62

MORRISON, Dorothy
Singles: 7-inch

BUDDAH 3-5   70
ELEKTRA 4-6   69
LPs: 10/12-inch 33rpm
BUDDAH 10-15   70
  Also see HAWKINS, Edwin, Singers

MORRISON, Junie
Singles: 7-inch

ISLAND 2-4   84
  Also see JUNIE

MORRISON, Van
(Van Morrison and the Chieftains)
Singles: 7-inch

BANG 4-8   67-68
MERCURY 2-4   85-90
SOLID GOLD 2-4   73
WARNER 2-5   70-83
LPs: 10/12-inch 33rpm
BANG (BLP-218 "Blowin' Your Mind") 20-25   67
  (Monaural.)
BANG (BLPS-218 "Blowin' Your Mind")25-30   67
  (Stereo. White label. Has 45 rpm version of
  Brown-Eyed Girl, with "makin' love in the green
  grass behind the stadium" lyric.)
BANG (BLPS-218 "Blowin' Your Mind")25-30   67
  (Stereo. White label. Has edited *Brown-Eyed Girl*,
  with "laughin' and a runnin' behind the stadium"
  lyric.)
BANG (BLPS-218 "Blowin' Your Mind")10-15   70
  (Yellow label.)
BANG (400 "T.B. Sheets") 10-15   74
LONDON 10-15   74
MERCURY 5-10   85-90
WARNER 8-15   68-83
  Also see THEM

MORRISSEY
LPs: 10/12-inch 33rpm

SIRE 5-8   88-91

MORROW, Buddy, and His Orchestra
Singles: 78rpm

MERCURY 3-5   54-57
RCA 3-5   50-57

Singles: 7-inch

EPIC 4-6   64
MERCURY 4-8   54-62
RCA 5-10   50-59
U.A. 4-8   68
WING 4-8   55-56
EPs: 7-inch 33/45rpm
MERCURY 5-10   54-61
RCA 5-10   52-61
LPs: 10/12-inch 33rpm
EPIC (Except 24095 and 26095) 5-15   64-65
EPIC (24095 "Big Band Beatlemania") 15-25   64
  (Monaural.)
EPIC (26095 "Big Band Beatlemania") 20-30   64
  (Stereo.)
MERCURY 10-20   54-62
RCA (2000 and 2100 series) 10-20   59-60
RCA (2200 and series) 8-15   60
RCA (3100 and 3200 series) 15-30   52-54
  (10-inch LPs.)
U.A. 5-10   68
WING 10-20   56

MORSE, Ella Mae
(Ella Mae Morse and Freddie Slack)
Singles: 78rpm

CAPITOL 3-5   50-56
Singles: 7-inch
CAPITOL (1600 through 3400 series) . 5-10   50-56
EPs: 7-inch 33/45rpm
CAPITOL 10-20   54-55
LPs: 10/12-inch 33rpm
CAPITOL (H-513 "Barrelhouse Boogie
  and the Blues") 75-125   54
  (10-inch LP.)
CAPITOL (T-513 "Barrelhouse Boogie
  and the Blues") 50-75   55
CAPITOL (898 "Morse Code") 50-75   57
CAPITOL (1802 "Hits") 30-45   62

MORSE, Steve, Band
LPs: 10/12-inch 33rpm

MCA 5-8   89
MUSICIAN/ELEKTRA 5-8   84
  Also see DIXIE DREGS
  Also see KANSAS

MOSBY, Johnny and Jonie
Singles: 7-inch

CAPITOL 3-6   67-73
CHALLENGE 5-10   60
COLUMBIA 4-8   62-66
STARDAY 4-6   65
TOPPA 5-8   61
Picture Sleeves
CAPITOL 3-5   70
LPs: 10/12-inch 33rpm
CAPITOL 8-12   68-71
COLUMBIA 10-15   65
HARMONY 5-10   70

MOSS, Bill
Singles: 7–inch
BELL 3-5   69

MOST, Donny
Singles: 7–inch
U.A. 3-5   76-77
VENTURE 3-5   78
Picture Sleeves
U.A. 3-5   76
LPs: 10/12–inch 33rpm
U.A. 8-12   76

MOST, Mickie
Singles: 7–inch
LAWN (263 "Sea Cruise") 10-20   64

MOTELS
Singles: 7–inch
CAPITOL 2-5   79-85
Picture Sleeves
CAPITOL 2-4   85
LPs: 10/12–inch 33rpm
CAPITOL 5-10   79-85
<small>Members: Martha Davis; Martin Jourard; Jeff Jourard; Brian Glascock; Tim McGovern; Mike Goodroe.</small>

MOTHER EARTH
Singles: 7–inch
MERCURY 4-8   68-69
REPRISE 3-5   70
U.A. 5-10   68
LPs: 10/12–inch 33rpm
MERCURY 10-20   68-70
REPRISE 10-15   71
U.A. 15-20   68
<small>Member: Tracy Nelson.
Also see NELSON, Tracy</small>

MOTHER'S FINEST
Singles: 12–inch 33/45rpm
EPIC 4-8   77-79
Singles: 7–inch
EPIC 3-5   76-79
LPs: 10/12–inch 33rpm
ATLANTIC 5-10   81
EPIC 5-10   76-79
RCA 8-12   72
<small>Also see KENNEDY, Joyce</small>

MOTHERLODE
Singles: 7–inch
BUDDAH 4-6   69
LPs: 10/12–inch 33rpm
BUDDAH 10-15   69-72

MOTHERS of INVENTION
(Mothers)
Singles: 7–inch
BIZARRE/REPRISE 10-15   70
DISCREET 6-10   73
VERVE 10-20   66-68

Promotional Singles
BIZARRE/REPRISE 12-15   70
DISCREET 8-10   73
VERVE 15-20   66-68
EPs: 7–inch 33/45rpm
REPRISE (332 "Uncle Meat") 35-40   69
(Promotional issue only.)
LPs: 10/12–inch 33rpm
BIZARRE (2024 "Uncle Meat") 25-35   69
(Blue label. With 12-page booklet.)
BIZARRE (2024 "Uncle Meat") 15-25   69
(Blue label. Without booklet.)
BIZARRE (2028 "Weasles Ripped
My Flesh") 15-25   70
(Blue label.)
BIZARRE (2042 "The Mothers Live/
Fillmore East") 15-25   71
(Blue label.)
BIZARRE (2075 "Just Another
Band from L.A.") 15-25   72
(Blue label.)
BIZARRE (2093 "Grand Wazoo") ... 15-25   72
(Blue label.)
BIZARRE (6370 "Burnt Weeny
Sandwich") 30-40   69
(Blue label. With folder of bonus photos.)
BIZARRE (6370 "Burnt Weeny
Sandwich") 10-20   69
(Blue label. Without folder of photos.)
DISCREET (2149 "Over-Nite
Sensation") 10-20   73
DISCREET (MS4-2149 "Over-Nite
Sensation") 30-40   73
(Quadrophonic.)
MGM (112 "Mothers of Invention") ... 30-40   70
MGM (4754 "Worst of the Mothers") . 25-35   71
REPRISE 8-12   73-74
(Reissues of Bizarre catalog.)
VERVE (5005 "Freak Out!") 75-125   66
(Monaural. With mail-order "Freak Out - Hot Spots"
map/poster offer printed on inside of cover.)
VERVE (V6-5005 "Freak Out!") 50-100   66
(Stereo. With mail-order "Freak Out - Hot Spots"
map/poster offer printed on inside of cover.)
VERVE (5005 "Freak Out!") 50-100   67
(Monaural. Without mail-order map/poster offer
printed on inside of cover.)
VERVE (V6-5005 "Freak Out!") 40-80   67
(Stereo. Without mail-order map/poster offer
printed on inside of cover.)
VERVE (5013 "Absolutely Free") 50-75   67
(Monaural.)
VERVE (V6-5013 "Absolutely Free") . 40-60   67
(Stereo.)
VERVE (5045 "We're Only in It
for the Money") 50-75   67
(Monaural. With "Only Money" insert.)

VERVE (V6-5045 "We're Only in It
for the Money") 50-75   67
(Stereo. With "Only Money" insert.)
VERVE (5068 "Mothermania") 20-40   69
VERVE (5074 "XXXX of the Mothers") 20-25   69
Note: price range of Verve LPs is for copies on the
blue and the black labels as well as white
MGM/Verve labels.
WARNER 8-10   77
Promotional LPs
BIZARRE (2024 "Uncle Meat") 40-60   69
BIZARRE (2028 "Weasles Ripped
My Flesh") 35-45   70
BIZARRE (2042 "The Mothers Live/
Fillmore East") 35-45   71
BIZARRE (2075 "Just Another
Band from L.A.") 30-40   72
BIZARRE (2093 "Grand Wazoo") 30-40   72
BIZARRE (6370 "Burnt Weeny
Sandwich") 30-30   69
VERVE (5005 "Freak Out!") 100-200   66
VERVE (5013 "Absolutely Free") . . . 75-125   67
VERVE (5045 "We're Only in It
for the Money") 75-125   67
VERVE (5068 "Mothermania") 50-100   69
VERVE (5074 "XXXX of
the Mothers") 50-100   69
Members: Frank Zappa; Jimmy Carl Black; Roy Estrada; Ray
Collins; Elliot Ingber; Jim Pons; Lowell George.
Also see CAPTAIN BEEFHEART
Also see DUKE, George
Also see LEAVES
Also see LITTLE FEAT
Also see MISSING PERSONS
Also see PRESTON, Billy
Also see RUBEN and the Jets
Also see TURTLES
Also see ZAPPA, Frank

MOTIVATION
Singles: 7–inch
DE-LITE 2-4   83

MOTLEY CRUE
Singles: 7–inch
ELEKTRA 2-4   83-88
Picture Sleeves
ELEKTRA 2-4   85
LPs: 10/12–inch 33rpm
ELEKTRA 5-10   82-89
LEATHÜR ("Too Fast for Love") 50-75   81
(Black lettering on cover.)
LEATHÜR ("Too Fast for Love") 25-50   81
(White lettering on cover.)
WEA/ELEKTRA (60395 "Helter
Skelter") 10-15   84
(Picture disc. Price includes poster.)
Member: Vince Neil; Nikki Sixx; Mick Mars; Tommy Lee.

MOTORHEAD
Singles: 7–inch
MERCURY 2-4   80-83

LPs: 10/12–inch 33rpm
EMI AMERICA 5-8   85
GWR/PROFILE 5-8   86-87
MERCURY 5-8   80-83
Members: Ian "Lemmy" Kilmister; Phil Campbell; Pete Gill; Mick
"Wurzel" Burston.
Also see GLITTER BAND
Also see HAWKWIND
Also see SAXON

MOTORS
Singles: 7–inch
VIRGIN 3-5   77-80
LPs: 10/12–inch 33rpm
VIRGIN 8-10   77-80
Also see TCHAIKOVSKY, Bram

MOTT
Singles: 7–inch
COLUMBIA 3-5   75-76
LPs: 10/12–inch 33rpm
COLUMBIA 5-10   75-76
Also see MOTT the HOOPLE

MOTT the HOOPLE
Singles: 7–inch
ATLANTIC 4-6   70
COLUMBIA 3-5   72-74
LPs: 10/12–inch 33rpm
ATLANTIC 12-18   70-74
COLUMBIA 10-15   72-75
Member: Ian Hunter.
Also see BRITISH LIONS
Also see HUNTER, Ian
Also see MOTT

MOTTOLA, Tony
LPs: 10/12–inch 33rpm
COMMAND 10-15   62-65
PROJECT 3 5-10   67-70

MOUNTAIN
Singles: 7–inch
WINDFALL 3-6   69-71
LPs: 10/12–inch 33rpm
COLUMBIA 10-15   73-74
SCOTTI BROTHERS 5-8   85
WINDFALL 10-15   69-72
Members: Leslie West; Corky Laing; Steve Knight; Felix
Pappalardi; David Perry.
Also see WEST, Leslie

MOUSKOURI, Nana
Singles: 7–inch
BELL 3-5   72-74
FONTANA 4-8   62-71
MERCURY 5-8   60
PRESIDENT 5-8   61
RIVERSIDE 4-8   62
LPs: 10/12–inch 33rpm
BELL 5-10   73
FONTANA 10-20   62-69
Also see BELAFONTE, Harry, and Nana Mouskouri
Also see HAYWARD, Justin

MOUTH & MacNEAL
Singles: 7–inch
PHILIPS .... 3-5　　72
Picture Sleeves
PHILIPS .... 3-5　　72
LPs: 10/12–inch 33rpm
PHILIPS .... 10-12　72-73
Members: Will Duyn; Maggie MacNeal.

MOUZON, Alphonse
(Alphonse Mouzon Featuring Carol Dennis; Alphonze Mouzon)
Singles: 12–inch 33/45rpm
PRIVATE I .... 4-6　　84
Singles: 7–inch
BLUE NOTE .... 3-5　73-74
HIGHRISE .... 2-4　　82
PRIVATE I .... 2-4　　84
LPs: 10/12–inch 33rpm
BLUE NOTE .... 5-10　73-76
HIGHRISE .... 5-8　　82
PAUSA .... 5-8　　81
PRIVATE I .... 5-8　　84

MOUZON, Alphonse, and Larry Coryell
LPs: 10/12–inch 33rpm
ATLANTIC .... 5-10　　77
Also see CORYELL, Larry
Also see MOUZON, Alphonse

MOVE
Singles: 7–inch
A&M .... 5-10　67-69
CAPITOL .... 10-15　　70
DERAM .... 5-10　　67
MGM .... 8-10　　71
U.A. .... 4-8　72-73
LPs: 10/12–inch 33rpm
A&M (3181 "Shazam") .... 5-8　　82
A&M (3625 "Best of the Move") ..... 15-20　74
A&M (4259 "Shazam") .... 20-25　　69
CAPITOL .... 15-25　　71
PICKWICK 10-15
U.A. .... 10-15　　73
Members: Jeff Lynne; Roy Wood; Bev Bevan; Denny Cordell; Richard Tandy; Carl Wayne; Rick Price; Trevor Burton; Ace Kefford.
Also see LYNNE, Jeff
Also see WOOD, Roy

MOVING PICTURES
Singles: 7–inch
NETWORK .... 3-5　　82
LPs: 10/12–inch 33rpm
NETWORK .... 5-8　　82

MOYET, Alison
Singles: 12–inch 33/45rpm
COLUMBIA .... 4-6　　85
Singles: 7–inch
COLUMBIA .... 2-4　　85
LPs: 10/12–inch 33rpm
COLUMBIA .... 5-8　85-87

Also see YAZ

MOZART, Mickey, Quintet
Singles: 7–inch
ROULETTE .... 5-8　59-61

MR: see MISTER

MRS. MILLER: see MILLER, Mrs.

MTUME
(James Mtume)
Singles: 12–inch 33/45rpm
EPIC .... 4-8　79-86
Singles: 7–inch
EPIC .... 2-5　78-87
LPs: 10/12–inch 33rpm
EPIC .... 5-8　78-86

MUDDY WATERS: see WATERS, Muddy

MUGWUMPS
(Mugwump Establishment)
Singles: 7–inch
WARNER .... 5-10　64-67
LPs: 10/12–inch 33rpm
WARNER (W-1697 "Mugwumps") ... 15-25　67
(Monaural.)
WARNER (WS-1697 "Mugwumps") .. 20-30　67
(Stereo.)
Members: Cass Elliot; Denny Doherty; James Hendricks; John Sebastian; Zal Yanovsky.
Also see ELLIOT, Cass
Also see SEBASTIAN, John

MUHAMMAD, Idris
Singles: 12–inch 33/45rpm
FANTASY .... 4-6　　83
Singles: 7–inch
FANTASY .... 3-5　80-83
KUDU .... 3-5　77-78
PRESTIGE .... 3-5　　72
LPs: 10/12–inch 33rpm
FANTASY .... 5-8　　83
KUDU .... 8-10　76-77
PRESTIGE .... 8-10　　72

MULDAUR, Maria
Singles: 7–inch
REPRISE .... 3-5　73-76
WARNER .... 3-5　78-79
LPs: 10/12–inch 33rpm
MYRRH .... 5-8　　82
REPRISE .... 8-12　73-76
TAKOMA .... 5-8　　80
WARNER .... 5-10　78-79

MULL, Martin
(Martin Mull Orchestra)
Singles: 7–inch
ABC .... 3-5　　77
CAPRICORN .... 3-5　72-77
ELEKTRA .... 3-5　　79
LPs: 10/12–inch 33rpm
ABC .... 8-10　77-78

CAPRICORN 8-12	73	
ELEKTRA 5-10	79	
MCA 5-8		

MULLIGAN, Gerry
(Gerry Mulligan Quartet)
Singles: 7-Inch

PACIFIC JAZZ 4-6	61	
PHILIPS 4-6	64	
VERVE 4-8	60	

EPs: 7-Inch 33/45rpm

CAPITOL 30-45	53	
COLUMBIA 10-20	59	
EMARCY 10-20	56	
PACIFIC JAZZ 25-50	53-57	
PRESTIGE (1317 "Gerry Mulligan Blows") 50-100	52	
PRESTIGE (1318 "Gerry Mulligan Blows") 50-100	52	
U.A. 10-20	58	

LPs: 10/12-Inch 33rpm

A&M 8-12	72	
ABC-PAR (225 "Jazz Concerto") ... 75-100	58	
BLUE NOTE 5-8	81	
CTI 8-12	75	
CAPITOL (H-439 "Gerry Mulligan") 150-200	53	
(10-inch LP.)		
CAPITOL (691 "Modern Sounds") .. 75-125	56	
(One side is by Shorty Rogers.)		
CAPITOL (2000 series) 20-35	63	
CAPITOL (11000 series) 8-12	72	
CHIAROSCURO 5-10	77	
COLUMBIA (1307 through 1932) 20-35	59-63	
(Monaural.)		
COLUMBIA (8116 through 8732) 25-45	59-63	
(Stereo.)		
COLUMBIA (34000 series) 5-10	77	
CROWN 10-20	63-64	
DRG 5-8	80	
EMARCY (1000 series) 5-8	81	
EMARCY (36056 "Gerry Mulligan Sextet") 75-100	56	
EMARCY (36101 "Mainstream") ... 75-100	57	
GRP 5-8	83	
GENE NORMAN PRESENTS (3 "Gerry Mulligan Quartet") 100- 200	52	
(10-inch LP.)		
GENE NORMAN PRESENTS (26 "Gerry Mulligan/ Chet Baker / Buddy DeFranco") ...50-75	57	
GENE NORMAN PRESENTS (56 "Gerry Mulligan/ Chet Baker / Buddy DeFranco") ...20-40	61	
INNER CITY 5-8	80	
KIMBERLY 20-30	63	
LIMELIGHT (82000 series) 12-25	65-66	
(Monaural.)		
LIMELIGHT (86000 series) 15-30	65-66	
(Stereo.)		
MERCURY (20453 "Profile") 40-60	59	
ODYSSEY 10-20	68	

PACIFIC JAZZ (1 "Gerry Mulligan Quartet") 150-250	53	
(10-inch LP.)		
PACIFIC JAZZ (2 "Gerry Mulligan Quartet") 100-250	53	
(10-inch LP.)		
PACIFIC JAZZ (5 "Gerry Mulligan") 100-200	53	
(10-inch LP.)		
PACIFIC JAZZ (10 "Gerry Mulligan")100-200	54	
(10-inch LP.)		
PACIFIC JAZZ (1201 "California Concert") 100-125	55	
PACIFIC JAZZ (1207 "Original Quartet") 75-100	55	
PACIFIC JAZZ (1210 "Paris Concert") 75-100	56	
PACIFIC JAZZ (1228 "Mulligan at Storyville") 75-100	57	
PACIFIC JAZZ (1237 "Songbook") . 75-100	57	
PACIFIC JAZZ (1241 "Reunion") ... 75-100	57	
PACIFIC JAZZ (10000 and 20000 series) 10-20	66	
PAUSA 5-10	76	
PHILIPS 10-20	63-64	
PRESTIGE (003 "Mulligan Plays Mulligan") 5-8	82	
PRESTIGE (120 "Gerry Mulligan Blows") 200-300	52	
(10-inch LP.)		
PRESTIGE (141 "Mulligan Too Blows") 200-300	53	
(10-inch LP.)		
PRESTIGE (7006 "Gerry Plays Mulligan") 75-100	56	
(Yellow label.)		
PRESTIGE (7251 "Historically Speaking") 30-40	63	
(Yellow label.)		
SUNSET 10-15	66	
TRIP 6-12	75-76	
U.A. (4006 "I Want to Live") 30-40	58	
(Monaural.)		
U.A. (4006 "I Want to Live") 40-50	58	
(Stereo.)		
V.S.P 10-20	66	
VERVE 20-45	58-60	
(Reads "Verve Records, Inc." at bottom of label.)		
VERVE 10-25	61-72	
(Reads "MGM Records - A Division Of Metro-Goldwyn-Mayer, Inc." at bottom of label.)		
VERVE 5-12	73-84	
(Reads "Manufactured By MGM Record Corp.," or mentions either Polydor or Polygram at bottom of label.)		
WHO'S WHO in JAZZ 5-8	78	
WING 10-20	67	
WORLD PACIFIC (1241 "Reunion") . 50-75	58	
WORLD PACIFIC (1253 "Annie Ross Sings with Mulligan") 50-75	59	

Also see BRUBECK, Dave, and Gerry Mulligan
Also see GETZ, Stan, and Gerry Mulligan

MULLIGAN, Gerry, and Paul Desmond
(Gerry Mulligan / Paul Desmond)
LPs: 10/12-Inch 33rpm

FANTASY (220 "Gerry Mulligan/
Paul Desmond") 75-100   56
(Colored vinyl.)
RCA (2642 "Two of a Mind") 35-55   62
VERVE (8246 "Gerry Mulligan/
Paul Desmond") 40-60   58
(Reads "Verve Records, Inc." at bottom of label.)
VERVE (8246 "Gerry Mulligan/
Paul Desmond") 25-35   62
(Reads "MGM Records - A Division Of
Metro-Goldwyn-Mayer, Inc." at bottom of label.)
Also see DESMOND, Paul

MULLIGAN, Gerry, and Johnny Hodges
LPs: 10/12-Inch 33rpm

VERVE 30-40   60
(Reads "Verve Records, Inc." at bottom of label.)
VERVE 15-25   62
(Reads "MGM Records - A Division of
Metro-Goldwyn-Mayer, Inc." at bottom of label.)
Also see HODGES, Johnny

MULLIGAN, Gerry, and Thelonious Monk
LPs: 10/12-Inch 33rpm

MILESTONE 8-12   82
RIVERSIDE (247 "Mulligan
Meets Monk") 50-75   57
RIVERSIDE (1106 "Mulligan
Meets Monk") 40-60   58
Also see MONK, Thelonious

MULLIGAN, Gerry, and Oscar Peterson
LPs: 10/12-Inch 33rpm

VERVE (8235 "Gerry and Oscar
at Newport") 50-80   57
VERVE (8559 "Gerry and Oscar
at Newport") 30-40   63
(Monaural.)
VERVE (68559 "Gerry and Oscar
at Newport") 30-40   63
(Stereo.)
Also see MULLIGAN, Gerry
Also see PETERSON, Oscar

MUNDY, Nick
Singles: 7-Inch

COLUMBIA 2-4   84

MUNGO JERRY
Singles: 7-Inch

BELL 3-5   71-73
FLASHBACK 3-5   73
JANUS 3-5   70-71
PYE 3-5   72-75
LPs: 10/12-Inch 33rpm
JANUS 10-15   70

MUNICH MACHINE
Singles: 7-Inch

CASABLANCA 3-5   78
LPs: 10/12-Inch 33rpm
CASABLANCA 5-10   78

MUPPETS
(Sesame Street Muppets)
Singles: 7-Inch

ATLANTIC 2-4   79-81
SESAME STREET 2-4   78
Picture Sleeves
ATLANTIC 2-4   79-81
SESAME STREET 2-4   78
LPs: 10/12-Inch 33rpm
ARISTA 5-8   77
ATLANTIC 5-8   79-81
COLUMBIA 5-10   70-72
SESAME STREET 5-8   78
WARNER 5-10   71
Also see DENVER, John, and the Muppets
Also see ERNIE / Sesame Street Kids
Also see HENSON, Jim
Also see KERMIT / Fozzie Bear

MURAD, Jerry: see HARMONICATS

MURDOCK, Lydia
Singles: 12-Inch 33/45rpm

TEEN 4-6   83
Singles: 7-Inch
TEEN 2-4   83

MURDOCK, Shirley
Singles: 12-Inch 33/45rpm

ELEKTRA 4-6   86
Singles: 7-Inch
ELEKTRA 2-4   86-88
LPs: 10/12-Inch 33rpm
ELEKTRA 5-8   87-88
Also see ZAPP

MURE, Billy
**(Billy Mure and the Wild-Cats; Billy Mure and the
Trumpeteers; Billy Mure and the 7 Karats)**
Singles: 78rpm

RCA 4-6   57-58
Singles: 7-Inch
DANCO 4-6   65
EVEREST 4-8   60
MGM 3-6   60-66
PARIS 4-8   60
RCA 5-10   57-58
RIVERSIDE 4-6   63
SRG 4-6   61
SPLASH 5-8   58
STRAND 4-6   61
EPs: 7-Inch 33/45rpm
RCA 8-15   58
LPs: 10/12-Inch 33rpm
EVEREST 15-20   60-61
KAPP 15-20   61
MGM 15-20   59-66

RCA 25-30   57-58
STRAND 15-20   61
SUNSET 10-12   67
U.A. (3031 "Bandstand Record Hop") 30-40   59
   Also see TRUMPETEERS
   Also see WILD-CATS

MURE, Billy and Benny
Singles: 7–inch
MGM 4-8   64

MURMAIDS
(Mermaids)
Singles: 7–inch
CHATTAHOOCHEE 4-8   63-69
LIBERTY 4-8   68
LPs: 10/12–inch 33rpm
CHATTAHOOCHEE 8-10   81

MURPHEY, Michael
(Michael Martin Murphey)
Singles: 7–inch
A&M 3-5   72
CAPITOL 3-5   74
EMI AMERICA 2-4   84-85
EPIC 3-5   74-79
LIBERTY 2-4   82-84
WARNER 2-4   86
Picture Sleeves
EPIC 3-5   74
LPs: 10/12–inch 33rpm
A&M 8-10   72-73
EMI AMERICA 5-8   84-85
EPIC 8-12   74-78
LIBERTY 5-8   82-83
WARNER 5-8   86
   Also see DENVER, John
   Also see LEWIS & CLARKE

MURPHY, Eddie
Singles: 12–inch 33/45rpm
COLUMBIA 4-6   83-85
Singles: 7–inch
COLUMBIA 2-4   83-86
Picture Sleeves
COLUMBIA 2-4   83-85
LPs: 10/12–inch 33rpm
COLUMBIA (Except picture discs) 5-8   82-86
COLUMBIA (1763 "Comedian") 10-15   83
(Promotional Picture disc.)
COLUMBIA (9C9-39151 "Comedian") 10-12   83
(Picture disc.)

MURPHY, Peter
LPs: 10/12–inch 33rpm
BEGGAR'S BANQUET 5-8   88-90

MURPHY, Walter
(Walter Murphy and the Big Apple Band)
Singles: 12–inch 33/45rpm
PRIVATE STOCK 4-8   77
Singles: 7–inch
MCA 2-4   82

PRIVATE STOCK 3-5   76-77
LPs: 10/12–inch 33rpm
MCA 5-8   82
PRIVATE STOCK 5-10   76-77

MURPHYS
Singles: 7–inch
VENTURE 2-4   82

MURRAY, Anne
Singles: 7–inch
CAPITOL 2-5   70-86
Picture Sleeves
CAPITOL 2-4   80-86
LPs: 10/12–inch 33rpm
CAPITOL (Except "Let's Keep It
  That Way" picture disc) 5-10   70-87
CAPITOL ("Let's Keep It That Way") . 50-75   78
(Picture disc. Promotional issue only. One of a
four-artist, four-LP set.)
   Also see CAMPBELL, Glen, and Anne Murray
   Also see CAMPBELL, Glen / Anne Murray / Kenny Rogers /
    Crystal Gayle
   Also see WINCHESTER, Jesse

MURRAY, Anne, and Dave Loggins
Singles: 7–inch
CAPITOL 2-4   85
   Also see LOGGINS, Dave
   Also see MURRAY, Anne

MURRAY, Mickey
Singles: 7–inch
SSS INT'L 4-8   67-68
LPs: 10/12–inch 33rpm
FEDERAL 8-12   71
SSS INT'L 10-15   67

MURRAY, Mickey and Clarence
Singles: 7–inch
SSS INT'L 4-8   68
   Also see MURRAY, Mickey

MUSCLE SHOALS HORNS
Singles: 7–inch
ARIOLA AMERICA 3-5   77
BANG 3-5   76
MONUMENT 2-4   83
LPs: 10/12–inch 33rpm
ARIOLA AMERICA 5-10   77
BANG 8-10   76
MONUMENT 5-8   83

MUSIC EXPLOSION
Singles: 7–inch
ATTACK (1404 "Little Black Egg") ... 10-20   66
LAURIE 5-10   67-69
LPs: 10/12–inch 33rpm
LAURIE 20-30   67
   Members: Jamie Lyons; Don Atkins; Bob Avery; Rick Nesta;
   Butch Stahl.
   Also see BLOOM, Bobby
   Also see KASENETZ - KATZ SINGING ORCHESTRAL CIRCUS

MUSIC MACHINE
Singles: 7–inch
BELL 5-10   69
ORIGINAL SOUND 5-10   66-67
WARNER 5-10   68
Picture Sleeves
ORIGINAL SOUND (82 "Hey Joe") .. 15-25   67
LPs: 10/12–inch 33rpm
ORIGINAL SOUND (5015 "Turn on
  the Music Machine") 20-30   66
  (Monaural.)
ORIGINAL SOUND (8875 "Turn on
  the Music Machine") 75-100   66
  (Stereo.)
  Members: Sean Bonniwell; Mark Landon; Keith Olsen; Ron
  Edgar; Doug Rhodes.

MUSIC MAKERS
Singles: 7–inch
GAMBLE 4-8   67-68
LPs: 10/12–inch 33rpm
GAMBLE 12-18   68

MUSICAL YOUTH
Singles: 12–inch 33/45rpm
MCA 4-6   82-84
Singles: 7–inch
MCA 2-4   82-84
LPs: 10/12–inch 33rpm
MCA 5-8   82-84

MUSIQUE
Singles: 12–inch 33/45rpm
PRELUDE 5-10   78
Singles: 7–inch
PRELUDE 3-5   78-79
LPs: 10/12–inch 33rpm
PRELUDE 5-10   78

MUSTANGS
Singles: 7–inch
KEETCH 5-10   64
PROViDENCE 8-12   63-64
SURE SHOT 5-10   64
VEST 4-8
LPs: 10/12–inch 33rpm
PROVIDENCE (1 "Dartel Stomp") ... 35-45   64

MYERS, Alicia
Singles: 12–inch 33/45rpm
MCA 4-6   81-85
Singles: 7–inch
MCA 2-4   81-85
LPs: 10/12–inch 33rpm
MCA 5-8   84

MYLES, Billy
Singles: 78rpm
EMBER 10-15   57
Singles: 7–inch
COLLECTABLES 2-4
EMBER 10-20   57

KING 5-10   60

MYRICK, Gary, and the Figures
Singles: 7–inch
EPIC 2-4   83-84
LPs: 10/12–inch 33rpm
EPIC 5-8   83-84

MYSTIC MERLIN
Singles: 7–inch
CAPITOL 3-5   80-82
LPs: 10/12–inch 33rpm
CAPITOL 5-10   80-82

MYSTIC MOODS ORCHESTRA
Singles: 7–inch
PHILIPS 4-6   66-70
SOUNDBIRD 3-5   75-78
WARNER 3-5   72-73
LPs: 10/12–inch 33rpm
MFSL 20-40   78
PHILIPS 5-10   66-70
SOUNDBIRD 5-10   75-78
WARNER 5-10   72-73

MYSTICS
Singles: 7–inch
AMBIENT SOUND 3-5   82
COLLECTABLES 2-4
LAURIE (3028 "Don't Take the Stars") 10-15   59
LAURIE (3028 "Hushabye") 10-15   59
LAURIE (3028-S "Hushabye") 30-40   59
  (Stereo.)
LAURIE (3047 through 3086) 10-15   59
LAURIE (3104 "Sunday Kind of Love") 15-20   61
LPs: 10/12–inch 33rpm
AMBIENT SOUND 5-8   82
COLLECTABLES 6-8   87
  Also see GARRETT, Scott

MYSTICS / Passions
LPs: 10/12–inch 33rpm
LAURIE 5-10   79
  Also see MYSTICS
  Also see PASSIONS

MYSTIQUE
Singles: 7–inch
CURTOM 3-5   77
LPs: 10/12–inch 33rpm
CURTOM 5-10   77
  Member: Ralph Johnson.
  Also see C.O.D.s
  Also see IMPRESSIONS

N

N.C.C.U.
Singles: 12–inch 33/45rpm
U.A. 4-8   77
Singles: 7–inch
U.A. 3-5   77
LPs: 10/12–inch 33rpm
U.A. 5-10   77

NRBQ
(New Rhythm and Blues Quintet)
Singles: 7–inch
BEARSVILLE 3-5   83
BUDDAH 3-5   74
COLUMBIA 4-8   69
KAMA SUTRA 4-6   73
MERCURY 4-6   78
RED ROOSTER 3-6   77
ROUNDER 3-5   80-83
VIRGIN 3-5   89-90
Picture Sleeves
RED ROOSTER 3-5   77
ROUNDER 3-5   80
EPs: 7–inch 33/45rpm
ROUNDER 5-10   82
LPs: 10/12–inch 33rpm
ANNUIT COEPTIS 10-15   76
BEARSVILLE 5-8   83
KAMA SUTRA 10-15   72-73
MERCURY 8-12   78
COLUMBIA 10-15   69
RED ROOSTER 8-10   77-83
ROUNDER 5-10   79-80
VIRGIN 5-8   89
Members: Terry Adams; G.T. Stanley; Jody St. Nicholas; Steve Ferguson; Don Adams.
  Also see ANDERSON, Al
  Also see DAVIS, Skeeter, and NRBQ
  Also see PERKINS, Carl, and NRBQ

NV
Singles: 12–inch 33/45rpm
SIRE 4-6   83-84
Singles: 7–inch
SIRE 2-4   83-84

N.W.A.
N.W.A. 5-8   89-90

NABORS, Jim
Singles: 7–inch
COLUMBIA 3-5   65-74
RANWOOD 2-4   77
LPs: 10/12–inch 33rpm
COLUMBIA 5-15   65-75
HARMONY 5-10   71
RANWOOD 4-8   76-82

NAIROBI and the Awesome Foursome
Singles: 7–inch
STREETWISE 2-4   82

NAJEE
LPs: 10/12–inch 33rpm
EMI 5-8   87-90

NAKED EYES
Singles: 12–inch 33/45rpm
EMI AMERICA 4-6   83-84
Singles: 7–inch
EMI AMERICA 2-4   83-84
LPs: 10/12–inch 33rpm
EMI AMERICA 5-8   83-84
Members: Pete Byrne; Rob Fisher.

NAPOLEON XIV
(Jerry Samuels)
Singles: 7–inch
ERIC 3-5   76
WARNER (5800 series) 5-10   66
WARNER (7700 series) 4-6   73
LPs: 10/12–inch 33rpm
WARNER (W-1661 "They're Coming
to Take Me Away") 50-60   66
(Monaural.)
WARNER (W-1661 "They're Coming
to Take Me Away") 75-100   66
(White label. Promotional issue only.)
WARNER (WS-1661 "They're Coming
to Take Me Away") 75-100   66
(Stereo.)

NASH, Graham
Singles: 7–inch
ATLANTIC (2000 series) 3-5   71-73
ATLANTIC (89000 series) 2-4   86
CAPITOL 3-5   79-80
LPs: 10/12–inch 33rpm
ATLANTIC (7000 series) 8-12   71-73
ATLANTIC (81000 series) 5-8   86
CAPITOL 8-10   80
  Also see CROSBY, David, and Graham Nash
  Also see CROSBY, STILLS & NASH
  Also see HOLLIES
  Also see YOUNG, Neil, and Graham Nash

NASH, Johnny
Singles: 12–inch 33/45rpm
EPIC 4-8   79
Singles: 7–inch
ABC-PAR 5-10   57-61
ARGO 4-8   64-65
ATLANTIC 4-8   66
BABYLON 4-6   69
EPIC 3-5   72-80
GROOVE 4-8   63-64
JAD 4-6   68-70
JANUS 3-5   70
JODA 4-8   65-66
MGM 4-8   66-67

WARNER	4-8	62-63

Picture Sleeves

ABC-PAR	5-10	59-60
GROOVE	5-8	63-64

EPs: 7–inch 33/45rpm

ABC-PAR	10-20	58-61

LPs: 10/12–inch 33rpm

ABC-PAR	15-25	58-61
ARGO	15-20	64
CADET	10-15	73
EPIC	10-15	72-74
JAD	10-20	68-69

Also see ANKA, Paul, George Hamilton IV and Johnny Nash

NASH, Johnny, and Kim Weston
Singles: 7–inch

BABYLON	4-6	69

Also see NASH, Johnny
Also see WESTON, Kim

NASHVILLE BRASS: see DAVIS, Danny

NASHVILLE TEENS
Singles: 7–inch

LONDON	5-10	64-65
MGM	5-10	65-67
U.A.	3-5	72

LPs: 10/12–inch 33rpm

LONDON (407 "Tobacco Road")	40-50	64
(Stereo.)		
LONDON (3407 "Tobacco Road")	50-60	64
(Monaural.)		

Members: Arthur Sharp; John Allen; Roger Groom; Ray Phillips; Barry Jenkins.

NATASHA
Singles: 12–inch 33/45rpm

EMERGENCY	4-6	83

NATIONAL LAMPOON
Singles: 7–inch

BLUE THUMB	4-6	72-73
EPIC (193 "Have a Kun-Fu Christmas")	2-4	75
(Promotional issue only.)		
LABEL 21	3-5	78-80

Picture Sleeves

EPIC (193 "Have a Kung-Fu Christmas")	4-6	75
(Promotional issue only.)		
LABEL 21	3-5	78-80

EPs: 7–inch 33/45rpm

EPIC (1095 "A History of the Beatles")	10-15	75
(Promotional issue only.)		

LPs: 10/12–inch 33rpm

BANANA	10-15	72-74
BLUE THUMB	10-15	72-74
EPIC	8-12	75-76
IMPORT	8-10	77
LABEL 21 (Except PIC-2001)	5-8	78-80
LABEL 21 (PIC-2001 "That's Not Funny		
That's Sick")	10-15	80
(Picture disc.)		
NATIONAL LAMPOON	15-20	74

PASSPORT	5-8	82
VISA	5-8	78

Members: John Belushi; Chevy Chase; Melissa Manchester; Tony Hendra; Jim Payne; John Lopresti.
Also see BELUSHI, John
Also see MANCHESTER, Melissa

NATIVE
Singles: 7–inch

RCA	3-5	80

LPs: 10/12–inch 33rpm

RCA	5-10	80

NATURAL FOUR
Singles: 7–inch

ABC	4-6	69
CURTOM	3-5	74-76

LPs: 10/12–inch 33rpm

CURTOM	8-12	74-75

NATURALS
Singles: 7–inch

CALLA	3-5	71
MOTOWN	3-5	72

NATURE ZONE
Singles: 7–inch

LONDON	3-5	76

NATURE'S DIVINE
Singles: 7–inch

INFINITY	3-5	79

LPs: 10/12–inch 33rpm

INFINITY	5-10	79

NATURE'S GIFT
Singles: 7–inch

ABC	3-5	74

NAUGHTON, David
Singles: 7–inch

RSO	3-5	78-79

NAYLOR, Jerry
Singles: 7–inch

COLUMBIA	3-6	68-71
HITSVILLE	3-5	76
JEREMIAH	3-5	79
MC	3-5	78
MGM	3-5	71-72
MELODYLAND	3-5	74-75
OAK	3-5	80
PACIFIC CHALLENGER	3-5	82
SKLYA	8-12	61-62
SMASH	4-8	65
TOWER	4-8	65-68
WARNER	3-5	79
WEST	2-4	86

Also see ALLAN, Davie
Also see CRICKETS
Also see HONDELLS

NAYOBE
Singles: 12–inch 33/45rpm

FEVER	4-6	85-86

Singles: 7–inch
FEVER 2-4   85-86

NAZARETH
Singles: 7–inch
A&M 3-5   73-80
MCA 2-4   83-84
WARNER 3-5   71
Picture Sleeves
A&M 3-5   75-80
LPs: 10/12–inch 33rpm
A&M 5-10   73-82
MCA 5-8   83-84
WARNER 8-12   72
Members: Dan McCafferty; Pete Agnew; Darrell Sweet; Manny Charlton.

NAZTY
Singles: 7–inch
MANKIND 3-5   76
LPs: 10/12–inch 33rpm
MANKIND 5-10   76

NAZZ
Singles: 7–inch
VERY RECORD (001 "Lay Down and Die,
Goodbye") 750-1000   67
Members: Vince "Alice Cooper" Furnier; M. Bruce; G. Buxton; D. Dunaway; T. Speer.
Also see COOPER, Alice

NAZZ
Singles: 7–inch
SGC (001 "Hello It's Me") 8-12   68
(Yellow label.)
SGC (001 "Hello It's Me") 4-8   68
(Green label.)
SGC (006 "Not Wrong Long") 5-10   69
SGC (009 "Some People") 5-10   69
Picture Sleeves
SGC 6-12   68
Promotional Singles
SGC (001 "Hello It's Me") 10-20   68
SGC (006 "Not Wrong Long") 10-15   69
SGC (009 "Some People") 10-15   69
SGC (009 "Kicks") 15-25   70
LPs: 10/12–inch 33rpm
SGC (5001 "Nazz") 30-50   68
SGC (5002 "Nazz-Nazz") 40-60   69
(Black vinyl.)
SGC (5002 "Nazz-Nazz") 50-100   69
(Colored vinyl. Pink and orange label. SGC logo is blue. Identification number is 671531.)
SGC (5002 "Nazz-Nazz") 75-100   69
(Colored vinyl. Mail-order edition. Red and orange label. SGC logo is purple. Identification number is 671531-MO.)
SGC (5004 "Nazz III") 30-50   71
Members: Todd Rundgren; Robert Antoni; Carson Van Osten.
Also see RUNDGREN, Todd

N'COLE
Singles: 7–inch
MILLENNIUM 3-5   78

NDUGU and the Chocolate Jam Company
Singles: 7–inch
EPIC 3-5   80

NECROPOLIS
LPs: 10/12–inch 33rpm
BOMP 5-8   88

NEELY, Sam
Singles: 7–inch
A&M 3-5   74-75
CAPITOL 3-5   72-73
ELEKTRA 3-5   77
MCA 2-4   83
LPs: 10/12–inch 33rpm
A&M 8-10   74
CAPITOL 8-12   72-73

NEIGHBORHOOD
Singles: 7–inch
BIG TREE 4-8   70
BULLET (102269 "Why Can't
You See") 15-25   69
LPs: 10/12–inch 33rpm
BIG TREE 10-15   70

NEIL & JACK
Singles: 7–inch
DUEL (508 "You Are My
Love at Last") 100-200   62
DUEL (517 "I'm Afraid") 100-200   62
Members: Neil Diamond; Jack Parker.
Also see DIAMOND, Neil

NEIL and the Shocking Pinks:
see YOUNG, Neil

NEKTAR
Singles: 7–inch
PASSPORT 3-5   74-75
LPs: 10/12–inch 33rpm
PASSPORT 8-12   74-76
POLYDOR 8-10   77
VISA 8-10   78

NELSON, Jimmy
Singles: 78rpm
CHESS 10-20   53
RPM 10-20   53
Singles: 7–inch
ALL BOY 5-10   62
CHESS (1587 "Free and Easy Mind") 25-40   53
CHESS (1800 series) 4-8   63
RPM (385 "Meet Me With
Your Black Dress On") 25-40   53
RPM (389 "Second Hand Fool") 25-40   53
RPM (397 "Mean Poor Girl") 25-40   53
Also see TURNER, Joe / Jimmy Nelson

NELSON, Karen, and Billy T.
Singles: 7–inch
AMHERST 8-10   77

NELSON, Phyllis
Singles: 12–inch 33/45rpm
CARRERE 4-6   85-86
Singles: 7–inch
CARRERE 2-4   85-86
LPs: 10/12–inch 33rpm
CARRERE 5-8   86

NELSON, Rick
(Rick Nelson and the Stone Canyon Band; Ricky Nelson)
Singles: 12–inch 33/45rpm
CAPITOL 5-10   82
Singles: 78rpm
IMPERIAL 25-75   57-58
VERVE 50-75   57
Singles: 7–inch
DECCA 4-8   63-72
CAPITOL 3-5   82
EPIC 3-5   77-86
IMPERIAL (5463 "Be-Bop Baby") ... 20-30   57
(Maroon label.)
IMPERIAL (5463 "Be-Bop Baby") ... 10-15   58
(Black label.)
IMPERIAL (5483 "Stood Up") 15-25   57
(Maroon label.)
IMPERIAL (5483 "Stood Up") 10-15   58
(Black label.)
IMPERIAL (5503 "Believe What
You Say") 10-20   58
IMPERIAL (5528 "Poor Little Fool") .. 10-20   58
IMPERIAL (5545 "Lonesome Town") . 10-20   58
(Black vinyl.)
IMPERIAL (5545 "Lonesome Town")150-200
(Colored vinyl.)
IMPERIAL (5565 "It's Late") 10-20   59
IMPERIAL (5595 "Just a
Little Too Much") 10-15   59
IMPERIAL (5614 "Mighty Good") 10-15   59
IMPERIAL (5663 "Young Emotions") . 10-15   60
IMPERIAL (5685 "I'm Not Afraid") ... 10-15   60
IMPERIAL (5707 "You Are the
Only One") 10-15   60
IMPERIAL (5741 "Travelin' Man") 8-12   61
(Black vinyl.)
IMPERIAL (5741 "Travelin' Man") . 150-200   61
(Colored vinyl. Promotional issue only.)
IMPERIAL (5770 through 5935) 8-15   61-63
IMPERIAL (5958 "A Long Vacation") .. 5-10   63
(Black vinyl.)
IMPERIAL (5958 "A Long Vacation") . 50-75   63
(Colored vinyl.)
IMPERIAL (5985 "Time After Time") ... 8-12   63
IMPERIAL (66000 series) 8-15   63-64
LIBERTY 2-4
MCA 3-5   73-75

VERVE (10047 "A Teenager's
Romance") 15-25   57
VERVE (10070 "You're My One
and Only Love") 15-25   57
(Flip is by Barney Kessell.)
Picture Sleeves
DECCA 8-18   63-70
EPIC 3-5   86
IMPERIAL (5483 "Stood Up") 20-30   57
IMPERIAL (5503 "Believe What
You Say") 20-30   58
IMPERIAL (5545 "Lonesome
Town") 15-25
IMPERIAL (5565 "It's Late") 15-25   59
IMPERIAL (5595 "Just a
Little Too Much") 15-25   59
IMPERIAL (5614 "Mighty Good") 15-25   59
IMPERIAL (5663 "Young Emotions") . 15-20   60
IMPERIAL (5685 "I'm Not Afraid") ... 15-20   60
IMPERIAL (5707 "You Are the
Only One") 15-20   60
IMPERIAL (5741 "Travelin' Man") ... 10-20   61
IMPERIAL (5770 through 5935) 10-20   61-63
MCA 3-5   86
EPs: 7–inch 33/45rpm
DECCA (4419 "For Your Sweet Love") 25-45   63
(Jukebox issue.)
DECCA (4460 "Best Always") 25-45   65
(Jukebox issue.)
IMPERIAL (153/154/155 "Ricky") ... 35-55   58
(Price is for any of three volumes.)
IMPERIAL (157/158 "Ricky Nelson") . 35-55   58
(Price is for either of two volumes.)
IMPERIAL (159/160/161 "Ricky
Sings Again") 35-55   58
(Price is for any of three volumes.)
IMPERIAL (162/163/164 "Songs
By Ricky") 35-55   59
(Price is for any of three volumes.)
IMPERIAL (165 "Ricky
Sings Spirituals") 40-60   60
VERVE (5048 "Ricky") 75-100   57
(Has one track by Barney Kessell.)
LPs: 10/12–inch 33rpm
CAPITOL 5-8   81
DECCA (DL-4419 through DL-4944) . 20-30   63-67
(Monaural.)
DECCA (DL7-4419 through
DL7-4944) 25-40   63-67
(Stereo.)
DECCA (75014 through 75391) 15-25   68-72
EPIC 8-15   77-86
EPIC/NU-DISK 10-15   81
IMPERIAL (9048 "Ricky") 50-80   57
("Imperial" across top of label.)
IMPERIAL (9048 "Ricky") 15-20   64
("IR-Imperial" logo on left.)
IMPERIAL (9050 "Ricky Nelson") ... 45-65   58
("Imperial" across top of label.)

IMPERIAL (9061 "Ricky Sings Again") 40-50   59
(Monaural.)
IMPERIAL (9082 "Songs by Ricky") . . 40-50   59
(Monaural.)
IMPERIAL (9122 "More Songs
by Ricky") 30-50   60
(Monaural.)
IMPERIAL (9152 "Rick Is 21") 30-40   61
(Monaural.)
IMPERIAL (9167 "Album Seven") . . . 25-35   62
(Monaural.)
IMPERIAL (9218 "Best Sellers") 25-35   63
(Monaural.)
IMPERIAL (9223 "It's Up to You") 25-35   63
(Monaural.)
IMPERIAL (9232 "Million Sellers
by Rick Nelson") 20-30   63
(Monaural.)
IMPERIAL (9244 "A Long Vacation") . 20-30   63
(Monaural.)
IMPERIAL (9251 "Rick Nelson
Sings for You") 20-30   63
(Monaural.)
IMPERIAL (12059 "More Songs
by Ricky") 40-60   60
(Stereo. Black vinyl.)
IMPERIAL (12059 "More Songs
by Ricky") 300-400   60
(Stereo. Colored vinyl.)
IMPERIAL (12090 "Ricky
Sings Again") 20-30   64
(Stereo.)
IMPERIAL (12071 "Rick Is 21") 35-45   61
(Stereo.)
IMPERIAL (12082 "Album Seven") . . 30-40   62
(Stereo.)
IMPERIAL (12218 "Best Sellers") 30-40   63
(Stereo.)
IMPERIAL (12223 "It's Up to You") . . . 30-40   63
(Stereo.)
IMPERIAL (12232 "Million Sellers
By Rick Nelson") 25-35   64
(Stereo.)
IMPERIAL (12244 "A Long
Vacation") 20-30   63
(Stereo.)
IMPERIAL (12251 "Rick Nelson
Sings for You") 20-30   64
(Stereo.)
LIBERTY 5-8   81-83
MCA (Except 1517) 10-15   73-74
MCA (1517 "The Decca Years") 5-10   82
MCA/SILVER EAGLE 5-10   86
MGM (4256 "Teen Time") 15-25   65
RHINO 5-8   85
SESSIONS (1003 "Ricky Nelson
Story") 15-25   79
(Three-LP mail-order offer.)
SUNSET 10-20   66-68

U.A. (330 "Very Best
of Rick Nelson") 10-12   75
U.A. (1004 "Ricky") 8-10   80
U.A. (9960 "Legendary
Masters") 15-25   71
VERVE (2083 "Teen Time") 150-200   57
(Also has tracks by Randy Sparks; Gary Williams,
Jeff Allen, Rock Murphy, and Barney Kessel.)
Members: James Burton; Joe Osborn; Randy Meisner; Al Kemp;
Steve Duncan.
Also see GRAPPELLI, Stephane, and Barney Kessel
Also see MARTIN, Dean, and Ricky Nelson
Also see MEISNER, Randy
Also see MOON, Keith
Also see RIVERS, Johnny / Ricky Nelson / Randy Sparks

THEATRE
PROMOTION RECORD

JACK LEMMON   RICKY NELSON
plays   sings

KB-760   45 rpm

DO YOU KNOW WHAT IT MEANS
TO MISS NEW ORLEANS?
From The Soundtrack of
THE WACKIEST SHIP IN THE ARMY
A Fred Kohlmar Prod. - A Columbia Pictures Release
Broadcasting and/or sale of this
record prohibited

NELSON, Rick, and Jack Lemmon
Singles: 7–inch
THEATRE PROMOTION RECORD (760 "Do
You Know What It Means to
Miss New Orleans") 100-150   60
(Promotional issue, for theatre play only.)

NELSON, Rick / Joannie Sommers / Dona Jean Young
LPs: 10/12–inch 33rpm
DECCA (DL-4836 "On the Flip Side") 20-30   66
(Monaural.)
DECCA (DL7-4836 "On the Flip Side") 25-35   66
(Stereo.)
Also see NELSON, Rick
Also see SOMMERS, Joannie

NELSON, Sandy
Singles: 7–inch
COLLECTABLES 2-4
ERA 3-5   72
IMPERIAL 4-8   61-69
LIBERTY 2-4
ORIGINAL SOUND 10-15   59
U.A. 3-5   74
EPs: 7–inch 33/45rpm
IMPERIAL 10-20   65
(Stereo jukebox "Little LPs.")

LPs: 10/12–inch 33rpm

IMPERIAL (Except 9105/12044) 10-25	61-69
IMPERIAL (9105 "Teen Beat") 20-30	60
(Monaural.)	
IMPERIAL (12044 "Teen Beat") 20-30	60
(Stereo.)	
LIBERTY 5-10	82-83
SKYCLAD 5-8	89
SUNSET 10-20	66-70
U.A. 8-12	75
Also see TEDDY BEARS	

NELSON, Tracy

Singles: 7–inch

ATLANTIC 3-5	75
CAPITOL 3-5	77
MCA 3-5	75

LPs: 10/12–inch 33rpm

ADELPHI 5-10	83
ATLANTIC 8-12	74
COLUMBIA 10-12	73
FLYING FISH 5-10	78-80
MCA 8-10	75
PRESTIGE (7303 "Deep Are	
the Roots") 15-20	65
PRESTIGE (7726 "Deep Are	
the Roots") 8-12	69
REPRISE 10-12	72
Also see MOTHER EARTH	
Also see NELSON, Willie and Tracy	

NELSON, Tyka

Singles: 7–inch

COOLTEMPO 2-4	88

NELSON, Willie

Singles: 7–inch

AMERICAN GOLD 3-5	76
ATLANTIC 3-5	73-75
BETTY 10-15	64
BELLAIRE (107 "Night Life") 15-25	63
(Black vinyl.)	
BELLAIRE (107 "Night Life") 25-50	63
(Colored vinyl.)	

WILLIE NELSON RECORDS
Vancouver, Washington

15-628-A
Granite BMI

Vocal By
Willie Nelson

NO PLACE FOR ME
(W. Nelson)
WILLIE NELSON

BELLAIRE (5000 series) 3-5	76
CAPITOL 3-5	78
COLUMBIA 2-5	75-86
D 10-20	59-60
DOUBLE BARREL 4-8	
LIBERTY (55000 series) 5-10	61-64
LIBERTY (56000 series) 3-6	69
LONE STAR 3-5	78
MONUMENT (800 series) 4-6	64
RCA (0100 through 0800 series) ... 3-5	69-72
RCA (8500 through 9900 series) 4-6	65-71
RCA (10000 through 12000 series) 3-5	75-81
SONGBIRD 3-5	80
U.A. (600 series) 4-8	63
U.A. (700 through 1200 series) 3-5	76-78
WILLIE NELSON (628 "No Place	
for Me") 100-200	57

Picture Sleeves

RCA (12000 series) 3-5	81

LPs: 10/12–inch 33rpm

ACCORD 5-8	83
ALLEGIANCE 5-8	83
ATLANTIC 8-12	73-76
AUDIO FIDELITY (213 "Willie Nelson") 8-12	
(Picture disc.)	
AURA 5-8	83
CAMDEN 8-12	70-74
CASINO 8-10	84
COLUMBIA (30000 series, except	
38250 and picture discs) 5-15	75-86
COLUMBIA (38250 "Willie Nelson") . 60-100	83
(Ten-LP boxed set.)	
COLUMBIA (35305 "Stardust") 25-35	78
(Picture disc.)	
COLUMBIA (38258 "Always on	
My Mind") 15-25	83
(Picture disc. Promotional issue only.)	
COLUMBIA (39943 "Always on	
My Mind") 10-20	83
(Picture disc.)	
COLUMBIA (40000 series, except	
half-speed mastered) 5-10	85-90
COLUMBIA (40000 series, half-speed	
mastered) 20-35	82-83
(With "HC" prefix.)	
DELTA 5-8	82
EXACT 5-8	83
HBO (171010 "Willie Nelson	
and Family") 15-25	83
(Picture disc. Promotional issue only.)	
H.S.R.D. 8-10	84
HEARTLAND 10-15	87
HOT SCHATZ 5-10	84
LIBERTY (3239 "And Then I Wrote") . 25-35	62
(Monaural.)	
LIBERTY (7239 "And Then I Wrote") . 30-45	62
(Stereo.)	
LIBERTY (10000 series) 5-10	
LONE STAR 8-12	78

MCA 5-10	80	
PICKWICK 8-10		
PLANTATION 5-10	82	
POTOMAC 10-15	82	
PREMORE 5-10		
RCA (1100 through 3200 series) 5-10	75-79	

RCA (LPM-3400 through
   LPM-3900 series) 10-20 65-68
   (Monaural.)
RCA (LSP-3400 through
   LSP-4700 series) 10-25 65-72
   (Stereo.)
RCA (3600 through 4800 series) 4-8 80-83
   (With "AYL1" prefix.)

RCA/CANDELITE 8-10	80	
SHOTGUN 10-20	77	
SONGBIRD 5-10	80	
SUNSET 10-20	66	
TAKOMA 5-8	83	
TIME-LIFE (16000 series) 15-25	83	

   (Three-LP set.)
U.A. 8-12 73-78
   Also see CHARLES, Ray, and Willie Nelson
   Also see COCHRAN, Hank, and Willie Nelson
   Also see COE, David Allan, and Willie Nelson
   Also see DARRELL, Johnny / George Jones / Willie Nelson
   Also see DAVIS, Danny, and the Nashville Brass, and Willie
    Nelson
   Also see HAGGARD, Merle, and Willie Nelson
   Also see IGLESIAS, Julio, and Willie Nelson
   Also see JENNINGS, Waylon, and Willie Nelson
   Also see LEE, Brenda, and Willie Nelson
   Also see MEYERS, Augie
   Also see PRICE, Ray, and Willie Nelson

NELSON, Willie, and Kris Kristofferson
LPs: 10/12-inch 33rpm
COLUMBIA 5-8   84
   Also see KRISTOFFERSON, Kris

NELSON, Willie, and Johnny Lee
LPs: 10/12-inch 33rpm
QUICKSILVER 5-8   84

NELSON, Willie / Johnny Lee / Mickey Gilley
LPs: 10/12-inch 33rpm
PLANTATION 5-8   82
   Also see GILLEY, Mickey
   Also see LEE, Johnny

NELSON, Willie / Jerry Lee Lewis / Carl Perkins / David Allan Coe
LPs: 10/12-inch 33rpm
PLANTATION 5-10   75
   Also see COE, David Allan
   Also see LEWIS, Jerry Lee
   Also see PERKINS, Carl

NELSON, Willie, and Roger Miller
LPs: 10/12-inch 33rpm
COLUMBIA 5-8   82
   Also see MILLER, Roger

NELSON, Willie, and Dolly Parton
Singles: 7-inch
MONUMENT 2-4   82

   Also see PARTON, Dolly

NELSON, Willie and Tracy
Singles: 7-inch
ATLANTIC 3-5   74
   Also see NELSON, Tracy

NELSON, Willie, and Webb Pierce
Singles: 7-inch
COLUMBIA 2-4   82
LPs: 10/12-inch 33rpm
COLUMBIA 5-8   82
   Also see PIERCE, Webb

NELSON, Willie, and Leon Russell
Singles: 7-inch
COLUMBIA 3-5   79
LPs: 10/12-inch 33rpm
COLUMBIA 5-10   79
   Also see RUSSELL, Leon

NELSON, Willie / Faron Young
LPs: 10/12-inch 33rpm
ROMULUS 5-10
   Also see NELSON, Willie
   Also see YOUNG, Faron

NENA
Singles: 12-inch 33/45rpm
EPIC 4-6 83-84
Singles: 7-inch
EPIC 2-4 83-84
LPs: 10/12-inch 33rpm
EPIC 5-8   84

NEON PHILHARMONIC
Singles: 7-inch
MCA 3-5	76	
TRX 3-5	72	
WARNER 4-6	69-71	
LPs: 10/12-inch 33rpm
WARNER 10-15   69

NERO, Peter
Singles: 7-inch
ARIOLA AMERICA 2-5	76	
ARISTA 2-5	75	
COLUMBIA 3-5	69-73	
RCA 3-6	61-68	
Picture Sleeves
RCA 3-5 62-63
LPs: 10/12-inch 33rpm
ARISTA 5-10	75	
CAMDEN 5-10	67-73	
COLUMBIA 5-10	69-75	
CONCORD JAZZ 5-8	78	
HARMONY 5-10	71	
PREMIER 10-15	63	
RCA 5-15	61-76	
   Also see ANN-MARGRET
   Also see CRAMER, Floyd / Peter Nero / Frankie Carle

NERVOUS NORVUS
(Jimmy Drake; Nervous Norvus With Red Blanchard)
Singles: 78rpm
DOT . . . . 10-20　56-57
Singles: 7–inch
BIG BEN 10-15
DOT (15000 series) . . . . 10-20　56
(Maroon label.)
DOT (15000 series) . . . . 8-12　57
(Black label.)
DOT (16000 series) . . . . 4-8　65
EMBEE . . . . 10-15　59

NESMITH, Michael
(Michael Nesmith and the First National Band;
Michael Nesmith and the Second National Band)
Singles: 7–inch
EDAN (1001 "Just a Little Love") . . . . 50-75　65
ISLAND . . . . 3-5　77
OMNIBUS . . . . 15-25　63
PACIFIC ARTS . . . . 5-10　75-79
RCA . . . . 5-15　70-75
Picture Sleeves
RCA (0453 "Nevada Fighter") . . . . . . 10-15　71
LPs: 10/12–inch 33rpm
PACIFIC ARTS (101 "The Prison") . . . 20-30　78
(Boxed edition. With booklet.)
PACIFIC ARTS (101 "The Prison") . . . 10-15　78
(Standard LP. With booklet.)
PACIFIC ARTS (106 through 130) . . . 10-15　78-79
RCA . . . . 20-30　70-75
Promotional LPs
PACIFIC ARTS ("Conversation with Michael Nesmith
Music-Radio Special") . . . . 25-35　78
　Also see BLESSING, Michael
　Also see MONKEES
　Also see WICHITA TRAIN WHISTLE

NETTO, Loz
Singles: 7–inch
21 . . . . 2-4　83
LPs: 10/12–inch 33rpm
21 . . . . 5-8　82
　Also see SNIFF 'N the TEARS

NEVIL, Robbie
Singles: 12–inch 33/45rpm
MANHATTAN . . . . 4-6　86
Singles: 7–inch
EMI . . . . 2-4　88
MANHATTAN . . . . 2-4　86-87
LPs: 10/12–inch 33rpm
EMI . . . . 5-8　88
MANHATTAN . . . . 5-8　86

NEVILLE, Aaron
(Arron Neville)
Singles: 7–inch
AIRECORDS . . . . 4-8　63
BELL . . . . 4-8　68-69
HEAD 3-5
MERCURY . . . . 3-5　72-73

MINIT . . . . 5-10　60-63
PAR-LO . . . . 4-8　66-67
POLYDOR . . . . 3-5　77
SAFARI . . . . 4-8　67
LPs: 10/12–inch 33rpm
COLLECTABLES . . . . 6-8　88
MINIT (40007 "Like It 'Tis") . . . . 15-25　67
(Monaural.)
MINIT (40007 "Like It 'Tis") . . . . 15-25　67
(Stereo.)
PAR-LO (1 "Tell It Like It Is") . . . . 20-30　67
(Monaural.)
PAR-LO (1 "Tell It Like It Is") . . . . 25-35　67
(Stereo.)
　Also see NEVILLE BROTHERS
　Also see RONSTADT, Linda, and Aaron Neville

NEVILLE, Aaron / Toussaint McCall
Singles: 7–inch
TRIP 3-5
　Also see McCALL, Toussaint
　Also see NEVILLE, Aaron

NEVILLE, Ivan
LPs: 10/12–inch 33rpm
POLYDOR . . . . 5-8　88

NEVILLE BROTHERS
Singles: 7–inch
A&M . . . . 3-5　81-90
LPs: 10/12–inch 33rpm
A&M . . . . 5-10　81-90
BLACK TOP . . . . 5-10　86
CAPITOL (11865 "The Neville
Brothers") . . . . 20-30　78
EMI AMERICA . . . . 5-8　87
RHINO . . . . 5-8　87
SPINDLE TOP . . . . 5-8　87
　Members: Aaron Neville; Art Neville; Charles Neville; Cyril
　Neville.
　Also see METERS
　Also see NEVILLE, Aaron

NEW BIRTH
Singles: 7–inch
ARIOLA AMERICA . . . . 3-5　79
BUDDAH . . . . 3-5　75
RCA . . . . 3-5　71-75
WARNER . . . . 3-5　76-78
LPs: 10/12–inch 33rpm
ARIOLA AMERICA . . . . 5-10　79
BUDDAH . . . . 8-12　75
COLLECTABLES . . . . 5-10　88
RCA (Except APD1-0285
and LSP-4000 series) . . . . 5-10　73-82
RCA (APD1-0285 "It's Been
a Long Time") . . . . 15-25　74
(Quadrophonic.)
RCA (LSP-4000 series) . . . . 10-15　70-72
WARNER . . . . 8-12　76-77
　Members: Harvey Fuqua; Tony Churchill; Alan Frey; Robert
　Jackson; Joe Porter; Leslie Wilson; Mel Wilson.
　Also see HARVEY

NEW CACTUS BAND
Singles: 7–inch
ATCO 3-6   73
LPs: 10/12–inch 33rpm
ATCO 8-12   73
Members: Mike Pinera; Duane Hitchings; Manuel Bertematti;
Roland Robinson; Jerry Norris.
Also see CACTUS

NEW CENSATION
Singles: 7–inch
PRIDE 3-5   74-75
LPs: 10/12–inch 33rpm
PRIDE 8-12   74

NEW CHOICE
Singles: 7–inch
RCA 2-4   87

NEW CHRISTY MINSTRELS
Singles: 7–inch
COLUMBIA (42000 series) 4-8   62-63
COLUMBIA (43000 and 44000 series) .. 4-6   64-69
GREGAR 3-5   70-72
WARNER 3-5   79
Promotional Singles
COLUMBIA (Colored vinyl) 5-10   63-65
LPs: 10/12–inch 33rpm
COLUMBIA (1800 through 2500
   series) 10-20   62-66
   (Monaural.)
COLUMBIA (8600 through 9300
   series) 12-25   62-66
   (Stereo.)
COLUMBIA (9600 and 9700 series) .. 10-15   68
GREGAR 8-12   70
HARMONY 8-12   68-72
Members: Randy Sparks; Barry McGuire; Kenny Rogers; Mike
Settle; Thelma Lou Camacho; Terry Williams; Mickey Jones;
Jackie Miller; Gayle Caldwell.
Also see FIRST EDITION
Also see McGUIRE, Barry

NEW COLONY SIX
Singles: 7–inch
CENTAUR 4-8   66
MCA 3-6   74
MERCURY ("Attacking a Straw Man") 10-20   69
   (Promotional issue only. Number not known.)
MERCURY (72737 through 73004) 4-8   67-70
MERCURY (73063 "People and Me") . 8-15   70
MERCURY (73093 "Close Your Eyes
   Little Girl") 8-15   70
SENTAR 4-8   66-67
SUNLIGHT 3-5   71-72
TWILIGHT 3-5   73
Picture Sleeves
MERCURY 4-8   67-68
LPs: 10/12–inch 33rpm
MERCURY 20-30   68-69
SENTAR (101 "Breakthrough") ... 150-250   66
SENTAR (3001 "Colonization") 35-50   67

Members: Ronnie Rice; Ray Graffia; Craig Kemp; Jerry
Kollenberg; Pat McBride; Chick James; Billy Herman; Chuck
Lobes; Wally Kemp.

NEW EDITION
Singles: 12–inch 33/45rpm
MCA 4-6   84-86
STREETWISE 4-6   83
Singles: 7–inch
MCA (Black vinyl) 2-4   84-88
MCA (Colored vinyl) 3-5   85
STREETWISE 5-8   83
Picture Sleeves
MCA 2-5   84-88
LPs: 10/12–inch 33rpm
MCA 5-8   84-88
STREETWISE 5-8   83
Member: Johnny Gill.
Also see GILL, Johnny
Also see KING DREAM CHORUS and Holiday Crew

NEW ENGLAND
Singles: 7–inch
ELEKTRA 3-5   80-81
INFINITY 3-5   79
LPs: 10/12–inch 33rpm
ELEKTRA 5-10   80-81
INFINITY 5-10   79

NEW ENGLAND CONSERVATORY RAGTIME ENSEMBLE
Singles: 7–inch
ANGEL.......................... 2-4   80
LPs: 10/12–inch 33rpm
ANGEL.......................... 5-8   73
GOLDEN CREST 5-10   75

NEW ESTABLISHMENT
Singles: 7–inch
COLGEMS 5-8   69
MERCURY 4-8   67

NEW GUYS on the BLOCK
Singles: 7–inch
SUGAR HILL 2-4   83

NEW HOLLYWOOD ARGYLES
Singles: 7–inch
KAMMY 5-10   66
Also see HOLLYWOOD ARGYLES

NEW HOPE
Singles: 7–inch
JAMIE 4-8   69-71
LPs: 10/12–inch 33rpm
JAMIE (3034 "The New Hope") 20-30   69
LIGHT 8-10   72

NEW HORIZONS
Singles: 7–inch
COLUMBIA 2-4   83
LPs: 10/12–inch 33rpm
COLUMBIA 5-8   83

NEW JERSEY MASS CHOIR
Singles: 12–inch 33/45rpm
SAVOY 4-6   85
Also see FOREIGNER

NEW KIDS on the BLOCK
Singles: 12–inch 33/45rpm
COLUMBIA 4-6   86
Singles: 7–inch
COLUMBIA 2-4   86-90
Picture Sleeves
COLUMBIA 2-4   88
LPs: 10/12–inch 33rpm
COLUMBIA 5-8   86-90

NEW KINGSTON TRIO
Singles: 7–inch
CAPITOL 3-6   71
Also see KINGSTON TRIO

NEW MARKETTS
(Danny Welton and the New Marketts)
Singles: 7–inch
CALLIOPE 3-6   77
FARR 3-6   76-77
SEMINOLE 3-6   76
LPs: 10/12–inch 33rpm
CALLIOPE 8-12   77
Also see MARKETTS

NEW ORDER
Singles: 12–inch 33/45rpm
FACTUS 4-6   83
QWEST 4-6   85
STREETWISE 4-6   83
Singles: 7–inch
QWEST 2-4   85-89
STREETWISE 2-4   83
LPs: 10/12–inch 33rpm
QWEST (Except 25621) 5-8   85-89
QWEST (25621 "Substance") 8-12   87

NEW RIDERS of the Purple Sage
Singles: 7–inch
COLUMBIA 3-5   71-74
MCA 3-5   76-77
LPs: 10/12–inch 33rpm
A&M 5-8   81
BUDDAH 8-12   75
COLUMBIA 10-15   71-75
MCA 8-10   76-77
RELIX 5-8   86-87
Members: Skip Battin; David Turbert. Assorted Grateful Dead
members guested on Columbia and Relix issues.
Also see GRATEFUL DEAD
Also see KINGFISH

NEW ROTARY CONNECTION
LPs: 10/12–inch 33rpm
CHESS 8-12   71
Also see ROTARY CONNECTION

NEW SEEKERS
Singles: 7–inch
ELEKTRA 3-5   70-72
MGM/VERVE 3-5   72-73
Picture Sleeves
MGM/VERVE 3-5   72-73
EPs: 7–inch 33/45rpm
COCA-COLA 5-10   69
(Promotional issue only.)
LPs: 10/12–inch 33rpm
ELEKTRA 10-12   71-72
MGM/VERVE 8-10   73
Member: Keith Potger.
Also see SEEKERS

NEW VAUDEVILLE BAND
Singles: 7–inch
FONTANA 3-6   66-68
LPs: 10/12–inch 33rpm
FONTANA 10-15   67

NEW VENTURES: see VENTURES

NEW YORK CITI PEECH BOYS
Singles: 12–inch 33/45rpm
GARAGE 4-6   83-84
ISLAND 4-6   83-84
Singles: 7–inch
ISLAND 2-4   83-84
LPs: 10/12–inch 33rpm
ISLAND 5-8   84

NEW YORK CITY
Singles: 7–inch
CHELSEA 3-5   73-75
LPs: 10/12–inch 33rpm
CHELSEA 10-15   73-77
Also see CADILLACS
Also see FIVE SATINS

NEW YORK COMMUNITY CHOIR
Singles: 7–inch
RCA 3-5   77

NEW YORK DOLLS
Singles: 7–inch
MERCURY 3-5   73-76
Picture Sleeves
MERCURY 4-8   73
LPs: 10/12–inch 33rpm
MERCURY (675 "New York Dolls") . . 20-25   73
MERCURY (1001 "Too Much
Too Soon") 15-20   74
REACH OUT INT'L 5-10   81
Members: David Johansen; Jerry Nolan; Arthur Kane; Johnny
Thudners; Sylvain Sylvain.
Also see JOHANSEN, David
Also see SYLVAIN SYLVAIN
Also see W.A.S.P.

NEW YORKERS
Singles: 7–inch
WALL (547 "Miss Fine") 15-25   61
WALL (548 "Tears in My Eyes") 15-25   61

Members: Fred Parris; Richard Freeman; Wesley Forbes; Louis Peebles; Silvester Hopkins.
Also see FIVE SATINS

NEW YOUNG HEARTS
Singles: 7–inch
ZEA 3-5 70

NEWBEATS
Singles: 7–inch
ABC 3-5 74
HICKORY 4-8 64-72
PLAYBOY 3-5 74
LPs: 10/12–inch 33rpm
HICKORY (LP-120 "Bread and
  Butter") 25-45 65
  (Monaural.)
HICKORY (LPS-120 "Bread and
  Butter") 35-55 65
  (Stereo.)
HICKORY (LP-122 "Big Beat Sound") 25-35 65
  (Monaural.)
HICKORY (LPS-122 "Big Beat
  Sound") 30-40 65
  (Stereo.)
HICKORY (LP-128 "Run Baby Run") . 25-35 65
  (Monaural.)
HICKORY (LPS-128 "Run Baby Run") 30-40 65
  (Stereo.)
Members: Larry Henley; Dean Mathis; Mark Mathis.
Also see DEAN & MARC

NEWBERRY, Booker, III
Singles: 12–inch 33/45rpm
BOARDWALK 4-6 83
Singles: 7–inch
BOARDWALK 2-4 83
OMNI 2-4 86

NEWBURY, Mickey
Singles: 7–inch
ELEKTRA 3-5 71-73
HICKORY 4-8 65-68
MERCURY 3-6 69-70
RCA 3-6 68-70
Picture Sleeves
RCA 3-6 68
LPs: 10/12–inch 33rpm
ABC/HICKORY 5-10 77-79
MCA 5-8
ELEKTRA 8-10 71-75
MERCURY 10-12 69
RCA 10-12 68-72

NEWCLEUS
Singles: 12–inch 33/45rpm
SUNNYVIEW 4-6 83-86
Singles: 7–inch
SUNNYVIEW 2-4 83-86
LPs: 10/12–inch 33rpm
SUNNYVIEW 5-8 84-86

NEWCOMERS
Singles: 7–inch
GIGOLO 4-8 65
STAX 3-5 71
TRUTH 3-5 74-75
VOLT 3-6 69
Members: Terry Bartlett; Bert Brown; William Sumlin.
Also see KWICK

NEWHART, Bob
LPs: 10/12–inch 33rpm
HARMONY 10-15 69
WARNER (1300 through 1500 series) 20-30 60-65
WARNER (1600 through 1700 series) 15-25 66-67

NEWLEY, Anthony
Singles: 7–inch
KAPP 4-6 69
LONDON 4-8 58-63
MGM 3-5 71-74
RCA 4-8 66-67
U.A. 3-5 76-77
WARNER 4-6 68
LPs: 10/12–inch 33rpm
BELL 8-10 71
LONDON 10-20 62-66
MGM 8-12 71-73
RCA 10-20 64-69
U.A. 5-10 77

NEWMAN, Jimmy C.
(Jimmy Newman; Jimmy C. Newman and Cajun Country)
Singles: 78rpm
DOT 5-10 54-57
Singles: 7–inch
DECCA 4-8 60-71
DOT (Except 15766) 5-15 54-57
DOT (15766 "Carry On") 50-75 58
MGM 5-8 58-60
MONUMENT 3-5 72
PLANTATION 3-5 76-80
SHANNON 3-5 73
EPs: 7–inch 33/45rpm
DECCA 5-10 64
LPs: 10/12–inch 33rpm
CROWN 8-12
DECCA 10-20 62-70
DELTA 5-8 82
DOT 10-20 66
LA LOUISANNE 5-8
MGM 15-25 59-62
PICKWICK/HILLTOP 8-12
PLANTATION 5-10 77-81
SWALLOW 5-8

NEWMAN, Jimmy C., Danny Davis and the Nashville Brass
Singles: 7–inch
RCA 2-4 80
Also see DAVIS, Danny
Also see NEWMAN, Jimmy C.

NEWMAN, Randy
Singles: 78rpm
REPRISE (0284 "I Think It's
  Gonna Rain Today") 8-10   78
(Promotional issue only.)
Singles: 7-inch
CHELSEA 3-5   74
DOT 4-8   62
REPRISE 3-6   68-78
WARNER 2-5   77-85
LPs: 10/12-inch 33rpm
EPIC (147 "Peyton Place") 20-30   65
(TV Soundtrack.)
REPRISE (Except 6286) 5-10   70-88
REPRISE (6286 "Randy Newman") .. 10-20   68
(Cover pictures Randy in sweater and coat.)
REPRISE (6286 "Randy Newman") .. 10-15   68
(Cover picture is a close-up of Randy.)
WARNER 5-10   77-85
  Also see BISHOP, Stephen
  Also see EAGLES
  Also see McVIE, Christine
  Also see RONSTADT, Linda
  Also see SEGER, Bob

NEWMAN, Randy, and Paul Simon
Singles: 7-inch
WARNER 3-5   83
  Also see NEWMAN, Randy
  Also see SIMON, Paul

NEWMAN, Ted
Singles: 78rpm
REV 5-10   57
Singles: 7-inch
REV 5-10   57

NEWMAN, Thunderclap
Singles: 7-inch
MCA 2-4
TRACK (2000 series) 4-8   69-70
TRACK (60000 series) 3-5   75
LPs: 10/12-inch 33rpm
ATLANTIC/TRACK 10-20   70
MCA/TRACK 5-10   73
  Members: Andy Newman; Jimmy McCulloch; Speedy Keen.
  Also see McCARTNEY, Paul

NEWSOME, Bobby
Singles: 7-inch
SPRING 3-5   72

NEWSOME, Frankie
Singles: 7-inch
GWP 4-6   69

NEWTON, Juice
Singles: 7-inch
CAPITOL 3-5   78-84
RCA 2-4   84-86
Picture Sleeves
CAPITOL 3-5   78-84
RCA 2-4   84-85

LPs: 10/12-inch 33rpm
CAPITOL 5-10   78-84
RCA 5-8   84-86
  Also see RABBITT, Eddie, and Juice Newton

NEWTON, Juice, and Silver Spur
Singles: 7-inch
CAPITOL 3-5   77
RCA 3-5   75-76
LPs: 10/12-inch 33rpm
CAPITOL (11000 series) 8-10   77
CAPITOL (16000 series) 5-8   81
RCA (1000 series) 8-12   75
RCA (4000 series) 5-8   81
  Also see NEWTON, Juice

NEWTON, Wayne
Singles: 7-inch
ARIES II 3-5   79-80
CAPITOL (Except 5338) 4-8   63-71
CAPITOL (5338 "Comin' on
  Too Strong") 10-20   64
(With Bruce Johnston and Terry Melcher.)
CHALLENGE 4-8   64
CHELSEA 3-5   72-76
GEORGE (7777 "Little White
  Cloud That Cried") 10-15   62
MGM 3-6   68
20TH FOX 3-5   78
WARNER 3-5   70-77
Picture Sleeves
CAPITOL 4-8   65-66
LPs: 10/12-inch 33rpm
AIRES II 5-8   79-80
CAMDEN 5-10   74
CAPITOL (573 "Wayne Newton") ... 15-25   70
(Three-LP set.)
CAPITOL (T-1973 through T-2797) .. 10-20   63-67
(Monaural.)
CAPITOL (ST-1973 through ST-2797) 15-25   63-67
(Stereo.)
CAPITOL (SM-2300 series) 5-8   75
CAPITOL (11000 series) 5-8   79
CAPITOL (16000 series) 5-8   80
CHELSEA 5-10   72
MGM 6-12   68
MUSICOR 5-8   79
20TH FOX 5-8   78
  Also see BRUCE & TERRY

NEWTON BROTHERS
(Newton Brothers Featuring Wayne)
Singles: 7-inch
CAPITOL (4236 "The Real Thing") .. 60-80   59
GEORGE (7778 "Little Jukebox") .. 15-20   61
GEORGE (7780 "I Still Love You") .. 10-15   61
LAMA (7794 "I Was Born
  When You Kissed Me") 25-50   63
  Members: Wayne Newton; Jerry Newton.
  Also see NEWTON RASCALS

NEWTON RASCALS
Singles: 7-inch
RANGER RECORDS (401 "If the Easter Bunny
  Knew the Fun He'd Have on Xmas") 15-25   58
  (Issued with a paper insert picturing 12-year-old
  Wayne and 14-year-old Jerry as "The Rascals in
  Rhythm." Value of insert is about the same as for
  disc.)
  Members: Wayne Newton; Jerry Newton.
   Also see NEWTON, Wayne
   Also see NEWTON BROTHERS

NEWTON-JOHN, Olivia
Singles: 12-inch 33/45rpm
MCA (Except 1150) 4-6   81-84
MCA (1150 "Twist of Fate") 5-10   83
  (Promotional issue only.)
Singles: 7-inch
GEFFEN 2-4   89
KIRSHNER (5005 "Goin' Back") 10-15   70
MCA (Except 40043) 2-5   73-88
MCA (40043 "Take Me Home
  Country Roads") 5-10   73
RSO 3-5   78
UNI (55281 "If Not for You") 5-10   71
UNI (55304 "Banks of the Ohio") 4-8   71
UNI (55317 "What Is Life") 4-8   72
UNI (55348 "Just a Little too Much") .. 8-12   72
Promotional Singles
MCA (1810 "Deeper Than the Night") 25-30   79
  (Picture disc. Promotional issue only.)
WHAT'S IT ALL ABOUT 25-50   74
Picture Sleeves
MCA (Except 40418) 2-5   73-84
MCA (40418 "Please Mr. Please") 6-10   75
EPs: 7-inch 33/45rpm
MCA 12-15   73
  (Promotional issues only.)
LPs: 10/12-inch 33rpm
GEFFEN 5-8   89
MCA (389 "Let Me Be There" 10-12   73
MCA (411 "If You Love Me,
  Let Me Know") 12-15   74
  (With I Love You, I Honestly Love You. Note longer
  title.)
MCA (411 "If You Love Me,
  Let Me Know") 8-10   74
  (With I Honestly Love You. Note shorter title.)
MCA (2000 and 3000 series) 8-10   75-78
MCA (5000 and 6000 series) 5-8   80-83
MCA (37000 series) 5-8   80-83
MFSL 25-50   80
UNI (73117 "If Not for You") 50-75   71
  (Cover depicts a field scene.)
UNI (73117 "If Not for You") 20-30   71
  (Field scene removed from cover.)
  Also see DENVER, John, and Olivia Newton-John
  Also see FOSTER, David, and Olivia Newton-John
  Also see TOMORROW
  Also see WILSON, Carl

NEWTON-JOHN, Olivia, and the Electric Light Orchestra
Singles: 7-inch
MCA (41285 "Xanadu") 3-5   80
Picture Sleeves
MCA (41285 "Xanadu") 3-5   80
LPs: 10/12-inch 33rpm
MCA (6100 "Xanadu") 8-10   80
MCA (10384 "Xanadu") 750-1000   80
  (Picture disc. Promotional issue only. Also has Cliff
  Richard, Gene Kelly and the Tubes.)
  Also see ELECTRIC LIGHT ORCHESTRA
  Also see RICHARD, Cliff
  Also see TUBES

NEWTON-JOHN, Olivia, and Andy Gibb
Singles: 12-inch 33/45rpm
POLYDOR (104 "Rest Your
  Love-on Me") 10-15   79
Singles: 7-inch
RSO 3-5   80
  Also see GIBB, Andy

NEWTON-JOHN, Olivia, and Cliff Richard
Singles: 7-inch
MCA 3-5   80
Picture Sleeves
MCA 3-5   80
  Also see RICHARD, Cliff

NEWTON-JOHN, Olivia, and John Travolta
Singles: 7-inch
RSO 3-5   78
Picture Sleeves
RSO 3-5   78
  Also see NEWTON-JOHN, Olivia
  Also see TRAVOLTA, John

NEXT MOVEMENT
Singles: 7-inch
NUANCE 2-4   84

NICE
Singles: 7-inch
IMMEDIATE 4-8   68
MERCURY 3-5   70-71
LPs: 10/12-inch 33rpm
CHARISMA 8-12
COLUMBIA 8-12
IMMEDIATE 10-15   68-71
MERCURY 10-12   70-72
SIRE 10-12   75
  Members: Keith Emerson; Lee Jackson; Brian Davison; Joe
  Harriot; Davy O'List.
  Also see EMERSON, Keith, and the Nice

NICHOLAS, Paul
Singles: 7-inch
COLUMBIA 3-5   74
RSO 3-5   76-78
LPs: 10/12-inch 33rpm
RSO 5-10   77

NICHOLS, Mike, and Elaine May
Singles: 7–inch
MERCURY 3-6
LPs: 10/12–inch 33rpm
MERCURY 15-30   59-72

NICK & ELVIS
Singles: 12–inch 33/45rpm
COLUMBIA 4-8   84
Members: Nick Lowe; Elvis Costello.
Also see COSTELLO, Elvis
Also see LOWE, Nick

NICKIE LEE: see LEE, Nickie

NICKS, Stevie
Singles: 12–inch 33/45rpm
MODERN 4-8   81-86
Singles: 7–inch
MODERN 2-5   81-89
Picture Sleeves
MODERN 2-5   81-86
LPs: 10/12–inch 33rpm
MFSL (121 "Bella Donna") 20-30   84
MODERN 5-10   81-89
Also see BUCKINGHAM NICKS
Also see EGAN, Walter
Also see FLEETWOOD MAC
Also see LOGGINS, Kenny, and Stevie Nicks
Also see STEWART, John

NICKS, Stevie, and Don Henley
Singles: 7–inch
MODERN 3-5   81
Also see HENLEY, Don

NICKS, Stevie, and Tom Petty and the Heartbreakers
Singles: 7–inch
MODERN 3-5   81-86
Also see NICKS, Stevie
Also see PETTY, Tom, and the Heartbreakers

NICOLE
Singles: 12–inch 33/45rpm
PORTRAIT 4-6   85-86
Singles: 7–inch
EPIC 2-4   88
PORTRAIT 2-4   85-86
LPs: 10/12–inch 33rpm
PORTRAIT 5-8   86

NIELSEN - PEARSON BAND
Singles: 7–inch
CAPITOL 3-5   80-83
EPIC 3-5   78
LPs: 10/12–inch 33rpm
CAPITOL 5-10   80-81
EPIC 5-10   78
Members: Reid Nielsen; Mark Pearson.

NIGHT
Singles: 7–inch
PLANET 3-5   79-81

Picture Sleeves
PLANET 3-5   80-81
LPs: 10/12–inch 33rpm
PLANET 5-10   79-80
Members: Chris Thompson; Nicky Hopkins; Derek Austin; Bill Payne; Michael McDonald; Vince Melamed; Steve Porcaro; James Johnson.
Also see THOMPSON, Chris, and Night

NIGHT RANGER
Singles: 7–inch
BOARDWALK 2-4   83
MCA 2-4   83-87
LPs: 10/12–inch 33rpm
BOARDWALK 5-10   82
CAMEL 5-8   88
MCA 5-10   83-87

NIGHTCRAWLERS
Singles: 7–inch
KAPP 5-10   66-67
LEE (1012 "Little Black Egg") 10-20   66
LPs: 10/12–inch 33rpm
KAPP (3520 "Little Black Egg") 30-50   67

NIGHTHAWK
Singles: 7–inch
QUALITY 3-5   82

NIGHTHAWKS
LPs: 10/12–inch 33rpm
ADELPHI 6-12   76-82
ALADDIN (101 "Rock and Roll") 50-75   75
CHESAPEAKE (Black vinyl) 5-10   83
CHESAPEAKE (Colored vinyl) 10-15   83
VARRICK 5-10   83
MERCURY 5-10   80
Members: Mark Wenner; Jim Thackery.

NIGHTINGALE, Maxine
Singles: 7–inch
A&M 3-5   81
HIGHRISE 3-5   82
RCA 3-5   80
U.A. 3-5   76
WINDSONG 3-5   79
LPs: 10/12–inch 33rpm
HIGHRISE 5-10   82
U.A. 5-10   76-79
WINDSONG 5-10   80

NIGHTINGALE, Maxine, and Jimmy Ruffin
Singles: 7–inch
HIGHRISE 3-5   82
Also see NIGHTINGALE, Maxine
Also see RUFFIN, Jimmy

NIGHTINGALE, Ollie
Singles: 7–inch
MEMPHIS 3-5   71
PATHFINDER 3-5   78
PRIDE 3-5   72-73
LPs: 10/12–inch 33rpm
PRIDE 8-12   73

NIGHTNOISE
LPs: 10/12–inch 33rpm
WINDHAM HILL 5-8   88

NILE, Willie
Singles: 7–inch
ARISTA 3-5   80-81
LPs: 10/12–inch 33rpm
ARISTA 5-10   80-81

Excerpts from
the album "The Point!"
Nilsson
Produced by Nilsson

RCA

STEREO
SPS-45-248
APKA-4801

Not For Sale

1. Dunbar Music
   Golden Syrup
   Music, BMI
2. Dunbar
   Music, BMI
   1. 2:20
   2. 2:38

1–LIFE LINE (Nilsson)
2–POL'Y HIGH (Nilsson)
Arranged and conducted by
George Tipton

NILSSON
(Harry Nilsson and the New Salvation Singers)
Singles: 7–inch
POLYDOR 2-4   85
RCA 3-6   67-77
TOWER (100 series) 5-8   64-65
TOWER (500 series) 4-6   69
Picture Sleeves
RCA 3-6   74-77
EPs: 7–inch 33/45rpm
RCA (248 "Excerpts from *The Point*) . . 8-10   71
(Promotional issue only.)
LPs: 10/12–inch 33rpm
51 WEST 5-8
MUSICOR 8-10   77
POLYDOR 5-8   85
RCA (0097 through 0817,,
   except "APD1" series) 8-12   73-75
RCA ("APD1" series) 10-20   74-75
(Quadrophonic.)
RCA (1003 "The Point") 10-12   71
(With Davy Jones and Mickey Dolenz.)
RCA (1031 through 3811) 5-10   76-80
RCA (3874 "Pandemonium
   Shadow Show") 15-20   67
RCA (3956 "Aerial Ballet") 10-20   68
RCA (4197 through 4717) 8-12   69-72
RAPPLE 8-12   74
SPRINGBOARD 5-10   78
TOWER (5095 "Spotlight") 10-15   69
Promotional LPs
RCA (567 "Scatalogue") 30-40
RCA ("Pandemonium
   Shadow Show - Boxed Set") 50-75   67
(With photos and inserts.)
Also see CHER & NILSSON

Also see DOLENZ, Mickey
Also see JONES, Davy
Also see STARR, Ringo, and Harry Nilsson

NIMOY, Leonard
Singles: 7–inch
DOT 8-12   67-69
LPs: 10/12–inch 33rpm
CAEDMON 10-15
DOT 25-50   67-69
JRT ("The Mysterious Golem") 20-40   82
PARAMOUNT 20-40   74
PICKWICK 15-25
SEARS 15-25

9TH CREATION
Singles: 7–inch
HILLTAK 3-5   79-80
PRELUDE 3-5   77
LPs: 10/12–inch 33rpm
PRELUDE 8-10   77
RITE TRACK 10-12

9.9
Singles: 12–inch 33/45rpm
RCA 4-6   85-86
Singles: 7–inch
RCA 2-4   85-86
LPs: 10/12–inch 33rpm
RCA 5-10   85

999
Singles: 7–inch
POLYDOR 3-5   81
LPs: 10/12–inch 33rpm
PVC 5-10   79
POLYDOR 5-10   80-81

1910 FRUITGUM COMPANY
Singles: 7–inch
ATTACK 4-8   70
BUDDAH 4-8   67-69
SUPER K 4-8   70
LPs: 10/12–inch 33rpm
BUDDAH 15-25   68-70
Also see KASENETZ - KATZ SINGING ORCHESTRAL CIRCUS

1910 FRUITGUM COMPANY / Lemon Pipers
LPs: 10/12–inch 33rpm
BUDDAH 15-20   68-70
Also see LEMON PIPERS
Also see 1910 FRUITGUM COMPANY

NINO and the Ebb Tides
Singles: 7–inch
MADISON (162 "Those Oldies
   But Goodies") 20-30   61
MADISON (166 "Juke Box
   Saturday Night") 15-20   61
MALA (480 "Linda Lou") 10-15   64
MARCO (105 "Someday") 20-30   61
MR. PEACOCK (102 "Wished
   I Was Home") 10-20   61
MR. PEACOCK (117 "Lovin' Time") . . 10-15   62

MR. PEEKE (123 "Tonight") 10-15   63
RECORTE (405 "Puppy Love") 20-30   58
RECORTE (408 "The Real Meaning
  of Christmas") 100-125   58
RECORTE (409 "I'm Confessin") 20-30   58
RECORTE (413 "I Love Girls") 20-30   58
Member: Nino Aiello.

NINO and the Ebb Tides / Miss Frankie Nolan
Singles: 7-inch
MADISON (151 "A Week
  from Sunday") 10-20   61
Also see NINO and the Ebb Tides

NITEFLYTE
Singles: 7-inch
ARIOLA AMERICA 3-5   79-81
LPs: 10/12-inch 33rpm
ARIOLA AMERICA 5-10   79-81
Also see JOHNSON, Howard

NITE-LITERS
Singles: 7-inch
RCA 3-5   71-72
LPs: 10/12-inch 33rpm
RCA 8-12   71-72

NITTY GRITTY DIRT BAND
(Dirt Band)
Singles: 7-inch
LIBERTY (1000 series) 3-5   81-84
LIBERTY (50000 series) 4-8   67-70
U.A. 3-5   71-80
WARNER 2-4   84-86
Picture Sleeves
LIBERTY (1000 series) 3-5   81-84
LIBERTY (50000 series) 8-12   67
U.A. 3-5   71-80
EPs: 7-inch 33/45rpm
U.A. (69 "All the Good Times") 20-30   71
(Promotional issue only. Includes script and
booklet.)
LPs: 10/12-inch 33rpm
LIBERTY (1100 series) 5-10   81
LIBERTY (3501 "Nitty Gritty
  Dirt Band") 15-20   67
(Monaural.)
LIBERTY (7501 "Nitty Gritty
  Dirt Band") 15-25   67
(Stereo.)
LIBERTY (7501 through 7611) 10-20   67-69
LIBERTY (7642 "Uncle Charlie") .. 100-125   70
(Gatefold promotional edition. Includes two bonus
singles, photos and booklet.)
LIBERTY (LST-7642 "Uncle Charlie") 10-20   70
LIBERTY (LATO-7642 "Uncle Charlie") . 5-8
U.A. (117 "Interview") 15-25   75
(Promotional issue only.)
U.A. (UA-LA184 "Stars and
  Stripes Forever") 10-20   74
U.A. (LWB-184 "Stars and
  Stripes Forever") 8-10

U.A. (469 "Dream") 8-12   75
U.A. (469 "Dream - Programmers
  Guide") 15-25   75
(Promotional issue only.)
U.A. (UA-LA670 "Dirt
  Silver and Gold") 15-20   76
U.A. (LKCL-670 "Dirt,
  Silver and Gold") 10-12
U.A.(854 through 1042) 5-10   78-80
U.A. (5500 series) 8-12   71
U.A. (9800 series) 8-10   72
UNIVERSAL 8-12   89
WARNER 5-10   84-86
Also see SKAGGS, Ricky

NITTY GRITTY DIRT BAND and Roy Acuff
Singles: 7-inch
U.A. 3-5   71

NITTY GRITTY DIRT BAND and Linda Ronstadt
Singles: 7-inch
U.A. 3-5   79
Also see NITTY GRITTY DIRT BAND
Also see RONSTADT, Linda

NITZINGER
(John Nitzinger)
Singles: 7-inch
CAPITOL 3-5   72-73
20TH FOX 3-5   76
LPs: 10/12-inch 33rpm
CAPITOL 8-12   72-73
20TH FOX 8-10   76
Members: John Nitzinger; Bugs Henderson.

NITZSCHE, Jack
Singles: 7-inch
FANTASY 3-5   76
MCA 3-5   78
REPRISE 4-8   63-65
Picture Sleeves
REPRISE (20,202 "Lonely Surfer") .. 15-25   63
LPs: 10/12-inch 33rpm
MCA 8-10   78
REPRISE (2000 series) 8-12   73
REPRISE (6100 series) 15-25   63-64
REPRISE (6200 series) 10-20   66

NIVENS, Pamela
Singles: 7-inch
SUN VALLEY 3-5   83

NIX, Don
Singles: 7-inch
CREAM 3-5   76
ELEKTRA 3-5   71
LPs: 10/12-inch 33rpm
CREAM 5-10   79
ELEKTRA 8-12   71
ENTERPRISE 8-10   73

NIXON, Mojo, and Skid Roper
LPs: 10/12–inch 33rpm
ENIGMA 5-8   87-89

NOBLE, Nick
Singles: 78rpm
MERCURY 4-8   56-57
WING 4-8   55-56
Singles: 7–inch
CAPITOL 3-5   73
CHESS 4-8   63-64
CHURCHILL 3-5   77
CORAL 4-8   59-66
DATE 4-6   67-68
EPIC 3-5   77
LIBERTY 4-8   62-63
MERCURY 5-10   56-57
TMS 3-5   79
20TH FOX 4-8   65
WING 5-10   55-56
LPs: 10/12–inch 33rpm
COLUMBIA 8-12   69
LIBERTY 10-15   63
WING 10-20   60

NOBLES, Cliff
(Cliff Nobels and Co.)
Singles: 7–inch
ATLANTIC 4-8   66-67
PHIL L.A. of SOUL 4-6   68-69
JAMIE 3-5   72
ROULETTE 3-5   73
LPs: 10/12–inch 33rpm
MOON SHOT 8-10
PHIL L.A. of SOUL 10-15   68
Also see MFSB

NOCERA
Singles: 7–inch
SLEEPING BAG 2-4   86-87

NOEL
Singles: 7–inch
4TH and B'WAY 2-4   87-88
LPs: 10/12–inch 33rpm
4TH and B'WAY 5-8   88

NOGUEZ, Jacky, and His Orchestra
Singles: 7–inch
JAMIE 4-8   59-60
Picture Sleeves
JAMIE 5-10   60
LPs: 10/12–inch 33rpm
JAMIE 10-20   60

NOLAN: see PORTER, Nolan

NOLAN, Kenny
Singles: 7–inch
CASABLANCA 3-5   79-80
DOT 4-8   68
FORWARD 4-8   69
HIGHLAND 4-8   68

LION 3-5   72
MGM 3-5   71
POLYDOR 3-5   78
20TH FOX 3-5   76-77
LPs: 10/12–inch 33rpm
CASABLANCA 5-10   79
POLYDOR 5-10   78
20TH FOX 5-10   77

NORDINE, Ken
Singles: 7–inch
DOT (16000 series) 8-12   59
LPs: 10/12–inch 33rpm
BLUE THUMB 8-12   72
DECCA (8550 "Concert in the Sky") . 40-50   57
DOT (3075 through 3301) 30-50   57-60
(Monaural.)
DOT (25115 through 25301) 30-50   58-60
(Stereo.)
DOT (25880 "Best of Word Jazz") ... 10-20   67
HAMILTON 20-30   59
PHILIPS 15-25   67
Also see VAUGHN, Billy

NORMA
Singles: 12–inch 33/45rpm
ERC 4-6   83

NORMA JEAN
(Norma Jean Wright)
Singles: 12–inch 33/45rpm
BEARSVILLE 4-8   79-80
Singles: 7–inch
BEARSVILLE 3-5   78-80
LPs: 10/12–inch 33rpm
BEARSVILLE 5-10   78
Also see CHIC

NORMAN, Jimmy
(Jimmy Norman and the Hollywood Teeners; Jimmy Norman and the Viceroys)
Singles: 7–inch
DOT 8-12   59
FUN 8-12   60
GOOD SOUND 5-10   61
JOSIE 4-8   68
LITTLE STAR 5-10   62-63
MERCURY 4-8   67
MUN RAB 8-12   59
POLO 4-8   64
RAY STAR 5-10   61-62
SAMAR 4-8   66
LPs: 10/12–inch 33rpm
BADCAT 5-10
Also see CHARGERS
Also see COASTERS
Also see DYNA-SORES
Also see HARLEM RIVER DRIVE

NORMAN, Jimmy, and Dorothy Berry
Singles: 7–inch
LITTLE STAR 5-10   62

NORMAN, Jimmy / Willie "The Moon Man" Echols
Singles: 7–inch
GOOD SOUND 5-10   61

NORMAN, Jimmy, and the O'Jays
Singles: 7–inch
LITTLE STAR 5-10   63
Also see NORMAN, Jimmy
Also see O'JAYS

NORTH, Freddie
Singles: 7–inch
A-BET 4-8   67-69
CAPITOL 4-8   62
RIC 4-8   64
MANKIND 3-5   71-76
PHILLIPS INT'L 5-10   61
LPs: 10/12–inch 33rpm
A-BET 8-10
MANKIND 8-12   71-75
PHONORAMA 5-8

NORTHCOTT, Tom
Singles: 7–inch
UNI 3-5   71
WARNER 4-8   67-69
LPs: 10/12–inch 33rpm
UNI 8-12   71

NORTHERN LIGHT
Singles: 7–inch
COLUMBIA 3-5   75
GLACIER 3-5   75-77

NORVUS, Nervous: see NERVOUS NORVUS

NORWOOD, Dorothy
(Dorothy Norwood and the Norwood Singers)
Singles: 7–inch
GRC 3-5   72-75
JEWEL 3-5   78
SAVOY 4-8   63-69
LPs: 10/12–inch 33rpm
JEWEL 5-10   78
SAVOY 8-18   63-83

NOTATIONS
Singles: 7–inch
C.R.A. 3-5   73
GEMIGO 3-5   75-76
MERCURY 3-5   77
TWINIGHT 3-5   70
LPs: 10/12–inch 33rpm
GEMIGO 8-12   76
Members: Clifford Curry; Bobby Thomas; Lasalle Matthews;
Jimmy Stroud; Walter Jones.

NOVA, Aldo
Singles: 12–inch 33/45rpm
PORTRAIT 5-8   82
Singles: 7–inch
PORTRAIT 2-5   82

LPs: 10/12–inch 33rpm
PORTRAIT 5-10   82-83

NOVAS
Singles: 7–inch
PARROT (45005 "The Crusher") 30-50   64
TWIN TOWN (713 "Nova's Coaster") 25-35   65

NOVELLE, Jay
Singles: 12–inch 33/45rpm
EMERGENCY 4-6   84

NOVO COMBO
Singles: 7–inch
POLYDOR 3-5   82
LPs: 10/12–inch 33rpm
POLYDOR 5-10   81-82
Member: Mike Shrieve.
Also see SANTANA

NU SHOOZ
Singles: 7–inch
ATLANTIC 2-4   86-88
LPs: 10/12–inch 33rpm
ATLANTIC 5-8   86-88
Members: Valerie Day; John Smith.

NU TORNADOS
Singles: 7–inch
CARLTON 5-10   58-59
FELSTED 5-10   59

NUANCE
(Featuring Vikki Love)
Singles: 12–inch 33/45rpm
4TH and BROADWAY 4-6   84-85
Singles: 7–inch
4TH and BROADWAY 2-4   84-85
Also see LOVE, Vikki, with Nuance

NUCLEAR ASSULT
LPs: 10/12–inch 33rpm
I.R.S. 5-8   88
IN-EFFECT 5-8   89
UNDER ONE FLAG (21 "Survive") ... 8-12   88
(Picture disc.)

NUGENT, Ted
(Ted Nugent and the Amboy Dukes; Ted Nugent and
Brian Howe)
Singles: 7–inch
ATLANTIC 2-5   84-88
DISCREET 3-5   74
EPIC 3-5   76-80
LPs: 10/12–inch 33rpm
ATLANTIC 5-10   82-88
DISCREET 8-10   74
EPIC (Except 607) 8-15   75-81
EPIC (607 "State of Shock") 15-25   79
(Picture disc.)
MAINSTREAM (10-01 "Ted Nugent
and the Amboy Dukes") 5-10   82
MAINSTREAM (421 "Ted Nugent
and the Amboy Dukes") 8-12

POLYDOR (4035 "Survival of
the Fittest") 10-20   71
  Also see AMBOY DUKES
  Also see BAD COMPANY

NUGGETS
Singles: 7–inch
MERCURY 2-4   79
LPs: 10/12–inch 33rpm
MERCURY 5-10   79

NUMAN, Gary
(Gary Numan and the Tubeway Army)
Singles: 7–inch
ATCO 3-5   79-81
LPs: 10/12–inch 33rpm
ATCO 5-10   79-81

NUMONICS
Singles: 7–inch
HODISK 3-5   84

NUNN, Bobby
(Bobby Nunn and the Robbins)
Singles: 78rpm
MODERN (807 "Rockin") 50-100   51
  Also see BYRD, Bobby
  Also see COASTERS
  Also see LITTLE ESTHER and Bobby Nunn
  Also see ROBINS

NURSERY SCHOOL
Singles: 12–inch 33/45rpm
EPIC 4-6   83

NUTMEGS
Singles: 78rpm
HERALD 20-30   55-57
Singles: 7–inch
COLLECTABLES 2-4
FLASHBACK 3-5   65
HERALD (452 "Story Untold") 20-35   55
HERALD (459 "Ship of Love") 15-25   55
HERALD (466 "Whispering
  Sorrows") 20-30   55
HERALD (475 "Key to the Kingdom") 25-35   56
HERALD (492 "A Love So True") 20-25   56
HERALD (538 "My Story") 25-35   59
HERALD (574 "Rip Van Winkle") 10-20   62
LANA 3-5
TEL (1014 "A Dream of Love") 50-75   60
TIMES SQUARE (6 "Let Me Tell You") 15-20   63
  (Colored vinyl:)
TIMES SQUARE (14 "The Way
  Love Should Be") 10-15   63
TIMES SQUARE (27 "Down
  in Mexico") 10-15   64
TIMES SQUARE (103 "You're Crying") 10-15   64
EPs: 7–inch 33/45rpm
HERALD (452 "The Nutmegs") ... 150-200   60
LPs: 10/12–inch 33rpm
COLLECTABLES 5-10   84
RELIC 8-10

Members: Leroy Griffin; Jimmy Tyson; Leroy McNeil; James
"Sonny" Griffin; Bill Emery; Ed Martin; Sonny Washburn; Harold
Jones.

NUTMEGS / Admirations
Singles: 7–inch
TIMES SQUARE (19 "Down
to Earth") 10-15   64

NUTMEGS / Volumes
Singles: 7–inch
TIMES SQUARE (22 "Why Must We
Go to School") 10-15   63
  Also see NUTMEGS
  Also see VOLUMES

NUTTY SQUIRRELS
Singles: 7–inch
COLUMBIA 5-10   60
HANOVER 5-10   59-60
RCA 4-8   64
Picture Sleeves
COLUMBIA 10-15   60
HANOVER 10-15   59
EPs: 7–inch 33/45rpm
HANOVER 15-25   60
LPs: 10/12–inch 33rpm
COLUMBIA 20-25   61
HANOVER (8014 "The Nutty
Squirrels") 25-35   60
MGM 15-25   64

NYLONS
Singles: 7–inch
OPEN AIR 3-5   82-87
LPs: 10/12–inch 33rpm
OPEN AIR 5-10   85-87
WINDHAM HILL 5-8   89
  Members: Claude Morrison; Marc Connors; Paul Cooper; Arnold
  Robinson.

NYRO, Laura
Singles: 7–inch
COLUMBIA 3-6   68-71
VERVE/FOLKWAYS 4-8   66-67
VERVE/FORECAST 4-6   68-69
Picture Sleeves
COLUMBIA 4-8   68
LPs: 10/12–inch 33rpm
COLUMBIA 5-15   68-84
VERVE/FOLKWAYS 10-20   67
VERVE/FORECAST 10-15   69
  Also see LABELLE, Patti

NYTRO
Singles: 12–inch 33/45rpm
WHITFIELD 4-8   79
Singles: 7–inch
WHITFIELD 3-5   76-79
LPs: 10/12–inch 33rpm
WHITFIELD 5-10   77-79

O

O., Jerry: see JERRY O

O ROMEO
Singles: 12–inch 33/45rpm
BOB CAT 4-6   83
OH MY 4-6   84
Members: Lorilee Svedberg; Dora Suppes; Terry Weinberg.

O.M.D.
Singles: 12–inch 33/45rpm
A&M 4-6   84
Singles: 7–inch
A&M 2-4   84

O.R.S.
LPs: 10/12–inch 33rpm
SALSOUL 5-10   79

OAK
Singles: 7–inch
MERCURY 3-5   79-80
Also see PINETTE, Rick, and Oak

OAK RIDGE BOYS
(Oak Ridge Quartet; Oaks)
Singles: 7–inch
ABC 2-5   78-79
ABC/DOT 3-5   77
CADENCE 8-12   59
COLUMBIA 3-5   73-76
HEARTWARMING 3-5   71
IMPACT 3-5   71
MCA 2-5   79-90
WARNER 4-8   63
LPs: 10/12–inch 33rpm
ABC 5-10   78-79
ABC/DOT 8-10   77
ACCORD 5-10   81-82
CADENCE (3019 "The Oak
  Ridge Quartet") 35-55   58
CANAAN 8-15   66
COLUMBIA 5-10   74-83
EXACT 5-10   83
51 WEST 5-8
HEARTWARMING 5-8   71-74
INTERMEDIA 5-8
MCA 5-10   80-86
NASHVILLE 8-10   70
OUT of TOWN DIST. 5-10   82
PHONORAMA 5-10
POWER PAK 5-10
PRIORITY 5-10   82
SKYLITE 10-20   64-66
STARDAY 10-20   65
U.A. 10-20   66
WARNER 10-20   63

Members: William Golden; Duane Allen; Rich Sterban; Joe Bonsall; Steve Sanders.
  Also see LEE, Brenda, and the Oak Ridge Boys
  Also see MANDRELL, Barbara, and the Oak Ridge Boys

OAKEY, Philip:
see MORODER, Giorgio, and Philip Oakey

OAS, Holly
Singles: 12–inch 33/45rpm
DND 4-6   84

O'BANION, John
Singles: 7–inch
ELEKTRA 3-5   81
LPs: 10/12–inch 33rpm
ELEKTRA 5-10   81

O'BRYAN
(O'Bryan Burnette)
Singles: 12–inch 33/45rpm
CAPITOL 4-6   82-86
Singles: 7–inch
CAPITOL 2-4   82-87
LPs: 10/12–inch 33rpm
CAPITOL 5-8   82-86

OCASEK, Ric
Singles: 12–inch 33/45rpm
GEFFEN 4-6   83
Singles: 7–inch
GEFFEN 2-4   83-86
LPs: 10/12–inch 33rpm
GEFFEN 5-8   83-86
Also see CARS

OCEAN
Singles: 7–inch
KAMA SUTRA 3-5   71-72
LPs: 10/12–inch 33rpm
KAMA SUTRA 8-12   71-72

OCEAN, Billy
Singles: 12–inch 33/45rpm
EPIC 4-8   80-82
JIVE 4-6   84-86
Singles: 7–inch
ARIOLA AMERICA 3-5   76
EPIC 3-5   77-82
JIVE 2-4   84-89
LPs: 10/12–inch 33rpm
EPIC 5-10   81-82
JIVE 5-8   84-89

OCHS, Phil
(Phil Ochs with the Pan African Ngembo Rumba Band)
Singles: 7–inch
A&M 5-10   67-73
SPARKLE (9966 "Bwatue") 3-5   91
(Canadian. 1,000 numbered copies made.)
Picture Sleeves
SPARKLE (9966 "Bwatue") 3-5   91
(Canadian. 1,000 numbered copies made.)

Singles: 7–inch

ARGO	4-8	59
MGM	5-10	53-56
SEVILLE	4-8	59-60

LPs: 10/12–inch 33rpm

GOLDEN CREST	15-25	56

ODDS & ENDS

Singles: 7–inch

RED BIRD	5-10	66
SOUTHBAY	4-6	
TODAY	4-6	71-72

O'DELL, Brooks

Singles: 7–inch

GOLD	4-8	63

O'DELL, Kenny

Singles: 7–inch

ABC	3-5	73
CAPRICORN	3-5	73-79
KAPP	3-5	72
MAR-KAY	5-10	65
VEGAS	4-8	67-68
WHITE WHALE	4-6	69

LPs: 10/12–inch 33rpm

CAPRICORN	5-10	74-78
VEGAS	15-25	68

ODETTA

(Odetta and Larry; Odetta Holmes)

Singles: 7–inch

DUNHILL	4-6	69
RCA	4-8	63
RIVERSIDE	4-8	62
VANGUARD	5-10	59
VERVE/FOLKWAYS	4-6	66
VERVE/FORECAST	4-6	68

EPs: 7–inch 33/45rpm

FANTASY (4017/4018 "Odetta and Larry")	15-20	54
(Price is for either of two volumes.)		

LPs: 10/12–inch 33rpm

EVEREST	5-10	73
FANTASY (15 "Odetta and Larry")	40-60	54
(10–inch LP.)		
FANTASY (3252 "Odetta"	35-50	58
(Colored vinyl.)		
POLYDOR	5-10	70
RCA	10-20	62-66
RIVERSIDE (400 series)	15-25	62
RIVERSIDE (3000 series)	10-15	68
RIVERSIDE (9400 series)	20-30	62
TRADITION (1010 "Odetta Sings Ballads and Blues")	25-35	57
TRADITION (1025 "At the Gate of Horn")	20-30	58
TRADITION (1052 "Best of Odetta")	10-15	67
(Monaural.)		
TRADITION (2052 "Best of Odetta")	10-20	67
(Stereo.)		

U.A.	5-10	76
VANGUARD	10-20	59-67
VERVE/FOLKWAYS	10-15	67

ODYSSEY

Singles: 12–inch 33/45rpm

RCA	4-8	77-82

Singles: 7–inch

MOWEST	3-5	72
RCA	3-5	77-82

LPs: 10/12–inch 33rpm

MOWEST	10-12	72
RCA	8-10	77-82

Members: Lillian Lopez; Louise Lopez.

OFARIM, Esther and Abraham

(Esther Ofarim; Esther and Abi Ofarim)

Singles: 7–inch

PHILIPS	4-6	64-68

LPs: 10/12–inch 33rpm

CAPITOL	5-10	68
PHILIPS	5-15	63-70

OFF BROADWAY USA

Singles: 7–inch

ATLANTIC	3-5	80

LPs: 10/12–inch 33rpm

ATLANTIC	5-10	80

OFFITT, Lillian

Singles: 78rpm

EXCELLO	5-10	57

Singles: 7–inch

CHIEF	8-12	60
EXCELLO	10-20	57

OH ROMEO: see O ROMEO

O'HEARN, Patrick

LPs: 10/12–inch 33rpm

PRIVATE	5-8	88

O'HENRY, Lenny

(Lenny O'Henry and the Short Stories)

Singles: 7–inch

ABC-PAR	10-15	61
ATCO	5-10	64-67
SMASH	5-10	63

OHIO EXPRESS

(Ohio Ltd.)

Singles: 7–inch

ATTACK	3-6	70
BUDDAH	4-6	68-73
CAMEO	5-8	67
ERIC	3-5	78
SUPER K	4-6	69-70

LPs: 10/12–inch 33rpm

BUDDAH	10-20	68-70
CAMEO (20,000 "Beg, Borrow and Steal")	20-30	68

Also see IVY LEAGUE

Also see KASENETZ - KATZ SINGING ORCHESTRAL CIRCUS

Also see REUNION

Also see 10CC

OHIO LTD: see OHIO [...]

OHIO PLAYERS

Singles [...]

AIR CITY		
ARISTA		
BOARDWALK		
CAPITOL		
COMPASS		
MERCURY		
TANGERINE		
TRACK		
WESTBOUND		

LPs: 10/12–inch 33rpm

ACCORD	5-10	81
ARISTA	5-10	79
BOARDWALK	5-10	81
CAPITOL (192 "Observations in Time")	10-20	69
CAPITOL (11291 "The Ohio Players")	8-12	74
MERCURY	8-12	74-78
TRIP	8-10	72
U.A.	8-10	75
WESTBOUND	8-12	72-75

Also see JUNIE

OINGO BOINGO

Singles: 12–inch 33/45rpm

A&M	4-8	81
MCA	4-6	85-86

Singles: 7–inch

A&M	3-5	81-83
MCA	2-4	85-86

LPs: 10/12–inch 33rpm

A&M	5-10	81-89
I.R.S.	5-10	80
MCA	5-8	85-90

Members: Danny Elfman; Steve Bartek; John Hernandez; Dale
Turner; Kerry Hatch; Richard Gibbs.

O'JAYS

Singles: 12–inch 33/45rpm

PHILADELPHIA INT'L	4-8	83

Singles: 7–inch

ALL PLATINUM	3-5	74
APOLLO	5-10	63
ASTROSCOPE	3-5	74
BELL	3-6	67-73
EPIC	2-4	83
IMPERIAL	4-8	63-66
LIBERTY	3-5	81
LITTLE STAR	5-10	63
MINIT	4-8	67
NEPTUNE	3-6	69-70
PHILADELPHIA INT'L	2-5	72-87
SARU	3-5	71
TSOP	3-5	80-81

LPs: 10/12–inch 33rpm

BELL (6014 "Back on Top")	10-20	68
BELL (6082 "The O'Jays")	8-12	73

O'JAYS / Moment[...]

LPs: 10/12–[...]

STANG	8-12	74

Also see MOMENTS
Also see O'JAYS

O'KAYSIONS

Singles: 7–inch

ABC	4-8	68
COTILLION	3-5	70
NORTH STATE (1001 "Girl Watcher")	20-30	68
ROULETTE	3-5	68

Picture Sleeves

NORTH STATE (1001 "Girl Watcher")	25-45	68

LPs: 10/12–inch 33rpm

ABC (664 "Girl Watcher")	15-25	68

Member: Donnie Weaver.

O'KEEFE, Danny

Singles: 7–inch

ATLANTIC	3-5	75
JERDEN	4-8	66
SIGNPOST	3-5	72
WARNER	3-5	77-78

Picture Sleeves

WARNER	3-5	77-78

LPs: 10/12–inch 33rpm

ATLANTIC	8-12	73-75
COTILLION	10-15	70
FIRST AMERICAN	8-10	
SIGNPOST	10-12	72
WARNER	5-10	77-79

OLA and the Janglers

Singles: 7–inch

GNP/CRESCENDO	4-8	68-69
LONDON	4-8	67

LPs: 10/12–inch 33rpm

GNP/CRESCENDO	15-20	69

Member: Ola Hakansson.

...IE & JERRY
Singles: 12-inch 33/45rpm
POLYDOR 4-6   84-85
Singles: 7-inch
POLYDOR 2-4   84-85
Members: Ollie Brown; Jerry Knight.
Also see KNIGHT, Jerry

OLLIE and the Nighingales
Singles: 7-inch
STAX 4-8   68
LPs: 10/12-inch 33rpm
STAX 10-15   69

OLSON, Rocky
Singles: 7-inch
CHESS 10-15   59

OLSSON, Nigel
Singles: 7-inch
BANG 3-5   78-79
COLUMBIA 3-5   78
ROCKET 3-5   75
UNI 3-5   71-72
LPs: 10/12-inch 33rpm
BANG 5-10   79-80
COLUMBIA 5-10   78
ROCKET 8-12   73-75
UNI 8-12   71
Also see JOHN, Elton

OLYMPIC RUNNERS
Singles: 7-inch
LONDON 3-5   74-77
POLYDOR 3-5   79
LPs: 10/12-inch 33rpm
LONDON 8-10   74-77
POLYDOR 5-10   79

OLYMPICS
Singles: 7-inch
ABC 3-5   73
ARVEE (Except 5031) 5-10   59-65
ARVEE (5031 "Stay Where You Are") 15-25   59-65
COLLECTABLES 2-4
DEMON 5-10   58-60
DUO DISC 4-8   64
ERIC 2-4
JUBILEE 4-8   69
LIBERTY 4-8   63
LOMA 4-8   65
MGM 3-5   73
MIRWOOD 4-8   66-67
PARKWAY 4-8   68
TITAN 10-20   61
TRI DISC 5-10   63
WARNER 3-5   70
EPs: 7-inch 33/45rpm
ARVEE (423 "Doin' the Hully Gully") 50-75   60
LPs: 10/12-inch 33rpm
ARVEE (423 "Doin' the Hully Gully") 75-150   60

...obert

Dea...
(Prom...
includes...
members o...d. Price also
LP covers, an...d, a letter about
...OUND (02 and 0... several miniature
...d Heads")... ...ertising posters.)
...or both dis...

Dea... 20-30   75
(Price is fo...scs, without inserts. Divide in
half for either one of the two records.)
Also see GRATEFUL DEAD
Also see OLD and in the Way

OLDFIELD, Mike
(Mike and Sally Oldfield)
Singles: 7-inch
EPIC 3-5   81-82
VIRGIN 3-5   73-82
LPs: 10/12-inch 33rpm
EPIC 5-10   81-82
VIRGIN (Except 2001) 5-15   73-88
VIRGIN (2001 "Tubular Bells") . 10-12   73
(Picture disc.)

OLIVER
(Bill Oliver Swofford)
Singles: 7-inch
CREWE 3-5   69-70
JUBILEE 4-6   69
LIBERTY 3-5
PARAMOUNT 3-5   73
PEOPLE SONG 3-5   82
U.A. 3-5   70-71
Picture Sleeves
CREWE 4-6   69
LPs: 10/12-inch 33rpm
CREWE 10-15   69-70
U.A. 8-12   71
Also see BILLY & SUE

OLIVER, David
Singles: 7-inch
MERCURY 3-5   78-80
LPs: 10/12-inch 33rpm
MERCURY 5-10   78-79

OLIVOR, Jane
Singles: 7-inch
COLUMBIA. 2-5   77-85
LPs: 10/12-inch 33rpm
...OLUMBIA 5-10   77-85

ARVEE (424 "Dance By the Light
  of the Moon") 75-125   61
ARVEE (429 "Party Time") 75-125   61
EVEREST 5-10   81
MIRWOOD (M-7003 "Something Old
  Something New") 20-30   66
  (Monaural.)
MIRWOOD (MS-7003 "Something Old
  Something New") 25-35   66
  (Stereo.)
POST 8-10
RHINO 5-8
TRI-DISC (1001 "Do the Bounce") ... 30-50   63
  Members: Walter Ward; Eddie Lewis; Melvin King; Charles
  Figer; Julius McMichaels.
  Also see PARAGONS
  Also see REYNOLDS, Jody / Olympics

100 PROOF Aged in Soul
Singles: 7-inch
HOT WAX 3-6   69-72
LPs: 10/12-inch 33rpm
HOT WAX 10-15   70-73

101 NORTH
Singles: 7-inch
CAPITOL 2-4   88
LPs: 10/12-inch 33rpm
CAPITOL 5-8   88

101 STRINGS
Singles: 7-Inch
SOMERSET 3-5   59
LPs: 10/12-Inch 33rpm
SOMERSET 5-10   59-61
STEREO FIDELITY 5-10   59-61

ONE on ONE
Singles: 7-inch
KEE WEE 2-4   84

1 PLUS 1
Singles: 7-inch
M.O.C. 4-8   66

ONE WAY
(Featuring Al Hudson)
Singles: 12-inch 33/45rpm
MCA 4-6   82-86
Singles: 7-inch
MCA 3-5   79-87
LPs: 10/12-inch 33rpm
MCA 5-10   79-86
  Also see HUDSON, Al

O'NEAL, Alexander
Singles: 12-inch 33/45rpm
TABU 4-6   85-86
Singles: 7-inch
TABU 2-4   85-90
Picture Sleeves
TABU 2-4   85
LPs: 10/12-inch 33rpm
TABU 5-8   85-90

Also see CHERRELLE

ONO, Yoko
(Yoko Ono and the Plastic Ono Band)
Singles: 12-inch 33/45rpm
POLYDOR 5-10   85-86
Singles: 7-Inch
APPLE 4-8   71-73
GEFFEN 3-5   81
POLYDOR 3-5   82-86
Promotional Singles
APPLE (OYB-1 "Open Your Box") . 400-600   70
APPLE (1853 "Now Or Never") 25-30   72
APPLE (1867 "Woman Power") 20-25   73
GEFFEN 5-8   81
POLYDOR 4-6   82-86
Picture Sleeves
APPLE (1853 "Now Or Never") 8-12   72
GEFFEN 2-4   81
LPs: 10/12-inch 33rpm
APPLE 15-20   71-73
GEFFEN 5-10   81
POLYDOR 5-10   82-86
Promotional LPs
GEFFEN (934 "Walking on Thin Ice") 20-25   81
GEFFEN (975 "No No No") 25-30   81
  Also see LENNON, John

OPUS SEVEN
Singles: 7-inch
SOURCE 3-5   79
LPs: 10/12-inch 33rpm
SOURCE 5-10   79

OPUS 10
Singles: 7-inch
PANDISC 2-4   85

ORBISON, Roy
(Roy Orbison and the Teen Kings; Roy Orbison and the Candymen; Roy Orbison and the Roses; Roy Orbison and Friends)
Singles: 78rpm
SUN 30-50   56-57
Singles: 7-inch
ASYLUM 3-5   78-79
COLLECTABLES 2-4   85
MGM 4-8   65-73
MGM CELEBRITY SCENE (CSN9-5 "Roy
  Orbison") 50-75   66
  (Boxed set of five singles with bio insert and title
  strips.)
MERCURY 4-8   74
MONUMENT (409 "Paper Boy") 20-30   59
MONUMENT (412 "Uptown") 15-20   59
MONUMENT (421 through 467) 8-12   60-62
MONUMENT (800 and 900 series) ... 5-10   63-66
MONUMENT (500 series) 4-8   63
MONUMENT (8600 series) 3-5   76
MONUMENT (8900 series) 3-5   72
MONUMENT (45000 series) 3-5   76-77
RCA (7381 "Sweet and Innocent") ... 20-30   58

RCA (7447 "Jolie") 20-30   59
SSS/SUN 3-5
SUN (242 "Ooby Dooby") 20-30   56
SUN (251 "Rockhouse") 20-30   56
SUN (265 "Sweet and Easy
  to Love") 20-30   56
SUN (284 "Chicken Hearted") 20-30   58
SUN (353 "Sweet and Easy to Love") . 8-10   61
  (Yellow label.)
SUN (353 "Sweet and Easy to Love") 10-15   61
  (White label. Promotional issue only.)
Picture Sleeves
MGM 8-12   65-67
MONUMENT (400 series) 10-20   60-62
MONUMENT (800 series) 10-15   63-64
EPs: 7–inch 33/45rpm
MONUMENT (2 "Crying") 20-30   62
  (Compact 33, "Special Promotional Six-Pac.")
STARS INC. (101 "Roy Orbison and
  the Teen Kings") 300-400   59
  (Promotional issue, distributed to fan club
  members.)
LPs: 10/12–inch 33rpm
ACCORD 5-8   81
ASYLUM 5-8   78-79
BUCKBOARD 8-10
CANDLELITE MUSIC 10-15
DESIGN 10-15
HALLMARK 10-12
MGM (E-4308 through E-4514) 15-20   65-67
  (Monaural.)
MGM (SE-4308 through SE-4514) . . . 20-30   65-67
  (Stereo.)
MGM (4636 through 4934) 10-20   69-73
MERCURY 8-12   75
MONUMENT (4002 "Lonely and
  Blue") 100-150   61
  (Monaural.)
MONUMENT (14002 "Lonely and
  Blue") 125-200   61
  (Stereo.)
MONUMENT (4007 "Crying" 30-35   62
  (Monaural.)
MONUMENT (14007 "Crying") 45-50   62
  (Stereo.)
MONUMENT (4009 "Greatest Hits") . 25-30   62
  (Monaural.)
MONUMENT (14009 "Greatest Hits") 35-40   62
  (Stereo.)
MONUMENT (6600 series) 8-10
MONUMENT (7600 "Regeneration") . . 8-10   76
MONUMENT (8000 "Greatest Hits") . 20-25   63
  (Monaural.)
MONUMENT (18000 "Greatest Hits") 30-35   63
  (Stereo. Apparently the number of this LP was
  changed when Monument switched from the
  4000/14000 series to the 8000/18000 series.)
MONUMENT (8003 "In Dreams") 20-25   63
  (Monaural.)

MONUMENT (18003 "In Dreams") . . 30-35   63
  (Stereo.)
MONUMENT (8024 "More Greatest
  Hits") 20-25   64
  (Monaural.)
MONUMENT (18024 "More Greatest
  Hits") 25-30   64
  (Stereo.)
MONUMENT (8035 "Orbisongs") . . . 15-20   65
  (Monaural.)
MONUMENT (18035 "Orbisongs") . . 20-25   65
  (Stereo.)
Note: For the sake of continuity, the preceding
  14000 and 18000 series stereo issues, requiring
  separate pricing, are listed directly below their
  4000 and 8000 series mono counterpart.
MONUMENT (8023 "Early Orbison") . 20-25   64
MONUMENT (18023 "Early Orbison") 20-30   64
MONUMENT (8045 "Very Best") 15-20   66
  (Blue cover.)
MONUMENT (18045 "Very Best") . . . 15-25   66
  (Blue cover.)
MONUMENT (8045 "Very Best") 12-15   66
  (Purple cover.)
MONUMENT (18045 "Very Best") . . . 12-18   66
  (Purple cover.)
MONUMENT (38384 "All-Time
  Greatest Hits") 8-10   82
RHINO 5-8   88
SPECTRUM 15-20
SSS/SUN 5-10   69
SUN (1260 "Rock House") 200-225   61
SUNNYVALE 8-10   77
TRIP 8-10   74
VIRGIN 6-12   88-89
    Also see CANDYMEN
    Also see DRIFTERS / Lesley Gore / Roy Orbison / Los Bravos
    Also see GOLDSBORO, Bobby
    Also see JAN & DEAN / Roy Orbison / 4 Seasons / Shirelles
    Also see LEWIS, Jerry Lee / Roger Miller / Roy Orbison
    Also see PERKINS, Carl, Jerry Lee Lewis, Roy Orbison &
      Johnny Cash
    Also see TEEN KINGS
    Also see TRAVELING WILBURYS

ORBISON, Roy / Bobby Bare / Joey Powers
LPs: 10/12–inch 33rpm
CAMDEN 15-25   64
    Also see BARE, Bobby
    Also see POWERS, Joey

ORBISON, Roy, and Emmylou Harris / Craig Hundley
Singles: 7–inch
WARNER 3-5   80
    Also see HARRIS, Emmylou

ORBISON, Roy, and K.D. Lang
Singles: 7–inch
VIRGIN 2-4   87
    Also see LANG, K.D.
    Also see ORBISON, Roy

ORBIT
Singles: 12–inch 33/45rpm
QUALITY/RFC 4-6   82-84
Singles: 7–inch
QUALITY/RFC 2-4   82-84
Member: Carol Hall.

ORCHESTRAL MANOEUVERS in the Dark
(OMD)
Singles: 12–inch 33/45rpm
A&M 4-6   85-86
Singles: 7–inch
A&M 2-4   84-86
EPIC 3-5   82-83
LPs: 10/12–inch 33rpm
A&M 5-8   84-88
EPIC 5-10   82-83

ORIGINAL ANIMALS: see ANIMALS

ORIGINAL CADILLACS
Singles: 78rpm
JOSIE 10-15   57
Singles: 7–inch
JOSIE 10-15   57-58
Members: Earl Carroll; Earl Wade; Charles Brooks; Bobby
Phillips; Junior Glanton; Roland Martinez.
Also see CADILLACS

ORIGINAL CAST
(Featuring Kacey Cisyk)
Singles: 7–inch
ARISTA 3-5   77

ORIGINAL CASTE
(Featuring Dixie Lee Innes)
Singles: 7–inch
DOT 4-8   68
T-A 4-8   69-70
LPs: 10/12–inch 33rpm
T-A 10-20   70

ORIGINAL CASUALS
(Featuring Gary Mears)
Singles: 7–inch
BACK BEAT 8-12   58
EPs: 7–inch 33/45rpm
BACK BEAT (40 "Three Kisses
Past Midnight") 50-70   58

ORIGINALS
Singles: 7–inch
MOTOWN 3-5   75
PHASE II 2-5   81
SOUL (35029 through 35061) 4-8   67-69
SOUL (35066 through 35119) 4-6   69-76
LPs: 10/12–inch 33rpm
FANTASY 5-10   78-79
MOTOWN 5-10   74-80
SOUL 8-15   69-76
Members: Ty Hunter; Henry Dixon; Joe Stubbs; Walt Gaines;
C.P. Spencer; Freddie Gorman.
Also see HUNTER, Ty
Also see VOICE MASTERS

ORIGINALS and Jermaine Jackson
Singles: 12–inch 33/45rpm
MOTOWN 4-8   76
Also see JACKSON, Jermaine
Also see ORIGINALS

ORIOLES
(Sonny Til and the Orioles)
Singles: 78rpm
IT'S a NATURAL (5000 "It's Too
Soon to Know") 50-100   48
JUBILEE (5000 "It's too Soon
to Know") 25-50   48
JUBILEE (5001 "Dare to Dream") . . . 25-50   48
JUBILEE (5001 "Lonely Christmas") . 25-50   48
JUBILEE (5002 "Please Give My
Heart a Break") 25-50   49
JUBILEE (5005 "Tell Me So") 25-50   49
JUBILEE (5008 "I Challenge
Your Kiss") 25-50   49
JUBILEE (5009 "A Kiss and a
Rose") 25-50   49
JUBILEE (5016 "So Much") 25-50   49
JUBILEE (5017 "What Are You
Doing New Year's Eve") 25-50   49
JUBILEE (5018 "Would You Still
Be the One in My Heart") 25-50   50
JUBILEE (5025 "At Night") 25-50   50
JUBILEE (5026 "Moonlight") 25-50   50
JUBILEE (5028 "You're Gone") 25-50   50
JUBILEE (5031 "I'd Rather Have You
Under the Moon") 25-50   50
JUBILEE (5037 "I Need You So") . . . 40-60   50
JUBILEE (5040 "I Cross My Fingers") 20-35   50
JUBILEE (5045 "Oh Holy Night") 25-50   50
JUBILEE (5057 "Would I Love You") . 20-35   51
JUBILEE (5061 "I'm Just a Fool
in Love") 20-35   51
Note: At least ten of the above 78rpm singles were
reissued around 1951 on 45s. It's likely that others in
the 5001-5061 series appeared on early '50s Jubilee
45s, but those listed below are the only ones we can
verify.
JUBILEE (5061 through 5231) 10-25   51-56
VEE JAY 10-15   56-57
Singles: 7–inch
ABNER (1016 "Sugar Girl") 25-50   58
CHARLIE PARKER 5-10   62-63
COLLECTABLES 2-4
JUBILEE (5000 "It's Too Soon
to Know") 500-750   51
JUBILEE (5005 "Tell Me So") 500-750   51
JUBILEE (5016 "So Much") 400-600   51
JUBILEE (5017 "What Are You
Doing New Year's Eve") 400-600   51
JUBILEE (5025 "At Night") 400-600   51
JUBILEE (5040 "I Cross My
Fingers") 300-500   51
JUBILEE (5045 "Oh Holy Night") . . 250-350   51

JUBILEE (5051 "I Miss You So") .. 300-500   51
(Black vinyl.)

JUBILEE (5051 "I Miss You So") .. 500-750   51
(Colored vinyl.)

JUBILEE (5055 "Pal of Mine") 300-500   51

JUBILEE (5061 "I'm Just a Fool
in Love") 300-500   51

JUBILEE (5065 "Baby, Please
Don't Go") 250-350   51
(Black vinyl.)

JUBILEE (5065 "Baby, Please
Don't Go") 500-750   51
(Colored vinyl.)

JUBILEE (5071 "When You're
Not Around") 250-350   51

JUBILEE (5074 "Trust in Me") 250-350   52

JUBILEE (5082 "It's Over Because
We're Through") 250-350   52

JUBILEE (5084 "Barfly") 200-300   52

JUBILEE (5092 "Don't Cry Baby") . 200-300   52
(Black vinyl.)

JUBILEE (5092 "Don't Cry Baby") . 400-600   52
(Colored vinyl.)

JUBILEE (5102 "You Belong to Me")250-350   52

JUBILEE (5107 "I Miss You So") .. 150-250   53
(Reissued in 1963, using the same catalog
number, but credited to Sonny Til and the Orioles.
Black vinyl.)

JUBILEE (5107 "I Miss You So") .. 400-600   53
(Colored vinyl.)

JUBILEE (5108 "Teardrops on
My Pillow") 150-250   53
(Black vinyl.)

JUBILEE (5108 "Teardrops on
My Pillow") 400-600   53
(Colored vinyl.)

JUBILEE (5115 "Bad Little Girl") .. 100-150   53

JUBILEE (5120 "I Cover the
Waterfront") 100-150   53
(Black vinyl.)

JUBILEE (5120 "I Cover the
Waterfront") 300-500   53
(Colored vinyl.)

JUBILEE (5122 "Crying in
the Chapel") 30-50   53

JUBILEE (5127 "In the Mission of
St. Augustine") 30-50   53

JUBILEE (5134 "There's No
One But You") 30-50   54

JUBILEE (5137 "Secret Love") 30-50   54

JUBILEE (5143 "Maybe You'll
Be There") 50-75   54

JUBILEE (5154 "In the Chapel in
the Moonlight") 30-50   54

JUBILEE (5161 "If You Believe") 30-50   54

JUBILEE (5172 "Runaround") 30-50   54

JUBILEE (5177 "I Love You Mostly") . 25-40   55

JUBILEE (5189 "I Need You Baby") .. 25-40   55

JUBILEE (5221 "Please Sing My
Blues Tonight") 25-35   55

JUBILEE (5231 "Angel") 30-50   56

JUBILEE (5363 "Tell Me So") 5-10   59

JUBILEE (5384 "First of Summer") ... 5-10   60
Note: There may be other Jubilee colored vinyl
issues, but those noted here are ones we've verified.
Also, some Jubilee tracks, such as *Crying in the
Chapel*, were reissued as by Sonny Til and the
Orioles. Those are found in the "Til" section.

VEE JAY (196 "Happy Till the Letter") 15-25   56

VEE JAY (228 "For All We Know") ... 15-25   56

VEE JAY (244 "Sugar Girl") 25-35   57

Picture Sleeves

JUBILEE (5017 "What Are You Doing
New Year's Eve") 150-250   54
(Sleeve for 78 rpm.)

JUBILEE (5017 "What Are You Doing
New Year's Eve") 300-400   54
(Sleeve for 45 rpm.)

JUBILEE (5045 "Oh Holy Night") .. 300-400   54
(Both Jubilee sleeves were issued in late 1954 and
sold with 1954 pressings, actually second
pressings of both. These were blue script Jubilee
labels with the line under the logo.)

LANA 3-5   63

EPs: 7–inch 33/45rpm

JUBILEE (5000 "The Orioles
Sing") 750-1000   53

LPs: 10/12–inch 33rpm

BIG A RECORDS (2001 "Greatest
All Time Hits") 20-30   69

CHARLIE PARKER (816 "Modern
Sounds") 50-75   62

COLLECTABLES 5-10   84

MURRAY HILL 30-40
(Five-LP set.)

ROULETTE 5-10
Members: Sonny Til; Alex Sharp; George Nelson; John Reed;
Tom Gaither; Charles Harris; Greg Carroll; Billy Adams; Jerry
Holman; Al Russell; Jerry Rodriguez; Bill Taylor.
Also see CADILLACS / Orioles
Also see TIL, Sonny

ORION, P.J., and the Magnates
LPs: 10/12–inch 33rpm
MAGNATE (122459 "P.J. Orion and
the Magnates") 75-125

ORION the HUNTER
Singles: 7–inch
PORTRAIT 2-4   84-85
LPs: 10/12–inch 33rpm
PORTRAIT 5-8   84
Member: Barry Goudreau.
Also see BOSTON

ORLANDO, Tony
Singles: 12–inch 33/45rpm
CASABLANCA 5-10   79
Singles: 7–inch
ATCO 4-8   65

CAMEO 4-8   67
CASABLANCA 3-5   79-80
EPIC (9000 series) 5-10   61-64
Promotional Singles
EPIC (55299 "Happy Times Are
Here to Stay") 8-12   61
LPs: 10/12–inch 33rpm
EPIC (611 "Bless You") 35-40   61
(Stereo.)
EPIC (3808 "Bless You") 35-40   61
(Monaural.)
EPIC (33785 "Before Dawn") 10-12   75
CASABLANCA 5-10   79-80
Picture Sleeves
EPIC 5-10   61-62
Also see WIND

ORLANDO, Tony, and Dawn
Singles: 7–inch
ARISTA 3-5   75
BELL 3-5   71-74
ELEKTRA 3-5   75-78
LPs: 10/12–inch 33rpm
ARISTA 8-10   75-76
ASYLUM 8-10   75
BELL (6000 series) 10-12   70-71
BELL (1000 series) 8-10   73-75
ELEKTRA 8-10   75-78
KORY 8-10   74-77
Also see DAWN
Also see ORLANDO, Tony

ORLEANS
Singles: 7–inch
ABC 3-5   73
ASYLUM 3-5   75-77
INFINITY 3-5   79
LPs: 10/12–inch 33rpm
ABC 10-12   73-78
ASYLUM 8-10   75-76
INFINITY 5-10   79
RADIO 5-8   82
Member: John Hall.
Also see HALL, John

ORLONS
Singles: 7–inch
ABC 4-8   67
CALLA 4-8   66
CAMEO (198 "I'll Be True") 30-40   61
CAMEO (211 "Mr. 21") 30-40   62
CAMEO (218 through 384) 5-10   62-65
Picture Sleeves
CAMEO 5-10   62-64
LPs: 10/12–inch 33rpm
CAMEO (1020 "Wah Watusi") 30-60   62
CAMEO (1033 "All the Hits") 25-50   62
CAMEO (1041 "South Street") 25-50   63
CAMEO (1054 "Not Me") 25-50   63
CAMEO (1061 "Biggest Hits") 25-50   63
CAMEO (1073 "Memory Lane") 25-50   63

Members: Shirley Brickley; Rosetta Hightower; Steve Caldwell; Marlena Davis.

ORLONS / Dovells
LPs: 10/12–inch 33rpm
CAMEO (1067 "Golden Hits") 25-50   63
Also see DOVELLS
Also see ORLONS

ORPHEUS
Singles: 7–inch
MGM 4-6   68-69
LPs: 10/12–inch 33rpm
BELL 10-12   71
MGM 10-15   68-69

ORRALL, Robert Ellis
(Robert Ellis Orrall and Carlene Carter)
Singles: 7–inch
RCA 3-5   81-83
LPs: 10/12–inch 33rpm
RCA 5-10   81-83
Also see CARTER, Carlene

OSAMU
LPs: 10/12–inch 33rpm
A&M 5-8   88
ISLAND 8-10   77

OSBORNE, Jeffrey
Singles: 12–inch 33/45rpm
A&M 4-6   82-86
Singles: 7–inch
A&M 2-5   82-88
ARISTA 2-4   90
LPs: 10/12–inch 33rpm
A&M 5-10   82-88
ARISTA 5-8   90
Also see KENNEDY, Joyce, and Jeffrey Osborne
Also see L.T.D.
Also see WARWICK, Dionne, and Jeffrey Osborne

OSBORNE & GILES
LPs: 10/12–inch 33rpm
RED LABEL 5-8   85
Members: Billy Osborne; A.Z. Giles.

OSBORNE BROTHERS
(Osborne Brothers and Red Allen)
Singles: 7–inch
CMH 2-4   80
DECCA 3-6   63-72
MCA 3-5   73-75
MGM (100 series) 3-5   64
MGM (12000 and 13000 series) 4-8   59-63
EPs: 7–inch 33/45rpm
MGM 10-15   59
LPs: 10/12–inch 33rpm
CMH 5-10   76-82
CORAL 5-10   73
DECCA 10-20   65-72
MCA 5-10   73-75
MGM (100 series) 5-10   70
MGM (3700 series) 25-35   59

MGM (4000 series) 15-25   62-63
ROUNDER 5-8
SUGAR HILL 5-8   84
Members: Bobby Osborne; Sonny Osborne.

OSBOURNE, Ozzy
Singles: 7–inch
CBS ASSOCIATED 2-4   83-86
JET 3-5   82
LPs: 10/12–inch 33rpm
CBS ASSOCIATED 5-8   83-90
JET 5-10   81-82
PRIORITY 5-8   90
Also see BLACK SABBATH
Also see FORD, Lita, and Ozzy Osbourne

OSBOURNE, Ozzy, and Randy Rhoads
LPs: 10/12–inch 33rpm
CBS ASSOC 5-8   87

OSIBISA
Singles: 7–inch
DECCA 3-5   72
ISLAND 3-5   76-77
MCA 2-4
WARNER 3-5   73-74
LPs: 10/12–inch 33rpm
BUDDAH 8-10   73
DECCA 10-12   71-72
ISLAND 8-10   77
MCA 5-8
WARNER 8-10   73-74

OSIRIS
Singles: 7–inch
INFINITY 3-5   79
WARNER 3-5   79
LPs: 10/12–inch 33rpm
INFINITY 5-10   79
WARNER 5-10   79

OSKAR, Lee
Singles: 7–inch
ELEKTRA 3-5   78-81
U.A. 3-5   76
LPs: 10/12–inch 33rpm
ELEKTRA 5-10   78-79
U.A. 8-10   76
Also see WAR

OSMOND, Donny
Singles: 7–inch
MGM 3-5   71-75
POLYDOR 3-5   76-78
Picture Sleeves
MGM 3-5   71-75
LPs: 10/12–inch 33rpm
CAPITOL 5-8   89-90
MGM 8-10   71-74
POLYDOR 5-10   76-77
Also see OSMONDS

OSMOND, Donny and Marie
Singles: 7–inch
MGM 3-5   74-75
POLYDOR 3-5   76-78
LPs: 10/12–inch 33rpm
MGM 8-10   74-75
POLYDOR 5-10   76-78
Also see OSMOND, Donny
Also see OSMOND, Marie

OSMOND, Jimmy
(Little Jimmy Osmond)
Singles: 7–inch
MGM 3-5   70-75
MERCURY 3-5   78
LPs: 10/12–inch 33rpm
MGM 8-10   72
Also see OSMONDS

OSMOND, Marie
Singles: 7–inch
CAPITOL 2-5   85-88
ELEKTRA 3-5   82-84
MGM 3-5   73-75
POLYDOR 3-5   76-78
RCA 3-5   84
Picture Sleeves
MGM 3-5   73-75
POLYDOR 3-5   77
RCA 3-5   84
LPs: 10/12–inch 33rpm
CAPITOL 5-8   85-88
MGM 8-12   73-75
POLYDOR 5-8   77
Also see OSMOND, Donny and Marie
Also see OSMONDS
Also see SEALS, Dan, and Marie Osmond

OSMOND, Marie, and Paul Davis
Singles: 7–inch
CAPITOL 2-4   86-88
Also see DAVIS, Paul
Also see OSMOND, Marie

OSMONDS
(Osmond Brothers)
Singles: 7–inch
BARNABY 4-6   68-69
EMI AMERICA 2-4   85-86
ELEKTRA 3-5   82-83
MGM (13126 through 14159) 4-6   63-70
MGM (14193 through 14831) 3-5   70-75
MERCURY 3-5   79
POLYDOR 3-5   76-77
UNI (55015 "I Can't Stop") 4-8   67
UNI (55276 "I Can't Stop") 3-5   71
WARNER/CURB 3-5   83-85
Picture Sleeves
MGM 3-5   73-74
LPs: 10/12–inch 33rpm
EMI AMERICA 5-8   86
ELEKTRA 5-10   82

MGM (7 "Preview: the Osmond
  Brothers") 15-20
  (Promotional issue only.)
MGM (4100 and 4200 series) 15-25   63-65
MGM (4724 through 5012) 8-12   70-75
MERCURY 5-10   79
METRO 10-20   65
POLYDOR 5-10   76-77
WARNER/CURB 5-8   83-85
  Members: Donny Osmond; Alan Osmond; Merrill Osmond;
  Wayne Osmond; Jimmy Osmond; Marie Osmond.
  Also see CURB, Mike
  Also see OSMOND, Donny
  Also see OSMOND, Jimmy
  Also see OSMOND, Marie

OSMONDS, Steve Lawrence and Eydie Gorme
Singles: 7–inch
MGM 3-5   72
  Also see LAWRENCE, Steve, and Eydie Gorme
  Also see OSMONDS

O'SULLIVAN, Gilbert
Singles: 7–inch
EPIC 3-5   77-81
MAM 3-5   71-76
Picture Sleeves
MAM 3-5   72
LPs: 10/12–inch 33rpm
EPIC 5-10   81
MAM 10-15   72-73

OTIS, Johnny
(Johnny Otis Show; Johnny Otis and the Peacocks;
Johnny Otis Quintette)
Singles: 78rpm
CAPITOL 10-20   57
DIG 10-20   55-57
EXCELSIOR 15-25   45-47
MERCURY 10-20   51-53
PEACOCK (Except 1625) 10-20   52
PEACOCK (1625 "Young Girl") 15-25   52
REGENT 10-20   50-51
SAVOY 10-20   50-54
Singles: 7–inch
CAPITOL (3799-3802 "The Johnny
  Otis Show") 350-400   57
  (Four discs with special four-pocket cover.)
CAPITOL (3799 through 3802) 10-20   57
  (Individual records without cover.)
CAPITOL (3852 through 4326,
  except 4168) 8-12   58-60
CAPITOL (4168 "Castin' My Spell") .. 10-15   59
  (Monaural.)
CAPITOL (S-4168 "Castin' My Spell") 20-30   59
  (Stereo.)
DIG 15-25   55-59
ELDO (105 "The New Bo Diddley") ... 5-10   60
ELDO (153 "Long Distance") 4-8   67
EPIC 3-5   70
HAWK SOUND 3-5   75

KENT 3-5   69
KING 5-8   61-63
MERCURY (8263 "Oopy Doo") ... 30-50   51
MERCURY (8273 "Goomp Blues") .. 30-50   51
MERCURY (8289 "Call Operator 210") 30-50   52
MERCURY (8295 "Gypsy Blues") ... 30-50   52
MERCURY (70038 "Why Don't You
  Believe Me") 30-50   52
MERCURY (70050 "The Love Bug
  Boogie") 30-50   52
OKEH 4-6   69
PEACOCK (1625 "Young Girl") 40-60   52
PEACOCK (1636 "Shake It") 25-45   52
PEACOCK (1648 "Sittin' Here
  Drinkin") 25-45   52
PEACOCK (1675 "Butterball") 25-45   52
SAVOY 15-25   50-54
EPs: 7–inch 33/45rpm
CAPITOL (940 "Johnny Otis Show") 50-100   58
CAPITOL (1134 "Johnny Otis") 50-75   59
LPs: 10/12–inch 33rpm
ALLIGATOR 5-10   82
BLUES SPECTRUM 10-15
CAPITOL (940 "Johnny Otis Show") 100-200   58
DIG (104 "Rock and Roll
  Hit Parade") 300-500   57
  (Gold cover.)
Counterfeits of Dig 104 exist, some of which have
a yellow cover and are easy to spot. Some others,
however, have the gold cover. Regardless, the
discs of originals are noticeably thicker than is
used on the fakes.
EPIC 10-15   70-71
JAZZ WORLD 5-10   78
KENT 10-20   70
SAVOY 5-10   78-80
Referenced below are some of the artists who
performed with the Johnny Otis Show, or with
whom he or his orchestra appears.
  Also see ADAMS, Marie
  Also see FREEMAN, Ernie
  Also see JACQUET, Illinois
  Also see McNEELY, Big Jay
  Also see WATSON, Johnny

OTIS, Johnny, and Preston Love
Singles: 7–inch
KENT 3-5   70
  Also see OTIS, Shuggie, and Preston Love

OTIS, Johnny, Orchestra, with Little Esther and Mel Walker
Singles: 78rpm
REGENT (1036 "I Dream") 15-25   51
SAVOY 15-25   50-51
Singles: 7–inch
REGENT (1036 "I Dream") 50-75   51
SAVOY (750 "Cupid's Boogie") 50-75   50
SAVOY (775 "Love Will
  Break Your Heart") 50-75   51
  Also see LITTLE ESTHER and Mel Walker

OTIS, Johnny, Quintette, with Little Esther and the Robins
Singles: 78rpm
SAVOY 25-50   50
Singles: 7–inch
SAVOY (731 "Double Crossing
  Blues") 75-100   50
  Also see LITTLE ESTHER
  Also see OTIS, Johnny
  Also see ROBINS

OTIS, Shuggie
Singles: 7–inch
EPIC 3-5   70-75
LPs: 10/12–inch 33rpm
EPIC 10-15   70-75
  Also see KOOPER, Al, and Shuggie Otis

OTIS, Shuggie, and Preston Love
Singles: 7–inch
KENT 3-5   70
  Also see OTIS, Johnny, and Preston Love
  Also see OTIS, Shuggie

OTIS & CARLA
Singles: 7–inch
ATCO 4-6   69
STAX 4-8   67-68
LPs: 10/12–inch 33rpm
STAX 10-20   67
  Members: Otis Redding; Carla Thomas.
  Also see REDDING, Otis
  Also see THOMAS, Carla

OUTLAWS
Singles: 7–inch
ARISTA 3-5   75-83
LPs: 10/12–inch 33rpm
ARISTA 5-10   75-83
PASHA 5-8   86
PEAR 8-12   84
  Members: Hughie Thomason; Henry Paul; Billy Jones; Freddy
  Salem; Rick Cua; David Dix; Harvey Dalton Arnold; Frank
  O'Keefe; Monte Yoho.
  Also see PAUL, Henry, Band

OUTLAWS
Singles: 7–inch
PASHA 2-4   86
LPs: 10/12–inch 33rpm
PASHA 5-8   86

OUTPUT
Singles: 12–inch 33/45rpm
CBS ASSOCIATED 4-6   83
Singles: 7–inch
CBS ASSOCIATED 3-5   83
TUFF CITY 2-4   84

OUTSIDERS
Singles: 7–inch
BELL 4-6   70
CAPITOL 4-8   66-68
KAPP 4-6   70

Picture Sleeves
CAPITOL 5-10   66-67
LPs: 10/12–inch 33rpm
CAPITOL 15-25   66-67
  Members: Sonny Geraci; Bill Bruno; Tom King; Rickey Baker;
  Merdin Madsen.
  Also see CLIMAX

OVATIONS
Singles: 7–inch
ANDIE (5017 "My Lullabye") 15-25   60
BARRY (101 "The Day We Fell
  in Love") 20-25   61
EPIC (9470 "Oh What a Day") 25-30   61

OVERKILL
Singles: 7–inch
SST 2-4   86
LPs: 10/12–inch 33rpm
SST 5-8   86

OVERKILL
LPs: 10/12–inch 33rpm
ATLANTIC 5-8   86

OVERLANDERS
Singles: 7–inch
HICKORY 10-15   64-66
MERCURY 5-10   63

OVERTON, C.B.
Singles: 7–inch
SHOCK 3-5   78

OVERTONES
LPs: 10/12–inch 33rpm
TWIN/TONE 5-8   88

OWEN, B.
Singles: 7–inch
JANUS 3-5   70

OWEN, Reg, and His Orchestra
Singles: 7–inch
PALETTE 4-6   58-62
LPs: 10/12–inch 33rpm
PALETTE 15-25   59-60

OWENS, Buck
(Buck Owens and the Buckaroos)
Singles: 78rpm
CAPITOL 10-20   57
Singles: 7–inch
CAPITOL (2000 through 4000 series) .. 3-5   67-75
  (Orange label.)
CAPITOL (3824 "Come Back") 10-15   57
  (Purple label.)
CAPITOL (3957 "Sweet Thing") 10-15   58
  (Purple label.)
CAPITOL (4000 series) 5-10   59-63
  (Purple or orange/yellow label.)
CAPITOL (5000 series) 3-6   63-67
CHESTERFIELD (44223 "Leavin'
  Dirty Tracks") 10-20

HILLTOP (6027 "Hot Dog") 25-50
NEW STAR (6418 "Hot Dog") 100-150
PEP (105 "Down on the
   Corner of Love") 20-30   56
PEP (106 "Right After the Dance") . . . 20-30   56
PEP (109 "There Goes My Love") . . . 20-30   57
STARDAY (588 "Down on the
   Corner of Love") 5-10   61
STARDAY (5000 series) 4-6   64
WARNER (Except 8316) 3-5   76-80
WARNER (8316 "World
   Famous Holiday Inn") 5-10   77
WARNER (8316 "World
   Famous Paradise Inn") 3-5   77
Picture Sleeves
CAPITOL 5-10   66-69
EPs: 7-inch 33/45rpm
CAPITOL 10-25   61-65
LPs: 10/12-inch 33rpm
CAPITOL (100 through 400 series) . . . 8-12   68-70
CAPITOL (500 series, except 574) . . . 8-10   70
CAPITOL (600 through 800 series) . . . 5-10   70-72
CAPITOL (574 "Buck Owens") 15-25   70
   (Three-LP set.)
CAPITOL (T-1482 through T-1989) . . 30-40   61-63
   (Monaural.)
CAPITOL (ST-1482 through ST-1989) 35-50   61-63
   (Stereo.)
CAPITOL (DT-1400 series) 8-12   69
CAPITOL (2100 through 2700
   series) 12-25   64-67
CAPITOL (2800 through 2900
   series) 10-15   68
CAPITOL (2980 "Buck Owens
   Minute Masters") 30-40   66
   (Promotional issue only.)
CAPITOL (11000 series) 5-8   72-78
HALL of MUSIC 8-12
LA BREA (8017 "Buck Owens") . . . 100-150   61
OUT of TOWN DIST 5-8   82
PICKWICK/HILLTOP 5-10   78
STARDAY (172 "Fabulous Country Music
   Sound of Buck Owens") 30-40   62
STARDAY (300 series) 15-20   64-65
STARDAY (400 series) 8-12   75
TIME-LIFE 5-10   82
TRIP 5-8   76
WARNER 5-10   76-77
   Also see JONES, Corky
   Also see JONES, George / Buck Owens / David Houston /
    Tommy Hill.

OWENS, Buck, and Emmylou Harris
Singles: 7-inch
WARNER 2-4   79
   Also see HARRIS, Emmylou

OWENS, Buck, and Susan Raye
Singles: 7-inch
CAPITOL 3-5   70-73

LPs: 10/12-inch 33rpm
CAPITOL 5-10   70-73
   Also see RAYE, Susan

OWENS, Buck / Faron Young / Ferlin Husky
LPs: 10/12-inch 33rpm
PICKWICK/HILLTOP 10-15   65
   Also see HUSKY, Ferlin
   Also see OWENS, Buck
   Also see YOUNG, Faron

OWENS, Donnie
(Donny Owens)
Singles: 7-inch
ARA 4-8
GUYDEN 5-10   58-59
TREY 5-10   60

OWENS, Gwen
Singles: 7-inch
BIG TREE 3-5   79
JOSIE 4-6   69

OWENS, Tony
Singles: 7-inch
SOUL SOUND 4-8   67
SOULIN' 4-8   67

OXO
Singles: 7-inch
GEFFEN 2-4   83
LPs: 10/12-inch 33rpm
GEFFEN 5-8   83

OZARK MOUNTAIN DAREDEVILS
Singles: 7-inch
A&M 3-5   74-78
COLUMBIA 3-5   80
Picture Sleeves
A&M 3-5   75-76
LPs: 10/12-inch 33rpm
A&M 8-12   73-78
COLUMBIA 5-10   80

OZO
Singles: 7-inch
DJM 3-5   76
LPs: 10/12-inch 33rpm
DJM 5-10   76

OZONE
Singles: 7-inch
MOTOWN 3-5   80-83
LPs: 10/12-inch 33rpm
MOTOWN 5-10   80-83

P

P.F.M.
(Premiata Forneria Marconi)
Singles: 7–inch
ASYLUM 3-5   76-77
MANTICORE 3-5   73-75
LPs: 10/12–inch 33rpm
ASYLUM 5-10   76-77
MANTICORE 8-12   73-74
PETERS INT'L 5-10   76

P CREW
Singles: 7–inch
PRELUDE 2-4   83

P. FUNK ALL-STARS
Singles: 12–inch 33/45rpm
UNCLE JAM 4-6   84
Singles: 7–inch
CBS ASSOCIATED 2-4   83
HUMP 3-5   82
UNCLE JAM 2-4   84
LPs: 10/12–inch 33rpm
CBS ASSOCIATED 5-8   84
UNCLE JAM 5-8   84

PG&E:
see PACIFIC GAS and Electric

PABLO CRUISE
Singles: 7–inch
A&M 2-5   75-84
Picture Sleeves
A&M 2-5   77-84
LPs: 10/12–inch 33rpm
A&M 5-10   75-84
MFSL (029 "A Place in the Sun") 15-25   79
(Half-speed mastered.)
NAUTILUS 10-20   81
Members: Dave Jenkins; Steven Price; Cory Lerios; Bud Cockrell.
Also see IT'S a BEAUTIFUL DAY

PACIFIC GAS and Electric
(PG&E; Pacific Gas and Electric Blues Band)
Singles: 7–inch
BRIGHT ORANGE 5-10   68
COLUMBIA 3-6   69-72
POWER 5-10   69
LPs: 10/12–inch 33rpm
ABC 8-10
BRIGHT ORANGE (701 "Get It On") . 40-80   68
COLUMBIA 8-12   69-73
POWER 10-15   69
Also see SEEGER, Pete, and Pacific Gas and Electric

PACK, David
Singles: 7–inch
WARNER 2-4   86
LPs: 10/12–inch 33rpm
WARNER 5-8   86
Also see AMBROSIA
Also see McDONALD, Michael
Also see PARSONS, Alan, Project

PACKERS
Singles: 7–inch
HBR 4-8   66
IMPERIAL 4-6   69
PURE SOUL MUSIC 4-8   65
TANGERINE 4-8   68
LPs: 10/12–inch 33rpm
IMPERIAL 10-15   68
PURE SOUL MUSIC 15-20   66

PAGAN, Bruni
Singles: 7–inch
ELEKTRA 3-5   79

PAGAN, Ralfi
Singles: 7–inch
FANIA 3-5   71

PAGE, Gene
Singles: 7–inch
ARISTA 3-5   78-80
ATLANTIC 3-5   74-75
LPs: 10/12–inch 33rpm
ARISTA 5-10   78-80
ATLANTIC 8-12   74-75

PAGE, Jimmy
LPs: 10/12–inch 33rpm
GEFFEN 5-8   88
SWAN SONG 5-10   82
Also see CLAPTON, Eric, Jeff Beck and Jimmy Page
Also see FIRM
Also see HERMAN'S HERMITS
Also see HONEYDRIPPERS
Also see LED ZEPPELIN
Also see LORD SUTCH
Also see STEWART, Al
Also see WILLIE and the Poor Boys
Also see YARDBIRDS

PAGE, Jimmy, and Sonny Boy Williamson
LPs: 10/12–inch 33rpm
SPRINGBOARD 10-20   72
Also see WILLIAMSON, Sonny Boy, and the Yardbirds

PAGE, Patti
Singles: 78rpm
MERCURY 5-10   48-58
Singles: 7–inch
AVCO 3-5   74-75
COLUMBIA 4-6   63-70
EPIC 3-5   73
MERCURY (5000 series) 8-15   50-52
MERCURY (70000 through 72000
series) 5-10   52-63
MERCURY (73000 series) 3-5   71

PLANTATION 3-5   81-82

Picture Sleeves

MERCURY 5-15   54-63

EPs: 7–inch 33/45rpm

MERCURY 5-15   51-61

LPs: 10/12–inch 33rpm

ACCORD 5-10   82
CANDLELITE 8-12
COLUMBIA 8-18   63-70
EMARCY (102 "East Side, West Side") 50-80
EMARCY (36074 "In the Land
   of Hi Fi") 40-60   56
   (No Mercury logo on cover or label.)
EMARCY (36074 "In the Land
   of Hi Fi") 40-60   58
   (Reissue, with Mercury logo on cover and label.)
EXACT 5-8   80
HARMONY 5-10   69-70
MERCURY (100 series) 8-12   69
MERCURY (20000 series) 15-30   55-64
   (Monaural.)
MERCURY (25000 series) 20-40   50-54
   (10–inch LPs.)
MERCURY (60000 series) 15-30   58-64
   (Stereo.)
MERCURY (61000 series) 5-10   71
PLANTATION 5-10   81
WING 10-20   63-65
   Also see MARTIN, Dean / Patti Page

PAGE, Patti, and Tom T. Hall
Singles: 7–inch
MERCURY 3-5   72
   Also see HALL, Tom T.
   Also see PAGE, Patti

PAGES
Singles: 7–inch
CAPITOL 3-5   81
EPIC 3-5   79-80
LPs: 10/12–inch 33rpm
CAPITOL 5-10   81
EPIC 5-10   78-79

Members: Richard Page; Steve George; Russell Battelene; Jerry
Manfredi; Peter Leinheiser.
   Also see MR. MISTER

PAIGE, Sharon
(Sharon Paige and Harold Melvin and the Bluenotes)
Singles: 7–inch
PHILADELPHIA INT'L 3-5   75
SOURCE 3-5   80
   Also see MELVIN, Harold

PAINTER
Singles: 7–inch
ELEKTRA 3-5   73
LPs: 10/12–inch 33rpm
ELEKTRA 8-12   73

PALLAS, Laura
Singles: 12–inch 33/45rpm
TVI 4-6   84

PALMER, Robert
Singles: 12–inch 33/45rpm
ISLAND 4-6   83-86
Singles: 7–inch
ISLAND 2-5   75-86
LPs: 10/12–inch 33rpm
EMI 5-8   88-90
ISLAND (Except 819) 5-10   75-86
ISLAND (819 "Secrets") 35-40   79
   (Picture disc. Promotional issue only.)
   Also see POWER STATION

PAMPLEMOUSSE, LE:
see LE PAMPLEMOUSSE

PANIC BUTTON
Singles: 7–inch
CHALOM 4-8   68
GAMBLE 4-6   69

PAONE, Nicola
Singles: 7–inch
ABC-PAR 3-6   59
CADENCE 3-6   59
EPs: 7–inch 33/45rpm
CADENCE 5-10   59
LPs: 10/12–inch 33rpm
ABC-PAR 10-20   59-60
ROULETTE 10-15   65

PAPER LACE
Singles: 7–inch
BANG 3-5   72
MERCURY 3-5   74-75
LPs: 10/12–inch 33rpm
MERCURY 8-10   74

PARACHUTE CLUB
Singles: 12–inch 33/45rpm
RCA 4-6   83
Singles: 7–inch
RCA 2-4   83
LPs: 10/12–inch 33rpm
RCA 5-8   83

PARADE
Singles: 7–inch
A&M 4-8   67-69
Member: Jerry Riopelle.

PARADISE EXPRESS
Singles: 12–inch 33/45rpm
FANTASY 4-8   78-81
Singles: 7–inch
FANTASY 3-5   78-81
LPs: 10/12–inch 33rpm
FANTASY 5-10   78

PARADONS
Singles: 7–inch
COLLECTABLES 2-4
ERA 3-5   72
MILESTONE (2003 "Diamonds
  and Pearls") 15-20   60
  (Maroon label.)
MILESTONE (2003 "Diamonds
  and Pearls") 10-15   60
  (Red label.)
MILESTONE (2003 "Diamonds
  and Pearls") 5-10   60
  (Green label.)
MILESTONE (2005 "Bells Ring") 15-20   60
MILESTONE (2015 "I Had a Dream") 25-35   62
TUFFEST (102 "Never Again") 75-125   61
WARNER (5186 "Take All of Me") ... 10-15   61
Members: Bill Myers; Chuck Weldon; Wes Tyler; Bill Powers.

PARAGONS
Singles: 7–inch
ABC 3-5   73
BUDDAH 3-5   75
COLLECTABLES 2-4
MUSIC CLEF (3001 "Time After Time") 10-15   63
MUSICRAFT (1102 "Wedding Bells") . 10-20   60
TAP (500 "If") 15-25   61
TAP (503 "Begin the Beguine") 15-25   61
TAP (504 "If You Love Me") 15-25   61
TIMES SQUARE (9 "So You
  Will Know") 10-15   63
VIRGO 2-4   72-73
WINLEY (215 "Florence") 20-35   57
  (With "Winley" in 3⁄16-inch letters.)
WINLEY (215 "Florence") 10-15   61
  (With "Winley" in 1⁄4-inch letters.)
WINLEY (220 "Let's Start All
  over Again") 20-35   57
  (With "Winley" in 3⁄16-inch letters.)
WINLEY (220 "Let's Start All
  over Again") 10-15   61
  (With "Winley" in 1⁄4-inch letters.)
WINLEY (223 "Two Hearts Are
  Better Than One") 30-40   58
  (With "Winley" in 3⁄16-inch letters.)
WINLEY (223 "Two Hearts Are
  Better Than One") 10-15   61
  (With "Winley" in 1⁄4-inch letters.)

WINLEY (227 "Twilight"
  /"The Wows of Love") 75-100   58
  (Note spelling error on "Vows.")
WINLEY (227 "Twilight"
  /"The Vows of Love") 20-35   58
  (With "Winley" in 3⁄16-inch letters.)
WINLEY (227 "Twilight"
  /"The Vows of Love") 10-15   61
  (With "Winley" in 1⁄4-inch letters.)
WINLEY (228 "So You Will Know") .. 25-35   59
  (With "Winley" in 3⁄16-inch letters.)
WINLEY (228 "So You Will Know") .. 10-15   61
  (With "Winley" in 1⁄4-inch letters.)
WINLEY (236 "Darling, I Love You") . 25-35   59
WINLEY (240 "So You Will Know") .. 15-25   60
WINLEY (250 "Kneel and Pray") 15-25   61
LPs: 10/12–inch 33rpm
COLLECTABLES 6-8   86
LOST-NITE 5-10   81
RARE BIRD (8002 "Simply
  the Paragons") 35-45
  Members: Julius McMichaels; Mack Starr; Al Brown; Don Travis;
  Ben Frazier; Bill Witt; Rick Jackson.
  Also see HARPTONES / Paragons
  Also see JESTERS / Paragons
  Also see OLYMPICS

PARAGONS / Samohl Serenaders
Singles: 7–inch
CENTURY CUSTOM (19317 "Surf
  Drums") 20-30
  Members: Mike Faulkner; Forrest Peque.

PARAMOR, Norrie, and His Orchestra
Singles: 78rpm
ESSEX 3-6   53
Singles: 7–inch
ESSEX 5-10   53
EPs: 7–inch 33/45rpm
CAPITOL 8-15   56
LPs: 10/12–inch 33rpm
CAPITOL 10-25   55-66
ESSEX 10-20   54
HAYNES and SBARRA 5-10   79

PARAMOURS
Singles: 7–inch
MOONGLOW (214 "There She Goes") 10-15   62
  (Black vinyl.)
MOONGLOW (214 "There She Goes") 20-30   62
  (Colored vinyl.)
SMASH (1701 "That's the
  Way We Love") 10-15   61
SMASH (1718 "Cutie Cutie") 10-15   61
  Members: Bill Medley; Bobby Hatfield.
  Also see RIGHTEOUS BROTHERS

PARIS
Singles: 7–inch
CAPITOL 3-5   76
LPs: 10/12–inch 33rpm
CAPITOL 8-12   76

Members: Bob Welch; Glen Cornick; Bernie Marsden; Thom
Mooney.
  Also see WELCH, Bob

PARIS SISTERS
Singles: 78rpm
DECCA 5-10   54-58
IMPERIAL 5-10   57-58
Singles: 7-inch
ABC 3-5   73
CAPITOL 4-8   68
COLLECTABLES 2-4
DECCA 5-10   54-58
ERIC 2-4
GNP/CRESCENDO 4-8   68
GREGMARK 8-12   61-62
IMPERIAL 5-10   57-58
MGM 4-8   64
MERCURY 4-8   64-65
REPRISE 4-8   66-67
Picture Sleeves
MGM 10-20   64
MERCURY 8-10   64
LPs: 10/12-inch 33rpm
REPRISE (R-6259 "Everything
  Under the Sun") 15-20   67
  (Monaural.)
REPRISE (RS-6259 "Everything
  Under the Sun") 20-25   67
  (Stereo.)
SIDEWALK 12-18
UNIFILMS 10-15
  Members: Priscilla Paris; Sherrell Paris; Albeth Paris.
  Also see ALLAN, Davie
  Also see PRISCILLA

PARKAYS
Singles: 7-inch
ABC-PAR 5-10   61
FONTANA 4-8   65

PARKER, Bobby
Singles: 7-inch
AMANDA 5-10   60
V-TONE 4-8   61

PARKER, Fess
(Fess Parker and Buddy Ebsen)
Singles: 78rpm
COLUMBIA 4-6   55
DISNEYLAND 4-6   57
Singles: 7-inch
BUENA VISTA 4-8   63
CASCADE 5-10   59
COLUMBIA 5-10   55
DISNEYLAND 5-10   57
GUSTO 4-8   63
RCA 4-8   64-69
Picture Sleeves
BUENA VISTA 5-10   63
DISNEYLAND 5-10   57
RCA 4-8   64

EPs: 7-inch 33/45rpm
COLUMBIA (2031 "Indian Fighter") . . 20-25   55
COLUMBIA (2032 "Davy Crockett
  Goes to Congress") 20-25   55
COLUMBIA (2033 "At the Alamo") . . . 20-25   55
LPs: 10-inch 33rpm
COLUMBIA (666 "Davy
  Crockett") 50-75   55
DISNEYLAND (1200 series) 10-20   64-65
DISNEYLAND (1300 series) 5-10   70
DISNEYLAND (1900 series) 10-20   63
DISNEYLAND (3007 "Yarns
  and Songs") 25-35   55
DISNEYLAND (3900 series) 10-20   64
HARMONY 10-20   60
RCA 10-20   64

PARKER, Graham
(Graham Parker and Rumour; Graham Parker and the
Shot)
Singles: 7-inch
ARISTA 2-5   79-83
MERCURY 3-5   76-77
Picture Sleeves
ARISTA 3-5   80-83
LPs: 10/12-inch 33rpm
ARISTA 5-10   78-83
ELEKTRA 5-8   85
MERCURY 5-10   77-78
RCA 5-8   88-89
Promotional LPs
ARISTA (41 "Mercury Poisoning") . . . 25-35   78
ARISTA (63 "Live Sparks") 25-35   79
  Also see RUMOUR
  Also see SPRINGSTEEN, Bruce

PARKER, Little Junior
(Junior Parker; Little Junior and His Blue Flames;
Little Junior Parker and the Blue Blowers)
Singles: 78rpm
DUKE 10-15   54-58
MODERN (864 "Bad Women,
  Bad Whiskey") 20-40   52
Singles: 7-inch
ABC 3-5   73
BLUE ROCK 4-6   68-69
CAPITOL 3-5   71
DUKE (137 "Backtrackin") 25-35   55
DUKE (300 series) 5-10   59-66
DUKE (400 series) 4-8   67
MCA 2-4
MERCURY 4-8   66-68
MINIT 4-8   69
LPs: 10/12-inch 33rpm
ABC 8-10   76
BLUE ROCK 10-15   69
BLUESWAY 8-12   73
CAPITOL 10-15   70
DUKE (76 "Driving Wheel") . . 60-100   62
  (Cover pictures a Cadillac.)

DUKE (76 "Driving Wheel") 35-55   62
(Cover pictures a Wagon Wheel.)
DUKE (83 "Best of Junior Parker") 8-10   74
MCA 5-8
MERCURY 12-20   67
MINIT 10-15   69
   Also see BLAND, Bobby / Little Junior Parker
   Also see LITTLE JUNIOR'S BLUE FLAMES

PARKER, Little Junior, with Bill Johnson's Blue Flames
Singles: 78rpm
DUKE 10-20   54
Singles: 7-inch
DUKE (120 "Dirty Friend Blues") 30-50   54
DUKE (127 "Please Baby Blues") ... 30-50   54

PARKER, Little Junior, and Jimmy McGriff
LPs: 10/12-inch 33rpm
CAPITOL 10-15   71
U.A. 10-15   71
   Also see McGRIFF, Jimmy
   Also see PARKER, Little Junior

PARKER, Little Willie, and Lorenzo Smith
Singles: 7-inch
MAR-VEL 4-8   64

PARKER, Paul
Singles: 12-inch 33/45rpm
MEGATONE 4-6   83

PARKER, Ray, Jr.
(Ray Parker, Jr. and Raydio)
Singles: 12-inch 33/45rpm
ARISTA 4-6   84-85
Singles: 7-inch
ARISTA (Except 1035) 2-5   80-85
ARISTA (1035 "Christmas Time Is Here") 3-5   82
(Promotional issue only.)
FLASHBACK 2-4   82
GEFFEN 2-4   87
Picture Sleeves
ARISTA (Except 1035) 2-4   80-85
ARISTA (1035 "Christmas Time Is Here") 3-5   82
(Promotional issue only.)
LPs: 10/12-inch 33rpm
ARISTA 5-8   80-85
GEFFEN 5-8   87
   Members: J.D. Nicholas; Arnell Carmichael; Jack Ashford; Ollie Brown.
   Also see RAYDIO

PARKER, Robert
Singles: 7-inch
HEAD 3-5   72
IMPERIAL 4-8   62
ISLAND 3-5   75-76
NOLA 4-8   66-67
RON 5-10   59-60
SILVER FOX 4-6   69

LPs: 10/12-inch 33rpm
NOLA (1001 "Barefootin") 20-30   66
(Monaural.)
NOLA (S-1001 "Barefootin") 30-40   66
(Stereo.)
   Also see BO, Eddie

PARKER, Winfield
Singles: 7-inch
ARCTIC 4-6   69
GSP 3-5   72
RU-JAC 4-6   68
SPRING 3-5   71

PARKING METER
Singles: 12-inch 33/45rpm
ATLANTIC 4-6   84
Singles: 7-inch
ATLANTIC 3-5   84

PARKS, Michael
Singles: 7-inch
MGM 3-5   70
LPs: 10/12-inch 33rpm
MGM 10-15   69-70
VERVE 8-12   71

PARLET
Singles: 7-inch
CASABLANCA 3-5   78-80
LPs: 10/12-inch 33rpm
CASABLANCA 5-10   79

PARLET and Jeanette Washington
Singles: 7-inch
CASABLANCA 3-5   80
   Also see WASHINGTON, Baby

PARLIAMENT
(Parliament Thang)
Singles: 12-inch 33/45rpm
CASABLANCA 4-6   78
Singles: 7-inch
CASABLANCA 3-5   74-81
INVICTUS 3-5   70-71
SOULTOWN 3-5
LPs: 10/12-inch 33rpm
CASABLANCA (Except NBPIX-7125) . 5-10   74-80
CASABLANCA (NBPIX-7125 "Motor
Booty Affair") 10-15   79
(Picture disc.)
INVICTUS 8-12   70
   Also see BOOTSY'S RUBBER BAND
   Also see BRIDES of FUNKENSTEIN
   Also see PARLIAMENTS
   Also see WORRELL, Bernie

PARLIAMENTS
Singles: 7-inch
ATCO 3-5   69
REVILOT 4-8   67-68
   Also see CLINTON, George, Band
   Also see FUNKADELIC
   Also see PARLIAMENT

PARR, John
Singles: 12–inch 33/45rpm
ATLANTIC 4-6   86
Singles: 7–inch
ATLANTIC 2-4   84-86
LPs: 10/12–inch 33rpm
ATLANTIC 5-8   84-86

PARRIS, Fred
(Fred Parris and the Satins; Fred Parris and the
Scarlets; Fred Parris and Black Satin; Fred Parris and
the Restless Hearts; Fred Paris)
Singles: 7–inch
ATCO 5-10   66
BIRTH 4-8
BUDDAH 3-5   75
CANDLELITE 5-10   63
CHECKER 5-10   65
ELEKTRA 3-5   82
GREEN SEA 5-10   66
KLIK (7905 "She's Gone") 60-80   58
MAMA SADIE 4-8   67
RCA (9200 series) 4-8   67
(In 1968, a different Freddie Paris recorded for
RCA. Note different spelling.)
LPs: 10/12–inch 33rpm
BUDDAH 30-50   75
ELEKTRA 10-15   82
Also see FIVE SATINS
Also see PARIS, Freddie

PARRISH, Dean
(Dean Parish)
Singles: 7–inch
BOOM 4-8   66
LAURIE 4-8   67
MUSICOR 4-8   65

PARRISH, Man
Singles: 7–inch
SUGAR SCOOP 2-4   85
LPs: 10/12–inch 33rpm
IMPORTE 5-8   83

PARSONS, Alan, Project
Singles: 7–inch
ARISTA 2-5   77-89
20TH FOX 3-5   76
LPs: 10/12–inch 33rpm
ARISTA (111 "No Gambler") 15-20   80
ARISTA (140 "Complete Audio
   Guide") 75-100   82
   (Eight-LP boxed set.)
ARISTA (4000 series) 5-10   78
ARISTA (7002 I Robot") 5-10   77
ARISTA (8000 series, except 8263) ... 5-8   83-89
ARISTA (8263 "Vulture Culture") 5-8   85
ARISTA (PD-8263 "Vulture Culture") . 20-25   85
   (Picture disc. Promotional issue only.)
ARISTA (9000 series) 5-10   79-82
20TH FOX (508 "Tales of
   Mystery and Imagination") ... 15-25   76
   (Includes eight-page booklet.)
20TH FOX (508 "Tales of
   Mystery and Imagination") 8-12   76
20TH FOX (539 "Tales of
   Mystery and Imagination") 5-10   77
MFSL (084 "I Robot") 25-50   82
MFSL/UHQR (084 "I Robot") 75-100   82
   (Boxed set.)
MFSL (175 "Best of the Alan
   Parsons Project) 15-25   85
Members: Alan Parsons; David Paton; Stuart Tosh; Eric
Woolfson; Lenny Zakatek; Ian Bairnson; B.J. Cole; Stuart Elliott;
Colin Blunstone; Allan Clarke; Andrew Powell; John Miles; Gary
Brooker; Christopher Rainbow; Duncan Mackay; Richard Cottle;
Laurie Cottle; Geoff Barradale.
   Also see AMBROSIA
   Also see BROWN, Arthur
   Also see CLARKE, Alan
   Also see HOLLIES
   Also see MILES, John
   Also see PACK, David
   Also see PILOT
   Also see VITAMIN Z

PARSONS, Bill
(Bobby Bare)
Singles: 7–inch
ABC 3-5   73
COLLECTABLES 2-4
FRATERNITY (835 "The All
   American Boy") 10-15   58
FRATERNITY (838 "Educated
   Rock and Roll") 8-12   59
   Also see BARE, Bobby

PARSONS, Gram
(Gram Parsons and the Fallen Angels)
Singles: 7–inch
REPRISE 3-5   73
SIERRA 3-5   79
EPs: 7–inch 33/45rpm
SIERRA 8-10   82
   (Promotional issue only.)
LPs: 10/12–inch 33rpm
REPRISE 8-12   73

SHILOH 10-15   73
SIERRA 5-10   79-82
   Also see BYRDS
   Also see FLYING BURRITO BROTHERS
   Also see HARRIS, Emmylou

PARTLAND BROTHERS
Singles: 7–inch
MANHATTAN 2-4   87
LPs: 10/12–inch 33rpm
MANHATTAN 5-8   87

PARTON, Dolly
Singles: 12–inch 33/45rpm
RCA (Black vinyl) 4-6   78-83
RCA (Colored vinyl) 8-10   78
Singles: 7–inch
GOLDBAND (1086 "Puppy Love") ... 20-30   59
MERCURY (71982 "It's Sure
   Gonna Hurt") 10-20   62
MONUMENT (800 through 1000
   series) 4-8   65-68
RCA (0100 and 0200 series) 3-5   69-76
RCA (5000 series) 2-4   86
RCA (9500 through 9900 series) 3-5   68-71
RCA (10000 through 14000 series) ... 2-5   74-87
Promotional Singles
RCA (Colored vinyl) 3-8   77-85
Picture Sleeves
RCA 3-5   69-85
LPs: 10/12–inch 33rpm
ALSHIRE 8-12   69-71
CAMDEN 5-10   72-78
COLUMBIA 5-8   87
MONUMENT (7600 series) 5-10   78
MONUMENT (8085 "Hello, I'm
   Dolly") 15-20   67
MONUMENT (18000 series) 12-20   67
MONUMENT (18100 series) 8-15   70
MONUMENT (31000 series) 8-15   72
MONUMENT (33000 series) 8-10   75
RCA (0033 through 5000 series) 5-12   73-87
   (With "AFL1," "AHL1," "APD1," "APL1," or "AYL1"
   prefix.)
RCA (CPL1-3413 "Great Balls
   of Fire") 15-20   79
   (Picture disc.)
RCA (3900 through 4700 series) 8-15   68-72
   (With "LPM" or "LSP" prefix.)
RCA (4422 "Greatest Hits") 25-50   82
   (Without Islands in the Stream.)
RCA (4422 "Greatest Hits") 5-8   82
   (With Islands in the Stream.)
RCA (5000 series) 5-8   84
SOMERSET 10-20   63-68
STEREO-FIDELITY 10-20   63-68
TIME-LIFE 5-8   81
   Also see HARRIS, Emmylou
   Also see NELSON, Willie, and Dolly Parton
   Also see PHILLIPS, Bill, and Dolly Parton
   Also see ROGERS, Kenny, and Dolly Parton

Also see WAGONER, Porter, and Dolly Parton

PARTON, Dolly / George Jones
LPs: 10/12–inch 33rpm
STARDAY (429 "Dolly Parton and
   George Jones") 30-40   68
   Also see JONES, George

PARTON, Dolly, Linda Ronstadt, and Emmylou Harris
LPs: 10/12–inch 33rpm
WARNER 5-8   87
   Also see HARRIS, Emmylou
   Also see RONSTADT, Linda

PARTON, Dolly / Kitty Wells
LPs: 10/12–inch 33rpm
EXACT 5-8   80
   Also see PARTON, Dolly
   Also see WELLS, Kitty

PARTRIDGE FAMILY
(Featuring David Cassidy)
Singles: 7–inch
BELL 3-5   70-73
Picture Sleeves
BELL 3-5   70-73
LPs: 10/12–inch 33rpm
BELL 8-12   70-74
   Also see CASSIDY, David

PASSIONS
Singles: 7–inch
ABC-PAR 8-10   63
AUDICON 10-20   59-61
COLLECTABLES 2-4
DIAMOND (146 "16 Candles") 15-25   63
DORE 10-15   58
JUBILEE 8-12   61
LAURIE 3-5
OCTAVIA (8005 "Aphrodite") 100-150   62
   Members: Jim Gallagher; Tony Armato; Al Galione; Vince
   Acerno; Louis Rotondo.
   Also see MYSTICS / Passions

PASSPORT
Singles: 7–inch
ATCO 3-5   76
ATLANTIC 3-5   78
LPs: 10/12–inch 33rpm
ATCO 8-12   74-77
ATLANTIC 5-10   78-82
REPRISE 8-12   72

PASTEL SIX
Singles: 7–inch
CHATTAHOOCHEE 5-10   65
DOWNEY 10-20   62-63
ERA 3-5   72
ZEN 10-20   62
ZENITH 10-20   63
LPs: 10/12–inch 33rpm
ZEN (1001 "Cinnamon Cinder") 50-100   62
   Member: Sonny Patterson.

PASTELS
Singles: 7-inch
ARGO (5287 "Been So Long") 10-20   58
ARGO (5297 "You Don't Love
Me Anymore") 15-25   58
ARGO (5314 "So Far Away") 10-20   58
CADET 3-5
CHESS 3-5   73
MASCOT (123 "Been So Long") ... 75-125   57
  Members: Big Dee Irwin; Richard Travis; Tony Thomas; J.B.
  Wellington.
  Also see IRWIN, Big Dee

PASTORIUS, Jaco
LPs: 10/12-inch 33rpm
WARNER 5-8   81-83
  Also see WEATHER REPORT

PAT and the Satellites
Singles: 7-inch
ATCO 8-12   59
  Members: Pat Otts; King Curtis; Wayne Lips.
  Also see KING CURTIS

PAT and the Wildcats
Singles: 7-inch
CRUSADER 4-8   64

PATE, Johnny
(Johnny Pate Trio)
Singles: 78rpm
FEDERAL 4-8   57
GIG 4-8   56
Singles: 7-inch
ARGO 4-6   64
FEDERAL 5-10   57-59
GIG 10-15   56
LPs: 10/12-inch 33rpm
GIG 40-50   56
KING (561 "Jazz Goes Ivy League") . 30-50   58
  (Monaural.)
KING (KSD-561 "Jazz Goes
  Ivy League") 50-75   59
  (Stereo.)
KING (584 "Swingin' Flute") 30-50   58
KING (611 "A Date
  with Johnny Pate") 30-50   58
SALEM 25-35   58
STEPHENY (4002 "Johnny Pate
  At the Blue Note") 45-55   57

PATIENCE & PRUDENCE
Singles: 78rpm
LIBERTY 5-10   56
Singles: 7-inch
CHATTAHOOCHEE 4-8   64-65
LIBERTY 8-12   56
U.A. 3-5
  Also see CLIFFORD, Mike, and Patience and Prudence

PATRIS
Singles: 12-inch 33/45rpm
EMERGENCY 4-6   85

PATTERSON, Kellee
Singles: 7-inch
SHADYBROOK 3-5   75-77
LPs: 10/12-inch 33rpm
SHADYBROOK 5-10   76-79
  Shadybrook may also be shown as Shady Brook
  (two words).

PATTI and the Emblems:
see PATTY and the Emblems

PATTON, Robbie
Singles: 7-inch
ATLANTIC 2-4   83-85
BACKSTREET 3-5   79
LIBERTY 3-5   81
LPs: 10/12-inch 33rpm
ATLANTIC 5-8   85
LIBERTY 5-10   81

PAUL, Billy
Singles: 12-inch 33/45rpm
PHILADELPHIA INT'L 4-8   79
Singles: 7-inch
FINCH 8-12   60
PHILADELPHIA INT'L 3-5   71-81
LPs: 10/12-inch 33rpm
GAMBLE 10-20   67
NEPTUNE 10-15   70
PHILADELPHIA INT'L 5-10   71-80
  Also see PHILADELPHIA INTERNATIONAL ALL STARS

PAUL, Henry, Band
Singles: 7-inch
ATLANTIC 3-5   79-81
LPs: 10/12-inch 33rpm
ATLANTIC 5-10   79-81
  Also see OUTLAWS

PAUL, Les
(Les Paul Trio)
Singles: 78rpm
CAPITOL 4-8   50-53
DECCA 4-8   54
Singles: 7-inch
CAPITOL 5-10   50-53
DECCA 5-10   54
EPs: 7-inch 33/45rpm
DECCA 10-20   50-53
LPs: 10/12-inch 33rpm
CAPITOL (200 series) 5-10   77
CAPITOL (16000 series) ....
DECCA (5018 "Hawaiian
  Paradise") 50-100   49
  (10-inch LP.)
DECCA (5376 "Galloping Guitars") .. 50-75   52
  (10-inch LP.)
DECCA (8589 "More of Les") 30-50   57
GLENDALE 5-8   78
LONDON 6-12   68-79
VOCALION 6-12   68
  Also see ATKINS, Chet, and Les Paul

PAUL, Les, and Mary Ford
Singles: 78rpm
CAPITOL 4-8   50-57
Singles: 7-inch
CAPITOL 5-10   50-57
COLUMBIA 4-8   58-64
Picture Sleeves
COLUMBIA 4-8   58-64
EPs: 7-inch 33/45rpm
CAPITOL 10-20   50-57
LPs: 10/12-inch 33rpm
CAPITOL (SM-200 series) 5-8   78
CAPITOL (H-226 through H-577) 30-50   50-55
(10–inch LPs.)
CAPITOL (T-226 through T-802) 25-35   55-57
CAPITOL (T-1400 and T-1500 series) 15-25   60-61
(Monaural.)
CAPITOL (ST-1400 and
ST-1500 series) 20-30   60-61
(Stereo.)
CAPITOL (11000 series) 5-10   74
COLUMBIA 10-20   61-63
HARMONY 8-12   61-65
Also see PAUL, Les

PAUL, Pope: see POPE PAUL

PAUL & PAULA
Singles: 7-inch
LE CAM (300 series) 3-5   74-82
LE CAM (99 "The Beginning of Love") . 8-12   63
PHILIPS (40000 series) 4-8   62-66
PHILIPS (44000 series) 3-5
UNI 4-8   68
U.A. 3-5   70
Picture Sleeves
PHILIPS 8-12   63-64
LPs: 10/12-inch 33rpm
PHILIPS (200078 "For Young Lovers") 25-40   63
(Monaural.)
PHILIPS (200089 "We Go Together")   25-40   63
(Monaural.)
PHILIPS (200101 "Holiday for Teens") 25-40   63
(Monaural.)
PHILIPS (600078 "For Young Lovers") 25-50   63
(Stereo.)
PHILIPS (600089 "We Go Together")   25-50   63
(Stereo.)
PHILIPS (600101 "Holiday for Teens") 25-50   63
(Stereo.)
Members: Ray Hildebrand; Jill Jackson.
Also see CHANNEL, Bruce / Paul & Paula
Also see JILL & RAY

PAULETTE SISTERS
Singles: 78rpm
CAPITOL 4-8   55
Singles: 7-inch
CAPITOL 5-10   55
CONTEMPO 4-8   63
DECCA 4-6

RIBBON 4-8   60
20TH FOX 4-8   61

PAULSEN, Pat
LPs: 10/12-inch 33rpm
MERCURY 8-15   68-70

PAUPERS
Singles: 7-inch
VERVE/FOLKWAYS 5-10   66-67
VERVE/FORECAST 4-8   67-68
Picture Sleeves
VERVE 5-10   67
LPs: 10/12-inch 33rpm
VERVE/FORECAST 10-20   67-68

PAVLOV'S DOG
Singles: 7-inch
COLUMBIA 3-5   76
LPs: 10/12-inch 33rpm
ABC 10-15   75
COLUMBIA 8-12   75-76
Members: David Surkamp; Mike Abebe; Murray Krugman;
Sandy Pearlman; Mike Safron; Richard Stockton; David
Hamilton; Doug Rayburn; Steve Scorfina; Bill Bruford.
Also see YES

PAVONE, Rita
Singles: 7-inch
RCA 4-8   63-66
Picture Sleeves
RCA 4-8   64-65
LPs: 10/12-inch 33rpm
RCA 10-20   64-67

PAVAROTTI, Luciano
Singles: 7-inch
LONDON 2-4   79-84
LPs: 10/12-inch 33rpm
LONDON 5-8   76-84

PAXTON, Tom
Singles: 7-inch
ASYLUM 3-5   70
ELEKTRA 4-8   69
REPRISE 3-5   71
LPs: 10/12-inch 33rpm
ANCHOR 8-12
ELEKTRA 10-15   64-71
FLYING FISH 5-8
PRIVATE STOCK 8-10   75
REPRISE 10-15   71-73

PAYCHECK, Johnny
Singles: 7-inch
ABC 3-5   74
CUTLASS 3-5   72
EPIC 3-5   71-82
HILLTOP 5-10   64-66
LITTLE DARLIN' (008 through 0072) ... 4-8   66-69
LITTLE DARLIN' (7000 series) 3-5   78-79
MERCURY 2-5   86

LPs: 10/12–inch 33rpm

ACCORD	5-10	82
ALLEGIANCE	5-10	83
CENTRON	8-15	70
EPIC	5-10	71-83
EXCELSIOR	5-8	80
GUSTO	5-10	83
IMPERIAL	5-10	80
LITTLE DARLIN' (0500 through 0700 series)	5-10	79-80
LITTLE DARLIN' (8000 series)	10-20	66-69
LITTLE DARLIN' (10000 series)	8-12	79
MERCURY	5-8	86
PICKWICK/HILLTOP	5-10	72

Also see HAGGARD, Merle, and Johnny Paycheck
Also see JENNINGS, Waylon / Johnny Paycheck
Also see JONES, George, and Johnny Paycheck
Also see YOUNG, Donny

PAYCHECK, Johnny, and Jody Miller
Singles: 7–inch

EPIC	3-5	72

Also see MILLER, Jody
Also see PAYCHECK, Johnny

PAYNE, Freda
Singles. 12–inch 33/45rpm

CAPITOL	4-8	79

Singles: 7–inch

ABC	3-5	75
ABC-PAR	4-8	62-63
CAPITOL	3-5	77-78
DUNHILL	3-5	74
IMPULSE	4-8	63
INVICTUS	3-6	69-73
MGM	4-8	66
SUTRA	3-5	82

Picture Sleeves

CAPITOL	3-5	77-78
INVICTUS	3-5	71-73

LPs: 10/12–inch 33rpm

ABC	8-10	75
CAPITOL	5-10	78-79
DUNHILL	8-10	74
IMPULSE	15-25	64
INVICTUS	10-15	70-72
MGM	10-20	66-70
U.S.A.	10-15	71

PAYNE, Scherrie
Singles: 12–inch 33/45rpm

MEGATONE	4-6	84

Singles: 7–inch

ALTAIR	3-5	
INVICTUS	3-5	72
MOTOWN	3-5	80
SUPERSTAR INT'L	3-5	

Also see GLASS HOUSE
Also see SUPREMES

PAYTON, Lawrence
Singles: 7–inch

DUNHILL	3-5	73-74

Also see FOUR TOPS

PEACHES & HERB
Singles: 7–inch

COLUMBIA	3-5	71-74
DATE	4-6	66-70
MCA	3-5	77
MERCURY	3-5	73

Picture Sleeves

DATE	4-8	67-68

LPs: 10/12–inch 33rpm

DATE	10-20	67-68
EPIC	8-10	79
MCA	8-10	77

Members: Francine Barker; Herb Fame.

PEACHES & HERB
Singles: 12–inch 33/45rpm

POLYDOR	4-8	78-79

Singles: 7–inch

COLUMBIA	3-5	83
POLYDOR	3-5	78-83

LPs: 10/12–inch 33rpm

POLYDOR	5-10	78-81

Members: Linda Green; Herb Fame.

PEANUT BUTTER CONSPIRACY
Singles: 7–inch

CHALLENGE	5-8	69
COLUMBIA	8-10	67
VAULT	10-15	66

LPs: 10/12–inch 33rpm

CHALLENGE (200 "For Children of All Ages")	20-25	69
COLUMBIA (2654 "Peanut Butter Conspiracy Is Spreading") (Monaural.)	20-25	67
COLUMBIA (2790 "The Great Conspiracy") (Monaural.)	20-30	68
COLUMBIA (9454 "Peanut Butter Conspiracy Is Spreading") (Stereo.)	25-30	68
COLUMBIA (9590 "The Great Conspiracy") (Stereo.)	20-25	68
COLUMBIA (38000 series)	8-10	82

Members: Sandi Robison; Alan Brackett; Lance Fent; Bill Wolf; Jim Voight; John Merrill.

PEANUT BUTTER CONSPIRACY / Ashes / Chambers Brothers
LPs: 10/12–inch 33rpm

VAULT (113 "West Coast Love-In")	15-25	68

Also see CHAMBERS BROTHERS

PEARL, Leslie
Singles: 7–inch

RCA	3-5	82

PEARL HARBOR
(Pearl Harbor and the Explosions)
Singles: 7–Inch
WARNER 3-5   80-81
LPs: 10/12–Inch 33rpm
WARNER 5-10   80-81

PEARLETTES
Singles: 7–inch
CRAIG 8-12   61
VEE JAY 8-10   61-62

PEARLS BEFORE SWINE
Singles: 7–inch
ESP (4554 "Drop Out") 20-30   67
REPRISE 5-10   69-70
LPs: 10/12–inch 33rpm
ADELPHI 5-10   80
ESP 15-25   67-68
REPRISE 10-15   69-71
Members: Tom Rapp; Richard Alderson; Bob Elizabeth; Warren
Smith; Charlie McCoy; Lane Lender; Wayne Harley.

PEARSON, Duke
Singles: 7–inch
BLUE NOTE 4-8   60-66
LPs: 10/12–inch 33rpm
ATLANTIC 10-20   66
BLUE NOTE 25-40   59-61
(Label gives New York street address for Blue Note
Records.)
BLUE NOTE 20-30   63-64
(Label reads "Blue Note Records Inc. - New York,
USA.")
BLUE NOTE 10-20   66-74
(Label shows Blue Note Records as a division of
either Liberty or United Artists.)
PRESTIGE 10-15   70

PEARSON, Mr. Danny
Singles: 7–inch
UNLIMITED GOLD 3-5   78
LPs: 10/12–inch 33rpm
UNLIMITED GOLD 5-10   79

PEBBLES
Singles: 7–inch
MCA 2-4   87-88
LPs: 10/12–inch 33rpm
MCA 5-8   87-90

PEDICIN, Mike
(Michael Pedicin, Jr; Mike Pedicin Quintet)
Singles: 78rpm
CAMEO 5-10   57
MALVERN 10-20   57
RCA 5-10   56
Singles: 12–inch 33/45rpm
PHILADELPHIA INT'L 4-8   79-82
Singles: 7–inch
ABC-PAR 5-10   62

APOLLO (534 "Hey Pop
Give Me the Keys") 25-35   59
CAMEO 5-10   57
FEDERAL 8-12   61
MALVERN (100 "The Dickie-Doo") .. 10-20   57
PHILADELPHIA INT'L 3-5   79-82
RCA 5-10   56
20TH FOX 4-8
EPs: 7–inch 33/45rpm
RCA 15-25   56
("General Electric Flash Blub Limited Edition.")
LPs: 10/12–inch 33rpm
APOLLO (484 "Musical Medicine") .. 50-75   59
PHILADELPHIA INT'L 5-10   79

PEDRICK, Bobby
(Bobby Pedrick Jr.)
Singles: 7–inch
BIG TOP 8-12   58-60
DUEL 5-10   62-63
MGM 4-8   65
SHELL 15-20   60
VERVE (10402 "Maybe") 40-50   66
Also see JOHN, Robert

PEEBLES, Ann
Singles: 7–inch
HI 3-6   69-78
MOTOWN 2-4   82
LPs: 10/12–inch 33rpm
HI 8-12   69-75
MOTOWN 5-8   82

PEEK, Dan
Singles: 7–inch
LAMB and LION 3-5   79
SONGBIRD 3-5   79
Also see AMERICA

PEEK, Paul
Singles: 7–inch
COLUMBIA 4-8   66
FAIRLANE 10-15   61
MERCURY 4-8   62-63
NRC 10-20   58-60
1-2-3 4-6   69

PEEL, David, and the Lower East Side
Singles: 7–inch
APPLE (6498 "F Is Not a Dirty Word")50-100   72
(Promotional issue only.)
APPLE (6545 "Hippie from
New York City") 50-100   72
(Promotional issue only.)
ORANGE 4-6   77
ORANGE PEEL (70078PD "Interview")10-15   80
LPs: 10/12–inch 33rpm
APPLE (3391 "The Pope
Smokes Dope") 40-60   72
ELEKTRA 12-15   68-70
ORANGE 8-12   77

PEEL, David, and the Lower East Side / John Lennon & Yoko Ono
Singles: 7–inch
ORANGE (8374 "Amerika") 3-5   90
(Promotional bonus with book purchase.)
ORANGE (789001 "Ballad of
New York City") 3-5   87
Picture Sleeves
ORANGE (8374 "Amerika") 3-5   90
(Promotional bonus with book purchase.)
Also see LENNON, John
Also see PEEL, David, and the Lower East Side

PEELS
Singles: 7–inch
KARATE 4-8   66
LPs: 10/12-inch 33rpm
KARATE (5402 "Juanita Banana") . . . 55-65   66
(Monaural.)
KARATE (5402 "Juanita Banana") . . . 65-75   66
(Stereo.)

PEEPLES
Singles: 7–inch
MERCURY 2-4   88

PEERCE, Jan
Singles: 7–inch
BLUEBIRD 4-6   60
RCA 5-10   51
U.A. 4-6   63
EPs: 7–inch 33/45rpm
RCA 5-10   51
LPs: 10/12-inch 33rpm
RCA (Except 2900 series) 10-20   51
RCA (2900 series) 5-10   78
U.A. 5-15   63-65
VANGUARD 5-15   63-67

PEGGY LEE: see LEE, Peggy

PENDERGRASS, Teddy
Singles: 12–inch 33/45rpm
PHILADELPHIA INT'L 4-8   78-82
Singles: 7–inch
ASYLUM 2-4   84-88
ELEKTRA 2-4   88-90
PHILADELPHIA INT'L 2-5   77-84
LPs: 10/12-inch 33rpm
ASYLUM 5-8   84-86
ELEKTRA 5-8   88-90
EPIC 5-10   83
PHILADELPHIA INT'L (30000 series,
except JZ-30595) 5-10   77-84
PHILADELPHIA INT'L (JZ-30595 "Life Is
a Song") 20-25   78
(Picture disc. Promotional issue only.)
PHILADELPHIA INT'L (40000
series) 10-15   82
(Half-speed mastered.)
Also see HOUSTON, Whitney
Also see MELVIN, Harold

Also see MILLS, Stephanie, and Teddy Pendergrass
Also see PHILADELPHIA INTERNATIONAL ALL STARS

PENDULUM
Singles: 7–inch
VENTURE 3-5   80
LPs: 10/12–inch 33rpm
VENTURE 5-10   81

PENGUINS
(Penguins Featuring Cleve Duncan; Penquins)
Singles: 78rpm
ATLANTIC 10-20   57
DOOTO 15-25   57
DOOTONE 20-30   54-55
WING 10-15   56
Singles: 7–inch
ATLANTIC (1132 "Pledge of Love") . . 10-20   57
DOOTO (348 "Earth Angel") 8-10   62
(Reissue of DooTONE 348.)
DOOTO (428 "That's How Much
I Need You") 25-30   57
DOOTO (432 "Let Me Make Up
Your Mind") 25-30   58
DOOTO (435 "Do Not Pretend") 25-30   58
(Dootone 345 is found in the following section:
PENGUINS / Dootsie Williams Orchestra.)
DOOTONE (348 "Earth Angel") 50-75   54
(Red label.)
DOOTONE (348 "Earth Angel") 40-50   54
(Maroon label.)
DOOTONE (348 "Earth Angel") 35-45   54
(Blue label.)
DOOTONE (348 "Earth Angel") 20-30   54
(Black label.)
DOOTONE (353 "Love Will Make
Your Mind Go Wild") 40-50   54
(Red label.)
DOOTONE (353 "Love Will Make
Your Mind Go Wild") 30-40   54
(Maroon label.)
DOOTONE (353 "Love Will Make
Your Mind Go Wild") 20-30   54
(Blue label.)
DOOTONE (353 "Love Will Make
Your Mind Go Wild") 15-20   54
(Black label.)
DOOTONE (362 "Kiss a
Fool Goodbye") 20-40   55
GLENVILLE 4-6
MERCURY (70610 "Be Mine Or
Be a Fool") 20-30   55
MERCURY (70654 "It Only Happens
with You") 20-25   55
MERCURY (70703 "Devil That
I See") 20-30   55
MERCURY (70762 "Christmas
Prayer") 40-50   55

MERCURY (70799 "My Troubles Are
Not at an End") 25-35   56
(Maroon label.)
MERCURY (70799 "My Troubles Are
Not at an End") 15-20   56
(Black label.)
MERCURY (70943 "Earth Angel") . . . 20-25   56
MERCURY (71033 "Will You Be Mine")15-25   57
ORIGINAL SOUND (27 "Memories of
El Monte") 30-40   63
ORIGINAL SOUND (54 "Heavenly
Angel") 15-25   63
POWER 4-8
SUN STATE (001 "Believe Me") 10-20   62
WING (90076 "Peace of Mind") 15-20   56
Picture Sleeves
POWER 5-10
EPs: 7-inch 33/45rpm
DOOTO (241/243/244 "Cool, Cool
Penguins") 15-25   59
(Price is for any of three volumes.)
DOOTONE (201 "The Penguins") . . 50-100   55
LPs: 10/12-inch 33rpm
DOOTO (242 "Cool, Cool
Penguins") 150-250   59
(Yellow label with red lettering. Full-color cover.)
DOOTO 10-15
(Multi-color label.)
Members: Cleve Duncan; Curtis Williams; Dexter Tisby; Bruce
Tate; Randy Jones; Ted Harper; Walter Saulsberry.
Also see JULIAN, Don, and the Meadowlarks
Also see VICEROYS

PENGUINS / Dootsie Williams Orchestra
Singles: 78rpm
DOOTONE (345 "Nore Ain't No
News Today") 20-40   54
Singles: 7-inch
DOOTONE (345 "Nore Ain't No
News Today") 75-100   54

PENGUINS / Meadowlarks / Medallions / Dootones
LPs: 10/12-inch 33rpm
DOOTONE (204 "Best in
Rhythm and Blues") 50-80   57
(Flat maroon label.)
DOOTONE (204 "Best in
Rhythm and Blues") 10-20
(Glossy label. Colored vinyl pressings are
bootlegs.)
Also see PENGUINS

PENGUINS
Singles: 7-inch
DONNA 10-15   61
ERIC 2-4
FLEET INT'L (100 "To Be Loved") . . . 50-75   60
JAMIE 10-15   61-62
SPECIALTY 10-20   58

PENTAGONS / Earl Phillips
Singles: 7-inch
OLDIES 45 4-6   64
Also see PENTAGONS

PENTANGLE
Singles: 7-inch
REPRISE 4-8   68-69
TRANSATLANTIC 4-6
LPs: 10/12-inch 33rpm
REPRISE 10-20   68-72
Members: Jacqui McShee; Bert Jansch; Danny Thompson; John
Renbourn; Terry Cox.

PEOPLE
Singles: 7-inch
CAPITOL 5-10   67-69
PARAMOUNT 4-8   69-70
POLYDOR 3-5   71
ZEBRA (102 "Come Back Beatles") . . 5-10   78
(Includes a note suggesting the Beatles reunite.)
LPs: 10/12-inch 33rpm
CAPITOL 20-30   68-69
PARAMOUNT 10-20   69-70
Members: Larry Norman; Robb Levin; Tom Tucker; John Tristao;
Gene Mason; Geoff Levin.

PEOPLE'S CHOICE
Singles: 7-inch
CASABLANCA 3-5   80
PALMER 4-8   67
PHIL-L.A. of SOUL 3-5   71-73
PHILADELPHIA INT'L 3-5   71
PHILIPS 4-6   69
TSOP 3-5   74-77
LPs: 10/12-inch 33rpm
CASABLANCA 5-10   80
DECCA 10-15   69
PHILADELPHIA INT'L 5-10   78
TSOP 8-10   75-76
Members: Roger Andrews; Guy Fiske; David Thompson; Bob
Eli; Frankie Brunson.
Also see MFSB

PEPPERMINT, Danny, and the Jumping Jacks
Singles: 7-inch
CARLTON 5-10   61
LPs: 10/12-inch 33rpm
CARLTON (LP-20001 "Danny
Peppermint") 25-35   62
(Monaural.)
CARLTON (STLP-20001 "Danny
Peppermint") 35-50   62
(Stereo.)
Member: Danny Lamego.

PEPPERMINT HARRIS
(Peppermint Harris with Cross Town Blues Band;
Harrison Nelson)
Singles: 78rpm
ALADDIN 10-20   51-52
CASH 10-15   54
MODERN 10-15   51

MONEY 10-15   54
SITTIN' in WITH 5-10   50-51
X 15-25   55
Singles: 7–inch
ALADDIN (3097 "I Got Loaded") 30-50   51
(Black vinyl.)
ALADDIN (3097 "I Got Loaded") .. 100-200   51
(Colored vinyl.)
ALADDIN (3107 "Have Another Drink
and Talk to Me") 30-50   51
ALADDIN (3108 "P. H. Blues") 30-50   51
ALADDIN (3130 "Right Back On") ... 30-50   52
ALADDIN (3141 "There's a Dead
Cat on the Line") 30-50   52
ALADDIN (3154 "I Sure Do Miss
My Baby") 30-50   51
ALADDIN (3177 "Wasted Love") 30-50   51
ALADDIN (3183 "Don't Leave
Me All Alone") 30-50   53
ALADDIN (3206 "I Never Get
Enough of You") 30-50   51
CASH (1003 "Cadillac Funeral") ... 25-45   54
DART 10-15   60
DUKE 10-15   60
JEWEL 4-8   65-68
LUNAR 3-5
MODERN (936 "Bye, Bye, Fare
Thee Well") 25-45   51
MONEY (214 "Cadillac Funeral") 25-45   54
SITTIN' in WITH (543 "Rainin' in
My Heart") 50-90   51
X (0142 "I Need Your Lovin') 50-75   55
LPs: 10/12–inch 33rpm
TIME (5 "Peppermint Harris") 35-45   62
Also see REED, Jimmy / Peppermint Harris

PEPPERMINT RAINBOW
Singles: 7–inch
DECCA 4-6   68-69
Picture Sleeves
DECCA 4-8   69
LPs: 10/12–inch 33rpm
DECCA 10-20   69

PEPPERMINT TROLLEY COMPANY
Singles: 7–inch
ACTA 8-12   67-68
VALIANT 10-15   66
LPs: 10/12–inch 33rpm
ACTA 15-20   68

PEPPERS
Singles: 7–inch
BIG TREE 3-5   75
EVENT 3-5   74-75
LPs: 10/12–inch 33rpm
EVENT 8-12   74

PEPSI & SHIRLIE
Singles: 7–inch
POLYDOR 2-4   87

LPs: 10/12–inch 33rpm
POLYDOR 5-8   88

PERCELLS
Singles: 7–inch
ABC-PAR 5-10   63-64

PERCY & THEM
Singles: 7–inch
PLAYBOY 3-5   73

PERFECT, Christine
(Christine McVie)
Singles: 7–inch
EPIC 4-8   69
LPs: 10/12–inch 33rpm
SIRE (6000 series) 5-8   77
SIRE (7000 series) 8-10   76
Also see McVIE, Christine

PERICOLI, Emilio
Singles: 7–inch
VESUVIUS 4-6   62
WARNER 4-6   62-63
Picture Sleeves
WARNER 4-6   62
LPs: 10/12–inch 33rpm
WARNER 10-20   63-66
VESUVIUS 10-20   62

PERKINS, Al
Singles: 7–inch
ATCO 4-6   69-70
HI 3-5   72
U.S.A. 4-8   64-65

PERKINS, Carl
(Carl Perkins and the C.P. Express)
Singles: 78rpm
FLIP (501 "Movie Magg") 100-200   55
SUN (224 "Gone Gone Gone") 20-30   56
SUN (234 through 287) 10-20   56-57
Singles: 7–inch
AMERICA/SMASH 3-5   86
COLUMBIA (3-41000 and 3-42000
series) 20-40   60-62
(Compact 33 Singles.)
COLUMBIA (4-41000 through 4-43000
series) 10-20   58-64
COLUMBIA (4-44000 and 4-45000
series) 5-10   64-72
DECCA 5-10   63-64
DOLLIE 5-10   67
FLIP (501 "Movie Magg") 300-400   55
JET 3-5   79
MERCURY 4-6   73-77
SSS/SUN 3-5
SUN (224 "Gone Gone Gone") 45-60   56
SUN (234 through 287) 15-25   56-58
Picture Sleeves
COLUMBIA (41131 "Pink
Pedal Pushers") 25-45   58

COLUMBIA (42405 "Hollywood
City") 20-30   62
COLUMBIA (42514 "Hambone") 40-60   62
EPs: 7–inch 33/45rpm
COLUMBIA (12341 "Whole Lotta
Shakin") 200-300   58
SUN (115 "Blue Suede Shoes") ... 100-200   58
LPs: 10/12–inch 33rpm
ACCORD 5-10   82
ALBUM GLOBE 8-12
ALLEGIANCE 5-10   84
COLUMBIA (1234 "Whole Lotta
Shakin") 100-200   58
COLUMBIA (9800 series) 10-20   69
DESIGN 10-15
DOLLIE 10-20   67
GRT/SUNNYVALE 8-12   77
HARMONY 8-12   72
JET 8-10   78
KOALA 5-10   80
MERCURY 8-12   73
ROUNDER 5-10   89
SSS/SUN 5-10   69-84
SUEDE 8-10   81
SUN (1225 "Dance Album") 500-750   57
SUN (1225 "Teen Beat") 200-250   61
(Repackage of *Dance Album*.)
TRIP 8-10   74
UNIVERSAL 5-10   89
TRIP 8-12   74
　Also see McCARTNEY, Paul
　Also see NELSON, Willie / Jerry Lee Lewis / Carl Perkins /
　　David Allan Coe
　Also see YOUNG, Faron / Carl Perkins / Claude King

PERKINS, Carl / Sonny Burgess
LPs: 10/12–inch 33rpm
SSS/SUN 5-10

**PERKINS, Carl, Jerry Lee Lewis, Roy
Orbison & Johnny Cash**
LPs: 10/12–inch 33rpm
AMERICA 20-30   86
(Mail-order edition. Has souvenir booklet and audio
cassette with interviews of the singers.)
AMERICA/SMASH 5-10   86
　Also see CASH, Johnny, Carl Perkins & Jerry Lee Lewis
　Also see LEWIS, Jerry Lee, Carl Perkins & Charlie Rich
　Also see ORBISON, Roy

PERKINS, Carl, and NRBQ
Singles: 7–inch
COLUMBIA 3-5   70
LPs: 10/12–inch 33rpm
COLUMBIA 10-15   70
　Also see NRBQ
　Also see PERKINS, Carl

PERKINS, George
(George Perkins and the Silver Stars)
Singles: 7–inch
SILVER FOX 4-8   69
SOUL POWER 3-6   72

LPs: 10/12–inch 33rpm
CRYIN' in the STREETS 8-12   77

PERKINS, Joe
Singles: 7–inch
BERRY 4-8
MUSICOR 4-8   65
SOUND STAGE 7 4-8   63

PERKINS, Tony
Singles: 78rpm
RCA 5-10   57
Singles: 7–inch
RCA 8-12   57
Picture Sleeves
RCA 10-20   57
LPs: 10/12–inch 33rpm
EPIC (3394 "Tony Perkins") 25-35   57
RCA (1679 "From My Heart") 20-30   58
RCA (LPM-1853 "On a
Rainy Afternoon") 20-30   58
RCA (LSP-1853 "On a
Rainy Afternoon") 30-40   58

PERKINS, Tony / James Dean
Singles: 78rpm
RAINBO (5-21-57 "Dean and
Perkins") 30-50   57
(Flexi, picture disc.)
　Also see PERKINS, Tony

PERRY, Greg
Singles: 7–inch
ALFA 2-4   82
CASABLANCA 3-5   74-75
CHESS 4-8   68
RCA 3-5   77
LPs: 10/12–inch 33rpm
CASABLANCA 8-12   75

PERRY, Jeff
Singles: 7–inch
ARISTA 3-5   75-76
EPIC 3-5   77

PERRY, Joe, Project
Singles: 7–inch
COLUMBIA 3-5   80-81
LPs: 10/12–inch 33rpm
COLUMBIA 5-10   80-81
MCA 4-8   83
　Also see AEROSMITH

PERRY, Linda
Singles: 7–inch
MAINSTREAM 3-5   73

PERRY, Roxy
Singles: 12–inch 33/45rpm
PERSONAL 4-6   83

PERRY, Steve
Singles: 7–inch
COLUMBIA 2-4   84-85

LPs: 10/12–inch 33rpm

COLUMBIA 5-8   84-85
   Also see JOURNEY
   Also see LOGGINS, Kenny, and Steve Perry
   Also see U.S.A. for AFRICA

PERRY & SANLIN
Singles: 7–inch

CAPITOL 3-5   80

LPs: 10/12–inch 33rpm

CAPITOL 5-10   80

PERSIANS
Singles: 7–inch

ABC 4-8   68
CAPITOL 3-5   71-72
GWP 3-6   69-70

PERSON, Houston
Singles: 7–inch

WESTBOUND 3-5   75-76

PERSUADERS
Singles: 7–inch

ATCO 4-8   71-75
CALLA 3-5   77
WIN OR LOSE 3-5   71-72

LPs: 10/12–inch 33rpm

ATCO 8-12   73-74
CALLA 8-10   77
WIN OR LOSE 10-15   72

PERSUASIONS
Singles: 7–inch

A&M 3-5   74-75
CAPITOL 3-5   71-72
CATAMOUNT 3-5
MCA 3-5   73
REPRISE 3-5   70
TOWER 4-8   65-66

LPs: 10/12–inch 33rpm

A&M 10-15   74
CAPITOL 10-20   71-72
ELEKTRA 10-12   77
FLYING FISH 5-10   79
MCA 8-12   73
ROUNDER 5-8
STRAIGHT 15-25   70
   Members: Jerry Lawson; Jimmy Hayes; Jayotis Washington; Joe
   Russell; Herb Rhoad.

PET SHOP BOYS
Singles: 12–inch 33/45rpm

EMI 4-6 86-87

Singles: 7–inch

EMI 2-4 86-90

LPs: 10/12–inch 33rpm

EMI 5-8 86-90
   Members: Neil Tennant; Chris Lowe.
   Also see SPRINGFIELD, Dusty

PETER & GORDON
Singles: 7–inch

CAPITOL 4-8   64-69

Picture Sleeves

CAPITOL 5-10   64-67

LPs: 10/12–inch 33rpm

CAPITOL (T-2115 through T-2882) .. 10-20   64-68
   (Monaural.)
CAPITOL (ST-2115 through ST-2882) 12-25   64-68
   (Stereo.)
CAPITOL (SM-2549 "Best of
   Peter & Gordon") 5-10   77
CAPITOL (SN-16084 "Best of
   Peter & Gordon") 5-8   80
   Members: Peter Asher; Gordon Waller.

PETER & GORDON / Lettermen
Singles: 7–inch

CAPITOL CREATIVE PRODUCTS ... 5-10   66
   (Fritos Company promotional issue.)
   Also see LETTERMEN
   Also see PETER & GORDON

PETER, PAUL & MARY
Singles: 7–inch

"EUGENE McCARTHY for
   PRESIDENT" 10-20   68
   (Promotional issue only. No label name used.)
WARNER (5000 series) 4-8   62-66
WARNER (7000 series) 3-6   67-70

Picture Sleeves

WARNER 4-8   62-64

EPs: 7–inch 33/45rpm

WARNER 5-10   63-64
   (Jukebox issues only.)

LPs: 10/12–inch 33rpm

GOLD C. 5-8   87
WARNER (1449 through 1648) 20-30   62-66
   (Quality of pressing is vital to grading with this
   Warner series. Poor fidelity pressings, regardless
   of visual grade, cannot be considered near-mint.)
WARNER (1700 through 2552) 8-15   67-70
   (Gold or gray labels.)
WARNER (3000 series) 5-10   77-78
   Members: Peter Yarrow; Paul Stookey; Mary Travers.
   Also see STOOKEY, Paul
   Also see TRAVERS, Mary
   Also see YARROW, Peter

PETERS, Bernadette
Singles: 7–inch

ABC-PAR 4-8   65
COLUMBIA 4-8   67
MCA 3-5   78-81
U.A. 5-10   62

Picture Sleeves

MCA 3-5   80-81

LPs: 10/12–inch 33rpm

MCA 5-10   80-81

PETERSEN, Paul
Singles: 7–inch

ABC 3-5   74
COLPIX (Except 720) 5-10   62-65

COLPIX (720 "She Rides with Me") .. 25-35   64
(With the Beach Boys.)
ERIC 2-4
MCA 2-4
MOTOWN 4-6   67-68
Picture Sleeves
COLPIX (663 "My Dad") 10-15   62
LPs: 10/12–inch 33rpm
COLPIX (CP-429 "Lollipops
and Roses") 15-25   62
(Monaural.)
COLPIX (SCP-429 "Lollipops
and Roses") 25-35   62
(Stereo.)
COLPIX (CP-442 "My Dad") 15-25   63
(Monaural.)
COLPIX (SCP-442 "My Dad") 25-35   63
(Stereo.)
  Also see BEACH BOYS
  Also see DARREN, James / Shelly Fabares / Paul Petersen

PETERSEN, Paul, and Shelly Fabares
Singles: 7–inch
COLPIX 5-10   62
  Also see FABARES, Shelly
  Also see PETERSEN, Paul

PETERSON, Bobby
(Bobby Peterson Quintet)
Singles: 7–inch
ATLANTIC 4-8   62
V-TONE 5-10   59-60

PETERSON, Lucky, Blues Band
Singles: 7–inch
TODAY 3-5   71
LPs: 10/12–inch 33rpm
TODAY 10-15   71

PETERSON, Oscar
(Oscar Peterson Trio)
Singles: 78rpm
CLEF 4-6   53-56
MERCURY 4-8   51-52
NORGRAN 4-6   55
VERVE 4-8   57
Singles: 7–inch
CLEF 5-10   53-56
LIMELIGHT 4-6   65-66
MERCURY (8900 series) 5-10   51-52
MERCURY (72000 series) 4-6   64
MERCURY (89000 series) 5-10   52-53
NORGRAN 5-10   55
PRESTIGE 4-6   69
VERVE 4-8   57-64
EPs: 7–inch 33/45rpm
CLEF 20-40   52-53
RCA (3006 "This Is Oscar Peterson") 75-125   51
LPs: 10/12–inch 33rpm
BASF 8-12   74-76
CLEF (106 "Piano Solos") 100-150   52
(10–inch LP.)

CLEF (107 "At Carnegie Hall") 100-150   52
(10–inch LP.)
CLEF (110 "Collates") 100-150   52
(10–inch LP.)
CLEF (116 "Oscar Peterson
Quartet") 100-150   52
(10–inch LP.)
CLEF (119 "Oscar Peterson
Plays Pretty") 100-150   52
(10–inch LP.)
CLEF (127 "Collates, No. 2") 75-125   53
(10–inch LP.)
CLEF (145 "Oscar Peterson
Sings") 75-125   54
(10–inch LP.)
CLEF (155 "Oscar Peterson
Plays Pretty, No. 2") 75-125   54
(10–inch LP.)
CLEF (168 "Oscar Peterson
Quartet, No. 2") 75-125   55
(10–inch LP.)
CLEF (600 series) 50-75   53-56
EMARCY 8-12   76
LIMELIGHT (1000 series) 5-8   82
LIMELIGHT (82000 and 86000 series) 10-20   65-67
MGM (100 series) 8-12   70
MPS 8-12   72-76
MERCURY (20975 "Trio+One") 20-30   64
(Monaural.)
MERCURY (60975 "Trio+One") 25-35   64
(Stereo.)
METRO 10-15   65
PABLO 6-12   75-83
PAUSA 5-10   79-81
PRESTIGE 8-15   69-74
RCA (3006 "This Is
Oscar Peterson") 200-250   51
(10–inch LP.)
TRIP 5-8   75-76
VSP 10-20   66-67
VERVE 25-50   56-60
(Reads "Verve Records, Inc." at bottom of label.)
VERVE 10-25   61-72
(Reads "MGM Records - A Division of
Metro-Goldwyn-Mayer, Inc." at bottom of label.)
VERVE 5-15   73-83
(Reads "Manufactured By MGM Record Corp.," or
mentions either Polydor or Polygram at bottom of
label.)
WING 8-12   67
  Also see ARMSTRONG, Louis, and Oscar Peterson
  Also see BASIE, Count, and Oscar Peterson
  Also see FITZGERALD, Ella, and Oscar Peterson
  Also see GETZ, Stan, and Oscar Peterson
  Also see HUBBARD, Freddie, and Oscar Peterson
  Also see MULLIGAN, Gerry, and Oscar Peterson
  Also see RIDDLE, Nelson

PETERSON, Ray
Singles: 7–inch
CLOUD 9 3-5   75

DECCA 3-5	71
DUNES 5-10	60-63
MGM 4-8	64-66
POLYDOR 3-5	
RCA (47-7000 series) 10-15	58-60
RCA (47-8000 series) 4-8	64
RCA (61-7578 "My Blue Angel") 15-25	60
(Stereo.)	
RCA (61-7745 "Tell Laura I Love Her") 15-25	60
(Stereo.)	
RCA (61-7779 "Teenage Heartache") 15-25	60
(Stereo.)	
REPRISE 4-6	69
UNI 3-5	70

Picture Sleeves

DUNES (2002 "Corrina Corrina") 8-12	60
MGM (13269 "Oh No") 5-10	64
MGM (13336 "House Without	
Windows") 5-10	64
RCA (7635 "Goodnight My Love") 8-12	59

EPs: 7–inch 33/45rpm

RCA (4367 "Tell Laura I Love Her") . . 40-60	60

LPs: 10/12–inch 33rpm

CAMDEN 10-20	66
DECCA 8-12	71
MGM 20-30	64-65
RCA (LPM-2297 "Tell Laura	
I Love Her") 40-60	60
(Monaural.)	
RCA (LSP-2297 "Tell Laura	
I Love Her") 60-80	60
(Stereo.)	
UNI 10-15	70

PETITE
Singles: 7–inch

YORK'S 2-4	86

PETS
Singles: 78rpm

ARWIN 5-10	58

Singles: 7–inch

ARWIN 5-10	58
Member: Seph Acre.	

PETTUS, Giorge
Singles: 7–inch

MCA 2-4	87-88

PETTY, Frank, Trio
Singles: 78rpm

MGM 3-5	50-57

Singles: 7–inch

MGM 4-8	50-57

EPs: 7–inch 33/45rpm

MGM 5-10	50-57

LPs: 10/12–inch 33rpm

MGM 10-20	50-57

PETTY, Norman, Trio
Singles: 78rpm

ABC-PAR 4-8	57

COLUMBIA (Except 41039) 4-8	57
COLUMBIA (41039 "Moondreams") . 25-50	57
(With Buddy Holly on guitar.)	
NOR VA JAK 5-10	57
X 4-6	54-55

Singles: 7–inch

ABC-PAR 5-10	57
COLUMBIA (Except 41039) 5-10	57
COLUMBIA (41039 "Moondreams") . 40-60	57
(With Buddy Holly on guitar.)	
FELSTED 4-8	62
JARO 5-10	60
NOR VA JAK (Except 1325) 15-20	57-59
NOR VA JAK (1325 "True Love	
Ways") 25-35	60
NORMAN 5-10	60
X 5-10	54-55

EPs: 7–inch 33/45rpm

COLUMBIA (2139 "Four Hits") 15-25	58
COLUMBIA (10921 "Moondreams") 50-100	58
X 15-25	55

LPs: 10/12–inch 33rpm

COLUMBIA (1092 "Moondreams") . 50-100	58
TOP RANK (R-639 "Petty for	
Your Thoughts") 20-30	60
(Monaural.)	
TOP RANK (RS-639 "Petty for	
Your Thoughts") 30-40	60
(Stereo.)	
VIK (1073 "Corsage") 30-45	57
Members: Norman Petty; Vi Petty; Jack Petty.	
Also see HOLLY, Buddy	

PETTY, Tom, and the Heartbreakers
Singles: 7–inch

BACKSTREET 2-5	79-83
MCA 2-4	85-87
SHELTER 3-5	77-78

Picture Sleeves

BACKSTREET 2-5	79-83
MCA 2-4	85
SHELTER 3-5	77-78

LPs: 10/12–inch 33rpm

BACKSTREET 5-10	79-82
MCA 5-8	85-87
SHELTER 8-15	76-78

Promotional LPs

SHELTER (12677 "Official Live 'Leg") 15-25	76
SHELTER (52029 "You're Gonna	
Get It") 15-25	78
(Colored vinyl.)	
Also see DYLAN, Bob, and the Heartbreakers / Michael Rubini	
Also see NICKS, Stevie, and Tom Petty and the Heartbreakers	
Also see TRAVELING WILBURYS	

PHANTOM LIMBS
LPs: 10/12–inch 33rpm

ROMANCE 5-8	83-86
Members: Jim Parks; Jeff Keenan; Peter "Splat" Catalanotte.	

PHANTOM, ROCKER & SLICK
Singles: 7–inch
EMI AMERICA 3-5   85-86
LPs: 10/12–inch 33rpm
EMI AMERICA 5-10   85-86
Members: Jim Phantom; Lee Rocker; Earl Slick.
Also see STRAY CATS

PHELPS, James
(Jimmy Phelps and the Du-Ettes)
Singles: 7–inch
ARGO 4-8   65
CADET 4-8   66
FONTANA 4-8   66-67
MECCA 5-10   60
PARAMOUNT 3-5   71-72

PHILADELPHIA INTERNATIONAL ALL STARS
Singles: 7–inch
PHILADELPHIA INT'L 3-5   77
Members: Archie Bell; the O'Jays; Billy Paul; Teddy
Pendergrass; Lou Rawls; Dee Dee Sharpe.
Also see BELL, Archie
Also see MFSB
Also see O'JAYS
Also see PAUL, Billy
Also see PENDERGRASS, Teddy
Also see RAWLS, Lou
Also see SHARPE, Dee Dee

PHILADELPHIA STORY
Singles: 7–inch
H&L 3-5   77

PHILHARMONICS
Singles: 7–inch
CAPRICORN 3-5   77
LPs: 10/12–inch 33rpm
CAPRICORN 5-10   77

PHILLINGANES, Greg
Singles: 12–inch 33/45rpm
PLANET 4-6   85
Singles: 7–inch
PLANET 2-4   81-85
LPs: 10/12–inch 33rpm
PLANET 5-8   81-85

PHILLIPS, Anthony
Singles: 7–inch
PASSPORT 3-5   77-78
LPs: 10/12–inch 33rpm
PASSPORT 5-10   77-78
Also see GENESIS

PHILLIPS, Bill, and Dolly Parton
Singles: 7–inch
DECCA (31901 "Put It
Off Until Tomorrow") 5-10   66
LPs: 10/12–inch 33rpm
DECCA (4792 "Put It
Off Until Tomorrow") 15-20   66
(Monaural.)

DECCA (74792 "Put It
Off Until Tomorrow") 20-25   66
(Stereo.)
Also see PARTON, Dolly

PHILLIPS, Esther, and Joe Beck
LPs: 10/12–inch 33rpm
KUDU 8-10   76
Also see BECK, Joe
Also see LITTLE ESTHER

PHILLIPS, John
Singles: 7–inch
ATCO 3-5   74
COLUMBIA 3-5   73
DUNHILL 3-5   70
LPs: 10/12–inch 33rpm
DUNHILL 10-15   70
Also see MAMAS and the Papas

PHILLIPS, Little Esther:
see LITTLE ESTHER

PHILLIPS, Phil
(Phil Phillips with the Twilights)
Singles: 7–inch
CLIQUE 4-8   66
KHOURY'S (711 "Sea of Love") 60-90   59
MERCURY (10021 "Verdi Mae") 10-20   59
(Stereo.)
MERCURY (71000 series) 5-10   59-61

PHILLIPS, Shawn
Singles: 7–inch
A&M 3-5   70-75
ASCOT 4-8   64
LPs: 10/12–inch 33rpm
A&M 8-12   70-77
RCA 5-10   78-81

PHILLIPS, Stu
Singles: 7–inch
CAPITOL 3-5   73
COLPIX 10-20   62
MCA 3-5   78
PARAGON 3-5   76
SMASH 8-12   66
Also see HOLLYRIDGE STRINGS

PHILLIPS, Wes
Singles: 12–inch 33/45rpm
QUALITY 4-6   84
Singles: 7–inch
QUALITY 2-4   84

PHILLY CREAM
Singles: 12–inch 33/45rpm
WMOT 4-8   79
Singles: 7–inch
FANTASY 3-5   79
WMOT 3-5   79
LPs: 10/12–inch 33rpm
WMOT 5-10   79

PHILLY DEVOTIONS
Singles: 7–inch
COLUMBIA 3-5   75-76

PHOTOGLO, Jim
(Photoglo)
Singles: 7–inch
CASABLANCA 3-5   83
20TH FOX 3-5   80-81
LPs: 10/12–inch 33rpm
CASABLANCA 5-10   83
20TH FOX 5-10   80-81

PIAF, Edith
Singles: 78rpm
CAPITOL 4-8   56-58
COLUMBIA 4-8   50-52
Singles: 7–inch
CAPITOL 5-10   56-61
COLUMBIA 5-10   50-52
EPs: 7–inch 33/45rpm
ANGEL 5-15
COLUMBIA 5-15   50-52
DECCA (6000 series) 5-15
LPs: 10/12–inch 33rpm
ANGEL 20-40   55-56
CAPITOL 5-20   59-82
COLUMBIA (Except 37000 series) ... 20-40   50-56
COLUMBIA (37000 series) 5-10   81
DECCA (6000 series) 20-40   54
DISCOS 20-30   56
PHILIPS 10-20   64-67
RCA 10-15   64
VOX 20-40   53

PIANO RED
(Willie Perryman)
Singles: 78rpm
CHECKER 10-20   58
GROOVE 10-15   54-57
RCA 10-20   50-57
Singles: 7–inch
CHECKER (911 "Get Up Mare") 15-25   58
GROOVE 10-30   54-57
JAX 8-12   59
RCA (0099 "Rockin' with Red") 50-75   50
(Colored vinyl.)
RCA (0106 "The Wrong YoYo") 25-50   50
RCA (0118 "Jumpin' the Boogie") ... 25-50   51
RCA (0130 "Baby What's Wrong") ... 25-50   51
RCA (4265 "Let's Have a Good Time") 25-50   51
RCA (4380 "Hey Good Lookin") 25-50   51
RCA (4524 "Bouncin' with Red") ... 25-50   52
RCA (4766 "Sales Tax Boogie") 25-50   52
RCA (4957 "Voo Doopee Doo") 25-50   52
RCA (5101 "I'm Gonna
Rock Some More") 20-35   52
RCA (5224 "I'm Gonna
Tell Everybody") 20-35   53
RCA (5337 "Your Mouth's Got a Hole") 20-35   52

RCA (5544 "Right and Ready") 20-35   52
RCA (6000 and 7000 series) 15-25   57-58
EPs: 7–inch 33/45rpm
GROOVE (3 "Jump Man, Jump") 40-60   56
GROOVE (10026/27/28 "Piano Red
in Concert") 35-50   56
(Price is for any of three volumes.)
RCA (587 "Rockin' with Red") 50-100   54
RCA (5091 "Rockin' with Red") 40-60   59
(Black label.)
RCA (5091 "Rockin' with Red") 50-100   59
(Maroon label.)
LPs: 10/12–inch 33rpm
ARHOOLIE 8-10
BLACK LION 8-10   76
GROOVE (1002 "Piano Red
in Concert") 150-250   56
KING 10-15   70
RCA 8-10   74

PICKETT, Bobby
(Bobby "Boris" Pickett and the Crypt-Kickers)
Singles: 12–inch 33/45rpm
EASY STREET 4-8   84
Singles: 7–inch
ANTHEM 3-5
ATMOSPHERE 5-10   65
CAPITOL 5-10   63-64
EASY STREET 3-5   84
GARPAX (1 "Monster Mash") 8-12   62
GARPAX (724 "I'm Down to
My Last Heartbreak") 5-10
GARPAX (44000 series) 5-10   62-64
LONDON 3-5
METROMEDIA (0089 "Me and My
Mummy") 4-8   68
METROMEDIA (9989 "Me and My
Mummy") 3-6   73
PARROT 4-8   70-73
RCA 5-10   64
WHITE WHALE 4-8   70
Picture Sleeves
GARPAX 10-20   62-63
LPs: 10/12–inch 33rpm
GARPAX (GP-67001 "Monster Mash") 30-50   62
(Monaural.)
GARPAX (SGP-67001 "Monster
Mash") 50-75   62
(Stereo.)
PARROT 10-20   73

PICKETT, Wilson
Singles: 7–inch
ATLANTIC (2200 through 2400 series) . 4-8   64-67
ATLANTIC (2500 through 2900 series) . 3-6   68-72
BIG TREE 3-5   78
CORREC-TONE (501 "Let Me
Be Your Boy") 25-45   62
CUB 10-15   62
DOUBLE-L 5-10   63

EMI AMERICA	3-5	79-81
MOTOWN	2-4	87
RCA	3-5	73-74
ROWE/AMI	5-10	66
("Play Me" Sales Stimulator promotional issue.)		
VERVE	4-8	65
WICKED	3-5	75-76

LPs: 10/12-inch 33rpm

ATLANTIC (Except 8100 series)	10-15	69-73
ATLANTIC (8100 series)	15-20	65-68
BIG TREE	5-10	78
BROOKVILLE	8-12	77
DOUBLE-L (DL-8300 "It's Too Late")	25-35	63
(Monaural.)		
DOUBLE-L (SDL-8300 "It's Too Late")	30-40	63
(Stereo.)		
EMI AMERICA	5-10	79-81
RCA	8-12	73-77
WAND	10-15	68
WICKED	8-12	76
Also see FALCONS		

PICKETT, Wilson / Sam and Dave
LPs: 10/12-inch 33rpm

ATLANTIC (ST-136 "Excerpts from *Hey Jude*)	15-25	69
(Promotional issue for in-store use.)		
Also see PICKETT, Wilson		
Also see SAM & DAVE		

PICKETTYWITCH
Singles: 7-inch

JANUS	3-5	70
PYE	3-5	71

LPs: 10/12-inch 33rpm

JANUS	8-12	70
Member: Polly Brown.		
Also see BROWN, Polly		

PICTURE PERFECT
Singles: 7-inch

ATLANTIC	2-4	87

PIECES of a DREAM
Singles: 12-inch 33/45rpm

ELEKTRA	4-6	84

Singles: 7-inch

ELEKTRA	3-5	81-84
MANHATTAN	2-4	88

LPs: 10/12-inch 33rpm

ELEKTRA	5-10	81-84
MANHATTAN	5-8	86

PIECES of EIGHT
Singles: 7-inch

A&M	5-10	67-68
ACTION	5-10	
MALA	5-10	68
Also see SWINGIN' MEDALLIONS		

PIERCE, Webb
Singles: 78rpm

DECCA	5-10	51-52

4 STAR	8-12	51-52

Singles: 7-inch

DECCA (28000 through 30000 series)	10-20	52-59
DECCA (31000 through 33000 series)	4-8	59-73
DECCA (46000 series)	8-12	51-52
4 STAR	10-15	51-52
KING	5-10	60
MCA	3-5	73-74
PLANTATION	3-5	75-77
SOUNDWAVES	2-4	83

EPs: 7-inch 33/45rpm

DECCA	10-20	53-65

LPs: 10/12-inch 33rpm

CORAL	5-10	73
DECCA (181 "Webb Pierce Story")	20-30	64
(Includes booklet.)		
DECCA (DL-4015 "Webb with a Beat")	25-35	60
(Monaural.)		
DECCA (DL7-4015 "Webb with a Beat")	3050	60
(Stereo.)		
DECCA (DL-4079 through 4964)	10-25	60-67
DECCA (DL7-4079 through 4964)	15-30	60-67
DECCA (5536 "Wandering Boy")	40-60	53
(10 Inch LP.)		
DECCA (8129 "Webb Pierce")	30-50	55
DECCA (8295 "Wandering Boy")	30-50	56
DECCA (8728 "Just Imagination")	30-50	57
DECCA (DL-8889 "Bound for the Kingdom")	20-25	59
(Monaural.)		
DECCA (DL7-8889 "Bound for the Kingdom")	25-35	59
(Stereo.)		
DECCA (DL-8899 "Webb!")	25-35	59
(Monaural.)		
DECCA (DL7-8899 "Webb!")	30-40	59
(Stereo.)		
DECCA (74000 series)	8-12	68
ERA	8-10	77
KING (648 "The One and Only Webb Pierce")	35-50	59
MCA	5-12	73-78
PICKWICK/HILLTOP	10-15	65
PLANTATION	5-8	76-77
SEARS	8-12	
SKYLITE	5-8	77
VOCALION	5-15	66-70
Also see NELSON, Willie, and Webb Pierce		

PIERCE, Webb / Loretta Lynn
LPs: 10/12-inch 33rpm

PHILCO/MCA	15-25	69
Also see LYNN, Loretta		

PIERCE, Webb / Wynn Stewart
LPs: 10/12-inch 33rpm

DESIGN	10-20	62
Also see STEWART, Wynn		

LPs: 10/12–inch 33rpm

ELEKTRA 5-10   79
Members: Mie; Kei.

PIPEDREAM
Singles: 12–inch 33/45rpm

ZOO YORK 4-6   84
LPs: 10/12–inch 33rpm

ABC 5-10   78

PIPER, Wardell
Singles: 7–inch

MIDSONG INT'L 3-5   79-80

PIPKINS
Singles: 7–inch

CAPITOL 3-6   70
LPs: 10/12–inch 33rpm

CAPITOL 10-15   70
Member: Chester Pipkin.
Also see ALLEY CATS

PIPS
Singles: 7–inch

BRUNSWICK (55048 "Whistle
My Love") 50-75   58
CASABLANCA 3-5   77-78
EVERLAST 4-8   63
FURY 5-10   62
HUNTOM (2510 "Every Beat of
My Heart") 100-125   61
VEE JAY 5-10   61
LPs: 10/12–inch 33rpm

CASABLANCA 5-10   77-78
Members: Gladys Knight; Merald Knight; William Guest; Edward Guest.
Also see KNIGHT, Gladys

PIRATES
(Temptations)
Singles: 7–inch

MEL-O-DY (105 "Mind over Matter") . 25-50   62
Also see TEMPTATIONS

PITNEY, Gene
Singles: 7–inch

COLLECTABLES 2-4
EPIC 3-5   77
ERIC 2-4
FESTIVAL (25002 "Please Come
Back Baby") 10-20   61
MUSICOR (1000 series) 5-10   60-65
MUSICOR (1100 through 1400
series) 4-8   65-72
Picture Sleeves

MUSICOR (1000 series) 5-10   60-65
MUSICOR (1100 through 1400
series) 4-8   66-69
EPs: 7–inch 33/45rpm

MUSICOR (500 "Looking Through
the Eyes of Love") 15-20   65
(Issued without cover. Promotional issue only.)

LPs: 10/12–inch 33rpm

COLUMBIA HOUSE 10-15
(Columbia Record Club release.)
EVEREST 5-8   81
MUSIC DISC 10-15   69
MUSICOR (2001 through 2008) 15-25   62-64
MUSICOR (2015 through 2134) 15-20   64-67
MUSICOR (3001 through 3008) 20-30   62-64
MUSICOR (3015 through 3134) 15-25   64-67
MUSICOR (3148 through 3183) 10-15   67-70
MUSICOR (5026 "This Is Gene
Pitney") 15-20   68
(Columbia Record Club issue.)
MUSICOR (5600 series) 8-10   78
RHINO 5-8   85
SPRINGBOARD 5-10   76
TRIP 5-10   76
51 WEST 5-10   79
Also see BRYAN, Billy
Also see JAMIE and JANE
Also see JONES, George, and Gene Pitney

PITNEY, Gene, and Melba Montgomery
Singles: 7–inch

MUSICOR 4-8   65
LPs: 10/12–inch 33rpm

BUCKBOARD 8-10   76
MUSICOR 15-20   66
Also see MONTGOMERY, Melba

PITNEY, Gene / Newcastle Trio
LPs: 10/12–inch 33rpm

DESIGN 8-12
Also see PITNEY, Gene

PIXIES THREE
Singles: 7–inch

MERCURY 8-12   63-64
Picture Sleeves

MERCURY (72130 "Birthday Party") . 10-20   63
MERCURY (72208 "Cold,
Cold Winter") 15-20   63
MERCURY (72288 "It's Summertime") 10-20   64
LPs: 10/12–inch 33rpm

MERCURY (20912 "Party") 50-75   64
(Monaural.)
MERCURY (60912 "Party") 75-100   64
(Stereo.)
Members: Debra Swisher; Midge Bollinger; Kay McCool.

PIZANI, Frank
Singles: 78rpm

BALLY 5-10   57
Singles: 7–inch

AFTON 5-10   59
BALLY 5-10   57
WARWICK 5-10   59
Also see HIGHLIGHTS

PLACE, Mary Kay
Singles: 7–inch

COLUMBIA 3-5   76-78

MERCURY (70948 "You'll Never
Never Know") 10-15   56
MERCURY (71011 "One in a Million") 10-15   56
MERCURY (71032 "I'm Sorry") 10-20   56
(Maroon label.)
MERCURY (71032 "I'm Sorry") 8-12   56
(Black label.)
MERCURY (71093 "My Dream") 10-20   56
(Maroon label.)
MERCURY (71093 "My Dream") 8-12   56
(Black label.)
MERCURY (71184 through 71904) ... 8-12   57-61
MERCURY (71921 through 72359) 4-8   62-64
MUSICOR 4-8   66-71
OWL 3-5   73
POWER 4-8

Picture Sleeves
MERCURY 10-15   60-64

EPs: 7–inch 33/45rpm
FEDERAL (378 The Platters Sing
for Only You") 300-400   56
KING (378 "The Platters") 100-200   56
KING (651 "The Platters") 100-200   56
MERCURY 25-50   56-61

LPs: 10/12–inch 33rpm
CANDLELITE 15-25
EVEREST 5-10   81
FEDERAL (549 "The Platters") 300-500   57
51 WEST 5-8
KING (651 "The Platters") 75-125   59
MERCURY (4000 series) 5-8   82
MERCURY (8000 series) 5-8
MERCURY (20146 through 20366) .. 25-50   56-58
MERCURY (20410 through 20983) .. 15-30   59-65
(Monaural.)
MERCURY (60043 through 60983) .. 20-40   59-65
(Stereo.)
MUSIC DISC 10-12   69
MUSICO (1002 "Only You") 8-10   70
MUSICOR (2000 and 3000 series) .. 10-15   66-69
MUSICOR (4600 series) 10-12   77
PICKWICK 8-10
RHINO 8-12
SPRINGBOARD 8-10   76
TRIP 8-10   76
WING 10-20   62-67
    Members: Tony Williams; David Lynch; Herb Reed; Linda Hayes;
    Sandra Dawn; Nate Nelson; Sonny Turner; Zola Taylor; Paul
    Robi; Alex Hodge.
    Also see HAYES, Linda, and the Platters
    Also see LITTLE ANTHONY and the Imperials / Platters

PLATTERS / Exotic Guitars
LPs: 10/12–inch 33rpm
GUEST STAR 10-15   64
    Also see EXOTIC GUITARS

PLATTERS / Inez & Charlie Foxx / Jive Five / Tommy Hunt
LPs: 10/12–inch 33rpm
MUSICOR 10-20   67

Also see FOXX, Inez
Also see HUNT, Tommy
Also see JIVE FIVE

PLATTERS '65
Singles: 7–inch
ENTREE 4-8   65
    Also see PLATTERS

PLAYBOYS
Singles: 7–inch
ABC-PAR 8-12   59
ACE 4-8   64
CAMEO (142 "Over the Weekend") .. 10-15   58
CATALINA 10-20   64
CHANCELLOR 5-10   61-62
DOLTON 5-10   59
HEARTBEAT 4-8
IMPERIAL 5-10   59
JEWEL 4-8   64
LEGATO (101 "Mope De Mope") 10-20   63
MARTINIQUE (101 "Over the
Weekend") 15-25   58
MARTINIQUE (400 "Please
Forgive Me") 15-25   59
MERCURY 10-15   57
RIK 5-10   59
SOUVENIR 5-10   59
TITAN 4-8   65

PLAYER
Singles: 7–inch
CASABLANCA 3-5   80
RCA 3-5   82
RSO 3-5   77-78
LPs: 10/12–inch 33rpm
CASABLANCA 5-10   80
RCA 5-10   81
RSO 5-10   77-78
    Also see BANDANA

PLAYERS ASSOCIATION
Singles: 12–inch 33/45rpm
VANGUARD 4-8   79-80
Singles: 7–inch
VANGUARD 3-5   77-80
LPs: 10/12–inch 33rpm
VANGUARD 5-10   77-80

PLAYMATES
Singles: 78rpm
ROULETTE 5-10   57
Singles: 7–inch
ABC-PAR 4-8   63-64
BELL 3-5   71
COLPIX 4-8   64-65
CONGRESS 4-8   65
ROULETTE 8-12   57-63
LPs: 10/12–inch 33rpm
FORUM 15-25   60
ROULETTE 20-30   57-61
    Members: Donny Conn; Morey Carr; Chic Hetti.

PLEASURE
Singles: 12–inch 33/45rpm
FANTASY 4-8 76-80
Singles: 7–inch
FANTASY 3-5 76-80
RCA 2-4 82-83
LPs: 10/12–inch 33rpm
FANTASY 5-10 76-80
RCA 5-8 82

PLEASURE, King
Singles: 78rpm
ALADDIN 4-8 57
JUBILEE 4-8 55
PRESTIGE 4-8 52-55
Singles: 7–inch
ALADDIN 10-15 57
HI-FI 5-8 60
JUBILEE 10-15 55
PRESTIGE (100 series) 4-8 60
PRESTIGE (800 and 900 series) 10-20 52-55
U.A. 5-10 62
LPs: 10/12–inch 33rpm
HI-FI (425 "Golden Days") 35-55 60
PRESTIGE (208 "King Pleasure
  Sings") 75-125 55
  (10–inch LP.)
PRESTIGE (7128 "King Pleasure
  Sings") 50-75 57
U.A. (14031 "Mr. Jazz") 30-40 62
  (Monaural.)
U.A. (15031 "Mr. Jazz") 35-50 62
  (Stereo.)

PLEASURE and the Beast
Singles: 12–inch 33/45rpm
AIRWAVE 4-6 84

PLEIS, Jack, and His Orchestra
Singles: 7–inch
ATCO 4-6 65
COLUMBIA 4-6 61
DECCA 5-10 53-60
LONDON 5-10 50-51
RANWOOD 3-5 76
EPs: 7–inch 33/45rpm
DECCA 5-10 55-57
LPs: 10/12–inch 33rpm
CAMEO 10-20 63
COLUMBIA 10-15 61
DECCA 10-20 55-57
RANWOOD 5-8 76

PLIMSOULS
Singles: 12–inch 33/45rpm
BOMP 5-8 80
Singles: 7–inch
BOMP 3-5 80
GEFFEN 2-4 83
SHAKY CITY 3-5

Picture Sleeves
BOMP 3-5 80
SHAKY CITY 3-5
LPs: 10/12–inch 33rpm
GEFFEN 5-8 83
PLANET 5-10 81

PLUSH
Singles: 7–inch
RCA 3-5 82
LPs: 10/12–inch 33rpm
RCA 5-10 82

P-NUT GALLERY
Singles: 7–inch
BUDDAH 3-5 71

POCKETS
Singles: 7–inch
ARC 4-6 79
COLUMBIA 4-6 77-78
LPs: 10/12–inch 33rpm
ARC 5-10 79
COLUMBIA 5-10 77-78

POCO
Singles: 7–inch
ABC 3-5 75-79
ATLANTIC 2-4 82-84
EPIC 3-6 69-75
MCA 2-5 79-82
Picture Sleeves
EPIC 3-6 70-72
MCA 3-5 80
LPs: 10/12–inch 33rpm
ABC 8-12 75-78
ATLANTIC 5-8 82-84
EPIC (26460 through 30753) 10-15 69-71
EPIC (31601 through 36210) 5-10 71-81
MCA 5-10 80-82
MFSL (020 "Legend") 25-50 78
RCA 5-8 89
Members: Richie Furay; Jim Messina; Rusty Young; Timothy
Schmit; Paul Cotton.
  Also see BUFFALO SPRINGFIELD
  Also see EAGLES
  Also see FURAY, Richie
  Also see ILLINOIS SPEED PRESS
  Also see MEISNER, Randy
  Also see MESSINA, Jim
  Also see SCHMIT, Timothy B.

POETS
Singles: 7–inch
CHAIRMAN 5-10 63
SYMBOL 5-10 66
TRY ME 4-8 63
VEEP 4-8 68
  Also see MAIN INGREDIENT

POETS
Singles: 7–inch
DYNO VOX 4-8 64

POINT BLANK
Singles: 7–inch
ARISTA 3-6   76-77
MCA 3-5   79-81
LPs: 10/12–inch 33rpm
ARISTA 5-10   76-77
MCA 5-8   79-82

POINTER, Anita
Singles: 7–inch
RCA 2-4   87-88

POINTER, Anita, and Earl Thomas Conley
Singles: 7–inch
RCA 2-4   86
   Also see POINTER SISTERS

POINTER, Bonnie
Singles: 12–inch 33/45rpm
MOTOWN 4-8   78-81
PRIVATE I 4-6   84-85
Singles: 7–inch
MOTOWN (Black vinyl) 3-5   78-81
MOTOWN (Colored vinyl) 4-6   78-81
PRIVATE I 2-4   84-85
Promotional Singles
MOTOWN (Colored vinyl) 4-8   78
LPs: 10/12–inch 33rpm
MOTOWN 5-10   78-79
PRIVATE I 5-8   84
   Also see POINTER SISTERS

POINTER, June
Singles: 12–inch 33/45rpm
PLANET 4-6   83-84
Singles: 7–inch
PLANET 2-4   83-84
LPs: 10/12–inch 33rpm
PLANET 5-8   83

POINTER, Noel
Singles: 12–inch 33/45rpm
U.A. 4-6   77
Singles: 7–inch
BLUE NOTE 3-5   77
LIBERTY 3-5   81
U.A. 3-5   78-80
LPs: 10/12–inch 33rpm
BLUE NOTE 5-10   77
LIBERTY 5-8   81
U.A. 5-8   78-80

POINTER SISTERS
Singles: 12–inch 33/45rpm
PLANET 4-8   78-85
RCA 4-6   85-86
Singles: 7–inch
ABC 3-5   75-78
ATLANTIC 3-5   72
BLUE THUMB 3-5   73-78
MCA 2-4   87
PLANET 2-5   78-85

RCA 2-4   85-88
Picture Sleeves
PLANET 2-5   78-85
RCA 2-4   85-88
LPs: 10/12–inch 33rpm
BLUE THUMB 8-12   73-77
MCA 5-10   81
PLANET 5-10   78-84
RCA 5-8   85-88
   Members: Bonnie Pointer; Anita Pointer; Ruth Pointer; June Pointer.
   Also see MEMPHIS HORNS
   Also see POINTER, Anita, and Earl Thomas Conley
   Also see POINTER, Bonnie
   Also see POINTER, June

POISON
Singles: 12–inch 33/45rpm
ROULETTE 4-8   76
Singles: 7–inch
ROULETTE 3-5   75-76
LPs: 10/12–inch 33rpm
ROULETTE 5-10   76

POISON
Singles: 7–inch
CAPITOL 2-4   87
ENIGMA 2-4   86-87
LPs: 10/12–inch 33rpm
CAPITOL 5-8   86-90
ENIGMA 5-8   86-88
   Members: Bret Michaels; Rikki Rocket; C.C. DeVille; Bobby Dall.

POISON DOLLYS
LPs: 10/12–inch 33rpm
PVC 5-8   86

POLICE
Singles: 7–inch
A&M (Except 25000 and picture
  discs) 3-5   79-84
A&M (25000 "De Do Do Do,
  De Da Da Da") 3-5   80
  (Spanish/Japanese language version.)
A&M (2096 "Roxanne") 25-35   79
  (Picture disc. Promotional issues only.)
A&M (4401 "Don't Stand So Close") . 15-25   81
  (Picture disc. Promotional issues only.)
SIRE 2-4   86
Picture Sleeves
A&M (Except 25000) 3-5   79-84
A&M (25000 "De Do Do Do,
  De Da Da Da") 4-6   80
LPs: 10/12–inch 33rpm
A&M (Except 3713) 5-15   79-86
A&M (3713 "Reggatta de Blanc") ... 10-20   79
  (Two 10–inch LPs. Includes poster. Promotional
  issue only.)
NAUTILUS 10-20   81
   Members: Gordon "Sting" Sumner; Andy Summers; Stewart Copeland.
   Also see COPELAND, Stewart
   Also see FRIPP, Robert, and Andy Summers

Also see STING

POLITICIANS
Singles: 7–inch
HOT WAX 3-5   72
LPs: 10/12–inch 33rpm
HOT WAX 8-12   72
Members: McKinley Jackson.

POLNAREFF, Michel
Singles: 12–inch 33/45rpm
ATLANTIC 4-8   76
Singles: 7–inch
ATLANTIC 3-5   76
4 CORNERS (141 "Time Will Tell") . . . 8-12   67
KAPP 4-8   65-66
LPs: 10/12–inch 33rpm
ATLANTIC 8-10   75
4 CORNERS 10-15   67

PONDEROSA TWINS + ONE
Singles: 7–inch
ASTROSCOPE 3-5   72
HOROSCOPE 3-5   71
LPs: 10/12–inch 33rpm
HOROSCOPE 8-12   71

PONI-TAILS
Singles: 78rpm
ABC-PAR 10-20   57
MARC 10-15   57
POINT 10-15   57
Singles: 7–inch
ABC 3-5   73
ABC-PAR 10-20   57-60
MCA 2-4
MARC 10-15   57
POINT 10-15   57

PONSAR, Serge
Singles: 12–inch 33/45rpm
WARNER 4-6   83
Singles: 7–inch
WARNER 2-4   83

PONTY, Jean-Luc
Singles: 7–inch
ATLANTIC 2-5   76-85
LPs: 10/12–inch 33rpm
ATLANTIC 5-10   75-85
BLUE NOTE 5-10   76-81
MPS 5-10   72-73
PACIFIC JAZZ 8-18   68-78
PAUSA 5-10   80
PRESTIGE 8-15   70
WORLD PACIFIC 15-25   69

POOLE, Brian
(Brian Poole and the Tremeloes)
Singles: 7–inch
DATE 5-10   66
LONDON 5-10   63
MONUMENT 5-10   64-65

LPs: 10/12–inch 33rpm
AUDIO FIDELITY 15-25   66-67
Also see TREMELOES

POP, Iggy
(Iggy and the Stooges)
Singles: 12–inch 33/45rpm
A&M 4-8   86
Singles: 7–inch
A&M 2-4   86
RCA 3-5   77
SIAMESE 3-6   77
EPs: 7–inch 33/45rpm
BOMP 5-10   78
LPs: 10/12–inch 33rpm
A&M 5-8   86
ANIMAL 5-10   82
ARISTA 8-12   79-81
BOMP (1018 "Kill City") 10-15   78
  (Black vinyl.)
BOMP (1018 "Kill City") 20-30   78
  (Colored vinyl.)
COLUMBIA 10-20   73
ENIGMA 5-8   84
IMPORT 8-10   77
INVASION 8-10   83
RCA 5-10   77-78
VIRGIN 5-8   90
Also see BOWIE, David / Iggy Pop
Also see STOOGES

POP, Iggy, and James Williamson
EPs: 7–inch 33/45rpm
BOMP 5-10   78
LPs: 10/12–inch 33rpm
BOMP 5-10   78
Also see POP, Iggy

POP TARTS
Singles: 7–inch
FUNTONE USA 5-10   88
Members: Fenton Pop Tart; Randy Pop Tart; C.P. Roth; Alan Bezoz; Gabriel Rotello; Simon Girl.

POP TOPS
Singles: 7–inch
ABC 3-5   71
CALLA 4-8   68

POPE JOHN XXIII
LPs: 10/12–inch 33rpm
MERCURY 5-10   63

POPE JOHN PAUL II
LPs: 10/12–inch 33rpm
BETHLEHEM 5-8   79
INFINITY 5-8   79
VOX CHRISTIANA 5-8   79

POPE PAUL VI
LPs: 10/12–inch 33rpm
AMY 5-10   65
AUDIO FIDELITY 5-10   65
MGM 5-10   65

20TH FOX 5-10   64

POPPIES
Singles: 7–inch
EPIC 4-8   66
Picture Sleeves
EPIC 5-10   66
LPs: 10/12–inch 33rpm
EPIC 20-30   66
   Member: Dorothy Moore.
   Also see MOORE, Dorothy

POPPY FAMILY
Singles: 7–inch
LONDON 3-5   70-72
LPs: 10/12–inch 33rpm
LONDON 10-15   70-71
   Members: Susan Jacks; Terry Jacks.
   Also see JACKS, Susan
   Also see JACKS, Terry

PORTER, David
Singles: 7–inch
ENTERPRISE 3-5   70-72
LPs: 10/12–inch 33rpm
ENTERPRISE 8-12   70-72
   Also see HAYES, Isaac and David Porter

PORTER, Nolan
(N.F. Porter; Nolan)
Singles: 7–inch
ABC 3-5   73
LIZARD 3-5   71
LPs: 10/12–inch 33rpm
LIZARD 8-12   71

PORTNOY, Gary
Singles: 7–inch
APPLAUSE 2-4   83
EARTHTONE 2-4   84
Picture Sleeves
EARTHTONE 3-5   84

POSEY, Sandy
Singles: 7–inch
AUDIOGRAPH 2-4   83
COLUMBIA 3-5   71-72
MGM 4-6   66-67
POLYDOR 2-4   83
WARNER 3-5   78-79
Picture Sleeves
MGM 4-8   66-67
LPs: 10/12–inch 33rpm
COLUMBIA 5-10   72
51 WEST 5-8   83
GUSTO 5-8
MGM 8-15   66-70

POSEY, Sandy / Skeeter Davis
LPs: 10/12–inch 33rpm
GUSTO 5-8
   Also see DAVIS, Skeeter
   Also see POSEY, Sandy

POST, Mike
(Mike Post Coalition)
Singles: 7–inch
BELL 3-5   71
ELEKTRA 2-4   81-82
EPIC 3-5   77
MGM 3-5   75
MUSIC FACTORY 4-6   68
POLYDOR 2-4   87
REPRISE 4-6   65-66
WARNER 3-6   69
Picture Sleeves
ELEKTRA 3-5   81-82
LPs: 10/12–inch 33rpm
ELEKTRA 5-8   82
RCA 5-8   83
MGM 5-10   75
POLYDOR 5-8   87
WARNER 8-12   69

POTLIQUOR
Singles: 7–inch
CAPITOL 3-5   79
JANUS 3-5   72
LPs: 10/12–inch 33rpm
CAPITOL 5-10   79
JANUS 10-15   70-73

POURCEL, Franck
(Franck Pourcel's French Fiddles)
Singles: 7–inch
BLUE 3-5   69
CAPITOL 4-8   59-64
IMPERIAL 3-6   66-68
PARAMOUNT 3-5   71-73
EPs: 7–inch 33/45rpm
CAPITOL 5-10   59
LPs: 10/12–inch 33rpm
ATCO 5-10   69
CAPITOL 5-20   56-79
IMPERIAL 5-15   66-68
PARAMOUNT 5-8   70-73
WESTMINSTER 10-25   54-55

POUSETTE - DART BAND
Singles: 7–inch
CAPITOL 3-5   76-79
LPs: 10/12–inch 33rpm
CAPITOL 5-10   76-80
   Member: Jon Pousette-Dart.

POWELL, Adam Clayton
LPs: 10/12–inch 33rpm
JUBILEE 10-15   67

POWELL, Bobby
Singles: 7–inch
JEWEL 4-8   67
WHIT 3-8   65-71
LPs: 10/12–inch 33rpm
EXCELLO 8-12   73

POWELL, Cozy
Singles: 7-Inch
CHRYSALIS 3-5   74
Also see BECK, Jeff
Also see EMERSON, LAKE & POWELL

POWELL, Jane
Singles: 78rpm
VERVE 4-6   56
Singles: 7-Inch
RANWOOD 3-5   68
VERVE 4-8   56
LPs: 10/12-Inch 33rpm
COLUMBIA 15-30   55-57
LION 10-20   59
MGM 20-40   55
VERVE 20-35   56

POWER STATION
Singles: 12-Inch 33/45rpm
CAPITOL 4-6   85
Singles: 7-Inch
CAPITOL 2-4   85
LPs: 10/12-Inch 33rpm
CAPITOL 5-8   85
Members: Andy Taylor; John Taylor; Robert Palmer.
Also see DURAN DURAN
Also see PALMER, Robert
Also see TAYLOR, Andy
Also see TAYLOR, John

POWERS, Joey
(Joey Powers' Flower)
Singles: 7-Inch
AMY 5-10   63-67
MGM 5-10   65
RCA (8000 series) 4-8   62
RCA (9700 series) 3-6   69
LPs: 10/12-Inch 33rpm
AMY 15-25   64
Also see ORBISON, Roy / Bobby Bare / Joey Powers

POWERS, Tom
Singles: 7-Inch
BIG TREE 3-5   77

POWERSOURCE
Singles: 7-Inch
POWERVISION 2-4   87

POZO - SECO SINGERS
(Pozo Seco; Susan Taylor and the Pozo Seco Singers)
Singles: 7-Inch
CERTRON 3-5   70
COLUMBIA 4-8   65-70
EDMARK 10-20   65
LPs: 10/12-Inch 33rpm
CERTRON 10-15   70
COLUMBIA 10-20   66-68
Mombers: Don Williams; Susan Taylor; Lofton Kline.
Also see WILLIAMS, Don

PRADO, Perez, and His Orchestra
Singles: 78rpm
RCA 4-6   50-58

Singles: 7-Inch
RCA 4-10   50-64
U.A. 3-6   64
Picture Sleeves
RCA 5-10   59
EPs: 7-Inch 33/45rpm
BELL (2 "Perez Prado") 5-10
RCA 8-15   54-61
LPs: 10/12-Inch 33rpm
CAMDEN 10-15   60
RCA 5-10   76
(With "ANL1" prefix.)
RCA 10-30   54-72
(With "LPM," "LSP" or "VPS" prefix.)
SPRINGBOARD 5-10   77
U.A. 10-15   65-68
Also see CLOONEY, Rosemary, and Perez Prado
Also see HIRT, Al / Henry Mancini / Perez Prado

PRATT, Andy
Singles: 7-Inch
COLUMBIA 3-5   73
NEMPEROR 3-5   76-77
LPs: 10/12-Inch 33rpm
COLUMBIA 8-12   73
NEMPEROR 5-10   76-79
POLYDOR 10-15   70
Also see SPRINGSTEEN, Bruce / Andy Pratt

PRATT - McCLAIN
Singles: 7-Inch
REPRISE 3-5   76-77
LPs: 10/12-Inch 33rpm
DUNHILL 8-12   73
REPRISE 8-10   76
Members: Truett Pratt; Jerry McClain.

PRECISIONS
Singles: 7-Inch
ATCO 4-8   69
D-TOWN 4-8   65
DREW 5-10   66-68
HEN-MAR 3-5   73

PRELUDE
Singles: 7-Inch
ISLAND 3-5   74
PYE 3-5   75
LPs: 10/12-Inch 33rpm
ISLAND 8-10   74
PYE 8-10   75

PRELUDES FIVE
(Preludes)
Singles: 7-Inch
PIK (231 "Don't You Know") 15-20   61

PREMIATA FORNERIA MARCONI: see P.F.M.

PREMIERS
Singles: 7-Inch
FARO 5-10   64-67
FINE 4-8

LEO 5-10   64
WARNER 4-8   64

LPs: 10/12–inch 33rpm

WARNER 15-25   64

PRENTISS, Lee
Singles: 12–inch 33/45rpm

MSB 4-6   83

PREPARATIONS
Singles: 7–inch

HEART and SOUL 4-8   68

PRESIDENTS
Singles: 7–inch

DELUXE 4-8   69
HOLLYWOOD 4-8   68
SUSSEX 3-5   70-71

LPs: 10/12–inch 33rpm

SUSSEX 10-15   70

PRESLEY, Elvis
Singles: 78rpm
(Commercial and Promotional)

RCA (6357 "Mystery Train") 100-150   55
RCA (6380 "That's All Right") 100-150   55
RCA (6381 "Good Rockin'
  Tonight") 100-150   55
RCA (6382 "Milkcow Blues Boogie") 100-150   55
RCA (6383 "Baby, Let's Play
  House") 100-150   55
RCA (6420 "Heartbreak Hotel") 75-100   56
  (Black label.)
RCA (6420 "Heartbreak Hotel") ... 400-500   56
  (White label. Promotional issue only.)
RCA (6540 "I Want You, I
  Need You, I Love You") 75-100   56
  (Black label.)
RCA (6540 "I Want You, I
  Need You, I Love You") 400-500   56
  (White label. Promotional issue only.)
RCA (6604 "Don't Be Cruel") 75-100   56
  (Black label.)
RCA (6604 "Don't Be Cruel") 400-500   56
  (White label. Promotional issue only.)
RCA (6636 "Blue Suede Shoes") ... 75-100   56
  (Black label.)
RCA (6637 "I Got a Woman") 75-100   56
  (Black label.)
RCA (6638 "I'm Gonna Sit
  Right Down and Cry") 75-100   56
  (Black label.)
RCA (6639 "Tryin' to Get to You") ... 75-100   56
  (Black label.)
RCA (6640 "Blue Moon") 75-100   56
  (Black label.)
RCA (6641 "Money Honey") 75-100   56
  (Black label.)
RCA (6642 "Lawdy Miss Clawdy") .. 75-100   56
  (Black label.)

RCA (6643 "Love Me Tender") 75-100   56
  (Black label.)
RCA (6643 "Love Me Tender") 400-500   56
  (White label. Promotional issue only.)
RCA (6800 "Too Much") 75-100   57
  (Black label.)
RCA (6800 "Too Much") 400-500   57
  (White label. Promotional issue only.)
RCA (6870 "All Shook Up") 75-100   57
  (Black label.)
RCA (6870 "All Shook Up") 400-500   57
  (White label. Promotional issue only.)
RCA (7000 "Teddy Bear") 75-100   57
  (Black label.)
RCA (7000 "Teddy Bear") 400-500   57
  (White label. Promotional issue only.)
RCA (7035 "Jailhouse Rock") 75-100   57
  (Black label.)
RCA (7035 "Jailhouse Rock") 400-500   57
  (White label. Promotional issue only.)
RCA (7150 "Don't") 75-100   58
RCA (7240 "Wear My Ring
  Around Your Neck") 75-100   58
RCA (7280 "Hard Headed Woman") 75-125   58
RCA (7410 "One Night") 400-500   58
ROYAL ("Elvis Presley Show") 150-250   56
  (Single-sided disc, issued to radio stations to
  promote Elvis in concert. Includes an excerpt of
  Heartbreak Hotel.)
SUN (209 "That's All Right") 400-500   54
SUN (210 "Good Rockin' Tonight") 400-500   54
SUN (215 "Milkcow Blues Boogie") 450-550   55
SUN (217 "Baby Let's Play House") 400-500   55
SUN (223 "Mystery Train") 400-500   55
Notes: All Elvis RCA and Sun 78s were
simultaneously issued on 45rpm singles. For 78rpm
plastic soundsheets and flexi-discs, see a separate
section that follows. RCA and Sun 78s can be found
with many label variations. Sun promotional singles
were marked with the word "sample" rubber stamped
on the label.

Singles: 7–inch
(Commercial)

COLLECTABLES 2-4   86-87
RCA (0088 "Raised on Rock") 4-6   73
RCA (0130 "How Great Thou Art") ... 15-20   69
RCA (0196 "Take Good Care of Her") .. 3-5   74
RCA (0280 "If You Talk in Your Sleep") . 3-5   74
RCA (0572 "Merry Christmas Baby") . 12-15   71
RCA (0619 "Until It's Time
  for You to Go") 3-5   72
RCA (0651 "He Touched Me") 3-5   72
RCA (0651 "He Touched Me") 100-150   72
  (Has the *He Touched Me* side pressed at about
  35rpm instead of 45. These copies—the result of a
  production error—were commercial issues. The
  flip, *Bosom of Abraham*, plays at 45rpm.)
RCA (0672 "An American Trilogy") ... 10-20   72

RCA (0769 "Burning Love") 3-5   72
(Orange label.)
RCA (0769 "Burning Love") 75-100   72
(Gray label.)
RCA (0815 "Separate Ways") 3-5   71
RCA (0910 "Steamroller Blues") 3-5   73
RCA (1017 "It's Only Love") 3-5   71
RCA (2458 "My Boy"/"Loving Arms") 400-500   74
(Produced in the U.S. for European distribution.)
RCA (6357 "Mystery Train") 30-40   55
RCA (6380 "That's All Right") 30-40   55
RCA (6381 "Good Rockin' Tonight") .. 30-40   55
RCA (6382 "Milkcow Blues Boogie") . 30-40   55
RCA (6383 "Baby, Let's Play House") 30-40   55
RCA (6420 "Heartbreak Hotel") 20-30   56
RCA (6540 "I Want You, I
Need You, I Love You") 20-30   56
RCA (6604 "Don't Be Cruel") 20-30   56
RCA (6636 "Blue Suede Shoes") 30-40   56
RCA (6637 "I Got a Woman") 30-40   56
RCA (6638 "I'm Gonna Sit
Right Down and Cry") 30-40   56
RCA (6639 "Tryin' to Get to You") 30-40   56
RCA (6640 "Blue Moon") 30-40   56
RCA (6641 "Money Honey") 30-40   56
RCA (6642 "Lawdy Miss Clawdy") ... 30-40   56
(Dog is pictured on label.)
RCA (6642 "Lawdy Miss Clawdy") . 150-200   56
(Dog is not shown on label.)
RCA (6643 "Love Me Tender") 20-30   56
RCA (6800 "Too Much") 20-30   57
(Dog is pictured on label.)
RCA (6800 "Too Much") 150-200   57
(Dog is not shown on label.)
RCA (6870 "All Shook Up") 20-30   57
RCA (7000 "Teddy Bear") 20-30   57
RCA (7035 "Jailhouse Rock") 20-30   57
Note: All RCA singles from 6357 through 7035 can
be found on various black labels, with or without a
horizontal silver line.
RCA (7150 "Don't") 10-15   58
RCA (7240 "Wear My Ring
Around Your Neck") 10-15   58
RCA (7280 "Hard Headed Woman") . 10-15   58
RCA (7410 "One Night") 10-15   58
RCA (7506 "I Need Your
Love Tonight") 10-15   59
RCA (7600 "A Big Hunk O' Love") ... 10-15   59
RCA (47-7740 "Stuck on You") 8-10   60
RCA (61-7740 "Stuck on You") 250-300   60
(Living Stereo.)
RCA (47-7777 "It's Now Or Never") ... 8-10   60
RCA (61-7777 "It's Now Or Never") 300-400   60
(Living Stereo.)
RCA (47-7810 "Are You
Lonesome To-night") 8-10   60
RCA (61-7810 "Are You
Lonesome To-night") 300-400   60
(Living Stereo.)

RCA VICTOR COMPACT SINGLE 33

57-7992
Gladys Music
In:., ASCAP   Produce
N2W'-1307   Sieve Sholes
2:23

GOOD LUCK CHARM
(Aaron Schroeder-Wally Gold)

ELVIS PRESLEY
with The Jordanaires

RCA (37-7850 "Surrender") 400-500   61
(Compact 33 Single.)
RCA (47-7850 "Surrender") 8-10   61
RCA (61-7850 "Surrender") 300-400   61
(Living Stereo.)
RCA (68-7850 "Surrender") 1000-1500   61
(Stereo Compact 33 Single.)
RCA (37-7880 "I Feel So Bad") .. 500-1000   61
(Compact 33 Single.)
RCA (47-7880 "I Feel So Bad") 8-10   61
RCA (37-7908 "His Latest
Flame") 1000-2000   61
(Compact 33 Single.)
RCA (47-7908 "His Latest Flame") ... 8-10   61
RCA (37-7968 "Can't Help
Falling in Love") 2000-4000   61
(Compact 33 Single.)
RCA (47-7968 "Can't Help
Falling in Love") 8-10   61
RCA (37-7992 "Good Luck
Charm") 3000-5000   62
(Compact 33 Single.)
RCA (47-7992 "Good Luck Charm") .. 8-10   62
RCA (8041 "She's Not You") 8-10   62
RCA (8100 "Return to Sender") 8-10   62
RCA (8134 "One Broken
Heart for Sale") 8-10   63
RCA (8188 "Devil in Disguise") 50-100   63
(Flip side title is incorrectly shown as Please Don't
Drag That String ALONG.)
RCA (8188 "Devil in Disguise") 6-10   63
(Flip side title correctly shown as Please Don't
Drag That String AROUND.)
RCA (8243 "Bossa Nova Baby") 6-10   63
RCA (8307 "Kissin' Cousins") 6-10   64
RCA (8360 "Viva Las Vegas") 6-10   64
RCA (8400 "Such a Night") 6-10   64
RCA (8440 "Ask Me") 6-10   64
RCA (8500 "Do the Clam") 6-10   65
RCA (8585 "Easy Question") 5-8   65
RCA (8657 "I'm Yours") 5-8   65
RCA (8740 "Tell Me Why") 5-8   65

RCA (8780 "Frankie and Johnny") 5-8   66
RCA (8870 "Love Letters") 5-8   66
RCA (8941 "Spinout") 5-8   66
RCA (8950 "If Everyday
   Was Like Christmas") 5-8   66
RCA (9056 "Indescribably Blue") 5-8   67
RCA (9115 "Long Legged Girl") 5-8   67
RCA (9287 "There's Always Me") 5-8   67
RCA (9341 "Big Boss Man") 5-8   67
RCA (9465 "U.S. Male") 5-8   68
RCA (9547 "Your Time
   Hasn't Come Yet Baby") 5-8   68
RCA (9600 "You'll Never Walk Alone") . 5-10   68
RCA (9610 "Almost in Love") 5-8   68
   Note: Commercial issues of all RCA singles from
   6357 through 9600 are on black labels.
RCA (9670 "If I Can Dream") 3-5   68
RCA (9731 "Memories") 3-5   69
RCA (9741 "In the Ghetto") 3-5   69
RCA (9747 "Clean Up
   Your Own Back Yard") 3-5   69
RCA (9764 "Suspicious Minds") 3-5   69
RCA (9768 "Don't Cry Daddy") 3-5   69
RCA (9791 "Kentucky Rain") 3-5   70
RCA (9835 "The Wonder of You") 3-5   70
RCA (9873 "I've Lost You") 3-5   70
RCA (9916 "You Don't Have
   to Say You Love Me") 3-5   70
RCA (9960 "I Really Don't
   Want to Know") 3-5   70
RCA (9980 "Where Did They Go Lord") . 3-5   71
RCA (9985 "Life") 3-5   71
RCA (9998 "I'm Leavin") 3-5   71
   Note: RCA numbers in the 10000 to 14000 series with
   a "GB" prefix are Gold Standards and are listed in a
   separate Gold Standard Singles section.
RCA (10074 "Promised Land") 3-5   74
   (Orange label.)
RCA (10074 "Promised Land") 20-25   74
   (Gray label.)
RCA (10191 "My Boy") 3-5   75
   (Orange label.)
RCA (10191 "My Boy") 8-10   75
   (Tan or brown label.)
RCA (10278 "T-r-o-u-b-l-e") 3-5   75
   (Orange label.)
RCA (10278 "T-r-o-u-b-l-e") 8-10   75
   (Tan label.)
RCA (10401 "Bringing It Back") 45-55   75
   (Orange label.)
RCA (10401 "Bringing It Back") 3-5   75
   (Tan label.)
RCA (10601 "For the Heart") 3-5   76
   (Tan label.)
RCA (10601 "For the Heart") 90-100   76
   (Black label.)

RCA (10857 "Moody Blue") 3-5   76
   (Black vinyl. Colored vinyl 45s of *Moody Blue,* were
   experimental and are listed in the Promotional
   Singles section that follows.)
RCA (10998 "Way Down") 3-5   77
RCA (11099 through 11113) 2-4   77
   (Discs in this series were originally packaged in
   either 11301 and/or 11340, both of which are
   boxed sets of singles with sleeves.)
RCA (11165 "My Way") 3-5   77
   (Flip side shown as *America.*)
RCA (11165 "My Way") 15-20   77
   (Fith flip side shown as *America the Beautiful.*)
RCA (11212 "Softly, As I Leave You") .. 3-5   78
RCA (11301 "15 Golden Records") .. 45-55   77
   (Boxed set of 15 Elvis singles with picture sleeves.)
RCA (11320 "Teddy Bear") 3-5   78
RCA (11340 "20 Golden Hits") 65-75   77
   (Boxed set of 10 Elvis singles with picture sleeves.)
RCA (11533 "Are You Sincere") 3-5   79
RCA (11679 "I Got a Feelin'
   in My Body") 12-15   79
   (With production and backing credits shown on
   label.)
RCA (11679 ("I Got a Feelin'
   in My Body") 3-5   79
   (With backing credits removed, leaving only
   production credits.)
RCA (12158 "Guitar Man") 3-5   81
RCA (12205 "Lovin' Arms") 3-5   81
RCA (13058 "You'll Never Walk Alone") . 3-5   82
RCA (13351 "The Elvis Medley") 3-5   82
RCA (13500 "I Was the One") 3-5   83
RCA (13547 "Little Sister") 3-5   83
RCA (13875 "Baby, Let's Play House") 20-40   84
   (Colored vinyl.)
RCA (13885 through 13890) 2-4   84
   (Discs in this series were originally packaged in
   13897, *Golden Singles, Vol. I.* May include jukebox
   title strips.)
RCA (13891 through 13896) 2-4   84
   (Discs in this series were originally packaged in
   13898, *Golden Singles, Vol. II.* May include
   jukebox title strips.)
RCA (13897 "Golden Singles, Vol. I") 10-15   84
   (Package of six colored vinyl singles with sleeves.)
RCA (13898 "Golden Singles, Vol. II") 10-15   84
   (Package of six colored vinyl singles with sleeves.)
RCA (13929 "Blue Suede Shoes") ... 10-15   84
   (Colored vinyl. Incorrectly shows *Blue Suede
   Shoes* as stereo and *Promised Land* as mono.)
RCA (13929 "Blue Suede Shoes") 8-12   84
   (Colored vinyl. Correctly shows *Blue Suede Shoes*
   as mono and *Promised Land* as stereo.)
RCA (14090 "Always on My Mind") ... 8-12   85
   (Colored vinyl.)
RCA (14237 "Merry Christmas Baby") 10-15   85
   (Black vinyl.)

RCA (14237 "Merry Christmas Baby") 10-15   85
(Colored vinyl.)

Note: RCA numbers in the 10000-14000 series with a "GB" prefix are Gold Standard Series and are listed in a separate Gold Standard Singles section. Regular series issues are in the preceding section.

SUN (209 "That's All Right") 400-500   54
SUN (210 "Good Rockin' Tonight") . 400-500   54
SUN (215 "Milkcow Blue Boogie") . 450-550   55
SUN (217 "Baby Let's Play House") 400-500   55
SUN (223 "Mystery Train") 400-500   55
TRIBUTE (501 "A Tribute to
Elvis Presley") 50-100   56

(Has Elvis plus guest appearances by Edward R. Murrow, Steve Allen, Ed Sullivan, Danny Kaye, Jimmy Durante, Gabriel Heater, Sid Ceaser, Liberace, Mantovani, Jack Benny, Gene Vincent, Gloria DeHaven, Nat King Cole, Nelson Eddy, and Jane Russell.)

Note: Plastic soundsheets or flexi-discs are listed in a separate section that follows.

Picture Sleeves
(Commercial and Promotional)

LAUREL (41 623 "Treat
Me Nice") 3000-5000   57

(Pictures Elvis but credits Vince Everett. A black and white sleeve made as a prop for the *Jailhouse Rock* film. The printed sheets have no reverse side, but are applied to a randomly selected EP. No Laurel records of this title exist.)

PECA ("Could I Fall in Love") ... 2000-2500   66

(Pictures Elvis but credits Guy Lambert with George and His G-Men. A full color sleeve made as a prop for the *Double Trouble* film. No Peca records of this title exist.)

RCA (76 "Don't"/"Wear My Ring
Around Your Neck") 1000-1500   60
(Promotional issue only.)

RCA (0088 "Raised on Rock") 8-12   73
RCA (118 "King of the
Whole Wide World") 150-200   62
(Promotional issue only.)

RCA (0130 "How Great Thou Art") .. 75-100   69
RCA (162 "How Great Thou Art") .. 100-150   67
(Promotional issue only.)

RCA (0196 "I've Got a Thing
About You Baby") 8-12   74
RCA (0280 "If You Talk in Your Sleep") 8-12   74
RCA (0572 "Merry Christmas Baby") . 20-30   71
RCA (0619 "Until It's Time
for You to Go") 8-12   71
RCA (0651 "He Touched Me") 40-50   71
RCA (0672 "An American Trilogy") ... 15-25   72
RCA (0769 "Burning Love") 8-12   72
RCA (0815 "Separate Ways") 8-12   71
RCA (0910 "Steamroller Blues") 8-12   73
RCA (1017 "It's Only Love") 8-12   71

RCA (6540 "I Want You, I
Need You, I Love You") 350-450   56
(Cartoon "This Is His Life" series. Promo only.)

RCA (6604 "Don't Be Cruel") 65-75   56
(Shows *Don't Be Cruel* c/w *Hound Dog*.)

RCA (6604 "Hound Dog") 55-65   56
(Shows *Hound Dog* c/w *Don't Be Cruel*.)

RCA (6643 "Love Me Tender") 100-150   56
(Black and white sleeve.)

RCA (6643 "Love Me Tender") 60-75   56
(Black and green sleeve.)

RCA (6643 "Love Me Tender") 35-45   56
(Black and dark pink sleeve.)

RCA (6643 "Love Me Tender") 30-35   56
(Black and light pink sleeve.)

RCA (6800 "Too Much") 40-60   57
RCA (6870 "All Shook Up") 40-60   57
RCA (7000 "Teddy Bear") 40-60   57
RCA (7035 "Jailhouse Rock") 40-60   57
(Sleeve only.)

RCA/MGM "Jailhouse Rock") 500-750   57
(MGM *Jailhouse Rock* film preview invitation ticket. A promotional item for the media, the ticket came wrapped around a commercial single and sleeve. Deduct $200 to $250 if ticket stub is detached.)

RCA (7150 "Don't") 40-50   58
RCA (7240 "Wear My Ring
Around Your Neck") 40-50   58
RCA (7280 "Hard Headed Woman") . 35-45   58
RCA (7410 "One Night") 35-45   58
RCA (7506 "I Need Your
Love Tonight") 150-200   59
(Has advertising for the *Elvis Sails* EP on reverse.)

RCA (7506 "I Need Your
Love Tonight") 25-35   59
(Has a listing of Elvis EPs and 45s on reverse.)

RCA (7600 "A Big Hunk O' Love") ... 25-35   59
RCA (7740 "Stuck on You") 15-25   60
RCA (7777 "It's Now Or Never") 15-25   60
RCA (7810 "Are You
Lonesome To-night") 15-25   60

RCA (37-7850 "Surrender") 300-500   61
(Compact 33 Single sleeve.)
RCA (47-7850 "Surrender") 15-20   61
RCA (37-7880 "I Feel So Bad") .. 500-1000   61
(Compact 33 Single sleeve.)
RCA (47-7880 "I Feel So Bad") 15-25   61
RCA (37-7908 "His Latest
Flame") 1000-2000   61
(Compact 33 Single sleeve.)
RCA (47-7908 "His Latest Flame") ... 15-25   61
RCA (37-7968 "Can't Help
Falling in Love") 2000-4000   61
(Compact 33 Single sleeve.)
RCA (47-7968 "Can't Help
Falling in Love") 15-20   61
RCA (37-7992 "Good Luck
Charm") 3000-5000   62
(Compact 33 Single sleeve.)
RCA (47-7992 "Good Luck Charm") .. 15-25   62
RCA (8041 "She's Not You") 15-20   62
RCA (8100 "Return to Sender") 15-20   62
RCA (8134 "One Broken
Heart for Sale") 15-20   63
RCA (8188 "Devil in Disguise") 15-20   63
RCA (8243 "Bossa Nova Baby") 15-20   63
RCA (8307 "Kissin' Cousins") 15-20   64
RCA (8360 "Viva Las Vegas") 15-20   64
RCA (8400 "Such a Night") 15-20   64
RCA (8440 "Ask Me") 15-20   64
RCA (8500 "Do the Clam") 15-20   65
RCA (8585 "Easy Question") 15-20   65
RCA (8657 "I'm Yours") 15-20   65
RCA (8740 "Tell Me Why") 15-20   65
RCA (8780 "Frankie and Johnny") ... 15-20   66
RCA (8870 "Love Letters") 15-20   66
RCA (8941 "Spinout") 15-20   66
RCA (8950 "If Everyday
Was Like Christmas") 15-20   66
RCA (9056 "Indescribably Blue") 15-20   67
RCA (9115 "Long Legged Girl") 15-20   67
RCA (9287 "There's Always Me") 15-20   67
RCA (9341 "Big Boss Man") 15-20   67
RCA (9425 "Guitar Man") 10-20   68
RCA (9465 "U.S. Male") 10-20   68
RCA (9547 "Your Time
Hasn't Come Yet Baby") 10-20   68
RCA (9600 "You'll Never Walk Alone") 35-45   68
RCA (9610 "Almost in Love") 10-15   68
RCA (9670 "If I Can Dream") 10-15   68
RCA (9731 "Memories") 10-15   69
RCA (9741 "In the Ghetto") 10-15   69
RCA (9747 "Clean Up
Your Own Back Yard") 10-15   69
RCA (9764 "Suspicious Minds") 8-12   69
RCA (9768 "Don't Cry Daddy") 8-12   69
RCA (9791 "Kentucky Rain") 8-12   70
RCA (9835 "The Wonder of You") 8-12   70
RCA (9873 "I've Lost You") 8-12   70

RCA (9916 "You Don't
Have to Say You Love Me") 8-12   70
RCA (9960 "I Really Don't
Want to Know") 8-12   70
RCA (9980 "Where Did They Go Lord") 8-15   71
RCA (9985 "Life") 20-30   71
RCA (9998 "I'm Leavin") 8-15   71
RCA (10074 "Promised Land") 8-10   74
RCA (10191 "My Boy") 8-10   75
RCA (10278 "T-r-o-u-b-l-e") 8-10   75
RCA (10401 "Bringing It Back") 8-12   75
RCA (10601 "For the Heart") 8-10   76
RCA (10857 "Moody Blue") 6-10   76
RCA (10998 "Way Down") 6-10   77
RCA (11099 through 11113) 2-4   77
(Sleeves in this series were originally packaged in
either RCA 11301 and/or 11340, both boxed sets
of singles with sleeves.)
RCA (11165 "My Way") 6-10   77
(Flip side title shown as *America*.)
RCA (11165 "My Way") 15-25   77
(Flip side title shown as *America the Beautiful*.)
RCA (11212 "Softly, As I Leave You") . 5-10   78
RCA (11320 "Teddy Bear") 5-10   78
RCA (11533 "Are You Sincere") 5-10   79
RCA (11679 "I Got a Feelin'
in My Body") 5-10   79
RCA (12158 "Guitar Man") 5-10   81
RCA (13058 "You'll Never Walk Alone") 5-10   82
RCA (13302 "The Impossible
Dream") 75-100   82
(Promotional issue only.)
RCA (13351 "The Elvis Medley") 5-10   82
RCA (13500 "I Was the One") 5-10   83
RCA (13547 "Little Sister") 5-10   83
RCA (13875 "Baby, Let's Play House") 20-40   84
RCA (13885 through 13896) 2-4   84
(Sleeves in this series were originally packaged in
RCA 13897 and 13898, *Golden Singles*.)
RCA (13929 "Blue Suede Shoes") 5-10   84
RCA (14090 "Always on My Mind") ... 5-10   85
RCA (14237 "Merry Christmas Baby") . 8-12   85
Notes:There may be slight price differences between
"Coming Soon" and "Ask For" variations. Likewise for
variations in colors and paper stock used. Often, the
difference is simply which one is needed to complete
a run. Regardless, sleeve variations within the price
range given do not require separate listings. If the
value varies beyond the given range, a separate
listing will be added. Sleeves for the RCA "447" Gold
Standard Series are listed in a separate section
following the Gold Standard Singles. A slight
premium—perhaps $2 to $5—may be placed on
RCA's "Living Stereo" paper sleeves. These were
used for many different RCA stereo singles and were
not exclusively an Elvis item.

Gold Standard Singles with "447" prefix
(Commercial)

RCA (0600 through 0639) 10-20   59-64
(Black label, dog on top.)
RCA (0600 through 0639) 5-10   65-66
(Black label, dog on side.)
RCA (0600 through 0639) 10-20   68-69
(Orange label.)
RCA (0600 through 0639) 4-8   70-74
(Red label.)
RCA (0600 through 0639) 2-4   77
(Black label, dog near top.)
RCA (0640 through 0642) 20-25   64
(Black label, dog on top.)
RCA (0640 through 0642) 5-10   65-66
(Black label, dog on side.)
RCA (0640 through 0642) 4-8   70-74
(Red label.)
RCA (0643 "Crying in the Chapel") ... 5-10   65
(Black label, dog on side.)
RCA (0643 "Crying in the Chapel") 4-8   70-74
(Red label.)
RCA (0643 "Crying in the Chapel") 2-4   77
(Black label, dog near top.)
RCA (0644 through 0646) 25-35   65
(Black label, dog on top.)
RCA (0644 through 0646) 5-8   65
(Black label, dog on side.)
RCA (0644 through 0646) 15-25   68-69
(Orange label.)
RCA (0644 through 0646) 4-8   70-74
(Red label.)
RCA (0644 through 0646) 2-4   77
(Black label, dog near top.)
RCA (0647 through 0650) 5-10   65
(Black label, dog on side.)
RCA (0647 through 0650) 4-8   70-74
(Red label.)
RCA (0647 through 0650) 2-4   77
(Black label, dog near top.)
RCA (0651 and 0652) 10-12   66
(Black label, dog on side.)
RCA (0651 and 0652) 4-8   70-74
(Red label.)
RCA (0653 through 0658) 5-10   66-68
(Black label, dog on side.)
RCA (0653 through 0658) 4-8   70-74
(Red label.)
RCA (0653 through 0658) 2-4   77
(Black label, dog near top.)
RCA (0659 "Indescribably Blue") 10-15   70
(Red label.)
RCA (0660 "Long Legged Girl") 25-35   70
(Red label.)
RCA (0661 "Judy") 10-15   70
(Red label.)
RCA (0662 "Big Boss Man") 8-10   70
(Red label.)

RCA (0663 through 0685) 4-8   70-73
(Red label.)
RCA (0663 through 0685) 2-4   77
(Black label, dog near top.)
RCA (0720 "Blue Christmas") 10-15   64
(Black label, dog on top.)

Gold Standard Singles with "GB" prefix
(Commercial)

RCA (10156 through 10489) 4-8   75-76
(Red label.)
RCA (10156 through 10489) 2-4   77
(Black label, dog near top.)
RCA (11326 through 13275) 2-4   77
(Black label, dog near top.)
Gold Standard promotional singles are in numerical sequence in the section for Promotional Singles.

Gold Standard Picture Sleeves

RCA (0601 "That's All Right") 50-60   64
RCA (0602 "Good Rockin' Tonight") .. 50-60   64
RCA (0605 "Heartbreak Hotel") 50-60   64
RCA (0608 "Don't Be Cruel") 50-60   64
RCA (0618 "All Shook Up") 50-60   64
RCA (0639 "Kiss Me Quick") 20-25   64
RCA (0643 "Crying in the Chapel") .. 15-20   65
RCA (0647 "Blue Christmas") 20-25   65
(Pictures Elvis on a Christmas card among wrapped gifts.)
RCA (0647 "Blue Christmas") 8-10   77
(Pictures Elvis in a circle among colored ornaments.)
RCA (0650 "Puppet on a String") 20-25   65
RCA (0651 "Joshua Fit the Battle") .. 50-75   66
RCA (0652 "Milky White Way") 50-75   66
RCA (0651 and 0652 "Special Easter Programming Kit") 600-750   66
(Picture sleeve-mailer. Contained both 1966 Easter singles, *Joshua Fit the Battle* and *Milky White Way* in their sleeves and an Easter greeting card from Elvis. Price is for the complete kit.)
RCA (0651 and 0652 "Special Easter Programming Kit") 300-400   66
(Picture sleeve-mailer only.)
RCA (0720 "Blue Christmas") 30-35   64

Promotional Singles

CREATIVE RADIO ("Elvis 10th Anniversary"/
"The Elvis Hour") 15-20   87
(Demonstration disc, promoting the syndicated 10th anniversary radio special.)
CREATIVE RADIO ("Memories of Elvis"/
"The Elvis Hour") 15-20   87
(Demonstration disc, promoting the syndicated 10th anniversary radio special.)
For *Elvis 50th Birthday Special,* see PRESLEY, Elvis / Buddy Holly.
For *The Elvis Hour,* see PRESLEY, Elvis / Gary Owens.

CREATIVE RADIO ("Nearer My God
to Thee") 5-10   89
(Promotional souvenir only. Issued as a bonus
single with the LP, *Between Takes with Elvis*.)

PARAMOUNT PICTURES (1800 "Blue
Hawaii") 300-500   61
(Single-sided pressing. Issued only to select
theatres, designed for lobby play. Has excerpts of
songs from the film.)

PARAMOUNT PICTURES (2017 "Girls! Girls!
Girls!") 500-750   64
(Issued only to select theatres, designed for lobby
play.)

PARAMOUNT PICTURES (2413
"Roustabout") 2000-2500   64
(Issued only to select theatres, designed for lobby
play. Has an otherwise unreleased alternate take.)

RCA (15 "Old Shep") 600-700   56

RCA (76 "Don't"/"Wear My Ring
Around Your Neck") 500-750   60
(Issued with special sleeve, listed in the Picture
Sleeves section.)

RCA (0088 "Raised on Rock") 8-10   73
(Yellow label.)

RCA (118 "King of the Whole
Wide World") 175-225   62
(Issued with a special sleeve, listed in the Picture
Sleeves section.)

RCA (0130 "How Great Thou Art") ... 25-30   69
(Yellow label.)

RCA (139 "Roustabout") 200-250   64

RCA (162 "How Great Thou Art") .. 125-150   67
(Issued with a special sleeve, listed in the Picture
Sleeves section.)

RCA (0196 "I've Got a
Thing About You Baby") 8-10   74
(Yellow label.)

RCA (0280 "If You Talk in Your Sleep") 8-10   74
(Yellow label.)

RCA (0517 "Little Sister") 100-125   83
(12-inch single.)

RCA (0572 "Merry Christmas Baby") . 12-15   71
(Yellow label.)

RCA (0601 "That's All Right") 50-75   64
(White label.)

RCA (0602 "Good Rockin' Tonight") .. 50-75   64
(White label.)

RCA (0605 "Heartbreak Hotel") 50-75   64
(White label.)

RCA (0608 "Don't Be Cruel") 50-75   64
(White label.)

RCA (0618 "All Shook Up") 50-75   64
(White label.)

RCA (0619 "Until It's Time
for You to Go") 10-12   72
(Yellow label.)

RCA (0639 "Kiss Me Quick") 20-25   64
(White label.)

RCA (0643 "Crying in the Chapel") .. 15-20   65
(White label.)

RCA (0647 "Blue Christmas") 25-30   65
(White label.)

RCA (0650 "Puppet on a String") 25-30   65
(White label.)

RCA (0651 "Joshua Fit the Battle") .. 30-40   66
(White label.)

RCA (0652 "Milky White Way") 30-40   66
(White label. See Gold Standard Picture Sleeves
section for special mailing sleeve used with 0651
and 0652.)

RCA (0651 "He Touched Me") 45-55   72
(Yellow label.)

RCA (0672 "An American Trilogy") ... 12-15   72
(Yellow label.)

RCA (0720 "Blue Christmas") 25-30   64
(White label.)

RCA (0769 "Burning Love") 8-10   72
(Yellow label.)

RCA (0808 "Blue Christmas") .. 1000-1500   57

RCA (0815 "Separate Ways") 8-10   72
(Yellow label.)

RCA (0910 "Steamroller Blues") 8-10   73
(Yellow label.)

RCA (6357 "Mystery Train") 200-300   55
(White "Record Prevue" label.)

RCA (8360 "Viva Las Vegas") 20-25   64
(White label.)

RCA (8400 "Such a Night") 2000-3000   64
(White label.)

RCA (8440 "Ask Me") 20-25   64
(White label.)

RCA (8500 "Do the Clam") 20-25   65
(White label.)

RCA (8585 "It Feels So Right") 20-25   65
(White label.)

RCA (8657 "I'm Yours") 20-25   65
(White label.)

RCA (8740 "Tell Me Why") 20-25   65
(White label.)

RCA (8780 "Frankie and Johnny") ... 20-25   66
(White label.)

RCA (8870 "Love Letters") 20-25   66
(White label.)

RCA (8941 "Spinout") 20-25   66
(White label.)

RCA (8950 "If Everyday
Was Like Christmas") 20-35   66
(White label.)

RCA (9056 "Indescribably Blue") 20-25   67
(White label.)

RCA (9115 "Long Legged Girl") 20-25   67
(White label.)

RCA (9287 "There's Always Me") ... 20-25   67
(White label.)

RCA (9341 "Big Boss Man") 20-25   67
(White label.)

RCA (9425 "Guitar Man") 15-20   68
(Yellow label.)
RCA (9465 "U.S. Male") 15-20   68
(Yellow label.)
RCA (9547 "Your Time
Hasn't Come Yet Baby") 15-20   68
(Yellow label.)
RCA (9600 "You'll Never Walk Alone") 15-20   68
(Yellow label.)
RCA (9610 "Almost in Love") 10-15   68
(Yellow label.)
RCA (9670 "If I Can Dream") 10-15   68
(Yellow label.)
RCA (9731 "Memories") 10-15   69
(Yellow label.)
RCA (9741 "In the Ghetto") 10-15   69
(Yellow label.)
RCA (9747 "Clean Up
Your Own Back Yard") 10-15   69
(Yellow label.)
RCA (9764 "Suspicious Minds") 10-15   69
(Yellow label.)
RCA (9768 "Don't Cry Daddy") 10-15   69
(Yellow label.)
RCA (9791 "Kentucky Rain") 10-15   70
(Yellow label.)
RCA (9835 "The Wonder of You") . . . 10-15   70
(Yellow label.)
RCA (9873 "I've Lost You") 10-15   70
(Yellow label.)
RCA (9916 "You Don't
Have to Say You Love Me") 10-15   70
(Yellow label.)
RCA (9960 "I Really Don't
Want to Know") 10-15   70
(Yellow label.)
RCA (9980 "Where Did
They Go Lord") 10-15   71
(Yellow label.)
RCA (9985 "Life") 10-15   71
(Yellow label.)
RCA (9998 "I'm Leavin") 10-15   71
(Yellow label.)
RCA (10074 "Promised Land") 8-10   74
(Yellow label.)
RCA (10191 "My Boy") 8-10   75
(Yellow label.)
RCA (10278 "T-r-o-u-b-l-e") 8-10   75
(Yellow label.)
RCA (10401 "Bringing It Back") 8-10   75
(Yellow label.)
RCA (10601 "Hurt") 8-10   76
(Yellow label.)
RCA (10857 "Moody Blue") 6-10   76
(Yellow label. Black vinyl.)
RCA (10857 "Moody Blue") 900-1000   76
(Experimental colored vinyl pressings. Not
intended for distribution.)
RCA (10951 "Let Me Be There") . . 100-125   77

RCA (10998 "Way Down") 125-150   77
(White label.)
RCA (10998 "Way Down") 6-10   77
(Yellow label.)
RCA (11165 "My Way") 6-10   77
(Yellow label.)
RCA (11212 "Softly, As I Leave You") . 6-10   78
(Yellow label.)
RCA (11320 "Teddy Bear") 6-10   78
(Yellow label.)
RCA (11533 "Are You Sincere") 6-10   79
(Yellow label.)
RCA (11679 "I Got a
Feelin' in My Body") 6-10   79
(Yellow label.)
RCA (12158 "Guitar Man") 6-10   81
(Yellow label. Black vinyl.)
RCA (12158 "Guitar Man") 200-300   81
(Yellow label. Colored vinyl.))
RCA (12205 "Lovin' Arms") 6-10   81
(Yellow label. Black vinyl.)
RCA (12205 "Lovin' Arms") 200-300   81
(Yellow label. Colored vinyl.)
RCA (13058 "You'll Never Walk Alone") 6-10   82
(Yellow label.)
RCA (13302 "The Impossible
Dream") 75-100   82
RCA (13351 "The Elvis Medley") 6-10   82
(Yellow label. Black vinyl.)
RCA (13351 "The Elvis Medley") . . 200-300   82
(Gold label. Colored vinyl.)
RCA (13500 "I Was the One") 6-10   83
(Yellow label. Black vinyl.)
RCA (13500 "I Was the One") 200-300   83
(Yellow label. Colored vinyl.)
RCA (13547 "Little Sister") 6-10   83
(Yellow label. Black vinyl.)
RCA (13547 "Little Sister") 175-200   83
(Blue label. Colored vinyl.)
RCA (13875 "Baby, Let's
Play House") 150-200   84
(Gold label. Colored vinyl.)
RCA (13929 "Blue Suede Shoes) 6-10   84
(Gold label. Colored vinyl.)
RCA (14090 "Always on My Mind") . . . 6-10   85
(Gold label. Colored vinyl.)
RCA (14237 "Merry Christmas Baby") . 6-10   85
Note: Elvis 50th Anniversary singles—RCA 13875
through 14237—used the same gold label for both
commercial and promotional issues. Promo singles
have "Not For Sale" printed on the label.
RCA (4-834-115 "I'll Be Back") . 7500-10000   66
(White label. Single-sided disc. Reads "For Special
Academy Consideration Only." Quantity made is
unknown; however, only two are now known to
exist. Made for submission to the Academy of
Motion Picture Arts and Sciences.

ROYAL CARIBBEAN CRUISE LINES (12690
"Follow That Dream - Take 2") 10-20   90
(Souvenir disc for Elvis cruise passengers.)

UNITED STATES AIR FORCE (125 "It's Now
Or Never"): see PRESLEY, Elvis / Jaye P.
Morgan.

UNITED STATES AIR FORCE (159 "Surrender"):
see PRESLEY, Elvis / Lawrence Welk.

WHAT'S IT ALL ABOUT (78 "Life"): see PRESLEY,
Elvis / Helen Reddy

WHAT'S IT ALL ABOUT (1840 "Elvis
Presley") 70-75   80

WHAT'S IT ALL ABOUT (3025 "Elvis
Presley") 50-60   82
Note: Plastic soundsheets and flexi-discs are listed
in a separate section that follows. Promotional 78s
are included with Singles: 78rpm,, at the beginning
of the Presley section.

Plastic Soundsheets/Flexi-discs

EVA-TONE (38713 "Elvis Speaks! The
Truth About Me") 30-40
(Eva-Tone number is not on label but is etched in
the trail-off.)

EVA-TONE (52578 "The King Is Dead
Long Live the King") 90-100   78

EVA-TONE (831942 "50,000,000 Elvis
Fans Weren't Wrong!") 5-10   83

EVA-TONE (726771 "The Elvis Presley
Story") 5-10   77

EVA-TONE (1037710 "Elvis Live") ... 30-40   78
(Price for magazine, titled Collector's Issue, with
bound-in soundsheet.)

EVA-TONE (1037710 "Elvis Live") ... 15-20   78
(Price for soundsheet only.)

EVA-TONE (1227785 "Thompson
Vocal Eliminator") 15-20   78
(Has segments of songs by three artists including
Elvis.)

EVA-TONE (10287733 "Elvis: Six
Hour Special") 15-20   77

EVA-TONE/RCA ("Love Me Tender") . 25-35   74
(Price for April 1974 issue of Teen Magazine with
bound-in soundsheet.)

EVA-TONE/RCA ("Love Me Tender") . 15-25   74
(Price for soundsheet only.)

LYNCHBURG AUDIO ("The Truth
About Me") 125-150   56
(Lynchburg Audio number is not on label but is
etched in the trail-off.)

RAINBO ("Elvis Speaks - In
Person") 300-325   56
(Price for magazine, Elvis Answers Back, with
78rpm flexi-disc still attached to front cover.)

RAINBO ("Elvis Speaks - In
Person") 100-125   56
(Price for flexi-disc only.)

RAINBO ("The Truth About Me") .. 300-325   56
(Price for magazine, Elvis Answers Back, with
78rpm paper flexi-disc still attached to front cover.)

RAINBO ("The Truth About Me") .. 100-125   56
(Price for flexi-disc only.)
Note: All soundsheets and flexi-discs were used for
some type of promotional purpose.

EPs: 7-inch 33/45rpm
(Commercial and Promotional)

RCA (15 Extended Plays) 800-1000   55
(Set of 10 discs. No box or cover is known to exist
for this package. For just the Elvis EP from this set,
see RCA 9089.)

RCA (19 "The Sound of
Leadership") 1800-2200   56
(Boxed set of eight discs. Includes inserts and
custom inner sleeves. For just the Elvis EP from
this set, see RCA 9113. Promotional issue only.)

RCA (22 "Elvis Presley") 800-1000   56
("Elvis" in dark pink letters on front cover. Two-EP
bonus promotional item. Discs are numbered 9121
and 9122.)

RCA (22 "Elvis Presley") 750-950   56
("Elvis" in light pink letters on front cover. Two-EP
bonus promotional item. Discs are numbered 9121
and 9122.)

RCA (23 "Elvis Presley") 2000-2500   56
(Three-EP bonus promotional item. Discs are
numbered 9123, 9124 and 9125.)

RCA (26 "Great Country/
Western Hits") 800-1000   56
(Boxed set of 10 discs. Includes inserts and
custom inner sleeves. For just the Elvis EP from
this set, see RCA 9141.)

RCA (27 "Save-On Records") 250-300   56
(Various artists sampler. Promotional issue only.)

RCA (37 "Perfect for Parties") 80-120   56
(Various artists sampler. Issued with paper sleeve.
Promotional issue only. Issued with paper
envelope/sleeve. Promotional issue only.)

RCA (39 "Dealers' Prevue") 900-1200   57
(Various artists sampler. Issued with paper
envelope/sleeve. Promotional issue only.)

RCA (61 Extended Play Sampler) 1000-1500   57
(Various artists EP sampler. Not issued with
sleeve. Promotional issue only.)

RCA (121 "RCA Family
Record Center") 1500-2000   62
(Various artists sampler. Not issued with sleeve.
Promotional issue only.)

RCA (128 "Elvis By Request") 50-60   61

RCA (747 "Elvis Presley") 140-160   56
(Black label, without dog.)

RCA (747 "Elvis Presley") 75-100   56
(Black label, dog on top. Has song title strip across
the top of front cover.)

RCA (747 "Elvis Presley") 50-70   65
(Black label, dog on side.)

RCA (747 "Elvis Presley") 60-90   69
(Orange label.)

RCA (747 "Blue Suede Shoes") ... 550-650   56
(Temporary paper sleeve for 1956 issue of
EPA-747. Price is for sleeve only.)

RCA (821 "Heartbreak Hotel") 200-250   56
(Black label, without dog.)

RCA (821 "Heartbreak Hotel") 75-100   56
(Black label, dog on top. Has song title strip across
the top of front cover.)

RCA (821 "Heartbreak Hotel") 50-70   65
(Black label, dog on side.)

RCA (821 "Heartbreak Hotel") 60-90   69
(Orange label.)

RCA (830 "Elvis Presley") 75-100   56
(Black label, dog on top. Has song title strip across
the top of front cover.)

RCA (830 "Elvis Presley") 200-250   56
(Black label, without dog.)

RCA (830 "Elvis Presley") 50-70   65
(Black label, dog on side.)

RCA (830 "Elvis Presley") 60-90   69
(Orange label.)

RCA (940 "The Real Elvis") 75-100   56
(Black label, dog on top. Has song title strip across
the top of front cover.)

RCA (940 "The Real Elvis") 200-250   56
(Black label, without dog. Reissued as Gold
Standard 5120.)

RCA (965 "Any Way You Want Me") 75-100   56
(Black label, dog on top. Has song title strip across
the top of front cover.)

RCA (965 "Any Way You Want Me") 200-250   56
(Black label, without dog.)

RCA (965 "Any Way You Want Me") . 50-70   65
(Black label, dog on side.)

RCA (965 "Any Way You Want Me") . 60-90   69
(Orange label.)

RCA (992 "Elvis, Vol. 1") 75-100   56
(Black label, dog on top. Has song title strip across
the top of front cover.)

RCA (992 "Elvis, Vol. 1") 200-250   56
(Black label, without dog.)

RCA (992 "Elvis, Vol. 1") 50-70   65
(Black label, dog on side.)

RCA (992 "Elvis, Vol. 1") 60-90   69
(Orange label.)

RCA (993 "Elvis, Vol. 2") 75-100   56
(Black label, dog on top. Has song title strip across
the top of front cover.)

RCA (993 "Elvis, Vol. 2") 200-250   56
(Black label, without dog.)

RCA (993 "Elvis, Vol. 2") 50-70   65
(Black label, dog on side.)

RCA (993 "Elvis, Vol. 2") 60-90   69
(Orange label.)

RCA (994 "Strictly Elvis") 75-100   56
(Black label, dog on top. Has song title strip across
the top of front cover.)

RCA (994 "Strictly Elvis") 200-250   56

(Black label, without dog.)

RCA (994 "Strictly Elvis") 50-70   65
(Black label, dog on side.)

RCA (994 "Strictly Elvis") 60-90   69
(Orange label.)

RCA (1254 "Elvis Presley") 500-600   56
(Black label, without dog. Two EP set.)

RCA (1254 "Elvis Presley") 300-400   56
(Black label, dog on top. Two EP set.)

RCA (1254 "Most Talked-About
New Personality") 1800-2000   56
(Two EPs, also numbered 0793 and 0794, in a
single pocket paper sleeve. Promotional issue only.
Add $50 to $75 if accompanied by a copy of
Dee-Jay Digest.)

RCA (1254 "Most Talked-About
New Personality") 400-500   56
(Price for the two EPs without the sleeve. Either
disc would be worth about half the amount shown
for both. Discs, numbered 0793 and 0794, are
untitled. Promotional issue only.)

RCA (1-1515 "Loving You, Vol. 1") .. 75-100   57
(Black label, dog on top. Has song title strip across
the top of front cover.)

RCA (1-1515 "Loving You, Vol. 1") ... 50-70   65
(Black label, dog on side.)

RCA (1-1515 "Loving You, Vol. 1") ... 60-90   69
(Orange label.)

RCA (2-1515 "Loving You, Vol. 2") .. 75-100   57
(Black label, dog on top. Has song title strip across
the top of front cover.)

RCA (2-1515 "Loving You, Vol. 2") ... 50-70   65
(Black label, dog on side.)

RCA (2-1515 "Loving You, Vol. 2") ... 60-90   69
(Orange label.)

RCA (2006 "Aloha from Hawaii") 60-75   74
(Includes sheet of 10 title strips. Made for jukebox
operators only.)

RCA (4006 "Love Me Tender") 200-250   56
(Black label, without dog. Has song title strip
across the top of front cover.)

RCA (4006 "Love Me Tender") 75-100   56
(Black label, dog on top. Has song title strip across
the top of front cover.)

RCA (4006 "Love Me Tender") 50-70   65
(Black label, dog on side.)

RCA (4006 "Love Me Tender") 60-90   69
(Orange label.)

RCA (4041 "Just for You") 200-250   57
(Black label, without dog. Has EP title strip across
the top of front cover.)

RCA (4041 "Just for You") 75-100   57
(Black label, dog on top. Has EP title strip across
the top of front cover.)

RCA (4041 "Just for You") 50-70   65
(Black label, dog on side.)

RCA (4041 "Just for You") 60-90   69
(Orange label.)

RCA (4054 "Peace in the Valley") .. 75-100   57
(Black label, dog on top. Has EP title strip across
the top of front cover. Reissued as Gold Standard
5121.)

RCA (4108 "Elvis Sings
Christmas Songs") 75-100   57
(Black label, dog on top. Has EP title strip across
the top of front cover.)

RCA (4108 "Elvis Sings
Christmas Songs") 50-70   65
(Black label, dog on side.)

RCA (4108 "Elvis Sings
Christmas Songs") 60-90   69
(Orange label.)

RCA (4114 "Jailhouse Rock") 65-85   57
(Black label, dog on top.)

RCA (4114 "Jailhouse Rock") 50-70   65
(Black label, dog on side.)

RCA (4114 "Jailhouse Rock") 60-90   69
(Orange label.)

RCA (4319 "King Creole") 75-100   58
(Reissued as Gold Standard 5122.)

RCA (4321 "King Creole Vol. 2") 65-85   58
(Black label, dog on top.)

RCA (4321 "King Creole Vol. 2") 50-70   65
(Black label, dog on side.)

RCA (4321 "King Creole Vol. 2") 60-90   69
(Orange label.)

RCA (4325 "Elvis Sails") 75-100   58
(Reissued as Gold Standard 5157.)

RCA (4340 "Christmas with Elvis") .. 75-100   58
(Black label, dog on top.)

RCA (4340 "Christmas with Elvis") ... 50-70   65
(Black label, dog on side.)

RCA (4340 "Christmas with Elvis") ... 60-90   69
(Orange label.)

RCA (4368 "Follow That Dream") 70-90   62
(Black label, dog on top. Playing times are
incorrectly listed for three of the four tracks: *Follow
That Dream* shown as 1:35, should be 1:38; *Angel*
shown as 2:35, should be 2:40; and *I'm Not the
Marrying Kind* shown as 1:49, should be 2:00.)

RCA (4368 "Follow That Dream") 50-70   62
(Black label, dog on top. All playing times are
correctly shown.)

RCA (4368 "Follow That Dream") ... 75-100   62
(Promotional issue only. Marked "Not For Sale.")

RCA (4368 "Follow That Dream") .. 125-160   62
(Special paper sleeve, issued to radio stations and
jukebox operators. Promotional issue only. Price is
for sleeve only.)

RCA (4368 "Follow That Dream") 50-70   65
(Black label, dog on side.)

RCA (4368 "Follow That Dream") 60-90   69
(Orange label.)

RCA (4371 "Kid Galahad") 60-80   62
(Black label, dog on top.)

RCA (4371 "Kid Galahad") 50-70   65
(Black label, dog on side.)

RCA (4371 "Kid Galahad") 60-90   69
(Orange label.)

RCA (4382 "Viva Las Vegas") 65-85   64
(Black label, dog on top.)

RCA (4382 "Viva Las Vegas") 50-70   65
(Black label, dog on side.)

RCA (4382 "Viva Las Vegas") 60-90   69
(Orange label.)

RCA (4383 "Tickle Me") 50-70   65
(Black label, dog on side.)

RCA (4383 "Tickle Me") 60-90   69
(Orange label.)

RCA (4387 "Easy Come, Easy Go") . 50-70   67
(Black label, dog on side.)

RCA (4387 "Easy Come, Easy Go") 100-150   67
(White label. Promotional Issue Only.)

RCA (5088 "A Touch of Gold,
Vol. I") 425-500   59
(Maroon label.)

RCA (5088 "A Touch of Gold, Vol. I") 75-100   59
(Black label, dog on top. Add $15 to $25 if
accompanied by "I am a loyal Elvis fan" insert
card.)

RCA (5088 "A Touch of Gold, Vol. I") . 50-70   65
(Black label, dog on side.)

RCA (5088 "A Touch of Gold, Vol. I") . 60-90   69
(Orange label.)

RCA (5101 "A Touch of Gold,
Vol. II") 425-500   59
(Maroon label.)

RCA (5101 "A Touch of Gold, Vol. II") 75-100   59
(Black label, dog on top. Add $15 to $25 if
accompanied by "I am a loyal Elvis fan" insert
card.)

RCA (5101 "A Touch of Gold, Vol. II") 50-70   65
(Black label, dog on side.)

RCA (5101 "A Touch of Gold, Vol. II") 60-90   69
(Orange label.)

RCA (5120 "The Real Elvis") 500-600   59
(Maroon label. Reissue of 940.)

RCA (5120 "The Real Elvis") 55-75   59
(Black label, dog on top.)

RCA (5120 "The Real Elvis") 50-70   65
(Black label, dog on side.)

RCA (5120 "The Real Elvis") 60-90   69
(Orange label.)

RCA (5121 "Peace in the Valley") . 500-600   59
(Maroon label. Reissue of 4054.)

RCA (5121 "Peace in the Valley") ... 60-80   59
(Black label, dog on top.)

RCA (5121 "Peace in the Valley") ... 50-70   65
(Black label, dog on side.)

RCA (5121 "Peace in the Valley") ... 60-90   69
(Orange label.)

RCA (5122 "King Creole") 800-1000   59
(Maroon label. Reissue of 4319.)

RCA (5122 "King Creole") 60-80   59
(Black label, dog on top.)

RCA (5122 "King Creole") 50-70   65
(Black label, dog on side.)
RCA (5122 "King Creole") 60-90   69
(Orange label.)
RCA (5141 "A Touch of
Gold, Vol. 3") 425-500   60
(Maroon label.)
RCA (5141 "A Touch of Gold, Vol. 3") 75-100   60
(Black label, dog on top.)
RCA (5141 "A Touch of Gold, Vol. 3") . 50-70   65
(Black label, dog on side.)
RCA (5141 "A Touch of Gold, Vol. 3") . 60-90   69
(Orange label.)
RCA (5157 "Elvis Sails") 50-70   65
(Black label, dog on top. Reissue of 4325.)
RCA (5157 "Elvis Sails") 50-70   65
(Black label, dog on side.)
RCA (5157 "Elvis Sails") 60-90   69
(Orange label.)
RCA (8705 "TV Guide
Presents Elvis") 800-1200   56
(Price for disc only. Insert sheets are priced
separately below. No sleeve or special cover exists
for this disc. Promotional issue only.)
RCA (8705 "TV Guide
Presents Elvis") 50-100   56
(Price for "Elvis Exclusively" gray insert.)
RCA (8705 "TV Guide
Presents Elvis") 100-200   56
(Price for *Elvis Exclusively* pink insert, with
suggested continuity.)
RCA (9089 "SPD-15 Elvis EP") ... 750-900   56
(Black label. The Elvis disc from SPD-15.)
RCA (9089 "SPD-15 Elvis EP") ... 600-700   56
(Gray label. The Elvis disc from SPD-15. Gray
label pressings were for jukebox operators.)
RCA (9113 "SPD-19 Elvis EP") ... 750-800   56
(The Elvis disc from SPD-19, *The Sound of
Leadership*.)
RCA (9141 "SPD-26 Elvis EP") ... 200-250   56
(Black label. The Elvis disc from SPD-15, *Great
Country/Western Hits*.)
TUPPERWARE (11973 "Tupperware's
Hit Parade") 50-75   73
(Various artists sampler. Promotional issue only.)
Notes: Unless listed and priced separately, all EP
values include both disc and cover with
approximately half of the total attached to each.
Some of the rarer pieces that are often traded
individually (disc or sleeve), as well as those sleeves
that have an exceptionally higher value than their
disc, are listed separately in this section. All EPs in
the 5000 series are Gold Standard Series issues
although none are identified as such on the labels,
only on the covers. Remember, if you don't find the
EP in this section it may contain two, three or four
artists, and will be listed following the Presley LP
section.

LPs: 10/12–inch 33rpm
(Commercial and Promotional)

ABC RADIO (1003 "Elvis
Memories") 475-575   78
(Three-LP boxed set. Add $25 to $50 if
accompanied by a 16-page programmer's booklet
and four pages of additional information. Issued
only to radio stations. Add $40 to $50 if
accompanied by a 7–inch reel tape, with spots and
promotional announcements. Highlights of this
program were issued on Michelob 810.)
ATV (1 "In the Beginning") 25-35   80
(Various artists collection.)
A&M (3930 "Heart of Dixie") 10-15   89
(Various artists collection.)
ASSOCIATED BROADCASTERS (1001
"Legend of a King") 125-150   80
(White label. Advance pressing.)
ASSOCIATED BROADCASTERS (1001
"Legend of a King") 25-30   80
(Picture disc. First pressings are numbered from
3000 through 6000. Number appears under "Side
One" on the disc itself. Cover is standard, die-cut,
picture disc cover. Has several spelling errors on
back cover, including "idle" for idol and
"Jordinaires" instead of Jordanaires.)
ASSOCIATED BROADCASTERS (1001
"Legend of a King") 20-25   80
(Picture disc. Second pressings are numbered
from 6001 through 9000. Most of the spelling
errors were corrected on this cover.)
ASSOCIATED BROADCASTERS (1001
"Legend of a King") 15-20   80
(Picture disc. Third pressings are numbered from
00001 through 02999 and 09001 through 15000.
Cover errors have all been corrected.)
ASSOCIATED BROADCASTERS (1001
"Legend of a King") 10-12   84
(Picture disc. Fourth pressings are also numbered
from 3000 through 6000, but were packaged in a
clear plastic sleeve instead of a conventional
cover.)
ASSOCIATED BROADCASTERS (1001
"Legend of a King") 8-10   85
(Picture disc. Discs are not numbered. Packaged
in a plastic sleeve.)
ASSOCIATED BROADCASTERS ("Legend
of a King") 200-250   85
(Three hour, three-LP set. Not boxed. Price
includes six pages of cue sheets. Available to radio
stations only.)
ASSOCIATED BROADCASTERS ("Legend
of a King") 300-350   85
(Same as above, but packaged in a specially
printed box.)

ASSOCIATED BROADCASTERS ("Legend
of a King") 300-350   86
(Three-LP boxed set, same as above except time
on segment 1-B is increased from 14:25 to 15:15
in order to include a Johnny Bernero interview.)
ASSOCIATED PRESS (1977 "The
World in Sound") 80-100   78
(News highlights of 1977, including coverage of
Elvis' death.)
BEALE STREET (1 "Rebirth of
Beale Street") 200-225   83
(Various artists collection. Promotional issue only.)
BOXCAR ("Having Fun with
Elvis on Stage") 100-125   74
(No number used. Sold in conjunction with Elvis'
concert appearances. Reissued as RCA
CPM1-0818.)
CBS SONGS (101 "Radio's Million
Performance Songs") 40-50   84
(Various artists collection. Promotional issue only.)
CAEDMON (1572 "On the Record") . . 60-80   78
(Various artists collection.)
CAMDEN (2304 "Flaming Star") 15-18   69
(First issued as RCA PRS-279, reissued in 1975
as Pickwick 2304.)
CAMDEN (2408 "Let's Be Friends") . . 15-18   70
(Reissued in 1975 as Pickwick 2408.)
CAMDEN (2428 "Elvis' Christmas
Album") 15-18   70
(Eight songs on this LP were first issued on RCA
LOC-1035. Reissued in 1975 as Pickwick 2428.)
CAMDEN (2440 "Almost in Love") . . . 25-30   70
(With Stay Away Joe.)
CAMDEN (2440 "Almost in Love") . . . 15-18   73
(Stay Away replaces Stay Away Joe. Reissued in
1975 as Pickwick 2440.)
CAMDEN (2472 "You'll Never
Walk Alone") 15-18   71
(Reissued in 1975 as Pickwick 2472.)
CAMDEN (2518 "C'mon Everybody")   15-18   71
(Reissued in 1975 as Pickwick 2518.)
CAMDEN (2533 "I Got Lucky") 15-18   71
(Reissued in 1975 as Pickwick 2533.)
CAMDEN (2567 "Elvis Sings Hits
from His Movies") 15-18   72
(Reissued in 1975 as Pickwick 2567.)
CAMDEN (2595 "Burning Love") 20-30   72
(Add $25 to $35 if accompanied by the bonus 8x10
Elvis photo. Reissued in 1975 as Pickwick 2595.)
CAMDEN (2611 "Separate Ways") 15-18   73
(Reissued in 1975 as Pickwick 2611.)
CENTURY 21 PRODUCTIONS ("Epic of
the '70s") 150-200   76
(Six-LP program of '70s songs by various artists.
Promotional issue only. Not issued with a special
cover.)

COLLECTOR'S EDITION (505 "All-Time
Christmas Favorites") 250-275   78
(Five LP boxed set. Various artists collection, with
one side of one disc by Elvis.)
COUNTRY CROSSROADS (32-83 "Country
Crossroads") 50-100   83
(Various artists collection. Promotional issue only.)
COUNTRY SESSIONS U.S.A. (122 "Best of
Country Sessions U.S.A.") 50-75   83
(Various artists collection. Promotional issue only.)
COUNTRY SESSIONS U.S.A. (126 "A Tribute
to Elvis") 225-250   83
(Price includes cue sheets. Promotional issue only.)
CREATIVE RADIO ("Elvis
Remembered") 100-125   78
(Three-LP set. Price includes six insert pages.
Advance copies of this set, which was not issued
with a special cover or package, were with plain
white, handwritten, labels. These copies may be
valued at $150 to $250. Promotional issue only.)
CREATIVE RADIO ("Elvis, the
Country Side") 75-85   84
(Two-LP set. Promotional issue only.)
CREATIVE RADIO ("Elvis 50th
Anniversary") 250-275   85
(Six-LP set. Price includes seven pages of
programming instructions and cues. Packaged in a
plain, unprinted box. Promotional issue only.)
CREATIVE RADIO ("Elvis 10th
Anniversary") 150-175   87
(Six-LP set. Price includes eight pages of
programming instructions and cues. Packaged in a
custom printed box. Promotional issue only.)
CREATIVE RADIO ("Christmas with
Elvis") 25-30   87
(Promotional issue only. Not issued with special
cover.)
CREATIVE RADIO ("Birthday Tribute
To Elvis") 25-30   88
(Promotional issue only. Not issued with special
cover.)
CREATIVE RADIO ("The Elvis Hour")   10-12   86-88
(Price is for any of the weekly discs in this series.
The first 52 discs in the series have been selling as
a set for $450 to $475. Promotional issues only.)
CREATIVE RADIO ("Demo of 10
Creative Radio Programs") 25-30
(Includes segments of The Elvis Hour, 10th
Anniversary Special and Memories of Elvis, along
with portions of other shows by other artists.
Promotional issue only.)
CREATIVE RADIO (E1 "Elvis Exclusive
Interview") 175-200   88
(Price for complete 1956 Little Rock concert
copies. Only the first 100 copies were pressed with
the full concert. The only way to visually identify
these is to check the disc. On the full concert
pressings, the grooves take up nearly the entire
disc.)

CREATIVE RADIO (E1 "Elvis Exclusive
Interview") 20-30   88
(Has edited concert songs. On this pressing the
grooves occupy only about two-thirds of the disc.)
CREATIVE RADIO ("Between Takes
with Elvis") 150-250   89
(Three-LP set. Promotional issue only. Though not
packaged inside covers—shrink wrapped at the
factory—each LP set came with the bonus single,
Nearer My God to Thee/You Gave Me a Molehill.)
Note: On any of the above listings, Creative Radio
may be shown as Creative Radio Shows or Creative
Radio Network.)
CURRENT AUDIO MAGAZINE (1 "Elvis: Press
Conference") 45-55   72
(Various artists collection.)
DIAMOND P. PRODUCTIONS ("Reflections
of Elvis") 350-400   77
(Three LP set. Various artists collection.)
DICK CLARK (402 "Rock, Roll and
Remember") 100-150   77
(Six LPs. Various artists collection. Promotional
issue only.)
DICK CLARK ("Rock, Roll and
Remember, 1982") 140-170   82
(Four LPs. Various artists collection. Promotional
issue only.)
DICK CLARK ("Rock, Roll and
Remember, 1985") 140-170   85
(Four LPs. Various artists collection. Promotional
issue only.)
DRAKE-CHENAULT ("Elvis: a Three
Hour Special") 300-350   77
(Three-LP boxed set. Includes three pages of cue
sheets.)
DRAKE-CHENAULT ("Golden Years
of Country") 150-250   80
(25 LPs. Various artists collection. Promotional
issue only.)
EMR ENTERPRISES (8 "The Age
of Rock") 100-125   69
(Various artists. Promotional issue only.)
EARTH NEWS ("August 29, 1977") 325-375   77
(Promotional issue only. Price includes one-page
letter.)
ELEKTRA (60107 "Diner") 10-20   82
(Soundtrack.)
FRANKLIN MINT (4 "The Official Grammy
Award Winners") 150-200   85
(Boxed set of four colored vinyl discs. One in a
series of 14 boxed sets, but only this one (titled
The Great Singers) has Elvis. Includes booklet.)
GOLDEN EDITIONS LIMITED (1 "The
First Year") 8-15   79
(Print in upper corners on front cover is in white.
Label Is black. Add $5 to $8 if accompanied by a
12-page booklet and one-page copy of the 1954
Elvis/Scotty Moore contract.)

GOLDEN EDITIONS LIMITED (101 "The
First Year") 15-25   79
(Print in upper corners on front cover is in gold.
Label is white. Add $5 to $8 if accompanied by a
12-page booklet and one-page copy of the 1954
Elvis/Scotty Moore contract. Most of the material
on this LP was previously issued on HALW 00001.)
GREAT NORTHWEST (4005 "The Elvis
Tapes") 10-15   77
(These interviews were repackaged on Starday
995.)
GREAT NORTHWEST (4006 "The King
Speaks") 8-10   77
(This press conference was first issued as Green
Valley 2001.)
GREEN VALLEY (2001 "Elvis 1961
Press Conference") 30-50   77
(Cover is thin, soft stock and does not have black
bar on spine. Label does not have the catalog
number on it.)
GREEN VALLEY (2001 "Elvis 1961
Press Conference") 12-15   77
(Cover is standard stock and has black bar on
spine. Label has the catalog number on it.
Repackaged as one half of Green Valley
2001/2003. It was later repackaged as Great
Northwest 4006.)
GREEN VALLEY (2001/2003 "Elvis Speaks
to You") 25-30   78
(GV-2001 was first issued as a single LP.)
HALW (00001 "The First Years") 25-30   78
(Repackaged in 1979 on Golden Editions 1.)
HEARTLAND/RCA (1072/4 "Unforgettable
Fifties") 18-22   88
(Four LPs. TV mail-order, various artists collection.)
INTERNATIONAL HOTEL PRESENTS
ELVIS—1969 1000-1500   69
(Custom gift box prepared by Col. Parker and RCA
for International Hotel guests. Originally contained:
RCA LPM-4088 and LSP-4155, three 8x10 Elvis
photos, RCA Elvis catalog, calendar and a
nine-page letter. Price is for complete set but box
itself represents 90-95% of value.)
INTERNATIONAL HOTEL PRESENTS
ELVIS—1970 1000-1500   70
(Custom gift box prepared by Col. Parker and RCA
for International Hotel guests. Originally contained:
RCA LSP-6020 and 45-9791, one 8x10 Elvis
photo, photo album, RCA Elvis catalog, calendar,
menu and letter. Price is for complete set but box
itself represents 90-95% of value.)
K-TEL (9900 "Elvis Love Songs") . . . 15-20   81
LOUISIANA HAYRIDE (3061 "The
Beginning Years") 300-350   84
(White label advance pressing from RCA,
Indianapolis, where this LP was manufactured.)

LOUISIANA HAYRIDE (3061 "The
Beginning Years") 15-25   84
(Price includes 20-page *D.J. Fontana Remembers
Elvis* booklet, a four sheet copy of Elvis' Hayride
contract and a 10x10 *Presleyana, Second Edition*
flyer, all of which represent about $5 to $10 of the
value. Selections from this LP are also on the
Music Works 3601 and 3602.)
LOUISIANA HAYRIDE (8454 "The
Louisiana Hayride") 550-650   76
(Yellow label. A program of various artists including
Elvis. Issued to radio stations only.)
LOUISIANA HAYRIDE (8454 "The
Louisiana Hayride") 300-325   81
(Gold label. A program of various artists including
Elvis.)
LOWERY GROUP (1 "25 Golden
Years") 40-60   80
(Two-LP, various artists collection. Promotional
issue only.)
MCA ("MCA Music") 40-60
(No number used. Four-LP set with excerpts of 200
songs by various artists.)
MFSL (059 "From Elvis in Memphis") . 30-50   82
(First issued as RCA LSP-4155.)
MARCH of DIMES (0653 "Discs
for Dimes") 1400-1600   56
(Various artist, 16–inch disc. Promotional issue
only. Includes 16 pages of notes.)
MARCH of DIMES (0657 "Disc Jockey
Interviews") 1400-1600   56
(Various artist, 16–inch disc. Promotional issue
only. Includes scripts and notes.)
MARVENCO (101 "1954-1955, The
Beginning") 10-15   88
(Has material perviously issued on Golden Editions
101.)
MEDIA ENTERTAINMENT ("The King's
Gold") 50-75   85
(Three reel-to-reel tapes, issued only to radio
stations. Price includes cue sheets. Not known to
exist on disc.)
MICHELOB (810 "Highlights of
Elvis Memories") 175-200   78
(A Michelob in-house promotional issue only.
Elvis Memories was first issued on ABC Radio
1003.
MORE MUSIC (333-72 "A Chronology of
American Music") 500-600   72
(21-LP set of number one songs by various artists.
For radio stations only. Not issued with any special
box or package.)
MUSIC WORKS (3601 "The First
Live Recordings") 8-10   84
(This material was first issued on Louisiana
Hayride 3061.)
MUSIC WORKS (3602 "Hillbilly Cat") . 8-10   84
(This material was first issued on Louisiana
Hayride 3061.)

MUTUAL ("Super Songs") 30-50
(Various artists collection. Promotional issue only.)
MUTUAL BROADCAST SYSTEM (4082 "The
Frantic Fifties") 250-300   59
(Various artists collection. Promotional issue only.)
NEW WORLD (207 "Country Music in
the Modern Era") 50-70   77
(Various artists collection. Promotional issue only.)
OAK (1003 "Vintage 1955") 70-100   91
ORIGINAL SOUND RECORDINGS (11 "Rock
Rock Rock") 40-50   72
(Various artists collection.)
PAIR (1010 "Double Dynamite") 20-25   82
(First issued as Pickwick 5001.)
PAIR (1037 "Remembering Elvis") ... 20-25   83
PICKWICK (1 "We're Playing
Your Song") 20-40   80
(Various artists collection.)
PICKWICK (2304 "Flaming Star") 8-10   75
(First issued as RCA PRS-279.)
PICKWICK (2408 "Let's Be Friends"
black vinyl) 8-10   75
(First issued as Camden 2408.)
PICKWICK (2408 "Let's Be Friends"
colored vinyl) 500-600
(Experimental pressing only. There is no colored
vinyl commercial or promotional edition of this
issue.)
PICKWICK (2428 "Elvis' Christmas
Album") 8-10   75
(First issued as Camden 2428.)
PICKWICK (2428 "Elvis' Christmas
Album") 15-25   86
(Has RCA Special Products on label and cover.)
PICKWICK (2440 "Almost In Love") .. 8-10   75
(First issued as Camden 2440.)
PICKWICK (2472 "You'll Never
Walk Alone") 8-10   75
(First issued as Camden 2472.)
PICKWICK (2518 "C'mon
Everybody") 8-10   75
(First issued as Camden 2518.)
PICKWICK (2533 "I Got Lucky") 8-10   75
(First issued as Camden 2533.)
PICKWICK (2567 "Elvis Sings Hits
from His Movies") 8-10   75
(First issued as Camden 2567.)
PICKWICK (2595 "Burning Love") 8-10   75
(First issued as Camden 2595.)
PICKWICK (2611 "Separate Ways") .. 8-10   75
(First issued as Camden 2611.)
PICKWICK (5001 "Double Dynamite") 25-30   75
(Repackaged in 1982 as Pair 1010.)
PICKWICK (7007 "Frankie and
Johnny") 10-12   76
(First issued as RCA 3553.)
PICKWICK (7064 "Mahalo from
Elvis") 15-20   78

PLAYBOY (7473 "The Playboy Music Hall
of Fame Winners") 175-225   78
(Three-LP, various artists collection.)

PREMORE (589 "Early Elvis") 5-10   89
(Mail-order album from the Solo Cup Company.)

PROMO ("All Time Greats, Vol. 1") . . 20-30
(Various artists collection.)

PROMO ("All Time Greats, Vol. 3") . . 20-30
(Various artists collection.)

RCA (EPC-1 "Special Christmas
Program" Reel Tape) 300-325   67
(Price includes programming inserts, which
represent $25-35 of the value. This show was
never issued commercially on disc. Any 10–inch
red vinyl LPs of this material with the EPC-1
number are unauthorized.)

RCA (TB-1 "A Collectors Edition") . 100-150   76
(Five-LP boxed set. Various artists collection.)

RCA (0001 "Robert W.
Sarnoff") 1500-2000   73
(Various artists collection. Promotional issue only.)

RCA (4 Untitled RCA Sampler) . . 1000-1500   56
(Various artists collection. Promotional issue only.)

RCA (10 Untitled RCA Sampler) . . 900-1200   58
(Various artists collection. Promotional issue only.)

RCA (010 "Elvis! His Greatest Hits") 400-450   79
(White box edition. Eight-LP boxed set, sold
mail-order by *Reader's Digest.*)

RCA (010 "Elvis! His Greatest Hits") . 40-60   83
(Yellow box edition. Seven-LP boxed set, sold
mail-order by *Reader's Digest.* See RCA 181 for
the bonus LP offered with this set.)

RCA (27 "August 1959 Sampler") 750-1000   59
(Various artists collection. Promotional issue only.)

RCA (0034 "QSP Presents a
Gift of Music") 40-60   84
(Various artists collection. Promotional issue only.)

RCA RBA-040: see READER'S DIGEST 040

RCA (54 "October Christmas
Sampler") 600-750   59
(Various artists collection. Promotional issue only.)

RCA (0056 "Elvis") 40-50   73
(Mustard color label. Cover shows "Brookville
Records" in upper right. A mail-order LP offer.)

RCA (0056 "Elvis") 20-25   73
(Blue label. Cover doesn't show "Brookville
Records." Mail-order LP offer. Repackaged in 1978
and titled *Elvis Commemorative Album.*)

RCA (0056 "Elvis Commemorative
Album") 75-80   78
(Price includes a "Registered Certificate of
Ownership." A mail-order LP offer. First titled *Elvis,*
using the same catalog number.)

RCA (59-7 "February Sampler") . . . 600-800   59
(Various artists collection. Promotional issue only.)

RCA (66 "Christmas Programming
from RCA") 1000-1200   59
(Various artists collection. Includes paper
sleeve/cover. Promotional issue only.)

RCA (072 "Great Hits of 1956-57") . . 10-20   87
(Offered as a bonus LP from *Reader's Digest,* with
the purchase of one of their non-Elvis boxed sets.)

RCA (0086 "Brightest Stars
of Christmas") 30-50   74
(Various artists collection. JC Penny promotional
issue only.)

RCA (96 "October 1960 Popular
Stereo Sampler") 500-750   60
(Various artists collection. Promotional issue only.)

RCA (0108 "E-Z Country No. 2") . . 250-300   55
(Various artists collection. 10–inch LP. Promotional
issue only.)

RCA (141 "October '61
Pop Sampler") 500-750   61
(Various artists collection. Promotional issue only.)

RCA (0168 "Elvis in Hollywood") 35-45   76
(Add $10 to $15 is accompanied by a 20-page
photo booklet.)

RCA (181 "Elvis Sings
Inspirational Favorites") 15-20   83
(Special Products, Reader's Digest mail-order
bonus LP for buyers of the 1983 edition of RCA
010. Price includes 24-page Reader's Digest
Music catalog.)

RCA (191 "Elvis, the Legend
Lives On") 40-45   86
(Seven-LP boxed set, sold mail-order by Reader's
Digest. Includes booklet.)

RCA (0197 "E-Z Pop No. 6") 250-300   56
(Various artists collection. 10–inch LP. Promotional
issue only.)

RCA (0199 "E-Z Country No. 3") . . 250-300   56
(Various artists collection. 10–inch LP. Promotional
issue only.)

RCA (215 "30 Years of No. 1
Country Hits") 40-55   86
(Seven-LP boxed set. Various artists collection.)

RCA (219 "September '63
Pop Sampler") 500-750   63
(Various artists collection. Promotional issue only.)

RCA (242 "Elvis Sings
Country Favorites") 20-30   84
(Bonus LP from Reader's Digest, given with the
purchase of their seven-disc boxed set, *The Great
Country Entertainers.*—which has no Elvis cuts.)

RCA (247 "December '63
Pop Sampler") 500-750   63
(Various artists collection. Promotional issue only.)

RCA (0263 "The Elvis Presley Story") 30-40   77
(Special Products five-LP boxed set. A Candelite
Music mail-order offer.)

RCA (0264 "Songs of Inspiration") . . . 10-15   77
(Special Products issue. A Candelite Music
mail-order bonus LP for buyers of RCA 0263.)

RCA (272 "April '64 Pop Sampler") 500-750   64
(Various artists collection. Promotional issue only.)

RCA (279 "Singer Presents Elvis") . . . 70-80   68
(Reissued in 1969 as Camden 2304 and in 1975
as Pickwick 2304.)

RCA (0283 "Elvis, Including Fool") . . . 50-60   73

RCA (331 "April '65 Pop Sampler") 500-750   65
(Various artists collection. Promotional issue only.)

RCA (0341 "Legendary
Performer, Vol. 1") 20-25   74
(With die-cut cover. Add $5 to $10 if accompanied
by *The Early Years* booklet.)

RCA (0341 "Legendary
Performer, Vol. 1") 5-10   83
(With standard cover—not die-cut.)

RCA (0341 "Legendary
Performer, Vol. 1") 800-1000   78
(Picture discs of the 0341 material but with pictures
from any of about six different LP covers pressed
on the disc. RCA in-house, experimental items.)

RCA (347 "August '65
Pop Sampler") 500-750   65
(Various artists collection. Promotional issue only.)

RCA (0347 "Memories of Elvis") 35-45   78
(Special Products five-LP boxed set. A Candelite
Music mail-order offer. Add $8 to $10 if
accompanied by a 16-page booklet and an Elvis
print. Not all sets were issued with the print and
booklet.)

RCA (0348 "Greatest Show on Earth") 10-12   78
(Special Products issue. A Candelite Music
mail-order bonus LP for buyers of RCA 0347.)

RCA (0388 "Raised on Rock") 15-20   73
(Orange label.)

RCA (0388 "Raised on Rock") 8-10   77
(Black label.)

RCA (403 "April '66 Pop Sampler") 500-750   66
(Various artists collection. Promotional issue only.)

RCA (0401 RCA Radio Victrola
Division Spots") 750-1000   56
(Single-sided disc with four 50-second radio
commercials for RCA's Victrolas, as well as for the
SPD-22 and SPD-23 EPs that were offered as a
bonus. Elvis is the announcer on all of the spots,
which include excerpts of some of his songs.
Issued only to radio stations scheduling the spots.)

RCA (0412 "The Legendary
Recordings") 30-40   79
(Special Products six-LP boxed set. A Candelite
Music mail-order offer.)

RCA (0413 "Greatest Moments
in Music") 10-15   80
(Special Products issue. A Candelite Music
mail-order bonus LP for buyers of RCA 0412.)

RCA (0437 "Rock 'N Roll Forever") . . 10-15   81
(Candelite Music mail-order LP offer.)

RCA (461 "Special Palm
Sunday Programming") 500-600   67
(Add $75 to $100 if accompanied by a
programming packet. Promotional issue only.)

RCA (0461 "The Legendary Magic") . 10-15   80
(Candelite Music mail-order LP offer.)

RCA (CPL1-0475 "Good Times") 15-20   74

VICTOR (AFL1-0475 "Good Times") . . 8-10   77

RCA (0561 "Country Gold") 20-25   82
(Various artists collection.)

RCA (571 "Madison Square
Garden") 250-300   72
(Two-LP, double pocket issue. Promotional issue
only. Commercially issued as RCA LSP-4776.)

RCA (DJL1-0606 "On Stage
in Memphis") 250-275   74
(Banded edition. Promotional issue only.)

RCA (CPL1-0606 "On Stage
in Memphis") 15-18   74
(Orange label.)

RCA (CPL1-0606 "On Stage
in Memphis") 10-15   76
(Tan label.)

RCA (APD1-0606 "On Stage
in Memphis") 120-130   74
(Quadradisc. Orange label.)

RCA (AFL1-0606 "On Stage
in Memphis") 8-10   77

RCA (0608 "Happy Holidays Vol. 18") . 8-12   83
(Various artists collection.)

RCA (0632 "The Elvis Presley
Collection") 50-60   84
(Special Products three-LP boxed set, produced
for Candelite Music. Includes booklet. A mail-order
LP offer.)

RCA (DPL1-0647 "Elvis Country") . . . 15-20   84
(Special Products issue for ERA Records.)

RCA (DPK1-0679 "Savage
Young Elvis") 5-10   84
(Cassette tape of a package that was never
available on LP. Price is for tape still attached to
12x12 photo card.)

RCA (0704 "Elvis, HBO Special") . . . 25-35   84
(Includes color poster. Special Products issue for
HBO cable TV subscribers. This material was first
issued as RCA LPM-4088.)

RCA (0710 "Elvis: 50 Years, 50 Hits") 20-25   85
(Three-LP set. Offered by TV mail-order and
through the RCA Record Club.)

RCA (0713 "Happy Holidays Vol. 20") . 8-12   85
(Various artists collection.)

RCA (0716 "A Christmas Treasury
from Avon") 8-12   85
(Various artists collection.)

RCA (0728 "Elvis, His Songs of
Faith and Inspiration") 15-18   86
(Two LP, mail-order offer.)

RCA (0739 "Happy Holidays Vol. 21") . 8-12   86
(Various artists collection.)

RCA (0751 "Avon Valentine
Favorites") 12-18   86
(Various artists collection.)

RCA (DPL1-0803 "Celebrate the
    Season with Tupperware") 20-40   87
    (Various artists collection.)
RCA (CPM1-0818 "Having Fun with
    Elvis on Stage") 15-20   74
    (Orange label.)
RCA (CPM1-0818 "Having Fun with
    Elvis on Stage") 10-15   76
    (Tan label.)
RCA (AFM1-0818 "Having Fun with
    Elvis on Stage") 8-10   77
    (First issued on Boxcar without a catalog number.)
RCA (0835 "Elvis Presley
    Interview Record") 75-100   84
    (Promotional issue only.)
RCA (0842 "The Stars of Christmas") 15-25   88
    (Various artists collection.)
RCA (0868 "Coming Home") 10-20   88
    (Various artists collection.)
RCA (APL1-0873 "Promised Land") .. 15-18   75
    (Orange label.)
RCA (APL1-0873 "Promised Land") .. 10-15   76
    (Tan label.)
RCA (AFL1-0873 "Promised Land") ... 8-10   77
RCA (APD1-0873 "Promised Land") 100-125   75
    (Quadradisc. Orange label.)
RCA (APD1-0873 "Promised Land") . 40-50   77
    (Quadradisc. Black label.)
RCA (ANL1-0971 "Pure Gold") 15-18   75
    (Orange label.)
RCA (ANL1-0971 "Pure Gold") 10-15   76
    (Yellow label.)
RCA (ANL1-0971 "Pure Gold") 8-10   77
    (Black label.)
    Reissued in 1980 as AYL2-4732.
RCA (1001 "The Sun Collection") 20-25   75
    (Label does not have "Starcall" on it. Back cover
    pictures other LPs.)
RCA (1001 "The Sun Collection") 15-20   75
    (Label has "Starcall" on it. Back cover with liner
    notes. This English import was distributed
    throughout the U.S. It was repackaged in 1976 as
    RCA 1675.)
RCA (LOC-1035 "Elvis'
    Christmas Album") 475-525   57
    (With gold foil, gift-giving sticker.)
RCA (LOC-1035 "Elvis'
    Christmas Album") 350-400   57
    (Without gold foil, gift-giving sticker. Repackaged in
    1958 as RCA 1951, in 1970 as Camden 2428 and
    in 1985 as RCA 5486. This LP may be found with
    either gold or silver print on the spine.)
RCA (APL1-1039 "Today") 15-18   75
    (Orange label.)
RCA (APL1-1039 "Today") 10-15   76
    (Tan label.)
RCA (AFL1-1039 "Today") 8-10   77
RCA (APD1-1039 "Today") 100-125   75
    (Quadradisc. Orange label.)

RCA (APD1-1039 "Today") 40-50   77
    (Quadradisc. Black label.)
RCA (LPM-1254 "Elvis Presley") .. 100-125   56
    (Monaural. Black label, "Long Play" at bottom.
    Cover has catalog number in upper right corner.)
RCA (LPM-1254 "Elvis Presley") 50-75   63
    (Black label, "Mono" at bottom. Cover has catalog
    number on left.)
RCA (LPM-1254 "Elvis Presley") 25-50   64
    (Black label, "Monaural" at bottom. Cover has
    catalog number on left.)
RCA (LSP-1254e "Elvis Presley") . 150-200   62
    (Stereo. Black label, all print on label is silver.)
RCA (LSP-1254e "Elvis Presley") ... 25-50   64
    (Black label, RCA logo is white, other label print is
    silver.)
RCA (LSP-1254e "Elvis Presley") ... 20-30   68
    (Orange label.)
RCA (LSP-1254e "Elvis Presley") ... 10-20   76
    (Tan label.)
RCA (AFL1-1254e "Elvis Presley") ... 8-15   77
    (Digitally remastered in 1984 on RCA 5198.)
RCA (ANL1-1319 "His Hand in Mine") 10-15   76
    (First issued as LPM/LSP-2328.)
RCA (1349 "Legendary
    Performer, Vol. 2") 50-65   76
    (Does not have the false starts and outtakes on
    Such a Night and *Cane and a High Starched
    Collar*. Mistakenly has only the complete take of
    both songs. Add $5 to $10 if accompanied by *The
    Early Years Continued* booklet.)
RCA (1349 "Legendary
    Performer, Vol. 2") 20-25   76
    (With die-cut cover. Add $5 to $10 if accompanied
    by *The Early Years Continued* booklet.)
RCA (1349 "Legendary
    Performer, Vol. 2") 5-10   83
    (With standard cover—not die-cut.)
RCA (LPM-1382 "Elvis") 750-1000   56
    (Monaural. Black label, "Long Play" at bottom.
    Cover has catalog number in upper right corner.
    Has an otherwise unreleased [on vinyl] alternate
    take of *Old Shep*. These usually have either a
    "15S," "17S" or "19S" following the identification
    number stamped in the vinyl trail-off.)
RCA (LPM-1382 "Elvis") 200-250   56
    (Black label, selections numbered as "Band 1"
    through "Band 6.")
RCA (LPM-1382 "Elvis") 100-125   56
    (Black label, "Long Play" at bottom. Cover has
    catalog number in upper right corner.)
RCA (LPM-1382 "Elvis") 45-55   63
    (Black label, "Mono" at bottom. Cover has catalog
    number on left.)
RCA (LPM-1382 "Elvis") 25-30   64
    (Black label, "Monaural" at bottom. Cover has
    catalog number on left.)
RCA (LSP-1382e "Elvis") 75-85   62
    (Stereo. Black label, all print on label is silver.)

RCA (LSP-1382e "Elvis") 25-30   64
(Black label, RCA logo is white, other print on label
is silver.)
RCA (LSP-1382e "Elvis") 10-20   68
(Orange label.)
RCA (LSP-1382e "Elvis") 10-15   76
(Tan label.)
RCA (AFL1-1382e "Elvis") 8-10   77
(Digitally remastered in 1984 on RCA 5199.)
RCA (APL1-1506 "From Elvis
Presley Boulevard") 12-15   76
RCA (AFL1-1506 "From Elvis
Presley Boulevard") 8-10   77
RCA (LPM-1515 "Loving You") 100-125   57
(Monaural. Black label, "Long Play" at bottom.
Cover has catalog number in upper right corner.)
RCA (LPM-1515 "Loving You") 45-55   63
(Black label, "Mono" at bottom. Cover has catalog
number on left.)
RCA (LPM-1515 "Loving You") 25-30   64
(Black label, "Monaural" at bottom. Cover has
catalog number on left.)
RCA (LSP-1515e "Loving You") 75-85   62
(Stereo. Black label, all print on label is silver.)
RCA (LSP-1515e "Loving You") 25-30   64
(Black label, RCA logo is white, other label print is
silver.)
RCA (LSP-1515e "Loving You") 10-20   68
(Orange label.)
RCA (LSP-1515e "Loving You") 10-15   76
(Tan label.)
RCA (AFL1-1515e "Loving You") 5-10   77
RCA (APM1-1675 "The Sun
Sessions") 12-15   76
RCA (AFM1-1675 "The Sun
Sessions") 8-10   77
(First issued as RCA HY-1001 and was reissued in
1981 as RCA AYM2-4893.)
RCA (LPM-1707 "Elvis' Golden
Records") 100-125   58
(Monaural. Black label, "Long Play" at bottom.
Cover has catalog number in upper right corner
and LP title in light blue letters.)
RCA (LPM-1707 "Elvis' Golden
Records") 45-55   63
(Black label, "Mono" at bottom. Cover has catalog
number on left and LP title in white letters.)
RCA (LPM-1707 "Elvis' Golden
Records") 25-30   64
(Black label, "Monaural" at bottom. Cover has
catalog number on left.)
RCA (LSP-1707e "Elvis' Golden
Records") 75-85   62
(Stereo. Black label, all print on label is silver.)
RCA (LSP-1707e "Elvis' Golden
Records") 25-30   64
(Black label, RCA logo is white, other label print is
silver.)

RCA (LSP-1707e "Elvis' Golden
Records") 10-20   68
(Orange label.)
RCA (LSP-1707e "Elvis' Golden
Records") 10-15   76
(Tan label.)
RCA (AFL1-1707e "Elvis' Golden
Records") 8-10   77
RCA (AQL1-1707e "Elvis' Golden
Records") 5-10   79
(Digitally remastered in 1984 on RCA 5196.)
RCA (1785 "WRCA Plays
the Hits") 300-350   76
(Various artists collection. Promotional issue only.)
RCA (LPM-1884 "King Creole") ... 100-125   58
(Monaural. Black label, "Long Play" at bottom.
Cover has catalog number in upper right corner.
Add $75-100 if accompanied by an 8x10 black and
white bonus photo of Elvis in uniform.)
RCA (LPM-1884 "King Creole") 45-55   63
(Black label, "Mono" at bottom. Cover has catalog
number on left.)
RCA (LPM-1884 "King Creole") 25-30   64
(Black label, "Monaural" at bottom. Cover has
catalog number on left.)
RCA (LSP-1884e "King Creole") 75-85   62
(Stereo. Black label, all print on label is silver.)
RCA (LSP-1884e "King Creole") 25-30   62
(Black label, RCA logo is white, other label print is
silver.)
RCA (LSP-1884e "King Creole") 10-20   68
(Orange label.)
RCA (LSP-1884e "King Creole") 10-15   76
(Tan label.)
RCA (AFL1-1884e "King Creole") 8-10   77
(Reissued in 1980 as RCA AYL2-4733.)
RCA (ANL1-1936 "Wonderful World
of Christmas") 5-10   77
(First issued as RCA LSP-4579.)
RCA (LPM-1951 "Elvis'
Christmas Album") 90-100   58
(Monaural. Black label, "Long Play" at bottom.
Cover has catalog number in upper right corner.)
RCA (LPM-1951 "Elvis'
Christmas Album") 45-55   63
(Black label, "Mono" at bottom. Cover has catalog
number on left.)
RCA (LPM-1951 "Elvis'
Christmas Album") 25-30   64
(Black label, "Monaural" at bottom. Cover has
catalog number on left.)
RCA (LSP-1951e "Elvis'
Christmas Album") 25-30   64
(Stereo. Black label, RCA logo is white, other label
print is silver.)

RCA (LSP-1951e "Elvis'
Christmas Album") 20-25   68
(Orange label. Repackage of RCA LOC-1035. It
was repackaged in 1970 as Camden 2428 and
again in 1985 as RCA AFM1-5486.)

RCA (1981 "Felton Jarvis
Talks About Elvis") 200-250   81
(Price includes three script sheets. Add $25 to $50
if accompanied by silver and black *Guitar Man*
engraved Elvis belt buckle.)

RCA (LPM-1990 "For LP
Fans Only") 100-125   59
(Monaural. Black label, "Long Play" at bottom.
Cover has catalog number in upper right corner.)

RCA (LPM-1990 "For LP Fans Only") 45-55   63
(Black label, "Mono" at bottom. Cover has catalog
number on left.)

RCA (LPM-1990 "For LP Fans Only") 25-30   65
(Black label, "Monaural" at bottom. Cover has
catalog number on left.)

RCA (LSP-1990e "For LP Fans Only") 25-30   65
(Stereo. Black label, RCA logo is white, other label
print is silver.)

RCA (LSP-1990e "For LP Fans Only") 10-20   68
(Orange label.)

RCA (LSP-1990e "For LP Fans Only") 10-15   76
(Tan label.)

RCA (AFL1-1990e "For LP Fans Only") 8-10   77

RCA (LPM-2011 "A Date with Elvis") 300-500   59
(Monaural. Black label, "Long Play" at bottom. Has
gatefold cover and 1960 calendar. With "New
Golden Age of Sound" wrap-around banner.)

RCA (LPM-2011 "A Date with Elvis") 150-175   59
(Black label, "Long Play" at bottom. Has gatefold
cover and 1960 calendar, but does not have "New
Golden Age of Sound" banner.)

RCA (LPM-2011 "A Date with Elvis") . 45-55   65
(Black label, "Mono" at bottom. Cover has catalog
number on left.)

RCA (LPM-2011 "A Date with Elvis") . 25-30   65
(Black label, "Monaural" at bottom. Cover has
catalog number on left.)

RCA (LSP-2011e "A Date with Elvis") 25-30   65
(Stereo. Black label, RCA logo is white, other label
print is silver.)

RCA (LSP-2011e "A Date with Elvis") 10-20   68
(Orange label.)

RCA (LSP-2011e "A Date with Elvis") 10-15   76
(Tan label.)

RCA (AFL1-2011e "A Date with Elvis") . 8-10   77

RCA (LPM-2075 "Elvis' Golden
Records, Vol. 2") 100-125   59
(Monaural. Black label, "Long Play" at bottom.
Cover has catalog number in upper right corner.)

RCA (LPM-2075 "Elvis' Golden
Records, Vol. 2") 45-55   63
(Black label, "Mono" at bottom. Cover has catalog
number on left.)

RCA (LPM-2075 "Elvis' Golden
Records, Vol. 2") 25-30   64
(Black label, "Monaural" at bottom. Cover has
catalog number on left.)

RCA (LSP-2075e "Elvis' Golden
Records, Vol. 2") 75-85   62
(Stereo. Black label, all print on label is silver.)

RCA (LSP-2075e "Elvis' Golden
Records, Vol. 2") 25-30   64
(Black label, RCA logo is white, other label print is
silver.)

RCA (LSP-2075e "Elvis' Golden
Records, Vol. 2") 10-20   68
(Orange label.)

RCA (LSP-2075e "Elvis' Golden
Records, Vol. 2") 10-15   76
(Tan label.)

RCA (AFL1-2075e "Elvis' Golden
Records, Vol. 2") 8-10   77
(May also be shown as *50,000,000 Elvis Presley
Fans Can't Be Wrong*. Digitally remastered in 1984
on RCA 5197.)

RCA (2227 "The Great Performances")10-20   90

RCA (LPM-2231 "Elvis Is Back") .. 100-150   60
(Monaural. Black label, "Long Play" at bottom. No
song titles printed on cover. May have a yellow
sticker on cover showing song titles.)

RCA (LPM-2231 "Elvis Is Back") 45-55   63
(Black label, "Mono" at bottom. Cover has catalog
number on left.)

RCA (LPM-2231 "Elvis Is Back") 25-30   64
(Black label, "Monaural" at bottom. Cover has
catalog number on left.)

RCA (LSP-2231 "Elvis Is Back") .. 120-160   60
(Stereo. Black label, "Living Stereo" at bottom. No
song titles printed on cover. May have a yellow
sticker on cover showing song titles.)

RCA (LSP-2231 "Elvis Is Back") 25-30   64
(Black label, RCA logo is white, other label print is
silver.)

RCA (LSP-2231 "Elvis Is Back") 10-20   68
(Orange label.)

RCA (LSP-2231 "Elvis Is Back") 10-15   76
(Tan label.)

RCA (AFL1-2231 "Elvis Is Back") 8-10   77

RCA (LPM-2256 "G.I. Blues") 100-125   60
(Monaural. Black label, "Long Play" at bottom. Add
$15 to $25 if accompanied by "Elvis Is Back" inner
sleeve.)

RCA (LPM-2256 "G.I. Blues") 45-55   63
(Black label, "Mono" at bottom.)

RCA (LPM-2256 "G.I. Blues") 25-30   64
(Black label, "Monaural" at bottom.)

RCA (LSP-2256 "G.I. Blues") 100-125   60
(Stereo. Black label, "Living Stereo" at bottom.
Add $15 to $25 if accompanied by "Elvis Is Back"
inner sleeve.)

RCA (LSP-2256 "G.I. Blues") 25-30   64
(Black label, RCA logo is white, other label print is silver.)
RCA (LSP-2256 "G.I. Blues") 10-20   68
(Orange label.)
RCA (LSP-2256 "G.I. Blues") 10-15   76
(Tan label.)
RCA (AFL1-2256 "G.I. Blues") 8-10   77
(Reissued in 1980 as RCA AYL2-4735.)
RCA (APL1-2274 "Welcome to
My World") 10-15   77
RCA (AFL1-2274 "Welcome to
My World") 8-10   77
RCA (AQL1-2274 "Welcome to
My World") 5-10   79
RCA (LPM-2328 "His Hand in Mine") . 75-90   60
(Monaural. Black label, "Long Play" at bottom.)
RCA (LPM-2328 "His Hand in Mine") . 40-50   63
(Black label, "Mono" at bottom.)
RCA (LPM-2328 "His Hand in Mine") . 25-30   64
(Black label, "Monaural" at bottom.)
RCA (LSP-2328 "His Hand in Mine") 90-100   60
(Stereo. Black label, "Living Stereo" at bottom.)
RCA (LSP-2328 "His Hand in Mine") . 25-30   64
(Black label, RCA logo is white, other label print is silver.)
RCA (LSP-2328 "His Hand in Mine") . 10-20   68
(Orange label.)
RCA (LSP-2328 "His Hand in Mine") . 10-15   76
(Tan label.)
(Repackaged in 1976 as RCA ANL1-1319 and in 1981 as RCA AYM2-4935.)
RCA (2347 "Elvis-Greatest Hits,
Vol. One") 10-15   81
(Has embossed letters on front cover.)
RCA (2347 "Elvis-Greatest Hits,
Vol. One") 5-10   83
(Standard cover print—not embossed.)
RCA (LPM-2370 "Something for
Everybody") 75-90   61
(Monaural. Black label, "Long Play" at bottom. Back cover promotes Compact 33s.)
RCA (LPM-2370 "Something for
Everybody") 40-50   63
(Black label, "Mono" at bottom.)
RCA (LPM-2370 "Something for
Everybody") 25-30   64
(Black label, "Monaural" at bottom.)
RCA (LSP-2370 "Something for
Everybody") 90-100   61
(Stereo. Black label, "Living Stereo" at bottom. Back cover promotes Compact 33s.)
RCA (LSP-2370 "Something for
Everybody") 25-30   64
(Black label, RCA logo is white, other label print is silver.)
RCA (LSP-2370 "Something for
Everybody") 10-20   68
(Orange label.)

RCA (LSP-2370 "Something for
Everybody") 10-15   76
(Tan label.)
RCA (AFL1-2370 "Something for
Everybody") 8-10   77
(Reissued in 1981 as RCA AYM1-4116.)
RCA (LPM-2426 "Blue Hawaii") 75-90   61
(Monaural. Black label, "Long Play" at bottom.)
RCA (LPM-2426 "Blue Hawaii") 40-50   63
(Black label, "Mono" at bottom.)
RCA (LPM-2426 "Blue Hawaii") 25-30   64
(Black label, "Monaural" at bottom.)
RCA (LSP-2426 "Blue Hawaii") 90-100   61
(Stereo. Black label, "Living Stereo" at bottom.)
RCA (LSP-2426 "Blue Hawaii") 25-30   64
(Black label, RCA logo is white, other label print is silver.)
RCA (LSP-2426 "Blue Hawaii") 10-20   68
(Orange label.)
RCA (LSP-2426 "Blue Hawaii") 10-15   76
(Tan label.)
RCA (AFL1-2426 "Blue Hawaii") 8-10   77
(Reissued in 1981 as RCA AYL2-4683.)
RCA (AFL1-2428 "Moody Blue") 1000-1200   77
(Colored vinyl—any color other than blue. Experimental production discs for RCA in-house use only.)
RCA (AFL1-2428 "Moody Blue") 10-12   77
(Blue vinyl.)
RCA (AFL1-2428 "Moody Blue") .. 125-150   77
(Black vinyl.)
RCA (AQL1-2428 "Moody Blue") 8-10   79
RCA (LPM-2523 "Pot Luck") 75-90   62
(Monaural. Black label, "Long Play" at bottom.)
RCA (LPM-2523 "Pot Luck") 40-50   63
(Black label, "Mono" at bottom.)
RCA (LPM-2523 "Pot Luck") 25-30   64
(Black label, "Monaural" at bottom.)
RCA (LSP-2523 "Pot Luck") 90-100   62
(Stereo. Black label, "Living Stereo" at bottom.)
RCA (LSP-2523 "Pot Luck") 25-30   64
(Black label, RCA logo is white, other label print is silver.)
RCA (LSP-2523 "Pot Luck") 10-20   68
(Orange label.)
RCA (LSP-2523 "Pot Luck") 10-15   76
(Tan label.)
RCA (AFL1-2523 "Pot Luck") 8-10   77
RCA (APL1-2558 "Harum Scarum") .. 8-10   77
(First issued as RCA LPM/LSP-3468. Reissued in 1980 as RCA AYL2-4734.)
RCA (APL1-2560 "Spinout") 8-10   77
(First issued as RCA LPM/LSP-3702. Reissued in 1980 as RCA AYL2-4684.)
RCA (APL1-2564 "Double Trouble") .. 8-10   77
(First issued as RCA LPM/LSP-3787.)
RCA (APL1-2565 "Clambake") 8-10   77
(First issued as RCA LPM/LSP-3893.)

RCA (APL1-2568 "It Happened at
the World's Fair") 8-10   77
(First issued as RCA LPM/LSP-2697.)

RCA (APL2-2587 "Elvis in Concert") . 15-20   77
RCA (CPL2-2587 "Elvis in Concert") 12-15   82

RCA (LPM-2621 "Girls! Girls! Girls!") . 75-90   62
(Monaural. Black label, "Long Play" at bottom.)

RCA (LPM-2621 "Girls! Girls! Girls!") . 40-50   63
(Black label, "Mono" at bottom.)

RCA (LPM-2621 "Girls! Girls! Girls!") . 25-30   64
(Black label, "Monaural" at bottom.)

RCA (LSP-2621 "Girls! Girls! Girls!") 90-100   62
(Stereo. Black label, "Living Stereo" at bottom.)

RCA (LSP-2621 "Girls! Girls! Girls!") . 25-30   64
(Black label, RCA logo is white, other label print is
silver.)

RCA (LSP-2621 "Girls! Girls! Girls!") . 10-20   68
(Orange label.)

RCA (LSP-2621 "Girls! Girls! Girls!") . 10-15   76
(Tan label.)

RCA (AFL1-2621 "Girls! Girls! Girls!") . 8-10   77

RCA (CPD2-2642 "Aloha from
Hawaii") 15-20   75
(Orange label.)

RCA (CPD2-2642 "Aloha from
Hawaii") 10-12   77
(Black label. First issued as RCA VPSX-6089.)

RCA (LPM-2697 "It Happened at the
World's Fair") 75-90   63
(Monaural. Black label, "Long Play" at bottom. Add
$100 to $125 if accompanied by an 8x10 bonus
color photo.)

RCA (LPM-2697 "It Happened at the
World's Fair") 40-50   63
(Black label, "Mono" at bottom.)

RCA (LPM-2697 "It Happened at the
World's Fair") 25-30   64
(Black label, "Monaural" at bottom.)

RCA (LSP-2697 "It Happened at the
World's Fair") 90-100   63
(Stereo. Black label, "Living Stereo" at bottom.
Add $100 to $125 if accompanied by an 8x10
bonus color photo.)

RCA (LSP-2697 "It Happened at the
World's Fair") 25-30   64
(Black label, RCA logo is white, other label print is
silver. Reissued in 1977 as RCA APL1-2568.)

RCA (LPM-2756 "Fun in Acapulco") . . 60-70   63
(Monaural. Black label, "Mono" at bottom.)

RCA (LPM-2756 "Fun in Acapulco") . . 25-30   64
(Black label, "Monaural" at bottom.)

RCA (LSP-2756 "Fun in Acapulco") . . 60-70   63
(Stereo. Black label, all print on label is silver.)

RCA (LSP-2756 "Fun in Acapulco") . . 25-30   64
(Black label, RCA logo is white, other label print is
silver.)

RCA (LSP-2756 "Fun in Acapulco") . . 10-20   68
(Orange label.)

RCA (LSP-2756 "Fun in Acapulco") . . 10-15   76
(Tan label.)

RCA (AFL1-2756 "Fun in Acapulco") . . 8-10   77

RCA (LPM-2765 "Elvis' Golden
Records, Vol. 3") 90-100   63
(Monaural. Black label, "Mono" at bottom.)

RCA (LPM-2765 "Elvis' Golden
Records, Vol. 3") 25-30   64
(Black label, "Monaural" at bottom.)

RCA (LSP-2765 "Elvis' Golden
Records, Vol. 3") 90-100   63
(Stereo. Black label, all print on label is silver.)

RCA (LSP-2765 "Elvis' Golden
Records, Vol. 3") 25-30   64
(Black label, RCA logo is white, other label print is
silver.)

RCA (LSP-2765 "Elvis' Golden
Records, Vol. 3") 10-20   68
(Orange label.)

RCA (LSP-2765 "Elvis' Golden
Records, Vol. 3") 10-15   76
(Tan label.)

RCA (AFL1-2765 "Elvis' Golden
Records, Vol. 3") 8-10   77

RCA (AFL1-2772 "He Walks
Beside Me") 8-10   77

RCA (LPM-2894 "Kissin' Cousins") 100-150   64
(Monaural. Black label, "Mono" at bottom. *Does not*
picture film cast in lower right corner photo on
cover.)

RCA (LPM-2894 "Kissin' Cousins") . . 60-70   64
(Black label, "Mono" at bottom. Pictures film cast in
lower right corner photo on cover.)

RCA (LPM-2894 "Kissin' Cousins") . . 25-30   64
(Black label, "Monaural" at bottom.)

RCA (LSP-2894 "Kissin' Cousins") 100-150   64
(Stereo. Black label, all print on label is silver.
Does not picture film cast in lower right corner
photo on cover.)

RCA (LSP-2894 "Kissin' Cousins") . . 60-70   64
(Black label, all print on label is silver. Pictures film
cast in lower right corner photo on cover.)

RCA (LSP-2894 "Kissin' Cousins") . . 25-30   64
(Black label, RCA logo is white, other label print is
silver.)

RCA (LSP-2894 "Kissin' Cousins") . . 10-20   68
(Orange label.)

RCA (LSP-2894 "Kissin' Cousins") . . 10-15   76
(Tan label.)

RCA (LSP-2894 "Kissin'
Cousins") 1000-1200   77
(Blue vinyl. Experimental pressing only.)

RCA (AFL1-2894 "Kissin' Cousins") . . . 8-10   77
(Reissued in 1981 as RCA AYM1-4115.)

RCA (CPL1-2901 "Elvis Sings
for Children") 8-10   78
(Includes "Special Memories" greeting card.)

RCA (LPM-2999 "Roustabout") 60-70   64
(Monaural. Black label, "Mono" at bottom.)

RCA (LPM-2999 "Roustabout") 25-30   65
(Black label, "Monaural" at bottom.)

RCA (LSP-2999 "Roustabout") 500-600   64
(Stereo. Black label. All print on label—including RCA logo—is silver.)

RCA (LSP-2999 "Roustabout") 25-30   64
(Black label, RCA logo is white, other label print is silver.)

RCA (LSP-2999 "Roustabout") 10-20   68
(Orange label.)

RCA (LSP-2999 "Roustabout") 10-15   76
(Tan label.)

RCA (AFL1-2999 "Roustabout") 8-10   77

RCA (3078 "Legendary
Performer, Vol. 3") 15-20   78
(Picture disc. Add $5 to $10 if accompanied by
Yesterdays booklet. May be found with the actual
disc pressed on either blue or black vinyl. Also
issued on standard black vinyl as 3082.)

RCA (3082 "Legendary
Performer, Vol. 3") 8-12   78
(Add $5 to $10 if accompanied by *Yesterdays*
booklet. Also issued on a picture disc, as RCA
3078.)

RCA (3279 "Our Memories of Elvis") .. 8-10   79

RCA (LPM-3338 "Girl Happy") 40-50   65
(Monaural.)

RCA (LSP-3338 "Girl Happy") 40-50   65
(Stereo. Black label.)

RCA (LSP-3338 "Girl Happy") 10-20   68
(Orange label.)

RCA (LSP-3338 "Girl Happy") 10-15   76
(Tan label.)

RCA (AFL2-4338 "Girl Happy") 8-10   77

RCA (3448 "Our Memories
of Elvis Vol. 2") 8-10   79
(A sampling of these tracks is on RCA 3455, *Pure
Elvis*.)

RCA (LPM-3450 "Elvis for Everyone") 35-45   65
(Monaural.)

RCA (LSP-3450 "Elvis for Everyone") 35-45   65
(Stereo. Black label.)

RCA (LSP-3450 "Elvis for Everyone") 10-20   68
(Orange label.)

RCA (LSP-3450 "Elvis for Everyone") 10-15   76
(Tan label.)

RCA (AFL2-4450 "Elvis for Everyone") 8-10   77
Reissued in 1982 as RCA AYL1-4232.

RCA (3455 "Pure Elvis") 275-325   79
(Cover reads "Pure Elvis," but label shows "Our
Memories of Elvis - Vol. 2." Promotional issue only.)

RCA (LPM-3468 "Harum Scarum") .. 35-50   65
(Monaural. Add $55 to $75 if accompanied by
bonus 12x12 photo.)

RCA (LSP-3468 "Harum Scarum") ... 35-50   65
(Stereo. Add $55 to $75 if accompanied by bonus
12x12 photo. Reissued in 1977 as RCA
APL1-2558 and in 1980 as RCA AYL2-4734.)

RCA (LPM-3553 "Frankie and
Johnny") 35-50   66
(Monaural. Add $55 to $75 if accompanied by
bonus 12x12 print.)

RCA (LSP-3553 "Frankie and
Johnny") 35-50   66
(Stereo. Add $55 to $75 if accompanied by bonus
12x12 print. Reissued in 1977 as RCA APL1-2559.
A repackage appeared in 1976 on Pickwick 7007.)

RCA (LPM-3643 "Paradise
Hawaiian Style") 35-45   66
(Monaural.)

RCA (LSP-3643 "Paradise
Hawaiian Style") 35-45   66
(Stereo. Black label.)

RCA (LSP-3643 "Paradise
Hawaiian Style") 10-20   68
(Orange label.)

RCA (LSP-3643 "Paradise
Hawaiian Style") 10-15   76
(Tan label.)

RCA (AFL2-4643 "Paradise
Hawaiian Style") 8-10   77

RCA (AYL2-4683 "Blue Hawaii") 5-10   80
(First issued as RCA LPM/LSP-2426.)

RCA (AYL2-4684 "Spinout") 5-10   80
(First issued as RCA LPM/LSP-3702, reissued in
1977 as RCA APL1-2560.)

RCA (CPL8-3699 "Elvis
Aron Presley") 80-100   80
(Eight-LP boxed set. Add $5 to $10 if accompanied
by 20-page booklet.)

RCA (CPL8-3699 "Elvis
Aron Presley") 450-500   80
(REVIEWER SERIES edition. Silver sticker on
back also identifies the Reviewer Series copy as
"NS-3699." Add $5 to $10 if accompanied by
20-page booklet.)

RCA (CPK8-3699 "Elvis
Aron Presley") 80-100   80
(Four-cassette boxed set. Add $10 to $20 if
accompanied by 20-page booklet and eight 12x12
Elvis photos.)

RCA (CPS8-3699 "Elvis
Aron Presley") 100-125   80
(Four 8-track boxed set. Add $10 to $20 if
accompanied by 20-page booklet and eight 12x12
Elvis photos. *Excerpts* of songs in this set
appeared on RCA 3729. *Selections* from this LP
are on RCA 3781.)

RCA (LPM-3702 "Spinout") 35-50   66
(Monaural. Add $55 to $75 if accompanied by
bonus 12x12 photo.)

RCA (LSP-3702 "Spinout") 35-50   66
(Stereo. Add $55 to $75 if accompanied by bonus
12x12 photo. Reissued in 1977 as APL1-2560.)

RCA (3729 "Elvis Aron
Presley," Excerpts) 100-125   80
(Has 37 excerpts from RCA 3699. Promotional
issue only.)
RCA (AYL2-4732 "Pure Gold") 5-10   80
(First issued as RCA ANL1-0971.)
RCA (AYL2-4733 "King Creole") 5-10   80
(First issued as RCA LSP-1884.)
RCA (AYL2-4734 "Harum Scarum") ... 5-10   80
(First issued as RCA LPM/LSP-3468.)
RCA (AYL2-4735 "G.I. Blues") 5-10   80
(First issued as RCA LPM/LSP-2256.)
RCA (LPM-3758 "How Great
Thou Art") 40-50   67
(Monaural.)
RCA (LSP-3758 "How Great
Thou Art") 35-45   67
(Stereo. Black label.)
RCA (LSP-3758 "How Great
Thou Art") 10-20   68
(Orange label.)
RCA (LSP-3758 "How Great
Thou Art") 10-15   76
(Tan label.)
RCA (AFL2-4758 "How Great
Thou Art") 8-10   77
RCA (3781 "Elvis Aron
Presley," Selections) 100-125   80
(Has 12 selections from RCA 3699. Promotional
issue only.)
RCA (LPM-3787 "Double Trouble") .. 40-50   67
(Monaural. Front cover reads "Special Bonus Full
Color Photo." Add $25 to $35 if accompanied by
bonus 7x9 photo.)
RCA (LPM-3787 "Double Trouble") .. 30-40   68
("Special Bonus Full Color Photo" is replaced by
"Trouble Double.")
RCA (LSP-3787 "Double Trouble") ... 40-50   67
(Stereo. Front cover reads "Special Bonus Full
Color Photo." Add $25 to $35 if accompanied by
bonus 7x9 photo. Black label.)
RCA (LSP-3787 "Double Trouble") ... 30-40   68
("Special Bonus Full Color Photo" is replaced by
"Trouble Double.")
RCA (LSP-3787 "Double Trouble") ... 10-20   68
(Orange label.)
RCA (LSP-3787 "Double Trouble") ... 10-15   76
(Tan label.)
(Reissued in 1977 as RCA APL1-2564.)
RCA (AYL2-4892 "Elvis in Person") ... 5-10   81
(First issued as RCA LSP-4428.)
RCA (LPM-3893 "Clambake") 150-200   67
(Monaural. Add $30 to $40 if accompanied by
bonus 12x12 photo. Reissued in 1977 as RCA
APL1-2565.)
RCA (LSP-3893 "Clambake") 30-50   67
(Stereo. Add $30 to $40 if accompanied by bonus
12x12 photo. Reissued in 1977 as RCA
APL1-2565.)

RCA (AYM2-4893 "The Sun Sessions") 5-10   81
(First issued as RCA APM1-1675.)
RCA (AYM2-4894 "Elvis TV Special") . 5-10   81
(First issued RCA LPM-4088.)
RCA (3917 "Guitar Man") 8-12   81
(Includes a "This Is Elvis" flyer. Producer Felton
Jarvis talks about Elvis and the making of this LP
on RCA 1981.)
RCA (LPM-3921 "Elvis' Gold
Records, Vol. 4") 800-1000   68
(Monaural.) RCA (LSP-3921 "Elvis' Gold
Records, Vol. 4") 60-90   68
(Stereo. Black label.)
RCA (LSP-3921 "Elvis' Gold
Records, Vol. 4") 10-20   68
(Orange label.)
RCA (LSP-3921 "Elvis' Gold
Records, Vol. 4") 10-15   76
(Tan label.)
RCA (AFL2-4921 "Elvis' Gold
Records, Vol. 4") 8-10   77
RCA (AYM2-4935 "His Hand
in Mine") 5-10   81
(First issued as RCA LPM/LSP-2328.)
RCA (AYL2-4956 "That's The
Way It Is") 5-10   81
First issued as RCA LSP-4460.
RCA (LPM-3989 "Speedway") 850-950   68
(Monaural. Add $25 to $50 if accompanied by
bonus 8x10 photo.)
RCA (LSP-3989 "Speedway") 35-45   68
(Stereo. Black label. Add $25 to $50 if
accompanied by bonus 8x10 photo.)
RCA (LSP-3989 "Speedway") 10-20   68
(Orange label.)
RCA (LSP-3989 "Speedway") 10-15   76
(Tan label.)
RCA (AFL2-4989 "Speedway") 8-10   77
RCA (4031 "This Is Elvis") 10-15   80
RCA (LPM-4088 "Elvis
TV Special") 15-20   68
(Orange label. Rigid disc.)
RCA (LPM-4088 "Elvis TV Special") . 10-15   72
(Orange label. Flexible disc.)
RCA (LPM-4088 "Elvis TV Special") . 10-15   76
(Tan label.)
RCA (AFM1-4088 "Elvis TV Special") . 8-10   77
(Reissued in 1981 as RCA AYM2-4894.
Repackaged for HBO as RCA 0704.)
RCA (AYL1-4114 "That's The
Way It Is") 5-10   81
(First issued as RCA LSP-4445.)
RCA (AYM1-4115 "Kissin' Cousins") .. 5-10   81
(First issued as RCA LPM/LSP-2894.)
RCA (AYM1-4116 "Something for
Everybody") 5-10   81
(First issued as RCA LPM/LSP-2370.)

RCA (LSP-4155 "From Elvis
in Memphis") 20-25   69
(Orange label. Rigid disc. Add $30 to $40 if
accompanied by 8x10 Elvis photo.)
RCA (LSP-4155 "From Elvis
in Memphis") 10-15   72
(Orange label. Flexible disc.)
RCA (LSP-4155 "From Elvis
in Memphis") 10-15   69
(Tan label.)
RCA (AFL1-4155 "From Elvis
in Memphis") 8-10   77
(A half-speed mastered issue of this LP was
released in 1982 as MFSL 059.)
RCA (AYL1-4232 "Elvis for Everyone") 5-10   82
(First issued as RCA LPM/LSP-3450.)
RCA (4351 "60 Years of
Country Music") 10-20   82
(Various artists collection.)
RCA (LSP-4362 "On Stage") 15-20   70
(Orange label. Rigid disc.)
RCA (LSP-4362 "On Stage") 10-15   72
(Orange label. Flexible disc.)
RCA (LSP-4362 "On Stage") 10-15   76
(Tan label.)
RCA (AFL1-4362 "On Stage") 10-12   77
RCA (AQL1-4362 "On Stage") 5-10   83
RCA (4395 "Memories of Christmas") . 8-10   82
RCA (LSP-4428 "Elvis in Person") .. 15-20   70
(Orange label.)
RCA (LSP-4428 "Elvis in Person") ... 10-15   76
(Tan label.)
RCA (AFL1-4428 "Elvis in Person") 8-10   77
(First released as half of RCA LSP-6020, then
reissued in 1981 as RCA AYL2-4892.)
RCA (LSP-4429 "Elvis Back
in Memphis") 15-20   70
(Orange label.)
RCA (LSP-4429 "Elvis Back
in Memphis") 10-15   76
(Tan label.)
RCA (AFL1-4429 "Elvis Back
in Memphis") 8-10   77
(First issued as half of RCA LSP-6020.)
RCA (LSP-4445 "That's the Way It Is") 15-20   70
(Orange label.)
RCA (LSP-4445 "That's the Way It Is") 10-15   76
(Tan label.)
RCA (LSP-4445 "That's the Way It Is") 8-10   77
(Black label.)
RCA (AFL1-4445 "That's the
Way It Is") 8-10   77
(Reissued in 1981 as RCA AYL1-4114.)
RCA (LSP-4460 "Elvis Country") 15-20   71
(Orange label. Add $10 to $15 if accompanied by
7x9 Elvis photo.)
RCA (LSP-4460 "Elvis Country") 10-15   76
(Tan label.)

RCA (AFL1-4460 "Elvis Country") 8-10   77
(Reissued in 1981 as RCA AYL2-4956.)
RCA (LSP-4530 "Love Letters") 25-40   71
(Orange label. Full title, *Love Letters From Elvis*,
on TWO lines on front cover.)
RCA (LSP-4530 "Love Letters") 20-35   71
(Orange label. Full title, *Love Letters From Elvis*,
on THREE lines on front cover.)
RCA (LSP-4530 "Love Letters") 10-15   76
(Tan label.)
RCA (AFL1-4530 "Love Letters") 8-10   77
(Reissued in 1981 as RCA AYL2-4956.)
RCA (AHL1-4530 "The Elvis Medley") . 8-10   82
RCA (LSP-4579 "Wonderful World
of Christmas") 20-25   71
(Orange label. Add $4 to $8 if accompanied by a
5x7 Elvis postcard. Reissued in 1977 as RCA
ANL1-1936.)
RCA (LSP-4671 "Elvis Now") 50-60   72
(Has white titles/times sticker on front cover.
Promotional issue only.)
RCA (LSP-4671 "Elvis Now") 15-18   72
(Orange label.)
RCA (LSP-4671 "Elvis Now") 10-15   76
(Tan label.)
RCA (AFL1-4671 "Elvis Now") 8-10   77
RCA (LSP-4690 "He Touched Me") .. 50-60   72
(Has white titles/times sticker on front cover.
Promotional issue only.)
RCA (LSP-4690 "He Touched Me") .. 15-18   72
(Orange label.)
RCA (LSP-4690 "He Touched Me") .. 10-15   76
(Tan label.)
RCA (AFL1-4690 "He Touched Me") .. 8-10   77
RCA (4678 "I Was the One") 8-10   83
RCA (LSP-4776 "Madison
Square Garden") 50-60   72
(Orange label. Has white programming stickers
applied to front cover. Promotional issue only.)
RCA (LSP-4776 "Madison
Square Garden") 15-20   72
(Orange label.)
RCA (LSP-4776 "Madison
Square Garden") 10-15   76
(Tan label.)
RCA (AQL1-4776 "Madison
Square Garden") 8-10   77
RCA (4809 "A Country
Christmas" Vol. 2) 8-10   83
RCA (4848 "Legendary
Performer, Vol. 4") 8-10   83
(Price includes a 12-page *Memories of the King*
booklet.)
RCA (4941 "Elvis' Gold Records,
Vol. 5") 5-10   84
RCA (5172 "A Golden Celebration") . 40-50   84
(Six-LP boxed set. Price includes custom inner
sleeves and an envelope containing an 8x10 Elvis
photo and a 50th Anniversary flyer.)

RCA (5172 "A Golden Celebration") . . 15-20   84
(Special "Advance Cassette" boxed set sampler.)
RCA (5182 "Rocker") 5-10   84
RCA (5196 "Elvis' Golden Records") . . 5-10   84
(Digitally remastered, quality mono pressing. Price
includes gold "The Definitive Rock Classic" banner.
First issued as RCA LPM-1707.)
RCA (5197 "Elvis' Gold Records,
Vol. 2") 5-10   84
(Digitally remastered, quality mono pressing. Price
includes gold "The Definitive Rock Classic" banner.
First issued as RCA LPM-2075.)
RCA (5198 "Elvis Presley") 5-10   84
(Digitally remastered, quality mono pressing. Price
includes gold "The Definitive Rock Classic" banner.
First issued as RCA LPM-1254.)
RCA (5199 "Elvis") 5-10   84
(Digitally remastered, quality mono pressing. Price
includes gold "The Definitive Rock Classic" banner.
First issued as RCA LPM-1382.)
RCA (5353 "A Valentine Gift for You") . 8-10   85
(Colored vinyl.)
RCA (5353 "A Valentine Gift for You") . 5-10   85
(Black vinyl.)
RCA (5418 "Reconsider Baby") 5-10   85
RCA (5430 "Always on My Mind") 5-10   85
RCA (5463 "Rock and Roll,
the Early Days") 8-12   85
(Various artists collection.)
RCA (5486 "Elvis' Christmas Album") . . 5-10   85
(Colored vinyl.)
RCA (5486 "Elvis' Christmas Album") . 20-40   85
(Black vinyl. Thus far, all black vinyl copies
discovered were packaged with stickers reading
"pressed on green vinyl.")
RCA (5600 "Return of the Rocker") . . . 5-10   86
RCA (5697 "Special Christmas
Programming") 800-1000   67
(Promotional issue only.)
RCA (5800 "Best of the '50s") 8-10   86
(Various artists collection.)
RCA (5802 "Best of the '60s") 8-10   86
(Various artists collection.)
RCA (5837 "Best of the '70s") 8-10   86
(Various artists collection.)
RCA (5838 "Best of the '50s,
'60s and '70s") 8-10   86
(Various artists collection.)
RCA (LSP-6020 "From Memphis
to Vegas") 30-40   69
(Orange label. Incorrectly shows writers of *Words*
as Tommy Boyce and Bobby Hart. Also shows
writer of *Suspicious Minds* as Frances Zambon.
Add $20 to $40 if accompanied by two 8x10, black
and white Elvis photos.)

RCA (LSP-6020 "From Memphis
to Vegas") 20-30   69
(Orange label. Correctly shows writers of *Words* as
Barry, Robin and Maurice Gibb, and writer of
Suspicious Minds as Mark James. Add $20 to $40
if accompanied by two 8x10 Elvis photos.)
RCA (LSP-6020 "From Memphis
to Vegas") 15-20   76
(Tan label.)
RCA (LSP-6020 "From Memphis
to Vegas") 10-15   77
(Black label. Each of the two LPs in this set was
reissued individually, *Elvis in Person at the
International Hotel* as LSP-4428 and *Elvis Back in
Memphis* as LSP-4429, both in 1970.)
RCA (VPSX-6089 "Aloha from
Hawaii") 1500-2000   73
(Has "Chicken of the Sea" sticker on cover.
Quadradisc and contents stickers also are on
cover. A promotional in-house issue by the Van
Camps Company.)
RCA (VPSX-6089 "Aloha from
Hawaii") 300-350   73
(Has white titles/times sticker on front cover.
Promotional issue only.)
RCA (VPSX-6089 "Aloha from
Hawaii") 75-100   73
(Has Quadradisc and contents stickers on cover.
Red/orange label.)
RCA (VPSX-6089 "Aloha from
Hawaii") 25-30   74
(Has Quadradisc/RCA logo in lower right corner of
front cover. Titles are printed on back cover.
Orange label.)
RCA (VPSX-6089 "Aloha from
Hawaii") 25-30   76
(Tan label. Issued through the RCA Record Club
as RCA 213736 and later (1977) as RCA
CPD2-2642.)
RCA (6221 "The Memphis Record") . 10-15   87
(Includes a bonus color 15x22 poster and *Elvis
Talks* LP flyer.)
RCA (6313 "Elvis Talks!") 10-15   87
(Mail-order LP offer.)
RCA (6382 "Number One Hits") 8-10   87
(Includes a bonus color 15x22 poster and *Elvis
Talks* LP flyer.)
RCA (6383 "Top Ten Hits") 10-12   87
(Includes a bonus color 15x22 poster and *Elvis
Talks* LP flyer.)
RCA (LPM-6401 "Worldwide 50
Gold Hits, Vol. 1") 60-75   70
(Orange label. Four-LP boxed set. Add $30 to $40
if accompanied by a 16-page Elvis photo booklet.)
RCA (LPM-6401 "Worldwide 50
Gold Hits, Vol. 1") 30-40   76
(Tan label.)

RCA (LPM-6401 "Worldwide 50
Gold Hits, Vol. 1") 20-25   77
(Black label. Two of the LPs in this set were
repackaged for the RCA Record Club in 1974 as
RCA 213690 and the other two in 1978 as RCA
214657.)

RCA (LPM-6402 "Worldwide 50
Gold Hits, Vol. 2") 60-75   71
(Orange label. Four-LP boxed set. Add $25 to $50
if accompanied by an Elvis print, and an envelope
with piece of material.)

RCA (LPM-6402 "Worldwide 50
Gold Hits, Vol. 2") 30-40   76
(Tan label. With bonus items shown as included.)

RCA (LPM-6402 "Worldwide 50
Gold Hits, Vol. 2") 25-35   76
(Tan label. No bonus items shown as being
included.)

RCA (LPM-6402 "Worldwide 50
Gold Hits, Vol. 2") 20-25   77
(Black label. Two of the LPs in this set were
repackaged for the RCA Record Club in 1978 as
RCA 214567.)

RCA (6414 "The Complete
Sun Sessions") 10-15   87
(Includes a bonus color 15x22 poster and *Elvis
Talks* LP flyer.)

RCA (6738 "Essential Elvis") 5-10   88
RCA (6985 "The Alternate Aloha") 5-10   88
RCA (7004 "14 #1 Country Hits") 5-10   85
(Various artists collection.)

RCA (7013 "The Best of Christmas") . . 5-10   85
(Various artists collection.)

RCA (7031 "Elvis Forever") 25-35   74
(TV mail-order offer.)

RCA (8372 "Mistletoe and Memories") 10-20   88
(Various artists collection.)

RCA (9681 "E-Z Pop No. 5") 250-300   55
(Various artists collection. Promotional issue only.)

RCA (7065 "Canadian Tribute") 10-12   78
(Price includes photo inner-sleeve. Canadian
issues of this LP had the same number but are
clearly marked on back cover as Canadian.)

RCA (8468 "Elvis in Nashville") 5-10   88
RCA (8533 "Heartbreak Hotel") 10-15   88
(Soundtrack. Various artists collection.)

RCA (9586 "Elvis Gospel") 5-10   89
RCA (9589 "Stereo '57,
Essential Elvis, Vol. 2") 5-10   89
RCA (213690 "Worldwide 50
Gold Hits, Parts 1&2") 75-100   74
(Orange label. RCA Record Club issue only.)

RCA (213690 "Worldwide 50
Gold Hits, Parts 1&2") 25-30   76
(Tan label. RCA Record Club issue only.)

RCA (213690 "Worldwide 50
Gold Hits, Parts 1&2") 12-15   77
(Black label. RCA Record Club issue only. The two
discs in this set were first issued as half of RCA
LPM-6401.)

RCA (213736 "Aloha from Hawaii") . . 45-55   73
(Orange label.)

RCA (213736 "Aloha from Hawaii") . . 18-20   76
(Tan label.)

RCA (214657 "Worldwide 50
Gold Hits," Parts 3&4") 12-15   78
(RCA Record Club issue only. The two discs in this
set were first issued as half of RCA LPM-6401.)

RCA (233299 "Country Classics") . . . 20-25   80
(RCA Record Club issue only.)

RCA (234340 "From Elvis with Love") 20-25   78
(RCA Record Club issue only.)

RCA (244047 "Legendary Concert
Performances") 20-25   78
(RCA Record Club issue only.)

RCA (244069 "Country
Memories") 20-25   78
(RCA Record Club issue only.)

READER'S DIGEST (040 "Easy Listening Hits
of the '60s and '70s") 20-30   89
(Various artists collection. Seven-LP boxed set.
Includes booklet.)

RHINO (71103 "The Sun Story") 10-15   86
(Various artists collection.)

RHINO ("Billboard Top
Rock 'N' Roll Hits) 5-10   89
(Various artists collections. Price is for any volume
in the series.)

SSS-SHELBY SINGLETON MUSIC (1 "Songs
for the Seventies") 300-400   69
(Various artists collection. Promotional issue only.)

SESSIONS (0887 "Those
Fabulous '50s") 20-25   89
(Various artists collection.)

SILHOUETTE (10001/10002
"Personally Elvis") 20-25   79

STARDAY (995 "Interviews with
Elvis") 30-50   78
(Previously issued on Great Northwest 4005.)

SUN (1001 "The Sun Years") 75-80   77
(Light yellow label, "Memphis" at bottom. Light
yellow cover with light brown printing.)

SUN (1001 "The Sun Years") 15-20   77
(Darker yellow label, four target circles. Dark
yellow cover with dark brown printing.)

SUN (1001 "The Sun Years") 20-25   77
(White cover with brown printing.)

TM ("The Presley Years") 100-200   81
(12-LP boxed syndicated radio show. Includes
script and cue sheets.)

TIME-LIFE (106 "Elvis Presley:
1954-1961") 15-18   86
(Three-LP boxed set, part of the *Rock'N'Roll Era*
series of sets available from Time-Life by
mail-order. Includes brochure.)

TIME-LIFE (107 "The Time-Life
Treasury of Christmas") 15-20   86
(Three-LP boxed set. Various artists collection.)

TIME-LIFE (108 "The Time-Life
Treasury of Christmas, Vol. 2") 15-20   87
(Three-LP boxed set. Various artists collection.)

TIME-LIFE (109 "Country Christmas) . 15-20   88
(Three-LP boxed set. Various artists collection.)

TIME-LIFE (126 "Elvis the King") 20-30   89
(Two-LP boxed set.)

TIME-LIFE (127 "Songs of Faith
and Inspiration") 15-25   89
(Three-LP boxed set. Various artists collection.)

WATERMARK ("The Elvis Presley
Story," 1975) 800-900   75
(13-LP set. White label, pink letters. Includes a
48-page operations manual. Promotional issue
only. Not issued with a special cover or package.)

WATERMARK ("The Elvis Presley
Story," 1977) 700-800   77
(13-LP set. White label, pink letters. Includes a
48-page operations manual, which represents
about $100 of the value. Promotional issue only.
Not issued with a special cover or package.)

WELK (3002 "Blue Christmas") 60-80   84
(Various artists collection. Promotional issue only.)

WELK ("Sound Ideas") 50-70   86
(Five LPs. Various artists collection. Promotional
issue only.)

WESTWOOD ONE ("A Golden
Celebration") 200-250   84
(Three-LP boxed set. Price includes instructions
and cue sheets, which represent $5-10 of the
value. Issued to radio stations only.)

WORLD of ELVIS PRESLEY 50-100   83
(A one hour weekly radio show, on discs numbered
program 1 through program 30. The show ceased
operation after 30 programs. Each disc was
accompanied by a single cue sheet. Price is for
any one of the discs.)

- **Notes:** Prefix letters or numbers are used on some LP
  listings in order to more quickly identify the variations
  available.
- A few items that have no label name are listed by title,
  such as the International Hotel boxed sets.
- Beginning in 1961, many Elvis LPs had a separate sticker,
  promoting such things as certain songs or bonus photos.
  When not listed separately in this edition, a premium of
  10%-20% could be placed on LPs with these original
  stickers.
- LPs with a sticker applied over the catalog number, showing a new number, are valued approximately the same
  as those without the sticker.

- Any album identified as a "Various artists collection" is one
  containing at least one Elvis track, and having no less than
  four other artists.
- Some albums were pressed with the "Dog Near Top" label
  using the older LSP prefix, prior to being switched to the
  AFL1 series. These are not listed separately since there
  seems to be no consequential price difference between
  the two.
- If you don't find a record in the preceding sections, it may
  contain two, three or four artists, and is listed in a section
  that follows.
- Separate publications in our price guide series provide a
  far more in-depth study of Elvis collectibles. For more
  information, simply write the author and request a complete listing of other available books.

Also see ALLEN, Steve
Also see AUDREY
Also see BLACK, Bill
Also see BLOSSOMS
Also see COLE, Nat "King"
Also see CRAMER, Floyd
Also see CRICKETS
Also see DURANTE, Jimmy
Also see HARRIS, Emmylou
Also see KERR, Anita
Also see LIBERACE
Also see MANTOVANI
Also see MILSAP, Ronnie
Also see MOORE, Bob
Also see RANDOLPH, Boots
Also see REED, Jerry
Also see RUSSELL, Jane
Also see SINATRA, Nancy
Also see SWEET INSPIRATIONS
Also see VINCENT, Gene

PRESLEY, Elvis / Beatles
Singles: 7-inch

OSBORNE ENTERPRISES ("The 1967
Elvis Medley") 3-5   88
(Flip side is titled *The #1 Hits Medley, 1956-69.*)

OSBORNE ENTERPRISES ("The 1967
Elvis Medley") 4-8   89
(Flip side is titled *The #1 Hits Medley, 1956-70.*)

LPs: 10/12-inch 33rpm

UNITED DISTRIBUTORS (2382 "Lightning
Strikes Twice") 25-50   81
(Promotional issue only. Has five songs by each
artist.)
Also see BEATLES

PRESLEY, Elvis / Martha Carson / Lou Monte / Herb Jeffries
EPs: 7-inch 33/45rpm

RCA (2 "Dealer's Prevue") 900-1200   57
(Issued with paper envelope/sleeve. Promotional
issue only.)

PRESLEY, Elvis / Jean Chapel
EPs: 7-inch 33/45rpm

RCA (7 "Love Me Tender") 150-200   56
(Not issued with a special sleeve or cover.
Promotional issue only.)

PRESLEY, Elvis / Buddy Holly
Singles: 7–inch
CREATIVE RADIO ("Elvis 50th
Birthday Special") 10-20   85
(Demonstration disc. A promotional issue.)
Also see HOLLY, Buddy

PRESLEY, Elvis / Fear
LPs: 10/12–inch 33rpm
DISCONET (309 "The Original Elvis
Presley Medley"/"Fear Medley") ... 25-50   80
(Promotional issue only.)

PRESLEY, Elvis / David Keith
Singles: 7–inch
RCA (8760 "Heartbreak Hotel") 50-100   88
(White label. Promotional issue only.)
RCA (8760 "Heartbreak Hotel") 3-5   88
(Red label. Printing on both sides of label.)
RCA (8760 "Heartbreak Hotel") 4-8   88
(Red label. Printing on Elvis side only.)
RCA (8760 "Heartbreak Hotel") 4-8   88
(Red label. Printing on David Keith side only.)
Picture Sleeves
RCA (8760 "Heartbreak Hotel") 50-100
(Pictures RCA's Butch Waugh. Promotional issue
only.)
RCA (8760 "Heartbreak Hotel") 4-8   88
Also see KEITH, David

PRESLEY, Elvis / Vaughn Monroe / Gogi Grant / Robert Shaw
EPs: 7–inch 33/45rpm
RCA (3736 "Pop Transcribed
30 Sec. Spot") 500-600   58
(Not issued with a special sleeve or cover.
Promotional issue only.)

PRESLEY, Elvis / Jaye P. Morgan
Singles: 7–inch
UNITED STATES AIR FORCE (125 "It's
Now Or Never") 300-400   61
(Add $30 TO $50 if accompanied by printed,
cardboard mailing box. Issued only to radio
stations.)
EPs: 7–inch 33/45rpm
RCA (992 and 689 "Elvis/Jaye P.
Morgan") 3500-4000   56
(Two-EP set, with 992 by Presley and 689 by Jaye
P. Morgan coupled together in a promotional
double-pocket package. Since the discs were
standard pressings, at least 95% of the value here
is represented by the custom EP cover.)
Also see MORGAN, Jaye P.

PRESLEY, Elvis / Gary Owens
Singles: 7–inch
CREATIVE RADIO ("The Elvis Hour") 20-30   86
(Demonstration disc. A promotional issue.)

PRESLEY, Elvis / Helen Reddy
Singles: 7–inch
WHAT'S IT ALL ABOUT (78 "Life") .. 45-55   77
(Issued only to radio stations.)
Also see REDDY, Helen

PRESLEY, Elvis / Dinah Shore
EPs: 7–inch 33/45rpm
RCA (56 "Too Much") 150-200   57
(Not issued with a special sleeve or cover.
Promotional issue only.)
Also see SHORE, Dinah

PRESLEY, Elvis / Frank Sinatra / Nat King Cole
EPs: 7–inch 33/45rpm
CREATIVE RADIO ("Elvis
Remembered") 40-45   79
(Promotional demonstration disc.)
Also see COLE, Nat "King"
Also see SINATRA, Frank

PRESLEY, Elvis / Hank Snow / Eddy Arnold / Jim Reeves
RCA (12 "Old Shep") 1700-2000   56
(Issued with a paper, "WOHO Featuring RCA
Victor" sleeve. Promotional only.)
Also see ARNOLD, Eddy
Also see REEVES, Jim
Also see SNOW, Hank

PRESLEY, Elvis / Lawrence Welk
Singles: 7–inch
UNITED STATES AIR FORCE (159
"Surrender") 300-400   61
(Add $30 TO $50 if accompanied by printed,
cardboard mailing box. Issued only to radio
stations.)
Also see WELK, Lawrence

PRESLEY, Elvis / Hank Williams
LPs: 10/12–inch 33rpm
SUNRISE MEDIA (3011 "History of
Country Music") 10-20   81
(Has four songs by each artist.)
Also see PRESLEY, Elvis
Also see WILLIAMS, Hank

PRESSURE
Singles: 7–inch
LAX 3-5   79-80
LPs: 10/12–inch 33rpm
LAX 5-10   79

PRESSURE DROP
Singles: 12–inch 33/45rpm
TOMMY BOY 4-6   82
Singles: 7–inch
TOMMY BOY 3-5   82

PRESTON, Billy
Singles: 12–inch 33/45rpm
MEGATONE 4-6   84
MONTAGE 4-6   84

Singles: 7-inch

A&M	3-5	72-78
APPLE/AMERICOM (433 "That's the Way		
God Planned It")	150-250	69
(Four-inch flexi, "pocket disc.")		
APPLE	5-10	69-72
CAPITOL	4-8	66-69
CONTRACT	8-12	61
MOTOWN	3-5	79-82
VEE JAY	5-10	65

Picture Sleeves

A&M	4-8	73-75
APPLE	5-10	69-70

LPs: 10/12-inch 33rpm

A&M	8-12	71-82
APPLE	10-20	69-72
BUDDAH	10-15	69
CAPITOL	10-15	66
(With "ST" prefix.)		
CAPITOL	6-10	75
(With "SM" prefix.)		
DERBY (701 "16-Year-Old Soul")	50-75	63
EXODUS	15-20	65
GNP/CRESCENDO	10-15	73
MOTOWN	5-10	79-82
MYRRH	5-10	78
PEACOCK	8-12	73
SPRINGBOARD	5-10	78
TRIP	8-12	73
VEE JAY	15-25	65-66

Also see BEATLES
Also see MOTHERS of INVENTION

PRESTON, Billy, and Syreeta
Singles: 7-inch

MOTOWN	3-5	79-81
TAMLA	3-5	80

LPs: 10/12-inch 33rpm

MOTOWN	5-10	79-81

Also see PRESTON, Billy
Also see SYREETA

PRESTON, Johnny
Singles: 7-inch

ABC	3-6	68-73
HALL/HALL WAY	4-8	64-66
IMPERIAL	4-8	63
MERCURY	5-10	59-62
TCF	4-8	65

Picture Sleeves

MERCURY	8-12	60-62

EPs: 7-inch 33/45rpm

MERCURY (3397 "Johnny Preston")	30-50	60

LPs: 10/12-inch 33rpm

MERCURY (20592 "Running Bear")		
(Monaural.)	50-70	60
MERCURY (20609 "Come Rock		
with Me")		
(Monaural.)	50-70	60
MERCURY (60250 "Running Bear")		
(Stereo. Black label)	60-80	60
MERCURY (60250 "Running Bear")		
(Chicago "Skyline" label)	8-12	81
MERCURY (60609 "Come Rock		
with Me")		
(Stereo.)	60-80	60
WING (12246 "Running Bear")		
(Monaural.)	20-30	63
WING (16246 "Running Bear")		
(Stereo.)	25-35	63

PRESTON, Mike
Singles: 7-inch

LONDON	5-8	58-63

PRESTON, Terry
(Ferlin Husky)
Singles: 78rpm

CAPITOL	5-10	52-53

Singles: 7-inch

CAPITOL	10-20	52-53

Also see HUSKY, Ferlin

PRETENDERS
(Featuring Chrissie Hynde)
Singles: 7-inch

SIRE	2-5	79-90

Picture Sleeves

SIRE	3-5	80-83

LPs: 10/12-inch 33rpm

SIRE	5-10	80-90

Also see UB40

PRETTY BOY
(Don Covay; With Johnny Fuller's Band)
Singles: 78rpm

ATLANTIC (1147 "Bip Bop Bip")	30-40	57
BIG	30-40	57
RHYTHM (1768 "I'm Bad")	30-40	54

Singles: 7-inch

ATLANTIC (1147 "Bip Bop Bip")	50-75	57
BIG (617 "Switchin'		
in the Kitchen")	50-75	57

Also see COVAY, Don
Also see KING CURTIS

PRETTY MAIDS
LPs: 10/12-inch 33rpm

EPIC	5-10	87

PRETTY POISON
Singles: 12-inch 33/45rpm

MONTAGE	4-6	84
SVENGALI	4-6	84

Singles: 7-inch

MONTAGE	2-4	84
SVENGALI	2-4	84
VIRGIN	2-4	87-88

LPs: 10/12-inch 33rpm

VIRGIN	5-10	88

PRETTY THINGS
Singles: 7-inch

FONTANA	5-10	64-66
LAURIE	4-8	68

SWAN SONG 3-5   75-76
     LPs: 10/12–inch 33rpm
FONTANA (27544 "Pretty Things") . . . 35-55   66
  (Monaural.)
FONTANA (67544 "Pretty Things") . . . 35-55   66
  (Stereo.)
MOTOWN 10-15   76
RARE EARTH (506 "S.F. Sorrow") . . . 15-25   69
  (With standard square cover.)
RARE EARTH (506 "S.F. Sorrow") . . . 20-40   69
  (With rounded-top cover. Promotional issue.)
RARE EARTH (515 "Parachute") 15-20   70
RARE EARTH (549 "Rare Earth") 8-12   76
  (Reissue of material from 506 and 515.)
SIRE 8-10   76
SWAN SONG 8-10   75-76
WARNER 8-10   73-80
    Also see GREEN, Jack

PRETTY TONY
(Tony Butler)
     Singles: 7–inch
MUSIC 2-4   84

PREVIN, Andre
(Andre Previn and David Rose's Orchestra)
     Singles: 78rpm
MODERN 3-5   51
     Singles: 7–inch
COLUMBIA 3-6   60-64
DECCA 3-6   61
MGM 4-8   59
MODERN 10-20   51
RCA 3-5   67
     EPs: 7–inch 33/45rpm
MGM 5-10   59
     LPs: 10/12–inch 33rpm
ALLEGIANCE 5-8   84
ANGEL 5-8   80-81
CAMDEN 5-10   64
COLUMBIA 10-20   60-65
CONTEMPORARY 15-30   57-60
DECCA (4000 series) 8-15   61-63
  (Decca LP numbers in this series preceded by a
  "7" or a "DL-7" are stereo issues.)
DECCA (8000 series) 20-40   55-56
EVEREST 5-10   70
HARMONY 5-10   67
MFSL 20-40   82
MGM 10-15   59-64
METRO JAZZ 10-20   59
MONARCH (203 "All Star Jazz") 60-80   54
  (10–inch LP.)
MONARCH (204 "Andre Previn
  Plays Duke") 60-80   54
  (10–inch LP.)
ODYSSEY 8-12   68
RCA (1000 series) 5-10   75
  (With an "ARL1" prefix.)

RCA (1000 series) 20-45   54
  (With an "LPM" prefix.)
RCA (1356 "Three Little Words") 40-60   56
RCA (2900 series) 6-12   67
RCA (3002 ("Andre Previn
  Plays Harry Warren") 75-100   51
  (10–inch LP.)
RCA (3400 through 3800 series) 10-20   65-67
U.A. (5200 series) 5-10   71
VERVE 15-25   63
    Since publication of *The Official Price Guide to Movie/TV Soundtracks and Original Cast Albums*, with over 8,000 listings, this guide has dropped many soundtracks, including some by this artist.
    Also see ANDREWS, Julie, and Andre Previn / Vic Damone / Jack Jones / Marian Anderson
    Also see DAY, Doris, and Andre Previn
    Also see ROSE, David
    Also see SHORE, Dinah, and Andre Previn

PREYER, Ron
     Singles: 7–inch
SHOCK 3-5   78

PRICE, Alan
(Alan Price Set)
     Singles: 7–inch
COTILLION 4-8   69
EPIC 2-4   84
JET 3-5   77-79
PARROT 5-10   66-68
WARNER 3-5   72
     LPs: 10/12–inch 33rpm
ACCORD 5-10   82
JET 8-12   77-80
PARROT 15-25   68
TOWNHOUSE 5-10   81
WARNER 8-12   73
    Also see ANIMALS

PRICE, Lloyd
(Lloyd Price Orchestra; Lloyd Price and the Dukes)
     Singles: 78rpm
ABC-PAR 10-20   57
KRC (587 "Just Because") 30-40   57
SPECIALTY 10-15   55-56
     Singles: 7–inch
ABC 3-6   67-73
ABC-PAR (Monaural) 8-12   57-60
ABC-PAR (S-9972 "Stagger Lee") . . . 20-30   59
  (Stereo.)
ABC-PAR (S-9997 "Where Were You") 20-30   59
  (Stereo.)
COLLECTABLES 2-4
DOUBLE-L 5-10   63-66
GSF 3-5   72-73
JAD 4-8   68
KRC (Except 587) 8-12   57-59
KRC (587 "Just Because") 40-50   57
LPG 3-5   76
LUDIX 4-6
MCA 2-4

PRICE, Priscilla

Singles: 7–inch

PRICE, Ray
(Ray Price and the Cherokee Cowboys)

Singles: 78rpm

Singles: 7–inch

DIMENSION	2-4	81-82
MONUMENT	2-5	78-79
MYRRH	2-4	74-75
STEP ONE	2-4	85-86
WARNER	2-4	82-83
WORD	2-4	78

Picture Sleeves

COLUMBIA	3-5	66

EPs: 7–inch 33/45rpm

COLUMBIA (1700 through 2800 series)	15-25	53-57
COLUMBIA (8556 "Ray Price")	10-20	
COLUMBIA (10000 through 14000 series)	10-20	57-60
(White label. Promotional issue only.)		

LPs: 10/12–inch 33rpm

ABC/DOT	6-12	75-77
COLUMBIA (28 "The World of Ray Price")	8-12	70
COLUMBIA (1015 "Ray Price Sings Heart Songs")	30-40	57
COLUMBIA (1148 "Talk to Your Heart")	25-35	58
COLUMBIA (1400 through 2600 series)	10-25	60-67
(Monaural)		
COLUMBIA (8200 through 9400 series)	15-30	60-67
(Stereo)		
COLUMBIA (9700 through 9900 series)	8-12	68-70
COLUMBIA (10000 series)	5-10	73
COLUMBIA (30000 through 37000 series)	5-10	70-81
DIMENSION	5-8	81
51 WEST	5-8	84
HARMONY	8-15	66-71
MONUMENT	5-10	79
MYRRH	5-8	74
RADIANT	5-8	81
STEP ONE	5-10	86
WARNER	5-8	83
WORD	5-8	77

Also see ROBBINS, Marty / Johnny Cash / Ray Price

PRICE, Ray / Lefty Frizzell / Carl Smith
LPs: 10/12–inch 33rpm

COLUMBIA (1257 "Greatest Western Hits")	15-25	59
(Monaural.)		
COLUMBIA (8776 "Greatest Western Hits")	15-25	63
(Stereo.)		

Also see FRIZZELL, Lefty
Also see SMITH, Carl

PRICE, Ray / Johnny Horton / Carl Smith / George Morgan
EPs: 7–inch 33/45rpm

COLUMBIA (2157 "4 Big Hits")	20-25	60

Also see HORTON, Johnny
Also see SMITH, Carl

PRICE, Ray, and Willie Nelson
Singles: 7–inch

COLUMBIA	2-4	80

LPs: 10/12–inch 33rpm

COLUMBIA	5-8	80

Also see NELSON, Willie
Also see PRICE, Ray

PRIDE, Charley
(Country Charley Pride; Charley Pride and the Pridesmen)
Singles: 7–inch

RCA (0100 through 0500 series)	4-8	66-69
RCA (0600 through 0900 series)	3-5	72-73
RCA (8700 and 8800 series)	4-8	66
RCA (9000 through 9900 series)	3-6	66-71
RCA (10000 through 14000, except 11736)	2-5	74-86
RCA 11736 "Dallas Cowboys")	3-5	79
(Black label.)		
RCA 11736 "Dallas Cowboys")	8-12	79
(Gray and blue label. Special Dallas Cowboys Edition.)		

Picture Sleeves

RCA	3-5	71-74

EPs: 7–inch 33/45rpm

RCA	5-10	
(Jukebox issues.)		

LPs: 10/12–inch 33rpm

CAMDEN	5-10	72
RCA (Except LPM/LSP 3700 through 4800 series)	5-10	74-86
RCA (3700 through 4800 series)	10-20	66-73
(With "LPM" or "LSP" prefix.)		

Also see DAVE & SUGAR

PRIMA, Louis
(Louis Prima and His Orchestra)
Singles: 78rpm

COLUMBIA	4-6	52-53
DECCA	4-8	54
HIT	5-10	44-45
MERCURY	4-8	50
ROBIN HOOD	4-8	50
SAVOY	4-8	53

Singles: 7–inch

ABC	3-6	68-74
BUENA VISTA	3-6	66-74
CAPITOL	4-8	62
COLUMBIA	5-10	52-53
DECCA	5-10	54
DOT	4-8	59-62
HBR	4-6	66
KAMA SUTRA	4-6	66
MERCURY	5-10	50
PRIMA	4-8	63-64
ROBIN HOOD	5-10	50
SAVOY	5-10	53
U.A.	3-6	67

EPs: 7–inch 33/45rpm
CAPITOL	5-10	56
JUBILEE	5-10	55
VARSITY	6-12	54

LPs: 10/12–inch 33rpm
BUENA VISTA	8-18	65-74
CAPITOL	10-20	56-62
DE-LITE	5-10	68
DOT	10-15	60
HBR	5-12	66
HAMILTON	5-10	65
MERCURY (25000 series)	20-35	53
(10–inch LPs.)		
PRIMA	5-8	72-76
RONDO/RONDOLETTE	10-20	59
U.A.	5-10	67

PRIMA, Louis, and Keely Smith
Singles: 7–inch
CAPITOL	4-8	58-59
DOT	4-8	59-61

Picture Sleeves
CAPITOL (4063 "That Old Black Magic")5-10	.58	
(Sleeve has a die-cut center hole)		
DOT	5-10	59

EPs: 7–inch 33/45rpm
CAPITOL	5-10	58
DOT	4-8	60

LPs: 10/12–inch 33rpm
CAPITOL	5-8	75
(With "SM" prefix.)		
CAPITOL	15-25	58-61
(With "T" or "ST" prefix.)		
DOT	15-25	59-60
Also see SMITH, Keely		

PRIMETTES
(Supremes)
Singles: 7–inch
LUPINE (120 "Tears of Sorrow")	200-250	61
Also see SUPREMES		

PRINCE
(Prince and the Revolution)
Singles: 12–inch 33/45rpm
PAISLEY PARK	4-6	85-91
WARNER	5-10	81-84

Promotional 12–inch Singles
PAISLEY PARK	10-20	85-92
WARNER	15-30	78-84

Singles: 7–inch
PAISLEY PARK	2-5	85-92
WARNER (Except 29286 and 29174)	3-8	78-84
WARNER (29286 "When Doves Cry")	3-5	84
(Black vinyl.)		
WARNER (29286 "When Doves Cry")	10-15	84
(Colored vinyl.)		
WARNER (29174 "Purple Rain")	3-5	84
(Black vinyl.)		
WARNER (29174 "Purple Rain")	10-15	84
(Colored vinyl.)		

Promotional Singles
PAISLEY PARK (Except 2939 and 29052)	4-8	85-92
PAISLEY PARK (2939 "Hot Thing")	15-25	87
PAISLEY PARK (29052 "Paisley Park")	15-25	85
WARNER (Except 29286, 29174 and 29746)	3-8	78-84
WARNER (29286 "When Doves Cry")	5-8	84
(Black vinyl.)		
WARNER (29286 "When Doves Cry")	15-25	84
(Colored vinyl.)		
WARNER (29174 "Purple Rain")	5-8	84
(Black vinyl.)		
WARNER (29174 "Purple Rain")	15-25	84
(Colored vinyl.)		
WARNER (29746 "Little Red Corvette")	5-10	83
(Black vinyl.)		
WARNER (29746 "Little Red Corvette")	10-15	83
(Picture disc.)		

Picture Sleeves
PAISLEY PARK	3-6	85-89
WARNER	4-10	79-84

LPs: 10/12–inch 33rpm
PAISLEY PARK	5-8	85-90
WARNER (Except 25110 and 25677)	5-10	78-89
WARNER (25110 "Purple Rain")	5-10	84
(Black vinyl.)		
WARNER (25110 "Purple Rain")	30-40	84
(Colored vinyl.)		
WARNER (25677 "Black Album")	1000-2000	87
(Promotional issue only.)		
Also see E., Sheila		

PRINCE BUSTER
(Prince Buster and the Sea Busters)
Singles: 7–inch
AMY	4-8	64
ATLANTIC	4-8	64
PHILIPS	4-8	67
RCA	4-8	67
STELLAR	4-8	64

LPs: 10/12–inch 33rpm
RCA	10-20	67

PRINCE HAROLD
Singles: 7–inch
MERCURY	4-8	66
SPRING	4-8	67
VERVE	4-8	67

PRINCE LA LA
Singles: 7–inch
AFO	5-10	61-62

PRINCESS
Singles: 12–inch 33/45rpm
NEXT PLATINUM	4-6	85-86

POLYDOR 4-6   86
Singles: 7–inch
POLYDOR 2-4   86-87

PRINCIPATO, Tom
LPs: 10/12–inch 33rpm
POWERHOUSE 5-8   88

PRINCIPLE, Jamie
Singles: 12–inch 33/45rpm
PERSONA 4-6   85

PRINE, John
Singles: 7–inch
ASYLUM 3-5   78
ATLANTIC 3-5   71-75
OH BOY (Colored vinyl) 3-5   81-86
LPs: 10/12–inch 33rpm
ASYLUM 5-10   78-80
ATLANTIC 8-12   71-76
OH BOY 5-8   84-86

PRINE, John / Daryl Hall & John Oates / Barnaby Bye / Delbert & Glen
EPs: 7–inch 33/45rpm
ATLANTIC (195 "Something for
Nothing") 5-8   73
Also see DELBERT & GLEN
Also see HALL, Daryl, and John Oates
Also see PRINE, John

PRISCILLA
(Priscilla Paris; With Davie Allan)
Singles: 7–inch
YORK 5-10   67
LPs: 10/12–inch 33rpm
HAPPY TIGER 8-12
YORK (4005 "Priscilla Sings Herself") 20-30   67
Also see ALLAN, Davie
Also see PARIS SISTERS

PRISM
Singles: 7–inch
ARIOLA AMERICA 3-5   77-79
CAPITOL 3-5   82
LPs: 10/12–inch 33rpm
ARIOLA AMERICA (Except 50034) .. 10-15   77-79
ARIOLA AMERICA (50034 "Live
Tonite") 15-25   78
(Promotional issue only.)
CAPITOL 5-10   80-82

PRISTER, Jerome "Secret Weapon"
TUFF CITY 2-4   88

PROBY, P.J.
Singles: 7–inch
IMPERIAL 4-8   64
LIBERTY 5-10   61-68
LONDON 4-8   64
SURFSIDE 8-12   65
Picture Sleeves
LIBERTY 8-12   67

LPs: 10/12–inch 33rpm
LIBERTY 15-25   65-68
Also see FOCUS and P.J. Proby

PROCESS and the Doo Rags
Singles: 7–inch
COLUMBIA 2-4   85-87

PROCOL HARUM
Singles: 7–inch
A&M 4-8   67-72
CHRYSALIS 3-5   73-77
DERAM 4-8   67
Picture Sleeves
A&M 3-6   72-73
CHRYSALIS 3-5   73
LPs: 10/12–inch 33rpm
A&M (Except 4294 and 8053) 8-12   68-73
A&M (4294 "Broken Barricades") 12-15   71
(With die-cut gatefold cover.)
A&M (4294 "Broken Barricades") 10-12   72
(With standard cover.)
A&M (8053 "Procol Harum Lives") ... 30-40
(Promotional issue only.)
CHRYSALIS 8-10   73-77
DERAM (16008 "Procol Harum") 50-75   67
(Monaural. With bonus poster, which represents
$15 to $20 of the value.)
DERAM (18008 "Procol Harum") 50-75   67
(Stereo. With bonus poster, which represents $15
to $20 of the value.)
Members: Gary Brooker; Robin Trower.
Also see TROWER, Robin

PRODUCERS
Singles: 7–inch
PORTRAIT 3-5   81-82
LPs: 10/12–inch 33rpm
PORTRAIT 5-10   81-82

PROFESSOR FUNK and His Eighth Street Funk Band
Singles: 7–inch
ROXBURY 3-5   73

PROFESSOR MORRISON'S LOLLIPOP:
see MORRISON, Professor

PROFILES
Singles: 7–inch
BAMBOO 4-8   69
DUO 4-8   68

PROJECT FUTURE
Singles: 12–inch 33/45rpm
CAPITOL 4-6   83
Singles: 7–inch
CAPITOL 2-4   83

PROPHECY
Singles: 7–inch
AIRBORNE 3-5
ALL PLATINUM 3-5   74
MAINSTREAM 3-5   75

Picture Sleeves

AIRBORNE 3-5
Members: Mack Wolfman; Bernie Taylor.

PROPHETS, Thee: see THEE PROPHETS

PROTHEROE, Brian
Singles: 7-inch

CHRYSALIS 3-5   75
LPs: 10/12-inch 33rpm
CHRYSALIS 8-12   75-76

PROVINE, Dorothy
Singles: 7-inch

WARNER 3-6   61
LPs: 10/12-inch 33rpm
WARNER 15-25   60-61

PROVINE, Dorothy, and Joe "Fingers" Carr
LPs: 10/12-inch 33rpm

WARNER 15-25   60-62
Also see CARR, Joe "Fingers"

PRUETT, Jeanne
(Jean Pruett)
Singles: 7-inch

AUDIOGRAPH 2-4   83
DECCA 3-6   68-72
IBC 2-5   79-80
MCA 3-5   73-77
MERCURY 3-5   78
PAID 2-4   81
RCA 4-6   63-64
LPs: 10/12-inch 33rpm
ALLEGIANCE 5-8   84
AUDIOGRAPH 5-8   83
DECCA 8-12   72
IBC 5-10   79
MCA 5-10   73-75
OUT of TOWN DIST 5-10   82
Also see ROBBINS, Marty, and Jeanne Pruett

PRYOR, Richard
Singles: 7-inch

LAFF 3-5   80
WARNER 4-6   76-79
LPs: 10/12-inch 33rpm
DOVE 10-15   68
LAFF 5-10   71-81
PARTEE 5-10   74
REPRISE 6-12   68-77
TIGER LILY 5-10   77
WARNER 5-10   76-85

PRYSOCK, Arthur
Singles: 78rpm

DECCA 4-8   52-54
MERCURY 4-8   54-55
Singles: 7-inch
BETHLEHEM 3-5   72
DECCA (25000 series) 4-8   65
DECCA (27000 through 29000 series) . 5-10   52-54
DECCA (31000 series) 4-8   64-65

GUSTO 3-5   79
KING 3-6   69-71
MCA 3-5   78
MGM 3-5   70
MERCURY 5-10   54-55
OLD TOWN (100 series) 3-5   73-76
OLD TOWN (1000 series) 4-8   59-60
(Light blue label.)
OLD TOWN (1000 series) 3-5   76-77
(Dark blue or black label.)
OLD TOWN (1100 series) 4-6   61-66
VERVE 3-6   66-69
LPs: 10/12-inch 33rpm
DECCA 15-20   64-65
KING 8-12   69-71
MCA 5-10   78
OLD TOWN (100 series) 20-30   60-62
OLD TOWN (2000 series) 15-25   62-65
OLD TOWN (12000 series) 5-10   73-77
POLYDOR 5-10   77
VERVE 10-20   66-69
Also see ECKSTINE, Billy / Arthur Prysock
Also see JOHNSON, Buddy

PRYSOCK, Arthur, and Count Basie
Singles: 7-inch

VERVE 3-6   66
LPs: 10/12-inch 33rpm
VERVE 15-20   66
Also see BASIE, Count

PRYSOCK, Arthur / Leroy Bivins
LPs: 10/12-inch 33rpm

GUEST STAR 5-10   64
Also see PRYSOCK, Arthur

PSEUDO ECHO
Singles: 7-inch

RCA 2-4   87
LPs: 10/12-inch 33rpm
RCA 5-8   87

PSYCHEDELIC FURS
Singles: 12-inch 33/45rpm

COLUMBIA 4-6   84-86
Singles: 7-inch
COLUMBIA 2-5   80-89
LPs: 10/12-inch 33rpm
COLUMBIA 5-10   80-89
Members: Tim Butler; Richard Butler; John Ashton; Mars
Williams; Paul Garisto; Marty Williamson.

PUBLIC IMAGE LTD.
Singles: 12-inch 33/45rpm

VIRGIN 4-6   87
LPs: 10/12-inch 33rpm
ELEKTRA 5-8   86
ISLAND 8-10   80
VIRGIN 5-8   87-89
WARNER 8-10   81
Also see SEX PISTOLS

PUCKETT, Gary
(Gary Puckett and the Union Gap; Union Gap
Featuring Gary Puckett)
Singles: 7–inch
COLUMBIA 4-8   67-72
Picture Sleeves
COLUMBIA 5-10   67-69
LPs: 10/12–inch 33rpm
BACK-TRAC 5-8   85
COLUMBIA 10-20   68-71
51 WEST 5-10   82
HARMONY 8-12   72
Also see CHATER, Kerry

PULLINS, Leroy
Singles: 7–inch
KAPP 4-8   66

PUMPKIN
(Pumpkin and the Profile All-Stars)
Singles: 12–inch 33/45rpm
PROFILE 4-6   84
Singles: 7–inch
PROFILE 2-4   84

PUPPETS
Singles: 12–inch 33/45rpm
QUALITY/RFC 4-6   84
Singles: 7–inch
QUALITY/RFC 2-4   84

PURDIE, Pretty
(Bernard Purdie)
Singles: 7–inch
COLUMBIA 4-6   69
DATE 4-8   67-68
LPs: 10/12–inch 33rpm
DATE 10-20   67
FLYING DUTCHMAN 8-12   73
PRESTIGE 8-12   71

PURE ENERGY
Singles: 12–inch 33/45rpm
PRISM 4-6   80-84
Singles: 7–inch
PRISM 3-5   80-84

PURE LOVE & PLEASURE
Singles: 7–inch
DUNHILL 3-5   70
LPs: 10/12–inch 33rpm
DUNHILL 10-15   70

PURE PRAIRIE LEAGUE
Singles: 7–inch
RCA 3-5   72-79
CASABLANCA 3-5   80-81
EPIC 3-5   77
LPs: 10/12–inch 33rpm
CASABLANCA 5-10   80-81
RCA 6-12   72-80
Also see AMERICAN FLYER

PURIFY, James and Bobby
Singles: 7–inch
BELL 4-8   66-69
CASABLANCA 3-5   74-75
MERCURY 3-5   76-77
LPs: 10/12–inch 33rpm
BELL 10-20   66-67
MERCURY 8-12   77
Members: James Purify; Bobby Dickey.

PURIM, Flora
LPs: 10/12–inch 33rpm
MILESTONE 5-10   74-77
WARNER 5-10   77-78
Also see HART, Mickey, Airto and Flora Purim

PURPLE REIGN
Singles: 7–inch
GO-RILLA 4-8   75
PRIVATE STOCK 3-5   75

PURSELL, Bill
Singles: 7–inch
COLUMBIA 3-6   62-66
DOT 3-5   69
EPIC 3-5   67
LPs: 10/12–inch 33rpm
COLUMBIA 8-15   63-65

PUSH
LPs: 10/12–inch 33rpm
MOON 10-15

PYRAMIDS
Singles: 7–inch
BEST 15-25   63
(Label makes no mention of distributed by London.)
BEST 8-12   63-64
(Label reads, "Distributed By London.")
CEDWICKE (13005 "Midnight Run") . 20-30   64
CEDWICKE (13006 "Contact") 20-30   64
Picture Sleeves
BEST (13002 "Penetration") 20-30   63
LPs: 10/12–inch 33rpm
BEST (36501 "Penetration") 75-125   64
WHAT 5-8   83

PYTHON LEE JACKSON
Singles: 7–inch
GNP/CRESCENDO 4-6   72
LPs: 10/12–inch 33rpm
GNP/CRESCENDO 10-15   72
Member: Rod Stewart.
Also see SMALL FACES
Also see STEWART, Rod

Q

Q
Singles: 7–inch
EPIC 3-5   77
LPs: 10/12–inch 33rpm
EPIC 8-10   77
Members: Robert Peckman; Don Garvin.
Also see JAGGERZ

QUADRANT SIX
Singles: 12–inch 33/45rpm
ATLANTIC 4-6   83
Singles: 7–inch
ATLANTIC 2-4   83

QUAITE, Christine
Singles: 7–inch
WORLD ARTISTS 5-8   64

QUAKER CITY BOYS
Singles: 7–inch
SWAN 5-10   58-59

QUANDO QUANDO
Singles: 12–inch 33/45rpm
FACTORY 4-6   83

QUARTER NOTES
Singles: 78rpm
DOT 5-10   57
Singles: 7–inch
DOT 10-20   57
GUYDEN 10-15   63
IMPERIAL 5-10   60
RCA 5-10   58
WIZZ 10-20   59

QUARTERFLASH
Singles: 12–inch 33/45rpm
GEFFEN 4-6   81-82
Singles: 7–inch
GEFFEN 3-5   81-85
WARNER 3-5   82
Picture Sleeves
GEFFEN 3-5   83
LPs: 10/12–inch 33rpm
GEFFEN 5-10   81-85

QUARTERMAN, Joe, and Free Soul
Singles: 7–inch
GSF 3-5   72-74
MERCURY 3-5   74

QUARTZ
Singles: 7–inch
MARLIN 3-5   78
POLYDOR 3-5   79

LPs: 10/12–inch 33rpm
POLYDOR 5-10   79

QUATEMAN, Bill
Singles: 7–inch
COLUMBIA 3-5   72-73
RCA 3-5   77-78
LPs: 10/12–inch 33rpm
COLUMBIA 8-10   73
RCA 5-10   77-78

QUATRO, Suzi
(Susie Quatro)
Singles: 7–inch
ARISTA 3-5   75
BELL 3-5   73-74
BIG TREE 3-5   76
DREAMLAND 3-5   80-81
RAK 5-10   72-74
RSO 3-5   79
Picture Sleeves
DREAMLAND 3-5   80
LPs: 10/12–inch 33rpm
ARISTA 8-10   75
BELL 10-12   74
DREAMLAND 5-10   80
RSO 5-10   79

QUATRO, Suzi, and Chris Norman
Singles: 7–inch
RSO 3-5   79
Also see QUATRO, Suzi
Also see SMOKIE

QUAZAR
Singles: 7–inch
ARISTA 3-5   78
LPs: 10/12–inch 33rpm
ARISTA 5-10   78

QUEEN
Singles: 12–inch 33/45rpm
CAPITOL 4-8   84-86
Singles: 7–inch
CAPITOL 2-5   84-86
ELEKTRA 3-6   74-82
Picture Sleeves
CAPITOL 3-5   84
ELEKTRA 4-6   77-82
LPs: 10/12–inch 33rpm
CAPITOL 5-10   84-89
ELEKTRA (Except 5064) 6-12   73-82
ELEKTRA (5064 "Queen") 20-30   73
(Quadrophonic.)
HOLLYWOOD 5-8   91
MFSL 35-50   82
Members: Freddie Mercury; John Deacon; Brian May; Roger
Taylor.
Also see MAY, Brian
Also see MERCURY, Freddie
Also see TAYLOR, Roger

QUEEN & DAVID BOWIE
Singles: 7–inch
ELEKTRA 3-5   81
Picture Sleeves
ELEKTRA 3-5   81
   Also see BOWIE, David
   Also see QUEEN

QUEENSRYCHE
Singles: 7–inch
EMI 2-4 83-86
LPs: 10/12–inch 33rpm
EMI (Except 01435) 5-8   83-90
EMI (01436 "Operation Mind Crime") . 20-25   88

? AND the MYSTERIANS
(Question Mark and the Mysterians)
Singles: 7–inch
ABKCO 2-4
CAMEO 4-8   66-67
CAPITOL 5-10   68
CHICORY (410 "Talk Is Cheap") 10-20   67
LUV 4-6   73
PA-GO-GO (102 "96 Tears") 75-125   66
SUPER K 4-8   69
TANGERINE 4-8
LPs: 10/12–inch 33rpm
CAMEO (2004 "96 Tears") 50-100   66
CAMEO (2006 "Action") 50-100   67
   Members: Rudy Martinez; Robert Martinez; Frank Rodriguez;
   Larry Borjas; Bob Balderamma; Frank Lugo.

QUICK
Singles: 12–inch 33/45rpm
EPIC 4-6   82
PAVILLION 4-6   81
Singles: 7–inch
EPIC (37000 series) 3-5   82
PAVILLION 3-5   81
LPs: 10/12–inch 33rpm
EPIC 5-10   82

QUICKEST WAY OUT
Singles: 7–inch
WARNER 3-5   75-76

QUICKSILVER
(Quicksilver Messinger Service)
Singles: 7–inch
CAPITOL 4-8   68-76
LPs: 10/12–inch 33rpm
CAPITOL (120 "Happy Trails") 20-30   69
CAPITOL (288 "Quicksilver
  Messenger Service") 30-50   69
CAPITOL (391 through 819) 10-25   69-71
CAPITOL (2904 "Quicksilver
  Messenger Service") 20-30   68
CAPITOL (11000 series) 10-15   72-75
CAPITOL (16000 series) 5-10   80
   Also see HOPKINS, Nicky
   Also see JEFFERSON AIRPLANE
   Also see MILLER, Steve / Band / Quicksilver Messenger Service
   Also see VALENTI, Dino

QUIET RIOT
Singles: 12–inch 33/45rpm
PASHA 4-6   83-85
Singles: 7–inch
CBS 2-4   83
PASHA 2-4   83-86
LPs: 10/12–inch 33rpm
PASHA (Except 8Z8-39203) 5-10   83-88
PASHA (8Z8-39203 "Mental Health") . 10-12   83
(Picture disc.)

QUINELLA
Singles: 7–inch
BECKET 3-5   81

QUINN, Carmel
Singles: 78rpm
COLUMBIA 3-5   55-56
Singles: 7–inch
COLUMBIA 5-10   55-56
DOT 4-6   64
HEADLINE 4-8   59-62
EPs: 7–inch 33/45rpm
COLUMBIA 8-12   55
LPs: 10/12–inch 33rpm
CAMDEN 10-15   65
COLUMBIA 15-25   55-56
DOT 10-15   65
HEADLINE 10-20   59-62

Red Top

Myra Music
BMI

Time 2:39

DOWN THE AISLE OF LOVE
(The Quin-Tones)
THE QUIN-TONES
RT 108

QUIN-TONES
Singles: 7–inch
COLLECTABLES 2-4
HUNT (321 "Down the Aisle
  of Love") 10-20   58
HUNT (322 "Down the Aisle
  of Love") 15-25   58
RED TOP (108 "Down the Aisle
  of Love") 30-40   58
  (Blue label.)
RED TOP (108 "Down the Aisle
  of Love") 10-15
  (Red label.)

R

RCR
Singles: 7–inch
RADIO 3-5   80
Members: Donna Rhodes; Charles Chalmers; Sandy Rhodes.

R.E.M.
Singles: 7–inch
EVA-TONE (105900 "Dark Globe") ... 5-10
(Promotional issue only.)
HIBTONE (Radio Free Europe") 50-75   81
I.R.S. 3-6   82-87
Picture Sleeves
I.R.S. 4-8   82-86
EPs: 7–inch 33/45rpm
I.R.S. 5-10   82
LPs: 10/12–inch 33rpm
I.R.S. 5-10   82-88
WARNER 5-8   88-90
Members: J. Michael Stipe; Bill Berry; Peter Buck; Mike Mills.
Singles: 7–inch
EPIC (Except 10000 and 11000 series) . 2-5   75-90
EPIC (10000 and 11000 series) 3-5   72-74
Picture Sleeves
EPIC 3-5   80-85
EPs: 7–inch 33/45rpm
CSP 4-8   81
(Nestles candy promotional issue.)
LPs: 10/12–inch 33rpm
EPIC (Except 40000 series) 6-12   71-90
EPIC (40000 series) 12-15   81-82
(Half-speed mastered.)
Promotional LPs
EPIC (643 "Nine Lives") 15-20
Members: Kevin Cronin; Neal Doughty; Al Gratzer; Bruce Hall;
Terry Luttrell.
Also see MAY, Brian

R.J.'S LATEST ARRIVAL
(Ralph James)
Singles: 7–inch
ARIOLA AMERICA 3-5   79
ATLANTIC 2-4   85
BUDDAH 3-5   81
LARC 2-4   83
EMI MANHATTAN 2-4   88
MANHATTAN 2-4   87
QUALITY/RFC 2-4
SUTRA 3-5   81
ZOO YORK 3-5   82
LPs: 10/12–inch 33rpm
ARIOLA AMERICA 5-10   79
ATLANTIC 5-8   85

RABBITT, Eddie
Singles: 7–inch
DATE 4-6   68

ELEKTRA 3-5   74-83
RCA 2-4   86
20TH FOX 4-8   64
WARNER 2-4   83-85
Picture Sleeves
ELEKTRA 3-5   81
LPs: 10/12–inch 33rpm
ELEKTRA 5-10   75-82
RCA 5-8   86
WARNER 5-8   84-85

RABBITT, Eddie, and Crystal Gayle
Singles: 7–inch
ELEKTRA 3-5   82
Also see GAYLE, Crystal

RABBITT, Eddie, and Juice Newton
Singles: 7–inch
RCA 2-4   86
Also see NEWTON, Juice
Also see RABBITT, Eddie

RABIN, Trevor
Singles: 7–inch
CHRYSALIS 3-5   78-80
LPs: 10/12–inch 33rpm
CHRYSALIS 5-10   78-80
ELEKTRA 5-8   89

RACE
Singles: 7–inch
OCEAN FRONT 2-4   83

RACING CARS
Singles: 7–inch
CHRYSALIS 3-5   77-78
LPs: 10/12–inch 33rpm
CHRYSALIS 5-10   77-78

RADIANCE
(Radiance with Andrea Stone)
Singles: 12–inch 33/45rpm
ARE 'N BE 4-6   83
Singles: 7–inch
WARNER 2-4   85

RADIANTS
(Maurice McAlister and the Radiants; Maurice and the
Radiants)
Singles: 7–inch
CHESS 4-8   62-69
ERIC 2-4
TWINIGHT 3-5   71
Members: Maurice McAlister; Wallace Sampson; Jerome
Brooks; Elzie Butler; Green McLauren; Frank McCollum;
Leonard Caston, Jr; James Jameson; Mitchell Bullock; Victor
Caston.

RADIATORS
Singles: 7–inch
EPIC 2-4   87-89
LPs: 10/12–inch 33rpm
EPIC 5-8   87-89
Members: Dave Malone; Frank Bua; Reggie Scanlan; Ed Volker;
Camile Baudoin; Glenn Sears.

RADICE, Mark
Singles: 7–inch
U.A. 3-5   76
LPs: 10/12–inch 33rpm
ROADSHOW 8-12   77

RADIO HEART
(Featuring Gary Numan)
Singles: 7–inch
CRITIQUE 2-4   87
LPs: 10/12–inch 33rpm
CRITIQUE (Black vinyl) 5-8   87
CRITIQUE (Picture discs) 8-12   87

RADNER, Gilda
Singles: 7–inch
WARNER 3-5   79-80
LPs: 10/12–inch 33rpm
WARNER 5-10   79

RAE, Fonda
(Fonda Raye)
Singles: 12–inch 33/45rpm
POSSE 4-6   83
VANGUARD 4-6   82
Singles: 7–inch
VANGUARD 2-4   82
Also see WISH

RAE, Robbie
Singles: 7–inch
QUALITY 2-4   83

RAELETTES
(Raeletts; Raelets)
Singles: 7–inch
TRC 3-5   70
TANGERINE 3-6   67-73
LPs: 10/12–inch 33rpm
TRC 8-12   71-72
TANGERINE 8-12   72
Also see CHARLES, Ray
Also see TURNER, Ike and Tina

RAES
Singles: 7–inch
A&M 3-5   78
LPs: 10/12–inch 33rpm
A&M 5-10   79

RAFFERTY, Gerry
Singles: 7–inch
BLUE THUMB 3-5   72
LIBERTY 2-4   82
SIGNPOST 3-5   72
U.A. 3-5   77-80
Picture Sleeves
U.A. 3-5   77-78
LPs: 10/12–inch 33rpm
BLUE THUMB 8-10   73-78
LIBERTY 5-8   82
MFSL 25-50   81
U.A. 8-10   78-80

VISA 5-10   78
Also see STEALERS WHEEL

RAG DOLLS
Singles: 7–inch
MALA 8-12   65
Member: Jean Thomas.

RAG DOLLS / Caliente Combo
Singles: 7–inch
PARKWAY 5-10   64
Also see RAG DOLLS

RAHEEM
LPs: 10/12–inch 33rpm
A&M 5-8   88

RAIDERS, and Paul Revere:
see REVERE, Paul, and the Raiders

RAIK'S PROGRESS
Singles: 7–inch
LIBERTY (55930 "Sewer Rat
Love Chant") 15-20   66

RAIL
Singles: 7–inch
EMI AMERICA 2-4   84
LPs: 10/12–inch 33rpm
EMI AMERICA 5-8   84
PASSPORT 5-8

RAILHEAD
Singles: 12–inch 33/45rpm
WAX-TRAX 5-8   87
Singles: 7–inch
WAX-TRAX 2-4   87

RAILWAY CHILDREN
LPs: 10/12–inch 33rpm
VIRGIN 5-8   87

RAINBOW
Singles: 7–inch
MERCURY 3-5   82-83
POLYDOR 3-5   79
LPs: 10/12–inch 33rpm
MERCURY 5-10   82-86
OYSTER 8-12   77
POLYDOR 5-10   78-81
Member: Ritchie Blackmore.
Also see ALCATRAZZ
Also see BLACKMORE'S RAINBOW
Also see CAREY, Tony
Also see GLOVER, Roger

RAINDROPS
Singles: 7–inch
JUBILEE 8-12   63-65
VIRGO 3-5   73
LPs: 10/12–inch 33rpm
JUBILEE (J-5023 "The Raindrops") .. 30-50   63
(Monaural.)
JUBILEE (SJ-5023 "The Raindrops") 50-75   63
(Stereo.)
MURRAY HILL 5-8

Members: Jeff Barry; Ellie Greenwich. (Third person pictured on LP cover did not sing with the group.)
   Also see GREENWICH, Ellie

RAINES, Rita
Singles: 78rpm
DEED 4-8   56
Singles: 7–inch
DEED 5-10   56

RAINMAKERS
Singles: 7–inch
MERCURY 2-4   86
LPs: 10/12–inch 33rpm
MERCURY 5-8   86-87

RAINWATER, Marvin
Singles: 78rpm
CORAL 5-10   56
MGM (Except 12240 and 12370) 5-10   55-57
MGM (12240 "Hot and Cold") 10-15   56
MGM (12370 "Get off the Stool") 10-15   56
Singles: 7–inch
BRAVE 4-6   63-67
CORAL 8-12   56
HILLTOP 5-10
MGM (12000 and 12100 series) 10-20   55
MGM (12240 "Hot and Cold") 30-40   56
MGM (12313 "Why Did You Have
   to Go and Love Me") 10-20   56
MGM (12370 "Get off the Stool") 30-40   56
MGM (12412 through 12938) 5-10   57-60
NU TRAYL 3-5   76
U.A. 4-6   65-66
WARNER 3-5   69-70
WARWICK 5-10   61
EPs: 7–inch 33/45rpm
MGM (1464/1465/1466 "Songs by
   Marvin Rainwater") 15-25   57
   (Price is for any of three volumes.)
LPs: 10/12–inch 33rpm
CROWN 15-25
MGM (3534 "Songs by
   Marvin Rainwater") 75-125   57
MGM (3721 "With a Heart
   With a Beat") 75-125   58
MGM (4046 "Gonna Find Me
   a Bluebird") 50-100   62
MOUNT VERNON 8-10
SPINORAMA 8-10
   Also see DEAN, Jimmy / Marvin Rainwater
   Also see FRANCIS, Connie, and Marvin Rainwater

RAINY DAZE
Singles: 7–inch
CHICORY 10-15   67
UNI 4-8   67
WHITE WHALE 4-8   68
LPs: 10/12–inch 33rpm
UNI 15-20   67

RAITT, Bonnie
Singles: 7–inch
CAPITOL 2-4   89-91
WARNER 2-4   72-86
LPs: 10/12–inch 33rpm
CAPITOL 5-8   89-91
WARNER 6-12   71-86

RAITT, Bonnie / Gilley's "Urban Cowboy" Band
Singles: 7–inch
FULL MOON/ASYLUM 3-5   80
Picture Sleeves
FULL MOON/ASYLUM 3-5   80
   Also see RAITT, Bonnie

RAKE
Singles: 7–inch
PROFILE 2-4   83

RALKE, Don
(Big Sound of Don Ralke)
Singles: 78rpm
CROWN 3-6   55
Singles: 7–inch
CROWN 4-8   55
DRUM BOY 3-6   66
REAL 4-8   56
WARNER 4-6   59-64
LPs: 10/12–inch 33rpm
CROWN 10-20   55
WARNER 10-20   59-60
   Also see BYRNES, Edward
   Also see JAN & ARNIE

RALPH, Sheryl Lee
Singles: 12–inch 33/45rpm
NYM 4-6   84-85
Singles: 7–inch
NYM 2-4   84-85

RAM JAM
Singles: 12–inch 33/45rpm
EPIC 5-10   77
Singles: 7–inch
EPIC 3-5   77-78
LPs: 10/12–inch 33rpm
EPIC 8-12   77-78
   Also see LEMON PIPERS

RAMA
Singles: 12–inch 33/45rpm
SUGARSCOOP 4-6   84

RAMATAM
Singles: 7–inch
ATLANTIC 3-5   72-73
LPs: 10/12–inch 33rpm
ATLANTIC 10-15   72-73
   Also see PINERA, Mike

RAMBEAU, Eddie
Singles: 7–inch
BELL 3-5   69

DYNA VOICE 4-8		65-66
SWAN 4-8		61-62
20TH FOX 4-8		64
VIRGO 2-4		73

LPs: 10/12-inch 33rpm

DYNO VOICE 15-25		65

Also see MARCY JO and Eddie Rambeau

RAMBLERS
Singles: 7-inch

ADDIT 8-12		60

RAMBLERS
Singles: 7-inch

ALMONT 10-20		64
SIDEWINDERS 10-20		64

RAMIN, Sid, and Orchestra
LPs: 10/12-inch 33rpm

RCA 8-12		63

SUEDE RECORDS
NATCHEZ, MISS.
UNBREAKABLE
45 R.P.M.
RECORD NO.
SD 1401
SO 283
C & S Music
Time 2:20
LITTLE GIRL
(Ramistella)
JOHNNY RAMISTELLA
AND ORCHESTRA

RAMISTELLA, Johnny
(Johnny Rivers)
Singles: 7-inch

SUEDE (1401 "Little Girl") 50-100		58

Also see RIVERS, Johnny

RAMONES
Singles: 7-inch

RSO 3-5		81
SIRE 5-10		76-80

Picture Sleeves

SIRE 8-12		77

EPs: 7-inch

SIRE (805 "Rock 'N Roll High School") 10-15		79
(Promotional issue only.)		

LPs: 10/12-inch 33rpm

SIRE (Except 6063 and 7528) 5-8		76-89
SIRE (6063 "Road to Ruin") 8-12		78
(Black vinyl.)		
SIRE (6063 "Road to Ruin") 15-25		78
(Yellow vinyl.)		
SIRE (7528 "Leave Home") 15-25		77
(Has *Carbona Not Glue*, which is not on reissues.)		

RAMRODS
Singles: 7-inch

AMY 8-12		60-62
PLYMOUTH 10-20		64-66
QUEEN 8-12		62

RAMRODS
Singles: 7-inch

RAMPAGE 3-5		72

RANDAZZO, Teddy
(Teddy Randazzo and All 6)
Singles: 7-inch

ABC-PAR 4-8		59-62
COLPIX 4-8		62-63
DCP 4-8		64-66
MGM 4-8		66
VERVE/FOLKWAYS 4-8		67
VIK 5-10		58

LPs: 10/12-inch 33rpm

ABC-PAR 20-30		61-62
MGM 15-20		66
VIK (1121 "I'm Confessing") 30-50		58

Also see CHUCKLES
Also see THREE CHUCKLES

RAN-DELLS
Singles: 7-inch

RSVP 8-12		64
CHAIRMAN 8-12		63-64

Picture Sleeves

CHAIRMAN (4403 "Martian Hop") . . . 15-25		63

RANDOLPH, Boots
(Homer Randolph)
Singles: 7-inch

MONUMENT 2-5		61-83
PALO ALTO 2-4		
RCA 4-8		59-61

Picture Sleeves

MONUMENT 5-10		64

LPs: 10/12-inch 33rpm

CAMDEN 10-20		64
GUEST STAR 5-10		64
MONUMENT (Except 8000 and 18000 series) 6-12		71-82
MONUMENT (8000 and 18000 series) 10-20		63-71
PALO ALTO 5-8		
RCA 15-25		60

Also see ANN-MARGRET
Also see ATKINS, Chet, Floyd Cramer and Boots Randolph
Also see FRANCIS, Connie
Also see HALEY, Bill / Boots Randolph
Also see HIRT, Al, and Boots Randolph
Also see KNIGHTSBRIDGE STRINGS
Also see LEE, Brenda
Also see PRESLEY, Elvis

RANDOLPH, Cookie "Chainsaw"
Singles: 7-inch

93-KDKB 2-4		86

RANDY and the Rainbows
Singles: 7-inch
B.T. PUPPY 5-8	67
LAURIE 3-5	
MIKE 5-10	66
RUST (Except 5059) 8-12	63-64
RUST (5059 "Denise") 20-25	63
(Blue label.)	
RUST (5059 "Denise") 5-10	63
(Rust and white label.)	

LPs: 10/12-inch 33rpm
AMBIENT SOUND 8-10	82
MAGIC CARPET 8-10	

Members: Dominick "Randy" Safuto; Frank Safuto; Mike Zero; Sal Zero; Ken Arcipowski.

RANK & FILE
Singles: 7-inch
SLASH 2-4	83-84

LPs: 10/12-inch 33rpm
SLASH 5-8	83-84

Also see SEATRAIN

RANKIN, Billy
Singles: 7-inch
A&M 2-4	84

LPs: 10/12-inch 33rpm
A&M 5-8	84

RANKIN, Kenny
(Ken Rankin)
Singles: 7-inch
ABC-PAR 4-8	61
COLUMBIA 4-8	63-65
DECCA 5-10	58-60
LITTLE DAVID 3-5	73-77
MERCURY 4-6	68-69

Picture Sleeves
MERCURY 5-8	68

LPs: 10/12-inch 33rpm
ATLANTIC 5-10	80
LITTLE DAVID 8-10	72-77
MERCURY 10-15	67-69

RANKING ROGER
LPs: 10/12-inch 33rpm
I.R.S. 5-8	88

RAPPIN' DUKE
Singles: 12-inch 33/45rpm
TOMMY BOY 4-6	86

RARE BIRD
Singles: 7-inch
ABC 3-5	72
POLYDOR 3-5	73-74
PROBE 3-5	70

LPs: 10/12-inch 33rpm
ABC 8-10	72
POLYDOR 8-10	73-74
PROBE 10-12	70

RARE EARTH
Singles: 7-inch
MOTOWN 3-5	81
PRODIGAL 2-4	78
RARE EARTH 2-4	70-76
VERVE 4-8	68

Picture Sleeves
RARE EARTH 4-6	71-73

LPs: 10/12-inch 33rpm
MOTOWN 5-8	81
PRODIGAL 5-8	77-78
RARE EARTH (Except 507) 8-12	70-76
RARE EARTH (507 "Get Ready") 8-12	69
(With standard square cover.)	
RARE EARTH (507 "Get Ready") . . . 30-40	69
(With rounded-top cover. Promotional issue.)	
VERVE 10-20	68

RARE ESSENCE
Singles: 12-inch 33/45rpm
FANTASY 4-8	82

RASCALS
(Young Rascals)
Singles: 7-inch
ATLANTIC (Except 2428) 4-8	65-70
ATLANTIC (2428 "Groovin' [Italian]") 10-20	67
(Backed with Groovin' in Spanish.)	
COLUMBIA 3-5	71-72

Picture Sleeves
ATLANTIC 5-10	66-70

EPs: 7-inch 33/45rpm
ATLANTIC (190 "Time Peace") 10-15	68
(Promotional issue only.)	

LPs: 10/12-inch 33rpm
ATLANTIC (137 "Freedom Suite") . . . 20-30	69
(Promotional issue only.)	
ATLANTIC (901 "Freedom Suite") . . . 20-30	69
(Without cut corner or BB holes.)	
ATLANTIC (901 "Freedom Suite") . . . 10-20	69
(With cut corner or BB holes.)	
ATLANTIC (8123 through 8148) 15-25	66-67
ATLANTIC (8169 through 8276) 10-15	68-71
COLUMBIA 8-12	71-72
PAIR 8-10	86
RHINO 5-8	87

Members: Felix Cavaliere; Ed Brigati; Dino Danelli; Gene Cornish; David Brigati.
Also see BULLDOG
Also see CAVALIERE, Felix
Also see DEE, Joey
Also see FOTOMAKER
Also see SWEET INSPIRATIONS

(YOUNG) RASCALS / Buggs / Four Seasons / Johnny Rivers
LPs: 10/12-inch 33rpm
CORONET (283 "The Young Rascals") 15-25	66

Also see 4 SEASONS
Also see RIVERS, Johnny

(YOUNG) RASCALS / Isley Brothers
LPs: 10/12–inch 33rpm
DESIGN (253 "Young Rascals
and the Isley Brothers") 15-25
Also see ISLEY BROTHERS
Also see RASCALS

RASPBERRIES
Singles: 7–inch
CAPITOL 4-6   72-74
Picture Sleeves
CAPITOL 5-10   72-73
LPs: 10/12–inch 33rpm
CAPITOL (11036 through 11329) 15-20   72-74
CAPITOL (11524 "Raspberries'
Best") 8-12   76
CAPITOL (16095 "Raspberries'
Best") 5-10   80
Members: Eric Carmen; Wally Bryson; Dave Smalley; Jim
Bonfanti.
Also see CARMEN, Eric
Also see FOTOMAKER

RATCHELL
Singles: 7–inch
DECCA 3-5   72
LPs: 10/12–inch 33rpm
DECCA 10-15 71-72

RATIONALS
Singles: 7–inch
A SQUARE 10-20   66
CAMEO 10-20   66-67
CAPITOL 5-10   68
CREWE 4-8   69
DANBY'S ("Turn On") 25-35
(No number used.)
GENESIS 4-8
LPs: 10/12–inch 33rpm
CREWE (1334 "Rationals") 15-25 69
Also see SRC / Rationals

RATT
Singles: 7–inch
ATLANTIC 2-4   84-87
TIME COAST 3-5   83-84
LPs: 10/12–inch 33rpm
ATLANTIC 5-8   84-90
TIME COAST 5-10   83-84

RATTLES
Singles: 7–inch
LONDON 3-5
MERCURY 5-10   66
PROBE 4-6   70
LPs: 10/12–inch 33rpm
MERCURY (21127 "Greatest Hits") .. 30-40 67
(Monaural.)
MERCURY (61127 "Greatest Hits") .. 40-60 67
(Stereo.)
Also see SEARCHERS / Rattles

RAVAN, Genya
Singles: 7–inch
COLUMBIA 3-5   71-72
DE LITE 3-5   75
DUNHILL 3-5   73
20TH FOX 3-5   78-79
LPs: 10/12–inch 33rpm
COLUMBIA 8-12   72
DUNHILL 8-12   73
20TH FOX 5-10   78-79
Also see TEN WHEEL DRIVE

RAVEN
Singles: 7–inch
RAMPART 3-5
LPs: 10/12–inch 33rpm
ATLANTIC 5-8   85-86

RAVEN, Marcia
Singles: 12–inch 33/45rpm
PROFILE 4-6   83
Singles: 7–inch
PROFILE 3-5   83

RAVENS
Singles: 78rpm
ARGO 10-20 56-57
CHECKER 10-15 57
COLUMBIA 50-80 50-51
HUB 30-40 46
KING 25-35 48-49
JUBILEE 5-10   55-56
MERCURY 15-25 51-55
OKEH (6825 "Whiffenpoof Song") .. 50-100 51
OKEH (6843 "That Old Gang
of Mine") 50-100 51
OKEH (6888 "Mam'selle") 50-100 52
NATIONAL 40-60 47-51
RENDITION (5001 "Write Me
a Letter") 20-30 51
Singles: 7–inch
ARGO (5255 "Kneel and Pray") 25-35 56
ARGO (5261 "A Simple Prayer") 50-75 56
ARGO (5276 "That'll be the Day") ... 15-25 57
ARGO (5284 "Here Is My Heart") ... 15-25 57
CHECKER (871 "That'll Be
the Day") 10-15 57
COLUMBIA (1-903 "Time Takes
Care of Everything") 400-500 50
(Compact 33 Single.)
COLUMBIA (6-903 "Time Takes
Care of Everything") 350-450 50
COLUMBIA (1-925 "My Baby's
Gone") 350-450 50
(Compact 33 Single.)
COLUMBIA (6-925 "My Baby's
Gone") 350-450 50
COLUMBIA (39112 "You Don't Have to
Drop a Heart to Break It") 200-300 51

COLUMBIA (39194 "You're Always
in My Dreams") 200-300   51
COLUMBIA (39408 "You Foolish
Thing") 600-700   51
JUBILEE 15-25 55-56
MERCURY (5764 "There's No
Use Pretending") 100-200   51
MERCURY (5800 "Begin the
Beguiine") 75-125   52
MERCURY (5853 "Why Did
You Leave") 75-125   52
MERCURY (8291 "Write Me
One Sweet Letter") 50-75   52
MERCURY (8296 "Too Soon") 50-75   52
MERCURY (70060 "Don't Mention
My Name") 75-100   52
MERCURY (70119 "Come a
Little Bit Closer") 50-75   53
MERCURY (70213 "Who'll Be
the Fool") 50-75   53
MERCURY (70240 "Without a Song") 50-75   53
MERCURY (70307 "September
Song") 50-75   54
MERCURY (70330 "Lonesome Road") 50-75   54
MERCURY (70413 "Love Is
No Dream") 100-150   54
(Pink label.)
MERCURY (70413 "Love Is
No Dream") 50-75   54
(Black label.)
MERCURY (70505 "White
Christmas") 100-150   54
(Pink label.)
MERCURY (70505 "White Christmas") 50-75   54
(Black label.)
MERCURY (70554 "Write Me
a Letter") 100-150   55
(Pink label.)
MERCURY (70554 "Write Me
a Letter") 50-75   55
(Black label.)
NATIONAL (9111 "Count
Every Star") 1000-1500   50
OKEH (6825 "Whiffenpoof Song") . 350-450   51
OKEH (6843 "That Old Gang
of Mine") 350-450   51
OKEH (6888 "Mam'selle") 200-300   52
SAVOY 10-15   58
TOP RANK 10-20   59
VIRGO 3-5   72

EPs: 7-inch 33/45rpm
KING (310 "The Ravens Featuring
Jimmy Ricks") 300-400   54
RENDITION (104 "Ol Man
River") 300-450   52

LPs: 10/12-inch 33rpm
HARLEM HITPARADE 10-12   75
REGENT (6062 "Write Me a Letter") 100-150   57
(Green label.)

REGENT (6062 "Write Me a Letter") . 50-75
(Red label.)
SAVOY 10-15   78
Members: Warren Suttles; Ollie Jones; Joe Van Loan; Jimmy
Ricks; Leonard Puzey; Maithe Marshall; Joe Medlin; Louis
Heyward; James Stewart; Louis Frazier; Tom Evans; James Van
Loan; David Bowers; Paul Van Loan; Rich Cannon; Bob
Kornegay; Willis Sanders; Willie Ray.
Also see CUES

RAVENS and Dinah Washington
Singles: 78rpm
MERCURY (8257 "Out in the
Cold Again") 15-25   51
Singles: 7-inch
MERCURY (8257 "Out in the
Cold Again") 40-60   51
Also see WASHINGTON, Dinah

RAVENS / Three Clouds
Singles: 78rpm
KING 25-35   48-49
Also see RAVENS

RAW SILK
Singles: 7-inch
WEST END 3-5   82

RAWLS, Lou
Singles: 12-inch 33/45rpm
PHILADELPHIA INT'L 4-8   79
Singles: 7-inch
ARISTA 3-5   75
BELL 3-5   74
CANDIX 5-10   60-61
CAPITOL 3-8   61-70
EPIC 2-4   82-85
GAMBLE 2-4   87
MGM 3-5   71-73
PHILADELPHIA INT'L 2-5   76-81
SHAR-DEE 8-12   60
Picture Sleeves
CAPITOL 4-8   67
LPs: 10/12-inch 33rpm
ALLEGIANCE 5-8   84
BELL 8-10   74
CAPITOL (Except 1700 through
2900 series) 5-12   69-77
CAPITOL (1700 through 2900 series) 12-25   63-68
EPIC 5-8   82-83
MGM 8-10   71-73
PHILADELPHIA INT'L 5-10   76-80
POLYDOR 8-10   76
Also see COOKE, Sam
Also see PHILADELPHIA INTERNATIONAL ALL STARS
Also see VEGA, Tata

RAWLS, Lou, and Les McCann Ltd.
Singles: 7-inch
CAPITOL 4-6   62
LPs: 10/12-inch 33rpm
CAPITOL 5-8   75
(With "SM" prefix.)

CAPITOL .... 20-30　　62
(With "T" or "ST" prefix.)
Also see McCANN, Les
Also see RAWLS, Lou

RAY, Baby: see BABY RAY

RAY, Diane
Singles: 7–inch
MERCURY .... 4-8　　63-64
Picture Sleeves
MERCURY .... 10-15　　63
LPs: 10/12–inch 33rpm
MERCURY .... 20-30　　64

RAY, Don
Singles: 7–inch
POLYDOR .... 3-5　　78
LPs: 10/12–inch 33rpm
POLYDOR .... 5-10　　78

RAY, Harry
Singles: 7–inch
SUGAR HILL .... 2-4　　82-83
LPs: 10/12–inch 33rpm
SUGAR HILL .... 5-8　　83
Also see RAY, GOODMAN & BROWN

RAY, James
Singles: 7–inch
CAPRICE .... 5-10　　61-62
CONGRESS .... 4-8　　63-64
DYNAMIC .... 4-8　　62
LPs: 10/12–inch 33rpm
CAPRICE (LP-1002 "James Ray") ... 40-60　　62
(Monaural.)
CAPRICE (SLP-1002 "James Ray") 75-100　　62
(Stereo.)
Also see GRANT, Janie

RAY, Johnnie
(Johnnie Ray and the Four Lads)
Singles: 78rpm
COLUMBIA .... 4-8　　57
OKEH .... 5-10　　52
Singles: 7–inch
CADENCE .... 5-10　　60
COLUMBIA (39000 and 41000 series) . 5-15　　52-60
DECCA .... 4-6　　63-64
GROOVE .... 4-6　　64
LIBERTY .... 4-8　　62
OKEH (6809 "Wiskey and Gin") ..... 15-25　　51
OKEH (6840 "Cry") .... 10-15　　51
OKEH RHYTHM & BLUES (6840
"Cry") .... 15-25　　51
U.A. .... 4-8　　61
Picture Sleeves
COLUMBIA .... 10-20　　57
EPs: 7–inch 33/45rpm
COLUMBIA .... 10-20　　52-59
EPIC .... 10-20　　52-54
LPs: 10/12–inch 33rpm
COLUMBIA (961 "The Big Beat") .... 35-45　　57

COLUMBIA (1385 "On the Trail") .... 15-25　　59
(Monaural.)
COLUMBIA (2510 "I Cry for You") ... 30-50　　56
(10 Inch LP.)
COLUMBIA (6199 "Johnnie Ray") ... 35-55　　51
(10 Inch LP.)
COLUMBIA (8180 "On the Trail") .... 20-30　　59
(Stereo.)
EPIC (1120 "Johnnie Ray") .... 30-50　　55
(10–inch LP.)
HARMONY .... 5-10　　71
SUNSET .... 10-15　　66
Also see DAY, Doris, and Johnnie Ray
Also see FOUR LADS

RAY, Johnnie, and Timi Yuro
Singles: 7–inch
LIBERTY .... 4-8　　61
Also see RAY, Johnnie
Also see YURO, Timi

RAY, Ricardo
Singles: 7–inch
ALEGRE .... 4-6　　68

RAY and BOB
Singles: 7–inch
LEDO .... 5-10　　62
Members: Ray Swayne; Bob Appleberry.

RAY, GOODMAN & BROWN
Singles: 7–inch
EMI AMERICA .... 2-4　　87
PANORAMIC .... 2-4　　84
POLYDOR .... 3-5　　80-81
LPs: 10/12–inch 33rpm
POLYDOR .... 5-10　　80-81
Members: Harry Ray; Al Goodman; Bill Brown.
Also see MOMENTS
Also see RAY, Harry

RAYBURN, Margie
Singles: 78rpm
ALMA .... 4-8　　54
LIBERTY .... 4-8　　56-57
S&G .... 4-8　　54
Singles: 7–inch
ALMA .... 5-10　　54
CAPITOL .... 4-6　　65
CHALLENGE .... 4-8　　61
DOT .... 4-8　　62-66
LIBERTY .... 5-10　　56-62
S&G .... 5-10　　54
Picture Sleeves
LIBERTY .... 10-15　　57
LPs: 10/12–inch 33rpm
LIBERTY (3126 "Margie") .... 20-25　　59
(Monaural.)
LIBERTY (7126 "Margie") .... 25-35　　59
(Stereo.)

RAYDIO
(Featuring Ray Parker Jr.)
Singles: 7-inch
ARISTA 3-5   78-79
Picture Sleeves
ARISTA 3-5   78-79
LPs: 10/12-inch 33rpm
ARISTA 5-10   78-79
Also see KNIGHT, Jerry
Also see PARKER, Ray, Jr.

RAYE, Fonda: see RAE, Fonda

RAYE, Susan
Singles: 7-inch
CAPITOL 3-6   69-76
U.A. 2-5   76-77
WESTEXAS 2-4   85-86
Picture Sleeves
CAPITOL 3-5   71
LPs: 10/12-inch 33rpm
CAPITOL 8-12   70-76
U.A. 5-10   77
Also see OWENS, Buck, and Susan Raye

RAY-O-VACS
Singles: 78rpm
ATCO 5-10   57
COLEMAN 5-10   49
DECCA 4-8   50-53
JOSIE 5-10   54
JUBILEE 5-10   52
KAISER 5-10   56
Singles: 7-inch
ATCO 10-15   57
DECCA 10-20   50-53
JOSIE 15-20   54
JUBILEE 15-20   52
KAISER 15-20   56
SHARP 15-25   60
Members: Lester Harris; Herb Milliner.

RAYS
Singles: 78rpm
CAMEO 10-20   57-58
CHESS 10-20   55-57
XYZ (Except 100 and 102) 4-8   58-61
XYZ (100 "My Steady Girl") 10-20   57
XYZ (102 "Silhouettes") 10-20   57
Singles: 7-inch
ABKCO 2-4
AMY 3-5   64
ARGO 3-5
CAMEO (117 "Silhouettes") 10-15   57
CAMEO (128 "Triangle") 15-20   58
CAMEO (133 "Rags to Riches") 15-25   57
CHESS (1613 "Tippity Top") 15-20   55
CHESS (1678 "Second Fiddle") 15-25   57
PERRI (1004 "Are You Happy Now") . 15-25   62
(With Frankie Valli.)
XYZ (100 "My Steady Girl") 35-45   57

XYZ (102 "Silhouettes") 75-100   57
(Gray label.)
XYZ (102 "Silhouettes") 30-40   57
(Blue label.)
XYZ (106 "Souvenirs of Summertime") 30-40   58
XYZ (600 "Why Do You Look
the Other Way") 30-40   59
XYZ (605 "Mediterranean Moon") ... 25-30   59
XYZ (607 "Magic Moon") 25-30   60
(Blue label.)
XYZ (607 "Magic Moon") 10-15   60
(Red label.)
XYZ (608 "Old Devil Moon") 10-15   60
XYZ (2001 "Souvenirs
of Summertime") 25-35   58
(First issued in 1958 on XYZ 106.)
EPs: 7-inch 33/45rpm
CHESS (5120 "The Rays") 15-200   58
Members: Harold "Hal" Miller; Walter Ford; David Jones; Harry James.

RAYS
Singles: 7-inch
EMI MANHATTAN 2-4   87

RAZE
Singles: 7-inch
COLUMBIA 2-4   88

RAZOR'S EDGE
Singles: 7-inch
POW 8-12   66-67
POWER (4932 "Get Yourself
Together") 15-25   67

RAZZY: see BAILEY, Razzy

REA, Chris
Singles: 7-inch
COLUMBIA 3-5   82
GEFFEN 2-4   89-90
MOTOWN 2-4   87
RCA 2-4   84
U.A. 3-5   78-79
Picture Sleeves
U.A. 3-5   78
LPs: 10/12-inch 33rpm
COLUMBIA 5-8   80-82
GEFFEN 5-8   89-90
RCA 5-8   84
U.A. 5-8   78
Also see WILLIE and the Poor Boys

READ, John Dawson
Singles: 7-inch
CHRYSALIS 3-5   75
LPs: 10/12-inch 33rpm
CHRYSALIS 5-10   75-76

READY for the WORLD
Singles: 12-inch 33/45rpm
MCA 4-6   84-86

Singles: 7–inch
MCA 2-4   84-87
Picture Sleeves
MCA 2-4   85
LPs: 10/12–inch 33rpm
MCA 5-8   86-88

REAL LIFE
Singles: 12–inch 33/45rpm
CURB/MCA 4-6   83-86
Singles: 7–inch
CURB/MCA 2-4   83-86
LPs: 10/12–inch 33rpm
CURB/MCA 5-8   83-89

REAL ROXANNE
(With Hitman Howie Tee)
Singles: 12–inch 33/45rpm
SELECT 4-6   85-86

REAL THING
Singles: 12–inch 33/45rpm
BELIEVE in a DREAM 4-6   81
EPIC 4-8   79
Singles: 7–inch
BELIEVE in a DREAM 3-5   81
EPIC 3-5   79
U.A. 3-5   76-77
WHIZ 4-6   69
LPs: 10/12–inch 33rpm
U.A. 5-10   76

REAL to REEL
Singles: 12–inch 33/45rpm
ARISTA 4-6   83-84
Singles: 7–inch
ARISTA 2-4   83-84
LPs: 10/12–inch 33rpm
ARISTA 5-8   83

REAVES, Paulette
Singles: 7–inch
BLUE CANDLE 3-5   77-78

REBELS
Singles: 7–inch
MAR-LEE (0094 "Wild Weekend") . . . 20-40   60
SWAN 10-15   62-63
Also see BUFFALO REBELS
Also see ROCKIN' REBELS

REBENNACK, Mac
Singles: 7–inch
A.F.O. (309 "One Naughty Flat") 15-25   62
ACE (611 "Good Times") 15-25   61
REX (1008 "Storm Warning") 30-50   59
Also see DR. JOHN

RECORD, Eugene
Singles: 12–inch 33/45rpm
WARNER 4-8   79
Singles: 7–inch
WARNER 3-5   77-79

LPs: 10/12–inch 33rpm
WARNER 5-10   77-79
Also see CHI-LITES

RECORDS
Singles: 7–inch
VIRGIN 3-5   79-81
Picture Sleeves
VIRGIN 3-5   79-81
EPs: 7–inch 33/45rpm
VIRGIN 3-6   79
(Issued as a bonus with Virgin LP 13130, *The Records*.)
LPs: 10/12–inch 33rpm
VIRGIN 8-10   79-82

RED HOT CHILI PEPPERS
Singles: 12–inch 33/45rpm
EMI AMERICA 4-6   85
Singles: 7–inch
EMI AMERICA 2-4   84-85
WARNER 2-4   91
LPs: 10/12–inch 33rpm
EMI AMERICA 5-8   84-85
EMI MANHATTAN 5-8   87
WARNER 5-8   91
Members: Anthony Kiedis; Jack Irons; Hillel Slovak; Mike Balzary; John Frusciante; Chad Smith.

RED RIDER
Singles: 7–inch
CAPITOL 2-5   80-86
Picture Sleeves
CAPITOL 2-5   80-84
LPs: 10/12–inch 33rpm
CAPITOL 5-10   80-86
Member: Tom Cochrane.
Also see COCHRANE, Tom, and Red Rider

RED RIVER DAVE
(Dave McEnery)
Singles: 7–inch
COPYRIGHT 4-8   61
SAVOY 4-8   60-65
EPs: 7–inch 33/45rpm
VARSITY 5-10
LPs: 10/12–inch 33rpm
BLUEBONNET 8-12
CONTINENTAL 10-20   62
PLACE 10-15
SUTTON 5-10

RED ROCKERS
Singles: 12–inch 33/45rpm
COLUMBIA 4-6   84-85
Singles: 7–inch
COLUMBIA 2-4   84-85
LPs: 10/12–inch 33rpm
COLUMBIA 5-8   83

RED 7
LPs: 10/12–inch 33rpm
MCA 5-8   85-87

REDBONE
Singles: 7-inch
EPIC 3-5   71-74
RCA 3-5   78
LPs: 10/12-inch 33rpm
ACCORD 5-10   82
EPIC 8-15   70-75
RCA 5-10   77
Members: Pat Vegas; Lolly Vegas.

REDBONE, Leon
Singles: 78rpm
WARNER 5-10   78
(Promotional issue only.)
Singles: 7-inch
EMERALD CITY 3-5   81
WARNER 3-5   77-78
LPs: 10/12-inch 33rpm
ACCORD 8-12   82
EMERALD CITY 8-12   81
WARNER 10-20 77-78

REDD, Sharon
Singles: 12-inch 33/45rpm
PRELUDE 4-6   81-83
Singles: 7-inch
COLUMBIA 3-5   78
PRELUDE 3-5   81-83
VEEP 4-8   67
LPs: 10/12-inch 33rpm
COLUMBIA 5-10   78
PRELUDE 5-8   82

REDD, Sharon, Ula Hedwig and Charlotte Crossley
Singles: 7-inch
COLUMBIA 3-5   77-78
Also see MIDLER, Bette
Also see REDD, Sharon

REDD HOT
(Redd Hott)
Singles: 7-inch
VENTURE 3-5   81-82
Members: Kevin "Flash" Ferrell; Robert Parson; Daryl Simmons; Greg Russell; De Morris Smith.
Also see MANCHILD

REDD KROSS
LPs: 10/12-inch 33rpm
BIT 5-8   87
POSH BOY 5-10   85-86

REDDING, Gene
Singles: 7-inch
HAVEN 3-5   74

REDDING, Otis
(Otis Redding and the Pinetoppers; Otis Redding and the Pinetones)
Singles: 7-inch
ATCO 3-6   68-71
BETHLEHEM 10-15 64
CONFEDERATE 10-20 62

FINER ARTS 4-8
KING 3-6   68
ORBIT (135 "Shout Bamalama") 50-75 61
STAX 4-6   68
STONE 4-8
VOLT 5-10 62-68
EPs: 7-inch 33/45rpm
VOLT 10-20 66
LPs: 10/12-inch 33rpm
ATCO (33-161 "Pain in My Heart") .. 50-70 64
(Monaural.)
ATCO (SD-33-161 "Pain in My Heart") 60-80 64
(Stereo.)
ATCO (200 series) 10-15 68-69
ATCO (300 series) 8-12   70
ATCO (801 "Best of Otis Redding") .. 10-20 72
(Currently available, using the same catalog number.)
ATLANTIC 5-10   82
VOLT (Except 411) 20-35 65-68
VOLT (411 "Soul Ballads") 35-45 65
(Monaural.)
VOLT (411 "Soul Ballads") 40-50 65
(Stereo.)
Also see BAR-KAYS

REDDING, Otis / Little Joe Curtis
LPs: 10/12-inch 33rpm
ALSHIRE 8-12   68
SOMERSET 8-12   68

REDDING, Otis / Jimi Hendrix
LPs: 10/12-inch 33rpm
REPRISE (2029 "Otis Redding/The Jimi Hendrix Experience") 10-15 70
REPRISE (93371 "Otis Redding/The Jimi Hendrix Experience") 15-20 70
(Same as 2029, but with different front cover. Disc reads "Music from the Monterey Pop Soundtrack.")
Also see HENDRIX, Jimi

REDDING, Otis / Carla Thomas / Sam & Dave / Eddie Floyd
LPs: 10/12-inch 33rpm
STAX (722 "Stax/Volt Revue, Vol. 2") 15-25 67
Also see FLOYD, Eddie
Also see OTIS & CARLA
Also see REDDING, Otis
Also see SAM & DAVE
Also see THOMAS, Carla

REDDINGS
Singles: 12-inch 33/45rpm
BELIEVE in a DREAM 4-8   83
Singles: 7-inch
BELIEVE in a DREAM 3-5   80-83
POLYDOR 2-4   85-88
LPs: 10/12-inch 33rpm
BELIEVE in a DREAM 5-10   80-83
POLYDOR 5-8   85
Members: Otis Redding III; Dexter Redding; Mark Locket.

REDDS and the Boys
Singles: 7–inch
4TH and BROADWAY 3-5   85

REDDY, Helen
Singles: 12–inch 33/45rpm
CAPITOL 4-6   79
Singles: 7–inch
CAPITOL 3-5   71-81
FONTANA 3-6   68
MCA 3-5   81-83
LPs: 10/12–inch 33rpm
CAPITOL 5-10   71-81
MCA 5-8   81-83
  Also see PRESLEY, Elvis / Helen Reddy

REDEYE
Singles: 7–inch
PENTAGRAM 3-5   70-71
LPs: 10/12–inch 33rpm
PENTAGRAM 10-15   70-71
  Members: Doug "Red" Mark; David Hodkins; Bobby Bereman;
  Bill Kman.
  Also see SUNSHINE COMPANY

REDJACKS
Singles: 7–inch
APT (25006 "Big Brown Eyes") 10-15   58
OKLAHOMA (5005 "Big Brown Eyes") 30-50   58

REDNOW, Eivets
(Stevie Wonder)
Singles: 7–inch
GORDY 5-10   68
LPs: 10/12–inch 33rpm
GORDY (932 "Eivets Rednow") 25-30   68
  Also see WONDER, Stevie

REDWAY, Michael
(Mike Redway)
Singles: 7–inch
LONDON 4-8   64
PHILIPS 3-5   73

REED, Clarence:
see REID, Clarence

REED, Dan, Network
LPs: 10/12–inch 33rpm
MERCURY 5-8   88-89

REED, Dean
Singles: 7–inch
CAPITOL 8-12   59-61
IMPERIAL 5-10   61

REED, Denny
Singles: 7–inch
ASPIRE 3-5   77
DOT 4-8   62
MCI 10-20   60
TREY 10-15   60-61
TOWER 4-8   65
U.A. 5-10   61

REED, Jerry
(Jerry Reed and the Hully Girlies)
Singles: 78rpm
CAPITOL 5-10   55-56
Singles: 7–inch
CAPITOL 10-20   55-56
COLUMBIA 5-10   61-63
NRC 5-10   59
RCA (Except 8500 through 9700) 3-5   69-85
RCA (8500 through 9700) 4-6   65-69
Picture Sleeves
COLUMBIA 8-10   61
RCA 2-4   72-85
LPs: 10/12–inch 33rpm
CAMDEN 5-10   72-74
HARMONY 8-12   71
PICKWICK/HILLTOP 5-10
RCA (Except "LPM" and "LSP" series) 5-10   73-83
RCA ("LPM" and "LSP" series) 8-18   67-73
  Also see HART, Freddie / Sammi Smith / Jerry Reed
  Also see JENNINGS, Waylon, and Jerry Reed
  Also see PRESLEY, Elvis

REED, Jerry, and Chet Atkins
LPs: 10/12–inch 33rpm
RCA 8-12   72
  Also see ATKINS, Chet
  Also see REED, Jerry

REED, Jimmy
Singles: 78rpm
CHANCE (1142 "High and
  Lonesome") 40-60   53
VEE JAY (100 through 119) 15-30   53-54
VEE JAY (132 through 153) 10-15   55
VEE JAY (168 through 275) 15-30   53-58
Singles: 7–inch
ABC 3-5   73
ABC-PAR 4-8   66
BLUESWAY 3-6   67
CHANCE (1142 "High and
  Lonesome") 300-400   53
  (Reissue of Vee Jay 100.)
COLLECTABLES 2-4
EXODUS 4-8   66
TRIP 3-5
VEE JAY (100 "High and
  Lonesome") 125-175   53
  (Black vinyl.)
VEE JAY (100 "High and
  Lonesome") 250-350   53
  (Colored vinyl.)
VEE JAY (105 "I Found My Baby") 100-150   53
  (Black vinyl.)
VEE JAY (105 "I Found My Baby") 200-300   53
  (Colored vinyl.)
VEE JAY (119 "You Don't Have
  to Go") 30-40   54
  (Black vinyl.)

U.A. (3000 and 6000 series) 10-20   65-71

REEVES, Del, and Bobby Goldsboro
Singles: 7–inch
U.A. 3-6   65-71
LPs: 10/12–inch 33rpm
U.A. 10-20   68
Also see GOLDSBORO, Bobby

REEVES, Del / Red Sovine
LPs: 10/12–inch 33rpm
EXACT 5-8   80
Also see SOVINE, Red

REEVES, Del, and Billie Jo Spears
Singles: 7–inch
U.A. 3-5   76
LPs: 10/12–inch 33rpm
LIBERTY 5-8   82
U.A. 5-10   76
Also see REEVES, Del
Also see SPEARS, Billie Jo

REEVES, Dianne
Singles: 7–inch
BLUE NOTE 2-4   87
LPs: 10/12–inch 33rpm
BLUE NOTE 5-8   88
EMI 5-8   90

REEVES, Jim
Singles: 78rpm
ABBOTT 10-20   53-55
FABOR 10-15   54
RCA 5-10   55-57
Singles: 7–inch
ABBOTT (100 series, except 116) ... 10-25   53-55
(Black vinyl.)
ABBOTT (116 "Mexican Joe") 15-25   53
(Black vinyl.)
ABBOTT (116 "Mexican Joe") 35-50   53
(Colored vinyl.)
ABBOTT (3000 series) 10-20   55
ABBOTT (4000 series) 4-8
FABOR 10-15   54
RCA (0100 through 0800 series) 3-6   69-74
RCA (6200 through 7500 series) 5-10   55-59
RCA (7600 through 9900 series) 3-8   59-71
RCA (10000 through 13000 series) 3-5   75-84
Picture Sleeves
RCA (Except 8252) 5-10   60-65
RCA (8252 "Señor Santa Claus") 10-15   63
EPs: 7–inch 33/45rpm
RCA (Except 1256) 25-45   56-61
RCA (1256 "Singing Down the Lane") 50-100   56
LPs: 10/12–inch 33rpm
ABBOTT (5001 "Jim Reeves
   Sings") 750-1000   56
CAMDEN (Except 500 and 600 series) 5-15   64-73
CAMDEN (500 and 600 series) 10-20   60-63
GUEST STAR 10-15   64
HISTORY of COUNTRY MUSIC 6-10   72

PAIR 8-12   82
PICKWICK 5-10   72
PICKWICK/HILLTOP 5-10   74
RCA (0039 through 4800 series) 5-10   73-83
(With "AHL1," "ANL1," "APL1," "AYL1" or "CPL1"
prefix.)
RCA (0587 "Golden Collection") 30-35
(Special Products, five-LP set.)
RCA (LPM-1256 "Singing Down
   the Lane") 100-150   56
RCA (LPM-1410 "Bimbo") 40-60   57
RCA (LPM-1576 "Jim Reeves") 40-50   57
RCA (LPM-1685 "Girls I Have Known") 30-40   58
RCA (LPM-1950 "God be with You") . 25-30   58
(Monaural.)
RCA (LSP-1950 "God be with You") . 30-40   58
(Stereo.)
RCA (LPM-2001 through LPM-2339) . 15-25   59-61
(Monaural.)
RCA (LSP-2001 through LSP-2339) . 20-30   59-61
(Stereo.)
RCA (LPM-2487 through LPM-3903) . 10-20   62-67
RCA (LSP-2487 through LSP-3903) . 12-25   62-67
RCA (LPM-3987 "A Touch of
   Sadness") 40-50   68
(Monaural.)
RCA (LSP-3987 "A Touch of
   Sadness") 10-15   68
(Stereo.)
RCA (LSP-4000 through LPS-4700) .. 8-15   68-72
READER'S DIGEST (210 "Unforgettable
   Jim Reeves") 40-50   76
(Six-LP set.)
Also see CRAMER, Floyd
Also see KERR, Anita
Also see PRESLEY, Elvis / Hank Snow / Eddy Arnold / Hank
   Snow

REEVES, Jim, and Deborah Allen
Singles: 7–inch
RCA 2-5   79-80

REEVES, Jim, and Patsy Cline
Singles: 7–inch
MCA 3-5   82
RCA 3-5   81
LPs: 10/12–inch 33rpm
MCA 5-10   82
RCA 5-10   81
Also see CLINE, Patsy

REEVES, Jim / Alvadean Coker
Singles: 78rpm
ABBOTT 10-20   54
Singles: 7–inch
ABBOTT 15-25   54

REEVES, Jim / Hugi and Lugi Chorus
Singles: 7–inch
U.S.A.F. (89 "In a Mansion
   Stands My Love") 20-30
(Promotional issue only.)

REISMAN, Joe, and His Orchestra
Singles: 78rpm
RCA 2-4   55-57
Singles: 7–inch
LANDA 4-6   61
RCA 4-8   55-59
ROULETTE 4-6   59-60
EPs: 7–inch 33/45rpm
RCA 5-10   56
LPs: 10/12–inch 33rpm
CAMDEN 5-10   72
RCA 10-20   56
ROULETTE 10-15   59-60

REJOICE
Singles: 7–inch
DUNHILL 4-6   68-69
LPs: 10/12–inch 33rpm
DUNHILL 10-15   69

RENAISSANCE
Singles: 7–inch
CAPITOL 3-5   72-73
SIRE 2-5   76-78
LPs: 10/12–inch 33rpm
CAPITOL 8-12   72-78
ELEKTRA (74068 "Renaissance") ... 15-25   69
I.R.S. 5-8   81-83
MFSL 20-40   82
SIRE 8-10   74-79
SINGCORD 8-10   76-77
SOVEREIGN 8-12   73
> Members: John Tout; Mike Dunford; Jim McCarty; Annie Haslam; Keith Relf; Jon Camp; Terry Sullivan; Louis Cennamo; Jane Relf.
> Also see ARMAGEDDON
> Also see HASLAM, Annie

RENAISSANCE
Singles: 7–inch
RANWOOD 3-5   71
LPs: 10/12–inch 33rpm
RANWOOD 5-10   70

RENAY, Diane
Singles: 7–inch
ATCO 5-10   62-63
DICE (8018 "Navy Blue") 15-20   87
ERIC 2-4
FONTANA 5-10   69
MGM (13335 "I Had a Dream") 10-20   64
NEW VOICE 5-10   65
REX (293 "Maybe") 15-25
20TH FOX 5-10   64
U.A. (50048 "Please Gypsy") 10-15   66
LPs: 10/12–inch 33rpm
20TH FOX (TF-3133 "Navy Blue") ... 25-40   64
  (Monaural.)
20TH FOX (TFS-3133 "Navy Blue") .. 30-50   64
  (Stereo.)

RENDER, Rudy
Singles: 78rpm
LONDON 4-6   49-51
Singles: 7–inch
DOT 4-8   60-61
EDISON INT'L 4-8   59
LONDON 5-10   51

RENE, Della
Singles: 7–inch
AIRWAVE 3-5   81

RENE, Google
(Google Rene and His Combo)
Singles: 78rpm
CLASS 4-8   57-58
Singles: 7–inch
CLASS 4-8   57-66
KAPP 4-6   62
NEW BAG 4-6   67
REED 5-10   60
RENDEZVOUS 4-8   60
Picture Sleeves
RENDEZVOUS 5-10   60
LPs: 10/12–inch 33rpm
CLASS 15-25   59-63

RENE, Henri, and His Orchestra
Singles: 78rpm
RCA 2-5   51-56
STANDARD 2-5   52-53
Singles: 7–inch
DECCA 3-6   62
IMPERIAL 4-8   59
RCA 4-8   51-56
STANDARD 4-8   52-53
Picture Sleeves
RCA 5-10   55
EPs: 7–inch 33/45rpm
CAMDEN 5-10   54-57
RCA 5-10   53-56
LPs: 10/12–inch 33rpm
CAMDEN 10-20   54-57
KAPP 5-10   67
RCA (Except 3000 series) 10-20   56-61
RCA (3000 series) 15-25   53
  (10–inch LPs.)
> Also see BELL SISTERS

RENE & ANGELA
Singles: 12–inch 33/45rpm
MERCURY 4-6   85-86
Singles: 7–inch
CAPITOL 3-5   80-83
MERCURY 2-4   85-86
LPs: 10/12–inch 33rpm
CAPITOL 5-10   80-83
MERCURY 5-8   85-86

RENE & RAY
Singles: 7–inch
DONNA 5-10   62

RENE & RENE
Singles: 7–inch

ABC 3-5	73
ABC-PAR 4-8	65
ARU 4-8	64
CERTRON 3-5	71
COBRA 4-8	65
COLUMBIA 4-8	64
EPIC 3-6	69
FALCON 4-8	68
JOX 5-10	64-66
WHITE WHALE 3-6	68-69

Picture Sleeves

COLUMBIA 4-8	64

LPs: 10/12–inch 33rpm

EPIC 10-15	69
WHITE WHALE 10-15	68

Members: Rene Ornelas; J. Ramirez.

RENEGADE
Singles: 7–inch

ALLIED ARTISTS 2-4	86

LPs: 10/12–inch 33rpm

ALLIED ARTISTS 5-8	86

Member: Luis Cardenas.

RENFRO, Anthony C., Orchestra
Singles: 7–inch

RENFRO 3-5	76

RENO, Mike, and Ann Wilson
Singles: 7–inch

COLUMBIA 3-5	84

Also see LOVERBOY
Also see WILSON, Ann

RENTE, Damon
LPs: 10/12–inch 33rpm

TBA 5-8	86

REO, Diamond: see DIAMOND REO

REPARATA and the Delrons
Singles: 7–inch

KAPP 5-10	69-70
MALA 5-10	67-68
RCA 10-15	65-67
WORLD ARTISTS 5-10	64-65

LPs: 10/12–inch 33rpm

AVCO EMBASSY 10-20	70
WORLD ARTISTS (3006 "Whenever a Teenager Cries") 40-60	65

Members: Mary Aiese; Sheila Reillie; Carol Drobnicki; Nanette Licari; Lorraine Mazzola; Cookie Sirico.

REPLACEMENTS
Singles: 7–inch

SIRE 2-5	85-90
TWIN TONE 3-5	82-84

LPs: 10/12–inch 33rpm

SIRE 5-10	85-90
TWIN/TONE 5-10	84

Promotional LPs

SIRE ("Interview with Paul Westerberg") 20-25	85

Member: Paul Westerberg.

RENRUT, Icky
(Ike Turner)
Singles: 7–inch

STEVENS (104 "Jack Rabbit") 25-35	59
STEVENS (107 "Hey-Hey") 25-35	59

Also see TURNER, Ike

RESTIVO, Johnny
Singles: 7–inch

EPIC 5-10	62
RCA (Except 7559) 5-10	60
(Monaural.)	
RCA (47-7559 "The Shape I'm In") . . . 5-10	59
(Monaural.)	
RCA (61-7559 "The Shape I'm In") . . 15-25	59
(Stereo.)	
20TH FOX 8-12	61

Picture Sleeves

RCA 10-20	60
20TH FOX 10-20	61

LPs: 10/12–inch 33rpm

RCA (LPM-2149 "Oh Johnny") 25-35	59
(Monaural.)	
RCA (LSP-2149 "Oh Johnny") 40-50	59
(Stereo.)	

Also see KING CURTIS

RESTLESS HEART
Singles: 7–inch

RCA 2-4	87-90

LPs: 10/12–inch 33rpm

RCA 5-8	87-90

RETURN to FOREVER
Singles: 7–inch

COLUMBIA 3-5	77-79
POLYDOR 3-5	75

LPs: 10/12–inch 33rpm

COLUMBIA 5-10	76-79
ECM 8-10	75
POLYDOR 8-12	73-75

Members: Chick Corea; Lenny White; Stanley Clarke; Al DiMeola.
Also see CLARKE, Stanely
Also see COREA, Chick
Also see DI MEOLA, Al
Also see WHITE, Lenny

REUNION
Singles: 7–inch

MR. G. 4-8	68
RCA 3-5	74-75

Also see OHIO EXPRESS

REVELATION
Singles: 7–inch

COMBINE 4-8	67
HANDSHAKE 3-5	80-82
MERCURY 3-5	70

MUSIC FACTORY	4-8	68
RCA	3-5	79
RSO	3-5	76

LPs: 10/12-inch 33rpm

HANDSHAKE	5-10	82
MERCURY	8-12	70
RCA	5-10	79

REVELS

Singles: 7-inch

NORGOLDE (103 "Dead Man's Stroll")	25-50	59
NORGOLDE (103 "Midnight Stroll")	10-15	59
NORGOLDE (104 "Foo Man Choo")	10-20	59

REVERE, Paul, and the Raiders
(Paul Revere and the Raiders Featuring Mark Lindsay; Raiders)

Singles: 7-inch

COLUMBIA (10000 series)	3-5	75
COLUMBIA (42814 through 42373)	5-10	63-65
COLUMBIA (43375 "Steppin' Out") (Black vinyl.)	4-8	65
COLUMBIA (43375 "Steppin' Out") (Colored vinyl. Promotional issue only.)	15-25	65
COLUMBIA (43461 "Just Like Me") (Black vinyl.)	4-8	65
COLUMBIA (43461 "Just Like Me") (Colored vinyl. Promotional issue only.)	15-25	65
COLUMBIA (43556 "Kicks") (Black vinyl.)	4-8	66
COLUMBIA (43556 "Kicks") (Colored vinyl. Promotional issue only.)	15-25	66
COLUMBIA (43678 "Hungry") (Black vinyl.)	4-8	66
COLUMBIA (43678 "Hungry") (Colored vinyl. Promotional issue only.)	15-25	66
COLUMBIA (43810 "The Great Airplane Strike") (Black vinyl.)	4-8	66
COLUMBIA (43810 "The Great Airplane Strike") (Colored vinyl. Promotional issue only.)	15-25	66
COLUMBIA (43907 "Good Thing") (Black vinyl.)	4-8	67
COLUMBIA (43907 "Good Thing") (Colored vinyl. Promotional issue only.)	15-25	67
COLUMBIA (44018 through 45898)	3-6	68-73
COLUMBIA (105499 "SS 396"/ "Corvair Baby") (Promotional issue only.)	8-12	66
DRIVE	3-5	76
GARDENA	15-25	60-62
JERDEN (807 "So Fine")	10-15	66
RAIDER	5-10	82
SANDE (101 "Louie Louie")	25-35	63
20TH FOX	3-5	76

Picture Sleeves

COLUMBIA	6-12	66-69

EPs: 7-inch 33/45rpm

JERDEN (JRLS-7004 "In the Beginning") (Jukebox issue only. Includes title strips.)	25-45	66

LPs: 10/12-inch 33rpm

BACK-TRAC	5-8	85
COLUMBIA (12 "Two Great Selling LPs")	15-20	69
COLUMBIA (462 "Greatest Hits")	20-25	67
COLUMBIA (2307 through 2721) (Monaural.)	20-30	65-67
COLUMBIA (2755 "Christmas Present and Past") (Monaural.)	40-60	67
COLUMBIA (2805 "Goin' to Memphis") (Monaural.)	20-30	68
COLUMBIA (9107 through 9521) (Stereo.)	25-40	65-67
COLUMBIA (9555 "Christmas Present and Past") (Stereo.)	40-60	67
COLUMBIA (9605 "Goin' to Memphis") (Stereo.)	20-25	68
COLUMBIA (9665 through 9964)	10-20	68-70
COLUMBIA (30000 series)	8-15	71-76
COLUMBIA SPECIAL PRODUCTS (141714 "The Judge") (Promotional issue only.)	150-200	
HARMONY	10-15	70-72
GARDENA (1000 "Like Long Hair")	250-300	61
JERDEN (7004 "In the Beginning")	75-125	66
PICKWICK	10-15	
RAIDER	10-15	82
SANDE (1001 "Paul Revere and the Raiders")	250-300	63
SEARS	40-50	

(Special Products Sears promotional issue.)
Members: Mark Lindsay; Freddy Weller; Paul Revere; Keith Allison; Joe Correro Jr; Carl Driggs; Omar Martinez; Doug Heath; Ron Foos; Danny Krause.
Also see BROTHERHOOD
Also see CYRKLE / Paul Revere and the Raiders
Also see LINDSAY, Mark
Also see UNKNOWNS
Also see WELLER, Freddy

REX, T.: see T-REX

REYNOLDS, Burt

Singles: 7-inch

MCA	3-5	80
MERCURY	3-5	73-74

Picture Sleeves

MCA	3-5	80

LPs: 10/12-inch 33rpm

MERCURY	8-12	73

REYNOLDS, Debbie

Singles: 78rpm

CORAL	4-6	57

MGM	4-6	55-59

Singles: 7-inch

ABC	3-5	74
ABC-PAR	4-8	65
BEVERLY HILLS	3-5	72
CORAL	5-10	57-58
DOT	4-8	59-63
JANUS	3-5	70
MCA	2-4	
MGM (11000 and 12000 series)	5-10	55-59
MGM (13000 series)	4-8	63-66
PARAMOUNT	3-5	73

Picture Sleeves

MGM	8-15	58-66

EPs: 7-inch 33/45rpm

CORAL	10-20	58
MGM	10-20	55

LPs: 10/12-inch 33rpm

DOT (Except 25295)	15-20	59-63
DOT (25295 "Am I That Easy to Forget") (Black vinyl.	15-25	60
DOT (25295 "Am I That Easy to Forget") (Colored vinyl.	35-45	60
MGM	12-25	60-66
METRO	10-15	65

Also see CARPENTER, Carleton, and Debbie Reynolds
Also see FISHER, Eddie, and Debbie Reynolds

REYNOLDS, Jeannie
Singles: 7-inch

CASABLANCA	3-5	75

REYNOLDS, Jody
Singles: 78rpm

DEMON (1507 "Endless Sleep")	15-25	58

Singles: 7-inch

ABC	3-5	73
BRENT	4-8	63
COLLECTABLES	2-4	
DEMON	10-20	58-59
PULSAR	3-6	69
SMASH	4-8	63
TITAN	4-8	66

LPs: 10/12-inch 33rpm

TRU-GEMS	8-10	78

Also see CASEY, Al
Also see CLARK, Sanford

REYNOLDS, Jody, and Bobbie Gentry
Singles: 7-inch

TITAN	4-8	67

Also see GENTRY, Bobbie

REYNOLDS, Jody / Olympics
Singles: 7-inch

DEMON	10-20	58
LIBERTY	4-8	63
TITAN	4-8	62

Picture Sleeves

DEMON (1801 "Endless Sleep")	15-25	58

Also see OLYMPICS

REYNOLDS, L.J.
(L.J. Reynolds and the Chocolate Syrup)
Singles: 12-inch 33/45rpm

CAPITOL	4-6	82

Singles: 7-inch

CAPITOL	3-5	81-82
FANTASY	2-4	85-87
LAW-TON	3-5	71-72
MAINSTREAM	4-6	69
MERCURY	2-4	84

LPs: 10/12-inch 33rpm

CAPITOL	5-10	81-82
MERCURY	5-8	84

Also see DRAMATICS

REYNOLDS, Lawrence
Singles: 7-inch

COLUMBIA	3-5	72
WARNER	3-6	69-70

LPs: 10/12-inch 33rpm

WARNER	8-12	69

RHEINS, Robert
Singles: 7-inch

RHEINS	3-5	59

EPs: 7-inch 33/45rpm

RHEINS	4-8	59

LPs: 10/12-inch 33rpm

MISTLETOE	5-8	75
RHEINS	5-15	58-63
U.A.	5-8	72-74

RHINOCEROS
Singles: 7-inch

ELEKTRA	4-6	69-70

LPs: 10/12-inch 33rpm

ELEKTRA	10-20	68-70

Members: Alan Gerber; Billy Mundi; Michael Fonfara; John
Finley; Danny Weis; Jerry Penrod; Peter Hodgson.
Also see EARTH OPERA

RHODES, Emitt
Singles: 7-inch

DUNHILL	3-5	70-73

LPs: 10/12-inch 33rpm

A&M	10-15	70
DUNHILL	8-12	70-73

Also see MERRY-GO-ROUND

RHODES, Todd
Singles: 78rpm

KING	5-10	48-54
MODERN	5-10	49
SENSATION (Except 6)	10-20	47-49
SENSATION (6 "Blues for the Red Boy")	25-35	47
VITACOUSTIC	10-20	47

Singles: 7-inch

KING (4469 "Gin Gin Gin")	40-50	51
KING (4486 "Good Man")	20-30	51

KING (4509 "Your Daddy's Doggin'
Around") 20-30   51
(Black vinyl.)
KING (4509 "Your Daddy's Doggin'
Around") 50-70   51
(Colored vinyl.)
KING (4528 "Rocket 69") 40-60   52
KING (4556 through 4601) 10-20   52-53
(Lavern Baker is the vocalist on one side of each
of the four King issues in the 4556-4601 series)
KING (4648 through 4775) 5-10   53-54
EPs: 7–Inch 33/45rpm
KING 30-40   52-54
LPs: 10/12-Inch 33rpm
KING (88 "Todd Rhodes Plays
the Hits") 75-100   53
KING (658 "Dance Music") 35-55   60
Also see BAKER, Lavern

RHYTHM CORPS
LPs: 10/12–inch 33rpm
PASHA 5-8   88

RHYTHM HERITAGE
Singles: 12–inch 33/45rpm
ABC 4-8   78
Singles: 7–inch
ABC 3-5   75-78
LPs: 10/12–inch 33rpm
ABC 5-10   76-77

RHYTHM MAKERS
Singles: 7–inch
VIGOR 3-5   76
LPs: 10/12–inch 33rpm
VIGOR 8-10   76

RHYZE
Singles: 7–inch
SAM 3-5   80
20TH FOX 3-5   81
LPs: 10/12–inch 33rpm
20TH FOX 5-10   81

RIBBONS
Singles: 7–inch
ERA 3-5   72
MARSH 10-15   63
PARKWAY 5-10   64

RICH, Buddy
(Buddy Rich Band)
Singles: 78rpm
CLEF 4-8   54
NORGRAN 4-8   55-56
Singles: 7–Inch
ARGO 4-8   61
CLEF 5-10   54
EVEREST 3-5   71
GROOVE MERCHANT 3-5   74
MCA 2-4   81
NORGRAN 5-10   55-56

PACIFIC JAZZ 3-6   66-67
RCA 3-5   76
EPs: 7-Inch 33/45rpm
NORGRAN 20-40   54-56
LPs: 10/12-Inch 33rpm
ARGO (676 "Playtime") 35-45   61
CLEF (684 "Gene Krupa
and Buddy Rich") 100-150   56
EMARCY 10-20   65-76
GREAT AMERICAN GRAMOPHONE . . 5-8   78
GROOVE MERCHANT 5-10   74-75
GRYPHON 5-10   79
LIBERTY 8-12   70
MCA 5-8   81
MERCURY (126 "Buddy Rich Story") 10-20   69
MERCURY (20448 "Rich vs. Roach") 50-75   59
(Monaural.)
MERCURY (20451 "Richcraft") 50-75   60
(Monaural.)
MERCURY (20461 "The Voice
Is Rich") 40-60   60
(Monaural.)
MERCURY (60133 "Rich vs. Roach") 60-85   59
(Stereo.)
MERCURY (60136 "Richcraft") 60-85   60
(Stereo.)
MERCURY (60144 "The Voice
Is Rich") 45-65   60
(Stereo.)
NORGRAN (26 "Swingin") 75-125   54
NORGRAN (1031 "Sing and Swing") . 60-80   55
NORGRAN (1038 "Buddy Rich and
Sweets Edison") 60-80   55
NORGRAN (1052 "Swingin") 60-80   55
NORGRAN (1078 "Wailing") 50-75   56
NORGRAN (1086 "One for Basie") . . 50-75   56
PACIFIC JAZZ (Except 10000 series) . 8-18   66-70
PACIFIC JAZZ (10000 series) 5-8   81
PAUSA 5-8
RCA 8-12   72-77
ROOST 10-20   66
TRIP 8-10   76
VSP 10-15   67
VERVE (2009 "Buddy Rich
Sings Johnny Mercer") 50-75   57
VERVE (8129 "Buddy Rich and
Sweets Edison") 50-75   57
VERVE (8142 "Swingin") 50-75   57
VERVE (8168 "Wailin") 50-75   57
VERVE (8176 "One for Basie") 50-75   57
VERVE (8285 "In Miami") 50-75   58
VERVE (8425 "Blue Caravan") 30-40   62
VERVE (8471 "Burnin' Beat") 30-40   62
(Monaural.)
VERVE (8484 "Drum Battle: Gene Krupa
and Buddy Rich") 25-40   62
VERVE (68471 "Burnin' Beat") 35-45   62
(Stereo.)
VERVE (68778 "Super Rich") 10-15   69

VERVE (68824 "Monster") 10-15   73
WHO'S WHO in JAZZ 5-10   78
WING 8-12   69
WORLD PACIFIC 10-15   68
  Also see DAVIS, Sammy, Jr., and Buddy Rich
  Also see TORME, Mel

RICH, Buddy, and Max Roach
LPs: 10/12-inch 33rpm
MERCURY 5-10   81
  Also see RICH, Buddy

RICH, Charlie
Singles: 7-inch
ARISTA 3-5   80
COLUMBIA 2-4   82
EPIC 3-5   70-81
ELEKTRA 3-5   78-81
GROOVE 4-8   63-64
HI 4-8   66-67
MERCURY 3-5   73-74
PHILLIPS INT'L 10-20   59-63
RCA (Except 8000 series) 3-5   74-77
RCA (8000 series) 4-8   64-65
SSS/SUN 3-5
SMASH 4-8   65-66
U.A. 3-5   78-80
Picture Sleeves
GROOVE (0020 "She Loved Everybody
  But Me") 10-20   63
EPs: 7-inch 33/45rpm
EPIC (1099 "Silver Linings") 8-12   76
  (Promotional issue only.)
LPs: 10/12-inch 33rpm
BUCKBOARD 8-10
CAMDEN 8-10   70-74
EPIC (Except 139) 6-12   68-78
EPIC (139 "Everything You
  Wanted to Hear") 15-20   76
  (Promotional issue only.)
ELEKTRA 5-10   80
51 WEST 5-10
GROOVE (G-1000 "Charlie Rich") ... 25-50   64
  (Monaural.)
GROOVE (GS-1000 "Charlie Rich") .. 35-60   64
  (Stereo.)
HARMONY 8-10   73
HI (Except 32037) 8-10   74-77
HI (32037 "Charlie Rich") 15-25   67
HILLTOP 8-10
MERCURY 10-15   74
PHILLIPS INT'L (1970 "Lonely
  Weekends") 400-500   60
PHONORAMA 5-8
POWER PAK 8-10   74
RCA (Except 3000 series) 8-10   73-77
RCA (3000 series) 15-25   65-66
SSS/SUN 5-10   69-79
SMASH 15-25   65-66
TRIP 8-10   74

U.A. 5-10   78-79
WING 10-15   69
  Also see CASH, Johnny
  Also see LEWIS, Jerry Lee, Carl Perkins and Charlie Rich
  Also see SHERIDAN, Bobby

RICHARD, Cliff
(Cliff Richard and the Drifters; Cliff Richard and the
Shadows)
Singles: 12-inch 33/45rpm
EMI AMERICA 4-8   83
Singles: 7-inch
ABC-PAR 10-15   59-61
BIG TOP 4-8   62
CAPITOL 10-15   59
DOT 4-8   62
EMI AMERICA 3-5   79-84
EPIC 4-8   63-67
MONUMENT 3-5   70-72
ROCKET 3-5   76-79
SIRE 3-5   73
UNI 4-6   68-69
WARNER 4-6   69
Picture Sleeves
EMI AMERICA 3-5   80-81
EPIC 5-10   63-66
LPs: 10/12-inch 33rpm
ABC-PAR (ABC-321 "Cliff Sings") ... 25-35   60
  (Monaural.)
ABC-PAR (ABCS-321 "Cliff Sings") .. 35-45   60
  (Stereo.)
ABC-PAR (ABC-391 "Listen to Cliff") . 25-35   61
  (Monaural.)
ABC-PAR (ABCS-391 "Listen to Cliff") 35-45   61
  (Stereo.)
EMI AMERICA 5-10   79-83
EPIC 15-25   63-65
ROCKET 5-10   76-78
  Also see NEWTON-JOHN, Olivia, and the Electric Light
  Orchestra
  Also see NEWTON-JOHN, Olivia, and Cliff Richard
  Also see SHADOWS

RICHARD, Little: see LITTLE RICHARD

RICHARDS, Diane
Singles: 7-inch
ZOO YORK 2-4   83

RICHARDS, Turley
Singles: 7-inch
ATLANTIC 3-5   80
COLUMBIA 4-8   66-67
EPIC 3-5   76-78
KAPP 4-8   68
MGM 4-8   64
20TH FOX 4-8   65
WARNER 3-5   70
Picture Sleeves
COLUMBIA 4-8   66
LPs: 10/12-inch 33rpm
ATLANTIC 5-10   80

EPIC	5-10	76
20TH FOX	10-20	65
WARNER	10-15	70-71

RICHARDSON, Jape
(Jape Richardson and His Japettes)
Singles: 78rpm

MERCURY	10-20	57

Singles: 7-inch

MERCURY (71219 "Beggar to a King")	15-25	57
MERCURY (71312 "Teenage Moon")	10-20	58

Also see BIG BOPPER

RICHIE, Lionel
Singles: 12-inch 33/45rpm

MOTOWN	4-8	83-86

Singles: 7-inch

MOTOWN	2-4	82-87

LPs: 10/12-inch 33rpm

MOTOWN	5-8	82-86

Also see COMMODORES
Also see ROSS, Diana, and Lionel Ritchie
Also see U.S.A. for AFRICA

RICHIE, Lionel, and Alabama
Singles: 12-inch 33/45rpm

MOTOWN (195 "Special Motown Service to Country Radio")	8-12	86
(Promotional issue only.)		

Singles: 7-inch

MOTOWN	2-4	86

Also see ALABAMA
Also see RICHIE, Lionel

RICHIE'S ROOM 222 GANG
Singles: 7-inch

SCEPTER	3-5	71

RICHMOND EXTENSION
Singles: 7-inch

SILVER BLUE	3-5	74

RICK and the Keens
Singles: 7-inch

AUSTIN (303 "Peanuts")	35-50	61
JAMIE (1219 "Your Turn to Cry")	10-15	62
LE CAM (721 "Peanuts")	25-35	61
LE CAM (133 "Darla")	15-25	61
SMASH (1705 "Peanuts")	10-15	61
TOLLIE (9016 "Darla")	10-15	64
TROY	20-30	

RIDDLE, Nelson, and His Orchestra
Singles: 78rpm

CAPITOL	3-5	53-57

Singles: 7-inch

CAPITOL	3-8	53-62
EPIC	3-6	67
LIBERTY	3-6	67
REPRISE	3-6	63-66
20TH FOX	3-6	66
VERVE	4-8	59

Picture Sleeves

CAPITOL	5-10	60

EPIC	4-8	67

EPs: 7-inch 33/45rpm

CAPITOL	8-15	55-59
VERVE	6-12	59

LPs: 10/12-inch 33rpm

ALSHIRE	5-10	70-71
CAPITOL	5-20	55-78
DAYBREAK	5-8	73
HARMONY	5-10	69
LIBERTY	5-10	67
MPS	5-10	73
PICKWICK	5-10	65
REPRISE	5-15	63-65
SOLID STATE	5-10	67
SUNSET	5-10	68
U.A.	5-10	68
VERVE	5-15	59

Since publication of *The Official Price Guide to Movie/TV Soundtracks and Original Cast Albums,* with over 8,000 listings, this guide has dropped many soundtracks, including some by this artist.
Also see FITZGERALD, Ella
Also see MARTIN, Dean / Nelson Riddle
Also see PETERSON, Oscar

RIDGWAY, Stan
Singles: 7-inch

I.R.S.	2-4	86

LPs: 10/12-inch 33rpm

I.R.S.	5-8	86

Also see WALL of VOODOO

RIGHT CHOICE
Singles: 7-inch

MOTOWN	2-4	88

RIGHT KIND
Singles: 7-inch

GALAXY	4-8	68

RIGHTEOUS BROTHERS
Singles: 7-inch

HAVEN	3-5	74-76
MGM	3-5	78-79
MGM CELEBRITY SCENE (8 "Righteous Brothers")	35-45	66
(Boxed set of five singles with bio insert and jukebox title strips.)		
MOONGLOW	5-10	63-66
PHILLES	5-10	64-66
POLYDOR	3-5	
VERVE	4-8	65-70

Picture Sleeves

PHILLES	8-12	65-66
VERVE	5-10	66-67

LPs: 10/12-inch 33rpm

HAVEN	10-15	74-75
MGM	10-15	70-73
MOONGLOW (1001 "Right Now")	20-30	63
MOONGLOW (1002 "Some Blue Eyed Soul")	20-30	64
MOONGLOW (1003 "This Is New")	20-30	65

MOONGLOW (1004 "Best of
the Righteous Brothers) 20-30   66
PHILLES (4007 "You've Lost
That Lovin' Feeling) 25-45   64
PHILLES (4008 "Just Once
in My Live") 25-45   65
PHILLES (4009 "Back to Back") 25-45   65
VERVE (5001 "Soul and Inspiration") 15-20   66
VERVE (5004 "Go Ahead and Cry") .. 15-20   66
VERVE (5010 "Sayin' Something") .. 15-20   67
VERVE (5020 "Greatest Hits") 15-20   67
VERVE (5031 "Souled Out") 15-20   66
VERVE (5058 "One for the Road") ... 15-20   68
VERVE (5076 "Re-Birth") 15-20   69
Members: Bill Medley; Bobby Hatfield.
Also see HATFIELD, Bobby
Also see MEDLEY, Bill
Also see PARAMOURS
Also see SONNY & CHER / Righteous Brothers / Lettermen

RILEY, Billy
(Billy Lee Riley; Billy Riley and His Little Green Men)
Singles: 78rpm
SUN 15-25   56-57
Singles: 7-inch
ATLANTIC 3-6   68
BRUNSWICK (55085 "Rockin' on
the Moon") 150-250   58
ENTRANCE 3-5   72
GNP/CRESCENDO 4-8   66
HIP 4-8   68
HOME of the BLUES (233 "Flip, Flop
and Fly") 20-30   61
MERCURY 5-10   64-65
MOJO 4-8   67
SUN (245 "Rock with Me Baby") 50-75   56
SUN (260 "Flying Saucers
Rock and Roll") 50-75   57
SUN (277 "Red Hot") 25-50   57
SUN (289 "Wouldn't You Know") 10-20   58
SUN (313 "No Name Girl") 10-20   58
SUN (322 "Got the Water Boiling") ... 50-75   59
SSS/SUN 4-6   69-70
LPs: 10/12-inch 33rpm
CROWN 15-20   63
GNP/CRESCENDO 15-20   66
MERCURY 15-20   64-65
MOJO 15-20   79

RILEY, Cheryl Pepsii
LPs: 10/12-inch 33rpm
COLUMBIA 5-8   88

RILEY, Jeannie C.
Singles: 7-inch
CAPITOL 3-6   69
CROSS COUNTRY 2-4   79
GARPAX 2-4   80
GOD'S COUNTRY 3-5   75
MCA 2-4   82
MGM 3-5   71-74

MERCURY 3-5   74
PLANTATION (Black vinyl) 2-4   68-72
PLANTATION (Colored vinyl) 4-8   68-72
WARNER 3-5   76
Picture Sleeves
PLANTATION 4-8   68-72
EPs: 7-inch 33/45rpm
PLANTATION 5-10   68
LPs: 10/12-inch 33rpm
ALBUM GLOBE 5-8
CAPITOL 8-12   69
CROSS COUNTRY 5-10   79
HSRD/PLEASANT SOUNDS 5-8   82
HEARTWARMING 4-8   79
LITTLE DARLIN' 10-15   68
MGM 5-10   72-74
OUT of TOWN DIST 5-8   82
PLANTATION 5-12   68-82
POWER PAK 5-8
SONGBIRD 4-8   81-83
TRIP 8-12   74

RIMSHOTS
Singles: 7-inch
A-1 (4000 "Soul Train") 4-6
STANG 3-5   76-77
LPs: 10/12-inch 33rpm
STANG 5-10   76

RINGS
Singles: 7-inch
MCA 3-5   81
LPs: 10/12-inch 33rpm
MCA 5-10   81

RINKY-DINKS
(Featuring Bobby Darin)
Singles: 7-inch
ATCO (6121 "Early in the Morning") . 20-25   58
Also see DARIN, Bobby

RIOS, Augie
(Augie Rios and the Notations)
Singles: 7-inch
MGM 4-8   60-64
METRO 5-10   58-59
SHELLEY 10-20   63-64

RIOS, Miguel
Singles: 7-inch
A&M 3-5   70
LPs: 10/12-inch 33rpm
A&M 10-15   70

RIOT
Singles: 7-inch
MOTOWN 3-5   74
LPs: 10/12-inch 33rpm
CBS 5-8   88
CAPITOL 5-8   80-82
ELEKTRA 5-8   81-82
FIRE-SIGN (87001 "Rock City") 15-25   78

| MOTOWN | 8-10 | 74 |
| QUALITY/RFC | 5-8 | 84 |

RIP CHORDS
Singles: 7-inch

COLUMBIA (42687 "Here I Stand")	10-15	63
COLUMBIA (42812 "Gone")	10-15	63
(Black vinyl.)		
COLUMBIA (42812 "Gone")	20-30	63
(Colored vinyl. Promotional issue only.)		
COLUMBIA (42921 "Hey Little Cobra")	10-15	63
(Black vinyl.)		
COLUMBIA (42921 "Hey Little Cobra")	20-30	63
(Colored vinyl. Promotional issue only.)		
COLUMBIA (43035 "Three Window Coupe")	10-15	64
(Black vinyl.)		
COLUMBIA (43035 "Three Window Coupe")	20-30	64
(Colored vinyl. Promotional issue only.)		
COLUMBIA (43093 "One-Piece, Topless Bathing Suit")	10-15	64
COLUMBIA (43221 "Don't Be Scared")	10-15	64
COLUMBIA (3-42000 series)	10-20	63
(Compact 33 singles.)		

Picture Sleeves

COLUMBIA (42687 "Here I Stand")	15-25	63
(Promotional issue only.)		
COLUMBIA (42812 "Gone")	15-25	63

LPs: 10/12-inch 33rpm

COLUMBIA (2151 "Hey Little Cobra")	25-35	64
(Monaural.)		
COLUMBIA (2216 "Three Window Coupe")	30-40	64
(Monaural.)		
COLUMBIA (8951 "Hey Little Cobra")	25-35	64
(Stereo.)		
COLUMBIA (9016 "Three Window Coupe")	30-40	64
(Stereo.)		

Members: Bruce Johnston; Terry Melcher; Phil Stewart; Ernie Bringas; Steve Barri; Phil Sloan; Glen Campbell; Hal Blaine; Tommy Tedesco.
Also see BRUCE & TERRY
Also see CAMPBELL, Glen

RIPERTON, Minnie
Singles: 12-inch 33/45rpm

EPIC	4-8	77

Singles: 7-inch

CAPITOL	3-5	79-81
EPIC	3-5	74-77
GRT	3-5	72
JANUS	3-5	75-76

LPs: 10/12-inch 33rpm

ACCORD	5-8	82
CAPITOL	5-10	79-81

EPIC	10-12	74-77
51 WEST	5-8	
GRT	10-15	70
JANUS	8-12	74

Also see JONES, Quincy
Also see ROTARY CONNECTION

RIPPINGTONS Featuring Russ Freeman
LPs: 10/12-inch 33rpm

GRP	5-8	89
PASSPORT	5-8	88

Member: Steve Reid.

RIPPLE
Singles: 7-inch

GRC	3-5	73-75
SALSOUL	3-5	77-78

LPs: 10/12-inch 33rpm

GRC	8-10	74
SALSOUL	5-8	77

RIPPLES and Waves Plus Michael
(Jackson Five)
Singles: 7-inch

STEELTOWN (688 "Let Me Carry Your School Books")	50-80	69
(Mono. "Steeltown" is in all upper case letters on label.)		
STEELTOWN (688 "Let Me Carry Your School Books")	75-100	69
(Stereo. "Steeltown" is in upper and lower case letters.)		

Also see JACKSONS

RITCHARD, Cyril
LPs: 10/12-inch 33rpm

RIVERSIDE	8-15	61-62

RITCHIE FAMILY
Singles: 12-inch 33/45rpm

MARLIN	4-8	76
RCA	4-6	82

Singles: 7-inch

CASABLANCA	3-5	79-80
MARLIN	3-5	76-78
RCA	2-4	82-83
20TH FOX	3-5	75

LPs: 10/12-inch 33rpm

CASABLANCA	5-10	79-80
MARLIN	5-10	76-78
RCA	5-8	82
20TH FOX	5-10	75

RITENOUR, Lee
Singles: 7-inch

ELEKTRA	2-4	81-82
EPIC	3-5	76-80

Picture Sleeves

ELEKTRA	2-4	81

LPs: 10/12-inch 33rpm

ELEKTRA	5-8	78-84
EPIC	5-10	76-80
GRP	5-8	85

JVC 5-10	78	
MFSL 15-25	85	
MUSICIAN 5-8	82	
Also see GRUSIN, Dave		

RITTER, Tex

Singles: 78rpm

CAPITOL 3-8	50-57	
CHAMPION 10-20		
CONQUEROR 10-20		

Singles: 7-inch

CAPITOL (1100 through 3900 series) . 5-10	50-58	
(Purple labels.)		
CAPITOL (2000 through 4000 series) .. 3-6	68-76	
(Orange labels.)		
CAPITOL (4000 through 5900 series) .. 4-8	58-67	

Picture Sleeves

CAPITOL 4-8	68	

EPs: 7-inch 33/45rpm

CAPITOL (Except 431) 5-10	59-60	
CAPITOL (431 "Tex Ritter Sings") 15-25	53	

LPs: 10/12-inch 33rpm

ALBUM GLOBE 5-8		
BUCKBOARD 5-8		
CAPITOL (213 through 467) 8-12	69-71	
CAPITOL (971 "Songs from		
the Western Screen") 40-50	58	
CAPITOL (1100 "Psalms") 20-30	59	
CAPITOL (T-1292 "Blood on		
the Saddle") 20-30	60	
(Monaural.)		
CAPITOL (ST-1292 "Blood on		
the Saddle") 25-35	60	
(Stereo.)		
CAPITOL (SM-1292 "Blood on		
the Saddle") 5-10	78	
CAPITOL (1623 through 2800) 10-20	61-68	
CAPITOL (W-1562 "The Lincoln		
Hymns") 25-30	61	
(Monaural.)		
CAPITOL (SW-1562 "The Lincoln		
Hymns") 30-35	61	
(Stereo.)		
CAPITOL (4004 "Cowboy Favorites") 50-75	53	
(10-inch LP.)		
CORONET 8-12		
HILLTOP 10-15		
LA BREA (8036 "Jamboree") 30-40	62	
PICKWICK/HILLTOP 6-12	66-68	
SHASTA 8-12		
SPIN-O-RAMA 8-12		
Also see KENTON, Stan, and Tex Ritter		

RIVERA, Hector

Singles: 7-inch

BARRY 3-6	66	

LPs: 10/12-inch 33rpm

EPIC 10-15	61	
WING 10-15	60	

RIVERS, Joan

LPs: 10/12-inch 33rpm

BUDDAH 5-10	69	
GEFFEN 5-8	83	
WARNER 10-15	65	

RIVERS, Johnny
(Johnny Ramistella)

Singles: 7-inch

ATLANTIC 3-5	74	
BIG TREE 3-5	77-78	
CAPITOL 4-8	62-64	
CHANCELLOR 8-12	61-62	
CORAL 5-10	64	
CUB (9047 "Everyday") 10-20	59	
CUB (9058 "Answer Me My Love") .. 10-15	60	
DEE DEE 10-15	59	
EPIC 3-5	75-76	
ERA 5-10	61	
GONE (5026 "Baby Come Back") ... 20-30	58	
GUYDEN (2003 "Hole in the Ground") 10-15	58	
GUYDEN (2110 "Hole in the Ground") .. 4-8	64	
IMPERIAL 4-8	64-70	
MGM 5-8	64	
RSO 3-5	80	
RIVERAIRE 10-20	59	
ROULETTE (4565 "Baby Come Back") 8-12	64	
ROWE/AMI 5-10	66	
("Play Me" Sales Stimulator promotional issue.)		
SOUL CITY (Except 008) 3-5	76-77	
SOUL CITY (008 "Slow Dancing") 4-8	77	
U.A. (Except 700 series) 3-5	71-73	
U.A. (700 series) 4-8	64	

Picture Sleeves

IMPERIAL 5-10	64-69	
U.A. 3-5	71	

LPs: 10/12-inch 33rpm

ATLANTIC 8-10	74	
BIG TREE 8-10	77	
CAPITOL (T-2161 "Sensational		
Johnny Rivers") 35-50	64	
(Monaural.)		
CAPITOL (ST-2161 "Sensational		
Johnny Rivers") 50-75	64	
(Stereo.)		
CUSTOM 8-12		
EPIC 8-10	75	
GUEST STAR 10-15	64	
IMPERIAL 10-20	64-70	
LIBERTY 5-8	82	
PICKWICK 8-10		
PRIORITY 5-8	83	
RSO 5-10	80	
SEARS (417 "Mr. Teenage") 20-30		
(Special Products issue for Sears stores)		
SOUL CITY 8-10	77	
SUNSET 8-12	67-69	
U.A. (Except UAL, UAS		
and UXS series) 5-10	73-75	

U.A. (UAL-3386 "Go Johnny Go") . . . 20-25   64
(Monaural.)
U.A. (UAS-6386 "Go Johnny Go") . . . 20-30   64
(Stereo.)
U.A. (UAS-5532 "Homegrown") 10-15   71
U.A. (UAS-5650 "L.A. Reggae") 10-15   72
U.A. (UXS-93 "Johnny Rivers") 12-15   72
  Also see JONES, Tom / Freddie and the Dreamers / Johnny
  Rivers
  Also see RAMISTELLA, Johnny
  Also see WILSON, Brian

RIVERS, Johnny / Ricky Nelson / Randy Sparks

LPs: 10/12–inch 33rpm

MGM (E-4256 "Johnny Rivers, Ricky Nelson,
Randy Sparks") 20-25   64
(Monaural.)
MGM (SE-4256 "Johnny Rivers, Ricky Nelson,
Randy Sparks") 20-30   64
(Stereo.)
  Also see NELSON, Ricky
  Also see RASCALS / Buggs / Four Seasons / Johnny Rivers
  Also see RIVERS, Johnny
  Also see SIMON, Paul

RIVERS, Johnny / 4 Seasons / Jerry Butler / Jimmy Soul

LPs: 10/12–inch 33rpm

GLADWYNNE (2004 "Shindig
Hullabaloo Spectacular") 10-20   65
  Also see BUTLER, Jerry
  Also see 4 SEASONS
  Also see SOUL, Jimmy

RIVIERAS

Singles: 7–inch

COED (503 "Count Every Star") 20-25   58
COED (508 "Moonlight Serenade") . . 20-25   58
COED (513 through 561 10-20   59-61
COED (592 "Moonlight Cocktails") 5-10   64
COLLECTABLES 2-4
ERIC 2-4
LOST-NITE 3-5

LPs: 10/12–inch 33rpm

POST 10-15
  Members: Ronald Cook; Homer Dunn; Andy Jones; Charles
  Allen.

RIVIERAS

Singles: 7–inch

LANA 2-4
RIVIERA 5-10   63-65

LPs: 10/12–inch 33rpm

RIVIERA (701 "Campus Party") 50-100   64
USA (102 "Let's Have a Party") 50-100   64
  Members: Marty Fortson; Paul Dennert; Otto Nuss; Doug Gean;
  Joe Pennell.

RIVINGTONS

Singles: 7–inch

A.R.E. AMERICAN 10-15   64
BATON MASTER 4-8
COLUMBIA 5-10   66

J.D 3-5   76
LADERA 3-5
LIBERTY (Except 55610) 5-10   62-64
LIBERTY (55610 "Cherry") 20-30   63
QUAN 4-8   67
RCA 4-8   69
REPRISE 4-8   64
VEE JAY 4-8   64-65
WAND 3-5   73

Picture Sleeves

LIBERTY (55553 "The Bird's
the Word") 15-25   63

LPs: 10/12–inch 33rpm

LIBERTY (3282 "Doin' the Bird") 50-60   63
(Monaural.)
LIBERTY (7282 "Doin' the Bird") 50-75   63
(Stereo.)
LIBERTY (10184 "Papa-Oom
Mow-Mow") 5-10   82
  Members: Carl White; Al Frazier; Sonny Harris; Turner Wilson;
  Darryl White.

RIX, Jerry

Singles: 7–inch

A.V.I. 3-5   77

ROAD

Singles: 7–inch

KAMA SUTRA 4-6   68-71
NATURAL RESOURCES 3-5   72

LPs: 10/12–inch 33rpm

KAMA SUTRA 10-15   69-71
NATURAL RESOURCES 10-12   72
  Members: Jerry Hudson; Phil Hudson; Joseph Hesse; Jim
  Hesse; Ralph Parker; Nick Distefano.

ROAD APPLES

Singles: 7–inch

MUMS 3-5   75
POLYDOR 3-5   75

ROB BASE and D.J. EZ-Rock
(Rob Base)

Singles: 7–inch

PROFILE 2-4   88

LPs: 10/12–inch 33rpm

PROFILE 5-8   88

ROBBINS, Marty

Singles: 78rpm

COLUMBIA 5-15   52-58

Singles: 7–inch

COLUMBIA (02000 and 03000 series) . 2-4   81-83
COLUMBIA (10305 through 11425) . . . 3-5   76-81
COLUMBIA (20965 through 21324) . . 15-30   52-54
COLUMBIA (21351 "That's All Right") 25-35   54
COLUMBIA (21352 through 21414) . . 10-15   54-55
COLUMBIA (21446 "Maybellene") . . . 25-35   55
COLUMBIA (21461 "Pretty Mama") . . 20-30   55
COLUMBIA (21477 "Tennessee
Toddy") 30-40   56

COLUMBIA (21508 "Singing the
Blues") 10-20   56
COLUMBIA (21545 "Singing the
Blues") 10-15   56
COLUMBIA (30000 series) 10-20   60
(Compact 33 stereo singles.)
COLUMBIA (40679 "Long Tall Sally") . 30-40   56
COLUMBIA (40706 "Respectfully
Miss Brooks") 20-30   56
COLUMBIA (40815 through 41408) . . . 5-15   57-59
COLUMBIA (41511 through 43770) 4-8   59-66
COLUMBIA (43845 through 45775) . . . 3-6   67-73
DECCA 4-6   72
MCA 3-5   73-75

Picture Sleeves

COLUMBIA (40815 through 41408) . . 10-20   57-59
COLUMBIA (41511 through 43770) . . . 5-10   59-66

EPs: 7-Inch 33/45rpm

COLUMBIA (1785 "Marty Robbins") . . 20-40   56
COLUMBIA (2116 "Singing the
Blues") 20-40   56
COLUMBIA (2134 "A White
Sport Coat") 20-30   57
COLUMBIA (2153 "Marty Robbins") . . 15-25   56
COLUMBIA (2808 "Marty Robbins") . . 20-30   57
COLUMBIA (2814 "Marty Robbins") . . 10-20   58
COLUMBIA (9761/9762/9763 "The Song
of Robbins") 10-20   57
(Price is for any of three volumes.)
COLUMBIA (10000 through 14000
series) 10-20   57-60

LPs: 10/12-inch 33rpm

ARTCO (110 "Best of Marty Robbins") 40-50   73
(Covers shows 110, label has 644.)
CANDLELITE 8-12   77
COLUMBIA (15 "Marty's Country") . . . 10-15   69
COLUMBIA (31 "Open-End Columbia
Artists Interviews") 35-50
(Promotional issue only.)
COLUMBIA (32 "Columbia Artists Interviews
with Frank Jones") 50-75
(Includes 42-page booklet. Promotional issue only.)
COLUMBIA (237 "Saddle Tramp") . . . 25-35   66
(Columbia Record Club issue.)
COLUMBIA (445 "Bend in the River") 35-45   68
(Columbia Record Club issue.)
COLUMBIA (890 "Marty Robbins
Gold") 8-10   75
COLUMBIA (976 "The Song
of Robbins") 25-35   57
COLUMBIA (1087 "Song of
the Islands") 25-35   57
COLUMBIA (1189 "Marty Robbins") . . 25-35   58
COLUMBIA (1256 "Return of
the Gunfighter") 15-20   69
(Columbia "Country Star" series.)
COLUMBIA (1325 "Marty's Greatest
Hits") 15-25   59

COLUMBIA (1349 "Gunfighter Ballads
and Trail Songs") 15-25   59
COLUMBIA (1481 "More Gunfighter Ballads
and Trail Songs") 15-25   60
COLUMBIA (1599 "Marty's Greatest
Hits") 15-20   69
(Columbia "Country Star" series issue.)
COLUMBIA (1635 "More Greatest
Hits") 15-25   61
COLUMBIA (1666 "Just a Little
Sentimental") 15-25   61
COLUMBIA (1801 "Marty After
Midnight") 40-50   62
COLUMBIA (1855 "Portrait of Marty") 25-35   62
(With bonus portrait of Marty.)
COLUMBIA (1855 "Portrait of Marty") 15-25   62
(Without bonus portrait of Marty.)
COLUMBIA (1918 "Devil Woman") . . 15-20   62
COLUMBIA (2016 "The Heart of
Marty Robbins") 80-100   69
(Columbia "Country Star" series issue.)
COLUMBIA (2040 "Hawaii's
Calling Me") 20-30   62
COLUMBIA (2072 "Return of
the Gunfighter") 15-20   63
COLUMBIA (2167 "Island Woman") . 35-40   64
COLUMBIA (2220 "R.F.D.") 40-50   64
COLUMBIA (2304 "Turn the Lights
Down Low") 15-25   65
COLUMBIA (2448 "What God
Has Done") 15-20   65
COLUMBIA (2527 "The Drifter") 10-20   66
COLUMBIA (2563 "What God
Has Done") 15-20   69
(Columbia "Country Star" series issue.)
COLUMBIA (2601 "Rock'n Roll'n
Robbins") 500-600   56
(10-inch LP.)
COLUMBIA (2645 "My Kind
of Country") 15-20   67
COLUMBIA (2725 "Tonight Carmen") 10-20   67

COLUMBIA (2735 "Christmas with
Marty Robbins") 20-30   67
COLUMBIA (2762 "More Gunfighter Ballads
and Trail Songs") 15-20   69
(Columbia "Country Star" series issue.)
COLUMBIA (2817 "By The Time I
Get to Phoenix") 20-30   68
COLUMBIA (3557 "The Drifter") 15-20   69
(Columbia "Country Star" series issue.)
COLUMBIA (3867 "My Kind
of Country") 15-20   69
(Columbia "Country Star" series issue.)
COLUMBIA (5489 "Tonight Carmen")   15-20   69
(Columbia "Country Star" series issue.)
COLUMBIA (5498 "Christmas with
Marty Robbins") 15-20   69
(Columbia "Country Star" series issue.)
COLUMBIA (5812 "Marty") 20-40   72
(Five-LP set. Columbia Special Products issue.)
COLUMBIA (6994 "I Walk Alone") ... 15-20   69
(Columbia "Country Star" series issue.)
COLUMBIA (CS-8158 "Gunfighter Ballads
and Trail Songs") 15-25   59
COLUMBIA (PC-8158 "Gunfighter Ballads
and Trail Songs") 5-10
COLUMBIA (CS-8272 "More Gunfighter Ballads
and Trail Songs") 15-25   60
COLUMBIA (PC-8272 "More Gunfighter Ballads
and Trail Songs") 5-10
COLUMBIA (CS-8435 "More Greatest
Hits") 15-20   61
COLUMBIA (PC-8435 "More Greatest
Hits") 5-10
COLUMBIA (8466 "Just a Little
Sentimental") 15-25   61
COLUMBIA (8601 "Marty After
Midnight") 40-50   62
COLUMBIA (8655 "Portrait of Marty")   25-35   62
(With bonus portrait of Marty.)
COLUMBIA (8655 "Portrait of Marty")   15-25   62
(Without bonus portrait.)
COLUMBIA (8718 "Devil Woman") .. 15-20   62
COLUMBIA (8840 "Hawaii's
Calling Me") 20-30   62
COLUMBIA (8872 "Return of
the Gunfighter") 15-20   63
COLUMBIA (8976 "Island Woman") .. 35-40   64
COLUMBIA (CS-9020 "R.F.D.") 40-50   64
COLUMBIA (CSRP-9020 "R.F.D.") 8-10
(Columbia Special Products issue.)
COLUMBIA (9104 "Turn the Lights
Down Low") 20-30   65
COLUMBIA (CS-9248 "What God
Has Done") 15-20   65
COLUMBIA (ACS-9248 "What God
Has Done") 5-10
(Columbia Special Products issue.)
COLUMBIA (9327 "The Drifter") 10-20   66

COLUMBIA (9421 "The Song
of Robbins") 30-40   67
COLUMBIA (9445 "My Kind
of Country") 15-25   67
COLUMBIA (9525 "Tonight Carmen")   10-20   67
COLUMBIA (9535 "Christmas with
Marty Robbins") 10-20   67
COLUMBIA (9617 "By the Time I
Get to Phoenix") 8-12   68
COLUMBIA (9725 "I Walk Alone") 8-15   68
COLUMBIA (9811 "It's a Sin") 20-30   69
COLUMBIA (9978 "My Woman, My Woman,
My Wife") 8-12   70
COLUMBIA (10022 through 10579) ... 8-10   73-75
(Columbia's Limited Edition series. All Have an
"LE" prefix.)
COLUMBIA (10980 "Christmas with
Marty Robbins") 15-20   70
(Columbia Special Products issue.)
COLUMBIA (11222 "Marty's Greatest
Hits") 5-10   75
COLUMBIA (11311 "By the Time I
Get to Phoenix") 5-10   70
(Columbia Special Products issue.)
COLUMBIA (11513 "By the Time I
Get to Phoenix") 15-20   71
(Columbia Special Products issue.)
COLUMBIA (12416 "Marty Robbins'
Own Favorites") 12-15   74
(Special Products issue for Vaseline Hair Tonic.)
COLUMBIA (13358 "Christmas with
Marty Robbins") 5-10   72
(Columbia Special Products issue.)
COLUMBIA (14035 "Legendary
Music Man") 8-12   77
(Columbia Special Products issue.)
COLUMBIA (14613 "Best of Marty
Robbins") 5-10   78
(Columbia Special Products issue.)
COLUMBIA (15594 "Number One
Cowboy") 5-10   81
(Columbia Special Products issue.)
COLUMBIA (15812 "Marty Robbins'
Best") 5-10   82
(Columbia Special Products issue.)
COLUMBIA (16561 "Reflections") 5-10   82
(Columbia Special Products issue.)
COLUMBIA (16578 "Classics") 15-20   83
(Three-LP set. Columbia Special Products issue.)
COLUMBIA (16914 "Country
Classics") 5-10   83
(Columbia Special Products issue.)
COLUMBIA (17120 "Sincerely") 5-10   83
(Columbia Special Products issue.)
COLUMBIA (17136 "Forever Yours") .. 5-10   83
(Columbia Special Products issue.)
COLUMBIA (17137 "That Country
Feeling") 5-10   83
(Columbia Special Products issue.)

COLUMBIA (17138 "Banquet
of Songs") 5-10   83
(Columbia Special Products issue.)
COLUMBIA (17159 "The Great
Marty Robbins") 5-10   83
(Columbia Special Products issue.)
COLUMBIA (17206 "The Legendary
Marty Robbins") 5-10   83
(Columbia Special Products issue.)
COLUMBIA (17209 "Country Cowboy") 5-10   83
(Columbia Special Products issue.)
COLUMBIA (17367 "Song of
the Islands") 5-10   83
(Columbia Special Products issue.)
COLUMBIA (30000 through 40000
series) 5-12 70-86
DECCA 8-12   72
GUSTO/COLUMBIA 8-10   81
HARMONY (Except 31258) 8-15 69-72
HARMONY (31258 "Song of
the Islands") 20-25   72
K-TEL 8-10   77
MCA 6-12 73-74
ORBIT 8-10   84
PICKWICK 5-10
READER'S DIGEST (054 "Greatest
Hits") 20-30   83
(Five-LP set.)
SUNRISE MEDIA 5-10   81
TIME-LIFE 5-10   81
Also see SMITH, Carl / Lefty Frizzell / Marty Robbins

ROBBINS, Marty / Johnny Cash / Ray Price
LPs: 10/12–inch 33rpm
COLUMBIA 8-10   70
Also see CASH, Johnny
Also see PRICE, Ray

ROBBINS, Marty, and Jeanne Pruett
Singles: 7–inch
AUDIOGRAPH 2-4   83
Also see PRUETT, Jeanne
Also see ROBBINS, Marty

ROBBINS, Rockie
Singles: 7–inch
A&M 3-5 79-81
MCA 2-4   85
Picture Sleeves
A&M 3-5   80
LPs: 10/12–inch 33rpm
A&M 5-10 80-81
MCA 5-8   85

ROBBS
Singles: 7–inch
ATLANTIC 4-8   68
DUNHILL 4-8 69-70
MERCURY 5-10 66-67
Picture Sleeves
MERCURY 8-12   67

LPs: 10/12–inch 33rpm
MERCURY (21130 "The Robbs") 20-25   67
(Monaural.)
MERCURY (61130 "The Robbs") 20-30   67
(Stereo.)

ROBERT & JOHNNY
Singles: 78rpm
OLD TOWN 10-15   57
Singles: 7–inch
COLLECTABLES 2-4
OLD TOWN 10-15 57-62
Members: Robert Carr; Johnny Mitchell.

ROBERT & JOHNNY / Fiestas
Singles: 7–inch
ATCO 3-5
Also see FIESTAS
Also see ROBERT & JOHNNY

ROBERTA LEE: see LEE, Roberta

ROBERTINO
Singles: 7–inch
KAPP 4-6   61
LPs: 10/12–inch 33rpm
KAPP 10-20 61-62

ROBERTS, Austin
Singles: 7–inch
ARISTA 3-5   78
CHELSEA 3-5 72-75
COLLECTABLES 2-4
GUSTO 2-4
PHILIPS 4-6 68-71
PRIVATE STOCK 3-5 75-76
LPs: 10/12–inch 33rpm
CHELSEA 8-12 72-73
PRIVATE STOCK 6-10   75

ROBERTS, John
Singles: 7–inch
DUKE 4-8 67-69

ROBERTS, Lea
Singles: 7–inch
MINIT 4-8   69
U.A. 3-5 74-75

ROBERTSON, Don
Singles: 78rpm
CAPITOL 3-5 56-57
Singles: 7–inch
CAPITOL 4-8 56-59
MONUMENT 3-5 66-76
RCA 3-8 61-68
LPs: 10/12–inch 33rpm
RCA 10-15   65

ROBERTSON, Robbie
LPs: 10/12–inch 33rpm
GEFFEN 5-8   87

ROBEY

Singles: 12–inch 33/45rpm

SILVER BLUE 4-6   84-85

Singles: 7–inch

SILVER BLUE 3-5   84-85

ROBIC, Ivo

Singles: 7–inch

LAURIE 4-8   59-60
PHILIPS 3-6   62

ROBIN, Cock: see COCK ROBIN

ROBIN, Tina

Singles: 78rpm

CORAL 5-10   57

Singles: 7–inch

CORAL 5-10   57-59
MERCURY 4-8   61-63

ROBINS

(Robbins)

Singles: 78rpm

ALADDIN (3031 "Don't Like the
  Way You're Doing") 150-200   49
ATCO 5-15   55
CROWN 25-50   54
RCA 25-50   53
RECORDED in HOLLYWOOD (112 "Bayou
  Baby Blues") 100-150   51
RECORDED in HOLLYWOOD (121 "Falling
  Star") 100-150   51
SAVOY 15-25   50
SCORE 20-30   49
SPARK 15-25   54-55
WHIPPET 10-20   56-57

Singles: 7–inch

ARVEE 8-12   60
ATCO (6059 "Smokey Joe's Cafe") .. 15-25   55
CROWN (106 "I Made a Vow") 150-200   54
CROWN (120 "Key to My Heart") .. 150-200   54
GONE (5101 "Baby Love") 15-25   61
KNIGHT (2001 "Quarter to Twelve") . 15-25   58
KNIGHT (2008 "It's Never Too Late") 35-55   58
RCA (5175 "A Fool Such As I") 200-300   53
RCA (5271 "All Night Baby") 175-225   53
RCA (5434 "How Would You Know")175-225   53
RCA (5486 "My Baby Done
  Told Me") 100-150   53
RCA (5489 "Ten Days in Jail") 75-100   53
RCA (5564 "Don't Stop Now") 75-100   53
SPARK (103 "Riot in Cell Block No. 9")40-50   54
SPARK (107 "Framed") 40-50   54
SPARK (110 "If Teardrops
  Were Kisses") 75-125   55
SPARK (113 "One Kiss") 75-125   55
SPARK (116 "I Must Be Dreaming") .. 50-75   55
SPARK (122 "Smokey Joe's Cafe") 100-125   55
WHIPPET (100 "Cherry Lips") 25-35   56
WHIPPET (200 "Cherry Lips") 15-25   56
WHIPPET (201 "Hurt Me") 20-30   56

WHIPPET (203 "Since I First
  Met You") 20-30   56
WHIPPET (206 "A Fool in Love") 20-30   57
WHIPPET (208 "Every Night") 20-30   57
WHIPPET (211 "In My Dreams") ... 20-30   57
WHIPPET (212 "You Wanted Fun") .. 20-30   58

LPs: 10/12–inch 33rpm

GNP/CRESCENDO 5-10   75
WHIPPET (703 "Rock 'N' Roll
  with the Robins") 300-400   58
  Members: Ty Terrell; Bobby Nunn; Carl Gardner; Bill Richards;
  Grady Chapman; H.B. Barnum; Roy Richards; Richard Berry.
  Also see BARNUM, H.B.
  Also see COASTERS
  Also see NUNN, Bobby
  Also see OTIS, Johnny, Quintette, with Little Esther and the
  Robins

ROBINS / Mel Walker and the Bluenotes

Singles: 78rpm

REGENT (1016 "I'm Not Falling
  in Love with You") 25-35   50
  Also see ROBINS

ROBINS, Jimmy

Singles: 7–inch

KENT 4-8   68

ROBINSON, Alvin

Singles: 7–inch

ATCO 4-8   68
BLUE CAT 5-10   65
JOE JONES 4-8   66
RED BIRD 5-10   64
TIGER 4-8   64

ROBINSON, Dutch

Singles: 7–inch

CBS ASSOCIATED 2-4   84-85

ROBINSON, Ed

Singles: 7–inch

COTILLION 3-5   70

ROBINSON, Floyd

Singles: 7–inch

DOT 4-8   61-62
GROOVE 4-8   64
JAMIE 4-8   61
RCA 5-10   59-60
U.A. 5-10   63-66

EPs: 7–inch 33/45rpm

RCA (4350 "Makin' Love") 20-30   59

LPs: 10/12–inch 33rpm

RCA (LPM-2162 "Floyd Robinson") .. 20-30   60
  (Monaural.)
RCA (LSP-2162 "Floyd Robinson") .. 30-40   60
  (Stereo.)

ROBINSON, Freddy

Singles: 7–inch

CHECKER 4-8   66
LIBERTY 3-5   70
LIMELIGHT 5-10   58

MERCURY 5-10   58
PACIFIC JAZZ 3-5   69-70
QUEEN 4-8   61
WORLD PACIFIC 3-5   70
LPs: 10/12-inch 33rpm
ENTERPRISE 8-12   71
PACIFIC JAZZ 10-15   69-70
Also see HOWLING WOLF

ROBINSON, J.P.
Singles: 7-inch
ALSTON 3-6   68-69

ROBINSON, Jackie
Singles: 7-inch
ARIOLA AMERICAN 3-5   76

ROBINSON, Roscoe
(Rosco Robinson)
Singles: 7-inch
ATLANTIC 3-5   69
FAME 3-5   70
PAULA 3-5
SOUND STAGE 7 4-8   67-69
WAND 4-8   66-67

ROBINSON, Smokey
(William Robinson)
Singles: 7-inch
TAMLA 3-5   73-86
MOTOWN 2-4   87-88
LPs: 10/12-inch 33rpm
MOTOWN 5-10   82-90
TAMLA 5-12   73-86
Also see JAMES, Rick, and Friend
Also see MIRACLES
Also see ROSS, Diana, Stevie Wonder, Marvin Gaye & Smokey
    Robinson
Also see TEMPTATIONS
Also see U.S.A. for AFRICA
Also see VANITY / Smokey Robinson

ROBINSON, Smokey, and Barbara Mitchell
Singles: 7-inch
TAMLA 3-5   83
Also see HIGH INERGY
Also see ROBINSON, Smokey

ROBINSON, Stan
Singles: 7-inch
AMY 5-10   60-61
MONUMENT 5-10   59
TOTSY (601 "Start to Jump") 75-100

ROBINSON, Tom, Band
Singles: 7-inch
HARVEST 3-5   78-79
I.R.S. 3-5   80
LPs: 10/12-inch 33rpm
HARVEST 5-10   78-79
I.R.S. 5-8   80

ROBINSON, Vicki Sue
Singles: 12-inch 33/45rpm
PROFILE 8-12   83-84

Singles: 7-inch
PROFILE 2-4   83-84
RCA 3-5   76-77
LPs: 10/12-inch 33rpm
PROFILE 5-8   83
RCA 5-10   76-81

ROBINSON, Wanda
LPs: 10/12-inch 33rpm
PERCEPTION 5-10   71

ROBOTNICK, Alexander
Singles: 7-inch
SIRE 3-5   85

ROCCA, John
Singles: 12-inch 33/45rpm
STREETWISE 4-6   84
Singles: 7-inch
STREETWISE 2-4   84
Also see FREEZ

ROCHELL
Singles: 12-inch 33/45rpm
WARNER 4-6   85
Singles: 7-inch
WARNER 2-4   85

ROCHELL and the Candels
Singles: 7-inch
CHALLENGE (9158 "Each Night") . . . 40-50   62
CHALLENGE (9191 "Let's Run Away
    and Get Married") 15-25   62
COLLECTABLES 2-4
SWINGIN' (623 "Once Upon a Time") 10-15   60
SWINGIN' (634 "So Far Away") 10-15   61
SWINGIN' (640 "Peg O' My Heart") . . 10-15   61
SWINGIN' (652 "Long Time Ago") . . . 10-15   62
Members: Rochell Henderson; Johnny Wyatt.

ROCHES
LPs: 10/12-inch 33rpm
WARNER 5-10   79-82
Members: Maggie Roche; Terre Roche; Suzzy Roche.
Singles: 7-inch
BUDDAH 4-8   68

ROCK FLOWERS
Singles: 7-inch
WHEEL 4-8   71-73
LPs: 10/12-inch 33rpm
WHEEL 10-15   71-72

**ROCK MASTER SCOTT and the Dynamic
Three**
Singles: 12-inch 33/45rpm
REALITY 4-6   84-85
Singles: 7-inch
REALITY 2-4   84-85

ROCK SQUAD
Singles: 12-inch 33/45rpm
TOMMY BOY 4-6   85

ROCK STEADY CREW
Singles: 12–inch 33/45rpm
ATLANTIC 4-6   83-84
Singles: 7–inch
ATLANTIC 2-4   83-84

ROCK-A-TEENS
Singles: 7–inch
DORAN (3515 "Who-Hoo") 40-60   59
ROULETTE (4192 "Who-Hoo") 10-15   59
ROULETTE (4217 "Doggone It Baby") 15-20   60
LPs: 10/12–inch 33rpm
MURRAY HILL 5-10
ROULETTE (R-25109 "Woo-Hoo") . 75-100   60
(Monaural.)
ROULETTE (SR-25109 "Woo-Hoo") 100-125   60
(Stereo.)

ROCKER'S REVENGE
Singles: 12–inch 33/45rpm
STREETWISE 4-6   83-84
Singles: 7–inch
STREETWISE 3-5   82-84

ROCKET
Singles: 12–inch 33/45
QUALITY/RFC 4-6   83
LPs: 10/12–inch 33rpm
QUALITY/RFC 5-8   83

ROCKETS
Singles: 7–inch
RSO 3-5   79
TORTOISE INT'L 3-5   77-78
LPs: 10/12–inch 33rpm
ELEKTRA 5-10   81
RSO 5-10   79-80
TORTOISE INT'L 8-12   77
Also see DETROIT

ROCKIN' Rs
Singles: 7–inch
STEPHENY (1842 "Walking You
to School") 15-25   60
TEMPUS (1507 "Heat") 15-20   59
TEMPUS (1515 "Mustang") 15-20   60
TEMPUS (7541 "The Beat") 20-30   59
VEE JAY 5-10   60

ROCKIN' REBELS
Singles: 7–inch
ABC 3-5   73
ERIC 2-4
ITZY (8 "Wild Weekend") 15-25
STORK (3 "Bongo Blue Beat") 10-15   64
SWAN 8-12   62-63
LPs: 10/12–inch 33rpm
SWAN (509 "Wild Weekend") 50-100   63
Members: Tom Gorman; Paul Balon; Mickey Kipler; Jim Kipler.
Also see BUFFALO REBELS
Also see HOT-TODDYS
Also see REBELS

ROCKINGHAM, David, Trio
Singles: 7–inch
JOSIE 4-8   63-64

ROCKPILE
Singles: 7–inch
COLUMBIA 3-5   80
EPs: 7–inch 33/45rpm
COLUMBIA (1219 "Nick Lowe and
Dave Edmunds") 3-5   80
(Bonus EP, issued with the LP *Seconds of
Pleasure*.)
LPs: 10/12–inch 33rpm
COLUMBIA (36886 "Seconds of
Pleasure") 5-10   80
(Includes the bonus EP, 1219, *Nick Lowe & Dave
Edmunds*.)
Members: Nick Lowe; Dave Edmunds.
Also see CARTER, Carlene
Also see LOWE, Nick, and Dave Edmunds
Also see McCARTNEY, Paul / Rochestra / Who / Rockpile

ROCKWELL
Singles: 12–inch 33/45rpm
MOTOWN 4-6   84-86
Singles: 7–inch
MOTOWN 2-4   84-86
LPs: 10/12–inch 33rpm
MOTOWN 5-8   84-86
Also see JACKSON, Michael

ROCKY FELLERS
Singles: 7–inch
DONNA 5-10   63
PARKWAY 5-10   62
SCEPTER 5-10   62-63
WARNER 4-8   64-65
Picture Sleeves
SCEPTER (1254 "Like the
Big Guys Do") 10-15   63
LPs: 10/12–inch 33rpm
SCEPTER (SP-512 "Killer Joe") 25-35   63
(Monaural.)
SCEPTER (SPS-512 "Killer Joe") ... 30-40   63
(Stereo.)
Members: Eddie; Albert; Tony; Junior; Pop.

ROD
Singles: 7–inch
PRELUDE 3-5   80

RODGERS, Eileen
Singles: 78rpm
COLUMBIA 3-6   56-57
Singles: 7–inch
COLUMBIA 5-10   56-60
KAPP 4-6   61
EPs: 7–inch 33/45rpm
COLUMBIA 5-10   58
LPs: 10/12–inch 33rpm
COLUMBIA 15-25   58
Also see MITCHELL, Guy / Eileen Rodgers

RODGERS, Jimmie

Singles: 78rpm

ROULETTE 5-10	57	

Singles: 7-inch

A&M 3-6	67-70	
ABC 3-5	73	
DOT 4-8	62-67	
EPIC 3-5	71-72	
RCA 3-5	73-75	
ROULETTE (Except "SSR" series) ... 5-10	57-61	
ROULETTE (SSR-4158 "Ring-a-Ling-a-Lario") 10-20	59	
(Stereo.)		
ROULETTE (SSR-4218 "T.L.C.") 10-20	60	
(Stereo.)		
ROULETTE (SSR-8001 "Bo Diddley") 15-25	59	
(Stereo.)		
ROULETTE (SSR-8007 "Froggy Went A-Courtin") 10-20	59	
(Stereo.)		
SCRIMSHAW 3-5	78	

Picture Sleeves

DOT 4-8	62-64	
ROULETTE 8-12	58-61	

EPs: 7-inch 33/45rpm

ROULETTE 10-20	57-60	

LPs: 10/12-inch 33rpm

A&M 8-15	67-70	
DOT 10-20	62-67	
FORUM 10-20	60	
HAMILTON 10-20	64-65	
RCA 8-12	73-75	
ROULETTE (25020 through 25057) . 20-30	57-59	
ROULETTE (R-25071 through R-25199) 10-20	59-63	
(Monaural.)		
ROULETTE (SR-25071 through SR-25199) 15-25	59-63	
(Stereo.)		
ROULETTE (42000 series) 5-10		
SCRIMSHAW 5-10	78	

RODGERS, Michael

Singles: 7-inch

WTG 2-4	88	

RODGERS, Nile

Singles: 12-inch 33/45rpm

WARNER 4-6	85	

Singles: 7-inch

WARNER 2-4	85	

LPs: 10/12-inch 33rpm

MIRAGE 5-10	84	
WARNER 5-8	85	
Also see CHIC		
Also see HONEYDRIPPERS		

RODGERS, Paul

Singles: 7-inch

ATLANTIC 3-5	83	

LPs: 10/12-inch 33rpm

ATLANTIC 5-10	83	
Also see BAD COMPANY		
Also see FIRM		
Also see FREE		

RODNEY-O — JOE COOLEY

LPs: 10/12-inch 33rpm

ATLANTIC 5-8	90	
EGYPT 5-8	89	

RODRIGUEZ, Johnny

Singles: 7-inch

COLUMBIA 3-5	80	
EPIC 3-5	79-84	
MERCURY 3-6	72-79	

Picture Sleeves

MERCURY 3-5	77	

LPs: 10/12-inch 33rpm

EPIC 5-10	80-84	
K-TEL 5-10	77	
MERCURY 5-12	73-79	

RODWAY

(Steve Rodway)

Singles: 7-inch

MILLENNIUM 3-5	82	

LPs: 10/12-inch 33rpm

MILLENNIUM 5-10	82	

ROE, Tommy

(Tommy Roe and the Satins; Tommy Roe and the Flamingos; Tommy Roe and the Roemans)

Singles: 7-inch

ABC 4-8	66-71	
ABC-PAR 5-10	62-66	
JUDD (1018 "Caveman") 15-25	60	
JUDD (1022 "Sheila") 25-45	62	
MCA 2-4		
MCA/CURB 2-4	86	
MGM/SOUTH 3-5	72-73	
MARK IV (001 "Caveman") 25-50	60	
MERCURY 3-5	86	
MONUMENT 3-5	72-77	
ROULETTE 3-5		
TRUMPET (1401 "Caveman") 50-75	60	
WARNER 3-5	78-80	

Picture Sleeves

ABC 4-8	66-70	
ABC-PAR (10362 "Susie Darlin") 8-12	62	

LPs: 10/12-inch 33rpm

ABC (594 through 762) 10-15	67-72	
ABC-PAR (ABC-423 through ABC-574) 20-35	62-66	
(Monaural.)		
ABC-PAR (ABCS-423 through ABCS-575) 25-40	62-66	
(Stereo.)		
ACCORD 5-10	82	
GUSTO 5-10		
MCA 5-10	82	
MONUMENT 8-12	76-77	

ROE, Tommy / Bobby Rydell / Ray Stevens
LPs: 10/12–inch 33rpm
DESIGN (178 "Young Lovers") 15-25   63
  Also see RYDELL, Bobby
  Also see STEVENS, Ray

ROE, Tommy / Al Tornello
LPs: 10/12–inch 33rpm
DIPLOMAT 10-20

ROE, Tommy / Bobby Lee Trammell
LPs: 10/12–inch 33rpm
CROWN 15-20   63
  Also see ROE, Tommy

ROGER
(Roger Featuring Shirley Murdock; Roger Troutman)
Singles: 7–inch
REPRISE 2-4   87-88
WARNER 3-5   81-85

LPs: 10/12–inch 33rpm
REPRISE 5-8   87
WARNER 5-10   81-84
  Also see SCRITTI POLITTI / Roger
  Also see ZAPP

ROGERS, D.J.
Singles: 12–inch 33/45rpm
COLUMBIA 4-8   79
Singles: 7–inch
ARC 3-5   79-80
COLUMBIA 3-5   78-80
RCA 3-5   75-76
LPs: 10/12–inch 33rpm
COLUMBIA 5-10   78-80
RCA 5-10   76-77
SHELTER 5-10   77
  Also see RUSHEN, Patrice, and D.J. Rogers

ROGERS, Dann
Singles: 7–inch
IA 3-5   79

ROGERS, Eric, and His Orchestra
LPs: 10/12–inch 33rpm
LONDON/PHASE 4 5-15   61-66

ROGERS, Jimmy
(Jimmy Rogers and His Trio; Jimmy Rogers and His Rocking Four)
Singles: 78rpm
CHESS 10-25   50-57
Singles: 7–inch
CHESS (1506 "I Used to Have
  a Woman") 50-100   52
CHESS (1519 "The Last Time") 50-100   52
CHESS (1543 "Left Me with
  a Broken Heart") 50-75   53
CHESS (1574 "Chicago Bound") 50-75   54
CHESS (1616 "You're the One") 40-60   55
CHESS (1643 "If It Ain't Me") 40-60   56
CHESS (1659 "One Kiss") 40-60   57
CHESS (1721 "My Last Meal") 20-30   59

LPs: 10/12–inch 33rpm
CHESS 8-12
  Also see WATERS, Muddy

ROGERS, Jimmy, and Freddy King
LPs: 10/12–inch 33rpm
SHELTER 8-10   73
  Also see KING, Freddy
  Also see ROGERS, Jimmy

ROGERS, Julie
Singles: 7–inch
MEGA 3-5   72
MERCURY 4-8   64-66
Picture Sleeves
MERCURY 5-10   65
LPs: 10/12–inch 33rpm
MEGA 5-10   72
MERCURY 15-25   65

ROGERS, Kenny
(Kenneth Rogers)
Singles: 7–inch
CARLTON (454 "That Crazy Feeling") 25-50   58
CARLTON (468 "For You Alone") 25-50   58
KEN-LEE (102 "Jole Blon") 50-100
LIBERTY 2-4   80-86
MERCURY 5-10   66
RCA 2-4   84-86
U.A. 3-5   76-80
Picture Sleeves
LIBERTY 2-4   80-86
RCA 2-4   84-86
U.A. 3-5   76-80
LPs: 10/12–inch 33rpm
LIBERTY 5-10   80-85
MFSL 20-30   81
QSP 5-10   84
RCA 5-8   84-87
REPRISE 5-8   89
U.A. (Except 934) 5-8   76-80
U.A. (934 "The Gambler) 5-10   78
U.A. (934 "The Gambler) 50-75   78
(Picture disc. Promotional issue only. One of a
four-artist, four-LP set.)

Also see CAMPBELL, Glen / Anne Murray / Kenny Rogers / Crystal Gayle
Also see EASTON, Sheena, and Kenny Rogers
Also see U.S.A. for AFRICA

ROGERS, Kenny, and Kim Carnes
Singles: 7–inch
U.A. 3-5   80
Picture Sleeves
U.A. 3-5   80
Also see CARNES, Kim

ROGERS, Kenny, Kim Carnes and James Ingram
Singles: 7–inch
RCA 2-4   84
Also see INGRAM, James
Also see ROGERS, Kenny, and Kim Carnes

ROGERS, Kenny, and Dolly Parton
Singles: 7–inch
RCA 2-4   83-85
Also see PARTON, Dolly

ROGERS, Kenny, and Nickie Ryder
Singles: 7–inch
RCA 2-4   86

ROGERS, Kenny, and the First Edition
Singles: 7–inch
JOLLY ROGER 3-5   72-73
REPRISE 4-8   68-72
LPs: 10/12–inch 33rpm
JOLLY ROGERS 8-12   72-73
REPRISE 10-25   69-72
Members: Kenny Rogers; Mike Settle; Terry Williams; Mickey Jones; Kin Vassey; Mary Arnold.
Also see FIRST EDITION

ROGERS, Kenny, and Dottie West
Singles: 7–inch
U.A. 3-5   78-79
LPs: 10/12–inch 33rpm
U.A. 5-10   78-80
LPs: 10/12–inch 33rpm
Also see ROGERS, Kenny
Also see WEST, Dottie

ROGERS, Lee
Singles: 7–inch
D-TOWN 4-8   64-65
INSTANT 3-5   72
LOADSTONE 3-5   72
MAHS 4-8
PLATINUM SOUND 3-5   79
PREMIUM STUFF 4-8   67
WHEELSVILLE 4-8   66

ROGERS, Roy
(Roy Rogers & Dale Evans; Roy Rogers and the Sons of the Pioneers)
Singles: 78rpm
DECCA 10-20   40-44
RCA 5-15   45-57
Singles: 7–inch
CAPITOL 3-5   70-71

MCA 2-4   80
NEW DISC 8-12   56
RCA (Except 215) 5-15   51-52
RCA (215 "Souvenir Album") 20-40   49
(Boxed set of three colored vinyl 45s.)
20TH FOX 3-5   74-75
EPs: 7–inch 33/45rpm
BLUEBIRD 10-20
RCA (Except 3041) 10-20   50-57
RCA (3041 "Souvenir Album") 25-50   52
LPs: 10/12–inch 33rpm
BLUEBIRD 15-25   59
CAMDEN 10-20   60-75
CAPITOL 10-20   62-72
GOLDEN 10-20   62
PICKWICK 5-10
RCA (1439 "Sweet Hour of Prayer") . 20-30   57
RCA (3041 "Souvenir Album") 30-60   52
(10–inch LP.)
RCA (3168 "Hymns of Faith") 25-45   54
(10–inch LP.)
20TH FOX 5-10   75
WORD 4-8   73-77

ROGERS, Timmie
(Timmie "Oh Yeah" Rogers; Timmie Rogers and the Excelsior Hep Cats; Timmie Rogers and the Stomp Russell Trio; Timmy Rogers; Super Soul Brother Alias Clark Dark.)
Singles: 78rpm
CAMEO 5-15   57-58
CAPITOL 5-10   53
EXCELSIOR 10-20   45
MAJESTIC 10-20   46
MERCURY 10-15   54
REGIS 10-20   45
VARSITY 10-20
Singles: 7–inch
CADET 3-5   71
CAMEO 5-10   57-58
CAPITOL 5-10   53
EPIC 4-8   65-66
MERCURY (70451 "If I Give My Heart to You") 15-25   54
PARKWAY 5-10   60
PARTEE 3-5   73
PHILIPS 4-8   62
SIGNATURE 5-10   60
LPs: 10/12–inch 33rpm
EPIC 15-20   65
PARTEE 10-15   73
PHILIPS 15-20   63

ROLLE, Ralph
Singles: 12–inch 33/45rpm
STREETWISE 4-6   85
Singles: 7–inch
STREETWISE 2-4   85

ROLLERS
Singles: 7–inch

LIBERTY 5-10   61
Member: Al Wilson.
Also see WILSON, Al

ROLLERS
Singles: 7–inch

ARISTA 3-5   79
LPs: 10/12–inch 33rpm

ARISTA 5-10   79
Also see BAY CITY ROLLERS

ROLLIN, Dana
Singles: 7–inch

TOWER 4-8   67

ROLLING STONES
Singles: 12–inch 33/45rpm

ATCO (4616 "Miss You") 10-15   79
ROLLING STONES (70 "Hot Stuff") .. 45-55   76
(Promotional issue only.)
ROLLING STONES (119 "Miss You") . 15-20   78
(Promotional issue only.)
ROLLING STONES (253 "If I Was
a Dancer") 12-15   79
(Promotional issue only.)
ROLLING STONES (367 "Emotional
Rescue") 15-20   80
(Promotional issue only.)
ROLLING STONES (397 "Start
Me Up") 15-20   81
(Promotional issue only. Price includes special
cover.)
ROLLING STONES (574 "She Was
Hot") 12-15   84
(Promotional issue only.)
ROLLING STONES (685 "Undercover
of the Night") 20-25   83
(White label. Promotional issue only.)
ROLLING STONES (685 "Undercover
of the Night") 12-15   83
(Yellow label. Promotional issue only.)
ROLLING STONES (692 "Too Much
Blood") 15-20   85
(Promotional issue only. Price includes special
cover.)
ROLLING STONES (2275 "Harlem
Shuffle") 8-10   86
(Price includes special cover.)
ROLLING STONES (2275 "Harlem
Shuffle") 10-12   86
(Promotional issue only. Price includes special
cover.)
ROLLING STONES (2340 "One Hit") .. 8-10   86
(Price includes color cover.)
ROLLING STONES (2340 "One Hit") . 20-25   86
(Price includes black and white cover. Promotional
issue only.)
ROLLING STONES (4609 "Miss You") 8-10   78
(Price includes special cover.)

ROLLING STONES (4616 "Miss You"/
"Hot Stuff") 12-15   78
ROLLING STONES (96902 "Too
Much Blood") 8-10   85
(Price includes special cover.)
ROLLING STONES (96978 "Undercover of
the Night") 8-10   83
(Price includes special cover.)
Singles: 7–inch

ABKCO (4701 "I Don't Know Why") 4-8   75
ABKCO (4702 "Out of Time") 4-8   75
LONDON (901 through 910) 3-6   66-69
LONDON (9641 "Stoned") 500-1000   64
LONDON (9657 "Not Fade Away") ... 8-12   64
(Purple and white label.)
LONDON (9657 "Not Fade Away") 4-6   65
(Blue and white swirl label.)
LONDON (9682 "Tell Me") 5-10   64
(Purple and white label.)
LONDON (9682 "Tell Me") 4-6   65
(Blue and white swirl label.)
LONDON (9687 "It's All Over Now") .. 5-10   64
(Purple and white label.)
LONDON (9687 "It's All Over Now") ... 4-6   65
(Blue and white swirl label.)
LONDON (9708 "Time Is on My Side") 5-10   64
(Purple and white label.)
LONDON (9708 "Time Is on My Side") . 4-6   65
(Blue and white swirl label.)
LONDON (9725 "Heart of Stone") 5-10   65
(Purple and white label.)
LONDON (9725 "Heart of Stone") 4-6   65
(Blue and white swirl label.)
LONDON (9741 "The Last Time") 5-10   65
(Purple and white label.)
LONDON (9741 "The Last Time") 4-6   65
(Blue and white swirl label.)
LONDON (9766 "Satisfaction") 5-10   65
LONDON (9792 "Get off of My Cloud") 5-10   65
LONDON (9808 "As Tears Go By") ... 5-10   65
LONDON (9823 "19th Nervous
Breakdown") 5-10   66
ROLLING STONES (Except 99724) .. 3-5   71-86
ROLLING STONES (99724 "Miss
You"/"Too Tough") 10-15   78
Picture Sleeves

LONDON (901 "Paint It Black") 10-20   66
LONDON (902 "Mother's
Little Helper") 10-20   66
LONDON (903 "Have You Seen Your
Mother Baby, Standing in
the Shadows") 15-20   66
LONDON (904 "Ruby Tuesday") 10-20   67
LONDON (905 "Dandelion") 80-100   67
LONDON (906 "She's a Rainbow") .. 10-20   67
LONDON (908 "Jumpin' Jack Flash") 10-15   68
LONDON (909 "Street Fighting
Man") 2500-3500   68
LONDON (910 "Honky Tonk Women") 10-15   69

LONDON (9657 "Not Fade Away") . . . 50-75   64
LONDON (9682 "Tell Me") 40-60   64
LONDON (9687 "It's All Over Now") . . 30-50   64
LONDON (9708 "Time Is on My Side") 25-35   64
LONDON (9725 "Heart of Stone") . 150-250   65
LONDON (9741 "The Last Time") . . . 25-35   65
LONDON (9766 "Satisfaction") 40-60   65
LONDON (9808 "As Tears Go By") . . 15-20   65
LONDON (9823 "19th Nervous
  Breakdown") 15-25   66
ROLLING STONES (Except 228, 316
  and 19309) 3-5   78-86
ROLLING STONES (228 "Time Waits
  for No One") 15-25   76
  (Promotional issue only.)
ROLLING STONES (316 "Before They
  Make Me Run") 15-25   78
  (Promotional issue only.)
ROLLING STONES (19309 "Beast of
  Burden") 300-400   78

Promotional Singles

ABKCO (4701 "I Don't Know Why") . . . 5-10   75
ABKCO (4702 "Out of Time") 5-10   75
LONDON (901 through 910) . . . 15-25   66-69
LONDON (9641 "Stoned") 400-500   64
LONDON (9657 "Not Fade Away") . . . 40-60   64
LONDON (9682 "Tell Me") 15-25   64
LONDON (9687 "It's All Over Now") . . 15-25   64
LONDON (9708 "Time Is on My Side") 15-25   64
LONDON (9725 "Heart of Stone") . . . 15-25   65
LONDON (9741 "The Last Time") . . . 15-25   65
LONDON (9766 "Satisfaction") 10-20   65
LONDON (9792 "Get off of My Cloud") 10-20   65
LONDON (9808 "As Tears Go By") . . 10-20   65
LONDON (9823 "19th Nervous
  Breakdown") 10-20   66
ROLLING STONES (228 "Time Waits
  for No One") 15-25   76
ROLLING STONES (316 "Before They
  Make Me Run") 15-25   78
ROLLING STONES (05000 series) . . . 5-10   86
ROLLING STONES (19000 through 21301,
  except 19307) 6-10   71-82
ROLLING STONES (19307 "Miss You"/
  Far Away Eyes") 5-10   78
ROLLING STONES (19307 "Far Away Eyes"/
  Far Away Eyes") 50-75   78
ROLLING STONES (90000 series,
  except 99724) 4-6   82-85
ROLLING STONES (99724 "Miss
  You"/"Miss You") 10-20   78

EPs: 7–inch 33/45rpm

ATLANTIC (900 "Exile on
  Main Street") 35-45   72
  (Jukebox issue only.)
ATLANTIC (5901 "Goats Head Soup") 35-45   73
  (Jukebox issue only.)
LONDON (34 "Rolling Stones Now") 100-150   64
  (Jukebox issue only.)

LONDON (37 "Out of Our Heads")   100-150   64
  (Jukebox issue only.)
LONDON (43 "December's
  Children") 100-150   64
  (Jukebox issue only.)
LONDON (54 "Their Satanic
  Majesties Request") 100-200   64
  (Jukebox issue only.)
ROLLING STONES (287 "The
  Rolling Stones") 35-45   77
  (Promotional issue only.)

LPs: 10/12–inch 33rpm

ABKCO (ANA-1 "Metamorphosis") . . 15-20   75
ABKCO (MPD-1 "Songs of the
  Rolling Stones") 150-200   75
  (Promotional issue only.)
ABKCO (0268 "Greatest Hits") 20-25   75
  (TV mail-order offer.)
ABKCO (1218 "Singles Collection") . . 15-25   89
  (Four-LP set.)
CRAWDADDY ("Rolling Stones
  Tour Special") 150-200   76
  (Promotional issue to college radio stations only.)
D.I.R. (312 "King Biscuit
  Flower Hour") 150-200   80
  (Promotional issue only.)
D.I.R. (325 "King Biscuit
  Flower Hour") 150-200   80
  (Promotional issue only.)
INS RADIO (1003 "It's Here Luv") . . 75-125   65
LONDON (1 "Big Hits") 15-25   66
  (Monaural.)
LONDON (2 "Their Satanic
  Majesties Request") 50-100   67
  (Monaural. Has 3-D cover.)
LONDON (2 "Their Satanic
  Majesties Request") 20-30   67
  (Stereo.)
  (With 3-D cover.)
LONDON (2 "Their Satanic
  Majesties Request") 10-15   70
  (Stereo.)
  (With standard cover.)
LONDON (3 "Through the Past
  Darkly") 8-10   69
LONDON (4 "Let It Bleed") 10-20   69
  (With bonus poster.)
LONDON (4 "Let It Bleed") 8-10   69
  (Without poster.)
LONDON (5 "Get Your Ya-Yas
  Out") 8-10   70
LONDON (375 "The Rolling
  Stones") 30-50   64
  (Stereo. Add $75 to $100 if accompanied by a 12"
  x 12" bonus, color photo. Cover has printed note
  about photo at lower left. With "Full Frequency
  Range Recording" label.)

LONDON (375 "The Rolling
Stones") 8-10   65
(No mention of photo on cover. Does not have "Full
Frequency Range Recording" on label.)
LONDON (402 "12 x 5") 30-50   64
(Stereo. With "Full Frequency Range Recording"
label.)
LONDON (402 "12 x 5") 8-10   65
(Does not have "Full Frequency Range Recording"
on label.)
LONDON (420 "Rolling Stones Now") 30-50   65
(Stereo. With "Full Frequency Range Recording"
label.)
LONDON (420 "Rolling Stones Now") . 8-10   65
(Does not have "Full Frequency Range Recording"
on label.)
LONDON (429 "Out of Our Heads") . . 30-50   65
(Stereo. With "Full Frequency Range Recording"
label.)
LONDON (429 "Out of Our Heads") . . . 8-10   65
(Does not have "Full Frequency Range Recording"
on label.)
LONDON (451 "December's
Children") 30-50   65
(Stereo. With "Full Frequency Range Recording"
label.)
LONDON (451 "December's Children") 8-10   65
(Does not have "Full Frequency Range Recording"
on label.)
LONDON (476 "Aftermath") 8-10   66
(Stereo.)
LONDON (493 "Got Live If You
Want It") 8-10   66
(Stereo.)
LONDON (499 "Between the Buttons") 8-10   67
(Stereo.)
LONDON (509 "Flowers") 8-10   67
(Stereo.)
LONDON (539 "Beggars Banquet") . . . 8-10   68
(All songs are shown as written by Jagger and
Richard.)
LONDON (539 "Beggars Banquet") . . . 8-10   68
(*Prodigal Son* is shown as written by Rev. Wilkins.)
LONDON (606/7 "Hot Rocks") 10-12   71
LONDON (626/7 "More Hot Rocks") . 10-12   72
LONDON (3375 "The Rolling
Stones") 75-100   64
(Monaural. With "Full Frequency Range
Recording" label. Add $75 to $100 if accompanied
by a 12" x 12" bonus, color photo. Cover has
printed note about photo at lower left.)
LONDON (3375 "The Rolling Stones") 30-40   65
(Does not have "Full Frequency Range Recording"
on label.)
LONDON (3375 "The Rolling
Stones") 400-600   64
(White label, monaural. Promotional issue only.)

LONDON (3402 "12 x 5") 50-75   64
(Monaural. With "Full Frequency Range
Recording" label.)
LONDON (3402 "12 x 5") 30-40   65
(Does not have "Full Frequency Range Recording"
on label.)
LONDON (3420 "Rolling Stones
Now") 50-75   65
(Monaural. With "Full Frequency Range
Recording" label.)
LONDON (3420 "Rolling Stones Now") 30-40   65
(Does not have "Full Frequency Range Recording"
on label.)
LONDON (3429 "Out of Our Heads") 50-75   65
(Monaural. With "Full Frequency Range
Recording" label.)
LONDON (3429 "Out of Our Heads") 30-40   65
(Does not have "Full Frequency Range Recording"
on label.)
LONDON (3451 "December's
Children") 50-75   65
(Monaural. With "Full Frequency Range
Recording" label.)
LONDON (3451 "December's
Children") 30-40   65
(Does not have "Full Frequency Range Recording"
on label.)
LONDON (3476 "Aftermath") 20-30   66
(Monaural.)
LONDON (3493 "Got Live If You
Want It") 20-30   66
(Monaural.)
LONDON (3499 "Between the
Buttons") 20-30   67
(Monaural.)
LONDON (3509 "Flowers") 20-30   67
(Monaural.)
MFSL (1 "Rolling Stones") 250-300   85
(11-LP boxed set, includes booklet, postcard and
alignment tool.)
MFSL (060 "Sticky Fingers") 20-40   82
MFSL (087 "Some Girls") 20-40   82
MUTUAL BROADCASTING SYSTEM ("The Rolling
Stones: Past and Present") 800-1200   84
(12-LP boxed set, issued only to radio stations.
Price includes programming sheets.)
ROLLING STONES (2900 "Exile on
Main St.") 10-15   72
(Add $3 to $5 if accompanied by sheet of 12 bonus
postcards.)
ROLLING STONES (9001 "Love You
Live") 10-15   77
ROLLING STONES (16015 "Emotional
Rescue") 5-10   80
ROLLING STONES (16028 "Sucking in
the Seventies") 5-10   81
ROLLING STONES (16052 "Tattoo
You") 5-10   81

ROLLING STONES (39108 "Some
Girls") 10-15   78
(With all girls' faces shown.)
ROLLING STONES (39108 "Some
Girls") 5-10   78
(Not all girls' faces shown. Cover is "Under
Construction.")
ROLLING STONES (39113 "Still Life") . 5-10   82
ROLLING STONES (40250 "Dirty
Work") 5-10   86
ROLLING STONES (45333 "Steel
Wheels") 5-10   89
ROLLING STONES (59100 "Sticky
Fingers") 8-10   71
(Yellow label.)
ROLLING STONES (59100 "Sticky
Fingers") 150-250   71
(White label. Promotional issue only.)
ROLLING STONES (59101 "Goats
Head Soup") 8-10   73
ROLLING STONES (79101 "It's Only
Rock and Roll") 8-10   74
ROLLING STONES (79102 "Made in
the Shade") 8-10   75
ROLLING STONES (79104 "Black
and Blue") 8-10   76
ROLLING STONES (90120
"Undercover") 5-10   83
ROLLING STONES (90176 "Rewind") . 5-10   84
WESTWOOD ONE ("The Rolling
Stones Special") 175-225   82
(Promotional issue only.)
Members: Mick Jagger; Keith Richards; Bill Wyman; Brian
Jones; Charlie Watts; Mick Taylor; Ron Wood.
   Also see BEACH BOYS
   Also see FAITHFUL, Marianne
   Also see HOPKINS, Nicky
   Also soo JAGGER, Mick
   Also see JONES, Brian
   Also see TAYLOR, Mick
   Also see WILLIE and the Poor Boys
   Also see WOOD, Ron
   Also see WYMAN, Bill

ROMAN HOLIDAY
Singles: 7–inch
JIVE 2-4   83-85
LPs: 10/12–inch 33rpm
JIVE 5-10   83

ROMANTICS
Singles: 12–inch 33/45rpm
NEMPEROR 4-8   83-85
Singles: 7–inch
BOMP 4-6   78
NEMPEROR 3-5   80-85
SPIDER 8-12   77
EPs: 7–inch 33/45rpm
BOMP 5-8   78
LPs: 10/12–inch 33rpm
NEMPEROR 5-10   80-85

ROMEO & JULIET
Singles: 7–inch
CAPITOL 3-5   69

ROMEO VOID
Singles: 12–inch 33/45rpm
COLUMBIA 4-6   82-84
Singles: 7–inch
COLUMBIA 2-4   82-84
LPs: 10/12–inch 33rpm
COLUMBIA 5-8   82-84
415 8-10   82

ROMEO'S DAUGHTER
LPs: 10/12–inch 33rpm
JIVE 5-8   88

ROMEOS
Singles: 7–inch
MARK II 4-8   67
LPs: 10/12–inch 33rpm
MARK II 15-20   67
Members: Kenny Gamble; Thom Bell; Roland Chambers; Winnie
Walford; Karl Chambers.

RON & BILL
Singles: 7–inch
ARGO (5350 "It") 25-35   59
TAMLA (54025 "It") 35-45   60
Members: Ron White; Bill "Smokey" Robinson.
   Also see MIRACLES

RONDELLS
(Ron-Dells; Rondels)
Singles: 7–inch
ABC-PAR 4-8   65
DOT (16000 series) 8-12   63-64
DOT (17000 series) 4-8   70
SHALIMAR 8-12   63
XPRESS 5-10

RONDELS
Singles: 7–inch
AMY 8-12   61-62
NOTE 8-12   61

RONDO, Don
Singles: 78rpm
DECCA 3-5   55
JUBILEE 3-5   56-57
Singles: 7–inch
ATLANTIC 4-8   63
CARLTON 4-8   60-61
DECCA 5-10   55
JUBILEE 5-10   56-66
ROULETTE 4-8   59-60
TRIP 3-5
TUBA 4-6   65
U.A. 4-6   66-67
VIRGO 3-5   72
LPs: 10/12–inch 33rpm
JUBILEE 10-20   57-58
VOCALION 5-10   70

RONETTES
(Ronnettes)

Singles: 7–inch

A&M	5-10	69
BUDDAH	5-10	73-74
COLPIX (646 "I'm Gonna Quit While I'm Ahead")	30-40	62
MAY (114 "Silhouettes")	30-40	63
MAY (138 "The Memory")	30-40	63
PAVILLION	3-5	82
PHILLES	10-15	63-66

Promotional Singles

A&M	8-12	69
BUDDAH	10-15	73-74
COLPIX (646 "I'm Gonna Quit While I'm Ahead")	30-40	62
MAY (114 "Silhouettes")	30-40	63
MAY (138 "The Memory")	30-40	63
PAVILLION	4-8	82
PHILLES	10-20	63-66

Picture Sleeves

PHILLES (123 "Walking in the Rain")	25-35	64
PHILLES (126 "Born to Be Together")	25-35	65
PHILLES (128 "Is This What I Get for Loving You")	25-40	65

LPs: 10/12–inch 33rpm

COLPIX (486 "The Ronettes, Featuring Veronica") (Blue label. Monaural.)	50-100	65
COLPIX (486 "The Ronettes, Featuring Veronica") (Gold label. Monaural.)	75-150	65
COLPIX (486 "The Ronettes, Featuring Veronica") (Blue label. Stereo.)	60-75	65
COLPIX (486 "The Ronettes, Featuring Veronica") (Gold label. Stereo.)	100-200	65
COLPIX (486 "The Ronettes, Featuring Veronica") (White label. Promotional issue only.)	75-100	65
PHILLES (4006 "Presenting the Fabulous Ronettes") (Blue label. Monaural.)	100-125	64
PHILLES (4006 "Presenting the Fabulous Ronettes") (Yellow label. Monaural.)	75-150	64
PHILLES (4006 "Presenting the Fabulous Ronettes") (Yellow label with red print. Stereo.)	200-300	64
PHILLES (4006 "Presenting the Fabulous Ronettes") (Yellow label with black print. Stereo issue through Capitol Record Club.)	200-250	64
MURRAY HILL	5-10	86

Members: Veronica Bennett-Spector; Estelle Bennett; Nedra Talley-Ross.
Also see RONNIE and the Relatives
Also see SPECTOR, Ronnie

RONETTES / Crystals / Darlene Love
Singles: 7–inch

PAVILLION (1354 "Phil Spector's Christmas Medley") (Promotional issue only.)	3-5	81

RONETTES / Crystals / Darlene Love / Bob B. Soxx and the Blue Jeans
EPs: 7–inch 33/45rpm

PHILLES ("Christmas EP")	20-40	63

LPs: 10/12–inch 33rpm

APPLE (3400 "Phil Spector's Christmas Album")	10-12	72
PASSPORT (3604 "Phil Spector's Christmas Album")	5-8	85
PAVILLION	5-10	81
PHILLES (4005 "A Christmas Gift for You") (Blue label.)	50-100	63
PHILLES (4005 "A Christmas Gift for You") (Yellow and red label.)	40-60	63
WARNER/SPECTOR	8-12	

Phil Spector is heard speaking on this LP. The Apple and Passport LPs are reissues of the Philles album.
Also see BOB. B. SOXX and the Blue Jeans
Also see CRYSTALS
Also see LOVE, Darlene
Also see RONETTES

RONNIE and the Hi-Lites
Singles: 7–inch

ABC-PAR	10-15	65
COLLECTABLES	2-4	
ERIC	2-4	
JOY	10-15	62
RAVEN (8000 "Valerie") (Black label.)	10-15	63
RAVEN (8000 "Valerie") (White label. Promotional issue only.)	15-25	63
WIN	10-15	63

RONNIE and the Relatives
(Ronnettes)
Singles: 7–inch

COLPIX (601 "I Want a Boy")	30-40	61

MAY (111 "My Guiding Angel") 50-75   62
Also see RONETTES

RONNY and the Daytonas
Singles: 7–inch
MALA 6-12   64-66
RCA 5-10   66-68
SHOW-BIZ 8-12   68
Picture Sleeves
RCA (8896 "All American Girl") 15-25   66
LPs: 10/12–inch 33rpm
MALA (4001 "G.T.O.") 50-100   64
MALA (4002 "Sandy") 20-35   66
(Monaural.)
MALA (4002-S "Sandy") 75-100   66
(Stereo.)
Members: John "Bucky" Wilkin; Buzz Cason.

RONSON, Mick
LPs: 10/12–inch 33rpm
RCA 8-12   74
Also see HUNTER, Ian, and Mick Ronson

RONSTADT, Linda
(Linda Ronstadt and the Stone Poneys)
Singles: 7–inch
ASYLUM 2-5   73-85
CAPITOL (2004 "Different Drum") 5-10   67
CAPITOL (2110 "Up to My Neck
in High Muddy Water") 10-15   68
CAPITOL (2195 "Some of
Shelly's Blues") 5-10   68
CAPITOL (2438 "Dolphins") 5-10   69
CAPITOL (2767 "Lovesick Blues") 4-8   70
CAPITOL (2846 through 4050) 3-6   70-75
CAPITOL (5838 "All the
Beautiful Things") 8-12   67
CAPITOL (5910 "Evergreen") 5-10   67
ELEKTRA 3-5   75-78
SIDEWALK (937 "So Fine") 75-100   66
(With Davie Allan.)
Picture Sleeves
ASYLUM 3-5   78-82
CAPITOL (2110 "Up to My Neck
in High Muddy Water") 15-25   68
LPs: 10/12–inch 33rpm
ASYLUM (Except 401 and 60489) 5-10   73-86
ASYLUM (401 "Living in the U.S.A.") . 10-15   78
(Picture disc.)
ASYLUM (60489 "'Round Midnight") . 10-15   86
CAPITOL (208 through 635) 10-15   69-72
CAPITOL (2000 series) 12-18   68
CAPITOL (11000 series) 8-12   74-77
CAPITOL (16000 series) 5-10   80
ELEKTRA 5-10   80-87
MFSL 15-20   85
Also see ALLAN, Davie
Also see CASH, Johnny / Roy Clark / Linda Ronstadt
Also see CHRISTMAS SPIRIT
Also see EAGLES
Also see GLASS, Phillip
Also see NEWMAN, Randy

Also see NITTY GRITTY DIRT BAND and Linda Ronstadt
Also see PARTON, Dolly, Linda Ronstadt, and Emmylou Harris
Also see STONE PONEYS

RONSTADT, Linda, and Emmylou Harris
Singles: 7–inch
ASYLUM 3-5   75
Also see HARRIS, Emmylou

RONSTADT, Linda, and James Ingram
Singles: 7–inch
MCA 3-5   86
Also see INGRAM, James

RONSTADT, Linda, and Aaron Neville
LPs: 10/12–inch 33rpm
ELEKTRA 5-8   89
Also see NEVILLE, Aaron
Also see RONSTADT, Linda

ROOFTOP SINGERS
Singles: 7–inch
ATCO 4-6   67
VANGUARD 4-8   62-65
Picture Sleeves
VANGUARD 5-10   63
LPs: 10/12–inch 33rpm
VANGUARD 10-20   63-65
Members: Erik Darling; Lynne Taylor; Bill Svanoe.
Also see TARRIERS

ROOMATES
Singles: 7–inch
ADDIT (2211 "Making Believe") 10-15   60
CAMEO (233 "A Sunday Kind
of Love") 15-25   62
CANADIAN AMERICAN (166 "My
Heart") 15-25   64
COLLECTABLES 2-4
PHILIPS (40105 "Gee") 10-20   63
PHILIPS (40153 "The Nearness
of You") 20-25   63
PHILIPS (40153 "The Nearness
of You") 15-20   64
PROMO (2211 "Making Believe") ... 10-15   64
VALMOR (8 "Glory of Love") 8-12   61
VALMOR (10 "Band of Gold") 8-12   61
VALMOR (13 "My Foolish Heart") ... 10-15   61
Also see CATHY JEAN and the Roomates

ROQ-IN ZOO
Singles: 12–inch 33/45rpm
MOTOWN 4-6   86
Singles: 7–inch
MOTOWN 2-4   86

ROS, Edmundo, and His Orchestra
Singles: 78rpm
LONDON 3-5   51-57
Singles: 7–inch
LONDON 4-8   51-63
EPs: 7–inch 33/45rpm
CORAL 5-10   54
LONDON 5-10   52-59

LPs: 10/12-inch 33rpm

CORAL	8-15	54
LONDON	5-15	52-78

ROSCOE & MABLE
Singles: 7-inch

CHOCOLATE CITY	3-5	77

ROSE, Andy
(Andy Rose and the Thorns)
Singles: 7-inch

AAMCO	10-20	58
CORAL	5-10	59-62
EMBER	4-8	64
GOLDEN CREST	4-8	64

ROSE, Biff
Singles: 7-inch

BUDDAH	3-5	71
TETRAGRAMMATON	3-5	68-70

LPs: 10/12-inch 33rpm

BUDDAH	8-12	71
TETRAGRAMMATON	10-15	68-69
U.A.	8-12	73

ROSE, David, and His Orchestra
Singles: 78rpm

MGM	3-5	50-57

Singles: 7-inch

CAPITOL	3-6	66-69
MGM	3-8	50-67

Picture Sleeves

MGM	4-8	56-62

EPs: 7-inch 33/45rpm

KAPP	5-10	59
MGM	5-10	51-58
ROYALE	5-10	

LPs: 10/12-inch 33rpm

CAPITOL	8-15	66-69
DINO	5-10	72
KAPP	10-20	59-61
LION	10-20	59
MCA	5-8	83
MGM	5-20	51-70
METRO	5-15	65-66

Also see PREVIN, Andre

ROSE BROTHERS
Singles: 12-inch 33/45rpm

MUSCLE SHOALS	4-6	86

Singles: 7-inch

MUSCLE SHOALS	2-4	86-88

LPs: 10/12-inch 33rpm

MUSCLE SHOALS	5-8	86

Members: Bob Rose; Larry Rose; Kenny Rose; Greg Rose.

ROSE COLORED GLASS
Singles: 7-inch

BANG	3-5	71

ROSE GARDEN
Singles: 7-inch

ATCO	4-8	67-68

LPs: 10/12-inch 33rpm

ATCO	15-20	68

ROSE ROYCE
Singles: 12-inch 33/45rpm

MONTAGE	4-8	84

Singles: 7-inch

C&R	2-4	84
MCA	3-5	76-77
OMNI	2-4	86-87
WHITFIELD	3-5	77-82

LPs: 10/12-inch 33rpm

EPIC	5-8	82
MCA	5-10	76
WHITFIELD	5-10	77-81

ROSE TATOO
Singles: 7-inch

MIRAGE	3-5	80-82

LPs: 10/12-inch 33rpm

MIRAGE	5-10	80-82

ROSELLI, Jimmy
Singles: 7-inch

RIC	4-8	65
U.A.	4-6	65-69

LPs: 10/12-inch 33rpm

RIC	10-15	65
U.A.	5-12	65-72

ROSIE
(Rosie and the Originals)
Singles: 7-inch

ABC	3-5	73
HIGHLAND	10-20	60-61
BRUNSWICK	10-20	61

LPs: 10/12-inch 33rpm

BRUNSWICK (54102 "Lonley Blue Nights") (Monaural.)	40-60	61
BRUNSWICK (754102 "Lonley Blue Nights") (Stereo.)	50-80	61

ROSS, Charlie
Singles: 7-inch

BIG TREE	3-5	75-76

ROSS, Diana
Singles: 12-inch 33/45rpm

MOTOWN	5-10	78-80

Singles: 7-inch

MOTOWN	3-6	70-81
RCA	2-5	81-87

Picture Sleeves

MOTOWN	3-6	70-81

EPs: 7-inch 33/45rpm

MOTOWN (7588 "Sneak Preview from Lady Sings the Blues") (Promotional issue only.)	8-12	72

LPs: 10/12–inch 33rpm
DORAL (104 "Diana Ross") 150-200
(Promotional mail-order issue, from Doral
cigarettes.)
KORY 8-10   77
MOTOWN (100 series) 5-10   81-83
MOTOWN (711 through 907) 8-12   70-78
MOTOWN (923 "The Boss") 5-10   79
(Black vinyl.)
MOTOWN (923 "The Boss") 10-20   79
(Colored vinyl. Promotional issue only.)
MOTOWN (951 through 960) 6-12   81
MOTOWN (5000 series) 5-10   83
MOTOWN (6000 series) 6-12   83-89
PARAMOUNT (181/182 "Lady Sings
the Blues") 35-50   72
(An "MRA Multiple Record Album, serving the
requirements of both radio and TV stations," this
LP has a 15-minute interview with Diana Ross.
Includes scripts. Promotional issue only.)
RCA 5-10   81-87
Also see DENVER, John / Diana Ross
Also see GAYE, Marvin, and Diana Ross
Also see IGLESIAS, Julio, and Diana Ross
Also see SUPREMES
Also see TEMPTATIONS
Also see U.S.A. for AFRICA

ROSS, Diana, and Bill Cosby / Diana Ross with the Jackson Five
EPs: 7–inch 33/45rpm
MOTOWN 5-10   70
Also see COSBY, Bill
Also see JACKSONS

ROSS, Diana, and Michael Jackson
Singles: 7–inch
MCA 3-5   78
Picture Sleeves
MCA 3-5   78
Also see JACKSON, Michael

ROSS, Diana, and Lionel Richie
Singles: 7–inch
MOTOWN 3-5   81
POLYGRAM ("Dreaming of You") 10-15   81
(Promotional issue only. No number given.)
Also see RICHIE, Lionel

ROSS, Diana, Stevie Wonder, Marvin Gaye & Smokey Robinson
Singles: 7–inch
MOTOWN (1455 "Pops, We Love You") 3-5   79
(Black vinyl.)
MOTOWN (1455 "Pops, We Love You") 5-10   79
(Heart shaped disc. Red vinyl.)
MOTOWN (1455 "Pops, We Love You") 5-10   79
(Green vinyl. Promotional issue only.)
LPs: 10/12–inch 33rpm
MOTOWN 5-10   79
Also see DIAMOND, Neil / Diana Ross and the Supremes
Also see GAYE, Marvin
Also see ROBINSON, Smokey

Also see ROSS, Diana
Also see WONDER, Stevie

ROSS, Jack
Singles: 7–inch
DOT 4-8   61-63
ROMAL 5-10   61
LPs: 10/12–inch 33rpm
DOT (3429 "Cinderella") 15-25   62

ROSS, Jackie
Singles: 7–inch
BRUNSWICK 4-8   67-68
CAPITOL 3-5   76
CHESS 4-8   64
FOUNTAIN 4-6   69
GSF 3-5   72-73
MERCURY 3-5   70-71
SCEPTER 3-5   72
LPs: 10/12–inch 33rpm
CHESS (1489 "Full Bloom") 15-25   64

ROSS, Jimmy
Singles: 7–inch
RFC 3-5   81

ROSS, Spencer
Singles: 7–inch
COLUMBIA 4-6   59-60
LPs: 10/12–inch 33rpm
COLUMBIA 10-20   60

ROSSINGTON - COLLINS BAND
Singles: 7–inch
MCA 2-5   80-88
LPs: 10/12–inch 33rpm
MCA 5-10   80-88
Members: Gary Rossington; Al Collins.
Also see LYNYRD SKYNYRD

ROTA, Nino
Singles: 7–inch
PARAMOUNT 3-5   72
U.A. 3-5   72

ROTARY CONNECTION
Singles: 7–inch
CADET CONCEPT 4-6   68-70
LPs: 10/12–inch 33rpm
CADET CONCEPT 15-25   68-70
Member: Minnie Riperton.
Also see NEW ROTARY CONNECTION
Also see RIPPERTON, Minnie

ROTH, David Lee
Singles: 7–inch
WARNER 2-4   85-90
LPs: 10/12–inch 33rpm
WARNER 5-10   85-90
Also see BEACH BOYS
Also see VAN HALEN

ROUGH DIAMOND
Singles: 7–inch
ISLAND 3-5   77

LPs: 10/12–inch 33rpm

ISLAND . . . . 8-10　　77
　Members: Byron Britton; Geoff Britton.
　Also see URIAH HEEP

ROUGH TRADE
Singles: 7–inch
BOARDWALK . . . . 3-5　　82
LPs: 10/12–inch 33rpm
UMBRELLA . . . . 10-15　　77

ROUND ROBIN
Singles: 7–inch
CAPITOL . . . . 4-8　　67
DOMAIN . . . . 5-10　　63-65
SHOT . . . . 4-8　　66
LPs: 10/12–inch 33rpm
CHALLENGE (620 "Land of
　1000 Dances") . . . . 15-25　　65
DOMAIN (101 "Greatest Dance Hits
　Slauson Style") . . . . 25-35　　64

ROUND ROBINS / Joe Cenna
Singles: 7–inch
BELL 4-8

ROUNDTREE
Singles: 12–inch 33/45rpm
ISLAND . . . . 4-8　　78
Singles: 7–inch
ISLAND . . . . 3-5　　78

ROUNDTREE, Richard
Singles: 7–inch
ARTISTS of AMERICA . . . . 3-5　　76
MGM . . . . 3-5　　73
VERVE . . . . 3-5　　72-73
LPs: 10/12–inch 33rpm
MGM . . . . 8-12　　72

ROUSSOS, Demis
Singles: 7–inch
BIG TREE . . . . 3-5　　74-75
MGM . . . . 3-5　　73
MERCURY . . . . 3-5　　76-78
LPs: 10/12–inch 33rpm
BIG TREE . . . . 8-12　　74-75
MGM . . . . 10-15　　72
MERCURY . . . . 5-10　　76-78

ROUTERS
Singles: 7–inch
WARNER . . . . 4-8　　62-64
LPs: 10/12–inch 33rpm
MERCURY . . . . 10-15　　73
WARNER (1490 "Let's Go") . . . . 20-30　　63
WARNER (1524 "1963's Great
　Instrumental Hits") . . . . 20-30　　63
WARNER (1559 "Charge!") . . . . 20-30　　64
WARNER (1595 "Chuck Berry
　Songbook") . . . . 20-30　　65
　Members: Joe Saraceno; Rene Hall; Mike Gordon. Ed Kay.

ROUX, Le: see LE ROUX

ROVER BOYS
Singles: 78rpm
ABC-PAR . . . . 4-8　　56
CORAL . . . . 4-8　　54
Singles: 7–inch
ABC . . . . 3-5　　73
ABC-PAR . . . . 5-10　　56
CORAL . . . . 5-10　　54
RCA . . . . 4-8　　59
U.A. . . . . 4-8　　61
　Member: Billy Albert.

ROVERS
Singles: 7–inch
EPIC . . . . 3-5　　81
LPs: 10/12–inch 33rpm
CLEVELAND INT'L . . . . 5-10　　81-82
　Also see IRISH ROVERS

ROWANS
Singles: 7–inch
ASYLUM . . . . 3-5　　75-76
COLUMBIA . . . . 3-5　　72-73
LPs: 10/12–inch 33rpm
ASYLUM . . . . 8-10　　75-77
COLUMBIA . . . . 10-15　　72
　Members: Peter Rowan; Chris Rowan; Lorin Rowan.
　Also see GARCIA, Jerry
　Also see OLD and in the Way

ROWLES, John
Singles: 7–inch
KAPP . . . . 3-6　　68-71
UNI . . . . 3-6　　68
LPs: 10/12–inch 33rpm
KAPP . . . . 10-15　　69-71

ROXANNE with UTFO
Singles: 12–inch 33/45rpm
SELECT . . . . 4-6　　85
Singles: 7–inch
SELECT . . . . 2-4　　85
　Also see UTFO

ROXY MUSIC
Singles: 7–inch
ATCO . . . . 3-6　　75-80
WARNER . . . . 2-5　　82-83
Promotional Singles
ATCO . . . . 4-8　　75-80
WARNER . . . . 3-5　　82-83
Picture Sleeves
WARNER . . . . 3-5　　82-83
LPs: 10/12–inch 33rpm
ATCO (Except 106 and 8114) . . . . 8-15　　74-83
ATCO (106 "Country Life") . . . . 20-35　　75
　(Cover pictures two women in their underwear.)
ATCO (106 "Country Life") . . . . 8-15　　75
　(The two women are not pictured on cover.)
ATCO (8114 "Manifesto") . . . . 20-25　　75
　(Picture disc. Promotional issue only.)

ATLANTIC 8-10	74	
REPRISE (2114 "Roxy Music") 15-25	72	
WARNER (Except 2696) 5-10	82-83	
WARNER (2696 "For Your Pleasure") 15-25	73	

Member: Bryan Ferry.
Also see ENO, Brian
Also see FERRY, Bryan
Also see MANZANERA, Phil

ROY, Barbara
Singles: 12–inch 33/45rpm

ASCOT 4-6	84

Singles: 7–inch

RCA 2-4	86

Also see ECSTASY, PASSION & PAIN

ROY C.
(Roy Charles Hammond)
Singles: 7–inch

ALAGA 3-5	71	
BLACK HAWK 4-8	65-66	
MERCURY 3-5	73-77	
SHOUT 4-6	66	
UPTOWN 4-6	66	

LPs: 10/12–inch 33rpm

MERCURY 8-12	77

Also see GENIES

ROYAL, Billy Joe
Singles: 7–inch

ALL WOOD 5-10	62	
ATLANTIC (2300 series) 4-8	66	
ATLANTIC (89000 series) 2-4	85-86	
ATLANTIC AMERICA 3-5	86-88	
COLUMBIA (43305 "Down in the Boondocks") 4-8	65	
(Black vinyl.)		
COLUMBIA (43305 "Down in the Boondocks") 10-20	65	
(Colored vinyl. Promotional issue only.)		
COLUMBIA (43390 "I Knew You When") 4-8	65	
(Black vinyl.)		
COLUMBIA (43390 "I Knew You When") 10-20	65	
(Colored vinyl. Promotional issue only.)		
COLUMBIA (43465 through 45620) 4-8	65-72	
FAIRLANE 8-12	61-62	
KAT FAMILY 3-5	81	
MGM/SOUTH 3-5	73	
MERCURY 3-5	80	
PLAYER'S 5-10	65	
PRIVATE STOCK 3-5	78	
SCEPTER 3-5	76	
TOLLIE 5-10	64	

Picture Sleeves

TOLLIE 8-12	64

LPs: 10/12–inch 33rpm

ATLANTIC AMERICA 5-10	86	
BRYLEN 5-10		
COLUMBIA 15-25	65-69	
51 WEST 5-10	83	
KAT FAMILY 5-10	81	

MERCURY 5-10	80	

Also see FARGO, Donna, and Billy Joe Royal

ROYAL GUARDSMEN
Singles: 7–inch

LAURIE 4-8	66-69	

LPs: 10/12–inch 33rpm

LAURIE 10-20	67-68	

Members: Chris Nunley; Barry Winslow.

ROYAL HOUSE
Singles: 7–inch

IDLERS WAR 2-4	88

ROYAL JOKERS
Singles: 78rpm

ATCO 8-12	55-56	
HI-Q 10-15	57	

Singles: 7–inch

ATCO (6052 "You Tickle Me Baby") .. 25-35	55	
ATCO (6062 "Don't Leave Me, Fanny") 20-30	55	
ATCO (6077 "She's Mine, All Mine") . 25-35	55	
FORTUNE (560 "You Tickle Me Baby") 15-20	63	
FORTUNE (840 "Sweet Little Angel") 20-25	57	
HI-Q (5004 "September in the Rain") . 25-30	57	

ROYAL PHILHARMONIC ORCHESTRA
(Conducted by Louis Clark)
Singles: 7–inch

RCA 2-4	81-83	

LPs: 10/12–inch 33rpm

RCA 5-8	81-83	

ROYAL SCOTS DRAGOON GUARDS
Singles: 7–inch

RCA 3-5	72	

LPs: 10/12–inch 33rpm

RCA 5-10	72	

ROYAL TEENS
Singles: 78rpm

ABC-PAR 5-10	57-58	
POWER (215 "Short Shorts") 20-30	57	

Singles: 7–inch

ABC 3-5	73	
ABC-PAR 8-12	57-58	
ALLNEW (1415 "Royal Twist") 10-15	62	
ASTRA 5-10		
CAPITOL 8-12	59-60	
JUBILEE (5418 "Royal Twist") 5-10	62	
MCA 2-4		
MIGHTY (111 "Leotards") 10-15	58	
MIGHTY (112 "Cave Man") 15-25	59	
MIGHTY (200 "My Memories of You") 20-30	58	
MUSICOR 4-8	69-70	
POWER (215 "Short Shorts") 40-00	57	
SWAN (4200 "I'll Love You Till the End of Time") 25-35	65	
TCF 5-10	65	

LPs: 10/12–inch 33rpm

DEMAND 10-15	

MUSICOR 10-15   70
TRU-GEMS 8-10   75
  Members: Bob Gaudio; Al Kooper; Buddy Randell; Joey Villa;
  Billy Crandall; Tom Austin; Tony Grochowski.
  Also see 4 SEASONS
  Also see KOOPER, Al

ROYALCASH
Singles: 12-inch 33/45rpm
SUTRA 4-6   83
Singles: 7-inch
SUTRA 3-5   83

ROYALETTES
Singles: 7-inch
CHANCELLOR 8-12   62-63
MGM 5-10   64-66
ROULETTE 5-10   67
WARNER 5-10   64
LPs: 10/12-inch 33rpm
MGM 15-25   65-66

ROYALS
Singles: 78rpm
FEDERAL (12064 "Every Beat
  of My Heart") 50-75   52
FEDERAL (12077 "Starting from
  Tonight") 50-75   52
FEDERAL (12088 "Moonrise") 40-60   52
FEDERAL (12098 "A Love in
  My Heart") 30-50   52
FEDERAL (12113 "Are You
  Forgetting") 25-50   52
FEDERAL (12121 "The Shrine
  of St. Cecilia") 25-50   53
FEDERAL (12133 "Get It") 15-25   53
FEDERAL (12150 "Hey Miss Fine") .. 15-25   53
FEDERAL (12160 "That's It") 15-25   54
FEDERAL (12169 "Work with
  Me Annie") 20-30   54
Singles: 7-inch
FEDERAL (12064 "Every Beat
  of My Heart") 250-350   52
  (Black vinyl.)
FEDERAL (12064 "Every Beat
  of My Heart") 500-700   52
  (Colored vinyl.)
FEDERAL (12077 "Starting from
  Tonight") 400-500   52
FEDERAL (12088 "Moonrise") 350-400   52
FEDERAL (12098 "A Love in
  My Heart") 300-350   52
FEDERAL (12113 "Are You
  Forgetting") 250-300   52
FEDERAL (12121 "The Shrine
  of St. Cecilia") 250-300   53
FEDERAL (12133 "Get It") 75-100   53
FEDERAL (12150 "Hey Miss Fine") . 60-80   53
FEDERAL (12160 "That's It") 60-80   54
FEDERAL (12169 "Work with
  Me Annie") 40-60   54

FEDERAL (12177 "Give It Up") 25-35   54
  (White label. Test pressing only. Commercial
  copies credit "The Midnighters, Formally Known as
  the Royals.")
GUSTO 3-5
  Federal titles reissued as by the Midnighters are
  found in their section.
  Members: Henry Booth; Hank Ballard; Charles Sutton; Lawson
  Smith; Alonzo Tucker; Sonny Woods.
  Also see BALLARD, Hank
  Also see MIDNIGHTERS

ROYALTONES
Singles: 7-inch
ABC 3-5   73
GOLDISC 10-15   60-61
JUBILEE (Blue label) 5-10   58-59
JUBILEE (Black label) 4-6   62
MALA 4-8   63-64
PENTHOUSE 25-35   59
ROULETTE 3-5   71
VIRGO 3-5   72

ROYALTY
Singles: 7-inch
W.B. 2-4   88

RUBBER BAND
Singles: 7-inch
ABC 4-8   66
COLUMBIA 4-8   66-67
REPRISE 4-8   67

RUBBER RODEO
Singles: 7-inch
MERCURY 3-5   84-85
LPs: 10/12-inch 33rpm
MERCURY 5-10   85

RUBEN and the Jets
(Mothers of Invention)
Singles: 7-inch
VERVE (10632 "Any Way the
  Wind Blows") 20-30   68
VERVE (10632 "Deseri") 20-30   68
LPs: 10/12-inch 33rpm
VERVE (5055 "Crusin' with Ruben
  and the Jets") 30-40   68
  (Issued with three paper inserts, any of which can
  add $15 to $25 to the value.)
  Also see MOTHERS of INVENTION

RUBEN and the Jets
Singles: 7-inch
MERCURY 3-5   73
LPs: 10/12-inch 33rpm
MERCURY 10-12   73
  Member: Ruben Guevara; Johnny Martinez; Tony Duran; Robert
  Zamora; Bob Roberts; Robert Camarena; Jim Sherwood.

RUBETTES
Singles: 7-inch
MCA 3-5   76
POLYDOR 3-5   74-75

LPs: 10/12–inch 33rpm

MCA	6-10	76

RUBICON

Singles: 7–inch

20TH FOX	3-5	78-79

LPs: 10/12–inch 33rpm

20TH FOX	5-10	78-79

Also see SLY and the Family Stone

RUBINOOS

Singles: 12–inch 33/45rpm

WARNER	4-6	83

Singles: 7–inch

BESERKLEY	3-5	77-79
WARNER	2-4	84

Picture Sleeves

BESERKLEY	3-5	77-79

LPs: 10/12–inch 33rpm

BESERKLEY	5-10	77-79

Also see KIHN, Greg, Band / Earthquake / Modern Lovers / Rubinoos
Member: Jon Rubin.

RUBY and the Party Gang

Singles: 7–inch

GAMBLE	3-5	72
LAW-TON	3-5	71

RUBY and the Romantics

Singles: 7–inch

A&M	4-6	69
ABC	4-8	67-68
KAPP	5-10	62-67
MCA	2-4	

Picture Sleeves

KAPP	5-10	63-64

LPs: 10/12–inch 33rpm

ABC	10-20	68
KAPP	15-25	63-67
MCA	5-10	

Members: Ruby Nash; Edward Roberts; Ronald Mosley; Leroy Fann; George Lee.

RUFFIN, David

Singles: 7–inch

CHECK MATE	10-20	61-62
MOTOWN	3-6	69-76
WARNER	2-5	79-80

LPs: 10/12–inch 33rpm

MOTOWN (100 and 200 series)	5-10	82
MOTOWN (600 series)	10-15	69
MOTOWN (700 and 800 series)	8-10	73-76
WARNER	8-10	77-80

Also see HALL, Daryl, John Oates, David Ruffin and Eddie Kendrick
Also see NIGHTINGALE, Maxine, and Jimmy Ruffin
Also see TEMPTATIONS
Also see VOICE MASTERS

RUFFIN, David, and Eddie Kendricks

Singles: 7–inch

RCA	2-4	87-88

Also see KENDRICKS, Eddie

RUFFIN, David and Jimmy
(Ruffin Brothers)

Singles: 7–inch

SOUL	3-6	70

LPs: 10/12–inch 33rpm

MOTOWN	5-10	80
SOUL	10-12	70

Also see RUFFIN, David
Also see RUFFIN, Jimmy

RUFFIN, Jimmy

Singles: 12–inch 33/45rpm

EPIC	4-8	77

Singles: 7–inch

EPIC	2-4	77
MIRACLE	20-25	61
MOTOWN	3-5	
RSO	3-5	80
SOUL	4-6	64-71

LPs: 10/12–inch 33rpm

RSO	5-8	80
SOUL	10-15	67-69

Also see RUFFIN, David and Jimmy

RUFFNER, Mason

LPs: 10/12–inch 33rpm

CBS ASSOC	5-8	87

RUFUS
(Rufus Featuring Chaka Khan)

Singles: 12–inch 33/45rpm

WARNER	4-6	83-84

Singles: 7–inch

ABC	3-5	74-78
ATLANTIC	3-5	74
BEARSVILLE	3-5	75
EPIC	3-5	70-71
MCA (Except picture discs)	2-5	79-81
MCA (9162 "Party 'Til You're Broke")	20-25	81
(Picture disc. Promotional issue only.)		
MCA (9288 "Do You Love		
What You Feel")	20-25	81
(Picture disc. Promotional issue only.)		
WARNER	2-4	83-84

LPs: 10/12–inch 33rpm

ABC (Except picture discs)	8-10	73-78
ABC (AA-1049 "Street Player")	20-25	78
(Picture disc. Promotional issue only.)		
ABC (AA-1098 "Numbers")	15-20	79
(Picture disc. Promotional issue only.)		
COMMAND	8-10	74-75
MCA	5-10	79-82
WARNER	5-8	83

Also see AMERICAN BREED
Also see KHAN, Chaka

RUFUS & CARLA

Singles: 7–inch

SATELLITE	10-15	60
STAX	4-8	64-65

Members: Rufus Thomas; Carla Thomas.
Also see THOMAS, Carla
Also see THOMAS, Rufus

RUGBYS
Singles: 7–inch
AMAZON (Except 1)	4-8	69-70
AMAZON (1 "You, I")	4-8	69
(Black vinyl.)		
AMAZON (1 "You, I")	8-12	69
(Colored vinyl. Promotional issue only.)		
SMASH	5-10	65
TOP DOG	5-10	

LPs: 10/12–inch 33rpm
AMAZON	10-20	70

RUMBLERS
Singles: 7–inch
DOT	5-10	63-64
DOWNEY	10-20	63-65
HIGHLAND (1026 "Intersection")	20-30	62

LPs: 10/12–inch 33rpm
DOT (3509 "Boss")	20-25	63
(Monaural.)		
DOT (25509 "Boss")	25-30	63
(Stereo.)		
DOWNEY (DLP-1001 "Boss")	40-60	63
(Monaural.)		
DOWNEY (DLPS-1001 "Boss")	50-75	63
(Stereo.)		

Members: Adrian Lloyd; Johnny Kirkland; Bob Jones; Wayne Matteson; Mike Kelishes; Greg Crowner.

RUMOUR
Singles: 7–inch
ARISTA	3-5	79
MERCURY	3-5	78

LPs: 10/12–inch 33rpm
ARISTA	5-10	79
MERCURY	8-10	77

Also see PARKER, Graham

RUN - D.M.C.
Singles: 12–inch 33/45rpm
PROFILE	4-6	83-86
QUALITY/RFC	4-6	83

Singles: 7–inch
PROFILE	2-4	83-88

LPs: 10/12–inch 33rpm
PROFILE	5-8	84-90

Members: Joe "Run" Simmons; Daryll McDaniels; Jason Mizell.
Also see AEROSMITH
Also see KING DREAM CHORUS and Holiday Crew
Also see KRUSH GROVE ALL STARS

RUNAWAYS
Singles: 7–inch
MERCURY	4-6	76-77

LPs: 10/12–inch 33rpm
MERCURY	10-15	76-77
RHINO (250 "Little Lost Girls")	5-8	82
RHINO (250 "Little Lost Girls")	10-15	82
(Picture disc.)		

Members: Joan Jett; Cherie Currie; Lita Ford; Sandy West; Vicki Blue.
Also see FORD, Lita
Also see JETT, Joan, and the Blackhearts

RUNDGREN, Todd
(Todd Rundgren's Utopia)
Singles: 7–inch
BEARSVILLE (Except 0003)	3-5	77-83
BEARSVILLE (0003 "I Saw the Light")	5-10	72
(Black vinyl.)		
BEARSVILLE (0003 "I Saw the Light")	10-15	72
(Colored vinyl.)		

LPs: 10/12–inch 33rpm
BEARSVILLE (524 "Todd Rundgren Radio Show")	40-50	
(Promotional issue only.)		
BEARSVILLE (597 "Radio Interview")	120-130	81
(Promotional issue only.)		
BEARSVILLE (788 "Todd Rundgren Radio Sampler")	25-40	79
(Promotional issue only.)		
BEARSVILLE (2066 "Something/ Anything")	10-12	72
BEARSVILLE (2066 "Something/ Anything")	150-200	72
(Colored vinyl. Price includes lyrics insert.)		
BEARSVILLE (2133 "A Wizard/ A True Star")	5-10	73
BEARSVILLE (3522 "Healing")	8-10	81
(Price includes the bonus single, *Time Heals*.)		
BEARSVILLE (6952 "Todd")	12-15	74
(Price includes bonus poster.)		
BEARSVILLE (6957 "Initiation")	8-10	75
BEARSVILLE (6961 "Another Live")	10-12	75
BEARSVILLE (6963 "Faithful")	8-10	76
BEARSVILLE (6965 "Ra")	10-12	77
BEARSVILLE (6970 "Oops, Wrong Planet")	10-12	77
BEARSVILLE (6981 "Hermit of Mink Hollow")	5-8	78
BEARSVILLE (6986 "Back to the Bars")	8-10	78
BEARSVILLE (23732 "Ever Popular Tortured Artist Effect")	5-8	83

Also see NAZZ
Also see RUNT
Also see TYLER, Bonnie
Also see UTOPIA

RUNNER
Singles: 7–inch
ISLAND	3-5	79

LPs: 10/12–inch 33rpm
ISLAND	5-10	79

Members: Steve Gould; Mickie Feat; David Dowle; Allan Merrill.

RUNT
(Featuring Todd Rundgren)
Singles: 7–inch
AMPEX	5-10	70
BEARSVILLE	4-8	71

LPs: 10/12–inch 33rpm
AMPEX (10105 "Runt")	100-150	70
(With *Say No More* and a full-length version of *Baby Let's Swing*.)		

AMPEX (10105 "Runt") 50-100   70
  (Does not have *Say No More*. Has *Baby Let's*
  Swing as part of a medley.)
AMPEX (10116 "The Ballad of
  Todd Rundgren") 50-100   71
WARNER 5-8   85-91
  Also see RUNDGREN, Todd

RUSH
Singles: 7–inch
MERCURY 2-5   75-87
Picture Sleeves
MERCURY 3-5   81
EPs: 7–inch 33/45rpm
MERCURY 5-10   80
LPs: 10/12–inch 33rpm
ATLANTIC 5-8   89
MERCURY (1000 through 4000 series,
  except 1300) 5-8   74-82
MERCURY (1300 "Hemispheres") ... 10-20   78
  (Picture disc.)
MERCURY (7000 series) 8-12   76-81
MERCURY (9000 series) 10-15   76-81
MERCURY (800000 series) 5-8   84-88
  Members: Geddy Lee; Neil Peart; Alex Lifeson.

RUSH, Bobby
Singles: 7–inch
ABC 3-6   68
CHECKER 4-8   67
GALAXY 3-5   71
JEWEL 4-8
PHILADELPHIA INT'L 3-5   79
SALEM 3-6   69
TOP 3-5
LPs: 10/12–inch 33rpm
PHILADELPHIA INT'L 5-10   79

RUSH, Jennifer
Singles: 7–inch
EPIC 2-4   86
LPs: 10/12–inch 33rpm
EPIC 5-8   86-87

RUSH, Jennifer, and Elton John
Singles: 7–inch
EPIC 2-4   87
  Also see JOHN, Elton

RUSH, Merrilee
(Merrilee Rush and the Turnabouts)
Singles: 7–inch
AGP 3-6   69-70
BELL 4-8   68
GTP 4-8   68
MERRILIN 4-8
RURO 4-6
SCEPTER 3-5   71
SPHERE SOUND 3-5
U.A. 3-5   77-78
LPs: 10/12–inch 33rpm
BELL 10-20   68

LIBERTY 5-8   82
U.A. 8-10   77

RUSH, Otis
Singles: 78rpm
COBRA 5-10   56-57
Singles: 7–inch
CHESS 5-10   60
COBRA 10-20   56-59
COTILLION 4-6   69
DUKE 5-10   62
LPs: 10/12–inch 33rpm
BLUE HORIZON 10-15   68-70
BULLFROG 8-10   77
COTILLION 10-15   69
DELMARK 5-10   75-79
  Also see KING, Albert, and Otis Rush

RUSH, Tom
Singles: 7–inch
COLUMBIA 3-5   72-74
ELEKTRA 4-6   66-70
PRESTIGE 4-8   64
LPs: 10/12–inch 33rpm
COLUMBIA 6-12   70-76
ELEKTRA 8-15   65-70
FANTASY 5-10   72
LY CORNU 15-20
PRESTIGE 10-20   64-68

RUSHEN, Patrice
Singles: 12–inch 33/45rpm
ELEKTRA 4-8   79-84
Singles: 7–inch
ARISTA 2-4   87
ELEKTRA 3-5   80-84
PRESTIGE 3-5   76
Picture Sleeves
ELEKTRA 3-5   80
LPs: 10/12–inch 33rpm
ARISTA 5-8   87
ELEKTRA 5-10   78-84
PRESTIGE 5-10   75-80

RUSHEN, Patrice, and D.J. Rogers
Singles: 7–inch
ELEKTRA 3-5   80
  Also see ROGERS, D.J.
  Also see RUSHEN, Patrice

RUSS, Lonnie
Singles: 7–inch
4J 5-10   62

RUSSELL, Bobby
(Bobby Russell and the Beagles; Bobby and Sadie
Russell)
Singles: 7–inch
COLUMBIA 3-5   73-74
D 5-10   60
ELF 4-6   68-69
FELSTED 5-10   59
FILLY-COLT 3-5   78

RUSSELL, Brenda
Singles: 7–inch

RUSSELL, Lee
(Leon Russell)
Singles: 7–inch

RUSSELL, Leon
(Leon Russell and the Shelter People; Leon Russell and the New Grass Revival)
Singles: 7–inch

RUSSELL, Leon and Mary
Singles: 7–inch

RUSSELL, Sam
Singles: 7–inch

RUSSO, Charlie
Singles: 7–inch

RUTH, Babe: see BABE RUTH

RUTHERFORD, Mike
Singles: 7–inch

RUTLES
Singles: 12–inch 33/45rpm

RYAN, Barry
Singles: 7–inch

RYAN, Charlie
(Charlie Ryan and the Timberline Riders; Charlie Ryan and the Livingston Brothers)
Singles: 7–inch

RYDELL, Bobby
Singles: 7–inch

CAMEO ("Steel Pier") 15-20
(No number used. Single-sided, promotional issue
from the Steel Pier in Atlantic City.)
CAMEO (160 "Please Don't
Be Mad") 10-15   59
CAMEO (164 "All I Want Is You") 10-15   59
CAMEO (167 through 186) 5-10   59-61
CAMEO (190 through 361) 4-8   61-65
CAMEO (1070 "Forget Him"/
"A Message from Bobby") 8-12   63
(Packaged as a bonus single with *Top Hits of
1963*.)
CAPITOL 4-8   64-66
P.I.P. 3-5   76
PERCEPTION 3-5   74
RCA 3-5   70
REPRISE 4-6   68
TIME 5-8   59
VEKO (731 "Fatty Fatty") 20-25   58
VENISE (201 "Fatty Fatty") 10-20   62
Picture Sleeves
CAMEO 5-15   59-64
CAPITOL 5-10   64
EPs: 7-inch
CAPITOL 10-20   65
LPs: 10/12-inch 33rpm
CAMEO (1006 "We Got Love") 40-80   59
CAMEO (1007 "Bobby Sings,
Bobby Swings") 20-30   60
CAMEO (1009 "Bobby's Biggest
Hits") 40-50   61
(Gatefold cover. With 12 x 12 photo insert.)
CAMEO (1009 "Bobby's Biggest
Hits") 30-35   61
(Gatefold cover. Without 12 x 12 photo.)
CAMEO (1009 "Bobby's Biggest
Hits") 15-20   62
(Standard cover. Some copies with 1009 on the
cover may have Cameo 1008 on the disc.)
CAMEO (1010 through 1055) 15-25   61-63
CAMEO (1070 "Top Hits of 1963
Sung by Robby Rydell") 20-30   63
(With bonus single *Forget Him/A Message from
Bobby.*)
CAMEO (1070 "Top Hits of 1963
Sung By Robby Rydell") 15-20   63
(Without bonus single.)
CAMEO (1080 "Forget Him") 15-20   64
CAMEO (2000 series) 15-20
CAMEO (4017 "An Era Reborn") 15-25   64
CAPITOL (2281 "Somebody
Loves You") 15-20   65
DESIGN 10-15
P.I.P. 8-12   76
SPINORAMA 10-15
STRAND (1120 "Bobby Rydell
Sings") 25-35   60
Also see CHECKER, Chubby, and Bobby Rydell

Also see CHRISTIE, Lou / Len Barry and the Dovells / Bobby
Rydell / Tokens
Also see ROE, Tommy / Bobby Rydell / Ray Stevens

RYDER, John and Anne
Singles: 7-inch
DECCA 4-6   69
LPs: 10/12-inch 33rpm
DECCA 10-15   70

RYDER, Mitch
(Mitch Ryder and the Detroit Wheels)
Singles: 7-inch
ABC 3-5   73
AVCO EMBASSY 3-6   70
DOT 4-6   69
DYNO VOICE 4-8   67-68
ERIC 2-4
NEW VOICE (Except 820) 4-8   65-68
NEW VOICE (820 "Sock It to Me-Baby")5-10   67
(With "Feels like a punch" lyrics.)
NEW VOICE (820 "Sock It to Me-Baby") 4-6   67
(With "Hits me like a punch" lyrics.)
RIVA............................ 2-4   83
VIRGO 2-4   73
Picture Sleeves
NEW VOICE 4-8   67
LPs: 10/12-inch 33rpm
CREWE 12-15
DOT 12-15   69
DYNO VOICE 10-20   67
NEW VOICE 20-30   66-68
RIVA......................... 5-8   83
ROULETTE 5-10
SEEDS and STEMS 5-10   78-80
VIRGO 8-10   73
Members: Mitch Ryder; Joe Kubert; Jim McCallister; Jim
McCarty; Johnny Badanjek.
Also see DETROIT

RYLES, John Wesley
Singles: 7-inch
ABC/DOT 3-5   77
COLUMBIA 4-6   68-70
GRT 3-5   70
MCA 3-5   79-83
MUSIC MILL 3-5   75-76
PLANTATION 3-5   72-73
PRIMERO 3-5   82
RCA 3-5   74
LPs: 10/12-inch 33rpm
ABC 5-10   78
ABC/DOT 8-10   77
COLUMBIA 10-15   69
MCA........................... 5-10   79-83
PLANTATION 5-10   77

S

S.O.S. BAND
Singles: 12–Inch 33/45rpm
TABU 4-6   80-89
Singles: 7–Inch
TABU 2-5   80-89
LPs: 10/12–Inch 33rpm
TABU 5-10   80-89

S.O.U.L.
Singles: 7–Inch
MUSICOR 3-5   71-74
LPs: 10/12–Inch 33rpm
MUSICOR 8-12   72

SRC
(Scott Richard Case)
Singles: 7–Inch
A SQUARE (301 "I'm So Glad") 10-20   67
BIG CASINO 4-8   71
CAPITOL 5-10   68-69
LPs: 10/12–Inch 33rpm
CAPITOL (134 "Milestones") 25-40   69
CAPITOL (273 "Travelers Tale") 15-25   69
CAPITOL (2991 "SRC") 40-65   68

SRC / Rationals
Singles: 7–Inch
A SQUARE (402 "Get the Picture") . . 10-20   67
Also see RATIONALS
Also see SRC

S.S.O.
Singles: 7–Inch
SHADY BROOK 3-5   75-76

SSQ
Singles: 12–Inch 33/45rpm
ENIGMA 4-6   84
Singles: 7–Inch
ENIGMA 2-4   84
LPs: 10/12–Inch 33rpm
ENIGMA 5-8   84
Also see ST. JAMES, Jon

SAAD, Sue, and the Next
Singles: 7–Inch
PLANET 3-5   80
LPs: 10/12–Inch 33rpm
PLANET 5-10   80

SACCO
(Lou Christie)
Singles: 12–Inch 33/45rpm
LIFESONG (81775 "People Theme") . . 8-10   78
Singles: 7–Inch
LIFESONG (81775 "People Theme") . 30-50   78
Also see CHRISTIE, Lou

SAD CAFE
Singles: 7–Inch
A&M 3-5   78-79
SWAN SONG 3-5   81
Picture Sleeves
SWAN SONG 3-5   81
LPs: 10/12–Inch 33rpm
A&M 5-10   78-79
SWAN SONG 5-10   81
Members: Paul Young; Doreen Chanter; Irene Chanter; John Stimpson; Vic Emerson; Ian Wilson; Ashley Mulford; Lenni Zaksen.
Also see MIKE + the MECHANICS
Also see YOUNG, Paul

SADANE, Marc
(Sadane)
Singles: 7–Inch
WARNER 3-5   81-82
Picture Sleeves
WARNER 3-5   81
LPs: 10/12–Inch 33rpm
WARNER 5-10   81

SADE
Singles: 12–Inch 33/45rpm
PORTRAIT 4-6   84-86
Singles: 7–Inch
EPIC 2-4   88
PORTRAIT 2-4   84-86
LPs: 10/12–Inch 33rpm
EPIC 5-8   88
PORTRAIT 5-8   85-86

SADLER, Barry
(S/SGT. Barry Sadler)
Singles: 7–Inch
GAS 3-5   78
RCA 4-6   66-67
Picture Sleeves
RCA 5-10   66-67
LPs: 10/12–Inch 33rpm
RCA 10-20   66-67
VETERAN 8-12   74
Also see ANN-MARGRET

SAFARIS
(With the Phantom's Band)
Singles: 7–Inch
ELDO 10-20   60-61
Members: Jimmy Stephens; Sheldon Breier.

SA-FIRE
LPs: 10/12–Inch 33rpm
CUTTING 5-8   88

SAGA
Singles: 7–Inch
POLYDOR 3-5   79
PORTRAIT 3-5   82-85
LPs: 10/12–Inch 33rpm
ATLANTIC 5-8   87
POLYDOR 5-10   79
PORTRAIT 5-10   82-85

SAGER, Carole Bayer
(Carole Bayer)
Singles: 7–inch
BOARDWALK 3-5	81
ELEKTRA 3-5	77-78
METROMEDIA 3-5	72
Picture Sleeves
| BOARDWALK .... 3-5 | 81 |
LPs: 10/12–inch 33rpm
| BOARDWALK .... 5-10 | 81 |
| ELEKTRA .... 5-10 | 77-78 |

SAGITTARIUS
Singles: 7–inch
| COLUMBIA .... 5-10 | 67-69 |
| TOGETHER .... 5-10 | 68-69 |
LPs: 10/12–inch 33rpm
BACK-TRAC 5-10	85
COLUMBIA (9644 "Present Tense") .. 15-25	68
TOGETHER (1002 "Blue Marble") ... 20-30	69

Members: Gary Usher; Glen Campbell; Bruce Johnston; Terry Melcher; Curt Boetcher
Also see BRUCE & TERRY
Also see CAMPBELL, Glen

SAHL, Mort
Singles: 7–inch
GNP/CRESCENDO 3-5	73
REPRISE 3-6	61
VERVE 4-8	60
LPs: 10/12–inch 33rpm
GNP/CRESCENDO 5-10	73
MERCURY 8-12	67
REPRISE 10-20	61
VERVE 10-20	59-64

Also see MARTIN, Dean

SAHM, Doug
(Doug Sahm and the Mex Trip; Doug Sahm and the Texas Tornados)
Singles: 7–inch
ABC/DOT 4-6	76
ATLANTIC 5-10	73
CASABLANCA (0828 "Roll with the Punches") 10-20	75
CHRYSALIS 3-5	81
COBRA (116 "Just a Moment") 40-50	61
CRAZY CAJUN 3-5	74
HARLEM (107 "Why, Why, Why") ... 20-35	60
HARLEM (108 "Baby, Tell Me") 20-30	60
(Black vinyl.)	
HARLEM (108 "Baby, Tell Me") 40-60	60
(Colored vinyl. Promotional issue only.)	
HARLEM (116 "Just a Moment") 40-50	61
PERSONALITY (260 "Baby, What's on Your Mind") 30-50	59
PLAYBOY 3-5	76
RENNER (212 "Big Hat") 20-30	61
(Black vinyl.)	
RENNER (212 "Big Hat") 50-75	61
(Colored vinyl. Promotional issue only.)	

RENNER (215 "Baby, What's on Your Mind") 20-30	61
(Black vinyl.)	
RENNER (215 "Baby, What's on Your Mind") 50-75	61
(Colored vinyl. Promotional issue only.)	
RENNER (226 "Just Because") 20-30	62
RENNER (232 "Cry") 20-30	63
RENNER (240 "Lucky Me") 20-30	63
RENNER (247 "Mr. Kool") 20-30	64
SATIN (100 "Crazy Daisy") 30-50	59
SOFT (1031 "Cry") 20-30	65
SWINGIN' (625 "Why, Oh Why") 15-25	60
TEXAS RECORD (108 "Henrietta") .. 10-20	76
WARNER 3-5	74
WARRIOR (507 "Crazy Daisy") 40-60	58
Picture Sleeves
| CHRYSALIS .... 3-5 | 81 |
LPs: 10/12–inch 33rpm
ANTONE'S 5-8	88
ATLANTIC 8-12	73
HARLEM 8-10	79
MERCURY 10-20	73
TAKOMA 5-10	80
WARNER 10-20	74

Also see BROMBERG, David
Also see DR. JOHN
Also see DYLAN, Bob
Also see SIR DOUGLAS QUINTET

SAHM, Doug, and Augle Meyers
Singles: 7–inch
| TEARDROP .... 2-4 | 83 |
Picture Sleeves
| TEARDROP .... 3-5 | 83 |

Also see SAHM, Doug

SAILCAT
Singles: 7–inch
| ELEKTRA .... 3-5 | 72-73 |
LPs: 10/12–inch 33rpm
| ELEKTRA .... 10-15 | 72 |

SAIN, Oliver
Singles: 7–inch
ABET 3-5	71-77
BOBBIN 4-8	62
HCRC 3-5	82
VANESSA 5-10	
LPs: 10/12–inch 33rpm
| ABET (400 series) .... 8-12 | 71-73 |
| ABET (8700 series) .... 5-10 | 77 |

ST. JAMES, Jon
Singles: 12–inch 33/45rpm
| EMI AMERICA .... 4-6 | 84 |
Singles: 7–inch
| EMI AMERICA .... 2-4 | 84 |
LPs: 10/12–inch 33rpm
| EMI AMERICA .... 5-10 | 84 |

Also see SSQ

ST. PETERS, Crispian
Singles: 7–inch
JAMIE 4-8   66-68
LPs: 10/12–inch 33rpm
JAMIE (3027 "The Pied Piper") 20-30   66

ST. ROMAIN, Kirby
Singles: 7–inch
INETTE 4-8   63-64
TEARDROP 4-8   64

SAINT TROPEZ
Singles: 12–inch 33/45rpm
BUTTERFLY 4-8   77-79
DESTINY 4-6   82
Singles: 7–inch
BUTTERFLY 3-5   77-79
DESTINY 2-4   82
LPs: 10/12–inch 33rpm
BUTTERFLY (Black vinyl) 5-10   77-79
BUTTERFLY (Colored vinyl) 10-15   77-79
DESTINY 5-10   82

SAINTE-MARIE, Buffy
Singles: 7–inch
ABC 3-5   76
MCA 3-5   74-75
VANGUARD 3-8   65-72
LPs: 10/12–inch 33rpm
ABC 5-10   76
MCA 5-10   74-75
VANGUARD 8-15   64-74

SAKAMOTO, Kyu
Singles: 7–inch
CAPITOL 4-6   63-64
EMI 2-4   75
LPs: 10/12–inch 33rpm
CAPITOL 10-20   63

SALES, Soupy
Singles: 7–inch
ABC-PAR 5-10   65
CAPITOL 5-10   66
MOTOWN 4-6   69
REPRISE 5-10   62
Picture Sleeves
CAPITOL 10-15   66
LPs: 10/12–inch 33rpm
ABC-PAR 15-25   64-65
MOTOWN 10-15   69
REPRISE 15-25   61-62

SALSOUL ORCHESTRA
Singles: 12–inch 33/45rpm
SALSOUL 4-6   78-83
Singles: 7–inch
SALSOUL 2-5   75-83
LPs: 10/12–inch 33rpm
SALSOUL 5-10   75-83
Also see CHARO
Also see HOLLOWAY, Loleatta

SALT-N-PEPA
Singles: 7–inch
NEXT PLATEAU 2-4   87-90
LPs: 10/12–inch 33rpm
NEXT PLATEAU 5-8   87-90

SALVAGE
Singles: 7–inch
ODAX 3-5   71

SALVO, Sammy
Singles: 78rpm
RCA 5-10   57
Singles: 7–inch
DOT 5-10   60
HICKORY 5-10   61-63
IMPERIAL 5-10   59-60
MARK V 5-10
RCA 8-12   57-59

SAM, Butch, and the Station Band
Singles: 7–inch
PRIVATE I 2-4   85

SAM & BILL
Singles: 7–inch
DECCA 4-8   67
JODA 4-8   65-66
Members: Sam Gary; Bill Johnson.

SAM & DAVE
Singles: 7–inch
ATLANTIC 3-6   68-71
ROULETTE 4-8   62-66
STAX 4-8   65-68
U.A. 3-5   74-75
LPs: 10/12–inch 33rpm
ATLANTIC (8205 "I Thank You") 15-20   68
ATLANTIC (8218 "Best of Sam
   & Dave") 8-12   69
GUSTO 5-10
ROULETTE (25323 "Sam & Dave") .. 15-25   66
STAX (708 "Hold On I'm Coming") .. 20-30   66
STAX (712 "Double Dynamite") 20-30   66
STAX (725 "Soul Men") 20-30   67
U.A. 8-12   74-75
Members: Sam Moore; Dave Prater.
Also see PICKETT, Wilson / Sam & Dave
Also see REDDING, Otis / Carla Thomas / Sam & Dave / Eddie
   Floyd
Also see STARS on 45 (Featuring Sam & Dave)

SAM the SHAM and the Pharaohs
(Sam the Sham Revue; Sam; Sam Samudio)
Singles: 7–inch
DINGO (001 "Haunted House") 20-30   64
MGM (13000 series) 5-10   64-69
MGM (14000 series) 3-5   73
POLYDOR 2-4
TUPELO (2982 "Betty and Dupree") . 20-30   63
WARRIOR 20-30
XL (905 "Signifyin' Monkey") 15-25   64
XL (906 "Wooly Bully") 30-50   65

Picture Sleeves

MGM 8-12   65-67

LPs: 10/12–inch 33rpm

MGM 15-25   65-68

SAMI JO
(Sami Jo Cole)

Singles: 7–inch

FAME 3-5   71-72
MGM 3-5   74-75
POLYDOR 3-5   76

LPs: 10/12–inch 33rpm

MGM 5-10   74-75

SAMPLE, Joe

Singles: 7–inch

ABC 3-5   78-79
MCA 2-4   80-83

LPs: 10/12–inch 33rpm

ABC 5-10   78-79
MCA 5-8   81-83
MFSL 25-50   78
WARNER 5-8   89
Also see CRUSADERS

SAN REMO GOLDEN STRINGS

Singles: 7–inch

GORDY 3-6   67
RIC-TIC 4-8   65-66

LPs: 10/12–inch 33rpm

GORDY 10-15   67-68
RIC-TIC 10-20   66

SAN SEBASTIAN STRINGS
(Rod McKuen with the San Sebastian Strings)

Singles: 7–inch

WARNER 3-6   67-73

LPs: 10/12–inch 33rpm

WARNER (Except 2754) 8-15   67-75
WARNER (2754 "Spring, Summer,
  Winter, Autumn") 15-20   73
  (Four-LP set.)
  Also see McKUEN, Rod

SANBORN, David

Singles: 12–inch 33/45rpm

WARNER 4-8   81-85

Singles: 7–inch

REPRISE 2-4   88
WARNER 3-5   76-87

LPs: 10/12–inch 33rpm

REPRISE 5-8   88
WARNER 5-10   76-87
Also see JAMES, Bob, and David Sanborn

SANDALS

Singles: 7–inch

WORLD PACIFIC (415 "Theme from
  Endless Summer) 10-15   64
WORLD PACIFIC (421 "Always") 15-25   64
WORLD PACIFIC (77000 series) 8-12   65-67

LPs: 10/12–inch 33rpm

WORLD PACIFIC (WP-1832 "Endless
  Summer") 20-25   66
  (Monaural. Soundtrack)
WORLD PACIFIC (ST-1832 "Endless
  Summer") 25-30   66
  (Stereo. Soundtrack)
  Members: John Blakely; Danny Brawner; John Gibson; Gaston
  Georis; Walter Georis.

SANDERS, Felicia

Singles: 78rpm

COLUMBIA 3-5   52-57

Singles: 7–inch

COLUMBIA 5-10   52-57
DECCA 4-8   59-61
MGM 4-8   65
TIME 4-8   60

EPs: 7–inch 33/45rpm

COLUMBIA 8-12   55-56

LPs: 10/12–inch 33rpm

COLUMBIA 15-25   55-57
SPECIAL EDITIONS 5-10   67
TIME 10-15   60-64
Also see FAITH, Percy
Also see VALE, Jerry, Peggy King and Felicia Sanders

SANDERS, Pharoah

Singles: 7–inch

ARISTA 3-5   78

LPs: 10/12–inch 33rpm

ARISTA 5-10   78
IMPULSE 10-15   69-74
INDIA NAVIGATION 5-10   77
NOVUS 5-10   81
THERESA 5-12   80-81
TRIP 8-12   71

SANDLER, Tony, and Ralph Young
(Sandler and Young)

Singles: 7–inch

CAPITOL 3-6   66-70

LPs: 10/12–inch 33rpm

A.V.I. 5-10   79
CAPITOL 5-15   66-78
Also see CAMPBELL, Glen / Lettermen / Ella Fitzgerald /
Sandler & Young

SANDPEBBLES

Singles: 7–inch

ABC 3-5   73
CALLA 4-8   67-69
Also see C and the Shells

SANDPIPERS

Singles: 7–inch

A&M 3-6   66-72
KISMET 4-8   66
TRU-GLOW-TOWN 4-8   66

LPs: 10/12–inch 33rpm

A&M 8-15   66-73

SANDS, Evie
Singles: 7–inch
ABC-PAR	4-8	63-64
A&M	3-6	68-70
BLUE CAT	5-10	65
CAMEO	4-6	66-68
GOLD	4-8	64
HAVEN	3-5	75-76
RCA	3-5	79

LPs: 10/12–inch 33rpm
A&M	10-15	69
HAVEN	8-10	74
RCA	5-10	79

SANDS, Jodie
Singles: 78rpm
BERNLO	4-8	57
CHANCELLOR	4-8	57
TEEN	5-10	55

Singles: 7–inch
ABC	3-5	74
ABC-PAR	4-8	62-63
BERNLO	8-12	57
CHANCELLOR	5-10	57-59
PARIS	5-10	60-61
SIGNATURE	5-10	59
TEEN	10-20	55
THOR	5-10	59

SANDS, Tommy
(Tommy Sands and the Raiders)
Singles: 78rpm
CAPITOL	5-10	57
RCA	6-12	54-56

Singles: 7–inch
ABC-PAR	4-8	63-64
CAPITOL (3639 through 4082)	8-12	57-58
CAPITOL (4160 through 4580)	5-10	59-61
IMPERIAL	4-8	66-67
LIBERTY	4-8	65
RCA	10-15	54-56
SUPERSCOPE	3-6	69

Picture Sleeves
CAPITOL	10-15	58-59

EPs: 7–inch 33/45rpm
CAPITOL	15-25	57-59

LPs: 10/12–inch 33rpm
BRUNSWICK	8-10	78
CAPITOL (848 "Steady Date")	35-45	57
CAPITOL (929 "Sing Boy Sing")	35-45	58
CAPITOL (1081 "Sands Storm")	30-40	58
CAPITOL (T-1123 "This Thing Called Love") (Monaural.)	25-30	59
CAPITOL (ST-1123 "This Thing Called Love") (Stereo.)	30-35	59
CAPITOL (T-1239 "When I'm Thinking of You") (Monaural.)	25-30	59
CAPITOL (ST-1239 "When I'm Thinking of You") (Stereo.)	30-35	59
CAPITOL (T-1364 "Sands at the Storm") (Monaural.)	20-30	60
CAPITOL (ST-1364 "Sands at the Sands") (Stereo.)	25-35	60
CAPITOL (T-1426 "Dream with Me") (Monaural.)	20-30	60
CAPITOL (ST-1426 "Dream with Me") (Stereo.)	25-35	60

Also see ANNETTE and Tommy Sands

SANFORD - TOWNSEND BAND
Singles: 7–inch
WARNER	3-5	77-79

LPs: 10/12–inch 33rpm
WARNER	5-10	78-79

Members: Ed Sanford; John Townsend.

SANG, Samantha
Singles: 7–inch
ATCO	4-6	69
PRIVATE STOCK	3-5	77-78
U.A.	3-5	79

LPs: 10/12–inch 33rpm
PRIVATE STOCK	5-10	77-78
U.A.	5-10	79

Also see BEE GEES

SANS, Billie
Singles: 7–inch
INVICTUS	3-5	71

SANTA ESMERALDA:
see ESMERALDA, Santa

SANTAMARIA, Mongo
(Mongo Santamaria and His Afro-Latin Group)
Singles: 12–inch 33/45rpm
TAPPAN ZEE	4-8	79

Singles: 7–inch
ATLANTIC	3-6	69-72
BATTLE	4-8	63
COLLECTABLES	2-4	
COLUMBIA	4-6	64-69
FANTASY	4-8	61-62
RIVERSIDE	4-8	62-66
TAPPAN ZEE	3-5	79
VAYA	3-5	73

LPs: 10/12–inch 33rpm
ATLANTIC	8-12	70
BATTLE	15-25	63
COLUMBIA	5-15	65-79
FANTASY	10-25	59-62

(Many Fantasy LPs are still available, using original catalog numbers in the 8000 series. The 3000 series is mono and out of print.)

MILESTONE	6-12	73-76
PRESTIGE	6-12	72

RIVERSIDE 10-20   62-66
VAYA 6-12   73-74

SANTANA
(Carlos Santana)
Singles: 12-inch 33/45rpm
COLUMBIA 4-6   85
Singles: 7-inch
COLUMBIA 2-5   69-90
Picture Sleeves
COLUMBIA 3-5   70-82
LPs: 10/12-inch 33rpm
COLUMBIA 5-12   69-90
Members: Devadip Carlos Santana; Armando Peraza; Graham Lear; David Margen; Richard Baker; Alex Ligertwood; Orestes Vilato; Raul Rekow.
Also see AZTECA
Also see BOOKER T. and the MGs
Also see COLTRANE, Alice, and Carlos Santana
Also see ESCOVEDO, Coke
Also see FABULOUS THUNDERBIRDS
Also see FRANKLIN, Aretha
Also see HAGAR, SCHON, AARONSON, SHRIEVE
Also see HANCOCK, Herbie
Also see NOVO COMBO

SANTANA, Carlos, and Buddy Miles
Singles: 7-inch
COLUMBIA 3-5   72
LPs: 10/12-inch 33rpm
COLUMBIA 6-12   72
Also see MILES, Buddy
Also see SANTANA

SANTANA, Jorge
Singles: 7-inch
TOMATO 3-5   78-79
Also see MALO

SANTIAGO
Singles: 7-inch
AMHERST 3-5   76

SANTO & JOHNNY
Singles: 7-inch
CANADIAN AMERICAN 5-10   59-66
ERIC 2-4
IMPERIAL 4-8   67-68
U.A. 4-8   66
Picture Sleeves
CANADIAN AMERICAN 6-12   60-64
LPs: 10/12-inch 33rpm
CANADIAN AMERICAN 20-40   59-64
IMPERIAL 10-20   67-69
Members: Santo Farina; Johnny Farina.

SANTOS, Larry
Singles: 7-inch
ATLANTIC (2250 "Someday") 10-20   64
CASABLANCA 3-5   76-77
EVOLUTION 4-6   69-71
LPs: 10/12-inch 33rpm
CASABLANCA 8-10   77
EVOLUTION 10-15   69
Also see 4 SEASONS

SAPPHIRES
Singles: 7-inch
ABC 3-5   73
ABC-PAR 5-10   64-66
COLLECTABLES 2-4
ERIC 2-4
ITZY (5 "Who Do You Love") 20-30   63
SWAN 8-10   63-64
LPs: 10/12-inch 33rpm
SWAN (513 "Who Do You Love") ... 40-60   64
Members: Carol; George; Joe.

SARDUCCI, Father Guido
Singles: 7-inch
A&M 3-5   74
WARNER 2-4   80
LPs: 10/12-inch 33rpm
WARNER 5-10   80

SARIDIS, Saverio
Singles: 7-inch
U.A. 3-6   66
WARNER 4-8   61-62
Picture Sleeves
WARNER 4-8   61
LPs: 10/12-inch 33rpm
WARNER 10-20   62

SARSTEDT, Peter
Singles: 7-inch
SIRE 3-5   78
U.A. 3-5   72
WORLD PACIFIC 4-6   69
LPs: 10/12-inch 33rpm
U.A. 8-12   71
WORLD PACIFIC 10-15   69

SASS
Singles: 7-inch
20TH FOX 3-5   77

SATELLITE, Billy: see BILLY SATELLITE

SATISFACTIONS
Singles: 7-inch
CHESAPEAKE (610 "We Will
Walk Together") 15-25   63
IMPERIAL 10-15   66
LIONEL 3-5   70-71
1-2-3 4-6   69
SMASH 4-8   66-67

SATTERFIELD, Esther
Singles: 7-inch
A&M 3-5   76
LPs: 10/12-inch 33rpm
A&M 5-10   76

SATURDAY NIGHT BAND
Singles: 7-inch
PRELUDE 3-5   78
LPs: 10/12-inch 33rpm
PRELUDE 5-10   78

SAULSBERRY, Rodney
Singles: 7–inch

ALLEGIANCE 2-4   84-85
RYAN 2-4   88

SAUNDERS, Merl
(Merle Saunders and Heavy Turbulence)
Singles: 7–inch

FANTASY 4-8   64-69
GALAXY 3-5   71
LPs: 10/12–inch 33rpm
FANTASY 10-20   68-73
 Also see FOGERTY, Tom
 Also see GARCIA, Jerry

SAUNDERS, Red
(Red Saunders Featuring Delores Hawkins)
Singles: 78rpm

BLUE LAKE 4-8   54
OKEH 5-10   51-53
SAVOY 10-15   45
SULTAN 10-15   46
SUPREME 5-10   49
Singles: 7–inch
BLUE LAKE (Colored vinyl) 10-15   54
OKEH (6000 series, except 6862) 6-12   51-53
OKEH (6862 "Hambone") 25-35   52
 (With Dee Clark.)
OKEH (7000 series) 4-8   63
Picture Sleeves
OKEH (7000 series) 5-10   63
 Also see CLARK, Dee

SAVAGE GRACE
Singles: 7–inch

REPRISE 3-5   70-71
LPs: 10/12–inch 33rpm
REPRISE 10-15   70-71

SAVALAS, Telly
Singles: 7–inch

MCA 3-5   74-75
LPs: 10/12–inch 33rpm
AUDIO FIDELITY 5-10   75
MCA 5-10   74-76

SAVATAGE
Singles: 7–inch

ATLANTIC 2-4   86-90
LPs: 10/12–inch 33rpm
ATLANTIC 5-8   86-90

SAVOY, Ronnie
Singles: 7–inch

CANDELO 5-10   59
EPIC 4-8   63-64
GONE 5-10   59
MGM 5-10   60-61
PHILIPS 4-8   62-63
WINGATE 4-8   65

SAVOY BROWN
(Savoy Brown Blues Band)
Singles: 7–inch

LONDON 3-5   74-75
PARROT 3-6   69-73
TOWN HOUSE 3-5   81
LPs: 10/12–inch 33rpm
LONDON (600 and 700 series) 8-10   74-77
LONDON (50000 "Best of Savoy Brown") 5-8   77
PARROT 10-15   68-73
 (Many Parrot LPs are currently available using
 original catalog numbers.)
TOWN HOUSE (Except 7562) 8-12   81
TOWN HOUSE (7562 "Prime Cuts") . 10-15   81
 (Promotional issue only.)
 Also see FOGHAT
 Also see PHILLIPS, Warren, and the Rockets

SAWYER, Ray
Singles: 7–inch

CAPITOL 3-5   76-79
SANDY (1030 "Rockin' Satellite") . . . 20-30   60
SANDY (1037 "I'm Gonna Leave") . . 10-20   61
LPs: 10/12–inch 33rpm
CAPITOL 8-10   76
 Also see DR. HOOK

SAWYER BROWN
Singles: 7–inch

CAPITOL/CURB 3-5   84-90
LPs: 10/12–inch 33rpm
CAPITOL/CURB 5-10   85-90

SAWYER BROWN and "Cat" Joe Bonsall
Singles: 7–inch

CAPITOL/CURB 2-4   86
 Also see SAWYER BROWN

SAXON
Singles: 7–inch

CARRERE 3-5   83-84
LPs: 10/12–inch 33rpm
CAPITOL 5-10   83-87
 Also see MOTORHEAD

SAYER, Leo
Singles: 7–inch

WARNER 3-5   73-84
LPs: 10/12–inch 33rpm
WARNER 6-10   75-84

SCAFFOLD
Singles: 7–inch

BELL 4-8   68
WARNER 3-5   74
LPs: 10/12–inch 33rpm
BELL (6018 "Thank U Very Much") . . 25-30   68
 Members: Mike McGear; Roger McGough; John Gorman; Mike
 Vickers; Lol Creme; Andy Roberts; Zoot Money.
 Also see GODLEY, Kevin, and Lol Creme

SCAGGS, Boz
Singles: 7–inch

ATLANTIC 4-8   69

COLUMBIA 2-5 71-81
FULL MOON 3-5 81
Picture Sleeves
COLUMBIA 3-5 76-81
EPs: 7-inch 33/45rpm
COLUMBIA 5-10 76
LPs: 10/12-inch 33rpm
ATLANTIC (8239 "Boz Scaggs") 8-12 69
ATLANTIC (19166 "Boz Scaggs") 5-8 78
COLUMBIA (Except 40000 series) 6-10 71-80
COLUMBIA (40463 "Other Roads") 5-8 88
COLUMBIA (43920 "Silk Degrees") . . 15-20 80
(Half-speed mastered.)
Promotional LPs
COLUMBIA (203 "The Boz Scaggs
Sampler") 10-20 76
Also see MILLER, Steve, Band

SCALES, Harvey
(Harvey Scales and the Seven Sounds)
Singles: 7-inch
CASABLANCA 3-5
CHESS 3-5 70
MAGIC TOUCH 4-8 67-68
MERCURY 3-6 69
STAX 3-5
LPs: 10/12-inch 33rpm
CASABLANCA 5-10 79

SCANDAL
(Scandal Featuring Patty Smyth)
Singles: 12-inch 33/45rpm
COLUMBIA (Except 8C8-39905) 4-6 82-85
COLUMBIA (8C8-39905 "Warrior") . . 10-15 82
(Picture disc.)
Singles: 7-inch
COLUMBIA 2-5 82-85
LPs: 10/12-inch 33rpm
COLUMBIA 5-10 82-85

SCARBURY, Joey
Singles: 7-inch
BELL 3-5 71-73
BIG TREE 3-5 73
COLUMBIA 3-5 77-79
ELEKTRA 3-5 81
LIONEL 3-5 71
PLAYBOY 3-5 74
RCA 2-4 84
REENA 4-6 68
Picture Sleeves
ELEKTRA 3-5 81
LPs: 10/12-inch 33rpm
ELEKTRA 5-10 81

SCARLET & BLACK
LPs: 10/12-inch 33rpm
VIRGIN 5-8 88

SCHAFER, Kermit
Singles: 78rpm
JUBILEE 5-10 56

Singles: 7-inch
JUBILEE (5258 "Rock Around
the Blooper") 10-15 56
LPs: 10/12-inch 33rpm
AUDIO FIDELITY 8-12 69
JUBILEE 10-20 58-63
KAPP 8-12 68-70
KING 10-15 64
MCA 5-10 74-77
Kermit Schafer has released numerous comedy
albums of "Bloopers," which we have not
attempted to list.

SCHENKER, Michael, Group
Singles: 7-inch
CHRYSALIS 3-5 80-83
LPs: 10/12-inch 33rpm
CHRYSALIS 5-10 80-83
Also see ALCATRAZZ
Also see UFO

SCHIFRIN, Lalo
Singles: 12-inch 33/45rpm
CTI 5-10 76
TABU 4-8 78-79
Singles: 7-inch
A&M 3-5 75
CTI 3-5 76-77
DOT 3-5 67
MCA 2-5 77-83
MGM 4-6 63-70
PABLO 3-5 77
PARAMOUNT 4-6 69
TABU 2-5 78-79
TETRAGRAMMATON 4-6 69
20TH FOX 3-5 74-75
U.A. 3-5 70
VERVE 4-6 63-71
WARNER 3-6 68-69
LPs: 10/12-inch 33rpm
AUDIO FIDELITY 5-15 62-68
CTI 5-10 76-77
COLPIX 10-20 64
DOT (25852 "There's a Whole Lalo
Schifrin Goin' On") 10-15 68
MCA (5000 series) 5-10 81
MGM 5-15 63-70
ROULETTE 10-15 62
TABU 5-10 79
TICO 10-20 60
VERVE (Except 8624) 10-20 63-69

SCHILLING, Nina
Singles: 12-inch 33/45rpm
MOBY DICK 4-6 84

SCHILLING, Peter
Singles: 12-inch 33/45rpm
ELEKTRA 4-6 83
Singles: 7-inch
ELEKTRA 3-5 83

LPs: 10/12–inch 33rpm

ELEKTRA 5-10   83

SCHMIT, Timothy B.
Singles: 7–inch

FULL MOON 3-5   82
MCA 2-4   87
LPs: 10/12–inch 33rpm

ASYLUM 5-10   84
MCA 5-8   87
Also see EAGLES
Also see POCO

SCHNEIDER, Fred, and the Shake Society
Singles: 12–inch 33/45rpm

WARNER 4-6   84
Singles: 7–inch

WARNER 2-4   84

SCHNEIDER, John
Singles: 7–inch

MCA 2-4   84-86
SCOTTI BROS 3-5   81-83
Picture Sleeves

MCA 2-4   84-86
SCOTTI BROS 3-5   81-83
LPs: 10/12–inch 33rpm

MCA 5-8   84-86
SCOTTI BROS 5-10   81-83

SCHNEIDER, John, and Jill Michaels
Singles: 7–inch

SCOTTI BROS 2-4   83
Also see SCHNEIDER, John

SCHON, Neal, and Jan Hammer
LPs: 10/12–inch 33rpm

COLUMBIA 5-10   81-83
Also see HAGAR, SCHON, AARONSON, SHRIEVE
Also see HAMMER, Jan
Also see JOURNEY

SCHOOLBOYS
Singles: 78rpm

OKEH 5-10   56-57
Singles: 7–inch

JUANITA (103 "Angel of Love") 60-80   58
OKEH (7076 "Please Say
  You Want Me") 20-25   56
  (Purple label.)
OKEH (7076 "Please Say
  You Want Me") 10-15   57
  (Yellow label.)
OKEH (7085 "Mary") 15-25   57
OKEH (7090 "Carol") 15-25   57
  (Purple label.)
OKEH (7090 "Carol") 15-25   57
  (White label. Promotional issue only.)
OKEH (7090 "Carol") 10-15   57
  (Yellow label.)
Members: Les Martin; Jim Edwards; Roger Hayes; Jim McKay;
Renaldo Gamble.
EPs: 7–inch 33/45rpm

MAGIC CARPET 5-10

Also see CADILLACS

SCHOOLEY D
LPs: 10/12–inch 33rpm

JIVE 5-8   88

SCHORY, Dick
(Dick Schory's Percussion Pops Orchestra)
LPs: 10/12–inch 33rpm

RCA 5-15   59-63

SCHUMANN, Walter
(Voices of Walter Schumann)
Singles: 78rpm

CAPITOL 3-5   52
RCA 3-5   53-56
Singles: 7–inch

CAPITOL 4-6   52
RCA 4-6   53-56
EPs: 7–inch 33/45rpm

CAPITOL 5-10   52
RCA 5-10   53-56
LPs: 10/12–inch 33rpm

CAPITOL 5-15   52
RCA 5-15   53-56

SCHURR, Diane
LPs: 10/12–inch 33rpm

GRP 5-8   88-90

SCHWARTZ, Eddie
Singles: 7–inch

ATCO 3-5   81-82
LPs: 10/12–inch 33rpm

ATCO 5-10   82

SCORPIONS
Singles: 7–inch

MERCURY 2-4   79-85
RCA 3-5   74-80
LPs: 10/12–inch 33rpm

MERCURY 5-8   79-90
RCA 5-10   74-84
Members: Klaus Meine; Francis Bucholz; Matt Jabs; Herman
Rarebell; Uli Roth; Rudolf Schenker.

SCOTT, Billy
Singles: 78rpm

CAMEO 5-10   57
Singles: 7–inch

CAMEO 8-12   57-58
EVEREST 5-10   59

SCOTT, Bobby
Singles: 78rpm

ABC-PAR 5-10   56
Singles: 7–inch

ABC 3-5   73
ABC-PAR 8-12   56

SCOTT, Christopher
(Sir Christopher Scott)
LPs: 10/12–inch 33rpm

DECCA 5-10   69-70

SCOTT, Linda
Singles: 7–inch
CANADIAN AMERICAN	8-12	61-62
CONGRESS	5-10	62-64
ERIC	2-4	
KAPP	5-10	64-66
RCA	4-8	68

EPs: 7–inch 33/45rpm
CONGRESS (1005 "Starlight Starbright")	25-35	62
CONGRESS (3001 "Linda Scott")	25-35	62

(Promotional issue only. Issued with picture insert, but not with cover.)

LPs: 10/12–inch 33rpm
CANADIAN AMERICAN (CALP-1005 "Starlight Starbright")	35-45	61

(Monaural.)
CANADIAN AMERICAN (SCALP-1005 "Starlight Starbright")	40-50	61

(Stereo.)
CANADIAN AMERICAN (CALP-1007 "Great Scott")	35-45	62

(Monaural.)
CANADIAN AMERICAN (SCALP-1007 "Great Scott")	40-50	62

(Stereo.)
CONGRESS (3001 "Linda")	25-35	62
KAPP (3424 "Hey Look at Me Now")	25-35	65

SCOTT, Marilyn
Singles: 7–inch
BIG TREE	3-5	77
MERCURY	2-4	83-85

LPs: 10/12–inch 33rpm
ATCO	5-10	79
MERCURY	5-8	83

SCOTT, Millie
(Mildred Scott)
Singles: 7–inch
4TH and BROADWAY	2-4	86-87

SCOTT, Neal
(Neal Scott and the Concords; Neil Scott; Neil Bogart)
Singles: 7–inch
CAMEO	5-10	67
CLOWN	10-15	60
COMET	10-15	62
HERALD	10-15	63
PORTRAIT	8-12	61-62

SCOTT, Peggy
Singles: 7–inch
SSS INT'L	4-8	69

SCOTT, Peggy, and Jo Jo Benson
Singles: 7–inch
SSS INT'L	4-8	68-69
SUN	3-5	

LPs: 10/12–inch 33rpm
AVI	5-10	84

SSS INT'L	10-15	69

Also see SCOTT, Peggy

SCOTT, Rena
Singles: 7–inch
BUDDAH	3-5	79
EPIC	3-5	72-74
SEDONA	2-4	88

SCOTT, Tom
(Tom Scott and the L.A. Express; Tom Scott and the California Dreamers)
Singles: 12–inch 33/45rpm
SIRE	4-6	83

Singles: 7–inch
A&M	3-5	72
ATLANTIC	3-5	83
COLUMBIA	3-5	79
IMPULSE	4-6	68
ODE	3-5	74-79
SIRE	2-4	83

LPs: 10/12–inch 33rpm
COLUMBIA	5-10	78-81
EPIC/ODE	5-8	84
IMPULSE	20-30	68
ODE	8-10	74-77
MUSICIAN	5-10	82
RCA	5-10	81

Also see CLAYTON, Merry
Also see HARRISON, George

SCOTT-HERON, Gil
Singles: 7–inch
ARISTA	2-5	75-84

LPs: 10/12–inch 33rpm
ARISTA	6-12	75-84
FLYING DUTCHMAN (100 through 0600 series)	8-15	71-74
FLYING DUTCHMAN (3800 series)	5-8	80

SCOTT-HERON, Gil, and Brian Jackson
Singles: 7–inch
ARISTA	3-5	75-80

LPs: 10/12–inch 33rpm
ARISTA	6-12	75-80
STRATA-EAST	8-15	74

Also see SCOTT-HERON, Gil

SCREAMIN' BLUE MESSIAHS
LPs: 10/12–inch 33rpm
ELEKTRA	5-8	87

SCRITTI POLITTI
Singles: 12–inch 33/45rpm
WARNER	4-6	84-86

Singles: 7–inch
WARNER	2-4	84-86

LPs: 10/12–inch 33rpm
WARNER	5-8	84-86

SCRITTI POLITTI / Roger
Singles: 7–inch
WARNER	2-4	88

Also see ROGER

Also see SCRITTI POLITTI

SCRUFFY the CAT
LPs: 10/12-Inch 33rpm
RELATIVITY 5-8   88

SCRUGGS, Earl
(Earl Scruggs Revue)
Singles: 7-inch
COLUMBIA 3-5   70-83
LPs: 10/12-Inch 33rpm
COLUMBIA 5-10   73-83
Also see FLATT, Lester, and Earl Scruggs
Also see HALL, Tom T., and Earl Scruggs
Also see SKAGGS, Ricky

SEA, Johnny
(Johnny Seay)
Singles: 7-inch
CAPITOL 4-6   61
COLUMBIA 3-5   67-69
NRC 4-8   59-60
PHILIPS 3-5   64-65
VIKING 3-5   70-71
WARNER 3-6   66-67
Picture Sleeves
COLUMBIA 3-5   68
LPs: 10/12-inch 33rpm
GUEST STAR 8-12   66
PHILIPS 10-15   64-65
PICKWICK/HILLTOP 8-12   65
WARNER 10-20   66

SEA LEVEL
Singles: 7-inch
ARISTA 3-5   80
CAPRICORN 3-5   77-79
LPs: 10/12-inch 33rpm
ARISTA 5-10   80
CAPRICORN 5-10   77-80
Also see ALLMAN BROTHERS BAND

SEALS, Dan
(England Dan Seals)
Singles: 7-inch
ATLANTIC 3-5   80-82
EMI AMERICA 2-4   84-86
LIBERTY 2-4   83-84
LPs: 10/12-inch 33rpm
ATLANTIC 5-10   80-82
EMI AMERICA 5-8   84-86
LIBERTY 5-8   83
Also see ENGLAND DAN & JOHN FORD COLEY

SEALS, Dan, and Marie Osmond
Singles: 7-inch
CAPITOL 2-4   85
Also see OSMOND, Marie
Also see SEALS, Dan

SEALS & CROFTS
Singles: 7-inch
T.A. 4-6   69-71
WARNER 3-5   71-80

LPs: 10/12-inch 33rpm
T.A. 20-25   69-70
WARNER (Except 2809) 6-12   71-80
WARNER (2809 "Seals and
  Crofts I and II") 10-12   74
Members: Jimmy Seals; Dash Crofts.
Also see CHAMPS

SEARCHERS
Singles: 7-inch
ERIC 2-4
KAPP 5-10   64-67
LIBERTY (55646 "Sugar and Spice") . 8-12   63
LIBERTY (55689 "Sugar and Spice") . 5-10   63
MERCURY 5-10   63
RCA 4-6   71-72
SIRE 3-5   80-81
Picture Sleeves
KAPP (577 "Needles and Pins") 10-20   64
KAPP (609 "Some Day We're
  Gonna Live Again") 10-20   64
LPs: 10/12-inch 33rpm
KAPP 20-30   64-66
MERCURY (20914 "Hear! Hear!") . 25-35   64
  (Monaural. Red label.)
MERCURY (20914 "Hear! Hear!") . . . 40-60   64
  (White label. Promotional issue only.)
MERCURY (60914 "Hear! Hear!") . . . 25-35   64
  (Stereo. Red label.)
MERCURY (60914 "Hear! Hear!") . . . 40-60   64
  (White label. Promotional issue only.)
PYE 10-12   76
SIRE 8-10   80-81

SEARCHERS / Rattles
LPs: 10/12-inch 33rpm
MERCURY (20994 "The Searchers Meet
  the Rattles) 35-45   65
  (Monaural. Red label.)
MERCURY (20994 "The Searchers Meet
  the Rattles) 50-75   65
  (White label. Promotional issue only.)
MERCURY (60994 "The Searchers Meet
  the Rattles) 35-45   65
  (Stereo. Red label.)
MERCURY (60994 "The Searchers Meet
  the Rattles) 50-75   65
  (White label. Promotional issue only.)
Also see RATTLES
Also see SEARCHERS

SEASE, Marvin
LPs: 10/12-inch 33rpm
LONDON 5-8   87

SEATRAIN
Singles: 7-inch
A&M 4-8   68
CAPITOL 3-6   71-72
WARNER 3-5   73
LPs: 10/12-inch 33rpm
A&M 10-15   69

CAPITOL (800 series) 8-12   71
CAPITOL (16000 series) 5-10   80
WARNER 8-10   73
    Also see BLUES PROJECT
    Also see RANK & FILE

SEAWIND
Singles: 7-inch
A&M 3-5   80-82
CTI 3-5   77-78
HORIZON 3-5   79
LPs: 10/12-inch 33rpm
A&M 5-10   80-82
CTI 5-10   77-78
HORIZON 5-10   79

SEAY, Johnny: see SEA, Johnny

SEBASTIAN, John
Singles: 7-inch
KAMA SUTRA 4-6   68-70
MGM 4-6   68-70
REPRISE 3-5   70-77
Picture Sleeves
KAMA SUTRA 4-8   69
LPs: 10/12-inch 33rpm
KAMA SUTRA 10-15   70
MGM 10-15   69-70
REPRISE 8-12   70-76
    Also see LOVIN' SPOONFUL
    Also see MUGWUMPS
    Also see SIMPSONS

SECO, Pozo, Singers:
  see POZO SECO SINGERS

SECOND VERSE
Singles: 7-inch
IX CHAINS 3-5   74

SECRET TIES
Singles: 7-inch
NIGHT WAVE 2-4   86

SECRET WEAPON
Singles: 7-inch
PRELUDE 3-5   82-83

SECRETS
Singles: 7-inch
DCP 4-8   65
OMEN 4-8   66
PHILIPS 8-12   63-64
Picture Sleeves
PHILIPS 10-15   64

SEDAKA, Neil
(Neil Sedaka and the Marvels)
Singles: 7-inch
DECCA (30520 "Laura Lee") 40-60   57
ELEKTRA 3-5   77-80
GUYDEN (2004 "Ring-a-Rockin") ... 35-45   58
KIRSHNER 2-4   72-80
LEGION (133 "Ring-a-Rockin") 50-75   58
MCA 3-5   75-84

MGM 3-5   73
PYRAMID (623 "Oh Delilah") 10-15   62
RCA (7408 "The Diary") 8-12   58
  (Black label.)
RCA (7408 "The Diary") 10-20   58
  (White, photo label. Promotional issue only.)
RCA (7473 "I Go Ape") 10-15   59
RCA (47-7595 "Oh Carol") 5-10   59
  (Monaural.)
RCA (61-7595 "Oh Carol") 15-25   59
  (Stereo.)
RCA (47-7709 "Stairway to Heaven") . 5-10   60
  (Monaural.)
RCA (61-7709 "Stairway to Heaven") 15-25   60
  (Stereo.)
RCA (47-7781 "Run Sampson Run") .. 5-10   60
  (Monaural.)
RCA (61-7781 "Run Sampson Run") . 15-25   60
  (Stereo.)
RCA (37-7829 "Calendar Girl") 15-25   60
  (Compact 33 Single.)
RCA (47-7829 "Calendar Girl") 5-10   60
  (Monaural.)
RCA (61-7829 "Calendar Girl") 15-25   60
  (Stereo.)
RCA (37-7874 "Little Devil") 15-25   61
  (Compact 33 Single.)
RCA (47-7874 "Little Devil") 5-10   61
RCA (37-7922 "Sweet Little You") ... 15-25   61
  (Compact 33 Single.)
RCA (47-7922 "Sweet Little You") 5-10   61
RCA (37-7957 "Happy Birthday
  Sweet Sixteen") 15-25   61
  (Compact 33 Single.)
RCA (47-7957 "Happy Birthday
  Sweet Sixteen") 5-10   61
RCA (37-8007 "King of Clowns") 15-25   62
  (Compact 33 Single.)
RCA (47-8007 "King of Clowns") 5-10   62
RCA (37-8007 "King of Clowns") ... 15-25   62
  (Compact 33 Single.)
RCA (8046 through 9004) 4-8   62-66
ROCKET 3-5   74-76
S.G.C. 4-6   68-69
Picture Sleeves
RCA 5-15   60-65
EPs: 7-inch 33/45rpm
RCA (105 "Neil's Best") 15-25   61
  (Compact 33 Double.)
RCA (135 "Little Devil") 15-25   61
  (Compact 33 Double.)
RCA (4334 "I Go Ape") 30-40   59
RCA (4353 "Oh Carol") 25-35   59
LPs: 10/12-inch 33rpm
ACCORD 5-10   81
CAMDEN 8-12
ELEKTRA 5-10   77-81
51 WEST 5-8
INTERMEDIA 5-8   85

KIRSHNER 10-15 71-72
MCA 5-10 84
RCA (AFL1 and APL1 series) 8-10 75-78
RCA (ANL1 series) 5-10 75-79
RCA (VPL1 series) 8-12 76
RCA (LPM-2035 "Neil Sedaka") 35-45 59
  (Monaural.)
RCA (2035 "Neil Sedaka") 50-100 59
  (Stereo.)
RCA (LPM-2317 through LPM-2627) . 20-30 61-62
  (Monaural.)
RCA (LSP-2317 through LSP-2627) . 25-35 61-62
  (Stereo.)
RCA (10181 "Smile") 15-20 66
ROCKET 8-10 74-77
  Also see ANKA, Paul / Sam Cooke / Neil Sedaka
  Also see COOKE, Sam / Rod Lauren / Neil Sedaka / Browns
  Also see JOHN, Elton
  Also see KING CURTIS
  Also see SIMON, Paul
  Also see 10CC
  Also see WILLOWS

SEDAKA, Neil and Dara
Singles: 7–inch
ELEKTRA 3-5 80
MCA 2-4 84
  Also see SEDAKA, Dara

SEDAKA, Neil, and the Tokens
LPs: 10/12–inch 33rpm
GUEST STAR 10-20
VERNON 10-15

SEDAKA, Neil, and the Tokens / Coins
LPs: 10/12–inch 33rpm
CROWN 10-20 63

SEDAKA, Neil, and the Tokens / Angels / Jimmy Gilmer and the Fireballs
LPs: 10/12–inch 33rpm
ALMOR (105 "Teen Bandstand") 15-25
  Also see ANGELS
  Also see GILMER, Jimmy
  Also see SEDAKA, Neil
  Also see TOKENS

SEEDS
(Featuring Sky Saxon)
Singles: 7–inch
GNP/CRESCENDO (354 "Can't Seem to
  Make You Mine"/"Daisy Mae") 5-10 65
GNP/CRESCENDO (354 "Can't Seem to
  Make You Mine"/"I Tell Myself") 4-8 67
GNP/CRESCENDO (364 "Your Pushing
  too Hard") 8-12 65
  (Reissued on 372 as *Pushing too Hard*, with a
  different flip, *Try to Understand*.)
GNP/CRESCENDO (370 "The Other
  Place") 5-10 65
GNP/CRESCENDO (372 through 422) . 4-8 66-69
MGM 8-12 69-70

Picture Sleeves
GNP/CRESCENDO (354 "Can't Seem to
  Make You Mine"/"I Tell Myself") 10-20 67
GNP/CRESCENDO (383 "Mr.
  Farmer") 10-20 67
GNP/CRESCENDO (394 "A Thousand
  Shadows") 10-20 67
LPs: 10/12–inch 33rpm
GNP/CRESCENDO (2023 through
  2043) 20-30 66-67
  (All Seeds LPs, except 2043, *Raw and Alive*, were
  reissued with original catalog numbers. First issue,
  red label, 1960s LPs have, "GNP/Crescendo," on a
  horizontal line. Reissues have the label name in a
  circular manner on the label.)
GNP/CRESCENDO (2100 series) 5-10 77
  Also see FULLER, Bobby / Seeds

SEEGER, Pete
Singles: 7–inch
COLUMBIA 4-6 63-67
FOLKWAYS 5-10 59
PIONEER 4-8 60
LPs: 10/12–inch 33rpm
ARAVEL 10-20 63-64
ARCHIVE of FOLK MUSIC 10-15 65
BROADSIDE 10-20 63
CAPITOL 10-20 64-67
COLUMBIA 10-20 63-72
DISC 10-20 64
FOLKWAYS 8-20 59-75
  (Black vinyl.)
FOLKWAYS (7610 "Animal Folk
  Songs") 25-30
  (Colored vinyl.)
HARMONY 5-10 68-70
ODYSSEY 8-12 68
OLYMPIC 5-10 73
PHILIPS 10-20 63
STINSON (57 "Pete Seeger Concert") 20-30 54
  (10–inch LP.)
STINSON (90 "Pete") 5-10 70
TRADITION 5-10 73
VANGUARD 6-12 78
VERVE/FOLKWAYS 10-20 65
WARNER 5-10 79
  Also see SEEGERS
  Also see WEAVERS

SEEGER, Pete, and Arlo Guthrie
LPs: 10/12–inch 33rpm
REPRISE 8-12 75
WARNER 5-10 81
  Also see GUTHRIE, Arlo

SEEGER, Pete, and Pacific Gas and Electric
LPs: 10/12–inch 33rpm
COLUMBIA (3540 "Tell Me That You Love
  Me, Junie Moon") 10-15 70
  (Soundtrack.)
  Also see PACIFIC GAS & ELECTRIC

SEEGERS
LPs: 10/12–inch 33rpm
PRESTIGE 10-20   65
   Members: Pete Seeger; Peggy Seeger; Mike Seeger; Barbara
   Seeger; Penny Seeger.
   Also see SEEGER, Pete

SEEKERS
Singles: 7–inch
ATMOS 5-8   65
CAPITOL 4-6   65-68
MARVEL 5-8   65
Picture Sleeves
CAPITOL 5-10   65
LPs: 10/12–inch 33rpm
CAPITOL (100 series) 8-12   69
CAPITOL (2000 series) 10-20   65-67
CAPITOL (16000 series) 5-10   80
MARVEL 15-20   65
   Members: Judy Durham; Keith Potger.
   Also see JAMES, Sonny / Seekers
   Also see NEW SEEKERS

SEELY, Jeannie
Singles: 7–inch
CHALLENGE 4-6   64-65
COLUMBIA 3-5   77-78
DECCA 3-5   69-73
MCA 3-5   73-75
MONUMENT 3-5   66-68
LPs: 10/12–inch 33rpm
DECCA 6-12   69-70
HARMONY 5-10   72
MCA 5-8   73
MONUMENT 6-12   66-77
   Also see GREENE, Jack, and Jeannie Seely

SEGAL, George
(George Segal and the Imperial Jazzband)
Singles: 7–inch
FLYING DUTCHMAN 3-5   74
PHILIPS 4-6   67
LPs: 10/12–inch 33rpm
PHILIPS 10-20   67
SIGNATURE 5-10   74

SEGER, Bob
(Bob Seger and the Last Heard; Bob Seger System;
Bob Seger and the Silver Bullet Band)
Singles: 7–inch
ABKCO 3-6   72-75
CAMEO (438 "East Side Story") 10-20   66
CAMEO (444 "Sock It to
   Me Santa") 15-25   66
CAMEO (465 "Persecution Smith") . . 10-20   66
CAMEO (473 "Vagrant Winter") 10-20   66
CAMEO (494 "Heavy Music") 8-12   67
CAPITOL (Except 2000 series) 2-5   71-86
CAPITOL (2000 series) 4-8   68-70
HIDEOUT (1013 "East Side Story") . . 20-30   66
HIDEOUT (1014 "Persecution Smith") 20-30   66
MCA 2-4   87

PALLADIUM 3-6   71-74
REPRISE 3-6   72
Promotional Singles
CAPITOL (Colored vinyl) 4-8   78
CAPITOL (9878 "Shame on the Moon") 3-6   82
   (This was an edited version, at 4:22, and not the
   promo single of 5187, which ran 4:55.)
Picture Sleeves
CAPITOL 2-5   78-84
LPs: 10/12–inch 33rpm
CAPITOL (ST-172 "Ramblin' Gamblin'
   Man") 15-25   69
CAPITOL (SM-172 "Ramblin' Gamblin'
   Man") 8-10   75
CAPITOL (ST-236 "Noah") 50-70   69
CAPITOL (SKAO-499 "Mongrel") 15-25   70
CAPITOL (SM-499 "Mongrel") 8-10   75
CAPITOL (ST-731 "Brand New
   Morning") 30-50   71
CAPITOL (8433 "Live Bullet,
   Consensus Cuts") 20-30   75
   (Promotional issue only.)
CAPITOL (11000 series, except
   11557 and 11904) 6-12   75-78
CAPITOL (ST-11557 "Night Moves") . . 5-10   78
CAPITOL (ST-11557 "Night Moves") . 30-40   78
   (Picture disc. Promotional issue only.)
CAPITOL (SW-11904 "Stranger in
   Town") 5-10   78
CAPITOL (SEAX-11904 "Stranger in
   Town") 15-20   79
   (Picture disc.)
CAPITOL (12000 series) 6-10   80-86
CAPITOL (16000 series) 5-8   80
INNER VIEW ("Demonstration Record
   Bob Seger") 15-25   76
   (Promotional issue only.)
MFSL (034 "Night Moves") 25-50   79
MFSL (127 "Against the Wind") 20-30   85
PALLADIUM (1006 "Smokin' O.P.'s") . 15-25   72
PALLADIUM (2126 "Back in '72") . . . 50-75   73
REPRISE 10-15   72-74
   Also see BEACH BUMS
   Also see BROWNSVILLE STATION
   Also see NEWMAN, Randy

SELECTOR
Singles: 7–inch
CHRYSALIS 3-5   79-81
LPs: 10/12–inch 33rpm
CHRYSALIS 5-10   79-81

SELF, Ronnie
Singles: 78rpm
ABC-PAR 10-20   56
COLUMBIA 10-20   57
Singles: 7–inch
ABC-PAR (9714 "Pretty Bad Blues") 60-100   56
ABC-PAR (9768 "Sweet Love") 50-75   56
AMY 4-8   68

COLUMBIA (Except 41241) 15-25   57-58
COLUMBIA (41241 "Petrified") 75-125   58
DECCA 5-10   59-62
KAPP 4-8   63
EPs: 7–inch 33/45rpm
COLUMBIA (2149 "Ain't I'm a Dog") 175-200   57

SELLARS, Marilyn
Singles: 7–inch
MEGA 3-5   74-77
ZODIAC 3-5   76-77
LPs: 10/12–inch 33rpm
MEGA 5-10   74-77
ZODIAC 5-10   77

SEMBELLO, Michael
Singles: 12–inch 33/45rpm
CASABLANCA 4-6   83
WARNER 4-6   83-84
Singles: 7–inch
A&M 2-4   86
CASABLANCA 3-5   83
GEFFEN 2-4   85
WARNER 3-5   83-84
LPs: 10/12–inch 33rpm
A&M 5-8   86
MCA 5-8   85
WARNER 5-10   83

SENATOR BOBBY
Singles: 7–inch
RCA 4-8   67
Also see HARDLY WORTHIT PLAYERS

SENATOR McKINLEY:
see HARDLY WORTHIT PLAYERS

SENAY, Eddy
Singles: 7–inch
SUSSEX 3-5   72-73
LPs: 10/12–inch 33rpm
SUSSEX 8-12   72

SENECA, Joe
Singles: 7–inch
EVEREST 5-10   59-60

SEÑOR SOUL
Singles: 7–inch
DOUBLE SHOT 4-8   67-68
WHIZ 3-6   69-70
LPs: 10/12–inch 33rpm
DOUBLE SHOT 10-15   68-69

SENSATIONS
(Yvonne Baker and the Sensations)
Singles: 78rpm
ATCO 8-12   55
Singles: 7–inch
ARGO 5-10   61-62
ATCO 15-25   55
CHESS 3-5   73
JUNIOR 8-12   62-64

TOLLIE 5-10   64
LPs: 10/12–inch 33rpm
ARGO (4022 "Let Me In") 50-75   63
Also see MILLS, Yvonne, and the Sensations

SEQUENCE
Singles: 7–inch
SUGAR HILL 3-5   80-82
LPs: 10/12–inch 33rpm
SUGAR HILL 5-10   81

SERENDIPITY SINGERS
Singles: 7–inch
PHILIPS 4-8   64-66
U.A. 3-5   67-69
Picture Sleeves
PHILIPS 4-8   64-66
LPs: 10/12–inch 33rpm
PHILIPS 10-20   64-65
WING 8-12   68

SERIOUS INTENTION
Singles: 12–inch 33/45rpm
EASY STREET 4-6   84

SESAME STREET KIDS: see ERNIE

SETZER, Brian
Singles: 7–inch
EMI 2-4   86-88
LPs: 10/12–inch 33rpm
EMI 5-8   86-88
Also see STRAY CATS

SEVELLE, Taja
Singles: 7–inch
PAISLEY PARK 2-4   87
REPRISE 2-4   87-88

707
Singles: 7–inch
BOARDWALK 3-5   82
CASABLANCA 3-5   80
LPs: 10/12–inch 33rpm
BOARDWALK 5-10   82
CASABLANCA 5-10   80

7A3
Singles: 7–inch
GEFFEN 2-4   88
LPs: 10/12–inch 33rpm
GEFFEN 5-8   88

SEVEN SEAS
Singles: 7–inch
GLADES 3-5   75

SEVENTH WONDER
(7th Wonder)
Singles: 12–inch 33/45rpm
CASABLANCA 4-6   80
PARACHUTE 4-8   79
Singles: 7–inch
ABET 3-5   73
CASABLANCA 3-5   80

CHOCOLATE CITY 3-5   80
PARACHUTE 3-5   78-79
LPs: 10/12–inch 33rpm
CHOCOLATE CITY 5-10   80
PARACHUTE 5-10   78-79

SEVERINSEN, Doc, Orchestra
(Doc Severinsen and the Dodge City Boys; Tonight Show Band With Doc Severinsen)
Singles: 7–inch
COMMAND 3-5   65-70
EPIC 4-6   59-76
FRONTLINE 2-4   80
RCA 2-4   72-73
Picture Sleeves
COMMAND 3-5   70
LPs: 10/12–inch 33rpm
ABC 5-10   71-73
AMHERST 5-8   86
COMMAND 5-15   61-73
EPIC 5-8   76-81
EVEREST 5-8   78
JUNO 5-10   70-79
MCA 4-8   82
RCA 5-10   71
Also see MANCINI, Henry, and Doc Severinsen

SEVILLE, David
(Ross Bagdasarian)
Singles: 78rpm
LIBERTY 4-8   56-57
Singles: 7–inch
LIBERTY 5-10   56-61
Picture Sleeves
LIBERTY (55079 "Gotta Get
  to Your House") 10-15   57
EPs: 7–inch 33/45rpm
LIBERTY (1003 "The Witch Doctor") . 25-45   57
LPs: 10/12–inch 33rpm
LIBERTY (3073 "The Music of
  David Seville") 25-35   57
LIBERTY (3092 "The Witch Doctor") . 35-45   58
Also see CHIPMUNKS

SEVILLES
Singles: 7–inch
CAL-GOLD 8-12   62
GALAXY 8-12   63-64
J.C. 10-20   60-61

SEX PISTOLS
Singles: 7–inch
WARNER 3-6   78
LPs: 10/12–inch 33rpm
WARNER 5-10   77
Also see PUBLIC IMAGE LTD.
Also see SIOUXSIE and the Banshees

S-EXPRESS
Singles: 7–inch
CAPITOL 2-4   88

SEXTON, Ann
Singles: 7–inch
DASH 3-5   77
MONUMENT 3-5   77
SEVENTY SEVEN 3-5   72-74
SOUND STAGE 3-5   77

SEXTON, Charlie
Singles: 7–inch
MCA 2-4   86-89
LPs: 10/12–inch 33rpm
MCA 5-8   86-89

SEXTON, Charlie, and Ron Wood
LPs: 10/12–inch 33rpm
MCA 5-8   84
Also see SEXTON, Charlie
Also see WOOD, Ron

SEYMOUR, Phil
Singles: 7–inch
BOARDWALK 3-5   81
LPs: 10/12–inch 33rpm
BOARDWALK 5-10   81
Also see TEXTONES
Also see TWILLEY, Dwight, Band

SHA NA NA
Singles: 7–inch
KAMA SUTRA 3-5   70-75
SUTRA 3-5   74
LPs: 10/12–inch 33rpm
ACCORD 5-10   81-83
BUDDAH 5-10   77
CSP 8-12   78
EMUS 8-12   78
K-TEL 5-10   81
KAMA SUTRA 10-15   69-76
NASHVILLE 5-10   80
Members: Lennie Baker; Jon "Bowzer" Bauman; Johnny Contardo; Denny Green; Henry Gross; Jocko Marcellino; Danny McBride; Scott Powell; David-Allan "Chico" Ryan "Screamin' Scott Simon; Donny York.
Also see GROSS, Henry
Also see TRAVOLTA, John / Sha Na Na

SHACK
Singles: 7–inch
VOLT 3-5   71

SHACKLEFORDS
Singles: 7–inch
CAPITOL 4-6   66
LHI 4-6   67-68
MERCURY 4-8   63
LPs: 10/12–inch 33rpm
CAPITOL 10-20   66
MERCURY 15-25   63
Members: Lee Hazlewood; Marty Cooper; Al Stone; Garcia Nitzsche.
Also see HAZLEWOOD, Lee
Also see MOMENTS

SHADES of BLUE
Singles: 7-inch
COLLECTABLES 2-4
IMPACT 4-8   66-67
SHADES 4-8   68
LPs: 10/12-inch 33rpm
IMPACT (101 "Happiness Is") 25-30   66
(Monaural.)
IMPACT (101 "Happiness Is") 30-40   66
(Stereo.)

SHADES of LOVE
Singles: 7-inch
VENTURE 3-5   82

SHADOW
Singles: 7-inch
ELEKTRA 3-5   79-81
LPs: 10/12-inch 33rpm
ELEKTRA 5-10   79-81

SHADOWFAX
Singles: 7-inch
WINDHAM HILL 3-5   82
LPs: 10/12-inch 33rpm
CAPITOL 5-8   88
PASSPORT 8-10   76
WINDHAM HILL 5-8   82-86

SHADOWS of KNIGHT
Singles: 7-inch
ATCO 8-12   69
COLUMBIA/AURAVISION ("Potato
Chip") 30-50
(5-inch, promotional flexi-disc.)
DUNWICH (116 "Gloria") 10-15   66
(Label makes no reference to distribution by Atco.)
DUNWICH (116 "Gloria") 5-10   66
(Label reads "Distributed by Atco.")
DUNWICH (122 through 167) 5-10   66-67
SUPER K 5-10   69
TEAM 5-10   68
Picture Sleeves
DUNWICH (122 "Oh Yeah") 15-20   66
DUNWICH (128 "Bad Little Woman") . 20-30   66
LPs: 10/12-inch 33rpm
DUNWICH (666 "Gloria") 50-100   66
DUNWICH (667 "Back Door Men") . 50-100   66
SUPER K (6002 "The Shadows
of Knight") 15-25   69

SHAFTO, Bobby
Singles: 7-inch
RUST 5-8   64-65

SHAKATAK
Singles: 12-inch 33/45rpm
POLYDOR 4-6   82-84
Singles: 7-inch
POLYDOR 2-4   82-84
LPs: 10/12-inch 33rpm
POLYDOR 5-8   82

SHALAMAR
Singles: 12-inch 33/45rpm
COLUMBIA 4-6   84-85
SOLAR 4-6   79-85
Singles: 7-inch
COLUMBIA 2-4   84-85
MCA 2-4   84
SOLAR 3-5   78-87
SOUL TRAIN 3-5   77
Picture Sleeves
SOLAR 3-5   83
LPs: 10/12-inch 33rpm
SOLAR 5-10   78-85
SOUL TRAIN 5-10   77
Members: Howard Hewett; Jody Watley; Jeffrey Daniel.
Also see HEWETT, Howard

SHANGO
Singles: 12-inch 33/45rpm
CELLULOID 4-8   83
Singles: 7-inch
A&M 4-6   69
CELLULOID 2-4   83
GNP/CRESCENDO 3-6   69
LPs: 10/12-inch 33rpm
A&M 10-15   69
DUNHILL 8-12   70
Also see BAMBAATAA, Afrika

SHANGRI-LAS
(Shangra-Las)
Singles: 7-inch
COLLECTABLES 2-4
ERIC 2-4
MERCURY 4-8   66-67
RED BIRD 5-10   64-66
SSS INT'L 3-5
SCEPTER 10-15   65
SMASH 10-20   63
SPOKANE 10-20   64
TRIP 2-4
LPs: 10/12-inch 33rpm
BACK-TRAC 5-10   85
COLLECTABLES 5-10   83
MERCURY (21099 "Golden Hits of
the Shangri-las") 20-30   66
(Monaural.)
MERCURY (21099 "Golden Hits of
the Shangri-las") 50-75   66
(Shown as monaural but plays in true stereo.)
MERCURY (61099 "Golden Hits of
the Shangri-las") 25-35   66
(Stereo.)
POST 10-12
RED BIRD (101 "Leader of the Pack") 30-50   65
RED BIRD (104 "Shangri-Las '65") . 50-100   65
RED BIRD (104 "I Can Never Go
Home Anymore") 50-85   65
Members: Mary Weiss; Marge Ganser; Mary Ann Ganser.

SHANK, Bud
Singles: 78rpm
GOOD TIME JAZZ 4-6   54
Singles: 7–inch
GOOD TIME JAZZ 5-10   54
PACIFIC JAZZ 3-6   61-70
WORLD PACIFIC 3-6   64-68
EPs: 7–inch 33/45rpm
NOCTURNE (3/4 "The Bud Shank
  Quintet") 50-75   53
  (Price is for either volume.)
PACIFIC JAZZ 20-30   54-58
LPs: 10/12–inch 33rpm
CONCORD JAZZ 5-8   76
CROWN 10-20   63
KIMBERLY 10-20   63
NOCTURNE (2 "The Bud Shank
  Quintet") 125-175   53
  (10–inch LP.)
PACIFIC JAZZ (14 "Bud Shank
  with Three Trombones") 50-100   54
  (10–inch LP.)
PACIFIC JAZZ (20 "Bud Shank
  and Bob Brookmeyer") 50-100   55
  (10–inch LP.)
PACIFIC JAZZ (4 through 89) 15-25   60-65
  (12–inch LPs.)
PACIFIC JAZZ (404 "Jazz Swings
  Broadway") 30-50   57
PACIFIC JAZZ (411 "The Swing's
  to TV") 30-50   57
PACIFIC JAZZ (1205 "Bud Shank
  and Shorty Rogers") 30-60   55
PACIFIC JAZZ (1213 "Strings and
  Trombones") 30-50   56
PACIFIC JAZZ (1215 "The Bud
  Shank Quartet") 30-50   56
PACIFIC JAZZ (1219 "Jazz at
  Cal-Tech") 30-50   56
PACIFIC JAZZ (1226 "Flute 'N
  Oboe") 30-50   57
PACIFIC JAZZ (1230 "The Bud
  Shank Quartet") 30-50   57
PACIFIC JAZZ (10000 and 20000
  series) 5-15   66-81
SUNSET 8-12   66
WORLD PACIFIC (1000 through
  1200 series) 20-40   58-60
WORLD PACIFIC (1400 series) 15-30   61-63
WORLD PACIFIC (1800 series) 15-20   64-67
WORLD PACIFIC (21000 series) 10-20   66-68
  Also see FOLKSWINGERS
  Also see LONDON, Julie, and the Bud Shank Quintet

SHANKAR, Ravi
Singles: 7–inch
APPLE 4-8   71
DARK HORSE 3-5   75
WORLD PACIFIC 4-8   59-68

Picture Sleeves
APPLE (1838 "Joi Bangla") 20-25   71
LPs: 10/12–inch 33rpm
ANGEL 10-15   67
APPLE 8-15   71-73
CAPITOL 8-15   67-72
COLUMBIA 8-15   66-68
DARK HORSE 5-10   74-76
FANTASY 8-12   73
PRESTIGE 8-12   68
SPARK 5-10   73
WORLD PACIFIC 10-20   59-69
  Also see BEATLES
  Also see HARRISON, George

SHANNON
(Marty Wilde)
Singles: 7–inch
EPIC/MAGNET 3-5   75
HERITAGE 4-6   69
  Also see WILDE, Marty

SHANNON
(Shannon Greene)
Singles: 12–inch 33/45rpm
EMERGENCY 4-6   83-84
MIRAGE 4-6   84-85
Singles: 7–inch
ATLANTIC 2-4   86
EMERGENCY 3-5   83-84
MIRAGE 3-5   84-85
LPs: 10/12–inch 33rpm
MIRAGE 5-10   84-85

SHANNON, Del
Singles: 7–inch
AMY 4-8   64-65
BERLEE 5-10   63-64
BIG TOP 8-15   61-63
COLLECTABLES 2-4
DUNHILL 4-8   69
ERIC 2-4
ISLAND 3-5   75
LANA 3-5

STEREO Runaway with Del Shannon

LIBERTY 5-10   66-68
NETWORK 3-5   81-82
TERRIFIC 3-5
WARNER 3-5   85
Picture Sleeves
LIBERTY 8-12   68
LPs: 10/12–inch 33rpm
AMY 20-40   64-65
BIG TOP (1303 "Runaway") 50-100   61
(Monaural.)
BIG TOP (1303 "Runaway") 400-600   61
(Stereo.)
BIG TOP (1308 "Little Town Flirt") ... 40-60   63
BUG 5-10   85
DOT 15-25   67
LIBERTY 15-20   66-68
NETWORK/ELEKTRA 5-10   81
PHOENIX 20 5-10   80
PICKWICK 8-10
POST 10-15
SIRE 10-15   75
SUNSET 10-15   70
U.A. 10-15   73
Also see HONDELLS / Del Shannon / Martha and the Vandellas

SHANNON, Jackie
(Jackie Shannon and the Cajuns; Jackie DeShannon)
Singles: 7–inch
DOT (15928 "Just Another Lie") 15-20   59
FRATERNITY (836 "Just Another Lie") 10-15   59
P.J. (101 "Trouble") 30-40   59
SAGE (290 "Just Another Lie") 20-30   59
SAND (330 "Trouble") 20-30   59
Also see DE SHANNON, Jackie

SHANTE, Roxanne
Singles: 12–inch 33/45rpm
POP ART 4-6   85
Singles: 7–inch
POP ART 2-4   85
LPs: 10/12–inch 33rpm
POP ART 5-8   85
Also see JAMES, Rick, and Roxanne Shante

SHANTELLE
Singles: 7–inch
PANDISC 4-6   85

SHAPIRO, Helen
Singles: 7–inch
CAPITOL 5-10   61-62
EPIC 4-8   62-63
JANUS 3-5   70
MUSICOR 4-6   65
TOWER 4-6   67
Picture Sleeves
EPIC 4-8   62
LPs: 10/12–inch 33rpm
EPIC 10-20   63

SHA-RAE, Billy
(Sha-Rae)
Singles: 7–inch
BAY-UKE 5-10   61-62
HOUR GLASS 3-5
LAURIE 3-5
SPECTRUM 3-5   71
Also see HEBB, Bobby / Billy Sha-Rae

SHARKEY, Feargal
Singles: 12–inch 33/45rpm
A&M 4-6   86
Singles: 7–inch
A&M 2-4   86
LPs: 10/12–inch 33rpm
A&M 5-8   86

SHARKS
Singles: 7–inch
MCA 3-5   73-74
LPs: 10/12–inch 33rpm
MCA 8-12   73-74

SHARP, Dee Dee
(Dee Dee Sharp Gamble)
Singles: 7–inch
ABKCO 3-5   83-84
ATCO 4-8   66-68
CAMEO 4-8   62-66
FAIRMOUNT 4-8   66
GAMBLE 4-8   68
PHILADELPHIA INT'L 3-5   77-81
TSOP 3-5   76
Picture Sleeves
CAMEO 5-10   62-65
LPs: 10/12–inch 33rpm
CAMEO 20-30   62 63
PHILADELPHIA INT'L 8-10   75-81
Also see CHECKER, Chubby, and Dee Dee Sharp
Also see KING, Ben E., and Dee Dee Sharp
Also see PHILADELPHIA INTERNATIONAL ALL STARS

SHARPE, Mike
Singles: 7–inch
LIBERTY 4-8   66-69
LPs: 10/12–inch 33rpm
LIBERTY 10-20   67-69

SHARPE, Ray
(Ray Sharpe and the Blues Whalers; Ray Sharpe and
the Soul Set)
Singles: 7–inch
A&M 3-5   71
ATCO 4-8   66
DOT 5-10   59
FLYING HIGH 3-5
GAREX 5-10   63
GREGMARK 5-10   62
HAMILTON 8-12   59
JAMIE (Except 1128) 5-10   58-60
JAMIE (1128 "Linda Lu"/
"Monkey's Uncle") 10-15   59

JAMIE (1128 "Linda Lu"/
"Red Sails In the Sunset") 5-10   59
(Note different flip side.)
LHI 4-6
MONUMENT 4-8   65
PARK AVE 4-8
SOCK and SOUL 4-8
TREY 5-10   61
LPs: 10/12–inch 33rpm
AWARD (711 "Welcome Back") 25-50
Also see KING CURTIS

SHARPEES
Singles: 7–inch
ONE-DERFUL 5-10   65-66
Members: Herbert Reeves; Vernon Guy; Stacy Johnson.

SHARPLES, Bob
(Bob Sharples' Living Strings)
Singles: 78rpm
LONDON 3-5   56-57
Singles: 7–inch
LONDON 4-6   56-61
LPs: 10/12–inch 33rpm
CAMDEN 5-10   60
LONDON 5-15   61-64
METRO 5-10   65

SHAW, Georgie
Singles: 78rpm
DECCA 3-5   53-56
Singles: 7–inch
DECCA 4-8   53-56
EPs: 7–inch 33/45rpm
DECCA 5-10   56
LPs: 10/12–inch 33rpm
DECCA 10-20   53-56
Also see KALLEN, Kitty, and Georgie Shaw

SHAW, Marlena
Singles: 12–inch 33/45rpm
COLUMBIA 4-8   79
SOUTH BAY 4-6   83
Singles: 7–inch
BLUE NOTE 3-5   72-76
CADET 4-6   66-69
COLUMBIA 3-5   77-79
SOUTH BAY 3-5   83
Picture Sleeves
CADET 4-8   67
LPs: 10/12–inch 33rpm
BLUE NOTE 8-12   72-75
CADET 10-15   68-69
COLUMBIA 5-10   77-79

SHAW, Robert, Chorale
Singles: 78rpm
RCA 3-5   50-58
Singles: 7–inch
RCA 4-8   50-62
EPs: 7–inch 33/45rpm
RCA 5-10   54-56

LPs: 10/12–inch 33rpm
ALMANAC 5-10   66
CAMDEN 5-10   64
RCA 5-15   50-70
VICTROLA 4-8   70

SHAW, Roland, Orchestra
Singles: 78rpm
LONDON 3-5   56-57
Singles: 7–inch
LONDON 3-6   56-67
LPs: 10/12–inch 33rpm
LONDON 5-10   64-78

SHAW, Sandie
Singles: 7–inch
MERCURY 4-8   64
RCA 3-6   68-70
REPRISE 4-8   64-67
LPs: 10/12–inch 33rpm
REPRISE 15-20   65-66

SHAW, Timmy
Singles: 7–inch
JAMIE 4-8   61-62
SCEPTER 3-5   73
WAND 4-8   63-64

SHAW, Tommy
Singles: 7–inch
A&M 2-4   84-85
LPs: 10/12–inch 33rpm
A&M 5-8   84-85
Also see STYX

SHAWN, Damon
Singles: 7–inch
WESTBOUND 3-5   73

SH-BOOMS
(Chords)
Singles: 78rpm
CAT 10-15   55
VIK 10-15   57
Singles: 7–inch
ATCO (6213 "Sh-Boom") 8-12   61
ATLANTIC (2074 "Blue Moon") 10-20   60
CAT (117 "Could It Be") 25-30   55
VIK (0295 "I Don't Want to
Set the World on Fire") 15-25   57
Also see CHORDS

SHEAR, Jules
Singles: 12–inch 33/45rpm
EMI AMERICA 4-6   84-85
Singles: 7–inch
EMI AMERICA 2-4   84-85
LPs: 10/12–inch 33rpm
EMI AMERICA 5-8   83

SHEARING, George, Quintet
Singles: 78rpm
CAPITOL 3-5   55-57
MGM 3-6   50-56

Singles: 7-Inch

CAPITOL	3-8	55-67
LONDON	3-6	63
MGM	5-10	50-56
SHEBA	3-5	71

EPs: 7-Inch 33/45rpm

CAPITOL	5-10	55-60
MGM	5-10	51-55

LPs: 10/12-Inch 33rpm

ARCHIVE of FOLK MUSIC	6-12	68
BASF	5-10	73
CAPITOL (Except 648 through 1628)	5-15	62-77
CAPITOL (648 through 1628)	10-25	55-61
CONCORD JAZZ	5-8	80-82
DISCOVERY (3002 "George Shearing Qunitet") (10-inch LP.)	30-50	50
EVEREST	5-10	69
LION	10-20	59
MGM (90 "A Touch of Genius") (10-inch LP.)	20-40	51
MGM (155 "I Hear Music") (10-inch LP.)	20-40	52
MGM (226 "When Lights Are Low") (10-inch LP.)	20-40	53
MGM (252 "An Evening with George Shearing") (10-inch LP.)	20-40	55
MGM (100 series)	5-10	70
MGM (3000 series)	15-25	55-60
MGM (4000 series)	10-20	62-63
MPS	5-10	74-75
METRO	10-15	65
PAUSA	5-8	79-82
SAVOY (12093 "Midnight on Cloud 69")	15-25	57
SAVOY (15003 "Piano Solo") (10-inch LP.)	30-50	51
SHEBA	5-10	71-76
VSP	10-15	66-67

Also see COLE, Cozy
Also see COLE, Nat "King," and George Shearing
Also see COLE, Natalie
Also see LEE, Peggy, and George Shearing

SHEARING, George and the Montgomery Brothers

Singles: 7-Inch

JAZZLAND	3-6	62

LPs: 10/12-Inch 33rpm

JAZZLAND (55 "George Shearing and the Montgomery Brothers) (Cover pictures Shearing with the three brothers.)	25-40	61
JAZZLAND (55 "George Shearing and the Montgomery Brothers) (Cover pictures a woman.)	15-25	62
RIVERSIDE	5-10	82

Also see MONTGOMERY BROTHERS
Also see SHEARING, George, Quintet
Also see WILSON, Nancy, & George Shearing

SHEEN, Bobby

Singles: 7-Inch

CAPITOL	4-8	66-69
CHELSEA	3-5	75
DIMENSION	4-8	65
LIBERTY	5-10	62
WARNER	3-5	72

Also see ALLEY CATS
Also see BOB B. SOXX and the Blue Jeans

SHEEP

Singles: 7-Inch

BOOM	10-20	66

Also see STRANGELOVES

SHEILA
(Sheila and B. Devotion)

Singles: 7-Inch

CARRERE	3-5	80-81
CASABLANCA	3-5	78

Picture Sleeves

CARRERE	3-5	80-81

Promotional Singles

CARRERE (37675 "Little Darlin") (Price includes special sleeve.)	4-6	81

LPs: 10/12-Inch 33rpm

CARRERE	5-10	80
CASABLANCA	5-10	78

SHEILA E: see E., Sheila

SHELLEY, Pete
(Peter Shelley)

Singles: 12-inch 33/45rpm

ARISTA	4-6	82-83

Singles: 7-Inch

ARISTA	2-4	82-83
BELL	3-5	74

LPs: 10/12-Inch 33rpm

ARISTA	5-8	82-83

Also see BUZZCOCKS

SHELLS

Singles: 78rpm

CANDLELITE (436 "Baby Oh Baby") (Colored vinyl.)	5-10	72
JOHNSON	10-15	57

Singles: 7-Inch

ABC	3-5	75
BOARDWALK	3-5	75
COLLECTABLES	2-4	
END (1022 "Pretty Little Girl")	50-100	58
END (1050 "Whispering Winds")	25-40	59
GONE (5103 "Pretty Little Girl")	10-20	61
JOHNSON (099 "My Cherie")	4-6	72
JOHNSON (104 "Baby Oh Baby"/ "Angel Eyes")	20-30	57
(Has selection number, 104, centered between the horizontal lines on the right side of label.)		

JOHNSON (104 "Baby Oh Baby"/
"What's in an Angel Eyes") 8-12   60
(The 1960 issue label has two parallel lines with
one thinner than the other. These lines are both
the same thickness on the '57 issue. MOST 1957
issues have the shorter flip side title, but ALL 1960
issues have the longer title.)
JOHNSON (106 "Pleading No More") 75-100   58
JOHNSON (107 "Explain It to Me") .. 10-20   61
JOHNSON (109 "Better Forget Him") 10-20   61
JOHNSON (110 "In the Dim of
the Dark") 10-20   61
JOHNSON (112 "Sweetest One") ... 15-25   61
JOHNSON (119 "Deep in My Heart") . 20-25   62
JOHNSON (120 "A Toast on
Your Birthday") 20-25   62
JOHNSON (127 "On My Honor") 30-40   63
JOHNSON (332 "Explain It to Me") ... 8-12   61
JOSIE (912 "Deep in My Heart") 10-15   63
ROULETTE (4156 "She Wasn't Meant
for Me") 15-25   59
SELSOM 5-10   65
SNOWFLAKE (1959 "If You Were
Gone from Me"/"Misty") 10-20   64
(Blank, orange labels.)
SOUNDS from the SUBWAY 3-5   77
(Colored vinyl.)
LPs: 10/12–inch 33rpm
CANDLELITE 10-12
JUBILEE 10-15
Members: Nathaniel Burknight; Shade Alston; Bobby Nurse;
Danny Small; Gus Geter; Roy Jones.
Also see DUBS / Shells

SHELTO, Steve
Singles: 12–inch 33/45rpm
SAM 4-6   83

SHELTON, Anne
Singles: 78rpm
COLUMBIA 4-6   56
Singles: 7–inch
COLUMBIA 5-10   56
EPIC 4-8   59

SHELTON, Ricky Van
Singles: 7–inch
COLUMBIA 2-4   86-91
LPs: 10/12–inch 33rpm
COLUMBIA 5-8   87-91

SHELTON, Roscoe
Singles: 7–inch
BATTLE 4-8   62-63
EXCELLO 5-10   59-61
SIMS 4-8   64-65
SOUND STAGE 7 4-8   65-68
LPs: 10/12–inch 33rpm
EXCELLO (8002 "Roscoe Shelton") . 40-50   61
SOUND STAGE 7 15-20   66

SHEP and the Limelites
(Featuring James Sheppard)
Singles: 7–inch
ABC 3-5   73
HULL (Except 770) 10-20   61-65
HULL (770 "A Party for Two") 20-30   65
ROULETTE 3-5   73
LPs: 10/12–inch 33rpm
HULL (1001 "Our Anniversary") ... 300-400   62
ROULETTE (25350 "Our Anniversary")35-45   67
Also see HEARTBEATS
Also see HEARTBEATS / Shep and the Limelites

SHEPARD, Jean
Singles: 78rpm
CAPITOL 3-5   53-57
Singles: 7–inch
CAPITOL 5-10   53-61
(Purple labels.)
CAPITOL 3-8   61-72
(Orange or orange/yellow labels.)
MERCURY 3-5   72
SCORPION 2-4   78
U.A. 3-5   73-77
EPs: 7–inch 33/45rpm
CAPITOL 5-10   56-61
LPs: 10/12–inch 33rpm
CAPITOL (100 through 800 series) ... 5-10   69-71
CAPITOL (700 through 1200 series) . 15-25   56-59
(With a "T" prefix.)
CAPITOL (1500 through 2900 series) 10-15   61-68
CAPITOL (11000 series) 5-10   72-79
MERCURY 5-10   71
PICKWICK/HILLTOP 5-12   67-68
POWER PAK 5-8
U.A. 5-10   73-76

SHEPARD, Jean, and Ferlin Huskey
Singles: 78rpm
CAPITOL 3-5   53
Singles: 7–inch
CAPITOL 4-8   53
Also see HUSKY, Ferlin
Also see SHEPARD, Jean

SHEPARD SISTERS:
see SHEPHERD SISTERS

SHEPPARD, T.G.
Singles: 7–inch
COLUMBIA 2-4   85
HITSVILLE 3-5   76
MELODYLAND 3-5   74-75
WARNER 2-4   77-85
LPs: 10/12–inch 33rpm
COLUMBIA 5-8   85
CURB 5-8   84
HITSVILLE 5-10   76
MELODYLAND 8-10   75-76
WARNER 5-8   78-83
Also see COLLINS, Judy, and T.G. Sheppard
Also see EASTWOOD, Clint, and T.G. Sheppard

SHEPPARD SISTERS:
see SHEPHERD SISTERS

SHERBET
(Sherbs)
Singles: 7–inch
ATCO 3-5   81
MCA 3-5   76-77
LPs: 10/12–inch 33rpm
ATCO 5-10   80-82
MCA 5-10   76-77

SHERBS: see SHERBET

SHERIDAN, Bobby
(Charlie Rich)
Singles: 7–inch
SUN (354 "Red Man") 10-15   61
Also see RICH, Charlie

SHERIDAN, Tony and the Beat Brothers:
see BEATLES

SHERIFF
Singles: 7–inch
CAPITOL 3-5   83
LPs: 10/12–inch 33rpm
CAPITOL 5-8   83
OBSERVATORY 6-10   79

SHERMAN, Allan
(Allan Sherman and Friends)
Singles: 7–inch
RCA 3-6   68
WARNER 4-8   63-66
Picture Sleeves
WARNER 4-8   63-64
LPs: 10/12–inch 33rpm
JUBILEE 10-20   62
RCA (Except 310) 10-15   64
RCA (310 "Alan Sherman and You") . 20-30 64
(Promotional issue only. Includes 25-page script,
letter from Allan and a comments postcard.)
RHINO 5-8   85-86
WARNER 10-20   62-65

SHERMAN, Bobby
Singles: 7–inch
CAMEO 4-8   66
CONDOR 4-8   69
DECCA 5-10   64-65
DOT 4-8   63
EPIC 4-8   67
GRT 3-5   76
JANUS 3-5   75
METROMEDIA 3-5   69-73
PARKWAY 5-10   65
STARCREST 5-10   62
Picture Sleeves
DECCA 8-12   65
METROMEDIA 3-5   69-72

EPs: 7–inch 33/45rpm
METROMEDIA ("Bobby Sherman") 4-8   70
(Flexi-disc.)
LPs: 10/12–inch 33rpm
METROMEDIA 8-12   69-73

SHERMAN, Joe, and His Orchestra
(Joe Sherman and the Arena Brass)
Singles: 78rpm
KAPP 3-5   56-57
Singles: 7–inch
EPIC 3-5   65-66
KAPP 4-6   56-61
WORLD ARTISTS 3-6   63-65
LPs: 10/12–inch 33rpm
COLUMBIA 5-10   68
EPIC 5-10   66
RCA 5-10   67
WORLD ARTISTS 5-12   63-64

SHERRYS
Singles: 7–inch
GUYDEN 8-12   62-63
MERCURY 5-10   64
ROBERTS 5-10
LPs: 10/12–inch 33rpm
GUYDEN (503 "At the Hop") 75-125 62

SHERWOOD, Roberta
Singles: 78rpm
DECCA 3-5   56-57
Singles: 7–inch
DECCA 4-8   56-64
DUNHILL 3-6   68
HAPPY TIGER 3-6   69
HARMON 3-6   62-63
KING 3-5   71-72
MCA 3-5   73
OLEN 4-6   65
EPs: 7–inch 33/45rpm
DECCA 5-10   56-59
LPs: 10/12–inch 33rpm
ABC-PAR 5-15   63-64
DECCA 8-18   56-65
HARMONY 5-15   63
KING 5-8   70
VOCALION 5-10   66-68

SHIELDS
Singles: 7–inch
DOT (136 "You Cheated") 20-25 66
(Colored vinyl. Promotional issue only.)
DOT (15805 "You Cheated") 10-15 58
DOT (15856 "I'm Sorry Now") 15-20 58
DOT (15940 "Play the Game Fair") . 15-20 59
TENDER (513 "You Cheated") 30-40 58
(Label does NOT read "Dist. By Dot.")
TENDER (513 "You Cheated") 15-20 58
(Label reads "Dist. By Dot.")
TENDER (518 "I'm Sorry Now") 25-35 59
TENDER (521 "Play the Game Fair") 25-35 59

TRANSCONTINENTAL (1013 "The Girl
Around the Corner") 75-100   60

LPs: 10/12–inch 33rpm

BRYLEN 5-10
    Members: Frankie Ervin; Charles Wright; Nathaniel Wilson.
    Also see WRIGHT, Charles

SHINDOGS

Singles: 7–inch

VIVA 4-8   66
WARNER 4-8   65
    Members: Delaney Bramlet; Bonnie Bramlett.
    Also see DELANEY & BONNIE

SHINEHEAD

LPs: 10/12–inch 33rpm

ELEKTRA 5-8   88-90

SHIRELLES

Singles: 7–inch

COLLECTABLES 2-4
BLUE ROCK 4-8   68
DECCA 10-20   58-61
ERIC 2-4
GUSTO 2-4
RCA 5-10   71-73
SCEPTER (1203 "Dedicated to
the One I Love") 15-25   59
SCEPTER (1203 "Dedicated to
the One I Love") 10-15   59
SCEPTER (1205 through 1208) 15-20   59-60
(White label.)
SCEPTER (1205 through 1208) 10-15   59-60
(Red label.)
SCEPTER (1211 "Tomorrow") 20-25   60
SCEPTER (1211 "Will You
Love Me Tomorrow") 10-15   60
(Note longer title.)
SCEPTER (1217 through 12217) 5-10   61-68
TIARA (6112 "I Met Him
on a Sunday") 100-125   57
U.A. 3-5   70-71

Picture Sleeves

SCEPTER 10-20   63

LPs: 10/12–inch 33rpm

BACK-TRAC 5-10   85
EVEREST 5-10   81
GUSTO 5-10
PHOENIX 5-10   81
PRICEWISE 15-25
RCA 10-15   71-72
RHINO 5-8   85
SCEPTER (SRM-501 "Tonight's the
Night") 60-80   61
(Monaural.)
SCEPTER (SPS-501 "Tonight's the
Night") 75-100   61
(Stereo.)
SCEPTER (502 through 562) 25-40   61-67
SCEPTER (599 "Remember
When") 15-20   72

SPRINGBOARD 8-10   72
U.A. 10-15   71-75
    Members: Shirley Jackson-Alston; Beverly Lee; Doris
    Coley-Jackson; Addie "Micki" Harris-McFadden.
    Also see 4 SEASONS / Shirelles
    Also see JAN & DEAN / Roy Orbison / 4 Seasons / Shirelles
    Also see KING, Carole
    Also see SHIRLEY and the Shirelles

SHIRELLES and King Curtis

LPs: 10/12–inch 33rpm

SCEPTER (505 "A Twist Party") 25-35   62
    Also see KING CURTIS
    Also see SHIRELLES

SHIRLEY, Donald
(Don Shirley Trio)

Singles: 7–inch

BARNABY 2-4   76
CADENCE 4-8   60-64
COLUMBIA 3-6   68-69

LPs: 10/12–inch 33rpm

ATLANTIC 5-12   72
AUDIO FIDELITY 10-25   59
CADENCE 15-30   55-63
COLUMBIA 10-15   65-69

SHIRLEY & COMPANY
(Shirley Goodman)

Singles: 7–inch

VIBRATION 3-5   75-76

LPs: 10/12–inch 33rpm

VIBRATION 8-10   75
    Also see SHIRLEY & LEE

SHIRLEY & LEE

Singles: 78rpm

ALADDIN (3152 through 3205) 10-20   52-57

Singles: 7–inch

ABC 2-4   73
ALADDIN (3153 "I'm Gone") 50-75   52
ALADDIN (3173 "Baby") 40-60   53
ALADDIN (3192 "Shirley's Back") .. 30-50   53
ALADDIN (3205 "Two Happy People") 25-40   53
ALADDIN (3222 "Why Did I") 25-40   53
ALADDIN (3244 "Confessin") 25-40   54
ALADDIN (3258 "Comin' Over") 25-40   54
ALADDIN (3289 "Feel So Good") ... 15-25   55
ALADDIN (3302 "Lee's Dream") 15-25   55
ALADDIN (3313 "That's What I'll Do") 20-30   55
ALADDIN (3325 "Let the
Good Times Roll") 10-20   56
ALADDIN (3338 "I Feel Good") 10-20   56
ALADDIN (3362 "When I Saw You") . 10-20   57
ALADDIN (3369 "I Want to Dance") .. 10-20   57
ALADDIN (3380 "Rock All Night") ... 10-20   57
ALADDIN (3390 "Rockin' with
the Clock") 10-20   57
ALADDIN (3405 "I'll Thrill You") 10-20   57
ALADDIN (3418 "Everybody's
Rockin") 10-20   58
ALADDIN (3432 "All I Want to
Do Is Cry") 10-20   58

ALADDIN (3455 "True Love") 10-20   59
IMPERIAL 5-10   62-63
LIBERTY 2-4
U.A. 3-5   73
WARWICK 5-10   60-61

LPs: 10/12–inch 33rpm
ALADDIN (807 "Let the Good
  Times Roll") 300-400   56
IMPERIAL (9179 "Let the Good
  Times Roll") 50-75   62
SCORE (4023 "Let the Good
  Times Roll") 100-150   57
U.A. 20-25   73-74
WARWICK (2028 "Let the Good
  Times Roll") 75-100   61
  Members: Shirley Goodman; Leonard Lee.
  Also see ADAMS, Faye / Little Esther / Shirley & Lee
  Also see SHIRLEY & COMPANY

SHIRLEY & SQUIRRELY
Singles: 7–inch
GRT 3-5   76
LPs: 10/12–inch 33rpm
GRT 5-10   76
  Also see SHIRLEY, SQUIRRELY & MELVIN

SHIRLEY and the Shirelles
(Featuring Shirley Alston)
Singles: 7–inch
BELL 5-8   69
  Also see SHIRELLES

SHIRLEY, SQUIRRELY & MELVIN
Singles: 7–inch
EXCELSIOR 2-4   81
Picture Sleeves
EXCELSIOR 3-5   81
LPs: 10/12–inch 33rpm
EXCELSIOR 5-10   81
  Also see SHIRLEY & SQUIRRELY

SHOCK
Singles: 7–inch
DOWNTOWN 3-5   78
  (Colored vinyl.)
Picture Sleeves
DOWNTOWN 3-5   78
EPs: 7–inch 33/45rpm
IMPACT 8-10   78
  (Colored vinyl. Issued with a paper sleeve.)
  Members: Paul Lesperance; Steve Reiner; Kip Brown; Gaylord.

SHOCK
Singles: 12–inch 33/45rpm
FANTASY 4-6   81-83
Singles: 7–inch
FANTASY 2-4   81-83
LPs: 10/12–inch 33rpm
FANTASY 5-10   81-82

SHOCK-A-RA
Singles: 7–inch
FUTURE 2-4   88

SHOCKED, Michelle
LPs: 10/12–inch 33rpm
MERCURY 5-8   88-89

SHOCKING BLUE
Singles: 7–inch
BUDDAH 3-5   71
COLOSSUS 3-6   69-71
MGM 3-5   72-73
Picture Sleeves
COLOSSUS 4-6   69-70
LPs: 10/12–inch 33rpm
COLOSSUS 10-20   70

SHOES
Singles: 7–inch
BOMP 3-5   78
ELEKTRA 3-5   79
Picture Sleeves
ELEKTRA 3-5   79
EPs: 7–inch 33/45rpm
BOMP 5-10   78
LPs: 10/12–inch 33rpm
BLACK VINYL 8-12
ELEKTRA 5-10   77-82
PVC 5-10   78

SHONDELL, Troy
(Troy Shondel; Troy Shundell; Gary Shelton)
Singles: 7–inch
BRITE STAR 3-5   73-74
COLLECTABLES 2-4
COMMERCIAL 3-5   78
DECCA 4-8   64
EVEREST 4-8   62-64
GAYE (2010 "This Time") 20-25   61
GOLDCREAST (161 "This Time") ... 15-20   61
  (Company name is misspelled on label.)
GOLDCREST (161 "This Time") 10-15   61
LIBERTY 5-10   61-62
LUCKY 3-5   75
MASTER 10-15
RIC 4-8   65
SUNSHINE 3-5   76
TRX 4-8   67-69
TELESONIC 3-5   80-81
3 RIVERS 4-8
WRITERS & ARTISTS (001 "This
  Time") 25-35   61
LPs: 10/12–inch 33rpm
EVEREST (1206 "Many Sides") 25-35   63
STAR-FOX 10-15
SUNSET 10-15   67

SHONDELLS / Rod Bernard / Warren Storm / Skip Stewart
LPs: 10/12–inch 33rpm
LA LOUISIANNE (109 "At the
  Saturday Hop") 50-75   64
  Also see BERNARD, Rod
  Also see STORM, Warren

SHONDELLS
(Featuring Tommy James)
Singles: 7–inch
RED FOX (110 "Hanky Panky") 15-25   66
SELSOM (102 "Why Do Fools
  Fall in Love") 10-20   65
SNAP (101 "Pretty Little Red Bird") .. 25-45   63
SNAP (102 "Hanky Panky") 50-75   63
  (Makes no mention of distribution by Red Fox
  Records.
SNAP (102 "Hanky Panky") 20-25   65
  (Reads, "Distributed by Red Fox Records.")
  Also see JAMES, Tommy

SHO-NUFF
Singles: 12–inch 33/45rpm
MALACO 4-6   81-84
Singles: 7–inch
MALACO 2-4   81-84
STAX 3-5   78-79
LPs: 10/12–inch 33rpm
STAX 5-10   78

SHOOTING STAR
Singles: 7–inch
EPIC 2-4   82
VIRGIN 3-5   80
Picture Sleeves
VIRGIN 3-5   80
LPs: 10/12–inch 33rpm
ENIGMA 5-8   89
EPIC 5-8   81-83
VIRGIN 5-10   80-82

SHORE, Dinah
Singles: 78rpm
BLUEBIRD 5-10   40-42
RCA 3-6   50-57
VICTOR 4-8   42-46
Singles: 7–inch
CAPITOL 4-6   60-62
DECCA 3-5   69
MERCURY 3-5   74
PROJECT 3 3-6   67-68
RCA 5-10   50-57
Picture Sleeves
RCA 8-12   53
EPs: 7–inch 33/45rpm
CAMDEN 5-10   56
CAPITOL 4-8   59
COLUMBIA 4-8   59
RCA 5-15   51-57
LPs: 10/12–inch 33rpm
BAINBRIDGE 5-8   82
CAMDEN 5-10   59-60
CAPITOL (1200 series) 10-20   59-60
CAPITOL (1354 "Dinah Sings Some
  Blues with Red Norvo") ... 20-30   60
CAPITOL (1600 and 1700 series) ... 10-20   62

COLUMBIA (6000 series) 20-40   50-51
  (10–inch LPs.)
COLUMBIA (34000 series) 5-10   77
DECCA 5-10   69
HARMONY 5-10   59-60
NABISCO ("Nabisco Invitational") ... 15-20   83
  (Picture disc. Promotional issue only.)
PROJECT 3 5-10   68
RCA (11 "Tangos") 25-35   51
RCA (1100 and 1200 series) 20-30   55-56
RCA (3000 series) 20-30   53-54
  (10–inch LPs.)
REPRISE 10-15   65
  Also see KINGSTON TRIO / Dinah Shore
  Also see MARTIN, Dean

SHORE, Dinah, and Andre Previn
LPs: 10/12–inch 33rpm
CAPITOL 15-25   60
  Also see PREVIN, Andre
  Also see SHORE, Dinah

SHORR, Mickey, and the Cutups
Singles: 7–inch
TUBA 5-10   62

SHORROCK, Glenn
Singles: 7–inch
CAPITOL 2-4   83
  Also see LITTLE RIVER BAND

SHORT, Bobby
LPs: 10/12–inch 33rpm
ATLANTIC 10-20   59-72

SHORTER, Wayne
LPs: 10/12–inch 33rpm
BLUE NOTE 20-30   62
  (Label reads "Blue Note Records Inc. - New York,
  USA.")
BLUE NOTE 15-20   66
  (Label shows Blue Note Records as a division of
  either Liberty or United Artists.)
COLUMBIA 5-10   75
VEE JAY (Maroon label) 30-40   60
VEE JAY (Black label) 20-30   61-62
  Also see WEATHER REPORT

SHOT in the DARK
Singles: 7–inch
RSO 3-5   81
LPs: 10/12–inch 33rpm
RSO 5-10   81
  Members: Peter White; Bryan Savage; Krysia Kristianne; Robin
  Lamble; Adam Yurman.
  Also see STEWART, Al

SHOTGUN
Singles: 12–inch 33/45rpm
MONTAGE 4-6   82
Singles: 7–inch
ABC 3-5   77-79
MCA 3-5   80
MONTAGE 3-5   82

LPs: 10/12-inch 33rpm

ABC	5-10	77-79
MCA	5-10	79-80
MONTAGE	5-10	82

SHOW STOPPERS
(Showstoppers)

Singles: 7-inch

AMBER	5-10	63
COLLECTABLES	2-4	
COLUMBIA	10-15	66-67
HERITAGE	4-6	68
SHOWTIME	4-8	67

LPs: 10/12-inch 33rpm

COLLECTABLES	5-10	

SHOWBOYS

Singles: 12-inch 33/45rpm

PROFILE	4-6	86

Singles: 7-inch

PROFILE	2-4	86

SHOWDOWN

Singles: 7-inch

HONEY BEE	3-5	77

LPs: 10/12-inch 33rpm

HONEY BEE	5-10	77

SHOWMEN

Singles: 7-inch

AIRECORDS	10-20	
AMY	4-8	68
BB	4-8	67
IMPERIAL	5-10	64
LIBERTY	3-5	70-81
MINIT	8-15	61-63
SWAN	5-10	65-66

Member: General Johnson.
Also see JOHNSON, General
Also see THOMAS, Irma / Ernie K-Doe / Showmen / Benny Spellman

SHRIEKBACK

Singles: 12-inch 33/45rpm

ARISTA	4-6	84
WARNER	4-6	83

Singles: 7-inch

WARNER	2-4	83

LPs: 10/12-inch 33rpm

ISLAND	5-8	87-88
WARNER	5-8	83

Members: Barry Andrews; David Allen.
Also see GANG of FOUR
Also see XTC

SHUNDEL, Troy: see SHONDELL, Troy

SIBERRY, Jane

Singles: 7-inch

OPEN AIR	2-4	86

LPs: 10/12-inch 33rpm

OPEN AIR	5-8	86

SIDE EFFECT

Singles: 12-inch 33/45rpm

FANTASY	4-6	78-81

Singles: 7-inch

ELEKTRA	2-4	80-82
FANTASY	3-5	75-81

LPs: 10/12-inch 33rpm

ELEKTRA	5-8	80-82
FANTASY	5-8	75-81

Member: Miki Howard.
Also see HOWARD, Miki

SIDEKICKS

Singles: 7-inch

RCA	4-8	66-67

LPs: 10/12-inch 33rpm

RCA	10-20	66

SIEGEL, Dan

Singles: 7-inch

CRS ASSOC	2-4	88

SIEGEL - SCHWALL BAND

Singles: 7-inch

DEUTSCHE GRAMMOPHON	3-5	73
WOODEN NICKEL	3-5	72-74

LPs: 10/12-inch 33rpm

VANGUARD	12-25	66-70
WOODEN NICKEL	15-30	72-74

Members: Corky Siegel; Jim Schwall.
Also see SIEGEL, Corky

SIFFRE, Labi

Singles: 7-inch

CHINA	2-4	87

SIGLER, Bunny
(Mr. Emotions)

Singles: 12-inch 33/45rpm

SALSOUL	4-6	80

Singles: 7-inch

BEE	5-10	59
CRAIG	4-8	61
DECCA	3-6	65-67
GOLD MINE	3-5	78-79
NEPTUNE	4-8	
PARKWAY	4-6	67-69
PHILADELPHIA INT'L	3-5	71-76
SALSOUL	3-5	80

LPs: 10/12-inch 33rpm

GOLD MIND	5-10	78-79
PARKWAY	10-20	67
SALSOUL	5-10	80

Also see HOLLOWAY, Loleatta, and Bunny Sigler
Also see MASON, Barbara, and Bunny Sigler

SIGUE SIGUE SPUTNIK

Singles: 12-inch 33/45rpm

MANHATTAN	4-6	86

Singles: 7-inch

MANHATTAN	2-4	86

LPs: 10/12-inch 33rpm

MANHATTAN	5-10	86

Member: Tony James.
Also see GENERATION X

SILAS, Alfie
(Alfie)
Singles: 7–inch
MOTOWN	2-4	84-86
RCA	2-4	82-84
LPs: 10/12–inch 33rpm
MOTOWN	5-8	85
RCA	5-8	82-84

Also see KING, Bobby

SILENCERS
Singles: 7–inch
PRECISION	3-5	80
LPs: 10/12–inch 33rpm
PRECISION	5-10	80-81

SILENCERS
Singles: 7–inch
RCA	2-4	87
LPs: 10/12–inch 33rpm
RCA	5-8	87-90

SILENT UNDERDOG
Singles: 12–inch 33/45rpm
PROFILE	4-6	85

SILHOUETTES
Singles: 78rpm
EMBER	10-20	57
JUNIOR	20-40	57
Singles: 7–inch
ABC	3-5	73
ACE (552 "I Sold My Heart to the Junkman")	12-15	58
COLLECTABLES	2-4	
EMBER (1029 "Get a Job") (Red label.)	10-15	57
EMBER (1029 "Get a Job") Black label.)	4-8	60
EMBER (1032 "Headin' for the Poorhouse")	10-15	58
EMBER (1037 "Bing Bong") (Shiny red label.)	50-75	58
EMBER (1037 "Bing Bong") (Flat red label.)	10-15	58
FLASHBACK	3-5	65
IMPERIAL	5-10	62
JUNIOR (391 "Get a Job") (Brown label.)	150-200	57
JUNIOR (391 "Get a Job") (Blue label.)	75-100-200	57
JUNIOR (396 "I Sold My Heart to the Junkman")	30-40	58
JUNIOR (400 "Evelyn")	100-150	59
JUNIOR (993 "Your Love")	15-25	63
LPs: 10/12–inch 33rpm
GOODWAY (100 "Get a Job")	100-150	68

Also see HORTON, Bill, and the Silhouettes

SILK
Singles: 7–inch
ABC	3-5	69
DECCA	3-5	71
LPs: 10/12–inch 33rpm
ABC	10-15	69

Member: Michael Stanley.
Also see STANLEY, Michael, Band

SILK
Singles: 12–inch 33/45rpm
PHILADELPHIA INT'L	4-8	79-80
Singles: 7–inch
PHILADELPHIA INT'L	3-5	79-80
PRELUDE	3-5	77
PYE	3-5	76
LPs: 10/12–inch 33rpm
ARISTA	5-10	77
PHILADELPHIA INT'L	5-10	79

Member: Debra Henry.
Also see BUTLER, Jerry, and Debra Henry

SILK, J.M.
Singles: 12–inch 33/45rpm
D.J. INT'L	4-6	85

SILKIE
Singles: 7–inch
FONTANA	4-8	65-66
LPs: 10/12–inch 33rpm
FONTANA (27548 "You've Got to Hide Your Love Away") (Monaural.)	20-30	65
FONTANA (67548 "You've Got to Hide Your Love Away") (Stereo.)	25-35	65

Also see BEATLES

SILVA-TONES
(Bob Silva and the Silva-Tones)
Singles: 78rpm
ARGO	5-10	57
MONARCH	10-15	57
Singles: 7–inch
ARGO (5281 "That's All I Want from You")	10-15	57
MONARCH (615 "That's All I Want from You") (Yellow label.)	25-30	57
MONARCH (615 "That's All I Want from You") (Black label.)	15-20	57

SILVER
Singles: 7–inch
ARISTA	3-5	76-77
LPs: 10/12–inch 33rpm
ARISTA	8-10	76

Members: John Batdorf; Brent Mydland.
Also see BATDORF, John
Also see GRATEFUL DEAD

SILVER, Horace, Quintet
Singles: 78rpm
BLUE NOTE 4-8   54-57
Singles: 7-Inch
BLUE NOTE (300 through 1000 series) . 3-5   73-77
BLUE NOTE (1600 and 1700 series) ... 4-8   54-61
BLUE NOTE (1800 and 1900 series) ... 4-6   61-69
LPs: 10/12-Inch 33rpm
BLUE NOTE (1518 "Horace Silver
  Quintet") 40-60   56
  (Label gives New York street address for Blue Note
  Records.)
BLUE NOTE (1518 "Horace Silver
  Quintet") 20-30
  (Label gives New York street address for Blue Note
  Records.)
BLUE NOTE (1520 "New Faces") ... 40-60   56
  (Label gives New York street address for Blue Note
  Records.)
BLUE NOTE (1520 "New Faces") ... 20-30
  (Label reads "Blue Note Records Inc. - New York,
  U.S.A.")
BLUE NOTE (1562 "Stylings") 40-60   57
  (Label gives New York street address for Blue Note
  Records.)
BLUE NOTE (1562 "Stylings") 20-30
  (Label reads "Blue Note Records Inc. - New York,
  U.S.A.")
BLUE NOTE (1562 "Stylings") 15-20
  (Label shows Blue Note Records as a division of
  Liberty.)
BLUE NOTE (1589 "Further
  Explorations") 40-60   58
  (Label gives New York street address for Blue Note
  Records.)
BLUE NOTE (1589 "Further
  Explorations") 20-30
  (Label reads "Blue Note Records Inc. - New York,
  U.S.A.")
BLUE NOTE (1589 "Further
  Explorations") 15-20
  (Label shows Blue Note Records as a division of
  Liberty.)
BLUE NOTE (4000 series) 30-40   59-60
  (Label gives New York street address for Blue Note
  Records.)
BLUE NOTE (4000 series) 59-65
  (Label reads "Blue Note Records Inc. - New York,
  U.S.A.")
BLUE NOTE (4000 series) 15-20   66-68
  (Label shows Blue Note Records as a division of
  either
BLUE NOTE (5018 "New Faces") .. 75-125   53
  (10-inch LP.)
BLUE NOTE (5034 "Horace Silver
  Trio") 75-125   54
  (10-inch LP.)

BLUE NOTE (5058 "Horace Silver
  Quintet") 75-125   55
  (10-inch LP.)
BLUE NOTE (5062 "Horace Silver
  Quintet") 75-125   55
  (10-inch LP.)
BLUE NOTE (84000 series) 30-40   59-60
  (Label gives New York street address for Blue Note
  Records.)
BLUE NOTE (84000 series) 59-65
  (Label reads "Blue Note Records Inc. - New York,
  U.S.A.")
BLUE NOTE (84000 series) 10-20   66-80
  (Label shows Blue Note Records as a division of
  either
EPIC (3326 "Silver's Blue") 75-100   57
EPIC (16006 "Silver's Blue") 60-80   58
  Also see STITT, Sonny, Kai Winding and Horace Silver

SILVER, Horace, Quintet, and Stanley Turrentine
LPs: 10/12-Inch 33rpm
BLUE NOTE 10-15   68
  Also see SILVER, Horace, Quintet
  Also see TURRENTINE, Stanley

SILVER APPLES
Singles: 7-Inch
KAPP 4-6   68-69
LPs: 10/12-Inch 33rpm
KAPP 10-15   68-69

SILVER CONDOR
Singles: 7-Inch
COLUMBIA 2-4   81
Picture Sleeves
COLUMBIA 3-5   81
LPs: 10/12-Inch 33rpm
COLUMBIA 5-10   81
  Members: Joe Cerisano; Earl Slick; John Corey; Claude Pepper;
  Jay Davis.

SILVER CONVENTION
Singles: 7-Inch
MIDLAND INT'L 3-5   75-77
MIDSONG INT'L 3-5   77-78
Picture Sleeves
MIDLAND INT'L 3-5   76
LPs: 10/12-Inch 33rpm
MIDLAND INT'L 5-10   75-77
MIDSONG INT'L 5-10   77
  Member: Penny McLean.
  Also see McLEAN, Penny

SILVER PLATINUM
Singles: 7-Inch
SRI............................. 3-5   81
SPECTOR 3-5   81
LPs: 10/12-Inch 33rpm
SPECTOR 5-10   81

SILVER, PLATINUM & GOLD
Singles: 7–inch
FARR 3-5   76-77
WARNER 3-5   74-75
LPs: 10/12–inch 33rpm
NEPTUNE 5-10   82

SILVERADO
Singles: 7–inch
PAVILLION 3-5   81
RCA 3-5   77
LPs: 10/12–inch 33rpm
PAVILLION 5-10   81
RCA 5-10   77

SILVERSPOON, Dooley
Singles: 7–inch
COTTON 3-5   74-75

SILVERSTEIN, Shel
Singles: 7–inch
COLUMBIA 3-5   71-75
ELEKTRA 5-10   60
RCA 4-6   69-70
LPs: 10/12–inch 33rpm
ATLANTIC (8072 "Inside Folk Songs") 20-30   63
  (Monaural.)
ATLANTIC (SD-8072 "Inside
  Folk Songs") 25-35   63
  (Stereo.)
ATLANTIC (8200 series) 10-15   70
CADET 15-25   65-66
COLUMBIA 5-12   72-84
CRESTVIEW 15-25   63
ELEKTRA (176 "Hairy Jazz") 30-40   59
  (Monaural.)
ELEKTRA (7-176 "Hairy Jazz") 40-50   59
  (Stereo.)
FLYING FISH 5-8   80
JANUS 8-12   73
PARACHUTE (Except 20512) 5-10   78
PARACHUTE (20512 "Selected Cuts
  from Songs and Stories") 15-20   78
  (Promotional issue only.)
RCA 10-15   69

SILVETTI
Singles: 7–inch
SALSOUL 3-5   77
LPs: 10/12–inch 33rpm
SALSOUL 5-10   77

SIMEONE, Harry, Chorale
Singles: 7–inch
COLUMBIA 3-5   66-67
KAPP 3-5   64-68
MERCURY 3-5   62-64
MISTLETOE 2-4   74
20TH FOX 3-5   58-79
Picture Sleeves
MERCURY 4-6   62

20TH FOX 4-8   58-63
Promotional Picture Sleeve
20TH FOX (121 "The Little
  Drummer Boy") 5-10   58
  (This "Prepare to Be Enchanted" sleeve was sent
  only to radio stations.)
LPs: 10/12–inch 33rpm
DECCA 5-15   62-64
KAPP 5-10   65
MERCURY 5-15   63-64
MISTLETOE 4-8   73
MOVIETONE 5-10   67
20TH FOX 5-15   58-79
WING 5-10   69

SIMMONS, Aleese
Singles: 7–inch
ORPHEUS 2-4   88

SIMMONS, Gene
(Jumpin' Gene Simmons; Morris Gene Simmons)
Singles: 7–inch
AGP 4-8
CHECKER 8-12   60
EPIC 3-5   70
DELTUNE 3-5   78
HI 4-8   61-67
HURSHEY 3-5   73
MALA 4-8   68
SANDY 4-8
SUN (299 "Drinkin' Wine") 25-35   58
TUPELO 4-8
LPs: 10/12–inch 33rpm
HI (2018 "Jumpin' Gene Simmons") . 20-25   64
  (Monaural.)
HI (32018 "Jumpin' Gene Simmons") 25-30   64
  (Stereo.)

SIMMONS, Gene
Singles: 7–inch
CASABLANCA 2-4   78-79
LPs: 10/12–inch 33rpm
CASABLANCA (Except PIX 7120) ... 20-30   78-80
CASABLANCA (PIX 7120 "Gene
  Simmons") 40-50   79
  (Picture disc.)
  Also see KISS

SIMMONS, Patrick
Singles: 12–inch 33/45rpm
ELEKTRA 4-8   83
Singles: 7–inch
ELEKTRA 3-5   83
LPs: 10/12–inch 33rpm
ELEKTRA 5-10   83
  Also see DOOBIE BROTHERS
  Also see EAGLES

SIMMONS, Simtec
Singles: 7–inch
INNOCATION 3-5   75

SIMMS, John and Arthur
Singles: 7-inch
CASABLANCA 3-5   80
LPs: 10/12-inch 33rpm
CASABLANCA 5-10   80

SIMMS TWINS: see SIMS TWINS

SIMON, Carly
Singles: 7-inch
ARISTA 2-4   86-90
COLUMBIA 3-5   73
ELEKTRA 3-5   71-79
EPIC 2-4   85-86
MIRAGE 3-5   82
WARNER 3-5   80-83
Picture Sleeves
ARISTA (9525 "Coming Around Again") . 4-8   86
(Pictures Meryl Streep and Jack Nicholson.)
ARISTA (9525 "Coming Around Again") . 3-5   86
(Pictures Carly Simon.)
ELEKTRA 3-5   75-79
WARNER 3-5   80-83
LPs: 10/12-inch 33rpm
ARISTA 5-8   86-90
ELEKTRA 5-10   71-79
EPIC 5-8   85-86
WARNER 5-10   80-83
   Also see JAGGER, Mick
   Also see SIMON SISTERS

SIMON, Carly, and James Taylor
Singles: 7-inch
ELEKTRA 3-5   74-78
   Also see SIMON, Carly
   Also see TAYLOR, James

SIMON, Joe
(Joe Simon and the Checkmates; Joe Simon and the Mainstreeters)
Singles: 7-inch
COMPLEAT 3-5
DOT 4-8   64
HUSH 5-10   60-62
IRRAL 4-8   63
MONUMENT 3-5   70-72
POSSE 3-5   81-82
SOUND STAGE 7 3-6   66-72
SPRING 3-5   69-75
VEE JAY 4-8   64-65
Picture Sleeves
SPRING 3-5   71-73
LPs: 10/12-inch 33rpm
BUDDAH 10-15   69
POSSE 5-8   81-82
SOUND STAGE 7 8-15   67-75
SPRING 8-12   71-78
   Also see GOLDEN TONES

SIMON, Lowrell
Singles: 12-inch 33/45rpm
ZOO YORK 4-6   81

Singles: 7-inch
ZOO YORK 3-5   81
   Also see LOWRELL

SIMON, Paul
(Paul Simon and Urubamba; Paul Simon and Los Incas)
Singles: 7-inch
COLUMBIA 3-5   72-77
WARNER 2-4   80-90
Picture Sleeves
COLUMBIA 3-8   73-77
WARNER 3-5   80
LPs: 10/12-inch 33rpm
COLUMBIA (Except C5X and 43000
series) 6-12   72-77
COLUMBIA (C5X-37581 "Paul Simon's
Collected Works") 30-40   81
(Five-LP set.)
COLUMBIA (43000 series) 15-20   81
(Half-speed mastered.)
DMG (1 "Songs of Paul Simon") 15-20   75
(Also has tracks by Simon & Garfunkel, Aretha
Franklin, Yes, the Crykle, and Booker T. & the
MGs. Promotional issue only.)
DMG (2 "Songs of Paul Simon - Easy
Listening Collection") 10-15   75
(Promotional issue only.)
MCP (8027 "Paul Simon Plus")
WARNER 5-10   80-90
   Also see BOOKER T. and the MGs
   Also see CYRKLE
   Also see DION
   Also see 4 SEASONS
   Also see FRANKLIN, Aretha
   Also see KANE, Paul
   Also see LANDIS, Jerry
   Also see NEWMAN, Randy, and Paul Simon
   Also see ORLANDO, Tony
   Also see RIVERS, Johnny
   Also see SEDAKA, Neil
   Also see SIMON & GARFUNKEL
   Also see TAYLOR, True
   Also see TICO and the Triumphs
   Also see U.S.A. for AFRICA
   Also see VALERY, Dana
   Also see YES

SIMON, Paul, and Phoebe Snow
(With the Jessy Dixon Singers)
Singles: 7-inch
COLUMBIA 3-5   75
   Also see SNOW, Phoebe

SIMON & GARFUNKEL
Singles: 7-inch
ABC-PAR (10788 "This Is My Story")   10-15   66
COLUMBIA (10000 series) 3-5   75
COLUMBIA (11000 series) 5-8   66
COLUMBIA (43396 "The Sounds
of Silence") 4-8   65
COLUMBIA (43396 "The Sounds
of Silence") 30-40   65
(Colored vinyl. Promotional issue only.)

COLUMBIA (43511 "Homeward Bound") 4-8   66
COLUMBIA (43511 "Homeward
Bound") 30-40   66
(Colored vinyl. Promotional issue only.)
COLUMBIA (43617 "I Am a Rock") 4-8   66
COLUMBIA (43617 "I Am a Rock") .. 30-40   66
(Colored vinyl. Promotional issue only.)
COLUMBIA (43728 through 45663) 4-8   66-75
TEEN SCOOP (789 "Visits with
Simon & Garfunkel") 10-20   66
(*Teen Scoop* magazine bonus soundsheet.)
WARNER 3-5   82

Picture Sleeves
COLUMBIA 5-10   66-75

EPs: 7–inch 33/45rpm
COLUMBIA 10-20   68-69
(Jukebox issues only.)

LPs: 10/12–inch 33rpm
COLUMBIA (CL-2249 "Wednesday
Morning 3 A.M.") 10-20   64
(Monaural.)
COLUMBIA (CL-2469 "Sounds of
Silence") 10-20   66
(Monaural.)
COLUMBIA (CL-2563 "Parsley, Sage
Rosemary and Thyme") 10-20   66
(Monaural.)
COLUMBIA (OS-3180 "The
Graduate") 12-15   68
(Soundtrack.)
COLUMBIA (CS-9049 "Wednesday
Morning 3 A.M.") 10-15   64
(Stereo.)
COLUMBIA (PC-9049 "Wednesday
Morning 3 A.M.") 5-10
(Stereo.)
COLUMBIA (CS-9269 "Sounds of
Silence") 10-15   66
(Stereo.)
COLUMBIA (CS-9363 "Parsley, Sage
Rosemary and Thyme") 10-15   66
(Stereo.)
COLUMBIA (PC-9363 "Parsley, Sage
Rosemary and Thyme") 5-10
COLUMBIA (KCS-9529 "Bookends") . 10-15   68
COLUMBIA (PC-9529 "Bookends") ... 5-10
COLUMBIA (9914 "Bridge over
Troubled Water") 10-15   70
COLUMBIA (30995 "Bridge over
Troubled Water") 10-20   71
(Quadrophonic.)
COLUMBIA (31350 "Greatest Hits") ... 5-10   72
COLUMBIA (37587 "Simon & Garfunkel's
Collected Works") 30-40   81
(Five-LP set.)
COLUMBIA (41350 "Greatest Hits") .. 10-15   81
(Half-speed mastered.)
COLUMBIA (49914 "Bridge over
Troubled Water") 10-20   80
(Half-speed mastered.)

MFSL (173 "Bridge over
Troubled Water") 15-20   85
OFFSHORE 10-15
PICKWICK (3059 "Hit Sound of Simon
& Garfunkel") 50-75   66
SEARS (435 "Simon & Garfunkel") .. 20-30
WARNER 5-8   82
Members: Paul Simon; Art Garfunkel.
Also see GARFUNKEL, Art
Also see SIMON, Paul
Also see TOM & JERRY

SIMON SAID
Singles: 7–inch
ATCO 3-5   75-76
ROULETTE 3-5   75

SIMON SISTERS
Singles: 7–inch
COLUMBIA (02600 series) 2-4   82
COLUMBIA (45000 series) 3-5   73
KAPP 4-8   64-65

LPs: 10/12–inch 33rpm
COLUMBIA (21525 "Lobster
Quadrille") 10-15   69
COLUMBIA (21539 "Simon Sisters
Sing for Children") 10-12   73
COLUMBIA (24506 "Lobster
Quadrille") 15-20   69
(Special childrens' book edition.)
COLUMBIA (37000 series) 5-10   82
KAPP 15-25   64
WARNER 5-10   80
Members: Carly Simon; Lucy Simon.
Also see DOOBIE BROTHERS / Kate Taylor and the
Simon-Taylor Family
Also see SIMON, Carly

SIMONE, Nina
Singles: 7–inch
BETHLEHEM 3-8   59-70
CTI 3-5   78
COLPIX 4-8   59-63
PHILIPS 4-6   64-66
RCA 3-6   67-71
TRIP 2-4   72

EPs: 7–inch 33/45rpm
BETHLEHEM 5-10   59

LPs: 10/12–inch 33rpm
ACCORD 5-10   80
BETHLEHEM 20-30   59
CTI 5-10   78-79
COLPIX 15-30   59-66
PHILIPS 10-20   64-69
QUINTESSENCE 5-10   80
RCA 8-15   67-76
STROUD 5-10   73
TRIP 5-10   72-77
UPFRONT 5-10   72
VERSATILE 5-10   78
Also see LYNNE, Gloria / Nina Simone / Billie Holiday

SIMONE, Nina, Chris Connor and Carmen McRae
LPs: 10/12-inch 33rpm
BETHLEHEM 20-30   60
  Also see CONNOR, Chris
  Also see McRAE, Carmen
  Also see SIMONE, Nina

SIMPLE MINDS
Singles: 12-inch 33/45rpm
A&M 4-6   82-86
Singles: 7-inch
A&M 2-4   82-86
Picture Sleeves
A&M 3-5   84
LPs: 10/12-inch 33rpm
A&M 5-10   82-91
PVC 8-10   79
  Members: John Giblin; Charles Burchill; Jim Kerr; Michael MacNeil; Mel Gaynor.

SIMPLY RED
Singles: 12-inch 33/45rpm
ELEKTRA 4-6   85-86
Singles: 7-inch
ELEKTRA 2-4   85-89
LPs: 10/12-inch 33rpm
ELEKTRA 5-8   85-89

SIMPSON, Paul
(Paul Simpson Connection)
Singles: 12-inch 33/45rpm
EASY STREET 4-6   85
STREETWISE 4-6   83
Singles: 7-inch
STREETWISE 2-4   83

SIMPSON, Valerie
Singles: 7-inch
TAMLA 3-5   71-72
LPs: 10/12-inch 33rpm
TAMLA 8-10   71-77
  Also see ASHFORD & SIMPSON

SIMPSONS
Singles: 7-inch
GEFFEN 2-4   91
LPs: 10/12-inch 33rpm
GEFFEN (24308 "Sing the Blues") 5-8   90
  Members: Dan Castellaneta; Julie Kavner; Nancy Cartwright; Yeardley Smith; Matt Groening. With: Harry Shearer; Ron Taylor; Harry Shearer; Buster Poindexter; Joe Walsh; B.B. King; John Sebastian; D.J. Jazzy Jeff; Andrew Gold; Dr. John.
  Also see D.J. JAZZY JEFF and the Fresh Prince
  Also see DR. JOHN
  Also see GOLD, Andrew
  Also see KING, B.B.
  Also see SEBASTAIN, John
  Also see WALSH, Joe

SIMS, Joyce
Singles: 7-inch
SLEEPING BAG 2-4   86-88

SIMS, Marvin L.
Singles: 7-inch
KAREN 4-6   69
MELLOW 4-8   66-67
MERCURY 3-5   72
REVUE 4-6   68-69

SIMS TWINS
(Simms Twins)
Singles: 7-inch
ABKCO 3-5
CROSSOVER 3-5   74
KENT 3-5   71
PARKWAY 4-8   68
SAR 5-10   61-62
SPECIALTY 3-5

SIMTEC & WYLIE
Singles: 7-inch
MISTER CHAND 3-5   70-72
SHAMA 3-6   69-70
LPs: 10/12-inch 33rpm
MISTER CHAND 8-12   71-72
  Also see KRYSTAL GENERATION
  Also see SOUTHSIDE MOVEMENT

SINATRA, Frank
Singles: 78rpm
BLUEBIRD 30-50   42-43
BRUNSWICK (8443 "From the Bottom of My Heart") 100-150   39
  (With Harry James and His Orchestra)
CAPITOL 5-10   53-58
COLUMBIA 5-15   39-52
  (With Harry James and His Orchestra)
RCA ("Oh Look at Me Now") 50-100
  (Promotional issue only. Numbered edition of 1,000 issued.)
Singles: 7-inch
CAPITOL (2450 "Lean Baby") 15-25   53
CAPITOL (2500 through 4800 series) . 5-15   53-62
COLUMBIA (100 through 900 series) 30-50   50-52
  (Microgroove 33 single series.)
COLUMBIA (38000 and 39000 series) 5-10   50-51

"HIGH HOPES with JACK KENNEDY"/
  "Jack Kennedy All the Way" 150-250   60
  (Presidential campaign promotional issue only. No
  label name or artist shown, only titles.)
REPRISE (45 "Gunga Din") 30-50   66
  (Promotional issue only.)
REPRISE (0249 through 1335) 3-8   64-75
REPRISE (20001 through 20151) 4-8   61-63
REPRISE (20157 "California") 50-100   63
  (White label. Promotional issue only.)
REPRISE (20157 "California") 100-200   77
  (Brown label. Promotional issue only.)
REPRISE (29000 series) 2-4   82
REPRISE (49000 series) 3-5   80-83
REPRISE/CAL NEVADA LODGE (101
  "Ring-A-Ding-Ding") 30-40   61

Picture Sleeves

REPRISE (0249 through 1300 series) . 5-15   64-76
REPRISE (20001 through 20151) ... 10-20   61-63
REPRISE/CAL NEVADA LODGE (101
  "Ring-A-Ding-Ding") 50-75   61
  (Promotional souvenir, available from the lodge.)
SINATRA 2-4   75

EPs: 7–Inch 33/45rpm

CAPITOL 15-30   54-61
COLUMBIA 20-40   50-59
RCA (3000 series) 40-60   52
RCA (5000 series) 15-25   60

LPs: 10/12–Inch 33rpm

CAMDEN 5-10   72-73
CAPITOL ("Radio/TV Sampler") ... 200-250   58
  (Number unknown. Yellow label. Promotional issue
  only.)
CAPITOL (200 and 300 series) 8-15   69
CAPITOL (H-488 through H-581) 20-40   54-55
  (10–inch LPs.)
CAPITOL (T-488 through T-1164) ... 20-30   54-59
CAPITOL (581 through 1676) 5-15   61-78
  (With "DT," "DW," "SM," "STBB," "SW," or "W"
  prefix.)
CAPITOL (T-1221 through T-1676) .. 10-20   59-62
  (Monaural.)
CAPITOL (ST-1221 through ST-1676) 10-20   59-62
  (Stereo.)
CAPITOL (1729 "Love and Things") .. 10-20   62
CAPITOL (1762 "Great Years") 20-30   62
  (Three-LP set.)
CAPITOL (1825 through 2700) 10-20   62-67
CAPITOL (2814 "Deluxe Set") 35-50   67
  (Six-LP set.)
CAPITOL (11000 and 12000 series) .. 5-10   74-80
CAPITOL (16000 series) 5-8   80-82
COLUMBIA (6 "The Frank Sinatra
  Story") 10-20   58
COLUMBIA (42 "Essential
  Frank Sinatra") 15-30   67
COLUMBIA (606 through 803) 15-25   55-57
COLUMBIA (842 "Essential Frank
  Sinatra") 15-30   67

COLUMBIA (855 through 1448) 12-25   57-60
COLUMBIA (2400 and 2500 series) .. 8-15   66
  (12–inch LPs.)
COLUMBIA (2500 series) 15-30   55
  (10–inch LPs.)
COLUMBIA (2900 series) 5-10   69
COLUMBIA (6000 series) 30-60   50-54
  (10–inch LPs. Some LPs in this series have paper
  sleeves.)
COLUMBIA (9200 and 9300 series) .. 8-15   66
COLUMBIA (10000 series) 5-10   73
COLUMBIA (31000 series) 5-10   72
HARMONY 5-12   66-71
MFSL (1 "Frank Sinatra") 300-400   85
  (16-LP boxed set. Includes booklet and alignment
  tool.)
MFSL (100 series) 15-30   84-86
ODYSSEY 8-15   68
QWEST 5-8   84
RCA (400 through 1500 series) 5-10   72-76
RCA (3000 series) 20-40   52
  (10–inch LP.)
RCA (4300 series) 8-12   82
RCA (4700 series) 4-8   83
REPRISE (1001 through 1024) 10-20   61-68
REPRISE (1025 through 1034) 8-12   68-72
REPRISE (2020 through 2275) 5-15   64-77
REPRISE (2300 "Trilogy") 15-25   80
  (Three-LP set.)
REPRISE (2305 "She Shot Me Down") . 5-8   81
REPRISE (6000 series) 10-15   65
SINATRA 5-10   75
  Also see ALI, Muhammad, and Frank Sinatra
  Also see ANTHONY, Ray
  Also see CROSBY, Bing, and Frank Sinatra
  Also see DAY, Doris and Frank Sinatra
  Also see DORSEY, Tommy, Orchestra
  Also see JAMES, Harry
  Also see KINGSTON TRIO / Frank Sinatra
  Also see PRESLEY, Elvis / Frank Sinatra / Nat King Cole
  Also see VINCENT, Gene / Frank Sinatra / Sonny James / Ron
   Goodwin
  Also see ZENTER, Si

SINATRA, Frank, and the Charioteers
Singles: 78rpm

COLUMBIA 5-10   45
  Also see CHARIOTEERS

SINATRA, Frank, and Count Basie
LPs: 10/12–Inch 33rpm

REPRISE 10-20   63-66
  Also see BASIE, Count

SINATRA, Frank / Nat King Cole
EPs: 7–Inch 33/45rpm

CAPITOL (500 "Witchcraft") 35-55   58
  (Promotional issue only.)
  Also see COLE, Nat King

SINATRA, Frank, and Duke Ellington
Singles: 7–Inch

REPRISE 3-5   68

LPs: 10/12–inch 33rpm
REPRISE 8-15   68
Also see ELLINGTON, Duke

SINATRA, Frank, and Antonio Carlos Jobim
LPs: 10/12–inch 33rpm
REPRISE 8-15   67-71
Also see JOBIM, Antonio Carlos

SINATRA, Frank, and Keely Smith
Singles: 7–inch
CAPITOL 4-8   58
Also see SMITH, Keely

SINATRA, Frank, Bing Crosby and Dean Martin
Singles: 7–inch
REPRISE (20,217 "The Oldest Established
[Permanent Floating Crap Game
in New York]) 10-20   62
Picture Sleeves
REPRISE (20,217 "The Oldest Established
[Permanent Floating Crap Game
in New York]) 25-45   62

SINATRA, Frank, Sammy Davis Jr. and Dean Martin
Singles: 7–inch
REPRISE (20,128 "Me and My Shadow/
Sam's Song") 3-5   62
Picture Sleeves
REPRISE (20,128 "Me and My Shadow/
Sam's Song") 5-10   62
LPs: 10/12–inch 33rpm
LATIMER (247-17 "Summit Meeting at
the 500 Club") 200-300   64
(Promotional issue only. Issued with three different,
paste-on covers.)

SINATRA, Frank, Dean Martin, Sammy Davis Jr., and Bing Crosby
LPs: 10/12–inch 33rpm
REPRISE (5031 "The Summit") . . 500-1000   64
(British issue only. Listed mainly to dispell rumors
that such an LP does not exist.)
Also see CROSBY, Bing
Also see DAVIS, Sammy, Jr.
Also see MARTIN, Dean

SINATRA, Frank and Nancy
(Sinatra Family)
Singles: 7–inch
REPRISE 3-6   66-71
LPs: 10/12–inch 33rpm
REPRISE 8-15   69
Members: Sinatra Family included Frank Sinatra, Frank Jr.,
Nancy and Tina.
Also see SINATRA, Nancy

SINATRA, Nancy
Singles: 7–inch
ELEKTRA 3-5   80
PRIVATE STOCK 3-5   75-77
RCA 3-5   72-73

REPRISE 3-6   61-71
Picture Sleeves
REPRISE 4-8   62-67
EPs: 7–inch 33/45rpm
REPRISE 10-12   66
(Jukebox issue only.)
LPs: 10/12–inch 33rpm
RCA 8-10   72
REPRISE 15-30   66-72
Also see BARRY, John
Also see MARTIN, Dean
Also see PRESLEY, Elvis
Also see SINATRA, Frank and Nancy
Also see TILLIS, Mel, and Nancy Sinatra

SINATRA, Nancy, and Lee Hazlewood
Singles: 7–inch
PRIVATE STOCK 3-5   76
RCA 3-5   72
REPRISE 4-8   67-68
LPs: 10/12–inch 33rpm
RCA 8-10   72
REPRISE 10-15   68
Also see HAZLEWOOD, Lee
Also see SINATRA, Nancy

SINCLAIR, Gordon
Singles: 7–inch
AVCO 3-5   74

SINFIELD, Pete
Singles: 7–inch
MANTICORE 3-5   73
LPs: 10/12–inch 33rpm
MANTICORE 8-10   73

SINGING BELLS
Singles: 7–inch
MADISON 5-10   60

SINGING DOGS
(Don Charles Presents the Singing Dogs)
Singles: 78rpm
RCA 3-5   55
Singles: 7–inch
RCA 3-6   55-72
Picture Sleeves
RCA 5-10   55-56

SINGING NUN
(Janine Deckers)
Singles: 7–inch
PHILIPS 3-5   63-64
Picture Sleeves
PHILIPS 4-8   63-64
LPs: 10/12–inch 33rpm
PHILIPS 5-15   63-69

SINGLE BULLET THEORY
Singles: 7–inch
NEMPEROR 2-4   83
LPs: 10/12–inch 33rpm
NEMPEROR 5-8   83

SINGLETON, Charlie
Singles: 7–inch
ARISTA 2-4   85
LPs: 10/12–inch 33rpm
ARISTA 5-8   85
Also see CAMEO
Also see COBHAM, Billy

SINGLETON, Charlie, and Modern Man
Singles: 7–inch
EPIC 2-4   87-88

SINNAMON
Singles: 12–inch 33/45rpm
BECKET 4-6   82-83
JIVE 4-6   84
Singles: 7–inch
BECKET 2-4   82-83

SIOUXSIE and the Banshees
Singles: 12–inch 33/45rpm
GEFFEN 4-6   84-86
PVC 4-8   80-82
Singles: 7–inch
GEFFEN 2-4   84-86
PVC 3-5   80-82
POLYDOR 3-5   79
LPs: 10/12–inch 33rpm
GEFFEN 5-8   84-90
PVC 5-10 80-82
POLYDOR 8-10 79
Also see SEX PISTOLS

SIR CHAUNCEY
(Ernie Freeman)
Singles: 7–inch
PATTERN 5-10 60
WARNER 3-6   60
Also see FREEMAN, Ernie

SIR DOUGLAS QUINTET
(Sir Douglas Band)
Singles: 7–inch
ATLANTIC 4-8   73
CASABLANCA (0828 "Roll with
   the Punches") 5-15 75
MERCURY 3-5   71
PACEMAKER (260 "Sugar Bee") 15-20 64
PHILIPS 3-5   70-71
SMASH 4-8   68-70
TRIBE 5-10 65
   (No Indian on label.)
TRIBE 4-8   65-67
   (Label pictures Indian.)
Picture Sleeves
PHILIPS 3-5   70-71
LPs: 10/12–inch 33rpm
ACCORD 5-10 82
ATLANTIC 10-15 73
MERCURY 10-15 72
PHILIPS 10-15 70-71
SMASH 15-30 68-70

TAKOMA 5-10 80-83
TRIBE (47001 "Best of Sir
   Douglas Quintet") 40-60 66
   Members: Doug Sahm; Augie Meyers; Jack Barber; Leon
   Baety; John Perez; Frank Morin; Jim Stallings.
   Also see AMIGOS DE MUSICA
   Also see ATWOOD the ELECTRIC ICEMAN
   Also see CASCADES / Sir Douglas Quintet
   Also see DEVONS
   Also see GOLDIE, Don
   Also see LIGHT, J.J.
   Also see LONG, Joey
   Also see MEYERS, Augie
   Also see ROCKY and the Border Kings
   Also see SAHM, Doug

SIR LORD BALTIMORE
Singles: 7–inch
MERCURY 3-5   70-71
LPs: 10/12–inch 33rpm
MERCURY 8-12 70-71

SIR MIX-A-LOT
Singles: 7–inch
NASTYMIX 2-4   88-90
LPs: 10/12–inch 33rpm
NASTYMIX 5-8   88-90

SIREN
Singles: 7–inch
MIDSONG INT'L 3-5   79
LPs: 10/12–inch 33rpm
ELEKTRA 8-10 71
DANDELION 10-12 70

SIRENNE, Gianni
Singles: 12–inch 33/45rpm
ATLANTIC 4-6   84
Singles: 7–inch
ATLANTIC 2-4   84

SISTER & BROTHERS
Singles: 7–inch
CALLA 3-5   71
UNI 3-5   70

SISTER SLEDGE
Singles: 12–inch 33/45rpm
ATLANTIC 4-6   85
COTILLION 4-8   79-83
Singles: 7–inch
ATCO 3-5   73-75
ATLANTIC 2-4   85
COTILLION 3-5   76-83
LPs: 10/12–inch 33rpm
ATCO 8-10 75
ATLANTIC 5-8   85
COTILLION 5-10 76-83

SISTERS LOVE
Singles: 7–inch
A&M 3-5   69-71
MOWEST 3-5   73

SISTERS of MERCY
LPs: 10/12-inch 33rpm
ELEKTRA 5-8   88-90

SIX TEENS
Singles: 78rpm
FLIP 5-10   56-57
Singles: 7-inch
FLIP (Except 338 and 346) 10-15   56-60
FLIP (338 "Baby-O") 15-20   58
FLIP (346 "Why Do I Go to School") . 15-20   58
Members: Trudy Williams; Louise Williams; Ed Wells; Bev Pecot; Ken Sinclair; Darrell Lewis.
Also see TRUDY & LOUISE

SIX TEENS / Donald Woods / Richard Berry
LPs: 10/12-inch 33rpm
FLIP (1001 "12 Flip Hits") 50-75   59
Also see BERRY, Richard
Also see WOODS, Donald

SKA KINGS
Singles: 7-inch
ATLANTIC 4-8   64

SKAGGS, Ricky
Singles: 7-inch
EPIC 2-5   81-86
ROUNDER 3-5   80
SUGAR HILL 3-5   80
LPs: 10/12-inch 33rpm
EPIC 5-10   81-86
ROUNDER 5-10   82
SUGAR HILL 5-10   79-80
WEL DUN 6-12   78
Also see NITTY GRITTY DIRT BAND
Also see SCRUGGS, Earl

SKELLERN, Peter
Singles: 7-inch
LONDON 3-5   72
PRIVATE STOCK 3-5   75
LPs: 10/12-inch 33rpm
LONDON 5-10   76

SKELTON, Red
Singles: 78rpm
MGM 4-6   56
Singles: 7-inch
CBS/BURGER KING ("Pledge of
  Allegiance") 8-12   69
  (Promotional paper soundsheet.)
COLUMBIA 3-6   69
MGM 5-10   56
LPs: 10/12-inch 33rpm
LIBERTY 10-15   65-66

SKHY, A.B: see A.B. SKHY

SKIP & FLIP
Singles: 7-inch
BRENT 5-10   59-62
CALIFORNIA 3-5   63
COLLECTABLES 2-4

ERIC 2-4
TIME 5-10   61
Members: Clyde Batton; Gary Paxton.
Also see GARY & CLYDE
Also see PAXTON, Gary
Also see PLEDGES

SKIP and the Casuals
Singles: 7-inch
D.C. INT'L 3-5   74

SKIPWORTH & TURNER
Singles: 12-inch 33/45rpm
4TH and BROADWAY 4-6   85
WARNER 4-6   86
Singles: 7-inch
4TH and BROADWAY 2-4   85
WARNER 2-4   86
LPs: 10/12-inch 33rpm
WARNER 5-8   86
Members: Rodney Skipworth; Philip Turner.

SKOOL BOYZ
Singles: 12-inch 33/45rpm
COLUMBIA 4-6   84-85
Singles: 7-inch
COLUMBIA 2-4   84-85
DESTINY 3-5   81-82
LPs: 10/12-inch 33rpm
DESTINY 5-10   81
Also see TRIPLE "S" CONNECTION

SKRATCH
Singles: 12-inch 33/45rpm
PASSION 4-6   85

SKWARES
Singles: 7-inch
MERCURY 2-4   88

SKY
Singles: 7-inch
RCA 3-5   71-72
LPs: 10/12-inch 33rpm
RCA 10-12   70-71

SKY
Singles: 7-inch
ARISTA 3-5   81
LPs: 10/12-inch 33rpm
ARISTA 8-10   81
Member: Doug Fieger.
Also see KNACK

SKYLARK
Singles: 7-inch
CAPITOL 3-5   72-73
LPs: 10/12-inch 33rpm
CAPITOL 8-10   72-74
Members: Donny Gerrard; Carl Graves.
Also see GERRARD, Donny
Also see GRAVES, Carl

SKYLINERS
Singles: 7-inch
ATCO (6270 "Since I Fell for You") .. 15-25   63

CALICO 45 RPM / Calico Publishing Co. (ASCAP) / 103 / VOCAL / SINCE I DON'T HAVE YOU / (J. Rock - The Skyliners) / THE SKYLINERS / LENNY MARTIN AND THE ORCHESTRA / CALICO RECORDS INC. PITTSBURGH, PA.

CALICO 10-20	59-60	
CAMEO (215 "Three Coins in the Fountain") 15-25	62	
CAPITOL 3-5	75	
CLASSIC ARTISTS 3-5	90	
COLPIX (188 "I'll Close My Eyes") ... 20-30	61	
COLPIX (613 "Close Your Eyes") 20-30	61	
JUBILEE 8-12	65-66	
ORIGINAL SOUND 3-5		
TORTOISE INT'L 4-8	78	
VIRGO 3-5	73	
VISCOUNT 8-12	62	

LPs: 10/12–inch 33rpm

CALICO (3000 "The Skyliners") ... 150-200	59	
KAMA SUTRA (2026 "Once Upon a Time") 15-25	71	
ORIGINAL SOUND (8873 "Since I Don't Have You") 20-30	63	
TORTOISE INT'L 8-10	78	

Members: Jimmy Beaumont; Janet Vogel; Wally Lester; Jack Taylor; Joe Verscharen.
Also see BEAUMONT, Jimmy

SKYNYRD, Lynyrd: see LYNYRD SKYNYRD

SKYY

Singles: 12–inch 33/45rpm

CAPITOL 4-6	86	
SALSOUL 4-8	79-85	

Singles: 7–inch

CAPITOL 2-4	86	
SALSOUL 3-5	79-85	

LPs: 10/12–inch 33rpm

ATLANTIC 5-8	89	
CAPITOL 5-8	86	
SALSOUL 5-10	79-83	

SLADE

Singles: 7–inch

CBS ASSOCIATED 2-4	84-85	
COTILLION 3-5	71-72	
POLYDOR 3-5	72-73	
REPRISE 3-5	73	
WARNER 3-5	73-76	

LPs: 10/12–inch 33rpm

CBS ASSOCIATED 5-8	84-85	
COTILLION 10-15	70	
POLYDOR 8-10	72-73	
REPRISE 10-12	73	
WARNER 8-10	74-76	

Also see AMBROSE SLADE

SLADES

Singles: 7–inch

DOMINO 15-25	58-61	
LIBERTY 8-12	58	

Also see SPADES

SLATKIN, Felix, Orchestra

Singles: 7–inch

LIBERTY 4-6	60-62	

LPs: 10/12–inch 33rpm

ANGEL 5-10	72	
CAPITOL 10-15	59	
LIBERTY 10-15	60-64	
SUNSET 5-10	66-68	
U.A. 5-10	71	

SLAVE

(Slave-Arrington)

Singles: 12–inch 33/45rpm

COTILLION 4-6	83	

Singles: 7–inch

COTILLION 2-5	77-84	
ICHIBAN 2-4	86-87	

LPs: 10/12–inch 33rpm

COTILLION 5-10	77-84	
ICHIBAN 5-8	86	

Member: Steve Arrington.
Also see ARRINGTON, Steve
Also see AURRA
Also see DEJA

SLAY, Emitt

(Emitt Slay Trio; Emitt Slay's Slayriders with Sweetie Dolores)

Singles: 78rpm

SAVOY 8-12	52-53	

Singles: 7–inch

CHECKER (898 "Honey Bun") 25-50	58	
J.V.B. 8-12	59	
SAVOY 15-25	52-53	

SLAY, Frank, and His Orchestra

Singles: 7–inch

SCA 3-6	63	
SWAN 4-8	61	

Also see CANNON, Freddy

SLAYER

Singles: 7–inch

METAL BLADE 2-4	85	

LPs: 10/12–inch 33rpm

DEF AMERICAN 5-8	90	
DEF JAM 5-8	86-88	
ENIGMA/METAL BLADE 5-8	85	

SLEDGE, Percy
Singles: 7–inch
ATLANTIC 4-8   66-72
CAPRICORN 3-5   74-76
MONUMENT 3-5   83
LPs: 10/12–inch 33rpm
ATLANTIC 10-20   66-69
CAPRICORN 8-10   74-75
MONUMENT 5-10   83
   Also see JACKSON, Chuck / Percy Sledge

SLEDGE, Sister: see SISTER SLEDGE

SLEEPY KING
Singles: 7–inch
AWAKE 10-15
JOY 5-10   61

SLICK
Singles: 12–inch 33/45rpm
FANTASY 4-6   80
Singles: 7–inch
FANTASY 3-5   80
LPs: 10/12–inch 33rpm
FANTASY 5-10   80
WMOT 5-10   79

SLICK, Grace
(Grace Slick and the Great Society)
Singles: 7–inch
GRUNT 4-6   72-74
RCA 3-5   80-81
Picture Sleeves
RCA 3-5   80
LPs: 10/12–inch 33rpm
COLUMBIA (CS-9624 "Conspicuous
  Only") 20-30   68
COLUMBIA (PC-9624 "Conspicuous
  Only") 5-10
COLUMBIA (CS-9702 "How It Was") . 15-20   68
COLUMBIA (30459 "Collector's Item") 10-15   71
GRUNT 8-12   74
HARMONY 10-15   71
RCA 5-10   80-83
Promotional LPs
RCA ("*Dreams* Interview") 25-30   80
RCA (3922 "*Wrecking Ball* Interview) . 20-30   81
RCA (3923 "Special Radio Series") .. 10-15   81
RCA (13708 "Interview LP") 5-10
   Also see CROSBY, David
   Also see GREAT!! SOCIETY!!
   Also see JEFFERSON AIRPLANE
   Also see KANTNER, Paul, and Grace Slick

SLIM, Guitar: see GUITAR SLIM

SLIM, Tarheel: see TARHEEL SLIM

SLIM and ANN:
  see TARHEEL SLIM & LITTLE ANN

SLIM HARPO: see HARPO, Slim

SLINGSHOT
Singles: 12–inch 33/45rpm
QUALITY/RFC 4-6   83
Singles: 7–inch
QUALITY/RFC 2-4   83

SLOAN, P.F.
(Phil Sloan)
Singles: 7–inch
ATCO 4-6   69
DUNHILL 4-8   65-67
MART 8-12   60
MUMS 3-5   72
LPs: 10/12–inch 33rpm
ATCO 10-15   68
DUNHILL 10-20   65-66
MUMS 8-10   72
   Also see FANTASTIC BAGGIES
   Also see IMAGINATIONS
   Also see INNER CIRCLE
   Also see STREET CLEANERS

SLONIKER, Mark
LPs: 10/12–inch 33rpm
SANDSTONE 5-8   88

SLY
(Sly Stone; Sly Stewart)
Singles: 7–inch
AUTUMN 5-10   65
   Also see SLY and the Family Stone
   Also see STEWART, Sly

SLY & ROBBIE
Singles: 7–inch
ISLAND 2-4   86-87
LPs: 10/12–inch 33rpm
ISLAND 5-8   86-87
   Members: Sly Dunbar; Robbie Shakespeare.

SLY and the Family Stone
Singles: 12–inch 33/45rpm
EPIC 4-8   79
Singles: 7–inch
EPIC 3-6   67-75
WARNER 2-5   79-85
Picture Sleeves
EPIC 3-6   68-70
LPs: 10/12–inch 33rpm
EPIC (264 "Everything You Always
  Wanted to Hear") 10-20   76
  (Promotional issue only.)
EPIC (26000 series) 10-15   67-69
EPIC (KE-30325 "Greatest Hits") 8-12   70
EPIC (PE-30325 "Greatest Hits") 5-10
EPIC (EQ-30325 "Greatest Hits") ... 25-50   73
  (Quadrophonic. Has some true stereo tracks that
  were rechanneled on earlier issues.)
EPIC (30335 through 37071) 5-10   70-81
WARNER 5-10   79-83
   Members: Sylvester "Sly Stone" Stewart; Rose Stone; Larry
   Graham; Fred Stone; Gregg Errico; Jerry Martini.
   Also see BANKS, Rose
   Also see GRAHAM, Larry

Also see RUBICON
Also see SLY
Also see STONE, Sly

SLY FOX
Singles: 12–inch 33/45rpm
CAPITOL .... 4-6　85-86
Singles: 7–inch
CAPITOL .... 2-4　85-86
LPs: 10/12–inch 33rpm
CAPITOL .... 5-8　86
Members: Mike Camacho; Gary Cooper.

SMALL, Karen
Singles: 7–inch
VENUS .... 4-8　66

SMALL, Millie
(Blue Beat Girl)
Singles: 7–inch
ATCO .... 5-10　65
ATLANTIC .... 5-10　64
BRIT .... 5-10　65
SMASH .... 4-8　64
LPs: 10/12–inch 33rpm
SMASH .... 15-25　64

SMALL FACES
Singles: 7–inch
IMMEDIATE .... 5-10　67-68
PRESS .... 8-12　65-68
RCA .... 8-12　66
WARNER .... 4-8　70-75
Picture Sleeves
IMMEDIATE .... 10-15　68
WARNER .... 5-10　73
LPs: 10/12–inch 33rpm
ABKCO .... 8-12　73
ACCORD .... 5-10　82
ATLANTIC .... 8-10　77-78
COMPLEAT .... 5-8　86
IMMEDIATE (002 "There Are But
　Four Small Faces") .... 20-30　68
IMMEDIATE (008 "Ogden's Nut
　Gone Flake") .... 20-30　68
IMMEDIATE (4225 "Ogden's Nut
　Gone Flake") .... 10-15　73
MGM .... 10-15　74
PRIDE .... 10-15　72-73
SIRE 10-15
WARNER .... 10-15　70
Members: Steve Marriott; Ronnie Lane.
　Also see FACES
　Also see HUMBLE PIE
　Also see LANE, Ronnie
　Also see MARRIOTT, Steve
　Also see McLAGAN, Ian
　Also see PYTHON LEE JACKSON

SMASH PALACE
Singles: 7–inch
EPIC .... 2-4　86
LPs: 10/12–inch 33rpm
CBS .... 5-8　85

SMITH
Singles: 7–inch
DUNHILL .... 3-5　69-70
ROULETTE 2-4
Picture Sleeves
DUNHILL .... 4-8　69
LPs: 10/12–inch 33rpm
DUNHILL .... 10-15　69-70
Member: Gayle McCormack.
　Also see McCORMACK, Gayle

SMITH, Betty
(Betty Smith Group)
Singles: 7–inch
ECHO (584 "Oh Yeah") 20-30
LONDON .... 5-10　58

SMITH, Bobby
LPs: 10/12–inch 33rpm
RIPSAW .... 5-8　87
Members: Danny Gatton; Johnny Castle; Mitch Collins.

SMITH, Bro
Singles: 7–inch
BIG TREE .... 3-5　76
Picture Sleeves
BIG TREE .... 3-5　76

SMITH, Cal
Singles: 7–inch
DECCA .... 3-5　70-73
KAPP .... 3-6　66-70
PLAID .... 4-8　60
MCA .... 2-4　73-79
SOUNDWAVES .... 2-4　82
STEP ONE .... 2-4　86
LPs: 10/12–inch 33rpm
CORAL .... 5-10　73
DECCA .... 8-12　72
KAPP .... 8-15　66-70
MCA .... 5-10　73-77

SMITH, Carl
(Carl Smith and the Tunesmiths)
Singles: 78rpm
COLUMBIA .... 4-6　51-57
Singles: 7–inch
ABC/HICKORY .... 3-5　76-78
COLUMBIA (20000 and 21000 series)　5-10　51-56
COLUMBIA (40000 through 45000
　series) .... 3-8　56-72
HICKORY .... 3-5　74-76
Picture Sleeves
COLUMBIA .... 5-10　59
EPs: 7–inch 33/45rpm
COLUMBIA .... 6-12　57-58
LPs: 10/12–inch 33rpm
ABC/HICKORY .... 5-10　77-78
COLUMBIA (31 "Anniversary Album") . 8-12　70
COLUMBIA (900 through 1100 series)　15-25　57-58
COLUMBIA (1500 through 2600
　series) .... 10-20　60-67

COLUMBIA (2579 "Carl Smith") 35-50   56
(10–inch LP.)
COLUMBIA (8300 through 9800
series) 10-20   60-72
(12–inch LPs.)
COLUMBIA (9023 "Sentimental
Songs") 30-40   54
(10–inch LP.)
COLUMBIA (9026 "Softly and
Tenderly") 30-40   54
(10–inch LP.)
COLUMBIA (10000 series) 5-10   73
COLUMBIA (30000 series) 5-10   70-84
GUSTO 5-8   80
HICKORY 5-10   75
HARMONY 5-15   64-72
LAKE SHORE 5-10
Also see PRICE, Ray / Lefty Frizzell / Carl Smith
Also see PRICE, Ray / Johnny Horton / Carl Smith / George
Morgan

SMITH, Carl / Lefty Frizzell / Marty Robbins
LPs: 10/12–inch 33rpm
COLUMBIA (2544 "Carl, Lefty
and Marty") 200-300   56
(10–inch LP.)
Also see FRIZZELL, Lefty
Also see ROBBINS, Marty
Also see SMITH, Carl

SMITH, Connie
Singles: 7–inch
COLUMBIA 3-5   73-77
EPIC 2-4
MONUMENT 2-5   77-83
RCA 3-6   64-74
Picture Sleeves
RCA 4-6   67
LPs: 10/12–inch 33rpm
CAMDEN 5-10   67-72
COLUMBIA 5-10   73-77
MONUMENT 5-8   77-78
RCA (0100 through 1200 series) 5-10   73-75
RCA (3300 through 4800 series) 8-15   65-73

SMITH, Dawson
Singles: 7–inch
ROADSHOW/SCEPTER 3-5   75

SMITH, Effie
Singles: 78rpm
ALADDIN 5-15   46-53
G&G 10-15   45
GEM 10-15   45
MILTONE 8-12   47
VITA 5-10   56
Singles: 7–inch
ALADDIN 15-25   53
DUO DISC 4-8   64-65
EEE CEE 4-6   68
SPOT 5-10   59
VITA 10-20   56

LPs: 10/12–inch 33rpm
JUBILEE 15-25   66
Also see CARPENTER, Ike
Also see SQUIRES

SMITH, Frankie
Singles: 12–inch 33/45rpm
WMOT 4-6   81
Singles: 7–inch
WMOT 3-5   81
LPs: 10/12–inch 33rpm
WMOT 5-10   81

SMITH, Hank, and the Nashville Playboys / Bud Roman and the Topppers / "Scat" Benny
(George Jones)
EPs: 7–inch 33/45rpm
HOLLYWOOD HIT CLUB (280 "Heartbreak
Hotel") 30-50   56
TOPS (280 "Heartbreak Hotel") 30-40   56
Also see JONES, George

SMITH, Helene
Singles: 7–inch
DEEP CITY 4-8   68
PHIL-L.A. of SOUL 4-8   67-69

SMITH, Huey
(Huey Smith and His Band; Huey "Piano" Smith and His Clowns; Huey Smith and the Pitter Pats)
ACE 5-10   56-58
SAVOY 10-15   54
Singles: 7–inch
ABC 3-5   73
ACE (521 through 571) 10-15   56-59
ACE (584 through 672) 5-10   60-65
COLLECTABLES 2-4
CONSTELLATION 4-8   63
COTILLION 3-5   72
IMPERIAL 5-10   61
INSTANT 4-8   68-69
SAVOY (1113 "You Made Me Cry") .. 40-60   54
VIN 5-10   60
EPs: 7–inch 33/45rpm
ACE (104 "Having Fun") 50-75   59
LPs: 10/12–inch 33rpm
ACE (1004 "Having Fun") 75-125   59
ACE (1015 "For Dancing") 50-100   61
ACE (1027 "Twas the Night
Before Christmas") 50-100   62
ACE (2021 "Rock and Roll Revival") . 25-35   74
GRAND PRIX 10-20
Also see FORD, Frankie
Also see MARCHAN, Bobby, and the Clowns

SMITH, Hurricane
Singles: 7–inch
CAPITOL 3-5   72-73
EMI 3-5   74
LPs: 10/12–inch 33rpm
CAPITOL 8-10   72

SMITH, Jerry
(Jerry Smith and His Pianos)
Singles: 7-inch
ABC	3-5	69
AD	4-8	59-61
CHART	4-6	67
DECCA	3-5	70-72
RANWOOD	3-5	73-78
RICE	4-6	67
SOUND STAGE 7	4-8	65

LPs: 10/12-inch 33rpm
ABC	5-10	69
DECCA	5-10	70-72
RANWOOD	5-8	73-75

Also see DIXIEBELLES
Also see MAGIC ORGAN

SMITH, Jimmy
Singles: 7-inch
BLUE NOTE	4-8	56-63
MGM	2-4	78
MERCURY	2-4	77
PRIDE	3-5	74
VERVE	3-6	62-73

LPs: 10/12-inch 33rpm
BLUE NOTE	25-50	56-60
(Label gives New York street address for Blue Note Records.)		
BLUE NOTE	15-25	61-63
(Label reads "Blue Note Records Inc. - New York, USA.")		
BLUE NOTE	10-20	66-73
(Label shows Blue Note Records as a division of either Liberty or United Artists.)		
COBBLESTONE	6-12	72
ELEKTRA	5-10	82-83
GUEST STAR	8-12	64
INNER CITY	5-10	81
MGM	8-12	70
MERCURY	5-10	77-78
METRO	8-15	67
MOJO	5-10	75
PRIDE	5-10	74
SUNSET	5-10	70
VERVE	10-25	63-72
(Reads "MGM Records - A Division of Metro-Goldwyn-Mayer, Inc." at bottom of label.)		
VERVE	5-10	73-84
(Reads "Manufactured By MGM Record Corp.," or mentions either Polydor or Polygram at bottom of label.)		

Also see BURRELL, Kenny, and Jimmy Smith

SMITH, Jimmy, and Wes Montgomery
LPs: 10/12-inch 33rpm
VERVE	10-20	66-69

Also see MONTGOMERY, Wes
Also see SMITH, Jimmy

SMITH, Kate
Singles: 78rpm
COLUMBIA	3-6	27-46
VICTOR	3-6	38-42
MGM	3-5	48

Singles: 7-inch
ATLANTIC	3-5	74
MGM	2-4	78
RCA	3-5	63-68
TOPS	4-6	60

Picture Sleeves
RCA	4-8	63-64

EPs: 7-inch 33/45rpm
MGM	4-8	52-57
RCA	4-8	59

LPs: 10/12-inch 33rpm
CAMDEN	4-8	70-73
CAPITOL	5-15	54-57
COLUMBIA (6000 series)	10-20	50
(10-inch LPs.)		
HARMONY	5-12	57
KAPP	5-15	58
LION	5-12	57-60
MGM	5-15	52-66
METRO	5-10	67
RCA	5-12	63-80

SMITH, Keely
Singles: 78rpm
CAPITOL	3-5	56-58

Singles: 7-inch
ATLANTIC	3-5	67
CAPITOL	4-8	56-58
DOLTON	3-5	64
DOT	4-6	59-62
RCA	3-6	66-71
REPRISE	3-6	63-66

Picture Sleeves
DOT	4-8	60

EPs: 7-inch 33/45rpm
CAPITOL	4-8	58-59
DOT	4-8	60

LPs: 10/12-inch 33rpm
CAPITOL	5-15	58-75
DOT	10-15	59-62
HARMONY	5-10	69
REPRISE	8-15	63-65

Also see PRIMA, Louis, and Keely Smith
Also see SINATRA, Frank, and Keely Smith

SMITH, Leslie, and Merry Clayton
Singles: 7-inch
ELEKTRA	3-5	82

Also see CLAYTON, Merry

SMITH, Lonnie Liston
(Lonnie Liston Smith and the Cosmic Echoes)
Singles: 12-inch 33/45rpm
COLUMBIA	4-8	79

Singles: 7-inch
COLUMBIA	3-5	78-80

DOCTOR JAZZ 2-4   83
FLYING DUTCHMAN 3-5   75-76
RCA 3-5   77
LPs: 10/12-inch 33rpm
COLUMBIA 5-10   78-79
DOCTOR JAZZ 5-8   83
FLYING DUTCHMAN 6-12   73-76
RCA 5-10   76-77

SMITH, O.C.
(Ocie Smith)
Singles: 78rpm
CADENCE 4-8   56-57
MGM 4-8   56
Singles: 7-inch
BIG TOP 4-8   60
CADENCE 5-10   56-57
CARIBOU 3-5   76-77
CITATION 5-10   59
COLUMBIA 3-6   66-74
FAMILY 3-5   80
GORDY 3-5   82
MGM 5-10   56
MOTOWN 3-5   82
RENDEZVOUS 2-4   86-87
SHADYBROOK 2-4   78
SOUL WEST 3-5   72
SOUTH BAY 2-4   82
Picture Sleeves
COLUMBIA 3-6   69
LPs: 10/12-inch 33rpm
CARIBOU 5-10   79
COLUMBIA 8-12   67-74
HARMONY 8-10   71
MGM 8-10   72
MOTOWN 5-10   82
SOUTH BAY 5-8   82

SMITH, Patti
(Patti Smith Group)
Singles: 7-inch
ARISTA 3-5   76-79
MER (601 "Hey Joe") 50-75   74
SIRE 3-5   77
Picture Sleeves
ARISTA 4-8   78
LPs: 10/12-inch 33rpm
ARISTA 6-12   75-88
Members: Patti Smith; Ivan Kral; Jay Dee Daugherty; Lenny
Kaye; Allen Lanier; Richard Sohl; Andy Paley.
Also see KAYE, Lenny
Also see PALEY BROTHERS

SMITH, Ray
Singles: 7-inch
ABC 3-5   73
CELEBRITY CIRCLE 4-8   64
CINNAMON 3-5   73-74
COLLECTABLES 2-4
CORONA 3-5   75-77
DIAMOND 4-8   65

HEART (250 "Gone Baby, Gone") . 150-200
INFINITY 5-10   61
JUDD 8-12   59-61
NU-TONE 4-8   64
SMASH 4-8   62
SSS INT'L 3-5
SSS/SUN 3-5
SUN (298 "Right Behind You Baby") . 10-20   58
SUN (308 "Why Why Why") 10-15   59
SUN (319 through 375) 6-12   59-62
TOLLIE 8-10   64
TOPPA 4-8   62
VEE JAY 4-8   64
WARNER 4-8   63
WIX 3-5   78
LPs: 10/12-inch 33rpm
BOOT 5-10   78
COLUMBIA 20-25   63
JUDD (701 "Travelin' with Ray") .. 150-250   60
T (56062 "Best of Ray Smith") 20-30
WIX 10-15
Also see DONNER, Ral / Ray Smith / Bobby Dale

SMITH, Ray / Pat Cupp
LPs: 10/12-inch 33rpm
CROWN 15-25   63
Also see CUPP, Pat
Also see SMITH, Ray

SMITH, Rex
Singles: 7-inch
COLUMBIA 3-5   76-81
Picture Sleeves
COLUMBIA 3-5   79-80
LPs: 10/12-inch 33rpm
COLUMBIA 5-10   76-81
Also see REX

SMITH, Rex, and Rachel Sweet
Singles: 7-inch
COLUMBIA 3-5   81
Picture Sleeves
COLUMBIA 3-5   81
Also see SMITH, Rex
Also see SWEET, Rachel

SMITH, Richard Jon
Singles: 12-inch 33/45rpm
JIVE 4-6   83
Singles: 7-inch
JIVE 2-4   83
LPs: 10/12-inch 33rpm
JIVE 5-8   83

SMITH, Roger
Singles: 7-inch
JEROME 4-8   61
WARNER 5-10   59
Picture Sleeves
WARNER 10-15   59
LPs: 10/12-inch 33rpm
WARNER (1305 "Beach Romance") . 30-40   59

SMITH, Sammi
Singles: 7-inch
COLUMBIA	3-6	67-69
CYCLONE	3-5	79
ELEKTRA	3-5	75-78
MEGA	3-5	70-76
SOUND FACTORY	2-4	80-82
STEP ONE	2-4	86
TRIP	2-4	74
ZODIAC	2-4	76

Picture Sleeves
MEGA	3-5	70

LPs: 10/12-inch 33rpm
CYCLONE	5-8	79
ELEKTRA	5-10	76-78
HARMONY	5-10	71
MEGA	5-10	70-75
TRIP	5-8	74
U.A.	5-10	75
ZODIAC	5-8	76

Also see HART, Freddie / Sammi Smith / Jerry Reed

SMITH, Somethin,' and the Redheads
Singles: 78rpm
EPIC	3-5	54-57

Singles: 7-inch
EPIC	5-8	54-59
MGM	4-6	61

Picture Sleeves
EPIC	5-10	58

EPs: 7-inch 33/45rpm
EPIC	10-20	59

LPs: 10/12-inch 33rpm
EPIC	10-20	59
MGM	10-15	61

SMITH, Tab
(Tab Smith and His Band)
Singles: 78rpm
ARCO	4-6	48
ATLANTIC	5-10	52
CHESS	4-8	52
DECCA	5-8	44
EBONY	4-6	46
HARLEM	5-8	46
HUB	4-6	45-46
KING	4-8	46
MANOR	4-6	44-48
QUEEN	4-6	46
REGIS	5-8	44
SOUTHERN	4-6	46
20TH CENTURY	4-6	45
UNITED	4-8	51-57

Singles: 7-inch
ARGO	5-10	58-59
ATLANTIC	10-20	52
B&F	4-8	61
CHECKER	4-8	59
CHESS	10-15	52
KING (4000 series)	10-15	52

KING (5000 series)	4-8	60-61
UNITED (Black vinyl)	10-15	51-57
UNITED (Colored vinyl)	15-25	51

EPs: 7-inch 33/45rpm
KING	10-15	54

LPs: 10/12-inch 33rpm
CHECKER	15-25	59
UNITED (001 "Music Styled by Tab Smith")	30-35	
UNITED (003 "Red Hot and Cool Blue Moods")	20-30	

Also see POMUS, Doc

SMITH, Verdelle
Singles: 7-inch
CAPITOL	4-8	66-67
COLUMBIA	4-8	65
JANUS	3-5	75

Picture Sleeves
COLUMBIA	4-8	65

LPs: 10/12-inch 33rpm
CAPITOL	15-25	66
JANUS	8-10	75

SMITH, Vince
Singles: 7-inch
FOUR WINDS	2-4	86-88

LPs: 10/12-inch 33rpm
FOUR WINDS	5-10	87-88

SMITH, Warren
Singles: 78rpm
SUN	10-20	57

Singles: 7-inch
LIBERTY	4-8	60-64
MERCURY	4-6	68
SUN (239 "Rock 'N' Roll Ruby")	20-30	56
SUN (250 "Ubangi Stomp")	15-20	56
SUN (268 through 314)	10-15	57-59
SSS/SUN	3-5	80
WARNER	5-10	59

LPs: 10/12-inch 33rpm
LIBERTY (3199 "First Country Collection") (Monaural.)	35-45	61
LIBERTY (7199 "First Country Collection") (Stereo.)	40-60	61

SMITH, Whistling Jack
Singles: 7-inch
DERAM	4-6	67-69

LPs: 10/12-inch 33rpm
DERAM	10-15	67

SMITH CONNECTION
Singles: 7-inch
MUSIC MERCHANT	3-5	73

SMITHEREENS
Singles: 7-inch
CAPITOL/ENIGMA	2-4	88

ENIGMA 3-5   85-86
LPs: 10/12–inch 33rpm
CAPITOL/ENIGMA 5-8   88-89
ENIGMA 5-10   85-89
Members: Pat Dinizio; Jim Babjak; Dennis Diken; Mike Mesaros.

SMITHS
Singles: 12–inch 33/45rpm
SIRE 4-6   84-86
Singles: 7–inch
SIRE 2-4   84-88
LPs: 10/12–inch 33rpm
SIRE 5-8   84-88
Members: Andy Rourke; Mike Joyce.
Also see O'CONNOR, Sinead

SMOKE CITY
Singles: 7–inch
EPIC 2-4   84-85

SMOKE RING
Singles: 7–inch
BUDDAH 4-8   69

SMOKE RINGS
Singles: 7–inch
DOT 4-8   66

SMOKESTACK LIGHTNIN'
Singles: 7–inch
BELL 4-6   68-70
WHITE WHALE 4-6   67
LPs: 10/12–inch 33rpm
BELL 10-15   69

SMOKIE
(Smokey)
Singles: 7–inch
MCA 3-5   75
RSO 3-5   76-79
LPs: 10/12–inch 33rpm
MCA 8-10   75
RSO 5-10   76-79
Member: Chris Norman.
Also see QUATRO, Suzi, and Chris Norman

SMOTHERS, Dick
Singles: 7–inch
MERCURY (72717 "Saturday Night
at the World") 10-20   67
Picture Sleeves
MERCURY (72717 "Saturday Night
at the World") 15-25   67
Also see SMOTHERS BROTHERS

SMOTHERS BROTHERS
Singles: 7–inch
MERCURY (72323 through 72182) 4-8   62-63
Picture Sleeves
MERCURY (72483 "Three Song") 5-10   64
MERCURY (72519 "The Toy Song") . . 5-10   65
SMOTHERS INCORPORATED ("The
Christmas Bunny") 25-35   69
(No number used. Promotional issue only.)

EPs: 7–inch 33/45rpm
MERCURY (104 "Comedy Hour") . . . 10-15   68
(Promotional issue only.)
MERCURY (628 "Two Sides") 10-20   62
LPs: 10/12–inch 33rpm
MERCURY (20 "Best of the
Smothers Brothers") 25-35   64
(Promotional issue only.)
MERCURY (25 "Brothers
Smothers Month") 25-35   64
(Promotional issue only. Open-end interview.)
MERCURY (20000 series) 10-20   61-68
(Monaural.)
MERCURY (60000 series) 12-25   61-68
(Stereo.)
Members: Dick Smothers; Tom Smothers.
Also see SMOTHERS, Dick
Also see WILLIAMS, Mason / Smothers Brothers

SNAIL
Singles: 7–inch
CREAM 3-5   78-79
LPs: 10/12–inch 33rpm
CREAM 5-10   78-79

SNEAKER
Singles: 7–inch
HANDSHAKE 3-5   81-82
LPs: 10/12–inch 33rpm
HANDSHAKE 5-10   81

SNEED, Lois
Singles: 7–inch
CAPITOL 3-5   73

SNELL, Annette
Singles: 7–inch
DIAL 3-5   73-74
EPIC 3-5   77

SNIFF 'N' the TEARS
Singles: 7–inch
ATLANTIC 3-5   79-80
MCA 3-5   81
LPs: 10/12–inch 33rpm
ATCO 5-10   79
ATLANTIC 5-10   79-80
MCA 5-10   81

Also see NETTO, Loz

SNOW, Hank
Singles: 78rpm
BLUEBIRD 15-30
RCA 5-10   49-57
Singles: 7-inch
RCA (0100 and 0900 series) 3-5   69-74
(Orange labels.)
RCA (0300 and 0400 series) 8-12   50-51
(Gray labels.)
RCA (4346 through 7748) 5-10   52-60
RCA (7803 through 9907) 3-6   61-70
RCA (10000 and 11000 series) 2-5   74-80
Picture Sleeves
RCA 4-8   63
EPs: 7-inch 33/45rpm
RCA (295 through 1113) 12-25   54-56
RCA (1156 "Old Doc Brown") 35-45   55
RCA (1200 series) 20-30   55
RCA (1400 series) 15-25   57
RCA (3000 and 3100 series) 30-50   52-53
RCA (4000 series) 15-20   58
RCA (5000 series) 12-25   58-60
LPs: 10/12-inch 33rpm
CAMDEN 8-15   59-74
HANK SNOW SCHOOL of MUSIC
(1149/50 "The Guitar") 175-225   58
(Special issue from the Hank Snow School of
Music. Includes guitar instruction booklet.)
PICKWICK 5-10   75-76
RCA (0134 "Living Legend") 100-125   78
(RCA Special Products issue.)
RCA (0162 through 0908) 5-10   73-75
RCA (1004 "I'm Movin' On") 15-20   82
(RCA Special Products issue.)
RCA (1052 through 3511) 5-10   75-79
(With ""AHL1, "ANL1" or APL1" prefix.)
RCA (1113 "Just Keep-A-Movin") 25-35   55
(With "LPM" prefix.)
RCA (1156 "Old Doc Brown") 150-175   55
RCA (1233 through 1861) 25-45   55-58
RCA (2043 through 4708) 10-25   60-72
RCA (3026 "Country Classics") 50-75   52
(10-inch LP.)
RCA (3070 "Hank Snow Sings") 50-75   52
(10-inch LP.)
RCA (3131 "Hank Snow Salutes
Jimmie Rodgers") 50-75   53
(10-inch LP.)
RCA (3267 "Country Guitar") 50-75   53
(10-inch LP.)
RCA (3000 and 3100 series) 40-60   52-54
(10-inch LPs.)
RCA (6014 "This Is My Story") 20-30   66
READER'S DIGEST (216 "I'm
Movin' On") 125-150
(6-LP set.)
Also see MARTIN, Janis / Hank Snow

Also see PRESLEY, Elvis / Hank Snow / Eddy Arnold / Hank
Snow

SNOW, Hank, and Chet Atkins
Singles: 78rpm
RCA 4-8   55
Singles: 7-inch
RCA (5900 series) 5-10   55
LPs: 10/12-inch 33rpm
RCA (2952 "Reminiscing") 20-30   64
RCA (4254 "By Special Request") ... 20-30   70
Also see ATKINS, Chet

SNOW, Hank / Hank Locklin / Porter Wagoner
LPs: 10/12-inch 33rpm
RCA (2723 "Three Country
Gentlemen") 15-25   63
Also see LOCKLIN, Hank
Also see SNOW, Hank
Also see WAGONER, Porter

SNOW, Phoebe
Singles: 7-inch
COLUMBIA 3-5   76-78
MIRAGE 3-5   81
SHELTER 3-5   74-75
LPs: 10/12-inch 33rpm
COLUMBIA 5-10   76-81
ELEKTRA 5-8   89
MCA 5-10   79
MIRAGE 5-10   81
SHELTER 8-10   74
Also see GOODMAN, Steve, and Phoebe Snow
Also see JEFFREYS, Garland, and Phoebe Snow
Also see SIMON, Paul, and Phoebe Snow

SNUFF
Singles: 7-inch
WARNER/CURB 2-4   83

SOBER, Errol
Singles: 7-inch
ABC 3-5   74
ABNAK 3-5   70
BELL 3-5   72
CAPITOL 3-5   76
NUMBER ONE 3-4   79

SOCCIO, Gino
Singles: 12-inch 33/45rpm
ATLANTIC 4-6   80-84
WARNER/RFC 4-6   79-80
Singles: 7-inch
ATLANTIC 3-5   80-84
WARNER/RFC 3-5   79-82
LPs: 10/12-inch 33rpm
ATLANTIC 5-10   80-84
WARNER/RFC 5-10   79-80

SOFFICI, Piero
Singles: 7-inch
JUBILEE 4-6   61
KIP 4-6   61

SOFT CELL
Singles: 12–inch 33/45rpm
SIRE 4-6   82
Singles: 7–inch
SIRE 3-5   82
Picture Sleeves
SIRE 3-5   82
LPs: 10/12–inch 33rpm
ACCORD 5-10   82
SIRE 5-10   82-83
Members: Marc Almond; David Ball.
Also see ALMOND, Marc

SOFT MACHINE
Singles: 7–inch
PROBE 4-6   69
LPs: 10/12–inch 33rpm
ACCORD 5-10   82
COLUMBIA 8-12   70-73
COMMAND 12-18   73
PROBE (4500 "The Soft Machine") .. 20-30   68
(With movable parts cover.)
PROBE (4500 "The Soft Machine") .. 15-20   69
(With standard cover.)
PROBE (4505 "The Soft
Machine, Vol. 2") 15-25   69
RECKLESS 5-10   88
Also see WYATT, Robert

SOFTONES
(Soft Tones)
Singles: 7–inch
AVCO 3-5   73-75
H&L 3-5   77
Picture Sleeves
H&L 3-5   77

SOLARIS
Singles: 7–inch
DANA 3-5   80
LPs: 10/12–inch 33rpm
DANA 5-10   80

SOLO
Singles: 12–inch 33/45rpm
NEXT PLATINUM 4-6   84

SOME, Belouis: see BELOUIS SOME

SOMMER, Bert
Singles: 7–inch
BUDDAH 3-5   71
CAPITOL 3-5   77-78
ELEUTHERA 3-5   70
LPs: 10/12–inch 33rpm
BUDDAH 8-12   71
CAPITOL 8-10   77
ELEUTHERA 10-15   70

SOMMERS, Joanie
Singles: 7–inch
ABC 3-5   78
CAPITOL 4-6   67

COLUMBIA 4-8   66
HAPPY TIGER 3-5   70
WARNER (107 "Sommers' Hot,
Sommers' Here") 10-15   60
(Promotional issue only.)
WARNER (5000 series) 4-8   60-65
WARNER (7000 series) 3-5   68
LPs: 10/12–inch 33rpm
COLUMBIA 10-20   66
DISCOVERY 5-10   83
WARNER 15-25   59-62
Also see BYRNES, Edd "Kookie," with Joanie Sommers and the
Mary Kaye Trio
Also see NELSON, Rick / Joanie Sommers / Dona Jean Young

SOMMERS, Joanie, and Laurindo Almeida
LPs: 10/12–inch 33rpm
WARNER 15-25   64
Also see ALMEIDA, Laurindo
Also see SOMMERS, Joanie

SOMMERS, Ronny
(Sonny Bono)
Singles: 7–inch
SWAMI (1001 "Don't Shake
My Tree") 10-20   61
Also see SONNY

SONICS
Singles: 7–inch
BOMP 3-5   80
BURDETTE 3-5   75
ETIQUETTE 10-15   64-66
JERDEN 5-10   66-67
PICCADILLY 8-10   68
UNI 5-10   67
LPs: 10/12–inch 33rpm
BOMP 8-10   80
BUCKSHOT 10-12
ETIQUETTE (024 "Here Are
the Sonics") 100-150   66
ETIQUETTE (024 "Here Are
the Sonics") 5-10   84
(Reissues the 1984 date on back cover.)
ETIQUETTE (027 "The Sonics
Boom") 100-150   67
FIRST AMERICAN 8-12   80
JERDEN (7007 "Introducing
the Sonics") 100-150   67
Member: Gerry Roslie; Andy Parypa; Larry Parypa; Rob Lind;
Bob Bennett.

SONICS / Wailers
Singles: 7–inch
ETIQUETTE 10-15   65

SONICS / Wailers / Galaxies
LPs: 10/12–inch 33rpm
ETIQUETTE (ETALB-025 "Merry
Christmas") 100-150   66
ETIQUETTE (025 "Merry
Christmas") 5-10   84
(Reissues the 1984 date on back cover.)

ETIQUETTE (028 "The Northwest
  Collection") 125-150
  (Six-LP boxed set.)
    Also see SONICS
    Also see WAILERS

SONNY
(Sonny Bono)
Singles: 7–inch
ATCO 4-8   65-67
HIGHLAND 5-10   63
MCA 3-5   72-74
SPECIALTY 3-8   65-72
LPs: 10/12–inch 33rpm
ATCO 12-20   67
    Also see CHRISTY, Don
    Also see SOMMERS, Ronny
    Also see SONNY & CHER

SONNY & CHER
Singles: 7–inch
ATCO 4-8   65-70
KAPP 3-6   71-72
MCA 3-5   73-74
REPRISE 5-10   64-65
VAULT (916 "The Letter") 10-15 65
WARNER 3-5   77
Picture Sleeves
VAULT (916 "The Letter") 10-15 65
EPs: 7–inch 33/45rpm
ATCO 8-12   65
    (Jukebox issues only.)
REPRISE 15-25   65
LPs: 10/12–inch 33rpm
ATCO 12-20   65-72
KAPP 10-15   71-72
MCA 8-12   73-74
TVP 8-10   77
    Members: Salvatore Bono; Cher LaPiere.
    Also see CAESAR & CLEO
    Also see CHER
    Also see SONNY

SONNY & CHER / Righteous Brothers / Lettermen
LPs: 10/12–inch 33rpm
REPRISE (6177 "Baby Don't Go") ... 25-35   65
    (Credited to, "Sonny & Cher and Friends.")
    Also see RIGHTEOUS BROTHERS
    Also see SONNY & CHER

SONS of CHAMPLIN
(Sons)
Singles: 7–inch
ARIOLA AMERICA 3-5   75-77
CAPITOL 4-6   69-70
COLUMBIA 3-5   73
GOLDMINE 8-12
VERVE 5-10   67
LPs: 10/12–inch 33rpm
ARIOLA AMERICA 8-10   75-77
CAPITOL 10-20   69
COLUMBIA 10-15   73

Also see CHAMPLIN, Bill

SOPHISTICATED LADIES
Singles: 7–inch
MAYHEW 3-5   77

SOUL: see S.O.U.L.

SOUL, David
Singles: 7–inch
MGM 4-6   66-67
PARAMOUNT 3-5   70
PRIVATE STOCK 3-5   77
LPs: 10/12–inch 33rpm
PRIVATE STOCK 8-10   77

SOUL, Jimmy
(Jimmy Soul and the Chants)
Singles: 7–inch
S.P.Q.R. 5-10   62-65
20TH FOX 4-8   63
Picture Sleeves
S.P.Q.R. 10-15   62-63
LPs: 10/12–inch 33rpm
S.P.Q.R. (16001 "If You Wanna
  Be Happy") 40-50   63
    Also see BENTON, Brook / Chuck Jackson / Jimmy Soul
    Also see RIVERS, Johnny / 4 Seasons / Jerry Butler / Jimmy
    Soul

SOUL, Jimmy / Belmonts
LPs: 10/12–inch 33rpm
SPINORAMA 20-25   63
    Also see BELMONTS
    Also see SOUL, Jimmy

SOUL ASYLUM
LPs: 10/12–inch 33rpm
TWIN/TONE 5-8   88
    Members: Dan Murphy; Grant Young; Dave Pirner; Karl Mueller.

SOUL BROTHERS SIX
Singles: 7–inch
ATLANTIC 4-8   67-69
PHIL-L.A. of SOUL 3-5   72-74

SOUL CHILDREN
Singles: 12–inch 33/45rpm
STAX 4-8   78-79
Singles: 7–inch
EPIC 3-5   75-76
STAX 3-6   69-74
LPs: 10/12–inch 33rpm
EPIC 8-10   76
STAX 8-12   69-79

SOUL CLAN
Singles: 7–inch
ATLANTIC 4-8   68
Picture Sleeves
ATLANTIC 4-8   68
LPs: 10/12–inch 33rpm
ATCO 10-15
    Members: Solomon Burke; Arthur Conley; Don Covay; Ben E.
    King; Joe Tex.
    Also see BURKE, Solomon

Also see CONLEY, Arthur
Also see COVAY, Don
Also see KING, Ben E.
Also see TEX, Joe

SOUL DOG
Singles: 7-inch
AMHERST 3-5   76
LPs: 10/12-inch 33rpm
AMHERST 8-12   77

SOUL GENTS
(Soul Generation)
Singles: 7-inch
EBONY SOUNDS 3-5   72-74
FROS RAY 3-6   68-71
LPs: 10/12-inch 33rpm
EBONY SOUNDS 8-12   72

SOUL RUNNERS
Singles: 7-inch
MO SOUL 4-8   66-67

SOUL SEARCHERS
Singles: 7-inch
POLYDOR 3-5   75
SUSSEX 3-5   72-74
LPs: 10/12-inch 33rpm
SUSSEX 8-12   73-74

SOUL SISTERS
Singles: 7-inch
GUYDEN 4-8   62
KAYO 4-8   63
SUE 4-8   64-65
VEEP 4-8   68
LPs: 10/12-inch 33rpm
SUE (1022 "I Can't Stand It") 25-35   64

SOUL SURVIVORS
Singles: 7-inch
ATCO 4-8   68-69
CRIMSON 4-8   67-68
DECCA 4-8   67
PHILADELPHIA INT'L 3-5   76
TSOP 3-5   74-75
LPs: 10/12-inch 33rpm
ATCO 12-18   69
CRIMSON 15-25   67
TSOP 8-10   75
Members: Richard Ingui; Charles Ingui; Kenny Jeremiah.

SOUL TORNADOS
Singles: 7-inch
BURT 4-8   69

SOUL TRAIN GANG
Singles: 7-inch
SOUL TRAIN 3-5   75-77
LPs: 10/12-inch 33rpm
SOUL TRAIN 8-10   76

SOULE, George
Singles: 7-inch
LA LOUISIANNE 4-8   65

FAME 3-5   73
TETRAGRAMMTON 3-6   69

SOULE, George, and Ava Aldridge
Singles: 7-inch
MCA 3-5   78
Also see SOULE, George

SOULFUL STRINGS
Singles: 7-inch
CADET 3-6   66-73
LPs: 10/12-inch 33rpm
CADET 8-10   67-73

SOUND EXPERIENCE
Singles: 7-inch
SOULVILLE 3-5   74

SOUNDGARDEN
EPs: 7-inch 33/45rpm
"SCREAMING LIFE" 5-8   87
(Colored vinyl.)
LPs: 10/12-inch 33rpm
A&M 5-8   89
Members: Chris Cornell; Hiro Yamamoto; Matthew Cameron;
Kim Thayil.

SOUNDS of SUNSHINE
Singles: 7-inch
P.I.P. 3-5   76
RANWOOD 3-5   71-73
LPs: 10/12-inch 33rpm
P.I.P. 5-10   76
RANWOOD 5-10   71-72

SOUNDS ORCHESTRAL
Singles: 7-inch
PARKWAY 3-6   62-66
LPs: 10/12-inch 33rpm
PARKWAY 8-15   62-67

SOUPY SALES: see SALES, Soupy

SOURIRE, Soeur: see SINGING NUN

SOUTH, Joe
(Joe South and the Believers)
Singles: 7-inch
A&M 4-6   68
ALL WOOD 5-10   62
APT 4-8   65
CAPITOL 3-6   67-75
COLUMBIA 4-6   67
FAIRLANE 5-10   61-62
ISLAND 3-5   75
MGM 4-8   63-64
NRC (Except 002) 6-12   58-60
NRC (002 "I'm Snowed") 20-30   58
LPs: 10/12-inch 33rpm
ACCORD 5-10   81
CAPITOL 8-15   68-72
ISLAND 10-12   70
MINE 10-12   70
Also see CHIPS

SOUTH, Joe / Dells
LPs: 10/12–inch 33rpm
APPLE 15-25   71
   Also see DELLS
   Also see SOUTH, Joe

SOUTH SHORE COMMISSION
Singles: 7–inch
WAND 3-5   75-76

SOUTHCOTE
Singles: 7–inch
BUDDAH 3-6   74

SOUTHER, J.D.
(John David Souther)
Singles: 7–inch
ASYLUM 3-5   74-76
COLUMBIA 3-5   79
WARNER 2-4   85
LPs: 10/12–inch 33rpm
ASYLUM 8-10   72-76
COLUMBIA 5-10   79
WARNER 5-8   85
   Also see TAYLOR, James, and J.D. Souther
   Also see TILLOTSON, Johnny, and J.D. Souther

SOUTHER - HILLMAN - FURAY BAND
Singles: 7–inch
ASYLUM 3-5   74-75
LPs: 10/12–inch 33rpm
ASYLUM 8-10   74-75
   Members: J. D. Souther; Chris Hillman; Richie Furay.
   Also see FURAY, Richie
   Also see HILLMAN, Chris
   Also see SOUTHER, J.D.

SOUTHERN, Jeri
Singles: 78rpm
CAPITOL 3-5   59
Singles: 7–inch
CAPITOL 4-8   59
DECCA........................ 5-10   51-58
EPs: 7–inch 33/45rpm
DECCA........................ 5-10   55-56
LPs: 10/12–inch 33rpm
CAPITOL 10-20   59
DECCA........................ 15-25   55-58
ROULETTE 10-20   57-59

SOUTHERN BELL SINGERS
Singles: 7–inch
VEE JAY 4-8   63

SOUTHERN COMFORT
Singles: 7–inch
CAPITOL 3-5   71-72
COTILLION 4-6   69
LPs: 10/12–inch 33rpm
BRYLEN 5-8
CAPITOL 10-12   71
COLUMBIA 10-12   70
SIRE 12-15   69
   Also see MATTHEWS' SOUTHERN COMFORT

SOUTHERN COOKIN'
Singles: 7–inch
POLYDOR 3-5   79
LPs: 10/12–inch 33rpm
POLYDOR 5-10   79

SOUTHROAD CONNECTION
Singles: 12–inch 33/45rpm
U.A. 4-8   79-80
Singles: 7–inch
LIBERTY 3-5   80
MAHOGANY 3-5   78
U.A. 3-5   79-80
LPs: 10/12–inch 33rpm
U.A. 5-10   80

SOUTHSIDE JOHNNY and the Asbury Jukes
(Jukes; Southside Johnny and the Jukes; Southside Johnny)
Singles: 7–inch
ATLANTIC 2-4   86
EPIC 3-5   77-78
MERCURY 3-5   79
MIRAGE....................... 2-4   83-84
LPs: 10/12–inch 33rpm
ATLANTIC 5-8   86
CYPRESS 5-8   88
EPIC 8-10   76-79
MERCURY 5-10   79-81
MIRAGE....................... 5-8   83-84
   Also see FIVE SATINS

SOUTHSIDE MOVEMENT
Singles: 7–inch
20TH FOX 3-5   74-75
WAND 3-5   73
LPs: 10/12–inch 33rpm
20TH FOX 5-10   75
WAND 8-10   73
   Also see SIMTEC & WYLIE

SOUTHWEST F.O.B.
Singles: 7–inch
GPC 4-8   68
HIP 5-10   68-69
LPs: 10/12–inch 33rpm
HIP (7001 "Smell of Incense") 25-35   69
   Members: Dan Seals; John Ford Coley.
   Also see ENGLAND DAN & JOHN FORD COLEY
   Also see THESE FEW

SOVINE, Red
Singles: 78rpm
DECCA (Except 30239) 3-6   54-66
DECCA (30239 "Juke Joint Johnny") .. 8-12   57
MGM 3-6   50-53
Singles: 7–inch
CHART 3-5   71-75
DECCA (Except 30239) 4-8   54-66
DECCA (30239 "Juke Joint Johnny") . 10-20   57
GUSTO 3-5   79-80
MGM 5-10   50-53

SOXX, Bob B.:
   see BOB B. SOXX and the Blue Jeans

SPACE

SPACEMEN
   (Space Men)

SPADES
   (Slades)

SPADES
   (Thirteenth Floor Elevators)

SPAIN, Joanne

SPANDAU BALLET

SPANIELS
   (Spanials)

VEE JAY (107 "Goodnite Sweetheart,
Goodnite") 250-300   53
(Colored vinyl.)
VEE JAY (116 "Play It Cool") 50-75   54
(Black vinyl.)
VEE JAY (116 "Play It Cool") 250-350   54
(Colored vinyl.)
VEE JAY (131 "Do-Wah") 40-60   55
(Black vinyl.)
VEE JAY (131 "Do-Wah") 250-350   55
(Colored vinyl.)
VEE JAY (154 "You Painted Pictures") 40-50   55
VEE JAY (154 "Painted Picture") 30-40   55
(Shown as by the Spanials. Note different title.)
VEE JAY (178 "False Love") 75-100   56
VEE JAY (189 "Dear Heart") 75-100   56
VEE JAY (202 "Since I Fell for You") 75-100   56
VEE JAY (229 through 328) 30-45   56-58
VEE JAY (342 "People Will
Say We're in Love") 50-75   59
VEE JAY (350 "I Know") 20-25   60
LPs: 10/12–inch 33rpm
LOST-NITE (19 "The Spaniels") 5-10   81
LOST-NITE (137 "The Spaniels") 15-20
VEE JAY (1002 "Goodnite, It's
Time to Go") 200-300   59
(Maroon label.)
VEE JAY (1002 "Goodnite, It's
Time to Go") 75-100   61
(Black label.)
VEE JAY (1024 "The Spaniels") ... 200-250   60
UPFRONT 10-20
Members: Pookie Hudson; Jerry Gregory; Ernest Warren; Willie
Jackson; Opal Courtney; James Cochran; Carl Rainge; Don
Porter; Andy Magruder; Bill Carey.
Also see HUDSON, Pookie

SPANKY & OUR GANG
Singles: 7–inch
EPIC 3-5   75-76
MERCURY 4-8   67-69
Picture Sleeves
MERCURY 4-8   67-68
EPs: 7–inch 33/45rpm
MERCURY (90 "Like to Get
to Know You") 10-20   67
(Promotional issue only. Issued with paper sleeve.)
LPs: 10/12–inch 33rpm
EPIC 8-10   75
MERCURY 10-20   67-71
Members: Elaine "Spanky" McFarlane; Lefty Baker; Malcolm
Hale; Nigel Pickering; John Seiter.

SPARKLETONES, with Joe Bennett:
see BENNETT, Joe, and the Sparkletones

SPARKS
Singles: 12–inch 33/45rpm
ATLANTIC 4-6   84
Singles: 7–inch
ATLANTIC 2-4   82-84
BEARSVILLE 3-5   72

COLUMBIA 3-5   78
ELEKTRA 3-5   79
FINE ARTS 2-4   88
ISLAND 3-5   73-76
RCA 3-5   81
LPs: 10/12–inch 33rpm
ATLANTIC 5-10   82-84
BEARSVILLE 12-15   72-73
COLUMBIA (Black vinyl) 8-10   77
COLUMBIA (Colored vinyl) 12-15   77
ELEKTRA 8-10   79
ISLAND 8-10   74-76
RCA 5-10   81
Members: Ron Mael; Russell Mael.
Also see HALFNELSON

SPARKS and Jane Wiedlin
Singles: 12–inch 33/45rpm
ATLANTIC 4-6   83
Singles: 7–inch
ATLANTIC 3-5   83
Also see SPARKS
Also see WIEDLIN, Jane

SPEARS, Billie Jo
Singles: 7–inch
CAPITOL 3-5   68-71
LIBERTY 2-4   81
PARLIAMENT 2-4   84
U.A. (Except 50000 series) 2-5   74-80
U.A. (50000 series) 3-6   66-67
LPs: 10/12–inch 33rpm
CAPITOL 5-15   68-79
LIBERTY 5-8   81
PICKWICK/HILLTOP 5-8
U.A. 5-10   75-80
Also see REEVES, Del, and Billie Jo Spears

SPECIAL AKA
Singles: 12–inch 33/45rpm
CHRYSALIS 4-6   84
Singles: 7–inch
CHRYSALIS 2-4   84
LPs: 10/12–inch 33rpm
CHRYSALIS 5-8   84
Also see SPECIALS

SPECIAL DELIVERY
Singles: 7–inch
MAINSTREAM 3-5   75-76
SHIELD 3-5   77-78
Member: Terry Huff.

SPECIALS
Singles: 7–inch
CHRYSALIS 3-5   79-80
Picture Sleeves
CHRYSALIS 3-5   79
LPs: 10/12–inch 33rpm
CHRYSALIS 5-10   80
Also see FUN BOY THREE
Also see SPECIALS AKA

SPECTOR, Ronnie
(Ronnie Spector and the Ronettes; Ronnie Spector
and the E Street Band)
Singles: 7-inch
ALSTON 5-8   78
APPLE 5-10   70-71
BUDDAH 4-6   74
EPIC/CLEVELAND INT'L 5-10   77
COLUMBIA 2-4   87
POLISH 3-5   80
TOM CAT (Black vinyl) 3-5   75-76
TOM CAT (Colored vinyl) 5-8   75
    (Promotional issues only.)
WARNER./SPECTOR 3-5   76
Picture Sleeves
APPLE 8-10   71
COLUMBIA 3-5   87
EPIC/CLEVELAND INT'L 5-10   77
LPs: 10/12-inch 33rpm
POLISH 8-12   80
    Also see MONEY, Eddie, and Ronnie Spector
    Also see RONETTES
    Also see SPRINGSTEEN, Bruce
    Also see VERONICA

SPELLBINDERS
Singles: 7-inch
COLUMBIA 4-8   65-66
DATE 4-8   67
MIRAMAR 4-8
LPs: 10/12-inch 33rpm
COLUMBIA 10-20   66

SPELLBOUND
Singles: 7-inch
EMI AMERICA 3-5   78
LPs: 10/12-inch 33rpm
EMI AMERICA 5-10   78

SPELLMAN, Benny
Singles: 7-inch
ACE 5-10   61
ALON 4-8   66
ATLANTIC 4-8   65
MINIT 5-10   62
SANSU 4-8   67
WATCH 4-8   64
    Also see K-DOE, Ernie
    Also see THOMAS, Irma / Ernie K-Doe / Showmen / Benny
    Spellman

SPENCE, Judson
LPs: 10/12-inch 33rpm
ATLANTIC 5-8   88

SPENCER, Sonny
Singles: 7-inch
MEMO 10-20   59
MUSIC HALL 5-10
ONDA 15-25

SPENCER, Tracie
Singles: 7-inch
CAPITOL 2-4   88-91
LPs: 10/12-inch 33rpm
CAPITOL 5-8   88-91

SPENCER & SPENCER
Singles: 7-inch
ARGO 5-10   59
GONE 10-15   59

SPERRY, Steve
Singles: 7-inch
MERCURY 3-5   77

SPHEERIS, Chris
LPs: 10/12-inch 33rpm
COLUMBIA 5-8   88

SPHEERIS, Jimmie
Singles: 7-inch
COLUMBIA 3-5   72
EPIC 3-5   75
LPs: 10/12-inch 33rpm
EPIC 8-10   75

SPIDER
Singles: 7-inch
CAPITOL 3-5   72
LPs: 10/12-inch 33rpm
CAPITOL 8-12   72

SPIDER
Singles: 7-inch
DREAMLAND 3-5   80-81
Picture Sleeves
DREAMLAND 3-5   80
LPs: 10/12-inch 33rpm
DREAMLAND 5-10   80-81

SPIDERS
Singles: 78rpm
IMPERIAL 10-20   54-57
Singles: 7-inch
IMPERIAL (5265 "I Didn't
    Want to Do It") 40-60   53
IMPERIAL (5280 "Tears Began
    to Flow") 50-60   54
IMPERIAL (5291 "I'm Searching") . . . 50-60   54
IMPERIAL (5305 "The Real Thing") . . 30-40   54
IMPERIAL (5318 "She Keeps
    Me Wondering") 30-40   54
IMPERIAL (5331 "That's Enough") . . 25-35   55
IMPERIAL (5344 "Am I the One") . . . 20-30   55
IMPERIAL (5354 "Bells in My Heart") 40-60   55
    (Red label.)
IMPERIAL (5354 "Bells in My Heart") 10-15   57
    (Black label.)
IMPERIAL (5366 "Is It True") 40-60   55
    (Blue label.)
IMPERIAL (5366 "Is It True") 20-30   55
    (Red label.)

IMPERIAL (5676 through 5739) 12-25   59-61
OWL 3-5   73
LPs: 10/12-inch 33rpm
IMPERIAL (9142 "I Didn't Want
  to Do It") 150-250   61
Member: Chuck Carbo.
Also see CARBO, Chuck

SPIDERS
Singles: 7-inch
MASCOT (112 "Why Don't
  You Love Me") 750-1000   65
SANTA CRUZ (003 "Don't Blow
  Your Mind") 300-400   66
Member: Alice Cooper.
Also see COOPER, Alice

SPIDERS from MARS
Singles: 7-inch
PYE 3-5   76
LPs: 10/12-inch 33rpm
PYE 8-10   76
Also see BOWIE, David

SPIN
Singles: 7-inch
ARIOLA AMERICA 3-5   76
LPs: 10/12-inch 33rpm
ARIOLA AMERICA 8-10   76

SPINAL TAP
Singles: 7-inch
POLYDOR 2-4   84
LPs: 10/12-inch 33rpm
POLYDOR 5-8   84
Also see CREDIBILITY GAP

SPINNERS
Singles: 7-inch
ATLANTIC 3-5   72-85
MOTOWN (1000 and 1100 series) 4-8   64-68
MOTOWN (1200 series) 3-5   73
TRI-PHI 8-12   61-62
V.I.P. 4-6   70
LPs: 10/12-inch 33rpm
ATLANTIC 6-10   73-84
MOTOWN (Except 639) 5-10   73-82
MOTOWN (639 "The Original
  Spinners") 15-20   67
PICKWICK 8-10   76
V.I.P. 10-15   70
Members: Bobby Smith; Henry Fambrough; Pervis Jackson; Bill
Henderson; G.C. Cameron; Philippe Wynne; Reese Palmer; Jim
Knowland; Ed Edwards; Chester Simmons.
Also see ABBA / Spinners / Firefall / England Dan and John
  Ford Coley
Also see CAMERON, G.C.
Also see MARQUEES
Also see WARWICK, Dionne, and the Spinners

SPIRAL STARECASE
Singles: 7-inch
COLUMBIA 4-6   69-70
LPs: 10/12-inch 33rpm
COLUMBIA 15-20   69

Member: Pat Upton.

SPIRIT
Singles: 12-inch 33/45rpm
MERCURY 4-6   84
Singles: 7-inch
EPIC 3-6   70-74
MERCURY 3-5   75-76
ODE 4-8   68-70
POTATO 3-5   78
RHINO 2-4   81
Picture Sleeves
EPIC 4-8   74
POTATO 2-4   78
LPs: 10/12-inch 33rpm
EPIC 8-12   70-73
MERCURY (Except 818514) 10-15   75-77
MERCURY (818514 "Spirit of '84") 5-8   84
ODE (44003 "Spirit") 20-25   68
  (Monaural.)
ODE (44004 "Spirit") 15-20   68
  (Stereo.)
ODE (44014 "The Family That
  Plays Together") 10-20   68
ODE (44016 "Clear") 10-15   69
POTATO 10-15
RHINO 5-8   81
Members: Jay Ferguson; Randy California; Mark Andes; Ed
Cassidy; John Locke; John Arliss.
Also see FERGUSON, Jay
Also see HEART
Also see YELLOW BALLOON

SPLINTER
Singles: 7-inch
DARK HORSE 3-6   74-77
LPs: 10/12-inch 33rpm
DARK HORSE 8-10   74-77
Members: Bill Elliott; Bob Purvis.
Also see ELLIOTT, Bill, and the Elastic Oz Band

SPLIT ENZ
Singles: 7-inch
A&M (Except AMS-8128) 3-5   80-84
A&M (AMS-8128 "Shark Attack") 40-60   82
  (Picture disc. Promotional issue only.)
Picture Sleeves
A&M 3-5   81
EPs: 7-inch 33/45rpm
A&M (4848 "I Don't Want to Dance") . 15-25   81
  (Picture disc. Promotional issue only.)
LPs: 10/12-inch 33rpm
A&M 5-10   80-84
CHRYSALIS 8-10   77
Members: Tim Finn; Neil Finn.
Also see CROWDED HOUSE
Also see FINN, Tim

SPLIT IMAGE
Singles: 12-inch 33/45rpm
CAPITOL 4-6   84

SPOKESMEN
Singles: 7–inch
DECCA 4-8   65-66
WINCHESTER 4-8   67
LPs: 10/12–inch 33rpm
DECCA 25-30   65
Members: Johnny Madara; David White.
Also see MADARA, Johnny

SPOOKY TOOTH
Singles: 7–inch
A&M 4-6   69
MALA 5-10   68
ISLAND 3-5   72
LPs: 10/12–inch 33rpm
A&M 10-15   69-73
ACCORD 5-10   82
BELL 15-20   68
ISLAND 8-10   73-74
Members: Gary Wright; Mike Harrison; Luther Grosvenor.
Also see BOXER
Also see GROSVENOR, Luther
Also see HARRISON, Mike
Also see WRIGHT, Gary

SPOONBREAD
Singles: 7–inch
STANG 3-5   72

SPOONIE GEE
Singles: 12–inch 33/45
CBS ASSOCIATED 4-6   83
Singles: 7–inch
CBS ASSOCIATED 3-5   83
TUFF CITY 3-5   83

SPORTS
Singles: 7–inch
ARISTA 3-5   79
LPs: 10/12–inch 33rpm
ARISTA 5-10   79-80

SPRING
Singles: 7–inch
U.A. (50848 "Now That Everything's
  Been Said") 10-15   71
U.A. (50907 "Good Time") 25-30   72
LPs: 10/12–inch 33rpm
U.A. 15-25   72
Members: Marilyn Wilson; Diane Rovell.
Also see AMERICAN SPRING
Also see HONEYS

SPRINGERS
Singles: 7–inch
WAY OUT 5-8   65

SPRINGFIELD, Dusty
Singles: 7–inch
ATLANTIC 3-6   68-71
CASABLANCA 3-5   82
DUNHILL 3-5   73
PHILIPS 4-8   63-68
20TH FOX 3-5   80

U.A. 3-5   77-79
Picture Sleeves
PHILIPS 5-10   64-67
ATLANTIC 4-6   68
LPs: 10/12–inch 33rpm
ATLANTIC 10-15   69-70
CASABLANCA 5-8   82
DUNHILL 8-10   73
PHILIPS 12-20   64-67
U.A. 5-10   78-79
WING 10-15   68
Also see HONDELLS / Dusty Springfield
Also see PET SHOP BOYS
Also see SPRINGFIELDS

SPRINGFIELD, Rick
Singles: 12–inch 33/45rpm
RCA 4-6   83-84
Singles: 7–inch
CAPITOL 3-6   72-73
CHELSEA 3-5   76-77
COLUMBIA 3-5   74
MERCURY 2-4   84-85
RCA 3-5   81-85
Picture Sleeves
CAPITOL 4-8   72
MERCURY 3-5   84
RCA 3-5   81-85
LPs: 10/12–inch 33rpm
CAPITOL (11000 series) 15-20   72-73
CAPITOL (16000 series) 5-10   81
CHELSEA 8-12   76
COLUMBIA (KC-32000 series) 10-15   73
COLUMBIA (PC-32000 series) 5-8
MERCURY 5-8   84
RCA 5-10   80-88

SPRINGFIELD, Rick, and Randy Crawford
Singles: 7–inch
RCA 3-5   84
Also see CRAWFORD, Randy
Also see SPRINGFIELD, Rick

SPRINGFIELDS
Singles: 7–inch
PHILIPS 4-6   62-63
LPs: 10/12–inch 33rpm
PHILIPS 15-25   62-63
Members: Dusty Springfield; Tom Springfield; Tim Field.
Also see SPRINGFIELD, Dusty

SPRINGSTEEN, Bruce
(Bruce Springsteen and the E Street Band)
Singles: 12–inch 33/45rpm
COLUMBIA (1332 "Santa Claus
  Is Comin' to Town") 30-40   81
(White label. Promotional issue only.)
COLUMBIA (2007 "I'm on Fire") 20-25   85
(Red label. Black and white cover. Promotional
issue only.)

COLUMBIA (2082 "Glory Days") 20-25   85
(Red label. Black and white cover. Promotional
issue only.)
COLUMBIA (2174 "I'm Goin' Down") . 20-25   85
(Red label. Black and white cover. Promotional
issue only.)
COLUMBIA (2233 "My Hometown") .. 20-25   85
(Red label. Black and white cover. Promotional
issue only.)
COLUMBIA (05028 "Dancing in
the Dark") 5-8   84
COLUMBIA (05028 "Dancing in
the Dark") 20-30   84
(Black and white cover. Promotional issue only.)
COLUMBIA (05028 "Dancing in
the Dark") 15-25   84
(Promotional issue with color cover and gold
promo stamp.)
COLUMBIA (05087 "Cover Me") 5-8   84
COLUMBIA (05147 "Born in the U.S.A.") 4-6   84
COLUMBIA (05147 "Born in
the U.S.A.") 15-20   84
(White label. Promotional issue only.)

Singles: 7-inch

COLUMBIA (03243 "Hungry Heart") ... 3-5   84
COLUMBIA (04463 "Dancing in
the Dark") 3-5   84
COLUMBIA (04561 "Cover Me") 3-5   84
COLUMBIA (04680 "Born in the U.S.A.") 3-5   84
COLUMBIA (04772 "I'm on Fire") 3-5   85
COLUMBIA (04924 "Glory Days") 3-5   85
COLUMBIA (05606 "I'm Goin' Down") .. 3-5   85
COLUMBIA (05728 "My Hometown") ... 3-5   85
COLUMBIA (06432 "War") 3-4   86
COLUMBIA (06657 "Fire") 3-4   87
COLUMBIA (07595 "Brilliant Disguise") . 3-4   87
COLUMBIA (07663 "Tunnel of Love") .. 3-4   87
COLUMBIA (07726 "One Step Up") 3-4   88
COLUMBIA (08400 series) 3-4   88
(Columbia Hall of Fame series.)
COLUMBIA (10209 "Born to Run") 4-8   75
COLUMBIA (10274 "Tenth Avenue
Freeze-Out") 5-10   75
COLUMBIA (10763 "Prove It All Night") . 5-8   78
COLUMBIA (10801 "Badlands") 3-6   78
COLUMBIA (11391 "Hungry Heart") 3-4   80
COLUMBIA (11431 "Fade Away"/
"To Be True") 20-30   81
COLUMBIA (11431 "Fade Away"/
"Be True") 3-4   81
COLUMBIA (33323 "Born to Run") 3-6   76
(Red label. Columbia Hall of Fame series.)
COLUMBIA (33323 "Born to Run") 2-4   84
(Gray label. Columbia Hall of Fame series.)
COLUMBIA (45805 "Blinded by
the Light") 150-250   73
COLUMBIA (45864 "Spirit in
the Night") 300-500   73

Promotional Singles: 7-inch

COLUMBIA (1332 "Santa Claus Is
Comin' to Town") 10-15   81
COLUMBIA (04463 "Dancing in
the Dark") 8-10   84
COLUMBIA (04561 "Cover Me") 6-10   84
COLUMBIA (04680 "Born in
the U.S.A.") 6-10   84
COLUMBIA (04772 "I'm on Fire") 6-10   85
COLUMBIA (04924 "Glory Days") 6-10   85
COLUMBIA (05606 "I'm Goin' Down") . 6-10   85
COLUMBIA (05728 "My Hometown") . 6-10   85
COLUMBIA (06432 "War") 5-8   86
COLUMBIA (07595 "Brilliant Disguise") . 5-8   87
COLUMBIA (07663 "Tunnel of Love") .. 5-8   87
COLUMBIA (07726 "One Step Up") 5-8   88
COLUMBIA (10209 "Born to Run") .. 25-35   75
(With large letters on label.)
COLUMBIA (10209 "Born to Run") .. 15-20   75
(With small letters on label.)
COLUMBIA (10274 "Tenth Avenue
Freeze-Out") 15-20   75
COLUMBIA (10763 "Prove It
All Night") 15-20   78
COLUMBIA (10801 "Badlands") 15-20   78
COLUMBIA (11391 "Hungry Heart") . 15-20   80
COLUMBIA (11431 "Fade Away") ... 10-15   81
COLUMBIA (45805 "Blinded by
the Light") 45-55   73
COLUMBIA (45864 "Spirit in
the Night") 35-45   73

Picture Sleeves

COLUMBIA (1332 "Santa Claus
Is Comin' to Town") 15-20   81
(Promotional issue only.)
COLUMBIA (04463 "Dancing in
the Dark") 5-10   84
COLUMBIA (04561 "Cover Me") 5-10   84
COLUMBIA (04680 "Born in
the U.S.A.") 5-10   84
COLUMBIA (04772 "I'm on Fire") 5-10   85
COLUMBIA (04924 "Glory Days") 5-10   85
COLUMBIA (05606 "I'm Goin' Down") . 5-10   85
COLUMBIA (05728 "My Hometown") . 5-10   85
COLUMBIA (06432 "War") 4-8   86
COLUMBIA (07595 "Brilliant Disguise") . 4-8   87
COLUMBIA (07663 "Tunnel of Love") .. 4-8   87
COLUMBIA (07726 "One Step Up") 4-8   88
COLUMBIA (11391 "Hungry Heart") ... 4-8   80
COLUMBIA (11431 "Fade Away") 3-6   81
COLUMBIA (45805 "Blinded By
the Light") 100-150   73

LPs: 10/12-inch 33rpm

COLUMBIA (KC-31903 "Greetings
from Asbury Park") 15-20   73
COLUMBIA (PC-31903 "Greetings
from Asbury Park") 8-12   75
COLUMBIA (JC-31903 "Greetings
from Asbury Park") 5-8   78

COLUMBIA (KC-32432 "The Wild Innocent
and the E Street Shuffle") 15-18   73
COLUMBIA (PC-32432 "The Wild Innocent
and the E Street Shuffle") 10-15   73
COLUMBIA (JC-32432 "The Wild Innocent
& the E Street Shuffle") 5-8   78
COLUMBIA (PC-33795 "Born to Run") 25-30   75
(Credits show Jon Landau as "John.")
COLUMBIA (PC-33795 "Born to Run") 15-20   75
(Has "Jon" correction strip applied to cover.)
COLUMBIA (PC-33795 "Born to Run")   8-12   75
(Has "Jon" correction printed on cover.)
COLUMBIA (JC-33795 "Born to Run") . . 5-8   78
COLUMBIA (JC-35318 "Darkness on
the Edge of Town") 5-8   78
COLUMBIA (36854 "The River") 10-15   80
COLUMBIA (38358 "Nebraska") 5-8   82
COLUMBIA (38653 "Born in the U.S.A.") 5-8   84
COLUMBIA (40558 "Bruce Springsteen
and the E Street Band
Live, 1975-85") 30-40   86
(Includes 36-page booklet.)
COLUMBIA (40999 "Tunnel of Love") . . 5-8   87
COLUMBIA (HC-43795 "Born to Run") 25-35   80
(Half-speed mastered.)
COLUMBIA (HC-45318 "Darkness on
the Edge of Town") 25-35   81
(Half-speed mastered.)

Promotional LPs

COLUMBIA (978 "As Requested Around
the World") 30-40   81
COLUMBIA (1957 "Born in
the U.S.A.") 20-30   84
COLUMBIA (31903 "Greetings
from Asbury Park") 35-45   73
(White label.)
COLUMBIA (32432 "The Wild Innocent
and the E Street Shuffle") 35-45   73
(White label.)
COLUMBIA (33795 "Born to Run") . 300-500   75
(With "script" title cover.)
COLUMBIA (33795 "Born to Run") ... 40-50   75
(White label.)
COLUMBIA (JC-35318 "Darkness on
the Edge of Town") 30-40   78
(White label.)
COLUMBIA (PAL-35318 "Darkness on
the Edge of Town") 75-100   78
(Picture disc.)
COLUMBIA (36854 "The River") 25-35   80
(White label.)
COLUMBIA (38358 "Nebraska") 15-25   82
(White label.)
COLUMBIA (38653 "Born in
the U.S.A.") 15-20   84
(White label.)
    Also see BONDS, Gary "U.S."
    Also see CLEMONS, Clarence
    Also see LITTLE STEVEN and the Disciples of Soul

Also see PARKER, Graham
Also see SPECTOR, Ronnie
Also see THOMPSON, Robbin, Band
Also see U.S.A. for AFRICA

SPRINGSTEEN, Bruce / Albert Hammond / Loudon Wainwright, III / Taj Mahal
Singles: 7-inch
COLUMBIA/PLAYBACK (AS-52 "The
Circus Song") 50-75   73
Picture Sleeves
COLUMBIA/PLAYBACK (AS-52 "The
Circus Song") 40-60   73
    Also see HAMMOND, Albert
    Also see TAJ MAHAL
    Also see WAINWRIGHT, Loudon, III

SPRINGSTEEN, Bruce / Andy Pratt
Singles: 7-inch
COLUMBIA/PLAYBACK (AS-45 "Blinded
by the Light") 35-45   73
Picture Sleeves
COLUMBIA/PLAYBACK (AS-45 "Blinded
by the Light") 10-15   73
    Also see PRATT, Andy

SPRINGSTEEN, Bruce / Johnny Winter / Hollies
Singles: 7-inch
COLUMBIA/PLAYBACK (AS-66
"Rosalita") 30-50   73
Picture Sleeves
COLUMBIA/PLAYBACK (AS-66
"Rosalita") 15-25   73
    Also see HOLLIES
    Also see SPRINGSTEEN, Bruce
    Also see WINTER, Johnny

SPRINGWELL
Singles: 7-inch
PARROT 3-5   71

SPUNK
Singles: 7-inch
GOLD COAST 3-5   81
LPs: 10/12-inch 33rpm
GOLD COAST 5-10   81

SPYDER-D
(Spyder-D and D.J. Divine
Singles: 12-inch 33/45rpm
PROFILE 4-6   84-86

SPYRO GYRA
Singles: 7-inch
AMHERST 3-5   78
INFINITY 3-5   79
MCA 3-5   80-85
Picture Sleeves
INFINITY 3-5   79
LPs: 10/12-inch 33rpm
AMHERST 5-10   78
GRP 5-8   90-91
INFINITY 5-10   79
MCA (5000 series) 5-10   80-86

MCA (6000 series)	8-10	84-89
MCA (42000 series)	5-8	87

Members: Chet Catallo; Jay Beckenstein.

SPYS

Singles: 7–inch

EMI AMERICA	3-5	82

LPs: 10/12–inch 33rpm

EMI AMERICA	5-10	82

Also see FOREIGNER

SQUEEZE
(U.K. Squeeze)

Singles: 7–inch

A&M	2-5	79-87

Picture Sleeves

A&M	3-5	80

LPs: 10/12–inch 33rpm

A&M (Except 3413 and 4687)	5-10	79-89
A&M (3413 "Squeeze")	10-20	72
A&M (4687 "U.K. Squeeze")	10-15	78
I.R.S.	5-8	90

Members: Chris Difford; Glenn Tilbrook; Jools Holland; Gilson
Lavis; Keith Wilkinson; Andy Metcalfe.
Also see CARRACK, Paul
Also see DIFFORD & TILBROOK
Also see HOLLAND, Jools, and the Millionaires

SQUIER, Billy

Singles: 7–inch

CAPITOL	2-5	80-91

Picture Sleeves

CAPITOL	2-5	80-86

LPs: 10/12–inch 33rpm

CAPITOL	5-10	80-91

Also see PIPER

SQUIRE, Chris

Singles: 7–inch

ATLANTIC	3-5	76

LPs: 10/12–inch 33rpm

ATLANTIC	8-10	76

Also see YES

STACEY Q
(Stacey Swain)

Singles: 12–inch 33/45rpm

ATLANTIC	4-6	86-87

Singles: 7–inch

ATLANTIC	2-4	86-88
ON the SPOT	2-4	87

LPs: 10/12–inch 33rpm

ATLANTIC	5-8	86-88

STACKHOUSE, Ruby
(Ruby Andrews)

Singles: 7–inch

KELLMAC	4-8	65

Also see ANDREWS, Ruby

STACKRIDGE

Singles: 7–inch

DECCA	3-5	71-72
MCA	3-5	73
ROCKET	3-5	76

SIRE	3-5	74-75

LPs: 10/12–inch 33rpm

DECCA	10-12	71
MCA	8-10	73
ROCKET	5-10	76
SIRE	8-10	74-75

Member: Mutter Slater.

STAFFORD, Jim

Singles: 7–inch

COLUMBIA	2-4	84
ELEKTRA	3-5	80-81
ISLAND	3-5	74
MGM	3-5	73-75
POLYDOR	3-5	75-78
TOWNHOUSE	3-5	82
WARNER	3-5	76-80

LPs: 10/12–inch 33rpm

MGM	8-10	74-75
POLYDOR	5-10	76

STAFFORD, Jo

Singles: 78rpm

CAPITOL	3-8	43-50
COLUMBIA	3-5	50-57

Singles: 7–inch

COLPIX	4-6	62
COLUMBIA	5-10	50-60
DECCA	4-6	68
DOT	4-6	65
REPRISE	4-6	63

EPs: 7–inch 33/45rpm

CAPITOL	5-15	50-57
COLUMBIA	5-15	50-59

LPs: 10/12–inch 33rpm

BAINBRIDGE	5-8	82
CAPITOL (H-75 through H-435) (10–inch LPs.)	20-40	50-53
CAPITOL (T-197 through T-435)	15-25	55
CAPITOL (T-1653 through T-2166) (Monaural.)	10-20	62-64
CAPITOL (ST-1653 through ST-2166) (Stereo.)	12-25	62-64
CAPITOL (9014 "Songs of Faith") (10–inch LP.)	20-30	54
CAPITOL (11000 series)	5-8	79
COLUMBIA (584 through 1339) (Monaural.)	15-25	54-59
COLUMBIA (1561 "Jo Plus Jazz") (Monaural.)	30-50	60
COLUMBIA (2500 series) (10–inch LPs.)	15-30	55
COLUMBIA (6000 series) (10–inch LPs.)	20-35	50-54
COLUMBIA (8080 "I'll Be Seeing You") (Stereo.)	20-30	59
COLUMBIA (8139 "Ballad of the Blues") (Stereo.)	20-30	59

COLUMBIA (8361 "Jo Plus Jazz") ... 40-60   60
(Stereo.)
DECCA 10-15   68
DOT 10-15   66
TRIBUTE 5-10   71
VOCALION 8-12   68-69
> Also see LAINE, Frankie, and Jo Stafford
> Also see MacRAE, Gordon, and Jo Stafford
> Also see PIED PIPERS
> Also see WESTON, Paul

STAFFORD, Terry
Singles: 7–inch
ATLANTIC 3-5   73-74
COLLECTABLES 2-4
CRUSADER 4-8   64
ERIC 2-4
FIRSTLINE 3-5   81
MGM 3-5   71
MELODYLAND 3-5   75
MERCURY 4-8   66
SIDEWALK 4-8   66-67
TERRIFIC 3-5
WARNER 3-6   69
LPs: 10/12–inch 33rpm
ATLANTIC 8-12   73
CRUSADER (1001 "Suspicion!") 20-25   64
(Monaural)
CRUSADER (1001 "Suspicion!") 25-35   64
(Stereo)
> Also see ALLAN, Davie

STAIRSTEPS
Singles: 7–inch
BUDDAH 3-5   71-72
DARK HORSE 3-5   75-76
> Also see FIVE STAIRSTEPS

STALLION
Singles: 7–inch
CASABLANCA 3-5   77-78
LPs: 10/12–inch 33rpm
CASABLANCA 5-10   77-78

STALLONE, Frank
Singles: 12–inch 33/45rpm
RSO 4-6   83
Singles: 7–inch
POLYDOR 2-4   84-85
SCOTTI BROS 3-5   80
LPs: 10/12–inch 33rpm
POLYDOR 5-8   84

STAMPEDERS
Singles: 7–inch
BELL 3-5   71
CAPITOL 3-5   73
FLASHBACK 2-4   74
MGM 4-8   68
QUALITY 3-5   76
LPs: 10/12–inch 33rpm
BELL 10-15   71
CAPITOL 8-12   73-74

PRIVATE STOCK/QUALITY 8-10   76
> Also see WOLFMAN JACK

STAMPLEY, Joe
Singles: 7–inch
ABC 3-5   77
ABC/DOT 3-5   75-76
CHESS (1798 "Creation
of Love") 10-20   63
COLUMBIA 3-4   81-84
DOT 3-5   70-74
EPIC 2-5   75-86
IMPERIAL 5-10   59
PARAMOUNT 3-5   70
PAULA 3-5   74
LPs: 10/12–inch 33rpm
ABC 5-10   77
ABC/DOT 8-12   74-76
ACCORD 5-10   82
COLUMBIA 5-10   81-84
EPIC 5-10   75-83
PHONORAMA 5-10
> Also see UNIQUES

STANDELLS
Singles: 7–inch
COLLECTABLES 2-4
LIBERTY 10-20   64
MGM 10-20   65
SUNSET 10-20   66
TOWER 10-20   66-68
VEE JAY 10-20   65
Picture Sleeves
TOWER 15-20   67
VEE JAY 15-25   65
LPs: 10/12–inch 33rpm
LIBERTY (3384 "In Person at P.J.'s" . 40-50   64
(Monaural.)
LIBERTY (7384 "In Person at P.J.'s" . 50-60   64
(Stereo.)
RHINO 5-8
SUNSET (1136 "Live and
Out of Sight") 15-25   66
(Monaural.)
SUNSET (5136 "Live and
Out of Sight") 20-30   66
(Stereo.)
TOWER (T-5027 "Dirty Water") 40-50   66
(Monaural.)
TOWER (ST-5027 "Dirty Water") 50-60   66
(Stereo.)
TOWER (T-5044 "Why Pick on Me") . 40-50   66
(Monaural.)
TOWER (ST-5044 "Why Pick on Me") 50-60   66
(Stereo.)
TOWER (T-5049 "Hot Ones") 40-50   66
(Monaural.)
TOWER (ST-5049 "Hot Ones") 50-60   66
(Stereo.)
TOWER (T-5098 "Try It") 40-50   66

TOWER (ST-5098 "Try It") 50-60   66
  Members: Dick Dodd; Larry Tamblyn; Gary Lane; Tony
  Valentino; Dave Burke.
  Also see DODD, Dick
  Also see SLLEDNATS
  Also see TAMBLYN, Larry

STANDLEY, Johnny
Singles: 78rpm
CAPITOL 3-5   52-56
Singles: 7-inch
CAPITOL 5-10   52-56
MAGNOLIA 20-25   60

STANKY - BROWN GROUP
Singles: 7-inch
SIRE 3-5   76-78
LPs: 10/12-inch 33rpm
SIRE 8-10   76-78

STANLEY, Michael, Band
Singles: 7-inch
ARISTA 3-5   78-79
EMI AMERICA 3-5   80-83
EPIC 3-5   77
TUMBLEWEED 3-5   72-73
LPs: 10/12-inch 33rpm
ARISTA 5-8   78-79
EMI AMERICA 5-8   80-83
EPIC 8-10   75-76
MCA 10-12   73
TUMBLEWEED 8-12   73
  Also see TREE STUMPS
  Also see SILK

STANLEY, Pamala
Singles: 12-inch 33/45rpm
KOMANDER 4-6   83
MIRAGE 4-6   84-85
TSR 4-6   84
Singles: 7-inch
EMI AMERICA 3-5   79
MIRAGE 2-4   84-85
LPs: 10/12-inch 33rpm
EMI AMERICA 5-10   79

STANLEY, Paul
Singles: 7-inch
CASABLANCA 3-5   78
LPs: 10/12-inch 33rpm
CASABLANCA (Except PIX 7123) . . . 20-30   78-80
CASABLANCA (PIX 7123 "Gene
  Simmons") 40-50   79
  (Picture disc.)
  Also see KISS

STAPELTON - MORLEY EXPRESSION
Singles: 7-inch
DUNHILL 4-6   67
LPs: 10/12-inch 33rpm
DUNHILL 10-15   67

STAPLE SINGERS
(Staples)
Singles: 7-inch
ABC 3-5   73
CURTOM 3-5   75-77
EPIC 3-6   64-71
PRIVATE I 2-4   84-86
RIVERSIDE 4-6   62-63
SHARP 4-8   60
STAX 3-6   68-74
20TH FOX 3-5   81
VEE JAY 4-8   59-62
WARNER 3-5   76-80
LPs: 10/12-inch 33rpm
BUDDAH 5-10   69
CREED 5-10   73
CURTOM 5-10   76
EPIC 8-12   65-71
EVEREST 8-12   68-69
FANTASY 5-10   73
51 WEST 5-8
GOSPEL 5-15   59
HARMONY 5-10   72
MILESTONE 5-10   75
PRIVATE I 5-8   84-86
RIVERSIDE 10-15   62-65
STAX 5-10   68-81
20TH FOX 5-10   81
TRIP 5-10   71-77
VEE JAY 10-15   59-63
WARNER 5-10   76-78
  Members: Mavis Staples; Roebuck Staples; Cleo Staples;
  Yvonne Staples.
  Also see STAPLES, Mavis

STAPLES, Mavis
Singles: 7-inch
CURTOM 3-5   77
PHONO 2-4   84
VOLT 3-5   70-72
WARNER 2-4   79-86
LPs: 10/12-inch 33rpm
VOLT 8-12   69-70
WARNER 5-10   79-86
  Also see BELL, William, and Mavis Staples
  Also see FLOYD, Eddie, and Mavis Staples
  Also see STAPLE SINGERS

STAPLETON, Cyril, and His Orchestra
Singles: 78rpm
LONDON 3-5   51-63
MGM 3-5   55-56
Singles: 7-inch
DECCA 3-6   67
LONDON 4-8   51-63
MGM 4-8   55-56
STAGE 3-6   62
EPs: 7-inch 33/45rpm
LONDON 4-8   55-57
MGM 4-8   55-56

LPs: 10/12–inch 33rpm

IMPERIAL 5-10   61
LONDON 5-15   55-59
MGM 5-15   55-56
RICHMOND 5-15   59-61

STARBUCK
Singles: 7–inch

A.V.I. 2-4   84
ATCO 3-5   73
ELEKTRA 3-5   71
PRIVATE STOCK 3-5   76-77
U.A. 3-5   78-79

LPs: 10/12–inch 33rpm

PHONORAMA 5-10
PRIVATE STOCK 8-10   76
U.A. 8-10   78

Members: Bruce Blackman; James Cobb; Ken Crysler; Sloan Hayes; Dave Shaver; Bo Wagner.
Also see KORONA

STARCASTLE
Singles: 7–inch

EPIC 3-5   76-78

LPs: 10/12–inch 33rpm

EPIC (Except PAL-34935) 5-10   76-79
EPIC (PAL-34935 "Citadel") 40-50   79
(Promotional issue only.)

STARCHER, Buddy
Singles: 7–inch

BOONE 3-6   66
DECCA 3-6   66
HEARTWARMING 3-5   67
STARDAY 4-8   59-66

EPs: 7–inch 33/45rpm

4 STAR 5-10
STARDAY 5-10   61

LPs: 10/12–inch 33rpm

BLUEBONNET 8-12
DECCA 8-15   66
HEARTWARMING 5-10   68
STARDAY 8-15   62-66

STARGARD
Singles: 12–inch 33/45rpm

WARNER 4-8   79-81

Singles: 7–inch

MCA 3-5   77-78
WARNER 3-5   79-81

LPs: 10/12–inch 33rpm

MCA 5-10   78-82
WARNER 5-10   79-81

STARGAZE
Singles: 12–inch 33/45rpm

T.N.T. 4-8   83

STARK & McBRIEN
Singles: 7–inch

RCA 3-5   74-76

LPs: 10/12–inch 33rpm

RCA 8-10   75

Members: Fred Stark; Rod McBrien.

STARLAND VOCAL BAND
Singles: 7–inch

WINDSONG 3-5   76-80

LPs: 10/12–inch 33rpm

WINDSONG 8-10   76-80

Members: Bill Danoff; Taffy Danoff.
Also see BILL & TAFFY

STARLETS
Singles: 7–inch

ASTRO 15-20   60

Also see ANGELS

STARLETS
Singles: 7–inch

LUTE (5909 "I'm So Young") 15-20   60
PAM 8-12   61

Members: Maxine Edwards; Bernice Williams; Liz Walker.
Also see BLUE BELLES

STARLETS
Singles: 7–inch

TOWER 5-10   65

Member: Davie Allan.
Also see ALLAN, Davie

STARLETS
Singles: 7–inch

CHESS 4-8   67-68

STARPOINT
Singles: 12–inch 33/45rpm

BOARDWALK 4-6   83
CHOCOLATE CITY 4-8   80-82
ELEKTRA 4-6   83-85

Singles: 7–inch

BOARDWALK 2-4   83
CHOCOLATE CITY 3-5   80-82
ELEKTRA 2-4   83-87

LPs: 10/12–inch 33rpm

CHOCOLATE CITY 5-10   80-82
ELEKTRA 5-8   83-87

Also see DAWSON, Cliff, and Renee Diggs

STARR, Edwin
Singles: 12–inch 33/45rpm

20TH FOX 4-8   77-80

Singles: 7–inch

CASABLANCA 2-4   84
GRANITE 3-5   75-76
GORDY (Black vinyl) 3-6   67-71
GORDY (Colored vinyl) 5-8
(Promotional issues only.)
MONTAGE 2-4   82
MOTOWN 3-5   73-74
RIC-TIC 4-8   65-66
SOUL 3-5   72-73
20TH FOX 2-5   77-84

LPs: 10/12–inch 33rpm

GORDY 10-15   69-71
GRANITE 8-10   75
MOTOWN 8-10   73-82

20TH FOX 8-10   77-81
  Also see HOLIDAYS

STARR, Edwin, and Blinky
Singles: 7-inch
GORDY 4-6   69
LPs: 10/12-inch 33rpm
GORDY 10-15   69
  Also see STARR, Edwin

STARR, Kay
Singles: 78rpm
CAPITOL 3-6   48-57
CORONET 10-20
MODERN 10-20   49
RCA 3-5   55-57
RONDOLETTE 10-20
Singles: 7-inch
ABC 3-5   67-68
CAPITOL (936 through 2887) 5-10   50-54
CAPITOL (4000 and 5000 series) 3-8   58-64
DOT 3-6   68
GNP/CRESCENDO 3-5   74-75
HAPPY TIGER 3-5   70
RCA (0100 series) 3-5   73
RCA (6000 and 7000 series) 4-8   55-59
Picture Sleeves
CAPITOL 4-8   62
EPs: 7-inch 33/45rpm
CAPITOL 5-15   50-61
RCA 5-10   55-58
LPs: 10/12-inch 33rpm
ABC 5-15   68
CAMDEN 10-20   60-61
CAPITOL (H-211 "Songs by
  Kay Starr") 40-60   50
  (10-inch LP.)
CAPITOL (T-211 "Songs by
  Kay Starr") 20-40   55
CAPITOL (H-415 "The Hits of
  Kay Starr") 20-35   53
  (10-inch LP.)
CAPITOL (211 through 1200) 15-25   53-59

CAPITOL (400 through 900 series) ... 5-15   63-75
  (With "DT" or "SM" prefix.)
CAPITOL (1300 series) 15-25   60
CAPITOL (T-1438 "Kay Starr,
  Jazz Singer") 20-30   60
  (Monaural.)
CAPITOL (ST-1438 "Kay Starr,
  Jazz Singer") 25-35   60
  (Stereo.)
CAPITOL (1468 through 2100 series) 10-20   61-64
CAPITOL (11000 series) 5-10   74-79
CORONET 10-20   63
CRYSTALETTE (4500 "Kay Starr
  Sings") 50-100   52
  (10-inch LP.)
GNP/CRESCENDO 5-10   74-75
LIBERTY (3280 "Swingin' with
  the Starr") 15-25   63
LIBERTY (9001 "Swingin' with
  the Starr") 35-45   56
RCA (1100 through 1700 series) 15-25   55-57
RONDO-LETTE 20-30   58

STARR, Kay, and Count Basie
LPs: 10/12-inch 33rpm
MCA 5-8   83
PARAMOUNT 10-15   69
  Also see BASIE, Count

STARR, Kay, and Tennessee Ernie Ford
Singles: 78rpm
CAPITOL 3-5   50-56
Singles: 7-inch
CAPITOL 5-10   50-56
EPs: 7-inch 33/45rpm
CAPITOL 5-15   56
  Also see FORD, Tennessee Ernie

STARR, Kay / Erroll Garner
LPs: 10/12-inch 33rpm
CROWN 15-30   57
MODERN 25-35   56
  Also see GARNER, Erroll
  Also see STARR, Kay

STARR, Kenny
Singles: 7-inch
MCA 3-5   73-78
SRO 3-5   82
S.S. TITANIC 2-4   81
LPs: 10/12-inch 33rpm
MCA 5-10   75
SRO 5-10   82
  Also see LYNN, Loretta

STARR, Lucille
Singles: 7-inch
A&M 4-6   66
ALMO 4-8   64-65
EPIC 4-6   67-69
LPs: 10/12-inch 33rpm
EPIC 8-12   69
  Also see BOB & LUCILLE

Also see CANADIAN SWEETHEARTS

STARR, Randy
Singles: 78rpm
DALE 4-8   57
Singles: 7-Inch
DALE 8-12   57-59
MAYFLOWER 5-10   59
Also see ISLANDERS

STARR, Randy, and Frank Metis
LPs: 10/12-Inch 33rpm
MAYFLOWER 15-25   59
Also see STARR, Randy

STARR, Ringo
Singles: 12-Inch 33/45rpm
ATLANTIC (93 "Drowning in the
   Sea of Love") 15-20   77
   (Promotional issue only.)
Singles: 7-Inch
APPLE (1831 "It Don't Come Easy") ... 4-8   71
APPLE (1849 "Back Off Boogaloo") .. 10-15   72
   (With a blue apple on the label.)
APPLE (1849 "Back Off Boogaloo") 4-6   73
   (With a green apple on the label.)
APPLE (1865 "Photograph") 3-5   73
APPLE (1870 "You're Sixteen") 5-8   73
   (With standard apple label.)
APPLE (1870 "You're Sixteen") 4-6   73
   (With 5-point star label.)
APPLE (1872 "Oh My My") 4-6   74
APPLE (1876 "Only You") 4-6   74
APPLE (1880 "No No Song") 4-6   75
APPLE (1882 "It's All Down to
   Goodnight Vienna") 4-6   75
APPLE (2969 "Beaucoups of Blues") ... 4-8   70
ATLANTIC (3361 "Dose of Rock 'N' Roll")5-8   76
ATLANTIC (3371 "Hey Baby") 8-12   76
ATLANTIC (3412 "Drowning in
   the Sea of Love") 10-20   77
ATLANTIC (3429 "Wings") 8-12   77
BOARDWALK (130 "Wrack My Brain") . 3-5   81
BOARDWALK (134 "Private Property") . 3-5   82
CAPITOL (Orange label) 4-8   75
CAPITOL (Purple label) 3-5   78
CAPITOL (Black label) 2-4   83
PORTRAIT (70015 "Lipstick Traces") .. 5-10   78
PORTRAIT (70018 "Heart on
   My Sleeve") 4-8   78
Picture Sleeves
APPLE (1826 "Beaucoups of Blues") . 25-35   70
   (With the 2969 catalog number mistakenly shown
   as Apple 1826.)
APPLE (1831 "It Don't Come Easy") . 10-15   71
APPLE (1849 "Back Off Boogaloo") .. 10-15   72
APPLE (1865 "Photograph") 8-12   73
APPLE (1870 "You're Sixteen") 8-12   73
APPLE (1876 "Only You") 5-10   74
APPLE (1882 "It's All Down to
   Goodnight Vienna") 8-10   75

APPLE (2969 "Beaucoups of Blues")   12-18   70
   (With the catalog number correctly shown.)
BOARDWALK (130 "Wrack My Brain") . 3-5   81
Promotional Singles
APPLE (1831 "It Don't Come Easy") . 15-20   71
APPLE (1849 "Back Off Boogaloo") . 35-45   72
   (White label.)
APPLE (1865 "Photograph") 20-30   73
APPLE (1870 "You're Sixteen") 20-30   73
APPLE (1872 "Oh My My") 20-30   74
APPLE (1876 "Only You") 20-30   74
APPLE (1880 "No No Song") 20-30   75
APPLE (1882 "It's All Down to
   Goodnight Vienna") 20-30   75
APPLE (1882 "Oo-Wee") 25-30   75
ATLANTIC (3361 "Dose of
   Rock 'N' Roll") 20-30   76
   (White label.)
ATLANTIC (3361 "Dose of
   Rock 'N' Roll") 10-15   76
   (Blue label.)
ATLANTIC (3371 "Hey Baby") 20-30   76
   (White label.)
ATLANTIC (3371 "Hey Baby") 10-15   76
   (Red-white and blue labels.)
ATLANTIC (3371 "Hey Baby") 25-35   76
   (Single-sided disc.)
ATLANTIC (3412 "Drowning in the
   Sea of Love") 10-20   77
ATLANTIC (3429 "Wings") 20-25   77
   (White label.)
ATLANTIC (3429 "Wings") 10-12   77
   (Red-white and blue labels.)
BOARDWALK (130 "Wrack My Brain") 8-12   81
BOARDWALK (134 "Private Property") 8-12   82
PORTRAIT (70015 "Lipstick Traces") . 8-12   78
PORTRAIT (70018 "Heart on
   My Sleeve") 8-12   78
LPs: 10/12-Inch 33rpm
APPLE (3365 "Sentimental Journey") 10-15   70
APPLE (3368 "Beaucoups of Blues") 10-15   70
APPLE (3417 "Goodnight Vienna") .. 10-15   75
APPLE (3422 "Blast from Your Past") 10-15   75
APPLE (3413 "Ringo") 15-20   73
   (Includes a 20-page booklet.)
APPLE (3413 "Ringo") 10-15   73
   (With 4:05 version of Six O'Clock.)
ATLANTIC (18193 "Ringo's
   Rotogravure") 8-12   76
ATLANTIC (19108 "Ringo the 4th") ... 8-12   77
BOARDWALK (33246 "Stop and
   Smell the Roses") 8-10   81
CAPITOL 5-12   80-81
PORTRAIT (35378 "Bad Boy") 8-10   78
Promotional LPs
APPLE (3413 "Ringo") 100-125   73
   (With 5:26 version of Six O'Clock. Some copies list
   the track at 5:26 though it actually runs only 4:05.)

ATLANTIC (18193 "Ringo's
Rotogravure") 10-20   76
(With programming sticker on front cover.)
ATLANTIC (19108 "Ringo the 4th") .. 10-20   77
(With programming sticker on front cover.)
PORTRAIT (35378 "Bad Boy") 25-30   78
(Labels reads "Advance Promotion.")
PORTRAIT (35378 "Bad Boy") 15-20   78
(Labels reads "Demonstration, Not For Sale.")
Also see BEATLES
Also see CLAPTON, Eric
Also see FRAMPTON, Peter
Also see JOHN, Elton
Also see LOMAX, Jackie
Also see NILSSON

STARS ON
(Stars on 45; Stars on Long Play)
Singles: 12–inch 33/45rpm
RADIO 5-8   81-82
Singles: 7–inch
RADIO 3-5   81-82
TWENTY-ONE 2-4   83
LPs: 10/12–inch 33rpm
RADIO 5-10   81-82
TWENTY-ONE 5-8   83

STARS on 45 Featuring Sam and Dave
Singles: 7–inch
TWENTY-ONE 2-4   85
Also see SAM & DAVE

STARSHINE
Singles: 12–inch 33/45rpm
PRELUDE 4-6   83
Singles: 7–inch
PRELUDE 2-4   83

STARSHIP
(Jefferson Starship)
Singles: 7–inch
GRUNT 2-4   85-87
LPs: 10/12–inch 33rpm
GRUNT 5-8   85-87
Also see JEFFERSON STARSHIP

STARSKI, Love Bug
Singles: 7–inch
ATLANTIC 2-4   85

STARZ
Singles: 7–inch
CAPITOL 3-5   76-79
Picture Sleeves
CAPITOL 3-5   76-79
LPs: 10/12–inch 33rpm
CAPITOL (Black vinyl) 8-10   76-78
CAPITOL (Colored vinyl) 12-15   77
VIOLATION 5-8   83
Member: Richie Ranno; Joe Dube; Brendan Harkin.
Also see RANNO, Richie

STATE of GRACE
Singles: 12–inch 33/45rpm
PROFILE 4-6   83

Singles: 7–inch
PROFILE 2-4   83

STATLER BROTHERS
Singles: 7–inch
COLUMBIA 4-6   64-69
MERCURY 2-5   70-86
LPs: 10/12–inch 33rpm
COLUMBIA (CL-2000 series) 15-25   66-67
(Monaural.)
COLUMBIA (CS-9000 series) 12-25   66-69
(Stereo.)
COLUMBIA (PC-9000 series) 5-8
COLUMBIA (31000 series) 5-10
51 WEST 5-8
HARMONY 6-12   71-73
MERCURY 5-10   71-86
PRIORITY 5-8   82
TIME-LIFE 5-8   81
Members: Harold Reid; Don Reid; Lew DeWitt; Phil Balsley;
Jimmy Fortune.
Also see CASH, Johnny

STATON, Candi
Singles: 7–inch
FAME 3-6   69-73
L.A. 2-4   81
SUGAR HILL 2-4   82
WARNER 3-5   74-80
LPs: 10/12–inch 33rpm
FAME 8-12   70-72
SUGAR HILL 5-8   82
WARNER 8-10   74-80
Also see SOURCE, and Candi Staton

STATON, Dakota
Singles: 78rpm
CAPITOL 4-8   55-63
Singles: 7-inch
CAPITOL 4-8   55-63
GROOVE MERCHANT 3-5   72
EPs: 7-inch 33/45rpm
CAPITOL 5-15   58-60
LPs: 10/12-inch 33rpm
CAPITOL (800 through
1600 series) 20-40   58-63
HALF MOON 5-8   83
LONDON 10-15   67
U.A. 10-20   63-64
VERVE 8-12   71

STATUES
Singles: 7–inch
LIBERTY 10-20   60
Member: Garry Miles.
Also see MILES, Garry

STATUS QUO
Singles: 7–inch
A&M 3-5   73-74
CADET/CONCEPT 4-8   68-69
CAPITOL 3-5   75-77
JANUS 3-5   72

WORLD JAZZ 4-8   81

STEINBERG, David
Singles: 7–inch
COLUMBIA 3-5   74
LPs: 10/12–inch 33rpm
COLUMBIA 5-10   74-75
ELEKTRA 5-10   70
UNI 8-15   68

STEINMAN, Jim
Singles: 7–inch
EPIC/CLEVELAND INT'L 3-5   81
LPs: 10/12–inch 33rpm
EPIC/CLEVELAND INT'L 5-10   81

STEPHENS, Tennyson
(Tenison Stephens)
Singles: 7–inch
ARIES 4-6   69
CHESS 4-6   69
BACK BEAT 4-8   61
Also see HUGHES, Rheta, and Tennyson Stephens
Also see UPCHURCH, Phil, and Tennyson Stephens

STEPHENSON, Van
Singles: 7–inch
HANDSHAKE 3-5   81
MCA 2-4   84
LPs: 10/12–inch 33rpm
HANDSHAKE 5-10   81
MCA 5-8   84

STEPPENWOLF
Singles: 7–inch
ABC 3-5   70
DUNHILL 4-8   67-71
IMMEDIATE 4-8   67
MCA 2-4
MUMS 3-5   74-75
ROULETTE 3-5
Picture Sleeves
DUNHILL 4-8   71
MUMS 3-5   74
EPs: 7–inch 33/45rpm
DUNHILL 5-10   68
(Jukebox issues only.)
LPs: 10/12–inch 33rpm
ABC 8-12   75-76
ALLEGIANCE 5-8
DUNHILL 15-30   68-73
EPIC 8-12   75-76
MCA 5-10   79
MUMS 8-10   74
Members: John Kay; Goldy McJohn; Michael Monarch; Jerry
Edmonton; Nick St. Nicholas.
Also see HARD TIMES
Also see KAY, John
Also see SPARROWS

STEPTOE
Singles: 12–inch 33/45rpm
FANTASY 4-6   82

Singles: 7–inch
FANTASY 3-5   82

STEREO FUN INC.
Singles: 12–inch 33/45rpm
MOBY DICK 4-6   83

STEREOS
Singles: 7–inch
MINK (22 "Memory Lane") 10-20   59
(*Memory Lane* was reissued later in 1959, showing
the group as the Tams. the same track was again
issued in 1963, shown as by the Tams and then by
the Hippies.)
Also see HIPPIES / Reggie Harrison
Also see TAMS

STEREOS
Singles: 7–inch
CADET 4-8   67-68
COLLECTABLES 2-4   86
CUB (Except 9106) 10-20   61
CUB (9106 "Do You Love Me") 10-15   62
(Black vinyl.)
CUB (9106 "Do You Love Me") 25-35   62
(Black vinyl.)
GIBRALTAR (105 "A Love for You") . . 20-25   59
(Dark blue label.)
GIBRALTAR (105 "A Love for You") . . 10-15   59
(Light blue label.)
WORLD ARTISTS 10-15   63

STERLING, Michael
Singles: 7–inch
SUCCESS 2-4   83

STETSAPHONIC
Singles: 7–inch
TOMMY BOY 2-4   87

STEVE & EYDIE:
see LAWRENCE, Steve, and Eydie Gorme

STEVENS, April
Singles: 78rpm
RCA 4-8   51-52
SOCIETY 10-15   50
Singles: 7–inch
A&M 3-5   72
ATCO 4-6   65
CONTRACT 4-8   61
IMPERIAL 4-8   59-65
KING 4-6   64
MGM 4-6   67
RCA 5-10   51-52
VERVE 3-5   71
EPs: 7–inch 33/45rpm
KING 10-20   54
LPs: 10/12–inch 33rpm
IMPERIAL 15-20   61-64
LIBERTY 5-8   83
Also see APRIL
Also see TEMPO, Nino, and April Stevens

STEVENS, April / Marg Phelan
LPs: 10/12-inch 33rpm
AUDIO LAB 15-20   59
Also see STEVENS, April

STEVENS, Cat
Singles: 12-inch 33/45rpm
A&M 5-8   77
Singles: 7-inch
A&M 3-5   70-79
DERAM 4-6   66-72
Picture Sleeves
A&M 3-5   71-78
EPs: 7-inch 33/45rpm
A&M 8-10   70
(Jukebox issue only.)
LPs: 10/12-inch 33rpm
A&M 5-10   69-84
DERAM 10-15   67-72
LONDON 5-10   78
MFSL (035 "Tea for the Tillerman") .. 15-20   79
MFSL/UHQR (035 "Tea for the
Tillerman") 30-40   79
(Boxed set.)

STEVENS, Connie
Singles: 7-inch
BELL 4-8   70-72
MGM 10-15   68
PARAMOUNT ("Why Can't He
Care for Me") 35-50   58
(Promotional issue only. No actual label name or
number is shown, but this may have been
distributed by Paramount to promote the film,
Rock-A- Bye Baby, in which Connie starred.)
WARNER (Except 5092) 5-10   59-66
WARNER (5092 "Apollo") 10-20   59
Picture Sleeves
WARNER (5159 "Too Young
to Go Steady") 15-25   60
LPs: 10/12-inch 33rpm
HARMONY 10-20   69
WARNER (1208 "Conchetta") 40-50   58
WARNER (1335 through 1460) 20-40   59-62
Also see BYRNES, Edward

STEVENS, Dodie
Singles: 7-inch
CRYSTALETTE 8-12   59
DOLTON 4-8   63
DOT 4-8   59-62
IMPERIAL 4-8   63
Picture Sleeves
CRYSTALETTE (724 "Pink
Shoe Laces") 20-30   59
LPs: 10/12-inch 33rpm
DOT 20-30   60-61

STEVENS, Ray
(Ray Stevens and the Merry Melody Singers)
Singles: 7-inch
BARNABY 3-5   70-76
CAPITOL 8-12   58-59
MCA 2-4   85-89
MERCURY (66 "Butch Barbarian") ... 5-10   64
(Promotional issue only.)
MERCURY (71000 and 72000 series) .. 4-8   61-68
MERCURY (810000 series) 3-5   83
MONUMENT 4-8   65-69
NRC 5-10   59-60
PREP 10-15   57
PRIORITY 2-4
RCA 3-5   81-82
WARNER/AHAB 3-5   76-79
Picture Sleeves
BARNABY 4-6   70
MCA 3-5   86
MERCURY 10-15   61-64
WARNER/AHAB 3-5   79
EPs: 7-inch 33/45rpm
MERCURY (85 "Ray Stevens") 10-15   62
(Promotional issue only. Not issued with cover.)
LPs: 10/12-inch 33rpm
BARNABY 8-10   70-78
MCA 5-8   85-89
MERCURY (0732 "1,837 Seconds
of Humor") 50-75   62
MERCURY (0732 "Ahab the Arab") .. 20-25   62
(Reissue of 1,837 Seconds of Humor.)
MERCURY (0828 "This Is Ray
Stevens") 20-30   63
MERCURY (61272 "The Best of
Ray Stevens") 10-15   70
MERCURY (810000 series) 5-8   83
MONUMENT 10-15   66-69
PRIORITY 5-8   82
RCA 5-10   80-82
WARNER 5-10   76-79
WING 10-15   68
Also see ARCHIES
Also see 4 SEASONS / Ray Stevens
Also see HENHOUSE FIVE PLUS TOO
Also see ROE, Tommy / Bobby Rydell / Ray Stevens

STEVENS, Ray / Hal Winters
LPs: 10/12-inch 33rpm
CROWN 12-18   63
Also see STEVENS, Ray

STEVENS, Shakin'
Singles: 7-inch
EPIC 3-5   81-84
LPs: 10/12-inch 33rpm
EPIC 5-10   81-84

STEVENSON, B.W.
Singles: 7-inch
MCA 3-5   80
PRIVATE STOCK 3-5   78

RCA 3-5   73
WARNER 3-5   77-78
LPs: 10/12–inch 33rpm
MCA 5-10   80
RCA 5-10   72-77
WARNER 5-10   77

STEVIE B
Singles: 7–inch
LMR 2-4   87-90
LPs: 10/12–inch 33rpm
LMR 5-8   87

STEWART, Al
Singles: 7–inch
ARISTA 3-5   78-82
ENIGMA 2-4   88
JANUS 3-5   74-77
Picture Sleeves
JANUS 3-5   74
LPs: 10/12–inch 33rpm
ARISTA (Except 40) 5-10   78-81
ARISTA (40 "The Live Radio Concert") 25-35   80
  (Promotional issue only.)
EPIC 20-25   70
JANUS 10-15   74-77
MFSL (009 "Year of the Cat") 30-60   78
MFSL (082 "Time Passages") 20-30   82
  Also see PAGE, Jimmy
  Also see SHOT in the DARK

STEWART, Amii
Singles: 12–inch 33/45rpm
ARIOLA 4-8   79
EMERGENCY 4-6   85
Singles: 7–inch
ARIOLA 3-5   79
EMERGENCY 2-4   85
LPs: 10/12–inch 33rpm
ARIOLA AMERICA 5-10   79
HANDSHAKE 5-8   81

STEWART, Amii, and Johnny Bristol
Singles: 7–inch
HANDSHAKE 3-5   80
  Also see BRISTOL, Johnny
  Also see STEWART, Amii

STEWART, Andy
Singles: 7–inch
CAPITOL 4-6   62
EPIC 4-6   64
WARWICK 4-8   61
LPs: 10/12–inch 33rpm
CAPITOL 5-15   62-72
EPIC 5-15   64-68
GREEN LINNET 4-8   83
WARWICK 15-25   61

STEWART, Baron
Singles: 7–inch
U.A. 3-5   75

LPs: 10/12–inch 33rpm
U.A. 8-10   75

STEWART, Billy
Singles: 78rpm
ARGO 8-12   56
Singles: 7–inch
ARGO 8-12   56
CHESS 4-8   62-73
ERIC 2-4
U.A. 4-8   61
LPs: 10/12–inch 33rpm
CADET 8-10   74
CHESS 15-25   65-67

STEWART, Billy, and the Marquees
Singles: 7–inch
OKEH (7095 "Baby, You're
  My Only Love") 50-75   57
  Also see STEWART, Billy

STEWART, Bobby
Singles: 12–inch 33/45rpm
WARNER 4-6   83
Singles: 7–inch
WARNER 2-4   83

STEWART, Dave, and Barbara Gaskin
Singles: 7–inch
PLATINUM 3-5   81

STEWART, Gary
(Gary Stewart & Dean Dillon)
Singles: 7–inch
CORY (101 "Walk On Boy") 10-20
DECCA 3-5   71
KAPP 3-6   68-70
MCA 3-5   75
RCA 3-5   73-83
Picture Sleeves
RCA 3-5   82
LPs: 10/12–inch 33rpm
MCA 4-8   75
RCA 5-10   75-83

STEWART, Jermaine
Singles: 12–inch 33/45rpm
ARISTA 4-6   84-86
Singles: 7–inch
ARISTA 2-4   84-88
LPs: 10/12–inch 33rpm
ARISTA 5-8   85-88

STEWART, John
Singles: 7–inch
ALLEGIANCE 3-4
CAPITOL 4-6   69
RCA 3-5   73-75
RSO 3-5   77-80
WARNER 3-5   71
LPs: 10/12–inch 33rpm
ALLEGIANCE 5-8
CAPITOL 10-15   69-70

RCA	5-10	73-75
RSO	5-10	77-80
SHIP	5-8	87
WARNER	8-12	71

Also see BUCKINGHAM, Lindsey
Also see KINGSTON TRIO
Also see NICKS, Stevie

STEWART, John, and Buffy Ford
LPs: 10/12–inch 33rpm

CAPITOL	10-15	68

STEWART, John, and Nick Reynolds
LPs: 10/12–inch 33rpm

TAKOMA	5-10

Also see KINGSTON TRIO
Also see STEWART, John

STEWART, John, and Scott Engel:
see ENGEL, Scott, and John Stewart

STEWART, Mel
Singles: 12–inch 33/45rpm

MERCURY	4-6	83

Singles: 7–inch

MERCURY	2-4	83

STEWART, Rod
(Rod Stewart and the Faces)
Singles: 12–inch 33/45rpm

WARNER	5-10	78-82

Singles: 7–inch

GEFFEN	2-4	87
GNP/CRESCENDO	3-5	73
MERCURY	4-8	70-76
PRESS (8722 "Good Morning Little Schoolgirl")	15-25	65
PRIVATE STOCK	3-5	76
WARNER	2-4	75-86

Picture Sleeves

MERCURY	5-10	72-73
WARNER	3-5	75-86

LPs: 10/12–inch 33rpm

ACCORD	5-8	81
MERCURY (Except 61000 series)	8-12	71-76
MERCURY (61000 series)	10-20	69-70
MFSL	25-50	81
PRIVATE STOCK	8-10	77
SPRINGBOARD	8-12	72
TRIP	8-10	77
WARNER (Except BSP-3276)	5-10	75-88
WARNER (BSP-3276 "Blondes Have More Fun"")	10-15	79
(Picture disc.)		

Also see BECK, Jeff, and Rod Stewart
Also see PYTHON LEE JACKSON

STEWART, Sandy
Singles: 78rpm

EPIC	3-5	54
OKEH	3-5	53
20TH CENTURY	3-5	54
X	3-5	55

Singles: 7–inch

ATCO	4-8	59
COLPIX	4-8	62-63
DCP	3-6	64
EAST WEST	4-8	58
EPIC	5-10	54
OKEH	5-10	53
20TH CENTURY	5-10	54
U.A.	4-8	60-61
X	5-10	55

Picture Sleeves

COLPIX	5-10	62

LPs: 10/12–inch 33rpm

COLPIX	10-20	63

STEWART, Wynn
(Wynn Stewart and the Tourists)
Singles: 78rpm

CAPITOL	3-5	56-57

Singles: 7–inch

ATLANTIC	3-4	74
CAPITOL (2000 series)	3-5	67-71
CAPITOL (3000 series)	5-10	56-57
CAPITOL (5000 series)	4-8	62-67
CHALLENGE	4-8	59-64
4 STAR	3-4	80
JACKPOT	10-15	59
PLAYBOY	3-5	75-76
PRETTY WORLD	2-4	85
RCA	3-5	72-73
WINS	3-5	79

Picture Sleeves

CAPITOL	4-8	67-69

LPs: 10/12–inch 33rpm

CAPITOL	5-15	67-75
PICKWICK/HILLTOP	5-12	67
PLAYBOY	5-10	76
STARDAY	8-12	68
WRANGLER (1006 "Wynn Stewart")	20-30	62

Also see PIERCE, Webb / Wynn Stewart

STILLS, Stephen
(Stephen Stills and Manassas)
Singles: 7–inch

ATLANTIC	3-5	70-73
COLUMBIA	3-5	75-78

Picture Sleeves

ATLANTIC	3-5	71

LPs: 10/12–inch 33rpm

ATLANTIC	5-10	70-84
COLUMBIA (Except PCQ-33575)	5-10	75-78
COLUMBIA (PCQ-33575 "Stills")	10-15	75
(Quadrophonic.)		

Also see BLOOMFIELD, Mike, Al Kooper & Steve Stills
Also see BUFFALO SPRINGFIELD
Also see CROSBY, STILLS & NASH
Also see JEFFERSON AIRPLANE
Also see STILLS - YOUNG BAND

STILLS - YOUNG BAND
Singles: 7–inch

REPRISE	3-5	77

LPs: 10/12–inch 33rpm

REPRISE 5-10   76
   Members: Stephen Stills; Neil Young.
   Also see STILLS, Stephen
   Also see YOUNG, Neil

STILLWATER

Singles: 7–inch

CAPRICORN 3-5   77-78

LPs: 10/12–inch 33rpm

CAPRICORN 5-10   78-79

STING
(Gordon Sumner)

Singles: 12–inch 33/45rpm

A&M 4-6   85-87

Singles: 7–inch

A&M 2-4   85-90
ABC 3-5   78

Picture Sleeves

A&M 2-4   85-87

LPs: 10/12–inch 33rpm

A&M 5-8   85-90
ABC 5-10   78
   Also see BAND AID
   Also see POLICE

STIRLING SILVER

Singles: 7–inch

COLUMBIA 3-5   76

STITES, Gary

Singles: 7–inch

CARLTON 10-15   59-60
EPIC 4-8   66
MADISON 10-15   60-61
MR. PEEKE 8-12   62

LPs: 10/12–inch 33rpm

CARLTON (STLP-120 "Lonely
  for You") 40-50   60
  (Monaural.)
CARLTON (STLP-120 "Lonely
  for You") 50-75   60
  (Stereo.)

STITT, Sonny

Singles: 7-Inch

ARGO 4-8   58-65
ATLANTIC 4-6   63
CADET 3-5   74
CATALYST 3-5   77
ENTERPRISE 3-5   69
IMPULSE 4-6   64
PRESTIGE 3-6   63-69
ROULETTE 4-6   65-67
WINGATE 4-6   65
WORLD PACIFIC 4-6   63

EPs: 7-Inch 33/45rpm

PRESTIGE 10-25   53

LPs: 10/12-Inch 33rpm

ARGO 20-40   58-65
ATLANTIC 15-30   62-64

CADET 10-25   65-74
CATALYST 5-10   76-77
CHESS 8-12   76
COLPIX 10-20   66
EVEREST 5-8   82
FLYING DUTCHMAN 5-10   75-76
IMPULSE 15-25   63-64
JAMAL 8-12   71
JAZZLAND 20-40   62
JAZZTONE (1231 "Early Modern") . . 40-60   56
JAZZTONE (1263 "Early Modern") . . 30-50   57
MUSE 5-10   73-82
PACIFIC JAZZ 20-30   63
PAULA 5-10   74
PRESTIGE (060 "Kaleidoscope") 5-10   83
PRESTIGE (103 "Sonny Stitt
  Plays") 100-150   51
  (10–inch LP.)
PRESTIGE (111 "Mr. Saxophone") 100-150   51
  (10–inch LP.)
PRESTIGE (126 "Favorites") 100-150   52
  (10–inch LP.)
PRESTIGE (148 "Favorites") 100-150   53
  (10–inch LP.)
PRESTIGE (7000 series) 25-50   56-64
  (Yellow label.)
PRESTIGE (7000 series) 10-25   65-70
  (Blue labels.)
PRESTIGE (10000 series) 8-12   71-74
PRESTIGE (20000 series) 8-15   74
ROOST (418 "At the Hi Hat") 150-250   52
  (10–inch LP.)
ROOST (1200 series) 30-50   56
ROOST (2200 series) 15-35   57-66
ROULETTE 10-25   65-70
SAVOY (9006 "Be-Bop") 100-150   53
  (10–inch LP.)
SOLID STATE 10-15   69
TRIP 8-12   73
UPFRONT 5-10   77
VERVE 25-50   57-59
  (Reads "Verve Records, Inc." at bottom of label.)
VERVE 12-25   62-72
  (Reads "MGM Records - A Division Of
  Metro-Goldwyn-Mayer, Inc." at bottom of label.)
VERVE 5-10   73-84
  (Reads "Manufactured By MGM Record Corp." or
  mentions either Polydor or Polygram at bottom of
  label.)
   Also see AMMONS, Gene, and Sonny Stitt

STITT, Sonny, Kai Winding and Horace Silver
LPs: 10/12–inch 33rpm

ROOST (415 "From the Pen
  of Johnny Richards") 150-250   52
  (10–inch LP.)
   Also see AMMONS, Gene, and Sonny Stitt
   Also see SILVER, Horace
   Also see WINDING, Kai

STOKES, Simon T.
(Simon Stokes and the Nighthawks)
Singles: 7-inch
CASABLANCA 3-5   74
ELEKTRA 3-6   69-70
IN SOUND 4-8   68
U.A. 3-5   77
LPs: 10/12-inch 33rpm
MGM 10-15   70
SPINDIZZY 8-12   73
U.A. 6-10   77

STOLOFF, Morris
(Morris Stoloff Conducts the Columbia Studio
Orchestra)
Singles: 78rpm
DECCA 3-5   56
MERCURY 3-5   54
Singles: 7-inch
COLPIX 4-8   59
DECCA 4-8   56
MERCURY 4-8   54
REPRISE 3-6   65
LPs: 10/12-inch 33rpm
DECCA 5-15   56
WARNER (1416 "Fanny") 25-35   61
(Soundtrack.)

STOMPERS
Singles: 7-inch
GONE (5120 "Stompin' Around
the Christmas Tree") 30-50   61
LANDA 10-15   61-62
MERCURY (72000 series) 5-10   63

STOMPERS
Singles: 7-inch
BOARDWALK 2-4   83
MERCURY (880000 series) 2-4   84
LPs: 10/12-inch 33rpm
MERCURY 5-8   84

STONE
Singles: 7-inch
WEST END 3-5   82

STONE, Cliffie
(Cliffie Stone Singers)
Singles: 78rpm
CAPITOL (Except 2910) 3-5   50-57
CAPITOL (2910 "Blue Moon of
Kentucky") 4-8   54
Singles: 7-inch
CAPITOL (Except 2910) 4-10   50-69
CAPITOL (2910 "Blue Moon of
Kentucky") 10-20   54
TOWER 3-6   67
LPs: 10/12-inch 33rpm
CAPITOL (100 through 300 series) .. 5-10   68-69
CAPITOL (1000 through 1600 series) 20-40   58-62
CAPITOL (2100 series) 10-20   64
TOWER 10-15   67

STONE, Kirby, Four
(Kirby Stone Quartet)
Singles: 78rpm
COLUMBIA .... : 3-5   57
Singles: 7-inch
COLUMBIA 4-8   57-65
MGM 4-6   67
WARNER 4-6   63-64
LPs: 10/12-inch 33rpm
COLUMBIA .... : .. 10-20   58-62
WARNER 10-15   63-64
Members: Kirby Stone; Edward Hall; Michael Gardner; Larry
Foster.

STONE, Sly
(Sylvester "Sly Stone" Stewart)
Singles: 12-inch 33/45rpm
EPIC 4-8   80
Singles: 7-inch
EPIC 3-5   75-79
LPs: 10/12-inch 33rpm
EPIC 5-10   79
Also see JOHNSON, Jesse
Also see SLY and the Family Stone

STONE CITY BAND
Singles: 7-inch
GORDY 3-5   80-83
LPs: 10/12-inch 33rpm
GORDY 5-10   80-83
Also see JAMES, Rick

STONE FURY
Singles: 7-inch
MCA 2-4   84
LPs: 10/12-inch 33rpm
MCA 5-8   84

STONE PONEYS
(Stone Poneys Featuring Linda Ronstadt)
Singles: 7-inch
CAPITOL 5-10   67
Picture Sleeves
CAPITOL 5-10   67
LPs: 10/12-inch 33rpm
CAPITOL (2600 and 2700 series) ... 20-30   67
Also see RONSTADT, Linda

STONEBOLT
Singles: 7-inch
PARACHUTE 3-5   78-79
RCA 3-5   80
LPs: 10/12-inch 33rpm
PARACHUTE 5-10   78
RCA . : 5-10   80

STONEY & MEAT LOAF
Singles: 7-inch
RARE EARTH 3-5   71
LPs: 10/12-inch 33rpm
PRODIGAL 5-10   78
RARE EARTH 10-15   71
Also see MEAT LOAF

STOOGES
(Featuring Iggy Pop)
Singles: 7–inch
ELEKTRA 5-10   69-70
LPs: 10/12–inch 33rpm
ELEKTRA 15-25   69-70
  Also see POP, Iggy

STOOKEY, Paul
Singles: 7–inch
ERIC 3-5
WARNER 3-5   71-72
LPs: 10/12–inch 33rpm
NEWPAX 5-8
WARNER 8-10   71
  Also see PETER, PAUL & MARY

STOREY SISTERS
Singles: 7–inch
BATON 10-15   58
CAMEO 10-15   58
MERCURY 8-12   59

STORIES
Singles: 7–inch
ERIC 3-5
KAMA SUTRA 3-5   72-74
RADIOACTIVE GOLD 3-5   74
LPs: 10/12–inch 33rpm
KAMA SUTRA 8-12   72-73
  Members: Ian Lloyd; Michael Brown.
  Also see LEFT BANKE
  Also see LLOYD, Ian

STORM
Singles: 7–inch
PHI KAPPA 3-5   74
LPs: 10/12–inch 33rpm
CAPITOL 5-8   83
MCA 5-10   77

STORM, Billy
(Billy Storm and the Valiants)
Singles: 7–inch
ATLANTIC 10-15   60-61
BUENA VISTA 4-8   63
COLUMBIA 5-10   59
ENSIGN 8-12   59
GREGMARK 4-8   61
HBR 4-8   66
INFINITY 4-8   62-63
LOMA 4-8   64-65
ODE 4-8   69
Picture Sleeves
HBR 5-10   66
LPs: 10/12–inch 33rpm
BUENA VISTA (3315 "Billy Storm") .. 25-50   63
FAMOUS (504 "This Is the Night") ... 20-30   69
  Also see VALIANTS

STORM, Gale
Singles: 78rpm
DOT 4-8   55-56

Singles: 7–inch
DOT (Maroon label) 8-15   55-56
DOT (Black label) 4-8   57-60
DOT (Orange label) 3-5
Picture Sleeves
DOT 10-20   58
EPs: 7–inch 33/45rpm
DOT 15-25   55-56
LPs: 10/12–inch 33rpm
DOT 25-35   56-59
HAMILTON 10-15   66
MCA 5-10   82

STORM, Warren
Singles: 7–inch
ATCO 3-6   68
DOT 4-8   61
KINGFISH 4-8
NASCO 5-10   58-60
ROCKO 10-15
SINCERE 10-15
SOUTH STAR 2-4   83
STARFLITE 3-5   79
ZYNN 10-20
  Also see SHONDELLS / Rod Bernard / Warren Storm / Skip
  Stewart

STRAIT, George
Singles: 7–inch
MCA 2-5   81-91
LPs: 10/12–inch 33rpm
MCA 5-10   81-91

STRAKER, Nick, Band
Singles: 7–inch
PRELUDE 3-5   82
LPs: 10/12–inch 33rpm
PRELUDE 5-10   82

STRANGE, Billy
(Billy Strange and the Telstars; Billy Strange and the
Transients)
Singles: 78rpm
CAPITOL 3-5   54-55
DECCA 3-5   55
Singles: 7–inch
BUENA VISTA 4-8   62-63
CAPITOL 5-10   54-55
COLISEUM 4-8   63
DECCA 5-10   55
GNP/CRESCENDO 4-8   64-65
LIBERTY 4-8   61-62
TOWER 4-6   69
LPs: 10/12–inch 33rpm
COLISEUM 10-20   62
GNP/CRESCENDO 5-15   63-75
HORIZON 10-15   63
SUNSET 8-10   68
SURREY 10-15   65
TRADITION 8-12   68
  Also see CAMPBELL, Glen, and Billy Strange

STRANGELOVES
Singles: 7–inch
BANG 5-10   65-67
SIRE 4-8   68
SWAN 8-10   64
LPs: 10/12–inch 33rpm
BANG (BLP-211 "I Want Candy") 35-45   65
(Monaural.)
BANG (BLPS-211 "I Want Candy") .. 45-65   65
(Stereo.)
Members: Bob Feldman; Jerry Goldstein; Richie Gottehrer.
Also see McCOYS
Also see SHEEP

STRANGERS
Singles: 7–inch
TITAN 10-20   59-60
Member: Joel Hill.

STRAWBERRY ALARM CLOCK
Singles: 7–inch
ALL AMERICAN (373 "Incense and
Peppermints") 25-50   67
MCA 2-4
UNI (Except 55218) 5-15   67-70
UNI (55218 "California Day") 10-20   70
LPs: 10/12–inch 33rpm
BACK-TRAC 5-10   85
UNI 20-40   67-70
VOCALION 15-20   71
Members: Randy Seol; Ed King.
Also see LYNYRD SKYNYRD
Also see WHO / Strawberry Alarm Clock

STRAWBS
Singles: 7–inch
A&M 4-8   68-75
ARISTA 3-5   78
OYSTER 3-5   76-77
LPs: 10/12–inch 33rpm
A&M 8-15   71-78
ARISTA 5-10   78
OYSTER 8-10   76-77
Also see DENNY, Sandy, and the Strawbs
Also see WAKEMAN, Rick

STRAY CATS
Singles: 7–inch
EMI AMERICA 2-5   82-86
Picture Sleeves
EMI AMERICA 2-5   82-84
LPs: 10/12–inch 33rpm
EMI (91401 "Blast Off") 5-10   89
EMI AMERICA (17070 "Built for Speed")5-10   82
EMI AMERICA (17102 "Rant'n Rave with
the Stray Cats") 5-10   83
Members: Brian Setzer; Lee Rocker; Slim Jim Phantom; Brian
McDonald; Gary Barnacle; Lee Allen.
Also see ALLEN, Lee
Also see PHANTOM, ROCKER & SLICK
Also see SETZER, Brian

STREEK
Singles: 7–inch
COLUMBIA 3-5   81
LPs: 10/12–inch 33rpm
COLUMBIA 5-10   81

STREET, Janey
Singles: 7–inch
ARISTA 2-4   84
LPs: 10/12–inch 33rpm
ARISTA 5-8   84-85

STREET CHRISTIANS
Singles: 7–inch
P.I.P. 3-5   73

STREET PEOPLE
Singles: 7–inch
MUSICOR 4-6   69-70
VIGOR 3-5   75-77
MUSICOR 12-18   70
PICKWICK 8-10   72
Also see HOLMES, Rupert

STREET PLAYERS
Singles: 7–inch
ARIOLA AMERICA 3-5   79
LPs: 10/12–inch 33rpm
ARIOLA AMERICA 5-10   79

STREETS
Singles: 7–inch
ATLANTIC 2-4   83-84
EPIC 3-5   79
LPs: 10/12–inch 33rpm
ATLANTIC 5-8   83-84
EPIC 5-10   79
Member: Steve Walsh.
Also see KANSAS

STREISAND, Barbra
Singles: 12–inch 33/45rpm
COLUMBIA (White labels) 12-25   79-85
(Promotional issues only.)
Singles: 7–inch
ARISTA 4-6   75
COLUMBIA (04000 and 05000 series) . 2-4   83-86
COLUMBIA (10000 and 11000 series) .. 2-5   76-80
COLUMBIA (3-42648 "My Coloring
Book") 20-30   62
(Compact 33 Single.)
COLUMBIA (4-42648 "My Coloring
Book") 8-12   62
COLUMBIA (42631 "Happy Days
Are Here Again") 5-10   63
COLUMBIA (42965 through 43469) 4-6   64-65
COLUMBIA (43518 through 46024) 3-5   66-74
Promotional Singles
COLUMBIA (04000 and 05000 series) . 2-5   83-86
COLUMBIA (10000 and 11000 series) .. 2-5   76-80

COLUMBIA (4-42648 "My Coloring
Book") 15-25   62
COLUMBIA (42631 "Happy Days Are
Here Again") 10-15   63
COLUMBIA (42965 through 43469) ... 5-10   64-65
COLUMBIA (43518 through 46024) 4-8   66-74
Picture Sleeves
COLUMBIA (Except 43000 series) 3-5   73-84
COLUMBIA (43000 series) 4-8   66
LPs: 10/12-inch 33rpm
ARISTA 8-10   75
CAPITOL (2059 "Funny Girl") 10-20   64
COLUMBIA (1779 "The Legend of
Barbra Streisand") 30-40   83
(Promotional, one-hour interview program.)
COLUMBIA (CL-2007 through
CL-2682) 15-25   63-67
(Monaural. Black vinyl.)
COLUMBIA (2054 "The Second Barbra
Streisand Album") 30-50   63
(Colored vinyl. Promotional issue only.)
COLUMBIA (2478 "Color Me Barbra") 30-50   66
(Colored vinyl. Promotional issue only.)
COLUMBIA (3220 "Funny Girl") 10-15   68
COLUMBIA (CS-8807 through
CS-9482) 15-25   63-67
(Stereo. Black vinyl.)
COLUMBIA (8854 "The Second Barbra
Streisand Album") 40-60   63
(Colored vinyl. Promotional issue only.)
COLUMBIA (9278 "Color Me Barbra") 40-60   66
(Colored vinyl. Promotional issue only.)
COLUMBIA (9710 through 9968) 10-15   68-70
COLUMBIA (PC-8000 and
PC-9000 series) 5-8
COLUMBIA (JC-9000 series) 5-8
COLUMBIA (30086 through 45369) ... 5-15   70-89
20TH FOX 10-15   69
Also see ARLEN, Harold, with "Friend"

STREISAND, Barbra, and Kim Carnes
Singles: 7-inch
COLUMBIA 2-4   84
Also see CARNES, Kim

STREISAND, Barbra, and Neil Diamond
Singles: 7-inch
COLUMBIA 3-5   78
Also see DIAMOND, Neil

STREISAND, Barbra, and Barry Gibb
Singles: 7-inch
COLUMBIA 3-4   80-81
Also see GIBB, Barry

STREISAND, Barbra, and Donna Summer
Singles: 12-inch 33/45rpm
COLUMBIA/CASABLANCA 8-10   79
(Promotional issue only. Issued with special cover.)
Singles: 7-inch
COLUMBIA 3-5   79

Picture Sleeves
COLUMBIA 3-5   79
Also see STREISAND, Barbra
Also see SUMMER, Donna

STRIKERS
Singles: 7-inch
PRELUDE 3-5   81
LPs: 10/12-inch 33rpm
PRELUDE 5-10   81

STRING-A-LONGS
Singles: 7-inch
ATCO (6694 "Popi") 4-8   69
(Reportedly recorded by the Fireballs but credited
to the String-A-Longs.)
DOT 5-10   62-65
WARWICK (Except 603 and 606) 5-10   61-62
WARWICK (603 "Wheels"/
"Tell the World") 10-15   60
WARWICK (603 "Wheels"/"Am I
Asking too Much") 5-10   61
WARWICK (606 "Tell the World") 10-15   61
LPs: 10/12-inch 33rpm
ATCO (241 "World Wide Hits") 15-25   68
(Reportedly recorded by the Fireballs but credited
to the String-A-Longs.)
DOT 15-25   62-66
WARWICK (W-2036 "Pick-A-Hit") ... 40-50   61
(Monaural.)
WARWICK (WST-2036 "Pick-A-Hit") . 50-75   61
(Stereo.)
Members: Keith McCormick; Jimmy Tores.
Also see FIREBALLS

STROKE
Singles: 12-inch 33/45rpm
OMNI 4-6   85

STROLLERS
Singles: 7-inch
CARLTON (546 "There's No
One But You") 15-25   61

STRONG, Barrett
Singles: 7-inch
ANNA 15-20   60
ATCO 4-8   62

CAPITOL 3-5   75
EPIC 3-5   73
MOTOWN 2-4
TAMLA (54027 "Money") 30-40   60
  (With horizontal lines on label.)
TAMLA (54027 "Money") 10-15   60
  (With Tamla globe logo on label.)
TAMLA (54029 "Money") 50-60   60
  (With horizontal lines on label.)
TAMLA (54033 "Whirlwind") 5-10   60
TAMLA (54035 "Money and Me") 8-12   61
TAMLA (54043 "Misery") 20-30   61
TOLLIE 5-10   64

Picture Sleeves

EPIC 3-5   73

LPs: 10/12–inch 33rpm

CAPITOL 8-10   74

STRUNK, Jud
(Jud Strunk and the Coplin Kitchen Band)
Singles: 7–inch

CAPITOL 3-5   74
COBURT 3-5   71
COLUMBIA 3-5   70
MCA 3-5   77
MGM 3-5   72-73
MELODYLAND 3-5   75-76

LPs: 10/12–inch 33rpm

COLUMBIA 6-12   70
HARMONY 5-10   73
MCA 5-10   77
MGM 5-10   71-73

STRYPER
LPs: 10/12–inch 33rpm

ENIGMA 5-8   84-90
  Members: Michael Sweet; Oz Fox; Tim Gaines; Robert Sweet.

STUDENTS
Singles: 7–inch

ARGO (5386 "I'm So Young") 8-12   61
CADET 4-6   65
CHECKER (902 "I'm So Young") 10-15   58
CHECKER (1004 "My Vow to You") ... 8-10   61
CHESS 3-5   73
COLLECTABLES 2-4
NOTE (10012 "I'm So Young") 150-200   58
NOTE (10019 "My Vow to You") ... 150-200   58
RED TOP (100 "My Heart Is
  an Open Door") 100-150   57
  (Blue label.)
RED TOP (100 "My Heart Is
  an Open Door") 25-35   58
  (Red label.)
  Members: Leroy King; Emerson "Rocky" Brown; Rich Havens.

STUFF
Singles: 7–inch

WARNER 3-5   76-80

LPs: 10/12–inch 33rpm

WARNER 5-10   76-80

STUFF 'N' RAMJETT
Singles: 7–inch

CHELSEA 3-5   76

STYLE COUNCIL
Singles: 7–inch

GEFFEN 2-4   84-85
POLYDOR 2-4   83-88

LPs: 10/12–inch 33rpm

GEFFEN 5-8   84-85
POLYDOR 5-8   83-88
  Also see BAND AID
  Also see JAM

STYLERS
Singles: 78rpm

GOLDEN CREST 5-8   57
JUBILEE 4-8   55-57

Singles: 7–inch

GOLDEN CREST 8-12   57-58
JUBILEE 5-10   55-57

STYLISTICS
Singles: 7–inch

AMHERST 3-4   85
AVCO 3-5   70-76
H&L 3-5   76-79
MERCURY 3-5   79
PHILADELPHIA INT'L 3-5   82
STREETWISE 2-4   84-86
TSOP 3-4   80-84

Picture Sleeves

AVCO 3-5   76

LPs: 10/12–inch 33rpm

AVCO 5-10   71-75
H&L 5-10   76-79
MERCURY 5-10   78-79
PHILADELPHIA INT'L 5-10   82
STREETWISE 5-8   84-86
TSOP 5-10   80-81
  Members: Russell Tompkins, Jr.; Airrion Love; Herb Murrell;
  James Dunn; James Smith.

STYX
Singles: 7–inch

A&M 2-5   76-84
PARAMOUNT 3-5   71-72
RCA 3-5   76
WOODEN NICKEL 3-5   72-78

Picture Sleeves

A&M 3-5   77-84

LPs: 10/12–inch 33rpm

A&M (Except PR-4724) 5-10   75-84
A&M (PR-4724 "Pieces of Eight") ... 10-15   79
MFSL (026 "Grand Illusion") 25-50   79
NAUTILUS 10-15   81
RCA 5-10   72-82
WOODEN NICKEL 8-10   72-77

Promotional LPs

A&M (8431 "Styx Radio Special") ... 15-25   77
  (Two-LP set.)

A&M (17053 "Styx Radio Special") .. 35-40   78
(Three-LP set.)
Members: Dennis DeYoung; James Young; Tommy Shaw; John
Panozzo; Chuck Panozzo.
Also see DE YOUNG, Dennis
Also see SHAW, Tommy

SUAVE'
Singles: 7–inch
CAPITOL 2-4   88
LPs: 10/12–inch 33rpm
CAPITOL 5-8   88

SUE ANN
Singles: 7–inch
WARNER 3-5   81
LPs: 10/12–inch 33rpm
WARNER 5-10   81

SUGAR BABES
Singles: 7–inch
MCA 2-4   87

SUGAR BILLY
Singles: 7–inch
FAST TRACK 3-5   75
LPs: 10/12–inch 33rpm
FAST TRACK 5-10   75

SUGAR CUBES
LPs: 10/12–inch 33rpm
ELEKTRA 5-8   88-89

SUGARHILL GANG
Singles: 12–inch 33/45rpm
SUGAR HILL (Except 542) 5-10   80-85
SUGAR HILL (542 "Rapper's Delight") 20-30   79
Singles: 7–inch
SUGAR HILL 2-5   79-85
LPs: 10/12–inch 33rpm
SUGAR HILL 5-10   80-85
Also see FURIOUS FIVE and the Sugarhill Gang

SUGARLOAF
(Sugarloaf with Jerry Corbetta)
Singles: 7–inch
BRUT 3-5   73-74
CLARIDGE 3-5   74-76
LIBERTY 3-5   70-71
U.A. 3-5   71
Picture Sleeves
BRUT 4-6   73-74
LIBERTY 4-6   71
LPs: 10/12–inch 33rpm
BRUT 8-10   73
CLARIDGE 8-10   75
LIBERTY 10-15   70-71
Members: Jerry Corbetta; Bob Webber.

SUICIDAL TENDENCIES
Singles: 7–inch
FRONTIER 2-4   84
LPs: 10/12–inch 33rpm
CAROL 5-8   87

EPIC 5-8   88-90
JANA 8-10   86

SULTON, Kaslm
Singles: 7–inch
EMI AMERICA 3-5   82
LPs: 10/12–inch 33rpm
EMI AMERICA 5-10   82

SUMMER, Donna
Singles: 12–inch 33/45rpm
CASABLANCA 5-8   78-80
GEFFEN 4-8   80-86
MERCURY 4-8   83
OASIS 5-10   75-76
Singles: 7–inch
CASABLANCA 3-5   75-80
GEFFEN 3-4   80-87
OASIS 3-6   75-76
Picture Sleeves
GEFFEN 3-5   80-84
OASIS 3-6   76
LPs: 10/12–inch 33rpm
ATLANTIC 5-8   89
CASABLANCA (Except 20110) 5-10   75-80
CASABLANCA (20110 "Once Upon
a Time") 12-15   77
(Promotional issue only.)
GEFFEN 5-10   80-87
MERCURY 5-10   83
OASIS 6-12   75-76
Also see BROOKLYN DREAMS
Also see MORODER, Giorgio
Also see STREISAND, Barbra, and Donna Summer

SUMMER, Henry Lee
LPs: 10/12–inch 33rpm
CBS ASSOCIATED 5-8   88-89

SUMMERS, Andy, and Robert Fripp:
see FRIPP, Robert, and Andy Summers

SUMMERS, Bill
(Bill Summers and Summers Heat)
Singles: 12–inch 33/45rpm
MCA 4-6   81-84
Singles: 7–inch
MCA 3-5   81-84
PRESTIGE 3-5   77-80
LPs: 10/12–inch 33rpm
MCA 5-10   81
Also see HANCOCK, Herbie

SUN
Singles: 7–inch
AIR CITY 2-4   84
CAPITOL 3-5   76-82
Picture Sleeves
CAPITOL 3-5   76-82
LPs: 10/12–inch 33rpm
CAPITOL 5-10   77-82

SUN, Joe
Singles: 7-inch
A.M.I. 2-4   85
ELEKTRA 3-4   82-83
OVATION 3-5   78-80
LPs: 10/12-inch 33rpm
ELEKTRA 5-8   82-83
OVATION 5-10   78-80

SUNBEAR
Singles: 7-inch
SOUL TRAIN 3-5   77
LPs: 10/12-inch 33rpm
SOUL TRAIN 5-10   77

SUNDANCE
(Featuring Kevin Stevenson)
Singles: 7-inch
FATIMA 2-4   87

SUNDOWN COMPANY
Singles: 7-inch
POLYDOR 3-5   76

SUNFIRE
Singles: 12-inch 33/45rpm
WARNER 4-6   82
Singles: 7-inch
WARNER 3-5   82
LPs: 10/12-inch 33rpm
WARNER 5-10   82

SUNGLOWS
(Sunny and the Sunglows; Sunny and the Sunliners;
Sunny Ozuna and the Sunliners)
Singles: 7-inch
DISCO GRANDE (1021 "Peanuts") .. 10-20   65
KEY LOC 4-8   66
OKEH 5-10   61
RPR 4-6   69
SUNGLOW 5-10   62-66
TEAR DROP 4-8   63-64
LPs: 10/12-inch 33rpm
KEY LOC 10-20   66
SUNGLOW (103 "Peanuts") 25-35   65
TEAR DROP (2000 "Talk to Me") 30-50   63

SUNNY and the Sunglows/Sunliners
see SUNGLOWS

SUNNYSIDERS
Singles: 78rpm
KAPP 3-5   55-57
MARQUEE 3-5   55-56
Singles: 7-inch
KAPP 3-8   55-60
MARQUEE 3-8   55-56
NRC 3-6   60
ZENITH 3-6   60
EPs: 7-inch 33/45rpm
KAPP 4-8   56
LPs: 10/12-inch 33rpm
KAPP 5-15   56

SUNRAYS
Singles: 7-inch
TOWER 5-10   64-67
WARNER 5-10   62
Picture Sleeves
TOWER 15-20   67
LPs: 10/12-inch 33rpm
TOWER (5017 "Andrea") 50-100   66
Members: Rick Henn; Bryon Case; Vince Hozier; Ed Medora;
Marty DiGiovanni.
Also see ALLAN, Davie / Eternity's Children / Main Attraction /
Sunrays

SUNRISE
LPs: 10/12-inch 33rpm
CRUNCH 8-10   74
Also see CREACH, Papa John

SUNRIZE
Singles: 7-inch
BOARDWALK 3-4   82

SUNSHINE BAND:
see KC and the Sunshine Band

SUNSHINE COMPANY
Singles: 7-inch
IMPERIAL 4-8   67-68
LPs: 10/12-inch 33rpm
IMPERIAL 10-15   67-68
Members: Doug "Red" Mark; Maury Manseau; Larry Sims; Merle
Bregante; Mary Nance.
Also see REDEYE

SUPER LOVER CEE & CASANOVA RUD
LPs: 10/12-inch 33rpm
ELEKTRA 5-8   88

SUPER MAX
Singles: 7-inch
VOYAGE 3-5   79

SUPER NATURE
Singles: 12-inch 33/45rpm
POP ART 4-6   85

SUPERBS
Singles: 7-inch
COLLECTABLES 2-4
DORE 10-20   64-67
HERITAGE (103 "Rainbow of Love") . 25-35   61

SUPERIOR MOVEMENT
Singles: 7-inch
CHYCAGO INT'L 3-5   81-82
LPs: 10/12-inch 33rpm
CHYCAGO INT'L 5-10   82

SUPERLATIVES
Singles: 7-inch
UPTITE 4-8   66
WESTBOUND 4-6   69

SUPERSAX
LPs: 10/12-inch 33rpm
CAPITOL 5-10   73-74

SUPERTRAMP
Singles: 12–inch 33/45rpm
A&M 4-6   82-85
Singles: 7–inch
A&M 3-5   71-85
Picture Sleeves
A&M 3-5   77-85
LPs: 10/12–inch 33rpm
A&M 8-12   70-87
MFSL (005 "Crime of the Century") .. 30-60   78
MFSL/UHQR (005 "Crime of
the Century") 50-100   78
(Boxed set.)
MFSL (045 "Breakfast in America") .. 25-50   80
Members: Rick Davies; Roger Hodgson; Doug Thomson; Bob
Benberg; John Helliwell.
Also see HODGSON, Roger

SUPREMES
(Diana Ross and the Supremes)
Singles: 12–inch 33/45rpm
MOTOWN 6-10   79-81
Singles: 7–inch
GEORGE ALEXANDER INC. (1079 "The Only
Time I'm Happy") 30-40   65
(Special premium record. Has a Supremes
interview on the flip.)
MOTOWN (400 series) 2-4
MOTOWN (1027 "Your Heart
Belongs to Me") 15-25   62
MOTOWN (1034 "Let Me Go the
Right Way") 15-20   62
MOTOWN (1040 "My Heart Can't Take
It No More") 25-35   63
MOTOWN (1044 "A Breath Taking, First Sight
Soul Shaking, One Night Love Making, Next
Day Heart Breaking Guy") 25-30   63
MOTOWN (1044 "A Breath Taking Guy") 5-8   63
(Reissue, with shorter title.)
MOTOWN (1051 "When the Lovelight Starts
Shining Through His Eyes") 5-8   63
MOTOWN (1054 "Run, Run, Run) ... 15-25   64
MOTOWN (1060 through 1156) 4-8   64-69
MOTOWN/TOPPS (1 "Baby Love") .. 50-75   67
MOTOWN/TOPPS (2 "Stop in the
Name of Love") 50-75   67
MOTOWN/TOPPS (3 "Where Did Our
Love Go") 50-75   67
MOTOWN/TOPPS (15 "Come See
About Me") 50-75   67
MOTOWN/TOPPS (16 "My World
Is Empty Without You") 50-75   67
(Topps Chewing Gum promotional item.
Single-sided, cardboard, flexi, picture disc. Issued
with generic paper sleeve.)
TAMLA (54038 "I Want a Guy") 70-90   61
TAMLA (54045 "Buttered Popcorn") .. 35-45   61
Picture Sleeves
MOTOWN (1027 "Your Heart
Belongs to Me") 30-40   62

MOTOWN (1074 through 1137) 5-12   64-68
(In this series, only 1074, 1075, 1080, 1097, 1101,
and 1137 were issued with sleeves.)
Promotional Singles
AMERICAN INT'L PICTURES ("Dr. Goldfoot
and the Bikini Machine") 20-40   66
(Single-sided disc, used to promote the film of the
same name.)
EEOC ("Things Are Changing") 15-30   65
MOTOWN (1027 through 1054) 10-15   62-64
MOTOWN (1060 through 1156) 5-8   64-69
(Black vinyl.)
MOTOWN (Colored vinyl) 10-20   65
TOPPS 5-15   67
(Cardborad flexi-discs from the makers of Topps
chewing gum.)
EPs: 7–inch 33/45rpm
MOTOWN 20-25   64
LPs: 10/12–inch 33rpm
MOTOWN (100 and 200 series) 5-10   80-82
MOTOWN (606 "Meet the
Supremes") 200-300   63
(Front cover pictures each member sitting on a
chair.)
MOTOWN (606 "Meet the Supremes") 30-35   63
(Front cover pictures the head of each group
member.)
MOTOWN (621 through 638) 20-30   64-65
MOTOWN (643 through 708) 15-25   66-70
MOTOWN (794 "Anthology") 15-20   74
(Three-LP set. Includes 12-page booklet.)
MOTOWN (900 series) 5-10   75
MOTOWN (5000 series, except 5381) . 5-10   83-84
MOTOWN (5381 "25th Anniversary") 15-20   86
(Three-LP set. Includes 12-page booklet.)
NATURAL RESOURCES 5-10   78
Members: Diana Ross; Mary Wilson; Florence Ballard; Cindy
Birdsong.
Also see DIAMOND, Neil / Diana Ross and the Supremes
Also see PRIMETTES
Also see ROSS, Diana
Also see WILSON, Mary

SUPREMES
Singles: 7–inch
MOTOWN (400 series) 2-4
MOTOWN (1162 through 1415) 3-5   70-77
LPs: 10/12–inch 33rpm
MOTOWN (102 "Touch") 15-20   71
(Open-end interview LP. Price includes script.
Promotional issue only.)
MOTOWN (702 through 904) 6-12   70-78
Members: Jean Terrell; Mary Wilson; Cindy Birdsong.
Also see PAYNE, Scherrie
Also see TERRELL, Jean

SUPREMES and the Four Tops
Singles: 7–inch
MOTOWN (400 series) 2-4
MOTOWN (1100 series) 3-5   70-71

EPs: 7–inch 33/45rpm

MOTOWN (717 "Magnificant Seven") . 5-15   70
(Jukebox issue.)

LPs: 10/12–inch 33rpm

MOTOWN (100 series) 5-10   82
MOTOWN (700 series) 10-15   70-71
Also see FOUR TOPS

SUPREMES and the Temptations
Singles: 7–inch

MOTOWN (400 series) 2-4
MOTOWN (1100 series) 4-8   68-69
Picture Sleeves

MOTOWN 5-10   68
LPs: 10/12–inch 33rpm

MOTOWN (100 series) 5-10   82
MOTOWN (600 series) 10-15   68-69
Also see SUPREMES
Also see TEMPTATIONS

SURF TRIO
LPs: 10/12–inch 33rpm

VOXX 5-8   87-88

SURFACE
Singles: 12–inch 33/45rpm

COLUMBIA 4-6   86
SALSOUL 4-6   83
Singles: 7–inch

COLUMBIA 2-4   86-90
SALSOUL 2-4   83
LPs: 10/12–inch 33rpm

COLUMBIA 5-8   86-90

SURFARIS
Singles: 7–inch

ABC 2-4   74
CHANCELLOR 5-8   63
DFS (11 "Wipe Out") 200-300   63
DECCA 5-10   63-66
DOT (Except 144 and 16479) 5-10   65-67
DOT (144 "Wipe Out") 4-6   66
(Black vinyl.)
DOT (144 "Wipe Out") 25-30   66
(Colored vinyl. Promotional issue only.)
DOT (16479 "Wipe Out") 4-8   63
FELSTED 5-10   64
MCA 2-4
PRINCESS (50 "Wipe Out") 25-50   63
(Short version, same as Dot issue. Has "RE-1"
etched in the vinyl trail-off.)
PRINCESS (50 "Wipe Out") 50-75   63
(Long version. Does not have "RE-1" etched in the
vinyl trail-off.)
REGANO 5-10   63
UNIVERSAL (965 "Wipe Out") 20-40   63
EPs: 7–inch 33/45rpm

DECCA (2765 "Wipe Out") 20-40   63
LPs: 10/12–inch 33rpm

DECCA 25-45   63-65

DOT (535 "Wipe Out") 30-45   63
(Front cover reads "The Original Hit Version, Wipe
Out.")
DOT (535 "Wipe Out") 25-35   63
(Front cover reads "Wipe Out and Surfer Joe and
Other Popular selections By Other Instrumental
Groups." The Surfaris are heard only on *Wipe Out*
and *Surfer Joe*. Other tracks on this LP are by the
Challengers.)
DIPLOMAT 15-25
PICKWICK 10-15   78
Members: Ron Wilson; Jim Fuller; Jim Pash; Pat Connolly; Bob
Berryhill; Ken Forssi. Though not actual members, Richie
Podolor, Chuck Girard and Gary Usher made appearances on
Surfaris releases.
Also see BEACH BOYS / Dick Dale / Surfaris / Surf Kings
Also see DALE, Dick / Surfaris / Fireballs
Also see GIRARD, Chuck
Also see PODOLOR, Dickie
Also see USHER, Gary

SURFARIS / Biscaynes
Singles: 7–inch

NORTHRIDGE 10-20   63
REPRISE 8-12   63

SURFARIS / Challengers
Singles: 7–inch

DOT 5-10   65
Also see CHALLENGERS
Also see SURFARIS

SURRETT, Alfonzo
Singles: 7–inch

MCA 3-5   80

SURVIVOR
Singles: 12–inch 33/45rpm

SCOTTI BROS 4-6   79-86
Singles: 7–inch

CASABLANCA 2-4   84
SCOTTI BROS 3-5   80-88
Picture Sleeves

SCOTTI BROS 3-5   84
LPs: 10/12–inch 33rpm

SCOTTI BROS (Except 362) 5-10   79-88
SCOTTI BROS (362 "Rebel Girl") . . . 10-12   80
(Promotional issue only.)
Members: Jim Peterik; Jim Jameson.

SURVIVORS
Singles: 7–inch

CAPITOL (5102 "Pamela Jean") . . 150-200   64
Members: Brian Wilson; Dave Nowlen; Bob Norberg; Rich
Peterson.
Also see BEACH BOYS

SUSAN
Singles: 7–inch

RCA 3-5   79
SCEPTER 3-5   70
LPs: 10/12–inch 33rpm

RCA 5-10   79

SUTCH, Screaming Lord: see LORD SUTCH

SUTHERLAND BROTHERS
(Sutherland Brothers and Quiver)
Singles: 7–inch
COLUMBIA 3-5   75-79
ISLAND 3-5   72-73
LPs: 10/12–inch 33rpm
COLUMBIA 6-10   75-76
ISLAND 6-10   72-74

SUTTON, Glenn
Singles: 7–inch
ABC 3-5   73
EPIC 4-6   67
MGM 4-8   64-65
MERCURY 2-5   78-86
LPs: 10/12–inch 33rpm
MERCURY 5-8   79
Also see KELLUM, Murray / Glenn Sutton

SUTTON, Mike and Brenda
Singles: 7–inch
SAM 3-5   81-82

SUTTONS
Singles: 7–inch
ROCSHIRE 2-4   84
LPs: 10/12–inch 33rpm
ROCSHIRE 5-8   84

SUZY and the Red Stripes
(Linda McCartney and Wings)
Singles: 12–inch 33/45rpm
CAPITOL (15244 "Seaside Woman") . 10-20   86
EPIC (361 "Seaside Woman") 20-30   77
(Promotional issue only.)
Singles: 7–inch
CAPITOL (5608 "Seaside Woman") 3-6   86
EPIC (50403 "Seaside Woman") 4-8   77
Promotional Singles
EPIC (50403 "Seaside Woman") 30-40   77
(Colored vinyl.)
EPIC (50403 "Seaside Woman") 35-45   77
(Black vinyl. White label, states "Advance
Promotion")
EPIC (50403 "Seaside Woman") 40-50   77
(Black vinyl. White label, no mention of "Advance
Promotion")
Also see McCARTNEY, Paul

SUZY Q
Singles: 7–inch
ATLANTIC 3-5   81

SVENSSON, Bo
LPs: 10/12–inch 33rpm
GOLDEN BOY 5-8   88

SWALLOWS
Singles: 78rpm
AFTER HOURS (104 "My Baby") 50-75   54
KING (4466 "Since You've
Been Away") 50-100   51

KING (4458 "Will You Be Mine") ... 50-100   51
KING (4466 "Since You've
Been Away") 100-150   51
KING (4501 "Eternally") 40-60   51
KING (4515 "Tell Me Why") 40-60   51
KING (4525 "Beside You") 30-50   52
KING (4533 "I Only Have
Eyes for You") 40-60   52
KING (4579 "Where Do I
Go from Here") 40-60   52
KING (4612 "Laugh") 30-50   53
KING (4632 "Nobody's Lovin' Me") .. 30-50 53
KING (4656 "Trust Me") 30-50   53
KING (4676 "I'll Be Waiting") 30-50   53
Singles: 7–inch
AFTER HOURS (104 "My Baby") . 300-400   54
GUSTO 2-4
KING (4458 "Will You Be Mine") .. 400-600   51
KING (4501 "Eternally") 400-500   51
(Black vinyl.)
KING (4501 "Eternally") 600-750   51
(Colored vinyl.)
KING (4515 "Tell Me Why") 600-750   51
KING (4525 "Beside You") 100-200   52
KING (4533 "I Only Have
Eyes for You") 300-400   52
KING (4579 "Where Do I
Go from Here") 300-400   52
KING (4612 "Laugh") 150-250   53
KING (4632 "Nobody's Lovin' Me") 150-250   53
KING (4656 "Trust Me") 100-200   53
KING (4676 "I'll Be Waiting") 150-200   53
Members: Junior Denby; Ed Rich; Earl Hurley; Fred Johnson;
Norris Mack; Dee Bailey; Buddy Bailey; Irving Turner; Al France;
Cal Kollette.

SWALLOWS
Singles: 7–inch
FEDERAL 15-25   58

SWAMP DOGG
(Jerry Williams; Swamp Dogg with the Riders of the
New Funk)
Singles: 7–inch
ALA 3-4   82
ATOMIC ARTS 3-5   79
BRUT 3-5   73
CANYON 3-5   70
CREAM 3-5   73
ELEKTRA 3-5   72
ISLAND 3-5   73
MUSICOR 3-5   77
RARE BULLET 3-4   83-85
ROKER 3-5   71
STONEDOGG 3-5   73
SWAMP DOGG PRESENTS 3-5   72
WIZARD 3-5   77
LPs: 10/12–inch 33rpm
ALA 5-10   82
CANYON 10-20   70
CREAM 6-10   72

ELEKTRA	8-12	71
ISLAND	6-10	73
MUSICOR	5-10	77
TAKOMA	5-10	81
WAR BRIDE	5-10	82
WIZARD	5-10	78

Also see WILLIAMS, Jerry, Jr.

SWAN, Billy
Singles: 7–inch

A&M	3-5	78-79
COLUMBIA	3-5	76-77
EPIC	3-4	81-83
MGM	5-10	68
MERCURY	2-4	86
MONUMENT	4-6	66-76
RISING SONS	4-6	67

LPs: 10/12–inch 33rpm

A&M	5-10	78
COLUMBIA/MONUMENT	5-10	77
EPIC	5-10	81
MONUMENT	5-10	74-78

SWANN, Bettye
Singles: 7–inch

A-BET	3-5	72-74
ATLANTIC	3-5	72-76
BIG TREE	3-5	
CAPITOL	3-6	68-70
FAME	3-5	71
MONEY	4-8	65-67

Picture Sleeves

CAPITOL	3-5	69

LPs: 10/12–inch 33rpm

A-BET	8-10	72
ATLANTIC	8-10	72-75
CAPITOL	10-12	69
MONEY	10-20	67

Also see DEES, Sam, and Bettye Swann

SWANS
Singles: 7–inch

CAMEO (302 "The Boy with the Beatle Hair")	25-35	64
SWAN	8-12	63

SWANSON, Brad, and His Whispering Organ Sound
LPs: 10/12–inch 33rpm

THUNDERBIRD	5-10	69

SWAYZE, Patrick
(Featuring Wendy Fraser)
Singles: 7–inch

RCA	2-4	87

Picture Sleeves

RCA	3-5	87

SWEAT, Keith
Singles: 7–inch

ELEKTRA	2-4	87
VINTERTAINMENT	2-4	88-90

LPs: 10/12–inch 33rpm

VINTERTAINMENT	5-8	88-90

SWEAT BAND
Singles: 7–inch

UNCLE JAM	3-5	80

LPs: 10/12–inch 33rpm

UNCLE JAM	5-10	80

Also see BOOTSY'S RUBBER BAND

SWEATHOG
Singles: 7–inch

COLUMBIA	3-5	71

LPs: 10/12–inch 33rpm

COLUMBIA	8-10	71-72

SWEENEY, Jimmy
(Jimmy Sweeney and the Varieteers)
Singles: 78rpm

HICKORY (1004 "Deep Blues")	20-40	53
TENNESSEE	5-10	50

Singles: 7–inch

BUCKLEY (1101 "She Wears My Ring")	5-10	62
COLUMBIA	5-10	59
DATE	4-6	
HICKORY (1004 "Deep Blues")	100-150	53
HICKORY (1136 "She Wears My Ring")	10-15	53

SWEENY TODD
Singles: 7–inch

LONDON	4-8	76

LPs: 10/12–inch 33rpm

LONDON (694 "If Wishes Were Horses")	20-25	77

Members: Bryan Guy Adams; Nick Gilder.
Also see ADAMS, Bryan
Also see GILDER, Nick

SWEET
Singles: 7–inch

BELL	3-5	71-74
CAPITOL	3-5	75-79

LPs: 10/12–inch 33rpm

BELL	10-20	73
CAPITOL (Except 16000 series)	8-10	75-79
CAPITOL (16000 series)	5-8	80-82
KORY	8-10	77

Promotional LPs

CAPITOL (8849 "Short and Sweet")	20-30	78
CAPITOL (11129 "Cut Above the Rest")	45-55	79

(Boxed set, containing the LP, 8-track and cassette issues of *Cut Above the Rest*, plus a group photo and biography.)

SWEET, Rachel
Singles: 12–inch 33/45rpm

STIFF/COLUMBIA	10-15	79

(Promotional issue only.)
Singles: 7–inch

COLUMBIA	3-5	81-83
DERRICK	3-5	76-78

STIFF/COLUMBIA 3-5   79-80
   LPs: 10/12-inch 33rpm
ARC 5-10   81
COLUMBIA 5-10   81-82
STIFF/COLUMBIA 5-10   79-80
   Also see SMITH, Rex, and Rachel Sweet

SWEET CREAM
   Singles: 12-inch 33/45rpm
SHADYBROOK 4-8   78
   Singles: 7-inch
SHADYBROOK 3-5   78

SWEET DREAMS
   Singles: 7-inch
ABC 3-5   74

SWEET G.
   Singles: 12-inch 33/45rpm
FEVER 4-6   83

SWEET INSPIRATIONS
   Singles: 12-inch 33/45rpm
RSO 4-8   79
   Singles: 7-inch
ATLANTIC 3-8   67-71
CARIBOU 3-5   77
RSO 3-5   79
STAX 3-5   73-74
   LPs: 10/12-inch 33rpm
ATLANTIC 10-12   68-70
RSO 5-10   79
STAX 8-10   73
   Members: Cissy Houston; Sylvia Shemwell; Myrna Smith;
   Estelle Brown.
   Also see FRANKLIN, Aretha
   Also see HOUSTON, Cissy
   Also see PRESLEY, Elvis
   Also see RASCALS

SWEET MUSIC
   Singles: 7-inch
WAND 3-5   76

SWEET OBSESSION
   Singles: 7-inch
EPIC 2-4   88
   LPs: 10/12-inch 33rpm
EPIC 5-8   88

SWEET SENSATION
   Singles: 7-inch
PYE 3-5   74-75
   LPs: 10/12-inch 33rpm
ATCO 5-8   88-90
PYE 6-10   75

SWEET TEE
   Singles: 7-inch
PROFILE 2-4   88
   LPs: 10/12-inch 33rpm
PROFILE 5-8   88

SWEET THUNDER
   Singles: 7-inch
FANTASY 3-5   78-79
WMOT 3-5   79
   LPs: 10/12-inch 33rpm
WMOT 5-10   78

SWEETWATER
   Singles: 7-inch
REPRISE 3-6   68-71
   LPs: 10/12-inch 33rpm
REPRISE 10-15   68-71

SWING OUT SISTER
   Singles: 7-inch
MERCURY 2-4   87
   LPs: 10/12-inch 33rpm
FONTANA 5-8   89
MERCURY 5-8   87

SWINGIN' MEDALLIONS
   Singles: 7-inch
CAPITOL 4-8   68
COLLECTABLES 2-4
DOT 5-10   65
4 SALE (002 "Double Shot") 20-30   66
1-2-4 3-5   70
SMASH 4-8   66-67
   LPs: 10/12-inch 33rpm
SMASH 25-35   66
   Also see PIECES of EIGHT

SWINGING BLUE JEANS
   Singles: 7-inch
IMPERIAL 5-10   64-67
   LPs: 10/12-inch 33rpm
IMPERIAL (9261 "Hippy Hippy
  Shake") 50-75   64
  (Monaural.)
IMPERIAL (12261 "Hippy Hippy
  Shake") 30-50   64
  (Stereo.)
LIBERTY 5-10   82

SWINGLE SINGERS
   LPs: 10/12-inch 33rpm
COLUMBIA 4-6   76
PHILIPS 5-10   63-72

SWISS MOVEMENT
   Singles: 7-inch
CASABLANCA 4-6   74
PERKY (101 "Spoonful") 20-30   68
RCA 3-5   73
   LPs: 10/12-inch 33rpm
RCA 8-12   73

SWITCH
   Singles: 7-inch
GORDY (Black vinyl) 3-4   78-82
GORDY (Colored vinyl) 4-8   78-82
  (Promotional issues only.)
TOTAL EXPERIENCE 2-4   82-84

LPs: 10/12–inch 33rpm

GORDY	5-10	78-81
TOTAL EXPERIENCE	5-8	82-84

Also see DECO

SYBIL

Singles: 7–inch

NEXT PLATEAU	2-4	87-89

LPs: 10/12–inch 33rpm

NEXT PLATEAU	5-8	87-89

SYKES, Keith

Singles: 7–inch

BACKSTREET	3-5	80

LPs: 10/12–inch 33rpm

BACKSTREET	5-10	80
MIDLAND INT'L	8-10	77
VANGUARD	10-12	70-71

SYLVAIN SYLVAIN

Singles: 7–inch

RCA	3-5	79

LPs: 10/12–inch 33rpm

RCA	5-10	79

Also see NEW YORK DOLLS

SYLVERS

Singles: 12–inch 33/45rpm

CASABLANCA	4-8	79
GEFFEN	4-6	84-85
SOLAR	4-6	81-82

Singles: 7–inch

CAPITOL	3-5	75-78
CASABLANCA	3-5	78-79
GEFFEN	2-4	84-85
MGM	3-5	72-74
PRIDE	3-5	72-73
SOLAR	3-4	81-82
VERVE	3-5	71

Picture Sleeves

GEFFEN	3-4	84-85

LPs: 10/12–inch 33rpm

CAPITOL	5-10	75-78
CASABLANCA	5-10	78-79
CONCEPT	5-10	81
GEFFEN	5-8	84
MGM	8-10	72-74
PRIDE	8-10	72-73
SOLAR	5-10	81

Members: Foster Sylvers; Edmund Sylvers; Pay Sylvers; Angie
Sylvers.
Also see SYLVERS, Edmund
Also see SYLVERS, Foster

SYLVERS, Edmund

Singles: 7–inch

CASABLANCA	3-5	80

LPs: 10/12–inch 33rpm

CASABLANCA	5-10	80

Also see SYLVERS

SYLVERS, Foster

Singles: 7–inch

MGM	3-5	73
PRIDE	3-5	73

LPs: 10/12–inch 33rpm

MGM	6-10	74
PRIDE	8-10	73

Also see SYLVERS

SYLVESTER

(Sylvester James)

Singles: 12–inch 33/45rpm

FANTASY	4-8	78-79
MEGATONE	4-6	83-86

Singles: 7–inch

FANTASY (Black vinyl)	3-5	78-79
FANTASY (Colored vinyl)	4-8	78-79
(Promotional issues only.)		
HONEY	3-5	80-81
MEGATONE	2-4	83-86
WARNER	2-4	87

LPs: 10/12–inch 33rpm

FANTASY	5-10	78-81
HONEY	5-10	80-81
MEGATONE	5-8	83-86
WARNER	5-8	87

SYLVESTER, Tony, and the New Ingredient

Singles: 7–inch

MERCURY	3-5	76

SYLVIA

(Sylvia Vanderpool; Sylvia Robinson)

Singles: 12–inch 33/45rpm

SUGARHILL	4-6	82
VIBRATION	4-8	77

Singles: 7–inch

ALL PLATINUM	3-5	74
STANG	3-5	70
SUGARHILL	3-5	81
VIBRATION	3-5	73-78

LPs: 10/12–inch 33rpm

SUGARHILL	5-10	81
VIBRATION	6-10	73-78

Also see LITTLE SYLVIA
Also see MICKEY & SYLVIA
Also see TURNER, Ike and Tina

SYLVIA and Ralfi Pagan

Singles: 7–inch

VIBRATION	3-5	73

Also see SYLVIA

SYLVIA

(Sylvia Kirby Allen)

Singles: 7–inch

RCA	2-4	81-86

Picture Sleeves

RCA	3-4	81-86

LPs: 10/12–inch 33rpm

RCA	5-10	81-86

SYLVIA and Michael Johnson
Singles: 7–inch

RCA 2-4   86
    Also see JOHNSON, Michael
    Also see SYLVIA

SYLVIA, Margo, and the Tune Weavers:
see TUNE WEAVERS

SYMBA
Singles: 7–inch

VENTURE 3-5   80

SYMBOL 8
Singles: 7–inch

SHOCK 3-5   77-78

SYMS, Sylvia
Singles: 78rpm

ATLANTIC 3-5   52-53
DECCA.......................... 3-5   56-57
Singles: 7–inch
ATLANTIC 4-8   52-53
COLUMBIA 4-6   59-65
DECCA.......................... 3-8   56-64
PRESTIGE 3-6   67
RORI 4-6   62
EPs: 7–inch 33/45rpm
ATLANTIC 5-15   56
DECCA.......................... 5-15   55
LPs: 10/12–inch 33rpm
A&M 5-10   78
ATLANTIC (137 "Songs by
   Sylvia Syms")................. 50-75   53
   (10–inch LP.)
ATLANTIC (1243 "Songs by
   Sylvia Syms")................. 20-40   56
   (Has Atlantic logo at top of label.)
ATLANTIC (1243 "Songs by
   Sylvia Syms")................. 15-25   60
   (Has Atlantic logo on side of label.)
ATLANTIC (18000 series) 5-10   76
COLUMBIA 20-30   60
DECCA (8188 "Sylvia Sings") 35-45   55
DECCA (8639 "Song of Love") 30-40   58
KAPP 15-25   61
MOVIETONE 10-15   67
PRESTIGE 12-25   65-67
REPRISE 5-10   82
20TH FOX 10-20   64
VERSION (103 "After Dark") 35-50   54
   (10–inch LP.)

SYNDICATE of SOUND
Singles: 7–inch

BELL 4-8   66-67
BUDDAH 3-5   70
CAPITOL 3-6   69
DEL-FI (4304 "Prepare for Love") ... 10-15   66
HUSH (228 "Little Girl") 20-30   66
SCARLET (5-3 "Prepare for Love") .. 15-25   66

LPs: 10/12–inch 33rpm
BELL (LP-6001 "Little Girl") 25-35   66
   (Monaural.)
BELL (SLP-6001 "Little Girl") 30-45   66
   (Stereo.)
PERFORMANCE 5-8   88
   Members: Jim Sawyers; Bob Gonzalez; John Sharkey; Don
   Baskin; John Duckworth; Larry Roy; Carl Scott; Barrie
   Thompson; Dennis Tracy.

SYNERGY
Singles: 7–inch
PASSPORT 3-5   76
LPs: 10/12–inch 33rpm
PASSPORT (Black vinyl) 5-10   75-84
PASSPORT (Clear vinyl) 8-12   78

SYREETA
(Syreeta Wright)
Singles: 7–inch
MOTOWN 3-5   74-80
MOWEST 3-5   72
TAMLA 3-5   80-83
LPs: 10/12–inch 33rpm
MOTOWN 5-10   74-81
MOWEST 8-12   72
TAMLA 5-10   77-81
   Also see PRESTON, Billy, and Syreeta

SYSTEM
Singles: 12–inch 33/45rpm
MIRAGE........................ 4-6   83-86
Singles: 7–inch
ATCO 2-4   88
ATLANTIC 2-4   87
MIRAGE........................ 2-4   83-86
LPs: 10/12–inch 33rpm
ATLANTIC 5-8   87
MIRAGE........................ 5-10   83-86

SZABO, Gabor
Singles: 7–inch
BLUE THUMB 3-5   70
BUDDAH 3-5   70
CTI 3-5   73
IMPULSE 3-5   66-68
MERCURY 3-5   76-77
REPRISE 3-5   73
SKYE 3-6   68-70
LPs: 10/12–inch 33rpm
BLUE THUMB 8-12   70
BUDDAH 8-12   70
CTI 8-12   73-74
IMPULSE 10-20   66-70
MCA 5-8   82
MERCURY 5-10   76
SALVATION 5-10   75
SKYE 8-12   68-70
   Also see HORNE, Lena, and Gabor Szabo
   Also see WOMACK, Bobby

T

T. REX
(Tyrannosaurus Rex)
Singles: 7–inch
A&M 5-10   68
BLUE THUMB 4-8   71-72
CASABLANCA 3-5   75
REPRISE 3-6   71-74
LPs: 10/12–inch 33rpm
A&M (3000 series) 10-15   72
A&M (4000 series) 15-20   68
BLUE THUMB 10-20   71-72
CASABLANCA 8-10   74
REPRISE 8-12   71-73
Members: Marc Bolan; Jack Green.
Also see BOLAN, Marc
Also see GREEN, Jack

TFO
Singles: 7–inch
VENTURE 3-5   80-81

T.H.P. ORCHESTRA
Singles: 7–inch
ATLANTIC 3-5   79
BUTTERFLY (Black vinyl) 2-4   77-78
BUTTERFLY (Colored vinyl) 3-5   77-78
LPs: 10/12–inch 33rpm
ATLANTIC 5-8   79
BUTTERFLY 8-10   77

TKA
(Total Knowledge in Action)
Singles: 12–inch 33/45rpm
TOMMY BOY 4-6   86
Singles: 7–inch
TOMMY BOY 2-4   86-88
LPs: 10/12–inch 33rpm
TOMMY BOY 5-8   86-88

TKO
Singles: 7–inch
INFINITY 3-5   79
LPs: 10/12–inch 33rpm
INFINITY 5-10   79

T.M.G.
Singles: 7–inch
ATCO 3-5   79
LPs: 10/12–inch 33rpm
ATCO 5-10   79

TMP BAND
Singles: 7–inch
CRITIQUE 2-4   86

TNT BAND
Singles: 7–inch
COTIQUE 3-5   69

T.S.U. TORONADOS
Singles: 7–inch
ATLANTIC 4-6   68-69
VOLT 3-5   69-70

TTF
(Today, Tomorrow, Forever)
Singles: 7–inch
CURTOM 3-5   80
GOLD COAST 3-5   81
RSO 3-5   80
LPs: 10/12–inch 33rpm
GOLD COAST 5-10   81

T.Z.
Singles: 12–inch 33/45rpm
STREET SOUND 4-6   83

TA MARA and the Seen
Singles: 12–inch 33/45rpm
A&M 4-6   85-86
Singles: 7–inch
A&M 2-4   85-88
LPs: 10/12–inch 33rpm
A&M 5-8   85

TA'BOO
Singles: 12–inch 33/45rpm
ACME 4-6   84

TACO
(Taco Ockerse)
Singles: 12–inch 33/45rpm
RCA 4-6   83-84
Singles: 7–inch
RCA 2-4   83-84
LPs: 10/12–inch 33rpm
RCA 5-8   83-84

TAFF, Russ
Singles: 7–inch
HORIZON 2-4   85-86
LPs: 10/12–inch 33rpm
MYRRH 5-8

TAIL GATORS
LPs: 10/12–inch 33rpm
RESTLESS 5-8   88
WRESTLER 5-8   87

TAJ MAHAL
Singles: 7–inch
COLUMBIA (10000 series) 3-5   75
COLUMBIA (44000 series) 4-8   67-69
COLUMBIA (45000 series) 3-6   69-74
Picture Sleeves
COLUMBIA 4-8   67
LPs: 10/12–inch 33rpm
COLUMBIA 6-12   68-81
WARNER 5-10   77

Also see SPRINGSTEEN, Bruce / Albert Hammond / Loudon Wainwright III / Taj Mahal

TAKA BOOM: see BOOM, Taka

TALK TALK
Singles: 12–inch 33/45rpm
EMI AMERICA 4-8   82-86
Singles: 7–inch
EMI AMERICA 3-5   82-86
LPs: 10/12–inch 33rpm
EMI AMERICA 5-10   82-86

TALKING HEADS
Singles: 12–inch 33/45rpm
SIRE 4-8   79-86
Singles: 7–inch
SIRE 2-5   77-88
Picture Sleeves
SIRE 3-5   78-85
LPs: 10/12–inch 33rpm
SIRE (Except 23771) 5-10   77-88
SIRE (23771 "Speaking in Tongues") . 20-30
(Promotional issue only.)
WARNER (104 "Live on Tour") 25-45   79
(Promotional issue only.)
Members: David Byrne; Jerry Harrison; Tina Weymouth; Brian Eno; Robert Fripp.
Also see BYRNE, David
Also see TOM TOM CLUB

TAMI SHOW
Singles: 7–inch
CHRYSALIS 2-4   88

TAMPA RED
(Hudson Whittaker)
Singles: 78rpm
BLUEBIRD 10-20   44-45
RCA (20-0000 and 22-0000 series) . . 10-15   45-48
Singles: 78rpm
BLUEBIRD 15-25   44-45
RCA 5-15   45-54
Singles: 7–inch
RCA (47-4000 and 47-5000 series) . . 25-35   51-54
RCA (50-0000 series) 40-60   49-51
LPs: 10/12–inch 33rpm
BLUEBIRD 10-15   75
BLUES CLASSICS 5-10
PRESTIGE BLUESVILLE 20-35   61-62
YAZOO 10-15

TAMS
Singles: 7–inch
MINK (22 "Memory Lane") 20-30   59
(*Memory Lane* was first issued in 1959, showing the group as the Stereos. The same track was reissued in 1963, shown first as by the Tams and then by the Hippies.)
PARKWAY (863 "Memory Lane") 10-15   63
Also see HIPPIES / Reggie Harrison
Also see STEREOS

TAMS
Singles: 7–inch
ABC 3-6   68-73
ABC-PAR 4-8   63-64
APT/ABC 3-5   72
ARLEN 5-10   62-63
CAPITOL 3-6   71
COLLECTABLES 2-4
COMPLEAT 3-5   83
DAISY 5-10
DUNHILL 3-5   71
GENERAL AMERICAN 8-10   62
GUSTO 3-5   80
1-2-3 3-5   70
KING 4-8   65
MCA 2-4
RIPETE 3-5   82
ROULETTE 2-4
SOUTH 3-5   73
SWAN 8-12   60
WONDER 3-5   82
LPs: 10/12–inch 33rpm
ABC 10-15   67-69
ABC-PAR 20-30   64
BRYLEN 5-10   84
CAPITOL 5-10   79
COMPLEAT 5-8   83
1-2-3 8-10   70
SOUNDS SOUTH 8-10   77
Members: Joe Pope; Charles Pope; Floyd Ashton; Robert Lee Smith; Horace Key; Albert Cottle.

TANEGA, Norma
Singles: 7–inch
ABC 3-5   73
ERIC 2-4
NEW VOICE 4-8   66-67
VIRGO 2-4   73
LPs: 10/12–inch 33rpm
NEW VOICE 15-20   66

TANGERINE DREAM
Singles: 7–inch
EMI AMERICA 2-4   84
VIRGIN 3-5   75-77
LPs: 10/12–inch 33rpm
EMI AMERICA 5-8   84
ELEKTRA 5-10   81
MCA 5-10   77-86
VIRGIN 8-12   74-77
Members: Peter Baumann; Chris Franks; Ed Froese.
Also see BAUMANN, Peter

TANGERINE DREAM / Jon Anderson / Bryan Ferry
LPs: 10/12–inch 33rpm
MCA (6165 "Legend") 8-10   86
(Soundtrack.)
Also see ANDERSON, Jon
Also see FERRY, Bryan
Also see TANGERINE DREAM

TANNER, Gary
    Singles: 7–inch
20TH FOX 3-5   78

TANNER, Marc, Band
    Singles: 7–inch
ELEKTRA 3-5   79
PRIVATE I 2-4
    LPs: 10/12–inch 33rpm
ELEKTRA 5-10 78-80
PRIVATE I 5-10

TANTRUM
    Singles: 7–inch
OVATION 3-5   79
    LPs: 10/12–inch 33rpm
OVATION 5-10   79

TARHEEL SLIM
(Alden Bunn)
    Singles: 78rpm
FIRE 20-30 59-60
    Singles: 7–inch
FIRE 15-25 59-60
FURY 15-25   59
    Also see BUNN, Allen
    Also see LOVERS

TARHEEL SLIM & LITTLE ANN
(Slim & Ann; Slim & Little Ann; Tarheel Slim & Lil'
Annie)
    Singles: 78rpm
FIRE 20-30 59-60
    Singles: 7–inch
ATCO 5-10   63
FIRE 15-25 59-62
PORT 4-8   65
    Also see TARHEEL SLIM

TARNEY - SPENCER BAND
    Singles: 7–inch
A&M 3-5 78-81
PRIVATE STOCK 3-5   76
    LPs: 10/12–inch 33rpm
A&M 5-10 78-79
    Members: Alan Tarney; Trevor Spencer.

TARRIERS
    Singles: 78rpm
GLORY 5-10   56
    Singles: 7–inch
DECCA 4-8 63-64
GLORY 8-12   56
U.A. 5-10   59
    LPs: 10/12–inch 33rpm
ATLANTIC 15-25   60
DECCA 10-20 62-64
GLORY (1200 "The Tarriers") 40-50   57
KAPP 10-20   63
U.A. 15-25   59
    Members: Erik Darling; Alan Arkin; Bob Carey.
    Also see MARTIN, Vince
    Also see ROOFTOP SINGERS
    Also see WEISSBERG, Eric

TASSELS
    Singles: 7–inch
AMY 4-8   66
MADISON 10-15   59

TASTE
    Singles: 7–inch
ATCO 3-5 69-70
    LPs: 10/12–inch 33rpm
ATCO 10-15 69-70
    Member: Rory Gallagher.
    Also see GALLAGHER, Rory

TASTE of HONEY
    Singles: 12–inch 33/45rpm
CAPITOL (Except 9572) 4-8 78-79
CAPITOL (9572 "Sukiyaki") 8-10   80
  (Fan shaped disc. Promotional issue only.)
MCA 4-6   84
    Singles: 7–inch
CAPITOL 3-5 78-82
MCA 2-4   84
    Picture Sleeves
CAPITOL 3-5 78-82
    LPs: 10/12–inch 33rpm
CAPITOL 5-10 78-82
    Members: Janice Marie Johnson; Hazel Payne.
    Also see FELDER, Wilton
    Also see JOHNSON, Janice Marie

TATE, Howard
    Singles: 7–inch
TURNTABLE 4-6 69-70
VERVE 4-8 66-68
    LPs: 10/12–inch 33rpm
ATLANTIC 10-20   69
TURNTABLE 8-10
VERVE 10-20 67-68

TATE, Tommy
    Singles: 7–inch
JACKSON SOUND 3-5   70
KOKO 3-5 72-76
OKEH 4-8   66

TAVARES
    Singles: 12–inch 33/45rpm
CAPITOL 4-8 77-79
RCA 4-6 82-84
    Singles: 7–inch
CAPITOL 3-5 73-80
RCA 2-4 82-84
    LPs: 10/12–inch 33rpm
CAPITOL 8-10 73-81
RCA 5-10 82-83

TAWATHA
    Singles: 7–inch
EPIC 2-4   87

TAXXI
    Singles: 7–inch
FANTASY 3-5   82

LPs: 10/12–inch 33rpm
FANTASY 5-10   82
MCA 5-8   85

TAYLOR, Alex
Singles: 7–inch
BANG 3-5   78-79
CAPRICORN 3-5   71
DUNHILL 3-5   74
LPs: 10/12–inch 33rpm
CAPRICORN 8-10   71
DUNHILL 8-10   74

TAYLOR, Andy
Singles: 12–inch 33/45rpm
ATLANTIC 4-6   86
Singles: 7–inch
ATLANTIC 2-4   86
MCA 2-4   86-87
LPs: 10/12–inch 33rpm
MCA 5-8   87
  Also see DURAN DURAN
  Also see POWER STATION

TAYLOR, Austin
Singles: 7–inch
LAURIE 5-10   60-61
  Also see TAYLOR, Ted

TAYLOR, B.E., Group
Singles: 12–inch 33/45rpm
EPIC 4-6   84
Singles: 7–inch
EPIC 2-4   84-86
MCA 3-5   83-84
LPs: 10/12–inch 33rpm
MCA 5-10   82

TAYLOR, Bobby
(Bobby Taylor and the Vancouvers)
Singles: 7–inch
BUDDAH 3-5   72
GORDY 4-8   68-69
INTEGRA 8-12   68
PLAYBOY 3-5   75
SUNFLOWER 3-5   72
TOMMY 3-5   73
LPs: 10/12–inch 33rpm
GORDY 10-20   68-69
  Members: Bobby Taylor; Wes Henderson; Eddie Patterson;
  Robbie King; Ted Lewis; Tommy Chong.
  Also see CHEECH & CHONG

TAYLOR, Debbie
Singles: 7–inch
ARISTA 3-5   75-76
DECCA 4-6   68
GWP 4-6   69
POLYDOR 3-5   74
TODAY 3-5   72
LPs: 10/12–inch 33rpm
TODAY 6-10   72

TAYLOR, Felice
Singles: 7–inch
KENT 4-6   68
MUSTANG 4-8   67

TAYLOR, Gary
Singles: 7–inch
VIRGIN 2-4   88

TAYLOR, Gloria
Singles: 7–inch
COLUMBIA 3-5   74
GLO-WHIZ 4-6   69
SILVER FOX 4-6   69

TAYLOR, James
(James Taylor and the Original Flying Machine)
Singles: 7–inch
APPLE (1805 "Carolina in My
  Mind"/"Taking It In") 200-300   69
  (Promotional issue.)
APPLE (1805 "Carolina in My
  Mind"/"Something's Wrong") 5-10   70
  (Note different flip side.)
APPLE (1805 "Carolina in My
  Mind"/"Something's Wrong") 20-30   70
APPLE (4675 "More Apples,
  Radio Co-Op Ads") 125-175   69
  (Single-sided disc. Promotional issue only.)
CAPITOL 3-5   76
COLUMBIA 2-5   77-88
EUPHORIA 3-5   71
WARNER 3-5   70-76
LPs: 10/12–inch 33rpm
APPLE 10-15   69-70
COLUMBIA 5-10   77-88
EUPHORIA 12-15   71
TRI 8-10   73
WARNER 8-10   70-77
  Also see DOOBIE BROTHERS, James Hall and James Taylor
  Also see DOOBIE BROTHERS / Kate Taylor and the
    Simon-Taylor Family
  Also see FLYING MACHINE
  Also see GARFUNKEL, Art
  Also see KING DREAM CHORUS and Holiday Crew
  Also see SIMON, Carly, and James Taylor

TAYLOR, James, and J.D. Souther
Singles: 7–inch
COLUMBIA 3-5   81
  Also see SOUTHER, J.D.
  Also see TAYLOR, James

TAYLOR, John
Singles: 12–inch 33/45rpm
CAPITOL 4-6   86
Singles: 7–inch
CAPITOL 2-4   86
LPs: 10/12–inch 33rpm
CAPITOL 5-8   86
  Also see DURAN DURAN
  Also see POWER STATION

TAYLOR, Johnnie
(Johnny Taylor)
Singles: 7–inch
BEVERLY GLEN 3-5   82
COLUMBIA 3-5   76-80
DERBY 4-8   63-64
MALACO 2-4   83-87
RCA 3-5   77
SAR (Except 131) 5-10   61-65
SAR (131 "Never Never") 15-25   61
STAX 3-6   66-77
LPs: 10/12–inch 33rpm
BEVERLY GLEN 5-10   82
COLUMBIA 6-10   76-81
MALACO 5-8   83-86
RCA 8-10   77
STAX 6-10   67-83

TAYLOR, Johnnie, and Carla Thomas
Singles: 7–inch
STAX 3-6   69
Also see TAYLOR, Johnnie
Also see THOMAS, Carla

TAYLOR, Kate
Singles: 7–inch
COLUMBIA 3-5   77-79
COTILLION 3-5   71
LPs: 10/12–inch 33rpm
COLUMBIA 5-10   78-79
COTILLION 5-10   71
Also see DOOBIE BROTHERS / Kate Taylor and the
Simon-Taylor Family

TAYLOR, Koko
(Cocoa Taylor)
Singles: 7–inch
CHECKER 4-8   66-68
U.S.A. 5-10   63
LPs: 10/12–inch 33rpm
ALLIGATOR 5-10   76-81
CHESS 10-12   69-72

TAYLOR, Little Johnny
Singles: 7–inch
GALAXY 4-8   63-64
RONN 3-5   71-79
LPs: 10/12–inch 33rpm
BEVERLY GLEN 5-8   87
GALAXY 15-25   63
RONN 5-10   72-79

TAYLOR, Little Johnny, and Ted Taylor
LPs: 10/12–inch 33rpm
RONN 5-10   73
Also see TAYLOR, Little Johnny
Also see TAYLOR, Ted

TAYLOR, Livingston
Singles: 7–inch
CAPRICORN 3-5   70-73
EPIC 3-5   78-80

LPs: 10/12–inch 33rpm
ATCO 5-8   8-1270
CAPRICORN 5-10   71-79
EPIC 5-10   78
Also see DOOBIE BROTHERS / Kate Taylor and the
Simon-Taylor Family

TAYLOR, Mick
Singles: 7–inch
COLUMBIA 3-5   79
LPs: 10/12–inch 33rpm
COLUMBIA 5-10   79
Also see MAYALL, John
Also see ROLLING STONES

TAYLOR, R. Dean
Singles: 7–inch
AUDIO MASTER (1 "At the High
School Dance") 75-150   60
BARRY (3023 "At the High
School Dance") 50-100   60
(Canadian.)
FARR 3-5   76
JANE 3-5   77
MALA 5-10   62
MOTOWN 3-5
RAGAMUFFIN 3-5   79
RARE EARTH 3-5   70-72
20TH FOX 3-5   81
V.I.P. 4-8   65-68
Picture Sleeves
RARE EARTH 3-5   71
LPs: 10/12–inch 33rpm
RARE EARTH 10-15   70

TAYLOR, Roger
Singles: 7–inch
CAPITOL 2-4   84
ELEKTRA 3-5   81
LPs: 10/12–inch 33rpm
CAPITOL 5-8   84
ELEKTRA 5-10   81
Also see ARCADIA
Also see QUEEN

TAYLOR, Ted
Singles: 7–inch
ALARM 3-5   76
APT 4-8   62
ATCO 4-8   65-66
DADE 4-8   63
DUKE 5-10   59
EPIC 4-8   66
GOLD EAGLE 4-8   61
JEWEL 4-8   66-67
OKEH 4-8   62-65
RONN 4-6   67-72
SONCRAFT 4-8   61
TOP RANK 5-10   60-61
WARWICK 4-8   61
LPs: 10/12–inch 33rpm
OKEH 15-25   63-66

MCA 5-10   78
RONN 5-10   69-72
  Also see CADETS
  Also see TAYLOR, Austin
  Also see TAYLOR, Little Johnny and Ted Taylor

TAYLOR, True
(Paul Simon)
Singles: 7-inch
BIG (614 "Teenage Fool") 20-40   58
  Also see SIMON, Paul

T-BONES
Singles: 7-inch
LIBERTY 4-8   64-66
EPs: 7-inch 33/45rpm
LIBERTY .... 5-10 '   65
  (Jukebox issues only.)
LPs: 10/12-inch 33rpm
LIBERTY 15-25   64-66
SUNSET 10-15   66
  Members: Dan Hamilton; Gene Pello; Joe Frank Carollo; Tom
  Reynolds; Judd Hamilton; Richard Torres; George Dee.
  Also see HAMILTON, JOE FRANK & REYNOLDS

TCHAIKOVSKY, Bram
Singles: 7-inch
ARISTA 3-5   81
POLYDOR 3-5   79
LPs: 10/12-inch 33rpm
ARISTA 5-10   81
POLYDOR 5-10   79-80
  Also see MOTORS

T-CONNECTION
Singles: 12-inch 33/45rpm
CAPITOL 4-6   81-84
Singles: 7-inch
CAPITOL 3-5   81-84
DASH 3-5   77-79
LPs: 10/12-inch 33rpm
CAPITOL 5-10   81-84
DASH 5-10   77-79

TEARDROP EXPLODES
Singles: 7-inch
MERCURY 3-5   81-82
LPs: 10/12-inch 33rpm
MERCURY 5-10   81-82

TEARS for FEARS
Singles: 12-inch 33/45rpm
MERCURY 4-6   83-86
Singles: 7-inch
MERCURY 2-4   83-86
LPs: 10/12-inch 33rpm
FONTANA 5-8   89
MERCURY 5-8   83-86
SELECT ONE 12-18

TEASE
Singles: 12-inch 33/45rpm
EPIC 4-6   86
RCA 4-6   83
Singles: 7-inch
EPIC 2-4   86-88
RCA 2-4   83
LPs: 10/12-inch 33rpm
EPIC 5-8   86
RCA 5-8   83

TECHNIQUE
Singles: 12-inch 33/45rpm
ARIAL 4-6   83

TECHNIQUES
Singles: 78rpm
ROULETTE 4-8   57
Singles: 7-inch
ROULETTE 5-10   57-58
STARS 15-25   57

TEDDY and the Twilights
Singles: 7-inch
SWAN 10-15   62

TEDDY BEARS
Singles: 7-inch
COLLECTABLES 2-4
DORE 8-12   58-59
IMPERIAL 10-20   58-59
LPs: 10/12-inch 33rpm
IMPERIAL (9067 "The Teddy
  Bears Sing") 150-250   59
  (Monaural.)
IMPERIAL (12010 "The Teddy
  Bears Sing") 350-450   59
  (Stereo.)
  Members: Phil Spector; Annette Kleinbard; Marshall Leib.
  Also see NELSON, Sandy

TEE, Willie
Singles: 7-inch
A.F.O. 5-10   62
ATLANTIC 4-8   65
CAPITOL 4-6   68-70
GATOR 3-5   71

NOLA 5-10   65
U.A. 3-5   76
LPs: 10/12-inch 33rpm
CAPITOL 10-15   69
U.A. 5-10   76

TEE SET
Singles: 7-inch
COLLECTABLES 2-4
COLOSSUS 3-5   70-71
Picture Sleeves
COLOSSUS 3-5   70
LPs: 10/12-inch 33rpm
COLOSSUS 10-15   70

TEEGARDEN & VAN WINKLE
Singles: 7-inch
ATCO 4-8   68
PLUMM 3-6   70
WESTBOUND 3-6   69-72
Picture Sleeves
WESTBOUND 3-5   70
LPs: 10/12-inch 33rpm
ATCO 10-15   68
WESTBOUND 8-12   69-72
Members: David Teegarden; Skip Knape.

TEEN DREAM
(Teen Dream with Valentino)
Singles: 7-inch
WARNER 2-4   87-88

TEEN KINGS
Singles: 78rpm
JE-WEL (101 "Ooby Dooby") 200-300   56
Singles: 7-inch
JE-WEL (101 "Ooby Dooby") 400-600   56
(May read "Vocal Roy Oribson," instead of
"Orbison," on some labels.)
Members: Roy Orbison; Johnny "Peanuts" Wilson; Billy Par Ellis;
James Monroe; Jack Kennelly.
Also see ORBISON, Roy

TEEN QUEENS
Singles: 78rpm
RPM 5-10   56-57
Singles: 7-inch
ANTLER 5-10   60-61
COLLECTABLES 2-4
KENT 4-8   61
RCA 5-10   58
RPM 10-20   56-57
Picture Sleeves
ANTLER 10-20   60
LPs: 10/12-inch 33rpm
CROWN (5022 "Eddie My Love") ... 50-100   56
CROWN (5373 "The Teen Queens") . 20-30   63
UNITED 8-12
Members: Rose Collins; Betty Collins.

TEENA MARIE:
see MARIE, Teena

TEENAGERS
Singles: 78rpm
GEE (1046 "Flip-Flop") 5-10   57
Singles: 7-inch
END (1071 "Crying") 30-40   60
END (1076 "Can You Tell Me") 20-30   60
GEE (1046 "Flip-Flop") 10-20   57
ROULETTE (4086 "Broken Heart") .. 35-45   58
Members: Billy Lobrano; Herman Santiago; Sherman Garnes;
Jim Merchant; Joe Negroni.
Also see LYMON, Frankie

TEMPER
Singles: 12-inch 33/45rpm
MCA 4-6   84
Singles: 7-inch
MCA 2-4   84

TEMPO, Nino
(Nino Tempo and 5th Ave. Sax)
Singles: 7-inch
A&M 3-5   73-74
RCA 5-10   59-60
TOWER 4-6   67
U.A. 5-10   60
LPs: 10/12-inch 33rpm
A&M 8-10   74
ATCO 10-15   66
Also see ARCHIES
Also see KINGBEES

TEMPO, Nino, and April Stevens
Singles: 7-inch
A&M 3-5   72-75
ABC 3-5   73
ATCO 4-8   62-66
BELL 3-6   69
CHELSEA 3-5   76
MARINA 3-5   72
WHITE WHALE 4-6   66-68
LPs: 10/12-inch 33rpm
ATCO 10-15   63-66
CAMDEN 10-15   64
WHITE WHALE 10-15   69
Also see STEVENS, April
Also see TEMPO, Nino

TEMPOS
Singles: 78rpm
KAPP 8-12   57
Singles: 7-inch
CLIMAX 10-15   59
KAPP 10-20   57-58
PARIS 10-15   59
ROULETTE 3-5

TEMPREES
Singles: 7-inch
EPIC 3-5   76
STAX 2-4   84
WE PRODUCE 2-4   72-74
LPs: 10/12-inch 33rpm
STAX 5-8   84

WE PRODUCE 5-10 72-74

TEMPTATIONS
Singles: 7-inch
GOLDISC (3001 "Barbara") 15-25 60
  Black label.)
GOLDISC (3001 "Barbara") 10-15 60
  Multi-color label.)
ROULETTE 3-5 71

TEMPTATIONS
Singles: 7-inch
ATLANTIC 3-5 77-78
GORDY (1631 through 1933) 2-4 82-88
GORDY (7001 "Dream Come True") . 20-25 62
GORDY (7010 "Paradise") 15-20 62
GORDY (7015 "I Want a Love
  I Can See") 10-15 63
GORDY (7020 "May I Have This
  Dance") 8-12 63
GORDY (7028 through 7074) 4-8 64-68
GORDY (7081 through 7213) 3-6 68-81
MIRACLE (5 "Oh Mother of Mine") ... 60-75 61
MIRACLE (12 "Check Yourself") 15-25 62
MOTOWN 2-4 84-87
MOTOWN/TOPPS (4 "My Girl") 50-75 67
MOTOWN/TOPPS (13 "The Way You
  Do the Things You Do") 50-75 67
  (Topps Chewing Gum promotional item.
  Single-sided, cardboard flexi, picture disc. Issued
  with generic paper sleeve.)
Picture Sleeves
GORDY (Except 7038) 4-8 66-70
GORDY (7038 "My Girl") 15-20 65
LPs: 10/12-inch 33rpm
ATLANTIC 5-10 77-78
GORDY (911 through 927) 15-25 64-68
GORDY (938 through 1006) 8-15 68-80
GORDY (6000 series) 5-8 82-86
KORY 8-10 77
MOTOWN (100 and 200 series) 5-10 81-82
MOTOWN (782 "Anthology") 15-20 73
  (Three-LP set. Includes 12-page color booklet.)

MOTOWN (998 "Give Love at
  Christmas") 12-18 80
  (Promotional issue only.)
MOTOWN (5389 "25th Anniversary") 10-15 86
  (Includes eight-page color booklet.)
MOTOWN (6246 "Together Again") 5-8 87
NATURAL RESOURCES 5-10 78
  Members: David Ruffin; Eddie Kendricks; Melvin Franklin; Otis
  Williams; Paul Williams; Damon Harris; Dennis Edwards.
  Also see EDWARDS, Dennis
  Also see FOUR TOPS / Temptations
  Also see HARRIS, Damon
  Also see KENDRICKS, Eddie
  Also see LANDS, Liz, and the Temptations
  Also see PIRATES
  Also see ROBINSON, Smokey
  Also see ROSS, Diana
  Also see RUFFIN, David
  Also see SUPREMES and the Temptations

TEMPTATIONS and the Four Tops
LPs: 10/12-inch 33rpm
MOTOWN (134 "Battle of
  the Champions") 10-20
  (Promotional issue only.)
SILVER EAGLE 5-10 87
  Also see FOUR TOPS

TEMPTATIONS and Rick James
Singles: 12-inch 33/45rpm
GORDY 4-6 82
Singles: 7-inch
GORDY 2-4 82
  Also see JAMES, Rick

TEMPTATIONS / Stevie Wonder
LPs: 10/12-inch 33rpm
TAMLA (101 "The Sky's the Limit") .. 15-25 71
  (Promotional issue only.)
  Also see TEMPTATIONS
  Also see WONDER, Stevie

10CC
Singles: 7-inch
MERCURY 3-5 75-77
POLYDOR 3-5 78
UK 3-5 72-74
Picture Sleeves
MERCURY 5-8 75-77
LPs: 10/12-inch 33rpm
MERCURY 10-15 75-77
POLYDOR 5-8 78-79
UK 10-15 73-75
WARNER 8-10 80
  Members: Kevin Godley; Lol Creme; Graham Gouldman; Eric
  Stewart; Paul Burgess;
Rick Fenn; Tony O'Malley; Stuart Tosh.
  Also see GODLEY, Kevin, and Lol Creme
  Also see HOTLEGS
  Also see KASENETZ - KATZ SINGING ORCHESTRAL CIRCUS
  Also see KOKOMO
  Also see OHIO EXPRESS
  Also see PILOT
  Also see SEDAKA, Neil
  Also see WAX

10DB
Singles: 7–inch
CRUSH 2-4   88

10 SPEED
Singles: 12–inch 33/45rpm
QUALITY/RFC 4-6   83
Singles: 7–inch
QUALITY/RFC 3-5   83

10,000 MANIACS
LPs: 10/12–inch 33rpm
ELEKTRA 5-8   87-90

TEN WHEEL DRIVE
Singles: 7–inch
CAPITOL 3-5   73
POLYDOR 4-6   69-71
LPs: 10/12–inch 33rpm
CAPITOL 8-10   73
POLYDOR 10-12   69-71
Member: Genya Ravan.
Also see RAVAN, Genya
Also see ZAGER, Michael, Band

TEN YEARS AFTER
Singles: 7–inch
COLUMBIA 3-5   71-73
DERAM 4-6   68-70
LPs: 10/12–inch 33rpm
CHRYSALIS 5-10   83-89
COLUMBIA 8-12   71-76
DERAM 8-12   68-75
LONDON 5-10   77
Member: Alvin Lee.
Also see LEE, Alvin

TENANT, Jimmy: see TENNANT, Jimmy

TENDER SLIM
Singles: 7–inch
GREY CLIFF 5-10   59
HERALD 4-8   62

TENNANT, Jimmy
(Jimmy Velvet; Jimmy Tenant)
Singles: 7–inch
AMP 5-10   59
WARWICK 10-15   60
Also see VELVET, Jimmy

TENNESSEE ERNIE:
see FORD, "Tennessee" Ernie

TENNILLE, Toni
Singles: 7–inch
MIRAGE 3-5   84
LPs: 10/12–inch 33rpm
GAIA 5-8   87
MIRAGE 5-8   84
Also see CAPTAIN & TENNILLE

TEPPER, Robert
Singles: 7–inch
SCOTTI BROTHERS 2-4   85-86

LPs: 10/12–inch 33rpm
SCOTTI BROTHERS 5-8   85-86

TERRELL, Jean
Singles: 7–inch
A&M 3-5   78
LPs: 10/12–inch 33rpm
A&M 8-10   78
Also see SUPREMES

TERRELL, Tammi
Singles: 7–inch
MOTOWN 4-8   65-69
LPs: 10/12–inch 33rpm
MOTOWN (200 series) 5-8   82
MOTOWN (600 series) 12-15   67
Also see GAYE, Marvin, and Tammi Terrell
Also see JACKSON, Chuck, and Tammi Terrell
Also see MONTGOMERY, Tammy

TERRY, Sonny
(Sonny "Hootin" Terry and His Night Owls; Sonny
Terry and His Buckshot Five)
Singles: 78rpm
ASCH 10-20   45
CAPITOL 5-15   47-50
GOTHAM 8-12   51
GRAMERCY 8-12   52
GROOVE 5-10   54-55
HARLEM 10-15   52
JACKSON 10-15   52
JAX 10-15
JOSIE 10-15   56
OLD TOWN 10-15   56
RCA 5-10   53
RED ROBIN 15-25   53
SAVOY 8-12   48
SOLO 10-15   49
Singles: 7–inch
CAPITOL (931 "Telephone Blues") .. 50-75   50
CHOICE 5-10   61
GOTHAM (517 "Baby, Let's
   Have Some Fun") 20-30   51
GOTHAM (518 "Harmonica Rumbo") 20-30   51
GRAMERCY (1004 "Hootin' Blues") . 25-35   52
   (Black vinyl.)
GRAMERCY (Colored vinyl) 50-75   52
   (Colored vinyl.)
GROOVE 15-25   54-55
HARLEM (2327 "Dangerous Woman") 40-50   52
JACKSON (2302 "That Woman
   Is Killing Me") 50-100   52
   (Colored vinyl.)
JAX (305 "I Don't Worry") 50-100
   (Colored vinyl.)
JOSIE 10-20   56
OLD TOWN 10-20   56
RCA (5492 "Hootin' and Jumpin") ... 20-30   53
RCA (5577 "Sonny Is Drinkin") 20-30   53
RED ROBIN (110 "Harmonica Hop") 75-125   53

LPs: 10/12–inch 33rpm

ARCHIVE of FOLK MUSIC 15-25	65	
EVEREST 5-10		
PRESTIGE BLUESVILLE 20-30	61-63	
WASHINGTON (702 "Talkin' About the Blues") 25-35	61	

Most of the Sonny Terry sessions included Brownie McGhee on guitar.
Also see BAGBY, Doc
Also see HOPKINS, Lightnin,' and Sonny Terry
Also see McGHEE, Brownie, and Sonny Terry

TERRY, Todd, Project
LPs: 10/12–inch 33rpm

FRESH 5-8   88

TERRY, Tony
Singles: 7–inch

EPIC 2-4   87-90

LPs: 10/12–inch 33rpm

EPIC 5-8   87-91

TESLA
Singles: 7–inch

GEFFEN 2-4   87-90

LPs: 10/12–inch 33rpm

GEFFEN 5-8   87-90

TESTAMENT
LPs: 10/12–inch 33rpm

MEGAFORCE 5-8   88-90

TETES NOIRES
EPs: 7–inch 33/45rpm

RAPUNZEL 4-6   85

LPs: 10/12–inch 33rpm

RAPUNZEL 5-10   85
ROUNDER 5-8   87

Members: Jennifer Holt; Cindy Bartell; Renee Kayon; Camille Gage; Polly Alexander; Angela Frucci.

TEX, Joe
(Joe Tex and the Class Mates)
Singles: 78rpm

KING 5-10   55-57

Singles: 12–inch 33/45rpm

EPIC 4-8   77

Singles: 7–inch

ACE 5-10	58-60	
ANNA 5-10	60-61	
ATLANTIC 3-5	72	
CHECKER 4-8	63	
DIAL (1000 series) 3-6	71-76	
DIAL (2800 series) 3-5	78	
DIAL (3000 series) 4-8	61-64	
DIAL (4000 series) 4-6	64-69	
EPIC 3-5	77-79	
HANDSHAKE 3-5	81	
JALYNNE 5-10	61	
KING 10-15	55-57	

LPs: 10/12–inch 33rpm

ACCORD 5-8	82	
ATLANTIC 10-15	65-72	

CHECKER 12-18	64	
DIAL 8-10	72-79	
EPIC 5-10	77-78	
KING 12-18	65	
LONDON 5-10	79	
PARROT 12-18	65	
PRIDE 8-10	73	

Members: Mike Appell; Rod Bristow.
Also see KELLY, Paul
Also see SOUL CLAN

TEXANS
Singles: 7–inch

GOTHIC 10-20	61	
INFINITY 10-20	61	
JOX 8-12	64	
VEE JAY 4-8	65	

Members: Dorsey Burnette; Johnny Burnette.
Also see BURNETTE, Johnny and Dorsey

TEXAS "GUITAR" SLIM
(Johnny Winter)
Singles: 7–inch

JIN (174 "Broke and Lonely") 30-50   62
(This same number was used for *Something's Wrong*, by Rockin' Sidney.)
MOON-LITE 75-100   60
Also see GUITAR SLIM
Also see WINTER, Johnny

TEXAS SLIM
(John Lee Hooker)
Singles: 78rpm

KING 5-10   48-50
Also see HOOKER, John Lee

TEXTONES
Singles: 7–inch

GOLD MOUNTAIN 2-4   84
I.R.S./FAULTY PRODUCTS 3-5   80

LPs: 10/12–inch 33rpm

GOLD MOUNTAIN 5-8   84
Members: Carla Olson; Mark Cuff; Kathy Valentine; David Provost; George Callins; Phil Seymour; Tom Morgan; Joe Read.
Also see DREAM SYNDICATE
Also see GO-GOs
Also see SEYMOUR, Phil

THE
(The The)
Singles: 12–inch 33/45rpm
EPIC 4-6   84-89
SIRE 4-6   84
Singles: 7–inch
EPIC 2-4   84-85
LPs: 10/12–inch 33rpm
EPIC 5-8   84-89

THEE MIDNITERS
Singles: 7–inch
CHATTAHOOCHEE 5-10   65-66
UNI 4-8   69
WHITTIER 4-8   66-68
LPs: 10/12–inch 33rpm
CHATTAHOOCHEE 20-30   65
RHINO 5-8   83
WHITTIER 15-20   66-67

THEE PROPHETS
Singles: 7–inch
KAPP 4-8   69
LPs: 10/12–inch 33rpm
KAPP 15-20   69

THEM
(Featuring Van Morrison)
Singles: 7–inch
HAPPY TIGER 4-6   69-70
KING 8-10   65
LOMA 5-8   66
LONDON 2-4
PARROT (Except 365) 5-10   64-66
PARROT (365 "Gloria") 10-15   65
(Copies with later copyright dates are reissues.
Later released on Parrot 9727.)
RUFF 8-10   67
SULLY 15-20
TOWER 4-8   67-69
LPs: 10/12–inch 33rpm
HAPPY TIGER (1004 "Them") 20-30   69
HAPPY TIGER (1012 "In Reality") ... 20-30   71
LONDON 5-10   77
PARROT (61005 "Them") 50-100   65
(Cover does NOT emphasize *Gloria*.)
(Monaural.)
PARROT (61005 "Them") 30-35   65
(Cover emphasizes *Gloria*.)
(Monaural.)
PARROT (61008 "Them Again") 25-30   66
(Monaural.)
PARROT (71005 "Them") 50-100   65
(Cover does NOT emphasize *Gloria*.)
(Stereo.)
PARROT (71005 "Them") 30-35   65
(Cover emphasizes *Gloria*.)
(Stereo.)
PARROT (71008 "Them Again") 25-30   66
(Stereo.)

PARROT (71053 "Them Featuring
Van Morrison") 12-15   72
TOWER (5104 "Now and Them") ... 25-35   68
TOWER (5116 "Time Out") 25-35   68
Members: Van Morrison; Billy Harrison; Alan Henderson; Peter
Bardens; J. McAuley; John Stark.
Also see MORRISON, Van

THEO VANESS
Singles: 7–inch
PRELUDE 3-5   79
LPs: 10/12–inch 33rpm
PRELUDE 5-10   79

THEODORE, Mike, Orchestra
Singles: 7–inch
WESTBOUND 3-5   77-79
LPs: 10/12–inch 33rpm
WESTBOUND 5-10   77-79

THERESA
Singles: 7–inch
RCA 2-4   87-88

THEY MIGHT BE GIANTS
LPs: 10/12–inch 33rpm
BAR NONE 5-8   88
ELEKTRA 5-8   90

THIN LIZZY
Singles: 12–inch 33/45rpm
WARNER 4-8   78
(Promotional issues only.)
Singles: 7–inch
LONDON 3-5   73
MERCURY 3-5   76-77
VERTIGO 3-5   75
WARNER 3-5   78-79
Picture Sleeves
VERTIGO 3-5   75
LPs: 10/12–inch 33rpm
LONDON (500 and 600 series) 10-15   71
LONDON (50000 series) 5-10   77
MERCURY 8-12   76-77
VERTIGO 10-12   74-75
WARNER 5-10   78-84
Members: Philip Lynott; Gary Moore; Brian Robertson.
Also see MOORE, Gary

THINK
Singles: 7–inch
BIG TREE 3-5   74
COLUMBIA 4-8   68-69
LAURIE 3-5   71
LPs: 10/12–inch 33rpm
LAURIE 8-10   72
Member: Lou Stallman.

THIRD POWER
Singles: 7–inch
BARON 5-10
VANGUARD 4-6   70
LPs: 10/12–inch 33rpm
VANGUARD 10-15   70

THIRD RAIL
Singles: 7–inch
CAMEO 4-8   66
EPIC 3-6   67-69
LPs: 10/12–inch 33rpm
EPIC 20-30   67

THIRD WORLD
Singles: 12–inch 33/45rpm
COLUMBIA 4-6   81-82
ISLAND 4-8   78-80
Singles: 7–inch
ABRAXAS 3-5   76
COLUMBIA 3-5   81-85
ISLAND 3-5   79
LPs: 10/12–inch 33rpm
COLUMBIA 5-8   81-85
ISLAND 5-10   76-80
MERCURY 5-8   89
   Also see WONDER, Stevie

13TH FLOOR ELEVATORS
Singles: 7–inch
CONTACT (5269 "You're Gonna
   Miss Me") 50-75   66
   (First issue of *You're Gonna Miss Me*.)
HBR (492 "You're Gonna Miss Me") . . 40-50   66
   (Third issue of *You're Gonna Miss Me*.)
INTERNATIONAL ARTISTS (107 "You're
   Gonna Miss Me") 10-20   66
   (Second issue of *You're Gonna Miss Me*.)
INTERNATIONAL ARTISTS (111 through
   130) 10-20   66-68
LPs: 10/12–inch 33rpm
INTERNATIONAL ARTISTS (1 "Psychedelic
   Sounds") 75-100   67
   (Does NOT have "Masterfonics" stamped in the
   vinyl trail-off.)
INTERNATIONAL ARTISTS (5 "Easter
   Everywhere") 40-60   67
   (Does NOT have "Masterfonics" stamped in the
   vinyl trail-off.)
INTERNATIONAL ARTISTS (8 "Live") 40-60   68
   (Does NOT have "Masterfonics" stamped in the
   vinyl trail-off.)
INTERNATIONAL ARTISTS (9 "Bull of
   the Woods") 40-60   68
   (Does NOT have "Masterfonics" stamped in the
   vinyl trail-off.)
INTERNATIONAL ARTISTS 10-20   79
   (Reissues. With "Masterfonics" stamped in the
   vinyl trail-off.)
INTERNATIONAL ARTISTS (White
   Label) 150-225   67-68
   (Promotional issues only.)
TEXAS ARCHIVE 8-10   85
   Members: Roky Erickson; Tommy Hall; Stacy Sutherland; John
   Ike Walton; Benny Thurman.
   Also see SPADES

.38 SPECIAL
Singles: 7–inch
A&M 2-5   77-88
CAPITOL 2-5   84
Picture Sleeves
A&M 3-5   80-83
LPs: 10/12–inch 33rpm
A&M 5-10   77-88
CAPITOL 5-8   84
   Member: Dave Van Zandt.

THOMAS, B.J.
(B.J. Thomas and the Triumphs)
Singles: 7–inch
ABC 3-5   75
BRAGG (103 "Billy and Sue") 15-20   66
CLEVELAND INT'L 2-4   83
COLLECTABLES 2-4
COLUMBIA 2-4   83-86
HICKORY 4-8   66
MCA 3-5   77-82
MYRRH 2-4   77-81
PACEMAKER 10-15   66
PARAMOUNT 3-5   73-74
SCEPTER (12100 series) 4-8   66-67
SCEPTER (12200 through 12364) 3-6   68-72
SCEPTER (21000 series) 3-5   73-74
VALERIE 4-8
Picture Sleeves
MCA 3-5   79
LPs: 10/12–inch 33rpm
ABC 5-10   74-77
ACCORD 5-10   81-82
BUCKBOARD 5-10
CLEVELAND INT'L 5-10   83
COLUMBIA 5-8   86
DORAL 15-25
   (Promotional mail-order issue, from Doral
   cigarettes.)
EXACT 5-10   80
EXCELSIOR 5-10   80
EVEREST 5-10   81

BILLY AND SUE
(Mark Charron)

BRAGG
BRAGG-TYCO BMI
45-103-2
11 Porter:Engineer
Time: 2:66

B. J. THOMAS
And The Triumphs
B-103

MFG. BY BRAGG RECORD CORP. NASHVILLE, TENNESSEE, U.S.A.

51 WEST	5-10	79
HICKORY	20-30	66
MCA	5-10	77-82
MCA/SONGBIRD	5-10	80
MYRRH	5-8	78-83
PACEMAKER (3001 "B.J. Thomas and the Triumphs")	40-50	66
PARAMOUNT	5-10	73-74
PHOENIX 20	5-10	81
PICKWICK	5-8	78
PRIORITY	5-8	83
SCEPTER	8-12	69-73
SPRINGBOARD	5-10	73-79
STARDAY	5-10	77
TRIP	5-10	76
U.A.	5-10	74

Also see EDDY, Duane

THOMAS, B.J., and Ray Charles
Singles: 7–inch

COLUMBIA	2-4	85

Also see CHARLES, Ray
Also see THOMAS, B.J.

THOMAS, Carla
Singles: 7–inch

ATLANTIC	4-8	60-65
SATELLITE (104 "Gee Whiz Look at His Eyes")	40-50	60
STAX	3-8	65-72

Picture Sleeves

STAX	4-8	67

EPs: 7–inch 33/45rpm

STAX	10-15	66

(Jukebox issues only.)

LPs: 10/12–inch 33rpm

ATLANTIC (8057 "Gee Whiz")	20-30	61
ATLANTIC (8232 "Best of Carla Thomas")	10-15	69
STAX	10-15	66-71

Also see BELL, William, and Carla Thomas
Also see OTIS and CARLA
Also see REDDING, Otis / Carla Thomas / Sam & Dave / Eddie Floyd
Also see RUFUS & CARLA
Also see TAYLOR, Johnnie, and Carla Thomas

THOMAS, Evelyn
Singles: 12–inch 33/45rpm

TSR	4-6	84

Singles: 7–inch

CASABLANCA	3-5	78
TSR	3-5	84
VANGUARD	3-5	85

LPs: 10/12–inch 33rpm

A.V.I.	5-10	79
CASABLANCA	5-10	78

THOMAS, Gene
Singles: 7–inch

HICKORY	3-5	71
TRX	3-6	69
U.A.	4-8	61-65

VENUS	10-15	61-62

Also see GENE & DEBBE

THOMAS, Ian
Singles: 7–inch

ATLANTIC	3-5	78
CHRYSALIS	3-5	75
JANUS	3-5	73-74
MERCURY	2-4	84

LPs: 10/12–inch 33rpm

ATLANTIC	5-10	78
JANUS	8-10	73
MERCURY	5-8	84

THOMAS, Irma
Singles: 7–inch

BANDY	4-8	
CANYON	3-5	70
CHESS	4-6	68
COTILLION	3-5	71-72
FUNGUS	3-5	73
IMPERIAL	4-8	64-66
MINIT	4-8	61-63
RCS	3-5	79-81
ROKER	3-5	71
RON	5-10	59-60

LPs: 10/12–inch 33rpm

FUNGUS	8-10	73
IMPERIAL (266 "Wish Someone Would Care")	20-30	64
IMPERIAL (302 "Take a Look")	15-20	66
RCS	5-10	80

Also see BROWN, Maxine / Irma Thomas

THOMAS, Irma / Ernie K-Doe / Showmen / Benny Spellman

MINIT (0004 "New Orleans, Home of the Blues, Vol. 2")	15-20	64

Also see K-DOE, Ernie
Also see SHOWMEN
Also see SPELLMAN, Benny

THOMAS, Jamo, and the Party Brothers
Singles: 7–inch

CHESS	4-8	66
DECCA	4-8	68
SOUND STAGE 7	4-8	67
THOMAS	4-8	66

THOMAS, Joe
Singles: 78rpm

KING	5-10	49-51
MERCURY	5-10	51

Singles: 7–inch

KING (4460 "Jumpin' Joe")	15-25	51
KING (4474 "You're Just My Kind")	15-25	51
MERCURY (8268 "Everybody Loves My Baby")	15-25	51

THOMAS, Joe
Singles: 7–inch

GROOVE MERCHANT	3-5	76
LRC	3-5	77-79

SUE 4-8   64
LPs: 10/12–inch 33rpm
LRC 5-10   77-78
TODAY 6-12   72

THOMAS, Joe, and Bill Elliott
LPs: 10/12–inch 33rpm
SUE 15-25   64
Also see THOMAS, Joe

THOMAS, Jon
(John Thomas)
Singles: 78rpm
CHECKER 5-10   55
Singles: 7–inch
ABC-PAR 5-10   60-61
CHECKER 10-15   55
JUNIOR 4-8   64
VEEP 4-8   67-68
LPs: 10/12–inch 33rpm
ABC-PAR 20-30   60
MERCURY 15-25   63

THOMAS, Leone
Singles: 7–inch
DON 3-5   76

THOMAS, Lillo
Singles: 12–inch 33/45rpm
CAPITOL 4-6   83-85
Singles: 7–inch
CAPITOL 2-4   83-87
LPs: 10/12–inch 33rpm
CAPITOL 5-8   83-85

THOMAS, Lillo, and Melba Moore
Singles: 7–inch
CAPITOL 3-5   84
Also see MOORE, Melba
Also see THOMAS, Lillo

THOMAS, Nolan
Singles: 12–inch 33/45rpm
EMERGENCY 4-6   84-85
Singles: 7–inch
MIRAGE 3-5   84-85

THOMAS, Pat
Singles: 7–inch
MGM 3-5   62-63
VERVE 3-5   62-64
Picture Sleeves
MGM 3-6   62
LPs: 10/12–inch 33rpm
MGM 10-20   62-64
STRAND 10-20   61

THOMAS, Philip-Michael
Singles: 7–inch
ATLANTIC 3-5   85

THOMAS, Ray
Singles: 7–inch
THRESHOLD 3-5   75-76

LPs: 10/12–inch 33rpm
THRESHOLD (Except 102) 8-10   75-76
THRESHOLD (102 "Ray Thomas Discusses
   From Mighty Oaks") 15-25   75
   (Promotional issue only.)
Also see MOODY BLUES

THOMAS, Rufus
(Rufus "Bearcat" Thomas; Rufus Thomas Jr.)
Singles: 12–inch 33/45rpm
A.V.I. 4-8   78
Singles: 78rpm
CHESS 15-25   52
STAR TALENT 20-30   50
SUN (181 "Bear Cat [Answer to
   Hound Dog]") 40-60   53
   (With subtitle.)
SUN (181 "Bear Cat") 30-40   53
   (Without subtitle.)
SUN (188 "Tiger Man") 40-60   53
Singles: 7–inch
A.V.I. 3-5   77-78
ARTISTS of AMERICA 3-5   76
HI 3-5   78
METEOR (5039 "I'm Steady
   Holdin' On") 100-150   56
STAX (100 and 200 series) 4-8   62-68
STAX (0010 through 0236) 3-6   68-75
SUN (181 "Bear Cat [Answer to
   Hound Dog]") 100-150   53
   (With subtitle.)
SUN (181 "Bear Cat") 75-100   53
   (Without subtitle.)
SUN (188 "Tiger Man") 100-150   53
LPs: 10/12–inch 33rpm
A.V.I. 5-10   77-78
ARTISTS of AMERICA 8-10   76
GUSTO 5-10   80
STAX (Except 704) 6-15   70-79
STAX (704 "Walking the Dog") 15-20   63
Also see RUFUS and CARLA

THOMAS, Tasha
Singles: 7–inch
ATLANTIC 3-5   78-79

THOMAS, Timmy
Singles: 12–inch 33/45rpm
GOLD MOUNTAIN 4-6   84
SPECTOR 4-6   83
Singles: 7–inch
GLADES 3-5   72-77
GOLD MOUNTAIN 2-4   84-85
GOLDWAX 4-8   67
MARLIN 3-5   80-81
SPECTOR 2-4   83
TM 3-5   78
LPs: 10/12–inch 33rpm
GLADES 8-10   72-76
GOLD MOUNTAIN 5-8   84

THOMAS, Vaneese
Singles: 7–inch

GEFFEN 2-4   87

THOMPSON, Chris, and Night
Singles: 7–inch

PLANET 3-5   79
Also see MANN, Manfred
Also see NIGHT

THOMPSON, Hank
(Hank Thompson and the Brazos Valley Boys)
Singles: 78rpm

CAPITOL 4-8   47-57
GLOBE (34 "Whoa Sailor") 35-50   46
Singles: 7–inch

ABC 2-5   75-79
ABC/DOT 3-5   74-77
CAPITOL (1000 through 3000 series) . 5-15   50-58
CAPITOL (4000 and 5000 series) 4-8   58-66
CHURCHILL 2-4   83
DOT 3-5   68-74
MCA 2-4   79-80
WARNER 3-6   66-67
Picture Sleeves

CAPITOL 4-8   61
EPs: 7–inch 33/45rpm

CAPITOL 10-20   53-59
LPs: 10/12–inch 33rpm

ABC 5-8   78
ABC/DOT 5-10   74-77
CAPITOL (H-418 "Songs of
the Brazos Valley") 50-75   53
(10–inch LP.)
CAPITOL (T-418 "Songs of
the Brazos Valley") 30-50   55
CAPITOL (H-618 "North of
the Rio Grande") 50-75   53
(10–inch LP.)
CAPITOL (T-618 "North of
the Rio Grande") 30-50   55
CAPITOL (H-729 "New Recordings") . 50-75   53
(10–inch LP.)
CAPITOL (T-729 "New Recordings") . 30-50   55
CAPITOL (T-826 "Hank!") 30-40   57
CAPITOL (T-975 "Dance Ranch") 30-40   58
CAPITOL (T-1111 through T-2154) ... 15-25   59-64
(Monaural.)
CAPITOL (ST-1111 through ST-2154) 15-30   59-64
(Stereo.)
CAPITOL (SM-2000 series) 5-8   75
CAPITOL (T-2274 through T-2800) .. 10-20   65-67
(Monaural.)
CAPITOL (ST-2274 through ST-2826) 10-25   65-67
(Stereo.)
CAPITOL (H-9111 "Favorites") 50-100   50
(10–inch LP.)
CAPITOL (11000 series) 5-8   79
CHURCHILL 5-8   84
DOT 5-15   68-74

GUSTO 5-8   80
PICKWICK/HILLTOP 5-15   67-68
TOWER 8-15   68
WACO 8-10

THOMPSON, Kay
Singles: 78rpm

CADENCE 3-5   56
MGM 3-5   54-55
Singles: 7–inch

CADENCE 4-8   56
MGM 4-8   54-55

THOMPSON, Richard
Singles: 7–inch

HANNIBAL 2-4   83
POLYDOR 2-4   85-86
REPRISE 3-5   72
LPs: 10/12–inch 33rpm

CAPITOL 5-8   88
HANNIBAL 5-8   83
POLYDOR 5-8   85-86
REPRISE 8-10   72
Also see FAIRPORT CONVENTION

THOMPSON, Richard and Linda
Singles: 7–inch

CHRYSALIS 3-5   78
ISLAND 3-5   74-75
LPs: 10/12–inch 33rpm

CHRYSALIS 5-10   78
ISLAND 5-10   74-75
Also see THOMPSON, Richard

THOMPSON, Robbin, Band
Singles: 7–inch

NEMPEROR 3-5   76-77
OVATION 3-5   80
LPs: 10/12–inch 33rpm

NEMPEROR 5-10   76
OVATION 5-10   80
Also see SPRINGSTEEN, Bruce

THOMPSON, Roy
Singles: 7–inch

OKEH 4-8   66-67

THOMPSON, Sonny
Singles: 78rpm

CHART 5-10   56
KING 5-10   50-57
Singles: 7–inch

CHART 10-20   56
KING (4500 through 5300 series) 5-10   52-60
KNIGHT 4-8   61
EPs: 7–inch 33/45rpm

KING 20-40   52-54
LPs: 10/12–inch 33rpm

KING (568 "Moody Blues") 75-100   58
KING (655 "Mellow Blues") 50-75   59
Also see KING, Freddie / Lulu / Sonny Thompson

THOMPSON, Sue
Singles: 78rpm
DECCA	5-10	55
MERCURY	5-10	51-54

Singles: 7–inch
DECCA	10-15	55
GUSTO	2-4	
HICKORY (Except 1100 and 1200 series)	3-6	66-76
HICKORY (1100 and 1200 series)	4-8	61-65
MERCURY	10-20	51-54

Picture Sleeves
HICKORY	5-8	64

LPs: 10/12–inch 33rpm
HICKORY (Except 104 through 121)	8-15	69-74
HICKORY (104 through 121)	15-25	62-65
WING	10-15	66

Also see GIBSON, Don, and Sue Thompson
Also see LUMAN, Bob, and Sue Thompson

THOMPSON TWINS
Singles: 12–inch 33/45rpm
ARISTA	4-6	83-86

Singles: 7–inch
ARISTA	2-4	82-87

Picture Sleeves
ARISTA	3-5	84

LPs: 10/12–inch 33rpm
ARISTA	5-10	82-87

Members: Tom Bailey; Alannah Currie; Joe Leeway; Chris Bell.
Also see GENE LOVES JEZEBEL

THOMSON, Ali
Singles: 7–inch
A&M	3-5	80-81

LPs: 10/12–inch 33rpm
A&M	5-10	80

THORNE, David
(David Throne)
Singles: 7–inch
ADMIRAL	4-8	64-65
CHOICE	5-10	60
RIVERSIDE	4-8	62
SAVOY	5-10	59

THORNTON, Big Mama:
see THORNTON, Willie Mae

THORNTON, Fonzi
Singles: 12–inch 33/45rpm
RCA	4-6	83

Singles: 7–inch
RCA	2-4	83

LPs: 10/12–inch 33rpm
RCA	5-8	83

THORNTON, Willie Mae
(Big Mama Thornton)
Singles: 78rpm
PEACOCK	5-15	52-57

Singles: 7–inch
ABC	3-5	73
ARHOOLIE	4-6	68

BAY TONE	8-12	61
GALAXY	4-8	66
KENT	4-8	65
MERCURY	3-6	69
PEACOCK (Maroon label)	25-35	52
PEACOCK (Red label)	15-25	53-55
PEACOCK (White label)	10-15	56-57
(White label numbers below 1676 are reissues, which Peacock continued carrying in their catalog through the '70s.)		
SOTOPLAY	5-10	65

LPs: 10/12–inch 33rpm
ARHOOLIE	10-15	66-67
BACK BEAT	20-25	70
MERCURY	10-15	69-70
PENTAGRAM	10-12	71
ROULETTE	10-15	70
VANGUARD	8-10	74-75

THOROGOOD, George, and the Destroyers
Singles: 12–inch 33/45rpm
EMI	4-6	83-85

Singles: 7–inch
EMI	2-4	82-86
MCA	3-5	79
ROUNDER	3-5	78-80

LPs: 10/12–inch 33rpm
EMI	5-8	82-91
MCA	5-10	79
ROUNDER	5-10	77-80

THORPE, Billy
Singles: 7–inch
CAPRICORN	3-5	79
POLYDOR	3-5	79
PASHA (Except "Retail Teaser")	2-4	85
PASHA ("Retail Teaser")	4-8	85

LPs: 10/12–inch 33rpm
CAPRICORN	15-20	79
ELEKTRA	5-8	80
PASHA	8-12	82-85
POLYDOR	5-8	79

THREE CHUCKLES
(Featuring Teddy Randazzo)
Singles: 78rpm
BOULEVARD (100 "Runaround")	10-15	53
VIK	4-8	56
X	4-8	54-56

Singles: 7–inch
BOULEVARD (100 "Runaround")	45-55	53
CLOUD	4-6	66
VIK	5-10	56
X	10-15	54-56

EPs: 7–inch 33/45rpm
RCA (192/193/194 "Three Chuckles")	10-20	55
(Price is for any of three volumes.)		
VIK (4 "Three Chuckles")	15-25	57
(Promotional issue only. Not issued with cover.)		

LPs: 10/12–inch 33rpm
VIK (1067 "Three Chuckles") 50-100   55
    Members: Teddy Randazzo; Phil Benti; Tom Romano; Russ
    Gilberto.
    Also see CHUCKLES
    Also see RANDAZZO, Teddy

THREE DEGREES
Singles: 7–inch
ARIOLA AMERICA 3-5   78-80
EPIC 3-5   76
METROMEDIA 4-6   69
NEPTUNE 3-5   70
PHILADELPHIA INT'L 3-5   73-76
ROULETTE 3-5   70-73
SWAN 6-12   64-66
WARNER 4-8   68
LPs: 10/12–inch 33rpm
ARIOLA AMERICA 5-10   78-81
EPIC 8-10   77
PHILADELPHIA INT'L 8-10   74-76
ROULETTE 10-15   70-75
    Also see MFSB

THREE DOG NIGHT
(3 Dog Night)
Singles: 7–inch
ABC 3-5   70-76
DUNHILL (Except 4168) 3-6   69-75
DUNHILL (4168 "Nobody") 5-8   68
PASSPORT 2-4   83
Picture Sleeves
DUNHILL (Except 4168) 2-5   70
DUNHILL (4168 "Nobody") 20-30   68
    (Promotional issue only.)
LPs: 10/12–inch 33rpm
ABC 8-12   75-76
COMMAND 10-15   74-75
DUNHILL (50048 through 50068) ... 10-15   68-69
DUNHILL (50078 "It Ain't Easy") 15-20   70
    (Cover pictures nude people.)
DUNHILL (50078 "It Ain't Easy") 10-12   70
    (Cover doesn't show nudes.)
DUNHILL (50088 through 50158) ... 10-15   70-73
DUNHILL (50168 "Hard Labor") 15-20   74
    (With baby delivery cover.)
DUNHILL (50168 "Hard Labor") 10-12   74
    (With Band-Aid cover.)
DUNHILL (50178 "Joy to the World") .. 8-10   74
MCA 5-8   82
PASSPORT 5-8   83
    Members: Danny Hutton; Cory Wells; Chuck Negron.
    Also see HUTTON, Danny

3 FRIENDS
Singles: 7–inch
CAL-GOLD (169 "Blue Ribbon
    Baby") 50-100   61
IMPERIAL 10-20   61

THREE Gs
Singles: 7–inch
COLUMBIA 5-10   58-61

THREE GRACES / Wailers
EPs: 7–inch 33/45rpm
GOLDEN CREST (88601/2 "Four Songs
    on 45 rpm") 75-125   60
    (Issued with paper sleeve-mailer. Both sides have
    label pictures.)
    Also see WAILERS

THREE MAN ISLAND
Singles: 7–inch
CHRYSALIS 5-8   88

THREE MILLION
Singles: 12–inch 33/45rpm
COTILLION 4-6   84-84
Singles: 7–inch
COTILLION 3-5   83-84

3 OUNCES of LOVE
Singles: 7–inch
MOTOWN 3-5   78
LPs: 10/12–inch 33rpm
MOTOWN 5-10   78

THREE PLAYMATES
Singles: 7–inch
SAVOY 8-12   58
    Also see PLAYMATES

THREE SUNS
Singles: 78rpm
RCA 2-5   50-57
Singles: 7–inch
RCA 4-8   50-64
EPs: 7–inch 33/45rpm
RCA 5-10   50-61
ROYALE 5-10
VARSITY 5-10   52
LPs: 10/12–inch 33rpm
CAMDEN 5-15   60-64
MUSICOR 5-10   66
RCA 5-20   50-76
RONDO 5-15   59
ROYALE 10-15
VARSITY 10-20   50-52
    Members: Al Nevins; Marty Nevins; Art Dunn.

THRILLS
Singles: 7–inch
G&P 3-5   80-81
LPs: 10/12–inch 33rpm
G&P 5-10   80-81

THUNDER, Johnny
Singles: 7–inch
ABC 3-5   74
CALLA 4-6   69
DIAMOND 4-8   62-68
EPIC 5-10   59
U.A. 3-5   70

Picture Sleeves

DIAMOND 8-12		63

LPs: 10/12–inch 33rpm

DIAMOND (D-5001 "Loop De Loop") . 25-35		63
(Monaural.)		
DIAMOND (SD-5001 "Loop De Loop") 35-45		63
(Stereo.)		
REAL RECORDS 10-15		
Also see ARCHIES / Johnny Thunder		

THUNDER, Johnny, and Ruby Winters
Singles: 7–inch

DIAMOND 4-8	67-68	
Also see THUNDER, Johnny		
Also see WINTERS, Ruby		

THUNDER, Margo
Singles: 7–inch

HAVEN 3-5		74

THUNDERCLAP NEWMAN:
see NEWMAN, Thunderclap

THUNDERFLASH
Singles: 7–inch

JAMPOWER 3-5		83

THUNDERKLOUD, Billy, and the Chieftones
Singles: 7–inch

POLYDOR 3-5	76-77	
20TH FOX 3-5	74-75	

LPs: 10/12–inch 33rpm

SUPERIOR 8-12		74
20TH FOX 6-12	74-75	

THURSTON, Bobby
Singles: 7–inch

PRELUDE 3-5		80

TIA
Singles: 7–inch

RCA 2-4		87

TIC TOC
Singles: 12–inch 33/45rpm

RCA 4-6		84

Singles: 7–inch

RCA 2-4		84

LPs: 10/12–inch 33rpm

RCA 5-8		84

TICO and the Triumphs
(Featuring Paul Simon)
Singles: 7–inch

AMY (835 "Motorcycle") 15-25		62
AMY (845 "Wild Flower") 15-25		62
AMY (860 "Cry Little Boy") 15-25		62
AMY (876 "Cards of Love") 30-40		62
MADISON (169 "Motorcycle") 20-30		61
Also see SIMON, Paul		

TIERRA
Singles: 7–inch

ASI 3-5		80
BOARDWALK 3-5	80-82	

SALSOUL 3-5		81
MCA 3-5		79
TODY 3-5		

LPs: 10/12–inch 33rpm

ASI 5-10		80
BOARDWALK 5-10		80
SALSOUL 5-10		81
Members: Salas Brothers.		
Also see EL CHICANO		

TIFFANY
Singles: 7–inch

MCA 2-4	87-88	

LPs: 10/12–inch 33rpm

MCA 5-8	87-88	

TIGGI CLAY
Singles: 7–inch

MOROCCO 2-4		84

LPs: 10/12–inch 33rpm

MOROCCO 5-8		84

TIGHT FIT
Singles: 12–inch 33/45rpm

ARISTA 4-6		81
JIVE 4-6		81

Singles: 7–inch

ARISTA 3-5		81
JIVE 3-5		81

TIJUANA BRASS: see ALPERT, Herb

TIL, Sonny
(Sonny Til and the Orioles)
Singles: 7–inch

JUBILEE (5363 "At Night") 8-12		59
JUBILEE (5383 "Come on Home") ... 8-12		60
JUBILEE (5394 "Night and Day") 40-60		60
JUBILEE (6001 "Crying in the Chapel") 8-12		59
RCA 4-6	69-72	
ROULETTE 5-10		58

LPs: 10/12–inch 33rpm

DOBRE 5-10		78
RCA 10-15	70-71	
Also see McGRIFF, Edna, and Sonny Til		
Also see ORIOLES		

'TIL TUESDAY
Singles: 7–inch

EPIC 2-4	85-88	

LPs: 10/12–inch 33rpm

EPIC 5-8	85-88	
Members: Aimee Mann; Michael Hausman; Robert Holmes;		
Joey Pesce.		

TILLMAN, Bertha
Singles: 7–inch

BRENT (7029 "Oh My Angel") 15-20		62
BRENT (7032 "I Wish") 20-30		62

TILLOTSON, Johnny
Singles: 7–inch

AMOS 3-5	69-70	
BARNABY 3-5		76

BUDDAH 3-5   71-73
CADENCE (1300 series) 5-10   58-61
CADENCE (1400 series) 4-8   61-63
COLUMBIA 3-5   73-75
ERIC........................... 2-4
MGM 4-8   63-68
REWARD 2-4   82-84
U.A. 3-5   76-77
Picture Sleeves
CADENCE 10-15   60
MGM 5-8   63-66
EPs: 7–inch 33/45rpm
CADENCE (114 "Dreamy Eyes") 25-35   60
CADENCE (33-1 "This Is
Johnny Tillotson") 15-25   61
CADENCE (33-2 "Music by
Johnny Tillotson") 15-25   61
LPs: 10/12–inch 33rpm
ACCORD 5-10   82
AMOS 10-15   69
BARNABY 8-10   77
BUDDAH 10-15   72
CADENCE 25-40   61-63
EVEREST 5-8   82
METRO 10-15   66
MGM 12-20   64-71
ROWE/AMI.................... 5-8   66
("Play Me" Sales Stimulator promotional issue.)
U.A. 8-10   77
Also see IVAN / Johnny Tillotson

TILLOTSON, Johnny / J.D. Souther
Singles: 7–inch
BUDDAH 3-5   71
Also see SOUTHER, J.D.
Also see TILLOTSON, Johnny

TIM TAM and the Turn-Ons
Singles: 7–inch
PALMER (5002 "Wait a Minute") 8-12   66
PALMER (5003 "Cheryl Ann") 15-20   66
PALMER (5006 "Kimberly") 20-25   66
PALMER (5014 "Don't Say Hi") 5-10   67

TIMBUK 3
Singles: 7–inch
I.R.S. 2-4   86-88
LPs: 10/12–inch 33rpm
I.R.S. 5-8   86-88

TIME
Singles: 12–inch 33/45rpm
WARNER 4-6   82-84
Singles: 7–inch
WARNER 3-5   81-84
LPs: 10/12–inch 33rpm
PAISLEY PARK 5-8   90
WARNER 5-8   81-84
Members: Morris Day; Jesse Johnson; Jimmy Jam; Monte Moir;
Jellybean Johnson; Stacy Adams; Terry Lewis.
Also see DAY, Morris
Also see JOHNSON, Jesse

Also see VANITY 6

TIME BANDITS
Singles: 12–inch 33/45rpm
COLUMBIA 4-6   85

TIME ZONE
Singles: 12–inch 33/45rpm
CELLULOID 4-6   84

TIMELORDS
Singles: 7–inch
TVT 2-4   88

TIMES TWO
LPs: 10/12–inch 33rpm
REPRISE 5-8   88

TIMETONES
Singles: 7–inch
ATCO (6201 "I've Got a Feeling") ... 15-25   61
TIMES SQUARE (26 "Sunday Kind
of Love") 15-20   64
TIMES SQUARE (34 "House Where
Lovers Dream") 30-40   64
TIMES SQUARE (421 "Here in
My Heart") 20-30   61
TIMES SQUARE (421 "In My Heart") . 8-10   61
(Note shortened title.)
Member: Slim Rose.

TIMEX SOCIAL CLUB
Singles: 12–inch 33/45rpm
DANYA......................... 4-6   86
JAY 4-6   86
Singles: 7–inch
DANYA......................... 2-4   86-87
JAY 2-4   86

TIN TIN
Singles: 12–inch 33/45rpm
SIRE 4-6   81-83
Singles: 7–inch
ATCO 3-5   71
LPs: 10/12–inch 33rpm
ATCO 10-15   70-71
Members: Steve Kipner; Steve Groves.

TINA B.
Singles: 12–inch 33/45rpm
ATLANTIC 4-8   82
ELEKTRA 4-6   83
Singles: 7–inch
ATLANTIC 3-5   82
ELEKTRA 2-4   83
LPs: 10/12–inch 33rpm
ATLANTIC 5-10   82
ELEKTRA 5-8   83

TINDLEY, George
(George Tindley and the Modern Red Caps; George
Tinley)
Singles: 7–inch
EMBER 5-10   60

TOKENS

Singles: 78rpm
MELBA (104 "While I Dream") 10-15   56

Singles: 7-inch
ABC 3-5   73
ATCO 3-5   74
B.T. PUPPY 4-8   64-69
BELL 3-5   72
BUDDAH 4-6   69-70
LAURIE 10-15   63
MELBA (104 "While I Dream") 25-35   56
RCA (37-7000 and 37-8000 series) .. 15-25   61-62
  (Compact 33 Singles.)
RCA (47-7000 and 47-8000 series) ... 6-12   61-65
WARNER 4-8   67-69
WARWICK 10-15   61

Picture Sleeves
B.T. PUPPY 8-12   66
RCA 10-15   61-63
WARNER 3-6   67

LPs: 10/12-inch 33rpm
B.T. PUPPY 15-20   66-78
BUDDAH 15-20   70
RCA 20-30   61-66
WARNER 20-25   67
  Members: Jay Siegal; Mitchell Margo; Philip Margo; Henry Medress.
  Also see CHRISTIE, Lou / Len Barry and the Dovells / Bobby Rydell / Tokens
  Also see SEDAKA, Neil

TOKENS / Happenings

LPs: 10/12-inch 33rpm
B.T. PUPPY 15-25   67
  Also see HAPPENINGS
  Also see TOKENS

TOLBERT, Israel "Popper Stopper"

Singles: 7-inch
WARREN 3-5   70-71

LPs: 10/12-inch 33rpm
WARREN 8-12   71

TOM & JERRIO

Singles: 7-inch
ABC-PAR 4-8   65
  Members: Eddie Thomas; Jerry Murray.

TOM & JERRY

Singles: 78rpm
BIG 10-15   58

Singles: 7-inch
ABC-PAR (10363 "Surrender,
  Please Surrender") 15-25   62
ABC-PAR (10788 "This Is My Story") . 10-15   66
BIG (613 "Hey, Schoolgirl") 15-25   57
BIG (616 "Two Teenagers") 20-30   58
BIG (618 "Don't Say Goodbye") 20-30   58
BIG (621 "Baby Talk") 40-60   58
EMBER (1094 "I'm Lonesome") 25-35   59
HUNT (319 "Don't Say Goodbye") ... 20-25   58
KING (5167 "Hey, Schoolgirl") 35-45   58
  Members: Paul Simon; Art Garfunkel.

Also see SIMON & GARFUNKEL

TOM & JERRY / Ronnie Lawrence

Singles: 7-inch
BELL (120 "Baby Talk") 20-30   71
  Also see TOM & JERRY

TOM TOM CLUB

Singles: 12-inch 33/45rpm
SIRE 4-8   81-83

Singles: 7-inch
SIRE 3-5   81-89

LPs: 10/12-inch 33rpm
SIRE 5-10   81-89
  Also see TALKING HEADS

TOMLIN, Lily

Singles: 7-inch
POLYDOR 3-5   73-75

LPs: 10/12-inch 33rpm
ARISTA 5-8   77
POLYDOR 5-10   71-75

TOMLINSON, Michael

Singles: 7-inch
CYPRESS 2-4   88

TOMMY TUTONE

Singles: 7-inch
COLUMBIA 3-5   80-83

LPs: 10/12-inch 33rpm
COLUMBIA (Except 1461) 5-10   80-83
COLUMBIA (1461 "Alive and Almost
  Dangerous") 10-15   82
  (Promotional issue only.)

TOMORROW'S EDITION

Singles: 7-inch
ATLANTIC 3-5   82
GANG 3-5   75

TOMORROW'S PROMISE

Singles: 7-inch
CAPITOL 3-5   73-74
MERCURY 3-5   75

TOMPALL and the Glaser Brothers
(Tompall and the Glasers; Tompall Glaser)

Singles: 7-inch
DECCA 4-8   59-65
ELEKTRA 2-5   80-81
MGM 3-6   66-71
RICH 8-12   61
ROBBINS 10-20   57

LPs: 10/12-inch 33rpm
ABC 8-10   77
DECCA (DL-4041 "This Land") 35-45   60
  (Monaural.)
DECCA (DL7-4041 "This Land") 40-50   60
  (Stereo.)
ELEKTRA 5-10   81
MGM 8-15   67-75
U.A. 25-35   66
VOCALION 8-12   67

TOMS, Gary
(Gary Toms' Empire)
Singles: 12–inch 33/45rpm

MCA	4-8	77

Singles: 7–inch

MCA	3-5	77
MERCURY	3-5	78
P.I.P.	3-5	75-76

LPs: 10/12–inch 33rpm

MCA	5-10	77
MERCURY	5-10	78
P.I.P.	5-10	75

TONE LOC
LPs: 10/12–inch 33rpm

DELICIOUS	5-8	89

TONES
Singles: 7–inch

CRIMINAL	3-5	83

TONEY, Oscar, Jr.
Singles: 7–inch

BELL	4-8	67-69
CAPRICORN	3-5	
KING	4-8	64

LPs: 10/12–inch 33rpm

BELL	10-20	67

TONEY LEE: see LEE, Toney

TONY & CAROL
Singles: 7–inch

ROULETTE	3-5	72

TONY & JOE
Singles: 7–inch

DORE	4-8	61-62
ERA	5-10	58
FLYTE	5-10	59
GARDENA	5-10	60

Members: Tony Savonne; Joe Saraceno.
Also see BEACH BOYS / Tony & Joe

TONY, BOB & JIMMY
Singles: 7–inch

CAPITOL	4-8	62

Members: Tony Butala; Bob Engemann; Jim Pike.
Also see LETTERMEN

TONY! TONI! TONE!
Singles: 7–inch

WING	2-4	88-90

TOO SHORT
LPs: 10/12–inch 33rpm

DANGEROUS	5-8	89
JIVE	5-8	90

TOOTS and the Maytals
Singles: 12–inch 33/45rpm

MANGO	4-6	82

Singles: 7–inch

MANGO	2-5	76-82

LPs: 10/12–inch 33rpm

ISLAND	5-8	75
MANGO	5-10	76-82

Members: Toots Hibbert; Nathaniel Mathias; Releigh Gordon;
Paul Douglas; Jackie Jackson; Winston Wright.
Also see WINWOOD, Steve

TOP SHELF
Singles: 7–inch

LO LO	4-6	69-70
SOUND TOWN	3-5	80

TORCH
Singles: 12–inch 33/45rpm

PACIFIC	4-6	83

TORCHSONG
Singles: 12–inch 33/45rpm

I.R.S.	4-6	83-84

Singles: 7–inch

I.R.S.	2-4	83-84

LPs: 10/12–inch 33rpm

I.R.S.	5-8	83

TORME, Mel
(Mel Torme and the Meltones)
Singles: 78rpm

BETHLEHEM	3-6	56-57
CAPITOL (1000 and 2000 series)	4-8	50-53

Singles: 7–inch

ATLANTIC	4-6	62-64
BETHLEHEM	5-10	56-58
CAPITOL (1000 and 2000 series)	5-10	50-53
(Purple labels.)		
CAPITOL (2000 series)	3-6	69-70
(Orange labels.)		
COLUMBIA	3-6	64-67
CORAL	5-10	53-56
LIBERTY	3-6	68
VERVE	4-8	59-61

EPs: 7–inch 33/45rpm

CAPITOL	5-15	50
P.R.I. (9 "The Touch of Your Lips")	5-10	

LPs: 10/12–inch 33rpm

ATLANTIC (8000 series)	12-25	62-64
ATLANTIC (18000 series)	5-10	75
ATLANTIC (80000 series)	5-8	83
BETHLEHEM (34 "It's a Blue World")	25-50	55
BETHLEHEM (52 "Mel Torme")	25-50	56
BETHLEHEM (4000 series)	10-20	65
BETHLEHEM (6000 series)	20-40	58-60
(Maroon labels.)		
BETHLEHEM (6000 series)	5-10	77-78
(Gray labels.)		
CAPITOL (200 "California Suite")	25-50	50
(10–inch LP.)		
CAPITOL (300 and 400 series)	8-12	69-70
COLUMBIA (2000 series)	10-20	64-66
(Monaural.)		
COLUMBIA (9000 series)	10-20	64-66
(Stereo.)		

CONCORD JAZZ 5-8   82
CORAL (57012 "At the Crescendo") . 40-60   54
CORAL (57044 "Musical Sounds") . . . 40-60   54
EVEREST 5-10   76
GLENDALE 5-8   78-79
GRYPHON 5-8   79
LIBERTY 8-15   68
MGM (552 "Songs By Mel Torme") . . 50-75   52
  (10-inch LP.)
MAYFAIR 25-35   58
METRO 10-20   65
MUSICRAFT 5-8   83
STRAND 12-25   60
VERVE 20-35   58-60
  (Reads "Verve Records, Inc." at bottom of label.)
VERVE 10-20   61-72
  (Reads "MGM Records - A Division of
  Metro-Goldwyn-Mayer, Inc." at bottom of label.)
VERVE 5-10   73-84
  (Reads "Manufactured By MGM Record Corp.," or
  mentions either Polydor or Polygram at bottom of
  label.)
VOCALION 5-10   70
  Also see CROSBY, Bing, and Mel Torme
  Also see LEE, Peggy, and Mel Torme
  Also see RICH, Buddy
  Also see WHITING, Margaret

TORNADER
Singles: 7-inch
POLYDOR 3-5   77

TORNADOES
Singles: 7-inch
LONDON 4-8   62-63
TOWER 4-8   65
LPs: 10/12-inch 33rpm
LONDON 25-35   62-63
  Members: Heinz Burt; Alan Caddy; Clem Cattini; George
  Bellamy.

TOROK, Mitchell
**(Mitchell Torok and the Louisiana Hayride Band;
Mitchell Torok and the Matches)**
Singles: 78rpm
ABBOTT 5-10   53-54
DECCA 5-10   57-59
Singles: 7-inch
ABBOTT 5-15   53-54
CAPITOL 4-8   62-63
DECCA 5-10   57-59
GUYDEN 5-10   59-60
INETTE 4-8   63
MERCURY 4-8   61
RCA 4-8   65
REPRISE 4-6   66-67
Picture Sleeves
GUYDEN 10-20   59-60
LPs: 10/12-inch 33rpm
GUYDEN (502 "Caribbean") 25-35   60
  (Monaural.)

GUYDEN (ST-502 "Caribbean") 35-50   60
  (Stereo.)
REPRISE 10-15   66

TORONTO
Singles: 7-inch
NETWORK 3-5   82
SOLID GOLD 3-5
LPs: 10/12-inch 33rpm
A&M 5-10   80-81
NETWORK 5-10   82
SOLID GOLD 5-10

TORRANCE, George
**(George Torrance and the Naturals; Georgie Torrance
and the Dippers)**
Singles: 7-inch
DUO DISC 4-8   66
EPIC 5-10   61
KING 5-10   60
SHOUT 4-6   68

TORRANCE, Richard
(Richard Torrance and Eureka)
Singles: 7-inch
CAPITOL 3-5   77-79
SHELTER 3-5   75
LPs: 10/12-inch 33rpm
CAPITOL 5-10   77
SHELTER 5-10   74-75

TOSH, Peter
Singles: 12-inch 33/45rpm
EMI AMERICA 4-6   83
Singles: 7-inch
COLUMBIA 3-5   76-77
EMI AMERICA 3-5   81-84
ROLLING STONES 3-5   78-79
Picture Sleeves
ROLLINS STONES 3-6   78
EPs: 7-inch 33/45rpm
COLUMBIA 4-8   76
  (Promotional only.)
LPs: 10/12-inch 33rpm
COLUMBIA 5-10   76-77
EMI AMERICA 5-8   81-84
ROLLING STONES 5-10   79

TOSH, Peter, and Mick Jagger
Singles: 7-inch
ROLLING STONES (19308 "Don't
  Look Back") 4-6   78
  (With "Rolling Stones" at top of label.)
ROLLING STONES (19308 "Don't
  Look Back") 3-5   78
  (Without "Rolling Stones" at top of label.)
Promotional Singles
ROLLING STONES (130 "Don't
  Look Back") 10-20   78
ROLLING STONES (7500 "Don't
  Look Back") 5-10   78

LPs: 10/12–Inch 33rpm
ROLLING STONES 5-10   78
  Also see JAGGER, Mick
  Also see MARLEY, Bob, and the Wailers

TOTAL COELO
Singles: 12–Inch 33/45rpm
CHRYSALIS 4-6   83
Singles: 7–Inch
CHRYSALIS 2-4   83
Picture Sleeves
CHRYSALIS 3-5   83

TOTAL CONTRAST
Singles: 12–Inch 33/45rpm
LONDON 4-6   85-86
Singles: 7–Inch
LONDON 2-4   85-88
LPs: 10/12–Inch 33rpm
LONDON 5-8   86

TOTO
Singles: 12–Inch 33/45rpm
COLUMBIA 4-8   79-85
Singles: 7–Inch
COLUMBIA 2-5   78-86
Promotional Singles
COLUMBIA (ZSS-165008 "Hold
  the Line") 10-20   78
  (Licorice Pizza picture disc.)
COLUMBIA (ZSS-165008 "Hold
  the Line") 20-30   78
  (KRBE picture disc.)
COLUMBIA (ZSS-165008 "Hold
  the Line") 20-30   78
  (Roxy Invitation picture disc.)
LPs: 10/12–Inch 33rpm
COLUMBIA (9C9-39911 "Isolation") ... 8-12   84
  (Picture disc.)
COLUMBIA (PJC-35317 "Toto") 20-30   79
  (Picture disc.)
COLUMBIA (37928 "Toto IV") 20-30   82
  (Picture disc. Promotional issue only.)
COLUMBIA (PD-36813 "Turn Back") . 20-30   79
  (Picture disc. Promotional issue only.)
COLUMBIA (30000 series
  except picture discs) 5-10   78-86
COLUMBIA (47728 "Toto IV") 10-15   83
  (Half-speed mastered.)
POLYDOR 5-8   84
  Members: Steve Porcaro; David Paich; Steve Lukather; David
  Hungate; Jeffrey Porcaro; Bobby Kimball.
  Also see VOICES of AMERICA / U.S.A. for Africa

TOUCH
Singles: 7–Inch
ATCO 3-5   80-81
BRUNSWICK 3-5   77
COLISEUM ..../........ 4-6   69
LECASVER 5-8   69
PUBLIC (103 "No Shame") 5-10

LPs: 10/12–Inch 33rpm
ATCO 5-10   80
COLISEUM 15-20   68
  Member: Don Gallucci.
  Also see DON and the Goodtimes

TOUCH
Singles: 7–Inch
SUPERTRONICS 2-4   87

TOUCH of CLASS
Singles: 12–Inch 33/45rpm
NEXT PLATINUM 4-6   84
Singles: 7–Inch
ATLANTIC 3-5   82
MIDLAND INT'L 3-5   75-77
ROADSHOW 3-5   79-84
LPs: 10/12–Inch 33rpm
MIDLAND INT'L 5-10   76
ROADSHOW 5-10   79

TOURISTS
Singles: 7–Inch
EPIC 3-5   80
LPs: 10/12–Inch 33rpm
EPIC 5-10   81
  Members: Annie Lennox; David Stewart; Ed Chin; Pete
  Coombes; Jim Toomey.
  Also see EURYTHMICS

TOWER of POWER
Singles: 7–Inch
COLUMBIA 3-5   76-78
SAN FRANCISCO 4-8   64-73
WARNER 3-5   72-75
LPs: 10/12–Inch 33rpm
COLUMBIA 5-10   76-79
SAN FRANCISCO 10-15   71
WARNER 8-10   72-76
  Also see LITTLE FEAT
  Also see WILLIAMS, Lenny

TOWNES, Carol Lynn
Singles: 12–Inch 33/45rpm
POLYDOR 4-6   84-85
Singles: 7–Inch
POLYDOR 2-4   84-85
LPs: 10/12–Inch 33rpm
POLYDOR 5-8   84

TOWNS, Eddie
(ET)
Singles: 12–Inch 33/45rpm
TOTAL EXPERIENCE 4-6   86
Singles: 7–Inch
TOTAL EXPERIENCE 2-4   86
LPs: 10/12–Inch 33rpm
TOTAL EXPERIENCE 5-8   86

TOWNSEND, Ed
Singles: 7–Inch
CAPITOL 5-8   58-59
CHALLENGE 4-8   61-62
DYNASTY 4-8   60

TRAMMPS

Singles: 7–inch

ATLANTIC	3-5	75-80
BUDDAH	3-5	72-76
ERIC	3-5	78
GOLDEN FLEECE	3-5	73-75
VENTURE	3-5	83

Picture Sleeves

ATLANTIC	3-5	77

LPs: 10/12–inch 33rpm

ATLANTIC	5-10	76-80
BUDDAH	5-10	75
GOLDEN FLEECE	5-10	75
PHILADELPHIA INT'L	5-10	77

Also see MFSB

TRANSVISION VAMP

LPs: 10/12–inch 33rpm

UNI	5-8	88

TRANS-X

Singles: 12–inch 33/45rpm

ATCO	4-6	86
MIRAGE	4-6	86

Singles: 7–inch

ATCO	2-4	86

TRAPEZE

Singles: 7–inch

PAID	3-5	81
THRESHOLD	3-5	72
WARNER	3-5	74-75

LPs: 10/12–inch 33rpm

PAID	5-10	81
POLYDOR ("Medusa")	40-60	71
(Number not known.)		
SHARK	8-10	
THRESHOLD (2 "Trapeze")	25-50	71
THRESHOLD (4 "Medusa")	75-100	71
THRESHOLD (11 "Final Swing")	25-50	71
WARNER	8-10	74-75

Also see DEEP PURPLE

TRASHMEN

Singles: 7–inch

ARGO	10-15	66
BEAR	10-20	66
ERA	3-5	72
ERIC	2-4	
GARRETT	10-20	63-64
LANA	3-5	
METROBEAT	10-15	68
TRIBE	10-15	66

Picture Sleeves

GARRETT (4012 "Whoa Dad")	15-25	64
GARRETT (4013 "Real Live Doll") ...	20-30	64

LPs: 10/12–inch 33rpm

GARRETT (GA-200 "Surfin' Bird") ...	50-75	64
(Monaural.)		
GARRETT (GAS-200 "Surfin' Bird")	100-150	64
(Stereo.)		

Members: Tony Andreason; Bob Reed; Dal Winslow; Steve Wahrer.

TRASHMEN / Castaways

Singles: 7–inch

SOMA	4-6	

Also see TRASHMEN

TRAVELING WILBURYS

Singles: 7–inch

WILBURY	2-5	88-89

Picture Sleeves

WILBURY	3-6	88-89

LPs: 10/12–inch 33rpm

WILBURY	8-10	88-90

Members: George Harrison; Bob Dylan; Roy Orbison; Tom Petty; Jeff Lynne.
Also see DYLAN, Bob
Also see HARRISON, George
Also see LYNNE, Jeff
Also see ORBISON, Roy
Also see PETTY, Tom, and the Heartbreakers

TRAVERS, Mary

Singles: 7–inch

CHRYSALIS	3-5	78-79
WARNER	3-5	71-73

LPs: 10/12–inch 33rpm

CHRYSALIS	5-10	78
WARNER	6-12	71-74

Also see DENVER, John
Also see PETER, PAUL & MARY

TRAVERS, Pat
(Pat Travers Band; Pat Travers' Black Pearl)

Singles: 7–inch

POLYDOR	3-5	77-80

LPs: 10/12–inch 33rpm

POLYDOR	5-10	76-84

TRAVIS, McKinley

Singles: 7–inch

PRIDE	3-5	70

TRAVIS, Randy
(Randy Traywick)

Singles: 7–inch

WARNER	2-4	85-91

LPs: 10/12–inch 33rpm

WARNER	5-8	85-91

Also see TRAYWICK, Randy

SANDY
RECORD COMPANY   Mobile, Ala.
Box 248

1033 - MS
Time 2:05
Burnt Oak
Pub. Co.- BMI

45 - RPM
Vocal

TELL HIM NO
(T. Pritchett)

TRAVIS & BOB
1017

TRAVIS & BOB
Singles: 7-inch
BIG TOP 4-8   60
MERCURY 4-8   61
SANDY (1017 "Tell Him No") 8-15   59
(No "Distributed By Dot" on label.)
SANDY (1017 "Tell Him No" 5-8   59
(Has "Distributed By Dot" on label)
SANDY (1019 through 1029) 5-10   59
Members: Travis Pritchett; Bob Weaver.

TRAVOLTA, Joey
Singles: 7-inch
CASABLANCA 3-5   78-79
MILLENIUM 3-5   78
Picture Sleeves
MILLENNIUM 3-5   78
LPs: 10/12-inch 33rpm
CASABLANCA 5-10   78-79
MILLENNIUM 5-10   78

TRAVOLTA, John
Singles: 7-inch
MIDLAND INT'L 3-5   76-80
RCA 3-5   77
RSO 3-5   78-79
Picture Sleeves
MIDLAND INT'L (Except 10623) 3-5   76-80
MIDLAND INT'L (10623 "Let Her In") . . . 4-8   76
RCA 3-5   77
RSO 3-5   78-79
LPs: 10/12-inch 33rpm
MIDLAND INT'L 5-10   76-77
MIDSONG INT'L 5-10   78
Also see NEWTON-JOHN, Olivia, and John Travolta

TRAVOLTA, John / Sha Na Na
Singles: 7-inch
RSO 3-5   78
Also see SHA NA NA
Also see TRAVOLTA, John

TRAYWICK, Randy
Singles: 7-inch
PAULA 3-6   78
Also see TRAVIS, Randy

TREASURES
Singles: 7-inch
EPIC 3-5   77
MERCURY 3-5   76
LPs: 10/12-inch 33rpm
EPIC 5-10   77

TREAT HER RIGHT
LPs: 10/12-inch 33rpm
RCA 5-8   88

TREE SWINGERS
Singles: 7-inch
GUYDEN 8-12   60

TREMELOES
Singles: 7-inch
DJM 3-5   74-75
EPIC 4-8   66-70
Picture Sleeves
EPIC 4-8   67
LPs: 10/12-inch 33rpm
DJM 8-10   74
EPIC 15-25   67-68
Also see POOLE, Brian

TRIBE
Singles: 7-inch
ABC 3-5   73-74
C&CT 3-5   71
LPs: 10/12-inch 33rpm
ABC 5-10   73-74
FARR 5-10   77
PICKWICK 10-15   75

TRINERE
Singles: 7-inch
JAMPACKED 2-4   85-87
LPs: 10/12-inch 33rpm
JAMPACKED 5-8   86

TRINERE / Freestyle / Debbie Deb
LPs: 10/12-inch 33rpm
PANDISC 5-8   89
Also see DEBBIE DEB
Also see FREESTYLE
Also see TRINERE

TRIO+ :
see LEWIS, Jerry Lee, Carl Perkins & Charlie Rich

TRIPLE "S" CONNECTION
Singles: 12-inch 33/45rpm
20TH FOX 4-6   79-80
Singles: 7-inch
20TH FOX 3-5   79-80
LPs: 10/12-inch 33rpm
20TH FOX 5-10   79
Also see SKOOL BOYZ

TRIUMPH
Singles: 7-inch
MCA (Black vinyl) 2-4   85-86
MCA (Colored vinyl) 3-5   85-86
RCA 2-5   78-84
LPs: 10/12-inch 33rpm
MCA 5-8   85-87
RCA 5-10   78-84
Members: Mike Levine; Gil Moore; Rik Emmett.

TRIUMVIRAT
Singles: 7-inch
CAPITOL 3-5   79
LPs: 10/12-inch 33rpm
CAPITOL 5-10   74-80
HARVEST 10-12   74

TRIXXX
Singles: 12–inch 33/45rpm
COTILLION 4-6   86
Singles: 7–inch
COTILLION 2-4   86

TROGGS
Singles: 7–inch
ATCO 5-10   66-67
BELL 3-5   73
FONTANA 4-8   66-69
PAGE ONE 3-6   69-70
PRIVATE STOCK 3-5   77
PYE 3-5   75-76
LPs: 10/12–inch 33rpm
ATCO (33-193 "Wild Thing") 35-45   66
  (Monaural.)
ATCO (SD-33-193 "Wild Thing") 25-35   66
  (Stereo.)
FONTANA 20-30   66-68
LIBERTY 20-30   66
MKC 8-10   80
PRIVATE STOCK 10-15   76
PYE 10-15   75
SIRE 10-15   76

TROLLS
Singles: 7–inch
ABC 4-8   66-67
RUFF 5-10   66
WARRIOR 4-8
LPs: 10/12–inch 33rpm
SMASH 10-15   69

TROLLS
Singles: 7–inch
U.S.A. 10-15   68

TROOP
Singles: 7–inch
ATLANTIC 2-4   88-90
LPs: 10/12–inch 33rpm
ATLANTIC 5-8   88-90

TROOPER
Singles: 7–inch
LEGEND 3-5   75-77
MCA 3-5   77-78
LPs: 10/12–inch 33rpm
LEGEND 8-10   75-76
MCA 5-10   78-80
RCA 5-8   82

TROPEA
Singles: 7–inch
MARLIN 3-5   76-77
LPs: 10/12–inch 33rpm
MARLIN 8-10   76-77

TROUBADOURS DU ROI BAUDOUIN
LPs: 10/12-inch 33rpm
PHILIPS 5-10   63-69

TROUBLE
Singles: 7–inch
AL and the KIDD 3-5   80
U.A. 3-5   77
LPs: 10/12–inch 33rpm
U.A. 8-10   77

TROUBLE FUNK
Singles: 12–inch 33/45rpm
ISLAND 4-6   85-86
SUGAR HILL 4-6   82
Singles: 7–inch
D.E.T.T. 2-4   83
ISLAND 2-4   85-86
LPs: 10/12–inch 33rpm
ISLAND 5-8   86
SUGAR HILL 5-8   82

TROUTMAN, Tony
Singles: 7–inch
GRAM-O-PHONE 3-5   75
T. MAIN 2-4   82-83

TROWER, Robin
Singles: 7–inch
CHRYSALIS 3-5   72-78
LPs: 10/12–inch 33rpm
ATLANTIC 5-8   88
CHRYSALIS 5-12   73-82
GNP/CRESCENDO 5-8   83-86
  Also see BRUCE, Jack, and Robin Trower
  Also see PROCOL HARUM

TROY, Benny
(Benny Troy and Maze)
Singles: 7–inch
DE-LITE 3-5   75
20TH FOX 3-5

TROY, Doris
Singles: 7–inch
APPLE 4-6   70
ATLANTIC 4-8   63-65
CALLA 4-8   66
CAPITOL 4-8   67
MIDLAND INT'L 3-5   76
LPs: 10/12–inch 33rpm
APPLE 15-20   70
ATLANTIC 20-25   64

TROYER, Eric
Singles: 7–inch
CHRYSALIS 3-5   80
LPs: 10/12–inch 33rpm
CHRYSALIS 5-10   80

TRUE, Andrea
(Andrea True Connection)
Singles: 7–inch
BUDDAH 3-5   76-78
ERIC 3-5   78
LPs: 10/12–inch 33rpm
BUDDAH 5-10   76-78

TRUE LOVE
Singles: 7–inch
CRITIQUE 2-4   87

TRUMPETEERS
Singles: 7–inch
SPLASH 4-8   59
Member: Billy Mure.
Also see MURE, Billy

TRUSSELL
Singles: 7–inch
ELEKTRA 3-5   80
LPs: 10/12–inch 33rpm
ELEKTRA 5-10   80

TRUTH
Singles: 7–inch
DEVAKI 3-5   80-81
ROULETTE 3-5   74-75
LPs: 10/12–inch 33rpm
PARAGON 5-10   78
ROULETTE 5-10   75

TRYTHALL, Gil
Singles: 7–inch
ATHENA 3-6   69-70
LPs: 10/12–inch 33rpm
ATHENA 5-10   69-70
PANDORA 5-8   81

TUBES
Singles: 12–inch 33/45rpm
CAPITOL 4-6   83
Singles: 7–inch
A&M 3-5   75-79
CAPITOL 2-4   81-85
Picture Sleeves
CAPITOL 3-5   81
LPs: 10/12–inch 33rpm
A&M 5-10   75-81
CAPITOL 5-8   81-85
Members: Fee Waybill; Roger Steen.
Also see NEWTON-JOHN, Olivia, and the Electric Light
  Orchestra
Also see WAYBILL, Fee

TUCKER, Junior
Singles: 7–inch
GEFFEN 2-4   83
LPs: 10/12–inch 33rpm
GEFFEN 5-8   83

TUCKER, Louise
Singles: 7–inch
ARISTA 2-4   . 83
LPs: 10/12–inch 33rpm
ARISTA 5-8   83

TUCKER, Marshall:
see MARSHALL TUCKER BAND

TUCKER, Tanya
Singles: 7–inch
ARISTA 3-5   82-84

CAPITOL 2-4   85-88
COLUMBIA 3-5   72-77
MCA 3-5   75-81
Picture Sleeves
COLUMBIA 3-6   72-75
MCA 3-5   75-81
LPs: 10/12–inch 33rpm
ARISTA 5-8   82-84
CAPITOL 5-8   86
COLUMBIA ("KC" series) 5-10   72-75
COLUMBIA ("PC" series) 5-8   77
MCA 5-10   75-81
Also see CAMPBELL, Glen, and Tanya Tucker
Also see HARRIS, Emmylou

TUCKER, Tommy
Singles: 7–inch
CHECKER 4-8   64-67
FESTIVAL 4-8   66
HI 5-10   59-60
RCA (47-7838 "Return of
  the Teenage Queen") 5-10   61
RCA (37-7838 "Return of
  the Teenage Queen") 10-20   61
  (Compact 33 Single.)
RCA (68-7838 "Return of
  the Teenage Queen") 15-25   61
  (Stereo Compact 33 Single.)
SUNBEAM 5-10   59
XL 4-8   66
LPs: 10/12–inch 33rpm
CHECKER (2990 "Hi-Heel Sneakers") 15-25   64

TUFANO & GIAMMERSE
Singles: 7–inch
ODE 3-5   73-76
LPs: 10/12–inch 33rpm
EPIC/ODE 8-10   76-77
ODE 10-15   73-74
Members: Dennis Tufano; Carl Giammerese.
Also see BUCKINGHAMS

TUFF DARTS
Singles: 7–inch
SIRE 3-5   78
LPs: 10/12–inch 33rpm
SIRE 5-10   78

TULL, Jethro: see JETHRO TULL

TUNE ROCKERS
Singles: 7–inch
PET 5-10   58
U.A. 5-10   58

TUNE WEAVERS
(Margo Sylvia and the Tune Weavers)
Singles: 78rpm
CASA GRANDE 10-15   57
CHECKER 8-10   57
Singles: 7–inch
CASA GRANDE (101 "Little Boy") ... 20-25   59

CASA GRANDE (3038 "My
　Congratulations Baby") .... 20-25　60
CASA GRANDE (4037 "Happy,
　Happy Birthday Baby") .... 35-50　57
CASA GRANDE (4038 "I Remember
　Dear") .... 20-25　57
CASA GRANDE (4040 "There Stands
　My Love") .... 20-30　58
CHECKER (872 "Happy,
　Happy Birthday Baby") .... 15-20　57
　(Checkerboard top label.)
CHECKER (872 "Happy,
　Happy Birthday Baby") .... 5-8　58
　(No Checkerboard at top.)
CHECKER (1007 "Congratulations on
　Your Wedding") .... 15-20　62
CHESS .... 3-5　73
CLASSIC ARTISTS .... 3-5　88-89
COLLECTABLES 2-4
ERIC 2-4

LPs: 10/12-inch 33rpm
CASA GRANDE 10-15
　Members: Margo Sylvia; Charlotte Davis; Gil Lopez; John Sylvia.

TUNETOPPERS:
see BROWN, Al, and His Tunetoppers

TUNNELL, Jimi
Singles: 12-inch 33/45rpm
MCA .... 4-6　84
Singles: 7-inch
MCA .... 2-4　84

TURBANS
Singles: 78rpm
HERALD .... 10-20　55-57
MONEY .... 20-25　55
Singles: 7-inch
ABC .... 3-5　73
COLLECTABLES 2-4
FLASHBACK .... 3-5　65
HERALD (458 "When You Dance") .. 20-30　55
　(Script print/flag logo.)
HERALD (458 "When You Dance") .. 10-15
　(Block print logo.)
HERALD (459 "Sister Sookey") ..... 15-20　55
HERALD (478 "I'm Nobody's") ...... 20-30　56

HERALD (486 "All of My Love") ..... 20-25　56
HERALD (495 "Valley of Love") ..... 20-25　57
HERALD (510 "Congratulations") ... 20-30　57
　(Script print/flag logo.)
HERALD (510 "Congratulations") .... 8-12　57
　(Block print logo.)
HERALD (510 "Congratulations") ... 25-35　57
　(Single sided. Promotional issue only.)
HI-OLDIES 2-4
IMPERIAL (5807 "Six Questions") ... 20-30　61
IMPERIAL (5828 "This Is My Story") . 15-20　62
IMPERIAL (5847 "I Wonder") .... 10-15　62
MONEY (209 "No, No Cherry") .... 75-100　55
PARKWAY (820 "When You Dance") . 10-20　61
RED TOP (115 "I Promise You Love") 25-35　59
ROULETTE .... 10-15　60-61

LPs: 10/12-inch 33rpm
COLLECTABLES .... 5-8　84
LOST-NITE .... 5-10　81
RELIC 10-15
　Members: Al Banks; Matt Platt; Andrew Jones; Charles Williams.

TURNER, Ike
(Ike Turner and the Kings of Rhythm)
Singles: 78rpm
CHESS .... 10-20　51
FEDERAL .... 5-10　57
FLAIR .... 8-12　52
RPM .... 10-15　52
Singles: 7-inch
ARTISTIC .... 8-10　59
COBRA .... 8-10　59
FEDERAL .... 10-15　57
FLAIR (1040 "Cubano Jump") ...... 25-35　52
FLAIR (1059 "Cuban Get Away") .... 25-35　52
KING .... 5-10　61
LIBERTY .... 3-5　70
RPM (356 "You're Driving Me Insane") 25-50　52
SUE (100 series) .... 4-8　66
SUE (700 series) .... 8-12　59
U.A. .... 3-5　71-74
LPs: 10/12-inch 33rpm
CROWN .... 20-25　63
POMPEII .... 10-15　69
U.A. .... 6-12　72-73
　Also see BLAND, Bobby, and Ike Turner
　Also see BRENSTON, Jackie
　Also see RENRUT, Icky

TURNER, Ike and Bonnie
Singles: 78rpm
RPM .... 10-15　52
Singles: 7-inch
RPM (362 "Looking for a Baby") .... 25-50　52

TURNER, Ike & Tina
(Ike & Tina Turner and the Ikettes; Ike & Tina Turner
and Home Grown Funk)
Singles: 7-inch
A&M .... 4-6　69
BLUE THUMB .... 3-5　69-71

COLLECTABLES 2-4		
FANTASY 3-5	80	
INNIS 3-6	68-71	
KENT (400 series) 4-8	64	
KENT (4500 series) 3-5	70	
LIBERTY 3-5	70-71	
LOMA 4-8	65	
MINIT 3-6	69-70	
MODERN 4-8	65	
PHILLES 8-12	66	
POMPEII 3-6	68-70	
SONJA 4-8	63-64	
SUE (100 series) 4-8	65-66	
SUE (700 series) 5-10	60-63	
TRC 3-5	71	
TANGERINE 4-8	66	
U.A. 3-5	71-75	
WARNER 4-8	64	

Picture Sleeves

POMPEII 4-8	69	
WARNER 5-10	64	

LPs: 10/12–inch 33rpm

A&M (3179 "River Deep, Mountain High") 5-10	82	
A&M (4178 "River Deep, Mountain High") 10-20	69	
ABC 8-10		
ACCORD 5-10	81	
BLUE THUMB 8-12	69-73	
CAPITOL (500 series) 5-10	75	
(With "SM" prefix.)		
CAPITOL (500 series) 10-15	69	
(With "ST" prefix.)		
CENCO 15-20		
COLLECTABLES 5-8	88	
FANTASY 5-10	80	
HARMONY (11000 series) 10-12	69	
HARMONY (30000 series) 8-10	71	
KENT 15-25	61-64	
LIBERTY (7000 series) 10-12	70	
LIBERTY (51000 series) 5-8	85	
LOMA 10-20	66	
MINIT 10-15	69	
PHILLES (4011 "River Deep, Mountain High") 1000-2000	66	
(Covers for a U.S. pressing have not yet been verified. British pressings [London/Philles SHU-8298] do exist with covers.)		
PICKWICK 5-10		
POMPEII 10-15	68-69	
SUE (2001 "The Sound of Ike & Tina Turner") 60-80	61	
SUE (2003 "Dance with Ike & Tina Turner's Kings of Rhythm") 50-75	62	
(Instrumentals by Ike & Tina Turner's band.)		
SUE (2004 "Dynamite") 50-75	63	
SUE (2005 "Don't Play Me Cheap") . . 50-75	63	
SUE (2007 "It's Gonna Work Out Fine") 50-75	63	

SUE (1038 "Greatest Hits") 35-45	65	
SUNSET 8-10	69-70	
UNART 5-10		
U.A. 8-12	71-78	
UNITED SUPERIOR 8-10		
WARNER 10-20	65-69	

   Also see BLAND, Bobby, and Ike Turner
   Also see IKETTES
   Also see RAELETTES
   Also see SYLVIA
   Also see TURNER, Tina

TURNER, Jesse Lee
Singles: 7–inch

CARLTON 5-10	59	
FRATERNITY 5-10	59	
GENE NORMAN PRESENTS (184 "All You Gotta Do") 4-8	62	
GENE NORMAN PRESENTS (188 "Shotgun Boogie") 40-60	62	
IMPERIAL 5-10	60	
SUDDEN 4-6		
TOP RANK 5-10	60	

Picture Sleeves

CARLTON 10-15	59	
FRATERNITY (855 "Teenage Misery") 35-50	59	

TURNER, Joe
(Big Joe Turner; Joe Turner and His Blues Kings; Joe Turner with Pete Johnson and His Orchestra)
Singles: 78rpm

ALADDIN (3013 "Morning Glory") . . 50-100	49	
ALADDIN (3070 "Back Breaking Baby") 50-100	50	
ATLANTIC 5-10	51-57	
BAYOU 10-20	53	
COLONY 5-10	52	
CORAL (65000 series) 5-10	48	
DECCA 5-10	41-56	
DOOTONE (305 "I Love Ya, I Love Ya, I Love Ya") 50-75	51	
DOWN BEAT 8-12	48	
EXCELSIOR 5-10	49	
FIDELITY 5-10	51-52	
FREEDOM 5-10	50	
IMPERIAL 5-10	50	
MGM 5-10	48-50	

Down Beat

153-B   VOCAL JOE TURNER

CHRISTMAS DATE BOOGIE
(Joe Turner)

JOE TURNER and PETE JOHNSON
with
Orchestral Accompaniment

NATIONAL 5-15	46-51
RPM 15-25	51
SWING BEAT 10-20	49
VOCALION 10-20	39

Singles: 7-inch

ATLANTIC (939 "Chains of Love") ... 40-60	51
ATLANTIC (949 "Bump Miss Susie") 35-45	51
ATLANTIC (960 "Sweet Sixteen") ... 30-40	52
ATLANTIC (970 "Don't You Cry") 25-35	52
ATLANTIC (982 "Don't You Cry") 20-30	52
ATLANTIC (1001 "Honey Hush") 15-25	53
ATLANTIC (1016 "TV Mama") 20-30	53
ATLANTIC (1026 through 1184) 10-20	54-58
ATLANTIC (2000 series) 5-10	59-60
BAYOU (015 "The Blues Jumped a Rabbit") 75-125	53
BLUESWAY 4-8	67
CORAL (62000 series) 4-8	64
DECCA (29000 series) 10-20	55-56
KENT 3-5	69-71
RPM (345 "Ridin' Blues") 50-75	51
RONN 4-6	69

EPs: 7-inch 33/45rpm

ATLANTIC (536 "Joe Turner Sings") 30-40	55
ATLANTIC (565 "Joe Turner") 30-40	56
ATLANTIC (586 "Joe Turner") 30-40	56
ATLANTIC (606 "Rock with Joe Turner") 30-40	56
EMARCY (6132 "Joe Turner and Pete Johnson") 35-45	56

LPs: 10/12-inch 33rpm

ARHOOLIE 15-20	62
ATCO 8-10	71
ATLANTIC (1234 "Boss of the Blues") 50-75	58
ATLANTIC (1332 "Big Joe Rides Again") 40-60	60
ATLANTIC (8005 "Joe Turner") .... 50-100 (Black label.)	57
ATLANTIC (8005 "Joe Turner") ..... 30-50 (Red label.)	59
ATLANTIC (8023 "Rockin' the Blues")50-100 (Black label.)	58
ATLANTIC (8023 "Rockin' the Blues") 30-50 (Red label.)	59
ATLANTIC (8033 "Big Joe Is Here") . 50-100 (Black label.)	59
ATLANTIC (8033 "Big Joe Is Here") .. 30-50 (Red label.)	59
ATLANTIC (8081 "Best of Joe Turner")25-40	63
ATLANTIC (8812 "Boss of the Blues") . 5-10	81
BIG TOWN 5-10	78
BLUES SPECTRUM 10-12	
BLUESWAY 8-12	67-73
CHIARDSCURO 8-10	76
CLASSIC JAZZ 5-10	79
EMARCY (36014 "Joe Turner with Pete Johnson") 75-125	56

INTERMEDIA 5-8	83-84
LMI 8-10	74
MCA 5-10	80
PABLO 5-10	76-83
SAVOY (14012 "Blues Can Make You Happy") 50-100	58
SAVOY (14106 "Carless Love") 30-40	64
SAVOY (2223 "Big Joe Is Here") 5-10	77
UNITED 8-10	

Also see KING CURTIS

TURNER, Joe / Jimmy Nelson
LPs: 10/12-inch 33rpm

CROWN 15-25	62

Also see NELSON, Jimmy
Also see TURNER, Joe

TURNER, Ruby
(Ruby Turner Featuring Jonathan Butler)
Singles: 7-inch

JIVE 2-4	86

LPs: 10/12-inch 33rpm

JIVE 5-8	86

TURNER, Sammy
(Sammy Turner and the Twisters)
Singles: 7-inch

BIG TOP (3007 and 3016) 5-10	59
BIG TOP (3029 "Always") .... 5-10 (Monaural.)	59
BIG TOP (S-3029 "Always") .... 15-25 (Stereo.)	59
BIG TOP (3032 through 3070) 5-10	60-61
BIG TOP (3089 "Falling") 10-15	61
ERIC 2-4	
MILLENNIUM 2-4	78
MOTOWN 10-15	64
PACIFIC (3016 "Lavender Blue") 25-35	59
20TH FOX 4-8	65
VERVE 4-8	66

LPs: 10/12-inch 33rpm

BIG TOP (1301 "Lavender Blue Moods") .... 20-30 (Monaural.)	60
BIG TOP (ST-1301 "Lavender Blue Moods") .... 25-35 (Stereo.)	60

Also see KING CURTIS

TURNER, Spyder
Singles: 7-inch

KWANZA 3-5	73
MGM 3-8	66-71
POLYDOR 2-4	84
WHITFIELD 3-5	78-79

LPs: 10/12-inch 33rpm

MGM 15-20	67
WHITFIELD 5-10	78-79

Also see BRISTOL, Johnny, and Spyder Turner

TURNER, Tina
Singles: 12-inch 33/45rpm

CAPITOL 4-6	84-87

Singles: 7–inch

CAPITOL	2-4	84-89
POMPEII	4-8	68
U.A.	3-5	75-78
WAGNER	3-5	79

Picture Sleeves

CAPITOL	2-5	84-87

LPs: 10/12–inch 33rpm

CAPITOL	5-8	84-89
FANTASY	5-10	
SPRINGBOARD	8-10	72
U.A. (Except 200)	8-10	75-78
U.A. (200 "Tina Turner Turns the Country On")	10-15	67
WAGNER	5-8	79

Also see ADAMS, Bryan, and Tina Turner
Also see BASS, Fontella, and Tina Turner
Also see BOWIE, David
Also see CLAPTON, Eric, and Tina Turner
Also see JOHN, Elton / Tina Turner
Also see TURNER, Ike & Tina
Also see U.S.A. for AFRICA

TURNER, Titus

Singles: 78rpm

ATLANTIC	4-8	57

Singles: 7–inch

ATCO	4-8	64
ATLANTIC	8-12	57
COLUMBIA	4-8	63
ENJOY	4-8	62-63
GLOVER (Except 202)	5-10	59-60
GLOVER (202 "When the Sergeant Comes Marching Home")	10-20	60
GUARANTEED	4-8	61-62
JAMIE	4-8	61
JOSIE	4-6	68-69
KING (Monaural)	5-10	57-61
KING (Stereo)	10-20	59
MURBO	4-8	65
OKEH (6844 through 7038)	15-25	52-54
OKEH (7200 series)	4-8	66
PHILIPS	4-8	67
WING	10-15	55

LPs: 10/12–inch 33rpm

JAMIE	25-35	61

TURRENTINE, Stanley

Singles: 7-inch

BLUE NOTE	3-8	61-69
CTI	3-5	72
ELEKTRA	2-4	79-81
FANTASY	2-5	74-78
IMPULSE	3-5	67

LPs: 10/12-inch 33rpm

BAINBRIDGE	5-8	81
BLUE NOTE	25-50	60-61

(Label gives New York street address for Blue Note Records.)

BLUE NOTE	15-30	62-65

(Label reads "Blue Note Records Inc. - New York, U.S.A.")

BLUE NOTE	8-18	65-85

(Label shows Blue Note Records as a division of either Liberty or United Artists.)

CTI	8-12	71-75
ELEKTRA	5-8	79-81
FPM	5-8	75
FANTASY	8-12	74-78
IMPULSE	8-15	67-78
MAINSTREAM	15-25	65
PRESTIGE	6-12	70-71
SUNSET	8-12	69
TIME	25-50	62-63
UPFRONT	6-12	72

Also see GILBERTO, Astrud, and Stanley Turrentine
Also see HUBBARD, Freddie, and Stanley Turrentine
Also see SILVER, Horace, Quintet, and Stanley Turrentine

TURTLES

Singles: 7–inch

COLLECTABLES	2-4	
WHITE WHALE	4-8	65-70

Picture Sleeves

WHITE WHALE	4-8	66-69

LPs: 10/12–inch 33rpm

RHINO (Except RNPD-901)	5-8	82-86
RHINO (RNPD-901 "Turtles 1968")	8-10	83
SIRE	10-15	74
TRIP	5-10	
WHITE WHALE	15-30	65-71

Members: Howard Kaylan; Mark Volman; Don Murray; Chuck Portz; Al Nichol; Jim Tucker; John Barbata; John Seiter; Jim Pons; Chip Douglas.
Also see CHRISTMAS SPIRIT
Also see LEAVES
Also see MOTHERS of INVENTION

TURZY, Jane

Singles: 78rpm

DECCA	3-5	51-54

Singles: 7–inch

DECCA	4-8	51-54

TUTONE, Tommy: see TOMMY TUTONE

TUXEDO JUNCTION

Singles: 12–inch 33/45rpm

BUTTERFLY	4-8	78-80

Singles: 7–inch

BUTTERFLY (Black vinyl)	3-5	78-80

LPs: 10/12–inch 33rpm

BUTTERFLY (Black vinyl)	5-10	77-79
BUTTERFLY (Colored vinyl)	10-12	77

(Promotional issues only.)

TWENNYNINE

Singles: 7–inch

ELEKTRA	3-5	79-81

LPs: 10/12–inch 33rpm

ELEKTRA	5-10	79-81

Member: Lenny White.
Also see WHITE, Lenny

20-20
Singles: 7–inch
PORTRAIT 3-5   79
EPs: 7–inch 33/45rpm
BOMP 5-10
LPs: 10/12–inch 33rpm
ENIGMA 5-8   83
PORTRAIT 5-10   79-81

21ST CENTURY
Singles: 7–inch
RCA 3-5   75

TWILIGHT 22
Singles: 12–inch 33/45rpm
VANGUARD 4-6   83-84
Singles: 7–inch
VANGUARD 2-4   83-84
LPs: 10/12–inch 33rpm
VANGUARD 5-8   84

TWILLEY, Dwight, Band
Singles: 7–inch
ARISTA 3-5   77-79
EMI AMERICA 2-4   82-84
SHELTER 3-5   75-76
Picture Sleeves
SHELTER 3-5   75-76
LPs: 10/12–inch 33rpm
ARISTA 5-10   77-79
EMI AMERICA 5-8   82-84
SHELTER 5-10   75-76
Also see SEYMOUR, Phil

TWIN IMAGE
Singles: 12–inch 33/45rpm
CAPITOL 4-6   84-85
Singles: 7–inch
CAPITOL 2-4   84-85
LPs: 10/12–inch 33rpm
CAPITOL 5-8   84

TWINS
Singles: 12–inch 33/45rpm
QUALITY/RFC 4-6   83

TWISTED SISTER
Singles: 7–inch
ATLANTIC 2-4   83-86
LPs: 10/12–inch 33rpm
ATLANTIC 5-8   83-87
Member: Dee Snider.

TWITTY, Conway
Singles: 78rpm
MERCURY 10-15   57
Singles: 7–inch
ABC-PAR (10507 "Go On and Cry") .. 5-10   63
ABC-PAR (10550 "My Baby Left Me") 10-15   64
DECCA 3-6   65-72
ELEKTRA 2-4   82-83
MCA 2-5   73-82
MGM (500 series) 3-5   78

MGM (12000 and 13000 series) 5-10   58-62
MGM (14000 series) 3-5   71-72
MGM (50000 series) 15-25   58-59
(Stereo.)
MERCURY 15-25   57-58
MUSIGRAM 3-5
(Flexi-disc.)
POLYDOR 2-4
WARNER 2-4   83-86
Picture Sleeves
ELEKTRA 2-5   82
MGM 10-20   58-62
EPs: 7–inch 33/45rpm
MGM 15-25   58-59
LPs: 10/12–inch 33rpm
ACCORD 5-10   82
ALLEGIANCE 5-8   84
CANDLELITE 10-12
CORAL 5-8   73
DECCA 8-15   66-72
DEMAND 8-12   72
ELEKTRA 5-8   82-83
MCA 5-12   73-85
MGM (110 "Conway Twitty") 10-15   70
MGM (3744 "Conway Twitty Sings") . 50-75   59
MGM (E-3786 "Saturday Night with
  Conway Twitty") 30-50   59
  (Monaural.)
MGM (SE-3786 "Saturday Night with
  Conway Twitty") 50-75   59
  (Stereo.)
MGM (E-3818 "Lonely Blue Boy") ... 30-50   60
  (Monaural.)
MGM (SE-3818 "Lonely Blue Boy") .. 50-75   60
  (Stereo.)
MGM (E-3849 "Conway Twitty's
  Greatest Hits") 30-50   60
  (Monaural. Black label. With gatefold cover and
  poster.)
MGM (SE-3849 "Conway Twitty's
  Greatest Hits") 40-60   60
  (Stereo. With gatefold cover and poster.)
MGM (3849 "Conway Twitty's
  Greatest Hits") 10-15   68
  (Blue and yellow label. With standard cover.)
MGM (E-3907 "The Rock and
  Roll Story") 30-40   61
  (Monaural.)
MGM (SE-3907 "The Rock and
  Roll Story") 40-60   61
  (Stereo.)
MGM (E-3943 "The Conway Twitty
  Touch") 20-30   61
  (Monaural.)
MGM (E-3943 "The Conway Twitty
  Touch") 30-40   61
  (Stereo.)
MGM (E-4019 through E-4217) 20-30   62-64
  (Monaural.)

MGM (SE-4019 through SE-4217) ... 25-35   62-64
  (Stereo.)
MGM (4650 through 4884) 10-15   69-73
METRO 15-25   65
OPRYLAND (12636 "Conway Twitty,
  Then and Now") 60-80
  (Six-LP set. Promotional issue only.)
PICKWICK 10-15   72
TEE VEE 5-10   78
TROLLY CAR 5-10
WARNER 5-8   83-86

TWITTY, Conway, and Loretta Lynn
Singles: 7–inch
DECCA 3-5   71-72
MCA 2-4   73-81
LPs: 10/12–inch 33rpm
DECCA 8-15   71-72
MCA 5-10   73-84
TVP 8-12   76
  Also see LYNN, Loretta
  Also see TWITTY, Conway

2 LIVE CREW
Singles: 7–inch
LUKE SKYWALKER 2-4   88-90
LPs: 10/12–inch 33rpm
LUKE SKYWALKER 5-8   87-90

2 of CLUBS
Singles: 7–inch
FRATERNITY 4-8   66-67

TWO SISTERS
Singles: 12–inch 33/45rpm
SUGARSCOOP 4-6   83

TWO TONS O' FUN
(Two Tons)
Singles: 12–inch 33/45rpm
FANTASY 4-6   80
Singles: 7–inch
FANTASY 3-5   80
HONEY 3-5   80-81
LPs: 10/12–inch 33rpm
FANTASY 5-8   80
HONEY 5-8   80
  Members: Martha Wash; Izora Armstead.
  Also see WEATHER GIRLS

TYCOON
Singles: 7–inch
ARISTA 3-5   79
LPs: 10/12–inch 33rpm
ARISTA 5-10   78-81

TYLER, Bonnie
Singles: 7–inch
CHRYSALIS 3-5   77
COLUMBIA 2-4   83-86
RCA 3-5   78-79
LPs: 10/12–inch 33rpm
CHRYSALIS 8-12   77

COLUMBIA 5-8   83-86
RCA 5-10   78-81
  Also see RUNDGREN, Todd

TYLER, Frankie
(Frankie Valli)
Singles: 7–inch
OKEH (7103 "I Go Ape") 50-75   58
Promotional Singles
OKEH (7103 "I Go Ape") 40-60   58
  Also see VALLI, Frankie

TYMES
Singles: 7–inch
ABKCO 3-5
COLUMBIA 4-6   68-70
MGM 4-8   66
PARKWAY (Except 871) 4-8   63-64
PARKWAY (871 "So in Love") 8-12   63
PARKWAY (871 "So Much
  in Love") 4-8   63
RCA 3-5   74-77
WINCHESTER 4-8   67
Picture Sleeves
PARKWAY 5-10   63-64
LPs: 10/12–inch 33rpm
ABKCO 5-10   74
COLUMBIA 10-15   69
PARKWAY 20-40   63-64
RCA 8-10   74-77
  Members: George Williams Jr; Donald Banks; Al Berry; Norman
  Burnett; George Hilliard.

TYNER, McCoy
(McCoy Tyner Trio)
Singles: 7–inch
COLUMBIA 2-4   82
IMPULSE 4-6   65
LPs: 10/12–inch 33rpm
BLUE NOTE 8-15   66-76
COLUMBIA 5-8   82
FPM 5-8   75
IMPULSE 10-20   62-78
MCA 5-8   81
MILESTONE 5-12   72-82
PAUSA 5-8   82

TYRANNOSAURUS REX: see T-REX

TYZIK
(Jeff Tyzik)
Singles: 12–inch 33/45rpm
POLYDOR 4-6   84
Singles: 7–inch
CAPITOL 2-4   82
POLYDOR 2-4   84
LPs: 10/12–inch 33rpm
CAPITOL 5-8   82
POLYDOR 5-8   84

U

UB40
(UB40 with Chrissie Hynde)
Singles: 12-inch 33/45rpm
A&M 4-6   83-86
Singles: 7-inch
A&M 2-4   83-88
LPs: 10/12-inch 33rpm
A&M 5-8   83-88
VIRGIN 5-8   89
  Also see PRETENDERS

UFO
Singles: 7-inch
CHRYSALIS 2-5   73-86
LPs: 10/12-inch 33rpm
CHRYSALIS 5-12   74-86
RARE EARTH 10-15   71
  Also see SCHENKER, Michael, Group

U.K.
Singles: 7-inch
POLYDOR 3-5   78-79
LPs: 10/12-inch 33rpm
POLYDOR 5-10   78-79
  Members: John Wetton; Eddie Jobson; Terry Bozzio; Bill Bruford;
  Allan Holdsworth.

U.K. SQUEEZE: see SQUEEZE

U.S.A.- EUROPEAN CONNECTION
Singles: 7-inch
MARLIN 3-5   78-79
LPs: 10/12-inch 33rpm
MARLIN 5-10   78-79

U.S.A. for AFRICA
Singles: 12-inch 33/45rpm
COLUMBIA 4-6   85
Singles: 7-inch
COLUMBIA 2-4   85
LPs: 10/12-inch 33rpm
COLUMBIA 5-8   85
  Members: Dan Aykroyd; Kim Carnes; Ray Charles; Bob Dylan;
  Daryl Hall; James Ingram; Michael Jackson; Jean-Michael Jarre;
  Al Jarreau; Waylon Jennings; Billy Joel; Quincy Jones; Cyndi
  Lauper; Huey Lewis; Kenny Loggins; Bette Midler; Steve Perry;
  Lionel Richie; Smokey Robinson; Kenny Rogers; Diana Ross;
  Paul Simon; Bruce Springsteen; Tina Turner; Dionne Warwick;
  Stevie Wonder.
  Also see CARNES, Kim
  Also see CHARLES, Ray
  Also see DYLAN, Bob
  Also see HALL, Daryl
  Also see INGRAM, James
  Also see JACKSON, Michael
  Also see JARRE, Jean-Michael
  Also see JARREAU, Al
  Also see JENNINGS, Waylon
  Also see JOEL, Billy
  Also see JONES, Quincy

  Also see LAUPER, Cyndi
  Also see LEWIS, Huey, and the News
  Also see LOGGINS, Kenny
  Also see MIDLER, Bette
  Also see PERRY, Steve
  Also see RICHIE, Lionel
  Also see ROBINSON, Smokey
  Also see ROGERS, Kenny
  Also see ROSS, Diana
  Also see SIMON, Paul
  Also see SPRINGSTEEN, Bruce
  Also see TURNER, Tina
  Also see VOICES of AMERICA / U.S.A. for AFRICA
  Also see WARWICK, Dionne
  Also see WONDER, Stevie

UTFO
Singles: 12-inch 33/45rpm
SELECT 4-6   85-86
Singles: 7-inch
SELECT 2-4   85-89
LPs: 10/12-inch 33rpm
SELECT 5-8   85-89
  Also see ROXANNE with UTFO

U2
Singles: 12-inch 33/45rpm
ISLAND 4-6   83
Singles: 7-inch
ISLAND 3-5   81-89
Picture Sleeves
ISLAND 3-5   81-89
LPs: 10/12-inch 33rpm
ISLAND 5-10   81-89
  Members: Paul "Bono Vox" Hewson; David "The Edge" Evan;
  Adam Clayton; Larry Mullen.
  Also see BAND AID

UBIQUITY
Singles: 7-inch
ELEKTRA 3-5   78
LPs: 10/12-inch 33rpm
ELEKTRA 5-10   78
  Also see AYERS, Roy

UGGAMS, Leslie
Singles: 7-inch
ATLANTIC 3-6   65-70
COLUMBIA 4-8   59-64
GORDY 3-5   76
MGM 5-10   54-55
SONDAY 3-5   71
EPs: 7-inch 33/45rpm
MGM 5-10   54
LPs: 10/12-inch 33rpm
ATLANTIC 5-15   66-69
COLUMBIA 10-25   59-63
MOTOWN 5-10   75
SONDAY 5-10   72

ULLANDA
Singles: 7-inch
OCEAN 3-5   79

ULLMAN, Tracey
Singles: 7–inch
MCA 3-5   84-85
LPs: 10/12–inch 33rpm
MCA 5-10   84

ULTIMATE
Singles: 7–inch
CASABLANCA 3-5   78-80
LPs: 10/12–inch 33rpm
CASABLANCA 5-10   78-80

ULTIMATE SPINACH
Singles: 7–inch
MGM 4-8   68-69
LPs: 10/12–inch 33rpm
MGM 20-30   68-69

ULTRAMAGNETIC MC'S
LPs: 10/12–inch 33rpm
NEXT PLATEAU 5-8   88

ULTRAVOX
Singles: 12–inch 33/45rpm
CHRYSALIS 4-6   83
Singles: 7–inch
ANTILLES 3-5   78-80
CHRYSALIS 2-4   80-84
ISLAND 8-10   77
LPs: 10/12–inch 33rpm
ANTILLES 5-10   78-80
CHRYSALIS 5-8   80-84
ISLAND 8-10   77
Also see BAND AID

UMILANI, Piero
Singles: 7–inch
ARIEL 3-5   69
LPs: 10/12–inch 33rpm
ARIEL 8-12   69

UNCLE DOG
Singles: 7–inch
MCA 3-5   73
LPs: 10/12–inch 33rpm
MCA 6-10   73

UNCLE LOUIE
Singles: 7–inch
MARLIN 3-5   79
LPs: 10/12–inch 33rpm
MARLIN 5-10   78

UNDERGROUND SUNSHINE
Singles: 7–inch
INTREPID 4-6   69
LPs: 10/12–inch 33rpm
INTERPID 10-15   69

UNDERTONES
Singles: 7–inch
CAPITOL 2-4   84
HARVEST 3-5   81
SIRE 3-5   80

LPs: 10/12–inch 33rpm
CAPITOL 5-8   84
HARVEST 5-10   81
SIRE 5-10   80
Member: Feargal Sharkey.

UNDERWOOD, Veronica
Singles: 7–inch
PHILLY WORLD 2-4   85

UNDERWORLD
Singles: 7–inch
SIRE 2-4   88
LPs: 10/12–inch 33rpm
SIRE 5-8   88

UNDISPUTED TRUTH
Singles: 12–inch 33/45rpm
WHITFIELD 4-8   77-79
Singles: 7–inch
GORDY 3-5   71-75
MOTOWN 2-4
WHITFIELD 3-5   76-79
LPs: 10/12–inch 33rpm
GORDY 8-10   71-75
WHITFIELD 5-10   77-79
Members: Joe Harris; Brenda Evans; Billie Calvin; Carl Smalls.
Also see BOOM, Taka
Also see DRAMATICS

UNICORN
Singles: 7–inch
CAPITOL 3-5   74-77
LPs: 10/12–inch 33rpm
CAPITOL 8-10   74-77

UNIFICS
Singles: 7–inch
FOUNTAIN 3-5   71
KAPP 4-8   68-69
MCA 2-4
Picture Sleeves
KAPP 4-8   68-69
LPs: 10/12–inch 33rpm
KAPP 10-15   68

UNION GAP: see PUCKET, Gary

UNIPOP
Singles: 7–inch
KAT FAMILY 2-4   82
LPs: 10/12–inch 33rpm
KAT FAMILY 5-8   82

UNIQUE
Singles: 12–inch 33/45rpm
PRELUDE 4-6   83
Singles: 7–inch
PRELUDE 2-4   83

UNIQUES
Singles: 7–inch
PARAMOUNT 3-5   70-72
PAULA 4-6   65-70

LPs: 10/12–inch 33rpm
PAULA 10-20   66-70
  Members: Joe Stampley; Bobby Stampley; Jim Woodfield; Mike
  Love; Ray Mills; Bobby Sims; Ronnie Weiss.
  Also see STAMPLEY, Joe

UNIT 4+2
Singles: 7–inch
LONDON 4-8   65-66
LPs: 10/12–inch 33rpm
LONDON (427 "Unit 4+2") 25-35   65
  (Monaural.)
LONDON (3427 "Unit 4+2") 25-40   65
  (Stereo.)
  Member: Russ Ballard.
  Also see BALLARD, Russ

UNITED STATES AIR FORCE BAND
LPs: 10/12–inch 33rpm
RCA 5-10   63

UNITED STATES MARINE BAND
LPs: 10/12–inch 33rpm
RCA 5-10   63

UNITED STATES NAVY BAND
LPs: 10/12–inch 33rpm
RCA 5-10   63

UNITED STATES of AMERICA
LPs: 10/12–inch 33rpm
COLUMBIA (9619 "United States
  of America") 15-25   68
  Members: Dorothy Moskowitz; Joseph Byrd; Gordon Marron;
  Rand Forbes; Craig Woodson.

UNITS
Singles: 12–inch 33/45rpm
EPIC 4-6   83-84
UPROAR 4-6   83
Singles: 7–inch
EPIC 2-4   84
LPs: 10/12–inch 33rpm
EPIC 5-8   84

UNIVERSAL ROBOT BAND
Singles: 7–inch
RED GREG 3-5   77
LPs: 10/12–inch 33rpm
RED GREG 5-10   77
  Also see KLEEER

UNKNOWNS
Singles: 7–inch
MARLIN 4-8   67
PARROT 4-8   66
SHIELD 4-8
LPs: 10/12–inch 33rpm
SIRE 8-10   81
INVASION 8-10   83
  Member: Keith Allison.
  Also see REVERE, Paul, and the Raiders

UNLIMITED TOUCH
Singles: 12–inch 33/45rpm
PRELUDE 4-6   81-84

Singles: 7–inch
PRELUDE 3-5   81-84
LPs: 10/12–inch 33rpm
PRELUDE 5-10   81-84
  Also see LORBER, Jeff

UP with PEOPLE
LPs: 10/12–inch 33rpm
PACE 5-8   66-70

UPBEATS
Singles: 7–inch
JOY 10-12   58-59
PREP 10-15   57-58
SWAN 10-15   58

UPCHURCH, Phil
(Phil Upchurch Combo)
Singles: 7–inch
BOYD 5-10   61
GOLDEN FLEECE 3-5   74
MARLIN 2-4   79
U.A. 4-8   61-62
LPs: 10/12–inch 33rpm
BLUE THUMB 8-10   73
BOYD 20-30   61
CADET 8-10   69
MILESTONE 5-8
U.A. 15-20   61-62
  Also see REED, Jimmy

UPCHURCH, Phil, and Tennyson Stephens
LPs: 10/12–inch 33rpm
KUDU 8-10   75
  Also see UPCHURCH, Phil

UPFRONT
Singles: 12–inch 33/45rpm
SILVER CLOUD 4-6   83

URGENT
Singles: 7–inch
MANHATTAN 2-4   85

URIAH HEEP
Singles: 7–inch
CHRYSALIS 3-5   78
MERCURY 3-5   70-83
WARNER 3-5   73-78
Picture Sleeves
MERCURY 3-5   70-82
LPs: 10/12–inch 33rpm
CHRYSALIS 5-10   78-79
MERCURY 5-10   70-83
WARNER 5-10   73-81
  Also see HENSLEY, Ken
  Also see ROUGH DIAMOND

UTOPIA
Singles: 7–inch
BEARSVILLE 3-5   76-80
NETWORK 2-4   82
PASSPORT 2-4   84-85

LPs: 10/12-inch 33rpm
BEARSVILLE 5-10   80-82
KENT 10-15   73
NETWORK 8-10   82
PASSPORT 5-8   84-85
Members: Todd Rundgren; Willie Wilcox; Roger Powell; Kasim
Sulton.
Also see CASSIDY, Shaun, and Todd Rundgren's Utopia
Also see RUNDGREN, Todd

V

V.S.O.P.
LPs: 10/12-inch 33rpm
COLUMBIA 5-10   77
Members: Herbie Hancock; Wayne Shorter; Freddie Hubbard;
Tony Williams.

VACELS
Singles: 7-inch
KAMA SUTRA 4-8   65

VALADIERS
Singles: 7-inch
GORDY (7003 "While I'm Away") 25-30   62
GORDY (7013 "I Found a Girl") 25-30   63
MIRACLE (6 "Greetings") 35-45   61
MIRACLE (6 "Greetings [This
Is Uncle Sam]") 20-30   61
(Note longer title.)

VALE, Jerry
Singles: 78rpm
COLUMBIA 3-5   51-57
Singles: 7-inch
BUDDAH 3-5   78
COLUMBIA 3-8   51-74
Picture Sleeves
COLUMBIA 4-8   64-65
EPs: 7-inch 33/45rpm
COLUMBIA 5-10   56-59
LPs: 10/12-inch 33rpm
COLUMBIA 5-15   58-75
HARMONY 5-10   69-74

VALE, Jerry, Peggy King and Felicia Sanders
LPs: 10/12-inch 33rpm
COLUMBIA 10-20   56
Also see KING, Peggy
Also see SANDERS, Felicia
Also see VALE, Jerry

VALENS, Ritchie
Singles: 12-inch 33/45rpm
DEL-FI 15-25
Singles: 7-inch
ABC 3-5   74
DEL-FI 15-25   58
(Solid green label with black print.)

DEL-FI 10-15   58-60
(With rows of circles on label.)
ERIC 2-4
GOODIES 2-4
KASEY 5-10
LANA 2-4
Picture Sleeves
DEL-FI (4114 "That's My Little Suzie") 15-25   59
DEL-FI (4117 "Little Girl") 20-35   59
(With explanatory "Concerning This Record" insert.)
DEL-FI (4117 "Little Girl") 15-25   59
(Without insert.)
DEL-FI (4128 "Stay Beside Me") 15-25   60
EPs: 7-inch 33/45rpm
DEL-FI (1 "Ritchie Valens") 50-75   59
(Promotional issue only.)
DEL-FI (101 "Ritchie Valens") 50-75   59
DEL-FI (111 "Ritchie Valens
Sings") 50-75   59
LPs: 10/12-inch 33rpm
DEL-FI (1201 "Ritchie Valens") 60-80   59
DEL-FI (1206 "Ritchie") 60-80   59
DEL-FI (1214 "Ritchie Valens
in Concert") 100-200   61
DEL-FI (1225 "Greatest Hits") 40-60   63
DEL-FI (1247 "Greatest Hits, Vol. 2") . 40-60   65
GUEST STAR 15-25   64
MGM 10-15   70
RHINO (Except 2798) 5-8   81-87
RHINO (2798 "History of
Ritchie Valens") 20-25   81
Also see ALLENS, Arvee

VALENS, Ritchie / Jerry Kole
LPs: 10/12-inch 33rpm
CROWN (5336 "Ritchie Valens
and Jerry Kole") 20-30   63

VALENTE, Caterina
Singles: 78rpm
DECCA 3-5   54-57
Singles: 7-inch
DECCA 5-10   54-59
LONDON 3-6   60-68
RCA 4-8   59
TELEFUNKEN 4-8   59
EPs: 7-inch 33/45rpm
DECCA 5-10   55
LPs: 10/12-inch 33rpm
DECCA 5-15   55-64
LONDON 5-15   59-72
RCA 5-15   61

VALENTE, Dino
Singles: 7-inch
ELEKTRA 5-8   64
LPs: 10/12-inch 33rpm
EPIC 15-20   68
Also see QUICKSILVER MESSENGER SERVICE

VALENTI, John
Singles: 7–inch
ARIOLA AMERICA 3-5   76-77

VALENTIN, Dave
Singles: 7–inch
GRP 3-5   80-81
LPs: 10/12–inch 33rpm
GRP 5-10   80-81

VALENTINE, Lezil
Singles: 7–inch
ALL PLATINUM 3-6   68

VALENTINE BROTHERS
Singles: 12–inch 33/45rpm
SOURCE 4-6   78
Singles: 7–inch
A&M 2-4   84
BRIDGE 2-4   82
SOURCE 3-5   79
LPs: 10/12–inch 33rpm
A&M 5-8   84
BRIDGE 5-8   82
SOURCE 5-10   79

VALENTINO, Danny
Singles: 7–inch
CONTRAST 4-8   67
MGM 5-10   59-60

VALENTINO, Mark
Singles: 7–inch
SWAN.......................... 5-10   62-63
(Shown as "Mark Valentinon" on some pressings.)
LPs: 10/12–inch 33rpm
SWAN (508 "Mark Valentino") 30-50   63

VALENTINOS
Singles: 7–inch
ABKCO 3-5
ASTRA 4-8
CHESS......................... 4-8   66
CLEAN 3-5   73
JUBILEE 4-6   68-69
SAR 5-10   62-64
Members: Bobby Womack; Curtis Womack.
Also see WOMACK, Bobby
Also see WOMACK BROTHERS

VALENTION, Mark: see VALENTINO, Mark

VALERIE & NICK
Singles: 7–inch
GLOVER 5-10   64
Members: Valerie Simpson; Nick Ashford.
Also see ASHFORD & SIMPSON

VALERY, Dana
Singles: 7–inch
ABC 4-6   68-69
COLUMBIA 8-10   67
LIBERTY 3-5   70
PHANTOM 3-5   75

SCOTTI BROS 3-5   79
Picture Sleeves
PHANTOM 3-5   75
Also see SIMON, Paul

VALIANTS
(Featuring Billy Storm)
Singles: 78rpm
KEEN 10-15   57
Singles: 7–inch
KEEN (4008 "Temptation of My Heart")25-30   58
KEEN (4026 "Please Wait My Love")   30-40   58
KEEN (34004 "This Is the Night") ... 15-25   57
KEEN (34007 "Lover Lover") 15-25   58
KEEN (82120 "This Is the Night") ... 10-15   60
SHAR-DEE (703 "Dear Cindy") 40-50   59
(No mention of distribution by London.)
SHAR-DEE (703 "Dear Cindy") 20-30   59
(Label reads "Distributed by London.")
Also see STORM, Billy

VALINO, Joe
Singles: 78rpm
U.A. 4-8   57
VIK 4-8   56
Singles: 7–inch
BANDBOX 4-8   61
CROSLEY 4-8   59-60
DEBUT 3-6   67-68
RCA 4-8   59
U.A. 5-10   57-58
VIK 5-10   56
Picture Sleeves
U.A. (101 "Legend of the Lost") 20-30   57
LPs: 10/12–inch 33rpm
DEBUT 8-12   67

VALJEAN
(Valjean Johns)
Singles: 7–inch
CARLTON 4-6   62-63
Picture Sleeves
CARLTON 4-8   62
LPs: 10/12–inch 33rpm
CARLTON 15-20   62-63

VALLEY, Frankie: see VALLI, Frankie

VALLI, Frankie
(Frankie Valley and the Travelers; Frankie Valle;
Frankie Vally; Frankie Vallie and the Romans)
Singles: 10/12–inch 33/45rpm
MOTOWN 15-20   73
PRIVATE STOCK 10-15   77
Singles: 7–inch
CINDY (3012 "Real") 75-100   59
COLLECTABLES 2-4
CORONA (1234 "My Mother's
Eyes") 300-500   53
DECCA (30994 "Please Take
a Chance") 75-100   59

MERCURY (70381 "Forgive and
Forget") 100-125   54
(Maroon label.)
MERCURY (70381 "Forgive and
Forget") 50-75   54
(Black label.)
MOTOWN 8-12   73
MOWEST 5-10   72
PHILIPS (40407 through 45098) 4-8   66-70
PHILIPS (40661 and 40680) 10-12   69-70
PRIVATE STOCK 3-5   74-78
RSO 3-5   78
SMASH 5-10   65-66
WARNER/CURB 3-5   78-80

Promotional Singles
BOB CREWE PRESENTS (1 "The Girl
I'll Never Know") 25-35   69
DECCA (30994 "Please Take
a Chance") 50-75   59
MERCURY (70381 "Forgive and
Forget") 50-75   54
MOWEST (5025 "The Night") 12-15   71
PHILIPS 8-12   66-70
PRIVATE STOCK 8-10   74-78
SMASH 8-12   65-66

Picture Sleeves
PHILIPS 10-15   66-69

LPs: 10/12-inch 33rpm
MOTOWN (100 series) 5-8   81
MOTOWN (800 series) 8-12   75
MCA 5-10   79-80
PHILIPS (200247 "Solo") 30-40   67
(Monaural.)
PHILIPS (600000 series) 20-25   67-68
(Stereo.)
PRIVATE STOCK 8-10   75-78
WARNER 8-10   78
Also see BEACH BOYS with Frankie Valli and the 4 Seasons
Also see FOUR LOVERS
Also see 4 SEASONS
Also see TYLER, Frankie

VALLI, Frankie, and Chris Forde
Singles: 7-inch
MCA 3-5   80

VALLI, Frankie, and Cheryl Ladd
Singles: 7-inch
CAPITOL 3-5   82
Also see LADD, Cheryl
Also see VALLI, Frankie

VALLI, June
Singles: 78rpm
RCA 3-5   52-56
Singles: 7-inch
ABC-PAR 4-6   63
DCP 4-6   64
MERCURY 4-8   58-61
RCA 5-10   52-56
U.A. 4-6   62
Picture Sleeves
MERCURY 4-8   61
EPs: 7-inch 33/45rpm
RCA 5-10   55-56
LPs: 10/12-inch 33rpm
AUDIO FIDELITY 5-10   69
MERCURY 8-15   60
RCA 12-25   55-56
Also see ZABACH, Florian

VALLIE, Frankie: see VALLI, Frankie

VALLY, Frankie: see VALLI, Frankie

VALUMES
(Volumes)
Singles: 7-inch
CHEX (1000 "I Love You") 75-125   62
Also see VOLUMES

VAN & TITUS
Singles: 7-inch
ELF 4-8   68

VANCE, Paul
Singles: 7-inch
ROULETTE 4-8   62
SCEPTER 4-8   66
LPs: 10/12-inch 33rpm
SCEPTER 10-20   66
Also see LEE & PAUL

VANDENBERG
(Adrian Vandenberg)
Singles: 7-inch
ATCO 2-4   83-84
LPs: 10/12-inch 33rpm
ATCO 5-8   83-84

VANDERPOOL, Sylvia: see LITTLE SYLVIA

VANDROSS, Luther
Singles: 12-inch 33/45rpm
EPIC 4-6   82-85
Singles: 7-inch
COTILLION 3-5   76

EPIC 2-5   81-90
Picture Sleeves
EPIC 2-4   85-87
LPs: 10/12–inch 33rpm
EPIC 5-10   81-90
Also see BOWIE, David
Also see CHANGE
Also see LYNN, Cheryl, and Luther Vandross
Also see WARWICK, Dionne, and Luther Vandross

VANDROSS, Luther, and Gregory Hines
Singles: 7–inch

EPIC 2-4   87
Also see HINES, Gregory

VAN DYKE, Leroy
Singles: 78rpm

DOT (Except 15698) 4-8   56-57
DOT (15698 "Leather Jacket") 20-30   57
Singles: 7–inch
ABC 3-5   74-75
ABC/DOT 3-5   75-77
DECCA 3-5   70-72
DOT (Except 15698) 5-10   56-57
DOT (15698 "Leather Jacket") 50-75   57
KAPP 4-6   68-70
MCA 3-5   73
MERCURY 4-8   61-64
PLANTATION 3-5   78
SUN 3-5   79
WARNER 4-6   65-67
Picture Sleeves
MERCURY 5-8   64
LPs: 10/12–inch 33rpm
DECCA 8-10   72
HARMONY 8-12   69
KAPP 8-15   68-69
MCA 5-10   73
MERCURY 12-25   62-64
PLANTATION 5-10   77-79
SUN 5-8   74
WARNER 10-15   65-66
WING 8-15   65-66

VAN DYKES
Singles: 7–inch

DELUXE (6193 "Bells Are Ringing") . . 10-15   61
DONNA (1333 "Gift of Love") 20-30   60
FELSTED (8565 "Once Upon
  a Dream") 15-20   59
SPRING (1113 "Gift of Love") 60-75   59

VAN DYKES
Singles: 7–inch

HUE 10-15   65
MALA 5-8   65-67
LPs: 10/12–inch 33rpm
BELL 15-20   67
Members: Ron Tandy; Wenzon Mosley; Jimmy May.

VANGELIS
Singles: 7–inch

POLYDOR 2-4   81

RCA 3-5   78
Picture Sleeves
POLYDOR 3-5   81
LPs: 10/12–inch 33rpm
POLYDOR 5-10   81-86
RCA 5-10   78-82
Also see JON & VANGELIS

VANGUARDS
Singles: 7–inch

LAMP 3-5   70
WHIZ 4-6   69

VAN HALEN
Singles: 12–inch 33/45rpm

WARNER 4-6   83-84
Singles: 7–inch
WARNER 2-5   78-90
Picture Sleeves
WARNER 2-4   78-84
LPs: 10/12–inch 33rpm
WARNER 5-10   78-90
WARNER/LOONEY TUNES (705 "Van
  Halen") 10-20   78
(Colored vinyl. Promotional issue only.)
Members: David Lee Roth; Edward Van Halen; Alex Van Halen;
Michael Anthony; Sammy Hagar.
  Also see HAGAR, Sammy
  Also see MAY, Brian
  Also see ROTH, David Lee
  Also see VAN HALEN, Edward

VAN HALEN, Edward
LPs: 10/12–inch 33rpm

MCA 5-8   86
Also see VAN HALEN

VANILLA FUDGE
Singles: 7–inch

ATCO 4-8   67-70
LPs: 10/12–inch 33rpm
ATCO (200 and 300 series) 15-20   67-69
ATCO (90000 series) 5-10   82
Also see BECK, BOGERT & APPICE

VANILLI, Milli: see MILLI VANILLI

VANITY
(Denise Matthews)
Singles: 12–inch 33/45rpm

MOTOWN 4-6   84-86
Singles: 7–inch
MOTOWN 2-4   84-86
LPs: 10/12–inch 33rpm
MOTOWN 5-8   84-86
Also see VANITY 6

VANITY / Smokey Robinson
LPs: 10/12–inch 33rpm

MOTOWN (179 "Superstar
  Interviews") 10-15   84
(Promotional issue only.)
  Also see ROBINSON, Smokey
  Also see VANITY

VANITY FARE
Singles: 7–inch
BRENT	4-8	67
DJM	3-5	75
PAGE ONE	3-6	68-70
SOMA	8-12	68
20TH FOX	3-5	73

LPs: 10/12–inch 33rpm
PAGE ONE	10-15	70

VANITY 6
Singles: 12–inch 33/45rpm
WARNER	4-6	82-83

Singles: 7–inch
WARNER	2-4	82-83

LPs: 10/12–inch 33rpm
WARNER	5-8	82

Member: Denise Matthews.
Also see APOLLONIA 6
Also see TIME
Also see VANITY

VANN, Teddy
Singles: 7–inch
CAPITOL	3-6	67
COLUMBIA	4-8	61
END	5-10	59
JUBILEE	4-8	62
ROULETTE	4-8	60
TRIPLE-X	5-10	60

VANNELLI, Gino
Singles: 12–inch 33/45rpm
HME	4-6	85

Singles: 7–inch
A&M	3-5	74-79
ARISTA	3-5	81-82
CBS ASSOCIATES	2-4	85-87
HME	2-4	85

Picture Sleeves
A&M	3-5	76-79
ARISTA	3-5	81-82

LPs: 10/12–inch 33rpm
A&M (3600 series)	5-10	74
A&M (3700 series)	5-8	81
A&M (4000 series)	8-10	74-78
ARISTA	5-10	81-82
CBS ASSOCIATES	5-8	87
HME	5-10	85
MFSL	20-35	80
NAUTILUS	15-20	81

(Half-speed mastered.)

VAN SHELTON, Ricky:
see SHELTON, Ricky Van

VAN TIEGHEM, David
Singles: 12–inch 33/45rpm
WARNER	4-6	84

Singles: 7–inch
WARNER	2-4	84

LPs: 10/12–inch 33rpm
WARNER	5-8	84

VANWARMER, Randy
Singles: 7–inch
BEARSVILLE	3-5	79

LPs: 10/12–inch 33rpm
BEARSVILLE	5-10	79-83

VAN ZANT, Johnny, Band
Singles: 7–inch
POLYDOR	3-5	80-82

LPs: 10/12–inch 33rpm
ATLANTIC	5-8	90
POLYDOR	5-10	80-82

VAPORS
Singles: 7–inch
LIBERTY	3-5	81
U.A.	3-5	80

LPs: 10/12–inch 33rpm
LIBERTY	5-10	81
U.A.	5-10	80

VASEL, Marianne, and Erich Storz
Singles: 7–inch
MERCURY	4-8	58

LPs: 10/12–inch 33rpm
DANA	10-20	59

VAUGHAN, Frankie
Singles: 7–inch
COLUMBIA	4-8	59-60
EPIC	4-8	58
PHILIPS	3-6	62-66

LPs: 10/12–inch 33rpm
COLUMBIA	10-20	60
PHILIPS	10-15	62

VAUGHAN, Sarah
Singles: 78rpm
COLUMBIA	3-6	49-53
CONTINENTAL	5-10	45
MGM (Except 71)	3-6	50-51
MGM (71 "Sarah Vaughan Sings")	40-60	51
(Four disc boxed set.)		
MERCURY	3-6	53-57
MUSICRAFT	4-8	47-48

Singles: 7–inch
ATLANTIC	2-5	81
COLUMBIA (38000 and 39000 series)	5-10	51-53
MGM (10000 and 30000 series)	5-10	50-51
MAINSTREAM	3-5	71-74
MERCURY (70000 series)	4-8	53-66
ROULETTE	4-6	60-64
WARNER	2-5	81

Picture Sleeves
MERCURY	4-8	65

EPs: 7–inch 33/45rpm
ATLANTIC (527 "Sarah Vaughan Sings")	30-40	55
COLUMBIA	10-20	50-56

EMARCY 10-20	54-56
MGM 10-20	52-55
MERCURY 8-15	53-59

LPs: 10/12–inch 33rpm

ALLEGRO 5-10	
ATLANTIC 5-8	81
COLUMBIA (660 "After Hours") 35-45	55
COLUMBIA (745 "Sarah in Hi-Fi") 35-45	55
COLUMBIA (914 "Linger Awhile") . . . 25-35	57
COLUMBIA (6133 "Sarah Vaughan") 50-100	50
(10–inch LP.)	
COLUMBIA (37000 series) 5-8	82
CONCORD 15-25	56
EMARCY (400 series) 8-12	77
EMARCY (1000 series) 5-10	81
EMARCY (26005 "Images") 50-75	54
(10–inch LP.)	
EMARCY (36000 series) 30-40	54-57
EVEREST 5-10	70-76
HARMONY 5-15	59-69
MGM (165 "Tenderly") 50-100	51
(10–inch LPs.)	
MGM (544 "Sarah Vaughan Sings") . 50-100	54
(10–inch LP.)	
MGM (3274 "My Kinda Love") 50-75	55
MAINSTREAM 6-12	71-75
MERCURY (100 "Great Songs") 25-35	57
MERCURY (101 "Gershwin Songs") . 25-35	57
MERCURY (1000 series) 5-8	82
MERCURY (20000 series) 15-30	58-64
MERCURY (21000 series) 10-20	65-67
(Monaural.)	
MERCURY (25188 "Divine Sarah") . . 60-80	53
(10–inch LPs)	
MERCURY (60000 series) 15-25	59-64
MERCURY (61000 series) 10-25	65-67
(Stereo.)	
METRO 8-15	65
MUSICRAFT 5-8	83-84
PABLO 5-10	78-82
REMINGTON (1024 "Hot Jazz") . . . 50-100	53
(10–inch LP.)	
RIVERSIDE (2511 "Sarah Vaughan	
Sings") 40-60	55
RONDO 20-40	59
RONDOLETTE 20-40	59
ROULETTE (100 series) 8-15	71
ROULETTE (52000 series,	
except 52082) 10-25	60-67
(Black vinyl.)	
ROULETTE (52082 "You're Mine") . . 15-25	62
(Black vinyl.)	
ROULETTE (52082 "You're Mine") . . 35-55	62
(Colored vinyl.)	
SCEPTER 5-10	74
SUTTON 5-10	
TRIP 5-10	74-76
WING 5-15	63-68

Also see BASIE, Count, Sarah Vaughan and Joe Williams

Also see ECKSTINE, Billy, and Sarah Vaughan
Also see LEGRAND, Michel
Also see WASHINGTON, Dinah, and Sarah Vaughan

VAUGHAN, Sarah, and Quincy Jones
LPs: 10/12–inch 33rpm

MERCURY 15-25	59

Also see JONES, Quincy
Also see VAUGHAN, Sarah

VAUGHAN, Stevie Ray
(Stevie Ray Vaughn and Double Trouble)
Singles: 7–inch

COLUMBIA 2-4	87
EPIC 2-4	85

LPs: 10/12–inch 33rpm

COLUMBIA 5-8	87
EPIC (Except 8E8-39609) 5-10	84-89
EPIC (8E8-39609 "Couldn't Stand	
the Weather") 10-15	84
(Picture disc.)	

VAUGHAN BROTHERS
LPs: 10/12–inch 33rpm

EPIC 5-8	89

Members: Stevie Ray Vaughan; Jimmie Vaughan.
Also see FABULOUS THUNDERBIRDS
Also see VAUGHAN, Stevie Ray

VAUGHN, Billy, Orchestra
Singles: 78rpm

DOT 2-5	54-57

Singles: 7–inch

ABC 2-4	74
DOT 3-8	54-70
PARAMOUNT 2-4	70-72

Picture Sleeves

DOT 3-8	58-67

EPs: 7–inch 33/45rpm

DOT 4-8	55-59

LPs: 10/12–inch 33rpm

ABC 5-8	74
DOT 5-15	55-70
HAMILTON 5-10	65-66
MCA 5-8	83
MISTLETOE 4-8	76
MUSICOR 4-8	77
PARAMOUNT 5-8	70-74
PICKWICK 5-8	68
RANWOOD 4-8	83

Also see HILLTOPPERS
Also see NORDINE, Ken

VAUGHN, Denny
Singles: 78rpm

KAPP 3-5	56

Singles: 7–inch

KAPP 4-8	56

BOBBY VEE

Stayin' In
and
More Than
I Can Say

VEE, Bobby
(Bobby Vee and the Shadows; Bobby Vee and the Eligibles; Bobby Vee and the Strangers; Bobby Vee and the Johnny Mann Singers; Robert Thomas Velline)

Singles: 7–inch
COGNITO 3-5		81
LIBERTY (3331 "How Many Tears") .. 20-25		61
(Stereo Compact 33 Single.)		
LIBERTY (55208 "Suzie Baby") 10-20		59
LIBERTY (55234 through 55325) 5-8		60-61
LIBERTY (55234 through 56208) 3-6		61-70
SHADYBROOK 3-5		75-77
SOMA (1110 "Susie Baby") 30-50		59
U.A. 3-5		71-78

Picture Sleeves
LIBERTY 5-10		60-68

EPs: 7–inch 33/45rpm
LIBERTY 25-35		60-62
U.A. 10-12		72

LPs: 10/12–inch 33rpm
LIBERTY (3165 through 3534) 20-30		60-67
(Monaural.)		
LIBERTY (7165 through 7534) 20-40		60-67
(Stereo.)		
LIBERTY (7554 through 7612) 10-20		67-69
LIBERTY (10000 series) 5-8		84
SUNSET 10-15		66-67
U.A. (300 series) 8-10		73
U.A. (1000 series) 5-8		80

VEE, Bobby / Johnny Burnette / Ventures / Fleetwoods

LPs: 10/12–inch 33rpm
LIBERTY (5503 "Teensville") 20-30		61
Also see BURNETTE, Johnny
Also see FLEETWOODS

VEE, Bobby, and the Crickets
Singles: 7–inch
LIBERTY 4-8		62

Picture Sleeves
LIBERTY 10-15		60-63

LPs: 10/12–inch 33rpm
LIBERTY 20-25		62
Also see CRICKETS

VEE, Bobby, and the Ventures
LPs: 10/12–inch 33rpm
LIBERTY 20-25		63
Also see VEE, Bobby
Also see VENTURES

VEGA, Suzanne
Singles: 7–inch
A&M 2-4		85-90

LPs: 10/12–inch 33rpm
A&M 5-8		85-90

VEGA, Tata
Singles: 12–inch 33/45rpm
TAMLA 4-8		79

Singles: 7–inch
TAMLA 3-5		76-80

LPs: 10/12–inch 33rpm
TAMLA 5-10		76-80
Also see RAWLS, Lou

VEJTABLES
Singles: 7–inch
AUTUMN 5-10		65-66
UPTOWN 4-8		67

VELAIRES
Singles: 7–inch
BRENT 5-10		
HI-MAR 4-8		65
JAMIE 10-15		61-62
MERCURY 5-10		69
PALMS (730 "Summertime Blues") .. 30-60		61
RAMCO 5-10		

VELEZ, Martha
Singles: 7–inch
MCA 2-4		80
POLYDOR 3-5		73
SIRE 3-5		69-76

LPs: 10/12–inch 33rpm
SIRE (7000 series) 8-10		74-76
SIRE (97000 series) 10-12		69

VELLINE, Robert Thomas:
see VEE, Bobby

VELOURS
Singles: 78rpm
ONYX (Except 508) 15-25		56-57
ONYX (508 "Romeo") 35-50		57

Singles: 7–inch
CUB 10-20		58-59
END 10-15		61
GOLDISC 15-20		60
GONE (5092 "Can I Come Over Tonight") 10-15		60
ONYX (501 "My Love Come Back") 100-150		56
ONYX (508 "Romeo") 150-250		57
ONYX (512 "Can I Come Over Tonight") 50-100		57

ONYX (515 "This Could Be
the Night") 40-60   57
ONYX (520 "Remember") 40-60   58
ORBIT (9001 "Remember") 20-30   58
ROULETTE 3-5
STUDIO (9902 "I Promise") 25-30   59
   Members: Jerry Ramos; Pete Winston; John Pearson; Don
   Heywood; John Cheetom; Charles Moffett; Keith Williams;
   Troyce Key.
   Also see KEY, Troyce

VELS
Singles: 12-inch 33/45rpm
MERCURY 4-6   84-85
Singles: 7-inch
MERCURY 2-4   84-85
LPs: 10/12-inch 33rpm
MERCURY 5-8   84

VELVELETTES
Singles: 7-inch
I.P.G. 4-8   63
SOUL 4-8   66
V.I.P. 4-8   64-65
   Members: Carolyn Gill, Sandra Tilley; Betty Kelly.
   Also see MARTHA and the Vandellas

VELVET, Jimmy
(Jimmy Velvet Five; James Velvet; Jimmy Velvit)
Singles: 7-inch
ABC-PAR 4-8   63-64
BELL 4-8   67
CAMEO 4-8   67
CORREC-TONE 5-10   62
CUB 5-10   61-62
DIVISION 5-10   61
PHILIPS 4-8   65
ROYAL AMERICAN 4-6   69
TOLLIE 4-8   64
U.A. 4-6   68
VELVET 5-10   61
VELVET TONE 4-8   65-67
LPs: 10/12-inch 33rpm
VELVET TONE 10-20   67
   Also see TENNANT, Jimmy

VELVET UNDERGROUND
Singles: 12-inch 33/45rpm
POLYGRAM 5-10   85
Singles: 7-inch
ASPEN ("Loop") 20-40   66
   (Single-sided soundsheet. Promotional issue only.)
COTILLION (44107 "Who Loves
the Sun") 20-40   71
INDEX ("Interview") 20-40   67
   (Single-sided picture disc soundsheet. Promotional
   issue only.)
MGM (14057 "What Goes On") 25-50   69
VERVE (10560 "White Light/
White Heat") 25-50   68
LPs: 10/12-inch 33rpm
COTILLION (9034 "Loaded") 15-20   70

COTILLION (9500 "Live") 15-20   70
MGM (131 "Velvet Underground") 8-10   71
MGM (4950 " Archetypes") 10-15   69-74
MERCURY (7504 "Velvet
Underground") 12-15   72
PRIDE 10-15   73
VERVE (5046 "White Light/
White Heat") 30-40   67
VERVE (800000 series) 5-10   84-85
   Members: Lou Reed; John Cale; Sterling Morrison; Maureen
   Tucker; Doug Yule.
   Also see AMERICAN FLYER
   Also see CALE, John
   Also see REED, Lou

VELVET UNDERGROUND & NICO
Singles: 7-inch
VERVE (10427 "All Tomorrow's
Parties") 25-50   66
(Blue label.)
VERVE (10427 "All Tomorrow's
Parties") 50-75   66
(White label. Promotional issue only.)
VERVE (10466 "Sunday Morning") . . 25-50   66
Picture Sleeves
VERVE (10427 "All Tomorrow's
Parties") 100-150   66
(Promotional issue only.)
LPs: 10/12-inch 33rpm
VERVE (5008 "Velvet Underground
& Nico") 100-150   67
(Monaural. With banana sticker on front cover.
Back cover pictures an upside-down torso of a
man behind the photo of Andy Warhol. Thus far, all
copies meeting this description have been mono.)
VERVE (5008 "Velvet Underground
& Nico") 50-75   67
(Stereo. With adhesive banana sticker on front
cover. If a stereo copy with the upside-down male
torso photo behind Andy Warhol exists, its value
would approximately double.)
VERVE (5008 "Velvet Underground
& Nico") 50-100   67
(With banana sticker on front cover. Back cover
has a sticker above the photo of the group on
stage, which reads: "The Velvet Underground and
Nico.")
VERVE (5008 "Velvet Underground
& Nico") 30-60   67
(With adhesive banana sticker on front cover. Does
not picture the upside-down male torso.)
VERVE (5008 "Velvet Underground
& Nico") 25-35   67
(No banana sticker on front cover.)
VERVE (800000 series) 5-10   84
   Also see NICO
   Also see VELVET UNDERGROUND

VELVETS
Singles: 7-inch
MONUMENT (400 series) 8-10   61-62

MONUMENT (800 and 900 series) 3-5   63-66
PLAID 5-8   59
20TH FOX 5-8   59
Member: Virgil Johnson.

VELVIT, Jimmy: see VELVET, Jimmy

VENETIANS
Singles: 7-inch
CHRYSALIS 2-4   87

VENTURES
Singles: 12-inch 33/45rpm
TRIDEX (1245 "Surfin' and Spyin") 5-8   81
(With vocals by Charlotte Caffey and Jane Weidlin.)
Singles: 7-inch
BLUE HORIZON 10-20   59-60
DOLTON 4-8   61-66
LIBERTY 3-6   66-70
TRIDEX 3-5   81
U.A. 3-5   70-78
Picture Sleeves
DOLTON 5-10   60-66
EPs: 7-inch 33/45rpm
DOLTON 20-25   60
LPs: 10/12-inch 33rpm
AWARD 8-12   84
DOLTON (2003 "Walk Don't Run") ... 25-35   60
(Light blue label. Monaural.)
DOLTON (2003 "Walk Don't Run") ... 15-25   61
(Dark blue label. Monaural.)
DOLTON (2004 through 2050) 20-25   61-67
(Monaural.)
DOLTON (8003 "Walk Don't Run") ... 30-40   60
(Light blue label. Stereo.)
DOLTON (8003 "Walk Don't Run") ... 20-30   61
(Dark blue label. Stereo.)
DOLTON (8004 through 8050) 20-30   61-67
(Stereo.)
DOLTON (17000 series) 15-20   65-66
LIBERTY (2000 and 8000 series) ... 10-20   67-70
LIBERTY (10000 series) 5-10   81-84
LIBERTY (35000 series) 10-15   70
SUNSET 10-15   66-71
TRIDEX 5-10   81-83
U.A. 10-15   71-77

Members: Don Wilson; Bob Bogle; Mel Taylor; Nokie Edwards;
Jerry McGee; Skip Moore; Howie Johnson.
  Also see GO-GOs
  Also see LOPEZ, Trini, with the Ventures & Nancy Ames
  Also see VEE, Bobby, and the Ventures

VENUS, Vic
Singles: 7-inch
BUDDAH 4-8   69

VERA, Billy
(Billy Vera and the Contrasts; Billy Vera and the
Beaters; Billy Vera and Blue Eyed Soul)
Singles: 7-inch
ATLANTIC 4-6   68-69
FLAVOR 10-15   64
MIDSONG 3-5   75-76
ORANGE 4-8   73
RHINO 2-4   86-87
RUST 10-20   62
LPs: 10/12-inch 33rpm
ALFA 5-10   81
ATLANTIC 10-15   68
MACOLA 5-8   87
MIDSONG INT'L 8-12   77
RHINO 5-8   86
Also see BILLY and the Beaters

VERA, Billy and Judy Clay
Singles: 7-inch
ATLANTIC 4-8   67-68
LPs: 10/12-inch 33rpm
ATLANTIC 10-15   68
Also see CLAY, Judy

VERA LYNN: see LYNN, Vera

VERLAINE, Tom
Singles: 7-inch
ELEKTRA 3-5   80
WARNER 3-5   81-84
LPs: 10/12-inch 33rpm
ELEKTRA 5-10   80
WARNER 5-10   81-84

VERNE, Larry
Singles: 7-inch
COLLECTABLES 2-4
ERA 5-8   60-64
Picture Sleeves
ERA 10-15   60
LPs: 10/12-inch 33rpm
ERA (104 "Mister Larry Verne") 25-35   60

VERONICA
(Veronica "Ronnie" Spector)
Singles: 7-inch
PHIL SPECTOR (1 "So Young") 25-35   64
PHIL SPECTOR (2 "Why Don't They
  Let Us Fall in Love") 25-35   64
Also see SPECTOR, Ronnie

VERTICAL HOLD
Singles: 7-inch
CRIMINAL 2-4   88

VIA AFRIKA
Singles: 12–inch 33/45rpm
EMI AMERICA 4-6   84
Singles: 7–inch
EMI AMERICA 2-4   84
LPs: 10/12–inch 33rpm
EMI AMERICA 5-8   84

VIBRATIONS
Singles: 7–inch
ABC 3-5   74
ATLANTIC 4-8   63-64
BET (1 "So Blue") 50-100   60
CHECKER (Except 954 and 987) . . . 10-15   60-63
CHECKER (954 "So Blue") 20-25   60
CHECKER (987 "All My Love
   Belongs to You") 25-30   61
CHESS 3-5   74
EPIC 4-8   68
MANDALA 3-5   72
NEPTUNE 4-6   69-70
OKEH 4-8   64-68
LPs: 10/12–inch 33rpm
CHECKER (2978 "Watusi") 30-50   61
MANDALA 10-15   72
OKEH 25-35   65-69
   Also see JAYHAWKS
   Also see MARATHONS

VICKY D
Singles: 7–inch
SAM 2-4   82

VICTIMS FAMILY
LPs: 10/12–inch 33rpm
MORDAM 5-8   88

VIDAL, Maria
Singles: 12–inch 33/45rpm
EMI AMERICA 4-6   84
Singles: 7–inch
EMI AMERICA 2-4   84
   Also see CHILD, Desmond, and Rouge

VIDEEO
Singles: 7–inch
H.C.R.C. 3-5   82

VIDELS
(Vi-Dels)
Singles: 7–inch
COLLECTABLES 2-4
DUSTY DISC 5-8
JDS (5004 "Mister Lonely") 15-25   60
   (Gray label.)
JDS (5004 "Mister Lonely") 10-15   60
   (Multi-color label.)
JDS (5005 "She's Not Coming Home") 15-25   60
   (Gray label.)
JDS (5005 "She's Not Coming Home") 10-15   60
   (Multi-color label.)
KAPP (361 "Streets of Love") 10-20   61
KAPP (405 "A Letter from Ann") 25-35   61

MEDIEVAL 8-10   59
MUSICNOTE (117 "We Belong
   Together") 20-30   63
RHODY (2000 "Be My Girl") 30-40   59
   Members: Pete Anders; Vinnie Poncia.

VIEW from the HILL
Singles: 7–inch
CAPITOL 2-4   88

VIGRASS & OSBORNE
Singles: 7–inch
EPIC 3-5   74
UNI 3-5   72
LPs: 10/12–inch 33rpm
EPIC 8-10   74
UNI 8-15   71
   Members: Paul Vigrass; Gary Osborne.

VILLAGE PEOPLE
Singles: 12–inch 33/45rpm
CASABLANCA 4-8   78-79
Singles: 7–inch
CASABLANCA 3-5   78-79
RCA 3-5   81
Picture Sleeves
CASABLANCA 3-5   78-79
RCA 3-5   81
LPs: 10/12–inch 33rpm
CASABLANCA (Except
   NBPIX series) 5-10   77-80
CASABLANCA (NBPIX series) 10-15   78
   (Picture discs.)
RCA 5-10   81
   Members: Victor Willis; Alexander Briley; Felipe Rose; Randy
   Jones; David Hodo; Glenn Hughes.

VILLAGE SOUL CHOIR
Singles: 7–inch
ABBOTT 3-5   69-70

VILLAGE STOMPERS
Singles: 7–inch
EPIC 3-6   63-67
Picture Sleeves
EPIC 4-8   63-65
LPs: 10/12–inch 33rpm
EPIC 10-20   63-67
   Also see VINTON, Bobby, and the Village Stompers

VINCENT, Gene
(Gene Vincent and His Blue Caps)
Singles: 78rpm
CAPITOL 10-20   56-57
Singles: 7–inch
CAPITOL (3450 through 3617) 12-25   56-57
CAPITOL (3678 "B-I-Bickey
   Bi-Bo-Bo-Go") 20-30   57
CAPITOL (3763 through 4665) 10-20   57-61
CHALLENGE 10-20   66-67
FOREVER 10-20   69-70
KAMA SUTRA 5-10   70-73

PLAYGROUND (100 "Story of
the Rockers") 100-150   68
Picture Sleeves
CAPITOL (4237 "Right Now") 800-1000   60
Promotional Singles
CAPITOL (White label) 20-40   56-61
EPs: 7–inch 33/45rpm
CAPITOL (438 "Dance to the Bop") 150-200   57
(Promotional issue only. Not issued with cover.)
CAPITOL (764 "Bluejean Bop") 75-125   57
(Price is for any of three volumes.)
CAPITOL (811 "Gene Vincent
and His Bluecaps") 75-125   57
(Price is for any of three volumes.)
CAPITOL (970 "Gene Vincent Rocks
and the Bluecaps Roll") 75-125   58
(Price is for any of three volumes.)
CAPITOL (985 "Hot Rod Gang") . . 350-400   58
(Green label. Soundtrack.)
CAPITOL (985 "Hot Rod Gang") . . 400-450   58
(White label. Promotional issue.)
CAPITOL (1059 "Record Date") 75-125   58
(Price is for any of three volumes.)
LPs: 10/12–inch 33rpm
CAPITOL (DKAO-380 "Gene Vincent's
Greatest") 15-25   69
CAPITOL (SM-380 "Gene Vincent's
Greatest") 5-10   78
CAPITOL (764 "Bluejean Bop") . . . 200-300   56
CAPITOL (811 "Gene Vincent and
His Blue Caps") 200-300   57
CAPITOL (970 "Gene Vincent
Rocks") 200-300   58
CAPITOL (1059 "Gene Vincent
Record Date") 200-300   58
CAPITOL (1207 "Sounds Like
Gene Vincent") 200-300   59
CAPITOL (1342 "Crazy Times") . . . 150-250   60
CAPITOL (11000 series) 8-12   74
CAPITOL (16000 series) 5-10   81
DANDELION 10-20   70
KAMA-SUTRA 10-20   70-71
ROLLIN' ROCK 5-10   80-81
Also see CHAMPS
Also see MEYERS, Augie
Also see PRESLEY, Elvis

VINCENT, Gene / Frank Sinatra / Sonny James / Ron Goodwin
EPs: 7–inch 33/45rpm
CAPITOL (437 "Special Hit
Pressing") 50-100   57
(Promotional issue only. Not issued with cover.)
Also see GOODWIN, Ron
Also see JAMES, Sonny
Also see SINATRA, Frank

VINCENT, Vinnie, Invasion
LPs: 10/12–inch 33rpm
CHRYSALIS 5-8   86-88
Also see KISS

VINTON, Bobby
(Bobby Vinton Orchestra)
Singles: 7–inch
ABC 3-5   74-77
ALPINE 10-15   59
DIAMOND 4-8   62
ELEKTRA 3-5   78
EPIC (9000 series) 4-8   60-66
(Black vinyl.)
EPIC (9000 series) 8-10   64
(Colored vinyl.)
EPIC (10000 series) 3-6   66-75
LARC 2-4   83
TAPESTRY 2-5   79-82
Picture Sleeves
EPIC 3-8   62-72
TAPESTRY 3-5   80
EPs: 7–inch 33/45rpm
EPIC 6-12   63-64
LPs: 10/12–inch 33rpm
ABC 8-10   74-77
COLUMBIA 8-10   73
EPIC (500 series) 20-25   60
EPIC (3000 series) 15-20   60
EPIC (20000 series) 8-15   62-70
(Black vinyl.)
EPIC (20468 "Blue on Blue") 20-40   63
(Colored vinyl. Promotional issue only.)
EPIC (30000 series) 5-10   72-79
HARMONY 5-10   70
TAPESTRY 5-10   80

VINTON, Bobby, and the Village Stompers
LPs: 10/12–inch 33rpm
EPIC 10-20   66
Also see VILLAGE STOMPERS
Also see VINTON, Bobby

VIO-LENCE
LPs: 10/12–inch 33rpm
MECHANIC 5-8   88

VIPERS
Singles: 12–inch 33/45rpm
MIDNIGHT 4-6   88
Singles: 7–inch
MIDNIGHT 2-4   84-88
LPs: 10/12–inch 33rpm
MIDNIGHT 5-8   84-88
PVC 5-8   85
SKYCLAD 5-8   89
Members: David Andrew Mann; Graham May; Paul Monroe
Martin; Patrick Allen Brown; Jonithan Adam Weiss; John
Englland; Bill McGarvey; Anders Thomsen.
Also see FLESHTONES

VIRTUES
(Frank Virtue and the Virtues; Frank Virtuoso and the Virtues)
Singles: 7–inch
ABC 3-5   73
ABC-PAR 5-10   59

B.V.D.	5-10	
FAYETTE	4-8	64
HIGHLAND	10-15	60
HUNT (Monaural)	5-10	59
HUNT (Stereo)	15-25	59
SURE (500 series)	8-12	59
SURE (1700 series)	4-8	62
VIRNON	5-10	60
VIRTUE	4-6	66-69
WYNNE	5-10	60

LPs: 10/12–inch 33rpm

STRAND	20-25	60
WYNNE	25-30	60

VISAGE

Singles: 12–inch 33/45rpm

POLYDOR	4-6	80-82

Singles: 7–inch

POLYDOR	3-5	81

LPs: 10/12–inch 33rpm

POLYDOR	5-10	80-82

VISCOUNTS
(Vicounts)

Singles: 7–inch

AMY	4-8	65-66
CORAL	4-8	66-67
MADISON	5-10	59-61
MR. PEACOCK	4-8	61
MR. PEEKE	4-8	63

LPs: 10/12–inch 33rpm

AMY (8008 "Harlem Nocturne")	20-30	65
MADISON (1001 "The Viscounts")	50-75	60

Members: Bobby Spievak; Joe Spievak; Harry Haller; Larry Vecchio; Clark Smith.

VISUAL

Singles: 12–inch 33/45rpm

PRELUDE	4-6	83-84

Singles: 7–inch

PRELUDE	2-4	83-84

VITALE, Joe

Singles: 7–inch

ASYLUM	3-5	81-82
ATLANTIC	3-5	74

LPs: 10/12–inch 33rpm

ASYLUM	5-10	81
ATLANTIC	5-10	74

Also see EAGLES
Also see WALSH, Joe

VITAMIN E

Singles: 7–inch

BUDDAH	3-5	77

VITAMIN Z

Singles: 12–inch 33/45rpm

GEFFEN	4-6	85

Singles: 7–inch

GEFFEN	2-4	85

LPs: 10/12–inch 33rpm

GEFFEN	5-8	85

Member: Geoff Barradale.
Also see PARSONS, Alan, Project

VITO and the Salutations

Singles: 7–inch

APT (25079 "Walkin")	25-35	65
BOOM	10-15	66
CRYSTAL BALL	3-5	78
HERALD	15-20	63-64
KRAM (1202 "Your Way")	30-40	62
RAYNA (5009 "Gloria")	20-25	62
RED BOY	8-12	66
REGINA (1320 "Get a Job")	15-25	64
RUST	10-15	66
SANDBAG	4-8	68
WELLS (1008 "Can I Depend on You") (Black vinyl.)	15-20	64
WELLS (1008 "Can I Depend on You") (Colored vinyl.)	20-30	64

LPs: 10/12–inch 33rpm

RED BOY (200 "Greatest Hits")	20-30	81

Members: Vito Balsamo; Shelly Buchansky; Randy Silverman; Len Citrin; Frank Fox.

VIXEN

Singles: 7–inch

EMI	2-4	88-90

Picture Sleeves

EMI	2-4	88

LPs: 10/12–inch 33rpm

EMI	5-8	88-90

VOCALEERS

Singles: 78rpm

RED ROBIN	20-40	52

Singles: 7–inch

OLD TOWN	10-15	60
OLDIES 45	4-6	65
PARADISE (113 "I Need Your Love So Bad")	15-25	59
RED ROBIN (113 "Be True")	150-200	52
RED ROBIN (114 "Is It a Dream")	100-150	52
RED ROBIN (119 "I Walk Alone")	150-200	53
RED ROBIN (125 "Will You Be True")	150-200	54
RED ROBIN (132 "Angel Face")	100-150	54
TWISTIME (11 "A Golden Tear")	10-20	62
VEST (832 "Hear My Plea")	40-60	60

Members: Joe Duncan; Curtis Dunham; Ted Williams; Mel Walton; Bill Walker; Lamarr Cooper; Joe Powell; Richard Blandon; Leo Fuller; Curtis Blandon; Caesar Williams.
Also see LITTLE ESTHER & Junior with the Johnny Otis Orchestra / Johnny Otis Orchestra with the Vocaleers

VOCALEERS / Mango Jones

Singles: 7–inch

OLDIES 45	4-6	65

Also see VOCALEERS

VOGUES

Singles: 7–inch

ABC	3-5	73
ABC-PAR	4-8	65

ASTRA 3-5   73
BELL 3-5   71
BLUE STAR (229 "You're the One") .. 10-20   65
CASCADE 5-10   59
CO & CE 4-8   65-67
DOT 8-12   58-59
GUSTO 2-4
MGM 4-8   67
MAINSTREAM 3-5   72
REPRISE 3-6   68-71
REVUE 4-8   68
SUN 3-5   79
20TH FOX 3-5   73

LPs: 10/12–inch 33rpm

CO & CE 25-35   65-66
51 WEST 5-10
PICKWICK 8-10   71
REPRISE 10-15   68-70
SSS INT'L 5-10   77
Members: Bob Bush; Bill Burkette; Hugh Geyer; Chuck Blasko; Don Miller.

VOICE MASTERS
Singles: 7–inch

ANNA (101 "Hope and Pray") 15-25   59
ANNA (102 "Needed") 15-25   59
ANNA (103 "Hit and Run Away") 15-20   59
BAMBOO 4-8   68
Members: Ty Hunter; C.P. Spencer; Lamont Dozier; David Ruffin; Freddie Gorman.
Also see DOZIER, Lamont
Also see HUNTER, Ty
Also see ORIGINALS
Also see RUFFIN, David

VOICES of AMERICA / U.S.A. for Africa
Singles: 7–inch

EMI AMERICA 2-4   86
Also see TOTO
Also see U.S.A. for AFRICA

VOICES of EAST HARLEM
Singles: 7–inch

ELEKTRA 3-5   70-72
JUST SUNSHINE 3-5   73-74

LPs: 10/12–inch 33rpm

ELEKTRA 8-10   70
JUST SUNSHINE 5-10   73-74

VOLCANOS
Singles: 7–inch

ARCTIC 4-8   65-67
VIRTUE 3-5   70

VOLLENWEIDER, Andreas
Singles: 12–inch 33/45rpm

CBS/COLUMBIA 4-6   86
Singles: 7–inch
CBS/COLUMBIA 2-4   86
LPs: 10/12–inch 33rpm
CBS/COLUMBIA 5-8   84-89

VOLTAGE BROTHERS
Singles: 12–inch 33/45rpm

MTM 4-6   86
Singles: 7–inch
LIFESONG 2-4   78
MTM 2-4   86
LPs: 10/12–inch 33rpm
LIFESONG 5-8   78
MTM 5-8   86

VOLUMES
Singles: 7–inch

ABC 3-5   73
AMERICAN ARTS 4-8   64-65
CHEX 10-20   62
IMPACT 4-8   66
INFERNO 4-8   67-68
JUBILEE 6-12   63
OLD TOWN (1154 "Why") 10-20   64
VIRGO 3-5   73

LPs: 10/12–inch 33rpm

RELIC 5-10   85
Also see NUTMEGS / Volumes
Also see VALUMES

VONTASTICS
Singles: 7–inch

CHESS 4-8   67
ST. LAWRENCE 4-8   65-66
SATELLITE 5-10   65

VOUDOURIS, Roger
Singles: 7–inch

WARNER 3-5   78-79
LPs: 10/12–inch 33rpm
WARNER 5-10   79

VOXPOPPERS
Singles: 7–inch

AMP 3 (1004 "Wishing for Your Love") 20-25   58
MERCURY 8-12   58
POPLAR 10-15   58
VERSAILLES (200 "A Blessing
   After All") 20-25   59
EPs: 7–inch 33/45rpm
MERCURY (3391 "The
   Voxpoppers") 50-100   58

VOYAGE
Singles: 7–inch

ATLANTIC 3-5   82
MARLIN 3-5   78-79
LPs: 10/12–inch 33rpm
ATLANTIC 5-8   82
MARLIN 5-10   78

VOYEUR
Singles: 7–inch

MCA 2-4   85

W

W.A.G.B.
Singles: 7–inch
STREET SOUNDS 2-4   82

W.A.S.P.
Singles: 7–inch
CAPITOL 2-4   84-89
Picture Sleeves
CAPITOL 2-4   84-87
LPs: 10/12–inch 33rpm
CAPITOL 5-8   84-89
Members: Blackie Lawless; Randy Piper; Chris Holmes; Steve Riley.
Also see NEW YORK DOLLS

WA WA NEE
Singles: 7–inch
EPIC 2-4   87
LPs: 10/12–inch 33rpm
EPIC 5-8   87

WACKERS
Singles: 7–inch
BOMP 3-5   75
ELEKTRA 3-5   71-73
LPs: 10/12–inch 33rpm
ELEKTRA 5-10   71-72

WADE, Adam
Singles: 7–inch
COED 5-8   59-61
EPIC 4-6   62-66
KIRSHNER 3-5   77
REMEMBER 4-6   69
WARNER 4-6   67-68
Picture Sleeves
COED 5-10   60-61
EPIC 4-8   62-63
LPs: 10/12–inch 33rpm
COED 20-25   60
EPIC 15-20   62
KIRSHNER 5-10   77

WADSWORTH MANSION
Singles: 7–inch
SUSSEX 3-5   70
LPs: 10/12–inch 33rpm
SUSSEX 10-20   71
Some Sussex issues showed the group as "Wadsworth Manison."

WAGNER, Jack
Singles: 7–inch
QWEST 2-4   84-87
LPs: 10/12–inch 33rpm
QWEST 5-8   84-87

WAGONER, Porter
Singles: 78rpm
RCA 3-6   56-57
Singles: 7–inch
RCA (0013 through 1007) 3-6   69-74
RCA (5600 through 7638) 5-10   54-59
RCA (7708 through 9979) 3-8   60-71
RCA (10124 through 11998) 2-5   74-79
WARNER 2-4   82-83
EPs: 7–inch 33/45rpm
RCA 8-15   56
LPs: 10/12–inch 33rpm
ACCORD 5-8   82
CAMDEN 5-15   63-73
H.S.R.D. 15-25   81
PICKWICK 5-10   75-77
RCA (Except 1300 through 2900 series) 5-15   66-79
RCA (1358 "A Satisfied Mind") 30-40   56
RCA (LPM-2447 through
LPM-2960) 10-20   62-65
(Monaural.)
RCA (LSP-2447 through
LSP-2960) 15-25   62-65
(Stereo.)
TUDOR 5-8   84
WARNER 5-8   83
Also see SNOW, Hank / Hank Locklin / Porter Wagoner

WAGONER, Porter, and Skeeter Davis
LPs: 10/12–inch 33rpm
RCA 10-20   62
Also see DAVIS, Skeeter

WAGONER, Porter, and Dolly Parton
Singles: 7–inch
RCA 3-6   67-71
LPs: 10/12–inch 33rpm
RCA (Except 3926 through 4841) 5-10   74-80
RCA (LPM-3926 "Just Between
You and Me") 30-40   68
(Monaural.)
RCA (LSP-3926 through LSP-4841) . 10-20   68-73
Also see PARTON, Dolly
Also see WAGONER, Porter

WAIKIKIS
Singles: 7–inch
KAPP 3-6   64-68
PALETTE 3-6   62-63
LPs: 10/12–inch 33rpm
BOOT 5-8   78
KAPP 8-15   64-69
MCA 5-8

WAILERS
Singles: 7–inch
BELL 4-8   67
ETIQUETTE 4-8   63-66
GOLDEN CREST 10-15   59
(Label pictures the group.)
GOLDEN CREST 5-10   60-64
(No picture on label.)

IMPERIAL	4-8	64
U.A.	4-8	67
VIVA	4-6	67

LPs: 10/12-inch 33rpm

BELL	10-15	68
ETIQUETTE (1 "The Fabulous Wailers at the Castle")	75-100	66
ETIQUETTE (022 "The Wailers and Company")	40-60	66
ETIQUETTE (023 "Wailers Wailers Everywhere")	75-100	66
ETIQUETTE (026 "Out of Our Tree")	40-60	

Reissues of Etiquette LPs have a 1980s date on back cover.

ETIQUETTE (1100 series)	5-8	86
GOLDEN CREST (3075 "The Fabulous Wailers") (Color cover.)	50-75	60
GOLDEN CREST (3075 "The Fabulous Wailers") (Black and white cover.)	40-60	60
GOLDEN CREST (3075 "The Wailers Wail")	25-35	
IMPERIAL	15-20	64
U.A. (3557 "Outburst!") (Monaural.)	25-35	67
U.A. (6557 "Outburst!") (Stereo.)	35-45	67

Members: Kent Morrill; Robin Roberts; Gail Harris; Mark Marush; Rich Dangel; John "Buck" Ormsby; Mike Burk; Neil Anderson; Ron Gardner; Dave Roland.
Also see MORRILL, Kent
Also see SONICS / Wailers
Also see SONICS / Wailers / Galaxies
Also see THREE GRACES / Wailers

Loudon Wainwright III: Unrequited

WAINWRIGHT, Loudon, III
Singles: 7-inch

ARISTA	3-5	76-78
COLUMBIA	3-5	73

LPs: 10/12-inch 33rpm

ARISTA	5-10	76-78
ATLANTIC	10-15	70-71
COLUMBIA ("KC" series)	10-15	72-73
COLUMBIA ("PC" series)	5-10	75

ROUNDER	5-10	80-83

Also see SPRINGSTEEN, Bruce / Albert Hammond / Loudon Wainwright, III / Taj Mahal

WAITE, John
Singles: 12-inch 33/45rpm

EMI AMERICA	4-6	84

Singles: 7-inch

CHRYSALIS	2-4	82-85
EMI AMERICA	2-4	84-87

Picture Sleeves

EMI AMERICA	2-5	84-87

LPs: 10/12-inch 33rpm

CHRYSALIS	5-8	82
EMI AMERICA	5-8	84-87

Also see BABYS

WAITRESSES
Singles: 7-inch

ANTILLES	3-5	80
POLYDOR	2-4	82

LPs: 10/12-inch 33rpm

POLYDOR	5-8	82-83

WAITS, Tom
Singles: 7-inch

ASYLUM	3-5	74
ELEKTRA	2-4	83
ISLAND	2-4	83-88

LPs: 10/12-inch 33rpm

ASYLUM	5-10	73-80
ELEKTRA	5-8	83
ISLAND	5-8	83-88

Also see GAYLE, Crystal, and Tom Waits

WAKELY, Jimmy
Singles: 78rpm

CAPITOL	3-5	50-52
CORAL	3-5	53-55
DECCA	3-5	55-57
JIMMY WAKELY SOUVENIR	5-10	

Singles: 7-inch

ARTCO	3-5	74
CAPITOL (1300 through 2100 series)	5-10	50-52
CORAL	4-8	53-55
DECCA	3-8	55-70
DOT	3-6	66
SHASTA (100 series)	3-6	58-67
SHASTA (200 series)	3-4	71

Picture Sleeves

SHASTA	5-10	58

EPs: 7-inch 33/45rpm

CAPITOL	10-20	50-53
CORAL	10-15	54
DECCA	8-12	58

LPs: 10/12-inch 33rpm

ALBUM GLOBE	5-10	81
CAPITOL	20-40	50-53
CORAL	4-8	73
DANNY	8-10	
DECCA (8400 through 8600 series)	20-35	56-57
DECCA (75000 through 78000 series)	8-18	67-70

DOT 10-15   66
MCA 4-8
MCR 5-10   74
SHASTA 5-15   58-75
TOPS 10-15
VOCALION 5-10   68-70
   Also see CHANDLER, Karen, and Jimmy Wakely
   Also see WHITING, Margaret, and Jimmy Wakely

WAKELIN, Johnny, and the Kinshasa Band
Singles: 7–inch

PYE 3-5   75

WAKEMAN, Rick
**(Rick Wakeman with the London Symphony
Orchestra and English Chamber Choir; Rick
Wakeman and the English Rock Ensemble)**
Singles: 7–inch

A&M 3-5   73
LPs: 10/12–inch 33rpm
A&M (3000 series) 5-10   74
A&M (4000 series) 5-12   73-77
A&M (6000 series) 10-15   79
   Also see DALTREY, Roger, and Rick Wakeman
   Also see STRAWBS
   Also see YES

WALDEN, Narada Michael
(Narada)
Singles: 12–inch 33/45rpm

ATLANTIC 4-6   82-83
WARNER 4-6   85
Singles: 7–inch
ATLANTIC 3-5   77-83
REPRISE 2-4   88
WARNER 2-4   85
LPs: 10/12–inch 33rpm
ATLANTIC 5-10   79-83

WALDEN, Narada Michael, and Patti Austin
Singles: 7–inch

WARNER 2-4   85
   Also see AUSTIN, Patti

WALDMAN, Wendy
Singles: 7–inch

EPIC 2-4   82-83
WARNER 3-5   77-78
LPs: 10/12–inch 33rpm
EPIC 5-8   82-83
WARNER 5-10   78

WALDO
Singles: 7–inch

COLUMBIA 3-5   82
LPs: 10/12–inch 33rpm
COLUMBIA 5-10   82

WALKER, Billy
Singles: 78rpm

COLUMBIA 3-6   54-56
Singles: 7–inch
CAPRICE 3-4   79
COLUMBIA (21000 series) 5-10   54-56

COLUMBIA (40000 series) 4-8   56-60
COLUMBIA (42000 and 43000 series) . 4-6   61-65
DIMENSION 2-4   83
MCA 3-5   77
MGM 3-5   70-74
MRC 3-4   78
MONUMENT 3-6   66-70
RCA 3-5   75-76
SCORPION 3-4   78
TALL TEXAN 3-4   83
Picture Sleeves
COLUMBIA 4-8   63-67
LPs: 10/12–inch 33rpm
COLUMBIA 10-20   63-69
GUSTO 5-8
H.S.R.D. 5-10   84
HARMONY 8-15   64-70
MGM 6-12   70-74
MONUMENT 8-18   66-72
RCA 5-10   75-76

WALKER, Billy, and Barbara Fairchild
Singles: 7–inch

PAID 3-5   81
LPs: 10/12–inch 33rpm
PAID 5-10   81
   Also see FAIRCHILD, Barbara

WALKER, Bobbi
Singles: 7–inch

CASABLANCA 3-5   80

WALKER, Boots
Singles: 7–inch

PROVIDENCE 4-6   66
RUST 4-8   67-68

WALKER, David T.
Singles: 7–inch

ODE 3-5   73-76
REVUE 4-6   69-69
ZEA 3-5   70
LPs: 10/12–inch 33rpm
ODE 8-10   74-76
REVUE 10-15   68-69

WALKER, Gloria
(Gloria Walker and the Chevelles)
Singles: 7–inch

FLAMING ARROW 4-8   68-69
PEOPLE 3-5

WALKER, Jerry Jeff
Singles: 7–inch

ATCO 3-6   68-70
MCA 2-5   73-80
LPs: 10/12–inch 33rpm
ATCO (Except 297) 15-20   68-70
ATCO (297 "Five Years Gone") 30-50   69
DECCA 10-12   72
ELEKTRA 8-10
MCA 5-10   73-80

SOUTH COAST 5-10   81
VANGUARD 10-12   69

WALKER, Jimmy
Singles: 7–inch
BUDDAH 3-5   75
LPs: 10/12–inch 33rpm
BUDDAH 8-10   75

WALKER, Junior
(Junior Walker and the All Stars; Junior Walker and
All the Stars)
Singles: 12–inch 33/45rpm
WHITFIELD 4-8   79
Singles: 7–inch
HARVEY 5-10   62-64
MOTOWN 2-4   83
SOUL 5-10   65
(With black band on label, printed over "Distributed
By Bell Records.")
SOUL (Except 35003) 3-6   65-76
(Without black band.)
SOUL (35003 "Monkey Jump") 5-8   64
WHITFIELD 3-5   79
Picture Sleeves
SOUL 4-8   65-66
LPs: 10/12–inch 33rpm
MOTOWN (Except 700 series) 5-10   80-83
MOTOWN (700 series) 8-12   74
SOUL (701 through 721) 10-15   65-70
SOUL (725 through 750) 8-10   70-78
WHITFIELD 5-10   79

WALKER BROTHERS
Singles: 7–inch
SMASH 4-8   64-66
Picture Sleeves
SMASH 5-10   65-66
LPs: 10/12–inch 33rpm
SMASH 20-25   66-67
Members: Scott Engel; John Maus; Gary Leeds.

WALL of VOODO
Singles: 12–inch 33/45rpm
I.R.S. 4-6   83
Singles: 7–inch
I.R.S. 3-5   81-83
LPs: 10/12–inch 33rpm
I.R.S. 5-10   81-83
Member: Stan Ridgway.
Also see COPELAND, Stewart, and Stan Ridgway
Also see RIDGWAY, Stan

WALLACE, Jerry
(Jerry Wallace and the Jewels)
Singles: 78rpm
ALLIED 4-8   54
CHALLENGE 5-10   57
Singles: 7–inch
ALLIED 5-10   54
BMA 3-5   77-78
CHALLENGE (1000 series) 8-12   57

CHALLENGE (9100 series) 4-8   61-63
CHALLENGE (59013 through 59098) . 5-10   58-60
CHALLENGE (59200 series) 4-8   63-65
CLASS 5-10   53
DECCA 3-5   71-72
DOOR KNOB 3-5   80
ERIC 2-4
4-STAR 3-5   78-79
GLENOLDEN 3-6   68
GUSTO 2-4
LIBERTY 3-5   67-70
MCA 2-4   73-74
MGM 3-5   75
MERCURY (Except 72000 series) 5-10   55-56
MERCURY (72000 series) 4-8   64-66
TOPS 5-10   53
U.A. 3-5   72-75
VOGUE 8-12   52
WING 5-10   56
Picture Sleeves
CHALLENGE (59013 through
59098) 8-12   58-60
CHALLENGE (59200 series) 4-8   63-65
EPs: 7–inch 33/45rpm
CHALLENGE 15-25   60
LPs: 10/12–inch 33rpm
BMA 8-10   77
CHALLENGE (606 "Just Jerry") 30-35   59
CHALLENGE (612 "There She
Goes") 20-25   61
CHALLENGE (616 "Shutters and
Boards") 15-20   63
CHALLENGE (619 "In the Misty
Moonlight") 15-20   64
CHALLENGE (2002 "Greatest Hits") . 10-15   69
DECCA 8-12   71
4-STAR 5-8   83
LIBERTY 10-12   68
MCA 8-10   73-74
MGM 8-10   75
MERCURY 10-15   66
U.A. 8-12   72-75
WING 10-12   68
Also see BARE, Bobby / Donna Fargo / Jerry Wallace

WALLACE, Jerry / Soul Surfers
Singles: 7–inch
CHALLENGE 4-8   64
Also see WALLACE, Jerry

WALLACE BROTHERS
Singles: 7–inch
JEWEL 4-6   68-69
SIMS 4-8   63-67
LPs: 10/12–inch 33rpm
SIMS 15-20   65

WALSH, James, Gypsy Band
Singles: 7–inch
RCA 3-5   78-79

LPs: 10/12–inch 33rpm

RCA	5-10	79

Also see GYPSY

WALSH, Joe

Singles: 7–inch

ABC	3-5	75-78
ASYLUM	3-5	78-81
DUNHILL	3-5	73-75
FULL MOON	3-5	80
MCA	3-5	79

LPs: 10/12–inch 33rpm

ABC	5-10	76-78
ASYLUM	5-10	78-81
COMMAND	8-12	74-75
DUNHILL	8-10	72-74
MCA	5-10	79
WARNER	5-8	83-87

Also see EAGLES
Also see JAMES GANG
Also see SIMPSONS
Also see VITALE, Joe

WALSH, Steve

Singles: 7–inch

KIRSHNER	3-5	80

LPs: 10/12–inch 33rpm

KIRSHNER	5-10	80

Also see KANSAS

WAMMACK, Travis

Singles: 7–inch

ARA	4-8	64-65
ATLANTIC	4-8	66
CAPRICORN	3-5	75
FAME	3-5	72-73
FRATERNITY (103 "Rock and Roll Blues")	50-100	58

LPs: 10/12–inch 33rpm

CAPRICORN	5-10	75
FAME	8-12	72
PHONORAMA	5-10	

WANDERERS

Singles: 78rpm

ONYX	10-15	57
ORBIT	10-15	58
SAVOY (1109 "We Could Find Happiness")	20-40	53

Singles: 7–inch

CUB	10-25	58-62
MGM	8-12	62
ONYX (518 "Thinking of You")	30-40	57
ORBIT (9003 "Teenage Quarrel")	20-30	58
SAVOY (1109 "We Could Find Happiness")	200-300	53
U.A.	5-10	62

Members: Ray Pollard; Bob Yarborough; Sheppard Grant; Frank Joyner.

WANDERLEY, Walter

Singles: 7–inch

A&M	3-5	69

GNP/CRESCENDO	3-4	81
TOWER	3-6	66-67
VERVE	3-6	66-68
WORLD PACIFIC	3-6	66

LPs: 10/12–inch 33rpm

A&M	5-10	69
CAPITOL	10-15	63
GNP/CRESCENDO	5-8	81
PHILIPS	8-12	67
TOWER	8-15	66-67
VERVE	8-15	66-68
WORLD PACIFIC	8-15	66-67

Also see GILBERTO, Astrud

WANG CHUNG
(Huang Chung)

Singles: 12–inch 33/45rpm

GEFFEN	4-6	84

Singles: 7–inch

GEFFEN	2-4	84-89

LPs: 10/12–inch 33rpm

ARISTA	5-8	83
GEFFEN	5-8	84-89

WANSEL, Dexter

Singles: 12–inch 33/45rpm

PHILADELPHIA INT'L	4-8	79

Singles: 7–inch

PHILADELPHIA INT'L	3-5	76-79

LPs: 10/12–inch 33rpm

PHILADELPHIA INT'L	5-10	76-79

WAR

Singles: 12–inch 33/45rpm

MCA	4-8	78-79

Singles: 7–inch

BLUE NOTE	3-5	77
COCO PLUM	2-4	85
LAX	3-5	81
MCA	3-5	77-82
PRIORITY	2-4	87
RCA	3-5	82-83
U.A.	3-6	71-78
WAR	3-5	77

Picture Sleeves

MCA	3-5	77
U.A.	3-5	71-75

LPs: 10/12–inch 33rpm

ABC	8-10	76
BLUE NOTE	8-10	76
MCA	5-10	77-82
PRIORITY	5-8	87
RCA	5-10	82-83
U.A. (Except 103)	8-10	71-78
U.A. (103 "Radio Free War")	15-20	74

(Colored vinyl. Promotional issue only.)
Members: Howard Scott; Lonnie Jordan; Dee Allen; B.B. Dickerson; Lee Oskar; Charles Miller; Harold Brown.
Also see BURDON, Eric, and War
Also see JORDAN, Lonnie
Also see OSKAR, Lee

WARD, Anita
Singles: 7–inch
JUANA 3-5   79
LPs: 10/12–inch 33rpm
JUANA 5-10   79

WARD, Billy, and the Dominoes
Singles: 78rpm
DECCA 5-10   56-57
FEDERAL (12105 "I'd Be Satisfied") . 10-20   52
FEDERAL (12106 "Yours Forever") . . 10-20   52
FEDERAL (12114 "Pedal Pushin'
  Papa") 20-40   52
FEDERAL (12129 "These Foolish
  Things") 15-25   53
FEDERAL (12139 through 12380) 5-15   53-57
Singles: 7–inch
ABC-PAR 10-15   60
DECCA 10-20   56-57
FEDERAL (12105 "I'd Be
  Satisfied") 100-150   52
FEDERAL (12106 "Yours Forever") 100-150   52
FEDERAL (12114 "Pedal Pushin'
  Papa") 100-150   52
FEDERAL (12129 "These Foolish
  Things") 150-200   53
  (Gold top label.)
FEDERAL (12129 "These Foolish
  Things") 50-75   53
  (Silver top label.)
FEDERAL (12129 "These Foolish
  Things") 10-20   53
  (Green label.)
FEDERAL (12139 "Where Now,
  Little Heart") 40-50   53
FEDERAL (12162 "My Baby's 3-D") . . 40-60   53
FEDERAL (12178 "Tootsie Roll") 40-50   54
FEDERAL (12184 "Handwriting
  on the Wall") 30-40   54
FEDERAL (12193 "Above
  Jacob's Ladder") 20-30   54
FEDERAL (12209 "Can't Do
  Sixty No More") 40-50   55
FEDERAL (12218 "Cave Man") 20-30   55
FEDERAL (12263 "Bobby Sox
  Baby") 20-30   57
FEDERAL (12301 "St. Louis Blues") . 20-30   57
GUSTO 3-5
JUBILEE (5163 "Come to Me, Baby") 10-20   54
JUBILEE (5213 "Sweethearts
  on Parade") 10-20   55
KING (1280 "Rags to Riches") 25-35   53
KING (1281 "Christmas in Heaven") . 40-50   53
KING (1342 "A Little Lie") 20-30   54
KING (1364 "Three Coins
  in the Fountain") 20-30   55
KING (1368 "Little Things
  Mean a Lot") 20-30   54
KING (1492 "Learnin' the Blues") 20-30   55

CHRISTMAS IN HEAVEN
(Billy Ward)
BILLY WARD
And His Dominoes

KING (1502 "Over the Rainbow") . . . 20-30   55
KING (5322 through 6016) 8-15   60-61
LIBERTY 8-15   57-62
RO-ZAN 10-15   62
Picture Sleeves
LIBERTY (55071 "Stardust") 15-25   57
EPs: 7–inch 33/45rpm
DECCA (2549 "Billy Ward and
  His Dominoes") 50-75   58
FEDERAL (212 "Billy Ward and
  His Dominoes, Vol. 1") 75-100   55
  (Silver top label.)
FEDERAL (262 "Billy Ward and
  His Dominoes, Vol. 2") 75-100   55
  (Silver top label.)
FEDERAL (269 "Billy Ward and
  His Dominoes, Vol. 3") 75-100   55
  (Silver top label.)
FEDERAL (212 "Billy Ward and
  His Dominoes, Vol. 1") 25-50   57
  (Green label.)
FEDERAL (262 "Billy Ward and
  His Dominoes, Vol. 2") 25-50   57
  (Green label.)
FEDERAL (269 "Billy Ward and
  His Dominoes, Vol. 3") 25-50   57
  (Green label.)
LIBERTY (3083 "Yours Forever") 25-40   59
  (Price is for any of three volumes.)
LPs: 10/12–inch 33rpm
DECCA (8621 "Billy Ward and
  His Dominoes") 75-125   58
FEDERAL (94 "Billy Ward and
  His Dominoes") 1000-2000   54
  (10–inch LP.)
FEDERAL (548 "Billy Ward and
  His Dominoes") 400-800   57
FEDERAL (559 "Clyde McPhatter with Billy
  Ward and His Dominoes") 500-750   57
KING (548 "Billy Ward and
  His Dominoes") 75-100   58
KING (559 "Clyde McPhatter with Billy
  Ward and His Dominoes") 100-200   61

KING (733 "Billy Ward and His Dominoes Featuring
  Clyde McPhatter & Jackie Wilson") . 50-60   61
KING (952 "24 Songs") 20-30   66
KING/GUSTO 5-10
LIBERTY (3056 "Sea of Glass") 40-60   58
LIBERTY (3083 "Yours Forever") 40-60   59
LIBERTY (3113 "Pagan Love Song") . 40-60   59
  (Monaural.)
LIBERTY (7113 "Pagan Love Song") . 50-75   59
  (Stereo.)
  Members: Clyde McPhatter; Jackie Wilson; Billy Ward; Gene
  Mumford; Milton Merle; Milton Grayson; William Lamont; Cliff
  Givens.
  Also see DOMINOES
  Also see WILSON, Jackie

WARD, Dale
Singles: 7–inch
BIG WAY 4-8
BOYD 4-8   62-65
DOT (16000 series) 4-8   63-65
DOT (17000 series) 3-5   71-72
MONUMENT 4-6   66-69
PARAMOUNT 4-6   69-70
Picture Sleeves
BOYD 10-20   62
  Also see WARD, Robin

WARD, Joe
Singles: 78rpm
KING 4-6   55-56
Singles: 7–inch
KING 8-12   55-56

WARD, Robin
Singles: 7–inch
DOT 4-8   63-64
SONGS UNLIMITED 4-8   63
Picture Sleeves
SONGS UNLIMITED 5-10   63
LPs: 10/12–inch 33rpm
DOT (3555 "Wonderful Summer") . . . 25-35   63
  (Monaural.)
DOT (25555 "Wonderful Summer") . . 35-45   63
  (Stereo.)
  Also see MARTINDALE, Wink, and Robin Ward
  Also see WARD, Dale

WARD, Singin' Sammy
Singles: 7–inch
SOUL 4-8   64
TAMLA (54030 "What Makes You
  Love Him") 25-35   61
  (With horizontal lines.)
TAMLA (54030 "What Makes You
  Love Him") 15-25   61
  (With Tamla globe logo.)
TAMLA (54049 "What Makes You
  Love Him") 15-25   62
TAMLA (54057 "Everybody Knows It") 30-35   62
TAMLA (54071 "Part Time Love") 5-10   62

WARE, Leon
Singles: 7–inch
ELEKTRA 3-5   81
FABULOUS 3-5   79
U.A. 3-5   72
LPs: 10/12–inch 33rpm
FABULOUS 5-10   79
GORDY 5-10   76
U.A. 8-12   72

WARINER, Steve
LPs: 10/12–inch 33rpm
MCA 5-8   87

WARING, Fred
(Fred Waring & The Pennsylvanians)
Singles: 78rpm
CAPITOL 3-5   57-58
DECCA 3-6   50-57
Singles: 7–inch
CAPITOL 3-6   57-59
DECCA 3-8   50-68
REPRISE 3-6   64
EPs: 7–inch 33/45rpm
CAPITOL 4-8   57-58
DECCA 5-10   50-59
LPs: 10/12–inch 33rpm
CAPITOL 5-15   57-69
DECCA 5-20   50-68
HARMONY 5-10   69
MCA 5-8   77
MEGA 5-8   71
REPRISE 5-15   64-65
RCA 5-10   68

WARNES, Jennifer
(Jennifer Warren)
Singles: 12–inch 33/45rpm
20TH FOX ("It Goes Like
  It Goes") 4-8   79
  (Shown as by Jennifer Warnes. No catalog number
  used.)
20TH FOX (379 "It Goes
  Like It Goes") 5-10   79
  (Shown as by Jennifer Warren.)
Singles: 7–inch
ARISTA 2-4   77-82
PARROT 3-6   68
WARNER 3-5   83
LPs: 10/12–inch 33rpm
ARISTA 5-10   76-82
CYPRESS 5-8   87
REPRISE 5-10   72
  Also see COCKER, Joe, and Jennifer Warnes
  Also see JENNIFER
  Also see MEDLEY, Bill, and Jennifer Warnes

WARP 9
Singles: 12–inch 33/45rpm
PRISM 4-6   83-84
Singles: 7–inch
PRISM 2-4   83-84

WARREN, Jennifer: see WARNES, Jennifer

WARREN, Rusty
Singles: 7–inch
JUBILEE 5-10   60
EPs: 7–inch 33/45rpm
JUBILEE 10-15   62
LPs: 10/12–inch 33rpm
GNP/CRESCENDO 5-12   74-77
JUBILEE 10-20   60-68

WARRIOR, Jade: see JADE WARRIOR

WARWICK, Dee Dee
(Dee Dee Warwick and the Dixie Flyers)
Singles: 7–inch
ATCO 4-6   70-71
BLUE ROCK 4-8   65
HURT 4-8   66
JUBILEE 4-8   63
MERCURY 3-6   66-69
PRIVATE STOCK 3-6   75
SUTRA 3-5
TIGER 4-8   64
LPs: 10/12–inch 33rpm
ATCO 8-12   70
HERITAGE SOUND 5-8   83
MERCURY 10-15   67-69

WARWICK, Dionne
(Dionne Warwicke)
Singles: 12–inch 33/45rpm
ARISTA 4-6   84
Singles: 7–inch
ARISTA 2-4   79-90
COLLECTABLES 2-4
ERIC 2-4
MUSICOR 3-5   77
SCEPTER (1200 series) 4-8   62-65
SCEPTER (12000 series) 3-5   65-71
WARNER 3-5   72-78
Picture Sleeves
SCEPTER 3-5   63-71
LPs: 10/12–inch 33rpm
ARISTA 5-8   79-90
CIRCA 5-8
EVEREST 5-8   81
51 WEST 5-8
MFSL 25-50   82
MUSICOR 5-10   77
PHOENIX 5-8   81
RHINO 5-8
SCEPTER (Except 200) 10-15   64-72
SCEPTER (200 "March Is Dionne
Warwick Month") 20-25   67
(Promotional issue only.)
U.A. 8-10   74
TRIP 8-10   76
WARNER 8-10   72-77
Also see BACHARACH, Burt / Glen Campbell / Dionne Warwick
Also see DIONNE and Friends
Also see GIBB, Barry

Also see HAYES, Isaac, and Dionne Warwick
Also see MATHIS, Johnny, and Dionne Warwick
Also see U.S.A. for AFRICA
Also see WONDER, Stevie / Dionne Warwick

WARWICK, Dionne, and Howard Hewett
ARISTA 2-4   88
Also see HEWETT, Howard

WARWICK, Dionne, and Glenn Jones
Singles: 7–inch
ARISTA 2-4   85
Also see JONES, Glenn

WARWICK, Dionne, and Kashif
Singles: 7–inch
ARISTA 2-4   87
Also see KASHIF

WARWICK, Dionne, and Jeffrey Osborne
Singles: 7–inch
ARISTA 2-4   87
Also see OSBORNE, Jeffrey

WARWICK, Dionne, and the Spinners
Singles: 7–inch
ATLANTIC 3-5   74
Also see SPINNERS

WARWICK, Dionne, and Luther Vandross
Singles: 7–inch
ARISTA 2-4   83
Also see VANDROSS, Luther
Also see WARWICK, Dionne

WAS (NOT WAS)
Singles: 12–inch 33/45rpm
ISLAND 4-6   82
Singles: 7–inch
GEFFEN 2-4   83
ISLAND 3-5   81-82
ZE 2-4   82
LPs: 10/12–inch 33rpm
CHRYSALIS 88-90
GEFFEN 5-8   83
ISLAND 5-8   81
Members: Don Fagenson; David Weiss.

WASHINGTON, Baby
(Jeanette Washington; Justine Washington)
Singles: 7–inch
ABC-PAR 4-8   61
A.V.I. 3-5   78
CHECKER 5-10   59
CHESS 3-5   70
COLLECTABLES 2-4
COTILLION 3-6   69-70
J&S 5-10   59
MASTER FIVE 3-5   73-75
NEPTUNE 10-15   60-61
SIXTH AVENUE 3-5   76
SUE 4-8   62-67
LPs: 10/12–inch 33rpm
A.V.I 5-10   78
COLLECTABLES 5-8   87-88
SUE 20-35   63-65

WASHINGTON, Jeanette:
see WASHINGTON, Baby

WASHINGTON, Jerry
Singles: 7–inch
EXCELLO 3-5   73

WATANABE KAZUMI
LPs: 10/12–inch 33rpm
GRAMA VISION 5-8   88

WATERBOYS
Singles: 7–inch
ISLAND 3-4   83
LPs: 10/12–inch 33rpm
CHRYSALIS 5-8   88-90
ISLAND 5-10   83

WATERS, Freddie
Singles: 7–inch
KARI 3-5   81
OCTOBER 3-5   77

WATERS, Muddy
Singles: 78rpm
ARISTOCRAT (406 "Sneakin' and
Cryin'") 25-35   50
ARISTOCRAT (412 "Rollin' and
Tumblin'") 25-35   50
ARISTOCRAT (1302 "Gypsy Woman") 25-35   48
ARISTOCRAT (1305 "I Can't Be
Satisfied") 25-35   48
ARISTOCRAT (1306 "Train Fare
Home") 25-35   48
ARISTOCRAT (1307 "You're Gonna
Miss Me") 25-35   49
ARISTOCRAT (1310 "Streamline
Woman") 25-35   49
ARISTOCRAT (1311 "Little Geneva") . 25-35   49
CHESS 5-15   50-55
Singles: 7–inch
CHESS (1509 "Country Boy") 40-50   52
CHESS (1514 "Looking for My Baby") 40-50   52
CHESS (1526 "Standing Around
Crying") 40-50   52
CHESS (1537 "She's All Right") 40-50   53
CHESS (1542 "Who's Gonna Be
Your Sweet Man") 40-50   52
CHESS (1550 "Blow, Wind, Blow") . . 30-40   53
CHESS (1560 "I'm Your Hootchie
Coochie Man") 30-40   53
CHESS (1571 "Just Make Love
to Me") 30-40   54
CHESS (1579 "I'm Ready") 15-25   54
CHESS (1585 "I'm a Natural
Born Lover") 15-25   54
CHESS (1596 "I Want to Be Loved") . 15-25   55
CHESS (1600 series) 5-15   55-59
CHESS (1700 series) 5-10   59-61
CHESS (1800 and 1900 series) 4-8   62-66
CHESS (2000 series) 3-8   67-73

LPs: 10/12–inch 33rpm
BLUE SKY 5-10   77-81
CADET CONCEPT 10-15   68-69
CHESS (127 "Fathers and Sons") . . . 15-20   69
CHESS (1427 "The Best of
Muddy Waters") 50-100   57
CHESS (1444 "Muddy Waters
Sings Big Bill") 40-60   60
CHESS (1449 "Muddy Waters
at Newport") 20-30   64
CHESS (1483 "Folk Singer") 15-25   64
CHESS (1500 series) 10-20   66-71
CHESS (50012 through 50023) 6-12   72-73
CHESS (50033 "Fathers and Sons") . 10-15   75
CHESS (60006 "McKinley
Morganfield") 10-12   71
CHESS (60013 through 60035) 6-12   72-75
DOUGLAS 10-15   68
MUSE 5-10   73
TESTAMENT 10-12
    Also see BRENSTON, Jackie
    Also see COTTON, James
    Also see ROGERS, Jimmy
    Also see WELLS, Junior
    Also see WINTER, Johnny

WATERS, Muddy, and Howlin' Wolf
LPs: 10/12–inch 33rpm
CHESS 8-10   74
    Also see DIDDLEY, Bo, Howlin' Wolf and Muddy Waters
    Also see HOWLIN' WOLF
    Also see WATERS, Muddy

WATERS, Patty
LPs: 10/12–inch 33rpm
ESP 10-15   66

WATERS, Roger
(With Madeline Bell, Katie Kissoon, Eric Clapton and
Doreen Chanter; Roger Waters and the Bleeding
Heart Band)
Singles: 12–inch
COLUMBIA 4-6   84
Singles: 7–inch
COLUMBIA 3-4   84
LPs: 10/12–inch 33rpm
COLUMBIA 5-10   84-87
    Also see BELL, Madeline
    Also see CLAPTON, Eric
    Also see KISSOON, Mac and Katie
    Also see PINK FLOYD

WATKINS, Tip
Singles: 7–inch
H&L 3-5   77

WATLEY, Jody
Singles: 7–inch
MCA 2-4   87-89
LPs: 10/12–inch 33rpm
MCA 5-8   87-89

WATSON, Doc
Singles: 7–inch
POPPY 3-5   72-74

U.A. 3-5   75-79
LPs: 10/12-inch 33rpm
FLYING FISH 5-8   81
FOLKWAYS 10-20   63-69
LIBERTY 5-8   83
POPPY 6-12   72
U.A. 8-15   75-76
VANGUARD 8-18   64-77
VERVE/FOLKWAYS 10-15   66
Also see FLATT, Lester, Earl Scruggs and Doc Watson

WATSON, Johnny
(Johnny Guitar Watson; Young John Watson; Johnny
Watson Trio)
Singles: 78rpm
FEDERAL 10-20   53-54
KEEN 5-10   57
RPM 5-10   55-56
Singles: 7-inch
ALL STAR 10-15   58
ARVEE 10-15   60
CLASS 10-15   59
DJM 3-5   77
ESCORT 4-8
FANTASY 3-5   73-75
FEDERAL (12120 "Highway 60") 50-75   53
FEDERAL (12131 "Motor Head Baby")50-75   53
FEDERAL (12143 "I Got Eyes") 50-75   53
FEDERAL (12157 "What's Going On") 50-75   53
FEDERAL (12175 "Half Pint
 of Whiskey") 50-75   54
FEDERAL (12183 "Gettin' Drunk") ... 50-75   54
GOTH 10-15   60
KEEN 10-20   57
KENT 5-10   60
KING 4-8   61-64
OKEH 4-8   66-67
RPM 10-20   55-56
VALLEY VUE 2-4   84
LPs: 10/12-inch 33rpm
A&M 5-10   81
BIG TOWN 8-10   77
CADET 10-15   67
CHESS (1490 "Blues/Soul") 30-50   64
DJM 5-10   76-81
FANTASY 5-10   73-81
KING (857 "Johnny Guitar Watson") . 50-75   63
OKEH 10-15   67
MCA 5-10   81
Also see BLAND, Bobby / Johnny Guitar Watson
Also see OTIS, Johnny
Also see WATSONIAN INSTITUTE
Also see WILLIAMS, Larry, and Johnny Watson

WATSON, Young John: see WATSON, Johnny

WATSONIAN INSTITUTE
Singles: 7-inch
DJM 3-5   78
LPs: 10/12-inch 33rpm
DJM 5-10   78
Also see WATSON, Johnny

WATTS, Ernie
Singles: 7-inch
QWEST 3-4   82
LPs: 10/12-inch 33rpm
QWEST 5-10   82

WATTS, Noble
(Noble "Thin Man" Watts and His Rhythm Sparks;
Noble Watts Quintet; Nobel Watts with Paul
"Hucklebuck" Williams)
Singles: 78rpm
BATON 5-10   57
DELUXE 5-10   54
Singles: 7-inch
BATON 8-12   57
BRUNSWICK 4-8   68
CLAMIKE 4-8   63-64
CUB 5-10   60
DELUXE 8-12   54
Also see WILLIAMS, Paul

WATTS, Noble, and June Bateman
Singles: 7-inch
ENJOY 4-8   63
Also see WATTS, Noble

WATTS 103rd ST. RHYTHM BAND
(Featuring Charles Wright)
Singles: 7-inch
KEYMEN 4-8   67
WARNER 4-8   68-71
LPs: 10/12-inch 33rpm
WARNER 10-15   68-71
Also see WRIGHT, Charles

WAX
Singles: 12-inch 33/45rpm
RCA 4-6   86
Singles: 7-inch
RCA 2-4   81-86
LPs: 10/12-inch 33rpm
COTILLION 5-10   80
RCA 5-8   81-86
Members: Graham Gouldman; Andrew Gold.
Also see GOLD, Andrew
Also see 10CC

WAYBILL, Fee
Singles: 7-inch
CAPITOL 2-4   84
LPs: 10/12-inch 33rpm
CAPITOL 5-8   84
Also see TUBES

WAYLON & WILLIE:
see JENNINGS, Waylon, and Willie Nelson

WAYNE, Bobby
Singles: 78rpm
MERCURY 4-6   51-54
Singles: 7-inch
MERCURY 5-10   51-54
EPs: 7-inch 33/45rpm
MERCURY 5-10   53

WAYNE, James
(James Waynes; Wee Willie Wayne)
Singles: 78rpm

ALADDIN	5-10	54
IMPERIAL	5-15	51-57
MILLION	5-10	54
PEACOCK	5-10	57
SITTIN' in WITH	5-15	51-52

Singles: 7-inch

ANGELTONE	5-10	60
ALADDIN	20-30	54
IMPERIAL (5200 series)	20-40	53
IMPERIAL (5300 series)	15-25	55
IMPERIAL (5600 and 5700 series)	4-8	60-61
MILLION	20-30	54
PEACOCK	10-15	57

LPs: 10/12-inch 33rpm

IMPERIAL (9144 "Travelin' Mood")	50-75	61

Also see CHARLES, Ray / Arbee Stidham / Li'l Son Jackson / James Wayne

WAYNE, John
Singles: 7-inch

CASABLANCA	2-4	79
RCA	3-5	73

LPs: 10/12-inch 33rpm

RCA (3000 series)	5-10	79-81
RCA (4800 series)	8-12	73

WAYNE, Thomas
(Thomas Wayne and the DeLons)
Singles: 7-inch

CAPEHART	4-8	61
CHALET	3-5	69
COLLECTABLES	2-4	
ERIC	2-4	
FERNWOOD (Except 106)	10-20	59-60
FERNWOOD (106 "You're the One That Done It")	50-75	58
MERCURY (71287 "You're the One That Done It")	30-50	58
MERCURY (71454 "You're the One That Done It")	20-30	59
OLDIES 45	4-6	64
PHILLIPS INT'L	5-10	62
RACER	4-8	65
SANTO	5-10	62

WAYNE, Wee Willie: see WAYNE, James

WAYNES, James: see WAYNE, James

WE FIVE
Singles: 7-inch

A&M	4-8	65-69
MGM	3-5	73
VAULT	4-8	67
VERVE	3-5	68-73

LPs: 10/12-inch 33rpm

A&M	15-20	65-69
A.V.I.	5-10	77
VAULT	10-15	70

Members: Mike Stewart; Pete Fullerton; Beverly Bivens; Bob Jones; Jerry Burgan.

WE the PEOPLE
Singles: 7-inch

CHALLENGE	10-20	66-67
DAVEL	3-5	75
IMPERIAL	4-6	69
LION	3-5	72-74
MAP CITY	3-6	69
RCA	10-15	67
REENA	3-6	68
VERVE	3-5	71

WEAPONS of PEACE
Singles: 7-inch

PLAYBOY	3-5	76-77

LPs: 10/12-inch 33rpm

PLAYBOY	5-10	77

Also see HENDERSON, Finis

WEATHER GIRLS
Singles: 12-inch 33/45rpm

COLUMBIA	4-6	83-85

Singles: 7-inch

COLUMBIA	3-4	83-85

LPs: 10/12-inch 33rpm

COLUMBIA	5-10	84

Also see TWO TONS O' FUN

WEATHER REPORT
Singles: 7-inch

COLUMBIA	3-5	73-84

LPs: 10/12-inch 33rpm

ARC/COLUMBIA	5-10	78-82
COLUMBIA	5-10	71-86

Also see PASTORIUS, Jaco
Also see SHORTER, Wayne

WEATHERLY, Jim
Singles: 7-inch

ABC	3-5	76-77
BUDDAH	3-5	74-75
ELEKTRA	3-5	79-80
ERIC	3-5	78
RCA	3-5	72-74
20TH FOX	4-8	65

Picture Sleeves

BUDDAH	3-5	74

LPs: 10/12-inch 33rpm

ABC	5-10	77
BUDDAH	5-10	74-75
RCA	8-12	72

WEATHERS, Carl
Singles: 7-inch

MIRAGE	3-5	81

WEATHERS, Oscar
Singles: 7-inch

BLUE CANDLE	3-5	73
TOP & BOTTOM	3-6	69-72

WEAVER, Dennis
(Dennis Weaver and the Good Time People)
Singles: 7–inch

CASCADE 5-10	59
CENTURY CITY 3-6	69
EVA 4-8	63
IM'PRESS 3-5	72
OVATION 3-5	75
WARNER 4-8	63

LPs: 10/12–inch 33rpm

IM'PRESS 8-10	72
OVATION 5-10	75

WEAVERS
(Weavers With Gordon Jenkins' Orchestra)
Singles: 78rpm

DECCA 3-5	50-57

Singles: 7–inch

DECCA (27000 through 29000 series) . 5-10	50-55
DECCA (31000 series) 4-8	62
NSD 3-5	82
VANGUARD 4-8	60-62

EPs: 7–inch 33/45rpm

DECCA 5-15	51-52

LPs: 10/12–inch 33rpm

DECCA (173 "Best of the Weavers") . 10-15	65
(Monaural.)	
DECCA (7173 "Best of the Weavers") 10-15	65
(Stereo.)	
DECCA (5285 "Folk Songs") 20-40	51
(10–inch LP.)	
DECCA (5373 "Merry Christmas") ... 20-40	52
(10–inch LP.)	
DECCA (74277 "Weavers Gold") 10-15	70
VANGUARD (15-16 "Greatest Hits") .. 8-12	71
VANGUARD (2000 series) 10-20	59-63
VANGUARD (3000 through 6000	
series) 8-15	67-70
VANGUARD (9000 series) 12-25	56-63
VANGUARD (9100 series) 10-20	65

Members: Pete Seeger; Lee Hays; Fred Hellerman; Ronnie Gilbert.
Also see JENKINS, Gordon, and His Orchestra
Also see SEEGER, Pete

WEB
LPs: 10/12–inch 33rpm

DERAM 10-15	68

WEB, Ebony: see EBONEE WEBB

WEBB, Jack
(Jack Webb and Jazz Combo)
EPs: 7–inch 33/45rpm

RCA (0342/3 "The Christmas Story") . 15-25	
RCA (1126 "Pete Kelly's Blues") 20-35	55

LPs: 10/12–inch 33rpm

RCA (1126 "Pete Kelly's Blues") 25-40	55
RCA (2040 "Pete Kelly's Blues") 15-25	59
WARNER 10-20	58

Members: Jack Webb; Matty Matlock; Dick Cathcart; Nick Fatool; Elmer "Moe" Schneider; George Van Eps; Ray Sherman; Jud DeNaut.

WEBB, Paula
Singles: 7–inch

WESTBOUND 3-5	75

WEBER, Joan
Singles: 78rpm

COLUMBIA 3-5	54-56

Singles: 7–inch

COLUMBIA 5-10	54-56
CROSLEY 4-6	63
MAPLE 4-6	61

EPs: 7–inch 33/45rpm

COLUMBIA 5-10	55

WEDNESDAY
Singles: 7–inch

BUDDAH 3-5	75
CELEBRATION 3-5	76
SKY 3-5	76
SUSSEX 3-5	73-74

LPs: 10/12–inch 33rpm

SUSSEX 8-10	74

WEE GEE
Singles: 7–inch

COTILLION 3-5	80
JUNEY 3-5	78

WEEKS & CO.
Singles: 12–inch 33/45rpm

SALSOUL 4-6	83

Singles: 7–inch

CHEZ RO 3-5	81
SALSOUL 2-4	83

LPs: 10/12–inch 33rpm

SALSOUL 5-8	83

WEIDER, John
LPs: 10/12–inch 33rpm

ANCHOR 8-10	76
GOLD CASTLE 5-8	88

Also see ANIMALS
Also see FAMILY

WEIR, Bob
Singles: 7–inch

ARISTA (315 "Bombs Away") 3-5	77
ARISTA (336 "I'll Be Doggone") 8-12	77
(Promotional issue only.)	
WARNER 3-5	72

LPs: 10/12–inch 33rpm

ARISTA 5-10	78
WARNER (2627 "Ace") 25-30	72

Also see BOBBY and the Midnites
Also see GRATEFUL DEAD
Also see KINGFISH

WEIR, Frank, Orchestra
Singles: 78rpm

CAPITOL 2-5	56
COLUMBIA 2-5	57

LONDON 2-5 54-57
Singles: 7-inch
CAPITOL 4-8 56
COLUMBIA 4-8 57
LONDON 4-8 54-63
EPs: 7-inch 33/45rpm
LONDON 5-10 54-55
LPs: 10/12-inch 33rpm
COLUMBIA 10-20 57
LONDON 10-20 54

WEISBERG, Tim
Singles: 7-inch
A&M 3-5 71-79
MCA 3-5 79
U.A. 3-5 77-80
LPs: 10/12-inch 33rpm
A&M 5-10 73-79
MCA 5-10 79-80
NAUTILUS 10-15 80
U.A. 5-10 77-78
Also see FOGELBERG, Dan, and Tim Weisberg

WEISSBERG, Eric
(Eric Weissberg and Steve Mandell; Eric Weissberg and Marshall Brickman)
Singles: 7-inch
WARNER 3-5 72-73
LPs: 10/12-inch 33rpm
ELEKTRA 15-25 63
WARNER 5-10 73
Also see TARRIERS

WELCH, Bob
Singles: 7-inch
CAPITOL 3-5 77-81
RCA 3-4 81-83
Picture Sleeves
CAPITOL 3-5 81
LPs: 10/12-inch 33rpm
CAPITOL (Except 16000 series) 8-10 77-80
CAPITOL (16000 series) 5-8 80-82
RCA 5-10 81-83
Promotional LPs
CAPITOL (11663 "French Kiss") 25-30 79
(Picture disc.)
Also see FLEETWOOD MAC
Also see PARIS

WELCH, Lenny
Singles: 7-inch
ATCO 3-5 72
BARNABY 3-5 76
BIG TREE 3-5 78-83
CADENCE (Except 1422) 5-10 59-64
CADENCE (1422 "Congratulations
Baby") 10-20 62
COLUMBIA 4-6 67
COMMONWEALTH UNITED 4-6 69
DECCA 5-10 59
KAPP 4-8 65-67
MAINSTREAM 3-5 73-74

MERCURY 4-6 68
ROULETTE 3-5 71
LPs: 10/12-inch 33rpm
CADENCE 15-25 64
COLUMBIA 10-20 65
KAPP 10-20 66-67

WELK, Lawrence, and His Orchestra
Singles: 78rpm
CORAL 2-4 50-57
MERCURY 2-4 50-55
Singles: 7-inch
CORAL 2-5 50-66
DOT 2-5 59-67
MERCURY 2-5 50-55
RANWOOD 2-4 68-77
Picture Sleeves
CORAL 4-8 56
EPs: 7-inch 33/45rpm
CORAL 4-8 50-58
DOT 3-6 59-60
MERCURY 4-8 50-55
LPs: 10/12-inch 33rpm
CORAL 5-15 50-65
DECCA 5-10 72
DOT 5-15 59-67
HAMILTON 4-8 64-66
HARMONY 4-8 68-70
MCA 4-8 74-76
RANWOOD 4-8 68-85
SUNNYVALE 4-6 79
TRADITION 4-8 75
VOCALION 4-8 59-70
WING 4-8 60-62
Also see HODGES, Johnny, and Lawrence Welk
Also see HUDSON, Emperor Bob, and Lawrence Welk
Also see LENNON SISTERS
Also see PRESLEY, Elvis / Lawrence Welk

WELLER, Freddy
Singles: 7-inch
ABC/DOT 3-5 75
APT 4-8 65
COLUMBIA 3-6 69-80
DORE 5-10 61
LPs: 10/12-inch 33rpm
COLUMBIA 5-10 69-80
EPIC 8-10 74
51 WEST 5-8
Also see REVERE, Paul, and the Raiders

WELLES, Orson
LPs: 10/12-inch 33rpm
MEDIARTS 8-12 70
Also see CROSBY, Bing, and Orson Welles

WELLS, Brandi
Singles: 7-inch
WMOT 3-5 81-82

WELLS, Jean
Singles: 7-inch
ABC-PAR 4-8 65

CALLA 4-8   67-68
VOLARE 4-6   69

WELLS, Junior
(Junior Wells and His Eagle Rockers; Junior Wells'
Chicago Blues Band)
Singles: 78rpm
STATES 10-20   52-53
Singles: 7–Inch
BLUE ROCK 4-8   68-69
BRIGHT STAR 4-8   66-67
CHIEF 8-15   57-62
PROFILE 5-10   59-60
SHAD 5-10   59
STATES (122 "Cut That Out") 75-125   52
(Colored vinyl.)
STATES (134 "Hodo Man") 75-125   53
(Colored vinyl.)
STATES (139 "Lawdy Lawdy") 75-125   53
(Colored vinyl.)
STATES (143 "So All Alone") 75-125   53
(Colored vinyl.)
U.S.A. 4-8   63-64
VANGUARD 4-8   67
LPs: 10/12–Inch 33rpm
BLUE ROCK 10-12   68
DELMARK 10-15   66-69
VANGUARD 10-15   66-68
Also see COTTON, James, Carey Bell, Junior Wells, and Billy
Branch
Also see WATERS, Muddy

WELLS, Junior, and Buddy Guy
LPs: 10/12–Inch 33rpm
ATCO 8-12   72
BLIND PIG 5-8   82
INTERMEDIA 5-8
Also see GUY, Buddy
Also see WELLS, Junior

WELLS, Kitty
Singles: 78rpm
DECCA 3-6   52-57
Singles: 7–Inch
CAPRICORN 3-5   74-76
DECCA (28000 and 29000 series) 5-10   52-56
DECCA (30000 through 32000 series) .. 3-8   56-71
MCA 2-4   73
RUBOCA 2-5   79-80
Picture Sleeves
DECCA 4-6   69
EPs: 7–Inch 33/45rpm
DECCA 5-15   55-65
LPs: 10/12–Inch 33rpm
CAPRICORN 6-10   74
DECCA (174 "The Kitty Wells Story") . 15-25   63
(Monaural. Includes booklet.)
DECCA (7-174 "The Kitty Wells Story") 20-30   63
(Stereo. Includes booklet.)
DECCA (4075 through 4929) 10-25   61-67
(Monaural.)

DECCA (7-4075 through 7-4929) ... 15-30   61-67
(Stereo.)
DECCA (7-4961 through 7-5350) ... 10-15   68-72
(Stereo.)
DECCA (8293 "Country Hit Parade") . 35-45   56
(Monaural.)
DECCA (7-8293 "Country Hit Parade") 10-15   68
(Stereo.)
DECCA (8552 "Winner of Your Heart") 35-45   56
DECCA (7-8552 "Winner of
Your Heart") 10-15   65
DECCA (8732 "Lonely Street") 30-40   58
(Monaural.)
DECCA (7-8732 "Lonely Street") 10-15   65
(Stereo.)
DECCA (8858 "Dust on the Bible") .. 25-35   59
(Monaural.)
DECCA (7-8858 "Dust on the Bible") . 10-15   68
(Stereo.)
DECCA (8888 "After Dark") 30-40   59
(Monaural.)
DECCA (7-8888 "After Dark") 10-15   68
(Stereo.)
DECCA (8979 "Kitty's Choice") 25-35   59
(Monaural.)
DECCA (7-8979 "Kitty's Choice") 30-40   59
(Stereo.)
EXACT 5-10   80
IMPERIAL HOUSE 5-10   80
KOALA 5-10   79
MCA 4-8   73-83
MISTLETOE 5-8
PICKWICK/HILLTOP 5-10
ROUNDER 5-8   82
RUBOCA 8-12   79
SUFFOLK MARKETING 5-10   80
VOCALION 8-15   66-69
Also see PARTON, Dolly / Kitty Wells
Also see PIERCE, Webb, and Kitty Wells

WELLS, Kitty, and Roy Drusky
Singles: 7–Inch
DECCA 4-8   60
Also see DRUSKY, Roy

WELLS, Kitty, and Red Foley
Singles: 78rpm
DECCA 3-5   54
Singles: 7–Inch
DECCA 3-8   54-69
EPs: 7–Inch 33/45rpm
DECCA 8-12   59
LPs: 10/12–Inch 33rpm
DECCA 12-25   61-67
Also see FOLEY, Red
Also see WELLS, Kitty

WELLS, Mary
Singles: 12–Inch 33/45rpm
EPIC 4-8   82

Singles: 7–Inch

ATCO	4-8	66-67
EPIC	2-4	82
JUBILEE	4-6	68-71
MOTOWN (1003 "Bye Bye Baby")	15-25	60
(Pink label.)		
MOTOWN (1011 "I Don't Want to		
Take a Chance")	10-20	61
(Pink label.)		
MOTOWN (1011 "I Don't Want to		
Take a Chance")	8-12	61
(Blue label.)		
MOTOWN (1024 through 1056)	5-10	62-64
REPRISE	3-5	71-74
20TH FOX	4-8	64-66

Picture Sleeves

MOTOWN (1003 "Bye Bye Baby")	25-35	61
MOTOWN (1011 "I Don't Want to		
Take a Chance")	20-25	61
MOTOWN (1024 "The One Who		
Really Loves You")	10-20	62
MOTOWN (1032 "You Beat Me to		
the Punch")	8-12	62
20TH FOX (590 "He's a Lover")	5-10	65

LPs: 10/12–Inch 33rpm

ALLEGIANCE	5-10	84
ATCO	15-20	66
EPIC	5-10	81
51 WEST	5-8	83
JUBILEE	10-20	68
MOTOWN (100 and 200 series)	5-10	82
MOTOWN (600 "Mary Wells")	75-125	61
(White label with blue print.)		
MOTOWN (605 "The One Who		
Really Loves You")	40-60	62
MOTOWN (607 through 653)	20-30	63-66
MOVIETONE	15-20	66
POWER PAK	5-8	
20TH FOX	20-30	65
Also see GAYE, Marvin, and Mary Wells		

WELLS, Terri
Singles: 12–Inch 33/45rpm
PHILLY WORLD	4-6	84

Singles: 7–Inch
PHILLY WORLD	2-4	84

WERNER, David
Singles: 7–Inch
EPIC	3-5	79
RCA	3-5	74-76

LPs: 10/12–Inch 33rpm
EPIC	5-10	79
RCA	5-10	75

WERNER, Max
Singles: 7–Inch
RADIO	3-5	81
Also see KAYAK		

WESLEY, Fred
(Fred Wesley and the Horny Horns; Fred Wesley and the J.B.s)
Singles: 7–Inch
ATLANTIC	3-5	77
PEOPLE	3-5	72-74
RSO	3-5	80

LPs: 10/12–Inch 33rpm
ATLANTIC	8-10	77
Also see BROWN, James, Band		

WEST, Belinda
Singles: 7–Inch
PANORAMA	3-5	80

WEST, Dr:
see DR. WEST'S MEDICINE SHOW and Junk Band

WEST, Dottie
Singles: 7–Inch
ATLANTIC	4-8	62
LIBERTY	2-4	80-82
RCA (Except 8000 series)	3-6	66-81
RCA (8000 series)	4-8	63-66
STARDAY (500 series)	4-8	60-61
STARDAY (700 series)	3-6	65
U.A.	3-4	76-80

Picture Sleeves
LIBERTY	3-5	80-81

LPs: 10/12–Inch 33rpm
CAMDEN	5-10	71-73
COLUMBIA	5-10	80
LIBERTY	5-8	81-82
NASHVILLE	8-12	
PICKWICK	5-10	75
RCA	8-18	65-75
STARDAY	10-20	64-65
U.A.	5-10	73-80
Also see DEAN, Jimmy, and Dottie West		
Also see GIBSON, Don, and Dottie West		
Also see REEVES, Jim, and Dottie West		
Also see ROGERS, Kenny, and Dottie West		

WEST, Dottie / Melba Montgomery
LPs: 10/12–Inch 33rpm
STARDAY	10-20	65
Also see MONTGOMERY, Melba		
Also see WEST, Dottie		

WEST, Leslie
(Leslie West Band)
Singles: 7–inch
PHANTOM 3-5   75-76
LPs: 10/12–inch 33rpm
PHANTOM 8-10   75-76
WINDFALL 10-15   69
Also see JAGGER, Mick
Also see MOUNTAIN
Also see WEST, BRUCE & LAING

WEST, Mae
Singles: 78rpm
BRUNSWICK 10-20   33
Singles: 7–inch
MGM 3-5   73
PLAZA 4-8   62
TOWER 4-8   66
20TH FOX (6718 "Hard to Handle") .. 15-30   70
EPs: 7–inch 33/45rpm
DECCA (838 "The Fabulous
    Mae West") 50-75   55
    (Three-EP set.)
LPs: 10/12–inch 33rpm
DAGONET 10-15   66
DECCA (9016 "The Fabulous
    Mae West") 40-60   55
DECCA (79016 "The Fabulous
    Mae West") 10-15   70
MGM 10-15   72
TOWER 15-25   66
Also see FIELDS, W.C.

WEST, BRUCE & LAING
Singles: 7–inch
COLUMBIA 3-5   73
LPs: 10/12–inch 33rpm
COLUMBIA 8-10   74
COLUMBIA/WINDFALL 8-12   72-74
Members: Leslie West; Jack Bruce; Corky Laing.
Also see BRUCE, Jack
Also see MOUNTAIN
Also see WEST, Leslie

WEST STREET MOB
Singles: 12–inch 33/45rpm
SUGAR HILL 4-6   81-83
Singles: 7–inch
SUGAR HILL 3-4   81-83
LPs: 10/12–inch 33rpm
SUGAR HILL 5-10   82

WESTON, Kim
Singles: 7–inch
ENTERPRISE 3-5   74
GORDY 4-8   65-66
MGM 4-8   67-68
MIKIM 3-5   71-72
PEOPLE 3-5   69-70
PRIDE 3-5   70
TAMLA 4-8   63-65

Picture Sleeves
MGM 4-8   67
LPs: 10/12–inch 33rpm
ENTERPRISE 8-10   74
MGM 15-20   67-68
VOLT 10-12   71
Also see GAYE, Marvin, and Kim Weston
Also see NASH, Johnny, and Kim Weston

WESTON, Paul, Orchestra
Singles: 78rpm
CAPITOL 2-5   45-57
COLUMBIA 2-4   50-56
Singles: 7–inch
CAPITOL 4-8   57-60
COLUMBIA 4-8   50-56
EPs: 7–inch 33/45rpm
COLUMBIA 5-10   50-56
LPs: 10/12–inch 33rpm
CAPITOL 5-15   57-61
COLUMBIA 5-15   50-56
CORINTHIAN 4-8   78
HARMONY 4-8   72
Also see STAFFORD, Jo

WET WET WET
LPs: 10/12–inch 33rpm
UNI............................. 5-8   88

WET WILLIE
Singles: 7–inch
CAPRICORN 3-5   74-78
EPIC 3-5   77-79
LPs: 10/12–inch 33rpm
CAPRICORN 5-10   71-78
EPIC 5-10   78-79
Member: Jimmy Hall.
Also see HALL, Jimmy

WHALUM, Kirk
LPs: 10/12–inch 33rpm
COLUMBIA 5-8   88

WHAM!
(Wham! U.K.)
Singles: 12–inch 33/45rpm
COLUMBIA 4-6   82-86
Singles: 7–inch
COLUMBIA 2-4   83-86
Picture Sleeves
COLUMBIA 3-5   82-86
LPs: 10/12–inch 33rpm
COLUMBIA (Except 40062) 5-8   83-86
COLUMBIA (40062 "Make It Big") 8-10   84
(Picture disc.)
Members: George Michael; Andrew Ridgely.
Also see MICHAEL, George

WHATNAUTS
(Whatnauts and the Whatnaut Band)
Singles: 7–inch
A&I 3-5   70
GSF 3-5   73
HARLEM INT'L 2-4   82

STANG 3-5   71
LPs: 10/12–inch 33rpm
STANG 10-20   70-71

WHEELER, Billy Edd
Singles: 7–inch
CAPITOL 3-5   75-76
KAPP 4-8   63-68
NSD 2-4   80-81
RCA 3-5   70-73
RADIO CINEMA 3-5   79
U.A. 3-6   69
Picture Sleeves
KAPP 4-8   67
LPs: 10/12–inch 33rpm
AVALANCHE 8-10   73
FLYING FISH 5-10   79
KAPP 10-20   64-68
MONITOR 15-25   61-62
RCA 8-10   71
U.A. 8-15   69

WHEN in ROME
LPs: 10/12–inch 33rpm
VIRGIN 5-8   88

WHIRLWIND
Singles: 12–inch 33/45rpm
ROULETTE 4-8   77
Singles: 7–inch
ROULETTE 3-5   76

WHISPERS
Singles: 12–inch 33/45rpm
SOLAR 4-6   80-84
Singles: 7–inch
COLLECTABLES 2-4
DORE 4-8   65-66
FONTANA 4-8   66
JANUS 3-5   70-75
SOLAR 2-4   79-88
SOUL CLOCK 3-5   69-70
SOUL TRAIN 3-5   75-77
LPs: 10/12–inch 33rpm
ACCORD 5-10   81
ALLEGIANCE 5-8   84
CAPITOL 5-8   90
DORE 5-10   80
JANUS 8-10   72-75
SOLAR 5-10   78-87
SOUL TRAIN 5-10   76-77
Members: Walter Scott; Wallace Scott; Nicholas Caldwell;
Marcus Hudson; Leaveil DeGree.
Also see LUCAS, Carrie, and the Whispers

WHISTLE
Singles: 12–inch 33/45rpm
SELECT 4-6   86
Singles: 7–inch
SELECT 2-4   86-88
LPs: 10/12–inch 33rpm
SELECT 5-8   86

WHITCOMB, Ian
(Ian Whitcomb and Bluesville; Ian Whitcomb and
Somebody's Chyldren)
Singles: 7–inch
JERDEN 5-10   64-65
TOWER 4-8   65-68
U.A. 3-5   73
Picture Sleeves
TOWER 4-8   66
LPs: 10/12–inch 33rpm
FIRST AMERICAN 5-10   78-82
SIERRA 5-10   80
TOWER 15-20   65-68
U.A. 8-10   72

WHITE, Artie "Blues Boy"
Singles: 7–inch
ALTEE 3-5   77
RONN 3-5

WHITE, Barry
(Barry White with Love Unlimited and the Love
Unlimited Orchestra; Barry White and Glodean)
Singles: 12–inch 33/45rpm
20TH FOX 4-8   73-78
UNLIMITED GOLD 4-6   83
Singles: 7–inch
A&M 2-4   87
BRONCO 4-8   67
CASABLANCA 3-5
20TH FOX 3-5   73-78
UNLIMITED GOLD 3-4   79-83
LPs: 10/12–inch 33rpm
A&M 5-8   87
20TH FOX (Except 1) 5-10   73-81
20TH FOX (1 "Barry White
Radio Special") 10-15
(Promotional issue only.)
UNLIMITED GOLD 5-10   79-82
Also see BOB & EARL
Also see LOVE UNLIMITED

WHITE, Barry, and the Atlantics / Atlantics
Singles: 7–inch
FARO 5-10   63
Also see WHITE, Barry

WHITE, Danny
Singles: 7–inch
ABC-PAR 4-8   64
ATLAS 4-8   66
DECCA 4-8   66-67
DOT 4-8   61
FRISCO 4-8   62
KING (5122 "That's My Doll") 20-30   58
ROCKY COAST 3-5   77
SSS INT'L 3-6   69

WHITE, Karyn
LPs: 10/12–inch 33rpm
WARNER 5-8   88

WHITE, Kitty
Singles: 78rpm
DECCA	3-5	51
MERCURY	3-5	55-56

Singles: 7-inch
CLOVER	3-6	66
DECCA	5-10	51
DOT	4-8	60
GNP/CRESCENDO	4-8	59
MERCURY	4-8	55-56

EPs: 7-inch 33/45rpm
EMARCY	5-15	54
PACIFIC JAZZ	8-15	54

LPs: 10/12-inch 33rpm
EMARCY	30-40	54
CLOVER	6-12	66
MERCURY	20-30	55
PACIFIC JAZZ	30-40	54-55

WHITE, Lenny
Singles: 7-inch
ELEKTRA	3-5	78-83
NEMPEROR	3-5	76

LPs: 10/12-inch 33rpm
ELEKTRA	5-8	78-83
NEMPEROR	8-10	75-77

Also see RETURN to FOREVER
Also see TWENNYNINE

WHITE, Maurice
Singles: 12-inch 33/45rpm
COLUMBIA	4-6	86

Singles: 7-inch
COLUMBIA	2-4	85-86
GOLD	8-12	59
PRIDE	5-10	60

LPs: 10/12-inch 33rpm
COLUMBIA	5-8	85-86

WHITE, Tony Joe
(Tony Joe White and the Mojos)
Singles: 7-inch
ARISTA	3-5	79
CASABLANCA	3-5	80
COLUMBIA	2-4	83-85
J-BECK	5-8	
MONUMENT	4-8	67-70
20TH FOX	3-5	76

LPs: 10/12-inch 33rpm
CASABLANCA	5-10	80
COLUMBIA	5-8	83
MONUMENT	8-15	69-70
20TH FOX	5-10	77
WARNER	8-10	71-73

WHITE LION
LPs: 10/12-inch 33rpm
ATLANTIC	5-8	87-90
GRAND SLAM	5-8	88

WHITE PLAINS
Singles: 7-inch
DERAM	3-5	70-71
LONDON	3-5	

LPs: 10/12-inch 33rpm
DERAM	10-15	70

Members: Roger Greenaway; Roger Cook.
Also see DAVID & JONATHAN

WHITE WOLF
Singles: 7-inch
RCA	2-4	85-86

LPs: 10/12-inch 33rpm
RCA	5-8	85-86

WHITEHEAD, Charles
(Charlie Whitehead and the Swamp Dogg Band)
Singles: 7-inch
ISLAND	3-5	75

LPs: 10/12-inch 33rpm
FUNGUS	10-15	
WIZARD	5-10	78

WHITEHEAD, John
Singles: 7-inch
MERCURY	2-4	88

WHITEHEAD, Kenny and Johnny
Singles: 12-inch 33/45rpm
PHILADELPHIA INT'L	4-6	86

Singles: 7-inch
PHILADELPHIA INT'L	2-4	86

LPs: 10/12-inch 33rpm
PHILADELPHIA INT'L	5-8	86

Also see KENNY & JOHNNY

WHITEMAN, Paul, Orchestra
Singles: 78rpm
CAPITOL	3-5	42-43
COLUMBIA	3-6	28-32
CORAL	2-5	50-56
DECCA	3-5	38-39
VICTOR	3-8	20-36

Singles: 7-inch
CORAL	3-6	50-56

EPs: 7-inch 33/45rpm
CORAL	4-8	50-56

LPs: 10/12-inch 33rpm
CAPITOL	5-10	62
CORAL	5-15	50-56
GRAND AWARD	5-15	56-59
RCA	4-8	68-69
WESTMINSTER	4-8	74

WHITESNAKE
Singles: 12-inch 33/45rpm
GEFFEN	4-6	86

Singles: 7-inch
GEFFEN	2-4	82-89
MIRAGE	3-5	80
U.A.	3-5	79

Picture Sleeves
MIRAGE	3-5	80

LPs: 10/12–inch 33rpm

GEFFEN	5-8	82-89
MIRAGE	5-10	80-81
U.A.	5-10	79

Members: David Coverdale; Jon Lord; Aynsley Dunbar; John Sykes; Neil Murray; Tommy Aldridge; Rudy Sarzo; Vivian Campbell; Adrian Vandenberg.
Also see DEEP PURPLE

WHITFIELD, David

Singles: 78rpm

LONDON	2-5	53-57

Singles: 7–inch

LONDON	3-8	53-63

EPs: 7–inch 33/45rpm

LONDON	4-8	54

LPs: 10/12–inch 33rpm

LONDON	5-15	54-66

WHITING, Margaret

Singles: 78rpm

CAPITOL	3-5	46-56
DOT	3-5	57

Singles: 7–inch

CAPITOL	5-10	50-56
DOT	4-8	57-59
LONDON	3-6	66-70
VERVE	4-6	60

EPs: 7–inch 33/45rpm

CAPITOL	5-10	50-56

LPs: 10/12–inch 33rpm

CAPITOL	12-25	50-56
DOT	8-18	57-67
HAMILTON	5-15	59-65
LONDON	5-15	67-68
VERVE	10-20	60

Also see MARTIN, Dean, and Margaret Whiting
Also see TORME, Mel

WHITING, Margaret, and Jimmy Wakely

Singles: 78rpm

CAPITOL	3-5	50

Singles: 7–inch

CAPITOL	5-10	50

EPs: 7–inch 33/45rpm

CAPITOL	8-15	53

LPs: 10/12–inch 33rpm

PICKWICK	8-12	67

Also see WHITING, Margaret
Also see WAKELY, Jimmy

WHITLOCK, Bobby

Singles: 7–inch

DUNHILL	3-5	72

LPs: 10/12–inch 33rpm

CAPRICORN	8-10	76
DUNHILL	10-12	72

Also see BELL, Maggie, and Bobby Whitlock
Also see DELANEY & BONNIE
Also see DEREK and the Dominoes

WHITMAN, Slim

Singles: 78rpm

IMPERIAL	3-8	52-57

Singles: 7–inch

CLEVELAND INT'L	3-4	80-82
EPIC	2-4	84
IMPERIAL (5000 series)	4-8	61-63
IMPERIAL (8000 through 8200 series)	5-10	52-58
IMPERIAL (8300 series)	4-8	59-60
IMPERIAL (50000 series)	3-5	70-71
IMPERIAL (65000 and 66000 series)	3-8	61-69
U.A.	3-8	70-77

EPs: 7–inch 33/45rpm

IMPERIAL	30-50	54-65
RCA (3217 "Slim Whitman Sings and Yodels")	100-150	54

LPs: 10/12–inch 33rpm

CAMDEN	8-12	66
CLEVELAND INT'L	5-10	80-81
EPIC	5-8	84
IMPERIAL (3004 "America's Favorite Folk Artist")	400-500	54
(10–inch LP.)		
IMPERIAL (9000 series)	25-40	56-60
(Maroon or black label with "Imperial" at top.)		
IMPERIAL (9000 series)	8-15	66
(Black label with "Imperial" on left side.)		
IMPERIAL (9100 series)	20-30	60-62
(Black label with "Imperial" at top.)		
IMPERIAL (9100 series)	8-15	66
(Black label with "Imperial" on left side.)		
IMPERIAL (9200 and 9300 series)	12-25	63-67
IMPERIAL (12100 series)	15-25	62
(Black label with "Imperial" at top.)		
IMPERIAL (12100 series)	8-15	66
(Black label with "Imperial" on left side.)		
IMPERIAL (12200 and 12300 series)	12-25	65-68
IMPERIAL (12400 series)	8-12	68-69
LIBERTY	5-10	80-82
PICKWICK	5-10	
RCA (3217 "Slim Whitman Sings and Yodels")	250-350	54
RCA (3700 series)	5-8	80
SUFFOLK MARKETING	8-12	79-82
SUNSET	8-12	66-70
U.A.	6-12	70-80

Also see WILLIAMS, Hank / Slim Whitman

WHITNEY, Marva

Singles: 7–inch

KING	4-6	67-69
T-NECK	3-5	70

LPs: 10/12–inch 33rpm

KING	8-12	69

Also see BROWN, James, and Marva Whitney

WHITNEY, Marva, and Ellie Taylor

Singles: 7–inch

EXCELLO	3-5	72

Also see WHITNEY, Marva

WHITTAKER, Roger

Singles: 7–inch

MAIN STREET	2-4	84

RCA 2-5   70-86

Picture Sleeves

RCA 3-5   80

LPs: 10/12–inch 33rpm

MAIN STREET 5-8   84
RCA 5-12   70-86

WHO

Singles: 7–inch

ATCO (6409 "Substitute") 20-30   67
ATCO (6509 "Substitute") 15-25   67
DECCA (31725 "I Can't Explain") 15-20   64
DECCA (31801 "Anyway Anyhow
  Anywhere") 15-25   65
DECCA (31877 "My Generation") ... 15-25   65
DECCA (31988 "The Kids Are Alright") 15-25   66
DECCA (32058 "I'm a Boy") 15-25   66
DECCA (32114 "Happy Jack") 8-12   67
DECCA (32156 "Pictures of Lily") 8-12   67
DECCA (32206 "I Can See for Miles") . 5-10   67
DECCA (32288 "Call Me Lightning") .. 8-12   68
DECCA (32362 "Magic Bus") 5-10   68
DECCA (32465 "Pinball Wizard") 4-8   69
DECCA (32519 "I'm Free") 4-8   69
DECCA (32670 "The Seeker") 5-10   70
DECCA (32708 "Summertime Blues") . 5-10   70
DECCA (32729 "See Me, Feel Me") ... 5-10   70
DECCA (32737 "Young Man Blues") . 50-75   70
DECCA (32846 "Won't Get Fooled
  Again") 5-10   71
DECCA (32888 "Behind Blue Eyes") . 5-10   71
DECCA (32983 "Join Together") 5-10   72
DECCA (33041 "The Relay") 5-10   72
LIFE 20-30
MCA 3-5   74-79
POLYDOR 3-5   75-79
TRACK 4-8   72-74
WARNER 3-5   81-83

Picture Sleeves

DECCA (32114 "Happy Jack") 10-20   67
DECCA (32465 "Pinball Wizard") 8-12   69
DECCA (32729 "See Me, Feel Me") ... 8-12   70
DECCA (32737 "Young Man Blues") 75-125   70
POLYDOR 4-6   75-79
WARNER 3-5   81-83

LPs: 10/12–inch 33rpm

DWJ ("Musical Biography") 30-50   78
  (Promotional issue only. Not issued with cover.)
DECCA (DL-4664 "My Generation") . 50-75   66
  (Monaural.)
DECCA (DL-4664 "My Generation") . 75-100   66
  (White label. Promotional issue only.)
DECCA (DL7-4664 "My Generation") . 40-60   66
  (Stereo.)
DECCA (DL-4892 "Happy Jack") 50-75   67
  (Monaural.)
DECCA (DL-4892 "Happy Jack") ... 75-100   67
  (White label. Promotional issue only.)

DECCA (DL7-4892 "Happy Jack") ... 40-60   67
  (Stereo.)
DECCA (DL-4950 "The Who Sell Out") 30-40   67
  (Monaural.)
DECCA (DL-4950 "The Who Sell
  Out") 50-75   67
  (White label. Promotional issue only.)
DECCA (DL7-4950 "The Who Sell
  Out") 20-30   67
  (Stereo.)
DECCA (DL-5064 "Magic Bus") 25-30   68
  (Monaural. White label. Promotional issue only.)
DECCA (DL7-5064 "Magic Bus") 25-30   68
DECCA (DXW-7205 "Excerpts
  from Tommy") 100-150   69
  (Monaural. White label. Promotional issue only.
  Includes 12-page booklet.)
DECCA (DXSW-7205 "Tommy") 25-35   69
  (Stereo. Includes 12-page booklet.)
DECCA (79175 "Live at Leeds") 50-75   70
  (White label. Promotional issue only.)
DECCA (79175 "Live at Leeds") 20-30   70
DECCA (79182 "Who's Next") 15-20   71
DECCA (79184 "Meaty Beaty Big
  and Bouncy") 15-20   71
MCA (1987 "Who Are You") 15-25   78
MCA (2000 series) 15-25   74
MCA (2161 "The Who By Numbers") .. 8-10   75
MCA (3050 "Who Are You") 8-10   78
  (Black vinyl.)
MCA (3050 "Who Are You") 15-20   78
  (Colored vinyl.)
MCA (5000 series) 5-8   83-85
MCA (6000 series) 10-12   74
MCA (8000 series) 10-12   84
MCA (10004 "Quadrophenia") 10-12   81
MCA (10005 "Tommy") 10-12   77
MCA (11005 "The Kids Are Alright") .. 10-12   79
MCA (12001 "Hooligans") 10-12   81
MCA (14950 "Who Are You") 12-15   79
  (Picture disc.)
MCA (19501 "Join Together") 8-12   90
MCA (37000 series) 5-8   79
MFSL 15-25   84
TRACK (2126 "Odds and Sods") 10-20   74
  (Includes insert.)
TRACK (4000 series) 10-12   74
TRACK (10004 "Quadrophenia") 15-20   73
  (Includes 44-page booklet.)
WARNER 5-10   81-82
  Members: Roger Daltrey; Pete Townshend; John Entwistle; Keith
  Moon; Kenny Jones.
  Also see DALTREY, Roger
  Also see ENTWISTLE, John
  Also see McCARTNEY, Paul / Rochestra / Who / Rockpile
  Also see MOON, Keith
  Also see TOWNSHEND, Pete

WHO / Strawberry Alarm Clock
LPs: 10/12–inch 33rpm
DECCA (734586 "The Who/Strawberry
 Alarm Clock") 50-75   69
 (Philco-Ford Special Products promotional issue.)
 Also see STRAWBERRY ALARM CLOCK
 Also see WHO

WHODINI
Singles: 12–inch 33/45rpm
JIVE 4-6   84-86
Singles: 7–inch
JIVE 2-4   82-87
LPs: 10/12–inch 33rpm
JIVE 5-8   84-87
 Members: Jalil Hutchins; John Fletcher; Drew Carter.
 Also see JACKSON, Millie
 Also see KING DREAM CHORUS and Holiday Crew

WHOLE DARN FAMILY
Singles: 7–inch
SOUL INT'L 3-5   76-77
LPs: 10/12–inch 33rpm
SOUL INT'L 8-10   76

WHOLE OATS
Singles: 7–inch
ATLANTIC 4-8   72
 Members: Daryl Hall; John Oates.
 Also see HALL, Daryl, and John Oates

WICHITA TRAIN WHISTLE
Singles: 7–inch
DOT 5-8   68
LPs: 10/12–inch 33rpm
DOT 15-20   68
PACIFIC ARTS 8-10   78
 Member: Michael Nesmith.
 Also see NESMITH, Michael

WIDE BOY AWAKE
Singles: 12–inch 33/45rpm
RCA 4-6   83
Singles: 7–inch
RCA 3-5   83
LPs: 10/12–inch 33rpm
RCA 5-10   83

WIDOWMAKER
Singles: 7–inch
JET 3-5   76-77
LPs: 10/12–inch 33rpm
U.A. 8-10   76-77
 Members: John Butler; Aerial Bender.

WIEDLIN, Jane
Singles: 7–inch
I.R.S. 2-4   85
LPs: 10/12–inch 33rpm
EMI............................ 5-8   88
I.R.S. 5-8   85
 Also see GO GOs
 Also see SPARKS and Jane Wiedlin

WIER, Rusty
Singles: 7–inch
ABC 3-5   74
COLUMBIA 3-5   76
COMPLEAT 2-4   83-84
20TH FOX 3-5   75-76
LPs: 10/12–inch 33rpm
ABC 8-12   74
COLUMBIA 8-10   76
20TH FOX 8-10   75

WIGGINS, Spencer
Singles: 7–inch
FAME 3-6   69-70
GOLDWAX 4-8   66-69

WILCOX, Eddie, Orchestra
(Featuring Sunny Gale)
Singles: 78rpm
DERBY 3-6   52
Singles: 7–inch
DERBY 10-15   52
 (Colored vinyl.)
 Also see GALE, Sunny

WILCOX, Harlow
(Harlow Wilcox and the Oakies)
Singles: 7–inch
PLANTATION 4-6   69
SSS INT'L 3-5
LPs: 10/12–inch 33rpm
PLANTATION 5-10   70-71

WILD, Jack
Singles: 7–inch
BUDDAH 3-5   71
CAPITOL 3-5   70
Picture Sleeves
CAPITOL 3-5   70

WILD CHERRY
Singles: 12–inch 33/45rpm
EPIC 4-8   76-79
Singles: 7–inch
A&M............................ 3-5   75
BROWN BAG 3-5   72-73
EPIC/SWEET CITY 3-5   76-79
LPs: 10/12–inch 33rpm
EPIC/SWEET CITY 5-10   76-79
 Members: Robert Parissi; Allen Wentz; Ronald Beitle; Bryan Bassett.

WILD COUNTRY
Singles: 7–inch
LSI (75-12-1 "Sweet Country
 Woman") 15-25   70
LPs: 10/12–inch 33rpm
LSI (0275 "Wild Country") 500-1000   70
 Members: Randy Owen; Jeff Cook; Teddy Gentry; John B. Vartanian.
 Also see ALABAMA

WILD MAGNOLIAS
Singles: 7–inch
POLYDOR 3-5   74
LPs: 10/12–inch 33rpm
POLYDOR 8-10   ·74

WILD MAN STEVE
(Steve Gallon)
LPs: 10/12–inch 33rpm
RAW 5-12   69-70

WILD ONES
Singles: 7–inch
MAINLINE 4-8   65
MALA 4-8   67
U.A. 4-8   65-66
LPs: 10/12–inch 33rpm
U.A. 15-20   65
Also see ANTELL, Peter

WILD TURKEY
Singles: 7–inch
CHRYSALIS 3-5   72-73
REPRISE 3-5   72
LPs: 10/12–inch 33rpm
CHRYSALIS 8-10   72-73
REPRISE 8-12   72
Also see JETHRO TULL

WILD-CATS
Singles: 7–inch
U.A. (154 "Gazachstahagen") 5-10   58
(Monaural.)
U.A. (169 "King Size Guitar") 5-10   59
U.A. (1154 "Gazachstahagen") 15-25   58
(Stereo.)
LPs: 10/12–inch 33rpm
U.A. (3031 "Bandstand Record Hop")
Also see MURE, Billy

WILDE, Danny
LPs: 10/12–inch 33rpm
GEFFEN 5-8   88

WILDE, Eugene
Singles: 12–inch 33/45rpm
PHILLY WORLD 4-6   84-86
Singles: 7–inch
MCA 2-4   86
PHILLY WORLD 2-4   84-86
LPs: 10/12–inch 33rpm
PHILLY WORLD 5-8   84-86

WILDE, Kim
Singles: 12–inch 33/45rpm
MCA 4-6   85
Singles: 7–inch
EMI AMERICA 3-5   82
MCA 2-4   85-88
LPs: 10/12–inch 33rpm
EMI AMERICA 5-10   82
MCA 5-8   85-87

WILDE, Marty
Singles: 7–inch
BELL 3-5   74
EPIC 5-10   58-60
LPs: 10/12–inch 33rpm
EPIC (575 "Wilde About Marty") 30-40   60
(Stereo.)
EPIC (3686 "Bad Boy") 30-40   60
EPIC (3711 "Wilde About Marty") 25-35   60
(Monaural.)
Also see SHANNON

WILDER, Matthew
Singles: 12–inch 33/45rpm
PRIVATE I 4-6   83-85
Singles: 7–inch
PRIVATE I 2-4   83-85
LPs: 10/12–inch 33rpm
PRIVATE I 5-8   83-85

WILDFIRE
Singles: 7–inch
CASABLANCA 3-5   77

WILDWEEDS
Singles: 7–inch
CADET 4-8   67-68
CADET CONCEPT 4-8   68
VANGUARD 3-5   71
LPs: 10/12–inch 33rpm
VANGUARD 10-15   70
Also see ANDERSON, Al

WILEY, Ed
(With Teddy Reynolds and King Tut)
Singles: 78rpm
SITTIN' in WITH (Except 545) 10-15   50
Singles: 7–inch
ATLANTIC (959 "So Glad I'm Free") 50-100   51
SITTIN' in WITH (545 "Cry, Cry
Baby") 75-125   50
Members: Teddy Reynolds; King Tut.

WILEY, Michelle
Singles: 7–inch
20TH FOX 3-5   77

WILL and the Kill
LPs: 10/12–inch 33rpm
MCA 5-8   88

WILL to POWER
Singles: 7–inch
EPIC 2-4   87-90
LPs: 10/12–inch 33rpm
EPIC 5-8   87-90

WILLESDEN-DODGERS
Singles: 12–inch 33/45rpm
JIVE 4-6   83
Singles: 7–inch
JIVE 3-4   83

WILLIAMS, Andre
(Andre Williams and the Don Juans; Andre Williams
and the Five Dollars; Andre Williams and Diablos;
Andre "Bacon Fat" Williams with the Inspirations;
Andre "Mr. Rhythm" Williams)
Singles: 78rpm
EPIC	5-10	57
FORTUNE	5-10	55-57

Singles: 7-inch
AVIN	4-8	66
CHECKER	4-8	68-69
EPIC	8-12	57
FORTUNE	10-20	55-58
SPORT	4-8	67
WINGATE	4-8	66

LPs: 10/12-inch 33rpm
FORTUNE	5-8	86

WILLIAMS, Andre, and Gino Parks
Singles: 7-inch
FORTUNE	5-10	60

Also see WILLIAMS, Andre

WILLIAMS, Andy
Singles: 12-inch 33/45rpm
COLUMBIA	4-6	79

Singles: 78rpm
CADENCE	3-6	56-57

Singles: 7-inch
CADENCE	4-8	56-64
COLUMBIA	3-6	61-79

Picture Sleeves
CADENCE	5-10	59
COLUMBIA	3-5	61-76

EPs: 7-inch
CADENCE	8-15	57-59
COLUMBIA	5-10	62-66

(Jukebox issues only.)
LPs: 10/12-inch 33rpm
CADENCE	15-30	58-62
COLUMBIA	5-15	62-77

WILLIAMS, Andy and David
Singles: 7-inch
BARNABY	3-5	74-75
KAPP	3-5	72-73

LPs: 10/12-inch 33rpm
KAPP	5-10	72

WILLIAMS, Anson
Singles: 7-inch
CHELSEA	3-5	77

Picture Sleeves
CHELSEA	3-5	77

WILLIAMS, Billy
(Billy Williams Quartet)
Singles: 78rpm
CORAL	3-6	54-57

Singles: 7-inch
CORAL (61200 through 61800 series)	5-10	54-57
CORAL (61900 through 65500 series)	4-8	58-64

MCA	2-4	
MGM (10000 and 11000 series)	5-10	50-52
MGM (12000 series)	5-8	57
MERCURY	5-10	52-54

EPs: 7-inch 33/45rpm
CORAL	15-25	57
MGM	15-25	57
MERCURY	15-25	53-55

LPs: 10/12-inch 33rpm
CORAL (57184 "Billy Williams")	35-45	57
CORAL (57251 "Half Sweet Half Beat")	30-40	59
CORAL (57343 "The Billy Williams Revue")	30-40	60
MGM (3400 "The Billy Williams Quartet")	35-45	57
MERCURY (20317 "Oh Yeah!")	35-45	58
WING (12131 "Vote for Billy Williams")	30-40	59

Members: Billy Williams; Claude Riddick; John Ball; Eugene
Dixon.

WILLIAMS, Bobby Earl
Singles: 7-inch
IV CHAINS	3-5	74

WILLIAMS, Carol
Singles: 7-inch
SALSOUL	3-5	76

WILLIAMS, Danny
Singles: 7-inch
PILOT	4-8	62
U.A.	4-8	61-66

LPs: 10/12-inch 33rpm
U.A.	15-25	63-66

WILLIAMS, Deniece
Singles: 12-inch 33/45rpm
COLUMBIA	4-8	77-86

Singles: 7-inch
ARC	2-5	79-82
COLUMBIA	2-5	76-87
TODDLIN' TOWN	4-8	

LPs: 10/12-inch 33rpm
ARC	5-10	79-82
COLUMBIA	5-10	76-86

Also see MATHIS, Johnny, and Deniece Williams
Also see WONDER, Stevie

WILLIAMS, Diana
Singles: 7-inch
CAPITOL	3-5	76
LITTLE GEM	3-5	77

WILLIAMS, Don
Singles: 7-inch
ABC	3-5	75-78
ABC/DOT	3-5	74-77
CAPITOL	2-4	86
DOT	3-5	74
JMI	3-5	72-74
MCA	2-4	79-85

LPs: 10/12–inch 33rpm

ABC (Except 28) 5-10   77-78
ABC (28 "Don Williams") 10-15   77
(Promotional issue only.)
ABC/DOT 8-10   74-77
CAPITOL 5-8   86
JMI 15-20   73-74
MCA (Except 44) 5-10   75-85
MCA (44 "Expressions") 15-20   78
(Picture disc.)
Also see POZO SECO SINGERS

WILLIAMS, Esther
Singles: 7–inch
FRIENDS & CO 3-5   76-78

WILLIAMS, Geoffrey
Singles: 7–inch
ATLANTIC 2-4   88

WILLIAMS, Hank
(Hank Williams and the Drifting Cowboys; Hank Williams as "Luke the Drifter;" Hank and Audrey Williams)
Singles: 78rpm
MGM 5-10   47-55
STERLING (201 "Calling You") ... 200-400   47
STERLING (204 "Wealth Won't
Save Your Soul") 150-300   47
STERLING (208 "I Don't Care") ... 150-250   47
STERLING (210 "Pan American") . 150-250   47
Singles: 7–inch
MGM (10000 and 11000 series) 10-20   50-55
MGM (12000 series) 5-15   55-59
MGM (13000 series) 3-6   64-67
EPs: 7–inch 33/45rpm
ARHOOLIE 4-6   83
(Not issued with cover.)
MGM (100 and 200 series) 25-50   52-54
MGM (1000 through 1600 series) 15-30   55-60
LPs: 10/12–inch 33rpm
BLAINE HOUSE 15-20   72
BOLL WEEVIL 8-12   76
COLUMBIA (5616 "Hank Williams
Treasury") 35-45
(Four-LP set from the Columbia House record club.)
GOLDEN COUNTRY 5-8
MGM (2 "36 of Hank Williams'
Greatest Hits") 80-100   57
(Three-LP set.)
MGM (4 "36 More of Hank
Williams' Greatest Hits") 80-100   58
(Three-LP set.)
MGM (100 and 200 series) 50-100   52-54
(10–inch LPs.)
MGM (240-2 "24 Karat Hits,
Hank Williams") 15-20   68
MGM (1000 series) 8-10   76
(Special Products issue.)

MGM (3200 through 3900 series) ... 25-50   55-61
(With "E" prefix.)
MGM (3200 through 3900 series) ... 10-20   63-70
(With "SE" prefix.)
MGM (4000 through 4700 series,
except 4267) 10-20   63-71
MGM (4267 "The Hank Williams
Story") 50-75   66
(Four-LP set.)
MGM (4900 through 5400 series) 5-10   75-77
METRO 10-15   65-67
POLYDOR 6-12   83-84
SUNRISE MEDIA 8-10   81
TIME-LIFE 5-8   82
Also see PRESLEY, Elvis / Hank Williams

WILLIAMS, Hank / Slim Whitman
LPs: 10/12–inch 33rpm
SUNRISE MEDIA 8-10   81
Also see WHITMAN, Slim

WILLIAMS, Hank, and Hank Williams, Jr.
LPs: 10/12–inch 33rpm
MGM (4200 series) 15-25   65
MGM (4300 through 4900 series) ... 10-15   66-74
Also see WILLIAMS, Hank, Jr.

WILLIAMS, Hank, Jr.
(Hank Williams, Jr. and the Cheatin' Hearts; Hank Williams, Jr. With the Mike Curb Congregation; Hank Williams, Jr. and Lois Johnson)
Singles: 7–inch
CONSOL 10-20
(Promotional issue from Consolidation Coal.)
ELEKTRA/CURB 2-4   79-82
MGM (13000 series) 4-8   64-68
MGM (14000 series) 2-5   68-76
WARNER/CURB (Except 8000 series) . 2-4   82-91
WARNER/CURB (8000 series) 2-4   77-78
Picture Sleeves
MGM (13000 series) 5-10   64-68
LPs: 10/12–inch 33rpm
CURB 5-8   83-84
ELEKTRA 5-8   79-83
MGM (Except 5009) 10-20   64-76
MGM (5009 "Hank Williams Jr.
and Friends") 40-60   76
WARNER 5-10   77-87
WARNER/CURB 5-8   85-91
Also see BOCEPHUS
Also see CHARLES, Ray, and Hank Williams Jr.
Also see FRANCIS, Connie, and Hank Williams Jr.
Also see JENNINGS, Waylon, and Hank Williams Jr.
Also see WILLIAMS, Hank, and Hank Williams Jr.

WILLIAMS, James "D-Train"
Singles: 12–inch 33/45rpm
COLUMBIA 4-6   86
Singles: 7–inch
COLUMBIA 2-4   86-88
LPs: 10/12–inch 33rpm
COLUMBIA 5-8   86
Also see "D" TRAIN

WILLIAMS, Jeanette
Singles: 7–inch
BACK BEAT 3-5   66-69

WILLIAMS, Jerry
(Jerry Williams, Jr.)
Singles: 7–inch
CALLA 3-5   66-67
COTILLION 2-4   69
8730 RECORDS 3-5   67
MUSICOR 3-5   68
V-TONE 4-6   63
  Also see SWAMP DOGG
  Also see WILLIAMS, Little Jerry

WILLIAMS, John, Orchestra
Singles: 7–inch
ARISTA 2-4   77-80
COLUMBIA 2-4   83
MCA 2-4   74-76
RCA 2-4   79
20TH FOX 2-4   77-78
WARNER 2-4   79
Picture Sleeves
ARISTA 2-4   77
20TH FOX 2-4   78
WARNER 2-4   79
LPs: 10/12–inch 33rpm
CAPITOL 5-10   71
COLUMBIA (31091 "Changes") 5-10   71
COLUMBIA (37000 series) 5-8   81
DISCOVERY 4-8   84
RCA 5-8   77
  Since publication of *The Official Price Guide to Movie/TV
  Soundtracks and Original Cast Albums*, with over 8,000 listings,
  this guide has dropped many soundtracks, including some by this
  artist.
  Also see BOSTON POPS ORCHESTRA

WILLIAMS, Johnny
(John Lee Hooker)
Singles: 78rpm
GOTHAM 6-10   50-52
PRIZE (704 "Miss Rose Mae") 15-20   49
STAFF (704 "Miss Rose Mae") 15-20   50
STAFF (710 "Wandering Blues") 15-20   50
STAFF (718 "Prison Bound") 15-20   50
SWING TIME 6-10   50
  Also see HOOKER, John Lee

WILLIAMS, Johnny
Singles: 7–inch
BASHIE 2-4   70
CUB 2-4   68
PHILADELPHIA INT'L 2-4   73

WILLIAMS, L.C.
(L.C. Williams Orchestra; L.C. Williams With Conney's
Combo)
Singles: 78rpm
BAYOU 10-15   53
FREEDOM 8-12   49-50
GOLD STAR 10-15   48

IMPERIAL 5-8   52
JAX 8-10   52
MERCURY 5-8   52
SITTIN' in WITH 8-10   52
Singles: 7–inch
BAYOU 30-40   53

WILLIAMS, Larry
(Larry Williams and His Band)
Singles: 7–inch
CHESS 4-6   59-60
MERCURY 3-5   63
OKEH 3-5   66-67
SMASH 3-5   66
SPECIALTY (SPBX series) 12-15   85
  (Boxed set of six colored vinyl 45s.)
SPECIALTY (597 through 658) 5-10   57-59
SPECIALTY (665 through 682) 4-6   59-60
VENTURE 3-5   68
Picture Sleeves
SPECIALTY 10-20   58
LPs: 10/12–inch 33rpm
OKEH 10-15   67
SPECIALTY (2109 "Here's Larry
  Williams") 40-50   59
SPECIALTY (2158 "Unreleased Larry
  Williams") 6-10   88
  (With Art Neville.)
  Also see COOKE, Sam / Lloyd Price / Larry Williams / Little
  Richard

WILLIAMS, Larry, and Johnny Watson
Singles: 7–inch
OKEH (7300 "Nobody") 15-25   67
  (With Kaleidoscope.)
  Also see KALEIDOSCOPE
LPs: 10/12–inch 33rpm
OKEH 10-15   67
  Also see LARRY & JOHNNY
  Also see WATSON, Johnny
  Also see WILLIAMS, Larry

WILLIAMS, Lee
(Lee Williams and the Moonrays; Lee Williams and
the Cymbals; Lee "Shot" Williams)
Singles: 7–inch
CARNIVAL 3-5   66-69
FEDERAL 3-5   63-64
KING 8-10   60
SHAMA 2-4   69

WILLIAMS, Lenny
Singles: 12–inch 33/45rpm
ABC 4-6   78
ROCSHIRE 4-6   83-84
Singles: 7–inch
ABC 2-4   77-78
KNOBHILL 2-4   86
MCA 2-4   79-81
MOTOWN 2-4   75
ROCSHIRE 2-4   83-84

LPs: 10/12–inch 33rpm

ABC 8-10	77-78	
MCA 5-8	79-81	
MOTOWN 8-10	75	
ROCSHIRE 5-8	83-84	
WARNER 8-12	74	

Also see G., Kenny, and Lenny Williams
Also see TOWER of POWER

WILLIAMS, Linda
Singles: 7–inch

ARISTA 2-4	79	

WILLIAMS, Little Jerry
Singles: 7–inch

ACADEMY 4-6	64	
CALLA 3-5	65-66	
COTILLION 3-5	69	
LOMA 3-5	64	
SOUTHERN SOUND 4-6	64-65	

Also see WILLIAMS, Jerry

WILLIAMS, Mason
Singles: 7–inch

WARNER 2-4	68-71	

LPs: 10/12–inch 33rpm

EVEREST 6-12	69	
FLYING FISH 5-8	78	
VEE JAY 10-20	64	
WARNER 6-12	68-71	

WILLIAMS, Mason, and Mannheim Steamroller
LPs: 10/12–inch 33rpm

AMERICAN G. 5-8	87	

WILLIAMS, Mason / Smothers Brothers
EPs: 7–inch 33/45rpm

WARNER/SEVEN ARTS (283 "Scope Box") 20-40	70	

(Promotional issue only.)
Also see SMOTHERS BROTHERS
Also see WILLIAMS, Mason

WILLIAMS, Maurice
(Maurice Williams and the Zodiacs)
Singles: 7–inch

ATLANTIC 2-4	70	
COLLECTABLES 2-4		
DEESU 3-5	67	
ERIC 2-4		
FLASHBACK 2-4	65	
HERALD 4-6	60-62	
OWL 2-4	73	
SEA HORN 3-5	64	
SELWYN (5121 "College Girl") 20-40	59	
SPHERE SOUND 3-5	65	
VEE JAY 3-6	65	
VEEP 2-4	69	

LPs: 10/12–inch 33rpm

COLLECTABLES 6-8	84	
HERALD (1014 "Stay") 50-100	61	
RELIC 10-12		

SNYDER 25-30		
SPHERE SOUND 15-20	66	

Also see GLADIOLAS

WILLIAMS, Mike
Singles: 7–inch

ATLANTIC 3-6	65-66	
KING 3-6	66	

WILLIAMS, Otis
(Otis Williams and the Midnight Cowboys)
Singles: 7–inch

DELUXE (6100 series) 4-6	59	
KING 3-5	60-64	
OKEH 3-5	66	
STOP 2-4	71	

LPs: 10/12–inch 33rpm

POWER PAK 8-10	74	
STOP 8-12	71	

Also see CHARMS

WILLIAMS, Paul
(Paul Williams and His Orchestra)
Singles: 78rpm

CAPITOL 3-5	55	
CLEF 4-6	52	
GROOVE 4-8	54	
JAX 4-8	54	
JOSIE 3-6	56	
RAMA 15-30	55	
SAVOY 4-6	49-57	

Singles: 7–inch

ASCOT 3-5	62	
CAPITOL 5-10	55	
GROOVE 10-15	54	
JAX (Colored vinyl) 25-30	54	
JOSIE 6-10	56	
RAMA (167 "Ring-A-Ling") 50-75	55	

(Vocalist not credited, but believed to be Little Willie John.)

SAVOY (1100 series) 4-6	54-59	
VEE JAY 4-6	57	

Also see JOHN, Little Willie
Also see McNEELY, Big Jay / Paul Williams
Also see McPHERSON, Wyatt "Earp," and Paul Williams
Also see WATTS, Noble

WILLIAMS, Paul
Singles: 7–inch

A&M 2-4	72-77	
PAID 2-4	81	
PORTRAIT 2-4	79	
REPRISE 2-4	70	

LPs: 10/12–inch 33rpm

A&M 6-10	71-77	
PAID 5-8	81	
PORTRAIT 5-8	79	
REPRISE 8-12	70	

WILLIAMS, Robin
Singles: 12–inch 33/45rpm

CASABLANCA 4-6	79	

WILLIS, Timmy
Singles: 7-inch
JUBILEE 2-4   69
VEEP 3-5   68

WILLIS "The Guard" and Vigorish
Singles: 7-inch
HANDSHAKE 3-5   80
Members: Jerry Buckner; Gary Garcia.
Also see BUCKNER & GARCIA

WILL-O-BEES
Singles: 7-inch
DATE 3-5   67
SGC 3-5   68-69

WILLOWS
Singles: 78rpm
MELBA (Except 102) 5-10   56-57
MELBA (102 "Church Bells
  Are Ringing") 15-25   56
MELBA (102 "Church Bells May Ring) . 5-10   56
Singles: 7-inch
ABC 2-4   73
COLLECTABLES 2-4
MELBA (Except 102) 15-20   56-57
MELBA (102 "Church Bells
  Are Ringing") 50-60   56
MELBA (102 "Church Bells May Ring) 10-15   56
Members: Tony Middleton; Richard Davis; Ralph Martin; Joe
Martin; John Steele; Richard Simon; Dotty Martin.
Also see SEDAKA, Neil

WILMER and the the Dukes
Singles: 7-inch
APHRODISIAC 3-5   69
LPs: 10/12-inch 33rpm
APHRODISIAC 10-15   69
Member: Wilmer Alexander Jr.

WILSON, Al
Singles: 7-inch
BELL 2-4   70
BELL GOLD 2-4
CAROUSEL 2-4   71
PLAYBOY 2-4   76
ROADSHOW 2-4   79
ROCKY ROAD 2-4   72-75
SOUL CITY 3-5   67-69
LPs: 10/12-inch 33rpm
PLAYBOY 8-10   76
ROADSHOW 5-8   79
ROCKY ROAD 8-10   73-74
SOUL CITY 10-15   69
Also see ROLLERS

WILSON, Ann
(Ann Wilson and the Daybreaks)
Singles: 7-inch
CAPITOL 2-4   86
TOPAZ 10-15   67
Also see HEART
Also see RENO, Mike, and Ann Wilson

WILSON, Ann, Robin Zander
Singles: 7-inch
CAPITOL 2-4   88
Also see WILSON, Ann

WILSON, Bobby
Singles: 7-inch
BUDDAH 2-4   75
CHAIN 2-4   73

WILSON, Brian
Singles: 7-inch
CAPITOL (5610 "Caroline, No") 12-18   66
SIRE (27694 "Melt Away") 3-5   88
SIRE (27814 "Love and Mercy") 3-5   88
SIRE (28350 "Let's Go to
  Heaven in My Car") 3-5   87
Promotional Singles
SIRE (27694 "Melt Away") 4-8   88
SIRE (27787 "Night Time") 4-8   88
SIRE (27814 "Love and Mercy") 4-8   88
SIRE (28350 "Let's Go to
  Heaven in My Car") 5-10   87
Picture Sleeves
SIRE (27787 "Night Time") 8-12   88
SIRE (27814 "Love and Mercy") 4-8   88
SIRE (28350 "Let's Go to
  Heaven in My Car") 4-8   87
LPs: 10/12-inch 33rpm
SIRE (3248 "Brian Wilson: Words
  and Music") 15-20   88
SIRE (225669 "Brian Wilson") 5-10   88
Also see BEACH BOYS
Also see BERRY, Jan
Also see BLOSSOMS
Also see CAMPBELL, Glen
Also see CASTELLS
Also see DE SHANNON, Jackie
Also see HONDELLS
Also see RIVERS, Johnny

WILSON, Brian, and Mike Love
Singles: 7-inch
BROTHER (1002 "Gettin' Hungry") . . 15-25   67
Also see WILSON, Brian

WILSON, Carl
Singles: 7-inch
CARIBOU 2-4   81-83
LPs: 10/12-inch 33rpm
CARIBOU 5-8   81-82
Also see BEACH BOYS
Also see CASSIDY, David
Also see KING HARVEST
Also see NEWTON-JOHN, Olivia

WILSON, Dennis
Singles: 7-inch
CARIBOU 4-6   77
LPs: 10/12-inch 33rpm
CARIBOU 10-15   77
Also see BEACH BOYS

WILSON, Flip
Singles: 7–inch
FLIP WILSON (SK-1 "Flip Wilson") ... 5-10
(Promotional issue only. No title or label shown.)
LITTLE DAVID 2-4   72-75
LPs: 10/12–inch 33rpm
ATLANTIC 8-15   67-68
IMPERIAL 10-20   61
LITTLE DAVID 5-10   70-72
MINIT 8-15   68
SUNSET 8-10   70

WILSON, Hank
(Leon Russell)
Singles: 7–inch
SHELTER 2-4   73-74
LPs: 10/12–inch 33rpm
SHELTER 8-10   73
Also see RUSSELL, Leon

WILSON, J. Frank
(J. Frank Wilson and the Cavaliers)
Singles: 7–inch
ABC 2-4   73
APRIL 3-5
CHARAY 3-5   69
COLLECTABLES 2-4
ERIC 2-4
JOSIE 4-8   64-65
LE CAM (500 series) 2-4   81
LE CAM (722 "Last Kiss") 15-25   64
LE CAM (1000 series) 4-8   65
LE CAM (12000 series) 2-4
SOLLY 3-5   66
TAMARA 8-15   64
VIRGO 2-4   72
LPs: 10/12–inch 33rpm
DILL PICKEL 8-10   71
JOSIE (4006 "Last Kiss") 40-50   64

WILSON, Jackie
Singles: 78rpm
BRUNSWICK 5-10   57
Singles: 7–inch
BRUNSWICK (7-38000 series) 10-20   60
(Stereo compact 33 singles.)
BRUNSWICK (55024 through 55086) . 8-12   57-58
BRUNSWICK (55105 through 55165) .. 5-8   58-59
BRUNSWICK (55166 through 55236) .. 4-6   60-62
BRUNSWICK (55238 through 55504) .. 2-5   63-73
COLUMBIA 2-4   87
ERIC 2-4   83
GUSTO 2-4
Picture Sleeves
BRUNSWICK (55166 through 55236) . 8-12   60-62
BRUNSWICK (55238 through 55467) .. 4-8   63-72
COLUMBIA 2-4   87
EPs: 7–inch 33/45rpm
BRUNSWICK 20-35   59-63

LPs: 10/12–inch 33rpm
BRUNSWICK (111 "Solid Gold") 10-15
(Brunswick Special Products, mail-order offer.)
BRUNSWICK (54045 "Lonely
Teardrops") 50-100   59
BRUNSWICK (54042 "He's So
Fine") 50-100   59
BRUNSWICK (54050 "So Much") ... 40-80   60
BRUNSWICK (54055 "Jackie Sings
the Blues") 30-50   60
BRUNSWICK (54058 "My Golden
Favorites") 30-40   60
BRUNSWICK (54059 "A Woman, a
Lover, a Friend") 30-40   60
BRUNSWICK (54100 "You Ain't
Heard Nothin' Yet") 25-30   61
BRUNSWICK (54101 "By Request") . 25-30   61
BRUNSWICK (54105 "Body & Soul") 25-30   62
BRUNSWICK (54108 "At the Copa") . 25-30   62
BRUNSWICK (54110 through
54130) 20-25   63-67
(Beginning with 54050, Brunswick indicated stereo
LPs with a "7" preceding the catalog number.
Numbers after 54130 were available as stereo
issues only and are shown here as the 75000
series.)
BRUNSWICK (754138 through
754167) 15-20   68-71
BRUNSWICK (754185 through
754212) 10-15   72-77
COLUMBIA 5-8   87
DISCOVERY 8-10   78
EPIC 10-12   83
Also see WARD, Billy, and the Dominoes
Also see WILSON, Sonny

WILSON, Jackie, and Lavern Baker
Singles: 7–inch
BRUNSWICK 3-5   65
Also see BAKER, Lavern

WILSON, Jackie, and Count Basie
Singles: 7–inch
BRUNSWICK 3-5   68
LPs: 10/12–inch 33rpm
BRUNSWICK 15-20   68
Also see BASIE, Count

WILSON, Jackie, and the Chi-Lites
Singles: 7–inch
BRUNSWICK 2-4   75
Also see CHI-LITES

WILSON, Jackie, and Linda Hopkins
Singles: 7–inch
BRUNSWICK 3-5   62-65
EPs: 7–inch 33/45rpm
BRUNSWICK 15-20   63
LPs: 10/12–inch 33rpm
BRUNSWICK 25-35   68
Also see HOPKINS, Linda
Also see WILSON, Jackie

WILSON, Mary
Singles: 7–inch
MOTOWN 2-4   79
LPs: 10/12–inch 33rpm
MOTOWN 5-8   79
Also see SUPREMES

WILSON, Meri
Singles: 7–inch
GRT 2-4   77
LPs: 10/12–inch 33rpm
GRT 5-10   77

WILSON, Murray
(Murry Wilson)
Singles: 7–inch
CAPITOL 5-10   67
LPs: 10/12–inch 33rpm
CAPITOL 25-50 67

WILSON, Nancy
Singles: 12–inch 33/45rpm
CAPITOL 4-8   79
Singles: 7–inch
CAPITOL (Except 4000 and 5000 series) 2-5   68-79
CAPITOL (4000 and 5000 series) 3-6   59-67
Picture Sleeves
CAPITOL 4-8   65
LPs: 10/12–inch 33rpm
ASI 5-8   81
CAPITOL (100 through 800 series) . . . 5-12   69-71
CAPITOL (1300 through 1700 series) 15-30   59-62
CAPITOL (1800 through 2900 series) . 8-18   63-68
(With "T," "ST" or "SKAO" prefix.)
CAPITOL (1800 through 2900 series) . 5-8   78
(With "SM" prefix.)
CAPITOL (11000 and 12000 series) . . 5-10   74-80
CAPITOL (16000 series) 5-8   80
COLUMBIA 5-8   84
Also see CAPITOL'S MYSTERY ARTIST
Also see LEWIS, Ramsey

WILSON, Nancy, and Julian "Cannonball" Adderley
Singles: 7–inch
CAPITOL 2-5   62
LPs: 10/12–inch 33rpm
CAPITOL (1657 "Nancy Wilson and
Cannonball Adderley") 15-25   62
(With "T" or "ST" prefix.)
CAPITOL (1657 "Nancy Wilson and
Cannonball Adderley") 5-8   75
(With "SM" prefix.)
CAPITOL (16000 series) 4-8   81
Also see ADDERLEY, Cannonball

WILSON, Nancy, and George Shearing
Singles: 7–inch
CAPITOL 2-5   61
LPs: 10/12–inch 33rpm
CAPITOL (1524 "Swingin's Mutual") . 15-25   61
(With "T" or "ST" prefix.)

CAPITOL (1524 "Swingin's Mutual") . . . 5-8   75
(With "SM" prefix.)
Also see SHEARING, George
Also see WILSON, Nancy

WILSON, Phill
Singles: 7–inch
HURON 3-5   61

WILSON, Precious
Singles: 7–inch
JIVE 2-4   86
LPs: 10/12–inch 33rpm
JIVE 5-8   86

WILSON, Shanice
Singles: 7–inch
A&M 2-4   87-88
LPs: 10/12–inch 33rpm
A&M 5-8   87

WILSON, Sonny
(Jackie Wilson)
Singles: 78rpm
DEE GEE (4000 "Rainy Day
Blues") 30-50   52
DEE GEE (4001 "Danny Boy") 30-50   52
Singles: 7–inch
DEE GEE (4000 "Rainy Day
Blues") 50-100 52
DEE GEE (4001 "Danny Boy") 50-100 52
Also see WILSON, Jackie

WILSON, Timothy
Singles: 7–inch
BLUE ROCK 2-4   69
BUDDAH 3-5   67-68
VEEP 3-5   65

WILSON BROTHERS
Singles: 7–inch
ATCO 2-4   79
LPs: 10/12–inch 33rpm
ATCO 5-8   79

WILTON PLACE STREET BAND
Singles: 7–inch
ISLAND 2-4   77

WINAN, BeBe and CeCe
Singles: 12–inch 33/45rpm
CAPITOL 4-6   87
Singles: 12–inch 33/45rpm
CAPITOL 2-4   87
LPs: 10/12–inch 33rpm
CAPITOL 5-8   87-89

WINBUSH, Angela
Singles: 7–inch
MERCURY 2-4   87-89
LPs: 10/12–inch 33rpm
MERCURY 5-8   87-89

WINCHESTER, Jesse
Singles: 7–inch
AMPEX 2-4   70
BEARSVILLE 2-4   76-81
LPs: 10/12–inch 33rpm
BEARSVILLE/AMPEX 15-20   70
BEARSVILLE 6-10   71-81
Promotional LPs
BEARSVILLE (692 "Live at the Bijou") 20-25   75
BEARSVILLE (693 "Live at the
    Bijou/Live Interview") 30-40   75
   Also see HARRIS, Emmylou
   Also see LARSON, Nicolette
   Also see MURRAY, Anne

WIND
Singles: 7–inch
LIFE 4-6   69
LPs: 10/12–inch 33rpm
LIFE 15-20   69
   Member: Tony Orlando.
   Also see COOL HEAT
   Also see ORLANDO, Tony

WIND in the WILLOWS
Singles: 7–inch
CAPITOL 4-6   68
LPs: 10/12–inch 33rpm
CAPITOL (2956 "The Wind in
   the Willows") 40-75   68
   Members: Deborah Harry; Paul Klein; Peter Brittain; Anton
   Carysforth; Steve DePhillips.
   Also see HARRY, Debbie

WINDING, Kai, and His Orchestra
(Kai Winding and J.J. Johnson)
Singles: 7–inch
BETHLEHEM 2-4   60
COLUMBIA 2-5   56-59
IMPULSE 2-4   61
MGM 2-4   78
VERVE 2-4   62-67
EPs: 7–inch 33/45rpm
COLUMBIA 5-15   58-59
SAVOY 10-20   53
LPs: 10/12–inch 33rpm
A&M 8-12   68
COLUMBIA (900 through 1300 series) 15-30   56-59
COLUMBIA (8100 series) 15-25   59
GLENDALE 5-8   76-77
IMPULSE 15-25   61
JAZZTONE 20-35   56
PICKWICK 5-10   65-70
ROOST (400 series) 60-80   52
   (10–inch LPs.)
SAVOY (9000 series) 50-75   53
   (10–inch LPs.)
VERVE 10-25   61-67
   (Reads "MGM Records - a Division of
   Metro-Goldwyn-Mayer, Inc." at bottom of label.)

VERVE 5-10   73-84
   (Reads "Manufactured By MGM Record Corp.," or
   mentions either Poly dor or Polygram at bottom of
   label.)
WHO'S WHO in JAZZ 5-8   78
   Also see STITT, Sonny, Kai Winding and Horace Silver

WINDJAMMER
Singles: 7–inch
MCA 2-4   83-85
LPs: 10/12–inch 33rpm
MCA 5-8   83

WINDSTORM
Singles: 7–inch
POLYDOR 2-4   80

WINDY CITY
Singles: 7–inch
CHI-SOUND 2-4   77
KELLI-ARTS 2-4   80

WINE, April: see APRIL WINE

WING and a Prayer Fife and Drum Corps
Singles: 7–inch
WING and a PRAYER 2-4   75-77
LPs: 10/12–inch 33rpm
WING and a PRAYER 5-8   76-77

WINGER
LPs: 10/12–inch 33rpm
ATLANTIC 5-8   88-90

WINGFIELD, Pete
Singles: 7–inch
ISLAND 2-4   75-77
LPs: 10/12–inch 33rpm
ISLAND 5-8   75

WINGS
Singles: 7–inch
DUNHILL 3-5   68
LPs: 10/12–inch 33rpm
DUNHILL 10-12   68

WINNERS
Singles: 7–inch
ARIOLA-AMERICA 2-4   78
LPs: 10/12–inch 33rpm
ARIOLA-AMERICA 5-8   78
ROADSHOW 5-10   78

WINSTON, George
Singles: 7–inch
WINDHAM HILL 2-4
LPs: 10/12–inch 33rpm
WINDHAM HILL 5-8   83-88

WINSTONS
Singles: 7–inch
METROMEDIA 2-4   69
LPs: 10/12–inch 33rpm
METROMEDIA 8-12   69

WINTER, Edgar
(Edgar Winter Group; Edgar Winter's White Trash)
Singles: 12–inch 33/45rpm
BLUE SKY 4-6   80
BODY ROCK 4-6   83
Singles: 7–inch
BLUE SKY 2-4   75-81
EPIC 2-4   70-75
LPs: 10/12–inch 33rpm
BACK-TRAC 5-8   85
BLUE SKY 6-10   75-81
EPIC 10-15   70-75
   Also see DERRINGER, Rick
   Also see HARTMAN, Dan
   Also see MONTROSE, Ronnie
   Also see WINTER, Johnny and Edgar

WINTER, Jimmy: see WINTER, Johnny

KRCo

RCo 107
Vocal
107-A

ONE NIGHT OF LOVE
(Johnny Winter)
JOHNNY WINTER
and
THE CRYSTALIERS

WINTER, Johnny
(Johnny Winter and the Crystaliers; Jimmy Winter)
Singles: 7–inch
ATLANTIC 5-10   64
BLUE SKY 2-4   75
COLUMBIA 2-4   69-74
FROLIC 20-30
GRT 3-5   69
IMPERIAL 3-5   69
KRCO (107 "One Night of Love") 50-75   61
MGM 4-6   65
PACEMAKER 5-8   66
SONOBEAT 5-8   68
TODD 8-10   63
Picture Sleeves
SONOBEAT 50-75   68
(Some sleeves picture the Vulcan Gas Co., an
Austin nightclub, and those are at the high end of
the price range given. Sleeves that do not picture
the club are priced at the lower end.)
LPs: 10/12–inch 33rpm
ACCORD 5-8   81
ALLIGATOR 5-8   84-85
BLUE SKY 6-10   74-80
BUDDAH 10-15   69

CBS ASSOCIATED 5-8
COLUMBIA (9800 and 9900 series) . 15-20   69
COLUMBIA (30000 through
  33000 series) 10-15   70-75
CRAZY CAJUN 8-10
GRT 10-15   69
IMPERIAL 15-20   69
JANUS 10-12   69-70
SONOBEAT ("Progressive
  Blues Experiment") 100-150   68
(Limited edition autographed issue.)
SONOBEAT ("Progressive
  Blues Experiment") 75-125   68
(Limited edition, but not autographed.)
U.A. 8-10   73-74
   Also see GREAT BELIEVERS
   Also see GUITAR SLIM
   Also see JOHNNY and the Jammers
   Also see SPRINGSTEEN, Bruce / Johnny Winter / Hollies
   Also see TEXAS "GUITAR" SLIM
   Also see WATERS, Muddy

WINTER, Johnny and Edgar
Singles: 7–inch
BLUE SKY 2-4   76
CASCADE 35-45   64
LPs: 10/12–inch 33rpm
BLUE SKY (Except 242) 5-8   76
BLUE SKY (242 "Johnny and Edgar Winter
  Discuss *Together*") 10-20   76
(Promotional issue only.)
   Also see WINTER, Edgar
   Also see WINTER, Johnny

WINTER, Paul
(Paul Winter and Winter Consort; Paul Winter Sextet)
Singles: 7–inch
A&M 2-4   69-77
COLUMBIA 2-5   62
EPIC 2-4   72-73
LPs: 10/12–inch 33rpm
A&M 8-12   69-78
COLUMBIA 10-20   62-65
EPIC 8-10   72
LIVING MUSIC 5-8   83-86
   Also see WINTER CONSORT

WINTER, Ruby: see WINTERS, Ruby

WINTER CONSORT
Singles: 7–inch
A&M 3-5   69
   Also see WINTER, Paul

WINTERHALTER, Hugo, and His Orchestra
Singles: 78rpm
RCA 2-4   50-57
Singles: 7–inch
ABC-PAR 2-4   63
COLUMBIA 2-4   50
KAPP 2-4   64-65
MUSICOR 2-4   68-70
RCA 2-4   50-63

EPs: 7–inch 33/45rpm

RCA	3-6	50-59

LPs: 10/12–inch 33rpm

ABC-PAR	4-8	63
CAMDEN	4-8	69-72
KAPP	4-8	65
MUSIC DISC	4-8	69
MUSICOR	5-10	68-71
RCA	5-15	50-77
TRIP	4-8	76

Also see HEYWOOD, Eddie

WINTERS, Robert, and Fall
Singles: 7–inch

BUDDAH	2-4	80-81
CASABLANCA	2-4	82-84

LPs: 10/12–inch 33rpm

BUDDAH	5-8	80-81
CASABLANCA	5-8	82-83

WINTERS, Ruby
(Ruby Winter)

Singles: 7–inch

CERTRON	2-4	71
DIAMOND	3-5	66-69
MILLENNIUM	2-4	78
POLYDOR	2-4	73-75

LPs: 10/12–inch 33rpm

MILLENNIUM	5-8	78

Also see THUNDER, Johnny, and Ruby Winters

WINWOOD, Steve
Singles: 7–inch

ISLAND	2-4	77-87
U.A.	3-5	71
VIRGIN	2-4	88

Picture Sleeves

ISLAND	2-4	80-84

LPs: 10/12–inch 33rpm

ISLAND	5-8	77-87
U.A. (9950 "Winwood")	20-30	71
(With liner notes by Bobby Abrahms.)		
U.A. (9964 "Winwood")	10-15	71
(Without liner notes.)		
VIRGIN	5-8	88-90

Also see BAKER, Ginger
Also see BLIND FAITH
Also see DAVIS, Spencer
Also see TOOTS and the Maytals
Also see TRAFFIC
Also see YAMASHTA, Stomu

WIRE TRAIN
Singles: 12–inch 33/45rpm

COLUMBIA	4-6	84

Singles: 7–inch

COLUMBIA	2-4	84

LPs: 10/12–inch 33rpm

COLUMBIA	5-8	84-87

WISH
(Featuring Fonda Rae)
Singles: 12–inch 33/45rpm

KN	4-6	84

Singles: 7–inch

PERSONAL	2-4	84-85

Also see RAE, Fonda

WISHBONE ASH
Singles: 7–inch

ATLANTIC	2-4	77
DECCA	2-4	71-72
MCA	2-4	73-77

LPs: 10/12–inch 33rpm

ATLANTIC	6-10	76
DECCA (Except 1922)	10-15	71-72
DECCA (1922 "Live from Memphis")	15-20	72
(Promotional issue only.)		
MCA	5-8	73-82

Also see FOGHAT

WITCH QUEEN
Singles: 7–inch

ROADSHOW	2-4	79

LPs: 10/12–inch 33rpm

ROADSHOW	5-8	79

WITHERS, Bill
Singles: 12–inch 33/45rpm

COLUMBIA	4-6	79

Singles: 7–inch

COLUMBIA	2-4	75-85
SUSSEX	2-4	71-75

Picture Sleeves

SUSSEX	2-4	72

LPs: 10/12–inch 33rpm

COLUMBIA	5-8	75-85
SUSSEX	8-12	71-75

Also see WASHINGTON, Grover, Jr.
Also see WOMACK, Bobby, and Bill Withers

WITHERSPOON, Jimmy
(Jimmy Witherspoon and Groove Holmes; Jimmy
Witherspoon with Jay McShann and His Band; Jimmy
Witherspoon and Ben Webster; Jimmy Witherspoon
with Panama Francis and the Savoy Sultans)
Singles: 78rpm

CHECKER	5-10	54-55
FEDERAL	5-10	52-53
DOWN BEAT	5-8	48-49
MODERN (665 through 845)	4-6	49-51
RCA	4-8	57
SUPREME	5-8	48-49
SWING BEAT	4-8	49
SWING TIME	4-6	51

Singles: 7–inch

ABC	2-4	71
BLUE NOTE	2-4	75
BLUESWAY	2-4	69
CAPITOL	2-4	74
CHECKER (Black vinyl)	15-20	54-55
CHECKER (Colored vinyl)	50-75	54

FEDERAL	15-20	52-53
GNP/CRESCENDO	4-6	59
HI FI	4-6	60
KENT	2-4	71
KING	3-5	65
MODERN (857 through 903)	15-20	52-53
PACIFIC JAZZ	3-5	62
PRESTIGE	3-5	63-65
RCA	5-8	57
REPRISE	3-5	61-64
RIP	5-8	58
VEE JAY	4-6	59
VERVE	3-5	66-67
WORLD PACIFIC	4-6	59

LPs: 10/12–inch 33rpm

ABC	8-10	70
BLUE NOTE	8-10	75
BLUESWAY	8-10	69-73
CAPITOL	8-10	74
CONSTELLATION	15-20	64
CROWN (215 "Jimmy Witherspoon		
Sings the Blues")	15-20	61
(Black Vinyl.)		
CROWN (215 "Jimmy Witherspoon		
Sings the Blues")	20-40	61
(Colored Vinyl.)		
FANTASY	10-12	72
HI FI	20-30	59
INNER CITY	5-8	81
MCA	5-8	83
MUSE	5-8	83
OLYMPIC	8-10	73
PRESTIGE	10-15	64-69
(Many Prestige LPs remain currently available,		
using original catalog numbers.)		
RCA (1048 "Goin' to		
Kansas City Blues")	6-10	75
RCA (1639 "Goin' to		
Kansas City Blues")	30-40	58
REPRISE	20-30	61-62
SURREY	12-15	65
UNITED	8-10	
VERVE (5000 series)	12-15	66-68
VERVE (8000 series)	8-10	74
VERVE/FOLKWAYS (3011 "Blues		
Box")	25-30	66
WORLD PACIFIC	20-30	59-61

Also see BURDON, Eric, and Jimmy Witherspoon
Also see FREEMAN, Ernie
Also see HOLMES, Richard "Groove"
Also see McSHANN, Jay

WITHERSPOON, Jimmy, and the Lamplighters

Singles: 78rpm

FEDERAL	10-20	52

Singles: 7–inch

FEDERAL (12156 "Sad Life")	25-50	52
FEDERAL (12173 "24 Sad Hours") ..	25-50	52

WITHERSPOON, Jimmy, and the Quintones

Singles: 78rpm

ATCO	5-10	57

Singles: 7–inch

ATCO	10-20	57

WITHERSPOON, Jimmy / Eddie Vinson

LPs: 10/12–inch 33rpm

KING (634 "Battle of the		
Blues, Vol. 3")	200-300	59

Also see WITHERSPOON, Jimmy

WITT, Joachim

Singles: 12–inch 33/45rpm

W.E.A. INTERNATIONAL	4-6	84

WITTER, Jimmy

Singles: 7–inch

ELVIS (900 "If You Love		
My Woman")	150-175	
NEPTUNE	20-35	61
U.A.	8-10	61

WOLCOTT, Charles, Orchestra

Singles: 7–inch

MGM	2-4	60

WOLF
(Bill Wolfer)

Singles: 7–inch

CONSTELLATION	2-4	81-83

LPs: 10/12–inch 33rpm

CONSTELLATION	5-8	83

WOLF, Howlin: see HOWLIN' WOLF

WOLF, Peter

Singles: 12–inch 33/45rpm

EMI AMERICA	4-6	84-85

Singles: 7–inch

EMI AMERICA	2-4	84-87

LPs: 10/12–inch 33rpm

EMI AMERICA	5-8	84-87
MCA	5-8	90

Also see FRANKLIN, Aretha
Also see GEILS, J., Band

WOLF, Peter, and Mick Jagger

Singles: 12–inch 33/45rpm

EMI AMERICA	8-10	84

Singles: 7–inch

EMI AMERICA	2-4	84

LPs: 10/12–inch 33rpm

EMI AMERICA	8-10	84

Also see JAGGER, Mick
Also see WOLF, Peter

WOLFMAN JACK
(Bob Smith)

Singles: 7–inch

WOODEN NICKEL	2-4	72-73

LPs: 10/12–inch 33rpm

COLUMBIA	8-10	75
WOODEN NICKEL	8-10	72-73

Also see FLASH CADILLAC and the Continental Kids

Also see GUESS WHO
Also see STAMPEDERS

WOLFMAN JACK and the Wolf Pack
Singles: 7–inch
BREAD (71 "Wolfman Boogie") 25-30   65
BREAD (73 "New Orleans") 25-30   65
LPs: 10/12–inch 33rpm
BREAD (170 "Wolfman Jack
and the Wolf Pack") 50-75   65

WOMACK, Bobby
(Bobby Womack and Brotherhood; Bobby Womack
and Peace)
Singles: 12–inch 33/45rpm
ELEKTRA/WOMACK 4-6   83
Singles: 7–inch
ARISTA 2-4   79
ATLANTIC 3-5   67
BEVERLY GLEN 2-4   81-84
CHECKER 3-5   65
COLUMBIA 2-4   76-78
COLUMBIA/BROTHERHOOD 2-4   76-77
ELEKTRA/WOMACK 2-4   83
LIBERTY 2-4   70
MCA 2-4   86
MINIT 2-4   67-70
U.A. 2-4   71-76
EPs: 7–inch 33/45rpm
U.A. 10-15   72
(Promotional issue only.)
LPs: 10/12–inch 33rpm
ARISTA 5-8   79
BEVERLY GLEN 5-8   81-84
COLUMBIA 8-10   75-78
COLUMBIA/BROTHERHOOD 8-10   76
ELEKTRA/WOMACK 5-8   83
LIBERTY (7600 series) 8-10   70
LIBERTY (10000 series) 5-8
MCA 5-8   85
MINIT 10-12   68-70
U.A. 8-10   71-76
Also see BROTHERHOOD
Also see FELDER, Wilton, and Bobby Womack
Also see SZABO, Gabor
Also see VALENTINOS
Also see WOMACK BROTHERS

WOMACK, Bobby, and Patti Labelle
Singles: 7–inch
BEVERLY GLEN 2-4   84
Also see LABELLE, Patti
Also see WOMACK, Bobby

WOMACK, Bobby, and Bill Withers
Singles: 7–inch
U.A. 2-4   75
Also see WITHERS, Bill

WOMACK & WOMACK
Singles: 7–inch
ELEKTRA 2-4   84-85
LPs: 10/12–inch 33rpm
ELEKTRA 5-8   84-85

Members: Linda Womack; Cecil Womack.

WOMACK BROTHERS
Singles: 7–inch
SAR 4-6   61
Also see VALENTINOS
Also see WOMACK, Bobby

WOMBLES
Singles: 7–inch
COLUMBIA 2-4   74-75
LPs: 10/12–inch 33rpm
COLUMBIA 8-10   74
Member: Mike Batt.

WOMENFOLK
Singles: 7–inch
RCA 2-4   64-66
LPs: 10/12–inch 33rpm
RCA 10-15   63-66

WONDER, Stevie
(Little Stevie Wonder)
Singles: 12–inch 33/45rpm
MOTOWN 4-6
TAMLA 4-6
Singles: 7–inch
MOTOWN 2-4   84-88
MOTOWN/TOPPS (8 "Fingertips
Part 2") 50-75   67
MOTOWN/TOPPS (10 "Uptight") 50-75   67
(Topps Chewing Gum promotional item.
Single-sided, cardboard flexi, picture disc. Issued
with generic paper sleeve.)
TAMLA (1600 through 1800 series) 2-4   82-86
TAMLA (54061 "I Call It Pretty Music")   8-12   62
TAMLA (54074 "Contract on Love") 5-8   63
TAMLA (54080 "Fingertips") 3-5   63
TAMLA (54086 "Workout Stevie,
Workout") 3-5   63
TAMLA (54090 "Castles in the Sand") .. 4-6   64
TAMLA (54096 "Hey Harmonica Man") . 3-5   64
TAMLA (54103 "Happy Street") 8-12   64
TAMLA (54119 through 54139) 3-5   65-66
TAMLA (54142 "Someday at
Christmas") 6-10   66
TAMLA (54147 through 54323) 2-4   67-81
(Black vinyl.)
TAMLA (54147 through 54323) 4-8   69-78
(Colored vinyl. Promotional issues only.)
MOTOWN 2-4   82
Picture Sleeves
TAMLA (54061 "I Call It Pretty Music") 12-25   62
TAMLA (54080 through 54096) 4-8   63-64
TAMLA (54136 through 54317) 2-5   66-80
EPs: 7–inch 33/45rpm
TAMLA (340 "Something Extra for
Songs in the Key of Life") 10-15   76
LPs: 10/12–inch 33rpm
MOTOWN (100 and 200 series) 5-8   82
MOTOWN (800 series) 12-15   77
MOTOWN (6000 series) 5-8   84-91

TAMLA (232 "Tribute to Uncle Ray") . 50-65   63
TAMLA (233 "The Jazz Soul of
    Stevie Wonder") 50-65   63
TAMLA (240 "Little Stevie Wonder") .. 40-50   63
TAMLA (232 through 255) 30-40   63-64
TAMLA (268 through 279) 15-20   66-67
TAMLA (281 "Someday at
    Christmas") 30-40   67
TAMLA (282 through 371) 10-15   68-79
TAMLA (373 "Hotter Than July") 5-8   80
TAMLA (6000 series) 10-12   82-85

Promotional LPs

MOTOWN (PR-77 "Hotter Than July") 10-15   80
TAMLA (PR-61 "Stevie Wonder's Journey
    Through the Secret Life of Plants") . 10-15   79
TAMLA (PR 98/99 "Radio Programmer's
    Special") 15-20
    Also see CHARLENE and Stevie Wonder
    Also see DIONNE and Friends
    Also see JACKSONS
    Also see McCARTNEY, Paul, and Stevie Wonder
    Also see REDNOW, Eivets
    Also see ROSS, Diana, Stevie Wonder, Marvin Gaye & Smokey
        Robinson
    Also see TEMPTATIONS / Stevie Wonder
    Also see THIRD WORLD
    Also see U.S.A. for AFRICA
    Also see WILLIAMS, Deniece

WONDER, Stevie / John Denver
Singles: 7–inch

WHAT'S IT ALL ABOUT 4-8   80
    (Public service, radio station issue.)
    Also see DENVER, John

WONDER, Stevie, and Michael Jackson
Singles: 7–inch

MOTOWN 2-4   88
    Also see JACKSON, Michael

WONDER, Stevie, and Clarence Paul
(Little Stevie Wonder & Clarence Paul)
Singles: 7–inch

TAMLA 25-35   62

WONDER, Stevie / Dionne Warwick
LPs: 10/12–inch 33rpm

MOTOWN 5-8   84
    Also see WARWICK, Dionne
    Also see WONDER, Stevie

WONDER BAND
Singles: 7–inch

ATCO 2-4   79

LPs: 10/12–inch 33rpm

ATCO 5-8   79

WONDER LAND, Alice:
see ALICE WONDER LAND

WONDER WHO?
(4 Seasons)
Singles: 7–inch

COLLECTABLES 2-4
PHILIPS 3-5   65-67
VEE JAY 12-15   64

Picture Sleeves

PHILIPS 15-20   65-67
    Also see 4 SEASONS

WOO, Gerry
Singles: 7–inch

POLYDOR 2-4   87-88

WOOD, Bobby
Singles: 7–inch

CHALLENGE 3-5   62
CINNAMON 2-4   74
JOY 3-5   63-65
LUCKY ELEVEN 2-4   73
MALA 3-5   66
MGM 2-4   67-69
SUN 3-5   63

LPs: 10/12–inch 33rpm

JOY 10-15   64

WOOD, Brenton
Singles: 7–inch

BRENT 3-5   66
CREAM 2-4   76-78
DOUBLE SHOT 2-4   67-71
MR. WOOD 2-4   72-73
PRESIDENT 4-6   60
PROPHESY 2-4   73
WAND 8-12   64
WARNER 2-4   75

LPs: 10/12–inch 33rpm

CREAM 5-8   77
DOUBLE SHOT 12-15   67

WOOD, Del
Singles: 78rpm

DECCA 2-4   53-54
MERCURY 2-4   62-64
RCA 2-4   55-59
REPUBLIC 2-4   51-54
TENNESSEE 3-6   51

Singles: 7–inch

CHART 2-4   71-72
DECCA 3-5   53-54
MERCURY 2-4   62-64
RCA 2-5   55-59
REPUBLIC 3-8   51-54
TENNESSEE 5-10   51

EPs: 7–inch 33/45rpm

RCA 5-12   55-60
REPUBLIC 4-10   54-57

LPs: 10/12–inch 33rpm

CAMDEN 5-12   62-64
COLUMBIA 8-12   66
MERCURY 5-12   62-64
RCA 5-15   55-60
REPUBLIC 5-15   54-57
VOCALION 5-10

WOOD, Lauren
Singles: 7–inch

WARNER 2-4   79-81

Picture Sleeves
WARNER 2-4   81
LPs: 10/12–inch 33rpm
WARNER 5-8   81
Also see McDONALD, Michael

WOOD, Ron

Singles: 7–inch
COLUMBIA 2-4   79
WARNER 2-4   75-76
LPs: 10/12–inch 33rpm
COLUMBIA 5-8   79-81
WARNER 8-10   74-75
Also see BECK, Jeff, Ronnie Wood & Rod Stewart
Also see FACES
Also see ROLLING STONES
Also see SEXTON, Charlie, and Ron Wood

WOOD, Ron, and Ronnie Lane
(With Pete Townshend)
LPs: 10/12–inch 33rpm
ATCO (126 "Mahoney's Last Stand") . 10-15   76
(Soundtrack.)
Also see TOWNSHEND, Pete, and Ronnie Lane
Also see WOOD, Ron

WOOD, Roy
(Roy Wood's Wizzard; Roy Wood Wizzo Band)
Singles: 7–inch
U.A. 2-4   73-76
LPs: 10/12–inch 33rpm
U.A. 8-10   73-74
WARNER 5-8   79
Members: Roy Wood; Rick Price; Nick Pentelow; Mike Burney;
Keith Smart; Charlie Grima; Bill Hunt; Bob Brady.
Also see ELECTRIC LIGHT ORCHESTRA
Also see MOVE

WOODBURY, Woody
LPs: 10/12–inch 33rpm
STEREODDITIES 10-25   59-63

WOODENTOPS
Singles: 7–inch
COLUMBIA 2-4   86
LPs: 10/12–inch 33rpm
COLUMBIA 5-8   86

WOODS, Maceo
(Rev. Maceo and the Christian Tabernacle Choir)
Singles: 78rpm
VEE JAY (100 series) 3-5   55-56
Singles: 7–inch
ABC 2-4   73
VEE JAY (100 series) 4-8   55-56
VOLT 2-4   69
LPs: 10/12–inch 33rpm
GOSPEL TRUTH 4-8   72-74
SAVOY 4-8   76-83
STAX 4-8   78
TRIP 4-8   73
VEE JAY 5-15   60-65
VOLT 5-12   69

WOODS, Ren
Singles: 7–inch
ARC 2-4   79
ELEKTRA 2-4   82

WOODS, Stevie
Singles: 7–inch
COTILLION 2-4   81-83
LPs: 10/12–inch 33rpm
COTILLION 5-8   81-82

WOODS EMPIRE
Singles: 12–inch 33/45rpm
TABU 4-6   81
Singles: 7–inch
TABU 2-4   81
LPs: 10/12–inch 33rpm
TABU 5-8   81

WOOLEY, Sheb
Singles: 78rpm
MGM 3-5   55-57
Singles: 7–inch
MGM (12000 series) 4-6   55-61
MGM (13000 series) 3-5   61-68
MGM (14000 series) 2-4   68-75
POLYDOR 2-4
Picture Sleeves
MGM 4-8   59-62
EPs: 7–inch 33/45rpm
MGM 10-20 56-58
LPs: 10/12–inch 33rpm
MGM (3299 "Sheb Wooley") 20-25   56
MGM (4136 through 4026) 15-20 61-62
MGM (4275 through 4615) 8-15 65-69
Also see COLDER, Ben

WOOLIES
Singles: 7–inch
DUNHILL 3-5   66-67
SPIRIT 5-8   66
LPs: 10/12–inch 33rpm
SPIRIT 20-30   66

WOOLLEY, Bruce, and the Camera Club
Singles: 7–inch
COLUMBIA 2-4   80
Picture Sleeves
COLUMBIA 2-4   80
LPs: 10/12–inch 33rpm
COLUMBIA 5-8   80

WORD of MOUTH
(Featuring D.J. Cheese)
Singles: 12–inch 33/45rpm
BEAUTY and the BEAST 4-6   85
PROFILE 4-6   86

WORLD CLASS WRECKIN' CRU
Singles: 7–inch
KRU'CUT 2-4   88

WORLD PARTY
Singles: 7–inch
CHRYSALIS 2-4   86-87
LPs: 10/12–inch 33rpm
CHRYSALIS 5-8   86
ENSIGN 5-8   90

WORLD PREMIER
Singles: 12–inch 33/45rpm
CAPITOL 4-6   84
Singles: 7–inch
CAPITOL 2-4   84

WORLD'S FAMOUS SUPREME TEAM
Singles: 12–inch 33/45rpm
ISLAND 4-6   84
Singles: 7–inch
ISLAND 2-4   84

WORRELL, Bernie
Singles: 7–inch
ARISTA 2-4   79
LPs: 10/12–inch 33rpm
ARISTA 5-8   79
Also see PARLIAMENT

WORTH, Marion
Singles: 7–inch
CHEROKEE 3-5   59
COLUMBIA 2-4   60-67
DECCA 2-4   67-70
GUYDEN 3-5   59-60
Picture Sleeves
COLUMBIA 3-5   61-62
LPs: 10/12–inch 33rpm
COLUMBIA 10-20 63-64
DECCA 8-12   67

WRABIT
Singles: 7–inch
MCA 2-4   82
LPs: 10/12–inch 33rpm
MCA 5-8   82

WRAY, Bill
Singles: 7–inch
ABC 2-4   79

WRAY, Link
(Link Wray and His Ray Men; Link Wray and His Wray Men; Link Ray)
Singles: 78rpm
CADENCE 5-8   58
Singles: 7–inch
ATLAS 4-6   62
BARNABY 2-4   76
CADENCE 5-8   58
EPIC 5-8   59-61
HEAVY 3-5   68
KAY 50-65 58
MR. G 3-5   69
OKEH 3-5   67
POLYDOR 2-4   70-74

RUMBLE 15-20 61
SWAN (4137 "Jack the Ripper") 6-10   63
SWAN (4154 "Week End") 5-8   63
SWAN (4163 through 4187) 4-6   63-64
SWAN (4201 "Good Rockin' Tonight") 10-15 65
SWAN (4211 through 4232) 4-6   65
SWAN (4239 "Ace of Spades") 10-12 65
SWAN (4244 "The Batman Theme") ... 5-8   66
SWAN (4261 "Ace of Spades") 8-10   66
SWAN (4273 through 4282) 3-5   66-67
Picture Sleeves
EPIC 20-35 59
LPs: 10/12–inch 33rpm
EPIC (3661 "Link Wray and the Wraymen") 40-50 60
POLYDOR 8-10   71-74
RECORD FACTORY 20-25 74
SWAN 50-60 63
VERMILLION 20-25 75
VISA 5-8   79-80
Also see DUDLEY, Dave / Link Wray
Also see GORDON, Robert

WRAY, Link / Red Saunders
Singles: 7–inch
OKEH (7100 series) 4-6   63
OKEH (7200 series) 3-5   67

WRAY, Lucky
(Link Wray)
Singles: 78rpm
STARDAY 6-12   56
Singles: 7–inch
STARDAY (500 series) 20-25 56
STARDAY (600 series) 50-75 57

WRAY, Vernon
(With Link Wray)
LPs: 10/12–inch 33rpm
VERMILLION 20-25
Also see WRAY BROTHERS

WRAY BROTHERS
(Wray Family)
Singles: 7–inch
INFINITY 6-10   62
LAWN 6-10   63
Members: Link Wray; Doug Wray; Vernon Wray.
Also see WRAY, Link

WRECKING CREW
Singles: 12–inch 33/45rpm
ERECT 4-6   83
Singles: 7–inch
ERECT 2-4   83
SOUND of FLORIDA 2-4   83

WRIGHT, Bernard
Singles: 12–inch 33/45rpm
ARISTA 4-6   83
Singles: 7–inch
ARISTA 2-4   83-84
GRP 2-4   81-82

MANHATTAN 2-4   86
LPs: 10/12-inch 33rpm
ARISTA 5-8   83
GRP 5-8   81
MANHATTAN 5-8   86

WRIGHT, Betty
Singles: 12-inch 33/45rpm
EPIC 4-6   81
JAMAICA 4-6   84-85
Singles: 7-inch
ALSTON 2-4   68-79
ATCO 2-4   83
EPIC 2-4   81-83
FIRST STRING 2-4   86
JAMAICA 2-4   84-85
MS. B. 2-4   88
LPs: 10/12-inch 33rpm
ALSTON 6-10   72-79
ATCO 10-15   68
COLLECTABLES 6-8   88
EPIC 5-8   81-83
MS. B. 5-8   88
   Also see ALAIMO, Steve, and Betty Wright
   Also see BROWN, Peter, and Betty Wright
   Also see KC and the Sunshine Band

WRIGHT, Billy
Singles: 78rpm
SAVOY (710 through 761) 4-6   49-50
Singles: 7-inch
CARROLLTON 4-6   59
SAVOY (776 "Mean Old Wine") 15-20   51
SAVOY (827 "Drinkin' and Thinkin") ... 8-12   52

WRIGHT, Charles, and the Watts 103rd Street Rhythm Band
Singles: 7-inch
ABC 2-4   75
DUNHILL 2-4   73-74
WARNER 2-4   70-71
LPs: 10/12-inch 33rpm
ABC 6-10   75
DUNHILL 6-10   73-74
WARNER 8-12   70-72
   Also see SHIELDS
   Also see WATTS 103RD STREET RHYTHM BAND

WRIGHT, Dale
(Dale Wright and the Rock-Its; Dale Wright with the Wright Guys and the Dons)
Singles: 7-inch
ALCAR 8-10   60
FRATERNITY 10-15   58-59

WRIGHT, Duke
Singles: 7-inch
MOOLA 4-6   60

WRIGHT, Gary
(Gary Wright & Spooky Tooth)
Singles: 7-inch
A&M 2-4   70-72

WARNER 2-4   75-81
LPs: 10/12-inch 33rpm
A&M 8-12   70-76
WARNER 5-8   75-81
   Also see SPOOKY TOOTH
   Also see WRIGHT'S WONDERWHEEL

WRIGHT, O.V.
Singles: 7-inch
ABC 2-4   75-76
BACK BEAT 3-5   65-74
GOLDWAX 4-6   64
HI 2-4   76-79
LPs: 10/12-inch 33rpm
BACK BEAT 10-15   65-72
HI 5-8   78-79

WRIGHT, Priscilla
Singles: 78rpm
UNIQUE 3-6   55
Singles: 7-inch
20TH FOX 4-6   59
UNIQUE 5-8   55

WRIGHT, Ruben
Singles: 7-inch
CAPITOL 3-5   64-67
WYNNE 3-5   60

WRIGHT, Ruby
Singles: 78rpm
FRATERNITY 3-6   57
Singles: 7-inch
FRATERNITY 4-6   57
KING (Monaural) 3-5   59
KING (Stereo) 4-8   59

WRIGHT, Ruby, and Dick Pike
Singles: 7-inch
KING (5192 "Three Stars") 8-10   59
   Also see WRIGHT, Ruby

WRITERS
Singles: 12-inch 33/45rpm
COLUMBIA 4-6   79
Singles: 7-inch
COLUMBIA 2-4   78-79
LPs: 10/12-inch 33rpm
COLUMBIA 5-8   79

WUF TICKET
Singles: 12-inch 33/45rpm
PRELUDE 4-6   81
Singles: 7-inch
PRELUDE 2-4   81

WYCOFF, Michael
Singles: 12-inch 33/45rpm
RCA 4-6   83
Singles: 7-inch
RCA 2-4   80-84
LPs: 10/12-inch 33rpm
RCA 5-8   83
   Also see CLAYTON, Merry

WYLIE, Richard
(Richard "Popcorn" Wylie)
Singles: 7-inch
ABC	2-4	75
EPIC	3-5	62-63
KAREN	2-4	68
MOTOWN	30-40	61
SOUL	2-4	71
Picture Sleeves
EPIC	4-8	62
LPs: 10/12-inch 33rpm
ABC	8-10	74

WYMAN, Bill
Singles: 12-inch 33/45rpm
A&M (12041 "Je Suis Un Rock Star")	6-10	81
Singles: 7-inch
A&M (2367 "Je Suis Un Rock Star")	2-4	81
ROLLING STONES	4-6	74-75
Promotional Singles
A&M (2367 "Je Suis Un Rock Star")	4-6	81
A&M (12041 "Je Suis Un Rock Star")	15-20	81
(12-inch single.)		
Picture Sleeves
A&M (2367 "Je Suis Un Rock Star")	3-5	81
LPs: 10/12-inch 33rpm
ROLLING STONES	8-10	74-76

WYMAN, Bill / Rolling Stones
Singles: 7-inch
LONDON (907 "In Another Land")	4-6	67
Promotional Singles
LONDON (907 "In Another Land")	8-10	67
Picture Sleeves
LONDON (907 "In Another Land")	10-15	67
Also see ROLLING STONES
Also see WYMAN, Bill

WYND CHYMES
Singles: 7-inch
RCA	2-4	82-83
LPs: 10/12-inch 33rpm
RCA	5-8	82

WYNETTE, Tammy
Singles: 7-inch
EPIC (Except 1)	2-5	66-86
EPIC (1 "The Wonders You Perform")	4-8	70
(Colored vinyl. Promotional issue only.)		
Picture Sleeves
EPIC	2-4	69-76
LPs: 10/12-inch 33rpm
COLUMBIA	5-10	73
EPIC	5-15	68-86
HARMONY	5-10	70-71
TIME-LIFE	5-8	81
Also see CASH, Johnny / Tammy Wynette
Also see HOUSTON, David, and Tammy Wynette
Also see JONES, George, and Tammy Wynette
Also see LYNN, Loretta / Tammy Wynette

WYNNE, Philippe
Singles: 12-inch 33/45rpm
FANTASY	4-6	83
Singles: 7-inch
COTILLION	2-4	77
FANTASY	2-4	83
SUGAR HILL	2-4	83
UNCLE JAM	2-4	80
LPs: 10/12-inch 33rpm
COTILLION	5-8	77

X

X, Malcolm: see MALCOLM X
XTC
Singles: 7-inch
EPIC	2-4	82
GEFFEN (Except "PRO" series)	2-4	83-89
GEFFEN ("PRO" series)	3-5	83-84
(Promotional issues only.)		
RSO	2-4	81
VIRGIN	2-4	79-81
LPs: 10/12-inch 33rpm
EPIC	5-10	82
GEFFEN	5-8	84-89
RSO	5-10	
VIRGIN	5-10	78-82
Members: Andy Partridge; Barry Andrews; Colin Moulding; Terry Chambers; Dave Gregory.
Also see DUKES of STRATOSPHERE

XAVIER
(Xavier Smith)
Singles: 12-inch 33/45rpm
LIBERTY	4-6	82
Singles: 7-inch
LIBERTY	2-4	82
LPs: 10/12-inch 33rpm
LIBERTY	5-8	82

XAVION
Singles: 7-inch
ASYLUM	2-4	84-85
LPs: 10/12-inch 33rpm
ASYLUM	5-8	84

XENA
Singles: 12-inch 33/45rpm
EMERGENCY	4-6	83

X-25 BAND
Singles: 7-inch
H.C.R.C	2-4	82

Y

EPIC (34491 "Yardbirds' Great Hits") .. 8-10   77
EPIC (38455 "The Yardbirds") 5-8   83
EPIC (48455 "The Yardbirds") 12-15   83
(Half-speed mastered.)
MERCURY (21271 "Eric Clapton and the Yardbirds
Live with Sonny Boy Williamson") .. 20-30   66
(Monaural.)
MERCURY (61271 "Eric Clapton and the Yardbirds
Live with Sonny Boy Williamson") .. 30-40   66
(Stereo.)
RHINO 6-10   82-86
SPRINGBOARD 8-10   72
    Members: Eric Clapton; Jeff Beck; Keith Relf; Jimmy Page; Jim
    McCarty; Chris Dreja.
    Also see ARMAGEDDON
    Also see BECK, Jeff
    Also see BOX of FROGS
    Also see CACTUS
    Also see CLAPTON, Eric
    Also see PAGE, Jimmy
    Also see WILLIAMSON, Sonny Boy

YARROW, Peter
Singles: 7-inch
WARNER 2-4   68-75
LPs: 10/12-inch 33rpm
WARNER 8-10   72-75
    Also see PETER, PAUL & MARY

YAZ
(Yazoo)
Singles: 12-inch 33/45rpm
SIRE 4-6   82-84
Singles: 7-inch
SIRE 2-4   82-84
LPs: 10/12-inch 33rpm
SIRE 5-8   82-83
    Members: Alison Moyet; Vince Clarke.
    Also see MOYET, Alison

YAZZ and the Plastic Population
Singles: 7-inch
ELEKTRA 2-4   88

YELLO
Singles: 12-inch 33/45rpm
ELEKTRA 4-6   83-85
RALPH 5-8   81
STIFF 4-8
Singles: 7-inch
ELEKTRA 2-4   83-85
MERCURY 2-4   87-89
RALPH 2-4   81
STIFF (Picture discs) 4-8
LPs: 10/12-inch 33rpm
ELEKTRA 5-8   83-85
MERCURY 5-8   87-89
RALPH 8-10   81

YELLOW BALLOON
Singles: 7-inch
CANTERBURY 4-6   67-68
LPs: 10/12-inch 33rpm
CANTERBURY 15-20   67

Members: Alex Valdez; Don Grady; Don Braucht; Forrest Green;
Paul Cannella; Darryl Dragon.
    Also see CAPTAIN & TENNILLE
    Also see SPIRIT

YELLOW JACKETS
Singles: 7-inch
SMASH 3-5   68

YELLOW MAGIC ORCHESTRA
Singles: 12-inch 33/45rpm
A&M 4-6   80
Singles: 7-inch
A&M 2-4   80
HORIZON 2-4   80
LPs: 10/12-inch 33rpm
A&M 5-8   80-81
HORIZON 5-8   80

YELLOWMAN
Singles: 12-inch 33/45rpm
COLUMBIA 4-6   84
Singles: 7-inch
COLUMBIA 2-4   84
LPs: 10/12-inch 33rpm
COLUMBIA 5-8   84

YES
Singles: 12-inch 33/45rpm
ATCO 4-6   83-86
Singles: 7-inch
ATCO 2-4   83-87
ATLANTIC (Black vinyl) 2-4   70-78
ATLANTIC (Colored vinyl) 4-8   70-78
Promotional Singles
ATLANTIC 3-6   70-78
LPs: 10/12-inch 33rpm
ARISTA 5-8   91
ATCO 5-8   83-87
ATLANTIC (100 series) 12-15   73
ATLANTIC (500 series) 8-12   80
ATLANTIC (900 series) 12-15   74
ATLANTIC (7000 series) 10-12   71-72
ATLANTIC (8000 series) 10-15   69-71
ATLANTIC (16000 through
19000 series) 5-10   74-82
MFSL 25-50   82
Promotional LPs
ATLANTIC ("Solos") 10-15   76
    Members: Jon Anderson; Rick Wakeman; Steve Howe; Chris
    Squire; Tony Kaye; Alan White; Bill Bruford; Patrick Moraz; Geoff
    Downes; Trevor Horn.
    Also see ANDERSON, Jon
    Also see BANKS, Peter
    Also see BUGGLES
    Also see HOWE, Steve, Band
    Also see KING CRIMSON
    Also see MORAZ, Patrick
    Also see PAVLOV'S DOG
    Also see SIMON, Paul
    Also see WAKEMAN, Rick

YIPES
Singles: 7-inch
MILLENNIUM 2-4   79-80

LPs: 10/12–inch 33rpm

MILLENNIUM 5-8 79-80

YOAKAM, Dwight
Singles: 7–inch

OAK 15-25   86
REPRISE 2-4   86-90

LPs: 10/12–inch 33rpm

OAK ("Guitars, Cadillacs") 800-1000   86
(Number not known.)
REPRISE 5-8   86-90

YORK, Dave, and the Beachcombers
Singles: 7–inch

LANCELOT 8-12   62
P.K.M. 4-6   62

YORK, Rusty
Singles: 7–inch

CAPITOL 3-5   61
CHESS 5-8   59
GAYLORD 3-5   63
KING (5100 series) 5-8   58
KING (5500 series) 4-6   61-62
NOTE 20-30   59
P.J 10-15   59
SAGE 10-15   60
   Also see MACK, Lonnie, and Rusty York

YOST, Dennis
Singles: 7–inch

MGM 2-4   75
ROBOX 2-4   81

LPs: 10/12–inch 33rpm

ACCORD 5-8   81
ROBOX 5-8   82
   Also see CLASSICS IV

YOU KNOW WHO GROUP
Singles: 7–inch

CASUAL 4-6   65
4 CORNERS 4-6   64

LPs: 10/12–inch 33rpm

INTERNATIONAL ALLIED 15-20   65

YOUNG, Barry
Singles: 7–inch

COLUMBIA 2-4   66
DOT 3-5   65-66
EVA 3-6   63
HOOKS BROTHERS 2-4   66

Picture Sleeves

COLUMBIA 3-6   66

LPs: 10/12–inch 33rpm

DOT 10-20   65

YOUNG, Donny
Singles: 7–inch

DECCA (Except 31077) 10-15   61
DECCA (31077 "Shakin' the Blues") . 20-25   60
MERCURY 5-10   61-62
TODD 4-8   64
   Also see PAYCHECK, Johnny

YOUNG, Faron
(Faron Young and Margie Singleton)
Singles: 78rpm

CAPITOL 3-6   53-57

Singles: 7–inch

CAPITOL (2200 through 3900 series) .. 4-8   53-58
CAPITOL (4000 through 4800 series) .. 3-5   58-62
MCA 2-4   79-80
MERCURY 2-4   63-78

Picture Sleeves

CAPITOL 3-6   61
MERCURY 2-5   62-68

EPs: 7–inch 33/45rpm

CAPITOL 8-15   54-61

LPs: 10/12–inch 33rpm

ALBUM GLOBE 5-8   81
ALLEGIANCE 5-8   84
CAPITOL (700 series) 30-40   57
CAPITOL (1000 series) 20-25   58-59
CAPITOL (1100 series) 30-40   59
CAPITOL (1400 through 2500 series) 12-25   60-66
(With "T," "DT" or "ST" prefix.)
CAPITOL (1500 series) 5-8   75
(With "SM" prefix.)
CASTLE 5-8
EXACT 5-8   80
FARON YOUNG 15-20
MCA 4-8   79-83
MARY CARTER PAINTS (1000 "Faron
   Young Sings on Stage") 35-45
(Promotional issue only.)
MERCURY 5-15   63-77
PICKWICK/HILLTOP 8-12   66-68
SEARS 8-12
TOWER 12-15   66-68
WING 8-12   68
   Also see ATKINS, Chet / Faron Young
   Also see NELSON, Willie / Faron Young
   Also see OWENS, Buck / Faron Young / Ferlin Husky

YOUNG, Faron / Carl Perkins / Claude King
LPs: 10/12–inch 33rpm

PICKWICK/HILLTOP 8-15   65
   Also see KING, Claude
   Also see PERKINS, Carl

YOUNG, Georgie
(Georgie Young and the Rockin' Bocs; George Young)
Singles: 7–inch

CAMEO 4-6   58-59
CHANCELLOR 3-5   61
COLUMBIA (42773 "Supercar") 10-20   63
FORTUNE 5-8   57
MERCURY (71259 "Can't
   Stop Me") 30-40   58
PACE SETTER 5-8
SWAN 4-6   60

YOUNG, Jesse Colin
(Jesse Colin Young with the Youngbloods)
Singles: 7–inch

ELEKTRA	2-4	78
REPRISE	2-4	73
WARNER	2-4	70-77

LPs: 10/12–inch 33rpm

CAPITOL (2000 series)	20-25	64
CAPITOL (11000 series)	8-10	74
CAPITOL (16000 series)	5-8	80
ELEKTRA	5-8	78
MERCURY (61005 "Young Blood")	20-25	65
MERCURY (61273 "Two Trips")	10-15	70
WARNER	8-10	72-77

Also see YOUNGBLOODS

YOUNG, John Paul
Singles: 7–inch

ARIOLA AMERICA	2-4	75-76
SCOTTI BROTHERS	2-4	78

LPs: 10/12–inch 33rpm

SCOTTI BROTHERS	5-8	78

YOUNG, Karen
Singles: 7–inch

WEST END	2-4	78

YOUNG, Kathy
(Kathy Young and the Innocents)
Singles: 7–inch

COLLECTABLES	2-4	
ERA	2-4	72
ERIC	2-4	
INDIGO	10-15	60-62
MONOGRAM	8-10	62
STARFIRE	3-6	79
VIRGO	2-4	72

Picture Sleeves

INDIGO	6-12	60-61

LPs: 10/12–inch 33rpm

INDIGO (504 "The Sound of Kathy Young")	50-100	61

Also see CHRIS & KATHY
Also see INNOCENTS

YOUNG, Neil
(Neil Young and Crazy Horse; Neil and the Shocking Pinks; Neil Young and the Bluenotes)
Singles: 12–inch 33/45rpm

GEFFEN	4-6	86

Singles: 7–inch

GEFFEN	2-4	83-86
REPRISE (0785 through 0898)	3-5	68-70
REPRISE (0911 through 1396)	2-4	70-79
REPRISE (49000 series)	2-4	79-81

Picture Sleeves

REPRISE	2-4	78-81

EPs: 7–inch 33/45rpm

REPRISE	10-15	72

(Jukebox issue only.)

LPs: 10/12–inch 33rpm

GEFFEN	5-8	83-87
REPRISE (2000 series, except 2257 and 2296)	5-8	72-90
REPRISE (2257 "Decade")	12-15	77
REPRISE (2296 "Live Rust")	10-12	79
REPRISE (6317 "Neil Young")	40-50	68
(Front cover does NOT show Neil Young's name.)		
REPRISE (6317 "Neil Young")	8-12	68
(Front cover has Neil Young's name on it.)		
REPRISE (6349 "Everybody Knows This Is Nowhere")	10-12	69
REPRISE (6383 "After the Gold Rush")	10-12	70
REPRISE (6480 "Journey Through the Past")	12-15	72
WARNER	5-10	72-79

Also see BUFFALO SPRINGFIELD
Also see CASCADES
Also see CRAZY HORSE
Also see CROSBY, STILLS, NASH & YOUNG
Also see HARRIS, Emmylou
Also see LARSON, Nicolette
Also see STILLS - YOUNG BAND

YOUNG, Neil, and Jim Messina
Singles: 7–inch

REPRISE	3-5	70

Also see MESSINA, Jim

YOUNG, Neil, and Graham Nash
Singles: 7–inch

REPRISE	2-4	72

Also see NASH, Graham
Also see YOUNG, Neil

YOUNG, Nelson
Singles: 7–inch

LUCKY	60-75	59
MADISON	25-30	
RUBY	25-35	57

YOUNG, Paul
Singles: 12–inch 33/45rpm

COLUMBIA	4-6	83-86

Singles: 7–inch

COLUMBIA	2-4	83-86
EPIC	2-4	74

LPs: 10/12–inch 33rpm

COLUMBIA	5-8	84-90

Also see BAND AID
Also see MIKE + the MECHANICS
Also see SAD CAFE

YOUNG, Retta
Singles: 7–inch

ALL PLATINUM	2-4	75

YOUNG, Tommie
Singles: 7–inch

MCA	2-4	78
SOUL POWER	2-4	73-75

LPs: 10/12–inch 33rpm

MCA	5-8	78

YOUNG, Val
Singles: 12–inch 33/45rpm
GORDY 4-6   85-86
Singles: 7–inch
AMHERST 2-4   87
GORDY 2-4   85-86
LPs: 10/12–inch 33rpm
GORDY 5-8   85-86

YOUNG, Victor
Singles: 78rpm
DECCA 2-4   50-57
Singles: 7–inch
DECCA 2-4   50-57
EPs: 7–inch 33/45rpm
DECCA 3-6   50-57
LPs: 10/12–inch 33rpm
DECCA 5-15 50-59
Also see CROSBY, Bing
Also see GARLAND, Judy

YOUNG AMERICANS
LPs: 10/12–inch 33rpm
ABC 5-10 69

YOUNG & COMPANY
Singles: 7–inch
BRUNSWICK 2-4   81
RCA 2-4   69
LPs: 10/12–inch 33rpm
BRUNSWICK 5-8   81

YOUNG FRESH FELLOWS
Singles: 7–inch
POPLLAMA 2-4   85-86
EPs: 7–inch 33/45rpm
POPLLAMA 3-5   87
LPs: 10/12–inch 33rpm
POPLLAMA 5-8   84-86
POPLLAMA/FRONTIER 5-8   87
Members: Scott McCaughey; Tad Hutchison; Jim Sangster;
Chuck Carroll.

YOUNG HEARTS
Singles: 7–inch
AVCO EMBASSY 2-4   70
MINIT 3-5   68-69
20TH FOX 2-4   74-75
LPs: 10/12–inch 33rpm
MINIT 10-12 69

YOUNG HOLT UNLIMITED
(Young-Holt Trio)
Singles: 7–inch
BRUNSWICK 2-4   66-69
COTILLION 2-4   70-71
ERIC 2-4 83
PAULA 2-4   73
LPs: 10/12–inch 33rpm
ATLANTIC 8-10   73
BRUNSWICK 10-15 67-69
COTILLION 8-10   70-71
PAULA 5-8   73

Members: Eldee Young; Isaac Holt.
Also see LEWIS, Ramsey

YOUNG RASCALS: see RASCALS

YOUNG VANDALS
Singles: 7–inch
T-NECK 2-4   70

YOUNGBLOOD, Lonnie
Singles: 7–inch
FAIRMOUNT 3-5   67
LOMA 3-5   67-68
RADIO 2-4   81
SHAKAT 2-4   74
TURBO 2-4   71-73
LPs: 10/12–inch 33rpm
RADIO 5-8   81
TURBO 8-10   71
Also see HENDRIX, Jimi, and Lonnie Youngblood

YOUNGBLOODS
(Featuring Jesse Colin Young)
Singles: 7–inch
MERCURY 5-8   66-69
RCA 4-6   66-71
WARNER/RACCOON 2-4   70-72
Picture Sleeves
RCA 4-6   66
LPs: 10/12–inch 33rpm
RCA (3000 series) 5-8   80
  (With "ALY1" prefix.)
RCA (3000 series) 12-15   67
  (With "LPM" or "LSP" prefix.)
RCA (4000 series) 10-15 69-71
  (With "LPM" or "LSP" prefix.)
RCA (6000 series) 12-15   72
WARNER/RACOON 10-12 70-72
Members: Jesse Colin Young; Jerry Corbit; Joe Cauer; Lowell
"Banana" Levinger.
  Also see BOWIE, David / Joe Cocker / Youngbloods
  Also see YOUNG, Jesse Colin

YOUNGHEARTS
Singles: 7–inch
ABC 2-4   77
CANTERBURY 3-5   67
20TH FOX 2-4   73-76
LPs: 10/12–inch 33rpm
ABC 5-8   77
20TH FOX 8-10   73-74

YURO, Timi
Singles: 7–inch
LIBERTY (55000 series) 3-5   61-64
LIBERTY (56000 series) 2-4   68
MERCURY 2-4   64-67
PLAYBOY 2-4   75
EPs: 7–inch 33/45rpm
LIBERTY 8-12   61
  (Jukebox issues only.)
LPs: 10/12–inch 33rpm
COLGEMS 8-10   68

LIBERTY (Except 7500 series) 15-20   61-63
LIBERTY (7500 series) 8-10   68
MERCURY 10-15   65
SUNSET 6-12   66-70
U.A. 5-8   75-76
WING 8-10   68
   Also see RAY, Johnnie, and Timi Yuro

YUTAKA
Singles: 7-inch
ALFA 2-4   81
Picture Sleeves
ALFA 2-4   81
LPs: 10/12-inch 33rpm
ALFA 5-8   81
   Also see AUSTIN, Patti

Z

ZZ TOP
Singles: 12-inch 33/45rpm
WARNER 4-6   84-86
Singles: 7-inch
LONDON 2-4   70-77
SCAT 5-8
WARNER 2-4   80-86
Picture Sleeves
LONDON 2-4   75
LPs: 10/12-inch 33rpm
LONDON (Except 1001) 8-12   71-77
LONDON (1001 "World Wide
  Texas Tour") 12-15   76
  (Promotional issue only.)
WARNER 5-8   79-90
   Members: Bill Gibbons; Frank Beard; Dusty Hill.

ZABACH, Florian
Singles: 78rpm
DECCA 2-4   51-54
MERCURY 2-4   56-57
Singles: 7-inch
CADENCE 2-4   61
DECCA 2-4   51-54
MERCURY 2-4   56-58
EPs: 7-inch 33/45rpm
DECCA 4-8   51-54
MERCURY 3-6   56-58
LPs: 10/12-inch 33rpm
DECCA 5-15   51-65
MERCURY 5-15   56-60
VOCALION 4-8   63-66
WING 4-8   63
   Also see VALLI, June

ZACHARIAS, Helmut
(Helmut Zacharias' Magic Violins)
Singles: 78rpm
DECCA 2-4   56-57

Singles: 7-inch
CAPITOL 2-4   69
DECCA 2-4   56-64
EPs: 7-inch 33/45rpm
DECCA 3-6   56-58
LPs: 10/12-inch 33rpm
CAPITOL 4-8   69
DECCA 5-15   56-61
PHILIPS 4-8   62
RCA 4-8   66

ZACHERLE, John
(Zacherle; Zacherley; John Zacherle "Cool Ghoul")
Singles: 7-inch
ABKCO 2-4
CAMEO 5-8   58
COLPIX 4-6   64
ELEKTRA 4-6   60
PARKWAY 3-5   62
LPs: 10/12-inch 33rpm
CRESTVIEW 25-35   63
ELEKTRA 25-35   60
PARKWAY 25-35   62-63

ZADORA, Pia
(Pia Zadora and the London Symphony Orchestra)
Singles: 12-inch 33/45rpm
MCA 4-6   83
Singles: 7-inch
CURB 2-4   83
ELEKTRA 2-4   82-83
MCA 2-4   83-84
WARNER 2-4   78
LPs: 10/12-inch 33rpm
CBS ASSOCIATED 5-8   86
ELEKTRA 5-8   82
   Also see CHRISTIE, Lou, and Pia Zadora
   Also see JACKSON, Jermaine, and Pia Zadora

ZAGER, Michael, Band
Singles: 12-inch 33/45rpm
CBS ASSOCIATED 4-6   84
COLUMBIA 4-6   79
Singles: 7-inch
BANG 2-4   78
CBS ASSOCIATED 2-4   84
PRIVATE STOCK 2-4   78
LPs: 10/12-inch 33rpm
COLUMBIA 5-8   79
PRIVATE STOCK 5-8   78
   Also see TEN WHEEL DRIVE

ZAGER, Michael, Moon Band, and Peabo Bryson
Singles: 7-inch
BANG 2-4   76
   Also see BRYSON, Peabo
   Also see ZAGER, Michael, Band

ZAGER & EVANS
Singles: 7-inch
RCA 3-5   69-70

LIBERTY 2-4   59-67
RCA 2-4   64-66
Picture Sleeves
LIBERTY 2-5   62
EPs: 7–inch 33/45rpm
LIBERTY 5-8   59-67
LPs: 10/12–inch 33rpm
BEL CANTO 8-15   59
LIBERTY 5-15   59-67
RCA 5-10   65-66
SUNSET 5-10   66
Also see DENNY, Martin
Also see MANN, Johnny, Singers
Also see MARTIN, Dean / Patti Page
Also see SINATRA, Frank

ZEPHYR
Singles: 7–inch
PROBE 5-8   70
WARNER 2-4   70
Promotional Singles
PROBE 10-12   70
LPs: 10/12–inch 33rpm
PROBE 30-40   69
RED SNEAKERS 5-10   82
WARNER 25-30   71-72
Members: Candy Givens; Tommy Bolin.
Also see BOLIN, Tommy

ZEPPELIN, Led:
see LED ZEPPELIN

ZEVON, Warren
(Zevon)
Singles: 7–inch
ASYLUM 2-4   76-80
LPs: 10/12–inch 33rpm
ASYLUM 5-8   76-82
IMPERIAL 10-12   70
VIRGIN 5-8   87
Members: Richard Hayward; Kenny Gradney; Greg Beck; Karen Childs.
Also see LITTLE FEAT
Also see LYME & CYBELLE

ZILL, Pat
Singles: 7–inch
BIG C 3-5   62
ERA 3-5   63
INDIGO 3-5   61
SAND 5-8   61

ZINGARA
Singles: 7–inch
WHEEL 2-4   80-81
LPs: 10/12–inch 33rpm
WHEEL 5-8   81

ZINO
Singles: 12–inch 33/45rpm
PACIFIC 6 4-6   84

ZION BAPTIST CHURCH CHOIR
Singles: 7–inch
MYRRH 5-8   73

ZODIAC MINDWARP and the Love Reaction
LPs: 10/12–inch 33rpm
VERTIGO 5-8   88

ZOMBIES
Singles: 7–inch
DATE 3-5   68-69
EPIC 2-4   74
ERIC 2-4   83
LONDON 2-4
PARROT 4-6   64-66
Picture Sleeves
PARROT 10-20   65
LPs: 10/12–inch 33rpm
BACK-TRAC 5-8   85
DATE (4013 "Odessey and Oracle") . 20-25   68
(No promotional mention of *Time of the Season* on front cover.)
DATE (4013 "Odessey and Oracle") . 15-20   68
(With promo for *Time of the Season* on front cover.)
EPIC 10-12   74
LONDON 10-15   69
PARROT 30-35   65
RHINO 5-8
Members: Colin Blunstone; Rod Argent.
Also see ARGENT

ZOOM
Singles: 7–inch
MCA 2-4   83
POLYDOR 2-4   81-82
LPs: 10/12–inch 33rpm
A&M 8-10   74
MCA 5-8   83
POLYDOR 5-8   81

ZULEMA
(Zulema Cusseaux)
Singles: 7–inch
LE JOINT 2-4   78-79
RCA 2-4   74-76
SUSSEX 2-4   72-73
LPs: 10/12–inch 33rpm
LE JOINT 5-8   78
RCA 5-8   75-76
SUSSEX 8-10   72-74

ZWOL
(Walter Zwol)
Singles: 7–inch
EMI AMERICA (Except 8905) 2-4   78-79
EMI AMERICA (8905 "New York City") . 4-8   78
(Alternate version on white vinyl. Promotional issue only.)
LPs: 10/12–inch 33rpm
EMI AMERICA 5-8   78-79

DIRECTORY of
BUYERS and SELLERS

After learning the current value of their old records, some collectors will decide it's time to offer them for sale; others will decide they would like to purchase out-of-print records and build their collection of the oldies.

Still others will simply want to keep track of some of the latest products, supplies and services available to music collectors.

Regardless of whether you are moving in or out of the hobby, or just curious as to what's going on, let our Buyers and Sellers Directory point you in the right direction. There's something for everyone here — from dealers who want to buy as well as sell records, to sources for record care and storage products, to publications vital to the marketplace.

For infomation about advertising in the Buyers and Sellers Directory section of future record guides, contact the author (address on page 5).

958

959

964

RECORDS

New & Used—'50s to Now!
4741 N. Central Ave.
Phoenix, Arizona 85012
(602) 274-2660

WE BUY COLLECTIBLES!

ABOUT THE AUTHOR

A side from being an avid collector of records for over thirty-five years, Jerry Osborne has also been producing record price guides and reference books full time since 1975. His published works on music now number about fifty—probably more than anyone else in the entire world. Like the Energizer Bunny, however, he's still going and going, with several new titles released each year.

In addition, Jerry writes the popular, syndicated weekly newspaper column, "Mr. Music," answering a wide assortment of readers' questions on music and records. The column is distributed nationwide by World Features Syndicate.

Over the years, Osborne founded, published and then sold two internationally distributed magazines for record collectors: *Record Digest* and *DISCoveries,* the latter of which is still being published monthly by a Michigan company.

Jerry's influence and involvement in record collecting has been chronicled in virtually every major magazine and newspaper in the country, including: *Reader's Digest, The Wall Street Journal, USA Today, People Magazine, Esquire, Woman's Day, Oui, National Enquirer, Money, Changing Times, Photoplay, High Fidelity, Billboard, Cash Box, Music City News,* and *Rolling Stone.*

He is a frequent guest on major radio and TV talk shows, discussing the world of record collecting. Among these have been "Good Morning America," "The Today Show," and The Nashville Network, plus too many local and regional shows to count.

In the early '80s, Jerry served as a technical advisor and consultant for the critically acclaimed ABC-TV nostalgic news-magazine program, "Our World." He also worked as a consultant on several HBO specials and for CBS-TV's "West 57th Street."

Jerry Osborne is the author of several other House of Collectibles titles, including: *The Official® Price Guide to Records; The Official® Price Guide to Movie/TV Soundtracks and Original Cast Albums,* and *The Official® Price Guide to Memorabilia of Elvis Presley and the Beatles.*

No one person has been more responsible—directly or indirectly—for the amazing growth of the hobby of music collecting.

♪ ROCK WITH THE LEGENDS! ♪

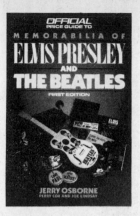

Experts JERRY OSBORNE ("Mr. Music"; author of *The Official® Price Guide to Records*), PERRY COX, and JOE LINDSAY don't miss a beat in *The Official® Price Guide to Memorabilia of Elvis Presley and The Beatles*. This is the first book ever to bring two of the greatest names in rock 'n' roll history together — a nostalgic compilation of the astounding array of memorabilia that make Elvis and The Beatles the cultural idols they remain today.

☆ Over 200 photos…eight-page color insert…fully indexed!

TAKE A MAGICAL MYSTERY TOUR THROUGH THIS BOOK!